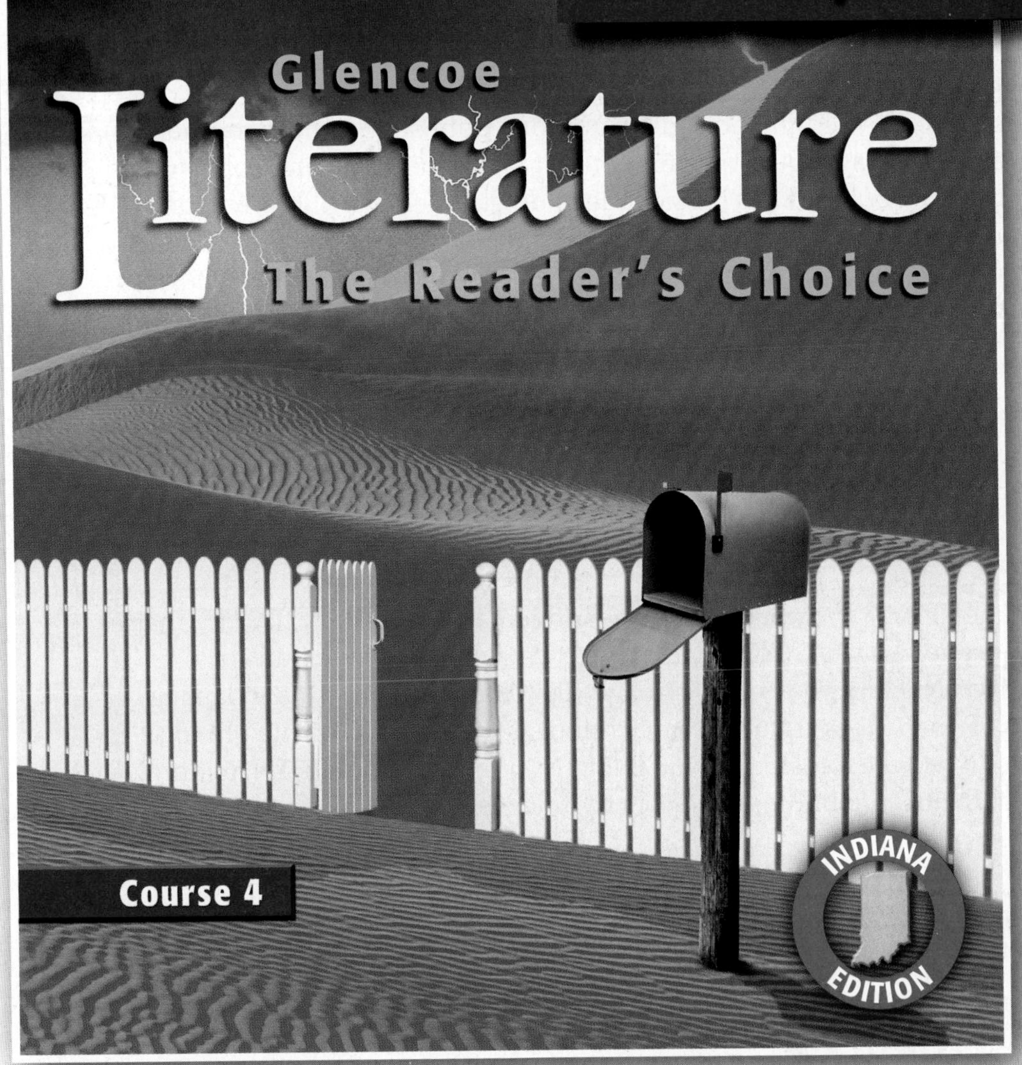

PROGRAM CONSULTANTS

Jeffrey D. Wilhelm, PhD

Douglas Fisher, PhD

Beverly Ann Chin, PhD

Jacqueline Jones Royster, DA

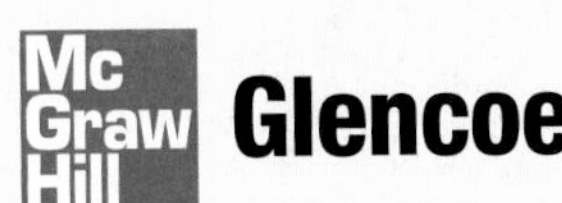

New York, New York Columbus, Ohio Chicago, Illinois Woodland Hills, California

ACKNOWLEDGMENTS

Grateful acknowledgment is given authors, publishers, photographers, museums, and agents for permission to reprint the following copyrighted material. Every effort has been made to determine copyright owners. In case of any omissions, the Publisher will be pleased to make suitable acknowledgments in future editions.

Acknowledgments continued on page R100.

Image credits:
IN5 age fotostock/SuperStock; **IN6** Bridgeman Art Library; **IN7** (t)Charles and Josette Lenars/CORBIS, (b)Private Collection/Bridgeman Art Library; **IN56** file photo; **IN57** image 100/Alamy Images; **IN60** Banana Stock/Punch Stock; **IN61** David Schmidt/Masterfile; **IN62** file photo; **IN64** Pixtal/age fotostock; **IN66 IN68 IN70 IN74** file photo; **IN76** John L. Santa; **IN96G** file photo; **IN96H** Getty Images.

The McGraw·Hill Companies

Send all inquiries to:
Glencoe/McGraw-Hill
8787 Orion Place
Columbus, OH 43240-4027

ISBN: (student edition) 978-0-07-878180-3
MHID: (student edition) 0-07-878180-9
ISBN: (teacher edition) 978-0-07-878184-1
MHID: (teacher edition) 0-07-878184-1

Printed in the United States of America.

1 2 3 4 5 6 7 8 9 071/043 12 11 10 09 08 07

Senior Program Consultants

Jeffrey D. Wilhelm, PhD, a former middle and secondary school English and reading teacher, is currently Professor of Education at Boise State University. He is the author or coauthor of numerous articles and several books on the teaching of reading and literacy, including award-winning titles such as *You Gotta BE the Book* and *Reading Don't Fix No Chevys.* He also works with local schools as part of the Adolescent Literacy Project and recently helped establish the National Writing Project site at Boise State University.

Douglas Fisher, PhD, is Professor of Language and Literacy Education and Director of Professional Development at San Diego State University, where he teaches English language development and literacy. He also serves as Director of City Heights Educational Pilot, which won the Christa McAuliffe Award from the American Association of State Colleges and Universities. He has published numerous articles on reading and literacy, differentiated instruction, and curriculum design. He is coauthor of the book *Improving Adolescent Literacies: Strategies That Work* and coeditor of the book *Inclusive Urban Schools.*

Program Consultants

Beverly Ann Chin, PhD, is Professor of English, Director of the English Teaching Program, former Director of the Montana Writing Project, and former Director of Composition at the University of Montana in Missoula. She currently serves as a Member at Large of the Conference of English Leadership. Dr. Chin is a nationally recognized leader in English language arts standards, curriculum, and assessment. Formerly a high school teacher and an adult education reading teacher, Dr. Chin has taught in English language arts education at several universities and has received awards for her teaching and service.

Jacqueline Jones Royster, DA, is Professor of English and Senior Vice Provost and Executive Dean of the Colleges of Arts and Sciences at The Ohio State University. She is currently on the Writing Advisory Committee of the National Commission on Writing and serves as chair for both the Columbus Literacy Council and the Ohioana Library Association. In addition to the teaching of writing, Dr. Royster's professional interests include the rhetorical history of African American women and the social and cultural implications of literate practices. She has contributed to and helped to edit numerous books, anthologies, and journals.

Special Consultant

FOLDABLES **Dinah Zike, MEd,** was a classroom teacher and a consultant for many years before she began to develop Foldables™—a variety of easily created graphic organizers. Zike has written and developed more than 150 supplemental books and materials used in classrooms worldwide. Her *Big Book of Books and Activities* won the Teachers' Choice Award.

Glencoe National Reading and Language Arts Advisory Council

Mary A. Avalos, PhD
Assistant Department Chair, Department of Teaching and Learning
Research Assistant Professor, Department of Teaching and Learning
University of Miami
Coral Gables, Florida

Wanda J. Blanchett, PhD
Associate Dean for Academic Affairs and Associate Professor of Exceptional Education
School of Education
University of Wisconsin–Milwaukee
Milwaukee, Wisconsin

William G. Brozo, PhD
Professor of Literacy
Graduate School of Education
College of Education and Human Development
George Mason University
Fairfax, Virginia

Nancy Drew, EdD
LaPointe Educational Consultants
Corpus Christi, Texas

Susan Florio-Ruane, EdD
Professor
College of Education
Michigan State University
East Lansing, Michigan

Sharon Fontenot O'Neal, PhD
Associate Professor
Texas State University
San Marcos, Texas

Nancy Frey, PhD
Associate Professor of Literacy in Teacher Education
School of Teacher Education
San Diego State University
San Diego, California

Victoria Gentry Ridgeway, PhD
Associate Professor
Reading Education
Clemson University
Clemson, South Carolina

Kimberly Lawless, PhD
Associate Professor
Curriculum, Instruction and Evaluation
College of Education
University of Illinois at Chicago
Chicago, Illinois

William Ray, MA
Lincoln-Sudbury Regional High School
Sudbury, Massachusetts

Janet Saito-Furukawa, MEd
Literacy Coach
Washington Irving Middle School
Los Angeles, California

Bonnie Valdes, MEd
Independent Reading Consultant
CRISS Master Trainer
Largo, Florida

INDIANA TEACHER REVIEWERS

Heather Bontratger
Language Arts Teacher
NorthWood Middle School
Wakarusa, Indiana

Heather Coy
Language Arts Department Chair
Harrison High School
Evansville, Indiana

Kristin Cramer
Language Arts Teacher
NorthWood Middle School
Wakarusa, Indiana

Judith Ann Gibson
English Teacher
Lawrence North High School
Indianapolis, Indiana

Fred Fox
Language Arts Teacher
Doe Creek Middle School
New Palestine, Indiana

John Houser
Language Arts Department Chair
Snider High School
Fort Wayne, Indiana

Dina Koble
Language Arts Teacher
NorthWood Middle School
Wakarusa, Indiana

Sherri Pankratz
English Teacher
Carmel High School
Carmel, Indiana

Madelyn Russell
Literature Teacher
Thompkins Middle School
Evansville, Indiana

Instructional Planning and Support

Correlation to the Indiana Academic Standards

Indiana Academic Standards	*Glencoe Literature,* Course Four
Standard 1 READING: Word Recognition, Fluency, and Vocabulary Development	
9.1 Word Recognition involves the understanding of the basic features of words: word parts, patterns, relationships, and origins. Students use phonics, context clues, and a growing knowledge of English and other languages to determine the meaning of words and become fluent readers.	
Vocabulary and Concept Development	
9.1.1 Identify and use the literal and figurative meanings of words and understand the origins of words.	Author's Language and Style 349, 1163 Literary Element 588, 594, 599, 653, 745 Literary Element Review 625, 806 Quickwrite 862 Reading Strategy 979, 1185 Responding and Thinking Critically 540, 593 Vocabulary Practice 42, 174, 278, 334, 406, 444, 449, 522, 850, 924, 1020, 1086, 1162, 1202 Vocabulary Workshop 1022, 1073 Writing About Literature 1185
9.1.2 Distinguish between what words mean literally and what they imply and interpret what the words imply.	Author's Language and Style 407, 1163, 1247 Literature Groups 745 Reading Strategy 476 Responding and Thinking Critically 41, 521, 527, 531, 535, 555, 579, 607, 625, 631 Vocabulary Practice 599, 1257 Vocabulary Workshop 434, 875, 1186
9.1.3 Use knowledge of mythology (Greek, Roman, and other mythologies) to understand the origin and meaning of new words.	Vocabulary Workshop 1022, 1073
Standard 2 READING: Comprehension and Analysis of Nonfiction and Informational Text	
9.2 Comprehension involves understanding grade-level-appropriate material. Students develop strategies such as asking questions; making predictions; and identifying and analyzing structure, organization, perspective, and purpose. After Grade 5, the focus is on informational texts.	
Structural Features of Informational and Technical Materials	
9.2.1 Analyze the structure and format of reference or functional workplace documents, including the graphics and headers, and explain how authors use the features to achieve their purposes.	Preview the Article 88, 429, 537, 808, 1030, 1224

Indiana Academic Standards	*Glencoe Literature,* Course Four
9.2.2 Prepare a bibliography of reference materials for a report using a variety of public documents, such as consumer, government, workplace and others.	Writing Handbook R35–40 Writing Workshop 1094–1101, 1099
Analysis of Grade-Level-Appropriate Nonfiction and Informational Text	
9.2.3 Generate relevant questions about readings on issues or topics that can be researched.	Internet Connection 120, 361, 392, 428, 595, 626, 1066, 1163 Writing Workshop 1093
9.2.4 Synthesize the content from several sources or works by a single author dealing with a single issue; paraphrase the ideas and connect them to other sources and related topics to demonstrate comprehension.	Comparing the Big Idea 378, 477 Interdisciplinary Activity 531 Learning for Life 915 Responding and Thinking Critically 476, 564, 811 Writing About Literature 445
9.2.5 Demonstrate use of technology by following directions in technical manuals.	Internet Connection 120, 361, 392, 428, 595, 626, 1066, 1163
9.2.8 Make reasonable statements and draw conclusions about a text, supporting them with accurate examples.	Reading Strategy 320, 325 Responding and Thinking Critically 92, 317, 333, 405, 443, 476, 485
Expository (Informational) Critique	
9.2.6 Critique the logic of functional documents (such as an appeal to tradition or an appeal to force) by examining the sequence of information and procedures in anticipation of possible reader misunderstandings.	Quickwrite 437 Reading Strategy 447, 808
9.2.7 Evaluate an author's argument or defense of a claim by examining the relationship between generalizations and evidence, the comprehensiveness of evidence, and the way in which the author's intent affects the structure and tone of the text.	Literary Element 462 Literary Element Review 486 Reading Strategy 242, 439, 444, 447, 449, 451, 457, 479, 486, 886, 1138, 1224 Responding and Thinking Critically 456, 1140 Writing About Literature 457, 463, 476

Indiana Academic Standards	*Glencoe Literature,* Course Four
Standard 3 READING: Comprehension and Analysis of Literary Text	
9.3 Response to grade-level-appropriate literature includes identifying story elements such as character, theme, plot, and setting, and making connections and comparisons across texts. Literary response enhances students' understanding of history, culture, and the social sciences.	
Structural Features of Literature	
9.3.1 Explain the relationship between the purposes and the characteristics of different forms of dramatic literature (including comedy, tragedy, and dramatic monologue).	Listening and Speaking 925 Unit Introduction 688
9.3.2 Compare and contrast the presentation of a similar theme or topic across genres (different types of writing) to explain how the selection of genre shapes the theme or topic.	Comparing Authors' Beliefs 146, 551, 818, 1177 Comparing Authors' Culture 863 Comparing Author's Meaning 1029 Comparing Author's Purpose 378, 642 Comparing the Big Idea 146, 378, 551, 642, 818, 863, 1029, 1177 Comparing Conflict 863 Comparing Description 1177 Comparing Sound Devices 642 Comparing Structure 551 Comparing Theme 146, 818, 1029 Comparing Tone 378 Quickwrite 1028 Reading Strategy 1048 Responding and Thinking Critically 246, 540, 564, 889, 1052, 1140
Analysis of Grade-Level-Appropriate Literary Text	
9.3.3 Analyze interactions between characters in a literary text and explain the way those interactions affect the plot.	Discussion Starter 861 Literary Element 119, 174, 203 Literary Element Review 119, 835 Reading Strategy 161, 174, 268, 891, 903, 916, 1036, 1046 Responding and Thinking Critically 20, 41, 53, 63, 85, 119, 120, 129, 141, 157, 173, 185, 202, 215, 240, 277, 657, 721, 773, 789, 805, 834, 850, 874, 884, 903, 915, 923, 979, 993, 1007, 1019, 1045, 1064, 1072, 1077, 1085, 1090, 1148, 1161, 1173, 1184, 1245 Writing About Literature 836

Indiana Academic Standards	*Glencoe Literature,* Course Four
9.3.4 Determine characters' traits by what the characters say about themselves in narration, dialogue, and soliloquy (when they speak out loud to themselves).	Literary Element 141, 255, 773, 924, 1007, 1077, 1173, 1201 Literary Element Review 157, 203, 325, 835, 1148, 1201, 1246 Literature Groups 836 Quickwrite 107, 1028 Reading Strategy 109, 119, 134, 141, 189, 203, 722, 745, 891, 903, 924, 1166, 1173, 1228, 1246 Responding and Thinking Critically 53, 75, 85, 141, 173, 215, 254, 267, 631, 646, 652, 660, 745, 850, 874, 915, 923, 1019, 1077, 1090, 1135, 1173 Visual Literacy 923 Writing About Literature 131, 175, 721, 789, 1021, 1077, 1086, 1202
9.3.5 Compare works that express a universal theme and provide evidence to support the views expressed in each work.	Comparing the Big Idea 146, 378, 551, 642, 818, 863, 1029, 1177 Comparing Theme 146, 818, 1029
9.3.6 Analyze and trace an author's development of time and sequence, including the use of complex literary devices, such as foreshadowing (providing clues to future events) or flashbacks (interrupting the sequence of events to include information about an event that happened in the past).	Literary Element 53, 1136, 1222, 1246 Reading Strategy 45, 54, 980, 993 Responding and Thinking Critically 53, 173, 993 Visual Literacy 1135
9.3.7 Recognize and understand the significance of various literary devices, including figurative language, imagery, allegory (the use of fictional figures and actions to express truths about human experiences), and symbolism (the use of a symbol to represent an idea or theme), and explain their appeal.	Literary Element 131, 579, 588, 594, 599, 603, 653, 745, 1072, 1184 Literary Element Review 229, 625, 806 Literature Groups 175, 745 Primary Visual Artifact 129 Quickwrite 550, 575, 621, 862 Reading Strategy 543, 545, 567, 570, 590, 594, 774, 789, 959, 979, 1068, 1072, 1179, 1185 Responding and Thinking Critically 267, 521, 527, 531, 535, 545, 555, 569, 579, 593, 599, 603, 607, 617, 652 Writing About Literature 523, 599, 654, 1185
9.3.8 Interpret and evaluate the impact of ambiguities, subtleties, contradictions, and ironies in a text.	Literary Element 86, 789 Literary Element Review 103, 462 Reading Strategy 886 Responding and Thinking Critically 85, 215, 889, 1257 Writing About Literature 131, 807, 1185

Indiana Academic Standards	*Glencoe Literature,* Course Four
9.3.9 Explain how voice and the choice of a narrator affect characterization and the tone, plot, and credibility of a text.	Literary Element 229, 240, 255, 278, 527 Literary Element Review 216, 267, 278, 333, 594, 1020, 1046 Reading Strategy 529, 531, 644, 647 Responding and Thinking Critically 333, 646 Writing About Literature 230, 374, 579, 631, 1047, 1137
9.3.10 Identify and describe the function of dialogue, soliloquies, asides, character foils, and stage designs in dramatic literature. • Dialogue: a conversation between two characters • Soliloquies: long speeches in which characters, on stage alone, reveal inner thoughts aloud • Asides: words spoken by characters directly to the audience • Character foils: characters who are used as contrast to another character • Stage designs: directions and drawings for the setting of a play	Literary Element 721, 773, 850 Literary Element Review 835, 924 Performing 885 Reading Strategy 891, 903, 916 Responding and Thinking Critically 850 Unit Introduction 688 Writing About Literature 874
Literary Criticism	
9.3.11 Evaluate the aesthetic qualities of style, including the impact of diction and figurative language on tone, mood, and theme.	Author's Language and Style 217, 230, 349, 407, 836, 925, 1021, 1163, 1247 Literary Element 64, 216, 267, 278, 360 Literary Element Review 86, 462, 535, 570, 646, 806, 1201, 1222 Reading Strategy 364, 374, 525, 527, 553, 555, 586, 588 Writing About Literature 217, 318, 392, 407, 588, 631, 773, 1047, 1223, 1257
9.3.12 Analyze the way in which a work of literature is related to the themes and issues of its historical period.	Author's Language and Style 1247 Daily Life and Culture 277, 324, 390, 443, 569, 652, 805, 1019 Interdisciplinary Activity 230 Internet Connection 361 Literary Element 333 Literary Element Review 75, 360 Reading Strategy 328, 334, 352, 361, 560, 915, 1143, 1149 Responding and Thinking Critically 173, 246, 277, 317, 443, 462, 603, 693, 957 Writing About Literature 158, 241, 334, 885, 1066

Indiana Academic Standards	*Glencoe Literature,* Course Four
9.3.13 Explain how voice, persona, and the choice of narrator affect the mood, tone, and meaning of text.	Literary Element 229, 278, 527 Literary Element Review 267, 594, 1046 Reading Strategy 529, 531, 644, 647 Writing About Literature 374, 579, 1047
Standard 4 WRITING: Processes and Features	
9.4 The writing process includes prewriting, drafting, editing, and revising. Students progress through these stages to write clear, coherent, and focused paragraphs and essays.	
Organization and Focus	
9.4.1 Discuss ideas for writing with classmates, teachers, and other writers and develop drafts alone and collaboratively.	Writing About Literature 21, 43, 54, 65, 76, 87, 104, 120, 131, 158, 175, 186, 204, 217, 230, 241, 256, 268, 279, 318, 326, 334, 349, 361, 392, 399, 407, 414, 428, 445, 457, 463, 487, 523, 536, 571, 595, 613, 618, 626, 647, 654, 807, 836, 885, 925, 1021, 1047, 1066, 1086, 1091, 1137, 1149, 1163, 1185, 1202, 1223, 1247, Writing Workshop 283–284, 491–492, 665–666, 929–930, 1261–1262
9.4.2 Establish a coherent thesis that conveys a clear perspective on the subject and maintain a consistent tone and focus throughout the piece of writing.	Writing About Literature 21, 43, 54, 65, 76, 186, 279, 318, 326, 334, 361, 374, 392, 399, 428, 487, 536, 571, 613, 1086, 1149, 1185, 1247 Writing Workshop 930, 1095
9.4.3 Use precise language, action verbs, sensory details, and appropriate modifiers.	Revising Check 407 Writing Workshop 668
9.4.13 Establish coherence within and among paragraphs through effective transitions, parallel structures, and similar writing techniques.	Grammar Workshop 350, 1087 Writing Workshop 1100
Research Process and Technology	
9.4.4 Use writing to formulate clear research questions and to compile information from primary and secondary print or Internet sources.	Writing Workshop 1093–1094
9.4.5 Develop the main ideas within the body of the composition through supporting evidence, such as scenarios, commonly held beliefs, hypotheses, and definitions.	Writing Workshop 283, 286, 932, 1096, 1100
9.4.6 Synthesize information from multiple sources, including almanacs, microfiche, news sources, in-depth field studies, speeches, journals, technical documents, and Internet sources.	Interdisciplinary Activity 230, 1021 Internet Connection 595, 1066 Learning for Life 613, 915 Writing About Literature 445

Indiana Academic Standards	*Glencoe Literature,* Course Four
9.4.7 Integrate quotations and citations into a written text while maintaining the flow of ideas.	Learning for Life 915 Writing About Literature 487 Writing Workshop 933, 1101
9.4.8 Use appropriate conventions for documentation in text, notes, and bibliographies, following the formats in specific style manuals.	Writing Handbook R35–40
9.4.9 Use a computer to design and publish documents by using advanced publishing software and graphic programs.	Speaking, Listening, and Viewing Workshop 1103
Evaluation and Revision	
9.4.10 Review, evaluate, and revise writing for meaning, clarity, content, and mechanics.	Revising Check 43, 65, 87, 131, 175, 204, 217, 230, 256, 279, 326, 349, 392, 407, 445, 487, 523, 571, 595, 613, 654, 807, 836, 925, 1021, 1047, 1066, 1137, 1163, 1223, 1247 Writing About Literature 21, 43, 54, 65, 76, 87, 104, 120, 131, 158, 175, 186, 204, 217, 230, 241, 256, 268, 279, 318, 326, 334, 349, 361, 392, 399, 407, 414, 428, 445, 457, 463, 487, 523, 536, 545, 571, 595, 613, 618, 626, 647, 654, 807, 836, 885, 925, 1021, 1047, 1066, 1086, 1091, 1137, 1149, 1163, 1185, 1202, 1223, 1247, 1257 Writing Workshop 286, 494, 668, 932, 1100, 1264
9.4.11 Edit and proofread one's own writing, as well as that of others, using an editing checklist with specific examples of corrections of frequent errors.	Writing Workshop 286–287, 494–495, 668–669, 932–933, 1100–1101, 1264–1265
9.4.12 Revise writing to improve the logic and coherence of the organization and perspective, the precision of word choice, and the appropriateness of tone by taking into consideration the audience, purpose, and formality of the context.	Writing Workshop 286, 494, 668, 932, 1100, 1264

Indiana Academic Standards	*Glencoe Literature,* Course Four
Standard 5 WRITING: Applications (Different Types of Writing and Their Characteristics)	
9.5 Through the exploration of different types of writing and the characteristics of each, students become proficient at narrative (stories), expository (informational), descriptive (sensory), persuasive (emotional appeal), argumentative (logical defense), and technical writing. Writing demonstrates an awareness of the audience (intended reader) and purpose for writing.	
9.5.1 Write biographical or autobiographical narratives or short stories that: • describe a sequence of events and communicate the significance of the events to the audience. • locate scenes and incidents in specific places. • describe with specific details the sights, sounds, and smells of a scene and the specific actions, movements, gestures, and feelings of the characters; in the case of short stories or autobiographical narratives, use interior monologue (what the character says silently to self) to show the character's feelings. • pace the presentation of actions to accommodate changes in time and mood.	Quickwrite 575, 1026, 1123, 1174, 1189 Test Preparation and Practice 1111 Writing About Literature 230, 527, 1163, 1257 Writing Workshop 488–495, 662–669
9.5.2 Write responses to literature that: • demonstrate a comprehensive grasp of the significant ideas of literary works. • support statements with evidence from the text. • demonstrate an awareness of the author's style and an appreciation of the effects created. • identify and assess the impact of ambiguities, nuances, and complexities within the text.	Interdisciplinary Activity 399 Internet Connection 595 Literary Criticism 654, 1137 Quickwrite 475, 517, 691, 862, 1028, 1055 Test Preparation and Practice 679, 943, 1275 Writing About Literature 21, 131, 175, 326, 361, 487, 527, 559, 588, 603, 626, 721, 789, 836, 903, 1047, 1077 Writing Workshop 280–287

Indiana Academic Standards	*Glencoe Literature,* Course Four
9.5.3 Write expository compositions, including analytical essays, summaries, descriptive pieces, or literary analyses that: • gather evidence in support of a thesis (position on the topic), including information on all relevant perspectives. • communicate information and ideas from primary and secondary sources accurately and coherently. • make distinctions between the relative value and significance of specific data, facts, and ideas. • use a variety of reference sources, including word, pictorial, audio, and Internet sources, to locate information in support of topic. • include visual aids by using technology to organize and record information on charts, data tables, maps, and graphs. • anticipate and address readers' potential misunderstandings, biases, and expectations. • use technical terms and notations accurately.	Comparing Author's Purpose 378 Comparing the Big Idea 146, 818, 1177 Literary Criticism 21, 279 Test Preparation and Practice 297 Unit Introduction 306, 952 Writing About Literature 43, 54, 65, 76, 87, 104, 120, 158, 186, 204, 217, 241, 256, 268, 279, 318, 334, 349, 392, 399, 407, 414, 428, 445, 449, 457, 463, 523, 536, 545, 555, 571, 595, 599, 613, 631, 654, 661, 773, 807, 850, 874, 885, 925, 993, 1021, 1025, 1066, 1072, 1086, 1137, 1149, 1173, 1185, 1202 Writing Workshop 281–287, 926–933, 1092–1101
9.5.4 Write persuasive compositions that: • organize ideas and appeals in a sustained and effective fashion with the strongest emotional appeal first and the least powerful one last. • use specific rhetorical (communication) devices to support assertions, such as appealing to logic through reasoning; appealing to emotion or ethical belief; or relating a personal anecdote, case study, or analogy. • clarify and defend positions with precise and relevant evidence, including facts, expert opinions, quotations, expressions of commonly accepted beliefs, and logical reasoning. • address readers' concerns, counterclaims, biases, and expectations.	Learning for Life 1247 Literary Criticism 1137 Quickwrite 437, 469 Test Preparation and Practice 505 Writing About Literature 463, 487, 626 Writing Workshop 1258–1265

Indiana Academic Standards	*Glencoe Literature,* Course Four
9.5.5 Write documents related to career development, including simple business letters and job applications that: • present information purposefully and in brief to meet the needs of the intended audience. • follow a conventional business letter, memorandum, or application format.	Learning for Life 613 Writing Handbook R41–44
9.5.6 Write technical documents, such as a manual on rules of behavior for conflict resolution, procedures for conducting a meeting, or minutes of a meeting that: • report information and express ideas logically and correctly. • offer detailed and accurate specifications. • include scenarios, definitions, and examples to aid comprehension. • anticipate readers' problems, mistakes, and misunderstandings.	Interdisciplinary Activity 1021 Learning for Life 915 Unit Introduction 8
9.5.7 Use varied and expanded vocabulary, appropriate for specific forms and topics.	Unit Introduction 688, 1120 Vocabulary Workshop 434 Writing About Literature 175, 647
9.5.8 Write for different purposes and audiences, adjusting tone, style, and voice as appropriate.	Interdisciplinary Activity 1091 Internet Connection 626 Learning for Life 76, 618, 915 Quickwrite 437, 575, 955 Unit Introduction 8 Writing About Literature 487, 527, 559, 603, 647, 789, 1091 Writing Workshop 494

Indiana Academic Standards	*Glencoe Literature,* Course Four
Research Application	
9.5.9 Write or deliver a research report that has been developed using a systematic research process (defines the topic, gathers information, determines credibility, reports findings) and that: • uses information from a variety of sources (books, technology, multimedia), distinguishes between primary and secondary documents, and documents sources independently by using a consistent format for citations. • synthesizes information gathered from a variety of sources, including technology and one's own research, and evaluates information for its relevance to the research questions. • demonstrates that information that has been gathered has been summarized, that the topic has been refined through this process, and that conclusions have been drawn from synthesizing information. • demonstrates that sources have been evaluated for accuracy, bias, and credibility. • organizes information by classifying, categorizing, and sequencing, and demonstrates the distinction between one's own ideas from the ideas of others, and includes a bibliography (Works Cited).	Writing Workshop 1092–1101
Standard 6 WRITING: English Language Conventions	
9.6 Conventions include the grade-level-appropriate mechanics of writing, such as penmanship, spelling, grammar, capitalization, punctuation, sentence structure, and manuscript form.	
Grammar and Mechanics of Writing	
9.6.1 Identify and correctly use clauses, both main and subordinate; phrases, including gerund, infinitive, and participial; and the mechanics of punctuation, such as semicolons, colons, ellipses, and hyphens.	Author's Language and Style 43, 175, 204, 279, 326, 523, 595, 807, 1047, 1137, 1223 Grammar Workshop 218, 350, 408, 812, 1141 Writing Workshop 669, 933, 1101, 1265

Indiana Academic Standards	*Glencoe Literature,* Course Four
9.6.2 Demonstrate an understanding of sentence construction, including parallel structure, subordination, and the proper placement of modifiers, and proper English usage, including the use of consistent verb tenses.	Author's Language and Style 65, 87, 131, 836 Grammar Workshop 159, 218, 408, 812 Writing Workshop 287, 669
Manuscript Form	
9.6.3 Produce legible work that shows accurate spelling and correct use of the conventions of punctuation and capitalization.	Writing Workshop 287, 495, 669, 933, 1101, 1265
9.6.4 Apply appropriate manuscript conventions – including title page presentation, pagination, spacing, and margins – and integration of source and support material by citing sources within the text, using direct quotations, and paraphrasing.	Writing Workshop 1092–1101
Standard 7 LISTENING AND SPEAKING: Skills, Strategies, and Applications	
9.7 Response to oral communication includes careful listening and evaluation of content. Speaking skills, such as phrasing, pitch, and tone are developed in conjunction with such strategies as narration, exposition, description, and persuasion and are applied to students' delivery of oral presentations.	
Comprehension	
9.7.1 Summarize a speaker's purpose and point of view and ask questions concerning the speaker's content, delivery, and attitude toward the subject.	Literary Element 486 Speaking, Listening, and Viewing Workshop 289 Visual Literacy 485
Organization and Delivery of Oral Communication	
9.7.2 Choose appropriate techniques for developing the introduction and conclusion in a speech, including the use of literary quotations, anecdotes (stories about a specific event), and references to authoritative sources.	Speaking, Listening, and Viewing Workshop 671, 935, 1102–1103

Indiana Academic Standards	*Glencoe Literature,* Course Four
9.7.3 Recognize and use elements of classical speech forms (including the introduction, transitions, body, and conclusion) in formulating rational arguments and applying the art of persuasion and debate.	Listening and Speaking 445, 463 Literary Element Review 444 Speaking, Listening, and Viewing Workshop 1103, 1266–1267
9.7.4 Use props, visual aids, graphs, and electronic media to enhance the appeal and accuracy of presentations.	Listening and Speaking 131 Speaking, Listening, and Viewing Workshop 289, 497, 1102–1103, 1267
9.7.5 Produce concise notes for extemporaneous speeches (speeches delivered without a planned script).	Listening and Speaking 104, 1149 Speaking, Listening, and Viewing Workshop 496, 670, 935 Unit Introduction 8, 952, 1120
9.7.6 Analyze the occasion and the interests of the audience and choose effective verbal and nonverbal techniques (including voice, gestures, and eye contact) for presentations.	Listening and Speaking 217 Performing 204, 334, 647, 807, 885, 1086, 1223 Speaking, Listening, and Viewing Workshop 497, 671, 935, 1103, 1267
Analysis and Evaluation of Oral and Media Communications	
9.7.7 Make judgments about the ideas under discussion and support those judgments with convincing evidence.	Listening and Speaking 463 Speaking, Listening, and Viewing Workshop 934–935, 1266–1267 Unit Introduction 688
9.7.8 Compare and contrast the ways in which media genres (including televised news, news magazines, documentaries, and online information) cover the same event.	Listening and Speaking 925
9.7.9 Analyze historically significant speeches (such as Abraham Lincoln's "House Divided" speech or Winston Churchill's "We Will Never Surrender" speech) to find the rhetorical devices and features that make them memorable.	Author's Language and Style 445 Listening and Speaking 445 Literary Element 444 Writing About Literature 445

Indiana Academic Standards	*Glencoe Literature,* Course Four
9.7.10 Assess how language and delivery affect the mood and tone of the oral communication and make an impact on the audience.	Author's Language and Style 487 Listening and Speaking 334, 607 Speaking, Listening, and Viewing Workshop 496–497, 671, 935, 1102–1103, 1266–1267
9.7.11 Evaluate the clarity, quality, effectiveness, and general coherence of a speaker's important points, arguments, evidence, organization of ideas, delivery, choice of words, and use of language.	Listening and Speaking 349 Speaking, Listening, and Viewing Workshop 289
9.7.12 Analyze the types of arguments used by the speaker, including argument by causation, analogy (comparison), authority, emotion, and the use of sweeping generalizations.	Literary Element 486 Literary Element Review 486
9.7.13 Identify the artistic effects of a media presentation and evaluate the techniques used to create them (comparing, for example, Shakespeare's *Romeo and Juliet* with Franco Zefferelli's film version).	Listening and Speaking 925
Speaking Applications	
9.7.14 Deliver narrative presentations that: • narrate a sequence of events and communicate their significance to the audience. • locate scenes and incidents in specific places. • describe with specific details the sights, sounds, and smells of a scene and the specific actions, movements, gestures, and feelings of characters. • time the presentation of actions to accommodate time or mood changes.	Listening and Speaking 326 Speaking, Listening, and Viewing Workshop 496–497

Indiana Academic Standards	*Glencoe Literature,* Course Four
9.7.15 Deliver expository (informational) presentations that: • provide evidence in support of a thesis and related claims, including information on all relevant perspectives. • convey information and ideas from primary and secondary sources accurately and coherently. • make distinctions between the relative value and significance of specific data, facts, and ideas. • include visual aids by employing appropriate technology to organize and display information on charts, maps, and graphs. • anticipate and address the listeners' potential misunderstandings, biases, and expectations. • use technical terms and notations accurately.	Learning for Life 618 Speaking, Listening, and Viewing Workshop 1102–1103
9.7.16 Apply appropriate interviewing techniques: • prepare and ask relevant questions. • make notes of responses. • use language that conveys maturity, sensitivity, and respect. • respond correctly and effectively to questions. • demonstrate knowledge of the subject or organization. • compile and report responses. • evaluate the effectiveness of the interview.	Listening and Speaking 131
9.7.17 Deliver oral responses to literature that: • advance a judgment demonstrating a comprehensive understanding of the significant ideas of works or passages. • support important ideas and viewpoints through accurate and detailed references to the text and to other works. • demonstrate awareness of the author's writing style and an appreciation of the effects created. • identify and assess the impact of ambiguities, nuances, and complexities within the text.	Literature Groups 523 Speaking, Listening, and Viewing Workshop 288–289, 934–935

Indiana Academic Standards	*Glencoe Literature,* Course Four
9.7.18 Deliver persuasive arguments (including evaluation and analysis of problems and solutions and causes and effects) that: • structure ideas and arguments in a coherent, logical fashion from the hypothesis to a reasonable conclusion, based on evidence. • contain speech devices that support assertions (such as by appeal to logic through reasoning; by appeal to emotion or ethical belief; or by use of personal anecdote, case study, or analogy). • clarify and defend positions with precise and relevant evidence, including facts, expert opinions, quotations, expressions of commonly accepted beliefs, and logical reasoning. • anticipate and address the listener's concerns and counterarguments.	Listening and Speaking 104, 463 Speaking, Listening, and Viewing Workshop 1266–1267
9.7.19 Deliver descriptive presentations that: • establish a clear point of view on the subject of the presentation. • establish the presenter's relationship with the subject of the presentation (whether the presentation is made as an uninvolved observer or by someone who is personally involved). • contain effective, factual descriptions of appearance, concrete images, shifting perspectives, and sensory details.	Speaking, Listening, and Viewing Workshop 670–671

BOOK OVERVIEW

Reference Section

CONTENTS

"Its walls had been lined with human remains . . ."

—Edgar Allan Poe

— PART 2 — *Rewards and Sacrifices* 105

> *"If I lost, I would bring shame on my family."*
> —Amy Tan

— PART 3 — *Dreams and Reality* 205

"America was far, far away on the other side of the ocean, at the edge of the world."

—Isaac Bashevis Singer

UNIT TWO NONFICTION

"Mr. Booth, President Lincoln has been shot . . . And—oh, Mr. Booth—they say your brother John has done it!"

—James Cross Giblin

— PART 2 — On the Move 379

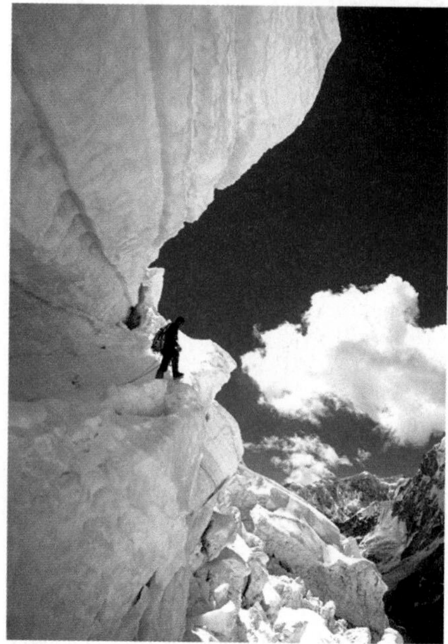

". . . I observed my own slide from reality with a blend of fascination and horror."

—Jon Krakauer

— PART 3 — FINDING COMMON GROUND

"Begin with that most terrifying of all things, a clean slate."
—Anna Quindlen

". . . if day
has to become night
this is a beautiful way."

—E. E. Cummings

"How dreary—to be—Somebody!"
—Emily Dickinson

> *"I can read regret in her fingers untangling snarls . . ."*
>
> —Chitra Banerjee Divakaruni

"O, that I were a glove upon that hand, that I might touch that cheek!"

—William Shakespeare

"*I been looking for a girl every Saturday night of my life.*"

—Paddy Chayefsky

UNIT FIVE

Epic and Myth

"The gods have tried me in a thousand ways."

—Homer

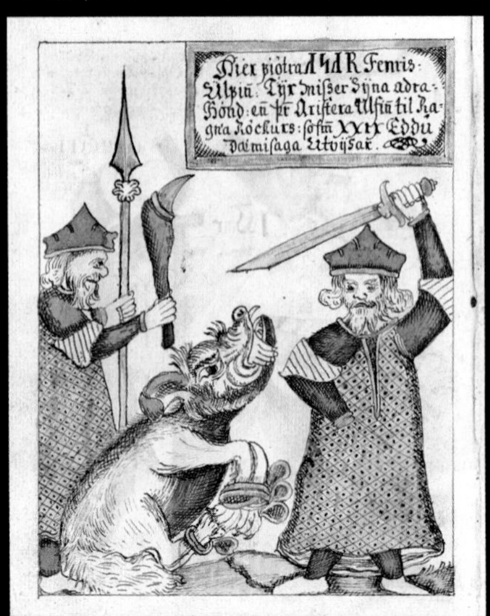

"His great, red eyes burned with fury, the black hair bristled on his back, and he gnashed his teeth until the foam flew."

—Olivia Coolidge

UNIT SIX Genre Fiction

— PART 1 — Our World and Beyond

"*Two wizards in one town,*" *he said.* "*Bad!*"

—Ursula K. Le Guin

— PART 2 — Revealing the Concealed

"*He does not believe in ghosts, consequently he never encounters them.*"

—Ellery Queen

Reference Section

SELECTIONS BY GENRE

Fiction

Short Story

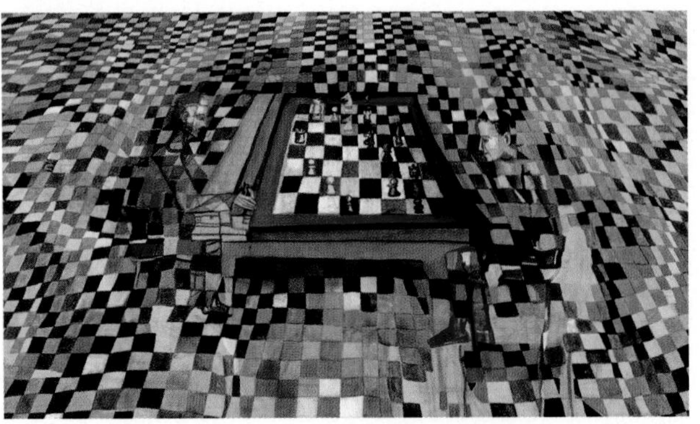

Modern Fable/Parable

Myth

Novel

Poetry

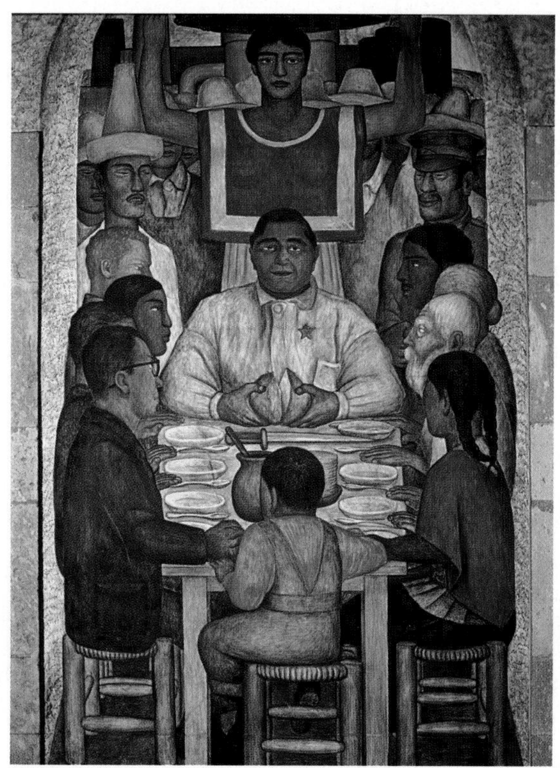

Ballad

Epic

Drama

Tragedy

Comedy

Modern Drama

Nonfiction and Informational Text

Biography, Autobiography, or Memoir

Essay

Interview

Journal

Letter

Movie Review

Speech

Graphic Novel

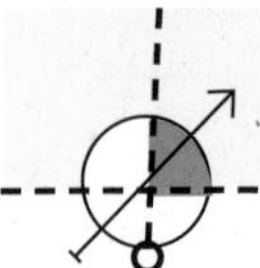

PERSPECTIVES

Award-winning nonfiction book excerpts and primary source documents

TIME

High-interest magazine articles

Comparing Literature *Across Genres*

UNIT ONE

UNIT TWO

UNIT THREE

FEATURES

UNIT FOUR

UNIT FIVE

UNIT SIX

Comparing Literature: *Different Viewpoints*

UNIT TWO

LITERARY FOCUS

LITERARY HISTORY

INDEPENDENT READING

TEST PREPARATION AND PRACTICE

SKILLS WORKSHOPS

Writing Workshops

Speaking, Listening, and Viewing Workshops

Grammar Workshops

Vocabulary Workshops

Organization

The literature selections you will read are organized by literary element and genre into six units: The Short Story, Nonfiction, Poetry, Drama, Epic and Myth, and Genre Fiction.

Each unit contains the following:

A **UNIT INTRODUCTION** provides valuable background information that will help make your reading experience more meaningful.

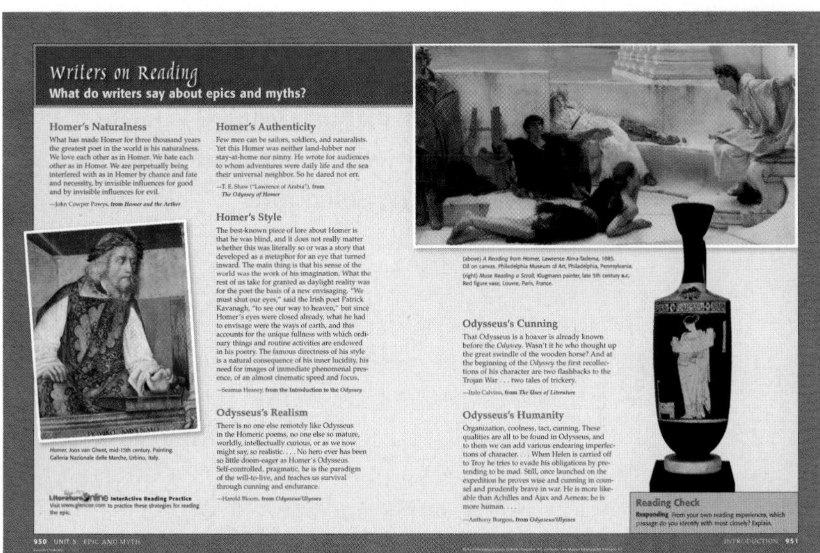

Writers on Reading
What do writers say about epics and myths?

Homer's Naturalness
What has made Homer for three thousand years the greatest poet in the world is his naturalness. We love each other as in Homer. We hate each other as in Homer. We are perpetually being interfered with as in Homer by chance and fate and necessity, by invisible influences for good and by invisible influences for evil.

—John Cowper Powys, from *Homer and the Aether*

Homer's Authenticity
Few men can be sailors, soldiers, and naturalists. Yet this Homer was neither land-lubber nor stay-at-home nor ninny. He wrote for audiences to whom adventures were daily life and the sea their universal neighbor. So he dared not err.

—T. E. Shaw ("Lawrence of Arabia"), from *The Odyssey of Homer*

Homer's Style
The best-known piece of lore about Homer is that he was blind, and it does not really matter whether this was literally so or was a story that developed as a metaphor for an eye that turned inward. The main thing is that his sense of the world was the work of his imagination. What the rest of us take for granted as daylight reality was for the poet the basis of a new envisaging. "We must shut our eyes," said the Irish poet Patrick Kavanagh, "to see our way to heaven," but since Homer's eyes were closed already, what he had to envisage were the ways of earth, and this accounts for the unique fullness with which ordinary things and routine activities are endowed in his poetry. The famous directness of his style is a natural consequence of his inner lucidity, his need for images of immediate phenomenal presence, of an almost cinematic speed and focus.

—Seamus Heaney, from the Introduction to the *Odyssey*

Homer, Joos van Ghent, mid-15th century. Painting. Galleria Nazionale delle Marche, Urbino, Italy.

Odysseus's Realism
There is no one else remotely like Odysseus in the Homeric poems, no one else so mature, worldly, intellectually curious, or as we now might say, so realistic. . . . No hero ever has been so little doom-eager as Homer's Odysseus. Self-controlled, pragmatic, he is the paradigm of the will-to-live, and teaches us survival through cunning and endurance.

—Harold Bloom, from *Odysseus/Ulysses*

Literature Online InterActive Reading Practice Visit www.glencoe.com to practice these strategies for reading the epic.

(above) *A Reading from Homer,* Lawrence Alma-Tadema, 1885. Oil on canvas. Philadelphia Museum of Art, Philadelphia, Pennsylvania.
(right) *Muse Reading a Scroll,* Klugmann painter, late 5th century B.C. Red figure vase, Louvre, Paris, France.

Odysseus's Cunning
That Odysseus is a hoaxer is already known before the *Odyssey.* Wasn't it he who thought up the great swindle of the wooden horse? And at the beginning of the *Odyssey* the first recollections of his character are two flashbacks to the Trojan War . . . two tales of trickery.

—Italo Calvino, from *The Uses of Literature*

Odysseus's Humanity
Organization, coolness, tact, cunning. These qualities are all to be found in Odysseus, and to them we can add various endearing imperfections of character. . . . When Helen is carried off to Troy he tries to evade his obligations by pretending to be mad. Still, once launched on the expedition he proves wise and cunning in counsel and prudently brave in war. He is more likeable than Achilles and Ajax and Aeneas; he is more human. . . .

—Anthony Burgess, from *Odysseus/Ulysses*

Reading Check
Responding From your own reading experiences, which passage do you identify with most closely? Explain.

950 UNIT 5 EPIC AND MYTH

INTRODUCTION 951

- **GENRE FOCUS** defines the literary elements that make up a unit.
- **THE LITERARY ANALYSIS MODEL** uses an example to help you identify different literary elements and analyze their use within the text.
- **WRITERS ON READING** gives you genre-specific reading tips from famous authors.

Why do I need this book?

Glencoe Literature, The Reader's Choice is more than just a collection of stories, poems, nonfiction articles, and other literary works. Every unit is built around **Big Ideas,** concepts that you will want to think about, talk about, and maybe even argue about. Big Ideas help you become part of an important conversation. You can join in lively discussions about who we are, where we have been, and where we are going.

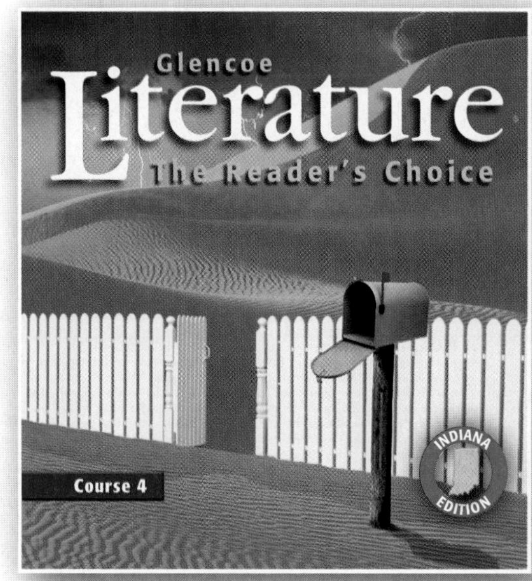

BEFORE YOU READ

The Lady, or the Tiger?

MEET FRANK R. STOCKTON

At the height of his success, Frank R. Stockton was considered a major literary figure in the United States; writer William Dean Howells considered Stockton to be second in importance only to Mark Twain. Stockton's body of work fills twenty-three volumes and includes stories, novels, and nonfiction. Yet today, this writer is known primarily for his story, "The Lady, or the Tiger?"

Launching a Career Stockton enjoyed writing during his school days; however, his father hoped that he would become a doctor. Stockton chose another path entirely: wood engraving, a popular way to illustrate stories and articles at the time. Still, Stockton continued to write and began to publish his short stories.

As the wood engraving business gave way to other types of illustrations, Stockton focused his attention on writing and publishing. His early works were mainly written for children. In 1867, he published a short story called "Ting-a-Ling," which he later turned into a book. A fanciful tale about an elf-like character, "Ting-a-Ling" captured the attention of Mary Mapes Dodge, an author and editor of the time. After she was named editor of *St. Nicholas*, a new magazine for children, Dodge invited Stockton to join her staff.

St. Nicholas was a new

The Story That Created a Stir In 1878, Stockton left the magazine because of his failing eyesight, but he continued to write. Within a few years, he published several more books. Still, Stockton's novels never earned attention equal to that which he gained in 1882, when he published a short story in *Century Magazine*. That story was "The Lady, or the Tiger?"

The story not only created a stir at the time but for years afterward. It was later turned into an operetta, a play, a movie, and a recording. The story's unusual ending created a flurry of letters to the author that continued throughout his life. A well-known poet, Robert Browning, wrote a poem about the ending and scholars debated the issue, but Stockton kept quiet.

Stockton continued to publish humorous and fanciful novels, but few are still read today. The year after his death, a twenty-three-volume collection of his fiction was published. However, after a lifetime of writing, Stockton's name is

12 UNIT 1 THE SHORT STORY

LITERATURE PREVIEW

Connecting to the Story

Would you trust your life to a friend? Before you read the story, think about the following questions:

- Which is a stronger emotion—love or jealousy?
- How completely can one person ever know and understand another?

Building Background

During the Middle Ages in England, guilt or innocence was decided through a practice known as an ordeal. An accused person was physically tested, and the outcome determined guilt or innocence. The accusers believed that supernatural forces controlled what happened. For instance, in the ordeal by water, the accused person was tied up and thrown into deep water. A person who floated was thought to be guilty; a person who sank was considered innocent. Unfortunately, those who sank often drowned before they could be hauled back up.

Setting Purposes for Reading

Big Idea **Matters of Life and Death**

As you read this story, notice how the characters value life and death in different ways.

Literary Element **Conflict**

Every story revolves around a **conflict**, or struggle between opposing forces. A conflict can be external or internal. An external conflict is one between a character and an outside force, such as another character, nature, society, or fate. An internal conflict takes place within the mind of a character who is torn between different courses of action.

- See Literary Terms Handbook, p. R4.

Literature Online Interactive Literary Elements Handbook To review or learn more about the literary elements, go to www.glencoe.com.

READING PREVIEW

Reading Strategy **Summarizing**

Summarizing is stating only the main ideas of a selection in a logical sequence and in your own words. When you summarize a story, include the main characters, the setting, the conflict, important plot details, and the resolution.

Reading Tip: Tracking Main Ideas Use a chart to record the important details that you want to include in a summary.

Setting	Characters	Conflict	Resolution
A long time ago; in a kingdom			

Vocabulary

impartial (im pär′ shəl) *adj.* not favoring one side more than another; fair; p. 15 *An honest judge is impartial.*

emanate (em′ ə nāt′) *v.* to come forth; p. 15 *We never heard any sound emanate from that room.*

dire (dīr) *adj.* dreadful; terrible; p. 15 *Breaking certain rules can have dire consequences.*

fervent (fur′ vənt) *adj.* having or showing great intensity of feeling; passionate; p. 16 *The coach was a fervent believer in practicing every day in order to improve.*

novel (nov′ əl) *adj.* new and unusual; p. 16 *Since that older method seldom works, try a more novel approach.*

Vocabulary Tip: Multiple-Meaning Words Many words have more than one meaning. Use context to help determine a word's correct meaning.

13

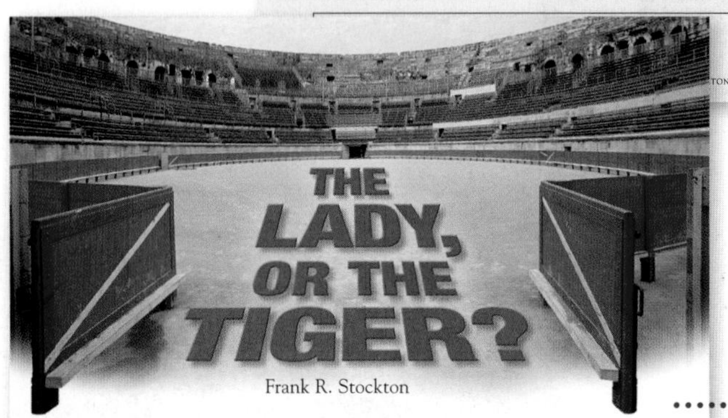

Frank R. Stockton

In the very olden time, there lived a semibarbaric king, whose ideas, though somewhat polished and sharpened by the progressiveness of distant Latin neighbors, were still large, florid, and untrammeled,[1] as became the half of him which was barbaric. He was a man of exuberant fancy, and, withal, of an authority so irresistible that, at his will, he turned his varied fancies into facts. He was greatly given to self-communing; and, when he and himself agreed upon any thing, the thing was done. When every member of his domestic and political systems moved smoothly in its appointed course, his nature was bland and genial;[2] but whenever there was a little hitch, and some of his orbs got out of their orbits, he was blander and more genial still, for nothing pleased him so much as to make the crooked straight, and crush down uneven places.

Among the borrowed notions by which his barbarism had become semified[3] was that of the public arena, in which, by exhibitions of manly and beastly valor, the minds of his subjects were refined and cultured.

But even here the exuberant and barbaric fancy asserted itself.[4] The arena of the king was built, not to give the people an opportunity of hearing the rhapsodies[5] of dying gladiators, nor to enable them to view the inevitable conclusion of a conflict between religious opinions and hungry jaws, but for purposes far better adapted to widen and

1. The king's ideas are somewhat uncivilized (*semibarbaric*); they are very showy (*florid*) and unrestrained (*untrammeled*).
2. The king himself is generally agreeable and mild (*bland*) and pleasantly cheerful (*genial*).
3. *Semified* is a made-up word meaning "reduced in half or made partial."
4. Here, *asserted itself* means "exercised its influence; insisted on being recognized."
5. *Rhapsodies* are enthusiastic expressions of emotion.

Literary Element Conflict *How does this passage suggest a future conflict?*

14 UNIT 1 THE SHORT STORY

Reading and hinking

The main selections in your textbook are arranged in three parts.

- Start with **BEFORE YOU READ.** Learn valuable background information about the selection and preview the skills and strategies that will guide your reading.

MEET THE AUTHOR presents a detailed biography of the writer whose work you will read and analyze.

LITERATURE PREVIEW AND READING PREVIEW list the basic tools you will use to read and analyze the selection.

- Next, read the **LITERATURE SELECTION.** As you flip through the selections, you will notice that parts of the text are highlighted in different colors. At the bottom of the page are color-coded questions that relate to the highlighted text. Yellow represents a *Big Idea,* magenta represents a *Literary Element,* and blue represents a *Reading Strategy.* These questions will help you gain a better understanding of the text.

- Wrap up the selection with **AFTER YOU READ.** Explore what you have learned through a wide range of reading, thinking, vocabulary, and writing activities.

AFTER YOU READ

RESPONDING AND THINKING CRITICALLY

Respond

1. What was your reaction to the ending of the story? How would your reaction be different if you knew what was behind the door on the right?

Recall and Interpret

2. (a)In the kingdom described in the story, what happens when a person is accused of a crime? (b)Why do the members of the community support this method?
3. (a)What is the young man's crime? (b)Why are his actions considered criminal?
4. (a)What does the princess do when the young man is in the arena? (b)What motive does she have for sending him to his death, and what motive does she have for saving his life?

Analyze and Evaluate

5. The story is told from the third-person point of view at the beginning. How does the point of view change, and what is the effect of this change?
6. Why do you think the story ends with a question instead of an answer?
7. Most stories end by telling the readers what happened to the main characters. This story lets the readers decide what happens. What is your opinion of this type of ending? Explain.

Connect

8. In what ways is the king's justice similar to flipping a coin to decide an important question?
9. Big Idea **Matters of Life and Death** At what point is the young man's fate actually decided? Explain.

LITERARY ANALYSIS

Literary Element Conflict

Conflict is the engine that drives most stories—it sets the action in motion. Many stories, like this one, contain more than one type of conflict. Characters may struggle against other characters and outside forces, but they may also struggle with themselves. A character may find himself or herself torn between two choices, for example, even as he or she battles some enemy. When a character struggles against an outside force, it is called an external conflict. On the other hand, when a character battles with himself or herself, it is called an internal conflict. Think about the conflicts in this story and then answer the following questions.

1. What conflicts does the young man have? Are his conflicts internal or external? Support your answers with details from the story.
2. Why is the princess's internal conflict so central to the story?

Review: Plot

As you learned on pages 10–11, **plot** is the sequence of events in a story. It begins with the exposition, or the introduction of the characters, setting, and situation.

Partner Activity Meet with another classmate and discuss which plot details in the exposition of "The Lady, or the Tiger?" are most important to understanding the story. Use those details to fill in the story map parts.

Place

Time

Characters

Situation

20 UNIT 1 THE SHORT STORY

Vocabulary

VOCABULARY WORDS that may be new or difficult to you are chosen from most selections. They are introduced on the **BEFORE YOU READ** page. Each word is accompanied by its pronunciation, its part of speech, its definition, and the page number on which it appears. The vocabulary word is also used in a sample sentence. Vocabulary words are highlighted in the Literature Selection.

VOCABULARY PRACTICE On the **AFTER YOU READ** pages, you will be able to practice using the vocabulary words in an exercise. This exercise will show you how to apply a vocabulary strategy to understand new or difficult words.

ACADEMIC VOCABULARY Many of the **AFTER YOU READ** pages will also introduce you to two words that are frequently used in academic work. You will be prompted to apply the definitions of these words to answer questions about the selection that you have just read.

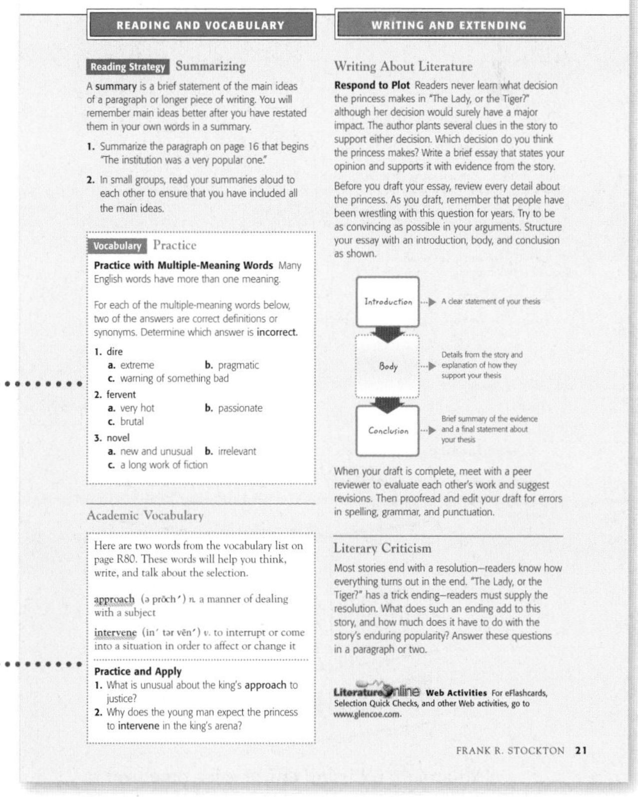

READING AND VOCABULARY

Reading Strategy Summarizing

A **summary** is a brief statement of the main ideas of a paragraph or longer piece of writing. You will remember main ideas better after you have restated them in your own words in a summary.

1. Summarize the paragraph on page 16 that begins "The institution was a very popular one."
2. In small groups, read your summaries aloud to each other to ensure that you have included all the main ideas.

Vocabulary Practice

Practice with Multiple-Meaning Words Many English words have more than one meaning.

For each of the multiple-meaning words below, two of the answers are correct definitions or synonyms. Determine which answer is **incorrect**.

1. dire
   a. extreme b. pragmatic
   c. warning of something bad
2. fervent
   a. very hot b. passionate
   c. brutal
3. novel
   a. new and unusual b. irrelevant
   c. a long work of fiction

Academic Vocabulary

Here are two words from the vocabulary list on page R80. These words will help you think, write, and talk about the selection.

approach (ə prōch′) *n.* a manner of dealing with a subject

intervene (in′ tər vēn′) *v.* to interrupt or come into a situation in order to affect or change it

Practice and Apply

1. What is unusual about the king's **approach** to justice?
2. Why does the young man expect the princess to **intervene** in the king's arena?

WRITING AND EXTENDING

Writing About Literature

Respond to Plot Readers never learn what decision the princess makes in "The Lady, or the Tiger?" although her decision would surely have a major impact. The author plants several clues in the story to support either decision. Which decision do you think the princess makes? Write a brief essay that states your opinion and supports it with evidence from the story.

Before you draft your essay, review every detail about the princess. As you draft, remember that people have been wrestling with this question for years. Try to be as convincing as possible in your arguments. Structure your essay with an introduction, body, and conclusion as shown.

When your draft is complete, meet with a peer reviewer to evaluate each other's work and suggest revisions. Then proofread and edit your draft for errors in spelling, grammar, and punctuation.

Literary Criticism

Most stories end with a resolution—readers know how everything turns out in the end. "The Lady, or the Tiger?" has a trick ending—readers must supply the resolution. What does such an ending add to this story, and how much does it have to do with the story's enduring popularity? Answer these questions in a paragraph or two.

LiteratureOnline **Web Activities** For eFlashcards, Selection Quick Checks, and other Web activities, go to www.glencoe.com.

FRANK R. STOCKTON 21

Writing Workshops

Each unit in *Glencoe Literature, The Reader's Choice* includes a Writing Workshop. The workshop walks you through the writing process as you work on an extended piece of writing related to the unit.

- You will create writing goals and apply strategies to meet them.
- You will pick up tips and polish your critical skills as you analyze professional and workshop models.
- You will focus on mastering specific aspects of writing, including organization, grammar, and vocabulary.
- You will use a rubric to evaluate your own writing.

Revising

Peer Review Once you complete your draft, exchange papers with a partner. Your partner should note if you have consistently used the first-person point of view, and if you have used details to elaborate. Also, your partner can evaluate how you keep your audience interested by making suggestions for dialogue and for developing a conflict.

Use the rubric below to evaluate your essay.

Rubric: Writing an Autobiographical Narrative

- ☑ Does your introduction create suspense or draw interest?
- ☑ Do you use the first-person point of view?
- ☑ Do you elaborate using narrative details that develop the plot?
- ☑ Do you use chronological order, or another clear organizational pattern?
- ☑ Do you use dialogue to make your narrative more immediate for your audience?
- ☑ Do you effectively communicate the significance of the memory?

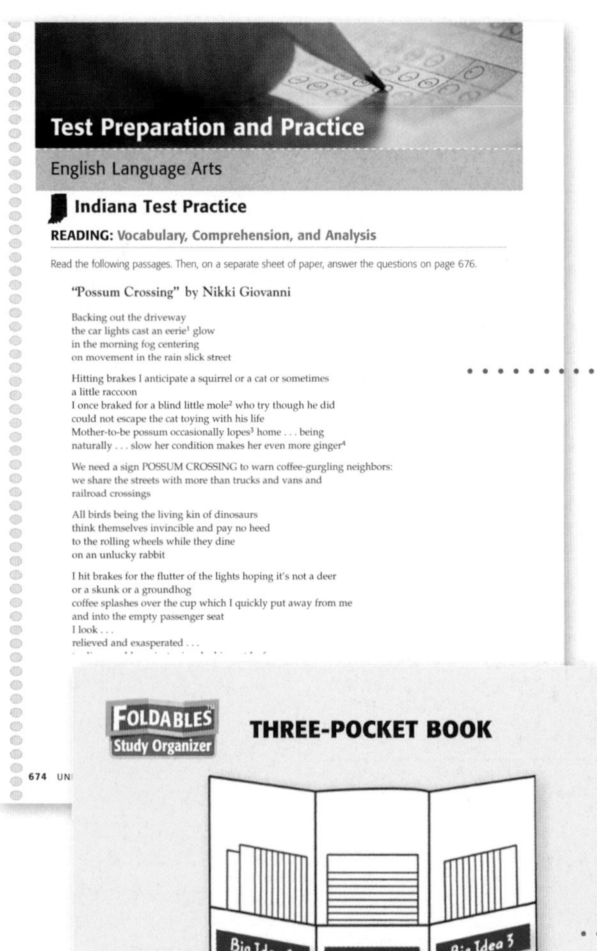

Test Preparation and Practice

English Language Arts

Indiana Test Practice

READING: Vocabulary, Comprehension, and Analysis

Read the following passages. Then, on a separate sheet of paper, answer the questions on page 676.

"Possum Crossing" by Nikki Giovanni

Backing out the driveway
the car lights cast an eerie[1] glow
in the morning fog centering
on movement in the rain slick street

Hitting brakes I anticipate a squirrel or a cat or sometimes
a little raccoon
I once braked for a blind little mole[2] who try though he did
could not escape the cat toying with his life
Mother-to-be possum occasionally lopes[3] home . . . being
naturally . . . slow her condition makes her even more ginger[4]

We need a sign POSSUM CROSSING to warn coffee-gurgling neighbors:
we share the streets with more than trucks and vans and
railroad crossings

All birds being the living kin of dinosaurs
think themselves invincible and pay no heed
to the rolling wheels while they dine
on an unlucky rabbit

I hit brakes for the flutter of the lights hoping it's not a deer
or a skunk or a groundhog
coffee splashes over the cup which I quickly put away from me
and into the empty passenger seat
I look . . .
relieved and exasperated . . .

674 UN

You might try using this graphic organizer to keep track of the three Big Ideas in this unit.

Indiana Test Preparation and Practice

At the end of each unit, you will be tested on the literature, reading, and vocabulary skills you have just learned. Designed to simulate Indiana's standardized tests, this test will give you the practice you need to succeed while providing an assessment of how well you have met the unit objectives.

Organizing Information

Graphic organizers—such as Foldables™, diagrams, and charts—help you keep your information and ideas organized.

SCAVENGER HUNT

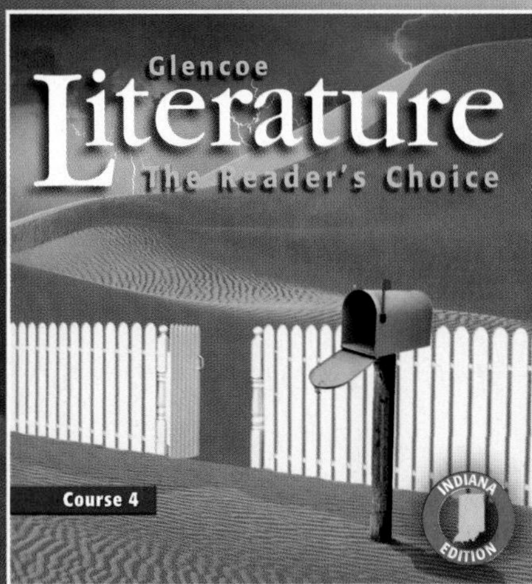

Glencoe's ***Reader's Choice*** contains a wealth of information. The trick is to know where to look to access that information. If you go through this scavenger hunt, either alone or with teachers or parents, you will quickly learn how the textbook is organized and how to get the most out of your reading and study time.

Let's get started!

1. How many units and parts are there in this book?
   Six units and fifteen parts
2. What is the difference between the Glossary and the Index?
   The Glossary lists vocabulary words and definitions. The Index lists skills, authors, titles, art, and artists.
3. There is a section on Test-Taking Strategies in the Reference Section in the back of the textbook. Where else in the book can you find help for test preparation?
   In the Test Preparation and Practice section at the end of each unit
4. If you wanted to find a definition of the term *allegory*, where would you look?
   In the Literary Terms Handbook at the back of the book
5. Where can you find the Big Ideas for each unit of the book? At the beginning of each unit and part
6. In what special feature would you find biographical information about a specific author?
   Meet the Author in the Before You Read pages
7. If you want to find all of the selections in the book that are short stories, where would you look? In the Selections by Genre section at the front of the book
8. The Web site for the book is referred to throughout the book. What sort of information does the Web site contain that might help you? Additional information about the literature and the authors
9. Which of the book's main features will provide you with the strategies for developing your writing skills?
   The Writing Workshops

After you answer all the questions, meet with a partner or a small group to compare answers.

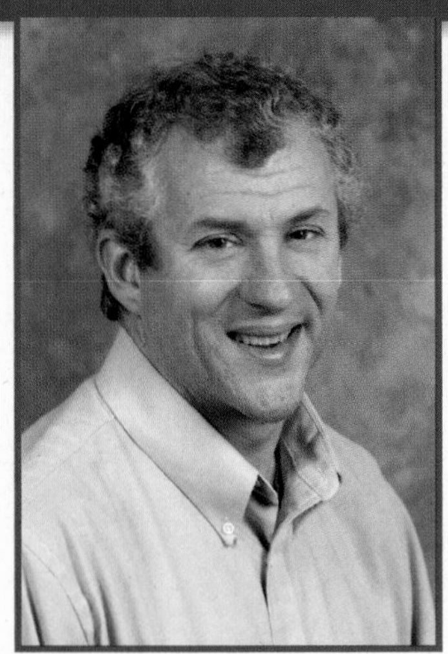

RESEARCH-BASED CLASSROOM SOLUTIONS

Philosophy Statement

Glencoe Literature: The Reader's Choice

by Jeffrey D. Wilhelm, PhD
Professor of English Education, Boise State University

Glencoe Literature: The Reader's Choice is a uniquely powerful program for helping to engage and teach your students. Why? It is an inquiry-based program, featuring differentiated instruction and using an integrated "Big Ideas" approach.

An Inquiry-Based Approach

Inquiry is a research-based approach that gives students significant reasons or purposes for reading. It is the most powerful instructional treatment for both engaging students and assisting them to learn essential concepts and strategies. Based on his review of research, George Hillocks has famously argued that all reading and writing are forms of inquiry and that they are best taught and learned through inquiry. ***The Reader's Choice*** provides a historical, cultural, and social context for every literary selection, thereby producing a framework for inquiry and discovery. This kind of inquiry not only informs students' thinking about the literature but also informs their thinking about issues in our contemporary world.

Differentiated Instruction

All classroom teachers understand that their students bring different interests and abilities to class. They have different motivations and needs. However, in most classrooms, every student is asked to do the same thing at the same time. With an inquiry-based approach, individual students can read texts that are appropriate to their interests and abilities, engage in more or less practice with particular strategies, work in different small groups, and yet still be part of the common classroom project of pursuing an inquiry. In fact, with this type of learning environment, difference becomes an asset and a resource, because those who read different things and learn different concepts and strategies have a unique contribution to offer the group (Wilhelm 2006). In ***The Reader's Choice,*** we introduce various resources, such as graphic novels and informational texts, which appeal to a variety of learners' needs and can be used with individual students or small groups. We also suggest ways to pursue various selections and activities with students so that the power of differentiation can be tapped.

The Big Ideas

The Reader's Choice also employs the exclusive **Big Ideas** approach that organizes, motivates, and guides student learning. The **Big Ideas,** which guide each unit, are personally relevant to students and socially significant in the world. Teachers can achieve curricular coherence because all instructional materials, whether conceptual or procedural, are organized around understanding the central ideas. For example, stories and poems that were once taught in isolation from each other now inform each other as they address the central guiding ideas. Using this approach, students are much more likely to understand important concepts that they can apply both to their lives and to their future reading and writing.

Motivation

Motivating students is the greatest challenge facing teachers today, particularly when it comes to reading and writing. The seminal research of John Guthrie (2002), my own award-winning research on boys and literacy development (Smith and Wilhelm 2002, 2006), and various national reports and reviews have demonstrated this.

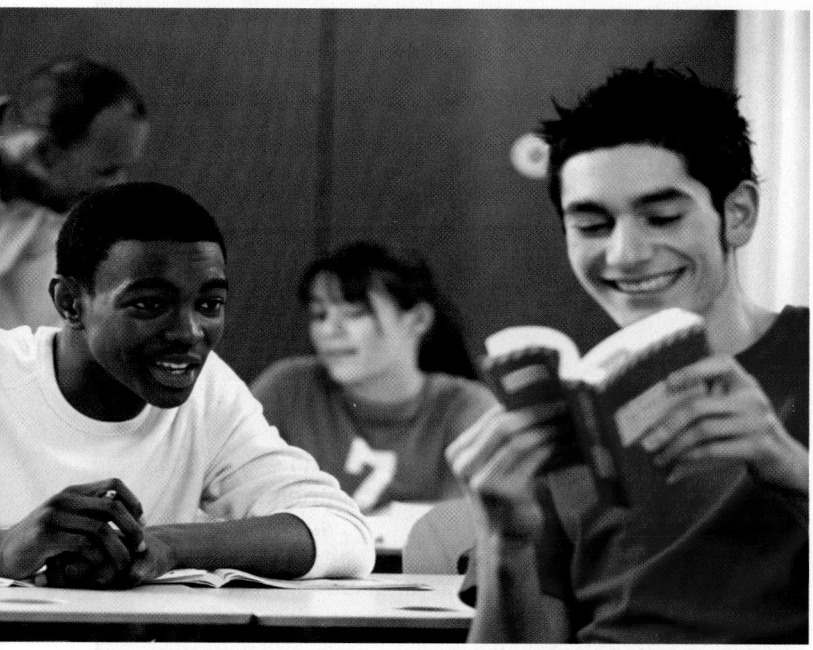

When Michael Smith and I undertook our studies of boys' literacy, we found that before students would engage with a literacy task, they needed to understand the purpose and to know that they would receive the necessary assistance for success. They also needed to know that they would become more competent in obvious ways, that they would be able to exert more control over their own lives as a result, and that they would engage in social activity. The research of Czikszentmihalyi (1990), Gee (2003), and others indicates that these conditions are also crucial for the learning of young women. ***The Reader's Choice*** is designed first and foremost to meet these motivational prerequisites to engagement and learning.

Works Cited

Applebee, A. N., Burroughs, R., and Stevens, A. S. 2000. Shaping Conversations: A study of continuity and coherence in high school literature curricula. *Research in the Teaching of English* 34:396–429.

Brown, J., Collins, A., and DuGuid, P. 1989. Situated cognition and the culture of learning. *Educational Researcher* 18, 32–42.

Caskey, M. 2006. The evidence for core curriculum—past and present. *Middle School Journal* (37)3, 48–54.

Csikszentmihalyi, M. 1990. Flow: *The Psychology of Optimal Experience.* New York: Harper & Row.

Gee, J. 2003. *What Video Games Have to Teach Us About Learning and Literacy.* New York: Palgrave Macmillan.

Guthrie, J. 2002. Classroom contexts for engaged reading: An overview. http://www.cori.umd.edu/Research/Papers/Classroom.htm.

Hidi, S., and Harackiewicz, J. M. 2000. Motivating the academically unmotivated: A critical issue for the twenty-first century. *Review of Educational Research* 70, 151–180.

Hillocks, G. 1995. *Teaching Writing as Reflective Practice.* New York: Teachers College Press.

Hillocks, G., Jr. 1999. *Ways of Teaching/Ways of Learning.* New York: Teachers College Press.

Jacobs, Heidi Hayes. 1989. *Interdisciplinary Curriculum: Design and implementation.* Washington, DC: ASCD.

Smith, M. W., and Wilhelm, J. D. 2006 *Going with the Flow: How to engage boys (and girls) in their literacy learning.* Portsmouth, NH: Heinemann.

Smith, M. W., and Wilhelm, J. D. 2002 *Reading Don't Fix No Chevys: Literacy in the lives of young men.* Portsmouth, NH: Heinemann.

Tyler, R. 1949. *Basic Principles of Curriculum and Instruction.* Chicago: University of Chicago Press.

Wertsch, J. 1998. *Mind as Action.* New York: Oxford University Press.

Wiggins, G., and McTighe, J. 2003. *Understanding by Design.* Washington, DC: ASCD.

Wilhelm, J. D., Baker, T., and Dube-Hackett, J. 2001. *Strategic Reading.* Portsmouth, NH: Heinemann.

Wilhelm, J. D. 2006. *Inquiring Minds Learn to Read and Write: Inquiry, questioning and discussion strategies to improve reading and writing.* New York: Scholastic.

The *Reading Next* Report

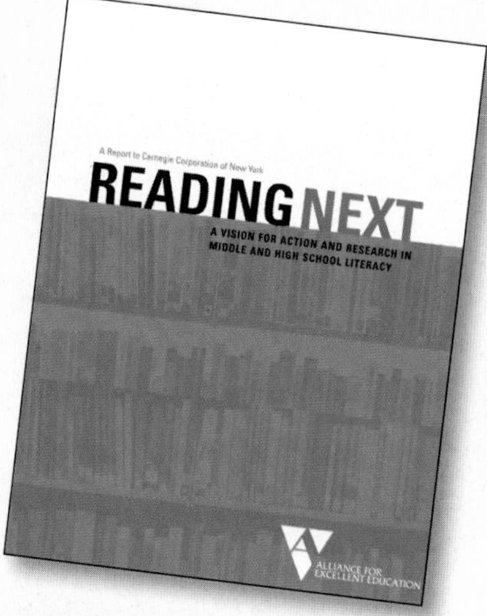

What Is the Focus of the Report?

In 2004 the Carnegie Corporation released *Reading Next—A Vision for Action and Research in Middle and High School Literacy: A Report to Carnegie Corporation of New York.* Authored by Harvard researchers Gina Biancarosa and Dr. Catherine Snow and published by the Alliance for Excellent Education in Washington, D.C., the report responds to the growing literacy crisis among middle and high school students.

The contours of this problem are troubling. For example, in the United States today, more than eight million students in grades 4–12 lack the ability to read proficiently (U.S. DOE 2003). Every day, more than three thousand students drop out of high school (Alliance for Excellent Education 2003)—largely because they lack the literacy skills to keep up (Kamil 2003; Snow and Biancarosa 2003). Only seventy percent of high school students graduate on time, and fewer than sixty percent of all African American and Latino students get their diplomas (Greene 2002). Clearly, these numbers paint a picture of a system in crisis.

The driving force behind the *Reading Next* report is simple. Students who lack literacy skills face serious disadvantages in almost every aspect of their lives—at school, at work, and in the community. Research indicates that most middle and high school readers decode well; that is, they are able to sound out the words on a given page of text. However, many of these readers are unable to conceptualize what they read or to connect new words and ideas to those they already know. Unable to comprehend the various texts they encounter, these students quickly fall behind in the three areas—school, work, and community—that matter most.

The *Reading Next* report draws attention to this problem and seeks to dispel the outdated notion that struggling and reluctant middle and high school readers are unable to benefit from literacy instruction. Instead, the report asserts, these students can and *do* benefit—significantly—from literacy instruction. According to the report, educators and other interested parties should, then, work hard to develop effective literacy programs for struggling middle and high school students.

Why Is the *Reading Next* Report Important?

The report identifies fifteen characteristics of an effective literacy program. The first nine characteristics, or recommendations, are instructional—ideas and activities that teachers can implement. The remaining six are infrastructural—ideas and activities that can be realized at the schoolwide level or in the student's home or community.

According to the report, effective literacy programs for struggling readers share the following **instructional** components:

1. **Direct, explicit comprehension instruction,** or teaching core reading strategies
2. **Effective instructional principles embedded in content,** or teaching students to use reading skills in all content areas
3. **Motivation and self-directed learning,** or motivating students to read (now and after graduation), and to become independent, lifelong learners
4. **Text-based collaborative learning,** or teaching students to interact with one another vis-à-vis a variety of texts
5. **Strategic tutoring,** or giving students intense, individualized instruction when necessary
6. **Diverse texts,** or using texts whose genre, topic, and level of difficulty vary
7. **Intensive writing,** or offering instruction that relates to the writing tasks students will perform at the high school level and beyond
8. **A technology component,** or using technology as a tool for and topic of literacy instruction
9. **Ongoing formative assessment of students,** or conducting frequent, informal assessments of student progress under current instructional practices

The report also notes that effective literacy programs share the following **infrastructural** components:

10. **Extended time for literacy,** or offering two to four hours of interdisciplinary (cross-classroom and cross-content area) literacy instruction per day
11. **Professional development,** or offering long-term and ongoing support for teachers
12. **Ongoing summative assessment of students and programs,** or evaluating students and educators in order to build accountability and improve systems
13. **Teacher teams,** or forming interdisciplinary groups that discuss and are accountable for students' progress
14. **Leadership,** or the execution of program goals by teachers and principals who understand their students and their reading and writing curriculum
15. **A comprehensive and coordinated literacy program,** or the formation of a literacy program that draws strength from various disciplines, departments, and community organizations

Glencoe Literature: The Reader's Choice and the *Reading Next* Report

The *Reading Next* report recommends nine instructional improvements, and ***The Reader's Choice*** program equips teachers to implement all of them—when, where, and how they choose. Developed with these improvements in mind, ***The Reader's Choice*** gives teachers the instructional tools they need to help students in the ways that matter most.

The *Reading Next* Report recommends...	*The Reader's Choice* features...
direct, explicit comprehension instruction.	**Before You Read** pages, which clearly teach reading skills, literary elements and analysis, and vocabulary development.
effective instructional principles embedded in content.	**Vocabulary Workshops, Grammar Workshops, Writing Workshops**, which focus on the teach-model-practice-assess mode of instruction.
motivation and self-directed learning.	**Independent Reading** pages, which motivate students to explore literary works on their own.
text-based collaborative learning.	several types of partner and group activities, which encourage students to work together and share opinions about the text.
strategic tutoring.	peer review activities in the **Writing Workshops**, which give students the opportunity to work in small mentoring groups.
diverse texts.	a wide range of literary selections from various genres.
intensive writing.	**Writing Workshops** and **Writing About Literature** activities, which help students develop the connection between reading and writing.
a technology component.	a variety of technology-based components, such **Glencoe.online** products, the ***Student Works* CD-ROM,** and the ***Skill Arcade* CD-ROM,** which help students build proficiency.
ongoing formative assessment of students.	end-of-unit **Test Preparation and Practice** pages, which that are designed to gauge students' mastery of reading, writing, and vocabulary skills.

RESEARCH-BASED CLASSROOM SOLUTIONS

Inquiry-Based Learning

The Power of Inquiry for Teaching Reading and Writing

by Jeffrey D. Wilhelm, PhD
Professor of English Education,
Boise State University

The late MIT physicist Jerrold Zaccharias once defined education as "the raising of questions worth arguing about." As my research has shown, many students would agree (Smith and Wilhelm 2003). They do not want to "play guess what the teacher already knows"—they want to pursue questions that really matter to them personally and in the world.

Our foremost educators since John Dewey's time have argued against information-transmission modes of instruction and for "hands-on" and "minds-on" learning. Surveys of students and research in the field support the use of inquiry approaches instead of information transmission. Inquiry approaches have been shown to improve student engagement, attitude, achievement, and learning in a wide spectrum of areas.

What Is Inquiry?

Inquiry is the problem-oriented exploration of questions that drive and organize the disciplines. Through inquiry students learn essential concepts and strategies for doing work and applying understanding in the real world. They engage in the same kinds of conversations, problem solving, and applications that real practitioners do and make use of the same tools.

Finding out about existing information is part of true inquiry, but it is only the initial step. Inquirers then proceed to many other steps that help them interpret, generate, and shape information into knowledge. Human beings want to make meanings, not just receive them. Students want to be agents and actors in the world and do not want their actions dictated by teachers' directions and past ways of understanding. They want to mark their own identities, not merely take on other people's identities, ideas, and ways of doing things.

Inquiry-oriented, active, discussion-based learning, particularly when abetted by a purposeful curriculum of connected activities, works to build deep understandings over time and an emphasis on high academic achievement.

Inquiry-Based Learning and *Glencoe Literature: The Reader's Choice*

There are numerous advantages to using the inquiry approach (see Hillocks 1999; Wiggins and McTighe 1998). Here we'll touch briefly on what seem to me to be the most important: motivation, context, and curricular coherence.

Motivation

In my own research (Smith and Wilhelm 2002, 2006; Wilhelm and Friedemann 1998), I've found that inquiry approaches organized around essential questions that embed reading and composing as meaningful inquiry-oriented activities have many benefits. These include increased student engagement, comprehension, better behavior and assignment completion, and deeper learning. In ***Glencoe Literature: The Reader's Choice,*** each unit is organized around the **Big Ideas,** designed to make learning matter to students in immediate ways.

Context

Many of the reading, composing, and language activities in ***The Reader's Choice*** are organized around real problems and issues, providing a meaningful context for students. Grammar, vocabulary, and reading and writing strategies are taught in the context of immediate use and are in service to reading or composing something that is personally relevant and that addresses the inquiry question.

Curricular Coherence

Inquiry teaching characterizes what Applebee, Burroughs, and Stevens (2000) call an *integrated* curriculum, that is, a curriculum in which students develop a set of skills, strategies, or tools that they apply with increasing sophistication across a range of activities. Everything that is learned is learned sequentially and in an integrated way by addressing the **Big Ideas.** Through inquiry a congruence of means and ends is achieved (Wiggins and McTighe 1998). Reading and writing help students personally address historically and socially significant issues. Likewise, grammar is taught in the context of the literary selections and students' own writing so that it is situated and meaningful. Care has been taken to teach grammatical constructs when it will help students with the kinds of writing they are engaged in at that time. In this way, reading and writing become integrated as forms of inquiry taught in a context of inquiry. By using this exciting approach, your students will see all of the benefits that accompany inquiry approaches.

Works Cited

Please Note: Some elements of this white paper appear in *Going with the Flow,* Smith and Wilhelm, and *Inquiring Minds Learn to Read and Write,* Wilhelm. Used with permission. Interested readers can find fuller treatments of the ideas presented here, along with relevant supporting research, by referring to these books.

Applebee, A. N., Burroughs, R., and Stevens, A. S. 2000. Shaping Conversations: A study of continuity and coherence in high school literature curricula. *Research in the Teaching of English* 34:396–429.

Dewey, J. 1916. *Democracy in Education.* New York: The Free Press.

Hillocks, G., Jr. 1999. *Ways of Thinking, Ways of Teaching.* New York: Teachers College Press.

Smith, M. W., and Wilhelm, J. D. 2002 *Reading Don't Fix No Chevys: Literacy in the lives of young men.* Portsmouth, NH: Heinemann.

Smith, M. W. and Wilhelm, J. D. 2006. *Going with the Flow: How to engage boys (and girls) in their literacy learning.* Portsmouth, NH: Heinemann.

Wiggins, G., and McTighe, J. 1998. *Understanding by Design.* Alexandria, VA: ASCD.

Wilhelm, J. D. 2003. *Reading IS Seeing.* New York: Scholastic.

Wilhelm, J. D., and Friedemann, P. 1998. *Hyperlearning: Where projects, inquiry, and technology meet.* York, ME: Stenhouse.

RESEARCH-BASED CLASSROOM SOLUTIONS

Differentiated Instruction

Meeting the Diverse Needs of Our Students

by Douglas Fisher, PhD
Professor of Education and Director of Professional Development, San Diego State University

Today's classroom contains students from a variety of backgrounds and with a variety of learning styles, strengths, and challenges. With careful planning, you can address the needs of all students in the literature classroom, using ***Glencoe Literature: The Reader's Choice.*** The basis for this planning is differentiated learning.

Differentiated Instruction Is a Key to Access

To differentiate instruction, teachers must acknowledge and react accordingly to students' differences in background knowledge, interests, needs, learning styles and preferences, and current reading, writing, and English language skills. The general guidelines for differentiating instruction include:

- **Linking assessment with instruction** Assessments should occur before, during, and after instruction to ensure that the curriculum is aligned with what students do and do not know. Using assessments in this way allows you to plan instruction for whole groups, small groups, and individual students.
- **Clarifying key concepts and generalizations** Students need to know what is essential and how this information can be used in their future learning. In addition, students need to develop a sense of the **Big Ideas**—historical, cultural, or social concepts that structure each unit in ***The Reader's Choice.***
- **Emphasizing critical and creative thinking** The content, process, and products used or assigned in the classroom should require that students think about what they are learning. While some students may require support, additional motivation, varied tasks, materials, or equipment, the overall focus on critical and creative thinking allows for all students to participate in the lesson.
- **Including teacher- and student-selected tasks** A differentiated classroom includes both teacher- and student-selected activities and tasks. At some points in the lesson, the teacher must provide instruction and assign learning activities. At other points, students should be provided choices in how they engage with the content. This balance increases motivation, engagement, and learning.

Supporting Individual Students

The vast majority of students will thrive in a classroom based on differentiated instruction. However, wise teachers recognize that no single option will work for all students and that there may be students who require unique systems of support to be successful.

Tips for Instruction

The following tips for instruction can support your efforts to help all students reach their maximum potential.

- Survey students to discover their individual differences. Use interest inventories of their unique talents so you can encourage contributions in the classroom.
- Be a model for respecting others. Adolescents crave social acceptance. The student with learning differences is especially sensitive to correction and criticism, particularly when it comes from a teacher. Your behavior will set the tone for how students treat one another.
- Expand opportunities for success. Provide a variety of instructional activities that reinforce skills and concepts.
- Establish measurable objectives and decide how you can best help students meet them.
- Celebrate successes and make note of and praise "work in progress."
- Keep it simple. Point out problem areas if doing so can help a student effect change. Avoid overwhelming students with too many goals at one time.
- Assign cooperative group projects that challenge all students to contribute to solving a problem or creating a product.

How Do I Reach Students with Learning Disabilities?

- Provide support and structure. Clearly specify rules, assignments, and responsibilities.
- Practice skills frequently. Use games and drills to help maintain student interest.
- Incorporate many modalities into the learning process. Provide opportunities to say, hear, write, read, and act out important concepts and information.
- Link new skills and concepts to those already mastered.
- If possible, allow students to record answers on audiotape.
- Allow extra time to complete assessments and assignments.
- Let students demonstrate proficiency with alternative presentations, including oral reports, role plays, art projects, and musical presentations.
- Provide outlines, notes, or tape recordings of lecture material.
- Pair students with peer helpers and provide class time for pair interaction.

How Do I Reach English Language Learners?

- Remember that students' ability to speak English does not reflect their academic abilities.
- Try to incorporate the students' cultural experiences into your instruction. The help of a bilingual aide may be effective.
- Avoid any references in your instruction that could be construed as cultural stereotypes.
- Preteach important vocabulary and concepts.
- Encourage students to preview text, such as noting headings, before they begin reading.
- Remind students not to ignore graphic organizers, photographs, and maps since there is much information in these visuals.
- Use artifacts and photographs whenever possible to build background knowledge and understanding. An example of this would be coins in a foreign currency or a raw cotton ball to reinforce cotton's importance in history.

How Do I Reach Gifted Students?

- Make arrangements for students to take selected subjects early and to work on independent projects.
- Ask "what if" questions to develop high-level thinking skills. Establish an environment safe for risk taking in your classroom.
- Emphasize concepts, theories, ideas, relationships, and generalizations about the content.
- Promote interest in the past by inviting students to make connections to the present.
- Let students express themselves in alternate ways such as creative writing, acting, debates, simulations, drawing, or music.
- Provide students with a catalog of helpful resources, listing things such as agencies that provide free or inexpensive materials, appropriate community services and programs, and community experts who might be called upon to speak to your students.
- Assign extension projects that allow students to solve real-life problems related to their communities.

References

Fisher, D. 2005. The missing link: standards, assessment, and instruction. *Voices From the Middle.* 13(2), 8–11.

McTighe, J., Seif, E., and Wiggins, G. 2004. You can teach for meaning. *Educational Leadership* 62(1), 26-30.

Pflaum, S. W., and Bishop, P. A. 2004. Student perceptions of reading engagement: learning from the learners. *Journal of Adolescent and Adult Literacy* 48(3), 202–213.

Tomlinson, C. A., and McTighe, J. 2006. *Integrating Differentiated Instruction & Understanding by Design: Connecting content and kids.* Alexandria, VA: ASCD.

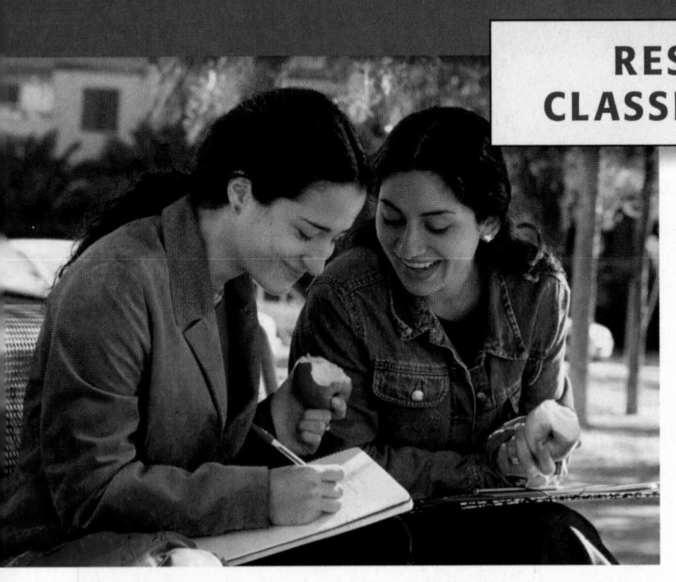

RESEARCH-BASED CLASSROOM SOLUTIONS

Content Literacy

Ensuring that Students Access the Text to Build Reading, Writing, and Thinking Skills

by Douglas Fisher, PhD,
Professor of Education
and Director of Professional Development,
San Diego State University

Considerable research evidence exists regarding "what works" in helping students understand difficult concepts and content. The evidence to date clearly indicates that teachers must activate students' background and prior knowledge, teach students how to take notes and use graphic organizers, focus on vocabulary, and help students develop their thinking through writing. As such, our instructional goals are multifaceted. Students must read, write, speak, listen, and view in order to understand the content. This requires that we provide content literacy instruction that is evidence based and results in increased achievement.

Activating Background and Prior Knowledge

Decades of research strongly suggest that learning is dependent on attention and interest. When we have and hold students' attention and interest, they think about the content of our classes, and they learn. To gain their attention, we have to activate both background knowledge and prior knowledge (Dochy, Segers, & Buehl 1999).

Although they are sometimes used interchangeably, *background knowledge* and *prior knowledge* are different yet complementary ideas. Background knowledge is the information that students have because of who they are and what they have experienced. Prior knowledge is the information that students should know based on their participation in previous schooling experiences. Activating and building both background and prior knowledge focus students' attention on the topic at hand, a powerful way to begin a standards-aligned unit of study.

Note Taking

The ability to take and organize notes is a significant predictor of student success. Notes serve an external storage function, which builds comprehension and understanding of the content. Over time, and with instruction, students not only use their notes for external storage of information, but also for encoding their ideas. Pauk (1974) has observed that note taking is a critical skill for college success. Peverly, Brobst, Graham, and Shaw (2003) showed that background knowledge and note taking were significant predictors of success on tests.

In other words, note taking is a critical skill. But the question remains: what kind of note-taking system works? According to a number of studies, a two-column format, such as Cornell note taking, is effective (Fisher, 2001). With this format, students take notes and complete the tasks on the right side of the page while the left side provides a guide to key points. These key points help students quickly find information, locate references, and study for exams. As Faber, Morris, and Lieberman (2000) found, the Cornell note-taking system increases comprehension (and test scores!).

Graphic Organizers

Graphic organizers, such as concept maps, semantic webs, and cause-and-effect charts, also help students visually organize information presented in text format (Fisher, Frey, & Williams 2002). In addition, graphic organizers are a good way to summarize information and will aid students in remembering and recalling content (Irwin-DeVitis & Pease 1995; Wilson 2002).

Graphic organizers have been used successfully by many different kinds of learners, including English language learners, struggling readers, students with disabilities, and students who are gifted and talented. The usefulness of graphic organizers is well documented, and they are a powerful way to ensure that students learn and understand content.

Vocabulary

The vocabulary demands in secondary schools are intense. Students are expected to learn thousands of words per year in multiple content areas. In a study of secondary students, Espin and Foegen (1996) found vocabulary to be a significant predictor of content-area performance. Farket and Elmore (1992) found vocabulary knowledge to be a stronger predictor of reading comprehension than most other variables, even cognitive ability.

When researchers study successful students, they often find that vocabulary knowledge is an important factor in student learning (Martino & Hoffman 2002). Teachers must ensure that their students develop the specialized and technical vocabulary to discuss the discipline, as well as the generalized vocabulary to convey their thinking about the subjects they study.

Writing to Learn

Writing is an excellent way to learn. Did you know that we all clarify our thinking when we write? Students often say that they didn't know what they thought until they wrote it down. Writing not only helps students clarify their thinking but also provides the teacher with information about what students do and do not understand (Fisher & Frey 2004). However, the writing prompts must be constructed to ensure that students engage and think as they write.

Quality writing prompts remind students to do what good readers automatically do: summarize information, predict what's coming next, make connections between their lives and the text, question the information in the text and the author of the text, clarify information and ideas, visualize what the text has to say, and make inferences or draw conclusions from facts and ideas (Harvey & Goudvis 2000).

Summary

In short, learning is language based. To comprehend academic content, students must engage in a number of reading, writing, speaking, listening, and viewing activities. These activities must be grounded in well-developed content, and they must be accessible for students. Not all strategies are created equal. There are specific instructional strategies and techniques that enjoy a firm research base. The topics, ideas, approaches, and strategies outlined in this paper and in the references below will ensure that students become increasingly literate as they learn valuable content information.

Works Cited

Dochy, F., Segers, M., and Buehl, M. M. 1999. The relationship between assessment practices and outcomes of studies: The case of research on prior knowledge. *Review of Educational Research* 69:145–186.

Espin, C. A., and Foegen, A. 1996. Validity of general outcome measures for predicting secondary students' performance on content-area tasks. *Exceptional Children* 62:497–514.

Faber, J. E., Morris, J. D., and Lieberman, M. G. 2000. The effect of note taking on ninth grade students' comprehension. *Reading Psychology* 21:257–270.

Fisher, D. 2001. "We're moving on up": Creating a schoolwide literacy effort in an urban high school. *Journal of Adolescent & Adult Literacy* 45:92–101.

Fisher, D., and Frey, N. 2004. *Improving adolescent literacy: Strategies at work.* Upper Saddle River, NJ: Merrill Prentice Hall.

Fisher, D., Frey, N., and Williams, D. 2002. Seven literacy strategies that work. *Educational Leadership* 60(3):70–73.

Harvey, S., and Goudvis, A. 2000. *Strategies That Work: Teaching comprehension to enhance understanding.* York, ME: Stenhouse.

Irwin-DeVitis, L., and Pease, D. 1995. Using graphic organizers for learning and assessment in middle level classrooms. *Middle School Journal* 26(5):57–64.

Martino, N. L., and Hoffman, P. R. 2002. An investigation of reading and language abilities of college freshmen. *Journal of Research in Reading* 25:310–318.

Pauk, W. 1974. *How to study in college.* Boston: Houghton Mifflin.

Peverly, S. T., Brobst, K. E., Graham, M., and Shaw, R. 2003. College adults are not good at self-regulation: A study on the relationship of self-regulation, note taking, and test taking. *Journal of Educational Psychology* 95:335–346.

Wilson, E. 2002. Literature and literacy in the social studies classroom: Strategies to enhance social studies instruction. *Southern Social Studies Journal* 28(1):45–57.

RESEARCH-BASED CLASSROOM SOLUTIONS

Vocabulary Development

Teaching and Learning Vocabulary in *The Reader's Choice* Program

by Sharon F. O'Neal, PhD
Associate Professor, Texas State University

What Is Vocabulary?

At first, this question seems simple. Vocabulary is our knowledge of words and their corresponding meanings. These are the words we use when we speak and write. These are the words we understand when we listen and read. Our job as teachers is simply to decide which words are important and help our students learn them.

However, the question becomes more complicated when we begin to think about the gradations of understanding our students bring to the printed page. Sometimes a student just barely knows a word, and she may or may not be able to figure out the meaning of the word in context. Another student may know the meaning of a word only in a single context. Finally, another student may have a full and rich understanding of a vocabulary word in multiple contexts. This student can even use the context to figure out the definition of a word that she is not sure about.

As teachers of the language arts, we want our students to build that base of established, known words in multiple contexts. Current research has shed light on the essential importance of vocabulary knowledge and vocabulary strategies across content areas and throughout life.

Why Is Vocabulary Instruction Important?

Vocabulary is the first key connection to literacy. All of the oral language that surrounds young children will play a part in their understanding of words when they begin to read. Middle and high school students also make connections between and among their experiences and knowledge and the words on a page. The talk that surrounds that text may be critical to understanding text. Reading vocabulary is crucial for understanding texts at all levels. But what about the student who speaks a language other than English? How can we build his vocabulary so that he can comprehend the selections in a literature text?

In some classrooms, it is common to have students who speak other languages in the home. Understandably, students who are learning English while simultaneously trying to learn content often lag behind in English reading success. Such struggles are frequently due to lack of word knowledge. In addition, studies have shown that vocabulary instruction may be more important to test performance than prior knowledge of content is (Jimenez et al., 1996). Studies indicate that English language learners (ELL's) make gains in vocabulary development and reading comprehension if they receive an enriched program in vocabulary development (August, et al., 2006).

Yet students who struggle with reading usually avoid reading and therefore encounter fewer words in context. If reading skills are stalled at earlier grade levels, vocabulary growth may stop altogether. Such students may be stuck in a vicious cycle. They read less because they know fewer words, and they know fewer words because they read less. The goal of ***The Reader's Choice*** is to entice all readers to come to the page: those who scarcely know the language of literature, those who may know the meanings of words in limited contexts, and those who have a full and rich understanding of what the English language has to offer.

How Does *The Reader's Choice* Address Vocabulary Instruction?

The average student's reading vocabulary increases by between 3,000 and 5,000 words per year. Such acquisition results in a reading vocabulary of 25,000 words by the end of middle school and 50,000 words by the end of high school for the successful student (Graves 2000). If students are to flourish in school, they must acquire 4,000 new words per year. Many words can be learned through wide and varied reading experiences, but some words must be learned through direct instruction. ***The Reader's Choice*** offers teachers and students both short- and long-term strategies.

Short-term strategies include providing the teacher with key words prior to reading the selection. Glencoe has mined both the fiction and nonfiction selections for those vocabulary words that are most critical for understanding the reading passage. Students are pre-taught words through discussions and activities such as categorizing words and making personal connections to the unique words found in the text.

In addition to offering instruction that leads to the immediate understanding of the selected text, ***The Reader's Choice*** also values the importance of providing students with strategies they can use on their own. Such long-term goals include direct instruction in the meaning of prefixes and suffixes and how the addition of such word parts alters the meaning of the base words. Precise directions for using context and reference materials are emphasized as well. In other words, it is not enough just to teach a list of words. Readers need to know the structure of text and the relationship among words.

Students must understand the larger concepts related to selected vocabulary words. In ***The Reader's Choice,*** students' background knowledge is continually tapped and built so that they are better prepared for reading. Students must know many things about words—their literal meanings, their various connotations, and their semantic associates (synonyms and antonyms, for example). Both depth and breadth of word knowledge are examined. Teachers can assess word knowledge through a variety of products including journal entries, word maps, and word banks. These provide practice for the learner and inform the teacher about the progress of the learner.

Throughout the program, ***The Reader's Choice*** is sensitive to the importance of wide exposure to vocabulary. As a result, multiple opportunities are provided to read related texts in varied content areas. Teachers and students will find bibliographies of additional readings related to the text provided throughout the program.

Works Cited

August, D., Carlo, M., Lively, T., McLaughlin, B., and Snow, C. 2006. Promoting the vocabulary growth of English learners. In T. Young and M. Hadaway (Eds.) *Supporting the Development of English Learners: Increasing success in all classrooms.* Newark, DE: International Reading Association.

Graves, M. F. 2000. A vocabulary program to complement and bolster a middle grade comprehension program. In B. Taylor, M. Graves, and P. van den Broek (Eds.) *Reading for Meaning: Fostering comprehension in the middle grades.* Newark, DE: International Reading Association.

Jimenez, R., Garcia, G., and Pearson, P. 1996. The reading strategies of Latino/a students who are successful English readers: Opportunities and obstacles. *Reading Research Quarterly* 31:31–61.

RESEARCH-BASED CLASSROOM SOLUTIONS

Writing

by Jacqueline Jones Royster, DA
Professor of English and Senior Vice Provost and Executive Dean of the College of Arts and Sciences, The Ohio State University

As both art and artifact, writing is a flexible tool that can work dynamically with other elements of instruction to enhance both learning and performance. The collection of texts and activities in *Glencoe Literature: The Reader's Choice* offers a theoretically and pedagogically sound way to address the challenges of developing the writing and related skills of students in the classroom. Writing activities are generously incorporated throughout each thematic unit for a variety of purposes. The series takes into account contemporary trends in both scholarship and practice and sets forth features that offer much potential for success.

Writing to Make Personal Connections with Reading Selections

Through journaling and other writing activities in *The Reader's Choice,* students have a mechanism for responding to whatever they read and making sense of the details. Writing can help students express personal connections with ideas, images, and experiences; discover ways to go beyond their own connections toward broader implications; and note critical distinctions between their own experiences and the content of the reading selections.

Writing to Experiment as Creative Thinkers

We as teachers accomplish an important cultural task when we help students move from viewing themselves as just consumers of other people's writing to seeing themselves as producers of writing. The creative writing activities in *The Reader's Choice* encourage students to write in many genres and to compose and present their work through various media. With these writing activities, students can explore varied roles and diverse points of view as a way to think seriously about what it means to produce literature.

Writing to Understand Form and Function

Through the **Writing Workshops** in *The Reader's Choice,* students gain direct experience producing various forms and genres of writing. The genre knowledge students build helps them to see writing as having structure and organization as shaped by audience, purpose, and context. Throughout *The Reader's Choice,* writing activities reinforce students' understanding of form and function by asking them to try their own hand at writing reflective essays, literary analyses, historical investigations, autobiographical sketches, persuasive speeches, short stories, and other distinctive forms.

Writing to Develop Thinking Skills

Writing helps students think about what a text says and does and whether it is successful. Students can sort through ideas, weigh the impact and consequences of language choices, and use these assessments to make informed judgments about what works in written expression and why.

The writing activities in *The Reader's Choice* foster students' abilities to think like literary critics. The **Literary Criticism, You're the Critic,** and **Primary Source Quotation** activities, for example, use scholarly quotations to prompt students to write thoughtful analyses of the selections. Through writing, students can express what appeals to them as readers and explain how authors achieve particular effects, justifying their interpretations by providing examples and evidence from the text. Students may also investigate the broader meaning of texts through research and writing. By gathering and synthesizing information from primary and secondary sources, students can discover the historical, political, or cultural context of a literary work.

Writing to Communicate Effectively

The act of writing itself—writing frequently for many purposes and in various genres—hones students' abilities as writers and communicators. Through activities, workshops, and assessments, *The Reader's Choice* provides ample practice for developing writing skills. For example, the Writing Workshops at the end of each theme guide students through the writing process and focus on particular moments of engagement—

prewriting, drafting, revising, editing/proofreading, and publishing/presenting.

In addition, complete annotated **Writing Models**—both student workshop models and professional models—help teachers and students focus on these **Traits of Strong Writing:**

- **Ideas** The message or the theme and the details that develop it
- **Organization** The arrangement of main ideas and supporting details
- **Voice** A writer's unique way of using tone and style
- **Word Choice** The vocabulary a writer uses to convey meaning
- **Sentence Fluency** The smooth rhythm and flow of sentences in length and style
- **Conventions** Correct spelling, grammar, usage, and mechanics
- **Presentation** The way words and design elements look on a page

Writing to Master Standard English Conventions

The Reader's Choice provides two paths for achieving mastery of grammar, usage, and mechanics:

- **Point-of-Use Approach** In both the Student and Teacher Wraparound editions, **Grammar Workshops** and **Author's Language and Style** activities help teachers review a skill in grammar, usage, or mechanics while linking that skill to an author's application of it in a literary work, thus giving students a "real-world" example from which to learn.
- **Systematic Approach** Teachers may use the ***Language Handbook*** in the **Reference Section** of *The Reader's Choice* to study English language conventions systematically, moving methodically through instruction in skills such as identifying parts of speech, using modifiers correctly, and enhancing sentence fluency through sentence combining.

Writing to Prepare for the Real World

Many writing activities in *The Reader's Choice* ask students to draft career-related or public documents in response to literature. For example, students might write a brochure about a poetic setting, an interview with a character from a short story, or a news broadcast on an author's life. The ***Business Writing Handbook*** focuses on business and technical documents, such as résumés, memos, and business e-mails. In addition, students are regularly asked to conduct research for informal essays and formal research reports and to use widely accepted conventions for citing and documenting sources.

To prepare students for the **Advanced Placement** examination and for college work, activities such as **Literary Analysis** and **Writing About Literature** require students to write analyses of works of literature and the literary elements that shape them. These kinds of writing help sharpen students' understandings of audience and purpose and enhance their abilities to write clearly and coherently for situations they will encounter beyond high school.

Recommended Readings

Benson, C., and Christian, S., (Eds.) 2002. *Writing to Make a Difference: Classroom projects for community change.* New York: Teachers College Press.

Branscombe, N. A., Goswami, D., and Schwartz, J., (Eds.) 1992. *Students Teaching, Teachers Learning.* Portsmouth, NH: Boynton/Cook.

Dean, D. 2006. *Strategic Writing: The writing process and beyond in the secondary English classroom.* Urbana, IL: NCTE.

Golub, J. N. 2000. *Making Learning Happen: Strategies for an interactive classroom.* Urbana, IL: NCTE.

Mitchell, D., and Christenbury, L. 2000. *Both Art and Craft: Teaching ideas that spark learning.* Urbana, IL: NCTE.

The National Commission on Writing in America's Schools and Colleges. 2003. *The Neglected* "R." New York: The College Entrance Examination Board.

Shanahan, T. (Ed.) 1994. *Teachers Thinking, Teachers Knowing: Reflections on literacy and language education.* Urbana, IL: NCTE.

RESEARCH-BASED CLASSROOM SOLUTIONS

English Language Learners

by Mary A. Avalos, PhD
Assistant Department Chair and Research Assistant Professor, Department of Teaching and Learning, University of Miami

English language learners are a growing population in our schools. During the 2000–2001 academic year, more than 4.5 million English language learners were enrolled in U.S. public schools (McREL 2003). The growth of culturally and linguistically diverse populations is expected to continue through this decade. Immigrants come to the United States for various reasons—some to escape political or economic oppression, others to seek higher-paying wages or provide a higher standard of living for their families. Although shifting demographics have a greater impact on certain regions of the United States, all teachers should be prepared to teach all students.

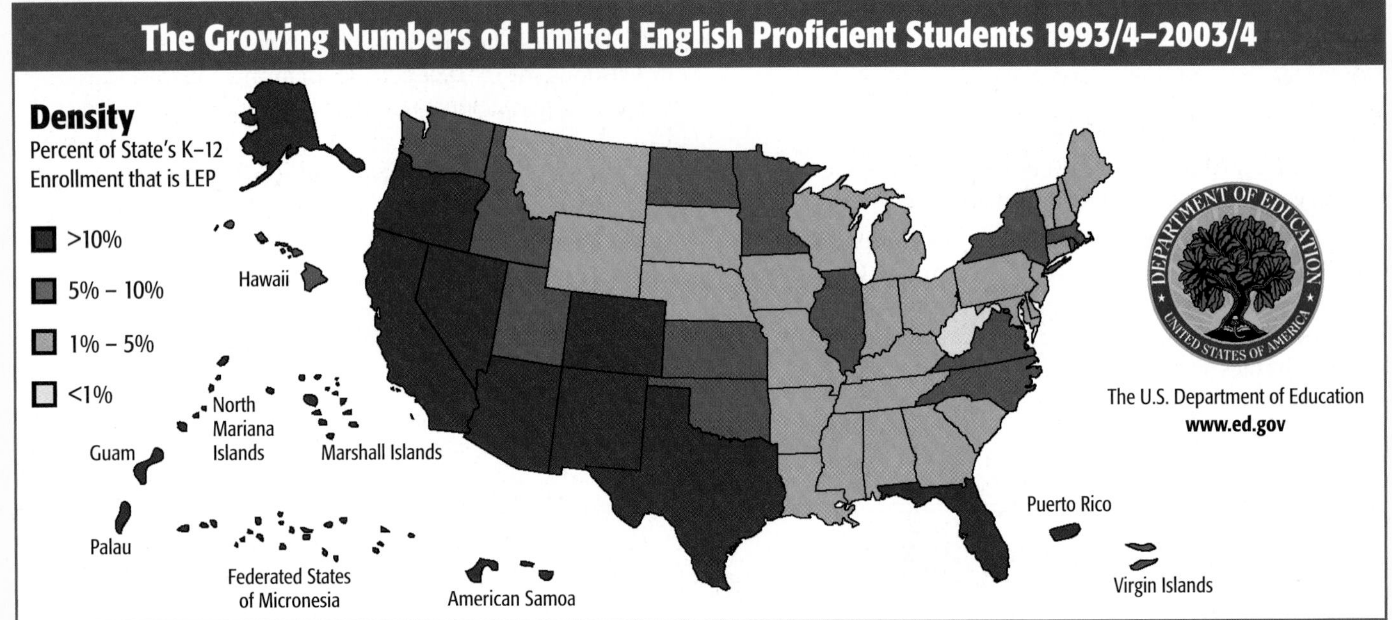

Meeting the Challenge

There are challenges specific to teaching English language learners, who must learn content while learning to read, write, and speak a new language. English language learners' literacy proficiency in their first language, or L1, will impact their literacy acquisition of a second language, or L2. (Au 1993; Cummins 2003; Hudelson 1984; Snow 1990), particularly if the L1 is similar to the L2.

English language learners make an easier transition between L1 and L2 if both languages share a similar writing system.

Writing System	Example
Alphabetic	English, French, Spanish, Italian
Syllabic	Cherokee
Logographic	Chinese

To provide effective instruction, teachers should build upon what English language learners know about language and literacy knowledge. Teachers should also consider English language learners' cultural traits, such as those related to celebration and mourning rituals, child-rearing practices, and food. Try to incorporate the students' cultural experiences into your teaching.

Gauging Levels of Language Proficiency

A common misconception is that English language learners are ready to proceed to mainstream instruction with little or no support once they are able to converse using everyday language. In reality, there are three levels of language proficiency as labeled by Cummins (2003).

Level of Language Proficiency	Example
Basic Interpersonal Conversation Skills (BICS)	ability to talk about daily activities, make requests, and retell a personal story or event
Discrete Language Skills	knowledge of phonological awareness, grammar rules, or conventions of writing in the learner's first language
Cognitive Academic Language Proficiency (CALP)	the ability to read and understand technical or subject area texts with low frequency words of Latin or Greek origin

By learning about language-acquisition processes, teachers can better meet the needs of English language learners.

Several instructional features of ***Glencoe Literature: The Reader's Choice*** help English language learners develop higher levels of language proficiency. Note the following examples.

1. analyzing the reading selections to facilitate comprehension of low frequency vocabulary, as well as identified vocabulary words for study
2. prompting students to activate prior knowledge before/while reading to make connections between the reader and the text
3. integrating literary elements throughout the selections to provide meaningful prompts in context
4. setting objectives to ensure that all students receive high quality, standards-based instruction
5. contextualizing writing, grammar, and spelling instruction throughout the program

All of these examples increase teacher awareness of text- and reader-based features as teachers instruct English language learners. This approach to instruction, in turn, better meets the unique needs of English language learners as they learn content and language together.

Works Cited

Au, K. H. 1993. *Literacy Instruction in Multicultural Settings.* Orlando, FL: Harcourt Brace College Publishers.

Cummins, J. 2003. Reading and the bilingual student: Fact and friction. In G. G. Garcia (Ed.) *English Learners: Reaching the highest level of English literacy.* Newark, DE: International Reading Association.

Hudelson, S. 1984. "Kan yu ret an rayt en ingles": Children become literate in English as a second language. *TESOL Quarterly* 18:221–238.

Mid-continent Research for Education and Learning. Fall 2003. English language learners and the No Child Left Behind Act. *Changing Schools: A newsletter from the Central Region Educational Laboratory* Retrieved from the Internet on February 17, 2006: http://www.mcrel.org/PDF/ChangingSchools/5032NL_CSfall2003.pdf#search='percentage%20of%20English%20language%20learners%20in%20U.S.%20schools

Snow, C.E. 1990. Rationales for native language instruction in the education of language minority children: Evidence from research. In A. Padilla, H. Fairchild, and C. Valadez (Eds.) *Bilingual education: Issues and strategies.* pp. 60-74. Newbury Park, CA: Sage.

Jamestown Education

Support for All Readers

For over 35 years, Jamestown Education has made its primary focus helping all readers become better readers. The Jamestown programs shown here are based on the latest research in adolescent literacy and on over 35 years of experience reaching adolescent readers. Each of these programs can help you build a comprehensive and well-coordinated literary program.

Jamestown Literature: An Adapted Reader

- Grade Levels 6–10
- Reading Levels 3–8
- Instructional Support:
  This series provides grade-specific collections of literature adapted to lower reading levels. Providing struggling readers with alternative versions of canon literature offers an additional opportunity to differentiate instruction. Look for the image of *Jamestown Literature: An Adapted Reader* in the Teacher's Wraparound Edition. This reference means you can find the same selection in both *Glencoe Literature: The Reader's Choice* and *Jamestown Literature.*

In the Spotlight™

- Reading Levels 2–10
- Instructional Support:
  This eight-book series provides your students with engaging and motivating biographies to read while building their reading skills and vocabulary development. In each graduated unit, students are guided before, during, and after reading, with comprehension, skill, and vocabulary reinforcement, as well as writing exercises.

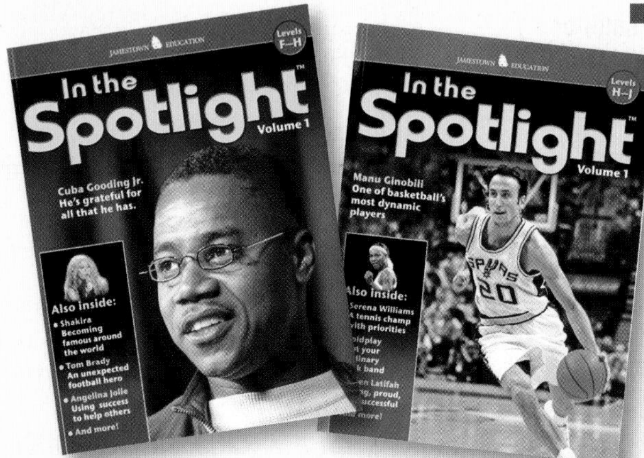

Timed Readings, Timed Readings Plus, Timed Readings in Literature

- Reading Levels 1–13+
- Instructional Support:
  Each series (ten books in each) helps your students increase both reading rate and comprehension. The fiction and nonfiction passages of uniform length are designed for systematic classroom practice to improve reading rate and comprehension of text.

Reading Fluency

- Reading Levels 1–10
- Instructional Support:
  This seven-book series helps your students read smoothly, accurately, and expressively. Students work in pairs to provide immediate feedback and self-assessment. Author Camille Blachowicz states that "the ability to read fluently is highly correlated with many other measures of reading competence."

Jamestown Reading Improvement

- Reading Levels 4–10
- Instructional Support:
  Authored by renowned reading expert Edward Fry, this eight-book series focuses on helping build your students' comprehension, vocabulary, and study skills. Repeated practice with targeted exercises ensures mastery of valuable reading skills.

Critical Reading Series

- Reading Levels 2–8
- Instructional Support:
  This 27-book, high-interest series, written at three reading spans, encourages your reluctant readers to build a love for nonfiction and focuses on critical reading skills. Topics ranging from *Fateful Journeys* to *Weird Science* to *Heroes* draw students in and give them ample opportunities to master the important skills found on both state and national tests.

Jamestown Reading Navigator

Jamestown Reading Navigator is an online and print-based intervention program built upon the latest research in adolescent literacy, *Reading Next*. Here are the key objectives of the online version, available to students 24 hours a day from anywhere they can connect to the Web.

- Increase student achievement through direct, explicit instruction in comprehension strategies and modeling of good reading practices.
- Motivate and engage reluctant readers with a student-directed, self-paced learning environment enriched with interactive activities and media.
- Provide built-in formative and summative assessment to help teachers track student progress and make instructional decisions.

RESEARCH-BASED CLASSROOM SOLUTIONS

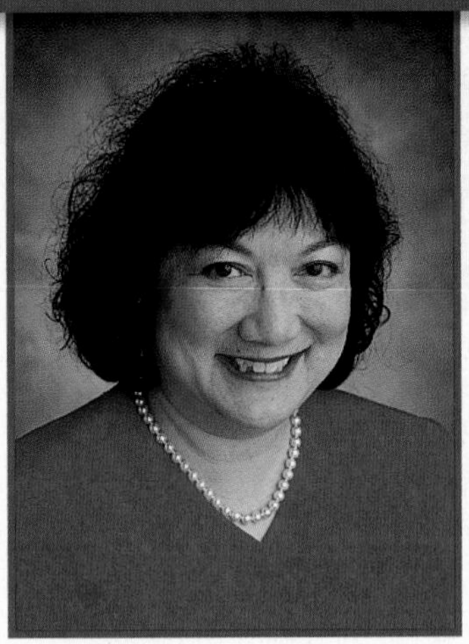

Assessment

by Beverly Ann Chin, PhD
Professor of English, Director of English Teaching Program, University of Montana

What Is Assessment?

Assessment is the process of gathering information about student learning. The purpose of assessment is to provide evidence on what and how well students are learning in the English language arts. The best assessments clearly reflect learning objectives, instructional strategies, and curriculum standards.

Formative assessments—or assessments *for* learning—are ongoing opportunities for students to gain information about themselves and their learning processes. Teachers use formative assessments during the instructional units to help students discover their own areas of strength and areas for improvement in the English language arts.

Summative assessments—or assessments *of* learning—occur at the end of a unit of study and summarize what students have learned and how well they have met the learning objectives. Summative assessments are more formal, culminating experiences and often include student demonstrations or performances of their learning.

How Does *The Reader's Choice* Integrate Assessment?

Glencoe Literature: The Reader's Choice carefully weaves assessment *for* learning and assessment *of* learning throughout the instructional units.

We provide numerous opportunities to help students access information about their learning progress. Formative assessments, such as **Selection and Unit Assessments** and **Interactive Tutor Self-Assessments,** give information about what students are learning and help teachers differentiate or modify their instruction. These assessments *for* learning are diagnostic and enable teachers to provide more support and resources for students during the instructional unit.

The Reader's Choice also provides multiple methods of summative and performance assessments, including:

- assessment by learning objectives
- rubrics for assessing student writing, listening, and speaking

Each of these assessments *of* learning gives teachers and students a clear summary of what students have learned and how well they have met the learning objectives for the unit.

Through formative and summative assessments, English language arts teachers gain valuable information and insight into their students' understandings of and appreciations for literature. By using assessments that align with the learning objectives and curriculum standards, we empower our students to become learners who are able to set goals, monitor their learning processes, and reflect on their growth as readers, writers, speakers, and listeners.

References

Marzano, R. J., Pickering, D. J., & McTighe, J. 1993. *Assessing Student Outcomes.* Alexandria, VA: Association for Supervision and Curriculum Development.

Stiggins, R. J. 2001. *Student-involved Classroom Assessment* (3rd ed.). Upper Saddle River, NJ: Prentice-Hall.

Stiggins, R. J., Arter, J. A., Chappuis, J., & Chappuis, S. 2004. *Classroom Assessment for Student Learning: Doing It Right—Using It Well.* Portland, OR: Assessment Training Institute.

Wiggins, G., & McTighe, J. 1998. *Understanding by Design.* Alexandria, VA: Association of Supervision and Curriculum Development.

Technology Use

Electronic Technologies: *Everything* to Do with Literacy

by Jeffrey D. Wilhelm, PhD, Professor of English Education, Boise State University

What Is Technology?

A technology can be defined as any tool that extends our human abilities—that helps us accomplish our work more effectively. Literacy is the ability to use the most powerful tools to exchange information and to communicate, which humans do in a variety of deep and complex ways.

Neil Postman (1992) cautions that we must learn how best to use technology for our purposes or we are doomed to be used by the technology. Many critics of computers in schools argue that this is what happens: Computers are often used as expensive ways to implement old and ineffective ways of teaching. Further, students often lose sight of the nature of technology as a tool, using it instead for its own sake.

However, there is an alternative—the kind of technology use offered in ***Glencoe Literature: The Reader's Choice.*** By using technological applications in our inquiry-based program, students find information, organize data, develop new data and understandings, and design and represent new understandings.

The rewards of this kind of technological instruction are great. First, the purposeful use of such technologies motivates students. It fosters engagement, collaboration, and substantive learning (Smith and Wilhelm 2002, 2006; Wilhelm, 2006). Students learn to use the Internet, hypermedia, and other applications in a meaningful context. The technology also supports traditional ways of reading and composing as students converse through Web logs and e-mail, find information on the Internet, organize and analyze data electronically, and use video and computers to construct documents that can be shared through other electronic means. This kind of curriculum has been shown to have many positive effects, particularly for students often considered reluctant or "at-risk" (Wilhelm and Friedemann 1998).

How Does *The Reader's Choice* Integrate Technology?

In ***The Reader's Choice,*** technology is used to improve reading, composing, and learning. Technology features, such as ***Skills Arcade,*** **Interactive Tutor Self-Assessments, Vocabulary PuzzleMakers,** and **eWorkbooks,** reflect these principles, fostering inquiry and deep understanding.

Seymour Papert (1996), the world's foremost authority on computers and learning, writes that "the computer is the world's greatest construction kit." He agrees that literacy is intimately involved in technology and its critical use. He argues that schools that do not make meaningful use of the computer are failing our kids. Critical use, he tells us, can occur only if students find and design knowledge with technology. This kind of work is what Papert calls "hard fun," and it leads to powerful and exciting forms of learning. We have provided the context and support for this kind of learning in the text you hold in your hands. Turn the page and get ready for some "hard fun" of your own.

Works Cited

Beck, C., and Kosnick, C. 2004. Constructivist accounts of learning. In K. Leithwood, et al. (Eds.) *Teaching for Deep Understanding.* pp.13–21. Toronto: EFTP/OISE.

Papert, S. 1996. *The Connected Family.* Atlanta, GA: Longstreet Press.

Postman, N. 1992. *Technopoly: The surrender of culture to technology.* New York: Vintage.

Smith, M. W., and Wilhelm, J. D. 2002 *Reading Don't Fix No Chevys: Literacy in the lives of young men.* Portsmouth, NH: Heinemann.

Smith, M. W., and Wilhelm, J. D. 2006 *Going with the Flow: How to engage boys (and girls) in their literacy learning.* Portsmouth, NH: Heinemann.

Wilhelm, J. D. 2006. *Inquiring Minds Learn to Read and Write: Inquiry, questioning and discussion strategies to improve reading and writing.* New York: Scholastic.

Wilhelm, J. D., and Friedemann, P. 1998. *Hyperlearning: Where projects, inquiry, and technology meet.* York, ME: Stenhouse.

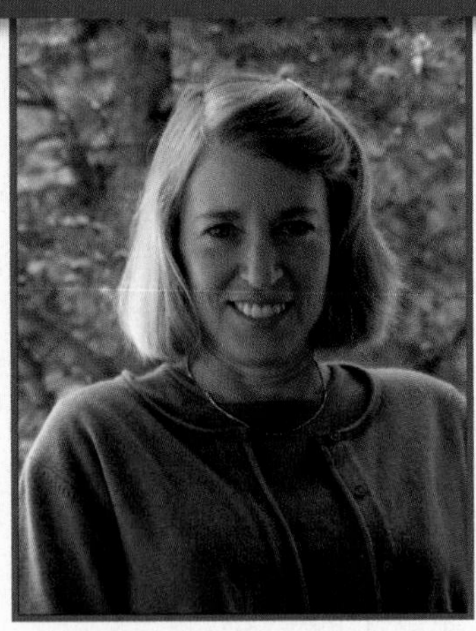

RESEARCH-BASED CLASSROOM SOLUTIONS

Project CRISS

by Carol M. Santa, PhD
Original developer of Project CRISS,
Director of Education at the Montana Academy

What is CRISS?

CRISS stands for Creating Independence through Student-owned Strategies. It is a staff development program that I created in collaboration with middle and high school teachers in Kalispell, Montana.

The CRISS Philosophy

Project CRISS is more than a collection of learning strategies. Its underlying power rests not on the individual strategies but on the teaching philosophy behind them. This philosophy integrates work from cognitive psychology, social learning theory, and neurological research about how the brain learns. It includes the overlapping principles in the chart below.

A Systematic Approach

Project CRISS is a valuable basis for instruction. It provides a systematic approach for using what we now know about teaching and learning. The following chart lists questions we continually need to ask ourselves while we are teaching. Use this chart to monitor your efforts to incorporate CRISS principles into your teaching.

CRISS Principles	The CRISS Philosophy	Yes	No	Somewhat
Background knowledge	Did I assist students in thinking about what they already knew about the topic before beginning the unit? Did I develop necessary concepts before students read?			
Purpose setting	Did my students have a clear purpose about what they were going to learn before beginning the lesson?			
Author's craft	Can my students use the author's style of presentation to facilitate their understanding?			
Active involvement	Were my students engaged in the topic? Did I help students become actively involved in their learning?			
Discussion	Did my students have opportunities to talk about what they were learning?			
Organization	Did my students organize information in a variety of ways?			
Writing	Did my students write about what they were learning?			
Teacher modeling	Did I do enough teacher modeling of learning strategies so that students could begin using them on their own?			

Guide to Readability

Throughout the teacher materials in your Teacher Wraparound Edition, you will encounter DRP readability measures assigned to the reading selections in ***The Reader's Choice.*** You will also find readability scores based on the Lexile Framework® for Reading and the Dale-Chall Readability Formula. You can use these scores to select reading materials that are suitable for your entire class or for individual students.

Degrees of Reading Power® (DRP)

DRP values indicate the readability of prose text. The higher the value, the more difficult the text. The scale ranges from 1 to 100; commonly encountered English text tends to fall somewhere between 25 and 85. Although middle school texts have an average difficulty of 56, and high school texts have an average difficulty of 62, no single readability level is appropriate for each grade level. Rather, a typical classroom has materials with a range of readability levels available for use—some intended for less proficient readers, some for average readers, and some for stronger readers. The following chart shows the average DRP readability range for materials widely available for use at each grade. Some materials you might use, however, will certainly fall outside of the range for your particular grade.

Grade	DRP Readability Ranges
6	51–61
7	52–62
8	53–64
9	53–65
10	51–68
11	56–67
12	57–68

The Lexile® Framework

A Lexile measure assigned to a text is the specific number that describes the reading demands of the text. The typical Lexile Scale ranges from 200 to 1700 Lexiles. As with the DRP measures, there is not a direct translation from a specific Lexile measure to a specific grade level. Within any classroom, there will be a range of readers and a range of materials to be read. The levels shown on the following chart indicate the approximate range of Lexile scores for 50 percent of the materials found in a typical grade-level classroom. For example, the middle half of the instructional materials typically found in a sixth-grade classroom ranges in difficulty from about 850L to 1050L.

Grade	Text Measures (from Lexile Framework Map)
6	850L to 1050L
7	950L to 1075L
8	1000L to 1100L
9	1050L to 1150L
10	1100L to 1200L
11 and 12	1100L to 1300L

Dale-Chall Readability Formula

The idea behind this formula is that readers typically find it easier to read, process, and recall a passage if the words and sentences are familiar and grade appropriate. The Dale-Chall Formula assesses the difficulty of a passage by computing two different values from the text. The first measure is the average number of words per sentence. The second measure is the percentage of words in the passage not found on the grade-appropriate Dale Word List. The following chart shows the average Dale-Chall readability scores for grades 5 through 12.

Grade	Dale-Chall Readability Ranges
5–6	5.0 to 5.9
7–8	6.0 to 6.9
9–10	7.0 to 7.9
11–12	8.0 to 8.9

* Degrees of Reading Power, DRP, and TASA are registered trademarks of Touchstone Applied Science Associates, Inc. (TASA). Lexile is a registered trademark of MetaMetrics, Inc.

SCOPE AND SEQUENCE

The charts on these and the following two pages provide an overview of the scope and sequence for Glencoe ***The Reader's Choice—Course 4.*** For a detailed scope and sequence of skills, see the chart preceding the numbered part of each unit in the Teacher Wraparound Edition. Refer also to the Index of Skills (pages R83–R91) for a comprehensive listing of all skills and concepts taught in ***The Reader's Choice—Course 4.***

○ = Introduce/Teach ● = Review

	UNIT 1	UNIT 2	UNIT 3	UNIT 4	UNIT 5	UNIT 6
Literary Criticism						
Analayzing Literature in Context						
Historical Approach	○	●	●	●	●	●
Artistic Approach		○	●		●	
Biographical Approach		○		●		
Literary Genres						
Oral Tradition Forms						
Song					○	
Myth, Folklore, and Legend				○	●	●
Fiction						
Short Story	○		●	●	●	●
Novel Excerpt		○	●		●	
Nonfiction						
Autobiography or Memoir		○				
Biography	○	●	●			
Magazine Article	○	●	●	●	●	●
Newspaper Article		○				●
Speech		○				
Informational Text	○	●	●	●	●	●
Public Document		○				
Journal or Diary			○			
Letter		○				

○ = Introduce/Teach ● = Review

	UNIT 1	UNIT 2	UNIT 3	UNIT 4	UNIT 5	UNIT 6
Poetry						
Narrative poem	○	●	●	●	●	●
Ballad					○	
Epic	○				●	
Drama						
Comedy				○		
Tragedy				○		
Literary Elements						
Literary Structure						
Plot	○			●	●	●
Setting	○	●	●	●		●
Characters	○	●		●	●	●
Point of View	○	●				●
Theme	○	●	●	●	●	
Voice and Tone	○	●	●		●	●
Author's Purpose	○	●	●	●	●	●
Literary Language						
Imagery	○	●	●	●	●	●
Symbolism	○		●		●	
Figures of Speech			○	●	●	●
Sound Devices	○		●	●		
Diction	○		●	●	●	
Rhetorical Strategies		○	●			

○ = Introduce/Teach ● = Review

	UNIT 1	UNIT 2	UNIT 3	UNIT 4	UNIT 5	UNIT 6
Reading Skills						
Strategies						
Analyzing	○	●	●	●	●	●
Clarifying		○	●			
Drawing Conclusions		○	●	●		
Making Inferences	○		●	●		●
Making Predictions	○			●		
Monitoring Comprehension		○	●			
Paraphrasing	○		●			
Previewing	○	●	●	●	●	●
Questioning	○		●	●		
Recognizing Bias	○	●				
Summarizing	○	●				●
Synthesizing	○	●	●	●	●	●
Vocabulary Development						
Analogies	○	●	●	●	●	●
Antonyms				○	●	●
Context Clues	○	●	●	●	●	●
Denotation and Connotation			○	●		●
Multiple-Meaning Words	○					
Prefixes and Suffixes	○	●	●	●	●	
Synonyms	○	●	●	●		●
Word Roots	○	●	●	●	●	●

○ = Introduce/Teach ● = Review

	UNIT 1	UNIT 2	UNIT 3	UNIT 4	UNIT 5	UNIT 6
Writing and Grammar						
Types of Writing						
Response to Literature	○	●	●	●	●	●
Autobiographical Narrative		○				
Reflective Essay			○			
Literary Analysis	○	●	●	●		●
Research Report			○	●	●	●
Editorial						○
Writing Process						
Prewriting, Drafting, Revising, Editing and Proofreading, Presenting	○	●	●	●	●	●
Traits of Strong Writing	○	●	●	●	●	●
Grammar, Usage, and Mechanics						
Parts of Speech	○	●	●	●		
Capitalization and Punctuation	○		●		●	●
Sentence Structure	○	●	●	●	●	●
Listening, Speaking, and Viewing						
Oral Response to Literature	○	●	●	●	●	
Narrative Presentation		○				
Reflective Presentation			○			
Literary Analysis				○		
Expository Presentation					○	
Persuasive Presentation						○

TEACHER WRAPAROUND EDITION WALKTHROUGH

To Teachers

Welcome to the Teacher Wraparound Edition of ***Glencoe Literature: The Reader's Choice—Course 4.*** We have created this teacher edition based on input from experienced teachers and educational consultants. Teaching suggestions, background information, point-of-use strategies, leveled activities for differentiated instruction, and more—all are conveniently "wrapped" around every page of the reduced student text.

INTRODUCING UNIT ONE

Focus

BELLRINGER

Bellringer Options
Literature Launcher Video
Daily Language Practice Transparency 1

Or **say:** Identify some reasons why people tell and retell stories. *(Students may suggest that stories help us make sense of the world and allow us to go places we could never actually go to or experience things we could not normally do.)*

Objectives for the Unit Introduction

- To identify and interpret various literary elements used in the short story (SE)
- To analyze the effects that these literary elements have upon the reader (SE)
- To analyze short stories for the ways in which authors inspire the reader to share emotions (SE)

Toyota Taxi, 2005. P. J. Crook. Acrylic on canvas, 116.8 x 152.4 cm.

Teaching Support

The point-of-use strategies, activities, learning objectives, and informative notes in the side columns support and guide your approach to standards-based instruction.

Unit Introduction Skills

The web diagram summarizes the skills of a major literary genre taught in the Student Edition and the Teacher Wraparound Edition.

Unit Introduction Skills

The Short Story

Reading Skills
- Reading the Short Story (SE p. 2)
- Reading Journal (TWE p. 2)
- Solving Problems (TWE p. 8)

Listening/Speaking/Viewing Skills
- Defining Literary Term (SE p. 8)
- Creating a Timeline (SE p. 8)
- Telling a Story (TWE p. 6)

Writing Skills/Grammar
- Creating a Dictionary (SE p. 8)
- Writing a News Report (TWE p. 4)

Literary Elements
- Plot and Setting (SE p. 2)
- Character and Theme (SE pp. 2–3)
- Narrator and Voice (SE p. 3)

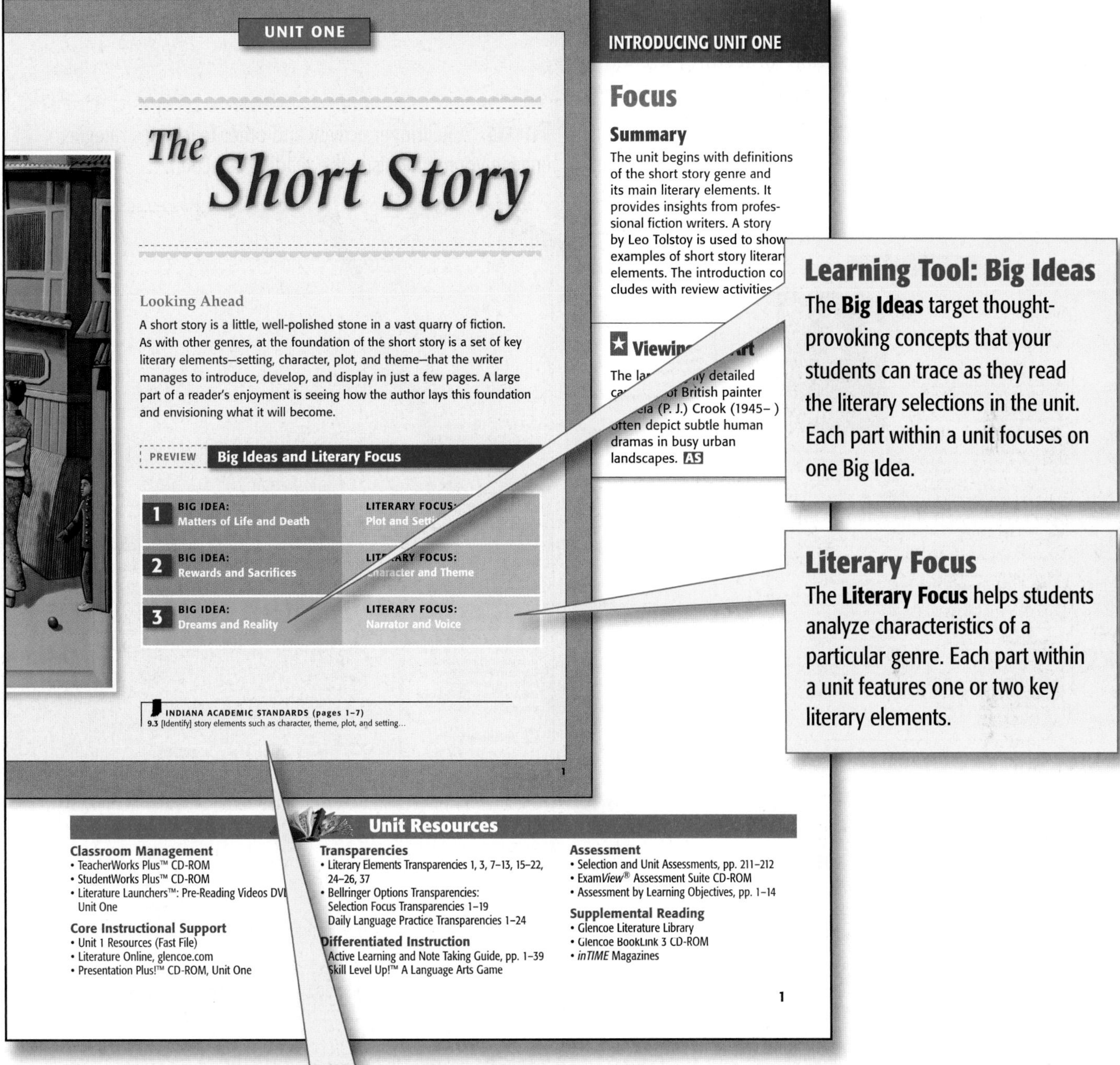
UNIT ONE

The Short Story

Looking Ahead

A short story is a little, well-polished stone in a vast quarry of fiction. As with other genres, at the foundation of the short story is a set of key literary elements—setting, character, plot, and theme—that the writer manages to introduce, develop, and display in just a few pages. A large part of a reader's enjoyment is seeing how the author lays this foundation and envisioning what it will become.

PREVIEW **Big Ideas and Literary Focus**

1	BIG IDEA: Matters of Life and Death	LITERARY FOCUS: Plot and Setting
2	BIG IDEA: Rewards and Sacrifices	LITERARY FOCUS: Character and Theme
3	BIG IDEA: Dreams and Reality	LITERARY FOCUS: Narrator and Voice

INDIANA ACADEMIC STANDARDS (pages 1–7)
9.3 [Identify] story elements such as character, theme, plot, and setting...

1

INTRODUCING UNIT ONE

Focus

Summary

The unit begins with definitions of the short story genre and its main literary elements. It provides insights from professional fiction writers. A story by Leo Tolstoy is used to show examples of short story literary elements. The introduction concludes with review activities.

Viewing the Art

The largely detailed canvases of British painter Pamela (P. J.) Crook (1945–) often depict subtle human dramas in busy urban landscapes. AS

Unit Resources

Classroom Management
- TeacherWorks Plus™ CD-ROM
- StudentWorks Plus™ CD-ROM
- Literature Launchers™: Pre-Reading Videos DVD, Unit One

Core Instructional Support
- Unit 1 Resources (Fast File)
- Literature Online, glencoe.com
- Presentation Plus!™ CD-ROM, Unit One

Transparencies
- Literary Elements Transparencies 1, 3, 7–13, 15–22, 24–26, 37
- Bellringer Options Transparencies: Selection Focus Transparencies 1–19, Daily Language Practice Transparencies 1–24

Differentiated Instruction
- Active Learning and Note Taking Guide, pp. 1–39
- Skill Level Up!™ A Language Arts Game

Assessment
- Selection and Unit Assessments, pp. 211–212
- Exam*View*® Assessment Suite CD-ROM
- Assessment by Learning Objectives, pp. 1–14

Supplemental Reading
- Glencoe Literature Library
- Glencoe BookLink 3 CD-ROM
- *inTIME* Magazines

1

Learning Tool: Big Ideas

The **Big Ideas** target thought-provoking concepts that your students can trace as they read the literary selections in the unit. Each part within a unit focuses on one Big Idea.

Literary Focus

The **Literary Focus** helps students analyze characteristics of a particular genre. Each part within a unit features one or two key literary elements.

Indiana Academic Standards

Each lesson features correlations to the **Indiana Academic Standards.** These correlations let students know which standards the lesson will help them master.

Lesson Support: Structure of Reading Selections

The Teacher Wraparound Edition for reading selections in *Glencoe Literature: The Reader's Choice* is organized in a three-part structure—*Focus, Teach,* and *Assess.*

Focus A Bellringer activity and other teaching strategies engage your students in the reading selection.

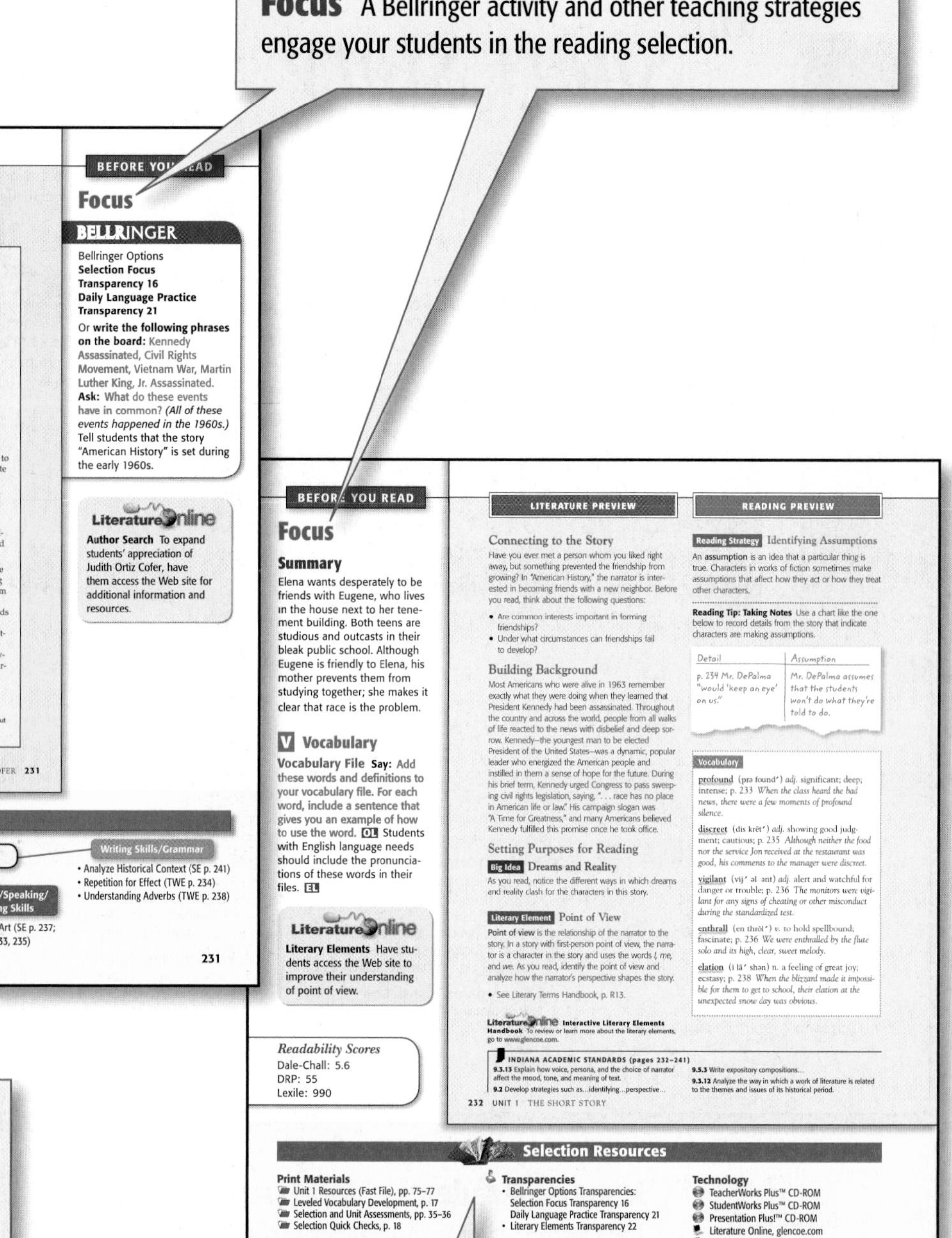

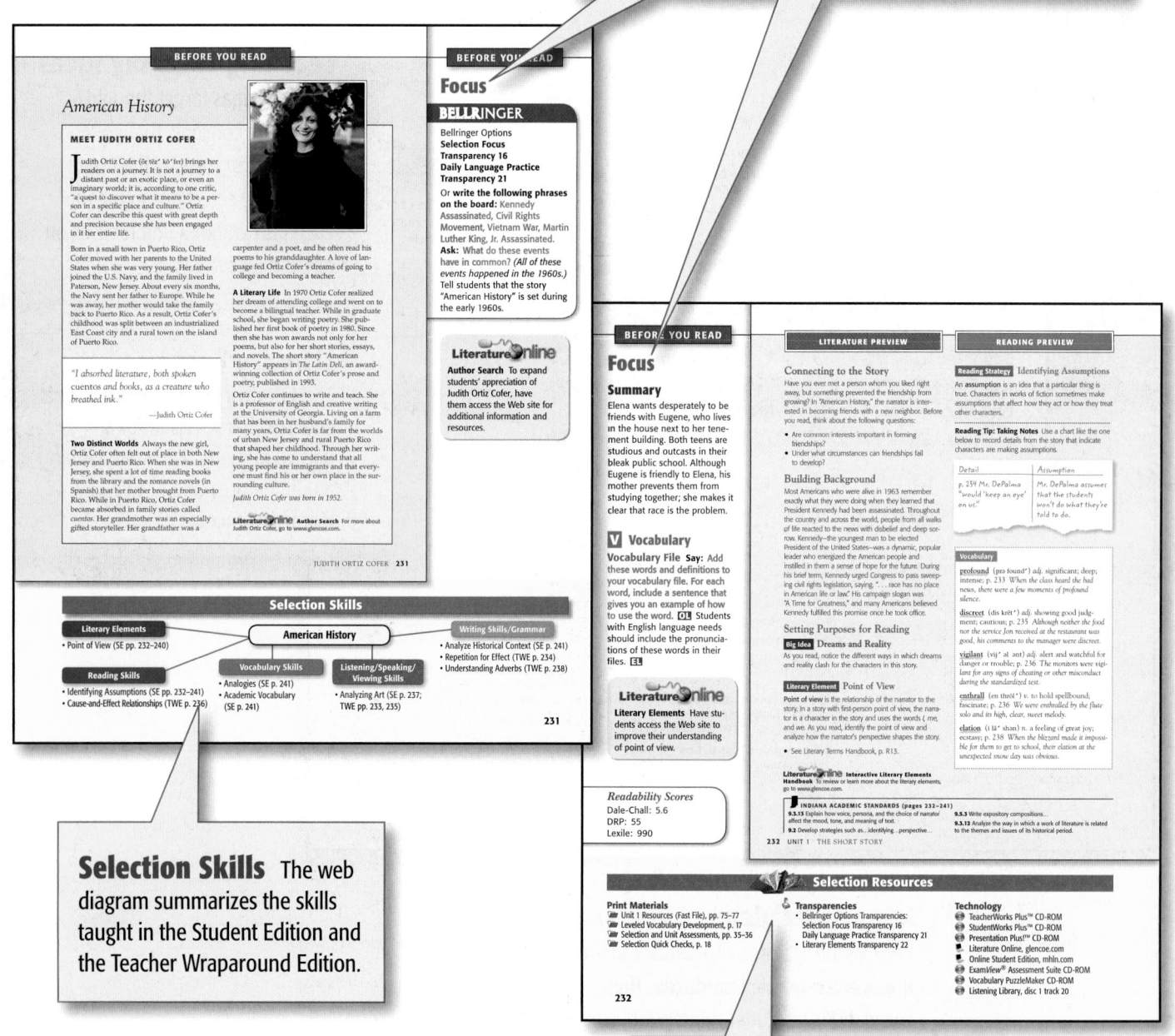

Selection Skills The web diagram summarizes the skills taught in the Student Edition and the Teacher Wraparound Edition.

Selection Resources This handy chart lists resources you can use to teach, reinforce, extend, and assess the lessons for each selection.

Teach Leveled activities stimulate learning and motivation.

The Big Idea Thought-provoking statements prompt students to explore the Big Idea in context to the reading selection.

Assess Answers to questions are provided.

View in Chambers Street, 1936. O. Louis Guglielmi. Oil on canvas, 30 1/4 × 24 1/4 in. The Newark Museum, New Jersey.

AMERICAN HISTORY

Judith Ortiz Cofer

I once read in a *Ripley's believe it or not* column that Paterson, New Jersey, is the place where the Straight and Narrow (streets) intersect. The Puerto Rican tenement[1] known as El Building was one block up from Straight. It was, in fact, the corner of Straight and Market; not "at" the corner, but the corner.

At almost any hour of the day, El Building was like a monstrous jukebox, blasting out *salsas*[2] from open windows as the residents, mostly new immigrants just up from the island,[3] tried to drown out whatever they were currently enduring with loud music. But the day President Kennedy was shot, there was a **profound** silence in El Building; even the abusive tongues of viragoes,[4] the cursing of the unemployed, and the screeching of small children had been somehow muted. President Kennedy was a saint to these people. In fact, soon his photograph would be hung alongside the Sacred Heart[5] and over the spiritist altars that many women kept in their apartments. He would become part of the hierarchy of martyrs[6] they prayed to for favors that only one who had died for a cause would understand.

On the day that President Kennedy was shot, my ninth grade class had been out in

1. A *tenement* is a run-down apartment building, generally with low rent.
2. *Salsas* are Latin American dance tunes.
3. When the writer refers to "the island" in this story, she is referring to Puerto Rico, an island in the Caribbean Sea, which is a self-governing commonwealth of the United States.
4. *Viragoes* (vi rä' gōz) are bad-tempered, scolding women who, here, use coarse or insulting (*abusive*) language.
5. The *Sacred Heart* is a picture of the wounded heart of Jesus, sometimes encircled in a crown of thorns and giving off rays of golden light.
6. The *hierarchy* (hī' ə rär' kē) of *martyrs* (mär' tərz) is the ranking of those who have suffered or died for their religion.

Literary Element Point of View *What point of view does the writer use for this story? How do you know?* L

Vocabulary

profound (prə fo[und]') *adj.* significant; deep; intense

Teach

Big Idea

Dreams and Reality Say: Keep these questions in mind as you read: What dreams and realities have you shared with new friends? How would you react if authority figures, such as parents and teachers, tried to interfere with your dreams? OL

L Literary Element

Point of View Answer: *The writer establishes a first-person point of view by starting with the word I.* OL

Viewing the Art

Many of O. Louis Guglielmi's (1906–1956) paintings were created while he worked with the Works Progress Administration. The WPA was set up by the federal government during the Great Depression to help Americans make ends meet. Guglielmi's paintings are noted for their strong colors and unusual perspective. AS

CheckPoint

Use the CheckPoint questions on Presentation Plus! to monitor students' comprehension. These questions can be used with interactive response keypads for immediate student feedback.

Academic Standards

The Additional Support activity on p. 233 covers the following standard:

English Language Coach: **9.1.2** Distinguish between what words mean literally and what they imply and interpret what the words imply.

English Lang[ua]ge Coach

Understanding Connotation Ask: Do you think Elena's nickname, Skinn[y] Bones, is an insult or a compliment? Explain that *skinny* can have either negative or positive connotation[s]—implied meaning—depending [on] context. Prompt students to [...] situation in which the nam[e] [...] be [co]mplimentary *(if a person had wanted [t]o lose weight).* As students continue to read, ask them to consider the connotation of expressions and of stylistic conventions, such as the use of quotes around "a conference" on page 237. Invite pairs of students to identify other examples. EL

AFTER YOU R[EA]D

Assess

1. Accept reasonable answers.
2. (a) A ninth-grade Puerto Rican girl, Paterson, New Jersey, November 22, 1963 (b) She feels embarrassed by it.
3. (a) The house next door (b) She finds normalcy and comfort in their daily routines.
4. (a) She is invited to Eugene's house. His mother sends her home. (b) She may have been racially prejudiced.
5. To contrast with her message and underline her cruelty
6. Accept answers supported by details.
7. The title refers to the assassination, the subject Elena and Eugene plan to study, and the country's history of racial division.
8. Assassination shattered the dreams of those who believed in Kennedy; life in the tenement eclipsed the parents' dream of a beach house; Elena's dreams of Eugene's friendship are shattered by his mother's prejudice.

AFTER YOU READ

RESPONDING AND THINKING CRITICALLY

Respond

1. How do you feel about what happens to the narrator at Eugene's house?

Recall and Interpret

2. (a)Who is telling the story, and when and where is the story set? (b)How does the narrator feel about her home?
3. (a)What does Elena enjoy looking at from her window? (b)In your opinion, why is Elena interested in the daily habits of the old Jewish couple and later of Eugene's family?
4. (a)Why does Elena feel particularly happy on the day the story takes place and particularly sorrowful that night? (b)What factors might have led Eugene's mother to react as she did to Elena? Use details from the story to support your opinion.

Analyze and Evaluate

5. A character trait is a habit, a physical attribute, or an attitude that helps define a character. Why might Ortiz Cofer have given Eugene's mother the character traits of a face like a doll and a tiny, sweet-sounding voice?
6. Do you think the author expressed the feelings of a ninth-grade girl realistically? Support your response with details from the story as well as from your own experience.
7. In your opinion, why might the writer have titled this story "American History"?

Connect

8. Big Idea **Dreams and Reality** Describe three ways in which dreams are overshadowed by reality in this story.

LITERARY ANALYSIS

Literary Element Point of View

The choice of **point of view** can greatly influence how a story unfolds. A writer will usually choose a narrator whose point of view effectively communicates the main ideas and themes.

1. How does the first-person point of view in "American History" shape how readers feel about the interactions between people of different cultures or ethnic groups?
2. If Ortiz Cofer had chosen to tell this story from the point of view of one of the adults, how might that choice have changed the focus of the story?

Review: Setting

As you learned on pages 10–11, **setting** is the time and place in which the events of a literary work occur. Setting also includes the ideas, customs, beliefs, and values of the time and place.

Group Activity Work with a small group to create a web diagram listing details the writer gives in "American History" to evoke the setting of El Building in 1963, home to many Puerto Ricans who have moved to Paterson, New Jersey. Try to include at least one example for each category in the web below.

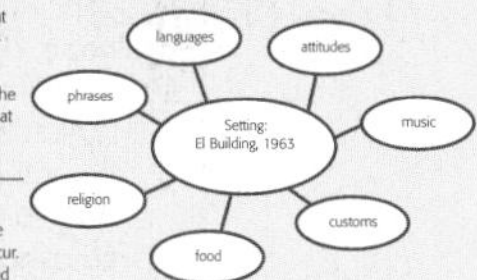

Literary Element

1. First-person helps readers empathize with ethnic groups facing prejudice.
2. The focus might be the assassination.

Review: Setting

Attitudes: Stick with your own ethnic group
Customs: *luto* (silent mourning)
Phrases: moony or *enamorada*
Languages: Spanish
[...]ns, pork chops
[...]st altars

Color-Coded Highlighting The legend below explains the kinds of color coding.

- Big Idea
- Literary Element
- Reading Strategy
- Vocabulary

Indiana Academic Standards The Additional Support activities are correlated to the **Indiana Academic Standards.** These correlations show the specific standards addressed in each activity.

Informational Text

The wide range of informational text in ***Glencoe Literature: The Reader's Choice*** broadens student reading to include more than just poetry, short stories, and plays.

Perspectives Award-winning book excerpts provide students with the in-depth information they need to explore the cultural, political, historical, and literary contexts of a reading selection.

HISTORICAL PERSPECTIVE
Informational Text

Focus

Summary

This passage from *A Thousand Days* begins with the author hearing the news that President Kennedy was shot in the head. The author then lists the responses of many people in America and around the world to the death of an American President.

Teach

Big Idea

Dreams and Reality Many people saw the young, energetic President as a source of hope. His assassination left some feeling that the American dream had been damaged if not altogether destroyed.
Ask: Why would Kennedy's assassination demoralize so many people across the country? *(People hoped Kennedy would improve their lives. Also, the reality of violence is shocking to many.)* OL

Readability Scores
Dale-Chall: 8.4
DRP: 61
Lexile: 1020

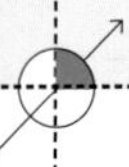

HISTORICAL PERSPECTIVE on *American History*
Informational Text

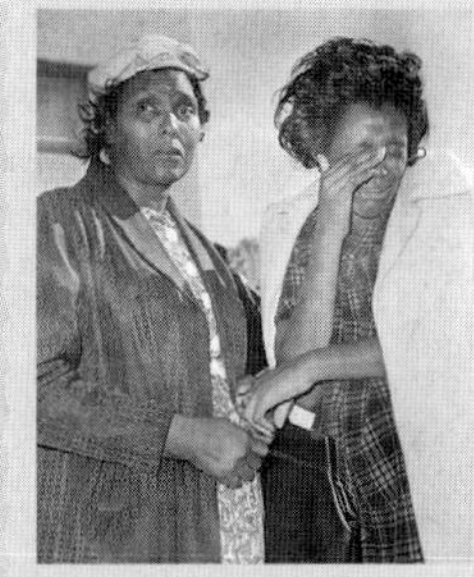

The Drums of Washington

Arthur M. Schlesinger Jr.

Pulitzer Prize Winner

Building Background

John F. Kennedy, who in 1960 was the youngest person ever elected president of the United States, is revered for his charisma and vision. Despite crises abroad, the Kennedy administration managed to make progress in foreign and domestic policy. During Kennedy's presidency, Arthur M. Schlesinger Jr. served as his adviser and later as a special assistant for Latin American affairs. In this excerpt, Schlesinger explores the grief that overwhelmed the world upon the assassination of President Kennedy on November 22, 1963.

Set a Purpose for Reading

Read to discover the reactions of people around the world to the assassination of President Kennedy.

Reading Strategy

Recognizing Bias

When you read to determine if the author has an inclination toward a certain opinion or position, you are **recognizing bias.** As you read "The Drums of Washington," take note of any statements made by Schlesinger that suggest bias.

On Friday morning I had flown to New York with Katharine Graham,[1] whose husband Philip had died three months before, for a luncheon with the editors of her magazine *Newsweek.* Kenneth Galbraith[2] had come down from Cambridge for the occasion. We were still sipping drinks before luncheon in an amiable mood of Friday-before-the-Harvard-Yale game relaxation when a young man in shirtsleeves entered the room and said, a little tentatively, "I am sorry to break in, but I think you should know that the President has been shot in the head in Texas." For a flash one thought this was some sort of ghastly office joke. Then we knew it could not be and huddled desperately around the nearest television. Everything was confused and appalling. The minutes dragged along. Incomprehensible bulletins came from the

1. *Katharine Graham* (1917–2001) was an owner and publisher of news media, including the *Washington Post.*
2. *Kenneth Galbraith* (1908–) is an economist who served as an ambassador to India and an adviser during the Kennedy administration.

Additional Support

Skills Practice

VOCABULARY: Negative Prefixes
The writer uses several words that begin with a negative prefix. *In-*, *im-*, *il-*, and *ir-* are all examples of negative prefixes. Usually, these word parts mean "not," "without," or "the opposite of" and reverse the meaning of the words to which they are attached. When the news bulletins about President Kennedy were *incomprehensible,* it means the writer could not understand what he was hearing. Have partners scan the passage, find other examples of words with negative prefixes, and figure out the meanings of the words. OL

Teaching Support **Skills Practice** in the bottom channel targets content areas for building your students' proficiency and provides strategies to introduce, teach, and reinforce concepts.

TIME articles Linked to a Big Idea, an author, or a reading selection, these articles deliver the facts on topical issues.

Informational Text

TIME

Focus

Summary

John Beiler and his friends, Mike and Tom, go hunting on Alaska's Afognak Island. While alone, John breaks his leg. Stranded, he spends the night battling hypothermia, dehydration, and pain. At dawn, ravens overhead reveal his location. A helicopter flies John to a hospital. Although he spends Thanksgiving there, John is grateful to have survived his ordeal.

Teach

Preview the Article

Answers:

1. Excitement and a sense of danger
2. The final subhead is "Just in Time," which indicates that the outcome is probably positive.

Readability Scores

Dale-Chall: 7.1

DRP: 56

Lexile: 900

Informational Text

Media Link to Matters of Life and Death

Preview the Article

In "Shattered," deer hunter John Beiler separates from his friends and ends up alone in the snow banks of Alaska with an injured leg, waiting for rescue.

1. Read the *deck*, or the sentence in large type that appears underneath the title. What emotions do you think the writer wants the reader to feel while reading this article?
2. Skim the boldfaced subheadings that appear in the article. Based on these, what do you think will be the outcome of the article?

Set a Purpose for Reading

Read to discover the events of John Beiler's survival tale and what he learned from it.

Reading Strategy

Identifying Problem and Solution

Identifying problem and solution involves asking these questions:

- What is the main problem?
- Who is experiencing it?
- What solutions are tried?
- What happens as a result?

As you read, take notes on the main problem presented in the article and the steps taken for it to be solved. Use a chart like the one below.

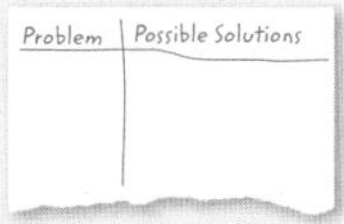

ACADEMIC STANDARDS (pages 88–92)

9.2.1 Analyze the structure and format of ...documents, including...headers...

TIME

Shattered

A terrible fall leaves a lone deer hunter with a shattered leg in the middle of brown-bear country. Now night is falling and nobody knows where he is.

By CHISTOPHER BATIN

JOHN BEILER LIKED HUNTING SITKA BLACKTAIL DEER ON Alaska's Afognak Island. He loved the otter-filled bays, the scenic rock cliffs, the salmon streams, and just about all of the island's many natural wonders. Except one.

Afognak Island has a dark side. Typhoon winds can hammer the coastline without mercy for days at a time. Huge coastal brown bears roam the dark rain forests and salmon streams. Even hunters who are prepared for disasters often die or get seriously injured. For John Beiler, misfortune happened to others but not to him. Or so he thought.

At daybreak, Beiler and his hunting buddies Mike and Tom eyed the steep slopes of Mount Paramanof, rising 2,100 feet above their tidewater base camp. It was Thanksgiving week, and they were looking forward to blacktail steaks and mashed potatoes smothered in gravy. The hunters planned a several-hour climb to an alpine meadow where big bucks lived.

Beiler, who liked to hunt hillsides alone, left his buddies and crossed a marsh near the base of a steep cliff. He was a muscular, big-boned man, well suited to hunting the mountains. Although his rubber boots with tread soles didn't offer the best traction going uphill, they kept his feet dry as he crossed creeks and swamps.

By late afternoon, a light rain had filled the alpine landscape with the pungent-sweet smell of wet tundra. The approaching ★ storm had caused the deer to hole up in thickets, and the dark outline of the beach below would take an hour to reach. Beiler walked faster so he could meet up with his friends before dark.

The hillside's grass and rotting plants were as slick as greased ice. Leaning farther back for balance on the steep slope, he felt his right foot slide on an ice patch and shoot out from under him. He hit the ground with a jarring slam.

Beiler paused for a few moments to regain his breath. He tried to stand. Something wasn't right.

The sole of his left boot faced

Additional Support

See also Active Learning and Note Taking Guide, pp. 15–23.

Skills Practice

READING: Cause and Effect Point out to students that the author builds the story through cause and effect.

Ask: What is the main cause and effect of the story? *(Students may say that Beiler goes off on his own–cause–thereby causing him to break his leg and fight for his life–effect.)* Ask students to design a cause-and-effect graphic organizer for the story. Students should include details such as the ravens' flocking, leading to Beiler, being found; the ship, seeking shelter from the storm, leading to the hunters' being able to radio for help. OL

Unit Resources

These well-organized, easy-to-read pages, preceding each unit of the Teacher Wraparound Edition, provide resources you need to plan and present the selections and features.

UNIT TWO

Unit Resources

Glencoe Literature: The Reader's Choice offers a comprehensive package of tools to optimize student learning and the teaching experience. Each resource has been designed to assist students in specific areas and to offer instructional support for teachers. While all of these areas are covered in the core textbook, some students may need extra practice or additional help in specific areas. The resource package is designed so that you, the teacher, can choose which items will best assist your students. You may also use these resources as homework assignments and for assessment purposes. The following are resources recommended for use with Unit Two.

Key for Unit Resource

- Blackline Master
- Workbook
- Supplemental Text
- CD-ROM
- DVD
- Transparency
- Web-based

Essential Instructional Support

FAST FILE UNIT 2 RESOURCES

Reading and Literature
- Unit Introduction, pp. 1–2
- The Big Idea Foldable, pp. 3–4
- The Big Idea School-Home Connection, p. 5
- The Big Idea School-Home Connection (Spanish), p. 6
- Challenge Planner, pp. 7–10
- Academic Vocabulary Development, pp. 11–13
- Comparing Literature Graphic Organizers, pp. 34, 73
- Literary Elements, pp. 17, 20, 23, 27, 31, 35, 41, 44, 47, 51, 54, 61, 64, 67, 70, 74, 77
- Reading Strategies, pp. 18, 21, 24, 26, 28, 32, 36, 42, 45, 48, 52, 55, 57, 62, 65, 68, 71, 75, 78
- Active Reading Graphic Organizers, pp. 84–93
- Selection Vocabulary Practice, pp. 19, 22, 25, 29, 33, 37, 43, 46, 49, 53, 56, 63, 66, 69, 72, 76, 79
- Literary Focus, pp. 39, 59

Writing, Grammar, and Spelling
- Spelling Practice, p. 80
- Grammar Workshop, pp. 30, 50
- Writing Workshop Graphic Organizer, p. 81

Speaking, Listening, and Viewing
- Speaking, Listening, and Viewing Activities, pp. 82–83

English Language Learners
- English Language Coach Review, pp. 16, 40, 60

DIFFERENTIATED INSTRUCTION
- Active Learning and Note Taking Guide, pp. 40–77
- Leveled Vocabulary Development, pp. 21–37
- Skill Level Up!™ A Language Arts Game
- Listening Library Audio CD, disc 1, tracks 25–47
- Glencoe BookLink 3
- Vocabulary PuzzleMaker
- Literature Library Vocabulary PuzzleMaker

ASSESSMENT

- Selection and Unit Assessments, pp. 45–82, 213–214
- Selection Quick Checks, pp. 23–41
- Selection Quick Checks (Spanish), pp. 23–41
- Assessment by Learning Objectives, pp. 15–25
- Rubrics for Assessing Student Writing, Listening and Speaking, pp. 6–7, 28–29
- Standardized Test Preparation and Practice
- Glencoe Online Essay Grader
- Interactive Tutor: Self-Assessment
- Exam*View*® Assessment Suite
- Literature Library Exam*View*® Assessment

297C

UNIT TWO RESOURCES

Additional Instructional Support

LITERATURE AND READING
- Active Learning and Note Taking Guide, pp. 40–77
- *inTIME* Magazines
- Glencoe Literature Library
- Literature Launchers: Pre-Reading Videos
- Literature Classics

WRITING, GRAMMAR, AND SPELLING
- REAL Success in Writing: Research and Reports
- Writing Constructed Responses
- Spelling Power eWorkbook
- Revising with Style eWorkbook
- Sentence Diagraming eWorkbook
- Grammar and Composition Handbook
- Grammar and Language Workbook
- Grammar & Language eWorkbook

PROFESSIONAL DEVELOPMENT
- Professional Development Package

TRANSPARENCIES
- Read Aloud, Think Aloud Transparencies 11–26
- Bellringer Options Transparencies
  - Selection Focus Transparencies 20–27
  - Daily Language Practice Transparencies 25–45
- Grammar and Language Transparencies 4, 67, 76
- Writing Workshop Transparencies 11–15
- Visual Literacy/Fine Art Transparencies

ENGLISH LANGUAGE LEARNER
- English Language Coach, Unit Resources (Fast File)
- *inTIME* Magazines (Spanish)
- Spanish Listening Library

TECHNOLOGY
- TeacherWorks Plus™
- StudentWorks Plus™
- Literature Launchers: Pre-Reading Videos
- Vocabulary PuzzleMaker
- Literature Library Vocabulary PuzzleMaker
- Skill Level Up!™ A Language Arts Game
- glencoe.com
- Presentation Plus!™
- Exam*View*™ Assessment Suite
- Literature Library Exam*View*™ Assessment Suite
- Listening Library Audio CD, disc 1, tracks 25–47
- Interactive Tutor: Self-Assessment
- Glencoe BookLink 3
- Online Student Edition, mhln.com
- Glencoe Online Essay Grader
- Grammar and Language eWorkbook
- Revising with Style eWorkbook
- Sentence Diagraming eWorkbook
- Spelling Power eWorkbook
- Literature Classics
- Spanish Listening Library

297D

REAL Success: Reading Excellence at All Levels

Glencoe REAL Success is a suite of new reading and language arts products designed to foster reading excellence at all levels.

Look for TWE point-of-use references for these specific products that will help your students succeed in reading this Unit.

- *Jamestown Literature: An Adapted Reader*
- REAL Success in Writing: Research and Reports
- Skill Level Up!™ A Language Arts Game
- CheckPoint PowerPoint™ slides
- Literature/Reading support at Glencoe Web site

inTIME

A lively collection of articles drawn from issues of the TIME family of magazines helps students develop the skills they need to interact with informational text in a meaningful way. Each of the news stories, feature articles, reviews, profiles, and essays in the magazine connect to an author, work, or theme in *Glencoe Literature: The Reader's Choice.* See the *inTIME* Teacher's Guide for specific connections to each unit and for reproducible student worksheets designed to develop students' reading and critical thinking skills.

Literature Launchers

Set the scene with Glencoe's Literature Launchers, engaging pre-reading video segments that introduce each unit. Each Unit Launcher brings the literature to life, featuring expert testimony and archival stills and footage from the time.

Insert your Glencoe Literature Launchers into your DVD player. Select the Unit 2 Launcher from the menu to introduce Nonfiction.

Teacher Wraparound Edition Key

Level Appropriate Code

AL = Activities for students working above grade level
OL = Activities for students working at grade level
BL = Activities for students working below grade level
EL = Activities for English language learners
AS = Information for all students

Teacher Wraparound Prompts

R Reading Skill These activities help you teach reading

...y.

...**ary** These activities help students comprehend

...ate them into reading.

BI Big Idea These activities and questions prompt students to explore the Big Idea.

L Literary Element These activities and questions help students comprehend selections and learn more about each genre.

★ Enrichment Additional activities and information involving art appreciation and history.

Additional Glencoe Resources

Dinah Zike's Foldables™

Foldables™ are three-dimensional, interactive graphic organizers that help students practice basic writing skills, review key vocabulary terms, and answer Big Ideas. Every unit contains a Foldable™ activity. You can find the pattern and directions for the Unit 2 Foldable™ in the Unit 2 Resources Fast File booklet. You can use the Foldables™ as they are presented or modify them to suit the needs of your students.

Literature Online

For a wealth of online resources that support the instruction in Unit 2, students and teachers can visit our Web site at glencoe.com. Students will find additional learning, practice, and assessment opportunities such as these, which are noted in the student text:

- Author Search
- Big Idea Overview and Activity
- Interactive Literary Elements Handbook
- Study Central
- Unit Assessment
- Web Activities
- Writing Models

Teachers will find planning and instructional tools that include the following:

- Book Lesson Plans
- Web Activity Lesson Plans
- Teacher Forum
- Professional Resources

Go to glencoe.com to see the entire selection of *Glencoe Literature* online resources.

Glencoe's Presentation Plus!™, a multimedia teaching tool, lets you present dynamic lessons that will engage your students. Using Microsoft PowerPoint®, you can customize the presentations to create your own personalized lessons. Use CheckPoint questions with interactive response keypads to get immediate student feedback during lessons, to increase student participation, and to assess student comprehension.

Glencoe Literature Library

The collection of hardcover books includes full-length novels, novellas, plays, and works of nonfiction. Each volume consists of at least one complete extended-length reading accompanied by several related readings from a broad range of genres. A separate Study Guide for each *Glencoe Literature Library* book provides teaching notes and reproducible activity pages for students. Glencoe Literature Library titles that complement this unit include:

- ***Great Expectations with Related Readings*** by Charles Dickens
- ***. . . And the Earth Did Not Devour Him with Related Readings*** by Tomás Rivera
- ***To Kill a Mockingbird with Related Readings*** by Harper Lee

Glencoe BookLink

Use the Glencoe BookLink 3 CD-ROM, a database of more than 26,700 titles, to *create customized reading lists* for your students.

- Search for award-winning titles (e.g., Newbery Award winners, Coretta Scott King Award winners, and Caldecott Medal winners) and for books on several state recommended reading lists.
- Find Degrees of Reading Power™ (DRP) and Lexile™ readability scores for all selections.
- Organize reading lists by students' reading level, author, genre, theme, or area of interest.
- Get a brief summary of each selection.

You can find recommended leveled readings for this unit with Independent Reading (see pages 498 and 499).

Online Essay Grader

Use Glencoe's online essay grader powered by SkillWriter™ to score your students' writing and to provide individualized feedback to each student automatically.

You and your students can visit glencoe.com to link to the essay grader. *Students* can enter their essays and receive feedback on demand. *You* can manage demographic data, assign tests, and generate individual student and aggregated reports. The essay grader can help you

- save time with automatic scoring and individualized feedback.
- supplement in-class writing instruction using guided writing practice.

Classroom Resources

Unit Resources

Fast File Booklets

These blackline master booklets provide all the teaching materials you need to reinforce the content in each unit of ***Glencoe Literature: The Reader's Choice.*** One to two pages of each booklet focus on the following topics or skills:

- Unit Introduction
- The Big Idea Foldables™
- The Big Idea: School-Home Connection (English and Spanish versions)
- Unit Challenge: Planner and Rubrics
- Academic Vocabulary Practice
- Literary History
- Comparing Literature Graphic Organizers
- Literary Focus
- Literary Elements
- Key Reading Skills
- Spelling Practice
- Selection Vocabulary Development
- English Language Coach Reviews
- Grammar Practice
- Writing Workshop Graphic Organizers
- Active Reading Graphic Organizers
- Listening, Speaking, and Viewing Activities

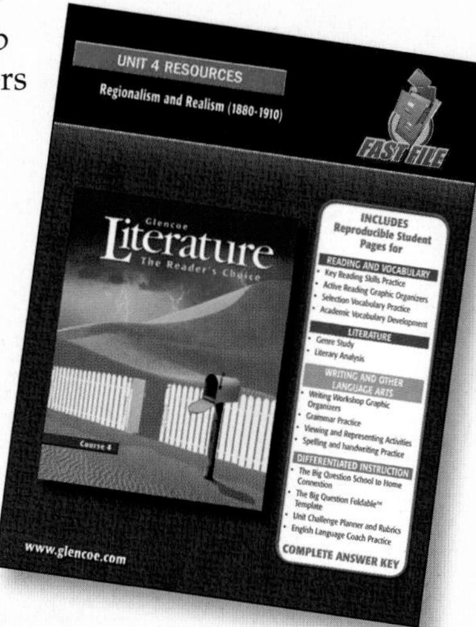

Literature and Reading

Active Learning and Note Taking Guide SE

This set of consumable workbooks provides structured outline support for students to use before, during, and after reading and helps them focus on key concepts and information. Activities include interactive exercises on literary elements and vocabulary for writing about literature. The workbooks are offered in four versions:

- **Grade-Level Active Learning and Note Taking Guide** Addresses students who are reading at grade level.
- **Enriched Active Learning and Note Taking Guide** Challenges students to develop a basic understanding of the skills.
- **Adapted Active Learning and Note Taking Guide** Helps students who are reading one or two grades below grade level.
- **ELL Active Learning and Note Taking Guide** Coaches English language learners to master the content.

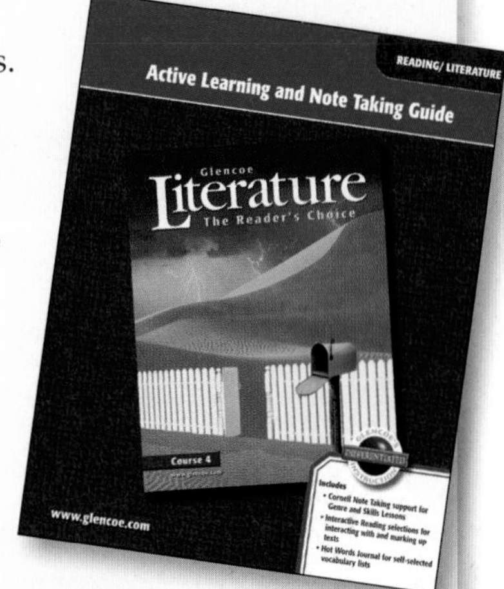

Literature Library

Glencoe Literature Library offers an extensive collection of hardcover books that help you encourage your students to read independently. Choose from among the more than 120 full-length literary works—novels, novellas, plays, and nonfiction. Each book includes related readings from a broad range of genres. Support your teaching with these technology products:

- ***Literature Library* Exam*View*® *Assessment Suite* CD** Offers you the flexibility to create customized tests for all the literary works included in the *Glencoe Literature Library* collection.
- **Literature Library Vocabulary PuzzleMaker** Allows you to create crossword puzzles, word-search puzzles, and jumble puzzles based on vocabulary selected from the *Glencoe Literature Library* collection.

Ethnic Anthologies

This collection of anthologies with teacher guides broadens students' reading and understanding of American literature. Encourage your students to study classic and contemporary authors from diverse ethnic and cultural backgrounds.

- **African American Literature**
- **Asian American Literature**
- **Hispanic American Literature**
- **Native American Literature**

inTIME Magazine

These high-interest collections of articles drawn from issues of *TIME* magazine and other Time, Inc., publications help students develop reading strategies to interact with informational text. The *inTIME* magazines are available in both English and Spanish and include teacher guides.

Literature Launchers: Pre-Reading Videos/DVD

Each of the engaging video segments on this DVD brings the literature to life, providing both visual and historical context for every unit.

Literature Classics CD-ROM

Glencoe Literature Classics CD-ROM brings a collection of more than 1,100 additional classic literature selections directly to your classroom—accessible by author, title, date, genre, country, course/grade level, and Big Idea. Genre Focus Lesson Plans with blackline masters are also provided.

Writing

REAL Success in Writing: Research and Reports

These blackline masters reinforce and extend the coverage of research presented in the Student Edition.

Writing Constructed Responses

This sourcebook with blackline masters helps students effectively respond to short-essay questions.

Differentiated Instruction

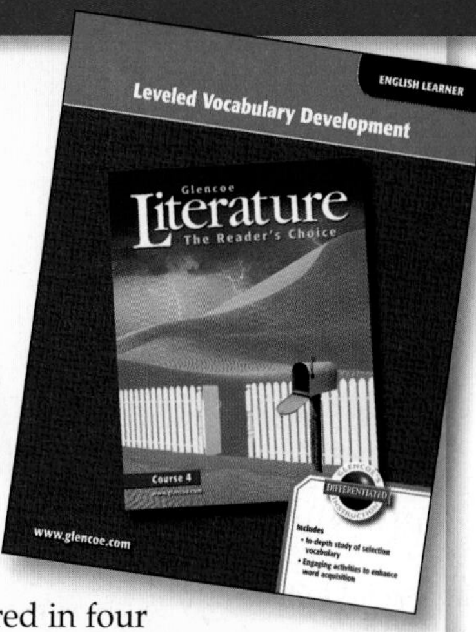

Leveled Vocabulary Development

These blackline masters provide practice on selection vocabulary. The booklet is offered in four versions:

- **Leveled Vocabulary Grade Level**
- **Leveled Vocabulary Enriched**
- **Leveled Vocabulary Adapted**
- **Leveled Vocabulary English Language Learner**

Vocabulary PuzzleMaker

This easy-to-use program lets you create crossword puzzles, word search puzzles, and jumble puzzles in an instant. To generate your puzzles, choose from selection and academic vocabulary (in both English and Spanish) and any of the terms included in the Literary Terms Handbook.

Listening Library Audio CD

The *Listening Library* Audio CD contains engaging recordings of all the selections in ***Glencoe Literature: The Reader's Choice.*** These will help students improve overall comprehension and reading fluency.

Spanish Listening Library Audio CD

Provide valuable support to your English language learners with the *Spanish Listening Library* Audio CD. This CD includes Spanish translations of key selections and Spanish summaries of virtually all selections.

Skill Level Up!™ A Language Arts Game CD-ROM

Skill Level Up! A Language Arts Game offers an innovative approach to language arts and reading skills practice, assessment, and remediation.

Glencoe BookLink 3 CD-ROM

Use the *Glencoe BookLink 3* CD-ROM, a database of more than 26,700 titles, to create customized reading lists for your students. Search for award-winning titles and for books on several state-recommended reading lists.

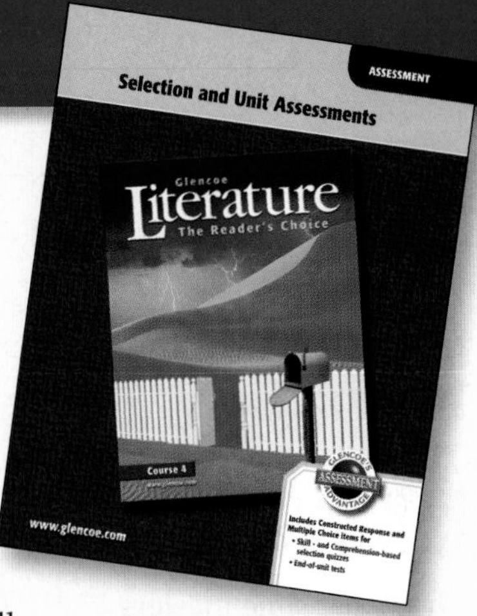

Assessment

Selection and Unit Assessments

This assessment tool contains comprehensive tests and answer keys for all selections and units.

Exam*View*® Assessment Suite

With the Test Generator, you can quickly create customized unit- or selection-based assessments. Use the unit exams or the selection-specific exams provided in both English and Spanish on this CD-ROM, or create your own questions.

Selection Quick Check

These short-answer questions serve as a quick way to assess students' basic comprehension of a selection. (Spanish and English)

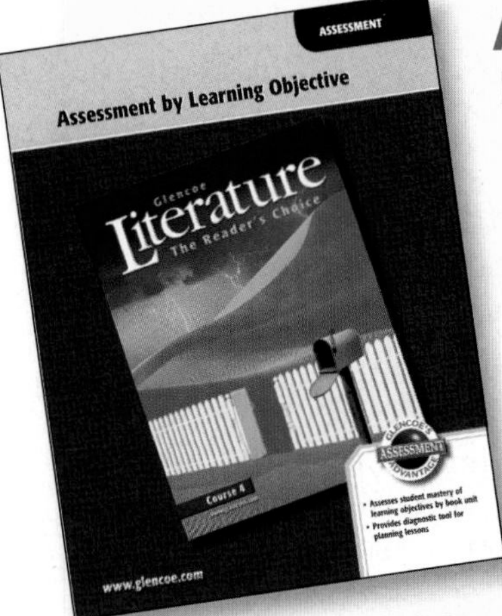

Assessment by Learning Objectives

These booklets help you assess learning objectives related to reading strategy, literary element, genre, or literary period or movement.

Rubrics for Assessing Student Writing, Listening, and Speaking

In structured assessment activities with evaluation rubrics, students apply their understanding of book selections to real-world situations.

Standardized Test Prep and Practice

This assessment tool contains exercises and activities that get students ready for the high-stakes standardized exams.

Interactive Tutor: Self-Assessment

This software allows students to review unit-based skills at their own pace and provides immediate prescriptive feedback. You can monitor student progress using the software's reporting system.

Professional Development

This package of materials, designed to help teachers manage their time and present engaging class sessions, includes the following:

- **Literature Lesson Plans** help teachers develop well-organized approaches for presenting all selections, such as Unit Openers, Perspectives pieces, *TIME* magazine articles, and Writing Workshops.
- **Block Scheduling Guide** contains block scheduling charts with pacing suggestions, model lessons, and general teaching strategies.

Technology Resources

StudentWorks™ Plus CD-ROM

StudentWorks™ Plus contains everything that your students need on one easy-to-use CD-ROM—the complete Student Edition, text in audio, access to all student workbooks, links to online activities and resources, and unit-based PowerPoint projects.

Online Student Edition

Showcasing the interactive versions of McGraw-Hill textbooks, mhln.com offers the same content as the printed text, with multimedia-enhanced content. Games, interactivities, and other items are correlated directly to each page.

TeacherWorks™ Plus CD-ROM

TeacherWorks™ Plus contains a suite of easy-to-use and effective tools designed to help you develop lesson plans, manage daily activities, access all textbook materials, and utilize resources on the Internet.

Exam*View*® Assessment Suite

With the Test Generator, you can quickly create customized unit- or selection-based assessments. Use the unit exams or the selection-specific exams provided in both English and Spanish on this CD-ROM, or create your own questions.

Skill Level Up!™ A Language Arts Game CD-ROM

Skill Level Up!™ A Language Arts Game offers an innovative approach to language arts and reading skills practice, assessment, and remediation.

Presentation Plus!™ CD-ROM

This multimedia application enables teachers to present dynamic lessons for every unit and selection in *Glencoe Literature*. The PowerPoint multimedia presentations can be edited and customized for teacher lesson planning.

Vocabulary PuzzleMaker CD-ROM

This easy-to-use program lets you create crossword puzzles, word-search puzzles, and jumble puzzles in an instant. To generate your puzzles, choose from selection and academic vocabulary (in both English and Spanish), and any of the terms included in the Literary Terms Handbook.

Literature Classics CD-ROM

Glencoe Literature Classics CD-ROM brings a collection of more than 1,100 additional classic literature selections directly to your classroom—accessible by author, title, date, genre, country, course/grade level, and Big Idea. Genre Focus Lesson Plans with blackline masters are also provided.

Literature Library Exam*View*® Assessment Suite CD-ROM

This software offers you the flexibility to create customized tests for all the literary works included in the *Glencoe Literature Library* collection.

Literature Library PuzzleMaker CD-ROM

This easy-to-use software allows you to create crossword puzzles, word-search puzzles, and jumble puzzles based on vocabulary selected from the *Glencoe Literature Library* collection.

Literature Launchers: Pre-Reading Videos DVD

Each of the engaging video segments on this DVD brings the literature to life, providing both visual and historical context for every unit.

Listening Library Audio CD

The *Listening Library* Audio CD contains engaging recordings of all the selections in ***Glencoe Literature: The Reader's Choice.*** These recordings will help students improve overall comprehension and reading fluency.

Spanish Listening Library Audio CD

Provide valuable support to your English language learners with the *Spanish Listening Library* Audio CD. This CD includes Spanish translations of key selections and Spanish summaries of virtually all selections.

Glencoe BookLink 3 CD-ROM

Use the *Glencoe BookLink 3* CD-ROM, a database of more than 26,700 titles, to create customized reading lists for your students. Search for award-winning titles and for books on several state-recommended reading lists.

Glencoe Online Essay Grader

Improve student writing and save time with Glencoe's Online Essay Grader, powered by SkillWriter™. Glencoe's Online Essay Grader will score your students' Writing Workshop assignments and provide individualized feedback automatically.

Internet Resources (glencoe.com)

For online resources that support the instruction in *Glencoe Literature,* students and teachers can visit our Web site at **glencoe.com**. Students will find additional learning, practice, and assessment opportunities.

Transparencies

- **Read Aloud, Think Aloud Transparencies** model active reading.
- **Bellringer Option Transparencies** include warm-up exercises to engage students and provide a quick review of previously taught activities.
- **Literary Analysis Transparencies** help reinforce literary elements that are the focus of each lesson.
- **Grammar and Writing Workshop Transparencies** help reinforce the skills taught in the Grammar and Writing workshops in the Student Edition.
- **Visual Literacy Arts Transparencies** enhance a strong humanities approach to literature and help students analyze visual representations of literary concepts and characters.

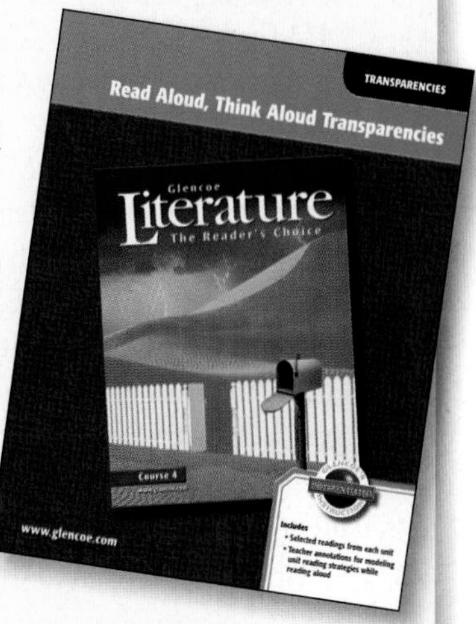

Glencoe Resources for Independent Reading

Foster a lifelong love of reading by encouraging your students to read independently. The following resources can help students improve their critical thinking skills, vocabulary, and ability to connect with literature. Have your students maintain reading lists to keep track of their progress. Parents or guardians can review the lists to help students set manageable goals.

Glencoe Literature Library

Below is a sampling from our collection of hardcover books, which includes full-length novels, novellas, plays, and works of nonfiction. Each *Glencoe Literature Library* volume consists of at least one complete extended-length reading accompanied by several related readings from a broad range of genres. Works include short stories, poems, essays, or informational articles. In addition, a separate Study Guide for each *Glencoe Literature Library* book provides teaching notes and reproducible activity pages for students. Students may also find these activity pages at **www.glencoe.com**.

The Adventures of Huckleberry Finn by Mark Twain **DRP 54***
All Quiet on the Western Front by Erich Maria Remarque **DRP 52**
. . . And the Earth Did Not Devour Him by Tomas Rivera **DRP 52**
Animal Farm by George Orwell **DRP 60**
The Autobiography of Benjamin Franklin by Benjamin Franklin **DRP 64**
The Autobiography of Miss Jane Pittman by Ernest J. Gaines **DRP 49**
The Awakening by Kate Chopin **DRP 58**
Beowulf
Billy Budd by Herman Melville **DRP 68**
The Bridge of San Luis Rey by Thornton Wilder **DRP 55**
The Brothers Karamazov by Fyodor Dostoevsky **DRP 55**
The Canterbury Tales by Geoffrey Chaucer **DRP 59**
The Chosen by Chaim Potok **DRP 56**
A Country Doctor by Sarah Orne Jewett **DRP 59**
Cyrano de Bergerac by Edmond Rostand
Ethan Frome by Edith Wharton **DRP 59**
Fallen Angels by Walter Dean Myers **DRP 47**
Frankenstein by Mary Shelley **DRP 64**
Great Expectations by Charles Dickens **DRP 60**
Gulliver's Travels by Jonathan Swift **DRP 67**
Hamlet by William Shakespeare
Heart of Darkness and *The Secret Sharer* by Joseph Conrad **DRP 58**
A House for Mr Biswas by V. S. Naipaul **DRP 58**
The House of the Seven Gables by Nathaniel Hawthorne **DRP 65**
The Importance of Being Earnest by Oscar Wilde
Invisible Man by Ralph Ellison **DRP 57**
Jane Eyre by Charlotte Brontë **DRP 61**
Julius Caesar by William Shakespeare
The Jungle by Upton Sinclair **DRP 59**
The Mayor of Casterbridge by Thomas Hardy **DRP 60**
The Metamorphosis by Franz Kafka **DRP 57**
A Midsummer Night's Dream by William Shakespeare
My Ántonia by Willa Cather **DRP 57**
Narrative of the Life of Frederick Douglass by Frederick Douglass **DRP 62**
Nectar in a Sieve by Kamala Markandaya **DRP 56**
Night by Elie Wiesel **DRP 51**
One Day in the Life of Ivan Denisovich by Aleksandr Solzhenitsyn **DRP 56**
Our Town by Thornton Wilder
Picture Bride by Yoshiko Uchida **DRP 55**

***Degrees of Reading Power**® DRP values indicate the readability of prose text. The higher the value, the more difficult the text. Though the scale ranges from 0 to 100, texts widely available for use at grades nine through twelve typically range from 53 to 68. Some materials, however, may certainly fall outside of this range.

Pride and Prejudice by Jane Austen **DRP 61**
A Raisin in the Sun by Lorraine Hansberry
The Red Badge of Courage by Stephen Crane **DRP 60**
The Return of the Native by Thomas Hardy **DRP 61**
The Scarlet Letter by Nathaniel Hawthorne **DRP 67**
Sense and Sensibility by Jane Austen **DRP 63**
A Separate Peace by John Knowles **DRP 59**
Silas Marner by George Eliot **DRP 55**
The Souls of Black Folk by W. E. B. Du Bois **DRP 66**
The Story of My Life by Helen Keller **DRP 59**
The Strange Case of Dr Jekyll and Mr Hyde by Robert Louis Stevenson **DRP 63**
A Tale of Two Cities by Charles Dickens **DRP 62**
The Tempest by William Shakespeare
Things Fall Apart by Chinua Achebe **DRP 56**
The Time Machine and *The War of the Worlds* by H. G. Wells **DRP 59**
To Kill a Mockingbird by Harper Lee **DRP 51**
Walden by Henry David Thoreau **DRP 62**
The Way to Rainy Mountain by N. Scott Momaday **DRP 55**
Wuthering Heights by Emily Brontë **DRP 61**
The Yearling by Marjorie Kinnan Rawlings **DRP 53**

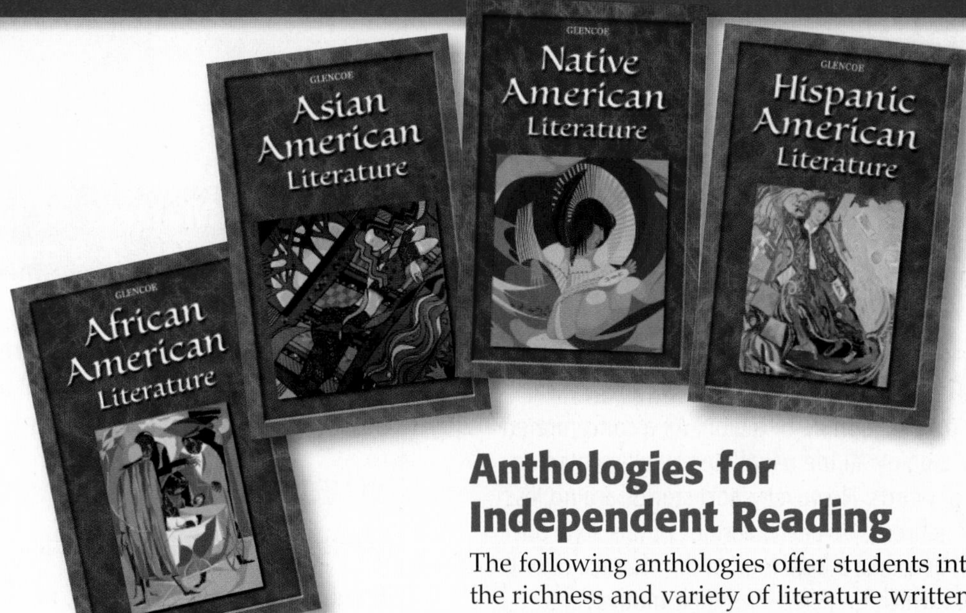

Anthologies for Independent Reading

The following anthologies offer students introductions to the richness and variety of literature written by African, Asian, Hispanic, and Native Americans. A Teacher's Guide for each anthology suggests answers to questions accompanying each selection to help further student discussion.

- *Glencoe African American Literature*
- *Glencoe Asian American Literature*
- *Glencoe Hispanic American Literature*
- *Glencoe Native American Literature*

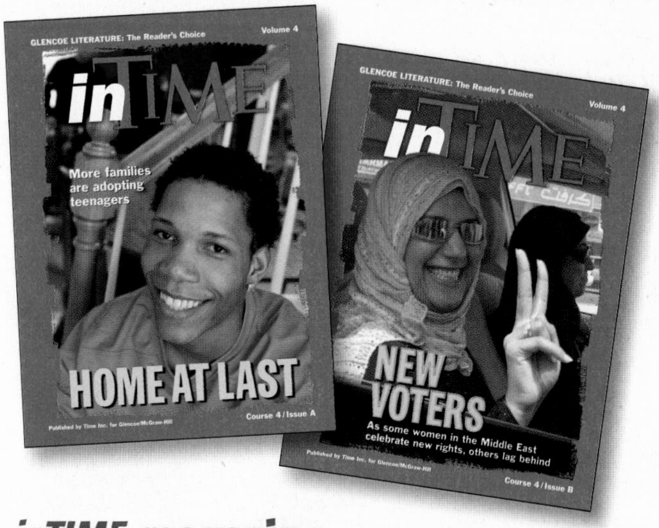

inTIME magazine

This lively collection of articles drawn from issues of *TIME* helps students develop the skills they need to interact with informational text in a meaningful way. Each of the news stories, feature articles, reviews, profiles, and essays connects to an author, a reading selection, or a Big Idea in ***Glencoe Literature: The Reader's Choice.*** The magazines are available in both English and Spanish editions. In addition, a separate Teacher Guide, including lessons and reproducible student worksheets designed to develop students' reading and critical thinking skills, accompanies each magazine.

Unit at a Glance

The Short Story

About the Unit

Short stories are gems in the mine of fiction. As a concentrated form, a writer must employ all the usual literary elements in a shortened amount of words. However, short stories are no less complex than other genres. The particularities of this style are explored in this unit and take a long look at the characters of the stories, the setting in which they live, and their motivations.

Unit Introduction
Building Background
2–3 days

Part 1: Matters of Life and Death
7–8 days

Part 1 is concerned with the most dire of themes—life and death. The literary focus for this part is plot and setting. A chart showing the core skills taught in this Part appears on pages 9A–9B.

SELECTIONS AND FEATURES

Part 2: Rewards and Sacrifices
8–10 days

Part 2 explores the themes of rewards and sacrifices for characters in short stories. The literary elements of theme and character are also emphasized. A chart showing the core skills taught in this Part appears on pages 105A–105B.

SELECTIONS AND FEATURES

LITERARY FOCUS: Character and Theme pp. 106–107

Amy Tan, "Rules of the Game" pp. 108–120

O. Henry, "The Gift of the Magi" pp. 121–131

Comparing Literature Across Genres
Julia Alvarez, "Liberty"
Elizabeth Wong, "The Struggle to Be an All-American Girl"
Linda Pastan, "Grudnow"
pp. 132–146

Eugenia Collier, "Sweet Potato Pie" pp. 147–158

Grammar Workshop: Sentence Structure p. 159

James Hurst, "The Scarlet Ibis" pp. 160–175

W. D. Wetherell, "The Bass, the River, and Sheila Mant" pp. 176–186

Vocabulary Workshop: Multiple-Meaning Words p. 187

Truman Capote, "A Christmas Memory" pp. 188–204

Part 3: Dreams and Reality
7–8 days

Part 3 contrasts dreams with reality as described in fiction. Additionally, the literary focus for this part explores the question, "How do narrator, point of view, and voice affect a story?" A chart showing the core skills taught in this Part appears on pages 205A–205B.

SELECTIONS AND FEATURES

LITERARY FOCUS: Narrator and Voice pp. 206–207

James Thurber, "The Secret Life of Walter Mitty" pp. 208–217

Grammar Workshop: Sentence Structure p. 218

Guy de Maupassant, "The Necklace" pp. 219–230

Judith Ortiz Cofer, "American History" pp. 231–241

HISTORICAL PERSPECTIVE on **American History**: Arthur M. Schlesinger Jr., "The Drums of Washington" pp. 242–246

Mark Twain, "Bakers Bluejay Yarn" pp. 247–256

Diana Garcia, "The Flat of the Land" pp. 257–268

Isaac Bashevis Singer, "The Son from America" pp. 269–279

End-of-Unit Features
5–6 Days

Writing Workshop: Response to Literature
pp. 280–287

Speaking, Listening, and Viewing Workshop:
Oral Response to Literature
pp. 288–289

INDEPENDENT READING
pp. 290–291

Test Preparation and Practice
pp. 292–297

Unit Resources

Glencoe Literature: The Reader's Choice offers a comprehensive package of tools to optimize student learning and the teaching experience. Each resource has been designed to assist students in specific areas and to offer instructional support for teachers. While all of these areas are covered in the core textbook, some students may need extra practice or additional help in specific areas. The resource package is designed so that you, the teacher, can choose which items will best assist your students. You may also use these resources as homework assignments and for assessment purposes. The following are resources recommended for use with Unit One.

Key for Unit Resource

- Blackline Master
- Workbook
- Supplemental Text
- CD-ROM
- DVD
- Transparency
- Web-based

Essential Instructional Support

FAST FILE UNIT 1 RESOURCES

Reading and Literature

- Unit Introduction, pp. 1–2
- The Big Idea Foldable, pp. 3–4
- The Big Idea School-Home Connection, p. 5
- The Big Idea School-Home Connection (Spanish), p. 6
- Challenge Planner, pp. 7–10
- Academic Vocabulary Development, pp. 11–13
- Comparing Literature Graphic Organizers, p. 48
- Literary Elements, pp. 17, 20, 23, 26, 29, 32, 36, 42, 45, 49, 52, 56, 59, 62, 68, 72, 75, 79, 82, 85
- Reading Strategies, pp. 18, 21, 24, 27, 30, 33, 35, 37, 43, 46, 50, 53, 57, 60, 63, 69, 73, 76, 78, 80, 83, 86
- Active Reading Graphic Organizers, pp. 92–101
- Selection Vocabulary Practice, pp. 19, 22, 25, 28, 31, 34, 38, 44, 47, 51, 54, 58, 61, 64, 70, 74, 77, 81, 84, 87
- Literary Focus, pp. 15, 40, 66

Writing, Grammar, and Spelling

- Spelling Practice, p. 88
- Grammar Practice, pp. 55, 71
- Writing Workshop Graphic Organizer, p. 89

Speaking, Listening, and Viewing

- Speaking, Listening, and Viewing Activities, pp. 90–91

English Language Learners

- English Language Coach Review, pp. 16, 41, 67

DIFFERENTIATED INSTRUCTION

- Active Learning and Note Taking Guide pp. 1–39
- Leveled Vocabulary Development, pp. 1–20
- Skill Level Up!™ A Language Arts Game
- Listening Library Audio CD, disc 1, tracks 1–24
- Glencoe BookLink 3
- Vocabulary PuzzleMaker
- Literature Library Vocabulary PuzzleMaker

ASSESSMENT

- Selection and Unit Assessments, pp. 1–44, 211–212
- Selection Quick Checks, pp. 1–22
- Selection Quick Checks (Spanish), pp. 1–22
- Assessment by Learning Objectives, pp. 1–14
- Rubrics for Assessing Student Writing, Listening and Speaking, pp. 4–5, 26–27
- Standardized Test Preparation and Practice
- Glencoe Online Essay Grader
- Interactive Tutor: Self-Assessment
- Exam*View*® Assessment Suite
- Literature Library Exam*View*® Assessment

Additional Instructional Support

LITERATURE AND READING

- Active Learning and Note Taking Guide, pp. 1–39
- *inTIME* Magazines
- Glencoe Literature Library
- Literature Launchers: Pre-Reading Videos
- Literature Classics

WRITING, GRAMMAR, AND SPELLING

- REAL Success in Writing: Research and Reports
- Writing Constructed Responses, pp. 1–26, 42–47, 54
- Spelling Power eWorkbook
- Revising with Style eWorkbook
- Sentence Diagraming eWorkbook
- Glencoe Grammar and Composition Handbook
- Grammar and Language Workbook
- Grammar and Language eWorkbook

PROFESSIONAL DEVELOPMENT

- Professional Development Package

TRANSPARENCIES

- Read Aloud, Think Aloud Transparencies 1–10
- Bellringer Options Transparencies
  - Selection Focus Transparencies 1–19
  - Daily Language Practice Transparencies 1–24
- Grammar and Language Transparencies 3, 5, 10
- Writing Workshop Transparencies 6–10
- Visual Literacy/Fine Art Transparencies

ENGLISH LANGUAGE LEARNER

- English Language Coach, Unit Resources (Fast File)
- *inTIME* Magazines (Spanish)
- Spanish Listening Library

TECHNOLOGY

- TeacherWorks Plus™
- StudentWorks Plus™
- Literature Launchers: Pre-Reading Videos
- Vocabulary PuzzleMaker
- Literature Library Vocabulary PuzzleMaker
- Skill Level Up!™ A Language Arts Game
- glencoe.com
- Presentation Plus! ™
- Exam*View*™ Assessment Suite
- Literature Library Exam*View*™ Assessment Suite
- Listening Library
- Interactive Tutor: Self-Assessment
- Glencoe BookLink 3
- Online Student Edition, mhln.com
- Glencoe Online Essay Grader
- Grammar and Language eWorkbook
- Revising with Style eWorkbook
- Sentence Diagraming eWorkbook
- Spelling Power eWorkbook
- Literature Classics
- Spanish Listening Library

Additional Glencoe Resources

Dinah Zike's Foldables™

Foldables™ are three-dimensional, interactive graphic organizers that help students practice basic writing skills, review key vocabulary terms, and answer Big Ideas. Every unit contains a Foldable™ activity. You can find the pattern and directions for the Unit 1 Foldable™ in the Unit 1 Resources Fast File booklet. You can use the Foldables™ as they are presented or modify them to suit the needs of your students.

For a wealth of online resources that support the instruction in Unit 1, students and teachers can visit our Web site at glencoe.com. Students will find additional learning, practice, and assessment opportunities such as these, which are noted in the student text:

- Author Search
- Big Idea Overview and Activity
- Interactive Literary Elements Handbook
- Study Central
- Unit Assessment
- Web Activities
- Writing Models

Teachers will find planning and instructional tools that include the following:

- Book Lesson Plans
- Web Activity Lesson Plans
- Teacher Forum
- Professional Resources

  Go to glencoe.com to see the entire selection of *Glencoe Literature* online resources.

Glencoe's Presentation Plus!™, a multimedia teaching tool, lets you present dynamic lessons that will engage your students. Using Microsoft PowerPoint®, you can customize the presentations to create your own personalized lessons. Use CheckPoint questions with interactive response keypads to get immediate student feedback during lessons, to increase student participation, and to assess student comprehension.

Glencoe Literature Library

The collection of hardcover books includes full-length novels, novellas, plays, and works of nonfiction. Each volume consists of at least one complete extended-length reading accompanied by several related readings from a broad range of genres. A separate Study Guide for each *Glencoe Literature Library* book provides teaching notes and reproducible activity pages for students. Glencoe Literature Library titles that complement this unit include:

- ***A Separate Peace with Related Readings*** by John Knowles
- ***Winter Thunder with Related Readings*** by Mari Sandoz
- ***The Metamorphosis with Related Readings*** by Franz Kafka

GLENCOE BOOKLINK

Use the Glencoe BookLink 3 CD-ROM, a database of more than 26,700 titles, to *create customized reading lists* for your students.

- Search for award-winning titles (e.g., Newbery Award winners, Coretta Scott King Award winners, and Caldecott Medal winners) and for books on several state recommended reading lists.
- Find Degrees of Reading Power™ (DRP) and Lexile™ readability scores for all selections.
- Organize reading lists by students' reading level, author, genre, theme, or area of interest.
- Get a brief summary of each selection.

You can find recommended leveled readings for this unit with Independent Reading (see pages 290 and 291).

Online Essay Grader

Use Glencoe's online essay grader powered by SkillWriter™ to score your students' writing and to provide individualized feedback to each student automatically.

You and your students can visit glencoe.com to link to the essay grader. *Students* can enter their essays and receive feedback on demand. *You* can manage demographic data, assign tests and generate individual student and aggregated reports. The essay grader can help you

- Save time with automatic scoring and individualized feedback.
- Supplement in-class writing instruction using guided writing practice.

REAL Success: Reading Excellence at All Levels

Glencoe REAL Success is a suite of new reading and language arts products designed to foster reading excellence at all levels.

Look for TWE point-of-use references for these specific products that will help your students succeed in reading this Unit.

- *Jamestown Literature: An Adapted Reader*
- REAL Success in Writing: Research and Reports
- Skill Level Up!™ A Language Arts Game
- CheckPoint PowerPoint™ slides
- Literature/Reading support at Glencoe Web site

Literature Launchers

Set the scene with Glencoe's Literature Launchers, engaging pre-reading video segments that introduce each unit. Each Unit Launcher brings the literature to life, featuring expert testimony and archival stills and footage from the time.

Insert your Glencoe Literature Launchers into your DVD player. Select the Unit 1 Launcher from the menu to introduce The Short Story.

A lively collection of articles drawn from issues of the TIME family of magazines helps students develop the skills they need to interact with informational text in a meaningful way. Each of the news stories, feature articles, reviews, profiles, and essays in the magazine connects to an author, work, or theme in *Glencoe Literature: The Reader's Choice.* See the *inTIME* Teacher's Guide for specific connections to each unit and for reproducible student worksheets designed to develop students' reading and critical thinking skills.

Teacher Wraparound Edition Key

Level Appropriate Code

AL = Activities for students working above grade level

OL = Activities for students working at grade level

BL = Activities for students working below grade level

EL = Activities for English language learners

AS = Information for all students

Teacher Wraparound Prompts

R Reading Skill These activities help you teach reading skills and vocabulary.

V Vocabulary These activities help students comprehend words and incorporate them into reading.

BI Big Idea These activities and questions prompt students to explore the Big Idea.

L Literary Element These activities and questions help students comprehend selections and learn more about each genre.

★ Enrichment Additional activities and information involving art appreciation and history.

Professional Development Center

From Your Authors:

Teaching Literary Analysis: Short Stories

Build Background Partner conversations are frequently used to engage students in conversations about the themes or topics they will be studying in their English classroom. During partner conversations, students share what they know or have experienced about a specific topic. In doing so, students use vocabulary common with the reading selections. These conversations also build interest for students, as they want to know how other people react to situations they have experienced. Before reading "The Gift of the Magi" by O. Henry, have students discuss with a partner the most valuable gift they have ever received. As students have conversations about their own gifts, they will share experiences and use vocabulary that may also be present in the story. In this way, they will have a connection to the story that will make it more interesting to them.

Develop Historical Perspective Reading short stories allows students to understand and appreciate the experiences of others, including those who lived in another time and place. As they read, students can keep a log of different characters and their perspectives—either as stated by the author or inferred by the reader—as these characters interact with one another or with the events in the story. While reading "American History" by Judith Ortiz Cofer, ask students to keep a log of what Elena thinks and feels, how she interacts with other characters, and how she reacts to the historical event that occurs. Ask students to compare Elena's experiences and feelings to their own.

Jacqueline Jones Royster and Beverly Chin

Teacher to Teacher

Sylvia Barnhill
North Pitt High School
Bethel, North Carolina

Before beginning a unit on short stories, I review the basic elements of fiction. For some students, this is a refresher, but for others, it may be an introduction. To make this a nonthreatening experience for everyone, I use the familiar childhood story "Little Red Riding Hood." We read the story aloud in class and examine how many elements of fiction appear in it. Students complete a written analysis of the story, which is something they do for every story we read during the unit. Now armed with the basics, students apply this knowledge as we move into literature that demands them to read and comprehend at higher levels. Students' analysis sheets are collected and put into a three-ring binder, which becomes their study guide for the unit test.

Teacher Chat Room

Making Literature Come Alive

Before you begin this unit or sometime during the unit, talk with other teachers about ways they have taught short stories. Have a lunch-time discussion group or an after-school hour for professional development and discuss the following questions and answers from our authors:

How do I make short stories interesting to high school students?

- Choose topics that resonate with the lived experiences of high school students.
- Choose selections that make students consider the ethical dimensions of a problem—high school students are developing their ethical belief systems.
- Allow students to analyze the actions of people who are both similar to and different from them.
- Ask students what they would do if they were one of the characters. For example, ask students to consider what it would be like to have Anna of the Flying Avalons for a mother as they read "The Leap" by Louise Erdrich. Ask students how having a mother who had been part of a trapeze act in the circus would affect their childhood and their perspective of their mother.

How do I show students that literary analysis can heighten their enjoyment of short stories?

- Remind students that authors use literacy devices to help the reader.
- Ask students to consider the role of the author and the author's purpose for writing.
- Share your own reactions to the mood and tone of the story with students. Ask students which words the author uses to establish the mood or tone. For example, when reading Richard Connell's "The Most Dangerous Game," you may ask students how the suspenseful mood is created. How does this mood affect the pacing of the story?
- Discuss the motivation readers have for reading short stories. By analyzing literature, readers can better understand their reactions to literary works. For example, when reading "The Necklace" by Guy de Maupassant, have students examine how Mathilde's unfortunate experience affects her view of the world; why is this experience compelling for readers?

How can graphic novels help students better understand the structure of short stories?

- Graphic novels can be used to understand how narratives are organized and structured. Using graphic novels, students can often visually identify the parts of plot, such as exposition, climax, and resolution.
- Some graphic novels use sequential visual art to convey a particular perspective. Analyzing perspective in a graphic novel helps students develop this skill that they can then use in reading short stories. While students are reading "The Secret Life of Walter Mitty" by James Thurber, have them analyze Walter's perspective by creating a graphic novel portraying the events in the story from his viewpoint.

Focus

BELLRINGER

Bellringer Options
Literature Launcher Video
Daily Language Practice Transparency 1

Or **say:** Identify some reasons why people tell and retell stories. *(Students may suggest that stories help us make sense of the world and allow us to go places we could never actually go to or experience things we could not normally do.)*

Objectives for the Unit Introduction

- To identify and interpret various literary elements used in the short story (SE)
- To analyze the effects that these literary elements have upon the reader (SE)
- To analyze short stories for the ways in which authors inspire the reader to share emotions (SE)

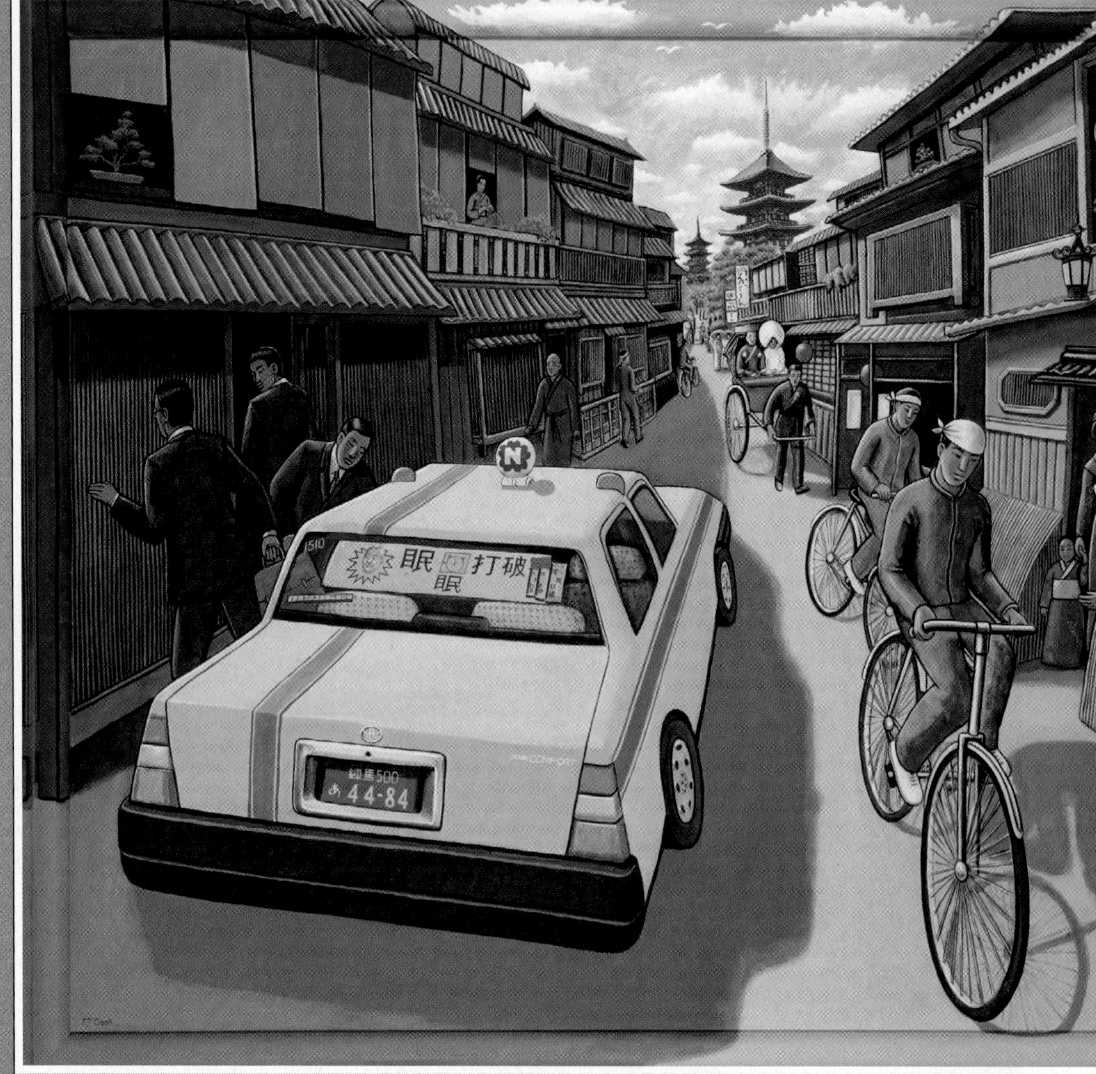

Toyota Taxi, 2005. P. J. Crook. Acrylic on canvas, 116.8 x 152.4 cm. 

Unit Introduction Skills

The Short Story

Reading Skills
- Reading the Short Story (SE p. 2)
- Reading Journal (TWE p. 2)
- Solving Problems (TWE p. 8)

Listening/Speaking/Viewing Skills
- Defining Literary Term (SE p. 8)
- Creating a Timeline (SE p. 8)
- Telling a Story (TWE p. 6)

Writing Skills/Grammar
- Creating a Dictionary (SE p. 8)
- Writing a News Report (TWE p. 4)

Literary Elements
- Plot and Setting (SE p. 2)
- Character and Theme (SE pp. 2–3)
- Narrator and Voice (SE p. 3)

The Short Story

Looking Ahead

A short story is a little, well-polished stone in a vast quarry of fiction. As with other genres, at the foundation of the short story is a set of key literary elements—setting, character, plot, and theme—that the writer manages to introduce, develop, and display in just a few pages. A large part of a reader's enjoyment is seeing how the author lays this foundation and envisioning what it will become.

PREVIEW **Big Ideas and Literary Focus**

	BIG IDEA:	LITERARY FOCUS:
1	Matters of Life and Death	Plot and Setting
2	Rewards and Sacrifices	Character and Theme
3	Dreams and Reality	Narrator and Voice

INDIANA ACADEMIC STANDARDS (pages 1–7)
9.3 [Identify] story elements such as character, theme, plot, and setting...

Focus

Summary

The unit begins with definitions of the short story genre and its main literary elements. It provides insights from professional fiction writers. A story by Leo Tolstoy is used to show examples of short story literary elements. The introduction concludes with review activities.

Viewing the Art

The large, highly detailed canvases of British painter Pamela (P. J.) Crook (1945–) often depict subtle human dramas in busy urban landscapes. AS

Unit Resources

Classroom Management
- TeacherWorks Plus™ CD-ROM
- StudentWorks Plus™ CD-ROM
- Literature Launchers™: Pre-Reading Videos DVD, Unit One

Core Instructional Support
- Unit 1 Resources (Fast File)
- Literature Online, glencoe.com
- Presentation Plus!™ CD-ROM, Unit One

Transparencies
- Literary Elements Transparencies 1, 3, 7–13, 15–22, 24–26, 37
- Bellringer Options Transparencies:
  Selection Focus Transparencies 1–19
  Daily Language Practice Transparencies 1–24

Differentiated Instruction
- Active Learning and Note Taking Guide, pp. 1–39
- Skill Level Up!™ A Language Arts Game

Assessment
- Selection and Unit Assessments, pp. 211–212
- Exam*View*® Assessment Suite CD-ROM
- Assessment by Learning Objectives, pp. 1–14

Supplemental Reading
- Glencoe Literature Library
- Glencoe BookLink 3 CD-ROM
- *inTIME* Magazines

Teach

- Point out that there are six literary elements students should know before they read the selections in Unit One. An excerpt from a story from the unit illustrates each literary element. OL
- Invite volunteers to read aloud the explanation of each literary term and then the literary example beside it. Take time to point out how the excerpt illustrates the literary element. OL

★ Language History

Plot *Plot* is a word with many meanings, including "a scheme or plan," "a piece of land," and "a graph." The literary meaning—"the sequence of events in a story"—was first used in the seventeenth century. The word's origin as a literary term is unknown. AS

Genre Focus: Short Story

What are the elements that shape a short story?

African author Chinua Achebe describes perfectly the give-take-give relationship between reader and writer by saying, "people create stories create people; or rather stories create people create stories." Literary elements like plot, setting, and voice help strengthen this link between author and audience and serve to sharpen and intensify the reading experience.

Plot and Setting

Sequence of Events

★ **Plot** is the sequence of events that ties the beginning of a story to its end. An important part of any plot is **conflict:** the struggle between two or more forces that must be resolved by the end of the narrative.

> When all the people had assembled in the galleries, and the king, surrounded by his court, sat high up on his throne of royal state on one side of the arena, he gave a signal, a door beneath him opened, and the accused subject stepped into the amphitheater.
>
> —Frank R. Stockton, **from "The Lady, or the Tiger?"**

Time and Place

Setting is a story's time and place. It includes concrete aspects of a story, such as the location, the weather, and the time of year. Setting can also include abstractions such as the ideas, customs, values, and beliefs of a particular time and place.

> At the most remote end of the crypt there appeared another less spacious. Its walls had been lined with human remains, piled to the vault overhead, in the fashion of the great catacombs of Paris. Three sides of this interior crypt were ornamented in this manner.
>
> —Edgar Allan Poe, **from "The Cask of Amontillado"**

Character and Theme

Individuals

Characters are the people, animals, and other individuals in a story. Most stories have one or more main characters that drive the plot forward and a set of minor characters that support the action.

> My mother's face, usually sternly set, changed with the varying nuances of her emotion, its plane shifting, shaped by the soft highlights of the sanctuary, as she progressed from subdued "amen" to a loud "Help me, Jesus" wrung from the depths of her gaunt frame.
>
> —Eugenia Collier, **from "Sweet Potato Pie"**

Additional Support

Skills Practice

READING: Reading Journal
Encourage students to keep a journal for recording their responses as they read. Explain that a turning point in a story is a moment when a character decides or does something that has a major effect on the outcome of the story. Suggest students keep a list of such turning points in their journals and record their responses to them under the following headings: **Pros and Cons of Decision/Action, What I Would Have Done, How the Story Would Change.** OL

Message

L The **theme** is the main idea, or message, in a literary work. Theme is not the subject of a story but is an insight about life or human nature. Sometimes stories have a **stated theme,** which is expressed directly. More often, however, a story has an **implied theme,** which the author reveals through setting, point of view, and the actions of the characters.

Poor Sheila! Before the month was over, the spell she cast over me was gone, but the memory of that lost bass haunted me all summer and haunts me still. There would be other Sheila Mants in my life, other fish, and though I came close once or twice, it was those secret, hidden tuggings in the night that claimed me, and I never made the same mistake again. ★

—W. D. Wetherell, **from "The Bass, the River, and Sheila Mant"**

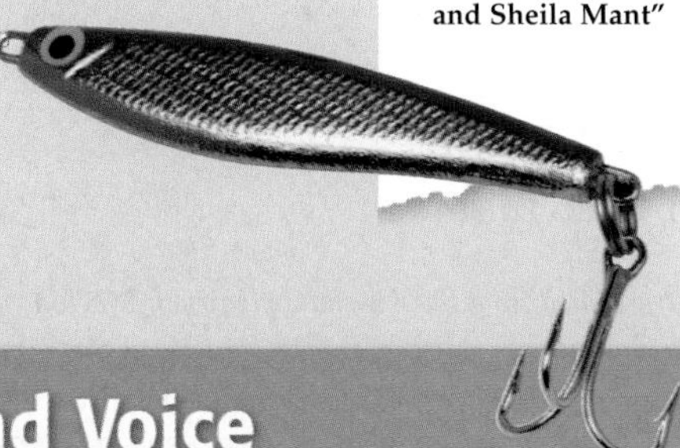

Narrator and Voice

Point of View

A **narrator** is the person who tells a story. The narrator can be an outside observer or a character in the story. The relationship of the narrator to the story is called **point of view.** In a story with first-person point of view, the narrator is a character in the story. In a story with third-person limited point of view, the narrator reveals the thoughts, feelings, and observations of only one character. In a story with third-person omniscient point of view, the narrator stands outside the story and comments on the action.

Pandemonium broke loose in the courtroom. A woman's scream rose above the bedlam and suddenly a lovely, dark-haired girl was in Walter Mitty's arms. The District Attorney struck at her savagely. Without rising from his chair, Mitty let the man have it on the point of the chin.

—James Thurber, **from "The Secret Life of Walter Mitty"**

Language Choices

Voice is the distinctive use of language that conveys the writer's or narrator's personality to the reader. Sometimes voice is determined by the author's or narrator's word choices. In other cases, voice is determined by tone, an author's attitude toward his or her subject matter or audience, and mood, the emotional quality of a literary work.

The light through the large kitchen window of his house told me that El Building blocked the sun to such an extent that they had to turn lights on in the middle of the day. I felt ashamed about it. But the white kitchen table with the lamp hanging just above it looked cozy and inviting. I would soon sit there, across from Eugene.

—Judith Ortiz Cofer, **from "American History"**

LiteratureOnline **Study Central** Visit www.glencoe.com to review the elements that shape a short story.

Teach

L Literary Element

Theme Help students identify themes by comparing them to the morals of Aesop's fables. Ask students to recall a fable such as "The City Mouse and the Country Mouse." Briefly discuss its moral.

Say: Like the moral of a fable, the theme of a story is its main idea or message and provides insight into human nature. **OL**

★ Writer's Technique

Sentence Complexity and Voice Students should notice the last sentence of the excerpt by W. D. Wetherell. The sentence is compound-complex. It combines two independent clauses with a dependent clause. By using this structure, Wetherell shows the connections between the narrator's ideas. **AS**

Study Central Have students visit the Web site for resources that will help them to review the short story genre.

Differentiated Instruction

Setting a Purpose Encourage students to set a purpose for reading, such as noticing how a paragraph shows a story's theme or plot. After they finish reading, have them check their comprehension by asking a question based on their reading purpose; for instance: How did this paragraph show the theme or plot? **BL**

Academic Standards

Additional Support activities on pp. 2 and 3 cover the following standards:

Skills Practice: **9.3** [Identify] story elements such as…plot… **9.5.2** Write responses to literature that support statements with evidence from the text…

Differentiated Instruction: **9.3** [Identify] story elements such as…theme [and] plot…

Teach

R Reading Strategy

Visualizing Explain that Tolstoy uses specific details to help readers picture the setting and the action.
Ask: What details help you imagine the monkey? *(The words and phrases* large, capering, silly faces, *and* aped *create a vivid picture)* Encourage students to jot down details that help them visualize as they read. OL

★ Writer's Technique

Tolstoy's Sentence Structure Note that most of Tolstoy's sentences in the first half of the story begin with a subject and verb, rather than with introductory phrases or clauses. The emphasis of the sentences is on the story's action. As a result, the story resembles a news report or a sportscaster's play-by-play. The sentences in the last four paragraphs are more complex. They begin with dependent clauses that are descriptive, slowing the action of the story. AS

Literary Analysis Model

How do literary elements function in a short story?

The Russian writer Leo Tolstoy (1828–1910) is considered one of the world's greatest authors. Although he is best known for his epic novels *War and Peace* and *Anna Karenina,* Tolstoy also wrote essays, plays, and short stories. "The Jump" is considered one of his finest short stories.

The Jump

by Leo Tolstoy

translated from the Russian by Miriam Morton

APPLYING Literary Elements

Setting
The first lines offer information about *place:* aboard a ship.

A ship had sailed around the world and was on its homeward journey. The weather was calm and everyone was on deck. A large monkey was capering about amidst the crowd, amusing everybody. She tumbled here and there, made silly faces, and aped the people. It was clear that she knew that she was funny and therefore carried on even more. R

She jumped over to a twelve-year-old boy, the son of the ship's captain, and snatched his hat from his head, put it on her own, and quickly scampered up the mast. Everyone laughed, and the boy didn't know whether to laugh or be angry.

The monkey perched on the bottom crossbeam of the mast, took off the hat and began to tear it with her teeth and paws. She seemed to be doing it to spite the boy. She pointed at him and made funny faces.

Character
Notice the contrast between the playful, amusing monkey and the angry, threatening boy.

The boy shouted at her and threatened her with his fist, but she kept tearing the hat, doing it even harder. The sailors laughed louder, the boy flushed with anger, threw off his jacket, and went after the monkey on the mast. In an instant he had climbed the rope ladder to the first crossbeam. But just as the boy was about to grab his hat from her, the monkey quickly climbed even higher. ★

"You won't get away with this," the boy cried out, and climbed after the monkey. The animal lured him on, scrambling still higher, to the top of the high mast.

Up there, holding fast to a rope with one foot, the monkey stretched out her body, extended her long arm, and hung the torn cap on the end of the highest crossbeam. Then she reached the very tip of the mast and sat there making faces, baring her teeth, and enjoying her victory.

Narrator
Tolstoy's narrator is an unbiased observer, which adds a sense of realism to the story.

There was a space of about six feet between the boy and the end of the crossbeam where his hat was hanging now. To reach it, he would have to let go of both the rope and the mast. He was so upset by now that, forgetting all danger, he stepped onto this highest crossbeam, balancing himself the best he could with his arms.

Additional Support

Skills Practice

WRITING: Writing a News Report Review the structure of news reports. Note that the first paragraph always answers the most important questions—*Who? What? When? Where?* Later paragraphs discuss why and how the event happened. Challenge students to use details from Tolstoy's story as the basis of a news report. Students may quote from the story and write a headline. Ask volunteers to read their reports to the class. OL

All the people on deck had been watching the chase between the captain's son and the monkey. But when they saw the son let go of the rope and step out on the crossbeam, they froze with terror. If he lost his balance and fell to the deck, he would be killed. Or even if he somehow reached the end of the crossbeam and got his hat, it would be hard for him to turn around and get back to the mast.

They were looking on in silence, waiting to see what would happen, when someone in the crowd suddenly cried out in panic. The boy heard the cry, looked down, and teetered.

Just then the captain of the ship, the boy's father, came out of his cabin. He was holding a rifle for shooting seagulls. When he saw his son teetering on the uppermost crossbeam, he at once aimed the gun at him, shouting, "Jump! Jump into the water! Or I'll shoot!"

The boy hesitated, not understanding.

"Jump! One, two . . ."

As soon as his father cried "three," the boy stepped out and dived into the sea.

Like a cannonball his body hit the water, but before the waves could cover him, twenty brave seamen had jumped from the ship into the sea. Within forty seconds—they seemed like eternity—the body of the boy came to the surface. The seamen grabbed him and brought him back on board.

After a few long minutes water began to come from his mouth and nose, and he began to breathe.

When the captain saw this, he uttered a choked cry, and he hurried away to his cabin so that no one would see him weep.

Plot

As a way of heightening suspense, the narrator tells the events of the story in the order in which they occurred.

Theme L

On the surface, the father's order to jump seems heartless. Only after the boy has recovered does the reader understand the extent of the father's love. Then the theme—sometimes drastic measures are necessary—becomes clear.

Leo Tolstoy with his grandchildren. ★

Reading Check

Evaluating What is the most memorable part of this story? Why?

Teach

Reading Check

Answer: *Students should support their answers with details from the story.*

L Literary Element

Theme Remind students that a theme expresses an idea about the world or human nature.
Ask: What is the theme of the story? *(Guide students to see how the story illustrates the complexity of a father's intense feelings for his son—he unselfconsciously explodes in rage yet seems ashamed of his deep tenderness.)* OL

★ Literary History

Leo Tolstoy Tolstoy was one of Russian literature's great realists. His novels and stories depict both the internal and external worlds of a broad range of characters—from aristocrats and soldiers to peasants—in precise detail. As Tolstoy grew older, his interest in worldly affairs waned. He became a pacifist and renounced his possessions. AS

Building Reading Fluency

Paired Reading Have partners choose a brief passage from the story and take turns reading it aloud to each other, using expression to suggest mood and emphasis. Students should evaluate their partner's reading technique and offer constructive comments. BL

Reading in the Real World

Citizenship Like Tolstoy, Gandhi and Martin Luther King Jr. believed that social change can occur without violence. Have students research the principle of nonviolence and write a journal entry about a citizen's responsibility to his or her society. OL

Academic Standards

Additional Support activities on pp. 4 and 5 cover the following standards:

Skills Practice: **9.5.2** Write responses to literature that demonstrate a comprehensive grasp of the significant ideas of literary works...

Building Reading Fluency: **9.7** [Develop] speaking skills...in conjunction with...strategies...[for] delivery of oral presentations.

Reading in the Real World: **9.5.3** Write expository compositions...that communicate information and ideas from primary and secondary sources accurately and coherently...

Teach

R Reading Strategy

Making Connections
Discuss the phrase "put yourself in my shoes." Emphasize that to connect to a story is to imagine yourself in the character's situation.
Ask: What element in fiction helps writer John Gardner put himself in a character's "shoes"? *(Sensory details)* OL

Viewing the Art

American painter Tom Blackwell (1938–) belongs to the photorealist school, a style of painting that began in the late 1960s. Blackwell's rendering of a reflection in a plate glass window typifies that movement's aim of capturing every detail of ordinary objects with the exactitude of a camera. AS

Writers on Reading

What do writers say about the short story?

Columbus Circle. Tom Blackwell. 

The Imagery of Fiction

The most important single notion in the theory of fiction I have outlined—essentially the traditional theory of our civilization's literature—is that of the vivid and continuous fictional dream. According to this notion, the writer sets up a dramatized action in which we are given the signals that make us "see" the setting, characters, and events; that is, he does not tell us about them in abstract terms, like an essayist, but gives us images that appeal to our senses—preferably all of them, not just the visual sense—so that we seem to move among the characters, lean with them against the fictional walls, taste the fictional gazpacho, smell the fictional hyacinths. R

—John Gardner, **from *The Art of Fiction***

Additional Support

Skills Practice

SPEAKING AND LISTENING: Telling a Story Illustrate Atwood's point about storytelling by telling "Little Red Riding Hood" twice—first badly, and then with style. In the first instance, speak in a flat voice, with awkward pauses, and omit key details. Then retell the story with animation and attention to detail. Ask students to identify the differences between the two stories and to explain why one of them was better than the other. OL

Recognizing Details

The truth is that the best preparation I could have had for a life as a novelist was life as a reporter. At a time when more impressionistic renderings of events were beginning to creep into the news pages, I learned to look always for the telling detail: the Yankees cap, the neon sign in the club window, the striped towel on the deserted beach. Those things that, taken incrementally, make a convincing picture of real life, and maybe get you onto page 1, too.

I learned to distinguish between those details that simply existed and those that revealed. Those telling details are the essence of fiction that feels real. The command of those details explains why Charles Dickens, a onetime reporter, has a byline for the ages.

I learned, from decades of writing down their words verbatim in notebooks, how real people talk. I learned that syntax and rhythm were almost as individual as a fingerprint, and that one quotation, precisely transcribed and intentionally untidied, could delineate a character in a way that pages of exposition never could.

—Anna Quindlen, **from "Eye of the Reporter, Heart of the Novelist"**

"When we read a story, we inhabit it."

—John Berger

The Reader's Voice

L Ever since I was first read to, then started reading to myself, there has never been a line read that I didn't *hear*. As my eyes followed the sentence, a voice was saying it silently to me. It isn't my mother's voice, or the voice of any person I can identify, certainly not my own. It is human, but inward, and it is inwardly that I listen to it. It is to me the voice of the story or the poem itself. The cadence, whatever it is that asks you to believe, the feeling that resides in the printed word, reaches me through the reader-voice. I have supposed, but never found out, that this is the case with all readers—to read as listeners—and with all writers, to write as listeners. It may be part of the desire to write. The sound of what falls on the page begins the process of testing it for truth, for me. Whether I am right to trust so far I don't know. By now I don't know whether I could do either one, reading or writing, without the other.

—Eudora Welty, **from *One Writer's Beginnings*** 

Storytelling

Think of a simple joke; now think of the same joke told, first well and then badly. It's the timing, isn't it? And the gestures, the embellishments, the tangents, the occasion, the expression on the face of the teller, and whether you like him or not. Literary critics talking about fiction may call these things style, voice, and narrative technique and so forth, but you can trace them all back to that moment when the tribe or the family is sitting around the fire or the dinner table and the storyteller decides to add something, leave something out or vary the order of telling in order to make the story a little better. Writing on the page is after all just a notation, and all literature, like all music, is oral by nature.

—Margaret Atwood, **from *Second Words***

LiteratureOnline InterActive Reading Practice
Visit www.glencoe.com to practice these strategies for reading a short story.

Reading Check

Responding From your own reading experiences, which passage do you identify with most closely? Explain.

Teach

Reading Check

Answer: *Answers will vary. Make sure students give reasons for their responses.*

L Literary Element

Voice Explain that voice in a short story conveys the writer's or narrator's personality.
Ask: What does Welty's voice in the excerpt on page 7 suggest about her personality? *(Students may say that she sounds thoughtful and honest.)* **OL**

★ Literary History

Eudora Welty Eudora Welty (1909–2001) was an American short story writer and novelist. She won a Pulitzer Prize for her novel *The Optimist's Daughter* (1972). Her works are almost always set in the Deep South and reflect Southerners' culture, humor, and way of speaking. **AS**

InterActive Reading Have students access the Web site for more practice with reading strategies.

English Language Coach

Literary Terms Students may not know the literary terms the writers discuss—detail, syntax, voice, and narrative. Review how to use the *Literary Terms Handbook* at the back of the book. Encourage students to ask questions about unfamiliar terms and to keep a list of terms and their definitions. **EL**

Differentiated Instruction

Listening and Summarizing Less proficient readers may have trouble with the professional writers' diction and ideas. Read the writers' words aloud. Ask students to work together to paraphrase or summarize what each writer says about writing and reading. **BL**

Academic Standards

Additional Support activities on pp. 6 and 7 cover the following standards:

Skills Practice: **9.7.10** Assess how…delivery affect[s]…oral communication…

English Language Coach: **9.1** Use…a growing knowledge of English…to determine the meaning of words…

Differentiated Instruction: **9.7** [Respond] to oral communication [with] careful listening and evaluation of content…

Assess/Close

Guide to Reading a Short Story

Remind students to be active readers—to ask questions, make connections, and consider their own reactions as they read.

Elements of a Short Story

Encourage students to focus on the six literary elements described in the introduction as they read.

Activities

1. **Speaking/Listening** Students may want to start with one of the more straightforward elements, such as character, setting, or plot.
2. **Visual Literacy** Remind students that the plot events occur over the course of a few minutes.
3. **Writing** Invite students to illustrate their definitions. Remind them to refer to the *Literary Terms Handbook* on page R1.

FOLDABLES™ Study Organizer

Have students make and label the Foldable.™ Instruct them to write their reactions to each selection in the Reader Response Journal.

Wrap-Up

Guide to Reading a Short Story

- Preview a short story before you begin reading. Read the first sentence carefully, and then skim for key words and phrases.
- Watch for clues about character, setting, and theme as you read.
- Think about the chief conflict of the plot.
- Understand how the conflict is resolved.
- Think about what the story reminds you of in your own life or consider what it is that makes the story memorable.

Elements of a Short Story

- **Plot** is the sequence of events in a story.
- **Setting** is the time and place in which the action of a story occurs.
- **Theme** is the author's message, or insight about life or human nature.
- A **character** is an individual in a literary work.
- The **narrator** is the person who tells the story.
- **Voice** is the distinctive use of language that helps the reader understand the narrator's personality.

Activities

Use what you have learned about reading a short story to do one of these actvities.

1. **Speaking/Listening** Choose a literary term mentioned in the Unit 1 Genre Focus to present to the class. Define the term, and then offer examples. Keep in mind that visuals can add interest to your presentation.
2. **Visual Literacy** Create a timeline showing the major plot events in "The Jump." Label the event that marks the climax, or the point of highest emotion, of the story.
3. **Writing** Create a dictionary of literary terms that you can add to over the course of the year. Begin with the six you learned in this unit: plot, setting, theme, character, narrator, and voice. Define each term and provide examples from the unit or your own reading.

BOUND BOOK

Try using this study organizer to explore your personal responses to the selections you read in this unit.

INDIANA ACADEMIC STANDARDS (page 8)
9.3 [Identify] story elements such as character, theme, plot, and setting...

Additional Support

Skills Practice

READING: Solving Problems Explain that one strategy for reading stories is to think of them as a series of problems and solutions. A character has a problem and may or may not be able to solve it. Have groups of students reread "The Jump" and write down at least two problems and two attempted solutions from the story. Students should decide if the actions solved the problem or not. **OL**

PART 1

Matters of Life and Death

Saving the Man from the Sea, 2003. Susan Bower. Oil on Board, 48.2 x 41.9 cm. Private Collection. 

BIG IDEA

BI Danger can threaten us in many ways. Our pride, our happiness, our safety, even our lives can be at stake. In the short stories in Part 1, you will read about people who face life-and-death challenges, both real and imagined. As you read the short stories, ask yourself: What are effective ways to deal with danger?

Analyzing and Extending

BI Big Idea

Matters of Life and Death Direct students to read the text under the "Big Idea" heading. Elicit a definition of *danger.* Write students' responses on the board. Then challenge students to identify the danger depicted in the art.

Ask: What are effective ways to deal with danger? Return to this question after students have read selections and have them reconsider their answers. OL

★ Viewing the Art

Susan Bower (1953–) lives in Yorkshire, England, where she began painting in 1985. She paints chiefly in oil and uses a carefree and whimsical style to portray a variety of people. AS

English Language Coach

Building Background Ask students to identify the word in their native language that means "danger." Discuss various kinds of danger and how attitudes toward it may differ. Some enjoy danger and others avoid it at all costs. Encourage students to answer the question on page 9. EL

Differentiated Instruction

Danger and Plot Have students name stories or movies in which danger is a key element. Discuss how danger increases suspense and makes readers pay attention to the plot in order to find out what happens. BL

Academic Standards

Additional Support activities on pp. 8 and 9 cover the following standards:

Skills Practice: **9.3** [Identify] story elements such as…plot…

English Language Coach: **9.1** Use…other languages to determine the meaning of words…

Differentiated Instruction: **9.3** [Identify] story elements such as…theme [and] plot…

UNIT ONE

Part 1: Skills Scope and Sequence

Readability Scores Key
Dale-Chall/DRP/Lexile

PACING (DAYS) STANDARD	BLOCK	SELECTIONS AND FEATURES	LITERARY ELEMENTS
2 class sessions	1	"The Lady, or the Tiger?" by Frank R. Stockton **10.1/68/1260**, pp. 12–21	Conflict, SE pp. 13–20; TWE p. 18 Plot, SE p. 20
		"The Most Dangerous Game" by Richard Connell **6.2/50/740**, pp. 22–43	Suspense, SE pp. 23–42 Conflict, SE p. 42 Style, SE p. 43 Plot, SE p. 41; TWE p. 26 Setting, TWE p. 36
2 class sessions	1	"The Leap" by Louise Erdrich **6.4/64/1260**, pp. 44–54	Flashback, SE pp. 45–53 Setting, SE p. 53 Theme, TWE p. 52
		"The Cask of Amontillado" by Edgar Allan Poe **9.8/55/790**, pp. 55–65	Mood, SE pp. 56, 58–61, 64 Suspense, SE p. 64
		Vocabulary Workshop: Context Clues, p. 66	
2 class sessions	1	"Blues Ain't No Mockin Bird" by Toni Cade Bambara **6.8/53/960**, pp. 67–76	Dialect, SE pp. 68–75 Setting, SE p. 75
		"The Interlopers" by Saki **14.4/65/1230**, pp. 77–87	Irony, SE pp. 78–86 Mood, SE p. 86
1–2 class sessions	1	TIME magazine, "Shattered" by Christopher Batin **7.1/56/900**, pp. 88–92	Mood, TWE p. 90
		"The Garden of Stubborn Cats" by Italo Calvino **7.0/67/1140**, pp. 93–104	Description, SE pp. 94–103 Irony, SE p. 103

About the Part

Part 1 takes a look at stories in which characters' lives are at stake.

READING AND CRITICAL THINKING	VOCABULARY	WRITING AND GRAMMAR	LISTENING, SPEAKING, AND VIEWING
Summarizing, SE pp. 13–21 Paraphrase, TWE p. 14	Multiple-Meaning Words, SE pp. 13, 21 Academic Vocabulary, SE p. 21	Respond to Plot, SE p. 21 Literary Criticism, SE p. 21 Sentence Structure, TWE p. 16	Analyzing Art, SE p. 17; TWE p. 18
Predictions about Plot, SE pp. 23–42 Compare and Contrast, TWE p. 30 Draw Conclusions, TWE p. 32 Scanning, TWE p. 40	Word Origins, SE p. 42 Academic Vocabulary, SE p. 42 Clarifying Meaning, TWE p. 31 Etymology, TWE p. 34	Evaluate Author's Craft, SE p. 43 Math Activity, SE p. 43 Using Dashes, SE p. 43 Word Choice, TWE p. 38	Analyzing Art, SE p. 39; TWE pp. 24, 28, 33, 36
Identifying Sequence, SE pp. 45–54 Cause and Effect, TWE p. 46	Word Parts, SE p. 54 Academic Vocabulary, SE p. 54 Idioms, TWE p. 49	Compare and Contrast Events, SE p. 54 Infinitive Phrases, TWE p. 50	News Report, SE p. 54 Analyzing Art, TWE pp. 46, 49, 51
Paraphrasing, SE pp. 56, 57, 58, 61, 62, 64 Making a Chart, SE p. 56 Character, TWE p. 62	Context Clues, SE pp. 56, 64 Understanding Archaic Vocabulary, TWE p. 64	Analyze Sensory Details, SE p. 65 Evaluating Sentence Structure, SE p. 65 Inverted Sentences, SE p. 65	Analyzing Art, TWE p. 60 Group Activity, SE p. 63
	Recognizing Homonyms and Homophones, SE p. 66		
Analyzing Concrete Details, SE pp. 68–76 Taking Notes, SE p. 68	Analogies, SE p. 76 Academic Vocabulary, SE p. 76	Analyze Cultural Context, SE p. 76 Write a Memo, SE p. 76	Analyzing Art, SE p. 72; TWE p. 70 Presentation, TWE p. 72
Analyzing Cause-and-Effect Relationships, SE pp. 78–86 Listing Cause and Effect, SE p. 78	Practice with Analogies, SE p. 86 Word Groups, TWE p. 84	Analyze Setting, SE p. 87 Varying Sentence Length, SE p. 87 Diction, TWE p. 80	Analyzing Art, SE p. 82; TWE pp. 79, 80 Group Activity, SE p. 85 Literature Groups, SE p. 87
Identifying Problem and Solution, SE p. 88 Cause and Effect, TWE p. 88	Compound Words, TWE p. 89		
Visualizing, SE pp. 94–104 Sketching, SE p. 94 Point of View, TWE p. 96	Synonyms, SE pp. 94, 104 Academic Vocabulary, SE p. 104	Analyze Conflict, SE p. 104 Hyphens, TWE p. 98 Descriptive Writing, TWE p. 100	Analyzing Art, SE p. 96; TWE pp. 95, 99, 101 Oral Presentation, SE p. 104

Focus

BELLRINGER

Bellringer Options
Daily Language Practice Transparency 2

Or display images of various settings—the jungle, a beach, a farm, a city street, and a crowded concert hall.
Ask: How important is a setting in a story? How does the setting affect what happens in a story? Have students consider, as they read Part 1, why setting is important.

Teach

L Literary Element

Conflict Explain that conflict is essential to a good story. It creates the problem that a character has to solve.
Say: Think of a story you heard as a child, such as "Cinderella."
Ask: What was the conflict in that story? *(Cinderella longs to go to the ball but her stepmother forbids it.)* OL

Literary Elements Have students access the Web site to improve their understanding of plot and setting.

LITERARY FOCUS

Plot and Setting

How do plot and setting contribute to a story's meaning?

The events of a story and the way they unfold create both the author's meaning and the reader's pleasure. In "The Storyteller," by Saki, a bachelor is traveling in a railway carriage that also holds an aunt and her young nieces and nephew.

from *The Storyteller*

by Saki

In a low, confidential voice, interrupted at frequent intervals by loud, petulant questionings from her listeners, she began an unenterprising and deplorably uninteresting story about a little girl who was good, and made friends with every one on account of her goodness, and was finally saved from a mad bull by a number of rescuers who admired her moral character.

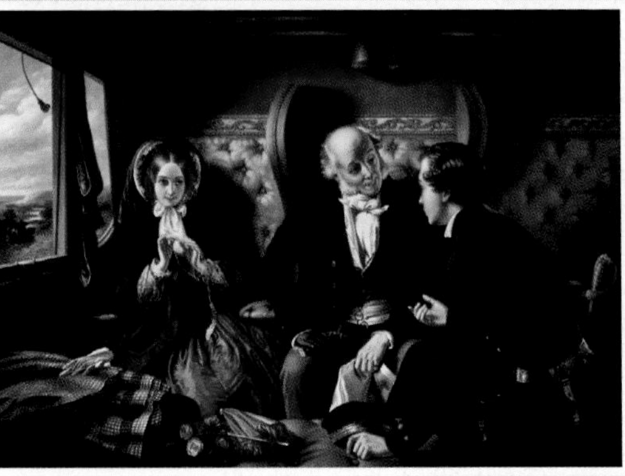

First Class–The Meeting. Abraham Soloman. Oil on Canvas, 54.5 x 76.3 cm. Southhampton City Art Gallery, Hampshire, UK.

Setting

Setting is a story's time and place. It includes simple attributes, like the location, the climate, and the time of year. Setting may also include more complex attributes, such as the historical context of the story and the ideas, customs, values, and beliefs of a particular time and place.

It was a hot afternoon, and the railway carriage was correspondingly sultry, and the next stop was at Templecombe, nearly an hour ahead.

Plot

Plot is the sequence of events in a story. A literary plot has five elements: **exposition, rising action, climax, falling action,** and **resolution.**

Climax
Exposition
Rising action
Falling action
Resolution

Conflict Most plots develop around a conflict, or struggle between two or more forces in a story. **External conflict** is the battle between a character and an outside force—nature, society, fate, or another character. **Internal conflict** is the battle within the mind of a character who is torn between different courses of action. L

"You don't seem to be a success as storyteller," said the bachelor suddenly from his corner.

The aunt bristled in instant defense.

Additional Support

Skills Practice

READING: Skimming Note that skimming means looking quickly through a text to find specific information. Remind students to use keywords, headings, and graphics as guides. Have them skim the story to answer these questions:

- What is setting? *(The time and place of a story)*
- What are the five parts of a plot? *(exposition, rising action, climax, falling action, resolution)* OL

Exposition During a plot's exposition, the author gives background information about the story and introduces the story's characters and setting. The exposition also introduces the main conflict.

The occupants of the carriage were a small girl, and a smaller girl, and a small boy. An aunt belonging to the children occupied one corner seat, and the further corner seat on the opposite side was occupied by a bachelor.

R **Rising Action** Rising action is the series of events that lead up to the climax, or most dramatic moment, of the story. The rising action in "The Storyteller" lies in the events of the bachelor's story about a little girl named Bertha who was "horribly good."

"She was so good," continued the bachelor, "that she won several medals for goodness which she always wore, pinned onto her dress. There was a medal for obedience, another medal for punctuality, and a third for good behavior. They were large metal medals and they clicked against one another as she walked."

Climax The climax is a story's most dramatic and revealing moment. It usually comes near the end of a story and satisfies the reader's curiosity about what happens.

The wolf was just moving away when he heard the sound of the medals clinking and stopped to listen; they clinked again in a bush quite near him. He dashed into the bush, his pale gray eyes gleaming with ferocity and triumph, and dragged Bertha out and devoured her to the last morsel.

Falling Action The falling action follows the climax and describes the results of the climax.

"The story began badly," said the smaller of the small girls, "but it had a beautiful ending."

"It is the most beautiful story that I ever heard," said the bigger of the small girls, with immense decision.

"It is the only beautiful story I have ever heard," said Cyril.

A dissenting opinion came from the aunt.

Resolution The resolution, or *denouement,* comes at the end of the falling action. Here, the author tells or suggests the outcome of the conflict.

"Unhappy woman!" he observed to himself as he walked down the platform of Templecombe station; "for the next six months or so those children will assail her in public with demands for an improper story!"

Quickwrite

A New Setting Think of your favorite fairy tale. Write a new version of the story in a different setting. Use one of these ideas or come up with one of your own.

1. "Little Red Riding Hood" in today's New York City
2. "Hansel and Gretel" in Hawaii
3. "Beauty and the Beast" on Mars in the distant future

LiteratureOnline Interactive Literary Elements Handbook Go to www.glencoe.com to review or learn more about plot and setting.

INDIANA ACADEMIC STANDARDS (pages 10–11)
9.3 [Identify] story elements such as…plot and setting…

Teach

R Reading Strategy

Draw Conclusions Ask: Why is it important for a story to have both a setting and a plot? *(Without a setting, readers will not be able to picture where and when events take place. Without a plot, the story will have no action.)* Challenge students to think of a story they have read or seen in movies or on television that lacked either setting or plot. Ask for their reactions. OL

Assess

Students' responses should identify which elements of a plot might be affected by the change in setting. For example, if "Little Red Riding Hood" were set in a large city, the main character might encounter a rat or a shifty criminal rather than a wolf.

English Language Coach

Analyzing Plot and Setting Make sure that English language learners comprehend the elements of setting and plot. Have them think of a story they have read or heard in their native language and then answer the following questions: *Where and when does the story take place? What happens in the story?* EL

Differentiated Instruction

Plot Diagram Advanced learners may enjoy applying the plot diagram to a favorite story. Have them create a diagram like the one on page 10 and then fill in the appropriate information. Ask volunteers to share their diagrams with the class. AL

Academic Standards

Additional Support activities on pp. 10 and 11 cover the following standards:

Skills Practice: **9.2.1** Analyze the structure and format of reference…documents, including the graphics and headers…

English Language Coach: **9.3** [Identify] story elements such as…plot, and setting…

Differentiated Instruction: **9.3** [Identify] story elements such as…plot…

Focus

BELLRINGER

Bellringer Options
Selection Focus Transparency 1
Daily Language Practice Transparency 3

Or ask students to share examples of difficult decisions they have made or have read about. **Ask:** What made the decision difficult? *(Students may mention lack of good options, too many good options, or another reason.)* What factors did you consider? *(Possible answers: likely advantages and disadvantages)* Have students consider as they read how the king, the princess, and the young man make their decisions.

Author Search To expand students' appreciation of Frank R. Stockton, have them access the Web site for additional information and resources.

BEFORE YOU READ

The Lady, or the Tiger?

MEET FRANK R. STOCKTON

At the height of his success, Frank R. Stockton was considered a major literary figure in the United States; writer William Dean Howells considered Stockton to be second in importance only to Mark Twain. Stockton's body of work fills twenty-three volumes and includes stories, novels, and nonfiction. Yet today, this writer is known primarily for his story, "The Lady, or the Tiger?"

Launching a Career Stockton enjoyed writing during his school days; however, his father hoped that he would become a doctor. Stockton chose another path entirely: wood engraving, a popular way to illustrate stories and articles at the time. Still, Stockton continued to write and began to publish his short stories.

As the wood engraving business gave way to other types of illustrations, Stockton focused his attention on writing and publishing. His early works were mainly written for children. In 1867, he published a short story called "Ting-a-Ling," which he later turned into a book. A fanciful tale about an elf-like character, "Ting-a-Ling" captured the attention of Mary Mapes Dodge, an author and editor of the time. After she was named editor of *St. Nicholas*, a new magazine for children, Dodge invited Stockton to join her staff.

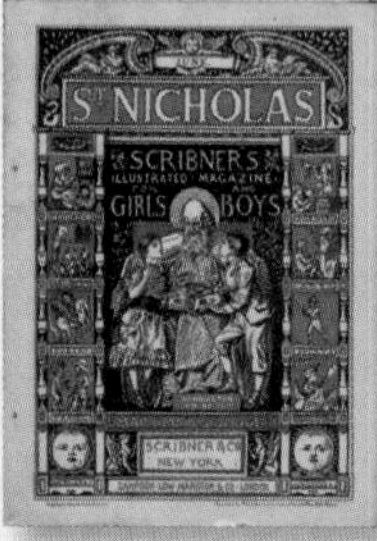

St. Nicholas was a new type of children's magazine. Earlier children's publications were blandly moralistic, but *St. Nicholas* was realistic and literary. Within a few years, it became one of the most successful children's magazines of its time.

The Story That Created a Stir In 1878, Stockton left the magazine because of his failing eyesight, but he continued to write. Within a few years, he published several more books. Still, Stockton's novels never earned attention equal to that which he gained in 1882, when he published a short story in *Century Magazine*. That story was "The Lady, or the Tiger?"

The story not only created a stir at the time but for years afterward. It was later turned into an operetta, a play, a movie, and a recording. The story's unusual ending created a flurry of letters to the author that continued throughout his life. A well-known poet, Robert Browning, wrote a poem about the ending and scholars debated the issue, but Stockton kept quiet.

Stockton continued to publish humorous and fanciful novels, but few are still read today. The year after his death, a twenty-three-volume collection of his fiction was published. However, after a lifetime of writing, Stockton's name is most closely linked with one brief story, which continues to delight and puzzle readers more than a century after it was written.

Frank R. Stockton was born in 1834 and died in 1902.

LiteratureOnline **Author Search** For more about Frank R. Stockton, go to www.glencoe.com.

Selection Skills

The Lady, or the Tiger?

Literary Elements
- Conflict (SE pp. 13–15, 20; TWE p. 18)
- Plot (SE p. 20; TWE p. 20)

Reading Skills
- Summarizing (SE pp. 13, 16, 18, 21)
- Paraphrase (TWE p. 14)

Vocabulary Skills
- Multiple-Meaning Words (SE pp. 13, 21)
- Academic Vocabulary (SE p. 21)
- Idioms (TWE p. 17)

Listening/Speaking/Viewing Skills
- Review: Plot (SE p. 20)
- Analyzing Art (SE p. 17; TWE p. 18)

Writing Skills/Grammar
- Writing About Literature (SE p. 21)
- Literary Criticism (SE p. 21)
- Sentence Length (TWE p. 15)
- Sentence Structure (TWE p. 16)

LITERATURE PREVIEW

Connecting to the Story

Would you trust your life to a friend? Before you read the story, think about the following questions:

- Which is a stronger emotion—love or jealousy?
- How completely can one person ever know and understand another?

Building Background

During the Middle Ages in England, guilt or innocence was decided through a practice known as an ordeal. An accused person was physically tested, and the outcome determined guilt or innocence. The accusers believed that supernatural forces controlled what happened. For instance, in the ordeal by water, the accused person was tied up and thrown into deep water. A person who floated was thought to be guilty; a person who sank was considered innocent. Unfortunately, those who sank often drowned before they could be hauled back up.

Setting Purposes for Reading

Big Idea Matters of Life and Death

As you read this story, notice how the characters value life and death in different ways.

Literary Element Conflict

Every story revolves around a **conflict,** or struggle between opposing forces. A conflict can be external or internal. An external conflict is one between a character and an outside force, such as another character, nature, society, or fate. An internal conflict takes place within the mind of a character who is torn between different courses of action.

- See Literary Terms Handbook, p. R4.

LiteratureOnline Interactive Literary Elements Handbook To review or learn more about the literary elements, go to www.glencoe.com.

READING PREVIEW

Reading Strategy Summarizing

Summarizing is stating only the main ideas of a selection in a logical sequence and in your own words. When you summarize a story, include the main characters, the setting, the conflict, important plot details, and the resolution.

Reading Tip: Tracking Main Ideas Use a chart to record the important details that you want to include in a summary.

Setting	Characters	Conflict	Resolution
A long time ago; in a kingdom			

Vocabulary

impartial (im pär′ shəl) *adj.* not favoring one side more than another; fair; p. 15 *An honest judge is impartial.*

emanate (em′ ə nāt′) *v.* to come forth; p. 15 *We never heard any sound emanate from that room.*

dire (dīr) *adj.* dreadful; terrible; p. 15 *Breaking certain rules can have dire consequences.*

fervent (fur′ vənt) *adj.* having or showing great intensity of feeling; passionate; p. 16 *The coach was a fervent believer in practicing every day in order to improve.*

novel (nov′ əl) *adj.* new and unusual; p. 16 *Since that older method seldom works, try a more novel approach.*

Vocabulary Tip: Multiple-Meaning Words Many words have more than one meaning. Use context to help determine a word's correct meaning.

INDIANA ACADEMIC STANDARDS (pages 13–21)

9.3.3 Analyze interactions between characters in a literary text and explain the way those interactions affect the plot.

9.2 Develop [reading] strategies...

9.5.3 Write expository compositions...

BEFORE YOU READ

Focus

Summary

The king's daughter is in love, but her father does not like her young man and sentences him to the arena. There, he must choose between two doors. Behind one is a man-eating tiger. Behind the other is a lady whom he will marry. The princess is jealous of the maiden behind the door, and she finds out which door conceals her. When the young man enters the arena, the princess gives him a signal. He opens the door she indicates. The reader is left to decide. Does the lady or the tiger emerge?

V Vocabulary

Vocabulary File Say: Add these words and definitions to your vocabulary file. For each word, include a sentence that gives you an example of how to use the word. **OL** Students with English language needs should include the pronunciations of these words in their files. **EL**

Literary Elements Have students access the Web site to improve their understanding of conflict.

Selection Resources

Print Materials
- Unit 1 Resources (Fast File), pp. 17–19
- Leveled Vocabulary Development, p. 1
- Selection and Unit Assessments, pp. 1–2
- Selection Quick Checks, p. 1

Transparencies
- Bellringer Options Transparencies: Selection Focus Transparency 1, Daily Language Practice Transparency 3
- Literary Elements Transparency 3

Technology
- TeacherWorks Plus™ CD-ROM
- StudentWorks Plus™ CD-ROM
- Presentation Plus!™ CD-ROM
- Literature Online, glencoe.com
- Online Student Edition, mhln.com
- Exam*View*® Assessment Suite CD-ROM
- Vocabulary PuzzleMaker CD-ROM
- Listening Library, disc 1 track 1

Teach

BI1 Big Idea

Matters of Life and Death
Say: Keep these questions in mind as you read: Why does a life-or-death trial appeal to the king? *(The king enjoys putting people at the mercy of a heartless and whimsical fate and uses this cruel spectacle to teach his subjects a lesson.)* Why do the king's subjects enjoy the life-or-death trial? *(The uncertainty is exciting.)* OL

L1 Literary Element

Conflict **Answer:** *The king is a tyrant who expects the whole world to bend to his will.* OL

★ Writer's Technique

Title Punctuation The question mark in the title "The Lady, or the Tiger?" is a clue to the decision around which the story will center. Punctuation often offers important clues to meaning. AS

Readability Scores
Dale-Chall: 10.1
DRP: 68
Lexile: 1260

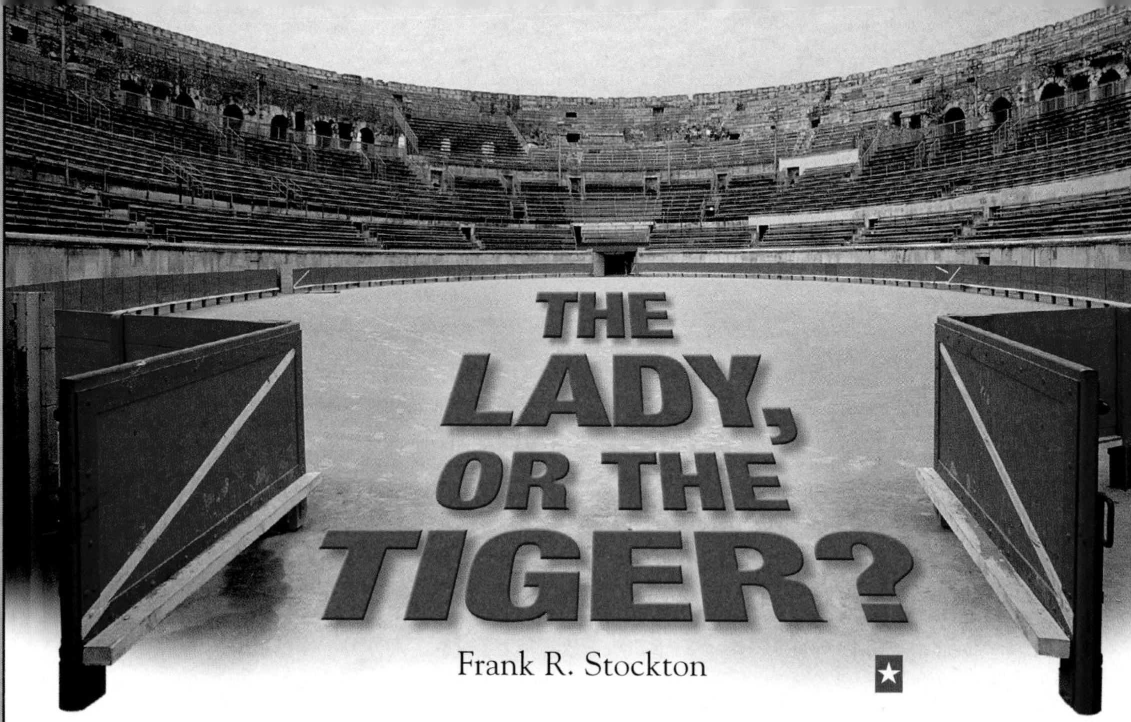

THE LADY, OR THE TIGER?

Frank R. Stockton ★

BI1 In the very olden time, there lived a semibarbaric king, whose ideas, though somewhat polished and sharpened by the progressiveness of distant Latin neighbors, were still large, florid, and untrammeled,[1] as became the half of him which was barbaric. He was a man of exuberant fancy, and, withal, of an authority so irresistible that, at his will, he turned his varied fancies into facts. He was greatly given to self-communing; and, when he and himself agreed upon any thing, the thing was done. When every member of his domestic and political systems moved smoothly in its appointed course, his nature was bland and genial;[2] but whenever there was a little hitch, and some of his orbs got out of their orbits, he was blander and more genial still, for nothing pleased him so much as to make the crooked straight, and crush down uneven places.

Among the borrowed notions by which his barbarism had become semified[3] was that of the public arena, in which, by exhibitions of manly and beastly valor, the minds of his subjects were refined and cultured.

But even here the exuberant and barbaric fancy asserted itself.[4] The arena of the king was built, not to give the people an opportunity of hearing the rhapsodies[5] of dying gladiators, nor to enable them to view the inevitable conclusion of a conflict between religious opinions and hungry jaws, but for purposes far better adapted to widen and

1. The king's ideas are somewhat uncivilized (*semibarbaric*); they are very showy (*florid*) and unrestrained (*untrammeled*).
2. The king himself is generally agreeable and mild (*bland*) and pleasantly cheerful (*genial*).
3. *Semified* is a made-up word meaning "reduced in half or made partial."
4. Here, *asserted itself* means "exercised its influence; insisted on being recognized."
5. *Rhapsodies* are enthusiastic expressions of emotion.

Literary Element Conflict *How does this passage suggest a future conflict?* L1

Additional Support

Skills Practice

READING: Paraphrase Remind students that paraphrasing is restating text in their own words. It can help them not only summarize but also more fully understand the text, especially in stories with elaborate language, such as this one. Have students work in small groups to paraphrase passages from the story. Have them begin by defining unfamiliar words and then replacing them with synonyms. OL develop the mental energies of the people. This vast amphitheater, with its encircling galleries, its mysterious vaults, and its unseen passages, was an agent of poetic justice, in which crime was punished, or virtue rewarded, by the decrees of an **impartial** and incorruptible chance.

When a subject was accused of a crime of sufficient importance to interest the king, public notice was given that on an appointed day the fate of the accused person would be decided in the king's arena,—a structure which well deserved its name; for, although its form and plan were borrowed from afar, its purpose **emanated** solely from the brain of this man, who, every barleycorn[6] a king, knew no tradition to which he owed more allegiance than pleased his fancy, and who ingrafted on every adopted form of human thought and action the rich growth of his barbaric idealism.

When all the people had assembled in the galleries, and the king, surrounded by his court, sat high up on his throne of royal state on one side of the arena, he gave a signal, a door beneath him opened, and the accused subject stepped out into the amphitheater.[7] Directly opposite him, on the other side of the enclosed space, were two doors, exactly alike and side by side. It was the duty and the privilege of the person on trial, to walk directly to these doors and open one of them. He could open either door he pleased: he was subject to no guidance or influence but that of the aforementioned impartial and incorruptible chance. If he opened the one, there came out of it a hungry tiger, the fiercest and most cruel that could be procured, which immediately sprang upon him, and tore him to pieces, as a punishment for his guilt. The moment that the case of the criminal was thus decided, doleful iron bells were clanged, great wails went up from the hired mourners posted on the outer rim of the arena, and the vast audience, with bowed heads and downcast hearts, wended slowly their homeward way, mourning greatly that one so young and fair, or so old and respected, should have merited so **dire** a fate.

But, if the accused person opened the other door, there came forth from it a lady, the most suitable to his years and station that his majesty could select among his fair subjects; and to this lady he was immediately married, as a reward of his innocence. It mattered not that he might already possess a wife and family, or that his affections might be engaged upon an object of his own selection: the king allowed no such subordinate arrangements to interfere with his great scheme of retribution and reward.[8] The exercises, as in the other instance, took place immediately, and in the arena. Another door opened beneath the king, and a priest, followed by a band of choristers, and dancing maidens blowing joyous airs on golden horns and treading an epithalamic measure, advanced to where the pair stood, side by side; and the wedding was promptly and cheerily solemnized.[9] Then the gay brass bells rang forth their merry peals, the people shouted glad hurrahs, and the innocent

6. The *barleycorn* is an old unit of measure equal to the width of one grain of barley—about a third of an inch. This phrase is similar to "every inch a king" and means that he was kingly in every way and in every part, top to bottom.

7. An *amphitheater* is a circular structure with rising tiers of seats around a central open space.

8. The king's plan for giving out punishment (*retribution*) and reward was of primary importance, and everything else was less important (*subordinate*), including family values.

9. *Epithalamic* (ep′ ə thə lā′ mik) refers to a song in honor of a bride and groom. When a wedding is *solemnized,* it is celebrated with a formal ceremony.

Literary Element Conflict *Based on this passage, what do you think the main conflict will be?* **L2**

Vocabulary

impartial (im pär′ shəl) *adj.* not favoring one side more than another; fair

emanate (em′ ə nāt′) *v.* to come forth

Big Idea Matters of Life and Death *What do these details suggest about the people's view of death and mourning?* **BI2**

Vocabulary

dire (dīr) *adj.* dreadful; terrible

Teach

L2 Literary Element

Conflict **Answer:** *A person on trial will have to choose between the two doors.* **OL**

BI2 Big Idea

Matters of Life and Death
Answer: *They put on a great show of emotion they did not really feel ("hired mourners").* **OL**

Cultural History

Roman Times The author may be alluding to the Romans, the "distant Latin neighbors" named on page 14. During the early years of Christianity, the Romans had a practice of putting Christians in the arena with lions, where they were mauled to death for their beliefs. **AS**

CheckPoint

Use the CheckPoint questions on Presentation Plus! to monitor students' comprehension. These questions can be used with interactive response keypads for immediate student feedback.

English Language Coach

Sentence Length English language learners may have difficulty with the story's long sentences. Read a particularly long or difficult sentence aloud, and then show students how to divide it into two or three shorter ones to aid comprehension. For example, "If he opened the one, there came out of it a hungry tiger. . . ." Have students choose another long sentence and rewrite it as two or more sentences, changing word order or adding words as necessary to clarify meaning. **EL**

Academic Standards

Additional Support activities on pp. 14 and 15 cover the following standards:

Skills Practice: **9.1** Use…context clues…to determine the meaning of words…

English Language Coach: **9.6.2** Demonstrate an understanding of sentence construction…

Teach

R Reading Strategy

Summarizing Answer: *A person accused of a crime comes into an arena with two doors. Behind one is a tiger and behind the other is a woman. The accused will either be devoured or married, depending on the door he chooses.* OL

BI Big Idea

Matters of Life and Death
Answer: *The young man's future will be decided; in one instant, he will "choose" life or death.* OL

★ Literary History

Fables/Fairy Tales The author uses phrases such as "as is usual in such cases" and "common to the conventional heroes of romance." These phrases reflect the style of fables and fairy tales, which have conventions such as the beautiful young maiden and the handsome young hero.
Ask: What other fairy tale conventions can you name? *(Possible answers: "Once upon a time" at the beginning; "They lived happily ever after" at the end.)* AS

man, preceded by children strewing flowers on his path, led his bride to his home.

This was the king's semibarbaric method of administering justice. Its perfect fairness is obvious. The criminal could not know out of which door would come the lady: he opened either he pleased, without having the slightest idea whether, in the next instant, he was to be devoured or married. On some occasions the tiger came out of one door, and on some out of the other. The decisions of this tribunal were not only fair, they were positively determinate:[10] the accused person was instantly punished if he found himself guilty; and, if innocent, he was rewarded on the spot, whether he liked it or not. There was no escape from the judgments of the king's arena.

The institution was a very popular one. When the people gathered together on one of the great trial days, they never knew whether they were to witness a bloody slaughter or a hilarious wedding. This element of uncertainty lent an interest to the occasion which it could not otherwise have attained. Thus, the masses were entertained and pleased, and the thinking part of the community could bring no charge of unfairness against this plan; for did not the accused person have the whole matter in his own hands?

This semibarbaric king had a daughter as blooming as his most florid fancies, and with a soul as **fervent** and imperious[11] as his own. ★ As is usual in such cases, she was the apple of his eye, and was loved by him above all humanity. Among his courtiers was a young man of that fineness of blood and lowness of station common to the conventional heroes of romance who love royal maidens. This royal maiden was well satisfied with her lover, for he was handsome and brave to a degree unsurpassed in all this kingdom; and she loved him with an ardor[12] that had enough of barbarism in it to make it exceedingly warm and strong. This love affair moved on happily for many months, until one day the king happened to discover its existence. He did not hesitate nor waver in regard to his duty in the premises. The youth was immediately cast into prison, and a day was appointed for his trial in the king's arena. This, of course, was an especially important occasion; and his majesty, as well as all the people, was greatly interested in the workings and development of this trial. Never before had such a case occurred; never before had a subject dared to love the daughter of a king. In after-years such things became commonplace enough; but then they were, in no slight degree, **novel** and startling.

The tiger-cages of the kingdom were searched for the most savage and relentless beasts, from which the fiercest monster might be selected for the arena; and the ranks of maiden youth and beauty throughout the land were carefully surveyed by competent judges, in order that the young man might have a fitting bride in case fate did not determine for him a different destiny. Of course, everybody knew that the deed with which the accused was charged had been done. He had loved the princess, and neither he, she, nor any one else thought of denying the fact; but the king would not think of allowing any fact of this kind to interfere with the workings of the tribunal, in which he took such great delight and satisfaction. No matter how the affair turned out, the youth would be disposed of; and the king would take an aesthetic pleasure in

10. Usually, *tribunal* refers to a group of judges or a place of judgment. Here, it is "the king's semibarbaric method of administering justice," and its outcome is absolutely final (*determinate*).
11. To be *imperious* is to be extremely proud and controlling.

Reading Strategy Summarizing *Summarize the king's "semibarbaric method of administering justice."* R

Vocabulary

fervent (fur′ vənt) *adj.* having or showing great intensity of feeling; passionate

12. *Ardor* means intense passion.

Big Idea Matters of Life and Death *How does this passage reflect matters of life and death?* BI

Vocabulary

novel (nov′ əl) *adj.* new and unusual

Additional Support

Skills Practice

WRITING: Sentence Structure On the board, write the sentence "Never before had such a case occurred; never before had a subject dared to love the daughter of a king." Explain the use of a semicolon to join independent clauses. BL

Have students find other examples in the story. Post these on the board and discuss them together. Then ask students to write their own sentences that contain two independent clauses joined by a semicolon. OL

Mona Vanna, 1866. Dante Gabriel Rossetti. Oil on canvas, 88.9 × 86.4 cm. Tate Gallery, London.
Viewing the Art: How would you describe this woman's personality? ★

princess loved him! What a terrible thing for him to be there!

As the youth advanced into the arena, he turned, as the custom was, to bow to the king: but he did not think at all of that royal personage; his eyes were fixed upon the princess, who sat to the right of her father. Had it not been for the moiety[13] of barbarism in her nature, it is probable that lady would not have been there; but her intense and fervid soul would not allow her to be absent on an occasion in which she was so terribly interested. From the moment that the decree had gone forth, that her lover should decide his fate in the king's arena, she had thought of nothing, night or day, but this great event and the various subjects connected with it. Possessed of more power, influence, and force of character than any one who had ever before been interested in such a case, she had done what no other person had done—she had possessed herself of the secret of the doors. She knew in which of the two rooms, that lay behind those doors, stood the cage of the tiger, with its open front, and in which waited the lady. Through these thick doors, heavily curtained with skins on the inside, it was impossible that any noise or suggestion should come from within to the person who should approach to raise the latch of one of them; but gold, and the power of a woman's will, had brought the secret to the princess. L2

watching the course of events, which would determine whether or not the young man had done wrong in allowing himself to love the princess.

The appointed day arrived. From far and near the people gathered, and thronged the great galleries of the arena; and crowds, unable to gain admittance, massed themselves against its outside walls. The king and his court were in their places, opposite the twin doors,—those fateful portals, so terrible in their similarity.

All was ready. The signal was given. A door beneath the royal party opened, and the lover of the princess walked into the arena. Tall, beautiful, fair, his appearance was greeted with a low hum of admiration and anxiety. Half the audience had not known so grand a youth had lived among them. No wonder the

13. A *moiety* (moi′ ə tē) means "a half."

Literary Element Conflict *How does this passage advance the central conflict of the story?* L1

Teach

L1 Literary Element

Conflict Answer: *The princess knows which door the tiger is behind, so she could use that information to save the young man.* OL

L2 Literary Element

Characterization Review princess characters from fairy tales students know.
Ask: How is the princess in this story typical of a conventional fairy tale princess? How does she differ? *(Like the conventional princess, she is beautiful. Unlike them, she is selfish and calculating.)* OL

★ Viewing the Art

Answer: *She appears to be haughty, rather cold and cunning, and someone who loves luxury.* OL

Dante Gabriel Rossetti (1828–1882) was a poet and an artist, who had little formal training in painting. Rossetti's paintings are better known for their brilliant colors than for their technical expertise. AS

English Language Coach

Idioms Model how to use context clues to define "fineness of blood" and "lowness of station," used to describe the young man. Explain that *blood* refers to inherited traits, while *station* refers to a family's social class. The first phrase is positive; the second is negative. EL

Reading in the Real World

Career Discuss contemporary jobs that are comparable to roles featured in the story, such as judge (the king) or athlete/performer (the young man). Have students read about such jobs in want ads or news articles. Ask students to write a brief job description for each job. OL

Academic Standards

Additional Support activities on pp. 16 and 17 cover the following standards:

Skills Practice: **9.6.1** Identify and correctly use clauses...and...semicolons...

English Language Coach: **9.1.1** Identify and use the...figurative meanings of words...

Reading in the Real World: **9.4.6** Synthesize information from multiple sources...

Teach

R Reading Strategy

Summarizing **Answer:** *The youth knows the princess very well; he foresaw that she would seek knowledge of what lay behind the door.* OL

L1 Literary Element

Conflict Discuss the highlighted passage.
Ask: What is the princess's inner conflict? *(She loves the young man but is torn by her selfish nature and hatred for her rival. The dilemma: death for her beloved or his loss to her rival.)* OL

★ Viewing the Art

Rosa Bonheur (1822–1899), a French painter and sculptor, was both trained and encouraged by her father. She first exhibited her work in 1841, when she was not yet twenty. Much of her work reflects her love of animals and her skill at observing nature. AS

Stalking Tiger, Rosa Bonheur (1822–99). Private collection, © Gavin Graham Gallery, London, UK. 

And not only did she know in which room stood the lady ready to emerge, all blushing and radiant, should her door be opened, but she knew who the lady was. It was one of the fairest and loveliest of the damsels of the court who had been selected as the reward of the accused youth, should he be proved innocent of the crime of aspiring to one so far above him; and the princess hated her. Often had she seen, or imagined that she had seen, this fair creature throwing glances of admiration upon the person of her lover, and sometimes she thought these glances were perceived and even returned. Now and then she had seen them talking together; it was but for a moment or two, but much can be said in a brief space; it may have been on most unimportant topics, but how could she know that? The girl was lovely, but she had dared to raise her eyes to the loved one of the princess; and, with all the intensity of the savage blood transmitted to her through long lines of wholly barbaric ancestors, she hated the woman who blushed and trembled behind that silent door.

When her lover turned and looked at her, and his eye met hers as she sat there paler and whiter than any one in the vast ocean of anxious faces about her, he saw, by that power of quick perception which is given to those whose souls are one, that she knew behind which door crouched the tiger, and behind which stood the lady. He had expected her to know it. He understood her nature, and his soul was assured that she would never rest until she had made plain to herself this thing, hidden to all other lookers-on, even to the king. L1 The only hope for the youth in which there was any element of certainty was based upon the success of the princess in discovering this

Reading Strategy Summarizing *Based on this passage, how would you summarize the relationship between the lovers?* R

Additional Support

Skills Practice

RESEARCH: Interviews Interviews are a useful way to gather information about any topic, including public displays of high drama. Have students prepare and dramatize interviews with the story characters. Suggest these strategies:

- Collect information about the interviewee and the topic.
- Write questions that ask for more than yes or no answers.
- Maintain eye contact, and listen.
- Ask clarifying questions as needed. Take notes or use a tape recorder.
- Check facts, including name spellings. OL

mystery; and the moment he looked upon her, he saw she had succeeded, as in his soul he knew she would succeed.

Then it was that his quick and anxious glance asked the question: "Which?" It was as plain to her as if he shouted it from where he stood. There was not an instant to be lost. The question was asked in a flash; it must be answered in another.

Her right arm lay on the cushioned parapet[14] before her. She raised her hand, and L2 made a slight, quick movement toward the right. No one but her lover saw her. Every eye but his was fixed on the man in the arena.

He turned, and with a firm and rapid step he walked across the empty space. Every heart stopped beating, every breath was held, every eye was fixed immovably upon that man. Without the slightest hesitation, he went to the door on the right, and opened it.

Now, the point of the story is this: Did the tiger come out of that door, or did the lady?

The more we reflect upon this question, the harder it is to answer. It involves a study of the human heart which leads us through devious mazes of passion, out of which it is difficult to find our way. Think of it, fair reader, not as if the decision of the question ★ depended upon yourself, but upon that hot-blooded, semibarbaric princess, her soul at a white heat beneath the combined fires of despair and jealousy. She had lost him, but who should have him?

How often, in her waking hours and in her dreams, had she started in wild horror, and covered her face with her hands as she thought of her lover opening the door on the other side of which waited the cruel fangs of the tiger!

But how much oftener had she seen him at the other door! How in her grievous reveries[15] had she gnashed her teeth, and torn her hair, when she saw his start of rapturous delight as he opened the door of the lady! How her soul had burned in agony when she had seen him rush to meet that woman, with her flushing cheek and sparkling eye of triumph; when she had seen him lead her forth, his whole frame kindled with the joy of recovered life; when she had heard the glad shouts from the multitude, and the wild ringing of the happy bells; when she had seen the priest, with his joyous followers, advance to the couple, and make them man and wife before her very eyes; and when she had seen them walk away together upon their path of flowers, followed by the tremendous shouts of the hilarious multitude, in which her one despairing shriek was lost and drowned!

Would it not be better for him to die at once, and go to wait for her in the blessed regions of semibarbaric futurity?

And yet, that awful tiger, those shrieks, that blood.

Her decision had been indicated in an instant, but it had been made after days and nights of anguished deliberation. She had known she would be asked, she had decided what she would answer, and, without the slightest hesitation, she had moved her hand to the right.

The question of her decision is one not to be lightly considered, and it is not for me to presume[16] to set myself up as the one person able to answer it. And so I leave it with all of you: Which came out of the opened door—the lady, or the tiger?

14. Here, the *parapet* is a low wall or railing around the royal "box seats."

15. Something that is *grievous* causes great grief or worry; *reveries* are daydreams.

16. *Presume* means "to take upon oneself without permission" or "to dare."

Big Idea Matters of Life and Death *How does this passage suggest that the trial feels like a matter of life and death for the princess?* BI

Teach

BI Big Idea

Matters of Life and Death
Answer: *Her shriek of protest upon imagining her lover married to another woman is "drowned" by the joyous shouts of the crowd, suggesting that seeing her lover with another woman would feel like dying.* OL

L2 Literary Element

Plot In most stories, the climax occurs at the point of greatest emotional intensity.
Ask: At what point in this story does the climax occur? *(The climax occurs when the princess gestures toward the right, and the young man opens the door.)* OL

★ Writer's Technique

Imagery Stockton uses imagery related to fire throughout the final passage of his story. Words such as "hot-blooded," "white heat," "fires of despair," "burned in agony," and "kindled" work together to create the emotional intensity the author seeks.
Ask: What does fire imagery suggest about emotions? *(The emotions are fierce and consuming.)* AS

English Language Coach

Style Point out the word "oftener." Clarify that this word is not correct grammatically. **Ask:** What would the correct language be? *(more often)* Explain that the author has made a style choice to use it, and point out that it fits with the archaic-sounding fairy tale language elsewhere in the story. EL

Differentiated Instruction

Body Language The lovers in the story communicate nonverbally at a crucial moment. Have students demonstrate gestures and facial expressions that communicate a specific meaning in certain situations, such as at an athletic event, in the classroom, or in a restaurant. BL

Academic Standards

Additional Support activities on pp. 18 and 19 cover the following standards:

Skills Practice: **9.7.16** Apply appropriate interviewing techniques: prepare and ask relevant questions; make notes of responses...

English Language Coach: **9.3.11** Evaluate the aesthetic qualities of style, including the impact of diction...

Differentiated Instruction: **9.7.6** Analyze the occasion and...choose effective... nonverbal techniques...

AFTER YOU READ

Assess

1. Students may like the author's ambiguous ending or prefer more resolution. Some may say a definite ending would be less intriguing; others might find this more satisfying.
2. (a) The accused person must choose between two doors concealing either a tiger that will kill him or a woman who will marry him. Chance governs his choice. (b) They find the trials exciting and entertaining, as well as fair, since the accused made the choice.
3. (a) Loving the king's daughter (b) His low position in society made him an unworthy suitor.
4. (a) Gesture toward the right (b) Jealousy; true, unselfish love
5. It becomes first person and uses *we* to include readers in the story.
6. Possible answer: To invite readers to ponder the conflict between love and jealousy
7. Students should support their opinions with reasons.
8. In both cases, chance alone determines the outcome.
9. Possible answers: when the princess makes her decision; only after the door opens. Students should give reasons.

Literary Element

1. External: which door to open; Internal: whether to believe the princess
2. Her decision governs if the young man lives or dies. Readers' view of her will affect their choice of resolution.

AFTER YOU READ

RESPONDING AND THINKING CRITICALLY

Respond

1. What was your reaction to the ending of the story? How would your reaction be different if you knew what was behind the door on the right?

Recall and Interpret

2. (a)In the kingdom described in the story, what happens when a person is accused of a crime? (b)Why do the members of the community support this method?
3. (a)What is the young man's crime? (b)Why are his actions considered criminal?
4. (a)What does the princess do when the young man is in the arena? (b)What motive does she have for sending him to his death, and what motive does she have for saving his life?

Analyze and Evaluate

5. The story is told from the third-person point of view at the beginning. How does the point of view change, and what is the effect of this change?
6. Why do you think the story ends with a question instead of an answer?
7. Most stories end by telling the readers what happened to the main characters. This story lets the readers decide what happens. What is your opinion of this type of ending? Explain.

Connect

8. In what ways is the king's justice similar to flipping a coin to decide an important question?
9. **Big Idea** **Matters of Life and Death** At what point is the young man's fate actually decided? Explain.

LITERARY ANALYSIS

Literary Element Conflict

Conflict is the engine that drives most stories—it sets the action in motion. Many stories, like this one, contain more than one type of conflict. Characters may struggle against other characters and outside forces, but they may also struggle with themselves. A character may find himself or herself torn between two choices, for example, even as he or she battles some enemy. When a character struggles against an outside force, it is called an external conflict. On the other hand, when a character battles with himself or herself, it is called an internal conflict. Think about the conflicts in this story and then answer the following questions.

1. What conflicts does the young man have? Are his conflicts internal or external? Support your answers with details from the story.
2. Why is the princess's internal conflict so central to the story?

Review: Plot

As you learned on pages 10–11, **plot** is the sequence of events in a story. It begins with the exposition, or the introduction of the characters, setting, and situation.

Partner Activity Meet with another classmate and discuss which plot details in the exposition of "The Lady, or the Tiger?" are most important to understanding the story. Use those details to fill in the story map parts.

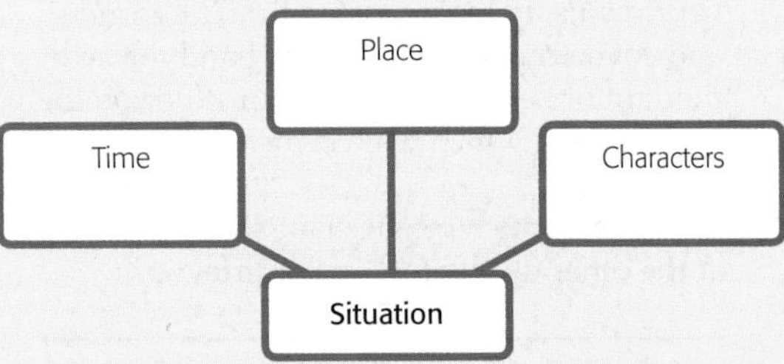

Review: Plot

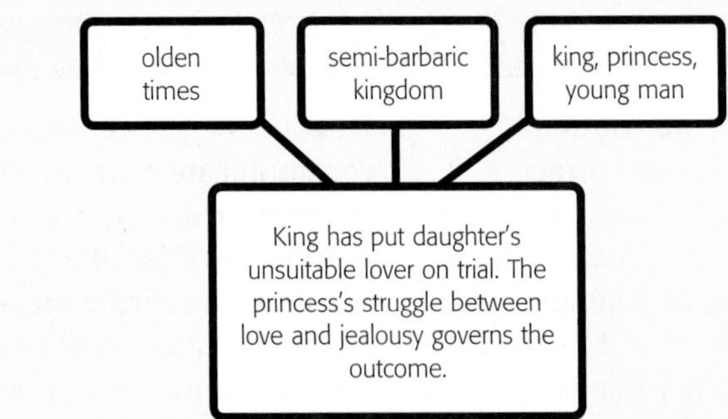

Reading Strategy Summarizing

A **summary** is a brief statement of the main ideas of a paragraph or longer piece of writing. You will remember main ideas better after you have restated them in your own words in a summary.

1. Summarize the paragraph on page 16 that begins "The institution was a very popular one."
2. In small groups, read your summaries aloud to each other to ensure that you have included all the main ideas.

Vocabulary Practice

Practice with Multiple-Meaning Words Many English words have more than one meaning.

For each of the multiple-meaning words below, two of the answers are correct definitions or synonyms. Determine which answer is **incorrect.**

1. dire
   - **a.** extreme
   - **b.** pragmatic
   - **c.** warning of something bad
2. fervent
   - **a.** very hot
   - **b.** passionate
   - **c.** brutal
3. novel
   - **a.** new and unusual
   - **b.** irrelevant
   - **c.** a long work of fiction

Academic Vocabulary

Here are two words from the vocabulary list on page R80. These words will help you think, write, and talk about the selection.

approach (ə prōch′) *n.* a manner of dealing with a subject

intervene (in′ tər vēn′) *v.* to interrupt or come into a situation in order to affect or change it

Practice and Apply

1. What is unusual about the king's **approach** to justice?
2. Why does the young man expect the princess to **intervene** in the king's arena?

Writing About Literature

Respond to Plot Readers never learn what decision the princess makes in "The Lady, or the Tiger?" although her decision would surely have a major impact. The author plants several clues in the story to support either decision. Which decision do you think the princess makes? Write a brief essay that states your opinion and supports it with evidence from the story.

Before you draft your essay, review every detail about the princess. As you draft, remember that people have been wrestling with this question for years. Try to be as convincing as possible in your arguments. Structure your essay with an introduction, body, and conclusion as shown.

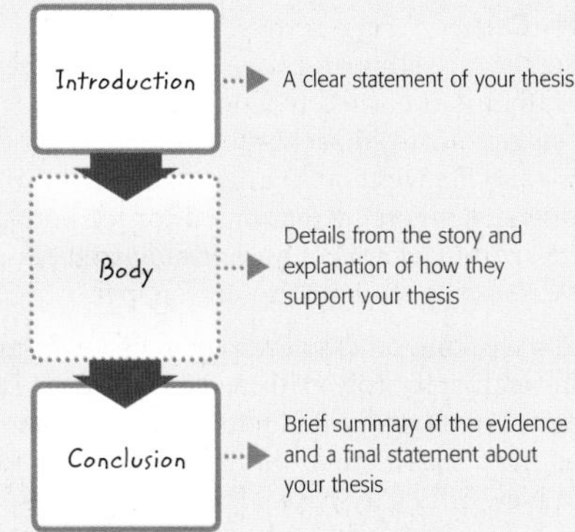

When your draft is complete, meet with a peer reviewer to evaluate each other's work and suggest revisions. Then proofread and edit your draft for errors in spelling, grammar, and punctuation.

Literary Criticism

Most stories end with a resolution—readers know how everything turns out in the end. "The Lady, or the Tiger?" has a trick ending—readers must supply the resolution. What does such an ending add to this story, and how much does it have to do with the story's enduring popularity? Answer these questions in a paragraph or two.

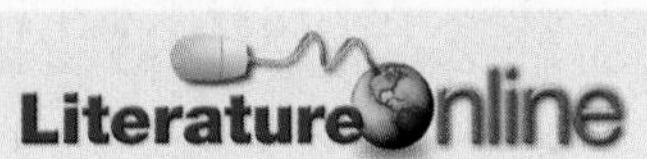
Web Activities For eFlashcards, Selection Quick Checks, and other Web activities, go to www.glencoe.com.

Assess

Reading Strategy

1. Summaries should contain the following: People loved the institution because its outcome was dramatic. No one could complain about fairness, because the accused determined the outcome.
2. In their discussions, students should distinguish main ideas and supporting details.

Vocabulary

1. b **2.** c **3.** b

Academic Vocabulary

1. The approach depended on chance; the accused made a choice, so it seemed fair.
2. He knows her nature and that she will learn the door secret.

Writing About Literature

Students' essays should

- tell which decision they think that the princess made
- include details from the story to support their opinions
- include an introduction with a clearly stated thesis

Literary Criticism

Students' responses should

- explain that the trick ending forces readers to consider the motivation of the princess
- indicate whether the ending or some other element is responsible for the story's popularity

CheckPoint

Use the CheckPoint questions on Presentation Plus! to check students' mastery of the selection. These questions can be used with interactive response keypads for immediate student feedback.

LiteratureOnline

Web Activities Have students access the Web site for interactive activities that will help them assess their understanding of the selection.

Focus

BELLRINGER

Bellringer Options
Selection Focus Transparency 2
Daily Language Practice Transparency 4

Or obtain a copy of the painting *The Hungry Lion* by Henri Rousseau. Have students study it and then discuss these questions. **Ask:** What hidden dangers do you see in the painting? *(There is a panther in the trees and other animals partially visible.)* How do dangers that you cannot see differ from those you can see? *(They add a component of the unknown, which heightens tension.)* Have students consider as they read what qualities help people cope with danger.

Author Search To expand students' appreciation of Richard Connell, have them access the Web site for additional information and resources.

BEFORE YOU READ

The Most Dangerous Game

MEET RICHARD CONNELL

Once asked when he began writing, Richard Connell said he could not remember a time when he did not write. His father edited the *Poughkeepsie News Press* in Poughkeepsie, New York, and young Richard began reporting on baseball games when he was only ten years old. For this, he was paid ten cents a game.

Early Career At age sixteen, Connell became the city editor for the newspaper. When his father was elected to Congress in 1910, seventeen-year-old Richard worked as his secretary. He went on to attend Harvard University, where he was an editor for both the *Harvard Lampoon,* a humor magazine, and the *Crimson*, a student-run newspaper.

While working on the newspaper, he wrote an editorial that sharply criticized a publisher. That editorial had unexpected effects: the publisher sued the *Crimson* but also offered Connell a job on a New York City paper. From there, Connell moved to a job in advertising. When World War I began, Connell enlisted. He continued to write during his enlistment, editing the camp weekly newspaper, *Gas Attack*.

"There is no greater bore than perfection."

—Richard Connell
from "The Most Dangerous Game"

After the war, Connell returned to advertising, but only for a very brief period, until a short story that he wrote was published. His career in advertising ended, and his career as a literary writer began.

A Writer's Life Connell was a prolific short-story writer, producing hundreds of stories for various U.S. and British magazines. These included the *Saturday Evening Post* and *Collier's*, both of which had a broad readership. Many of his stories, including "The Most Dangerous Game," were later turned into movies.

In 1925 Connell moved to California to focus on writing film scripts. He worked on a variety of films for several different studios. His film credits include *Meet John Doe, Presenting Lily Mars,* and *Seven Faces*. At the time of his death, he was working on a play.

Despite a varied career, Connell is best remembered for the story "The Most Dangerous Game," which has been the basis for more than half a dozen films. The first version, with the same title as the story, was filmed on the set of the 1933 movie *King Kong;* the film even used many of the actors who later appeared in *King Kong*. As a testament to the story's enduring popularity, a movie version was filmed in the late 1980s, decades after Connell's death, and more recently, the story was adapted for a Halloween episode of the television show *The Simpsons*.

Richard Connell was born in 1893 and died in 1949.

Literature Online **Author Search** For more about Richard Connell, go to www.glencoe.com.

Selection Skills

The Most Dangerous Game

Literary Elements
- Suspense (SE pp. 23–42)
- Conflict (SE p. 42)
- Style (SE p. 43)

Reading Skills
- Predictions About Plot (SE pp. 23–42)

Vocabulary Skills
- Word Origins (SE p. 42)
- Academic Vocabulary (SE p. 42)

Listening/Speaking/Viewing Skills
- Analyzing Art (SE pp. 28, 39; TWE pp. 24, 33, 36)

Writing Skills/Grammar
- Writing About Literature (SE p. 43)
- Interdisciplinary Activity (SE p. 43)
- Using Dashes (SE p. 43)
- Word Choice (TWE p. 38)
- Adverbs (TWE p. 39)

LITERATURE PREVIEW

Connecting to the Story

The protagonist in this story says, "The world is made up of two classes—the hunters and the huntees." As you read the story, think about that quotation and the following questions:

- What might the character mean?
- Into which class would you place yourself?
- What would happen if the two classes changed places?

Building Background

Years ago, before many species of large game animals became endangered, hunting for trophies was considered a great sport for "gentlemen and kings." Hunters would hire guides to take them into jungles, across grasslands, or to other wild places where they could stalk and shoot game. These adventurers were primarily interested in what they viewed as the "sport." They were not hunting for food, and usually kept only the animals' heads, which they mounted on the walls of their homes and hunting lodges.

Setting Purposes for Reading

Big Idea Matters of Life and Death

As you read this selection, notice how often you come across references to death and evil.

Literary Element Suspense

Suspense is a feeling of curiosity, uncertainty, or even dread about what is going to happen next in a story. Writers heighten the level of suspense by creating situations that threaten the central character and by raising questions in readers' minds about what will happen in a conflict. As you read "The Most Dangerous Game," notice each situation that might affect the central character. What about each situation makes you wonder what will happen?

- See Literary Terms Handbook, p. R17.

Literature Online **Interactive Literary Elements Handbook** To review or learn more about the literary elements, go to www.glencoe.com.

READING PREVIEW

Reading Strategy Making and Verifying Predictions About Plot

When you **make a prediction,** you make an informed guess about what is likely to happen in a story. The guess is educated because you combine clues in the text with your own knowledge. **Verifying predictions** is checking to see whether the predictions you made turn out to be correct.

Reading Tip: Tracking Predictions Use a simple chart to record and verify predictions.

Story Detail	Prediction	What Happens
Ship-Trap Island	the ship will be trapped	

Vocabulary

tangible (tan′ jə bəl) *adj.* capable of being touched or felt; p. 25 *The rainbow was so bright that it seemed tangible.*

discern (di surn′) *v.* to detect or recognize; to make out; p. 27 *Through the fog, he was able to discern a human figure.*

condone (kən dōn′) *v.* to excuse or overlook an offense, usually a serious one, without criticism; p. 31 *I cannot condone the use of force against unarmed people.*

imperative (im per′ ə tiv) *adj.* absolutely necessary; p. 36 *The swimmer knew it was imperative to reach shore quickly.*

zealous (zel′ əs) *adj.* very eager; enthusiastic; p. 37 *A zealous supporter of animal rights would not hunt for sport.*

INDIANA ACADEMIC STANDARDS (pages 23–43)

9.3.7 Recognize and understand the significance of various literary devices...

9.2 Develop strategies such as...making predictions...

9.5.3 Write expository compositions...

9.3.6 Analyze and trace an author's development of time and sequence, including the use of...foreshadowing...

BEFORE YOU READ

Focus

Summary

Sanger Rainsford, a famous hunter, falls from a yacht into the Caribbean. He swims ashore and discovers the mansion of General Zaroff. A hunter who preys on shipwrecked sailors, Zaroff proposes a game: If Zaroff cannot find and kill Rainsford in three days, he will transport him to the mainland. Unable to outwit Zaroff, Rainsford jumps into the sea and swims around the island to the mansion. The two duel; Rainsford kills Zaroff.

V Vocabulary

Vocabulary File **Say:** Add these words and definitions to your vocabulary file. For each word, include a sentence that gives you an example of how to use the word. **OL** Students with English language needs should include the pronunciations of these words in their files. **EL**

Literary Elements Have students access the Web site to improve their understanding of suspense.

Selection Resources

Print Materials
- Unit 1 Resources (Fast File), pp. 20–22
- Leveled Vocabulary Development, p. 2
- Selection and Unit Assessments, pp. 3–4
- Selection Quick Checks, p. 2

Transparencies
- Bellringer Options Transparencies: Selection Focus Transparency 2 Daily Language Practice Transparency 4
- Literary Elements Transparency 7

Technology
- TeacherWorks Plus™ CD-ROM
- StudentWorks Plus™ CD-ROM
- Presentation Plus!™ CD-ROM
- Literature Online, glencoe.com
- Online Student Edition, mhln.com
- Exam*View*® Assessment Suite CD-ROM
- Vocabulary PuzzleMaker CD-ROM
- Listening Library, disc 1 track 2

Teach

BI1 **Big Idea**

Matters of Life and Death

Say: Keep these questions in mind as you read: How does the desire to stay alive affect Rainsford's actions? *(It keeps him pushing the limits of his endurance.)* How does the life-or-death outcome affect the readers' experience? *(It heightens the suspense.)* OL

BI2 **Big Idea**

Matters of Life and Death

Answer: *For the hunted, it is not sport, but a matter of life and death.* OL

★ Viewing the Art

Belgian artist Henri Cleenewerck (1818–1901) was influenced by the Flemish old masters. His painting *A Hunter in the Cuban Jungle* reflects this. In addition to scenes in Cuba, Cleenewerck landscapes included locations in California and Europe. AS

Readability Scores

Dale-Chall: 6.2

DRP: 50

Lexile: 740

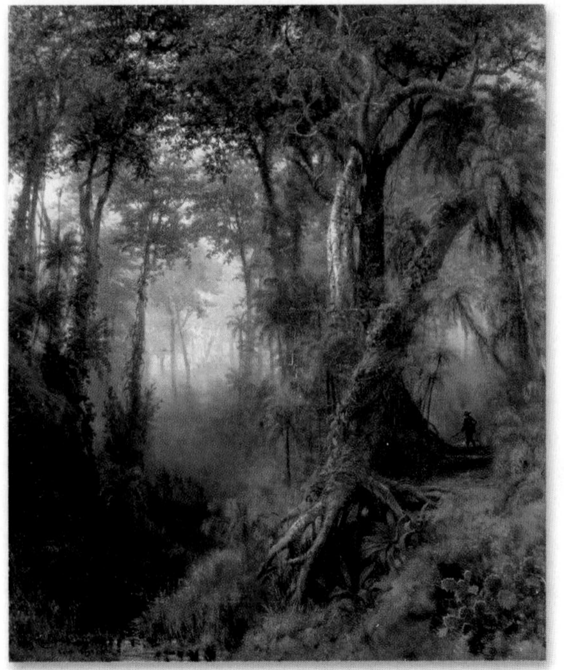

A Hunter in the Cuban Jungle, Sunrise, 1869. Henri Cleenewerck. Oil on canvas, 96.8 × 82.5 cm. Private Collection. ★

THE Most Dangerous GAME

Richard Connell

BI1 "Off there to the right—somewhere—is a large island," said Whitney. "It's rather a mystery—"

"What island is it?" Rainsford asked.

"The old charts call it 'Ship-Trap Island'," Whitney replied. "A suggestive name, isn't it? Sailors have a curious dread of the place. I don't know why. Some superstition—"

"Can't see it," remarked Rainsford, trying to peer through the dank tropical night that was palpable as it pressed its thick warm blackness in upon the yacht.

"You've good eyes," said Whitney, with a laugh, "and I've seen you pick off a moose moving in the brown fall bush at four hundred yards, but even you can't see four miles or so through a moonless Caribbean night."

"Nor four yards," admitted Rainsford. "Ugh! It's like moist black velvet."

"It will be light enough in Rio," promised Whitney. "We should make it in a few days. I hope the jaguar guns have come from Purdey's. We should have some good hunting up the Amazon. Great sport, hunting."

"The best sport in the world," agreed Rainsford.

"For the hunter," amended Whitney. "Not for the jaguar."

"Don't talk rot, Whitney," said Rainsford. "You're a big-game hunter, not a philosopher. Who cares how a jaguar feels?"

"Perhaps the jaguar does," observed Whitney.

"Bah! They've no understanding."

"Even so, I rather think they understand one thing—fear. The fear of pain and the fear of death."

Big Idea Matters of Life and Death *What does Whitney's statement suggest about his view of hunting?* BI2

Additional Support

Skills Practice

VIEWING: Critical Viewing Remind students that the artwork offers important clues to the readings. Suggest these strategies for using the artwork:

- Read background information and link it to the story.
- List words to describe the painting's mood, such as *eerie.*
- List the painting's colors and describe the scene.
- Ask how the painting relates to the story's plot or mood.

Have students apply this process to the painting on page 24 and the one on page 36 and share their results as a group. OL

"Nonsense," laughed Rainsford. "This hot weather is making you soft, Whitney. Be a realist. The world is made up of two classes—the hunters and the huntees. Luckily, you and I are hunters. Do you think we've passed that island yet?"

"I can't tell in the dark. I hope so."

"Why?" asked Rainsford.

"The place has a reputation—a bad one."

"Cannibals?" suggested Rainsford.

"Hardly. Even cannibals wouldn't live in such a God-forsaken place. But it's gotten into sailor lore,[1] somehow. Didn't you notice that the crew's nerves seemed a bit jumpy today?"

"They were a bit strange, now you mention it. Even Captain Nielsen—"

"Yes, even that tough-minded old Swede, who'd go up to the devil himself and ask him for a light. Those fishy blue eyes held a look I never saw there before. All I could get out of him was: 'This place has an evil name among seafaring men, sir.' Then he said to me, very gravely: 'Don't you feel anything?'—as if the air about us was actually poisonous. Now, you mustn't laugh when I tell you this—I did feel something like a sudden chill.

"There was no breeze. The sea was as flat as a plate-glass window. We were drawing near the island then. What I felt was a—a mental chill; a sort of sudden dread."

"Pure imagination," said Rainsford. "One superstitious sailor can taint the whole ship's company with his fear."

"Maybe. But sometimes I think sailors have an extra sense that tells them when they are in danger. Sometimes I think evil is a **tangible** thing—with wave lengths, just as sound and light have. An evil place can, so to speak, broadcast vibrations of evil. Anyhow, I'm glad we're getting out of this zone. Well, I think I'll turn in now, Rainsford."

"I'm not sleepy," said Rainsford. "I'm going to smoke another pipe up on the afterdeck."

"Good night, then, Rainsford. See you at breakfast."

"Right. Good night, Whitney."

> "Sometimes I think evil is a tangible thing . . ."

There was no sound in the night as Rainsford sat there but the muffled throb of the engine that drove the yacht swiftly through the darkness, and the swish and ripple of the wash of the propeller.

Rainsford, reclining in a steamer chair, indolently puffed on his favorite briar.[2] The sensuous drowsiness of the night was upon him. "It's so dark," he thought, "that I could sleep without closing my eyes; the night would be my eyelids—"

An abrupt sound startled him. Off to the right he heard it, and his ears, expert in such matters, could not be mistaken. Again he heard the sound, and again. Somewhere, off in the blackness, someone had fired a gun three times.

Rainsford sprang up and moved quickly to the rail, mystified. He strained his eyes in the direction from which the reports had come, but it was like trying to see through a blanket. He leaped upon the rail and balanced himself there, to get greater elevation; his pipe,

1. Accumulated traditions and beliefs about a particular subject are called *lore*.

2. *Indolently* means "lazily"; a *briar* is a tobacco pipe made from the fine-grained wood of the root of a Mediterranean shrub.

Reading Strategy Making and Verifying Predictions About Plot *What do you think will happen, and what clues help you make this prediction?* **R**

Literary Element Suspense *How does this statement generate suspense?* **L1**

Literary Element Suspense *What words in this passage increase your sense of unease?* **L2**

Vocabulary

tangible (tan′ jə bəl) *adj.* capable of being touched or felt

Teach

R Reading Strategy

Making and Verifying Predictions About Plot
Answer: *The story will involve hunting and the island. Clues include mentions of hunting, the title, and the island's name.* **OL**

L1 Literary Element

Suspense **Answer:** *The reader wonders why the place has an evil name.* **OL**

L2 Literary Element

Suspense **Answer:** *The word* evil *is used twice.* **OL**

English Language Coach

Superstitions Rainsford and Whitney discuss the superstitions about Ship-Trap Island. Superstitions are unscientific beliefs based on fear or ignorance. Many, such as fear of black cats, are specific to a culture. Many people make light of superstitions, as Whitney does. Have students discuss familiar superstitions. **EL**

Use the CheckPoint questions on Presentation Plus! to monitor students' comprehension. These questions can be used with interactive response keypads for immediate student feedback.

Academic Standards

Additional Support activities on pp. 24 and 25 cover the following standards:

Skills Practice: **9.3** [Identify] story elements such as…plot…and [make] connections…

English Language Coach: **9.1** Use…a growing knowledge of English and other languages to determine the meaning of words…

Teach

R1 Reading Strategy

Making and Verifying Predictions About Plot
Answer: *He will swim to the island, since the boat is out of reach. He will be stranded there.* OL

L1 Literary Element

Suspense **Answer:** *They introduce the threat of anguish and terror on the island.* OL

BI Big Idea

Matters of Life and Death
Answer: *Most students will infer that the animal was killed.* OL

L2 Literary Element

Suspense **Answer:** *It foreshadows the danger ahead, while leaving the reader to wonder about the specific nature of that threat.* OL

★ Writer's Technique

Setting The Caribbean Sea, a part of the Atlantic Ocean, is several degrees warmer than the waters farther north. Connell's use of the term *blood-warm* to describe a temperature that would usually seem inviting helps readers imagine Rainsford's fear. AS

striking a rope, was knocked from his mouth. He lunged for it; a short, hoarse cry came from his lips as he realized he had reached too far and had lost his balance. The cry was ★ pinched off short as the blood-warm waters of the Caribbean Sea closed over his head.

He struggled up to the surface and tried to cry out, but the wash from the speeding yacht slapped him in the face and the salt water in his open mouth made him gag and strangle. Desperately he struck out with strong strokes after the receding lights of the yacht, but he stopped before he had swum fifty feet. A certain cool-headedness had come to him; it was not the first time he had been in a tight place. There was a chance that his cries could be heard by someone aboard the yacht, but that chance was slender, and grew more slender as the yacht raced on. He wrestled himself out of his clothes, and shouted with all his power. The lights of the yacht became faint and ever-vanishing fireflies; then they were blotted out entirely by the night.

Rainsford remembered the shots. They had come from the right, and doggedly he swam in that direction, swimming with slow, deliberate strokes, conserving his strength. For a seemingly endless time he fought the sea. He began to count his strokes; he could do possibly a hundred more and then—

Rainsford heard a sound. It came out of the darkness, a high screaming sound, the sound of an animal in an extremity of anguish and terror.

He did not recognize the animal that made the sound; he did not try to; with fresh vitality he swam toward the sound. He heard it again; then it was cut short by another noise, crisp, staccato.

"Pistol shot," muttered Rainsford, swimming on.

Ten minutes of determined effort brought another sound to his ears—the most welcome he had ever heard—the muttering and growling of the sea breaking on a rocky shore. He was almost on the rocks before he saw them; on a night less calm he would have been shattered against them. With his remaining strength he dragged himself from the swirling waters. Jagged crags appeared to jut up into the opaqueness;[3] he forced himself upward, hand over hand. Gasping, his hands raw, he reached a flat place at the top. Dense jungle came down to the very edge of the cliffs. What perils that tangle of trees and underbrush might hold for him did not concern Rainsford just then. All he knew was that he was safe from his enemy, the sea, and that utter weariness was upon him. He flung himself down at the jungle edge and tumbled headlong into the deepest sleep of his life.

When he opened his eyes he knew from the position of the sun that it was late in the afternoon. Sleep had given him new vigor; a sharp hunger was picking at him. He looked about him, almost cheerfully.

"Where there are pistol shots, there are men. Where there are men, there is food," he thought. But what kind of men, he wondered, in so forbidding a place? An unbroken front of snarled and ragged jungle fringed the shore.

He saw no sign of a trail through the closely knit web of weeds and trees; it was easier to go along the shore, and Rainsford floundered along by the water. Not far from where he had landed, he stopped.

3. *Crags* are steep, rugged, protruding rocks or cliffs. Here, the crags jut up into the darkness *(opaqueness)* of the night.

Reading Strategy Making and Verifying Predictions About Plot *What do you think will happen to Rainsford?* R1

Literary Element Suspense *What effect do these details have on the plot?* L1

Big Idea Matters of Life and Death *Why does the pistol shot stop the sound?* BI

Literary Element Suspense *What does this detail add to the suspense of the story?* L2

Additional Support

Skills Practice

LITERARY ELEMENT: Plot To help students predict the action, review these plot elements:

- **Conflict:** struggle of the main character with opposing forces
- **Rising Action:** events arising from the conflict
- **Climax:** the high point
- **Falling Action:** events that follow the climax
- **Resolution:** outcome

Discuss the rising action.
Ask: Why does Rainsford go to the rail? *(He hears a sound.)* How does this advance the plot? *(It leads to him falling overboard.)* OL

Some wounded thing, by the evidence, a large animal, had thrashed about in the underbrush; the jungle weeds were crushed down and the moss was lacerated; one patch of weeds was stained crimson. A small, glittering object not far away caught Rainsford's eye and he picked it up. It was an empty cartridge.

★ "A twenty-two," he remarked. "That's odd. It must have been a fairly large animal, too. The hunter had his nerve with him to tackle it with a light gun. It's clear that the brute put up a fight. I suppose the first three shots I heard was when the hunter flushed his quarry[4] and wounded it. The last shot was when he trailed it here and finished it."

He examined the ground closely and found what he had hoped to find—the print of hunting boots. They pointed along the cliff in the direction he had been going. Eagerly he hurried along, now slipping on a rotten log or a loose stone, but making headway; night was beginning to settle down on the island.

Bleak darkness was blacking out the sea and jungle when Rainsford sighted the lights. He came upon them as he turned a crook in the coast line, and his first thought was that he had come upon a village, for there were many lights. But as he forged along he saw to his great astonishment that all the lights were in one enormous building—a lofty structure with pointed towers plunging upward into the gloom. His eyes made out the shadowy outlines of a palatial chateau;[5] it was set on a high bluff, and on three sides of it cliffs dived down to where the sea licked greedy lips in the shadows.

"Mirage," thought Rainsford. But it was no mirage, he found, when he opened the tall spiked iron gate. The stone steps were real enough; the massive door with a leering gargoyle for a knocker was real enough; yet above it all hung an air of unreality.

Visual Vocabulary
A *gargoyle* is an outlandish or grotesque carved figure.

He lifted the knocker, and it creaked up stiffly, as if it had never before been used. He let it fall, and it startled him with its booming loudness. He thought he heard steps within; the door remained closed. Again Rainsford lifted the heavy knocker, and let it fall. The door opened then, opened as suddenly as if it were on a spring, and Rainsford stood blinking in the river of glaring gold light that poured out. The first thing Rainsford's eyes **discerned** was the largest man Rainsford had ever seen—a gigantic creature, solidly made and black-bearded to the waist. In his hand the man held a long-barreled revolver, and he was pointing it straight at Rainsford's heart.

Out of the snarl of beard two small eyes regarded Rainsford.

"Don't be alarmed," said Rainsford, with a smile which he hoped was disarming.[6] "I'm no robber. I fell off a yacht. My name is Sanger Rainsford of New York City."

The menacing look in the eyes did not change. The revolver pointed as rigidly as if the giant were a statue. He gave no sign that he understood Rainsford's words, or that he had even heard them. He was dressed in uniform, a black uniform trimmed with gray astrakhan.[7]

4. *Quarry* is anything that is hunted or pursued, especially an animal.
5. A *palatial chateau* (sha tō′) is a magnificent, palace-like mansion.
6. *Disarming* means "tending to remove fear or suspicion; charming."
7. *Astrakhan* is the woolly skin of young lambs and is named after a region in Russia.

Literary Element Suspense *How does the author's word choice add suspense in this passage?* **L3**

Reading Strategy Making and Verifying Predictions About Plot *What do you think Rainsford will do now that he has found the footprints?* **R2**

Literary Element Suspense *What about this character increases suspense?* **L4**

Vocabulary
discern (di surn′) *v.* to detect or recognize; to make out

Teach

L3 Literary Element

Suspense Answer: Crushed, lacerated, *and* stained crimson *suggest physical violence.* **OL**

R2 Reading Strategy

Making and Verifying Predictions About Plot
Answer: *He will follow them to their source.* **OL**

L4 Literary Element

Suspense Possible answer: *Details such as the gun and his large size, menacing look, and lack of response to Rainsford's explanation add suspense.* **OL**

★ Cultural History

Hunting Guns Rainsford's reference to a "twenty-two" describes the caliber, or approximate size, of the cartridge, or shell case, used in a 22-caliber gun. The caliber of a gun is the inside diameter of its barrel measured in hundredths of an inch. Rainsford thinks only a bold hunter would use such a lightweight gun against big game. **AS**

Differentiated Instruction

Creating Maps Some students may benefit from visual orientation to the story setting. Display a map of the Caribbean.

Ask: What do you notice about the geography? *(There are many islands and a lot of water.)* Urge students to draw their own maps of areas described in the story. As they read, artistic students may want to illustrate their maps with drawings of Rainsford, his yacht, the island, and Zaroff's chateau. **AL**

Academic Standards
Additional Support activities on pp. 26 and 27 cover the following standards:
Skills Practice: **9.3** [Identify] story elements such as…plot, and setting…
Differentiated Instruction: **9.2.1** Analyze the structure and format of reference…documents, including the graphics and headers…

Teach

L1 Literary Element

Characterization Define *foil* as a character that strongly contrasts with another character. **Ask:** How does the man with the gun function as a foil for General Zaroff? *(He is rough, primitive-looking, and menacing. Zaroff is well-groomed, cultivated, and sophisticated.)* OL

★ Viewing the Art

Answer: *Accept reasonable answers.*

Paul Cézanne (1839–1906) strongly influenced modern painting. He developed his own unique brushstrokes. Although Cézanne borrowed from Impressionist elements, his work was too realistic to be considered Impressionist. AS

Le Château Noir, 1904–06. Paul Cezanne. Oil on canvas, 29 × 36¾ in. Gift of Mrs. David M. Levy. The Museum of Modern Art, New York.

Viewing the Art: Compare and contrast the chateau in the painting with the chateau described in the story. ★

"I'm Sanger Rainsford of New York," Rainsford began again. "I fell off a yacht. I am hungry."

The man's only answer was to raise with his thumb the hammer of his revolver. Then Rainsford saw the man's free hand go to his forehead in a military salute, and he saw him click his heels together and stand at attention. Another man was coming down the broad marble steps, an erect, slender man in evening clothes. He advanced to Rainsford and held out his hand.

In a cultivated voice marked by a slight accent that gave it added precision and deliberateness, he said: "It is a very great pleasure and honor to welcome Mr. Sanger Rainsford, the celebrated hunter, to my home." L1

Automatically Rainsford shook the man's hand.

"I've read your book about hunting snow leopards in Tibet, you see," explained the man. "I am General Zaroff."

Rainsford's first impression was that the man was singularly handsome; his second was that there was an original, almost bizarre quality about the general's face. He was a tall man past middle age, for his hair was a vivid white; but his thick eyebrows and pointed military mustache were as black as the night from which Rainsford had come. His eyes, too, were black and very bright. He had high cheek bones, a sharp-cut nose, a spare, dark face, the face of a man used to giving orders, the face of an aristocrat. Turning to the giant in uniform, the general made a sign. The giant put away his pistol, saluted, withdrew.

"Ivan is an incredibly strong fellow," remarked the general, "but he has the misfortune to be deaf and dumb. A simple fellow, but, I'm afraid, like all his race, a bit of a savage."

"Is he Russian?"

"He is a Cossack,"[8] said the general, and his smile showed red lips and pointed teeth. "So am I."

8. The *Cossacks* are a people of southern Russia (and, now, Kazakhstan). During czarist times, Cossack men were famous as horsemen in the Russian cavalry.

Additional Support

Academic Standards

The Additional Support activity on p. 28 covers the following standard:

Skills Practice: **9.2.4** Synthesize the content from several sources...; paraphrase the ideas...

Skills Practice

RESEARCH: Electronic Resources

Discuss how to use these sources of information about Cossacks.

- CD-ROM: Most libraries have encyclopedias on compact discs.
- Computerized catalogs: Computerized catalogs linking a network of public libraries enable users to borrow books from libraries in other cities and towns.
- Internet: Search engines or online encyclopedias can provide a starting point for research.

Have partners use one of these resources to research Cossacks and then present their findings orally OL or in a written report. AL

"Come," he said, "we shouldn't be chatting here. We can talk later. Now you want clothes, food, rest. You shall have them. This is a most restful spot."

Ivan had reappeared, and the general spoke to him with lips that moved but gave forth no sound.

"Follow Ivan, if you please, Mr. Rainsford," said the general. "I was about to have my dinner when you came. I'll wait for you. You'll find that my clothes will fit you, I think."

It was to a huge, beam-ceilinged bedroom with a canopied bed big enough for six men that Rainsford followed the silent giant. Ivan laid out an evening suit, and Rainsford, as he put it on, noticed that it came from a London tailor who ordinarily cut and sewed for none below the rank of duke.

The dining room to which Ivan conducted them was in many ways remarkable. There was a medieval magnificence about it; it suggested a baronial hall of feudal times with its oaken panels, its high ceiling, its vast refectory tables where twoscore men could sit down to eat.[9] About the hall were the mounted heads of many animals—lions, tigers, elephants, moose, bears; larger or more perfect specimens Rainsford had never seen. At the great table the general was sitting, alone.

"You'll have a cocktail, Mr. Rainsford," he suggested. The cocktail was surpassingly good; and, Rainsford noticed, the table appointments were of the finest—the linen, the crystal, the silver, the china.

They were eating *borscht*, the rich, red soup with whipped cream so dear to Russian palates. Half apologetically General Zaroff said: "We do our best to preserve the amenities of civilization here.[10] Please forgive any lapses. We are well off the beaten track, you know. Do you think the champagne has suffered from its long ocean trip?"

"Not in the least," declared Rainsford. He was finding the general a most thoughtful and affable host, a true cosmopolite.[11] But there was one small trait of the general's that made Rainsford uncomfortable. Whenever he looked up from his plate he found the general studying him, appraising him narrowly.

"Perhaps," said General Zaroff, "you were surprised that I recognized your name. You see, I read all books on hunting published in English, French, and Russian. I have but one passion in my life, Mr. Rainsford, and it is the hunt."

"You have some wonderful heads here," said Rainsford as he ate a particularly well cooked *filet mignon*. "That Cape buffalo[12] is the largest I ever saw."

"Oh, that fellow. Yes, he was a monster."

"Did he charge you?"

"Hurled me against a tree," said the general. "Fractured my skull. But I got the brute."

"I've always thought," said Rainsford, "that the Cape buffalo is the most dangerous of all big game."

For a moment the general did not reply; he was smiling his curious red-lipped smile. Then he said slowly: "No. You are wrong, sir. The Cape buffalo is not the most dangerous big game." He sipped his wine. "Here in my preserve on this island," he said in the same slow tone, "I hunt more dangerous game." ★

9. The words *medieval, baronial,* and *feudal* all relate to the Middle Ages. A *refectory table* might be found in a baron's castle; it is a long, wooden table with straight, heavy legs.

10. *Borscht* (bôrsht) is a soup made from beets. Here, *palates* means "tastes" or "likings," and *amenities* means "agreeable features" or "niceties."

11. *Affable* means "friendly and gracious." A *cosmopolite* (koz mop′ ə līt′) is a gracious and sophisticated person.

12. The African *Cape buffalo* is a large, often fierce buffalo with heavy, downward-curving horns.

Reading Strategy Making and Verifying Predictions About Plot *What do you predict will happen between Rainsford and General Zaroff?* **R1**

Big Idea Matters of Life and Death *What do all the mounted heads tell you about Zaroff?* **BI**

Reading Strategy Making and Verifying Predictions About Plot *Does this passage change your earlier prediction about General Zaroff? Explain.* **R2**

Literary Element Suspense *Why do phrases about dangerous game heighten the suspense?* **L2**

Teach

R1 Reading Strategy

Making and Verifying Predictions About Plot
Answer: *The two will get along well.* **OL**

BI Big Idea

Matters of Life and Death
Answer: *Zaroff hunts and kills for sport. He likes to have trophies made from the animals he kills, which means he is proud of his kills.* **OL**

R2 Reading Strategy

Making and Verifying Predictions About Plot
Answer: *Yes. Zaroff will most likely become a threat to Rainsford.* **OL**

L2 Literary Element

Suspense **Answer:** *Readers wonder what game is more dangerous than that mentioned and how this game will affect Rainsford.* **OL**

★ Language History

Game The term *game* refers both to wild animals hunted for sport and to an entertaining contest or sport. Both meanings derive from the Old English word for amusement or sport, *gamen.* **AS**

Differentiated Instruction

Medieval Times Point out the description of the dining room. Have students research medieval art and architecture, social systems, and standard of living. Then have them discuss in what respects the medieval look of the setting is or is not appropriate for General Zaroff. **AL**

English Language Coach

Characterization Have a student read aloud the description on page 28 of Rainsford's first impression of General Zaroff. Encourage students to share experiences of first impressions that later proved to be wrong. Have students predict if Zaroff will prove to be different and how. **EL**

Academic Standards

Additional Support activities on p. 29 cover the following standards:

Differentiated Instruction: **9.7.17** Deliver oral responses to literature that support…ideas and viewpoints through…references to the text and to other works…

English Language Coach: **9.3.3** Analyze interactions between characters…and explain the way those interactions affect the plot.

Teach

BI1 Big Idea

Matters of Life and Death
Answer: *He thinks of life as a game or a hunt. His goals are related to achieving hunting success.* OL

L1 Literary Element

Suspense **Answer:** *The reader is waiting to find out what the most dangerous game is and is chilled by Zaroff's boredom with hunting jaguars. This passage builds suspense by making the reader wonder what animal could possibly challenge this man.* OL

★ Cultural History

Russian Revolution After the revolution of 1917, many wealthy Russian aristocrats lost their money. Often they were forced to move to other countries and live in humble circumstances. AS

Rainsford expressed his surprise. "Is there big game on this island?"

The general nodded. "The biggest."

"Really?"

"Oh, it isn't here naturally, of course. I have to stock the island."

"What have you imported, general?" Rainsford asked. "Tigers?"

The general smiled. "No," he said. "Hunting tigers ceased to interest me some years ago. I exhausted their possibilities, you see. No thrill left in tigers, no real danger. I live for danger, Mr. Rainsford."

The general took from his pocket a gold cigarette case and offered his guest a long black cigarette with a silver tip; it was perfumed and gave off a smell like incense.

"We will have some capital hunting, you and I," said the general. "I shall be most glad to have your society."

"But what game—" began Rainsford.

"I'll tell you," said the general. "You will be amused, I know. I think I may say, in all modesty, that I have done a rare thing. I have invented a new sensation. May I pour you another glass of port?"

"Thank you, general."

The general filled both glasses, and said: "God makes some men poets. Some He makes kings, some beggars. Me He made a hunter. My hand was made for the trigger, my father said. He was a very rich man with a quarter of a million acres in the Crimea, and he was an ardent sportsman. When I was only five years old he gave me a little gun, specially made in Moscow for me, to shoot sparrows with. When I shot some of his prize turkeys with it, he did not punish me; he complimented me on my marksmanship. I killed my first bear in the Caucasus[13] when I was ten. My whole life has been one prolonged hunt. I went into the army—it was expected of noblemen's sons—and for a time commanded a division of Cossack cavalry, but my real interest was always the hunt. I have hunted every kind of game in every land. It would be impossible for me to tell you how many animals I have killed."

The general puffed at his cigarette.

"After the debacle in Russia I left the country, for it was imprudent for an officer of the Czar to stay there.[14] Many noble Russians lost everything. I, luckily, had invested heavily in American securities, so I shall never have to open a tearoom in Monte Carlo or drive a taxi in Paris. Naturally, I continued to hunt—grizzlies in your Rockies, crocodile in the Ganges, rhinoceroses in East Africa. It was in Africa that the Cape buffalo hit me and laid me up for six months. As soon as I recovered I started for the Amazon to hunt jaguars, for I had heard they were unusually cunning. They weren't." The Cossack sighed. "They were no match at all for a hunter with his wits about him, and a high-powered rifle. I was bitterly disappointed. I was lying in my tent with a splitting headache one night when a terrible thought pushed its way into my mind. Hunting was beginning to bore me! And hunting, remember, had been my life. I have heard that in America business men often go to pieces when they give up the business that has been their life."

"I live for danger, Mr. Rainsford."

13. *Crimea* (krī mē′ ə) is a region in the southern part of the former Russian empire near the Black Sea. *Caucasus* (kô′ kə səs) refers to both a region and a mountain range between the Black and Caspian Seas.

14. A *debacle* (di bä′ kəl) is a disastrous defeat. Zaroff refers to the 1917 revolution that overthrew the Czar, an event that made it unwise *(imprudent)* for him to stay in Russia.

Big Idea Matters of Life and Death *What general statement could you make about General Zaroff's life goals?* BI1

Literary Element Suspense *How does General Zaroff's discovery about jaguars build suspense in the story he is telling?* L1

Additional Support

Skills Practice

READING: Compare and Contrast Comparing and contrasting characters can help readers predict plot developments. For example, Zaroff talks a lot, while Rainsford says little. This suggests that Zaroff controls the situation so far.

Have students complete a Venn diagram about the two men. Discuss how they are the same and different. OL

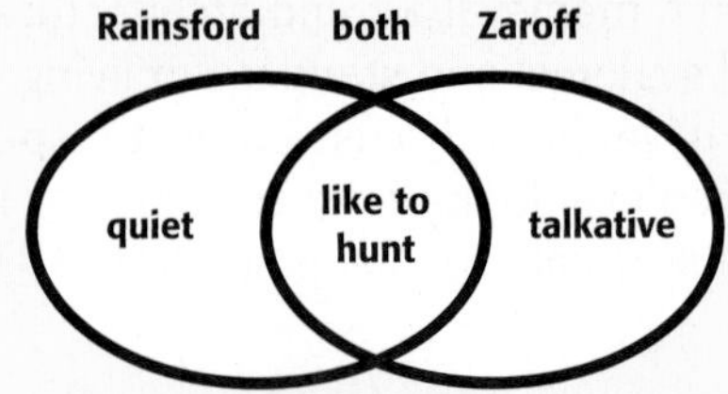

"Yes, that's so," said Rainsford.

The general smiled. "I had no wish to go to pieces," he said. "I must do something. Now, mine is an analytical mind, Mr. Rainsford. Doubtless that is why I enjoy the problems of the chase."

"No doubt, General Zaroff."

"So," continued the general, "I asked myself why the hunt no longer fascinated me. You are much younger than I am, Mr. Rainsford, and have not hunted as much, but you perhaps can guess the answer."

"What was it?"

"Simply this: hunting had ceased to be what you call 'a sporting proposition.' It had become too easy. I always got my quarry. Always. There is no greater bore than perfection."

"Instinct is no match for reason."

The general lit a fresh cigarette.

"No animal had a chance with me any more. That is no boast; it is a mathematical certainty. The animal had nothing but his legs and his V instinct. Instinct is no match for reason. When I thought of this it was a tragic moment for me, I can tell you."

Rainsford leaned across the table, absorbed in what his host was saying.

"It came to me as an inspiration what I must do," the general went on.

"And that was?"

The general smiled the quiet smile of one who has faced an obstacle and surmounted it with success. "I had to invent a new animal to hunt," he said.

"A new animal? You're joking."

"Not at all," said the general. "I never joke about hunting. I needed a new animal. I found one. So I bought this island, built this house, and here I do my hunting. The island is perfect for my purposes—there are jungles with a maze of trails in them, hills, swamps—"

Literary Element Suspense *How does General Zaroff continue to build suspense in the telling of his story?* **L2**

"But the animal, General Zaroff?"

"Oh," said the general, "it supplies me with the most exciting hunting in the world. No other hunting compares with it for an instant. Every day I hunt, and I never grow bored now, for I have a quarry with which I can match my wits."

Rainsford's bewilderment showed in his face.

"I wanted the ideal animal to hunt," explained the general. "So I said: 'What are the attributes of an ideal quarry?' And the answer was, of course: 'It must have courage, cunning, and, above all, it must be able to reason.'"

"But no animal can reason," objected Rainsford.

"My dear fellow," said the general, "there is one that can."

"But you can't mean—" gasped Rainsford.

"And why not?"

"I can't believe you are serious, General Zaroff. This is a grisly joke."

"Why should I not be serious? I am speaking of hunting."

"Hunting? Good God, General Zaroff, what you speak of is murder."

The general laughed with entire good nature. He regarded Rainsford quizzically. "I refuse to believe that so modern and civilized a young man as you seem to be harbors romantic ideas about the value of human life. Surely your experiences in the war—"

"Did not make me **condone** cold-blooded murder," finished Rainsford stiffly.

Reading Strategy Making and Verifying Predictions About Plot *What animal do you think Zaroff will name?* **R**

Big Idea Matters of Life and Death *What does General Zaroff imply about the effect of war on whether a person values life? Explain.* **BI2**

Vocabulary

condone (kən dōn′) *v.* to excuse or overlook an offense, usually a serious one, without criticism

Teach

V Vocabulary

Clarifying Meaning *Instinct* describes behavior that is inborn. For example, a baby animal knows without being taught to stay close to its mother. *Reason* refers to thinking and judgment. Humans, like animals, are often driven by instincts but have superior reasoning ability. **OL**

L2 Literary Element

Suspense **Answer:** *His telling of the story in a roundabout way that only hints at his meaning, and in an understated manner (with a "quiet smile") builds suspense.* **OL**

R Reading Strategy

Making and Verifying Predictions About Plot
Answer: *Zaroff will name humans.* **OL**

BI2 Big Idea

Matters of Life and Death
Answer: *Zaroff implies that people who have experienced war become desensitized to death and attach less value to human life.* **OL**

Differentiated Instruction

Making Inferences Review how to make inferences by using clues to figure out the author's meaning. Help students skim page 31 for clues to the fact that Zaroff hunts people. *("I had to invent a new animal to hunt," "So I said: 'What are the attributes of an ideal quarry?' And the answer was, of course: 'It must have courage, cunning, and, above all, it must be able to reason,'" "But no animal can reason," "there is one that can.")* **BL**

Academic Standards

Additional Support activities on pp. 30 and 31 cover the following standards:

Skills Practice: **9.3.3** Analyze interactions between characters in a literary text and explain the way those interactions affect the plot.

Differentiated Instruction: **9.3.4** Determine characters' traits by what the characters say about themselves in…dialogue…

Teach

BI1 Big Idea

Matters of Life and Death
Answer: *The weak die.* OL

L1 Literary Element

Characterization Ask: What do readers learn about General Zaroff through his dialogue? *(He is cruel and unfeeling; he discriminates among different ethnic and social classes of people. In general, he has no respect for human life.)* OL

R Reading Strategy

Making and Verifying Predictions About Plot
Answer: *Zaroff will become violent; he will hunt Rainsford.* OL

Cultural History

Social Darwinism "Life is for the strong" recalls the ideas of the nineteenth-century naturalist Charles Darwin. His theory of natural selection, or survival of the fittest, proposed that evolution tended to favor strength over weakness. Social Darwinism applied this theory to human society, proposing that it should weed out the unfit. AS

Laughter shook the general. "How extraordinarily droll you are!" he said. "One does not expect nowadays to find a young man of the educated class, even in America, with such a naive, and, if I may say so, mid-Victorian[15] point of view. It's like finding a snuff-box in a limousine. Ah, well, doubtless you had Puritan ancestors. So many Americans appear to have had. I'll wager you'll forget your notions when you go hunting with me. You've a genuine new thrill in store for you, Mr. Rainsford."

"Thank you, I'm a hunter, not a murderer."

"Dear me," said the general, quite unruffled, "again that unpleasant word. But I think I can show you that your scruples[16] are quite ill founded."

"Yes?"

"Life is for the strong, to be lived by the strong, and, if needs be, taken by the strong. The weak of the world were put here to give the strong pleasure. I am strong. Why should I not use my fist? If I wish to hunt, why should I not? I hunt the scum of the earth—sailors from tramp ships—lascars,[17] blacks, Chinese, whites, mongrels—a thoroughbred horse or hound is worth more than a score of them."

"But they are men," said Rainsford hotly.

"Precisely," said the general. "That is why I use them. It gives me pleasure. They can reason, after a fashion. So they are dangerous."

"But where do you get them?"

The general's left eyelid fluttered down in a wink. "This island is called Ship-Trap," he answered. "Sometimes an angry god of the high seas sends them to me. Sometimes, when Providence is not so kind, I help Providence a bit. Come to the window with me."

Rainsford went to the window and looked out toward the sea.

"Watch! Out there!" exclaimed the general, pointing into the night. Rainsford's eyes saw only blackness, and then, as the general pressed a button, far out to sea Rainsford saw the flash of lights.

The general chuckled. "They indicate a channel," he said, "where there's none; giant rocks with razor edges crouch like a sea monster with wide-open jaws. They can crush a ship as easily as I crush this nut." He dropped a walnut on the hardwood floor and brought his heel grinding down on it. "Oh, yes," he said, casually, as if in answer to a question, "I have electricity. We try to be civilized here."

"Civilized? And you shoot down men?"

A trace of anger was in the general's black eyes, but it was there for but a second, and he said, in his most pleasant manner: "Dear me, what a righteous young man you are! I assure you I do not do the thing you suggest. That would be barbarous. I treat these visitors with every consideration. They get plenty of good food and exercise. They get into splendid physical condition. You shall see for yourself tomorrow."

"What do you mean?"

"We'll visit my training school," smiled the general. "It's in the cellar. I have about a dozen pupils down there now. They're from the Spanish bark *San Lucar* that had the bad luck to go on the rocks out there. A very inferior lot, I regret to say. Poor specimens and more accustomed to the deck than to the jungle."

Visual Vocabulary
A *bark* has from three to five masts, all but one of which are rigged with four-sided sails. The last mast has both three- and four-sided sails.

15. Zaroff feels that Rainsford is quaint *(droll)*, innocent and unsophisticated *(naive)*, and old-fashioned *(mid-Victorian)*.
16. *Scruples* are beliefs about the morality or ethics of an act. To have scruples means you will not do something you believe is wrong.
17. *Lascars* are sailors from India.

Big Idea Matters of Life and Death *What happens to the weak in Zaroff's world?* BI1

Reading Strategy Making and Verifying Predictions About Plot *What do you think Zaroff will do?* R

Additional Support

Skills Practice

READING: Draw Conclusions
Students can draw conclusions or make judgments by combining prior knowledge with information from a text. Thus, they might reasonably conclude that a story about two teams running bases to score points is about baseball.

Have students reread the four paragraphs following "The general's left eyelid fluttered. . . ."
Ask: Where does General Zaroff get his prey? *(They come from nearby shipwrecks. Some wrecks occur naturally; Zaroff causes others with lights that lead ships onto rocks.)* OL

In 1901, Sir George Bulloughs of Lancashire, England, bought the Isle of Rhum for use as a sporting estate. The Trophy Room at Kinloch Castle, shown here, is a centerpiece of this Edwardian extravaganza, replete with stuffed deer heads, a white bearskin, and a piano. ★

He raised his hand, and Ivan, who served as waiter, brought thick Turkish coffee. Rainsford, with an effort, held his tongue in check.

"It's a game, you see," pursued the general blandly. "I suggest to one of them that we go hunting. I give him a supply of food and an excellent hunting knife. I give him three hours' start. I am to follow, armed only with a pistol of the smallest caliber and range. If my quarry eludes me for three whole days, he wins the game. If I find him"—the general smiled—"he loses."

"Suppose he refuses to be hunted?"

"Oh," said the general, "I give him his option, of course. He need not play that game if he doesn't wish to. If he does not wish to hunt, I turn him over to Ivan. Ivan once had the honor of serving as official knouter[18] to the Great White Czar, and he has his own ideas of sport. Invariably, Mr. Rainsford, invariably they choose the hunt."

"And if they win?"

The smile on the general's face widened. "To date I have not lost," he said. Then he added, hastily: "I don't wish you to think me a braggart, Mr. Rainsford. Many of them afford only the most elementary sort of problem. Occasionally I strike a tartar.[19] One almost did win. I eventually had to use the dogs."

"The dogs?"

"This way, please. I'll show you."

18. As the Czar's *knouter* (nou′ tər), Ivan was in charge of administering whippings and torture. A knout is a whip made of leather straps braided together with wires.
19. To *strike a tartar* is to take on someone who is stronger or abler.

Big Idea Matters of Life and Death *What do you think happens to someone who loses?* **BI2**

Literary Element Suspense *How does this statement increase the suspense?* **L2**

Teach

BI2 Big Idea

Matters of Life and Death
Answer: *The loser dies.* **OL**

L2 Literary Element

Suspense **Answer:** *The statement shows how dangerous Zaroff is and suggests that the game is rigged; it is not a fair contest.* **OL**

★ Viewing the Art

Kinloch Castle, on the Isle of Rhum in Scotland, is one of the best examples of an Edwardian country house. The castle was built between 1897 and 1901. *Kinloch* means "at the head of the loch"—in this case, referring to Loch Scresort. **AS**

Building Reading Fluency

Dialogue Have students practice reading dialogue to achieve fluency. Note that readers often must infer who the speaker is. Assign students portions of dialogue from page 33 and have them read the lines aloud. **BL**

Differentiated Instruction

Dramatization Invite volunteers to read dialogue aloud, using the tone, gesture, and facial expressions appropriate to the character. Then have them improvise dialogue for a scene set inside Rainsford's home. Discuss how changing the setting affects their portrayal of Zaroff. **AL**

Academic Standards

Additional Support activities on pp. 32 and 33 cover the following standards:

Skills Practice: **9.3** [Identify] story elements such as character...plot...

Building Reading Fluency: **9.7** [Develop] speaking skills...in conjunction with...strategies...[for] delivery of oral presentations.

Differentiated Instruction: **9.7.6** Analyze the occasion and...choose effective verbal and nonverbal techniques (including voice, gestures...) for presentations.

Teach

L1 Literary Element

Suspense Answer: *Like Rainsford, the reader knows that the general wants to show off his collection of human heads.* OL

BI1 Big Idea

Matters of Life and Death Answer: *These details show that Rainsford feels trapped and fears for his life. He is reminded of death in the eyes of the dogs and the sound of the pistol.* OL

R1 Reading Strategy

Making and Verifying Predictions About Plot Answer: *Poor hunting will probably leave the general bored and unsatisfied.* OL

★ Cultural History

Clothing Style Zaroff wears "the tweeds of a country squire." English landowners, who were often addressed with the title *squire,* favored trousers and jackets made from tweed, a rough multi-colored woolen fabric.

Ask: What does this choice of clothing say about Zaroff? *(Since wool seems impractical for the tropics, it suggests he is obsessed with his image.)* AS

The general steered Rainsford to a window. The lights from the windows sent a flickering illumination that made grotesque patterns on the courtyard below, and Rainsford could see moving about there a dozen or so huge black shapes; as they turned toward him, their eyes glittered greenly.

"A rather good lot, I think," observed the general. "They are let out at seven every night. If anyone should try to get into my house—or out of it—something extremely regrettable would occur to him." He hummed a snatch of song from the *Folies Bergère.*[20]

"And now," said the general, "I want to show you my new collection of heads. Will you come with me to the library?"

"I hope," said Rainsford, "that you will excuse me tonight, General Zaroff. I'm really not feeling well."

"Ah, indeed?" the general inquired solicitously.[21] "Well, I suppose that's only natural, after your long swim. You need a good, restful night's sleep. Tomorrow you'll feel like a new man, I'll wager. Then we'll hunt, eh? I've one rather promising prospect—" Rainsford was hurrying from the room.

"Sorry you can't go with me tonight," called the general. "I expect rather fair sport—a big, strong black. He looks resourceful—Well, good night, Mr. Rainsford; I hope you have a good night's rest."

The bed was good, and the pajamas of the softest silk and he was tired in every fiber of his being, but nevertheless Rainsford could not quiet his brain with the opiate of sleep. He lay, eyes wide open. Once he thought he heard stealthy steps in the corridor outside his room. He sought to throw open the door; it would not open. He went to the window and looked out. His room was high up in one of the towers. The lights of the chateau were out now, and it was dark and silent, but there was a fragment of sallow moon, and by its wan light he could see, dimly, the courtyard; there, weaving in and out in the pattern of shadow, were black, noiseless forms; the hounds heard him at the window and looked up, expectantly, with their green eyes. Rainsford went back to the bed and lay down. By many methods he tried to put himself to sleep. He had achieved a doze when, just as morning began to come, he heard, far off in the jungle, the faint report of a pistol.

General Zaroff did not appear until luncheon. He was dressed faultlessly in the tweeds of a country squire. He was solicitous about the state of Rainsford's health. ★

"As for me," sighed the general, "I do not feel so well. I am worried, Mr. Rainsford. Last night I detected traces of my old complaint."

To Rainsford's questioning glance the general said: "Ennui.[22] Boredom."

Then, taking a second helping of *Crêpes Suzette,* the general explained: "The hunting was not good last night. The fellow lost his head. He made a straight trail that offered no problems at all. That's the trouble with these sailors; they have dull brains to begin

Visual Vocabulary *Crêpes Suzette* (krāps′ so͞o zet′) are thin pancakes rolled and heated in a sweet sauce flavored with orange or lemon juice and brandy.

20. The *Folies Bergère* (fô lē′ ber zher′) is a music hall in Paris, famed for its variety shows.
21. *Solicitously* means "in a caring or concerned manner."
22. *Ennui* (än wē′)

Literary Element Suspense *What is particularly foreboding about General Zaroff's statement at this point in the story?* L1

Big Idea Matters of Life and Death *In what ways are the details of this paragraph significant?* BI1

Reading Strategy Making and Verifying Predictions About Plot *What effect will a poor hunt have on the general?* R1

Additional Support

Skills Practice

VOCABULARY: Etymology Explain that a word's etymology is its origin and history. Many English words come from other languages. Point out the word *ennui* on page 34. Explain that it comes from the French language. Zaroff uses many other French terms, such as *filet mignon* and *au revoir.* Learning a word's history can enrich a reader's understanding of the text. Have students look up the French words *rendezvous* and *tête-à-tête* in an English dictionary and share their meanings. OL Have students write a sentence about the story, using each of the words. AL with, and they do not know how to get about in the woods. They do excessively stupid and obvious things. It's most annoying. Will you have another glass of *Chablis,*[23] Mr. Rainsford?"

"General," said Rainsford firmly, "I wish to leave this island at once."

The general raised his thickets of eyebrows; he seemed hurt. "But, my dear fellow," the general protested, "you've only just come. You've had no hunting—"

"I wish to go today," said Rainsford. He saw the dead black eyes of the general on him, studying him. General Zaroff's face suddenly brightened.

He filled Rainsford's glass with venerable *Chablis* from a dusty bottle.

"Tonight," said the general, "we will hunt—you and I."

Rainsford shook his head. "No, general," he said, "I will not hunt."

The general shrugged his shoulders and delicately ate a hothouse grape. "As you wish, my friend," he said. "The choice rests entirely with you. But may I not venture to suggest that you will find my idea of sport more diverting[24] than Ivan's?"

He nodded toward the corner to where the giant stood, scowling, his thick arms crossed on his hogshead of a chest.

"You don't mean—" cried Rainsford.

"My dear fellow," said the general, "have I not told you I always mean what I say about hunting? This is really an inspiration. I drink to a foeman worthy of my steel—at last." The general raised his glass, but Rainsford sat staring at him.

"You'll find this game worth playing," the general said enthusiastically. "Your brain against mine. Your woodcraft against mine. Your strength and stamina against mine. Outdoor chess! And the stake is not without value, eh?"

"And if I win—" began Rainsford huskily.

"I'll cheerfully acknowledge myself defeated if I do not find you by midnight of the third day," said General Zaroff. "My sloop will place you on the mainland near a town." The general read what Rainsford was thinking.

"Oh, you can trust me," said the Cossack. "I will give you my word as a gentleman and a sportsman. Of course you, in turn, must agree to say nothing of your visit here."

"I'll agree to nothing of the kind," said Rainsford.

"Oh," said the general, "in that case—But why discuss that now? Three days hence we can discuss it over a bottle of *Veuve Cliquot,*[25] unless—"

The general sipped his wine. Then a businesslike air animated him. "Ivan," he said to Rainsford, "will supply you with hunting clothes, food, a knife. I suggest you wear moccasins; they leave a poorer trail. I suggest, too, that you avoid the big swamp in the southeast corner of the island. We call it Death Swamp. There's quicksand there. One foolish fellow tried it. The deplorable[26] part of it was that Lazarus followed him. You can imagine my feelings, Mr. Rainsford. I loved Lazarus; he was the finest hound in my pack. Well, I must beg you to excuse me now. I always take a siesta after lunch. You'll hardly have time for a nap, I fear. You'll want to start, no doubt. I shall not follow till dusk. Hunting at night is so much more exciting than by day, don't you think? Au revoir,[27] Mr. Rainsford, au revoir." General Zaroff, with a deep, courtly bow, strolled from the room.

23. *Chablis* (sha blē′) is a white wine.
24. *Diverting* means "entertaining" or "amusing."
25. *Veuve Cliquot* (vœv klē kō′) is a French champagne.
26. *Deplorable* means "very bad" or "regrettable."
27. *Au revoir* (ō rə vwär′) is French for "good-bye" or "until we meet again."

Reading Strategy Making and Verifying Predictions About Plot *What do you predict Rainsford will do?* R2

Big Idea Matters of Life and Death *Why might Rainsford's statement put him in danger?* BI2

Literary Element Suspense *How do General Zaroff's words here generate suspense?* L2

Teach

R2 Reading Strategy

Making and Verifying Predictions About Plot

Answer: *Rainsford will probably agree to the hunt rather than face certain death at Ivan's hands.* OL

BI2 Big Idea

Matters of Life and Death

Answer: *Zaroff will be determined to kill Rainsford rather than let him live to tell what Zaroff does on the island.* OL

L2 Literary Element

Suspense **Answer:** *The General's "au revoir" has two meanings—a casual "see you later" and a more ominous "until we meet again—when I have a gun pointed in your face." General Zaroff's casual attitude at such a tense moment for Rainsford also creates suspense.* OL

★ Cultural History

Moccasins Native Americans were some of the first people to wear moccasins: ankle-length or knee-length, heelless shoes made of deerskin. The upper parts of the shoes are often decorated with beads or embroidery. AS

English Language Coach

Figurative Language Explain to students that figurative language is used to evoke emotions and mental images. It has meaning beyond its literal definition. For example, a phrase such as "dead black eyes" does not mean that Zaroff's eyes are actually dead, but that they are as devoid of feeling as a dead person's eyes. Help students understand other examples of figurative language on pages 34–36: "fragment of sallow moon"; "hogshead of a chest"; "worthy of my steel"; and "sharp rowels of something very like panic." EL

Academic Standards

Additional Support activities on pp. 34 and 35 cover the following standards:

Skills Practice: **9.1.1** Identify and use the…meanings of words and understand the origins of words.

English Language Coach: **9.1.2** Distinguish between what words mean literally and what they imply and interpret what the words imply.

Teach

Viewing the Art

Scarred as a boy by the loss of his mother and a brother, Caspar David Friedrich (1774–1840) painted harsh, desolate landscapes. This painting suggests the isolation of the individual in the vastness of nature. **AS**

Sea Piece by Moonlight. Caspar David Friedrich. Oil on canvas, 25 × 33 cm. Museum der bildenden Künste, Leipzig, Germany.

Rainsford had fought his way through the bush for two hours. "I must keep my nerve. I must keep my nerve," he said through tight teeth.

He had not been entirely clear-headed when the chateau gates snapped shut behind him. His whole idea at first was to put distance between himself and General Zaroff, and, to this end, he had plunged along, spurred on by the sharp rowels[28] of something very like panic. Now he had got a grip on himself, had stopped, and was taking stock of himself and the situation. He saw that straight flight was futile; inevitably it would bring him face to face with the sea. He was in a picture with a frame of water, and his operations, clearly, must take place within that frame.

"I'll give him a trail to follow," muttered Rainsford, and he struck off from the rude path he had been following into the trackless wilderness. He executed a series of intricate loops; he doubled on his trail again and again, recalling all the lore of the fox hunt, and all the dodges of the fox. Night found him leg-weary, with hands and face lashed by the branches, on a thickly wooded ridge. He knew it would be insane to blunder on through the dark, even if he had the strength. His need for rest was **imperative** and he thought: "I have played the fox, now I must play the

28. A *rowel* is a wheel with sharp radiating points, as on the end of a rider's spur.

Vocabulary

imperative (im per ′ ə tiv) *adj.* absolutely necessary

Additional Support

Skills Practice

LITERARY ELEMENT: Setting Setting is the time and place of a story. In this story, setting plays an important role in creating suspense. Have students complete a Sensory Images web to describe the jungle on pages 36–37. Discuss how these images add to the suspense. **OL**

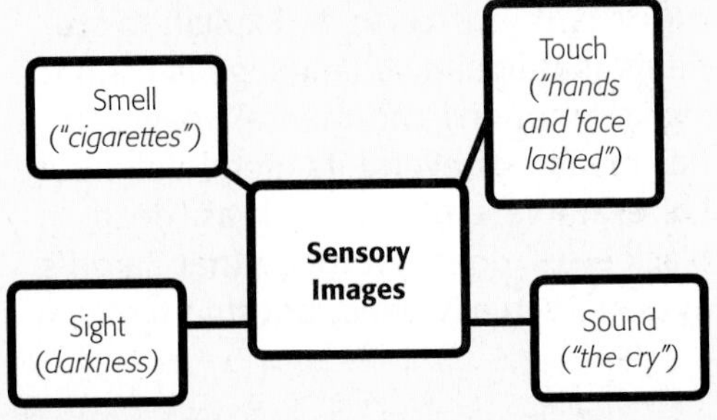

cat of the fable." A big tree with a thick trunk and outspread branches was near by, and, taking care to leave not the slightest mark, he climbed up into the crotch, and stretching out on one of the broad limbs, after a fashion, rested. Rest brought him new confidence and almost a feeling of security. Even so **zealous** a hunter as General Zaroff could not trace him there, he told himself; only the devil himself could follow that complicated trail through the jungle after dark. But, perhaps the general was a devil—

L1 An apprehensive night crawled slowly by like a wounded snake, and sleep did not visit Rainsford, although the silence of a dead world was on the jungle. Toward morning when a dingy gray was varnishing the sky, the cry of some startled bird focused Rainsford's attention in that direction. Something was coming through the bush, coming slowly, carefully, coming by the same winding way Rainsford had come. He flattened himself down on the limb, and through a screen of leaves almost as thick as tapestry, he watched. . . . That which was approaching was a man.

He was General Zaroff. He made his way along with his eyes fixed in utmost concentration on the ground before him. He paused, almost beneath the tree, dropped to his knees and studied the ground. Rainsford's impulse was to hurl himself down like a panther, but he saw that the general's right hand held something metallic—a small automatic pistol.

The hunter shook his head several times, as if he were puzzled. Then he straightened up and took from his case one of his black cigarettes; its pungent incenselike smoke floated up to Rainsford's nostrils.

Rainsford held his breath. The general's eyes had left the ground and were traveling inch by inch up the tree. Rainsford froze there, every muscle tensed for a spring. But the sharp eyes of the hunter stopped before they reached the limb where Rainsford lay; a smile spread over his brown face. Very deliberately he blew a smoke ring into the air; then he turned his back on the tree and walked carelessly away, back along the trail he had come. The swish of the underbrush against his hunting boots grew fainter and fainter.

The pent-up air burst hotly from Rainsford's lungs. His first thought made him feel sick and numb. The general could follow a trail through the woods at night; he could follow an extremely difficult trail; he must have uncanny powers; only by the merest chance had the Cossack failed to see his quarry.

Rainsford's second thought was even more terrible. It sent a shudder of cold horror through his whole being. Why had the general smiled? Why had he turned back?

Rainsford did not want to believe what his reason told him was true, but the truth was as evident as the sun that had by now pushed through the morning mists. The general was playing with him! The general was saving him for another day's sport! The Cossack was the cat; he was the mouse. Then it was that Rainsford knew the full meaning of terror.

"I will not lose my nerve. I will not." L3

He slid down from the tree, and struck off again into the woods. His face was set and he forced the machinery of his mind to function. Three hundred yards from his hiding place he stopped where a huge dead tree leaned precariously on a smaller, living one. Throwing off his sack of food, Rainsford took his knife from its sheath and began to work with all his energy.

The job was finished at last, and he threw himself down behind a fallen log a hundred

Literary Element Suspense *What words and images does the author use in this passage to heighten the suspense?* L2

Vocabulary

zealous (zel′ əs) *adj.* very eager; enthusiastic

Big Idea Matters of Life and Death *What makes this a good metaphor for Rainsford's situation?* BI

Teach

L1 Literary Element

Figurative Language Point out the highlighted text and urge students to visualize this image of the night. Have them define *apprehensive. (worried and fearful)*
Ask: Does this word literally describe the night? *(No, the image reflects Rainsford's fear.)* OL

L2 Literary Element

Suspense **Answer:** *Most students will say that "apprehensive," "like a wounded snake," and "a dead world" add to the suspense.* OL

BI Big Idea

Matters of Life and Death
Answer: *A cat will play with a mouse before killing it, just as Zaroff plays with Rainsford.* OL

L3 Literary Element

Characterization **Ask:** What traits has Rainsford shown in escaping Zaroff? *(Knowledge of the wilderness, quick thinking, ingenuity, and physical strength)* Point out the repetition of "I will not" in Rainsford's remark. Have a volunteer read the line aloud with emotion. Then **ask:** What does this remark suggest about Rainsford? *(Determination)* OL

English Language Coach

Background Students may need the following background in order to understand the story. Clarify that Rainsford refers on pages 36 and 37 to a fable by Aesop in which a fox challenges a cat to do tricks. The cat says that he does not know how to do tricks, but he knows how to do the most important things such as getting food and protecting himself. When some dogs come along, the fox continues acting "tricky" and is caught by the dogs. The cat simply climbs a tree, successfully avoiding capture. EL

Academic Standards

Additional Support activities on pp. 36 and 37 cover the following standards:

Skills Practice: **9.3** [Identify] story elements such as...setting...

English Language Coach: **9.3.7** Recognize and understand the significance of various literary devices...

Teach

R Reading Strategy

Making and Verifying Predictions About Plot
Answer: *He will be more determined and more careful.* OL

L1 Literary Element

Suspense **Answer:** *The detail about Death Swamp and the quicksand raises the question of how Rainsford can avoid death there.* OL

★ Literary History

Film Many movies, such as *The Fugitive, The Silence of the Lambs,* and Alfred Hitchcock's *North by Northwest,* have depicted manhunts. Like this story, these films center on a battle of wits and endurance between the fugitive and the pursuer. A film version of Connell's story was released in 1932. AS

feet away. He did not have to wait long. The cat was coming again to play with the mouse.

★ Following the trail with the sureness of a bloodhound came General Zaroff. Nothing escaped those searching black eyes, no crushed blade of grass, no bent twig, no mark, no matter how faint, in the moss. So intent was the Cossack on his stalking that he was upon the thing Rainsford had made before he saw it. His foot touched it, the general sensed his danger and leaped back with the agility of an ape. But he was not quick enough; the dead tree, delicately adjusted to rest on the cut living one, crashed down and struck the general a glancing blow on the shoulder as it fell; but for his alertness, he must have been smashed beneath it. He staggered, but he did not fall; nor did he drop his revolver. He stood there, rubbing his injured shoulder, and Rainsford, with fear again gripping his heart, heard the general's mocking laugh ring through the jungle.

"Rainsford," called the general, "if you are within sound of my voice, as I suppose you are, let me congratulate you. Not many men know how to make a Malay man-catcher. Luckily, for me, I, too, have hunted in Malacca.[29] You are proving interesting, Mr. Rainsford. I am going now to have my wound dressed; it's only a slight one. But I shall be back."

When the general, nursing his bruised shoulder, had gone, Rainsford took up his flight again. It was flight now, a desperate, hopeless flight, that carried him on for some hours. Dusk came, then darkness, and still he pressed on. The ground grew softer under his moccasins, the vegetation grew ranker, denser; insects bit him savagely. Then, as he stepped forward, his foot sank into the ooze. He tried to wrench it back, but the muck sucked viciously at his foot as if it were a giant leech. With a violent effort, he tore his feet loose. He knew where he was now. Death Swamp and its quicksand.

His hands were tight closed as if his nerve were something tangible that someone in the darkness was trying to tear from his grip. The softness of the earth had given him an idea. He stepped back from the quicksand a dozen feet or so and, like some huge prehistoric beaver, he began to dig.

Rainsford had dug himself in in France when a second's delay meant death. That had been a placid pastime compared to his digging now. The pit grew deeper; when it was above his shoulders, he climbed out and from some hard saplings cut stakes and sharpened them to a fine point. These stakes he planted in the bottom of the pit with the points sticking up. With flying fingers he wove a rough carpet of weeds and branches and with it he covered the mouth of the pit. Then, wet with sweat and aching with tiredness, he crouched behind the stump of a lightning-charred tree.

Visual Vocabulary A *sapling* is a young tree.

He knew that his pursuer was coming; he heard the padding sound of feet on the soft earth, and the night breeze brought him the perfume of the general's cigarette. It seemed to Rainsford that the general was coming with unusual swiftness; he was not feeling his way along, foot by foot. Rainsford, crouching there, could not see the general, nor could he see the pit. He lived a year in a minute. Then he felt an impulse to cry aloud with joy, for he heard the sharp crackle of the breaking branches as the cover of the pit gave way; he heard the sharp scream of pain as the pointed stakes found their mark. He leaped up from his place of concealment. Then he cowered back. Three feet from the pit a man was

29. The *Malay* are a people of southeast Asia, and *Malacca* (mə lak′ ə) is their home region.

Reading Strategy Making and Verifying Predictions About Plot *How do you think Zaroff will act after he returns, and why?* R

Literary Element Suspense *Why does this detail heighten the suspense?* L1

Additional Support

Skills Practice

WRITING: Word Choice Tell students that word choice helps authors craft engaging plots and characters as well as convey mood. Connell uses strong, specific, and vivid verbs throughout his story to advance these goals. Have students locate some examples on pages 38–39, such as *crouched, cowered, flee, panted, rumbled,* and *hissed.* Discuss how the verbs make the action realistic and exciting. Ask students to write two sentences describing a sport or physical activity, using specific, vivid verbs. Then have partners exchange papers and suggest additional vivid verbs. OL standing, with an electric torch in his hand.

"You've done well, Rainsford," the voice of the general called. "Your Burmese tiger pit has claimed one of my best dogs. Again you score. I think, Mr. Rainsford, I'll see what you can do against my whole pack. I'm going home for a rest now. Thank you for a most amusing evening."

At daybreak Rainsford, lying near the swamp, was awakened by a sound that made him know that he had new things to learn about fear. It was a distant sound, faint and wavering, but he knew it. It was the baying of a pack of hounds.

Rainsford knew he could do one of two things. He could stay where he was and wait. That was suicide. He could flee. That was postponing the inevitable. For a moment he stood there, thinking. An idea that held a wild chance came to him, and, tightening his belt, he headed away from the swamp.

Land's End–Cornwall, 1888. William Trost Richards. Oil on canvas, 62 × 50 in. The Butler Institute of American Art, Youngstown, Ohio.

Viewing the Art: What might it feel like to stand at the edge of cliffs like these? ★

The baying of the hounds drew nearer, then still nearer, nearer, ever nearer. On a ridge Rainsford climbed a tree. Down a watercourse, not a quarter of a mile away, he could see the bush moving. Straining his eyes, he saw the lean figure of General Zaroff; just ahead of him Rainsford made out another figure whose wide shoulders surged through the tall jungle weeds; it was the giant Ivan, and he seemed pulled forward by some unseen force; Rainsford knew that Ivan must be holding the pack in leash.

They would be on him any minute now. His mind worked frantically. He thought of a native trick he had learned in Uganda. He slid down the tree. He caught hold of a springy young sapling and to it he fastened his hunting knife, with the blade pointing down the trail; with a bit of wild grapevine he tied back the sapling. Then he ran for his life. The hounds raised their voices as they hit the fresh scent. Rainsford knew now how an animal at bay[30] feels.

He had to stop to get his breath. The baying of the hounds stopped abruptly, and Rainsford's heart stopped, too. They must have reached the knife.

He shinned excitedly up a tree and looked back. His pursuers had stopped. But the hope that was in Rainsford's brain when he climbed died, for he saw in the shallow valley that General Zaroff was still on his feet. But Ivan was not. The knife,

Literary Element Suspense *How do the short sentences add to the feeling of suspense?* L2

30. *At bay* refers to the position of a cornered animal that is forced to turn and confront its pursuers.

Teach

L2 Literary Element

Suspense **Answer:** *The short sentences speed up the pace and show how rapidly Rainsford must think. They add pressure and a feeling of panic to his decision.* OL

★ Viewing the Art

Answer: *Students may say it would feel frightening, exciting, or awe-inspiring.*

William Trost Richards (1833–1905) began drawing as a boy in Philadelphia. Though he left school to support his family, he was able to study art at the Pennsylvania Academy of Fine Arts. Many of his paintings depict the rugged coast of Cornwall, in southwestern England. Land's End, the subject of this painting, is England's southwesternmost point. AS

English Language Coach

Adverbs Remind students that the *-ly* ending often signals an adverb in English. Write examples such as "We walked quickly" and "Our flight was especially smooth" to show that the function of adverbs is to modify verbs and adjectives. Point out the adverb *frantically* on pages 39. Explain that although it adds a detail, the sentence makes sense without the adverb. Have students find at least three more adverbs and figure out their meanings from context or by analyzing word parts. EL

Academic Standards

Additional Support activities on pp. 38 and 39 cover the following standards:

Skills Practice: **9.4.3** Use precise language [and] action verbs...

English Language Coach: **9.1** Use...context clues...to determine the meaning of words...

Teach

R1 Reading Strategy

Making and Verifying Predictions About Plot

Answer: *Some students may predict his death, while others may predict that he will swim across the cove.* OL

BI Big Idea

Matters of Life and Death

Answer: *The phrase shows that Rainsford will not behave like a civilized man but rather as a beast in mortal peril; it suggests that he will show no mercy.* OL

R2 Reading Strategy

Evaluate Point out that the final fight between Rainsford and Zaroff is not described. **Ask:** Do you think this is effective? *(It is effective. The last sentence reveals the identity of the victor, but the actual fighting is left to the imagination.)* OL

★ Writer's Technique

Flash-Forward In the last sentence, the story jumps forward in time. A flash-forward is often marked by a blank line, series of asterisks, or text ornament. Connell does not mark the jump, which makes it more startling. Students may need to reread to figure out what happened. AS

driven by the recoil of the springing tree, had not wholly failed.

Rainsford had hardly tumbled to the ground when the pack took up the cry again.

"Nerve, nerve, nerve!" he panted, as he dashed along. A blue gap showed between the trees dead ahead. Ever nearer drew the hounds. Rainsford forced himself on toward that gap. He reached it. It was the shore of the sea. Across a cove he could see the gloomy gray stone of the chateau. Twenty feet below him the sea rumbled and hissed. Rainsford hesitated. He heard the hounds. Then he leaped far out into the sea. . . . R1

When the general and his pack reached the place by the sea, the Cossack stopped. For some minutes he stood regarding the blue-green expanse of water. He shrugged his shoulders. Then he sat down, took a drink of brandy from a silver flask, lit a cigarette, and hummed a bit from "Madame Butterfly."[31]

"Better luck another time."

General Zaroff had an exceedingly good dinner in his great paneled dining hall that evening. With it he had a bottle of *Pol Roger* and half a bottle of *Chambertin.* Two slight annoyances kept him from perfect enjoyment. One was the thought that it would be difficult to replace Ivan; the other was that his quarry had escaped him; of course the American hadn't played the game—so thought the general as he tasted his after-dinner liqueur. In his library he read. At ten he went up to his bedroom. He was deliciously tired, he said to himself, as he locked himself in. There was a little moonlight, so, before turning on his light, he went to the window and looked down at the courtyard. He could see the great hounds, and he called: "Better luck another time," to them. Then he switched on the light.

A man, who had been hiding in the curtains of the bed, was standing there.

"Rainsford!" screamed the general. "How in God's name did you get here?"

"Swam," said Rainsford. "I found it quicker than walking through the jungle."

The general sucked in his breath and smiled. "I congratulate you," he said. "You have won the game."

Rainsford did not smile. "I am still a beast at bay," he said in a low, hoarse voice. "Get ready, General Zaroff." BI

The general made one of his deepest bows. "I see," he said. "Splendid! One of us is to furnish a repast[32] for the hounds. The other will sleep in this very excellent bed. On guard, Rainsford. . . ." R2

He had never slept in a better bed, Rainsford decided. ★

31. *Madame Butterfly* is an Italian opera by Giacomo Puccini.

32. *Repast* means "meal" or "feast."

Reading Strategy Making and Verifying Predictions About Plot *What do you think will happen to Rainsford as a result of this jump?* R1

Big Idea Matters of Life and Death *What does the phrase "a beast at bay" suggest about Rainsford?* BI

Additional Support

Skills Practice

READING: Scanning Explain that scanning is the process of looking quickly through written material to find a specific piece of information. Readers use keywords, headings, or pictures to guide them to the information needed. Scanning is useful for answering the questions in chapter reviews or post-reading activities. Have students scan the story for answers to this question: What kind of door knocker did the general have? *(A gargoyle, p. 27)* Then have students suggest other questions and work in pairs to scan for answers. OL

AFTER YOU READ

RESPONDING AND THINKING CRITICALLY

Respond

1. Who did you think was more frightening, Ivan or General Zaroff? Explain.

Recall and Interpret

2. (a)How did Rainsford end up on Ship-Trap Island? (b)What is ironic about the comment, "All he knew was that he was safe from his enemy, the sea"?
3. (a)What solution had General Zaroff found to his problem of boredom with hunting? (b)Why is Zaroff excited to have Rainsford play his "game"?
4. (a)How did the game end? (b)What do you think Zaroff meant when he thought "the American hadn't played the game"?

Analyze and Evaluate

5. *Game* can mean both "a contest" and "an animal to be hunted." Use each definition to explain the possible meanings of the title.
6. Did Rainsford's knowledge, experience, and training as a hunter help him stay alive? Explain.
7. Did Rainsford do the right thing at the end of the story? Defend or criticize his act and explain your reasons.
8. Would you recommend this story to a friend? Why or why not?

Connect

9. **Big Idea** **Matters of Life and Death** In this story, what is the relationship between Zaroff and Rainsford, or the hunter and the hunted? Explain.

VISUAL LITERACY: Graphic Organizer

Reading a Plot Outline

The plots of most stories follow the same basic pattern; most plots include exposition, rising action that includes a conflict, climax, falling action, and resolution. However, the way each stage plays out may differ, depending on the specific story. A typical plot outline is shown here. On a separate piece of paper, modify the outline to reflect the plot of "The Most Dangerous Game." For example, you may make certain stages longer or shorter, or you may omit them altogether. Label your outline with story details so that a viewer can see which important events happen at each stage of the plot.

Group Activity Compare your plot outline with your classmates' to note similarities and dissimilarities. Then discuss the following questions:

1. What does the story gain by having a long exposition?
2. Which parts of the story contain suspense?
3. What makes the ending of this story different from many other stories?

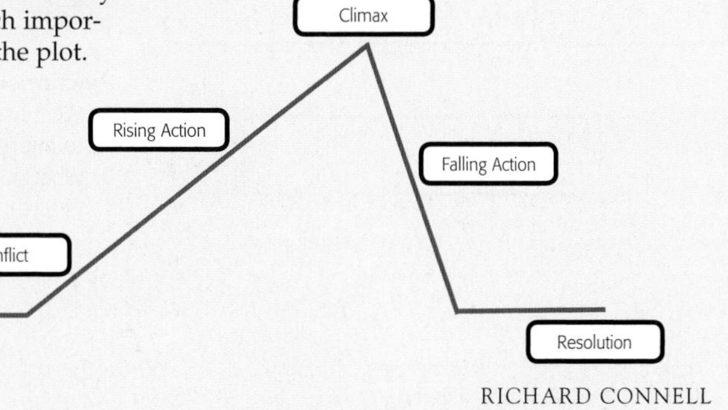

Visual Literacy

1. The long exposition builds suspense.
2. The entire story is filled with suspense.
3. The abruptness of the ending distinguishes the story. Also, the reader must infer what happened.

CheckPoint

Use the CheckPoint questions provided on Presentation Plus! to check students' mastery of the selection. These questions can be used with interactive response keypads for immediate student feedback.

AFTER YOU READ

Assess

1. Ivan: his size and skill at torture; Zaroff: his contempt for the weak, coolness in killing, and hunting skill
2. (a) He accidentally falls off a boat while passing the island. (b) The island is far more dangerous than the sea.
3. (a) Zaroff had begun to hunt men. (b) Zaroff recognizes Rainsford's experience and skill and feels challenged by the idea of hunting him.
4. (a) Rainsford, the hunted, kills Zaroff, the hunter. (b) Zaroff may have thought that Rainsford would have committed suicide rather than continue playing.
5. The contest is the "most dangerous" because the loser dies. Man is the "most dangerous" animal to hunt because man can outwit the hunter with reason.
6. Rainsford's knowledge helps because he uses tricks he had learned while hunting animals to elude and attack Zaroff.
7. Rainsford had no choice but to kill Zaroff, who would have killed him otherwise; Rainsford should have captured Zaroff and sought justice through legal means.
8. The story is worth reading. It is exciting and suspenseful.
9. Zaroff only feels alive when causing death. Rainsford can only live if Zaroff dies.

Academic Standards

The Additional Support activity on p. 40 covers the following standard:

Skills Practice: **9.2** Develop strategies such as [scanning]...

AFTER YOU READ

Assess

Literary Element

1. The superlative in the title makes readers wonder, "What is the *most* dangerous game?" The questions about what the island's name means and why sailors dread the place also add suspense.
2. Because the game occurs on an island, there is no escape. The thick, dangerous jungle and the nighttime hunting create a sense of foreboding.
3. His civilized appearance is only a veneer that hides the man's true motives and intentions. Readers are kept constantly guessing what he is up to.

Review: Conflict

External conflicts: Rainsford's struggles against the sea, the jungle, the quicksand, and Zaroff; Internal conflicts: Rainsford's battle to stay rational rather than succumb to fear; Main conflict: the life-and-death struggle between Rainsford and Zaroff; the story is driven by a combination of internal and external conflicts

Reading Strategy

1. Rainsford will try to leave the island; Rainsford will free the captives; Rainsford will stay to enjoy the chateau.

LITERARY ANALYSIS

Literary Element Suspense

Writers build **suspense** in several ways. For example, the writer may provide just enough information to keep the question "What will happen next?" burning in the reader's mind.

1. What information did the author include in the title and first three paragraphs to raise questions in readers' minds?
2. How does the setting add to the suspense? Consider not only where events take place but at what time of day.
3. In many ways, Zaroff is a very civilized person. How does the author use this characteristic to heighten the suspense of the story?

Review: Conflict

As you learned on p. 13, **conflict** is the struggle between opposing forces in a story. An external conflict exists when a character struggles against some outside force, such as another person, nature, society, or fate. An internal conflict is a struggle that takes place within a character's mind.

Partner Activity Meet with a classmate to discuss the conflicts in the story. Use a graphic like the one below to list internal and external conflicts. Create as many internal and external conflict boxes as you need. Discuss whether the story is driven primarily by internal conflicts, external conflicts, or a combination of both. Finally, identify the main conflict in the story and try to capture it in a phrase or short declarative sentence.

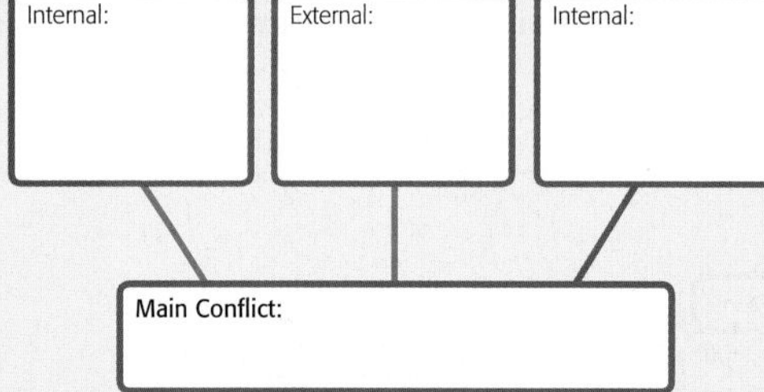

READING AND VOCABULARY

Reading Strategy Making and Verifying Predictions About Plot

Look again at the **prediction** chart that you made on page 23. How often were you correct about your predictions? Now look back at your incorrect predictions. Were there clues that you missed? Based on what you know from the story and from reviewing your predictions, consider what the future might hold in store for Rainsford.

1. The story ends abruptly. What do you think is likely to happen next?
2. What story clues support this prediction?

Vocabulary Practice

Practice with Word Origins A word's origins often give clues to its meaning. Match each vocabulary word with its corresponding origin word or word part. Use a dictionary if you need assistance.

1. tangible — a. Latin "to sift apart"
2. discern — b. Greek "ardor"
3. condone — c. Latin "to command"
4. imperative — d. Latin "to absolve"
5. zealous — e. Latin "to touch"

Academic Vocabulary

Here are two words from the vocabulary list on page R80. These words will help you think, write, and talk about the selection.

injure (in′ jər) *v.* to harm or cause bodily damage to

survey (sər vā′) *v.* to inspect or examine carefully

Practice and Apply

1. What useful bit of knowledge allows Rainsford to **injure** Zaroff?
2. What does Zaroff do after he **surveys** the water into which Rainsford leaps?

2. Rainsford's leaving: his earlier demand to leave; Freeing captives: his attitude about the value of human life and Zaroff's reference to a "training school"; Staying: comments about the beauty of the chateau and the bed's comfort

Vocabulary

1. e **2.** a **3.** d **4.** c **5.** b

Academic Vocabulary

1. Rainsford knew how to make a Malay man-catcher.
2. Zaroff sat down, had a drink and a smoke, and hummed a bit from "Madame Butterfly."

WRITING AND EXTENDING

Writing About Literature

Evaluate Author's Craft Connell often uses foreshadowing to create suspense. Foreshadowing means using text clues to hint at what will happen next. One example is the name of the island: Ship-Trap Island. The name suggests that this island may be dangerous.

Write a brief essay that evaluates the author's use of foreshadowing in the story. Begin by stating whether you think he uses the technique effectively or poorly. Relate how foreshadowing may have helped or hindered the building of suspense in the story. Support your opinion with specific examples from the story.

When you draft, follow the writing path shown here to help you organize your ideas.

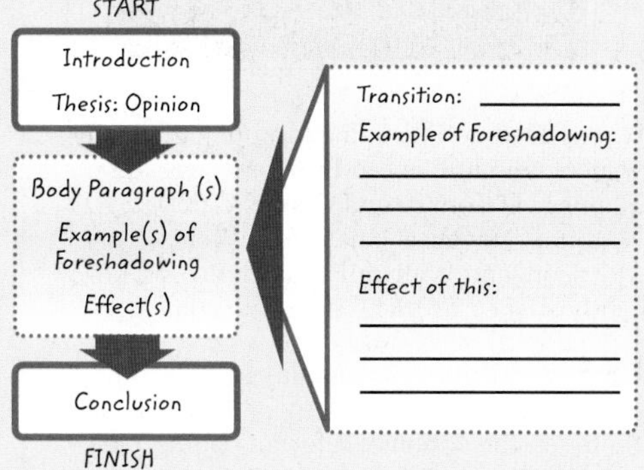

After you complete your draft, meet with a peer reviewer to evaluate each other's work and suggest revisions. Revise your draft and then proofread it for errors in spelling, grammar, and punctuation.

Interdisciplinary Activity: Mathematics

The story clearly indicates the passage of time from the opening scene to the closing scene. Create a daily schedule that lists all of the events as they occur each day and night. Use specific times when possible. Use your schedule to estimate how many hours pass from the time Rainsford falls from the ship to the time he confronts Zaroff in his bedroom. Afterward, compare your results with those of a partner and discuss any differences you notice between your schedules.

GRAMMAR AND STYLE

Connell's Language and Style

Using Dashes In "The Most Dangerous Game," Connell uses dashes to serve three different functions. He uses a dash to set off a summarizing statement from the rest of the sentence, to indicate an abrupt break in speech, and to indicate a pause in speech. The last two uses often appear in dialogue, because they make the characters' speech sound realistic.

Read these sentences from the story:

"The world is made up of two classes—the hunters and the huntees."

"But you can't mean—" gasped Rainsford.

"What I felt was a—a mental chill; a sort of sudden dread."

Scan the story for additional places where the author uses dashes. Copy the sentences in which you find them. Then note the function that the dash serves in each sentence: to set off a summary, to show an abrupt break, or to show a pause. Consider other techniques that Connell might have chosen instead, and decide why he may have chosen to use dashes in those places.

Activity Write three sentences of dialogue based on conversations that you have had recently. In your sentences, use a dash in each of the three ways described above. Try to make your dialogue sound realistic. Record your sentences and the functions of their dashes in a chart like the one below.

Sentence	Dash Function

Revising Check

Dashes Reread your essay on foreshadowing to review the punctuation. Are there places where dashes would be effective, or where you used them incorrectly? Revise accordingly.

Web Activities For eFlashcards, Selection Quick Checks, and other Web activities, go to www.glencoe.com.

AFTER YOU READ

Assess

Writing About Literature

Use these criteria when evaluating students' writing. Does the essay

- offer an opinion about how well or poorly the author used foreshadowing?
- relate how foreshadowing helped build suspense?
- contain specific examples from the story to support the opinion?
- contain an introduction and conclusion?

Interdisciplinary Activity

Students should determine that four nights and four days (about 96 hours) pass from the time Rainsford falls in the water until he appears in Zaroff's bedroom.

Connell's Language and Style

Students' dialogues should include at least three examples of dashes. Their charts should include a clear explanation of how each dash functions.

Revising Check

Remind students that dashes often function like commas or parentheses to set aside a piece of optional text. As they revise, urge students to read aloud and listen for places where pauses indicate an opportunity to add nonessential details.

Literature Online

Web Activities Have students access the Web site for interactive activities that will help them assess their understanding of the selection.

BEFORE YOU READ

Focus

BELLRINGER

Bellringer Options

Selection Focus Transparency 3
Daily Language Practice Transparency 5

Or obtain a copy of the painting *The Circus* by Georges Seurat. Have students study it and then discuss circus acts and the courage they require.

Ask: What do you think motivates people to take great risks, physical or otherwise? *(Students may mention a desire for fame, to save a loved one, or to feel excitement.)* Have students consider as they read what compels the narrator's mother toward heroism and how her heroism affects the narrator.

Author Search To expand students' appreciation of Louise Erdrich, have them access the Web site for additional information and resources.

BEFORE YOU READ

The Leap

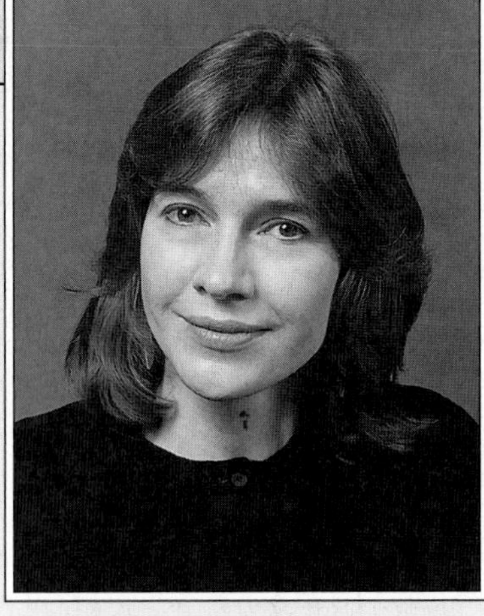

MEET LOUISE ERDRICH

Storytelling is as natural as breathing for Louise Erdrich. Part Chippewa, she attributes her passion for writing to her Native American roots.

Growing Up The oldest of seven children, Erdrich was born in Minnesota and raised in North Dakota, where both of her parents worked for the Bureau of Indian Affairs. Her father, of German descent, and her mother, born on the Turtle Mountain Ojibwe (Chippewa) Reservation, both encouraged her early writing efforts. Her father rewarded her by paying her five cents for each story she wrote, and her mother affirmed her daughter's talent by creating book covers for the stories.

Erdrich was one of the first women admitted to Dartmouth University, where she continued to write and where she also met her future husband, Michael Dorris, a professor of Native American Studies. She and Dorris became successful literary collaborators, as well as parents to six children. They also became well-known and respected voices of Native American culture.

"All of our searches involve trying to discover where we are from."

—Louise Erdrich

Genres and Influences While some of Erdrich's earliest published work is poetry, her writing falls into a wide range of genres. Her novels, which include *Love Medicine* and *The Beet Queen*, were bestsellers as well as critical successes. Her short stories appear in numerous collections and her essays are also widely read and acclaimed. Among the many writers who influenced Erdrich's work are Flannery O'Connor and Gabriel García Márquez. Novelists Jane Austen, Toni Morrison, and William Faulkner also significantly shaped Erdrich's style and content.

Themes Erdrich often employs Native American themes, and many of her stories center on the notion of returning home. One of her most important themes is personal identity, both within the family and within the culture. She writes often, as she does in "The Leap," about women's personal power and the sacred struggle of mothers.

Erdrich is the recipient of several prizes for her writing, including the Pushcart Prize for poetry and the National Book Critics Circle Award for fiction. Today, Erdrich continues to write and lives with her daughters in Minnesota, where she runs a small bookstore.

Louise Erdrich was born in 1954.

Literature Online **Author Search** For more about Louise Erdrich, go to www.glencoe.com.

44 UNIT 1 THE SHORT STORY

Selection Skills

The Leap

Literary Elements
- Flashback (SE pp. 45–53)
- Setting (SE p. 53)

Reading Skills
- Sequence (SE pp. 45–54; TWE p. 51)

Vocabulary Skills
- Word Parts (SE p. 54)
- Academic Vocabulary (SE p. 54)
- Idioms (TWE p. 49)

Listening/Speaking/Viewing Skills
- Learning for Life (SE p. 54)
- Analyzing Art (SE p. 51; TWE pp. 46, 49)

Writing Skills/Grammar
- Writing About Literature (SE p. 54)
- Infinitive Phrases (TWE p. 50)
- Compare and Contrast (SE p. 54)

LITERATURE PREVIEW

Connecting to the Story

At two different times in this story, the narrator's mother faces a situation in which someone's life is in imminent danger. Both times, she chooses to make a courageous leap. Before you read the story, think about the following questions:

- What personal qualities does it require to take a "leap" against great odds?
- Does the kind of leap the mother takes occur only in stories, or could it happen in real life?

Building Background

This story is set at a time when many of today's safety standards did not exist. In the past, most circus troupes performed in huge canvas tents that they carried around with them as they traveled from town to town. The canvas, however, like the sawdust that covered the dirt floors of the circus ring, was flammable, and circus tents sometimes became the scenes of terrible fires. In addition, many trapeze and high-wire performers did not use safety nets or belts during their acts.

Setting Purposes for Reading

Big Idea Matters of Life and Death

As you read, notice who or what in this story dies—and who or what is given new life. Consider how closely death and life are bound together as each part of the story unfolds.

Literary Element Flashback

A **flashback** is an interruption in the chronological order of the narrative to show an event that happened earlier. A flashback gives readers information that may help explain the main events of a story. As you read "The Leap," identify the main flashbacks and think about how the author uses them to deepen the intensity of the story.

- See Literary Terms Handbook, p. R7.

LiteratureOnline Interactive Literary Elements Handbook To review or learn more about the literary elements, go to www.glencoe.com.

READING PREVIEW

Reading Strategy Identifying Sequence

Identifying sequence is finding the logical order of ideas or events. Understanding the logical sequence of ideas in a piece helps you follow a writer's train of thought. As you read "The Leap," think about why the author may have chosen to present the events in the sequence that she did.

Reading Tip: Making a Sequence Chain Create a sequence chain to show the main events in the order they are presented in this story. Note that your chain will not show chronological order.

Narrator, sitting in her childhood home, has a sudden memory caused by . . .

↓

The newspaper article tells the story of the weather on that day, saying . . .

↓

The Avalons' circus act comes to an end when . . .

Vocabulary

commemorate (kə mem′ ə rāt′) *v.* to preserve the memory of; p. 47 *I chose to commemorate my grandfather's life by researching his past.*

extricate (eks′ trə kāt′) *v.* to release from entanglement or difficulty; to set free; p. 48 *John worked hard to extricate the animal from the trap.*

constricting (kən strikt′ ing) *adj.* restricting; limiting; p. 50 *The tiny space was constricting for the large man.*

perpetually (pər pech′ o͞o əl ē) *adv.* constantly; unceasingly; p. 50 *The busy waiters were perpetually moving from table to table.*

tentative (ten′ tə tiv) *adj.* hesitant; uncertain; p. 52 *The mother was thrilled when her toddler took her first tentative steps.*

INDIANA ACADEMIC STANDARDS (pages 45–54)

9.3.6 Analyze and trace an author's development of time and sequence, including the use of complex literary devices, such as...flashbacks...

9.2 Develop strategies such as...identifying and analyzing structure...

9.5.3 Write expository compositions...

BEFORE YOU READ

Focus

Summary

The narrator is living in her childhood home with her blind, elderly mother. She states that she owes her life to her mother three times. The first was before her own birth, when her mother survived a circus accident. While recovering in the hospital, her mother met a doctor whom she married. The narrator's birth is the second time her mother ensured her existence. On the third occasion, the narrator is a child trapped inside her burning home. Her mother leaps to the window from a tree and saves her.

V Vocabulary

Vocabulary File Say: Add these words and definitions to your vocabulary file. For each word, include a sentence that gives you an example of how to use the word. **OL** Students with English language needs should include the pronunciations of these words in their files. **EL**

Literary Elements Have students access the Web site to improve their understanding of flashback.

Selection Resources

Print Materials

- Unit 1 Resources (Fast File), pp. 23–25
- Leveled Vocabulary Development, p. 3
- Selection and Unit Assessments, pp. 5–6
- Selection Quick Checks, p. 3

Transparencies

- Bellringer Options Transparencies: Selection Focus Transparency 3, Daily Language Practice Transparency 5
- Literary Elements Transparency 37

Technology

- TeacherWorks Plus™ CD-ROM
- StudentWorks Plus™ CD-ROM
- Presentation Plus!™ CD-ROM
- Literature Online, glencoe.com
- Online Student Edition, mhln.com
- Exam*View*® Assessment Suite CD-ROM
- Vocabulary PuzzleMaker CD-ROM
- Listening Library, disc 1 track 3

Teach

BI1 **Big Idea**

Matters of Life and Death

Say: Keep these questions in mind as you read: How is the narrator's approach to life and death different from her mother's? *(It is measured and logical, whereas her mother's is instinctive and emotional.)* How are the two approaches the same? *(Both people want to live.)* **OL**

★ Viewing the Art

Marc Chagall (1887–1985) was born and grew up in Russia. He later lived in Paris and the United States. Chagall's work includes stage sets, a skill reflected in this painting's strong sense of place. The story's vividly described setting is suggested by the painting. **AS**

Readability Scores

Dale-Chall: 6.4

DRP: 64

Lexile: 1260

THE LEAP

Louise Erdrich

BI1 My mother is the surviving half of a blindfold trapeze act, not a fact I think about much even now that she is sightless, the result of encroaching and stubborn cataracts. She walks slowly through her house here in New Hampshire, lightly touching her way along walls and running her hands over knickknacks, books, the drift of a grown child's belongings and castoffs.

Au Cirque, 1976. Marc Chagall. Oil on canvas, 48 × 43¼ in. Private collection. ★

Additional Support

Academic Standards

The Additional Support activity on p. 46 covers the following standard:

Skills Practice: **9.3** [Identify] story elements such as…plot…

Skills Practice

READING: Cause and Effect

Remind students that causes make events happen, and effects are the results that occur. Clarify that events that occur in sequence may or may not be linked by cause and effect. In this story, the narrator says she is alive *because* of her mother's actions on three occasions. Have students use a cause-and-effect chart to trace this pattern as they read. Then discuss whether they agree with the narrator. **OL**

Cause	Effect

She has never upset an object or as much as brushed a magazine onto the floor. She has never lost her balance or bumped into a closet door left carelessly open.

It has occurred to me that the catlike precision of her movements in old age might be the result of her early training, but she shows so little of the drama or flair one might expect from a performer that I tend to forget the Flying Avalons. She has kept no sequined costume, no photographs, no fliers or posters from that part of her youth. I would, in fact, tend to think that all memory of double somersaults and heart-stopping catches had left her arms and legs were it not for the fact that sometimes, as I sit sewing in the room of the rebuilt house in which I slept as a child, I hear the crackle, catch a whiff of smoke from the stove downstairs, and suddenly the room goes dark, the stitches burn beneath my fingers, and I am sewing with a needle of hot silver, a thread of fire.

I owe her my existence three times. The first was when she saved herself. In the town square a replica tent pole, cracked and splintered, now stands cast in concrete. It **commemorates** the disaster that put our town smack on the front page of the Boston and New York tabloids.[1] It is from those old newspapers, now historical records, that I get my information. Not from my mother, Anna of the Flying Avalons, nor from any of her in-laws, nor certainly from the other half of her particular act, Harold Avalon, her first husband. In one news account it says, "The day was mildly overcast, but nothing in the air or temperature gave any hint of the sudden force with which the deadly gale would strike."

I have lived in the West, where you can see the weather coming for miles, and it is true that out here we are at something of a disadvantage. When extremes of temperature collide, a hot and cold front, winds generate instantaneously behind a hill and crash upon you without warning. That, I think, was the likely situation on that day in June. People probably commented on the pleasant air, grateful that no hot sun beat upon the striped tent that stretched over the entire center green. They bought their tickets and surrendered them in anticipation. They sat. They ate caramelized popcorn and roasted peanuts. There was time, before the storm, for three acts. The White Arabians of Ali-Khazar rose on their hind legs and waltzed. The Mysterious Bernie folded himself into a painted cracker tin, and the Lady of the Mists made herself appear and disappear in surprising places. As the clouds gathered outside, unnoticed, the ringmaster cracked his whip, shouted his introduction, and pointed to the ceiling of the tent, where the Flying Avalons were perched.

They loved to drop gracefully from nowhere, like two sparkling birds, and blow kisses as they threw off their plumed helmets and high-collared capes. They laughed and flirted openly as they beat their way up again on the trapeze bars. In the final vignette[2] of their act, they actually would kiss in midair, pausing, almost hovering as they swooped past one another. On the ground, between bows, Harry Avalon would skip quickly to the front rows and point out the smear of my mother's lipstick, just off the edge of his mouth. They made a romantic pair all right, especially in the blindfold sequence.

1. Here, *tabloids* are newspapers with pages half the size of an ordinary newspaper page. They contain brief news articles and many pictures.

2. A *vignette* (vin yet′) is a short scene, sketch, or incident.

Big Idea Matters of Life and Death *What might be the three reasons the narrator owes her life to her mother?* **BI2**

Reading Strategy Identifying Sequence *How is the narrator going to order the events of the story? How do you know?* **R**

Vocabulary

commemorate (kə mem′ ə rāt′) *v.* to preserve the memory of

Literary Element Flashback *How does this sentence serve as a transition from the narrator's present thoughts to her description of an event in the past?* **L**

Teach

BI2 Big Idea

Matters of Life and Death
Answer: *Most students will say that her mother gave birth to her. Accept other reasonable answers.* **OL**

R Reading Strategy

Identifying Sequence
Answer: *The narrator is going to describe the three events in chronological order. The phrase "the first time" is a clue.* **OL**

L Literary Element

Flashback **Answer:** *She describes what she now thinks the day in the past was like. This gives a smooth link from present to past.* **OL**

★ Cultural History

United States Climate
People in the western United States can see storms coming because flat, open spaces make the sky visible. In the East, hills, trees, and buildings block views of the sky. **AS**

CheckPoint

Use the CheckPoint questions on Presentation Plus! to monitor students' comprehension. These questions can be used with interactive response keypads for immediate student feedback.

English Language Coach

Build Background Share the Cultural History on page 47 with students, pointing out regions on a U.S. map. Then have English learners describe the landscape in their home country. Help students contrast: How easy is it to see the approaching weather in different places? **EL**

Reading in the Real World

Careers Have students find and read information about the work of a circus entertainer, firefighter, or physician. Invite them to share their findings briefly. Then ask them to explain how these jobs are similar; for example, each involves assuming responsibility for others' lives. **OL**

Academic Standards

Additional Support activities on p. 47 cover the following standards:

English Language Coach: **9.3** [Identify] story elements such as…setting, and make connections and comparisons…

Reading in the Real World: **9.2.4** Synthesize the content from several sources…

Teach

BI1 Big Idea

Matters of Life and Death
Answer: *The two will never kiss again because they will be separated forever by death.* OL

R Reading Strategy

Identifying Sequence
Answer: *It was in the past ("once said") but after the narrator was born.* OL

★ Writer's Technique

Motif A motif is a significant word, description, idea, or image that is repeated throughout a literary work and is related to its theme. In this story, Erdrich uses blindness as a motif. AS

That afternoon, as the anticipation increased, as Mr. and Mrs. Avalon tied sparkling strips of cloth onto each other's face and as they puckered their lips in mock kisses, lips destined "never again to meet," as one long breathless article put it, the wind rose, miles off, wrapped itself into a cone, and howled. There came a rumble of electrical energy, drowned out by the sudden roll of drums. One detail not mentioned by the press, perhaps unknown—Anna was pregnant at the time, seven months and hardly showing, her stomach muscles were that strong. It seems incredible that she would work high above the ground when any fall could be so dangerous, but the explanation—I know from watching her go blind—is that my mother lives comfortably in extreme elements. She is one with the constant dark now, just as the air was her home, familiar to her, safe, before the storm that afternoon.

From opposite ends of the tent they waved, blind and smiling, to the crowd below. The ringmaster removed his hat and called for silence, so that the two above could concentrate. They rubbed their hands in chalky powder, then Harry launched himself and swung, once, twice, in huge calibrated[3] beats across space. He hung from his knees and on the third swing stretched wide his arms, held his hands out to receive his pregnant wife as she dove from her shining bar.

It was while the two were in midair, their hands about to meet, that lightning struck the main pole and sizzled down the guy wires,[4] filling the air with a blue radiance that Harry Avalon must certainly have seen through the cloth of his blindfold as the tent buckled and the edifice[5] toppled him forward, the swing continuing and not returning in its sweep, and Harry going down, down into the crowd with his last thought, perhaps, just a prickle of surprise at his empty hands.

My mother once said that I'd be amazed at how many things a person can do within the act of falling. Perhaps, at the time, she was teaching me to dive off a board at the town pool, for I associate the idea with midair somersaults. But I also think she meant that even in that awful doomed second one could think, for she certainly did. When her hands did not meet her husband's, my mother tore her blindfold away. As he swept past her on the wrong side, she could have grasped his ankle, the toe-end of his tights, and gone down clutching him. Instead, she changed direction. Her body twisted toward a heavy wire and she managed to hang on to the braided metal, still hot from the lightning strike. Her palms were burned so terribly that once healed they bore no lines, only the blank scar tissue of a quieter future. She was lowered, gently, to the sawdust ring just underneath the dome of the canvas roof, which did not entirely settle but was held up on one end and jabbed through, torn, and still on fire in places from the giant spark, though rain and men's jackets soon put that out.

Three people died, but except for her hands my mother was not seriously harmed until an overeager rescuer broke her arm in **extricating** her and also, in the process, collapsed a portion of the tent bearing a huge buckle that knocked her unconscious. She was taken to the town hospital, and there she must have hemorrhaged,[6] for they kept her, confined to her bed,

3. Here, *calibrated* means "precisely timed and measured."
4. A *guy* is a rope, cord, or cable used for steadying, guiding, or holding something. In this case, *guy wires* hold the main pole of the tent steady.
5. An *edifice* is a building or other structure (here, the tent), especially a large, impressive one.
6. To *hemorrhage* (hem′ ər ij) is to bleed heavily or excessively—in this case, probably because of internal injuries.

Big Idea Matters of Life and Death *What is the meaning of the quote from the newspaper article?* BI1

Reading Strategy Identifying Sequence *Where would you place the conversation the narrator mentions here within the chronology of events described in the story so far?* R

Vocabulary

extricate (eks′ trə kāt′) *v.* to release from entanglement or difficulty; to set free

Additional Support

Skills Practice

RESEARCH: Develop Questions

Say: Answering questions beginning with *who, what,* and *when* can help you learn more about circus history, while answering questions beginning with *why* and *how* can help you analyze information. Have groups develop research questions about circus history. Offer these ideas:

- *Where* and *when* did circuses begin?
- *When* did they come to the United States?
- *How* have circuses changed over time?

Have groups share their questions. OL Challenge students to research the answer to one question. AL a month and a half before her baby was born without life.

Harry Avalon had wanted to be buried in the circus cemetery next to the original Avalon, his uncle, so she sent him back with his brothers. The child, however, is buried around the corner, beyond this house and just down **L** the highway. Sometimes I used to walk there just to sit. She was a girl, but I rarely thought of her as a sister or even as a separate person really. I suppose you could call it the egocentrism[7] of a child, of all young children, but I considered her a less finished version of myself.

When the snow falls, throwing shadows among the stones, I can easily pick hers out from the road, for it is bigger than the others and in the shape of a lamb at rest, its legs curled beneath. The carved lamb looms larger as the years pass, though it is probably only my eyes, the vision shifting, as what is close to me blurs and distances sharpen. In odd moments, I think it is the edge drawing near, the edge of everything, the unseen horizon we do not really speak of in the eastern woods. And it also seems to me, although this is probably an idle fantasy, that the statue is growing more sharply etched, as if, instead of weathering itself into a porous mass, it is hardening on the hillside with each snowfall, perfecting itself.

Au Nouveau Cirque, Papa Chrysanthème. After Henri de Toulouse-Lautrec. 1894–95. Louis Comfort Tiffany. Musée d'Orsay, Paris, France. ★

It was during her confinement in the hospital that my mother met my father. He was called in to look at the set of her arm, which was complicated. He stayed, sitting at her bedside, for he was something of an armchair traveler and had spent his war quietly, at an air force training grounds, where he became a specialist in arms and legs broken during parachute training exercises. Anna Avalon had been to many of the places he longed to visit—Venice, Rome, Mexico, all through France and Spain. She had no family of her own and was taken in by the Avalons, trained to perform from a very young age. They toured Europe before the war, then based themselves in New York. She was illiterate.

It was in the hospital that she finally learned to read and write, as a way of overcoming the boredom and depression of those weeks, and it was my father who insisted on teaching her. In

7. *Egocentrism* means "self-centeredness."

Big Idea Matters of Life and Death *What is the "unseen horizon" that the narrator mentions?* **BI2**

Teach

L Literary Element

Characterization Discuss techniques the author uses to characterize the narrator. Note the first-person point of view. **Ask:** How does this affect characterization? *(The reader's idea of the main character is based on the narrator's own thoughts.)* How would you describe the narrator? *(She is introspective, sensitive, and analytical. She is loving and appreciates her mother's love.)* **OL**

BI2 Big Idea

Matters of Life and Death
Answer: *Students should infer that the unseen horizon is death.* **OL**

★ Viewing the Art

French artist Henri de Toulouse-Lautrec (1864–1901) is known for his paintings of residents of the Montmartre area of Paris at the end of the nineteenth century. This is one of his works done in stained glass by Louis Comfort Tiffany (1848–1933), an American artist known for his work in that medium. **AS**

English Language Coach

Idioms Point out the phrase "armchair traveler" in the paragraph beginning "It was during her confinement . . ." on page 49.
Ask: Can people literally travel in an armchair? If not, what meaning does the phrase have? *(No; the phrase describes a person who reads and dreams about traveling while staying at home.)* Encourage students to keep a list of English idioms or figures of speech that cannot be taken literally. Have them draw a cartoon or use another clue to help them remember the meaning of each. **EL**

Academic Standards

Additional Support activities on pp. 48 and 49 cover the following standards:

Skills Practice: **9.2.3** Generate relevant questions about readings on...topics that can be researched.

English Language Coach: **9.3.7** Recognize and understand the significance of various literary devices, including figurative language...

Teach

L1 Literary Element

Character Point out the narrator's descriptions of her father, beginning with "Once my father and mother . . ." and include the cause of the fire. **Ask:** What is the father like? *(He is devoted to his wife—willing to ignore his own desires to live as she chooses—absent-minded, and hardworking.)* **OL**

R Reading Strategy

Identifying Sequence
Answer: *The narrator continues to present the past events in chronological order. The second time is the event she has just described: her parents' meeting at the hospital.* **OL**

L2 Literary Element

Flashback **Answer:** *This shows the importance of the circus episode in her life.* **OL**

return for stories of her adventures, he graded her first exercises. He bought her her first book, and over her bold letters, which the pale guides of the penmanship pads could not contain, they fell in love.

I wonder if my father calculated the exchange he offered: one form of flight for another. For after that, and for as long as I can remember, my mother has never been without a book. Until now, that is, and it remains the greatest difficulty of her blindness. Since my father's recent death, there is no one to read to her, which is why I returned, in fact, from my failed life where the land is flat. I came home to read to my mother, to read out loud, to read long into the dark if I must, to read all night.

L1 Once my father and mother married, they moved onto the old farm he had inherited but didn't care much for. Though he'd been thinking of moving to a larger city, he settled down and broadened his practice in this valley. It still seems odd to me, when they could have gone anywhere else, that they chose to stay in the town where the disaster had occurred, and which my father in the first place had found so **constricting.** It was my mother who insisted upon it, after her child did not survive. And then, too, she loved the sagging farmhouse with its scrap of what was left of a vast acreage of woods and hidden hay fields that stretched to the game park.

I owe my existence, the second time then, to the two of them and the hospital that brought them together. That is the debt we take for granted since none of us asks for life. It is only once we have it that we hang on so dearly.

I was seven the year the house caught fire, probably from standing ash. It can rekindle, and my father, forgetful around the house and **perpetually** exhausted from night hours on call, often emptied what he thought were ashes from cold stoves into wooden or cardboard containers. The fire could have started from a flaming box, or perhaps a buildup of creosote inside the chimney was the culprit.[8] It started right around the stove, and the heart of the house was gutted. The babysitter, fallen asleep in my father's den on the first floor, woke to find the stairway to my upstairs room cut off by flames. She used the phone, then ran outside to stand beneath my window.

When my parents arrived, the town volunteers had drawn water from the fire pond and were spraying the outside of the house, preparing to go inside after me, not knowing at the time that there was only one staircase and that it was lost. On the other side of the house, the superannuated[9] extension ladder broke in half. Perhaps the clatter of it falling against the walls woke me, for I'd been asleep up to that point.

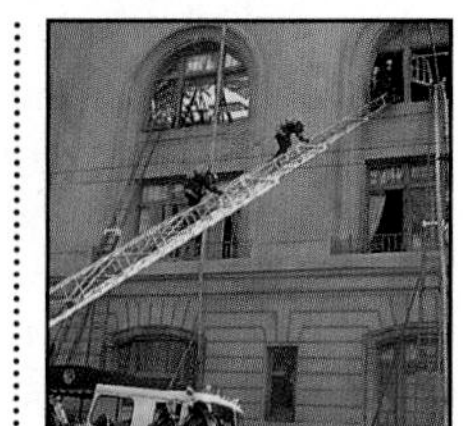

Visual Vocabulary An *extension ladder* has two or more sections joined together by a sliding mechanism that allows the ladder to be extended to its total length.

As soon as I awakened, in the small room that I now use for sewing, I smelled the smoke. I followed things by the letter then, was good at memorizing instructions, and so I did exactly what was taught in the second-grade home fire drill. I got up, I touched the back of my door before opening it. Finding it hot, I left it closed and stuffed my rolled-up rug beneath the crack. I did not hide under

Reading Strategy Identifying Sequence *How do the words "second time" remind you of the sequence in the story, and to what do they refer?* **R**

Vocabulary

constricting (kən strikt′ ing) *adj.* restricting; limiting

perpetually (pər pech′ o͞o əl ē) *adv.* constantly; unceasingly

8. *Creosote* (krē′ ə sōt′), an oily liquid that comes from the tar in wood and coal, would be a natural suspect as the *culprit,* or guilty party, in a chimney fire.
9. Something that is *superannuated* has been set aside as too old and out-of-date to use.

Literary Element Flashback *The author links this flashback to earlier details of the setting that launched her retelling of the circus episode. Why might she have done this?* **L2**

Additional Support

Skills Practice

GRAMMAR: Infinitive Phrases
Point out the sentence that begins "I came home to read to my mother . . ." **Say:** This sentence consists of a series of infinitive phrases: the infinitive form of the verb, plus *to.* An infinitive can be used in a sentence as a noun, an adjective, or an adverb. Remind students not to confuse infinitive phrases with prepositional phrases beginning with *to*, as in "to my mother." **OL** Challenge students to look for examples of infinitive phrases in the story. Have them tell whether the infinitive phrases are used as nouns, adjectives, or adverbs. **AL**

La Maternité, 1901. Pablo Picasso. Oil on burlap. Private collection.

Viewing the Art: How does this painting reflect the relationship of the mother and the daughter in the story? ★

Teach

★ Viewing the Art

Answer: *The painting portrays the love, warmth, and security that the mother in the story provides for her daughter.*

Pablo Picasso (1881–1973), one of the foremost painters of the twentieth century, adopted many different artistic styles in his career. Here, his work mirrors the story: the mother and child are depicted realistically, but the background, like the story setting, is perhaps a bit fantastical. AS

Differentiated Instruction

Sequence Less proficient readers may struggle with the flashbacks and time jumps in the narrative. Urge them to use a chronological sequence chain. This will help students stay oriented to the story sequence. BL

Reading in the Real World

Citizenship Newspapers often feature stories of daring rescues such as the one described in the story. Often the hero is a citizen inspired to help a stranger. Have students find and read such a story and then write a brief character description of the hero at its center. OL

Academic Standards

Additional Support activities on pp. 50 and 51 cover the following standards:

Skills Practice: **9.6.1** Identify...phrases, including...infinitive...

Differentiated Instruction: **9.3.6** Analyze and trace an author's development of time and sequence, including the use of...flashbacks...

Reading in the Real World: **9.5.1** Write biographical...narratives...that describe with specific details...the specific actions, movements, gestures, and feelings of the characters...

Teach

R Reading Strategy

Identifying Sequence
Answer: *1. Her mother asks her father to unzip her dress. 2. Her mother tears off her dress. 3. Her mother asks a man to lean the ladder against the tree. 4. He does so. 5. She climbs the ladder and then the tree.* OL

L Literary Element

Flashback **Answer:** *The change in verb tense indicates the end of the flashback as does the use of the word "then" in the second sentence to indicate the past.* OL

★ Language History

Outdated Terms The narrator's mother wears "drawers." These are ladies' undergarments that have legs almost to the knee. They may be narrow or wide, fancy or plain. AS

my bed or crawl into my closet. I put on my flannel robe, and then I sat down to wait.

Outside, my mother stood below my dark window and saw clearly that there was no rescue. Flames had pierced one side wall, and the glare of the fire lighted the massive limbs and trunk of the vigorous old elm that had probably been planted the year the house was built, a hundred years ago at least. No leaf touched the wall, and just one thin branch scraped the roof. From below, it looked as though even a squirrel would have had trouble jumping from the tree onto the house, for the breadth of that small branch was no bigger than my mother's wrist.

Standing there, beside Father, who was preparing to rush back around to the front of the house, my mother asked him to unzip her dress. When he wouldn't be bothered, she made him understand. He couldn't make his hands work, so she finally tore it off and stood there in her pearls and stockings. She directed one of the men to lean the broken half of the extension ladder up against the trunk of the tree. In surprise, he complied. She ascended. She vanished. Then she could be seen among the leafless branches of late November as she made her way up and, along her stomach, inched the length of a bough that curved above the branch that brushed the roof.

Once there, swaying, she stood and balanced. There were plenty of people in the crowd and many who still remember, or think they do, my mother's leap through the ice-dark air toward that thinnest extension, and how she broke the branch falling so that it cracked in her hands, cracked louder than the flames as she vaulted with it toward the edge of the roof, and how it hurtled down end over end without her, and their eyes went up, again, to see where she had flown.

I didn't see her leap through air, only heard the sudden thump and looked out my window. She was hanging by the backs of her heels from the new gutter we had put in that year, and she was smiling. I was not surprised to see her, she was so matter-of-fact. She tapped on the window. I remember how she did it, too. It was the friendliest tap, a bit **tentative,** as if she was afraid she had arrived too early at a friend's house. Then she gestured at the latch, and when I opened the window she told me to raise it wider and prop it up with the stick so it wouldn't crush her fingers. She swung down, caught the ledge, and crawled through the opening. Once she was in my room, I realized she had on only underclothing, a bra of the heavy stitched cotton women used to wear and step-in, lace-trimmed drawers. I remember feeling light-headed, of course, terribly relieved, and then embarrassed for her to be seen by the crowd undressed. ★

I was still embarrassed as we flew out the window, toward earth, me in her lap, her toes pointed as we skimmed toward the painted target of the fire fighter's net.

I know that she's right. I knew it even then. As you fall there is time to think. Curled as I was, against her stomach, I was not startled by the cries of the crowd or the looming faces. The wind roared and beat its hot breath at our back, the flames whistled. I slowly wondered what would happen if we missed the circle or bounced out of it. Then I wrapped my hands around my mother's hands. I felt the brush of her lips and heard the beat of her heart in my ears, loud as thunder, long as the roll of drums. ∾

Reading Strategy Identifying Sequence *Restate the sequence of events presented in this paragraph in your own words.* R

Literary Element Flashback *How do you know that the flashback is over?* L

Vocabulary
tentative (ten′ tə tiv) *adj.* hesitant; uncertain

Additional Support

The Additional Support activity on p. 52 covers the following standard:

Skills Practice: **9.3** [Identify] story elements such as character [and] theme…

Skills Practice

LITERARY ELEMENT: Theme Explain that theme is the main idea of a literary work, and it is often revealed gradually through plot, character, setting, imagery, and so on. In this story the narrator repeatedly mentions her mother's blindness and also refers to her own vision on page 49.

Ask: What do you think these references to vision suggest about the story's themes? *(The characters see clearly what they need to see, despite obstacles to literal sight. One theme might be that we see each other more clearly when we have some distance, perhaps created by age or blindness.)* OL

AFTER YOU READ

RESPONDING AND THINKING CRITICALLY

Respond

1. What do you think is the most dramatic event in this story? Give details to explain your choice.

Recall and Interpret

2. (a)What caused the disaster at the circus, and what happened to the Flying Avalons? (b)In your opinion, why didn't the mother save her costume or anything related to this period in her life?
3. (a)What happened to the narrator when she was seven? (b)What comparisons do you think the narrator would make between her life and her mother's? Provide evidence from the story to substantiate your claims.
4. (a)To what event or events in this story does the title refer? (b)To what, besides events in the story, might the title refer?

Analyze and Evaluate

5. How effective is the author at capturing the reader's attention with the opening passage of this story? Explain.
6. Is the mother primarily characterized by her words or by her actions? Support your answer with details from the story.
7. (a)What is the narrator's attitude toward her dead half-sister and how does it change over time? (b)What does information about this sibling add to the message of the story?

Connect

8. **Big Idea** **Matters of Life and Death** Both the narrator and her mother reacted to matters of life and death in this story. Did you find their reactions realistic? Explain.

LITERARY ANALYSIS

Literary Element Flashback

A **flashback** can take the form of an earlier event, a prior conversation, or a complete episode. Flashbacks help the reader understand characters as well as events. Often presented as a memory of the narrator, a flashback may be sparked by one or more cues, such as a sound or odor associated with a prior experience or a visit to a related setting.

1. How do a sound, an odor, and a certain setting work together to spark the narrator's memory at the beginning of "The Leap"?
2. What other sensory details help to reveal the similarities between the two main flashbacks in the story?
3. Which of her mother's character traits were displayed throughout the narrator's flashbacks? How did the author's choice to use flashbacks help to better portray these traits? Give reasons for your opinion.

Review: Setting

As you learned on pages 10–11, **setting** is the time and place in which the events of a literary work occur. Setting includes not only the physical surroundings, but also the ideas, customs, values, and beliefs of a particular time and place. Setting often helps create a work's mood.

Partner Activity Work with a classmate to record details of the setting. Create a chart like this one and complete it with details from the story.

	Times	Places
Past		
Present		

Literary Element

1. They remind the narrator of her rescue from the fire.
2. The stitches that burn the narrator's fingers, the mother's burned hands; the mother's grace in the circus, her rescue of the narrator; the falls of the unborn child and narrator, both held by the mother
3. Resilience, strength, grace, intuitiveness, balance, devotion; The reader sees the traits in action so they seem more real.

AFTER YOU READ

Assess

1. The circus event (the risky trapeze act and fierce storm); the rescue (deadly fire, amazing leap)
2. (a) Lightning hit the pole, sending Harry to his death. Anna saved herself. (b) She wanted to forget the death of her husband and baby.
3. (a) She was trapped inside her burning house. (b) Their lives seemed miraculous and dramatic; both survived deadly events.
4. (a) The mother's first leap to save herself and the one to save her daughter (b) A leap of faith, such as the mother's courage in starting a new life and the daughter's faith that her mother would save her
5. Its unusual details stimulate the reader's interest.
6. Actions; her grace and balance, rather than her words, are emphasized.
7. (a) The sister seems unreal at first but later becomes a more definite presence. (b) As people age, they can visualize death more clearly.
8. Their calm attitude was realistic. The mother was trained to take great risks; a child might not appreciate the danger she faced or the finality of death.

Review: Setting

Past: Time: Unnamed past—narrator's childhood and before; **Place:** Circus tent; Hospital; Cemetery; Burning house; **Present: Time:** Unnamed present—narrator's adulthood; **Place:** New Hampshire farmhouse—sewing room that was the narrator's childhood bedroom

AFTER YOU READ

Assess

Reading Strategy

1. Chronological: the circus fire; Nonchronological: the narrator recalling the smell of smoke; Chronological: the narrator's recollections; Nonchronological: the rescue of the narrator at age seven
2. Answers will vary: The flashback sequence is more interesting because it builds a detailed picture of the mother through dramatic events and weaves events together in unpredictable ways to surprise the reader.

Vocabulary

1. a **2.** c **3.** b **4.** a **5.** c

Academic Vocabulary

Students should point to specific details, such as her growing love for the doctor who was caring for her in the hospital, as well as her desire to learn to read and write.

Writing About Literature

Students' essays should

- clearly identify the similarities and differences between the two events
- use a logical organization to present similarities and differences
- include an introduction with a clearly stated thesis and a conclusion that summarizes and extends the thesis.

Learning for Life

News reports should

- accurately relate the facts of the house fire
- use vivid language to capture the drama of the moment

Literature Online

Web Activites Have students access the Web site for interactive activities that will help them assess their understanding of the selection.

CheckPoint

Use the CheckPoint questions on Presentation Plus! to check students' mastery of the selection. These questions can be used with interactive response keypads for immediate student feedback.

READING AND VOCABULARY

Reading Strategy Identifying Sequence

The **sequence** of events in "The Leap" is not chronological. Review the sequence chain you created as you read. Then, answer the following questions.

1. With what events does each sequence chain begin? What events end each sequence chain?
2. Which sequence do you think is more interesting? Give three reasons to support your opinion.

Vocabulary Practice

Practice with Word Parts Read the following questions and choose the best answer. Use a dictionary if you need help.

1. Which of the following words contains a prefix that can mean "out"?
   a. extricate **b.** tentative **c.** commemorate
2. Which of the following words contains a suffix that indicates a verb?
   a. perpetually **b.** tentative **c.** commemorate
3. Which of the following words contains a suffix that indicates an adverb?
   a. constricting **b.** perpetually **c.** extricate
4. Which of the following words has a root that suggests remembering?
   a. commemorate **b.** constricting **c.** extricate
5. Which of the following words has a suffix that can signal a verb or an adjective?
   a. tentative **b.** perpetually **c.** constricting

Academic Vocabulary

Here is a word from the vocabulary list on page R80.

sustain (sə stān′) *v.* to support or keep going; to keep up

Practice and Apply
What appears to **sustain** the narrator's mother after the tragedy at the circus tent?

WRITING AND EXTENDING

Writing About Literature

Compare and Contrast Events Erdrich writes of Anna's transformation from a career that most would call exciting and unusual to the life of a homemaker and an avid reader. Two events brought about this change—the accident that killed her first husband and child, and the healing that resulted in remarriage and having another daughter. Write a short essay describing the similarities and differences between these two events, and use this comparison to support your opinion of Anna's character.

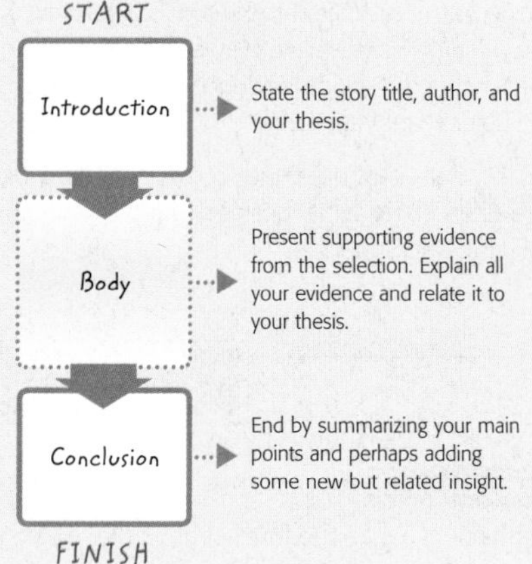

After you complete your draft, have a classmate read it and suggest revisions. Then proofread and edit your work for errors in spelling, grammar, and punctuation.

Learning for Life

The narrator quotes from a newspaper account of the circus fire. Imagine that you are a radio news reporter on the scene of the burning house. Create a news report to present the facts to your class. Make the report authentic, factual, and dramatic, while maintaining the objective perspective of a journalist.

Web Activities For eFlashcards, Selection Quick Checks, and other Web activities, go to www.glencoe.com.

BEFORE YOU READ

The Cask of Amontillado

MEET EDGAR ALLAN POE

Crumbling mansions, hearts that continue to beat after death, and insane killers are just a few of the ingredients in Edgar Allan Poe's fiction. His stories are not simple spine-tinglers, however. Poe travels deep into psychological territory, exploring guilt, rage, sorrow, madness, and fear.

A Loner Poe's life itself was a dark and often haunting tale. His parents were poverty-stricken actors. Poe's father left when Poe was two years old, and his mother died when he was three. Separated from his siblings, Poe was raised by John and Frances Allan. As Poe entered adolescence, he had a serious falling out with his foster father, who disapproved of his desire to write. Poe spent a few years in the army to try to regain his foster father's approval, but once it was clear that Allan was through with him, Poe moved to Baltimore and focused on writing.

> *"From childhood's hour I have not been*
> *As others were—I have not seen*
> *As others saw—"*
>
> —Edgar Allan Poe, "Alone"

Turmoil and Grief Poe began to write poetry as a teenager and published his first collection of poems in 1829. His short stories began appearing in magazines, and in 1833, one of his tales won a prize. This led to a job as a literary editor, a position that brought him great success, but which he lost due to his changeable nature and alcoholism. Most of the remainder of Poe's short life was spent in poverty and pain. He continued to work, but he did not achieve the public success he felt he deserved. Alcohol remained a problem, and he was often ill. He watched the love of his life, his wife Virginia Clemm, waste away and die from tuberculosis. Poe's loneliness, pain, and general inability to connect with others helped forge his uniquely dark vision.

A Literary Giant Poe's essays and reviews are still read today for their literary insights. His poetry, including such famous works as "The Raven" and "The Bells," lives on in countless collections of America's best writing. Perhaps most of all, his fictional works continue to frighten and delight readers worldwide.

Today, Poe is classified as an American Romantic writer, a detective fiction writer, and a Gothic writer. Some critics refer to Poe as the first truly modern writer because he probed the individual and the mystery of the self.

The work of English Romantic poet John Keats greatly influenced Edgar Allan Poe. Poe, in turn, influenced generations of detective fiction writers, short fiction writers, and poets. Nevertheless, he remains a unique voice in American letters. His vision of the dark side of life was all his own. Two years after his wife's death, he disappeared for five days in Baltimore, probably a victim of gang violence. A few days after his rescue, Poe died.

Edgar Allan Poe was born in 1809 and died in 1849.

LiteratureOnline **Author Search** For more about Edgar Allan Poe, go to www.glencoe.com.

BEFORE YOU READ

Focus

BELLRINGER

Bellringer Options
Selection Focus Transparency 4
Daily Language Practice Transparency 6

Or **write on the board:** *What scares you?* Engage students in a discussion of what they find frightening. Encourage them to consider a broad range of topics, including places, sounds, animals, and insects. Broaden the discussion to entertainment, such as movies and books. Discuss the paradox of enjoying being frightened.

LiteratureOnline

Author Search To expand students' appreciation of Edgar Allan Poe, have them access the Web site for additional information and resources.

Selection Skills

The Cask of Amontillado

Literary Elements
- Mood (SE pp. 56–64)
- Suspense (SE p. 64)

Reading Skills
- Paraphrasing (SE pp. 56–64)
- Making a Chart (SE p. 56)

Vocabulary Skills
- Context Clues (SE pp. 56, 64)
- Archaic Expressions (TWE p. 64)

Listening/Speaking/Viewing Skills
- Analyzing Art (TWE p. 60)
- Visual Literacy (SE p. 63)

Writing Skills/Grammar
- Analyze Sensory Details (SE p. 65)
- Evaluating Sentence Structure (SE p. 65)
- Inverted Sentences (SE p. 65)
- Writing Dialogue (TWE p. 60)

BEFORE YOU READ

Focus

Summary

The narrator, Montresor, vows to exact revenge on Fortunato for an unspecified insult. During carnival season, Montresor sees Fortunato, who has been drinking. He leads Fortunato into the catacombs beneath his palazzo. When they reach a niche in the cellar wall, Montresor chains Fortunato to the wall and fills in the niche with bricks and mortar. Before installing the final stone, Montresor throws a torch into the niche. At the story's end, he states that the crime has gone undetected for fifty years.

V Vocabulary

Vocabulary File Say: Add these words and definitions to your vocabulary file. For each word, include a sentence that gives you an example of how to use the word. **OL** Students with English language needs should include the pronunciations of these words in their files. **EL**

Literary Elements Have students access the Web site to improve their understanding of mood.

LITERATURE PREVIEW

Connecting to the Story

Most people have thoughts of revenge at least once in their lives. Before you read "The Cask of Amontillado," think about the following questions:

- What kinds of wrongs or injuries would make you want to take revenge?
- Do you think getting revenge makes people feel better or worse?

Building Background

This story is set during Carnival, an often uninhibited celebration involving costume parades, feasting, and other festivities. It takes place mainly in Roman Catholic regions during the weeks before Lent, a holy season of abstinence and prayer.

Much of this story is set in the catacombs of the Montresor (mon′ tre sor′) family, which were also used as a wine cellar. Catacombs are underground cemeteries that can descend as many as four stories below ground. The walls of the narrow passageways are lined with niches where bodies are placed. Catacombs are dark, damp, and often littered with the bones of those who were buried there long ago.

Setting Purposes for Reading

Big Idea Matters of Life and Death

As you read, think about the sensory details in the story that allow you to see, feel, hear, and even breathe the atmosphere of death.

Literary Element Mood

Mood is the emotional quality of a literary work. A writer's choice of language, subject matter, setting, and tone, as well as such sound devices as rhyme and rhythm, contribute to creating mood. As you read "The Cask of Amontillado," think about what emotions it evokes.

- See Literary Terms Handbook, p. R11.

LiteratureOnline Interactive Literary Elements Handbook To review or learn more about the literary elements, go to www.glencoe.com.

READING PREVIEW

Reading Strategy Paraphrasing

Paraphrasing is putting something into your own words. Unlike a summary, a paraphrase is usually about the same length as the original passage.

Reading Tip: Making a Chart Paraphrase difficult sentences, or parts of sentences, as you read.

Author's Words	My Paraphrase
p. 57 "The thousand injuries of Fortunato I had borne as I best could."	I had put up with the many wrongs Fortunato did to me as well as I could.

Vocabulary

preclude (pri klo͞od′) *v.* to prevent; to make impossible; p. 57 *Failing grades preclude the possibility of playing in Friday's basketball game.*

impunity (im pū′ nə tē) *n.* freedom from punishment, harm, or bad consequences; p. 57 *No one here knew him, so he thought he could lie with impunity.*

accost (ə kôst′) *v.* to approach and speak to, especially in an aggressive manner; p. 58 *The beggars accost and scare the shoppers.*

explicit (eks plis′ it) *adj.* definitely stated, clearly expressed; p. 59 *Ms. DePietro gave explicit instructions for each stage of the assignment.*

implore (im plôr′) *v.* to ask earnestly; to beg; p. 61 *Some parents implore their children to study.*

Vocabulary Tip: Context Clues Context clues are words and phrases that surround an unfamiliar word and provide clues to its meaning. Common types of context clues include synonyms, restatements, definitions, examples, explanations, and antonyms.

INDIANA ACADEMIC STANDARDS (pages 56–65)
9.3.11 Evaluate the aesthetic qualities of style, including the impact of diction and figurative language on...mood...
9.2 Develop [reading] strategies...
9.5.3 Write expository compositions...

Selection Resources

Print Materials
- Unit 1 Resources (Fast File), pp. 26–28
- Leveled Vocabulary Development, p. 4
- Selection and Unit Assessments, pp. 7–8
- Selection Quick Checks, p. 4

Transparencies
- Bellringer Options Transparencies: Selection Focus Transparency 4, Daily Language Practice Transparency 6
- Literary Elements Transparency 10

Technology
- TeacherWorks Plus™ CD-ROM
- StudentWorks Plus™ CD-ROM
- Presentation Plus!™ CD-ROM
- Literature Online, glencoe.com
- Online Student Edition, mhln.com
- Exam*View*® Assessment Suite CD-ROM
- Vocabulary PuzzleMaker CD-ROM
- Listening Library, disc 1 track 4

The Cask of Amontillado

Edgar Allan Poe

The thousand injuries of Fortunato[1] I had borne as I best could; but when he ventured upon insult, I vowed revenge. You, who so well know the nature of my soul, will not suppose, however, that I gave utterance to a threat. *At length* I would be avenged; this was a point definitively settled—but the very definitiveness with which it was resolved, **precluded** the idea of risk. I must not only punish, but punish with **impunity**. A wrong is unredressed when retribution overtakes its redresser. It is equally unredressed when the avenger fails to make himself felt as such to him who has done the wrong.[2]

It must be understood, that neither by word nor deed had I given Fortunato cause to doubt my good-will. I continued, as was my wont, to smile in his face, and he did not perceive that my smile *now* was at the thought of his immolation.[3]

He had a weak point—this Fortunato—although in other regards he was a man to

1. *Fortunato* (fôr′ to͞o nä′ tō)

Reading Strategy Paraphrasing *In your own words, explain what the narrator is saying.* **R**

Vocabulary

preclude (pri klo͞od′) *v.* to prevent; to make impossible

impunity (im pū′ nə tē) *n.* freedom from punishment, harm, or bad consequences

2. *[A wrong is . . . done the wrong.]* These sentences might be rephrased this way: "A wrong is not avenged if the avenger either is punished for taking revenge or does not make the wrongdoer aware that he is taking revenge."
3. Here, *immolation* means "death or destruction."

Big Idea Matters of Life and Death *What is the narrator's attitude toward the death of Fortunato?* **BI**

Teach

R Reading Strategy

Paraphrasing **Answer:** *You know me pretty well, so you know I never actually threatened him.* **OL** Ask students how this comment affects them as readers. *(Students may say that having the narrator treat them as close, personal friends lends the story an engaging air of intimacy.)* **AL**

BI Big Idea

Matters of Life and Death
Answer: *He smiles at the thought of it; it gives Montresor pleasure.*
Ask: How do this comment and others on the first page affect your feelings about the narrator? Have students point out specific examples to support their opinions. *(Students may say they feel he is evil, based on details that highlight his obsession and delight with revenge.)* **OL**

CheckPoint

Use the CheckPoint questions on Presentation Plus! to monitor students' comprehension. These questions can be used with interactive response keypads for immediate student feedback.

Readability Scores
Dale-Chall: 9.8
DRP: 55
Lexile: 790

English Language Coach

Sentence Structures English language learners may have particular difficulty with Poe's sentence structure. Have students pause and paraphrase at the end of each paragraph. Encourage students to discuss language and grammar they find unclear before continuing to the next section. **EL**

Differentiated Instruction

Story Elements Students may be unfamiliar with such story elements as carnival season, palazzos, and catacombs. Encourage students to research any unfamiliar story elements. Have students share their results with the class. **BL**

Academic Standards

Additional Support activities on p. 57 cover the following standards:

English Language Coach: **9.3.11** Evaluate the aesthetic qualities of style, including the impact of diction…

Differentiated Instruction: **9.2.4** Synthesize the content from several sources…; paraphrase the ideas…

Teach

L1 Literary Element

Irony Irony is the contrast between appearance and reality. **Ask:** Why is it ironic that Montresor says Fortunato is luckily met? *(Since Montresor plans to kill Fortunato, the meeting is hardly lucky for him.)* OL **Ask:** How else does Poe create wry humor in this line? *(The name Fortunato looks and sounds like* fortunate, *but is a play on words. Fortunato is doomed, rather than lucky.)* AL

L2 Literary Element

Mood **Answer:** *It is friendly, cordial, and enthusiastic.*

R Reading Strategy

Paraphrasing **Answer:** *Putting on my black mask and pulling my cape around me, I let him rush me home. Montresor is disguised so that no one will recognize him; he is making it seem as if Fortunato is in control of the situation.* OL

be respected and even feared. He prided himself on his connoisseurship[4] in wine. Few Italians have the true virtuoso spirit. For the most part their enthusiasm is adopted to suit the time and opportunity—to practice imposture upon the British and Austrian *millionnaires.* In painting and gemmary Fortunato, like his countrymen, was a quack—but in the matter of old wines he was sincere. In this respect I did not differ from him materially: I was skilful in the Italian vintages myself, and bought largely whenever I could.

"How remarkably well you are looking today!"

It was about dusk, one evening during the supreme madness of the carnival season, that I encountered my friend. He **accosted** me with excessive warmth, for he had been drinking much. The man wore motley.[5] He had on a tight-fitting parti-striped dress, and his head was surmounted by the conical cap and bells. I was so pleased to see him, that I thought I should never have done wringing his hand.

L1 I said to him: "My dear Fortunato, you are luckily met. How remarkably well you are looking today! But I have received a pipe of what passes for Amontillado,[6] and I have my doubts."

"How?" said he. "Amontillado? A pipe? Impossible! And in the middle of the carnival!"

"I have my doubts," I replied; "and I was silly enough to pay the full Amontillado price without consulting you in the matter. You were not to be found, and I was fearful of losing a bargain."

"Amontillado!"

"I have my doubts."

"Amontillado!"

"And I must satisfy them."

"Amontillado!"

"As you are engaged, I am on my way to Luchesi.[7] If anyone has a critical turn, it is he. He will tell me——"

"Luchesi cannot tell Amontillado from Sherry."

"And yet some fools will have it that his taste is a match for your own."

"Come, let us go."

"Whither?"

"To your vaults."

"My friend, no; I will not impose upon your good nature. I perceive you have an engagement. Luchesi—"

"I have no engagement;—come."

"My friend, no. It is not the engagement, but the severe cold with which I perceive you are afflicted. The vaults are insufferably damp. They are encrusted with niter."[8]

"Let us go, nevertheless. The cold is merely nothing. Amontillado! You have been imposed upon. And as for Luchesi, he cannot distinguish Sherry from Amontillado."

Thus speaking, Fortunato possessed himself of my arm. Putting on a mask of black silk, and drawing a *roquelaure* closely about my person, I suffered him to hurry me to my palazzo.[9]

Visual Vocabulary
A *roquelaure* (rôk ə lor′) is a knee-length cloak that was popular in the 1700s.

4. *Connoisseurship* (kon′ ə sur′ ship) is expert knowledge that qualifies one to pass judgment in a particular area.
5. *Motley* is the multicolored costume of a court jester or clown.
6. A *pipe* is a wine barrel that holds 126 gallons. *Amontillado* (ə môn′ tē yä′dō) is a kind of pale, dry sherry from Spain.
7. *Luchesi* (lo͞o kā′ sē)
8. *Niter* is a salt-like substance found in cool, damp places.
9. A *palazzo* (pə lät′ sō) is a mansion or palace.

Vocabulary

accost (ə kôst′) *v.* to approach and speak to, especially in an aggressive manner

Literary Element Mood *What is the mood in this opening exchange between the two main characters?* L2

Reading Strategy Paraphrasing *Paraphrase this sentence and explain what is happening.* R

Additional Support

Leveled Reading An adapted version of this selection is available on page 2 of Jamestown Literature: An Adapted Reader, grade 9.

Skills Practice

STUDY SKILLS: Research Direct students' attention to the last six lines on page 59. Ask what image they think the Montresor family coat of arms and motto present. *(Students may say that the family crest and motto are daunting.)* Challenge students to create their own coats of arms and family mottos. Assign students to research their family histories for clues to things they can include in their designs, such as symbols, names, places, and animals. OL Have students share their projects with the class, explaining their choice of imagery and the impressions they wanted to convey. AL

There were no attendants at home; they had absconded to make merry in honor of the time. I had told them that I should not return until the morning, and had given them **explicit** orders not to stir from the house. These orders were sufficient, I well knew, to insure their immediate disappearance, one and all, as soon as my back was turned.

I took from their sconces two flambeaux,[10] and giving one to Fortunato, bowed him through several suites of rooms to the archway that led into the vaults. I passed down a long and winding staircase, requesting him to be cautious as he followed. We came at length to the foot of the descent, and stood together on the damp ground of the catacombs of the Montresors.

The gait of my friend was unsteady, and the bells upon his cap jingled as he strode.

"The pipe?" said he.

"It is farther on," said I; "but observe the white web-work which gleams from these cavern walls."

He turned toward me, and looked into my eyes with two filmy orbs that distilled the rheum of intoxication.[11]

"Niter?" he asked, at length.

"Niter," I replied. "How long have you had that cough?"

"Ugh! ugh! ugh!—ugh! ugh! ugh!—ugh! ugh! ugh!—ugh! ugh! ugh!—ugh! ugh! ugh!"

My poor friend found it impossible to reply for many minutes.

"It is nothing," he said, at last.

"Come," I said, with decision, "we will go back; your health is precious. You are rich, respected, admired, beloved; you are happy, as once I was. You are a man to be missed. For me it is no matter. We will go back; you will be ill, and I cannot be responsible. Besides, there is Luchesi——"

"Enough," he said; "the cough is a mere nothing; it will not kill me. I shall not die of a cough."

"True—true," I replied; "and, indeed, I had no intention of alarming you unnecessarily; but you should use all proper caution. A draft of this Medoc[12] will defend us from the damps."

Here I knocked off the neck of a bottle which I drew from a long row of its fellows that lay upon the mold.

"Drink," I said, presenting him the wine.

He raised it to his lips with a leer. He paused and nodded to me familiarly, while his bells jingled.

"I drink," he said, "to the buried that repose[13] around us."

"And I to your long life."

He again took my arm, and we proceeded.

"These vaults," he said, "are extensive."

"The Montresors," I replied, "were a great and numerous family."

"I forget your arms."[14]

"A huge human foot d'or, in a field azure; the foot crushes a serpent rampant[15] whose fangs are imbedded in the heel."

"And the motto?"

"Nemo me impune lacessit."[16]

"Good!" he said.

---

10. *Sconces* are wall brackets that hold candles or torches, and *flambeaux* (flam′ bō′) are lighted torches.
11. *[filmy orbs . . . intoxication]* This phrase describes Fortunato's eyes as clouded and watery from excessive drinking.
12. *Medoc* (mā dôk′) is a French red wine. A *draft* is the amount taken in one swig or swallow.
13. To *repose* is to lie at rest, either sleeping or in death.
14. *Arms* is short for "coat of arms," an arrangement of figures and symbols on or around a shield that, along with a motto, represents one's ancestry.
15. The Montresor family's coat of arms includes a golden foot on a sky-blue background and a snake rising up.
16. The *motto* is Latin for "Nobody provokes me with impunity."

Big Idea Matters of Life and Death *What in the description of the setting creates an aura of death?* BI

Vocabulary

explicit (eks plis′ it) *adj.* definitely stated; clearly expressed

Literary Element Mood *How would you describe the mood of this passage? Explain.* L3

Teach

BI Big Idea

Matters of Life and Death
Answer: *The catacombs are underground cemeteries. Poe also mentions a long descent, giving the sense of being buried deep underground. He then reinforces this with the sensory detail of "damp ground" so that the reader smells and feels the surroundings.* OL

L3 Literary Element

Mood **Answer:** *The word* alarming *suggests danger, and the request to "use all proper caution" also suggests that danger is lurking.* OL

Differentiated Instruction

Visualizing Visual learners may benefit from expressing mood through a design project. Point out to students that color and shape create mood in art the way words do in writing. Instruct students to use abstract images and colors that reflect the mood of the story. Hold a class discussion about the projects. BL

Building Reading Fluency

Reading Aloud Note that when elaborate language is spoken aloud, it may be easier to understand. Assign two students to read aloud the dialogue between Fortunato and Montresor. Have a third student read the part of the narrator. BL

Academic Standards

Additional Support activities on pp. 58 and 59 cover the following standards:

Skills Practice: **9.2.4** Synthesize the content from several sources or works…; paraphrase the ideas and connect them to…related topics…

Differentiated Instruction: **9.3.11** Evaluate the aesthetic qualities of style, including the impact of diction and figurative language on…mood…

Building Reading Fluency: **9.7** [Develop] speaking skills…in conjunction with… strategies [for] delivery of oral presentations.

Teach

BI Big Idea

Matters of Life and Death

Answer: *The mention of bones brings to mind death, while the references to catacombs suggest being trapped and cut off from the outside world.* OL

Viewing the Art

The catacombs beneath Paris were originally limestone quarries. As churchyards began to fill, the quarries became catacombs, or underground cemeteries. They cover about 300 km under Paris and are estimated to hold from five to seven million graves. AS

The wine sparkled in his eyes and the bells jingled. My own fancy grew warm with the Medoc. We had passed through walls of piled bones, with casks and puncheons[17] intermingling, into the inmost recesses of the catacombs. I paused again, and this time I made bold to seize Fortunato by an arm above the elbow.

"The niter!" I said; "see, it increases. It hangs like moss upon the vaults. We are below the river's bed. The drops of moisture trickle among the bones. Come, we will go back ere it is too late. Your cough——"

"It is nothing," he said; "let us go on. But first, another draft of the Medoc."

I broke and reached him a flagon[18] of De Grâve. He emptied it at a breath. His eyes flashed with a fierce light. He laughed and threw the bottle upward with a gesticulation I did not understand.

I looked at him in surprise. He repeated the movement—a grotesque one.

"You do not comprehend?" he said.

"Not I," I replied.

"Then you are not of the brotherhood."

"How?"

"You are not of the masons."[19]

"Yes, yes," I said; "yes, yes."

"You? Impossible! A mason?"

"A mason," I replied.

"A sign," he said.

"It is this," I answered, producing a trowel from beneath the folds of my *roquelaure.*

"You jest," he exclaimed, recoiling a few paces. "But let us proceed to the Amontillado."

17. *Casks* and *puncheons* are large containers for storing liquids.

18. The *flagon* is a narrow-necked bottle with a handle.

Big Idea Matters of Life and Death *How do these details add to the growing sense of entrapment in the story?* BI

19. Here, *masons* is short for "Freemasons," an organization of stonecutters and bricklayers that was formed in the Middle Ages. By the time of this story, the masons had become a social group with secret rituals and signs.

Additional Support

Skills Practice

WRITING: Dialogue Have students review the dialogue between Fortunato and Montresor and identify the techniques Poe used to make it seem realistic. *(The characters speak in incomplete sentences; dashes at the end of a speech indicate pauses or interruptions; exclamation points add strong emotion to the characters' comments.)* Ask students to write a brief dialogue based on a recent conversation with a friend or family member. Stress using Poe's techniques to make the dialogue realistic. OL

"Be it so," I said, replacing the tool beneath the cloak, and again offering him my arm. He leaned upon it heavily. We continued our route in search of the Amontillado. We passed through a range of low arches, descended, passed on, and descending again, arrived at a deep crypt,[20] in which the foulness of the air caused our flambeaux rather to glow than flame.

At the most remote end of the crypt there appeared another less spacious. Its walls had been lined with human remains, piled to the vault overhead, in the fashion of the great catacombs of Paris. Three sides of this interior crypt were still ornamented in this manner. From the fourth the bones had been thrown down, and lay promiscuously upon the earth, forming at one point a mound of some size. Within the wall thus exposed by the displacing of the bones, we perceived a still interior recess, in depth about four feet, in width three, in height six or seven. It seemed to have been constructed for no especial use within itself, but formed merely the interval between two of the colossal supports of the roof of the catacombs, and was backed by one of their circumscribing walls of solid granite.

It was in vain that Fortunato, uplifting his dull torch, endeavored to pry[21] into the depth of the recess. Its termination the feeble light did not enable us to see.

"Proceed," I said; "herein is the Amontillado. As for Luchesi——"

"He is an ignoramus," interrupted my friend, as he stepped unsteadily forward, while I followed immediately at his heels. In an instant he had reached the extremity of the niche,[22] and finding his progress arrested by the rock, stood stupidly bewildered. A moment more and I had fettered[23] him to the granite. In its surface were two iron staples, distant from each other about two feet, horizontally. From one of these depended a short chain, from the other a padlock. Throwing the links about his waist, it was but the work of a few seconds to secure it. He was too much astounded to resist. Withdrawing the key I stepped back from the recess.

"Pass your hand," I said, "over the wall; you cannot help feeling the niter. Indeed it is *very* damp. Once more let me **implore** you to return. No? Then I must positively leave you. But I must first render you all the little attentions in my power." L2

"The Amontillado!" ejaculated my friend, not yet recovered from his astonishment.

"True," I replied; "the Amontillado."

As I said these words I busied myself among the pile of bones of which I have before spoken. Throwing them aside, I soon uncovered a quantity of building stone and mortar. With these materials and with the aid of my trowel, I began vigorously to wall up the entrance of the niche.

I had scarcely laid the first tier of the masonry when I discovered that the intoxication of Fortunato had in a great measure worn off. The earliest indication I had of this was a low moaning cry from the depth of the

"Indeed it is *very* damp."

20. A *crypt* is a burial chamber.
21. Here, *pry* means "to look closely; peer."

22. Here, the *extremity of the niche* (nich) is the farthest spot inside the recess.
23. *Fettered* means "bound with chains or shackles; restrained."

Literary Element Mood *How do details in this paragraph create a feeling of fear and horror?* L1

Reading Strategy Paraphrasing *Paraphrase these sentences.* R

Literary Element Mood *What action is occurring, and how does it contribute to the mood of the story?* L3

Vocabulary
implore (im plôr′) *v.* to ask earnestly; to beg

Teach

L1 Literary Element

Mood Answer: *The characters are now surrounded by signs of death. Bones are piled to the ceiling. It is disturbing that the dead have not been left in peace; one wall of bones has been torn down.* OL

R Reading Strategy

Paraphrasing Answer: *Fortunato's torch did not give much light, so his staring into the dark recess did no good. He could not see to the end.* OL

L2 Literary Element

Dialogue Ask: How has the dialogue changed? How does this contribute to the mood? *(Students may say that Montresor has gone from flattering Fortunato to mocking him. His delight in mocking Fortunato intensifies the horror.)* OL

L3 Literary Element

Mood Answer: *Montresor is burying Fortunato alive. This reinforces the horror that has been building throughout the story.* OL

English Language Coach

Context Clues Have English-language learners practice working with context clues by writing an original sentence that includes context clues for each new vocabulary word. Have partners swap sentences to see how effective their clues are. EL

Differentiated Instruction

Story Writing Challenge gifted and talented students to rewrite the story from Fortunato's point of view. Instruct students to try to emulate Poe's techniques for evoking a mood and creating realistic dialogue. Have students read their stories aloud in class. AL

Academic Standards

Additional Support activities on pp. 60 and 61 cover the following standards:

Skills Practice: **9.5.8** Write for different purposes and audiences, adjusting tone, style, and voice as appropriate.

English Language Coach: **9.1** Use…context clues…to determine the meaning of words…

Differentiated Instruction: **9.5.1** Write…short stories that describe with specific details the sights, sounds, and smells of a scene and the specific actions, movements, gestures, and feelings of the characters…

Teach

BI Big Idea

Matters of Life and Death

Answer: *Fortunato finally realizes that he will die in the crypt; he realizes Montresor's evil intent.* OL Point out to students that Fortunato never asks why Montresor is killing him. Ask students why they think this is. *(Students may say because he already knows or that he is too panicked to think that clearly.)* AL

R Reading Strategy

Paraphrasing Answer: *I echoed and added to the screams; I even screamed louder than Fortunato did. Then Fortunato stopped screaming. Montresor is mocking Fortunato.* OL

Use the CheckPoint questions on Presentation Plus! to check students' mastery of the selection. These questions can be used with interactive response keypads for immediate student feedback.

recess. It was *not* the cry of a drunken man. There was then a long and obstinate silence. I laid the second tier, and the third, and the fourth; and then I heard the furious vibrations of the chain. The noise lasted for several minutes, during which, that I might hearken to it with the more satisfaction, I ceased my labors and sat down upon the bones. When at last the clanking subsided, I resumed the trowel, and finished without interruption the fifth, the sixth, and the seventh tier. The wall was now nearly upon a level with my breast. I again paused, and holding the flambeaux over the mason-work, threw a few feeble rays upon the figure within.

Visual Vocabulary A *rapier* (rā′ pē ər) is a long, lightweight sword with a sharp point but no cutting edge.

A succession of loud and shrill screams, bursting suddenly from the throat of the chained form, seemed to thrust me violently back. For a brief moment I hesitated—I trembled. Unsheathing my rapier, I began to grope with it about the recess; but the thought of an instant reassured me. I placed my hand upon the solid fabric of the catacombs, and felt satisfied. I reapproached the wall. I replied to the yells of him who clamored. I re-echoed—I aided—I surpassed them in volume and in strength. I did this, and the clamorer grew still.

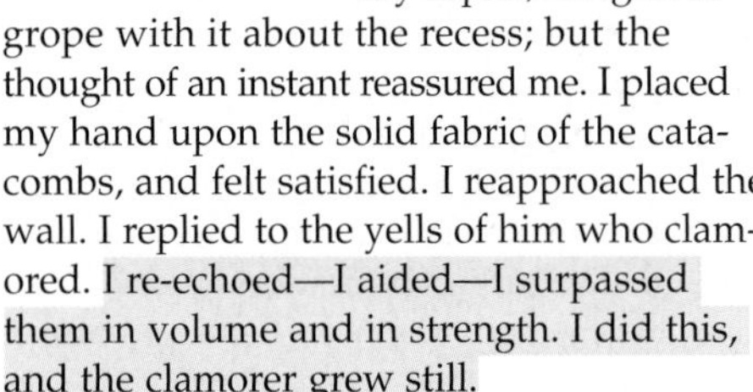

It was now midnight, and my task was drawing to a close. I had completed the eighth, the ninth, and the tenth tier. I had finished a portion of the last and the eleventh; there remained but a single stone to be fitted and plastered in. I struggled with its weight; I placed it partially in its destined[24] position. But now there came from out the niche a low laugh that erected the hairs upon my head. It was succeeded by a sad voice, which I had difficulty in recognizing as that of the noble Fortunato. The voice said——

"For the love of God, Montresor!"

"Ha! ha! ha!—he! he!—a very good joke indeed—an excellent jest. We will have many a rich laugh about it at the palazzo—he! he! he!—over our wine—he! he! he!"

"The Amontillado!" I said.

"He! he! he!—he! he! he!—yes, the Amontillado. But is it not getting late? Will not they be awaiting us at the palazzo, the Lady Fortunato and the rest? Let us be gone."

"Yes," I said, "let us be gone."

"For the love of God, Montresor!"

"Yes," I said, "for the love of God!"

But to these words I hearkened in vain for a reply. I grew impatient. I called aloud:

"Fortunato!"

No answer. I called again:

"Fortunato!"

No answer still. I thrust a torch through the remaining aperture and let it fall within. There came forth in return only a jingling of the bells. My heart grew sick—on account of the dampness of the catacombs. I hastened to make an end of my labor. I forced the last stone into its position; I plastered it up. Against the new masonry I re-erected the old rampart[25] of bones. For the half of a century no mortal has disturbed them. *In pace requiescat!*[26]

Big Idea Matters of Life and Death *What does Fortunato finally realize?* BI

Reading Strategy Paraphrasing *Paraphrase these lines, and then explain what Montresor is doing.* R

24. Here, *destined* means "intended for a particular purpose or use."
25. A *rampart* is a protective barrier or fortification.
26. *In pace requiescat* (in pä′ chā rek′ wē es kät′) is Latin for "May he rest in peace."

Additional Support

Academic Standards

The Additional Support activity on p. 62 covers the following standard:

Skills Practice: **9.3.4** Determine characters' traits by what the characters say about themselves…

Skills Practice

LITERARY ELEMENT: Character

Ask: What have you learned about Montresor's character? About Fortunato's? *(Students may say Montresor is obsessed and evil; Fortunato is foolish and narcissistic.)* Have students create graphic webs showing the character traits of each man. Have students include page numbers indicating where each trait is displayed. Discuss the webs in class. Have students discuss traits listed on their webs. Encourage students to add traits from the discussion to their webs. OL

AFTER YOU READ

RESPONDING AND THINKING CRITICALLY

Respond

1. What are one or two questions you would ask Montresor?

Recall and Interpret

2. (a)How does Montresor get Fortunato to come with him to his vaults? (b)What is Montresor's motive for leading Fortunato there?
3. (a)What kind of relationship does Montresor have with the people who take care of his home? (b)What does this reveal about him?
4. (a)Describe the conversation between Montresor and Fortunato as they walk in the catacombs. (b)What is ironic about Montresor's concern for Fortunato's health?
5. (a)Explain what happens to Fortunato at the end of the story. (b)In what ways is this a "perfect" crime?

Analyze and Evaluate

6. What details does Poe include to show Montresor as a cold-blooded killer? Do you think his portrayal is effective? Why or why not?
7. Why might Poe have chosen to write this story from the first-person point of view, describing only Montresor's thoughts and not Fortunato's?
8. (a)What is the moment of greatest horror in the story? (b)How well does Poe build up to this moment?

Connect

9. **Big Idea** **Matters of Life and Death** Is "The Cask of Amontillado" an effective horror story? Explain.

VISUAL LITERACY: Illustration

An Illustrator's Interpretation

Famed British illustrator Arthur Rackham created this image in 1935 to illustrate "The Cask of Amontillado." Study the illustration, looking carefully at the subject matter, the use of color, and the use of line. Think about the mood that Rackham creates.

Fortunado and Montresor, 1935. Arthur Rackham.

Group Activity Discuss the following questions with classmates. Use evidence from "The Cask of Amontillado" to support your answers.

1. How accurately does Rackham re-create the setting of "The Cask of Amontillado"? Consider the size of the niche, the number of levels of brick, the chains, the niter, and the bones. Also consider the lighting.
2. How accurately does Rackham re-create the characters? Consider the characters' clothing, the expressions on their faces, and their postures.
3. How well does Rackham capture the mood of this moment in the story? Explain.

AFTER YOU READ

Assess

1. "What was the insult that made you want to kill Fortunato?" or "Have you ever regretted your crime?"
2. (a) He tempts Fortunato to sample a fine wine. (b) To murder him
3. (a) His servants revile him. (b) He is hateful and manipulative.
4. (a) Montresor fusses over Fortunato's health and suggests turning back. (b) His real intent is murder.
5. (a) He is entombed behind a wall. (b) The crime goes undetected.
6. The premeditated crime is coldly and methodically carried out despite his victim's screams; he drops a torch into the niche to make the death more brutal. Most students will say the portrayal was effective.
7. It lets readers into a killer's mind.
8. (a) When Montresor starts to fill the niche or when he throws in the torch. (b) The gradual descent into the catacombs builds to the final horrible act.
9. The eerie setting, mad killer, and idea of being walled up alive will horrify some readers. Others might feel distanced by the unfamiliar setting and old-fashioned language.

Visual Literacy

1. Some may say the image looks too large; pictured niche might accommodate 14 rows of brick, rather than 11; niter and the chain near the waist look accurate; scene looks too bright, given that light was from a torch (not shown)
2. (a) Fortunato wears motley, cap, and bells as in story, but clothes should fit tighter; face and stance show his fear (b) Montresor's clothes look right, but inward-leaning posture suggests interest, not detachment; sword and trowel as in story
3. Some students may argue that adding light and color to such a darkly sinister moment detracts from the horror. Others may say that these features reflect Montresor's disturbing giddiness.

AFTER YOU READ

Assess

Literary Element

1. The dark mood foreshadows a monstrous act of revenge.
2. Poe uses specific, vivid words: *damp, cold, remote, crypt,* and *foulness.*
3. The connotations of colorful gaiety contrast with the gloomy vault and emphasize Montresor's evil glee.

Review: Suspense

Details That Create Suspense	Why They Create Suspense
Niter everywhere	Niter suggests sense of suffocation, death
Reach far end of crypt	No place left to go—and no Amontillado
Montresor's "heart grew sick"	Does he realize the horror of his crime? Will he really leave Fortunato?

Reading Strategy

1. They help by replacing words such as *flambeaux, rheum,* and *orbs* with familiar terms.
2. "Thus speaking, Fortunato possessed himself of my arm" might become "As he spoke, Fortunato took my arm."

Vocabulary

1. b **2.** a **3.** b **4.** b **5.** a

LITERARY ANALYSIS

Literary Element Mood

Mood is the feeling that an author creates in a literary work. The mood can suggest an emotion, such as fear or joy; it can also suggest the quality of a setting, such as gloom or airiness. For example, if Poe had described the catacombs as "peaceful" or "still," he would have created a quiet, restful mood.

1. Describe the overall mood that Poe creates in this story. In what way does the mood contribute to the story's suspense?
2. How does Poe create the mood? Point to specific examples throughout the story to support your answer.
3. What impact does the Carnival setting have on the mood of this story?

Review: Suspense

As you learned on page 23, **suspense** is a feeling of curiosity, uncertainty, or even dread about what will happen next in a story. Writers increase the level of suspense by creating a threat to the central character and raising questions in the reader's mind about the outcome of a conflict.

Partner Activity With a classmate, make a list of details that create suspense in the story and explain why they are suspenseful. Display your work in a two-column chart.

Details That Create Suspense	Why They Create Suspense
No one is home at the Montresor house.	No one can witness the crime.

READING AND VOCABULARY

Reading Strategy Paraphrasing

One reason it helps to **paraphrase** Poe's writing is that his diction, or word choice, can be difficult to understand. First, Poe uses many archaic words. Second, styles of Poe's day often dictated a more roundabout, academic, and ornate style than we use today. One aspect of this style was "fancy" vocabulary.

1. Look at footnotes 10 and 11 on page 59. Explain why footnotes and paraphrasing help you understand Poe's writing.
2. Choose a sentence from the story that requires paraphrasing primarily because of its difficult vocabulary. Then paraphrase the sentence.

Vocabulary Practice

Practice with Context Clues Read each of the following sentences and identify the words that provide a context clue for the meaning of the boldfaced vocabulary word.

1. Taking those lessons will **preclude** the possibility of your working on the newspaper, which meets at the same time.
   a. Taking those lessons
   b. which meets at the same time
2. Would Joe be punished, or would he commit the crime with **impunity?**
   a. be punished, or
   b. commit the crime
3. Some people greet you in a timid way, while others **accost** you.
   a. Some people
   b. in a timid way, while others
4. I have **explicit** instructions on how to get to the meet instead of a vague description like last time.
   a. how to get to the meet
   b. instead of a vague description
5. "Please, please, don't go to that party," Mrs. Weeks **implored.**
   a. Please, please,
   b. don't go to that party

Additional Support

Skills Practice

VOCABULARY: Archaic Expressions Help students skim the story for archaic words and list them on the board. Have students replace them with modern synonyms and add these synonyms to their vocabulary lists. **BL** Have the class tell a story using the archaic words. The first student picks a word and starts the story. The second student adds a sentence with a different word, and so on. **OL** Limit the story to a specific genre. **AL**

WRITING AND EXTENDING

Writing About Literature

Analyze Sensory Details "The Cask of Amontillado" is rich in sensory details. Write a brief essay analyzing how Poe uses sensory details to establish the setting.

Begin prewriting by identifying some of the sensory details.

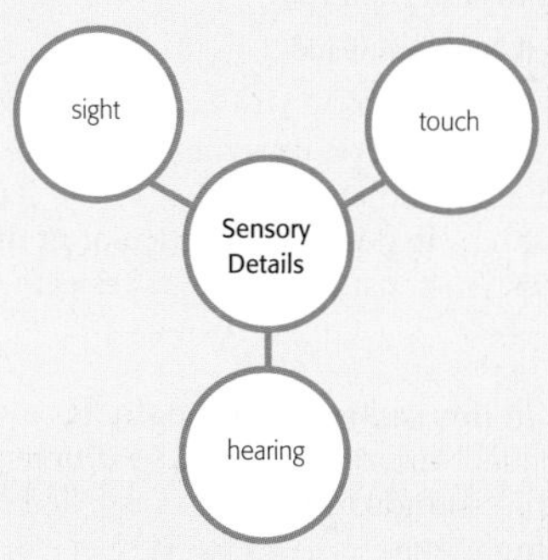

Use your prewriting to develop a thesis about how Poe uses sensory details to establish the setting of the story. Include your thesis in the introduction. In the body paragraphs, develop your thesis by presenting and explaining exact details from the story that show how Poe appeals to the reader's senses. Conclude your essay with a summary statement, as well as a final thought or insight into the story.

After you complete your draft, have a peer read it and suggest revisions. Then proofread your work for errors in spelling, grammar, and punctuation.

Reading Further

If you would like to read more by or about Edgar Allan Poe, you might enjoy these works:

Short Stories and Poems: *Edgar Allan Poe: Complete Tales & Poems,* edited by Wilbur Steward Scott, contains all the famous poems and stories and far more.

Reference: *Edgar Allan Poe A to Z: The Essential Reference to His Life and Work* by Dawn B. Sova, includes entries for all Poe's works; people, places, and events associated with him; and illustrations.

LiteratureOnline Web Activities For eFlashcards, Selection Quick Checks, and other Web activities, go to www.glencoe.com.

GRAMMAR AND STYLE

Poe's Language and Style

Evaluating Sentence Structure One way that Poe takes us deep into the long ago and far away is through his sentence structure. Although his sentences were not unusual for his literary era, many of them strike the contemporary reader as lengthy or curiously structured. One reason for this is that Poe used inverted sentences.

Inverted sentences are sentences with an unexpected word order. The most common kind of inverted sentence mixes up the usual expectations about sentence structure by placing the subject after the verb, as in this example:

	VERB	SUBJECT
Into the niche	stepped	Fortunato.

Poe inverts sentences, or creates unexpected word order, in other ways as well. Read this example from "The Cask of Amontillado."

"Its termination the feeble light did not enable us to see."

In this sentence, Poe places the direct object, *termination,* before the subject, *light*. This creates variety and emphasizes the word *termination*.

Activity Scan the story for other examples of inverted sentences. Note what has been inverted, or changed from the expected order, such as a subject after a verb, or an object before the subject. Decide what word or phrase the inverted structure emphasizes. Make a list to share with the class.

Revising Check

Inverted Sentences Using an inverted sentence can help you vary your sentences and add interest to your writing. This technique should be used sparingly, however. Find a place in your essay about sensory details where you might effectively use an inverted sentence. After you insert it, read the entire paragraph aloud to make sure it adds desirable variety to your paper and also reads smoothly.

AFTER YOU READ

Assess

Writing About Literature

Remind students that sensory details involve the five senses. Have volunteers describe eating a lemon. Write the descriptions on the board.
Ask: "Are your mouths watering?" Note how vivid sensory details can evoke physical reactions. OL

Poe's Language and Style

Remind students that varying the structure of their sentences will raise their scores for timed essays on standardized tests. Note that practicing sentence structure now will help them write essays with more varied, complex sentences without using too much time during the test. OL

Web Activities Have students access the Web site for interactive activities that will help them assess their understanding of the selection.

Reading in the Real World

Career Brainstorm career ideas suggested by the story, such as a detective or a building contractor. List them on the board. Have students choose a career from the list to research. Suggest including examples of well-known people in these careers from movies, TV, magazines, and books. Have students share their research with the class. Encourage students to interview someone in their chosen field. OL

Academic Standards

Additional Support activities on pp. 64 and 65 cover the following standards:
Skills Practice: **9.1.2** Distinguish between what words mean literally and what they imply and interpret what the words imply.
Reading in the Real World: **9.7.15** Deliver expository presentations that convey information and ideas from primary and secondary sources accurately and coherently... **9.7.16** Apply appropriate interviewing techniques...

Focus

Assign individual student groups a homonym word pair to use in sentences that include context clues. Have the groups share their sentences and add context suggested by the class. **OL**

Teach

Write on the board: *its, it's, your, you're.* Have students differentiate by breaking down each contraction.

Say: If the sentence calls for *it is,* use *it's.* If the sentence calls for *you are,* use *you're.* **OL**

Assess

1. (a) wine, (b) cellar, (c) led
2. (a) arm: *n.* a body part, a limb; *n.* a weapon; *v.* to equip with weaponry; *v.* to prepare for warfare or conflict
(b) ground: *n.* solid surface of the earth; *n.* soil or earth; *n.* an area of land designated for a particular purpose; *n.* a conductor that makes electrical connections with the earth; *v.* to place or cause to touch the ground; *v.* to connect to a ground
(c) lie: *v.* to recline; *v.* to give false information; *n.* a falsehood
(d) order: *n.* the arrangement of elements in a group; *n.* a command or direction; *v.* to command or instruct; *v.* to put in a methodical arrangement

Vocabulary Workshop

Context Clues

Recognizing Homonyms and Homophones

"In this respect, I did not differ from him materially."

—Edgar Allan Poe, from "The Cask of Amontillado"

Connecting to Literature In this sentence, Poe uses the homonym *respect.* **Homonyms** are words that sound alike and are spelled alike but have different meanings. Here, *respect* is a noun that means "particular or detail." Yet, *respect* is also a verb that means "to consider worthy of esteem or regard."

Poe also uses the homophone *not* in this sentence. **Homophones** are words that sound alike but are spelled differently and have different meanings and histories. A word that sounds like *not* but is spelled differently and has a different meaning is *knot.*

The English language is full of homonyms and homophones. Here are a few.

Homonym	Meaning
like	care for
like	nearly the same
Homophone	**Meaning**
principal	person with authority; head of a school; major
principle	basic truth, rule, policy, or law; moral conviction
sight	something seen; the ability to see
cite	to refer to; to acknowledge; to point out
site	a place; to locate

Commonly Confused Homophones

The most commonly confused homophones are *its* and *it's; your* and *you're; their, they're,* and *there;* and *to, too,* and *two.* Each time you use one of these words, be sure you have chosen the spelling that matches your intended meaning.

Test-Taking Tip

To determine the meaning of a homophone, use context clues. The part of speech can sometimes help you understand the intended meaning.

Reading Handbook
For more about vocabulary, see Reading Handbook, p. R19.

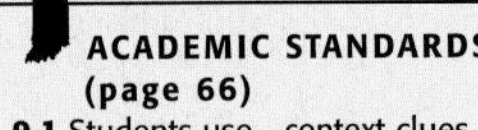

eFlashcards For eFlashcards and other vocabulary activities, go to www.glencoe.com.

Exercise

1. Choose the correct homophone to complete each sentence.
   a. Fortunato has expert knowledge about (whine, wine).
   b. Montresor takes Fortunato deeper into the (cellar, seller).
   c. Montresor has (lead, led) Fortunato to his death.
2. Use a dictionary to find more than one meaning for each homonym. Write at least two meanings.
   a. arm b. ground c. lie d. order

ACADEMIC STANDARDS (page 66)
9.1 Students use...context clues... to determine the meaning of words...

eFlashcards Have students access the Web site for more practice with recognizing homonyms and homophones.

Blues Ain't No Mockin Bird

MEET TONI CADE BAMBARA

Toni Cade Bambara once said that her mother never interrupted her if she was daydreaming. Bambara explained, "She recognized that as important work to do." Throughout her childhood, Bambara was encouraged to be creative, and she wrote on any slip of paper she could find. Growing up in Harlem in New York City, Bambara was drawn to the dramatic words of the people who spoke at the local Speaker's Corner. Bambara was also inspired by a portrait of poet Gwendolyn Brooks that hung in her Harlem library and by poet Langston Hughes, who spoke to the children reading there.

A New Name As a young girl, Bambara asserted her independence by changing her first name, Miltona, to Toni. She adopted the last name "Bambara" after seeing the name in a sketchbook in her great-grandmother's attic. (The Bambara are an African people in Mali who are well known for their carved wooden headdresses.)

> *"Words are to be taken seriously. . . . Words set things in motion."*
>
> —Toni Cade Bambara

Academia and Activism After receiving degrees in theater arts and American studies, Bambara taught at Rutgers University, Duke University, and Spelman College. Of her teaching, she said, "I'm a very seductive teacher, persuasive, infectious, overwhelming, irresistible. I worked hard in the classroom to teach students to critique me constantly, to protect themselves from my nonsense. . . . I would have to go into the classroom and beat them up for not taking me to the wall, for succumbing to mere charm and flash, when they should have been challenging me." During the turbulent years of the 1960s and 1970s, Bambara aligned herself with activists working to redress the injustices of American society. As part of that effort, she edited *The Black Woman,* an influential anthology that included selections from African American woman authors such as Nikki Giovanni, Audre Lorde, and Alice Walker.

Fiction and Film In 1972, Bambara published a collection of short stories entitled *Gorilla, My Love.* Of that collection, critic C. D. B. Bryan wrote, "Toni Cade Bambara tells me more about being black through her quiet, proud, silly, tender, hip, acute, loving stories than any amount of literary polemicizing could hope to do. She writes about love: a love for one's family, one's race, one's neighborhood, and it is the sort of love that comes with maturity and inner peace." Bambara published another short story collection, *The Sea Birds Are Still Alive,* in 1977 and a novel, *The Salt Eaters,* in 1980. In later years, she taught script writing at Scribe Video Center in Philadelphia. Bambara died from cancer at the age of fifty-six.

Toni Cade Bambara was born in 1939 and died in 1995.

Author Search For more about Toni Cade Bambara, go to www.glencoe.com.

Focus

BELLRINGER

Bellringer Options
Selection Focus Transparency 5
Daily Language Practice Transparency 7

Or prompt students to discuss the paparazzi. Note how famous people often object to being photographed by them. **Ask:** How would you feel if you were photographed without your consent? How do you think the photographer feels when taking such a picture? Discuss with students what they think is appropriate behavior for photographers.

Author Search To expand students' appreciation of Toni Cade Bambara, have them access the Web site for additional information and resources.

Selection Skills

Blues Ain't No Mockin Bird

Literary Elements
- Dialect (SE pp. 68–75; TWE p. 74)
- Setting (SE p. 75)

Reading Skills
- Concrete Details (SE pp. 68–76)

Vocabulary Skills
- Academic Vocabulary (SE p. 76)
- Analogies (SE p. 76)

Listening/Speaking/Viewing Skills
- Analyzing Art (SE pp. 70, 72)

Writing Skills/Grammar
- Analyze Cultural Context (SE p. 76)
- Write a Memo (SE p. 76)
- Double Negatives (TWE p. 70)

Study Skills/Research/Assessment
- Research the Blues (TWE p. 72)

BEFORE YOU READ

Focus

Summary

As the narrator plays with friends, Granny makes Christmas cakes on the back porch. Two men making a film for the county begin filming without her permission. Granny asks them to stop, but they don't. Granddaddy Cain returns from the woods with a chicken hawk he shot down. When the wounded hawk's mate swoops down, Granddaddy kills it with a hammer. Then he asks the men to leave, but they stay on. Only after he uses the hammer to smash the camera do they leave.

V Vocabulary

Vocabulary File **Say:** Add these words and definitions to your vocabulary file. For each word, include a sentence that gives you an example of how to use the word. **OL** Students with English language needs should also include the pronunciations of these words in their files. **EL**

Literary Elements Have students access the Web site to improve their understanding of dialect.

LITERATURE PREVIEW

Connecting to the Story

In Bambara's story, a rural African American family is suddenly confronted with two cameramen who enter their property without permission and start filming them. Before you read, think about the following questions:

- What would you say to someone who invaded your privacy?
- When is it not appropriate to photograph or film others?

Building Background

The great American style of music known as the blues was born in the rural southern United States. There, African musical traditions were transformed to create a new music that spoke to the sadness and joy in African American life. Though blues is commonly viewed as a music of lament, it expresses a full range of emotions, from despair to exhilaration.

The mockingbird is a songbird that mimics, or imitates, the songs of other birds. The mockingbird is highly territorial. It fiercely defends its nest and environment by swooping down on its enemies.

Setting Purposes for Reading

Big Idea Matters of Life and Death

As you read, try to determine what the adults in the family value most. Think about what the confrontation with the filmmakers reveals about the family's values.

Literary Element Dialect

People who live in a specific region or who belong to a specific group may use **dialect**, a variation of a standard language. Their speech may contain different sounds, words, or sentence structures from the speech used by other groups or in other regions. Writers use dialect to realistically portray the personality and speech of their characters.

- See Literary Terms Handbook, p. R5.

LiteratureOnline Interactive Literary Elements Handbook To review or learn more about the literary elements, go to www.glencoe.com.

READING PREVIEW

Reading Strategy Analyzing Concrete Details

In short stories, authors typically include specific, **concrete details** about the people and events they portray. These details help readers to visualize setting, make inferences about character, and understand plot. As you read the story, think about how concrete details help you gain a precise idea of the narrator, her family, their home, and their reactions to two unexpected visitors.

Reading Tip: Taking Notes Use a chart to record inferences you draw from the details.

Detail	Inference
The puddle had frozen over	The story is set in winter and it is cold outside

Vocabulary

paperweight (pāp′ ər wāt′) *n.* a heavy, often decorative object traditionally used to hold down loose papers; p. 69 *After the wind blew Terra's papers off her desk twice, she put to use the paperweight her father had given her.*

campaign (kam pān′) *n.* a series of related actions with the purpose of a specific goal, such as an election campaign; p. 70 *His campaign to become class president included a formal speech to the entire school.*

mortal (môrt′ əl) *adj.* deadly; p. 71 *During the joust, the knight received a mortal blow and died before sunset.*

molasses (mə las′ iz) *n.* a thick, dark brown syrup created by boiling down raw sugar; p. 74 *His father's cookie recipe uses both sugar and molasses.*

INDIANA ACADEMIC STANDARDS (pages 68–76)

9.3.7 Recognize and understand the significance of various literary devices...

9.2 Develop [reading] strategies...

9.5.3 Write expository compositions...

Selection Resources

Print Materials

- Unit 1 Resources (Fast File), pp. 29–31
- Leveled Vocabulary Development, p. 5
- Selection and Unit Assessments, pp. 9–10
- Selection Quick Checks, p. 5

Transparencies

- Bellringer Options Transparencies: Selection Focus Transparency 5, Daily Language Practice Transparency 7
- Literary Elements Transparency 12

Technology

- TeacherWorks Plus™ CD-ROM
- StudentWorks Plus™ CD-ROM
- Presentation Plus!™ CD-ROM
- Literature Online, glencoe.com
- Online Student Edition, mhln.com
- Exam*View*® Assessment Suite CD-ROM
- Vocabulary PuzzleMaker CD-ROM
- Listening Library, disc 1 track 5

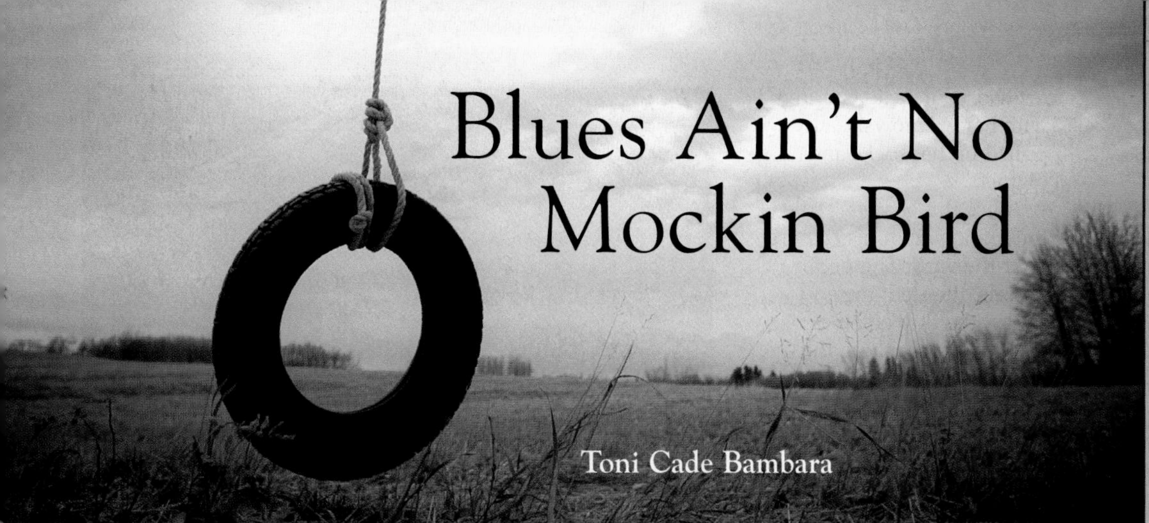

Blues Ain't No Mockin Bird

Toni Cade Bambara

The puddle had frozen over, and me and Cathy went stompin in it. The twins from next door, Tyrone and Terry, were swingin so high out of sight we forgot we were waitin our turn on the tire. Cathy jumped up and came down hard on her heels and started tap-dancin. And the frozen patch splinterin every which way underneath kinda spooky.

"Looks like a plastic spider web," she said. "A sort of weird spider, I guess, with many mental problems." But really it looked like the crystal **paperweight** Granny kept in the parlor. She was on the back porch, Granny was, making the cakes drunk. The old ladle dripping rum into the Christmas tins, like it used to drip maple syrup into the pails when we lived in the Judson's woods, like it poured cider into the vats when we were on the Cooper place, like it used to scoop buttermilk and soft cheese when we lived at the dairy.

"Go tell that man we ain't a bunch of trees."

"Ma'am?"

"I said to tell that man to get away from here with that camera." Me and Cathy look over toward the meadow where the men with the station wagon'd been roamin around all mornin. The tall man with a huge camera lassoed to his shoulder was buzzin our way.

"They're makin movie pictures," yelled Tyrone, stiffenin his legs and twistin so the tire'd come down slow so they could see.

"They're makin movie pictures," sang out Terry.

"That boy don't never have anything original to say," say Cathy grown-up.

By the time the man with the camera had cut across our neighbor's yard, the twins were out of the trees swingin low and Granny was onto the steps, the screen door bammin soft and scratchy against her palms. "We thought we'd get a shot or two of the house and everything and then—"

"Good mornin," Granny cut him off. And smiled that smile.

"Good mornin," he said, head all down the way Bingo does when you yell at him about the bones on the kitchen floor. "Nice place you got here, aunty. We thought we'd take a—"

Reading Strategy Analyzing Concrete Details *What do the details in this sentence tell you about the family?* **R1**

Vocabulary

paperweight (pāp′ ər wāt′) *n.* a heavy, often decorative object traditionally used to hold down loose papers

Reading Strategy Analyzing Concrete Details *Who is Bingo? How do you know?* **R2**

Teach

R1 Reading Strategy

Analyzing Concrete Details

Answer: *The details suggest the family has lived in many different places and that they lived off the land and local resources.* **OL**

R2 Reading Strategy

Analyzing Concrete Details

Answer: *Bingo is a dog. This is clear from the context clue "bones on the kitchen floor."* **OL**

CheckPoint

Use the CheckPoint questions on Presentation Plus! to monitor students' comprehension. These questions can be used with interactive response keypads for immediate student feedback.

Readability Scores

Dale-Chall: 6.8
DRP: 53
Lexile: 960

English Language Coach

Graphic Web Help English language learners understand Granny's anger by drawing a graphic web on the board with "Granny" in the center. As they read, have students contribute facts about Granny, her family, and her home that help explain her anger. Have students consider questions such as these: How wealthy is the family? Are they used to having their own home? What are food stamps, and how does Granny feel about them? How has Granny been treated by people outside the family in the past? **EL**

Academic Standards

The Additional Support activity on p. 69 covers the following standard:

English Language Coach: **9.3.3** Analyze interactions between characters…and explain the way those interactions affect the plot.

Teach

R1 Reading Strategy

Analyzing Concrete Details
Answer: *Students may say that Granny resents the invasion of privacy or that she is suspicious because of past unfair treatment.* OL

★ Viewing the Art

Answer: *Students might infer that this is the face of a strong woman, who will speak with her facial expressions and stand her ground. Granny couldn't stand being taken advantage of, which was the reason for many of her actions.*

Elizabeth Catlett (1915–), an American printmaker and sculptor, has fought for equality for African American people and other people of color through her art. AS

"Did you?" said Granny with her eyebrows. Cathy pulled up her socks and giggled.

"Nice things here," said the man, buzzin his camera over the yard. The pecan barrels, the sled, me and Cathy, the flowers, the printed stones along the driveway, the trees, the twins, the toolshed.

"I don't know about the thing, the it, and the stuff," said Granny, still talkin with her eyebrows. "Just people here is what I tend to consider."

Camera man stopped buzzin. Cathy giggled into her collar.

"Mornin, ladies," a new man said. He had come up behind us when we weren't lookin. "And gents," discoverin the twins givin him a nasty look. "We're filmin for the county," he said with a smile. "Mind if we shoot a bit around here?"

"I do indeed," said Granny with no smile. Smilin man was smiling up a storm. So was Cathy. But he didn't seem to have another word to say, so he and the camera man backed on out the yard, but you could hear the camera buzzin still. "Suppose you just shut that machine off," said Granny real low through her teeth, and took a step down off the porch and then another.

"Now, aunty," Camera said, pointin the thing straight at her.

"Your mama and I are not related."

Smilin man got his notebook out and a chewed-up pencil. "Listen," he said movin back into our yard, "we'd like to have a statement from you . . . for the film. We're filmin for the county, see. Part of the food stamp **campaign**. You know about the food stamps?"[1]

Granny said nuthin.

"Maybe there's somethin you want to say for the film. I see you grow your own vegetables," he smiled real nice. "If more folks did that, see, there'd be no need—"

Granny wasn't sayin nuthin. So they backed on out, buzzin at our clothesline and the twins' bicycles, then back on down to the meadow. The twins were danglin in the tire, lookin at Granny. Me and Cathy were waitin, too, cause Granny always got somethin to

Sharecropper, 1970. Elizabeth Catlett. Linoleum cut, 26 × 22 in. Hampton University Art Museum, VA.

Viewing the Art: How would you describe the personality of this woman? How might she be similar to or different from Granny? ★

1. *Food stamps* are coupons issued by the government to people with low incomes, who use the stamps, as if they were cash, to buy food at stores.

Reading Strategy Analyzing Concrete Details *Why is Granny unfriendly to the men?* R1

Vocabulary

campaign (kam pān′) *n.* a series of related actions with the purpose of a specific goal, such as an election campaign

Additional Support

Skills Practice

GRAMMAR AND LANGUAGE:

Double Negatives Remind students that in Standard American English, two negative words are not used together. Just as in math, two negatives cancel each other out. Point out that *barely, scarcely,* and *hardly* count as negatives. "I had scarcely no sleep" should be "I had no sleep" or "I had scarcely any sleep." Authors sometimes use double negatives in creating realistic regional dialect. Have students rewrite the following examples from the story, using say. She teaches steady with no let-up. "I was on this bridge one time," she started off. "Was a crowd cause this man was goin to jump, you understand. And a minister was there and the police and some other folks. His woman was there, too."

"What was they doin?" asked Tyrone.

"Tryin to talk him out of it was what they was doin. The minister talkin about how it was a **mortal** sin,[2] suicide. His woman takin bites out of her own hand and not even knowin it, so nervous and cryin and talkin fast."

"So what happened?" asked Tyrone.

"So here comes . . . this person . . . with a camera, takin pictures of the man and the minister and the woman. Takin pictures of the man in his misery about to jump, cause life so bad and people been messin with him so bad. This person takin up the whole roll of film practically. But savin a few, of course."

"Of course," said Cathy, hatin the person. Me standin there wonderin how Cathy knew it was "of course" when I didn't and it was *my* grandmother.

After a while Tyrone say, "Did he jump?"

"Yeh, did he jump?" say Terry all eager.

And Granny just stared at the twins till their faces swallow up the eager and they don't even care any more about the man jumpin. Then she goes back onto the porch and lets the screen door go for itself. I'm lookin to Cathy to finish the story cause she knows Granny's whole story before me even. Like she knew how come we move so much and Cathy ain't but a third cousin we picked up on the way last Thanksgivin visitin. But she knew it was on account of people drivin Granny crazy till she'd get up in the night and start packin. Mumblin and packin and wakin everybody up sayin, "Let's get on away from here before I kill me somebody." Like people wouldn't pay her for things like they said they would. Or Mr. Judson bringin us boxes of old clothes and raggedy magazines. Or Mrs. Cooper comin in our kitchen and touchin everything and sayin how clean it all was. Granny goin crazy, and Granddaddy Cain pullin her off the people, sayin, "Now, now, Cora." But next day loadin up the truck, with rocks all in his jaw, madder than Granny in the first place.

"I read a story once," said Cathy soundin like Granny teacher. "About this lady Goldilocks who barged into a house that wasn't even hers. And not invited, you understand. Messed over the people's groceries and broke up the people's furniture. Had the nerve to sleep in the folks' bed."

"Then what happened?" asked Tyrone. "What they do, the folks, when they come in to all this mess?"

"Did they make her pay for it?" asked Terry, makin a fist. "I'd've made her pay me."

I didn't even ask. I could see Cathy actress **R2** was very likely to just walk away and leave us in mystery about this story which I heard was about some bears.

"Did they throw her out?" asked Tyrone, like his father sounds when he's bein extra nasty-plus to the washin-machine man.

"Woulda," said Terry. "I woulda gone upside her head with my fist and—"

"You woulda done whatcha always do—go cry to Mama, you big baby," said Tyrone. So naturally Terry starts hittin on Tyrone, and next thing you know they tumblin out the tire and rollin on the ground. But Granny didn't say a thing or send the twins home or step

2. In some Christian teachings, a *mortal sin* is one so terrible that it causes the death of the soul and results in eternal damnation.

Big Idea Matters of Life and Death *What does Granny's story suggest about her values?* **BI**

Vocabulary
mortal (môrt′ əl) *adj.* deadly

Literary Element Dialect *What does the narrator mean when she says Granddaddy Cain had "rocks all in his jaw"?* **L1**

Literary Element Dialect *How does dialect help to characterize Terry and Tyrone?* **L2**

Teach

BI Big Idea

Matters of Life and Death
Answer: *Students may say that Granny values her dignity and demands respect.* **OL**

L1 Literary Element

Dialect **Answer:** *Students may say that the expression suggests that Granddaddy Cain is angrily clenching his jaw.* **OL**

R2 Reading Strategy

Analyzing Concrete Details
Ask: How does the narrator describe Cathy? *(Students may say that the narrator first says she sounds like "Granny teacher" and then calls her "Cathy actress.")* **OL**
Ask: Why do you think the narrator gives Cathy different titles? *(Students may say that the narrator is showing the different roles that Cathy takes on.)* **AL**

L2 Literary Element

Dialect **Answer:** *Students may say that dialect helps to realistically portray Terry and Tyrone as two young African American children in the South of the 1940s or 1950s.* **OL**

Standard American English: "That boy don't never have anything original to say." *(That boy doesn't ever have anything original to say.)* ". . . couldn't no train throw him off and couldn't nobody turn him round." *(. . . and no train could throw him off and nobody could turn him around.)* **OL**

Building Reading Fluency

Dialect Encourage students to read aloud and listen to regional dialect to improve comprehension. Assign parts and encourage students to speak with regional accents. Discuss how hearing the dialect helped them interpret the story. **BL**

Academic Standards
Additional Support activities on pp. 70 and 71 cover the following standards:
Skills Practice: **9.6.2** Demonstrate an understanding of sentence construction… and proper English usage…
Building Reading Fluency: **9.7.6** Analyze the occasion and…choose effective verbal…techniques…

Teach

Viewing the Art

Answer: *The settings are similar: a small, modest yet comfortable and cozy home in a peaceful rural setting.*

This painting is an example of folk art, artwork created by artists with little or no formal training. Folk artists often depict elements of everyday life. **AS**

out on the steps to tell us about how we can't afford to be fightin amongst ourselves. She didn't say nuthin. So I get into the tire to take my turn. And I could see her leanin up against the pantry table, starin at the cakes she was puttin up for the Christmas sale, mumblin real low and grumpy and holdin her forehead like it wanted to fall off and mess up the rum cakes.

Behind me I hear before I can see Granddaddy Cain comin through the woods in his field boots. Then I twist around to see the shiny black oilskin[3] cuttin through what little left there was of yellows, reds, and oranges. His great white head not quite round cause of this bloody thing high on his shoulder, like he was wearin a cap on sideways. He takes the shortcut through the pecan grove, and the sound of twigs snapping overhead and underfoot travels clear and cold all the way up to us. And here comes Smilin and Camera

3. Here, the *oilskin* is a coat made of cloth treated with oil to make it waterproof.

Our House, 1994. Jessie Coates. Acrylic on Masonite, 3½ × 5 in. Private collection.
Viewing the Art: How does this painting compare with the setting described in the story?

Additional Support

Skills Practice

RESEARCH AND STUDY SKILLS: Presentation Encourage students to gain insight into the story's title by doing a research project on the blues. Have students work in groups. After choosing a blues artist, they should research the artist's life and then give an oral presentation in class. Students should also include selections of the artist's music and explain why and how the music relates to the story. Finally, have each group discuss the importance of the story's title. **OL**

up behind him like they was goin to do somethin. Folks like to go for him sometimes. Cathy say it's because he's so tall and quiet and like a king. And people just can't stand it. But Smilin and Camera don't hit him in the head or nuthin. They just buzz on him as he stalks by with the chicken hawk slung over his shoulder, squawkin, drippin red down the back of the oilskin. He passes the porch and stops a second for Granny to see he's caught the hawk at last, but she's just starin and mumblin, and not at the hawk. So he nails the bird to the toolshed door, the hammerin crackin through the eardrums. And the bird flappin himself to death and droolin down the door to paint the gravel in the driveway red, then brown, then black. And the two men movin up on tiptoe like they was invisible or we were blind, one.

Visual Vocabulary
A *chicken hawk* is any hawk that preys on chickens.

"Get them persons out of my flower bed, R1 Mister Cain," say Granny moanin real low like at a funeral.

"How come your grandmother calls her husband 'Mister Cain' all the time?" Tyrone whispers all loud and noisy and from the city and don't know no better. Like his mama, Miss Myrtle, tell us never mind the formality as if we had no better breeding than to call her Myrtle, plain. And then this R2 awful thing—a giant hawk—come wailin up over the meadow, flyin low and tilted and screamin, zigzaggin through the pecan grove, breakin branches and hollerin, snappin past the clothesline, flyin every which way, flyin into things reckless with crazy.

"He's come to claim his mate," say Cathy fast, and ducks down. We all fall quick and flat into the gravel driveway, stones scrapin my face. I squinch my eyes open again at the hawk on the door, tryin to fly up out of her death like it was just a sack flown into by mistake. Her body holdin her there on that nail, though. The mate beatin the air overhead and clutchin for hair, for heads, for landin space.

The camera man duckin and bendin and runnin and fallin, jigglin the camera and scared. And Smilin jumpin up and down swipin at the huge bird, tryin to bring the hawk down with just his raggedy ole cap. Granddaddy Cain straight up and silent, watchin the circles of the hawk, then aimin the hammer off his wrist. The giant bird fallin, silent and slow. Then here comes Camera and Smilin all big and bad now that the awful screechin thing is on its back and broken, here they come. And Granddaddy Cain looks up at them like it was the first time noticin, but not payin them too much mind cause he's listenin, we all listenin, to that low groanin music comin from the porch. And we figure any minute, somethin in my back tells me any minute now, Granny gonna bust through that screen with somethin in her hand and murder on her mind. So Granddaddy say above the buzzin, but quiet, "Good day, gentlemen." Just like that. Like he'd invited them in to play cards and they'd stayed too long and all the sandwiches were gone and Reverend Webb was droppin by and it was time to go.

They didn't know what to do. But like Cathy say, folks can't stand Granddaddy tall and silent and like a king. They can't neither. The smile the men smilin is pullin the mouth back and showin the teeth. Lookin like the wolf man, both of them. Then Granddaddy holds his hand out—this huge hand I used to sit in when I was a baby and he'd carry me through the house to my mother like I

Reading Strategy Analyzing Concrete Details *How does the giant hawk behave as it approaches the family?* R3

Literary Element Dialect *How do Granddaddy Cain's words reflect the description of him?* L

Reading Strategy Analyzing Concrete Details *Why might the author have chosen to describe the men as "wolf man"?* R4

Teach

R1 Reading Strategy

Analyzing Concrete Details
Ask: How does this description of Granny add to the mood of scene? *(Students may say the comment "moanin' real low like at a funeral" shows her grim view of the situation.)* OL

R2 Reading Strategy

Infer Discuss what students think the hawks might represent in the story. *(Students may say the hawks are pests and predators like the filmmakers.)* OL

R3 Reading Strategy

Analyzing Concrete Details
Answer: *The hawk behaves unpredictably and violently.* OL

L Literary Element

Dialect **Answer:** *Students may say he acts and sounds dignified and authoritative.* OL

R4 Reading Strategy

Analyzing Concrete Details
Answer: *Students may say the description shows that they are predators.* OL

Reading in the Real World

Citizenship Have students look in the library or on the Internet for articles on invasion of privacy. Discuss the articles in class, addressing issues such as whether the public encourages invasion of privacy and how to remedy the situation. OL Have students debate the topic. One group should be pro-paparazzi and the other pro-privacy. Students should research current case law on privacy beforehand. AL

Academic Standards

Additional Support activities on pp. 72 and 73 cover the following standards:

Skills Practice: **9.7.15** Deliver expository... presentations that convey information and ideas from...sources accurately and coherently... **9.7.4** Use...electronic media to enhance the appeal and accuracy of presentations.

Reading in the Real World: **9.2.4** Synthesize the content from several sources or works...; paraphrase the ideas and connect them to...related topics...

Teach

BI Big Idea

Matters of Life and Death
Answer: *Students may say that Granddaddy values privacy and autonomy.* OL

L Literary Element

Dialect Point out to students that the two men's dialect is not significantly different from the family's dialect.
Ask: What point, if any, do you think the author was making by keeping the men's dialect similar to the family's? *(Some students may say that the two men look down on the family even though they speak in the same rural dialect. Others may say the similarity in dialect has more to do with the author's style than trying to make a point.)* OL

R Reading Strategy

Analyzing Concrete Details
Ask: Does the author think Cathy will write her story? *(Students may say no since she refers to Cathy as a dreamer.)* OL

was a gift on a tray. Like he used to on the trains. They called the other men just waiters. But they spoke of Granddaddy separate and said, The Waiter. And said he had engines in his feet and motors in his hands and couldn't no train throw him off and couldn't nobody turn him round. They were big enough for motors, his hands were. He held that one hand out all still and it gettin to be not at all a hand but a person in itself.

"He wants you to hand him the camera," Smilin whispers to Camera, tiltin his head to talk secret like they was in the jungle or somethin and come upon a native that don't speak the language. The men start untyin the straps, and they put the camera into that great hand speckled with the hawk's blood all black and crackly now. And the hand don't even drop with the weight, just the fingers move, curl up around the machine. But Granddaddy lookin straight at the men. They lookin at each other and everywhere but at Granddaddy's face.

"We filmin for the county, see," say Smilin. "We puttin together a movie for the food stamp program . . . filmin all around these parts. Uhh, filmin for the county."

"Can I have my camera back?" say the tall man with no machine on his shoulder, but still keepin it high like the camera was still there or needed to be. "Please, sir."

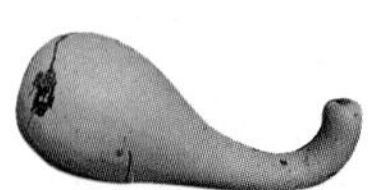
Visual Vocabulary
A *calabash* is a gourdlike fruit of a tropical American tree.

Then Granddaddy's other hand flies up like a sudden and gentle bird, slaps down fast on top of the camera and lifts off half like it was a calabash cut for sharing.

"Hey," Camera jumps forward. He gathers up the parts into his chest and everything unrollin and fallin all over. "Whatcha tryin to do? You'll ruin the film." He looks down into his chest of metal reels and things like he's protectin a kitten from the cold.

"You standin in the misses' flower bed," say Granddaddy. "This is our own place."

The two men look at him, then at each other, then back at the mess in the camera man's chest, and they just back off. One sayin over and over all the way down to the meadow, "Watch it, Bruno. Keep ya fingers off the film." Then Granddaddy picks up the hammer and jams it into the oilskin pocket, scrapes his boots, and goes into the house. And you can hear the squish of his boots headin through the house. And you can see the funny shadow he throws from the parlor window onto the ground by the string-bean patch. The hammer draggin the pocket of the oilskin out so Granddaddy looked even wider. Granny was hummin now—high, not low and grumbly. And she was doin the cakes again, you could smell the **molasses** from the rum.

"There's this story I'm goin to write one day," say Cathy dreamer. "About the proper use of the hammer."

"Can I be in it?" Tyrone say with his hand up like it was a matter of first come, first served.

"Perhaps," say Cathy, climbin onto the tire to pump us up. "If you there and ready."

Big Idea Matters of Life and Death *What does Granddaddy's explanation suggest about what he values?* BI

Vocabulary
molasses (mə las′ iz) *n.* a thick, dark brown syrup created by boiling down raw sugar

Additional Support

Academic Standards
The Additional Support activity on p. 74 covers the following standard:
Skills Practice: **9.1.2** Distinguish between what words mean literally and what they imply…

Skills Practice

GRAMMAR AND LANGUAGE: Colloquialisms Explain to students that regional colloquialisms are an important part of dialect. Explain that a colloquialism is informal speech or slang and have them add the word to their vocabulary lists. Brainstorm a list of regional colloquialisms with students, such as *y'all* for the South and *howdy* for the West. Challenge students to a Create Your Own Colloquialism contest. Instruct students that their slang should be appropriate for the classroom. Have students present their examples and vote on the best slang. OL

AFTER YOU READ

RESPONDING AND THINKING CRITICALLY

Respond

1. What images from the story linger in your mind?

Recall and Interpret

2. (a)Who is the narrator, or person telling the story? (b)What details reveal the narrator's relationship to other characters in the story?
3. (a)What are the two men doing on the Cain family's property? (b)How would you describe the men's initial attitude toward Granny and the rest of the family? Include details from the story in your answer.
4. (a)Summarize Granny's experience on the bridge. (b)What does Granny's story about the man's suicide attempt reveal about her and her reactions to the men with the camera?
5. (a)Explain what happens to the two hawks. (b)How are the hawks like the men with the cameras? Consider what kind of message the hawks' death might have sent to these men.

Analyze and Evaluate

6. The narrator says that Granny "always got something to say. She teaches steady with no let-up." (a)Does the narrator think Granny is a good teacher? (b)Do you think she is a good teacher? Support your opinion with evidence from the story.
7. Why do you think Toni Cade Bambara gave Granddaddy only fifteen words to say? Do you feel you got to know his character? Explain.
8. Do you think "Blues Ain't No Mockin Bird" is an appropriate title for this story? Explain.

Connect

9. **Big Idea** **Matters of Life and Death** Why might Granny and Granddaddy Cain feel that privacy is worth fighting for? Give details from the story in your answer.

LITERARY ANALYSIS

Literary Element Dialect

A **dialect** is a variation of a standard language. Dialects are spoken by people who live in specific regions or who belong to specific groups. Dialects often make use of vivid, sometimes startling, expressions.

1. Rewrite in Standard English each of the following examples of dialect from the story.

   (a)Granny always got somethin to say.

   (b)Let's get on away from here before I kill me somebody.

   (c)I woulda gone upside her head with my fist.

2. (a)How did the dialect affect your reading and understanding of the story? (b)How does dialect make the story's characters and events seem more real? Explain.

Review: Setting

As you learned on pages 10–11, **setting** is the time and place in which the events of a story occur. The history, customs, and beliefs of a place are also a part of setting. "Blues Ain't No Mockin Bird" is set in what is likely a poor rural county in the South during the late 1940s or 1950s. Bambara includes vivid details to help readers picture the Cain family home.

Partner Activity Imagine that you are in charge of preparing a film or television version of this story. With a partner, choose three important moments in the story. For each moment, create a storyboard—a picture portraying the setting, characters, and events of the moment you selected. Below each storyboard, record the details from the story that helped you to create the the storyboard.

Literary Element

1. (a) Granny always has something to say. (b) Let's go before I kill somebody. (c) I would have hit her on the side of her head with my fist.
2. The dialect adds liveliness and realism to characters.

Use the CheckPoint questions on Presentation Plus! to check students' mastery of the selection. These questions can be used with interactive response keypads for immediate student feedback.

AFTER YOU READ

Assess

1. Accept any reasonable answer that includes adequate support.
2. (a) The Cains' young granddaughter (b) Details such as the narrator's references to "Granny" and "Granddaddy"
3. (a) Making a film for the county's food stamp program (b) Presumptuous and rude
4. (a) Granny saw a man threatening to jump off a bridge. His minister and wife were trying to coax him down. A man took pictures of the incident, saving them in case the man jumped. (b) Granny thinks the two filmmakers are intrusive and exploitive.
5. (a) Granddaddy kills the first hawk because it preys on his chickens. The hawk's mate attacks the others and Granddaddy, who kills it with a hammer. (b) They are pests who prey on others. The message is that the men are unwelcome.
6. (a) She respects but she does not entirely understand Granny. (b) Granny is a wise teacher; or Granny fails to drive off the men.
7. His regal bearing and dramatic actions speak louder than words.
8. Students may say the title has something to do with realizing that it's wrong to exploit the serious troubles and hard times ("the blues") of other people.
9. They have probably known oppression and value their privacy, dignity, and self-sufficiency.

AFTER YOU READ

Assess

Reading Strategy

1. Students should support their answers.
2. Students should explain how the details they selected contribute to the meaning of the story.

Writing About Literature

Suggest to students that they can organize the details, using a graphic organizer. Have them jot down details on one side, then write their inferences based on cultural context on the other. Tell students to number the details in the order they will use them in the essay. Then have students begin writing their draft.

Learning for Life

Suggest to students that when writing a memo, it is important to keep your purpose and audience in mind. Since this memo is to a boss, its tone should be more formal than conversational. Discuss what students want to accomplish with the memo. Are they trying to avoid getting into trouble or proposing an alternative plan for a project?

Vocabulary

1. a **2.** b **3.** a **4.** b

READING AND VOCABULARY

Reading Strategy Analyzing Concrete Details

A writer uses **concrete details** to evoke ideas and images with precision. By examining the concrete details of a story, you can better understand the story's meaning. You can also deepen your appreciation for the author's skill in crafting the story.

1. List three details about Granny and explain what the details tell you about her experiences, feelings, and personality.
2. Describe a detail in the story that you found especially evocative or suggestive. Explain how the detail affects the story's meaning.

Vocabulary Practice

Practice with Analogies To complete an analogy, first decide what relationship exists in a pair of words. Then choose the word that creates the same relationship in a second pair of words. For each item below, choose the word that best completes the analogy.

1. wind : paperweight :: rain :
   a. umbrella **b.** sunshine **c.** sweater
2. drive : campaign :: competition :
   a. amusement **b.** tournament **c.** sport
3. injury : mortal :: mistake :
   a. extreme **b.** benign **c.** failing
4. syrup : molasses :: bird :
   a. song **b.** hawk **c.** flight

Academic Vocabulary

Here is a word from the vocabulary list on page R80.

income (in′kum′) *n.* money received from work, collection of rent, or investment

Practice and Apply
How does the Cain family obtain its **income**?

Literature Online Web Activities For eFlashcards, Selection Quick Checks, and other Web activities, go to www.glencoe.com.

WRITING AND EXTENDING

Writing About Literature

Analyze Cultural Context In some stories, the setting is a minor feature. In other stories, such as "Blues Ain't No Mockin Bird," the setting is crucial to an understanding of the plot. The **cultural context** of Bambara's story—the customs, beliefs, and relationships that typified the rural South during the 1940s and 1950s—is especially important. At that time and in that place, large disparities of wealth and power separated African Americans from whites. This situation was sustained by unfair laws, forcing African Americans to struggle for basic rights and respect. African Americans and whites had their own customs and beliefs as well as those they shared.

Write a brief essay in which you analyze the way in which cultural context helps to explain the story, especially the thoughts and actions of Granny, Granddaddy Cain, and the men with the camera. To begin organizing your first draft, compile details from the story and jot down your inferences about what these details may mean based on cultural context.

You may wish to organize your draft according to the plan below.

Introduction	Body	Conclusion
A thesis, or central idea, about the role of cultural context in the story	Details from the story that help reveal the influence of cultural context on the story's plot, characters, and other elements	A restatement of the thesis, a brief summation of evidence for the thesis, and a final thought about what the story suggests about the South during the 1940s and 1950s

After writing your draft, meet with a peer reviewer to evaluate each other's work and suggest revisions. Then proofread and edit your draft for errors in spelling, grammar, and punctuation.

Learning for Life

Think about the story from Camera and Smilin's point of view. How did they first perceive the Cain family, and what did they think after they left the family's property, unable to complete their assignment? Draft a memo Camera and Smilin might write to their boss explaining what happened and why.

Academic Vocabulary

The Cain family appears to have a farm, and Granny is making cakes to sell.

Web Activities Have students access the Web site for interactive activities that will help them assess their understanding of the selection.

The Interlopers

MEET SAKI

Miserable old women eaten by ferrets, little girls who torment adults by making up strange tales, a cat who learns to talk so it can repeat the unkind comments it overhears—these are the plots and characters from the pen of the writer known as Saki. The stories are often a delightful mix of humor, horror, and plot-twisting irony that can be grim but unforgettable.

"A most improper story to tell the young children! You have undermined the effect of years of careful teaching."

—Saki, from "The Storyteller"

The Early Years Hector Hugh Munro was born in the former British colony of Burma, the third of three children. His father was a member of the British military police. His mother died shortly after Hector's birth, so his father took the children to England. Leaving the children in the care of his two unmarried sisters, Hector's father returned to Burma. The aunts were extremely strict and rarely let the children play or go outside. Munro later related to his sister Ethel that he believed their unusual upbringing was responsible for their originality.

When Munro was twenty-three, he took a job in Burma (now Myanmar) with the military police. He contracted malaria, however, and was forced to return to England. While he was recuperating he decided to become a professional writer.

Saki Appears When Munro published *The Rise of the Russian Empire* in 1900, reviewers were quick to criticize his flippant style. However, the book contained elements that would survive in Saki's short stories: vivid descriptions of settings, scenes of pointless cruelty, and images of ferocious animals.

Munro then wrote a series of satiric pieces for a London newspaper. He began signing his work "Saki," a pseudonym he took from a twelfth-century Persian poem. He realized he had a talent for analyzing political intrigue, so he took a job as a foreign correspondent. The next few years found him traveling throughout Russia and Eastern Europe, moving from one war-torn spot to the next.

In 1908 Munro returned to England. By 1909 he was able to earn a living as a freelance writer. Although he wrote two novels, Munro remains best known for his short stories. His biographer, Charles Gillen, believes that Munro's stories continue to be popular because readers see "something familiar and pertinent in Munro's cynicism and unflattering view of humanity."

When World War I began in 1914, Munro announced, "I have always looked forward to the romance of a European war." He enlisted and became one of the millions of soldiers who endured trench duty on the front lines. On a dark winter morning in 1916, he gave away his position when he ordered a soldier to put out a cigarette. Seconds later, Munro was killed by a shot through the head.

Saki was born in 1870 and died in 1916.

Literature Online **Author Search** For more about Saki, go to www.glencoe.com.

Focus

BELLRINGER

Bellringer Options
Selection Focus Transparency 6
Daily Language Practice Transparency 8

Or **write on the board:** *Do you think humanity is basically warlike or peaceful?* Discuss whether most of humanity tends toward violence or peace.

Literature Online

Author Search To expand students' appreciation of Saki (aka Hector Hugh Munro), have them access the Web site for additional information and resources.

Selection Skills

The Interlopers

Literary Elements
- Irony (SE pp. 78–86)
- Mood (SE p. 86)

Reading Skills
- Analyzing Cause-and-Effect Relationships (SE pp. 78–86)
- Listing Cause and Effect (SE p. 78)

Vocabulary Skills
- Practice with Analogies (SE p. 86)
- Word Groups (TWE p. 84)

Listening/Speaking/Viewing Skills
- Analyzing Art (SE p. 82; TWE pp. 79, 80)
- Group Discussion (SE p. 87)

Writing Skills/Grammar
- Analyze Setting (SE p. 87)
- Varying Sentence Length (SE p. 87)

Study Skills/Research/Assessment
- You're the Critic (SE p. 85)

BEFORE YOU READ

Focus

Summary

The Gradwitz and Znaeym families have been fighting over a piece of forestland for generations. Ulrich von Gradwitz goes to the forest intent on catching Georg Znaeym poaching on his game and then killing him. When the two men meet, a tree falls on them. They reconcile as they lie pinned beneath the fallen tree, awaiting rescue. At the end of the story, they think they glimpse a rescue party but instead wolves appear.

V Vocabulary

Vocabulary File Say: Add these words and definitions to your vocabulary file. For each word, include a sentence that gives you an example of how to use the word. **OL** Students with English language needs should include the pronunciations of these words in their files. **EL**

Literary Elements
Have students access the Web site to improve their understanding of irony.

LITERATURE PREVIEW

Connecting to the Story

Have you ever experienced a sudden change in a relationship? Before you read "The Interlopers," think about the following questions:

- What are some things that can happen to change relationships?
- Have you ever found that taking the time to talk to someone changed your opinion about that person?

Building Background

"The Interlopers" takes place in the Carpathian Mountains, a mountain range in southeastern Europe. The time of the story is probably the early 1900s. In the eastern part of the Carpathians, great forests are home to bears, deer, wolves, lynx, boars, and other wild animals. Vast tracts of family-owned land in this region often included forest in addition to farmland, so that the owners could hunt.

Poachers are people who trespass on another person's land to hunt or fish, and they have long been a problem for landowners. Poaching has been a crime, sometimes punishable by death, for hundreds of years.

Setting Purposes for Reading

Big Idea Matters of Life and Death

As you read this story, think about the details that seem to lead to inevitable death or new life.

Literary Element Irony

Irony is the contrast or discrepancy between appearance and reality. There are several forms of irony. Situational irony is a contrast between what is expected and what actually happens. As you read, look for ways that Saki uses situational irony to convey meaning about life and death.

- See Literary Terms Handbook, p. R9.

LiteratureOnline Interactive Literary Elements Handbook To review or learn more about the literary elements, go to www.glencoe.com.

READING PREVIEW

Reading Strategy Analyzing Cause-and-Effect Relationships

A cause is that which makes something happen. An effect is what happens as a result of the cause. When you **analyze a cause-and-effect relationship,** you explore the causes or reasons behind thoughts, actions, or events, and examine the results of these thoughts, actions, or events. You may also find that an effect can in turn become the cause of the next effect. As you read, notice how cause and effect control the plot and outcome of Saki's story.

Reading Tip: Listing Cause and Effect Use a chart like the one below to record cause and effect in "The Interlopers."

Cause	Effect
p. 79: a long series of accusations	embittered relationships between the two families

Vocabulary

acquiesce (ak′ wē es′) *v.* to consent or agree to without protest; p. 79 *He would not acquiesce to our plans for a surprise party.*

pious (pī′ əs) *adj.* having either genuine or pretended religious devotion; p. 81 *His pious acts included generosity to the poor and care for the sick.*

endeavor (en dev′ ər) *n.* a serious or strenuous attempt to accomplish something; p. 83 *Despite their best endeavors, they could not rebuild the house in one day.*

languor (lang′ gər) *n.* weakness; fatigue; p. 83 *He could not explain the feeling of languor that made him want to sleep all day.*

reconciliation (rek′ ən sil′ ē ā′ shən) *n.* a settlement of a controversy or disagreement; p. 84 *Reconciliation between the two countries quickly brought an end to fighting.*

INDIANA ACADEMIC STANDARDS (pages 78–87)
9.3.8 Interpret and evaluate the impact of…ironies in a text.
9.2 Develop [reading] strategies…
9.5.3 Write expository compositions…
9.3 [Identify] story elements such as…setting…

Selection Resources

Print Materials
- Unit 1 Resources (Fast File), pp. 32–34
- Leveled Vocabulary Development, p. 6
- Selection and Unit Assessments, pp. 11–12
- Selection Quick Checks, p. 6

Transparencies
- Bellringer Options Transparencies: Selection Focus Transparency 6, Daily Language Practice Transparency 8
- Literary Elements Transparency 8

Technology
- TeacherWorks Plus™ CD-ROM
- StudentWorks Plus™ CD-ROM
- Presentation Plus!™ CD-ROM
- Literature Online, glencoe.com
- Online Student Edition, mhln.com
- Exam*View*® Assessment Suite CD-ROM
- Vocabulary PuzzleMaker CD-ROM
- Listening Library, disc 1 track 6

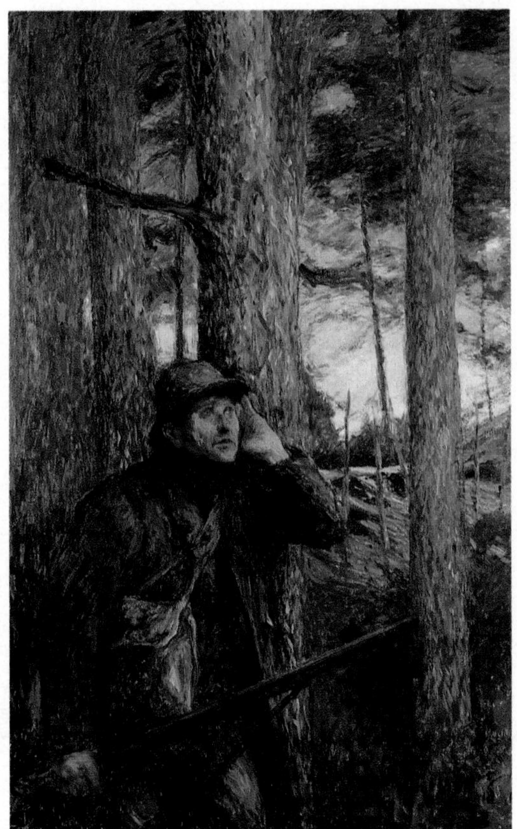

Poacher, 1894. Bruno Liljefors. Oil on canvas, 41 × 61 cm. Statens Konstmuseer, Stockholm. ★

THE INTERLOPERS

Saki (H. H. Munro)

In a forest of mixed growth somewhere on the eastern spurs of the Carpathians,[1] a man stood one winter night watching and listening, as though he waited for some beast of the woods to come within the range of his vision, and, later, of his rifle. But the game for whose presence he kept so keen an outlook was none that figured in the sportsman's calendar as lawful and proper for the chase; Ulrich von Gradwitz[2] patrolled the dark forest in quest of a human enemy.

The forest lands of Gradwitz were of wide extent and well stocked with game; the narrow strip of precipitous[3] woodland that lay on its outskirt was not remarkable for the game it harbored or the shooting it afforded, but it was the most jealously guarded of all its owner's territorial possessions. A famous lawsuit, in the days of his grandfather, had wrested[4] it from the illegal possession of a neighboring family of petty landowners; the dispossessed party had never **acquiesced** in the judgment of the Courts, and a long series of poaching affrays[5] and similar scandals had embittered the relationships between the families for three generations. The neighbor feud had grown into a personal one since Ulrich had come to be head of his family; if there was a man in the world whom he detested and wished ill to it was Georg

1. The *Carpathians* are a mountain range in southeastern Europe, and *spurs* are ridges of mountains that extend from the main range.
2. *Ulrich von Gradwitz* (o͞ol′ rik fōn gräd′ vitz)
3. *Precipitous* means "very steep."
4. *Wrested* means "taken as if by force."
5. *Affrays* are disruptive, public quarrels or disagreements.

Literary Element Irony *Explain how the description of the hunter and his game is an example of situational irony.* L

Reading Strategy Analyzing Cause-and-Effect Relationships *Why might it be significant that the feud became a "personal one"?* R

Vocabulary

acquiesce (ak′ wē es′) *v.* to consent or agree to without protest

Teach

L Literary Element

Irony Answer: *Readers expect him to be hunting an animal; instead, he is hunting a human being.* OL

R Reading Strategy

Analyzing Cause-and-Effect Relationships

Answer: *Because Ulrich takes it personally, he is less likely to let it go. Maintaining the feud is a matter of personal pride.* OL

★ Viewing the Art

Swedish artist Bruno Liljefors (1860–1939) is famous for his wildlife paintings. He painted outdoors in an effort to capture the true spirit of the natural world. His love of hunting is reflected in many of his paintings. Artistically, he was influenced by Impressionist and Japanese art. AS

CheckPoint

Use the CheckPoint questions on Presentation Plus! to monitor students' comprehension. These questions can be used with interactive response keypads for immediate student feedback.

Readability Scores

Dale-Chall: 14.4
DRP: 65
Lexile: 1230

Differentiated Instruction

Setting Ask student groups to pick a country that contains the Carpathian Mountains, such as Hungary, Romania, the Czech Republic, or the Ukraine. Each group should research its country and the effect of the mountains on the region, and share results and images. AL

Building Reading Fluency

Pronunciation Students may stumble over the unusual names in the story, which will slow down their reading. Instruct students to practice saying the names out loud until they are comfortable with them. BL

Academic Standards

Additional Support activities on p. 79 cover the following standards:

Differentiated Instruction: **9.7.15** Deliver expository (informational) presentations...

Building Reading Fluency: **9.1** Use phonics...and a growing knowledge of English and other languages to...become fluent readers.

Teach

BI Big Idea

Matters of Life and Death
Answer: *There are hunters in the forest, so the animals may be running for their lives.* OL

★ Viewing the Art

Gustave Courbet (1819–1877) is credited as an instigator and leader of the Realism art movement. Realism, as the term implies, relies on accurate depictions of subjects, with no embellishment. Courbet believed only in painting things that actually existed and that were of his time. AS

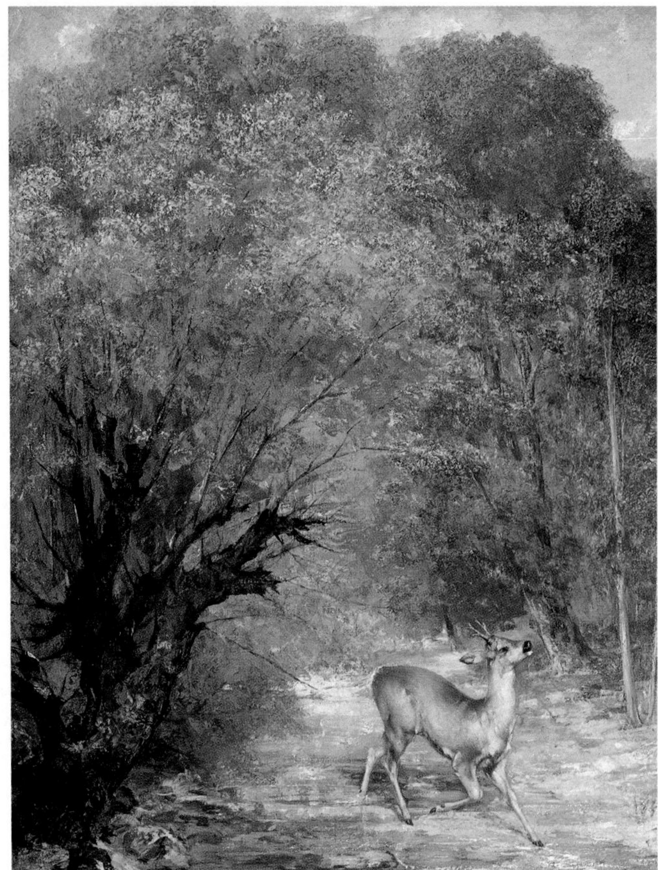

The Hunted Roe-Deer on the Alert, 1867. Gustave Courbet. Oil on canvas, 111 × 85 in. Musée d'Orsay, Paris, France. ★

Znaeym,[6] the inheritor of the quarrel and the tireless game-snatcher and raider of the disputed border-forest. The feud might, perhaps, have died down or been compromised if the personal ill-will of the two men had not stood in the way; as boys they had thirsted for one another's blood, as men each prayed that misfortune might fall on the other, and this wind-scourged[7] winter night Ulrich had banded together his foresters to watch the dark forest, not in quest of four-footed quarry,[8] but to keep a look-out for the prowling thieves whom he suspected of being afoot from across the land boundary. The roebuck, which usually kept in the sheltered hollows during a storm-wind, were running like driven things tonight, and there was movement and unrest among the creatures that were wont[9] to sleep through the dark hours. Assuredly there was a disturbing element in the forest, and Ulrich could guess the quarter from whence it came.

He strayed away by himself from the watchers whom he had placed in ambush on the crest of the hill, and wandered far down the steep slopes amid the wild tangle of undergrowth, peering through the tree-trunks and listening through the whistling and skirling[10] of the wind and the restless

6. *Georg Znaeym* (gā′ ôrg znē′ əm)
7. *Wind-scourged* means "wind-whipped."
8. *Quarry* (kwôr′ ē) refers to an animal—or anything—that is being hunted or pursued.
9. *Wont* means "accustomed" or "used to."
10. *Skirling* is any long, shrill sound, but the word originally referred to the sound of a bagpipe

Big Idea Matters of Life and Death *How does the description of the behavior of the animals in the forest relate to the big idea?* BI

Additional Support

Skills Practice

LITERARY ELEMENT: Imagery Point out to students how Saki's word choice contributes to the mood in the story.
Write on the board: *restless beating of the branches.*
Ask: What mood does this create? *(Students may say that* restless *suggests tension and* beating *foreshadows violence.)* Have students skim the story for vivid sensory images of the forest.
OL Ask students to write a paragraph describing the setting, using vivid sensory images. AL

beating of the branches for sight or sound of the marauders. If only on this wild night, in this dark, lone spot, he might come across Georg Znaeym, man to man, with none to witness—that was the wish that was uppermost in his thoughts. And as he stepped round the trunk of a huge beech he came face to face with the man he sought.

The two enemies stood glaring at one another for a long silent moment. Each had a rifle in his hand, each had hate in his heart and murder uppermost in his mind. The chance had come to give full play to the passions of a lifetime. But a man who has been brought up under the code of a restraining civilization cannot easily nerve himself to shoot down his neighbor in cold blood and without word spoken, except for an offense against his hearth[11] and honor. And before the moment of hesitation had given way to action a deed of Nature's own violence overwhelmed them both. A fierce shriek of the storm had been answered by a splitting crash over their heads, and ere[12] they could leap aside a mass of falling beech tree had thundered down on them. Ulrich von Gradwitz found himself stretched on the ground, one arm numb beneath him and the other held almost as helplessly in a tight tangle of forked branches, while both legs were pinned beneath the fallen mass. His heavy shooting-boots had saved his feet from being crushed to pieces, but if his fractures were not as serious as they might have been, at least it was evident that he could not move from his present position till some one came to release him. The descending twigs had slashed the skin of his face, and he had to wink away some drops of blood from his eyelashes before he could take in a general view of the disaster. At his side, so near that under ordinary circumstances he could almost have touched him, lay Georg Znaeym, alive and struggling, but obviously as helplessly pinioned[13] down as himself. All round them lay a thick-strewn wreckage of splintered branches and broken twigs.

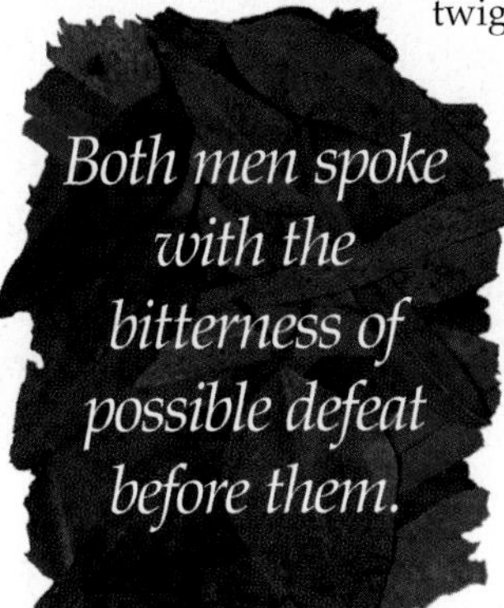
Both men spoke with the bitterness of possible defeat before them.

Relief at being alive and exasperation at his captive plight brought a strange medley of **pious** thank-offerings and sharp curses to Ulrich's lips. Georg, who was nearly blinded with the blood which trickled across his eyes, stopped his struggling for a moment to listen, and then gave a short, snarling laugh.

"So you're not killed, as you ought to be, but you're caught, anyway," he cried; "caught fast. Ho, what a jest, Ulrich von Gradwitz snared in his stolen forest. There's real justice for you!"

And he laughed again, mockingly and savagely.

"I'm caught in my own forest-land," retorted Ulrich. "When my men come to release us you will wish, perhaps, that you

11. Here, *hearth* is used figuratively to mean "home and family."

12. *Ere* (ār) is an old word for *before.*

13. To be *pinioned* is to be disabled by the binding of one's arms.

Literary Element Irony *Why is the appearance of Georg Znaeym unexpected?* **L1**

Reading Strategy Analyzing Cause-and-Effect Relationships *What causes the two men to hesitate instead of shooting immediately? What is the effect of their hesitation?* **R**

Literary Element Irony *What is ironic about the men's situation?* **L2**

Vocabulary

pious (pī′ əs) *adj.* having either genuine or pretended religious devotion

Teach

L1 Literary Element

Irony **Answer:** *Znaeym would know that Gradwitz was his enemy, and like the running deer, he should be trying to escape the hunter. Also, no hunter expects his prey to appear that suddenly.* **OL**

R Reading Strategy

Analyzing Cause-and-Effect Relationships

Answer: *Despite their mutual hatred, they are civilized men who hesitate to kill a fellow human in cold blood. During that moment of hesitation, a tree falls on them.* **OL**

L2 Literary Element

Irony **Answer:** *Each man thought that the other was the only enemy he had to worry about. Now both are trapped by a common "enemy," the tree.* **OL**

Differentiated Instruction

Visualizing Visual learners will have an easier time grasping vocabulary if they can "see" it. Instruct students to come up with images for their vocabulary words. Images can be literal, such as a picture of a bird, or more figurative, such as showing someone building a pyramid to represent endeavor. Have students bring the images to class and share their impressions of how the images relate to the words. Have students paste the images next to their vocabulary word as a memory aid. **BL**

Academic Standards

Additional Support activities on pp. 80 and 81 cover the following standards:

Skills Practice: **9.3.11** Evaluate the aesthetic qualities of style, including the impact of diction…on…mood…

Differentiated Instruction: **9.1.1** Identify and use the literal and figurative meanings of words…

Teach

R1 Reading Strategy

Analyzing Cause-and-Effect Relationships Georg and Ulrich both threaten to have their men kill the other. **Ask:** If Georg's men kill Ulrich, or Ulrich's men kill Georg, what will be the effect on the feud? *(Students may say that murder would intensify the feud. Others may say that the death of one of the men would end it.)* OL

BI Big Idea

Matters of Life and Death
Answer: *They are trapped by a tree, not by one another. Their men might be long in coming. What else, besides the fallen tree, might occur in this dangerous forest?* OL

★ Viewing the Art

Answer: *Students may say that the stark trees against a dark sky reflects the grim forest setting and the mood of menace and doom.*

William Fraser Garden (1856–1921) employed a technique known as photo-realism. Although this is a painting, its precise attention to detail makes it look like a photograph. AS

The Wood at Dusk. William Fraser Garden. Watercolor. Private collection.
Viewing the Art: How does this scene help you picture the setting of the story? ★

were in a better plight than caught poaching on a neighbor's land, shame on you."

Georg was silent for a moment; then he answered quietly:

"Are you sure that your men will find much to release? I have men, too, in the forest tonight, close behind me, and *they* will be here first and do the releasing. When they drag me out from under these damned branches it won't need much clumsiness on their part to roll this mass of trunk right over on the top of you. Your men will find you dead under a fallen beech tree. For form's sake I shall send my condolences to your family."

"It is a useful hint," said Ulrich fiercely. "My men had orders to follow in ten minutes' time, seven of which must have gone by already, and when they get me out—I will remember the hint. Only as you will have met your death poaching on my lands I don't think I can decently send any message of condolence to your family."

"Good," snarled Georg, "good. We fight this quarrel out to the death, you and I and our foresters, with no cursed interlopers[14] to come between us. Death and damnation to you, Ulrich von Gradwitz."

"The same to you, Georg Znaeym, forest-thief, game-snatcher."

Both men spoke with the bitterness of possible defeat before them, for each knew that it might be long before his men would seek him out or find him; it was a bare matter of chance which party would arrive first on the scene.

Both had now given up the useless struggle to free themselves from the mass of wood that

14. *Interlopers* are people who violate or interfere with the rights of another, such as by trespassing.

Big Idea Matters of Life and Death *Both men face death and threaten death at this moment. What about their situation suggests that life or death is not entirely in their own hands?* BI

Additional Support

Skills Practice

LITERARY ELEMENT: Dialogue
Ask: Do you feel the dialogue is realistic? *(Some may find the dialogue old-fashioned and stilted, while others might argue that it is appropriate to the story's setting.)* Have groups of students improvise various styles of dialogue, such as comic, western, or soap opera, for the class. OL Have students rewrite the dialogue in the style of their choosing and perform it for the class. AL

held them down; Ulrich limited his **endeavors** to an effort to bring his one partially free arm near enough to his outer coat-pocket to draw out his wine-flask. Even when he had accomplished that operation it was long before he could manage the unscrewing of the stopper or get any of the liquid down his throat. But what a Heaven-sent draught[15] it seemed! It was an open winter, and little snow had fallen as yet, hence the captives suffered less from the cold than might have been the case at that season of the year; nevertheless, the wine was warming and reviving to the wounded man, and he looked across with something like a throb of pity to where his enemy lay, just keeping the groans of pain and weariness from crossing his lips.

"Could you reach this flask if I threw it over to you?" asked Ulrich suddenly; "there is good wine in it, and one may as well be as comfortable as one can. Let us drink, even if tonight one of us dies."

"No, I can scarcely see anything; there is so much blood caked round my eyes," said Georg, "and in any case I don't drink wine with an enemy."

Ulrich was silent for a few minutes, and lay listening to the weary screeching of the wind. An idea was slowly forming and growing in his brain, an idea that gained strength every time that he looked across at the man who was fighting so grimly against pain and exhaustion. In the pain and **languor** that Ulrich himself was feeling the old fierce hatred seemed to be dying down.

He looked across with something like a throb of pity to where his enemy lay . . .

"Neighbor," he said presently, "do as you please if your men come first. It was a fair compact.[16] But as for me, I've changed my mind. If my men are the first to come you shall be the first to be helped, as though you were my guest. We have quarreled like devils all our lives over this stupid strip of forest, where the trees can't even stand upright in a breath of wind. Lying here tonight, thinking, I've come to think we've been rather fools; there are better things in life than getting the better of a boundary dispute. Neighbor, if you will help me to bury the old quarrel I—I will ask you to be my friend."

Georg Znaeym was silent for so long that Ulrich thought, perhaps, he had fainted with the pain of his injuries. Then he spoke slowly and in jerks.

"How the whole region would stare and gabble[17] if we rode into the market-square together. No one living can remember seeing a Znaeym and a von Gradwitz talking to one another in friendship. And what peace there would be among the forester folk if we ended our feud tonight. And if we choose to make peace among our people there is none other to interfere, no interlopers from outside. . . . You would come and keep the Sylvester night beneath my roof, and I would come and feast on some high day[18] at your castle. . . . I would never fire a shot on your land, save when you invited me as a guest; and you should come and shoot with me down in the marshes where the

15. *Draught* is the amount taken in one drink. The word is pronounced the same as, and is often spelled, *draft.*

16. Here, *compact* means "agreement."

17. *Gabble* means "to talk rapidly and foolishly; jabber."

18. *Sylvester night* refers to New Year's Eve festivities honoring Saint Sylvester who, according to legend, converted Constantine the Great to Christianity after curing him of leprosy. A *high day* is any holy day (or holiday) in the church calendar.

Literary Element Irony *What is ironic about Ulrich's change of heart?* **L**

Vocabulary

endeavor (en dev′ ər) *n.* a serious or strenuous attempt to accomplish something

languor (lang′ gər) *n.* weakness; fatigue

Reading Strategy Analyzing Cause-and-Effect Relationships *What effect do you think Ulrich's words will have on Georg?* **R2**

Teach

L Literary Element

Irony **Answer:** *It was Ulrich's becoming the head of his family that worsened the feud. No one would have imagined that his murderous hatred could fade.* **OL**

R2 Reading Strategy

Analyzing Cause-and-Effect Relationships

Answer: *Students may predict that Georg will gladly agree to end the feud. Others may predict that he will deny Ulrich a second time.* **OL**

Reading in the Real World

Citizenship Explain that poaching remains a serious problem in the modern world. Hunters poach game not only from private lands but also from wildlife preserves and national parks. Have students research poaching in today's world to learn about local efforts to protect wildlife and the challenges facing conservationists. Encourage students to discuss ways to overcome these challenges. **OL** Have students research poaching as a local problem and as a global issue and write a comparison of the two topics. **AL**

Academic Standards

Additional Support activities on pp. 82 and 83 cover the following standards:

Skills Practice: **9.3.11** Evaluate the aesthetic qualities of style, including the impact of diction...on tone, mood, and theme.

Reading in the Real World: **9.2.4** Synthesize the content from several sources or works...; paraphrase the ideas and connect them to...related topics to demonstrate comprehension.

Teach

R Reading Strategy

Analyzing Cause-and-Effect Relationships

Ask: Given what you know about the feud, do you believe Georg is sincere in his promises of friendship to Ulrich? *(Students may say Georg was swept up in the moment and may not follow through. Others may feel he has truly changed.)* OL

L1 Literary Element

Irony Answer: *Something will prevent their plan from being realized. Their men might attack before learning of their leaders' change of heart. Perhaps nature will again intervene.* OL

BI Big Idea

Matters of Life and Death

Answer: *The two men will most likely die. They might have escaped this fate if they had made peace sooner.* OL

Use the CheckPoint questions on Presentation Plus! to check students' mastery of the selection. These questions can be used with interactive response keypads for immediate student feedback.

wildfowl are. In all the countryside there are none that could hinder if we willed to **R** make peace. I never thought to have wanted to do other than hate you all my life, but I think I have changed my mind about things too, this last half-hour. And you offered me your wine-flask. . . . Ulrich von Gradwitz, I will be your friend."

For a space both men were silent, turning over in their minds the wonderful changes that this dramatic **reconciliation** would bring about. In the cold, gloomy forest, with the wind tearing in fitful gusts through the naked branches and whistling round the tree-trunks, they lay and waited for the help that would now bring release and succor[19] to both parties. And each prayed a private prayer that his men might be the first to arrive, so that he might be the first to show honorable attention to the enemy that had become a friend.

Presently, as the wind dropped for a moment, Ulrich broke silence.

"Let's shout for help," he said; "in this lull our voices may carry a little way."

"They won't carry far through the trees and undergrowth," said Georg, "but we can try. Together, then."

The two raised their voices in a prolonged hunting call.

"Together again," said Ulrich a few minutes later, after listening in vain for an answering halloo.

"I heard something that time, I think," said Ulrich.

"I heard nothing but the pestilential[20] wind," said Georg hoarsely.

There was silence again for some minutes, and then Ulrich gave a joyful cry.

"I can see figures coming through the wood. They are following in the way I came down the hillside."

Both men raised their voices in as loud a shout as they could muster.

"They hear us! They've stopped. Now they see us. They're running down the hill towards us," cried Ulrich.

> *"I can see figures coming through the wood."*

"How many of them are there?" asked Georg.

"I can't see distinctly," said Ulrich; "nine or ten."

"Then they are yours," said Georg; "I had only seven out with me."

"They are making all the speed they can, brave lads," said Ulrich gladly.

"Are they your men?" asked Georg. "Are they your men?" he repeated impatiently as Ulrich did not answer.

"No," said Ulrich with a laugh, the idiotic chattering laugh of a man unstrung with hideous fear.

"Who are they?" asked Georg quickly, straining his eyes to see what the other would gladly not have seen.

"Wolves."

19. To bring *succor* is to bring help, assistance, or relief.

Literary Element Irony *What irony is suggested by this passage?* **L1**

Vocabulary

reconciliation (rek′ ən sil′ ē ā′ shən) *n.* a settlement of a controversy or disagreement

20. Here, *pestilential* means "harmful" or "destructive."

Big Idea Matters of Life and Death *What fate awaits the two men? What might have kept the men from this fate?* **BI**

Additional Support

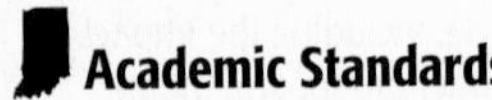

Academic Standards

The Additional Support activity on p. 84 covers the following standard:

Skills Practice: **9.1** Use…a growing knowledge of English and other languages to determine the meaning of words…

Skills Practice

VOCABULARY: Word Groups Tell students that creating word groups can help them learn vocabulary. Suggest that as they continue to add words to their vocabulary lists, they organize them into groups. They should group words with similar definitions together and create a name for the group. For example, a group of words related to happiness would constitute a happiness category. OL Students may also want group words based on their etymology. AL

AFTER YOU READ

RESPONDING AND THINKING CRITICALLY

Respond

1. (a)As you read the story, how did you think it would end? (b)What thoughts went through your mind at the end of the story?

Recall and Interpret

2. (a)What started the feud between the von Gradwitz and Znaeym families? (b)In your opinion, why do Ulrich and Georg hate each other so much?
3. (a)How does the men's relationship gradually change while they are trapped under the tree? (b)What causes the change in the men's relationship? Explain.
4. (a)Who are the figures that Ulrich sees coming through the forest? (b)What is ironic about the way the story ends?

Analyze and Evaluate

5. To whom or what might the title of this story refer?
6. Do Ulrich and Georg seem to meet by chance or by design? Explain your answer.
7. Saki is well known as a master of surprise endings, but he also drops hints to prepare a careful reader for the surprise. (a)What hints about the ending appear in "The Interlopers"? (b)How well has Saki prepared readers for the ending?

Connect

8. **Big Idea** **Matters of Life and Death** What does Ulrich's statement that "there are better things in life than getting the better of a boundary dispute" suggest about how the two men have spent their lives?

YOU'RE THE CRITIC: Different Viewpoints

What Makes Saki, Saki?

Read the two excerpts of literary criticism below. E. V. Knox notes how often Saki uses animals in his stories. Charles Gillen notes important features of Saki's surprise endings. Together, these comments will help you appreciate "The Interlopers."

> *"The wild things run riot. They peep out in every plot. They peer from the corner of every conversation. . . .One creature or another, exotic or domesticated, is always playing a part in these tales, and sometimes a decisive part, terrible or whimsical. . . .Here is a world in which time after time in the author's eyes, human beings are a little lower than the animals."*
>
> —E. V. Knox

> *"It is difficult to give examples of [the surprise ending] aspect of Munro's writing without relating the entire plot of the story in point, so tightly knit was the preparation and skilled placing of false scents; the surprise ending of the story must be considered in relation to every little thing that has occurred before it."*
>
> —Charles Gillen

Group Activity Discuss the following questions with classmates. Refer to the excerpts and cite evidence from "The Interlopers."

1. Do you agree with Knox that in this story "human beings are a little lower than the animals"? Explain.
2. How well do you think Gillen's points are illustrated in "The Interlopers"? Give examples from the story.
3. Which element do you find more interesting—Saki's use of animals or his surprise endings? Explain.

AFTER YOU READ

Assess

1. (a) Readers may have expected a "trick" ending. Others may have expected one man to be killed or that both would be saved. (b) Some may be startled or horrified by the end or hopeful that they may survive.
2. (a) Disputed ownership of the forestland (b) The feud was a family tradition.
3. (a) They decide to become friends. (b)Their life-or-death situation puts their pointless feud in perspective and creates a bond between them.
4. (a) Wolves (b) The men's conflict is about to destroy them just when they have finally resolved it.
5. Georg and his family trespassing on the Gradwitz land; Georg and Ulrich intruding in the wilderness; or the lurking wolves
6. By design; they are looking for each other.
7. (a) "The roebuck . . . were running like driven things," suggests danger; "disturbing element in the forest . . ." suggests lurking menace. Several mentions of *interlopers* emphasize the idea of an intrusion. (b) Some may argue that these hints are too subtle.
8. They have wasted their lives in a petty dispute.

You're the Critic

1. Some will note that animals such as wolves kill only to survive; human beings can murder, so they are worse than animals. Others will say the two men resolved their feud through reason and did not deserve to die.
2. Many will agree Saki skillfully weaves together a series of ominous hints and "false scents." For example, because the men repeatedly insist their comrades are nearby, the reader expects the figures on the hill to be a search party. References to restless animals and repetition of the word *interloper* also foreshadow the men's fate. The plot twists keep the reader guessing.
3. Some will find the element of surprise suspenseful and fun. Others may prefer the use of animals as symbols and in imagery.

AFTER YOU READ

Assess

Literary Element

1. Some may suggest that Saki wants readers to see the damage done by hatred and unresolved issues. He seems to warn readers to resolve conflicts before it is too late.
2. Students may say humans should recognize that they are part of a larger reality beyond their control. Both men felt in charge of the situation, but both soon learned they were at the mercy of chance and nature.

Review: Mood

Details should include visual images of restless forest creatures, sounds of the wind blowing and the branches beating, and the fact that the story takes place on a winter night. Students may mention such words and phrases from the story as *prowling, unrest, disturbing,* and *wild tangle of undergrowth.*
Conclusion: The mood is scary and foreboding.

Reading Strategy

1. Some may say that he is showing how stubborn resentment can cause people to lose perspective and act irrationally.

LITERARY ANALYSIS

Literary Element Irony

Writers use **irony** to express or show meaning without giving readers a lecture or tacking on a moral to the story. For instance, a startling example of situational irony occurs in "The Interlopers" when the men, having agreed to end their feud and believing they are on the verge of being rescued by their comrades, discover to their horror that the "rescuers" are wolves. Saki leaves it up to readers to determine what the irony suggests about human beings and the way they live—or die. The situational irony of the story is that both men think only of their human enemy, but do not realize that there are other elements that can determine their fates.

1. What do the numerous ironies in the story suggest about relationships between individuals?
2. What does the story's ironic ending suggest about human shortsightedness?

Review: Mood

As you learned on page 56, **mood** is the emotional quality of a literary work. A writer's choice of language, subject matter, setting, and tone contribute to creating mood.

Partner Activity Meet with another classmate and talk about what sort of mood Saki creates in "The Interlopers." Use a graphic like the one below to fill in descriptive details from the story and then form a conclusion about the mood based on those details.

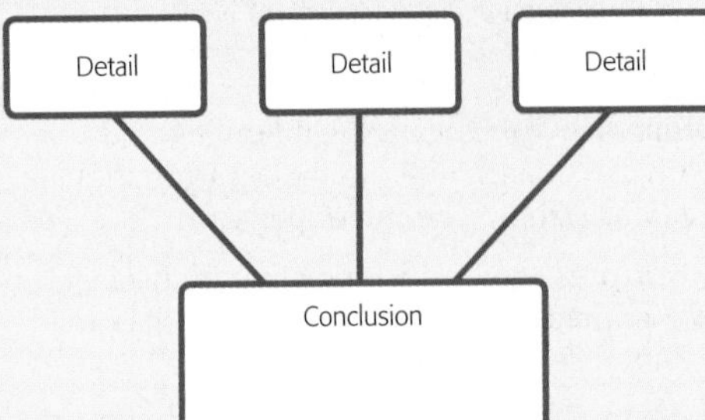

READING AND VOCABULARY

Reading Strategy Analyzing Cause-and-Effect Relationships

Saki shows readers several kinds of **cause-and-effect relationships** in "The Interlopers." One kind originates with actions of human beings, and the other depends on an act of nature. Both have far-reaching and deadly consequences for Ulrich and Georg.

1. What do you think Saki is trying to tell readers by showing the causes and effects of the feud between Ulrich and Georg?
2. A wild wind—nature's violence—causes a huge beech tree to fall on the men. (a)What is an ironically peaceful effect of this violence? (b)What do you think Saki might be suggesting about the relationship between people and nature by having the ultimate effect of the falling tree be death?

Vocabulary Practice

Practice with Analogies Analogies are comparisons based on the relationships between things or ideas. To complete an analogy, you must first decide what relationship exists in a pair of words. Then choose the word that creates the same relationship in a second pair of words. For each item below, choose the word that best completes the analogy.

1. nod : acquiesce :: frown :
   a. agree **b.** disapprove **c.** displease
2. handshake : welcome :: reconciliation :
   a. explanation **b.** truce **c.** approval
3. saint : pious :: thief :
   a. aloof **b.** benign **c.** dishonest
4. sleep : languor :: water :
   a. thirst **b.** revenge **c.** sand
5. endeavor : attempt :: custom :
   a. story **b.** habit **c.** flavor

2. (a) Trapped together, the men get to know each other and realize their conflict is pointless. (b) Some will say that no matter how powerful or prepared, any human can fall victim to unforeseen natural events.

Vocabulary

1. b **2.** b **3.** c **4.** a **5.** b

WRITING AND EXTENDING

Writing About Literature

Analyze Setting Saki uses many sensory details in describing the setting of "The Interlopers." Look at the chart you prepared for reviewing mood. Using those details, write a three-paragraph analysis of how the story's setting contributes to its mood.

As you draft, write from start to finish. Follow the writing path shown here to help you create an orderly, coherent arrangement of details for your first analysis.

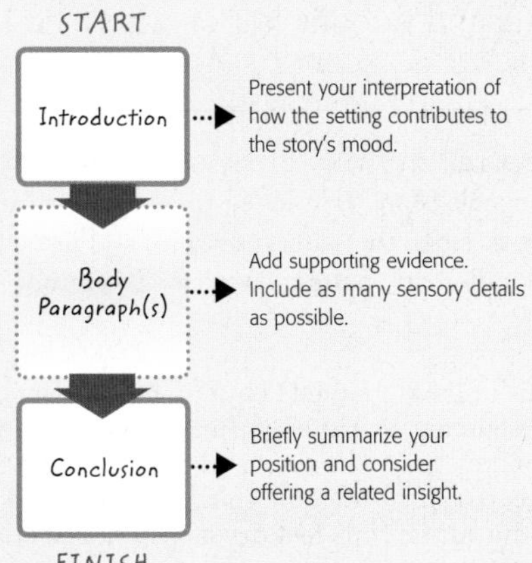

START
Introduction
Present your interpretation of how the setting contributes to the story's mood.
Body Paragraph(s)
Add supporting evidence. Include as many sensory details as possible.
Conclusion
Briefly summarize your position and consider offering a related insight.
FINISH

After you complete your draft, meet with a peer reviewer to evaluate each other's work and to suggest revisions. Then proofread and edit your draft for errors in spelling, grammar, and punctuation.

Literature Groups

What might have happened if the tree had not fallen on Ulrich and Georg? At the time of the accident, each man "had a rifle in his hand, each had hate in his heart and murder uppermost in his mind." In your group, discuss what you think might have happened had not "a deed of Nature's own violence overwhelmed them both." Support your opinion with evidence from the story. Share your ideas with the class.

Literature Online **Web Activities** For eFlashcards, Selection Quick Checks, and other Web activities, go to www.glencoe.com.

GRAMMAR AND STYLE

Saki's Language and Style

Varying Sentence Length Authors can make their writing more interesting by varying the length of sentences. For example, in the third paragraph of "The Interlopers," Saki uses three sentences. The first sentence is quite long. It describes the setting and develops a mood of increasing suspense. The second sentence, about half as long as the first, speeds up the flow of the paragraph and prepares readers for the short dramatic final sentence. By varying the length of his sentences, Saki holds the reader's attention and creates suspense and surprise. He avoids the monotony of too many long sentences in a row, as well as the choppy sound of too many short sentences.

You can record information in a chart about the variety of sentence length in a passage:

Sentence	Structure
First: "He strayed away..."	Long
Second: "If only on..."	Medium-length
Third: "And as he..."	Short

Activity Rewrite the following passage so that it has sentences of varying lengths. Feel free to rearrange ideas and add words or phrases.

> Ulrich lay pinned under the tree. He was suffering great pain. He looked over at Georg. His enemy was in the same predicament. Ulrich's great hatred for Georg began to melt away. He realized how stupid their quarrel really was. Ulrich decided to ask Georg to be his friend.

Revising Check

Sentence Length Sentence length is important to consider when revising your own writing. With a partner, go through your essay on setting and note places where varying sentence length would improve the flow of the paragraphs. Revise your draft to vary your sentence lengths.

AFTER YOU READ

Assess

Writing About Literature

Students' analyses should
- identify the sensory details that describe the setting
- discuss how setting details affect the mood of the story

Literature Groups

Encourage students to use evidence from the text to form their predictions of what would have happened. Some students will think that the men would have reconciled, citing their hesitancy to shoot. Others will think that only a fight to the death would have ended their feud.

Saki's Language and Style

Possible rewrite: Ulrich lay pinned under the tree, suffering great pain. He looked over at Georg. His enemy was in the same predicament. Ulrich's great hatred for Georg began to melt away. Realizing how stupid their quarrel really was, Ulrich decided to ask Georg to be his friend.

Revising Check

Remind students that they dealt with inverted sentences while working on "The Cask of Amontillado." Suggest that students review their notes on inverted sentences before completing the Sentence Length exercise.

Differentiated Instruction

Cause and Effect Fables are short tales with morals. The plot often shows cause-and–effect relationships. Read aloud some of Aesop's fables. Discuss the cause and effect seen in each. Have students write a fable that uses cause and effect. BL

English Language Coach

Definitions Remind students that many words contain clues that will help them remember the definitions. Note that *acquiesce* sounds similar to the word *yes*, which makes the definition ("to consent or agree") easy to remember. Encourage students to look for similar aids with new vocabulary. EL

Academic Standards

Additional Support activities on p. 87 cover the following standards:

Differentiated Instruction: **9.3** [Identify] story elements such as...plot, and...make connections and comparisons across texts...

English Language Coach: **9.1** Use...word parts, patterns, relationships, and origins...to determine the meaning of words...

Informational Text

TIME

Focus

Summary

John Beiler and his friends, Mike and Tom, go hunting on Alaska's Afognak Island. While alone, John breaks his leg. Stranded, he spends the night battling hypothermia, dehydration, and pain. At dawn, ravens overhead reveal his location. A helicopter flies John to a hospital. Although he spends Thanksgiving there, John is grateful to have survived his ordeal.

Teach

Preview the Article

Answers:

1. Excitement and a sense of danger
2. The final subhead is "Just in Time," which indicates that the outcome is probably positive.

Readability Scores
Dale-Chall: 7.1
DRP: 56
Lexile: 900

Informational Text

Media Link to Matters of Life and Death

Preview the Article

In "Shattered," deer hunter John Beiler separates from his friends and ends up alone in the snow banks of Alaska with an injured leg, waiting for rescue.

1. Read the *deck,* or the sentence in large type that appears underneath the title. What emotions do you think the writer wants the reader to feel while reading this article?
2. Skim the boldfaced subheadings that appear in the article. Based on these, what do you think will be the outcome of the article?

Set a Purpose for Reading

Read to discover the events of John Beiler's survival tale and what he learned from it.

Reading Strategy

Identifying Problem and Solution
Identifying problem and solution involves asking these questions:

- What is the main problem?
- Who is experiencing it?
- What solutions are tried?
- What happens as a result?

As you read, take notes on the main problem presented in the article and the steps taken for it to be solved. Use a chart like the one below.

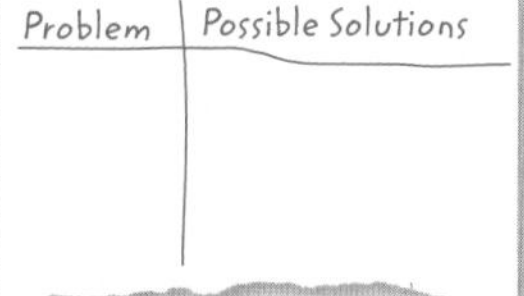

ACADEMIC STANDARDS (pages 88–92)
9.2.1 Analyze the structure and format of ...documents, including...headers...

TIME

Shattered

A terrible fall leaves a lone deer hunter with a shattered leg in the middle of brown-bear country. Now night is falling and nobody knows where he is.

By CHISTOPHER BATIN

JOHN BEILER LIKED HUNTING SITKA BLACKTAIL DEER ON Alaska's Afognak Island. He loved the otter-filled bays, the scenic rock cliffs, the salmon streams, and just about all of the island's many natural wonders. Except one.

Afognak Island has a dark side. Typhoon winds can hammer the coastline without mercy for days at a time. Huge coastal brown bears roam the dark rain forests and salmon streams. Even hunters who are prepared for disasters often die or get seriously injured. For John Beiler, misfortune happened to others but not to him. Or so he thought.

At daybreak, Beiler and his hunting buddies Mike and Tom eyed the steep slopes of Mount Paramanof, rising 2,100 feet above their tidewater base camp. It was Thanksgiving week, and they were looking forward to blacktail steaks and mashed potatoes smothered in gravy. The hunters planned a several-hour climb to an alpine meadow where big bucks lived.

Beiler, who liked to hunt hillsides alone, left his buddies and crossed a marsh near the base of a steep cliff. He was a muscular, big-boned man, well suited to hunting the mountains. Although his rubber boots with tread soles didn't offer the best traction going uphill, they kept his feet dry as he crossed creeks and swamps.

By late afternoon, a light rain had filled the alpine landscape with the pungent-sweet smell of wet tundra. The approaching storm had caused the deer to hole up in thickets, and the dark outline of the beach below would take an hour to reach. Beiler walked faster so he could meet up with his friends before dark.

The hillside's grass and rotting plants were as slick as greased ice. Leaning farther back for balance on the steep slope, he felt his right foot slide on an ice patch and shoot out from under him. He hit the ground with a jarring slam.

Beiler paused for a few moments to regain his breath. He tried to stand. Something wasn't right.

The sole of his left boot faced

Additional Support

See also Active Learning and Note Taking Guide, pp. 15–23.

Skills Practice

READING: Cause and Effect Point out to students that the author builds the story through cause and effect.
Ask: What is the main cause and effect of the story? *(Students may say that Beiler goes off on his own–cause–thereby causing him to break his leg and fight for his life–effect.)* Ask students to design a cause-and-effect graphic organizer for the story. Students should include details such as the ravens' flocking, leading to Beiler, being found; the ship, seeking shelter from the storm, leading to the hunters' being able to radio for help. **OL**

Rick Farrell

up, having slipped off in the fall. No big deal; he grabbed the boot top to pull it back on. His fingers slowed, then froze.

His foot was still inside the boot.

An Explosion of Pain

BI The horror of the moment paralyzed and confused him. He dug in his right heel and sat upright. There was no pain, yet the fall had snapped his leg in two places.

Beiler used his rifle barrel to straighten out his foot. The leg exploded in pain, taking away his breath and driving his head back in agony. He gritted his teeth and sucked air deep into his gut.

Long minutes passed before the pain lessened. The hill's steep angle made it impossible to move, so he took stock of the situation.

His survival gear consisted of a penlight, waterproof matches, three tea bags, a can of portable cooking fuel, aluminum foil, a candy bar, jerky, a knife, and 10 rounds of ammo. He was wearing a cap, gloves, a hoodless rubber-coated rain jacket, and the kind of waterproof pants used by fishers. Underneath he wore flannel-lined pants, cotton long johns, and a wool shirt. R

Beiler decided to tough it out and let his friends find him. Being in the open, he would have a clear shot at any brown bears that viewed him as an easy meal.

The wool clothing soaked up drizzle like a dry sponge. Beiler sliced off his yellow rain pants, first down one leg, then the other. He pulled the fabric over his head and curled up against the storm.

Informational Text
TIME

Teach

BI Big Idea

Matters of Life and Death
Ask: Why is it ironic that John Beiler is fighting for his survival in this story? *(Beiler is a hunter and went to the island to hunt deer. Instead, he is the one fighting for his life.)* OL

R Reading Strategy

Visualizing **Ask:** What do the details about Beiler's survival gear tell you about him? *(Students may say the details tell them that he is an experienced hunter and is well prepared for his trip.)* OL

Cultural History

Tundra Tundra comes from the Finnish word *tunturi,* meaning "arctic hill." Alpine tundra is one of two types of tundra in the world (the other is arctic) and is found at high altitudes on mountains. The tundra is characterized by cold temperatures, scarce vegetation, and permanently frozen ground called permafrost. AS

English Language Coach

Compound Words Remind English-language learners that compound words are formed by joining two words together to form a new word. Explain that by looking at the parts, the students can figure out the meaning of many compounds. Point out the word *tidewater* in the passage. Ask students to identify the component parts (*tide* and *water*). In this case, *tidewater* simply means water that is affected by the tides. Have students work in pairs to find other compound words in the passage. Have them practice splitting the compounds into parts to decipher their meanings. EL

Academic Standards

Additional Support activities on pp. 88 and 89 cover the following standards:

Skills Practice: **9.2** Develop strategies such as…identifying and analyzing… organization…

English Language Coach: **9.1** Use…word parts…to determine the meaning of words…

Teach

L1 Literary Element

Mood Point out to students that through the use of descriptive details, authors can set the mood in nonfiction just as they do in fiction.

Ask: What is the mood of the article? *(Students may say suspenseful or scary.)*

Ask: How do the descriptive details enhance the mood? Have students point out specific details in the story. *(Students may say that using details like "jarring slam," "twist grotesquely," and "fingers like claw hammers" creates tension.)* OL

Rick Farrell

Though he tried to hold his position, gravity kept biting away at his foothold, eroding the earthy stop under his right heel. He watched his injured leg twist grotesquely, then fold up like the edge of a pancake turned before its time. With teeth clenched tight, he eased uphill to straighten his leg. The pain swelled within him.

L1 Using his fingers like claw hammers, he dug up clumps of mud and grass from the partly frozen ground. He slid into the dip and used the roots there to fashion a mud and grass splint around his leg. Then he braced himself and fired three shots. The recoil from the rifle set off more unbearable pain. Far down on the beach, a three-shot reply sailed past him and echoed off the rocks.

They heard him!

Back at Camp

Thinking Beiler had killed a deer, Mike and Tom returned to camp to start supper and await his return.

Beiler was realistic. The forested mountainside was now too dark and dangerous for his friends to begin looking for him. He knew he was on his own until morning.

Back at camp, Tom and Mike had made a bonfire. It roared and crackled, and served as a beacon for Beiler to follow. They shot their hunting rifles repeatedly.

Finally, they heard a single shot and knew he was alive.

From the mountain, Beiler watched the massive storm churn Shelikof Strait into a ★ whitecapped frenzy. He saw a shrimp boat head for safety in the bay below. Soon after, a small runabout cut a wake to his hunting camp. No doubt his friends would ask the captain for help.

In the hours before midnight, steady rain and cold slowly numbed Beiler's legs and back. He was losing consciousness.

Beiler believed that if he fell asleep, he'd never wake up. He placed a tea bag in his mouth, steeping it in whatever saliva he could muster. The caffeine in the tea helped keep him awake. He sucked on the bags until the paper dissolved. Then he chewed on leaves and twigs. On the brushy alpine tundra, there was no wood.

Struggling to Survive

The cold rain trickled through his makeshift hood, inching through his underwear. He lit the cooking fuel and placed the hot metal can on his chest. Once warmed, he allowed the 50-knot gusts to put out the flame for a while.

He flashed his penlight to signal his location to anyone looking for him. The blackness failed to blink a reply. Around midnight, the last of the cooking fuel flickered out. His shivering became so intense that his gun barrel vibrated.

Additional Support

Skills Practice

LITERARY ELEMENT: Mood **Ask:** How is the mood important to this article? *(Students may say that the suspenseful atmosphere draws readers in and makes them want to finish the article or that it makes the article memorable.)* BL

Challenge students to write nonfiction articles with specific moods of their choosing. OL Instruct students to use heads, subheads, and a deck to enhance their stories and create consistent mood. AL

He twisted his mouth to catch rain. His clothes were soaked, yet he craved water. The wool gloves sopped up the puddles around him. With head back, he wrung every drop of the precious liquid into his mouth. A blast of rain pelted his face, and he prayed to survive the night.

The storm howled its opposition to the breaking dawn as the bay frothed in a tempest of whitecaps. The tops of hundred-year-old spruce trees whipped violently. Beiler had survived what seemed an eternity on this mountainside, and he was desperate for rescue.

Fifty yards away, a brush line snaked its way along the base of a shelf, taunting him with its promise of wood and fire. But the distance was just too great.

Survival became difficult. Hypothermia was a wrecking ball that continuously chipped away at his instinct for self-preservation, luring him into a world of neither pain nor cold. Beiler found an inner strength and calm thinking about his brothers, sisters, and family. He promised himself to give up his bad habits. And finally, he made his peace with his Maker, just in case.

Beiler snapped to full alert, fearful he had fallen asleep. Revitalized by the burst of adrenaline, he decided he was going to live. He wouldn't give up, no matter what.

The cold had left his leg and back muscles knotted up and useless. He pushed himself up with his arms, raising and balancing his torso on his numb, unbroken leg. Slowly he pushed himself upward and inched his broken leg forward. The world spun, and he hit the ground hard. He struggled to breathe as he slid and rolled headfirst for 20 feet before wedging into a clump of grass.

Beiler's left leg was as rigid as a wet towel and stuck out 90 degrees from his body. He gagged at the sight and would have vomited if he had had any food in his stomach.

A Long Crawl

Dragging his rifle, Beiler crawled to some brush 40 yards distant. His foot flopped and rotated as he did so. The pain stabbed him relentlessly, driving him crazy. But he kept crawling.

After reaching the brush, he reset his leg and took a breather. He cut pieces of wood and carefully arranged and tied them to his leg with strips of rain pant.

Meanwhile, at Mike and Tom's request, the shrimp boat captain radioed the Coast Guard that a hunter had spent a night on the mountain and was possibly in trouble. At the same time, the friends grabbed sleeping bags, food and water, and fired signal shots on the hillside below him.

Beiler knew they'd never see him in the brush. He tried to shout, but his throat was parched from thirst. Their rifle shots grew louder. He fired his last round, knowing that his rescue was now close at hand.

He tried to stand and again fell onto his back. Dazed, he looked up and witnessed a bizarre sight. Several ravens hovered over him on gusts of wind, performing an aerial circus of squawks and acrobatics. Mike and Tom saw the ravens and turned toward the commotion.

Beiler could hear shouts far off in the brush. He struggled to rise but couldn't. He was spent, exhausted. He gritted his teeth and slowly rose to his one good knee. If they passed him in the brush, it would be over.

With the gun as a crutch in his left hand, and the remnants of his yellow rain pants in his right, Beiler wobbled upright, teetered on one leg, and waved his pants and gun at the disappearing rescuers. His broken, cramped and tired limbs were unable to hold him, and he crumpled into a clump of broken flesh. He had given it everything he had.

Just in Time

It was enough. Mike and Tom saw him and busted through the brush to his side. Beiler's adrenaline surged at the sight of his rescuers, but he was in bad shape. Mike pulled out a candy

"Survival became difficult. Hypothermia was a wrecking ball that continuously chipped away at his instinct for self-preservation, luring him into a world of neither pain nor cold."

Informational Text

TIME

Teach

Cultural History

Shelikof Strait The Strait lies between mainland Alaska and Afognak Island. Much of the island is devoted to a state park, one of the first conservation areas in the United States. In addition to the salmon, bears, and deer mentioned in the story, Afognak Island State Park is also home to the endangered marbled murrelet. In continuing conservation efforts, more land has been added to the park since its 1892 inception. Currently, the park is about 75,000 acres and covers most of the northern and eastern sides of the island. AS

Reading in the Real World

Career Point out that Beiler's dramatic rescue results from a team effort. Invite students to research careers in the Coast Guard and in medicine, including rescue and trauma teams. Have students share their findings with the class. OL

Differentiated Instruction

Retelling To ensure that less proficient readers absorb the story, invite students to retell it in their own words. Have students go through each section, explaining the chain of events. Encourage students to ask questions. BL

Academic Standards

Additional Support activities on pp. 90 and 91 cover the following standards:

Skills Practice: **9.3** [Identify] story elements such as [mood]... **9.5.3** Write expository compositions, including...descriptive pieces... **9.6.4** Apply appropriate manuscript conventions...

Reading in the Real World: **9.7.15** Deliver expository (informational) compositions that convey information and ideas from... sources accurately and coherently.

Differentiated Instruction: **9.7.17** Deliver oral responses to literature that demonstrate an awareness of the author's writing style and an appreciation of the effects created...

Informational Text

TIME

Teach

L Literary Element

Dialogue **Ask:** What effect does adding dialogue near the end have? *(Some may say that it reinforces the fictionlike feeling of the article; others will say that it lends realism.)* OL

BI Big Idea

Matters of Life and Death
Ask: How does adding the detail about the dead man's clothes reinforce the life-and-death drama of the story? *(It reinforces how close Beiler came to dying and how easily he himself might have died.)* OL

Assess

1. Some students will appreciate that many people enjoy risky pursuits. Others will think he was foolhardy.
2. (a) Beiler's leg broke in two places. (b) The description of the leg looking "like the edge of a pancake turned before its time"
3. (a) A storm comes. (b) Beiler's survival is threatened by the conditions.
4. The story builds with Beiler's struggle. The discovery of his location is the climax.

bar, a fried-egg sandwich, and a cold soda. Beiler wolfed down the food. Ever so slowly, his limbs started to tingle with feeling.

Mike and Tom dressed him in a spare rain suit and roped both legs together from ankle to thigh. Even his head was lashed forward to keep his neck from catching a log and snapping. They numbed him with pain medication and started their climb down to camp.

Once in the heavy timber and out of the wind, Mike stayed with Beiler and got a fire going. Tom descended to base camp for more supplies and to summon help.

The hot spruce fire pierced Beiler's stupor and drew him like a moth. The heat blistered the back of his rain jacket. Mike kept rolling Beiler away from the fire. Incoherent and suffering from hypothermia, Beiler didn't care if he was on fire. He needed heat desperately.

Mike piled more green sticks on the fire, and soon they could hear the rescue helicopter overhead. Mike dragged his friend into the open.

Gusts of wind howled across the mountaintop, as the copter dangled the rescue basket in front of Mike. He caught it single-handedly and strapped Beiler in before finally patting him on the chest.

"You're okay, John," Mike shouted over the noise of the chopper's blades.

"Tie me in tight, little buddy," Beiler replied, and gave him a thumbs up. L

At Kodiak hospital, the doctor cut off the makeshift splint. Beiler's foot and leg flopped to the side. They cut off his wet, soiled clothes, set his leg, and treated him for hypothermia and dehydration.

Beiler spent Thanksgiving in the hospital, having cafeteria turkey instead of his blacktail venison. That weekend, with his leg in a full cast, he found himself with nothing to wear for his flight home to Fairbanks. A nurse brought him some clothes from a man who had recently died. BI

John thought about the many events that saved his life. A storm forced a fishing boat to seek shelter near their camp. The skipper had a radio that he used to call the Coast Guard for assistance. The ravens helped lead his buddies to his location. Had these things not happened, his clothes might have been the ones offered to someone else.

He hobbled upright on crutches out of the Kodiak hospital, a grateful man in borrowed clothes, having received a second chance at life.

—Updated 2005, from OUTDOOR LIFE, November 2004

RESPONDING AND THINKING CRITICALLY

Respond

1. Beiler decides to hunt alone on Afognak Island, knowing that hunters "often die or get seriously injured" while doing so. How did you react to his story knowing that he willingly takes such a risk?

Recall and Interpret

2. (a)What injury does Beiler suffer in the wildness? (b)What details make Beiler's pain come alive for the reader?
3. (a)How does the weather change while Beiler is waiting for his friends to find him? (b)How do descriptions of the weather build suspense?
4. This article unfolds with a plot similar to that of a short story. What do you think is the climax, or the moment of greatest suspense or emotional intensity, and why?

Analyze and Evaluate

5. Beiler faces an external conflict with nature. What internal conflict does he face? Support your answer with evidence from the text.
6. When Beiler is in the hospital, "a nurse brought him clothes from a man who had recently died." Why does the writer include this detail?
7. (a)What makes Beiler's story compelling? (b)Why do you think people are interested in stories about matters of life and death?

Connect

8. How is Beiler's experience in Alaska similar to what happens to Ulrich and Georg in "The Interlopers"? What other stories from this unit are similar to the story described in this article?

For additional assessment, see Selection and Unit Assessments, pp. 15–16.

5. The fear of losing his "instinct for self-preservation"
6. The detail is ironic. Beiler thinks that if he had not survived, his clothes would have been used in the same way. It also emphasizes the fragility of human life.
7. (a) Most will agree it was compelling because of the dramatic events and the vivid details, language, and imagery. (b) Some will say that such stories concern occurrences that do not happen to people every day. Others may say they remind people that life is precious.
8. Both men are hunters who find themselves in extreme conditions, where they become the hunted. Beiler's predator is nature, and Rainsford's predator is Zaroff.

The Garden of Stubborn Cats

MEET ITALO CALVINO

Readers all over the world are delighted by the wondrous and fantastic tales of Italo Calvino. Writers love Calvino's way of combining experiment with tradition, philosophy with emotion, and the everyday with the bizarre.

Influenced by Italy Calvino was born in Cuba to Italian parents. When he was young, his family moved back to Italy, where they lived on the Italian Riviera. Calvino's parents were botanists, plant experts who managed gardens for a living. Their scientific rigor and precision made an impression on Calvino. He developed a lifelong devotion to detail and a fascination with intricate structures.

Marked by War When Calvino was growing up, Italy was controlled by the fascist dictator Benito Mussolini. During World War II, Calvino belonged to a Resistance movement working to undermine the fascist government. After the war ended, he moved to Turin, earned a literature degree, and began a career as a writer. Eventually he settled in Paris, where he lived with his wife and daughter.

His experiences with dictatorship and war were one reason, perhaps, why Calvino retained strong feelings about justice and human rights. Not a man to avoid ambiguity or difficulty, he occasionally wrote essays exploring thorny political questions. But it was in his fiction that Calvino most fully developed his sensibility. In a series of *raccontini*, or "little tales," he honed his sharp wit and displayed his love for fables. Calvino's first novel, a realistic work about the war called *The Path to the Nest of Spiders*, won him a prestigious literary prize, the Premio Riccione.

> *"Humanity reaches as far as love reaches; it has no frontiers except those we give it."*
>
> —Italo Calvino

Experimenting Thereafter, Calvino abandoned realism for experiment and fantasy. Calvino admired the French writers of the Oulipo school, who conducted daring formal experiments in their writing. One Oulipo author, Georges Perec, wrote a novel without using the letter *e*. Calvino shared the Oulipo writers' intense concern with form but also maintained a love for entertainment and storytelling. Though no subject was too arcane for Calvino, heavy subjects did not dull the edge of his artistry. He managed to be entertaining whether exploring logical paradoxes, high mathematics, time travel, or gardens of stubborn cats.

Italo Calvino was born in 1923 and died in 1985.

Literature Online **Author Search** For more about Italo Calvino, go to www.glencoe.com.

Focus

BELLRINGER

Bellringer Options
Selection Focus Transparency 7
Daily Language Practice Transparency 9

Or **ask:** What do you think should happen to stray animals in the city? Discuss options for caring for strays, such as putting them in shelters for adoption, euthanizing them, or neutering them and then releasing them. Have students brainstorm possible solutions.

Author Search To expand students' appreciation of Italo Calvino, have them access the Web site for additional information and resources.

Selection Skills

The Garden of Stubborn Cats

Literary Elements
- Description (SE pp. 94–103)
- Irony (SE p. 103)

Reading Skills
- Visualizing (SE pp. 94–104)
- Sketching (SE p. 94)

Vocabulary Skills
- Academic Vocabulary (SE p. 104)
- Synonyms (SE pp. 94, 104)

Listening/Speaking/Viewing Skills
- Analyzing Art (SE p. 96; TWE pp. 95, 99, 101)

Writing Skills/Grammar
- Analyze Conflict (SE p. 104)
- Hyphens (TWE p. 98)

Study Skills/Research/Assessment
- Point-of-View (TWE p. 96)
- Research a Cause (TWE p. 102)

BEFORE YOU READ

Focus

Summary

During his lunch break, Marcovaldo follows a cat around the city. The tabby leads him to a restaurant. Marcovaldo snares a fish from the restaurant tank, and the cat steals the fish. Marcovaldo chases the cat to the garden of a small villa in the city. The property is a refuge for cats and other wildlife. Someone there steals his fish. When Marcovaldo confronts the Marchesa, she tells him the cats keep her prisoner. The Marchesa dies. The animals make it impossible to build on the property.

V Vocabulary

Vocabulary File Say: Add these words and definitions to your vocabulary file. For each word, include a sentence that gives you an example of how to use the word. **OL** Students with English language needs should include the pronunciations of these words in their files. **EL**

Literary Elements Have students access the Web site to improve their understanding of description.

LITERATURE PREVIEW

Connecting to the Story

This story describes a man who follows a cat to see where it goes. Before you read the story, think about the following questions:

- Have you ever followed, chased, or tracked an animal? Where did it lead you?
- What hidden places do you go to when you want to get away?

Building Background

A fable is a short, usually simple tale that teaches a moral lesson and often contains animal characters. Many cultures have very old fables that have been passed down through the years by one person telling them out loud to others. Calvino's work reflects his fascination with fables.

This story takes place in a large city, probably in Italy. The man in the story, Marcovaldo, takes a walk every day between noon and three, when the rest of the workers at his warehouse go home to eat. In Europe, the main meal of the day occurs in mid-afternoon. Many businesses close while workers go home to eat this meal with their families.

Setting Purposes for Reading

Big Idea Matters of Life and Death

As you read, notice how Calvino uses vivid settings and raucous characters to create a sense of teeming life.

Literary Element Description

Description is writing that helps readers imagine what characters see, hear, feel, taste, or touch. Notice the vivid description in this passage from "The Garden of Stubborn Cats": "To the sound of gypsy violins, partridges and quails swirled by on silver dishes balanced by the white-gloved fingers of waiters in tailcoats." Descriptive language can help bring a setting to life. As you read, notice vivid details that help you imagine the city of Calvino's story.

- See Literary Terms Handbook, p. R5.

LiteratureOnline Interactive Literary Elements Handbook To review or learn more about the literary elements, go to www.glencoe.com.

READING PREVIEW

Reading Strategies Visualizing

Visualizing is picturing a writer's ideas or descriptions in your mind's eye. Visualizing can help you better understand what an author is trying to show you or tell you in a story. Visualizing can also help you better remember what you read. To visualize, examine carefully how Calvino describes a person, a place, or a thing. Then ask yourself: What would this look like? Or: Can I see how the steps in this process would work?

Reading Tip: Sketching As you read, pause to visualize key descriptions. Note the descriptions that you find most striking. Record them in a simple 2-column chart. Include a brief description of the ideas or feelings each description evokes.

Vocabulary

ordain (ôr dān′) *v.* to appoint; to establish; p. 96 *The plan for a new town hall was ordained by the mayor.*

scrutinize (skrōōt′ ən īz′) *v.* to scan, inspect, or examine; p. 97 *Please scrutinize your contact information to be sure that it is correct.*

treacherous (trech′ ər əs) *adj.* marked by betrayal of fidelity, confidence, or trust; p. 98 *The council members considered the mayor's criticism of their proposal treacherous.*

degenerate (di jen′ ə rāt′) *v.* to decline or deteriorate; p. 101 *The council should not permit meetings to degenerate into counterproductive fighting.*

confiscate (kon′ fis kāt′) *v.* to seize or take away; p. 101 *The sports arena confiscates food purchased outside the park.*

Vocabulary Tip: Synonyms Synonyms are words that have the same or nearly the same meaning, such as *climb* and *ascend*. Note that synonyms must be the same part of speech.

INDIANA ACADEMIC STANDARDS (pages 94–104)

9.3.11 Evaluate the aesthetic qualities of style, including the impact of diction and figurative language on…mood…

9.2 Develop [reading] strategies…

9.5.3 Write expository compositions…

Selection Resources

Print Materials

- Unit 1 Resources (Fast File), pp. 36–38
- Leveled Vocabulary Development, p. 7
- Selection and Unit Assessments, pp. 15–16
- Selection Quick Checks, p. 8

Transparencies

- Bellringer Options Transparencies: Selection Focus Transparency 7; Daily Language Practice Transparency 9
- Literary Elements Transparency 11

Technology

- TeacherWorks Plus™ CD-ROM
- StudentWorks Plus™ CD-ROM
- Presentation Plus!™ CD-ROM
- Literature Online, glencoe.com
- Online Student Edition, mhln.com
- Exam*View*® Assessment Suite CD-ROM
- Vocabulary PuzzleMaker CD-ROM
- Listening Library, disc 1 track 8

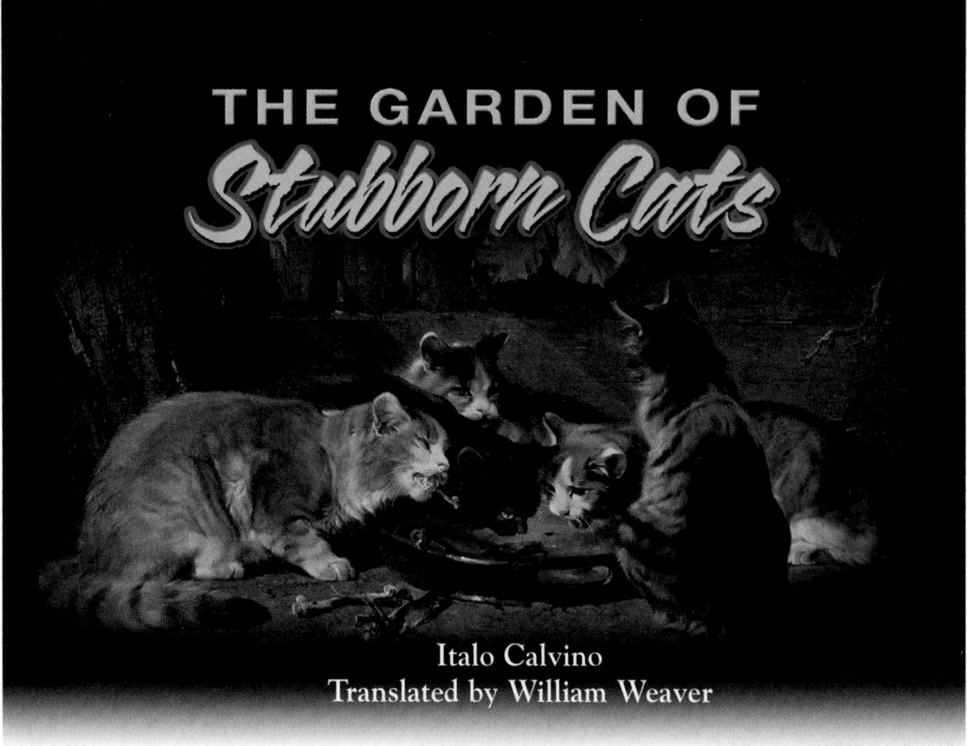

THE GARDEN OF
Stubborn Cats
Italo Calvino
Translated by William Weaver

Dinner Time. Julius Adam. Private collection. 

The city of cats and the city of men exist one inside the other, but they are not the same city. Few cats recall the time when there was no distinction: the streets and squares of men were also streets and squares of cats, and the lawns, courtyards, balconies, and fountains: you lived in a broad and various space. But for several generations now domestic felines have been prisoners of an uninhabitable city: the streets are uninterruptedly overrun by the mortal traffic of cat-crushing automobiles; in every square foot of terrain where once a garden extended or a vacant lot or the ruins of an old demolition, now condominiums loom up, welfare housing, brand-new skyscrapers; every entrance is crammed with parked cars; the courtyards, one by one, have been roofed by reinforced concrete and transformed into garages or movie houses or storerooms or workshops. And where a rolling plateau[1] of low roofs once extended, copings,[2] terraces, water tanks, balconies, skylights, corrugated-iron sheds, now one general superstructure rises wherever structures can rise; the intermediate differences in height, between the low ground of the street and the supernal[3] heaven of the penthouses, disappear; the cat of a recent litter seeks in vain the itinerary of its fathers, the point from which to make the soft leap from balustrade to cornice[4] to drainpipe, or for the quick climb on the roof-tiles. R

But in this vertical city, in this compressed city where all voids tend to fill up and every block of cement tends to mingle with other

Literary Element Description *How have people transformed the city?* L

1. A *plateau* is a level surface raised sharply above the surfaces surrounding it.
2. *Copings* are the top layer of masonry, sloped to carry off water.
3. *Supernal* means "of the sky" or "of heaven."
4. A *balustrade* is a row of vertical objects (such as posts or columns) topped by a railing. A *cornice* is horizontal molding projecting above the top of a wall.

Teach

L Literary Element

Description **Answer:** *Students may say that with the advent of cars and modern technology, the city has become crowded and hectic.* OL

R Reading Strategy

Visualizing Discuss how students see the city based on the description. Ask students if it reminds them of any cities they have visited or seen pictures of, and have them explain why. OL

Viewing the Art

Julius Adam (1826–1874) was a Bavarian lithographer and painter. His son, Julius Adam II, became famous for his paintings of felines. AS

CheckPoint

Use the CheckPoint questions on Presentation Plus! to monitor students' comprehension. These questions can be used with interactive response keypads for immediate student feedback.

English Language Coach

Multiple Words English language learners may find the strings of multiple adjectives and nouns in the descriptions challenging. In order to keep the words from becoming a blur, discuss the nuances of the words with the class. EL

Differentiated Instruction

Visualizing Visual learners will benefit from finding visual representations of Calvino's city. Assign students to use the Internet or the library to research city images. Have students bring images to class and create a collage that represents the city in both style and mood. BL

Academic Standards

Additional Support activities on p. 95 cover the following standards:

English Language Coach: **9.1.2** Distinguish between what words mean literally and what they imply and interpret what the words imply.

Differentiated Instruction: **9.4.6** Synthesize information from multiple sources, including...microfiche, news sources,...journals,...and Internet sources.

Teach

R Reading Strategy

Visualizing Answer: *Students' descriptions should be reasonable and might include typical alley descriptions.* OL

★ Viewing the Art

Answer: *Tall buildings, dark alleys and claustrophobic feeling reflect the story. The uncrowded street leading to a bright place differs.* AS

Painter and illustrator Mary Iverson often paints urban landscapes. She turns urban icons and ordinary objects, such as building cranes, into art.

Readability Scores
Dale-Chall: 7.0
DRP: 67
Lexile: 1140

Ironweed, 1995. Mary Iverson

Viewing the Art: How is the city in this image similar to and different from the city in the story? ★

blocks of cement, a kind of counter-city opens, a negative city, that consists of empty slices between wall and wall, of the minimal distances **ordained** by the building regulations between two constructions, between the rear of one construction and the rear of the next; it is a city of cavities, wells, air conduits, driveways, inner yards, accesses to basements, like a network of dry canals on a planet of stucco and tar, and it is through this network, grazing the walls, that the ancient cat population still scurries.

On occasion, to pass the time, Marcovaldo would follow a cat. It was during the work-break, between noon and three, when all the personnel[5] except Marcovaldo went home to eat, and he—who brought his lunch in his bag—laid his place among the packing-cases in the warehouse, chewed his snack, smoked a half-cigar, and wandered around, alone and idle, waiting for work to resume. In those hours, a cat that peeped in at a window was always welcome company, and a guide for new explorations. He had made friends with a tabby,[6] well fed, a blue ribbon around its neck, surely living with some well-to-do family. This tabby shared with Marcovaldo the habit of an afternoon stroll right after lunch; and naturally a friendship sprang up.

Following his tabby friend, Marcovaldo had started looking at places as if through the round eyes of a cat and even if these places were the usual environs of his firm he saw them in a different light, as settings for cattish stories, with connections practicable only by light, velvety paws. Though from the outside the neighborhood seemed poor in cats, every day on his rounds Marcovaldo made the acquaintance of some new face, and a miau, a hiss, a stiffening of fur on an arched back was enough for him to sense ties and intrigues and rivalries among them. At those moments he thought he had already pene-

5. *Personnel* are employees or staff.
6. A *tabby* is a cat with a striped coat.

Vocabulary

ordain (ôr dān′) *v.* to appoint; to establish

Reading Strategy Visualizing *From the details in this paragraph, how do you picture the "counter-city" of passageways that the cats travel in?* R

Additional Support

Skills Practice

READING: Point of View Help students explore Calvino's use of perspective by having them imagine an animal's point of view. Encourage them to pick an animal that interests them, whether it be an exotic species, such as a tiger, or a common pet, such as a dog. Students should research what a day in the animal's life is like. BL Have students write a short day-in-the-life-of description. OL Have students write the day-in-the-life story from the animal's point of view. AL trated the secrecy of the felines' society: and then he felt himself **scrutinized** by pupils that became slits, under the surveillance of the antennae of taut whiskers, and all the cats around him sat impassive as sphinxes, the pink triangles of their noses convergent on the black triangles of their lips, and the only things that moved were the tips of the ears, with a vibrant jerk like radar. They reached the end of a narrow passage, between squalid blank walls; and, looking around, Marcovaldo saw that the cats that had led him this far had vanished, all of them together, no telling in which direction, even his tabby friend, and they had left him alone. Their realm had territories, ceremonies, customs that it was not yet granted to him to discover.

On the other hand, from the cat city there opened unsuspected peepholes onto the city of men: and one day the same tabby led him to discover the great Biarritz Restaurant.

Anyone wishing to see the Biarritz Restaurant had only to assume the posture of a cat, that is, proceed on all fours. Cat and man, in this fashion, walked around a kind of dome, at whose foot some low, rectangular little windows opened. Following the tabby's example, Marcovaldo looked down. They were transoms[7] through which the luxurious hall received air and light. To the sound of gypsy violins, partridges and quails swirled by on silver dishes balanced by the white-gloved fingers of waiters in tailcoats. Or, more precisely, above the partridges and quails the dishes whirled, and above the dishes the white gloves, and poised on the waiters' patent-leather shoes, the gleaming parquet[8] floor, from which hung dwarf potted palms and tablecloths and crystal and buckets like bells with the champagne bottle for their clapper: everything was turned upside-down because Marcovaldo, for fear of being seen, wouldn't stick his head inside the window and confined himself to looking at the reversed reflection of the room in the tilted pane.

But it was not so much the windows of the dining-room as those of the kitchens that interested the cat: looking through the former you saw, distant and somehow transfigured,[9] what in the kitchens presented itself—quite concrete and within paw's reach—as a plucked bird or a fresh fish. And it was toward the kitchens, in fact, that the tabby wanted to lead Marcovaldo, either through a gesture of altruistic friendship or else because it counted on the man's help for one of its raids. Marcovaldo, however, was reluctant to leave his belvedere[10] over the main room: first as he was fascinated by the luxury of the place, and then because something down there had riveted his attention. To such an extent that, overcoming his fear of being seen, he kept peeking in, with his head in the transom.

In the midst of the room, directly under that pane, there was a little glass fish tank, a kind of aquarium, where some fat trout were swimming. A special customer approached, a man with a shiny bald pate,[11] black suit, black beard. An old waiter in tailcoat followed him, carrying a little net as if he were going to catch butterflies. The gentleman in black looked at the trout with a grave, intent air; then he raised one hand and with a slow, solemn gesture singled out a fish. The waiter dipped the net into the tank, pursued the appointed trout, captured it, headed for the

7. A *transom* is a small window, usually above a door or a larger window.

8. *Parquet* is patterned wood.

9. *Transfigured* means "given a new appearance" or "transformed."

10. A *belvedere* is an open, roofed gallery.

11. The *pate* is the top of the head.

Literary Element Description *How do the cats respond to Marcovaldo?* **L**

Big Idea Matters of Life and Death *What does this passage reveal about the lives of cats?* **BI**

Vocabulary

scrutinize (skrōōt′ ən īz′) *v.* to scan, inspect, or examine

Teach

L Literary Element

Description **Answer:** *The cats study him, but they remain as unreadable as sphinxes.* **OL**

BI Big Idea

Matters of Life and Death
Answer: *Marcovaldo is learning that the cats have secret places and routines unknown to humans.* **OL**

Cultural History

Cats Cats became domesticated in about 3000 B.C. The modern cat is believed to have descended from African and European wildcats. Although cats meow, hiss, and purr, they also communicate through the position of their tails. Today, domesticated cats inhabit every continent. **AS**

Building Reading Fluency

Descriptions Students may find the lengthy descriptions overwhelming and therefore tend to gloss over or skip the details. To ensure they've gleaned the information, have students read aloud and summarize what they've read at the end of each paragraph. **BL**

Academic Standards

Additional Support activities on pp. 96 and 97 cover the following standards:

Skills Practice: **9.5.1** Write...short stories that describe a sequence of events and communicate the significance of the events to the audience; describe with specific details the sights, sounds, and smells of a scene and the specific actions, movements, gestures, and feelings of the characters... use interior monologue...to show the character's feelings.

Building Reading Fluency: **9.3.7** Recognize and understand the significance of various literary devices, including figurative language [and] imagery...

Teach

L1 Literary Element

Description Answer: *The customer has selected a fresh fish. He now waits for it to be served.* OL

R1 Reading Strategy

Visualizing Answer: *Answers will vary. Students should envision a humorous scene of people dressed up dining in an expensive restaurant while a fish is reeled up over their heads.* OL

BI1 Big Idea

Matters of Life and Death
Answer: *The chase could be a matter of life and death for the cat because it needs food. For Marcovaldo, however, the chase seems less serious.* OL

kitchens, holding out in front of him, like a lance, the net in which the fish wriggled. The gentleman in black, solemn as a magistrate who has handed down a capital sentence, went to take his seat and wait for the return of the trout, sautéed "à la meunière."[12]

If I found a way to drop a line from up here and make one of those trout bite, Marcovaldo thought, I couldn't be accused of theft; at worst, of fishing in an unauthorized place. And ignoring the miaus that called him toward the kitchens, he went to collect his fishing tackle.

Nobody in the crowded dining room of the Biarritz saw the long, fine line, armed with hook and bait, as it slowly dropped into the tank. The fish saw the bait, and flung themselves on it. In the fray one trout managed to bite the worm: and immediately it began to rise, rise, emerge from the water, a silvery fish, it darted up high, over the laid tables and the trolleys of hors d'oeuvres, over the blue flames of the crêpes Suzette,[13] until it vanished into the heavens of the transom.

Marcovaldo had yanked the rod with the brisk snap of the expert fisherman, so the fish landed behind his back. The trout had barely touched the ground when the cat sprang. What little life the trout still had was lost between the tabby's teeth. Marcovaldo, who had abandoned his line at that moment to run and grab the fish, saw it snatched from under his nose, hook and all. He was quick to put one foot on the rod, but the snatch had been so strong that the rod was all the man had left, while the tabby ran off with the fish, pulling the line after it. **Treacherous** kitty! It had vanished.

But this time it wouldn't escape him: there was that long line trailing after him and showing the way he had taken. Though he had lost sight of the cat, Marcovaldo followed the end of the line: there it was, running along a wall; it climbed a parapet, wound through a doorway, was swallowed up by a basement . . . Marcovaldo, venturing into more and more cattish places, climbed roofs, straddled railings, always managed to catch a glimpse—perhaps only a second before it disappeared—of that moving trace that indicated a thief's path.

Now the line played out down a sidewalk, in the midst of the traffic, and Marcovaldo, running after it, almost managed to grab it. He flung himself down on his belly: there, he grabbed it! He managed to seize one end of the line before it slipped between the bars of a gate.

Beyond a half-rusted gate and two bits of wall buried under climbing plants, there was a little rank garden, with a small, abandoned-looking building at the far end of it. A carpet of dry leaves covered the path, and dry leaves lay everywhere under the boughs of the two plane-trees, forming actually some little mounds in the yard. A layer of leaves was yellowing in the green water of a pool. Enormous buildings rose all around, skyscrapers with thousands of windows, like so many eyes trained disapprovingly on that little square patch with two trees, a few tiles, and all those yellow leaves, surviving right in the middle of an area of great traffic.

And in this garden, perched on the capitals and balustrades, lying on the dry leaves of the flowerbeds, climbing on the trunks of the trees or on the drainpipes, motionless on their

12. *À la meunière* (a le me nyer′) is a French preparation in which food is rolled in flour, fried in butter, and sprinkled with lemon juice and chopped parsley.

13. *Hors d'oeuvres* (ôr durvz′) are appetizers served at the beginning of a meal. *Crêpes Suzette* (krāp so͞o zet′) are thin pancakes rolled or folded in a hot orange-flavored sauce.

Literary Element Description *From this description, what process do you infer Marcovaldo is viewing?* L1

Reading Strategy Visualizing *How do you visualize the events of this paragraph?* R1

Big Idea Matters of Life and Death *Does this chase evoke the sense of a life and death situation? Explain.* BI1

Vocabulary

treacherous (trech′ ər əs) *adj.* marked by betrayal of fidelity, confidence, or trust

Additional Support

Skills Practice

GRAMMAR AND LANGUAGE:

Hyphens Students are often confused by hyphenating. Point out to students Calvino's use of hyphens in his descriptions, such as "small, abandoned-looking building." Instruct students that when a compound adjective precedes a noun, they should use a hyphen. **Write on the board:** *thirty-year career.* Since the compound adjective *thirty-year* precedes the noun *career,* the adjective requires a hyphen. Have students go through the story and find other examples of hyphenated descriptions. BL four paws, their tails making a question-mark, seated to wash their faces, there were tiger cats, black cats, white cats, calico cats, tabbies, angoras, Persians,[14] house cats and stray cats, perfumed cats and mangy cats. Marcovaldo realized he had finally reached the heart of the cats' realm, their secret island. And, in his emotion, he almost forgot his fish.

It had remained, that fish, hanging by the line from the branch of a tree, out of reach of the cats' leaps; it must have dropped from its kidnapper's mouth at some clumsy movement, perhaps as it was defended from the others, or perhaps displayed as an extraordinary prize. The line had got tangled, and Marcovaldo, tug as he would, couldn't manage to yank it loose. A furious battle had meanwhile been joined among the cats, to reach that unreachable fish, or rather, to win the right to try and reach it. Each wanted to prevent the others from leaping: they hurled themselves on one another, they tangled in midair, they rolled around clutching each other, and finally a general war broke out in a whirl of dry, crackling leaves.

After many futile yanks, Marcovaldo now felt the line was free, but he took care not to pull it: the trout would have fallen right in the midst of that infuriated scrimmage of felines.

It was at this moment that, from the top of the walls of the gardens, a strange rain began to fall: fish-bones, heads, tails, even bits of lung and lights. Immediately the cats' attention was distracted from the suspended trout and they flung themselves on the new delicacies. To Marcovaldo, this seemed the right moment to pull the line and regain his fish. But, before he had time to act, from a blind of the little villa, two yellow, skinny hands darted out: one was brandishing scissors; the other, a frying pan. The hand with the scissors was raised above the trout, the hand with the frying pan was thrust under it. The scissors cut the line, the trout fell into the pan; hands, scissors and pan withdrew, the blind closed: all in the space of a second. Marcovaldo was totally bewildered. R2

The Garden, 1936. Pierre Bonnard. Musée Du Petit Palais, Paris, France. ★

14. *Calico cats* have blotched or spotted coats. *Angoras* are longhaired cats, frequently from Asia. *Persians* are longhaired cats from Turkey and Iran.

Literary Element Description *What information about the garden is given in this paragraph?* L2

Big Idea Matters of Life and Death *Why is it important to the cats that these "new delicacies" come raining down on them?* BI2

Teach

L2 Literary Element

Description Answer: *The garden is small, dirty, surrounded by skyscrapers, and full of cats.* OL

BI2 Big Idea

Matters of Life and Death
Answer: *Students should point out that these wild cats need food in order to survive in the city.* OL

R2 Reading Strategy

Visualizing Ask: Based on Calvino's description, what can you infer about the person who stole the fish? *(Students may say that the "yellow, skinny hands" indicate an elderly or sick person living in the villa.)* OL

★ Viewing the Art

Pierre Bonnard (1867–1947) created a new art style with line, color, and flat, patterned surfaces. His later works reveal vibrant use of color and interrelated forms.
Ask: Does this painting accurately represent the garden? Explain. *(Some may say it is more colorful and lacks animals and modern buildings; others may say the vibrancy suggests the animal life.)* AS

Assign students to write a one-paragraph description of the room, using compound adjectives and hyphenation. OL Have students volunteer sentences from their descriptions. Write the sentences on the board and have the class review whether the hyphenation is correct. AL

English Language Coach

Visualizing Nonnative English speakers may be unfamiliar with the types of cats referenced by Calvino and therefore may have trouble connecting to the images he presents. Have students research and bring in pictures of the various kinds of cats mentioned. EL

Academic Standards
Additional Support activities on pp. 98 and 99 cover the following standards:
Skills Practice: **9.6.1** Identify and correctly use…hyphens.
English Language Coach: **9.2.4** Synthesize the content from several sources or works…and connect…to…related topics…

Teach

BI Big Idea

Matters of Life and Death
Answer: *There are no other green spaces or patches of nature left in the city for the animals to go to other than this garden.* OL

L1 Literary Element

Style Discuss Calvino's sentence structure with students. **Ask:** How would you describe Calvino's writing style? *(Students may say that Calvino favors long, descriptive phrases and writes from a third-person point of view.)* Discuss with students the effect it has on the reader when Calvino adds shorter, exclamatory sentences among his longer, descriptive sentences. OL

"Are you also a cat lover?" A voice at his back made him turn round. He was surrounded by little old women, some of them ancient, wearing old-fashioned hats on their heads; others, younger, but with the look of spinsters; and all were carrying in their hands or their bags packages of leftover meat or fish, and some even had little pans of milk. "Will you help me throw this package over the fence, for those poor creatures?"

All the ladies, cat lovers, gathered at this hour around the garden of dry leaves to take the food to their protégés.[15]

"Can you tell me why they are all here, these cats?" Marcovaldo inquired.

"Where else could they go? This garden is all they have left! Cats come here from other neighborhoods, too, from miles and miles around . . ."

"And birds, as well," another lady added. "They're forced to live by the hundreds and hundreds on these few trees . . ."

"And the frogs, they're all in that pool, and at night they never stop croaking . . . You can hear them even on the eighth floor of the buildings around here."

"Who does this villa belong to anyway?" Marcovaldo asked. Now, outside the gate, there weren't just the cat-loving ladies but also other people: the man from the gas pump opposite, the apprentices from a mechanic's shop, the postman, the grocer, some passersby. And none of them, men and women, had to be asked twice: all wanted to have their say, as always when a mysterious and controversial subject comes up.

"It belongs to a Marchesa.[16] She lives there, but you never see her . . ."

15. Here, *protégé* (prō′ tə zhā′) refers to a person who is protected by someone more experienced.
16. *Marchesa* (mar kā′ zə) is a title for an Italian noblewoman.

Big Idea Matters of Life and Death *Why do the animals come to the garden?* BI

"She's been offered millions and millions, by developers, for this little patch of land, but she won't sell . . ."

"What would she do with millions, an old woman all alone in the world? She wants to hold on to her house, even if it's falling to pieces, rather than be forced to move . . ."

"It's the only undeveloped bit of land in the downtown area . . . Its value goes up every year . . . They've made her offers—"

"Offers! That's not all. Threats, intimidation, persecution . . . You don't know the half of it! Those contractors!"

"But she holds out. She's held out for years . . ."

"She's a saint. Without her, where would those poor animals go?"

"A lot she cares about the animals, the old miser! Have you ever seen her give them anything to eat?"

"How can she feed the cats when she doesn't have food for herself? She's the last descendant of a ruined family!"

"She hates cats! I've seen her chasing them and hitting them with an umbrella!"

"Because they were tearing up her flowerbeds!"

"What flowerbeds? I've never seen anything in this garden but a great crop of weeds!"

Marcovaldo realized that with regard to the old Marchesa opinions were sharply divided: some saw her as an angelic being, others as an egoist and a miser. L1

"It's the same with the birds; she never gives them a crumb!"

"She gives them hospitality. Isn't that plenty?"

"Like she gives the mosquitoes, you mean. They all come from here, from that pool. In the summertime the mosquitoes eat us alive, and it's all the fault of that Marchesa!"

"And the mice? This villa is a mine of mice. Under the dead leaves they have their burrows, and at night they come out . . ."

"As far as the mice go, the cats take care of them . . ."

Additional Support

Academic Standards

The Additional Support activity on p. 100 covers the following standard:

Skills Practice: **9.3.11** Evaluate the aesthetic qualities of style, including the impact of diction…on…mood…

Skills Practice

WRITING: Descriptive Writing
Discuss how good descriptive writing should lead to fully detailed visualization on the part of the reader. BL Divide students into three groups. Challenge students to use Calvino's descriptions to create the city, the cats' counter-city of passageways, and the garden with the villa. Instruct students to approach the project as if they are designing a set for a movie or a play. Invite them to use whatever medium they feel will best represent their interpretations of Calvino's world. OL

Head of an Old Woman. Bernardo Strozzi. Oil on canvas, 48.3 × 38.8 cm. The Barber Institute of Fine Arts, University of Birmingham, Alabama.

"Oh, you and your cats! If we had to rely on them . . ."

"Why? Have you got something to say against cats?"

Here the discussion **degenerated** into a general quarrel.

"The authorities should do something: **confiscate** the villa!" one man cried.

"What gives them the right?" another protested.

"In a modern neighborhood like ours, a mouse-nest like this . . . it should be forbidden . . ."

"Why, I picked my apartment precisely because it overlooked this little bit of green . . ."

"Green, hell! Think of the fine skyscraper they could build here!"

Marcovaldo would have liked to add something of his own, but he couldn't get a word in. Finally, all in one breath, he exclaimed: "The Marchesa stole a trout from me!"

The unexpected news supplied fresh ammunition to the old woman's enemies, but her defenders exploited it as proof of the indigence[17] to which the unfortunate noblewoman was reduced. Both sides agreed that Marcovaldo should go and knock at her door to demand an explanation.

It wasn't clear whether the gate was locked or unlocked; in any case, it opened, after a push, with a mournful creak. Marcovaldo picked his way among the leaves and cats, climbed the steps to the porch, knocked hard at the entrance.

At a window (the very one where the frying pan had appeared), the blind was raised slightly and in one corner a round, pale blue eye was seen, and a clump of hair dyed an undefinable color, and a dry skinny hand. A voice was heard, asking: "Who is it? Who's at the door?" the words accompanied by a cloud smelling of fried oil.

"It's me, Marchesa. The trout man," Marcovaldo explained. "I don't mean to trouble you. I only wanted to tell you, in case you didn't know, that the trout was stolen from me, by that cat, and I'm the one who caught it. In fact the line . . ."

"Those cats! It's always those cats . . ." the Marchesa said, from behind the shutter, with a shrill, somewhat nasal voice. "All my troubles come from the cats! Nobody knows what I go through! Prisoner night and day of those horrid beasts! And with all the refuse people throw over the walls, to spite me!"

"But my trout . . ."

"Your trout! What am I supposed to know about your trout!" The Marchesa's voice became almost a scream, as if she wanted to

Reading Strategy Visualizing *As they talk, what do you think the people in the group look like?* R

Vocabulary

degenerate (di jen′ ə rāt′) *v.* to decline or deteriorate
confiscate (kon′ fis kāt′) *v.* to seize or take away

17. *Indigence* is severe poverty or deprivation.

Literary Element Description *From the description in this paragraph, what impression do you get of the house?* L3

Teach

R Reading Strategy

Visualizing Answer: *Students should describe the women who were first described as well as an assortment of other city-dwellers.* OL

L2 Literary Element

Description Ask: What do you predict the Marchesa will actually be like? *(Students may say that she is an old woman and a hermit and therefore will be antisocial. Others may say that she will be warm and kind, because she keeps the villa for the cats.)* OL

L3 Literary Element

Description Answer: *Students may say that the house seems run-down.* OL

★ Viewing the Art

Italian artist Bernardo Strozzi (1581–1644) painted in both Genoa and Venice but got his nicknames "Il Cappuccino" (the Capuchin) and "Il Prete Genovese" (the Genovese priest) because of his time as a member of the Capuchin monastery. Strozzi combined the influences of such artists as Rubens, Caravaggio, and Van Dyck to create his own unique style. He is particularly known for his religious paintings and his portraits. AS

Reading in the Real World

Citizenship How much do students know about their community's history? Ask students what changes have occurred during their lifetimes and if they feel these changes are positive or negative. Assign students to research the history of their community, with particular emphasis on changes over the last 100 years, and hold a class discussion. Instruct students to write an op-ed piece focusing on whether they feel the modernization of their community is positive or negative. Instruct students to back their arguments with factual data from their reading. OL

Academic Standards

The Additional Support activity on p. 101 covers the following standards:

Reading in the Real World: **9.4.6** Synthesize information from multiple sources…
9.5.4 Write persuasive compositions that clarify and defend positions with…relevant evidence, including facts…

Teach

BI Big Idea

Matters of Life and Death
Ask: Do you feel that the fish is of life-and-death importance to the Marchesa? *(Students may say that she is so old, poor, and desperate that the fish means the difference between starving and eating. Others will feel that she's just being spiteful.)* OL

R Reading Strategy

Visualizing **Answer:** *Student descriptions should incorporate the round blue eyes and protruding teeth mentioned in the text.* OL

L Literary Element

Description **Answer:** *Some may say that it creates somber feelings. Others may say it is wryly humorous, because the creatures in the garden triumph over every effort by the humans to oust them.* OL

CheckPoint

Use the CheckPoint questions on Presentation Plus! to check students' mastery of the selection. These questions can be used with interactive response keypads for immediate student feedback.

BI drown out the sizzle of oil in the pan, which came through the window along with the aroma of fried fish. "How can I make sense of anything, with all the stuff that rains into my house?"

"I understand, but did you take the trout or didn't you?"

"When I think of all the damage I suffer because of the cats! Ah, fine state of affairs! I'm not responsible for anything! I can't tell you what I've lost! Thanks to those cats, who've occupied house and garden for years! My life at the mercy of those animals! Go and find the owners! Make them pay damages! Damages? A whole life destroyed! A prisoner here, unable to move a step!"

"Excuse me for asking: but who's forcing you to stay?"

From the crack in the blind there appeared sometimes a round, pale blue eye, sometimes a mouth with two protruding teeth; for a moment the whole face was visible, and to Marcovaldo it seemed, bewilderingly, the face of a cat.

"They keep me prisoner, they do, those cats! Oh, I'd be glad to leave! What wouldn't I give for a little apartment all my own, in a nice clean modern building! But I can't go out . . . They follow me, they block my path, they trip me up!" The voice became a whisper, as if to confide a secret. "They're afraid I'll sell the lot . . . They won't leave me . . . won't allow me . . . When the builders come to offer me a contract, you should see them, those cats! They get in the way, pull out their claws; they even chased a lawyer off! Once I had the contract right here, I was about to sign it, and they dived in through the window, knocked over the inkwell, tore up all the pages . . ."

All of a sudden Marcovaldo remembered the time, the shipping department, the boss. He tiptoed off over the dried leaves, as the voice continued to come through the slats of the blind, enfolded in that cloud apparently from the oil of a frying pan. "They even scratched me . . . I still have the scar . . . All alone here at the mercy of these demons . . ."

Winter came. A blossoming of white flakes decked the branches and capitals and the cats' tails. Under the snow, the dry leaves dissolved into mush. The cats were rarely seen, the cat lovers even less; the packages of fish-bones were consigned only to cats who came to the door. Nobody, for quite a while, had seen anything of the Marchesa. No smoke came now from the chimneypot of the villa.

One snowy day, the garden was again full of cats, who had returned as if it were spring, and they were miauing as if on a moonlight night. The neighbors realized that something had happened: they went and knocked at the Marchesa's door. She didn't answer: she was dead.

In the spring, instead of the garden, there was a huge building site that a contractor had set up. The steam shovels dug down to great depths to make room for the foundations, cement poured into the iron armatures,[18] a very high crane passed beams to the workmen who were making the scaffoldings. But how could they get on with their work? Cats walked along all the planks, they made bricks fall and upset buckets of mortar, they fought in the midst of the piles of sand. When you started to raise an armature, you found a cat perched on top of it, hissing fiercely. More treacherous pusses climbed onto the masons' backs as if to purr, and there was no getting rid of them. And the birds continued making their nests in all the trestles, the cab of the crane looked like an aviary[19]. . . And you couldn't dip up a bucket of water that wasn't full of frogs, croaking and hopping . . .

18. An *armature* is a framework.
19. *Trestles* are frames that serve as support. An *aviary* is a place where birds are kept.

Reading Strategy Visualizing *How do you picture the Marchesa?* R

Literary Element Description *What feeling is conveyed by this passage?* L

Additional Support

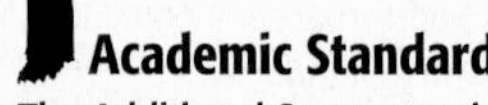

Academic Standards
The Additional Support activity on p. 102 covers the following standard:
Skills Practice: **9.7.15** Deliver expository... presentations that convey information and ideas from...sources accurately and coherently...

Skills Practice

STUDY SKILLS: Research and Connect Remind students that justice and human rights were important to Calvino. Challenge students to find a cause that inspires them. Have them research an organization that supports the cause and then write about it. Instruct students that they can choose anything, ranging from human rights to environmental organizations. Have students share their research with the class. OL Assign students to write a short story, using the cause and organization as their theme. The story can be an allegory, a fable, or simple fiction. AL

AFTER YOU READ

RESPONDING AND THINKING CRITICALLY

Respond

1. What was your reaction to the end of the story?

Recall and Interpret

2. (a)In the opening pages of the story, what does the author reveal about the city the story is set in? (b)Why are those details about the setting important?
3. (a)Who is Marcovaldo and what routine does he establish? (b)What sense do you get of Marcovaldo based on this routine?
4. (a)What happens when Marcovaldo goes to the Biarritz Restaurant? (b)Why might Marcovaldo not go to the restaurant and order the fish to eat?
5. (a)What is notable about the garden? (b)Why do people fight over the state of the garden?

Analyze and Evaluate

6. A story's **mood**—the feeling or emotion it creates—is important to its overall effect. How would you describe the mood of this story? In your answer, cite passages that create the mood.
7. How would you describe the "society" of cats presented in the story? How does it compare with the society of people presented? Explain.
8. Summarize the events at the end of the story. Do you think it is an effective ending? Explain.

Connect

9. **Big Idea** **Matters of Life and Death** (a)A **fable** is a short, simple tale that usually features animal characters and that teaches a lesson or moral. In what ways is this story like a fable? (b)What ideas about nature and city life do you think the author was trying to express through this story? Explain.

LITERARY ANALYSIS

Literary Element Description

A **description** is a detailed portrayal of a person, a place, a thing, or an event. The details of a description help you see, hear, and feel what is being described.

1. Reread the first two pages of the story. Identify five descriptive details about the city that helped you picture what Marcovaldo was seeing.
2. What details does Calvino use to describe the cats?
3. What details does he use to describe the garden and the Marchesa?

Double Cat Spread. Ditz. Private Collection.

Review: Irony

As you learned on page 78, **irony** is a contrast between what appears to be true and what is actually true, or between what is expected and what actually happens. When the reader of a story believes something is going to happen but the opposite happens instead, it is called situational irony.

Partner Activity With a partner, find two examples of irony in the story. To help you locate them, answer the questions below. Then share your results with the class.

1. What are two examples of moments in the story when you expected one thing to happen, but the opposite happened instead?
2. What effect did the irony create—for example, did it create humor or add meaning to the story?

Literary Element

1. Accept reasonable, well-supported answers.
2. The "pink triangles of their noses," and their tails "making a question-mark"
3. Details include the "half-rusted gate," the "small, abandoned-looking building," the "carpet of dry leaves," and the "green water of a pool."

Review: Irony

1. Accept all well-supported answers.
2. The irony promotes the message that nature prevails; it is also humorous.

AFTER YOU READ

Assess

1. Accept reasonable, well-supported answers.
2. (a) The city is a crowded, bustling, modern metropolis. (b) Those details are important to understanding the situation of the cats.
3. (a) He's a man who works at a warehouse shipping department and spends his lunch hour roaming the city with a cat. (b) Possibly adventurous, affable
4. (a) He takes a fish from the restaurant tank. The cat then steals the fish. (b) He doesn't seem like the typical Biarritz patron. It seems very expensive, and Marcovaldo brings a bag lunch to work.
5. (a) It's full of frogs, birds, and cats. (b) Some think it's the last natural refuge in the city; others believe it is a breeding ground for pests.
6. Possibly energetic, happy, or wistful; Answers should be supported.
7. Cats are intelligent creatures with their own routines and haunts. Students should support their answers.
8. The Marchesa dies. The garden and building are destroyed to erect a new building, but the animals impede the work. The ending fits because it shows the animals holding onto life.
9. (a) It's simple and entertaining; it centers on cats; it teaches a lesson. (b) "It is impossible to eliminate nature from the city; nature will assert its rights."

AFTER YOU READ

Assess

Reading Strategy

1. Students should support their answers.
2. Students may say it allows them to see the city through the cats' eyes.
3. Students should support their answers.

Vocabulary

1. b **2.** a **3.** b **4.** b

Academic Vocabulary

She hates the cats and wants to sell her home and leave.

Writing About Literature

Problems: a) Man is taking over animals' habitats; b) The tabby is hungry; c) The Marchesa wants to move; d) The animals need the garden.
Conflicts: a) Man v. animals; b) Marcovaldo v. the tabby; c) The Marchesa v. the cats; d) The contractor v. the cats
Outcome: a) Man wins, but the animals make a last stand; b) Marcovaldo gets the fish but loses it to the Marchesa; c) The Marchesa dies in her home; d) The animals stop construction

Listening and Speaking

Students should use graphic aids and practice with a small group beforehand.

READING AND VOCABULARY

Reading Strategy Visualizing

When you **visualize,** you picture a writer's ideas or descriptions in your mind's eye. Visualizing is one of the best ways to understand and remember information in fiction.

1. Take a moment to visualize Marcovaldo. In your own words, describe how you picture him.
2. How does visualizing help you better understand how the city looks to the cats?
3. How did visualizing help you clarify events in the story? Use specific details from the text to support your answer.

Vocabulary Practice

Practice with Synonyms Read the following sentences. Choose the best synonym for the boldfaced vocabulary word.

1. The decision to open the contest to all students was **ordained** by the senior council.
   a. considered **b.** established
2. We plan to **scrutinize** every order our shipping company receives.
   a. inspect **b.** revise
3. She was warned that her opponent's way of competing was **treacherous.**
   a. effective **b.** untrustworthy
4. The peaceful negotiation may **degenerate** into a squabble if that issue is raised.
   a. transform **b.** deteriorate

Academic Vocabulary

Here is a word from the vocabulary list on page R80.

emerge (i murj′) *v.* to become evident

Practice and Apply
What facts about the Marchesa **emerge** when Marcovaldo finally meets her?

WRITING AND EXTENDING

Writing About Literature

Analyze Conflict Most stories are based on a problem, or conflict, and its resolution. When characters struggle with an outside force, such as another person, society, fate, or a force of nature, it is called **external conflict.** Many stories have more than one conflict, but there is usually a primary conflict that the action of the story revolves around.

Write a brief essay explaining the main external conflict and one minor conflict in the story. In your essay, be sure to explain how the conflicts are resolved. Before beginning your essay, review the story and fill in a chart like the one shown to organize your thoughts.

Problem faced by a character(s)	Conflict suggested by the problem	Outcome of the conflict

Begin your essay by identifying the main external conflict in the story. Identify a minor conflict as well. In the body of your essay, explain these conflicts in detail, citing information from the story. Tell how the conflicts are resolved. Finish your essay with a final thought about what ideas the author may have wished to convey.

After you complete your draft, meet with a partner to review each other's work and to suggest revisions. Then proofread and edit your draft to correct errors in spelling, grammar, and punctuation.

Listening and Speaking

In the story, the cats roam freely through the streets of the city. In many cities, stray cats roam together and have places where they routinely go to eat or to hide. Do research at the library and on the Internet to learn more about urban populations of free-roaming dogs and cats. Create an oral presentation in which you summarize your research and give your own conclusions about what should be done about stray cats and dogs.

LiteratureOnline **Web Activities** For eFlashcards, Selection Quick Checks, and other Web activities, go to www.glencoe.com.

Additional Support

Web Activities Have students access the Web site for interactive activities that will help them assess their understanding of the selection.

Skills Practice

GRAMMAR AND LANGUAGE:

Vocabulary Encourage students to get a better grasp on their vocabulary words by making a game out of it. Have students work in groups to design crossword puzzles using this selection's academic vocabulary as well as words from the story. Have students practice with synonyms by using them to design the crossword puzzle clues. **OL** To make the crossword puzzles more challenging, instruct students to add vocabulary from previous Academic Vocabulary lists and other stories. **AL**

PART 2

Rewards and Sacrifices

Stepping into the American Dream. Xavier Cortada. Acrylic on canvas, 96 x 97¾ in. Private Collection. ★

BIG IDEA

BI Goals give purpose to life, and the struggles to attain them can bring both joy and heartache. The short stories in Part 2 deal with sacrifices people make as they strive to gain a reward or a goal. As you read the stories, ask yourself: Is the reward worth the characters' sacrifices?

Analyzing and Extending

BI Big Idea

Rewards and Sacrifices Have students read the text under the "Big Idea" head. Urge them to discuss their long-term and short-term goals. Ask them to make a connection between their desire to reach their goals and the scene depicted in the art. Challenge students to consider the question, "Is the reward of attaining a goal worth the sacrifices?" **OL**

★ Viewing the Art

Stepping into the American Dream was a mural created by Cuban American artist Xavier Cortada (1964–) in 2002 for the White House Conference on Minority Homeownership. Cortada specializes in large-scale public works, such as murals. For one mural in Miami, hundreds of people volunteered to paint. **AS**

English Language Coach

Build Vocabulary Write the word *goal* on the board and make sure that students know its pronunciation and meaning. Allow students to work in pairs or small groups to generate a list of eight to ten words that describe a person who is able to reach his or her goals. Ask groups to share their lists. **EL**

Differentiated Instruction

Illustrating Goals Invite students to draw images of someone reaching a goal. Ask students to write a caption beneath the image that explains the goal and the kind of effort required to reach it. **BL**

Academic Standards

Additional Support activities on pp. 104 and 105 cover the following standards:

Skills Practice: **9.1.1** Identify and use the literal...meanings of words...

English Language Coach: **9.1.1** Identify and use the literal...meanings of words...

Differentiated Instruction: **9.5.8** Write for different purposes and audiences...

Part 2: Skills Scope and Sequence

Readability Scores Key
Dale-Chall/DRP/Lexile

PACING (DAYS) STANDARD	BLOCK	SELECTIONS AND FEATURES	LITERARY ELEMENTS
1–2 class sessions	1	LITERARY FOCUS: Character and Theme, pp. 106–107	
		"Rules of the Game" by Amy Tan	Protagonist and Antagonist, SE pp. 109, 110, 115–119
3 class sessions	1–2	"The Gift of the Magi" by O. Henry **8.0/55/910**, pp. 121–131	Symbol SE pp. 122, 124, 125, 130 Plot, SE p. 130
		COMPARING LITERATURE Across Genres "Liberty" by Julia Alvarez **4.5/50/840**, pp. 132–141 "The Struggle to Be an All-American Girl" by Elizabeth Wong **7.6/59/1080**, pp. 142–143 "Grudnow" by Linda Pastan, pp. 144–146	Motivation, SE pp. 134, 136, 137, 140, 141 Foreshadowing, TWE p. 137 Conflict, TWE p. 143
1–2 class sessions	1	"Sweet Potato Pie" by Eugenia Collier **6.7/60/970**, pp. 147–158	Theme, SE pp. 148, 151–157 Character, SE p. 157
		Grammar Workshop: Sentence Structure, p. 159	
2 class sessions	1	"The Scarlet Ibis" by James Hurst **6.5/57/1070**, pp. 160–175	Characterization, SE pp. 161, 163–165, 167, 169–172, 174 Setting, SE p. 174 Similes, TWE p. 162
		"The Bass, the River, and Sheila Mant" by W. D. Wetherell **9.4/62/1110**, pp. 176–186	Motif, SE pp. 177–185 Plot, SE p. 185
		Vocabulary Workshop: Multiple-Meaning Words, p. 187	
1 class session	1	"A Christmas Memory" by Truman Capote **7.9/60/900**, pp. 188–204	Dialogue, SE pp. 189, 191, 194, 196–197, 201, 203 Character, SE p. 203 Imagery, TWE p. 194 Alliteration, TWE p. 200

About the Part

Part 2 explores the literary themes of rewards and sacrifices and the literary elements of theme and character.

READING AND CRITICAL THINKING	VOCABULARY	WRITING AND GRAMMAR	LISTENING, SPEAKING, AND VIEWING
Making Inferences About Characters,	Word Parts, SE p. 120	Analyze Setting, SE p. 120	Analyzing Art, SE p. 117;
Identifying Problem and Solution, SE pp. 122, 123, 125, 126, 128, 130	Synonyms, SE p. 130 Academic Vocabulary, SE p. 130	Character Analysis, SE p. 130 Sentence Structure, SE p. 131	Analyzing Art, SE p. 124, 127 Interview, SE p. 131
Responding to Characters, SE pp. 134–141; TWE p. 142 Previewing, TWE p. 134 Making Inferences, TWE p. 136		Analyzing Theme, SE p. 141 Essay on Sacrifices, SE p. 146 Using Articles, TWE p. 137 Dash, TWE p. 138 Infinitives, TWE p. 140	Analyzing Art, SE p. 139; TWE pp. 135, 145
Questioning, SE pp. 148, 149, 152, 154, 156, 157	Word Parts, SE pp. 148, 158 Academic Vocabulary, SE p. 158	Analyze Cultural Context, SE p. 158	Analyzing Art, SE pp. 149, 150, 155
		Avoiding Misplaced Modifiers, SE p. 159	
Comparing and Contrasting Characters, SE pp. 161–164, 166, 167, 169, 171, 174 Problem and Solution, TWE p. 164	Word Origins, SE pp. 161, 174	Respond to Character, SE p. 175 Using Prepositional Phrases, SE p. 175	Analyzing Art, SE pp. 165, 168; TWE p. 171 Literature Groups, SE p. 175 Readers' Theater, TWE p. 170
Connecting to Personal Experience, SE pp. 177–186	Analogies, SE pp. 177, 186 Academic Vocabulary, SE p. 186	Evaluating Author's Craft, SE p. 186	Analyzing Art, SE p. 180; TWE pp. 181, 184 Literature Groups, SE p. 186
	Multiple-Meaning Words, SE p. 187		
Analyzing Characterization, SE pp. 189, 191–193, 196, 198, 199, 201, 203	Analogies, SE pp. 189, 203 Academic Vocabulary, SE p. 203 Compound Words, TWE p. 190	Explore Author's Purpose, SE p. 204 Using Colons, SE p. 204 Description, TWE p. 192	Analyzing Art, SE p. 198; TWE pp. 190, 191, 194, 200 Group Activity, SE p. 202 Performing, SE p. 204 Design Elements, TWE p. 198

LITERARY FOCUS

Focus

BELLRINGER

Bellringer Options
Daily Language Practice Transparency 10
Or display images of characters from popular culture.
Ask: How would you describe these characters and their motivations? Have students consider what characters contribute to stories as they read the selections.

Teach

L Literary Element

Character Explain that many main characters in modern literature are flawed and morally ambiguous. Such protagonists are often referred to as antiheroes. Have students name heroes and antiheroes from stories or films. OL

★ Viewing the Cartoon

Cartoonist Bill Watterson (1958–) drew the comic strip *Calvin and Hobbes* from 1985 to 1995. AS

LITERARY FOCUS

Character and Theme

How do the traits and actions of characters help you understand a story's theme?

Have you ever had to describe someone, perhaps when telling a story or recalling an event? Fiction writers describe a character's appearance, personality, and actions to give the reader a better understanding of the character's motivations, to reveal what makes the character tick. All of the information about the characters in a story, taken together with the plot and setting, can also reveal something about the overall meaning of the story.

★

L Character

Characters are the people, animals, and other individuals in a work of fiction. The most important characters in a story are called **main characters.** Among these main characters, there is a single **protagonist.** The protagonist is the central character around whom the central conflict revolves. **Minor characters** are those who help or observe the protagonist solve the conflict.

> My mother imparted her daily truths so she could help my older brothers and me rise above our circumstances. We lived in San Francisco's Chinatown. Like most other Chinese children who played in the back alleys of restaurants and curio shops, I didn't think that we were poor.
>
> —Amy Tan, **from "Rules of the Game"**

Interactive Literary Elements Handbook Go to www.glencoe.com to review or learn more about character and theme.

Additional Support

Skills Practice

VOCABULARY: Character Words
Suggest students create flashcards to help them remember literary terms associated with character. Have them write the literary term on the front of a card and definitions and quotations or sketches on the back. Allow them to work in pairs to make and then use their flashcards. OL

Literature Online

Literary Elements Have students access the Web site to improve their understanding of character and theme.

Round and Flat Characters Writers create two kinds of characters. A **round character** is complex, like people you know. He or she thinks, acts, and talks in a convincing way. Like a real person, a round character has multiple and sometimes contradictory traits.

> I skipped through the rooms, down the echoing halls, shouting, "Mama, he smiled. He's all there! He's all there!" and he was.
>
> —James Hurst, **from "The Scarlet Ibis"**

A **flat character,** on the other hand, shows only one or two personality traits. In "Rules of the Game," Lau Po is a flat character. His only role in the story is to teach the protagonist how to be a better chess player. A **stereotype**, such as a cruel headmaster or a jealous lover, is a flat character of a familiar type.

Dynamic and Static Characters Another way to describe characters is by watching to see how they change. A **dynamic character** develops or changes over the course of the story. Usually the development or change is spurred by the central conflict of the story. Very often, the change results in a character's newfound understanding of himself or herself or others.

> The truth was that after Liberty arrived, I never played with the others. It was as if I had found my double in another species.
>
> —Julia Alvarez, **from "Liberty"**

Static characters are characters that do not undergo a change. Most characters in a story are static so as not to distract the reader from the significant changes that occur in the protagonist.

Theme R

The main idea, or message, of a literary work is called its **theme.** Keep in mind that a single work can have many themes, and that the theme of a story is different from its subject. The subject is what the story is about. The theme is the author's insight about life or human nature. "Rules of the Game" is about chess, but its theme addresses the generation gap that exists between mother and daughter.

> My mother had a habit of standing over me while I plotted out my games. I think she thought of herself as my protective ally. Her lips would be sealed tight, and after each move I made, a soft "Hmmmmph" would escape from her nose.
>
> "Ma, I can't practice when you stand there like that," I said one day. She retreated to the kitchen and made loud noises with the pots and pans.
>
> —Amy Tan, **from "The Rules of the Game"**

Sometimes a story will have a **stated theme,** meaning the author expresses the theme directly. For example, fables have a stated theme. Most literary works, however, have implied themes. An **implied theme** is revealed gradually through a variety of literary elements, including plot, character, setting, figurative language, and point of view.

Quickwrite

Charting Changes Think of a character from a story you know well. Using the graphic organizer below, describe how the character changes from the beginning of the story to the end.

Character Development

Beginning		Middle		End
	→		→	

INDIANA ACADEMIC STANDARDS (pages 106–107)

9.3.3 Analyze interactions between characters in a literary text and explain the way those interactions affect the plot.

9.3 [Identify] story elements such as character [and] theme...

Teach

R Reading Strategy

Making Inferences Say: Themes are rarely stated directly. You may have to "read between the lines" and review plot events to determine the story's message. When considering theme, try to complete the following sentences: "The message of the story is . . ." or "The point the writer wants to make is. . . ." OL

Assess

Students should fill their graphic organizers with details about the character in the stories they choose. In most cases, the character will demonstrate some kind of development over the course of the story. Challenge students to make a generalization about the character's growth or lack of growth.

English Language Coach

Learning the Short Story Elements Have English language learners choose a story from their own culture or from a movie and discuss it with a partner. Then have them list literary elements on note cards with brief definitions and examples from the story or movie they discussed. EL

Differentiated Instruction

Designing a Poster Ask spatial learners to create a poster that illustrates the different types of characters. The posters should be colorful and easy to read. Hang students' posters around the classroom. BL

Academic Standards

Additional Support activities on pp. 106 and 107 cover the following standards:

Skills Practice: **9.1** Use...relationships... and a growing knowledge of English... to determine the meaning of words...

English Language Coach: **9.3** [Identify] story elements such as character, theme, plot, and setting...

Differentiated Instruction: **9.5.7** Use varied and expanded vocabulary, appropriate for specific forms and topics.

Focus

BELLRINGER

Bellringer Options
Selection Focus Transparency 8
Daily Language Practice Transparency 11

Or ask students to describe their neighborhoods. *(Crowded, busy, public parks, businesses, vacant buildings, lots of traffic, quiet, noisy, etc.)* Have students consider as they read how their neighborhoods affect their lives just as the narrator's life is affected by her life in San Francisco's Chinatown.

Author Search To expand students' appreciation of Amy Tan, have them access the Web site for additional information and resources.

BEFORE YOU READ

Rules of the Game

MEET AMY TAN

Amy Tan's parents had very high expectations for her. "Of course, you will become a famous neurosurgeon," they said. In addition, they expected her to be a concert pianist in her spare time. Tan's parents were immigrants from China. Her father, John, came to the United States in 1947, and her mother, Daisy, fled here in 1949, just before the communist government came to power.

Tan remembers her father as playful, easygoing, and very loving. The pain and suffering of her mother's life in China, however, set the tone for the family. When Daisy became extremely unhappy, she had the urge to move to a new home. Tan's father always respected his wife's wishes. As a result, Tan attended eleven different schools, most in the San Francisco Bay area, before graduating from high school. The frequent moves made it hard for Tan to make close friends, and she was often lonely. However, to figure out how to fit in, she watched her classmates carefully. She would later draw on these observational skills when she began writing fiction.

> *"I enjoy the freedom to write whatever I feel like writing."*
>
> —Amy Tan

Tragedy Strikes When Tan was fifteen, a double tragedy transformed her life. Within several months, both her older brother and her father died of brain cancer. Tan's mother followed her pattern of moving the family to escape unhappiness. This time, she took Tan and her younger brother to Europe. First, they lived in the Netherlands. Later, they lived in Switzerland. Tan graduated from an international high school there and returned to the United States for college and graduate school.

Tan's first professional job after earning a master's degree in linguistics was working with young children who had language acquisition problems and other developmental delays. Later, she became a technical writer.

On the Path to Writing Fiction Although Tan had a successful career as a freelance technical writer, she began writing fiction as well. Eventually, she submitted her short story "Rules of the Game" to a publisher, along with an outline for a novel. Both were accepted, and Tan's first book, *The Joy Luck Club,* which incorporates "Rules of the Game," was published in 1989. *The Joy Luck Club* brought Tan overnight success. It was on the best-seller list for many months and has won many awards.

Tan has continued writing novels and has also written a memoir and two children's books. In addition, she is a vocalist in a rock band—Rock Bottom Remainders—that includes several other famous authors. This band tours the country and donates its profits to charity.

Amy Tan was born in 1952.

Literature Online **Author Search** For more about Amy Tan, go to www.glencoe.com.

Selection Skills

Rules of the Game

Literary Elements
- Protagonist and Antagonist (SE pp. 109, 111, 115–119)

Reading Skills
- Making Inferences About Characters (SE pp. 109, 111–116, 118, 120)

Vocabulary Skills
- Word Parts (SE p. 120)

Listening/Speaking/Viewing Skills
- Analyzing Art (SE p. 117; TWE p. 112)

Writing Skills/Grammar
- Essay on Setting (SE p. 120)
- Semicolons (TWE p. 116)

Study Skills/Research/Assessment
- Short Response (TWE p. 118)

LITERATURE PREVIEW

Connecting to the Story

One often hears of a "generation gap" that exists between people of different ages. Before you read "Rules of the Game," think about the following questions:

- What valuable lessons can parents teach their children?
- Are clashes between generations inevitable?

Building Background

Chess has been played for at least five hundred years, making it one of the oldest known board games. Like checkers, chess is a two-person game played on a board of sixty-four light and dark squares. The object of the game is to checkmate, or capture, the opponent's king. Chess players, like athletes, work their way up through the ranks by winning local, regional, national, and international tournaments. If they win enough tournaments at the international level, they reach grand master status.

Setting Purposes for Reading

Big Idea Rewards and Sacrifices

As you read, notice the sacrifices some of the characters make for others. Also notice sacrifices that the characters are unwilling to make for one another.

Literary Element Protagonist and Antagonist

The **protagonist** is the central character in a story. The **antagonist** is the character or force that opposes the protagonist. As you read "Rules of the Game," identify the protagonist and the antagonist.

- See Literary Terms Handbook, pp. R1 and R14.

Literature Online Interactive Literary Elements Handbook To review or learn more about the literary elements, go to www.glencoe.com.

READING PREVIEW

Reading Strategy Making Inferences About Characters

When you **make inferences about characters,** you pay attention to what the writer shows the characters doing and saying. Then you form ideas about their personality traits based on this evidence.

Reading Tip: Taking Notes Make a web diagram like the one below for each character in this story. Use the diagrams to help you make inferences about characters.

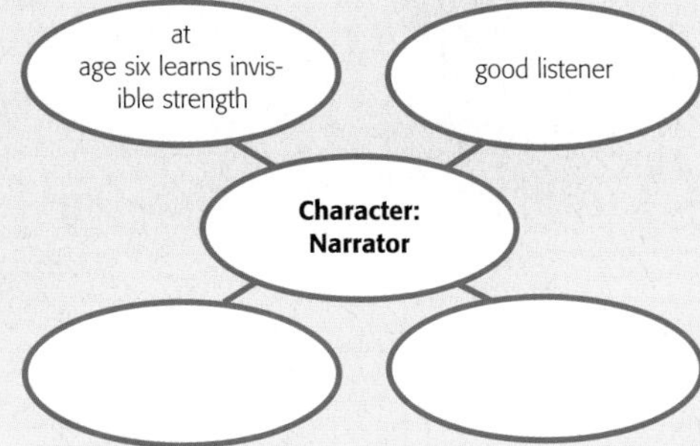

Vocabulary

impart (im pärt′) *v.* to make known; to tell; p. 110 *Jan decided to keep her plan to herself and impart it to no one.*

relent (ri lent′) *v.* to become less harsh or strict; to yield; p. 113 *At first, they didn't want the younger athletes to play on their softball team, but later they decided to relent.*

adversary (ad′ vər ser′ ē) *n.* an opponent or enemy; p. 114 *Although he was friendly to me off the field, he was my adversary during the game.*

benevolently (bə nev′ ə lənt lē) *adv.* kindly; p. 115 *The conductor nodded benevolently to the young musicians after a great performance.*

malodorous (mal ō′ dər əs) *adj.* bad-smelling; stinky; p. 117 *The old sofa became malodorous after we left it out in the rain.*

INDIANA ACADEMIC STANDARDS (pages 109–120)

9.3.3 Analyze interactions between characters...

9.3.4 Determine characters' traits by what the characters say about themselves in narration, dialogue, and soliloquy...

9.5.3 Write expository compositions, including analytical essays...

BEFORE YOU READ

Focus

Summary

Meimei is a Chinese-American girl growing up in San Francisco's Chinatown. She experiences a number of cultural clashes with her more traditional Chinese parents. These cultural differences worsen the generation gap between Meimei and her mother after Meimei becomes a chess champion.

V Vocabulary

Vocabulary File Say: Add these words and definitions to your vocabulary file. For each word, include a sentence that gives you an example of how to use the word. **OL** Students with English language needs should include the pronunciations of these words in their files. **EL**

Literary Elements Have students access the Web site to improve their understanding of protagonist and antagonist.

Selection Resources

Print Materials

- Unit 1 Resources (Fast File), pp. 42–44
- Leveled Vocabulary Development, p. 8
- Selection and Unit Assessments, pp. 17–18
- Selection Quick Checks, p. 9

Transparencies

- Bellringer Options Transparencies: Selection Focus Transparency 8 Daily Language Practice Transparency 11
- Literary Elements Transparency 13

Technology

- TeacherWorks Plus™ CD-ROM
- StudentWorks Plus™ CD-ROM
- Presentation Plus!™ CD-ROM
- Literature Online, glencoe.com
- Online Student Edition, mhln.com
- Exam*View*® Assessment Suite CD-ROM
- Vocabulary PuzzleMaker CD-ROM
- Listening Library, disc 1 track 9

Teach

BI1 Big Idea

Rewards and Sacrifices

Say: Keep these questions in mind as you read: Which type of game is being referred to in the title? *(Most students will say the game is chess; some may say the game is the art of winning arguments.)* What is the art of invisible strength? *(Possible answer: It may refer to being quiet but unyielding under pressure.)* OL

BI2 Big Idea

Rewards and Sacrifices

Answer: *The narrator has learned exactly what her mother has tried to teach her–to apply self-control; her mother rewards her silence by buying what she knows the narrator wants.* OL

Readability Scores

Dale-Chall: 7.3

DRP: 60

Lexile: 990

BI1 I was six when my mother taught me the art of invisible strength. It was a strategy for winning arguments, respect from others, and eventually, though neither of us knew it at the time, chess games.

"Bite back your tongue," scolded my mother when I cried loudly, yanking her hand toward the store that sold bags of salted plums. At home, she said, "Wise guy, he not go against wind. In Chinese we say, Come from South, blow with wind—poom!—North will follow. Strongest wind cannot be seen."

The next week I bit back my tongue as we entered the store with the forbidden candies. When my mother finished her shopping, she quietly plucked a small bag of plums from the rack and put it on the counter with the rest of the items.

My mother **imparted** her daily truths so she could help my older brothers and me rise above our circumstances. We lived in San Francisco's Chinatown.[1] Like most of the other Chinese children who played in the back alleys of restaurants and curio shops, I didn't think we were poor. My bowl was always full, three five-course meals every day, beginning with a soup full of mysterious things I didn't want to know the names of.

We lived on Waverly Place, in a warm, clean, two-bedroom flat that sat above a small Chinese bakery specializing in steamed pastries and dim sum.[2] In the early

Big Idea Rewards and Sacrifices *What has the narrator learned, and why does the mother respond the way she does?* BI2

1. *Chinatown* is a neighborhood or section of a city that is chiefly inhabited by Chinese people.
2. *Dim sum,* literally translated from the Chinese, means "dot-hearts," or "small treats that touch the heart." Dim sum foods are often bite-size dumplings, filled buns, or noodles.

Vocabulary

impart (im pärt′) *v.* to make known; to tell

Additional Support

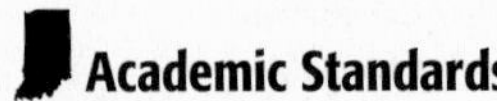

Academic Standards

The Additional Support activity on p. 110 covers the following standard:

Skills Practice: **9.3.3** Analyze interactions between characters…and explain the way those interactions affect the plot

Skills Practice

READING: Previewing This story deals with generational gaps that are part of the relationship between parents and children in all cultures. Ask students to answer these questions as they read:

- Why does Meimei's mother teach her children lessons called "daily truths"?
- What examples from the story are evidence of the generation gap between Meimei and her mother?

Tell students to read the story and note how the relationship between mother and daughter takes on the characteristics of a chess match. OL morning, when the alley was still quiet, I could smell fragrant red beans as they were cooked down to a pasty sweetness. By daybreak, our flat was heavy with the odor of fried sesame balls and sweet curried chicken crescents. From my bed, I would listen as my father got ready for work, then locked the door behind him, one-two-three clicks.

At the end of our two-block alley was a small sandlot playground with swings and slides well-shined down the middle with use. The play area was bordered by wood-slat benches where old-country people sat cracking roasted watermelon seeds with their golden teeth and scattering the husks to an impatient gathering of gurgling pigeons. The best playground, however, was the dark alley itself. It was crammed with daily mysteries and adventures. My brothers and I would peer into the medicinal herb shop, watching Old Li dole out onto a stiff sheet of white paper the right amount of insect shells, saffron-colored[3] seeds, and pungent[4] leaves for his ailing customers. It was said that he once cured a woman dying of an ancestral curse that had eluded the best of American doctors. Next to the pharmacy was a printer who specialized in gold-embossed wedding invitations and festive red banners. **L2**

Farther down the street was Ping Yuen Fish Market. The front window displayed a tank crowded with doomed fish and turtles struggling to gain footing on the slimy green-tiled sides. A hand-written sign informed tourists, "Within this store, is all for food, not for pet." Inside, the butchers with their bloodstained white smocks deftly gutted the fish while customers cried out their orders and shouted, "Give me your freshest," to which the butchers always protested, "All are freshest." On less crowded market days, we would inspect the crates of live frogs and crabs which we were warned not to poke, boxes of dried cuttlefish, and row upon row of iced prawns, squid, and slippery fish. The sand dabs[5] made me shiver each time; their eyes lay on one flattened side and reminded me of my mother's story of a careless girl who ran into a crowded street and was crushed by a cab. "Was smash flat," reported my mother.

Visual Vocabulary
A *prawn* is a large shrimp.

At the corner of the alley was Hong Sing's, a four-table café with a recessed stairwell in front that led to a door marked "Tradesmen." My brothers and I believed the bad people emerged from this door at night. Tourists never went to Hong Sing's, since the menu was printed only in Chinese. A Caucasian[6] man with a big camera once posed me and my playmates in front of the restaurant. He had us move to the side of the picture window so the photo would capture the roasted duck with its head dangling from a juice-covered rope. After he took the picture, I told him he should go into Hong Sing's and eat dinner. When he smiled and asked me what they served, I shouted, "Guts and duck's feet and octopus gizzards!" Then I ran off with my friends, shrieking with laughter as we scampered across the alley and hid in the entryway grotto of the China Gem Company, my heart pounding with hope that he would chase us. **L2**

My mother named me after the street that we lived on: Waverly Place Jong, my official name for important American documents.

3. Anything *saffron-colored* is orange-yellow.
4. Anything that is *pungent* has a sharp smell or taste.
5. The *sand dab* is a small Pacific Coast flatfish related to the flounder.
6. *Caucasian* refers to the group of people who make up what is loosely known as the white race.

Literary Element Protagonist and Antagonist *Who do you think will be the protagonist of this story? Why?* **L1**

Reading Strategy Making Inferences About Characters *What can you infer about the narrator from this description?* **R1**

Reading Strategy Making Inferences About Characters *What can you infer about the narrator from this incident?* **R2**

English Language Coach

Animal Names Write these animal names on the board: *pigeons, fish, turtles, frogs, crabs, cuttlefish, prawns, squid, sand dabs, octopus,* and *ducks.* Have students locate each and identify what it names, and then record words and definitions in their vocabulary notebooks. **EL**

Differentiated Instruction

Visualizing Ask student partners to choose a Chinatown location in the story. Have them reread the details about their location. Then pairs should draw a picture, or make a collage or a three-dimensional model of the location. Combine the projects to create Meimei's neighborhood. **BL**

Teach

L1 Literary Element

Protagonist and Antagonist **Answer:** *The little girl will be the protagonist because she tells the reader about herself.* **OL**

L2 Literary Element

Setting Point out how the writer vividly creates the setting in which the story takes place. Explain that giving these details draws readers into the story by helping them create mental pictures of the place in which events will unfold. Ask students which detail is most vivid to them. **OL**

R1 Reading Strategy

Making Inferences About Characters **Answer:** *She likes adventure and mystery; she appreciates small details of daily life.* **OL**

R2 Reading Strategy

Making Inferences About Characters **Answer:** *She is daring and playful. She likes to have adventures and take risks.* **OL**

Use the CheckPoint questions on Presentation Plus! to monitor students' comprehension. These questions can be used with interactive response keypads for immediate student feedback.

Academic Standards

Additional Support activities on p. 111 cover the following standards:

English Language Coach: **9.1.1** Identify and use the literal…meanings of words…

Differentiated Instruction: **9.3** [Identify] story elements such as…setting…

Teach

R1 Reading Strategy

Making Inferences About Characters **Answer:** *She expects herself, her family, and other Chinese people to set high goals and to strive for excellence in everything they do.* OL

★ Viewing the Art

Russian born Alek Rapoport (1933–1997) immigrated to San Francisco when forced to leave the Soviet Union. Considered a dissident artist, Rapoport concentrated on inner life and spiritual objects in his work. AS

Dragon's Gate, Chinatown, San Francisco, 1986. Alek Rapoport. Tempera and masonite, 101.6 × 94 in. Private collection. ★

But my family called me Meimei,[7] "Little Sister." I was the youngest, the only daughter. Each morning before school, my mother would twist and yank on my thick black hair until she had formed two tightly wound pigtails. One day, as she struggled to weave a hard-toothed comb through my disobedient hair, I had a sly thought.

I asked her, "Ma, what is Chinese torture?" My mother shook her head. A bobby pin was wedged between her lips. She wetted her palm and smoothed the hair above my ear, then pushed the pin in so that it nicked sharply against my scalp.

"Who say this word?" she asked without a trace of knowing how wicked I was being. I shrugged my shoulders and said, "Some boy in my class said Chinese people do Chinese torture."

"Chinese people do many things," she said simply. "Chinese people do business, do medicine, do painting. Not lazy like American people. We do torture. Best torture."

My older brother Vincent was the one who actually got the chess set. We had gone to the annual Christmas party held at the First Chinese Baptist Church at the end of the alley. The missionary ladies had put together a Santa bag of gifts donated by members of another church. None of the gifts had names on them. There were separate sacks for boys and girls of different ages.

One of the Chinese parishioners had donned a Santa Claus costume and a stiff paper beard with cotton balls glued to it. I think the only children who thought he was the real thing were too young to know that Santa Claus was not Chinese. When my turn came up, the Santa man asked me how old I

7. *Meimei* (mā′ mā)

Reading Strategy Making Inferences About Characters *What goals and values can you infer the mother has, based on what she says here?* R1

Additional Support

Skills Practice

READING: Evaluation An evaluation is a judgment. Both readers and characters make judgments. In the story, Meimei and her mother judge each other's behavior and motives. Have students chart their reactions and feelings toward Meimei and her mother. Ask students if their initial evaluations change by the end of the story. Have students give reasons for their answers. OL was. I thought it was a trick question; I was seven according to the American formula and eight by the Chinese calendar.[8] I said I was born on March 17, 1951. That seemed to satisfy him. He then solemnly asked if I had been a very, very good girl this year and did I believe in Jesus Christ and obey my parents. I knew the only answer to that. I nodded back with equal solemnity.

Having watched the other children opening their gifts, I already knew that the big gifts were not necessarily the nicest ones. One girl my age got a large coloring book of biblical characters, while a less greedy girl who selected a smaller box received a glass vial of lavender toilet water. The sound of the box was also important. A ten-year old boy had chosen a box that jangled when he shook it. It was a tin globe of the world with a slit for inserting money. He must have thought it was full of dimes and nickels, because when he saw that it had just ten pennies, his face fell with such undisguised disappointment that his mother slapped the side of his head and led him out of the church hall, apologizing to the crowd for her son who had such bad manners he couldn't appreciate such a fine gift.

As I peered into the sack, I quickly fingered the remaining presents, testing their weight, imagining what they contained. I chose a heavy, compact one that was wrapped in shiny silver foil and a red satin ribbon. It was a twelve-pack of Life Savers and I spent the rest of the party arranging and rearranging the candy tubes in the order of my favorites. My brother Winston chose wisely as well. His present turned out to be a box of intricate plastic parts; the instructions on the box proclaimed that when they were properly assembled he would have an authentic miniature replica of a World War II submarine.

Vincent got the chess set, which would have been a very decent present to get at a church Christmas party, except it was obviously used and, as we discovered later, it was missing a black pawn and a white knight. My mother graciously thanked the unknown benefactor,[9] saying, "Too good. Cost too much." At which point, an old lady with fine white, wispy hair nodded toward our family and said with a whistling whisper, "Merry, merry Christmas."

When we got home, my mother told Vincent to throw the chess set away. "She not want it. We not want it," she said, tossing her head stiffly to the side with a tight, proud smile. My brothers had deaf ears. They were already lining up the chess pieces and reading from the dog-eared instruction book.

I watched Vincent and Winston play during Christmas week. The chess board seemed to hold elaborate secrets waiting to be untangled. The chessmen were more powerful than Old Li's magic herbs that cured ancestral curses. And my brothers wore such serious faces that I was sure something was at stake that was greater than avoiding the tradesmen's door to Hong Sing's.

"Let me! Let me!" I begged between games when one brother or the other would sit back with a deep sigh of relief and victory, the other annoyed, unable to let go of the outcome. Vincent at first refused to let me play, but when I offered my Life Savers as replacements for the buttons that filled in for the missing pieces, he **relented.** He chose the flavors: wild

8. By the *Chinese calendar,* the day on which a baby is born is counted as its first birthday. By this method, then, Meimei was one year old on the day she was born.

9. A *benefactor* is someone who gives financial aid; here, it refers to the gift giver.

Big Idea Rewards and Sacrifices *What is Meimei's strategy for choosing the best present?* **BI**

Reading Strategy Making Inferences About Characters *How does what the mother says here contradict what she said earlier to the gift giver? What do her words reveal about her character?* **R2**

Vocabulary

relent (ri lent′) *v.* to become less harsh or strict; to yield

Teach

BI Big Idea

Rewards and Sacrifices

Answer: *Meimei chooses the gift that weighs the most.* **OL**

R2 Reading Strategy

Making Inferences About Characters

Answer: *She is gracious and shows good manners, even though she is insulted by the gift; she is proud and doesn't want to accept castoffs from others.* **OL**

Reading in the Real World

Citizenship Ask students to find magazine articles about family relationships between young people and their parents or grandparents. Have students discuss their articles in small groups. **OL**

Building Reading Fluency

Reading Aloud Tell student pairs to find favorite passages in the selection to read to each other. Have students practice individually before reading aloud. As partners read to each other, ask the listeners to note specific places where the reader was particularly effective and explain why. **BL**

Academic Standards

Additional Support activities on pp. 112 and 113 cover the following standards:

Skills Practice: **9.3.3** Analyze interactions between characters…

Reading in the Real World: **9.3** [Make] connections and comparisons across texts…

Building Reading Fluency: **9.7.10** Assess how…delivery affect[s] the mood and tone of the oral communication and make[s] an impact on the audience.

Teach

BI1 Big Idea

Rewards and Sacrifices
Answer: *She thinks the potential sacrifice of some of her candy will be well worth the reward of getting to play chess.* OL

R1 Reading Strategy

Making Inferences About Characters **Answer:** *She is determined, disciplined, and systematic. She seems to learn things quickly.* OL

L1 Literary Element

Foreshadowing An author often uses clues that hint at events that will occur later in the plot.
Ask: What is the author hinting at by making chess a metaphor for Meimei's real-life situation? *(Possible answer: The battle of wills between Meimei and her mother will continue beyond the story and into Meimei's future life.)* OL

BI2 Big Idea

Rewards and Sacrifices
Answer: *At the beginning of the story, she gets her mother to buy salted plums.* OL

cherry for the black pawn and peppermint for the white knight. Winner could eat both.

As our mother sprinkled flour and rolled out small doughy circles for the steamed dumplings that would be our dinner that night, Vincent explained the rules, pointing to each piece. "You have sixteen pieces and so do I. One king and queen, two bishops, two knights, two castles, and eight pawns. The pawns can only move forward one step, except on the first move. Then they can move two. But they can only take men by moving crossways like this, except in the beginning, when you can move ahead and take another pawn."

"Why?" I asked as I moved my pawn. "Why can't they move more steps?"

"Because they're pawns," he said.

"But why do they go crossways to take other men. Why aren't there any women and children?"

"Why is the sky blue? Why must you always ask stupid questions?" asked Vincent. "This is a game. These are the rules. I didn't make them up. See. Here. In the book." He jabbed a page with a pawn in his hand. "Pawn. P-A-W-N. Pawn. Read it yourself."

My mother patted the flour off her hands. "Let me see book," she said quietly. She scanned the pages quickly, not reading the foreign English symbols, seeming to search deliberately for nothing in particular.

"This American rules," she concluded at last. "Every time people come out from foreign country, must know rules. You not know, judge say, Too bad, go back. They not telling you why so you can use their way go forward. They say, Don't know why, you find out yourself. But they knowing all the time. Better you take it, find out why yourself." She tossed her head back with a satisfied smile.

I found out about all the whys later. I read the rules and looked up all the big words in a dictionary. I borrowed books from the Chinatown library. I studied each chess piece, trying to absorb the power each contained.

I learned about opening moves and why it's important to control the center early on; the shortest distance between two points is straight down the middle. I learned about the middle game and why tactics between two **adversaries** are like clashing ideas; the one who plays better has the clearest plans for both attacking and getting out of traps. I learned why it is essential in the endgame[10] to have foresight, a mathematical understanding of all possible moves, and patience; all weaknesses and advantages become evident to a strong adversary and are obscured[11] to a tiring opponent. I discovered that for the whole game one must gather invisible strengths and see the endgame before the game begins.

I also found out why I should never reveal "why" to others. A little knowledge withheld is a great advantage one should store for future use. That is the power of chess. It is a game of secrets in which one must show and never tell.

I loved the secrets I found within the sixty-four black and white squares. I carefully drew a handmade chessboard and pinned it to the wall next to my bed, where at night I would stare for hours at imaginary battles. Soon I no longer lost any games or

10. When played at the expert level, a chess game has three parts—the *opening,* the *middle game,* and the *endgame*—each with its own tactics and strategies.
11. When something is *obscured,* it is difficult to see or understand.

Big Idea Rewards and Sacrifices *How do you think Meimei feels about the potential sacrifices and rewards in this situation?* BI1

Reading Strategy Making Inferences About Characters *What does the way in which Meimei learns to play chess tell you about her character?* R1

Big Idea Rewards and Sacrifices *When did Meimei first use the art of invisible strength to get a reward?* BI2

Vocabulary
adversary (ad′ vər ser′ ē) *n.* an opponent or enemy

Additional Support

Skills Practice

READING: Repetition An author may repeat lines, words, or phrases to emphasize important ideas. Repetition also lends a sense of unity or continuity to the writing.

- Have students find examples of repetition on p. 114. *(Examples: I found out, I borrowed, I studied, I learned about, I learned why, I discovered, I loved.)*
- Ask students to explain what important ideas the author emphasizes by using repetition. *(Possible answer: She emphasizes the character's intense and focused desire to learn the game of chess and to excel as a player.)* OL

Life Savers, but I lost my adversaries. Winston and Vincent decided they were more interested in roaming the streets after school in their Hopalong Cassidy[12] cowboy hats.

On a cold spring afternoon, while walking home from school, I detoured through the playground at the end of our alley. I saw a group of old men, two seated across a folding table playing a game of chess, others smoking pipes, eating peanuts, and watching. I ran home and grabbed Vincent's chess set, which was bound in a cardboard box with rubber bands. I also carefully selected two prized rolls of Life Savers. I came back to the park and approached a man who was observing the game.

"Want to play?" I asked him. His face widened with surprise and he grinned as he looked at the box under my arm.

"Little sister, been a long time since I play with dolls," he said, smiling **benevolently**. I quickly put the box down next to him on the bench and displayed my retort.[13]

Lau Po, as he allowed me to call him, turned out to be a much better player than my brothers. I lost many games and many Life Savers. But over the weeks, with each diminishing roll of candies, I added new secrets. Lau Po gave me the names. The Double Attack from the East and West Shores. Throwing Stones on the Drowning Man. The Sudden Meeting of the Clan. The Surprise from the Sleeping Guard. The Humble Servant Who Kills the King. Sand in the Eyes of Advancing Forces. A Double Killing Without Blood.

12. *Hopalong Cassidy* is a fictional cowboy hero from early radio, movies, and television.
13. A *retort* (ri tôrt′) is a sharp, quick, witty reply.

Reading Strategy Making Inferences About Characters *Why do you think the narrator's brothers no longer want to play chess?* **R2**

Vocabulary

benevolently (bə nev′ ə lənt lē) *adv.* kindly

There were also the fine points of chess etiquette.[14] Keep captured men in neat rows, as well-tended prisoners. Never announce "Check" with vanity, lest someone with an unseen sword slit your throat. Never hurl pieces into the sandbox after you have lost a game, because then you must find them again, by yourself, after apologizing to all around you. By the end of the summer, Lau Po had taught me all he knew, and I had become a better chess player.

A small weekend crowd of Chinese people and tourists would gather as I played and defeated my opponents one by one. My mother would join the crowds during these outdoor exhibition games. She sat proudly on the bench, telling my admirers with proper Chinese humility,[15] "Is luck."

A man who watched me play in the park suggested that my mother allow me to play in local chess tournaments. My mother smiled graciously, an answer that meant nothing. I desperately wanted to go, but I bit back my tongue. I knew she would not let me play among strangers. So as we walked home I said in a small voice that I didn't want to play in the local tournament. They would have American rules. If I lost, I would bring shame on my family.

"Is shame you fall down nobody push you," said my mother.

During my first tournament, my mother sat with me in the front row as I waited for my turn. I frequently bounced my legs to unstick them from the cold metal seat of the folding chair. When my name was called, I leapt up. My mother unwrapped something in her lap. It was her *chang*,[16] a small tablet of red jade which

14. *Chess etiquette* (et′ i kit) refers to the accepted practices or manners involved in playing chess.
15. *Humility* is the quality of being humble or modest.
16. A *chang* is a good-luck charm.

Big Idea Rewards and Sacrifices *Why do you think chess etiquette requires self-control?* **BI3**

Literary Element Protagonist and Antagonist *To get her mother to agree to let her play in the tournament, what strategy does Meimei use?* **L2**

Teach

R2 Reading Strategy

Making Inferences About Characters **Answer:** *They do not like losing to their little sister.* **OL**

BI3 Big Idea

Rewards and Sacrifices
Answer: *The game of chess requires concentration. A lack of self-control would interfere with a player's ability to focus.* **OL**

L2 Literary Element

Protagonist and Antagonist
Answer: *She pretends to lack ambition, when she knows that her mother has high goals and strong ambitions. This shows the narrator is using clever strategies to get what she wants from her mother.* **OL**

Cultural History

U.S. Citizenship For an immigrant, becoming a U.S. citizen takes years. A person must first be a permanent resident for at least five years. Then, an applicant for citizenship must display knowledge of U.S. history and government, "the American rules" Meimei's mother mentions. **AS**

English Language Coach

Sharing Sayings Meimei's mother translates phrases from Chinese to English. Invite English learners to share favorite sayings from their home language, translate the sayings into English, and explain what they mean. Invite the class to share favorite sayings and their meanings. **EL**

Differentiated Instruction

Listening to Audiotape Allow less proficient readers to listen to a recorded version of the story with a partner. Partners should list things they do not understand. Then they should reread the text. Invite students to review parts of the recording as needed to enhance their comprehension. **BL**

Academic Standards

Additional Support activities on pp. 114 and 115 cover the following standards:

Skills Practice: **9.3.11** Evaluate the aesthetic qualities of style, including the impact of diction…on…theme.

English Language Coach: **9.1.1** Identify and use the…meanings of words and understand the origins of words.

Differentiated Instruction: **9.7** [Respond] to oral communication…[with] careful listening and evaluation of content…

Teach

L Literary Element

Protagonist and Antagonist
Answer: *Meimei and her mother are in conflict over the best strategies for chess games. Some students may suggest that the mother is applying life lessons to the game.* OL

R Reading Strategy

Making Inferences About Characters **Answer:** *The mother values her daughter's success greatly. She will release Meimei from family obligations to focus on chess.* OL

★ Writer's Technique

Personification This is a figure of speech in which an animal, object, force of nature, or idea is given human qualities or characteristics. Amy Tan uses this technique in the first and second complete paragraphs on this page.
Ask: What is the author personifying? *(The wind)* What is the wind doing? *(It is giving Meimei advice about how to win the chess match.)* AS

held the sun's fire. "Is luck," she whispered, and tucked it into my dress pocket. I turned to my opponent, a fifteen-year-old boy from Oakland. He looked at me, wrinkling his nose.

As I began to play, the boy disappeared, the color ran out of the room, and I saw only my white pieces and his black ones waiting on the other side. A light wind began blowing past my ears. It whispered secrets only I could hear.

"Blow from the South," it murmured. "The wind leaves no trail." I saw a clear path, the traps to avoid. The crowd rustled. "Shhh! Shhh!" said the corners of the room. The wind blew stronger. "Throw sand from the East to distract him." The knight came forward ready for the sacrifice. The wind hissed, louder and louder. "Blow, blow, blow. He cannot see. He ★ is blind now. Make him lean away from the wind so he is easier to knock down."

"Check," I said, as the wind roared with laughter. The wind died down to little puffs, my own breath.

My mother placed my first trophy next to a new plastic chess set that the neighborhood Tao[17] society had given to me. As she wiped each piece with a soft cloth, she said, "Next time win more, lose less."

"Ma, it's not how many pieces you lose," I said. "Sometimes you need to lose pieces to get ahead."

"Better to lose less, see if you really need."

At the next tournament, I won again, but it was my mother who wore the triumphant grin.

"Lost eight piece this time. Last time was eleven. What I tell you? Better off lose less!" I was annoyed, but I couldn't say anything.

I attended more tournaments, each one farther away from home. I won all games, in all divisions. The Chinese bakery downstairs from our flat displayed my growing collection of trophies in its window, amidst the dust-covered cakes that were never picked up. The day after I won an important regional tournament, the window encased a fresh sheet cake with whipped-cream frosting and red script saying, "Congratulations, Waverly Jong, Chinatown Chess Champion." Soon after that, a flower shop, headstone engraver, and funeral parlor offered to sponsor me in national tournaments. That's when my mother decided I no longer had to do the dishes. Winston and Vincent had to do my chores.

"Why does she get to play and we do all the work," complained Vincent.

"Is new American rules," said my mother. "Meimei play, squeeze all her brains out for win chess. You play, worth squeeze towel."

By my ninth birthday, I was a national chess champion. I was still some 429 points away from grand-master status, but I was touted as the Great American Hope, a child prodigy[18] and a girl to boot. They ran a photo of me in *Life* magazine next to a quote in which Bobby Fischer said, "There will never be a woman grand master." "Your move, Bobby," said the caption.

Visual Vocabulary
Considered to be one of the greatest players in the history of chess, American *Bobby Fischer* (1943–) became the youngest International Grandmaster at the age of fifteen.

The day they took the magazine picture I wore neatly plaited braids clipped with plastic barrettes trimmed with rhinestones. I was playing in a large high school auditorium that echoed with phlegmy coughs and the squeaky rubber

17. *Tao* is short for *Taoism* (dou′ iz′ əm), one of the main religions of China. It is based on a belief in harmony with nature and one's fellow human beings.

18. A *prodigy* (prod′ ə jē) is an extraordinarily gifted or talented person, especially a child.

Literary Element Protagonist and Antagonist *What conflict has arisen between Meimei and her mother?* L

Reading Strategy Making Inferences About Characters *What does this decision indicate about the mother and her values?* R

Additional Support

Skills Practice

GRAMMAR: Using Semicolons
Write: I turned the knob; the door was locked. **Rewrite:** I turned the knob, but the door was locked. Two related main clauses can be joined by a semicolon or by a coordinating conjunction such as *and, but, or, nor, yet,* and *for.* Have students change the following examples into sentences using a semicolon.

1. I rode my bike home, and my brother took the bus. *(home;)*
2. Efrain likes juice. Marita likes tea. *(juice;)*
3. We could search the Internet, or we could look in an encyclopedia. *(Internet;)* OL

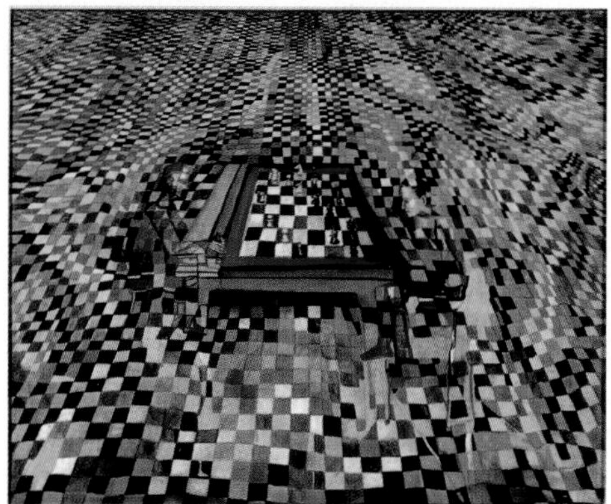

The Game of Chess, 1943. Maria Helena Vieira da Silva. Oil on canvas, 81 × 100 cm. Musée National d'Art Moderne, Centre Georges Pompidou, Paris.

Viewing the Art: In what ways does this painting capture Meimei's experiences while playing in chess tournaments? 

knobs of chair legs sliding across freshly waxed wooden floors. Seated across from me was an American man, about the same age as Lau Po, maybe fifty. I remember that his sweaty brow seemed to weep at my every move. He wore a dark, **malodorous** suit. One of his pockets was stuffed with a great white kerchief on which he wiped his palm before sweeping his hand over the chosen chess piece with great flourish.

In my crisp pink-and-white dress with scratchy lace at the neck, one of two my mother had sewn for these special occasions, I would clasp my hands under my chin, the delicate points of my elbows poised lightly on the table in the manner my mother had shown me for posing for the press. I would swing my patent leather shoes back and forth like an impatient child riding on a school bus. Then I would pause, suck in my lips, twirl my chosen piece in midair as if undecided, and then firmly plant it in its new threatening place, with a triumphant smile thrown back at my opponent for good measure.

I no longer played in the alley of Waverly Place. I never visited the playground where the pigeons and old men gathered. I went to school, then directly home to learn new chess secrets, cleverly concealed advantages, more escape routes.

But I found it difficult to concentrate at home. My mother had a habit of standing over me while I plotted out my games. I think she thought of herself as my protective ally. Her lips would be sealed tight, and after each move I made, a soft "Hmmmmph" would escape from her nose.

"Ma, I can't practice when you stand there like that," I said one day. She retreated to the kitchen and made loud noises with the pots and pans. When the crashing stopped, I could see out of the corner of my eye that she was standing in the doorway. "Hmmmph!" Only this one came out of her tight throat.

My parents made many concessions to allow me to practice. One time I complained that the bedroom I shared was so noisy that I couldn't think. Thereafter, my brothers slept in a bed in the living room facing the street. I said I couldn't finish my rice; my head didn't work right when my stomach was too full. I left the table with half-finished bowls and nobody complained. But there was one duty I couldn't avoid. I had to accompany my mother on Saturday market days when I had no tournament to play. My mother would proudly walk with me, visiting many shops, buying very little. "This my daughter Wavely Jong," she said to whoever looked her way.

One day, after we left a shop I said under my breath, "I wish you wouldn't do that, telling everybody I'm your daughter." My mother stopped walking. Crowds of people with heavy bags pushed past us on the sidewalk, bumping into first one shoulder, then another.

"Aiii-ya. So shame be with mother?" She grasped my hand even tighter as she glared at me.

I looked down. "It's not that, it's just so obvious. It's just so embarrassing."

Vocabulary

malodorous (mal ō′ dər əs) *adj.* bad-smelling; stinky

Big Idea Rewards and Sacrifices *What sacrifices does Meimei make to pursue chess? What rewards does she gain?* **BI**

Teach

BI Big Idea

Rewards and Sacrifices

Answer: *She has given up exploring her neighborhood and her normal child's play. She has gained attention from her family as well as local and national fame.* **OL**

Viewing the Art

Answer: *This painting reflects how Meimei becomes engrossed when she plays; all she can see are the white and black pieces on the chessboard. In the image, the world is filled by the geometric pattern of the chessboard.*

The work of Portugese-born artist Maria Helena Vieira da Silva (1908–1992) is often marked by a strong interest in perspective and its manipulation. *The Game of Chess* forcefully demonstrates this emphasis. **AS**

Differentiated Instruction

Dramatize Have students dramatize the scene in which Meimei and her mother argue to help them connect with the characters' emotions. Remind actors to use gestures and tone of voice to convey feeling and meaning. Discourage students from speaking with an accent. **AL**

Reading in the Real World

Citizenship With the help of a librarian or the *Reader's Guide to Periodical Literature,* students should look for information about real-life child prodigies who excel in academics, sports, art, music, or humanitarian efforts. Have students present their findings as part of a class discussion. **OL**

Academic Standards

Additional Support activities on pp. 116 and 117 cover the following standards:

Skills Practice: **9.6.1** Identify and correctly use [main] clauses…[and] semicolons…

Differentiated Instruction: **9.7.6** Analyze the occasion and…choose effective verbal and nonverbal techniques (including voice, gestures…) for presentations.

Reading in the Real World: **9.7.15** Deliver expository (informational) presentations that convey information and ideas from… sources accurately and coherently…

Teach

L1 Literary Element

Protagonist and Antagonist
Answer: *She is embarrassed by her mother's bragging; her mother thinks the narrator is embarrassed to be seen with her.* OL

R Reading Strategy

Making Inferences About Characters **Answer:** *Meimei might have been worried about what would happen because she blurted out her feelings to her mother, so she impulsively fled the situation.* OL

L2 Literary Element

Protagonist and Antagonist
Answer: *Meimei had to come home and her mother is treating her with anger and coldness.* OL

Use the CheckPoint questions on Presentation Plus! to check students' mastery of the selection. These questions can be used with interactive response keypads for immediate student feedback.

"Embarrass you be my daughter?" Her voice was cracking with anger.

"That's not what I meant. That's not what I said."

"What you say?"

I knew it was a mistake to say anything more, but I heard my voice speaking. "Why do you have to use me to show off? If you want to show off, then why don't you learn to play chess."

My mother's eyes turned into dangerous black slits. She had no words for me, just sharp silence.

I felt the wind rushing around my hot ears. I jerked my hand out of my mother's tight grasp and spun around, knocking into an old woman. Her bag of groceries spilled to the ground.

"Aii-ya! Stupid girl!" my mother and the woman cried. Oranges and tin cans careened down the sidewalk. As my mother stooped to help the old woman pick up the escaping food, I took off.

I raced down the street, dashing between people, not looking back as my mother screamed shrilly, "Meimei! Meimei!" I fled down an alley, past dark curtained shops and merchants washing the grime off their windows. I sped into the sunlight, into a large street crowded with tourists examining trinkets and souvenirs. I ducked into another dark alley, down another street, up another alley. I ran until it hurt and I realized I had nowhere to go, that I was not running from anything. The alleys contained no escape routes.

My breath came out like angry smoke. It was cold. I sat down on an upturned plastic pail next to a stack of empty boxes, cupping my chin with my hands, thinking hard. I imagined my mother, first walking briskly down one street or another looking for me, then giving up and returning home to await my arrival. After two hours, I stood up on creaking legs and slowly walked home.

The alley was quiet and I could see the yellow lights shining from our flat like two tiger's eyes in the night. I climbed the sixteen steps to the door, advancing quietly up each so as not to make any warning sounds. I turned the knob; the door was locked. I heard a chair moving, quick steps, the locks turning—click! click! click!—and then the door opened.

"About time you got home," said Vincent. "Boy, are you in trouble."

He slid back to the dinner table. On a platter were the remains of a large fish, its fleshy head still connected to bones swimming upstream in vain escape. Standing there waiting for my punishment, I heard my mother speak in a dry voice.

"We not concerning this girl. This girl not have concerning for us."

Nobody looked at me. Bone chopsticks clinked against the insides of bowls being emptied into hungry mouths.

I walked into my room, closed the door, and lay down on my bed. The room was dark, the ceiling filled with shadows from the dinnertime lights of neighboring flats.

In my head, I saw a chessboard with sixty-four black and white squares. Opposite me was my opponent, two angry black slits. She wore a triumphant smile. "Strongest wind cannot be seen," she said.

Her black men advanced across the plane, slowly marching to each successive level as a single unit. My white pieces screamed as they scurried and fell off the board one by one. As her men drew closer to my edge, I felt myself growing light. I rose up into the air and flew out the window. Higher and higher, above the alley, over the tops of tiled roofs, where I was gathered up by the wind and pushed up toward the night sky until everything below me disappeared and I was alone.

I closed my eyes and pondered my next move. ∾

Literary Element Protagonist and Antagonist *Why is Meimei embarrassed? Why does her mother think she is embarrassed?* L1

Reading Strategy Making Inferences About Characters *Why do you think Meimei runs away?* R

Literary Element Protagonist and Antagonist *Why do you think Meimei considers her mother the victor of their battle?* L2

Additional Support

Academic Standards

The Additional Support activity on p. 118 covers the following standard:

Skills Practice: **9.5.8** Write for different purposes and audiences…

Skills Practice

TEST PREPARATION: Short Response Explain that short-response questions often do not have one correct answer. Instead, an answer is generally judged by its insightfulness and the quality of textual evidence included. **Ask:** Which character did you most identify with? Have students write their answers using 3 to 5 lines. *(Possible answer: I identified with Meimei because she is a young girl who is trying to find her own identity as a person and wants to try new and different things. Her mother seems to want Meimei to conform to a lifestyle that she believes will suit Meimei best, with no input from her daughter.)* OL

AFTER YOU READ

RESPONDING AND THINKING CRITICALLY

Respond

1. With whom do you sympathize most at the end of the story, Meimei or her mother? Explain why.

Recall and Interpret

2. (a)What useful life lesson did Meimei's mother teach her when she was six years old? How did she learn it? (b)Explain how Meimei applies her mother's strategy to "winning arguments, respect for others, and . . . chess games."
3. (a)When does Meimei first become interested in chess? How does she learn to play the game? (b)In your opinion, why does Meimei enjoy chess so much? Support your answer with evidence from the story.
4. (a)How does Meimei trick her mother into letting her play in her first chess tournament? (b)How does this scene reveal that Meimei can "see the endgame before the game begins"?
5. (a)What conflict arises when the mother and daughter go shopping? (b)What are Meimei and her mother really arguing about when they are shopping? Explain.

Analyze and Evaluate

6. How does the mother feel about her daughter's success? How can you tell?
7. Do you think the mother is justified in being angry? Is Meimei? Support your opinion with examples from your own experience or with details from the story.
8. How is Meimei's relationship with her mother like a game of chess?

Connect

9. At the end of the story, Meimei considers her "next move." What move would you make if you were Meimei?
10. **Big Idea** **Rewards and Sacrifices** What sacrifices do the main characters in this story make to pursue rewards?

LITERARY ANALYSIS

Literary Element Protagonist and Antagonist

The **protagonist** and **antagonist** are important elements in this story. The action revolves around Meimei, the protagonist, who undergoes the main conflict. Readers are usually meant to identify with the protagonist and not with the antagonist.

1. Mrs. Jong is very supportive of Meimei's decision to play chess. What is the source of their conflict?
2. In what ways are Meimei and her mother victims of a "generation gap"?
3. Suppose the story had been told from the mother's point of view. Would Meimei still be the protagonist? Explain.

Review: Characters

As you learned on pages 106–107, **characters** are the people in the story. Meimei and her mother are the main characters in the story. Minor characters interact with the protagonist and antagonist to move the plot along.

Partner Activity Meet with a classmate to identify minor characters in this story. Discuss the roles they play in the plot. Make a chart like the one below to help you think about these characters.

Character	Role
Lau Po	teaches Meimei chess etiquette

Literary Element

1. Her mother brags about Meimei.
2. Meimei is comfortable with American customs, and her mother is suspicious of them.
3. Meimei would probably be the antagonist. Mrs. Jong would be the protagonist because readers would see the story through her eyes.

Review: Characters

Minor characters include the two brothers, Vincent and Winston, the father, and Lau Po, the man in the park. Have students devise questions about how they affect Meimei's motivation, ways of thinking, or character development.

AFTER YOU READ

Assess

1. Some may like Meimei's determination to be independent of her mother. Others may say the mother is doing her best.
2. (a) Her mother taught her the art of invisible strength. She bit her tongue and got results. (b) She withholds knowledge.
3. (a) Her brother receives a set for Christmas. She reads, studies strategies, plays her brothers, and then challenges a man in the park. (b) It is a game of secrets.
4. (a) She acts uninterested in playing. (b) She says the right thing to get what she wants.
5. (a) Meimei tells her mother to stop showing off. Her mother thinks Meimei is embarrassed by her. (b) Students may say the issue is "Whose success is this?"
6. The mother is very proud. She brags to everyone.
7. Some may say the mother isn't justified; she is controlling. Others may say Meimei is not justified; she is ungrateful.
8. They have an adversarial relationship. Both try to anticipate each other's next move.
9. Students might say Meimei should explain her feelings.
10. The parents sacrifice their traditional family values. Meimei and her mother sacrifice the good will between them.

AFTER YOU READ

Assess

Reading Strategy

1. At the beginning, she is six years old; when her brother receives the chess game, she is seven years old; she was a national champion by her ninth birthday; she was probably some months or even a year or two older at the story's end. All but the last age are given in the story.
2. Meimei learns how to apply the lesson of invisible strength she learns from her mother early in the story to personal interactions and her chess games. (Details: the salted plums incident, her new chess etiquette, not throwing chess pieces in the sandbox, her tactic for getting permission to play in tournaments, and how she wins her first tournament.) Meimei changes from being playful and childlike to becoming extremely focused on chess. (Detail: She comes straight home after school to study chess instead of playing and exploring.) She grows more arrogant. (Details: She complains about the noise in her bedroom, she does not follow family rules, and she rebels because her mother brags about her.)

Vocabulary

1. d **2.** b **3.** e **4.** a **5.** c

Academic Vocabulary

1. She plays against an older boy, uses the lesson of invisible strength, and wins easily.
2. Meimei has been successful in winning chess tournaments; her mother is proud of her and wants to help her continue winning.

READING AND VOCABULARY

Reading Strategy Making Inferences About Characters

As you read a work of literature, you can **make inferences** about a character's physical appearance, relationships with other characters, values, and motivations. Review the story and the web diagram you made about Meimei. Look for clues related to character development, or the ways a character changes.

1. How old is Meimei when each major event in the story occurs?
2. How does Meimei grow or change during the story? Describe the details that led you to make this inference.

Vocabulary Practice

Practice with Word Parts Use what you know about prefixes, root words, and suffixes to match each word on the left to a definition on the right. Use a dictionary if you need help.

1. impart	**a.** prefix means "well" or "good"
2. relent	**b.** root means "to bend"
3. adversary	**c.** prefix means "bad"
4. benevolently	**d.** prefix means "toward" or "into"
5. malodorous	**e.** root means "acting against"

Academic Vocabulary

Here are two words from the vocabulary list on page R80. These words will help you think, write, and talk about the selection.

participate (pär tis ə pāt′) *v.* to take part in something

primary (prī′ mər′ ē) *adj.* of first rank

Practice and Apply

1. What happens when Meimei **participates** in her first chess tournament?
2. In the middle of the story, why does Meimei's mother make Meimei's needs **primary**?

WRITING AND EXTENDING

Writing About Literature

Analyze Setting Amy Tan's "Rules of the Game" is rich with local color, or specific details that re-create the language, culture, and customs of a particular area. For example, notice how this sentence sets a scene:

"The play area was bordered by wood-slat benches where old-country people sat cracking roasted watermelon seeds with their golden teeth and scattering the husks to an impatient gathering of gurgling pigeons."

Review the story for passages in which the streets and alleyways of San Francisco's Chinatown come alive for you. Write a brief essay analyzing the effectiveness of the story's local color. As you draft your essay, be sure to:

- include at least three different examples of local color
- explain how these examples contribute to the mood of the story or aid your understanding of the characters and their conflicts
- discuss how these examples add to your enjoyment of the story

After you complete your draft, meet with a peer reviewer to evaluate each other's work and to suggest revisions. Pay close attention to the examples of local color and your explanations of how they enrich the story. After you have made your editorial revisions, proofread your essay for errors in grammar, spelling, and punctuation.

Internet Connection

Use the Internet to learn more about chess. See what you can uncover about the history of the game. How, for example, does today's game differ from the one played hundreds of years ago? What cultures are known to have played chess? You may also want to search for information about the rules of play and various strategies for the opening, the middle game, and the endgame.

LiteratureOnline **Web Activities** For eFlashcards, Selection Quick Checks, and other Web activities, go to www.glencoe.com.

Writing About Literature

Students' analyses should pick out three specific examples of local color. These might include the description of Waverly Place, the description of the different foods and meals, or the mother's way of speaking, among others. Analyses should address both how the details add to the mood or plot and how they increase enjoyment of the story.

Web Activities Have students access the Web site for interactive activities that will help them assess their understanding of the selection.

The Gift of the Magi

MEET O. HENRY

In the fall of 1903, O. Henry was living in a room at the small, rundown Hotel Marty in New York City. He had published a few stories in local magazines, but was still relatively unknown when editors at the *New York World* newspaper sent a young reporter to track down this mysterious writer. By the next day, O. Henry had an agreement with the newspaper to write one story a week for the magazine section of their Sunday edition. The *World* had the largest daily circulation in the world, and O. Henry's stories about New York life became immensely popular. By the time he left the newspaper after less than three years, O. Henry had established his reputation as a gifted storyteller and master of surprise endings.

"Life is made up of sobs, sniffles, and smiles, with sniffles predominating."

—O. Henry, from "The Gift of the Magi"

A Life of Twists O. Henry was the pen name used by William Sydney Porter, who was born in Greensboro, North Carolina. At the age of twenty, he moved to Austin, Texas, where he held a variety of jobs, eventually becoming a bank teller. He married and became a reporter and columnist for the *Houston Post*. After a few years, his wife was diagnosed with tuberculosis, and he was accused of embezzling from the bank where he worked. Some people have claimed that he was stealing money to help pay his wife's medical bills. O. Henry fled to Central America, but his wife was too ill to accompany him. Months later, when her condition worsened, he returned and turned himself in to the police. His wife soon died, and O. Henry spent three years in prison in Ohio. It was during his time in prison that he began writing the stories that would make him famous. W. S. Porter emerged from prison as O. Henry.

Success in the Big City In 1902 O. Henry moved to New York City and started trying to sell his stories. In a few years his luck changed for the better, and his position with the *New York World* helped make him a celebrated author. He published more than three hundred stories and gained worldwide acclaim. O. Henry's writing is admired for its colorful and realistic depictions of the everyday lives of New Yorkers. His stories are known for their plot twists and surprise endings. In fact, O. Henry's own life ended with a "twist"—his funeral was somehow scheduled in the same church at the same time as someone else's wedding! The O. Henry Award honors the authors of the best stories printed each year in American magazines.

O. Henry was born in 1862 and died in 1910.

LiteratureOnline **Author Search** For more about O. Henry, go to www.glencoe.com.

BEFORE YOU READ

Focus

BELLRINGER

Bellringer Options
Selection Focus Transparency 9
Daily Language Practice Transparency 12

Or **say:** Describe a time when you made a sacrifice in order to solve a problem. *(Student answers will vary, but they should draw from experiences in their own life.)*
Ask: What personal items would you have a hard time giving up? *(Student answers will vary, but they should explain why they would have a hard time giving it up.)*
Have students consider as they read how the characters in the story are willing to sacrifice for each other.

Author Search To expand students' appreciation of O. Henry, have them access the Web site for additional information and resources.

Selection Skills

The Gift of the Magi

Literary Elements
- Symbol (SE pp. 122, 124, 125, 130)
- Plot (SE p. 130)
- Point of View (TWE p. 126)

Reading Skills
- Identifying Problem and Solution (SE pp. 122, 123, 125, 126, 128, 130)

Vocabulary Skills
- Synonyms (SE p. 130)

Listening/Speaking/Viewing Skills
- Analyzing Art (SE pp. 124, 127; TWE p. 123)

Writing Skills/Grammar
- Respond to Characters (SE p. 131)
- Using Similes and Metaphors (TWE p. 126)

Study Skills/Research/Assessment
- Footnotes (TWE p. 123)

BEFORE YOU READ

Focus

Summary

On Christmas Eve, Della Young has very little cash and no gift for her husband Jim. She decides to sell her hair, the only valuable thing she has, to buy Jim a chain for his watch. Meanwhile, Jim sells his watch to buy Della hair combs she had been admiring. Jim and Della soon discover that each has sold his or her prized possession to give the other a gift that would enhance the now gone possessions.

V Vocabulary

Vocabulary File **Say:** Add these words and definitions to your vocabulary file. For each word, include a sentence that gives you an example of how to use the word. **OL** Students with English language needs should include the pronunciations of these words in their files. **EL**

Literary Elements Have students access the Web site to improve their understanding of symbol.

LITERATURE PREVIEW

Connecting to the Story

In "The Gift of the Magi," the main character comes up with a creative solution to her dilemma. Her solution, however, involves a sacrifice. Before you read the story, think about the following questions:

- What kinds of sacrifices have you made in order to solve a problem?
- What personal items would you have a hard time giving up and why?

Building Background

This story takes place in New York City around 1900. Most of the action occurs in the main characters' dingy, inexpensive flat, or apartment. The story begins on the afternoon of Christmas Eve and ends shortly after 7:00 PM the same day.

According to the gospel of Matthew in the New Testament of the Bible, the Magi (mā′ jī) were the three wise men who came from the East to visit the newborn baby Jesus. The Magi brought precious gifts of gold, frankincense, and myrrh for the child. Over time, the Magi have come to be associated with the practice of giving gifts.

Setting Purposes for Reading

Big Idea Rewards and Sacrifices

As you read, notice how the rewards for the characters' sacrifices are not what they expect.

Literary Element Symbol

A **symbol** is any object, person, place, or experience that represents something else, usually something abstract. For example, a wedding ring symbolizes marriage. As you read this story, examine how O. Henry develops symbolic meaning in everyday objects.

- See Literary Terms Handbook, p. R17.

Interactive Literary Elements Handbook To review or learn more about the literary elements, go to www.glencoe.com.

READING PREVIEW

Reading Strategy Identifying Problem and Solution

Why do people behave the way they do? Very often the decisions people make—in literature or in life—are the results of problems that they encounter. A **problem** is often the reason for a conflict. Whether insignificant or life-threatening, each of these problems requires a **solution** that will propel the action of the story. The solution is a character's response or answer to a problem. Identifying the main problem and its solution can help you understand a story's structure. As you read "The Gift of the Magi," consider the problems that both Della and Jim must solve.

Reading Tip: Tracking the Problem Use a flow chart like the one below to track the story's main problem.

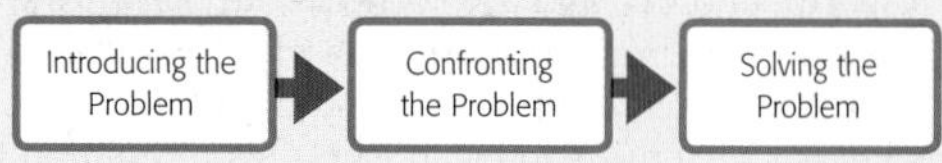

Vocabulary

imputation (im′ pyə tā′ shən) *n.* an accusation; p. 123 *He hadn't done anything wrong, so he didn't like the imputation.*

parsimony (pär′ sə mō′ nē) *n.* stinginess; p. 123 *Despite his great wealth, the man was known for his parsimony.*

depreciate (di prē′ shē āt′) *v.* to lessen the price or value of; p. 125 *The floodwater that soaked Anton's storage boxes depreciated his baseball card collection.*

prudence (prōōd′ əns) *n.* caution; good judgment; p. 126 *It was a dangerous place, and therefore her prudence was wise.*

INDIANA ACADEMIC STANDARDS (pages 122–131)

9.3.7 Recognize and understand the significance of various literary devices, including...symbolism...

9.2 Develop [reading] strategies...

9.5.2 Write responses to literature that...support statements with evidence from the text.

Selection Resources

Print Materials
- Unit 1 Resources (Fast File), pp. 45–47
- Leveled Vocabulary Development, p. 9
- Selection and Unit Assessments, pp. 19–20
- Selection Quick Checks, p. 10

Transparencies
- Bellringer Options Transparencies: Selection Focus Transparency 9 Daily Language Practice Transparency 12
- Literary Elements Transparency 20

Technology
- TeacherWorks Plus™ CD-ROM
- StudentWorks Plus™ CD-ROM
- Presentation Plus!™ CD-ROM
- Literature Online, glencoe.com
- Online Student Edition, mhln.com
- Exam*View*® Assessment Suite CD-ROM
- Vocabulary PuzzleMaker CD-ROM
- Listening Library, disc 1 track 10

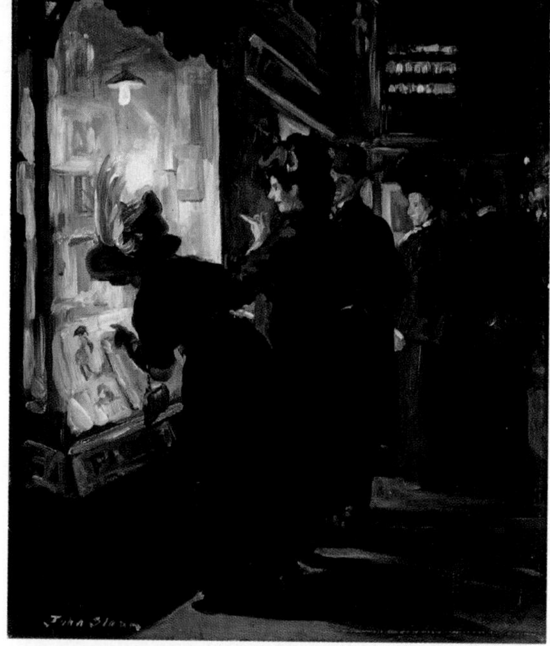

Picture Shop Window, 1907. John Sloan. Oil on canvas, 32 × 25⅛ in. Collection of The Newark Museum, Gift of Mrs. Felix Fuld, 1925. The Newark Museum, Newark, New Jersey.

The Gift of the Magi

O. Henry

One dollar and eighty-seven cents. That was all. And sixty cents of it was in pennies. Pennies saved one and two at a time by bulldozing the grocer and the vegetable man and the butcher until one's cheeks burned with the silent **imputation** of **parsimony** that such close dealing implied. Three times Della counted it. One dollar and eighty-seven cents. And the next day would be Christmas.

There was clearly nothing to do but flop down on the shabby little couch and howl. So Della did it. Which instigates[1] the moral reflection that life is made up of sobs, sniffles, and smiles, with sniffles predominating.

While the mistress of the home is gradually subsiding from the first stage to the second, take a look at the home. A furnished flat at $8 per week. It did not exactly beggar description, but it certainly had that word on the lookout for the mendicancy squad.[2]

In the vestibule below was a letter-box into which no letter would go, and an electric button from which no mortal finger could coax a ring. Also appertaining[3] thereunto was a card bearing the name "Mr. James Dillingham Young."

The "Dillingham" had been flung to the breeze during a former period of prosperity when its possessor was being paid $30 per

1. To *instigate* is to stir up or cause something to happen.

2. O. Henry is making a play on words here. To *beggar* is to defy or go past the limits of something. A *mendicancy squad* consists of the authorities who deal with mendicants, or beggars.

3. Here, *appertaining* means "belonging" or "relating."

Reading Strategy Identifying Problem and Solution
What problem does O. Henry present in this opening paragraph? R

Vocabulary

imputation (im′ pyə tā′ shən) *n.* an accusation

parsimony (pär′ sə mō′ nē) *n.* stinginess

Teach

Big Idea

Rewards and Sacrifices Have students keep these questions in mind as they read.
Ask: What problem is faced by both characters? *(Neither has money to buy a gift for the other.)* How do they solve their problem? *(They each give up something they care about.)* OL

R Reading Strategy

Identifying Problem and Solution **Answer:** *He establishes that Della is poor and does not have enough money to buy a Christmas present.* OL

★ Writer's Technique

Setting Writers often describe the time and place in which a story takes place to create an atmosphere or mood.
Ask: Why might O. Henry describe the apartment house vestibule? *(To show that the couple cannot afford to live in a nicer apartment.)* AS

Readability Scores
Dale-Chall: 8.0
DRP: 55
Lexile: 910

English Language Coach

Courtesy Titles Explain that *Mr.* is a courtesy title used before a man's name. *Mrs.* is a title for a married woman. *Miss* indicates an unmarried woman. *Ms.* may be used by any woman because it does not indicate marital status. Invite English learners to identify courtesy titles used in their home languages. EL

Differentiated Instruction

Footnotes Numbered footnotes in the selection correlate with footnotes at the bottom of the pages. These give information, such as definitions and pronunciation guides for difficult terms. Have one student read the story aloud, stopping at each footnote. Have a partner read the matching footnote aloud. BL

Academic Standards

Additional Support activities on p. 123 cover the following standards:

English Language Coach: **9.1.2** Distinguish between what words mean literally and what they imply and interpret what the words imply.

Differentiated Instruction: **9.2.1** Analyze the structure and format of…documents…and explain…purposes.

Teach

L1 Literary Element

Symbol **Answer:** *They symbolize Della's sadness and the gloomy mood.* OL

★ Viewing the Art

Answer: *Della and the woman in the picture both take pride in their long hair.*

Although he was a French impressionist, Edgar Degas (1834–1927) concentrated less on color and light and more on composition and form than many other impressionists. Among his best-known works are paintings that show people participating in everyday activities. AS

Woman at Her Toilet. Edgar Degas. Oil pastel on paper. The Hermitage, St. Petersburg, Russia.

Viewing the Art: What do you think Della and this woman each think about having long hair? ★

week. Now, when the income was shrunk to $20, the letters of "Dillingham" looked blurred, as though they were thinking seriously of contracting to a modest and unassuming[4] D. But whenever Mr. James Dillingham Young came home and reached his flat above he was called "Jim" and greatly hugged by Mrs. James Dillingham Young, already introduced to you as Della. Which is all very good.

Della finished her cry and attended to her cheeks with the powder rag. She stood by the window and looked out dully at a gray cat walking a gray fence in a gray backyard. Tomorrow would be Christmas Day, and she had only $1.87 with which to buy Jim a present. She had been saving every penny she could for months, with this result. Twenty dollars a week doesn't go far. Expenses had been greater than she had calculated. They always are. Only $1.87 to buy a present for Jim. Her Jim. Many a happy hour she had spent planning for something nice for him. Something fine and rare and sterling—

Literary Element Symbol *What do the things Della sees out the window symbolize?* L1

4. *Unassuming* means "not bold or boastful."

Additional Support

Leveled Reading An adapted version of this selection is available on page 34 of *Jamestown Literature: An Adapted Reader*, grade 9.

Skills Practice

READING: Cause and Effect
Characters' emotions are often important to the plot. In the "Gift of the Magi," Della's emotions change frequently. Students can gain insight into the story and the character of Della by identifying her emotions and their causes.

Have students complete a two-column chart, labeling one column *Emotion (Effect)* and the other *Triggering Event (Cause).* Encourage students to use specific terms, such as *frustration* and *rapture,* rather than general terms such as *sadness* and *happiness.* OL something just a little bit near to being worthy of the honor of being owned by Jim.

There was a pier-glass[5] between the windows of the room. Perhaps you have seen a pier-glass in an $8 flat. A very thin and very agile person may, by observing his reflection in a rapid sequence of longitudinal strips, obtain a fairly accurate conception of his looks. Della, being slender, had mastered the art.

Suddenly she whirled from the window and stood before the glass. Her eyes were shining brilliantly, but her face had lost its color within twenty seconds. Rapidly she pulled down her hair and let it fall to its full length.

Now, there were two possessions of the James Dillingham Youngs in which they both took a mighty pride. One was Jim's gold watch that had been his father's and his grandfather's. The other was Della's hair. Had the Queen of Sheba lived in the flat across the airshaft, Della would have let her hair hang out the window some day to dry just to **depreciate** Her Majesty's jewels and gifts. Had King Solomon[6] been the janitor, with all his treasures piled up in the basement, Jim would have pulled out his watch every time he passed, just to see him pluck at his beard from envy.

So now Della's beautiful hair fell about her, rippling and shining like a cascade of brown waters. It reached below her knee and made itself almost a garment for her. And then she did it up again nervously and quickly. Once she faltered for a minute and stood still while a tear or two splashed on the worn red carpet.

On went her old brown jacket; on went her old brown hat. With a whirl of skirts and with the brilliant sparkle still in her eyes, she fluttered out the door and down the stairs to the street.

Where she stopped the sign read: "Mme. Sofronie.[7] Hair Goods of All Kinds." One flight up Della ran, and collected herself, panting. Madame, large, too white, chilly, hardly looked the "Sofronie."

"Will you buy my hair?" asked Della.

"I buy hair," said Madame. "Take yer hat off and let's have a sight at the looks of it."

Down rippled the brown cascade.

"Twenty dollars," said Madame, lifting the mass with a practiced hand.

"Give it to me quick," said Della.

Oh, and the next two hours tripped by on rosy wings. Forget the hashed[8] metaphor. She was ransacking the stores for Jim's present.

She found it at last. It surely had been made for Jim and no one else. There was no other like it in any of the stores, and she had turned all of them inside out. It was a platinum fob chain simple and chaste[9] in design, properly proclaiming its value by substance alone and not by meretricious[10] ornamentation—as all good things should do. It was even worthy of

Visual Vocabulary
A *fob chain* is attached to a pocket watch and worn hanging from a pocket.

5. A *pier-glass* (pēr′ glas) is a tall, narrow mirror designed to be hung between two windows.
6. The Bible says that the *Queen of Sheba* visited *King Solomon,* bearing gifts that included great quantities of gold, spices, and jewels. Solomon is famous as the wisest and wealthiest man of his time.

Literary Element Symbol *What do the watch and hair represent?* **L2**

Vocabulary

depreciate (di prē′ shē āt′) *v.* to lessen the price or value of

7. *Mme. Sofronie* (mə dam′ sō frō′ nē)
8. O. Henry pokes fun at himself here. His metaphor is *hashed,* or mixed, because it combines parts of the familiar phrases "rose-colored glasses" and "on gossamer wings."
9. Here, *chaste* means "modest".
10. *Meretricious* means "cheap" or "showy".

Reading Strategy Identifying Problem and Solution *What do you think Della is going to do?* **R**

Teach

L2 Literary Element

Symbol Answer: *The watch is a symbol of continuity in Jim's family. Della's hair is a symbol of beauty. Both are a source of pride.* **OL**

R Reading Strategy

Identifying Problem and Solution Answer: *Della is going to do something with her hair, such as cut it off and sell it.* **OL**

CheckPoint

Use the CheckPoint questions on Presentation Plus! to monitor students' comprehension. These questions can be used with interactive response keypads for immediate student feedback.

Reading in the Real World

College Students in college may study literature on which movies have been based. For example, *The Gift of Love* was adapted from "The Gift of the Magi." Screenwriters may update stories for present-day audiences.

Ask students to decide how this story could be updated for a screenplay. Encourage them to consider these questions: *Where else could the story take place? What might be the couple's prized possessions? What gifts will they give each other? How else might they make sacrifices for each other?* Allow students to share their ideas during a class discussion. **OL**

Academic Standards

Additional Support activities on pp. 124 and 125 cover the following standards:

Skills Practice: **9.3** [Identify] story elements such as character…[and] plot…

Reading in the Real World: **9.7.17** Deliver oral responses to literature that advance a judgment demonstrating a comprehensive understanding of the significant ideas of works or passages…

Teach

BI1 Big Idea

Rewards and Sacrifices
Answer: *Della has probably put aside her feelings of loss regarding her hair when she sees the perfect fob chain for Jim's watch.* OL

L Literary Element

Point of View Explain to students that the story is being told in the third-person omniscient point of view. Discuss how the narrator uses the technique of addressing the reader directly. Have students find an example of this technique. *("Which is always a tremendous task, dear friends—a mammoth task.")* OL

BI2 Big Idea

Rewards and Sacrifices
Answer: *Students' answers will vary, but should include an explanation for their opinions.* OL

R1 Reading Strategy

Identifying Problem and Solution **Answer:** *Della is worried that Jim will not find her pretty without her long hair.* OL

The Watch. As soon as she saw it she knew that it must be Jim's. It was like him. Quietness and value—the description applied to both. Twenty-one dollars they took from her for it, and she hurried home with the 87 cents. With that chain on his watch Jim might be properly anxious about the time in any company. Grand as the watch was, he sometimes looked at it on the sly on account of the old leather strap that he used in place of a chain.

When Della reached home her intoxication gave way a little to **prudence** and reason. She got out her curling irons and lighted the gas and went to work repairing the ravages[11] made by generosity added to love. Which is always a tremendous task, dear friends—a mammoth task.

Within forty minutes her head was covered with tiny, close-lying curls that made her look wonderfully like a truant schoolboy. She looked at her reflection in the mirror long, carefully, and critically.

"If Jim doesn't kill me," she said to herself, "before he takes a second look at me, he'll say I look like a Coney Island[12] chorus girl. But what could I do—oh! what could I do with a dollar and eighty-seven cents?"

At 7 o'clock the coffee was made and the frying pan was on the back of the stove hot and ready to cook the chops.

11. *Ravages* means "destructive actions or their results." Here, it refers to the hasty cutting of Della's hair.
12. *Coney Island* is a famous beach and amusement park in Brooklyn, New York.

Big Idea Rewards and Sacrifices *How do you think Della feels about her sacrifice at this point?* BI1

Big Idea Rewards and Sacrifices *Do you agree with the narrator that generosity combined with love can cause damage that is difficult to repair?* BI2

Vocabulary
prudence (prōōd′ əns) *n.* caution; good judgment

Jim was never late. Della doubled the fob chain in her hand and sat on the corner of the table near the door that he always entered. Then she heard his step on the stair away down on the first flight, and she turned white for just a moment. She had a habit of saying little silent prayers about the simplest everyday things, and now she whispered: "Please God, make him think I am still pretty."

The door opened and Jim stepped in and closed it. He looked thin and very serious. Poor fellow, he was only twenty-two—and to be burdened with a family! He needed a new overcoat and he was without gloves.

> "I'm me without my hair, ain't I?"

Jim stopped inside the door, as immovable as a setter at the scent of quail. His eyes were fixed upon Della, and there was an expression in them that she could not read, and it terrified her. It was not anger, nor surprise, nor disapproval, nor horror, nor any of the sentiments that she had been prepared for. He simply stared at her fixedly with that peculiar expression on his face.

Della wriggled off the table and went for him.

"Jim, darling," she cried, "don't look at me that way. I had my hair cut off and sold it because I couldn't have lived through Christmas without giving you a present. It'll grow out again—you won't mind, will you? I just had to do it. My hair grows awfully fast. Say 'Merry Christmas!' Jim, and let's be happy. You don't know what a nice—what a beautiful, nice gift I've got for you."

"You've cut off your hair?" asked Jim, laboriously, as if he had not arrived at that patent[13] fact yet even after the hardest mental labor.

13. Here, Jim tries to grasp the obvious *(patent)* fact that Della has cut her hair.

Reading Strategy Identifying Problem and Solution *Della cut off her hair to buy a gift for Jim. What new problem has been caused by this solution?* R1

Additional Support

Skills Practice

WRITING: Similes and Metaphors
Writers often use similes and metaphors to describe something through comparison. These are figures of speech that compare seemingly unlike things. Similes use *like* or *as*; metaphors do not. Share examples such as the following: "Jim stopped inside the door, as immovable as a setter at the scent of quail."

Have students write a brief description of a person they know, including at least two similes and/or metaphors. OL

Teach

R2 Reading Strategy

Predict **Ask:** What do you think will be in the package? *(Possible answer: Based on the description, the gift will probably be some type of hair ornament–perhaps ribbons, a hair band, barrettes, or combs.)* OL

Cross Streets of New York, 1899. Everett Shinn. Charcoal, watercolor, pastel, white chalk, and Chinese white on paper, 21½ × 29¼ in. Corcoran Gallery of Art, Washington, D.C.

Viewing the Art: Look closely at this piece of art. How does the mood of this painting compare with the mood of "The Gift of the Magi"? ★

★ Viewing the Art

Answer: *The tenement buildings crowded together on a city street, the snow, and the pedestrians reflect the hustle-bustle mood of the day before Christmas and the setting of the story.*

Illustrator and painter Everett Shinn (1876–1953) was a member of the Ashcan School, a group of American artists working in the early twentieth century who realistically portrayed city life. AS

"Cut it off and sold it," said Della. "Don't you like me just as well, anyhow? I'm me without my hair, ain't I?"

Jim looked about the room curiously.

"You say your hair is gone?" he said, with an air almost of idiocy.

"You needn't look for it," said Della. "It's sold, I tell you—sold and gone, too. It's Christmas Eve, boy. Be good to me, for it went for you. Maybe the hairs of my head were numbered," she went on with a sudden serious sweetness, "but nobody could ever count my love for you. Shall I put the chops on, Jim?"

Out of his trance Jim seemed quickly to wake. He enfolded his Della. For ten seconds let us regard with discreet scrutiny some inconsequential object in the other direction.[14] Eight dollars a week or a million a year—what is the difference? A mathematician or a wit would give you the wrong answer. The Magi brought valuable gifts, but that was not among them. This dark assertion will be illuminated later on.[15]

Jim drew a package from his overcoat pocket and threw it upon the table. R2

"Don't make any mistake, Dell," he said, "about me. I don't think there's anything in the way of a haircut or a shave or a shampoo that could make me like my girl any less.

14. *[For ten seconds . . . other direction.]* O. Henry suggests that we give the couple privacy by examining some object on the other side of the room, as if we were physically in the couple's home.

15. *[This dark assertion . . . later on.]* O. Henry promises to explain, later, his statement in the preceding sentence.

English Language Coach

Contractions **Write on the board:** *I am* and *I'm.* Explain to English learners that a contraction is a shortened form of two words that uses apostrophes in the place of omitted letters. Have students write three contractions from pages 126–127 and the words they represent on a sheet of paper. EL

Building Reading Fluency

Expressive Reading Rereading the selection aloud will help students see the couple's love and also develop expressive reading skills. Have small groups of students take turns reading aloud using the appropriate tone of voice to communicate the characters' feelings. BL

Academic Standards

Additional Support activities on pp. 126 and 127 cover the following standards:

Skills Practice: **9.3.7** Recognize and understand the significance of various literary devices, including figurative language... **9.5.1** Write biographical... narratives...that describe with specific details the...characters...

English Language Coach: **9.1** [Use] word parts...and a growing knowledge of English...to determine the meaning of words...

Building Reading Fluency: **9.7** [Develop] speaking skills...in conjunction with... strategies...[for] delivery of oral presentations.

Teach

R Reading Strategy

Identifying Problem and Solution **Answer:** *She realizes that he bought her something she can no longer use because of the sacrifice she made to buy him a gift.* OL

BI Big Idea

Rewards and Sacrifices
Answer: *It suggests that Jim's and Della's gifts to each other were motivated by love. Jim and Della were poor, yet they found a way to give each other profound gifts. In the end, it was not the watch chain or the combs that mattered, but their willingness to make sacrifices for each other.* OL

CheckPoint

Use the CheckPoint questions on Presentation Plus! to check students' mastery of the selection. These questions can be used with interactive response keypads for immediate student feedback.

But if you'll unwrap that package you may see why you had me going a while at first."

White fingers and nimble tore at the string and paper. And then an ecstatic scream of joy; and then, alas! a quick feminine change to hysterical tears and wails, necessitating the immediate employment of all the comforting powers of the lord of the flat.

Visual Vocabulary
This *comb* is designed both to fasten and adorn a woman's hair. Ordinary combs are used only to smooth and arrange it.

For there lay The Combs—the set of combs, side and back, that Della had worshipped for long in a Broadway window. Beautiful combs, pure tortoise shell, with jewelled rims—just the shade to wear in the beautiful vanished hair. They were expensive combs, she knew, and her heart had simply craved and yearned over them without the least hope of possession. And now, they were hers, but the tresses that should have adorned the coveted[16] adornments were gone.

"Isn't it a dandy, Jim?"

But she hugged them to her bosom, and at length she was able to look up with dim eyes and a smile and say: "My hair grows so fast, Jim!"

And then Della leaped up like a little singed cat and cried, "Oh, oh!"

Jim had not yet seen his beautiful present. She held it out to him eagerly upon her open palm. The dull precious metal seemed to flash with a reflection of her bright and ardent spirit.

"Isn't it a dandy, Jim? I hunted all over town to find it. You'll have to look at the time a hundred times a day now. Give me your watch. I want to see how it looks on it."

Instead of obeying, Jim tumbled down on the couch and put his hands under the back of his head and smiled.

"Dell," said he, "let's put our Christmas presents away and keep 'em a while. They're too nice to use just at present. I sold the watch to get the money to buy your combs. And now suppose you put the chops on."

The Magi, as you know, were wise men—wonderfully wise men—who brought gifts to the Babe in the manger. They invented the art of giving Christmas presents. Being wise, their gifts were no doubt wise ones, possibly bearing the privilege of exchange in case of duplication. And here I have lamely related to you the uneventful chronicle of two foolish children in a flat who most unwisely sacrificed for each other the greatest treasures of their house. But in a last word to the wise of these days let it be said that of all who give gifts these two were the wisest. Of all who give and receive gifts, such as they are wisest. Everywhere they are wisest. They are the Magi.

16. *Coveted* means "strongly desired" or "wished for longingly."

Reading Strategy Identifying Problem and Solution *What problem does Della realize Jim was struggling with when he saw her cut hair?* R

Big Idea Rewards and Sacrifices *O. Henry is comparing the gifts that Jim and Della exchanged with the Magi's gifts. What does this comparison suggest about Jim's and Della's gifts?* BI

Additional Support

Academic Standards

The Additional Support activity on p. 128 covers the following standard:

Skills Practice: **9.3** [Identify] story elements such as character…[and] plot…

Skills Practice

READING: Charting Characters' Decisions In a selection, there are points at which a character makes a decision that affects the outcome of the story. O. Henry's story has two characters that make key decisions. Have students complete a chart like this one, and share their results in small groups. OL

Character: ______
Key Decision or Action: ______
What I Would Have Done: ______
How the Story Would Change: ______

AFTER YOU READ

RESPONDING AND THINKING CRITICALLY

Respond

1. Were you surprised by the outcome of the story? Why or why not?

Recall and Interpret

2. (a)Why is Della upset at the beginning of the story? (b)What does this tell you about her character?
3. (a)What do Della and Jim give up for each other, and what gifts do they buy for each other? (b)How are their choices ironic, or different from what is expected?
4. (a)What is Jim's initial reaction to Della when he arrives home? (b)How does this reaction create suspense?

Analyze and Evaluate

5. Della compares the watch chain to Jim: "Quietness and value—the description applied to both." Does this description apply to Jim when he enters the flat? Explain.
6. (a)According to the narrator, who were the Magi? (b)Why do you think the narrator refers to Della and Jim as the Magi?
7. During O. Henry's time, his stories were praised for their surprise endings and plot twists, but later generations of readers criticized these same techniques. What is your opinion of the surprise ending in this story? Explain your answer.

Connect

8. **Big Idea** **Rewards and Sacrifices** Even though neither Jim nor Della can use their gifts, how are they rewarded for their sacrifices?
9. Do you think the story's message is valuable to today's readers? Why or why not?

PRIMARY VISUAL ARTIFACT

Tortoiseshell Combs and a Platinum Fob Chain

The tortoiseshell combs and the platinum fob chain are objects that play a special role in "The Gift of the Magi." They have symbolic importance and add authenticity to the story's turn-of-the-century setting. Knowing what these objects look like and how they are used can add to your appreciation of the story.

1. How does the fob chain compare with the way that Jim has been carrying his watch?
2. How are the combs Della receives different from a regular comb?
3. If you were to write a modern-day version of this story, what gifts might you choose to replace these? Explain your choices.

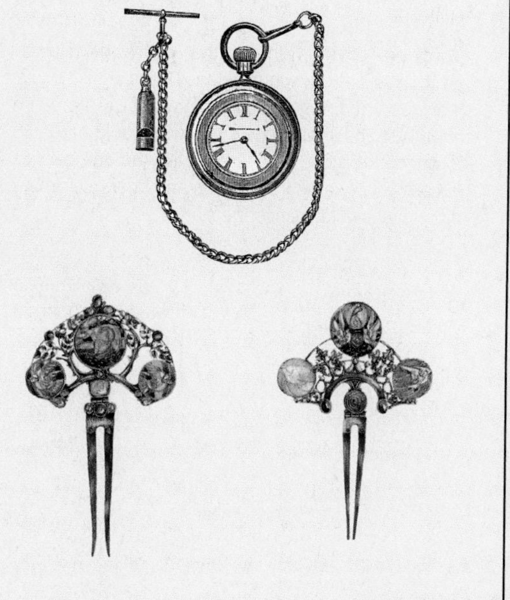

Primary Visual Artifact

1. Jim had been using a leather strap. Unlike the leather strap, the chain matches the watch and is made from similar materials. It also attaches more securely than the leather strap.
2. These combs are designed to fasten and adorn a woman's hair. They are expensive and jeweled. Ordinary combs are used only to smooth and arrange hair.
3. Students' answers should provide a brief explanation of why they chose the objects for their gifts.

AFTER YOU READ

Assess

1. Students should explain their answers.
2. (a) She does not have enough money to buy Jim the kind of gift he deserves. (b) Della is generous; she is poor but rich in love.
3. (a) Della gives up her hair. Jim gives up his watch. Della buys Jim a watch chain. Jim buys Della hair combs. (b) They each bought something to go with the thing that the other person sold.
4. (a) Jim stares fixedly at her with a peculiar expression. (b) Neither Della, nor the reader, knows how Jim will react. He might be angry, or he might not have noticed that Della cut her hair. Both reactions would drastically change our view of Jim and change the outcome of the story.
5. When Jim sees Della, he quietly tries to comprehend the changes he sees in Della. When he does respond, he is calm and comforting. He states that the changes would never diminish his feelings for her.
6. (a) According to the narrator, Jim and Della are the Magi. (b) Their selfless gifts were the wisest of all.
7. Students' answers should include a brief explanation of their reasoning.
8. They each learn how much the other sacrificed and how much they love each other.
9. Students' answers should include a brief explanation of their opinions.

AFTER YOU READ

Assess

Literary Element

1. Beauty is Della's most valuable asset, and cutting her prize feature symbolizes her willingness to sacrifice herself for Jim.
2. Time is what Jim gives of himself every day working, earning for the family. Selling his watch symbolizes his willingness to sacrifice his time, his connection to his family, and himself for Della.
3. Students may name the fob chain, the combs, or the Magi. Both the fob chain and combs symbolize Jim and Della's love for each other and their willingness to make sacrifices for one another. The Magi symbolize the giving of wise gifts. By comparing Della and Jim to the Magi, O. Henry is showing that their gifts were expressions of true love.

Review: Plot

Ask students to rewrite a part of the story using the new plot twist and share it with the class.

Reading Strategy

1. They can either buy very inexpensive gifts for each other or sacrifice something of their own to buy the gifts that they want to buy.

LITERARY ANALYSIS

Literary Element Symbol

After reading a story, you can identify its **symbols** by determining which objects or elements play an important role in the story. When an author focuses on an object or makes it a significant part of the story, that object may have a symbolic meaning. For example, a dove is often considered to be a symbol of peace. If a dove lands on the windowsill of a family in conflict, it might symbolize an end to the conflict and a fresh start for the family.

In "The Gift of the Magi," the symbols include Della's hair and Jim's pocket watch.

1. What does cutting Della's hair symbolize? Explain.
2. What does selling Jim's watch symbolize? Explain.
3. Look through the story and find one other item that works as a symbol. What is the item and what might it symbolize?

Review: Plot

As you learned on pages 10–11, **plot** is the sequence of events in a short story, novel, or drama. "The Gift of the Magi" is an example of a story that features a "plot twist," or surprise ending. Authors create plot twists by leading the reader to believe that something will happen and then having something unexpected happen instead.

Partner Activity With a partner, discuss other places in the story where you think a twist or surprise could have occurred. Together identify two places for a new plot twist and imagine how the twist would have changed the story. Using a chart like the one below, record your two new plot twists and briefly summarize how they would change the story.

Original Plot Event	New Plot Twist	How the Story Would Be Changed

READING AND VOCABULARY

Reading Strategy Identifying Problem and Solution

When a **problem** is presented in a story, there is usually more than one **solution** that a character can choose. The chosen solution often reveals something about a character.

1. What options do Della and Jim have for solving their Christmas gift problems?
2. What do their choices reveal about them?

Vocabulary Practice

Practice with Synonyms Synonyms are words that have the same or nearly the same meaning. Choose the synonym for each of the vocabulary words below.

1. imputation
   - **a.** cite
   - **b.** accusation
   - **c.** improvement
   - **d.** significant
2. parsimony
   - **a.** meanness
   - **b.** costliness
   - **c.** thriftiness
   - **d.** generosity
3. depreciate
   - **a.** reduce
   - **b.** appreciate
   - **c.** wane
   - **d.** devalue
4. prudence
   - **a.** irritation
   - **b.** caution
   - **c.** responsibility
   - **d.** haste

Academic Vocabulary

Here are two words from the vocabulary list on page R80. These words will help you think, write, and talk about the selection.

available (ə vā′ lə bəl) *adj.* present and ready for use; accessible

purchase (pər′ chis) *v.* to obtain in exchange for money or to acquire by effort

Practice and Apply

1. Why is selling her hair Della's only **available** option for making money?
2. Do you think that Della and Jim were using the gifts to **purchase** each other's love?

2. Their choice tells us they are generous and willing to sacrifice for the person they love.

Vocabulary

1. b **2.** c **3.** d **4.** b

Academic Vocabulary

1. Della and Jim are poor and unable to save money.
2. Students' answers may vary, but most will agree that Della and Jim were not trying to "buy" each other's love. Instead, they were trying to express their love through the gifts.

WRITING AND EXTENDING

Writing About Literature

Respond to Characters The narrator contradicts himself at the end of the story, saying first, "And here I have lamely related to you the uneventful chronicle of two foolish children in a flat who most unwisely sacrificed for each other the greatest treasures of their house." Then he says, "Let it be said that of all who give gifts these two were the wisest." Determine which of these statements is closer to your views about Della and Jim. Do you think that there might be truth in both statements? Write a brief essay explaining why you agree with the statement you chose. Make sure to use examples from the text to support your argument.

Before you begin writing, organize your thoughts in a two-column chart. In the left column list the reasons why you think Della and Jim are foolish, and in the right column list the reasons why you think they are wise. Use your chart as a reference as you write your essay.

Foolish	Wise

After completing your draft, meet with a peer reviewer to evaluate each other's work and to suggest revisions. Then proofread and edit your draft for errors in spelling, grammar, and punctuation.

Listening and Speaking

With a partner, interview several adults to find out about the greatest sacrifices they ever made for love. Ask for their permission to record their stories. Then select your favorite and play it for other students.

LiteratureOnline **Web Activities** For eFlashcards, Selection Quick Checks, and other Web activities, go to www.glencoe.com.

GRAMMAR AND STYLE

O. Henry's Language and Style

Varying Sentence Structure One way that O. Henry creates interest in his stories is by varying his sentences. He uses long and short sentences; simple, complex, and compound sentences; sentences with unexpected word order; and even sentence fragments. Note how varied the sentences are in this passage:

> As soon as she saw it she knew that it must be Jim's. It was like him. Quietness and value—the description applied to both. Twenty-one dollars they took from her for it, and she hurried home with the 87 cents.

The following chart lists the various sentence structures of this passage sentence by sentence:

Sentence	Structure
As soon as she saw it she knew that it must be Jim's.	Long
It was like him.	Short
Quietness and value—the description applied to both.	Complex
Twenty-one dollars they took from her for it, and she hurried home with the 87 cents.	Compound

Activity Rewrite the following passage, varying the sentence structures.

> You can give extra-special gifts. Extra-special gifts do not have to cost a lot of money. These gifts come from the heart. They do have a cost. They may require sacrifice. They show your love.

Revising Check

Sentence Structure Review your essay about Della and Jim. Do any sections seem dull or flat? Try rewriting them using varied sentence structure.

AFTER YOU READ

Assess

Writing About Literature

Students' essays should include
- a thesis statement that expresses their opinion clearly and concisely.
- a brief, well-reasoned explanation of their opinion.
- examples from the text that support their argument.
- a conclusion that convincingly restates their opinion.

Listening and Speaking

Students may wish to create a list of questions to use in encouraging the interviewee to tell the story.

O. Henry's Language and Style

Use this criteria when evaluating students' writing:

- Do students employ the type of sentence variety suggested by the chart?
- Does the sentence variety succeed in enhancing their essays?

Differentiated Instruction

Physically Disabled Allow students who have difficulty writing the option of using a tape recorder to tape their answers to the Assessment questions. OL

Web Activities Have students access the Web site for interactive activities that will help them assess their understanding of the selection.

Academic Standards

The Additional Support activity on p. 131 covers the following standards:

Differentiated Instruction: **9.3** [Identify] story elements such as character, theme, [and] plot... **9.7.3** Recognize and use elements of classical speech forms...in formulating rational arguments and applying the art of persuasion...

Focus

BELLRINGER

Bellringer Options
Daily Language Practice Transparency 13

Or display images of immigrants arriving in the United States at Ellis Island, San Francisco, and Florida.
Ask: What emotions might these people be experiencing? Why might these people have come to the United States? What are some reasons they may have for leaving their homelands?

Connecting to the Reading Selections

Have students share their responses to the opening questions. Then have them discuss what they already know about the history of immigrants to this country and the immigrants that continue to come to the United States today.

Comparing Literature *Across Genres*

Connecting to the Reading Selections

The United States is sometimes referred to as a nation of immigrants. Many immigrants come seeking greater political freedom; others seek better opportunities to support themselves and their families. With their bravery, ingenuity, and hard work, immigrants make contributions that vastly enrich the nation as a whole. The three works compared here—by Julia Alvarez, Elizabeth Wong, and Linda Pastan—explore the issues faced by people who leave behind their beloved homelands in order to build new lives and, in some cases, new identities.

COMPARING THE Big Idea Rewards and Sacrifices

Moving from one country to another can be exciting and rewarding. However, it can also be sad and painful. In these works, Julia Alvarez, Elizabeth Wong, and Linda Pastan suggest that for immigrants, moving to the United States is a very big step. Wanting to become part of a new country, yet remaining attached to their culture, immigrants must perform delicate balancing acts.

COMPARING Theme

The theme is the central message of a work of literature—an insight that readers can apply to their lives. Each of these writers uses literary elements to convey a theme about the experience of immigration to the United States.

COMPARING Author's Beliefs

Though these authors write of immigrants from very different places—the Dominican Republic, China, and Eastern Europe—each author suggests that how we have been brought up is deeply important to us. We cannot change our culture like clothing or discard it like old newspapers. Where we come from will stay with us—in one form or another—forever.

Selection Skills

Comparing Literature

Literary Elements
- Motivation (SE pp. 134, 136, 137, 138, 140, 141)
- Foreshadowing (TWE p. 137)
- Conflict (TWE p. 143)

Reading Skills
- Responding to Characters (SE pp. 134–141)
- Making Inferences (TWE pp. 135, 136)
- Previewing (TWE p. 134)

Listening/Speaking/Viewing Skills
- Analyzing Art (SE p. 139; TWE p. 135)

Writing Skills/Grammar
- Analyzing Theme (SE p. 141)
- Using Articles (TWE p. 137)
- Infinitives (TWE p. 140)
- Dashes (TWE p. 138)

Liberty

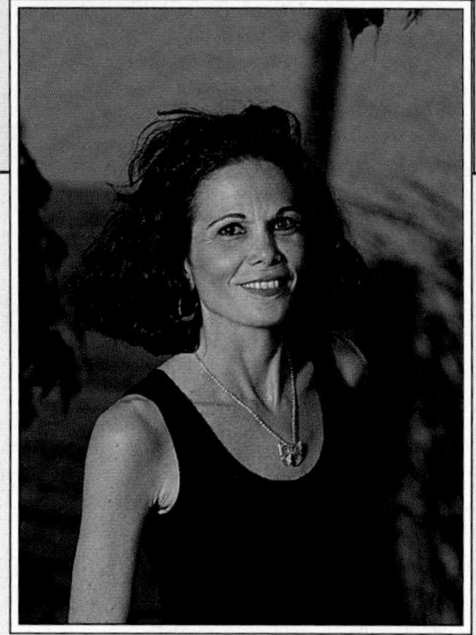

MEET JULIA ALVAREZ

At ten years old Julia Alvarez was a bewildered newcomer to the United States. Her family had recently escaped from the brutal regime of General Rafael Trujillo, military dictator of the Dominican Republic. In New York City, many miles away from the language and culture she grew up with, Alvarez felt out of place. "I looked around the schoolyard at unfriendly faces," she remembers.

A World of Words Unable to feel at home on the streets and playgrounds of New York City, Alvarez found a safe place in the world of words. "An English teacher asked us to write little stories about ourselves," she recalls. "I began to put into words some of what my life had been like in the Dominican Republic." Suddenly, Alvarez felt she had some control over her environment. "The boys in the schoolyard with ugly looks on their faces were not allowed into this world," she recalls.

"I found myself turning more and more to writing as the one place where I felt I belonged."

—Julia Alvarez

During high school and college, Alvarez dealt with problems by writing about them, and eventually she began to consider writing as a career. Her ambitions were startling for some people in her life. "I was raised in a very traditional, Old World family," she has explained, "so I never had thoughts about having a career. Moving to a new country, having to learn a new language, I got interested in words, and suddenly being in a world where there were books and encouragement of women to discover their talents contributed to my becoming a writer."

A Migrant Poet Alvarez graduated from Middlebury College in Vermont and received a graduate degree from Syracuse University. She then began her career as what she calls "a migrant poet." She began by teaching writing in prisons, retirement homes, and schools. "I would go anywhere," she told one interviewer. Finally she returned to Middlebury College, where she received tenure as a member of the English Department.

Writing from Experience Much of Alvarez's writing is about her homeland of the Dominican Republic and the lives of newcomers to the United States. Her first novel, *How the García Girls Lost Their Accents,* published in 1991, was an immediate success. It describes the struggles and successes of a family of Dominican immigrants. Alvarez's own three sisters saw many similarities between their experiences and those of the young women in the novel. "My sisters were a little taken aback," Alvarez admits. "But they're also very proud of me."

Julia Alvarez was born in 1950.

LiteratureOnline **Author Search** For more about Julia Alvarez, go to www.glencoe.com.

COMPARING LITERATURE

Focus

Big Idea

Rewards and Sacrifices As students read, have them consider how the narrator feels when she finds out her family is moving to a new country.

Ask: What would you give up in moving to a new place? What might you gain? *(Student answers will vary.)* Encourage volunteers who have made such a move to share the sacrifices and rewards of their experiences. OL

Author Search To expand students' appreciation of Julia Alvarez, have them access the Web site for additional information and resources.

Selection Resources

Print Materials
- Unit 1 Resources (Fast File), pp. 48–51
- Leveled Vocabulary Development, p. 10
- Selection and Unit Assessments, pp. 21–22
- Selection Quick Checks, p. 11

Transparencies
- Bellringer Options Transparencies: Daily Language Practice Transparency 13
- Literary Elements Transparency 16

Technology
- TeacherWorks Plus™ CD-ROM
- StudentWorks Plus™ CD-ROM
- Presentation Plus!™ CD-ROM
- Literature Online, glencoe.com
- Online Student Edition, mhln.com
- Exam*View*® Assessment Suite CD-ROM
- Vocabulary PuzzleMaker CD-ROM
- Listening Library, disc 1 tracks 11, 12, 13

COMPARING LITERATURE

BEFORE YOU READ

Focus

Summary

The narrator of this story, a young girl, has been hearing her parents talk about going to the United States. Her father, Papi, says he wants to go to school in the United States. Nothing seems to change until one day, with little warning, the children are told they will be leaving that very night for the United States. The narrator sees her world falling apart when she is told she must leave her pet dog, Liberty, behind.

V Vocabulary

Vocabulary File Say: Add these words and definitions to your vocabulary file. For each word, include a sentence that gives you an example of how to use the word. **OL** Students with English language needs should include the pronunciations of these words in their files. **EL**

Literary Elements Have students access the Web site to improve their understanding of motivation.

LITERATURE PREVIEW

Connecting to the Story

In "Liberty," a young girl is confused by the strange forces that are gripping the adult world around her. Before you read, think about the following questions:

- How did adults attempt to explain complicated circumstances to you when you were a child?
- Have you ever sacrificed something unwillingly, only to be thankful later that you did?

Building Background

Julia Alvarez does not name the country where "Liberty" takes place. It is likely, however, that the story is set in the Dominican Republic.

The Dominican Republic is a Spanish-speaking country in the Caribbean. It occupies the eastern two-thirds of the island of Hispaniola. From 1930 to 1961, the country fell under the power of Rafael Trujillo, a dictator whose family and friends dominated the economy and eliminated political freedoms. Trujillo's secret police abducted and tortured many people thought to be guilty of disloyalty to the president. Trujillo was eventually overthrown by members of his own army.

Setting Purposes for Reading

Big Idea Rewards and Sacrifices

As you read, reflect on the sacrifices one family makes as it leaves its home country for the United States.

Literary Element Motivation

Motivations are reasons or causes that a character acts in a certain way. To understand a character's motivation, think about what the character's words, thoughts, and actions reveal about the character's attitude toward the events in the story. Also think about what feelings it would make sense for a character to have, given the character's personality and background.

- See Literary Terms Handbook, p. R11.

Literature Online Interactive Literary Elements Handbook To review or learn more about the literary elements, go to www.glencoe.com.

READING PREVIEW

Reading Strategy Responding to Characters

Some of the most interesting people you will ever meet are to be found in books. Make the most of these amazing characters: Ask them questions. Argue with them. Give them advice. In other words, **respond to characters** you meet when you read, just as you respond to people you meet in real life.

Reading Tip: Recording Your Responses Use a chart like the one below to record your responses to characters you encounter while reading.

Character	Words, Thoughts, and Actions	My Response

Vocabulary

hyperactive (hī´ pər ak´ tiv) *adj.* overly energetic; very lively; p. 136 *Getting my hyperactive little brother to sit still for more than two minutes is next to impossible.*

distracted (dis trakt´ əd) *adj.* unable to pay attention; agitated; p. 136 *Distracted by thoughts of that evening's performance, Ara was unable to study.*

putrid (pū´ trid) *adj.* very nasty; disgusting; p. 137 *We threw out the rotten meat, but its putrid odor remained for days.*

admonition (ad´ mə nish´ ən) *n.* cautionary advice; warning; p. 137 *An admonition from a teacher is sometimes more effective than a scolding from a parent.*

inconsolable (in kən sō´ lə bəl) *adj.* heartbroken; impossible to comfort; p. 140 *The twins were inconsolable on hearing that the party had been canceled.*

INDIANA ACADEMIC STANDARDS (pages 134–141)
9.3.3 Analyze interactions between characters...
9.2 Develop [reading] strategies...
9.5.3 Write expository compositions, including analytical essays...

Additional Support

Skills Practice

READING: Previewing This story deals with the anguish and fears of a family on the brink of fleeing their homeland. It gives the reader a glimpse of the dangers the family faces if they stay and the risks they take by attempting to leave. Write these questions on the board for students to answer as they read:

- Why does Papi want to take his family to the United States?
- What is Mami's state of mind throughout the story?
- What sacrifices do family members make as they prepare to leave their homeland? **OL**

Liberty

Julia Alvarez

Papi came home with a dog whose kind we had never seen before. A black-and-white-speckled electric current of energy. It was a special breed with papers, like a person with a birth certificate. Mami just kept staring at the puppy with a cross look on her face. "It looks like a mess!" she said. "Take it back."

"Mami, it is a gift!" Papi shook his head. It would be an insult to Mister Victor, who had given us the dog. The American consul[1] wanted to thank us for all we'd done for him since he'd been assigned to our country.

"If he wanted to thank us, he'd give us our visas,"[2] Mami grumbled. For a while now, my parents had been talking about going to the United States so Papi could return to school. I couldn't understand why a grown-up who could do whatever he wanted would elect to go back to a place I so much wanted to get out of.

On their faces when they talked of leaving **R** there was a scared look I also couldn't understand.

"Those visas will come soon," Papi promised. But Mami just kept shaking her head about the dog. She had enough with four girls to take on puppies, too. Papi explained

The Burning Passion. Tsing-Fang Chen. Oil. 

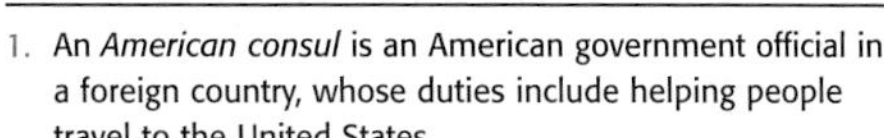

1. An *American consul* is an American government official in a foreign country, whose duties include helping people travel to the United States.
2. *Visas* are documents often necessary for traveling to other countries.

Teach

R Reading Strategy

Making Inferences Ask: Why do you think Mami and Papi seem scared when they talk about going to the United States? *(Possible inferences: Mami and Papi are fearful of what life may be like in the United States; Mami and Papi are fearful of what might happen when they try to leave their homeland.)* **OL**

★ Viewing the Art

This painting by Taiwanese-born artist Tsing-Fang Chen (1936–) is one of a series of works that commemorate the centennial of the Statue of Liberty. **AS**

Use the CheckPoint questions on Presentation Plus! to monitor students' comprehension. These questions can be used with interactive response keypads for immediate student feedback.

Readability Scores
Dale-Chall: 4.5
DRP: 50
Lexile: 840

Academic Standards

Additional Support activities on pp. 134 and 135 cover the following standards:

Skills Practice: **9.3.12** Analyze the way in which a work...is related to...issues of its historical period.

English Language Coach: **9.1** Use...a growing knowledge of English and other languages to determine the meaning of words...

Differentiated Instruction: **9.7.17** Deliver oral responses to literature that...[demonstrate] a comprehensive understanding of the significant ideas of...passages...

English Language Coach

Familiar Titles Have students discuss familiar or familial titles used among family members. Make a list of students' contributions on the board in as many languages as possible. **EL**

Differentiated Instruction

Reading in Small Parts Suggest that less proficient readers break the selection into small parts, such as one paragraph at a time. Have them read a paragraph aloud and then stop to paraphrase its main idea or central action. **BL**

Teach

L1 Literary Element

Motivation Answer: *Students may say that Papi wishes to be polite to the American consul or that for Papi, the dog symbolizes the United States or freedom.* OL

R1 Reading Strategy

Responding to Characters
Answer: *Answers will vary. Students may say that Mami is high-strung and Papi is kindhearted.* OL

L2 Literary Element

Motivation Answer: *Students may say Papi does not wish to be too public about his plans or to let his children know exactly what is going on. Papi's plans are dangerous because the country where the family lives is ruled by a dictatorship.* OL

R2 Reading Strategy

Responding to Characters
Answer: *Students may say that this scene creates compassion for the plight of Mami and Papi.* OL

COMPARING LITERATURE

that the dog would stay at the end of the yard in a pen. He would not be allowed in the house. He would not be pooping in Mami's orchid garden. He would not be barking until late at night. "A well-behaved dog," Papi concluded. "An American dog."

The little black-and-white puppy yanked at Papi's trouser cuff with his mouth. "What shall we call you?" Papi asked him.

"Trouble," Mami suggested, kicking the puppy away. He had left Papi's trousers to come slobber on her leg.

"We will call him Liberty. Life, liberty, and the pursuit of happiness." Papi quoted the U.S.A. Constitution. "Eh, Liberty, you are a lucky sign!"

Liberty barked his little toy barks and all us kids laughed. "Trouble." Mami kept shaking her head as she walked away. Liberty trotted behind her as if he agreed that that was the better name for him.

Mami was right, too—Liberty turned out to be trouble. He ate all of Mami's orchids, and that little **hyperactive** baton of a tail knocked things off the low coffee table whenever Liberty climbed on the couch to leave his footprints in among the flower prints. He tore up Mami's garden looking for buried treasure. Mami screamed at Liberty and stamped her foot. "Perro sin vergüenza!"[3] But Liberty just barked back at her.

"He doesn't understand Spanish," Papi said lamely. "Maybe if you correct him in English, he'll behave better!"

Mami turned on him, her slipper still in midair. Her face looked as if she'd light into him after she was done with Liberty. "Let him go be a pet in his own country if he wants instructions in English!" In recent weeks, Mami had changed her tune about going to the United States. She wanted to stay in her own country. She didn't want Mister Victor coming around our house and going off into the study with Papi to talk over important things in low, worried voices.

"All liberty involves sacrifice," Papi said in a careful voice. Liberty gave a few perky barks as if he agreed with that.

Mami glared at Papi. "I told you I don't want trouble—" She was going to say more, but her eye fell on me and she stopped herself. "Why aren't you with the others?" she scolded. It was as if I had been the one who had dug up her lily bulbs.

The truth was that after Liberty arrived, I never played with the others. It was as if I had found my double in another species. I had always been the tomboy, the live wire, the troublemaker, the one who was going to drive Mami to drink, the one she was going to give away to the Haitians. While the sisters dressed pretty and stayed clean in the playroom, I was out roaming the world looking for trouble. And now I had found someone to share my adventures.

"I'll take Liberty back to his pen," I offered. There was something I had figured out that Liberty had yet to learn: when to get out of Mami's way.

She didn't say yes and she didn't say no. She seemed **distracted**, as if something else was on her mind. As I led Liberty away by his collar, I could see her talking to Papi. Suddenly she started to cry, and Papi held her.

"It's okay," I consoled Liberty. "Mami doesn't mean it. She really does love you.

3. *Perro sin vergüenza* means "shameless dog."

Literary Element Motivation *Why does Papi want to keep the dog?* L1

Reading Strategy Responding to Characters *What are your first impressions of Mami and Papi?* R1

Vocabulary
hyperactive (hī′ pər ak′ tiv) *adj.* overly energetic; very lively

Literary Element Motivation *Why does Papi talk in low tones to Mister Victor and speak cautiously to Mami?* L2

Reading Strategy Responding to Characters *What feelings does this scene stir in you?* R2

Vocabulary
distracted (dis trakt′ əd) *adj.* unable to pay attention; agitated

Additional Support

Skills Practice

READING: Making Inferences
Explain that we make inferences every day based on available evidence, our knowledge, and our experience.
Say: Readers make inferences in a story by looking for subtle details that provide clues about characters and events. Have students answer these questions as they read:

- What inferences can you make about Mami?
- What can you infer about the relationship between the narrator and Liberty? OL

She's just nervous." It was what my father always said when Mami scolded me harshly.

At the back of the property stood Liberty's pen—a chain-link fence around a dirt square at the center of which stood a doghouse. Papi had built it when Liberty first came, a cute little house, but then he painted it a **putrid** green that reminded me of all the vegetables I didn't like. It was always a job to get Liberty to go into that pen.

Sure enough, as soon as he saw where we were headed, he took off, barking, toward the house, then swerved to the front yard to our favorite spot. It was a grassy knoll[4] surrounded by a tall hibiscus hedge. At the center stood a tall, shady samán tree. From there, no one could see you up at the house. Whenever I did something wrong, this was where I hid out until the punishment winds blew over. That was where Liberty headed, and I was fast behind on his trail.

Inside the clearing I stopped short. Two strange men in dark glasses were crouched behind the hedge. The fat one had seized Liberty by the collar and was pulling so hard on it that poor Liberty was almost standing on his hind legs. When he saw me, Liberty began to bark, and the man holding him gave him a yank on the collar that made me sick to my stomach. I began to back away, but the other man grabbed my arm. "Not so fast," he said. Two little scared faces—my own—looked down at me from his glasses.

"I came for my dog," I said, on the verge of tears.

"Good thing you found him," the man said. "Give the young lady her dog," he ordered his friend, and then he turned to me. "You haven't seen us, you understand?"

I didn't understand. It was usually I who was the one lying and grown-ups telling me to tell the truth. But I nodded, relieved when the man released my arm and Liberty was back in my hands.

"It's okay, Liberty." I embraced him when I put him back in his pen. He was as sad as I was. We had both had a hard time with Mami, but this was the first time we'd come across mean and scary people. The fat man had almost broken Liberty's neck, and the other one had left his fingerprints on my arm. After I locked up the pen, I watched Liberty wander back slowly to his house and actually go inside, turn around, and stick his little head out the door. He'd always avoided that ugly doghouse before. I walked back to my own house, head down, to find my parents and tell them what I had seen.

Overnight, it seemed, Mister Victor moved in. He ate all his meals with us, stayed 'til late, and when he had to leave, someone from the embassy was left behind "to keep an eye on things." Now, when Papi and Mister Victor talked or when the *tíos*[5] came over, they all went down to the back of the property near Liberty's pen to talk. Mami had found some wires in the study, behind the portrait of Papi's great-grandmother fanning herself with a painted fan. The wires ran behind a screen and then out a window, where there was a little box with lots of other wires coming from different parts of the house.

Mami explained that it was no longer safe to talk in the house about certain things. But the only way you knew what things those were was when Mami leveled her eyes on you as if she were pressing the off button on your mouth. She did this every time I asked her what was going on. ★

"Nothing," she said stiffly, and then she urged me to go outside and play. Forgotten were the **admonitions** to go study or I would flunk out of fifth grade. To go take a

4. A *knoll* is a hill.

5. *Tíos* means "uncles" in Spanish.

Literary Element Motivation *Why would the stranger say this to the narrator?* L3

Vocabulary

putrid (pū′ trid) *adj.* very nasty; disgusting

admonition (ad′ mə nish′ ən) *n.* cautionary advice; warning

Teach

L3 Literary Element

Motivation Answer: *Students may say that the visitors intend harm to the family and do not wish to be discovered.* OL

★ Writer's Technique

Foreshadowing A writer often gives clues to prepare readers for events that will happen later in a story.

Ask: What clues in the selection prepare readers for future events? *(Possible answers: the strange men and their warning to the narrator, Mr. Victor's presence in the narrator's home, the hidden wires, the adults' reluctance to talk inside the house, and Mami's emotional state.)* AS

English Language Coach

Using Articles Explain the use of articles. Point out that *a* or *an* is used when a topic is introduced: "I have a cat." *The* is used when the reader knows the thing or person referred to: "I like the cat." Give students a newspaper clipping with the articles blacked out. Have students fill in the appropriate articles. EL

Differentiated Instruction

Maintaining Focus Some students may be hampered by short attention spans. Suggest that students make a numbered list of events in the story as they read. If students take a break from reading, have them review the list each time before they resume reading the story. BL

Academic Standards

Additional Support activities on pp. 136 and 137 cover the following standards:

Skills Practice: **9.3.3** Analyze interactions between characters…

English Language Coach: **9.6.2** Demonstrate an understanding of sentence construction…

Differentiated Instruction: **9.3** [Identify] story elements such as…plot…

Teach

R1 Reading Strategy

Responding to Characters
Answer: *Students may say the narrator's actions are humorous and understandable.* OL

L1 Literary Element

Description Ask: What descriptive details about Mami share her tension with the reader? *(Possible details: flashed a bright smile, as if someone were taking her picture; performance of happiness; looked like she wanted to cry; company smile, between clenched teeth)* OL

L2 Literary Element

Motivation Answer: *Students may say that Mami wishes to reassure the children.* OL

R2 Reading Strategy

Responding to Characters
Answer: *Students may say the narrator's reaction is reasonable for a child. Others may say that they would not behave the same way, but would feel her deep sadness at having to leave a beloved pet behind.* OL

bath or the *microbios*[6] might kill me. To drink my milk or I would grow up stunted and with no teeth. Mami seemed absent and tense and always in tears. Papi was right—she was too nervous, poor thing.

I myself was enjoying a heyday of liberty. Several times I even got away with having one of Mister Victor's colas for breakfast instead of my boiled milk with a beaten egg, which Liberty was able to enjoy instead.

"You love that dog, don't you?" Mister Victor asked me one day. He was standing by the pen with Papi waiting for the uncles. He had a funny accent that sounded like someone making fun of Spanish when he spoke it.

I ran Liberty through some of the little tricks I had taught him, and Mister Victor laughed. His face was full of freckles—so that it looked as if he and Liberty were kin. I had the impression that God had spilled a lot of his colors when he was making American things.

Soon the uncles arrived and the men set to talking. I wandered into the pen and sat beside Liberty with my back to the house and listened. The men were speaking in English, and I had picked up enough of it at school and in my parents' conversations to make out most of what was being said. They were planning some hunting expedition for a goat with guns to be delivered by Mister Charlie. Papi was going to have to leave the goat to the others because his tennis shoes were missing. Though I understood the words—or thought I did—none of it made sense. I knew my father did not own a pair of tennis shoes, we didn't know a Mister Charlie, and who ever heard of hunting a goat?

As Liberty and I sat there with the sun baking the tops of our heads, I had this sense that the world as I knew it was about to end. The image of the two men in mirror glasses flashed through my head. So as not to think about them, I put my arm around Liberty and buried my face in his neck.

6. *Microbios* means "germs" in Spanish.

Reading Strategy Responding to Characters *What is your reaction to the narrator and the way in which she enjoys her freedom from Mami's scrutiny?* R1

Late one morning Mami gave my sisters and me the news. Our visa had come. Mister Victor had arranged everything, and that very night we were going to the United States of America! Wasn't that wonderful! She flashed us a bright smile, as if someone were taking her picture.

We stood together watching her, alarmed at this performance of happiness when really she looked like she wanted to cry. All morning aunts had been stopping by and planting big kisses on our foreheads and holding our faces in their hands and asking us to promise we would be very good. Until now, we hadn't a clue why they were so worked up.

Mami kept smiling her company smile. She had a little job for each of us to do. There would not be room in our bags for everything. We were to pick the one toy we wanted to take with us to the United States.

I didn't even have to think twice about my choice. It had suddenly dawned on me we were leaving, and that meant leaving *everything* behind. "I want to take Liberty." L1

Mami started shaking her head no. We could not take a dog into the United States of America. That was not allowed.

"Please," I begged with all my might. "Please, please, Mami, please." Repetition sometimes worked—each time you said the word, it was like giving a little push to the yes that was having a hard time rolling out of her mouth.

"I said no!" The bright smile on Mami's face had grown dimmer and dimmer. *"N–O."* She spelled it out for me in case I was confusing no with another word like yes. "I said a toy, and I mean a toy."

I burst into tears. I was not going to the United States unless I could take Liberty! Mami shook me by the shoulders and asked me between clenched teeth if I didn't understand we had to go to the United States or else.

Literary Element Motivation *Why does Mami try to seem happy?* L2

Reading Strategy Responding to Characters *How does the narrator's reaction strike you? Could you see yourself behaving this way in a similar situation?* R2

Additional Support

Skills Practice

WRITING: Dash Writers use a dash to signal a change in thought or to set off and emphasize supplemental information or parenthetical comments. Tell students to find where dashes are used on page 138. Ask students to discuss with a partner the effect of the dash in each case. Tell them to rewrite each sentence without using a dash. They may rephrase or use two sentences if they wish. Have them share their revised sentences with the class, compare them with the original sentences, and decide which version is more effective. OL

Portrait of Terrier. John Rabone Harvey. Private collection. John Noott Galleries, Broadway, Worcestershire, UK. 
Viewing the Art: Compare and contrast the dog pictured here with the dog described in the story.

COMPARING LITERATURE

Teach

★ Viewing the Art

Answer: *Liberty is "black-and-white-speckled" and very energetic. The breed is not given. The terrier is white with some brown on his ears and face. He sits quietly but alertly. Both seem to be intelligent and good companions.*

Portrait of Terrier was painted by British artist John Rabone Harvey (1862–1933). **AS**

Building Reading Fluency

Purposeful Reading Assign small, mixed-ability groups to prepare news stories about the narrator's predicament. Have students divide the story among them—beginning, middle, end—then reread their story section aloud to the group. Group members should work together to list each part's key events. **BL**

Differentiated Instruction

Summarizing Summarizing improves understanding and is valuable when reviewing for tests or organizing reports and papers. As students read longer works, they should record main ideas in notes or graphic organizers. Have students write summaries of this selection. Help them revise their summaries to include only main ideas. **BL**

Academic Standards

Additional Support activities on pp. 138 and 139 cover the following standards:

Skills Practice: **9.6.1** Identify and correctly use...the mechanics of punctuation...

Building Reading Fluency: **9.5.3** Write expository compositions...that communicate information and ideas from...sources accurately and coherently...

Differentiated Instruction: **9.5.2** Write responses to literature that support statements with evidence from the text...

Teach

L1 Literary Element

Motivation **Answer:** *Students may say that Tía Mimi's words are motivated by her desire to encourage her niece and help her get to the United States.* OL

L2 Literary Element

Motivation **Ask:** What motivates the narrator to free Liberty from his pen? *(Possible answer: She fears he will be harmed once her family leaves and the men in mirror glasses come to her home.)* OL

BI Big Idea

Rewards and Sacrifices
Answer: *Students may say that the narrator sacrifices the trusting friendship between her and her dog.* OL

Use the CheckPoint questions on Presentation Plus! to check students' mastery of the selection. These questions can be used with interactive response keypads for immediate student feedback.

But all I could understand was that a world without Liberty would break my heart. I was **inconsolable.** Mami began to cry.

Tía Mimi took me aside. She had gone to school in the States and always had her nose in a book. In spite of her poor taste in how to spend her free time, I still loved her because she had smart things to say. Like telling Mami that punishment was not the way to make kids behave. "I'm going to tell you a little secret," she offered now. "You're going to find liberty when you get to the United States."

"Really?" I asked.

She hesitated a minute, and then she gave me a quick nod. "You'll see what I mean," she said. And then, giving me a pat on the butt, she added, "Come on, let's go pack. How about taking that wonderful book I got you on the Arabian Nights?"

Late in the night someone comes in and shakes us awake. "It's time!"

Half asleep, we put on our clothes, hands helping our arms to go into the right sleeves, buttoning us up, running a comb through our hair.

We were put to sleep hours earlier because the plane had not come in.

But now it's time.

"Go sit by the door," we are ordered, as the hands, the many hands that now seem to be in control, finish with us. We file out of the bedroom, one by one, and go sit on the bench where packages are set down when Mami comes in from shopping. There is much rushing around. Mister Victor comes by and pats us on the head like dogs. "We'll have to wait a few more minutes," he says.

In that wait, one sister has to go to the bathroom. Another wants a drink of water. I am left sitting with my baby sister, who is dozing with her head on my shoulder. I lay her head down on the bench and slip out.

Through the dark patio down the path to the back of the yard I go. Every now and then a strange figure flashes by. I have said good-bye to Liberty a dozen times already, but there is something else I have left to do.

Sitting on the bench, I had an image of those two men in mirror glasses. After we are gone, they come onto the property. They smash the picture of Papi's great-grandmother fanning herself. They knock over the things on the coffee table as if they don't know any better. They throw the flowered cushions on the floor. They smash the windows. And then they come to the back of the property and they find Liberty.

Quickly, because I hear calling from the big house, I slip open the door of the pen. Liberty is all over me, wagging his tail so it beats against my legs, jumping up and licking my face.

"Get away!" I order sharply, in a voice he is not used to hearing from me. I begin walking back to the house, not looking around so as not to encourage him. I want him to run away before the gangsters come. L2

He doesn't understand and keeps following me. Finally I have to resort to Mami's techniques. I kick him, softly at first, but then, when he keeps tagging behind me, I kick him hard. He whimpers and dashes away toward the front yard, disappearing in areas of darkness, then reappearing when he passes through lighted areas. At the front of the house, instead of turning toward our secret place, he keeps on going straight down the drive, through the big gates, to the world out there.

He will beat me to the United States is what I am thinking as I head back to the house. I will find Liberty there, like Tía Mimi says. But I already sense it is a different kind of liberty my aunt means. All I can do is hope that when we come back—as Mami has promised we will—my Liberty will be waiting for me here.

Literary Element Motivation *What motivates Tía Mimi's words to the narrator?* L1

Vocabulary

inconsolable (in kən sō′ lə bəl) *adj.* heart-broken; impossible to comfort

Big Idea Rewards and Sacrifices *What sacrifice does the narrator make in order to keep Liberty safe?* BI

Additional Support

Academic Standards

The Additional Support activity on p. 140 covers the following standard:

Skills Practice: **9.6.1** Identify and correctly use…phrases, including…infinitive…

Skills Practice

GRAMMAR: Infinitives Infinitives are verb forms preceded by the word *to* and used as nouns, adjectives, or adverbs. Not all phrases beginning with *to* are infinitives; *to* may also introduce a prepositional phrase.

Write this sentence on the board: *To go* into a trance, the magician's subject needs *to abandon* conscious thought.

Have students write two pairs of questions and answers about the story. Each pair should contain one infinitive. Discuss students' examples. OL

AFTER YOU READ

RESPONDING AND THINKING CRITICALLY

Respond

1. What was your reaction at the end of this story? Explain.

Recall and Interpret

2. (a)What gift does the American consul give the narrator's family at the beginning of the story? (b)What else does the family hope to obtain from the consul?
3. (a)Who narrates, or tells, the story? (b)How would you describe the narrator?
4. (a)Whom does the narrator surprise in her favorite spot in the front yard? (b)What does the presence of these visitors tell the reader about the country in which the story takes place?
5. (a)How does Tía Mimi get the narrator to agree to go to the United States without her dog, Liberty? (b)What deeper meaning is there to her words? Explain.

Analyze and Evaluate

6. (a)How would you describe the narrator's mother and the attitudes of the other characters toward her? (b)What do you infer about why the mother behaves as she does? Explain.
7. How believable was the story's portrait of the young narrator? Cite examples from the story to support your answer.
8. Do you think that over the course of the story, the narrator grows or changes in any way? Explain.

Connect

9. **Big Idea** **Rewards and Sacrifices** (a)What sacrifices do the characters make over the course of the story? (b)What rewards do they hope to gain from these sacrifices? Explain whether you think the rewards are worth the cost.

LITERARY ANALYSIS

Literary Element Motivation

Characters almost always have a reason for behaving as they do. That is to say, there is generally **motivation** for their behavior. But this motivation is not always directly stated.

1. What is Papi's reason for naming the dog "Liberty"?
2. (a)Why does the narrator kick the dog to make it run away? (b)What might be the larger meaning of the narrator's wish at the end of the story to find the dog Liberty safe when she returns? Explain.

Writing About Literature

Analyze Theme This story gives readers a glimpse of life in a society where freedom is lacking. What statement do you think the author was making by writing the story? Write a brief essay in which you describe the story's theme, its central message or insight. Support your ideas about the theme with details from the story.

READING AND VOCABULARY

Reading Strategy Responding to Characters

When you react in a personal way to what you read, you enjoy your reading more and remember it better. What grabbed your attention as you read this story? For each of the following questions, write a few sentences explaining your response.

1. Which character did you find most interesting?
2. Which character did you find most irritating?
3. Which bit of dialogue, or words spoken by a character, did you find most memorable?
4. Which action seemed most important to you?

LiteratureOnline **Web Activities** For eFlashcards, Selection Quick Checks, and other Web activities, go to www.glencoe.com.

AFTER YOU READ

Assess

1. Students may say they hope the dog will be safe.
2. (a) A puppy (b) Visas for travel to the United States
3. (a) A young girl (b) Students may say she is rebellious and a tomboy.
4. (a) Two strange men (b) It suggests the country restricts its citizens and is unsafe.
5. (a) She says liberty awaited the narrator in the United States. (b) She means that the girl and her family will find freedom and safety.
6. (a) Students may say the mother is high-strung and grouchy. The father and narrator are gentle and indulgent towards her. (b) Students may infer that the mother is distraught about the family's unsafe situation and their impending attempt to flee.
7. Students may say the portrayal of a young girl gripped by forces beyond her comprehension was believable.
8. She has learned to understand the need to let go of her home and her beloved pet.
9. (a) They sacrifice their home; the girl sacrifices her dog. (b) They hope for freedom and safety; the girl hopes to safeguard her dog. Students should support opinions with text examples.

Literary Element

1. In honor of his goal of finding freedom in the United States
2. (a) She fears it will fall into the hands of the men who spied on the family. (b) This might refer to her desire to find her country safe when she returns.

Writing About Literature

Essays should explain the story's theme or message and give examples from the story that support the theme.

Reading Strategy

Students should support answers with reasoning and story details.

LiteratureOnline

Web Activities Have students access the Web site for interactive activities that will help them assess their understanding of the selection.

Focus

Summary

A girl and her brother of Chinese-American descent must attend Chinese school. The girl resists because she wants to be completely American. As an adult, she understands that her heritage is part of her.

Author Search To expand students' appreciation of Elizabeth Wong, have them access the Web site for additional information and resources.

Readability Scores
Dale-Chall: 7.6
DRP: 59
Lexile: 1080

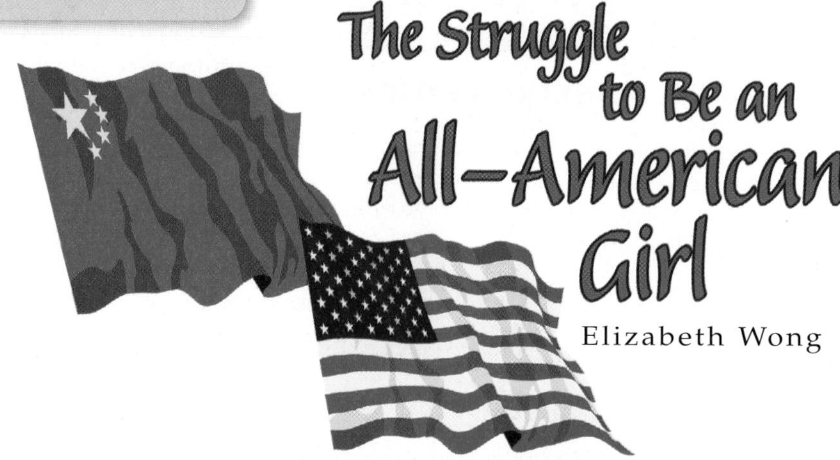

The Struggle to Be an All-American Girl

Elizabeth Wong

BEFORE YOU READ

Building Background

Elizabeth Wong has never stopped thinking and writing about the two cultures in which she spent her youth and the many cultures that make up the United States. "I am an American writer, of Chinese ancestry," she says, "blessed with a rich heritage of books and movies and food and people and languages from the world over, because, like it or not, that's the true inheritance, the true nature of America."

Elizabeth Wong was born in 1958.

Literature Online **Author Search** For more about Elizabeth Wong, go to www.glencoe.com.

It's still there, the Chinese school on Yale Street where my brother and I used to go. Despite the new coat of paint and the high wire fence, the school I knew ten years ago remains remarkably, stoically[1] the same.

Every day at 5 PM, instead of playing with our fourth- and fifth-grade friends or sneaking out to the empty lot to hunt ghosts and animal bones, my brother and I had to go to Chinese school. No amount of kicking, screaming, or pleading could dissuade my mother, who was solidly determined to have us learn the language of our heritage.

Forcibly, she walked us the seven long, hilly blocks from our home to school, depositing our defiant tearful faces before the stern principal. My only memory of him is that he swayed on his heels like a palm tree, and he always clasped his impatient twitching hands behind his back. I recognized him as a repressed maniacal child killer,[2] and knew that if we ever saw his hands we'd be in big trouble.

We all sat in little chairs in an empty auditorium. The room smelled like Chinese medicine, an imported faraway mustiness. Like ancient mothballs or dirty closets. I hated that smell. I favored crisp new scents. Like the soft French perfume that my American teacher wore in public school.

There was a stage far to the right, flanked by an American flag and the flag of the Nationalist Republic of China,[3] which was also red, white and blue but not as pretty.

1. *Stoically* here means "unaffected by outside influences."

2. The narrator uses the expression *repressed maniacal child killer* to humorously convey her childhood fear of her strict principal.

3. The *Nationalist Republic of China* is a country on the island of Taiwan. The People's Republic of China is on the mainland.

Additional Support

Skills Practice

READING: Comparing and Contrasting Have students compare and contrast the narrators of "Liberty" and "The Struggle to Be an All-American Girl." Guide students to set up graphic organizers. They can use Venn diagrams or simple charts to record similarities and differences. Allow time for students to share their comparisons. OL

Although the emphasis at the school was mainly language—speaking, reading, writing—the lessons always began with an exercise in politeness. With the entrance of the teacher, the best student would tap a bell and everyone would get up, kowtow,[4] and chant, *"Sing san ho,"* the phonetic for "How are you, teacher?"

L

Being ten years old, I had better things to learn than ideographs[5] copied painstakingly in lines that ran right to left from the tip of a *moc but*, a real ink pen that had to be held in an awkward way if blotches were to be avoided. After all, I could do the multiplication tables, name the satellites of Mars, and write reports on Little Women and Black Beauty. Nancy Drew, my favorite book heroine, never spoke Chinese.

The language was a source of embarrassment. More times than not, I had tried to disassociate myself from the nagging loud voice that followed me wherever I wandered in the nearby American supermarket outside Chinatown. The voice belonged to my grandmother, a fragile woman in her seventies who could outshout the best of the street vendors. Her humor was raunchy, her Chinese rhythmless, patternless. It was quick, it was loud, it was unbeautiful. It was not like the quiet, lilting romance of French or the gentle refinement of the American South. Chinese sounded pedestrian.[6] Public.

In Chinatown, the comings and goings of hundreds of Chinese on their daily tasks sounded chaotic and frenzied. I did not want to be thought of as mad, as talking gibberish. When I spoke English, people nodded at me, smiled sweetly, said encouraging words. Even the people in my culture would cluck and say that I'd do well in life. "My, doesn't she move her lips fast," they would say, meaning that I'd be able to keep up with the world outside Chinatown.

4. To *kowtow* means "to bow deeply and respectfully."
5. *Ideographs* are the symbols that make up traditional Chinese writing.
6. As used here, *pedestrian* means "ordinary."

My brother was even more fanatical than I about speaking English. He was especially hard on my mother, criticizing her, often cruelly, for her pidgin[7] speech—smatterings of Chinese scattered like chop suey in her conversation. "It's not 'What it is,' Mom," he'd say in exasperation. "It's 'What is it, what is it, what is it!'" Sometimes Mom might leave out an occasional "the" or "a," or perhaps a verb of being. He would stop her in midsentence: "Say it again, Mom. Say it right." When he tripped over his own tongue, he'd blame it on her: "See, Mom, it's all your fault. You set a bad example."

What infuriated my mother most was when my brother cornered her on her consonants, especially "r." My father had played a cruel joke on Mom by assigning her an American name that her tongue wouldn't allow her to say. No matter how hard she tried, "Ruth" always ended up "Luth" or "Roof."

After two years of writing with a *moc but* and reciting words with multiples of meanings, I finally was granted a cultural divorce. I was permitted to stop Chinese school.

I thought of myself as multicultural. I preferred tacos to egg rolls; I enjoyed Cinco de Mayo[8] more than Chinese New Year.

At last, I was one of you; I wasn't one of them.

Sadly, I still am.

7. *Pidgin* refers to a basic way of communicating, with a limited vocabulary and simplified grammar.
8. *Cinco de Mayo* means "fifth of May." It is a national holiday in Mexico.

Quickwrite

Reread the last two sentences of this selection. In two or three paragraphs, discuss the following questions: Who are the "you" and "them" that Wong refers to? What is the meaning of the last sentence?

COMPARING LITERATURE

Teach

L Literary Element

Conflict Explain that conflict is the main struggle between two opposing forces in a story. **Ask:** What is the conflict in this story? *(The narrator's desire to fit into American culture conflicts with her mother's determination that the children learn the language and customs of their Chinese heritage.)* OL

Quickwrite

Students' essays should explain that *you* refers to Americans. *Them* refers to people of Chinese heritage, such as her mother and grandmother. In the last line, the narrator, as an adult, seems to regret her resistance to Chinese culture.

CheckPoint

Use the CheckPoint questions on Presentation Plus! to check students' mastery of the selection. These questions can be used with interactive response keypads for immediate student feedback.

English Language Coach

Cultural Traditions Discuss cultural traditions mentioned in the selection: Chinese New Year, Cinco de Mayo, tacos, and egg rolls. **Ask:** Why does the narrator prefer celebrations and foods that are not part of her Chinese heritage? *(She wants to be a multicultural person, not a Chinese American.)* EL

Building Reading Fluency

Reading Aloud Reading this narrative aloud will clarify the narrator's conflict and help students develop expressive reading. Have students work in small groups and take turns reading portions of the selection, using tone of voice to communicate the narrator's feelings. BL

Academic Standards

Additional Support activities on pp. 142 and 143 cover the following standards:

Skills Practice: **9.3.2** Compare and contrast the presentation of a similar…topic across genres…to explain how the…genre shapes the…topic.

English Language Coach: **9.2.8** Make reasonable statements and draw conclusions about a text, supporting them with accurate examples.

Building Reading Fluency: **9.7** [Develop] speaking skills…in conjunction with…strategies…[for] delivery of oral presentations.

BEFORE YOU READ

Focus

Summary

An elderly man and his granddaughter discuss the European town he emigrated from. She asks why he left. She comments on the harshness of the scenes in his old photographs but then realizes that part of his heart still misses his homeland.

Author Search To expand students' appreciation of Linda Pastan, have them access the Web site for additional information and resources.

COMPARING LITERATURE

BEFORE YOU READ

Building Background

Linda Pastan is familiar with sacrifice. From the age of ten she knew that she wanted to write, but as a promising young poet just out of college she put her dream on hold in order to become a mother and housewife. "I was unhappy because I knew what I should be doing," she told an interviewer. With her children at school, Pastan returned to writing and after much hard work achieved recognition as a master of simple but intense poetry about housework, motherhood, love, growing older, dreams, and loss.

In "Grudnow," Pastan writes about her grandfather, who was born in Eastern Europe. Her elderly grandfather carried bittersweet memories of his homeland with him when he joined a flood of newcomers to the United States. Like other immigrants, he remained an inhabitant of two worlds—the one to which he had escaped and the one which he had access to only in memory.

Linda Pastan was born in 1932.

LiteratureOnline **Author Search** For more about Linda Pastan, go to www.glencoe.com.

Grudnow

Linda Pastan

When he spoke of where he came from,
my grandfather could have been
clearing his throat
of that name, that town
sometimes Poland, sometimes Russia,[1]
the borders penciled in
with a hand as shaky as his.
He left, I heard him say,
because there was nothing there.
I understood what he meant
when I saw the photograph
of his people standing
against a landscape emptied
of crops and trees, scraped raw
by winter. Everything
was in sepia,[2] as if the brown earth
had stained the faces,
stained even the air.
I would have died there, I think

1. The borders of Poland and Russia changed frequently during the nineteenth and twentieth centuries.
2. *Sepia* is the brown tint frequently seen in old photographs.

Additional Support

Skills Practice

READING: Paraphrasing Explain to students that paraphrasing can help improve their comprehension of the poem and enable them to pinpoint parts of the poem that may confuse them.

- Have students work in pairs to paraphrase the poem. Encourage them to restate the speaker's thoughts in their own words.
- After students finish paraphrasing, ask them to compare their results to the poem.
- Discuss the overall effect of the poem compared to the effect of their paraphrasing. **OL**

The Smith at Szeliwy, Poland, 1904. Robert Polhill Bevan. Oil on board, 26 × 37 cm. Private collection.

in childhood maybe
of some fever,
my face pressed for warmth
against a cow with flanks
like those of the great-aunts
in the picture. Or later
I would have died of history
like the others, who dug
their stubborn heels into that earth,
heels as hard as the heels
of the bread my grandfather tore
from the loaf at supper. He always
sipped his tea through a cube of sugar
clenched in his teeth, the way
he sipped his life here, noisily,
through all he remembered
that might have been sweet in Grudnow.

Discussion Starter

Meet with a small group to discuss what life in the old country was like for the grandfather of the speaker of "Grudnow." Consider what the grandfather himself says and what the details of the old photograph suggest about that place. Summarize your discussion for the rest of your class.

COMPARING LITERATURE

Teach

R Reading Strategy

Drawing Conclusions Ask students to draw conclusions about the quality of life in Grudnow. Have them use evidence from the poem to support their conclusions. *(Possible answer: Life was harsh and people were poor. Lines 10–18.)* OL

★ Viewing the Art

The paintings of British artist Robert Polhill Bevan (1865–1925) feature mainly outdoor scenes and were influenced by the work of the French painter Gauguin. AS

Discussion Starter

Discussions should touch on the the grandfather's description of the old country, the content of the old photographs, and what these tell about his reasons for leaving his homeland.

CheckPoint

Use the CheckPoint questions on Presentation Plus! to check students' mastery of the selection. These questions can be used with interactive response keypads for immediate student feedback.

Academic Standards

Additional Support activities on pp. 144 and 145 cover the following standards:

Skills Practice: **9.7.17** Deliver oral responses to literature that…[demonstrate] a comprehensive understanding of the significant ideas…

English Language Coach: **9.7.7** Make judgments about the ideas under discussion and support those judgments with evidence.

Differentiated Instruction: **9.7** [Develop] speaking skills…in conjunction with… strategies…[for] delivery of oral presentations.

English Language Coach

Group Discussions Help students develop strategies for following a group discussion. In small pre-discussion groups, students can write down ideas about a selection. Devise roles for those who are more comfortable listening than speaking, such as looking up dictionary meanings of words the group does not understand. EL

Differentiated Instruction

Drama Dramatic readings can provide students with another way to experience literature.

Have students choose a single work related to the Big Idea or theme to present as a dramatic reading. AL

Wrap-Up: Comparing Literature *Across Genres*

- *Liberty*
  Julia Alvarez
- *The Struggle to Be an All-American Girl*
  Elizabeth Wong
- *Grudnow*
  Linda Pastan

COMPARING THE **Big Idea** Rewards and Sacrifices

Writing Activity The narrator of "Liberty," the author of "The Struggle to Be an All-American Girl," and the grandfather in "Grudnow" all make sacrifices in order to create a life in the United States. Why are they willing to make such sacrifices? What do they gain in return? What do they lose in the process? Think about the issues that seem to be common to immigrants from many places. Then write a brief essay discussing the different facets of the immigrant experience as revealed by these works. Conclude your essay with your thoughts about the impact the immigrant experience has had on U.S. society.

Nostalgia Collage. Fred Otnes.

COMPARING Theme

Group Activity A genre is a category, or type, of literature. Though the selections compared here come from different genres—the first being fiction, the second nonfiction, and the third poetry—each of the selections conveys a theme, or message, about the subject of immigration. With a small group, discuss the following questions:

1. What message about immigration does each writer share with the reader?
2. For each selection, in what way did the characteristics of the genre help convey the writer's message?
3. Which of the selections, in your opinion, makes the most powerful statement about immigration? Support your answer with passages from the selections.

COMPARING Author's Beliefs

Partner Activity Julia Alvarez, Elizabeth Wong, and Linda Pastan each emphasize different aspects of the immigrant experience. What do the differences of emphasis reveal about the beliefs of these authors? With a partner, make inferences about each author's beliefs about the following:

- the importance of remembering one's origins
- the ways in which the United States is better or worse than other places
- the ways in which love for the United States might be combined with love for one's country of origin

Support your inferences with details from the selections. Then share your thoughts with your classmates.

INDIANA ACADEMIC STANDARDS (page 146)

9.3.2 Compare and contrast the presentation of a similar theme or topic across genres...

9.3.5 Compare works that express a universal theme...

9.5.3 Write expository compositions, including...essays...

Assess

Comparing the Big Idea

Critique student essays with these criteria:

- Do essays give reasons why immigrants make sacrifices to come to the United States?
- Do they tell what immigrants gain and sacrifice?
- Do essays conclude with students' ideas about the effects of immigrants on the United States?

Comparing Theme

1. Possible answers: Alvarez says immigration is driven by a need for liberty and safety; people should appreciate the freedoms in the United States. Wong says immigrants and their children must decide what to retain of their old culture; they should not give up their heritage. Pastan says immigrants may have good reasons for leaving their former countries, but their early experiences will lend richness and sweetness to their lives.
2. Possible answers: Fiction was a good way for Alvarez to convey the feelings of a family beginning a journey to a new place. Memoir may have been the best way for Wong to reveal her personal feelings. Poetry may have been an appropriate way to convey Pastan's delicate sentiments about gain and loss.
3. Answers will vary. Students should support their answers.

Comparing Author's Beliefs

Critique students' discussions on these criteria:

- Do discussions include each author's beliefs?
- Do discussions touch on remembering one's origins, sacrifices, and gains made by the immigrant and how the immigrant combines love of his/her homeland and the United States?

Sweet Potato Pie

MEET EUGENIA COLLIER

"Because racism is not over, writing still needs to define who we are. . . ." Eugenia Collier experienced racism firsthand as a young girl. The daughter of a doctor and an educator, she grew up in Baltimore, Maryland, where she attended segregated schools. After graduating with high honors from Howard University, earning her master's degree from Columbia University, and working as a public aid case worker for five years, Collier followed in her mother's footsteps by becoming a teacher.

The Educator Collier taught English at various colleges and universities in the metropolitan Baltimore-Washington, D.C., area. She was named one of the Outstanding Educators of America. Yet she herself continued to learn as well. "After a conventional Western-type education," Collier once stated, "I discovered the richness, the diversity, the beauty of my black heritage. This discovery has meant a coalescence of personal and professional goals. It has also meant a lifetime commitment."

"The fact of my blackness is the core and center of my creativity."

—Eugenia Collier

The Writer Collier merged her personal and professional lives by writing about the African American experience. In 1969 she won the Gwendolyn Brooks Award for Fiction for what is perhaps her most famous short story, "Marigolds." It tells the tale of a fourteen-year-old African American girl who comes of age in Maryland during the Great Depression. A one-act play based on her short story "Ricky" was staged in Chicago in 1976.

Collier has also written numerous critical essays about great African American authors such as Langston Hughes. In 1972, with collaborator Richard A. Long, she edited *Afro-American Writing: An Anthology of Prose and Poetry.* She herself has contributed poems as well as stories and articles to both scholarly and popular publications, including *Black World, TV Guide,* and the *New York Times.*

"A Lifetime Commitment" In 1976 Collier obtained her doctorate from the University of Maryland. She continued to teach as well as write and chaired the English Department at Morgan State University. Now retired, Collier's career has exhibited the "lifetime commitment" to her African American heritage that she has previously expressed.

Eugenia Collier was born in 1928.

LiteratureOnline **Author Search** For more about Eugenia Collier, go to www.glencoe.com.

Focus

BELLRINGER

Bellringer Options
Selection Focus Transparency 10
Daily Language Practice Transparency 14

Or discuss the meaning of the phrase "comfort food and family traditions." Ask students if they have comfort foods or favorite family traditions. Have volunteers share the meaning of these special foods and traditions.
Ask: Why do people have comfort foods and favorite traditions? Have students consider as they read what makes the sweet potato pie a special food for the narrator.

Author Search To expand students' appreciation of Eugenia Collier, have them access the Web site for additional information and resources.

Selection Skills

Sweet Potato Pie

Literary Elements
- Theme (SE pp. 148–157)
- Character (SE p. 157)

Reading Skills
- Questioning (SE pp. 148–158)

Vocabulary Skills
- Word Parts (SE pp. 148, 158)
- Academic Vocabulary (SE p. 158)

Listening/Speaking/Viewing Skills
- Analyzing Art (SE pp. 150, 155; TWE p. 149)
- Readers Theater (TWE p. 150)

Writing Skills/Grammar
- Analyze Cultural Context (SE p. 158)
- Proper Nouns (TWE p. 154)

Study Skills/Research/Assessment
- Research (TWE pp. 149, 153)

BEFORE YOU READ

Focus

Summary

Buddy was the youngest child of poor Southern sharecroppers. Now a college professor, Buddy drops in on his brother Charley's family in Harlem. He discovers that Charley, who sacrificed for Buddy all his life, will continue to do so forever.

V Vocabulary

Vocabulary File **Say:** Add these words and definitions to your vocabulary file. For each word, include a sentence that gives you an example of how to use the word. **OL** Students with English language needs should include the pronunciations of these words in their files. **EL**

Literary Elements Have students access the Web site to improve their understanding of theme.

Readability Scores

Dale-Chall: 6.7
DRP: 60
Lexile: 970

LITERATURE PREVIEW

Connecting to the Story

In Collier's story, family relationships are central. The support that Buddy, the narrator, receives from other members of his family—especially his older brother Charley—helps him overcome the poverty that grips his family and become a "somebody." Before you read the story, think about the following questions:

- What life experiences might cause a person to value status?
- In your experience, what suggests importance or status?

Building Background

Sharecropping was a farming system practiced in the South in the years between the Civil War and World War II. Landowners allowed formerly enslaved people to live on and farm a portion of their land in exchange for half the crop. If the landowners supplied equipment, animals, and seed, the sharecropper could keep only about one-third of the crop. The sale of that amount barely covered basic necessities and kept sharecropping families in poverty. In the 1940s mechanized cotton harvesters ended much of the need for sharecroppers, sending hundreds of thousands to seek work in cities.

Setting Purposes for Reading

Big Idea Rewards and Sacrifices

As you read "Sweet Potato Pie," notice what sacrifices the family members make, and think about what rewards they receive.

Literary Element Theme

The **theme** of a piece of literature is its central message about life or human nature. In some works, the theme is stated outright. In other works, the theme is implied and revealed gradually. As you read this story, look for details that suggest its central message or idea.

- See Literary Terms Handbook, pp. R17–R18.

 **Interactive Literary Elements Handbook** To review or learn more about the literary elements, go to www.glencoe.com.

READING PREVIEW

Reading Strategy Questioning

Reading is an active process that engages your mind as well as your eyes. One way to read actively is to ask yourself **questions** as you read. Asking questions and looking for the answers, or even predicting them, can help you read more actively and intelligently. It can also help you better remember what you have read. As you read, ask yourself questions and look for clues to the answers in the text.

Reading Tip: Taking Notes Use a chart to record your questions. Then check whether the question was answered or an answer was implied later in the text.

Question	Clues/Answer
Why is Buddy's love "seasoned with gratitude"?	His brother Charley gave up his childhood.

Vocabulary

collective (kə lek′ tiv) *adj.* having to do with a group of persons or things; common; shared; p. 150 *The collective opinion of the jury was that the woman was not guilty.*

antiquity (an tik′ wə tē) *n.* an ancient time or times; p. 151 *The pyramids of Egypt date back to antiquity.*

ubiquitous (ū bik′ wə təs) *adj.* seeming to be everywhere at once; p. 151 *Two days before the election, campaign posters were ubiquitous—in windows, along streets, on doors.*

futilely (fū′ til ē) *adv.* uselessly; vainly; hopelessly; p. 152 *The pedestrian futilely waved his arm at the taxicab as it sped by him.*

Vocabulary Tip: Word Parts Knowing what the parts of an unfamiliar word mean can help you determine the meaning of the entire word.

INDIANA ACADEMIC STANDARDS (pages 148–158)

9.3 [Identify] story elements such as...theme...

9.2 Develop strategies such as asking questions...

9.5.3 Write expository compositions, including analytical essays...that...make distinctions between the relative value and significance of specific data, facts, and ideas.

Selection Resources

Print Materials

- Unit 1 Resources (Fast File), pp. 52–54
- Leveled Vocabulary Development, p. 11
- Selection and Unit Assessments, pp. 23–24
- Selection Quick Checks, p. 12

Transparencies

- Bellringer Options Transparencies:
  Selection Focus Transparency 10
  Daily Language Practice Transparency 14
- Literary Elements Transparency 18

Technology

- TeacherWorks Plus™ CD-ROM
- StudentWorks Plus™ CD-ROM
- Presentation Plus!™ CD-ROM
- Literature Online, glencoe.com
- Online Student Edition, mhln.com
- Exam*View*® Assessment Suite CD-ROM
- Vocabulary PuzzleMaker CD-ROM
- Listening Library, disc 1 track 14

Sweet Potato Pie

Eugenia Collier

Midtown Mayhem, 1999. Patti Mollica. Acrylic & pastel on paper. Collection of the Artist. 

From up here on the fourteenth floor, my brother Charley looks like an insect scurrying among other insects. A deep feeling of love surges through me. Despite the distance, he seems to feel it, for he turns and scans the upper windows, but failing to find me, continues on his way. I watch him moving quickly—gingerly,[1] it seems to me—down Fifth Avenue and around the corner to his shabby taxicab. In a moment he will be heading back uptown.

I turn from the window and flop down on the bed, shoes and all. Perhaps because of what happened this afternoon or maybe just because I see Charley so seldom, my thoughts hover over him like hummingbirds. The cheerful, impersonal tidiness of this room is a world away from Charley's walk-up flat in Harlem[2] and a hundred worlds from the bare, noisy shanty where he and the rest of us spent what there was of childhood. I close my eyes, and side by side I see the Charley of my boyhood and the Charley of this afternoon, as clearly as if I were looking at a split TV screen. Another surge of love, seasoned with gratitude, wells up in me.

As far as I know, Charley never had any childhood at all. The oldest children of sharecroppers never do. Mama and Pa were shadowy figures whose voices I heard vaguely in the morning when sleep was shallow and whom I glimpsed as they left for the field before I was fully awake or as they trudged wearily into the house at night when my lids were irresistibly heavy.

They came into sharp focus only on special occasions. One such occasion was the day when the crops were in and the sharecroppers were paid. In our cabin there was so much excitement in the air that even I, the "baby," responded to it. For weeks we had been running out of things that we could neither grow nor get on credit. On the evening of that day we waited anxiously for our parents' return.

1. *Gingerly* means "with caution" or "carefully."
2. *Harlem* is a section of New York City mainly inhabited by African Americans and Hispanics.

Reading Strategy Questioning *What question might this statement lead you to ask?* **R**

Teach

Big Idea

Rewards and Sacrifices Tell students to keep these questions in mind as they read. **Ask:** What kind of relationship does the narrator have with Charley? *(He is Charley's younger brother.)* How does Charley's loving nature impact the life of the narrator? *(Charley cares for him as a father figure; he willingly makes sacrifices so the narrator can get an education.)* **OL**

R Reading Strategy

Questioning Answer: *Students will likely ask, "What happened this afternoon between the two characters?"* **OL**

Viewing the Art

Patti Mollica has created many urban street scenes, often set in New York City. Her work is characterized by bold colors. She sees the world as "a mosaic of shapes and color." **AS**

CheckPoint

Use the CheckPoint questions on Presentation Plus! to monitor students' comprehension. These questions can be used with interactive response keypads for immediate student feedback.

English Language Coach

Past Tense Write on the board *changed, toiled, looked, punished, comforted,* and *hunted.* **Say:** These words refer to actions in the past. Not all past tense verbs end in *-ed.* Have students write these past tense verbs: *rode, sent,* and *sang* and list their present tenses. **EL**

Reading in the Real World

Citizenship Have students find magazine or newspaper articles about young adults who have sacrificed to help their families or society. Ask students to answer these questions: Who is the subject of the article? What did the person do? Who benefited? What inspired the act? **OL**

Academic Standards

Additional Support activities on p. 149 cover the following standards:

English Language Coach: **9.6.2** Demonstrate an understanding of…proper English usage, including the use of…verb tenses.

Reading in the Real World: **9.2.8** Make reasonable statements…about a text…

Teach

L1 Literary Element

Theme Answer: *The description of the mother's face as beautiful and radiant despite her suffering is a clue to the theme of the story, which includes sacrifice.* OL

L2 Literary Element

Hero Ask: Do you think the mother and father qualify as heroes? Why or why not? *(Possible answer: Many students will say that they are heroes because they had the admirable trait of working hard for their children. Some students might answer that they are not heroes because they are not main characters.)* OL

Viewing the Art

Answer: *The family in the painting might look like Buddy's family, although there were more children in Buddy's family.*

Ellis Wilson (1899–1977) grew up in Maysfield, Kentucky, a small town in tobacco country. He painted people going about everyday activities—cutting lumber in the swamps, harvesting and picking tobacco, going to church and market, and dancing. AS

Field Workers. Ellis Wilson. Oil on masonite, 29¾ × 34⅞ in. National Museum of American Art, Washington, D.C.

Viewing the Art: How is your view of the narrator's family similar to or different from the family represented in this painting? 

Then we would cluster around the rough wooden table—I on Lil's lap or clinging to Charley's neck, little Alberta nervously tugging her plait,[3] Jamie crouched at Mama's elbow, like a panther about to spring, and all seven of us silent for once, waiting. Pa would place the money on the table—gently, for it was made from the sweat of their bodies and from their children's tears. Mama would count it out in little piles, her dark face stern and, I think now, beautiful. Not with the hollow beauty of well-modeled features but with the strong radiance of one who has suffered and never yielded.

"This for store bill," she would mutter, making a little pile. "This for c'llection. This for piece o'gingham . . ."[4] and so on, stretching the money as tight over our **collective** needs as Jamie's outgrown pants were stretched over my bottom. "Well, that's the crop." She would look up at Pa at last. "It'll do." Pa's face would relax, and a general grin flitted from child to child. We would survive, at least for the present. L2

The other time when my parents were solid entities was at church. On Sundays we would don our threadbare Sunday-go-to-meeting

3. A *plait* (plāt) is a braid or pigtail.

4. *Gingham* (ging′ əm) is checked, striped, or plaid cotton fabric.

Literary Element Theme *So far, what possible clues to the story's theme do you notice?* L1

Vocabulary

collective (kə lek′ tiv) *adj.* having to do with a group of persons or things; common; shared

Additional Support

Leveled Reading An adapted version of this selection is available on page 124 of *Jamestown Literature: An Adapted Reader*, grade 9.

Skills Practice

LISTENING AND SPEAKING: Readers Theater Readers theater is dramatic reading with minimal preparation. Readers can stand or sit in front of the audience, read from the book, and make eye contact with the audience.

- Have small groups of students prepare a dramatic reading of the text. Allow them to decide how to divide the text.
- Remind students to give their reading dramatic appeal by adjusting the following qualities of their voices as they read: volume, rate, pitch, and rhythm. OL

clothes and tramp, along with neighbors similarly attired, to the Tabernacle Baptist Church, the frail edifice of bare boards held together by God knows what, which was all that my parents ever knew of security and future promise.

Being the youngest and therefore the most likely to err, I was plopped between my father and my mother on the long wooden bench. They sat huge and eternal like twin mountains at my sides. I remember my father's still, black profile silhouetted against the sunny window, looking back into dark recesses of time, into some dim **antiquity**, like an ancient ceremonial mask. My mother's face, usually sternly set, changed with the varying nuances[5] of her emotion, its planes shifting, shaped by the soft highlights of the sanctuary, as she progressed from a subdued "amen" to a loud "Help me, Jesus" wrung from the depths of her gaunt frame.

My early memories of my parents are associated with special occasions. The contours of my everyday were shaped by Lil and Charley, the oldest children, who rode herd on the rest of us while Pa and Mama toiled in fields not their own. Not until years later did I realize that Lil and Charley were little more than children themselves.

Lil had the loudest, screechiest voice in the county. When she yelled, "Boy, you better git yourself in here!" you *got* yourself in there. It was Lil who caught and bathed us, Lil who fed us and sent us to school, Lil who punished us when we needed punishing and comforted us when we needed comforting. If her voice was loud, so was her laughter. When she laughed, everybody laughed. And when Lil sang, everybody listened.

5. A *nuance* (no͞o′ äns) is a slight shade of tone, expression, or meaning.

Big Idea Rewards and Sacrifices *What sacrifices have the parents in this family made?* **BI**

Vocabulary

antiquity (an tik′ wə tē) *n.* an ancient time or times

Charley was taller than anybody in the world, including, I was certain, God. From his shoulders, where I spent considerable time in the earliest years, the world had a different perspective: I looked down at tops of heads rather than at the undersides of chins. As I grew older, Charley became more father than brother. Those days return in fragments of splintered memory: Charley's slender dark hands whittling a toy from a chunk of wood, his face thin and intense, brown as the loaves Lil baked when there was flour. Charley's quick fingers guiding a stick of charred kindling over a bit of scrap paper, making a wondrous picture take shape—Jamie's face or Alberta's rag doll or the spare figure of our bony brown dog. Charley's voice low and terrible in the dark, telling ghost stories so delightfully dreadful that later in the night the moan of the wind through the chinks in the wall sent us scurrying to the security of Charley's pallet, Charley's sleeping form.

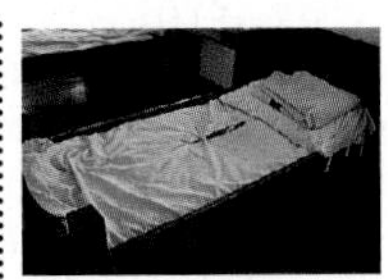

Visual Vocabulary
A *pallet* is a crude bed or mattress, usually filled with straw.

Some memories are more than fragmentary. I can still feel the *whap* of the wet dish rag across my mouth. Somehow I developed a stutter, which Charley was determined to cure. Someone had told him that an effective cure was to slap the stutterer across the mouth with a sopping wet dish rag. Thereafter whenever I began, "Let's g-g-g--," *whap!* from nowhere would come the **ubiquitous** rag. Charley would always insist, "I don't want hurt you none, Buddy—" and *whap* again. I don't know when or why I stopped stuttering. But I stopped.

Literary Element Theme *During his childhood, what did the narrator receive from Charley?* **L3**

Vocabulary

ubiquitous (ū bik′ wə təs) *adj.* seeming to be everywhere at once

Teach

BI Big Idea

Rewards and Sacrifices
Answer: *In order to support the children, the mother and father work long, hard hours and barely see their family.* **OL**

L3 Literary Element

Theme **Answer:** *Charley was a father figure for the narrator. He also was a brother to him and helped make the narrator's childhood happy.* **OL**

Building Reading Fluency

Learning New Words Have student pairs look up the meanings of words they do not understand. Partners should take turns rereading and paraphrasing passages with the unfamiliar words to gain understanding. Finally, partners should read the sections aloud, focusing on pronunciation and phrasing. **BL**

Differentiated Instruction

Role Playing Invite students to consider Buddy's personality and imagine how they would think, feel, and act in his situation. Have students write about their ideas in the form of a letter Buddy writes to his family as he is leaving home to go to college. **AL**

Academic Standards

Additional Support activities on pp. 150 and 151 cover the following standards:

Skills Practice: **9.7** [Develop] speaking skills…in conjunction with…strategies…[for] delivery of oral presentations.

Building Reading Fluency: **9.1** Use…context clues…to determine the meaning of words…

Differentiated Instruction: **9.5.2** Write responses to literature that support statements with evidence from the text… **9.6.4** Apply appropriate manuscript conventions…

Teach

R Reading Strategy

Questioning Answer: *Students may say the narrator received an education.* OL

BI Big Idea

Rewards and Sacrifices
Answer: *The family had worked in order for Buddy to succeed in school. His success was their reward.* OL

★ Writer's Technique

Using Dialect *Dialect* is a variation of a standard language spoken by a group of people, often within a particular region. Sentence structure, vocabulary, and pronunciation are affected by dialect. A writer uses dialect to enrich understanding of a character.

- Have a volunteer read aloud what Pa says to Buddy.
- Ask students to explain what Pa's language reveals about his character. AS

Already laid waste by poverty, we were easy prey for ignorance and superstition, which hunted us like hawks. We sought education feverishly—and, for most of us, **futilely**, for the sum total of our combined energies was required for mere brute survival. Inevitably each child had to leave school and bear his share of the eternal burden.

Eventually the family's hopes for learning fastened on me, the youngest. I remember—I *think* I remember, for I could not have been more than five—one frigid day Pa, huddled on a rickety stool before the coal stove, took me on his knee and studied me gravely. I was a skinny little thing, they tell me, with large, solemn eyes.

"Well, boy," Pa said at last, "if you got to depend on your looks for what you get out'n this world, you just as well lay down right now." His hand was rough from the plow, but gentle as it touched my cheek. "Lucky for you, you got a *mind*. And that's something ain't everybody got. You go to school, boy, get yourself some learning. Make something out'n yourself. Ain't nothing you can't do if you got learning."

Charley was determined that I would break the chain of poverty, that I would "be somebody." As we worked our small vegetable garden in the sun or pulled a bucket of brackish[6] water from the well, Charley would tell me, "You ain gon be no poor farmer, Buddy. You gon be a teacher or maybe a doctor or a lawyer. One thing, bad as you is you ain gon be no preacher."

I loved school with a desperate passion, which became more intense when I began to realize what a monumental struggle it was for my parents and brothers and sisters to keep me there. The cramped, dingy classroom became a battleground where I was victorious. I stayed on top of my class. With glee I out-read, out-figured, and out-spelled the country boys who mocked my poverty, calling me "the boy with eyes in back of his head"—the "eyes" being the perpetual holes in my hand-me-down pants.

As the years passed, the economic strain was eased enough to make it possible for me to go on to high school. There were fewer mouths to feed, for one thing: Alberta went North to find work at sixteen; Jamie died at twelve.

I finished high school at the head of my class. For Mama and Pa and each of my brothers and sisters, my success was a personal triumph. One by one they came to me the week before commencement bringing crumpled dollar bills and coins long hoarded, muttering, "Here, Buddy, put this on your gradiation clothes." My graduation suit was the first suit that was all my own.

On graduation night our cabin (less crowded now) was a frantic collage of frayed nerves. I thought Charley would drive me mad.

"Buddy, you ain pressed out them pants right . . . Can't you git a better shine on them shoes? . . . Lord, you done messed up that tie!"

Overwhelmed by the combination of Charley's nerves and my own, I finally exploded. "Man, cut it out!" Abruptly he stopped tugging at my tie, and I was afraid I had hurt his feelings. "It's okay, Charley. Look, you're strangling me. The tie's okay."

Charley relaxed a little and gave a rather sheepish chuckle. "Sure, Buddy." He gave my shoulder a rough joggle. "But you gotta look good. You *somebody*."

My valedictory address[7] was the usual idealistic, sentimental nonsense. I have forgotten what I said that night, but the sight of Mama

6. *Brackish* water tastes bad.

7. A *valedictory address* is a graduation speech, traditionally given by the class's highest-ranked student—the valedictorian.

Reading Strategy Questioning *"For most of us, futilely" implies that at least one child in the family did receive an education. Which one do you think received it?* R

Vocabulary
futilely (fū′ til ē) *adv.* uselessly; vainly; hopelessly

Big Idea Rewards and Sacrifices *How does this statement by the narrator relate to the theme of rewards and sacrifices?* BI

Additional Support

Skills Practice

READING: Contrasting Explain that contrasts are differences. The narrator describes people in his family by contrasting them so their differences stand out.

- List the characters' names on the board and ask students to identify their character traits. Example: Mother and Father are stern, hardworking; Lil is screechy-voiced, a caretaker; Charley is artistic; Buddy is smart; Bea is attentive and motherly.
- Have students discuss how contrasting helps readers visualize and understand characters. OL

and Pa and the rest is like a lithograph[8] burned on my memory; Lil, her round face made beautiful by her proud smile; Pa, his head held high, eyes loving and fierce; Mama radiant. Years later when her shriveled hands were finally still, my mind kept coming back to her as she was now. I believe this moment was the apex of her entire life. All of them, even Alberta down from Baltimore—different now, but united with them in her pride. And Charley, on the end of the row, still somehow the protector of them all. Charley, looking as if he were in the presence of something sacred.

As I made my way through the carefully rehearsed speech it was as if part of me were standing outside watching the whole thing—their proud, work-weary faces, myself wearing the suit that was their combined strength and love and hope: Lil with her lovely, low-pitched voice, Charley with the hands of an artist, Pa and Mama with God knows what potential lost with their sweat in the fields. I realized in that moment that I wasn't necessarily the smartest—only the youngest.

And the luckiest. The war came along, and I exchanged three years of my life (including a fair amount of my blood and a great deal of pain) for the GI Bill[9] and a college education. Strange how time can slip by like water flowing through your fingers. One by one the changes came—the old house empty at last, the rest of us scattered; for me, marriage, graduate school, kids, a professorship, and by now a thickening waistline and thinning hair. My mind spins off the years, and I am back to this afternoon and today's Charley—still long and lean, still gentle-eyed, still my greatest fan, and still determined to keep me on the ball.

I didn't tell Charley I would be at a professional meeting in New York and would surely visit; he and Bea would have spent days in fixing up, and I would have had to be company. No, I would drop in on them, take them by surprise before they had a chance to stiffen up. I was anxious to see them—it had been so long. Yesterday and this morning were taken up with meetings in the posh Fifth Avenue hotel—a place we could not have dreamed in our boyhood. Late this afternoon I shook loose and headed for Harlem, hoping that Charley still came home for a few hours before his evening run. Leaving the glare and glitter of downtown, I entered the subway which lurks like the dark, inscrutable *id*[10] beneath the surface of the city. When I emerged, I was in Harlem. ★

Whenever I come to Harlem I feel somehow as if I were coming home—to some mythic ancestral home. The problems are real, the people are real—yet there is some mysterious epic[11] quality about Harlem, as if all Black people began and ended there, as if each had left something of himself. As if in Harlem the very heart of Blackness pulsed its beautiful tortured rhythms. Joining the throngs of people that saunter Lenox Avenue late afternoons, I headed for Charley's apartment. Along the way I savored the panorama of Harlem—women with shopping bags trudging wearily home; little kids flitting saucily through the crowd; groups of adolescent boys striding boldly along—some boisterous, some ominously silent; tables of merchandise spread on the sidewalks with hawkers singing their siren songs[12] of irresistible bargains; a blaring microphone sending forth waves of words to draw passersby into a restless bunch around a slender young man whose eyes have seen Truth; defeated men standing around on street corners or sitting on steps, heads down, hands idle; posters announcing Garvey Day;[13] "Buy Black"

8. A *lithograph* is a picture printed by a process in which part of a flat surface is treated to retain ink, and part is treated to repel it.
9. The *G.I. Bill of Rights* provided educational and economic assistance to returning World War II soldiers.

10. In psychology, the *id* is the part of the personality that is associated with the most natural, primitive, and (to most people) mysterious drives for pleasure and satisfaction.
11. Here, *epic* means "majestic" or "heroic."
12. In mythology, *siren songs* were sung by sea nymphs, and sailors who heard these irresistible songs were drawn to their destruction.
13. *Garvey Day* is an unofficial holiday honoring Marcus Garvey (1887–1940), an African American leader during the 1920s.

Literary Element Theme *What did this insight help Buddy to understand about his family?* **L**

Teach

L Literary Element

Theme Answer: *It helped Buddy realize that his family had consciously chosen to sacrifice their own dreams and potential to help him. He was not the most gifted member of the family, but he was the luckiest.* **OL**

★ Writer's Technique

Figurative Language
Explain that writers often use figurative language to create powerful images in the reader's mind. To help students appreciate the simile "the subway which lurks like the dark, inscrutable *id* beneath the surface of the city," review the meaning of the word *id*.
Ask: How is the subway like the human id? *(Possible answer: The subway is deep, dark, and somewhat primitive when compared with the surface streets of the city.)* **AS**

English Language Coach

Mental Pictures Ask a volunteer to read aloud the paragraph that begins "Whenever I come to Harlem . . ." and ends ". . . a roaring fire from a single spark." Invite students to share their mental pictures they get from the details in this descriptive passage. Have students draw the images. **EL**

Differentiated Instruction

Research Have volunteers work together to prepare a report on Harlem. The report should expand on the author's description and contain current statistics and information. Allow time for the researchers to present their report and answer questions from the class. **AL**

Academic Standards
Additional Support activities on pp. 152 and 153 cover the following standards:
Skills Practice: **9.3** [Identify] story elements such as character…
English Language Coach: **9.3.7** Recognize and understand the significance of various literary devices, including…imagery…
Differentiated Instruction: **9.5.3** Write expository compositions, including…descriptive pieces…that communicate information…from…sources accurately and coherently…

Teach

BI Big Idea

Rewards and Sacrifices
Answer: *Charley had artistic talent but could never develop it nor get an education because he needed to work hard for the family and help raise his siblings. By doing so, he sacrificed any chance he had of living a better life when he got older.* OL

L1 Literary Element

Theme **Answer:** *He does not begrudge or resent Buddy at all, even though he sacrificed greatly to help him.* OL

R1 Reading Strategy

Questioning **Answer:** *Some students may wonder what Buddy's speech was about and how good a speaker he is. Others may wonder if Buddy is being humble so as not to make himself seem better than his family.* OL

stamped on pavements; store windows bright with things African; stores still boarded up, a livid[14] scar from last year's rioting. There was a terrible tension in the air; I thought of how quickly dry timber becomes a roaring fire from a single spark.

I mounted the steps of Charley's building—old and in need of paint, like all the rest—and pushed the button to his apartment. The graffiti on the dirty wall recorded the sexual fantasies of past visitors. Some of it was even a dialogue of sorts: Someone had scrawled, "Try Lola" and a telephone number, followed by a catalog of Lola's virtues. Someone else had written, "I tried Lola and she is a Dog." Charley's buzzer rang. I pushed open the door and mounted the urine-scented stairs.

"Well, do Jesus—it's Buddy!" roared Charley as I arrived on the third floor. "Bea! Bea! Come here, girl, it's Buddy!" And somehow I was simultaneously shaking Charley's hand, getting clapped on the back, and being buried in the fervor of Bea's gigantic hug. They swept me from the hall into their dim apartment.

"Lord, Buddy, what you doing here? Whyn't you tell me you was coming to New York?" His face was so lit up with pleasure that in spite of the inroads of time, he still looked like the Charley of years gone by, excited over a new litter of kittens.

"The place look a mess! Whyn't you let us know?" put in Bea, suddenly distressed.

"Looks fine to me, girl. And so do you!"

And she did. Bea is a fine-looking woman, plump and firm still, with rich brown skin and thick black hair.

"Mary, Lucy, look, Uncle Buddy's here!" Two neat little girls came shyly from the TV. Uncle Buddy was something of a celebrity in this house.

I hugged them heartily, much to their discomfort. "Charley, where you getting all these pretty women?"

We all sat in the warm kitchen, where Bea was preparing dinner. It felt good there. Beautiful odors mingled in the air. Charley sprawled in a chair near mine, his long arms and legs akimbo.[15] No longer shy, the tinier girl sat on my lap, while her sister darted here and there like a merry little water bug. Bea bustled about, managing to keep up with both the conversation and the cooking.

I told them about the conference I was attending and, knowing it would give them pleasure, I mentioned that I had addressed the group that morning. Charley's eyes glistened.

"You hear that, Bea?" he whispered. "Buddy done spoke in front of all them professors!"

"Sure I hear," Bea answered briskly, stirring something that was making an aromatic steam. "I bet he weren't even scared. I bet them professors learnt something, too."

We all chuckled. "Well anyway," I said, "I hope they did."

We talked about a hundred different things after that—Bea's job in the school cafeteria, my Jess and the kids, our scattered family.

"Seem like we don't git together no more, not since Mama and Pa passed on," said Charley sadly. "I ain't even got a Christmas card from Alberta for three-four year now."

"Well, ain't no two a y'all in the same city. An' everybody scratchin to make ends meet," Bea replied. "Ain't nobody got time to git together."

"Yeah, that's the way it goes, I guess," I said.

"But it sure is good to see you, Buddy. Say, look, Lil told me bout the cash you sent the children last winter when Jake was out of work all that time. She sure preciated it."

---

14. *Livid* can mean both "angry" and "bruised."

15. *Akimbo* (ə kim′ bō) means "being in a bent, bowed, or arched position."

Big Idea Rewards and Sacrifices *How does the description of where Charley lives tie in with the idea of sacrifice?* BI

Literary Element Theme *What admirable quality does Charley display here?* L1

Reading Strategy Questioning *What questions do you have at this point?* R1

Additional Support

Skills Practice

GRAMMAR: Proper Nouns Proper nouns name particular persons, places, things, or ideas. Write the following examples on the board: *Robert Smith, Houston, Empire State Building, Declaration of Independence.* Have students make a chart like the one shown. Ask them to scan the selection for proper nouns and write each in the correct column. OL

Names of People	
Names of Places	
Holidays	
Family Titles	
Religious Terms	

Rooftops (No. 1, This is Harlem), 1942–43. Jacob Lawrence. Gouache on paper, 14⅜ × 21⅞ in. Hirshhorn Museum and Sculpture Garden, Washington, D.C.

Viewing the Art: List three or four impressions about Harlem made by this scene. Does this picture fit Buddy's description of Harlem? Explain. ★

"Lord, man, as close as you and Lil stuck to me when I was a kid, I owed her that and more. Say, Bea, did I ever tell you about the time—" and we swung into the usual reminiscences.

They insisted that I stay for dinner. Persuading me was no hard job: fish fried golden, ham hocks and collard greens, corn bread—if I'd *tried* to leave, my feet wouldn't have taken me. It was good to sit there in Charley's kitchen, my coat and tie flung over a chair, surrounded by soul food and love.

R2 "Say, Buddy, a couple months back I picked up a kid from your school."

"No stuff."

"I axed him did he know you. He say he was in your class last year."

"Did you get his name?"

"No, I didn't ax him that. Man, he told me you were the best teacher he had. He said you were one smart cat!"

"He told you that cause you're my brother."

"Your *brother*—I didn't tell him I was your brother. I said you was a old friend of mine."

I put my fork down and leaned over. "What you tell him *that* for?"

Charley explained patiently as he had explained things when I was a child and had missed an obvious truth. "I didn't want your students to know your brother wasn't nothing but a cab driver. You *somebody*."

"You're a nut," I said gently. "You should've told that kid the truth." I wanted to say, I'm proud of you, you've got more on the ball than most people I know, I wouldn't have been anything at all except for you. But he would have been embarrassed.

Bea brought in the dessert—homemade sweet potato pie! "Buddy, I must of knew you were coming! I just had a mind I wanted to make some sweet potato pie."

There's nothing in this world I like better than Bea's sweet potato pie! "Lord, girl, how you expect me to eat all that?"

Literary Element Theme *What does this passage suggest about the message of the story?* L2

Teach

R2 Reading Strategy

Connecting Help students notice how Buddy's language becomes more like Charley's as they are speaking.

Ask: Why do you think Buddy starts using dialect when he is with Charley and Bea? *(Possible answer: Buddy is surrounded by his family, and he returns to speaking in a way that is more natural to him.)* OL

L2 Literary Element

Theme Answer: *Buddy realizes how much his family sacrificed for him and how much gratitude he feels toward Charley.* OL

★ Viewing the Art

Answer: *Students might point out the many buildings, the variety of venues, the people on the sidewalks, the liveliness–images that fit Buddy's description of Harlem.*

Jacob Lawrence (1917–2000) was one of the first painters to bring scenes of everyday African American life into mainstream consciousness. He painted images from his life experiences. His first concern was to convey a story; he was less interested in technique. AS

Differentiated Instruction

Standard vs. Nonstandard English

Ask students to review the dialogue on this page, paying close attention to the dialect.

- Have students choose a passage and rewrite the dialect as standard English.
- Ask students to read both the original and the rewritten passages aloud.
- Ask them to consider the effect each one has on the listener.
- Have students decide what effect the author wanted to convey by using dialect. AL

Academic Standards

Additional Support activities on pp. 154 and 155 cover the following standards:

Skills Practice: **9.6** [Use] appropriate mechanics of writing, such as...grammar...

Differentiated Instruction: **9.3.11** Evaluate the aesthetic qualities of style, including the impact of diction...on...theme.

Teach

R Reading Strategy

Questioning Answer: *Students may or may not be able to predict that Charley will try to stop Buddy from carrying the bag with the pie into the hotel.* OL

BI Big Idea

Rewards and Sacrifices
Answer: *This is important to Charley, who has sacrificed much more for Buddy.* OL

L Literary Element

Theme Ask: Why does Charley's action affect Buddy so strongly? *(It symbolizes a lifetime of familial love and sacrifice.)* OL

Use the CheckPoint questions on Presentation Plus! to check students' mastery of the selection. These questions can be used with interactive response keypads for immediate student feedback.

The slice she put before me was outrageously big—and moist and covered with a light, golden crust—I ate it all.

"Bea, I'm gonna have to eat and run," I said at last.

Charley guffawed. "Much as you et, I don't see how you gonna *walk,* let alone *run.*" He went out to get his cab from the garage several blocks away.

Bea was washing the tiny girl's face. "Wait a minute, Buddy, I'm gon give you the rest of that pie to take with you."

"Great!" I'd eaten all I could hold, but my spirit was still hungry for sweet potato pie.

Bea got out some waxed paper and wrapped up the rest of the pie. "That'll do you for a snack tonight." She slipped it into a brown paper bag.

I gave her a long good-bye hug. "Bea, I love you for a lot of things. Your cooking is one of them!" We had a last comfortable laugh together. I kissed the little girls and went outside to wait for Charley, holding the bag of pie reverently.

In a minute Charley's ancient cab limped to the curb. I plopped into the seat next to him, and we headed downtown. Soon we were assailed by the garish lights of New York on a sultry spring night. We chatted as Charley skillfully managed the heavy traffic. I looked at his long hands on the wheel and wondered what they could have done with artists' brushes.

We stopped a bit down the street from my hotel. I invited him in, but he said he had to get on with his evening run. But as I opened the door to get out, he commanded in the old familiar voice, "Buddy, you wait!" R

For a moment I thought my fly was open or something. "What's wrong?"

"What's that you got there?"

I was bewildered. "That? You mean this bag? That's a piece of sweet potato pie Bea fixed for me."

"You ain't going through the lobby of no big hotel carrying no brown paper bag."

"Man, you *crazy!* Of course I'm going—Look, Bea fixed it for me—*That's my pie*—"

Charley's eyes were miserable. "Folks in that hotel don't go through the lobby carrying no brown paper bags. That's *country*. And you can't neither. You *somebody,* Buddy. You got to be *right*. Now, gimme that bag."

"I want that pie, Charley. I've got nothing to prove to anybody—"

I couldn't believe it. But there was no point in arguing. Foolish as it seemed to me, it was important to him.

"You got to look *right,* Buddy. Can't nobody look dignified carrying a brown paper bag."

So finally, thinking how tasty it would have been and how seldom I got a chance to eat anything that good, I handed over my bag of sweet potato pie. If it was that important to him. BI

I tried not to show my irritation. "Okay, man—take care now." I slammed the door harder than I had intended, walked rapidly to the hotel, and entered the brilliant, crowded lobby.

"That Charley!" I thought. Walking slower now, I crossed the carpeted lobby toward the elevator, still thinking of my lost snack. I had to admit that of all the herd of people who jostled each other in the lobby, not one was carrying a brown paper bag. Or anything but expensive attaché cases or slick packages from exclusive shops. I suppose we all operate according to the symbols that are meaningful to us, and to Charley a brown paper bag symbolizes the humble life he thought I had left. I was *somebody.*

Visual Vocabulary
An *attaché* (at′ ə shā′) *case* is a slim briefcase.

I don't know what made me glance back, but I did. And suddenly the tears and laughter, toil and love of a lifetime burst around me like fireworks in a night sky. L

For there, following a few steps behind, came Charley, proudly carrying a brown paper bag full of sweet potato pie. ☙

Reading Strategy Questioning *Do you wonder why Charley is commanding Buddy to wait? What do you think he will say next?* R

Big Idea Rewards and Sacrifices *Why is Buddy willing to make this sacrifice for Charley?* BI

Additional Support

Academic Standards

Additional Support activities on pp. 156 and 157 cover the following standards:
Skills Practice: **9.3** Identify story elements…
Differentiated Instruction: **9.2.8** Make reasonable statements…

Skills Practice

READING: Problem and Solution

One strategy for reading stories is to think of them as a series of problems and solutions. There is a problem. The characters attempt to solve it. By the end of the story, the problem is solved or unresolved.

- Have students work in small groups to find and write down the problems and solutions in the selection, indicating whether each solution worked or not.
- Compile a master list in which the problems and solutions follow the sequence of events in the story. OL

AFTER YOU READ

RESPONDING AND THINKING CRITICALLY

Respond

1. What are your feelings about Buddy's family and the sacrifices they make to help Buddy succeed? Explain.

Recall and Interpret

2. (a)Who takes care of Buddy on a daily basis when he is a young boy? (b)How would you describe the relationship Buddy has with his siblings as he is growing up? Use details from the story to explain your response.
3. (a)What does Buddy accomplish that his parents and siblings do not? (b)What does Buddy mean when he says, "I wasn't necessarily the smartest—only the youngest."
4. (a)According to Buddy, what does the brown paper bag symbolize to Charley? (b)Why does Charley not mind carrying the paper bag?

Analyze and Evaluate

5. Charley withholds the truth about his identity from Buddy's former student. When Buddy hears this, he withholds the truth about his feelings for his brother. How are the brothers' decisions in keeping with their respective characters?
6. (a)When does Buddy speak in dialect, a variation of standard English, in this story? (b)Why might the author have chosen to have Buddy use dialect?

Connect

7. **Big Idea** **Rewards and Sacrifices** Explain what new insights into the concepts of reward and sacrifice you gained from reading the story "Sweet Potato Pie."

LITERARY ANALYSIS

Literary Element Theme

Some works have a **stated theme,** which is expressed directly. Other works have an **implied theme,** which is revealed gradually through events, dialogue, or description. A literary work may have more than one theme.

1. In your opinion, what is the central theme in "Sweet Potato Pie"? Is this theme stated or implied? Explain.
2. What details and descriptions in the story support the theme? Explain.

Review: Character

As you learned on pages 106–107, a **character** is an individual in a literary work. You have probably read short stories that featured characters with heroic qualities—characters whose personalities or deeds inspired your admiration. In your opinion, which character or characters in "Sweet Potato Pie" are heroic?

Partner Activity With a partner, go back through "Sweet Potato Pie" and use webs like the one shown to record details that reveal the characters' admirable qualities and deeds. Then discuss which character you consider to be the real hero of the story. Share your thoughts with the class.

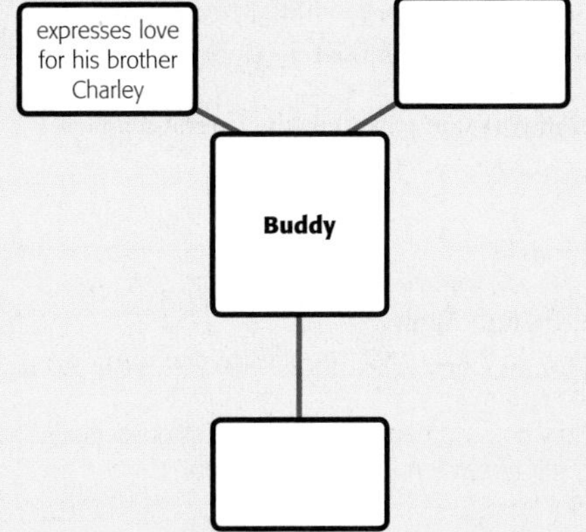

AFTER YOU READ

Assess

1. Students may think Charley and the rest of the family are warm, appealing, and admirable because they make such sacrifices for Buddy.
2. (a) Lil and Charley (b) Buddy sees his siblings—especially Lil and Charley—as parental figures and appreciates their care. He says, "Lil . . . punished us when we needed punishing and comforted us when we needed comforting," and "Charley became more father than brother."
3. (a) He completes his education. (b) His older siblings, who had to work in order to support the family and to cover Buddy's educational costs, had untapped potential.
4. (a) It symbolizes everything "country" and unsophisticated. (b) He is a "mere" cabdriver.
5. Students may say that Buddy and Charley have a special connection and try to protect each other.
6. (a) He speaks in dialect only when he is with Charley and Bea. (b) The author shows that Buddy can move between his two lives and that he has not completely changed.
7. Students may say they learned from Charley that true and loving sacrifice has no time limit.

Literary Element

1. The implied central theme is familial love and sacrifice.
2. Answers will vary, but may include: Buddy's family sacrifices everything so he can break free of their life of poverty and hard work.

Differentiated Instruction

Answering Questions Pair less proficient readers with more proficient readers. Have pairs read the questions before answering them.

Encourage students to clarify the meanings of unfamiliar words before answering the questions independently. BL

Review: Character

Students' character webs should include details and examples from the text that prove why the character is admirable. Encourage students to explain why they consider their choice the most heroic of all.

AFTER YOU READ

Assess

Reading Strategy

1. Sample questions: Plot: What happened this afternoon? Character: Why does the narrator visit Charley so seldom? Setting: Where is this impersonal, tidy room?
2. Students' responses will depend on the questions they have asked.

Vocabulary

1. ubiquity
2. collectively
3. antiquity
4. futilely

Academic Vocabulary

1. The parents carefully budget the small amount of money that they have and save what they can for their children's education.
2. To Buddy, the sweet potato pie represents comfort and tradition. To Charley, its bag represents a lack of status and sophistication. As a result, the brothers had a conflict over whether Buddy could carry it.

Writing About Literature

Students' essays should compare and contrast the qualities of the two types of African American life in the story. For example, the farming life in the South was poor and involved a lot of physical labor. The city of Harlem, on the other hand, is described as busy, exciting, and modern.

Interdisciplinary Activity

Encourage students to use library resources, including periodicals and online publications.

READING AND VOCABULARY

Reading Strategy Questioning

Active readers **ask questions** about the elements of fiction, such as the plot; the characters, their actions, and their motivations; and the setting.

1. Reread the second paragraph of "Sweet Potato Pie," beginning with "I turn from the window. . . ." Write three questions it might raise—one about plot, one about character, one about setting.
2. Work with a classmate to find clues and answers to your questions about the story.

Vocabulary Practice

Practice with Word Parts The suffix *–ity* turns adjectives into nouns. Likewise, the suffix *–ly* turns adjectives into adverbs. Choose the word that best completes each sentence.

antiquity collectively futilely ubiquity

1. The ____ of the pop star's photo was causing her to lose any sense of mystery.
2. We decided to pool our money and ____ sponsor the fundraiser.
3. The discovery of fire was monumental to the people of ____.
4. After ____ trying to win the game, the players slowly dragged themselves into the locker room.

Academic Vocabulary

Here are two words from the vocabulary list on page R80. These words will help you think, write, and talk about the selection.

economy (i kän′ ə mē′) *n.* the careful management of resources; thrift

item (ī′ təm) *n.* a separate thing in a grouping of things

Practice and Apply

1. How do Buddy's parents practice **economy** in their home?
2. How does an **item** of food cause a momentary conflict between Buddy and Charley?

WRITING AND EXTENDING

Writing About Literature

Analyze Cultural Context The narrator of "Sweet Potato Pie" describes life in a southern sharecropping family as well as a walk down a Harlem street to his brother's apartment building in New York City. Write an essay comparing and contrasting these two contexts of African American culture. Use evidence from the story as well as any personal experiences you may have had with rural or urban life.

Use a Venn diagram to help you generate and organize ideas.

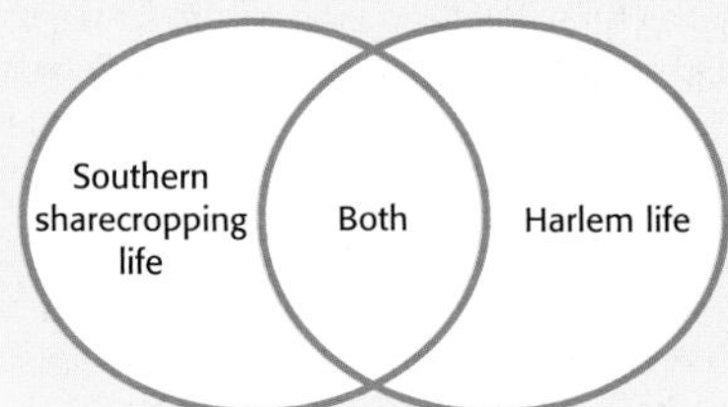

After completing your draft, meet with a peer reviewer to evaluate each other's work and suggest revisions. Then proofread and edit your draft for errors in spelling, grammar, and punctuation.

Interdisciplinary Activity: Science-Health

Sweet potato pie is a healthful, sweet ending to a meal. Research the nutrients this kind of pie contains, and then prepare a report for your class about the way the body uses these nutrients. You may wish to bake a sweet potato pie—and bring copies of the recipe—to share with your classmates.

Web Activities For eFlashcards, Selection Quick Checks, and other Web activities, go to www.glencoe.com.

Literature Online

Web Activities Have students access the Web site for interactive activities that will help them assess their understanding of the selection.

Academic Standards

The Additional Support activity on p. 159 covers the following standard:

English Language Coach: **9.6.2** Demonstrate an understanding of sentence construction…

Grammar Workshop

Sentence Structure

Avoiding Misplaced Modifiers

"Bea is a fine-looking woman, plump and firm still, with rich brown skin and thick black hair."

—Eugenia Collier, from "Sweet Potato Pie"

Connecting to Literature Eugenia Collier places modifiers where they belong: near or next to the words they modify. Look at the phrase "plump and firm still." It modifies, or tells more about, the word *woman*. Imagine, however, if the sentence had been written like this:

"Bea is a fine-looking woman with rich brown skin and thick black hair, plump and firm still."

In this sentence, the modifying phrase "plump and firm still" is a **misplaced modifier**. As is, it modifies *hair*. A misplaced modifier is a word or phrase that makes a sentence confusing because the modifier is in the wrong place.

To correct misplaced modifiers, think about what you want to say.

Problem 1 A misplaced phrase or group of words

Charley looks like an insect from the fourteenth floor.

Solution Move the word or phrase closer to the word it modifies.

From the fourteenth floor, Charley looks like an insect.

Problem 2 A misplaced word

The narrator only tells information about his family.

Solution Place modifiers such as *only* and *nearly* next to the word or words they modify.

The narrator tells information only about his family.

Exercise

Revise for Clarity Rewrite the following sentences, correcting any misplaced modifiers. If the sentence is correct, write *Correct.*

1. At Christmas time, Della has only $1.87, which isn't enough money for the right gift for Jim.
2. Della sells her hair to Madame Sofronie, which reaches below her knees.
3. Meanwhile, Jim sells his watch for Della for some hair combs.

Understanding Misplaced Modifiers

A **misplaced modifier** is a word or phrase that makes a sentence confusing because the modifier is in the wrong place.

Test-Taking Tip

If you are being tested on sentences, examine the modifiers. Remember that modifiers can be just one word, such as *only* or *nearly*; prepositional phrases; or other phrases and clauses, such as groups of words that begin with *who* or *that*. Then check to see if the modifiers are next to the words they are meant to modify.

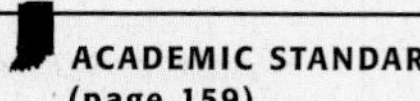

eWorkbooks To link to the Grammar and Language eWorkbook, go to www.glencoe.com.

ACADEMIC STANDARDS (page 159)

9.6.1 Identify and correctly use clauses, both main and subordinate...

9.6.2 Demonstrate an understanding of sentence construction...and the proper placement of modifiers...

Grammar Workshop

Sentence Structure

Focus

Write this sentence on the board: A few steps behind came a brown paper bag full of sweet potato pie proudly carried by Charley.
Rewrite it to read: A few steps behind came Charley, proudly carrying a brown paper bag full of sweet potato pie. Discuss how misplacing modifiers in a sentence can change the meaning.

Teach

Avoiding Misplaced Modifiers When correcting misplaced modifiers, students should reread to be sure that they make the correct change. Have students read Problem 1 and Solution 1. **Say:** You could also revise this sentence to read, *Charley, from the fourteenth floor, looks like an insect.* OL

Assess

Possible Rewrites:

1. Correct
2. Della sells her hair, which reaches below her knees, to Madame Sofronie.
3. Meanwhile, Jim sells his watch for some hair combs for Della.

eWorkbooks Have students access the Web site for more practice with avoiding misplaced modifiers.

English Language Coach

Syntax Help English learners understand that word order can be extremely important. Switching the order of two nouns that precede the verb usually does not change the meaning. For example, *The boy and the dog walked to the river* and *The dog and the boy walked to the river* have the same meaning. However, switching the order of the nouns that precede and follow the verb can change the meaning. For example, *The spider swallowed the fly* and *The fly swallowed the spider* have different meanings. EL

Focus

BELLRINGER

Bellringer Options
Selection Focus Transparency 11
Daily Language Practice Transparency 15

Or invite volunteers to share challenging or satisfying experiences they have had growing up with younger siblings. **Ask:** How have your feelings toward your siblings changed over time? Ask students to keep this discussion in mind as they read this story about a boy and his little brother.

Author Search To expand students' appreciation of James Hurst, have them access the Web site for additional information and resources.

BEFORE YOU READ

The Scarlet Ibis

MEET JAMES HURST

Brown magnolia petals, honeysuckle, and purple phlox: these are just a few of the flowers that might have grown on James Hurst's childhood farm and home in North Carolina. At the very least, they grew in his memory and served as inspiration for the glories of nature that appear in "The Scarlet Ibis." As a child, Hurst gained firsthand knowledge not only of nature's beauty but also of its fury. In the coastal South, he likely experienced a hurricane similar to the storm that blows the scarlet ibis far to the north in this story.

Not Only a Writer Hurst is a man of many experiences, talents, and careers. He holds a degree in chemical engineering from North Carolina State College and served in the army during World War II. To pursue his love of music, he studied at the Julliard School of Music in New York. He then went to Rome, where he lived for three years and continued to study music. When Hurst returned to the United States, he had a brief but unsuccessful career in opera. He then took a job at a large bank in New York City, where he worked for the next thirty-four years. Hurst was a bank employee by night and an author by day.

> *"Authors seldom understand what they write. That is why we have critics."*
>
> —James Hurst

During the 1950s and early 1960s, he published several short stories and a play. The pinnacle of his writing career occurred when the *Atlantic Monthly* published "The Scarlet Ibis" in 1960.

A Great Story "The Scarlet Ibis" was immediately heralded as a great piece of literature and has been reprinted in nearly every major literature textbook and in many anthologies. There are numerous reasons for its success. The beauty of the language, lure of the setting, emotional power of the plot, and the power of its two central symbols, the scarlet ibis and the swamp, have made it a favorite with readers and critics alike. Hurst himself, however, is modest about the story. While he admits that the setting is as much a character as either the narrator or his brother Doodle, Hurst leaves further interpretation to his readers.

At Home in North Carolina Today James Hurst still lives through "the clove of seasons" in North Carolina, on land not far from where he was born. Retired and living in the landscape that inspired his work, it seems likely that Hurst continues to believe—as he demonstrates in "The Scarlet Ibis"—in the power of nature and the beauty of the human spirit.

James Hurst was born in 1922.

LiteratureOnline **Author Search** For more about James Hurst, go to www.glencoe.com.

Selection Skills

The Scarlet Ibis

Literary Elements
- Characterization (SE pp. 161–174)
- Setting (SE p. 174)
- Similes (TWE p. 162)

Reading Skills
- Comparing and Contrasting Characters (SE pp. 161–174)
- Problem and Solution (TWE p. 164)
- Comparing and Contrasting (TWE p. 172)

Listening/Speaking/Viewing Skills
- Analyzing Art (SE pp. 165, 168; TWE p. 171)

Writing Skills/Grammar
- Respond to Character (SE p. 175)
- Prepositional Phrases (SE p. 175)
- Choosing Synonyms (TWE p. 166)
- Subjects and Predicates (TWE p. 168)

Vocabulary Skills
- Word Origins (SE p. 174)

LITERATURE PREVIEW

Connecting to the Story

Some brothers and sisters are very supportive of each other, while some compete or fight. Most have moments during which they are frustrated with one another. In "The Scarlet Ibis," a man wrestles with his childhood feelings about his younger brother. Before you read the story, think about the following questions:

- Can you imagine what it would feel like to be embarrassed by or ashamed of someone you care about?
- How might it feel to know that a close friend or family member felt embarrassed around you?

Building Background

This story is set on farmland in and around a swamp. Much of the story coincides with World War I, which was fought from 1914 to 1918.

A scarlet ibis is a tropical bird with bright red feathers; long, thin, red legs; a long, slender neck that can curve gracefully into an S-shape; a curved beak; and glossy black wing tips. The bird can reach a length of about twenty-three inches. It is native to South America but can occasionally be spotted in Florida and on the Gulf coast of Texas and Louisiana.

Setting Purposes for Reading

Big Idea Rewards and Sacrifices

As you read, think about all that the brothers gain from each other and all that they sacrifice for one another.

Literary Element Characterization

Characterization is the method a writer uses to reveal the personality of a character. A character can be revealed through the narrator's statements; through the character's words, thoughts, and actions; and through other characters' thoughts and comments. Characterization helps you understand a character's actions.

- See Literary Terms Handbook, p. R4.

LiteratureOnline Interactive Literary Elements Handbook To review or learn more about the literary elements, go to www.glencoe.com.

READING PREVIEW

Reading Strategy Comparing and Contrasting Characters

When you **compare and contrast characters,** you look for the similarities and differences between two or more characters in a literary work. In "The Scarlet Ibis," exploring similarities between the narrator and his brother Doodle will help you better understand the characters' motivations, the plot's events, and the story's themes.

Reading Tip: Making a Chart As you read, use a chart to organize your notes about the characters.

Narrator	Doodle
six years older than Doodle	six years younger than the narrator

Vocabulary

careen (kə rēn′) *v.* to tilt or sway while moving, as if out of control; p. 164 *The bicycle racers barely stay seated as they careen around the corner.*

serene (sə rēn′) *adj.* calm; peaceful; undisturbed; p. 167 *The water in the pond was still and serene.*

blighted (blīt′ əd) *adj.* damaged or spoiled; p. 168 *The blighted crops could not be sold.*

reiterate (rē it′ ə rāt′) *v.* to say again or do again; repeat; p. 170 *For most patients, doctors reiterate the same advice for staying healthy.*

precariously (pri kār′ ē əs lē) *adv.* dangerously; insecurely; p. 170 *The bundle was perched precariously on the shelf and seemed about to fall.*

Vocabulary Tip: Word Origins A word's origins are its history. Many words in English come from Latin, Greek, or French. Word origins can be found in a dictionary and are usually listed in brackets.

INDIANA ACADEMIC STANDARDS (pages 161–175)

9.3.4 Determine characters' traits by what the characters say about themselves in narration [and] dialogue...

9.3.3 Analyze interactions between characters...

9.5.2 Write responses to literature...

BEFORE YOU READ

Focus

Summary

The narrator tells about his childhood on a cotton farm in the Deep South between 1912 and 1918. His younger brother Doodle was expected to die in infancy but survives. The narrator has to lug Doodle everywhere, which is a burden in many ways. Over time, the boys become inseparable. Together, they conquer the seemingly impossible and push toward even greater feats. In the process, they must face limitations and cope with shame.

V Vocabulary

Vocabulary File Say: Add these words and definitions to your vocabulary file. For each word, include a sentence that gives an example of how to use the word. **OL** Students with English language needs should include the pronunciations of these words in their files. **EL**

Literary Elements Have students access the Web site to improve their understanding of characterization.

Selection Resources

Print Materials
- Unit 1 Resources (Fast File), pp. 56–58
- Leveled Vocabulary Development, p. 12
- Selection and Unit Assessments, pp. 25–26
- Selection Quick Checks, p. 13

Transparencies
- Bellringer Options Transparencies:
  Selection Focus Transparency 11
  Daily Language Practice Transparency 15
- Literary Elements Transparency 15

Technology
- TeacherWorks Plus™ CD-ROM
- StudentWorks Plus™ CD-ROM
- Presentation Plus!™ CD-ROM
- Literature Online, glencoe.com
- Online Student Edition, mhln.com
- Exam*View*® Assessment Suite CD-ROM
- Vocabulary PuzzleMaker CD-ROM
- Listening Library, disc 1 track 15

Teach

R1 Reading Strategy

Comparing and Contrasting Characters Answer: *The narrator is six years older.*
Ask: How does the narrator explain that Miss Leedie is different from his brother? *(Doodle is a "nice crazy"; Miss Leedie is a "crazy crazy.")* OL

★ Political History

President Woodrow Wilson Woodrow Wilson, to whom Miss Leedie wrote daily, served as the 28th president of the United States from 1913 to 1921. He led the country into World War I, and he also created and supported the League of Nations, forerunner of the United Nations, for which he received the Nobel Peace Prize. During his presidency, the 19th Amendment to the Constitution, giving women the right to vote, was passed and ratified. AS

Readability Scores
Dale-Chall: 6.5
DRP: 57
Lexile: 1070

Sunset Over the Marshes. Martin Johnson Heade.

THE SCARLET IBIS

James Hurst

It was in the clove[1] of seasons, summer was dead but autumn had not yet been born, that the ibis lit in the bleeding tree. The flower garden was stained with rotting brown magnolia petals and ironweeds grew rank[2] amid the purple phlox. The five o'clocks by the chimney still marked time, but the oriole nest in the elm was untenanted and rocked back and forth like an empty cradle. The last graveyard flowers were blooming, and their smell drifted across the cotton field and through every room of our house, speaking softly the names of our dead.

It's strange that all this is still so clear to me, now that that summer has long since fled and time has had its way. A grindstone stands where the bleeding tree stood, just outside the kitchen door, and now if an oriole sings in the elm, its song seems to die up in the leaves, a silvery dust. The flower garden is prim,[3] the house a gleaming white, and the pale fence across the yard stands straight and spruce. But sometimes (like right now), as I sit in the cool, green-draped parlor, the grindstone begins to turn, and time with all its changes is ground away—and I remember Doodle.

Doodle was just about the craziest brother a boy ever had. Of course, he wasn't a crazy crazy like old Miss Leedie, who was in love with President Wilson and wrote him a letter ★ every day, but was a nice crazy, like someone you meet in your dreams. He was born when I was six and was, from the outset, a disappointment. He seemed all head, with a tiny body which was red and shriveled like an old man's. Everybody thought he was

1. Here, a *clove* is a separation or split between two things.
2. Here, *rank* means "growing in vigorous, wild abundance."
3. Here, *prim* means "neat and trim."

Reading Strategy Comparing and Contrasting Characters *What differences between the narrator and his brother does the narrator point out?* R1

Additional Support

Leveled Reading An adapted version of this selection is available on page 82 of *Jamestown Literature: An Adapted Reader*, grade 9.

Skills Practice

LITERARY ELEMENT: Similes
A simile is a type of figurative language that uses *like* or *as* to compare two apparently unlike things. On page 163, the narrator says that Doodle would "collapse back onto the bed like an old worn-out doll."
Ask: What does Doodle have in common with a doll? *(He is limp and unable to sit up straight, like a doll that has lost its stuffing.)*

Have students identify and explain other similes on pages 162–163. *("rocked back and forth like an empty cradle," "body . . . like an old man's," "curtains . . . rustling like palmetto fronds," etc.)* OL going to die—everybody except Aunt Nicey, who had delivered him. She said he would live because he was born in a caul[4] and cauls were made from Jesus' nightgown. Daddy had Mr. Heath, the carpenter, build a little mahogany coffin for him. But he didn't die, and when he was three months old Mama and Daddy decided they might as well name him. They named him William Armstrong, which was like tying a big tail on a small kite. Such a name sounds good only on a tombstone.

L1

I thought myself pretty smart at many things, like holding my breath, running, jumping, or climbing the vines in Old Woman Swamp, and I wanted more than anything else someone to race to Horsehead Landing, someone to box with, and someone to perch with in the top fork of the great pine behind the barn, where across the fields and swamps you could see the sea. I wanted a brother. But Mama, crying, told me that even if William Armstrong lived, he would never do these things with me. He might not, she sobbed, even be "all there." He might, as long as he lived, lie on the rubber sheet in the center of the bed in the front bedroom where the white marquisette curtains billowed out in the afternoon sea breeze, rustling like palmetto fronds.

Visual Vocabulary
Palmetto fronds are the large, divided leaves of the palmetto, a small, ornamental palm tree.

It was bad enough having an invalid brother, but having one who possibly was not all there was unbearable, so I began to make plans to kill him by smothering him with a pillow. However, one afternoon as I watched him, my head poked between the iron posts of the foot of the bed, he looked straight at me and grinned. I skipped through the rooms, down the echoing halls, shouting, "Mama, he smiled. He's all there! He's all there!" and he was.

When he was two, if you laid him on his stomach, he began to try to move himself, straining terribly. The doctor said that with his weak heart this strain would probably kill him, but it didn't. Trembling, he'd push himself up, turning first red, then a soft purple, and finally collapse back onto the bed like an old worn-out doll. I can still see Mama watching him, her hand pressed tight across her mouth, her eyes wide and unblinking. But he learned to crawl (it was his third winter), and we brought him out of the front bedroom, putting him on the rug before the fireplace. For the first time he became one of us.

As long as he lay all the time in bed, we called him William Armstrong, even though it was formal and sounded as if we were referring to one of our ancestors, but with his creeping around on the deerskin rug and beginning to talk, something had to be done about his name. It was I who renamed him. When he crawled, he crawled backwards, as if he were in reverse and couldn't change gears. If you called him, he'd turn around as if he were going in the other direction, then he'd back right up to you to be picked up. Crawling backward made him look like a doodlebug,[5] so I began to call him Doodle, and in time even Mama and Daddy thought it was a better name than William Armstrong. Only Aunt Nicey disagreed. She said caul babies should be treated with special respect since they might turn out to be saints. Renaming my brother was perhaps the

4. The *caul* is a membrane, or layer of tissue, that sometimes clings to a baby's head at birth. It is thought by some to bring good luck and protection.

5. A *doodlebug* is the wormlike larva of the ant lion, which crawls backwards in order to dig a crater to trap ants and other insects.

Reading Strategy Comparing and Contrasting Characters *What differences between the narrator and his brother can you infer from this paragraph?* R2

Literary Element Characterization *What can you tell about the narrator based on his actions and words?* L2

Teach

L1 Literary Element

Ask: How does the narrator feel about the name given to the baby? *(He does not think the name is appropriate for the baby; it is too "big" for such a little baby.)* OL

R2 Reading Strategy

Comparing and Contrasting Characters **Answer:** *The narrator likes to run, jump, and climb; William Armstrong will never be able to do these things.*
Ask: How does the narrator feel about having a brother who is "different"? *(He is disappointed and ashamed.)* OL

L2 Literary Element

Characterization **Answer:** *He's thrilled to have a brother who will not embarrass him. His level of excitement shows that he was worried about his brother and didn't really want to harm him.* OL

CheckPoint

Use the CheckPoint questions on Presentation Plus! to monitor students' comprehension. These questions can be used with interactive response keypads for immediate student feedback.

English Language Coach

Names of Plants and Animals English learners will encounter many unfamiliar names of plants and animals. Challenge them to use context to determine whether the words fit the category *birds, insects,* or *plants.* Then invite them to look up the words in illustrated encyclopedias or nature guides. EL

Differentiated Instruction

Long Sentences Help students decode long sentences. Identify the main subject and verb (*He* and *might lie*) in the sentence on page 163 beginning "He might, as long as he lived. . . ." Students can then look at the phrases and clauses that give details. BL

Academic Standards

Additional Support activities on pp. 162 and 163 cover the following standards:

Skills Practice: **9.3.7** Recognize and understand the significance of various literary devices, including figurative language...

English Language Coach: **9.1** Use... context clues...to determine the meaning of words...

Differentiated Instruction: **9.6.2** Demonstrate an understanding of sentence construction...

Teach

BI Big Idea

Rewards and Sacrifices
Answer: *His brother cannot do the things the narrator can do. The narrator has to help his brother to do everything.* OL

L1 Literary Element

Characterization Answer: *The narrator has accepted the idea that he is stuck with his brother and willingly takes Doodle to a place they can both enjoy.*
Ask: How does the narrator treat his brother in the beginning? *(He is irritated with him and ignores his needs. He tries to discourage Doodle from wanting to come with him.)* OL

R Reading Strategy

Comparing and Contrasting Characters Answer: *The narrator can be cruel, as he is in this scene when he forces Doodle to look at and touch his own coffin.*
Ask: How does Doodle react to the way his brother treats him? *(Doodle does not get angry with his brother or return the cruelty. He tries to please his brother and to stay close to him.)* OL

kindest thing I ever did for him, because nobody expects much from someone called Doodle.

Although Doodle learned to crawl, he showed no signs of walking, but he wasn't idle. He talked so much that we all quit listening to what he said. It was about this time that Daddy built him a go-cart and I had to pull him around. At first I just paraded him up and down the piazza,[6] but then he started crying to be taken out into the yard and it ended up by my having to lug him wherever I went. If I so much as picked up my cap, he'd start crying to go with me and Mama would call from wherever she was, "Take Doodle with you."

He was a burden in many ways. The doctor had said that he mustn't get too excited, too hot, too cold, or too tired and that he must always be treated gently. A long list of don'ts went with him, all of which I ignored once we got out of the house. To discourage his coming with me, I'd run with him across the ends of the cotton rows and **careen** him around corners on two wheels. Sometimes I accidentally turned him over, but he never told Mama. His skin was very sensitive, and he had to wear a big straw hat whenever he went out. When the going got rough and he had to cling to the sides of the go-cart, the hat slipped all the way down over his ears. He was a sight. Finally, I could see I was licked. Doodle was my brother and he was going to cling to me forever, no matter what I did, so I dragged him across the burning cotton field to share with him the only beauty I knew, Old Woman Swamp. I pulled the go-cart through the saw-tooth fern, down into the green dimness where the palmetto fronds whispered by the stream. I lifted him out and set him down in the soft rubber grass beside a tall pine. His eyes were round with wonder as he gazed about him, and his little hands began to stroke the rubber grass. Then he began to cry.

"For heaven's sake, what's the matter?" I asked, annoyed.

"It's so pretty," he said. "So pretty, pretty, pretty."

After that day Doodle and I often went down into Old Woman Swamp. I would gather wildflowers, wild violets, honeysuckle, yellow jasmine, snakeflowers, and water lilies, and with wire grass we'd weave them into necklaces and crowns. We'd bedeck ourselves with our handiwork and loll about thus beautified, beyond the touch of the everyday world. Then when the slanted rays of the sun burned orange in the tops of the pines, we'd drop our jewels into the stream and watch them float away toward the sea.

There is within me (and with sadness I have watched it in others) a knot of cruelty borne by the stream of love, much as our blood sometimes bears the seed of our destruction, and at times I was mean to Doodle. One day I took him up to the barn loft and showed him his casket, telling him how we all had believed he would die. It was covered with a film of Paris green[7] sprinkled to kill the rats, and screech owls had built a nest inside it.

Doodle studied the mahogany box for a long time, then said, "It's not mine."

"It is," I said. "And before I'll help you down from the loft, you're going to have to touch it."

"I won't touch it," he said sullenly.

6. A *piazza* (pē äz′ ə) is a large covered porch.

7. *Paris green* is a poisonous green powder formerly used as a pesticide.

Big Idea Rewards and Sacrifices *Why does the narrator consider it a sacrifice to have to play with his brother?* BI

Vocabulary
careen (kə rēn′) *v.* to tilt or sway while moving, as if out of control

Literary Element Characterization *How has the narrator changed?* L1

Reading Strategy Comparing and Contrasting Characters *What qualities does the narrator have that are not evident in Doodle?* R

Additional Support

Skills Practice

READING: Problem and Solution
Most stories are built around a problem, or conflict, that needs to be solved. How the problem is solved makes up the story plot. Often, other smaller problems, in addition to the main problem, get solved along the way.

Write the following headings (but not the answers) on the board:
Main Problem: *(Brother wants Doodle to be a healthier and stronger playmate.)*
Solution: *(He treats Doodle roughly, hoping he will either stay at home or rise to the occasion.)*

A Wooded River Landscape, 1910. Peder Monsted. Oil on canvas, 43.25 × 43.25 cm. Private collection.
Viewing the Art: If the narrator had brought Doodle to a place like the one pictured, how might Doodle have reacted? ★

"Then I'll leave you here by yourself," I threatened, and made as if I were going down.

Doodle was frightened of being left. "Don't go leave me, Brother," he cried, and he leaned toward the coffin. His hand, trembling, reached out, and when he touched the casket he screamed. A screech owl flapped out of the box into our faces, scaring us and covering us with Paris green. Doodle was paralyzed, so I put him on my shoulder and carried him down the ladder, and even when we were outside in the bright sunshine, he clung to me, crying, "Don't leave me. Don't leave me."

Literary Element Characterization *How do the narrator's words and actions reveal two sides of his personality?* L2

Teach

L2 Literary Element

Characterization Answer: *The narrator's mean streak is revealed through his words, but his actions reveal his love.* OL

★ Viewing the Art

Answer: *On the basis of how Doodle reacted to Old Woman Swamp, he might react emotionally to this landscape. He is sensitive to beauty.*

Peder Monsted (1859–1941), an acclaimed Danish impressionist artist, was born in Grend, Denmark. He often worked in oil, painting portraits and landscapes such as this one. His paintings show his control of light and paint. He is best known for his scenes of snow-covered mountains and forests. AS

Related Problems: *(Brother doesn't want to take Doodle in the cart. Doodle hangs on and doesn't complain. Brother takes him and finds him to be a worthy companion.)*

After students complete the chart, discuss how problems and solutions affect the outcome of the story. OL

Differentiated Instruction

Illustrating Encourage students who have the ability to draw to illustrate at least one scene described on pages 164–165, such as Doodle in the go-cart, in the Old Woman Swamp, or in the barn loft. Have students share their pictures with the class. AL

Academic Standards

Additional Support activities on pp. 164 and 165 cover the following standards:

Skills Practice: **9.3** [Identify] story elements such as...plot...

Differentiated Instruction: **9.3** [Identify] story elements such as...setting...

Teach

BI1 Big Idea

Rewards and Sacrifices
Answer: *Seeing Doodle walk would make him proud, and knowing he is responsible would boost his ego. Also, if Doodle could walk, he would be less embarrassed by him.* OL

R1 Reading Strategy

Comparing and Contrasting Characters **Answer:** *They are united by the thrill and joy of success. They keenly feel the significance of the moment.*
Ask: Why is the narrator happy at the success? Why is Doodle happy? *(The narrator feels pride at the success, and now he does not have to carry Doodle. Doodle is happy because he is more independent and has pleased his brother.)* OL

★ Cultural History

Cotton It takes six to seven months for a cotton plant to mature. After about three months, white blossoms appear. After the blossoms fall off, small green pods, or bolls, containing the cotton fiber appear. When the ripened boll bursts open, revealing a white, fluffy ball of cotton, it is cotton-picking time. AS

When Doodle was five years old, I was embarrassed at having a brother of that age who couldn't walk, so I set out to teach him. We were down in Old Woman Swamp and it was spring and the sick-sweet smell of bay flowers hung everywhere like a mournful song. "I'm going to teach you to walk, Doodle," I said.

He was sitting comfortably on the soft grass, leaning back against the pine. "Why?" he asked.

I hadn't expected such an answer. "So I won't have to haul you around all the time."

"I can't walk, Brother," he said.

"Who says so?" I demanded.

"Mama, the doctor—everybody."

"Oh, you can walk," I said, and I took him by the arms and stood him up. He collapsed onto the grass like a half-empty flour sack. It was as if he had no bones in his little legs.

"Don't hurt me, Brother," he warned.

"Shut up. I'm not going to hurt you. I'm going to teach you to walk." I heaved him up again, and again he collapsed.

This time he did not lift his face up out of the rubber grass. "I just can't do it. Let's make honeysuckle wreaths."

"Oh yes you can, Doodle," I said. "All you got to do is try. Now come on," and I hauled him up once more.

It seemed so hopeless from the beginning that it's a miracle I didn't give up. But all of us must have something or someone to be proud of, and Doodle had become mine. I did not know then that pride is a wonderful, terrible thing, a seed that bears two vines, life and death. Every day that summer we went to the pine beside the stream of Old Woman Swamp, and I put him on his feet at least a hundred times each afternoon. Occasionally I too became discouraged because it didn't seem as if he was trying, and I would say, "Doodle, don't you *want* to learn to walk?"

He'd nod his head, and I'd say, "Well, if you don't keep trying, you'll never learn." Then I'd paint for him a picture of us as old men, white-haired, him with a long white beard and me still pulling him around in the go-cart. This never failed to make him try again.

Finally one day, after many weeks of practicing, he stood alone for a few seconds. When he fell, I grabbed him in my arms and hugged him, our laughter pealing through the swamp like a ringing bell. Now we knew it could be done. Hope no longer hid in the dark palmetto thicket but perched like a cardinal in the lacy toothbrush tree, brilliantly visible. "Yes, yes," I cried, and he cried it too, and the grass beneath us was soft and the smell of the swamp was sweet.

With success so imminent, we decided not to tell anyone until he could actually walk. Each day, barring rain, we sneaked into Old Woman Swamp, and by cotton-picking time ★ Doodle was ready to show what he could do. He still wasn't able to walk far, but we could wait no longer. Keeping a nice secret is very hard to do, like holding your breath. We chose to reveal all on October eighth, Doodle's sixth birthday, and for weeks ahead we mooned around the house, promising everybody a most spectacular surprise. Aunt Nicey said that, after so much talk, if we produced anything less tremendous than the Resurrection,[8] she was going to be disappointed.

At breakfast on our chosen day, when Mama, Daddy, and Aunt Nicey were in the dining room, I brought Doodle to the door in the go-cart just as usual and had them turn their backs, making them cross their hearts and hope to die if they peeked. I helped Doodle up, and when he was standing alone I let them look. There wasn't a sound as Doodle walked slowly across the room and sat down at his place at the table. Then

8. Here, the *Resurrection* refers to the Christian belief that Jesus rose from the dead after his burial.

Big Idea Rewards and Sacrifices *What benefit or reward does the narrator see in teaching Doodle to walk?* BI1

Reading Strategy Comparing and Contrasting Characters *How are the brothers alike at this moment?* R1

Additional Support

Skills Practice

WRITING: Choosing Synonyms
Read aloud this phrase: "So I won't have to haul you around." The author could have written, "So I won't have to carry you." In this case, *haul* is the better word choice because it evokes a certain image. Good writers choose synonyms for variety and to express precise meaning. Most synonyms have different shades of meaning.

Challenge students to explain the subtle differences between these pairs of synonyms: *right/correct; haste/hurry;* and *think/imagine.* Then have students use each word in a sentence. OL

Mama began to cry and ran over to him, hugging him and kissing him. Daddy hugged him too, so I went to Aunt Nicey, who was thanks praying in the doorway, and began to waltz her around. We danced together quite well until she came down on my big toe with her brogans, hurting me so badly I thought I was crippled for life.

Visual Vocabulary *Brogans* are sturdy, ankle-high shoes.

Doodle told them it was I who had taught him to walk, so everyone wanted to hug me, and I began to cry.

"What are you crying for?" asked Daddy, but I couldn't answer. They did not know that I did it for myself; that pride, whose slave I was, spoke to me louder than all their voices, and that Doodle walked only because I was ashamed of having a crippled brother.

Within a few months Doodle had learned to walk well and his go-cart was put up in the barn loft (it's still there) beside his little mahogany coffin. Now, when we roamed off together, resting often, we never turned back until our destination had been reached, and to help pass the time, we took up lying. From the beginning Doodle was a terrible liar and he got me in the habit. Had anyone stopped to listen to us, we would have been sent off to Dix Hill.[9]

My lies were scary, involved, and usually pointless, but Doodle's were twice as crazy. People in his stories all had wings and flew wherever they wanted to go. His favorite lie was about a boy named Peter who had a pet peacock with a ten-foot tail. Peter wore a golden robe that glittered so brightly that when he walked through the sunflowers they turned away from the sun to face him. When Peter was ready to go to sleep, the peacock spread his magnificent tail, enfolding the boy gently like a closing go-to-sleep flower, burying him in the gloriously iridescent,[10] rustling vortex.[11] Yes, I must admit it. Doodle could beat me lying.

Doodle and I spent lots of time thinking about our future. We decided that when we were grown we'd live in Old Woman Swamp and pick dog-tongue for a living. Beside the stream, he planned, we'd build us a house of whispering leaves and the swamp birds would be our chickens. All day long (when we weren't gathering dog-tongue) we'd swing through the cypresses on the rope vines, and if it rained we'd huddle beneath an umbrella tree and play stickfrog. Mama and Daddy could come and live with us if they wanted to. He even came up with the idea that he could marry Mama and I could marry Daddy. Of course, I was old enough to know this wouldn't work out, but the picture he painted was so beautiful and serene that all I could do was whisper Yes, yes.

Once I had succeeded in teaching Doodle to walk, I began to believe in my own infallibility and I prepared a terrific development program for him, unknown to Mama and Daddy, of course. I would teach him to run, to swim, to climb trees, and to fight. He, too, now believed in my infallibility, so we set the deadline for these accomplishments less than a year away,

9. *Dix Hill* refers to the state mental hospital in Raleigh, North Carolina.

10. The feathers are *iridescent,* or shimmering with rainbow colors.

11. A *vortex* is a whirling mass, like a whirlwind or whirlpool. Here, it is the wide funnel-shaped curve of the peacock's tail feathers.

Big Idea Rewards and Sacrifices *What does the narrator see as the reason, or reward, for teaching Doodle to walk? What do the adults probably think his reason is?* **BI2**

Reading Strategy Comparing and Contrasting Characters *Describe one possible reason for this difference between the two brothers.* **R2**

Literary Element Characterization *How has Doodle changed since the beginning of the story?* **L**

Vocabulary

serene (sə rēn′) *adj.* calm; peaceful; undisturbed

Teach

BI2 Big Idea

Rewards and Sacrifices
Answer: *The reward is no longer having to be ashamed of a crippled brother. The adults may think his reasons are less selfish—to help his brother.*
Ask: Do you think the narrator will be content with Doodle now that he has learned to walk? *(Now that the narrator has had a taste of success, he may continue to try to "improve" Doodle.)* **OL**

R2 Reading Strategy

Comparing and Contrasting Characters **Answer:** *Doodle has more need of a fictional world, as he faces disabilities in the real world. In his loneliness he has more time for an imaginative life.*
Ask: All the people in Doodle's "lies" have wings and fly. What does this say about Doodle's internal fantasies? *(His lies are well-imagined and express his dream of a world where people don't need to walk.)* **OL**

L Literary Element

Characterization **Answer:** *In addition to having learned to walk, Doodle now has confidence that his brother can succeed in teaching him.* **OL**

English Language Coach

Interpreting Point out the phrase "we took up lying" on page 167. Although the narrator continues to refer to the stories he and Doodle make up as "lies," they are actually just elaborate fantasies. Lying implies the attempt to deceive someone. **EL**

Differentiated Instruction

Creating Fantasies The boys' storytelling is just another shared activity, like playing in the swamp or swimming. Have partners make up a fantasy, like those created by the narrator and Doodle. Encourage students to write down and illustrate their fantasy, and share it with the class. **BL**

Academic Standards

Additional Support activities on pp. 166 and 167 cover the following standards:

Skills Practice: **9.5.7** Use varied and expanded vocabulary, appropriate for specific...topics.

English Language Coach: **9.1.2** Distinguish between what words mean literally and what they imply...

Differentiated Instruction: **9.5.1** Write... short stories that describe a sequence of events and communicate the significance of the events to the audience...

Teach

L1 Literary Element

Similes **Ask:** What similes are used on page 168? *(like a pot of gold; like the leaves; like a hawk)* Discuss what two things are being compared in each simile and how they are alike.

Viewing the Art

Answer: *The boys in the painting are shown enjoying a peaceful, idyllic time fishing in a boat. Like them, the boys in the story enjoyed a peaceful, idyllic summer, pursuing activities in a natural setting.*

Adam Albright was born in Monroe, Wisconsin. He was one of the first students of the prestigious Art Institute of Chicago, studying there from 1881 to 1883. Albright was noted for his landscapes, still lifes, and figures of country children, such as the boys shown in this image. AS

Young Fishermen in a Rowboat, 1909. Adam Emory Albright. Oil on canvas, 24 × 36 in. Private collection.
Viewing the Art: How does the mood of the painting reflect the mood of the boys' summer?

when, it had been decided, Doodle could start to school.

That winter we didn't make much progress, for I was in school and Doodle suffered from one bad cold after another. But when spring came, rich and warm, we raised our sights again. Success lay at the end of summer like a pot of gold, and our campaign got off to a good start. On hot days, Doodle and I went down to Horsehead Landing and I gave him swimming lessons or showed him how to row a boat. Sometimes we descended into the cool greenness of Old Woman Swamp and climbed the rope vines or boxed scientifically beneath the pine where he had learned to walk. Promise hung about us like the leaves, and wherever we looked, ferns unfurled and birds broke into song.

That summer, the summer of 1918, was **blighted.** In May and June there was no rain and the crops withered, curled up, then died under the thirsty sun. One morning in July a hurricane came out of the east, tipping over the oaks in the yard and splitting the limbs of the elm trees. That afternoon it roared back out of the west, blew the fallen oaks around, snapping their roots and tearing them out of the earth like a hawk at the

Vocabulary

blighted (blīt′ əd) *adj.* damaged or spoiled

Additional Support

Skills Practice

GRAMMAR: Subjects and Predicates The complete subject is the part of the sentence about which something is being said. The complete predicate has the verb and words that modify it or complete its meaning.

Write on the board:
Subject: Doodle and I
Predicate: went down to Horsehead Landing.

Have students write these sentences and underline each complete subject once and each complete predicate twice.

1. I heard a rain frog.
2. Wind and rain hurt the crops. OL

Visual Vocabulary
A *boll* is the rounded seed pod of the cotton plant.

entrails of a chicken. Cotton bolls were wrenched from the stalks and lay like green walnuts in the valleys between the rows, while the corn-field leaned over uniformly so that the tassels touched the ground. Doodle and I followed Daddy out into the cotton field, where he stood, shoulders sagging, surveying the ruin. When his chin sank down onto his chest, we were frightened, and Doodle slipped his hand into mine. Suddenly Daddy straightened his shoulders, raised a giant knuckly fist, and with a voice that seemed to rumble out of the earth itself began cursing heaven, hell, the weather, and the Republican Party.[12] Doodle and I, prodding each other and giggling, went back to the house, knowing that everything would be all right.

And during that summer, strange names were heard through the house: Château Thierry, Amiens, Soissons, and in her blessing at the supper table, Mama once said, "And bless the Pearsons, whose boy Joe was lost at Belleau Wood."[13]

So we came to that clove of seasons. School was only a few weeks away, and Doodle was far behind schedule. He could barely clear the ground when climbing up the rope vines and his swimming was certainly not passable. We decided to double our efforts, to make that last drive and reach our pot of gold. I made him swim until he turned blue and row until he couldn't lift an oar. Wherever we went, I purposely walked fast, and although he kept up, his face turned red and his eyes became glazed. Once, he could go no further, so he collapsed on the ground and began to cry.

"Aw, come on, Doodle," I urged. "You can do it. Do you want to be different from everybody else when you start school?"

"Does it make any difference?"

"It certainly does," I said. "Now, come on," and I helped him up.

As we slipped through dog days,[14] Doodle began to look feverish, and Mama felt his forehead, asking him if he felt ill. At night he didn't sleep well, and sometimes he had nightmares, crying out until I touched him and said, "Wake up, Doodle. Wake up."

It was Saturday noon, just a few days before school was to start. I should have already admitted defeat, but my pride wouldn't let me. The excitement of our program had now been gone for weeks, but still we kept on with a tired doggedness. It was too late to turn back, for we had both wandered too far into a net of expectations and had left no crumbs behind.

Daddy, Mama, Doodle, and I were seated at the dining-room table having lunch. It was a hot day, with all the windows and doors open in case a breeze should come. In the kitchen Aunt Nicey was humming softly. After a long silence, Daddy spoke. "It's so calm, I wouldn't be surprised if we had a storm this afternoon."

"I haven't heard a rain frog," said Mama, who believed in signs, as she served the bread around the table.

"I did," declared Doodle. "Down in the swamp."

12. Daddy probably curses the *Republican Party* because he, like most Southerners at the time of the story, was a Democrat.

13. *Château-Thierry* (shä tō tye rā′), *Amiens* (am ē ənz′), *Soissons* (swä sōn′), and *Belleau* (bel ō′) *Wood* were the sites of famous battles in France near the end of World War I.

14. *Dog days* are the hot, humid days of July and August.

Literary Element Characterization *What does this action reveal about Doodle and his relationship with his older brother?* **L2**

Reading Strategy Comparing and Contrasting Characters *How does the dialogue between the brothers reveal differences between them?* **R**

Big Idea Rewards and Sacrifices *What is Doodle sacrificing for his brother's plans?* **BI**

Literary Element Characterization *What might Doodle's words show about his character?* **L3**

Teach

L2 Literary Element

Characterization Answer: *Doodle reaches out to his brother for comfort and protection.*
Ask: How would you characterize Brother's treatment of Doodle? *(He appears to help Doodle, but he pushes him for his own satisfaction.)* **OL**

R Reading Strategy

Comparing and Contrasting Characters Answer: *Brother cares about Doodle's differences; Doodle does not.* **OL**

BI Big Idea

Rewards and Sacrifices
Answer: *Doodle may be sacrificing his health.* **OL**

L3 Literary Element

Characterization Answer: *He may be in tune with nature. Some students may say he is lying. His earlier "lies" are fanciful; this one is not.* **OL**

★ Language History

Dog Days The Egyptians, Greeks, and Romans thought the "dog star," Sirius, lent its heat to the sun. The Romans called hot days in July and August *caniculares dies* ("days of the dog"). People began using the term *dog days* for any long period of hot days. **AS**

Differentiated Instruction

Analyze and Interpret Have students work in pairs to chart Doodle's training program, using the following categories:
Purpose of program: *(to get Doodle ready for school)*
Program goals: *(to teach him to run, swim, climb trees, and fight)*
Deadline: *(before next autumn)*
Activities: *(swimming lessons, rowing practice, climbing vines, boxing)*
Obstacles: *(not enough time in winter, narrator goes to school, Doodle is often sick)* **BL**

Academic Standards

Additional Support activities on pp. 168 and 169 cover the following standards:
Skills Practice: **9.6.2** Demonstrate an understanding of sentence construction…
Differentiated Instruction: **9.3** [Identify] story elements such as…plot…

Teach

L1 Literary Element

Characterization Answer: *Doodle is greatly upset by what he sees. Perhaps he feels sympathy for the bird or views it as some kind of sign.* OL

L2 Literary Element

Characterization Answer: *This is the first time in the story that he takes the initiative.*
Ask: Why is it so important to him to bury the bird? *(Students may say he feels connected to nature and grief at the loss of the bird. He needs to give it a dignified burial.)* OL

★ Cultural History

Bird Identification Bird identification, or bird-watching, is a popular hobby in the United States. It requires binoculars and a field guide. Tropical birds caught in storms can end up far from their usual habitats. Some birds, such as Doodle's scarlet ibis, do not survive. AS

"He didn't," I said contrarily.

"You did, eh?" said Daddy, ignoring my denial.

"I certainly did," Doodle **reiterated,** scowling at me over the top of his iced-tea glass, and we were quiet again.

Suddenly, from out in the yard, came a strange croaking noise. Doodle stopped eating, with a piece of bread poised ready for his mouth, his eyes popped round like two blue buttons. "What's that?" he whispered.

I jumped up, knocking over my chair, and had reached the door when Mama called, "Pick up the chair, sit down again, and say excuse me."

By the time I had done this, Doodle had excused himself and had slipped out into the yard. He was looking up into the bleeding tree. "It's a great big red bird!" he called.

The bird croaked loudly again, and Mama and Daddy came out into the yard. We shaded our eyes with our hands against the hazy glare of the sun and peered up through the still leaves. On the topmost branch a bird the size of a chicken, with scarlet feathers and long legs, was perched **precariously.** Its wings hung down loosely, and as we watched, a feather dropped away and floated slowly down through the green leaves.

"It's not even frightened of us," Mama said.

"It looks tired," Daddy added. "Or maybe sick."

Doodle's hands were clasped at his throat, and I had never seen him stand still so long. "What is it?" he asked.

Daddy shook his head. "I don't know, maybe it's—"

At that moment the bird began to flutter, but the wings were uncoordinated, and amid much flapping and a spray of flying feathers, it tumbled down, bumping through the limbs of the bleeding tree and landing at our feet with a thud. Its long, graceful neck jerked twice into an S, then straightened out, and the bird was still. A white veil came over the eyes and the long white beak unhinged. Its legs were crossed and its clawlike feet were delicately curved at rest. Even death did not mar its grace, for it lay on the earth like a broken vase of red flowers, and we stood around it, awed by its exotic beauty.

"It's dead," Mama said.

"What is it?" Doodle repeated.

"Go bring me the bird book," said Daddy.

I ran into the house and brought back the bird book. As we watched, Daddy thumbed through its pages. "It's a scarlet ibis," he said, pointing to a picture. "It lives in the tropics—South America to Florida. A storm must have brought it here." ★

Sadly, we all looked back at the bird. A scarlet ibis! How many miles it had traveled to die like this, in *our* yard, beneath the bleeding tree.

"Let's finish lunch," Mama said, nudging us back toward the dining room.

"I'm not hungry," said Doodle, and he knelt down beside the ibis.

"We've got peach cobbler[15] for dessert," Mama tempted from the doorway.

Doodle remained kneeling. "I'm going to bury him."

"Don't you dare touch him," Mama warned. "There's no telling what disease he might have had."

"All right," said Doodle. "I won't."

Daddy, Mama, and I went back to the dining-room table, but we watched Doodle through the open door. He took out a piece

Literary Element Characterization *What do Doodle's actions show about him?* L1

Vocabulary

reiterate (rē it′ ə rāt′) *v.* to say again or do again; repeat

precariously (pri kār′ ē əs lē) *adv.* dangerously; insecurely

15. *Cobbler* is a deep-dish fruit pie with a thick top crust.

Literary Element Characterization *Has Doodle changed? Explain.* L2

Additional Support

Skills Practice

LISTENING AND SPEAKING:

Readers' Theater Readers' theater is a dramatic reading without actions. Readers stand or sit in front of the audience, read from a script or book, and make eye contact with the audience.

Have small groups give a dramatic reading of the text. Begin at "After a long silence, Daddy spoke," on page 169, and end at "'Specially *red* dead birds!" on page 171. Students should practice their parts before presenting their reading. Advise them to make their character come alive by adjusting the volume, rate, pitch, and rhythm of their voice. OL

Boy with Green Cap. Robert Henri. Oil on canvas. ★

Doodle didn't speak but nodded his head.

"Go wash your hands, and then you can have some peach cobbler," said Mama.

"I'm not hungry," he said.

"Dead birds is bad luck," said Aunt Nicey, poking her head from the kitchen door. "Specially *red* dead birds!"

As soon as I had finished eating, Doodle and I hurried off to Horsehead Landing. Time was short, and Doodle still had a long way to go if he was going to keep up with the other boys when he started school. The sun, gilded with the yellow cast of autumn, still burned fiercely, but the dark green woods through which we passed were shady and cool. When we reached the landing, Doodle said he was too tired to swim, so we got into a skiff and floated down the creek with the tide. Far off in the marsh a rail[16] was scolding, and over on the beach locusts were singing in the myrtle trees. Doodle did not speak and kept his head turned away, letting one hand trail limply in the water.

After we had drifted a long way, I put the oars in place and made Doodle row back against the tide. Black clouds began to gather in the southwest, and he kept watching them, trying to pull the oars a little

of string from his pocket and, without touching the ibis, looped one end around its neck. Slowly, while singing softly *Shall We Gather at the River,* he carried the bird around to the front yard and dug a hole in the flower garden, next to the petunia bed. Now we were watching him through the front window, but he didn't know it. His awkwardness at digging the hole with a shovel whose handle was twice as long as he was made us laugh, and we covered our mouths with our hands so he wouldn't hear.

When Doodle came into the dining room, he found us seriously eating our cobbler. He was pale and lingered just inside the screen door. "Did you get the scarlet ibis buried?" asked Daddy.

16. A *rail* is a small marsh bird.

Reading Strategy Comparing and Contrasting Characters *How does this scene underscore the differences between Doodle and his family?* **R**

Teach

R Reading Strategy

Comparing and Contrasting Characters **Answer:** *Doodle is moved by the death of the ibis and cannot eat, while the family is eating with great enthusiasm. Doodle seems more sensitive, or like a different species altogether.* **OL**

★ Viewing the Art

Robert Henri (1865–1929) painted portraits as well as realistic city scenes. Henri was a member of the Ashcan School, a group of painters portraying the stark realities of urban life. An influential art teacher, Henri believed that art should embody the spirit of its time. **AS**

Reading in the Real World

Career In the modern world, children with disabilities receive help from special educators. Their families might receive professional counseling in how to deal with the child's problems.

Have students who are interested in special-education careers read about children with physical and learning disabilities and the help that is available to them. Have them identify what specialists are employed in helping these children and then share their findings with the class. **OL**

Academic Standards

Additional Support activities on pp. 170 and 171 cover the following standards:

Skills Practice: **9.7.6** Analyze the occasion and...choose effective verbal... techniques...for presentations.

Reading in the Real World: **9.7.15** Deliver expository (informational) presentations that convey information and ideas from... sources accurately and coherently...

Teach

L1 Literary Element

Characterization Answer: *The narrator is still in control; he can still be insensitive and cruel; Doodle still looks to his brother for encouragement and approval.* OL

L2 Literary Element

Characterization Answer: *When the boys were in the loft, Doodle begged his brother not to leave him, and the narrator carried him down the ladder. Here, however, the narrator runs away from him. The narrator's pride and frustration have derailed his caring for his brother.*

The narrator is frank about his treatment of his brother, even when his cruelty leads to his brother's death. OL

faster. When we reached Horsehead Landing, lightning was playing across half the sky and thunder roared out, hiding even the sound of the sea. The sun disappeared and darkness descended, almost like night. Flocks of marsh crows flew by, heading inland to their roosting trees, and two egrets, squawking, arose from the oyster-rock shallows and careened away.

Doodle was both tired and frightened, and when he stepped from the skiff he collapsed onto the mud, sending an armada of fiddler crabs rustling off into the marsh grass. I helped him up, and as he wiped the mud off his trousers, he smiled at me ashamedly. He had failed and we both knew it, so we started back home, racing the storm. We never spoke (What are the words that can solder[17] cracked pride?), but I knew he was watching me, watching for a sign of mercy. The lightning was near now, and from fear he walked so close behind me he kept stepping on my heels. The faster I walked, the faster he walked, so I began to run. The rain was coming, roaring through the pines, and then, like a bursting Roman candle, a gum tree ahead of us was shattered by a bolt of lightning. When the deafening peal of thunder had died, and in the moment before the rain arrived, I heard Doodle, who had fallen behind, cry out, "Brother, Brother, don't leave me! Don't leave me!"

The knowledge that Doodle's and my plans had come to naught[18] was bitter, and that streak of cruelty within me awakened. I ran as fast as I could, leaving him far behind with a wall of rain dividing us. The drops stung my face like nettles, and the wind flared the wet glistening leaves of the bordering trees. Soon I could hear his voice no more.

I hadn't run too far before I became tired, and the flood of childish spite evanesced[19] as well. I stopped and waited for Doodle. The sound of rain was everywhere, but the wind had died and it fell straight down in parallel paths like ropes hanging from the sky. As I waited, I peered through the downpour, but no one came. Finally I went back and found him huddled beneath a red nightshade bush beside the road. He was sitting on the ground, his face buried in his arms, which were resting on his drawn-up knees. "Let's go, Doodle," I said.

He didn't answer, so I placed my hand on his forehead and lifted his head. Limply, he fell backwards onto the earth. He had been bleeding from the mouth, and his neck and the front of his shirt were stained a brilliant red.

"Doodle! Doodle!" I cried, shaking him, but there was no answer but the ropy rain. He lay very awkwardly, with his head thrown far back, making his vermilion[20] neck appear unusually long and slim. His little legs, bent sharply at the knees, had never before seemed so fragile, so thin.

I began to weep, and the tear-blurred vision in red before me looked very familiar. "Doodle!" I screamed above the pounding storm and threw my body to the earth above his. For a long long time, it seemed forever, I lay there crying, sheltering my fallen scarlet ibis from the heresy[21] of rain. ~

17. *Solder* (sod′ ər) means "to bond or repair."
18. *Naught* (nôt) means "nothing."

Literary Element Characterization *What fundamental difference between the brothers has not changed?* L1

Literary Element Characterization *How does the narrator's response to Doodle's cry compare with his response to a similar cry earlier in the story?* L2

19. *Evanesced* (ev′ ə nest′) means "faded away" or "vanished."
20. *Vermilion* is a bright red or scarlet color.
21. *Heresy* (her′ ə sē) is an action or opinion contrary to what is generally considered right, true, or proper.

Additional Support

Academic Standards

The Additional Support activity on p. 172 covers the following standard:

Skills Practice: **9.3.7** Recognize and understand the significance of various literary devices, including…symbolism…

Skills Practice

READING: Comparing and Contrasting Authors may use comparisons to make a point, to sharpen impressions, and to help the reader see the relationship between a symbol and the thing for which it stands. The narrator describes Doodle in death with details that remind the reader of the dead scarlet ibis. Have groups discuss how these details compare Doodle to the scarlet ibis (page 170).

- the "vermilion" stain on his neck and shirt
- the unusually long and slim appearance of his neck
- his fragile legs bent sharply OL

RESPONDING AND THINKING CRITICALLY

Respond

1. What emotions did you feel as you read the story? Why?

Recall and Interpret

2. (a)Name two things Doodle accomplishes despite the doctor's predictions. (b)What do Doodle's accomplishments reveal about his character?

3. (a)How is the narrator both kind and cruel to Doodle? (b)Why does the narrator set such high goals for Doodle?

4. (a)What happens to Doodle at the end of the story? (b)Do you think what happens to Doodle is the narrator's fault? Explain.

Analyze and Evaluate

5. (a)Why does the ibis die? (b)How does the death of the ibis serve as foreshadowing, or a clue that hints at later events in the plot?

6. (a)Why might Hurst have included references to World War I in the story? (b)Do these references enrich the story or move it away from its central focus? Explain.

7. (a)What emotions do you hear in the narrator's voice as he tells this story? (b)How do his word choices contribute to that tone? Cite three examples from the story to support your opinion.

Connect

8. Big Idea **Rewards and Sacrifices** What do the narrator and Doodle lose, or sacrifice, by being brothers, and what do they gain?

VISUAL LITERACY: Graphic Organizer

Using a Story Map

Copy the story map below and fill it in with as many details as you can. List minor and major characters as well as the settings of different scenes in the story. You may adjust the number of events.

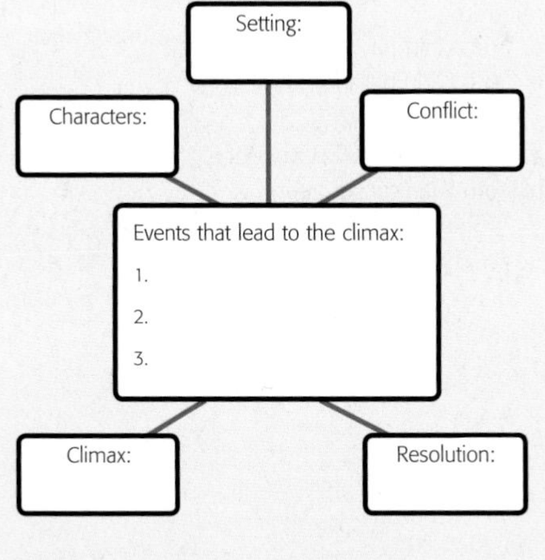

Group Activity Work with classmates to discuss and answer the following questions.

1. Use your story map to develop a summary of the story.
2. Use your story map and summary to reflect on the complexity of the story. Discuss what each of the following adds to the story:
   - the barn and cotton field settings
   - the Old Woman Swamp setting
   - settings that emphasize the change of season
   - the character of Aunt Nicey
   - the arrival of the scarlet ibis

Assess

1. Students may be upset, sad, or shocked at Doodle's death.

2. (a) He learns to crawl and to walk. (b) He has a strong will.

3. (a) He helps Doodle accomplish things but pushes him too hard. (b) He wants Doodle to be "normal" so he won't be embarrassed by him.

4. (a) He dies. (b) The narrator pushes him too hard and possibly hastens Doodle's death.

5. (a) It has been hurt in a storm. (b) The death hints at Doodle's death in the same storm.

6. (a) Hurst may want to call attention to a bloody war and the idea that brothers kill brothers during war. (b) This adds another level of tragic loss to the story.

7. (a) Students may hear a matter-of-fact, non-pitying tone in the child and sad regret in the adult. (b) Examples: the "tiny body which was red and shriveled like an old man's"; "Hope no longer hid in the dark palmetto thicket . . ."; "Promise hung about us. . . ."

8. Doodle died; the narrator lost faith in himself. They gained companionship. Doodle walked; the narrator gained satisfaction.

CheckPoint

Use the CheckPoint questions provided on Presentation Plus! to check students' mastery of the selection. These questions can be used with interactive response keypads for immediate student feedback.

Visual Literacy

1. Summaries should name time and place, main characters, the conflict, and all major events of the plot as they appear in the story map.

2. Students should note that the story is layered and complex. It shows the narrator's cruelty, the brothers' companionship, the sadness of changing seasons, superstitions and foreshadowing, and the ibis as a symbol of Doodle's fate.

AFTER YOU READ

Assess

Literary Element

1. Direct: He gives information about himself; he has a "knot of cruelty." Indirect: his thoughts and his actions show his character.
2. Direct: The narrator describes Doodle's physical appearance when he was born. Indirect: Doodle's words and actions reveal his character, such as his storytelling and taking his brother's hand when afraid.

Review: Setting

- beauty of natural world—stream, palmetto fronds, "green dimness," saw-tooth fern, soft rubber grass, tall pine: "the only beauty I knew"
- threat of natural world—high winds, hurricane, lightning; disabled children; injured birds
- symbolic qualities—Memory is a swamp with lush growth, but not everything there is good. A swamp is a place to get stuck; in the story, it is a place of both death and beauty; it is a memory the narrator escapes, especially in a certain season.

LITERARY ANALYSIS

Literary Element Characterization

In **direct characterization,** a narrator who is not a character in the story makes statements about a character, such as "he is smart" or "she runs a mining business." In **indirect characterization,** the writer reveals information about a character through his or her words, thoughts, and actions and through the comments and thoughts of other characters.

1. Is the characterization of the narrator of "The Scarlet Ibis" direct or indirect? Support your answer with examples from the story.
2. What methods of characterization are used to reveal Doodle's character? Provide examples from the text.

Review: Setting

As you learned on pages 10–11, **setting** is the time and place in which the events of a literary work occur. Setting includes not only physical surroundings, but also the ideas and customs of a place and time. In "The Scarlet Ibis," the setting is so vivid that it takes on a life of its own. This is one reason why Hurst personifies the swamp as Old Woman Swamp.

Partner Activity Meet with a partner to discuss the setting of the swamp. Make a web diagram like the one below and complete it with details or interpretations from the story.

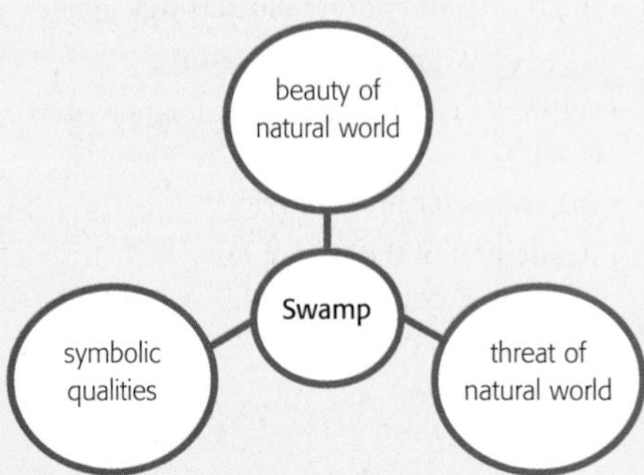

READING AND VOCABULARY

Reading Strategy Comparing and Contrasting Characters

In fiction, characters that have just one personality trait are called **flat characters,** whereas characters with varied and sometimes contradictory traits are called **round characters.** Likewise, a character that remains the same throughout the story is a **static character,** whereas a character that grows or changes during a story is a **dynamic character.**

1. Are the narrator and his brother flat or round characters? Cite evidence from the story to support your opinion.
2. Name one character in the story that is dynamic, and one that is static. Cite evidence from the story to support your opinion.

Vocabulary Practice

Practice with Word Origins Use a dictionary to identify the correct origins of the following words.

1. careen
   - **a.** from Latin for "keel of a ship"
   - **b.** from Middle English for "fall over"
2. serene
   - **a.** from Latin for "clear" or "cloudless"
   - **b.** from Greek for "quiet scene"
3. blight
   - **a.** from French for "ill"
   - **b.** origin unknown
4. reiterate
   - **a.** from Latin for "repeat"
   - **b.** from Old English for "tell again"
5. precariously
   - **a.** from Greek for "on the edge"
   - **b.** from Latin for "entreaty"

Reading Strategy

1. Both are round characters. The narrator is cruel and kind to Doodle; Doodle is generally accepting but sometimes frustrated and dejected.
2. Dynamic characters: the narrator and Doodle. The narrator looks back on his brother's life with adult understanding of his own cruelty. Doodle matures, but reverts to his early uncertainty at the end. Static characters: the parents and Aunt Nicey.

Vocabulary

1. a **2.** a **3.** b **4.** a **5.** b

WRITING AND EXTENDING

Writing About Literature

Respond to Character After the arrival of the scarlet ibis, the most significant event for Doodle in this story is learning to walk. Imagine that you are Doodle, and write a letter to your brother about this experience. Tell him how you felt before, during, and after you learned to walk. Write about negative as well as positive feelings.

To begin your prewriting, use a chart like the one below to identify some of your feelings and reactions.

Before	During	After

Use your prewriting ideas to develop separate paragraphs in your letter about each period of time and work chronologically. Conclude your letter with a summary statement or a final thought or insight that you want Brother to consider. Remember that your tone should be informal: you are writing to your own brother, who knows you better than anyone else.

After you complete your draft, have a partner read it and suggest revisions. Then proofread and edit your work for errors in spelling, grammar, and punctuation.

Literature Groups

A **symbol** is an object, person, place, or experience that represents something else. James Hurst has said that he chose the scarlet ibis as a symbol for Doodle. Discuss their similarities in appearance and in spirit. Consider Doodle's reaction to the bird and its death. Is the scarlet ibis a good symbol for Doodle? Why or why not? Share your conclusions with the class.

Literature Online **Web Activities** For eFlashcards, Selection Quick Checks, and other Web activities, go to www.glencoe.com.

GRAMMAR AND STYLE

Hurst's Language and Style

Using Prepositional Phrases In "The Scarlet Ibis," Hurst includes many flowing, descriptive sentences. Some have so many modifiers branching off from their verbs and nouns that they seem like the trailing vines of Old Woman Swamp. Hurst fleshes out his sentences with this much "growth" by using prepositional phrases. Read the sentence below, and notice how the prepositional phrases add necessary information as well as details that make the scene more vivid, interesting, or emotionally charged. Note, too, how the phrases help convey Hurst's nostalgic tone.

> The last graveyard flowers were blooming, and their smell drifted across the cotton field and through every room of our house, speaking softly the names of our dead.

Prepositional phrases work as modifiers in a sentence: they can tell which, whose, how, when, where, why, or to what extent. Study these examples of Hurst's use of prepositional phrases:

Prepositional Phrase	Word Modified	Tells
across the cotton field	drifted	where
through every room	drifted	where
of our dead	names	whose

Activity Use a chart like the one shown above to study other prepositional phrases from the story. Decide what each phrase adds to the meaning of the story, as well as how it helps to convey Hurst's tone.

Revising Check

Prepositional Phrases Using prepositional phrases can help you create more vivid imagery and convey a subtler tone. Work with a partner to find places in your letter where adding a prepositional phrase would make your letter more interesting, dramatic, or emotional. Revise your draft by adding a few well-chosen prepositional phrases.

AFTER YOU READ

Assess

Writing About Literature

Use these criteria to evaluate students' writing:

- Does the letter follow a chronological order of events?
- Is the tone informal and sincere, as if the letter were written to a brother?
- Does the letter conclude with a final thought or insight?

Literature Groups

Students' discussion should include specific points of comparison between Doodle and the scarlet ibis. Students should give details about Doodle's reaction to the bird's death and what this might imply. Students should offer reasons for their conclusion.

Hurst's Language and Style

The phrases add vivid details, create a nostalgic tone, and help the reader to understand where and when the events take place.

Sample answer:

Prepositional Phrase	Word Modified	Tells
in the dark palmetto thicket	hid	where
like a cardinal	perched	how
in the lacy toothbrush tree	cardinal	which
on hot days	went	when
to Horsehead Landing	went	where
of Old Woman Swamp	greenness	which

Revising Check

Use these criteria to evaluate students' writing:

- Does the writer show an understanding of prepositional phrases as modifiers?
- Do the prepositional phrases add necessary or vivid details?

Web Activities Have students access the Web site for interactive activities that will help them assess their understanding of the selection.

BEFORE YOU READ

Focus

BELLRINGER

Bellringer Options
Selection Focus Transparency 12
Daily Language Practice Transparency 16

Or **ask:** Have you ever observed someone pretending to be something that he or she was not in order to impress another person? What did you think of that person's behavior? As they read, students should observe how the main character behaves and the outcome of that behavior.

Author Search To expand students' appreciation of W. D. Wetherell, have them access the Web site for additional information and resources.

BEFORE YOU READ

The Bass, the River, and Sheila Mant

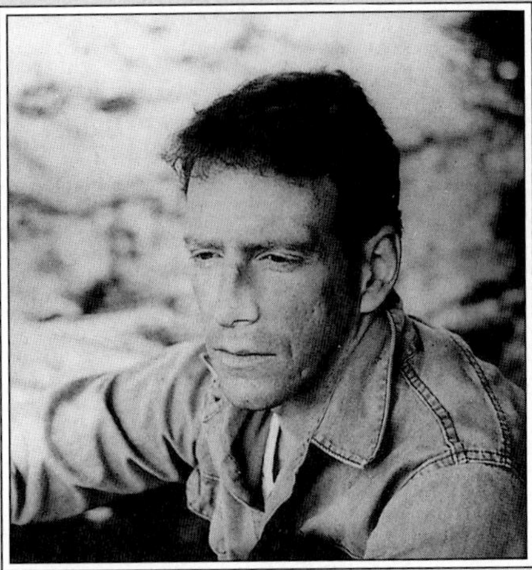

MEET W. D. WETHERELL

Author and fishing enthusiast W. D. Wetherell has been hooking readers since he first began publishing in the early 1980s. Born in a small town in New York, Wetherell was a shy child. By the time he was ten or eleven years old, he was interested in becoming a writer. Wetherell first wrote verse but soon switched to fiction, which he calls "the hardest kind of writing, the one demanding the most skill and imagination, the one you could really wrap a life around." Around the same time, Wetherell developed a passion for the outdoors of New England, and in particular for fishing. By the age of fourteen, Wetherell was spending many hours in solitary pursuit of big fish.

"Living modestly, with a certain leanness, brings joy unknown to those for whom money is no object."

—W. D. Wetherell

Early Career Wetherell wrote his first short story on the ping-pong table in his parents' basement at the age of nineteen. His early career was typical of that of many writers. He experienced eight long years of rejections before getting a piece accepted for publication. While attempting to make a living as a writer, Wetherell tried many jobs, from movie extra to tour guide. He refused to be deterred by early difficulties and eventually built a successful life as a writer. Wetherell has said that his work is "a testament of faith—in the power of art in general, and in the importance of fiction in particular."

The Country Life For many years, Wetherell has lived with his wife and two children in western New Hampshire, close enough to water to cast a fishing line. Without a computer or television, he lives a quiet life, enjoying the simple pleasures of fishing, watching the stars, reading poetry, and collecting local history.

In his work, Wetherell promotes a way of life that he believes is fast disappearing: a simple life spent in tune with nature. He calls himself "a walker in a sedentary age; a lover of quiet in a century that has the volume turned up full blast; a reader in a visual age; a writer in one that is increasingly aliterate."

To this day, Wetherell is an ardent fisherman and frequently writes about fishing. Much of his work is set in the places where Wetherell loves to fish—New Hampshire and Vermont.

Wetherell has published several novels as well as collections of short stories and essays. His work has earned him many prestigious awards, including the O. Henry Award for fiction.

W. D. Wetherell was born in 1948.

Literature Online **Author Search** For more about W. D. Wetherell, go to www.glencoe.com.

Selection Skills

The Bass, the River, and Sheila Mant

Literary Elements
- Motif (SE pp. 177–185)
- Plot (SE p. 185)

Reading Skills
- Connecting to Personal Experience (SE pp. 177–186)
- Previewing (TWE p. 178)
- Making Predictions (TWE p. 180)

Vocabulary Skills
- Analogies (SE p. 186; TWE p. 180)
- Academic Vocabulary (SE p. 186)

Writing Skills/Grammar
- Evaluating Author's Craft (SE p. 186)

Listening/Speaking/Viewing Skills
- Analyzing Art (SE p. 180; TWE pp. 182, 184)

LITERATURE PREVIEW

Connecting to the Story

Having a crush can make a person do unusual things. Before you read this story, think about the following questions:

- Under what circumstances would you quit your favorite hobby?
- Have you ever concealed something about yourself from someone you wanted to impress?

Building Background

The largemouth black bass of New England likes warm, slow-moving rivers and muddy-bottomed, weedy lakes. During the day it swims in the deeper shaded areas of the water, moving into shallower areas at night. The average largemouth bass lives about eight years, measures just over fourteen inches, and weighs one and one half pounds, but some bass weigh as much as eleven pounds. Most bass fishers are passionate about their sport: the fish are challenging to catch but delicious to eat. The river in the title of this story is the Connecticut River, which runs between New Hampshire and Vermont.

Setting Purposes for Reading

Big Idea Rewards and Sacrifices

At least once in our lives, most of us face a difficult choice between two attractive options. As you read, think about what the narrator in the story hopes to gain—and what he is willing to sacrifice to get it.

Literary Element Motif

A **motif** is a significant word, phrase, image, description, or idea repeated throughout a literary work. Motifs help to express a work's theme, or overall message. As you read, pay attention to ideas or images that recur throughout the story. Think about what larger truth the author may be hinting at by repeating these ideas.

- See Literary Terms Handbook, p. R11.

LiteratureOnline Interactive Literary Elements Handbook To review or learn more about the literary elements, go to www.glencoe.com.

READING PREVIEW

Reading Strategy Connecting to Personal Experience

When you **connect a story to your personal experience,** you link it to events in your own life or to other selections you have read. Connecting can help you to better appreciate and understand the story. As you read, think about what it feels like to experience an intense crush.

Reading Tip: Making a Chart As you read, make a chart to show the connections you share with characters and events in the story.

Detail	My Connection
p. 178 "... before July was over I had learned all her moods."	Most people will wait for a long time before they get up the nerve to ask a person out.

Vocabulary

pensive (pen′ siv) *adj.* thinking deeply, often sadly; p. 178 *Rowena was pensive as she studied the photograph of the forest fire.*

dubious (do͞o′ bē əs) *adj.* skeptical; feeling doubt; p. 181 *I was dubious when Lee claimed that she had jumped ten feet.*

surreptitiously (sur′ əp tish′ əs lē) *adv.* secretly or slyly; p. 182 *The child approached the cookie jar surreptitiously.*

inhibition (in′ i bish′ ən) *n.* a restraint on one's natural impulses; p. 182 *An inhibition prevented Jody from laughing in the presence of elders.*

lithe (līth) *adj.* limber; bending easily; p. 183 *The lithe gymnast easily bent forward to touch her toes.*

Vocabulary Tip: Analogies Analogies are comparisons based on relationships between things or ideas. To complete an analogy, decide what relationship exists in a pair of words. Choose the word that creates the same relationship in a second pair.

INDIANA ACADEMIC STANDARDS (pages 177–186)
9.3.7 Recognize...the significance of...literary devices...
9.2 Develop [reading] strategies...
9.5.3 Write expository compositions...that gather evidence in support of a thesis...

BEFORE YOU READ

Focus

Summary

A 14-year-old boy who is an avid fisherman develops a crush on Sheila Mant, the 17-year-old girl next door. As he paddles her in his canoe, Sheila announces that fishing is dumb, just as a fish attacks his lure. During the journey, the boy is torn between the girl of his dreams and the biggest bass he ever hooked. In the end, he makes a choice between the two and learns a valuable lesson about life and love.

V Vocabulary

Vocabulary File Say: Add these words and definitions to your vocabulary file. For each word, include a sentence that gives you an example of how to use the word. **OL** Students with English language needs should include the pronunciations of these words in their files. **EL**

Literary Elements Have students access the Web site to improve their understanding of motif.

Selection Resources

Print Materials
- Unit 1 Resources (Fast File), pp. 59–61
- Leveled Vocabulary Development, p. 13
- Selection and Unit Assessments, pp. 26–27
- Selection Quick Checks, p. 14

Transparencies
- Bellringer Options Transparencies: Selection Focus Transparency 12, Daily Language Practice Transparency 16
- Literary Elements Transparency 19

Technology
- TeacherWorks Plus™ CD-ROM
- StudentWorks Plus™ CD-ROM
- Presentation Plus!™ CD-ROM
- Literature Online, glencoe.com
- Online Student Edition, mhln.com
- Exam*View*® Assessment Suite CD-ROM
- Vocabulary PuzzleMaker CD-ROM
- Listening Library, disc 1 track 16

Teach

L1 Literary Element

Motif Answer: *Students may say that the bass, Sheila Mant, or both, may figure as a motif in the story.*
Ask: What does this first sentence suggest the story will be about? *(It may be about a summer love.)* OL

V Vocabulary

Multiple-Meaning Words Point out the multiple-meaning word *observant* on this page. One meaning is "conscientious about observing a custom or a rule."
Ask: What is another meaning of this word? Which definition applies to the word in this case?*(Another meaning is "alert, or quick to notice"; this definition fits the use on this page.)* OL

Use the CheckPoint questions on Presentation Plus! to monitor students' comprehension. These questions can be used with interactive response keypads for immediate student feedback.

Readability Scores
Dale-Chall: 9.4
DRP: 62
Lexile: 1110

The Bass, the River, and Sheila Mant

W. D. Wetherell

There was a summer in my life when the only creature that seemed lovelier to me than a largemouth bass was Sheila Mant. I was fourteen. The Mants had rented the cottage next to ours on the river; with their parties, their frantic games of softball, their constant comings and goings, they appeared to me denizens[1] of a brilliant existence.

"Too noisy by half," my mother quickly decided, but I would have given anything to be invited to one of their parties, and when my parents went to bed I would sneak through the woods to their hedge and stare enchanted at the candlelit swirl of white dresses and bright, paisley skirts.

Sheila was the middle daughter—at seventeen, all but out of reach. She would spend her days sunbathing on a float my Uncle Sierbert had moored in their cove, and before July was over I had learned all her moods. If she lay flat on the diving board with her hand trailing idly in the water, she was **pensive,** not to be disturbed. On her side, her head propped up by her arm, she was observant, considering those around her V with a look that seemed queenly and severe. Sitting up, arms tucked around her long, suntanned legs, she was approachable, but barely, and it was only in those glorious moments when she stretched herself prior to entering the water that her various suitors found the courage to come near.

These were many. The Dartmouth heavyweight crew[2] would scull[3] by her house on their way upriver, and I think all eight of

1. A *denizen* (den′ ə zən) is an inhabitant or occupant.
2. *Dartmouth heavyweight crew* refers to one of the rowing teams from Dartmouth College in Hanover, New Hampshire.
3. Here, *scull* means "propel by rowing."

Literary Element Motif *What clues to a possible motif, or recurring idea, does the first sentence of the story give you?* L1

Vocabulary
pensive (pen′ siv) *adj.* thinking deeply, often sadly

Additional Support

Skills Practice

READING: Previewing This story deals with a young man's conflict between wanting to impress a girl and denying something he loves. When the narrator gets what he thinks is a date with a girl he admires, he has to decide how much he will give up to impress her.

Have students think about these questions as they read:

- Have you ever had an intense crush on someone?
- What did you do—or would you do—to impress that person?
- Is there something you would not give up to impress that person? OL

them must have been in love with her at various times during the summer; the coxswain[4] would curse at them through his megaphone, but without effect—there was always a pause in their pace when they passed Sheila's float. I suppose to these jaded twenty-year-olds she seemed the incarnation of innocence and youth,[5] while to me she appeared unutterably suave, the epitome of sophistication.[6] I was on the swim team at school, and to win her attention would do endless laps between my house and the Vermont shore, hoping she would notice the beauty of my flutter kick, the power of my crawl. Finishing, I would boost myself up onto our dock and glance casually over toward her, but she was never watching, and the miraculous day she was, I immediately climbed the diving board and did my best tuck and a half for her, and continued diving until she had left and the sun went down and my longing was like a madness and I couldn't stop.

It was late August by the time I got up the nerve to ask her out. The tortured will-I's, won't-I's, the agonized indecision over what to say, the false starts toward her house and embarrassed retreats—the details of these have been seared from my memory, and the only part I remember clearly is emerging from the woods toward dusk while they were playing softball on their lawn, as bashful and frightened as a unicorn. Sheila was stationed halfway between first and second, well outside the infield. She didn't seem surprised to see me—as a matter of fact, she didn't seem to see me at all.

4. On a crew team, the *coxswain* (kok′ sən) steers the boat and directs the timing of the team's oar strokes.
5. The narrator imagines that the college men, being dulled by long experience *(jaded)* with women, see Sheila as the personification or purest form *(incarnation)* of adolescent innocence.
6. The narrator believes Sheila is polished and gracious *(suave)* beyond words *(unutterably)* and the *epitome* (i pit′ ə mē), or perfect example, of mature, worldly experience.

Reading Strategy Connecting to Personal Experience *How do you act when you want to impress someone?* **R**

"If you're playing second base, you should move closer," I said.

She turned—I took the full brunt of her long red hair and well-spaced freckles.

"I'm playing outfield," she said, "I don't like the responsibility of having a base."

"Yeah, I can understand that," I said, though I couldn't. "There's a band in Dixford tomorrow night at nine. Want to go?"

One of her brothers sent the ball sailing over the leftfielder's head; she stood and watched it disappear toward the river.

"You have a car?" she said, without looking up.

I played my master stroke. "We'll go by canoe."

I spent all of the following day polishing it. I turned it upside down on our lawn and rubbed every inch with Brillo, hosing off the dirt, wiping it with chamois until it gleamed as bright as aluminum ever gleamed.[7] About five, I slid it into the water, arranging cushions near the bow so Sheila could lean on them if she was in one of her pensive moods, propping up my father's transistor radio by the middle thwart[8] so we could have music when we came back. Automatically, without thinking about it, I mounted my Mitchell reel on my Pfleuger spinning rod and stuck it in the stern.

I say automatically, because I never went anywhere that summer without a fishing rod. When I wasn't swimming laps to impress Sheila, I was back in our driveway practicing casts, and when I wasn't practicing casts, I was tying the line to Tosca, our springer spaniel, to test the reel's drag, and when I wasn't doing any of those things, I was fishing the river for bass. **BI2**

7. *Brillo* is the brand name of a steel-wool pad used to scrub and clean, and *chamois* (sham′ ē) is a very soft, absorbent leather used to dry and polish.
8. In a canoe, a *thwart* is a brace running from side to side.

Big Idea Rewards and Sacrifices *Why is the narrator willing to sacrifice truthfulness?* **BI1**

Literary Element Motif *Why is fishing important to the narrator?* **L2**

Teach

R Reading Strategy

Connecting to Personal Experience **Answer:** *Answers will vary. Students may say they relate to the narrator's attempts to impress Sheila.* **OL**

BI1 Big Idea

Rewards and Sacrifices
Answer: *Perhaps the narrator's crush on Sheila is "like a madness," and he has lost all perspective.* **OL**

BI2 Big Idea

Rewards and Sacrifices
Have students read the bracketed passage.
Ask: Based on this passage, and what you have read so far about the narrator's feelings, do you think it would be a great sacrifice for him to give up fishing to impress Sheila? Why or why not? *(Some students may say it would not be a great sacrifice, since he has such a crush on Sheila; others may say fishing is very important to him; giving it up would be a great sacrifice.)* **OL**

L2 Literary Element

Motif **Answer:** *Students may say fishing is a contest of will for the narrator or that fishing represents the type of thoughtful life that the narrator values.* **OL**

English Language Coach

Building Background The setting for this story is a river on the border between the states of Vermont and New Hampshire. Ask volunteers to find it on a map. Invite students familiar with the region to talk about the climate and geography or help students use an atlas or other reference to find information.

Encourage volunteers to describe fishing methods used in their culture. Create a word web of fishing terms with students. **EL**

Academic Standards
Additional Support activities on pp. 178 and 179 cover the following standards:
Skills Practice: **9.2** Develop [reading] strategies…
English Language Coach: **9.3** [Identify] story elements such as…setting…

Teach

V Vocabulary

Analogies Refer students to the vocabulary word *dubious* and its definition on page 181. Then have students complete the following analogy:

dubious : certain :: solitude:

______

(Students may suggest words such as companionship *or* company.*)*

Ask: What is the relationship between the words in this analogy?*(These words are antonyms.)* OL

Viewing the Art

Answer: *Students may say that the quiet, sheltered scene showing a waterfront house, pier, and canoe are similar to the story setting they imagine.*

Award-winning artist Ed Labadie paints in watercolor and oil. He uses vivid colors and geometric shapes to create compelling compositions. His works include abstracts, outdoor scenes, and images of wildlife. AS

Country House with Canoe, 1996. Ed Labadie. Watercolor on paper, $17\frac{1}{2} \times 10\frac{1}{2}$ in. Collection of the artist. 

Viewing the Art: How well does the scene in this painting match how you imagine the story's setting?

Additional Support

Skills Practice

READING: Making Predictions

A prediction is an informed guess about what will happen in a story based upon personal experience and evidence from the text. Have students predict whether the narrator's "date" with Sheila will be a pleasant experience. Have them consider these questions:

- How has Sheila treated him up to this point in the story?
- What is the significance of her sitting with her back to him?
- What does Sheila's mention that Eric Caswell will be at the dance signify? OL

Too nervous to sit at home, I got in the canoe early and started paddling in a huge circle that would get me to Sheila's dock around eight. As automatically as I brought along my rod, I tied on a big Rapala plug, let it down into the water, let out some line and immediately forgot all about it.

It was already dark by the time I glided up to the Mants' dock. Even by day the river was quiet, most of the summer people preferring Sunapee or one of the other nearby lakes, and at night it was a solitude difficult to believe, a corridor of hidden life that ran between banks like a tunnel. Even the stars were part of it. They weren't as sharp anywhere else; they seemed to have chosen the river as a guide on their slow wheel toward morning, and in the course of the summer's fishing, I had learned all their names.

I was there ten minutes before Sheila appeared. I heard the slam of their screen door first, then saw her in the spotlight as she came slowly down the path. As beautiful as she was on the float, she was even lovelier now—her white dress went perfectly with her hair, and complimented her figure even more than her swimsuit.

It was her face that bothered me. It had V on its delightful fullness a very **dubious** expression.

"Look," she said. "I can get Dad's car."

"It's faster this way," I lied. "Parking's tense up there. Hey, it's safe. I won't tip it or anything."

She let herself down reluctantly into the bow. I was glad she wasn't facing me. When her eyes were on me, I felt like diving in the river again from agony and joy.

I pried the canoe away from the dock and started paddling upstream. There was an extra paddle in the bow, but Sheila made no move to pick it up. She took her shoes off, and dangled her feet over the side.

Ten minutes went by.

"What kind of band?" she said.

"It's sort of like folk music. You'll like it."

"Eric Caswell's going to be there. He strokes number four."[9]

"No kidding?" I said. I had no idea who she meant.

"What's that sound?" she said, pointing toward shore.

"Bass. That splashing sound?"

"Over there."

"Yeah, bass. They come into the shallows at night to chase frogs and moths and things. Big largemouths. *Micropetrus salmonides*,"[10] I added, showing off.

"I think fishing's dumb," she said, making a face. "I mean, it's boring and all. Definitely dumb."

Now I have spent a great deal of time in the years since wondering why Sheila Mant should come down so hard on fishing. Was her father a fisherman? Her antipathy[11] toward fishing nothing more than normal filial rebellion? Had she tried it once? A messy encounter with worms? It doesn't matter. What does, is that at that fragile moment in time I would have given anything not to appear dumb in Sheila's severe and unforgiving eyes.

She hadn't seen my equipment yet. What I *should* have done, of course, was push the canoe in closer to shore and carefully slide the rod into some branches where I could pick it up again in the morning. Failing that, I could have **surreptitiously** dumped the

9. Eric *strokes*, or rows, in the *number four* position in the racing scull.

10. The narrator probably means to say *Micropterus salmoides* (mī crop´ tə rəs sal moi´ dēz), the scientific name for the largemouth bass.

11. *Antipathy* (an tip´ ə thē) means "intense dislike."

Reading Strategy **Connecting to Personal Experience** *Can you imagine feeling the way the narrator is feeling? Explain.* R1

Vocabulary

dubious (dōō´ bē əs) *adj.* skeptical; feeling doubt

Reading Strategy **Connecting to Personal Experience** *Considering what you know of human nature, what do you predict will happen at the concert?* R2

Vocabulary

surreptitiously (sur´ əp tish´ əs lē) *adv.* secretly or slyly

Teach

R1 **Reading Strategy**

Connecting to Personal Experience **Answer:** *Students may say they have felt this way before.* **Ask:** Why do you think Sheila does not face the narrator in the boat? *(Students may suggest that Sheila is not really interested in the narrator. She just wants a ride to the dance.)* OL

R2 **Reading Strategy**

Connecting to Personal Experience **Answer:** *Students may predict Sheila will leave the narrator to spend time with Eric Caswell.* OL

Building Reading Fluency

Reading Dialogue Students can build reading fluency by working in groups of three to read the story aloud. Ask students to read from the first dialogue on page 181 through the end of the story. Have one student read the narrative. Have the other two read the dialogue spoken by the narrator and Sheila. Remind these students to use their voices to reflect what their character is thinking or feeling. Remind students that the story is told by an adult looking back on his experience as a boy. BL

Academic Standards

Additional Support activities on pp. 180 and 181 cover the following standards:

Skills Practice: **9.3.3** Analyze interactions between characters...and explain the way those interactions affect the plot.

Building Reading Fluency: **9.7** [Develop] speaking skills...in conjunction with... strategies...[for] delivery of oral presentations.

Teach

L1 Literary Element

Motif Answer: *Fishing represents the narrator's truest self, which he cannot escape even though he would like to appear otherwise for Sheila.* OL

R1 Reading Strategy

Connecting to Personal Experience Ask: How does Sheila respond to the explanation that the buzzing sound is bats? *(She shudders and takes her feet out of the water.)*

Ask: How would you respond? Why? *(Most students would respond the same way, because most people find bats distasteful.)*

Ask: What does Sheila's easy acceptance of the explanation tell you about her? *(She has never heard a bat or been around people fishing, or she would recognize the sound of the reel.)* OL

★ Viewing the Art

An early Impressionist, teacher and painter Fred Wagner (1864–1940) used a dark palette to represent the landscapes and industrial sites of Pennsylvania and New York City. His brushwork is associated with artist Robert Henri's influence. AS

The Carnival. Fred Wagner. Pastel. David David Gallery, Philadelphia. ★

whole outfit overboard, written off the forty or so dollars as love's tribute.[12] What I actually *did* do was gently lean forward, and slowly, ever so slowly, push the rod back through my legs toward the stern where it would be less conspicuous.

It must have been just exactly what the bass was waiting for. Fish will trail a lure sometimes, trying to make up their mind whether or not to attack, and the slight pause in the plug's speed caused by my adjustment was tantalizing enough to overcome the bass's **inhibitions.** My rod, safely out of sight at last, bent double. The line, tightly coiled, peeled off the spool with the shrill, tearing zip of a high-speed drill.

Four things occurred to me at once. One, that it was a bass. Two, that it was a big bass. Three, that it was the biggest bass I had ever hooked. Four, that Sheila Mant must not know.

"What was that?" she said, turning half around.

"Uh, what was what?"

"That buzzing noise."

"Bats."

She shuddered, quickly drew her feet back into the canoe. Every instinct I had told me to pick up the rod and strike back at the bass, but there was no need to—it was already solidly hooked. Downstream, an awesome distance downstream, it jumped clear of the water, landing with a concussion heavy enough to ripple the entire river. For a moment, I thought it was gone, but then the rod was bending again, the tip dancing into the water. Slowly, not making any motion that might alert Sheila, I reached down to tighten the drag.

While all this was going on, Sheila had begun talking and it was a few minutes before I was able to catch up with her train of thought.

"I went to a party there. These fraternity men. Katherine says I could get in there if I wanted. I'm thinking more of UVM or Bennington.[13] Somewhere I can ski."

The bass was slanting toward the rocks on the New Hampshire side by the ruins of Donaldson's boathouse. It had to be an old bass—a young one probably wouldn't have known the rocks were there. I brought the canoe back out into the middle of the river, hoping to head it off.

"That's neat," I mumbled. "Skiing. Yeah, I can see that."

"Eric said I have the figure to model, but I thought I should get an education first. I mean, it might be a while before I get started and all. I was thinking of getting my hair styled, more swept back? I mean, Ann-Margret?[14] Like hers, only shorter."

12. Here, a *tribute* is a payment showing devotion, respect, or gratitude.

13. *UVM* refers to the University of Vermont at Burlington; *Bennington* is a small, private college, also in Vermont.

14. *Ann-Margret* is an actress and singer who was a young, glamorous movie star at the time of the story.

Vocabulary

inhibition (in′ i bish′ ən) *n.* a restraint on one's natural impulses

Literary Element Motif *Why does fishing intrude upon the narrator's date with Sheila?* L1

Additional Support

Skills Practice

WRITING: Prepositional Phrases

Prepositional phrases can act as adjectives or adverbs.

Write: *The bass was slanting toward the rocks on the New Hampshire side.*

In the example, *toward the rocks* is an adverb phrase that tells where the bass was slanting. *On the New Hampshire side* is an adjective phrase modifying the noun *rocks.*

Ask students to write five sentences using two or more prepositional phrases in each. Have them use a single underline to indicate a phrase that acts as an adjective and a double underline to indicate a phrase that acts as an adverb. OL

She hesitated. "Are we going backwards?"

We were. I had managed to keep the bass in the middle of the river away from the rocks, but it had plenty of room there, and for the first time a chance to exert its full strength. I quickly computed the weight necessary to draw a fully loaded canoe backwards—the thought of it made me feel faint.

"It's just the current," I said hoarsely. "No sweat or anything."

I dug in deeper with my paddle. Reassured, Sheila began talking about something else, but all my attention was taken up now with the fish. I could feel its desperation as the water grew shallower. I could sense the extra strain on the line, the frantic way it cut back and forth in the water. I could visualize what it looked like—the gape of its mouth, the flared gills and thick, vertical tail. The bass couldn't have encountered many forces in its long life that it wasn't capable of handling, and the unrelenting tug at its mouth must have been a source of great puzzlement and mounting panic.

Me, I had problems of my own. To get to Dixford, I had to paddle up a sluggish stream that came into the river beneath a covered bridge. There was a shallow sandbar at the mouth of this stream—weeds on one side, rocks on the other. Without doubt, this is where I would lose the fish.

"I have to be careful with my complexion. I tan, but in segments. I can't figure out if it's even worth it. I wouldn't even do it probably. I saw Jackie Kennedy[15] in Boston and she wasn't tan at all."

Taking a deep breath, I paddled as hard as I could for the middle, deepest part of the bar. I could have threaded the eye of a needle with the canoe, but the pull on the stern threw me off and I overcompensated—the canoe veered left and scraped bottom. I pushed the paddle down and shoved. A moment of hesitation . . . a moment more . . . . The canoe shot clear into the deeper water of the stream. I immediately looked down at the rod. It was bent in the same, tight arc—miraculously, the bass was still on.

The moon was out now. It was low and full enough that its beam shone directly on Sheila there ahead of me in the canoe, washing her in a creamy, luminous glow. I could see the **lithe**, easy shape of her figure. I could see the way her hair curled down off her shoulders, the proud, alert tilt of her head, and all these things were as a tug on my heart. Not just Sheila, but the aura[16] she carried about her of parties and casual touchings and grace. Behind me, I could feel the strain of the bass, steadier now, growing weaker, and this was another tug on my heart, not just the bass but the beat of the river and the slant of the stars and the smell of the night, until finally it seemed I would be torn apart between longings, split in half. Twenty yards ahead of us was the road, and once I pulled the canoe up on shore, the bass would be gone, irretrievably gone. If instead I stood up, grabbed the rod and started pumping, I would have it—as tired as the bass was, there was no chance it could get away. I reached down for the rod, hesitated, looked up to where Sheila was stretching herself lazily toward the sky, her small breasts rising beneath the soft fabric of her dress, and the tug was too much for me, and quicker than it takes to write down, I pulled the penknife from my pocket and cut the line in half. L3

15. *Jackie Kennedy* (1929–1994), President John F. Kennedy's wife, was admired by many as a role model and style setter.

16. Here, Sheila's *aura* is a sort of atmosphere or quality that the narrator senses around her.

Big Idea Rewards and Sacrifices *What choice is the narrator struggling with?* BI

Literary Element Motif *What could be the deeper meaning of the bass's hold on the line?* L2

Reading Strategy Connecting to Personal Experience *If you had been in this situation, how would you have responded?* R2

Vocabulary

lithe (līth) *adj.* limber; bending easily

Teach

BI Big Idea

Rewards and Sacrifices
Answer: *He struggles to choose between impressing Sheila Mant and catching the large bass, thus revealing himself as a fisherman.*

Ask: How does each choice represent both a reward and a sacrifice? *(Impressing Sheila is a reward, but he must make the sacrifice of giving up the bass. Catching the bass is a reward, but he must sacrifice Sheila's good impression of him.)* OL

L2 Literary Element

Motif Answer: *It may represent the narrator's true life path or real feelings.* OL

L3 Literary Element

Motif Have students read the bracketed passage.

Ask: How does this passage counter the lure of the bass tugging on the narrator's line? *(Sheila's image in the moonlight, and what she represents, is an equal tug on the narrator.)* AL

R2 Reading Strategy

Connecting to Personal Experience Answer: *Answers will vary. Students may relate to the narrator's decision to prioritize his crush over his hobby.* OL

Reading in the Real World

Citizenship Have students find a magazine or newspaper article about a person who makes a material, emotional, or physical sacrifice for a loved one. Have small groups read and discuss their articles and answer these questions:

- Who is the article's subject?
- Faced with a conflict, what choice did the person make?
- Why did the person make a sacrifice?
- What positive results came about because of that sacrifice?
- What negative results or challenges came about? OL

Academic Standards

Additional Support activities on pp. 182 and 183 cover the following standards:

Skills Practice: **9.6.1** Identify and correctly use...phrases...

Reading in the Real World: **9.2.8** Make reasonable statements and draw conclusions about a text, supporting them with accurate examples.

Teach

BI Big Idea

Rewards and Sacrifices

Answer: *Students may say that the narrator's feelings for Sheila Mant were fleeting, but his feelings about fishing have remained with him all his life.* OL

★ Viewing the Art

American artist Winslow Homer (1836–1910) painted scenes of people interacting with nature and of the every-day life of nineteenth-century rural America. AS

Use the CheckPoint questions provided on Presentation Plus! to check students' mastery of the selection. These questions can be used with interactive response keypads for immediate student feedback.

Trout Fishing, Lake St. John 1895. Winslow Homer. William Wilkens Warren Fund. ★

With a sick, nauseous feeling in my stomach, I saw the rod unbend.

"My legs are sore," Sheila whined. "Are we there yet?"

Through a superhuman effort of self-control, I was able to beach the canoe and help Sheila off. The rest of the night is much foggier. We walked to the fair—there was the smell of popcorn, the sound of guitars. I may have danced once or twice with her, but all I really remember is her coming over to me once the music was done to explain that she would be going home in Eric Caswell's Corvette.

"Okay," I mumbled.

For the first time that night she looked at me, really looked at me.

"You're a funny kid, you know that?"

Funny. Different. Dreamy. Odd. How many times was I to hear that in the years to come, all spoken with the same quizzical, half-accusatory tone Sheila used then. Poor Sheila! Before the month was over, the spell she cast over me was gone, but the memory of that lost bass haunted me all summer and haunts me still. There would be other Sheila Mants in my life, other fish, and though I came close once or twice, it was these secret, hidden tuggings in the night that claimed me, and I never made the same mistake again. ~

Big Idea **Rewards and Sacrifices** *Why does the narrator call his decision to cut the fish off a mistake?* BI

Additional Support

Skills Practice

READING: Sequence Sequence refers to the order in which the author presents the plot details. Usually, these details appear in chronological, or time, order—the order in which they happened. Point out that in this story, the author presents the details in time order. However, at one point in the story—the canoe ride down the river—more than one event happens at the same time. Have students make two columns on the board as they identify what is happening in the canoe with Sheila and what is happening outside the canoe with the bass. OL

AFTER YOU READ

RESPONDING AND THINKING CRITICALLY

Respond

1. Did you find this story to be humorous, serious, or both? Explain.

Recall and Interpret

2. (a)How old is the narrator, and how old is Sheila Mant? (b)What makes Sheila so attractive to the narrator, and why is she "all but out of reach"?
3. (a)Which of the narrator's special hobbies or skills does he openly reveal to Sheila, and which does he keep secret? (b)How important is fishing to the narrator? Support your answer.
4. (a)How does the narrator's date with Sheila end? (b)The narrator says that there would be "other Sheila Mants" in his life. What does Sheila Mant come to represent for the narrator?

Analyze and Evaluate

5. How well does the story demonstrate the differences between the narrator and Sheila? Cite examples from the story.
6. What details does the author include to create sympathy for the narrator? Choose one passage that helps you feel sympathy for the narrator's actions. Explain why.
7. What theme, or overall message about life or human nature, do you think this story expresses? Explain.

Connect

8. **Big Idea** **Rewards and Sacrifices** (a)Do you think the narrator made the right choice in putting aside his interests for Sheila? Explain. (b)When do you think it is appropriate to put aside one's own interests for another, and when might it be wrong to do so? Explain.

LITERARY ANALYSIS

Literary Element Motif

In a short story, a **motif** is a recurring event, image, or idea. For example, a story about new beginnings may have repeated references to the rising sun. This image reinforces the idea of new beginnings because each new sunrise symbolizes the beginning of a new day and of new adventures. By paying attention to each occurrence of a motif, you will have a better understanding of a story's theme.

1. (a)Why do you think the author chooses fishing as a motif in a story about dating? (b)What does the motif of fishing help to suggest about following one's dreams or being true to oneself? Explain.
2. Which occurrences of the motif do you find particularly effective? Explain.

Review: Plot

As you learned on pages 10–11, in a story's plot, the falling action shows what happens to the characters after the climax. The resolution of the plot explains the final outcome of the story and ties up any loose ends.

1. What events make up this story's falling action?
2. In your opinion, is Sheila's comment that the narrator is a "funny kid" part of the falling action or part of the resolution? Why?
3. Did you find the resolution surprising, or was it predictable? Explain your answer.

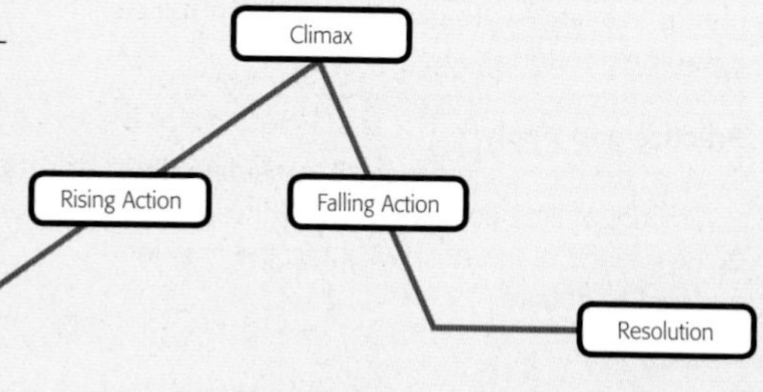

Literary Element

1. (a) Fishing is Wetherell's passion; he may be drawing from his life. (b) One should be true to oneself because it is impossible to bury one's deepest feelings.
2. Students should support answers with strong reasons and examples.

Review: Plot

1. They walk around and dance; Sheila says she is leaving with Eric.
2. It is part of the falling action because after that his crush continues for a while longer.
3. Most students will find his disillusionment predictable.

AFTER YOU READ

Assess

1. Students may find the subject serious but the treatment humorous.
2. (a) He is 14. She is 17. (b) She is lovely and three years older than the narrator.
3. (a) Reveals swimming; hides fishing (b) Very important; he spends most of his time at it.
4. (a) She goes home with Eric. (b) The temptation to gain others' approval at any cost
5. She is older and cares about her tan, college, and hair; she is a poor baseball player and a bad date. He is quiet and obsessed with her and fishing.
6. Students may say the author shows what it is like to be a sensitive, awkward adolescent with a crush.
7. The story expresses the value of following one's own inclinations.
8. (a) Possible answers: He was wrong because she was not a "better catch"; he was right because it would be rude to value fishing above another person. (b) Some may say putting one's own interests aside is noble, especially when it comes to taking care of others. Others may say that putting one's own interests aside is not noble if it allows another person to take advantage of the giver or if it contributes to a wrong the first person is committing.

Academic Standards

The Additional Support activity on p. 184 covers the following standard:

Skills Practice: **9.3.6** Analyze and trace an author's development of time and sequence...

AFTER YOU READ

Assess

Reading Strategy

1. Students should support their answers.
2. Students may say that unique abilities may make a person feel isolated but are rewarding.

Vocabulary

1. c **2.** a **3.** b **4.** c **5.** a

Academic Vocabulary

1. The narrator spent a **considerable** amount of time showing off his swimming and diving skills in order to impress Sheila.
2. The narrator has failed to **obtain** Sheila's affection or her approval.

Writing About Literature

Use these criteria when evaluating students' writing:

- Does the introduction include a clear thesis statement?
- Does the body include examples to support the thesis?
- Does the conclusion include a summary and a final thought or insight?

Web Activities Have students access the Web site for interactive activities that will help them assess their understanding of the selection.

READING AND VOCABULARY

Reading Strategy Connecting to Personal Experience

Making connections between the events of a story and your own experiences can help you better understand why characters behave as they do.

1. What about the narrator's feelings or experiences did you relate to most? Explain.
2. The narrator says that over the years, people have called him *funny, different, dreamy,* and *odd*. Have you ever felt that you were different from the people around you? Explain the advantages and disadvantages of having unique abilities or characteristics that others do not appreciate.

Vocabulary Practice

Practice with Analogies Choose the word that best completes each analogy.

1. **muscular : strength :: lithe :**
   a. cleverness **b.** dishonesty **c.** flexibility
2. **restraint : inhibition :: acknowledgement :**
   a. recognition **b.** termination **c.** distinction
3. **thinking : pensive :: thanking :**
   a. tentative **b.** appreciative **c.** talkative
4. **skeptic : dubious :: fan :**
   a. credulous **b.** imitative **c.** enthusiastic
5. **openly : surreptitiously :: abundantly :**
   a. scarcely **b.** regretfully **c.** unevenly

Academic Vocabulary

Here are two words from the vocabulary list on page R80.

considerable (kən sid′ər a bəl) *adj.* large

obtain (əb tān′) *v.* to get, usually as a result of planning or effort

Practice and Apply

1. What did the narrator spend a **considerable** amount of time doing to impress Sheila?
2. By the end of the story, what has the narrator failed to **obtain**?

WRITING AND EXTENDING

Writing About Literature

Evaluate Author's Craft In this story, W. D. Wetherell portrays a teenager experiencing a painful crush on a girl who may or may not like him. How effectively does Wetherell present this situation? In a brief essay, explain whether you find Wetherell's portrayal of the narrator's crush believable.

Begin your essay with a clear thesis statement that expresses your central idea about how well the author conveys the experience of having a crush. Then give evidence from the story to support your thesis. Structure your essay with an introduction, body, and conclusion as shown.

Introduction: A clear statement of your thesis about the author's skill in portraying a crush

↓

Body: Evidence from the story that illustrates your claims about the author's skill

↓

Conclusion: A summary of the evidence and a final statement about how accurately and believably the author portrays a crush

After you complete your draft, have a peer read it and suggest revisions. Then proofread and edit your work for errors in spelling, grammar, and punctuation.

Literature Groups

In a group, discuss the narrator's strong feelings about fishing and about Sheila Mant. Then survey your group members about the following question: Was the narrator's decision to cut the fish from the line romantic or foolish? Mark down each group member's opinion; then have each one take a turn defending his or her opinion to the group. After all members have had a chance to speak, survey the group again. Has anyone changed his or her mind? If so, why?

LiteratureOnline **Web Activities** For eFlashcards, Selection Quick Checks, and other Web activities, go to www.glencoe.com.

Literature Groups

Students may begin by making a two-column chart with the column heads *romantic* and *foolish.* Have them write specific reasons under the appropriate heading on the chart. Ask the group to review the chart before taking a final survey. Invite students who change their opinion to explain their reasons.

Vocabulary Workshop

Multiple-Meaning Words

Distinguishing Definitions

"She would spend her days sunbathing on a float my Uncle Sierbert had moored in their cove, and before July was over I had learned all her moods."

—W. D. Wetherell, "The Bass, the River, and Sheila Mant"

Connecting to Literature The word *float*, which can refer to a raft, the action of floating, or a drink made with ice cream and soda, is a multiple-meaning word. **Multiple-meaning words** are words that have several related definitions listed within a single dictionary entry.

Multiple-meaning words are common in English. Here are a few.

Word	Meanings	Examples
crawl	a crawling movement	Would the narrator *crawl* on hands and knees to get Sheila's attention?
	a particular swim stroke	The narrator swims the *crawl* in the cove.
figure	shape, outline, or form	Sheila's *figure* attracts the narrator.
	person or personality	Sheila is an important *figure* in the narrator's summer.
line	a strong cord with a hook used for fishing	During the boat ride, a large bass gets hooked on the narrator's *line*.
	a short letter or note	If Sheila sent the narrator a *line*, what would it say?
	a boundary	The narrator fails to draw a *line* between fishing and dating.

Exercise

Use context clues to determine the meaning of each underlined word. Write down this meaning. Then use a dictionary to write at least one additional meaning for the word.

1. The scarlet ibis is a symbol.
2. The bird is the bright red color of blood.
3. It has been blown off course and is far from its natural surroundings.
4. Doodle buries the ibis in the front yard.

Vocabulary Terms

A **multiple-meaning word** is a word that has several related definitions listed within a single dictionary entry.

Test-Taking Tip

To determine the intended use of a multiple-meaning word, look for context clues such as synonyms, antonyms, and examples.

Reading Handbook

For more about distinguishing between meanings, see Reading Handbook, p. R19.

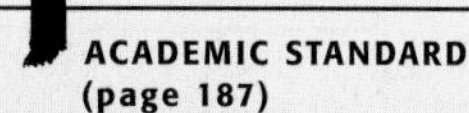

eFlashcards For eFlashcards and other vocabulary activities, go to www.glencoe.com.

ACADEMIC STANDARDS (page 187)

9.1.2 Distinguish between what words mean literally and what they imply and interpret what the words imply.

Focus

A multiple-meaning word may be used as more than one part of speech. For example, *float* can be a noun—a raft. It can be a verb—to go down a river.

Teach

Multiple-Meaning Words

Tell students to determine what part of speech the word is as it is used in the sentence. Then they should find context clues to the word's meaning.

Assess

1. Something used to represent something else; a written or printed sign used to represent an action or a relationship
2. Fluid circulated by the heart; a fluid that looks like blood, such as the juice of plants
3. The direction of movement; an area where a race is held
4. Ground around a building; an area where trains are switched or stored

eFlashcards Have students access the Web site for more practice in distinguishing definitions.

English Language Coach

Dictionary Use English learners may have difficulty using a dictionary, particularly when checking homographs. Help students review the entry for the word *yard.* Explain that *yard* is a homograph. It has two entries in the dictionary, with a different word origin for each. The first entry comes from a Middle English word meaning "rod or staff." The second comes from a Middle English word meaning "enclosure."

Review the definitions for each entry, noting the relation of the definitions to the word's origin. **EL**

Academic Standards

The Additional Support activity on p. 187 covers the following standard:

English Language Coach: **9.1** [Use] relationships, and origins…to determine the meaning of words…

Focus

BELLRINGER

Bellringer Options
Selection Focus Transparency 13
Daily Language Practice Transparency 17

Or show images of pairs of unlikely friends, such as an elderly person and a child, or a cat and a dog.

Ask: What is the definition of friendship? Encourage students to think about the meaning of friendship as they read this selection.

Author Search To expand students' appreciation of Truman Capote, have them access the Web site for additional information and resources.

BEFORE YOU READ

A Christmas Memory

MEET TRUMAN CAPOTE

For many people, Truman Capote was a flamboyant celebrity author who hobnobbed with the rich and famous. But he began with a talent honed in humble circumstances. Capote was shaped by a childhood spent in poverty in rural Alabama, an experience he wrote about for the rest of his life.

A Lonely Childhood Capote was born in New Orleans, Louisiana, to a salesman and a beauty queen. His parents soon divorced, and Capote was placed with relatives in Monroeville, Alabama. Life in the strict household was difficult for the young boy. He began writing for hours every day as a way to escape. With typical frankness, Capote said of those years, "I was so different from everyone, so much more intelligent and sensitive and perceptive. I was having fifty perceptions a minute to everyone else's five."

Capote's troubles during those years were eased by the loving care of an elderly cousin, Miss Sook Faulk. They were also softened by the presence of his best friend and next-door neighbor, Harper Lee, who eventually won a Pulitzer Prize for the novel *To Kill a Mockingbird.*

> "I always felt that nobody was going to understand me. . . . I guess that's why I started writing."
>
> —Truman Capote

When he was nine, Capote was enrolled in private schools in Connecticut and New York. Restless and ambitious, he left school at the age of seventeen to pursue a job at the prestigious literary magazine *The New Yorker.* His fame exploded with the publication of his first novel, *Other Voices, Other Rooms.* It caused a sensation with its fine, clear prose, its frank treatment of a young man's coming of age, and its jacket photograph of the handsome author.

Life as a Writer While he worked to solidify his reputation as a writer, Capote traveled and socialized. The glittering world of high society quickly welcomed the witty young man as one of its own. Capote was photographed vacationing in chalets in Switzerland and Italy. The publication of *In Cold Blood* in 1966 made him a wealthy man and started a new genre, the "nonfiction novel."

But wealth and acclaim were not enough for Capote, who, despite his bravado, was sensitive, self-critical, and prone to brooding about his painful childhood. Some friends felt that Capote's depression, combined with his love of the limelight, caused him to lose focus on his work. He eventually alienated many of his famous friends. During his last years, Capote was unwell and lonely.

What remains is a slim body of work that is remarkable for its insight and craft. An adept storyteller, Capote wove a compassionate understanding of character into intriguing, often suspenseful plots. His short story "A Christmas Memory" is considered a classic of the form.

Truman Capote was born in 1924 and died in 1984.

Literature Online **Author Search** For more about Truman Capote, go to www.glencoe.com

Selection Skills

A Christmas Memory

Literary Elements
- Dialogue (SE pp. 189–203)
- Character (SE p. 203)

Reading Skills
- Analyzing Characterization (SE pp. 189–203)

Vocabulary Skills
- Analogies (SE p. 203)
- Academic Vocabulary (SE p. 203)
- Compound Words (TWE p. 190)

Listening/Speaking/Viewing Skills
- Analyzing Art (SE p. 198; TWE pp. 190, 192, 193, 200)

Writing Skills/Grammar
- Author's Purpose (SE p. 204)
- Using Colons (SE p. 204)
- Description (TWE p. 192)

LITERATURE PREVIEW

Connecting to the Story

What personal qualities do you value in a best friend? Before you read the story, think about the following questions:

- Who has shown you love and kindness?
- What holidays from your childhood will you always remember?

Building Background

"A Christmas Memory" is set in rural Alabama in the early 1930s. During that time, poverty was widespread. The nation was reeling from the economic downturn known as the Great Depression. Rural areas in the South were especially hard hit. Many homes there did not yet have electricity or indoor plumbing. Some homes were still heated by fireplaces and lit by candles and oil lanterns, and cooking was done on large wood- or coal-burning stoves or on gas ranges. To remedy this situation, President Franklin D. Roosevelt introduced a program of rural electrification, as well as other programs intended to improve the U.S. economy.

In the story, a boy and his older relative make fruitcakes. A traditional Christmas dessert, fruitcake is a rich cake made with candied or dried fruits, nuts, spices, and sometimes a liquor, such as whiskey, sherry, or rum.

Setting Purposes for Reading

Big Idea Rewards and Sacrifices

As you read, think about the sacrifices that Buddy's friend makes so that others will be happy.

Literary Element Dialogue

Conversation between characters in a literary work is called **dialogue.** Dialogue brings characters to life by revealing their personalities as they react to other characters. Dialogue also helps advance the plot. As you read, notice what dialogue reveals about Capote's characters.

- See Literary Terms Handbook, p. R5.

Literature Online Interactive Literary Elements Handbook To review or learn more about the literary elements, go to www.glencoe.com.

READING PREVIEW

Reading Strategy Analyzing Characterization

A variety of methods can reveal the personality of a literary character. These methods are known as **characterization.** In direct characterization the writer states directly what a character's traits are. In indirect characterization the character's own words, thoughts, and actions, and what other characters think and say about the character, reveal the character's personality.

Reading Tip: Making a List As you read, list details that help you understand the characters.

Buddy	Buddy's friend	Haha Jones	Relatives
	"small and sprightly, like a bantam hen"		

Vocabulary

inaugurate (in ô′ gyə rāt′) *v.* to make a formal beginning; p. 191 *The university will inaugurate the term of its new president over the weekend.*

conspiracy (kən spir′ ə sē) *n.* the act of secretly planning together; p. 193 *The prosecutor discovered a conspiracy among several executives to conceal evidence of their company's wrongdoing.*

potent (pōt′ ənt) *adj.* having or exercising force, power, or authority; strong and powerful; p. 196 *Magnets have a potent attraction to metal.*

muse (mūz) *v.* to think or reflect, especially in an idle, dreamy manner; p. 197 *A daydreamer, Ivan likes to muse about his future possibilities.*

Vocabulary Tip: Analogies An analogy is a comparison that indicates the relationships between two objects or ideas. Developing a good vocabulary can help you succeed at completing analogies.

INDIANA ACADEMIC STANDARDS (pages 189–204)

9.3.3 Analyze interactions between characters...

9.3.4 Determine characters' traits by what the characters say about themselves...

9.5.3 Write...analytical essays...

BEFORE YOU READ

Focus

Summary

Truman Capote's memoir "A Christmas Memory" was inspired by Miss Sook Faulk, a distant cousin, who was his childhood best friend. The events unfold at Christmastime in rural Alabama. The boy, Buddy, is seven years old, and his friend is in her sixties. The two make and send fruitcakes, find and decorate a tree, and make gifts for the family.

V Vocabulary

Vocabulary File Say: Add these words and definitions to your vocabulary file. For each word, include a sentence that gives an example of how to use the word. OL Students with English language needs should include the pronunciations of these words in their files. EL

Literary Elements Have students access the Web site to improve their understanding of dialogue.

Selection Resources

Print Materials

- Unit 1 Resources (Fast File), pp. 62–64
- Leveled Vocabulary Development, p. 14
- Selection and Unit Assessments, pp. 29–30
- Selection Quick Checks, p. 15

Transparencies

- Bellringer Options Transparencies: Selection Focus Transparency 13 Daily Language Practice Transparency 17
- Literary Elements Transparency 17

Technology

- TeacherWorks Plus™ CD-ROM
- StudentWorks Plus™ CD-ROM
- Presentation Plus!™ CD-ROM
- Literature Online, glencoe.com
- Online Student Edition, mhln.com
- Exam*View*® Assessment Suite CD-ROM
- Vocabulary PuzzleMaker CD-ROM
- Listening Library, disc 1 track 17

Teach

Viewing the Art

Mary Adshead (1904–1995) illustrated books, designed postage stamps, painted in watercolors, created mosaics, and drew and sketched. Most significantly, Adshead was a talented muralist whose works remain on display throughout the United Kingdom. **AS**

CheckPoint

Use CheckPoint questions on Presentation Plus! to monitor students' comprehension. These questions can be used with interactive response keypads for immediate student feedback.

Readability Scores
Dale-Chall: 7.9
DRP: 60
Lexile: 900

Farmhouse Kitchen, 1941. Mary Adshead. Oil on board, 31 × 41cm. Private Collection, Sally Hunter Fine Art, London, UK.

A Christmas Memory

Truman Capote

Imagine a morning in late November. A coming of winter morning more than twenty years ago. Consider the kitchen of a spreading old house in a country town. A great black stove is its main feature; but there is also a big round table and a fireplace with two rocking chairs placed in front of it. Just today the fireplace commenced its seasonal roar.

A woman with shorn white hair is standing at the kitchen window. She is wearing tennis shoes and a shapeless gray sweater over a summery calico dress. She is small and sprightly, like a bantam hen; but, due to a long youthful illness, her shoulders are pitifully hunched. Her face is remarkable—not unlike Lincoln's, craggy like that, and tinted by sun and wind; but it is delicate too, finely boned, and her eyes are sherry-colored

Additional Support

Skills Practice

VOCABULARY: Compound Words
Fruitcake is a compound word made up of two words, each having its own meaning. Usually, you can find the meaning of a compound word by looking at the meaning of each part. Have students identify and define other compound words on pages 190–192. *(fireplace, windowpane, courthouse, cartwheel, out-of-doors, springtime, rattlesnake, buggyload, windfall, milk-glass, fireside, firelight.)* **OL**

and timid. "Oh my," she exclaims, her breath smoking the windowpane, "it's fruitcake weather!"

The person to whom she is speaking is myself. I am seven; she is sixty-something. We are cousins, very distant ones, and we have lived together—well, as long as I can remember. Other people inhabit the house, relatives; and though they have power over us, and frequently make us cry, we are not, on the whole, too much aware of them. We are each other's best friend. She calls me Buddy, in memory of a boy who was formerly her best friend. The other Buddy died in the 1880s, when she was still a child. She is still a child.

"I knew it before I got out of bed," she says, turning away from the window with a purposeful excitement in her eyes. "The courthouse bell sounded so cold and clear. And there were no birds singing; they've gone to warmer country, yes indeed. Oh, Buddy, stop stuffing biscuit and fetch our buggy. Help me find my hat. We've thirty cakes to bake."

It's always the same: a morning arrives in November, and my friend, as though officially **inaugurating** the Christmas time of year that exhilarates her imagination and fuels the blaze of her heart, announces: "It's fruitcake weather! Fetch our buggy. Help me find my hat."

The hat is found, a straw cartwheel corsaged with velvet roses out-of-doors has faded: it once belonged to a more fashionable relative. Together, we guide our buggy, a dilapidated baby carriage, out to the garden and into a grove of pecan trees. The buggy is mine; that is, it was bought for me when I was born. It is made of wicker, rather unraveled, and the wheels wobble like a drunkard's legs. But it is a faithful object; springtimes, we take it to the woods and fill it with flowers, herbs, wild fern for our porch pots; in the summer, we pile it with picnic paraphernalia[1] and sugar-cane fishing poles and roll it down to the edge of a creek; it has its winter uses, too: as a truck for hauling firewood from the yard to the kitchen, as a warm bed for Queenie, our tough little orange and white rat terrier who has survived distemper[2] and two rattlesnake bites. Queenie is trotting beside it now.

Three hours later we are back in the kitchen hulling a heaping buggyload of windfall pecans. Our backs hurt from gathering them: how hard they were to find (the main crop having been shaken off the trees and sold by the orchard's owners, who are not us) among the concealing leaves, the frosted, deceiving grass. Caarackle! A cheery crunch, scraps of miniature thunder sound as the shells collapse and the golden mound of sweet oily ivory meat mounts in the milk-glass bowl. Queenie begs to taste, and now and again my friend sneaks her a mite, though insisting we deprive ourselves. "We mustn't, Buddy. If we start, we won't stop. And there's scarcely enough as there is. For thirty cakes." The kitchen is growing dark. Dusk turns the window into a mirror: our reflections mingle with the rising moon as we work by the fireside in the firelight. At last, when the moon is quite high, we toss the final hull into the fire and, with joined sighs, watch it catch flame. The buggy is empty, the bowl is brimful.

We eat our supper (cold biscuits, bacon, blackberry jam) and discuss tomorrow. Tomorrow the kind of work I like best

Literary Element Dialogue *Based on this remark, what impression do you get of the woman's personality?* **L**

Reading Strategy Analyzing Characterization *What does the narrator mean when he says that his friend is still a child?* **R**

Vocabulary

inaugurate (in ô′gyə rāt′) *v.* to make a formal beginning

1. *Paraphernalia* (par′ə fər nāl′yə) means "equipment," or "things used in a particular activity."
2. Dogs (and some other mammals) can contract *distemper,* a highly contagious and sometimes fatal disease caused by a virus.

Big Idea Rewards and Sacrifices *Why does Buddy's friend feed the dog pecans while denying herself a taste?* **BI**

Teach

L Literary Element

Dialogue **Answer:** *Students may say that the woman seems likeable and excitable.*
Ask: What does "fruitcake weather" imply? *(It is nearing Christmastime and time to make fruitcakes.)* **OL**

R Reading Strategy

Analyzing Characterization
Answer: *His friend is still innocent and playful.*
Ask: How might her "long youthful illness" contribute to her child-like behavior? *(Her illness may have limited her mental development.)* **OL**

BI Big Idea

Rewards and Sacrifices
Answer: *She is willing to sacrifice her own pleasure; she is soft-hearted.* **OL**

English Language Coach

Holiday Traditions Some English learners may not be familiar with the Christmas traditions in the selection. Have students draw a two-column chart and copy story details in the first column. In the second column, they should write about holiday traditions in their homes. **EL**

Differentiated Instruction

Onomatopoeia The words *caarackle* and *crunch* name and imitate sounds. The use of sound words, or onomatopoeia, helps readers hear what is happening. Have students brainstorm other words that create sounds, write descriptive paragraphs using onomatopoeia, and read them aloud. **BL**

Academic Standards

Additional Support activities on pp. 190 and 191 cover the following standards:

Skills Practice: **9.1** [Use] word parts...to determine the meaning of words...

English Language Coach: **9.3** [Identify] story elements such as...setting...

Differentiated Instruction: **9.3.7** Recognize and understand the significance of various literary devices...

Teach

R1 Reading Strategy

Analyzing Characterization

Answer: *He enjoys shopping, cooking, and being a part of the activities his friend thinks up.*

Ask: Why is this friendship important to Buddy? *(The "relatives" seem cold and distant and do not provide warmth or affection; he does not mention other children his age. This is his only friendship and the only affection he gets.)* OL

Viewing the Art

Contemporary painter and photographer Ditz's work can be found in books, greeting cards, stationery products, ceramics and textiles. Born in Austria, Ditz has lived in England for over 30 years and has exhibited extensively. She usually favors animals in her artwork and even illustrated a book on cats. AS

Snow. Ditz. Private Collection.

begins: buying. Cherries and citron[3], ginger and vanilla and canned Hawaiian pineapple, rinds and raisins and walnuts and whiskey and oh, so much flour, butter, so many eggs, spices, flavorings: why, we'll need a pony to pull the buggy home.

But before these purchases can be made, there is the question of money. Neither of us has any. Except for skinflint sums[4] persons in the house occasionally provide (a dime is considered very big money); or what we earn ourselves from various activities: holding rummage sales, selling buckets of hand-picked blackberries, jars of homemade jam and apple jelly and peach preserves, rounding up flowers for funerals and weddings. Once we won seventy-ninth prize, five dollars, in a national football contest. Not that we know a fool thing about football. It's just that we enter any contest we hear about: at the moment our hopes are centered on the fifty-thousand-dollar Grand Prize being offered to name a new brand of coffee (we suggested "A.M."; and, after some hesitation, for my friend thought it perhaps sacrilegious,[5] the slogan "A.M.! Amen!"). To tell the truth, our only *really* profitable enterprise was the Fun and Freak Museum we conducted in a back-yard woodshed two summers ago. The Fun was a stereopticon[6] with slide views of Washington and New York lent us by a relative who had been to those places (she was furious when she discovered why we'd borrowed it); the Freak was a three-legged biddy chicken hatched by one of our own hens. Everybody hereabouts wanted to see that biddy: we charged grownups a nickel, kids two cents. And took in a good twenty dollars before the museum shut down due to the decease[7] of the main attraction.

But one way and another we do each year accumulate Christmas savings, a Fruitcake Fund. These moneys we keep hidden in an ancient bead purse under a loose board under the floor under a chamber pot[8] under

3. A *citron* is a large, thick-skinned, lemonlike fruit.
4. The relatives are stingy and miserly when they give only *skinflint sums.*

Reading Strategy Analyzing Characterization *What kinds of activities make Buddy happy?* R1

5. *Sacrilegious* (sak′ rə lij′ əs) means "showing disrespect for something sacred or cherished."
6. A *stereopticon* (ster′ ē op′ ti kən) is a device that projects two images, either overlapping or in quick succession, so that one fades into the other.
7. *Decease* means "death."
8. A *chamber pot* is a portable container used as a toilet.

Additional Support

Academic Standards

The Additional Support activity on p. 192 covers the following standard:

Skills Practice: **9.4.3** Use…sensory details…

Skills Practice

WRITING: Description Point out the vivid descriptions of money on page 193: "Dollar bills, tightly rolled and green as May buds," "Somber fifty-cent pieces," "bitter-odored pennies." These descriptions give the money character and interest. Have students write descriptive sentences about at least five ordinary objects they use every day but usually give little thought to, such as a pen or a bus pass. Challenge them to use language that appeals to the senses and to include similes, metaphors, personification, or alliteration. Invite students to share their descriptions with the class. OL my friend's bed. The purse is seldom removed from this safe location except to make a deposit, or, as happens every Saturday, a withdrawal; for on Saturdays I am allowed ten cents to go to the picture show. My friend has never been to a picture show, nor does she intend to: "I'd rather hear you tell the story, Buddy. That way I can imagine it more. Besides, a person my age shouldn't squander their eyes. When the Lord comes, let me see Him clear." In addition to never having seen a movie, she has never: eaten in a restaurant, traveled more than five miles from home, received or sent a telegram, read anything except funny papers and the Bible, worn cosmetics, cursed, wished someone harm, told a lie on purpose, let a hungry dog go hungry. Here are a few things she has done, does do: killed with a hoe the biggest rattlesnake ever seen in this county (sixteen rattles), dip snuff (secretly), tame hummingbirds (just try it) till they balance on her finger, tell ghost stories (we both believe in ghosts) so tingling they chill you in July, talk to herself, take walks in the rain, grow the prettiest japonicas[9] in town, know the recipe for every sort of old-time Indian cure, including a magical wart-remover.

Now, with supper finished, we retire to the room in a faraway part of the house where my friend sleeps in a scrap-quilt-covered iron bed painted rose pink, her favorite color. Silently, wallowing in the pleasures of **conspiracy,** we take the bead purse from its secret place and spill its contents on the scrap quilt. Dollar bills, tightly rolled and green as May buds. Somber fifty-cent pieces, heavy enough to weight a dead man's eyes.[10] Lovely dimes, the liveliest coin, the one that really jingles. Nickels and quarters, worn smooth as creek pebbles. But mostly a hateful heap of bitter-odored pennies. Last summer others in the house contracted to pay us a penny for every twenty-five flies we killed. Oh, the carnage[11] of August: the flies that flew to heaven! Yet it was not work in which we took pride. And, as we sit counting pennies, it is as though we were back tabulating dead flies. **R3** Neither of us has a head for figures; we count slowly, lose track, start again. According to her calculations, we have $12.73. According to mine, exactly $13. "I do hope you're wrong, Buddy. We can't mess around with thirteen. The cakes will fall. Or put somebody in the cemetery. Why, I wouldn't dream of getting out of bed on the thirteenth." This is true: she always spends thirteenths in bed. So, to be on the safe side, we subtract a penny and toss it out the window.

Of the ingredients that go into our fruitcakes, whiskey is the most expensive, as well as the hardest to obtain: State laws forbid its sale.[12] But everybody knows you can buy a bottle from Mr. Haha Jones. And the next day, having completed our more prosaic[13] shopping, we set out for Mr. Haha's business address, a "sinful" (to quote public opinion) fish-fry and dancing café down by the river. We've been there before, and on the same errand; but in previous years our dealings have been with Haha's wife, an iodine-dark Indian woman with brassy peroxided hair and a dead-tired disposition. ★ Actually, we've never laid eyes on her husband, though we've heard that he's an Indian too. A giant with razor scars across his cheeks. They call him Haha because he's so gloomy, a man who never laughs. As we approach his café (a large log

9. *Japonicas* (jə pon′ i kəz) are shrubs in the rose family, bearing bright red, pink, or white flowers.
10. The phrase *heavy enough to weight a dead man's eyes* refers to the custom of placing coins on the eyelids of a corpse to keep them closed.

Reading Strategy Analyzing Characterization *Why does the author include this list of details?* **R2**

Vocabulary

conspiracy (kən spir′ ə sē) *n.* the act of secretly planning together

11. *Carnage* is a great and bloody slaughter.
12. *[State laws forbid its sale.]* From 1920 to 1933, federal law prohibited the manufacture, sale, and consumption of alcoholic beverages.
13. *Prosaic* (prō zā′ ik) means "ordinary" or "commonplace."

Big Idea Rewards and Sacrifices *What sacrifices do Buddy and his friend make to achieve their goals?* **BI**

Teach

R2 Reading Strategy

Analyzing Characterization

Answer: *These details show her character: kind, generous, brave, in touch with nature.*

Ask: By including these details, what does the narrator reveal about himself? *(He reveals what he values and admires and that he is fond of his friend.)* **OL**

R3 Reading Strategy

Analyzing Characterization

Ask: Why do you think Buddy and his friend take no pride in killing flies? *(They may feel that taking life to earn money is somehow wrong, even if they are killing flies.)* **OL**

BI Big Idea

Rewards and Sacrifices

Answer: *They work hard to earn money, even doing distasteful things such as killing flies. They do not use the money for themselves, but spend it all on the cakes.* **OL**

★ Cultural History

Iodine and Peroxide

Iodine and its compounds are used in medicine as antiseptics. They are also used in the manufacture of dyes and have a dark reddish-violet color. Peroxide, also called hydrogen peroxide, is used as an antiseptic and to bleach hair and make it lighter in color. **AS**

Differentiated Instruction

Listening to Read-Aloud Listening to expressive reading will enhance comprehension for less-proficient readers. Tell students that as they listen, they are to remember three details. If some students cannot remember the details, they should write them down. Invite an expressive reader to read aloud from "They call him Haha . . . " (page 193) to "'just send me one of them fruitcakes instead'" (page 195). Ask students to share their three details with the class. **BL**

Academic Standards

The Additional Support activity on p. 193 covers the following standard:

Differentiated Instruction: **9.7** [Respond] to oral communication [with] careful listening and evaluation…

Teach

L Literary Element

Dialogue **Answer:** *It suggests that he has a sense of humor.*
Ask: How can you tell that Buddy's friend is nervous when she speaks to Mr. Haha? *(She speaks in "a whispery voice.")* OL

R Reading Strategy

Analyzing Characterization
Say: Mr. Haha has a reputation for being a scary and rough man.
Ask: What does Mr. Haha's response to their request tell the reader about him? *(He can be thoughtful and kind.)* What do the comments about Mr. Haha by Buddy's friend tell you about her character? *(She is not judgmental or prejudiced. She takes people at face value.)* OL

★ Viewing the Art

Anders Anderson-Lundby (1840?–1923) was a Danish artist famed for his paintings of winter landscapes. Ask students to compare the mood of the painting with the mood of the story.

The Golden Glow, 1886. Anders Anderson-Lundby. 

cabin festooned inside and out with chains of garish-gay[14] naked light bulbs and standing by the river's muddy edge under the shade of river trees where moss drifts through the branches like gray mist) our steps slow down. Even Queenie stops prancing and sticks close by. People have been murdered in Haha's café. Cut to pieces. Hit on the head. There's a case coming up in court next month. Naturally these goings-on happen at night when the colored lights cast crazy patterns and the Victrola wails. In the daytime Haha's is shabby and deserted. I knock at the door, Queenie barks, my friend calls: "Mrs. Haha, ma'am? Anyone to home?"

Visual Vocabulary
Victrola is the brand name of an early record player.

Footsteps. The door opens. Our hearts overturn. It's Mr. Haha Jones himself! And he *is* a giant; he *does* have scars; he *doesn't* smile. No, he glowers at us through Satan-tilted eyes and demands to know: "What you want with Haha?"

For a moment we are too paralyzed to tell. Presently my friend half-finds her voice, a whispery voice at best: "If you please, Mr. Haha, we'd like a quart of your finest whiskey."

His eyes tilt more. Would you believe it? Haha is smiling! Laughing, too. "Which one of you is a drinkin' man?" R

"It's for making fruitcakes, Mr. Haha. Cooking."

14. To be *festooned* is to have decorations that hang in loops or curves. Here, the *garish-gay* lights are bright and gaudy.

Literary Element Dialogue *What does this question suggest about Mr. Haha?* L

Additional Support

Skills Practice

LITERARY ELEMENT: Imagery
Imagery is descriptive or figurative language that creates an image or picture in the reader's mind. The author creates these images by using vivid details that appeal to the five senses: sight, sound, taste, touch, or smell.

Have students use a chart like the one below to list five images on page 194, stating the sense to which each appeals. OL

Image	Sense

This sobers him. He frowns. "That's no way to waste good whiskey." Nevertheless, he retreats into the shadowed café and seconds later appears carrying a bottle of daisy-yellow unlabeled liquor. He demonstrates its sparkle in the sunlight and says: "Two dollars."

R

We pay him with nickels and dimes and pennies. Suddenly, jangling the coins in his hand like a fistful of dice, his face softens. "Tell you what," he proposes, pouring the money back into our bead purse, "just send me one of them fruitcakes instead."

"Well," my friend remarks on our way home, "there's a lovely man. We'll put an extra cup of raisins in *his* cake."

The black stove, stoked with coal and firewood, glows like a lighted pumpkin. Eggbeaters whirl, spoons spin round in bowls of butter and sugar, vanilla sweetens the air, ginger spices it; melting, nose-tingling odors saturate the kitchen, suffuse the house, drift out to the world on puffs of chimney smoke. In four days our work is done. Thirty-one cakes, dampened with whiskey, bask on window sills and shelves.

My dancing shadow rollicks on the walls; our voices rock the chinaware . . .

Who are they for?

Friends. Not necessarily neighbor friends: indeed, the larger share is intended for persons we've met maybe once, perhaps not at all. People who've struck our fancy. Like President Roosevelt. Like the Reverend and Mrs. J. C. Lucey, Baptist missionaries to Borneo who lectured here last winter. Or the little knife grinder who comes through town twice a year. Or Abner Packer, the driver of the six o'clock bus from Mobile, who exchanges waves with us every day as he passes in a dust-cloud whoosh. Or the young Wistons, a California couple whose car one afternoon broke down outside the house and who spent a pleasant hour chatting with us on the porch (young Mr. Wiston snapped our picture, the only one we've ever had taken). Is it because my friend is shy with everyone *except* strangers that these strangers, and merest acquaintances, seem to us our truest friends? I think yes. Also, the scrapbooks we keep of thank-you's on White House stationery, time-to-time communications from California and Borneo, the knife grinder's penny post cards, make us feel connected to eventful worlds beyond the kitchen with its view of a sky that stops.

Now a nude December fig branch grates against the window. The kitchen is empty, the cakes are gone; yesterday we carted the last of them to the post office, where the cost of stamps turned our purse inside out. We're broke. That rather depresses me, but my friend insists on celebrating—with two inches of whiskey left in Haha's bottle. Queenie has a spoonful in a bowl of coffee (she likes her coffee chicory-flavored and strong). The rest we divide between a pair of jelly glasses. We're both quite awed at the prospect of drinking straight whiskey; the taste of it brings screwed-up expressions and sour shudders. But by and by we begin to sing, the two of us singing different songs simultaneously. I don't know the words to mine, just: *Come on along, come on along, to the dark-town strutters' ball.* But I can dance: that's what I mean to be, a tap-dancer in the movies. My dancing shadow rollicks[15] on the walls; our voices rock the chinaware; we giggle: as if unseen hands were tickling us. Queenie rolls on her back, her paws plow the air, something like a grin stretches her black lips. Inside myself, I feel

15. *Rollick* means "to play in a carefree, happy way."

Big Idea Rewards and Sacrifices *How does making fruitcakes help Buddy and his friend survive hard times?* BI

Teach

BI Big Idea

Rewards and Sacrifices

Answer: *It gives their lives excitement and helps them feel connected to people they like and admire.*

Ask: To what distant places are Buddy and his friend connected through their fruitcakes? *(California, Borneo, Washington, D.C., and Mobile)* OL

Cultural History

Chicory Chicory is a hardy blue-flowered plant that grows along roadsides and in vacant lots. It is used as a salad plant and is cultivated for its root, which is dried, ground, and mixed with coffee. When coffee was in short supply, chicory was mixed with coffee grounds to stretch the coffee supply. Especially in the South, people grew fond of chicory flavor in their coffee. AS

English Language Coach

Reading a Map Display a map of the world. Locate the town where Buddy and his friend live. (Capote grew up in Monroeville, Alabama.) Then point out the places mentioned: Borneo; California; Mobile, Alabama; and Washington, D.C. Have students identify the place nearest and most distant from Buddy's town. Use the map scale to measure the distances from Buddy's town to each place. EL

Academic Standards

Additional Support activities on pp. 194 and 195 cover the following standards:

Skills Practice: **9.3.7** Recognize and understand the significance of various literary devices, including…imagery…

English Language Coach: **9.2.1** Analyze the structure and format of reference…documents…

Teach

R Reading Strategy

Analyzing Characterization
Answer: *They are judgmental, narrow-minded, and unhelpful.*
Ask: What do the relatives imply when they say "remember Cousin Kate? Uncle Charlie, Uncle Charlie's brother-in-law?" *(They imply that these people were alcoholics and giving Buddy alcohol may lead to his "ruination" as well.)* OL

L1 Literary Element

Dialogue **Answer:** *He is loving.*
Ask: How does Buddy's friend respond to his words? *(She stops crying, brightens up, and begins planning where they can find a tree.)*
Ask: What does her response tell you about her? *(She is naturally cheerful, does not spend time feeling sorry for herself, and likes to have fun.)* OL

BI Big Idea

Rewards and Sacrifices
Ask: Why do you think Buddy and his friend are willing to suffer so many difficulties to find a tree? What does this tell you about them? *(The tree is important to them; they love Christmas and are excited about it. They are willing to suffer discomforts for the reward of the "perfect" tree.)* OL

warm and sparky as those crumbling logs, carefree as the wind in the chimney. My friend waltzes round the stove, the hem of her poor calico skirt pinched between her fingers as though it were a party dress: *Show me the way to go home*, she sings, her tennis shoes squeaking on the floor. *Show me the way to go home.*

Enter: two relatives. Very angry. **Potent** with eyes that scold, tongues that scald. Listen to what they have to say, the words tumbling together into a wrathful tune: "A child of seven! whiskey on his breath! are you out of your mind? feeding a child of seven! must be loony! road to ruination! remember Cousin Kate? Uncle Charlie? Uncle Charlie's brother-in-law? shame! scandal! humiliation! kneel, pray, beg the Lord!" R

Queenie sneaks under the stove. My friend gazes at her shoes, her chin quivers, she lifts her skirt and blows her nose and runs to her room. Long after the town has gone to sleep and the house is silent except for the chimings of clocks and the sputter of fading fires, she is weeping into a pillow already as wet as a widow's handkerchief.

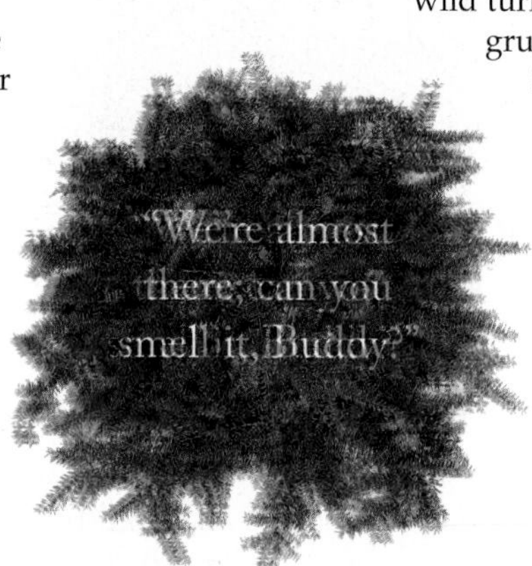
"We're almost
there; can you
smell it, Buddy?"

"Don't cry," I say, sitting at the bottom of her bed and shivering despite my flannel nightgown that smells of last winter's cough syrup, "don't cry," I beg, teasing her toes, tickling her feet, "you're too old for that."

"It's because," she hiccups, "I *am* too old. Old and funny."

"Not funny. Fun. More fun than anybody. Listen. If you don't stop crying you'll be so tired tomorrow we can't go cut a tree." L1

She straightens up. Queenie jumps on the bed (where Queenie is not allowed) to lick her cheeks. "I know where we'll find real pretty trees, Buddy. And holly, too. With berries big as your eyes. It's way off in the woods. Farther than we've ever been. Papa used to bring us Christmas trees from there: carry them on his shoulder. That's fifty years ago. Well, now: I can't wait for morning."

Morning. Frozen rime[16] lusters the grass; the sun, round as an orange and orange as hot-weather moons, balances on the horizon, burnishes[17] the silvered winter woods. A wild turkey calls. A renegade hog[18] grunts in the undergrowth. Soon, by the edge of knee-deep, rapid-running water, we have to abandon the buggy. Queenie wades the stream first, paddles across barking complaints at the swiftness of the current, the pneumonia-making coldness of it. We follow, holding our shoes and equipment (a hatchet, a burlap sack) above our heads. A mile more: of chastising thorns, burs and briers that catch at our clothes; of rusty pine needles brilliant with gaudy fungus and molted feathers. Here, there, a flash, a flutter, an ecstasy of shrillings remind us that not all the birds have flown south. Always, the path unwinds through lemony sun pools and pitch-black vine tunnels. Another BI

Reading Strategy Analyzing Characterization *From the relatives' words and actions, what ideas are you forming about them?* R

Vocabulary
potent (pō′ tənt) *adj.* having or exercising force, power, or authority; strong and powerful

16. The white coating formed on a surface by frost is called *rime.*
17. *Burnishes* means "polishes."
18. A *renegade hog* is one that has escaped its pen and run away.

Literary Element Dialogue *What does this conversation tell you about Buddy?* L1

Additional Support

Skills Practice

RESEARCH: Climate The author describes "frozen rime" on the grass and crossing streams of "pneumonia-making coldness" in search of a Christmas tree. What is winter like in Buddy's home?

Have students use an atlas or the Internet to locate weather data for Buddy's home, such as the average high and low winter temperatures. Point out that Capote lived in Monroeville, a town in southwestern Alabama. Have students compile the information in a chart and share it with the class. OL

BL creek to cross: a disturbed armada of speckled trout froths the water round us, and frogs the size of plates practice belly flops; beaver workmen are building a dam. On the farther shore, Queenie shakes herself and trembles. My friend shivers, too: not with cold but enthusiasm. One of her hat's ragged roses sheds a petal as she lifts her head and inhales the pine-heavy air. "We're almost there; can you smell it, Buddy?" she says, as though we were approaching an ocean.

And, indeed, it is a kind of ocean. Scented acres of holiday trees, prickly-leafed holly. Red berries shiny as Chinese bells: black crows swoop upon them screaming. Having stuffed our burlap sacks with enough greenery and crimson to garland a dozen windows, we set about choosing a tree. "It should be," **muses** my friend, "twice as tall as a boy. So a boy can't steal the star." The one we pick is twice as tall as me. A brave handsome brute that survives thirty hatchet strokes before it keels with a creaking rending cry. Lugging it like a kill, we commence the long trek out. Every few yards we abandon the struggle, sit down and pant. But we have the strength of triumphant huntsmen; that and the tree's virile, icy perfume revive us, goad us on. Many compliments accompany our sunset return along the red clay road to town; but my friend is sly and noncommittal[19] when passers by praise the treasure perched in our buggy: what a fine tree and where did it come from? "Yonder ways," she murmurs vaguely. Once a car stops and the rich mill owner's lazy wife leans out and whines: "Giveya two-bits cash for that ol tree." Ordinarily my friend is afraid of saying no; but on this occasion she promptly shakes her head: "We wouldn't take a dollar." The mill owner's wife persists. "A dollar, my foot! Fifty cents. That's my last offer. Goodness, woman, you can get another one." In answer, my friend gently reflects: "I doubt it. There's never two of anything."

Home: Queenie slumps by the fire and sleeps till tomorrow, snoring loud as a human.

A trunk in the attic contains: a shoebox of ermine tails (off the opera cape of a curious lady who once rented a room in the house), coils of frazzled tinsel gone gold with age, one silver star, a brief rope of dilapidated, undoubtedly dangerous candy-like light bulbs. Excellent decorations, as far as they go, which isn't far enough: my friend wants our tree to blaze "like a Baptist window," droop with weighty snows of ornament. But we can't afford the made-in-Japan splendors at the five-and-dime. So we do what we've always done: sit for days at the kitchen table with scissors and crayons and stacks of colored paper. I make sketches and my friend cuts them out: lots of cats, fish too (because they're easy to draw), some apples, some watermelons, a few winged angels devised from saved-up sheets of Hershey-bar tin foil. We use safety pins to attach these creations to the tree; as a final touch, we sprinkle the branches with shredded cotton (picked in August for this purpose). My friend, surveying the effect, clasps her hands together. "Now honest, Buddy. Doesn't it look good enough to eat?" Queenie tries to eat an angel.

After weaving and ribboning holly wreaths for all the front windows, our next project is the fashioning of family gifts. Tie-dye scarves for the ladies, for the men a home-brewed lemon and licorice and

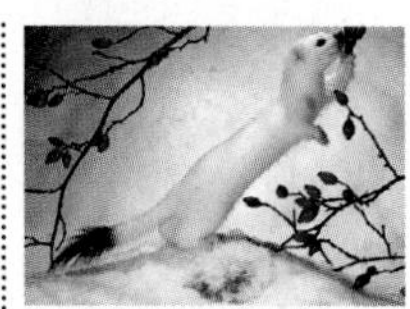

Visual Vocabulary
An *ermine* (ur′ min) is a weasel with a black-tipped tail. Its white fur is used for women's coats, often with black tails inserted at intervals for decorative effect.

19. Here, *noncommittal* means "not revealing thoughts, feelings, or other information."

Vocabulary
muse (mūz) *v.* to think or reflect, especially in an idle, dreamy manner

Literary Element Dialogue *What does this dialogue with the mill owner's wife suggest about relationships between people in the town?* L2

Teach

L2 Literary Element

Dialogue **Answer:** *It suggests that rich people in the town are used to treating poorer people as inferiors.*
Ask: What does the comment, "There's never two of anything" suggest about the way Buddy's friend views the world? *(She views it as a place of unique and wonderful things and values each thing for what it is.)* OL

Differentiated Instruction

Questioning Ask one member of a small group to read aloud the paragraph on page 196 beginning "Morning. Frozen rime. . . . " Have the group collaboratively answer these questions:

- Where is Buddy?
- What is the weather like?
- How many creeks do they cross?
- What animals do they see?

Ask students to imagine that they accompanied Buddy into the woods. Ask them to write a postcard to a friend about the adventure. If students wish, they may draw a picture of something they saw there. BL

Academic Standards
Additional Support activities on pp. 196 and 197 cover the following standards:
Skills Practice: **9.2.4** Synthesize the content from several sources…; paraphrase the ideas…
Differentiated Instruction: **9.2** Develop strategies such as asking questions… **9.5.2** Write responses to literature that demonstrate a comprehensive grasp of the significant ideas of literary works…

Teach

BI Big Idea

Rewards and Sacrifices
Answer: *She feels most rewarded by seeing her loved ones happy.* OL

R1 Reading Strategy

Analyzing Characterization
Answer: *She is both loving and fun.* OL

★ Viewing the Art

Answer: *It resembles the woods in which Buddy, his friend, and Queenie walked on their way to get a Christmas tree.*

Neil Welliver's paintings often have visual complexity, as in *The Birches.* Many painters wouldn't paint this scene because there is no focal point or path for the eye to follow. But Welliver feels nature should not be expected to organize itself to meet people's needs. AS

The Birches, 1977. Neil Welliver. Oil on canvas, 60 × 60 in. The Metropolitan Museum of Art, New York. ★
Viewing the Art: What does this painting add to your enjoyment of "A Christmas Memory"?

aspirin syrup to be taken "at the first Symptoms of a Cold and after Hunting." But when it comes time for making each other's gift, my friend and I separate to work secretly. I would like to buy her a pearl-handled knife, a radio, a whole pound of chocolate-covered cherries (we tasted some once, and she always swears: "I could live on them, Buddy, Lord yes I could—and that's not taking His name in vain"). Instead, I am building her a kite. She would like to give me a bicycle (she's said so on several million occasions: "If only I could, Buddy. It's bad enough in life to do without something *you* want; but confound it, what gets my goat is not being able to give somebody something you want *them* to have. Only one of these days I will, Buddy. Locate you a bike. Don't ask how. Steal it, maybe"). Instead, I'm fairly certain that she is building me a kite—the same as last year, and the year before: the year before that we exchanged slingshots. All of which is fine by me. For we are champion kite-fliers who study the wind like sailors; my friend, more accomplished than I, can get a kite aloft when there isn't enough breeze to carry clouds.

Christmas Eve afternoon we scrape together a nickel and go to the butcher's to buy Queenie's traditional gift, a good gnawable beef bone. The bone, wrapped in funny paper, is placed high in the tree near the silver star. Queenie knows it's there. She squats at the foot of the tree staring up in a trance of greed: when

Big Idea Rewards and Sacrifices *What does this remark reveal about the attitude of Buddy's friend toward rewards and sacrifices?* BI

Reading Strategy Analyzing Characterization *Why is Buddy's friend a good companion for a young boy?* R1

Additional Support

Skills Practice

VIEWING: Design Elements Help students understand why they feel a certain way when viewing a painting by discussing basic elements of art. For example, straight lines suggest order and direction; jagged, crossing lines can suggest fear or confusion.

Ask: What draws you into *The Birches*? What does the image make you feel? What do you think was the artist's attitude toward the subject? What are the clues? Students should support their opinions. OL bedtime arrives she refuses to budge. Her excitement is equaled by my own. I kick the covers and turn my pillow as though it were a scorching summer's night. Somewhere a rooster crows: falsely, for the sun is still on the other side of the world.

"Buddy, are you awake?" It is my friend, calling from her room, which is next to mine; and an instant later she is sitting on my bed holding a candle. "Well, I can't sleep a hoot," she declares. "My mind's jumping like a jack rabbit. Buddy, do you think Mrs. Roosevelt will serve our cake at dinner?" We huddle in the bed, and she squeezes my hand I-love-you. "Seems like your hand used to be so much smaller. I guess I hate to see you grow up. When you're grown up, will we still be friends?" I say always. "But I feel so bad, Buddy. I wanted so bad to give you a bike. I tried to sell my cameo[20] Papa gave me. Buddy"—she hesitates, as though embarrassed—"I made you another kite." Then I confess that I made her one, too; and we laugh. The candle burns too short to hold. Out it goes, exposing the starlight, the stars spinning at the window like a visible caroling that slowly, slowly daybreak silences. Possibly we doze; but the beginnings of dawn splash us like cold water; we're up, wide-eyed and wandering while we wait for others to waken. Quite deliberately my friend drops a kettle on the kitchen floor. I tap-dance in front of closed doors. One by one the household emerges, looking as though they'd like to kill us both; but it's Christmas, so they can't. First, a gorgeous breakfast: just everything you can imagine—from flapjacks and fried squirrel to hominy grits and honey-in-the-comb. Which puts everyone in a good humor except my friend and me. Frankly, we're so impatient to get at the presents we can't eat a mouthful.

"Buddy, the wind is blowing."

Well, I'm disappointed. Who wouldn't be? With socks, a Sunday school shirt, some handkerchiefs, a hand-me-down sweater and a year's subscription to a religious magazine for children. *The Little Shepherd.* It makes me boil. It really does.

My friend has a better haul. A sack of Satsumas,[21] that's her best present. She is proudest, however, of a white wool shawl knitted by her married sister. But she *says* her favorite gift is the kite I built her. And it *is* very beautiful; though not as beautiful as the one she made me, which is blue and scattered with gold and green Good Conduct stars; moreover, my name is painted on it, "Buddy."

"Buddy, the wind is blowing."

The wind is blowing, and nothing will do till we've run to a pasture below the house where Queenie has scooted to bury her bone (and where, a winter hence, Queenie will be buried, too). There, plunging through the healthy waist-high grass, we unreel our kites, feel them twitching at the string like sky fish as they swim into the wind. Satisfied, sun-warmed, we sprawl in the

20. A *cameo* is a piece of jewelry made from a precious or semiprecious stone that is carved in layers to produce a raised design, usually a woman's profile.

21. *Satsumas* are seedless tangerines native to Japan but now grown in parts of the United States and Mexico.

Literary Element Dialogue *What does this conversation tell you about how Buddy and his friend feel toward each other?* L

Reading Strategy Analyzing Characterization *What do the gifts reveal about the difference between Buddy's friend and the other relatives?* R3

Teach

L Literary Element

Dialogue Answer: *They love each other and rely on each other.* OL

R2 Reading Strategy

Analyzing Characterization
Ask: How does this action show that Buddy's friend is child-like? How would a normal adult behave in this situation? *(She is excited about Christmas morning and uses tricks to awaken the adults, as a child might do. A normal adult would be patient or would wake them deliberately.)* OL

R3 Reading Strategy

Analyzing Characterization
Answer: *The relatives do not know how to please him, or they care more about improving his character than giving him a special day. His friend is loving and thoughtful; she wants Buddy to feel special.*
Say: The word *says* is emphasized in the sentence, "But she *says* her favorite gift is the kite I built her."
Ask: What does this suggest? *(Buddy suspects she is lying to make him feel good.)* OL

English Language Coach

Synonyms Write on the board: The puppies were cavorting in the front yard. Explain that the verb *cavort* implies excited or playful running and hopping and is often used to describe children or animals at play.

Have English language learners work with more proficient English-speaking partners to look up five synonyms for *cavort* in a thesaurus and verify the meaning of each synonym in a dictionary. In their vocabulary file, have students record the synonyms and then write a sentence using each word. EL

Academic Standards
Additional Support activities on pp. 198 and 199 cover the following standards:
Skills Practice: **9.7.7** Make judgments about the ideas under discussion and support those judgments with convincing evidence.
English Language Coach: **9.1.2** Distinguish between what words mean literally and what they imply…

Teach

L1 Literary Element

Dialogue **Answer:** *She realizes that the day is perfect and she feels she is seeing God in everything around her.* OL

L2 Literary Element

Dialogue **Say:** On page 201, the author refers to his relatives as "Those Who Know Best." What does this show about his attitude toward them? *(His name for the relatives is ironic. He thinks of them collectively, not individually, and not fondly. They separated him from his friend and sent him to places where he was miserable.)* OL

★ Viewing the Art

Charles Burchfield (1893–1967) was interested in representational art at a time when most of the art world was not. In his watercolors, he concentrated on the expression of moods and emotions as well as on specific forces, including sound, heat, and movement. *Pussy Willow* was created in a period when he was painting in a realistic style. AS

Pussy Willows, 1936. Charles Burchfield. Watercolor on paper, 32$\frac{15}{16}$ × 25$\frac{1}{4}$ in. Munson-Williams-Proctor Institute Museum of Art, Utica, NY. ★

Additional Support

Skills Practice

LITERARY ELEMENT: Alliteration Alliteration is the repetition of sounds at the beginnings of words. Authors use this technique to emphasize words and ideas and to create a pleasing, rhythmic sound. In the last paragraph on page 201, ask students to identify the alliteration in the phrases "letting it loose like a kite" and "like hearts, a lost pair of kites hurrying toward heaven." Have them create alliteration by filling in the blanks in these phrases:

- a purse full of ____ *(pennies)*
- a ____ wind *(whispering west)*
- fruitcakes for ____ *(friends and family)* OL

grass and peel Satsumas and watch our kites cavort. Soon I forget the socks and hand-me-down sweater. I'm as happy as if we'd already won the fifty-thousand-dollar Grand Prize in that coffee-naming contest.

"My, how foolish I am!" my friend cries, suddenly alert, like a woman remembering too late she has biscuits in the oven. "You know what I've always thought?" she asks in a tone of discovery, and not smiling at me but a point beyond. "I've always thought a body would have to be sick and dying before they saw the Lord. And I imagined that when He came it would be like looking at the Baptist window: pretty as colored glass with the sun pouring through, such a shine you don't know it's getting dark. And it's been a comfort: to think of that shine taking away all the spooky feeling. But I'll wager it never happens. I'll wager at the very end a body realizes the Lord has already shown Himself. That things as they are"—her hand circles in a gesture that gathers clouds and kites and grass and Queenie pawing earth over her bone—"just what they've always seen, was seeing Him. As for me, I could leave the world with today in my eyes."

This is our last Christmas together.

L2 Life separates us. Those who Know Best decide that I belong in a military school. And so follows a miserable succession of bugle-blowing prisons, grim reveille-ridden[22] summer camps. I have a new home too. But it doesn't count. Home is where my friend is, and there I never go.

And there she remains, puttering around the kitchen. Alone with Queenie. Then alone. ("Buddy dear," she writes in her wild hard-to-read script, "yesterday Jim Macy's horse kicked Queenie bad. Be thankful she didn't feel much. I wrapped her in a Fine Linen sheet and rode her in the buggy down to Simpson's pasture where she can be with all her Bones . . .") For a few Novembers she continues to bake her fruitcakes single-handed; not as many, but some: and, of course, she always sends me "the best of the batch." Also, in every letter she encloses a dime wadded in toilet paper: "See a picture show and write me the story." But gradually in her letters she tends to confuse me with her other friend, the Buddy who died in the 1880s; more and more thirteenths are not the only days she stays in bed: a morning arrives in November, a leafless birdless coming of winter morning, when she cannot rouse herself to exclaim: "Oh my, it's fruitcake weather!"

And when that happens, I know it. A message saying so merely confirms a piece of news some secret vein had already received, severing from me an irreplaceable part of myself, letting it loose like a kite on a broken string. That is why, walking across a school campus on this particular December morning, I keep searching the sky. As if I expected to see, rather like hearts, a lost pair of kites hurrying toward heaven. ∾

22. *Reveille* (rev′ə lē) is the signal, usually played on a bugle, used to call soldiers to roll-call formation in the morning.

Literary Element Dialogue *Why is this day so special for Buddy's friend?* L1

Big Idea Rewards and Sacrifices *What do Buddy and his friend lose because of the decision to send him to military school?* BI

Reading Strategy Analyzing Characterization *The narrator visualizes a pair of kites. Why does he imagine them hurrying toward heaven?* R

Teach

BI Big Idea

Rewards and Sacrifices

Answer: *They lose their close companionship and ability to help each other.*

Ask: Who suffered most from their forced separation? *(Possible answers: She did, as Buddy seemed to be her only companion and the only one who treated her with respect; Buddy did, since he was young and alone in a hostile environment.)* OL

R Reading Strategy

Analyzing Characterization

Answer: *He may imagine he is accompanying his deceased friend to heaven.*

Say: The narrator says "some secret vein" tells him of his friend's death.

Ask: What is the meaning of the metaphor? What does it say about their relationship? *(Possible answers: He has an intuition of his friend's death because he was so close to her.)* OL

CheckPoint

Use the CheckPoint questions on Presentation Plus! to check students' mastery of the selection. These questions can be used with interactive response keypads for immediate student feedback.

Reading in the Real World

College Many young adults wish to attend college at the United States Military Academy at West Point or the United States Naval Academy at Annapolis. Both academies have long, proud traditions of preparing young people to become officers in the army, navy, and marine corps.

Have students read about West Point or Annapolis to learn about their history, their admission requirements, and their programs. Encourage students to share their information with the class. OL

Academic Standards

Additional Support activities on pp. 200 and 201 cover the following standards:

Skills Practice: **9.3.7** Recognize and understand the significance of various literary devices…

Reading in the Real World: **9.7.15** Deliver expository…presentations that convey information and ideas from…sources accurately and coherently…

AFTER YOU READ

Assess

1. (a) Possible answer: She seemed a likeable person with a child-like mind. (b) Possible answer: I grew to respect her child-like wisdom about how to live.
2. (a) They make fruitcakes. (b) They do it together, it gives them purpose, and it helps them to touch others.
3. (a) Relatives yell at her. (b) The relatives disapprove of Buddy and his friend.
4. (a) They give each other kites and fly the kites. (b) Possible answer: She feels the most perfect experiences in life are those that bring us closer to a loved one.
5. (a) He goes to military school, and his friend dies. (b) She was the only one who gave him unconditional love.
6. Students should support their answers.
7. (a) They may have felt he needed more supervision. (b) Possible answer: The decision was cruel or misguided.
8. Students may say Capote wanted to show the importance of unconditional love.
9. Possible answer: He learned the importance of sacrificing for others.

AFTER YOU READ

RESPONDING AND THINKING CRITICALLY

Respond

1. (a)How did you feel about Buddy's friend at the beginning of the story? (b)Did your opinion change by the end of the story? Explain.

Recall and Interpret

2. (a)What project do Buddy and his friend undertake each November? (b)Why is the project so special to Buddy and his friend?
3. (a)Why does Buddy's friend run to her room and cry in bed for a long time? (b)What kind of relationship seems to exist between the relatives in the house and Buddy and his friend?
4. (a)How do Buddy and his friend celebrate Christmas day together? (b)How do you interpret the friend's statement that she could "leave the world" with that day in her eyes? Explain.
5. (a)What leads to the permanent separation of Buddy and his friend? (b)Why is the memory of his friend so strong for Buddy?

Analyze and Evaluate

6. In your opinion, is this portrait of a friendship realistic and believable? Explain why or why not.
7. (a)Why might Buddy's relatives have sent him away to school, separating him from his friend? (b)What do you think of their decision?
8. What might Capote have wanted his audience to come away thinking or feeling after reading "A Christmas Memory"?

Connect

9. **Big Idea** **Rewards and Sacrifices** What lessons about sacrifice, friendship, and life in general does Buddy learn from his friend? Support your answer with evidence from the text.

YOU'RE THE CRITIC: Different Viewpoints

Was Capote a Top–Tier Writer?

As a stylist, Truman Capote is almost universally praised. However, critics disagree about whether he deserves a place in the pantheon of the greats. Some feel that he wrote a few works of excellence but never lived up to his full potential. Others think his novels and stories are masterpieces. Read the two excerpts of literary criticism below. Notice the differing assessments of Capote's overall greatness.

> *"I've been asked so many times about where you put Truman on some sort of literary ladder, and it's always seemed to me that the answer is probably the top of the second tier. The first tier would be taken up by the people who deal with grand themes."*
>
> —George Plimpton

> *"Truman Capote [was] the most perfect writer of my generation."*
>
> —Norman Mailer

Group Activity In a small group, discuss the following questions. Refer to the excerpts and cite evidence from "A Christmas Memory" for support.

1. (a)Do you agree with Plimpton that the greatest works treat "grand themes"? (b)Is it fair to say that "A Christmas Memory" treats a "grand theme"? Why or why not?
2. Which opinion of Capote, Mailer's or Plimpton's, strikes you as closest to the truth? Explain your answer.

You're The Critic

1. (a) Students should support their answers. (b) Students may say it has a theme about unconditional love. They may feel this theme is important enough to label "grand."
2. Students may say that Plimpton's answer is more balanced.

Academic Standards

The Additional Support activity on p. 203 covers the following standard:

Differentiated Instruction: **9.2.4** Synthesize the content from several sources or works…and connect…to…related topics…

LITERARY ANALYSIS

Literary Element Dialogue

Dialogue is the conversation between characters in a literary work. Capote uses dialogue in "A Christmas Memory" to portray details of life as it is lived moment by moment. The characters' dialogue sounds natural, flows smoothly, and satisfies readers' curiosity about the characters who are speaking. At key junctures, the dialogue helps advance the plot.

1. Reread the dialogue between Buddy's friend and Mr. Haha Jones. How does this conversation advance the plot of the story?
2. Reread the dialogue between Buddy and his friend that occurs after Buddy's friend goes to bed crying. Also reread the dialogue that occurs between them on Christmas Eve after bedtime. What do these conversations reveal about each character? Give details from the story in your answer.

Review: Character

As you learned on pages 106–107, a **character** is an individual in a literary work. Characters who reveal just one personality trait are called flat characters. Characters who show varied, and sometimes contradictory, traits are called round characters. Round characters tend to be more complex and realistic than flat characters.

Partner Activity With another classmate, look over the lists you used to record details about the story's characters. Discuss each character's personality and whether each character is flat or round.

Farmhouse Kitchen (detail), 1941. Mary Adshead. Oil on board, 31 × 41cm. Private Collection, Sally Hunter Fine Art, London, UK.

READING AND VOCABULARY

Reading Strategy Analyzing Characterization

By calling his story a "memory," Capote is able to write about real people who actually lived—while at the same time turning them into characters through the power of memory. He also creates the grown-up narrator who writes about his seven-year-old self, Buddy.

1. Identify two examples of direct characterization in the story. Explain what these examples help you understand about the character.
2. Give two examples of indirect characterization. Explain what these examples suggest about the character's personality.

Vocabulary Practice

Practice with Analogies Choose the word that best completes each analogy.

1. **inaugurate : complete :: enclose :**
   a. encircle **b.** release **c.** ensure
2. **conspiracy : plot :: legislation :**
   a. bill **b.** office **c.** governance
3. **potent : strong :: compelling :**
   a. boring **b.** fast-acting **c.** intriguing
4. **muse : disregard :: roam :**
   a. wander **b.** stay **c.** ramble

Academic Vocabulary

Here are two vocabulary words from the list on p. R80.

construct (kən strukt′) *v.* to build, form, or devise

positive (poz′ ə tiv) *adj.* confident; assured

Practice and Apply

1. How does the story demonstrate that people of differing ages can **construct** meaningful friendships?
2. Why does Buddy have a **positive** opinion of his friend?

AFTER YOU READ

Assess

Literary Element

1. As a result of the conversation with Haha Jones, Buddy and his friend are able to acquire the alcohol they need to complete the cakes.
2. Answers will vary. Students may say the dialogue reveals that the friend relies on Buddy almost as much as Buddy relies on the friend. The friend is innocent and sweet. Buddy is a loving, sensitive child. Students may also say that the dialogue reveals the characters' love for each other.

Review: Character

Students should include the following characters: Buddy: round; Buddy's friend: round; the two relatives: flat; woman in car: flat.

Reading Strategy

1. Students should find examples indicating that the narrator is explicitly telling readers about a character.
2. Students should find examples of a character's words, thoughts, and actions indirectly revealing an aspect of his or her personality.

Academic Vocabulary

1. Buddy, who is seven years old, and his friend, who is in her sixties, are able to construct a warm and loving relationship.
2. Buddy has a positive opinion of his friend because she treats him lovingly and is a fun companion.

Differentiated Instruction

Interpreting Clarify the critical observations of George Plimpton. Tell students that "grand themes" refer to universal themes in literature to which all human beings can relate, such as salvation or redemption, destructive passion, and loss. "Grand themes" are the subject of many works of world literature. BL

Vocabulary

1. b **2.** a **3.** c **4.** b

AFTER YOU READ

Assess

Writing About Literature

Use these criteria when evaluating students' writing:

- Does the essay explore the author's choice of title and short story form?
- Does the essay identify the tone and give specific examples of details as they relate to the author's purpose?
- Does the essay address the use of descriptive words?
- Does the essay contain a clear statement of the purpose or purposes of the author?

Performing

As students prepare their performance they should

- Choose a scene that reveals the character or the relationship between the two characters.
- Add dialogue as necessary to more fully reveal the personality of the characters.
- Be sure added dialogue is in keeping with the character's personality and the story.
- Practice the reading, using tone and inflections in keeping with the character and the dialogue.

WRITING AND EXTENDING

Writing About Literature

Explore Author's Purpose An author's purpose, or reason for writing, may be to entertain, to inform, or to persuade. Sometimes an author may have more than one purpose for writing. For example, you may find parts of "A Christmas Memory" entertaining, but Capote probably also wished to convey significant ideas about childhood, love, and memory.

Write a brief essay explaining what you think Capote's purposes were for writing the story. To begin, ask yourself questions like these:

Questions About Title
What might the title suggest about the nature of the topic and Capote's attitude toward it?
Questions About Form
For what purposes is the short story form most often used?
Questions About Tone
What is the nature of the tone: serious, formal, nostalgic, mocking? What might the tone suggest about the author's purpose?
Questions About Content
What types of details does the selection contain? For what purpose are such details most often used?
Questions About Language
Are there a lot of descriptive words? Why might an author use these words?

After you complete your draft, meet with a classmate to evaluate each other's work and to suggest revisions. Then proofread and edit your draft for errors in spelling, grammar, and punctuation.

Performing

Critic C. P. Farley wrote, "During the height of his fame, Capote loved to read 'A Christmas Memory' to enormous audiences that would come out to hear him read and bring several thousand people simultaneously to tears." When you hear a story read out loud or performed as a play, you often experience the story with new feeling and depth. With a group, select one scene of the story to perform. Write a script that includes the dialogue in the scene. After assigning roles and practicing reading your script out loud, perform your scene for the class.

GRAMMAR AND STYLE

Capote's Language and Style

Using Colons Colons are both punctuation marks and stylistic devices. Colons are often used to introduce a list, especially after statements that contain such words as *these, the following,* or *as follows.* Colons may also be used to introduce material that explains, illustrates, or restates preceding material. Finally, colons are used to introduce long or formal quotations.

In "A Christmas Memory," Capote employs colons to good effect. The use of colons helps to organize a diverse array of information into one compact segment:

> In addition to never having seen a movie, she has never: eaten in a restaurant, traveled more than five miles from home, received or sent a telegram, read anything except funny papers and the Bible, worn cosmetics, cursed, wished someone harm, told a lie on purpose, let a hungry dog go hungry.

Activity Find another sentence in the story in which Capote uses a colon. Copy the sentence to use as a model. Then use a chart like the one below to write three sentences about the story that contain colons. Explain the way that you used the colons—to introduce a list, to explain or restate previous material, or to introduce a quotation.

Sentence	Purpose of Colon

Revising Check

Colons The proper use of colons can help to improve the clarity and flow of your writing. With a partner, go through your essay about Capote's purpose for writing "A Christmas Memory" and note any quotations or lists of details that might be better introduced by a colon. Revise your draft as needed.

Literature Online **Web Activities** For eFlashcards, Selection Quick Checks, and other Web activities, go to www.glencoe.com.

Capote's Language and Style

Use these criteria when evaluating students' sentences:

- Do the sentences include colons in the appropriate place?
- Does the student correctly identify the purpose of the colon in each sentence?

Web Activities Have students access the Web site for interactive activities that will help them assess their understanding of the selection.

PART 3

Dreams and Reality

The Sleeping Gypsy, 1897. Henri Rousseau. Oil on canvas, 51 x 79 in. The Museum of Modern Art, New York. 

BIG IDEA

BI When reality intrudes on a person's dreams and daydreams, he or she must face choices. The actions taken then reveal much about his or her personality. In the short stories in Part 3, you will read about clashes between dreams and reality. As you read, ask yourself: How well do these dreams mesh with reality?

Analyzing and Extending

BI Big Idea

Dreams and Reality After students have read the text under the "Big Idea" head, discuss the distinction between dreams and reality. Then invite them to connect the Big Idea to the artwork. Challenge students to consider the question, "How well do dreams fit with reality?" Return to this question after students have read the selections and have them reconsider their answers. **OL**

★ Viewing the Art

The Sleeping Gypsy is the painting that secured the reputation of self-taught French painter Henri Rousseau (1844–1910). Rousseau was a public servant who took up painting at the age of 40. His unique style was at first dismissed by critics but embraced by the French avant-garde in the early 1900s. **AS**

English Language Coach

Comparing Cultures The relationship between dream and reality is not viewed the same way in every culture. Invite students who are familiar with non-Western cultures to talk about the place of dreams in the everyday world. As a class, make comparisons with modern American culture. **EL**

Differentiated Instruction

Dreams in Stories Invite advanced readers to think of literature in which dreams play an important part. Discuss how the dreams contributed to the works' meanings and how dreams often provide insight into a character's mind. **AL**

Academic Standards

Additional Support activities on p. 205 cover the following standards:

English Language Coach: **9.3** [Identify] story elements such as...theme...[to enhance] students' understanding of...culture...

Differentiated Instruction: **9.3.2** Compare and contrast...a similar theme or topic across genres...

UNIT ONE

Part 3: Skills Scope and Sequence

Readability Scores Key
Dale-Chall/DRP/Lexile

PACING STANDARD	(DAYS) BLOCK	SELECTIONS AND FEATURES	LITERARY ELEMENTS
1–2 class sessions	1	LITERARY FOCUS: Narrator and Voice, pp. 206–207	
		"The Secret Life of Walter Mitty" by James Thurber **3.2/52/700**, pp. 208–217	Diction, SE pp. 209, 210, 211, 212, 214, 216 Narrator, SE p. 216
		Grammar Workshop: Sentence Structure, p. 218	
2 class sessions	1	"The Necklace" by Guy de Maupassant **6.9/61/950**, pp. 219–230	Point of View, SE pp. 220, 223, 225, 229 Symbol, SE p. 229
		"American History" by Judith Ortiz Cofer **5.6/55/990**, pp. 231–241	Point of View, SE pp. 232–234, 236, 238–240 Setting, SE p. 240
2 class sessions	1	HISTORICAL PERSPECTIVE on American History: "The Drums of Washington" by Arthur M. Schlesinger Jr. **8.4/61/1020**, pp. 242–246	
		"Baker's Bluejay Yarn" by Mark Twain **7.3/57/980**, pp. 247–256	Persona, SE pp. 248, 251, 252, 255 Dialect, SE p. 255
2 class sessions	1	"The Flat of the Land" by Diana Garcia **7.9/61/1080**, pp. 257–268	Tone, SE pp. 258–267 Point of View, SE p. 267
		"The Son from America" by Isaac Bashevis Singer **3.8/54/760**, pp. 269–279	Style, SE pp. 270–275, 278 Voice, SE p. 278
2–3 class sessions	2–3	Writing Workshop: Response to Literature, pp. 280–287	
1 class session		Speaking, Listening, and Viewing Workshop: Oral Response to Literature, pp. 288–289	
2 class sessions		Test Preparation and Practice, pp. 292–297	

About the Part

Part 3 contrasts dreams with reality in short stories.

READING AND CRITICAL THINKING	VOCABULARY	WRITING AND GRAMMAR	LISTENING, SPEAKING, AND VIEWING
Visualizing, SE pp. 209, 212, 213, 214, 216	Synonyms, SE pp. 209, 216 Academic Vocabulary, SE p. 216	Analyze Diction, SE p. 216 Using Proper Nouns, SE p. 217	Analyzing Art, SE p. 210 Group Reading, SE p. 217
		Compound Subjects and Verbs, TWE p. 218	
Cause-and-Effect Relationships, SE pp. 220, 222, 225, 227, 229	Word Parts, SE p. 229	Apply Voice, SE p. 230 Using Adjectives, SE p. 230	Analyzing Art, SE p. 224; TWE p. 226
Identifying Assumptions, SE pp. 232, 234, 236, 238, 241 Cause-and-Effect Relationships, TWE p. 236	Practice with Analogies, SE p. 241 Academic Vocabulary, SE p. 241	Analyze Historical Context, SE p. 241 Repetition for Effect, TWE p. 234	Analyzing Art, SE p. 237; TWE pp. 233, 235 Literary Criticism, SE p. 241
Recognizing Bias, SE p. 242; TWE pp. 244, 245 Analyzing Details, TWE p. 244	Negative Prefixes, TWE p. 242		
Analyzing Language, SE pp. 248, 249, 252, 253, 255	Context Clues, SE pp. 248, 255 Academic Vocabulary, SE p. 255	Analyze Genre Elements, SE p. 256 Double Negatives, SE p. 256	Analyzing Art, SE p. 250
Analyzing Character and Setting, SE pp. 258–268 Sequencing Events, TWE p. 260	Word Parts: Negating Prefixes, SE p. 268 Connotations, TWE p. 265	Analyze Genre Elements, SE p. 268 Rhyming Poem, TWE p. 262	Analyzing Art, SE pp. 261, 264 Oral Report, SE p. 268
Making Inferences, TWE p. 272	Word Origins, SE p. 278 Academic Vocabulary, SE p. 278	Evaluate an Author's Craft, SE p. 279 Using Appositives, SE p. 279	Analyzing Art, TWE p. 275 Tone and Gesture, TWE p. 274
		Responding to a Short Story, SE pp. 280–287 Active Voice, TWE p. 284	
			Presenting in a Group Discussion, SE pp. 288–289
Test-Taking Strategies, TWE p. 292		Sentence Errors, TWE p. 296	

LITERARY FOCUS

Focus

BELLRINGER

Bellringer Options
Daily Language Practice Transparency 18

Or display photos or artwork that show different points of view—for example, views from great heights or ground level, close-ups, and wide-angle shots.

Ask: How does the point of view affect what we can see in these photographs? Why is point of view important? Have students consider as they read why an author chose to write from a particular point of view.

Teach

L Literary Element

Narrator's Point of View

Say: Point of view refers to the relationship of the narrator to the story. It determines the information that the reader gets. The first-person point of view, for example, gives readers access to the narrator's thoughts and feelings. Have students recall a story they have read recently and identify the point of view. OL

LITERARY FOCUS

Narrator and Voice

How do narrator, point of view, and voice affect a story?

Think of a narrator as a guide—someone who takes the reader from place to place, scene to scene, pointing out objects of interest along the way. The narrator may be a character in the story whose point of view and misunderstandings add suspense or interest to a story. Or, the narrator can be a trustworthy, reliable guide.

from *Baker's Bluejay Yarn*

by Mark Twain

Animals talk to each other, of course. There can be no question about that; but I suppose there are very few people who can understand them. I never knew but one man who could. I knew he could, however, because he told me so himself. He was a middle-aged, simple-hearted miner who had lived in a lonely corner of California, among the woods and mountains, a good many years, and had studied the ways of his only neighbors, the beasts and the birds, until he believed he could accurately translate any remark which they made. This was Jim Baker.

L Narrator

The **narrator** is the person who tells a story. The narrator can be a character in the story or an outside observer. The choice of a narrator is an important one to the author, for it influences how the story is revealed to the reader.

As far as I know, Charley never had any childhood at all. The oldest children of sharecroppers never do.

—Eugenia Collier, **from "Sweet Potato Pie"**

Additional Support

Skills Practice

WRITING: Changing Point of View

Tell students to think of a scene from a familiar story, such as a fairy tale or children's story. Then randomly assign points of view to students and have them rewrite the scene using the assigned perspective. Have students read their work aloud. OL

Literary Elements Have students access the Web site to improve their understanding of narrator and voice.

Point of View

First Person With a first-person narrator, the *I* in the story presents the point of view of only one character. The reader is restricted to the thoughts and feelings of that character alone.

> There was only one source of beauty and light for me that school year. The only thing I had anticipated at the start of the semester. That was seeing Eugene.
>
> —Judith Ortiz Cofer, **from "American History"**

A first-person narrator can be the protagonist, one of the minor characters, an outside observer, or a person who has heard the story second-hand. An unreliable first-person narrator is limited, perhaps by age or lack of awareness, in understanding all that is going on.

Third-Person Omniscient A third-person omniscient (all-knowing) narrator uses the pronouns *he* and *she* and usually is not a character in the story. This type of narrator can move from one place to another and back and forth through time. In addition, the omniscient narrator knows the characters' thoughts and feelings and may reveal details the characters themselves could not reveal.

> She dressed plainly because she could not afford fine clothes, but was as unhappy as a woman who has come down in the world; for women have no family rank or social class.
>
> With them, beauty, grace, and charm take the place of birth and breeding. Their natural poise, their instinctive good taste, and their mental cleverness are the sole guiding principles which make daughters of the common people the equals of ladies in high society.
>
> —Guy de Maupassant, **from "The Necklace"**

Third-Person Limited A third-person limited narrator knows the thoughts and feelings of only one character, usually the protagonist. The way people, places, and events appear to that character is the way they appear to the reader.

> "What are you driving so fast for?"
>
> "Hmm?" said Walter Mitty. He looked at his wife, in the seat beside him, with shocked astonishment. She seemed grossly unfamiliar, like a strange woman who had yelled at him in a crowd.
>
> —James Thurber, **from "The Secret Life of Walter Mitty"**

Voice

The distinctive use of language that conveys the author's or narrator's personality is called **voice.** In some cases, an author's voice will be determined by word choice. In other cases, the author's voice is determined by his or her attitude toward the subject or audience (tone) and by the overall emotional quality of the work (mood). **R**

> I did not know then that pride is a wonderful, terrible thing, a seed that bears two vines, life and death.
>
> —James Hurst, **from "The Scarlet Ibis"**

Quickwrite

Describing Author's Voice Think of a writer with a strong, distinctive voice. Describe this author's voice and the qualities that make it memorable.

LiteratureOnline Interactive Literary Elements Handbook Go to www.glencoe.com to review or learn more about narrator and voice.

INDIANA ACADEMIC STANDARDS (pages 206–207)

9.3.9 Explain how voice and the choice of a narrator affect characterization and the tone, plot, and credibility of a text.

9.3.13 Explain how voice, persona, and the choice of a narrator affect the mood, tone, and meaning of text.

LITERARY FOCUS

Teach

R Reading Strategy

Making Generalizations

Ask: How do narrator, point of view, and voice affect a story? *(Students should note that the point of view affects how much information is shared with the reader. It also affects voice. The narrator's voice is shaped by what he or she knows.)* **OL**

Assess

Students' answers should include adjectives that describe the author's voice. If students have trouble thinking of an author, remind them to review the stories they have read so far. Remind them to look at the author's choice of words, sentence length, and use of imagery to analyze the voice.

English Language Coach

Analyzing Narrator and Voice Have English language learners think of a story they have read or heard in their native language and then answer these questions: Who tells the story? *(narrator)* What is the overall tone that characterizes the story? *(voice)* **EL**

Differentiated Instruction

Matching Voice and Music Students who are musical will grasp how a writer's voice conveys a particular mood. Have them select music that expresses the same personality, mood, or tone as the voice in a story of their choosing. Students should play the music and explain their choice to the class. **AL**

Academic Standards

Additional Support activities on pp. 206 and 207 cover the following standards:

Skills Practice: **9.5.8** Write for different purposes...adjusting tone, style, and voice as appropriate.

English Language Coach: **9.3.13** Explain how voice...and...narrator affect the...tone...

Differentiated Instruction: **9.3.13** Explain how voice...affect[s] mood, tone...

Focus

BELLRINGER

Bellringer Options
Selection Focus Transparency 14
Daily Language Practice Transparency 19

Or have students brainstorm a list of things that they daydream about.

Ask: Do you daydream about things that could never come true, or things that could actually happen? Have students arrange their lists in two columns: things that could never come true and things that they could accomplish. Ask volunteers to share one of their daydreams with the class.

Author Search To expand students' appreciation of James Thurber, have them access the Web site for additional information and resources.

BEFORE YOU READ

The Secret Life of Walter Mitty

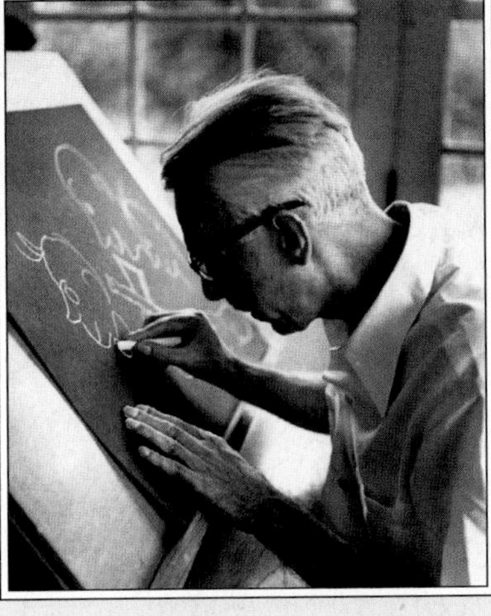

MEET JAMES THURBER

When he was six years old, James Thurber stood with an apple on his head while his older brother aimed a homemade arrow at the fruit. The arrow pierced Thurber's left eye, blinding him in that eye. Aside from that ill-advised decision to assist in his brother's re-creation of William Tell's famous act, Thurber had a relatively normal childhood in Columbus, Ohio.

A Working Writer Thurber's professional writing career began in 1920 when he took a job as a reporter for the *Columbus Dispatch.* In 1927, E. B. White, author of the children's classics *Stuart Little* and *Charlotte's Web,* helped Thurber get a job with *The New Yorker* magazine. For over thirty years, he delighted its readers with humorous stories, essays, fables, and cartoons.

> *"I write basically because it's so much fun."*
>
> —James Thurber

As Thurber aged, the vision in his right eye declined. As a result, he sometimes wrote with a black crayon on yellow paper, filling the page with just twenty words. His usual method of writing, however, was a mental process. Once he had worked out an idea in his mind, he would dictate his thoughts to a secretary, usually about two thousand words in an afternoon.

The Humorist James Thurber has been called the "funniest American writer of his day" and "one of the world's greatest humorists." However, some critics see Thurber's humor as far from lighthearted. In *Thurber: A Collection of Critical Essays,* John Updike wrote that "Thurber's genius was to make of our despair a humorous fable."

Thurber did not consider his humor gentle either. Instead, his stories are edgy and tense, typically reflecting the unsettling problems and disasters that befall humans. Much of his work was satire, a form of writing that ridicules people, practices, or institutions in order to point out their failings. Thurber's satire was social, not political. The institution of marriage was one of his chief targets. But many of his pieces are just plain fun. Thurber once said, "Humor is a serious thing. I like to think of it as one of our greatest earliest natural resources, which must be preserved at all cost."

In his later years, Thurber became increasingly pessimistic, most likely as a result of his ill health and blindness. During this time, his writing became more serious and lacked the humor and hope of his earlier works. He was a contributing writer to *The New Yorker* until the end of his life.

James Thurber was born in 1894 and died in 1961.

LiteratureOnline **Author Search** For more about James Thurber, go to www.glencoe.com.

Selection Skills

The Secret Life of Walter Mitty

Literary Elements
- Diction (SE pp. 209–216)
- Narrator (SE p. 216)

Reading Skills
- Visualizing (SE pp. 209–216)

Vocabulary Skills
- Synonyms (SE pp. 209, 216)
- Academic Vocabulary (SE p. 216)

Listening/Speaking/Viewing Skills
- Analyzing Art (SE p. 210; TWE p. 213)
- Visual Literacy (SE p. 215)

Writing Skills/Grammar
- Evaluate Author's Craft (SE p. 217)
- Using Proper Nouns (SE p. 217)
- Creating an Outline (TWE p. 214)
- Writing a Narrative (TWE p. 218)

LITERATURE PREVIEW

Connecting to the Story

Do you ever daydream? Thurber's short story is about a man who daydreams to escape reality. Before you read the story, think about the following questions:

- Under what circumstances can daydreams be constructive or rewarding?
- Can you think of circumstances when daydreams might be unhealthy or dangerous?

Building Background

This story depicts a person's daydreams about heroic real-life situations, but many of the details of these situations are invented. For example, one daydream includes an eight-engine Navy hydroplane, but there is no such thing. Its commander orders full strength from the turrets to get out of a storm, but turrets are structures on which guns rotate; they have nothing to do with engine power. Other invented details include a medical diagnosis of obstreosis in the ductal tract—a disease that cannot afflict humans in a part of the body that does not even exist—and a reference to a 50.80 caliber pistol, which in reality would be bigger than a cannon.

Setting Purposes for Reading

Big Idea Dreams and Reality

As you read, look for clues that separate Walter Mitty's real world from the world of his daydreams.

Literary Element Diction

Diction is a writer's choice of words and the arrangement of those words in phrases, sentences, or lines of a poem. As you read the story, examine how Thurber chooses his words carefully to convey character and to create a different tone and mood for each of Mitty's daydreams and for his real-life experiences.

- See Literary Terms Handbook, p. R5.

LiteratureOnline Interactive Literary Elements Handbook To review or learn more about the literary elements, go to www.glencoe.com.

READING PREVIEW

Reading Strategy Visualizing

Visualizing is picturing a writer's ideas or descriptions in the mind's eye. Descriptive details in "The Secret Life of Walter Mitty" help the reader visualize settings, characters, and events in Mitty's daydreams and in his real life.

Reading Tip: Gathering Details Use a chart to record details that will help you visualize details in the story.

First Daydream

What do I see?	What do I hear?	How do I feel?
commander in full-dress uniform	voice like thin ice breaking	confident, in control

Vocabulary

distraught (dis trôt′) *adj.* very upset; confused; p. 211 *She was distraught after the car accident.*

haggard (hag′ ərd) *adj.* having a worn and tired look; p. 211 *Anyone would look haggard after two days without sleep.*

craven (krā′ vən) *adj.* extremely cowardly; p. 212 *To let someone else take the punishment for his misdeeds was a truly craven act.*

pandemonium (pan′ də mō′ nē əm) *n.* wild uproar; p. 213 *When the mob began shouting and shoving, pandemonium ensued.*

disdainful (dis dān′ fəl) *adj.* showing scorn for something or someone regarded as unworthy; p. 214 *She gave her boss a disdainful look that showed no respect for his feelings.*

Vocabulary Tip: Synonyms Synonyms are words that have the same or similar meanings.

INDIANA ACADEMIC STANDARDS (pages 209–217)

9.3.11 Evaluate the aesthetic qualities of style, including the impact of diction...on tone [and] mood...

9.2 Develop [reading] strategies...

9.5.2 Write responses to literature that...demonstrate an awareness of the author's style and an appreciation of the effects created.

BEFORE YOU READ

Focus

Summary

Meek, ineffectual Walter Mitty has the world at his feet in his daydreams. He repeatedly drifts into this fantasyland during a shopping outing with his overbearing wife. However, the real world keeps intruding, as his wife, a police officer, a parking attendant, and even passersby interrupt his daydreams with duties he'd rather forget and remind him of mistakes caused by his inattention.

V Vocabulary

Vocabulary File Say: Add these words and definitions to your vocabulary file. For each word, include a sentence that gives you an example of how to use the word. **OL** Students with English language needs should include the pronunciations of these words in their files. **EL**

Literary Elements Have students access the Web site to improve their understanding of diction.

Selection Resources

Print Materials

- Unit 1 Resources (Fast File), pp. 68–70
- Leveled Vocabulary Development, p. 15
- Selection and Unit Assessments, pp. 31–32
- Selection Quick Checks, p. 16

Transparencies

- Bellringer Options Transparencies: Selection Focus Transparency 14; Daily Language Practice Transparency 19
- Literary Elements Transparency 26

Technology

- TeacherWorks Plus™ CD-ROM
- StudentWorks Plus™ CD-ROM
- Presentation Plus!™ CD-ROM
- Literature Online, glencoe.com
- Online Student Edition, mhln.com
- Exam*View*® Assessment Suite CD-ROM
- Vocabulary PuzzleMaker CD-ROM
- Listening Library, disc 1 track 18

Teach

Big Idea

Dreams and Reality Say: Why might it be easier to live in a daydream than in reality? *(In daydreams one can ignore one's problems and shortcomings.)* What effect can constant daydreaming have on one's life? *(It can result in blunders and keep a person from participating in real life.)* OL

L1 Literary Element

Diction Answer: *He is decisive and authoritative.* OL

Viewing the Art

British landscape artist George Horace Davis (1881–1963) painted aerial diagrams that were used to train pilots in the royal Air Force (RAF). **Answer:** *Students should compare their visualizations with the painting.* AS

Readability Scores

Dale-Chall: 3.3

DRP: 52

Lexile: 700

The Secret Life of Walter Mitty

James Thurber

"We're going through!" The Commander's voice was like thin ice breaking. He wore his full-dress uniform, with the heavily braided white cap pulled down rakishly[1] over one cold gray eye. "We can't make it, sir. It's spoiling for a hurricane, if you ask me."

"I'm not asking you, Lieutenant Berg," said the Commander. "Throw on the power lights! Rev her up to 8,500! We're going through!" The pounding of the cylinders increased: ta-pocketa-pocketa-pocketa-*pocketa-pocketa*. The Commander stared at the ice forming on the pilot window. He walked over and twisted a row of complicated dials. "Switch on No. 8 auxiliary!" he shouted. "Switch on No. 8 auxiliary!" repeated Lieutenant Berg. "Full strength in No. 3 turret!" shouted the Commander. "Full strength in No. 3 turret!" The crew, bending to their various tasks in the huge, hurtling eight-engined Navy hydroplane,[2] looked at each other and grinned. "The Old Man'll get us through," they said to

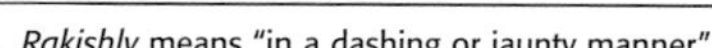

1. *Rakishly* means "in a dashing or jaunty manner."
2. A *hydroplane* is an airplane equipped with floats that allow it to take off from and land on water.

Literary Element Diction *What does the Commander's style of speaking tell you about him?* L1

Putting Out His Eyes, 1919. George Horace Davis. Oil. Imperial War Museum.

Viewing the Art: Is this how you picture the first scene of the story? Why or why not? 

Additional Support

Skills Practice

READING: Understanding Transitions Review Thurber's techniques for separating Mitty's two worlds, including the use of ellipses and the abrupt switch from criticism to flattery in dialogue and from flat to melodramatic description. Have students list clues from the dialogue and descriptions in a chart like the one shown here.

	Dialogue	Descriptions
Dream		
Reality		

OL

one another. "The Old Man ain't afraid of Hell!" . . .

"Not so fast! You're driving too fast!" said Mrs. Mitty. "What are you driving so fast for?"

"Hmm?" said Walter Mitty. He looked at his wife, in the seat beside him, with shocked astonishment. She seemed grossly unfamiliar, like a strange woman who had yelled at him in a crowd. "You were up to fifty-five," she said. "You know I don't like to go more than forty. You were up to fifty-five." Walter Mitty drove on toward Waterbury in silence, the roaring of the SN202 through the worst storm in twenty years of Navy flying fading in the remote, intimate airways of his mind. "You're tensed up again," said Mrs. Mitty. "It's one of your days. I wish you'd let Dr. Renshaw look you over."

Walter Mitty stopped the car in front of the building where his wife went to have her hair done. "Remember to get those overshoes while I'm having my hair done," she said. "I don't need overshoes," said Mitty. She put her mirror back into her bag. "We've been all through that," she said, getting out of the car. "You're not a young man any longer." He raced the engine a little. "Why don't you wear your gloves? Have you lost your gloves?" Walter Mitty reached in a pocket and brought out the gloves. He put them on, but after she had turned and gone into the building and he had driven on to a red light, he took them off again. "Pick it up, brother!" snapped a cop as the light changed, and Mitty hastily pulled on his gloves and lurched ahead. He drove around the streets aimlessly for a time, and then he drove past the hospital on his way to the parking lot.

Big Idea Dreams and Reality *What clues does Thurber provide to help you know there is a clash between dreams and reality here?* **BI1**

Literary Element Diction *How does Thurber's word choice here help convey Mitty's character?* **L2**

. . . "It's the millionaire banker, Wellington McMillan," said the pretty nurse. "Yes?" said Walter Mitty, removing his gloves slowly. "Who has the case?" "Dr. Renshaw and Dr. Benbow, but there are two specialists here, Dr. Remington from New York and Mr. Pritchard-Mitford from London. He flew over." A door opened down a long, cool corridor and Dr. Renshaw came out. He looked **distraught** and **haggard**. "Hello, Mitty," he said. "We're having the devil's own time with McMillan, the millionaire banker and close personal friend of Roosevelt. Obstreosis of the ductal tract. Tertiary. Wish you'd take a look at him." "Glad to," said Mitty.

In the operating room there were whispered introductions: "Dr. Remington, Dr. Mitty. Mr. Pritchard-Mitford, Dr. Mitty." "I've read your book on streptothricosis," said Pritchard-Mitford, shaking hands. "A brilliant performance, sir." "Thank you," said Walter Mitty. "Didn't know you were in the States, Mitty," grumbled Remington. "Coals to Newcastle,[3] bringing Mitford and me up here for a tertiary." "You are very kind," said Mitty. A huge, complicated machine, connected to the operating table, with many tubes and wires, began at this moment to go pocketa-pocketa-pocketa. "The new anesthetizer is giving way!" shouted an intern. "There is no one in the East who knows how to fix it!" "Quiet, man!" said Mitty, in a low, cool voice. He sprang to the machine, which was now going pocketa-pocketa-queep-pocketa-queep. He began fingering delicately a row of glistening dials. "Give me a fountain pen!"[4] he

3. Carrying *coals to Newcastle* would be a waste of time and energy, since Newcastle, England, is a coal-mining town.
4. A *fountain pen* has a reservoir or replaceable cartridge that automatically feeds a steady supply of ink to the nib, or pen point.

Big Idea Dreams and Reality *How does Thurber tie this daydream to what Mitty is experiencing in real life?* **BI2**

Vocabulary

distraught (dis trôt′) *adj.* very upset; confused

haggard (hag′ ərd) *adj.* having a worn and tired look

Teach

BI1 Big Idea

Dreams and Reality Answer: *Ellipses separate his daydreams from reality. In his fantasies, events are dramatic and he is always a hero; his real life is dull and he is always at fault.* **OL**

L2 Literary Element

Diction Answer: *"Hastily pulled on his gloves" suggests meek obedience. "Lurched ahead" suggests he is an incompetent driver.* **OL**

BI2 Big Idea

Dreams and Reality Answer: *This daydream is taking place in a hospital and Mitty is a doctor. In real life, Mitty has just driven past a hospital, and earlier his wife said he should see a doctor. In the daydream, Mitty removes his gloves slowly. In real life, he pulls on his gloves hastily.* **OL**

CheckPoint

Use the CheckPoint questions on Presentation Plus! to monitor students' comprehension. These questions can be used with interactive response keypads for immediate student feedback.

English Language Coach

Ellipses Help English language learners understand the use of ellipses in this selection. Explain that ellipses often indicate an unfinished thought or speech that trails off. In this selection, they serve as transitions between fantasy and reality. Ask students to mark the transitions with sticky notes. Then have students form small groups. Have group members take turns reading all the reality segments in sequence, followed by all the fantasy segments. Then ask students to share their reactions to the way Thurber structured the story. **EL**

Academic Standards

Additional Support activities on pp. 210 and 211 cover the following standards:

Skills Practice: **9.3.11** Evaluate the aesthetic qualities of style...

English Language Coach: **9.6.1** Identify... the mechanics of punctuation, such as...ellipses...

Teach

R1 Reading Strategy

Visualizing Answer: *The details "vaulted into the car" and "insolent skill" help create an image of a cocky young man whose skillful driving is intuitive. In contrast, Mitty drives in the wrong lane and is extremely cautious.* OL

L Literary Element

Diction Answer: *It creates a false sense of authenticity in Mitty's daydream.*
Ask: Why do you think Thurber puts so much nonsense into Mitty's fantasy dialogue? *(It contrasts with the heroic, commanding tone and context of the daydreams and reminds the reader that Mitty is making all this up.)* OL

★ Writer's Technique

Characterization Thurber gives readers a glimpse into Mitty's thought process about a real event and gives them a chance to draw a conclusion about what Mitty thinks of his true abilities. AS

snapped. Someone handed him a fountain pen. He pulled a faulty piston out of the machine and inserted the pen in its place. "That will hold for ten minutes," he said. "Get on with the operation." A nurse hurried over and whispered to Renshaw, and Mitty saw the man turn pale. "Coreopsis[5] has set in," said Renshaw nervously. "If you would take over, Mitty?" Mitty looked at him and at the **craven** figure of Benbow, who drank, and at the grave, uncertain faces of the two great specialists. "If you wish," he said. They slipped a white gown on him; he adjusted a mask and drew on thin gloves; nurses handed him shining . . . .

"Back it up, Mac! Look out for that Buick!" Walter Mitty jammed on the brakes. "Wrong lane, Mac," said the parking-lot attendant, looking at Mitty closely. "Gee. Yeh," muttered Mitty. He began cautiously to back out of the lane marked "Exit Only." "Leave her sit there," said the attendant. "I'll put her away." Mitty got out of the car. "Hey, better leave the key." "Oh," said Mitty, handing the man the ignition key. The attendant vaulted into the car, backed it up with insolent[6] skill, and put it where it belonged.

Visual Vocabulary
In some areas, people put *chains* on tires to provide better traction on ice and snow.

They're so damn cocky, thought Walter Mitty, walking along Main Street; they think they know everything. Once he had tried to take his chains off, outside New Milford, and he had got them wound around the axles. A man had had to come out in a wrecking car and unwind them, a young, grinning garageman. Since then Mrs. Mitty always made him drive to a garage to have the chains taken off. The next time, he thought, I'll wear my right arm in a sling; they won't grin at me then. I'll have my right arm in a sling and they'll see I couldn't possibly take the chains off myself. He kicked at the slush on the sidewalk. "Overshoes," he said to himself, and he began looking for a shoe store. ★

When he came out into the street again, with the overshoes in a box under his arm, Walter Mitty began to wonder what the other thing was his wife had told him to get. She had told him, twice, before they set out from their house for Waterbury. In a way he hated these weekly trips to town—he was always getting something wrong. Kleenex, he thought, Squibb's, razor blades? No. Toothpaste, toothbrush, bicarbonate, carborundum, initiative and referendum?[7] He gave it up. But she would remember it. "Where's the what's-its-name?" she would ask. "Don't tell me you forgot the what's-its-name." A newsboy went by shouting something about the Waterbury trial.

. . . "Perhaps this will refresh your memory." The District Attorney suddenly thrust a heavy automatic at the quiet figure on the witness stand. "Have you ever seen this before?" Walter Mitty took the gun and examined it expertly. "This is my Webley-Vickers 50.80," he said calmly. An excited buzz ran around the courtroom. The Judge rapped for order. "You are a crack shot with any sort of firearms, I believe?" said the District Attorney, insinuatingly.[8] "Objection!"

5. If *coreopsis* really has set in, the patient may need a gardener. This is the name of a daisy-like flowering plant.
6. *Insolent* means "so rude or proud as to be offensive."

Reading Strategy Visualizing *What details help you visualize the attendant? How does this image contrast with the image you formed of Mitty trying to park?* R1

Vocabulary
craven (krā′ vən) *adj.* extremely cowardly

7. Mitty's shopping list is partially nonsense: *Carborundum* is the brand name of an industrial compound used to grind and polish, an *initiative* is a procedure enabling voters to propose new laws, and a *referendum* is a direct popular vote on a public issue.
8. Here *insinuatingly* (in sin′ ū āt′ ing lē) means "in a way to suggest guilt."

Literary Element Diction *Why does Thurber include this reference to something that does not really exist?* L

Additional Support

Skills Practice

READING: Reviewing and Questioning Guide students to monitor comprehension by revisiting problematic sections. **Ask:** What happens to Mitty between the first and second paragraphs in the first column on page 212? *(In one paragraph he is a skilled doctor putting on a gown and gloves to do surgery. In the next paragraph, a parking attendant is yelling at him.)* What punctuation separates the two paragraphs? *(The paragraphs are separated by ellipses.)* How does Mitty change between paragraphs? *(Mitty goes from being respected to being humiliated.)* OL

Hotel Lobby, 1943. Edward Hopper. Oil on canvas, 82 × 103.5. cm Indianapolis Museum of Art.

shouted Mitty's attorney. "We have shown that the defendant could not have fired the shot. We have shown that he wore his right arm in a sling on the night of the fourteenth of July." Walter Mitty raised his hand briefly and the bickering attorneys were stilled. "With any known make of gun," he said evenly, "I could have killed Gregory Fitzhurst at three hundred feet *with my left hand.*" **Pandemonium** broke loose in the courtroom. A woman's scream rose above the bedlam and suddenly a lovely, dark-haired girl was in Walter Mitty's arms. The District Attorney struck at her savagely. Without rising from his chair, Mitty let the man have it on the point of the chin. "You miserable cur!" . . .[9]

"Puppy biscuit," said Walter Mitty. He stopped walking and the buildings of Waterbury rose up out of the misty courtroom and surrounded him again. A woman who was passing laughed. "He said 'Puppy biscuit,' " she said to her companion. "That man said 'Puppy biscuit' to himself." Walter Mitty hurried on. He went into an A&P,[10] not the first one he came to but a smaller one farther up the street. "I want some biscuit for small, young dogs," he said to the clerk. "Any special brand, sir?" The greatest pistol shot in the world thought a moment. "It says 'Puppies Bark for It' on the box," said Walter Mitty.

His wife would be through at the hairdresser's in fifteen minutes, Mitty saw in looking at his watch, unless they had trouble drying it; sometimes they had trouble drying it. She didn't like to get to the hotel first; she would want him to be there waiting for her as usual. He found a big leather chair in the lobby, facing a window, and he put the overshoes and the puppy biscuit on the floor beside it. He picked up an old copy of *Liberty* and sank down into the chair. "Can Germany Conquer the World Through the Air?" Walter Mitty looked at the pictures of bombing planes and of ruined streets.

9. A *cur* can be either a mean, rude person or a mixed-breed dog.

10. *A&P*, short for Atlantic & Pacific Tea Company, is a chain of grocery stores.

Vocabulary

pandemonium (pan′ də mō′ nē əm) *n.* wild uproar

Reading Strategy Visualizing *What details help you visualize this scene?* R2

Teach

R2 Reading Strategy

Visualizing Answer: *Details include repetition of the phrase "Puppy biscuit," the references to Waterbury and the A & P, and the mocking woman.*
Say: Thurber contrasts the melodramatic courtroom scene with the quietly mundane "puppy biscuit" episode to hilarious effect. What are some contrasting details that emphasize the difference between Mitty's two lives? *(Authority, action, passion, "raised his hand briefly," "crack shot," "pandemonium," girl in his arms) versus the mildness of puppies, his absent-minded dealings with the A & P clerk, mocking woman.)* Emphasize how well balanced the two scenes are. OL

Viewing the Art

American realist painter Edward Hopper (1882–1967) is known for his often stark scenes of everyday twentieth-century American life. His works often suggest that the figures depicted are alone, even if they are surrounded by others. AS

Differentiated Instruction

Monitoring Comprehension Remind less proficient readers to check their comprehension as they read. Encourage them to reread parts they find unclear and to ask and answer questions about characters and events. Have students record the events from Walter's "Fantasy World" and those from his "Real World" in a two-column chart like the one shown.

Fantasy World	Real World
The commander of a hydroplane has his crew flying at top speeds.	Mitty's wife tells him to drive more slowly, and he does what she asks.

BL

Academic Standards

Additional Support activities on pp. 212 and 213 cover the following standards:

Skills Practice: **9.3.6** Analyze and trace an author's development of time and sequence...

Differentiated Instruction: **9.2** Develop strategies such as asking questions...and identifying and analyzing...organization...

Teach

BI Big Idea

Dreams and Reality **Answer:** *Mitty was looking at pictures of bombing planes and ruined streets in the magazine* Liberty. OL

R Reading Strategy

Visualizing **Answer:** *Sounds include the cannon's pounding, machine guns' rat-tat-tatting, flame-throwers' pocketa-pocketa-pocketa, and Mitty's humming.* OL

L Literary Element

Diction **Answer:** *Even the revolving door appears to be ridiculing Mitty.* OL

Use the CheckPoint questions on Presentation Plus! to check students' mastery of the selection. These questions can be used with interactive response keypads for immediate student feedback.

. . . "The cannonading has got the wind up in young Raleigh, sir," said the sergeant. Captain Mitty looked up at him through tousled hair. "Get him to bed," he said wearily. "With the others. I'll fly alone." "But you can't, sir," said the sergeant anxiously. "It takes two men to handle that bomber and the Archies are pounding hell out of the air. Von Richtman's circus is between here and Saulier."[11] "Somebody's got to get that ammunition dump," said Mitty. "I'm going over. Spot of brandy?" He poured a drink for the sergeant and one for himself. War thundered and whined around the dugout and battered at the door. There was a rending of wood and splinters flew through the room. "A bit of a near thing," said Captain Mitty carelessly. "The box barrage[12] is closing in," said the sergeant. "We only live once, Sergeant," said Mitty, with his faint, fleeting smile. "Or do we?" He poured another brandy and tossed it off. "I never see a man could hold his brandy like you, sir," said the sergeant. "Begging your pardon, sir." Captain Mitty stood up and strapped on his huge Webley-Vickers automatic. "It's forty kilometers through hell, sir," said the sergeant. Mitty finished one last brandy. "After all," he said softly, "what isn't?" The pounding of the cannon increased; there was the rat-tat-tatting of machine guns, and from somewhere came the menacing pocketa-pocketa-pocketa of the new flame-throwers. Walter Mitty walked to the door of the dugout humming "Auprès de Ma Blonde."[13] He turned and waved to the sergeant. "Cheerio!" he said . . .

Something struck his shoulder. "I've been looking all over this hotel for you," said Mrs. Mitty. "Why do you have to hide in this old chair? How did you expect me to find you?" "Things close in," said Walter Mitty vaguely. "What?" Mrs. Mitty said. "Did you get the what's-its-name? The puppy biscuit? What's in that box?" "Overshoes," said Mitty. "Couldn't you have put them on in the store?" "I was thinking," said Walter Mitty. "Does it ever occur to you that I am sometimes thinking?" She looked at him. "I'm going to take your temperature when I get you home," she said.

They went out through the revolving doors that made a faintly derisive[14] whistling sound when you pushed them. It was two blocks to the parking lot. At the drugstore on the corner she said, "Wait here for me. I forgot something. I won't be a minute." She was more than a minute. Walter Mitty lighted a cigarette. It began to rain, rain with sleet in it. He stood up against the wall of the drugstore, smoking. . . . He put his shoulders back and his heels together. "To hell with the handkerchief," said Walter Mitty scornfully. He took one last drag on his cigarette and snapped it away. Then, with that faint, fleeting smile playing about his lips, he faced the firing squad; erect and motionless, proud and **disdainful**, Walter Mitty the Undefeated, inscrutable[15] to the last. ∾

11. Mitty blends fantasy with the realities of World War I. *Archies* was the British name for anti-aircraft guns and their shells. *Von Richtman* suggests Manfred von Richthofen, the German flying ace known as the Red Baron. *Saulier* appears to be a made-up name for a town in France.
12. *Box barrage* refers to artillery fire used to hold back the enemy or to protect one's own soldiers.
13. *"Auprès de Ma Blonde"* (ō prā də mä blōnd) is a French song ("Near My Blonde") that was popular during World War I.
14. *Derisive* (di rī′ siv) means mocking, jeering, or ridiculing.
15. *Inscrutable* (in skro͞o′ tə bəl) means "mysterious."

Big Idea Dreams and Reality *What triggers this daydream for Mitty?* BI

Reading Strategy Visualizing *What sounds help you create a vivid picture of this scene in your mind?* R

Literary Element Diction *Why do you think Thurber describes the sound of the door as "derisive"?* L

Vocabulary

disdainful (dis dān′ fəl) *adj.* showing scorn for something or someone regarded as unworthy

Additional Support

Skills Practice

WRITING: Creating an Outline
Have students write an outline of the selection's main ideas and details. Help students organize their outlines by noting that each of the fantasies and each real-life episode can be a main idea. Here is the beginning of a sample outline:

I. The Commander orders his crew to fly through bad weather.
   A. The Commander is fearless.
   B. His crew respects him.
II. Mitty's wife criticizes his driving.
   A. Mrs. Mitty wants the speed under forty.
   B. Mitty does what she says. OL

AFTER YOU READ

RESPONDING AND THINKING CRITICALLY

Respond

1. Did you identify with Walter Mitty as you read this story? Explain.

Recall and Interpret

2. (a)What does Mitty's wife ask him to do while she is at the hairdresser? (b)How does he feel about the errands, and why does he do them?
3. (a)What roles does Mitty play in his different daydreams? (b)What is ironic, or contradictory, about the way in which Mitty sees himself in his daydreams?
4. (a)Which of Mitty's traits causes his wife, the police officer, and the parking attendant to scold him? (b)Why do they treat him this way?
5. (a)How does Mitty's wife greet him at the hotel? (b)What does Mitty's conversation with his wife at the hotel tell you about their relationship?

Analyze and Evaluate

6. (a)What is the main conflict in the story? (b)Is the conflict resolved in a way that is satisfying to you? Why or why not?
7. (a)How does Thurber tie the beginning of the story to the ending? (b)Why do you think he does this?

Connect

8. **Big Idea** **Dreams and Reality** What is missing in Walter Mitty's real life that he tries to fulfill in his daydreams?

VISUAL LITERACY: Cartoon

Read the "Calvin and Hobbes" comic strip. Then consider how Calvin's daydream compares with Mitty's daydreams and in what ways the two characters are alike.

1. How are Calvin and Walter Mitty alike?
2. (a)How do Calvin's surroundings lead him into his daydream? (b)How do Mitty's surroundings lead him into daydreams?

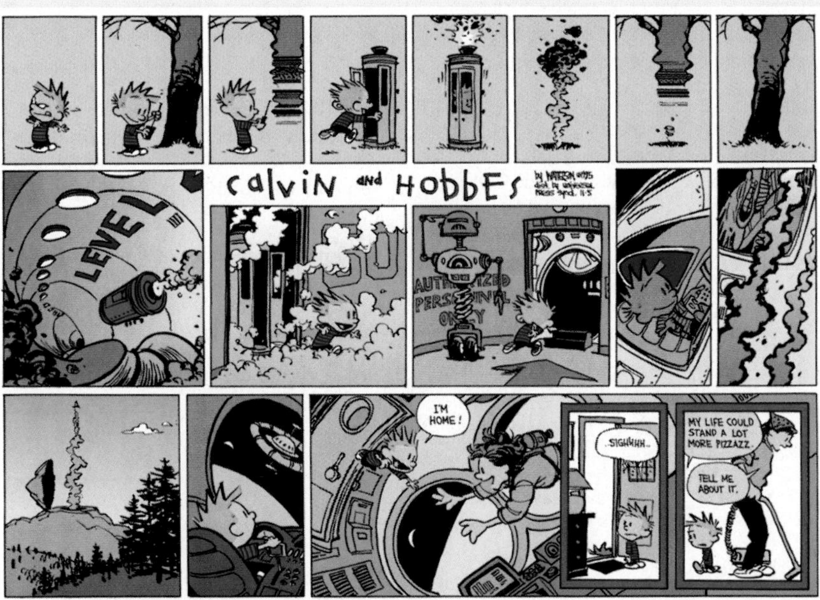

AFTER YOU READ

Assess

1. Accept reasonable answers supported by details from the text.
2. (a) To buy overshoes and puppy biscuits (b) He resents her demands but submits because he is meek and passive.
3. (a) A Navy flight commander, a surgeon, a wrongly accused defendant and crack shot, a World War I captain, and a man facing a firing squad (b) He is fearless and admired, the exact opposite of how he is viewed in real life.
4. (a) Inattentiveness (b) He never stands up for himself.
5. (a) She accuses him of being hard to find. (b) There is no real closeness or communication in their marriage.
6. (a) The conflict between his real life and his fantasy life (b) Accept any reasonable answer.
7. (a) It begins and ends in fantasy. (b) To show that Walter will cling to his fantasies to the end
8. Respect, excitement, power, admiration, and self-worth

Visual Literacy

Ask the groups to draw a Venn diagram in which to compare and contrast Calvin and Mitty.

1. They both dream of heroic adventures.
2. (a) Tree trunk turns into Calvin's space capsule. (b) View of hospital prompts surgeon fantasy; newsboy's cries lead to the murder trial sequence; magazine pictures of bombers inspire pilot daydream; leaning against wall prompts firing squad image.

Academic Standards

The Additional Support activity on p. 214 covers the following standard:

Skills Practice: **9.5.2** Write responses to literature that demonstrate a comprehensive grasp of the significant ideas of literary works…

AFTER YOU READ

Assess

Literary Element

1. The real Mitty is a chronically defeated sad sack.
2. Daydreams: "I'm not asking you," and "Quiet, man!" Wife: "Hmm?" and "Things close in." They show his divided character—the gap between his true self and what he would like to be.
3. Students may point to the Puppy biscuit incident and to Mitty's invention of a disease.

Review: Narrator

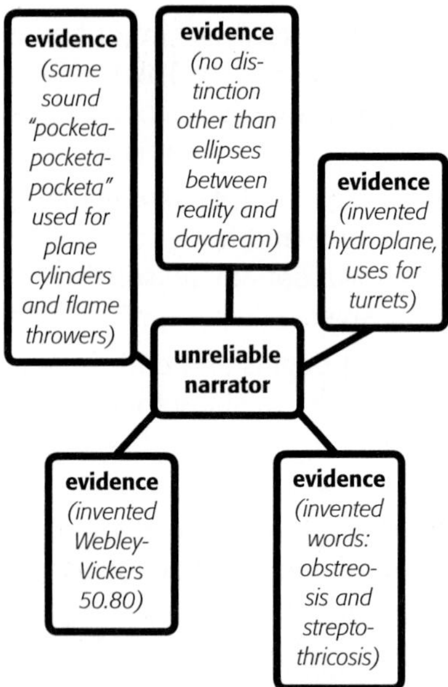

Reading Strategy

1. Images of Mitty as authoritative and admired (he silences the lawyers, "crack shot" girl's embrace) and wildly dramatic events (pandemonium, bedlam) are offset by opposing images of mildness, dullness, and mockery (puppies, A & P, laughing woman).
2. Accept answers that are well supported by sensory details.

LITERARY ANALYSIS

Literary Element Diction

Diction allows writers to establish setting, convey meaning, and create different tones, moods, and images. For example, in "The Secret Life of Walter Mitty," Thurber deliberately misuses real words such as *coreopsis*, which is a plant, not a disease, and *carborundum, initiative,* and *referendum*, which do not belong on a grocery list. This helps establish a humorous tone and, at the same time, reveals Mitty's daydreams as preposterous.

1. Reread the last line of the story. How do the adjectives used to describe Mitty compare with the way he really is?
2. Give examples of language Mitty uses to speak to others in his daydreams and language he uses to speak to his wife. What do these examples reveal about his character?
3. Besides the deliberate misuse of words, how does Thurber's diction contribute to the humorous tone of the story and help characterize Mitty as absurd and inept?

Review: Narrator

As you learned on pages 206–207, the **narrator** is the person who tells a story. An unreliable narrator presents an untrustworthy account of people and events. The narrator of "The Secret Life of Walter Mitty" shifts between the real world and Mitty's dream world. Does this shifting make the narrator unreliable?

Partner Activity Meet with a classmate and discuss how the story's narrator could be perceived as unreliable. Working with your partner, create a web diagram like the one below. Then fill it in with evidence that proves (or disproves) that the narrator is unreliable.

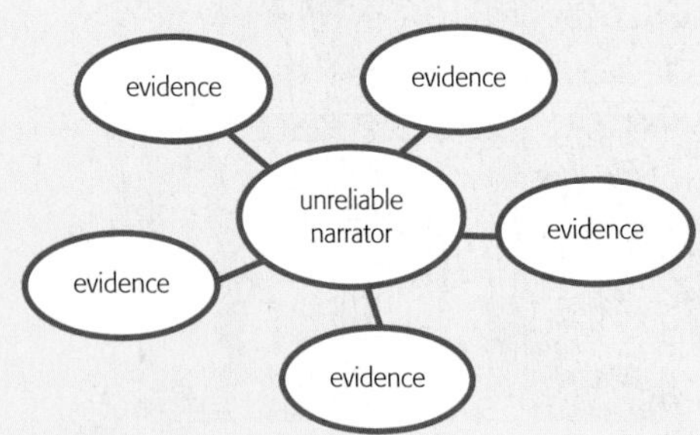

READING AND VOCABULARY

Reading Strategy Visualizing

By **visualizing** as you read, you can better understand what is happening and why. Review the sensory chart you created for visualizing important characters and events in the story.

1. Point out details that allow you to visualize the courtroom scene and the "puppy biscuit" scene. How does Thurber use these details to create parallels between the two scenes?
2. What scene in the story is most memorable to you? What specific details help you visualize this scene?

Vocabulary Practice

Practice with Synonyms Choose the synonym for each vocabulary word from "The Secret Life of Walter Mitty" listed in the first column. Use a dictionary or thesaurus if you need help.

1. craven	**a.** spineless	**b.** fear
2. pandemonium	**a.** stable	**b.** chaos
3. disdainful	**a.** haughty	**b.** proudly
4. distraught	**a.** agitated	**b.** peaceful
5. haggard	**a.** fresh	**b.** exhausted

Academic Vocabulary

Here are two words from the vocabulary list on page R80. These words will help you think, talk, and write about the selection.

respond (ri spond′) *v.* to react to a situation or event

constitute (kon′ stə to͞ot′) *v.* to make up a part or the whole of something

Practice and Apply

1. How does Walter Mitty **respond** to the crises that occur in his daydreams?
2. What elements would you say **constitute** a Walter Mitty daydream?

Vocabulary

1. a **2.** b **3.** a **4.** a **5.** b

Academic Vocabulary

1. He reacts by calmly taking command.
2. Heroism, drama, and excitement are the main elements of his daydreams.

WRITING AND EXTENDING

Writing About Literature

Evaluate Author's Craft Think about the way in which Thurber uses diction to create the real life and the daydream life of Walter Mitty. Write two or three paragraphs in which you state your opinion about how effectively Thurber uses diction to show the conflict between Mitty's two lives and how well he connects them. Use evidence and examples from the story to support your evaluation.

As you draft, write from start to finish. Use a chart like the one below to help you organize your thoughts.

	Event/Scene	Examples of Diction
Mitty's real life		
Mitty's daydream life		

After you complete your draft, meet with a peer reviewer to evaluate each other's work and to suggest revisions. Then proofread your draft for errors in spelling, grammar, and punctuation.

Listening and Speaking

With a small group, organize and present a dramatic reading of "The Secret Life of Walter Mitty." Select a director and a person to create sound effects, and then assign actors to play the different roles. (In order to perform the daydream sequences, some actors may need to play the parts of two or more characters.) Rehearse the story until you can perform it smoothly, focusing on volume, pacing, enunciation, eye contact, and gestures. Present your dramatic reading to the class.

GRAMMAR AND STYLE

Thurber's Language and Style

Using Proper Nouns A proper noun is the name of a particular person, place, thing, or idea. Proper nouns should always be capitalized. In "The Secret Life of Walter Mitty," James Thurber uses proper nouns to create a sense of realism in both Mitty's reality and his fantasies. Proper nouns add a sense of authenticity, whether or not the people or places actually exist. For example, note the capitalization of names and places in this sentence from the story.

". . . there are two specialists here, Dr. Remington from New York and Mr. Pritchard-Mitford from London."

Consider how much less effective it would have been if Thurber had used common nouns in the story instead of the following proper nouns:

Proper Noun	Common Noun
Wellington McMillan	man
Buick	car
Webley-Vickers 50.80	gun
Liberty	magazine

Activity Create a chart of your own, listing more proper nouns from the story. For each of Thurber's proper nouns, write a common noun that could be used in its place. Use your imagination to create common nouns for words Thurber made up, and do not forget to capitalize all proper nouns.

Revising Check

Proper Nouns Work with a partner to review the use of proper nouns in your essay about Thurber's diction. Revise your draft to include the appropriate proper nouns, and check that you have capitalized all proper nouns correctly.

LiteratureOnline **Web Activities** For eFlashcards, Selection Quick Checks, and other Web activities, go to www.glencoe.com.

AFTER YOU READ

Assess

Writing About Literature

Students' evaluations should

- identify specific examples of diction that characterize Mitty's real life and his daydreams.
- offer an opinion about how well Thurber uses diction to help readers understand the connection and conflict between Mitty in his real life and in his daydreams.

Listening and Speaking

Suggest that students consider the following techniques to indicate the dream sequences:

- perform in slower motion
- use music cues
- change the lighting
- use masks or other costume changes

Thurber's Language and Style

Students may choose answers such as:
Mrs. Mitty/wife or woman
SN202/plane
Dr. Benbow/doctor
New Milford or Waterbury/town
District Attorney/lawyer
A&P/supermarket

LiteratureOnline

Web Activities Have students access the Web site for interactive activities that will help them assess their understanding of the selection.

Differentiated Instruction

Essay Questions Essays are assessed more on how well the writer makes a point than on the writer's presenting a correct answer. Have students use these tips to plan their response to this question: What techniques does Thurber use to enable the reader to visualize and distinguish between Mitty's real and fantasy lives?

- Reread the test question to be sure you understand it.
- Write ideas on scrap paper.
- Start with a thesis statement, follow with supporting evidence, and end with a conclusion. AL

Academic Standards

The Additional Support activity on p. 217 covers the following standard:

Differentiated Instruction: **9.4.2** Establish a coherent thesis that conveys a clear perspective on the subject...

Focus

Write this sentence on the board: "Pick it up, brother!" snapped a cop as the light changed, and Mitty hastily pulled on his gloves and lurched ahead.
Discuss what makes this sentence compound and not a run-on.

Teach

Compound Subjects and Verbs Explain the difference between a compound sentence and compound subjects or verbs. Emphasize that a compound sentence is made up of two simple sentences, each of which has a subject and a verb. Note that compound subjects or verbs are not separated by a comma. OL

Assess

Possible rewrites:

1. Mitty is ordinary, but he imagines himself as extraordinary.
2. Mitty is running errands; he is daydreaming at the same time.
3. Mitty's wife tells him what to do, but she doesn't control his inner life.

Grammar Workshop

Sentence Structure

▶ **Run-on Sentences**
A **run-on sentence** is two or more complete sentences written incorrectly as a single sentence.

▶ **Test-Taking Tip**
Always check your writing on a test for run-on sentences. Look for two or more main clauses in a single sentence. Then check to be sure you have the correct punctuation.

▶ **Language Handbook**
For more about sentences, see Language Handbook, pp. R49–R50.

Avoiding Run-on Sentences

"He drove around the streets aimlessly for a time, and then he drove past the hospital on his way to the parking lot."

—James Thurber, from "The Secret Life of Walter Mitty"

Connecting to Literature James Thurber presents connected ideas in a **compound sentence**—a sentence with two or more main clauses. Sometimes, however, writers fail to correctly punctuate two or more main clauses. This creates a **run-on sentence,** two or more complete sentences written incorrectly as a single sentence.

Note the following run-on sentence problems and their solutions.

Problem 1 Two main clauses are separated with only a comma.

The doctor introduced himself, Mitty shook hands with him.

Problem 2 Two main clauses appear with no punctuation between them.

The machine doesn't operate correctly Mitty fixes it.

Solution A Make the sentence into two short sentences.

The doctor introduced himself. Mitty shook hands with him.

The machine doesn't operate correctly. Mitty fixes it.

Solution B Add a coordinating conjunction after a comma.

The doctor introduced himself, and Mitty shook hands with him.

The machine doesn't operate correctly, so Mitty fixes it.

Problem 3 A compound sentence is missing a comma.

The situation is serious but Mitty is confident.

Solution Add the comma before the coordinating conjunction.

The situation is serious, but Mitty is confident.

Literature Online
eWorkbooks To link to the Grammar and Language eWorkbook, go to www.glencoe.com.

Exercise

Rewrite these sentences, applying one of the solutions shown above.

1. Mitty is ordinary, he imagines himself as extraordinary.
2. Mitty is running errands he is daydreaming at the same time.
3. Mitty's wife tells him what to do but she doesn't control his inner life.

ACADEMIC STANDARDS (page 218)
9.6.2 Demonstrate an understanding of sentence construction...

Additional Support

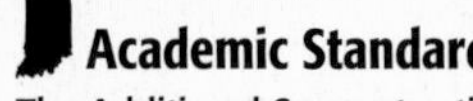

Academic Standards
The Additional Support activity on p. 218 covers the following standards:
Skills Practice: **9.6.2** Demonstrate an understanding of sentence construction... **9.5.1** Write...narratives... **9.4.11** Edit and proofread...

Skills Practice

WRITING: Writing a Narrative Have students reread selected paragraphs from the selection, noting compound and complex sentences. Copy examples onto the board and discuss the logic used in joining these clauses. Have students write a narrative paragraph in which Mitty daydreams he is a spy, including at least two run-on sentences. Students can then exchange papers, locate and correct the run-ons, and explain why they made these changes. Finally, have students read their own paragraphs aloud, using punctuation to cue appropriate pauses. OL

BEFORE YOU READ

The Necklace

MEET GUY DE MAUPASSANT

Guy de Maupassant (gē də mō pä sän′) ranks with the world's greatest short story writers and is one of the indispensable authors of French literature. Though he was the child of wealthy parents, he grew up among the children of peasants and sailors who lived near his mother's estates in northwestern France. Their hard-working lives and colorful language and customs captured the young Maupassant's imagination. When he went away to school, Maupassant spent occasional Sundays with the great French novelist Gustave Flaubert (goos täv′ flō bār′), his mother's childhood friend. Flaubert encouraged the young Maupassant's literary efforts and suggested that he experiment with poetry in order to practice clarity and concision.

From War to Writing The young Maupassant served in the Franco-Prussian War from late 1869 to July of 1871, an experience which gave him a strong distaste for war. Upon returning home, he became a government clerk, devoting his free time to writing. Flaubert helped Maupassant to join the flourishing Parisian literary scene, introducing Maupassant to such important writers as Émile Zola, Ivan Turgenev, and Henry James. At the age of thirty, Maupassant published his own work in a volume of stories by up-and-coming authors. Flaubert declared the story a masterpiece. Maupassant became famous and successful.

> *"She had been born for all the little niceties and luxuries of living."*
>
> —Guy de Maupassant, from "The Necklace"

Putting the working world behind him, Maupassant began to live extravagantly. He built himself a villa, purchased a boat, and traveled around Europe. Eventually his extravagances forced him into debt. To keep up with expenses, he began writing at a frenetic pace. Between 1880 and 1890, he authored three hundred short stories, six novels, three travel books, and his only volume of verse.

Life's Catastrophes Maupassant's own life experiences were reflected in his work. He wrote of middle-class strivers, peasants, soldiers, and ordinary people caught in disastrous or demeaning situations. Maupassant described his subject as life's "inexplicable, illogical, and contradictory catastrophes" and said that writing should aim not at "telling a story or entertaining us or touching our hearts but at forcing us to think and understand the deeper, hidden meaning of events." In addition to writing about the problems of ordinary people, Maupassant wrote probing horror stories that are named as influences by present-day artists such as director Oliver Stone and author Stephen King.

Maupassant's friends remarked on his sense of joie de vivre, or enjoyment of life. Many of his stories are humorous and warm-hearted. He captured a vital, colorful, charming, and sometimes heartbreaking France. For many, Maupassant epitomizes the polish and intelligence of French literature.

Guy de Maupassant was born in 1850 and died in 1893.

Literature Online **Author Search** For more about Guy de Maupassant, go to www.glencoe.com.

BEFORE YOU READ

Focus

BELLRINGER

Bellringer Options
Selection Focus Transparency 15
Daily Language Practice Transparency 20

Or **ask:** What are some items that people will go into debt to buy? *(Cars, houses, furniture, entertainment systems)* Why do people buy things that will cause them to go into debt? *(Financing a basic need such as a home or car is easier than buying outright. People who charge costly luxury items usually want instant gratification.)* Ask students to think about the emotional, as well as the economic, costs of debts as they read.

Author Search To expand students' appreciation of Guy de Maupassant, have them access the Web site for additional information and resources.

Selection Skills

The Necklace

Literary Elements
- Point of View (SE pp. 220, 223, 225, 229)

Reading Skills
- Analyzing Cause-and-Effect Relationships (SE pp. 220–229)
- Making Predictions (TWE p. 222)

Vocabulary Skills
- Word Parts (SE p. 229)

Listening/Speaking/Viewing Skills
- Analyzing Art (SE p. 224; TWE p. 226)

Writing Skills/Grammar
- Apply Voice (SE p. 230)
- Using Adjectives (SE p. 230)
- Synthesizing and Reporting (TWE p. 226)

BEFORE YOU READ

Focus

Summary

When Mathilde Loisel, a clerk's wife who dreams of wealth and glamour, is invited to a ball, she borrows a diamond necklace from a rich friend. Her social triumph turns into a disaster when she loses the necklace. The Loisels keep the loss a secret and borrow heavily to buy an identical piece. After ten years of toil and misery, they learn the borrowed jewels were fake.

V Vocabulary

Vocabulary File **Say:** Add these words and definitions to your vocabulary file. For each word, include a sentence that gives you an example of how to use the word. **OL** Students with English language needs should include the pronunciations of these words in their files. **EL**

Literary Elements Have students access the Web site to improve their understanding of point of view.

Readability Scores
Dale-Chall: 6.9
DRP: 61
Lexile: 950

LITERATURE PREVIEW

Connecting to the Story

"Honesty is the best policy" is a common saying. Why do people sometimes ignore this good advice? Before you read, think about the following questions:

- Do circumstances ever justify hiding the truth?
- How important is it to be proper and respectable?

Building Background

This story is set in Paris, France, in the late 1800s. At that time, a rigid class structure defined Parisian society. At the top of the social ladder were the aristocrats, who had enormous wealth, large estates, and many servants. Below this small, privileged group was a middle class consisting of merchants, clerks, and others, who generally lived in modest homes and could afford one or two servants. Although household budgets were often tight, custom forbade middle-class women from working outside the home. Below this class was the huge number of servants and peasants who worked for the rich or farmed the land. While the rich had annual incomes of hundreds of thousands of francs, the average worker earned less than nine hundred francs a year.

Setting Purposes for Reading

Big Idea Dreams and Reality

As you read the story, think about the reality that often lurks behind attractive appearances.

Literary Element Point of View

Point of view refers to the relationship of the narrator to the story. In a story with third-person omniscient, or all-knowing, point of view, the narrator is not a character in the story but someone who stands outside the story and comments on the action. A third-person omniscient narrator knows everything about the characters and the events and may reveal details that the characters themselves could not reveal. As you read, notice how third-person omniscient point of view helps to shape the story.

- See Literary Terms Handbook, p. R13.

LiteratureOnline Interactive Literary Elements Handbook To review or learn more about the literary elements, go to www.glencoe.com.

READING PREVIEW

Reading Strategy Analyzing Cause-and-Effect Relationships

A **cause-and-effect relationship** is made up of an event, or cause, and the result of the event, or the effect. When you analyze cause and effect, you look closely at the reasons events happen. To identify cause-and-effect relationships, ask yourself: What happened because of one event? What other effects and causes did the event lead to?

Reading Tip: Making a Cause-and-Effect Chain

As you read, keep track of the relationships between events by making a chain like the one shown.

Madame Loisel dreams of going to fashionable affairs.	→		→	

Vocabulary

incessantly (in ses′ ənt lē) *adv.* endlessly; constantly; p. 221 *The crickets would not stop chirping; they called out incessantly.*

disconsolate (dis kon′ sə lit) *adj.* so unhappy that nothing can comfort; hopeless and depressed; p. 222 *The fans were disconsolate when their team lost the game.*

aghast (ə gast′) *adj.* filled with fear, horror, or amazement; p. 225 *She was aghast at the possibility of failing the class.*

gamut (gam′ ət) *n.* the entire range or series of something; p. 226 *You can buy food dye in a gamut of colors, from black to red to white.*

privation (prī vā′ shən) *n.* the lack of the comforts or basic necessities of life; p. 226 *Their growing debts led to a life of privation.*

INDIANA ACADEMIC STANDARDS (pages 220–230)

9.3.13 Explain how voice, persona, and the choice of narrator affect the mood, tone, and meaning of text.

9.2 Develop strategies such as...analyzing...perspective...

9.5.1 Write biographical or autobiographical narratives...

Selection Resources

Print Materials
- Unit 1 Resources (Fast File), pp. 72–74
- Leveled Vocabulary Development, p. 16
- Selection and Unit Assessments, pp. 33–34
- Selection Quick Checks, p. 17

Transparencies
- Bellringer Options Transparencies: Selection Focus Transparency 15, Daily Language Practice Transparency 20
- Literary Elements Transparency 22

Technology
- TeacherWorks Plus™ CD-ROM
- StudentWorks Plus™ CD-ROM
- Presentation Plus!™ CD-ROM
- Literature Online, glencoe.com
- Online Student Edition, mhln.com
- Exam*View*® Assessment Suite CD-ROM
- Vocabulary PuzzleMaker CD-ROM
- Listening Library, disc 1 track 19

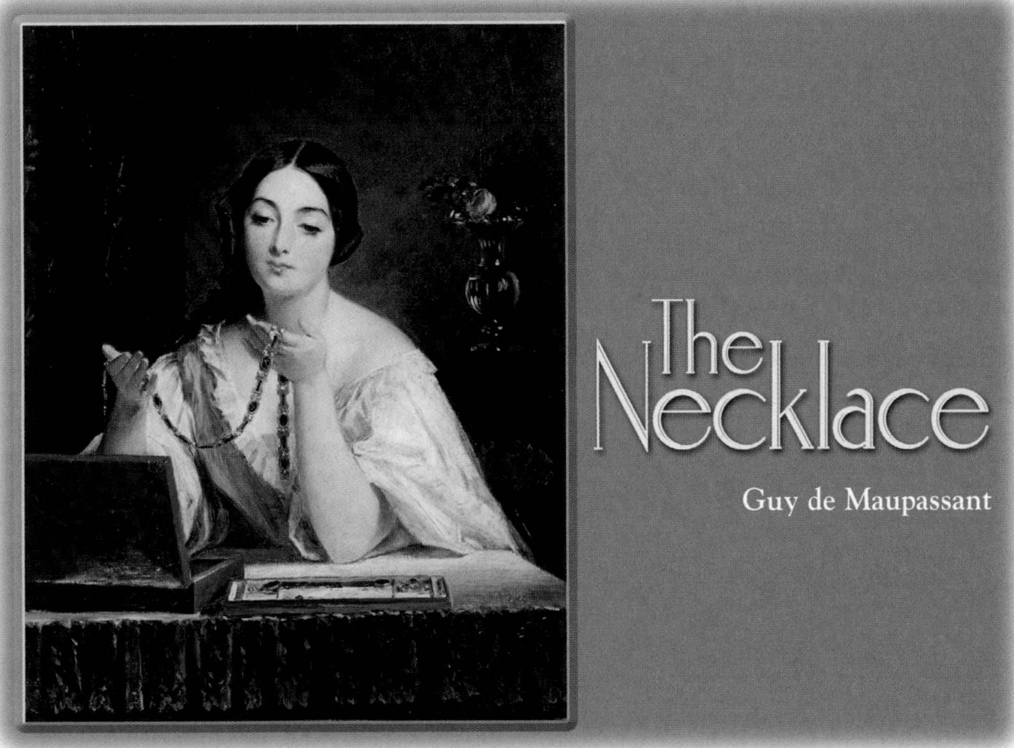

The Necklace

Guy de Maupassant

The Toilette. Charles Robert Leslie. Oil on panel, 12 × 10 in. Victoria and Albert Museum, London, England.

She was one of those pretty and charming girls, born, as if by an accident of fate, into a family of clerks. With no dowry,[1] no prospects, no way of any kind of being met, understood, loved, and married by a man both prosperous and famous, she was finally married to a minor clerk in the Ministry of Education.

She dressed plainly because she could not afford fine clothes, but was as unhappy as a woman who has come down in the world; for women have no family rank or social class. With them, beauty, grace, and charm take the place of birth and breeding. Their natural poise, their instinctive good taste, and their mental cleverness are the sole guiding principles which make daughters of the common people the equals of ladies in high society. **BI**

She grieved **incessantly,** feeling that she had been born for all the little niceties and luxuries of living. She grieved over the shabbiness of her apartment, the dinginess of the walls, the worn-out appearance of the chairs, the ugliness of the draperies. All these things, which another woman of her class would not even have noticed, gnawed at her and made her furious. The sight of the little Breton[2] girl who did her humble housework roused in ★

1. A *dowry* is money or property that a woman brings to her husband at the start of a marriage.

2. *Breton* (bret′ ən) refers to someone or something from the French province of Brittany.

Vocabulary

incessantly (in ses′ ənt lē) *adv.* endlessly; constantly

Teach

BI Big Idea

Dreams and Reality **Ask:** Why do some people pretend to be richer or more important than they really are? *(They are ashamed of or disappointed in their status in life.)* Why is accepting the reality of their lives so hard for such people? *(They are obsessed with appearances, desire admiration or attention, or lack self-worth.)* **OL**

★ Historical Note

Brittany Brittany is located on the northwestern coast of France. Originally settled by the Celts, Brittany became part of France in 1532. Many of its natives can still speak the Celtic language Breton. Brittany is famous for its many historic sites and Neolithic monuments. **AS**

CheckPoint

Use the CheckPoint questions on Presentation Plus! to monitor students' comprehension. These questions can be used with interactive response keypads for immediate student feedback.

English Language Coach

Understanding Pronoun References The author's reliance on pronouns to identify the characters may confuse some English language learners. Choose a difficult example and model how to identify the antecedents for various types of pronouns, including subject and object pronouns, possessives, and indefinite pronouns such as *one.* Encourage English learners to continue doing this as they read. **EL**

Academic Standards

The Additional Support activity on p. 221 covers the following standard:

English Language Coach: **9.6.2** Demonstrate an understanding of sentence construction…and proper English usage…

Teach

BI1 **Big Idea**

Dreams and Reality
Answer: *He is content with their circumstances; she despises them.* **OL**

R Reading Strategy

Analyzing Cause-and-Effect Relationships **Answer:** *He knows she craves a glamorous lifestyle and wants to please her. He thought she would be thrilled.*
Ask: Why does Mathilde react to her husband's surprise with scorn and irritation? *(The invitation is not enough; she wants the lifestyle that the other guests have. Her plain dress will reveal her true station.)* **OL**

★ Cultural Note

Sphinx According to myth, a Sphinx has the head of a woman and the body of a lion. Besides the Greek mythological Sphinx, there are famous statues of sphinxes in Egypt. The Great Sphinx of Giza, with the head of a pharaoh and the body of a lion, has become a national symbol of Egypt. **AS**

her disconsolate regrets and wild daydreams. She would dream of silent chambers, draped with Oriental tapestries and lighted by tall bronze floor lamps, and of two handsome butlers in knee breeches, who, drowsy from the heavy warmth cast by the central stove, dozed in large overstuffed armchairs.

She would dream of great reception halls hung with old silks, of fine furniture filled with priceless curios,[3] and of small, stylish, scented sitting rooms just right for the four o'clock chat with intimate friends, with distinguished and sought-after men whose attention every woman envies and longs to attract.

When dining at the round table covered for the third day with the same cloth, opposite her husband, who would raise the cover of the soup tureen, declaring delightedly, "Ah! a good stew! There's nothing I like better . . ." she would dream of fashionable dinner parties, of gleaming silverware, of tapestries making the walls alive with characters out of history and strange birds in a fairyland forest; she would dream of delicious dishes served on wonderful china, of gallant compliments whispered and listened to with a sphinxlike[4] smile as one eats the rosy flesh of a trout or nibbles at the wings of a grouse.

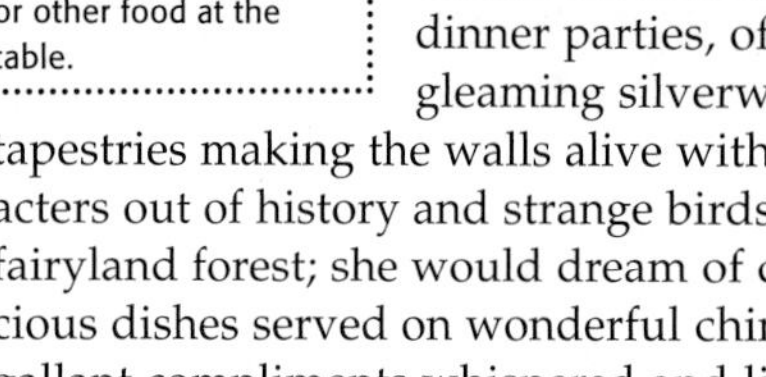

Visual Vocabulary
A *tureen* is a deep dish used for serving soup or other food at the table.

She had no evening clothes, no jewels, nothing. But those were the things she wanted; she felt that was the kind of life for her. She so much longed to please, be envied, be fascinating and sought after.

She had a well-to-do friend, a classmate of convent-school days whom she would no longer go to see, simply because she would feel so distressed on returning home. And she would weep for days on end from vexation,[5] regret, despair, and anguish.

Then one evening, her husband came home proudly holding out a large envelope.

"Look," he said, "I've got something for you."

She excitedly tore open the envelope and pulled out a printed card bearing these words:

"The Minister of Education and Mme. Georges Ramponneau beg M. and Mme. Loisel[6] to do them the honor of attending an evening reception at the Ministerial Mansion on Friday, January 18."

Instead of being delighted, as her husband had hoped, she scornfully tossed the invitation on the table, murmuring, "What good is that to me?"

"But, my dear, I thought you'd be thrilled to death. You never get a chance to go out, and this is a real affair, a wonderful one! I had an awful time getting a card. Everybody wants one: it's much sought after, and not many clerks have a chance at one. You'll see all the most important people there."

She gave him an irritated glance and burst out impatiently, "What do you think I have to go in?"

He hadn't given that a thought. He stammered, "Why, the dress you wear when we go to the theater. That looks quite nice, I think."

He stopped talking, dazed and distracted to see his wife burst out weeping. Two large tears slowly rolled from the corners of her eyes to the corners of her mouth; he gasped,

3. *Priceless curios* are rare or unusual ornamental objects that are very valuable.
4. *Sphinxlike* means "mysterious," referring to a creature in Greek mythology that killed anyone who could not answer its riddle.
5. Here, *vexation* means "distress."
6. *Georges Ramponneau* (ram pə nō′); *Loisel* (lwä zel′). The abbreviations *M.* and *Mme.* are the French versions of *Mr.* and *Mrs.* and stand for *Monsieur* (mə syœ′) and *Madame* (mə dam′).

Big Idea Dreams and Reality *How does the husband's attitude toward the reality of his family's life differ from his wife's?* **BI1**

Vocabulary
disconsolate (dis kon′ sə lit) *adj.* so unhappy that nothing can comfort; hopeless and depressed

Reading Strategy Analyzing Cause-and-Effect Relationships *Why does the husband go to great lengths to obtain the invitation? How does he expect his wife to react?* **R**

Additional Support

Skills Practice

READING: Making Predictions
Predicting plot developments emphasizes that narratives have logic and structure and also prompts students to consider what they already know as they read.

At the end of this page, **Ask:** What do you think will happen next? Encourage students to predict as many events as possible. Have them list their ideas and revise the predictions as they continue reading. **OL**

"Why, what's the matter? What's the trouble?"

By sheer will power she overcame her outburst and answered in a calm voice while wiping the tears from her wet cheeks:

"Oh, nothing. Only I don't have an evening dress and therefore I can't go to that affair. Give the card to some friend at the office whose wife can dress better than I can."

He was stunned. He resumed, "Let's see, Mathilde.[7] How much would a suitable outfit cost—one you could wear for other affairs too—something very simple?"

She thought it over for several seconds, going over her allowance and thinking also of the amount she could ask for without bringing an immediate refusal and an exclamation of dismay from the thrifty clerk.

Finally, she answered hesitatingly, "I'm not sure exactly, but I think with four hundred francs I could manage it."

He turned a bit pale, for he had set aside just that amount to buy a rifle so that, the following summer, he could join some friends who were getting up a group to shoot larks on the plain near Nanterre.

However, he said, "All right. I'll give you four hundred francs. But try to get a nice dress."

As the day of the party approached, Mme. Loisel seemed sad, moody, and ill at ease. Her outfit was ready, however. Her husband said to her one evening, "What's the matter? You've been all out of sorts for three days."

And she answered, "It's embarrassing not to have a jewel or a gem—nothing to wear on my dress. I'll look like a pauper:[8] I'd almost rather not go to that party."

He answered, "Why not wear some flowers? They're very fashionable this season. For ten francs you can get two or three gorgeous roses."

She wasn't at all convinced. "No . . . There's nothing more humiliating than to look poor among a lot of rich women."

But her husband exclaimed, "My, but you're silly! Go see your friend Mme. Forestier[9] and ask her to lend you some jewelry. You and she know each other well enough for you to do that."

She gave a cry of joy, "Why, that's so! I hadn't thought of it."

The next day she paid her friend a visit and told her of her predicament.

Mme. Forestier went toward a large closet with mirrored doors, took out a large jewel box, brought it over, opened it, and said to Mme. Loisel: "Pick something out, my dear."

At first her eyes noted some bracelets, then a pearl necklace, then a Venetian cross, gold and gems, of marvelous workmanship. She tried on these adornments in front of the mirror, but hesitated, unable to decide which to part with and put back. She kept on asking, "Haven't you something else?"

"Oh, yes, keep on looking. I don't know just what you'd like."

All at once she found, in a black satin box, a superb diamond necklace; and her pulse beat faster with longing. Her hands trembled as she took it up. Clasping it around her throat, outside her high-necked dress, she stood in ecstasy looking at her reflection.

"I'll look like a pauper: I'd almost rather not go to that party."

7. *Mathilde* (mä tēld′)

8. A *pauper* is a very poor person.

9. *Forestier* (fô res tyā′)

Literary Element Point of View *What does the narrator help the reader to fully appreciate about the husband's feelings for his wife?* **L**

Big Idea Dreams and Reality *What does Madame Loisel require in order to enjoy the party?* **BI2**

Teach

L Literary Element

Point of View **Answer:** *By revealing the husband's unspoken thoughts, the narrator enables readers to see how willing the husband is to sacrifice his own desires to please his wife.* **OL**

BI2 Big Idea

Dreams and Reality

Answer: *She must look as rich as the other guests.* **OL**

Differentiated Instruction

Personal Connections Some readers may not understand why Mathilde has so much trouble choosing a piece of jewelry. Prompt a discussion of her dilemma by raising questions about similar choices in students' lives. For example, **Say:** Imagine being really hungry and going into a restaurant where the menu lists all your favorite dishes. How would you feel? If you want the perfect outfit for a special event, would you rather shop in one nice store or go to all the best stores in town? *(Students may speak of feeling overwhelmed by too many options and reluctant to limit themselves to a single choice.)* **BL**

Academic Standards

Additional Support activities on pp. 222 and 223 cover the following standards:

Skills Practice: **9.3** [Identify] story elements such as...plot... **9.2** Develop strategies such as...making predictions...

Differentiated Instruction: **9.2** Develop [reading] strategies...

Teach

BI Big Idea

Dreams and Reality
Answer: *She looked lovely and was confident, vivacious, and charming.* OL

Viewing the Art

Answer: *(The luxurious setting, chandeliers, gilt trimmings, draperies, and splendid formal attire would excite her.)*

Julius L. Stewart (1855–1919) was the son of a wealthy American who lived in Europe. The social gatherings of the European elite inspired many of his paintings. AS

The Hunt Ball, 1885. Julius L. Stewart. Phototype, colored after a painting. Private collection.
Viewing the Art: What might Mme. Loisel find particularly exciting about this party?

Then she asked, hesitatingly, pleading, "Could I borrow that, just that and nothing else?"

"Why, of course."

She threw her arms around her friend, kissed her warmly, and fled with her treasure.

The day of the party arrived. Mme. Loisel was a sensation. She was the prettiest one there, fashionable, gracious, smiling, and wild with joy. All the men turned to look at her, asked who she was, begged to be introduced. All the Cabinet officials wanted to waltz with her. The minister took notice of her.

She danced madly, wildly, drunk with pleasure, giving no thought to anything in the triumph of her beauty, the pride of her success, in a kind of happy cloud composed of all the adulation,[10] of all the admiring glances, of all the awakened longings, of a sense of complete victory that is so sweet to a woman's heart.

She left around four o'clock in the morning. Her husband, since midnight, had been dozing in a small empty sitting room with three other gentlemen whose wives were having too good a time.

He threw over her shoulders the wraps he had brought for going home, modest garments of everyday life whose shabbiness clashed with the stylishness of her evening clothes. She felt this and longed to escape, unseen by the other women who were draped in expensive furs.

Loisel held her back.

"Hold on! You'll catch cold outside. I'll call a cab."

But she wouldn't listen to him and went rapidly down the stairs. When they were on the street, they didn't find a carriage; and they set out to hunt for one, hailing drivers whom they saw going by at a distance.

They walked toward the Seine,[11] disconsolate and shivering. Finally on the docks they

10. Here, *adulation* means "plentiful praise" or "flattery."

Big Idea **Dreams and Reality** *What reasons might there be for Madame Loisel's success at the party?* BI

11. The *Seine* (sen) is a river that flows through Paris.

Additional Support

Skills Practice

READING: Making Decisions The Loisels must make a decision quickly, for Mme. Forestier expects her necklace to be returned right away. Their decision to lie to buy time to correct the loss is made under emotional duress. Explain that sound decision-making requires an objective look at all possible outcomes. Have students think of a personal decision they must make and decide what steps to take in their decision-making process. Have them outline these steps, including their choices and realistic outcomes for each choice. OL found one of those carriages that one sees in Paris only after nightfall, as if they were ashamed to show their drabness during daylight hours.

It dropped them at their door in the Rue des Martyrs,[12] and they climbed wearily up to their apartment. For her, it was all over. For him, there was the thought that he would have to be at the Ministry at ten o'clock.

Before the mirror, she let the wraps fall from her shoulders to see herself once again in all her glory. Suddenly she gave a cry. The necklace was gone.

Her husband, already half undressed, said, "What's the trouble?"

She turned toward him despairingly, "I . . . I . . . I don't have Mme. Forestier's necklace."

"What! You can't mean it! It's impossible!"

They hunted everywhere, through the folds of the dress, through the folds of the coat, in the pockets. They found nothing.

He asked, "Are you sure you had it when leaving the dance?"

"Yes, I felt it when I was in the hall of the Ministry."

"But if you had lost it on the street we'd have heard it drop. It must be in the cab."

"Yes, quite likely. Did you get its number?"

"No. Didn't you notice it either?"

"No."

They looked at each other **aghast.** Finally Loisel got dressed again.

"I'll retrace our steps on foot," he said, "to see if I can find it."

And he went out. She remained in her evening clothes, without the strength to go to bed, slumped in a chair in the unheated room, her mind a blank.

Her husband came in about seven o'clock. He had had no luck.

He went to the police station, to the newspapers to post a reward, to the cab companies, everywhere the slightest hope drove him.

That evening Loisel returned, pale, his face lined; still he had learned nothing.

"We'll have to write your friend," he said, "to tell her you have broken the catch and are having it repaired. That will give us a little time to turn around."

She wrote to his dictation.

At the end of a week, they had given up all hope.

And Loisel, looking five years older, declared, "We must take steps to replace that piece of jewelry."

The next day they took the case to the jeweler whose name they found inside. He consulted his records. "I didn't sell that necklace, madame," he said. "I only supplied the case."

Then they went from one jeweler to another hunting for a similar necklace, going over their recollections, both sick with despair and anxiety.

They found, in a shop in Palais Royal, a string of diamonds which seemed exactly like the one they were seeking. It was priced at forty thousand francs. They could get it for thirty-six.

They asked the jeweler to hold it for them for three days. And they reached an agreement that he would take it back for thirty-four thousand if the lost one was found before the end of February.

Loisel had eighteen thousand francs he had inherited from his father. He would borrow the rest.

He went about raising the money, asking a thousand francs from one, four hundred from

12. A Paris street, *Rue des Martyrs* (rōō dā mär tēr′) translates as "Street of Martyrs." A *martyr* is a person who suffers greatly or sacrifices all for a belief, principle, or cause.

Literary Element Point of View *What details suggest the husband's down-to-earth simplicity?* **L**

Vocabulary

aghast (ə ast′) *adj.* filled with fear, horror, or amazement

Reading Strategy Analyzing Cause-and-Effect Relationships *What dilemma does the couple face because they cannot find the necklace?* **R**

Teach

L Literary Element

Point of View Answer: *The husband patiently waits with other husbands while Madame Loisel circulates at the party. He is not dazzled by glamorous affairs. His thoughts at the end of the night are on another day of labor.* **OL**

R Reading Strategy

Analyzing Cause-and-Effect Relationships

Answer: *They must decide whether to tell Madame Forestier the truth about losing the necklace or to find some alternative.* **OL**

★ Historical Note

Palais Royal The Palais Royal was orginally a theater that was part of Cardinal Richelieu's residence. After Richelieu's death, the Palais was inherited by Louis the XIII and became a royal property. Since then, the Palais has housed several theaters and has beeen used for entertainment purposes. **AS**

Differentiated Instruction

Summarizing Summarizing can help students keep track of characters, events, and other details as they read. First, students should identify the key characters and actions in a passage. They should then write down only the key points. Have students practice with the following passage: "Mme. Loisel experienced the horrible life the needy live. She played her part, however, with sudden heroism. That frightful debt had to be paid. She would pay it. She dismissed her maid; they rented a garret under the eaves." *(Mme. Loisel bravely resigned herself to a life of poverty to repay her debt.)* **BL**

Academic Standards

Additional Support activities on pp. 224 and 225 cover the following standards:

Skills Practice: **9.2** Develop [reading[strategies... **9.5.8** Write for different purposes and audiences...

Differentiated Instruction: **9.5.2** Write responses to literature that demonstrate a comprehensive grasp of the significant ideas of literary works...

Teach

BI1 Big Idea

Dreams and Reality
Answer: *He sacrifices his security and risks his reputation to replace the necklace.* OL

Viewing the Art

The Champs Élysées, one of the great Parisian boulevards, has traditionally been lined with luxury apartments, high-end boutiques, and a bustling swath of restaurants, cafés, theaters, museums, and parks.
Ask: What activities do you imagine took place on the Champs Élysées before it became a major thoroughfare for automobiles in the twentieth century? *(Students should use details of the painting to infer what the Champs Élysées would have been like in the late 1800s.)* AS

The Champs Élysées. Paris. Georges Stein. Gavin Graham Gallery, London, England. Private collection.

another, a hundred here, sixty there. He signed notes, made ruinous deals, did business with loan sharks, ran the whole **gamut** of moneylenders. He compromised the rest of his life, risked his signature without knowing if he'd be able to honor it, and then, terrified by the outlook for the future, by the blackness of despair about to close around him, by the prospect of all the **privations** of the body and tortures of the spirit, he went to claim the new necklace with the thirty-six thousand francs which he placed on the counter of the shopkeeper.

When Mme. Loisel took the necklace back, Mme. Forestier said to her frostily, "You should have brought it back sooner; I might have needed it."

She didn't open the case, an action her friend was afraid of. If she had noticed the substitution, what would she have thought? What would she have said? Would she have thought her a thief?

Mme. Loisel experienced the horrible life the needy live. She played her part, however, with sudden heroism. That frightful debt had to be paid. She would pay it. She dismissed her maid; they rented a garret under the eaves.[13]

She learned to do the heavy housework, to perform the hateful duties of cooking. She washed dishes, wearing down her shell-pink nails scouring the grease from pots and pans; she scrubbed dirty linen, shirts, and cleaning rags which she hung on a line to dry; she took the garbage down to the street each morning and brought up water, stopping on each landing to get her breath. And, clad like a peasant woman, basket on arm, guarding sou[14] by sou her scanty

Big Idea Dreams and Reality *How has Madame Loisel's dream turned into a difficult reality for her husband?* BI1

Vocabulary

gamut (am′ ət) n. the entire range or series of something

privation (prī vā′ shən) n. the lack of the comforts or basic necessities of life

13. A *garret under the eaves* would be a small attic apartment.
14. The *sou* (so͞o) is a French coin worth about one-twentieth of a franc.

Additional Support

Skills Practice

WRITING: Synthesizing and Reporting Maupassant regards the Loisels as heroic because they did what had to be done to pay their debt, no matter how hard or unpleasant. Have students find a recent story in a newspaper, magazine, or other source about a person whom they consider a hero. Have them share their stories in small groups, working together to list the actions and qualities that make a person heroic. Have the groups each write a report of their findings and then share their reports and participate in a class discussion. OL allowance, she bargained with the fruit dealers, the grocer, the butcher, and was insulted by them.

Each month notes had to be paid, and others renewed to give more time.

Her husband labored evenings to balance a tradesman's accounts, and at night, often, he copied documents at five sous a page.

And this went on for ten years.

Finally, all was paid back, everything including the exorbitant[15] rates of the loan sharks and accumulated compound interest.

Mme. Loisel appeared an old woman, now. She became heavy, rough, harsh, like one of the poor. Her hair untended, her skirts askew,[16] her hands red, her voice shrill, she even slopped water on her floors and scrubbed them herself. But, sometimes, while her husband was at work, she would sit near the window and think of that long-ago evening when, at the dance, she had been so beautiful and admired.

What would have happened if she had not lost that necklace? Who knows? Who can say? How strange and unpredictable life is! How little there is between happiness and misery!

Then one Sunday when she had gone for a walk on the Champs Élysées[17] to relax a bit from the week's labors, she suddenly noticed a woman strolling with a child. It was Mme. Forestier, still young-looking, still beautiful, still charming.

Mme. Loisel felt a rush of emotion. Should she speak to her? Of course. And now that everything was paid off, she would tell her the whole story. Why not?

She went toward her. "Hello, Jeanne."

The other, not recognizing her, showed astonishment at being spoken to so familiarly by this common person. She stammered, "But . . . madame . . . I don't recognize . . . You must be mistaken."

"No, I'm Mathilde Loisel."

Her friend gave a cry, "Oh, my poor Mathilde, how you've changed!"

"Yes, I've had a hard time since last seeing you. And plenty of misfortunes—and all on account of you!"

"Of me . . . How do you mean?"

"Do you remember that diamond necklace you loaned me to wear to the dance at the Ministry?"

"Yes, but what about it?"

"Well, I lost it."

"You lost it! But you returned it."

"I brought you another just like it. And we've been paying for it for ten years now. You can imagine that wasn't easy for us who had nothing. Well, it's over now, and I am glad of it."

Mme. Forestier stopped short. "You mean to say you bought a diamond necklace to replace mine?"

"Yes. You never noticed, then? They were quite alike."

And she smiled with proud and simple joy.

Mme. Forestier, quite overcome, clasped her by the hands. "Oh, my poor Mathilde. But mine was only paste.[18] Why, at most it was worth only five hundred francs!" ★

15. *Exorbitant* means "beyond what is reasonable or fair" or "excessive."
16. *Askew* (ə skyo͞o′) means "crooked" or "to one side."
17. The *Champs Élysées* (shän′ zā lē zā′) is a fashionable, tree-lined avenue in Paris.

18. Here, *paste* is a hard, brilliant glass used to make artificial jewels.

Big Idea Dreams and Reality *In what sense are Madame Loisel's worst fears coming true?* **BI2**

Reading Strategy Analyzing Cause-and-Effect Relationships *What happens to the couple because of Madame Loisel's losing the necklace?* **R**

Teach

BI2 Big Idea

Dreams and Reality

Answer: *She becomes the "pauper" she feared she would resemble at the ball.* **OL**

R Reading Strategy

Analyzing Cause-and-Effect Relationships

Answer: *They descend into a life of poverty and unceasing drudgery.* **OL**

★ Writer's Technique

Irony Irony is a figurative use of expression that occurs when an outcome is the opposite of what is expected. Maupassant creates irony in Mathilde's circumstances, her appearance, and her thinking. **AS**

CheckPoint

Use the CheckPoint questions on Presentation Plus! to check students' mastery of the selection. These questions can be used with interactive response keypads for immediate student feedback.

Building Reading Fluency

Preparing News Stories Encourage purposeful rereading by assigning small groups to prepare a news feature story about the Loisels' discovery of the mistake that ruined their lives. Students in each group should take turns reading sections of the story aloud, while the other group members list key events and pertinent details. Encourage students to imagine an outcome of the Loisels' discovery. (*For instance the owner might pay them for the necklace or they might sue her.*) Have each group present their stories to the class. **BL**

Academic Standards

Additional Support activities on pp. 226 and 227 cover the following standards:

Skills Practice: **9.4.6** Synthesize information from multiple sources… **9.5.3** Write expository compositions…that make distinctions between the relative value and significance of specific data, facts, and ideas…

Building Reading Fluency: **9.3** Identify story elements, such as character… **9.5.2** Write responses to literature that demonstrate a comprehensive grasp of the significant ideas of literary works; support statements with evidence from the text…

AFTER YOU READ

Assess

1. Students should support their answers.
2. (a) She longs for a life of luxury and attention. (b) She believes happiness comes from wealth, status, and admiration.
3. (a) Madame Loisel is depressed and refuses to go without the proper clothes. (b) His patient concern for his wife suggests he is loving, kind, and self-sacrificing.
4. (a) They acquire steep debts, which they labor for ten hard years to pay off. (b) Possible answers: fear that she will accuse them of theft; embarrassment
5. Accept any well-reasoned answer.
6. (a) She works hard and uncomplainingly. (b) She seemed idle and given to daydreaming and self-pity.
7. (a) The necklace could be seen as the immediate cause of both her greatest happiness and her worst misery. (b) Her vanity and shallow desires are the underlying cause of her unhappiness.
8. Students should support their answers.

AFTER YOU READ

RESPONDING AND THINKING CRITICALLY

Respond

1. Could you imagine feeling and acting as Madame Loisel does in the story? Why or why not?

Recall and Interpret

2. (a)At the beginning of the story, why is Madame Loisel unhappy with her life? (b)How would you characterize her ideas about what gives happiness in life?
3. (a)How does Madame Loisel react to the party invitation? (b)What do Monsieur Loisel's reactions to her suggest about him?
4. (a)How do the Loisels pay for the replacement necklace? (b)In your opinion, why do the Loisels decide not to tell Madame Forestier that they lost the necklace?

Analyze and Evaluate

5. Do you think the Loisels' efforts to replace the necklace are admirable or foolish? Give reasons for your opinion.
6. When she finds herself in debt, Madame Loisel "plays her part . . . with sudden heroism." (a)What does she do that might be called heroic? (b)Why might those actions seem surprising?
7. (a)To what extent is Madame Loisel's life molded by the necklace? (b)To what extent is her fate the result of her own personality? Explain.

Connect

8. **Big Idea** **Dreams and Reality** In your opinion, when are dreams for a better life beneficial, and when are they harmful? Explain.

YOU'RE THE CRITIC: Different Viewpoints

What Makes Maupassant's Writing Great?

Maupassant is almost universally praised by critics, but opinions differ as to what made him great. Critic Edward D. Sullivan calls attention to Maupassant's precise style. Maupassant's friend, the great French novelist Émile Zola, also praises Maupassant's style but stresses other qualities. Read the two excerpts from their literary criticism below. As you read, notice the different elements that the two writers choose to emphasize.

> *"Maupassant's greatest virtue lies in the fact that his narratives sustain the readers' interest and that he develops them with economy and concision, selecting. . . . the precisely pertinent details and excluding verbal flourishes or elaborate enumeration."*
>
> —Edward D. Sullivan

> *"He was understood because he had clarity, simplicity, moderation, and strength. He was loved because he possessed a laughing goodness; a profound satire which persists even through tears."*
>
> —Émile Zola

Group Activity Discuss the following questions with classmates. Refer to the excerpts and cite evidence from "The Necklace" for support.

1. (a)Which aspects of Maupassant's writing does Sullivan praise? (b)Which aspects of Maupassant's writing does Zola emphasize?
2. Which of the critical assessments most closely captures your own opinion? Cite evidence from the story.

You're the Critic

1. (a) Sullivan praises his economy, precision, and ability to entertain. (b) Zola praises not only his concise style but also his ironic yet moving portrayal of human weakness.
2. Students should support their answers with evidence from the text.

LITERARY ANALYSIS

Literary Element Point of View

Stories told from a **third-person omniscient point of view** are told by a narrator who is not a character in the story, but someone who stands outside the story and comments on the action. A third-person omniscient narrator knows everything about the characters and events but may withhold crucial information at various points in the story.

1. Think about how Maupassant makes use of the third-person omniscient point of view in this story. Why is the information revealed at the end so surprising? Explain.
2. The narrator comments in detail about both Madame and Monsieur Loisel. If these comments were removed from the story altogether, how might your perception of the story be different? Would you have greater, less, or the same amount of sympathy for the characters? Explain.

Review: Symbol

As you learned on page 122, a **symbol** is an object, person, place, or experience that represents something else, usually something abstract. In this story, for example, a fancy evening dress is a symbol of class and distinction. A symbol may have more than one meaning, or its meaning may change from the beginning to the end of a literary work.

Partner Activity Meet with a partner to consider the importance of the diamond necklace as a symbol in the story. Then work together to answer the following questions. When you are finished, share your thoughts with the class.

1. What does the necklace represent when Madame Loisel first sees it in its black satin box?
2. What does the necklace symbolize after Madame Loisel discovers that it is lost?
3. How does the meaning of the symbol change when it is revealed that the diamonds in the necklace were fake?

READING AND VOCABULARY

Reading Strategy Analyzing Cause-and-Effect Relationships

In a story, one event may have an effect that becomes the cause of still another effect. When causes and effects are related in this way, it leads to the formation of a chain of causes and effects.

1. What happens as a result of Madame Loisel's desire for luxury, entertainment, and attention?
2. What happens because the Loisels lose the necklace?
3. If the Loisels had confessed to losing the necklace, how might their lives have been different? Explain.

Vocabulary Practice

Practice with Word Parts Your knowledge of word roots can help you understand unfamiliar words. Read the roots and definitions below. Then use your knowledge of roots, as well as prefixes and suffixes, to pick the best definition for each of the boldfaced vocabulary words.

Latin Root: *cessare*—"delay"
Latin Root: *privare*—"to separate, deprive"
Latin Root: *solari*—"to console, soothe"

1. Ana waited for a break in the storm, but rain pounded down **incessantly.**
   a. cruelly **b.** constantly **c.** intermittently
2. They were **disconsolate** because the party would have to be held indoors.
   a. unhappy **b.** soothing **c.** angry
3. It is difficult to endure the **privation** of weeks spent living in a tent.
   a. necessity **b.** lack of escape
   c. lack of necessities

AFTER YOU READ

Assess

Literary Element

1. The narrator gives no hints that the necklace is a fake.
2. Possible answer: Without the comments, the reader would have too limited a view of the motivations and feelings of the characters. Students should support their answers.

Review: Symbol

1. It represents the life Madame Loisel desired.
2. Possible answers: A symbol of their ruin or of the life they will never have because of their debt
3. Possible answers: It then becomes a symbol of the emptiness of Mathilde's vanity and her illusions about happiness.

Reading Strategy

1. Madame Loisel's husband obtains an invitation to a glamorous party. Madame Loisel, wishing to look beautiful and rich, borrows a diamond necklace from a friend. When she loses the necklace, the Loisels go into debt to replace it.
2. Their lives are transformed. They must work for ten years to pay off the debt incurred from buying a replacement for the necklace.
3. Students may say that their lives would have been much better.

Vocabulary

1. b
2. a
3. c

AFTER YOU READ

Assess

Writing About Literature

Students' essays should

- be written from the first-person point of view.
- recount the negative consequences of borrowing or lending.
- tell what they learned from the experience, and compare or contrast their experience with Madame Loisel's.

Interdisciplinary Activity

Encourage students to use both print and online resources and to share their findings with the rest of the class.

Maupassant's Language and Style

Possible answers indicated in bold:

She would dream of **sumptuous** dinner parties, of **ornate** silverware, . . . of **exotic** birds in a forest, . . . of **delectable** dishes served on **delicate** china, of **wondrous** compliments whispered and listened to with a **dazzling** smile. . . .

WRITING AND EXTENDING

Writing About Literature

Apply Voice In writing, voice is the distinctive use of language that conveys the writer's or narrator's personality to the reader. Voice is created through elements of style such as sentence structure, word choice, and tone (the attitude expressed by the language). When you write, think about the effect you would like your words to have on the reader. By writing in a compelling voice, you will express your personality and create interest for the reader.

Write a brief essay about a time when you or someone you know got into trouble as a result of lending or borrowing something. Describe what happened and explain what you learned from the experience. How was the experience similar to or different from that of Madame Loisel's?

Write your essay from your own point of view—the first-person point of view. After you complete your draft, meet with a partner to review each other's work and to suggest revisions. Then proofread your draft for errors in spelling, grammar, and punctuation.

Interdisciplinary Activity: Social Studies

Using this story and the information provided in Before You Read, page 220, as a starting point, research women's roles in late nineteenth-century France. Investigate how class structure affected the way women lived and the things they valued. Then do research to find out what is similar and different about the way women live today. Use your personal experience to complement your research. Organize your ideas in a chart like the one below. If you wish, you may change the categories listed across the top of the chart. Compare your completed chart with those of others.

	Work	Money	Marriage
Nineteenth-century French women			
Women in the United States today			

GRAMMAR AND STYLE

Maupassant's Language and Style

Using Adjectives In "The Necklace," Maupassant uses vivid, precise adjectives to help create a strong mood. Consider, for example, how much less effective his description of Madame Loisel's desperate dreaming would have been without strong adjectives:

"She would dream of silent chambers, draped with Oriental tapestries and lighted by tall bronze floor lamps, and of two handsome butlers in knee breeches, who, drowsy from the heavy warmth cast by the central stove, dozed in large overstuffed armchairs."

Adjective	Word Modified
silent	chambers
Oriental	tapestries
tall	floor lamps
bronze	floor lamps
handsome	butlers

Activity Copy out the passage below, filling in the blanks with adjectives of your choosing. Choose adjectives that will create a mood of luxury. Then look at the passage in the story on page 222 to compare your choices with those of Guy de Maupassant.

She would dream of ______ dinner parties, of ______ silverware . . . of ______ birds in a ______ forest; she would dream of ______ dishes served on ______ china, of ______ compliments whispered and listened to with a ______ smile. . . .

Revising Check

Adjectives It is important to pay attention to your choice of words, including your choice of adjectives, when revising your own writing. With a partner, review your personal essay about borrowing and lending. Note places where adjectives could be changed or added to make your essay clearer and more vivid. Revise your draft accordingly. Use a thesaurus if necessary.

LiteratureOnline **Web Activities** For eFlashcards, Selection Quick Checks, and other Web activities, go to www.glencoe.com.

Additional Support

Academic Standards

The Additional Support activity on p. 230 covers the following standard:

Skills Practice: **9.5.2** Write responses to literature that demonstrate a comprehensive grasp of the significant ideas of literary works...

Skills Practice

TEST PREPARATION: Short Response Short-response questions may not have one correct answer. Instead, an answer may be judged by its insightfulness and the quality of the textual evidence used to support it.

Ask: Are the Loisels heroic? Explain. *(Possible answers: Mme. Loisel is not heroic. Her vanity creates the situation, so paying off the debt should be her responsibility. M. Loisel is heroic. He works hard and tries to make his wife happy. When she loses the necklace, he sacrifices much without complaint to pay off the debt.)* **OL**

BEFORE YOU READ

American History

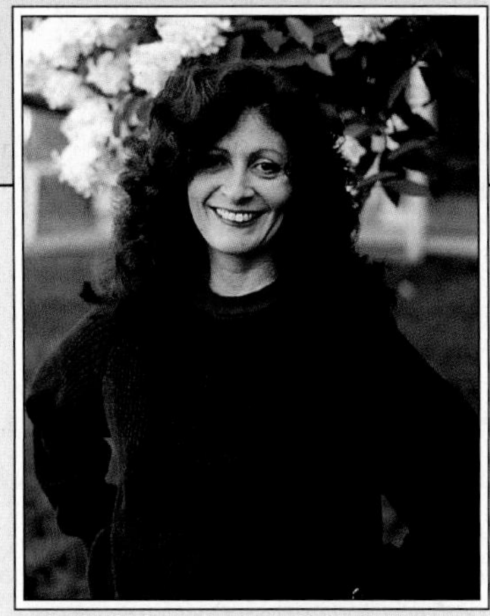

MEET JUDITH ORTIZ COFER

Judith Ortiz Cofer (ôr tēz′ kō′fer) brings her readers on a journey. It is not a journey to a distant past or an exotic place, or even an imaginary world; it is, according to one critic, "a quest to discover what it means to be a person in a specific place and culture." Ortiz Cofer can describe this quest with great depth and precision because she has been engaged in it her entire life.

Born in a small town in Puerto Rico, Ortiz Cofer moved with her parents to the United States when she was very young. Her father joined the U.S. Navy, and the family lived in Paterson, New Jersey. About every six months, the Navy sent her father to Europe. While he was away, her mother would take the family back to Puerto Rico. As a result, Ortiz Cofer's childhood was split between an industrialized East Coast city and a rural town on the island of Puerto Rico.

"I absorbed literature, both spoken cuentos *and books, as a creature who breathed ink."*

—Judith Ortiz Cofer

Two Distinct Worlds Always the new girl, Ortiz Cofer often felt out of place in both New Jersey and Puerto Rico. When she was in New Jersey, she spent a lot of time reading books from the library and the romance novels (in Spanish) that her mother brought from Puerto Rico. While in Puerto Rico, Ortiz Cofer became absorbed in family stories called *cuentos*. Her grandmother was an especially gifted storyteller. Her grandfather was a carpenter and a poet, and he often read his poems to his granddaughter. A love of language fed Ortiz Cofer's dreams of going to college and becoming a teacher.

A Literary Life In 1970 Ortiz Cofer realized her dream of attending college and went on to become a bilingual teacher. While in graduate school, she began writing poetry. She published her first book of poetry in 1980. Since then she has won awards not only for her poems, but also for her short stories, essays, and novels. The short story "American History" appears in *The Latin Deli*, an award-winning collection of Ortiz Cofer's prose and poetry, published in 1993.

Ortiz Cofer continues to write and teach. She is a professor of English and creative writing at the University of Georgia. Living on a farm that has been in her husband's family for many years, Ortiz Cofer is far from the worlds of urban New Jersey and rural Puerto Rico that shaped her childhood. Through her writing, she has come to understand that all young people are immigrants and that everyone must find his or her own place in the surrounding culture.

Judith Ortiz Cofer was born in 1952.

LiteratureOnline **Author Search** For more about Judith Ortiz Cofer, go to www.glencoe.com.

BEFORE YOU READ

Focus

BELLRINGER

Bellringer Options
Selection Focus Transparency 16
Daily Language Practice Transparency 21

Or **write the following phrases on the board:** Kennedy Assassinated, Civil Rights Movement, Vietnam War, Martin Luther King, Jr. Assassinated.
Ask: What do these events have in common? *(All of these events happened in the 1960s.)* Tell students that the story "American History" is set during the early 1960s.

Author Search To expand students' appreciation of Judith Ortiz Cofer, have them access the Web site for additional information and resources.

Selection Skills

American History

Literary Elements
- Point of View (SE pp. 232–240)

Reading Skills
- Identifying Assumptions (SE pp. 232–241)
- Cause-and-Effect Relationships (TWE p. 236)

Vocabulary Skills
- Analogies (SE p. 241)
- Academic Vocabulary (SE p. 241)

Listening/Speaking/Viewing Skills
- Analyzing Art (SE p. 237; TWE pp. 233, 235)

Writing Skills/Grammar
- Analyze Historical Context (SE p. 241)
- Repetition for Effect (TWE p. 234)
- Understanding Adverbs (TWE p. 238)

BEFORE YOU READ

Focus

Summary

Elena wants desperately to be friends with Eugene, who lives in the house next to her tenement building. Both teens are studious and outcasts in their bleak public school. Although Eugene is friendly to Elena, his mother prevents them from studying together; she makes it clear that race is the problem.

V Vocabulary

Vocabulary File **Say:** Add these words and definitions to your vocabulary file. For each word, include a sentence that gives you an example of how to use the word. **OL** Students with English language needs should include the pronunciations of these words in their files. **EL**

Literary Elements Have students access the Web site to improve their understanding of point of view.

Readability Scores

Dale-Chall: 5.6
DRP: 55
Lexile: 990

LITERATURE PREVIEW

Connecting to the Story

Have you ever met a person whom you liked right away, but something prevented the friendship from growing? In "American History," the narrator is interested in becoming friends with a new neighbor. Before you read, think about the following questions:

- Are common interests important in forming friendships?
- Under what circumstances can friendships fail to develop?

Building Background

Most Americans who were alive in 1963 remember exactly what they were doing when they learned that President Kennedy had been assassinated. Throughout the country and across the world, people from all walks of life reacted to the news with disbelief and deep sorrow. Kennedy—the youngest man to be elected President of the United States—was a dynamic, popular leader who energized the American people and instilled in them a sense of hope for the future. During his brief term, Kennedy urged Congress to pass sweeping civil rights legislation, saying, ". . . race has no place in American life or law." His campaign slogan was "A Time for Greatness," and many Americans believed Kennedy fulfilled this promise once he took office.

Setting Purposes for Reading

Big Idea Dreams and Reality

As you read, notice the different ways in which dreams and reality clash for the characters in this story.

Literary Element Point of View

Point of view is the relationship of the narrator to the story. In a story with first-person point of view, the narrator is a character in the story and uses the words *I, me,* and *we.* As you read, identify the point of view and analyze how the narrator's perspective shapes the story.

- See Literary Terms Handbook, p. R13.

LiteratureOnline Interactive Literary Elements Handbook To review or learn more about the literary elements, go to www.glencoe.com.

READING PREVIEW

Reading Strategy Identifying Assumptions

An **assumption** is an idea that a particular thing is true. Characters in works of fiction sometimes make assumptions that affect how they act or how they treat other characters.

Reading Tip: Taking Notes Use a chart like the one below to record details from the story that indicate characters are making assumptions.

Detail	Assumption
p. 234 Mr. DePalma "would 'keep an eye' on us."	Mr. DePalma assumes that the students won't do what they're told to do.

Vocabulary

profound (prə found′) *adj.* significant; deep; intense; p. 233 *When the class heard the bad news, there were a few moments of profound silence.*

discreet (dis krēt′) *adj.* showing good judgment; cautious; p. 235 *Although neither the food nor the service Jon received at the restaurant was good, his comments to the manager were discreet.*

vigilant (vij′ əl ənt) *adj.* alert and watchful for danger or trouble; p. 236 *The monitors were vigilant for any signs of cheating or other misconduct during the standardized test.*

enthrall (en thrôl′) *v.* to hold spellbound; fascinate; p. 236 *We were enthralled by the flute solo and its high, clear, sweet melody.*

elation (i lā′ shən) *n.* a feeling of great joy; ecstasy; p. 238 *When the blizzard made it impossible for them to get to school, their elation at the unexpected snow day was obvious.*

INDIANA ACADEMIC STANDARDS (pages 232–241)

9.3.13 Explain how voice, persona, and the choice of narrator affect the mood, tone, and meaning of text.

9.2 Develop strategies such as...identifying...perspective...

9.5.3 Write expository compositions...

9.3.12 Analyze the way in which a work of literature is related to the themes and issues of its historical period.

Selection Resources

Print Materials

- Unit 1 Resources (Fast File), pp. 75–77
- Leveled Vocabulary Development, p. 17
- Selection and Unit Assessments, pp. 35–36
- Selection Quick Checks, p. 18

Transparencies

- Bellringer Options Transparencies: Selection Focus Transparency 16 Daily Language Practice Transparency 21
- Literary Elements Transparency 22

Technology

- TeacherWorks Plus™ CD-ROM
- StudentWorks Plus™ CD-ROM
- Presentation Plus!™ CD-ROM
- Literature Online, glencoe.com
- Online Student Edition, mhln.com
- Exam*View*® Assessment Suite CD-ROM
- Vocabulary PuzzleMaker CD-ROM
- Listening Library, disc 1 track 20

View in Chambers Street, 1936. O. Louis Guglielmi. Oil on canvas, 30 1/4 × 24 1/4 in. The Newark Museum, New Jersey. ★

AMERICAN HISTORY

Judith Ortiz Cofer

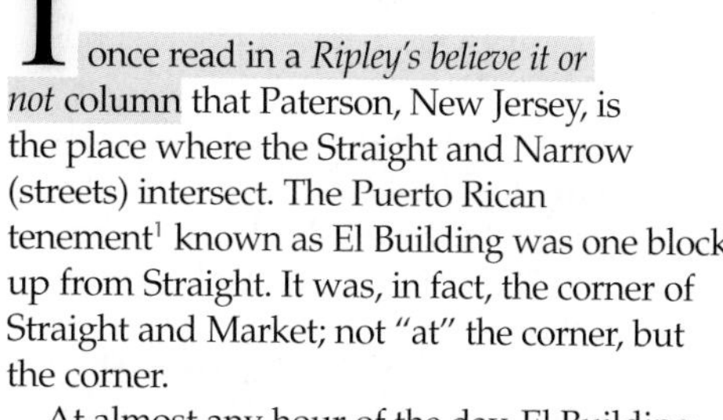

I once read in a *Ripley's believe it or not* column that Paterson, New Jersey, is the place where the Straight and Narrow (streets) intersect. The Puerto Rican tenement[1] known as El Building was one block up from Straight. It was, in fact, the corner of Straight and Market; not "at" the corner, but the corner.

At almost any hour of the day, El Building was like a monstrous jukebox, blasting out *salsas*[2] from open windows as the residents, mostly new immigrants just up from the island,[3] tried to drown out whatever they were currently enduring with loud music. But the day President Kennedy was shot, there was a **profound** silence in El Building; even the abusive tongues of viragoes,[4] the cursing of the unemployed, and the screeching of small children had been somehow muted. President Kennedy was a saint to these people. In fact, soon his photograph would be hung alongside the Sacred Heart[5] and over the spiritist altars that many women kept in their apartments. He would become part of the hierarchy of martyrs[6] they prayed to for favors that only one who had died for a cause would understand.

On the day that President Kennedy was shot, my ninth grade class had been out in

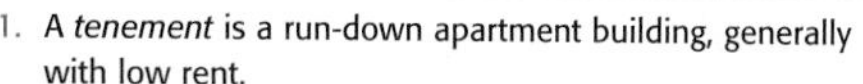

1. A *tenement* is a run-down apartment building, generally with low rent.
2. *Salsas* are Latin American dance tunes.
3. When the writer refers to "the island" in this story, she is referring to Puerto Rico, an island in the Caribbean Sea, which is a self-governing commonwealth of the United States.
4. *Viragoes* (vi rä′ gōz) are bad-tempered, scolding women who, here, use coarse or insulting (*abusive*) language.
5. The *Sacred Heart* is a picture of the wounded heart of Jesus, sometimes encircled in a crown of thorns and giving off rays of golden light.
6. The *hierarchy* (hī′ ə rär′ kē) *of martyrs* (mär′ tərz) is the ranking of those who have suffered or died for their religion.

Literary Element Point of View *What point of view does the writer use for this story? How do you know?* **L**

Vocabulary

profound (prə found′) *adj.* significant; deep; intense

Teach

Big Idea

Dreams and Reality Say: Keep these questions in mind as you read: What dreams and realities have you shared with new friends? How would you react if authority figures, such as parents and teachers, tried to interfere with your dreams? **OL**

L Literary Element

Point of View Answer: *The writer establishes a first-person point of view by starting with the word* I. **OL**

★ Viewing the Art

Many of O. Louis Guglielmi's (1906–1956) paintings were created while he worked with the Works Progress Administration. The WPA was set up by the federal government during the Great Depression to help Americans make ends meet. Guglielmi's paintings are noted for their strong colors and unusual perspective. **AS**

CheckPoint

Use the CheckPoint questions on Presentation Plus! to monitor students' comprehension. These questions can be used with interactive response keypads for immediate student feedback.

English Language Coach

Understanding Connotation Ask: Do you think Elena's nickname, Skinny Bones, is an insult or a compliment? Explain that *skinny* can have either a negative or positive connotation—or implied meaning—depending on the context. Prompt students to suggest a situation in which the name would be complimentary *(if a person had wanted to lose weight)*. As students continue to read, ask them to consider the connotation of expressions and of stylistic conventions, such as the use of quotes around "a conference" on page 237. Invite pairs of students to identify other examples. **EL**

Academic Standards

The Additional Support activity on p. 233 covers the following standard:

English Language Coach: **9.1.2** Distinguish between what words mean literally and what they imply and interpret what the words imply.

Teach

R1 Reading Strategy

Identifying Assumptions
Answer: *She assumes that the narrator's family eats a particular type of ethnic food.* OL

L Literary Element

Point of View **Answer:** *She reveals that she is a close observer of people and strongly empathizes with their feelings. Some students may also mention that the narrator seems to have a strong desire to be a part of a different family.* OL

the fenced playground of the Public School Number 13. We had been given "free" exercise time and had been ordered by our P.E.[7] teacher, Mr. DePalma, to "keep moving." That meant that the girls should jump rope and the boys toss basketballs through a hoop at the far end of the yard. He in the meantime would "keep an eye" on us from just inside the building.

It was a cold gray day in Paterson. The kind that warns of early snow. I was miserable, since I had forgotten my gloves and my knuckles were turning red and raw from the jump rope. I was also taking a lot of abuse from the black girls for not turning the rope hard and fast enough for them.

"Hey, Skinny Bones, pump it, girl. Ain't you got no energy today?" Gail, the biggest of the black girls who had the other end of the rope yelled, "Didn't you eat your rice and beans and pork chops for breakfast today?"

The other girls picked up the "pork chop" and made it into a refrain: "pork chop, pork chop, did you eat your pork chop?" They entered the double ropes in pairs and exited without tripping or missing a beat. I felt a burning on my cheeks, and then my glasses fogged up so that I could not manage to coordinate the jump rope with Gail. The chill was doing to me what it always did, entering my bones, making me cry, humiliating me. I hated the city, especially in winter. I hated Public School Number 13. I hated my skinny flat-chested body, and I envied the black girls who could jump rope so fast that their legs became a blur. They always seemed to be warm while I froze.

There was only one source of beauty and light for me that school year. The only thing I had anticipated at the start of the semester. That was seeing Eugene. In August, Eugene and his family had moved into the only house on the block that had a yard and trees. I could see his place from my window in El Building. In fact, if I sat on the fire escape I was literally suspended above Eugene's backyard. It was my favorite spot to read my library books in the summer. Until that August the house had been occupied by an old Jewish couple. Over the years I had become part of their family, without their knowing it, of course. I had a view of their kitchen and their backyard, and though I could not hear what they said, I knew when they were arguing, when one of them was sick, and many other things. I knew all this by watching them at mealtimes. I could see their kitchen table, the sink and the stove. During good times, he sat at the table and read his newspapers while she fixed the meals. If they argued, he would leave and the old woman would sit and stare at nothing for a long time. When one of them was sick, the other would come and get things from the kitchen and carry them out on a tray. The old man had died in June. The last week of school I had not seen him at the table at all. Then one day I saw that there was a crowd in the kitchen. The old woman had finally emerged from the house on the arm of a stocky middle-aged woman whom I had seen there a few times before, maybe her daughter. Then a man had carried out suitcases. The house had stood empty for weeks. I had had to resist the temptation to climb down into the yard and water the flowers the old lady had taken such good care of.

By the time Eugene's family moved in, the yard was a tangled mass of weeds. The father had spent several days mowing, and when he finished, I didn't see the red, yellow, and purple clusters that meant flowers to me from where I sat. I didn't see this family sit down at the kitchen table together. It was just the mother, a red-headed tall woman who wore a white uniform—

7. Here, *P.E.* stands for "physical education."

Reading Strategy Identifying Assumptions *What assumption does Gail make about the narrator and her family?* R1

Literary Element Point of View *What does the narrator reveal about herself through her description of the neighbors' house and family?* L

Additional Support

Leveled Reading An adapted version of this selection is available on page 16 of *Jamestown Literature: An Adapted Reader*, grade 9.

Skills Practice

WRITING: Repetition for Effect

Read aloud the passage on page 234: "I felt a burning . . . while I froze." Have students point out where repetition occurs. Ask them to explain the effect of repeating "I hated . . ." (*It emphasizes the strength of her emotion.*) Remind students that intentional repetition can build mood and underscore meaning. Unintentionally overused, it makes writing weak and boring. Have students use one of the following writing prompts to write a paragraph using repetition for effect.

1. The lecture was boring.
2. My _______ defines the word *cool.*
3. The wind never seems to stop. OL

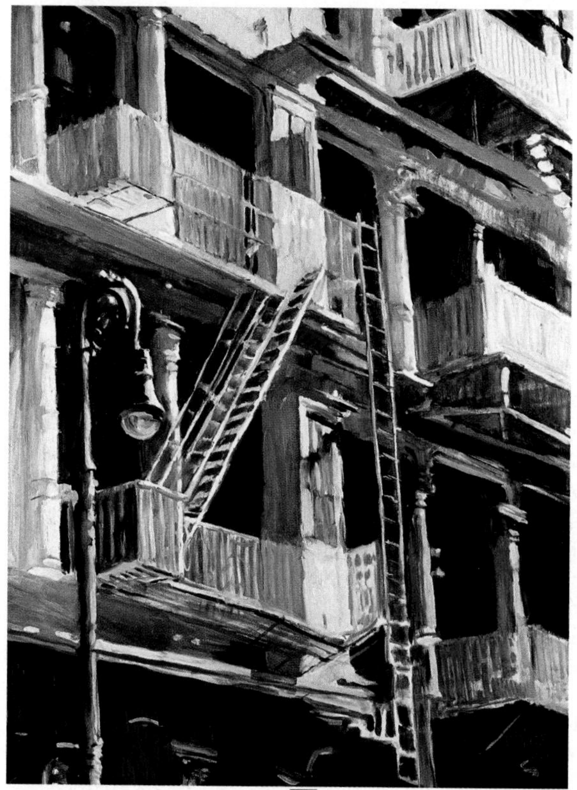

Soho Fire Escapes, 2001. Patti Mollica. ★

a nurse's, I guessed it was; the father was gone before I got up in the morning and was never there at dinner time. I only saw him on weekends when they sometimes sat on lawn chairs under the oak tree, each hidden behind a section of the newspaper; and there was Eugene. He was tall and blond, and he wore glasses. I liked him right away because he sat at the kitchen table and read books for hours. That summer, before we had even spoken one word to each other, I kept him company on my fire escape.

Once school started I looked for him in all my classes, but P.S. 13[8] was a huge, overpopulated place and it took me days and many **discreet** questions to discover that Eugene was in honors classes for all his subjects; classes that were not open to me because English was not my first language, though I was a straight A student. After much maneuvering I managed "to run into him" in the hallway where his locker was—on the other side of the building from mine—and in study hall at the library, where he first seemed to notice me but did not speak; and finally, on the way home after school one day when I decided to approach him directly, though my stomach was doing somersaults.

I was ready for rejection, snobbery, the worst. But when I came up to him, practically panting in my nervousness, and blurted out: "You're Eugene. Right?" He smiled, pushed his glasses up on his nose, and nodded. I saw then that he was blushing deeply. Eugene liked me, but he was shy. I did most of the talking that day. He nodded and smiled a lot. In the weeks that followed, we walked home together. He would linger at the corner of El Building for a few minutes then walk down to his two-story house. It was not until Eugene moved into that house that I noticed that El Building blocked most of the sun and that the only spot that got a little sunlight during the day was the tiny square of earth the old woman had planted with flowers.

I did not tell Eugene that I could see inside his kitchen from my bedroom. I felt

8. Here, *P.S.* stands for "public school."

Big Idea Dreams and Reality *Do you think that the narrator has a basis for forming such a positive impression of Eugene? Why or why not?* **BI1**

Reading Strategy Identifying Assumptions *Why do you think the narrator assumes that Eugene will reject her?* **R2**

Big Idea Dreams and Reality *Do you think that the narrator's beliefs about Eugene are rooted in reality, or not? Explain.* **BI2**

Vocabulary

discreet (dis krēt′) *adj.* showing good judgment; cautious

Teach

BI1 Big Idea

Dreams and Reality

Answer: *Some might think that she does because they both seem to be quiet and like to read; others may argue that she has only watched him and their backgrounds are different.* **OL**

R2 Reading Strategy

Identifying Assumptions

Answer: *She might assume that Eugene would reject her because of their racial differences or because he was not interested in her.* **OL**

BI2 Big Idea

Dreams and Reality

Answer: *They seem to be realistic, given that Eugene seems to be happy to talk with her.* **OL**

★ Viewing the Art

American contemporary illustrator and graphic designer Patti Mollica combines bold and vigorous use of color with composition influenced by strong graphic design to refect the energy of New York City. **AS**

Reading in the Real World

Citizenship Have students use a variety of sources to learn about Puerto Ricans and their contributions in the United States today. Some questions to guide their reading might include: How many Puerto Ricans live in the 48 contiguous United States? Where do they live? What is their average level of earnings and education? Who are some Puerto Rican men and women who have become famous? What contributions have Puerto Ricans made to art and entertainment? Have students report on their findings to the class. **OL**

Academic Standards

Additional Support activities on pp. 234 and 235 cover the following standards:

Skills Practice: **9.3.11** Evaluate the aesthetic qualities of style, including the impact of diction…on…mood… **9.5.8** Write for different purposes…adjusting…style… as appropriate.

Reading in the Real World: **9.7.15** Deliver expository (informational) presentations that convey information and ideas from… sources accurately and coherently…

Teach

L Literary Element

Point of View **Answer:** *The mother calls her by name. Since Elena is the narrator, revealing her name this way is more realistic than having her tell her name.* OL

BI1 Big Idea

Dreams and Reality
Answer: *The narrator has unpleasant memories of Puerto Rico and does not consider it her home; her parents remember it as paradise and dream about returning there.* OL

R Reading Strategy

Identifying Assumptions
Answer: *They assume Eugene is unsophisticated because he has a southern accent. They may have picked up this stereotype from movies or TV, without actually getting to know any southerners.* OL

dishonest, but I liked my secret sharing of his evenings, especially now that I knew what he was reading, since we chose our books together at the school library.

One day my mother came into my room as I was sitting on the windowsill staring out. In her abrupt way she said: "Elena, you are acting 'moony.' " *Enamorada*[9] was what she really said—that is, like a girl stupidly infatuated. Since I had turned fourteen and started menstruating my mother had been more **vigilant** than ever. She acted as if I was going to go crazy or explode or something if she didn't watch me and nag me all the time about being a señorita[10] now. She kept talking about virtue, morality, and other subjects that did not interest me in the least. My mother was unhappy in Paterson, but my father had a good job at the blue jeans factory in Passaic, and soon, he kept assuring us, we would be moving to our own house there. Every Sunday we drove out to the suburbs of Paterson, Clifton, and Passaic, out to where people mowed grass on Sundays in the summer and where children made snowmen in the winter from pure white snow, not like the gray slush of Paterson, which seemed to fall from the sky in that hue. I had learned to listen to my parents' dreams, which were spoken in Spanish, as fairy tales, like the stories about life in the island paradise of Puerto Rico before I was born. I had been to the Island once as a little girl, to grandmother's funeral, and all I remembered was wailing women in black, my mother becoming hysterical and being given a pill that made her sleep two days, and me feeling lost in a crowd of strangers all claiming to be my aunts, uncles, and cousins. I had actually been glad to return to the city. We had not been back there since then, though my parents talked constantly about buying a house on the beach someday, retiring on the island—that was a common topic among the residents of El Building. As for me, I was going to go to college and become a teacher.

But after meeting Eugene I began to think of the present more than of the future. What I wanted now was to enter that house I had watched for so many years. I wanted to see the other rooms where the old people had lived and where the boy I liked spent his time. Most of all, I wanted to sit at the kitchen table with Eugene like two adults, like the old man and his wife had done, maybe drink some coffee and talk about books. I had started reading *Gone with the Wind*.[11] I was **enthralled** by it, with the daring and the passion of the beautiful girl living in a mansion, and with her devoted parents and the slaves who did everything for them. I didn't believe such a world had ever really existed, and I wanted to ask Eugene some questions, since he and his parents, he had told me, had come up from Georgia, the same place where the novel was set. His father worked for a company that had transferred him to Paterson. His mother was very unhappy, Eugene said, in his beautiful voice that rose and fell over words in a strange, lilting way. The kids at school called him the Hick and made fun of the way he talked. I knew I was his only friend so far, and I liked that, though I felt sad for him sometimes. Skinny

9. *Enamorada* (en äm ′ ər ä ′ dä)
10. *Señorita* (sen′ yə rē ′ tə) is Spanish for *young lady.*

11. *Gone with the Wind* is a romantic novel about the South during and after the Civil War.

Literary Element Point of View *How does the author reveal the narrator's name? Why might the author have revealed it in this way?* L

Vocabulary
vigilant (vij′ əl ənt) *adj.* alert and watchful for danger or trouble

Big Idea Dreams and Reality *How do Elena's ideas and feelings about Puerto Rico contrast with those of her parents?* BI1

Reading Strategy Identifying Assumptions *What assumption do the other students make about Eugene? Why do you think that they make this assumption?* R

Vocabulary
enthrall (en thrôl′) *v.* to hold spellbound; fascinate

Additional Support

Skills Practice

READING: Cause-and-Effect Relationships Remind students that a cause is why something happened and an effect is what happened—the result. Note that a cause can lead to an effect, which itself can then be the cause of another effect, and so on. Have small groups of students construct chains of causes and effects using events from the story. Here are two possible starters:

1. Elena watches the new people in the little house.
2. Elena approaches Eugene directly.

Point out that students can build their chains by adding the word *because.* OL

Bones and the Hick was what they called us at school when we were seen together.

The day Mr. DePalma came out into the cold and asked us to line up in front of him was the day that President Kennedy was shot. Mr. DePalma, a short, muscular man with slicked-down black hair, was the science teacher, P.E. coach, and disciplinarian at P.S. 13. He was the teacher to whose homeroom you got assigned if you were a troublemaker, and the man called out to break up playground fights, and to escort violently angry teenagers to the office. And Mr. DePalma was the man who called your parents in for "a conference."

That day, he stood in front of two rows of mostly black and Puerto Rican kids, brittle from their efforts to "keep moving" on a November day that was turning bitter cold. Mr. DePalma, to our complete shock, was crying. Not just silent adult tears, but really sobbing. There were a few titters from the back of the line where I stood, shivering.

"Listen," Mr. DePalma raised his arms over his head as if he were about to conduct an orchestra. His voice broke, and he covered his face with his hands. His barrel chest was heaving. Someone giggled behind me.

"Listen," he repeated, "something awful has happened." A strange gurgling came from his throat, and he turned around and spit on the cement behind him.

"Gross," someone said, and there was a lot of laughter.

"The president is dead, you idiots. I should have known that wouldn't mean anything to a bunch of losers like you kids. Go home." He was shrieking now. No one moved for a minute or two, but then a big girl let out a "yeah!" and ran to get her books piled up with the others against the brick wall of the school building. The others followed in a mad scramble to get to their things before somebody caught on. It was still an hour to the dismissal bell.

A little scared, I headed for El Building. There was an eerie feeling on the streets. I looked into Mario's drugstore, a favorite hangout for the high school crowd, but there were only a couple of old Jewish men at the soda bar, talking with the short order cook in tones that sounded almost angry, but they were keeping their voices low. Even the traffic on one of the busiest intersections in Paterson—Straight Street and Park Avenue—seemed to be moving slower. There were no horns blasting that day. At El Building, the usual little group of unemployed men were not hanging out on the front stoop, making it difficult for women to enter the front door. No music spilled out from open doors in the hallway. When I walked into our apartment, I found my mother sitting in front of the grainy picture of the television set.

She looked up at me with a tear-streaked face and just said: *"Dios mío,"*[12] turning back to the set as if it were pulling at her eyes. I went into my room.

Flash—November 22, 1963, 1968. Andy Warhol. Silkscreen on paper, from a portfolio of 11 screenprints, colophon and text, 21 × 21 in. The Andy Warhol Foundation, Inc.

Viewing the Art: Can you imagine why Elena might think of Kennedy this way—in harsh colors and abstract shapes? Explain. ★

12. *Dios mío* (dē′ os mē′ ō) is Spanish for *My God.*

Big Idea Dreams and Reality *What is the narrator's mother watching? Based on what you already know, why is she so sad?* **BI2**

Teach

BI2 Big Idea

Dreams and Reality

Answer: *She is watching news coverage related to President Kennedy's assassination; she is very upset; the narrator noted earlier that Puerto Ricans in her building admired the President.* **OL**

★ Viewing the Art

Answer: *Harshness of color balances the starkness of the announcement and Elena's surroundings; like the shapes, Kennedy is an abstraction, or idea, to Elena. She does not feel a personal, emotional connection to Kennedy but realizes he is important to her community.*

Andy Warhol was the most innovative producer of Pop art, a form that features commonplace and commercial elements of technological society. According to Warhol, its intent is to bore the audience and show how dehumanizing life has become. **AS**

Differentiated Instruction

Writing and Performing a Skit

Have gifted students write a script for a skit based on the main idea of dreams destroyed by prejudice. Break students into small groups and have the groups assign each member a specific job, such as writer, editor, performers, and so on. Encourage students to use emotions like those found in the story and dialogue and movement to connect with the audience. Have the groups perform their skits for the class, and ask the class to provide feedback on the skits. **AL**

Academic Standards

Additional Support activities on pp. 236 and 237 cover the following standards:

Skills Practice: **9.3** [Identify] story elements such as...plot...

Differentiated Instruction: **9.5.8** Write for different purposes and audiences, adjusting tone, style, and voice as appropriate. **9.7.6** Analyze the occasion and the interests of the audience and choose effective verbal and nonverbal techniques...for presentations. **9.7** [Respond] to oral communication [with] careful listening and evaluation of content...

Teach

L1 Literary Element

Point of View Answer: *Experiencing the story through the narrator's eyes will prompt most students to empathize with her elation at realizing her dream of visiting Eugene's house rather than condemning her lack of involvement in the nation's mourning.* OL

R Reading Strategy

Identifying Assumptions

Answer: *She assumes they will reject her daughter.* OL

BI1 Big Idea

Dreams and Reality

Answer: *Students should mention the mother's ominous warning that Elena is heading for "humiliation and pain." The narrator is hoping that instead she and Eugene will enjoy their time together.* OL

Though I wanted to feel the right thing about President Kennedy's death, I could not fight the feeling of **elation** that stirred in my chest. Today was the day I was to visit Eugene in his house. He had asked me to come over after school to study for an American history test with him. We had also planned to walk to the public library together. I looked down into his yard. The oak tree was bare of leaves, and the ground looked gray with ice. The light through the large kitchen window of his house told me that El Building blocked the sun to such an extent that they had to turn lights on in the middle of the day. I felt ashamed about it. But the white kitchen table with the lamp hanging just above it looked cozy and inviting. I would soon sit there, across from Eugene, and I would tell him about my perch just above his house. Maybe I would.

In the next thirty minutes I changed clothes, put on a little pink lipstick, and got my books together. Then I went in to tell my mother that I was going to a friend's house to study. I did not expect her reaction.

"You are going out *today*?" The way she said "today" sounded as if a storm warning had been issued. It was said in utter disbelief. Before I could answer, she came toward me and held my elbows as I clutched my books.

"*Hija*,[13] the president has been killed. We must show respect. He was a great man. Come to church with me tonight."

She tried to embrace me, but my books were in the way. My first impulse was to comfort her, she seemed so distraught, but I had to meet Eugene in fifteen minutes.

"I have a test to study for, Mama. I will be home by eight."

"You are forgetting who you are, *Niña*.[14] I have seen you staring down at that boy's house. You are heading for humiliation and pain." My mother said this in Spanish and in a resigned tone that surprised me, as if she had no intention of stopping me from "heading for humiliation and pain." I started for the door. She sat in front of the TV, holding a white handkerchief to her face.

I walked out to the street and around the chain-link fence that separated El Building from Eugene's house. The yard was neatly edged around the little walk that led to the door. It always amazed me how Paterson, the inner core of the city, had no apparent logic to its architecture. Small, neat, single residences like this one could be found right next to huge, dilapidated apartment buildings like El Building. My guess was that the little houses had been there first, then the immigrants had come in droves, and the monstrosities had been raised for them—the Italians, the Irish, the Jews, and now us, the Puerto Ricans, and the blacks. The door was painted a deep green: *verde*, the color of hope. I had heard my mother say it: *Verde-Esperanza*.[15]

I knocked softly. A few suspenseful moments later the door opened just a crack. The red, swollen face of a woman appeared. She had a halo of red hair floating over a delicate ivory face—the face of a doll—with freckles on the nose. Her smudged eye makeup made her look unreal to me, like a mannequin seen through a warped store window.

13. *Hija* (ē′ hä) is Spanish for *daughter*.

14. *Niña* (nēn′ yä) is Spanish for *girl*.

15. Translated directly, *Verde-Esperanza* (vār′ dā es pe rän′ zə) is Green-Hope.

Literary Element Point of View *How does the writer's use of point of view influence how you react to the information given here?* L1

Vocabulary

elation (i lā′ shən) n. a feeling of great joy; ecstasy

Reading Strategy Identifying Assumptions *What assumption does Elena's mother make about Eugene and his family?* R

Big Idea Dreams and Reality *Why might seeing a sign of hope be especially important to the narrator at this moment?* BI1

Additional Support

Skills Practice

GRAMMAR: Understanding Adverbs

Explain to students that adverbs modify verbs, adjectives, or other adverbs by telling *when, where, how,* and *to what degree.* Write the following lines on the board: ". . . where he first seemed to notice me but did not speak; and finally, on the way home after school one day I decided to approach him directly. . . ." Discuss ways the adverbs add to the meaning of the sentence.

Have students locate other adverbs in the selection and write them, the word they modify, and the question that the adverb answers. OL

"What do you want?" Her voice was tiny and sweet-sounding, like a little girl's, but her tone was not friendly.

"I'm Eugene's friend. He asked me over. To study." I thrust out my books, a silly gesture that embarrassed me almost immediately.

"You live there?" She pointed up to El Building, which looked particularly ugly, like a gray prison with its many dirty windows and rusty fire escapes. The woman had stepped halfway out, and I could see that she wore a white nurse's uniform with "St. Joseph's Hospital" on the name tag.

"Yes. I do."

She looked intently at me for a couple of heartbeats, then said as if to herself, "I don't know how you people do it." Then directly to me: "Listen. Honey. Eugene doesn't want to study with you. He is a smart boy. Doesn't need help. You understand me. I am truly sorry if he told you you could come over. He cannot study with you. It's nothing personal. You understand? We won't be in this place much longer, no need for him to get close to people—it'll just make it harder for him later. Run back home now."

I couldn't move. I just stood there in shock at hearing these things said to me in such a honey-drenched voice. I had never heard an accent like hers except for Eugene's softer version. It was as if she were singing me a little song.

"What's wrong? Didn't you hear what I said?" She seemed very angry, and I finally snapped out of my trance. I turned away from the green door and heard her close it gently.

Our apartment was empty when I got home. My mother was in someone else's kitchen, seeking the solace[16] she needed. Father would come in from his late shift at midnight. I would hear them talking softly in the kitchen for hours that night. They would not discuss their dreams for the future, or life in Puerto Rico, as they often did; that night they would talk sadly about the young widow and her two children, as if they were family. For the next few days, we would observe *luto*[17] in our apartment; that is, we would practice restraint and silence—no loud music or laughter. Some of the women of El Building would wear black for weeks.

That night, I lay in my bed, trying to feel the right thing for our dead president. But the tears that came up from a deep source inside me were strictly for me. When my mother came to the door, I pretended to be sleeping. Sometime during the night, I saw from my bed the streetlight come on. It had a pink halo around it. I went to my window and pressed my face to the cool glass. Looking up at the light I could see the white snow falling like a lace veil over its face. I did not look down to see it turning gray as it touched the ground below. ∾

16. *Solace* is "relief from sorrow or disappointment;" it also means "comfort."

17. *Luto* (lo͞o′ tō) is Spanish for *mourning.*

Literary Element Point of View *How does the narrator's description of the building reflect her own mood at the moment?* **L2**

Big Idea Dreams and Reality *How does this passage reflect both dreams and realities?* **BI2**

Teach

L2 Literary Element

Point of View Answer: *Because this description of El Building comes from the narrator's point of view, the reader recognizes that it reflects her feelings of awkwardness and shame.* **OL**

BI2 Big Idea

Dreams and Reality

Answer: *When the narrator describes the suburbs, she mentions that the children play in white snow, unlike the gray slush she is used to in Paterson. The white snow represents dreams of a better life; the grey slush is the reality of her life now.* **OL**

CheckPoint

Use the CheckPoint questions on Presentation Plus! to check students' mastery of the selection. These questions can be used with interactive response keypads for immediate student feedback.

Differentiated Instruction

Emotional Vocabulary This story contains many words about emotions. Less proficient readers can relate to the climax of the story if they understand the emotional words in a familiar context. List the following words on the board and have students define each using a dictionary: *elation, distraught, disbelief, hope, humiliation.* Have them recall specific incidents when they felt these emotions, and then make up a sentence using each in a context that suggests this meaning. **BL**

Academic Standards

Additional Support activities on pp. 238 and 239 cover the following standards:

Skills Practice: **9.6.2** Demonstrate an understanding of sentence construction, including…the proper placement of modifiers, and proper English usage…

Differentiated Instruction: **9.1** Use…context clues, and a growing knowledge of English to determine the meaning of words…

AFTER YOU READ

Assess

1. Accept reasonable answers.
2. (a) A ninth-grade Puerto Rican girl, Paterson, New Jersey, November 22, 1963 (b) She feels embarrassed by it.
3. (a) The house next door (b) She finds normalcy and comfort in their daily routines.
4. (a) She is invited to Eugene's house. His mother sends her home. (b) She may have been racially prejudiced.
5. To contrast with her message and underline her cruelty
6. Accept answers supported by details.
7. The title refers to the assassination, the subject Elena and Eugene plan to study, and the country's history of racial division.
8. Assassination shattered the dreams of those who believed in Kennedy; life in the tenement eclipsed the parents' dream of a beach house; Elena's dreams of Eugene's friendship are shattered by his mother's prejudice.

AFTER YOU READ

RESPONDING AND THINKING CRITICALLY

Respond

1. How do you feel about what happens to the narrator at Eugene's house?

Recall and Interpret

2. (a)Who is telling the story, and when and where is the story set? (b)How does the narrator feel about her home?
3. (a)What does Elena enjoy looking at from her window? (b)In your opinion, why is Elena interested in the daily habits of the old Jewish couple and later of Eugene's family?
4. (a)Why does Elena feel particularly happy on the day the story takes place and particularly sorrowful that night? (b)What factors might have led Eugene's mother to react as she did to Elena? Use details from the story to support your opinion.

Analyze and Evaluate

5. A character trait is a habit, a physical attribute, or an attitude that helps define a character. Why might Ortiz Cofer have given Eugene's mother the character traits of a face like a doll and a tiny, sweet-sounding voice?
6. Do you think the author expressed the feelings of a ninth-grade girl realistically? Support your response with details from the story as well as from your own experience.
7. In your opinion, why might the writer have titled this story "American History"?

Connect

8. **Big Idea** **Dreams and Reality** Describe three ways in which dreams are overshadowed by reality in this story.

LITERARY ANALYSIS

Literary Element Point of View

The choice of **point of view** can greatly influence how a story unfolds. A writer will usually choose a narrator whose point of view effectively communicates the main ideas and themes.

1. How does the first-person point of view in "American History" shape how readers feel about the interactions between people of different cultures or ethnic groups?
2. If Ortiz Cofer had chosen to tell this story from the point of view of one of the adults, how might that choice have changed the focus of the story?

Review: Setting

As you learned on pages 10–11, **setting** is the time and place in which the events of a literary work occur. Setting also includes the ideas, customs, beliefs, and values of the time and place.

Group Activity Work with a small group to create a web diagram listing details the writer gives in "American History" to evoke the setting of El Building in 1963, home to many Puerto Ricans who have moved to Paterson, New Jersey. Try to include at least one example for each category in the web below.

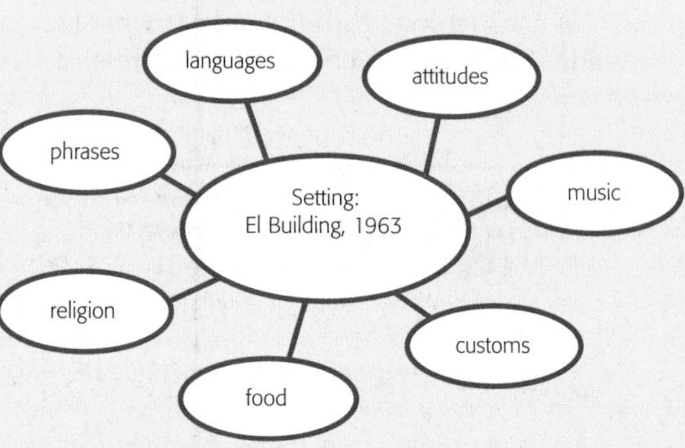

Literary Element

1. First-person helps readers empathize with ethnic groups facing prejudice.
2. The focus might be the assassination.

Review: Setting

Attitudes: Stick with your own ethnic group
Customs: *luto* (silent mourning)
Phrases: moony or *enamorada*
Languages: Spanish
Music: *salsas*
Food: rice, beans, pork chops
Religion: Spiritist altars

READING AND VOCABULARY

Reading Strategy Identifying Assumptions

What characters assume about each other is important for both the plot and the theme of "American History." Review the **assumptions** you identified in your chart that relate to different characters' attitudes toward each other.

1. What assumptions does Eugene's mother make about the narrator? How do her assumptions affect the plot of the story?
2. Do you think that the assumptions Eugene's mother makes about the narrator are valid? Why or why not?
3. What assumptions does Mr. DePalma make about the students? Do you think that his assumptions are correct? Explain.

Vocabulary Practice

Practice with Analogies Choose the word that best completes the analogy.

1. elation : pleasure :: terror :
   - **a.** happiness
   - **b.** fear
   - **c.** silliness
   - **d.** anger
2. interest : enthrall :: moisten :
   - **a.** dry
   - **b.** measure
   - **c.** select
   - **d.** soak
3. discreet : careless :: cautious :
   - **a.** careful
   - **b.** safe
   - **c.** reckless
   - **d.** distant
4. alert : vigilant :: happy :
   - **a.** overjoyed
   - **b.** penitent
   - **c.** sad
   - **d.** joyless

Academic Vocabulary

Here is a word from the vocabulary list on page R80.

appropriate (ə prō′ prē it) *adj.* especially suitable

Practice and Apply
Why does Elena's mother think that it is not **appropriate** for her to go out on the night of the story?

WRITING AND EXTENDING

Writing About Literature

Analyze Historical Context In your opinion, why did Ortiz Cofer choose the date November 22, 1963, as the setting for this story? Write a brief essay to explore the topic. (You may want to reread the Building Background section on page 232 before you begin writing.) Consider the following questions as you plan your essay:

- What did John F. Kennedy represent to many people in the United States?
- Based on details Ortiz Cofer presented, how did President Kennedy's death affect most adults in El Building? Other adults in the story?
- How did President Kennedy's death affect most of the young people in the story? Look for at least two details to help answer this question.
- In what way does President Kennedy's death serve as a symbol in the story?

After you complete your draft, exchange essays with a peer reviewer. Suggest ways to clarify each other's writing and organization. After you have made revisions to your essay, proofread and edit it to correct any errors in grammar, spelling, and punctuation.

Literary Criticism

Some works of literature are said to have universal appeal; in other words, any reader can find a personal connection or meaning in the text because he or she can relate to the experiences described. Reviewer Nancy Vasilakis writes that the narratives in Ortiz Cofer's book *An Island Like You: Stories of the Barrio* "have a universal resonance in the vitality, the brashness, the self-centered hopefulness, and the angst [anxiety] expressed by the teens." Working with a partner, make a list of examples of youthful vitality, brashness, self-centered hopefulness, and angst that you find in "American History." Then discuss whether you agree with Vasilakis's evaluation of Ortiz Cofer's appeal to teens.

LiteratureOnline Web Activities For eFlashcards, Selection Quick Checks, and other Web activities, go to www.glencoe.com.

AFTER YOU READ

Assess

Reading Strategy

1. She assumes that Elena is not good enough for her son and sends her home, ruining her plans and dreams.
2. Students should recognize the assumptions as unfair.
3. He assumes the students are apathetic, insensitive "losers." He is unfair to characterize all of them this way; most were probably confused by his display of emotion.

Vocabulary

1. b **2.** d **3.** c **4.** a

Academic Vocabulary

Her mother expected her to mourn and show respect for the slain president instead of socializing.

Writing About Literature

Students' analyses should

- describe how President Kennedy symbolized youth, idealism, and vigor.
- draw parallels between Kennedy's ideals and the dreams of minorities.
- comment on the sense of despair symbolized by Kennedy's death and the death of the narrator's dreams.
- use three to five examples from the story to reinforce these parallels.

Web Activities Have students access the Web site for interactive activities that will help them assess their understanding of the selection.

Literary Criticism

Suggest that students write an essay that takes a position on whether or not Cofer creates a universal appeal to teens in this story. Ask volunteers to share their essays with the class.

Focus

Summary

This passage from *A Thousand Days* begins with the author hearing the news that President Kennedy was shot in the head. The author then lists the responses of many people in America and around the world to the death of an American President.

Teach

Big Idea

Dreams and Reality Many people saw the young, energetic President as a source of hope. His assassination left some feeling that the American dream had been damaged if not altogether destroyed.
Ask: Why would Kennedy's assassination demoralize so many people across the country? *(People hoped Kennedy would improve their lives. Also, the reality of violence is shocking to many.)* **OL**

Readability Scores
Dale-Chall: 8.4
DRP: 61
Lexile: 1020

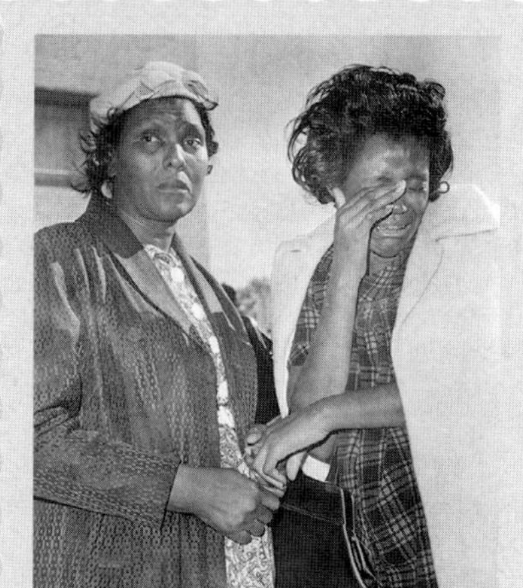

The Drums of Washington

Arthur M. Schlesinger Jr.

Pulitzer Prize Winner

Building Background

John F. Kennedy, who in 1960 was the youngest person ever elected president of the United States, is revered for his charisma and vision. Despite crises abroad, the Kennedy administration managed to make progress in foreign and domestic policy. During Kennedy's presidency, Arthur M. Schlesinger Jr. served as his adviser and later as a special assistant for Latin American affairs. In this excerpt, Schlesinger explores the grief that overwhelmed the world upon the assassination of President Kennedy on November 22, 1963.

Set a Purpose for Reading

Read to discover the reactions of people around the world to the assassination of President Kennedy.

Reading Strategy

Recognizing Bias

When you read to determine if the author has an inclination toward a certain opinion or position, you are **recognizing bias**. As you read "The Drums of Washington," take note of any statements made by Schlesinger that suggest bias.

On Friday morning I had flown to New York with Katharine Graham,[1] whose husband Philip had died three months before, for a luncheon with the editors of her magazine *Newsweek.* Kenneth Galbraith[2] had come down from Cambridge for the occasion. We were still sipping drinks before luncheon in an amiable mood of Friday-before-the-Harvard-Yale game relaxation when a young man in shirtsleeves entered the room and said, a little tentatively, "I am sorry to break in, but I think you should know that the President has been shot in the head in Texas." For a flash one thought this was some sort of ghastly office joke. Then we knew it could not be and huddled desperately around the nearest television. Everything was confused and appalling. The minutes dragged along. Incomprehensible bulletins came from the

1. *Katharine Graham* (1917–2001) was an owner and publisher of news media, including the *Washington Post.*
2. *Kenneth Galbraith* (1908–) is an economist who served as an ambassador to India and an adviser during the Kennedy administration.

Additional Support

See also Active Learning and Note Taking Guide, pp. 32–39.

Skills Practice

VOCABULARY: Negative Prefixes
The writer uses several words that begin with a negative prefix. *In-, im-, il-,* and *ir-* are all examples of negative prefixes. Usually, these word parts mean "not," "without," or "the opposite of" and reverse the meaning of the words to which they are attached. When the news bulletins about President Kennedy were *incomprehensible,* it means the writer could not understand what he was hearing. Have partners scan the passage, find other examples of words with negative prefixes, and figure out the meanings of the words. **OL**

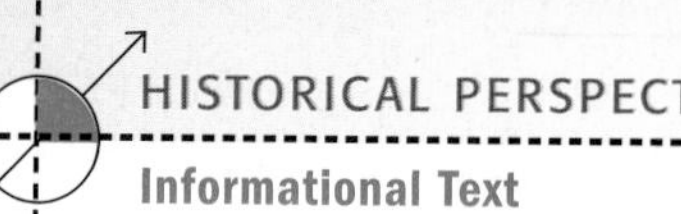

hospital. Suddenly an insane surge of conviction flowed through me: I felt that the man who had survived the Solomon Islands[3] and so much illness[4] and agony, who so loved life, embodied it, enhanced it, could not possibly die now. He would escape the shadow as he had before. Almost immediately we received the irrevocable word.

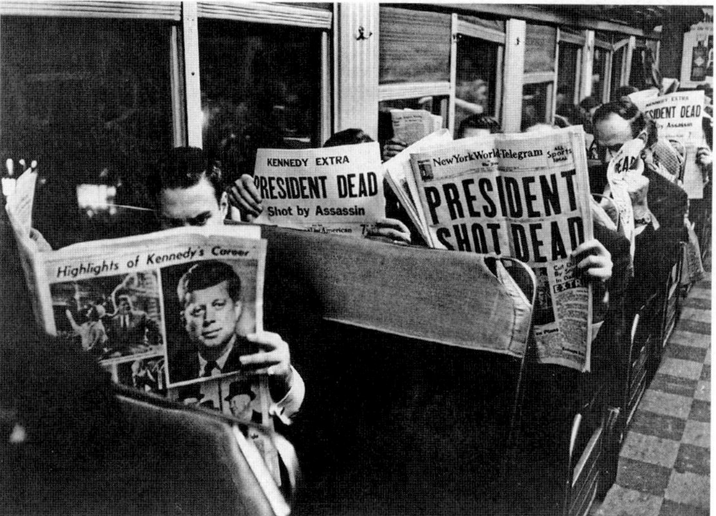

Commuters in New York read about Kennedy's assassination.

In a few moments Galbraith and I were on Katharine Graham's plane bound for Washington. It was the saddest journey of one's life. Bitterness, shame, anguish, disbelief, emptiness mingled inextricably in one's mind. When I stumbled, almost blindly, into the East Wing, the first person I encountered was Franklin D. Roosevelt Jr. In a short time I went with my White House colleagues to Andrews Field to await the return of Air Force One from Texas. A small crowd was waiting in the dusk, McNamara,[5] stunned and silent, Harriman,[6] haggard and suddenly looking very old, desolation everywhere. We watched incredulously as the casket was carefully lifted out of the plane and taken to the Naval Hospital at Bethesda. Later I went to my house in Georgetown. My weeping daughter Christina said, "Daddy, what has happened to our country? If this is the kind of country we have, I don't want to live here any more." The older children were already on their way back from college to Washington.

Still later I went back to the White House to await the last return. Around four in the morning the casket, wrapped in a flag, was brought from the Naval Hospital and placed on a stand in the East Room. Tapers were lit around the bier,[7] and a priest said a few words. Then Jacqueline approached the bier, knelt for a moment and buried her head in the flag. Soon she walked away. The rest of us waited for a little while in the great hall. We were beyond consolation, but we clung to the comradeship he had given us. Finally, just before daybreak, we bleakly dispersed into the mild night.

We did not grieve alone. Sorrow engulfed America and the world. At Harvard Yard the bells tolled in Memorial Church, a girl wept hysterically in Widener Library,[8] a student slammed a tree, again and again, with his fist.

3. Schlesinger is referring to Kennedy's service in the U.S. Navy. In 1943 Kennedy was seriously injured while commanding a patrol torpedo boat that was sunk by a Japanese destroyer in the Solomon Islands in the South Pacific.
4. The *illness* to which Schlesinger is referring is Addison's disease.
5. *Robert S. McNamara* (1916–) served as the U.S. Secretary of Defense from 1961 to 1968.
6. *W. Averell Harriman* (1891–1986) served as the assistant secretary for Far Eastern affairs from 1961 to 1963.
7. *Tapers* are candles. A *bier* is "the stand on which a coffin is placed before burial."
8. *Widener Library* is the main library at Harvard University.

Teach

R Reading Strategy

Recognizing Bias **Ask:** What is the mood in the first paragraph? *(Schlesinger and his friends are relaxed and happy.)* What causes the mood to change? *(A young man informs them that the President has been shot.)* Does Schlesinger's reaction to the news suggest bias? *(Schlesinger reacts by watching television, but the words he uses to describe how he felt are emotionally charged and suggest bias.)* OL

Political History

The Assassin Lee Harvey Oswald was the man who assassinated President Kennedy. Oswald, who was born in 1939 in New Orleans, served in the Marine Corps. On the same day as the assassination, Oswald also shot and killed a police officer who stopped to question him. AS

Differentiated Instruction

Using a Map Less proficient readers may have difficulty recognizing the names and places that Schlesinger refers to in this passage. Display a map of the world where students can see it. Have students take turns reading the passage out loud. When a new place is mentioned, locate the city, state, or country on the map and mark it with a pin. Explain that by including these references Schlesinger was suggesting that the whole world mourned the loss of President Kennedy. BL

Academic Standards

Additional Support activities on pp. 242 and 243 cover the following standards:

Skills Practice: **9.1** [Use] word parts...to determine the meaning of words...

Differentiated Instruction: **9.2.4** Synthesize the content from several sources or works...and connect...to...related topics...

Teach

R1 Reading Strategy

Recognizing Bias **Ask:** How does the writer suggest bias? *(Students may say he lists many people who shared his opinion of Kennedy.)* Why do you think the writer included comments by other political leaders? *(To add validity to his view of Kennedy)* How does describing Kennedy as a "young hero of far away, the slayer of the dragons of discrimination, poverty, ignorance, and war" show bias? *(It exaggerates Kennedy as a heroic figure.)* OL

Women in Germany place flowers next to a picture of John F. Kennedy to honor him after his death.

Alistair Cooke[14] spoke of "this sudden discovery that he was more familiar than we knew." "Is there some principle of nature," asked Richard Hofstadter,[15] "which requires that we never know the quality of what we have had until it is gone?" Around the land people sat desperately in front of television sets watching the bitter drama of the next four days. In Washington Daniel Patrick Moynihan, the Assistant Secretary of Labor, said, "I don't think there's any point in being Irish if you don't know that the world is going to break your heart eventually. I guess that we thought we had a little more time. . . . Mary McGrory[16] said to me that we'll never laugh again. And I said, 'Heavens, Mary. We'll laugh again. It's just that we'll never be young again.' "

Negroes mourned, and A. Philip Randolph[9] said that his "place in history will be next to Abraham Lincoln." Pablo Casals[10] mused that he had seen many great and terrible events in his lifetime—the Dreyfus case,[11] the assassination of Gandhi[12]—"but in recent history—and I am thinking of my own lifetime—there has never been a tragedy that has brought so much sadness and grief to as many people as this." "For a time we felt the country was ours," said Norman Mailer.[13] "Now it's theirs again." Many were surprised by the intensity of the loss.

In Ireland, "Ah, they cried the rain down that night," said a Fitzgerald of Limerick; he would not come back in the springtime. David Bruce reported from London, "Great Britain has never before mourned a foreigner as it has President Kennedy." As the news spread around London, over a thousand people assembled before the embassy in Grosvenor Square; they came in endless thousands in the next days to sign the condolence book. . . . In West Berlin people lighted candles in darkened windows. In Poland there was a spontaneous mass mourning by university students; church bells

9. *A. Philip Randolph* (1889–1979) was a trade unionist and civil rights leader who served as the first president of the Negro American Labor Council (1960–1966).
10. *Pablo Casals* (1876–1973) was a Spanish-born cellist and conductor who toured internationally.
11. The *Dreyfus case* occurred in 1894 in France, when an army officer, Captain Alfred Dreyfus, was sentenced to life imprisonment for selling military secrets to Germany. It was later discovered that another officer committed the crime, yet officials refused to reopen the case.
12. *Mohandas Gandhi* (1869–1948) led the Indian national movement by means of nonviolent protest to eliminate British rule in India.
13. *Norman Mailer* (1923–) is an American novelist who often criticizes totalitarianism.
14. *Alistair Cooke* (1908–2004) was a journalist who commented on history and culture.
15. *Richard Hofstadter* (1916–1970) was an American historian and recipient of two Pulitzer Prizes.
16. *Mary McGrory* (1918–2004) was a newspaper columnist who frequently wrote for the *Washington Post*. She was also a recipient of the Pulitzer Prize.

Additional Support

Skills Practice

READING: Analyzing Details Writers often give hints about a person by using vivid details to describe the individual's actions, words, and physical appearance. Readers may then draw conclusions about the individual's character, personality, or values on the basis of these details. This passage describes President Kennedy. "I felt that the man who had survived the Solomon Islands and so much illness and agony, who so loved life, embodied it, enhanced it, could not possibly die now. He would escape the shadow as he had before." These details reveal Kennedy's strength, resolve, and love of life.

tolled for fifteen minutes on the night of the funeral. In Yugoslavia Tito,[17] so overcome that he could hardly speak, phoned the American chief of mission; later he read a statement over the state radio and went in person to the embassy to sign the book. The national flag was flown at half-mast, and schools were instructed to devote one full hour to a discussion of the President's policies and significance. In Moscow Khrushchev[18] was the first to sign the book, and the Soviet television carried the funeral, including the service in the church.

Latin America was devastated. Streets, schools, housing projects were named after him, shrines set up in his memory; his picture, torn from the newspaper, hung on the walls of workers' shacks and in the hovels of the *campesinos.*[19] "For Latin America," said Lleras Camargo,[20] "Kennedy's passing is a blackening, a tunnel, a gust of cloud and smoke." Castro[21] was with Jean Daniel when the report came; he said, *"Es una mala noticia"* ("This is bad news"). In a few moments, with the final word, he stood and said, "Everything is changed. . . . I'll tell you one thing: at least Kennedy was an enemy to whom we had become accustomed." In Cambodia Prince Sihanouk ordered court mourning: "a light was put out," he later said, "which may not be re-lit for many years to come." In Indonesia flags flew at half-mast. In New Delhi people cried in the streets. In Algiers Ben Bella[22] phoned Ambassador Porter in tears and said, "I can't believe it. Believe me, I'd rather it happen to me than to him." In Guinea Sékou Touré[23] said, "I have lost my only true friend in the outside world." The embassy reported, "People expressed their grief without restraint, and just about everybody in Guinea seemed to have fallen under the spell of the courageous young hero of far away, the slayer of the dragons of discrimination, poverty, ignorance, and war." In N'zérékoré[24] in the back country, where one would hardly think they had heard of the United States let alone the American President, a group of natives presented a sum of money to their American pastor to buy, according to the custom of the Guerze people, a rush mat in which to bury President Kennedy. In Kampala Ugandans crowded the residence of the American Ambassador; others sat silently for hours on the lawns and hillsides waiting. In Mali, the most left-wing of African states, President Keita came to the embassy with an honor guard and delivered a eulogy. In the Sudan a grizzled old Bisharine tribesman told an American lawyer that it was terrible Kennedy's son was so young; "it will be a long time before he can be the true leader." *Transition,* the magazine of African intellectuals, said, "In this way was murdered the first real chance in this century for an intelligent and new leadership to the world. . . . More than any other person, he achieved the intellectual's ideal of a man in action. His death leaves us unprepared and in darkness."

In Washington grief was an agony. Somehow the long hours passed, as the new President took over with firmness and strength, but the roll of the drums, when we walked to St. Matthew's Cathedral on the frosty Monday, will sound forever in my ears, and the wildly twittering birds during the interment at Arlington[25] while the statesmen of the world looked on. It was all so grotesque and so incredible. One remembered Stephen Spender's poem:

17. *Josip Broz Tito* (1892–1980) was the president of the Communist Party of Yugoslavia from 1939 to 1980.
18. *Nikita Sergeyevich Khrushchev* was the premier of the Soviet Union from 1958 to 1964.
19. *Campesinos* is Spanish for "farmers."
20. *Alberto Lleras Camargo* (1906–1990) was the president of Colombia from 1945 to 1946 and 1958 to 1962.
21. *Fidel Castro* (c. 1926–) is the Cuban premier.
22. *Ahmed Ben Bella* (1918–) served as the first prime minister (1962–1963) and first president (1963–1965) of the Algerian republic.
23. *Sékou Touré* (1922–1984) served as the first president of the Republic of Guinea from 1958 to 1984.
24. *N'zérékoré* is a town in southeastern Guinea.
25. *Interment* means "the act of placing in a grave." Arlington refers to Arlington National Cemetery, in Virginia.

HISTORICAL PERSPECTIVE

Informational Text

Teach

R2 Reading Strategy

Recognizing Bias **Say:** A writer shows bias when he or she demonstrates a strong, personal, and sometimes unreasonable opinion. Readers should analyze how a writer's bias influences his or her writing. What bias is clear in this selection? *(Students may say that Schlesinger has a strong positive bias toward Kennedy because he worked with him and admired him.)*

Tell students to choose examples from the selection that reveal the author's bias and share them with the class. OL

★ Political History

The New President When the President of the United States dies, resigns, or is removed from office, the Vice President becomes President. Lyndon B. Johnson became President upon Kennedy's death and was later elected to a full term. AS

For practice, read the following passage to students and ask them what the details reveal about Kennedy's character. "It was all gone now—the life-affirming, life-enhancing zest, the brilliance, the wit, the cool commitment, the steady purpose . . . Kennedy transformed the American Spirit." OL

Building Reading Fluency

Expressive Reading Reading this selection aloud will convey the depth of Schlesinger's emotions and help students develop expressive reading skills. Assign small groups a paragraph from the selection. Have them take turns reading in a tone that communicates the writer's feelings. BL

Academic Standards

Additional Support activities on pp. 244 and 245 cover the following standards:

Skills Practice: **9.3** [Identify] story elements such as character… **9.2.8** Make reasonable statements and draw conclusions about a text, supporting them with accurate examples.

Building Reading Fluency: **9.7** [Develop] speaking skills…in conjunction with… strategies…[for] delivery of oral presentations.

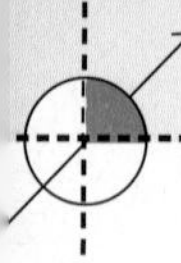

Assess

1. Students should be able to support their answer by explaining how the quotation established the mood of the time period described.
2. (a) His daughter had an intense reaction. She said, "If this is the kind of country we have, I don't want to live here anymore." (b) Accept any well-reasoned answer.
3. (a) Khrushchev was the first person in Moscow to sign the condolences book, and Castro said "This is bad news. Everything is changed. . . . I'll tell you one thing: at least Kennedy was an enemy to whom we had become accustomed." (b) Students should realize that in foreign relations, even with nations with whom the United States experienced tensions, President Kennedy commanded respect, and many foreign leaders liked him personally.
4. Students may feel he quotes too many people without providing enough background. Others may feel this approach conveys his sense that the whole world was affected by President Kennedy's assassination.

I think continually of those who were truly great. . . .
The names of those who in their lives fought for life,
Who wore at their hearts the fire's center.
Born of the sun they traveled a short while towards the sun,
And left the vivid air signed with their honor.

It was all gone now—the life-affirming, life-enhancing zest, the brilliance, the wit, the cool commitment, the steady purpose. . . .

Kennedy transformed the American spirit—and the response of his people to his murder, the absence of intolerance and hatred, was a monument to his memory. The energies he released, the standards he set, the purposes he inspired, the goals he established would guide the land he loved for years to come. Above all he gave the world for an imperishable moment the vision of a leader who greatly understood the terror and the hope, the diversity and the possibility, of life on this planet and who made people look beyond nation and race to the future of humanity. So the people of the world grieved as if they had terribly lost their own leader, friend, brother.

On December 22, a month after his death, fire from the flame burning at his grave in Arlington was carried at dusk to the Lincoln Memorial. It was fiercely cold. Thousands stood, candles in their hands; then, as the flame spread among us, one candle lighting the next, the crowd gently moved away, the torches flaring and flickering, into the darkness. The next day it snowed—almost as deep a snow as the inaugural blizzard. I went to the White House. It was lovely, ghostly, and strange.

It all ended, as it began, in the cold.

RESPONDING AND THINKING CRITICALLY

Respond

1. Schlesinger uses quotations from many people around the world. Which quotation do you think especially captured how people reacted to President Kennedy's assassination? Why?

Recall and Interpret

2. (a)How did Schlesinger's daughter react to the assassination of President Kennedy? (b)Do you think an American child living today would have a similar reaction to a U.S. president's assassination? Why or why not?
3. (a)How did the Soviet premier, Nikita Khrushchev, and Cuba's leader, Fidel Castro, react to President Kennedy's assassination? (b)During Kennedy's presidency, there was much tension between the United States and both Cuba and the Soviet Union. What do the reactions of Khrushchev and Castro say about how President Kennedy served in U.S. foreign relations?

Analyze and Evaluate

4. The author supports his opinion of President Kennedy by using quotations. Do you think this is effective? Why or why not?
5. This excerpt closes with the statement, "It all ended, as it began, in the cold." Literally, Schlesinger is referring to the day of President Kennedy's inauguration and the day of his assassination. What effect may he be trying to create?

Connect

6. Schlesinger in *Drums of Washington* and Judith Ortiz Cofer in "American History" both attempt to capture the mood of November 22, 1963, the day of President Kennedy's assassination. Which do you think is more effective and why?

INDIANA ACADEMIC STANDARDS (pages 242–246)
9.2.7 Evaluate an author's argument or defense of a claim...
9.2 Develop strategies such as...identifying...perspective...
9.3.2 Compare and contrast the presentation of a similar theme or topic across genres...

For additional assessment, see Selection and Unit Assessments, pp. 37–38.

5. Possible answers: He was using language to set a somber mood to influence the reaction of the reader; he was making a broader statement about Kennedy's presidency being a time when there was a different sort of energy and spirit leading the nation.
6. Possible answers: The perspective of someone their own age may be more accessible for some students; others may find the voice of a witness to that moment in history more compelling.

BEFORE YOU READ

Baker's Bluejay Yarn

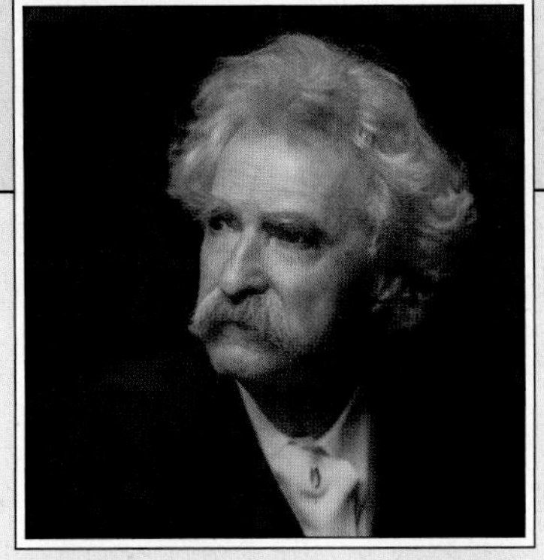

MEET MARK TWAIN

When Mark Twain died, the *Washington Post* wrote, "When one of its members dies, Congress adjourns in respect to his memory. Now that Mark Twain has passed away, the world will pause, if but for a moment, in its work and its play, its planning, and money-getting, to honor him. For thousands that never saw him felt that they knew him, and knew that they loved him." By capturing the experiences and everyday speech of ordinary people, by poking fun at the overly proud and mighty, and by finding humor and grace in every aspect of the human experience, Mark Twain became, for many readers and critics, the greatest American author of all time.

Child of the River Born Samuel Langhorne Clemens, Mark Twain grew up in Hannibal, Missouri, on the west bank of the Mississippi River. The mightiest river in the United States, it became the setting for many of Twain's literary works.

As a young boy, Mark Twain played on the banks of the river, listening to its sounds and watching the steamboats chug by. An alert and curious boy, he noticed every detail of the river and its colorful characters. The river was his education, and he would someday turn his childhood memories into literature.

> *"I have never let my schooling interfere with my education."*
>
> —Mark Twain

A Colorful Life When Twain was eleven, his father died, forcing the boy to find a job and help support his family. He worked odd jobs—as a delivery boy, grocery clerk, and blacksmith's helper—after school and during the summers, and at thirteen became a printer's apprentice. Then, at twenty-one, he fulfilled a lifelong goal: to become a pilot on a Mississippi riverboat. Twain loved this job and life on the river so much that he took as his pen name "Mark Twain," a riverboat pilot's term.

Twain's job as a steamboat pilot ended during the Civil War, when north-south traffic was banned on the Mississippi. Undaunted, he went off on another adventure, this time to search for gold in California. Luckily for readers, Twain was unsuccessful in his search. He settled in San Francisco, where he began a new career: that of journalist, fiction writer, and lecturer. In 1865 he published his first short story, "The Celebrated Jumping Frog of Calaveras County." The humorous tale was an instant hit. The works that followed brought Twain international fame and financial success.

In 1870 Twain married and settled in Hartford, Connecticut. There he wrote *The Adventures of Tom Sawyer* and *The Adventures of Huckleberry Finn*, the books that helped cement his reputation as America's greatest humorist. Despite the acclaim, Twain remained modest. "My books are water; those of the great geniuses are wine. Everybody drinks water," he wrote.

Mark Twain was born in 1835 and died in 1910.

BEFORE YOU READ

Focus

BELLRINGER

Bellringer Options
Selection Focus Transparency 17
Daily Language Practice Transparency 22

Or have students generate a list of several animal characters from stories and cartoons that they are familiar with. Write a few of these characters' names on the board.

Ask: What kinds of human character traits do we associate with this animal character?

Author Search To expand students' appreciation of Mark Twain, have them access the Web site for additional information and resources.

Selection Skills

Baker's Bluejay Yarn

Literary Elements
- Persona (SE pp. 248, 251, 252, 255)
- Dialect (SE p. 255)

Reading Skills
- Analyzing Language (SE pp. 248–255)

Vocabulary Skills
- Context Clues (SE pp. 248, 255)
- Academic Vocabulary (SE p. 255)
- Context Clues (TWE p. 250)

Listening/Speaking/Viewing Skills
- Analyzing Art (SE p. 250)

Writing Skills/Grammar
- Analysis of Genre Elements (SE p. 256)
- Double Negatives (SE p. 256)

Study Skills/Research/Assessment
- Test Preparation (TWE p. 252)

BEFORE YOU READ

Focus

Summary

In this humorous story, the behavior and mannerisms of blue jays are shown to be similar to the behavior and mannerisms of human beings. Told in the rich vernacular of the narrator Jim Baker, the story recounts the confusion that ensues when a blue jay attempts to store acorns in a "hole" that turns out to be the chimney of a house. The story spoofs the way people create dramas out of situations that are fundamentally absurd.

V Vocabulary

Vocabulary File Say: Add these words and definitions to your vocabulary file. For each word, include a sentence that gives you an example of how to use the word. **OL** Students with English language needs should include the pronunciations of these words in their files. **EL**

Literary Elements Have students access the Web site to improve their understanding of persona.

LITERATURE PREVIEW

Connecting to the Story

This story, which Twain based on a character he met while living in California, contains many examples of his precise character development and gruff humor. Before you read, think about the following questions:

- What characteristics do you tend to find in any group of people?
- What human foibles do you find humorous?

Building Background

With blue and white feathers, crested heads, and long blue tails, blue jays are easy to recognize. They are known for their loud, harsh voices. The blue jay has a distinctive call, which seems to say "Thief! Thief!" or "Jay! Jay!" or even "Cat! Cat!" Crows and magpies, fellow noisemakers, are related to blue jays.

Setting Purposes for Reading

Big Idea Dreams and Reality

By building his stories on exaggerated or fantastic elements, such as talking animals, Twain was able to gently hint at truths about human nature. As you read, notice the very human characteristics that Twain ascribes to blue jays.

Literary Element Persona

A **persona** is a narrator or character created by an author to tell a story. The personality of a persona differs from the author's personality. By having a persona tell a story, authors can write outrageous, funny, or rude comments that the author himself or herself would never say. The first two paragraphs of this story are told by a narrator. Thereafter, the story is told through the persona of Jim Baker. Notice what his commentary and humorous personality lend to the story.

- See Literary Terms Handbook, p. R13.

 **Interactive Literary Elements Handbook** To review or learn more about the literary elements, go to www.glencoe.com.

READING PREVIEW

Reading Strategy Analyzing Language

Readers love Twain's creative use of **language.** A man of the people, he loved the salty, freewheeling speech of miners, sailors, and farmers. Vernacular—the mode of expression people use every day in casual conversation—is important to Twain's writing. His masterly use of vernacular allows him to vividly portray everyday people and to suggest the energy and spirit of America. As you read, think about how Twain's use of vernacular helps to suggest a certain tone, or attitude, toward the blue jay's story.

Reading Tip: Taking Notes As you read, jot down striking words and expressions you come across. Think about the tone these words and expressions create.

Vocabulary

commonplace (kom ′ən plās′) *adj.* ordinary; not original or interesting; p. 251 *I thought the wooden table was commonplace, but it turned out to be a valuable antique.*

principle (prin′ sə pəl) *n.* a basic law, truth, or belief; p. 251 *My grandparents always told me to follow the principle of honesty.*

signify (sig′ nə fī′) *v.* to represent or mean; to indicate; p. 252 *Your nod of approval will signify that you agree.*

gratification (grat′ə fi kā′shən) *n.* the condition of being pleased or satisfied; p. 252 *I felt gratification when my uncle won the award for which I had nominated him.*

absurdity (ab sur′ də tē) *n.* something that is ridiculous; a piece of nonsense; p. 253 *To claim that gravity doesn't exist is an absurdity.*

Vocabulary Tip: Context Clues To figure out the meanings of unfamiliar words, look for context clues, or clues about meaning, in the words and phrases surrounding the unfamiliar word.

INDIANA ACADEMIC STANDARDS (pages 248–256)

9.3.13 Explain how...persona...affect[s] the mood, tone, and meaning of text.

9.3.11 Evaluate the...impact of diction...on tone...

9.5.3 Write...analytical essays...

Selection Resources

Print Materials
- Unit 1 Resources (Fast File), pp. 79–81
- Leveled Vocabulary Development, p. 18
- Selection and Unit Assessments, pp. 39–40
- Selection Quick Checks, p. 20

Transparencies
- Bellringer Options Transparencies: Selection Focus Transparency 17; Daily Language Practice Transparency 22
- Literary Elements Transparency 21

Technology
- TeacherWorks Plus™ CD-ROM
- StudentWorks Plus™ CD-ROM
- Presentation Plus!™ CD-ROM
- Literature Online, glencoe.com
- Online Student Edition, mhln.com
- Exam*View*® Assessment Suite CD-ROM
- Vocabulary PuzzleMaker CD-ROM
- Listening Library, disc 1 track 22

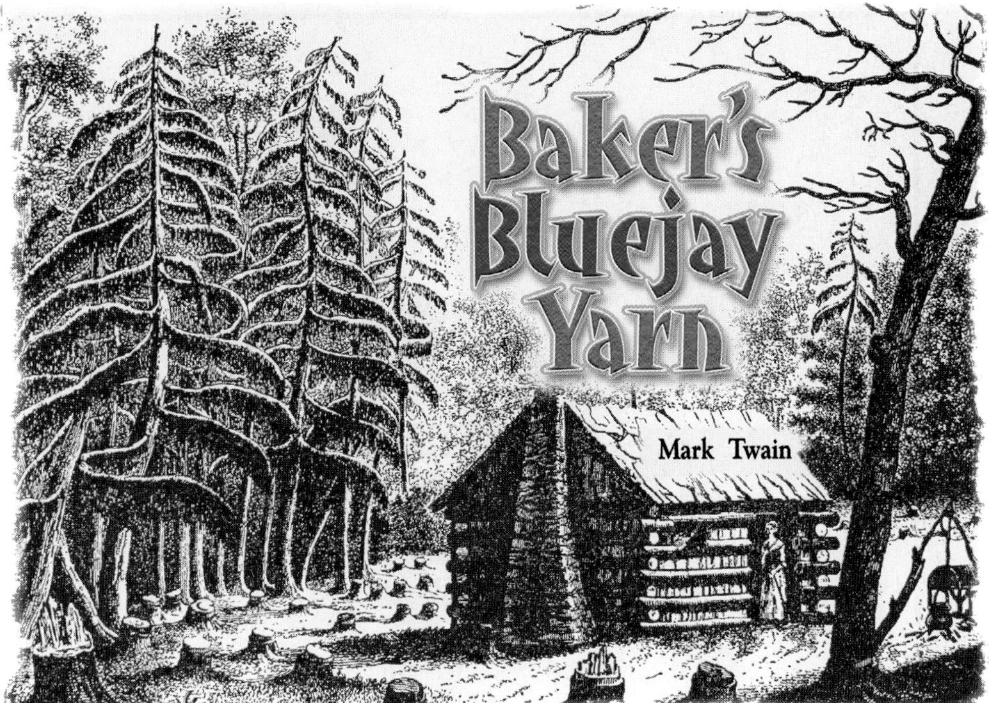

A frontier cabin, from *The Pageant of America, Vol. 3,* 1926. Ralph Henry Gabriel. Engraving. Private collection.

Animals talk to each other, of course. There can be no question about that; but I suppose there are very few people who can understand them. I never knew but one man who could. I knew he could, however, because he told me so himself. He was a middle-aged, simple-hearted miner who had lived in a lonely corner of California, among the woods and mountains, a good many years, and had studied the ways of his only neighbors, the beasts and the birds, until he believed he could accurately translate any remark which they made. This was Jim Baker.

According to Jim Baker, some animals have only a limited education, and use only very simple words, and scarcely ever a comparison or a flowery figure;[1] whereas, certain other animals have a large vocabulary, a fine command of language and a ready and fluent delivery; consequently these latter talk a great deal; they like it; they are conscious of their talent, and they enjoy "showing off." Baker said, that after long and careful observation, he had come to the conclusion that the bluejays were the best talkers he had found among birds and beasts. Said he:

"There's more *to* a bluejay than any other creature. He has got more moods, and more different kinds of feelings than other

1. A *flowery figure* is a fancy expression.

Reading Strategy Analyzing Language *How is the narrator's language like language you hear every day?* **R**

Big Idea Dreams and Reality *How might Jim Baker's description of animals be applied to humans?* **BI**

Teach

R Reading Strategy

Analyzing Language

Answer: *Students may say his basic vocabulary and informal tone sound similar to everyday language.* **OL**

BI Big Idea

Dreams and Reality

Answer: *People have different levels of education and abilities to express themselves.* **Ask:** Do you think it is unrealistic to attribute human qualities to animals? *(Some students may argue that animals and humans have many shared characteristics, while others will be skeptical of these connections.)* **OL**

Use the CheckPoint questions on Presentation Plus! to monitor students' comprehension. These questions can be used with interactive response keypads for immediate student feedback.

Readability Scores

Dale-Chall: 7.3
DRP: 57
Lexile: 980

English Language Coach

Vernacular Have pairs of English learners list examples of vernacular language from the story, such as ungrammatical usage or old-fashioned expressions. Explain that Twain's "errors" are deliberate and contribute to the narrator's persona. **EL**

Differentiated Instruction

Illustrations Have students create a series of illustrations for the story, including a picture of what happens to the blue jay's acorns. *(They fall into the chimney of a house.)* **BL**

Academic Standards

Additional Support activities on p. 249 cover the following standards:

English Language Coach: **9.3.11** Evaluate the aesthetic qualities of style, including the impact of diction…

Differentiated Instruction: **9.3** [Identify] story elements such as character…plot, and setting…

Teach

★ Viewing the Art

Answer: *Students should agree that the drawing of the blue jay is quite accurate, with many of the distinctive details clearly depicted.* **Ask:** How might the artist of a scientific drawing approach his subject differently from an artist who is painting or illustrating for another reason? *(Students should point out that the artist of a scientific drawing must depict his or her subject in precise detail, whereas another artist may take more freedom with the subject.)* **AS**

1. Blue Jay. 2. Yellow-Bird or Gold Finch. 3. Baltimore Bird. Academy of Natural Sciences of Philadelphia.

Viewing the Art: Based on the descriptions in the story, do you think this picture accurately portrays a blue jay? ★

Additional Support

Skills Practice

VOCABULARY: Context Clues

Explain that the expression *bristling with* means "full of." A metaphor is a comparison in which one thing is said to be another. Metaphors make language more colorful.

Ask: How does its context help you understand the meaning of the word "commonplace?" *(The context clues show what commonplace language is not: full of colorful language.)* As practice, ask students to make a list of commonplace objects. **OL**

creatures; and, mind you, whatever a bluejay feels, he can put into language. And no mere **commonplace** language, either, but rattling, out-and-out book-talk—and bristling with metaphor, too—just bristling! And as for command of language—why *you* never see a bluejay get stuck for a word. No man ever did. They just boil out of him! And another thing: I've noticed a good deal, and there's no bird, or cow, or anything that uses as good grammar as a bluejay. You may say a cat uses good grammar. Well, a cat does—but you let a cat get excited once; you let a cat get to pulling fur with another cat on a shed, nights, and you'll hear grammar that will give you the lockjaw. Ignorant people think it's the *noise* which fighting cats make that is so aggravating, but it ain't so; it's the sickening grammar they use. Now I've never heard a jay use bad grammar but very seldom; and when they do, they are as ashamed as a human; they shut right down and leave.

"You may call a jay a bird. Well, so he is, in a measure—because he's got feathers on him, and don't belong to no church, perhaps; but otherwise he is just as much a human as you be. And I'll tell you for why. A jay's gifts, and instincts, and feelings, and interests, cover the whole ground. A jay hasn't got any more **principle** than a Congressman. A jay will lie, a jay will steal, a jay will deceive, a jay will betray; and four times out of five, a jay will go back on his solemnest promise. The sacredness of an obligation[2] is a thing which you can't cram into no bluejay's head. Now, on top of all this, there's another thing; a jay can outswear any gentleman in the mines. You think a cat can swear. Well, a cat can; but you give a bluejay a subject that calls for his reserve-powers, and where is your cat? Don't talk to me—I know too much about this thing. And there's yet another thing; in the one little particular of scolding—just good, clean, out-and-out scolding—a bluejay can lay over anything, human or divine. Yes, sir, a jay is everything that a man is. A jay can cry, a jay can laugh, a jay can feel shame, a jay can reason and plan and discuss, a jay likes gossip and scandal, a jay has got a sense of humor, a jay knows when he is an ass just as well as you do—maybe better. If a jay ain't human, he better take in his sign, that's all. Now I'm going to tell you a perfectly true fact about some bluejays.

"When I first begun to understand jay language correctly, there was a little incident happened here. Seven years ago, the last man in this region but me moved away. There stands his house—been empty ever since; a log house, with a plank roof—just one big room, and no more; no ceiling—nothing between the rafters and the floor. Well, one Sunday morning I was sitting out here in front of my cabin, with my cat, taking the sun, and looking at the blue hills, and listening to the leaves rustling so lonely in the trees, and thinking of the home away yonder in the states, that I hadn't heard from in thirteen years, when a bluejay lit on that house, with an acorn in his mouth, and says, 'Hello, I reckon I've struck something.' When he spoke, the acorn dropped out of his mouth and rolled down the roof, of course, but he didn't care; his mind was all on the thing he had struck. It was a knot-hole in the roof. He cocked his head to one side, shut one eye and put the other one to the hole, like a possum looking down a jug; then he glanced up with his bright eyes, gave a wink or two

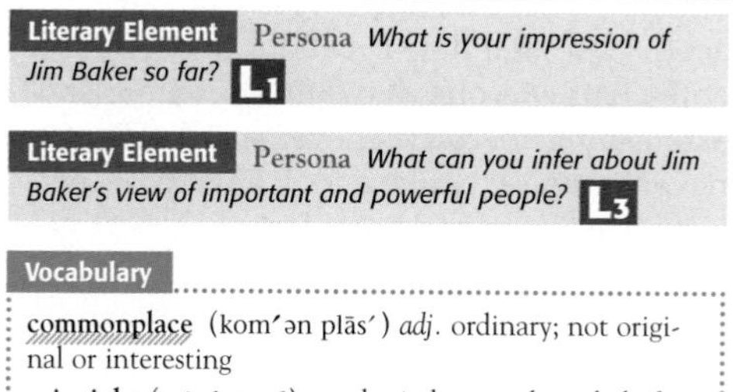

Literary Element Persona *What is your impression of Jim Baker so far?* L1

Literary Element Persona *What can you infer about Jim Baker's view of important and powerful people?* L3

Vocabulary

commonplace (kom′ən plās′) *adj.* ordinary; not original or interesting

principle (prin′sə pəl) *n.* a basic law, truth, or belief

2. Something that is *sacred* is holy, or deserving of great respect. Here, *obligation* means "a promise."

Teach

L1 Literary Element

Persona Answer: *Students may say that Jim Baker is salty, humorous, unpretentious, knowledgeable, and observant.* OL

L2 Literary Element

Persona Ask: What are some similarities that Jim Baker observes between blue jays and people? *(They will lie, steal, deceive, betray, break promises, swear, scold, and can show a full range of emotions.)* How seriously do you take these observations? How seriously do you take Baker in general? *(Many students will find Baker absurd, even if they agree with his observations.)* OL

L3 Literary Element

Persona Answer: *Students may say that Jim Baker views the important and powerful as no better than other people.* OL

Reading in the Real World

College College students may be asked to read and write not only in formal English but also in everyday, vernacular language.

Ask: Why would a writer choose to write in everyday language at times? *(To reflect common experience and everyday life)* OL

Differentiated Instruction

Cause and Effect Ask: Why does the jay drop the acorn? *(He opens his mouth to speak when he discovers a hole in the roof.)* After retrieving the acorn, why does he drop it in the hole? *(He wants to use the hole as a storage place.)* BL

Academic Standards

Additional Support activities on pp. 250 and 251 cover the following standards:

Skills Practice: **9.1** Use…context clues…to determine the meaning of words…

Reading in the Real World: **9.3.11** Evaluate the aesthetic qualities of style, including the impact of diction…

Differentiated Instruction: **9.3** [Identify] story elements such as…plot…

Teach

R1 Reading Strategy

Analyzing Language
Answer: *Students may say that his informal expressions make the blue jay seem endearingly human.* OL

L1 Literary Element

Persona Answer: *Students may say that Jim Baker is entertaining, larding his narrative with amusing digressions and anecdotes and creating suspense to pique the reader's interest.* OL

★ Literary History

Twain on Language
"A powerful agent is the right word. Whenever we come upon one of those intensely right words in a book or a newspaper the resulting effect is physical as well as spiritual, and electrically prompt."
—Mark Twain AS

with his wings—which **signifies gratification,** you understand—and says, 'It looks like a hole, it's located like a hole—blamed if I don't believe it is a hole!'

"Then he cocked his head down and took another look; he glances up perfectly joyful, this time; winks his wings and his tail both, and says, 'Oh, no, this ain't no fat thing, I reckon! If I ain't in luck!—why it's a perfectly elegant hole!' So he flew down and got that acorn, and fetched it up and dropped it in, and was just tilting his head back, with the heavenliest smile on his face, when all of a sudden he was paralyzed into a listening attitude and that smile faded gradually out of his countenance[3] like breath off'n a razor, and the queerest look of surprise took its place. Then he says, 'Why, I didn't hear it fall!' He cocked his eye at the hole again, and took a long look; raised up and shook his head; stepped around to the other side of the hole and took another look from that side; shook his head again. He studied a while, then he just went into the details—walked round and round the hole and spied into it from every point of the compass. No use. Now he took a thinking attitude on the comb of the roof[4] and scratched the back of his head with his right foot a minute, and finally says, 'Well, it's too many for *me,* that's certain; must be a mighty long hole; however, I ain't got no time to fool around here, I got to 'tend to business; I reckon it's all right—chance it, anyway.'

"So he flew off and fetched another acorn and dropped it in, and tried to flirt his eye to the hole quick enough to see what become of it, but he was too late. He held his eye there as much as a minute; then he raised up and sighed, and says, 'Confound it, I don't seem to understand this thing, no way; however, I'll tackle her again.' He fetched another acorn, and done his level best to see what become of it, but he couldn't. He says, 'Well, *I* never struck no such a hole as this before; I'm of the opinion it's a totally new kind of a hole.' Then he begun to get mad. He held in for a spell, walking up and down the comb of the roof and shaking his head and muttering to himself; but his feelings got the upper hand of him, presently, and he broke loose and cussed himself black in the face. I never see a bird take on so about a little thing. When he got through he walks to the hole and looks in again for half a minute; then he says, 'Well, you're a long hole, and a deep hole, and a mighty singular[5] hole altogether—but I've started in to fill you, and I'm d—d if I *don't* fill you, if it takes a hundred years!'

> 'Confound it, I don't seem to understand this thing, no way . . .'

"And with that, away he went. You never see a bird work so since you was born. He laid into his work, and the way he hove[6] acorns into that hole for about two hours and a half was one of the most exciting and astonishing spectacles I ever struck. He never stopped to take a look anymore—he just hove 'em in and went for more. Well, at last he could hardly flop his wings, he was so tuckered out. He comes a-drooping down, ★

3. A person's (or animal's) *countenance* is his or her face.
4. The *comb of the roof* is the ridge along the highest part.
5. If a thing is *singular,* it is unusual, remarkable, or one of a kind.
6. *Hove* is a past tense of *heave,* meaning "to lift and throw."

Reading Strategy Analyzing Language *How do informal expressions help to characterize the blue jay?* R1

Literary Element Persona *Do you enjoy Jim Baker's storytelling style? Explain.* L1

Vocabulary
signify (sig′ nə fī′) *v.* to represent or mean; to indicate
gratification (grat′ ə fi kā′ shən) *n.* the condition of being pleased or satisfied

Additional Support

Skills Practice

TEST PREPARATION: Short Responses Explain that short-response questions often do not have one correct answer. Instruct students to give an answer that is as comprehensive as possible, rather than focusing on something narrowly specific.

Ask: What personality traits does the blue jay share with some humans? *(Students may say the jay curses and shakes his head; he ponders and takes a chance; he is stubborn and has a bad temper.)* Explain that the best answer is the last because it has the widest focus. OL once more, sweating like an ice-pitcher, drops his acorn in and says, '*Now* I guess I've got the bulge on you by this time!' So he bent down for a look. If you'll believe me, when his head come up again he was just pale with rage. He says, 'I've shoveled acorns enough in there to keep the family thirty years, and if I can see a sign of one of 'em I wish I may land in a museum with a belly full of sawdust in two minutes!'

"He just had strength enough to crawl up on to the comb and lean his back agin the chimbly, and then he collected his impressions and begun to free his mind. I see in a second that what I had mistook for profanity in the mines was only just the rudiments,[7] as you may say.

"Another jay was going by, and heard him doing his devotions, and stops to inquire what was up. The sufferer told him the whole circumstance, and says, 'Now yonder's the hole, and if you don't believe me, go and look for yourself.' So this fellow went and looked, and comes back and says, 'How many did you say you put in there?' 'Not any less than two tons,' says the sufferer. The other jay went and looked again. He couldn't seem to make it out, so he raised a yell, and three more jays come. They all examined the hole, they all made the sufferer tell it over again, then they all discussed it, and got off as many leather-headed opinions about it as an average crowd of humans could have done.

"They called in more jays; then more and more, till pretty soon this whole region 'peared to have a blue flush about it. There must have been five thousand of them; and such another jawing and disputing and ripping and cussing, you never heard. Every jay in the whole lot put his eye to the hole and delivered a more chuckle-headed opinion about the mystery than the jay that went there before him. They examined the house all over, too. The door was standing half open, and at last one old jay happened to go and light on it and look in. Of course, that knocked the mystery galley-west[8] in a second. There lay the acorns, scattered all over the floor. He flopped his wings and raised a whoop. 'Come here!' he says, 'Come here, everybody; hang'd if this fool hasn't been trying to fill up a house with acorns!' They all came a-swooping down like a blue cloud, and as each fellow lit on the door and took a glance, the whole **absurdity** of the contract that that first jay had tackled hit him home and he fell over backward suffocating with laughter, and the next jay took his place and done the same.

"Well, sir, they roosted around here on the housetop and the trees for an hour, and guffawed over that thing like human beings. It ain't any use to tell me a bluejay hasn't got a sense of humor, because I know better. And memory, too. They brought jays here from all over the United States to look down that hole, every summer for three years. Other birds, too. And they could all see the point, except an owl that come from Nova Scotia to visit the Yo Semite,[9] and he took this thing in on his way back. He said he couldn't see anything funny in it. But then he was a good deal disappointed about Yo Semite, too."

7. The blue jay's bad language *(profanity)* earlier had been only the basics (the *rudiments*) of its knowledge of cursing.

8. To knock something *galley-west* is to knock it into complete ruin.

9. *Nova Scotia* is a province of eastern Canada. Across the continent, *Yo Semite* (usually spelled *Yosemite*) is the valley and national park in east central California.

Big Idea Dreams and Reality *In what ways is the character of the blue jay like that of a human?* **BI1**

Big Idea Dreams and Reality *What does this comparison say about people? Do you agree?* **BI2**

Reading Strategy Analyzing Language *How does this paragraph evoke the blue jays' hilarity?* **R2**

Vocabulary

absurdity (ab sur ʹ də tē) *n.* something that is ridiculous; a piece of nonsense

Teach

BI1 Big Idea

Dreams and Reality

Answer: *Students may say that the blue jay appears to stockpile food and gets frustrated, as a human does.* **OL**

BI2 Big Idea

Dreams and Reality

Answer: *Students may say that people in a crowd offer useless advice and conflicting opinions.* **OL**

R2 Reading Strategy

Analyzing Language

Answer: *Students may say that by describing the jays arriving one by one and laughing at what they see, the author evokes hilarity.* **OL**

CheckPoint

Use the CheckPoint questions on Presentation Plus! to check students' mastery of the selection. These questions can be used with interactive response keypads for immediate student feedback.

English Language Coach

Vernacular Speech English learners may have trouble identifying or understanding vernacular speech. As practice, have them make a list of vernacular expressions from their native language. Then ask them to translate these expressions into English and share them with the class. **EL**

Building Reading Fluency

Reading Vernacular Speech As practice, have students read sections of Twain's story aloud. Pay special attention to pronunciation, pacing, and emphasis, which will provide clues as to how well students understand what they are reading. **BL**

Academic Standards

Additional Support activities on pp. 252 and 253 cover the following standards:

Skills Practice: **9.3** [Identify] story elements such as character, theme, [and] plot...

English Language Coach: **9.1.1** Identify... the literal and figurative meanings of words...

Building Reading Fluency: **9.7** [Develop] speaking skills...in conjunction with... strategies...[for] delivery of oral presentations.

AFTER YOU READ

Assess

1. Students should support their answers.
2. (a) He is a miner from the West who has lived alone among the birds and beasts for years. (b) He understands the language of animals.
3. (a) In a hole in the roof of a house (b) The acorns disappear into the hole, which is the house's chimney.
4. (a) They are the best talkers in the animal world; they have more moods and feelings, better language and grammar skills than other animals. (b) It swears, scolds, laughs, and cries. Then it reasons, plans, discusses, and gossips.
5. They examine the hole, listen to the first jay's story, and discuss the problem.
6. Blue jays' emotions, cats' bad grammar, of jays' lack of principle, and of the first jay's reaction (his pondering, swearing, and hard work)
7. It shows the human tendency to become frustrated and upset in a crisis, and the way people cooperate to solve problems.
8. He shows both, touching on faults (dishonesty of politicians) and positive traits such as humor.
9. Tall tales entertain while imparting a lesson.

AFTER YOU READ

RESPONDING AND THINKING CRITICALLY

Respond

1. Was your reaction to this story more like the blue jay's or the owl's? Explain.

Recall and Interpret

2. (a)Who is Jim Baker? (b)What is his special talent?
3. (a)Where does the blue jay put the acorns? (b)Why is the blue jay unable to complete his task?
4. (a)According to Baker, what are some characteristics of blue jays? (b)Which of these characteristics does the blue jay display when he continues to bring and drop acorns?

Analyze and Evaluate

5. In what ways do the birds act like humans as they try to help the blue jay solve his problem?
6. A yarn is a far-fetched tale that uses exaggeration to create humor. What are some examples of humorous exaggeration in this story?
7. What does the story suggest about how human beings behave when faced with a problem?
8. In your opinion, what is Mark Twain's attitude toward people? Is it affectionate, critical, or both? Explain.

Connect

9. **Big Idea** **Dreams and Reality** People from many different times and places have spun tall tales, or yarns, such as this one. Why do you think people tell these tales? Explain your answer.

VISUAL LITERACY: Graphic Organizer

Using a Story Map

Yarns and tall tales are frequently built around a main character who faces a problem. Using a story map like the one on the right, list the characters in Baker's yarn, the problem faced by the main character, and the solution to the problem. Then think about what message about life or human nature is conveyed by the story.

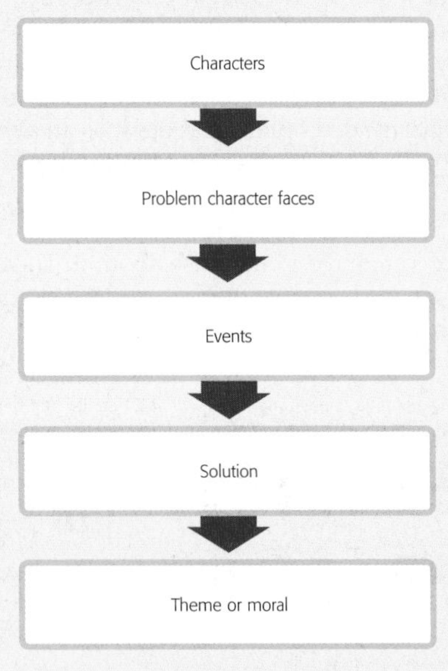

Group Activity Share your graphic organizer with a small group of classmates. Discuss the ways in which the characters and events of the story help to suggest an idea about life or human nature. Answer these questions:

1. (a)How do the blue jays show human strengths such as hard work and determination? (b)How do they show human failings such as pride, anger, and stubbornness?
2. (a)How is the problem in the story solved? (b)What moral or life lesson does this solution suggest?

Visual Literacy

1. (a) The first jay works hard to bury acorns and shows persistence. (b) The blue jay's initial unwillingness to stop demonstrates pride and stubbornness.
2. (a) The jays band together, and one realizes that the hole leads into the house. (b) The moral may be "two heads are better than one," or people make mistakes and need the help of others.

LITERARY ANALYSIS

Literary Element Persona

A **persona** is a character created by an author to tell a story. In "Baker's Bluejay Yarn," the use of a persona helps readers feel as if they were having their own encounter with a talkative, frank, and worldly man. As a reader, you might have felt as if you were sitting at the feet of a well-practiced storyteller.

1. From the details in the story, how do you imagine Jim Baker? Cite details from the story that help support your ideas.
2. Baker is full of contrasts: he displays enormous knowledge about the habits of animals and about their lore, yet his knowledge is conveyed through lively, informal, and sometimes ungrammatical speech. Why do you think Mark Twain created the persona of Jim Baker to tell this story?
3. What aspects of Baker's storytelling did you find the most humorous or witty? Explain.

Review: Dialect

As you learned on page 68, a **dialect** is a variation of language based on the way people speak in a particular region. In this story, the character of Jim Baker speaks in the dialect spoken by people living in the West during the 1800s. For example, he uses the expression "get to pulling fur" to mean "start fighting," and "I reckon" to mean "I suppose."

Partner Activity With a partner, use a chart like the one below to list three expressions from the story that are examples of dialect. Tell what each expression means. Then discuss how the story would be different if Baker had told it in Standard English rather than dialect.

Expression	Meaning

READING AND VOCABULARY

Reading Strategy Analyzing Language

Tone is the attitude an author has toward a subject or his or her audience.

1. (a)In your opinion, what is the overall tone of this story? (b)How does the use of vernacular—informal, everyday speech—help set the tone? Give examples of specific words and phrases that help create the tone.
2. Which parts of the story do you think are especially creative or well-phrased? Explain.

Vocabulary Practice

Practice with Context Clues Fill in each of the sentences below with the correct vocabulary word. Use context clues to determine the answer.

commonplace	principle	signify
gratification	absurdity	

1. Loyalty is a _______, or personal value, that most people subscribe to.
2. She felt a great sense of _______ when the teacher praised her speech.
3. It looks like a _______ watch, but it once belonged to Abraham Lincoln!
4. Let your hearty applause _______ your positive reaction to Delores's beautiful singing.
5. Mark Twain wrote about the silliness, even _______, of much human behavior.

Academic Vocabulary

Here are two words from the vocabulary list on page R80.

source (sôrs) *n.* the origin, or starting point, of an object, event, or characteristic

specific (spi sif′ik) *adj.* precise or exact

Practice and Apply

1. What is the **source** of the blue jay's problem?
2. What **specific** item does the blue jay drop into the hole?

AFTER YOU READ

Assess

Literary Element

1. He seems old, grizzled, experienced, salty, and entertaining, yet also innocent.
2. Students may say his language and his way of mixing realistic description with exaggeration help make the story entertaining.
3. Students should support their answers.

Review: Dialect

Students should share their expressions to compile a class chart.

Reading Strategy

1. (a) It is humorous or ironic. (b) Its use made the story seem informal and intimate. Students should support their answers with text examples.
2. Students should explain their answers.

Vocabulary

1. principle
2. gratification
3. commonplace
4. signify
5. absurdity

Academic Vocabulary

1. The hole he found was the chimney of a house.
2. He dropped acorns.

Assess

Writing About Literature

Students' essays should

- discuss three features of tall tales.
- contain examples of these features that relate to the selection.
- conclude with a brief summary of their essay and a comment on the genre.

Twain's Language and Style

Remind students that words such as *hardly, barely,* and *scarcely* are negatives. **Write on the board:** I barely had no time. Have students fix the sentence. (I barely had any time or I had not time.)

Interdisciplinary Activity

Ask students to include pictures of their birds in their presentation. If color photos are not readily available, suggest that students color in a black and white photocopy.

WRITING AND EXTENDING

Writing About Literature

Analyze Genre Elements As you have learned, many yarns can also be referred to as tall tales. Note these common features of tall tales:

- They are a type of folklore associated with the American West.
- They often contain wild exaggerations.
- They often have animal characters.
- They are often told in dialect.
- The main characters are often bold but foolish.

Write an essay in which you explain how "Baker's Bluejay Yarn" illustrates the common features of tall tales. Begin by making notes about aspects of the story that are common to tall tales. Then choose three features of tall tales to write about. You might organize your essay like this:

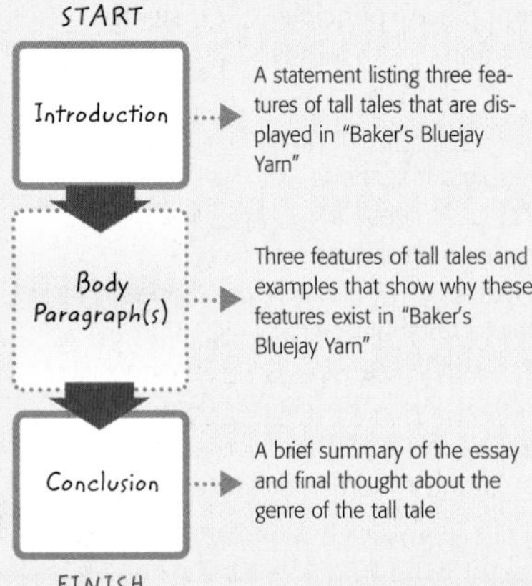
START
Introduction
A statement listing three features of tall tales that are displayed in "Baker's Bluejay Yarn"
Body Paragraph(s)
Three features of tall tales and examples that show why these features exist in "Baker's Bluejay Yarn"
Conclusion
A brief summary of the essay and final thought about the genre of the tall tale
FINISH

When you are finished, exchange your work with a partner. Critique each other's essays for effectiveness and accuracy. Then revise your essay on the basis of the feedback you receive. Proofread and edit it to correct any errors in spelling, grammar, or punctuation.

Interdisciplinary Activity: Science

Some birds, such as the blue jay, are common to many regions of the country. Research birds that are common in your area. Find out what they eat, when and where they migrate, and how their appearance changes from season to season. Discuss your findings with the class.

GRAMMAR AND STYLE

Twain's Language and Style

Using Double Negatives for Effect Double negatives occur when two negative words are used in the same clause, as in the sentence *I have never seen no desert.* The use of double negatives is considered grammatically incorrect. However, authors may choose to use double negatives to create specific effects within a text. For instance, some authors use double negatives to help convey the informal speech of their characters. Twain uses double negatives to convey the regional speech of people living in the West in the 1800s:

"You may call a jay a bird. Well, so he is, in a measure—because he's got feathers on him, and **don't** belong to **no** church, perhaps. . . . "

In the story, double negatives help lend humor to the thoughts and words of the blue jay:

"I **never** struck **no** such a hole as this before. . . . "

Authors may also use double negatives to create other effects. In a work of nonfiction, an author will sometimes include double negatives that occur in the speech of someone the author is quoting.

Activity Scan "Baker's Bluejay Yarn" for other examples of double negatives. Make a list of these examples and their effect on the tone of the story.

Revising Check

Double Negatives In formal writing and speech, double negatives should be avoided. When you notice a double negative in your own writing, correct it. The sentence below contains a double negative:

My little sister has not visited none of the Great Lakes.

To correct the sentence, eliminate one of the negative words:

My little sister has not visited **any** of the Great Lakes.

With a partner, go through your essay about "Baker's Bluejay Yarn" and the genre of the tall tale. Note any double negatives and revise your draft to correct them.

LiteratureOnline **Web Activities** For eFlashcards, Selection Quick Checks, and other Web activities, go to www.glencoe.com.

Web Activities Have students access the Web site for interactive activities that will help them assess their understanding of the selection.

The Flat of the Land

MEET DIANA GARCÍA

Diana García, who did not begin writing until her mid-thirties, says it is never too late to start doing something you love. Before beginning her writing career, García worked as an owner of an electronics store, a manager of a human resources department, and a sentencing consultant to criminal defense lawyers. "Coming to writing has been the greatest blessing of my life," she says.

In much of her work, García explores the experiences of migrant farm workers in California. García was born in Camp CPC in the San Joaquin Valley, a migrant labor camp that employed Mexicans and Mexican Americans in desperate need of jobs. García came to deeply appreciate the tenacity of the laborers, who worked long, hard hours for little pay in order to give their children a better life.

"For all would-be writers, begin now. Be alive to the swirl of life that surrounds you. Capture it in words and artwork."

—Diana García

Family Honor The workers who move from field to field with the seasons picking produce for America's tables have not always received fair treatment. When García was growing up, farm employers regularly forced grueling schedules on their workers and housed them in substandard conditions. "The labor contractor worked us through lunch without water," García wrote in one poem. Thanks to the efforts of labor leaders, such as celebrated activist César Chávez, over the past thirty years the working conditions of migrant laborers have slowly improved.

Literacy and Power The issues facing Latin American women are another source of motivation for García. She is especially interested in the fostering of educational opportunities for migrant laborers and their children. In her work, she describes the laborers as determined and caring people who manage to create beauty in the midst of squalor. "Even when Diana is documenting the lives of 'the anonymous poor' in migrant fields and in the barrios, she is able to make the harsh landscapes beautiful and transcendent," says writer Marilyn Chin.

García is the author of the acclaimed poetry collection *When Living Was a Labor Camp*, published in 2000. She has taught creative writing at Central Connecticut State University and the University of Freiburg in Freiburg, Germany. She currently teaches creative writing, contemporary world literatures, and Chicana-Chicano and Latina-Latino literature at California State University.

Diana García was born in 1950.

LiteratureOnline **Author Search** For more about Diana García, go to www.glencoe.com.

Focus

BELLRINGER

Bellringer Options
Selection Focus Transparency 18
Daily Language Practice Transparency 23

Or **ask:** Have you ever felt so overwhelmed by problems that you wished you could leave your old life behind and start fresh? What kind of world would you want to escape to? Have students consider as they read, why Amparo has chosen to live in an abandoned house in the remote desert.

Author Search To expand students' appreciation of Diana García, have them access the Web site for additional information and resources.

Selection Skills

The Flat of the Land

Literary Elements
- Tone (SE pp. 258–267)
- Point of View (SE p. 267)

Reading Skills
- Analyzing Character and Setting (SE pp. 258–268)
- Sequencing Events (TWE p. 260)

Vocabulary Skills
- Word Parts (SE p. 268)
- Academic Vocabulary (SE p. 268)

Listening/Speaking/Viewing Skills
- Analyzing Art (SE pp. 261, 264)
- Role-playing (TWE p. 266)

Writing Skills/Grammar
- Genre Elements (SE p. 268)
- Rhyming Poem (TWE p. 262)

Study Skills/Research/Assessment
- Learning About Mudflows (TWE p. 264)

BEFORE YOU READ

Focus

Summary

Amparo thinks she settles into the perfect hideout, an abandoned adobe house in California's San Joaquin Valley, until a steadily growing mudflow threatens to destroy her home. Faced with her home's destruction, Amparo learns to accept and appreciate the power of nature to affect her life.

V Vocabulary

Vocabulary File Say: Add these words and definitions to your vocabulary file. For each word, include a sentence that gives you an example of how to use the word. **OL** Students with English language needs should include the pronunciations of these words in their files. **EL**

Literary Elements Have students access the Web site to improve their understanding of tone.

LITERATURE PREVIEW

Connecting to the Story

Nature has many faces: some that are comforting, some that are disturbing, and some that are awe-inspiring. Before you read, think about these questions:

- Why do some people love powerful displays of nature, such as thunderstorms, while others are frightened by them?
- Can you imagine thinking of a storm as your friend?

Building Background

This story is set in recent times near the small town of Pixley, California, which is located about sixty miles south of the city of Fresno. In California, mudflows are a fairly common and often serious effect of heavy spring rains; they have caused houses to become dislodged from their foundations and topple down hills. In addition, California has numerous hot springs, some of which have bubbling mud pools.

Setting Purposes for Reading

Big Idea Dreams and Reality

Magical realism is a style of writing in which realistic details, events, settings, characters, and dialogue are interwoven with magical, bizarre, fantastic, or supernatural elements. As you read, notice how García uses both fantastic and realistic elements to tell her story.

Literary Element Tone

Tone is a reflection of the attitude a writer takes toward his or her subject matter. Tone is communicated through words and details that express particular emotions—for example, sadness, lightheartedness, or respect. As you read, think about what García's language suggests about the attitude she wishes to convey toward the story she is telling. Note that her tone may shift at certain points in the story.

- See Literary Terms Handbook, p. R18.

LiteratureOnline Interactive Literary Elements Handbook To review or learn more about the literary elements, go to www.glencoe.com.

READING PREVIEW

Reading Strategy Analyzing Character and Setting

The characters, or individuals, in a story are often as interesting and complicated as the people you meet in real life. To figure them out, you have to think about everything you know about them, just as you do with the people you meet in your own life. This process of assembling information in order to better understand something is called **analyzing.** When you read a story, you should analyze not only its characters, but also its setting—the time and place in which the story occurs. By paying attention to the details of setting throughout the story, you can better understand the meaning of the story.

Reading Tip: Taking Notes In this story, García reveals information about characters and setting through both bizarre and realistic details. As you read, use a two-column chart to record details about characters and setting and what the details suggest or reveal.

Vocabulary

impenetrable (im pen′ ə trə bəl) *adj.* inaccessible, or incapable of being pierced; p. 260 *We tried to enter the crowded concert area, but it was impenetrable.*

indiscernible (in′ di sur′ nə bəl) *adj.* difficult or impossible to see; p. 264 *At the lower right of the painting, the color shifts from blue to blue-green, but the change is almost indiscernible.*

belittle (bi lit′ əl) *v.* to cause to seem less important; to scorn; p. 265 *It is wrong to belittle others by making fun of their ideas.*

fluidity (flo͞o i′ də tē) *n.* the ability, as of a liquid, to flow and change shape; p. 266 *She increased the fluidity of the thick gravy by adding more broth.*

INDIANA ACADEMIC STANDARDS (pages 258–268)

9.3.11 Evaluate the aesthetic qualities of style, including the impact of diction and figurative language on tone...

9.3.3 Analyze interactions between characters...

9.5.3 Write...analytical essays...

Selection Resources

Print Materials
- Unit 1 Resources (Fast File), pp. 82–84
- Leveled Vocabulary Development, p. 19
- Selection and Unit Assessments, pp. 41–42
- Selection Quick Checks, p. 21

Transparencies
- Bellringer Options Transparencies: Selection Focus Transparency 18; Daily Language Practice Transparency 23
- Literary Elements Transparency 25

Technology
- TeacherWorks Plus™ CD-ROM
- StudentWorks Plus™ CD-ROM
- Presentation Plus!™ CD-ROM
- Literature Online, glencoe.com
- Online Student Edition, mhln.com
- Exam*View*® Assessment Suite CD-ROM
- Vocabulary PuzzleMaker CD-ROM
- Listening Library, disc 1 track 23

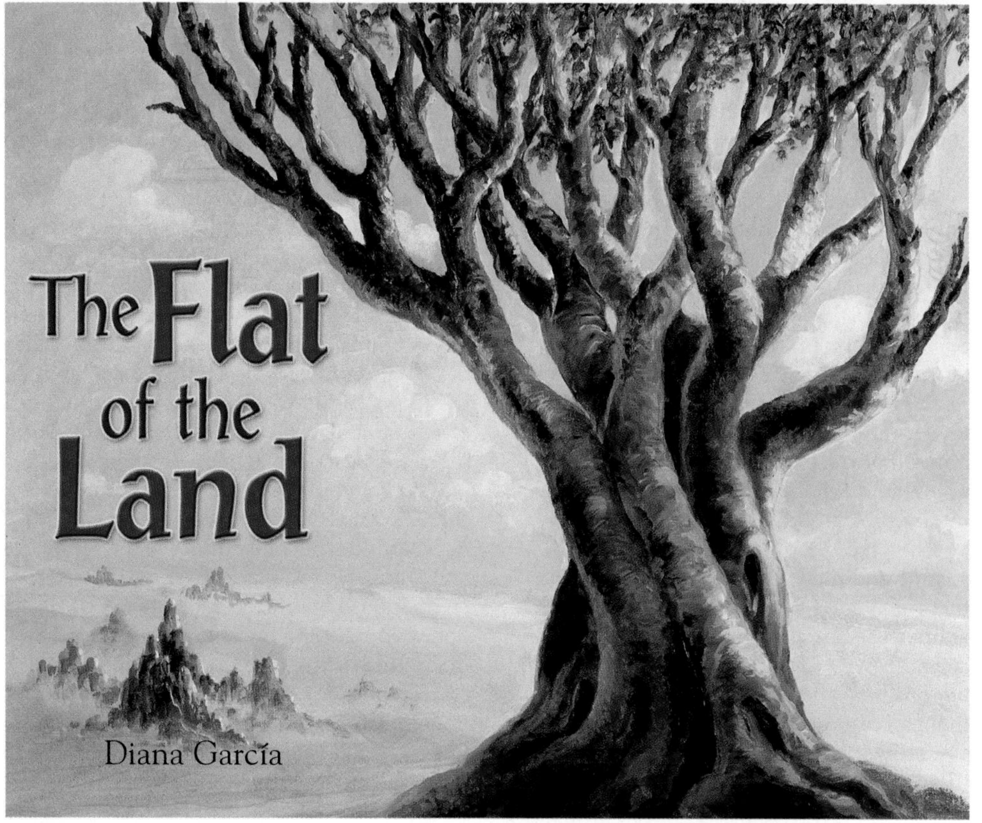

The Survivor. Yvonne Delvo. Private collection.

From the roof of her house, Amparo[1] gauged the tilt of the old water tower with the name "Pixley" faintly outlined on the side. It was hard to say how long the tower would still be visible: another week or two, depending on the mud's flow. Not that a missing tower would make any difference in a place where the only off-ramp was at least five miles west and the combination store and restaurant with its dusty lunch counter was on the abandoned side of old Highway 99. Maybe the girl with the blonde hair and freckles who worked at the store or the girl's mother or grandmother would notice when Amparo stopped coming in for an occasional skinny hamburger and greasy fries.

The first time the mud caught Amparo's attention, it looked like a harmless bubble in the ground. It was an April morning, and she'd been hanging the wash out to dry on the clothesline behind her house. She had scarcely paid attention when the mud burped at her, distracted at the time by the breeze whipping the clothes on the line and thinking that the shadowy clouds overhead might contain some rain.

That had been almost six months ago. Amparo turned and studied the flat expanse to the east and the Sequoia foothills in the distance. At the point where the mud had first appeared, the bubble had grown to the size of a pond. Here the land sank into itself and followed the outline of some long-ago river, a few scattered

1. *Amparo* (äm pär′ ō)

Reading Strategy Analyzing Character and Setting *What does this sentence tell you about the setting of the story?* R

Teach

R Reading Strategy

Analyzing Character and Setting **Answer:** *The setting seems ominous. Nature here, in the form of a mudflow, has the power to cover or knock down a water tower.* OL

★ Historic Note

Highway 99 Like historic Route 66, Highway 99 was one of the original U.S. highways. Created in 1926, Highway 99 ran North-South along the West Coast, from the Canadian to the Mexican borders. From the 1960s through the 1970s, it was decomissioned as the Interstate 5 freeway took its place. AS

Use CheckPoint questions on Presentation Plus! to monitor students' comprehension. These questions can be used with interactive response keypads for immediate student feedback.

Readability Scores
Dale-Chall: 7.9
DRP: 61
Lexile: 1080

English Language Coach

Learning Spanish Words English language learners whose native language is not Spanish may not recognize or understand the Spanish words in the selection. Have small groups, each with one Spanish speaker, list the Spanish words in this selection, define them, and give English translations. EL

Differentiated Instruction

Understanding Character Because the author does not explicitly describe Amparo's motivations, her actions and decisions may confuse some students. Pair less proficient readers to read the story together. Suggest they pause frequently to discuss questions such as *Why is Amparo acting this way? What is she feeling?* BL

Academic Standards

Additional Support activities on p. 259 cover the following standards:

English Language Coach: **9.1** Use…a growing knowledge of English and other languages to determine the meaning of words and become fluent readers.

Differentiated Instruction: **9.3** [Identify] story elements such as character…

Teach

L Literary Element

Tone Answer: *These words suggest a frightened or awed attitude. The overall feeling of the passage is ominous.* Suggest to students that by using the word *swallow,* the author makes the mud seem like a living creature.
Ask: What kind of creature does the mud seem like? *(Students may say the mud seems like a stalking predator.)* OL

BI Big Idea

Dreams and Reality Answer: *Students may say that Amparo is lonely and in need of friendship.* Tell students that Amparo's conversations suggest that she feels a special—almost magical—connection with nature. OL

cottonwoods the only clues to its crumbled banks. From this source, the mud had developed an easterly flow that skirted the stand of cottonwoods. Amparo wondered why the mud had left the trees untouched.

On the land next to hers, bulldozers had carved foundations for a style of house popular forty years earlier. From her roof, the excavations looked like archaeological digs.[2] By the time Amparo moved here, no one was left who could tell her why the development had been abandoned. All that remained of the original site was the water tower and the water main to her house. The only other trace of water was the mud; how else would the mud keep rising and spreading the way it did?

When the dimple of mud turned into a smile and then a six-inch wide crevice that threatened to swallow her clothesline, Amparo began to sense a possible threat to her hideaway. Up until now, she had kept her brothers and parents at bay[3] by giving them a Fresno post office box address. She visited them as often as twice a month so that they wouldn't press her for more information about where or how she was living. They seemed satisfied knowing she was living alone and that her disability income[4] was more than adequate for all her needs. She never talked about her son or her former husband, so they assumed she had laid those memories to rest. That damn mud, though, might spoil everything. At first she talked to it.

"What do you think you're doing? You have no business out here in this weather. The sun will bake you before the summer is over and then you'll have done all this work for nothing." When the sun didn't bake the oozing crack to a dry, light finish, she started asking, "Why don't you go downhill?"—indicating a direction opposite her house—"It's much easier than going uphill." The crack widened, its banks thickening and hardening, creating an **impenetrable** barrier within a few days' exposure to the sun.

Amparo trained herself not to think about the spreading mud. She listened to the Mexican stations on the radio. At night, she'd lie in bed and pretend the coyotes were talking to her instead of to the foothills and the jack rabbits. She'd answer, "Yes, manzanita[5] does make the best cover," and, "No, the easiest way to get yourself killed is to expose yourself." She rarely turned the lights on after dark, afraid someone might see the glow and learn she had discovered the house.

The house was no secret, really. A developer had built the two-story structure as a marketing device and then abandoned it as too expensive: adobe walls like those of a Pueblo ruin and energy supplied by an underground cable and a solar-powered generator. At one time, someone else must have lived here. Perhaps it had been a retired construction worker, some laborer or cement finisher destined to end his days sweeping dust from the compacted dirt floors and enjoying the cool feel of the dark tan walls, secure in the knowledge that no one would look for him here—no former wives or children with grandchildren to bother him.

Now it was Amparo's house. She washed her clothes in a wringer-washer like the one her mother had taught her to use when she was a little girl, like the one she had used when her son was born, the one in which

2. The word *archaeological* (är′ kē ə loj′ i kəl) refers to the scientific study of the past. Places where objects, such as bones, are dug up for study are called *digs* or *excavations.*
3. To keep *at bay* means to keep "at a distance."
4. *Disability income* is money paid by the government to people whose physical or mental impairment prevents them from holding jobs.

5. Several types of evergreen shrubs or small trees are known as *manzanita* (man′ zə nē′ tə).

Literary Element Tone *What attitude toward the mud flow is suggested by the author's use of the words "swallow" and "threat"?* L

Big Idea Dreams and Reality *Why might Amparo pretend that she is having conversations with the coyotes?* BI

Vocabulary

impenetrable (im pen′ ə trə bəl) *adj.* inaccessible, or incapable of being pierced

Additional Support

Skills Practice

READING: Sequencing Events The author sprinkles hints about Amparo's life throughout the story instead of revealing all the details up front. Have students map out the story on a timeline. In the middle of a horizontal line, they should label a vertical mark "Story Begins" and write "Amparo stands on roof wondering how long it will take the mud to knock down the tower." To the left, they can label a mark "Six Months Ago" and write "The mud looked like a harmless bubble in the ground." As they read, students should add information to the timeline. OL

Pink and Green, 1960. Georgia O'Keeffe. Oil on canvas, 30 × 16 in. The Georgia O'Keeffe Museum, Santa Fe, New Mexico.
Viewing the Art: What similarities do you see between this painting and the story's setting?

Teach

Viewing the Art

Answer: *Students may recognize details that remind them of the landscape in the story–the vast desert plain, the mountain ridge, the winding river that could be the mudflow.*

Pink and Green is an abstract painting by Georgia O'Keeffe (1887–1986), who was an American artist known for her paintings of flowers and other natural objects, such as animal bones and desert landscapes. She often used brilliant colors and simplified, abstract designs in her works.
Ask: What do you think this painting represents? Of what does it remind you? *(Students may suggest that the painting reminds them of a flowing river or a mountain range.)* AS

English Language Coach

Abstract and Concrete Words Help students understand the difference between the concrete and abstract words that appear in the story, such as *mud* and *foothills* (concrete) and *knowledge* and *secret* (abstract). Have students list concrete words in one column and abstract words in the other. EL

Differentiated Instruction

Illustrating the Story Invite spatial learners to select scenes that are particularly vivid and translate them into sketches or drawings. Challenge them to choose one or two sentences from the story to serve as captions to their illustrations. Ask volunteers to share their artwork with the class. BL

Academic Standards

Additional Support activities on pp. 260 and 261 cover the following standards:

Skills Practice: **9.3.6** Analyze and trace an author's development of time and sequence...

English Language Coach: **9.1** Use...a growing knowledge of English and other languages to determine the meaning of words...

Differentiated Instruction: **9.3** [Identify] story elements such as...setting...

Teach

R1 Reading Strategy

Analyzing Character and Setting Answer: *The house seems like a fortress.*
Ask: What does Amparo's choice of house tell you about her character? *(She feels vulnerable and is seeking a safe, secure place.)* OL

L Literary Element

Tone Possible answers: *The word choice gives the mud a human-like presence; it makes the mud seem playful; it makes it seem more dangerous, like flames.* OL

R2 Reading Strategy

Analyzing Character and Setting Answer: *Amparo has concluded that the mudflow is coming closer and will soon be covering the cottonwoods.* OL

she had washed his diapers. She admired, as if they were someone else's, the bookshelves carved into the sixteen-inch-thick walls of the living room and bedroom. When she felt the need for exercise, she'd run up and down the steps to the second floor loft and master bedroom, chanting "upstairs and downstairs and in my lady's chamber." And, of course, there was the six-inch plumbing throughout, wide enough to handle anything, even a pot of scorched beans.

Not that she ate much these days. She still enjoyed her plain Cream of Wheat for breakfast every morning—her *atole*,[6] she called it. For lunch and light snacks she had learned to eat seasonally, buying all her produce at the roadside stands along old Highway 99. There were almonds and raisins year-round; strawberries, peaches, tomatoes, and peppers during the summer. By early May she was tired of apples and oranges but with June came early corn and sometimes a melon or two. Dinner was always corn tortillas, beans, and rice. She made a pot of beans and another of rice every Sunday. Sometimes she'd toss some bits of chicken or beef along with a handful of garbanzos, some chopped onion, and cilantro[7] into the steaming rice. Her biggest craving was grease; once or twice a month she'd drive to Pixley for a hamburger and fries at the store's lunch counter.

The day the mud licked the left front tire of her old white Studebaker Lark station wagon, Amparo drove to the store for a "grease bomb"—that's what she called the hamburgers. It was the first official day of summer. By then, the mud-filled crevice was about twenty yards long, six inches wide, and about a foot-and-a-half deep. That day at the lunch counter she'd asked the young girl's mother, "Did they used to have a mud bath around here that you know of?"

"What do you mean, mud bath?" the woman had answered, poking a few loose strands of dark brown hair underneath one of the pink foam rollers on her head. At least the rollers worked better than the torn hair net the woman usually wore. "You mean the hot springs?"

Amparo checked her fries for stray hairs before she dipped them in ketchup. She knew about the dots on the map called Fountain Springs, California Hot Springs, and Miracle Springs. No water at any of them. "No, not water. Mud. Did they ever have mud baths over by the old water tower?" Amparo asked, trying not to sound too curious.

"No, no mud. This is a desert." The woman had a droning voice, like an old record player at slow speed. "The only water for mud would have to come from the creeks. We haven't had enough water for the creeks to run in almost ten years."

The woman's mother had interrupted, "The last time I saw the Chocolate River—that's the old riverbed over by your house—was when I was still a girl at home. That was about seventy years ago when the flash flood tore out the old road right after the war." Almost as an afterthought the old woman had added, "You know, a long time ago, when my grandmother's grandmother came here from Illinois, it was all tule marshland like Three Rivers."

Visual Vocabulary In the southwestern United States, *tule* (to͞o′ lē) refers to bulrushes, which are swamp plants in the grass family.

That was when Amparo began parking her Studebaker on the side of the house away from the cottonwoods.

After the mud ate the clothesline and then the smallest manzanita bush, the one farthest from the house, Amparo consoled herself with

6. *Atole* (ə tō′ lā) is a thin porridge or drink made with corn flour.
7. *Garbanzos* are chickpeas and *cilantro* is an herb.

Reading Strategy Analyzing Character and Setting *What kind of building does this house remind you of?* R1

Literary Element Tone *How does the use of the word "licked" affect your impression of the mud?* L

Reading Strategy Analyzing Character and Setting *Why does Amparo park her car somewhere else? What has she concluded about the place where she lives?* R2

Additional Support

Skills Practice

WRITING: Rhyming Poem Focus on the lyrics on page 263, pointing out how the lines rhyme. Remind students that rhyming words are easy to remember and are often used in poetry, songs, advertisements, and political slogans. Ask students to recall and, if possible, recite, rhyming poems and songs they learned when they were young children. Then invite students to write their own children's poem or song that uses rhyme. Ask volunteers to share their rhymes with the class. Discuss whether rhyming words alone make a song, poem, or slogan memorable. OL the thought that at least the muddy flow didn't interfere with her sewer line. By the Fourth of July, when the crevice reached a foot wide and the dried banks on each side made a slick sidewalk cooler than the surrounding earth, she had made some allowances for its existence. That night, she lit sparklers in the starlight. She jumped and danced from bank to bank, playing a cheery game, a combination of hopscotch and jump rope, remembering incantatory[8] lyrics from first grade.

Mother, Mother, I am sick.
Call the doctor, quick, quick, quick.
In comes the doctor, in comes the nurse,
In comes the lady with the alligator purse.
Out goes the doctor, out goes the nurse,
Out goes the lady with the alligator purse.

In the morning, the crevice was fifty yards long—Amparo estimated this from the thirty-foot foundations on each side of her lot—and anywhere from three to four feet deep, depending on where she pushed an old mop handle into the ground. Much more than four feet deep and Amparo wouldn't have anything long enough to measure the depth. As it was, when she pushed the mop handle into the section closest to the biggest manzanita bush, her fingers could touch the slowly rising mud.

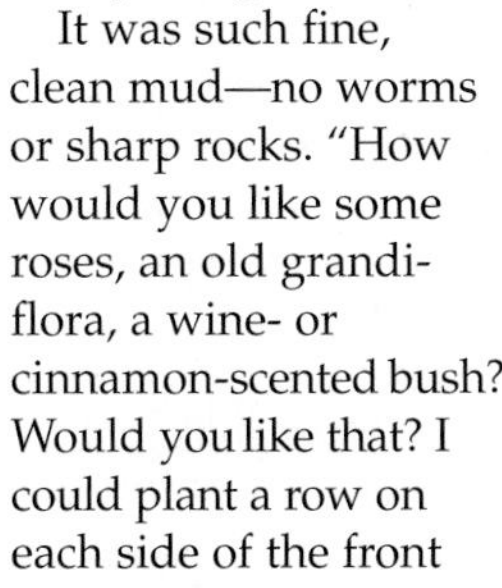

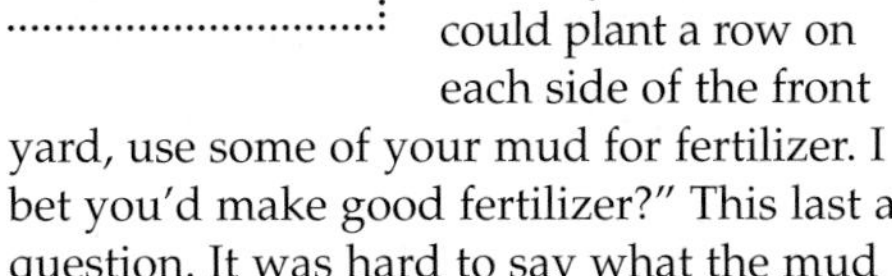

Visual Vocabulary
Grandiflora (gran′ də flôr′ ə) is a kind of rosebush; the word is Latin for "great flower."

It was such fine, clean mud—no worms or sharp rocks. "How would you like some roses, an old grandiflora, a wine- or cinnamon-scented bush? Would you like that? I could plant a row on each side of the front yard, use some of your mud for fertilizer. I bet you'd make good fertilizer?" This last a question. It was hard to say what the mud wanted.

8. This nursery rhyme is *incantatory* (in kan′ tə tôr′ ē) in that it has the quality of words spoken in casting a spell or performing a sacred ceremony.

On July 15, her forty-fifth birthday, Amparo washed her bathtub and sprayed it with rosewater. When the sun was at its highest, she started dragging buckets of warm mud to the tub, climbing the stairs to the master bathroom, careful not to slosh too much onto the floor. Not that it mattered. Once the mud set, it was hard to tell where the original dirt floor ended and the new layer of mud began.

Amparo patted the mud to remove any air pockets, then took off all her clothes. She combed her long, still mostly black hair until it sparked with static electricity. Carefully she packed mud into her hair, arranged the entire mass into a turban on top of her head. Then she delicately dipped her right toes into the mud. Thick, lukewarm liquid squeezed between her toes. She lowered herself into the tub and let the mud ooze above her knees, her belly button. Eyes closed, she finally sank to her chest and leaned her head against the back of the tub.

She thrilled to the sensation, like that of someone holding her without making contact. It was as if she had lost half her body weight. She felt an unnatural buoyancy,[9] an inability to touch the very bottom of the tub. With smooth, even strokes, she massaged a thick layer of mud on her face and behind her ears.

She felt her skin tighten as the mud dried. When the mud grew cooler than her body, she pulled the plug and watched the mud make its way down the drain in small gulps. Then she padded downstairs, mud dribbling in small clumps wherever she stepped too hard.

Amparo sat outside in the late afternoon sun, her legs stretched in front of her, the heat baking her body mask to a glossy finish. She studied the effect in the hand mirror. As long as she kept her body perfectly still,

9. *Buoyancy* (boi′ ən sē) is the ability or tendency to float or rise.

Reading Strategy Analyzing Character and Setting *Why might Amparo have decided to take a bath in the mud?* **R3**

Teach

R3 Reading Strategy

Analyzing Character and Setting **Answer:** *Students may remember Amparo asking the woman at the diner about mud baths earlier in the story, so it seems natural that Amparo would try one. Students may also suggest that Amparo is accepting the growing river of mud instead of fearing it.* **OL**

★ Writer's Technique

Personification Personification occurs when a writer gives an inanimate object the characteristics of a living thing. By having Amparo speak directly to the mud, the writer is treating the mud as if it were a character. Throughout the story, she gives the mud characteristics of a living creature—it licks, swallows, and moves. **AS**

Building Reading Fluency

Interpreting Descriptive Passages To increase student comprehension of descriptive passages, have them select a few paragraphs to read aloud. As they practice reading they should use their voices and pacing to convey the passage in a meaningful way. **BL**

Differentiated Instruction

Cause and Effect Have students explore cause and effect by posing this question: What events might lead to mudflows and landslides? Or, they could complete this statement: ______ *might cause landslides. Landslides in turn might cause* ______, *which in turn could cause* ______. **BL**

Academic Standards

Additional Support activities on pp. 262 and 263 cover the following standards:

Skills Practice: **9.5.8** Write for different purposes and audiences, adjusting tone, style, and voice as appropriate.

Building Reading Fluency: **9.7** [Develop] speaking skills…in conjunction with…strategies…[for] delivery of oral presentations.

Differentiated Instruction: **9.3** [Identify] story elements such as…plot…

Teach

L Literary Element

Tone Answer: *The mud seems healing.* OL

BI Big Idea

Dreams and Reality Answer: *Students may say that the author suggests that Amparo's powerful imagination allows her to make peace with the mud and even to view it as a friend.*

Ask: Why would Amparo share her food with the mud? *(Possible answers: She views the mud as a living creature. She accepts the mud and wants to care for it as if it were a child or a pet.)* OL

★ Viewing the Art

Answer: *Students may say that the image shows movement with ripples and texture like the mudflow in the story or that the colors and liquidity of the image is not like the mudflow.*

The works of German-born artist Susanne Schuenke range from abstract to realistic and attempt to deal with themes connected to nature and the modern human experience. AS

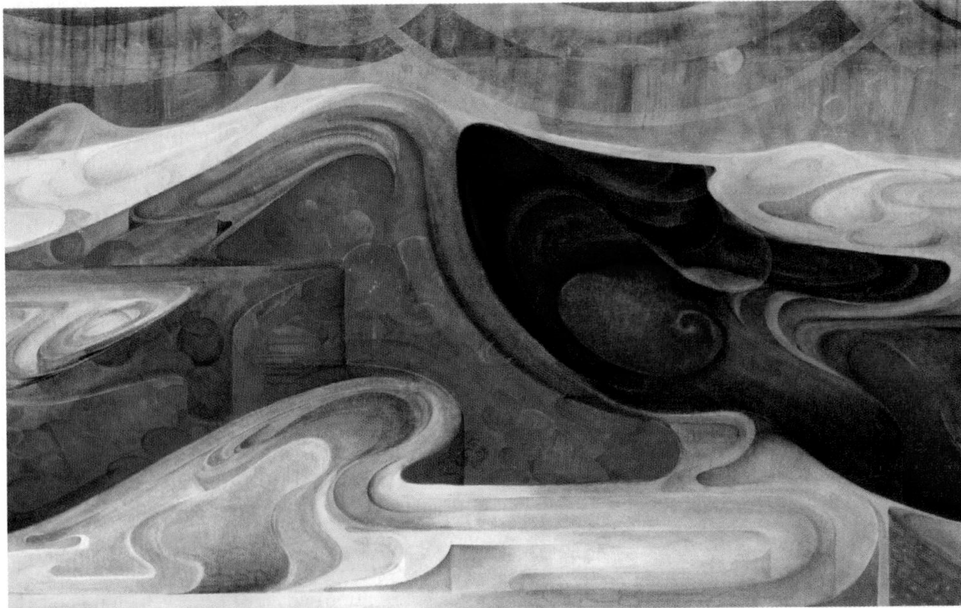

Life Forces, 1997. Susanne Schuenke. Oil and palladium leaf on linen.

Viewing the Art: In your opinion, what kind of movement is suggested by this painting? Do you think it reflects the movement of the mudflow? Why or why not? ★

she looked like an ancient statue. All the wrinkles were gone, the deep lines around her eyes and forehead, the cellulite.[10] And her back pain was gone.

Amparo stretched from her waist to touch her toes. Where the mud started to crack, she carefully peeled it away, conscious of the adhesive-like grip that caused her skin to redden wherever there was too much hair. Her skin had the firm smoothness of a ripened peach fresh from the tree. The pores on her nose had disappeared and her hair shone in the sunlight. She remembered how Sammy, her ex-husband, used to tell her that the first time he spotted her running her old black German shepherd in the park, the sun made her black-brown hair look like a comet. "How perfectly you've caught me," she told the mud, its slick surface stamped with the lines of her body. That night she fed the mud her leftover beans and rice.

In early August she spotted a possible hairline crack just to the right of the main crevice. She brushed the line with a manzanita branch and it seemed to go away. It was hard to say. By late August, when the hairline crack had lengthened to form a thin leg to a V, she was sure. This leg was aimed at the opposite corner of her house, and like the first leg, it pointed in the same direction. "Ahh, you want the foothills," she whispered.

At first, the mud's flow was **indiscernible** unless she sat for several minutes, her eyes focused on a mark she'd scratch into the

10. Fatty deposits, especially around the thighs and hips, are called *cellulite* (sel′ yə līt′).

Literary Element Tone *What feelings about the mud are evoked by this passage?* L

Big Idea Dreams and Reality *What does the author suggest about Amparo's imagination?* BI

Vocabulary

indiscernible (in′ di sur′ nə bəl) *adj.* difficult or impossible to see

Additional Support

Skills Practice

RESEARCH: Learning About Mudflows Students may be interested in learning about mudflows. Encourage them to use library resources and the Internet to formulate questions about mudflows and then answer them. For example, what is the difference between a mudflow and a mudslide? Is a mudslide the same thing as a landslide? How do mudflows and mudslides affect the landscape? Are mudflows or mudslides likely to affect the places where students live, visit, or have family? Have students write brief reports that include diagrams or other illustrations. Invite volunteers to share their findings with the class. OL still-damp sides of the widening cracks. Another trick she used to measure the mud's movement was to make little paper boats from old Christmas wrapping paper and watch them gently float and bob on the barely moving surface. By early October the mud flow was obvious—a steady movement east despite the three-year drought.

When she first found the house three years ago, its biggest attraction had been the roof, the easy access along the molded staircase that climbed in profile up the east wall of her second-floor bedroom to the roof escape. Amparo had always thought she would like to live in a house with a hidden staircase to some underground study; now she knew that her real dream had always been of such a skylight escape. She enjoyed climbing the stairs in the morning, sliding the double-construction skylights open. She'd clamber over the lip of the stairs and eat her *atole* on the roof, watching the day take hold. It was as if the house had been designed just for her.

Now she made the roof her lookout post; the mud would need guidance. "Foothills to the east, say 15 miles, straight flat land, hardly any sage," she announced her first day on the job. She listened to the mud's distinctive sound. She could hear it humming and swallowing, no longer baffled by its inability to lay claim to the house. There were no windows or doors on the east side of the first floor of the house. The mud waited at the weep holes[11] and joints, sensitive to the loosening of a corner as the house gave ground.

The coyotes' yips and cries grew more distinct. She counted how long it took their echoes to reach her, much as she would count the space between a thunderclap and a lightning flash. When they lurked too long she **belittled** them, smirking at their mangy coats, "Try a little mud in your fur. You'll kill a few fleas that way, I assure you," and "I once had a jacket with a red fox fur." She relented when they turned tail and skulked[12] away. The next night she left a pile of freshly grilled chicken breasts seasoned with rosemary. V

"Try a little mud in your fur. You'll kill a few fleas that way, I assure you."

On the day of the harvest moon, Amparo drove to the Fruit Patch produce stand and bought the last of the zucchini, now over a foot long and four inches in diameter. She chose a pumpkin the size of her head, as well as a garland of dried red New Mexico chili pods and a selection of Indian corn tied with twine.

At sunset, Amparo climbed to the roof and arranged the offerings on favorite plates. She poured a mixture of *atole* topped with raisins and walnuts in a mixing bowl. When the moon was full overhead, she placed the plates and bowl in a star-shaped pattern, one for her head, the others for her hands and feet. Then she lay on the roof enjoying the cool breeze overhead. ★

11. *Weep holes* are holes in a wall that allow water to drain out.

12. To *skulk* is to move so as to escape notice.

Reading Strategy Analyzing Character and Setting *Does this realization mark a change in Amparo's outlook? Explain.* R1

Reading Strategy Analyzing Character and Setting *In your opinion, why does Amparo leave chicken out?* R2

Vocabulary

belittle (bi lit′ əl) *v.* to cause to seem less important; to scorn

Teach

R1 Reading Strategy

Analyzing Character and Setting **Answer:** *Yes, she is less fearful now.* OL

V Vocabulary

Connotations Note that connotations are feelings associated with a word.

Ask: What are the connotations and the context of *lurked* and *skulked*? *(The words describe the coyotes' movements; they have negative connotations suggesting sneakiness or untrustworthiness.)* OL

R2 Reading Strategy

Analyzing Character and Setting **Answer:** *She feels sorry for the coyotes.* OL

★ Cultural History

Traditional Indian Food *Atole* is a porridge or mush made from cornmeal. It is a traditional food of the Indian people of northern Mexico. The Spanish word *atole* comes from the Nahuatl word *atolli.* AS

English Language Coach

Mexican Culture **Say:** As a child, García was influenced by Mexican and Mexican American culture. Have students share aspects of their own cultures that differ from American culture, such as traditions and ideas related to motherhood, marriage, or other elements of Amparo's past life. EL

Differentiated Instruction

Enacting a Scene Encourage students who are sensitive to the subtleties of language and movement to dramatize the final scenes. Have members of small groups choose acting or directing roles and then script and rehearse their scenes. Remind them to use voice and gesture to convey the feelings in the story. AL

Academic Standards

Additional Support activities on pp. 264 and 265 cover the following standards:

Skills Practice: **9.4.4** Use writing to formulate clear research questions and to compile information from…sources.

English Language Coach: **9.2** Develop [reading] strategies…

Differentiated Instruction: **9.7.6** Analyze the occasion and…choose effective verbal and nonverbal techniques (including voice, gestures…) for presentations.

Teach

R Reading Strategy

Analyzing Character and Setting **Answer:** *Students may say that Amparo used to take care of her husband and child.* OL

BI Big Idea

Dreams and Reality **Ask:** Are the events in this passage real or a dream? *(They seem to be really happening. Amparo awakes to find that the house was floating on a river of mud.)* OL

L Literary Element

Tone **Answer:** *Students may say that this description creates a sense of the mudflow's power, strength, and speed. The mudflow will not be stopped.*
Ask: What is the author's attitude toward the mud at the end of the story? *(The author is impressed by the strength and speed of the mud.)* OL

Use the CheckPoint questions on Presentation Plus! to check students' mastery of the selection. These questions can be used with interactive response keypads for immediate student feedback.

To the mud she tossed an inconsequential aside.[13] "Isn't it nice not to have to worry about cleaning and cooking and washing and worrying about someone all the time?" When the mud withdrew like a sulky child and refused to respond to her chatter, she confessed, "Yes, I give you credit for going uphill away from the riverbed. I never would have thought of that."

To the house she offered soothing counsel. "We'll ride it out together, the two of us. You'll see. I'll take good care of you." The mud hiccupped and poured a thick sheen over the lot. Amparo imagined how the land might have looked as an inland sea. "Just think of all that water." She felt the house shiver.

In Amparo's dreams that night, a stand of cottonwoods turned into a grove of ancient trees. Where a clothesline once twirled like a giant umbrella, clumps of tule rushes danced in the surge of a waxing moon.[14] In the distance, the flat roof of a house bobbed above the flat of the land that stretched toward the foothills.

And as she slept, the mud came close and caressed the base of the house. It told of the excitement of heat lightning cast on the horizon on summer evenings; of the tenderness of misty sighs heaved from a roiled[15] earth on snow-swept mornings; of a world best viewed from a height of 1500 feet.

In turn, the house recounted the thrill of water tumbling over a bed of smooth-ground gravel; of air so cold in autumn that spawning salmon gasped when they broke the surface.

House and mud lingered over shared secrets, reveling in this moment of discovery. The house openly admired the reflection of stars on the moist surface of the mud. In turn, the mud thrilled to the crusted surface of the house, each trowel-stroke another mystery to be explored.

In the predawn hours, Amparo awoke to the lurch of the house lifting and settling on a wide river of mud. House and mud paused as she clambered to the roof. They allowed her time to adjust her stance to the house's uncommon roll, then the house made a slow 180-degree turn from the old highway to the foothills.

Like a swimmer learning a new stroke, the house muscled through the mud, at first tentatively, then with increased **fluidity**. Loose pieces of masonry scattered as the house and mud picked up speed. The mud wash kicked up nearly one story high, flattening sage and manzanita.

"We're coming, we're coming, it won't be long before we're there," Amparo shouted to the hills. To the sun she complained, "We need some light over here. How do you expect us to see where we're going if you wait until six o'clock to get up?" To the house and mud she instructed, "Faster, go faster, we're almost there! Don't worry about me." As they drew closer, a cleft in the foothills parted, and house, mud, woman squeezed through in an eruption of closely contained forms, aiming for the tree-laced meadow above.

Through the temporary opening could be seen air so clear the sky looked like cut crystal, a passage so smooth that a traveler could press one hand against each side and never feel the moment of contact.

13. Something that is *inconsequential* neither follows from nor leads to anything important; it is insignificant. An *aside* is a remark not meant to be heard by everyone—or anyone.
14. A *waxing moon* gradually increases in size and brightness until it is full.
15. Here, *roiled* means "disturbed or stirred up."

Reading Strategy Analyzing Character and Setting *What does this suggest about Amparo's life before moving to the house?* R

Literary Element Tone *What sense of the mudflow is created by this description?* L

Vocabulary
fluidity (flo͞o i′ də tē) *n.* the ability, as of a liquid, to flow and change shape

Additional Support

Skills Practice

SPEAKING AND LISTENING:
Role-playing Discuss with students ways to make characters come alive during role-playing situations. List the following ideas on the board:

- Give the character a personality using tone of voice or word choice.
- Use facial expressions and gestures.
- Say and do things the character would say and do.

Invite small groups to enact and present a scene in which Amparo, the mudflow, and the house hold a conversation, using the story's descriptions of the mud and the house as the basis for their characterizations. OL

AFTER YOU READ

RESPONDING AND THINKING CRITICALLY

Respond

1. What thoughts went through your mind as you finished reading this story? Explain.

Recall and Interpret

2. (a)Describe the setting of the story, including Amparo's house, the immediate surroundings, and the nearby town. (b)Did you think there was beauty in the setting? Explain.
3. (a)What kind of life does Amparo lead? (b)Why might Amparo choose to live the way she does?
4. (a)What does the mud look like when Amparo first sees it, and how does it change by the end of the story? (b)Why is the formation and movement of the mud especially strange?
5. (a)Summarize the changes in Amparo's reactions to the mud. (b)How would you characterize her relationship with the mud?

Analyze and Evaluate

6. How does García's use of personification—figurative language that gives human qualities or characteristics to animals, objects, or ideas—affect your perceptions of the house and the mud? Explain.
7. Food and meal preparation are mentioned several times throughout the story. What meaning or effect do you think this adds to the story?
8. How would you explain the symbolic meaning of the story's ending?
9. In your opinion, did García succeed in creating a powerful and moving story? Explain why or why not.

Connect

10. **Big Idea** **Dreams and Reality** What did the magical or surreal elements of this story help to suggest about Amparo's state of mind? Explain.

LITERARY ANALYSIS

Literary Element Tone

Tone is the attitude a writer takes toward a subject, expressed through the words and details he or she uses. A writer's tone may convey a variety of attitudes, such as sympathy, objectivity, seriousness, irony, sadness, bitterness, or humor. For example, a good-bye between members of a family could express a combination of sadness about the parting and hopefulness about what is to come.

1. How would you describe the tone of this story? Make a list of at least five words or phrases from the story that help to convey the tone.
2. Tone can be used to help suggest a theme—a central message about life or human nature. What theme or themes does the tone of this story help to suggest? Explain.

Review: Point of View

As you learned on pages 206–207, **point of view** refers to the relationship of the narrator to the story. This story uses the third-person limited point of view, which means that the narrator reveals the thoughts, feelings, and observations of only one character, though other characters are mentioned.

Partner Activity Suspense is a feeling of curiosity, uncertainty, or even dread about what is going to happen next. How does the third-person limited point of view help to create suspense in this story? With a partner, go back over the story and record particularly suspenseful moments. Next, write down your thoughts about how the third-person limited point of view affected the suspense of the story. If the story had been told from a different point of view, would the level of suspense have been different? Share your thoughts with the class.

Literary Element

1. Students may say the tone is ominous, mysterious, suspenseful, or celebratory. Students should support their answers.
2. The tone supports the idea that the world can overwhelm a person's life.

Review: Point of View

Students should look at points in the story where they wondered what would happen next. The limited point of view helped hide the outcome of the story.

AFTER YOU READ

Assess

1. Students should support answers with evidence.
2. (a) Amparo lives in an adobe house in a desert. (b) Students should support answers.
3. (a) She is isolated, close to the land, and has no luxuries. (b) She wants to be left alone.
4. (a) The dimple becomes a fast-moving mud river. (b) It comes from nowhere and grows into a river. It flows uphill.
5. (a) She ignores, respects, and finally submits to it. She uses it as a bath and feeds it. (b) It is a curiosity, then a threat. She gives in to it.
6. The mud and the house seem like powerful beings but also Amparo's friends.
7. The food adds to the Southwestern setting and may symbolize Amparo's attempts to nurture herself.
8. The mud may symbolize Amparo's personal history. Like the mud, her troubles at first seem harmless but eventually carry her away. She takes strength from the mud and gives into it.
9. Students should support answers.
10. They make the reader wonder about her mental state and reveal her ability to find mystery in her surroundings.

Academic Standards

The Additional Support activity on p. 266 covers the following standard:

Skills Practice: **9.7.6** Analyze the occasion and…choose effective verbal and nonverbal techniques…

AFTER YOU READ

Assess

Reading Strategy

1. From details such as Amparo leaving food for the coyotes, students may conclude that Amparo is kind-hearted, although she has failed in her relationships with people. She now seems intent on avoiding others and concealing details of her life.
2. Students may say that nature becomes Amparo's closest companion. Her conversations with the house, mud, and coyotes; her offerings of food; and her decision to stay with the house all reveal the importance of nature to her.

Vocabulary

1. a **2.** b **3.** c **4.** a

Writing About Literature

Students' essays should

- clearly define magical realism.
- explain how the selection fits the criteria for the genre of magical realism.
- summarize the story's magical elements in the conclusion and explain how they affected their enjoyment as a reader.

Academic Vocabulary

Her desires for freedom and security are the basis of her decision to stay.

READING AND VOCABULARY

Reading Strategy Analyzing Character and Setting

In García's story, the main character, Amparo, has a close relationship to her house and to the natural world around her. By analyzing details about Amparo, her house, and the mud, you can better understand what happens to Amparo.

1. From details given in the story, what do you conclude about Amparo and about her relationships with other people?
2. What importance does nature come to have for Amparo? Support your answer by listing details from the story that reveal nature's importance for her.

Vocabulary Practice

Practice with Word Parts Each word below has either a prefix or suffix. Based on your knowledge of each word's definition and root, choose the best definition for the underlined word part.

1. <u>im</u>penetrable
a. not **b.** new **c.** degree

2. <u>in</u>discernible
a. toward **b.** not **c.** before

3. <u>be</u>little
a. degree **b.** again **c.** treat as

4. fluid<u>ity</u>
a. quality **b.** fit for **c.** the study of

Academic Vocabulary

Here is a word from the vocabulary list on page R80.

underlie (un′ dər lī′) *v.* to be under something as its foundation; to be at the basis of

Practice and Apply
What feelings **underlie** Amparo's decision to stay with the house?

LiteratureOnline **Web Activities** For eFlashcards, Selection Quick Checks, and other Web activities, go to www.glencoe.com.

WRITING AND EXTENDING

Writing About Literature

Analyze Genre Element The term magical realism is used to describe a style of writing in which realistic details, events, settings, characters, and dialogue are interwoven with magical, bizarre, fantastic, or supernatural elements. This style is especially prominent in Latin American literature.

How do you know that "The Flat of the Land" is an example of magical realism? Write a brief essay in which you identify both realistic and fantastic elements in the story. Then explain how the use of magical realism affected your enjoyment of the story.

Begin by reviewing the story to find at least three examples each of realistic elements and fantastic elements. Record the examples using a chart like the one shown.

Reality	Fantasy

Next, construct your essay. In your introduction, define magical realism in your own words. Then, in the body of your essay, explain why "The Flat of the Land" is a work of magical realism. Describe the imaginary or improbable situations that the story describes in a realistic manner. In your conclusion, summarize the magical elements of the story and explain how they affected your enjoyment of the story. As you construct your draft, use your chart for reference.

After you complete your draft, meet with a partner to evaluate each other's work and to suggest revisions. Then proofread your draft for errors in spelling, grammar, and punctuation.

Learning for Life

Do you think that stepping into a bathtub full of mud sounds horrible? Since ancient times, some people have believed that mud baths and facial mud packs are advantageous for overall health and a feeling of well-being. Research the history of and reasons for these beliefs. Draw conclusions about how and why mud might prove to be beneficial to the human body. Share your findings with the class.

Learning for Life

Students should prepare a brief oral report based on their findings. Their reports should contain three sections: history, reasons, and conclusions. Remind students that their conclusions should be based on the facts they discovered and their own feelings about the subject.

Web Activities Have students access the Web site for interactive activities that will help them assess their understanding of the selection.

The Son from America

MEET ISAAC BASHEVIS SINGER

"Of course, I believe in free will," Isaac Bashevis Singer once said. "I have no choice." This is the kind of sweetly humorous and delightfully human contradiction that marked his fiction, and, to some extent, his life.

Childhood in Poland Singer was born in a shtetl—a small, Jewish village—near Warsaw, Poland. When he was four, his family moved to Warsaw, where he spent most of his childhood. His father and both of his grandfathers were rabbis, and Singer passed his boyhood immersed in religious studies. The expectation was that he would be a rabbi, too, but at a very young age he began to have doubts about religion.

"The greatness of art is not to find what is common but what is unique."

—Isaac Bashevis Singer

Besides his constant reading, two experiences proved very important for the future writer. One was listening to the people who came to his father for advice on their poor street in Warsaw. The young Singer overheard their stories, their conflicts, and their individual and collective voices. Another important experience was living in his grandfather's village, Bilgoray, for three or four years when he was an adolescent. There, according to Singer, "the traditions of hundreds of years ago still lived," and he "learned a lot about Jewishness."

A Son from America In some ways, Singer himself became a "son from America." First, he did not follow the path his parents wanted him to pursue: instead of becoming a rabbi, he became a writer. He also left home for the United States—although with Hitler in power in Germany and conflict on the rise, leaving Europe was as much necessity as choice. In 1935, Singer joined his older brother who already worked in the United States as a writer.

Once in the United States, Singer wrote extensively. Working for the *Jewish Daily Forward,* he published one or two stories or chapters a week for more than forty years. All together, he wrote forty-five volumes of short stories, as well as novels, plays, autobiographies, and children's stories. Much of what he wrote was in Yiddish, a form of German spoken by Jews and descendants of Jews of central and eastern Europe. The only time he did not write was for a period of five to seven years following the death of his brother and the Holocaust.

A Lifetime of Achievement Singer received numerous awards, including the Nobel Prize in Literature in 1978. His short story collection *A Crown of Feathers,* which includes "The Son from America," won a National Book Award in 1974.

Isaac Bashevis Singer was born in 1904 and died in 1991.

Literature Online **Author Search** For more about Isaac Bashevis Singer, go to www.glencoe.com.

Focus

BELLRINGER

Bellringer Options
Selection Focus Transparency 19
Daily Language Practice Transparency 24

Or have students discuss this question: Are our memories of a place or a time in the past ever accurate, or do we tend to remember things as better—or worse—than they really were? As students read, they should consider the difference between Samuel's memory of his home village and the reality.

Literature Online

Author Search To expand students' appreciation of Isaac Bashevis Singer, have them access the Web site for additional information and resources.

Selection Skills

The Son from America

Literary Elements
- Style (SE pp. 270–278)
- Voice (SE p. 278)

Reading Skills
- Making Inferences About Theme (SE pp. 270–278)
- Making Inferences (TWE p. 272)

Vocabulary Skills
- Word Origins (SE p. 278)
- Academic Vocabulary (SE p. 278)

Listening/Speaking/Viewing Skills
- Analyzing Art (TWE p. 275)

Writing Skills/Grammar
- Evaluate Author's Craft (SE p. 279)
- Using Appositives (SE p. 279)

BEFORE YOU READ

Focus

Summary

Life in the tiny Polish village of Lentshin continues uneventfully, as it always has for Berl and his wife Berlcha. Then one day their son returns from the United States after 40 years, bearing gifts and modern ideas about wealth and happiness.

V Vocabulary

Vocabulary File **Say:** Add these words and definitions to your vocabulary file. For each word, include a sentence that gives you an example of how to use the word. **OL** Students with English language needs should include the pronunciations of these words in their files. **EL**

Literary Elements Have students access the Web site to improve their understanding of style.

LITERATURE PREVIEW

Connecting to the Story

Most children do not live the same lives as their parents lived. Before you read this story, think about the following questions:

- When you are an adult, what reasons might you have for staying in the place where you grew up? What reasons might you have for leaving it?
- Do you think the simpler life of earlier generations is superior to modern life?

Building Background

This story takes place in the fictional town of Lentshin, Poland, sometime between 1896 and 1917. The setting is the "old country": a deeply religious, traditional place where time seems to have stood still for generations. It is also a Jewish world in which the Sabbath (the holy day), the synagogue (the place of worship), and Jewish rites and rituals create the daily round of life. Thus, one of the main characters, Berlcha, lights candles on the Sabbath, makes a special braided bread for the Sabbath, and keeps two separate shelves for foodstuffs in her house—one for meat and one for dairy. All await the Messiah, whom they piously address in prayers such as "Come, My Groom." An important value in this culture is the preservation of Jewish identity over the generations.

Setting Purposes for Reading

Big Idea Dreams and Reality

As you read, consider what is dreamlike about this bygone world of the shtetl, as well as how it contrasts with ideas of "real" or modern life.

Literary Element Style

Style is all of the expressive qualities that distinguish an author's work, including word choice, the length and arrangement of sentences, and the use of figurative language and imagery. As you read the story, examine the choices Singer makes as he selects certain words and crafts his sentences and paragraphs.

- See Literary Terms Handbook, p. R17.

READING PREVIEW

Reading Strategy Making Inferences About Theme

A theme in fiction, poetry, or drama is the work's main idea or message. Sometimes, the reader has to **infer** the author's theme or to use his or her reason and experience to deduce what an author is saying indirectly. As you read "The Son from America," make inferences about the theme.

Reading Tip: Taking Notes Use a chart to help you make inferences about the theme.

Example	Inference
"But they never seemed to use the money. What for?"	Although the couple have little material wealth, they feel they have all that they need.

Vocabulary

mock (mok) *v.* to make fun of or ridicule; p. 271 *The mean boys mock the strange behaviors of the newcomer.*

contour (kon′toor) *n.* outline or general shape; p. 274 *When deciding where to place the house, the architect considered the contour of the land.*

benediction (ben′ə dik′shən) *n.* short prayer used as a blessing; p. 274 *The priest gave the benediction before the meal.*

bestow (bi stō′) *v.* to give as a gift; p. 276 *The parents bestow their greatest treasures on their children.*

tread (tred) *n.* step or footstep; p. 276 *We could barely hear the soft tread of the child's feet on the stairs.*

Literature Online **Interactive Literary Elements Handbook** To review or learn more about the literary elements, go to www.glencoe.com.

INDIANA ACADEMIC STANDARDS (pages 270–279)

9.3.11 Evaluate the aesthetic qualities of style...and theme.

9.2 Develop [reading] strategies...

9.5.2 Write responses to literature that...demonstrate an awareness of the author's style and...the effects created.

Selection Resources

Print Materials

- Unit 1 Resources (Fast File), pp. 85–87
- Leveled Vocabulary Development, p. 20
- Selection and Unit Assessments, pp. 43–44
- Selection Quick Checks, p. 22

Transparencies

- Bellringer Options Transparencies: Selection Focus Transparency 19; Daily Language Practice Transparency 24
- Literary Elements Transparency 24

Technology

- TeacherWorks Plus™ CD-ROM
- StudentWorks Plus™ CD-ROM
- Presentation Plus!™ CD-ROM
- Literature Online, glencoe.com
- Online Student Edition, mhln.com
- Exam*View*® Assessment Suite CD-ROM
- Vocabulary PuzzleMaker CD-ROM
- Listening Library, disc 1 track 24

The Son from America

Isaac Bashevis Singer

Mount Kosciusko, 1955. Konrad Winkler. Oil on canvas, 51 × 66 in. National Museum, Krakow, Poland.

The village of Lentshin was tiny—a sandy marketplace where the peasants of the area met once a week. It was surrounded by little huts with thatched roofs or shingles green with moss. The chimneys looked like pots. Between the huts there were fields, where the owners planted vegetables or pastured their goats.

In the smallest of these huts lived old Berl, a man in his eighties, and his wife, who was called Berlcha (wife of Berl). Old Berl was one of the Jews who had been driven from their villages in Russia and had settled in Poland. In Lentshin, they **mocked** the mistakes he made while praying aloud. He spoke with a sharp "r." He was short, broad-shouldered, and had a small white beard, and summer and winter he wore a sheepskin hat, a padded cotton jacket, and stout boots. He walked slowly, shuffling his feet. He had a half acre of field, a cow, a goat, and chickens.

The couple had a son, Samuel, who had gone to America forty years ago. It was said in Lentshin that he became a millionaire there. Every month, the Lentshin letter carrier brought old Berl a money order and a

Literary Element Style *What images and figurative language do you find in this passage?* **L**

Vocabulary

mock (mok) *v.* to make fun of or ridicule

Teach

L Literary Element

Style Answer: *Images include little huts with thatched roofs and mossy shingles. The simile compares chimneys to pots.*
Ask: What do the author's choice of image and words suggest about his writing style? *(Students may say that the writer's style is down-to-earth and honest.)* **OL**

Use CheckPoint questions on Presentation Plus! to monitor students' comprehension. These questions can be used with interactive response keypads for immediate student feedback.

Readability Scores
Dale-Chall: 3.8
DRP: 54
Lexile: 760

English Language Coach

Jewish Words English learners may be unfamiliar with words related to Jewish customs and traditions. Write on the board these words: *synagogue, czar, bris, gentile, Talmud, ruble, Kaddish, Gefilte,* and *Torah.* Have students find the definitions of these words in the footnotes. **EL**

Differentiated Instruction

Visualizing a Place Visualizing the world of Lentshin may be difficult for less proficient readers, but it is important for their understanding of the story. Have partners work together to read the story for details about its location, and then draw a picture that incorporates those details. **BL**

Academic Standards

Additional Support activities on p. 271 cover the following standards:

English Language Coach: **9.1** Use...a growing knowledge of English and other languages to determine the meaning of words...

Differentiated Instruction: **9.3** [Identify] story elements such as...setting...

Teach

L1 Literary Element

Style Answer: *It is short and informal. Although it is not dialogue, it reflects the way some people speak.*

Ask: Whose voice is reflected here? *(Students should realize that the voice could be that of Berl or of any person living in the village.)* OL

R Reading Strategy

Making Inferences About Theme Answer: *The reader can infer from the couple's modest lifestyle that the theme will concern the relative value of material possessions and the question of what is required to lead a good and happy life.* OL

BI Big Idea

Dreams and Reality

Answer: *Everything about them is beyond the realm of the parents' experience or understanding.* OL

letter that no one could read because many of the words were English. How much money Samuel sent his parents remained a secret. Three times a year, Berl and his wife went on foot to Zakroczym and cashed the money orders there. But they never seemed to use the money. What for? The garden, the cow, and the goat provided most of their needs. Besides, Berlcha sold chickens and eggs, and from these there was enough to buy flour for bread.

No one cared to know where Berl kept the money that his son sent him. There were no thieves in Lentshin. The hut consisted of one room, which contained all their belongings: the table, the shelf for meat, the shelf for milk foods, the two beds, and the clay oven. Sometimes the chickens roosted in the woodshed and sometimes, when it was cold, in a coop near the oven. The goat, too, found shelter inside when the weather was bad. The more prosperous villagers had kerosene lamps, but Berl and his wife did not believe in newfangled gadgets. What was wrong with a wick in a dish of oil? Only for the Sabbath would Berlcha buy three tallow candles at the store. In summer, the couple got up at sunrise and retired with the chickens. In the long winter evenings, Berlcha spun flax[1] at her spinning wheel and Berl sat beside her in the silence of those who enjoy their rest.

> Her face was yellowish and wrinkled like a cabbage leaf.

Once in a while when Berl came home from the synagogue[2] after evening prayers, he brought news to his wife. In Warsaw there were strikers who demanded that the czar abdicate.[3] A heretic by the name of Dr. Herzl had come up with the idea that Jews should settle again in Palestine.[4] Berlcha listened and shook her bonneted head. Her face was yellowish and wrinkled like a cabbage leaf. There were bluish sacks under her eyes. She was half deaf. Berl had to repeat each word he said to her. She would say, "The things that happen in the big cities!"

Here in Lentshin nothing happened except usual events: a cow gave birth to a calf, a young couple has a bris,[5] or a girl was born and there was no party. Occasionally, someone died. Lentshin had no cemetery, and the corpse had to be taken to Zakroczym. Actually, Lentshin had become a village with few young people. The young men left for Zakroczym, for Nowy Dwor, for Warsaw, and sometimes for the United States. Like Samuel's, their letters were illegible, the Yiddish mixed with the languages of the countries where they were now living. They sent photographs in which the men wore top hats and the women fancy dresses like squiresses.

Berl and Berlcha also received such photographs. But their eyes were failing and neither he nor she had glasses. They could barely make out the pictures. Samuel had sons and daughters with Gentile[6] names—and grandchildren who had married and had their own offspring. Their names were so strange that Berl and Berlcha could never

1. *Flax* is a fiber made from the stem of a plant.
2. A *synagogue* (sin′ə gog′) is a place for worship and religious instruction.
3. *Czar* is the title for Russian rulers until 1917. Russia ruled Poland at the time of the story. *Abdicate* means "to give up rule."
4. *Herzl* (1860–1904) refers to Dr. Theodor Herzl, the founder of Zionism, the movement to establish a Jewish state in Palestine, the biblical homeland of the Jews.
5. A *bris* is a Jewish ritual and celebration accompanying the birth of a male child.
6. A *Gentile* is a person who is not Jewish, usually someone who is Christian.

Literary Element Style *How does this sentence contribute to style?* L1

Reading Strategy Making Inferences About Theme *What details in these first paragraphs could you use to make inferences about the theme?* R

Big Idea Dreams and Reality *What makes these foreign places dreamlike to the parents who stay in Poland?* BI

Additional Support

Skills Practice

READING: Making Inferences
Although a U.S. resident at the time, Singer wrote this story in his native Yiddish. Note the contrast between dream and reality in his telling of the story.

Ask: Is Singer sentimental about the old country and its ways? How does he feel about American ways? Does he prefer one way of life to the other? Have students take notes as they read. Invite volunteers to share their inferences and the details supporting them. OL remember them. But what difference do names make? America was far, far away on the other side of the ocean, at the edge of the world. A Talmud[7] teacher who came to Lentshin had said that Americans walked with their heads down and their feet up. Berl and Berlcha could not grasp this. How was it possible? But since the teacher said so it must be true. Berlcha pondered for some time and then she said, "One can get accustomed to everything."

And so it remained. From too much thinking—God forbid—one may lose one's wits.

One Friday morning, when Berlcha was kneading the dough for the Sabbath loaves, the door opened and a nobleman entered. He was so tall that he had to bend down to get through the door. He wore a beaver hat and a cloak bordered with fur. He was followed by Chazkel, the coachman from Zakroczym, who carried two leather valises with brass locks. In astonishment Berlcha raised her eyes.

> From too much thinking—God forbid—one may lose one's wits.

The nobleman looked around and said to the coachman in Yiddish, "Here it is." He took out a silver ruble[8] and paid him. The coachman tried to hand him change but he said, "You can go now."

When the coachman closed the door, the nobleman said, "Mother, it's me, your son Samuel—Sam."

Berlcha heard the words and her legs grew numb. Her hands, to which pieces of dough were sticking, lost their power. The nobleman hugged her, kissed her forehead, both her cheeks. Berlcha began to cackle like a hen, "My son!" At that moment Berl came in from the woodshed, his arms piled with logs. The goat followed him. When he saw a nobleman kissing his wife, Berl dropped the wood and exclaimed, "What is this?"

The nobleman let go of Berlcha and embraced Berl. "Father!"

For a long time Berl was unable to utter a sound. He wanted to recite holy words that he had read in the Yiddish Bible, but he could remember nothing. Then he asked, "Are you Samuel?"

"Yes, Father, I am Samuel."

"Well, peace be with you." Berl grasped his son's hand. He was still not sure that he was not being fooled. Samuel wasn't as tall and heavy as this man, but then Berl reminded himself that Samuel was only fifteen years old when he had left home. He must have grown in that faraway country. Berl asked, "Why didn't you let us know that you were coming?"

"Didn't you receive my cable?" Samuel asked.

Berl did not know what a cable was.

Berlcha had scraped the dough from her hands and enfolded her son. He kissed her again and asked, "Mother, didn't you receive a cable?"

"What? If I lived to see this, I am happy to die," Berlcha said, amazed by her own words. Berl, too, was amazed. These were just the words he would have said earlier if he had been able to remember. After a while Berl came to himself and said, "Pescha, you will have to make a double Sabbath pudding ★ in addition to the stew."

It was years since Berl had called Berlcha by her given name. When he wanted to address her, he would say, "Listen," or

7. *Talmud* (täl′mood) is a collection of Jewish civil and religious laws. A Talmud teacher explains the complications of the law to the people.
8. A *ruble* (ro͞o′bəl) is a monetary unit in Russia and, in this case, Russian-occupied Poland.

Literary Element Style *What is unusual about this sentence? What effect does it have?* **L2**

Literary Element Style *Why might Singer have chosen to use so many references to animals when describing Berl and Berlcha?* **L3**

Teach

L2 Literary Element

Style Answer: *This sentence has an unexpected or inverted word order. The reversed word order puts more emphasis on Berlcha's astonishment.* **OL**

L3 Literary Element

Style Answer: *The connections between the characters and the animal reinforce the idea that the characters are simple, earthy people.* **OL**

★ Cultural History

The Jewish Sabbath The Sabbath, or day of rest, is an important Jewish tradition. The Jewish Sabbath is observed from sunset on each Friday to sunset on Saturday. On the Sabbath, Jews do not work but attend religious services and gather for a festive meal. Sabbath customs prohibit the handling of money or traveling. **AS**

English Language Coach

Using Time Order Explain that time order words and phrases, such as *when, a moment later,* and *for a long time,* help readers link events in the story. Have English language learners write down the time-order words and phrases they find on this page, along with the events that happen after each one. **EL**

Differentiated Instruction

Comparing Plots Many stories begin with the arrival of a stranger or a long-lost loved one. Have advanced students think of other works in which this device leads to a clash of ideas or cultures. In addition, have students write an alternative ending to Singer's story and share it with the class. **AL**

Academic Standards

Additional Support activities on pp. 272 and 273 cover the following standards:

Skills Practice: **9.2.8** Make reasonable statements and draw conclusions about a text, supporting them with accurate examples.

English Language Coach: **9.3.6** Analyze and trace an author's development of time and sequence...

Differentiated Instruction: **9.3.3** Analyze interactions between characters...and explain the way those interactions affect the plot. **9.5.2** Write responses to literature that demonstrate an awareness of the author's style...

Teach

R Reading Strategy

Making Inferences About Theme **Answer:** *It emphasizes the different life styles of the old couple and their son.*

L1 Literary Element

Style **Answer:** *Students may say that the goat represents the parents' rural culture. Others may say that it adds humor to an emotional moment.* OL

BI Big Idea

Dreams and Reality
Answer: *The snow covers everything, making it unrecognizable. The village seems wrapped in a white shroud, a world that time forgot.* OL

★ Language History

Gentile Pronounced jen′ tīl, the word literally means "nation" and comes from the Latin root *gens* for "race or people." Centuries ago, Jews applied the word to "heathens"—people who practiced polytheism. Later, it came to be used as a term for Christians. AS

"Say." It is the young or those from the big cities who call a wife by her name. Only now did Berlcha begin to cry. Yellow tears ran from her eyes, and everything became dim. Then she called out, "It's Friday—I have to prepare for the Sabbath." Yes, she had to knead the dough and braid the loaves. With such a guest, she had to make a larger Sabbath stew. The winter day is short and she must hurry.

Her son understood what was worrying her, because he said, "Mother, I will help you."

Berlcha wanted to laugh, but a choked sob came out. "What are you saying? God forbid."

The nobleman took off his cloak and jacket and remained in his vest, on which hung a solid-gold watch chain. He rolled up his sleeves and came to the trough. "Mother, I was a baker for many years in New York," he said, and he began to knead the dough.

"What! You are my darling son who will say Kaddish[9] for me." She wept raspingly. Her strength left her, and she slumped onto the bed.

Berl said, "Women will always be women." And he went to the shed to get more wood. The goat sat down near the oven; she gazed with surprise at this strange man—his height and his bizarre clothes.

The neighbors had heard the good news that Berl's son had arrived from America and they came to greet him. The women began to help Berlcha prepare for the Sabbath. Some laughed, some cried. The room was full of people, as at a wedding. They asked Berl's son, "What is new in America?" And Berl's son answered, "America is all right."

"Do Jews make a living?"

"One eats white bread there on weekdays."

"Do they remain Jews?" ★

"I am not a Gentile."

After Berlcha blessed the candles, father and son went to the little synagogue across the street. A new snow had fallen. The son took large steps, but Berl warned him, "Slow down."

In the synagogue the Jews recited "Let Us Exult" and "Come, My Groom." All the time, the snow outside kept falling. After prayers, when Berl and Samuel left the Holy Place, the village was unrecognizable. Everything was covered in snow. One could see only the **contours** of the roofs and the candles in the windows. Samuel said, "Nothing has changed here."

Berlcha had prepared gefilte fish,[10] chicken soup with rice, meat, carrot stew. Berl recited the **benediction** over a glass of ritual wine. The family ate and drank, and when it grew quiet for a while one could hear the chirping of the house cricket. The son talked a lot, but Berl and Berlcha understood little. His Yiddish was different and contained foreign words.

After the final blessing Samuel asked, "Father, what did you do with all the money I sent you?"

Berl raised his white brows. "It's here."

"Didn't you put it in a bank?"

"There is no bank in Lentshin."

"Where do you keep it?"

Berl hesitated. "One is not allowed to touch money on the Sabbath, but I will show you." He crouched beside the bed and began to shove something heavy. A boot appeared. Its top was stuffed with straw. Berl removed the straw and the son saw that the boot was full of gold coins. He lifted it.

9. *Kaddish* (kä′ dish) is a prayer, generally recited by mourners.

10. *Gefilte* (gə fil′ tə) *fish* is a preparation of minced fish and other ingredients shaped into balls or cakes.

Reading Strategy Making Inferences About Theme *How does this passage change or reinforce your ideas about the theme?* R

Literary Element Style *In your opinion, why might the author have chosen to give the goat human-like qualities here?* L1

Big Idea Dreams and Reality *What details make the village seem like a dream world?* BI

Vocabulary

contour (kon′ toor) *n.* outline or general shape

benediction (ben′ ə dik′ shən) *n.* short prayer used as a blessing

Additional Support

Skills Practice

SPEAKING AND LISTENING:

Expressing State of Mind Discuss the state of mind of the parents as well as of Samuel during their reunion. *(The parents are overwhelmed, surprised, and a little disbelieving; Samuel is expectant and joyful.)* Invite volunteers to demonstrate how each character would speak, move, and gesture to convey these feelings. Have groups of three act out the scene for the class. Remind students to base their performances on details from the text. OL

Shiviti, 19th century Jewish folk art from Poland. Collection of Isaac Einhorn, Tel Aviv, Israel. 

"Father, this is a treasure!" he called out.

"Well."

"Why didn't you spend it?"

"On what? Thank God, we have everything."

"Why didn't you travel somewhere?"

"Where to? This is our home."

L3 The son asked one question after the other, but Berl's answer was always the same: they wanted for nothing. The garden, the cow, the goat, the chickens provided them with all they needed. The son said, "If thieves knew about this, your lives wouldn't be safe."

"There are no thieves here."

"What will happen to the money?"

"You take it."

Literary Element Style *How does this single word convey a great deal of meaning?* L2

Slowly, Berl and Berlcha grew accustomed to their son and his American Yiddish. Berlcha could hear him better now. She even recognized his voice. He was saying, "Perhaps we should build a larger synagogue."

"The synagogue is big enough," Berl replied.

"Perhaps a home for old people."

"No one sleeps in the street."

The next day after the Sabbath meal was eaten, a Gentile from Zakroczym brought a paper—it was the cable. Berl and Berlcha lay down for a nap. They soon began to snore. The goat, too, dozed off. The son put on his cloak and his hat and went for a walk. He strode with his long legs across the marketplace. He stretched out a hand and touched a roof. He wanted to smoke a cigar, but he remembered it was forbidden on the Sabbath. He had a desire to talk to someone,

Teach

L2 Literary Element

Style Answer: *It seems to suggest he does not know what to say or do with so much money, while at the same time implying that for them this wealth is not really a treasure.*
Ask: What is ironic about Samuel's comment that "Nothing has changed here"? *(The village was just described as unrecognizable under the snow, but Samuel sees it as exactly the same.)* OL

L3 Literary Element

Style Ask: How is the narrator's style of speaking different from the character's style? *(Students should notice that the narrator is articulate and expressive, but the characters—particularly Berl and Berlcha—speak in short, direct sentences.)* OL

Viewing the Art

A *shiviti* is a decorative plaque or painting based on the verse, "I have set (*shiviti* in Hebrew) the Lord always before me." (Psalm 16:8). In the 18th and 19th centuries, these elaborate works of art often hung in synagogues and Jewish homes. AS

English Language Coach

Reading Dialogue Without Tags

Readers may have trouble identifying the speakers when the dialogue does not contain tags. Suggest that students work in trios to read aloud from "After the final blessing Samuel asked . . ." on p. 274 to "No one sleeps in the street." Before students begin, they should decide who will read the narrator's words, Samuel's words, and Berl's. Have students read the scene aloud, each taking one part. Afterward, ask students to summarize what was said. EL

Academic Standards

Additional Support activities on pp. 274 and 275 cover the following standard:

Skills Practice: **9.7.6** Analyze the occasion and…choose effective verbal and nonverbal techniques (including voice, gestures, and eye contact) for presentations.

English Language Coach: **9.7.17** Deliver oral responses to literature that demonstrate awareness of the author's writing style and an appreciation of the effects created…

Teach

R Reading Strategy

Making Inferences About Theme **Answer:** *They were completely content with what they had.* OL

BI Big Idea

Dreams and Reality
Answer: *Some students will say he is more in touch with the practical realities of today's world than his parents; others will argue that the parents' simpler existence is more authentic and meaningful.* OL

Use the CheckPoint questions on Presentation Plus! to check students' mastery of the selection. These questions can be used with interactive response keypads for immediate student feedback.

but it seemed that the whole of Lentshin was asleep. He entered the synagogue. An old man was sitting there, reciting psalms. Samuel asked, "Are you praying?"

"What else is there to do when one gets old?"

"Do you make a living?"

The old man did not understand the meaning of these words. He smiled, showing his empty gums, and then he said, "If God gives health, one keeps on living."

> "If God gives health, one keeps on living."

Samuel returned home. Dusk had fallen. Berl went to the synagogue for the evening prayers and the son remained with his mother. The room was filled with shadows.

Berlcha began to recite in a solemn singsong, "God of Abraham, Isaac, and Jacob,[11] defend the poor people of Israel and Thy name. The Holy Sabbath is departing; the welcome week is coming to us. Let it be one of health, wealth, and good deeds."

"Mother, you don't need to pray for wealth," Samuel said. "You are wealthy already."

Berlcha did not hear—or pretended not to. Her face had turned into a cluster of shadows.

In the twilight Samuel put his hand into his jacket pocket and touched his passport, his checkbook, his letters of credit. He had come here with big plans. He had a valise filled with presents for his parents. He wanted to **bestow** gifts on the village. He brought not only his own money but funds from the Lentshin Society in New York, which had organized a ball for the benefit of the village. But this village in the hinterland needed nothing. From the synagogue one could hear hoarse chanting. The cricket, silent all day, started again its chirping. Berlcha began to sway and utter holy rhymes inherited from mothers and grandmothers:

Thy holy sheep
In mercy keep,
In Torah[12] and good deeds;
Provide for all their needs,
Shoes, clothes, and bread
And the Messiah's ***tread.*** ∾

11. *Abraham, Isaac, and Jacob* are the original ancestors of the Jewish people. Abraham was the father of Isaac, who was the father of Jacob. They appear in the Torah and the Old Testament of the Bible.

12. *Torah* (tôr′ə) can be narrowly defined as the five books of Moses or broadly defined as a collection of Jewish texts including scripture and law.

Reading Strategy Making Inferences About Theme *In what ways are Berl and Berlcha wealthy?* R

Big Idea Dreams and Reality *Do you think Samuel represents the real world? Explain.* BI

Vocabulary

bestow (bi stō′) *v.* to give as a gift
tread (tred) *n.* step or footstep

Additional Support

Skills Practice

READING: Identifying Theme Some readers may need help to see that the story's key ideas are expressed in the scenes between Samuel and his father. Pose the following questions: *What is important to the characters of Berl and Samuel? What does Samuel learn? Which character does the author seem to value more?* Ask students to work together to articulate a theme based on their answers to the questions. *(Possible answer: People who live good, simple lives are really wealthy.)* OL

AFTER YOU READ

RESPONDING AND THINKING CRITICALLY

Respond

1. If you were Samuel, how would you feel about your visit to Lentshin?

Recall and Interpret

2. (a)Name five things that Berl and his wife own. (b)Why are there no thieves in Lentshin?
3. (a)When did the son leave home, and what happened to him since Berl and Berlcha last saw him? (b)Why does the son return?
4. (a)What does Samuel learn about the money that he has sent his parents? (b)Why is Samuel amazed at this fact?

Analyze and Evaluate

5. (a)There is some gentle humor in this story. Identify two examples. (b)What does the humor add to the story?
6. Do you think that the "holy rhyme" makes a good conclusion for the story?
7. In modern fiction, characters, motives, outcomes, and themes can be highly complex and ambiguous. Alternatively, in a folk story, the characters are often predictable and the outcome is clear. Do you think "The Son from America" is more like a folk tale or modern fiction? Explain using examples from the story.

Connect

8. **Big Idea** **Dreams and Reality** (a)In what ways does America seem like a dream to Berl and Berlcha? (b)In what ways does Lentshin seem to be a dreamlike or fantastic place to their son?

DAILY LIFE AND CULTURE

Life in a Polish Village Around 1900

The shtetls—the unique towns and villages that largely disappeared from Eastern Europe during the Holocaust—were small, closely interwoven communities. For Jews in the shtetl, the pattern of daily life was often unvarying and very much rooted in the rituals of religion. The synagogue was the center of community life. Ideas from outside the village, and especially from the secular, or nonreligious world, were usually regarded as heretical.

Many shtetls were market towns, and trade, along with farming, were their main economic bases. Grain was a major crop, and most peasants raised cattle, goats, pigs, chickens; harvested lumber from the forest; and grew their fruits and vegetables on small plots. In many shtetls, beginning in the nineteenth century, Russian rulers began taking away the lands of Jews and giving them to Christians, breaking ties to the land that Jews had had for generations.

Discuss the following questions with your classmates.

1. How well does the village described in "The Son from America" fit the factual description printed here? Find details in the story to support your opinion.
2. Which source gives you a better understanding of the life of Jews in a small European village around 1900: the passage on this page or Singer's story? Explain your answer.

Daily Life and Culture

1. The pattern of daily life is rooted in the rituals of religion. The synagogue is central to the villagers' lives. Ideas from outside the village are regarded as heretical. Berl and Berlcha farm their own land.
2. The story offers more insight; the passage gives more information.

AFTER YOU READ

Assess

1. Students may sympathize with Samuel's desire to share his wealth with the villagers.
2. (a) A half-acre, a cow, a goat, chickens, a table, two shelves, two beds, and an oven (b)There is nothing to steal; also the people do not consider themselves poor.
3. (a) Forty years ago; He went to the United States, became a baker, and had children and grandchildren. (b) To visit his parents and to provide for the community
4. (a) They never spent it. (b) He cannot understand why they would not want to "improve" their lives.
5. (a) The idea that "from too much thinking . . . one may lose one's wits"; the arrival of the cable one day after Samuel; the goat's "surprise" at Samuel; and Berl's suggestion that Samuel take the money (b) It entertains and provides insight into human nature.
6. Yes, it reinforces the importance and changelessness of tradition.
7. The story mixes these elements. Berlcha and Berl are predictable, and the ending of the story for them is clear. But the story is full of ambiguity. Both parents and child are sympathetic characters.
8. (a) It is a faraway land with strange ways and untold wealth. (b) It is stuck in time, untouched by the modern world

Academic Standards

The Additional Support activity on p. 276 covers the following standard:

Skills Practice: **9.3** [Identify] story elements such as theme…

AFTER YOU READ

Assess

Literary Element

1. It is set in a past time and place that no longer exists; Berl and Berlcha are flat characters; the ending for Berl and Berlcha is predictable.
2. (a) It is amused and affectionate. (b) He sees them as human—ignorant but good-hearted, pious, and kind.
3. (a) A third-person omniscient narrator (b) The narrator has access to the thoughts of all the characters.

Review: Voice

Students may point to additional examples, such as "The cricket, silent all day, started again its chirping" and "With such a guest, she had to make a larger Sabbath stew." Students should conclude that, in Yiddish, word order is often inverted.

Reading Strategy

1. That wealth and poverty are not absolute terms but are relative to the society in which one lives
2. Samuel's desire to improve the lives of the villagers by giving them money illustrates the theme that good intentions are often out of touch with reality.

LITERARY ANALYSIS

Literary Element Style

In fiction, **style** results from more than just choices a writer makes about words, images, and sentences. Decisions about the type of story told, the tone, and the narrator also contribute to style. Along with word choice, sentence structure, and other aspects of storytelling, these choices can help to reveal the author's attitude toward the subject as well as his or her purpose for writing.

1. Elements of a folktale include folk beliefs, a past or faraway setting, flat characters, and predictable endings. In what ways is this story like a folktale?
2. (a)What is the author's tone? (b)What does this tell you about his attitude toward the characters?
3. (a)Who tells the story? (b)How does this choice help the reader see more than one point of view?

Review: Voice

As you learned on pages 206–207, **voice** is the distinctive use of language that conveys the author's or narrator's personality to the reader. In "The Son from America," the narrator's voice is that of a Yiddish storyteller.

Partner Activity Work with a partner to find examples of things that are said in the story in a voice that sounds different to you from that of a typical American English speaker. From that list, draw a conclusion about Yiddish vocabulary, word order, or sentences.

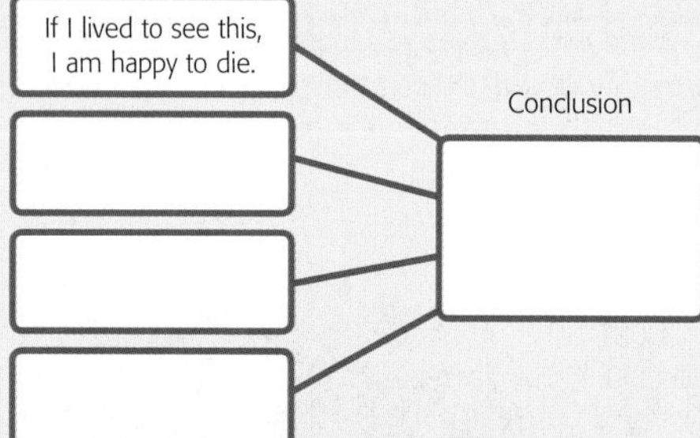

Examples
If I lived to see this, I am happy to die.
Conclusion

READING AND VOCABULARY

Reading Strategy Making Inferences About Theme

Most often, works have an **implied theme,** which is revealed gradually through events, dialogue, or description. Learning to accurately make inferences will allow you to find deeper meaning in any work of literature. Remember that it is possible for a literary work to have more than one theme.

1. What do you think is the primary theme in "The Son from America"?
2. What is one secondary, or minor, theme in the story? Point to specific passages in the story as evidence.

Vocabulary Practice

Practice with Word Origins Choose the language from which each term is derived. Use a dictionary to find word histories.

1. mock
   a. Middle English **b.** Algonquian
2. contour
   a. Italian and Latin **b.** Greek and Latin
3. benediction
   a. Greek **b.** Latin
4. bestow
   a. Middle English **b.** Greek
5. tread
   a. Italian **b.** Old English

Academic Vocabulary

Here is a word from the vocabulary list on page R80.

register (rej′is tər) *v.* to comprehend

Practice and Apply
Why does it take a while for Berl to **register** the identity of the "nobleman"?

Vocabulary

1. a **2.** a **3.** b **4.** a **5.** b

Academic Vocabulary

She does not recognize him because she has not seen him in forty years.

WRITING AND EXTENDING

Writing About Literature

Evaluate Author's Craft In "The Son from America," there are conflicts between the son and his parents, the young and old, and the city and the country. Yet, these clashes are described with a gentle and humorous tone, making them more pleasant and entertaining than negative and upsetting. Write an essay in which you evaluate Singer's craft in handling the meeting of two unlike worlds.

Begin by identifying and stating your evaluative judgment in a clear thesis statement. Then gather evidence from the story that supports your thesis. Present the evidence to support each of your main points, and be sure to explain how it relates to your thesis. When you draft, follow a plan like this one:

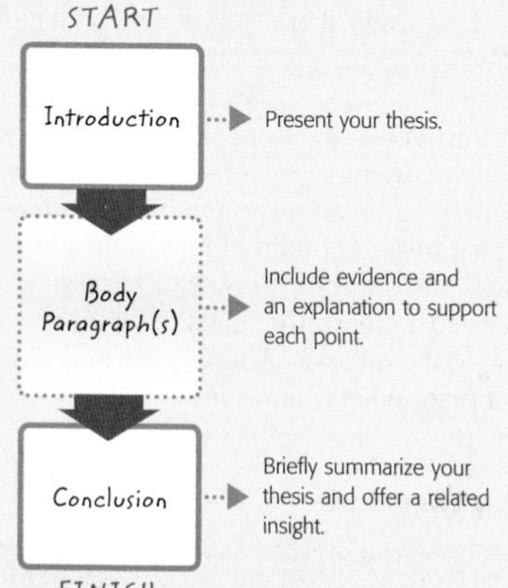
START
Introduction
Present your thesis.
Body Paragraph(s)
Include evidence and an explanation to support each point.
Conclusion
Briefly summarize your thesis and offer a related insight.
FINISH

After you complete your draft, have a peer read it and suggest revisions. Then proofread and edit your work for errors in spelling, grammar, and punctuation.

Literary Criticism

Critic Alfred Kazin said that the stories in the collection that includes "The Son from America" contained "imaginative splendor, wit, mischief and, not least, the now unbelievable life that Jews once lived in Poland." What would you say that "The Son from America" contains? Write a sentence or short review that credits the story with three qualities.

GRAMMAR AND STYLE

Singer's Language and Style

Using Appositives Singer adds information to some of his sentences by using appositives or appositive phrases. Appositives are words that follow and restate the noun or pronoun in a new way. For example, in this sentence, Singer uses an appositive phrase (a man in his eighties) to identify Berl:

"In the smallest of these huts lived old Berl, a man in his eighties."

In a sentence with an appositive, either the appositive or the noun or pronoun could stand alone as a subject or object, but together they supply added information. An appositive or appositive phrase is set off by commas if the information is not essential to the sentence.

Notice how these appositive phrases add detail to the sentences:

Sentence	Function of Appositive
The couple had a son, **Samuel,** who had gone to America forty years ago.	identifies son
Mother, it's me, **your son Samuel—Sam**.	identifies "me"

Activity Choose five nouns or pronouns from the story. Write sentences that include those nouns and pronouns as well as appositives or appositive phrases that identify them. Enclose the appositive in commas if it adds information to the sentence that is not necessary to understand the sentence or to identify the noun or pronoun.

Revising Check

Appositives Using appositives can add useful information to your writing. With a partner, go through your evaluative essay and note places where appositives or appositive phrases would help the reader identify the nouns and pronouns you use. Add the information, taking care to punctuate it correctly.

LiteratureOnline Web Activities For eFlashcards, Selection Quick Checks, and other Web activities, go to www.glencoe.com.

Revising Check

Remind students that appositives add information to a sentence but should not make the sentence cumbersome or overlong. Ask pairs of students to share examples of sentences both before and after they added appositives. Evaluate the changes as a class. Point out that not all changes are necessary or desirable.

AFTER YOU READ

Assess

Writing About Literature

Students' essays should

- contain a thesis statement and express an evaluative judgment about the writer.
- contain evidence from the story that supports the thesis.
- restate the thesis and offer insights into the writer's craft in the conclusion.

Literary Criticism

Students' may suggest in their sentences that the story provides a humorous but affectionate view of a backward village or that it honors old traditions in an increasingly modern world.

Singer's Language and Style

Possible nouns or pronouns: Sam, stew, Berl, synagogue. Possible sentences include:

- Sam, a good son, wants to help his parents.
- The stew, a special dinner, takes time to prepare.
- Berl, a farmer, lives a simple life.
- The synagogue, the center of community life, is covered in snow.

Web Activities Have students access the Web site for interactive activities that will help them assess their understanding of the selection.

Focus

BELLRINGER

Have students recall a favorite story. **Ask:** Why did the story become a favorite? Can you remember what you thought or felt the first time you read it? Ask students to reflect on their original response to their favorite story as they learn to write a response to literature.

Summary

In this workshop, students will write and present a response to literature. They will follow the stages of the writing process, including prewriting, drafting, revising, and editing. In addition, the workshop provides two mini-lessons, on including clear examples and correcting sentence fragments.

Writing Models Have students access the Web site for interactive writing models and writing guides.

The Writing Process

In this workshop, you will follow the stages of the writing process. At any stage, you may think of new ideas to include and better ways to express them. Feel free to return to earlier stages as you write.

- **Prewriting**
- **Drafting**
- **Revising**
  - Focus Lesson: Including Clear Examples
- **Editing and Proofreading**
  - Focus Lesson: Correcting Sentence Fragments
- **Presenting**

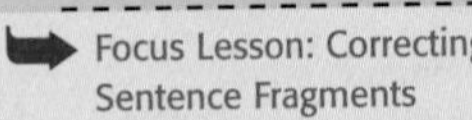

Writing Models For models and other writing activities, go to www.glencoe.com.

ACADEMIC STANDARDS (pages 280–287)

9.5.2 Write responses to literature...

9.4.1 Discuss ideas for writing with classmates...

9.4.10 Review, evaluate, and revise writing for meaning, clarity, content, and mechanics.

Writing Workshop

Response to Literature

Responding to a Short Story

"We had passed through walls of piled bones, with casks and puncheons intermingling, into the inmost recesses of the catacombs. I paused again, and this time I made bold to seize Fortunato by an arm above the elbow."

—Edgar Allan Poe, from "The Cask of Amontillado"

Connecting to Literature Edgar Allan Poe is known for writing stories with mood and atmosphere. His words often create a feeling of grim foreboding as they signal that a macabre event is about to happen. Readers of Poe's short stories have strong responses to them. How would you describe the effect the above passage has on you? To write a successful response to literature, you will need to learn the goals of writing a response and the strategies to achieve those goals. These goals and strategies form the defining features of a response to literature.

Rubric: Features of Responses to Literature

Goals	Strategies
To present your personal response to a story	☑ Focus on your own feelings or thoughts
To organize your response with an introduction, body, and conclusion	☑ Introduce your response ☑ Explain why you feel or think as you do ☑ Summarize your response
To use examples to support your response	☑ Provide vivid details and quotations ☑ Connect your examples to your response
To draw a conclusion	☑ Summarize your response ☑ Suggest an outcome based on your response

Academic Standards

The Additional Support activity on p. 281 covers the following standard:

English Language Coach: **9.5.2** Write responses to literature that demonstrate a comprehensive grasp of the...ideas...

Workshop Resources

Print Materials

- Unit 1 Resources (Fast File), pp. 88–91
- REAL Success in Writing
- Writing Constructed Responses, pp. 1–26, 42–47, 54
- Glencoe Literature Library

Transparencies

- Grammar and Language Transparencies 33, 36, 41
- Writing Workshop Transparencies 6–10

Technology

- Grammar & Language eWorkbook
- Revising with Style eWorkbook
- Sentence Diagraming eWorkbook
- Spelling Power eWorkbook
- Online Essay Grader, glencoe.com
- Literature Library Exam*View*™ Assessment Suite CD-ROM
- Literature Library Vocabulary PuzzleMaker CD-ROM

Assignment

Write a response to a short story that includes specific details and quotations to support a viewpoint about the characters, events, or setting. As you move through the stages of the writing process, keep your audience and purpose in mind.

Audience: peers, classmates, and teacher

Purpose: to express your response to a short story

Real-World Connection

Just as you respond to characters and events in real life, you respond to them in stories you read. Throughout your years in school, you will be assigned to write responses to literature. First connect to the story by relating it to your experiences, and then find evidence in the story to support your reaction.

Analyzing a Professional Model

In the following selection, Oscar Hijuelos describes his first reading of a short story that inspired him to become a writer. As you read the passage, note how Hijuelos uses descriptive details to describe the experience. Pay close attention to the comments in the margin. They point out features that you might want to include in your response.

"On 'The Aleph'" by Oscar Hijuelos ★

I first encountered "The Aleph" by the great Argentine writer Jorge Luis Borges one afternoon over twenty years ago, in 1973—I believe—when I was down on the Lower East Side visiting a friend, a young Armenian intellectual, such as one might meet at City College in those days. While he fiddled about in his kitchen (or walked his dog, or pleaded/conversed with his girlfriend on the telephone), I sat on his itchy, cat-haired, roach-egged couch, idly riffling through a pile of books that I had pulled from his shelves, among them a mildewed, jaundiced-looking, much-read-over pocketbook edition of *The Aleph and Other Stories* by Borges. Now, just a few days earlier I had been informed about the results of an aptitude test I had taken, the upshot being that I was apparently most suited for the profession of accounting. That well may have been my destiny, but I am happy (unhappy?) to report that the experience of reading "The Aleph" for the first of many times had a great effect upon me and my future; I have loved and will always love that story—and I will always be indebted to Borges for having written it—because, aside from its many wonderful qualities, it will always hold a special meaning for me: quite simply, "The Aleph" is the story that first inspired in me the desire to one day write.

Descriptive Details
Create a picture by using specific words and examples.

Personal Connection
Give your reaction to the work and explain its significance to your own life.

Teach

Big Idea

Dreams and Reality Ask: Have you ever become so involved in the fantasy world of a book or a movie that it seemed real to you? Discuss students' favorite works of fantasy, guiding them to recognize the role of concrete, realistic detail in creating a believable fantasy world.
Say: Think back on the selections you have read in this unit. Can you think of any examples of realistic, concrete details that helped to create a convincing fantasy world? *(Possible answer: detailed descriptions of blue jays' behavior in Twain's yarn)* **OL**

★ Literary History

Oscar Hijuelos In 1990, Hijuelos (1951–) became the first Hispanic to win the Pulitzer Prize in fiction. He received the award for his novel *The Mambo Kings Play Songs of Love,* which concerns two Cuban brothers who immigrate to New York in 1949 and become professional musicians. The novel was adapted into both a movie and a Broadway musical. Hijuelos was born and raised in New York City. He has written several other critically acclaimed novels.

English Language Coach

Understanding Personal Response Make sure that students understand that they are to write about their own responses to a story. Model a response: "I felt strongly about 'The Son from America' because my own family emigrated from Europe." Guide students through the responses to literature (p. 280). **EL**

Differentiated Instruction

Story Discussion Groups Have students who work best with others discuss with a small group stories they have read and their reactions to them. During the discussion, students should notice which stories generate the most excitement. Encourage students to take notes during their discussions. **AL**

Academic Standards

The Additional Support activity on p. 281 covers the following standard:

Differentiated Instruction: **9.7.17** Deliver oral responses to literature that advance a judgment...

Teach

Writing Skills

Main Idea Remind students that every piece of writing should have a main idea. **Ask:** What is the main idea of the professional model? *(Writers need to be aware of the contract they have with readers to tell the truth.)* OL

Writing Skills

Model Point out that Hijuelos was fascinated by the complexity of Borges's story: it has the characteristics of a love story, a horror tale, and a screenplay. Ask students to think of other stories that have the characteristics of more than one genre. *(Students may mention "The Scarlet Ibis," which combines poetic description with an emotional narrative.)*

★ Literary History

Jorge Luis Borges (1899–1986) was born in Argentina and became one of the greatest writers of the 1900s. He gained fame for his poems, essays, and short fiction. AS

Summary of Story
Summarize key elements of the story as a basis for your response.

As for the story itself, "The Aleph" is part love tale, told in a voice that is both obsessively introspective and delicately urbane; it has an undertone of near horror, like a ghost story—as in an Edgar Allan Poe tale, the object of the narrator's love, Beatriz Viterbo, exerts a great power long after she has been dead; it has a quite visual, nearly cinematic, narrative that is a pleasure to read.

Background Information
Include information about the author or the work that is relevant to your response.

Ironically, Borges, who suffered from a hereditary progressive blindness, had ★ often spoken about the influence of film upon his writing. In the economy and vividness of its details, it is instructive to young writers—note how effortlessly Borges suggests the shifting universe by opening with a most introspective and bemused narrator noticing yet another new brand of American cigarette being advertised on the billboards of Constitution Plaza in Buenos Aires. And it is quite funny—especially to writers—when, for example, the narrator, Borges himself, muses over the critical success of a decidedly second-rate talent, Carlos Argentino Daneri, who to the narrator's chagrin has risen to the top of the poet's profession while the narrator has not.

Conclusion
Conclude your response by making a general statement about the author's work or works with similar themes.

For a final note; without betraying the essence of the story, which is the "Aleph" itself, nor this story's spectacular climax, I will leave the reader with my sense that in this work, as in certain others—"Funes, the Memorious," for example—Borges is really writing about and paying tribute to the writer's consciousness, which, through its command of and access to the imagination and language, can contain and replicate everything that has existed or will ever exist in this universe.

The Result, 1924. William McCance. Oil on canvas, 69.8 x 90.1 cm. The Fleming-Wyfold Art Foundation, London.

Reading–Writing Connection Think about the writing techniques that you just encountered and try them out in your response to a short story.

Additional Support

Skills Practice

TEST PREPARATION: Understanding the Assignment In a test-taking situation, it is important that students understand exactly what kind of writing they need to provide. Remind them to read the assignment carefully, underlining key words or phrases before they begin prewriting. Provide practice by writing the following assignment on the board: *Write a response to a short story that includes specific details and quotations to support a viewpoint about the characters, events, or setting.*

As a class, review the assignment and underline key words. Have students summarize the assignment. OL

Prewriting

Gather Ideas As you prepare to write a response to a story, think about how the characters, events, and setting made you feel. Ask yourself what details are key to your response. You can use many different strategies:

- Relate the story to your own experience. Is the character in some way like you or someone you know? Has anything like this ever happened to you? Have you read other stories like this?
- Make a habit of keeping a response journal. Jot down notes in it while you are reading a story or book. You can go back and review these notes to write a response to the story.
- Consider the different elements in the story. You might react to a character, the plot, the setting, or the theme.
- Look for specific details in the story to use as support for your response.
- Use a chart to organize your thoughts about the story. Write an example or quote from the story in the left column and your response in the right column.

Example from story	My response to the example

Narrow Your Focus Before you begin drafting, choose a focus for your response. You might begin by deciding which literary element—characters, plot, setting, or theme—is most critical in the story. Then narrow your focus to a specific main idea that expresses your opinion or feelings.

Talk About Your Ideas To decide on a focus for your response, meet with a partner. Brainstorm by completing the sentence starters below.

I thought . . . .

I felt . . . .

I had looked at . . . .

I said to myself . . . .

Remember to keep your focus narrow. If your focus is too broad, it will not be manageable.

Consider the Reader

Help your reader understand your perspective. As you plan your response, develop a logical organization; choose words that are appropriate for your purpose and reflect your personal writing voice.

Test Prep

When writing a response to literature during a timed essay test, choose a focus and take a few minutes to make notes about your viewpoint. Keep in mind the importance of managing your time well so that you can write a complete response that is supported by examples from the story.

English Language Coach

Vivid Details English language learners may lack adequate specific vocabulary for describing the characteristics of a selection. Encourage them to replace words such as *great, good, okay,* and *liked* with words that provide concrete details. With students, brainstorm for a list of vivid and descriptive words connected to the plot, setting, and characters that evoke sights, sounds, and other sensory details. Challenge students to use a thesaurus or dictionary to add more descriptive words to their list and to use these in their responses. **EL**

Teach

Writing Process

Prewriting Explain that the purpose of most literary criticism is to inform or to persuade. Students should understand that they may do both in their own responses. They will inform readers of their responses and also try to convince readers to see the story through their eyes. **OL**

Writing Skills

The Contract Between a Writer and Readers

Answer: *Organization and word choice should be clear and should accurately reflect the events that took place or the points made in the writing. Provide evidence and factual details to support observations, assertions, and opinions.* **OL**

Writing Skills

Generating Examples

Encourage students to create a graphic organizer like the one on page 283 and to fill it in with as many examples as possible. Later they can choose the examples that are most interesting. They should look at their examples and identify common ideas. For example, all of the examples might involve one character. Seeing a commonality among the examples will help students formulate their main ideas. **OL**

Academic Standards

Additional Support activities on pp. 282 and 283 cover the following standards:

Skills Practice: **9.2** Develop strategies... [for] informational texts.

English Language Coach: **9.4.3** Use precise language...and appropriate modifiers.

Teach

Writing Process

Drafting Encourage students to devote one paragraph to each response from their prewriting graphic. They can rearrange the ideas in each paragraph as they revise; in the drafting stage they need not worry about organization. **OL**

Writing Skills

Summary of Story **Answer:** *Provides readers with an overview of the story.* **OL**

Writing Skills

Descriptive Details
Answer: *Helps readers visualize the flight of the trapeze artists and the husband's fall to his death.* **OL**

Writing Skills

Personal Connection
Answer: *The writer feels sympathy and empathy.* **OL**

Literary History

Louise Erdrich (1954–)
A writer whose best-known novels have focused on the intersection of Native American and Anglo cultures, Erdrich utilizes a rich mixture of dreams, myth, and reality. **AS**

Drafting

Put Your Thoughts Down on Paper Begin drafting your response using your plan as a guide. Occasionally look back at your unfinished draft and check that the details you include contribute to the main point you want to make about the story. If your writing is leading you in a new direction, you may want to follow it. Keep in mind that you can polish your response later.

Analyzing a Workshop Model

Here is a final draft of a response to a story. Read the response and answer the questions in the margin. Use the answers to these questions to guide you as you write.

My Response to "The Leap"

Summary of Story
Why is a summary important if you do not quote a passage?

"The Leap," by Louise Erdrich, is about a remarkable woman who risks her life to save her daughter. The mother has lost her eyesight as a result of cataracts, but even without sight her life is a reflection of precise vision and courage. Her dexterity and skill achieved as a young trapeze artist saved a life not once, but twice. Reading this story left me stunned by her courage and physical skill, and it convinced me that even when you are terrified, you can and do make life-and-death decisions.

Descriptive Details
How does the comparison of the trapeze artists to birds help readers visualize the scene?

I can only imagine how the narrator's mother must have felt to lose the man she loved and the father of her unborn baby girl. I could feel the love and trust these two people shared. They were "like two sparkling birds" passing each other so high in the air, pausing and kissing "as they swooped past one another" during their trapeze act. When the storm struck and lightning destroyed the main pole of the circus tent, the couple began to fall to their death. This woman made a split-second decision not to cling to the man she loved, but to save herself and the child growing within her. She "changed direction" in midair, and her husband fell to his death.

Personal Connection
How does the writer feel about the characters in the story?

The baby did not survive, but as the story continued, I became even more amazed by this courageous woman. Although talented and competent on the trapeze, she was illiterate. She was taught to read by her future husband during her recovery in the hospital. Books became a constant part of her life, and I found it tragic that life could be so unkind as to leave her without sight in the end. Yet I somehow think she always had enough inner strength to handle whatever she encountered.

Additional Support

Skills Practice

GRAMMAR: Active Voice Explain the difference between active and passive voice. **Say:** In active voice, the subject performs the action; in passive voice the subject is acted upon. Passive voice, the weaker voice, relies on linking verbs such as *am, is, was, were, be,* and *been.* Active voice relies on verbs.

Ask students to identify the sentences below as active or passive and to change the passive sentence to an active one.

1. She was taught to read by her future husband. *(passive; Her future husband taught her to read.)*
2. The woman acted quickly and decisively. *(active)* **OL**

Exposition

The mother remarried and had a daughter. Reading about how she saved her daughter from the fire in their home, when rescue seemed hopeless, left me with a feeling of awe. I couldn't believe it was possible to do something this brave. I was struck by how she took control of the situation. With no time to think about the consequences, this woman acted because it was necessary to save the life of her child. She climbed out on a tree branch near her daughter's window and jumped—flew—into the child's room. I could almost hear the tree branch as it broke, "so that it cracked in her hands, cracked louder than the flames as she vaulted with it toward the edge. . . ."

The story ends with a sentence that I needed to think about: "As you fall there is time to think." I guess there will be times in my life when I will have to make such quick, critical decisions. I just hope I will have as much strength and courage as the woman in this story when I need it most.

Narrative Details
Why is it important to give readers details of what happens in the story?

Elaboration
Why is this quotation an effective way to elaborate?

Conclusion
How does the writer conclude the response to "The Leap"?

Teach

Writing Skills

Narrative Details **Answer:** *Giving details of the story provides support for the writer's response.* OL

Writing Skills

Elaboration **Answer:** *The quotation supports the writer's image of the mother jumping from the branch and the sound of the branch when it cracks.* OL

Writing Skills

Conclusion **Answer:** *The writer concludes by acknowledging the character's strength and courage and expressing the possibility of applying those characteristics to his or her own life.* OL

Writing Skills

Punctuation Remind students of the importance of using correct punctuation in their writing. Note that the titles of short stories and poems should be set inside quotation marks and that titles of novels and films should be underlined or set in italics. Remind students that direct quotations from the original work of literature should appear in quotation marks too. Point out the quotations that appear in the second paragraph of the model. OL

English Language Coach

Time-Order Words Remind students to use time-order words when writing brief summaries of the story. Words such as *first, then, before,* and *afterwards* help link events in the story and help readers follow the narrative flow. Have students limit their summaries to just a sentence or two. EL

Differentiated Instruction

Learning Styles Students' learning styles may affect how they respond to literature. Visual learners may react to imagery, while interpersonal learners may focus on a story's insights. Encourage students to capitalize on their strengths. A visual learner might say, "The story's vivid images appeal to me." BL

Academic Standards

Additional Support activities on pp. 284 and 285 cover the following standards:

Skills Practice: **9.6.2** Demonstrate an understanding of...proper English usage...

English Language Coach: **9.4.3** Use precise language...

Differentiated Instruction: **9.5.2** Write responses to literature...

Teach

Writing Process

Revising Students may wish to read their drafts to a partner or into a tape recorder. They should read only what is written. If students find themselves rewriting as they read aloud, they should make a note of the revisions in the margins of their paper. **OL**

Writing Skill

Reconsidering Examples As they revise, students should make sure that the examples they provide actually support their points. Have students ask themselves these questions:

- What is my point here?
- What example do I provide to support my point?
- Why did I choose this example?
- Can I clearly explain how this example supports my point?
- Will readers understand the connection between my example and my point?

Students should also use the revising stage to consider the strength and arrangement of their ideas. **OL**

Revising

Traits of Strong Writing

Ideas message or theme and the details that develop it

Organization arrangement of main ideas and supporting details

Voice writer's unique way of using tone and style

Word Choice vocabulary a writer uses to convey meaning

Sentence Fluency rhythm and flow of sentences

Conventions correct spelling, grammar, usage, and mechanics

Presentation the way words and design elements look on a page

For more information on using the Traits of Strong Writing, see pages R32–R33 of the Writing Handbook.

Peer Review Exchange drafts with a classmate. Talk about the main idea in each paper. Then identify the organization, supporting details, and conclusion. Have your partner note any areas that could be improved. Refer to the traits of strong writing as you analyze the papers.

Use the rubric below to evaluate and strengthen your essay.

Rubric: Writing a Response to a Short Story

- ☑ Do you quote a passage or give a summary of the story?
- ☑ Do you make a personal connection to the story?
- ☑ Do you include descriptive and/or narrative details?
- ☑ Do you elaborate with quotes from the story?
- ☑ Does your elaboration provide effective support for your main idea?
- ☑ Do you state a conclusion?

Focus Lesson

Including Clear Examples

Your response should include examples that support your main point. These examples can be facts, explanations, vivid details, or descriptions. Your examples should clearly illustrate why you have responded to the story in a particular way. Here is a sentence from the Workshop Model. The revision shows the sentence followed by clear examples.

Draft:

I couldn't believe it was possible to do something this brave.

Revision:

I couldn't believe it was possible to do something this brave. With no time to think about the consequences, this woman acted because it was necessary to save the life of her child.[1] She climbed out on a tree branch near her daughter's window and jumped—flew—into the child's room.[2] I could almost hear the tree branch as it broke, "so that it cracked in her hands, cracked louder than the flames as she vaulted with it toward the edge. . . ."[3]

1: Explanation of the situation **2:** Vivid description of the action
3: Sensory imagery through descriptive details

Additional Support

Skills Practice

WRITING: Wordiness Wordy writing contains more words than are needed to convey an idea. It can result from awkward sentence structure, passive voice, and redundant expressions. Have students revise the following sentence: *Samuel is too materialistic and concerned with having money and wealth because of the fact that it is clear from the beginning that his family did not need anything that money could buy other than what they already had. (Samuel is too materialistic. It is clear that his family needed nothing that money could buy.)* Have students exchange drafts and circle any examples of wordiness they find. **OL**

Editing and Proofreading

Get It Right When you have completed the final draft of your essay, proofread for errors in grammar, usage, mechanics, and spelling. Refer to the Language Handbook, pages R46–R59, as a guide.

Focus Lesson

Correcting Sentence Fragments

A sentence fragment is a group of words that lacks a subject, a verb, or both. To correct the fragment, add the missing part. Sometimes a fragment is a subordinate clause. It needs to be rewritten as a complete sentence or added to a sentence.

Sentence Fragment:

When the storm struck and lightning destroyed the main pole of the circus tent.

Solution A: To avoid the fragment, rewrite it as a complete sentence.

The storm struck and lightning destroyed the main pole of the circus tent.

Solution B: Connect the fragment to a sentence and set it off with a comma.

When the storm struck and lightning destroyed the main pole of the circus tent, the couple began to fall to their death.

Managing Your Time

Did you allow enough time to edit and revise before your response was due? When you are under last-minute pressure, it is difficult to avoid mistakes. Remember that the writing process has steps that should be completed over the full period of time available for the assignment.

Presenting

The Final Touch Reread the assignment and any guidelines your teacher established for the number of words, the spacing, and the margins. Check to see if you have followed these exactly. Make sure you have identified the short story title and author. Remember that a neat paper free of errors in spelling, grammar, usage, and mechanics makes a good impression.

Writer's Portfolio

Place a clean copy of your response to a short story in your portfolio to review later.

Teach

Writing Process

Editing Remind students that although sentence fragments are often used in daily speech, they are not acceptable in formal writing situations, such as a response to literature. Tell students that every sentence in their essay should contain a subject and a verb—unless the sentence fragment is a direct quotation from the literature. OL

Writing Process

Presenting Showing pride in your work is one way of convincing others that you have something valuable to say. Attention to detail is the hallmark of an effective presentation. Have a partner look over your work to ensure that it looks neat and precise. OL

English Language Coach

Editing and Proofreading Encourage students to keep a log of the types of mistakes they often make in writing—particular misspellings or punctuation errors. Then tell students to work in pairs to go through their essays several times, each time looking for one kind of error on their lists. EL

Differentiated Instruction

Revising Help students who prefer to revise their work alone by suggesting these guidelines:

- Read your draft aloud.
- Put the draft aside for a day or two. Then return to it with fresh eyes.
- Read the draft several times, each time looking for one particular problem. BL

Academic Standards

Additional Support activities on pp. 286 and 287 cover the following standards:

Skills Practice: **9.4.12** Revise writing to improve...the precision of word choice...

English Language Coach: **9.4.11** Edit and proofread one's own writing, as well as that of others, using an editing checklist with specific examples of corrections of frequent errors.

Differentiated Instruction: **9.4.10** Review, evaluate, and revise writing for meaning, clarity, content, and mechanics.

Oral Response to Literature

Focus

Summary

In this workshop, students will learn how to plan and participate in an oral discussion of their responses to a short story.

Teach

Speaking Skills

Establishing Discussion Rules Students may feel more comfortable about participating in group discussions if some ground rules are provided. Share the following guidelines:

- Every group member must participate at least once.
- Ideas and comments such as "I liked it" or "I agree" must be supported with reasons.
- Participants who disagree with others' comments must not insult or dismiss them, but provide factual and/or textual support for their differing opinions.
- Students may not speak for more than two minutes at a time. OL

Speaking, Listening, and Viewing Workshop

Oral Response to Literature

Participating in a Group Discussion

Connecting to Literature Following a reading of "American History" in the town where it is set, author Judith Ortiz Cofer responded to a comment about the accuracy of a detail. Many contemporary authors read passages from their work and then respond to comments and questions from the audience. You respond to literature and to others' ideas when you participate in a group discussion.

Assignment Work in a small group to read and discuss "The Necklace" or another short story. Explain your feelings and thoughts about the main characters.

Planning for the Discussion

When you wrote your response to a short story, you were writing for an audience of readers. When you respond during a discussion, you address an audience of listeners. Plan ahead for a discussion to make sure you are ready to comment and respond to others in your group.

- Review the story.
- Make notes about your reactions to the characters and events in the story.
- Find examples, including details and quotations, to support your feelings and thoughts about the characters or events.

—Madame Loisel is unhappy because she is not rich.

p. 221 "She grieved incessantly, feeling that she had been born for all the little niceties and luxuries of living."

Additional Support

Skills Practice

LISTENING: Summarizing Remind students that a good way to remember ideas shared during a group discussion is to stop periodically and summarize or restate what has been discussed. Tell students to take notes or assign one of the group members the task of recording the main points of the discussion. At the end of the discussion, or at a logical stopping point, students should pause and summarize the main points of the discussion thus far. Have volunteers from each group share their summaries with the class. OL

Create a Graphic to Illustrate Your Response

As you prepare your response, consider making a visual to illustrate your point. Your visual might be a graphic organizer you draw on the board or on paper, or it might be a sketch that illustrates how you visualize a character.

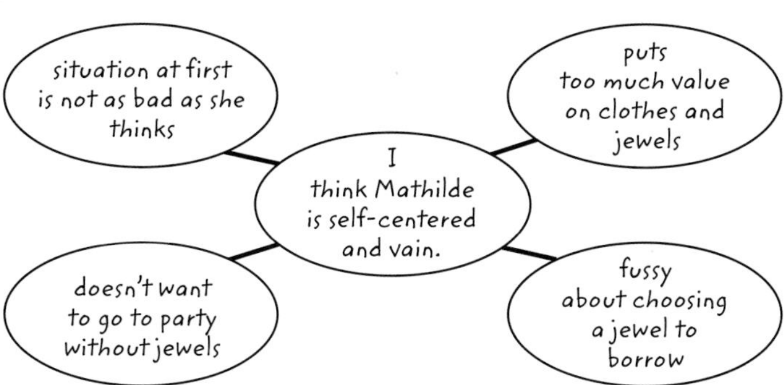

Summarize and Share Your Ideas

Share your responses with another small group. One way to do this is to choose someone to write notes on paper or on the board during the discussion. At the end of the discussion, review the notes and decide which should be included in the summary. Collaborate on a group summary, or choose a participant to write one.

Taking Part in a Discussion

If you have prepared well, you should be ready to offer comments in the group discussion and to respond to the comments of others. Use the following techniques as reminders of what to do during the discussion.

Techniques for Responding in a Discussion

☑ **Speak** Enunciate your words clearly and speak loudly enough to be heard easily.	☑ **Respond** Listen to others and respond to what they say.
☑ **Participate, Don't Monopolize** Offer your comments but give others a chance to speak.	☑ **Be Courteous** Do not act rudely or become angry when disagreeing with others.
☑ **Listen** Focus your attention on others when they are speaking.	☑ **Encourage Others to Speak** Ask an open-ended question to spark a response from the shy members of your group.

ACADEMIC STANDARDS (pages 288–289)

9.7.17 Deliver oral responses to literature...

9.7.7 Make judgments about the ideas under discussion...

Teach

Listening Skills

Group Discussion Students need to be good listeners as well as informed speakers. They should listen carefully to other ideas before speaking and should make sure that they do not repeat ideas that have been covered. Students should make sure that others have exhausted their ideas about the current subject before introducing a new idea. **OL**

Listening Skills

Discussion Assessment Ask students to write one- or two-paragraph assessments of their own and their peers' listening skills, answering these questions:

- Can I correctly summarize the discussion's main ideas?
- Did I understand what my peers were saying?
- Did I ask questions to clarify misunderstandings?
- Were other students attentive listeners? Why or why not?

Ask volunteers to submit their assessments. **OL**

English Language Coach

Oral Response Practice For several days before students participate in discussion groups, privately ask students questions such as "What do you think about the story?" If students say only that they liked or disliked the story, challenge them to elaborate on their ideas. **EL**

Differentiated Instruction

Discussion Leaders Invite students who are auditory learners or logical thinkers to lead the discussion. Leaders can guide students through their oral responses, keep track of time, note logical stopping points, and suggest questions or ideas to take the discussions in new directions. **AL**

Academic Standards

Additional Support activities on pp. 288 and 289 cover the following standards:

Skills Practice: **9.7** [Respond] to oral communication [with] careful listening and evaluation of content...

English Language Coach: **9.7.17** Deliver oral responses to literature that advance a judgment demonstrating a comprehensive understanding of the significant ideas of works or passages...

Differentiated Instruction: **9.7.1** Summarize a speaker's purpose and point of view and ask questions concerning the speaker's content...and attitude toward the subject.

Focus

Summary

In this lesson, students will read summaries of short story collections and novels that deal with a range of themes, including the challenges young people face as they grow up. Encourage students to read these selections and to think about how they portray the dreams and reality of young people.

Teach

Literary History

Lori Carlson Writer, editor, and translator Lori Carlson (1957–) is best known for works that celebrate Hispanic culture. She has produced an anthology of plays for young adults, written in English and Spanish, and a collection of poems, essays, and artworks by three generations of Hispanic artists. She has expressed interest in Asian and Native American cultures, and her goal is to help readers appreciate the variety of cultures that coexist in the United States. **AS**

INDEPENDENT READING

Short Stories and Novels

LIKE ANY GOOD NOVEL, A SHORT STORY CAN TAKE YOU TO NEW places or on new adventures. Along the way, it might give you new insights into human motivation and behavior. It might also make you laugh, ponder, praise, or cry out in horror. For more short stories on a range of themes, try the first three suggestions below. For novels that treat the Big Ideas of *Matters of Life and Death, Rewards and Sacrifices,* and *Dreams and Reality,* try the titles from the Glencoe Literature Library on the next page.

American Eyes: New Asian-American Short Stories

edited by Lori Carlson 

These ten short stories present the conflicts faced by Asian Americans whose families have immigrated from Taiwan, China, Japan, Korea, Vietnam, and other Asian nations. They explore issues of finding one's own identity in a new culture, as well as common universal themes such as the generation gap. They also look at American pop culture through the eyes of people who are seeing some of it for the first time. Conflicts range from the difficulties of growing up to the struggles of getting by financially.

An Island Like You: Stories from the Barrio

Judith Ortiz Cofer

Here are more stories about young people caught between two worlds: the one their parents left behind in Puerto Rico, and the one they now inhabit in Paterson, New Jersey. A different voice tells each story, though some characters reappear in different roles in other stories. The pages are packed with emotion: love and tenderness between generations; disappointment and rage; humor, hope, and friendship between teens; and dashed hopes and resentments. Everything is here from celebration to sorrow, but there are no neat and tidy endings.

Additional Support

Academic Standards

The Additional Support activity on p. 290 covers the following standard:

Skills Practice: **9.5.1** Write...narratives...that describe a sequence of events...

Skills Practice

WRITING: Teleplay Ask students to identify a favorite scene in John Knowles's *A Separate Peace* and to work independently or with a partner to turn it into a script for a movie or teleplay. Ask students to incorporate in their scenes as much of the original dialogue and details as possible. Then encourage students to perform or read aloud their scene for the class. If time allows, show students the same scene as it appears in the 1972 film version of the novel. Ask students to compare and contrast the different versions of the scenes. **OL**

CRITICS' CORNER

"Toni Cade Bambara's stories do more than paint a picture of black life in contemporary black settings. . . . Her characters achieve a personal identity as a result of their participation in the human quest for knowledge, which brings power. Bambara's skill as a writer saves her characters from being stereotypic cutouts."

—Martha M. Vertreace, from *American Women Writing Fiction: Memory, Identity, Family, Space*

Toni Cade Bambara

Gorilla, My Love

Toni Cade Bambara ★

This collection of fifteen short stories includes the well-known "Raymond's Run," the story of a young female track star who takes care of her older brother Raymond. The collection also includes "Happy Birthday," which describes the loneliness of a girl who celebrates her birthday by herself, and "Mississippi Ham Rider," which shows a Northern reporter trying to interview an old Southern blues guitar player. Most of the narrators are spirited young women.

From the Glencoe Literature Library

A Separate Peace

John Knowles

Two boys at a boarding school struggle with matters of life and death.

Winter Thunder

Mari Sandoz

Based on a real-life event, this gripping story of survival describes rewards and sacrifices.

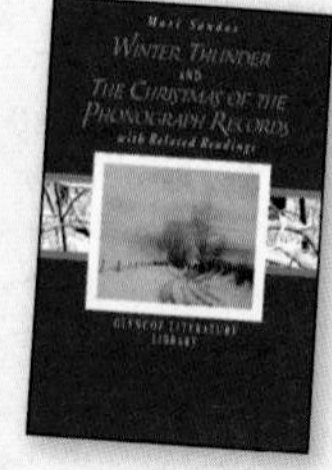

The Metamorphosis

Franz Kafka

One man straddles dreams and reality in a bizarre world.

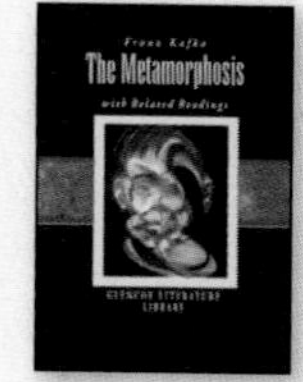

Teach

★ Literary History

Toni Cade Bambara Toni Cade was born in New York City in 1939. Cade became a writer before she finished college, adding Bambara to her pen name in honor of her great-grandmother. Most of her writings feature realistic portrayals of African American characters who are trying to figure out who they are and what their place is in the world. As a writer, one-time social worker, and community activist, Bambara saw writing as a force for positive social change. **AS**

Glencoe Literature Library

Glencoe Literature Library offers an extensive collection of hardcover books that help you encourage your students to read independently. Choose among the more than 120 full-length literary works—novels, novellas, plays, and nonfiction. Each book includes related readings from a broad range of genres. Go to glencoe.com for more information.

Building Reading Fluency

Comparing Passages Ask students to read a work described on pages 290 and 291 and then compare it with a selection in this unit. They should find common themes, details, or ideas in the two selections and then read the passages aloud to a small group. **OL**

Differentiated Instruction

Reading Conference Have students listen to recorded versions of the selections described on pages 290–291 as they read. Then encourage them to hold a reading conference to discuss what they read and heard. Prompt them by asking open-ended questions or challenging them to express their opinions. **BL**

Academic Standards

Additional Support activities on p. 291 cover the following standards:

Building Reading Fluency: **9.3.5** Compare works that express a universal theme… **9.7.13** Identify the artistic effects of a media presentation and evaluate the techniques used to create them…

Differentiated Instruction: **9.7** [Respond] to oral communication [with] careful listening and evaluation of content… **9.7.17** Deliver oral responses to literature that support… ideas and viewpoints through…references to the text and to other works…

Focus

BELLRINGER

Explain that students often may be asked to read a piece of fiction and to answer questions or write about it.

Ask: How would your approach to reading fiction change in a test situation? Have students list the elements they would pay attention to when reading fiction for a test. Review these lists and talk over any missing elements.

Test Preparation and Practice

English Language Arts

Indiana Test Practice

READING: Vocabulary, Comprehension, and Analysis

Read the following passage. Then, on a separate sheet of paper, answer the questions on page 294.

from "The Lumber Room"[1] by Saki (H. H. Munro)

"You are not to go into the gooseberry[2] garden," said the aunt, changing the subject.

"Why not?" demanded Nicholas.

"Because you are in disgrace," said the aunt loftily.

Now the gooseberry garden had two doors by which it might be entered, and once a small person like Nicholas could slip in there he could effectually disappear from view amid the masking growth of artichokes, raspberry canes, and fruit bushes. The aunt had many other things to do that afternoon, but she spent an hour or two in trivial gardening operations among flower beds and shrubberies, whence she could keep a watchful eye on the two doors that led to the forbidden paradise. She was a woman of few ideas, with immense powers of concentration.

Nicholas made one or two sorties[3] into the front garden, wriggling his way with obvious stealth of purpose towards one or other of the doors, but never able for a moment to evade the aunt's watchful eye. As a matter of fact, he had no intention of trying to get into the gooseberry garden, but it was extremely convenient for him that his aunt should believe that he had; it was a belief that would keep her on self-imposed sentry-duty[4] for the greater part of the afternoon. Having thoroughly confirmed and fortified her suspicions, Nicholas slipped back into the house and rapidly put into execution a plan of action that had long germinated in his brain. By standing on a chair in the library one could reach a shelf on which reposed a fat, important-looking key. The key was as important as it looked; it was the instrument which kept the mysteries of the lumber-room secure from unauthorized intrusion, which opened a way only for aunts and such-like privileged persons. The key turned stiffly in the lock, but it turned. The door opened, and Nicholas was in an unknown land, compared with which the gooseberry garden was a stale delight, a mere material pleasure.

Often and often Nicholas had pictured to himself what the lumber-room might be like, that region that was so carefully sealed from youthful eyes and concerning which no questions were ever answered. It came up to his expectations. In the first place it was large and dimly lit, one high window opening on to the forbidden garden being its only source of illumination. In the second place it was a storehouse of unimagined treasures. Such parts of the house as Nicholas knew best were rather bare and cheerless, but here there were wonderful things for the eye to feast on. First and foremost there was a piece of framed tapestry[5] that was evidently meant to be a fire-screen.[6] To Nicholas it was a living, breathing

[1]**lumber room:** storeroom

[2]**gooseberry:** tart edible berry that grows on a thorny shrub

[3]**sorties:** expeditions

[4]**sentry-duty:** standing guard and watching for danger

[5]**tapestry:** heavy woven fabric decorated with designs or pictures

[6]**fire-screen:** a protective screen placed in front of a fireplace

Reading

Test-Taking Strategies Tell students that most standardized tests are open-book tests; after reading a passage, they will be able to look back at it to find evidence or clues to answer questions. Write the following tips on the board to guide them through the process.

- Read the passage, stopping to paraphrase the information in your head.
- Read the question to be sure you understand what answer is needed.
- Eliminate answers that are incorrect.
- Look back at the passage for confirmation before marking your final choice.
- Mark your final answer. OL

story; he sat down on a roll of Indian hangings,[7] glowing in wonderful colors beneath a layer of dust, and took in all the details of the tapestry picture. A man, dressed in the hunting costume of some remote period, had just transfixed a stag[8] with an arrow; it could not have been a difficult shot because the stag was only one or two paces away from him; in the thickly growing vegetation that the picture suggested it would not have been difficult to creep up to a feeding stag, and the two spotted dogs that were springing forward to join in the chase had evidently been trained to keep to heel till the arrow was discharged. That part of the picture was simple, if interesting, but did the huntsman see, what Nicholas saw, that four galloping wolves were coming in his direction through the wood? There might be more than four of them hidden behind the trees, and in any case would the man and his dogs be able to cope with the four wolves if they made an attack? The man had only two arrows left in his quiver,[9] and he might miss with one or both of them; all one knew about his skill in shooting was that he could hit a large stag at a ridiculously short range. Nicholas sat for many golden minutes revolving the possibilities of the scene; he was inclined to think that there were more than four wolves and that the man and his dogs were in a tight corner.

. . . the voice of his aunt in shrill vociferation[10] of his name came from the gooseberry garden without. She had grown suspicious at his long disappearance, and had leapt to the conclusion that he had climbed over the wall behind the sheltering screen of the lilac bushes; she was now engaged in energetic and rather hopeless search for him among the artichokes and raspberry canes.

"Nicholas, Nicholas!" she screamed, "you are to come out of this at once. It's no use trying to hide there; I can see you all the time."

[7]**Indian hangings:** colorful fabrics from India designed to hang from a wall or window
[8]**stag:** adult male deer
[9]**quiver:** case for holding arrows
[10]**vociferation:** shouting

It was probably the first time for twenty years that anyone had smiled in that lumber-room.

Presently the angry repetitions of Nicholas' name gave way to a shriek, and a cry for somebody to come quickly. His aunt was still calling his name when he sauntered into the front garden.

"Who's calling?" he asked.

"Me," came the answer from the other side of the wall; "didn't you hear me? I've been looking for you in the gooseberry garden, and I've slipped into the rain-water tank.[11] Luckily there's no water in it, but the sides are slippery and I can't get out. Fetch the little ladder from under the cherry tree—"

"I was told I wasn't to go into the gooseberry garden," said Nicholas promptly.

"I told you not to, and now I tell you that you may," came the voice from the rain-water tank, rather impatiently.

"Your voice doesn't sound like aunt's," objected Nicholas; "you may be the Evil One tempting me to be disobedient. Aunt often tells me that the Evil One tempts me and that I always yield. This time I'm not going to yield."

"Don't talk nonsense," said the prisoner in the tank; "go and fetch the ladder."

"Will there be strawberry jam for tea?" asked Nicholas innocently.

"Certainly there will be," said the aunt, privately resolving that Nicholas should have none of it.

"Now I know that you are the Evil One and not aunt," shouted Nicholas gleefully; "when we asked aunt for strawberry jam yesterday she said there wasn't any. I know there are four jars of it in the store cupboard, because I looked, and of course you know it's there, but she doesn't, because she said there wasn't any. Oh, Devil, you HAVE sold yourself!"

There was an unusual sense of luxury in being able to talk to an aunt as though one was talking to the Evil One, but Nicholas knew, with childish discernment, that such luxuries were not

[11]**rain-water tank:** large container for holding water that has fallen as rain

Test Preparation and Practice

English Language Arts

Teach

Assessment Explain to students that this Test Preparation and Practice lesson is designed to develop test-taking strategies as well as to test their mastery of the skills covered in this unit. The lesson is modeled on tests they will be required to pass to be eligible to receive a high school diploma. Students will read one or two grade-level-appropriate selections and answer vocabulary, comprehension, and literary analysis questions, including multiple-choice, constructed-response, and extended-response items. In other sections, students' ability to use Standard English in their writing is assessed, and they are given an extended-writing prompt. **OL**

Assess

1. **C** is the correct answer. The aunt knows that Nicholas is a disobedient child.
2. **D** is the correct answer. The narration is not from the point of view of any one character, and it describes the thoughts of Nicholas and the aunt.
3. **B** is the correct answer. The hunter has shot the stag with an arrow.
4. **D** is the correct answer. Nicholas says things he does not mean.
5. **D** is the correct answer. The aunt had said there was no jam on the previous day, after which Nicholas checked the cupboard.
6. Rubric:

   2 points versions of two exemplars

   1 point version of one exemplar

   0 points other

   Exemplars:
   - The aunt is determined that Nicholas will not go into the gooseberry garden.
   - The aunt is determined that Nicholas will not have jam for tea.
   - The aunt is suspicious of Nicholas when he makes sorties into the front garden.
   - The aunt is suspicious of Nicholas's long disappearance from view.
   - The aunt is impatient when Nicholas refuses to enter the garden to rescue her.
   - The aunt is impatient when she must wait for someone to rescue her from the water tank.
7. Refer to the Reading Comprehension, Writing Applications, and Language Conventions rubrics provided by the State of Indiana Department of Education.

Student essays should include the following:
- clearly stated main ideas supported by quotations, examples, and details from the passage
- effective voice, word choice, and sentence variety
- effective presentation, with attention to grammar and spelling conventions

---

to be over-indulged in. He walked noisily away, and it was a kitchenmaid,[12] in search of parsley, who eventually rescued the aunt from the rain-water tank.

Tea that evening was partaken of in a fearsome silence. The aunt maintained the frozen muteness of one who has suffered undignified and unmerited detention in a rain-water tank for thirty-five minutes. As for Nicholas, he, too, was silent, in the absorption of one who has much to think about; it was just possible, he considered, that the huntsman would escape with his hounds while the wolves feasted on the stricken stag.

[12]**kitchenmaid:** female servant who works in a kitchen

---

1 The aunt assumes that Nicholas has gone into the gooseberry garden because

A she knows that he loves gooseberries
B she sees that the garden gate is open
C she had forbidden him to go there
D she cannot find him in the lumber room

2 You can tell that this passage is written from third-person point of view because the narrator

A reveals only what Nicholas thinks and feels
B is a character in the story
C tells only the aunt's thoughts and refers to her as "she"
D describes the thoughts of both main characters

3 Read this sentence from the passage.

> **A man, dressed in the hunting costume of some remote period, had just transfixed a stag with an arrow.**

Which of these BEST defines *transfixed* as it is used in this sentence?

A made motionless from awe
B pierced with a sharp instrument
C changed in appearance or structure
D fastened by piercing

4 Nicholas shouts gleefully to his aunt, "Now I know that you are the Evil One and not aunt." His words are an example of

A foreshadowing
B concern
C despair
D irony

5 Which of these events happened FIRST in the lives of the characters?

A Nicholas checks the cupboard for strawberry jam.
B The aunt promises Nicholas that there will be strawberry jam for tea.
C Nicholas asks his aunt, who is stuck in the rain-water tank, whether there will be strawberry jam for tea.
D The aunt tells Nicholas that there is no strawberry jam for tea.

6 All of these words describe the aunt. Choose a word and give TWO examples from the passage to support your choice.

determined suspicious impatient

7 Why does Nicholas say that his aunt is the "Evil One"? Write an expository essay in which you explain Nicholas's behavior. **In your expository essay, be sure to include at least TWO quotations from the passage to support your position.**

Use a separate sheet of paper to plan your writing.

Writing Checklist

The following checklist will help you write your essay. Be sure to

- ❏ brainstorm for ideas and develop a plan before you start writing
- ❏ organize your writing with an introduction, a body, and a conclusion
- ❏ pay attention to your word choice and voice
- ❏ edit for sentence fluency and conventions
- ❏ have a neat and organized presentation

WRITING: Writing Process

The following passage is part of a first draft of a student's research essay on Saki. Read the passage and use it to answer questions 8–11 on a separate sheet of paper.

> [1]Saki was the pen name of Hector Hugh Munro, he was born in 1870 at Burma. [2]His father was a member of the police force at the time that the country, called Myanmar now, is still part of the British Empire. [3]He was cared for in England by his grandmother and aunts. [4]The strictness of households like his became the subject of many of his stories. [5]His short stories made fun of Edwardian society. [6]He wrote several novels and wrote plays also.

8 Choose the BEST way to revise Sentence 1.

A Saki was the pen name of Hector Hugh Munro, born in 1870 Burma
B Saki was the pen name for Hector Hugh Munro, born in 1870 in Burma.
C Saki was the pen name of Hector Hugh Munro, who was born in 1870 in Burma.
D Saki is the pen name of Hector Hugh Munro, who was born in 1870 Burma.

9 The writer wants to replace the underlined phrase in Sentence 3 with a more formal expression. Which of these is the BEST replacement?

A introduced
B mentored
C indoctrinated
D nurtured

10 Choose the BEST way to combine Sentences 4 and 5.

A The strictness of households like his became the subject of many of his stories, and they made fun of Edwardian society.
B The strictness of households like his became the subject of many of his stories, which made fun of Edwardian society.
C The strictness of households like his, which made fun of Edwardian society, became the subject of many of his stories.
D The strictness of households like his became the subject of many of his stories, because they made fun of Edwardian society.

11 The Modern Language Association (MLA) recommends these guidelines for citing works used for reference.

1. List entries by author name. Write the author's last name first.
2. Underline the title of a book.
3. Place a colon between the place of publication and the name of the publisher.
4. Include the year of publication last.

The student who wrote the paragraph on Saki found the information in a book about the author's life. According to the MLA recommendations above, which is the correct way for the student to cite this source?

A Hemphill, Rose. Saki and His World. Boston 2002: Olive Press.
B Hemphill, Rose. Saki and His World. Boston—Olive Press, 2002.
C Rose Hemphill. Saki and His World. Boston: Olive Press, 2002.
D Hemphill, Rose. Saki and His World. Boston: Olive Press, 2002.

LiteratureOnline Unit Assessment To prepare for the Unit test, go to www.glencoe.com.

Test Preparation and Practice

English Language Arts

8. C is the correct answer. Sentence 1 contains a comma splice.

9. D is the correct answer. *Nurtured* means "to educate or further the development of."

10. B is the correct answer. It is the only option that retains the meaning of the two original sentences.

11. D is the correct answer. It is the only option that meets all four requirements.

Unit Assessment Have students access the Web site to prepare for the Unit One test.

Test Preparation and Practice

English Language Arts

Assess

12. **D** is the correct answer. An adverb clause at the beginning of a sentence should be followed by a comma.
13. **B** is the correct answer. A comma is the best choice to precede the participial phrase in this sentence.
14. **D** is the correct answer. Option A contains a comma splice.
15. **C** is the correct answer. The two main clauses have no punctuation between them.
16. **B** is the correct answer. Other verbs in the sentence are in the past tense.
17. **B** is the correct answer.
18. **D** is the correct answer. In titles, the first and last words, nouns, pronouns, verbs, adverbs, adjectives, and prepositions of more than four letters should be capitalized.

WRITING: English Language Conventions

Answer questions 12–18 on a separate sheet of paper.

12 Decide which punctuation mark is needed in the sentence.

Because of illness Munro quit the police force and returned to England.

A ;
B :
C .
D ,

13 Choose the sentence that is punctuated correctly.

A Munro also worked as a newspaper correspondent; reporting throughout Europe.
B Munro also worked as a newspaper correspondent, reporting throughout Europe.
C Munro also worked as a newspaper correspondent-reporting throughout Europe.
D Munro also worked as a newspaper correspondent: reporting throughout Europe

14 Choose the sentence that is correct and MOST clearly expressed.

A Three years later, illness forced Munro to quit, he returned to England.
B Three years later, illness forced Munro to quit, but he returned to England.
C Three years later, illness forced Munro to quit, and return to England.
D Three years later, illness forced Munro to quit, and he returned to England.

15 What type of an error has the writer of this sentence made?

Munro roved through Europe as a correspondent he permanently settled in London.

A spelling
B capitalization
C run-on sentence construction
D incorrect verb tense

16 Read this sentence.

After World War I began, Munro enlists in the army as an ordinary soldier even though his age exceeded the official limit.

Choose the group of words that BEST replaces the underlined part of the sentence.

A will enlist in
B enlisted in
C had enlisted in
D was enlisting in

17 Choose the word that is spelled correctly.

A insessantly
B incessantly
C incessently
D uncessantly

18 Read this sentence.

Munro's first book was patterned after The rise and fall of the Roman empire.

Which of the following is the BEST way to capitalize the underlined group of words?

A The Rise and Fall of The Roman Empire
B The rise and fall of the Roman Empire
C The Rise And Fall Of The Roman Empire
D The Rise and Fall of the Roman Empire

Writing

Evaluating Sentence Errors As experienced readers, students can evaluate whether a sentence contains a grammatical error without knowing exactly what the error is. Demonstrate by reading aloud the answer choices for question 14 as students follow along. Have students raise their hands if they think that something is wrong with a sentence. Ask students why they think the sentence is wrong. Tell students to read the sentences aloud in a quiet voice as they complete the section. Tell them to put a mark next to the sentences they think contain errors. **OL**

WRITING: Writing Applications

Complete the writing activity below. Do your planning and writing on separate sheets of paper.

Buy Books?

Read the writing prompt below and complete the writing activity.

> Suppose that your school is thinking about allowing a local bookstore to sell its products in your school. Think about the advantages and disadvantages of this proposed change.
>
> Write a persuasive article for your school newspaper in which you lobby for or against allowing the bookstore to do business in your school. Be sure to include strong, persuasive details to support your choice.

Be sure to include

- a statement of your opinion on the subject
- details that explain why you think as you do
- reasons that will persuade your readers to choose your position
- an introduction, a body, and a conclusion to your persuasive article

Use a separate sheet of paper to plan your writing. As you write, keep in mind that your essay will be evaluated for **ideas and content, organization, style, voice,** and **language conventions.**

Writing Checklist

Before you begin writing, be sure to

- ❑ brainstorm for ideas
- ❑ organize your ideas into a logical pattern
- ❑ develop a plan for an introduction, a body, and a conclusion

As you write your essay, be sure to

- ❑ describe the issue and clearly state your opinion
- ❑ provide reasons for your opinion
- ❑ discuss alternative opinions and show why you disagree with them
- ❑ end with a conclusion that restates your opinion

Assess

Assessment of writing prompts should focus on four elements:

- **Ideas and Content,** the message or theme and the details that develop it
- **Organization,** the arrangement of main ideas and supporting details
- **Style,** the word choices that a writer uses to convey meaning and the fluency, or rhythm and flow, of sentences
- **Voice,** the writer's unique way of using tone and style

Students' writing should also be assessed for correct **capitalization, punctuation, spelling, grammar and usage, paragraphing,** and **sentence structure.**

In addition, student essays should:

- fully complete the assigned task
- include complete, thorough, relevant, logically organized ideas
- exhibit correct word usage
- demonstrate exceptional writing technique
- use language and tone appropriate for the task and audience

Unit at a Glance

NONFICTION

About the Unit

Unit Two is about nonfiction, which includes everything from letters to memoirs. In this type of writing, it is important for the reader to trust the writer and it is the writer's job to make their writing believable and worthy of a reader's trust. As well as being true, the nonfiction piece should also be interesting. The variety of pieces presented in this section give the student ample room to see how nonfiction pieces can be accomplished successfully.

Unit Introduction
Building Background
2–3 days

Part 1: Looking into Lives
6–8 days

Part 1 includes selections that teach readers about the lives of others; specifically, the focus of this part is autobiography, biography, and memoir. A chart showing the core skills taught in this Part appears on pages 307A–307B.

SELECTIONS AND FEATURES

Part 2: On the Move
4–6 days

Part 2 includes personal and expository essays where the author shares personal experiences and also tries to convey a personal message to the reader. Selections in this section are by travel and adventure writers. A chart showing the core skills taught in this Part appears on pages 379A–379B.

SELECTIONS AND FEATURES

Part 3: Finding Common Ground
4–6 days

Part 3 includes persuasive essays and speeches. In this section, finding common ground between two opposing viewpoints is the biggest challenge. A chart showing the core skills taught in this Part appears on pages 435A–435B.

SELECTIONS AND FEATURES

End-of-Unit Features
5–6 days

Unit Resources

Glencoe Literature: The Reader's Choice offers a comprehensive package of tools to optimize student learning and the teaching experience. Each resource has been designed to assist students in specific areas and to offer instructional support for teachers. While all of these areas are covered in the core textbook, some students may need extra practice or additional help in specific areas. The resource package is designed so that you, the teacher, can choose which items will best assist your students. You may also use these resources as homework assignments and for assessment purposes. The following are resources recommended for use with Unit Two.

Key for Unit Resource

- Blackline Master
- Workbook
- Supplemental Text
- CD-ROM
- DVD
- Transparency
- Web-based

Essential Instructional Support

FAST FILE UNIT 2 RESOURCES

Reading and Literature

- Unit Introduction, pp. 1–2
- The Big Idea Foldable, pp. 3–4
- The Big Idea School-Home Connection, p. 5
- The Big Idea School-Home Connection (Spanish), p. 6
- Challenge Planner, pp. 7–10
- Academic Vocabulary Development, pp. 11–13
- Comparing Literature Graphic Organizers, pp. 34, 73
- Literary Elements, pp. 17, 20, 23, 27, 31, 35, 41, 44, 47, 51, 54, 61, 64, 67, 70, 74, 77
- Reading Strategies, pp. 18, 21, 24, 26, 28, 32, 36, 42, 45, 48, 52, 55, 57, 62, 65, 68, 71, 75, 78
- Active Reading Graphic Organizers, pp. 84–93
- Selection Vocabulary Practice, pp. 19, 22, 25, 29, 33, 37, 43, 46, 49, 53, 56, 63, 66, 69, 72, 76, 79
- Literary Focus, pp. 39, 59

Writing, Grammar, and Spelling

- Spelling Practice, p. 80
- Grammar Workshop, pp. 30, 50
- Writing Workshop Graphic Organizer, p. 81

Speaking, Listening, and Viewing

- Speaking, Listening, and Viewing Activities, pp. 82–83

English Language Learners

- English Language Coach Review, pp. 16, 40, 60

DIFFERENTIATED INSTRUCTION

- Active Learning and Note Taking Guide, pp. 40–77
- Leveled Vocabulary Development, pp. 21–37
- Skill Level Up!™ A Language Arts Game
- Listening Library Audio CD, disc 1, tracks 25–47
- Glencoe BookLink 3
- Vocabulary PuzzleMaker
- Literature Library Vocabulary PuzzleMaker

ASSESSMENT

- Selection and Unit Assessments, pp. 45–82, 213–214
- Selection Quick Checks, pp. 23–41
- Selection Quick Checks (Spanish), pp. 23–41
- Assessment by Learning Objectives, pp. 15–25
- Rubrics for Assessing Student Writing, Listening and Speaking, pp. 6–7, 28–29
- Standardized Test Preparation and Practice
- Glencoe Online Essay Grader
- Interactive Tutor: Self-Assessment
- Exam*View*® Assessment Suite
- Literature Library Exam*View*® Assessment

Additional Instructional Support

LITERATURE AND READING

- Active Learning and Note Taking Guide, pp. 40–77
- *inTIME* Magazines
- Glencoe Literature Library
- Literature Launchers: Pre-Reading Videos
- Literature Classics

WRITING, GRAMMAR, AND SPELLING

- REAL Success in Writing: Research and Reports
- Writing Constructed Responses
- Spelling Power eWorkbook
- Revising with Style eWorkbook
- Sentence Diagraming eWorkbook
- Grammar and Composition Handbook
- Grammar and Language Workbook
- Grammar & Language eWorkbook

PROFESSIONAL DEVELOPMENT

- Professional Development Package

TRANSPARENCIES

- Read Aloud, Think Aloud Transparencies 11–26
- Bellringer Options Transparencies
  - Selection Focus Transparencies 20–27
  - Daily Language Practice Transparencies 25–45
- Grammar and Language Transparencies 4, 67, 76
- Writing Workshop Transparencies 11–15
- Visual Literacy/Fine Art Transparencies

ENGLISH LANGUAGE LEARNER

- English Language Coach, Unit Resources (Fast File)
- *inTIME* Magazines (Spanish)
- Spanish Listening Library

TECHNOLOGY

- TeacherWorks Plus™
- StudentWorks Plus™
- Literature Launchers: Pre-Reading Videos
- Vocabulary PuzzleMaker
- Literature Library Vocabulary PuzzleMaker
- Skill Level Up!™ A Language Arts Game
- glencoe.com
- Presentation Plus!™
- Exam*View*™ Assessment Suite
- Literature Library Exam*View*™ Assessment Suite
- Listening Library Audio CD, disc 1, tracks 25–47
- Interactive Tutor: Self-Assessment
- Glencoe BookLink 3
- Online Student Edition, mhln.com
- Glencoe Online Essay Grader
- Grammar and Language eWorkbook
- Revising with Style eWorkbook
- Sentence Diagraming eWorkbook
- Spelling Power eWorkbook
- Literature Classics
- Spanish Listening Library

Additional Glencoe Resources

Dinah Zike's Foldables™

Foldables™ are three-dimensional, interactive graphic organizers that help students practice basic writing skills, review key vocabulary terms, and answer Big Ideas. Every unit contains a Foldable™ activity. You can find the pattern and directions for the Unit 2 Foldable™ in the Unit 2 Resources Fast File booklet. You can use the Foldables™ as they are presented or modify them to suit the needs of your students.

For a wealth of online resources that support the instruction in Unit 2, students and teachers can visit our Web site at glencoe.com. Students will find additional learning, practice, and assessment opportunities such as these, which are noted in the student text:

- Author Search
- Big Idea Overview and Activity
- Interactive Literary Elements Handbook
- Study Central
- Unit Assessment
- Web Activities
- Writing Models

Teachers will find planning and instructional tools that include the following:

- Book Lesson Plans
- Web Activity Lesson Plans
- Teacher Forum
- Professional Resources

Go to glencoe.com to see the entire selection of *Glencoe Literature* online resources.

Glencoe's Presentation Plus!™, a multimedia teaching tool, lets you present dynamic lessons that will engage your students. Using Microsoft PowerPoint®, you can customize the presentations to create your own personalized lessons. Use CheckPoint questions with interactive response keypads to get immediate student feedback during lessons, to increase student participation, and to assess student comprehension.

Glencoe Literature Library

The collection of hardcover books includes full-length novels, novellas, plays, and works of nonfiction. Each volume consists of at least one complete extended-length reading accompanied by several related readings from a broad range of genres. A separate Study Guide for each *Glencoe Literature Library* book provides teaching notes and reproducible activity pages for students. Glencoe Literature Library titles that complement this unit include:

- ***Great Expectations with Related Readings*** by Charles Dickens
- ***. . . And the Earth Did Not Devour Him with Related Readings*** by Tomás Rivera
- ***To Kill a Mockingbird with Related Readings*** by Harper Lee

Glencoe BookLink

Use the Glencoe BookLink 3 CD-ROM, a database of more than 26,700 titles, to *create customized reading lists* for your students.

- Search for award-winning titles (e.g., Newbery Award winners, Coretta Scott King Award winners, and Caldecott Medal winners) and for books on several state recommended reading lists.
- Find Degrees of Reading Power™ (DRP) and Lexile™ readability scores for all selections.
- Organize reading lists by students' reading level, author, genre, theme, or area of interest.
- Get a brief summary of each selection.

You can find recommended leveled readings for this unit with Independent Reading (see pages 498 and 499).

Online Essay Grader

Use Glencoe's online essay grader powered by SkillWriter™ to score your students' writing and to provide individualized feedback to each student automatically.

You and your students can visit glencoe.com to link to the essay grader. *Students* can enter their essays and receive feedback on demand. *You* can manage demographic data, assign tests, and generate individual student and aggregated reports. The essay grader can help you

- save time with automatic scoring and individualized feedback.
- supplement in-class writing instruction using guided writing practice.

REAL Success: Reading Excellence at All Levels

Glencoe REAL Success is a suite of new reading and language arts products designed to foster reading excellence at all levels.

Look for TWE point-of-use references for these specific products that will help your students succeed in reading this Unit.

- *Jamestown Literature: An Adapted Reader*
- REAL Success in Writing: Research and Reports
- Skill Level Up!™ A Language Arts Game
- CheckPoint PowerPoint™ slides
- Literature/Reading support at Glencoe Web site

Literature Launchers

Set the scene with Glencoe's Literature Launchers, engaging pre-reading video segments that introduce each unit. Each Unit Launcher brings the literature to life, featuring expert testimony and archival stills and footage from the time.

Insert your Glencoe Literature Launchers into your DVD player. Select the Unit 2 Launcher from the menu to introduce Nonfiction.

A lively collection of articles drawn from issues of the TIME family of magazines helps students develop the skills they need to interact with informational text in a meaningful way. Each of the news stories, feature articles, reviews, profiles, and essays in the magazine connect to an author, work, or theme in *Glencoe Literature: The Reader's Choice.* See the *inTIME* Teacher's Guide for specific connections to each unit and for reproducible student worksheets designed to develop students' reading and critical thinking skills.

Teacher Wraparound Edition Key

Level Appropriate Code

AL = Activities for students working above grade level

OL = Activities for students working at grade level

BL = Activities for students working below grade level

EL = Activities for English language learners

AS = Information for all students

Teacher Wraparound Prompts

R Reading Skill These activities help you teach reading skills and vocabulary.

V Vocabulary These activities help students comprehend words and incorporate them into reading.

BI Big Idea These activities and questions prompt students to explore the Big Idea.

L Literary Element These activities and questions help students comprehend selections and learn more about each genre.

★ Enrichment Additional activities and information involving art appreciation and history.

Professional Development Center

From Your Authors:

Jeffrey D. Wilhelm and Douglas Fisher

Teaching Literary Analysis: Nonfiction

Build Background Nonfiction, or informational text, relates to the physical, social, and biological world. As such, most students will have had experiences with the information contained in these readings. While students often have misconceptions about information or facts, they do have ideas about the ways in which the world operates. For example, high school students commonly report that the earth is closer to the sun during the summer and further away from the sun during the winter. While this is inaccurate, it is part of their "knowledge base." Using a KWL language chart that includes the headings "What I Know," "What I Want to Know," and "What I Learned," allows you to identify misconceptions students may have and to ensure that they have access to readings that address their knowledge base. Before reading the biographical stories in part one, have students create a KWL language chart and write down everything they know about the theme or topic of the story. For example, students may write what they know about Mount Everest or what they know about the dangers and intrigue of mountain climbing before reading the excerpt from "Into Thin Air" by Jon Krakauer. As students read the story, they can then confirm if their prior knowledge on the subject of mountain climbing was accurate or not.

Make Real World Connections Given that most students will have ideas, opinions, or factual information about the topics they'll be reading about in this unit, this is a good time to focus on making connections. Students should know that making connections is a strategy that good readers use as they read. Making connections with real world events allows readers to consider what they know and compare it with the information being presented by the author. Students should be encouraged to make connections and relate what they know about the world with the information being presented. Before reading "A New Generation of Americans," a speech given by President John F. Kennedy, ask students to discuss what they know about who President Kennedy was, what the historical climate was like during his term, the ideas that he presented and fought for during his term, and what happened to end his term in office. As students read, they will better relate to Kennedy's speech if they have made a connection to his life and how he was significant to American history.

Anna Mathews
Paris High School
Paris, Texas

Teacher to Teacher

When introducing a unit on nonfiction, I point out to my students that nonfiction takes different forms including (1) Exposition–explains, informs, defines, or clarifies by answering the questions "What is it? How does it work?" (2) Description–creates a mood and appeals to senses by answering the questions "What does it look like? What does it sound, smell, feel, or taste like?" (3) Narration–relates a series of events that answers the question "What happened?" (4) Persuasion–encourages the reader to believe or do something by answering the questions "How should I feel about this? What should I do about this?" We discuss how subjects change in focus when placed in these different forms. In groups, students choose a nonfiction topic and write about it using one of these assigned forms.

Teacher Chat Room

Making Literature Come Alive

Before you begin this unit or sometime during the unit, talk with other teachers about ways they have taught nonfiction. Have a lunch-time discussion group or an after-school hour for professional development and discuss the following questions and answers from our authors:

How can I encourage high school students to read biographies?

- In general, students enjoy reading about the experiences of other people, especially people who are like them or who have learned an important life lesson. As students read the excerpt from *All God's Children Need Traveling Shoes,* have them examine the life lessons learned by the author Maya Angelou as she describes some of her experiences in Ghana, Africa.
- In choosing biographies, select people that students know or people who are involved with topics or ideas that are interesting to high school students.
- When students read biographies, provide them with opportunities to consider how their life compares with the person they're reading about and how the time period in which the person lived influenced his or her life.

How can you help students discover possible biases in autobiographies?

- Have students read across texts to determine the accuracy of information. Students should read other accounts of the person's life.
- Students should also read public documents and historical period pieces to compare sources for their accuracy. Anytime students read an autobiography, encourage them to put the account into its historical context. When reading *Of Dry Goods and Black Bow Ties* by Yoshiko Uchida, have students investigate the historical atmosphere of the late-nineteenth and early-twentieth centuries.
- Have students examine the author's purpose to determine if the author is attempting to persuade or express opinions or if the author wants to describe or inform. For example, when students read "Only Daughter" by Sandra Cisneros, ask them to look carefully for the author's purpose. If the author is attempting to persuade, then students may find bias in the autobiography.

How can students learn to draw parallels between nonfiction narratives and fictional narratives?

- Students can use descriptive terms to compare and contrast fictional and nonfictional accounts. After students read *Put Down the Backpack* by Anna Quindlen, have them compare her speech to an excerpt from one of her fictional novels. Encourage students to create a Venn diagram to compare and contrast the descriptive words used in each selection.
- Students can also compare the traits, feelings, and motives of the central characters or people in the texts.

Focus

BELLRINGER

Bellringer Options
Literature Launcher Video
Daily Language Practice Transparency 25

Or **write on the board:** Why do people tell true stories?
Say: Identify some reasons why people write about their lives, the lives of others, and the world around them. *(Guide students to recognize that telling true stories helps people make sense of the world and preserve memories.)*

Objectives for the Unit Introduction

- To understand characteristics of different types of nonfiction (SE)
- To identify and explore literary elements significant to nonfiction (SE)
- To analyze the effect that these literary elements have upon the reader (SE)

The Three Graces. Freeman. Oil on canvas, 91.4 x 121.9 cm. Private Collection.

298

Unit Introduction Skills

Nonfiction

Literary Elements
- Autobiography and Biography (SE p. 300)
- Personal and Expository Essay (SE p. 301)
- Persuasive Essay and Speech (SE p. 301)

Reading Skills
- Reading Nonfiction (SE p. 300)
- Identifying Bias (TWE p. 302)
- Improving Comprehension (TWE p. 304)

Listening/Speaking/Viewing Skills
- Viewing the Art (TWE pp. 299, 300, 301, 304, 305)

Vocabulary Skills
- Spanish Words in Context (TWE p. 306)

Writing Skills/Grammar
- Autobiography (TWE p. 300)

NONFICTION

Looking Ahead

Nonfiction is truth in writing. It is the broadest category of literature and includes autobiographies, memoirs, biographies, letters, essays, speeches, and news articles, to name a few. All types of nonfiction concern real, rather than imaginary, subjects and are written, in part, to convey information to readers.

PREVIEW **Big Ideas and Literary Focus**

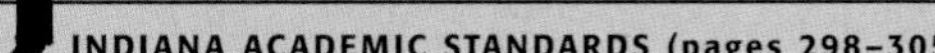

	BIG IDEA:	LITERARY FOCUS:
1	Looking into Lives	Autobiography and Biography
2	On the Move	Personal and Expository Essay
3	Finding Common Ground	Persuasive Essay and Speech

INDIANA ACADEMIC STANDARDS (pages 298–305)
9.2 Develop strategies such as asking questions; making predictions; and identifying and analyzing structure, organization, perspective, and purpose…

Focus

Summary

This unit identifies several kinds of nonfiction. An excerpt by Julia Alvarez is provided for students to read and analyze. Insights from professional writers of nonfiction are included. Activities to help students review the elements of nonfiction conclude the section.

★ Viewing the Art

American artist Kathryn Freeman specializes in painting figures in motion. Many of Freeman's paintings show ordinary places and people, but others have a magical or fairy tale quality. Her use of color and shading give her works a hazy, dreamlike atmosphere. AS

Unit Resources

Classroom Management
- TeacherWorks Plus™ CD-ROM
- StudentWorks Plus™ CD-ROM
- Literature Launchers™: Pre-Reading Videos DVD, Unit Two

Core Instructional Support
- Unit 2 Resources (Fast File)
- Literature Online, glencoe.com
- Presentation Plus!™ CD-ROM, Unit Two

Transparencies
- Literary Elements Transparencies 27, 34, 42
- Bellringer Options Transparencies: Selection Focus Transparencies 20–27 Daily Language Practice Transparencies 25–45

Differentiated Instruction
- Active Learning and Note Taking Guide, pp. 40–77
- Skill Level Up!™ A Language Arts Game

Assessment
- Selection and Unit Assessments, Unit Two, pp. 45–82, 213–214
- Exam*View*® Assessment Suite CD-ROM
- Assessment by Learning Objectives, pp. 15–25

Supplemental Reading
- Glencoe Literature Library
- Glencoe BookLink 3 CD-ROM
- *inTIME* Magazines

Teach

- Note that each of the selections that students will read illustrates one form of nonfiction.
- Invite volunteers to read each explanation and then the example beside it aloud. Point out how the excerpt illustrates the form.

★ Viewing the Art

Canadian artist Thomas Reid MacDonald (1908–1978) was primarily a portrait painter. While serving in Italy during World War II, he had the official job of painting his fellow soldiers' portraits. AS

Genre Focus: Nonfiction

What are the different types of nonfiction?

Nonfiction is the broadest category of literature. Autobiographies, biographies, memoirs, letters, essays, speeches, and news articles are just a few of the many types of nonfiction writing. All of these forms of prose concern real, rather than imaginary, subjects.

Nonfiction writers in particular know the importance of being clear. In addition, they understand that what they write must be of interest, or no one will want to read what they have to say. Even though nonfiction is about real people and real events, nonfiction writing can also be creative.

Autobiography and Biography

Writing About Oneself

An **autobiography** is the story of a person's life written by that person. Autobiographies are presented from the first-person point of view and may be based entirely on the writer's memory. A **memoir** is also about the person who has written it, but a memoir usually focuses on one experience or period in the person's life.

Once, several years ago, when I was just starting out my writing career, I was asked to write my own contributor's note for an anthology I was part of. I wrote: "I am the only daughter in a family of six sons. *That* explains everything."

—Sandra Cisneros, **from "Only Daughter"**

Night Travellers, 1943. Thomas Reid Macdonald. Oil on Canvas, 51.1 x 81.5 cm. Canadian War Museum, Ottawa. ★

Writing About Another

A **biography** is the story of a person's life written by someone other than that person. In addition to recounting the events of the subject's life, most biographers explore the person's reactions to those events and the effects they had on his or her personality.

My father came to America in 1906 when he was not yet twenty-one. Sailing from Japan on a small six-thousand-ton ship which was buffeted all the way by rough seas, he landed in Seattle on a bleak January day.

—Yoshiko Uchida, **from "Of Dry Goods and Black Bow Ties"**

Additional Support

Skills Practice

WRITING: Autobiography Have students write a one-page autobiography. Remind them to address the basic questions—*Who? What? Where? When? Why? How?* Ask volunteers to read their essays aloud. Discuss the different approaches writers took. Did they start with their birth and list events sequentially or focus on one portion of their life? After students read selections in the unit, have them reevaluate their methods. OL

Personal and Expository Essay

Formal and Informal Essays

An **essay** is a relatively short piece of nonfiction in which the writer explores a single topic from his or her own perspective. Essays can be formal or informal. The most common type of informal essay is the **personal essay,** in which the writer's purpose is to entertain or share personal experiences with the reader. Formal essays are more serious in tone. They include the **expository** (or explanatory) essay and the **persuasive** essay.

For *Sayonara,* literally translated, "Since it must be so," of all the good-byes I have heard is the most beautiful. Unlike *Auf Wiedersehens* and *Au revoirs*, it does not try to cheat itself by any bravado "Till we meet again," any sedative to postpone the pain of separation.

—Anne Morrow Lindbergh, **from "Sayonara"** R

Persuasive Essay and Speech

Writing to Persuade

One type of formal essay is the **persuasive essay** or speech. In persuasive writing, the writer tries to influence the reader's or listener's ideas or actions. A persuasive essay or speech may contain emotional appeals. However, a specific type of persuasive writing, known as **argument,** relies on logic, reason, and evidence to convince the reader.

"So let us begin anew—remembering on both sides that civility is not a sign of weakness, and sincerity is always subject to proof. Let us never negotiate out of fear. But let us never fear to negotiate."

—John F. Kennedy, **from *"A New Generation of Americans"***

Literature Online **Study Central** Visit www.glencoe.com to review the different types of nonfiction.

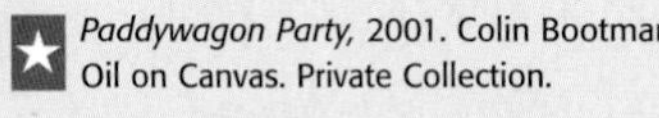

★ *Paddywagon Party,* 2001. Colin Bootman. Oil on Canvas. Private Collection.

Teach

R Reading Strategy

Recognize Facts and Opinions **Say:** Expository essays usually contain facts. Facts are provable statements.
Ask: What facts appear in the excerpt from "Sayonara"? (Sayonara *means "since it must be so.")*
Say: Essays may also contain opinions. Opinions are ideas or beliefs that cannot be proven, only argued.
Ask: What opinion is expressed in "Sayonara"? *(That the word* sayonara *is more beautiful than other words for "good-bye")* OL

★ Viewing the Art

Colin Bootman was born in Trinidad and came to the United States at an early age. Primarily an illustrator of children's books, he was inspired to draw by his first American comic book. AS

Literature Online

Study Central Have students visit the Web site for resources that will help them to review nonfiction.

English Language Coach

Identifying Nonfiction Encourage students to keep a list in their journals of the types of nonfiction and their characteristics. Encourage them to refer to the list to categorize the nonfiction selections they read. EL

Differentiated Instruction

Setting a Purpose Remind students as they read to set a purpose, such as, "I should notice what makes this paragraph expository or persuasive." After students read, they should ask a related question, such as, "How did the paragraph explain an idea or try to persuade me?" BL

Academic Standards

Additional Support activities on pp. 300 and 301 cover the following standards:

Skills Practice: **9.5.1** Write…autobiographical narratives…that describe a sequence of events and communicate the significance of the events to the audience…

English Language Coach: **9.5.8** Write for different purposes and audiences…

Differentiated Instruction: **9.2** Develop strategies such as asking questions…and identifying…purpose…

Teach

R1 Reading Strategy

Identifying the Main Idea

Say: In personal essays, the main idea may be stated directly or implied. If it is implied, you must pay attention to the details and consider what idea they support.

Ask: What is the main idea of the first paragraph of Alvarez's essay? *(Alvarez discovered something about herself by reading an author from another culture.)* **Ask:** Was the main idea stated or implied? *(It was stated in the first sentence.)* OL

★ Writer's Technique

Sentence Variety Note that one strategy Alvarez uses to keep readers' interest is to vary the lengths of her sentences. Most sentences are long. Occasionally she interrupts them with short sentences, such as, "Wow! The silence within me broke." The contrast makes readers pay attention. AS

LITERARY ANALYSIS MODEL

How do literary elements create meaning in nonfiction?

Because she spent half her childhood in the Dominican Republic and the other half in the United States, writer Julia Alvarez experienced firsthand how difficult it can be for a writer to find his or her "voice." In the essay that follows, Alvarez explains her roots as a writer and the joy she feels at being part of a *comunidad*—community—of authors. As you read, notice how she uses elements of the various types of nonfiction discussed on pages 302–303.

APPLYING Literary Elements

Autobiography

Alvarez's use of the first-person point of view is a clue that the selection may be an autobiography or a personal essay.

Personal Essay

Alvarez focuses on the lack of women authors represented in Latino writing. This focus is a clue that the selection is a personal essay, describing her thoughts about Latina writers.

from *On Finding a Latino Voice*

by Julia Alvarez

How I discovered a way into my bicultural, bilingual experience was paradoxically not through a Hispanic-American writer, but an Asian-American one. Soon after it came out, I remember picking up *The Woman Warrior* by Maxine Hong Kingston. I gobbled up the book and then I went back to the first page and read it through again. She addressed the duality of her experience, the Babel of voices in her head, the confusions and pressures of being a Chinese-American female. Wow! The silence within me broke.

With her as my model, I set out to write about my own experience as a Dominican American. And now that I had a name for what I had been experiencing, I could begin to understand it as not just my personal problem. I combed the bookstores and libraries. I discovered Latino writers I had never heard of: Piri Thomas, Ernesto Galarza, Rudolfo Anaya, Jose Antonio Villareal, Gary Soto. But I could not find any women among these early Latino writers.

The '80s changed all that. In 1983, Alma Gomez, Cherrie Moraga, and Mariana Romo-Carmona came out with *Cuentos: Stories by Latinas.* It was an uneven collection, but the introduction, titled "Testimonio," was like a clarion call: "We need *una literatura* that testifies to our lives, provides acknowledgement of who we are: an exiled people, a migrant people, *mujeres en la lucha*[1] . . . What hurts is the discovery of the measure of our silence. How deep it runs. How many of us are indeed caught, unreconciled between two languages, two political poles, and suffer the insecurities of that straddling."

1. *Mujeres en la lucha* is Spanish for "Women in the struggle."

Additional Support

Skills Practice

READING: Identifying Bias Explain that an author may express bias, or strong feelings for or against something. Have students practice identifying bias by answering the following questions:

- What does Alvarez think about the writers she mentions in the second paragraph? *(She is disappointed that they are all men.)*
- Is Alvarez in favor of identifying with one's culture? *(She thinks it is good to find a community and form a tradition.)* OL

The very next year Sandra Cisneros published her collection of linked stories, *The House on Mango Street;* Ana Castillo published her book of poems, *Women Are Not Roses;* I published *Homecoming.* Up at Bread Loaf,[2] I met Judith Ortiz Cofer and heard her read poems and stories that would soon find their way into her books of poems, stories, and essays and her novel *The Line of the Sun.* Cherrie Moraga, Helena Maria Viramontes, Denise Chavez. Suddenly there was a whole group of us, a tradition forming, a dialogue going on. And why not? If Hemingway and his buddies could have their Paris group and beat poets[3] their Black Mountain School,[4] why couldn't we Latinos and Latinas have our own made-in-the-U.S.A. boom? 

Still, I get nervous when people ask me to define myself as a writer.  I hear the cage of a definition close around me with its "subject matter," "style," "concerns." I find that the best way to define myself is through the stories and poems that do not limit me to a simple label, a choice. Maybe it is part of my immigrant uneasiness at the question, in whatever form, "Do you have something to declare?"[5] Maybe, too, after years of feeling caught between being a "real Dominican" and being American, I shy away from simplistic choices that will leave out an important part of who I am or what my work is about.

Certainly none of us serious writers of Latino origin wants to be a mere flash in the literary pan. We want to write good books that touch and move all our readers, not just those of our own particular ethnic background. And speaking for myself, I very much agree with the advice given to writers by Jean Rhys,[6] "Feed the sea, feed the sea." The little rivers dry up in the long run, but the sea grows. What matters is the great body of all that has been thought and felt and written by writers of different cultures, languages, experiences, classes, races.

At last, I have found a *comunidad* in the word that I had never found in a neighborhood in this country. By writing powerfully about our Latino culture, we are forging a tradition and creating a literature that will widen and enrich the existing canon. So much depends upon our feeling that we have a right and responsibility to do this.

2. *Bread Loaf* is an annual writers' conference held in Vermont.
3. The *beat poets* were part of a social and artistic movement that began in the 1950s. They withdrew from society and protested against social norms.
4. The *Black Mountain School* was a group of experimental poets in the 1950s that was centered in Black Mountain College in North Carolina.
5. The phrase *something to declare* is a pun. One sense of *declare* is to "state positively" or "announce." Another involves people entering the United States, who are required to "declare" to a customs agent any valuable property they are carrying and possibly to pay taxes on it.
6. Jean Rhys (1890–1979) was a West Indian novelist.

Personal and Expository Essay

Phrases like "the very next year" help the reader track the sequence of events Alvarez describes in her essay.

Persuasive Essay: Argument

Alvarez's thesis—that she and writers like her are forging a new tradition—appears at the end. Details in the preceding paragraphs support the thesis.

Reading Check

Analyzing What *comunidad* does Alvarez describe?

Teach

Reading Check

Answer: *A community where she can take pride in her heritage and can explore it in her writing*

R2 Reading Strategy

Evaluating Say: As you read nonfiction, you should evaluate whether the details support the writer's main idea.

Ask: What details support the author's idea that she "gets nervous when people ask *(her)* to define *(herself)*"? *(Her memory of having to declare each time she came back to the United States)* OL

Cultural History

Latinos in the United States The word *Latino* came into use after World War II to identify Latin-American people living in the United States. The word is generally interchangeable with *Hispanic.* Latinos come from a wide range of countries, including Mexico, the Caribbean, and Central and South America. Today, one eighth of the population of the United States identifies itself as Hispanic/Latino. AS

Building Reading Fluency

Paired Reading Alvarez's sentences vary in length. Reading passages aloud will help students appreciate the rhythm of her prose. Have them take turns with a partner. After each reading, students should ask questions and clarify meanings. BL

Reading in the Real World

Citizenship Invite students to research current trends that affect the U.S. Hispanic population. For example, they might learn about the Hispanic voting rate and compare it to that of other ethnic groups. Ask students to draw conclusions and share their findings with the class. OL

Academic Standards

Additional Support activities on pp. 302 and 303 cover the following standards:

Skills Practice: **9.2.7** Evaluate an author's argument or defense of a claim…

Building Reading Fluency: **9.2** Develop strategies such as asking questions…

Reading in the Real World: **9.2.8** Make reasonable statements and draw conclusions about a text, supporting them with accurate examples.

Teach

R1 Reading Strategy

Evaluating an Author Note that passages on this page are quotes from professional nonfiction writers.

Ask: Why is honesty so important to writer Joseph Epstein? *(Epstein says that nonfiction writers are responsible for writing and recording the truth. They must be honest or they are not writing nonfiction.)* OL

★ Viewing the Art

British artist Pamela (P. J.) Crook (1945–) paints crowded urban scenes that are full of real-life details. Her works often hint at dark personal dramas. AS

Writers on Reading

What do writers say about nonfiction?

"It's all storytelling, you know. That's what journalism is all about."

—Tom Brokaw

Honesty in Personal Essays

R What the personal essayist must do straightaway is establish his honesty. Honesty for a writer is rather different from honesty for others. Honesty, outside literature, means not lying, establishing trust through honorable conduct, absolute reliability in personal and professional dealings. In writing, honesty implies something rather different: it implies the accurate, altogether truthful, reporting of feelings, for in literature only the truth is finally persuasive and persuasiveness is at the same time the measure of truth. One might think this would be easy enough to do, but it isn't, especially when one is under the added pressure of making both the feelings and the reporting of them keenly interesting.

Two of the chief ways an essayist can prove interesting are, first, by telling readers things they already know in their hearts but have never been able to formulate for themselves; and, second, by telling them things they do not know and perhaps have never even imagined. Sometimes the personal essayist is announcing, in effect: "Please to notice that I am not so different from you in my feelings toward my father [music, food, sleep, aging, etc.]." When this happens, an amiable community is built up between essayist and audience. Sometimes the personal essayist is announcing, also in effect: "Something truly extraordinary has happened to me that I think you will find no less extraordinary than did I." When this happens, the reader, through the mediation of the essayist, finds his or her own experience enlarged.

—Joseph Epstein, **from "The Personal Essay: A Form of Discovery"**

Believability in Writing

For me, part of the pleasure of reading comes from the awareness that an author stands behind the scenes adroitly pulling the strings. But the pleasure quickly palls at painful reminders of that presence—the times when, for instance, I sense that the author strains to produce yet another clever metaphor. Then I stop believing in what I read, and usually stop reading. Belief is what a reader offers an author, what Coleridge famously called "That willing suspension of disbelief for the moment, which constitutes poetic faith." All writers have to find ways to do their work without disappointing readers into withdrawing belief.

I think that the nonfiction writer's fundamental job is to make what is true believable. But for some writers lately the job has clearly become more varied: to make believable what the writer thinks is true (if the writer wants to be scrupulous); to make believable what the writer

De Standaard, 20th century. P. J. Crook. Acrylic on canvas and wood. 40 x 51.97 in. 

Additional Support

Skills Practice

READING: Improving Comprehension Encourage students to keep notes on what they learn from nonfiction selections in their reading journals. Have them create a three-column list in their journals before they read each essay. They should label the columns **What I Know, What I Want to Know,** and **What I Learned.** After students finish reading, they should complete the final column. OL

Under the Elevated Tracks, 1989. Don Jacot. Louis K. Meisel Gallery, Inc. 

wishes were true (if the writer isn't interested in scrupulosity); or to make believable what the writer thinks might be true (if the writer couldn't get the story and had to make it up).

—Tracy Kidder, **from "Making it Believable"**

The Craft of the Biographer

In examining the lives of other people, one examines one's own. A biographer is, in a sense, a doppelgänger, a double goer; he becomes the shadow of his character. And an identity develops between the two, which may be loving, may be hypocritical. I think both these extremes are dangerous. If you love your subject, you end up writing soppy stuff. And if you hate your subject, it becomes unreadable for obvious reasons. So I think the best relationship that a biographer can have with his subject is one of mild affection. The interest must be there. One has to spend many years with this person, so you'd better make sure, up front, that it's going to be a congenial relationship.

—Edmund Morris, **from *Booknotes***

Where Life and Art Meet

The task of a biographer or autobiographer is to understand how the elements within the person he is writing about and the elements in the world surrounding that person both contributed to his formation. In the case of a literary man, however, we learn not only what made the man, but what made the artist. This makes a bridge between the everyday world and the world of literature, a connection not always obvious. But it is a connection of the most fundamental sort. Words cannot exist divorced from men; they depend on human experience for their symbolic value.

—Virginia Woolf, **from "How Should One Read a Book"** R2

 **Literature Online InterActive Reading Practice**
Visit www.glencoe.com to practice these strategies for reading nonfiction.

Reading Check

Responding From your own reading experiences, which passage do you identify with most closely? Explain.

Teach

Reading Check

Answers will vary. Make sure students support their responses with reasons.

R2 Reading Strategy

Making a Generalization

Ask: Based on the comments of these writers, what is a nonfiction writer's main purpose for writing? *(To depict the world truthfully)*

Ask: How are nonfiction writers different from fiction writers? *(Nonfiction writers are like reporters; they can only write about the facts. Fiction writers can invent content.)* OL

Viewing the Art

American artist Don Jacot (1949–) is best known for highly detailed paintings of urban life. The overlap of color and image in his works gives them the appearance of collages. AS

Interactive Reading Have students access the Web site for more practice with reading strategies.

English Language Coach

Unfamiliar Vocabulary Words in the writers' comments, such as *essayist, fundamental, doppelganger,* and *biographer,* may be unfamiliar to students. Ask them to identify any unfamiliar words. Remind them to use their knowledge of roots and suffixes to guess at the words' meanings. Allow students to confirm the words' meanings in a dictionary. EL

Academic Standards

Additional Support activities on pp. 304 and 305 cover the following standards:

Skills Practice: **9.2** Develop [reading] strategies… **9.2.8** Make reasonable statements and draw conclusions about a text…

English Language Coach: **9.1** [Use] word parts…to determine the meaning of words…

Assess/Close

Guide to Reading Nonfiction

Remind students to ask questions, make connections, and evaluate the writers' truthfulness as they read the selections.

Elements of Nonfiction

Explain that recognizing the types of nonfiction in the unit will help students set a purpose for reading.

FOLDABLES™ Study Organizer

Have students make and label the Layered-Look Book. As they read each selection in this unit, they can record notes under the question headings.

WRAP-UP

Guide to Reading Nonfiction

- When reading nonfiction, first determine what type of work you are reading.
- Try to identify the author's purpose. Is he or she writing to inform, to entertain, or to persuade?
- If the author's purpose is to inform, look for a thesis statement and support for the thesis.
- If the author's purpose is to entertain, look for literary elements, such as figurative language, dialogue, or suspense.
- If the author's purpose is to persuade, determine whether the author is presenting an argument, emotional appeals, or a combination of both.

Elements of Nonfiction

- **Nonfiction** is writing about real people and real events.
- An **autobiography** tells the story of the writer's own life.
- A **biography** tells the story of another person's life.
- An **essay** is a short work of nonfiction on a single topic. An essay can be **formal** or **informal.**
- Informal, or **personal,** essays are meant primarily to entertain. Formal essays are intended to explain, inform, or persuade.
- **Persuasive** essays and speeches are intended to change the way people act and think. Some persuasive essays and speeches contain arguments that persuade through logic, reason, and evidence.

Activities

Use what you have learned about reading nonfiction to complete one of these activities.

1. **Speaking/Listening** In small groups, discuss the excerpt from Julia Alvarez's essay "On Finding a Latino Voice." In your discussion, identify three events that helped the author find her voice.
2. **Visual Literacy** Create a Venn diagram to show the similarities and differences between autobiography and biography.
3. **Writing** Reread Alvarez's essay, noting specific word choices and structures the author uses. Write a short essay describing the effect of these choices on the essay as a whole.

LAYERED-LOOK BOOK

Reader's Questions
Who?
What?
Where?
When?
Why?

Try using this study organizer to jot down questions you have about the readings in this unit.

INDIANA ACADEMIC STANDARDS (page 306)

9.7.17 Deliver oral responses to literature...

9.5.2 Write responses to literature that...demonstrate an awareness of the author's style...

Activities

1. **Speaking/Listening** Students should include quotations and specific details from the text to support their ideas.
2. **Visual Literacy** Draw a Venn diagram on the board. Explain that shared characteristics should appear in the area where the circles overlap.
3. **Writing** Students should express a clear opinion or judgment.

PART 1

LOOKING INTO LIVES

The Quest. Tomar Levine. Watercolor on paper. Private collection. 

BIG IDEA

BI Writers create portraits that allow readers to look into the lives of people both familiar and exotic. The selections in this part look into the lives of people from all walks of life. As you read, ask yourself: In what ways are these people different from people I know, and in what ways are they similar?

Analyzing and Extending

BI Big Idea

Looking into Lives Have students read the text under the "Big Idea" head and study the artwork. Discuss why artists are interested in writing or painting other people's portraits. As students look at the artwork, have them answer the question at the bottom of the page. **OL**

★ Viewing the Art

Tomar Levine is known for his still-life paintings that feature shells, rocks, and bottles. The placement of these objects in each work is highly symbolic. He spends months on each painting. **AS**

English Language Coach

Building Background Review the term *portrait.* If possible, show students a variety of portraits from fine art and photography. Explain that a portrait captures a person at one point in his or her life, either formally posed or engaged in an activity. **EL**

Differentiated Instruction

Class Portraits Invite interested students to draw a self-portrait or a portrait of a classmate. Ask volunteers to show their works to the class. As a class, discuss each student's style and attention to detail. **AL**

Academic Standards

Additional Support activities on p. 307 cover the following standards:

English Language Coach: **9.1.1** Identify and use the literal…meanings of words…

Differentiated Instruction: **9.7.13** Identify the artistic effects of a media presentation…

UNIT TWO

Part 1: Skills Scope and Sequence

Readability Scores Key
Dale-Chall/DRP/Lexile

PACING (DAYS) STANDARD	BLOCK	SELECTIONS AND FEATURES	LITERARY ELEMENTS
1–2 class sessions	1	"Of Dry Goods and Black Bow Ties" by Yoshiko Uchida **6.7/62/1230**, pp. 310–318	Title, SE pp. 311–313, 315, 317 Biography, SE p. 317
		"Only Daughter" by Sandra Cisneros **5.7/57/900**, pp. 319–326	Author's Purpose, SE pp. 320, 321, 323, 325 Characterization, SE p. 325
1 class session	1	"A Brother's Crime" by James Cross Giblin **7.7/60/1110**, pp. 327–334	Historical Narrative, SE pp. 328, 329, 331, 333 Narrator, SE p. 333 Characterization, TWE p. 332
		VISUAL PERSPECTIVE on Abraham Lincoln: from *The Murder of Abraham Lincoln* by Rick Geary, pp. 335–339	
1 class session	1	from *The Story of My Life* by Hellen Keller **8.5/56/1030**, pp. 340–349	Anecdote, SE pp. 341, 343–345, 348 Author's Purpose, SE p. 348
		Grammar Workshop: Coherence p. 350	
3 class sessions	1–2	"Escape from Afghanistan" by Farah Ahmedi **5.8/54/820**, pp. 351–361	Tone, SE pp. 352, 353, 356, 358, 359, 360 Historical Narrative, SE p. 360
		COMPARING LITERATURE Across Genres "A Case of Cruelty" by James Herriot **5.8/57/1010**, pp. 362–374 "Ali" by W. S. Merwin, pp. 375–376 "A Friendly Welcome" by George Gordon, Lord Byron, pp. 377–378	Memoir, SE pp. 364, 366, 367, 369, 371, 372, 374 Tone, TWE p. 366

About the Part

Part 1 focuses on autobiography, biography, and memoir. This non-fiction literature teaches readers about the lives of others.

READING AND CRITICAL THINKING	VOCABULARY	WRITING AND GRAMMAR	LISTENING, SPEAKING, AND VIEWING
Analyzing Cause-and-Effect Relationships, SE pp. 311, 313, 315, 316, 318; TWE p. 312	Synonyms, SE pp. 311, 318 Academic Vocabulary, TWE p. 318	Analyze Tone, SE p. 318 Possessive Pronouns, TWE p. 316	Analyzing Art, SE p. 314 Literature Groups, SE p. 318
Drawing Conclusions About Author's Beliefs, SE pp. 320, 321, 323, 325	Analogies, SE p. 325 Academic Vocabulary, SE p. 325	Respond to Theme, SE p. 326 Using Compound Adjectives, SE p. 322	Role-playing, SE p. 326 Analyzing Art, TWE p. 321
Activating Prior Knowledge, SE pp. 328–330, 334	Word Origins, SE pp. 328, 334 Academic Vocabulary, SE p. 334	Analyze Historical Context, SE p. 334 Compound Verbs, TWE p. 330 Sentence Fragments, TWE p. 332	Performing, SE p. 334
Identifying Genre, SE p. 335 Connecting, TWE p. 337 Reading Aloud, TWE p. 338	Identifying and Using New Words, TWE p. 338		Preparing a Speech, TWE p. 336
Connecting to Personal Experience, SE pp. 341–343, 345, 346, 348 Comparing and Contrasting, TWE p. 342	Context Clues, SE pp. 341, 348 Academic Vocabulary, SE p. 348	Analyze Details, SE p. 349 Making Comparisons, SE p. 349 Adjectives, TWE pp. 344	Analyzing Art, SE pp. 342, 344 Sign Language, SE p. 349 Analyzing a Photo, TWE p. 343
		Placement of End Punctuation, TWE p. 350	
Analyzing Cultural Context, SE pp. 352–354, 356–358, 361 Sequence of Events, TWE p. 354	Context Clues, SE p. 361 Academic Vocabulary, SE p. 361	Respond to Theme, SE p. 361 Vivid Verbs, TWE p. 356	Analyzing Art, SE p. 358; TWE pp. 355, 357
Analyzing Style, SE pp. 364, 365, 368–370, 373, 374 Compare/Contrast in Nonfiction, TWE p. 372 Drawing Conclusions, TWE p. 376	Word Parts, SE p. 374 Applying Knowledge, TWE p. 364	Analyze Voice, SE p. 374 Essay on Author's Purpose, SE p. 378 Understanding Parallelism, TWE p. 366	Analyzing Art, SE p. 371 Group Activity, SE p. 378

LITERARY FOCUS

Focus

BELLRINGER

Bellringer Options
Selection Focus Transparency
Daily Language Practice Transparency 26
Or display an image of a famous public figure such as Abraham Lincoln.
Ask: What do you know about this person? How did you learn about him or her? *(Students may mention textbooks or biographies.)*

Teach

L Literary Element

Autobiography Remind students to be skeptical when they read autobiographies. Note that the writers are telling about their own lives and may try to present themselves in the best possible light.
Ask: How does Keller portray herself in the passage? *(Keller portrays herself as both ignorant and capable of great joy and curiosity.)* OL

LITERARY FOCUS

Autobiography and Biography

How do writers choose which details to include when they write about a real person?

Autobiography

An **autobiography** is the story of a person's life written by that person. Usually it is written in the first-person point of view. Most autobiographies are organized chronologically and reveal the events and ideas that shaped the writer's life.

Birth → Childhood → School years → Young adulthood → Adulthood

In this excerpt from her autobiography *The Story of My Life*, Helen Keller tells how she, a blind and deaf child, began to realize what words mean. Because Helen did not understand the difference between "mug" and "water," her teacher created an experience to help Helen understand the word *water.*

Someone was drawing water and my teacher placed my hand under the spout. As the cool stream gushed over one hand she spelled into the other the word water, first slowly, then rapidly. I stood still, my whole attention fixed upon the motions of her fingers. Suddenly I felt a misty consciousness as of something forgotten—a thrill of returning thought; and somehow the mystery of language was revealed to me. I knew then that "w-a-t-e-r" meant the wonderful cool something that was flowing over my hand. That living word awakened my soul, gave it light, hope, joy, set it free!

—Helen Keller, from *The Story of My Life* 

Literature Online **Interactive Literary Elements Handbook** Go to www.glencoe.com to review or learn more about autobiography and biography.

Additional Support

Literary Elements Have students access the Web site to improve their understanding of autobiography and biography.

Skills Practice

READING: Identifying Assumptions
Explain that an assumption is an idea accepted without proof, so it may or may not be true. Note that autobiographers as writers make assumptions about their audience and, as characters in their own story, make assumptions about the world. Ask students to answer the following questions:

- What assumption does Keller, the writer, have about her audience? *(She assumes people are interested in her life story.)*
- What assumption does Keller, the subject, have about the world? *(She assumes that she is the center of her own universe.)* OL

Memoir Like an autobiography, a **memoir** is a first-person account of a person's life written by that person. The chief difference between the two is that an autobiography is a more complete summation of a person's life. A memoir focuses on one period or significant episode in a person's life. For example, James Herriot has written a series of memoirs describing his life as a veterinarian.

The silvery haired old gentleman with the pleasant face didn't look the type to be easily upset, but his eyes glared at me angrily, and his lips quivered with indignation.

"Mr. Herriot," he said. I have come to make a complaint. I strongly object to your callousness in subjecting my dog to unnecessary suffering."

"Suffering? What suffering?" I was mystified.

"I think you know, Mr. Herriot. I brought my dog in a few days ago. He was very lame, and I am referring to your treatment on that occasion."

— James Herriot, **from "A Case of Cruelty"**

The Seaside, 1895–1905. Francois Flameng. ★

Biography

A **biography** is the account of a person's life written by someone other than that person. Unlike an autobiographer—who can write mostly from memory—biographers consult a variety of sources when gathering information about the subject. Most biographies are organized chronologically, and many reflect the attitude the author has toward his or her subject. Biographies can vary in length, from brief encyclopedia entries to works that span several volumes.

In his book *Good Brother, Bad Brother,* James Cross Giblin presents a biography about Edwin Booth, the brother of the man who assassinated Abraham Lincoln. In order to gather information for the biography, Giblin read documents such as newspaper articles and personal letters to and from Edwin Booth.

That night Edwin, who was staying at a friend's house in Boston, had trouble getting to sleep. But he still had no intimation of the shock that was in store for him the next morning. Without knocking first, his valet burst into his bedroom shortly after seven. Thrusting a newspaper in front of a dazed Edwin, the man exclaimed, "Mr. Booth, President Lincoln has been shot!" Before Edwin could absorb that terrible fact, the valet went on: "And—oh, Mr. Booth—they say your brother John has done it!"

—James Cross Giblin, **from "A Brother's Crime"** R

Quickwrite

Writing a Title Think of a famous person you find interesting. If you were to write a biography about the person, what title would you use? Write your title and then explain your choice.

INDIANA ACADEMIC STANDARDS (pages 308–309)
9.2 Develop strategies such as...identifying and analyzing structure, organization, perspective, and purpose...

Teach

R Reading Strategy

Identifying Bias Ask: In the excerpt from "A Brother's Crime," what does the author feel about his subject? *(The author makes the subject appear innocent; his shock at the news suggests his innocence.)* OL

★ Viewing the Art

Francois Flameng (1856–1923) was a French artist known for his portraits, historical paintings, and decorative work. He painted many ceilings and panels in buildings around the world. AS

Assess

Quickwrite

The title should reflect understanding of the person's accomplishments and reputation.

Differentiated Instruction

Understanding Emotions Students who are learning disabled may better understand the emotions in a text if they can hear the passage read aloud. Ask proficient readers to read the excerpts that appear on pages 308–309. Allow them time to practice reading and using their voices to express the excerpts' emotions accurately. BL

Academic Standards

Additional Support activities on pp. 308 and 309 cover the following standards:

Skills Practice: **9.2.8** Make reasonable statements and draw conclusions about a text...

Differentiated Instruction: **9.7** [Respond] to oral communication [with] careful listening and evaluation of content...

Focus

BELLRINGER

Bellringer Options
Selection Focus Transparency 20
Daily Language Practice Transparency 27

Or discuss students' concept of success. Invite small groups of students to compile a list of five different types of rewards that might stem from success. Start them off with some examples, such as personal fulfillment, financial security, and professional reputation.

Ask: What types of success do you think are most important to immigrants to the United States? *(Students may mention financial success or political freedom.)*

Author Search To expand students' appreciation of Yoshiko Uchida, have them access the Web site for additional information and resources.

BEFORE YOU READ

Of Dry Goods and Black Bow Ties

MEET YOSHIKO UCHIDA

The stories of millions of people who left their homes to seek better lives in the United States make up one of the most interesting chapters in American history. The parents of Yoshiko Uchida (yō shē′kō o͞o chē′dä), Dwight and Iku, were a part of this chapter. They immigrated to the United States from Japan.

Treated Like an Enemy Yoshiko Uchida was born in Alameda, California. Raised in the nearby community of Berkeley, Uchida finished high school early. She enrolled in college when she was only sixteen years old. In 1941, she was studying for final exams at the University of California in Berkeley when she learned that Japanese warplanes had bombed Pearl Harbor. Then the United States declared war on Japan.

"I write to celebrate our common humanity, for the basic elements of humanity are present in all our strivings."

—Yoshiko Uchida

Not long after, the United States government decided to imprison thousands of Japanese Americans. Citizens or not, those of Japanese heritage remained in "relocation centers" or internment camps for months or even years. Uchida and her family were among them. They had to leave everything behind and go to an internment camp. Until 1943, they lived in a remote, guarded camp in the Utah desert. Uchida later recalled this experience in *Journey to Topaz* and its sequel, *Journey Home.*

After Uchida was released in 1943, she earned a master's degree in education from Smith College in Massachusetts. She did not teach, however. Instead, she worked as a secretary during the day and wrote in the evenings. Uchida published her first book, *The Dancing Kettle and Other Japanese Folk Tales,* in 1949.

Visit to Japan In 1952, Uchida won a Ford Foundation research grant to study in Japan. Over a period of two years, she traveled around the country collecting folktales. She also learned about Japanese arts and crafts. As a result of her experiences in Japan, Uchida gained a deeper awareness of herself as a Japanese American. She also developed an increased "respect and admiration for the culture that had made my parents what they were."

Uchida eventually became an award-winning author of more than twenty children's books. They include *A Jar of Dreams, The Bracelet,* and *The Magic Purse.* Influenced by her heritage, she focused on Japanese American themes in her work. Uchida hoped that her books would help Asian American children "be aware of their history and culture." She wanted them "to understand some of the traditions, hopes, and values of the early immigrants." She also hoped her books would touch upon universal values and feelings common to all children.

Yoshiko Uchida was born in 1921 and died in 1992.

Literature Online **Author Search** For more about Yoshiko Uchida, go to www.glencoe.com.

Selection Skills

Of Dry Goods and Black Bow Ties

Literary Elements
- Title (SE pp. 311–313, 315, 317)
- Foreshadowing (TWE p. 315)
- Tone (TWE p. 316)

Vocabulary Skills
- Synonymns (SE p. 318)
- Academic Vocabulary (SE p. 318)

Reading Skills
- Analyzing Cause-and-Effect Relationships (SE pp. 311–318)
- Making Predictions (TWE p. 312)

Listening/Speaking/Viewing Skills
- Analyzing Art (SE p. 314)

Writing Skills/Grammar
- Analysis of Tone (SE p. 318)
- Commas in a Series (TWE p. 314)

Study Skills/Research/Assessment
- Research (TWE p. 315)

LITERATURE PREVIEW

READING PREVIEW

BEFORE YOU READ

Connecting to the Essay

In this selection, Uchida writes about success and failure in the lives of Japanese immigrants who came to live in the United States. Before you read the selection, think about the following questions:

- In your opinion, what does it mean to be successful?
- What obstacles do you think an immigrant might have to overcome?

Building Background

Although this autobiographical essay begins and ends in Berkeley, California, sometime after the mid-1940s, it mainly recalls events that happened between 1880 and 1929 in Seattle, Portland, and San Francisco. One event that is not directly discussed but that affected a central figure in this selection was a financial panic that triggered widespread selling of stocks on the New York Stock Exchange. This panic helped begin the Depression era in the United States. Many businesses failed at this time, including a dry goods store that Uchida's father had worked in. Dry goods are fabric, clothing, canned or packaged foods, and other nonperishable items. They were sold in "dry goods" stores before supermarkets became widespread in the late 1940s and 1950s.

Setting Purposes for Reading

Big Idea Looking into Lives

As you read, think about facts and details in the selection that bring to life the relationship between Uchida's father and Shozo Shimada, a successful Japanese American businessman.

Literary Element Title

The **title** is the name of a work of literature. Titles may express themes, highlight important details, or point to a central character or event. As you read this selection, pay attention to details that help you understand why Uchida chose her title.

- See Literary Terms Handbook, p. R18.

Literature Online **Interactive Literary Elements Handbook** To review or learn more about the literary elements, go to www.glencoe.com.

Reading Strategy Analyzing Cause-and-Effect Relationships

A **cause** is any event that leads to an **effect,** or result. For example, because Mr. Shimada can sew and speak Japanese, Japanese women come to his shop.

Reading Tip: Creating Organizers Use cause-and-effect diagrams like the one shown below to record other examples of cause-and-effect relationships that you find in this selection. You may have to add *Effect* boxes if a cause has more than one effect.

Cause
Mr. Shimada can sew and speak Japanese.
Effect
Japanese women come to his dress-making shop.

Vocabulary

confidant (kon′ fə dant′) *n.* a person to whom secrets are entrusted; p. 313 *My best friend is a true confidant; I can tell her anything.*

imposing (im pō′ zing) *adj.* impressive in appearance or manner; p. 314 *The pyramids in Egypt are imposing monuments.*

exhilarated (ig zil′ ə rāt′ əd) *adj.* cheerful, lively, or excited; p. 315 *The exhilarated cast took its final bow after a terrific performance.*

irreverent (i rev′ ər ənt) *adj.* showing a lack of proper respect; p. 316 *Jim felt that the unflattering jokes about our country's leaders were irreverent.*

Vocabulary Tip: Synonyms Synonyms are words that have the same or nearly the same meaning. Note that synonyms are always the same part of speech.

INDIANA ACADEMIC STANDARDS (pages 311–318)

9.3 [Identify] story elements...

9.2 Develop [reading] strategies such as...analyzing structure, organization, perspective, and purpose...

9.5.3 Write...analytical essays...

Focus

Summary

Yoshiko Uchida explores her father's relationship with his first employer, Mr. Shimada, a successful Japanese American businessman. Mr. Shimada says, "One never knows when one might be indebted to even the lowliest of beggars." Uchida's father never forgets Mr. Shimada's wisdom.

V Vocabulary

Vocabulary File Say: Add these words and definitions to your vocabulary file. For each word, include a sentence that gives you an example of how to use the word. **OL** Students with English language needs should include the pronunciation of these words in their files. **EL**

Literary Elements Have students access the Web site to improve their understanding of title.

Selection Resources

Print Materials
- Unit 2 Resources (Fast File), pp. 17–19
- Leveled Vocabulary Development, p. 21
- Selection and Unit Assessments, pp. 45–46
- Selection Quick Checks, p. 23

Transparencies
- Bellringer Options Transparencies: Daily Language Practice Transparency 27
- Literary Elements Transparency 108

Technology
- TeacherWorks Plus™ CD-ROM
- StudentWorks Plus™ CD-ROM
- Presentation Plus!™ CD-ROM
- Literature Online, glencoe.com
- Online Student Edition, mhln.com
- Exam*View*® Assessment Suite CD-ROM
- Vocabulary PuzzleMaker CD-ROM
- Listening Library, disc 1 track 25

Teach

R1 Reading Strategy

Predict Have students read the title and first paragraph. **Ask:** What do you think the essay will be about? Remind students to verify or revise their predictions as they read the rest of the essay. *(Students may predict that the essay will focus on the speaker's father and Mr. Shimada's influence on him.)* OL

L1 Literary Element

Title Answer: *The essay will be about the changes that have taken place in the author's father.* OL

BI1 Big Idea

Looking into Lives Answer: *It suggests he felt discouraged and isolated.* OL

CheckPoint

Use the CheckPoint questions on Presentation Plus! to monitor students' comprehension. These questions can be used with interactive response keypads for immediate student feedback.

Readability Scores

Dale-Chall: 6.7
DRP: 62
Lexile: 1230

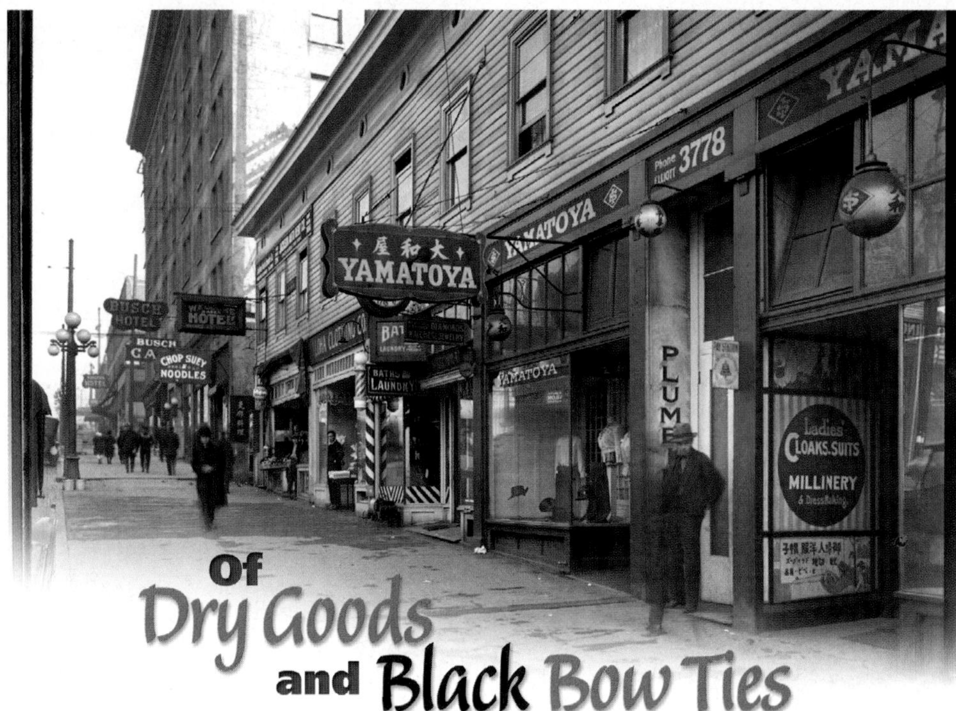

Of Dry Goods and Black Bow Ties

Yoshiko Uchida

Long after reaching the age of sixty, when my father was persuaded at last to wear a conservative four-in-hand tie,[1] it was not because of his family's urging, but because Mr. Shimada[2] (I shall call him that) had died. Until then, for some forty years, my father had always worn a plain black bow tie, a formality which was required on his first job in America and which he had continued to observe as faithfully as his father before him had worn his samurai[3] sword. R1

My father came to America in 1906 when he was not yet twenty-one. Sailing from Japan on a small six-thousand-ton ship which was buffeted all the way by rough seas, he landed in Seattle on a bleak January day. He revived himself with the first solid meal he had enjoyed in many days, and then allowed himself one day of rest to restore his sagging spirits. Early on the second morning, wearing a stiff new bowler,[4] he went to see Mr. Shozo Shimada to whom he carried a letter of introduction.

At that time, Shozo Shimada was Seattle's most successful Japanese businessman. He owned a chain of dry goods stores which extended not only from Vancouver to Portland, but to cities in Japan as well. He had come to America in 1880, penniless but enterprising, and sought work as a laborer. It wasn't long, however, before he saw the futility of trying to compete with American

1. A *four-in-hand tie* is a man's necktie that is tied in a slip knot with the ends hanging down vertically.
2. *Shimada* (shē mä′ dä)
3. In feudal Japan, the sword-carrying *samurai* (sam′ oo rī′) were an aristocratic class of warriors who valued honor above life itself.
4. A *bowler* is a hard, round hat with a narrow, curled brim.

Literary Element Title *Think about the title of the essay. What do you think this essay will be about?* L1

Big Idea Looking into Lives *How might this description reflect his mood, or how he feels when he arrives?* BI1

Additional Support

Leveled Reading An adapted version of this selection is available on page 248 of *Jamestown Literature: An Adapted Reader,* grade 9.

Skills Practice

READING: Analyzing Cause and Effect A cause is why something happened; an effect is what happened. Write the following example on the board: *Cause:* The narrator's father admired Mr. Shimada's modesty and success. *Effect:* He dedicated himself to following Mr. Shimada's rules. *Check:* The narrator's father dedicated himself to following Mr. Shimada's rules, because he admired his modesty and success. Have students find other examples of cause and effect and write them as *because* sentences. (*Sample: The women used Mr. Shimada as a banker because they considered him a trusted friend.*) OL laborers whose bodies were twice his in muscle and bulk. He knew he would never go far as a laborer, but he did possess another skill that could give him a start toward better things. He knew how to sew. It was a matter of expediency[5] over masculine pride. He set aside his shovel, bought a second-hand sewing machine, and hung a dressmaker's sign in his window. He was in business.

In those days, there were some Japanese women in Seattle who had neither homes nor families nor sewing machines, and were delighted to find a friendly Japanese person to do some sewing for them. They flocked to Mr. Shimada with bolts of cloth, elated to discover a dressmaker who could speak their native tongue and, although a male, sew western-styled dresses for them.

Mr. Shimada acquainted himself with the fine points of turning a seam, fitting sleeves, and coping with the slippery folds of satin, and soon the women ordered enough dresses to keep him thriving and able to establish a healthy bank account. He became a trusted friend and **confidant** to many of them and soon they began to bring him what money they earned for safekeeping.

"Keep our money for us, Shimada-san,"[6] they urged, refusing to go to American banks whose tellers spoke in a language they could not understand.

At first the money accumulated slowly and Mr. Shimada used a pair of old socks as a repository,[7] stuffing them into a far corner of his drawer beneath his union suits.[8] But after a time, Mr. Shimada's private bank began to overflow and he soon found it necessary to replenish his supply of socks. ★

He went to a small dry goods store downtown, and as he glanced about at the buttons, threads, needles, and laces, it occurred to him that he owed it to the women to invest their savings in a business venture with more future than the dark recesses of his bureau drawer. That night he called a group of them together.

"Think, ladies," he began. "What are the two basic needs of the Japanese living in Seattle? Clothes to wear and food to eat," he answered himself. "Is that not right? Every man must buy a shirt to put on his back and pickles and rice for his stomach."

The women marveled at Mr. Shimada's cleverness as he spread before them his fine plans for a Japanese dry goods store that would not only carry everything available in an American dry goods store, but Japanese foodstuff as well. That was the beginning of the first Shimada Dry Goods Store on State Street.

By the time my father appeared, Mr. Shimada had long since abandoned his sewing machine and was well on his way to becoming a business tycoon.[9] Although he had opened cautiously with such stock items as ginghams, flannel, handkerchiefs, socks, shirts, overalls, umbrellas, and ladies' silk and cotton stockings, he now carried tins of salt, rice crackers, bottles of soy sauce, vinegar, ginger root, fish-paste cakes, bean paste, Japanese pickles, dried mushrooms, salt fish, red beans, and just about every item of canned food that could be shipped from Japan. In addition, his was the first Japanese store to install a U.S. Post Office Station, and he therefore flew an American flag in front of the large sign that bore the name of his shop.

5. *Expediency* is a means of achieving a particular goal, or the quality of being appropriate to the end in view.
6. According to Japanese custom, the suffix *-san* (sän) is added after a person's name to express respect.
7. A *repository* is a place or object in which something may be stored for safekeeping.
8. *Union suits* are one-piece undergarments that combine a shirt with long pants.
9. A *tycoon* is a wealthy, powerful businessman.

Big Idea Looking into Lives *What does this passage tell you about the Japanese women who hired Mr. Shimada?* **BI2**

Vocabulary

confidant (kon′ fə dant′) *n.* a person to whom secrets are entrusted

Reading Strategy Analyzing Cause-and-Effect Relationships *What causes Mr. Shimada to establish a dry goods store?* **R2**

Literary Element Title *What does Mr. Shimada sell in his store? Why is this detail in the title of the essay?* **L2**

Teach

BI2 Big Idea

Looking into Lives **Answer:** *Students may say that the women's eagerness to adopt western-style dresses indicates they now think of themselves as Americans.* **OL**

R2 Reading Strategy

Analyzing Cause-and-Effect Relationships **Answer:** *He wanted to help the women profit from their investment and saw this as a good opportunity to fill a need in the Japanese emigrant community.* **OL**

L2 Literary Element

Title **Answer:** *He sold fabric, clothing, and packaged Japanese foods. Uchida's father worked in one of Mr. Shimada's dry goods stores.* **OL**

★ Writer's Technique

Humor Note that authors sometimes use humorous anecdotes as an engaging way to advance a narrative.
Ask: Why does the author tell the story about Mr. Shimada and his sock bank? *(The anecdote leads into an explanation of how he decided to open a dry goods store.)* **AS**

English Language Coach

Native Tongues English language learners may empathize with the desire of Mr. Shimada's customers to do business with a native Japanese speaker. Struggling to communicate in an unfamiliar language can be a difficult and isolating experience. Encourage students to discuss why they enjoy speaking in their native tongue and how they feel when they meet someone here who can speak their first language. **EL**

Academic Standards

Additional Support activities on pp. 312 and 313 cover the following standards:

Skills Practice: **9.3** [Identify] story elements such as…plot…

English Language Coach: **9.2** Develop [reading] strategies…

Teach

BI1 Big Idea

Looking into Lives Answer: *The details show how successful he is.* **OL**

★ Viewing the Photograph

Answer: *Students should note that the stores are of the same time period, the same general geographic area (the West coast), and both appear to sell Japanese goods.*

Photos taken between 1889 and the 1920s used nitrate-based film. Although black and white photos last longer, nitrate film degrades over time, becoming highly flammable and explosive. This film requires special care and storage. **AS**

Viewing the Photograph: How might this 1903 dry goods store in Sacramento, California, compare with Mr. Shimada's store? 

When my father first saw the big American flag fluttering in front of Mr. Shimada's shop, he was overcome with admiration and awe. He expected that Mr. Shozo Shimada would be the finest of Americanized Japanese gentlemen, and when he met him, he was not disappointed.

Although Mr. Shimada was not very tall, he gave the illusion of height because of his erect carriage. He wore a spotless black alpaca[10] suit, an immaculate[11] white shirt, and a white collar so stiff it might have overcome a lesser man. He also wore a black bow tie, black shoes that buttoned up the side and a gold watch whose thick chain looped grandly on his vest. He was probably in his fifties then, a ruddy-faced man whose hair, already turning white, was parted carefully in the center. He was an **imposing** figure to confront a young man fresh from Japan with scarcely a future to look forward to. My father bowed, summoned as much dignity as he could muster, and presented the letter of introduction he carried to him.

Mr. Shimada was quick to sense his need. "Do you know anything about bookkeeping?" he inquired.

"I intend to go to night school to learn this very skill," my father answered.

Mr. Shimada could assess a man's qualities in a very few minutes. He looked my father straight in the eye and said, "Consider yourself hired." Then he added, "I have a few basic rules. My employees must at all times wear a

10. *Alpaca* (al pak′ ə) is the fleece of the alpaca, a South American mammal related to the llama.
11. *Immaculate* (i mak′ yə lit) means "perfectly clean" or "spotless."

Big Idea Looking into Lives *What do these details reveal about Mr. Shimada?* **BI1**

Vocabulary

imposing (im pō′ zing) *adj.* impressive in appearance or manner

Additional Support

Skills Practice

GRAMMAR: Series Note the following passage: *My father bowed, summoned as much dignity as he could muster, and presented the letter of introduction he carried to him.* Review the use of commas between items in a series. Stress that items in a series may be phrases or clauses, or individual words. Have students write and punctuate three sentences about the following topics.

Recreation: *(I enjoy riding my bike, swimming in the lake, and flying kites.)*
Music: (*Our favorite styles of music include rock, blues, and classical.*)
Authors: (*My favorite authors are Amy Tan, Julia Alvarez, and Mark Twain.*) **OL**

clean white shirt and a black bow tie. They must answer the telephone promptly with the words, 'Good morning or good afternoon, Shimada's Dry Goods,' and they must always treat each customer with respect. It never hurts to be polite," he said thoughtfully. "One never knows when one might be indebted to even the lowliest of beggars."

My father was impressed with these modest words from a man of such success. He accepted them with a sense of mission and from that day was committed to white shirts and black bow ties, and treated every customer, no matter how humble, with respect and courtesy. When, in later years, he had his own home, he never failed to answer the phone before it could ring twice if at all possible.

My father worked with Mr. Shimada for ten years, becoming first the buyer for his Seattle store and later, manager of the Portland branch. During this time Mr. Shimada continued on a course of **exhilarated** expansion. He established two Japanese banks in Seattle, bought a fifteen-room house outside the dreary confines of the Japanese community and dressed his wife and daughter in velvets and ostrich feathers. When his daughter became eighteen, he sent her to study in Paris, and the party he gave on the eve of her departure, with musicians, as well as caterers to serve roast turkey, venison, baked ham, and champagne, seemed to verify rumors that he had become one of the first Japanese millionaires of America.

In spite of his phenomenal success, however, Mr. Shimada never forgot his early friends nor lost any of his generosity, and this, ironically enough, was his undoing. Many of the women for whom he had once sewn dresses were now well established, and they came to him requesting loans with which they and their husbands might open grocery stores and laundries and shoe repair shops. Mr. Shimada helped them all and never demanded any collateral.[12] He operated his banks on faith and trust and gave no thought to such common prudence as maintaining a reserve.[13]

When my father was called to a new position with a large Japanese firm in San Francisco, Mr. Shimada came down to Portland to extend personally his good wishes. He took Father to a Chinese dinner and told him over the peanut duck and chow mein that he would like always to be considered a friend.

"If I can ever be of assistance to you," he said, "don't ever hesitate to call." And with a firm shake of the hand, he wished my father well.

That was in 1916. My father wrote regularly to Mr. Shimada telling him of his new job, of his bride, and later, of his two children. Mr. Shimada did not write often, but each Christmas he sent a box of Oregon apples and pears, and at New Year's a slab of heavy white rice paste from his Seattle shop.

In 1929 the letters and gifts stopped coming and Father learned from friends in Seattle that both of Mr. Shimada's banks had failed. He immediately dispatched a letter to Mr. Shimada, but it was returned unopened. The next news he had was that Mr. Shimada had had to sell all of his shops. My father was now manager of the San Francisco branch of his firm. He wrote once more asking Mr. Shimada if there was anything he could do to help. The letter did not come back, but there was no reply, and my father did not write again. After all, how

12. A moneylender sometimes requires a borrower to provide *collateral:* something of equivalent value offered or promised as proof that a loan will be repaid.

13. A bank maintains a *reserve* of uninvested funds to meet possible demands or emergencies (such as a drop in the value of its invested funds).

Literary Element Title *Why do you think this detail is highlighted in the title of the essay?* L1

Reading Strategy Analyzing Cause-and-Effect Relationships *What are three effects of Mr. Shimada's success?* R1

Vocabulary

exhilarated (ig zil′ ə rāt′ əd) *adj.* cheerful, lively, or excited

Big Idea Looking into Lives *What positive traits and characteristics does Mr. Shimada have?* BI2

Reading Strategy Analyzing Cause-and-Effect Relationships *Why do Mr. Shimada's banks fail? What happens to Mr. Shimada's business as a result?* R2

Reading in the Real World

Citizenship Have each student find a print or online article that explores family, school, professional, personal, or other issues faced by recent U.S. immigrants. Have small groups of students use their research to answer questions such as these: *Who is the subject of the article? When did the person come to the United States? From where? Has the person's experience been mostly positive or mostly negative? What parts of his or her American experience have been positive? What parts have been negative?* OL

Teach

L1 Literary Element

Title Answer: *The black bow tie symbolizes Mr. Shimada's high standards and professionalism, which play a central role in shaping the attitudes of Uchida's father.* OL

L2 Literary Element

Foreshadowing While reflecting Shimada's philosophy, this statement also foreshadows events to come.
Ask: What might the author be hinting at by including this remark? *(That Shimada may fall on hard times)* OL

R1 Reading Strategy

Analyzing Cause-and-Effect Relationships Answer: *He established two banks, bought a mansion, and educated his daughter in Paris.* OL

BI2 Big Idea

Looking into Lives Answer: *He is intelligent, trusting, polite, hardworking, kind, generous, and loyal.* OL

R2 Reading Strategy

Analyzing Cause-and-Effect Relationships Answer: *He made loans without demanding collateral and did not maintain a reserve, which caused his bank to fail during the 1929 financial panic. He had to sell his shops as a result.* OL

Academic Standards

Additional Support activities on pp. 314 and 315 cover the following standards:
Skills Practice: **9.6.1** Identify and correctly use…the mechanics of punctuation…
Reading in the Real World: **9.2.8** Make reasonable statements and draw conclusions…

Teach

BI Big Idea

Looking into Lives Answer: *He is still loyal and respectful toward Shimada.* OL

R Reading Strategy

Analyzing Cause-and-Effect Relationships Answer: *He ended up a poor door-to-door salesman.* OL

L Literary Element

Tone The father's comment clearly conveys his great respect for Mr. Shimada.

Ask: How does the author convey her own feelings about Shimada? *(Always refers to him as Mr. Shimada; phrases such as "trusted friend and confidant," "never forgot his early friends nor lost any of his generosity" convey admiration.* OL If students have trouble, provide hints, such as, "What does the author call him?" "What words does the author use to describe him?" "What do these words suggest about the author's feelings about Shimada?" BL

CheckPoint

Use the CheckPoint questions on Presentation Plus! to check students' mastery of the selection. These questions can be used with interactive response keypads for immediate student feedback.

do you offer help to the head of a fallen empire? It seemed almost **irreverent.**

It was many years later that Mr. Shimada appeared one night at our home in Berkeley. In the dim light of the front porch my mother was startled to see an elderly gentleman wearing striped pants, a morning coat, and a shabby black hat. In his hand he carried a small black satchel. When she invited him inside, she saw that the morning coat was faded, and his shoes badly in need of a shine.

Visual Vocabulary
A *morning coat* is a man's jacket for formal daytime wear, traditionally worn with striped trousers and a top hat.

"I am Shimada," he announced with a courtly bow, and it was my mother who felt inadequate to the occasion. She hurriedly pulled off her apron and went to call my father. When he heard who was in the living room, he put on his coat and tie before going out to greet his old friend. BI

Mr. Shimada spoke to them about Father's friends in Seattle and about his daughter who was now married and living in Denver. He spoke of a typhoon that had recently swept over Japan, and he drank the tea my mother served and ate a piece of her chocolate cake. Only then did he open his black satchel.

"I thought your girls might enjoy these books," he said, as he drew out a brochure describing *The Book of Knowledge.*

"Fourteen volumes that will tell them of the wonders of this world." He spread his arms in a magnificent gesture that recalled his eloquence of the past. "I wish I could give them to your children as a personal gift," he added softly.

Without asking the price of the set, my father wrote a check for one hundred dollars and gave it Mr. Shimada.

Mr. Shimada glanced at the check and said, "You have given me fifty dollars too much." He seemed troubled for only a moment, however, and quickly added, "Ah, the balance is for a deposit, is it? Very well, yours will be the first deposit in my next bank."

"Is your home still in Seattle then?" Father asked cautiously.

"I am living there, yes," Mr. Shimada answered.

And then, suddenly overcome with memories of the past, he spoke in a voice so low he could scarcely be heard.

"I paid back every cent," he murmured. "It took ten years, but I paid it back. All of it. I owe nothing."

"You are a true gentleman, Shimada-san," L Father said. "You always will be." Then he pointed to the black tie he wore, saying, "You see, I am still one of the Shimada men."

That was the last time my father saw Shozo Shimada. Some time later he heard that he had returned to Japan as penniless as the day he set out for America.

It wasn't until the Christmas after we heard of Mr. Shimada's death that I ventured to give my father a silk four-in-hand tie. It was charcoal gray and flecked with threads of silver. My father looked at it for a long time before he tried it on, and then fingering it gently, he said, "Well, perhaps it is time now that I put away my black bow ties." ❧

Big Idea Looking into Lives *What does this action tell you about Uchida's father?* BI

Vocabulary
irreverent (i rev′ ər ənt) *adj.* showing a lack of proper respect

Reading Strategy Analyzing Cause-and-Effect Relationships *How does Mr. Shimada's life change after the Great Depression?* R

Additional Support

Skills Practice

GRAMMAR: Possessive Pronouns
Possessive pronouns show ownership and replace possessive nouns. Write the following possessive pronouns on the board in two columns: **Singular:** *my, mine, your, yours, his, her, hers, its.* **Plural:** *our, ours, your, yours, their, theirs.* Note that possessive pronouns do not have an apostrophe. Have students write ten sentences about someone or something that is special to them. They should use at least five different possessive pronouns and underline each one. OL

RESPONDING AND THINKING CRITICALLY

Respond

1. Describe your reaction to what happens to Mr. Shimada.

Recall and Interpret

2. (a)What happens after Japanese Americans in Mr. Shimada's neighborhood entrust him with their savings? (b)What traits and qualities do you think help Mr. Shimada become a success in business?
3. (a)Summarize what happens to Mr. Shimada and his businesses after the stock market crash of 1929. (b)Why does Mr. Shimada's generosity prove to be his "undoing"?
4. (a)When does the author's father decide it is time to put away his black bow ties? (b)Why might the author's father have continued to wear black bow ties even after he no longer worked for Mr. Shimada?

Analyze and Evaluate

5. What are the most important lessons that the author's father learned from his experience of working for Mr. Shimada?
6. In your opinion, is Mr. Shimada a shrewd or a naive businessman? Use evidence from the selection to support your answer.
7. What conclusions can you draw, based on your reading of this essay, about the impact of the stock market crash of 1929 and the Great Depression on the lives of Americans?

Connect

8. **Big Idea** **Looking into Lives** Would you want to work for a boss like Mr. Shimada? Explain.

LITERARY ANALYSIS

Literary Element Title

Many works of literature have a **title** that is linked to the work's central theme or to the traits of a major character. The link may be subtle or obvious. Often, writers attempt to select for their titles catchy, intriguing words and phrases to spark the readers' curiosity and interest. Consider your own first reaction to the title of this essay as well as the relationship between the title and the essay itself. Then answer the following questions.

1. In your opinion, why did Uchida give her essay the title "Of Dry Goods and Black Bow Ties"?
2. Do you think the title is effective? Explain.
3. If Uchida had invited you to think of a good title for this selection, what would you have suggested?

Review: Biography

As you learned on pages 308–309, a **biography** is an account of a person's life written by someone other than the subject.

Partner Activity With a partner, create a sequence chain like the one below, completing it with the most significant events from Mr. Shimada's life. Expand the chain to include as many events as necessary. Use your completed sequence chain to summarize the biography.

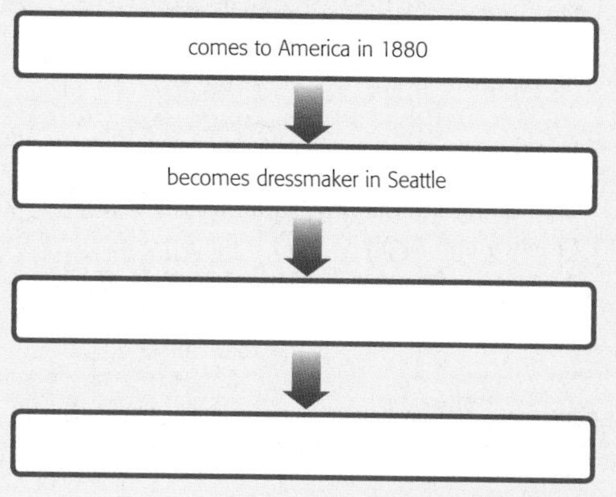

Assess

1. Students' answers should reflect an understanding of the tragedy of his fate.
2. (a) He invested their money in a dry goods store. (b) Hardworking, trustworthy, and perceptive about the needs of his community
3. (a) His banks failed, and he had to sell all his stores. (b) He loaned money without any guarantees of repayment.
4. (a) After Shimada's death (b) To emulate his professionalism and show his loyalty to his mentor
5. Generosity, loyalty, respect for others
6. Some may emphasize his shrewdness in capitalizing on business opportunities. Others will say he was naive to make loans without asking for collateral.
7. Answers should reflect understanding of its devastating impact on individuals and communities.
8. Students should identify his various qualities to support their answers.

Literary Element

1. It refers to the significance of Mr. Shimada and to a time now past.
2. Yes: it encapsulates the relationship between the father and Mr. Shimada.
3. Accept any reasonable answer.

Differentiated Instruction

Biography Students can expand their biography sequence chains by writing a one- or two-page biography of Mr. Shimada. **AL**

Review: Biography

Sample answers for chart:

1. invests money in store
2. opens bank
3. loses everything in stock market crash
4. pays back all the money he owes
5. returns to Japan

Academic Standards

Additional Support activities on pp. 316 and 317 cover the following standards:

Skills Practice: **9.6.2** Demonstrate an understanding of sentence construction...

Differentiated Instruction: **9.5.1** Write biographical...narratives...

AFTER YOU READ

Assess

Reading Strategy

Possible answers:

1. Therefore; when
2. Cause: The narrator's father rests and eats after his long oversea journey. Effect: His spirits are restored.
3. Cause: Shimada was generous and helpful. Effect: People trusted and relied on him. His banks failed because of unsecured loans.

Vocabulary

1. b **2.** b **3.** a **4.** a

Academic Vocabulary

The patrons of his dress shop helped finance Mr. Shimada's first store.

Writing About Literature

Students' essays should

- contain a clear thesis statement that identifies how Uchida feels about Mr. Shimada.
- include examples or words, phrases, and details that help communicate the writer's tone.

READING AND VOCABULARY

Reading Strategy Analyzing Cause-and-Effect Relationships

Sometimes, you will recognize **cause-and-effect relationships** in a work of literature because the author uses clue words such as *because, as a result, since, when,* or *therefore.* When you do recognize cause-and-effect relationships, determine whether the cause has one effect or more than one effect. Before you answer the following questions, review the cause-and-effect diagrams you created as you read this selection.

1. Identify two clue words that Uchida uses to signal cause-and-effect relationships in this essay.
2. Identify a cause-and-effect relationship in this essay that has one effect.
3. Identify a cause-and-effect relationship that has multiple effects.

Vocabulary Practice

Practice with Synonyms Choose the better synonym for each vocabulary word. Use a dictionary or a thesaurus if you need help.

1. imposing	**a.** big	**b.** grand
2. confidant	**a.** acquaintance	**b.** friend
3. exhilarated	**a.** elated	**b.** happy
4. irreverent	**a.** disrespectful	**b.** wrong

Academic Vocabulary

Here is a word from the vocabulary list on page R80. This word will help you think, talk, and write about the selection.

finance (fi nans′) *v.* to provide or raise the funds for

Practice and Apply
Who helped **finance** Mr. Shimada's first dry goods store?

Literature Online **Web Activities** For eFlashcards, Selection Quick Checks, and other Web activities, go to www.glencoe.com.

WRITING AND EXTENDING

Writing About Literature

Analyze Tone The tone of a work of literature is a reflection of a writer's attitude toward a subject. Authors convey tone through words and details that express emotions and that create an emotional response in the reader. Write a brief essay in which you analyze the tone of this biographical selection. First, identify how Uchida feels about Mr. Shimada, the subject of the essay. Then give examples of words, phrases, and details that Uchida uses to create and communicate this tone.

As you draft, state your thesis in the introduction, provide examples to support your analysis, and conclude with a summary of your main points. Follow the writing path shown here to help organize your essay.

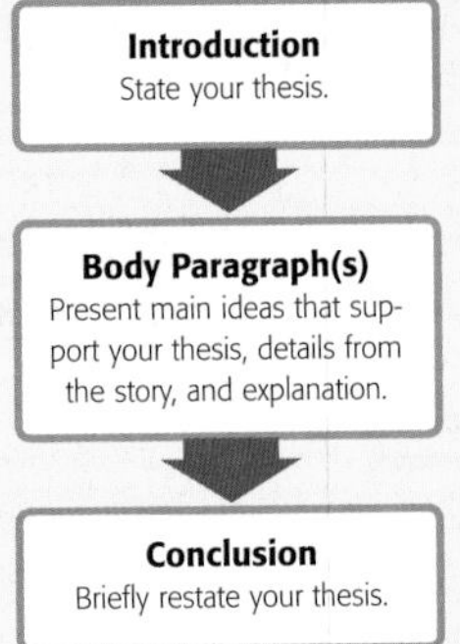

Introduction
State your thesis.
Body Paragraph(s)
Present main ideas that support your thesis, details from the story, and explanation.
Conclusion
Briefly restate your thesis.

After you complete your draft, meet with a peer reviewer to evaluate each other's work and to suggest revisions. Then proofread and edit your draft for errors in spelling, grammar, and punctuation.

Literature Groups

A **paradox** is an idea that includes two parts. Both parts are true but seem to contradict each other. With a small group, discuss these paradoxes that characterize Mr. Shimada:

- He appeared to be tall, but he was actually short.
- He was a success and a failure.

Identify facts that support the "truth" within each paradox and vote on which part of the paradox seems truer than the other. Share the results of your vote with the class.

Literature Groups

Suggest that students use a two-column chart to organize facts that support the two parts of each paradox. They should share their charts as well as their results with the class.

Web Activities Have students access the Web site for interactive activities that will help them assess their understanding of the selection.

BEFORE YOU READ

Only Daughter

MEET SANDRA CISNEROS

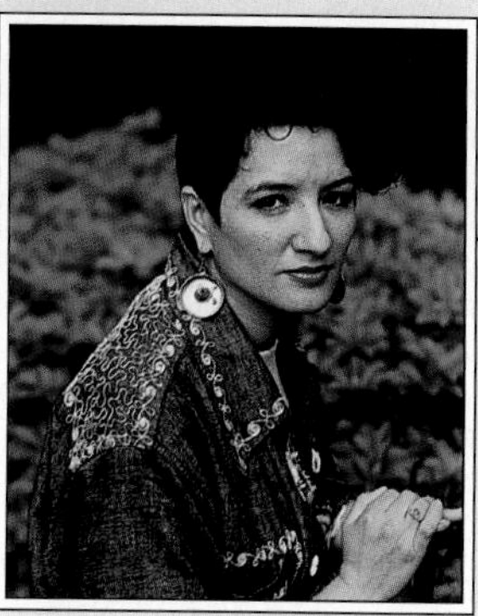

Sandra Cisneros says that coming from a Mexican American family gives her "two ways of looking at the world" and "twice as many words to pick from." Although Cisneros weaves Spanish words and phrases into her writing, she writes poetry and fiction primarily in English.

Poverty and Alienation Cisneros grew up in Chicago, Illinois, in a working-class Mexican American family. As she explains in her essay "Only Daughter," she was the only girl in a family of seven children. As a child, she experienced poverty firsthand. She also felt alienated because her family moved frequently between the United States and Mexico. As a result of moving and changing schools frequently, Cisneros had difficulty making friends and spent a lot of time alone.

While attending Catholic schools in Chicago, Cisneros studied hard, but she received poor grades. One reason was that she was too shy to speak up in class. As a young teenager, she began to write stories and poems to express her feelings and observations on paper.

Finding Her Voice After graduating from high school, Cisneros studied English at Loyola University in Chicago. Later, she attended graduate school at the University of Iowa where she earned a master's degree in poetry from the famed Iowa Writers' Workshop. While she was in graduate school, she realized that she wanted to write about her unique experiences as a Mexican American.

At this point in her life, Cisneros also began to write the vignettes that were later published in her acclaimed work of fiction *The House on Mango Street* (1984). In that collection of connected stories, as well as in her other writing, she focused on poor families—the people she "knew and loved but never saw in the pages of the books" that she borrowed from the library. As she portrayed life through the eyes of a female Mexican American protagonist, Cisneros culled her own identity for her themes and for elements of her style.

> *"I am a woman and a Latina. Those are the things that make my writing distinctive. Those are the things that give my writing power."*
>
> —Sandra Cisneros

A Writer's Life Despite the success of *The House on Mango Street*, which won the American Book Award, Cisneros struggled to earn a living after she finished graduate school. She worked as a high school teacher, a college recruiter, and a college professor while writing at night at her kitchen table. After she received a National Endowment for the Arts grant in 1988, Cisneros was able to work on *Woman Hollering Creek and Other Stories*, which was published in 1991. Since then, she has published a fourth book of poems, a children's book, and her first novel, *Caramelo*.

Sandra Cisneros was born in 1954.

Literature Online **Author Search** For more about Sandra Cisneros, go to www.glencoe.com.

BEFORE YOU READ

Focus

BELLRINGER

Bellringer Options
Selection Focus Transparency 21
Daily Language Practice Transparency 28

Or tell students that this selection focuses on family in an especially personal, vivid way. **Ask:** Does being a family's only daughter or son—or being an eldest, middle, or youngest child—affect a person's sense of who he or she is? Have small groups of students discuss the effect of family structure on their feelings about themselves or on someone they know.

Literature Online

Author Search To expand students' appreciation of Sandra Cisneros, have them access the Web site for additional information and resources.

Selection Skills

Only Daughter

Literary Elements
- Author's Purposes (SE pp. 320–321, 323, 325)
- Irony (TWE p. 322)

Reading Skills
- Drawing Conclusions About Author's Beliefs (SE pp. 320–321, 323, 326)

Vocabulary Skills
- Analogies (SE p. 325)
- Academic Vocabulary (SE p. 325)

Listening/Speaking/Viewing Skills
- Analyzing Art (SE p. 321)

Writing Skills/Grammar
- Response to Theme (SE p. 326)
- Compound Adjectives (SE p. 326)

BEFORE YOU READ

Focus

Summary

Sandra Cisneros is a young Mexican American woman who aspires to become a writer. She graduates from college, but, to her father's dismay, does not find a husband. After achieving professional recognition, she returns home with a published story. After reading the story, her father asks for copies for their relatives.

V Vocabulary

Vocabulary File **Say:** Add these words and definitions to your vocabulary file. For each word, include a sentence that gives you an example of how to use the word. **OL** Students with English language needs should include the pronunciations of these words in their files. **EL**

Literary Elements Have students access the Web site to improve their understanding of author's purpose.

LITERATURE PREVIEW

Connecting to the Essay

In this autobiographical essay, Cisneros discusses being the only daughter in her family. Before you read the selection, think about the following questions:

- Does being a family's only daughter or son affect who a person is? If so, how?
- How does being the eldest, middle, youngest, or only child in a family affect a person?

Building Background

This autobiographical essay was first published in *Glamour* magazine in 1990. In the essay, Cisneros recalls events that occurred during her childhood in Chicago, during her years in college, and during a visit to her parents at Christmas the year before this essay was written. She describes her relationship with her father, an upholsterer from Mexico, who acted as the head of her household and as the chief breadwinner for her family. She remembers him referring to his children as *"hijos"* (ēh′ ōs). In Spanish, *hijos* means "sons," but it also means "children." When Cisneros's father speaks directly to his daughter, he uses the feminine equivalent of the word *hijo,* which is *hija* (ē′ hä). He says *"mi'ja"* (mē′ hä), which is a shortening of *mi* and *hija*, meaning "my daughter."

Setting Purposes for Reading

Big Idea Looking into Lives

As you read, think about details in the selection that give readers an idea of what Cisneros's life was like as the only daughter in a large Mexican American family.

Literary Element Author's Purpose

An **author's purpose,** or reason for writing, may be to entertain, to persuade, to express opinions, to describe, or to inform. As you read this selection, pay attention to words, phrases, and details that help you determine Cisneros's purpose for writing.

- See Literary Terms Handbook, p. R3.

 **Interactive Literary Elements Handbook** To review or learn more about the literary elements, go to www.glencoe.com.

READING PREVIEW

Reading Strategy Drawing Conclusions About Author's Beliefs

When you draw a conclusion, you use a number of pieces of information to make a general statement about people, places, events, or ideas. By **drawing conclusions about an author's beliefs,** you can better understand and interpret how an author's ideas and opinions are related to what you are reading.

Reading Tip: Making a Chart Use a chart to list details that will help you draw conclusions about Cisneros's beliefs regarding the role of women, getting an education, and becoming a writer.

Role of Women	Getting an Education	Becoming a Writer
felt "erased" by her father	in fifth grade planned to go to college	aloneness was good for her

Vocabulary

anthology (an thol′ ə jē) *n.* a collection of written works, such as poems, stories, or essays, in a single book or set; p. 321 *My favorite story and Sam's favorite story are both in an anthology,* Best Short Stories About New England.

retrospect (ret′ rə spekt′) *n.* the act of looking back or thinking about the past; p. 322 *In retrospect the detective realized that he had missed an important clue.*

embroider (em broi′ dər) *v.* to make a story more interesting with imaginary details or exaggerations; p. 322 *Cal did not embroider his account of being lost at sea; the true story was thrilling enough.*

fulfill (fool fil′) *v.* to measure up to, or satisfy; to bring to pass; p. 322 *Dawn is determined to fulfill her dream of competing in the Olympics.*

INDIANA ACADEMIC STANDARDS (pages 320–326)

9.2.1 Analyze...structure and format...

9.2 Develop strategies such as...analyzing...purpose...

9.2.8 Make reasonable statements and draw conclusions...

9.5.2 Write responses to literature...

Selection Resources

Print Materials
- Unit 2 Resources (Fast File), pp. 20–22
- Leveled Vocabulary Development, p. 22
- Selection and Unit Assessments, pp. 47–48
- Selection Quick Checks, p. 24

Transparencies
- Bellringer Options Transparencies: Selection Focus Transparency 21, Daily Language Practice Transparency 28
- Literary Elements Transparency 35

Technology
- TeacherWorks Plus™ CD-ROM
- StudentWorks Plus™ CD-ROM
- Presentation Plus!™ CD-ROM
- Literature Online, glencoe.com
- Online Student Edition, mhln.com
- Exam*View*® Assessment Suite CD-ROM
- Vocabulary PuzzleMaker CD-ROM
- Listening Library, disc 1 track 26

Only Daughter

Sandra Cisneros

Woman in Cordilleran Night, 1996. Maria Eugenia Terrazas. Watercolor, 70 × 70 cm. Kactus Foto, Santiago, Chile.

Viewing the Art: How does the artist's use of color and lines affect the mood of this painting? Compare and contrast this woman with the narrator in this selection. ★

Once, several years ago, when I was just starting out my writing career, I was asked to write my own contributor's note for an **anthology** I was part of. I wrote: "I am the only daughter in a family of six sons. *That* explains everything."

Well, I've thought about that ever since, and yes, it explains a lot to me, but for the reader's sake I should have written: "I am the only daughter in a *Mexican* family of six sons." Or even: "I am the only daughter of a Mexican father and a Mexican-American mother." Or: "I am the only daughter of a working-class family of nine." All of these had everything to do with who I am today.

I was/am the only daughter and *only* a daughter. Being an only daughter in a family of six sons forced me by circumstance to spend a lot of time by myself because my brothers felt it beneath them to play with a *girl* in public. But that aloneness, that loneliness, was good for a would-be writer—it allowed me time to think and think, to imagine, to read and prepare myself.

Being only a daughter for my father meant my destiny would lead me to become someone's wife. That's what he believed. But when I was in the fifth grade and shared my plans for college with him, I was sure he understood. I remember my father saying, "*Qué bueno, mi'ja,*[1] that's good." That meant a lot to me, especially since my brothers thought the idea hilarious. What I didn't realize was that my father thought college was good for girls—good for finding a husband. After four years in college and two more in graduate school, and still no

1. *Qué bueno, mi'ja* (kā bwā′ nō mē′ hä)

Literary Element Author's Purpose *How do the first two paragraphs of the selection give you clues about the author's purpose for writing this essay?* L

Vocabulary

anthology (an thol′ ə jē) *n.* a collection of written works, such as poems, stories, or essays, in a single book or set

Reading Strategy Drawing Conclusions About Author's Beliefs *What conclusion can you draw about Cisneros's beliefs on what it takes to become a writer?* R

Teach

L Literary Element

Author's Purpose Answer: *She talks about her family and why she became a writer.* OL

R Reading Strategy

Drawing Conclusions About Author's Beliefs

Answer: *Students may conclude she thinks becoming a writer is a long, complex process.* OL

★ Viewing the Art

Answer: *The artist's use of color and definitive lines makes the woman in the painting stand out from her background—just as the author wants to "stand out."* AS

CheckPoint

Use the CheckPoint questions on Presentation Plus! to monitor students' comprehension. These questions can be used with interactive response keypads for immediate student feedback.

Readability Scores

Dale-Chall: 5.7
DRP: 57
Lexile: 900

English Language Coach

Mexican Culture Point out that Sandra Cisneros grew up in a household that was influenced by Mexican culture, which is different in many ways from U.S. culture. Have students discuss how their culture differs from U.S. culture. EL

Differentiated Instruction

Foreign Words Point out that Cisneros uses many Spanish words. Remind students to consult the footnotes to define these words. If there are any Spanish speakers, ask them to help with pronunciation. Point out that many Spanish words—such as *profesora*—have close English equivalents. BL

Academic Standards

Additional Support activities on p. 321 cover the following standards:

English Language Coach: **9.2** Develop strategies…[for] informational texts.

Differentiated Instruction: **9.1** Use phonics…and a growing knowledge of English and other languages to determine the meaning of words…

Teach

L1 Literary Element

Irony Ask: What are some clues that tell you that Cisneros is being ironic in this passage? *(She calls majoring in English "silly," and she asks a rhetorical question about "finding a nice professional" as a husband.)* OL

BI1 Big Idea

Looking into Lives Answer: *Their relationship is loving but not close.* OL

BI2 Big Idea

Looking into Lives Answer: *In some cultures, sons are more valued than daughters. Mr. Cisneros feels that people will be more impressed with him if he says all his children are sons.* OL

R1 Reading Strategy

Drawing Conclusions About Author's Beliefs

Ask: What does this passage suggest about the writer's feelings about the reading public? *(She regrets that most people are not interested in serious literature, but wants to write literature they will read.)* OL

husband, my father shakes his head even now and says I wasted all that education.

L1 In **retrospect**, I'm lucky my father believed daughters were meant for husbands. It meant it didn't matter if I majored in something silly like English. After all, I'd find a nice professional eventually, right? This allowed me the liberty to putter about **embroidering** my little poems and stories without my father interrupting with so much as a "What's that you're writing?"

But the truth is, I wanted him to interrupt. I wanted my father to understand what it was I was scribbling, to introduce me as "My only daughter, the writer." Not as "This is only my daughter. She teaches." *Es maestra*—teacher. Not even *profesora.*[2]

In a sense, everything I have ever written has been for him, to win his approval even though I know my father can't read English words, even though my father's only reading includes the brown-ink *Esto*[3] sports magazines from Mexico City and the bloody *¡Alarma!* magazines[4] that feature yet another sighting of *La Virgen de Guadalupe*[5] on a tortilla or a wife's revenge on her philandering husband[6] by bashing his skull in with a *molcajete* (a kitchen mortar[7] made of volcanic rock). Or the *fotonovelas,*[8] the little picture paperbacks with tragedy and trauma erupting from the characters' mouths in bubbles.

R1 My father represents, then, the public majority. A public who is disinterested in reading, and yet one whom I am writing about and for, and privately trying to woo.

When we were growing up in Chicago, we moved a lot because of my father. He suffered bouts of nostalgia.[9] Then we'd have to let go our flat, store the furniture with Mother's relatives, load the station wagon with baggage and bologna sandwiches and head south. To Mexico City.

We came back, of course. To yet another Chicago flat, another Chicago neighborhood, another Catholic school. Each time, my father would seek out the parish priest in order to get a tuition break, and complain or boast: "I have seven sons."

He meant *siete hijos,*[10] seven children, but he translated it as "sons." "I have seven sons." To anyone who would listen. The Sears Roebuck employee who sold us the washing machine. The short-order cook where my father ate his ham-and-eggs breakfasts. "I have seven sons." As if he deserved a medal from the state.

My papa. He didn't mean anything by that mistranslation, I'm sure. But somehow I could feel myself being erased. I'd tug my father's sleeve and whisper: "Not seven sons. Six! and *one daughter*."

When my oldest brother graduated from medical school, he **fulfilled** my father's dream that we study hard and use this—our heads, instead of this—our hands. Even now my father's hands are thick and yellow, stubbed by a history of hammer and nails

2. *Es maestra* (es mī äs ʹ trə); *profesora* (prō ʹ fes ō ʹ rə) means "professor."
3. *Esto* (äs ʹ tō)
4. The *¡Alarma!* magazines feature exciting stories about famous people, strange events, and shocking crimes.
5. *La Virgen de Guadalupe* (lä vēr ʹ hin dā gwä də loo ʹ pā), meaning "the Virgin of Guadalupe," is a name for Jesus' mother, Mary, the patron saint of Mexico.
6. A *philandering husband* is one who cheats on his wife.
7. A *molcajete* (mōl ʹ kə hā ʹ tā), or *kitchen mortar,* is a thick bowl used to crush substances, such as dried spices, into a powder or paste.
8. *fotonovelas* (fō ʹ tō nō vā ʹ läs)
9. *Nostalgia* is a sentimental longing for the past.
10. *Siete hijos* (sye ʹ tā ē ʹ hōs)

Big Idea Looking into Lives *How would you describe the relationship between Cisneros and her father?* BI1

Vocabulary

retrospect (ret ʹ rə spekt ʹ) *n.* the act of looking back or thinking about the past

embroider (em broi ʹ dər) *v.* to make a story more interesting with imaginary details or exaggerations

Big Idea Looking into Lives *Why does the author's father boast about having seven sons rather than seven children?* BI2

Vocabulary

fulfill (fool fil ʹ) *v.* to measure up to, or satisfy; to bring to pass

Additional Support

Leveled Reading An adapted version of this selection is available on page 236 of *Jamestown Literature: An Adapted Reader,* grade 9.

Skills Practice

GRAMMAR: Compound Adjectives

Write the following phrases on the board: would-be writer, working-class family, short-order cook. Point out that these compound adjectives use hyphens to show that together they act as a single adjective. Because they precede the noun, they are hyphenated.

Have students identify the words that should be hyphenated.

1. Anna is known as a very self reliant woman. (self-reliant)
2. Mrs. Williams is a well liked teacher. (well-liked)
3. Don lives in the second floor apartment. (second-floor) OL

and twine and coils and springs. "Use this," my father said, tapping his head, "and not this," showing us those hands. He always looked tired when he said it.

Wasn't college an investment? And hadn't I spent all those years in college? And if I didn't marry, what was it all for? Why would anyone go to college and then choose to be poor? Especially someone who had always been poor.

Last year, after ten years of writing professionally, the financial rewards started to trickle in. My second National Endowment for the Arts[11] Fellowship. A guest professorship at the University of California, Berkeley. My book, which sold to a major New York publishing house.

At Christmas, I flew home to Chicago. The house was throbbing, same as always: hot *tamales*[12] and sweet *tamales* hissing in my mother's pressure cooker, and everybody—my mother, six brothers, wives, babies, aunts, cousins—talking too loud and at the same time, like in a Fellini[13] film, because that's just how we are.

I went upstairs to my father's room. One of my stories had just been translated into Spanish and published in an anthology of Chicano[14] writing, and I wanted to show it to him. Ever since he recovered from a stroke two years ago, my father likes to spend his leisure hours horizontally. And that's how I found him, watching a Pedro Infante movie on Galavision[15] and eating rice pudding.

There was a glass filmed with milk on the bedside table. There were several vials of pills and balled Kleenex. And on the floor, one black sock and a plastic urinal that I didn't want to look at but looked at anyway. Pedro Infante was about to burst into song, and my father was laughing.

I'm not sure if it was because my story was translated into Spanish, or because it was published in Mexico, or perhaps because the story dealt with Tepeyac, the *colonia*[16] my father was raised in and the house he grew up in, but at any rate, my father punched the mute button on his remote control and read my story.

I sat on the bed next to my father and waited. He read it very slowly. As if he were reading each line over and over. He laughed at all the right places and read lines he liked out loud. He pointed and asked questions: "Is this So-and-so?" "Yes," I said. He kept reading.

When he was finally finished, after what seemed like hours, my father looked up and asked: "Where can we get more copies of this for the relatives?"

Of all the wonderful things that happened to me last year, that was the most wonderful. ∾

11. The *National Endowment for the Arts* is a U.S. government agency that awards money in the form of grants and fellowships to writers and other artists.
12. A *tamale* (tə mä′ lā) is a Mexican dish made of highly seasoned ground meat that is rolled in cornmeal dough, wrapped in corn husks, and steamed.
13. The movies of Italian director Federico *Fellini* (1920–1993) are often filled with strange characters and noisy, chaotic events.
14. *Chicano* (chi kä′ nō) means "Mexican American."
15. *Pedro Infante* (in fän′ tā) is a popular Mexican movie star who can occasionally be seen on *Galavision*, a Spanish-language, cable-television channel.
16. *Tepeyac* (tā pā yäk) is a district *(colonia)* of Mexico City.

Reading Strategy Drawing Conclusions About Author's Beliefs *Mr. Cisneros's beliefs about the purpose of education are clearly stated. What conclusion can you draw about Sandra Cisneros's beliefs about education?* **R2**

Literary Element Author's Purpose *Why do you think Cisneros tells this story about her father?* **L2**

Reading Strategy Drawing Conclusions About Author's Beliefs *Why is this experience important to Cisneros as a daughter, as a Mexican American woman, and as a writer?* **R3**

Teach

R2 Reading Strategy

Drawing Conclusions About Author's Beliefs

Answer: *She believes in the value of education for its own sake and not just for economic advancement.* **OL**

L2 Literary Element

Author's Purpose **Answer:** *The story shows that she achieved her goal and won her father's approval.* **OL**

R3 Reading Strategy

Drawing Conclusions About Author's Beliefs

Answer: *Cisneros finally gets the recognition she deserves from her father and feels proud that she is able to win over someone who ordinarily does not enjoy reading serious fiction. She has finally connected with her father in a way they can both understand.* **OL**

CheckPoint

Use the CheckPoint questions on Presentation Plus! to check students' mastery of the selection. These questions can be used with interactive response keypads for immediate student feedback.

English Language Coach

Using *Only* Draw students' attention to this sentence: "I was/am the only daughter and *only* a daughter." Have students paraphrase it. *(As the one girl in my family, I was always considered less important than my brothers.)* Note the two meanings of *only* and encourage students to think of synonyms such as *single* and *sole* and *merely, simply,* and *just.* **EL**

Academic Standards

Additional Support activities on pp. 322 and 323 cover the following standards:

Skills Practice: **9.6.1** Identify and correctly use...phrases...and hyphens.

English Language Coach: **9.1** Use...context clues...to determine the meaning of words...

AFTER YOU READ

Assess

1. Students' responses should give reasons for their reactions.
2. (a) Large, working-class Mexican American family. (b) Her desire to win her father's approval had the most impact on her development as a writer.
3. (a) He expected his sons to become well-paid professionals and his daughter to marry well. (b) Yes; his lack of interest let her work without interference, and his lack of support drove her to succeed. No; she succeeded in spite of his neglect.
4. (a) She is thrilled. (b) The story was translated into Spanish, published in Mexico, and it was about his home.
5. They do not really value writers or reading. The average person is more interested in financial success.
6. Confirms: Her family and her role in it shaped her development as a writer. Contradicts: She became a writer in spite of these facts.
7. It resulted in having solitude and time to think but also distanced her from father.
8. Possible answers: All children want this approval; culture, personality, gender, may affect how some feel.

AFTER YOU READ

RESPONDING AND THINKING CRITICALLY

Respond

1. How did you react to the author's experience as an only daughter?

Recall and Interpret

2. (a)Describe Cisneros's family. (b)In your opinion, why does Cisneros write more about her father in this essay than about any other family member?
3. (a)How was her father's attitude toward his daughter's college education different from his attitude toward his sons' educations? (b)Do you think that Cisneros was affected by his attitude? Explain why or why not, using details from the selection to support your answer.
4. (a)How does Cisneros react to her father's request for copies of her story? (b)In your opinion, why does the father react differently to the story she gives him at Christmas than to all the other work she has done?

Analyze and Evaluate

5. By writing "My father represents, then, the public majority," what might Cisneros be saying about her father—and about society? Explain.
6. "I am the only daughter in a family of six sons. *That* explains everything." In what ways does the essay confirm or contradict Cisneros's statement?
7. Explain how being the only daughter, and "only" a daughter, has proven to be both a positive and a negative experience for Cisneros.

Connect

8. Cisneros seeks approval from her father. In your experience, is this a goal that is specific to certain cultures or a common goal of all children? Explain.
9. **Big Idea** **Looking into Lives** How does the use of Spanish words, as well as the references to Mexican television, food, and magazines, help you look into Cisneros's life?

DAILY LIFE AND CULTURE

Social Change in the 1960s

In the late 1960s and early 1970s, Chicago had the third largest Mexican-origin population in the United States behind Los Angeles and San Antonio. Many Mexican Americans in urban areas faced unemployment, poverty, and racial discrimination. During the 1960s, these problems helped spark the Chicano movement, or the Mexican American struggle for political and civil rights. In part, this movement sought to improve education, gain voting rights, help migrant farm workers, and awaken cultural pride. During that period, some Mexican Americans also began to question traditional family structure and social roles.

Group Activity Discuss the following questions with classmates. Use evidence from "Only Daughter" to support your opinions.

1. Do you think Cisneros was influenced by political and social changes taking place in the 1960s and 1970s? Why or why not?
2. How might the Chicano movement have affected a young, aspiring writer like Cisneros? Explain your answer.

9. They bring to life the culture that helped shape her father's experience and her own.

Daily Life and Culture

1. Yes: Her independence and confidence suggest that she was influenced by the women's movement and the era's emphasis on cultural pride.
2. Some students may say it inspired Chicano writers to pursue their dreams. It also may have influenced their choice of subject matter.

LITERARY ANALYSIS

Literary Element Author's Purpose

Sometimes an author may have more than one **purpose** for writing. For example, you may find parts of "Only Daughter" entertaining, but Cisneros also had something important to say about being a daughter and the role of women in society.

1. In your opinion, what is Cisneros's primary purpose for writing this essay? Explain.
2. This work was published in *Glamour* magazine, which is read almost exclusively by women, many of whom are young and single. How might this information help you understand the author's purpose?

Review: Characterization

As you learned on page 161, an author reveals the personality of a character through **characterization**. In direct characterization, an author makes direct statements about a character. In indirect characterization, an author reveals a character through his or her words, thoughts, and actions and through what other characters think and say about that character.

Partner Activity With a partner, find details that reveal what Cisneros's father is like. Then complete a character web like the one below. When you are finished, identify the methods of characterization that Cisneros uses to bring her father to life in this autobiographical essay.

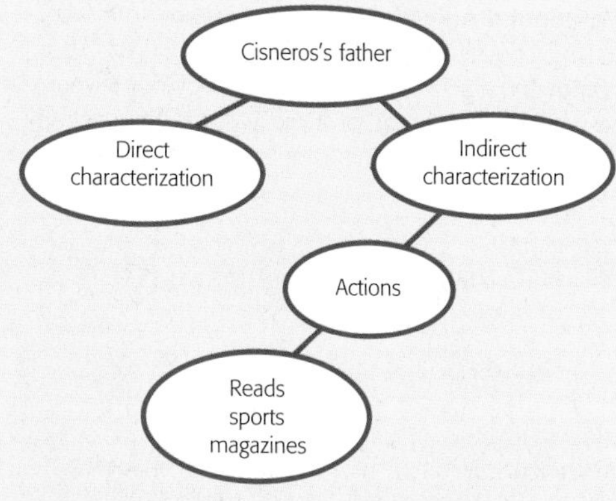

READING AND VOCABULARY

Reading Strategy Drawing Conclusions About Author's Beliefs

Drawing conclusions about an author's beliefs can help you understand the author's purpose for writing a literary work and better appreciate his or her choice of subject. Refer to the chart in which you listed facts and details in this selection about Cisneros's beliefs regarding the role of women, getting an education, and becoming a writer.

1. From the facts and details in your chart, what conclusion can you draw about Cisneros's beliefs on the role of women?
2. What conclusion can you draw about Cisneros's beliefs on getting an education?
3. What conclusion can you draw about Cisneros's beliefs on becoming a writer?

Vocabulary Practice

Practice with Analogies Complete each analogy below by identifying the relationship between the first pair of words and applying that relationship to the second pair of words.

1. **poem : anthology :: episode :**
   a. story **b.** series **c.** play
2. **embroider : exaggerate :: lie :**
   a. lesson **b.** deceive **c.** disagree
3. **retrospect : remember :: opinion :**
   a. believe **b.** fact **c.** debate
4. **fulfill : abandon :: succeed :**
   a. ascertain **b.** overcome **c.** fail

Academic Vocabulary

Here is a word from the vocabulary list on page R80. This word will help you think, talk, and write about the selection.

adequate (ad′ə kwət) *adj.* reasonably sufficient to satisfy a requirement

Practice and Apply
Does Cisneros provide **adequate** information for you to understand her father? Explain.

AFTER YOU READ

Assess

Literary Element

1. Possible answers: To show that daughters should be as valued as sons; to show that women's roles in society can extend beyond those of a wife, mother, and daughter.
2. Many young, single women face similar professional and personal struggles.

Review: Characterization

Sample details for web: direct—believes his daughter's destiny is to be a wife; indirect—words: says daughter wasted her education; moved family often to Mexico City; told priest he had seven sons; says "Use this."

Reading Strategy

1. She believes that women should be able to have a career and do not necessarily have to be wives and mothers.
2. Cisneros believes education is valuable for its own sake.
3. It requires preparation and struggle.

Vocabulary

1. b **2.** b **3.** a **4.** c

Academic Vocabulary

1. Students should say that she provides ample details and should give examples from the text.

AFTER YOU READ

Assess

Writing About Literature

Students' response essays should

- identify the theme of "Only Daughter."
- clearly state students' response to the theme in the introduction.
- use evidence from the selection to support their reasons for their responses.
- include a conclusion.

Listening and Speaking

Students should incorporate details from the text into their role-playing. Examples: Smile—When reading the lines he liked out loud; feel regret—when he says that she wasted all her education; ask questions—when he finished reading her essay.

Cisneros's Language and Style

Mexican-American mother
ham-and-eggs breakfasts
brown-ink Esto sports magazines

WRITING AND EXTENDING

Writing About Literature

Respond to Theme The implied theme of "Only Daughter" is that our culture, our personal experiences, and the time and place in which we grow up helps make us who we are. Do you agree or disagree with Cisneros's ideas and opinions? Write a brief essay in which you express your personal response to the theme of this selection.

Begin with an introduction in which you state the theme of "Only Daughter" and your response to it. In the body of your essay, explain your response using evidence from the selection. Conclude your essay with a summary of your response. Follow the writing path shown here to help you organize your essay.

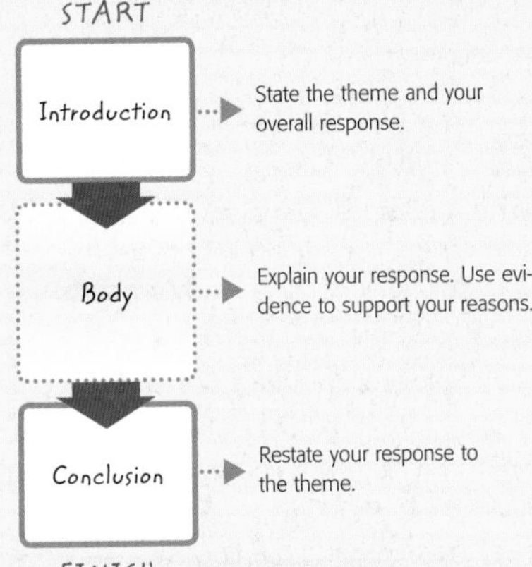
START
Introduction
State the theme and your overall response.
Body
Explain your response. Use evidence to support your reasons.
Conclusion
Restate your response to the theme.
FINISH

After completing your draft, meet with a peer reviewer to evaluate each other's work and to suggest revisions. Then proofread and edit your draft to correct errors in spelling, grammar, and punctuation.

Listening and Speaking

Review how Cisneros's father reacts when he reads his daughter's story in the anthology of Chicano writing (page 323). With a partner, role-play for the rest of the class how you think father and daughter might interact while he reads and reacts to her essay, "Only Daughter." Find places in the essay that might, for example, provoke him to smile, feel regret, or ask questions.

GRAMMAR AND STYLE

Cisneros's Language and Style

Using Compound Adjectives A compound adjective consists of two or more words that function as one adjective to modify or describe a noun or pronoun (for example, a dog that is *reddish brown*). When a compound adjective comes before the noun or pronoun it modifies, a hyphen shows that the words function together as a single adjective (a *reddish-brown* dog).

In "Only Daughter," Cisneros uses compound adjectives that are joined with a hyphen. For example, she writes, "But that aloneness, that loneliness, was good for a would-be writer." The compound adjective "would-be" refers to a person who, later in life, *would be* a writer.

Examples	Meaning
would-be writer	someone who *would be* a writer
working-class family	people who *work* for a living
short-order cook	someone who cooks individual, or *short*, *orders*

Activity Create a chart of your own, listing three other hyphenated compound adjectives that you find in "Only Daughter."

Revising Check

Compound Adjectives When you revise your own writing, check that you have correctly hyphenated any compound adjectives. Have a partner look over your response to the theme of "Only Daughter" to spot any compound adjectives that should be hyphenated.

LiteratureOnline **Web Activities** For eFlashcards, Selection Quick Checks, and other Web activities, go to www.glencoe.com.

Revising Check

Make sure that students, when revising their essays, understand that compound adjectives are hyphenated only when they appear before the word they modify.

Web Activities Have students access the Web site for interactive activities that will help them assess their understanding of the selection.

A Brother's Crime

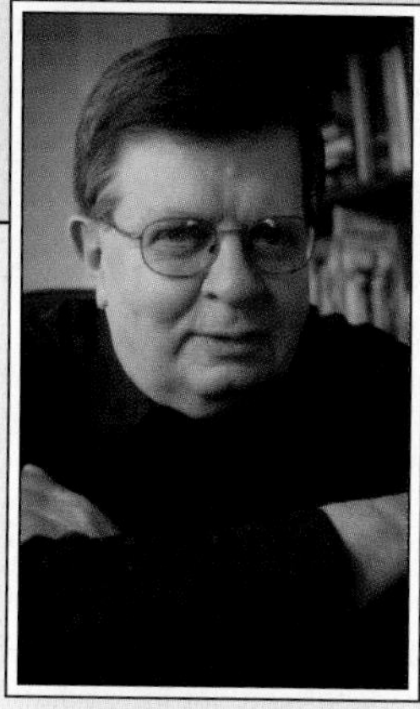

MEET JAMES CROSS GIBLIN

Who wants to write about the "bad guys" in history? James Cross Giblin does. He has already written about Adolf Hitler and John Wilkes Booth, Abraham Lincoln's assassin. He is currently working on the biography of Senator Joseph McCarthy, the man whose investigations of suspected Communists ruined so many lives in the 1950s. For Giblin, "bad guys"—who often see themselves as heroes—make terrific stories.

Theater Background Giblin, who wrote his own comic strips as a child, was more interested in acting than writing when he was in high school. After seeing a notice in a local newspaper, he auditioned for a role in a community play and got the part. After the play was over, he said, "I was hooked on the theater." In college, he studied drama and performed in many plays.

"I approach my nonfiction topics as if I were playing detective."

—James Cross Giblin

Giblin feels that his acting work actually helps him develop narrative interest and pacing in his nonfiction writing. "My training in the theater has given me a sense of drama that comes in handy when I'm trying to shape [my writing] in a way that will catch and hold the reader's attention," he says. He explains that actors ask themselves, "What is my character's chief goal, and how does he or she go about trying to achieve it?" This is similar, Giblin points out, to the biographer's job of determining his or her subject's motivations and inner life.

The Writing Life Because acting was an unpredictable career, Giblin started working as an editor. He enjoyed this career tremendously and discovered that he particularly liked working on books for young audiences. From editing, the transition to writing was natural, and in 1980, working with collaborator Dale Ferguson, Giblin published *The Scarecrow Book*. It was the beginning of a long list of nonfiction titles on topics ranging from skyscrapers and defensive walls to windows, pasteurized milk, and famous people.

Finding the Facts Giblin enjoys the research required to write a nonfiction book. Tracking down information seems to come naturally to him, and many critics have noted his thoroughness in this area. Giblin does not do his research exclusively in libraries. For his biography of Hitler, for example, he traveled across Europe twice.

Giblin asserts that he is not a professional historian, which he feels may be an advantage to his readers. As an amateur, he says, "I approach a subject on much the same level as my young readers, and we discover together what's interesting and important about it."

James Cross Giblin was born in 1933.

Literature Online **Author Search** For more about James Cross Giblin, go to www.glencoe.com.

Focus

BELLRINGER

Bellringer Options
Daily Language Practice Transparency 29

Or discuss with students the idea of family loyalties. Could there be a situation in which loyalty to a family member is severely tested?

Ask: What kind of situation might make you reconsider your loyalty to a member of your own family?

Author Search To expand students' appreciation of James Cross Giblin, have them access the Web site for additional information and resources.

Selection Skills

A Brother's Crime

Literary Elements
- Historical Narrative (SE pp. 328, 329, 331, 333)
- Narrator (SE p. 333)

Reading Skills
- Activating Prior Knowledge (SE pp. 328–330, 334)
- Identifying Genre (SE p. 335)

Vocabulary Skills
- Word Origins (SE p. 334)
- Academic Vocabulary (SE p. 334)

Listening/Speaking/Viewing Skills
- Analyzing a Graphic Novel (SE pp. 335–339)
- Performing (SE p. 334)

Writing Skills/Grammar
- Analysis of Historical Context (SE p. 334)

BEFORE YOU READ

Focus

Summary

In this historical narrative, the author describes the feelings and actions of Edwin Booth, brother of John Wilkes Booth. The narrative is set when Edwin learns that his younger brother, a fellow actor, has assassinated President Abraham Lincoln. Unlike his brother, Edwin is an admirer of Lincoln, and he knows that his life will never be the same again.

V Vocabulary

Vocabulary File Say: Add these words and definitions to your vocabulary file. For each word, include a sentence that gives you an example of how to use the word. **OL** Students with English language needs should include the pronunciation of these words in their files. **EL**

Literary Elements Have students access the Web site to improve their understanding of historical narrative.

LITERATURE PREVIEW

Connecting to the Text

In "A Brother's Crime," a man's life is changed by his brother's crime. Before you read the selection, think about the following questions:

- How would you deal with the news that a family member had committed a crime?
- How might your life change if someone close to you committed a terrible crime?

Building Background

Stage actors were the celebrities of the nineteenth century. Perhaps the greatest actor of his day was Edwin Booth, of whom one admiring critic wrote, "Edwin Booth has done more for the stage in America than any other man." Lincoln, who was an enthusiastic and regular theatergoer, saw Edwin Booth perform many times. Edwin's brother, John Wilkes Booth, was also an accomplished actor. When John Wilkes Booth shot Lincoln, he fired his shot from the president's box, jumped onto the stage, and cried out, *"Sic semper tyrannis."* This is the motto of the state of Virginia, which means "death always to tyrants." John Wilkes Booth, who believed that his actions were honorable, was easily recognized in what became his final role.

Setting Purposes for Reading

Big Idea Looking into Lives

Notice how Giblin uses contrast, as well as standard methods of characterization such as words and actions, to reveal Edwin Booth at this key moment in his life.

Literary Element Historical Narrative

A **historical narrative** is a work of nonfiction that tells the story of important historical events or developments. As you read the historical narrative that follows, note how you learn facts and gain insights into the lives of real people, as well as into the time period.

- See Literary Terms Handbook, p. R8.

 **Interactive Literary Elements Handbook** To review or learn more about the literary elements, go to www.glencoe.com.

READING PREVIEW

Reading Strategy Activating Prior Knowledge

Activating prior knowledge is considering what you already know about a person, place, idea, or event in a literary work and using that knowledge to deepen your understanding of what you are reading. As you read "A Brother's Crime," you can activate, or use, your prior knowledge of Lincoln, the Civil War, and human nature.

Reading Tip: Recording What You Know Record details about which you have prior knowledge.

Detail	Prior Knowledge
p. 329 "April 14, 1865"	This is near the end of the Civil War.

Vocabulary

premonition (prē′ mə nish′ ən) *n.* anticipation of an event without outside warning or reason; p. 329 *Dad had a premonition about the storm, so we all moved to higher ground.*

intimation (in′ tə mā′ shən) *n.* a suggestion or hint; p. 330 *The slight tic in the applicant's eye was the only intimation of his nervousness.*

calamity (kə lam′ ə tē) *n.* a disastrous event; p. 331 *The hurricane was a calamity for which few people were fully prepared.*

perpetrator (pur′ pə trā′ tər) *n.* one who commits a crime or other similar act; p. 331 *Police captured the perpetrator within hours.*

incriminating (in krim′ ə nāt′ ing) *adj.* showing involvement in a crime; p. 332 *Detectives found stolen goods and other incriminating items.*

Vocabulary Tip: Word Origins The origin of a word is its history. Many English words come from Latin, Greek, and earlier forms of the English language.

INDIANA ACADEMIC STANDARDS (pages 328–334)

9.2 Develop strategies such as...analyzing...purpose...

9.2.7 Evaluate...the way in which the author's intent affects the structure and tone of the text.

9.5.3 Write...analytical essays...

9.3.12 Analyze the way in which a work of literature is related to the themes and issues of its historical period.

Selection Resources

Print Materials
- Unit 2 Resources (Fast File), pp. 23–25
- Leveled Vocabulary Development, p. 23
- Selection and Unit Assessments, pp. 49–50
- Selection Quick Checks, p. 29

Transparencies
- Bellringer Options Transparencies: Daily Language Practice Transparency 27
- Literary Elements Transparency 31

Technology
- TeacherWorks Plus™ CD-ROM
- StudentWorks Plus™ CD-ROM
- Presentation Plus!™ CD-ROM
- Literature Online, glencoe.com
- Online Student Edition, mhln.com
- Exam*View*® Assessment Suite CD-ROM
- Vocabulary PuzzleMaker CD-ROM
- Listening Library, disc 1 track 27

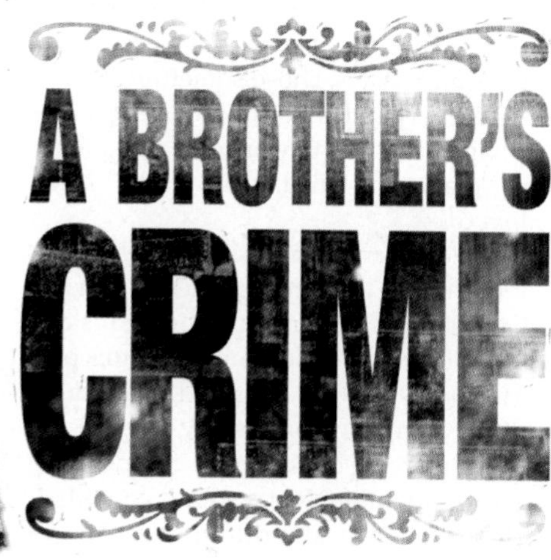

James Cross Giblin

Edwin Booth often had **premonitions** that something bad was going to happen. But there is no evidence that he had any advance warning on April 14, 1865, of the terrible event that was about to befall him and the nation. On that Friday—Good Friday[1]—Booth sat in his dressing room at the Boston Theatre, applying his makeup for the evening performance. The theater's manager had told him the house was sold out, and Booth wanted to give the crowd his best.

An air of eager expectation filled the auditorium as the audience members took their seats in the orchestra[2] or climbed the steep stairs to the balcony. Many had come just to see Booth, who, at thirty-one, was considered one of America's finest actors, if not the finest. But many others had come to celebrate the end of the Civil War. L2

The Sunday before, on April 9, the Confederate general, Robert E. Lee, had surrendered to the Union commander, Ulysses S. Grant, at the little town of Appomattox Courthouse in Virginia. Four years of increasingly bloody warfare had ended in victory for the North. Now, while the South mourned its loss, people all across the North rejoiced that the fighting was over. The Union flag—the American flag—flew everywhere, and red-white-and-blue bunting[3] decorated lampposts and storefronts in towns large and small.

On Good Friday, thousands of Northerners gave thanks for the victory by attending church services in the morning. That evening, theaters were packed in cities

1. *Good Friday* is the day that Christians observe as the anniversary of Christ's crucifixion.
2. Here, *orchestra* refers to a seating area on the first floor of a theater.
3. *Bunting* is loosely woven fabric or coarse muslin used for flags and other decorations.

Literary Element Historical Narrative *Identify the time, the place, and the person who is the subject of this historical narrative.* L1

Vocabulary

premonition (prē′ mə nish′ ən) *n.* anticipation of an event without outside warning or reason

Reading Strategy Activating Prior Knowledge *How did many Southerners feel at this time?* R

Teach

L1 Literary Element

Historical Narrative Answer: *The date is April 14, 1865 (Good Friday), and the place is the Boston Theatre. Edwin Booth is the subject of the narrative.* OL

L2 Literary Element

Historical Narrative Ask: How does the author of this narrative set the scene in historical context? *(He describes Booth as one of the finest actors of the day, and he refers specifically to the end of the Civil War in 1865.)* OL

R Reading Strategy

Activating Prior Knowledge
Answer: *Students may name emotions ranging from grief to violent resentment.* OL

CheckPoint

Use the CheckPoint questions on Presentation Plus! to monitor students' comprehension. These questions can be used with interactive response keypads for immediate student feedback.

Readability Scores
Dale-Chall: 7.7
DRP: 60
Lexile: 1110

English Language Coach

Articles Using *a, an,* and *the* may present a challenge to English language learners. Point out that *a* or *an* is used the first time a topic is introduced: "I saw a dog." *The* is used when the reader already knows the thing or person referred to: "I saw the dog." Have students copy a brief story from a newspaper or magazine, leaving blank spaces in place of the articles. Then have them exchange papers with a partner and fill in the appropriate articles. EL

Academic Standards
The Additional Support activity on p. 329 covers the following standard:
English Language Coach: **9.6.2** Demonstrate an understanding of…the proper placement of modifiers…

Teach

L1 Literary Element

Suspense Ask: What details does the author use in this paragraph to establish suspense? *(He refers to the packed theaters, and he interrupts the main thrust of the narrative by including details about Booth's choice of play. Perhaps significantly, Booth plays a starring role as the villain.)* OL

BI Big Idea

Looking into Lives Answer: *The details suggest that Booth was not overly dramatic or a person who wanted attention, but rather a restrained professional.* OL

R1 Reading Strategy

Activating Prior Knowledge Lincoln's wartime suspension of such constitutional rights as *habeas corpus* may have fed John Booth's suspicions.

Ask: Why might a president assume extraordinary powers in wartime? *(Possible response: To maintain order and to lead effectively in a time of crisis)* OL

R2 Reading Strategy

Activating Prior Knowledge Answer: *Most students will know that the more important stories are placed on the front page.* OL

throughout the North—and Boston was no exception. For the occasion, Edwin Booth, who was famed for his performances in Shakespeare's plays, chose something in a less classical vein. He decided to appear as the villain, Sir Edward Mortimer, in a melodrama[4] that never failed to please the crowd: *The Iron Chest.* ★

When Edwin made his entrance, clad[5] in black velvet, the audience greeted him with loud applause. Unlike most actors of his day, Booth never indulged in grand gestures or studied[6] poses. Instead, he acted in a more realistic style, relying on his low, intense voice and piercing dark eyes to compel the spectators' attention. Not a sound could be heard in the vast theater during the climactic death scene, when Booth, as Sir Edward, finally admitted his guilt. And at the end, he was brought back for curtain call after curtain call.

That night Edwin, who was staying at a friend's house in Boston, had trouble getting to sleep. But he still had no **intimation** of the shock that was in store for him the next morning. Without knocking first, his valet[7] burst into his bedroom shortly after seven. Thrusting a newspaper in front of a dazed Edwin, the man exclaimed, "Mr. Booth, President Lincoln has been shot!" Before Edwin could absorb that terrible fact, the valet went on: "And—oh, Mr. Booth—they say your brother John has done it!"

His brother John . . . how could that be? Edwin knew that John strongly supported the South and hated Abraham Lincoln. He'd often heard John state, without any evidence, that Lincoln would make himself king of the United States if the North won the war. The last time they'd been together, John had stormed out of the room when Edwin, whose sympathies were with the North, told him that he'd voted for Lincoln's re-election. Oh, John could be headstrong.[8] But to shoot the president—to try to kill him? That wasn't the brother he knew and loved.

Edwin grabbed the newspaper from the valet and quickly scanned the story of the shooting, which occupied the entire front page. It said that President Lincoln had been shot and gravely wounded in his box at Ford's Theatre in Washington, where he and his wife had gone to see a play. And there it was, the name of the attacker, who had been recognized at once by many in the audience. He was the dashing, dark-haired young actor who stirred many feminine hearts when he played Romeo in Shakespeare's *Romeo and Juliet* and other romantic roles: John Wilkes Booth.

Later, Edwin would write to a friend that when he saw his brother's name in print, he felt "as if I had been struck on the head by a hammer." As he struggled to comprehend the dreadful news, his mind was a jumble of worries and fears. He thought of his mother, at home in New York with his older sister, Rosalie. John had always been his mother's favorite; how would she deal with the news? Would she have the strength to go on? And where was John now? The newspaper said he had escaped—where had he gone?

While Edwin was still sorting out his reactions and trying to decide what to do, word came that Lincoln had lost his night-long battle for life. The president had died early that morning without ever regaining consciousness. Shortly after that,

4. A *melodrama* is a type of play that emphasizes action and dramatic effects over characterization and theme.
5. Here, *clad* means "dressed."
6. Here, *studied* means "carefully prepared."
7. A *valet* is a personal servant.
8. *Headstrong* means "impatient" or "unwilling to accept advice or control."

Big Idea Looking into Lives *What do these details suggest about Booth's personality?* BI

Vocabulary

intimation (in′ tə mā′ shən) *n.* a suggestion or hint

Reading Strategy Activating Prior Knowledge *What types of stories typically appear on the front pages of newspapers?* R2

Additional Support

Skills Practice

GRAMMAR: Compound Verbs A compound verb is made up of two or more simple verbs joined by a conjunction and having the same subject. The most commonly used conjunctions are *and* and *or.* The correlative conjunctions *neither . . . nor* and *both . . . and* may also join compound verbs. Point out the compound verb in the following example: "Edwin *grabbed* the newspaper from the valet and quickly *scanned* the story of the shooting. . . ." Have students practice writing sentences with compound verbs. They can write five sentences with simple verbs and then rewrite each sentence using compound verbs. OL a messenger arrived with a letter from the manager of the Boston Theatre. "My dear sir," the letter began. "A fearful **calamity** is upon us. The President of the United States has fallen by the hand of an assassin, and I am shocked to say suspicion points to one nearly related to you as the **perpetrator** of this horrid deed. God grant it may not prove so!"

R3 But the manager was taking no chances. He went on: "With this knowledge, and out of respect for the anguish which will fill the public mind as soon as the appalling[9] fact shall be fully revealed, I have concluded to close the Boston Theatre until further notice." The manager ended on a cool, impersonal note. "Please signify to me[10] your cooperation in this matter."

Edwin drafted a quick response to the manager's letter. It was written in the formal style of the time, but Edwin's feelings can be sensed between the lines. "With deepest sorrow and great agitation, I thank you for relieving me from my engagement[11] with yourself and the public," he wrote. "The news of the morning has made me wretched indeed, not only because I received the unhappy tidings of the suspicion of a brother's crime, but because a good man, and a most justly honored and patriotic ruler, has fallen by the hand of an assassin."

Edwin concluded the letter with a strong statement of his own loyalty and patriotism. "While mourning, in common with all other loyal hearts, the death of the President, I am oppressed by a private woe[12] not to be expressed in words. But whatever calamity

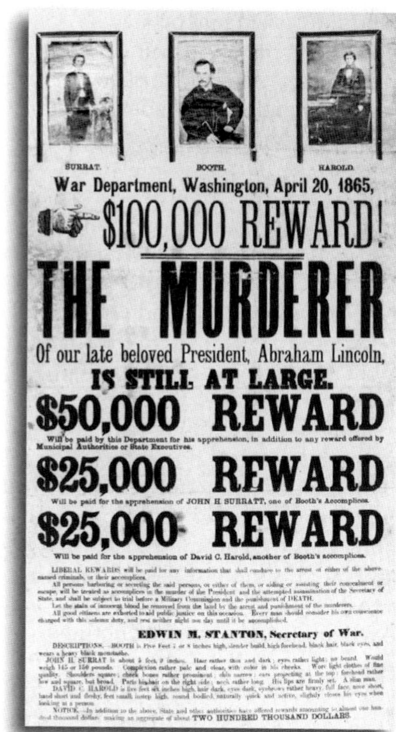

may befall me or mine, my country, one and indivisible, has my warmest devotion."

SURRAT.
BOOTH.
HAROLD.
War Department, Washington, April 20, 1865,
$100,000 REWARD!
THE MURDERER
Of our late beloved President, Abraham Lincoln,
IS STILL AT LARGE.
$50,000 REWARD
$25,000 REWARD
$25,000 REWARD
EDWIN M. STANTON, Secretary of War.

Now that the Boston Theatre was closed, Edwin had no reason to stay on in Boston. He decided to return to New York as soon as possible and sent a telegram to his mother saying he would take the midnight train and be home on Sunday morning. But he had to delay his departure. Federal marshals[13] wanted to question him about his relations with his brother and what, if anything, he knew about the assassination of the president. They also wanted to conduct a thorough search of his luggage.

Edwin did not keep a diary or journal, so there's no way of knowing what questions

9. *Appalling* means "horrifying."
10. *Signify to me* is an old-fashioned way of saying "Let me know of."
11. Here, *engagement* means "period of time working."
12. *Woe* is sorrow.

13. *Federal marshals* are law enforcement officers concerned with national issues.

Vocabulary

calamity (kə lam′ ə tē) *n.* a disastrous event

perpetrator (pur′ pə trā′ tər) *n.* one who commits a crime or other similar act

Literary Element Historical Narrative *How does this account differ from anything else you have read or heard about the events following Lincoln's assassination?* L2

Teach

R3 Reading Strategy

Evaluating Ask: Do you think the theater manager made the correct decision? Why or why not? *(Students may say that his fear of possible violence was well founded but that he could have written more tactfully to Edwin.)* OL

L2 Literary Element

Historical Narrative Answer: *This account gives a personal account of the assassin's brother, rather than an account of either Lincoln or John Wilkes Booth.* OL

Cultural Note

The Iron Chest George Colman the Younger wrote *The Iron Chest* in 1796, based on William Goodwin's popular 1794 novel, *Caleb Williams.* The play is a drama involving murder and deceit, with the lowly but good steward Willard (Caleb Williams) facing off with his villainous master, Sir Edward Mortimer. AS

Differentiated Instruction

Formal Style Edwin Booth's statements in his response to the manager of the Boston Theatre reveal his personal feelings, but the formality of his style may pose a challenge to some readers. Provide an opportunity to hear his words spoken. Play the audiotape for the class, or invite an expressive reader to read Edwin's letter aloud. Encourage students to raise their hands whenever they do not understand something. Pause and clear up the issue before going on. BL

Academic Standards

Additional Support activities on pp. 330 and 331 cover the following standards:

Skills Practice: **9.6.2** Demonstrate an understanding of…proper English usage…

Differentiated Instruction: **9.7.1** Summarize a speaker's purpose and…ask questions concerning the speaker's content…

Teach

L1 Literary Element

Characterization Ask: What does this passage reveal about Edwin's personality? *(He worked hard to gain a reputation for integrity, is sensitive to family ties, and is basically optimistic, even at a time of crisis.)* **OL**

BI Big Idea

Looking into Lives Answer: *Taking a midnight train and pulling his hat low suggest that he was worried about being recognized and injured.* **OL**

L2 Literary Element

Historical Narrative Although no one really knows what was on Edwin's mind, the writer offers his guesses, or conjectures, about Edwin's thoughts. **Ask:** Do you think these guesses are reasonable? Why or why not? *(Students may say yes because Edwin is known to have admired Lincoln, and he would naturally be concerned about his career.)* **OL**

CheckPoint

Use the CheckPoint questions on Presentation Plus! to check students' mastery of the selection. These questions can be used with interactive response keypads for immediate student feedback.

the authorities asked him or how he answered them. But an indication of his mood at this time can be glimpsed in a letter he wrote his friend Adam Badeau while waiting for permission to leave Boston.

L1 "You know, Ad, how I have labored to establish a name that all my friends would be proud of; how I have always toiled for the comfort and welfare of my family—and how loyal I have been from the first of this rebellion [the Civil War]. And you must feel deeply the agony I bear in thus being blasted in all my hopes by a villain [John] who seemed so lovable and in whom all his family found a source of joy in his boyish and confiding nature." Booth ended on a slightly more positive note: "I have a great deal to tell you of myself & the beautiful plans I had for the future—but must wait until my mind is more settled. I am half crazy now—"

The federal marshals found nothing **incriminating** in Edwin's trunks, or in his correspondence. He was not given clearance[14] to travel, though, until several prominent friends, including the governor of Massachusetts, spoke to the authorities on his behalf. At last, on Easter Sunday afternoon, he received official permission to leave Boston. His friend Orlando Tompkins volunteered to accompany him, and they reserved seats on the midnight train for New York. At that late hour, fewer people would be on the streets and there'd be less chance of Edwin being recognized.

The assassination had aroused strong feelings of outrage throughout the nation. Everyone who had any connection with John came under suspicion, and Edwin's friends feared that the hatred of his brother would rub off on him. Edwin shrugged off their worries. But before leaving for the railroad station, he pulled his wide-brimmed hat down low over his forehead so as to conceal as much of his face as possible.

He and Tompkins boarded the New York train without incident and found their seats in the nearly empty parlor car.[15] Exactly at midnight, the train pulled out of Boston's South Street Station and began the five-and-a-half-hour trip to New York. There's no way of knowing what was on Edwin's mind as he sat back in his seat and stared out into the darkness. No doubt his thoughts centered largely on his brother and the horrible thing he had done. But he must have wondered about his own future, too. Would he ever act again, or would audiences reject him because he was a Booth—the brother of the man who had killed President Lincoln?

A Booth. Earlier he had reminded Adam Badeau how hard he had labored to establish a name that he and all his friends would be proud of. He wasn't the first Booth to do so. Or the first Booth to make his reputation in the theater. His father, the actor Junius Brutus Booth, had emigrated from England in 1821 and, within a short time, had been recognized as one of the finest players American audiences had ever seen. L2

Edwin always spoke kindly of Junius—his gifted, eccentric,[16] lovable, and often maddening father. Junius had introduced him to the world of the theater and taught him much of what he knew about acting. Now, as he rode southward toward New York and an uncertain future, Edwin may have been wishing his father were still alive to offer advice and support.

14. Here, *clearance* means "permission from an authority."

15. A *parlor car* was a railroad car for which passengers paid extra fare in order to sit in individual chairs.

16. *Eccentric* means "odd."

Vocabulary

incriminating (in krim′ ə nāt′ ing) *adj.* showing involvement in a crime

Big Idea Looking into Lives *What does this action reveal about Edwin's true feelings?* **BI**

Additional Support

Academic Standards

The Additional Support activity on p. 332 covers the following standard:

Skills Practice: **9.6.2** Demonstrate an understanding of sentence construction…

Skills Practice

GRAMMAR: Sentence Fragments

Explain that writers sometimes use sentence fragments for effect. For example, in the next-to-last paragraph of the selection on page 332, Giblin uses two fragments: "A Booth," and "Or the first Booth to make his reputation in the theater." Have students correct the following fragments by joining them to the previous sentence or by adding missing parts of speech.

His father, Junius Booth. Had emigrated from England. *(His father, Junius Booth, had emigrated from England.)* **OL**

AFTER YOU READ

RESPONDING AND THINKING CRITICALLY

Respond

1. What was the most surprising or interesting thing you learned from this selection?

Recall and Interpret

2. (a)How did the audience respond to Edwin Booth during his last performance? (b)How did attitudes toward him change the next day?
3. (a)What did Edwin learn from his valet? (b)Why did this information shock him?
4. (a)What did the theater manager tell Edwin Booth? (b)What qualities did Edwin exhibit in his response to the manager?

Analyze and Evaluate

5. What is the author's attitude toward Edwin Booth? Cite details from the selection that support your opinion.
6. How well does Giblin show the effect of John's action on Edwin?
7. How credible do you think Giblin is as a source of information about the Booths? Do you think that he has any biases? Explain.

Connect

8. How would you defend Edwin Booth from someone who accused him of being just like his brother?
9. **Big Idea** **Looking into Lives** Why do you think Giblin chose to look into the life of Edwin Booth?

LITERARY ANALYSIS

Literary Element Historical Narrative

A **historical narrative** contains many elements found in fictional narratives. The people described in a historical narrative are real people, but they are also like characters in fiction: they have motives, and authors can reveal them through their words, actions, appearance, and other details. Like a fictional narrative, a historical narrative also includes events that are usually told in chronological order. Some historical narratives also include a central conflict, rising action, and a resolution.

1. What is the setting of Giblin's narrative?
2. What techniques does Giblin use to characterize the Booth brothers? Give examples.
3. What conflict(s) does Giblin present?

Review: Narrator

As you learned on pages 206–207, a **narrator** is the person or voice that tells a story. In "A Brother's Crime," the narrator uses a technique called interior monologue. This technique presents one character's thoughts as they occur to him or her. It is a monologue in the character's mind. Interior monologue allows the reader to get a more complete picture of a character by revealing thoughts and feelings that may not be obvious from a character's spoken dialogue or actions. Carefully examining the thoughts expressed in an interior monologue can help you to more fully understand a character.

Partner Activity With a partner, identify examples of interior monologue in the selection. Use a chart to record what each reveals about Edwin and/or John.

Interior Monologue	What It Shows About Edwin	What It Shows About John
"Would he ever act again . . . ?"	He is worried about his future.	

2. He describes their appearance, actions, and effect on audiences and portrays Edwin's thoughts in interior monologues and with quotations.
3. Edwin's internal conflict over whether to believe the accusation about his brother, and his external conflicts with those who associate him with his brother's crime.

Review: Narrator

Other examples of interior monologue appear on page 330 ("His brother John . . . How could that be?"; "how would she deal with the news?"). The monologue shows John's hatred of Lincoln, his tendency to be headstrong, and Edwin's concern for his mother.

AFTER YOU READ

Assess

1. Accept any reasonable answer.
2. (a) Entrance was applauded; received curtain calls (b) Lost his job and fell under suspicion
3. (a) His brother was accused of shooting Lincoln. (b) He had thought his brother incapable of such a crime.
4. (a) Tells Edwin the theater will close (b) Acts graciously, thanks manager, and expresses regret over Lincoln's death
5. Possible answer: Sympathetic: interior monologue shows his decency and compassion.
6. Possible answer: Details about Edwin's loss of his job, his questioning by authorities, and his abrupt nighttime departure clearly show the effect.
7. Possible answer: Seems credible: uses primary sources, makes reasonable inferences, notes that some facts remain unknown; Unbiased: humanizes killer by showing him through brother's eyes
8. Possible answer: Unlike John, he admires Lincoln and mourns his loss; responds to events in a calm, measured way, suggesting he is not like his "headstrong" brother.
9. Possible answer: To provide a fresh and intimate perspective on a famous event and to humanize the participants

Literary Element

1. The events occur in April of 1865 in Boston and on a train to New York.

AFTER YOU READ

Assess

Reading Strategy

1. Most students can probably recall hearing shocking news about someone they thought they knew well.
2. Students will probably recall similar worries of their own or of people they know.

Vocabulary

1. a **2.** a **3.** b **4.** a

Academic Vocabulary

Possible answers: That John Wilkes Booth thought that Lincoln would make himself king; that John Wilkes Booth had a brother

Writing About Literature

Students' essays should

- contain a clear thesis statement conveying what the text reveals about history
- include body paragraphs that summarize what readers learned about the historical context

READING AND VOCABULARY

Reading Strategy Activating Prior Knowledge

In "A Brother's Crime," James Cross Giblin assumes that you have **prior knowledge** of President Lincoln and the Civil War, but not of Edwin Booth. Nevertheless, you can use your prior knowledge about human nature to understand this historical figure. Review the chart you made as you read.

1. How does prior knowledge help you understand what Edwin Booth must have felt when he got the news of his brother's crime?
2. How does your understanding of people in general help you understand Edwin's concern for his family and fears for his future?

Vocabulary Practice

Practice with Word Origins Use your dictionary to look up and choose the correct origin for each of the following words.

1. premonition
   a. from Latin for "to name in advance"
   b. from Middle English for "warning"
2. intimation
   a. from Latin for "innermost"
   b. from Greek for "hint"
3. incriminating
   a. from Old English for "not" and "innocent"
   b. from Latin for "in" and "crime"
4. perpetrate
   a. from Latin for "through" and "to accomplish"
   b. from French for "to send forth"

Academic Vocabulary

Here is a word from the vocabulary list on page R80.

retain (ri tān′) *v.* to hold secure; to keep

Practice and Apply
Name two facts or ideas from this selection that you are likely to **retain.**

WRITING AND EXTENDING

Writing About Literature

Analyze Historical Context The historical context of a work is its time and place. In "A Brother's Crime," you learn facts not only about two brothers, but also about the world of 1865. For example, you learn a few facts about the theater, train travel, and how quickly news traveled. Write a brief essay in which you report on what you learned from this selection.

Prewrite by listing historical facts from the selection. Then write an analytical thesis based on them: that is, use details from the selection to arrive at a general statement of what the text reveals about the time period depicted in Giblin's narrative. Develop your draft by following this pattern:

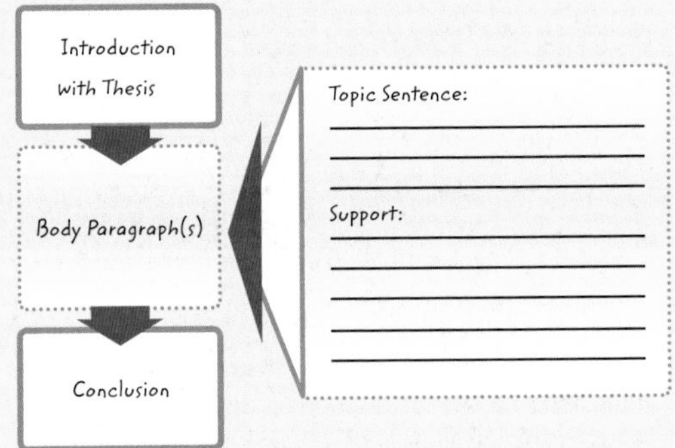

When your draft is complete, meet with a peer reviewer to evaluate each other's work and suggest revisions. Then proofread and edit your draft to correct errors in spelling, grammar, and punctuation.

Performing

Reread the scene in which Edwin first receives the news of his brother's crime. Examine Edwin's thoughts and actions. Then work with a partner to dramatize the scene. Write the characters' dialogue and add stage directions, or instructions to the actors on where and how to stand and what tone to use. Practice the scene before performing it for your classmates.

Web Activities For eFlashcards, Selection Quick Checks, and other Web activities, go to www.glencoe.com.

Additional Support

Performing

Students' scenes should

- include the facts, such as the valet entering with a newspaper and speaking to Booth
- include dramatic elements, such as gestures, intonation, and action, that show Edwin Booth's emotions

LiteratureOnline

Web Activities Have students access the Web site for interactive activities that will help them assess their understanding of the selection.

from
THE MURDER OF ABRAHAM LINCOLN
A CHRONICLE OF 62 DAYS IN THE LIFE OF THE AMERICAN REPUBLIC— MARCH 4 — MAY 4, 1865
WRITTEN AND ILLUSTRATED BY RICK GEARY
NBM ComicsLit

Building Background

Comic books have been an important part of U.S. popular culture since superheroes such as Superman and Batman first appeared in the late 1930s. In the 1970s, comic books took a new direction, which was soon referred to as the "graphic novel." Graphic novels have the same basic panel format as comic books and use the same visual techniques, such as speech balloons and inset panels. But the two forms differ in important ways. Graphic novels are longer than the standard comic book; they usually present only a single story; and they often deal with more realistic subject matter.

Rick Geary's graphic novel, *The Murder of Abraham Lincoln*, deals with the events immediately before and after the assassination of President Abraham Lincoln on April 14, 1865. This excerpt, which opens the novel, presents Lincoln's delivery of his Second Inaugural Address on March 4, 1865.

Set a Purpose for Reading

Read to experience a graphic novel interpretation of an important episode in Lincoln's life.

Reading Strategy

Identifying Genre

Like literature, visual art has different genres, or types, such as the portrait and the landscape. The comic is another visual genre. **Identifying genre** means recognizing the characteristic elements of a particular type of art. As you read Rick Geary's graphic novel, note how he uses elements of the comic book genre. Use a two-column chart like the one below to record your notes. **R**

Example	Genre Element
p. 337 The setting is established	boxed text over illustration

Reading in the Real World

Career Have students research careers that incorporate drawing skills, such as illustrators, graphic novelists, graphic designers, interior decorators, architects, and artists. Have each student present a brief report to the class on a drawing-related career of his or her choice. Make sure students include information on the training involved, types of assignments, and work environment. **OL**

Focus

Summary

The graphic novel tells the story of Lincoln's second inauguration, juxtaposing parts of Lincoln's speech with scenes depicting the reactions of his listeners. **OL**

R Reading Strategy

Identifying Genre Guide a discussion on the essential features of comics: panels of graphics that tell a story through both images and words. The words in comics, and in graphic novels, are set apart in bubbles called speech balloons. Have students examine and discuss some sample comics clipped from a daily newspaper. **OL**

Academic Standards

The Additional Support activity on p. 335 covers the following standard:

Reading in the Real World: **9.7.15** Deliver expository (informational) presentations that convey information and ideas from primary and secondary sources accurately and coherently…

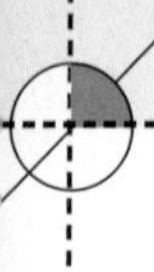

Teach

Historical Note

Salmon P. Chase Salmon Chase (1808–1873) helped form and lead the antislavery Liberty party. At various times a lawyer, governor of and senator from Ohio, and U.S. Secretary of the Treasury, Chase was nominated to the Supreme Court by President Lincoln. He eventually became Chief Justice. AS

Additional Support

See also Active Learning and Note Taking Guide, pp. 54–61.

Skills Practice

SPEAKING: Preparing a Speech
Have students imagine that they have been elected President of the United States. **Ask:** What would you say in your inaugural speech? Discuss with students what they think is appropriate to cover in an inaugural address and why. Instruct students to write an inaugural address as if they had been elected President. Have students present their speeches to the class. Discuss which speeches were the most effective and why. OL Ask students to include modern issues and their opinions about how these issues should be handled. AL

ON THE OCCASION CORRESPONDING TO THIS FOUR YEARS AGO, ALL THOUGHTS WERE ANXIOUSLY DIRECTED TO AN IMPENDING CIVIL WAR. ALL DREADED IT—ALL SOUGHT TO AVERT IT.

R1 THE COLD WINDS AND ANKLE-DEEP MUD OF THE CAPITAL DO LITTLE TO SUPPRESS THE ENTHUSIASM OF THE MULTITUDES IN ATTENDANCE.

BOTH PARTIES DEPRECATED WAR, BUT ONE OF THEM WOULD MAKE WAR RATHER THAN LET THE NATION SURVIVE, AND THE OTHER WOULD ACCEPT WAR RATHER THAN LET IT PERISH. AND THE WAR CAME.

EVERYONE CAN FEEL IT: AFTER FOUR BLOOD-SOAKED YEARS, THE TERRIBLE CONFLICT IS AT LAST COMING TO AN END.

ONE EIGHTH OF THE WHOLE POPULATION WERE COLORED SLAVES, NOT DISTRIBUTED GENERALLY OVER THE UNION, BUT LOCALIZED IN THE SOUTHERN PART OF IT. THESE SLAVES CONSTITUTED A PECULIAR AND POWERFUL INTEREST. ALL KNEW THAT THIS INTEREST WAS, SOMEHOW, THE CAUSE OF THE WAR. R2

NEWLY EMANCIPATED NEGROES AND OTHER RAGGED SURVIVORS HAVE SOUGHT REFUGE IN THE CAPITAL.

Teach

R1 Reading Strategy

Connecting Ask: How do the descriptions of the crowd's feelings enhance your reading of Lincoln's speech? *(Answers will vary. Students may say that understanding the responses of the crowd makes the speech more vibrant and real to them and helps them to empathize with the crowd and connect with the speech.)* OL

R2 Reading Strategy

Connecting Ask: How does the artwork relate to the written words? *(Students should note that the images illustrate Lincoln's speech.)*

Ask: How does this affect your understanding of the speech? *(Students may say that seeing the images clarifies what they are reading.)* OL

English Language Coach

Connecting Images and Text Point out to English language learners that they can use the images in the graphic novel to improve their comprehension of the written text. Have a student read Lincoln's speeches aloud. After each speech bubble has been read, discuss how that speech relates to the artwork. EL

Academic Standards

Additional Support activities on pp. 336 and 337 cover the following standards:

Skills Practice: **9.7.11** Evaluate the… effectiveness…of a speaker's important points… **9.7.2** Choose appropriate techniques for developing the introduction and conclusion in a speech…

English Language Coach: **9.2.1** Analyze the structure and format of…documents, including the graphics…and explain how authors use the features to achieve their purposes.

Teach

R1 Reading Strategy

Reading Aloud Invite volunteers to read the parts of President Lincoln and the narrator.

Ask: How does hearing the text aloud, while looking at the images, enhance your understanding? Engage students in a discussion of the advantages of hearing the text while viewing the images. OL

R2 Reading Strategy

Comprehension Ask: Why do you think some people found Lincoln to be "an object of scorn and deep loathing?" *(Students may cite the Civil War and Lincoln's emancipation of the slaves as reasons.)* OL

R1

R2

Additional Support

Academic Standards

Additional Support activities on pp. 338 and 339 cover the following standards:

Skills Practice: **9.5.7** Use varied and expanded vocabulary…

English Language Coach: **9.1** Use…word parts…to determine the meaning of words…

Skills Practice

VOCABULARY: Identifying and Using New Words Go through the graphic novel with students and make a list on the board of any unfamiliar or unclear words. Instruct students to work in pairs and use a dictionary or the Internet to find definitions for the words. Then have students use all the words in a short, fictional story written about the inauguration. OL Instruct students to write the story in first person, from the point of view of someone at the inauguration. AL

HIS MESSAGE TODAY IS ONE OF FORGIVENESS AND RECONCILIATION.
WITH MALICE TOWARD NONE; WITH CHARITY FOR ALL; WITH FIRMNESS IN THE RIGHT, AS GOD GIVES US TO SEE THE RIGHT, LET US STRIVE ON TO FINISH THE WORK WE ARE IN —
TO BIND UP THE NATION'S WOUNDS, TO CARE FOR HIM WHO SHALL HAVE BORNE THE BATTLE, AND FOR HIS WIDOW, AND FOR HIS ORPHAN —
TO DO ALL WHICH MAY ACHIEVE A JUST, AND A LASTING PEACE, AMONG OURSELVES AND WITH ALL NATIONS.

RESPONDING AND THINKING CRITICALLY

Respond

1. Considering both pictures and text, what words would you use to describe the way that Abraham Lincoln is presented in this excerpt?

Recall and Interpret

2. (a)What is the setting of page 336? (b)What is the effect of Geary's visual composition of this panel?
3. (a)What appears in the inset panel on page 336? (b)What storytelling purpose does the inset serve?

Analyze and Evaluate

4. (a)How does Geary arrange the speech balloons on pages 337 and 339? (b)What is the purpose of the arrangement in each case?
5. (a)How does Geary visually interrupt the presentation of Lincoln's Second Inaugural Address on page 337? (b)What effect does this interruption have?

Connect

6. How is the overall effect of this excerpt similar to and different from that of "A Brother's Crime"?

INDIANA ACADEMIC STANDARDS (pages 335–339)
9.3.2 Compare and contrast the presentation of a similar theme or topic across genres...

English Language Coach

Using Roots Remind students of the importance of using word roots to help them decipher vocabulary. Write the word *malice* on the blackboard.
Ask: What is the common root in this word? *(mal)* Underline *mal* in *malice* on the board.
Ask: What do you think *mal* means? *(Answers will vary. Students may say it means something negative.)* Instruct students that *mal* means *bad.* Therefore, words containing *mal* will have to do with something bad or negative. Have students note the word root in the notebooks. EL

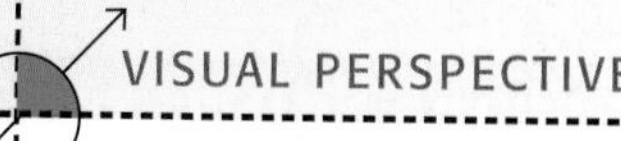
VISUAL PERSPECTIVE

Graphic Novel

Assess

1. Students should use such words as *heroic, noble, thoughtful, earnest, eloquent,* and *brave.*
2. (a) Lincoln's second inauguration outside the Capitol in Washington, D.C. (b) The vertical composition elevates the central figure of Lincoln, who stands above the spectators, by leading the eye up the Capitol's portico to the top of its dome.
3. (a) It shows Lincoln's hand on the Bible as he takes the oath of office. (b) The inset panel dramatizes the narrative.
4. (a) On page 337, the speech balloons connect Lincoln's words to panels illustrating the events he refers to. On page 339, the speech balloons divide the final part of Lincoln's speech into three parts that comprise his presidency's goals: finish the war, heal the country, and establish peace. (b) The arrangements show the context of Lincoln's words.
5. (a) Several panels show the hatred and violence directed at Lincoln throughout the war. (b) This foreshadows the President's assassination.
6. Both present Lincoln as heroic. Giblin concentrates on the assassin's single historically significant deed and its tragic effect on his brother. Geary focuses on Lincoln's last days and the national tragedies of the Civil War and the assassination.

For additional assessment, see Selection and Unit Assessments, pp. 51–52.

Focus

BELLRINGER

Bellringer Options
Selection Focus Transparency 22
Daily Language Practice Transparency 30

Or ask students to think about a time when they had a sudden realization—a moment when they felt as if they finally understood something about themself or about a subject they had been studying.

Ask: How did you feel at that moment? How did grasping this new concept affect you?

Author Search To expand students' appreciation of Helen Keller, have them access the Web site for additional information and resources.

from *The Story of My Life*

MEET HELEN KELLER

Blind and deaf since early childhood, Helen Keller became a symbol of all people who overcome seemingly impossible obstacles—both physical and societal. Though her achievements were recognized during her lifetime, only after Keller's death has society been able to fully appreciate her extraordinary life.

Breakthrough Helen Keller was born in Tuscumbia, Alabama. When she was nineteen months old, an undiagnosed illness left her both blind and deaf. Her heartbroken parents were not sure how to interact with her, and Helen, isolated in a world without sight, sound, or language, became more and more frustrated and uncontrollable. When she was seven years old, her parents learned of the Perkins School for the Blind and sent for a tutor. Soon Helen had a teacher who would change her life: Anne Sullivan.

Within a year of Sullivan's arrival, Keller had learned to read and write in braille. At age ten, she began learning speech. So rapid was Keller's progress that Sullivan was called "the miracle worker," which later became the title of a play about their relationship and accomplishments.

> *"Blindness has no limiting effect upon mental vision."*
>
> —Helen Keller

An Accomplished Author Keller's achievements catapulted her into the public eye. She met many famous people of her day, including President Grover Cleveland. In 1900 she entered Radcliffe College in Cambridge, Massachusetts, with Sullivan by her side. While at Radcliffe, Keller published her first autobiography, *The Story of My Life.* John Macy, a Harvard instructor and editor who eventually married Sullivan, helped Keller with the writing.

Keller graduated *cum laude* from Radcliffe in 1904. She wrote a total of fourteen books and hundreds of articles. Her writing was not always autobiographical: one of Keller's best-known books, *Teacher*, is about Sullivan, while other works deal with religion and politics.

Besides being an accomplished author, Keller was very active politically and socially. She spoke out for the rights of women and the disabled. She helped to abolish the practice of committing blind or deaf people to mental hospitals. She became living proof of her own philosophy—that people with disabilities can live rich and fulfilling lives.

Awards Keller carried her message around the world, earning not only the Presidential Medal of Freedom but also the Lebanese Medal of Merit, the French Legion of Honor, and the Brazilian Southern Cross, among others. "My work for the blind," she once wrote, "has never occupied a center in my personality. My sympathies are with all who struggle for justice."

Helen Keller was born in 1880 and died in 1968.

Literature Online **Author Search** For more about Helen Keller, go to www.glencoe.com.

Selection Skills

The Story of My Life

Literary Elements
- Anecdote (SE pp. 341, 343–345, 348)
- Author's Purpose (SE p. 348)

Reading Skills
- Connecting to Personal Experience (SE pp. 341–343, 345, 346, 348)
- Comparing and Contrasting (TWE p. 342)

Vocabulary Skills
- Context Clues (SE p. 348)
- Academic Vocabulary (SE p. 348)

Listening/Speaking/Viewing Skills
- Analyzing Art (TWE p. 342)

Writing Skills/Grammar
- Writing About Literature (SE p. 349)
- Adjectives (TWE p. 344)

LITERATURE PREVIEW

Connecting to the Text

One of the most important events in Helen Keller's life was her first connecting things with the words that name them. Before you read this excerpt from her autobiography, think about the following questions:

- What would it be like to live without language?
- How important are words in your life?

Building Background

Helen Keller first published *The Story of My Life* as a series of magazine articles that appeared in the *Ladies' Home Journal* in 1902. Keller used a braille machine to make notes for herself. Then, using a manual typewriter, she typed the first drafts, describing events in her life. Anne Sullivan and John Macy helped her put the material in chronological order. They pointed out "gaps," and she dictated transitions and revisions. A copy of the final manuscript was created in braille, so that Helen could read and approve it. *The Story of My Life* was incredibly popular and has been reissued multiple times since its original publication.

Setting Purposes for Reading

Big Idea Looking into Lives

As you read this selection, think about the unique challenges that shaped Helen Keller's life.

Literary Element Anecdote

An **anecdote** is a brief account of an interesting or significant occurrence. Writers often use anecdotes to illustrate their points, to get a reader's attention, to clarify their ideas, or to convey a story element, such as setting or rising action. As you read this excerpt from Keller's autobiography, focus on how anecdotes help you understand her message and life experiences.

- See Literary Terms Handbook, p. R1.

LiteratureOnline Interactive Literary Elements Handbook To review or learn more about the literary elements, go to www.glencoe.com.

READING PREVIEW

Reading Strategy Connecting to Personal Experience

To **connect to personal experience** is to use experiences in your own life to understand characters and events in literature. For example, you might better understand Keller's actions and feelings by considering how you act and feel when presented with a challenging or frustrating situation.

Reading Tip: Taking Notes Make connections between story details and your own life. Use a simple chart to note connections that you find.

Detail	My Personal Experience
Helen meets her teacher.	I remember one special teacher I had.

Vocabulary

traverse (trav′ ərs) *v.* to pass across or through; p. 345 *It was difficult to traverse the crowded dance floor.*

symmetrical (si met′ ri kəl) *adj.* exactly agreeing in size, form, and arrangement on both sides of something; p. 345 *The windows are symmetrical: they are the same size and the same distance from the door.*

verbatim (vər bā′ tim) *adv.* word for word; in exactly the same words; p. 346 *Are you paraphrasing what Keller said or quoting her verbatim?*

augment (ôg ment′) *v.* to become greater; increase; grow; p. 346 *These new stamps will augment my collection.*

Vocabulary Tip: Context Clues A word's context—the words and sentences around it—can help you determine its meaning.

INDIANA ACADEMIC STANDARDS (pages 341–349)

9.2.7 Evaluate...the way in which the author's intent affects the structure and tone of the text.

9.2 Develop [reading] strategies...

9.5.3 Write expository compositions, including analytical essays...that...make distinctions between the relative value and significance of specific data, facts, and ideas...

9.7.6 Analyze...and choose effective...nonverbal techniques... for presentations.

BEFORE YOU READ

Focus

Summary

Helen Keller describes her first encounter with her teacher, Annie Sullivan, as "the most important day I remember in all my life." Helen felt angry and lost until her teacher's gift of language freed her soul. She then threw herself enthusiastically into the great task of learning the words for everything around her, as well as the words for abstract concepts such as *think* and *love.*

V Vocabulary

Vocabulary File **Say:** Add these words and definitions to your vocabulary file. For each word, include a sentence that gives you an example of how to use the word. **OL** Students with English language needs should include the pronunciation of these words in their files. **EL**

Literary Elements Have students access the Web site to improve their understanding of anecdote.

Selection Resources

Print Materials

- Unit 2 Resources (Fast File), pp. 27–29
- Leveled Vocabulary Development, p. 24
- Selection and Unit Assessments, pp. 53–54
- Selection Quick Checks, p. 28

Transparencies

- Bellringer Options Transparencies: Selection Focus Transparency 22 Daily Language Practice Transparency 30
- Literary Elements Transparency 32

Technology

- TeacherWorks Plus™ CD-ROM
- StudentWorks Plus™ CD-ROM
- Presentation Plus!™ CD-ROM
- Literature Online, glencoe.com
- Online Student Edition, mhln.com
- Exam*View*® Assessment Suite CD-ROM
- Vocabulary PuzzleMaker CD-ROM
- Listening Library, disc 1 track 29

Teach

R1 Reading Strategy

Connecting to Personal Experience **Answer:** *Students may mention whispering, increased activity, or telephone calls.* OL

L1 Literary Element

Analogy Explain that an analogy is a similarity or resemblance shared between two otherwise dissimilar things. **Ask:** Identify the analogy used to explain Keller's situation in the moments before her teacher arrived. *(Her plight was similar to a ship lost in a dense fog: she waited for rescue, unable to determine how near it was.)* OL

CheckPoint

Use the CheckPoint questions on Presentation Plus! to monitor students' comprehension. These questions can be used with interactive response keypads for immediate student feedback.

Readability Scores
Dale-Chall: 8.5
DRP: 56
Lexile: 1030

from The Story of My Life

Helen Keller

Helen Keller at work on a braille typewriter. 

The most important day I remember in all my life is the one on which my teacher, Anne Mansfield Sullivan, came to me. I am filled with wonder when I consider the immeasurable contrasts between the two lives which it connects. It was the third of March, 1887, three months before I was seven years old.

On the afternoon of that eventful day, I stood on the porch, dumb, expectant. I guessed vaguely from my mother's signs and from the hurrying to and fro in the house that something unusual was about to happen, so I went to the door and waited on the steps. The afternoon sun penetrated the mass of honeysuckle that covered the porch, and fell on my upturned face. My fingers lingered almost unconsciously on the familiar leaves and blossoms which had just come forth to greet the sweet southern spring. I did not know what the future held of marvel or surprise for me. Anger and bitterness had preyed upon me continually for weeks and a deep languor[1] had succeeded this passionate struggle.

Have you ever been at sea in a dense fog, when it seemed as if a tangible white darkness shut you in, and the great ship, tense and anxious, groped her way toward the shore with plummet and sounding-line,[2] and L1

Reading Strategy Connecting to Personal Experience *How can you tell when something unusual is about to happen at your home or school?* R1

1. *Languor* is a lack of spirit, interest, energy, or activity.
2. A *sounding-line* is used to measure the depth of water. A *plummet*, or weight, at one end of the line sinks to the bottom; the resulting marks on the line show distance.

Additional Support

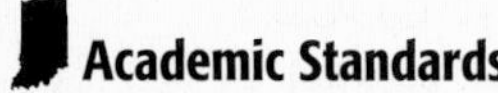

The Additional Support activity on p. 342 covers the following standard:

Skills Practice: **9.2** Develop strategies…[for] informational texts.

Skills Practice

READING: Comparing and Contrasting Note Keller's use of comparison and contrast, such as her contrasting of the language acquisition process of deaf children with that of hearing children.

Have students set up a comparison frame chart. As they read, they should list examples of how Helen learned certain words together with a corresponding example of how a hearing child might learn the same word. Have students share their examples and discuss how comparing and contrasting deepened their understanding of Helen's experience. OL you waited with beating heart for something to happen? I was like that ship before my education began, only I was without compass or sounding-line, and had no way of knowing how near the harbor was. "Light! give me light!" was the wordless cry of my soul, and the light of love shone on me in that very hour.

I felt approaching footsteps. I stretched out my hand as I supposed to my mother. Someone took it, and I was caught up and held close in the arms of her who had come to reveal all things to me, and, more than all things else, to love me.

The morning after my teacher came she led me into her room and gave me a doll. The little blind children at the Perkins Institution had sent it and Laura Bridgman[3] had dressed it; but I did not know this until afterward. When I had played with it a little while, Miss Sullivan slowly spelled into my hand the word "d-o-l-l." I was at once interested in this finger play and tried to imitate it. When I finally succeeded in making the letters correctly I was flushed with childish pleasure and pride. Running downstairs to my mother I held up my hand and made the letters for doll. I did not know that I was spelling a word or even that words existed; I was simply making my fingers go in monkey-like imitation. In the days that followed I learned to spell in this uncomprehending[4] way a great many words, among them *pin, hat, cup,* and a few verbs like *sit, stand,* and *walk.* But my teacher had been with me several weeks before I understood that everything has a name.

One day, while I was playing with my new doll, Miss Sullivan put my big rag doll into my lap also, spelled "d-o-l-l," and tried to make me understand that "d-o-l-l" applied to both. Earlier in the day we had had a tussle over the words "m-u-g" and "w-a-t-e-r." Miss Sullivan had tried to impress it upon me that "m-u-g" is *mug* and that "w-a-t-e-r" is *water,* but I persisted in confounding[5] the two. In despair she had dropped the subject for the time, only to renew it at the first opportunity. I became impatient at her repeated attempts and, seizing the new doll, I dashed it upon the floor. I was keenly delighted when I felt the fragments of the broken doll at my feet. Neither sorrow nor regret followed my passionate outburst. I had not loved the doll. In the still, dark world in which I lived there was no strong sentiment or tenderness. I felt my teacher sweep the fragments to one side of the hearth, and I had a sense of satisfaction that the cause of my discomfort was removed. She brought me my hat, and I knew I was going out into the warm sunshine. This thought, if a wordless sensation may be called a thought, made me hop and skip with pleasure.

We walked down the path to the well-house, attracted by the fragrance of the honeysuckle with which it was covered. Some one was drawing water and my teacher placed my hand under the spout. As the cool stream gushed over one hand she spelled into the other the word *water,* first slowly, then rapidly. I stood still, my whole attention fixed upon the motions of her fingers. Suddenly I felt a misty consciousness as of something forgotten—a thrill of returning thought; and somehow the mystery of language was revealed to me. I knew then that "w-a-t-e-r" meant the wonderful cool something that was flowing over my hand.

3. *Laura Bridgman* (1829–1889), a student of Dr. Samuel G. Howe of the Perkins Institution for the Blind, was the first deaf, blind, and mute person to be successfully educated in the United States.
4. *Uncomprehending* means "without understanding."

5. Here, *confounding* means "confusing" or "failing to understand the difference between."

Big Idea Looking into Lives *Why do you think Keller wanted to give readers this insight into her life?* BI

Literary Element Anecdote *What does this anecdote tell you about Helen's personality?* L2

Reading Strategy Connecting to Personal Experience *Besides feeling thrilled, what other feelings do people have when something suddenly becomes clear that was formerly hard to understand?* R2

Teach

BI Big Idea

Looking into Lives
Answer: *Students may suggest that Keller wanted readers to know how much and why she valued Sullivan.* OL

L2 Literary Element

Anecdote **Answer:** *Despite her frustration, Helen was innately curious and wanted to learn.* OL

L3 Literary Element

Setting **Ask:** What factors distinguish Keller's descriptions of setting? *(Students may notice that Keller often describes how things feel and smell. For example, she writes about how she felt Sullivan sweep away the fragments, how it felt going out into the warm sunshine, and the fragrance of honeysuckle.)* OL

R2 Reading Strategy

Connecting to Personal Experience **Answer:** *Students might mention feeling happy, gleeful, or eager for more.* OL

Viewing the Photo

The word *photography* comes from the Greek *photos* for "light" and *graphein* "to draw." In 1889, George Eastman revolutionized photography by developing a film that was both unbreakable and flexible, thereby replacing the hard plates previously in use. AS

English Language Coach

Italics (Underlining) Explain that italic type is slanted type used in printing. In typing and handwriting, underlining is used in place of italics. Italics are used with titles of books, foreign words and expressions, and words used to represent themselves. Have students underline the words that should be italicized.

1. In the excerpt from The Story of My Life, Helen Keller tells about learning the meaning of the word love.
2. What does the Latin expression e pluribus unum mean?
3. When he left the party, Peter said casually in French, "Au revoir!" EL

Academic Standards

The Additional Support activity on p. 343 covers the following standard:

English Language Coach: **9.6.1** Identify and correctly use...the mechanics of punctuation...

Teach

BI Big Idea

Looking into Lives
Answer: *They show how dark, confined, and limited Keller's world was before she learned language.* OL

L1 Literary Element

Anecdote **Answer:** *She feels more connected to the world around her and understands the consequences of her actions.* OL

L2 Literary Element

Simile **Ask:** Can you point out the simile Keller uses in these lines? *(Words make the world blossom, just as Aaron's rod in the Bible blossomed with flowers.)* OL

★ Cultural History

Braille The Braille reading system was created by Louis Braille (1809–1852) when he was 15 and a student at the Institute for Blind Youth in Paris, France. Raised dots are arranged in patterns in a "cell" of up to six dots. Each arrangement represents a letter, numeral, or symbol. With training, blind people can learn to "read" the dots with their fingertips. AS

Helen Keller reading braille. 

That living word awakened my soul, gave it light, hope, joy, set it free! There were barriers still, it is true, but barriers that could in time be swept away.

I left the well-house eager to learn. Everything had a name, and each name gave birth to a new thought. As we returned to the house every object which I touched seemed to quiver with life. That was because I saw everything with the strange, new sight that had come to me. On entering the door I remembered the doll I had broken. I felt my way to the hearth and picked up the pieces. I tried vainly to put them together. Then my eyes filled with tears; for I realized what I had done, and for the first time I felt repentance and sorrow.

Big Idea Looking into Lives *What do these words add to your understanding of Helen's life?* BI

Literary Element Anecdote *How does this anecdote show how Helen has changed?* L1

I learned a great many new words that day. I do not remember what they all were; but I do know that *mother, father, sister, teacher* were among them—words that were to make the world blossom for me, "like Aaron's rod,[6] with flowers." It would have been difficult to find a happier child than I was as I lay in my crib at the close of that eventful day and lived over the joys it had brought me, and for the first time longed for a new day to come. . . . L2

I had now the key to all language, and I was eager to learn to use it. Children who hear acquire language without any particular effort; the words that fall from others' lips they catch on the wing, as it were, delightedly, while the little deaf child must trap them by a slow and often painful process. But whatever the process, the result is

6. In the Bible, *Aaron's rod,* a wooden walking stick, miraculously blossoms and bears almonds.

Additional Support

Skills Practice

GRAMMAR AND LANGUAGE:

Adjectives Write this phrase on the board: a few early violets in the garden. Remind students that each underlined word is an adjective. An adjective modifies a noun or pronoun; that is, it tells *what kind, which one, how many,* or *how much.* Have students copy phrases from the selection and underline the adjective in each.

What kind: *(important day; something unusual)*

Which one: *(my upturned face)*

How many: *(three months; seven years)*

How much: *(whole attention)* OL

wonderful. Gradually from naming an object we advance step by step until we have **traversed** the vast distance between our first stammered syllable and the sweep of thought in a line of Shakespeare.

At first, when my teacher told me about a new thing I asked very few questions. My ideas were vague, and my vocabulary was inadequate; but as my knowledge of things grew, and I learned more and more words, my field of inquiry broadened, and I would return again and again to the same subject, eager for further information. Sometimes a new word revived an image that some earlier experience had engraved on my brain.

I remember the morning that I first asked the meaning of the word, "love." This was before I knew many words. I had found a few early violets in the garden and brought them to my teacher. She tried to kiss me: but at that time I did not like to have anyone kiss me except my mother. Miss Sullivan put her arm gently round me and spelled into my hand, "I love Helen."

"What is love?" I asked.

She drew me closer to her and said, "It is here," pointing to my heart, whose beats I was conscious of for the first time. Her words puzzled me very much because I did not then understand anything unless I touched it.

I smelled the violets in her hand and asked, half in words, half in signs, a question which meant, "Is love the sweetness of flowers?"

"No," said my teacher.

Again I thought. The warm sun was shining on us.

"Is this not love?" I asked, pointing in the direction from which the heat came. "Is this not love?"

It seemed to me that there could be nothing more beautiful than the sun, whose warmth makes all things grow. But Miss Sullivan shook her head, and I was greatly puzzled and disappointed. I thought it strange that my teacher could not show me love.

A day or two afterward I was stringing beads of different sizes in **symmetrical** groups—two large beads, three small ones, and so on. I had made many mistakes, and Miss Sullivan had pointed them out again and again with gentle patience. Finally I noticed a very obvious error in the sequence and for an instant I concentrated my attention on the lesson and tried to think how I should have arranged the beads. Miss Sullivan touched my forehead and spelled with decided emphasis, "Think."

In a flash I knew that the word was the name of the process that was going on in my head. This was my first conscious perception of an abstract[7] idea.

For a long time I was still—I was not thinking of the beads in my lap, but trying to find a meaning for "love" in the light of this new idea. The sun had been under a cloud all day, and there had been brief showers;

I thought it strange that my teacher could not show me love.

7. *Abstract* means "not concrete" or "unlike any specific example or thing."

Reading Strategy Connecting to Personal Experience *What do people who feel this tremendous thirst for knowledge typically do on a daily basis?* **R**

Vocabulary

traverse (trav′ ərs) *v.* to pass across or through

Literary Element Anecdote *Why is this a significant moment for Helen?* **L3**

Vocabulary

symmetrical (si met′ ri kəl) *adj.* exactly agreeing in size, form, and arrangement on both sides of something

Teach

R Reading Strategy

Connecting to a Personal Experience Answer: *They read and continually seek answers. For example, they look up unfamiliar words in a dictionary, ask questions, visit libraries, and search the Internet.* **OL**

L3 Literary Element

Anecdote Answer: *Knowing how to use words to express ideas and feelings is essential to learning and establishing relationships.* **OL**

Differentiated Instruction

Ornate Language Keller's use of ornate language to express complicated ideas and emotions may challenge some less proficient readers. Pair these readers with students who read at or above grade level and have them read silently, pausing at the end of each page to discuss the content. Or partners can take turns reading paragraphs aloud and then discuss the main idea of each one together. **BL**

Academic Standards

Additional Support activities on pp. 344 and 345 cover the following standards:

Skills Practice: **9.6.2** Demonstrate an understanding of...the proper placement of modifiers...

Differentiated Instruction: **9.2.8** Make reasonable statements and draw conclusions about a text, supporting them with accurate examples.

Teach

R Reading Strategy

Connecting to Personal Experience **Answer:** *Students may mention family celebrations or group experiences, such as thrilling performance or team efforts.* OL

BI Big Idea

Looking into Lives
Answer: *The statement shows that Keller is aware of what other people do not understand about the lives of deaf children.* OL

★ Writer's Technique

Author's Purpose
Ask: What does this passage suggest about Keller's purpose for writing? *(Possible answer: to help readers understand the challenges of hearing and visually impaired people)* AS

Use the CheckPoint questions on Presentation Plus! to check students' mastery of the selection. These questions can be used with interactive response keypads for immediate student feedback.

but suddenly the sun broke forth in all its southern splendor.

Again I asked my teacher, "Is this not love?"

"Love is something like the clouds that were in the sky before the sun came out," she replied. Then in simpler words than these, which at that time I could not have understood, she explained: "You cannot touch the clouds, you know; but you feel the rain and know how glad the flowers and the thirsty earth are to have it after a hot day. You cannot touch love either; but you feel the sweetness that it pours into everything. Without love you would not be happy or want to play."

The beautiful truth burst upon my mind—I felt that there were invisible lines stretched between my spirit and the spirits of others.

From the beginning of my education Miss Sullivan made it a practice to speak to me as she would speak to any hearing child; the only difference was that she spelled the sentences into my hand instead of speaking them. If I did not know the words and idioms[8] necessary to express my thoughts she supplied them, even suggesting conversation when I was unable to keep up my end of the dialogue.

★ This process was continued for several years; for the deaf child does not learn in a month, or even in two or three years, the numberless idioms and expressions used in the simplest daily intercourse.[9] The little hearing child learns these from constant repetition and imitation. The conversation he hears in his home stimulates his mind and suggests topics and calls forth the spontaneous[10] expression of his own thoughts. This natural exchange of ideas is denied to the deaf child. My teacher, realizing this, determined to supply the kinds of stimulus[11] I lacked. This she did by repeating to me as far as possible, **verbatim**, what she heard, and by showing me how I could take part in the conversation. But it was a long time before I ventured to take the initiative, and still longer before I could find something appropriate to say at the right time.
The deaf and the blind find it very difficult to acquire the amenities of conversation.[12] How much more this difficulty must be **augmented** in the case of those who are both deaf and blind! They cannot distinguish the tone of the voice or, without assistance, go up and down the gamut[13] of tones that give significance to words; nor can they watch the expression of the speaker's face, and a look is often the very soul of what one says.

8. *Idioms* (id′ ē əmz) are expressions whose meaning is different from the literal meaning of the words. Examples are "She's on the ball," "My stomach is in knots," and "The test is a piece of cake."
9. *Intercourse* is the exchange of thoughts, ideas, and feelings through conversation or other communication.

Reading Strategy Connecting to Personal Experience *What types of situations make you feel this type of connection to others?* R

10. *Spontaneous* means "arising from a natural impulse or cause" or "unplanned."
11. A *stimulus* is something that causes a response.
12. By *amenities of conversation* Keller means those things besides words, such as tone of voice or facial expression, that help communicate meaning.
13. Here, *gamut* means the "entire series" or "entire range" of possible tones or sounds.

Big Idea Looking into Lives *What does this statement add to your understanding of Keller's life?* BI

Vocabulary

verbatim (vər bā′ tim) *adv.* word for word; in exactly the same words

augment (ôg ment′) *v.* to become greater; increase; grow

Additional Support

Skills Practice

READING: Abstract and Concrete Words Keller talks about learning concrete words, such as *water* and *doll.* Explain that a concrete word names an object that can be recognized by the senses. The word *think* names an abstraction or idea—something that exists only as a mental construct or image. *Love, stubbornness, languor,* and other abstract words all name ideas, qualities, or characteristics. Direct students to create a two-column chart with one side labeled **Abstract** and the other **Concrete** and to list the two types of words as they read. OL

AFTER YOU READ

RESPONDING AND THINKING CRITICALLY

Respond

1. What questions would you want to ask Helen Keller or Anne Sullivan?

Recall and Interpret

2. (a)How does Keller describe her state of mind just before Sullivan arrived? (b)What do you suppose she means when she says that the wordless cry of her soul was "Light! give me light!"
3. (a)What is the first word Keller truly understands? (b)What changes inside the child when "the mystery of language [is] revealed" to her? Use details from the selection to support your response.
4. (a)How does Keller respond when Sullivan first introduces the word *love*? (b)Why were the words *think* and *love* important in her learning process?

Analyze and Evaluate

5. How and why was Keller's process of learning language different from that of a hearing child?
6. How well does Keller communicate the transition from a life without language to a world in which she can communicate with others? Give an example from the text to support your opinion.
7. Millions of readers and viewers have been moved by this part of Keller's life story. Explain what gives this segment such emotional power.

Connect

8. **Big Idea** **Looking into Lives** What examples of life's most important experiences do you find in this excerpt from Keller's autobiography?

PRIMARY SOURCE QUOTATION

A Feeling for Rhythm

During her lifetime, Helen Keller was often in the news. Read the following excerpt from the *New York Times* dated April 12, 1902, which discusses her book, *The Story of My Life*. As you read it, think about how Keller was taught.

> *"Miss Helen Keller, the deaf, dumb [speechless], and blind girl, whose extraordinary history has often been exploited in the newspapers, has prepared an account of her life. . . . Her book, which was written in sign language of the blind, is said to be remarkable for the excellence of its style. It shows that, though Miss Keller has never known the sound of speech, she has a feeling for rhythm in writing. Her composition has greatly astonished members of the Harvard faculty who take a deep interest in her. One of them attributes it directly to heredity; in no other way, he maintains, could it have been acquired."*

Partner Activity Discuss the following questions with a partner. Refer to the news article and cite evidence from the excerpt from *The Story of My Life* for support.

1. How did Anne Sullivan speak to Helen and teach her idiomatic speech?
2. Why do you think Keller had "a feeling for rhythm in writing"?
3. Do you agree or disagree with the Harvard faculty member's comment about heredity? Explain.

Helen Keller with Anne Sullivan

AFTER YOU READ

Assess

1. Accept any reasonable answer.
2. (a) Angry and isolated (b) She had no way to express her deep longing for understanding or even to articulate it for herself.
3. (a) *Water;* (b) She can relate to the world and begins to care about things outside herself, feeling regret, for example, over her broken doll.
4. (a) She cannot grasp the meaning. She tries to connect to something concrete. (b) They represent a higher level of thought and understanding.
5. Because she never heard words, she did not know they existed; a hearing child directly experiences words from birth.
6. Possible answer: Her progress seems remarkable. For example, she writes vividly, using many sensory details and thoughtful analogies.
7. Possible answers: Sullivan's creativity, patience, and dedication; Keller's strength, spirit, and remarkable achievements
8. Possible answers: Helen's ability to overcome great challenges; Sullivan's dedication to helping; the bond between a student and a great teacher

Primary Source Quotation

1. She spoke to Keller as she would to a hearing child, but spelled the words with sign language and supplied the words and idioms she did not know.
2. Sullivan repeated a great deal of information verbatim so that Keller was constantly surrounded by conversation.
3. Students should support their answers.

Academic Standards

The Additional Support activity on p. 346 covers the following standard:

Skills Practice: **9.1** [Use] relationships… and a growing knowledge of English…to determine the meaning of words…

AFTER YOU READ

Assess

Literary Element

1. Accept any reasonable answer supported by details from the text.
2. Accept any reasonable answer supported by details from the text.
3. Accept any reasonable answer supported by details from the text.

Review: Author's Purpose

Students may identify multiple purposes that Keller had for writing *The Story of My Life.* Responses may include: She wrote it to inform readers of how she learned; She wrote it to express her thoughts and feelings; She wrote it to persuade her audience that visually- and hearing-impaired people are capable of learning. Make sure that students support their answers with details from the text.

Web Activities Have students access the Web site for interactive activities that will help them assess their understanding of the selection.

LITERARY ANALYSIS

Literary Element Anecdote

An **anecdote** is a brief account of an interesting or amusing incident. An anecdote is often used to explain or support an idea, to entertain readers, or to reveal the personality of an author or another person.

1. Keller uses several anecdotes to show how she began to understand language, communication, and abstract thinking. Which anecdote did you find most effective for this purpose? Explain.
2. Which anecdote did you find the most amusing? Explain.
3. Which anecdote do you think best illustrates Keller's personality? Sullivan's personality? Explain.

Review: Author's Purpose

As you learned on page 320, **author's purpose** is the author's reason for writing. For example, the purpose may be to persuade, to express an opinion, or to inform. Sometimes an author may have more than one purpose for writing.

Partner Activity With a classmate, create a chart like the one below to find evidence that indicates Keller's purpose in writing *The Story of My Life*.

Evidence	Purpose
p. 343 "In the still, dark world in which I lived there was no strong sentiment or tenderness."	To describe her life before learning language

READING AND VOCABULARY

Reading Strategy Connecting to Personal Experience

In this story, a teacher moves a child out of a "dark" world into the "light" of language. Consider whether, in **your experience,** this is what teachers regularly do in their lives and work.

1. What qualities does Sullivan have that are important qualities for all teachers?
2. What is unusual or unique about the relationship between this teacher and child?
3. What might be unique about Keller as a pupil?

Vocabulary Practice

Practice with Context Clues Use context clues to choose the best meaning for each underlined word.

1. A cane helps a person without sight <u>traverse</u> an unfamiliar room.
   a. recreate **b.** cross **c.** avoid
2. Krista's painting is <u>symmetrical</u>–the image on the right is identical to the image on the left.
   a. balanced **b.** dull **c.** uneven
3. Although the parrot can repeat the phrase <u>verbatim</u>, it does not understand its meaning.
   a. all day **b.** out loud **c.** word for word
4. Parents' contributions <u>augmented</u> the school's small supply of soccer balls.
   a. increased **b.** decreased **c.** began

Academic Vocabulary

Here is a word from the vocabulary list on page R80. This word will help you think, write, and talk about the selection.

equivalent (i kwiv ʹə lənt) *n.* something equal in importance, value, or measure

Practice and Apply
What, for Helen, was the **equivalent** of spoken language?

Reading Strategy

1. Patience, persistence, caring, intelligence, creativity
2. They have a one-on-one relationship and spend all day together.
3. She was particularly perceptive, bright, and curious.

Vocabulary

1. b **2.** a **3.** c **4.** a

Academic Vocabulary

Signed language and touch

WRITING AND EXTENDING

Writing About Literature

Analyze Details Nonfiction can be vividly descriptive, and in this work, Keller takes pains to provide details about surroundings that she could neither see nor hear. Think about why she might have included these details.

Write a brief essay in which you state your opinion about why Keller includes sensory details in her writing. In the body of your essay, describe the types of details that she uses. Do some types of sensory impressions appear more than others? If so, consider why this might be so. As you gather ideas, use a sensory web to record the details that you notice. Use some of these details as evidence to support your idea.

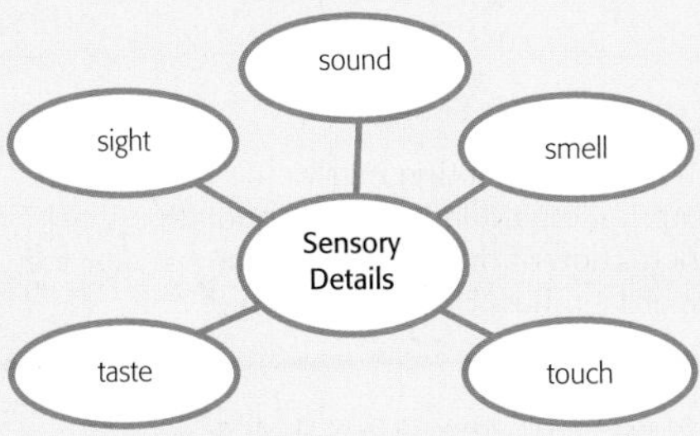

After you complete your draft, meet with a peer reviewer to evaluate each other's work and suggest revisions. Then edit and proofread your draft for errors in spelling, grammar, or punctuation.

Listening and Speaking

With a partner, research and learn the manual sign language that Anne Sullivan taught to Helen Keller. Then take turns spelling words into each other's hands. With eyes closed or blindfolded, the person "reading" the signs should try to identify each letter, say it aloud, and then pronounce the word spelled by the letters.

GRAMMAR AND STYLE

Keller's Language and Style

Making Comparisons Helen Keller realized that sighted, hearing people who can speak would have a hard time understanding her everyday world. To help her readers, Keller uses a number of comparisons. Some are analogies:

> Have you ever been at sea in a dense fog, when it seemed as if a tangible white darkness shut you in, and the great ship, tense and anxious, groped her way toward the shore . . . ?

At other times, however, Keller makes a direct comparison between her own life and the life of children who can see, hear, and speak:

> Children who hear acquire language without any particular effort; the words that fall from others' lips they catch on the wing, as it were, delightedly, while the little deaf child must trap them by a slow and often painful process.

Each comparison emphasizes particular aspects of the items being compared. The analogy about the ship emphasizes the sense of feeling lost and frightened; the other comparison emphasizes the difficulty deaf children have acquiring language.

Activity Find at least two additional comparisons in the selection. Write them out and explain what aspect of the situation is emphasized by using a comparison as opposed to a simple statement.

Revising Check

Comparisons Reread your essay about Keller's use of details with a partner to see if a comparison would strengthen one of the points you are trying to make. Revise your draft as necessary.

LiteratureOnline **Web Activities** For eFlashcards, Selection Quick Checks, and other Web activities, go to www.glencoe.com.

AFTER YOU READ

Assess

Writing About Literature

Students' essays should

- state an opinion about why Keller included sensory details
- identify specific details and the senses to which they appeal
- draw conclusions about why these senses were chosen

Listening and Speaking

Encourage students to use the Internet to research sign language and to learn more signs.

Keller's Language and Style

Students might choose these comparisons:

"words . . . make the world blossom"

"every object . . . quivered with life."

"traversed the vast distance between our first stammered syllable and the sweep of thought in a line of Shakespeare."

"a look is often the very soul of what one says."

Accept any reasonable explanation of what is emphasized by their comparison choices.

Revising Check

Students should review the details included in their sensory webs to determine whether comparisons would strengthen the effectiveness of the essays.

Differentiated Instruction

Tactile Learners Have tactile learners try an exercise in writing from Helen Keller's point of view. Have students work in pairs. Have them sit with their eyes closed and have one hand the other an object. With eyes closed, the first student should try to describe the object in as much detail as possible and to guess what it is. The second student should take notes on what is said. Have students switch places. Then have students write about their experience, focusing on how using senses other than sight affected the descriptions of the objects. BL

Academic Standards

The Additional Support activity on p. 349 covers the following standard:

Differentiated Instruction: **9.4.3** Use precise language,...sensory details, and appropriate modifiers.

Focus

Explain that dialogue, or direct discourse, quotes a speaker's exact words. Note that dialogue is enclosed in quotation marks and is often accompanied by speaker tags that identify who is talking. **Write an example such as the following on the board:** "What do you mean?" Rosalie asked.

Unlike dialogue, indirect discourse reports or describes rather than quotes what a person has said. **Write this example on the board:** Rosalie asked what he meant.

Teach

Placement of End Punctuation Emphasize that the placement of end punctuation with quotation marks depends on whether a question or an exclamation is, or is not, part of the quotation.

Assess

1. "Are you an only daughter?" Neil asked.
   "Yes, I am."
2. "Well, you might like this essay. It's by Sandra Cisneros."
3. "Oh, I think I already read that!"
4. "You're kidding!" Neil said. Marisa explained we had to read it in class.
5. "Did you enjoy it?" "I thought it was terrific!"

Grammar Workshop

Coherence

▶ **Writing Dialogue**

Dialogue is the exact words that characters exchange. Writers use **speaker tags** or tag lines to identify who is speaking in a dialogue.

▶ **Test-Taking Tip**

When you are writing or proofreading dialogue, always check for the end quotation mark. Writers often accidentally omit it.

▶ **Grammar Handbook**

For more about punctuating dialogue, see Language Handbook, pp. R53–R56.

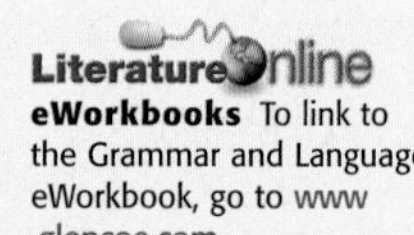

eWorkbooks To link to the Grammar and Language eWorkbook, go to www.glencoe.com.

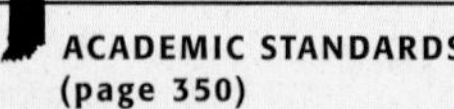

ACADEMIC STANDARDS (page 350)

9.6.1 Identify and correctly use... the mechanics of punctuation...

9.4.10 Review, evaluate, and revise writing for meaning, clarity...and mechanics.

Handling Dialogue

"'What is love?' I asked."

—Helen Keller, from *The Story of My Life*

Connecting to Literature Keller uses dialogue to break up long paragraphs, as well as to show her exact words. She encloses the words of each speaker in quotation marks and uses speaker tags or tag lines to identify the speakers. **Speaker tags** are phrases such as "she said" and "I replied." They identify who is speaking and often convey other information, such as tone of voice. Keller also follows specific rules for punctuating dialogue.

Examples

- Mr. Shimada asked, "Can you keep the books?"

Enclose the speaker's exact words in quotation marks and begin the speaker's statement with a capital letter. Place the end quotation mark after, not before, the end punctuation of the sentence. If the speaker tag comes before the speaker's words, follow it with a comma.

- "Yes, I can," my father answered.
- "May I have the chance to prove it?" my father added.

If the speaker tag comes after the speaker's words in a declarative sentence, follow the sentence with a comma. For an exclamatory or interrogative sentence, keep the exclamation point or question mark and do not add a comma.

- My father summoned his courage and asked Mr. Shimada, "Are you living in Seattle?"
  "Yes, I am," he replied.

Begin a new paragraph each time the speaker changes.

Exercise

Revise for Clarity Rewrite the dialogue below, which takes place between Neil and Marisa. Add punctuation, capitalization, indentation, and speaker tags as needed.

1. Are you an only daughter? Neil asked. Yes, I am.
2. Well, you might like this essay. It's by Sandra Cisneros.
3. Oh, I think I already read that!
4. You're kidding! Neil said. Marisa explained we had to read it in class.
5. Did you enjoy it? I thought it was terrific!

eWorkbooks Have students access the Web site for more practice with coherence.

Escape from Afghanistan

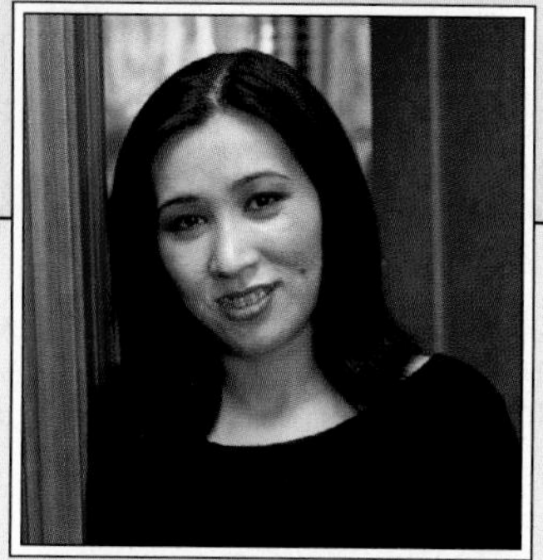

MEET FARAH AHMEDI

One day when Farah Ahmedi was in second grade and walking to school in her home city of Kabul, Afghanistan, she stepped on a landmine. At first, her parents thought she would die. Luckily, however, a humanitarian organization flew her to Germany for medical care. She spent two years there, all the time believing she would never walk again or see her family again. Ahmedi did lose one leg, and the other remained permanently rigid. Nevertheless, she was able to walk because of a prosthesis, or artificial replacement device.

Not long after Ahmedi returned to Afghanistan, she was out with her mother when a rocket hit her home in Kabul. Her father and two sisters were killed in the explosion. Her brothers left the country in order to avoid the Taliban, a militant Islamic group. Ahmedi never heard from them again. She and her mother were left full of grief and alone. When asked about her young life in Afghanistan, Ahmedi said she just wanted to get away.

"I was so scared. A lot of times I wonder why I didn't die. Those were hard times."

—Farah Ahmedi

Arrival in America During the time Ahmedi and her mother lived alone in Afghanistan, the Taliban gained control of the country. The Taliban government persecuted Ahmedi's ethnic group, the Hazara. Because Ahmedi's mother had a cousin in Pakistan who was willing to help them, they decided to flee their country. Ahmedi was only ten years old. After spending several years in a refugee camp in Pakistan, they were finally allowed to come to America in 2002, where Ahmedi entered high school at the age of fourteen.

A Contest Changes Her Life Only a couple years after Ahmedi's arrival, *Good Morning America* and the publisher Simon & Schuster offered a writing contest. It invited viewers to write their life stories. Ahmedi submitted an essay and was selected as one of three finalists. Then the publisher assigned a professional writer, Tamim Ansary, to write Ahmedi's story. Comfortable with Ansary, who was also from Afghanistan and spoke her native language of Farsi, Ahmedi spent five days recounting her story to him. The result was a full-length book. When viewers chose her book as the best, it was published as *The Story of My Life: An Afghan Girl on the Other Side of the Sky*. Ahmedi was also awarded a $10,000 prize and a ten-city book tour.

A Bright Future Ahmedi has visited the White House and met with First Lady Laura Bush. She has also been named a youth ambassador for the Adopt-a-Minefield Program. That organization works to clear landmines and help landmine survivors in the six most heavily mined countries in the world, one of which is Afghanistan. She is proud and happy to live in America, where she knows she has excellent opportunities for independence and education.

Farah Ahmedi was born in 1988.

Literature Online **Author Search** For more about Farah Ahmedi, go to www.glencoe.com.

Focus

BELLRINGER

Bellringer Options
Daily Language Practice Transparency 31

Or invite volunteers to give examples of regions where war, famine, or persecution has prompted people to flee to other countries either recently or in the past. *(Africa, Ireland, Germany)*

Ask: How would you feel if you suddenly had to leave your native country and live in exile? What hopes and fears might preoccupy your mind?

Literature Online

Author Search To expand students' appreciation of Farah Ahmedi, have them access the Web site for additional information and resources.

Selection Skills

Escape from Afghanistan

Literary Elements
- Tone (SE pp. 352–353, 356, 359–360)
- Historical Narrative (SE p. 360)

Reading Skills
- Analyzing Cultural Context (SE pp. 352–354, 356–358, 361)
- Sequence of Events (TWE p. 354)

Vocabulary Skills
- Context Clues (SE p. 361)
- Academic Vocabulary (SE p. 361)

Listening/Speaking/Viewing Skills
- Analyzing Art (SE p. 358; TWE pp. 355, 357)

Writing Skills/Grammar
- Response to Theme (SE p. 361)
- Vivid Verbs (TWE p. 356)
- Prepositional Phrases (TWE p. 358)

BEFORE YOU READ

Focus

Summary

In this suspenseful excerpt from her autobiography, Farah Ahmedi recounts how she and her mother made a harrowing journey across the border into Pakistan to escape persecution by the Taliban regime in Afghanistan and begin a new life.

V Vocabulary

Vocabulary File Say: Add these words and definitions to your vocabulary file. For each word, include a sentence that gives you an example of how to use the word. **OL** Students with English language needs should include the pronunciation of these words in their files. **EL**

Literary Elements Have students access the Web site to improve their understanding of tone.

LITERATURE PREVIEW

Connecting to the Autobiography

"Escape from Afghanistan" will give you insight into what it is like to escape one's own country in a time of war. Before you read the story, think about the following questions:

- How would you feel if you had to move to a new country with only a small bundle of belongings?
- How would you have dealt with the challenges that Ahmedi and her mother faced?

Building Background

Throughout its history, Afghanistan has suffered waves of political change. Landlocked and vulnerable to invasion, Afghanistan also lacks unity because of its mix of religions and cultures. About 85% of Afghans are Sunni Muslims. Shi'ite Muslims make up most of the remaining 15%. Afghans are also divided by language and ethnicity. The major ethnic group is the Pashtun—Sunnis who live mainly in the central and southern part of the country. When the Taliban took over in the 1990s, conflict between the Pashtun and other ethnic groups intensified and eventually led to the massacres of Shi'ite Muslims and other people. Until the end of the Taliban regime in 2001, thousands of Afghans left the country each year, most bound for Iran or Pakistan.

Setting Purposes for Reading

Big Idea Looking Into Lives

As you read, think about how Ahmedi's life has been a tale of survival against all odds.

Literary Element Tone

Tone is an author's attitude toward his or her subject matter. Tone is conveyed through elements such as word choice, punctuation, sentence structure, and figures of speech. As you read, think about how word choice reveals the author's feelings and attitudes.

- See Literary Terms Handbook, p. R18.

Literature Online Interactive Literary Elements Handbook To review or learn more about the literary elements, go to www.glencoe.com.

READING PREVIEW

Reading Strategy Analyzing Cultural Context

Analyzing cultural context is thinking about the time and place of a work, as well as the values of the people in that time and place, and determining how those factors affect the work. Understanding the cultural context will help you understand Ahmedi's story.

Reading Tip: Taking Notes As you read, make a list of details that show the time, place, values, or attitudes. Record conclusions you draw, inferences you make, or questions you ask based on those details.

Detail	Inferences/Conclusions/ Questions
p. 354 "a letter is hand-carried by some traveler"	Is this a place with no mail delivery? Is the author's mail censored?

Vocabulary

quandary (kwon′ drē) *n.* state of indecision or doubt; p. 353 *Lisa was in a quandary over which class to take.*

surge (surj) *v.* to move suddenly in a wave; p. 355 *The fans surge forward when the rock star comes on stage.*

pervade (pər vād′) *v.* to go through or fill every part of; p. 355 *After each win, joy pervades the locker room.*

stoke (stōk) *v.* to stir up; to cause to increase; p. 356 *Robert's part in the school prank stoked bad feelings in many of the faculty members.*

chide (chīd) *v.* to express disapproval; p. 359 *My parents chide me for putting off my homework until the last minute.*

INDIANA ACADEMIC STANDARDS (pages 352–361)
9.2.7 Evaluate...the way in which the author's intent affects the structure and tone of the text.
9.2 Develop [reading] strategies...
9.5.2 Write responses to literature...

Selection Resources

Print Materials
- Unit 2 Resources (Fast File), pp. 31–33
- Leveled Vocabulary Development, p. 25
- Selection and Unit Assessments, pp. 55–56
- Selection Quick Checks, p. 28

Transparencies
- Bellringer Options Transparencies: Daily Language Practice Transparency 31
- Literary Elements Transparency 25

Technology
- TeacherWorks Plus™ CD-ROM
- StudentWorks Plus™ CD-ROM
- Presentation Plus!™ CD-ROM
- Literature Online, glencoe.com
- Online Student Edition, mhln.com
- Exam*View*® Assessment Suite CD-ROM
- Vocabulary PuzzleMaker CD-ROM
- Listening Library, disc 1 track 30

ESCAPE from Afghanistan

Farah Ahmedi with Tamim Ansary

One day we got a letter, hand-carried to us by some traveler. Alas, it was not from my brothers. It came from my mother's cousin in Quetta, a city on the Pakistan side of the Afghan border. We had lost track of her and did not even know she was there, but somehow, six months after my father's death, she had heard about the event and about our **quandary**.

Come to Quetta, she wrote. *Get across the border somehow, and then come directly to Quetta. Do not tarry*[1] *in Peshawar.*[2] *That is a Taliban stronghold, a Pashtun city. You won't be welcome there. In fact, you will be in danger, for the Taliban come from that region, and they are prejudiced against Hazaras. Peshawar is a dangerous place for two Hazara women on their own. Do not even go into the city, if you can avoid it. Just come to Quetta.* And she gave directions for finding her house once we got to her city.

This cousin of my mother's had moved to Quetta some time ago. She had a settled life there. She had lost her husband, but she had a brother and two sons living in Turkmenistan.[3] Those men had gotten out of Afghanistan during the Communist era.[4] They had gone to Turkmenistan to study, and then, because the country had dissolved

1. Here, to *tarry* means "to delay" or "to stay longer than the minimum necessary."
2. *Peshawar* is the first major city in Pakistan below the Khyber Pass from Afghanistan.
3. *Turkmenistan* borders Afghanistan on the north.
4. The *Communist era* began in 1979 when the Soviets took control of Afghanistan. That occupation began the Afghanistan War, which lasted until 1989, devastating the country.

Literary Element Tone *What tone or attitude do you hear in this sentence?* L1

Vocabulary

quandary (kwon′ drē) n. state of indecision or doubt

Reading Strategy Analyzing Cultural Context *What appears to be part of the culture of Peshawar, Pakistan?* R

Teach

L1 Literary Element

Tone Answer: *The terse imperative sentence creates an urgent tone.* OL

R Reading Strategy

Analyzing Cultural Context
Answer: *There is prejudice against the Hazara and especially against Hazara women. There may be a threat of violence there.* OL

L2 Literary Element

Tone Ask: How would you describe the tone of this paragraph? *(The tone is factual and objective. There are many details but little personal commentary or emotional reaction.)* OL

CheckPoint

Use the CheckPoint questions on Presentation Plus! to monitor students' comprehension. These questions can be used with interactive response keypads for immediate student feedback.

Readability Scores
Dale-Chall: 5.8
DRP: 54
Lexile: 820

Differentiated Instruction

Visual Learners Students with acute spatial abilities respond well to descriptive passages such as the one on page 354 beginning "We made it to Jalalabad by bus" and ending ". . . back and forth like a ribbon along the riverbank." Encourage students to use that paragraph as the basis for a colorful drawing or painting. They may choose to illustrate the entire scene described, or they may select a portion of the scene. Later, hold a viewing and invite students to ask questions or make considerate comments about each other's pictures. BL

Academic Standards
The Additional Support activity on p. 353 covers the following standard:
Differentiated Instruction: **9.3** Identify story elements such as...setting...

Teach

R1 Reading Strategy

Analyzing Cultural Context
Answer: *It suggests that women cannot safely travel alone on buses there.* OL

BI1 Big Idea

Looking into Lives Ask: If you were in these travelers' position and had to choose just a few possessions to carry by hand, what would they be? *(Encourage students to offer support for their choices.)* OL

BI2 Big Idea

Looking into Lives Answer: *Their situation must be dire.* OL

R2 Reading Strategy

Analyzing Cultural Context
Ask students to visualize the "other bus station."
Ask: Why do you think the men in the vans acted this way? *(Possible answer: The rides they offered to the border were a violation of the law.)* OL

L2 into civil war, they had simply stayed. They now worked in that former Soviet republic and sent bits of money from time to time; that's what my mother's cousin lived on.

Well, we talked it over with our neighbors and decided that we had to do it. We made inquiries and learned that we could pay a man to serve as our escort on the bus to Jalalabad.[5] That would get us out of Taliban-dominated Kabul.[6] From Jalalabad to the border, we would be on our own. As for getting across the border, no one knew what that entailed. And as for making the journey from the border to Quetta, that was like asking how to get from one part of the moon to another part. No one could give us any advice on that subject. We would just have to figure things out when we got there.

This map shows the location of the cities and countries mentioned in the selection.

BI1 By the time we left Afghanistan, the warm days had come. We wrapped the few possessions we would take along in little cloth bundles. We could not take much, for we would have to carry whatever we took, and while I could not handle much of a load, my poor mother was in even worse shape. The day my father died, her asthma took a turn for the worse. Now she was rasping with every breath, and exertion of any kind tightened up her air passages. We had no medicine for her condition. When it got bad, all she could do was rest, so the last thing we needed was extra baggage.

We made it to Jalalabad by bus. We could not have gotten there any other way. The stretch of road between Kabul and Jalalabad goes over some of the country's steepest mountains, cutting through two rugged gorges. The Kabul River pours through those gorges in a series of thundering cataracts,[7] and the highway has been cut into nearly solid rock, folding back and forth, back and forth like a ribbon along the riverbank.

Once the road descended out of those gorges, the weather changed. The temperature rose. Now we were in the Jalalabad valley, which was dotted with groves of orange trees and lemon trees. The bus let us off in a crowded bazaar. We were frightened to be there alone and frightened to have to ask for advice and directions, but we addressed our questions to women as much as possible or to family groups that included women. In this way we found out how to get to the "other" bus station.

R2 This other bus station wasn't really a station. There was no building, no ticket booth, and no station agent—nothing like that. The

5. *Jalalabad* is the last major city in Afghanistan before the Khyber Pass. It is southeast of Kabul.
6. *Kabul* is the capital city of Afghanistan, located in the eastern part of the country.
7. *Gorges* are canyons or narrow passages through the land; *cataracts* are steep rapids.

Reading Strategy Analyzing Cultural Context *What does this tell you about the culture of Afghanistan?* R1

Big Idea Looking Into Lives *The author and her mother face incredible challenges. What does their willingness to forge ahead tell you about their situation?* BI2

Additional Support

Skills Practice

READING: Sequence of Events
Remind students that following the sequence, or order, in which events occur in a selection is important to understanding the text. Point out that the author may or may not use clue words such as *first, next, last,* and *then.*

Have students construct a timeline showing the events in the selection. Let them decide how to structure their timeline, or suggest that they use the following divisions:

Letter from mother's cousin
Bus rides to Jalalabad and to border
Three days at border
Traveling with Ghulam Ali to Pakistan OL

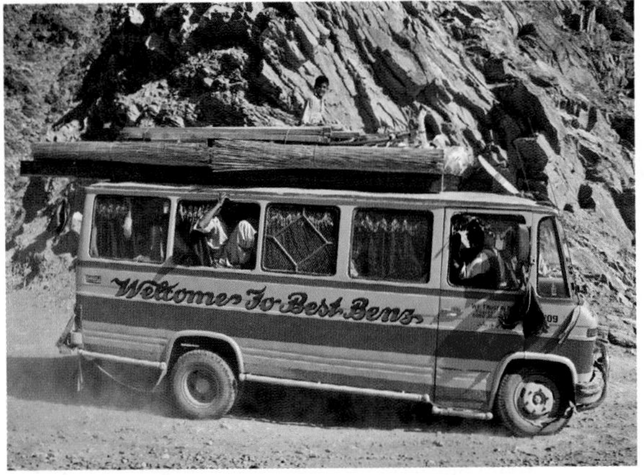

A passenger bus plies the rough road between Jalalabad and Kabul. ★

R2 so-called bus station looked like any other part of the bazaar: It was just a road lined on both sides with merchants' stalls. Along this strip of bazaar, however, men cruised back and forth in vans they owned, looking for people who wanted to go to the border. If you just stood at the curb, they pulled over and offered you a ride.

Before we got on, though, other people waiting there for rides advised us to get some plastic bags. We didn't know why, but we figured we had better do whatever other travelers were doing. They no doubt knew more than we did. Curiously enough, some of the stalls in that vicinity sold plastic bags as if this were a normal travel need.

Shortly after we took up our post by the side of the road, a van pulled over. Instantly, a crowd **surged** toward its door. People fought and threw elbows to get to the front so they could board. That's how it was at the "bus station." Only the most aggressive travelers got rides. Each van could carry ten or twelve people, if they squeezed; and they always squeezed. The drivers wanted to make as much money as they could. We were unable to get onto the first van. We could not get on the next one, either. By the third one, however, I saw what we needed to do, and taking my mother by the arm, I shoved and pushed with the others until we made it to the door of the van.

It wasn't all that far from Jalalabad to the border, but we were traveling in the heat of mid-afternoon. Dust boiled up around the car and got in through the windows. My mother began to wheeze and gasp. I worried that she might stop breathing right then and there, so I tried to shield her with my body, tried to keep the other passengers from pressing in on her so that she would have her own space to breathe out of. Meanwhile, the dust mingled with the sweat running down my face, turning to mud by the time it reached my chin. L

At that moment I discovered what the plastic bags were for: One of the men in the backseat vomited loudly, barely getting his awful stew into his bag. The nasty odor immediately **pervaded** the entire van. My nostrils puckered, and I felt my own vomit rising. I grabbed for my bag. Within minutes, all of us passengers were filling up our plastic bags. No, it wasn't far from Jalalabad to the border, just a couple of hours, but that ride felt like it would never end.

About half a mile from the border the van pulled over to the side of the road. "This is as far as we go," the driver said. "That's the

Big Idea Looking Into Lives *What does the description of this bus station tell you about the trip Ahmedi and her mother are taking?* BI3

Vocabulary

surge (surj) *v.* to move suddenly in a wave

Vocabulary

pervade (pər vād′) *v.* to go through or fill every part of

Teach

BI3 Big Idea

Looking into Lives Answer: *Their trip is obviously dangerous because they are relying on other people to help them. They are unsure where they are going and how exactly to get there.* OL

L Literary Element

Imagery Ask: To what two senses do the images in this passage appeal? *(sight and touch)* OL

★ Viewing the Art

Photographer Teru Kuwayama took this photograph on October 5, 2004, shortly before Afghanistan elected Hamid Karzai in its first democratic presidential election. The country also instituted a new constitution and a National Assembly. In spite of these government reforms, the Jalalabad Kabul road remains a dangerous travel route, targeted by terrorists. AS

English Language Coach

Developing Vocabulary Many words in the selection may be unfamiliar to English language learners. Direct students' attention to the paragraph on page 356 beginning "But at least it wasn't cold . . ." and ending "meant anybody harm." Note the words *hunkering, clotted, cheer, companionable,* and *folks.* Explain that context clues can often help readers figure out a word's meaning. Give pairs of students a stack of note cards. Have them write one vocabulary word (or other unfamiliar words from the text) on each note card. On the back of each card, they should write definitions from a dictionary. EL

Academic Standards

Additional Support activities on pp. 354 and 355 cover the following standards:

Skills Practice: **9.3.6** Analyze and trace an author's development of time and sequence...

English Language Coach: **9.1** Use... context clues and a growing knowledge of English...to determine the meaning of words...

Teach

L1 Literary Element

Tone **Answer:** *Worry, anxiety, and desperation* **OL**

R1 Reading Strategy

Analyzing Cultural Context
Answer: *Students might expect that they would cross the border in a vehicle, not on foot, and that the same transportation that they had on one side of the border would carry them through to their destination on the other side.* **OL**

L2 Literary Element

Tone **Answer:** *Although she is in an extremely difficult situation, she feels "blessed" in some ways, such as not being alone or too cold. She is emotional about the few positive things she experienced.* **OL**

border up ahead. You see those two buildings and the gate between them? That's it. If you can get through that gate, you're in Pakistan. About half a mile up the road on the other side, if you can get to the other side, you'll find other cars like this one offering rides to Peshawar."

Well, we got out and started trudging toward the border station. We were not alone. The whole stretch of road was filled with people hoping to get across the border that day—hundreds of families. I don't know how many. I wasn't counting. I didn't count. I was distracted by the scene I saw up ahead.

The gate to Pakistan was closed, and I could see that the Pakistani border guards were letting no one through. People were pushing and shoving and jostling up against that gate, and the guards were driving them back. As we got closer, the crowd thickened, and I could hear the roar and clamor at the gate. The Afghans were yelling something, and the Pakistanis were yelling back. My mother was clutching her side and gasping for breath, trying to keep up. I felt desperate to get through, because the sun was setting, and if we got stuck here, what were we going to do? Where would we stay? There was nothing here, no town, no hotel, no buildings, just the desert.

Yet we had no real chance of getting through. Big strong men were running up to the gate in vain. The guards had clubs, and they had carbines,[8] too, which they turned around and used as weapons. Again and again, the crowd surged toward the gate and the guards drove them back with their sticks and clubs, swinging and beating until the crowd receded. And after that, for the next few minutes, on our side of the border, people milled about and muttered and **stoked** their own impatience and worked up their rage, until gradually the crowd gathered strength and surged against that gate again, only to be swept back.

We never even got close to the front. We got caught up in the thinning rear end of the crowd, and even so, we were part of each wave, pulled forward, driven back. It was hard for me to keep my footing, and my mother was clutching my arm now, just hanging on, just trying to stay close to me, because the worst thing would have been if we had gotten separated. Finally, I saw that it was no use. We were only risking injury. We drifted back, out of the crowd. In the thickening dusk we could hear the dull roar of people still trying to get past the border guards, but we receded into the desert, farther and farther back from the border gate.

Night was falling, and we were stranded out there in the open.

But at least it wasn't cold; that was a blessing. And at least we were not alone. For that, too, I felt grateful. Hundreds of us were hunkering out there on the desert floor, in the shadows of the high hills that marked the border. We were clotted into family groups. Some groups managed to get fires going, which added a feeling of cheer. They chatted quietly around their fires, and we could hear their voices. There was something companionable about it, really. We were all just ordinary folks caught in a bad situation, sharing the same fate. No one there meant anybody harm.

Had I been alone, I would have felt frightened, but with that sea of families surrounding me, I felt safe, even if they were strangers. My mother and I had our little cloth bundles, in which we were each carrying some extra clothes, and we had our head scarves. We put

8. *Carbines* are a type of firearm.

Literary Element Tone *What emotions do you hear in the author's voice?* **L1**

Reading Strategy Analyzing Cultural Context *Does this description differ from what you would expect if you crossed an international border? Explain.* **R1**

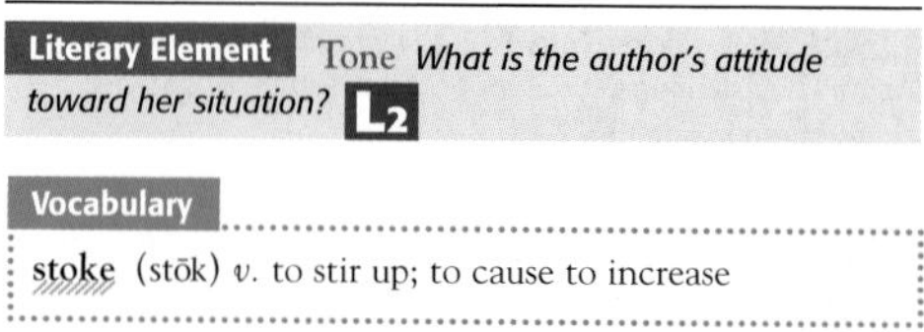

Literary Element Tone *What is the author's attitude toward her situation?* **L2**

Vocabulary

stoke (stōk) *v.* to stir up; to cause to increase

Additional Support

Skills Practice

WRITING: Vivid Verbs As students revise their work, urge them to focus on their word choices, particularly their verbs. By using precise, vivid verbs, students can dramatically improve the quality of their writing. Write this sentence on the board: Jean-Pierre set the sauté pan down on the stove and ran across the kitchen to answer the phone. Discuss how the sentence changes when it is revised: Jean-Pierre slammed the sauté pan down on the stove and charged across the kitchen to answer the phone. **OL**

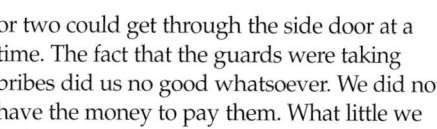

Mountains near Badakhshan, Afghanistan. 

those under our heads as pillows and slept under the stars. It wasn't bad. We did manage to catch some sleep.

Then dawn came, and we again had to make our way to the road and try to get across that border. What else could we do? We could not go back, nor could we stay in that wasteland indefinitely. We *had* to get through. But once again, the guards were keeping the gate closed, beating and hitting anyone who got close enough each time the crowd rushed.

On that second day, however, I learned that it was all a question of money. Someone told me about this, and then I watched closely and saw that it was true. Throughout the day, while some of the guards confronted the crowds, a few others lounged over to the side. People approached them quietly. Money changed hands, and the guards then let those people quietly through a small door to the side. Hundreds could have flowed through the main gate had it been opened, but only one or two could get through the side door at a time. The fact that the guards were taking bribes did us no good whatsoever. We did not have the money to pay them. What little we had we would need to get from Peshawar to Quetta. And so the second day passed.

Reading Strategy Analyzing Cultural Context *What do these details tell you about the guards at this border station?* **R2**

At the end of that day we found ourselves camping near a friendly family. We struck up a conversation with them. The woman told us that her husband, Ghulam Ali, had gone to look for another way across the border. He was checking out a goat path that supposedly went over the mountains several miles northeast of the border station. If one could get to Pakistan safely by that route, he would come back for his family. "You can go with us," the woman said.

Later that night her husband showed up. "It works," he said. "Smugglers use that path, and they bribe the guards to leave it unguarded. Of course, we don't want to run into any smugglers, either, but if we go late at night, we should be fine." **L3**

Teach

R2 Reading Strategy

Analyzing Cultural Context
Answer: *Smuggling is commonplace and accepted. Students may mention that it is not only at the official border that bribes are commonplace, but that most of the border guards are likely corrupt.* **OL**

L3 Literary Element

Dialogue Note that Ahmedi introduces dialogue, or direct quotations of the characters' words, at this turning point in the narrative.
Ask: Why do you think she uses this technique? *(Possible answer: To emphasize the conversation's importance and add immediacy)* **OL**

Viewing the Photograph

The Hindu Kush, an impressive and extreme mountain range, characterizes the geography of Afghanistan. The Hindu Kush spans 500 miles and spreads southwest into Afghanistan from Pakistan. Around 1500 B.C., people from Central Asia crossed through the range and brought with them the beginnings of Indo-Iranian languages. **AS**

Reading in the Real World

Citizenship Have students find an article online or in a newspaper or magazine that describes life in Afghanistan today. Have small groups of students use their research to answer questions such as these: *How has life in Afghanistan changed since the author left? After researching Afghanistan, what insight do you have in the author's decision to leave?* **OL**

Academic Standards

Additional Support activities on pp. 356 and 357 cover the following standards:

Skills Practice: **9.4.3** Use precise language [and] action verbs…

Reading in the Real World: **9.2.4** Synthesize the content from several sources or works…and connect…to…related topics…

Teach

R1 Reading Strategy

Analyzing Cultural Context

Answer: *The Islamic faith is a vital part of the culture. Even at the border crossing, there is a mosque. Despite the need for haste, prayers are observed.* OL

★ Viewing the Photograph

Answer: *Students might say that the image of the massed crowds behind the wire fence corresponds to Ahmedi's description.*

The terrain along the border between Afghanistan and Pakistan is rugged and mountainous; much of the border runs along the Hindu Kush mountain range. AS

Pakistani border security guards stand in front of the Pakistan-Afghanistan border to stop Afghan refugees, Wednesday, November 15, 2000, at Torkham border post, 55 kilometers (34 miles) northwest of Peshawar, northwestern Pakistan.

Viewing the Photograph: Based on Ahmedi's description, how well does this photo capture the scene at the border? ★

His wife then told him our story, and Ghulam Ali took pity on us. "Yes, of course you can come with us," he said. "But you have had two hard days. You will need some rest before you attempt this mountain crossing. Spend tonight here and sleep well, knowing that you will have nothing to do tomorrow except lounge around, rest, and catch your breath. Tomorrow, do not throw yourself against those border guards again. Let your only work be the gathering of your strength. Then tomorrow night we will all go over the mountain together, with God's grace. I will show you the way. If God wills it,[9] we will follow that smugglers' path to safety. You and your mother are in my care now."

So we spent the whole next day there. It was terribly warm and we had no water, but we walked a little way and found a mosque that refugees like us had built over the years, so that people waiting to get across the border would have a place to say their prayers. We got some water to drink at the mosque, and we said *namaz*[10] there too. Somehow we obtained a bit of bread as well. I can't remember how that turned up, but there it was, and we ate it. We sustained our strength. After sunset we lay down just as if we were going to spend another night. In fact, I did fall asleep for a while. Long after dark—or early the next morning, to be exact, before the sun came up—that man shook us awake. "It's time," he said.

We got up and performed our ablutions[11] quickly in the darkness, with just sand because that's allowed when you have no access to water. We said our prayers. Then Ghulam Ali began to march into the darkness with his family, and we trudged along silently behind them. After several miles the path began to climb, and my mother began to wheeze. Her asthma was pretty bad at this point, poor

9. Throughout the Muslim world, expressions that show an awareness of God are common. Here, typical phrases are used to show that people's fortunes are dependent on God's will or grace.

10. *Namaz* is prayer.

11. *Ablutions* refers to ritual washing before prayer.

Reading Strategy Analyzing Cultural Context *What does this tell you about the author's culture?* R1

Additional Support

Skills Practice

GRAMMAR: Prepositional Phrases Write the phrase *over the mountains* on the board. Explain that prepositional phrases consist of a preposition *(over)* and an object of the preposition *(mountains)*. Note that prepositional phrases often clarify spatial relationships: for example, Ahmedi uses the phrases *through the main gate, from Peshawar to Quetta, near a friendly family,* and *across the border.*

Have students write at least two prepositional phrases in sentences to clarify a spatial relationship. OL thing. No doubt, her anxiety made it worse, but in such circumstances how could she rid herself of anxiety? It was no use knowing that her difficulty was rooted in anxiety, just as it was no use knowing that we could have moved more quickly if we had possessed wings. Life is what it is. The path over that mountain was not actually very long, only a couple of miles. Steep as it was, we could have gotten over in little more than an hour if not for my mother. Because of her, we had to pause every few minutes, so our journey took many hours. **R2**

I myself hardly felt the exertion. I was walking quite well that day, quite athletically. I had that good prosthetic leg from Germany. The foot was a little worn by then, but not enough to slow me down. Thinking back, I'm puzzled, actually. How did I scale that mountain so easily? How did I climb down the other side? These days I find it hard to clamber up two or three flights of stairs, even. I don't know what made me so supple[12] and strong that day, but I felt no hardship, no anxiety or fear, just concentration and intensity. Perhaps my mother's problems distracted me from my own. That might account for it. Perhaps desperation gave me energy and made me forget the rigor of the climb. Well, whatever the reason, I scrambled up like a goat. The family we were following had a girl only a bit younger than me, and she was moving slowly. Her family used my example to chide her. They kept saying, "Look at that girl. She's missing a leg, and yet she's going faster than you. Why can't you keep up? Hurry now!"

That Ghulam Ali was certainly a good man, so patient with us and so compassionate. He had never seen us before, and yet when he met us, he said, "I will help you." That's the thing about life. You never know when and where you will encounter a spot of human decency. I have felt alone in this world at times; I have known long periods of being no one. But then, without warning, a person like Ghulam Ali just turns up and says, "I see you. I am on your side." Strangers have been kind to me when it mattered most. That sustains a person's hope and faith.

Anyway, climbing up that mountain on the Afghanistan side took some effort, but after we topped the crest, even my mother found the going down part fairly easy. We hardly stopped at all on the downward side. Going up took hours; coming down took minutes, or so it seemed.

As soon as we reached the bottom of the slope, Ghulam Ali told us we were now officially in Pakistan. We peered around. The landscape looked just the same here as it did back where we came from. And yet we were in Pakistan. We had escaped from Afghanistan. We started laughing. We couldn't stop. We tried to stop our mouths with our palms, and we could not do it. The laughter just insisted on bursting forth from us. Happiness filled our hearts. My mother's asthma disappeared without a trace for one whole hour. Yes, for one whole hour there, my mother could breathe. You might as well say we had been in prison for thirty years and had suddenly been released—that was the kind of joy we felt. **L3**

12. Here, *supple* means "able to adapt or respond to a new situation."

Literary Element Tone *What tone or attitude do you hear in this statement?* **L1**

Literary Element Tone *How do the author's word choices affect her tone in this passage?* **L2**

Vocabulary

chide (chīd) *v.* to express disapproval

Big Idea Looking Into Lives *How does the author draw the reader into the giddy happiness she felt on the other side of the mountain?* **BI**

Teach

R2 Reading Strategy

Making Inferences **Ask:** What can you infer about the narrator's attitude toward challenges in life? *(She believes confronting challenges may give a person energy and spirit.)* **OL**

L1 Literary Element

Tone **Answer:** *Students may hear resignation, acceptance, or endurance.* **OL**

L2 Literary Element

Tone **Answer:** *Her attitude is accepting, positive, and even good-humored. She compares her own climbing up the mountain to that of a goat.* **OL**

L3 Literary Element

Tone **Ask:** How does the tone at the end of the selection contrast with the tone at the beginning? *(End: exhilarated and jubilant; beginning: somber and foreboding)* **OL**

BI Big Idea

Looking into Lives **Answer:** *Her word choice and repeated mentions of the laughing draw the reader in, as does the repetition of her mother being able to breathe, along with the informal "Yes."* **OL**

Differentiated Instruction

Context Clues Explain that students can often use clues from context to determine a word's meaning. Write this example on the board: "I myself hardly felt the exertion." Note the word *athletically* in the next sentence. Explain that this word functions as a clue to the meaning of *exertion* ("physical effort").

Have students use context clues to define the underlined words in this passage:

1. ". . . clamber up two of three flights of stairs" *(climb with difficulty)*
2. "Perhaps my mother's problems distracted me from my own." *(diverted attention from)* **BL**

Academic Standards

Additional Support activities on pp. 358 and 359 cover the following standards:

Skills Practice: **9.6.1** Identify and correctly use…phrases…

Differentiated Instruction: **9.1** Use…context clues…to determine the meaning of words…

AFTER YOU READ

Assess

1. Accept any reasonable answer.
2. (a) From Kabul, Afghanistan, to Quetta, Pakistan; (b) They are in danger from the Taliban.
3. (a) They take a bus to Jalalabad and then continue in a van. (b) Possible answers: Need for male escort, armed border guards, unruly crowd at the border
4. (a) Ghulam Ali guides them along a smugglers' path through the mountains. (b) People have to bribe guards to get across. It was lucky to find someone who could help them across the border.
5. Mention of Taliban in both Afghanistan and Peshawar, Pakistan, and that they are hostile toward her people
6. Possible answer: Direct and factual
7. Vivid sensory details: van's stench, clamor and pressure of the frenzied throng, heat and dust of the desert
8. Accept reasonable answers.

CheckPoint

Use the CheckPoint questions on Presentation Plus! to check students' mastery of the selection. These questions can be used with interactive response keypads for immediate student feedback.

AFTER YOU READ

RESPONDING AND THINKING CRITICALLY

Respond

1. What part of this autobiography do you think you will remember longest? Why?

Recall and Interpret

2. (a)Where do the author and her mother start out, and where are they going? (b)What can you infer about why they are going?
3. (a)How do the author and her mother reach the border? (b)What details of the journey hint at danger?
4. (a)How do the author and her mother cross the border? (b)Why could they be considered lucky to have gotten across the border?

Analyze and Evaluate

5. How does the author make it clear that she and her mother faced problems in both Afghanistan and Pakistan?
6. How would you describe the style of the writing in this memoir? Explain.
7. How well does the author give you a "you-are-there" sense of the journey? Cite evidence from the text about what you can hear, see, smell, or otherwise experience through your senses.

Connect

8. **Big Idea** **Looking Into Lives** How are the challenges that the author faces similar to or different from your own?

LITERARY ANALYSIS

Literary Element Tone

A writer's **tone** can convey a variety of attitudes, such as sympathy, objectivity, or humor. The specific tone is often related both to the type of writing and its purpose. Often, first-person narratives, including autobiographies, are far more subjective and emotional than other types of nonfiction written in the third-person. An autobiographer can write for many purposes, including to inform, to reflect, to persuade, and to entertain.

1. Explain whether the tone of "Escape from Afghanistan" is serious or casual. Provide examples to support your opinion.
2. Name one other word that describes the author's tone. Give an example from the text to support your word choice.

Review: Historical Narrative

As you learned on page 328, a **historical narrative** is a work of nonfiction that tells the story of important historical events or developments.

Partner Activity Work with a classmate to record information you learn in this autobiography about Afghanistan during the Taliban regime. Use a cluster chart like this one.

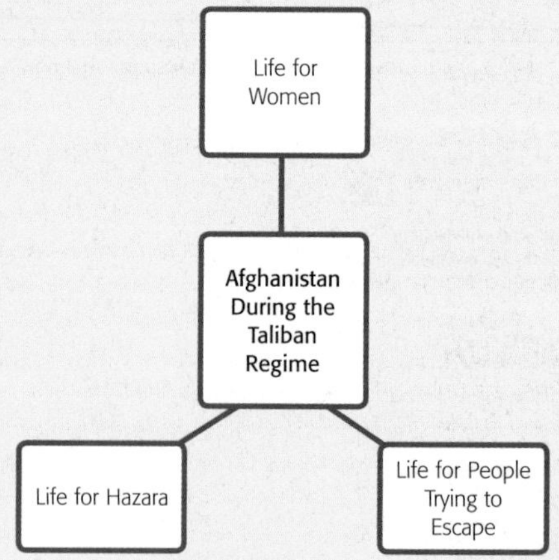

Literary Element

1. Serious: first-person view of life-or-death situation; includes frightening and suspenseful details such as the aggressive throng and armed border patrol
2. Possible answers: *Serious, reflective, hopeful;* answers should include supporting details from the text

Review: Historical Narrative

Sample answers for chart:
Life for Women: Need escort to travel
Life for Hazara: Hostility from the Taliban
Life for People Trying to Escape: No safe way across the border; must pay bribes or sneak across

READING AND VOCABULARY

Reading Strategy **Analyzing Cultural Context**

Much of what makes "Escape from Afghanistan" so interesting is that it is set in such a different world than the one most readers inhabit. Review the cultural details you noted as you read.

1. In what ways does this autobiography take you to a world that is different than the one you live in? List three or four examples.
2. How do the details about life in Afghanistan and the crossing to Pakistan interest you?

Vocabulary **Practice**

Practice with Context Clues Read each of the following sentences and then decide which of the choices reveals the best clues to the meaning of the word in boldface type.

1. Tyler is in a **quandary:** he cannot decide which pair of sneakers to buy.
   a. Tyler is **b.** he cannot decide
2. The crowd of protestors **surged** forward when the speaker appeared.
   a. The crowd of protestors **b.** appeared
3. Anxiety **pervaded** the stuck elevator, and everyone showed signs of stress.
   a. the stuck elevator **b.** everyone showed
4. The cheers grew louder as the touchdown **stoked** the fans' enthusiasm.
   a. grew louder **b.** touchdown
5. Ms. DiDario **chided** Leah for jaywalking.
   a. Ms. DiDario **b.** for jaywalking

Academic Vocabulary

Here is a word from the vocabulary list on page R80.

network (net′ wurk′) *n.* group of people with similar interests or goals

Practice and Apply
Who was the author's **network** of support?

WRITING AND EXTENDING

Writing About Literature

Respond to Theme One theme of Ahmedi's autobiography is the support of family and strangers. Write a brief essay explaining how and where this theme is presented and how you responded to it. Use evidence from the story to support your points.

Develop a working thesis statement for your paper. A working thesis statement presents the main idea you will support, but it may need revision when you finish drafting. Then gather evidence from the story that supports your thesis. Remember to introduce that evidence and explain it. Your plan of organization might look like this.

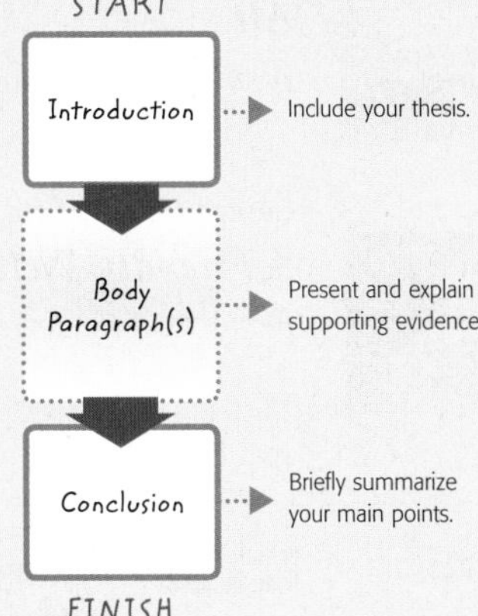
START
Introduction
Include your thesis.
Body Paragraph(s)
Present and explain supporting evidence.
Conclusion
Briefly summarize your main points.
FINISH

After you complete your draft, have a peer read it and suggest revisions. Then proofread and edit your work to correct errors in spelling, grammar, and punctuation.

Internet Connection

What effect have the many years of civil war, as well as the recent U.S. war against the Taliban, had on Afghan children? Use the Internet to find information. You might look for information about interrupted education, landmines, orphans, and refugees. Present your findings to the class.

LiteratureOnline **Web Activities** For eFlashcards, Selection Quick Checks, and other Web activities, go to www.glencoe.com.

LiteratureOnline

Web Activities Have students access the Web site for interactive activities that will help them assess their understanding of the selection.

AFTER YOU READ

Assess

Reading Strategy

1. Students may be unfamiliar with bazaars, ritual washing before prayer, and restrictions on women's freedom.
2. Accept any reasonable answer.

Vocabulary

1. b **2.** b **3.** b **4.** a **5.** b

Academic Vocabulary

Possible answers: mother's cousin, Ghulam Ali

Writing About Literature

Students' essays should

- contain a strong thesis statement expressing the main idea
- present evidence from the narrative that supports the thesis

Internet Connection

Students should deliver a concise summary of their findings, together with a description of the Web sites they consulted as sources in order to gather information on the effects of civil war in Afghanistan.

Focus

BELLRINGER

Bellringer Options
Selection Focus Transparency 23
Daily Language Practice Transparency 32

Or display images of different kinds of dogs.

Ask: What pets have you owned? What do they add to your life?

As students read the selections, ask them to think about the relationship of each dog with the people in each.

Connecting to the Reading Selections

Allow students to share their responses to the opening questions. Then have students discuss the key relationships in the lives of the characters in the selections they have read in this unit. Challenge them to examine the relationships of the dogs and their masters in the selections in this section.

Comparing Literature *Across Genres*

Connecting to the Reading Selections

What is the relationship between dogs and people? What do you think it should be? In the three selections that follow, you will read about abandoned and mistreated dogs who were given new lives, as well as about a watchdog's welcome.

James Herriot
A Case of Cruelty .... memoir 363
A dog lover meets a dog in need of love

W. S. Merwin
Ali .... poem 375
A small, rescued dog seems to take wing

George Gordon, Lord Byron
A Friendly Welcome .... poem 377
How sweet the watchdog's welcome is!

COMPARING THE Big Idea Looking into Lives

Dogs can be such dear companions. While some are just good friends, others fill deep and fundamental human needs. Each of the writers featured here offers a unique glimpse into the lives of dogs and their owners.

COMPARING Tone

Tone is a reflection of a writer's or a speaker's attitude toward the subject of a literary work. Tone is communicated through words and details that express particular emotions and that evoke an emotional response in the reader.

COMPARING Author's Purpose

Author's purpose is an author's reason for writing a literary work. An author's purpose for writing can inform his or her decisions about such choices as the tone, style, and genre. For example, an author who wants to persuade a specific group of people to do something may opt to give a speech written in a logical style.

Selection Skills

Comparing Literature

Literary Elements
- Memoir (SE pp. 364, 366, 367, 369, 371, 372, 374)
- Tone (TWE pp. 366, 370)
- Analyzing Style (TWE p. 373)

Reading Skills
- Analyzing Style (SE pp. 364, 365, 368–370, 373, 374)
- Applying Knowledge (TWE p. 364)

Vocabulary Skills
- Word Parts (SE p. 374)

Writing Skills/Grammar
- Essay on Voice (SE p. 374)

Listening/Speaking/Viewing Skills
- Analyzing Art (SE p. 371)

A Case of Cruelty

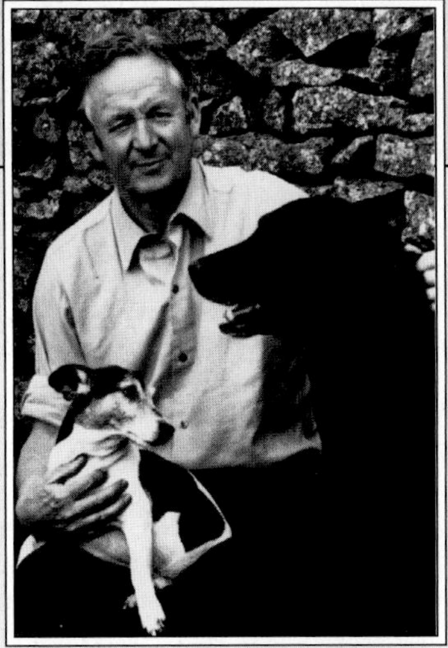

MEET JAMES HERRIOT

Cows having trouble giving birth, sheep with ear infections, and dogs who are disastrously overweight are among the many subjects of James Herriot's charming stories about his experiences as a country veterinarian in Yorkshire, England. In these stories, the problems and conflicts start with the animal, but quickly include people—and the full range of human personalities.

Getting Started as a Writer James Alfred Wight, who later took the pen name James Herriot, was born in England and spent most of his childhood living just outside Glasgow, Scotland. By the age of thirteen, he had already decided to become a country veterinarian. This job would allow him to treat both farm animals and house pets, such as cats and dogs. It would also allow him to combine his love of animals with his love of the countryside.

Although he often spoke to his wife about turning his experiences into stories, it was not until he was fifty that he began to write. He did not achieve immediate success. Herriot admits that those first stories were just plain bad, and that he had to teach himself how to write before he could do better. But do better he did. Eventually, he became a best-selling author and a popular sensation. In fact, his books about his life were considered a causal factor in a spike in applications to veterinary school, as well a spike in tourism in his little town in Yorkshire.

Simple Pleasures An employee and then a partner in a veterinary practice, Herriot took pleasure in his interactions with the local people and animals. He married, had two children, and continued working for as long as he was able. Even when he became rich and famous, he did not wish to live in any other place or any other way than he always had.

> *"I think it was the fact that I liked [my job] so much that made the writing just come out of me automatically."*
>
> —James Herriot

Accomplishments Herriot wrote twenty books, eight of which deal with his life as a veterinarian. Many others are books for children. More than sixty million copies of his works have sold worldwide. His books have also been turned into two films and a popular BBC television series. A museum and historic site have been built to honor his memory in his native village of Thirsk.

James Herriot was born in 1916 and died in 1995.

Literature Online **Author Search** For more about James Herriot, go to www.glencoe.com.

Teach

★ Cultural History

Tell students that scientific studies have shown that pets can have a profound influence on their human owners. Pets offer companionship, for example, with very few strings attached.

Ask: What qualities make a pet a good companion? What qualities make a human being a good pet owner?

Author Search To expand students' appreciation of James Herriot, have them access the Web site for additional information and resources.

Selection Resources

Print Materials
- Unit 2 Resources (Fast File), pp. 35–37
- Leveled Vocabulary Development, p. 26
- Selection and Unit Assessments, pp. 57–58
- Selection Quick Checks, p. 29

Transparencies
- Bellringer Options Transparencies: Selection Focus Transparency 23 Daily Language Practice Transparency 32
- Literary Elements Transparency 27

Technology
- TeacherWorks Plus™ CD-ROM
- StudentWorks Plus™ CD-ROM
- Presentation Plus!™ CD-ROM
- Literature Online, glencoe.com
- Online Student Edition, mhln.com
- Exam*View*® Assessment Suite CD-ROM
- Vocabulary PuzzleMaker CD-ROM
- Listening Library, disc 1 tracks 31, 32, 33

BEFORE YOU READ

Focus

Summary

Herriot's memoir recounts the case of Mrs. Donovan, an elderly busybody devastated by the death of her dog Rex. With deftly ironic humor, Herriot shows how Mrs. Donovan becomes rejuvenated when she takes charge of Roy, a badly neglected dog he rescued. Once the dog and Mrs. Donovan find each other, both gain new leases on life.

V Vocabulary

Vocabulary File Say: Add these words and definitions to your vocabulary file. For each word, include a sentence that gives you an example of how to use the word. **OL** Students with English language needs should include the pronunciation of these words in their files. **EL**

Literary Elements Have students access the Web site to improve their understanding of memoir.

COMPARING LITERATURE

LITERATURE PREVIEW

Connecting to the Memoir

In this story, Herriot brings together a human who needs a good dog and a dog who needs a good human. Before you read "A Case of Cruelty," think about the following questions:

- Have you ever had a pet or known someone who had a pet? How did the pet affect your or its owner's life?
- How important is it to feel needed?

Building Background

James Herriot's stories are autobiographical. They take place in Darrowby, a fictional town that many recognize as Thirsk, Herriot's hometown in Yorkshire, England. The stories take place in the 1940s and 1950s. At this time, veterinary science was far less sophisticated than it is now, but human nature was just the same. As a veterinarian, Herriot worked with a man he called Siegfried, who also appears in this selection.

In a veterinary practice, those who deal with small animals treat dogs, cats, and other pets. Those who deal with large animals typically treat farm animals such as horses, sheep, and cows.

Setting Purposes for Reading

Big Idea Looking into Lives

As you read, think about how Herriot concerns himself with both the physical and emotional lives of the people and animals of Darrowby.

Literary Element Memoir

A **memoir** is an account of an event or period in the author's life that emphasizes the author's personal experience of that event or period. Like an autobiography, a memoir is told from the first-person point of view.

- See Literary Terms Handbook, p. R10.

Literature Online **Interactive Literary Elements Handbook** To review or learn more about the literary elements, go to www.glencoe.com.

READING PREVIEW

Reading Strategy Analyzing Style

Analyzing style is looking carefully at the writer's word choice, sentences and paragraph structure, and use of figurative language and imagery in order to gain greater understanding of the author, the author's purpose, or the work itself.

Reading Tip: Making a Chart As you read, list interesting word choices, figures of speech, images, and particularly long, short, dense, or otherwise interesting sentences. Comment on what makes them expressive.

Interesting Language	Why/How It Is Expressive
p. 365 "his lips quivered with indignation"	Strong verb: *quivered* precise noun: *indignation*

Vocabulary

callousness (kal′ əs nes) *n.* state or attitude of feeling no emotion or sympathy; p. 365 *Jan viewed the family's loss with sympathy, but Brian viewed it with callousness.*

adamant (ad′ ə mənt) *adj.* rigidly determined; p. 366 *The teacher made it clear that she was adamant about her homework policy, and no exceptions were allowed.*

transcend (tran send′) *v.* to go beyond; p. 366 *Lee and Fran will transcend their personal differences to work together on the pledge drive.*

diligent (dil′ ə jənt) *adj.* steady, responsible; p. 367 *The diligent doctor gave thought to every possible diagnosis.*

placidly (plas′ id lē) *adv.* calmly, serenely; p. 373 *The quiet, contented child played placidly.*

INDIANA ACADEMIC STANDARDS (pages 364–374)

9.2.8 Make reasonable statements and draw conclusions about a text...

9.5.3 Write...analytical essays...

9.3.13 Explain how voice...affect[s] the mood, tone, and meaning of text.

Additional Support

Skills Practice

VOCABULARY: Applying Knowledge Have students become acquainted with the vocabulary list. Instruct students to find synonyms for each of the words on the list. Assign students to work in groups to create one- to two-page short stories in which they use all the words from the list. Instruct students that the topic of their stories should involve animals. **OL** Encourage students to use mythological animals or to create a fictional creature of their own as the subjects of their stories. Invite the groups to share their stories with the class. **AL**

Dog Lying Down (Dog Portrait), 1909. Franz Marc.

A Case of CRUELTY

James Herriot

The silvery haired old gentleman with the pleasant face didn't look the type to be easily upset, but his eyes glared at me angrily, and his lips quivered with indignation.

"Mr. Herriot," he said. "I have come to make a complaint. I strongly object to your **callousness** in subjecting my dog to unnecessary suffering." L

"Suffering? What suffering?" I was mystified.[1]

"I think you know, Mr. Herriot. I brought my dog in a few days ago. He was very lame, and I am referring to your treatment on that occasion."

I nodded. "Yes, I remember it well . . . but where does the suffering come in?"

"Well, the poor animal is going around with his leg dangling, and I have it on good authority that the bone is fractured and should have been put in plaster[2] immediately." The old gentleman stuck his chin out fiercely. L

"All right, you can stop worrying," I said. "Your dog has a radial paralysis[3] caused by a blow on the ribs, and if you are patient

1. *Mystified* means "bewildered."

Vocabulary

callousness (kal′ əs nes) *n.* state or attitude of feeling no emotion or sympathy

2. *Plaster* is a reference to a cast.
3. *Radial paralysis* is a loss of movement that has developed uniformly from a central point of injury.

Reading Strategy Analyzing Style *How does the author help you experience the "old gentleman"?* R

English Language Coach

Pronunciation Pronunciation guides in dictionaries can prove difficult for English language learners, who often need to hear how words actually sound. Give students note cards, and ask them to write unfamiliar words, one on each card, noting the page where it is found. Have students check the pronunciations in a dictionary, copy the definitions on the back of the cards, and ask a native English speaker to say each word. Encourage students to repeat each word several times. Then have them find the sentence in the selection that contains the word, read it aloud, and discuss the meaning of the sentence. EL

COMPARING LITERATURE

Teach

L Literary Element

Memoir Ask: What contribution do these exchanges of dialogue make to the atmosphere and tone of the memoir? *(Dialogue makes the memoir seem realistic and immediate.)* OL

R Reading Strategy

Analyzing Style Answer: *The reader can hear the old gentleman's voice and see him strike a somewhat aggressive pose.* OL

CheckPoint

Use the CheckPoint questions on Presentation Plus! to monitor students' comprehension. These questions can be used with interactive response keypads for immediate student feedback.

Readability Scores

Dale-Chall: 5.8
DRP: 57
Lexile: 1010

Academic Standards

Additional Support activities on pp. 364 and 365 cover the following standards:

Skills Practice: **9.1** Use…a growing knowledge of English…to determine the meaning of words… **9.1.3** Use knowledge of mythology…to understand the…meaning of new words.

English Language Coach: **9.1** Use phonics, context clues,…and a growing knowledge of English…to determine the meaning of words…

Teach

L1 Literary Element

Memoir **Answer:** *Only someone with a long-term, detailed knowledge of Darrowby could make such a general observation of Mrs. Donovan's omnipresence.* OL

BI Big Idea

Looking into Lives **Answer:** *Mrs. Donovan is a busybody; she is curious about everyone and everything that happens in town.* OL

L2 Literary Element

Tone **Ask:** How would you describe the tone in this passage? Name word choices that help create it. *(Ironic: "whole armory of medicines and remedies," "miracle-working condition powders," "unprecedented value," "uncanny ability," "what I had thought was my patient")* OL

and follow my treatment he'll gradually improve. In fact I think he'll recover completely."

"But he trails his leg when he walks."

"I know—that's typical, and to the layman[4] it does give the appearance of a broken leg. But he shows no sign of pain, does he?"

"No, he seems quite happy, but this lady seemed to be absolutely sure of her facts. She was **adamant**."

"Lady?"

"Yes," said the old gentleman. "She is very clever with animals, and she came around to see if she could help in my dog's convalescence. She brought some excellent condition powders[5] with her."

"Ah!" A blinding shaft pierced the fog in my mind. All was suddenly clear. "It was Mrs. Donovan, wasn't it?"

"Well . . . er, yes. That was her name."

Old Mrs. Donovan was a woman who really got around. No matter what was going on in Darrowby—weddings, funerals, house-sales—you'd find the dumpy little figure and walnut face among the spectators, the darting, black-button eyes taking everything in. And always, on the end of its lead, her terrier dog.

When I say "old," I'm only guessing, because she appeared ageless; she seemed to have been around a long time, but she could have been anything between fifty-five and seventy-five. She certainly had the vitality of a young woman because she must have walked vast distances in her dedicated quest to keep abreast of events. Many people took an uncharitable view of her acute curiosity, but whatever the motivation, her activities took her into almost every channel of life in the town. One of these channels was our veterinary practice.

Because Mrs. Donovan, among her other widely ranging interests, was an animal doctor. In fact I think it would be safe to say that this facet of her life **transcended** all the others.

She could talk at length on the ailments of small animals, and she had a whole armory of medicines and remedies at her command, her two specialities being her miracle-working condition powders and a dog shampoo of unprecedented value for improving the coat. She had an uncanny ability to sniff out a sick animal, and it was not uncommon when I was on my rounds to find Mrs. Donovan's dark, gypsy face poised intently over what I had thought was my patient, while she administered calf's foot jelly or one of her own patent nostrums.[6] L2

I suffered more than Siegfried because I took a more active part in the small animal side of our practice. I was anxious to develop this aspect and to improve my image in this field, and Mrs. Donovan didn't help at all. "Young Mr. Herriot," she would confide to my clients, "is all right with cattle and such like, but he don't know nothing about dogs and cats."

And of course they believed her and had implicit[7] faith in her. She had the irresistible mystic[8] appeal of the amateur, and on top of that there was her habit, particularly endearing in Darrowby, of never charging

4. Here, a *layman* is a person without specialized medical knowledge.
5. *Condition powders* are treatments or remedies in powdered form.
6. *Nostrums* can be effective medicines or quack remedies.
7. Here, *implicit* means "unquestioning."
8. Here, *mystic* means "mysterious."

Literary Element Memoir *How does this comment show the author's special knowledge about Darrowby?* L1

Big Idea Looking Into Lives *What kind of person is Mrs. Donovan? How does she live her life?* BI

Vocabulary

adamant (ad′ ə mənt) *adj.* rigidly determined

Vocabulary

transcend (tran send′) *v.* to go beyond

Additional Support

Skills Practice

GRAMMAR: Understanding Parallelism Using parallel construction helps create unity in a piece of writing. Writers do this by writing a series of words, phrases, or sentences that have similar grammatical form. An example of parallel construction occurs on page 366–367:

". . . [T]here was her habit, particularly endearing in Darrowby, of never charging for her advice, her medicines, her long periods of diligent nursing.

Point out that the three noun phrases in this sentence follow the same pattern. Have them look through this selection for sentences with parallel construction. OL

Beware of Dog, 1991. Reynard Milici. Louis K. Meisel Gallery, Inc.

for her advice, her medicines, her long periods of **diligent** nursing.

Older folk in the town told how her husband, an Irish farm worker, had died many years ago and how he must have had a "bit put away" because Mrs. Donovan had apparently been able to indulge all her interests over the years without financial strain. Since she inhabited the streets of Darrowby all day and every day, I often encountered her, and she always smiled up at me sweetly and told me how she had been sitting up all night with Mrs. So-and-so's dog that I'd been treating. She felt sure she'd be able to pull it through.

Literary Element Memoir *What do you hear in the narrator's tone as he tells about Mrs. Donovan? What does it tell you about the author's personality?* L3

Vocabulary

diligent (dil′ ə jənt) *adj.* steady, responsible

There was no smile on her face, however, on the day when she rushed into the surgery[9] while Siegfried and I were having tea. L4

"Mr. Herriot!" she gasped. "Can you come? My little dog's been run over!"

I jumped up and ran out to the car with her. She sat in the passenger seat with her head bowed, her hands clasped tightly on her knees. R

"He slipped his collar and ran in front of a car," she murmured. "He's lying in front of the school half way up Cliffend Road. Please hurry."

I was there within three minutes, but as I bent over the dusty little body stretched on the pavement, I knew there was nothing I could do. The fast-glazing eyes, the faint, gasping respirations, the ghastly pallor of

9. In Britain, *surgery* refers to a doctor's, vet's, or dentist's office.

Teach

L3 Literary Element

Memoir Possible Answer: *It conveys a hint of frustration but is a generally good-natured account of Herriot's adversary.* OL

L4 Literary Element

Atmosphere Ask: What sudden shift in the atmosphere or mood of the memoir occurs in this passage? *(The mood changes from ironic to urgent and critical.)* OL

R Reading Strategy

Compare/Contrast Ask: How does this description of Mrs. Donovan strikingly contrast with the initial one in the memoir? *(She seems totally crushed. All her energy and busybody behavior have drained away.)* OL

Differentiated Instruction

Connotations A word's connotations are its emotional associations and overtones as opposed to its denotation, or literal meaning. Note that writers often exploit the connotations of words to create atmospheric effects. Instruct students to read this passage on page 369. "But this garden was a wilderness . . . a dog sitting quietly."] Ask students to identify at least four words that connote shabbiness, sadness, neglect, or deterioration. *(Possible answers:* wilderness, chilling, desolation, gnarled, tangle, forsaken, ramshackle, peeling, rusted, mangle). AL

Academic Standards

Additional Support activities on pp. 366 and 367 cover the following standards:

Skills Practice: **9.6.2** Demonstrate an understanding of sentence construction, including parallel structure…

Differentiated Instruction: **9.1.2** Distinguish between what words mean literally and what they imply and interpret what the words imply.

Teach

BI Big Idea

Looking into Lives Answer: *Mrs. Donovan never went anywhere without the dog. She is a lonely widow, so this additional loss is devastating.* OL

R1 Reading Strategy

Analyzing Style Answer: *Students may say that he wants the reader to remember it or that he is closing this part of the story about Mrs. Donovan, and the statement gives it a feeling of finality.* OL

★ Cultural History

The U.S. counterpart to the R.S.P.C.A. is the American Society for the Prevention of Cruelty to Animals, or ASPCA. It was founded in 1866 through the efforts of Henry Bergh. AS

the mucous membranes[10] all told the same story.

"I'll take him back to the surgery and get some saline[11] into him, Mrs. Donovan," I said. "But I'm afraid he's had a massive internal hemorrhage.[12] Did you see what happened exactly?"

She gulped. "Yes, the wheel went right over him."

Ruptured liver, for sure. I passed my hands under the little animal and began to lift him gently, but as I did so, the breathing stopped, and the eyes stared fixedly ahead.

Mrs. Donovan sank to her knees, and for a few moments she gently stroked the rough hair of the head and chest. "He's dead, isn't he?" she whispered at last.

"I'm afraid he is," I said.

She got slowly to her feet and stood bewilderedly among the little group of bystanders on the pavement. Her lips moved, but she seemed unable to say any more.

I took her arm, led her over to the car and opened the door. "Get in and sit down," I said. "I'll run you home. Leave everything to me."

I wrapped the dog in my calving overall[13] and laid him in the boot[14] before driving away. It wasn't until we drew up outside Mrs. Donovan's house that she began to weep silently. I sat there without speaking till she finished. Then she wiped her eyes and turned to me.

"Do you think he suffered at all?"

"I'm certain he didn't. It was all so quick—he wouldn't know a thing about it."

She tried to smile. "Poor little Rex, I don't know what I'm going to do without him. We've traveled a few miles together, you know."

"Yes, you have. He had a wonderful life, Mrs. Donovan. And let me give you a bit of advice—you must get another dog. You'd be lost without one."

She shook her head. "No, I couldn't. That little dog meant too much to me. I couldn't let another take his place."

"Well I know that's how you feel just now, but I wish you'd think about it. I don't want to seem callous—I tell everybody this when they lose an animal, and I know it's good advice."

"Mr. Herriot, I'll never have another one." She shook her head again, very decisively. "Rex was my faithful friend for many years, and I just want to remember him. He's the last dog I'll ever have."

I often saw Mrs. Donovan around the town after this, and I was glad to see she was still as active as ever, though she looked strangely incomplete without the little dog on its lead. But it must have been over a month before I had the chance to speak to her.

It was on the afternoon that Inspector Halliday of the R.S.P.C.A.[15] rang me. ★

"Mr. Herriot," he said. "I'd like you to come and see an animal with me. A cruelty case."

"Right, what is it?"

"A dog, and it's pretty grim. A dreadful case of neglect." He gave me the name of a row of old brick cottages down by the river and said he'd meet me there.

Halliday was waiting for me, smart and business-like in his dark uniform, as I pulled up in the back lane behind the houses. He was a big, blond man with cheerful blue eyes, but he didn't smile as he came over to the car.

10. *Mucous membranes* are layers of tissues that line parts of the body such as the nose and mouth.
11. *Saline* is a salt solution.
12. A *massive internal hemorrhage* refers to extraordinary, abnormal bleeding inside the body.
13. A *calving overall* is a protective smock worn by a vet during the messy job of helping a cow give birth.
14. *Boot* is the British word for a car's trunk.
15. The *R.S.P.C.A.* is the Royal Society for the Prevention of Cruelty to Animals.

Big Idea Looking Into Lives *How has Mrs. Donovan's life changed at this moment?* BI

Reading Strategy Analyzing Style *Why do you think the author ends the paragraph with this particular statement?* R1

Additional Support

Skills Practice

GRAMMAR: Commas and Adjectives

Write the following phrase on the board: *big, blond man.* Explain that when a noun is modified by two or more adjectives of equal rank, a comma is used between the two modifiers: the man is big; he is also blond. Now write a second phrase: *bright red umbrella.* In this case the adjective *bright* modifies the second adjective, *red,* not the noun *umbrella:* the umbrella is not bright, but it is bright red. Have students punctuate the following phrases.

1. heavy dark clouds (*heavy, dark clouds*)
2. pale green plant (*no comma*)
3. fierce hot wind (*fierce, hot wind*) OL

"He's in here," he said and led the way towards one of the doors in the long, crumbling wall. A few curious people were hanging around, and with a feeling of inevitability I recognized a gnome-like brown face. Trust Mrs. Donovan, I thought, to be among those present at a time like this.

We went through the door into the long garden. I had found that even the lowliest dwellings in Darrowby had long strips of land at the back as though the builders had taken it for granted that the country people who were going to live in them would want to occupy themselves with the pursuits of the soil; with vegetable and fruit growing, even stock keeping[16] in a small way. You usually found a pig there, a few hens, often pretty beds of flowers.

But this garden was a wilderness. A chilling air of desolation hung over the few gnarled apple and plum trees standing among a tangle of rank[17] grass as though the place had been forsaken by all living creatures.

Halliday went over to a ramshackle wooden shed with peeling paint and a rusted corrugated iron roof. He produced a key, unlocked the padlock and dragged the door partly open. There was no window, and it wasn't easy to identify the jumble inside; broken gardening tools, an ancient mangle, rows of flower pots and partly used paint tins.[18] And right at the back, a dog sitting quietly.

L2 I didn't notice him immediately because of the gloom and because the smell in the shed started me coughing, but as I drew closer, I saw that he was a big animal, sitting very upright, his collar secured by a chain to a ring in the wall. I had seen some thin dogs, but this advanced emaciation reminded me of my textbooks on anatomy; nowhere else did the bones of pelvis, face and rib cage stand out with such horrifying clarity. A deep, smoothed out hollow in the earth floor showed where he had lain, moved about, in fact lived, for a very long time. L2

The sight of the animal had a stupefying[19] effect on me; I only half took in the rest of the scene—the filthy shreds of sacking scattered nearby, the bowl of scummy water.

"Look at his back end," Halliday muttered.

I carefully raised the dog from his sitting position and realized that the stench in the place was not entirely due to the piles of excrement. The hindquarters were a welter of pressure sores which had turned gangrenous, and strips of sloughing tissue hung down from them. There were similar sores along the sternum[20] and ribs. The coat, which seemed to be a dull yellow, was matted and caked with dirt.

The inspector spoke again. "I don't think he's ever been out of here. He's only a young dog—about a year old—but I understand he's been in this shed since he was an eight-week-old pup. Somebody out in the lane heard a whimper, or he'd never have been found."

I felt a tightening of the throat and a sudden nausea which wasn't due to the smell. It was the thought of this patient animal sitting starved and forgotten in the darkness and filth for a year. I looked again at the dog and saw in his eyes only a calm trust. Some dogs would have barked their heads off and soon been discovered, some would have become terrified and vicious, but this was one of the totally undemanding kind, the kind which

16. *Stock* is a shortened form of the word *livestock; stock keeping* is raising farm animals.
17. Here, *rank* means "overgrown."
18. *Tins* is a British term for cans.
19. Here, *stupefying* means "deadening to the senses."
20. The dog has a *welter*, or mass, of sores that have become dangerously infected, as well as dead tissue separating (*sloughing*) from its backsides. There are also similar sores along its *sternum*, or chest.

Literary Element Memoir *How does this comment show the author's personal response to the situation and his special knowledge about it?* L1

Reading Strategy Analyzing Style *How does Herriot's word choice in this description evoke a strong image?* R2

Teach

L1 Literary Element

Memoir Answer: *It implies he has some negative feelings toward Mrs. Donovan. It also shows he knows her well enough not to be surprised when she shows up.* OL

L2 Literary Element

Memoir Ask: What characteristics of his background and personality does the author reveal through these details? *(He shows keen powers of observation, describing the dog's posture and emaciation and the deep hollow in the floor. His mention of anatomy textbooks emphasizes his training and diagnostic skill.)* OL

R2 Reading Strategy

Analyzing Style Answer: *The phrases "filthy shreds" and "scummy water" evoke a strong image.* OL

English Language Coach

Synonyms Write this sentence on the board: The puppies were cavorting in the front yard. Explain that the verb *cavort* implies excited or playful running and hopping and is often used to describe children or animals at play.

Have English language learners work with a native English speaker to find five synonyms for *cavort* in a thesaurus and to verify the meaning of each synonym in a dictionary. Tell students to record the synonyms in their vocabulary notebooks, and then write a sentence using each word. EL

Academic Standards

Additional Support activities on pp. 368 and 369 cover the following standards:

Skills Practice: **9.6.1** Identify and correctly use…the mechanics of punctuation… **9.6.2** Demonstrate an understanding of… the proper placement of modifiers…

English Language Coach: **9.1.2** Distinguish between what words mean literally and what they imply and interpret what the words imply.

Teach

R1 Reading Strategy

Analyzing Style This passage is a turning point in the selection. **Ask:** What words does Herriot use to signal that something remarkable may be about to happen? *(Possible answers: immediately responded, pathetic dignity, held himself erect, calm eyes, friendly and unafraid)* OL

R2 Reading Strategy

Analyzing Style Answer: *He presents her first as a pair of eyes. He emphasizes her curiosity—or meddling.* OL

L1 Literary Element

Tone Ask: How would you describe the tone of this speech? Explain. *(The tone is tongue-in-cheek. The speaker has already shown himself to be in sympathy with the dog, and seems unlikely to put it down.)* OL

BI Big Idea

Looking into Lives Answer: *He knows the dog and Mrs. Donovan need each other, but he gently leads Mrs. Donovan to reach this conclusion herself.* OL

had complete faith in people and accepted all their actions without complaint. Just an occasional whimper perhaps as he sat interminably in the empty blackness which had been his world and at times wondered what it was all about.

"Well, Inspector, I hope you're going to throw the book at whoever's responsible," I said.

Halliday grunted. "Oh, there won't be much done. It's a case of diminished responsibility. The owner's definitely simple. Lives with an aged mother who hardly knows what's going on either. I've seen the fellow, and it seems he threw in a bit of food when he felt like it, and that's about all he did. They'll fine him and stop him keeping an animal in the future but nothing more than that."

"I see." I reached out and stroked the dog's head, and he immediately responded by resting a paw on my wrist. There was a pathetic dignity about the way he held himself erect, the calm eyes regarding me, friendly and unafraid. "Well, you'll let me know if you want me in court."

"Of course, and thank you for coming along." Halliday hesitated for a moment. "And now I expect you'll want to put this poor thing out of his misery right away."

I continued to run my hand over the head and ears while I thought for a moment. "Yes . . . yes, I suppose so. We'd never find a home for him in this state. It's the kindest thing to do. Anyway, push the door wide open will you so that I can get a proper look at him."

In the improved light I examined him more thoroughly. Perfect teeth, well-proportioned limbs with a fringe of yellow hair. I put my stethoscope on his chest, and as I listened to the slow, strong thudding of the heart, the dog again put his paw on my hand.

I turned to Halliday, "You know, Inspector, inside this bag of bones there's a lovely healthy golden retriever. I wish there was some way of letting him out."

As I spoke, I noticed there was more than one figure in the door opening.

A pair of black pebble eyes were peering intently at the big dog from behind the inspector's broad back. The other spectators had remained in the lane, but Mrs. Donovan's curiosity had been too much for her. I continued conversationally as though I hadn't seen her.

"You know, what this dog needs first of all is a good shampoo to clean up his matted coat."

"Huh?" said Halliday.

"Yes. And then he wants a long course of some really strong condition powders."

"What's that?" The inspector looked startled.

"There's no doubt about it," I said. "It's the only hope for him, but where are you going to find such things? Really powerful enough, I mean." I sighed and straightened up. "Ah well, I suppose there's nothing else for it. I'd better put him to sleep right away. I'll get the things from my car."

When I got back to the shed, Mrs. Donovan was already inside examining the dog despite the feeble remonstrances[21] of the big man.

"Look!" she said excitedly, pointing to a name roughly scratched on the collar. "His name's Roy." She smiled up at me. "It's a bit like Rex, isn't it, that name?"

"You know, Mrs. Donovan, now you mention it, it is. It's very like Rex, the way it comes off your tongue." I nodded seriously.

She stood silent for a few moments, obviously in the grip of a deep emotion, then she burst out.

"Can I have 'im? I can make him better, I know I can. Please, please let me have 'im!"

21. *Remonstrances* are protests.

Reading Strategy Analyzing Style *What words does Herriot use to portray Mrs. Donovan in this paragraph?* R2

Big Idea Looking Into Lives *How does the narrator show an understanding of both animals and people?* BI

Additional Support

Skills Practice

GRAMMAR: Understanding Idioms

Explain that an idiom is the use of a term that differs from its literal meaning. For example, *poor beggar, funny old stick,* and *get it* on page 371 are not meant literally. Have students define the following idioms. Discuss any clues that they may have used from the surrounding text.

1. Mrs. Donovan makes no bones about her desire to adopt the dog. *(does not pretend)*
2. Herriot suspected that the dog would do Mrs. Donovan good, and he was not wide of the mark. *(mistaken)* OL

Man and Dog Running. Holly Roberts.

Viewing the Art: How would you describe the relationship between human and dog shown here? How is it similar to or different from the relationship between Mrs. Donovan and Roy? ★

"Well I don't know," I said. "It's really up to the inspector. You'll have to get his permission."

Halliday looked at her in bewilderment, then he said: "Excuse me, Madam," and drew me to one side. We walked a few yards through the long grass and stopped under a tree.

"Mr. Herriot," he whispered, "I don't know what's going on here, but I can't just pass over an animal in this condition to anybody who has a casual whim. The poor beggar's had one bad break already—I think it's enough. This woman doesn't look a suitable person . . ."

I held up a hand. "Believe me, Inspector, you've nothing to worry about. She's a funny old stick, but she's been sent from heaven today. If anybody in Darrowby can give this dog a new life it's her."

Halliday still looked very doubtful. "But I still don't get it. What was all that stuff about him needing shampoos and condition powders?"

"Oh never mind about that. I'll tell you some other time. What he needs is lots of good grub, care, and affection, and that's just what he'll get. You can take my word for it."

"All right, you seem very sure." Halliday looked at me for a second or two then turned and walked over to the eager little figure by the shed.

I had never before been deliberately on the lookout for Mrs. Donovan: she had just cropped up wherever I happened to be, but now I scanned the streets of Darrowby anxiously day by day without sighting her. I didn't

Literary Element Memoir *What aspect of his personality does the author choose to focus on here? Do you find the first-person voice believable?* L2

Teach

L2 Literary Element

Memoir Answer: *He portrays himself as a dependable and trustworthy person who has influence with the townspeople. Most students will find the voice believable.* OL

★ Viewing the Art

Answer: *The running dog in the painting is healthy and devoted to its master. Mrs. Donovan nurses Roy back to health and an active life.*

Contemporary photographer and artist Holly Roberts uses photographs as the base layer for her art. She then paints over the photo to create her dreamlike paintings, drawings, and mixed media art. AS

Building Reading Fluency

Dialogue Students may find it difficult to follow a three-person dialogue. Assign three students to read aloud the conversation between Herriot, Mr. Halliday, and Mrs. Donovan that begins in the second column of page 370 and ends in the second column of page 371. Ask students to infer the emotions of each person involved in the conversation. BL

Academic Standards

Additional Support activities on pp. 370 and 371 cover the following standards:

Skills Practice: **9.1.2** Distinguish between what words mean literally...and interpret what the words imply.

Building Reading Fluency: **9.7** [Develop] speaking skills...in conjunction with... strategies...[for] delivery of oral presentations.

Big Idea

Looking into Lives Answer: *She is no longer all over town; she is no longer such a busybody.* OL

L Literary Element

Memoir Answer: *The words such as magnificence, rich, luxuriant, shining, glittered, and beautifully have positive connotations. The vet is glorying in the appearance of the dog.* OL

like it when Gobber Newhouse drove his bicycle determinedly through a barrier into a ten-foot hole where they were laying the new sewer and Mrs. Donovan was not in evidence among the happy crowd who watched the council workmen[22] and two policemen trying to get him out; and when she was nowhere to be seen when they had to fetch the fire engine to the fish and chip shop the night the fat burst into flames, I became seriously worried.

Maybe I should have called round to see how she was getting on with that dog. Certainly I had trimmed off the necrotic[23] tissue and dressed the sores before she took him away, but perhaps he needed something more than that. And yet at the time I had felt a strong conviction that the main thing was to get him out of there and clean him and feed him, and nature would do the rest. And I had a lot of faith in Mrs. Donovan—far more than she had in me—when it came to animal doctoring; it was hard to believe I'd been completely wrong.

"Haven't I made a difference to this dog!"

It must have been nearly three weeks, and I was on the point of calling at her home, when I noticed her stumping briskly along the far side of the market place, peering closely into every shop window exactly as before. The only difference was that she had a big yellow dog on the end of the lead.

I turned the wheel and sent my car bumping over the cobbles[24] till I was abreast of her. When she saw me getting out, she stopped and smiled impishly, but she didn't speak as I bent over Roy and examined him. He was still a skinny dog, but he looked bright and happy, his wounds were healthy and granulating[25] and there was not a speck of dirt in his coat or on his skin. I knew then what Mrs. Donovan had been doing all this time; she had been washing and combing and teasing at that filthy tangle till she had finally conquered it.

As I straightened up, she seized my wrist in a grip of surprising strength and looked up into my eyes.

"Now, Mr. Herriot," she said. "Haven't I made a difference to this dog!"

"You've done wonders, Mrs. Donovan," I said. "And you've been at him with that marvelous shampoo of yours, haven't you?"

She giggled and walked away, and from that day I saw the two of them frequently but at a distance, and something like two months went by before I had a chance to talk to her again. She was passing by the surgery as I was coming down the steps, and again she grabbed my wrist.

"Mr. Herriot," she said, just as she had done before. "Haven't I made a difference to this dog!"

I looked down at Roy with something akin to awe. He had grown and filled out, and his coat, no longer yellow but a rich gold, lay in luxuriant shining swathes over the well-fleshed ribs and back. A new, brightly studded collar glittered on his neck, and his tail, beautifully fringed, fanned the air gently. He was now a golden retriever in full magnificence. As I stared at him, he reared up, plunked his forepaws on my chest and looked into my face, and in his eyes I read plainly the same calm affection and trust I had seen in that black, noisome[26] shed.

"Mrs. Donovan," I said softly, "he's the most beautiful dog in Yorkshire." Then, because I knew she was waiting for it. "It's

22. The *council workmen* are laborers employed by the local government.
23. *Necrotic* means "dead."
24. *Cobbles* are stones; the road is cobblestone.
25. *Granulating* means "forming new tissues in the process of healing."
26. *Noisome* means "offensive" or "smelly."

Big Idea Looking Into Lives *How has Mrs. Donovan's life apparently changed?* BI1

Literary Element Memoir *How does the language in this paragraph show the author's attitude toward the dog and toward animals in general?* L

Additional Support

Skills Practice

READING: Compare/Contrast in Nonfiction Review how authors may use elements that compare or contrast to organize nonfiction narratives. Students will better understand what they read if they can identify what is being compared and contrasted. Have students identify the basic points of comparison and contrast between the first half of the memoir and the second half. *(Comparisons: Both the dog and Mrs. Donovan start out sad and alone and end up happy together. Contrast: the situation of both the dog and Mrs. Donovan at the beginning versus their happiness at the end.)* OL those wonderful condition powders. Whatever do you put in them?"

"Ah, wouldn't you like to know!" She bridled[27] and smiled up at me coquettishly and indeed she was nearer being kissed at that moment than for many years.

I suppose you could say that that was the start of Roy's second life. And as the years passed, I often pondered on the beneficent providence[28] which had decreed that an animal which had spent his first twelve months abandoned and unwanted, staring uncomprehendingly into that unchanging, stinking darkness, should be whisked in a moment into an existence of light and movement and love. Because I don't think any dog had it quite so good as Roy from then on.

His diet changed dramatically from odd bread crusts to best stewing steak and biscuit, meaty bones, and a bowl of warm milk every evening. And he never missed a thing. Garden fêtes, school sports, evictions, gymkhanas[29]—he'd be there. I was pleased to note that as time went on, Mrs. Donovan seemed to be clocking up an even greater daily mileage. Her expenditure on shoe leather must have been phenomenal, but of course it was absolute pie[30] for Roy—a busy round in the morning, home for a meal then straight out again; it was all go.

Mrs. Donovan didn't confine her activities to the town center; there was a big stretch of common land down by the river where there were seats, and people used to take their dogs for a gallop, and she liked to get down there fairly regularly to check on the latest developments on the domestic scene. I often saw Roy loping majestically over the grass among a pack of assorted canines, and when he wasn't doing that, he was submitting to being stroked or patted or generally fussed over. He was handsome, and he just liked people; it made him irresistible.

It was common knowledge that his mistress had bought a whole selection of brushes and combs of various sizes with which she labored over his coat. Some people said she had a little brush for his teeth, too, and it might have been true, but he certainly wouldn't need his nails clipped—his life on the roads would keep them down.

Mrs. Donovan, too, had her reward; she had a faithful companion by her side every hour of the day and night. But there was more to it than that; she had always had the compulsion to help and heal animals, and the salvation of Roy was the high point of her life—a blazing triumph which never dimmed.

I know the memory of it was always fresh because many years later I was sitting on the sidelines at a cricket match, and I saw the two of them; the old lady glancing keenly around her, Roy gazing **placidly** out at the field of play, apparently enjoying every ball. At the end of the match I watched them move away with the dispersing crowd; Roy would be about twelve then, and heaven only knows how old Mrs. Donovan must have been, but the big golden animal was trotting along effortlessly, and his mistress, a little more bent perhaps and her head rather nearer the ground, was going very well.

When she saw me, she came over, and I felt the familiar tight grip on my wrist.

"Mr. Herriot," she said, and in the dark probing eyes the pride was still as warm, the triumph still as bursting new as if it had all happened yesterday.

"Mr. Herriot, haven't I made a difference to this dog!" R2

27. Here, *bridled* means "drew back the head or chin."
28. *Beneficent providence* refers to the goodness of a greater power.
29. A *fête* is a party or festival; a *gymkhana* is an event featuring athletic contests.
30. Here, *pie* is a metaphor for a treat.

Reading Strategy Analyzing Style *How would you describe the style of this phrase?* R1

Big Idea Looking Into Lives *How does the dog change Mrs. Donovan's life?* BI2

Vocabulary

placidly (plas′ id lē) *adv.* calmly, serenely

COMPARING LITERATURE

Teach

R1 Reading Strategy

Analyzing Style **Answer:** *It is casual and colloquial.* OL

R2 Reading Strategy

Analyzing Style **Ask:** How does Herriot bring the memoir to a humorous and satisfying resolution? *(He repeats Mrs. Donovan's rhetorical question about the difference she has made to Roy, gently underscoring the irony of Mrs. Donovan's inability to see the even greater difference the dog has made to her.)*

BI2 Big Idea

Looking into Lives **Answer:** *The dog gives her a purpose and pride as well as companionship.* OL

CheckPoint

Use the CheckPoint questions on Presentation Plus! to check students' mastery of the selection. These questions can be used with interactive response keypads for immediate student feedback.

Differentiated Instruction

Compare/Contrast in Writing

Herriot uses details to describe Roy's early life and his life with Mrs. Donovan. Ask students to create a two-column chart, labeling the first column *First Year* and the second column *With Mrs. Donovan.* Have them copy phrases from the story into each column that describe Roy's life and condition. Then have students incorporate some of these details into a paragraph comparing and contrasting Roy's life before and after he is found. Suggest that they find and include one way in which Roy is the same in both situations. AL

Academic Standards

Additional Support activities on pp. 372 and 373 cover the following standards:

Skills Practice: **9.2** Develop strategies such as...identifying and analyzing... organization...

Differentiated Instruction: **9.5.2** Write responses to literature that demonstrate a comprehensive grasp of the significant ideas of literary works; that support statements with evidence from the text...

Assess

1. Accept reasonable answers.
2. (a) Herriot's treatment of his dog (b) Mrs. Donovan undermines his authority.
3. (a) Rex is killed by a car. (b) It was her companion.
4. (a) The dog has been left for a year in a dark shed. (b) Herriot determines that the dog and Mrs. Donovan are a perfect match.
5. (a) Through her critical words and her busybody ways (b) He creates a very believable character by describing her irritating behavior.
6. His description of the dog's condition is very effective.
7. He quotes Mrs. Donovan: "Haven't I made a difference to this dog?" He provides many details about Roy's changing appearance as he recovers.
8. Accept reasonable answers

Literary Element

1. It is written in the first person, and includes many details about the writer's relationships, thoughts, and feelings. It is not a typical memoir because it is told as if it were fiction.
2. Students should mention specific details related to Herriot's work and way of life.

LiteratureOnline

Web Activities Have students access the Web site for interactive activities that will help them assess their understanding of the selection.

COMPARING LITERATURE
AFTER YOU READ

RESPONDING AND THINKING CRITICALLY

Respond

1. Does either Herriot or Mrs. Donovan remind you of anyone you know? Explain.

Recall and Interpret

2. (a)What does the gentleman object to in the first scene of the story? (b)What does this scene tell you about James Herriot and Mrs. Donovan?
3. (a)What happens to Mrs. Donovan's dog Rex? (b)Why is this particularly awful for her?
4. (a)What is the "case of cruelty"? (b)How does Herriot act in the best interest of both the animal and Mrs. Donovan?

Analyze and Evaluate

5. (a)How does Herriot portray the character of Mrs. Donovan? Use examples from the story to support your answer. (b)How well does Herriot bring a small-town busybody to life?
6. How effectively does Herriot illustrate the case of cruelty for the reader?
7. How does Herriot show the positive effect of Roy on the owner and of the owner on Roy?

Connect

8. **Big Idea** **Looking Into Lives** Do you think this story is mainly about a case of cruelty, about Mrs. Donovan, or about the life of a vet in a small town? Explain.

LITERARY ANALYSIS

Literary Element Memoir

This story is a **memoir,** a first-person, true account that focuses on the author's personal experience of a particular time period or event in his or her life.

1. Which aspects of "A Case of Cruelty" make it a memoir? Is there anything in the story that is not typical of a memoir?
2. Memoirs draw heavily on the author's personal experiences. Cite three examples of details that only Herriot, the country veterinarian, would know or think to include.

Writing About Literature

Analyze Voice Herriot often portrays himself as the voice of authority. Herriot also portrays himself as warmhearted, clever, and wise, and, at times, confused, frustrated, or upset. Write an essay in which you analyze the ever-changing voice in "A Case of Cruelty." Remember to state in your thesis which voice you think is most effective, which is most predominant, or how the voice functions in this memoir.

LiteratureOnline **Web Activities** For eFlashcards, Selection Quick Checks, and other Web activities, go to www.glencoe.com.

READING AND VOCABULARY

Reading Strategy Analyzing Style

One aspect of **style** is figurative language and imagery. Figurative language includes similes, metaphors, and personification. It is used to describe and to convey ideas and emotions. Imagery is language that appeals to one or more of the five senses.

1. Find the first description of Mrs. Donovan on page 366. How does it contribute to Herriot's style?
2. Find another example of figurative language or imagery in this selection. Tell how these devices help bring the people, setting, or events to life.

Vocabulary Practice

Practice with Word Parts Choose the word that best answers each question. Use a dictionary as necessary.

1. Which word has a suffix that means "state of"?
   a. callousness **b.** adamant **c.** placidly
2. Which word has a root that refers to diamond?
   a. diligent **b.** adamant **c.** transcend
3. Which word has an adverb suffix?
   a. callousness **b.** placidly **c.** diligent

Reading Strategy

1. Imagery includes *dumpy little figure* and *walnut face. Black-button eyes* is a metaphor. The figurative language and imagery help the reader see Mrs. Donovan through Herriot's eyes.
2. Images such as the ramshackle wooden shed with peeling paint and a rusted iron roof bring the story to life.

Vocabulary

1. a **2.** b **3.** b

Writing About Literature

Students' essays should

- contain a thesis statement that relates to the most effective voice
- include body paragraphs supporting the choice made in the thesis statement

Ali

W. S. Merwin

BEFORE YOU READ

Building Background

Born in 1927, William Stanley Merwin grew up in Pennsylvania. When Merwin was a teenager, he met poet Ezra Pound, who advised him to write seventy-five lines of poetry a day and to learn foreign languages. He took this advice to heart. Merwin's early poems adhered to traditional narrative forms and regular meter patterns. By the 1960s, however, his poetry became more personal and his language became more relaxed. Over the years, Merwin became increasingly interested in ecology, and much of his poetry reflects his ideas about the relationship between people and nature. Merwin won the Pulitzer Prize for poetry in 1971.

LiteratureOnline **Author Search** For more about W. S. Merwin, go to www.glencoe.com.

Small dog named for a wing
never old and never young

abandoned with your brothers on a beach **L**
when you were scarcely weaned

taken home starving
by one woman with
too many to feed as it was

handed over to another
who tied you out back in the weeds
with a clothesline and fed you if she remembered

on the morning before the eclipse of the moon
I first heard about you over the telephone

only the swellings of insect bites
by then held the skin away from your bones

thin hair matted filthy the color of mud
naked belly crusted with sores
head low frightened silent watching

I carried you home and gave you milk and food
bathed you and dried you

Teach

L Literary Element

Apostrophe Remind students that in the technique known as apostrophe, a writer directly addresses someone who is not present or speaks to a nonhuman object or abstract quality. **Ask:** Which pronouns in these lines signal the poet's use of apostrophe? *(your* and *you)* **OL**

LiteratureOnline

Author Search To expand students' appreciation of W. S. Merwin, have them access the Web site for additional information and resources.

Differentiated Instruction

Less Proficient Readers Ask students to follow along while listening to an audio recording of the poem. Then encourage them to discuss what they have read and heard. Have small groups of students engage in a reading conference. Ask students to respond to open-ended questions that require them to discuss the statements and descriptions of the poem's speaker. Encourage students to connect the poem to their own experiences, and ask them to evaluate their feelings. **BL**

Academic Standards

The Additional Support activity on p. 375 covers the following standards:

Differentiated Instruction: **9.7** [Respond] to oral communication [with] careful listening and evaluation of content…
9.7.7 Make judgments about the ideas under discussion and support those judgments with convincing evidence.

Teach

L1 Literary Element

Simile Remind students that in a simile, a writer uses an explicit word such as *like, as,* or *resembles* to draw a comparison.
Ask: What is the comparative word in these lines? *(as)* What is being compared with what? *(The speaker compares Ali's "aerial grace" with that of a bird at the moment before flight.)* OL

L2 Literary Element

Tone **Ask:** How would you describe the speaker's tone in these lines? *(The tone might be described as compassionate or sad.)* OL

L3 Literary Element

Paradox Tell students that a paradox is a situation or statement with two parts that are true but seem to contradict each other.
Ask: How is the situation at the end of the poem paradoxical? *(Ali has died, but his owners continue to call him and hold him.)* OL

Quickwrite

Qualities might include grace, buoyancy, wisdom, hopefulness, lightness, and obedience.

dressed your sores and sat with you
in the sun with your wet head on my leg

we had one brother of yours already
and had named him for the great tree of the islands

we named you for the white shadows
behind your thin shoulders

and for the remainder of the desert
in your black muzzle lean as an Afghan's
and for the lightness of your ways
not the famished insubstance of your limbs

but even in your sickness and weakness
when you were hobbled with pain and exhaustion

an aerial grace a fine buoyancy
a lifting as in the moment before flight L1

I keep finding why that is your name

the plump vet was not impressed with you
and guessed wrong for a long time
about what was the matter

so that you could hardly eat
and never grew like your brother

small dog wise in your days

never servile never disobedient
and never far

standing with one foot on the bottom stair
hoping it was bedtime

standing in the doorway looking up
tail swinging slowly below sharp hip bones L2

toward the end you were with us whatever we did

the gasping breath through the night
ended an hour and a half before daylight

the gray tongue hung from your mouth L3
we went on calling you holding you

feeling the sudden height

Quickwrite

The speaker in this poem credits Ali with many qualities. Choose five of these qualities and write a paragraph describing what the qualities reveal about the speaker's feelings about the dog.

Additional Support

Skills Practice

READING: Drawing Conclusions
Point out that students can draw conclusions about characters and situations in a poem by noting how they are described. Have students consider the speaker's feelings toward the dog in "Ali." Ask what the speaker's words and actions suggest about his attitude. *(He is sympathetic and compassionate; he is deeply saddened when Ali dies.)* OL

BEFORE YOU READ

Building Background

Descended from two noble but flamboyant and violent families, George Gordon, Lord Byron, inherited his title and property at the age of ten when his great-uncle, known as the "Wicked Lord," died. Byron had been born with a clubfoot, and the physical suffering and acute embarrassment it caused him profoundly affected his temperament. To compensate for his condition, Byron succeeded in becoming a masterful swimmer, horseman, boxer, cricket player, and fencer.

After graduating from Cambridge University, Byron toured southern Europe and Asia Minor. While traveling, he worked his adventures into poetry. His books sold well, and he influenced art and fashion, as well as literature, with his flamboyant style. At twenty-eight, Byron left England, never to return. He spent most of the rest of his life in Italy.

LiteratureOnline Author Search For more about George Gordon, Lord Byron, go to www.glencoe.com.

Waiting for master. George Earl. Fine Art of Oakham, Leicestershire, Great Britain.

A Friendly Welcome

George Gordon, Lord Byron

'Tis sweet to hear the watch-dog's honest bark
Bay deep-mouthed welcome as we draw near home; L4
'Tis sweet to know there is an eye will mark
Our coming, and look brighter when we come. L5

Quickwrite

Name three specific words in this poem that convey delight and write a paragraph explaining how well these words convey the speaker's delight in his dog.

English Language Coach

Paraphrase Review any words that are unfamiliar or used in an uncommon way, such as *watchdog, bay, deep-mouthed,* and *mark.* Discuss with students the role of dogs in their native countries.

Ask: Do people have dogs as pets? Are dogs trained for special tasks such as watchdogs or seeing-eye dogs? Invite a volunteer to read aloud Byron's poem. Then have students paraphrase the poem in prose. Ask students to share their writing with the class and discuss the similarities and differences between their work and Byron's poem. EL

Teach

L4 Literary Element

Figurative Language **Ask:** How does Byron personify the watch-dog in these lines? *(The dog is described as "honest"; he bids the people returning home a "deep-mouthed welcome.")* OL

L5 Literary Element

Parallelism Ask students to explain how these lines illustrate the technique of parallelism. *(The phrase "look brighter when we come" echoes and balances the earlier phrase, "will mark our coming.")* OL

Quickwrite

Words might include *sweet, honest, welcome,* and *brighter.*

Author Search To expand students' appreciation of George Gordon, Lord Byron, have them access the Web site for additional information and resources.

Academic Standards

Additional Support activities on pp. 376 and 377 cover the following standards:

Skills Practice: **9.2.8** Make reasonable statements and draw conclusions about a text, supporting them with accurate examples.

English Language Coach: **9.1** Use…word parts…and a growing knowledge of English and other languages…to determine the meaning of words… **9.5.2** Write responses to literature that demonstrate a comprehensive grasp of the significant ideas of literary works… **9.3.2** Compare and contrast the presentation of a…topic across genres…to explain how the…genre shapes the…topic.

Comparing the Big Idea

Sample answer: Overlapping area of the Venn diagram: good dogs

"A Case of Cruelty": neglectful first owner
loving second owner
neglected dog
owner gains self-esteem through dog
dog gains a new life

"Ali": neglected dog
neglectful first owner
loving second owner
owner credits Ali with human and even spiritual qualities
owner feels loss of dog keenly
dog dies

"A Friendly Welcome":
proud owner
barking dog
watchdog
dog makes owner feel welcome

Comparing Tone

1. "A Case of Cruelty": certainty or authority; sympathy; heartache or sadness; joy or pride; "Ali": sadness, mystery; "A Friendly Welcome": satisfaction or contentment
2. In "A Case of Cruelty," the tone helps the reader understand the various people and their interactions, and especially the personality of the narrator. In "Ali," tone seems to give the dog poetic wings and is crucial for understanding the author's attitude toward the dog. In "A Friendly Welcome," the tone also goes hand in hand with the purpose. Tone is probably most important in "Ali" because the speaker credits the dog with so many qualities, including the ability to rise in flight.

Wrap-Up: Comparing Literature *Across Genres*

- *A Case of Cruelty* by James Herriot
- *Ali* by W. S. Merwin
- *A Friendly Welcome* by George Gordon, Lord Byron

COMPARING THE Big Idea Looking Into Lives

Partner Activity With a partner, discuss how the people and animals in these selections are alike and different. Then copy the Venn diagram below and work together to complete it.

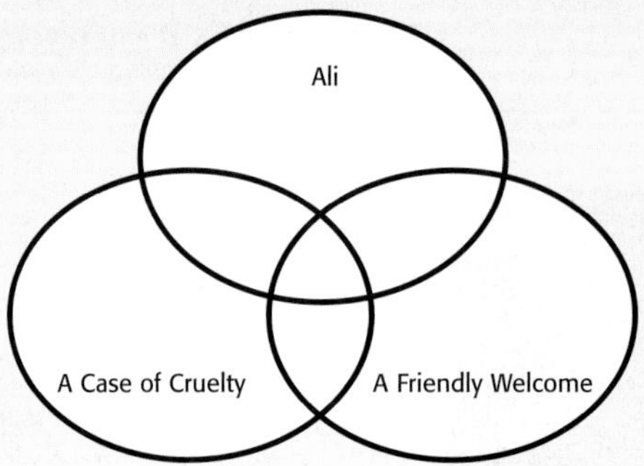

COMPARING Tone

Group Activity Short works of literature often have a single consistent tone. Longer works, however, may include many different scenes and each scene may have its own tone. Even a work that presents several tones, though, has one dominant tone that colors the entire work. In a small group, discuss the following questions. Cite evidence from the selections to support your ideas.

1. What is the dominant tone in each of the three selections?
2. How does the writer's tone help you appreciate both the people and animals in each piece? Do you think tone is more important in one of these selections than in the others? Explain.

COMPARING Author's Purpose

Writing Activity An author may have a single purpose for writing or a combination of purposes. To identify purpose, think about the details the author selects as well as the overall message or theme of the selection. Write a brief essay in which you compare and contrast the themes in at least two of the selections. Use a chart like the one below to help you get started.

Selection	Important Details	Overall Message or Theme	Author's Purpose(s)
"A Case of Cruelty""			
"Ali"			
"A Friendly Welcome"			

INDIANA ACADEMIC STANDARDS (page 378)

9.3.2 Compare and contrast the presentation of a similar theme or topic across genres...

9.3.5 Compare works that express a universal theme and provide evidence to support the views...in each work...

Comparing Author's Purpose

Selection	Important Details	Overall Message	Author's Purposes
"A Case of Cruelty"	description of mistreated dog; description of revived, well-treated dog	People and dogs help to complete each other's lives.	to entertain, to remember, to show the satisfactions of the life of a vet
"Ali"	references to flight and "sudden height" after death	Dogs can have human or even spiritual qualities.	to reflect, to express thoughts and feelings
"A Friendly Welcome"	the deep-mouthed baying	People and dogs respond joyfully to each other.	to express thoughts and feelings

PART 2

ON THE MOVE

Harbor, Lofoten, Norway, 1937. William Johnson. Smithsonian American Art Museum, Washington, DC. ★

BIG IDEA

BI The world and its richness is a favorite subject of essayists. Travel and adventure writers describe their travels in vivid detail and draw lessons from exploring the world or experiencing the wonders of nature. In the essays in Part 2, the writers not only tell of their experiences, they often offer personal messages—as if they were thinking aloud and talking only to you. As you read these essays, ask yourself: What message is the author trying to convey?

Analyzing and Extending

BI Big Idea

On the Move After students have read the text under the "Big Idea" heading, have them study the artwork. Note how the artist uses details to convey the place's appearance and mood. Lead a discussion in which students answer the question, "What is the artist trying to convey?" OL

★ Viewing the Art

African American artist William H. Johnson (1901–1970) studied at the National Academy of Art in Harlem, New York. After graduating, he moved to Paris and traveled around Europe, living in Denmark and Norway. In 1938, Johnson returned to the United States and devoted himself to depicting the lives of African Americans during the Depression. AS

English Language Coach

Building Vocabulary Write the word *adventure* on the board and review its pronunciation and meaning. Have partners list eight to ten words that describe a person who is adventurous. Make a master list on the board. EL

Differentiated Instruction

Sharing Adventure Stories Invite volunteers to talk about adventures they've experienced. Then, have students identify the elements of adventure stories—a conflict or problem, an interesting location, an unexpected turn of events, and high emotions. BL

Academic Standards

Additional Support activities on p. 379 cover the following standards:

English Language Coach: **9.1** Use... relationships...and a growing knowledge of English...to determine the meaning of words...

Differentiated Instruction: **9.3** [Identify] story elements...and make connections and comparisons across texts...

Part 2: Skills Scope and Sequence

Readability Scores Key
Dale-Chall/DRP/Lexile

PACING STANDARD	(DAYS) BLOCK	SELECTIONS AND FEATURES	LITERARY ELEMENTS
1–2 class sessions	1	from *All God's Children Need Traveling Shoes* by Maya Angelou **7.4/61/960**, pp. 382–392	Narrative Essay, SE pp. 384–391 Author's Purpose, SE p. 391 Setting, TWE p. 384
		"Field Trip" by Naomi Shihab Nye **5.5/58/1020**, pp. 393–399	Aphorism, SE pp. 394, 397, 398 Anecdote, SE p. 398
1–2 class sessions	1–2	"The Solace of Open Spaces" by Gretel Ehrlich **7.0/62/1130**, pp. 400–407	Descriptive Essay, SE pp. 401, 403, 406 Setting, SE p. 406
		Grammar Workshop: Sentence Structure, p. 408	
		"Sayonara" by Anne Morrow Lindbergh **9.1/59/1060**, pp. 409–414	Thesis, SE pp. 410–413 Descriptive Essay, SE p. 413
2 class sessions	1	from *Into Thin Air* By Jon Krakauer **9.4/64/1160**, pp. 415–426	Structure, SE pp. 416–427 Dialogue, SE p. 427 Idioms, TWE p. 420
		TIME, "Adventure to Antarctica" by Rob Johnson **7.0/61/1020**, pp. 429–433	Sensory Details, TWE p. 432
		Vocabulary Workshop: Technical Words, SE p. 434	

About the Part

Part 2 deals with travel, the motivations for it, and the difficulties that accompany it.

READING AND CRITICAL THINKING	VOCABULARY	WRITING AND GRAMMAR	LISTENING, SPEAKING, AND VIEWING
Identifying Problem and Solution, SE pp. 383–391 Making Inferences, TWE p. 386	Synonyms, SE p. 391	Analyze Style, SE p. 392 Possessive Pronouns, SE p. 392 Sentence Structure, TWE p. 385 Commas in a Series, TWE p. 388	Viewing Art, TWE pp. 386, 388 Group Activity, SE p. 390
Connecting to Personal Experience, SE pp. 394–399 Identifying Sequence, TWE p. 396	Analogies, SE pp. 394, 399 Academic Vocabulary, SE p. 399	Evaluate Author's Craft, SE p. 399	Interdisciplinary Activity: Art, SE p. 399
Visualizing, SE pp. 401–406 Cause and Effect, TWE p. 404	Word Origins, SE pp. 401, 406 Academic Vocabulary, SE p. 406	Analyze Mood, SE p. 407 Vivid Verbs, SE p. 407	Analyzing Art, SE p. 404 Group Activity, SE p. 405
		Adverb Clauses, SE p. 408 Sentence Variety, TWE p. 408	
Analyzing Rhetorical Devices, SE pp. 410, 412, 414	Analogies, SE pp. 410, 414 Academic Vocabulary, SE p. 414	Explore Author's Purpose, SE p. 414	Literature Groups, SE p. 414
Monitoring Comprehension, SE pp. 416–428 Cause and Effect, TWE p. 418 Problem and Solution, TWE p. 424	Word Parts, SE p. 428 Academic Vocabulary, SE p. 428 Idioms, TWE p. 420	Evaluate Author's Craft, SE p. 428 Signal Words, TWE p. 422	Analyzing Photographs, SE p. 419; TWE pp. 420, 426
Analyzing Text Structure, SE p. 429; TWE pp. 430–433 Previewing, TWE p. 430			
	Understanding Jargon, SE p. 434 Using Dictionaries, TWE p. 434		

LITERARY FOCUS

Focus

BELLRINGER

Bellringer Options
Daily Language Practice Transparency 33

Or present an example of an informative or persuasive essay from a newspaper.
Ask: Why do people read informative or persuasive essays? Why do newspapers print such essays? Have students consider their purpose for reading as they read the essays.

Teach

L Literary Element

Audience Explain that essay writers consider their audiences before they write. They think about what the audience will need or want to know. As students read these excerpts, have them identify the essays' likely audiences. OL

★ Viewing the Art

Elizabeth Barakah Hodges is an artist and educator who lives in Florida. She describes her work as "magic realism" and says she focuses on "the beauty of the spirit."

LITERARY FOCUS

Personal and Expository Essay

What is an essay?

L An **essay** is a short piece of nonfiction writing that usually deals with a single subject. But an essay can deal with virtually any subject in a variety of ways. Many essays, regardless of their type, share the author's thoughts about a subject or an experience.

In the excerpt in Part 2 from *All God's Children Need Traveling Shoes*, Maya Angelou tells of a weekend drive out of Accra to see the countryside of Ghana.

from *All God's Children Need Traveling Shoes*

by Maya Angelou

The too sweet aromas of flowers, the odors of freshly fried fish and stench from open sewers hung in my clothes and lay on my skin. Car horns blew, drums thumped. Loud radio music and the muddle of many languages shouted or murmured. I needed country quiet.

The Fiat was dependable, and I had a long weekend, money in my purse, and a working command of Fanti, so I decided to travel into the bush.

The essays in this part were written to inform or to share experiences with the reader. For example, in the above excerpt, Maya Angelou shares her impressions of the sights, sounds, and smells of Accra. Essays are generally categorized as **personal, expository,** or **persuasive.**

Africa, 1995. Elizabeth Barakah Hodges. Acrylic on canvas, 25 x 18 in. Private collection. ★

Additional Support

Literary Elements Have students access the Web site to improve their understanding of personal and expository essays.

Skills Practice

READING: Evaluating Credibility Remind students to consider the writer's credibility when reading nonfiction. A credible writer is one they can trust. Have students write these questions in a reading journal and ask them as they read the selections:

- What is the writer's motivation for writing?
- Is the author qualified to write on this topic?
- Is the author basing his or her ideas on facts that can be verified? OL

Personal Essays

Personal essays are usually informal in their language and tone. A personal essay often reflects on an incident in the writer's life. The writer may share a life lesson with the reader or perhaps reminisce about a past experience.

On the day Robert Kennedy was shot we found ourselves, numbed, staring at vats of creamy chocolate brew at the Judson Candy Factory. The air hung thickly around us. It didn't make much sense to consider all that work for something that wasn't even good for you.

R —Naomi Shihab Nye, **from "Field Trip"**

Expository Essays

The word *expository* is a derivative of the word *expose,* which means "to make known or explain." Whenever you write to inform, give directions, explain an idea, or make something clear, you are writing an **expository essay.**

The name Wyoming comes from an Indian word meaning "at the great plains," but the plains are really valleys, great arid valleys, sixteen hundred square miles, with the horizon bending up on all sides into mountain ranges. This gives the vastness a sheltering look.

Winter lasts six months here. Prevailing winds spill snowdrifts to the east, and new storms from the northwest replenish them. This white bulk is sometimes dizzying, even nauseating, to look at.

—Gretel Ehrlich, **from "The Solace of Open Spaces"**

Literature Online **Interactive Literary Elements Handbook** Go to www.glencoe.com to review or learn more about personal and expository essays.

Chefs in Paris, 2003. Pam Ingalls. 

Persuasive Essays

In a **persuasive essay,** the writer attempts to influence the reader to accept an idea, adopt a point of view, or perform an action. Persuasive writing may appeal to the reader's emotions. However, a type of persuasive writing called **argument** relies on reason, logic, and evidence to convince the reader. Most persuasive essays and speeches use a combination of argument and emotional appeal. You will encounter persuasive writing and speaking in Part 3 of this unit.

Quickwrite

Describing a Journey Describe your journey to school on a particular day. What main point will you make? What are your thoughts about your experience? Include details about what you see, hear, smell, taste, and touch that support your main point.

INDIANA ACADEMIC STANDARDS (pages 380–381)
9.5.1 Write...autobiographical narratives...that...describe with specific details the sights, sounds, and smells of a scene...

Teach

R Reading Strategy

Identifying Facts **Say:** In nonfiction, writers provide details that help the reader picture the setting and the people, but those details must be based in fact.

Ask: What details in Naomi Shihab Nye's essay can probably be verified as fact? *(The details about the vats at the factory and the workers' mood could be verified by talking to other people who were there.)* **OL**

★ Viewing the Art

Pam Ingalls began studying art with her father, the founder of the art department at Gonzaga University in Washington. She favors bold colors and simple subjects. Ingalls has won over 60 prizes for her work. **AS**

Assess

Quickwrite

Essays should include sensory details that bring the scene or events to life. Students should use the events to support a larger point about life and describe their thoughts and feelings.

Academic Standards

Additional Support activities on pp. 380 and 381 cover the following standards:

Skills Practice: **9.2** Develop strategies such as asking questions... **9.2.7** Evaluate an author's argument or defense of a claim...

Differentiated Instruction: **9.2.4** Synthesize the content from several sources or works...; paraphrase the ideas and connect them to...related topics to demonstrate comprehension.

Differentiated Instruction

Designing a Poster Ask spatial learners to create a poster that illustrates the different types of essays. Tell students that their posters should be colorful and easy to read. The posters should remind students of the different types of essays and their purposes. Display students' posters around the classroom. **BL**

Focus

BELLRINGER

Bellringer Options
Selection Focus Transparency 24
Daily Language Practice Transparency 34

Or discuss journeys students have taken to other states or countries, either physically or by reading a book or magazine. **Ask:** Why do you think people like to travel? *(Students may mention curiosity, family bonds, business, or sports.)* How are people different when traveling than when at home? *(Possible answer: They may be more adventurous; they may reinvent themselves a bit.)*

Author Search To expand students' appreciation of Maya Angelou, have them access the Web site for additional information and resources.

BEFORE YOU READ

from *All God's Children Need Traveling Shoes*

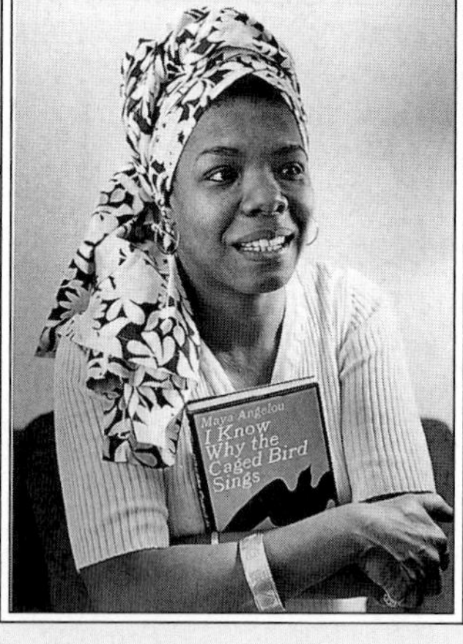

MEET MAYA ANGELOU

How many careers can one person have? Maya Angelou has been a cook, waitress, singer, actor, and dancer. She was the first female African American streetcar conductor in San Francisco. During the 1960s, she was a coordinator for the Southern Christian Leadership Conference and a voice of the Civil Rights Movement. She was a television and movie star, as well as a political activist for women's rights. She recently published a cookbook. On top of all that, she is an award-winning author.

Six Autobiographies Born in St. Louis, Missouri, Angelou spent much of her childhood in rural, racially segregated Stamps, Arkansas. She wrote eloquently about this and other periods of her life in a series of six autobiographical books. Of those books, *I Know Why the Caged Bird Sings* is the first and most famous. *All God's Children Need Traveling Shoes* is the fifth in the series. It recounts Angelou's years in Ghana, where she enrolled her son in college.

> *"[Travel] can introduce the idea that if we try to understand each other, we may even become friends."*
>
> —Maya Angelou

Angelou began writing autobiographies when she returned home from Ghana. One reason she wrote was because her friend James Baldwin, the African American novelist, encouraged her. Although Angelou never planned to write more than one volume, she published more and more books over the years. In addition to autobiographies, Angelou has published children's books, poetry, essays, plays, and film and television scripts.

On the Move Angelou has crossed the United States as well as other countries and continents to write, perform, appear on talk shows, receive honorary degrees, and fight for the rights of women and the underprivileged. A savvy traveler, Angelou speaks five languages in addition to English: Spanish, French, Italian, Arabic, and Fanti, a language spoken in Ghana. She knows that travel is not a cure for the world's problems, but she does think it has great potential for bringing people together.

Awards and Accomplishments Angelou has been honored in many ways. President Bill Clinton chose her to write and read a poem at his first inaugural ceremony in January 1993. Angelou was also chosen to write and read a poem for the fiftieth anniversary of the United Nations in 1995. She received the NAACP's Spingarn Medal in 1993. A dynamic speaker with a deep and rhythmic voice, Angelou remains a sought-after guest in every location from college campuses to the Oprah Winfrey show.

Maya Angelou was born in 1928.

Literature Online **Author Search** For more about Maya Angelou, go to www.glencoe.com.

Selection Skills

from All God's Children Need Traveling Shoes

Literary Elements
- Narrative Elements (SE pp. 383–391)
- Author's Purpose (SE p. 391)

Reading Skills
- Identifying Problem and Solution (SE pp. 383–391)

Vocabulary Skills
- Synonyms (SE p. 391)

Listening/Speaking/Viewing Skills
- Analyzing Art (SE p. 386; TWE p. 388)
- Group Activity (SE p. 390)

Writing Skills/Grammar
- Analyze Style (SE p. 392)
- Possessive Pronouns (SE p. 392)
- Commas in a Series (TWE p. 388)

Study Skills/Research/Assessment
- Internet Research (SE p. 392)

LITERATURE PREVIEW

Connecting to the Narrative Essay

When people travel, they often have a variety of experiences, both wonderful and disappointing. In *All God's Children Need Traveling Shoes* the author travels in Ghana. Before you read, think about the following questions:

- Have you ever gone someplace where you did not know anyone?
- How would you act if you were not sure you would be accepted among strangers?

Building Background

This selection takes place in the early 1960s in Ghana, a nation that lies on the Atlantic coast of West Africa. When fifteenth-century Portuguese explorers arrived in the region now known as Ghana, they found so much gold there that they named it the Gold Coast. From the 1500s to the 1850s, the Gold Coast was a center of the international slave trade. In 1957 the nation attained its independence and renamed itself Ghana.

Big Idea On the Move

As you read, think about what Angelou learned and felt during this part of her journey to Ghana.

Literary Element Narrative Essay

A **narrative essay** is a nonfiction story. In this short form, authors present a real time and place, real people as characters, and events that actually happened. Often a narrative essay includes a central conflict or problem, as well as a climax and resolution. Knowing that a literary work is a narrative essay can help you gain historical and/or general knowledge about other people, places, and events. As you read, note the elements of a narrative essay mentioned above.

- See Literary Terms Handbook, p. R12.

Interactive Literary Elements Handbook To review or learn more about the literary elements, go to www.glencoe.com.

READING PREVIEW

Reading Strategy Identifying Problem and Solution

Identifying problem and solution is looking for obstacles, conflicts, and problems and identifying how they are or can be solved. This process can help you better understand the purpose of a literary work and provide you with greater insight into its characters. As you read, identify the series of problems that arise as the narrator travels in Ghana and the solutions that she develops for those problems.

Reading Tip: Making a Chart As you read, use a chart to list problems and solutions.

Problem	Solution
The narrator cannot find a place to stay.	She asks a woman for help, and the woman guides her to the "old man."

Vocabulary

throng (thrông) *n.* a large number of people or things crowded together; p. 384 *Cars could not pass through the throng of tourists.*

pang (pang) *n.* a sudden sharp feeling of pain or distress; p. 385 *The woman felt a pang as she recalled the scene of the accident.*

suffuse (sə fūz′) *v.* to spread through or over; p. 385 *The smell of baking bread suffused the small house.*

impervious (im pur′vē əs) *adj.* incapable of being passed through, affected, or disturbed; p. 386 *The manager was impervious to the customer's complaints and refused to issue a refund.*

reverberate (ri vur′ bə rāt′) *v.* to echo; resound; p. 389 *The noise of the cars passing through the tunnel reverberated off its walls.*

INDIANA ACADEMIC STANDARDS (pages 383–392)

9.3 [Identify] story elements such as...plot ...

9.2 Develop [reading] strategies...

9.5.3 Write expository compositions, including analytical essays...that gather information in support of a thesis...

9.3.11 Analyze...style, including the impact of diction...

BEFORE YOU READ

Focus

Summary

During her stay in Ghana, the narrator is overcome with emotion at her thoughts about the slave dungeons. She stops overnight in the town of Dunkwa. A woman there brings the narrator to a private home. The narrator allows herself to be mistakenly identified as a Bambara from Liberia instead of an American and spends the night as an honored guest.

V Vocabulary

Vocabulary File Say: Add these words and definitions to your vocabulary file. For each word, include a sentence that gives you an example of how to use the word. **OL** Students with English language needs should include the pronunciations of these words in their files. **EL**

Literary Elements Have students access the Web site to improve their understanding of narrative essay.

Selection Resources

Print Materials
- Unit 2 Resources (Fast File), pp. 41–43
- Leveled Vocabulary Development, p. 27
- Selection and Unit Assessments, pp. 59–60
- Selection Quick Checks, p. 30

Transparencies
- Bellringer Options Transparencies: Selection Focus Transparency 24 Daily Language Practice Transparency 34
- Literary Elements Transparency 34

Technology
- TeacherWorks Plus™ CD-ROM
- StudentWorks Plus™ CD-ROM
- Presentation Plus!™ CD-ROM
- Literature Online, glencoe.com
- Online Student Edition, mhln.com
- Exam*View*® Assessment Suite CD-ROM
- Vocabulary PuzzleMaker CD-ROM
- Listening Library, disc 1 track 34

Teach

BI1 Big Idea

On the Move Say: Keep these questions in mind as you read: In what ways does Angelou enjoy traveling? *(She likes the sense of freedom.)* In what ways does she dislike her journey? *(She dislikes the city noise, and she is horrified by the remnants of slavery.)* **OL**

L1 Literary Element

Narrative Essay Possible answer: *Ghana has a colorful, diverse culture.* **OL**

BI2 Big Idea

On the Move Ask: What makes the narrator feel able to travel in the bush? *(She has plenty of money, she knows Fanti, the language of the bush, and she has a dependable car.)* **OL**

Cultural History

Cape Coast, Ghana
Historic Cape Coast has some of Ghana's best schools and museums. Cape Coast was the capital of the Gold Coast from 1700 to 1877. **AS**

Readability Scores
Dale-Chall: 7.4
DRP: 61
Lexile: 960

from All God's Children Need Traveling Shoes

Maya Angelou

BI1 Each morning Ghana's seven-and-one-half million people seemed to crowd at once into the capital city where the broad avenues as well as the unpaved rutted lanes became gorgeous with moving pageantry: bicycles, battered lorries, hand carts, American and European cars, chauffeur-driven limousines. People on foot struggled for right-of-way, white-collar workers wearing white knee-high socks brushed against market women balancing large baskets on their heads as they proudly swung their wide hips. Children, bright faces shining with palm oil, picked openings in the **throng**, and pretty young women in western clothes affected not to notice the attention they caused as they laughed together talking in the musical Twi language. Old men sat or stooped beside the road smoking homemade pipes and looking wise as old men have done eternally.

Vocabulary

throng (thrông) *n.* a large number of people or things crowded together

The too sweet aromas of flowers, the odors of freshly fried fish and stench from open sewers hung in my clothes and lay on my skin. Car horns blew, drums thumped. Loud radio music and the muddle of many languages shouted or murmured. I needed country quiet.

The Fiat was dependable, and I had a long weekend, money in my purse, and a working command of Fanti,[1] so I decided to travel into the bush. **BI2** I bought roasted plantain stuffed with boiled peanuts, a quart of Club beer and headed my little car west. The stretch was a highway from Accra to Cape Coast,[2] filled with trucks and private cars passing from lane to lane with abandon. People hung out of windows of the crowded mammie lorries,[3] and I could hear singing and shouting

1. *Fanti* (fan′ tē) is a dialect of Akan spoken by one of Ghana's many ethnic groups.
2. *Accra* is Ghana's capital and largest city; the town of *Cape Coast* is about 75 miles southwest of Accra.
3. *Mammie lorries* are small trucks or open-sided buses used for public transportation.

Literary Element Narrative Essay *What do these details reveal about Ghana?* **L1**

Additional Support

Skills Practice

LITERARY ELEMENT: Setting Review that setting includes the time and place of a work. In this story, the narrator visits new places, which produce strong reactions. She uses vivid details to create images of these places. Help students identify details in the following passages that help visualize the setting:

- page 384: first two paragraphs
- page 385: the paragraph beginning "I allowed the shapes . . ."

As they read, encourage students to note other vivid words and details that capture setting. **OL** when the drivers careened those antique vehicles up and down hills as if each was a little train out to prove it could.

I stopped in Cape Coast only for gas. Although many black Americans had headed for the town as soon as they touched ground in Ghana, I successfully avoided it for a year. Cape Coast Castle and the nearby Elmina Castle[4] had been holding forts for captured slaves. The captives had been imprisoned in dungeons beneath the massive buildings, and friends of mine who had felt called upon to make the trek reported that they felt the thick stone walls still echoed with old cries.

Visual Vocabulary
Found mostly in tropical Africa, *baobab* (bā′ ō bab′) *trees* have very broad trunks, thick branches, and large white flowers. They grow well on *savannahs,* which are open grasslands with scattered trees and shrubs.

The palm tree-lined streets and fine white stone buildings did not tempt me to remain any longer than necessary. Once out of the town and again onto the tarred roads, I knew I had not made a clean escape. Despite my hurry, history had invaded my little car. **Pangs** of self-pity and a sorrow for my unknown relatives **suffused** me. Tears made the highway waver and were salty on my tongue.

What did they think and feel, my grandfathers, caught on those green savannas, under the baobab trees? How long did their families search for them? Did the dungeon wall feel chilly and its slickness strange to my grandmothers, who were used to the rush of air against bamboo huts and the sound of birds rattling their grass roofs?

I had to pull off the road. Just passing near Cape Coast Castle had plunged me back into the eternal melodrama.[5]

There would be no purging,[6] I knew, unless I asked all the questions. Only then would the spirits understand that I was feeding them. It was a crumb, but it was all I had.

I allowed the shapes to come to my imagination: children passed tied together by ropes and chains, tears abashed, stumbling in dull exhaustion, then women, hair uncombed, bodies gritted with sand, and sagging in defeat. Men, muscles without memory, minds dimmed, plodding, leaving bloodied footprints in the dirt. The quiet was awful. None of them cried, or yelled, or bellowed. No moans came from them. They lived in a mute territory, dead to feeling and protest. These were the legions, sold by sisters, stolen by brothers, bought by strangers, enslaved by the greedy, and betrayed by history.

For a long time, I sat as in an open-air auditorium watching a troop of tragic players enter and exit the stage.

The visions faded as my tears ceased. Light returned and I started the car, turned off the main road, and headed for the interior. Using rutted track roads, and lanes a little larger than foot paths, I found the River Pra. The black water moving quietly, ringed with the tall trees, seemed enchanted. A fear of snakes kept me in the car, but I parked and watched the bright sun turn the water surface into a rippling cloth of lamé.[7] I passed through villages which were

4. *Cape Coast Castle* and *Elmina Castle* are two slave-trade era fortifications. The castles' dungeons held thousands of captured men, women, and children in chains as they awaited export to North America as slaves. The United Nations has designated the buildings as World Heritage Monuments.

5. *[eternal melodrama]* Angelou compares the experience of slavery to a play that never fails to stir the emotions deeply.

6. A *purging* is a removal of something that is unclean or undesirable.

7. *Lamé* (la mā′) is a fabric woven with metallic threads that give it a glittering appearance.

Vocabulary

pang (pang) *n.* a sudden sharp feeling of pain or distress

suffuse (sə fūz′) *v.* to spread through or over

Big Idea On the Move *What important connection came about because of this interruption in the narrator's journey?* **BI3**

Literary Element Narrative Essay *What happens in the narrative at this point and how do you know that something has changed?* **L2**

Teach

BI3 Big Idea

On the Move Answer: *The interruption helps the narrator connect with the experiences of the slaves and with her feelings about Cape Coast Castle's sad history.* **OL**

L2 Literary Element

Narrative Essay Answer: *The narrator resumes her trip to the "bush" by starting her car decisively and turning off the main road. In addition, restarting her journey may be a metaphor for resolving the emotions that Cape Coast evoked in the narrator.* **OL**

Use the CheckPoint questions on Presentation Plus! to monitor students' comprehension. These questions can be used with interactive response keypads for immediate student feedback.

English Language Coach

Sentence Structure Students may struggle with Angelou's long, detail-filled sentences. Help them identify the subject and verb in long sentences. After establishing the basic meaning, students can add back in descriptive modifiers. Have pairs complete the exercise with the same sentences, then share results. **EL**

Differentiated Instruction

Title Explain that Angelou traveled from Arkansas to Ghana to learn about her ancestors. Help students locate these places on a world map. Clarify that her title links people in both places as "God's children" and recognizes that it is hard to get from one place to the other—it takes traveling shoes. **BL**

Academic Standards

Additional Support activities on pp. 384 and 385 cover the following standards:

Skills Practice: **9.3** [Identify] story elements such as…setting…

English Language Coach: **9.6.2** Demonstrate an understanding of sentence construction…

Differentiated Instruction: **9.3** [Identify] story elements such as…theme [and] setting…

Teach

R1 Reading Strategy

Identifying Problem and Solution **Answer:** *The first sign of trouble is that the narrator cannot find a hotel and begins "to worry." She explains that she is short on gas and does not know the address of her student's family. Listing these unavailable solutions heightens the narrator's problem.* **OL**

★ Viewing the Art

Possible answer: *The colors in* Small Town in Africa *make it seem as if the town is in an area where the weather is hot and breezy.*

Irish-born Rosemary Woods reflects her Irish heritage in much of her artwork. She likes using rich colors. **AS**

Small Town in Africa. Rosemary Woods. **Viewing the Art:** How do the colors in this painting affect your sense of the place? ★

little more than collections of thatch huts, with goats and small children wandering in the lanes. The noise of my car brought smiling adults out to wave at me.

In the late afternoon, I reached the thriving town that was my destination. A student whom I had met at Legon had spoken to me often of the gold-mining area, of Dunkwa, his birthplace. His reports had so glowed with the town's virtues, and I had chosen that spot for my first journey.

My skin color, features, and the Ghana cloth I wore made me look like any young Ghanaian[8] woman. I could pass if I didn't talk too much.

As usual, in the towns of Ghana, the streets were filled with vendors selling their wares of tinned pat milk, hot spicy Killi Willis (fried, ripe plantain chips), Pond's cold cream, and antimosquito incense rings. Farmers were returning home, children returning from school. Young boys grinned at mincing[9] girls and always there were the market women, huge and **impervious.** I searched for a hotel sign in vain and as the day lengthened, I started to worry. I didn't have enough gas to get to Koforidua, a large town northeast of Dunkwa, where there would certainly be hotels, and I didn't have the address of my student's family. I parked the car a little out of the town center and stopped a woman carrying a bucket of water on her head and a baby on her back.

"Good day." I spoke in Fanti, and she responded. I continued, "I beg you, I am a stranger looking for a place to stay."

She repeated, "Stranger?" and laughed. "You are a stranger? No. No."

To many Africans only whites could be strangers. All Africans belonged somewhere,

8. *Ghanaian* (gä′ nə yən)

9. The *mincing* girls are trying to appear dainty and refined.

Reading Strategy Identifying Problem and Solution
When do you first realize that the narrator is in trouble and how does she convey the significance of her predicament? **R1**

Vocabulary

impervious (im pur′ vē əs) *adj.* incapable of being passed through, affected, or disturbed

Additional Support

Skills Practice

READING: Making Inferences
Making inferences means figuring out what an author means but does not directly state. Authors often provide clues for readers to piece together. For example, the villagers find the idea of one person from Accra (one Nkran) amusing. Point out clues that explain their reaction, such as the meaning of the word *Nkran,* which suggests millions of occupants living and building dwellings together.

Ask: How can you explain the villagers' reaction? *(If she is an "ant" from Nkran, it is funny to think she would be alone and without a dwelling.)* **OL**

to some clan. All Akan-speaking[10] people belong to one of eight blood lines (Abosua) and one of eight spirit lines (Ntoro).

I said, "I am not from here."

For a second fear darted in her eyes. There was the possibility that I was a witch or some unhappy ghost from the country of the dead. I quickly said, "I am from Accra." She gave me a good smile. "Oh, one Accra. Without a home." She laughed. The Fanti word *Nkran,* for which the capitol was named, means the large ant that builds ten-foot-high domes of red clay and lives with millions of other ants.

"Come with me." She turned quickly, steadying the bucket on her head, and led me between two corrugated tin shacks. The baby bounced and slept on her back, ★ secured by the large piece of cloth wrapped around her body. We passed a compound where women were pounding the dinner foo foo[11] in wooden bowls.

The woman shouted, "Look what I have found. One Nkran has no place to sleep tonight." The women laughed and asked, "One Nkran? I don't believe it."

"Are you taking it to the old man?"

"Of course."

"Sleep well, alone, Nkran, if you can." My guide stopped before a small house. She put the water on the ground and told me to wait while she entered the house. She returned immediately followed by a man who rubbed his eyes as if he had just been awakened.

He walked close and peered hard at my face. "This is the Nkran?" The woman was adjusting the bucket on her head.

"Yes, Uncle. I have brought her." She looked at me, "Good-bye, Nkran. Sleep in peace. Uncle, I am going." The man said, "Go and come, child," and resumed studying my face. "You are not Ga." He was reading my features.

A few small children had collected around his knees. They could barely hold back their giggles as he interrogated me.

"Aflao?"[12]

I said, "No."

"Brong-ahafo?"

I said, "No. I am—." I meant to tell him the truth, but he said, "Don't tell me. I will soon know." He continued staring at me. "Speak more. I will know from your Fanti."

"Well, I have come from Accra and I need to rent a room for the night. I told that woman that I was a stranger . . ."

He laughed. "And you are. Now, I know. You are Bambara from Liberia. It is clear you are Bambara." He laughed again. "I always can tell. I am not easily fooled." He shook my hand. "Yes, we will find you a place for the night. Come." He touched a boy at his right. "Find Patience Aduah, and bring her to me."

The children laughed and all ran away as the man led me into the house. He pointed me to a seat in the neat little parlor and shouted, "Foriwa, we have a guest. Bring beer." A small black woman with an imperial air entered the room. Her knowing face told me that she had witnessed the scene in her front yard.

She spoke to her husband. "And, Kobina, did you find who the stranger was?" She walked to me. I stood and shook her hand. "Welcome, stranger." We both laughed. "Now don't tell me, Kobina, I have ears, also. Sit down, Sister, beer is coming. Let me hear you speak."

We sat facing each other while her husband stood over us smiling. "You, Foriwa, you will never get it."

I told her my story, adding a few more words I had recently learned. She laughed

10. *Akan* (ä′ kän′) is the language spoken in southern Ghana; Fanti is a dialect of Akan.

11. *Foo foo* is a dough made from mashed yams, plantains, or other starchy fruits.

12. Here and in the next few paragraphs, the man guesses at Angelou's ethnic group in the mistaken belief that she is a native West African.

Literary Element Narrative Essay *What does the woman's response to the narrator suggest about her role in the narrative and the ensuing events?* **L**

Reading Strategy Identifying Problem and Solution *What are the complexities of the problem that the narrator has at this moment?* **R2**

Teach

L Literary Element

Narrative Essay Answer: *The woman's command to come with her implies that she has a solution to the narrator's problem. The unclear nature of the woman's solution may deepen the narrator's unease even as it develops the narrative.* **OL**

R2 Reading Strategy

Identifying Problem and Solution Answer: *The narrator finds it difficult to explain her identity as an African American in a country where only white people are considered strangers. This difficulty is heightened by the man's unwillingness to let her speak and assumption that he can figure out her identity.* **OL**

★ Cultural History

Clothing Both men and women in Ghana wear clothes made from brightly woven cloth. Women make blouses and sarong-type skirts from locally made cloth, while men wrap the cloth loosely around themselves. **AS**

English Language Coach

Figurative Language Help students build meaning for the phrase "fear darted in her eyes" on page 387. Point out that the phrase is an example of personification. By animating the emotion of fear, Angelou makes it more real for her readers. **EL**

Building Reading Fluency

Cultural Dialogue Note that the African people in this story speak with a rhythm that differs from the narrator's. For example, their sentences are shorter. Provide fluency practice by having pairs of students read aloud sections of dialogue between the narrator and the family. **BL**

Academic Standards

Additional Support activities on pp. 386 and 387 cover the following standards:

Skills Practice: **9.2.8** Make reasonable statements and draw conclusions about a text, supporting them with accurate examples.

English Language Coach: **9.3.7** Recognize and understand the significance of various literary devices, including figurative language...

Building Reading Fluency: **9.7** [Develop] speaking skills...in conjunction with strategies [for] delivery of oral presentations.

Teach

R1 Reading Strategy

Identifying Problem and Solution **Answer:** *The narrator is accepted as an African. Her happiness at this suggests that she does not feel "at home" in her American identity.* OL

R2 Reading Strategy

Identifying Problem and Solution **Answer:** *She has solved her problems of needing a place to stay and of finding an African identity for herself.* OL

★ Viewing the Art

Tilly Willis paints landscapes, still lifes, and portraits. Her work has been published in various media, including cards, books, and prints. Much of Willis's art is influenced by her travels to Africa, Russia, and the Middle East. AS

Calabash Girls, 1991. Tilly Willis. Oil on canvas. Private Collection. ★

grandly. "She is Bambara. I could have told you when Abaa first brought her. See how tall she is? See her head? See her color? Men, huh. They only look at a woman's shape."

Two children brought beer and glasses to the man who poured and handed the glasses around. "Sister, I am Kobina Artey; this is my wife Foriwa and some of my children."

I introduced myself, but because they had taken such relish in detecting my tribal origin I couldn't tell them that they were wrong. Or, less admirably, at that moment I didn't want to remember that I was an American. For the first time since my arrival, I was very nearly home. Not a Ghanaian, but at least accepted as an African. The sensation was worth a lie.

Voices came to the house from the yard.

"Brother Kobina," "Uncle," "Auntie."

Foriwa opened the door to a group of people who entered speaking fast and looking at me.

"So this is the Bambara woman? The stranger?" They looked me over and talked with my hosts. I understood some of their conversation. They said that I was nice looking and old enough to have a little wisdom. They announced that my car was parked a few blocks away. Kobina told them that I would spend the night with the newlyweds, Patience and Kwame Duodu. Yes, they could see clearly that I was a Bambara.

"Give us the keys to your car, Sister; someone will bring your bag."

I gave up the keys and all resistance. I was either at home with friends, or I would die wishing that to be so.

Later, Patience, her husband, Kwame, and I sat out in the yard around a cooking fire near to their thatched house which was much smaller than the Artey bungalow. They explained that Kobina Artey was not a chief, but a member of the village council, and all small matters in that area of Dunkwa were taken to him. As Patience stirred the stew in the pot, which was balanced over the fire, children and women appeared sporadiacally out of the darkness carrying covered plates. Each time Patience thanked the bearers and directed them to the house, I felt the distance narrow between my past and present.

In the United States, during segregation, black American travelers, unable to stay in hotels restricted to white patrons, stopped at churches and told the black ministers or deacons of their predicaments. Church officials would select a home and then inform the unexpecting hosts of the decision. There was never a protest, but the new hosts relied

Reading Strategy Identifying Problem and Solution
What problem is solved in this exchange with the Ghanaians, and what does this solution suggest about the narrator's sense of who she is? R1

Reading Strategy Identifying Problem and Solution
In what ways is this statement a solution to the narrator's earlier problems? R2

Additional Support

Skills Practice

WRITING: Commas in a Series
Point out the following phrases from the selection: *My skin color, features, and the Ghana cloth; fried plantain, dukuno, shrimp, fish cakes, and more.* Explain that in a series of three or more items, a comma is used after each item except the last. Write these categories on the board, and have students create a list for each category, using commas correctly.

- Recreational Activities *(skating, swimming, fishing, and hiking)*
- Kinds of Music *(pop, rock, blues, and folk)*
- Countries *(Japan, Brazil, and Spain)* OL

on the generosity of their neighbors to help feed and even entertain their guests. After the travelers were settled, surreptitious knocks would sound on the back door.

In Stamps, Arkansas, I heard so often, "Sister Henderson, I know you've got guests. Here's a pan of biscuits."

"Sister Henderson, Mama sent a half a cake for your visitors."

"Sister Henderson, I made a lot of macaroni and cheese. Maybe this will help with your visitors."

My grandmother would whisper her thanks and finally when the family and guests sat down at the table, the offerings were so different and plentiful, it appeared that days had been spent preparing the meal.

Patience invited me inside, and when I saw the table I was confirmed in my earlier impression. Groundnut stew, garden egg stew, hot pepper soup, *kenke, kotomre,* fried ★ plantain, *dukuno,* shrimp, fish cakes, and more, all crowded together on variously patterned plates.

In Arkansas, the guests would never suggest, although they knew better, that the host had not prepared every scrap of food, especially for them.

I said to Patience, "Oh, Sister, you went to such trouble."

She laughed, "It is nothing, Sister. We don't want our Bambara relative to think herself a stranger anymore. Come, let us wash and eat."

After dinner I followed Patience to the outdoor toilet, then they gave me a cot in a very small room.

In the morning I wrapped my cloth under my arms, sarong fashion, and walked with Patience to the bathhouse. We joined about twenty women in a walled enclosure that had no ceiling. The greetings were loud and cheerful as we soaped ourselves and poured buckets of water over our shoulders.

Patience introduced me. "This is our Bambara sister."

"She's a tall one all right. Welcome, Sister."

"I like her color."

"How many children, Sister?"

I apologized, "I only have one."

"One?"

"One?"

"One!" Shouts **reverberated** over the splashing water. I said, "One, but I'm trying."

They laughed. "Try hard, sister. Keep trying."

We ate leftovers from the last night feast and I said a sad good-bye to my hosts. The children walked me back to my car with the oldest boy carrying my bag. I couldn't offer money to my hosts, Arkansas had taught me that, but I gave change to the children. They bobbed and jumped and grinned.

"Good-bye, Bambara Auntie."

"Go and come, Auntie."

"Go and come."

I drove into Cape Coast before I thought of the gruesome castle and out of its environs before the ghosts of slavery caught me. Perhaps their attempts had been half-hearted. After all, in Dunkwa, although I let a lie speak for me, I had proved that one of their descendants, at least one, could just briefly return to Africa, and that despite cruel betrayals, bitter ocean voyages, and hurtful centuries, we were still recognizable.

Big Idea On the Move *How does the narrator's description of her meal at Dunkwa reveal the importance of travel to her?* **BI**

Literary Element Narrative Essay *How has the narrator's past helped her act appropriately in the present?* **L**

Vocabulary

reverberate (ri vur′bə rāt′) *v.* to echo; resound

Teach

BI Big Idea

On the Move Answer: *She recognizes the generosity of the Ghanaians and relates it to hospitality in her Arkansas hometown, specifically, when families took in African Americans banned from hotels by segregation. Travel illuminates her past and connects the two cultures.* **OL**

L Literary Element

Narrative Essay Answer: *She learned in childhood the appropriate way to act in similar situations.* **OL**

★ Cultural History

Food Corn, cassava, yams, and bananas are staples in most African regions. Groundnuts are the same as peanuts in the United States. Groundnut stew is made with okra, squash, groundnuts, and meat. **AS**

CheckPoint

Use the CheckPoint questions on Presentation Plus! to check students' mastery of the selection. These questions can be used with interactive response keypads for immediate student feedback.

English Language Coach

Dialect Point out the use of the term "Sister" throughout the selection. Explain that this is an example of dialect, or regional variety of a language with differences in vocabulary, grammar, and punctuation. Here, the phrase labels the narrator as one of a familiar group. Patience and her family consider the narrator to be one of their group—the group of Africans—and so they call her Sister. It does not mean that she is literally their sister. Ask students to find another similar label used in the selection. *(Auntie)* **EL**

Academic Standards

Additional Support activities on pp. 388 and 389 cover the following standards:

Skills Practice: **9.6.1** Identify and correctly use…the mechanics of punctuation…

English Language Coach: **9.1.2** Distinguish between what words mean literally and what they imply and interpret what the words imply.

AFTER YOU READ

Assess

1. Possible answers: Her pain and anger about slavery or her feelings of warmth and closeness toward the villagers; she evokes emotion by showing that travel illuminates critical aspects of identity and home.
2. (a) She has a vision of the slaves at the castle. (b) Yes, she avoided it to escape feelings of fear, anger, and sadness. She may resolve these feelings amongst the living of Dunkwa.
3. (a) Bambara from Liberia; they were proud of figuring it out; she wanted to be seen as an African. (b) She did not wish to be seen as American.
4. (a) The descendant of an African slave could return to Africa as an African. (b) The villagers give her a positive image to balance the negative one of African slaves.
5. (a) Her tears create a mood of pain and sadness. (b) She succeeds well. She creates a somber mood, shifts to buoyancy in Dunkwa, and then recalls the somber mood in the last lines.
6. (a) It shows that hospitality in the two places is alike. (b)The references connect the past and present, and Angelou's ancestors and present-day hosts.

AFTER YOU READ

RESPONDING AND THINKING CRITICALLY

Respond

1. Which emotion described in this selection could you relate to most? What specifically about the writing evokes this emotion?

Recall and Interpret

2. (a)Describe what happened when Angelou pulled her car off the road after passing Cape Coast Castle. (b)Do you think Angelou avoided entering Cape Coast Castle and, if so, why? What issues and emotions might Cape Coast Castle raise for her?
3. (a)What nationality do Kobina and Foriwa think Angelou is? What reason does she offer for not correcting them? (b)What unspoken reasons might Angelou have for not correcting her hosts when they misidentify her?
4. (a)What does Angelou feel that she proved in Dunkwa? (b)How do you think this resolution relates to her experience at Cape Coast Castle at the beginning of her journey?

Analyze and Evaluate

5. (a)How does the discussion of Cape Coast Castle introduce a new mood in this selection? (b)How well does Angelou succeed in creating this mood here and elsewhere in the selection?
6. (a)How is the information about Stamps, Arkansas, important in the story of Angelou's travels in Ghana? (b)How does that information make the selection more interesting?
7. Why might it have been important to Angelou to be seen as a Ghanaian woman?

Connect

8. **Big Idea** **On the Move** Do you think that traveling to Dunkwa was the only way that Angelou could have quieted the "ghosts of slavery"? Explain.

DAILY LIFE AND CULTURE

Life in Rural Ghana

In Ghana in the 1960s, most people lived in towns and villages that did not yet have electricity. Dirt roads and waterways connected them. In the greener, wealthier south, picturesque villages sat beneath trees and were surrounded by banana groves and coconut palms. In the dryer, poorer north, mud huts baked in the hot sun. In the villages and towns, women and girls carried water in buckets or pots, sometimes on their heads, from nearby streams or pipes; did washing by hand; pounded maize, cassava, and other starchy fruits and vegetables using a heavy mortar and pestle; and cooked over an open fire in the courtyard.

Group Activity Work with classmates to discuss and answer the following questions.

1. How full or complete a picture do you get of life and culture in Ghana in the early 1960s from Angelou's essay?
2. What do you learn from this feature about daily life and culture that is not stated in Angelou's essay?

7. She wants to be African and reclaim some of her stolen heritage.
8. Possible answer: Balancing the castle with a good experience helps her quiet the ghosts. She might have resolved her feelings by studying slavery at home.

Daily Life and Culture

1. The selection of details is not a complete picture, but readers can learn a lot about the city and country people.
2. Students should note they learn about the simple living conditions, including details about housing, cooking, and washing clothes.

LITERARY ANALYSIS

Literary Element Narrative Essay

A **narrative essay** often has story elements, including plot elements. Plot elements can include exposition (describing the time, place, and characters) as well as various events and rising action. Some, though not all, narrative essays also have a climax and resolution. A well-crafted plot is not as necessary in an essay, where the author's purpose is often to inform, as it is in a story, which is usually meant to entertain.

1. What do you learn from the exposition in this essay?
2. Do you think that this essay has a climax? Explain.
3. How does this narrative essay differ from a story? Use details from the essay to support your answer.

Review: Author's Purpose

As you learned on page 320, the **author's purpose** is the author's intent in writing a literary work. Authors typically write for one or more of the following purposes: to persuade, to inform, to explain, to entertain, or to describe.

Partner Activity Meet with a partner to discuss Angelou's purpose in writing this selection. Make a diagram like the one below. Complete it by listing three important points or main ideas of the essay. Draw a conclusion about Angelou's purpose based on the details.

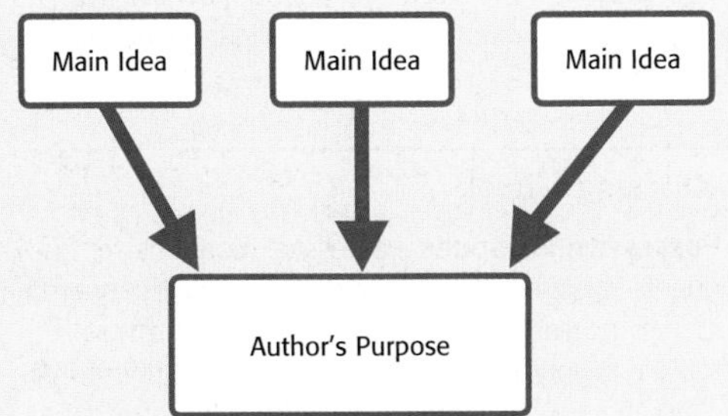

READING AND VOCABULARY

Reading Strategy Identifying Problem and Solution

In Angelou's narrative essay, some of the **problems and solutions** lead to new problems and solutions, creating a chain of events. Review the list of problems and solutions you created while reading this essay. Draw arrows in your chart to show which solutions led to new problems.

1. Which problems and solutions in this essay appear to lead to new problems?
2. In what way is the problem-solution structure of this essay related to the Big Idea of being "On the Move"? Use events from the narrative to support your answer.

Vocabulary Practice

Practice with Synonyms Synonyms are words that have the same or similar meanings. However, words that are synonyms may still have different shades of meaning. Note that synonyms are always the same part of speech. Read each sentence below. Choose the synonym for the underlined word.

1. He loved her so much he could not think of losing her without feeling a <u>pang</u>.
   a. twinge **b.** relief **c.** madness
2. The fragrance of the flowers <u>suffused</u> the house.
   a. diminished **b.** saturated **c.** overpowered
3. A good roof is <u>impervious</u> to rain.
   a. subject **b.** impressive **c.** resistant
4. She is slightly claustrophobic; a <u>throng</u> of people will make her nervous.
   a. room **b.** crowd **c.** meeting
5. Marisol's voice <u>reverberated</u> throughout the canyon.
   a. echoed **b.** whispered **c.** was heard

AFTER YOU READ

Assess

Literary Element

1. The city of Accra is a lively, bustling place, full of smells, with many people moving in various ways.
2. Possible answers: Yes, the climax occurs when she is being served dinner; no, there is no climax since she feels at home during her entire stay.
3. The characters and events are real. The essay is written from the first person point of view and has less suspense or tension than many stories.

Review: Author's Purpose

One main idea is centered on the busy city streets. Another main idea addresses what happened at the castle. A third main idea is concerned with the author and how she is like and unlike Ghanaian women. The author's pupose is to inform.

Vocabulary

1. a **2.** b **3.** c **4.** b **5.** a

Reading Strategy

1. Seeking a hotel: new problem of having to explain her identity; identified as a Bambara: new problem of not wanting to correct the proud host; giving up car keys: new problem of being at host's mercy; driving past Castle: new problem of emotions.
2. Being "on the move" entails difficulties, such as running out of gas, needing a place to stay, or searching for identity. It also brings solutions: getting past the castle literally and metaphorically, and feeling at home in Ghana.

AFTER YOU READ

Assess

Writing About Literature

Students' essays should

- state a thesis and provide supporting examples.
- provide insight into the author's style.
- analyze at least three sentences that exemplify clear, eloquent language.

Internet Connection

Suggest that students work in pairs to divide the research. They might also use online library databases, such as InfoTrac, that offer access to biography references.

Angelou's Language and Style

Possible answer: Market women balanced large baskets on their heads. *Their* replaces *the women's.* Patience and I sat in the yard behind her house. *Her* replaces *Patience's.* I drove into the city before I thought of the castle and out of its environs before the ghosts of slavery caught me. *Its* replaces *the castle's.*

WRITING AND EXTENDING

Writing About Literature

Analyze Style Maya Angelou is often praised for expressing deep thoughts in eloquent yet clear language. This sentence, with its parallel phrases, is an example: "These were the legions, sold by sisters, stolen by brothers, brought by strangers, enslaved by the greedy, and betrayed by history." Find other examples of eloquent, clear language in this selection, and write an essay in which you analyze them.

Begin your prewriting by identifying three examples and analyzing them.

	Sentence	My Analysis of Style
1.		
2.		
3.		

Use your prewriting ideas to develop three body paragraphs. Then write an introduction with a thesis statement that sums up what your analysis shows. Finally, add a formal conclusion that not only restates your main points but adds a fresh, but still related, insight or idea.

After you complete your draft, have a peer read it and suggest revisions. Then proofread and edit your work to correct errors in spelling, grammar, and punctuation.

Internet Connection

Much of Maya Angelou's writing is based on her own experiences. Use the Internet to learn more about her life and her writings. Find out what she has been doing recently and whether she has continued to write about her African roots. You might use a search engine to find sites dedicated to Angelou or look up online bookstores to find out more about her publications.

LiteratureOnline **Web Activities** For eFlashcards, Selection Quick Checks, and other Web activities, go to www.glencoe.com.

GRAMMAR AND STYLE

Angelou's Language and Style

Using Possessive Pronouns In this excerpt from *All God's Children Need Traveling Shoes,* Maya Angelou uses many possessive pronouns. Possessive pronouns show ownership. They take the place of possessive nouns and can be singular or plural.

Singular Possessive Pronouns	Plural Possessive Pronouns
my mine your yours his her hers its	our ours your yours their theirs

Notice the possessive pronoun in each of Angelou's sentences below and the possessive noun it replaces.

Angelou's Sentence	Possessive Noun Replaced
We sat facing each other while her husband stood over us smiling.	the woman's
A student whom I had met at Legon had spoken to me often of . . . Dunkwa, his birthplace.	the student's

Activity Make a chart like the one above with more examples from the story. Think about how the use of possessive pronouns helps to eliminate unnecessary repetition.

Revising Check

Possessive Pronouns Possessive pronouns are frequently misspelled or misused. Work with a partner to identify possessive pronouns and the nouns they replace in your analysis of Angelou's style. Refer to the chart above to be sure you have used the correct singular or plural form and spelling of each possessive pronoun. Edit as necessary.

LiteratureOnline

Web Activities Have students access the Web site for interactive activities that will help them assess their understanding of the selection.

Field Trip

MEET NAOMI SHIHAB NYE

Naomi Shihab Nye is the kind of writer who could show up at your school or local bookstore. She has been a visiting writer in hundreds of schools and she frequently gives readings. Energetic and always on the move, Nye has not only written in many different genres but has also been singer-songwriter and contributed to two PBS television series.

Published at Age Seven Born in St. Louis, Nye is the daughter of a Palestinian immigrant father and an American mother. She began writing at the age of six, and had her first poem accepted for publication by the age of seven. When she was in high school, her family moved to Jerusalem, where her father edited the *Jerusalem Times.* Nye wrote a column for the same paper. The family's stay in the Middle East ended abruptly, however, when the Six-Day War broke out, and they returned to the United States. Nye continued to publish, working her way from children's magazines to teen magazines and then literary journals.

Although Nye's first major published work was a book of poetry, she has also written essays, a novel for young adults, and many children's books. She has edited collections of poetry, including *This Same Sky,* an anthology of poems that includes one hundred twenty-nine poets from sixty-eight countries. More recently, she brought together poetry from the Middle East in a collection called *Nineteen Varieties of Gazelle.* A third collection called *I Feel a Little Jumpy around You* presents pairs of poems on the same topic, but written from male and female perspectives. It is aimed at teens and shows how gender differences affect people's lives.

On the Move "Field Trip" is part of a collection of essays called *Never In a Hurry.* It represents thirteen years of observation and personal experience with a variety of topics. Wandering is one theme of this book, which includes journeys to places as far away as Hawaii and India, and as close as the local print shop. Although Nye loves to explore mentally and calls travel a "recurrent theme" in her life, she does not think literal movement from place to place is a necessity for writing.

> *"I would adhere to Thoreau's idea that you can stay in your own backyard all your life and have plenty to write about."*
>
> —Naomi Shihab Nye

Today, Nye continues her personal journey in San Antonio, Texas. She writes, edits, and gives readings that take her audiences to new destinations and into new experiences.

Naomi Shihab Nye was born in 1952.

LiteratureOnline **Author Search** For more about Naomi Shihab Nye, go to www.glencoe.com.

Focus

BELLRINGER

Bellringer Options
Selection Focus Transparency 25
Daily Language Practice Transparency 35

Or have students discuss their expectations of a recent school event, such as a test, musical performance, or club activity. Have them contrast their expectations with the events.
Ask: How do expectations influence our behavior? *(They give us a guide to follow.)*
As they read, have students consider what the narrator likes and dislikes about having expectations.

Author Search To expand students' appreciation of Naomi Shihab Nye, have them access the Web site for additional information and resources.

Selection Skills

Field Trip

Literary Elements
- Aphorism (SE pp. 394–398)
- Anecdote (SE p. 398)

Reading Skills
- Connecting to Personal Experience (SE pp. 394–399)
- Identify Sequence (SE p. 396)

Vocabulary Skills
- Analogies (SE pp. 394, 399)
- Academic Vocabulary (SE p. 399)

Listening/Speaking/Viewing Skills
- Interdisciplinary Activity (SE p. 399)

Writing Skills/Grammar
- Evaluate Author's Craft (SE p. 399)

BEFORE YOU READ

Focus

Summary

In this essay, the author describes a school field trip to a printing office that takes an unexpected turn when the guide accidentally cuts off her finger. This experience leads the author to reflect on life experiences that turn out differently than she had expected.

V Vocabulary

Vocabulary File Say: Add these words and definitions to your vocabulary file. For each word, include a sentence that gives you an example of how to use the word. **OL** Students with English language needs should include the pronunciations of these words in their files. **EL**

Literature Online

Literary Elements Have students access the Web site to improve their understanding of aphorism.

LITERATURE PREVIEW

Connecting to the Essay

When unexpected things happen, how do people react to them? As you read the essay, think about the following questions:

- Does this story remind you in any way of field trips you have taken? If so, in what way? If not, why?
- In your opinion, how often do field trips have unexpected educational value?

Building Background

A commercial print shop is a place where written text and art are made into printed products such as business cards, stationery, brochures, posters, newspapers, magazines, and books. A print shop usually has many kinds of machines—including darkroom equipment, printing presses, computers, and photocopiers. It may also have an electric paper cutter that can trim more than five hundred sheets of paper with a single slice of its razor-sharp blade. In this essay, a class visits a print shop to see how pages are bound, or put together to make a book.

Setting Purposes for Reading

Big Idea On the Move

As you read, think about what the class is supposed to learn from the field trip, as well as what the class actually learns.

Literary Element Aphorism

An **aphorism** is a short, pointed statement that expresses a wise or clever observation about human experience. Other terms for aphorism include *saying, maxim,* and *adage*. This quotation from Robert Louis Stevenson is an example of an aphorism on the topic of travel: "To travel hopefully is a better thing than to arrive." As you read "Field Trip," identify the aphorisms that the author includes. Also consider what purpose they serve in the essay.

- See Literary Terms Handbook, p. R2.

Literature Online Interactive Literary Elements Handbook To review or learn more about the literary elements, go to www.glencoe.com.

READING PREVIEW

Reading Strategy Connecting to Personal Experience

Connecting to personal experience is linking what you read to your own life or to other selections. While reading "Field Trip," you may recall field trips that you have experienced or heard about, or events that surprised you or your friends.

Reading Tip: Taking Notes Take notes to show how you connect with details in the essay.

Detail	My Personal Connection
p. 395 "a large group of children on a field trip"	I've been responsible for groups of children as a camp counselor.

Vocabulary

severance (sev′ ər əns) *n.* the act of cutting off or apart; p. 395 *Part of the opening ceremony was the severance of a ribbon across the door.*

excruciating (iks kro͞o′ shē ā′ ting) *adj.* agonizing; intensely painful; p. 396 *Some dental work can result in excruciating pain.*

parched (pärcht) *adj.* severely dry; p. 397 *After a week without rain, the plants were parched.*

console (kən sōl′) *v.* to comfort someone experiencing sorrow or disappointment; p. 397 *Nothing could console Pam when her dog died.*

Vocabulary Tip: Analogies Analogies are comparisons based on the relationships between things or ideas. To complete an analogy, decide what relationship exists in a pair of words and create the same relationship in a second pair of words.

INDIANA ACADEMIC STANDARDS (pages 394–399)
9.3.7 Recognize and understand the significance of various literary devices...
9.3.5 Compare works that express a universal theme...
9.5.2 Write responses to literature...

Selection Resources

Print Materials
- Unit 2 Resources (Fast File), pp. 44–46
- Leveled Vocabulary Development, p. 28
- Selection and Unit Assessments, pp. 61–62
- Selection Quick Checks, p. 31

Transparencies
- Bellringer Options Transparencies: Selection Focus Transparency 25, Daily Language Practice Transparency 35
- Literary Elements Transparency 93

Technology
- TeacherWorks Plus™ CD-ROM
- StudentWorks Plus™ CD-ROM
- Presentation Plus!™ CD-ROM
- Literature Online, glencoe.com
- Online Student Edition, mhln.com
- Exam*View*® Assessment Suite CD-ROM
- Vocabulary PuzzleMaker CD-ROM
- Listening Library, disc 1 track 35

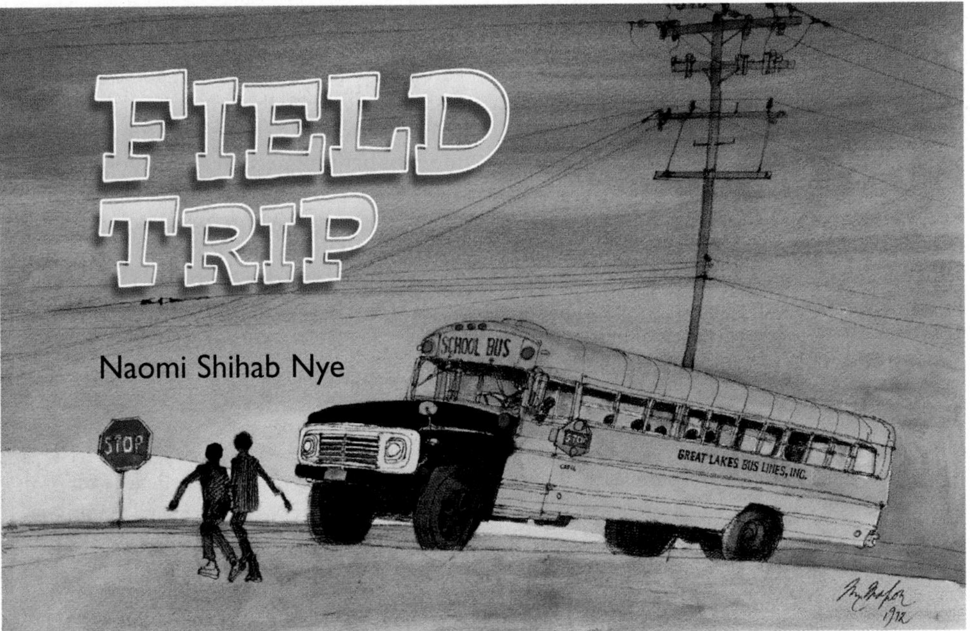

Busing. Franklin McMahon.

BI1 **O**nly once did I ever take a large group of children on a field trip. I took a creative writing workshop to a printing office to see how pages were bound together to make books, and our cheerfully patient guide chopped her finger off with a giant paper cutter.

I had not prepared the children for experiences beyond typeface, camera-ready copy, collation.[1] Standing toward the back like a shepherd, I felt their happy little backs stiffen at the moment of **severance.** A collective gasp rose from their throats as a blot of blood grew outward in a rapid pool, staining all the pages. Cupping her wounded hand against her chest, the woman pressed through the crowd, not screaming, but mouthing silently, "Hospital. Now. Let's go." The children stood motionless, suspended. The motion of the workers was like the flurry of feathers and wings when anyone steps too quickly into a chicken coop. People dialed, then asked one another why they were dialing. Couldn't they drive her to the hospital themselves? Someone at the emergency room said to place the severed finger on ice, and a man who, moments before, had been tediously pasting up layouts ran for ice.

One boy tugged my shirt and croaked, "The last thing she said was—you have to be very careful with this machine."

Someone dropped a ring of keys, and I immediately crawled around on the floor,

1. In the printing industry, a *typeface* is a style of letters to be printed, *camera-ready copy* is text and art arranged on a page, ready to be photographed for printing; and *collation* is the process of sorting pages into the correct order, by hand or machine.

Big Idea On the Move *In what way is a field trip an example of being "on the move"?* BI2

Vocabulary

severance (sev′ ər əns) *n.* the act of cutting off or apart

Reading Strategy Connecting to Personal Experience *How might your own reaction have been similar to or different from the students' reactions?* R

Teach

BI1 Big Idea

On the Move Say: Keep these questions in mind as you read: What are some risks of going to new places? *(Possible answer: meeting unpleasant people, getting lost, having accidents, being bored.)* What does the author learn about risk? *(She learns that chance plays a big role in life.)* OL

BI2 Big Idea

On the Move Answer: *A field trip is an example of being on the move because the class actually travels somewhere.* OL

R Reading Strategy

Connecting to Personal Experience Answer: *Students might say they would have been equally stunned by the awful sight.* OL

Readability Scores
Dale-Chall: 5.5
DRP: 58
Lexile: 1020

English Language Coach

Figurative Language Read aloud the simile that describes the workers' motion. When people walk into a chicken coop, they startle the chickens. The chickens flap their wings, which makes feathers fly into the air. The chickens move a lot but accomplish little, like the worried workers in the story. EL

Reading in the Real World

Citizenship Ask students to read safety signs in your school and community. If possible, have them visit local businesses and find safety signs posted for workers. Ask students to summarize their findings. Discuss how people can contribute to community safety. OL

Academic Standards
Additional Support activities on p. 395 cover the following standards:
English Language Coach: **9.3.7** Recognize and understand…literary devices…
Reading in the Real World: **9.2.4** Synthesize the content…

Teach

R1 Reading Strategy

Connecting to Personal Experience Answer: *Sometimes people react to difficult situations with grim humor.* OL

BI1 Big Idea

On the Move Possible answer: *Yes, parents may worry about their children being traumatized again; No, parents may feel their children learned a valuable life lesson.* OL

R2 Reading Strategy

Connecting to Personal Experience Answer: *Some students might think the accident was a rare event and not a reason to cancel future field trips; others might agree with Nye and be wary of future trips.* OL

★ Medical History

Reattachment Reattaching hand parts is challenging because hands are complex. They contain many nerves, bones, and connective tissues. After undergoing hand surgery, patients need physical therapy, in which they relearn how to use the injured hand. AS

reaching under a desk for them. It felt good to fall to my knees. For a second the stricken woman loomed above me, and I stuttered, apologizing for having distracted her from business, but she was distracted by something else.

"Honey, look at that thing!" she said, staring into the cup of ice where the index finger now rested like a rare archival specimen.[2] "It's turning white! If that finger stays white, I don't want it on my body!"

We laughed long and hard and straight, and the children stared, amazed. Had we lost our senses? That she could joke at such a moment, as the big fans whirred and the collating machines paused over vast mountains of stacked paper . . . I wanted to sing her blackness, the sweet twist of her joy, to call out to those boys and girls, "This, my friends, is what words can do for you—make you laugh when your finger rests in a plastic cup!"

But she went quickly off into the day, and I shuffled an extremely silent group of budding writers back onto our bus. I wanted to say something promising recovery, or praising our guide's remarkable presence of mind, but my voice seemed lost among the seats. No one would look at me.

Later I heard how they went home and went straight to their rooms. Some had nightmares. A mother called my assistant to say, "What in the world happened on that field trip? Sarah came over today, and she and Molly climbed up on the bed and just sobbed."

At our next meeting we forgot poetry and made get-well cards. Or come-together-again cards. May the seam hold. May the two become one. They thought up all kinds of things. I had been calling the printing office to monitor her progress, and the reports sounded good. The students had been gathering stories: someone's farmer-uncle whose leg was severed in a cornfield but who lived to see it joined; someone's brother's toe.

I went to her home with a bundle of hopeful wishes tied in loops of pink ribbon. She was wearing a terry-cloth bathrobe and sitting in a comfortable chair, her hand hugely bandaged.

She shook her head. "I guess none of those cute kids will ever become printers now, will they? Gee, I hope they don't stop reading and writing! And to think of it happening in front of such an interested audience! Oh, I feel just terrible about it."

Reading their messages made her chuckle. I asked what the doctors had said about the finger turning black again. She said they thought it would, but it might be slightly paler than the rest of her hand. And it would be stiff, for a long time, maybe forever. ★

She missed being at work; vacations weren't much fun when they came this unexpectedly. The pain had been **excruciating** at first but was easing now, and wasn't modern medicine incredible, and would I please thank those kids for their flowers and hearts!

Once I'd dreamed of visiting every factory in town, the mattress factory, the hot sauce factory, the assembly line for cowboy boots, but I changed my mind. Now I took my workshops out onto the schoolyard, but no farther. I made them look for buttons and feathers, I made them describe the ways men and women stood as they waited for a bus.

2. Archives (är′ kīvz) are a storage area, usually within a museum or a library, where documents or objects of historical or scientific interest are preserved. An *archival specimen*—such as a fossil or a rare book—is something kept in archives.

Reading Strategy Connecting to Personal Experience *Do you find this comment to be believable? Explain.* R1

Big Idea On the Move *Do you think the parents will think twice before allowing their children to go on another field trip? Explain.* BI1

Reading Strategy Connecting to Personal Experience *If you were Nye, how would you have reacted?* R2

Vocabulary

excruciating (iks kroo′ shē ā′ ting) *adj.* agonizing; intensely painful

Additional Support

Leveled Reading An adapted version of this selection is available on page 224 of *Jamestown Literature: An Adapted Reader*, grade 9.

Skills Practice

READING: Identifying Sequence Point out that several weeks or months transpire during the author's essay. She uses many sequence words, for example, *immediately, later,* and *at our next meeting.* Have students find other examples of sequence words, and use them to keep track of events. Provide pairs of events, and ask students to name the sequence in which they occur, for example: the author's visit to the printer at the hospital and her visit to the state mental hospital. *(1: state mental hospital; 2: printer)* OL

By the time our workshops ended that summer, we felt more deeply bonded than other groups I'd known. Maybe our sense of mortality linked us, our shared vision of the fragility of body parts. One girl went on to become one of the best young writers in the city. I'd like to think her hands were blessed by our unexpected obsession with hands.

Visual Vocabulary *David* (Davy) *Crockett*—pioneer, frontiersman, and Tennessee politician—became an American folk hero after being killed in 1836, while fighting to defend the Alamo against Mexican forces.

I continued to think about field trips in general. In San Antonio, school children are taken to the Hall of Horns, where legions[3] of exotic stuffed birds and beasts and fish stare back at them from glass habitats; to the missions, where the Indians' mounded bread ovens still rise from **parched** grass; and to the Alamo, where David Crockett's fork and fringed vest continue to reside. Here, we say, for your information, soak it up. See what you can learn.

It was not always predictable. At the state mental hospital, my high school health teacher unwittingly herded us into a room of elderly women who'd recently had lobotomies,[4] just after telling us doctors didn't do that to people anymore.

On the day Robert Kennedy[5] was shot we found ourselves, numbed, staring at vats of creamy chocolate brew at the Judson Candy Factory. The air hung thickly around us. It didn't make much sense to consider all that work for something that wasn't even good for you. A worker joked that a few of his friends had ended up in those vats, and no one smiled.

As a child I finally grew brave enough to plot a camping trip years after my friends had first done it—to Camp Fiddlecreek for Girl Scouts. I'd postponed such an adventure because of a profound and unreasonable fear of spiders. I felt certain a giant spider would crawl into my bedroll and entangle itself in my hair the moment I got there. The zipper on the sleeping bag would stick, and I would die, die, die. Luckily I finally decided a life without courage might be worse than death, so I packed my greenest duds and headed to the hills.

The first night I confided my secret fear to the girl who slept next to me. She said she'd always been more scared of snakes than spiders. I said, "Snakes, phooey!"

The next day while we were hiking, a group of donkeys broke out of a nearby field, ran at us, knocked me down, and trampled me. My leg swelled with three large, hard lumps. I could not walk. I would have to be driven back to the city for X rays. My friend leaned over my bruised face, smoothing back my bangs and **consoling** me. "Donkeys! Can you believe it? Who could ever dream a donkey would be so mean?"

So began a lifetime of small discoveries linked by a common theme: the things we worry about are never the things that happen. And the things that happen are the things we never could have dreamed. ★

3. Here, *legions* means "huge numbers."
4. *Lobotomies* are surgical operations in which nerve connections in the brain are cut in an attempt to control inappropriate behavior of certain mentally ill patients.
5. *Robert Kennedy* was assassinated while campaigning as a Democratic presidential candidate in 1968.

Big Idea On the Move *What learning experiences do field trips include?* **BI2**

Vocabulary

parched (pärcht) *adj.* severely dry

Literary Element Aphorism *Explain why this is an aphorism.* **L1**

Literary Element Aphorism *Restate this aphorism in your own words.* **L2**

Vocabulary

console (kən sōl′) *v.* to comfort someone experiencing sorrow or disappointment

Teach

BI2 Big Idea

On the Move **Answer:** *Field trips may include unexpected lessons; they can also contradict what people believe.* **OL**

L1 Literary Element

Aphorism **Answer:** *It is a brief statement that expresses wisdom about life or human experience.* **OL**

L2 Literary Element

Aphorism **Answer:** *There is no way to know what will happen. You may worry about one thing, and something else may be the problem.* **OL**

★ Cultural History

Aphorisms Historians trace aphorisms to Hippocrates, an ancient Greek scholar and physician, who used them in writing about the healing process. Today, we see aphorisms in many places, such as on the slips of paper inside fortune cookies. **AS**

English Language Coach

Proper Nouns Point out proper nouns in the essay: *San Antonio, Robert Kennedy, Camp Fiddlecreek for Girl Scouts.* Explain that proper nouns refer to specific people, places, or things and must be capitalized. Have students write three sentences using lower case for proper nouns, trade papers, and capitalize proper nouns correctly. **EL**

Differentiated Instruction

Get-Well Cards The children make get-well cards for the injured printer. Discuss customs for sending greeting cards. Suggest that students design get-well cards for the guide that reflect the essay details and an understanding of the printer's personality and sense of humor. **BL**

Academic Standards

Additional Support activities on pp. 396 and 397 cover the following standards:

Skills Practice: **9.3.6** Analyze and trace… time and sequence…

English Language Coach: **9.6** Use appropriate mechanics of writing, such as…grammar [and] capitalization…

Differentiated Instruction: **9.5.8** Write for different purposes and audiences…

AFTER YOU READ

Assess

1. Possible answers: the printer's accident; the camping trip incident
2. (a) The print shop explodes into chaos. (b) Disbelief
3. (a) At first, they are horrified. Later, some have nightmares. In time, they share hopeful stories of recovery. (b) Stories calm the children with positive outcomes. (c) Cards express their feelings.
4. (a) She sees women who have had lobotomies. The chocolate factory trip occurs the day Robert Kennedy is shot. (b) Students should note contrasts between outcome and expectations.
5. Students' answers should focus on Nye's word choice.
6. (a) The two main parts of the essay are 1) the accident in the print shop and its aftermath and 2) other field trips that contrast outcome and expectation. The order moves from most startling and developed to less important and developed. All the anecdotes lead to the concluding thesis. (b) Possible answer: Yes, it grabs readers' interest and supports the final thesis.
7. Possible answer: Yes, Nye draws wisdom about life—"pull[s] gold"—from the ordinary event of a field trip. However, the trip to the printer is not at all ordinary.
8. Students should use personal experience to support their opinions.

AFTER YOU READ

RESPONDING AND THINKING CRITICALLY

Respond

1. What part of this essay did you visualize or experience most vividly as you read?

Recall and Interpret

2. (a)How do the people in the print shop react to the accident? (b)What seems to be going on in the minds of the children, teacher, and coworkers at the moment of the accident?
3. (a)How do the children respond immediately after the incident and in the days that follow? (b)Why might the children have shared stories of similar events? (c)What purpose do their handcrafted cards serve?
4. (a)Name two unexpected things that happened to the author on other field trips or outings. (b)Choose one of the field trips the author describes in the essay and explain why the events might be considered ironic.

Analyze and Evaluate

5. Is this essay funny, serious, or both? Use examples from the text to explain your response.
6. (a)How does Nye structure her essay? That is, what parts does she include, and in what order does she put them? (b)Is this structure effective? Explain.
7. Critic Mary Logue says that Nye "often pulls gold from the ordinary." In your opinion, how well does "Field Trip" prove or disprove this statement? Use evidence from the essay in your response.

Connect

8. **Big Idea** **On the Move** Do you think that field trips are a necessary or important part of education? Use your own experiences to explain your opinion.

LITERARY ANALYSIS

Literary Element Aphorism

Because an **aphorism** often sums up the meaning of personal experience, it may be used in a nonfiction essay as a topic sentence, as a concluding thought, or as a thesis, or main idea. When an aphorism is used as a summary statement, the events and details of the essay may lead up to or follow the statement in order to develop and support it.

1. (a)What conclusion does the author draw about field trips, and by extension, about life? (b)Why is Nye's conclusion about field trips an aphorism?
2. Where does Nye state her aphorism about unexpected events? Why do you think she states it where she does?
3. How do Nye's examples lead up to and support or prove her aphorisms?

Review: Anecdote

As you learned on page 341, an **anecdote** is a brief account of an interesting event. Essayists often use anecdotes to support their opinions, clarify their ideas, get a reader's attention, or entertain.

Partner Activity Work with a classmate to record at least three anecdotes, or little stories, that Nye tells in this essay. Then draw a conclusion about her purpose for including the anecdotes.

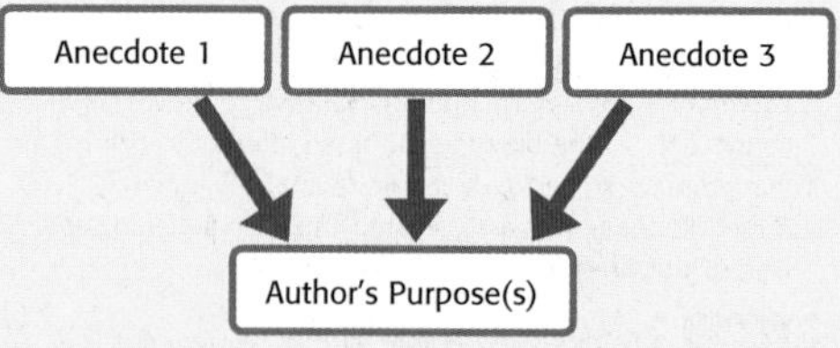

Literary Element

1. (a) People worry about things that don't happen, and must face things they never imagined. (b) It is a brief statement about human experience.
2. Nye's thesis concludes her essay. Readers can reach this conclusion, and Nye can state it dramatically.
3. They all took an unexpected turn.

Review: Anecdote

One anecdote is about the field trip to the print shop.

Another anecdote tells about a trip to the mental hospital.

A third anecdote describes a camping trip.

The author's purpose is to entertain and to express a truth about life.

READING AND VOCABULARY

Reading Strategy Connecting to Personal Experience

The central idea, or thesis, of this essay is a direct statement about human experience. Review the chart you created showing your personal connection to various details in the story. Then focus on the essay's thesis.

1. Do you agree with Nye's conclusion? What experiences in your own life support or disprove her conclusion?
2. What general statement about life would you make based on your own experiences with field trips? Explain.

Vocabulary Practice

Practice with Analogies Choose the word that best completes each analogy.

1. starving : hungry :: parched :
   a. sandy **b.** dry **c.** hot
2. scissors : severance :: ruler :
   a. inch **b.** length **c.** measurement
3. confine : release :: console :
   a. upset **b.** sympathize **c.** reveal
4. excellent : good :: excruciating :
   a. pleasant **b.** painful **c.** sharp
5. tediously : dully :: readily :
   a. eagerly **b.** slowly **c.** fully

Academic Vocabulary

Here are two words from the vocabulary list on page R80.

anticipate (an tis′ ə pāt′) *v.* expect and take steps to deal with

inevitable (i nev′ ə tə bəl) *adj.* destined to happen; unable to be avoided

Practice and Apply

1. According to Nye, when groups go on field trips, what can they **anticipate** will happen?
2. Was what happened in the print shop **inevitable?** Explain.

WRITING AND EXTENDING

Writing About Literature

Evaluate Author's Craft Did "Field Trip" hold your attention from beginning to end? Why or why not? Write an evaluation of the essay explaining why the work was successful or how it could be revised so that it would be compelling from beginning to end.

As you draft, follow this organizational plan:

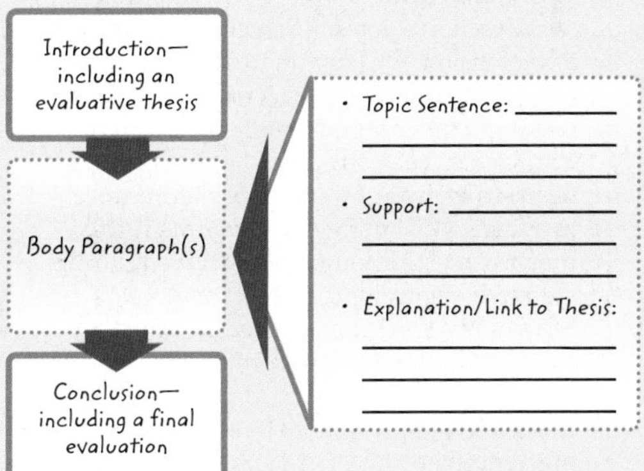

After you complete your draft, have a peer reviewer read it and suggest revisions. Then proofread and edit your work to correct errors in spelling, grammar, and punctuation.

Interdisciplinary Activity: Art

If "Field Trip" were a painting, what colors would be on the canvas? Which parts of the essay would best be represented by warm colors, such as red or orange? Which parts would best be represented by cool colors, such as blue or green? Photocopy the essay. Then, using colored pencils or markers and a color wheel for reference, shade or outline the passages with the appropriate color or colors. Finally, write a brief explanation of why the events or emotional contentof each passage led you to select particular colors.

LiteratureOnline **Web Activities** For eFlashcards, Selection Quick Checks, and other Web activities, go to www.glencoe.com.

AFTER YOU READ

Assess

Reading Strategy

1. Students should use their personal experience of field trips, camping trips, or other trips to support their answer.
2. Possible answer: Sometimes you need someone else to show you the places that end up important in your life.

Vocabulary

1. b **2.** c **3.** a **4.** b **5.** a

Academic Vocabulary

1. According to Nye, no one can truly anticipate what will happen on a field trip.
2. It was not inevitable. Instead, it was a random and highly unusual event.

Writing About Literature

Students' essays should

- have a clearly stated thesis.
- include several body paragraphs with supporting evidence for the thesis.
- link the evidence in a logical way to the thesis.
- provide a conclusion that summarizes the thesis and offers readers a new insight.

Interdisciplinary Activity

Before students begin, have them meet in groups to discuss the emotions and connotations associated with different colors.

LiteratureOnline

Web Activities Have students access the Web site for interactive activities that will help them assess their understanding of the selection.

BEFORE YOU READ

Focus

BELLRINGER

Bellringer Options
Selection Focus Transparency 26
Daily Language Practice Transparency 36

Or show students photographs of different landscapes, from hilly, contained places, such as New England, to wide-open places, such as Wyoming.
Ask: How are these places different? Which appeals to you? Why? *(Students should note differences in topography, color, vegetation, and light; students' preferences will vary.)* As they read, have students consider how the author's surroundings make her feel.

Author Search To expand students' appreciation of Gretel Ehrlich, have them access the Web site for additional information and resources.

BEFORE YOU READ

The Solace of Open Spaces

MEET GRETEL EHRLICH

Late in the summer of 1991, Gretel Ehrlich was walking with her dog out on her Wyoming ranch. Suddenly, after a brief vision, Ehrlich found herself lying on the ground. Her heart was racing and she could not talk or move her legs or arms. Ehrlich had been struck by lightning. She had been struck by lightning once before since arriving in Wyoming, but this time it was much worse. Although she survived, Ehrlich suffered serious injuries and spent years recovering. Ehrlich continued writing throughout those years, turning her near-fatal experience into a book, *A Match to the Heart*. Ehrlich has journeyed all over the world, writing about her travels in works of rich descriptive power.

Life on the Range Ehrlich was born on a horse ranch near Santa Barbara, California. After high school, she attended Bennington College in Vermont. With ambitions to become a filmmaker, Ehrlich went on to film school at UCLA and spent a decade working on films. Her work eventually brought her to Wyoming, where she recorded details of life on a 250,000-acre sheep and cattle ranch. In 1978, after the death of a loved one, Ehrlich decided to stay in Wyoming and become a full-time writer. Ehrlich's experiences there became the subject of a collection of essays, *The Solace of Open Spaces*, published in 1984.

"I like big, open, spare landscapes. There's lots of room. Nobody bothers you. . . . I feel as if I can think there."

—Gretel Ehrlich

World Traveler Ehrlich's books since then reveal her fascination with out-of-the-way, desolate places where the people are hardy and self-reliant. In Greenland, Ehrlich spent years living with the native people, the Inuit. She helped run a dog sled team, ate native foods such as polar bear, and lived through Arctic summers when the sun never set and Arctic winters when the sun never rose. She has also traveled extensively in Tibet, China, Japan, Africa, and South America. She is an adventurer with an admiration for world culture and a tireless thirst for travel.

Asked what advice she would give to aspiring writers of nonfiction, Ehrlich replied: "I would offer the same advice to anyone writing anything: read. Read widely of the best things written in every genre . . . poetry, prose, fiction, nonfiction, science. Just everything. . . . And I would also advise you to always be awake, aware, alive, observant. Neither grasping nor rejecting, just letting things soak in."

Gretel Ehrlich was born in 1946.

Literature Online **Author Search** For more about Gretel Ehrlich, go to www.glencoe.com.

Selection Skills

The Solace of Open Spaces

Literary Elements
- Descriptive Essay (SE pp. 401–406)
- Setting (SE p. 406)

Reading Skills
- Visualizing (SE pp. 401–406)
- Cause and Effect (TWE p. 404)

Vocabulary Skills
- Word Origins (SE pp. 401, 406)
- Academic Vocabulary (SE p. 406)

Listening/Speaking/Viewing Skills
- Analyzing Art (SE p. 404)
- Group Activity (SE p. 405)

Writing Skills/Grammar
- Analysis of Mood (SE p. 407)
- Using Vivid Verbs (SE p. 407)

Study Skills/Research/Assessment
- Reading Further (SE p. 407)

LITERATURE PREVIEW

Connecting to the Essay

The essay you are about to read describes life in a very sparsely populated place. Before you read, consider the following questions:

- Why do some people enjoy spending time in isolated places?
- How would you spend your time if you were staying somewhere far from people?

Building Background

The state of Wyoming—the setting of Ehrlich's memoir—is located in the western United States. The tenth largest state in terms of area, Wyoming has the smallest population of any state in the country. Wyoming's population density (the number of people per square mile) is lower than that of any other state except Alaska. Much of Wyoming is made up of badlands, areas marked by scant vegetation, unusual hill formations, mesas, and land sculpted by erosion. The keeping of large herds of livestock is a long tradition. Because of dry, arid conditions, the state is not suited to farming, but is excellent for ranching. It is also rich in mineral resources and has a significant mining industry.

Setting Purposes for Reading

Big Idea On the Move

As you read, notice how important travel is to the life of the rancher.

Literary Element Descriptive Essay

Descriptive essays use carefully selected details to help readers picture an object or place. In this essay, Ehrlich uses vivid details to describe life in Wyoming. Many of these details are sensory details, words that convey sensory experiences such as seeing, hearing, touching, tasting, and smelling. As you read, notice the sensory details.

- See Literary Terms Handbook, p. R5.

Literature Online Interactive Literary Terms Handbook To review or learn more about the literary elements, go to www.glencoe.com.

READING PREVIEW

Reading Strategy Visualizing

Visualizing is picturing a writer's ideas or descriptions in your mind's eye. Visualizing can help you better understand what an author is trying to show you or tell you. It can also help you remember what you read.

Reading Tip: Sketching As you read, pause to visualize the descriptions presented by Ehrlich. Jot down quick sketches of what you see in your mind's eye.

Vocabulary

replenish (ri plen′ ish) *v.* to fill, supply, or build up again; p. 402 *Please replenish the table with napkins when we run out.*

affluence (af′ lo͞o əns) *n.* wealth; abundance of property; p. 403 *Martha's expensive clothing was indicative of her affluence.*

haphazardly (hap′ haz′ ərd lē) *adv.* in a random or disorderly manner; p. 403 *The hats in the display window were placed haphazardly, as if someone had thrown them in the air and left them where they landed.*

fugitive (fū′ jə tiv) *adj.* intending flight; running away or fleeing; p. 404 *The fugitive goose flew far from the flock.*

Vocabulary Tip: Word Origins A word's origin can be determined by examining its history. To find a word's history, also called its etymology, refer to a dictionary. For example, the word *plateau* derives from the Middle French word *plat,* meaning "flat." Knowing this history makes it easier to determine and remember the meaning of *plateau*—an area of land that is higher than the surrounding land and has a flat surface.

INDIANA ACADEMIC STANDARDS (pages 401–407)

9.3.7 Recognize and understand the significance of…imagery…

9.2 Develop [reading] strategies…

9.5.3 Write expository compositions, including analytical essays…

9.3.13 Explain how voice…affect[s] the mood…of text.

BEFORE YOU READ

Focus

Summary

In this essay, the author describes her years in the open spaces of Wyoming. She vividly outlines the extremes of Wyoming weather, from arid summers to bitter cold winters. She focuses on how the solitude of Wyoming's open spaces affects the people there—they speak little and guard their feelings closely. She notes that solitude has nourished her and enabled her to see what is important in life.

V Vocabulary

Vocabulary File Say: Add these words and definitions to your vocabulary file. For each word, include a sentence that gives you an example of how to use the word. **OL** Students with English language needs should include the pronunciations of these words in their files. **EL**

Literary Elements Have students access the Web site to improve their understanding of descriptive essay.

Selection Resources

Print Materials
- Unit 2 Resources (Fast File), pp. 47–49
- Leveled Vocabulary Development, p. 29
- Selection and Unit Assessments, pp. 63–64
- Selection Quick Checks, p. 33

Transparencies
- Bellringer Options Transparencies: Selection Focus Transparency 26, Daily Language Practice Transparency 36
- Literary Elements Transparencies 11, 34

Technology
- TeacherWorks Plus™ CD-ROM
- StudentWorks Plus™ CD-ROM
- Presentation Plus!™ CD-ROM
- Literature Online, glencoe.com
- Online Student Edition, mhln.com
- Exam*View*® Assessment Suite CD-ROM
- Vocabulary PuzzleMaker CD-ROM
- Listening Library, disc 1 track 36

Teach

BI1 Big Idea

On the Move **Ask:** Why can't the author bring herself to leave Wyoming? *(Possible answer: She feels deeply attached to its solitude.)* How does staying turn out to be the same as going? How is movement involved in both choices? *(Possible answer: Staying involves a lot of moving, as going would have done.)* OL

R Reading Strategy

Visualizing **Answer:** *She is describing it from a distance, as if looking down from space and seeing the landscape of the whole state at once.* OL

★ Cultural History

Ranching Most ranches in the United States raise cattle or sheep. It takes a lot of land to grow the grass these animals eat, but on the wide-open spaces of Wyoming, the average ranch has roughly 3,350 acres. AS

Readability Scores
Dale-Chall: 7.0
DRP: 62
Lexile: 1130

The Solace of Open Places

Gretel Ehrlich

Landscape, 1950. Olive Fell. 19½ x 23⅓ in. Buffalo Bill Historical Center, Cody, Wyoming.

It's May and I've just awakened from a nap, curled against sagebrush[1] the way my dog taught me to sleep—sheltered from wind. A front is pulling the huge sky over me, and from the dark a hailstone has hit me on the head. I'm trailing a band of two thousand sheep across a stretch of Wyoming badlands, a fifty-mile trip that takes five days because sheep shade up in hot sun and won't budge until it's cool. Bunched together now, and excited into a run by the storm, they drift across dry land, tumbling into draws[2] like water and surge out again onto the rugged, choppy plateaus[3] that are the building blocks of this state. BI1

The name Wyoming comes from an Indian word meaning "at the great plains," but the plains are really valleys, great arid valleys, sixteen hundred square miles, with the horizon bending up on all sides into mountain ranges. This gives the vastness a sheltering look. ★

Winter lasts six months here. Prevailing winds spill snowdrifts to the east, and new storms from the northwest **replenish** them. This white bulk is sometimes dizzying, even nauseating, to look at. At twenty, thirty, and forty degrees below zero, not only does your car not work, but neither do your mind and body. The landscape hardens into a dungeon of

1. *Sagebrush* is a shrub that grows in the plains of the western United States.
2. *Draws* are shallow trenches worn into the earth by running water.
3. A *plateau* is an area of land with a level surface, raised sharply above nearby land.

Reading Strategy Visualizing *Visualize the land formation. From what perspective is Ehrlich describing the land?* R

Vocabulary

replenish (ri plen′ ish) *v.* to fill, supply, or build up again

Additional Support

Skills Practice

LITERARY ELEMENT: Metaphor/Simile Figurative language creates mental pictures for readers and helps essayists convey images through comparison. Similes are comparisons linked by *like* or *as.* Metaphors are comparisons without these links. Point out these examples from the selection:

- metaphor: *The landscape hardens into a dungeon of space.*
- simile: *I felt like the first person on earth, or the last.*

Have students list other metaphors and similes as they read. OL space. During the winter, while I was riding to find a new calf, my jeans froze to the saddle, and in the silence that such cold creates I felt like the first person on earth, or the last.

Today the sun is out—only a few clouds billowing. In the east, where the sheep have started off without me, the benchland tilts up in a series of eroded red-earthed mesas, planed flat on top by a million years of water; behind them, a bold line of muscular scarps rears up ten thousand feet to become the Big Horn Mountains.[4] A tidal pattern is engraved into the ground, as if left by the sea that once covered this state. Canyons curve down like galaxies to meet the oncoming rush of flat land.

To live and work in this kind of open country, with its hundred-mile views, is to lose the distinction between background and foreground. When I asked an older ranch hand to describe Wyoming's openness, he said, "It's all a bunch of nothing—wind and rattlesnakes—and so much of it you can't tell where you're going or where you've been and it don't make much difference." John, a sheepman I know, is tall and handsome and has an explosive temperament. He has a perfect intuition about people and sheep. They call him "Highpockets," because he's so long-legged; his graceful stride matches the distances he has to cover. He says, "Open space hasn't affected me at all. It's all the people moving in on it." The huge ranch he was born on takes up much of one county and spreads into another state; to put 100,000 miles on his pickup in three years and never leave home is not unusual. A friend of mine has an aunt who ranched on Powder River and didn't go off her place for eleven years. When her husband died, she quickly moved to town, bought a car, and drove around the States to see what she'd been missing.

Most people tell me they've simply driven through Wyoming, as if there were nothing to stop for. Or else they've skied in Jackson Hole, a place Wyomingites acknowledge uncomfortably because its green beauty and chic **affluence** are mismatched with the rest of the state. Most of Wyoming has a "lean-to" look. Instead of big, roomy barns and Victorian houses, there are dugouts, low sheds, log cabins, sheep camps, and fence lines that look like driftwood blown **haphazardly** into place. People here still feel pride because they live in such a harsh place, part of the glamorous cowboy past, and they are determined not to be the victims of a mining-dominated future.

Most characteristic of the state's landscape is what a developer euphemistically describes as "indigenous growth right up to your front door"—a reference to waterless stands of salt sage, snakes, jack rabbits, deerflies, red dust, a brief respite of wildflowers, dry washes, and no trees. In the Great Plains the vistas look like music, like Kyries[5] of grass, but Wyoming seems to be the doing of a mad architect—tumbled and twisted, ribboned with faded, deathbed colors, thrust up and pulled down as if the place had been startled out of a deep sleep and thrown into a pure light.

I came here four years ago. I had not planned to stay, but I couldn't make myself leave. John, the sheepman, put me to work immediately. It was spring, and shearing time. For fourteen days of fourteen hours

4. *Benchland* refers to a shelf of land interrupting slopes. *Mesas* are isolated bits of elevated land. A *scarp* is a steep slope or long cliff that usually results from erosion. The *Big Horn Mountains* extend from southern Wyoming into Montana.

5. A *Kyrie* is a repetitive prayer, often sung, in some Christian religions. The prayer repeats the phrase "Kyrie eleison," which is Greek for "Lord have mercy."

Big Idea On the Move *What kind of travel is a routine part of life on ranches in Wyoming?* **BI2**

Literary Element Descriptive Essay *In what way does Wyoming resemble the work of "a mad architect"?* **L**

Vocabulary

affluence (af′ lo͞o əns) *n.* wealth; abundance of property

haphazardly (hap′ haz′ ərd lē) *adv.* in a random or disorderly manner

Teach

BI2 Big Idea

On the Move Answer: *It is routine to walk long distances and drive many thousands of miles.* **OL**

L Literary Element

Descriptive Essay Answer: *The land is formed into intricate and fantastic structures.* **OL**

CheckPoint

Use the CheckPoint questions on Presentation Plus! to monitor students' comprehension. These questions can be used with interactive response keypads for immediate student feedback.

English Language Coach

Build Background Help students unfamiliar with the American west find Wyoming on a U.S. map. Show photos of the Wyoming landscape and the activities of cattle and sheep ranching. Ask students to share any knowledge they have of ranching. **EL**

Differentiated Instruction

Narrative Structure Point out the text "I came here four years ago." The author jumps back in time in order to provide background on her experience in Wyoming. She begins in present tense, then switches to past tense. Ask students to read slowly and reread as needed to keep track of events. **BL**

Academic Standards

Additional Support activities on pp. 402 and 403 cover the following standards:

Skills Practice: **9.3.7** Recognize and understand the significance of…literary devices, including figurative language…

English Language Coach: **9.3** [Identify] story elements such as…setting…

Differentiated Instruction: **9.3.6** Analyze and trace an author's development of time and sequence, including the use of…flashbacks…

Teach

R Reading Strategy

Visualizing Answer: *The land is sparse, and the towns and settlements look out of place.* OL

Viewing the Art

Answer: *The painting reflects Ehrlich's description of the wide-open landscape.*

Thomas Eakins (1844–1916) created precise, realistic paintings and photographs. He is well known for his boating scenes set in his native Philadelphia. AS

CheckPoint

Use the CheckPoint questions on Presentation Plus! to check students' mastery of the selection. These questions can be used with interactive response keypads for immediate student feedback.

Cowboys in the Badlands, 1888. Thomas Eakins.
Viewing the Art: How does this painting reflect Ehrlich's descriptions of Wyoming? ★

each, we moved thousands of sheep through sorting corrals to be sheared, branded, and deloused. I suspect that my original motive for coming here was to "lose myself" in new and unpopulated territory. Instead of producing the numbness I thought I wanted, life on the sheep ranch woke me up. The vitality of the people I was working with flushed out what had become a hallucinatory rawness inside me. I threw away my clothes and bought new ones; I cut my hair. The arid country was a clean slate. Its absolute indifference steadied me.

Sagebrush covers 58,000 square miles of Wyoming. The biggest city has a population of fifty thousand, and there are only five settlements that could be called cities in the whole state. The rest are towns, scattered across the expanse with as much as sixty miles between them, their populations two thousand, fifty, or ten. They are **fugitive**-looking, perched on a barren, windblown bench, or tagged onto a river or a railroad, or laid out straight in a farming valley with implement stores and a block-long Mormon church. In the eastern part of the state, which slides down into the Great Plains, the new mining settlements are boomtowns, trailer cities, metal knots on flat land.

Despite the desolate look, there's a coziness to living in this state. There are so few people (only 470,000) that ranchers who buy and sell cattle know one another statewide; the kids who choose to go to college usually go to the state's one university, in Laramie; hired hands work their way around Wyoming in a lifetime of hirings and firings. And despite the physical separation, people stay in touch, often driving two or three hours to another ranch for dinner.

Seventy-five years ago, when travel was by buckboard[6] or horseback, cowboys who were temporarily out of work rode the grub line—drifting from ranch to ranch, mending fences or milking cows, and receiving in exchange a bed and meals. Gossip and messages traveled this slow circuit with them, creating an intimacy between ranchers who were three and four weeks' ride apart. One old-time couple I know, whose turn-of-the-century homestead was used by an outlaw gang as a relay station for stolen horses, recall that if you were traveling, desperado or not, any lighted ranch house was a welcome sign. Even now, for someone who lives in a remote spot, arriving at a ranch or coming to town for supplies is cause for celebration. To emerge from isolation can be disorienting. Everything looks bright, new, vivid. After I had been herding sheep for only three days, the sound of the camp tender's pickup flustered me. Longing for human company, I felt a foolish grin take over my face; yet I had to resist an urgent temptation to run and hide.

Vocabulary

fugitive (fū′ jə tiv) *adj.* intending flight; running away or fleeing

6. A *buckboard* is a four-wheeled open carriage with a floor made of long, springy boards.

Reading Strategy Visualizing *From the descriptions in this paragraph, how do you visualize the towns and settlements in Wyoming?* R

Additional Support

Skills Practice

READING: Understanding Cause and Effect The author describes the impact of the weather on herself and the landscape around her. Have students use a cause/effect chart to list the four seasons and the impact of weather in each.

Weather	Impact
Spring	Houses destroyed by tornadoes, snow melts, full rivers destroy bridges

Ask students to explain which season's weather they would find most challenging. OL

RESPONDING AND THINKING CRITICALLY

Respond

1. What image or description in this essay did you find most powerful? Explain.

Recall and Interpret

2. (a)According to Ehrlich, what is the landscape like in Wyoming? (b)What element of the landscape seems to have the most importance for people who live in Wyoming?
3. (a)How does the author spend her time in Wyoming? (b)How would you describe the lifestyle of Wyomingites in general?
4. (a)Are the people Ehrlich describes friendly or quiet? (b)Does the landscape affect their personalities? Explain.

Analyze and Evaluate

5. In your opinion, what anecdote or story in the essay best explains what life is like in Wyoming? Explain.
6. (a)How does moving to Wyoming affect the author? (b)What details in the essay suggest the impact Wyoming has had on her?
7. The author's purpose is the author's reason for writing a work. In your opinion, what was Ehrlich's purpose for writing this essay? Explain.

Connect

8. **Big Idea** **On the Move** Is Wyoming the kind of place you would want to visit or live in someday? Use details from the essay to support your answer.

PRIMARY SOURCE QUOTATION

A Heart's Home

In interviews, Gretel Ehrlich has discussed her opinions of Wyoming, where she has lived for over seventeen years. Ehrlich has said, "I feel as if I can think there. Nobody's trying to be anything that they're not, and they don't really care who you are, particularly." To find out more about Ehrlich's feelings for Wyoming, read the quotation below.

> *"I think people find what [author] Edward Hoagland calls 'your heart's home.' I didn't move [to Wyoming] because I read a book about it; I just ended up there, and I found it suited me. I think it's good for people to just roam around. Stay where your car breaks down."*
>
> —Gretel Ehrlich

Group Activity Discuss the following questions with classmates. Refer to the quotation and cite evidence from "The Solace of Open Spaces" for support.

1. (a)How does "The Solace of Open Spaces" support Ehrlich's statement that "it's good for people to just roam around"? (b)What attributes of Wyoming make it Ehrlich's "heart's home"?
2. Why do you think that Ehrlich advises people to "stay where your car breaks down"?

AFTER YOU READ

Assess

1. Students should support their answers.
2. (a) Possible answer: It is sparse, with "hundred-mile views." (b) Possible answer: The vast distance between human settlements has the biggest effect on people.
3. (a) She spends her time working on ranches. (b) People in Wyoming work hard and spend a lot of time alone.
4. (a) The people are friendly because they are so isolated and need companionship, but they also are quiet because they are used to being alone. (b) The harsh landscape makes people proud and determined to protect the land.
5. Students should support their answers.
6. (a) Possible answer: Wyoming has "woken up" the author by giving her vitality and helping her see the world anew. (b) Students should support their answers.
7. Possible answer: She wished to write about Wyoming since many people drive through the state but do not stop to explore it.
8. Students should use passages and details from the essay to support their opinions.

Primary Source Quotation

1. Possible answers: (a) Ehrlich suggests that people in Wyoming become humble, wise, and more attuned to nature. (b) The silence, quiet, and open spaces of Wyoming, as well as the quirky warmth of its people, make Wyoming special to the author.
2. Possible answer: She thinks people should be adventurous and spontaneous. She believes chance encounters can lead to important and unexpected revelations about oneself.

Academic Standards

The Additional Support activity on p. 404 covers the following standard:

Skills Practice: **9.3** [Identify] story elements such as...plot, and setting...and [make] connections...

AFTER YOU READ

Assess

Literary Element

1. Students should support their answers.
2. (a–b) Students should support their answers.

Review: Setting

Possible answer: Details might include wide-open spaces and harsh climate. Inferences might be that life is lonely, challenging, and rewarding.

Reading Strategy

1. Students should support their answers.
2. Possible answer: The landscape was easier to visualize because the author used descriptive language so effectively.

Vocabulary

1. c
2. b
3. c
4. b

LITERARY ANALYSIS

Literary Element Descriptive Essay

A **descriptive essay** gives a carefully detailed portrayal of a place or a thing. Writers often use sensory details in their description to help readers understand what something looks like, sounds like, and feels like. Ehrlich uses sensory details to describe winter in Wyoming: "This white bulk is sometimes dizzying, even nauseating, to look at. . . . the landscape hardens into a dungeon of space."

1. List five descriptive details that help you picture Wyoming. Explain what you find interesting or evocative about the details.
2. (a)What details does Ehrlich use to describe ranches, settlements, and towns in Wyoming? (b)What details does she use to describe sheep herding and winter weather?

Review: Setting

As you learned on pages 10–11, **setting** is the time and place in which the events of a work occur. In addition to a place's physical characteristics, setting also includes the history, customs, and values of the people who live there.

Partner Activity With a partner, discuss Wyoming and its people as they are described in the essay. What would it be like to live in a place as spacious as Wyoming? What insights might you gain by living there? What lifestyle does it foster? With your partner, create a chart like the one shown. Use the chart to list details about Wyoming. Then record your inferences about how Wyoming might affect its residents.

Details	My Inferences About Life in Wyoming

READING AND VOCABULARY

Reading Strategy Visualizing

Visualizing is picturing a writer's ideas or descriptions in your mind's eye. Visualizing is one of the best ways to understand and remember information in an essay.

1. What pictures or images from "The Solace of Open Spaces" would you include in a documentary film about Wyoming? Explain.
2. As you read the essay, was it easier to visualize the people or the landscape? Explain.

Vocabulary Practice

Practice with Word Origins The origin, or etymology, of a word can be found in most dictionaries. It is usually listed after the pronunciation guide and part of speech designation. Use a dictionary to find the language from which each of the words originated.

1. replenish	**a.** Greek	**b.** Sanskrit	**c.** Latin
2. affluent	**a.** French	**b.** Latin	**c.** Greek
3. hazard	**a.** Latin	**b.** Norse	**c.** Arabic
4. fugitive	**a.** Slavic	**b.** Latin	**c.** Old English

Academic Vocabulary

Here are two words from the vocabulary list on page R80. These words will help you think, write, and talk about the selection.

scope (skōp) *n.* the range of one's perceptions, thoughts, or actions

capable (kāp′ ə bəl) *adj.* having the ability required for a specific task or accomplishment; qualified

Practice and Apply

1. According to Ehrlich, what is the **scope** of the intimacy between ranchers?
2. What difficulties are people in Wyoming **capable** of enduring?

Academic Vocabulary

1. The scope of intimacy between ranchers is narrow in that they do not share their feelings, but wide in that they help each other without hesitation.
2. People in Wyoming are capable of enduring harsh climate and lengthy isolation.

WRITING AND EXTENDING

Writing About Literature

Analyze Mood Mood is the emotional quality or atmosphere of a literary work. For instance, the mood of an essay might be apprehensive, joyful, or sad. Write a brief essay explaining how Ehrlich's subject matter, language, and tone contribute to the mood of "The Solace of Open Spaces." (Recall that tone is the attitude a writer expresses toward his or her subject matter.)

To generate ideas for your essay, use a web diagram like the one shown. Use the diagram to list details about the language, setting, and tone of the essay. Think about how these details help to create a mood.

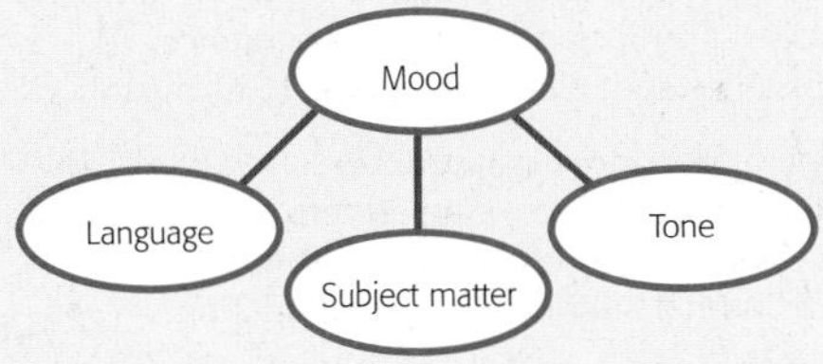

Refer to your diagram as you write your essay. After you complete your draft, meet with a peer reviewer to evaluate each other's work and to suggest revisions. Then proofread and edit your draft to correct errors in spelling, grammar, and punctuation.

Reading Further

Around the Globe After her time in Wyoming, Ehrlich traveled extensively in Greenland and China. If you would like to read more by Ehrlich, you might enjoy these works:

This Cold Heaven (2001) is Ehrlich's account of her time among the Inuit people of Greenland.

Questions of Heaven (1994) details Ehrlich's time in the foothills of the Himalayas in western China.

LiteratureOnline Web Activities For eFlashcards, Selection Quick Checks, and other Web activities, go to www.glencoe.com.

GRAMMAR AND STYLE

Ehrlich's Language and Style

Using Vivid Verbs The use of specific, vivid verbs can make an impact on readers and help them better visualize what a writer is describing. Vivid verbs can be more precise in their effect than commonplace verbs. In her essay, Ehrlich uses such verbs to create memorable descriptions. In the sentence below, note how one strong verb helps to make the description lively and evocative:

"Today the sun is out—only a few clouds *billowing*."

Consider how the sentence might read if Ehrlich had used a more commonplace verb:

"...only a few clouds *moving*."

"...only a few clouds *flowing*."

You may notice that *moving* and *flowing* lack the impact of *billowing*, which creates a more powerful image of the clouds.

Frequently used verbs often can be replaced by stronger, more vivid verbs. Look at the chart below which shows some common verbs and examples of vivid verbs that could be used instead.

Common Verbs	Vivid Verbs
yell walk eat	roar saunter devour

Activity Choose five other sentences from the essay. Underline vivid verbs in each sentence. If there are none, replace the common verb with one that is more descriptive. Use a thesaurus if you need help.

Revising Check

Vivid Verbs Review the essay you wrote in which you analyzed the mood of Ehrlich's essay. Do any of your verbs seem too commonplace? Are there places where a vivid verb would make your writing livelier or more precise? Insert more vivid verbs to improve your essay.

AFTER YOU READ

Assess

Writing About Literature

Students' essays should

- have a clearly identified mood.
- list supporting details that convey the stated mood.
- identify and discuss the subject matter and tone in Ehrlich's essay.
- describe the language Ehrlich uses.
- include a conclusion that summarizes the main thesis and provides insight for the reader.

Ehrlich's Language and Style

Remind students that verbs express the actions in a sentence. Vivid verbs help readers visualize the exact action, as the word *jog* offers a different image than *walk* or *run* or *move*. Pair students to brainstorm alternative verbs for the sentences that each partner has chosen.

Revising Check

Review with students the effectiveness of action verbs as opposed to linking verbs. Also discuss the importance of using precise verbs instead of commonplace verbs.

Web Activities Have students access the Web site for interactive activities that will help them assess their understanding of the selection.

Focus

Write on the board: Before I lived in Arkansas, I had a ranch in Wyoming. This sentence contains two parts. The first clause provides detail about the second clause but is not necessary to make a complete sentence.

Teach

Adverb Clauses Point out the second example. Clarify that adverb clauses need not appear at the beginning of sentences. **OL**

Assess

Exercise

1. Because they live in the land of cowboys, people from Wyoming feel (proud).
2. The landscape (hardens) when temperatures drop to ten or twenty below zero.
3. Although she hadn't planned to live there, Ehrlich (stayed) in Wyoming.

eWorkbooks Have students access the Web site for more practice with sentence structure.

Grammar Workshop

Sentence Structure

▸ **Punctuating Subordinate Clauses**

When a subordinate clause appears at the beginning of the sentence, use a comma to separate it from the main clause.

▸ **Test-Taking Tip**

To identify subordinate clauses on a test, look for subordinating conjunctions followed by a subject and a verb.

▸ **Subordinating Conjunctions**

after	if
although	since
as	so long as
as though	unless
because	until
before	when

▸ **Grammar Handbook**

For more on subordinate clauses, see Language Handbook, p. R50.

Literature Online

eWorkbooks To link to the Grammar and Language eWorkbook, go to www.glencoe.com.

ACADEMIC STANDARDS (page 408)

9.6.1 Identify and correctly use clauses, both main and subordinate...

9.6.2 Demonstrate an understanding of sentence construction, including... subordination...

Using Adverb Clauses

"After I had been herding sheep for only three days, the sound of the camp tender's pickup flustered me."

—Gretel Ehrlich, from "The Solace of Open Spaces"

Connecting to Literature Erhlich's sentence is made up of an independent, or main, clause: *the sound of the camp tender's pickup flustered me* and a subordinate, or dependent, clause: *after I had been herding sheep for only three days*. Both clauses contain a subject and a verb, but the dependent clause cannot stand alone as a sentence. Instead, it depends on the independent clause to complete its meaning.

An **adverb clause** is one type of dependent clause. Like an adverb, an adverb clause modifies a verb, an adjective, or an adverb and tells how, when, where, why, to what extent, or under what conditions. Like all subordinate clauses, it begins with a subordinating conjunction.

Examples

- Because Wyoming has wide-open spaces, some of its residents are lonely.
  [The underlined adverb clause tells why and modifies the adjective *lonely*.]
- One woman never left her ranch in Wyoming until her husband died.
  [The underlined adverb clause tells when and modifies the verb *left*.]

Exercise

Write a sentence that contains each group of elements. Underline each adverb clause you create, and circle the word it modifies.

1. **Clause:** they live in the land of cowboys
   Clause: people from Wyoming feel proud
   Subordinating conjunction: because
2. **Clause:** the landscape hardens
   Clause: temperatures drop to ten or twenty below zero
   Subordinating conjunction: when
3. **Clause:** she hadn't planned to live there
   Clause: Ehrlich stayed in Wyoming
   Subordinating conjunction: although

Additional Support

Academic Standards

The Additional Support activity on p. 408 covers the following standard:

Skills Practice: **9.6.1** Identify and correctly use clauses, both main and subordinate...

Skills Practice

WRITING: Sentence Variety Point out that adverb clauses, along with other subordinate clauses, allow writers to create sentence variety. They can place subordinate clauses at the beginning, middle, or end of a sentence. This helps to vary rhythm and avoid repetition. For example, the sentence beginning "Because Wyoming . . ." could begin "Some of its residents" and include the subordinate clause at the end. Have students exchange their answers with a partner, and rewrite the sentence to place the subordinate clause in a different place. **OL**

BEFORE YOU READ

Sayonara

MEET ANNE MORROW LINDBERGH

Imagine soaring high above the earth in a tiny single-engine plane—nothing but blue sky all around you and blue ocean water as far as the eye can see. That is how Anne Morrow Lindbergh spent much of the early years of her marriage to aviation pioneer Charles Lindbergh. In 1927 Charles became the first person to fly solo over the Atlantic Ocean, and he was greeted with worldwide adoration. Later that year, he was invited to visit Mexico by Dwight Morrow, the U.S. ambassador to that country. There he met Morrow's daughter, Anne.

The Daring Pilot Born in Englewood, New Jersey, Anne Morrow was a quiet girl who wrote poetry. She and Charles fell in love, and during their courtship, he taught her how to fly. The two married in 1929 after Anne graduated from college.

> *"Writing is thinking. It is more than living, for it is being conscious of living."*
>
> —Anne Morrow Lindbergh

Anne became an accomplished pilot, navigator, and radio operator. Together with Charles, she made historic flights all over the world, charting routes for the fledgling airline industry. The couple crisscrossed continents in their single-engine plane. In 1931 they flew an uncharted route over Canada, Alaska, and the northern Pacific Ocean to China. In 1933 the two completed a 30,000-mile survey of air routes over North and South Atlantic waters.

A Gifted Writer Anne's interest in aviation was matched by a devotion to writing. In fact, her flying was the source of inspiration for some of her work. In all, Anne wrote more than a dozen books and published five volumes of her diaries and letters. Her most popular and enduring work, however, was not about flying at all. In *Gift from the Sea,* Anne's quiet, contemplative nature was revealed in a series of essays about a woman's role in modern life.

Home Life/Public Life Anne gave birth to the first of her six children, Charles A. Lindbergh III, in 1930, a year after she married. In 1932, the young boy was kidnapped and murdered. The press sensationalized the crime and, later, the trial of the accused kidnapper. For the sake of their privacy and security, the Lindberghs left the United States to live in Europe. They went on to have five more children.

Once their children were grown, Anne and Charles began to travel again. They journeyed through Asia and Africa, working for conservation and the protection of endangered animals. In 1974, while residing on the Hawaiian island of Maui, Charles died. Anne moved back to the East Coast, where she lived until her death at the age of 94.

Anne Morrow Lindbergh was born in 1906 and died in 2001.

Literature Online **Author Search** For more about Anne Morrow Lindbergh, go to www.glencoe.com.

BEFORE YOU READ

Focus

BELLRINGER

Bellringer Options

Daily Language Practice Transparency 37

Or have students recall their parting words to a family member, friend, or teacher from the past few days.

Ask: How do your parting words differ from one situation to another? *(Students should recognize that they say good-bye in different ways.)*

As they read, have students consider why the author likes the good-bye "Sayonara."

Literature Online

Author Search To expand students' appreciation of Anne Morrow Lindbergh, have them access the Web site for additional information and resources.

Selection Skills

Sayonara

Literary Elements
- Thesis (SE pp. 410–413)
- Descriptive Essay (SE p. 413)

Reading Skills
- Analyzing Rhetorical Devices (SE pp. 410–414)

Vocabulary Skills
- Analogies (SE pp. 410, 414)
- Academic Vocabulary (SE p. 414)

Listening/Speaking/Viewing Skills
- Literature Groups (SE p. 414)

Writing Skills/Grammar
- Explore Author's Purpose (SE p. 414)
- Dashes/Parentheses (TWE p. 411)

BEFORE YOU READ

Focus

Summary

In this essay, the author describes her journey across Japan by train. She offers details about the Japanese countryside and culture, and pays particular attention to the way people conduct their farewells. When she departs a Japanese port by boat, the author considers how the Japanese good-bye—Sayonara—differs from and improves upon other good-byes.

V Vocabulary

Vocabulary File **Say:** Add these words and definitions to your vocabulary file. For each word, include a sentence that gives you an example of how to use the word. **OL** Students with English language needs should include the pronunciations of these words in their files. **EL**

Literary Elements Have students access the Web site to improve their understanding of thesis.

LITERATURE PREVIEW

Connecting to the Essay

Sayonara (sä′ yə nä′ rə) means "good-bye" in Japanese. In Lindbergh's essay "Sayonara," she describes a trip on which she hears, over and over again, family members saying good-bye to each other. Before you read the essay, think about the following questions:

- How does it feel to have to say good-bye to someone you love?
- Is one way of saying good-bye better than another?

Building Background

This descriptive essay is from *North to the Orient,* an account of the Lindberghs' 1931 trip to the Far East in their single-engine Lockheed plane. The young couple flew north over Canada and Alaska before turning south toward China. When the plane was damaged in China, the Lindberghs traveled by boat to Japan. They then had to travel by train across Japan to the ship that would carry them home to the United States. During the trip, the Lindberghs passed through the seaports Shanghai in China, and Yokohama in Japan.

Setting Purposes for Reading

Big Idea On the Move

As you read, think about the various ways of saying good-bye and the differences in their meanings.

Literary Element Thesis

A **thesis** is the main idea of an essay or other work of nonfiction. It is generally stated in one or two sentences. This brief summary is called the thesis statement. Identifying the thesis can help you better understand a work as a whole. As you read "Sayonara," look for clues that might help you to determine the thesis.

- See Literary Terms Handbook, p. R18.

 **Interactive Literary Elements Handbook** To review or learn more about the literary elements, go to www.glencoe.com.

READING PREVIEW

Reading Strategy Analyzing Rhetorical Devices

Rhetorical devices are stylistic techniques an author uses to express ideas, persuade, or evoke an emotional response. Rhetorical devices include repetition—repeating a sound, word, or phrase; analogy—explaining an unfamiliar idea by comparing it with a familiar one; juxtaposition—placing two or more distinct things side by side in order to compare or contrast them; and parallelism—using a series of similar grammatical structures. As you read, note instances of repetition, analogy, juxtaposition, and parallelism.

Reading Tip: Listening Use a chart to record instances of parallelism and of repetition of the word *Sayonara.* List who says the word and under what circumstances. Then note the effect the use of parallelism or repetition has on the essay as a whole.

Vocabulary

conglomerate (kən glom′ər it) *adj.* made up of separate parts collected together as one; p. 411 *The junk heap was a conglomerate pile of bottles, old tires, and other discarded material.*

unintelligible (un′ in tel′ ə jə bəl) *adj.* not able to be understood; p. 412 *Your voice sounds low and unintelligible on that cell phone.*

bravado (brə vä′dō) *n.* pretended courage or confidence; p. 412 *Although the boxer entered the ring with bravado, he had sweaty palms.*

Vocabulary Tip: Analogies An analogy is a type of comparison that is based on the relationships between things or ideas. For example, the word *good-bye* has the same relationship to *leave* (one says *good-bye* when one leaves) as *hello* has to *arrive* (one says *hello* when one arrives).

INDIANA ACADEMIC STANDARDS (pages 410–414)

9.2.8 Make reasonable statements and draw conclusions about a text, supporting them with accurate examples.

9.2 Develop [reading] strategies...

9.5.3 Write expository compositions...that gather evidence in support of a thesis...

Selection Resources

Print Materials
- Unit 2 Resources (Fast File), pp. 51–53
- Leveled Vocabulary Development, p. 30
- Selection and Unit Assessments, pp. 65–66
- Selection Quick Checks, p. 33

Transparencies
- Bellringer Options Transparencies: Daily Language Practice Transparency 37
- Literary Elements Transparency 34

Technology
- TeacherWorks Plus™ CD-ROM
- StudentWorks Plus™ CD-ROM
- Presentation Plus!™ CD-ROM
- Literature Online, glencoe.com
- Online Student Edition, mhln.com
- Exam*View*® Assessment Suite CD-ROM
- Vocabulary PuzzleMaker CD-ROM
- Listening Library, disc 1 track 37

Postcard for the Nippon Yusen Kaisha line, c. 1929. Private Collection.

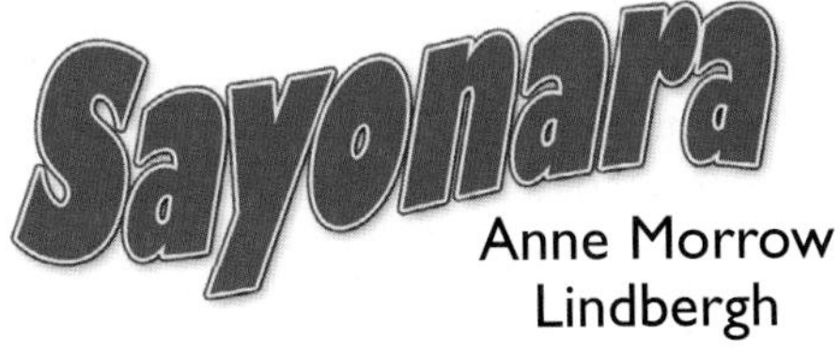

Sayonara

Anne Morrow Lindbergh

"Sayonara, Sayonara!" I was in my stateroom[1] but I could hear them, outside on the deck of the Japanese boat, calling to friends and relatives on the dock at Shanghai. "Sayonara"—up and down the gangplank and over the rails. A boatload of Japanese were leaving China for home, as we were. "Sayonara," the chains clanked and the warning whistle shook the boat. The voices outside rose in a flurry of noise, like a flock of frightened birds. But above the **conglomerate** sound there was always one voice, clean and sharp and individual and yet representative of the mass like that one face in the front line that holds the meaning of the whole crowd—one cry, "Sayonara." The impression was intensified perhaps because it was the one word of Japanese I understood—"Sayonara" ("Good-bye").

I was to hear it again, all along our trip home. For we crossed Japan by train from the southern tip to Yokohama, where we boarded the boat for America.

"Sayonara": the clatter of wooden clogs[2] along the station platform; the flutter of kimonos;[3] babies jogging on their mothers' backs; men carrying four or five small bundles tied up in different-colored furoshiki (squares of parti-colored silk or cotton); old women knocking along with their sticks, their brown faces hidden under enormous rooflike hats of straw; a man shouting his wares. We leaned out of the window at one of these stations and motioned to a vender for some tea. He poured out of his big tin into a little brown clay teapot like a child's toy, with a saucer for a lid and an inverted cup on top. "Two! Two!" we shouted and signaled as the train jerked forward, starting to pull out. The vender ran after us with another teapot swinging from its wire handle and pushed it in our window.

"Sayonara—Sayonara!" cried the passengers who had just stepped on board. A Japanese family across the aisle from us leaned out of the window to say a few last words. They occupied two long seats raised on a slight platform, separated from the next family by a partition. The mother and nurse

1. A *stateroom* is a private room aboard a ship.

2. Here, *clogs* refers to a type of sandal.

3. *Kimonos* (ki mō′ nōz) are loose gowns tied with a sash, part of the traditional costume worn by Japanese men and women.

Literary Element Thesis *Based on your reading so far, what do you think the thesis of this essay is?* **L**

Vocabulary

conglomerate (kən glom′ ər it) *adj.* made up of separate parts collected together as one

Teach

Big Idea

On the Move Say: Keep these questions in mind as you read: How does the author feel about traveling? *(Possible answer: She is fascinated by it.)* What aspects of traveling are most engaging to the author? *(She is engaged by the many sights and sounds of the culture and land around her.)* **OL**

L Literary Element

Thesis Possible answer: *The essay's thesis is that saying good-bye is difficult.* **OL**

★ Cultural History

Clothing Today, most Japanese dress in "Western style" clothes. At the time of Lindbergh's visit, however, more Japanese—especially women—may have worn traditional kimonos. **AS**

Readability Scores

Dale-Chall: 9.1
DRP: 59
Lexile: 1060

English Language Coach

Good-bye Ask students to share customs for saying good-bye in their home language or culture. Invite volunteers to translate into English the meaning of each good-bye they know. If students speak the languages cited in the essay, ask them to pronounce these good-byes. **EL**

Differentiated Instruction

Punctuation Point out the author's frequent use of dashes and parentheses. Both types of punctuation contain or separate information that is not essential to sentence meaning. Work through the examples to help students see how the details relate to the text. **BL**

Academic Standards

Additional Support activities on p. 411 cover the following standards:

English Language Coach: **9.1** Use…a growing knowledge of English and other languages to determine the meaning of words…

Differentiated Instruction: **9.6.1** Identify…the mechanics of punctuation…

Teach

R Reading Strategy

Analyzing Rhetorical Devices **Answer:** *She uses parallelism to convey her fondness for Japan.* OL

L Literary Element

Thesis **Answer:** *"Farewell" says too little; it hides the emotion of departure. Other terms say too much, but deny that people will be apart. She prefers Sayonara because it is an acceptance.* OL

★ Cultural History

Ship Farewells As recently as 2004—at the launch of a new cruise ship—passengers followed the custom of throwing streamers from the ocean liner. AS

CheckPoint

Use the CheckPoint questions on Presentation Plus! to check students' mastery of the selection. These questions can be used with interactive response keypads for immediate student feedback.

(or older sister) were dressed in Japanese kimonos, the father in Western business suit, the two little girls in green challis[4] suits with Irish-lace collars, and the baby in woolens. They had already kicked off their shoes, in Japanese fashion, and were squatting on their feet on the blue plush seats. They held the baby up to the window for the last good-bye—"Sayonara"; and then the monotonous doggerel rhythm of the train, quickening to a roar, drowned all noise. We were off.

It was good-bye for us too, as we rushed through Japan on our way to the boat. Good-bye to the rice fields terraced up a narrow gully in the hills; to thatched roofs and paper walls; to heavy-headed grain bent to a curve; to a field of awkward lotus leaves, like big elephant ears flapping on their tall stalks; to a white road leading up a hill to a pine grove and the flicker of red of a shrine gate. Good-bye to the little towns we rattled through, with their narrow cobbled streets lined with shops, open to the passerby except for fluttering blue-toweling curtains or bright paper and cloth flag-signs. Good-bye to blue paper umbrellas in the rain and little boys chasing dragon flies. R

Our real good-bye was not until the boat pulled out of the dock at Yokohama, when the crowd of Japanese leaning over the rails of the decks shot twirling strands of serpentine[5] across to those they had left behind on shore—a rain of bright fireworks. One end of these colored paper ribbons was held in the hands of those on deck; the other, by those on shore, until a brilliant multicolored web was spun between ship and shore. This and the shouts of conversation **unintelligible** to me, interlacing back and forth across the gap, made up a finely woven band—a tissue, intricately patterned and rich in texture which held together for a few more seconds those remaining and those departing. Then the gap of water slowly widening between dock and ship, the ribbons tautened and snapped, the broken and raveled ends twirling off idly into the water, floating away with the unfinished ends of sentences. And nothing could bridge the gap but "Sayonara!" ★

For *Sayonara,* literally translated, "Since it must be so," of all the good-byes I have heard is the most beautiful. Unlike the *Auf Wiedersehens* and *Au revoirs,* it does not try to cheat itself by any **bravado** "Till we meet again," any sedative to postpone the pain of separation. It does not evade the issue like the sturdy blinking *Farewell. Farewell* is a father's *good-bye.* It is—"Go out in the world and do well, my son." It is encouragement and admonition. It is hope and faith. But it passes over the significance of the moment; of parting it says nothing. It hides its emotion. It says too little. While *Good-bye* ("God be with you") and *Adios* say too much. They try to bridge the distance, almost to deny it. *Good-bye* is a prayer, a ringing cry. "You must not go—I cannot bear to have you go! But you shall not go alone, unwatched. God will be with you. God's hand will be over you" and even—underneath, hidden, but it is there, incorrigible—"I will be with you; I will watch you—always." It is a mother's *good-bye.* But Sayonara says neither too much nor too little. It is a simple acceptance of fact. All understanding of life lies in its limits. All emotion, smoldering, is banked up behind it. But it says nothing. It is really the unspoken good-bye, the pressure of a hand, "Sayonara." L

4. *Challis* (shal′ ē) is a lightweight cloth made of cotton or wool.
5. *Serpentine* are streamers of rolled colored paper that unwind when thrown.

Reading Strategy Analyzing Rhetorical Devices *What is the effect of Morrow's use of parallelism in this sentence?* R

Literary Element Thesis *What does the author mean by "too much" and "too little," and why does she prefer the term Sayonara?* L

Vocabulary

unintelligible (un′ in tel′ ə jə bəl) *adj.* not able to be understood

Vocabulary

bravado (brə vä′dō) *n.* pretended courage or confidence

Additional Support

Academic Standards

The Additional Support activity on p. 412 covers the following standard:

Skills Practice: **9.4.6** Synthesize information from multiple sources...

Skills Practice

RESEARCH: Setting Recall the background about Anne Morrow Lindbergh on page 409. Point out that the journey Lindbergh writes about occurred in the early 1930s, prior to World War II. Emphasize that Japan has changed dramatically since then. Have students do research to learn about Japan prior to and following World War II. Tell students to create a Venn diagram or other graphic device to show the contrasts revealed by their research. OL

AFTER YOU READ

RESPONDING AND THINKING CRITICALLY

Respond

1. Do you agree with Lindbergh that *Sayonara* is the most appropriate parting expression? Explain.

Recall and Interpret

2. (a)Reread the first paragraph. What are the voices being compared to? (b)How does the analogy contribute to the special importance attached to the word *Sayonara*?
3. (a)Why does Morrow say she was to hear the word *Sayonara* again and again? (b)Why do you think she uses the experience to make a generalization about life?
4. (a)What do the people on the boat deck do as the boat is leaving? (b)What does their action symbolize?
5. (a)What does *Sayonara* literally mean? (b)What does this meaning suggest about the Japanese view of life?

Analyze and Evaluate

6. In the passage beginning, ". . . the clatter of wooden clogs," the author uses parallel phrases: "babies jogging . . . men carrying . . . old women knocking. . . ." How does the first half of this paragraph differ from the second half, beginning, "We leaned out of the window"? Which style is more effective in describing the scene?
7. (a)Why does Lindbergh contrast the words *farewell* and *good-bye?* (b)Do you agree with her interpretations? Why or why not?
8. When the author says, "But it says nothing," does she really mean that *Sayonara* has no meaning? Explain.

Connect

9. **Big Idea** **On the Move** Although the idea of saying good-bye seems sad, the ending of the essay is neither sad nor happy. Why might this be important to Lindbergh?

LITERARY ANALYSIS

Literary Element Thesis

A **thesis** is the main idea of an essay or other work of nonfiction. A thesis may be stated directly, or it may be implied through the use of details. To determine the author's thesis, first identify the subject of the piece. Then use information from the text to determine the author's main point, or thesis, about the subject.

1. What is Lindbergh's thesis in "Sayonara"? Is the thesis implied or stated directly? Explain.
2. Did the author's thesis surprise you? If so, how?
3. How well does Lindbergh support the thesis? Use details from the text to support your opinion.

Review: Descriptive Essay

As you learned on page 401, a **descriptive essay** creates a picture in the mind of the reader of an actual person, object, or place. The essayist uses descriptive details and concrete language, which appeal to one or more of the senses, to create this picture.

Partner Activity Pair up with a classmate. Reread the scene at the train station. Note the specific details Lindbergh described, and classify each as a detail of sight or of sound. Then write a description of the overall impression these images give you.

AFTER YOU READ

Assess

1. Possible answers: *Sayonara* is best; different expressions suit particular situations.
2. (a) A flock of frightened birds (b) Contrasting the birds to *Sayonara* highlights the word's purity and simplicity.
3. (a) Because she is crossing Japan by train (b) She wants to express the pain and difficulty of separating from loved ones.
4. (a) Throw paper streamers to people on the dock (b) The action symbolizes separation as the streamers break.
5. (a) "Since it must be so" (b) The meaning suggests an acceptance of life as it is.
6. Possible answer: The first half is purely descriptive and contains parallelism. The second half uses phrases and no parallelism to recount an incident; First Half: provides more detail; Second Half: it reads like a story.
7. Possible answers: (a) She underscores the nuances of various departing sentiments. (b) The characterizations of how fathers and mothers feel is traditional and outdated.
8. She means that it is neutral, an acknowledgement of fact.
9. Lindbergh traveled a lot and no doubt said many good-byes. For her, good-bye was a "simple acceptance of fact."

Literary Element

1. Thesis: Although the word *Sayonara* is the most appropriate way to say good-bye, its true meaning is found in unspoken gestures beyond the word itself; the thesis is directly stated in the final paragraph.
2. Possible answer: The author's conclusion that the word "says nothing" was surprising. Stating the thesis at the end of the essay creates a dramatic effect.
3. Students should support their response with text evidence.

Review: Descriptive Essay

Possible answers: Sights: *babies jogging on mother's backs, men carrying different-colored bundles, brown faces under rooflike straw hats;* **Sounds:** *clatter of wooden clogs, sticks of old women knocking, man shouting;* The overall impression is one of noisy, colorful confusion.

AFTER YOU READ

Assess

Reading Strategy

1. Possible answer: The voices outside the boat in China rising like a flock of birds (similarity: sound)
2. Possible answer: The tangible web of streamers and the intangible web of back-and-forth shouts

Vocabulary

1. a
2. b
3. a
4. b

Academic Vocabulary

1. Lindbergh traveled by train.
2. It invokes God to watch over the one departing.

Writing About Literature

Students' essays should

- state Lindbergh's purpose to describe. A secondary purpose might be to inform or entertain.
- include two techniques she uses.
- include details that support the student's views.

READING AND VOCABULARY

Reading Strategy Analyzing Rhetorical Devices

The **rhetorical devices** of analogy and juxtaposition are methods of comparison. By using analogy, an author compares two dissimilar things by showing how they are similar. By using juxtaposition, an author compares or contrasts two distinct things placed side by side.

1. Find an example of analogy in "Sayonara." What two things are being compared? How are they similar?
2. Find an example of juxtaposition. What two things are juxtaposed? How are they similar or dissimilar?

Vocabulary Practice

Practice with Analogies Choose the word pair that best completes the analogy.

1. **conglomerate : individuals ::**
   a. team : players **b.** teacher : students
2. **monotonous : same ::**
   a. thoughtful : brainy **b.** various : different
3. **unintelligible : understand ::**
   a. hidden : see **b.** broken : mend
4. **bravado : nervousness ::**
   a. joy : emotion **b.** calmness : anxiety

Academic Vocabulary

Here are two words from the vocabulary list on page R80.

mode (mōd) *n.* a way or manner of doing, acting, or being

invoke (in vōk′) *v.* to call on for help, support, or blessing

Practice and Apply

1. What **mode** of travel did Lindbergh take across Japan?
2. According to Lindbergh, what does the parting expression *good-bye* **invoke**?

WRITING AND EXTENDING

Writing About Literature

Explore Author's Purpose An author's purpose in writing a descriptive essay is to describe a person, place, or object, but it might also be to entertain, to inform, or to persuade. Write an essay explaining what you think Lindbergh's purpose or purposes were in writing "Sayonara." Discuss two techniques she uses to achieve her purpose(s). Use evidence and examples from the essay as well as any related personal experiences to support your point.

Generate your ideas, and then organize them before you begin to write. Follow the organizational plan shown here for your essay:

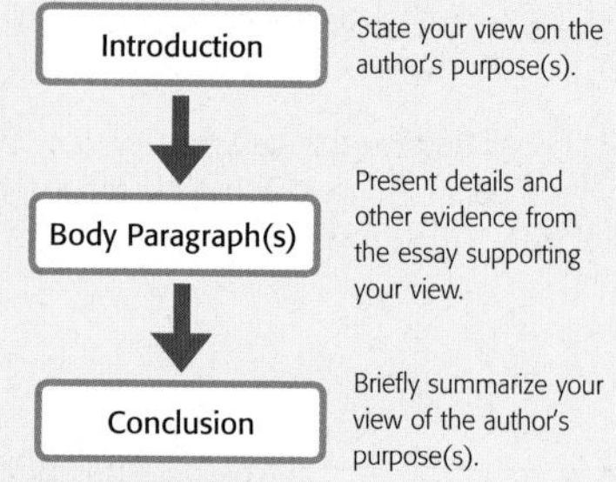

Introduction
State your view on the author's purpose(s).
Body Paragraph(s)
Present details and other evidence from the essay supporting your view.
Conclusion
Briefly summarize your view of the author's purpose(s).

After completing your draft, meet with a peer reviewer to evaluate each other's work and suggest revisions. Then proofread and edit your draft to correct errors in spelling, grammar, and punctuation.

Literature Groups

With three to five of your classmates, discuss the structure of Lindbergh's essay and whether you think it is effective. Key questions to discuss include the following: What structure does Lindbergh use in the first part of the essay? Does it effectively convey the description? Why or why not? What structure does she use at the end of the essay? Does it effectively convey her thesis? Why or why not? How do you personally respond to this structure as a reader? Support your views with reasons and details from the selection.

LiteratureOnline Web Activities For eFlashcards, Selection Quick Checks, and other Web activities, go to www.glencoe.com.

Literature Groups

Students' responses should

- identify the use of chronological order in the first part.
- note comparison and contrast at the end of the essay.
- support their views on the effectiveness of the structure with text examples.

LiteratureOnline

Web Activities Have students access the Web site for interactive activities that will help them assess their understanding of the selection.

from *Into Thin Air*

MEET JON KRAKAUER

Jon Krakauer went from being a recreational climber to a best-selling author: a tough mountain to scale. He got started as a writer when a mountain climbing club asked him to write an article about his ascent of three previously unclimbed Alaskan peaks. Three years later, a British magazine paid him to write another article, this time about climbing Devil's Thumb near Petersburg, Alaska. After that, Krakauer quit his carpentry job to become a freelance writer. His experience as a carpenter and commercial fisherman enabled him to write articles for *Architectural Digest* and *Smithsonian,* but he soon realized that only writing about the outdoors truly satisfied him.

Climbing and Writing Krakauer spent most of his childhood in Oregon, where he began climbing at age eight with his father. Krakauer never lost his love of climbing. After graduating from college, he spent part of each year working and the rest in the mountains. After publishing his first few articles, Krakauer turned to full-length books. His story of a young man who travels alone into the Alaskan wilderness, *Into the Wild,* became a bestseller.

Mount Everest In 1996 Krakauer was hired to write about how climbing Mount Everest was turning into a big business. Everyday adventurers would pay large sums for the thrill of saying they had climbed the world's tallest mountain. Krakauer admits that there were many reasons for not going but he could not resist the opportunity. He joined a climbing team led by the legendary Rob Hall. Hall, who had reached the top of Mount Everest seven times, would be one of several people to die on the May 1996 expedition.

Nevertheless, within a few years of the disaster he chronicles in *Into Thin Air,* Krakauer returned to climbing. He explains, "I'd give up writing before I gave up climbing."

> *"The plain truth is that I knew better but I went to Everest anyway."*
>
> —Jon Krakauer

Fact That Reads Like Fiction One reason for Krakauer's success as a writer is his ability to tell a story. In many ways, Krakauer works like a journalist. He takes volumes of notes and does extensive research. Yet his nonfiction work has the drama, the pacing, and the qualities of rising action—including suspense—that are found in fiction. His people are well-developed characters full of complex motives and emotions. Krakauer, who admits that he reads "a lot more fiction than nonfiction," adds that he works very hard to achieve these effects, sometimes taking days to hammer out a single sentence.

Jon Krakauer was born in 1954.

Literature Online **Author Search** For more about Jon Krakauer, go to www.glencoe.com.

BEFORE YOU READ

Focus

BELLRINGER

Bellringer Options
Daily Language Practice Transparency 38

Or show students photographs of remote natural locations, such as Mount Everest, Antarctica, and the Brazilian rainforest.
Ask: How would travel to all these places be similar? *(All are remote and hard to reach. All have potential dangers and amazing natural beauty.)*
As they read, have students consider how the author's journey to the summit of Mount Everest is like and unlike other journeys to remote natural locations.

Author Search To expand students' appreciation of Jon Krakauer, have them access the Web site for additional information and resources.

Selection Skills

***from* Into Thin Air**

Literary Elements
- Structure (SE pp. 416–427)
- Dialogue (SE p. 427)

Reading Skills
- Monitoring Comprehension (SE pp. 416–428)
- Cause and Effect (TWE p. 418)

Vocabulary Skills
- Word Parts (SE p. 428)
- Academic Vocabulary (SE p. 428)
- Idioms (TWE p. 420)

Listening/Speaking/Viewing Skills
- Viewing the Photograph (SE p. 419; TWE pp. 420, 426)

Writing Skills/Grammar
- Evaluate Author's Craft (SE p. 428)
- Signal Words (TWE p. 422)

Study Skills/Research/Assessment
- Internet Connection (SE p. 428)
- Reading for Information (TWE p. 426)

BEFORE YOU READ

Focus

Summary

In this excerpt from his memoir, the author describes his ascent to the summit of Mount Everest. On the journey up to the summit and back to the base camp, Krakauer records the many decisions that led to problems for him and his climbing mates. He looks back in an attempt to understand why he survives but 17 others do not after a storm catches the climbing party by surprise.

V Vocabulary

Vocabulary File Say: Add these words and definitions to your vocabulary file. For each word, include a sentence that gives you an example of how to use the word. **OL** Students with English language needs should include the pronunciations of these words in their files. **EL**

Literary Elements Have students access the Web site to improve their understanding of structure.

LITERATURE PREVIEW

Connecting to the Essay

In this excerpt from *Into Thin Air,* people risk their lives for the sake of adventure despite the record of tragedy and death on the world's highest mountain. Before you read the essay, think about the following questions:

- What is the riskiest adventure you have ever taken part in?
- What could motivate someone to put his or her life on the line in a place like Mount Everest?

Building Background

The lure of Mount Everest has long been a potent force for the world's best climbers. But the mountain has often proved deadly. At 29,028 feet, it claimed the lives of at least two dozen climbers before it was first successfully conquered in 1953. Besides ice, snow, steep rock faces, possible avalanches, and changing weather conditions, a central problem for all climbers is the "thin air," or lack of oxygen, at the mountain's higher elevations. Climbers must get used to the lack of oxygen by spending several weeks at a base camp, as well as at successive camps higher and higher up the mountain. Most also carry bottled oxygen. A regulator delivers oxygen from the bottle or canister, and climbers control the flow by turning a valve. If climbers do not get enough oxygen, they enter a state of hypoxia, which includes disorientation, dizziness, and hallucinations.

Setting Purposes for Reading

Big Idea On the Move

As you read, think about what it means to be on the move in one of the most dangerous places on earth.

Literary Element Structure

Structure is the particular order a writer uses to present ideas. Narratives commonly follow a chronological order. As you read the selection, think about the order in which Krakauer presents the events.

- See Literary Terms Handbook, p. R17.

LiteratureOnline Interactive Literary Elements Handbook To review or learn more about the literary elements, go to www.glencoe.com.

READING PREVIEW

Reading Strategy Monitoring Comprehension

Monitoring comprehension is thinking about whether you understand what you are reading. You can improve your comprehension by rereading or slowing down when the material is difficult. Keep asking yourself questions about central ideas, characters, and events. When you cannot answer a question, review and read at a slower pace.

Reading Tip: Rereading Record Keep a record of the parts you stop to reread. For each, jot down basic facts about who, what, where, when, why, and how.

Passage	Brief Summary
p. 419 First paragraph	Who—Krakauer; Where—at the top of Everest; What—a few snapshots, a few souvenirs; Why—in a hurry to get down the mountain

Vocabulary

tenuously (ten′ū əs lē) *adv.* uncertainly; shakily; p. 418 *The climber was perched tenuously on a crag above the cliff face.*

exacerbate (ig zas′ər bāt′) *v.* to make worse, more violent, or more bitter; p. 421 *The foul weather exacerbated Jane's headache.*

invincible (in vin′sə bəl) *adj.* not able to be beaten or overcome; p. 421 *Many people tried to beat Amanda at chess, but she was invincible.*

terrain (tə rān′) *n.* the physical features of the land; p. 423 *The team made slow progress over the rocky terrain.*

detachment (di tach′mənt) *n.* indifference; a state of being apart from; p. 424 *Steve's detachment was not unusual: he liked to be alone.*

INDIANA ACADEMIC STANDARDS (pages 416–428)
9.3.6 Analyze and trace an author's development of time and sequence...
9.2 Develop [reading] strategies...

Selection Resources

Print Materials
- Unit 2 Resources (Fast File), pp. 54–56
- Leveled Vocabulary Development, p. 31
- Selection and Unit Assessments, pp. 67–68
- Selection Quick Checks, p. 34

Transparencies
- Bellringer Options Transparencies: Daily Language Practice Transparency 38
- Literary Elements Transparency 36

Technology
- TeacherWorks Plus™ CD-ROM
- StudentWorks Plus™ CD-ROM
- Presentation Plus!™ CD-ROM
- Literature Online, glencoe.com
- Online Student Edition, mhln.com
- Exam*View*® Assessment Suite CD-ROM
- Vocabulary PuzzleMaker CD-ROM
- Listening Library, disc 1 track 38

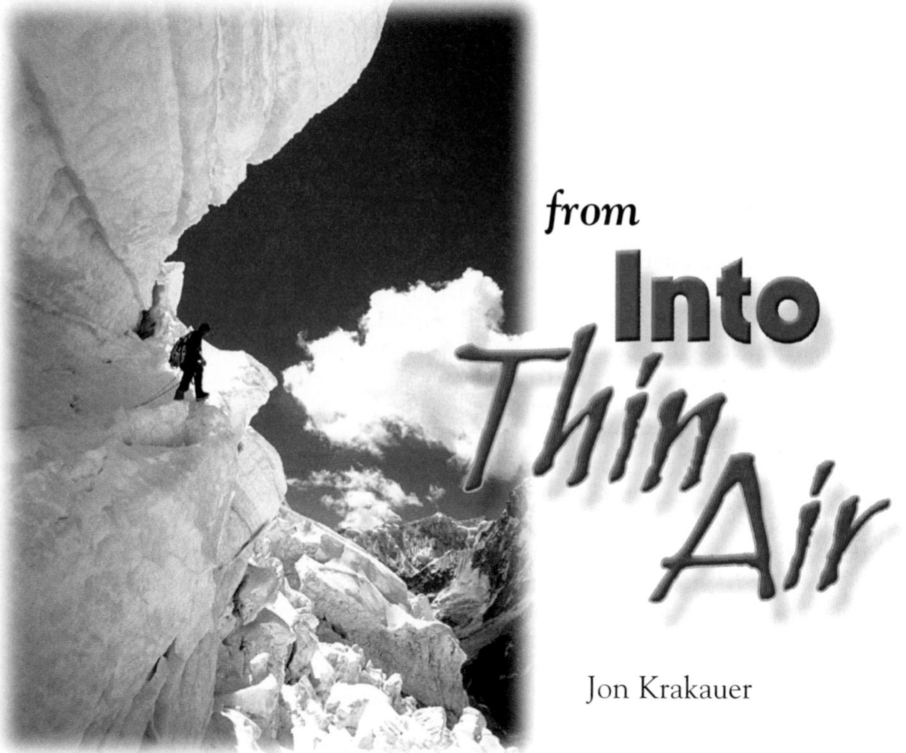

from Into Thin Air

Jon Krakauer

Near the top of Khumbu Icefall, Scott Fischer ascends the large overhanging serac known as the mouse trap, during the May 1996 ascent on Mount Everest.

In my backpack was a banner from *Outside* magazine, a small pennant emblazoned with a whimsical lizard that Linda, my wife, had sewn, and some other mementos[1] with which I'd intended to pose for a series of triumphant photos. Cognizant[2] of my dwindling oxygen reserves, however, I left everything in my pack and stayed on top of the world just long enough to fire off four quick shots of Andy Harris and Anatoli Boukreev posing in front of the summit survey marker. Then I turned to descend. About twenty yards below the summit I passed Neal Beidleman and a client of Fischer's named Martin Adams[3] on their way up. After exchanging a high five with Neal, I grabbed a handful of small stones from a wind-scoured patch of exposed shale, zipped the souvenirs into the pocket of my down suit, and hastened down the ridge.

A moment earlier I'd noticed that wispy clouds now filled the valleys to the south, obscuring all but the highest peaks. Adams—a small, pugnacious[4] Texan who'd gotten rich selling bonds during the booming 1980s—is an experienced airplane pilot who'd spent many hours gazing down on the tops of clouds; later he told me that he

1. *Mementos* are souvenirs.
2. Here, *cognizant* means "aware."

Literary Element Structure *What is the first thing Krakauer tells his readers?* **L**

3. Throughout this essay, Krakauer mentions the names of many other climbers, including guides Andy Harris, Anatoli Boukreev, Andy Fischer, and Neal Beidleman. He also mentions climbers who were led by these guides, including Martin Adams.
4. Here, *pugnacious* suggests someone who is not easy to get along with.

Teach

Big Idea

On the Move Say: Keep these questions in mind as you read: How do our surroundings contribute to our ability to be on the move? *(They affect how easy or difficult it is to move, and they can make it impossible to move.)* How do Krakauer's surroundings make it life-threatening to be on the move? *(They make him short of oxygen, subject to freezing temperatures, and at risk of falling.)* **OL**

L Literary Element

Structure Possible answer: *Krakauer first describes being on the top of Mount Everest.* **OL**

Use the CheckPoint questions on Presentation Plus! to monitor students' comprehension. These questions can be used with interactive response keypads for immediate student feedback.

Readability Scores
Dale-Chall: 9.4
DRP: 64
Lexile: 1160

Differentiated Instruction

Constructing Graphic Images To orient students to the setting, have them scan the images in the selection. Discuss setting elements, such as cumulonimbus clouds and shale, to confirm students' familiarity with them. Then encourage students to sketch Krakauer's route as they read. They can place icons or notes at key places on his journey. **BL**

Academic Standards
The Additional Support activity on p. 417 covers the following standard:
Differentiated Instruction: **9.3** [Identify] story elements such as...setting...

Teach

BI Big Idea

On the Move Answer: *Adams's experience as a pilot makes him recognize the approaching danger of the storm, while Krakauer remains focused on the danger of running out of oxygen.* **OL**

L Literary Element

Structure Answer: *Krakauer is still at the Hillary Step, 28,900 feet above sea level. He is describing the altitude's effects on him and the movement of the climbers around him.* **OL**

★ Cultural History

Sherpas Since Sherpas have lived in the Himalayas for centuries, they are acclimated to the thin air and are renowned for their high altitude physical ability. As Tibetan Buddhists, Sherpas are a distinct ethnic group within Nepalese society. **AS**

recognized these innocent-looking puffs of water vapor to be the crowns of robust thunderheads immediately after reaching the top. "When you see a thunderhead in an airplane," he explained, "your first reaction is to get out of there. So that's what I did."

But unlike Adams, I was unaccustomed to peering down at cumulonimbus cells from 29,000 feet, and I therefore remained ignorant of the storm that was even then bearing down. My concerns revolved instead around the diminishing supply of oxygen in my tank.

Fifteen minutes after leaving the summit I reached the top of the Hillary Step,[5] where I encountered a clot of climbers chuffing up the single strand of rope, and my descent came to an enforced halt.[6] As I waited for the crowd to pass, Andy arrived on his way down. "Jon," he asked, "I don't seem to be getting enough air. Can you tell if the intake valve to my mask is iced up?"

A quick check revealed a fist-sized chunk of frozen drool blocking the rubber valve that admitted ambient air into the mask from the atmosphere. I chipped it off with the pick of my ice ax, then asked Andy to return the favor by turning off my regulator in order to conserve my gas until the Step cleared. He mistakenly opened the valve instead of closing it, however, and ten minutes later all my oxygen was gone. My cognitive functions, which had been marginal before, instantly went into a nosedive. I felt like I'd been slipped an overdose of a powerful sedative.

I fuzzily remember Sandy Pittman climbing past as I waited, bound for the summit, followed an indeterminate time later by Charlotte Fox and then Lopsang Jangbu. Yasuko materialized next, just below my precarious stance, but was flummoxed[7] by the last and steepest portion of the Step. I watched helplessly for fifteen minutes as she struggled to haul herself up the uppermost brow of rock, too exhausted to manage it. Finally Tim Madsen, who was waiting impatiently directly below her, put his hands beneath her buttocks and pushed her to the top.

Rob Hall appeared not long after that. Disguising my rising panic, I thanked him for getting me to the top of Everest. "Yeah, it's turned out to be a pretty good expedition," he replied, then mentioned that Frank Fischbeck, Beck Weathers, Lou Kasischke, Stuart Hutchison, and John Taske had all turned back. Even in my state of hypoxic imbecility, it was obvious Hall was profoundly disappointed that five of his eight clients had packed it in—a sentiment that I suspected was heightened by the fact that Fischer's entire crew appeared to be plugging toward the summit. "I only wish we could have gotten more clients to the top," Rob lamented before continuing on his way.

Soon thereafter, Adams and Boukreev arrived on their way down, stopping immediately above me to wait for the traffic to clear. A minute later the overcrowding atop the Step intensified further as Makalu Gau, Ang Dorje, and several other Sherpas[8] came up the rope, followed by Doug Hansen and Scott Fischer. Then, finally, the Hillary Step was clear—but only after I'd spent more than an hour at 28,900 feet without supplemental oxygen. ★

By that point, entire sectors of my cerebral cortex seemed to have shut down altogether. Dizzy, fearing that I would black out, I was frantic to reach the South Summit, where my third bottle was waiting. I started **tenuously**

5. Named for Sir Edmund Hillary, *Hillary Step* is the last difficult ascent before the summit.
6. One of Krakauer's points is that there were so many climbers on the mountain that it was like a traffic jam.
7. *Flummoxed* means "confused."
8. *Sherpas* are people who live in the Himalayas and are hired to carry supplies and otherwise assist mountain climbers in their ascents.

Big Idea On the Move *How do Krakauer's and Adams's different travel experiences affect their assessment of the situation on Mount Everest?* **BI**

Literary Element Structure *Where is Krakauer? How is he using his location to tell his story?* **L**

Vocabulary
tenuously (ten ′ ū əs lē) *adv.* uncertainly; shakily

Additional Support

Skills Practice

READING: Cause and Effect
Krakauer's goal is partly to find out why people died on Mount Everest and why he didn't. He looks at causes and effects repeatedly. Causes are the reasons events happen, and effects are the results of causes. For example, Krakauer's panic is rising because he has run out of oxygen.

Ask students to read page 418 and look for other cause-and-effect relationships. Have them identify these in single sentences:

- _____ caused _____.
- _____ happened because of _____. **OL**

The summit ridge viewed from the South Summit in the early afternoon of May 10, 1996, as the climbers moved to the top. ★

Viewing the Photograph: What do you find most striking about this photograph? Explain.

Teach

★ Viewing the Photograph

Answer: *Students may say that it shows the final approach to the top of the world's highest mountain.*

The South Summit of Everest is located at 28,700 feet. Traditionally, this is the place where climbers decide to tackle the remaining challenges on the way to the summit, or turn around. **AS**

English Language Coach

Using a Dictionary Tell students that this selection contains many challenging words. Point out some vocabulary with which students may be unfamiliar. Direct students' attention to the word *ambient* in the third paragraph on page 418. Ask students what they think the word means, and then have them use a dictionary to look up the definition. Do the same for the following words: *cognitive, marginal, indeterminate, materialized, precarious, lamented,* and *cerebral cortex.* **EL**

Academic Standards

Additional Support activities on pp. 418 and 419 cover the following standards:

Skills Practice: **9.3** [Identify] story elements such as...plot...

English Language Coach: **9.1** Use...context clues and a growing knowledge of English to determine the meaning of words...

Teach

BI Big Idea

On the Move Possible answer: *The presence of other people has both hindered and helped Krakauer's movement. Without the traffic jam, he would not have run out of oxygen so soon. Without Mike Groom, he would have been stuck on Hillary Step.* OL

★ Viewing the Photograph

As a result of Everest's growing popularity with climbers, the mountain has become polluted. For example, the South Col at 26,000 feet is cluttered with items, such as bottles and climbing poles. *Col* is Welsh for "pass," and the South Col is the pass between Everest and Lhotse. AS

Doug Hansen approaching the summit, with Mike Groom descending behind. ★

down the fixed lines,[9] stiff with dread. Just below the step, Anatoli and Martin scooted around me and hurried down. Exercising extreme caution, I continued descending the tightrope of the ridge, but fifty feet above the oxygen cache the rope ended, and I balked at going farther without gas.

Over at the South Summit, I could see Andy Harris sorting through a pile of orange oxygen bottles. "Yo, Harold!"[10] I yelled, "Could you bring me a fresh bottle?"

"There's no oxygen here!" the guide shouted back. "These bottles are all empty!" This was disturbing news. My brain screamed for oxygen. I didn't know what to do. Just then, Mike Groom caught up to me on his way down from the summit. Mike had climbed Everest in 1993 without gas, and he wasn't overly concerned about going without. He gave me his oxygen bottle, and we quickly scrambled over to the South Summit.[11]

When we got there, an examination of the oxygen cache immediately revealed that there were at least six full bottles. Andy, however, refused to believe it. He kept insisting that they were all empty, and nothing Mike or I said could convince him otherwise.

The only way to know how much gas is in a canister is to attach it to your regulator and read the gauge; presumably this is how Andy had checked the bottles at the South

9. *Fixed lines,* also referred to later as *fixed ropes,* are ropes that have been put in place by others in the most challenging parts of the mountain. Climbers are supposed to clip a short safety tether to these ropes as they ascend or descend.

10. *Harold* was Andy Harris's nickname.

11. The *South Summit* is a short distance below Hillary Step.

Big Idea On the Move *How important is the presence of other people on Mount Everest to Krakauer's ability to move safely?* BI

Additional Support

Skills Practice

VOCABULARY: Idioms Tell students that a *gauge* is a meter that shows how much oxygen is in the tank. Pronounce the word and have them repeat after you. Explain that *fouled with ice* means "clogged with ice." The idiom *on the fritz* means "broken" or "working intermittently." Language historians think this phrase began after World War I. The Germans, who were often referred to by the common German name *Fritz,* were defeated. Therefore, something that didn't work was like the Germans. OL

Summit. After the expedition, Neal Beidleman pointed out that if Andy's regulator had become fouled with ice, the gauge might have registered empty even though the canisters were full, which would explain his bizarre obstinacy. And if his regulator was perhaps on the fritz and not delivering oxygen to his mask, that would also explain Andy's apparent lack of lucidity.[12]

This possibility—which now seems so self-evident—didn't occur to either Mike or me at the time, however. In hindsight,[13] Andy was acting irrationally and had plainly slipped well beyond routine hypoxia, but I was so mentally impeded myself that it simply didn't register.

My inability to discern the obvious was **exacerbated** to some degree by the guide-client protocol. Andy and I were very similar in terms of physical ability and technical expertise; had we been climbing together in a nonguided situation as equal partners, it's inconceivable to me that I would have neglected to recognize his plight.[14] But on this expedition he had been cast in the role of **invincible** guide, there to look after me and the other clients; we had been specifically indoctrinated not to question our guides' judgment. The thought never entered my crippled mind that Andy might in fact be in terrible straits—that a guide might urgently need help from me.

As Andy continued to assert that there were no full bottles at the South Summit, Mike looked at me quizzically. I looked back and shrugged. Turning to Andy, I said, "No big deal, Harold. Much ado about nothing." Then I grabbed a new oxygen canister, screwed it onto my regulator, and headed down the mountain. Given what unfolded over the hours that followed, the ease with which I abdicated responsibility—my utter failure to consider that Andy might have been in serious trouble—was a lapse that's likely to haunt me for the rest of my life.

Around 3:30 PM I left the South Summit ahead of Mike, Yasuko, and Andy, and almost immediately descended into a dense layer of clouds. Light snow started to fall. I could scarcely tell where the mountain ended and where the sky began in the flat, diminishing light; it would have been very easy to blunder off the edge of the ridge and never be heard from again. And the conditions only worsened as I moved down the peak.

At the bottom of the rock steps on the Southeast Ridge I stopped with Mike to wait for Yasuko, who was having difficulty negotiating the fixed ropes. He attempted to call Rob on the radio, but Mike's transmitter was working only intermittently and he couldn't raise anybody. With Mike looking after Yasuko, and both Rob and Andy accompanying Doug Hansen—the only other client still above us—I assumed the situation was under control. So as Yasuko caught up to us, I asked Mike's permission to continue down alone. "Fine," he replied. "Just don't walk off any cornices."[15]

About 4:45 PM, when I reached the Balcony[16]—the promontory at 27,600 feet on the Southeast Ridge where I'd sat watching the sunrise with Ang Dorje—I was shocked

12. *Lucidity* means "mental clarity."
13. *Hindsight* is the ability to see past events clearly and with wisdom, often in a way that was not possible at the time the events occurred.
14. Here, *plight* means "a dangerous condition or state."
15. *Cornices* are snowy, unsupported overhangs.
16. The *Balcony* is a projecting mass of land on the Southeast Ridge, the place where two of the faces or slopes of Mount Everest meet.

Reading Strategy Monitoring Comprehension *Monitor your comprehension by explaining Andy Harris's behavior. If necessary, reread.* **R1**

Vocabulary

exacerbate (ig zas ′ər bāt ′) *v.* to make worse, more violent, or more bitter

invincible (in vin ′sə bəl) *adj.* not able to be beaten or overcome

Reading Strategy Monitoring Comprehension *What does Krakauer mean by "a lapse"? Why will the lapse haunt him? If you are not sure of the answers, reread.* **R2**

Literary Element Structure *What clues are given here to chronological and spatial order?* **L**

Teach

R1 Reading Strategy

Monitoring Comprehension
Answer: *Andy thought all the oxygen bottles were empty at the time, but they were not. Reflecting on this later, Krakauer realizes that Harris was probably not getting enough oxygen.* **OL**

R2 Reading Strategy

Monitoring Comprehension
Answer: *The lapse was not realizing that Andy might have been in serious trouble. This will haunt him "given what unfolded over the hours that followed": a foreshadowing of disaster for Andy.* **OL**

L Literary Element

Structure **Answer:** *The time and location are both given. It is later in the day (the last mention of time was 3:30 PM) and lower on the mountain.* **OL**

Building Reading Fluency

Multiple Characters Krakauer includes a lot of dialogue, thus creating a storylike narrative in his memoir. Invite students to read aloud in character to clarify who is speaking and to gain oral fluency. Have pairs or groups review any unfamiliar vocabulary before reading a chosen passage. **BL**

Reading in the Real World

Careers Discuss jobs that may involve decisions that impact others' lives. Have students read about careers in law enforcement, fire safety, dangerous sports, or other jobs where a life decision might be made. Invite students to share their findings. **OL**

Academic Standards

Additional Support activities on pp. 420 and 421 cover the following standards:

Skills Practice: **9.1** [Use] relationships, and origins…to determine the meaning of words…

Building Reading Fluency: **9.7** [Develop] speaking skills…in conjunction with…strategies…[for] delivery of oral presentations.

Reading in the Real World: **9.7.15** Deliver expository (informational) presentations that convey information and ideas from…sources accurately and coherently…

Teach

BI Big Idea

On the Move Answer: *Beck is determined and perhaps irrational; he has climbed part of the mountain in an almost blind condition. This mountain is challenging even for sighted climbers.* OL

L Literary Element

Structure Answer: *He notes the coming darkness, the approach of night.*

Ask: How does the reference to night link readers to Beck's earlier discussion of his vision problem? *(Beck said earlier that he hoped his vision would clear in greater daylight. This implies the problem will get worse in fading light.)* OL

★ Medical History

Eye Surgery Nearsightedness, also called myopia, is the inability to see things in the distance. During radial keratotomy surgery, incisions are made in the cornea. This allows the cornea to flatten, bringing the focal point closer to the retina, and improving distance vision. AS

to encounter Beck Weathers, standing alone in the snow, shivering violently. I'd assumed that he'd descended to Camp Four[17] hours earlier. "Beck!" I exclaimed, "what are you still doing up here?"

Years earlier, Beck had undergone a radial keratotomy[18] to correct his vision. A side effect of the surgery, he discovered early in the Everest climb, was that the low barometric pressure that exists at high altitude caused his eyesight to fail. The higher he climbed, the lower the barometric pressure fell, and the worse his vision became.

The previous afternoon as he was ascending from Camp Three to Camp Four, Beck later confessed to me, "my vision had gotten so bad that I couldn't see more than a few feet. So I just tucked right behind John Taske and when he'd lift a foot I'd place my foot right in his bootprint."

Beck had spoken openly of his vision problem earlier, but with the summit in reach he neglected to mention its increasing severity to Rob or anyone else. His bad eyes notwithstanding, he was climbing well and feeling stronger than he had since the beginning of the expedition, and, he explained, "I didn't want to bail out prematurely."

Climbing above the South Col through the night, Beck managed to keep up with the group by employing the same strategy he'd used the previous afternoon—stepping in the footsteps of the person directly in front of him. But by the time he reached the Balcony and the sun came up, he realized his vision was worse than ever. In addition, he'd inadvertently rubbed some ice crystals into his eyes, lacerating both corneas.[19]

"At that point," Beck revealed, "one eye was completely blurred over, I could barely see out of the other, and I'd lost all depth perception. I felt that I couldn't see well enough to climb higher without being a danger to myself or a burden to someone else, so I told Rob what was going on."

"Sorry pal," Rob immediately announced, "you're going down. I'll send one of the Sherpas down with you." But Beck wasn't quite ready to give up his summit hopes: "I explained to Rob that I thought there was a pretty good chance my vision would improve once the sun got higher and my pupils contracted. I said I wanted to wait a little while, and then boogie on up after everybody else if I started seeing more clearly."

Rob considered Beck's proposal, then decreed, "O.K., fair enough. I'll give you half an hour to find out. But I can't have you going down to Camp Four on your own. If your vision isn't better in thirty minutes I want you to stay here so I know exactly where you are until I come back from the summit, then we can go down together. I'm very serious about this: either you go down right now, or you promise me you'll sit right here until I return."

"So I crossed my heart and hoped to die," Beck told me good-naturedly as we stood in the blowing snow and waning light. "And I've kept my word. Which is why I'm still standing here."

Shortly after noon, Stuart Hutchison, John Taske, and Lou Kasischke had gone past on their way down with Lhakpa and Kami, but Weathers elected not to accompany them. "The weather was still good," he explains, "and I saw no reason to break my promise to Rob at that point."

Now, however, it was getting dark and conditions were turning grim. "Come down with me," I implored. "It will be at least another two or three hours before Rob shows up. I'll be your eyes. I'll get you down, no problem." Beck was nearly persuaded to descend with me when I made the mistake of mentioning that Mike Groom was on his way down with Yasuko, a few minutes

17. *Camp Four* is the highest camp.
18. A *radial keratotomy* is surgery for nearsightedness.
19. The ice crystals cut the *cornea,* a clear layer that covers the iris and pupil, of each of Beck's eyes.

Big Idea On the Move *How would you describe Beck's desire to continue the climb?* BI

Literary Element Structure *How does Krakauer remind the reader of the chronological structure?* L

Additional Support

Skills Practice

WRITING: Signal Words Krakauer jumps back and forth in time to provide background about his fellow climbers. He uses chronological sequence words to orient readers. For example, he says *Years earlier,* before explaining the surgery Beck Weathers had and its impact on Beck's eyesight while on the climb. Ask students to find other examples of signal words that Krakauer uses to orient readers in time and space. Have students write a paragraph using at least two sequence words to orient readers. OL

Late in the afternoon during the descent from the summit of Mount Everest.

behind me. In a day of many mistakes, this would turn out to be one of the larger ones.

"Thanks anyway," Beck said. "I think I'll just wait for Mike. He's got a rope; he'll be able to short-rope[20] me down."

"O.K., Beck," I replied. "It's your call. I guess I'll see you in camp, then." Secretly, I was relieved that I wouldn't have to deal with getting Beck down the problematic slopes to come, most of which were not protected by fixed lines. Daylight was waning, the weather was worsening, my reserves of strength were nearly gone. Yet I still didn't have any sense that calamity[21] was around the corner. Indeed, after talking with Beck I even took the time to find a spent oxygen canister that I'd stashed in the snow on the way up some ten hours earlier. Wanting to remove all my trash from the mountain, I stuffed it into my pack with my other two bottles (one empty, one partially full) and then hurried toward the South Col, 1,600 feet below.

From the Balcony I descended a few hundred feet down a broad, gentle snow gully without incident, but then things began to get sketchy. The route meandered through outcroppings of broken shale blanketed with six inches of fresh snow. Negotiating the puzzling, infirm[22] **terrain** demanded unceasing concentration, an all-but-impossible feat in my punch-drunk state.

20. To *short-rope* is to pull a second climber along using a rope attached to a leading climber.
21. A *calamity* is a great loss.

22. Here, *infirm* means "not solid."

Reading Strategy Monitoring Comprehension
Describe the encounter between Krakauer and Beck. If necessary, reread. **R**

Vocabulary
terrain (tə rān′) *n.* the physical features of the land

Teach

R Reading Strategy

Monitoring Comprehension

Answer: *Krakauer urges Beck to descend with him but is relieved when Beck refuses. Krakauer does not feel the sense of urgency at this moment that he should have felt.* **OL**

Differentiated Instruction

VOCABULARY: Negating Prefixes

Explain that the prefixes *in-* and *im-* are examples of negating prefixes. Usually, they mean "not," "without," or "the opposite of," and reverse the meaning of the attached base word. When the terrain is "infirm," it is "not firm." Sometimes the letters *in* appear at the beginning of words, such as in *incident,* and are not negating prefixes but part of the base word. Have students find three words in the selection that begin with *in-, im-* or the other variations *il-* or *ir.* They should define those that begin with negating prefixes. **BL**

Academic Standards

Additional Support activities on pp. 422 and 423 cover the following standards:

Skills Practice: **9.3.6** Analyze and trace an author's development of time and sequence… **9.4.13** Establish coherence within and among paragraphs through effective transitions…

Differentiated Instruction: **9.1** [Use] word parts…to determine the meaning of words…

Teach

R1 Reading Strategy

Monitoring Comprehension
Answer: *Students may say that they knew what was coming (an earlier conversation between Adams and Krakauer on page 418 alludes to the storm), and so they could read at a fairly rapid pace.* OL

L1 Literary Element

Structure Point out the words "In the morning. . . ."
Ask: What do these words suggest about the order of events in this paragraph? *(They suggest a brief flashback to the morning's events.)* OL

★ Cultural History

Tenzing Norgay For more than 20 years, Tenzing Norgay climbed with expeditions trying to reach the summit of Mt. Everest. After reaching his goal in 1953, Norgay became a representative of the high altitude Sherpas. AS

Because the wind had erased the tracks of the climbers who'd gone down before me, I had difficulty determining the correct route. In 1993, Mike Groom's partner—Lopsang Tshering Bhutia, a skilled Himalayan climber who was a nephew of Tenzing Norgay's[23]—had taken a wrong turn in this area and fallen to his death. Fighting to maintain a grip on reality, I started talking to myself out loud. "Keep it together, keep it together, keep it together," I chanted over and over, mantra-like.[24] "This is way serious. Keep it together."

I sat down to rest on a broad, sloping ledge, but after a few minutes a deafening boom! frightened me back to my feet. Enough new snow had accumulated that I feared a massive slab avalanche had released on the slopes above, but when I spun around to look I saw nothing. Then there was another boom!, accompanied by a flash that momentarily lit up the sky, and I realized I was hearing the crash of thunder.

In the morning, on the way up, I'd made a point of continually studying the route on this part of the mountain, frequently looking down to pick out landmarks that would be helpful on the descent, compulsively memorizing the terrain: "Remember to turn left at the buttress that looks like a ship's prow.[25] Then follow that skinny line of snow until it curves sharply to the right." This was something I'd trained myself to do many years earlier, a drill I forced myself to go through every time I climbed, and on Everest it may have saved my life. By 6:00 PM, as the storm escalated into a full-scale blizzard with driving snow and winds gusting in excess of 60 knots,[26] I came upon the rope that had been fixed by the Montenegrins on the snow slope 600 feet above the Col. Sobered by the force of the rising tempest, I realized that I'd gotten down the trickiest ground just in the nick of time.

Wrapping the fixed line around my arms to rappel,[27] I continued down through the blizzard. Some minutes later I was overwhelmed by a disturbingly familiar feeling of suffocation, and I realized that my oxygen had once again run out. Three hours earlier when I'd attached my regulator to my third and last oxygen canister, I'd noticed that the gauge indicated that the bottle was only half full. I'd figured that would be enough to get me most of the way down, though, so I hadn't bothered exchanging it for a full one. And now the gas was gone.

I pulled the mask from my face, left it hanging around my neck, and pressed onward, surprisingly unconcerned. However, without supplemental oxygen, I moved more slowly, and I had to stop and rest more often.

The literature of Everest is rife[28] with accounts of hallucinatory experiences attributable to hypoxia and fatigue. In 1933, the noted English climber Frank Smythe observed "two curious looking objects floating in the sky" directly above him at 27,000 feet: "[One] possessed what appeared to be squat underdeveloped wings, and the other a protuberance[29] suggestive of a beak. They hovered motionless but seemed slowly to pulsate." In 1980, during his solo ascent, Reinhold Messner imagined that an invisible companion was climbing beside him. Gradually, I became aware that my mind had gone haywire in a similar fashion, and I observed my own slide from reality with a blend of fascination and horror.

I was so far beyond ordinary exhaustion that I experienced a queer **detachment** from my body, as if I were observing my descent

23. Tenzing Norgay and Edmund Hillary were the first climbers ever to reach the top of Mount Everest.
24. A *mantra* is a prayerlike repetition of syllables, words, or phrases for mystical purposes.
25. Krakauer describes a *buttress,* or a large, projecting rock, that looks like a *prow,* or the front part of a ship or boat.
26. *60 knots* is about 69 mph.
27. To *rappel* is to descend from a height by sliding down a rope.
28. Here, *rife* means "full of" or "overflowing with."
29. A *protuberance* is something that sticks out.

Reading Strategy Monitoring Comprehension *Did you slow down, speed up, or maintain the same reading rate as you read this paragraph? Explain.* R1

Vocabulary
detachment (di tach ′ mənt) *n.* indifference; a state of being apart from

Additional Support

Skills Practice

READING: Problem and Solution
Identifying problems and solutions can help students understand narrative nonfiction. Suggest these questions: What is the main problem? Who has the problem? What solutions are tried? What happens as a result?

Explain that Jon Krakauer discusses many problems—his own and others'—as he recounts his attempt to solve his problem of getting off the summit alive. Ask students to list at least three problems Krakauer discusses and then answer the questions about each. OL from a few feet overhead. I imagined that I was dressed in a green cardigan and wingtips. And although the gale was generating a windchill in excess of seventy below zero Fahrenheit, I felt strangely, disturbingly warm.

At 6:30, as the last of the daylight seeped from the sky, I'd descended to within 200 vertical feet of Camp Four. Only one obstacle now stood between me and safety: a bulging incline of hard, glassy ice that I would have to descend without a rope. Snow pellets borne by 70-knot gusts stung my face; any exposed flesh was instantly frozen. The tents, no more than 650 horizontal feet away, were only intermittently visible through the whiteout. There was no margin for error. Worried about making a critical blunder, I sat down to marshal[30] my energy before descending further.

Once I was off my feet, inertia[31] took hold. It was so much easier to remain at rest than to summon the initiative to tackle the dangerous ice slope; so I just sat there as the storm roared around me, letting my mind drift, doing nothing for perhaps forty-five minutes.

I'd tightened the drawstrings on my hood until only a tiny opening remained around my eyes, and I was removing the useless, frozen oxygen mask from beneath my chin when Andy Harris suddenly appeared out of the gloom beside me. Shining my headlamp in his direction, I reflexively recoiled when I saw the appalling condition of his face. His cheeks were coated with an armor of frost, one eye was frozen shut, and he was slurring his words badly. He looked in serious trouble. "Which way to the tents?" Andy blurted, frantic to reach shelter.

30. To *marshal* is to bring together in an effective way.
31. Here, *inertia* means "the tendency of a body at rest to remain at rest."

Literary Element Structure *Summarize how time and place have changed since the beginning of the essay.* L2

Big Idea On the Move *What is Andy's attitude toward the climb at this point?* BI

I pointed in the direction of Camp Four, then warned him about the ice just below us. "It's steeper than it looks!" I yelled, straining to make myself heard over the tempest. "Maybe I should go down first and get a rope from camp—" As I was in midsentence, Andy abruptly turned away and moved over the lip of the ice slope, leaving me sitting there dumbfounded.[32]

Scooting on his butt, he started down the steepest part of the incline. "Andy," I shouted after him, "it's crazy to try it like that! You're going to blow it for sure!" He yelled something back, but his words were carried off by the screaming wind. A second later he lost his purchase, flipped ass over teakettle, and was suddenly rocketing headfirst down the ice.

Two hundred feet below, I could just make out Andy's motionless form slumped at the foot of the incline. I was sure he'd broken at least a leg, maybe his neck. But then, incredibly, he stood up, waved that he was O.K., and started lurching[33] toward Camp Four, which, at the moment was in plain sight, 500 feet beyond.

I could see the shadowy forms of three or four people standing outside the tents; their headlamps flickered through curtains of blowing snow. I watched Harris walk toward them across the flats, a distance he covered in less than ten minutes. When the clouds closed in a moment later, cutting off my view, he was within sixty feet of the tents, maybe closer. I didn't see him again after that, but I was certain that he'd reached the security of camp, where Chuldum and Arita would doubtless be waiting with hot tea. Sitting out in the storm, with the ice bulge still standing between me and the tents, I felt a pang of envy. I was angry that my guide hadn't waited for me.

32. *Dumbfounded* means "so surprised that one cannot speak."
33. To *lurch* is to move in a sudden, irregular way.

Reading Strategy Monitoring Comprehension *Monitor your comprehension by telling who and what the preceding two paragraphs are about. If necessary, reread.* R2

Teach

L2 Literary Element

Structure Answer: *More than four hours have passed. He is within 200 vertical feet of his destination instead of at the top of the mountain.*
Ask: How do you know it is 6:00 PM and not 6:00 AM? *(He says "the last of the daylight seeped from the sky.")* OL

BI Big Idea

On the Move Answer: *Andy is near panic and wants the climb to be over.*
Ask: How does Andy's emotional state affect his judgment? *(He rushes down the slope without evaluating its steepness, and ends up falling.)* OL

R2 Reading Strategy

Monitoring Comprehension
Answer: *They are about Andy's almost miraculously safe descent, his making it almost (and presumably) to safety, and Krakauer's momentary jealousy of that fact.* OL

English Language Coach

Units of Measurement Enhance students' understanding of American units of measurement, such as Fahrenheit for temperature and feet for distance. Provide formulas for conversion (Celsius = (F−32) × 0.5555) or direct students to conversion web sites. Confirm comprehension by asking students to describe activities they would conduct at certain temperatures or to approximate travel that reflects certain distances. Clarify, if necessary, that Americans use a 12-hour time clock, beginning at midnight and noon. EL

Academic Standards

Additional Support activities on pp. 424 and 425 cover the following standards:

Skills Practice: **9.3** [Identify] story elements such as...plot...

English Language Coach: **9.1** Use...a growing knowledge of English and other languages to determine the meaning of words...

Teach

L Literary Element

Structure Answer: *He uses both orders throughout the essay. He only deviates to give background information about past climbers.* OL

★ Viewing the Photograph

This photograph was taken by Caroline Mackenzie, the Base Camp doctor for the expedition. Lack of oxygen (hypoxia), frostbite, and brain swelling are just some of the problems that face doctors on Everest. AS

Use the CheckPoint questions on Presentation Plus! to check students' mastery of the selection. These questions can be used with interactive response keypads for immediate student feedback.

Members of the ill-fated Mount Everest expedition led by Rob Hall (center right) and guide Scott Fischer (center left). John Krakauer is third from left. ★

My backpack held little more than three empty oxygen canisters and a pint of frozen lemonade; it probably weighed no more than sixteen or eighteen pounds. But I was tired, and worried about getting down the incline without breaking a leg, so I tossed the pack over the edge and hoped it would come to rest where I could retrieve it. Then I stood up and started down the ice, which was as smooth and hard as the surface of a bowling ball.

Fifteen minutes of dicey, fatiguing crampon[34] work brought me safely to the bottom of the incline, where I easily located my pack, and another ten minutes after that I was in camp myself. I lunged into my tent with my crampons still on, zipped the door tight, and sprawled across the frost-covered floor too tired to even sit upright. For the first time I had a sense of how wasted I really was: I was more exhausted than I'd ever been in my life. But I was safe. Andy was safe.[35] The others would be coming into camp soon. We'd done it. We'd climbed Everest. It had been a little sketchy there for a while, but in the end everything had turned out great.

It would be many hours before I learned that everything had not in fact turned out great—that nineteen men and women were stranded up on the mountain by the storm, caught in a desperate struggle for their lives.

34. *Crampons* are steel spikes attached to mountaineering boots to prevent sliding on ice and snow.

Literary Element Structure *How consistently does Krakauer use time and spatial order in this essay?* L

35. As Krakauer would realize later, he had mistaken Martin Adams for Andy Harris. In fact, Harris died on the climb while trying to help others reach safety.

Additional Support

Skills Practice

ASSESSMENT: Reading for Information Standardized test questions often assess students' basic comprehension, but questions may vary, depending on the type of excerpt. Suggest these strategies for types of reading:

- Stories: read for character and plot
- Nonfiction: read for main ideas and details
- Persuasive: read to find techniques, such as emotional appeals, or elements, such as bias

Ask: What strategies would you use for this selection? *(story and nonfiction)* OL

AFTER YOU READ

RESPONDING AND THINKING CRITICALLY

Respond

1. What part of this essay interested or startled you the most? Explain.

Recall and Interpret

2. (a)Where is Krakauer at the beginning of this selection? (b)How would you describe his mood or state of mind?
3. (a)What problems does Krakauer have with the climate on the mountain? (b)How do these problems lead to a crucial error on Krakauer's part?
4. (a)Where is Krakauer at the end of the selection? (b)Do you think Krakauer reaches this destination as a result of luck or skill? Explain.

Analyze and Evaluate

5. (a)What storytelling elements appear in this nonfiction selection? (b)How well does Krakauer tell the story of this part of the climb? Use evidence from the selection to back up your opinion.
6. How well does the author convey the dangers the climbers faced?
7. How does Krakauer let the reader know that there are too many people on the mountain and, perhaps, that there are people who should not have been there?

Connect

8. **Big Idea** **On the Move** How does this selection make you feel about the risks and rewards of climbing Mount Everest?

LITERARY ANALYSIS

Literary Element Structure

In this excerpt from *Into Thin Air,* Krakauer arranges the facts of his narrative in both spatial and chronological order. Spatial order shows the descent from the summit, while chronological order shows the passage of time.

1. Where is Krakauer at the beginning of the selection, and where is he at the end? State, in order, at least two places he stops along the way.
2. Explain how elevations, or heights measured in feet, provide a guide to the structure of this selection.
3. How much time would you guess elapses from the beginning of the action to the end? Cite evidence from the selection to support your answer.

Review: Dialogue

As you learned on page 189, **dialogue** is conversation between characters in a literary work. Dialogue is usually set off with quotation marks and dialogue tags, or markers that tell the reader who said what.

Partner Activity Work with a partner to record at least five examples of dialogue from the essay. For each one, identify the speakers, and reflect on the purpose of the dialogue. That is, tell whether the dialogue contributes to characterization, establishes mood, advances the action, helps develop a thesis or theme, or serves some other purpose.

Dialogue	Speakers	Purpose

Literary Element

1. beginning: the summit; end: at Camp Four; on the way down: the Hillary Step and the Balcony
2. Elevations are presented in descending order.
3. More than 5 and a half hours pass; students should calculate times based on the hours in the essay.

Review: Dialogue

Sample answers:

Andy Harris says, "I don't seem to be getting enough air." The purpose is to create a mood of danger, to show something about his character, and to advance the action.

Krakauer says, "Yo, Harold." The purpose is to show his goodwill toward Andy.

AFTER YOU READ

Assess

1. Possible answers: difficulties with oxygen; the bravery/recklessness of a near-blind climber wanting to continue
2. (a) At the top of Mount Everest (b) Eager to descend; his oxygen is running low
3. (a) The thin air deprives his brain of oxygen, and he gets dizzy and confused. (b) He fails to notice Andy Harris's advanced hypoxia.
4. (a) Safely in his tent at Camp Four (b) Both; he reaches camp ahead of the storm's worst; he is cautious and uses the fixed ropes.
5. (a) Characters, setting, events, rising action, suspense, and some foreshadowing (b) Possible answer: very well; vivid descriptions of Rob Hall, Martin Adams, and Andy Harris; details that convey the climb's dangers
6. Very well: descriptive language such as "any exposed flesh was instantly frozen;" dialogue that shows his fear ("Keep it together, keep it together,") and others' fear ("'Which way to the tents?' Andy blurted.")
7. Krakauer details his long wait at the Hillary Step because of "overcrowding," Beck's will despite near blindness, Yasuko's need to be boosted to the top, and his reaction to Andy's reckless final descent.
8. Possible answer: This essay clearly shows the extraordinary danger of such an adventure.

Academic Standards

The Additional Support activity on p. 426 covers the following standard:

Skills Practice: **9.2** Develop [reading] strategies...

AFTER YOU READ

Assess

Reading Strategy

1. Possible answer: The footnote about short-roping clarified the text.
2. Possible answer: Footnotes about the South Summit and the Balcony helped.

Vocabulary

1. b **2.** b **3.** a **4.** a **5.** b

Academic Vocabulary

1. You would need to know the height of Mount Everest and the elevation of Camp Four.
2. Krakauer recovered by getting a new canister of oxygen.

Writing About Literature

Students' essays should

- clearly state an evaluative judgment about Krakauer's memoir.
- provide evidence from the memoir to support their evaluation.
- develop at least three body paragraphs to present supporting evidence.
- conclude with a summarized thesis and additional insight.

Internet Connection

Point out that students may research a specific climber or expedition. Suggest that students conduct brief research independently, and then exchange suggestions for useful Web sites.

READING AND VOCABULARY

Reading Strategy Monitoring Comprehension

Krakauer assumes that his readers have some knowledge about mountaineering, Mount Everest, and the problems of thin air. Rereading, adjusting one's pace, and scanning for additional sources of information, such as footnotes and illustrations, can help in understanding difficult text.

1. Name at least one place where you slowed down to refer to a footnote.
2. Explain how the footnotes helped you understand the features of Mount Everest.

Vocabulary Practice

Practice with Word Parts Choose the word that answers each question. Use a dictionary if you need help.

1. Which word has a suffix used to form a noun?
   a. invincible **b.** detachment
2. Which word has a prefix that means "not"?
   a. terrain **b.** invincible
3. Which word has a Latin root meaning "earth"?
   a. terrain **b.** exacerbated
4. Which word has a suffix used to form a verb or adjective?
   a. exacerbated **b.** tenuously
5. Which word has a suffix that signals an adverb?
   a. detachment **b.** tenuously

Academic Vocabulary

Here are two words from the vocabulary list on page R80.

compute (kəm pūt′) *v.* to determine; to arrive at by using mathematics

recover (ri kuv′ər) *v.* to return to normal

Practice and Apply

1. What facts would you need to **compute** how far Krakauer descended?
2. How did Krakauer **recover** from his state of dizziness and mental confusion?

WRITING AND EXTENDING

Writing About Literature

Evaluate Author's Craft In this excerpt, Krakauer takes you to what mountaineers call "the death zone." How well does he lead you to the edge, or build suspense? Write an essay that states and supports your evaluative judgment.

Begin by identifying and stating your opinion in a clear thesis statement. Then gather evidence from the story that supports your thesis.

ESSAY STRUCTURE

Introductory paragraph with thesis

First body paragraph—first point in support of your thesis; examples and reasons to support your first point

Second body paragraph—second point in support of your thesis; examples and reasons to support your second point

Third body paragraph—third point in support of your thesis; examples and reasons to support your third point

Concluding paragraph

After you complete your draft, have a partner read it and suggest revisions. Then proofread and edit your work to correct errors in spelling, grammar, and punctuation.

Internet Connection

The history of human drama on Mount Everest is long and full of death and glory. Use the Internet to find out about other expeditions and climbers, such as George Leigh Mallory, Tom Hornbein and Willi Unsoeld, David Breashears, and Ed Viesturs. Report on their challenges and triumphs, including facts about their routes, the conditions of their ascents, and first-time feats.

LiteratureOnline Web Activities For eFlashcards, Selection Quick Checks, and other Web activities, go to www.glencoe.com.

LiteratureOnline

Literary Elements Have students access the Web site for interactive activities that will help them assess their understanding of the selection.

Media Link to On the Move

Preview the Article

In "Adventure to Antarctica," Rob Johnson shares his experiences of encountering danger when he and his team traveled to South Georgia Island in Antarctica.

1. What do you already know about Antarctica?
2. Read the *deck*, or the text in large type that appears underneath the title. What type of emotion do you think the author wants you to feel about the voyage he is about to describe?

Set a Purpose for Reading

Read to discover how Rob Johnson and his crew accomplish their goal and reap the rewards of doing so.

Reading Strategy

Analyzing Text Structure

Analyzing text structure involves recognizing the pattern of organization the author uses. The following selection's main pattern of organization is problem and solution. As you read the selection, identify the problem the author illustrates, and the possible solution or solutions he provides. Use a graphic organizer like the one below. **R**

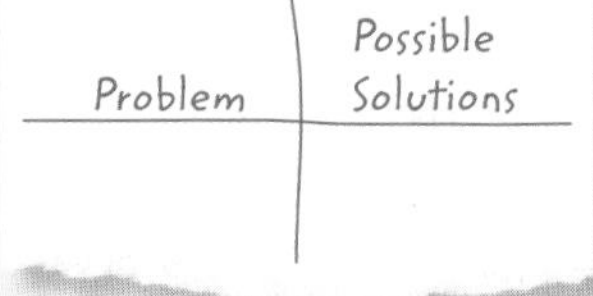

ACADEMIC STANDARDS (pages 429–433)

9.2.3 Generate relevant questions about readings on issues or topics that can be researched.

9.2 Develop [reading] strategies...

TIME

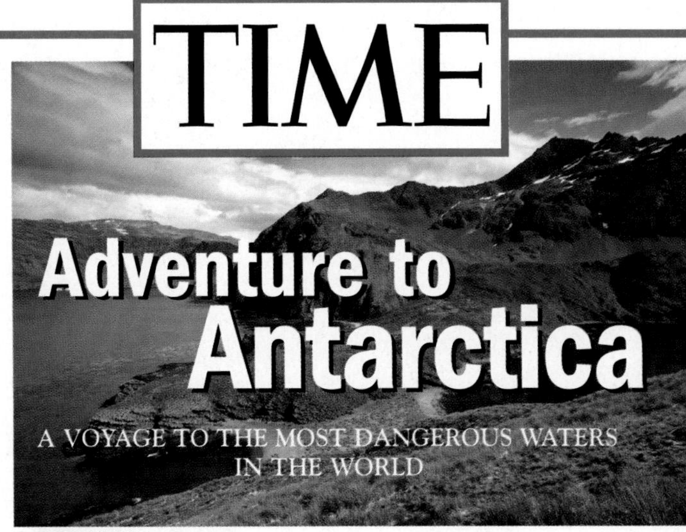

Adventure to Antarctica

A VOYAGE TO THE MOST DANGEROUS WATERS IN THE WORLD

By ROB JOHNSON

South Georgia Island, located in the South Atlantic Ocean, is the breeding ground of Antarctica. Birds and seals live and reproduce there. The island is also the site of the whaling industry in the Southern Ocean for much of the 20th century. This cold and windswept, rocky land is the final resting place and center of drama for the life of British explorer Sir Ernest Shackleton, who wanted to be the first person to cross the frozen continent.

Surrounded by ice and the most famous and dangerous waters in the world, South Georgia Island (SGI) represents the ultimate destination on Earth. With this in mind, I set my sights on sailing to her shores. But nearly 10 years of reading, planning, dreaming, and voyaging would pass before we cast off.

The first thing I had to do was to build *Shaman*, the ship that would take us on our adventure. Her design and construction became the cornerstone of the adventure. My vision of sailing to South Georgia Island became the tool I used to inspire the designer, project manager, boatbuilder, and sail maker as each joined me in creating this 88-foot sailing yacht. Everything about *Shaman* was created with the South Georgia mission in mind. We launched her in 1997, and every voyage aboard her—past many glaciers, through many storms—built my confidence for the passage to South Georgia.

The Management of Fear

To dream and consider is not the same as to act. Setting out on an expedition to SGI is challenging—the water temperature is 30 degrees Fahrenheit, winds are often stronger than 50 knots, and waves frequently reach a height of 50 feet.

We expected to hike on land that features elevation changes of 2,000 to 3,000 feet in a day's trek, and as much as 10,000 feet just a few miles from shore. Besides the weather and the

Informational Text TIME

Focus

Summary

Author Rob Johnson recounts his journey to Antarctica, inspired by his wish to see the final resting place of explorer Sir Ernest Shackleton. Johnson builds a boat, assembles a crew, and sets sail for Antarctica. Once there, the crew visits South Georgia Island, where Shackleton died, and Albatross Island. Johnson is deeply affected by his journey.

Teach

Preview the Article

1. Possible answer: Antarctica is a large, mostly uninhabited continent in the Southern Ocean at the South Pole.
2. Possible answer: The author creates an exciting mood by commenting on the perils of the story to come.

R Reading Strategy

Analyzing Text Structure

Problems may require many solutions and solutions can be multifaceted. Some problems are abstract, as in emotions such as fear. Others are concrete, as in staying aboard a ship in high seas. **OL**

Differentiated Instruction

Characters Although this article is nonfiction, it reads as if it were fiction. The character list is long. Have students construct a character web to keep all the people straight. In each cell, students can list the character's name and his or her role on the crew. **BL**

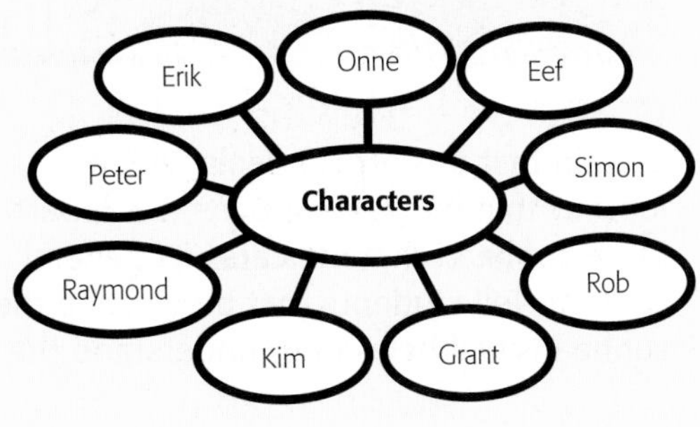

Readability Scores

Dale-Chall: 7.6

DRP: 61

Lexile: 1020

Academic Standards

The Additional Support activity on p. 429 covers the following standard:

Differentiated Instruction: **9.3** [Identify] story elements such as character...

Teach

BI Big Idea

On the Move Point out that Rob Johnson acknowledges that fear is a component of every journey. His goal was to use that fear in the service of the journey, rather than allowing it to detour the journey. OL

R1 Reading Strategy

Analyzing Text Structure
Say: As you read the subhead The Team, ask yourself how each crew member solves a particular problem. OL

★ Cultural History

Shaman Rob names his boat *Shaman,* a term that refers to a spiritual leader in many cultures. In some Asian and American Indian cultures, a shaman possesses healing powers. The term may also be used to suggest the power to control events, as perhaps Rob hoped for with his choice of name. AS

Onne Van Der Wal

land, there were other dangers to face. Animals, in this case fur seals, can bite, leaving a deadly infection, and South Georgia does not have a hospital.

Fear will always be present when risk and danger are real, yet too much fear can limit an adventure. Much pleasure, excitement, and achievement are lost if you give in to it. Yet you can't ignore fear. It is more dangerous to say it doesn't exist. BI

I believe that the central focus of expedition sailing is fear management. Are the boat, the equipment, the team, and the preparation thorough enough to manage the risk of a dangerous expedition? Does the crew get along and do they trust and support one another? How does the team work together to roll back the envelope of the fear that limits action—roll back, but not eliminate, fear to get the most from the experience?

The Team R1

I selected a team of nine people, including myself. Raymond Wroe Street and Kim Broas had been aboard *Shaman* for four years. They knew her inside out and were in charge of the mechanical and logistics preparations. Raymond's brother, Grant, and Simon Laight were the athletes. Grant was an experienced outdoorsman, hiker, and climber. We would need Simon's and Grant's help once we landed on the island. ★

Since the Southern Ocean is so dangerous, I needed experienced sailors, some of whom knew how to steer in heavy seas. An 88-foot sloop, such as *Shaman,* can reach speeds of 20 knots or more in the conditions that sailors find in the rough Southern Ocean. A mistake aboard a 100,000 pound yacht hurtling through

Additional Support

See also Active Learning and Note Taking Guide, pp. 66–73.

Skills Practice

READING: Previewing
Explain that this article deals with a journey that has several parts. Each part has a subhead that indicates its general content. Tell students that previewing the subheads will help them understand the selection. Encourage students to list all the subheads, and consider what each subhead adds to the main title. Then have students pause after each subsection to paraphrase. OL

The crew socialized with the residents of Albatross Island.

Onne Van Der Wal

confused seas at that speed can be costly.

Erik Soper had a strong spirit. He came to be known as Crean after the member of Shackleton's crew Tom Crean, who was at Shackleton's side throughout his voyage. Every job was his job in his mind. Erik proved to us all that we could do more.

THIS IS THE MOST AMAZING PLACE I HAVE EVER BEEN. IT WILL PROBABLY BE THE MOST AMAZING PLACE I WILL EVER GO.

Onne van der Wal was our photographer. He is a fine sailor and had sailed the Southern Ocean before. His skill as a seaman added to our confidence, and his pictures preserved our memories so we could share them forever.

Peter Wilson was the project manager in the building of *Shaman*, and an experienced seaman. He was formerly a captain and ocean racer. I was delighted that he had the chance to experience firsthand the ship which he had helped create.

We also needed knowledge of the island, its harbors, and its dangers. We were very fortunate to find a guide in Eef Willems. Eef had been to SGI several times, taking part in studies of the island's animal population. He also knew SGI's geology, animal life, wind conditions, and places to go for shelter. Eef had a very loving, enthusiastic, and encouraging way about her that was so important to her leadership. We could feel that she wanted us to stretch to see what she knew was waiting for us, and that she cared about our safety.

Departure R2

We left Ushuaia, Argentina, on February 7, 2003, and stopped briefly in Chile. Then we sailed out into the ocean, where light winds greeted us, eventually growing to 25 knots. We clipped along at 10–12 knots, at last on our way. Eef told us what we could expect during the 1,300-mile trip to SGI. Temperatures were cool and we spent time reviewing safety procedures. Everyone on deck had to wear a safety harness and be clipped to a tether so we wouldn't fall overboard. In addition, everyone on deck wore a life jacket and an emergency radio locator in case we *did* fall overboard!

Our trip was largely uneventful for 800 miles. Eef continued to tell stories about the island, which made us excited to see it. As we got closer, icebergs, 200 to 400 feet high, began to appear on the horizon. We were able to see the ice on radar, and during the daylight hours (about 19 hours of the day in the Antarctic summer), we could spot them in the distance. As the ice masses grew in number, Eef requested that we slow the boat to 5 knots or less during darkness. She also suggested that we put a crew member on the ship's bow during daylight as a lookout for ice. As excited as we were to reach the

Informational Text
TIME

Teach

R2 Reading Strategy

Analyzing Text Structure
Say: Each subhead identifies new problems. What are the problems in the section under the subhead Departure? *(Possible answers: not falling overboard; avoiding icebergs)* OL

Cultural History

Icebergs These massive islands of freshwater ice break off from glaciers and float across the ocean. The portion viewed above the water is a small fraction (one-seventh to one-tenth) of the entire iceberg. As a result, icebergs are extremely dangerous to ships. AS

English Language Coach

Build Background To help English learners visualize the land Johnson and his crew visit, review the animal names *fur seals, elephant seals,* and *penguins.* Explain that Steven Spielberg, mentioned on page 432 is a well-known film director. Johnson finds the scores to those films dramatic. The San Diego Zoo is a well-known zoo in California. Right Whale Island is named for a particular type of whale. One kind of Right Whale lives mostly south of the equator and may be where the island gets its name. EL

Academic Standards

Additional Support activities on pp. 430 and 431 cover the following standards:

Skills Practice: **9.2.1** Analyze the structure and format of…documents…and explain how authors use the features to achieve their purposes.

English Language Coach: **9.2** Develop [reading] strategies…

Teach

R1 Reading Strategy

Analyzing Text Structure
Ask: What personal characteristics does Shackleton use to solve his problems? *(Possible answer: courage, endurance, persistence, physical stamina)* OL

★ Cultural History

Heroic Era Ernest Shackleton went to Antarctica several times. On one journey in 1907, he and his crew traveled to within 100 nautical miles of the South Pole. They confirmed that the site was on actual land, not ice. These explorations occurred during an era of great exploration at the poles. Known as the Heroic Era, it features the race between Captain Scott and Roald Amundsen to reach the South Pole. Amundsen won the race. Scott made it but perished on the return trip. AS

island, we were all in favor of Eef's safer—if slower—approach.

Approach and First Landing

On a slightly hazy and overcast day, we sailed up to the northwest corner of the island toward Right Whale Bay. As we approached the anchorage, two things were clear. First, the symphony of animal cries was worthy of a Steven Spielberg movie. Fur seals, elephant seals, and penguins provided a continuous soundtrack. As dusk approached, we could make out the outlines of the many animals playing on the beach.

Second, our sense of smell told us that this place was different from any most of us had ever visited. Not even the monkey house at the San Diego Zoo could compare with this notification that animal life was abundant. In my journal of the day I wrote:

Animal cries were everywhere. Awe was in every pair of eyes I explored. The excitement of the romantic quest to the land of Shackleton had given way to that which was before our eyes and in our ears.

Ernest Henry Shackleton R1

Many times, close examination deflates the reputation of a heroic figure. In this case, though, the more we explored the experience of Shackleton, the more powerful his heroism became. Shackleton, who had hoped to be the first person to travel across Antarctica, had the sense to place the value of human life above his personal record of achievement. In the end he is all the more heroic for the choices he made.

In 1915, Shackleton's ship was crushed in the ice near Elephant Island, about 800 miles from a whaling center on SGI. To save his crew, the explorer and five of his strongest men sailed and rowed 800 miles in a 22-foot boat to get help from the whalers. As we visited the beach where Shackleton landed after his trip, and as we traced parts of his dangerous three-day hike across the island, we could see and feel how dismaying the task must have been to the men seeking help for their stranded crew.

Perhaps even more remarkable was that Shackleton returned to Elephant Island and rescued all of his team. Every one of them was alive after months of living on the ice, eating penguins, and burning seal blubber for warmth.

Shackleton died in 1922, aboard ship while docked at a harbor along SGI. On February 15, 2003, the 129th anniversary of Shackleton's birth, we visited his grave on South Georgia and had cake inscribed with the Shackleton family motto, "By Endurance We Conquer." Written on the back of the gravestone is the following: "I held that a man should strive to the uttermost for his life's set prize. —Robert Browning." ★

Albatross Island

We spent two days on Albatross Island playing with the wandering albatross, the largest existing bird species that can fly. This last stop was the most moving of experiences for me. I stood in the grass with my still and video cameras, and watched birds perform their mating dance. As they flew overhead, their 11-foot wingspan ripped the winds. At one point, two birds came up next to me. One of them nibbled on my glove. It then turned and sat down not 18 inches from my right thigh. I took off my glove and sat there petting its beautiful white-feathered back. Tears flowed down my cheeks. Tenderness and wonder filled my spirit.

After returning to *Shaman* I wrote in my journal: *I touched a bird and something in me was touched. At that moment, standing with Simon, Eef, Peter, and Onne, I could feel that I have completed what I came here to do. I cannot tell you what it is that I came here to do. But I know I have completed it. I am ready to come home. I do not entirely*

Onne Van Der Wal

Additional Support

Skills Practice

LITERARY ELEMENT: Sensory Details Johnson describes his surroundings and the trip with sensory details—sound, smell, touch, sight. Help students list these details in a chart:

Sounds	Sights	Smells	Touch
Van Morrison	eleven-foot wingspan	monkey house	nibbled on my glove

OL

know why I built this boat. I do not know why South Georgia Island was my ultimate destination from the beginning. When we took off, I expected it to be stimulating and, at times, stunning. But I did not know all of what I wanted to accomplish. I did not know either, early on, what would free my mind to set sail away from here feeling . . . . satisfied . . . . We have seen a lot, and the experience of this island has been significantly more powerful than I had expected. Even with high expectations, I do not know now why this moment with the wandering albatross completed my satisfaction, and I do not even know what it is that constitutes completeness. I just feel it. I can come home now.

Onne Van Der Wal (2)

Heading Home R2

The magnetic pull of family, business, and friendships grew increasingly strong. Snow was falling on the mountains as we left, and winds were moderate. Dolphins and albatross took turns as escorts, leading our parade toward home. Winds and seas continued to build as we crossed the rough waters.

This was our final test. Four times, waves crashing into the steering cockpit knocked the helmsman off of his feet. The power of the Southern Ocean lived up to the tales, and I knew we did not see the worst of its anger. *Shaman* was strong and the crew was capable, but we were aware that the sea could take us if it wanted to.

As we sailed north, the conditions eased and the temperatures warmed enough to let us step out of our woolies and wet gear. A beautiful sunrise and Van Morrison on the stereo brought relief to everyone.

That evening, we landed in Montevideo, Uruguay, and tied the ship to the dock. *Shaman* had safely completed that which she had been designed to do. It was the trip of a lifetime. I am so grateful.

—Updated 2005, from *Yachting*, October 2004

RESPONDING AND THINKING CRITICALLY

Respond

1. After reading about Johnson's travels, how would you describe his personality?

Recall and Interpret

2. (a)How long did Johnson prepare for the voyage? (b)How do you think the time he spent preparing affected his coping skills while on the voyage?
3. (a)What does Johnson think about fear? (b)Do you agree with his philosophy? Why or why not?
4. (a)What did Ernest Shackleton do to save his crew? (b)How do you think Shackleton's rescue efforts inspired Johnson's idea of a team?

Analyze and Evaluate

5. Why does Johnson describe each member of his team?
6. Why do you think Johnson points out the Shackleton family motto, "By Endurance We Conquer"? What does this say about Johnson's values?
7. Johnson wrote in his journal, "I could feel that I completed what I came here to do. I cannot tell you what it is that I came here to do. But I know I have completed it." Why may he have felt this?

Connect

8. Consider the article, "Adventure to Antarctica," and the excerpt from *Into Thin Air.* How does the team mentality differ in each selection?

Informational Text TIME

Teach

R2 Reading Strategy

Analyzing Text Structure
Direct students to the subhead Heading Home.
Ask: How does the subhead foreshadow the problem and solution of this subsection? *(The problem will be getting home, and it will probably be solved.)* **OL**

Assess

1. Possible answer: Johnson is an optimist because he set out to accomplish a difficult goal and led a team to achieve it.
2. (a) Close to ten years (b) The preparation helped prepare Johnson for any unexpected events.
3. (a) Fear should be managed, through preparation and by respecting danger. (b) Possible answers: Fear keeps you from truly feeling confident; true confidence accepts the unknown factors.
4. (a) Shackleton took his strongest men on a dangerous trip to get help for his stranded crew. (b) Johnson respected Shackleton's priority to protect his crew and the way the crew carried equal weight.
5. He wants to show that each individual on a team is important.
6. The motto inspires Johnson to adventure. He feels that endurance tests a person's will.
7. Johnson feels he has completed his goal of many years. The sense of completion comes also from his pleasure in Antarctica.
8. In "Adventure to Antarctica," each team member is assigned a specific task that benefits the team. In *Into Thin Air,* the hikers' tasks are more individual in nature. Also, this team has leaders with specific jobs.

For additional assessment, see Selection and Unit Assessments, pp. 69–70.

Academic Standards

The Additional Support activity on p. 432 covers the following standard:

Skills Practice: **9.3.7** Recognize and understand the significance of various literary devices, including...imagery...

Focus

Work with students to identify technical words or jargon and discuss their meanings. OL

Teach

Technical Words Recall that technical words can be specialized vocabulary, such as *spam,* or ordinary words used in specialized ways, such as *bug.* OL

Assess

Exercise

1. Mammie lorries; small trucks or buses; in Ghana, they are public transportation
2. Bambara; a native West African ethnic group; this term describes Angelou's host and the place she visits
3. *dukuno;* a kind of food; using this term gives a realistic view of West African life
4. Camera-ready copy; text that is ready to be photographed for printing
5. collation; process of putting pages in order; this term is used in a print shop to name a stage of production

Vocabulary Workshop

Technical Words

Understanding Jargon

"By 6:00 PM, as the storm escalated into a full-scale blizzard with driving snow and winds gusting in excess of 60 knots, I came upon the rope that had been fixed by the Montenegrins on the snow slope 600 feet above the Col."

—Jon Krakauer, from *Into Thin Air*

Connecting to Literature When Krakauer writes about mountain climbing, his language is full of words that climbers understand, such as references to fixed ropes and wind speeds. This specialized vocabulary is jargon. **Jargon** is any technical or specialized language specific to a particular sport, trade, hobby, or field. For example, the jargon of computer users includes terms like *bug, boot up, spam, Usenet,* and *blog*. The jargon of bodybuilders includes terms such as *rep, lats, mass,* and *set*.

Examples

Word	Meaning	Why the Word Is Used
intake valve	device used to control the flow of oxygen into an oxygen mask	Krakauer wore an oxygen mask, which he depended on to survive his climb.
cornice	a snowy, unsupported overhang on the mountain	Climbers who walked onto cornices could fall, possibly to their deaths.
the Balcony	a mass of land on the southwest side of Mount Everest where two of its faces, or slopes, meet	Krakauer relates different locations on the mountain and uses different times to retell the story of the climb.

Exercise

Identify jargon, or specialized vocabulary, in each sentence below. For each term, use a dictionary or context clues to find the meaning. Then give a reason why the author may have used the term.

1. In Ghana, Angelou sees people crowded into mammie lorries.
2. Angelou's hosts identify her as Bambara from Liberia.
3. At breakfast, Angelou is offered fish cakes, fried plantain, and *dukuno*.
4. At the print shop, Nye expected her students to see camera-ready copy.
5. Nye had prepared them to see the process of collation.

Technology Tip

To find specialized meanings online, use a search engine. Type *define:* and the term you want defined. For example, type *define: knot*, and several sites and/or definitions will appear. Different search engines will give different results, so if you do not find what you need immediately, try a different engine.

Test-Taking Tip

Always use context clues to determine the meaning of a term you think is jargon. Analyzing word parts can also help you determine meaning.

Reading Handbook

For more about vocabulary development, see Reading Handbook, p. R19.

eFlashcards For eFlashcards and other vocabulary activities, go to www.glencoe.com.

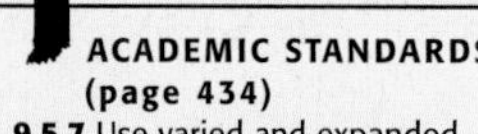

ACADEMIC STANDARDS (page 434)
9.5.7 Use varied and expanded vocabulary, appropriate for specific forms and topics.

Additional Support

eFlashcards Have students access the Web site for more practice with technical words.

Skills Practice

RESEARCH: Using Dictionaries
Review the use of dictionaries in decoding technical words. Explain that a location term may not be listed in a dictionary. Students should define the term in its ordinary use and apply this to context. For compound terms such as *camera-ready,* students should look for a definition of the entire term, if possible, or piece one together from definitions of the parts. OL

PART 3

FINDING COMMON GROUND

United Front (Un solo frente), ca. 1928. Diego Rivera. Mural, 6.69 x 5.28 ft. Court of Fiestas, Level 3, South Wall. Secretaria de Educacion Publica, Mexico City. ★

BIG IDEA

BI One of the most powerful forces in the world is that which comes about when people join with others who share their point of view. A major concern for citizens is how to get people to agree with one another and to join a common effort. The writers in Part 3 demonstrate their powers of persuasion. As you read these speeches, essays, and articles, ask yourself: How do you convince others to share your opinions? What do you do when someone does not agree with you?

Analyzing and Extending

BI Big Idea

Finding Common Ground Have students read the text under the "Big Idea" heading. Ask them to connect the idea of finding common ground to the artwork. Invite students to discuss how they deal with conflict. Return to this discussion later, after students have read selections from Part 3. Ask students to update their responses based on their reading. OL

★ Viewing the Art

United Front is a mural by the great Mexican artist Diego Rivera (1886–1957). Rivera revived the art of mural painting in his native country. Spurred by his interest in world politics, Rivera created huge murals that celebrated his heritage and depicted vibrant Mexican communities at work, at play, and at war. AS

English Language Coach

Comparing Cultures Persuasion is everywhere in mainstream American culture—in advertisements and newspapers. Invite students to talk about the way persuasion is handled in cultures they are familiar with. As a class, make comparisons with modern American culture. EL

Differentiated Instruction

Conflict in Stories Invite advanced readers to think of novels, plays, stories, or poems they have read in which one character persuades another to do or believe something unexpected or different. Ask students to talk about how the characters persuaded one another. AL

Academic Standards

Additional Support activities on pp. 434 and 435 cover the following standards:

Skills Practice: **9.2.1** Analyze the structure and format of reference…documents…

English Language Coach: **9.2.7** Evaluate an author's argument or defense of a claim by examining the relationship between generalizations and evidence, the comprehensiveness of evidence, and the way in which the author's intent affects the structure and tone of the text.

Differentiated Instruction: **9.3.3** Analyze interactions between characters…and explain the way those interactions affect the plot.

Part 3: Skills Scope and Sequence

Readability Scores Key
Dale-Chall/DRP/Lexile

PACING (DAYS) STANDARD	BLOCK	SELECTIONS AND FEATURES	LITERARY ELEMENTS
1–2 class sessions	1	"A New Generation of Americans" by John F. Kennedy **10.1/65/1360**, pp. 438–445	Rhetorical Devices, SE pp. 439, 441, 442, 444 Structure, SE p. 444
		"That One Man's Profit Is Another's Loss" by Michel de Montaigne **9.9/64/1140**, pp. 446–449	Antithesis, SE pp. 447, 448, 449
1–2 class sessions	1	"Daylight Saving" by Benjamin Franklin **10.3/62/1240**, pp. 450–457	Humor, SE pp. 451–456 Rhetorical Devices, SE pp. 456
		"The American Cause" by John Dos Passos **8.1/64/1460**, pp. 458–463	Persuasive Essay, SE pp. 459, 461, 462 Tone, SE p. 462
2 class sessions	1	COMPARING LITERATURE Different Viewpoints "Thoughts on Fenway Park" by Various Authors **7.4/59/930**, pp. 465–469 "Taxpayers Will Get a Return on Investment" by John L. Harrington **10.0/66/1260**, pp. 470–472 "Other Revenue Sources Should Be Pursued" by William M. Straus **8.6/67/1330**, pp. 473–477	Rhetorical Devices, SE pp. 466, 468, 471, 474, 476
		"Put Down the Backpack" by Anna Quindlen **7.4/57/1020**, pp. 478–487	Author's Purpose, SE pp. 479–486 Argument, SE p. 486
2–3 class sessions	2–3	Writing Workshop: Autobiographical Narrative, pp. 488–495	
1 class session		Speaking, Listening, and Viewing Workshop: Narrative Presentation, pp. 496–497	
2 class sessions		Test Preparation and Practice, pp. 500–505	

About the Part

Part 3 includes nonfiction literature attempting to persuade the reader about a subject.

READING AND CRITICAL THINKING	VOCABULARY	WRITING AND GRAMMAR	LISTENING, SPEAKING, AND VIEWING
Recognizing Bias, SE pp. 439, 441, 444	Word Origins, SE p. 444 Academic Vocabulary, SE p. 444	Compare and Contrast Speeches, SE p. 445 Creating Rhythm with Parallelism and Repetition, SE p. 445	Group Activity, SE p. 443 Listening to and Performing a Speech, SE p. 445
Analyzing Argument, SE pp. 447, 449	Word Origins, SE pp. 447, 449	Analyzing Genre Elements, SE p. 449	Analyzing Art, TWE p. 448
Evaluating Evidence, SE pp. 451, 453, 454, 457	Context Clues, SE p. 457	Evaluate Author's Craft, SE p. 457	Analyzing Art, SE p. 455
Distinguishing Fact and Opinion, SE pp. 459, 460, 463	Word Parts, SE p. 463 Academic Vocabulary, SE p. 463	Evaluate Author's Craft, SE p. 463	Debate, SE p. 463 Analyzing Art, TWE p. 460
Identifying Problem and Solution, SE pp. 466, 467, 469, 471, 474, 476 Comparing and Contrasting, TWE p. 468 Identifying Author's Purpose, TWE p. 470	Synonyms, SE p. 476	Respond to Arguments, SE p. 476 Comparison Essay, SE p. 477 Sentence Fragments, TWE p. 466 Persuasive Writing, TWE p. 472 Editorial, TWE p. 474	Group Activity, SE p. 477 Oral Presentation, SE p. 477 Analyzing Photographs, TWE pp. 467, 469, 471
Evaluating Credibility, SE pp. 479–481, 483, 486 Analyzing Arguments, TWE p. 480	Analogy, SE p. 486 Academic Vocabulary, SE p. 486	Respond to Thesis, SE p. 487 Juxtaposition, SE p. 487	Performing, SE p. 487 Analyzing Art, TWE pp. 483, 484
		Writing About a Memory, SE pp. 488–495	
Active Reading, TWE p. 500		Grammar Review, TWE p. 504	

Focus

BELLRINGER

Bellringer Options
Daily Language Practice Transparency 39

Or provide students with copies of an advertisement or a political flier.
Ask: How does the ad or flier make you feel? What does it make you think about? How does it try to influence you?

Teach

L Literary Element

Diction Ask: What words in Lincoln's address might make readers or listeners believe that the war is a worthy cause? *(Students may mention words and phrases such as "great civil war," "great battle-field," "brave men.")* OL

Literary Elements Have students access the Web site to improve their understanding of persuasive essays and speeches.

Persuasive Essay and Speech

What techniques make persuasive writing compelling?

On November 19, 1863, President Abraham Lincoln went to Gettysburg, Pennsylvania, to speak at the dedication of a cemetery that was to honor the Union war dead. One of Lincoln's goals in his speech was to persuade his audience to continue their support of the Civil War, no matter how terrible the losses.

Abraham Lincoln, 1864. William Willard. Oil on canvas, 61 x 45.5 cm. National Portrait Gallery, Smithsonian Institution, Washington, DC. ★

The Gettysburg Address

by Abraham Lincoln

Four score and seven years ago our fathers brought forth on this continent, a new nation, conceived in liberty, and dedicated to the proposition that all men are created equal. Now we are engaged in a great civil war, testing whether that nation or any nation so conceived and so dedicated, can long endure. We are met on a great battle-field of that war. We have come to dedicate a portion of that field, as a final resting place for those who here gave their lives that that nation might live. It is altogether fitting and proper that we should do this.

But, in a larger sense, we cannot dedicate—we cannot consecrate—we cannot hallow—this ground. The brave men, living and dead, who struggled here, have consecrated it, far above our poor power to add or detract. The world will little note, nor long remember what we say here, but it can never forget what they did here. It is for us the living, rather, to be here dedicated to the great task remaining before us—that from these honored dead we take increased devotion to that cause for which they here gave the last full measure of devotion—that we here highly resolve that these dead shall not have died in vain—that this nation, under God, shall have a new birth of freedom—and that government of the people, by the people, for the people shall not perish from the earth. L

Additional Support

Academic Standards

The Additional Support activity on p. 436 covers the following standard:
Skills Practice: **9.7.3** Recognize and use elements of classical speech forms…in formulating rational arguments…

Skills Practice

SPEAKING AND LISTENING: Speaking Persuasively Assign a mildly controversial topic to pairs of students (for example, all-year school or school uniforms). Students should choose pro or con and then take five minutes to think of an argument to support their stand. Students should then share their views with their partners. Listening partners should evaluate the speaker's effectiveness. OL

By speaking of the sacrifice of the fallen soldiers and emphasizing the importance of the cause—liberty not just for the United States but for the whole world—Lincoln made a strong persuasive speech in favor of continuing the war.

Persuasion Persuasion is writing that attempts to convince readers to think or act in a particular way. Writers of persuasive essays and speeches appeal to logic and reason, but they also appeal to emotion. Notice how Lincoln uses patriotic appeals in referring to the "honored dead" and "this nation, under God."

Argument Argument is a specific type of persuasive writing or speaking in which logic and evidence are used to appeal to the reader's or listener's reason. Notice for example how Lincoln employs logic in saying that the hallowed ground cannot be consecrated because it has already been consecrated by the dead soldiers.

An effective argument has four primary parts: (1) the assertion or opinion statement, (2) support for the assertion, (3) acknowledgement of opposing arguments, and (4) a recommendation. The four parts of an argument can come in any order, or they can be mixed together.

Assertion An assertion is a statement of belief. A good assertion is short, precise, and direct. The writer or speaker names the topic and then states his or her position.

> Let the word go forth from this time and place, to friend and foe alike, that the torch has been passed to a new generation of Americans–born in this century, tempered by war, disciplined by a hard and bitter peace, proud of our ancient heritage–and unwilling to witness or permit the slow undoing of those human rights to which this Nation has always been committed, and to which we are committed today at home and around the world.
>
> —John F. Kennedy, **from "A New Generation of Americans"** **R**

LiteratureOnline Interactive Literary Elements Handbook Go to www.glencoe.com to review or learn more about persuasive essays and speeches.

Evidence in support of an argument's assertion should be fact-based. It can come from a variety of sources, including research, expert opinion, and personal experience.

> When I quit the *New York Times* to be a full-time mother, the voices of the world said that I was nuts. When I quit it again to be a full-time novelist, they said I was nuts again. But I am not nuts. I am happy. I am successful on my own terms.
>
> —Anna Quindlen, **from "Put Down the Backpack"**

Refuting the opposing argument means anticipating what the opposition will say, and then explaining why these arguments are illogical, impractical, or unsound.

A good persuasive piece also includes a solution to the problem or a recommendation of what the reader or audience should do, think, or say as a result of the argument.

> Begin to say no to the Greek chorus that thinks it knows the parameters of a happy life when all it knows is the homogenization of human experience. Listen to that small voice from inside you, that tells you to go another way.
>
> —Anna Quindlen, **from "Put Down the Backpack"**

Quickwrite

Convincing Others Write an e-mail to a family member persuading him or her to allow you to go to an amusement park with friends. Then read what you wrote. Label the sentences in which you make the assertion, provide support, acknowledge opposing arguments, and make your recommendation.

INDIANA ACADEMIC STANDARDS (pages 436–437)

9.7.9 Analyze historically significant speeches...to find the rhetorical devices and features that make them memorable.

9.5.4 Write persuasive compositions...

9.5.8 Write for difference purposes and audiences...

Teach

R Reading Strategy

Evaluate Assertions Make sure that students understand the concept of assertion. **Ask:** What is the assertion in John F. Kennedy's inaugural speech? *(He is claiming that Americans are committed to supporting human rights all around the world.)* **OL**

★ Viewing the Art

President Lincoln (1809–1865) was the subject of many paintings such as this one by William Willard. Lincoln was also the first American president to be regularly photographed. **Ask:** What character traits does the portrait of Lincoln suggest? *(Poise, thoughtfulness, intelligence)* **AS**

Assess

Quickwrite

E-mails should contain an assertion, supporting facts, an opposing view, and a recommendation, all of which should be labeled. If students have trouble thinking of ideas, allow them to meet in groups to share their thoughts.

English Language Coach

Building Vocabulary Encourage English language learners to make a list of persuasive vocabulary words, including *argument, assertion, support, opinion,* and *recommendation.* Allow students time to look up the meanings and pronunciations of the words. **EL**

Differentiated Instruction

Role-Playing Invite students to model interpersonal problem solving. Present a situation, such as overcoming shyness. Have pairs of students act out a scene in which they deal with the problem using persuasive techniques. **AL**

Academic Standards

Additional Support activities on p. 437 cover the following standards:

English Language Coach: **9.1.1** Identify and use the literal...meanings of words...

Differentiated Instruction: **9.7.18** Deliver persuasive arguments...

BEFORE YOU READ

Focus

BELLRINGER

Bellringer Options
Daily Language Practice Transparency 40

Or display images of important people and events from the 1960s era, such as President Kennedy, the Cuban missile crisis, Martin Luther King Jr., the Civil Rights Movement, American and Russian space satellites, and astronaut Alan Shepard.

Literature Online

Author Search To expand students' appreciation of John F. Kennedy, have them access the Web site for additional information and resources.

BEFORE YOU READ

A New Generation of Americans

MEET JOHN F. KENNEDY

John F. Kennedy was the youngest person ever elected president of the United States. He was a positive leader who had many ideas about how to change the country for the better. Although his time in office ended tragically when he was assassinated, he accomplished much in his short presidency.

Kennedy was born in Brookline, Massachusetts. His father was a successful businessman who encouraged all nine of his children to try to win in whatever they might do. One of his father's favorite sayings was "Second place is a loser." Kennedy attended several universities and graduated from Harvard in 1940, shortly before the United States entered World War II.

> *"Change is the law of life. And those who look only to the past or present are certain to miss the future."*
>
> —John F. Kennedy

Soldier and Statesman Kennedy joined the Navy and served as a lieutenant during the war. In 1943, when he was a commander in the South Pacific, a Japanese destroyer sank his PT (patrol torpedo) boat. Kennedy led the ten other survivors to safety, despite his own serious injuries. The sailors spent three days afloat in the ocean, and Kennedy saved one of his wounded companions who was unable to swim. He gripped the other man's life jacket in his teeth and dragged him along for miles while swimming. For his bravery, Kennedy received recognition as a hero.

After the war ended, Kennedy became a Democratic Congressman, and he advanced to the Senate in 1953. Two years later he wrote a book, *Profiles in Courage,* about politicians who stay true to their principles despite difficult circumstances. This book was awarded the Pulitzer Prize for history.

Challenges as President Kennedy's popularity as a senator increased, and he decided to run for president. He won the presidential election in 1960. He called for new civil rights laws as well as additional government funding for education and better medical care. He also emphasized the need to help developing countries and started the Peace Corps, an organization that sends U.S. volunteers overseas.

Kennedy had to deal with threats from the Communist countries of Cuba and the Soviet Union. One significant event of his presidency was the Cuban missile crisis. In October of 1962, a terrifying situation developed when the Soviets tried to bring nuclear missiles to Cuba. The United States feared that Cuba might use them to attack the United States and start a nuclear war. Kennedy was able to resolve the situation peacefully, and the Russians removed the missiles. In return, the United States promised not to invade Cuba.

Kennedy was assassinated on November 22, 1963. He was shot while riding in a presidential motorcade during a campaign trip to Dallas, Texas.

John F. Kennedy was born in 1917 and died in 1963.

Literature Online **Author Search** For more about John F. Kennedy, go to www.glencoe.com.

Selection Skills

A New Generation of Americans

Literary Elements
- Rhetorical Devices (SE pp. 439, 441, 442, 444; TWE pp. 440–442)
- Structure (SE p. 444)

Vocabulary Skills
- Word Origins (SE p. 444)

Reading Skills
- Recognizing Bias (SE pp. 439, 441, 444; TWE p. 440)
- Identifying Author's Purpose (TWE p. 442)

Writing Skills/Grammar
- Using Dashes (TWE p. 440)
- Compare and Contrast Speeches (SE p. 445)

Listening/Speaking/Viewing Skills
- Listening and Performing a Speech (SE p. 445)

LITERATURE PREVIEW

Connecting to the Speech

In his inaugural address, Kennedy tries to inspire Americans to work together toward common goals for the good of their country. Before you read, think about the following questions:

- When is it necessary to compromise with someone with whom you disagree?
- What ideals and principles are so important to you that you would make sacrifices to protect them?

Building Background

Kennedy gave his inaugural address on January 20, 1961. World War II had ended less than twenty years before, and the hardships of war were still fresh in the nation's memory. Scientific progress in areas such as medicine and space exploration made the era a time of excitement–and uneasiness. The atomic bomb used to end the war had caused destruction unlike anything seen before. Many Americans feared the possibility of a nuclear war as tensions between the United States and the Soviet Union escalated. This conflict was known as the Cold War. The two countries were in an arms race, with each competing to accumulate more nuclear weapons than the other.

Setting Purposes for Reading

Big Idea Finding Common Ground

As you read, notice how Kennedy encourages Americans to focus on the aspects of their history and the common experiences that draw them together.

Literary Element Rhetorical Devices

Rhetorical devices are techniques that an author uses to create particular effects or to engage the attention of the reader. These devices use language in artistic ways that make passages more memorable as well as more persuasive. As you read, look for rhetorical devices and note their effects.

- See Literary Terms Handbook, p. R14.

LiteratureOnline Interactive Literary Elements Handbook To review or learn more about the literary elements, go to www.glencoe.com.

READING PREVIEW

Reading Strategy Recognizing Bias

Bias is a certain opinion or position on a topic that may stem from prejudice. An author who shows bias is inclined to think in a particular way and may have something to gain from the viewpoint he or she supports. Recognizing bias can help you evaluate a literary work with greater objectivity. As you read this selection, look for examples of bias.

Reading Tip: Making a Chart Use a chart to record instances of bias in Kennedy's address.

Passage	Bias
"human rights to which this nation has always been committed"	human rights have not always been protected in the United States

Vocabulary

venture (ven′ chər) *n.* an undertaking involving chance, risk, or danger; p. 441 *Though they were unsure of its chances for success, Mick's friends supported his business venture.*

negotiate (ni gō′ shē āt′) *v.* to discuss or compromise; p. 442 *The countries were able to negotiate a peace treaty.*

eradicate (i rad′ ə kāt′) *v.* to get rid of completely; p. 442 *Certain household pests are difficult to eradicate.*

testimony (tes′ tə mō′ nē) *n.* a solemn declaration; p. 442 *The witness gave testimony in court that showed that the incarcerated man had been innocent all along.*

INDIANA ACADEMIC STANDARDS (pages 439–445)

9.7.9 Analyze historically significant speeches...to find the rhetorical devices and features that make them memorable.

9.2.7 Evaluate an author's argument or defense of a claim...

9.5.3 Write...literary analyses that gather evidence in support of a thesis...

9.3.5 Compare works that express a universal theme...

BEFORE YOU READ

Focus

Summary

In his inaugural address, John F. Kennedy speaks about renewal and change. He pledges his allegiance to the beliefs of our American forefathers but serves notice that the world has changed, and there is a new generation of Americans. He proclaims that this new generation is ready and willing to take responsibility for preserving the ideals of equality and liberty. In his speech, Kennedy reaches out to all people and nations and implores them to join together to make a better world.

V Vocabulary

Vocabulary File Say: Add these words and definitions to your vocabulary file. For each word, include a sentence that gives you an example of how to use the word. **OL** Students with English language needs should include the pronunciations of these words in their files. **EL**

Literary Elements Have students access the Web site to improve their understanding of rhetorical devices.

Selection Resources

Print Materials
- Unit 2 Resources (Fast File), pp. 61–63
- Leveled Vocabulary Development, p. 32
- Selection and Unit Assessments, pp. 71–72
- Selection Quick Checks, p. 36

Transparencies
- Bellringer Options Transparencies: Daily Language Practice Transparency 40
- Literary Elements Transparency 42

Technology
- TeacherWorks Plus™ CD-ROM
- StudentWorks Plus™ CD-ROM
- Presentation Plus!™ CD-ROM
- Literature Online, glencoe.com
- Online Student Edition, mhln.com
- Exam*View*® Assessment Suite CD-ROM
- Vocabulary PuzzleMaker CD-ROM
- Listening Library, disc 1 track 40

Teach

BI1 **Big Idea**

Finding Common Ground
Say: Keep this question in mind as you read: How does Kennedy find common ground with his worldwide audience? *(He addresses each group directly, validating their importance.)* OL

BI2 **Big Idea**

Finding Common Ground
Answer: *The difficulties of war and of maintaining peace have brought Americans together and renewed their pride in their shared history.* OL

Readability Scores
Dale-Chall: 10.1
DRP: 65
Lexile: 1360

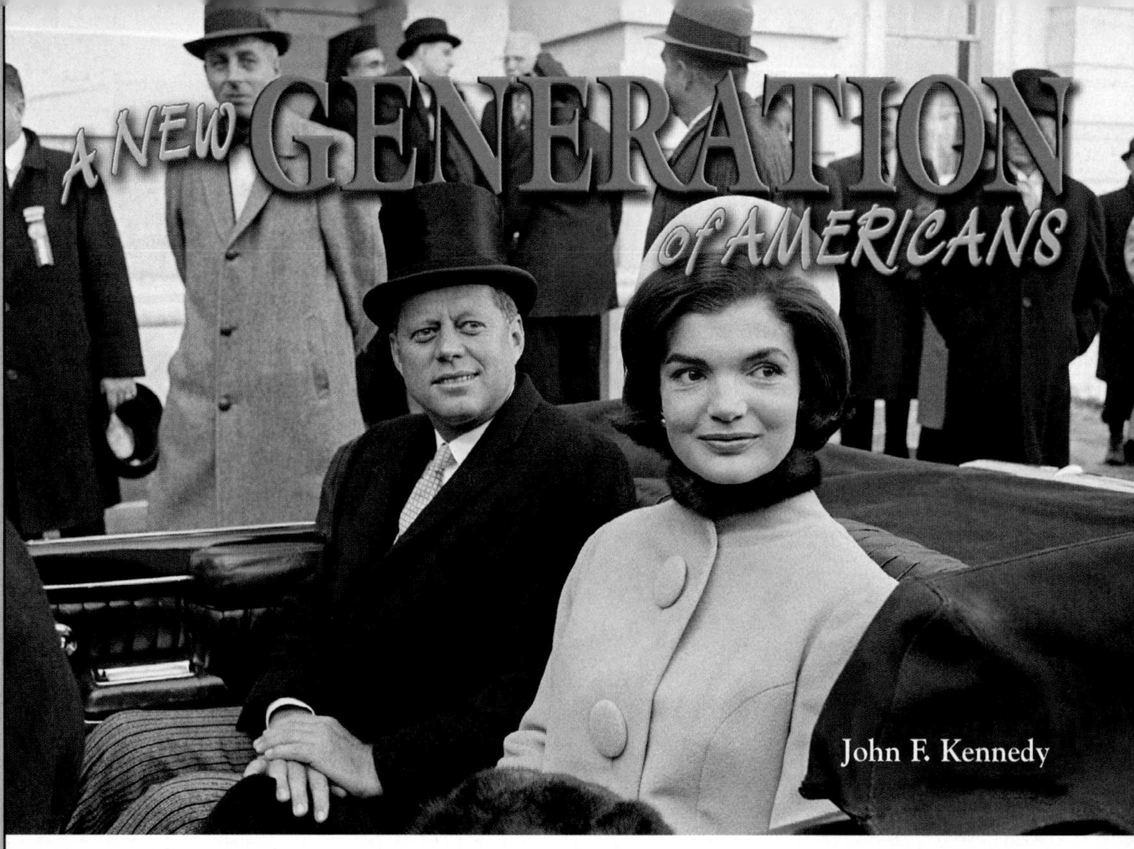

John F. Kennedy

BI1 We observe today not a victory of a party but a celebration of freedom—symbolizing an end as well as a beginning—signifying renewal as well as change. For I have sworn before you and Almighty God the same solemn oath our forebears[1] prescribed nearly a century and three quarters ago.

The world is very different now. For man holds in his mortal hands the power to abolish[2] all forms of human poverty and all forms of human life. And yet the same revolutionary beliefs for which our forebears fought are still at issue around the globe—the belief that the rights of man come not from the generosity of the state but from the hand of God.

We dare not forget today that we are the heirs of that first revolution. Let the word go forth from this time and place, to friend and foe alike, that the torch has been passed to a new generation of Americans—born in this century, tempered[3] by war, disciplined by a hard and bitter peace, proud of our ancient heritage—and unwilling to witness or permit the slow undoing of those human rights to which this nation has always been committed, and to which we are committed today at home and around the world.

1. *Forebears* are ancestors; Kennedy is referring here to the founders of the United States.
2. *Abolish* means "to end or destroy."

3. Here, *tempered* means "made stronger through hardship."

Big Idea Finding Common Ground *According to Kennedy, what was one of the effects of war on the people of the United States?* BI2

Additional Support

Skills Practice

GRAMMAR AND LANGUAGE: Using Dashes Dashes set off supplemental information that breaks up the flow of the text. Have students find places where dashes appear in the selection. Ask them to explain what effect the author achieved by interrupting the flow of the speech. *(Example: "The torch has been passed to a new generation of Americans–born in this century, tempered by war. . . ." The dash clarifies the group of Americans to which Kennedy refers.)* OL

Let every nation know, whether it wishes us well or ill, that we shall pay any price, bear any burden, meet any hardship, support any friend, oppose any foe to assure the survival and success of liberty.

This much we pledge—and more.

To those old allies whose cultural and spiritual origins we share, we pledge the loyalty of faithful friends. United, there is little we cannot do in a host of cooperative **ventures**. Divided, there is little we can do—for we dare not meet a powerful challenge at odds and split asunder.

To those new states whom we welcome to the ranks of the free, we pledge our word that one form of colonial control shall not have passed away merely to be replaced by a far more iron tyranny.[4] We shall not always expect to find them supporting our view. But we shall always hope to find them strongly supporting their own freedom—and to remember that, in the past, those who foolishly sought power by riding the back of the tiger ended up inside.

To those peoples in the huts and villages of half the globe struggling to break the bonds of mass misery, we pledge our best efforts to help them help themselves, for whatever period is required—not because the Communists may be doing it, not because we seek their votes, but because it is right. If a free society cannot help the many who are poor, it cannot save the few who are rich.

To our sister republics south of our border, we offer a special pledge—to convert our good words into good deeds—in a new alliance for progress—to assist free men and free governments in casting off the chains of poverty. But this peaceful revolution of hope cannot become the prey of hostile powers. Let all our neighbors know that we shall join with them to oppose aggression or subversion[5] anywhere in the Americas. And let every other power know that this hemisphere intends to remain the master of its own house.

To that world assembly of sovereign[6] states, the United Nations, our last best hope in an age where the instruments of war have far outpaced the instruments of peace, we renew our pledge of support—to prevent it from becoming merely a forum for invective[7]—to strengthen its shield of the new and the weak—and to enlarge the area in which its writ[8] may run.

Finally, to those nations who would make themselves our adversary, we offer not a pledge but a request: that both sides begin anew the quest for peace, before the dark powers of destruction unleashed by science engulf all humanity in planned or accidental self-destruction. L2

We dare not tempt them with weakness. For only when our arms are sufficient beyond doubt can we be certain beyond doubt that they will never be employed.

But neither can two great and powerful groups of nations take comfort from our present course—both sides overburdened by the cost of modern weapons, both rightly alarmed by the steady spread of the deadly atom, yet both racing to alter that uncertain balance of terror that stays the hand of mankind's final war. R2

So let us begin anew—remembering on both sides that civility is not a sign of weakness, and sincerity is always subject to proof.

4. *Tyranny* means "oppressive power."

Literary Element Rhetorical Devices *What is the effect of the repetitions in this passage?* L1

Reading Strategy Recognizing Bias *Who here defines what deeds are good and what constitutes progress?* R1

Vocabulary

venture (ven′ chər) *n.* an undertaking involving chance, risk, or danger

5. *Subversion* is a systematic attempt to overthrow a government.
6. Here, *sovereign* means "independent."
7. *Invective* means "insulting or abusive language."
8. A *writ* is a law or a formal written command or order. Kennedy is promising to help the United Nations extend its power.

Teach

L1 Literary Element

Rhetorical Devices Answer: *The repetitions make the passage more powerful or create a sense of urgency by adding emphasis.* OL

R1 Reading Strategy

Recognizing Bias Answer: *Kennedy and the United States define what progress would benefit these developing countries.* OL

L2 Literary Element

Tone Ask: What tone does Kennedy use to address "nations who would make themselves our adversary"? *(Possible answer: The tone is firm but not threatening; he asks nations to work together.)* OL

R2 Reading Strategy

Making an Inference Ask: What is Kennedy referring to in "mankind's final war"? *(The existence of nuclear weapons that could destroy life on Earth.)* OL

CheckPoint

Use the CheckPoint questions on Presentation Plus! to monitor students' comprehension. These questions can be used with interactive response keypads for immediate student feedback.

English Language Coach

Using a Dictionary It may be more helpful for English learners to hear how words sound than to use a pronunciation guide.

- Have students list unfamiliar words from the selection and use a dictionary to find each word's meaning.
- Pair students with English-proficient partners. Partners should practice pronouncing each word and discussing its meaning. EL

Academic Standards

Additional Support activities on pp. 440 and 441 cover the following standards:

Skills Practice: **9.4.10** Review [and] evaluate…writing for meaning, clarity,… and mechanics.

English Language Coach: **9.7** [Respond] to oral communication [with] careful listening and evaluation of content…

Teach

L1 Literary Element

Rhetorical Devices Answer: *His use of the same words in two consecutive sentences with opposite meanings emphasizes the importance of negotiation.* OL

L2 Literary Element

Rhetorical Devices Answer: *It emphasizes the difficulty of his goals.* OL

Use the CheckPoint questions on Presentation Plus! to check students' mastery of the selection. These questions can be used with interactive response keypads for immediate student feedback.

Let us never **negotiate** out of fear. But let us never fear to negotiate.

Let both sides explore what problems unite us instead of belaboring those problems which divide us. Let both sides, for the first time, formulate serious and precise proposals for the inspection and control of arms—and bring the absolute power to destroy other nations under the absolute control of all nations.

Let both sides seek to invoke[9] the wonders of science instead of its terrors. Together let us explore the stars, conquer the deserts, **eradicate** disease, tap the ocean depths, and encourage the arts and commerce.

Let both sides unite to heed in all corners of the earth the command of Isaiah[10]—to "undo the heavy burdens and to let the oppressed go free."

And if a beachhead[11] of cooperation may push back the jungle of suspicion, let both sides join in a new endeavor—not a new balance of power, but a new world of law, where the strong are just and the weak secure and the peace preserved.

All this will not be finished in the first one hundred days. Nor will it be finished in the first one thousand days, nor in the life of this administration, nor even perhaps in our lifetime on this planet. But let us begin.

In your hands, my fellow citizens, more than mine, will rest the final success or failure of our course. Since this country was founded, each generation of Americans has been summoned to give **testimony** to its national loyalty. The graves of young Americans who answered the call to service surround the globe.

Now the trumpet summons us again—not as a call to bear arms, though arms we need—not as a call to battle, though embattled[12] we are—but a call to bear the burden of a long twilight struggle, year in and year out, "rejoicing in hope, patient in tribulation"[13]—a struggle against the common enemies of man: tyranny, poverty, disease, and war itself.

Can we forge against these enemies a grand and global alliance, North and South, East and West, that can assure a more fruitful life for all mankind? Will you join in that historic effort?

In the long history of the world, only a few generations have been granted the role of defending freedom in its hour of maximum danger. I do not shrink from this responsibility—I welcome it. I do not believe that any of us would exchange places with any other people or any other generation. The energy, the faith, the devotion which we bring to this endeavor will light our country and all who serve it—and the glow from that fire can truly light the world.

And so, my fellow Americans, ask not what your country can do for you—ask what you can do for your country.

My fellow citizens of the world, ask not what America will do for you, but what together we can do for the freedom of man.

Finally, whether you are citizens of America or citizens of the world, ask of us here the same high standards of strength and sacrifice which we ask of you. With a good conscience our only sure reward, with history the final judge of our deeds, let us go forth to lead the land we love, asking his blessing and his help, but knowing that here on earth God's work must truly be our own.

9. To *invoke* means "to put into effect or operation."
10. *Isaiah* is a prophet in the Old Testament of the Bible.
11. A *beachhead* is an occupied area in an enemy country where troops and supplies can land.
12. *Embattled* means "prepared for battle."
13. A *tribulation* is a difficult experience.

Literary Element Rhetorical Devices *What technique does Kennedy use to make this passage memorable?* L1

Literary Element Rhetorical Devices *What is the effect of the repetition of the word* nor? L2

Vocabulary

negotiate (ni gō′ shē āt′) *v.* to discuss or compromise

eradicate (i rad′ ə kāt′) *v.* to get rid of completely

Vocabulary

testimony (tes′ tə mō′ nē) *n.* a solemn declaration

Additional Support

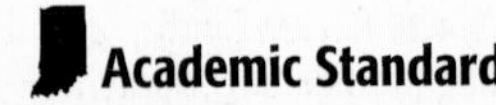

Academic Standards

The Additional Support activity on p. 442 covers the following standard:

Skills Practice: **9.2** Develop strategies such as… identifying…[author's] purpose.

Skills Practice

READING: Identifying Author's Purpose Explain that a speech can be written to entertain, inform, or persuade an audience. Sometimes the speaker can have more than one purpose.

Ask: What is Kennedy's main purpose in this speech? *(To persuade citizens to rededicate themselves to the ideals upon which the country was founded and to convince nations to work together to make life better for all mankind)*

Say: Kennedy also wants to inform. Have students find lines in the speech where Kennedy informs potential aggressors of the response of the United States to any threats. OL

RESPONDING AND THINKING CRITICALLY

Respond

1. (a)How does Kennedy's speech make you feel about the United States? (b)Do you agree with the way that he portrays the country?

Recall and Interpret

2. (a)According to Kennedy, in which ways has the world changed? (b)What does he expect of this new generation of Americans?
3. (a)What does Kennedy promise to the people of less developed countries? (b)How do you think his promises to these countries relate to his goals for the United States?
4. (a)What does Kennedy say are the common enemies of man? (b)How does he hope to make use of these common enemies?

Analyze and Evaluate

5. (a)What are the main arguments Kennedy uses to try to inspire the American people? (b)How persuasive is he in these arguments? Explain.
6. How does Kennedy present his attitude toward war in this speech? Support your answer with examples from the text.
7. (a)Kennedy says that "sincerity is always subject to proof." Does his speech strike you as sincere? (b)For what reasons might the writer of such a speech say something he did not really mean?

Connect

8. **Big Idea** **Finding Common Ground** (a) What groups of people does Kennedy encourage to find common ground? (b)What are some specific ways he mentions for this to be achieved?

DAILY LIFE AND CULTURE

Inaugurating a New Decade

President Kennedy inherited a sharply divided country. For the white American middle class, the 1950s were a time of stability and increased consumerism. For many African Americans, however, it was a time of racism and oppression. Happy nuclear families ate TV dinners while watching "Lassie" or "I Love Lucy," but there were fallout shelters in the yard, bomb drills in the classroom, young U.S. soldiers dying in Korea, and the creeping fear of Communism. In his inauguration speech, Kennedy expressed the hope that people would unite in order to dispel the increasing polarization of both the country and the world.

Group Activity Discuss the following questions with your classmates.

1. What do you know about the 1950s from popular culture, such as movies and television shows? What have your parents, grandparents, or other family members told you about life in the 1950s?
2. Compare and contrast life in the 1950s with life in the United States today.

A family gathers around the television in 1956.

AFTER YOU READ

Assess

1. (a) Students may say they feel proud or optimistic about the United States. (b) Some students may feel his portrayal is accurate; others may think he glosses over American failures.
2. (a) The world is different because people have the power to achieve more things, both good and bad, than they have before. (b) Americans will join together to use this power for the good of their country and the world.
3. (a) He promises to "help them help themselves, for whatever period is required." He pledges the United States will work with them to achieve freedom from tyranny and disease. (b) Students may say these are part of his vision of using American strength to create a better world.
4. (a) The common enemies are tyranny, poverty, disease, and war. (b) He hopes to use these common enemies of mankind as a rallying point to build a global alliance.
5. (a) He says Americans share experiences with people across the world who struggle for freedom because Americans fought for these same rights. Therefore, Americans must help developing countries and make sacrifices to preserve liberty around the world. (b) Answers will vary. Students should support opinions with examples from the text.
6. He thinks war is necessary, but only as a last resort; Increasing the nation's power and readiness for war may deter other countries.
7. (a) Some students may say he sounds sincere and uses sound reasoning. Others may distrust his patriotic and idealistic tone. (b) Students should note that the president was motivated to promote an optimistic vision in order to inspire people to support his plans.
8. (a) Americans and people from other countries, specifically developing nations and the Soviet Union. (b) He proposes working together against common problems or in the areas of science and art.

Daily Life and Culture

1. Answers will vary.
2. Answers will vary.

AFTER YOU READ

Assess

Literary Element

1. "both sides overburdened . . ."; "And so, my fellow Americans . . ."
2. The devices are emphatic, persuasive, or inspiring.
3. He begins each paragraph of a section with the same structure, such as, "To those new states . . ." Students should note how this adds to the speech's organization and impact.

Review: Structure

Invite students to compare their charts and read aloud each section of the speech.

Reading Strategy

1. As president, he is biased in favor of the U.S. and wants to present his country in a positive light. He hopes to gain support for his ideas.
2. Yes; his bias makes the speech less credible or no; bias does not affect the validity of his ideas

Vocabulary

1. c
2. a
3. f
4. b

LITERARY ANALYSIS

Literary Element Rhetorical Devices

A writer can draw from a wide variety of **rhetorical devices** to create a particular effect. Rhetorical devices are most often used to persuade or move an audience. Parallelism and repetition are examples of rhetorical devices that appear in Kennedy's address. Parallelism is the use of a series of words, phrases, or sentences that have a similar grammatical form. This sentence structure emphasizes the items that are arranged in a similar way. Repetition emphasizes words or phrases that appear more than once.

1. Examine Kennedy's speech to find one example of parallelism and one example of repetition.
2. For both passages you have chosen, describe how the rhetorical device is effective and what kind of reaction it is meant to evoke in the reader or listener.
3. How does Kennedy use parallelism on a large scale in his speech? What effect does this parallelism have on his speech as a whole?

Review: Structure

As you learned on page 416, **structure** is the particular order or pattern a writer uses to present ideas.

Partner Activity Work with a classmate to discuss the structure of Kennedy's speech. Create a chart similar to the one below. Fill in the first column with names for each section of the speech, such as *introduction* or *first main idea.* In the second column, note how long the section is. In the third column, summarize the main points presented in the section.

Section	Length	Main Points
Introduction	1st two paragraphs	The world is changing, and people have more power than before.

READING AND VOCABULARY

Reading Strategy Recognizing Bias

Most authors who write persuasively have a **bias** of some kind, simply because they have a point of view that they want the reader to adopt. Authors might also write with a slant, meaning they make something appear either better or worse than it actually is.

1. As president of the United States, in what ways is Kennedy likely to be biased? Do you notice examples of this kind of bias in the text?
2. Do you find that Kennedy's bias takes away from his credibility? Explain.

Vocabulary Practice

Practice with Word Origins If you look up *progress* in a dictionary, you can see that it comes from the Latin *progressus*, meaning "to advance or go forth." Match each vocabulary word below with its word of origin. Use a dictionary if you need help.

1. venture
2. negotiate
3. eradicate
4. testimony

a. *negotiare*
b. *testimonium*
c. *aventure*
d. *testum*
e. *negare*
f. *eradicare*

Academic Vocabulary

Here are two words from the vocabulary list on page R80. These words will help you think, write, and talk about the selection.

dynamic (dī nam′ik) *adj.* marked by productive activity or change

enhance (en hans′) *v.* to heighten, increase, or improve

Practice and Apply

1. In what ways does Kennedy's speech portray the early 1960s as a **dynamic** period in U.S. history?
2. How does the structure of Kennedy's speech **enhance** its persuasive power? Explain.

Academic Vocabulary

1. He emphasizes the potential for change and development.
2. Students may say the tight organization and use of parallelism makes his arguments more persuasive by highlighting logical connections.

Academic Standards

The Additional Support activity on p. 445 covers the following standard:

English Language Coach: **9.6.2** Demonstrate an understanding of...proper English usage...

WRITING AND EXTENDING

Writing About Literature

Compare and Contrast Speeches Every president of the United States gives an inauguration speech at the beginning of a term in office. How might a president with very different ideas from Kennedy address the American people? What characteristics do all inauguration speeches have in common?

Pick another inauguration speech to read or listen to and write a five-paragraph essay in which you compare and contrast it with Kennedy's speech. Before you begin drafting, take notes on which aspects of the speech are similar and which are different. You may want to organize your ideas in a Venn diagram like the one below.

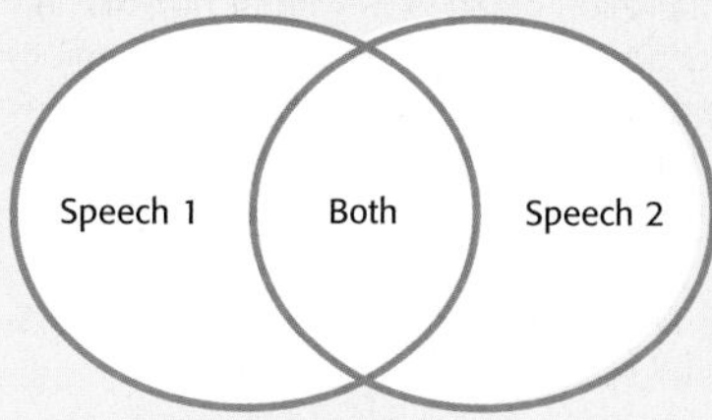

As you draft, make sure to provide plenty of supporting details for each speech to demonstrate their similarities and differences.

After completing your draft, meet with a peer reviewer to evaluate each other's work and to suggest revisions. Then proofread and edit your draft to correct errors in spelling, grammar, and punctuation.

Listening and Speaking

Listen to a recording of Kennedy giving his inaugural address, paying attention to his speaking style. Then perform all or part of the speech for your classmates. As you speak, focus on the persuasive and expressive elements of the speech. Vary your speed, volume, rhythm, and tone in accordance with the speech in order to fully communicate Kennedy's message to your audience.

LiteratureOnline **Web Activities** For eFlashcards, Selection Quick Checks, and other Web activities, go to www.glencoe.com.

GRAMMAR AND STYLE

Kennedy's Language and Style

Creating Rhythm with Parallelism and Repetition In his inauguration speech, Kennedy uses parallelism and repetition to create a certain rhythm. The rhythm of his speech, in turn, lends power to his ideas. In his conclusion, for example, parallelism gives his words a poetic rhythm that makes his message memorable:

"And so, my fellow Americans, ask not what your country can do for you—ask what you can do for your country."

"My fellow citizens of the world, ask not what America will do for you, but what together we can do for the freedom of man."

"Finally, whether you are citizens of America or citizens of the world, ask of us here the same high standards of strength and sacrifice which we ask of you."

Notice some of Kennedy's uses of repetition and parallelism:

Example	Literary Device
"Symbolizing an end as well as a beginning—signifying renewal as well as change . . ."	Parallelism
"Let us never negotiate out of fear. But let us never fear to negotiate."	Parallelism and Repetition

Activity Choose a passage of the speech where Kennedy uses parallelism. Paraphrase the passage and read it to a classmate. Discuss the differences between the two versions. Which is more effective?

Revising Check

Parallelism and Repetition Parallelism and repetition are important rhetorical devices to keep in mind when you revise your own writing. Read through your compare-and-contrast essay with a partner. Find places where you could add parallelism and repetition to create rhythmic and persuasive effects.

English Language Coach

Gender References **Ask:** To what does the word *man* refer in the second paragraph of Kennedy's speech? *(All people)* Discuss the use of masculine nouns and pronouns to refer to all genders. Ask students to list various meanings of the pronoun *he*. *(All people, a male, or when capitalized, God)* EL

Differentiated Instruction

Listening Students may better understand the emotional power of the speech if it is read aloud to them. Invite a volunteer to read the speech with emotion and conviction. Then have students discuss the emotions they felt as they listened. BL

AFTER YOU READ

Assess

Writing About Literature

Discuss ways students can organize their essays. They may devote one paragraph to each speech or focus instead on one part of all three speeches in each body paragraph. For example, they could compare the openings, structures, and conclusions of the speeches in separate paragraphs.

Listening and Speaking

Remind students to make eye contact with the audience, and to vary the volume and tone of their voice and the speed of their delivery.

Kennedy's Language and Style

Remind students that to fully evaluate a speech, they must hear it as well as read it. Techniques such as parallelism and repetition may be more powerful when heard aloud.

Revising Check

Remind students that parallelism and repetition can be used to connect ideas and demonstrate a logical progression of thought.

Web Activities Have students access the Web site for interactive activities that will help them assess their understanding of the selection.

Academic Standards

The Additional Support activity on p. 445 covers the following standard:

Differentiated Instruction: **9.7.9** Analyze historically significant speeches...to find the rhetorical devices and features that make them memorable.

BEFORE YOU READ

Focus

BELLRINGER

Bellringer Options
Daily Language Practice Transparency 41

Or ask students if they agree with the statement: *No gain can be made except at someone else's loss. (Students' answers will vary, but students should be able to support their opinions.)* Have students consider as they read how the author presents and supports his argument.

Author Search To expand students' appreciation of Michel de Montaigne, have them access the Web site for additional information and resources.

BEFORE YOU READ

That One Man's Profit Is Another's Loss

MEET MICHEL DE MONTAIGNE

An influential Renaissance thinker, humanist, and one of the world's greatest essayists, Michel de Montaigne (män tän′) had an unusual childhood. He was born near Bordeaux, France, to a wealthy merchant family and was educated according to his father's personal views, in an environment of gentle encouragement. He was taught Latin, the language of the educated in Europe at the time, and did not learn French until he was six years old. As a child, he was curious about everything, especially people and their motives. As an adult, he called into question many of the beliefs of his time.

Father of the Essay When Montaigne was six years old, he was sent to the famous humanist school, Collège de Guyenne. He went on to study law, and became a councilor in the Bordeaux parliament in 1554. In 1565 he married Françoise de la Chassaigne, the daughter of a parliament member. They had six daughters, but only the last child survived past infancy.

> *"I write to keep from going mad from the contradictions I find among mankind—and to work some of those contradictions out for myself."*
>
> —Michel de Montaigne

Three years after Montaigne married, his father died, and he inherited the family estate. He left his government position to settle at the family château where he began to write. Montaigne is called the "father of the familiar essay" because he revived the ancient literary form, named it (the French *essais* means "attempts"), and made it popular. Montaigne wrote about humankind by observing and analyzing his own behavior and opinions and comparing them with those of others. His essays cover a wide range of topics, such as how to read well, how to endure pain, and how to raise children. Montaigne traveled to Paris to present a copy of his famous *Essays* to the king, Henry III, in 1580.

A Progressive Thinker When drawing conclusions, Montaigne tried to use what he called his "natural judgment" rather than things he learned from books. He wrote in a clear, nontechnical style, and tried to humble his readers by calling attention to excessive pride. Montaigne wanted to challenge what other people accepted as truth. He pointed out the danger of believing in anything without thoroughly examining it. Living in an age when religious intolerance ran high, Montaigne thought that the beliefs and customs of different cultures should be respected.

Montaigne often borrowed and quoted from the works of other writers. Unlike other writers of his time, he structured his essays through free association. This distinctive style influenced later essayists, such as Francis Bacon and Ralph Waldo Emerson.

Michel de Montaigne was born in 1533 and died in 1592.

LiteratureOnline **Author Search** For more about Michel de Montaigne, go to www.glencoe.com.

Selection Skills

That One Man's Profit Is Another's Loss

Literary Elements
- Antithesis (SE pp. 447, 448, 449)

Reading Skills
- Analyzing Argument (SE pp. 447, 448, 449)
- Rereading (TWE p. 448)

Vocabulary Skills
- Word Origins (SE p. 449)

Listening/Speaking/Viewing Skills
- Analyzing Art (TWE p. 448)

LITERATURE PREVIEW

Connecting to the Essay

Have you ever wanted something even though you knew that getting it would mean a loss for someone else? Montaigne's essay about profit and loss explores the ways that one person's gain might have a negative effect on someone else. Before you read, think about the following questions:

- How might another person suffer because of something that you gain?
- Is it possible to be successful without taking advantage of others?

Building Background

The sixteenth century was the beginning of the modern era in Europe and was a time of ebb and flux. The population of Europe was growing quickly, and as the middle class grew, it became much more powerful. Most people were relatively prosperous. At the beginning of the century, even peasants could afford to eat meat.

Setting Purposes for Reading

Big Idea Finding Common Ground

As you read this essay, notice how Montaigne assumes that all people have certain traits in common.

Literary Element Antithesis

Antithesis is a contrasting relationship between two ideas. An author uses antithesis by placing two contrasting ideas together, often in parallel structure. Mentioning the two ideas next to each other highlights their differences. As you read, notice Montaigne's use of antithesis.

- See Literary Terms Handbook, p. R2.

Literature Online **Interactive Literary Elements Handbook** To review or learn more about the literary elements, go to www.glencoe.com.

READING PREVIEW

Reading Strategy Analyzing Argument

An **argument** is a technique an author uses to present an idea in a convincing way. Arguments use reasons and facts to support an idea or opinion. As you read the essay, think about what kinds of arguments Montaigne uses to persuade the reader.

Reading Tip: Taking Notes As you read the essay, note Montaigne's arguments and identify the supporting details. Create a web diagram like the one below. Write one of Montaigne's arguments in the center circle and fill the surrounding circles with supporting details.

Vocabulary

condemn (kən dem′) *v.* to declare to be wrong; to pronounce guilty; p. 448 *She condemned his cruelty to animals.*

contention (kən ten′ shən) *n.* a point advanced in a debate or argument; p. 448 *The speaker's contention was well supported and won the approval of the audience.*

vice (vīs) *n.* a moral fault or failing; p. 448 *She considered eating junk food a vice and decided to break her habit.*

Vocabulary Tip: Word Origins Many English words originated in other languages, such as Greek and Latin. For example, "profit" comes from the Latin *proficere*, which means "to advance."

INDIANA ACADEMIC STANDARDS (pages 447–449)

9.2.7 Evaluate an author's argument or defense of a claim by examining...the way in which the author's intent affects the structure and tone of the text.

9.2 Develop [reading] strategies...

9.5.3 Write expository compositions, including analytical essays...

BEFORE YOU READ

Focus

Summary

The speaker begins his speech with an anecdote about a man in ancient Greece who is condemned by another because he earns a living by selling funeral materials. The accuser claimed the man charged too much for his goods and made his profits from the deaths of many people. The speaker then ponders the question: Aren't all gains acquired at the expense of something or someone else?

V Vocabulary

Vocabulary File **Say:** Add these words and definitions to your vocabulary file. For each word, include a sentence that gives you an example of how to use the word. **OL** Students with English language needs should include the pronunciations of these words in their files. **EL**

Literary Elements Have students access the Web site to improve their understanding of antithesis.

Selection Resources

Print Materials

- Unit 2 Resources (Fast File), pp. 64–66
- Leveled Vocabulary Development, p. 33
- Selection and Unit Assessments, pp. 73–74
- Selection Quick Checks, p. 37

Transparencies

- Bellringer Options Transparencies: Daily Language Practice Transparency 41
- Literary Elements Transparency 44

Technology

- TeacherWorks Plus™ CD-ROM
- StudentWorks Plus™ CD-ROM
- Presentation Plus!™ CD-ROM
- Literature Online, glencoe.com
- Online Student Edition, mhln.com
- Exam*View*® Assessment Suite CD-ROM
- Vocabulary PuzzleMaker CD-ROM
- Listening Library, disc 1 tracks 41

Teach

L Literary Element

Antithesis Answer: *Yes; it contrasts gain and loss. Montaigne presents Demades's "ill-reasoned" idea and then argues that no profit can be made except at another's expense.* OL

★ Viewing the Art

Albert Hahn (1877–1918) was a Dutch artist known for his political cartoons, which were often critical of the militarism that he felt led to World War I. AS

Use the CheckPoint questions on Presentation Plus! to check students' mastery of the selection. These questions can be used with interactive response keypads for immediate student feedback.

Readability Scores
Dale-Chall: 9.9
DRP: 64
Lexile: 1140

That One Man's Profit Is Another's Loss

Michel de Montaigne

"The Man of the Century" (Caricature of entrepreneur), c.1890. Albert Hahn. Graphic art. ★

Demades the Athenian[1] **condemned** a man of his city whose trade was to sell what is needed for funerals, on the ground that he asked too high a profit, and that he could only make this profit by the death of a great many people. This seems an ill-reasoned judgment, since no profit can be made except at another's expense, and so by this rule we should have to condemn every sort of gain.

The merchant only thrives on the extravagance of youth; the farmer on the high price of grain; the architect on the collapse of houses; the officers of the law on men's suits[2] and **contentions;** even the honor and practice of ministers of religion depend on our deaths and our **vices.** No physician takes pleasure in the health even of his friends, says the ancient Greek comedy-writer,[3] no soldier in the peace of his city, and so on. And what is worse, let anyone search his heart and he will find that our inward wishes are for the most part born and nourished at the expense of others.

As I was reflecting on this, the fancy came upon me that here nature is merely following her habitual policy. For natural scientists hold that the birth, nourishment, and growth of each thing means the change and decay of something else:

> *Nam quodcumqus suis mutatum finibus exit,*
> *continuo hoc mors est illius, quod fuit ante.*[4]

1. *Demades the Athenian* was a character in Seneca's essay *Beneficiis*. Montaigne takes many ideas in his essay from the ancient Greek writer Seneca.
2. Here, *suits* refers to processes in a court for the recovery of a right or claim.
3. Montaigne is referring to Philemon, an ancient Greek writer of comedies.
4. "Whenever a thing changes and alters its nature, at that moment comes the death of what it was before." This sentence is a quotation from the Roman philosopher Lucretius (c. 96–c. 55 BC).

Literary Element Antithesis *Is this statement an antithesis? Explain.* 

Vocabulary

condemn (kən dem′) *v.* to declare to be wrong; to pronounce guilty
contention (kən ten′ shən) *n.* a point advanced in a debate or argument
vice (vīs) *n.* a moral fault or failing

Additional Support

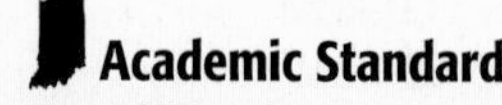

Academic Standards
The Additional Support activity on p. 448 covers the following standard:
Skills Practice: **9.2** Develop [reading] strategies…

Skills Practice

READING: Rereading Rereading will help students understand and interpret the selection. As they reread, ask them to take notes on the following:

- main idea
- supporting details
- author's purpose and tone
- rhetorical and literary devices
- unfamiliar words

Invite students to share their findings in a class discussion of these topics. OL

AFTER YOU READ

RESPONDING AND THINKING CRITICALLY

Respond

1. Do you agree with Montaigne's ideas about profit and loss? Explain your answer.

Recall and Interpret

2. (a)Why does Demades the Athenian criticize the funeral director? (b)How does Demades' complaint set the stage for Montaigne's declaration?
3. (a)What does Montaigne say anyone will find if he searches his own heart? (b)What does Montaigne's statement tell you about his view of human nature?
4. (a)According to Montaigne, what is the natural result of birth and growth? (b)Compare his earlier depiction of profit and loss with this view of nature.

Analyze and Evaluate

5. (a)What does Montaigne mean when he says that "No physician takes pleasure in the health even of his friends"? (b)How would you describe Montaigne's tone in this sentence?
6. In the last paragraph of the essay, Montaigne writes, "As I was reflecting on this, the fancy came upon me. . . ." What effect do the content, tone, and language of this sentence have on the reader?
7. Are you convinced by Montaigne's arguments in this essay? Explain using examples from the text.

Connect

8. **Big Idea** **Finding Common Ground** How does Montaigne employ the idea of nature as a way to establish common ground?

LITERARY ANALYSIS

Literary Element Antithesis

Authors use **antithesis** to make comparisons more powerful and to more clearly define the contrasting relationship between two things. Antithesis can lead the reader to certain conclusions or opinions.

1. Where does Montaigne use antithesis to try to lead the reader to a certain conclusion? Explain using examples from the essay.
2. In what ways is Montaigne's whole essay based on antithesis?

Writing about Literature

Analyze Genre Elements "That One Man's Profit Is Another's Loss" is a formal essay. This kind of persuasive writing is generally serious and logically organized. How well does Montaigne's essay fit this criteria? How does he balance formal and informal elements? Write a short essay analyzing Montaigne's form and technique.

LiteratureOnline **Web Activities** For eFlashcards, Selection Quick Checks, and other Web activities, go to www.glencoe.com.

READING AND VOCABULARY

Reading Strategy Analyzing Argument

The kinds of statements, reasons, and facts that an author uses to support an **argument** differ depending on the purpose of his essay or literary work. In order to persuade, an author must hone his or her argument by choosing only reasons that are certain to have a great impact on the reader.

1. What kinds of reasons or facts does Montaigne use to support his main argument?
2. What kind of support in this essay do you find most persuasive? Explain.

Vocabulary Practice

Practice with Word Origins Match each vocabulary word with the definition of its Latin root word. Use a dictionary if you need help.

1. condemn	a. to stretch (*contendere*)
2. contention	b. fault (*vitium*)
3. vice	c. to damn (*condemnare*)

Writing About Literature

Essays should include specific details to support students' opinions.

Vocabulary

1. c 2. a 3. b

Reading Strategy

1. He examines jobs that most people would not find distasteful and shows how each profession gains from loss. He states that this theory agrees with the laws of nature.
2. Answers will vary.

AFTER YOU READ

Assess

1. Some students may say when people trade money for services, both parties gain.
2. (a) The funeral director profits from people's deaths. (b) By highlighting this "ill-reasoned judgment," Montaigne makes his position sound reasonable.
3. (a) Our deepest wishes are "born and nourished at the expense of others." (b) He is pessimistic; he thinks people care only about their own interests.
4. (a) In nature when one thing is born or grows, another thing decays. (b) His ideas about profit and loss are in harmony with nature's "habitual policy."
5. (a) A physician who cares about profit loses if anyone is healthy. (b) humorous; he exaggerates to make a point
6. This line strikes a casual and conversational tone, as if his conclusion occurred to him spontaneously.
7. Answers will vary.
8. He appeals to the "habitual policy" of nature for the truth of his statement. Laws of nature include growth and decay; the laws also apply to profit and loss.

Literary Element

1. He shows the reader how most professions profit. He focuses on negative aspects of jobs so readers will find them ruthless.
2. The title has an antithesis. The theme, that one person's profit is another's loss, is an antithesis.

BEFORE YOU READ

Focus

BELLRINGER

Bellringer Options
Daily Language Practice Transparency 42

Or invite students to name their favorite comedian or comedy show on television.
Ask: Why does the comedian or television show appeal to you? As they read, have students consider the characteristics of humor and why people respond to humor.

Author Search To expand students' appreciation of Benjamin Franklin, have them access the Web site for additional information and resources.

BEFORE YOU READ

Daylight Saving

MEET BENJAMIN FRANKLIN

Born in Boston, Massachusetts, in 1706, Benjamin Franklin attended school for only two years before beginning work in his father's shop. When his brother James returned from England in 1718 and set up a printing shop, Franklin became James's apprentice. Franklin developed a great love of books. In fact, he would eventually establish America's first public library.

Literary Career When Franklin was sixteen, he began to write anonymously for the *New England Courant*, a newspaper that James had started. Franklin wrote under the pseudonym "Silence Dogood," thinking that his brother would not take his work seriously. In 1723 Franklin moved to Philadelphia, where he established a printing shop in 1728. One year later he purchased a local newspaper, the *Pennsylvania Gazette*. Franklin wrote a political editorial which soon made the paper famous.

Franklin married Deborah Read Rogers in 1730, and they raised three children, two of whom survived to adulthood. Two years later, Franklin started writing and publishing what became known as *Poor Richard's Almanack*, which was extremely popular for its engaging prose and useful information.

Scientist and Revolutionary Franklin busied himself conducting scientific experiments. During his lifetime, he was better known for his scientific achievements than for his writing accomplishments. For example, he devised a new way of printing paper money to make counterfeiting more difficult, and he designed the "Pennsylvania fireplace," which heated houses much more efficiently than other fireplaces. He also made many important discoveries concerning electricity and invented the grounding rod, which protected buildings from lightning strikes.

> *"If you would not be forgotten, as soon as you are dead, either write things worth reading, or do things worth the writing."*
>
> —Benjamin Franklin

Franklin was also an important figure in the struggle to achieve American independence from England. He was elected Speaker of the Pennsylvania House in 1764 and became one of the chief spokespersons for the colonies. In 1776 he served on the committee to draft the Declaration of Independence and then went to France as an ambassador. While there he negotiated the Treaty of Paris, which formally ended the American Revolutionary War. He is considered by many historians to be the most celebrated early American after George Washington.

Benjamin Franklin was born in 1706 and died in 1790.

LiteratureOnline **Author Search** For more about Benjamin Franklin, go to www.glencoe.com.

Selection Skills

Daylight Saving

Literary Elements
- Humor (SE pp. 451, 453, 455, 456
- Rhetorical Devices (SE p. 456)
- Personification (TWE p. 452)

Reading Skills
- Evaluating Evidence (SE pp. 451, 453, 454, 457)
- Problem and Solution (TWE p. 454)

Vocabulary Skills
- Context Clues (SE p. 457)

Writing Skills/Grammar
- Evaluate Author's Craft (SE p. 457)

Listening/Speaking/Viewing Skills
- Analyzing Art (SE p. 455)

LITERATURE PREVIEW

Connecting to the Essay

Franklin's humorous letter to the editor describes his "discovery" of early morning sunlight. Before you read this essay, think about the following questions:

- When have you shared a humorous incident with your friends and family members to convince them of something?
- How could you use humor to convince someone that an idea or discovery of yours is important?

Building Background

Daylight saving time, the system by which people change their clocks in the spring and fall, comes from an idea of Franklin's. The system was not seriously suggested, however, until 1907, when German William Willett proposed moving clocks forward twenty minutes on each of four consecutive Sundays in April and moving clocks back twenty minutes on each of four consecutive Sundays in September. His proposal met with a great deal of criticism. By the 1960s in the United States, most people observed daylight saving time according to local customs and laws.

Setting Purposes for Reading

Big Idea Finding Common Ground

As you read Franklin's letter, notice how he finds common ground with his readers as he argues the benefits of using the full duration of sunlight.

Literary Element Humor

Humor is the quality of a literary work that makes the characters, situations, or events seem funny or ridiculous. Recognizing an author's use of humor can help you determine how serious a selection is, as well as whether it is fictional or factual. As you read, note how and consider why Franklin uses humor in his writing.

- See Literary Terms Handbook, p. R8.

Literature Online **Interactive Literary Elements Handbook** To review or learn more about the literary elements, go to www.glencoe.com.

READING PREVIEW

Reading Strategy Evaluating Evidence

Evidence consists of facts and details that an author uses in order to support an argument. Recognizing evidence can help you evaluate whether an author's argument is credible. As you read Franklin's letter, think about the kinds of evidence he uses and how well this evidence supports the claims, or main points, of his argument.

Reading Tip: Making a Chart Create a chart like the one below to help you track Franklin's use of evidence. In the left column, list important claims. In the right column, note evidence in support of these points.

Claim	Supporting Evidence
It gets light earlier in the summer.	Franklin observed over several days the times of sunrise, and the almanac gave the same information.

Vocabulary

negligently (neg′ li jənt lē) *adv.* in a carelessly inattentive manner; p. 453 *The babysitter negligently allowed the children to go swimming alone.*

subsequent (sub′ sə kwənt) *adj.* following in time, order, or place; p. 453 *After working on their first research paper, the students hoped that subsequent assignments would be easier.*

obstinately (ob′ stə nit lē) *adv.* stubbornly; in spite of reason or persuasion; p. 454 *His friend obstinately refused to change his plans.*

prudent (pro͞od′ ənt) *adj.* showing wisdom and good judgment; p. 455 *She asked the advice of a prudent friend before making a big decision.*

INDIANA ACADEMIC STANDARDS (pages 451–457)

9.3.8 Interpret and evaluate the impact of…ironies in a text.

9.2.7 Evaluate an author's argument or defense of a claim by examining…the comprehensiveness of evidence…

9.5.3 Write expository compositions, including…literary analyses that gather evidence in support of a thesis…

BEFORE YOU READ

Focus

Summary

While visiting France, Benjamin Franklin witnesses the unveiling of a new type of lamp. A discussion follows about how economical using the lamp will be. A satisfactory conclusion is not reached. Franklin writes a humorous letter to the *Journal of Paris* describing the problem and a wonderful discovery he has made about the sun that will be the solution to the problem of saving daylight.

V Vocabulary

Vocabulary File Say: Add these words and definitions to your vocabulary file. For each word, include a sentence that gives you an example of how to use the word. **OL** Students with English language needs should include the pronunciations of these words in their files. **EL**

Literary Elements Have students access the Web site to improve their understanding of humor.

Selection Resources

Print Materials

- Unit 2 Resources (Fast File), pp. 67–69
- Leveled Vocabulary Development, p. 34
- Selection and Unit Assessments, pp. 75–76
- Selection Quick Checks, p. 38

Transparencies

- Bellringer Options Transparencies: Daily Language Practice Transparency 42
- Literary Elements Transparency 109

Technology

- TeacherWorks Plus™ CD-ROM
- StudentWorks Plus™ CD-ROM
- Presentation Plus!™ CD-ROM
- Literature Online, glencoe.com
- Online Student Edition, mhln.com
- Exam*View*® Assessment Suite CD-ROM
- Vocabulary PuzzleMaker CD-ROM
- Listening Library, disc 1 track 42

Teach

BI1 Big Idea

Finding Common Ground
Say: Keep these questions in mind as you read: What is the purpose of Franklin's letter? *(To provide information in a humorous way about saving money on lighting.)* How does Franklin use humor to make his point? *(He uses humor to poke fun at the people discussing the issue because they are oblivious to a simple solution.)* OL

BI2 Big Idea

Finding Common Ground
Answer: *He mentions people's desire to save money. The title connects saving money and "saving" daylight.* OL

L1 Literary Element

Personification Personification gives human qualities or characteristics to animals, forces of nature, or ideas.
Ask: How does Franklin use personification in his letter? *(He personifies the sun as a male person.)* OL

Readability Scores
Dale-Chall: 10.3
DRP: 62
Lexile: 1240

Shakespeare's Bed, 2003. Pam Ingalls.

Daylight Saving

Benjamin Franklin

BI1 MESSIEURS,[1]

You often entertain us with accounts of new discoveries. Permit me to communicate to the public, through your paper, one that has lately been made by myself, and which I conceive may be of great utility.

I was the other evening in a grand company, where the new lamp of Messrs. Quinquet and Lange was introduced, and much admired for its splendor; but a general inquiry was made, whether the oil it consumed was not in proportion to the light it afforded, in which case there would be no saving in the use of it. No one present could satisfy us in that point, which all agreed ought to be known, it being a very desirable thing to lessen, if possible, the expense of lighting our apartments, when every other article of family expense was so much augmented.

I was pleased to see this general concern for economy, for I love economy exceedingly.

I went home, and to bed, three or four hours after midnight, with my head full of the subject. An accidental sudden noise waked me about six in the morning, when I was surprised to find my room filled with light; and I imagined at first, that a number of those lamps had been brought into it; but, rubbing my eyes,

1. *Messieurs* (mes′ ərz), abbreviated as *Messrs.*, is the plural of *Monsieur* (mə syœ′), the French equivalent of the English title "Mister."

Big Idea Finding Common Ground *What common concern does Franklin mention here, and how is it related to the title of the essay?* BI2

Additional Support

Skills Practice

RESEARCH: Science Students may know that hours of daylight and darkness vary during the year with the changing seasons. Our seasons are the result of the tilt of Earth's axis.

- Have students compare hours of daylight and hours of darkness during winter and summer months.
- Have students check local newspapers for a listing of times the sun rises and sets in your area. OL

I perceived the light came in at the windows. I got up and looked out to see what might be the occasion of it, when I saw the sun just rising above the horizon, from whence he poured his rays plentifully into my chamber, my domestic[2] having **negligently** omitted, the preceding evening, to close the shutters. L1

I looked at my watch, which goes very well, and found that it was but six o'clock; and still thinking it something extraordinary that the sun should rise so early, I looked into the almanac,[3] where I found it to be the hour given for his rising on that day. R1 I looked forward, too, and found he was to rise still earlier every day till towards the end of June; and that at no time in the year he retarded his rising so long as till eight o'clock. Your readers, who with me have never seen any signs of sunshine before noon, and seldom regard the astronomical[4] part of the almanac, will be as much astonished as I was, when they hear of his rising so early; and especially when I assure them, *that he gives light as soon as he rises.* I am convinced of this. I am certain of my fact. One cannot be more certain of any fact. I saw it with my own eyes. And, having repeated this observation the three following mornings, I found always precisely the same result.

Yet it so happens, that when I speak of this discovery to others, I can easily perceive by their countenances,[5] though they forbear expressing it in words, that they do not quite believe me. One, indeed, who is a learned natural philosopher, has assured me that I must certainly be mistaken as to the circumstance of the light coming into my room; for it being well known, as he says, that there could be no light abroad at that hour, it follows that none could enter from without; and that of consequence, my windows being accidentally left open, instead of letting in the light, had only served to let out the darkness; and he used many ingenious arguments to show me how I might, by that means, have been deceived. I owned[6] that he puzzled me a little, but he did not satisfy me; and the **subsequent** observations I made, as above mentioned, confirmed me in my first opinion.

This event has given rise in my mind to several serious and important reflections. I considered that, if I had not been awakened so early in the morning, I should have slept six hours longer by the light of the sun, and in exchange have lived six hours the following night by candlelight; and, the latter being a much more expensive light than the former, my love of economy induced me to muster up what little arithmetic I was master of, and to make some calculations, which I shall give you, after observing that utility is, in my opinion the test of value in matters of invention, and that a discovery which can be applied to no use, or is not good for something, is good for nothing.

I took for the basis of my calculation the supposition that there are one hundred thousand families in Paris, and that these families consume in the night half a pound of bougies, or candles, per hour. I think this is a moderate allowance, taking one family with another; for though I believe some consume less, I know that many consume a great deal more. Then estimating seven hours per day as the medium quantity between the time of the sun's rising

2. A *domestic* is a household servant.
3. An *almanac* is a publication that gives the times of sunrise and sunset, the cycles of the moon, and the weather, among other things.
4. The *astronomical* part of the almanac refers to information about the sun, moon, and stars.
5. Here, *countenance* means "face."
6. Here, *own* means "admit."

Big Idea Finding Common Ground *Why do you think that Franklin includes himself with the readers here?* BI3

Reading Strategy Evaluating Evidence *Why might Franklin feel it necessary to give evidence of this point?* R2

Literary Element Humor *How does Franklin treat his natural philosopher friend's "logical" argument? What was your reaction?* L2

Vocabulary

negligently (neg′ li jənt lē) *adv.* in a carelessly inattentive manner

Vocabulary

subsequent (sub′ sə kwənt) *adj.* following in time, order, or place

Teach

R1 Reading Strategy

Evaluating Evidence

Ask: How does Franklin support his claim that the sun was supposed to rise at six o'clock? *(He looked at his watch and in an almanac.)* OL

BI3 Big Idea

Finding Common Ground

Answer: *He may not wish to appear smarter than others; saying that his readers will be as astonished as he was is humorous.* OL

R2 Reading Strategy

Evaluating Evidence

Answer: *He supports an obvious point to create a humorous tone. His letter depends on this "discovery;" all points that follow are based on it.* OL

L2 Literary Element

Humor **Answer:** *He pokes fun at the argument by treating it as scientific. The idea that he "let out the darkness" because the shutters were open is absurd.* OL

Building Reading Fluency

Student Partners Reading aloud with a partner can improve fluency. Pair students and have partners take turns listening to each other read a paragraph from the selection. Invite students to discuss the parts they find amusing. BL

Use the CheckPoint questions on Presentation Plus! to monitor students' comprehension. These questions can be used with interactive response keypads for immediate student feedback.

Academic Standards

Additional Support activities on pp. 452 and 453 cover the following standards:

Skills Practice: **9.2.4** Synthesize the content from several sources or works…and connect…to…related topics…

Building Reading Fluency: **9.7** [Respond] to oral communication [with] careful listening and evaluation of content…

Teach

R1 Reading Strategy

Making an Inference
Ask: Why does Franklin calculate how much money and tallow might be saved if people rose earlier in the day? *(He claims to be inspired by his love of economy, but he may be using the numbers as another element of humor.)* OL

R2 Reading Strategy

Evaluating Evidence
Answer: *Some students may state that Franklin's math weakens his argument. The fact that Franklin uses estimates and the less valuable* livres tournois *to get a final number five times larger than if he had used the Paris currency adds to Franklin's humor but not his argument.* OL

L1 Literary Element

Humor Answer: *His suggestion serves to engage readers in a funny or comical way.* OL

and ours, he rising during the six following months from six to eight hours before noon, and there being seven hours of course per night in which we burn candles, the account will stand thus;—

In the six months between the 20th of March and the 20th of September, there are

Nights 183
Hours of each night in which we burn candles. 7
Multiplication gives for the total number of hours 1,281
These 1,281 hours multiplied by 100,000, the number of inhabitants, give. 128,100,000
One hundred twenty-eight millions and one hundred thousand hours, spent at Paris by candlelight, which, at half a pound of wax and tallow[7] per hour, gives the weight of 64,050,000
Sixty-four millions and fifty thousand of pounds, which, estimating the whole at the medium price of thirty sols[8] the pound, makes the sum of ninety-six millions and seventy-five thousand livres tournois[9]. 96,075,000

R1 An immense sum! that the city of Paris might save every year, by the economy of using sunshine instead of candles. If it should be said, that people are apt to be **obstinately** attached to old customs, and that it will be difficult to induce them to rise before noon, consequently my discovery can be of little use; I answer, *Nil desperandum.*[10] I believe all who have common sense, as soon as they have learnt from this paper that it is daylight when the sun rises, will contrive to rise with him; and, to compel the rest, I would propose the following regulations; First. Let a tax be laid of a louis[11] per window, on every window that is provided with shutters to keep out the light of the sun.

Second. Let the same salutary[12] operation of police be made use of, to prevent our burning candles, that inclined us last winter to be more economical in burning wood; that is, let guards be placed in the shops of the wax and tallow chandlers,[13] and no family be permitted to be supplied with more than one pound of candles per week.

Third. Let guards also be posted to stop all the coaches, &c. that would pass the streets after sunset, except those of physicians, surgeons, and midwives.

Fourth. Every morning, as soon as the sun rises, let all the bells in every church be set ringing; and if that is not sufficient?, let cannon be fired in every street, to wake the sluggards[14] effectually, and make them open their eyes to see their true interest.

All the difficulty will be in the first two or three days; after which the reformation will be as natural and easy as the present irregularity; for, *ce n'est que le premier pas qui coûte.*[15] Oblige a man to rise at four in the morning, and it is more than probable he will go willingly to bed at eight in the evening; and, having had eight hours sleep, he will rise more willingly at four in the morning following. But this sum of ninety-six millions and seventy-five thousand livres is not the whole of what may be saved

7. *Tallow* is a white, nearly solid fat from cattle and sheep that is used to make soap and candles.
8. A *sol* was a French unit of currency.
9. *Livres tournois* refers to currency coined in Tours, a provincial French city in west-central France along the Loire River. This currency was worth one-fifth less than the money made in Paris.
10. *Nil desperandum* means "Never despair" in Latin.
11. A *louis* was a French unit of currency.
12. *Salutary* means "beneficial."
13. A *chandler* is a maker or seller of tallow, wax candles, or soap.
14. A *sluggard* is a habitually lazy person.
15. *Ce n'est que le premier pas qui coûte* means "It is only the first step that counts" in French.

Reading Strategy Evaluating Evidence *How does Franklin's math strengthen or weaken his argument? Explain.* R2

Vocabulary
obstinately (ob′ stə nit lē) *adv.* stubbornly; in spite of reason or persuasion

Literary Element Humor *What does this humorous suggestion add to Franklin's argument?* L1

Additional Support

Skills Practice

READING: Problem and Solution
Most prose literature is built around a problem, or conflict, that must be resolved. How the problem is solved makes up the plot of the story. Sometimes there are secondary problems that get solved along the way.

- Have students write the following column headings on a sheet of paper: *Main Problem, Solution, Related Problems.*
- Ask students to identify the main problem and solution, as well as related problems and solutions.
- Discuss how the problems and solutions contribute to the final outcome. OL

Starry Night, Aries, 1888. Vincent Van Gogh. Musee d'Orsay, Paris, France. 
Viewing the Art: What forms of light appear in this painting? Explain.

by my economical project. You may observe, that I have calculated upon only one half of the year, and much may be saved in the other, though the days are shorter. Besides, the immense stock of wax and tallow left unconsumed during the summer, will probably make candles much cheaper for the ensuing winter, and continue them cheaper as long as the proposed reformation shall be supported.

For the great benefit of this discovery, thus freely communicated and bestowed by me on the public, I demand neither place, pension, exclusive privilege, nor any other reward whatever. I expect only to have the honor of it. And yet I know there are little, envious minds, who will, as usual, deny me this and say, that my invention was known to the ancients, and perhaps they may bring passages out of the old books in proof of it. I will not dispute with these people, that the ancients knew not the sun would rise at certain hours; they possibly had, as we have, almanacs that predicted it; but it does not follow thence, that they knew *he gave light as soon as he rose.* This is what I claim as my discovery. If the ancients knew it, it might have been long since forgotten; for it certainly was unknown to the moderns, at least to the Parisians, which to prove, I need use but one plain simple argument. They are as well instructed, judicious,[16] and **prudent** a people as exist anywhere in the world, all professing, like myself, to be lovers of economy; and, from the many heavy taxes required from them by the necessities of the state, have surely an abundant reason to be economical. I say it is impossible that so sensible a people, under such circumstances, should have lived so long by the smoky, unwholesome, and enormously expensive light of candles, if they had really known, that they might have had as much pure light of the sun for nothing. I am, &c.
A SUBSCRIBER

16. *Judicious* means "using good judgment."

Literary Element Humor *How is this statement humorous? What purpose does it serve?* L2

Vocabulary

prudent (pro͞od′ ənt) *adj.* showing wisdom and good judgment

Teach

L2 Literary Element

Humor Answer: *The statement is humorous because the idea that the sun could rise and not give light is ridiculous. Getting the reader to laugh at this by crediting Franklin as a clever "scientist" serves to avoid blaming the Parisians for not realizing how obvious the idea of daylight saving should have been all along.* OL

Viewing the Art

Answer: *Direct light appears from the stars and the lights on shore. Indirect light appears as a reflection of the moonlight on the waves and a reflection of the shore lights in the water.*

Although 1888 saw the maturation of Van Gogh's technique, it was also a year of great mental turmoil for him. In December, he suffered a psychotic episode resulting in the infamous incident where he cut off part of his own ear. AS

CheckPoint

Use the CheckPoint questions on Presentation Plus! to check students' mastery of the selection. These questions can be used with interactive response keypads for immediate student feedback.

English Language Coach

Borrowed Words Point out the words *ce n'est que le premier pas qui coûte,* on page 454 and explain that the words are italicized because they are French words. When foreign words are accepted into English, they are not italicized. Pair English learners with English-speaking classmates. Have partners compile lists of borrowed words. Challenge students to identify words that took on English spellings and pronunciations and words that kept their original spellings. EL

Academic Standards

Additional Support activities on pp. 454 and 455 cover the following standards:

Skills Practice: **9.3** [Identify] story elements such as...plot...

English Language Coach: **9.1** Use...a growing knowledge of English and other languages to determine the meaning of words...

AFTER YOU READ

Assess

1. Students should distinguish between our daylight saving time and Franklin's parody.
2. (a) They do not believe him. (b) He teases others, but also mocks himself.
3. (a) People may be attached to old customs and find it hard to get up early. (b) He wants to highlight the ease of this transition.
4. (a) As wise people, they would have risen early and passed on such knowledge. (b) The ancients knew economics and most of Franklin's reasons save money.
5. His tone and use of detail add to the humor. Examples: He describes his gradual realization of the light source; he did not realize at once it was the sun.
6. His arguments state the obvious, but include facts as well.
7. (a) His essay is humorous, yet his letter explains that people waste daytime light and nighttime candles. He pokes fun at those who dispute his discovery's usefulness, and exaggerates ways to implement his plan. His discovery's economic benefits are real. (b) Answers will vary.
8. He makes fun of himself as well as them.

AFTER YOU READ

RESPONDING AND THINKING CRITICALLY

Respond

1. How does Franklin's essay affect your thoughts on our country's current daylight saving time program?

Recall and Interpret

2. (a)Franklin describes sharing his discovery with several people. How do they react to his news? (b)How does the way he talks about these people relate to his purpose for writing the essay?
3. (a)What are the only difficulties that Franklin sees in beginning a citywide program of daylight saving? (b)Why might he mention these difficulties?
4. (a)How does Franklin show that he "knows" the ancients did not perceive that the sun "gave light as soon as he rose"? (b)How do these reasons relate to what he considers the most important motive for proposing daylight saving?

Analyze and Evaluate

5. How does the way that Franklin narrates his discovery of early morning sunlight add to the humor of the essay?
6. Franklin says that a discovery that is not useful is good for nothing. How convincing is he in portraying daylight saving as useful?
7. (a)How does Franklin balance serious and humorous elements in his essay? (b)Do you take him seriously in spite of his humorous style? Explain.

Connect

8. **Big Idea** **Finding Common Ground** How does Franklin establish common ground with his audience?

LITERARY ANALYSIS

Literary Element Humor

Humor is often used to point out human failings and the ironies of everyday life. Humorous devices include sarcasm, exaggeration, puns, and verbal irony. Humor that is ironic presents a statement that is the opposite of what is true, or the opposite of what the author really means.

1. How does Franklin use humor to point out human failings?
2. What is an example of exaggeration in Franklin's letter?
3. Where does Franklin use verbal irony?

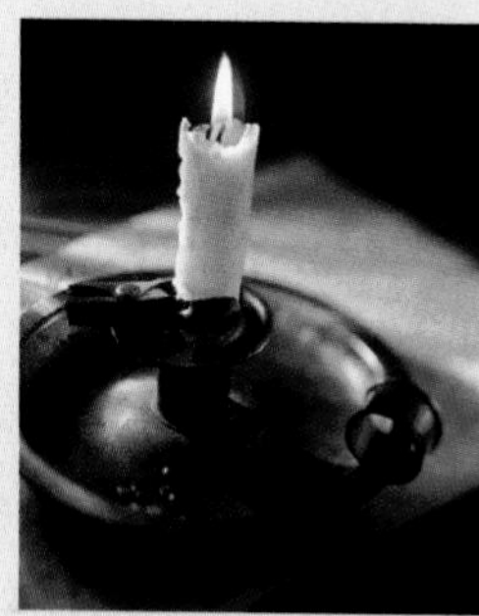

Review: Rhetorical Devices

As you learned on page 439, **rhetorical devices** are techniques that an author uses in order to heighten a particular effect or engage the attention of the reader. One of these techniques is the deliberate repetition of sentence structures, which is called parallelism.

Partner Activity With a classmate, look through Franklin's letter to find examples of parallelism. Use a chart like the one below to record the examples and their effects.

Example of Parallelism	Effect
"I looked at my watch" "I looked into the almanac" "I looked forward, too"	Humorous—he seems to need a lot of evidence that the sun comes up in the morning, something we all know.

Literary Element

1. He says that it might be difficult to convince people to rise before noon. He gives exaggerated examples of laws and measures.
2. Possible answer: His surprise upon waking at six in the morning and finding his room full of light.
3. He insists that his realization about the sun is an ingenious discovery.

Review: Rhetorical Devices

Students' answers will vary. They should include the effects of each example of parallelism.

READING AND VOCABULARY

Reading Strategy Evaluating Evidence

Evidence supports an author's ideas or opinions. Different types of evidence include statements, statistics, observations, or examples that can be proven. When **evaluating evidence,** it is important to consider whether an author's facts come from reliable sources.

1. Describe two kinds of evidence that Franklin uses in his letter. How effective is this evidence in persuading the reader?
2. On what does Franklin base his statistical evidence? Does he refer to any sources?

Vocabulary Practice

Practice with Context Clues Use context clues in each sentence to determine the meaning of the boldfaced word.

1. He **negligently** forgot to check the safety of the machinery, which led to an accident.
   a. hurriedly
   b. confusedly
   c. irresponsibly
2. The introduction to his speech was very interesting, but his **subsequent** points were less than inspiring.
   a. complicated
   b. following
   c. boring
3. Merle refused to learn to type correctly and **obstinately** kept typing in her own, much slower way.
   a. stubbornly
   b. frustratingly
   c. inexpertly
4. She wanted to start skiing down steep slopes immediately, but she made the more **prudent** decision to practice on gentler slopes first.
   a. hasty
   b. comfortable
   c. wise

LiteratureOnline Web Activities For eFlashcards, Selection Quick Checks, and other Web activities, go to www.glencoe.com.

WRITING AND EXTENDING

Writing About Literature

Evaluate Author's Craft When you evaluate an author's craft, you analyze his or her use of sentence structure, word choice, literary elements, and other technical aspects of writing. Write an essay in which you evaluate Benjamin Franklin's use of anecdote and antithesis. Remember that an anecdote is a brief account of an interesting incident, and antithesis is the juxtaposition of contrasting ideas.

Before you begin writing, create two web diagrams like the one below to organize your ideas. Use one web for anecdote and one for antithesis. In the center of each diagram, write the name of the technique. In the space around the web, list examples of Franklin's use of the technique.

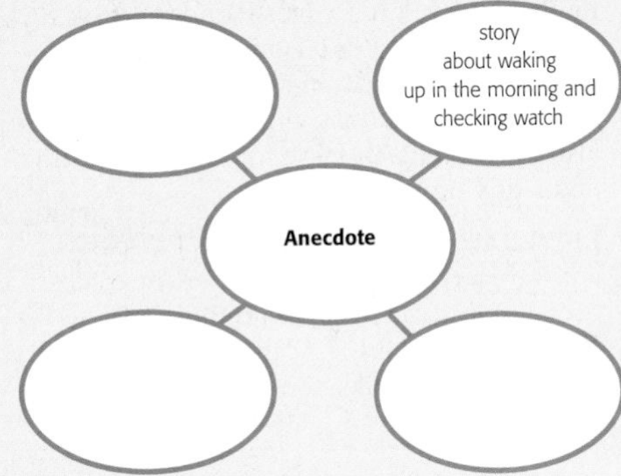

After completing your first draft, discuss your essay with a classmate and evaluate each other's work. Then proofread and edit your work for mistakes in spelling, grammar, and punctuation.

Reading Further

To learn more about Benjamin Franklin's discoveries or to read more of his humorous writings, you might enjoy the following books:

Poor Richard's Almanack was Franklin's most popular work. The book is full of Franklin's famous sayings, funny stories, and both practical and humorous information.

Franklin: Writings, edited by J. A. Leo Lemay, includes Franklin's autobiography, several of his essays, and writings about his inventions.

AFTER YOU READ

Assess

Reading Strategy

1. Students may point out the observational and statistical evidence that Franklin uses, such as the time the sun rises in the morning, or when he tries to persuade the reader of how much money could be saved from daylight saving time. Students may point out that statistics help to support an argument, even a humorous one.
2. Franklin bases his statistical evidence on his own calculations, but he refers to his almanac to confirm the early time of the sunrise.

Vocabulary

1. c **2.** b **3.** a **4.** c

Writing About Literature

Students may wish to brainstorm with a partner to complete the web diagrams. Point out that they do not need to include all the information from their diagrams when writing their essays.

Web Activities Have students access the Web site for interactive activities that will help them assess their understanding of the selection.

Differentiated Instruction

Short-Response Questions Short-response questions often do not have one correct answer. Instead, an answer is judged by its insight and the quality of textual evidence used to support it. Ask students to answer these questions using three to five lines:

- Why did Benjamin Franklin use humor to present his ideas about daylight saving?
- What is your favorite part of the selection? Why?

Have students discuss their responses with a partner. BL

Academic Standards

The Additional Support activity on p. 457 covers the following standard:

Differentiated Instruction: **9.2.8** Make reasonable statements and draw conclusions about a text, supporting them with accurate examples.

BEFORE YOU READ

Focus

BELLRINGER

Bellringer Options
Daily Language Practice Transparency 43

John Dos Passos lived in the United States in the early twentieth century. Before reading, have students brainstorm a list of advantages of living in the United States in the twenty-first century. After they read the selection, have students compare their list with the author's list.

Author Search To expand students' appreciation of John Dos Passos, have them access the Web site for additional information and resources.

BEFORE YOU READ

The American Cause

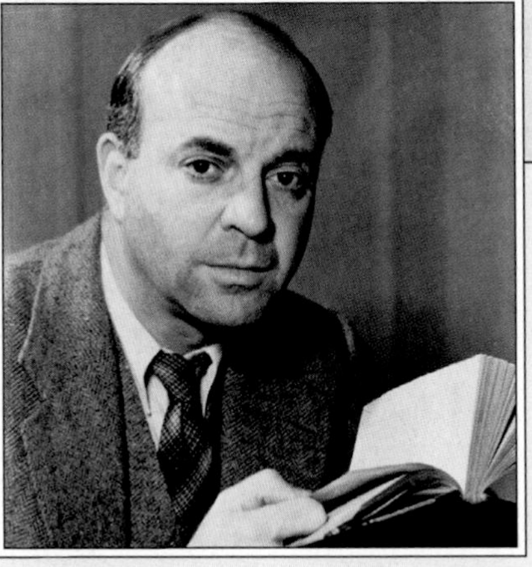

MEET JOHN DOS PASSOS

John Dos Passos's childhood encouraged him to study his country from an outsider's point of view. In his lifetime of writing, Dos Passos explored and reported changes in U.S. society, politics, and history.

John Roderigo Dos Passos was born in Chicago. His father worked as a prominent corporate lawyer. His mother traveled extensively, taking her son with her to Mexico, England, and Europe. Dos Passos later claimed he had a "hotel childhood" because he traveled so much. In those years, he developed a love of Europe, especially France. He also developed a passion for reading, writing, and studying languages.

In 1912, at the age of fifteen, Dos Passos entered Harvard University. There he established a close friendship with the poet E. E. Cummings. In 1917, the writings of both appeared in the collection *Eight Harvard Poets.*

> *"I was thoroughly embarked on an effort to keep up a contemporary commentary on history's changes."*
>
> —John Dos Passos

Social and Political Interests During World War I, Dos Passos served as an ambulance driver in France and Italy. He based his first novel, *One Man's Initiation—1917,* which appeared in 1920, on his wartime experiences. A second book, *Three Soldiers,* published in 1921, explored the bitterness men felt while serving in the armed forces. It gained attention as a significant war novel.

During the 1920s, Dos Passos traveled overseas. He spent time in Paris with American writers such as Ernest Hemingway and F. Scott Fitzgerald. He began to earn his living by writing—producing travel essays, poems, plays, and fiction. He took an interest in political protests and social causes. He wrote about labor unions, strikes, and the changing structure of U.S. industry.

Literary Career In 1925, Dos Passos established his literary reputation with his novel *Manhattan Transfer.* In the novel, he experimented with new writing techniques and created characters that reflected U.S. social orders. In the 1930s, Dos Passos published his trilogy *U.S.A.,* which critics praised as a landmark work of literature. For Dos Passos, the novel was a tool for encouraging political action.

Later in life, Dos Passos grew more conservative in his outlook and turned to writing about history. He published books about Thomas Jefferson and other historical figures, as well as another trilogy, *District of Columbia.*

However, the politics and culture of the United States continued to be a major focus in his writing. He spent the last years of his life in Virginia with his family.

John Dos Passos was born in 1896 and died in 1970.

LiteratureOnline **Author Search** For more about John Dos Passos, go to www.glencoe.com.

Selection Skills

The American Cause

Literary Elements
- Persuasive Essay (SE pp. 459, 460, 462)
- Tone (SE p. 462)

Reading Skills
- Distinguishing Fact and Opinion (SE pp. 459, 460, 463)

Vocabulary Skills
- Context Clues (TWE p. 460)

Writing Skills/Grammar
- Evaluate Author's Craft (TWE p. 463)

Listening/Speaking/Viewing Skills
- Analyzing Art (TWE p. 460)

LITERATURE PREVIEW

Connecting to the Essay

A group of German students asked John Dos Passos why they should admire the United States. Before you read his response, think about the following questions:

- Is it important to feel patriotic? Why or why not?
- In your opinion, what is admirable about the United States?

Building Background

Dos Passos wrote "The American Cause" in 1955, as he neared the age of sixty. He had witnessed two World Wars and was well aware of the challenges faced by the young Germans he addressed. Their country was still redefining itself after losing World War II (1939–1945) to the Allied Powers of the United States, Great Britain, France, and the Soviet Union. When Dos Passos's essay was published, Germany lacked political and economic stability. By contrast, the United States was enjoying a postwar boom in its economy and population.

Setting Purposes for Reading

Big Idea Finding Common Ground

As you read, notice what Dos Passos believes the German students might find they have in common with people in the United States.

Literary Element Persuasive Essay

A **persuasive essay** is an essay that employs techniques designed to convince an audience to think or act in a certain way. These techniques might include cause-and-effect reasoning or appeals to logic, emotion, ethics, or authority. Reading a persuasive essay gives the reader an opportunity to consider the arguments presented and use them to form his or her own opinion. As you read, notice the kinds of techniques used by Dos Passos.

- See Literary Terms Handbook, p. R13.

LiteratureOnline **Interactive Literary Elements Handbook** To review or learn more about the literary elements, go to www.glencoe.com.

READING PREVIEW

Reading Strategy Distinguishing Fact and Opinion

A fact is information that can be proven. An opinion is a personal interpretation. **Distinguishing fact and opinion** as you read will help you form your own opinions. As you read, determine if the author's statements are facts or opinions.

Reading Tip: Taking Notes Use a chart like the one shown to record details in the essay.

Detail	Fact or Opinion	Possible Effect
I didn't tell them that they should admire the United States for the victories of our armed forces. . .	Opinion: Dos Passos suggests that U.S. war victories are not the most admirable thing about the nation.	Encourages reader to consider the effects of national aggression.

Vocabulary

negations (ni gā′ shənz) *n.* acts of denying; negative statements or denials; p. 460 *The governor gave carefully worded negations when asked about her decision to cut education funding.*

estuaries (es′ cho͞o er′ ēz) *n.* places where rivers feed into the sea; p. 461 *They recorded the widths of the estuaries when mapping the ocean.*

inherent (in her′ ənt) *adj.* existing naturally in someone or something; p. 461 *All human beings have an inherent right to be treated with respect.*

unstratified (un strat′ ə fīd) *adj.* not structured into different social classes; p. 461 *An unstratified society treats all people as equals.*

INDIANA ACADEMIC STANDARDS (pages 459–463)

9.2.7 Evaluate an author's argument or defense of a claim...

9.2 Develop [reading] strategies...

9.5.3 Write expository compositions, including...literary analyses that gather evidence in support of a thesis...

BEFORE YOU READ

Focus

Summary

An American author is asked by a group of German students to give them reasons why they should admire the United States. He suggests that they admire the United States not for what it has achieved, but for what it has the potential to become.

V Vocabulary

Vocabulary File Say: Add these words and definitions to your vocabulary file. For each word, include a sentence that gives you an example of how to use the word. **OL** Students with English language needs should include the pronunciations of these words in their files. **EL**

Literary Elements Have students access the Web site to improve their understanding of a persuasive essay.

Selection Resources

Print Materials

- Unit 2 Resources (Fast File), pp. 70–72
- Leveled Vocabulary Development, p. 35
- Selection and Unit Assessments, pp. 77–78
- Selection Quick Checks, p. 39

Transparencies

- Bellringer Options Transparencies: Daily Language Practice Transparency 43
- Literary Elements Transparencies 34, 39, 42

Technology

- TeacherWorks Plus™ CD-ROM
- StudentWorks Plus™ CD-ROM
- Presentation Plus!™ CD-ROM
- Literature Online, glencoe.com
- Online Student Edition, mhln.com
- Exam*View*® Assessment Suite CD-ROM
- Vocabulary PuzzleMaker CD-ROM
- Listening Library, disc 1 track 43

Teach

R Reading Strategy

Distinguishing Fact and Opinion **Answer:** *This passage includes fact and opinion statements. Whether a car is shinier is an opinion, but the number of appliances or the amount of travel in a given country could be calculated and compared with similar figures from other countries.* OL

Viewing the Art

Painter, writer, philosopher, art historian, and visionary Dr. Tsing-Fang Chen created the Post-Modern art style called Neo-Iconography. Dr. Chen's work focuses on humanism, love, tolerance and peace. Dr. Chen received a Global Tolerance Award at the United Nations for his work.

Ask: The title of this work is *Liberty in Cubism (III)*. What do you think it expresses about liberty? *(Accept reasonable responses.)* AS

Readability Scores

Dale-Chall: 8.1

DRP: 64

Lexile: 1460

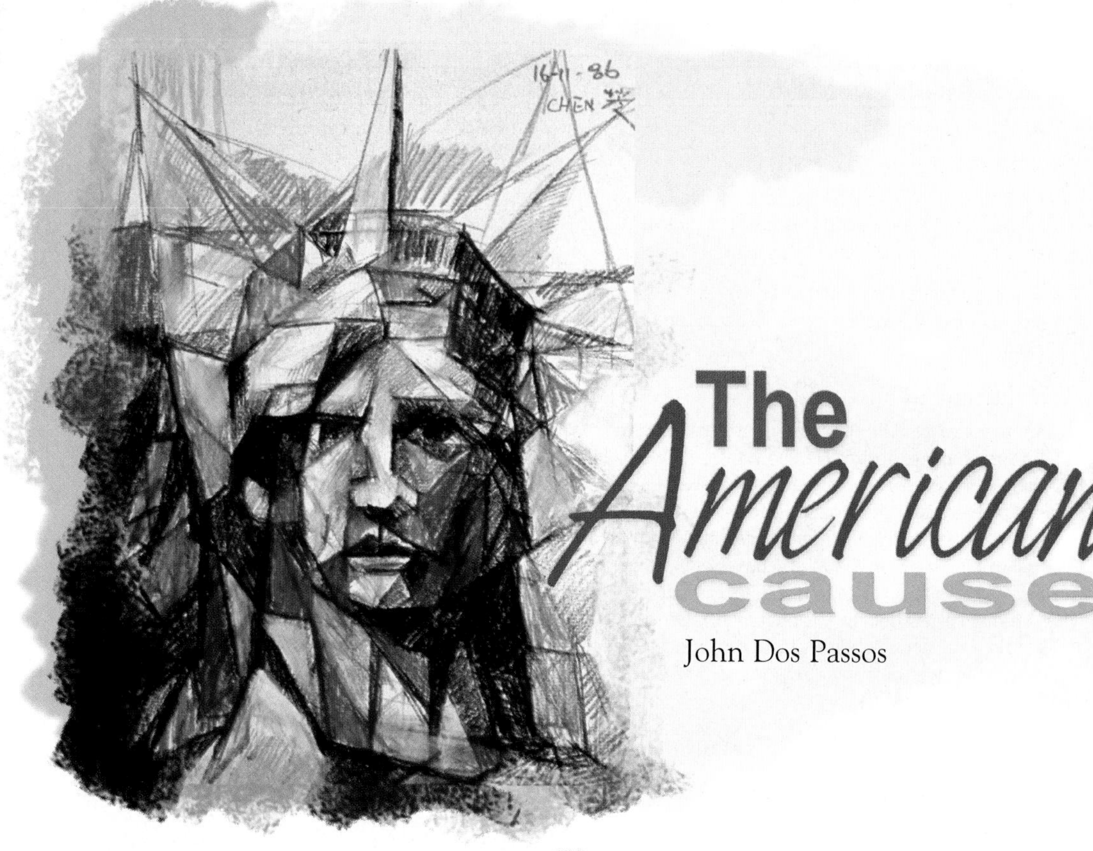

The American Cause

John Dos Passos

Liberty in Cubism (III). Tsing-Fang Chen. Mixed media on paper. 

Not long ago I received a letter from some German students asking me to explain to them in three hundred words why they should admire the United States. "Young people in Germany," they wrote, "as in other places in the world are disillusioned, weary of pronouncements on the slogan level. They are not satisfied with **negations,** they have been told over and over again what to hate and what to fight. . . . They want to know what to be and what to do."

This is what I didn't tell them: I didn't tell them that they should admire the United States for the victories of our armed forces or because we had first developed the atomic bomb or the hydrogen bomb, or because we had shinier automobiles or more washing machines and deep freeze[1] or more televisions or ran up more passenger miles of airplane travel a year than any other people in the world. I didn't tell them to admire us for getting more productive work done with less back

Vocabulary

negations (ni gā′ shənz) *n.* acts of denying; negative statements or denials

1. A *deep freeze* is a very large, stand-alone freezer that can store a considerable amount of frozen food.

Reading Strategy Distinguishing Fact and Opinion
Does this passage include statements of fact or opinion? How do you know? R

Additional Support

Skills Practice

VOCABULARY: Context Clues
Students may need support in understanding some of the words in this selection. As students read the selection, suggest that they list words that are unfamiliar. Allow students to work in pairs to find context clues for the terms on their lists. If students are unable to unlock the meaning of a word, have them refer to a dictionary. After looking up the word, they should return to the selection and identify clues in the sentence. OL

breaking than any other people in the world or for our high wages, or our social security system.[2] I didn't tell them to admire us because our popular leaders had the sweetest smiles before the television cameras or because we lived on a magnificent continent that offered an unbelievable variety of climates, mountains, plains, rivers, **estuaries,** seashores. Some of these are very good things but they are not things that would help them "to know what to be and what to do."

This is what I told them: I told them they should admire the United States not for what we were but for what we might become. Self-governing democracy[3] was not an established creed, but a program for growth. I reminded them that industrial society was a new thing in the world and that although we Americans had gone further than any people in spreading out its material benefits we were just beginning, amid crimes, illusions, mistakes, and false starts, to get to work on how to spread out what people needed much more: the sense of belonging, the faith in human dignity, the confidence of each man in the greatness of his own soul without which life is a meaningless servitude.[4] I told them to admire our failures because they might contain the seeds of great victories to come, not of the victories that come through massacring men, women, and children, but of the victories that come through overcoming the evil **inherent** in mankind through urgent and warmhearted use of our best brains. I told them to admire us for our foolish trust in other peoples, for our failure to create an empire when empire building was easy. I told them to admire us for our still **unstratified** society, where every man has the chance, if he has the will and the wit, to invent his own thoughts and to make his own way. I told them to admire us for the hope we still have that there is enough goodness in man to use the omnipotence[5] science has given him to ennoble[6] his life on earth instead of degrading it. Self-government, through dangers and distortions and failures, is the American cause. Faith in self-government, when all is said and done, is faith in the eventual goodness of man.

2. *Social security system* refers to the U.S. government program in which a portion of workers' wages is shared with people who are aided by the system.
3. *Democracy* is a system of government in which all citizens are free to participate by voting.
4. *Servitude* is submission to another person's will; a person in servitude has little or no independence.
5. *Omnipotence* means "state of being all powerful."
6. *Ennoble* means "to make noble" or "to elevate."

Literary Element Persuasive Essay *How does Dos Passos's repetition of this phrase help keep you interested in reading further?* **L**

Vocabulary

estuaries (es′ cho͞o er′ ēz) *n.* places where rivers feed into the sea

Big Idea Finding Common Ground *Why might Dos Passos refer to U.S. failures in his response to the German students?* **BI**

Vocabulary

inherent (in her′ənt) *adj.* existing naturally in someone or something

unstratified (un strat′ ə fīd) *adj.* not structured into different social classes

Teach

L Literary Element

Persuasive Essay Answer: *This statement is the opposite of what the reader would expect and it creates interest.* **OL**

BI Big Idea

Finding Common Ground
Answer: *Students should be aware that in 1955, the Germans were still suffering from defeat in World War II. Some students may recognize that by mentioning the failures of the United States, Dos Passos may hope to show the German students that they share common ground with people in the United States. He may also be encouraging them to learn from Germany's failures.* **OL**

CheckPoint

Use the CheckPoint questions on Presentation Plus! to monitor students' comprehension. These questions can be used with interactive response keypads for immediate student feedback.

English Language Coach

Building Background Newcomers to the United States may not be familiar with its history. Give students an overview of the time period in which the selection was written—postwar. Explain what the author means by the term *industrial society.* **EL**

Differentiated Instruction

Author's Purpose Some students may not grasp the author's purpose for *not* telling the German students about American achievements. Have students discuss why the author thought that boasting was not the best approach to use in his persuasive essay. **BL**

Academic Standards

Additional Support activities on pp. 460 and 461 cover the following standards:

Skills Practice: **9.1** Use…context clues and a growing knowledge of English…to determine the meaning of words…

English Language Coach: **9.3.12** Analyze the way in which a work…is related to…issues of its historical period.

Differentiated Instruction: **9.2** Develop strategies such as…identifying…[author's] purpose…

AFTER YOU READ

Assess

1. Yes, the nation is still evolving as changes occur.
2. (a) Military victories, powerful weapons, automobiles, high wages, and U.S. leadership (b) Military actions and material concerns are not things to be proud of. He stresses character, morality, and dignity.
3. (a) A sense of belonging, faith in human dignity, and confidence in the greatness of the human soul (b) These are harder to obtain than things you can buy.
4. (a) Self-government (b) Democracy is "a program for growth"; the nation's potential for ethical growth is admirable. Faith in self-government equals faith in human goodness.
5. Students may say that U.S. society is unstratified, since people still have "the chance . . . to invent [their] own thoughts and to make [their] own way." Others may say racial and class inequalities disprove this argument.
6. (a) Military victories (b) Victory is fighting evil and defeating morally undesirable traits.
7. Failures might have seeds of victories to come; we can learn from our mistakes.
8. U.S. citizens or all of humanity

CheckPoint

Use the CheckPoint questions on Presentation Plus! to check students' mastery of the selection. These questions can be used with interactive response keypads for immediate student feedback.

AFTER YOU READ

RESPONDING AND THINKING CRITICALLY

Respond

1. Is Dos Passos's essay still relevant today? Explain.

Recall and Interpret

2. (a)List three "very good things" Dos Passos says he excludes from his list of things to admire. (b)What do these exclusions suggest about Dos Passos's political and social views?
3. (a)What do people need more than material benefits, according to Dos Passos? (b)How easy is it to obtain these things?
4. (a)According to Dos Passos, what is the basic American cause? (b)How does this cause relate to his point that the United States should be admired for "what we might become"?

Analyze and Evaluate

5. Dos Passos argues that American society is "unstratified." Is this argument valid? Why or why not?
6. (a)What does Dos Passos mean by "not the victories that come through massacring men, women, and children"? (b)What does this phrase reveal about his definition of victory?
7. Why does Dos Passos insist that some U.S. failures are admirable?

Connect

8. **Big Idea** **Finding Common Ground** Dos Passos is answering a question posed by a group of German students. Who is the larger audience? Explain your reasoning.

LITERARY ANALYSIS

Literary Element Persuasive Essay

The author of a **persuasive essay** relies on appeals to both logic and emotion. A good persuasive writer anticipates the possible concerns and objections of the audience. The writer then uses this insight to directly address possible arguments. Sometimes this means admitting mistakes early on in order to avoid opposition later.

1. At times Dos Passos seems biased against industrial society. At other times, he seems to advocate industrial society. Identify one example of each point of view. How do they relate to his overall message?
2. (a)What assumption lies beneath Dos Passos's belief in "the evil inherent in mankind"? (b)How does this evil relate to what Dos Passos sees as the common human goal?

Review: Tone

As you learned on page 352, **tone** is the reflection of a writer's attitude toward his or her subject matter. Tone is conveyed through word choice, punctuation, sentence structure, and figures of speech. A writer's tone might communicate a variety of attitudes, including sympathy, anger, and humor.

Partner Activity With a classmate, discuss the tone of "The American Cause." Working with your partner, create a two-column chart. In the left-hand column, record passages from the text that demonstrate a particular tone. In the right-hand column, label each example with a descriptive adjective.

Passage	Tone
our popular leaders had the sweetest smiles	Ironic

Literary Element

1. He alternates between disgust and pride at U.S. accomplishments. The United States' material wealth is not as important as the wealth of human potential that it, as an industrial society, represents.
2. (a) Evil is an inescapable part of people. (b) If not for this evil, there would be no motivation to work together for the common good.

Review: Tone

Allow time in class for students to share their completed charts and discuss the tone the author creates.

READING AND VOCABULARY

WRITING AND EXTENDING

Reading Strategy Distinguishing Fact and Opinion

In order to **distiguish fact and opinion,** review the chart you made as you read the essay. Decide which details relate to the past, which focus on the future, and which are easiest to disprove.

1. Dos Passos argues that the best days for the United States lie in the future. Is this a fact or an opinion? Explain your answer.
2. Identify three details from the essay that are based on facts.

Vocabulary Practice

Practice with word parts The fundamental element of a word, without prefixes or suffixes, is the root. In the word *heroic*, for example, the root is *hero*. The suffix *–ic* changes *hero*, a noun, into an adjective. Use a dictionary to find the Latin root for each vocabulary word listed below.

1. negations	**a.** gates	**b.** negatus
2. estuaries	**a.** estar	**b.** aestus
3. inherent	**a.** here	**b.** inhaerens
4. unstratified	**a.** stratem	**b.** ratify

Academic Vocabulary

Here are two words from the vocabulary list on page R80.

advocate (ad′ və kāt′) *v.* to argue in favor of a cause

concentrate (kon′ sən trāt′) *v.* to increase the strength or intensity of; to focus or gather

Practice and Apply
1. What does Dos Passos **advocate** about peace?
2. Why does Dos Passos **concentrate** on "what we might become"?

Writing About Literature

Evaluate Author's Craft In this essay, Dos Passos uses repetition and juxtaposition to try to persuade his audience that certain things are more admirable about the United States than others. Repetition is a literary device in which words, phrases, and sentences are repeated for emphasis. Juxtaposition is the placing of two or more distinct things side by side in order to compare and contrast. Write a short essay in which you explain how repetition and juxtaposition contribute to Dos Passos's effectiveness or lack of effectiveness in convincing his audience that his ideas are sound. Use evidence from "The American Cause" to support your claims.

Before you begin drafting, graph elements from the essay to help you organize your response:

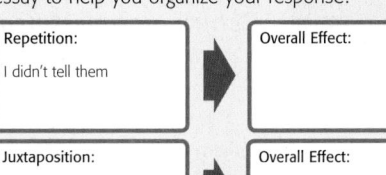

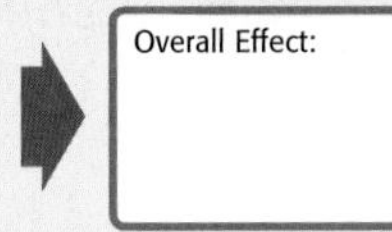

Repetition: I didn't tell them	Overall Effect:
Juxtaposition: not for what we were but for what we might become	Overall Effect:

After you complete your draft, meet with a peer reviewer. Discuss revisions that would improve your essay's power to persuade. When your revisions are complete, proofread and edit your draft to correct errors in spelling, grammar, and punctuation.

Listening and Speaking

Create two teams to debate the pros and cons of the United States as outlined in "The American Cause." Take ideas from the essay that support your side of the argument. In an organized debate, allow each team member to present an argument.

LiteratureOnline **Web Activities** For eFlashcards, Selection Quick Checks, and other Web activities, go to www.glencoe.com.

AFTER YOU READ

Assess

Reading Strategy

1. Students must conclude that this is an opinion, since the future is unknown.
2. Many of the details from the second paragraph can be proven and are therefore facts.

Vocabulary

1. b **2.** b **3.** b **4.** a

Academic Vocabulary

1. Students should infer that he writes of war with horror and disgust, and that he appeals to what is best in human nature in order to create peace.
2. He finds many mistakes and failures in the past, but he still hopes that the basic goodness of American ideals will reveal itself in the future.

Writing About Literature

Students' essays should
- identify examples of repetition and juxtaposition
- clearly state the effects of each of the examples
- evaluate the effectiveness of the literary devices

Listening and Speaking

Students should outline their arguments beforehand. Suggest that they use supporting details from the article in their arguments.

Reading in the Real World

Citizenship Have student volunteers write an essay responding to students in a foreign country. In it, students should explain why the United States should be admired now, in the twenty-first century. **OL**

Web Activities Have students access the Web site for interactive activities that will help them assess their understanding of the selection.

Academic Standards

The Additional Support activity on p. 463 covers the following standard:

Reading in the Real World: **9.5.4** Write persuasive compositions that clarify and defend positions with…relevant evidence, including facts…

Focus

BELLRINGER

Bellringer Options
Daily Language Practice Transparency 44
Or display images of Fenway Park from the past and present. Discuss students' experiences in a sports stadium or at a match or a game.
Ask: Why are sports fans so dedicated to their favorite teams? Why do some people have an emotional attachment to Fenway Park?

Connecting to the Reading Selections

Allow students to share their responses to the opening question. Then have students discuss what they know about the social, communal, and economic value of living near a sports stadium.

Comparing Literature: *Different Viewpoints*

Connecting to the Reading Selections

Many cities throughout the United States have faced this dilemma: What should be done about aging sports stadiums that lack the features team owners claim are essential to modern sports franchises? Many fans argue passionately for the preservation of their beloved stadiums. Others urge that new facilities are needed for teams to survive. In the works compared here, writers argue for and against the demolition of historic Fenway Park, home of the Boston Red Sox.

Various authors
Thoughts on Fenway Park .... persuasive text **467**
A variety of opinions about keeping or demolishing Fenway Park

John L. Harrington
Taxpayers Will Get a Return on Investment .... persuasive text **470**
A CEO's appeal for help from the taxpayers

William M. Straus
Other Revenue Sources Should Be Pursued .... persuasive text **473**
A state representative argues that the Red Sox need to find their own financing

COMPARING THE Big Idea Finding Common Ground

Is it always possible to find common ground? In these selections, authors express some agreement about the problems caused by the aging Fenway Park. They also express disagreement about the best way to address those problems.

COMPARING Persuasion

The art of persuasion is the art of convincing someone to adopt a certain belief or to take a certain action. For instance, you might try to persuade your friends that one candidate for class president is better than another, or you might try to persuade your parents to watch a particular movie. In these selections, authors make different kinds of appeals to persuade readers to adopt their ideas.

COMPARING Author's Viewpoint

The author's viewpoint is the author's opinion about, or approach to, an issue. In persuasive writing, the author's viewpoint helps shape both form and content, both what the author says and how he or she says it.

Selection Skills

Comparing Literature

Reading Skills
- Identifying Problem and Solution (SE pp. 466, 467, 469, 471, 474, 476)
- Comparing and Contrasting (TWE p. 468)
- Identifying Author's Purpose (TWE p. 470)

Literary Elements
- Rhetorical Devices (SE pp. 466, 468, 471, 474, 476; TWE pp. 467, 472)

Listening/Speaking/Viewing Skills
- Analyzing Art (TWE pp. 467, 469, 471)

Writing Skills/Grammar
- Sentence Fragments (TWE p. 466)
- Persuasive Writing (TWE p. 472)
- Editorial (TWE p. 474)

Vocabulary Skills
- Synonyms (SE p. 476)

Persuasive Text

READING AND ANALYZING PERSUASIVE TEXT

An **argument** is a type of persuasive writing in which logic or reason is used to try to influence the reader's ideas or actions. When reading an argument, it is important to be cautious about its claims. First, determine the author's position. Then identify the structure of the argument. Is the structure logical? Does the author provide strong evidence to support his or her opinions?

The Structure of an Argument At its most basic, an argument consists of a specific position plus evidence supporting that position. The strongest argument is a logical one, which means that the argument is structured in such a way that it makes sense. An argument can be structured logically by the use of either inductive or deductive reasoning.

Inductive reasoning involves drawing a general conclusion from a series of specific facts. When scientists draw conclusions based on data from experiments and observations, they are using inductive reasoning. The chart below shows how inductive reasoning led some scientists to conclude that Earth had been hit by a meteorite.

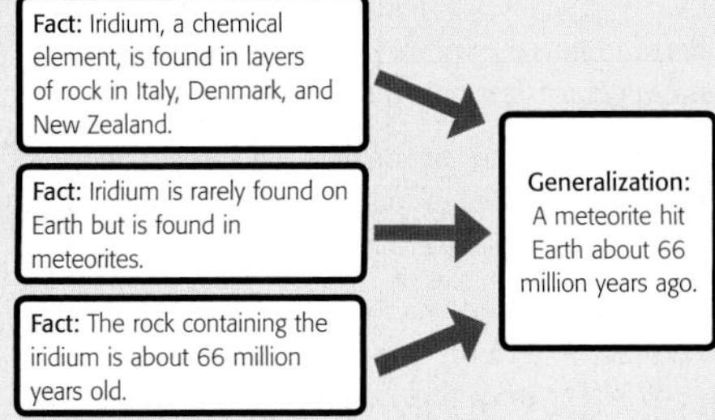

Fact: Iridium, a chemical element, is found in layers of rock in Italy, Denmark, and New Zealand.
Fact: Iridium is rarely found on Earth but is found in meteorites.
Fact: The rock containing the iridium is about 66 million years old.
Generalization: A meteorite hit Earth about 66 million years ago.

Deductive reasoning begins with a generalization and then applies that generalization to a specific example, or set of examples, to arrive at a conclusion. The chart below outlines the deductive reasoning used by the people who left Love Canal, a community in upstate New York, when they discovered that it had been built on a toxic waste dump.

Generalization: Toxic chemical waste is dangerous to humans.

↓

Fact: Love Canal is located on top of a layer of toxic waste.

↓

Conclusion: Love Canal is a dangerous place to live.

Common Pitfalls Most arguments involve both inductive and deductive reasoning. When analyzing arguments, be aware of faulty reasoning in the form of hasty generalizations and invalid assumptions. Hasty generalizations occur when a conclusion goes further than the evidence permits. For example, if you saw a group of drummers who were boys, you might reason inductively that only boys play drums, but your reasoning would be incorrect because it is based on too small a sample of drummers.

In deductive reasoning, the chain of reasoning can be invalidated by an incorrect statement. For example, consider this line of reasoning: *To attract top-notch students, a school needs a good science program; our school wants to attract top-notch students; therefore, we need to improve our science program.* Not everyone may agree with the first assumption. In this case, the reasoning is well-constructed but the conclusion is not necessarily true.

As you review an argument, also be sure to examine the evidence the author provides for his or her claims. Is the evidence credible? Does the evidence, in fact, support the author's opinions?

COMPARING LITERATURE

BEFORE YOU READ

Focus

R Reading Strategy

Author's Viewpoint Have students attempt to identify the author's opinion about the issue at hand. Remind students that in persuasive writing, the author wants to convince the reader that his or her viewpoint is correct.

Ask: What clues do you find in the selection to tell you about the author's viewpoint? *(The writers have specific opinions and present arguments to support these viewpoints.)* **OL**

Selection Resources

Print Materials
- Unit 2 Resources (Fast File), pp. 74–76
- Leveled Vocabulary Development, p. 36
- Selection and Unit Assessments, pp. 79–80
- Selection Quick Checks, p. 40

Transparencies
- Bellringer Options Transparencies: Daily Language Practice Transparency 44
- Literary Elements Transparencies 39, 42

Technology
- TeacherWorks Plus™ CD-ROM
- StudentWorks Plus™ CD-ROM
- Presentation Plus!™ CD-ROM
- Literature Online, glencoe.com
- Online Student Edition, mhln.com
- Exam*View*® Assessment Suite CD-ROM
- Vocabulary PuzzleMaker CD-ROM
- Listening Library, disc 1 tracks 44, 45, 46

BEFORE YOU READ

Focus

Summary

Sportswriters, the CEO of the Boston Red Sox, and a member of the Massachusetts House of Representatives speak out about the fate of Fenway Park, a landmark sports stadium in Massachusetts. Conflicting perspectives are presented: Save Fenway because of its historic and nostalgic value or build a new stadium, which would help provide funds and field a top team; let the state help with the funding or let private funds carry most of the cost. The selections introduce the reader to a variety of rhetorical devices.

V Vocabulary

Vocabulary File Say: Add these words and definitions to your vocabulary file. For each word, include a sentence that gives you an example of how to use the word. **OL** Students with English language needs should include the pronunciations of these words in their files. **EL**

Literary Elements Have students access the Web site to improve their understanding of rhetorical devices.

LITERATURE PREVIEW

Connecting to the Text

Public spaces can inspire deep feelings. For instance, if you grew up attending games at a particular baseball stadium, that stadium might seem like an old friend. Before you read, think about the following questions:

- What public building or other public space has special meaning for you, and why?
- What would it mean to you if that place were destroyed or replaced?

Building Background

In 1999 the Yawkey Trust, then-owner of the Boston Red Sox, proposed that a new stadium be built to replace Fenway Park. Many Red Sox fans were shocked and dismayed at the thought of their team playing home games anywhere other than Fenway Park. The Red Sox have been playing home games at Fenway Park since the stadium opened on April 20, 1912. Because the stadium is small, fans are close to the game as it is being played. The field is real grass, and the scoreboards are still hand-operated. Behind the scoreboards is a room where all the players throughout Fenway's history have signed their names on the walls. The short left field ends at a thirty-seven-foot wall called the Green Monster.

Setting Purposes for Reading

Big Idea Finding Common Ground

As you read the arguments about Fenway Park, notice that even writers with differing opinions can agree on certain points.

Literary Element Rhetorical Devices

Rhetorical devices are ways in which authors support their arguments and persuade their audiences. Such devices include appeals to logic, emotion, ethics, and authority.

- See Literary Terms Handbook, p. R14.

Literature Online Interactive Literary Elements Handbook To review or learn more about the literary elements, go to www.glencoe.com.

READING PREVIEW

Reading Strategy Identifying Problem and Solution

Most persuasive writing is concerned with **identifying a problem** and proposing a **solution** to that problem. As you read, consider how various writers approach the issue surrounding Fenway Park. To what extent do they agree that Fenway has problems? For the problems identified, what solutions do they propose?

Reading Tip: Taking Notes Use a chart to record the problems and solutions discussed in the articles about Fenway Park.

Problem: Fenway Park is a small, old stadium that cannot keep up with modern stadiums.		
Solution: Raise tax money to build a new stadium.	Solution:	Solution:

Vocabulary

cathedral (kə thē′ drəl) *n.* a large, important church; sometimes used to describe something of great importance; p. 467 *The redwood forests of California are nature's cathedrals.*

nostalgia (nos tal′ jə) *n.* a feeling of longing experienced when remembering the past; an overly sentimental feeling; p. 468 *As they listened to music from the 1980s, a wave of nostalgia washed over them.*

staggering (stag′ ər ing) *adj.* shocking; overwhelming; p. 471 *When I returned from vacation, I found a staggering tower of bills.*

magnitude (mag′ nə to͞od′) *n.* great size, volume, or extent; importance; significance; p. 475 *The bride had never in her life seen a cake of such magnitude.*

INDIANA ACADEMIC STANDARDS (pages 466–476)

9.2.6 Critique the logic of functional documents (such as an appeal to tradition or an appeal to force)...

9.2 Develop [reading] strategies...

9.5.2 Write responses to literature that demonstrate a comprehensive grasp of the significant ideas of literary works...

Additional Support

Skills Practice

GRAMMAR: Sentence Fragments

Explain that writers sometimes use sentence fragments for effect, but in general, students should make sure the sentences they write are complete sentences that have subjects and verbs.

Have students correct the following sentence fragments.

1. I swim every day. Get exercise.
2. Jeff learned to type. Works faster. **OL**

Thoughts on Fenway Park

Babe Ruth, Ernie Shore, Rube (George) Foster, and Del Gainer rest on the edge of their dugout during a game at Fenway Park, ca. 1915. ★

In 2000 sportscasters were invited to respond to the question, "Should Fenway Park be replaced?" Following are some of their responses.

Jayson Stark

No. Please. I may not be Paul Volcker,[1] but I understand modern baseball economics. And I'm tired of baseball's inclination to bulldoze its history in the name of economics. To me, places like Fenway and Wrigley and Yankee Stadium[2] aren't mere ballparks. They're national historic monuments. So we should no more consider blowing up Fenway than we would Independence Hall.[3]

I've seen the way players react after entering Fenway for the first time. They go knock on the Monster, climb inside the scoreboard, wander up to sit in The Ted Williams Seat[4] in the bleachers, think about Babe Ruth and Ty Cobb[5] dressing in the same clubhouse they now occupy. It's awesome. Believe me, nobody reacts this way when they enter Stade Olympique[6] for the first time.

So rather than tear down these cathedrals,

1. *Paul Volcker* is a financial expert who has served as undersecretary of the U.S. Treasury and president of New York's Federal Reserve Bank.
2. *Wrigley Field* and *Yankee Stadium* are located respectively in Chicago and New York City.
3. *Independence Hall* is the building in Philadelphia, Pennsylvania, in which the Declaration of Independence and the Constitution were signed.
4. *The Ted Williams Seat* is the seat in the stands at Fenway where Ted Williams's longest home run (also the longest ever hit in Fenway) landed. The seat back is red, which sets it apart from the other green seats.
5. *Ty Cobb* played baseball for the Detroit Tigers between 1905 and 1926. He is still considered one of baseball's greatest players.
6. The *Stade Olympique* is the large, modern stadium that housed the Montreal Expos baseball team until 2005.

Reading Strategy Identifying Problem and Solution *What solution is the author rejecting here?* 

Vocabulary

cathedral (kə thē′ drəl) *n.* a large, important church; sometimes used to describe something of great importance

English Language Coach

Sports Across Cultures Newcomers to the United States may be unfamiliar with baseball. They may understand the concept of a national sport. In most countries, soccer is the most popular sport. In some countries, such as India, cricket (a game similar to baseball) is popular. Ask students to describe a popular sport in their homeland. Prompt students to talk about how sports can help bring people from various backgrounds and cultures together. Have them share information about their favorite teams and players. EL

Teach

R Reading Strategy

Identifying Problem and Solution **Answer:** *He rejects decisions based on money rather than the sport's rich history.* OL

★ Viewing the Photograph

This photograph, taken in about 1915, shows how long baseball has been a part of U.S. culture. Baseball evolved from much earlier ball games but was systematized in the early nineteenth century. Its present form is generally attributed to Alexander Cartwright, but there has been some controversy regarding this identification over the years. AS

CheckPoint

Use the CheckPoint questions on Presentation Plus! to monitor students' comprehension. These questions can be used with interactive response keypads for immediate student feedback.

Readability Scores

Dale-Chall: 7.4
DRP: 59
Lexile: 930

Academic Standards

Additional Support activities on pp. 466 and 467 cover the following standards:

Skills Practice: **9.6.2** Demonstrate an understanding of sentence construction...

English Language Coach: **9.2** Develop [reading] strategies...

Teach

BI1 Big Idea

Finding Common Ground
Ask: What device does Campbell use to connect with readers? *(He uses a personal anecdote about his favorite ballpark to prove he understands how fans feel about Fenway.)* OL

BI2 Big Idea

Finding Common Ground
Answer: *Campbell tries to appeal to both sides through a compromise.* OL

L Literary Element

Rhetorical Devices
Answer: *It appeals to emotion. He says Fenway's replacement is "inevitable." He implies "Save Fenway" groups are not moving into "the 21st century." These statements cannot be proven.* OL

R1 Reading Strategy

Draw a Conclusion
Ask: Why is Kurkjian certain the park will be replaced? *(Fenway will need many more seats and luxury suites to generate profits.)* OL

the people who run the sport need to work with these teams to figure out ways to preserve their great ballparks and still keep them economically viable.[7] There is no equivalent to Fenway in *any* other sport. And it ought to dawn on our leaders one of these days that baseball needs to capitalize on[8] places like Fenway, not abandon them. The NFL has a new-stadium fund. Shouldn't baseball have an *old*-stadium fund?

Dave Campbell

Yes, Fenway should be replaced. I know it's tough for the fans in New England. I grew up in Michigan and Tiger Stadium[9] was the ultimate institution for me; it was my Fenway. It was the stadium I grew up in, with all the memories and **nostalgia** involved. Tiger Stadium was a wonderful sea of green and had a magical charm about it. In fact, Fenway and Tiger opened the exact same day—April 20, 1912. BI1

Unfortunately, the bottom line in today's economy is that you have to create a stadium that can generate a lot of revenue from places other than ticket sales. Right now, the Red Sox have the most expensive ticket prices in baseball and that is because they only have 33,000 seats. They need to have a stadium with corporate luxury suites; and I mean real, top-notch suites, not those things they threw up like a glorified backstop in recent years.

In Detroit they revamped[10] everything. There is nothing in the new stadium that reminds you of Tiger Stadium. But it doesn't have to be that way. Build a new stadium for the Red Sox and find a way to keep the Green Monster.

There was a tremendous amount of opposition to tearing down Tiger Stadium. They had all kinds of "Save Tiger" groups, just like they do in Boston now. The bottom line is Fenway Park is, like Tiger Stadium was, antiquated,[11] old, and probably getting to the point of unsafe. "Save Fenway" groups only put off the inevitable. It's time to move into the 21st century.

Tim Kurkjian

Absolutely not. There is so much history and tradition at Fenway, I would hate to see it go. I know it's getting a little old, and I know I sit in the press box and not behind some pole obstructing my view in the stands, but every time I walk in that place, I think about Ted Williams and Babe Ruth, and that stuff is really important. Even if they build a park to look just like it, it won't be the same.

Financially, I understand why new parks are necessities. Today's game is built around luxury suites, big-time corporate backing, and over 40,000 seats; and Fenway doesn't have any of those. The only way to make Fenway a financially viable park is to tear it down and build a new one. I know Fenway will be replaced eventually, and I'll be sad when it is. R1

7. *Viable* means "able to be done."
8. Here, *capitalize on* means "treat as an asset rather than as an expense."
9. *Tiger Stadium* was the stadium for the Detroit Tigers baseball team until 1999.
10. *Revamped* means "altered" or "renovated."
11. *Antiquated* means "out of date."

Vocabulary

nostalgia (nos tal′ jə) *n.* a feeling of longing experienced when remembering the past; an overly sentimental feeling

Big Idea Finding Common Ground *In this passage, to whom is the author trying to appeal?* BI2

Literary Element Rhetorical Devices *Does this part of the writer's argument appeal to logic, emotion, ethics, or authority? How can you tell?* L

Additional Support

Skills Practice

READING: Comparing and Contrasting Students should compare and contrast each writer's opinion to better understand how they use rhetorical devices to make an argument. Ask students to:

- take notes to show similarities and differences in each argument
- indicate whether writers appeal to logic or emotions
- evaluate the credibility of evidence offered by the writers

Students should add information on other writers as they read. OL

A Fenway Park vendor wears a shirt honoring former Red Sox player Ted Williams, who died in 2002.

Brian McRae
From a nostalgic standpoint, you can't tear down Fenway. But from an economic standpoint, the Red Sox are losing so much money, they need to get a new ballpark. The amount of money it costs just to maintain Fenway is amazing. The way the economics of baseball are today, if the Red Sox don't get a new stadium, 10 years from now it will be hard for them to compete and put a championship-caliber[12] team on the field. I think the fans would rather see a championship-caliber team in a new park than a last-place team in an old, broken-down Fenway Park. It's inevitable.

R3 **Rob Dibble**
No. There are very few old-time structures left in the league. In the NL, it's Wrigley; in the AL,[13] it's Yankee Stadium and Fenway. Those parks are monuments and are like museums. Babe Ruth, Yaz,[14] Ted Williams . . . great players have walked across that field. I love the historical aspect of baseball and the history of Fenway makes saving it worth more than any economic downside.

12. *Caliber* means "degree of excellence or importance."
13. *NL* stands for National League, and *AL* stands for American League. These are the two leagues that make up Major League Baseball (MLB).
14. *Yaz* refers to Carl Yastrzemski, the Red Sox player who replaced Ted Williams as left fielder in 1961.

Reading Strategy Identifying Problem and Solution *What problem and solution does the writer present in this sentence?* R2

There is enough technology to refurbish[15] the stadium without having to tear it down. You should be able to rebuild it from within. I understand that, economically, something has to be done. And the facilities aren't the greatest; the locker rooms are way too small. It needs to be upgraded in the worst way, but it's difficult to imagine Fenway not existing.

Buck Martinez
Yes. Fenway Park should be replaced because the locker-room facilities, the fan-comfort facilities and the concession stands are all antiquated. But when they replace it, they have to pay particular attention to keeping the new park as close to what it is now as possible. Fenway Park is baseball history and a remarkable baseball setting. They would make a terrible mistake if they don't include the Green Monster in whatever new ballpark is built. But the economics of the game today dictate that they need more luxury boxes and more fan amenities[16] because that is the way the game is headed.

Quickwrite

The sportswriters who responded to the question "Should Fenway Park be replaced?" gave a variety of opinions. Choose the response you think is the strongest and write a paragraph explaining why you chose it.

15. *Refurbish* means "to restore to the original state"; or "to renovate."
16. *Amenities* are benefits that make places more attractive to customers.

Teach

R2 Reading Strategy

Identifying Problem and Solution **Answer:** *It is too expensive to maintain Fenway. This leaves less money to pay players, which could lead to a weak team. A new stadium would allow the hiring of a "championship-caliber team."* OL

R3 Reading Strategy

Distinguishing Fact and Opinion **Ask:** Is Dibble's statement fact or opinion? *(Opinion)* OL

Quickwrite

Remind students to refer to specific points in the text to support their choice.

Viewing the Photograph

Ted Williams (1918–2002), who wore number 9 for the Boston Red Sox, was one of baseball's all-time greatest hitters. Although two major injuries and military service kept him from playing for nearly five seasons, Williams hit 521 home runs and was twice selected Most Valuable Player. AS

English Language Coach

Footnotes Explain to English-language learners that a footnote in a prose selection is numbered in both the text and at the bottom of the page. Remind students that footnotes are used because a book cannot explain every reference or definition within a text.

Have English learners work with English-proficient students to suggest additional words and phrases they think should be footnoted. Have students use their dictionaries to write footnotes for their additions. EL

Academic Standards
Additional Support activities on pp. 468 and 469 cover the following standards:
Skills Practice: **9.2.7** Evaluate an author's argument or defense of a claim…
English Language Coach: **9.2.1** Analyze the structure and format of…documents…and explain…purposes.

BEFORE YOU READ

Teach

R1 Reading Strategy

Evaluating Evidence

Ask: What concrete evidence is given about the team's commitment to build a new stadium? *(The team is committing over $350 million to the project.)* OL

Author Search To expand students' appreciation of John L. Harrington, have them access the Web site for additional information and resources.

Readability Scores
Dale-Chall: 10.0
DRP: 66
Lexile: 1260

COMPARING LITERATURE

Taxpayer$ Will Get A Return On Inve$tment

John L. Harrington

BEFORE YOU READ

Building Background

John L. Harrington was a young accounting professor at Boston College in 1970 when he was hired as controller by the president of baseball's American League. Three years later, he became treasurer of his hometown Red Sox. He never returned to academia. Harrington stayed with the Red Sox and served as Chief Executive Officer from 1992 to 2001. During that time, Fenway Park was expanded and refurbished, and the spring training site was moved to a state-of-the-art facility in Fort Myers, Forida. In an interview, Harrington said, "People refer to the Red Sox as an institution and look on me as a caretaker. And that's fine with me." The following article, which originally appeared in 2000, was excerpted from the official Web site of the Boston Red Sox.

Literature Online **Author Search** For more about John L. Harrington, go to www.glencoe.com.

With all of the talk and discussions today surrounding our new ballpark project, I wanted to communicate directly with you to update you on recent developments in our effort to build a new ballpark—the step we believe is essential to the future of the Boston Red Sox.

The Red Sox have committed to privately finance the entire new ballpark. We will put more private dollars into the new ballpark than any sports team in history has put into its facility. In absolute dollar terms, at the costs we face today, we are committing to over $350 million for the new ballpark. R1 Furthermore, we will take responsibility for any cost overruns involved in the park's construction.

Additional Support

Academic Standards

The Additional Support activity on p. 470 covers the following standard:

Skills Practice: **9.2** Develop strategies such as…identifying…[author's] purpose…

Skills Practice

READING: Identifying Author's Purpose Review with students the purpose an author may have for writing a speech: to inform, to persuade, to entertain.

As they read have students analyze the speech, paragraph by paragraph. Ask students to record where the author informs the reader and where he attempts to persuade the reader. OL

This is not easy for us. To raise this **staggering** amount will require us to use a combination of ticket revenues, in-park marketing and advertising revenues, up-front payments for club seats and suites, deposits from season-ticket holders, naming rights,[1] and revenue from major league baseball and our limited partners.

By taking this approach, we will be required to consider certain steps that I have been very reluctant to think about, such as naming rights and season ticket deposits. Our reluctance has stemmed from our desire to protect you, our fans. I recognize that many fans care deeply about their season tickets and about the name of the ballpark. But we do not think we can ask for the first public dollar until we have shown our willingness to consider every possible private dollar.

As you know, the Red Sox do not have the limitless pockets that some suggest we have. Our financial objective, carried forward from the Yawkey years,[2] is to break even—not to turn a profit. Because I run a trust[3] and not a traditional profit-making enterprise, and because the mandate[4] of that trust was to serve the best interests of the baseball team, we plow all our revenues back into the Red Sox organization.

The twin goals of the organization that we must balance are the fielding of a strong, competitive team and the preservation of Red Sox baseball as affordable family entertainment.

1. Sponsors who make very large contributions to an organization are sometimes given *naming rights,* or the opportunity to name a piece of property, such as a ball park, theater, or stadium.
2. *The Yawkey years* refers to the time period during which the Red Sox were owned by Tom Yawkey (1933–1976).
3. Here, *trust* means "a corporation legally responsible for managing the money or property of another person."
4. A *mandate* is an official duty or order.

Literary Element Rhetorical Devices *For what rhetorical purpose does the author bring up the subject of naming rights?* **L1**

Vocabulary

staggering (stag′ ər ing) *adj.* shocking; overwhelming

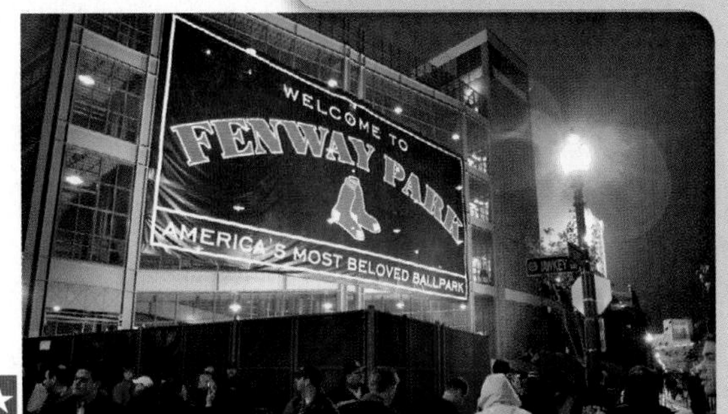

These goals are increasingly difficult in Fenway Park, the oldest and smallest park in the major leagues. We have stayed competitive, but we have maxed out ticket prices. Frankly, ticket prices are much higher than we'd like them to be, but we have no other way to raise revenue to field a team. In the economics of today's baseball, in a tiny ballpark, these twin goals are in conflict.

To meet our goal of fielding a competitive team, we must bear in mind that much of our competition plays in ballparks substantially built by their host municipalities.[5] This means that they enjoy a competitive advantage over us.

So be it. We want to play baseball here in Massachusetts, in Boston, in the Fenway, and we accept the political realities that go along with that.

But to play here for another hundred years we do need the kinds of public investments that have been made here in Massachusetts in the past. We believe that those public investments are justified by the return to the state and the city—in hard economic benefits, in increased income, sales, hotel and property taxes, and in the quality of life that a major league baseball team helps bring to a city.

5. Here, *host municipalities* are the towns or cities in which the teams play.

Reading Strategy Identifying Problem and Solution *According to the author, if ticket prices were reduced, what new problem might arise?* **R2**

Literary Element Rhetorical Devices *Which of these examples appeal to logic? Explain.* **L2**

Teach

L1 Literary Element

Rhetorical Devices **Answer:** *To remind readers that if they do not push for public funding, naming rights will have to be sold. He might seem to be appealing to logic, but he is actually making a veiled appeal to fans' emotions.* **OL**

R2 Reading Strategy

Identifying Problem and Solution **Answer:** *Fans might not have a winning team—or any team at all—to cheer for.* **OL**

L2 Literary Element

Rhetorical Devices **Answer:** *Increased income, sales, and hotel and property taxes are examples that appeal to logic because they are measurable. Quality of life is not as easily measured; it is subjective.* **OL**

Viewing the Photograph

In 2004 fans were overjoyed when the Red Sox finally won the World Series. The team hadn't won since they traded Babe "the Bambino" Ruth 86 years earlier. The dry spell was referred to as "The Curse of the Bambino." **AS**

English Language Coach

Context Clues Have English learners preview the selection. Ask them to list unfamiliar words they find. Have them write an operational definition for each word using context clues. Then have students look up the meaning of the words and make necessary changes. **EL**

Building Reading Fluency

Coaching Partners Invite student pairs to practice reading the speech. Partners should coach each other on the use of volume, tone, expression, and reading pace. Have students take turns recording their reading of the speech and then comment on places where the delivery was especially successful. **BL**

Academic Standards

Additional Support activities on p. 471 cover the following standards:

English Language Coach: **9.1** Use…context clues and a growing knowledge of English to determine the meaning of words…

Building Reading Fluency: **9.7** [Respond] to oral communication [with] careful listening and evaluation of content…

Teach

R1 Reading Strategy

Making an Inference
Ask: How does the writer use the timeline of the legislature's session to press for a decision? *(Possible answer: He implies that the project could be delayed for years and cost more if a decision is not made. Everyone will then lose the benefits from a new stadium.)* OL

L Literary Element

Rhetorical Devices
Ask: How does the writer attempt to manipulate the reader? *(Possible answer: He tries to create urgency by saying this "may be the last chance.")* OL

BI1 Big Idea

Finding Common Ground
Answer: *He first says the owners are open to other options and stresses the need for consensus. Then he presses for the decision he wants; consensus is less important than adopting the plan.* OL

The Red Sox also bring a special return through the ownership arrangement: the Yawkey Foundation[6] will be the biggest beneficiary of any future sale of the team, and Yawkey Foundation charities—educational, health care, and youth programs—will receive millions of dollars. That ownership arrangement, and that public benefit, is uniquely different from every other sports team in Massachusetts, and probably unique in American sports. . . .

We need assistance from the city we have called home for a hundred years, consistent with the steps the city has taken on other projects like the Convention Center. As Boston did with the Convention Center, the Red Sox need for the city to acquire the land and prepare the site. We believe this investment is more than justified by the economic benefits the Red Sox will generate in a new park, but we understand the city needs some revenue streams to support their investment.

R1 This legislative session has about eight weeks left. Last year's legislation for the new Patriots[7] stadium was passed in three weeks. But this year's window of opportunity closes on July 31, and if action is not taken by then, the opening date will be pushed back another year, or several years. That in turn means higher interest rates, construction costs, and possibly years without the benefits the new ballpark will bring to the fans, the team, the city, and the state.

Time is not on our side, and doing nothing is not an option. Fenway was built in 1912. We started trying to build a new ballpark in 1965, and have invested close to $100 million in Fenway maintenance and upkeep since then. In competitiveness—baseball survival—terms, we are one of the last teams in baseball still trying to build a new ballpark. New ballparks put teams like the Orioles and Indians back into contention,[8] and other cities followed: twenty-six of the other twenty-nine major league teams have either built new ballparks or are in the planning stages. If we do nothing, we will be left behind.

This legislative session may be the last chance to build this in the way we want it built. L Since Tom Yawkey bought this team more than sixty-five years ago, there has been an extraordinary relationship with this community, which has made this team one of the most beloved sports franchises[9] in the world. We know how people feel about the Red Sox, and we feel the same way about Boston. The Boston Red Sox have never contemplated any other way to run this team or this franchise.

There's more than one way to finance a ballpark project, but the best overall financing plan is the one that is acceptable to all the essential parties—the team, the city, and the state. We are open to any reasonable plan that can achieve a consensus[10] agreement in time for action in this legislative session.

The Boston Red Sox are prepared to do what we must to make this new park a reality. We ask you and our other fans and friends to speak out on this issue, let your public officials know how you feel, and encourage them to show the same kind of leadership they've shown in the past on similar projects.

Discussion Starter

Harrington presents several reasons for both building a new ballpark and using tax money to pay for it. With a group of classmates discuss Harrington's main points. Does your group agree with him? What arguments can you make to counter his proposal?

6. *The Yawkey Foundation* is a charitable organization that comprises Tom Yawkey's Foundation I and Jean Yawkey's Foundation II.
7. The *Patriots* are the New England Patriots football team, who play their home games at Gillette Stadium in Foxborough, Massachusetts.
8. Here, *contention* means "competition."
9. *Sports franchises* are professional teams that compete in a league.
10. Here, *consensus* means "among all members of a group."

Big Idea Finding Common Ground *What attitude is the author expressing here? Why?* BI1

Additional Support

Skills Practice

WRITING: Persuasive Writing
Review that persuasive writing tries to convince someone to adopt a certain belief or action.

- Ask students to write a persuasive essay about an issue relevant to them.
- Have students present their essays to the class for critiquing.

Have students use these questions to critique their essays: Is the author's purpose clearly stated? Does the author find common ground with the audience? Does the author appeal to both logic and emotion when making an argument? OL

William M. Straus

BEFORE YOU READ

R2
BI2

Building Background

After earning a law degree from Georgetown University, William M. Straus served as an Assistant District Attorney in Bristol County, Massachusetts, for six years. He has represented the 10th Bristol District in the Massachusetts state House of Representatives since 1992. One of his special concerns is protecting drinking water supplies and the unique coastal areas of southeastern Massachusetts. Straus grew up in South Orange, New Jersey, and remains a loyal Yankees fan. Nevertheless, he says he loves to see a game at Fenway Park. The following article was excerpted from the Web site of the New Bedford, Massachusetts, *Standard-Times* newspaper and originally appeared in 2000.

Literature Online **Author Search** For more about William M. Straus, go to www.glencoe.com.

Teach

R2 Reading Strategy

Analyzing an Argument
Have students prepare a For/Against chart to record the author's arguments. OL

BI2 Big Idea

Finding Common Ground
Say: As you read, answer this question: What is Straus's position on building a new stadium? *(He wants more financial research analyzed before a decision is made.)* OL

Literature Online

Author Search To expand students' appreciation of William M. Straus, have them access the Web site for additional information and resources.

Readability Scores
Dale-Chall: 8.6
DRP: 67
Lexile: 1330

English Language Coach

Difficult Words This selection contains difficult terms, such as *financing, credit, negotiation, maximizing,* and *revenue stream.* English learners should consult outside resources for words not defined in footnotes. Pair English learners with English-proficient students. Have partners prepare a three-column chart with the column headings: *Word, Definition,* and *Use in Speech.* Students should use a dictionary to complete a chart entry for each unfamiliar word. EL

Academic Standards
Additional Support activities on pp. 472 and 473 cover the following standards:
Skills Practice: **9.5.4** Write persuasive compositions that...use specific rhetorical (communication) devices to support assertions, such as appealing to logic through reasoning; appealing to emotion...
English Language Coach: **9.1** Use...context clues, and a growing knowledge of English to determine the meaning of words...

Teach

BI1 Big Idea

Finding Common Ground **Answer:** *To convince readers that this decision affects him, too.* OL

R1 Reading Strategy

Making an Inference **Ask:** Why does Straus comment on the deadline? *(The deadline is a ploy to force a quick decision.)* OL

R2 Reading Strategy

Identifying Problem and Solution **Answer:** *The estimates by Red Sox owners are low, and the city will have to pay more.* OL

R3 Reading Strategy

Scan for Information **Ask:** What two areas does Straus want the Red Sox to rethink? *(Private sources of money and a plan for reimbursing taxpayers.)* OL

L Literary Element

Rhetorical Devices **Answer:** *People should not let love of the team cloud their judgment in money matters. The phrase "natural tendency" softens his criticism. The words* emotional *and* nostalgic *appeal to readers' logic.* OL

COMPARING LITERATURE

There's something different in the air in Massachusetts whenever the discussion involves major league sports and stadiums. In 1993 we saw this play out with the financing of the FleetCenter[1] and last year with the Patriots and their whirlwind trip to Connecticut and back.[2]

And now it is the Red Sox's turn at bat. To its credit, the team has stated clearly its intention to remain in Boston with no threat to go elsewhere. In addition, the Red Sox contribution to the welfare of Massachusetts and its citizens has been exemplary,[3] whether in the field of charity or as a business neighbor.

Although the need for a new ballpark has been discussed for nearly twenty years, it was only in May that the team first went public with hard numbers on a request for taxpayer help. In a familiar negotiation approach, the Sox also stated that the deal had to be done by July 31, before the end of this year's legislative session. The imposition[4] of artificial deadlines usually doesn't help resolve negotiations, particularly when the deadline is set by someone who is asking for more than $200 million. R1

Unfortunately, the Red Sox request fell short in a number of respects. As of now, they are, in the phrase of the moment, "sharpening their pencils" to reduce the taxpayer's exposure in the costs of developing a new stadium. A quick review of the numbers helps explain the problem with the Red Sox's initial request.

The Sox priced the project at $627 million. The team was to provide $352 million to build the stadium, the city of Boston was being asked for $140 million for site acquisition and related costs, and the state of Massachusetts would put up $135 million for building two parking garages, utilities,[5] and road and subway improvements near the park.

The real cost of the subway and road projects, projected at around $50 million by the Red Sox, is more likely to come in at about $100 million. Even more disturbing is that the Sox did not identify the borrowing costs to the state or city for coming up with this amount of money. Given the current bond capacity[6] of the state, and the fact that this fall's ballot contains tax-cut proposals reducing annual state revenues by at least $1.5 billion, the carrying costs of the Sox proposal are a serious concern.

I believe there are two broad areas that caused this plan to fail and unless they are confronted in the next proposal by the Red Sox, will continue to plague the completion of the project.

First, have all private revenue sources been pursued? We are dealing with a private for-profit business enterprise. While public help for businesses in Massachusetts has occurred before, the private contribution is to be maximized. R3 The natural tendency to view sports teams in emotional or nostalgic terms cannot overwhelm other considerations.

1. The *FleetCenter* was the former name of a Boston sports arena that hosts hockey and basketball games as well as concerts and other events. The arena is now called the TD Banknorth Garden.
2. *Their whirlwind trip to Connecticut and back* refers to the time in which the Patriots football team left Boston briefly because the state legislature would not finance improvements to the Patriots' old stadium.
3. *Exemplary* means "so good that others should use it as an example."
4. *Imposition* means "an unreasonable request."
5. *Utilities* refer to services, such as water and electricity, that a city provides to homes and businesses.
6. *Bond capacity* refers to a way in which city, state, and federal governments borrow money for public projects. They sell bonds to citizens to raise funds and pay back the money, with interest, at a later date.

Big Idea Finding Common Ground *What does the author hope to do by using the word we?* BI1

Reading Strategy Identifying Problem and Solution *According to the author, what is the problem with the Red Sox's plan for paying for a new stadium?* R2

Literary Element Rhetorical Devices *What does the author mean here? How does his word choice affect his message?* L

Additional Support

Skills Practice

WRITING: Editorial Have students write a letter to the editor about the fate of Fenway Park. Remind students that their information comes from what they have read in this Comparing Literature section and from class discussions.

- Remind students to clearly present their point of view and provide credible evidence for their arguments.
- Allow volunteers to present their essays in class. OL

When tax increment financing[7] is used in our region or other parts of the state, some balance of local return is analyzed and weighed.

In this case, the Sox plan has not considered a number of other private sources of money that have been employed around the country for financing stadium projects. Naming rights to the stadium is the most obvious example which so far has been missing; published reports indicate that in some cases, companies have paid nearly $100 million for multiyear agreements for the right to name a facility. Another potential source of revenue is the inclusion of new private partners in the project. It has also been reported that other businesses might agree to help finance the $81 million in parking garages in return for their use outside of the eighty or so game dates needed by the Sox.

Companies have paid nearly $100 million for the right to name a facility.

Another private source of funds may be the private land owners whose land the Sox are asking be taken by the city of Boston in eminent domain[8] proceedings. And finally, many teams have raised money by selling private licenses for long-term seat ownership by the fans who attend the games. Until these avenues are exhausted, the Sox will have a hard time coming to the taxpayers for help.

The second broad area for the Sox to consider is the question of repayment to the taxpayers for the money put up by the state. The Sox proposed that they retain most of the revenue stream from the parking garage, which was to be built entirely by the state. This simply will not work. Assuming that it is even appropriate for the state to build a facility that private parties might be just as willing to construct, there seems to be no logic in simply handing over future income to the team from parking revenues. . . .

Some public assistance for a project of this **magnitude** can be justified by the overall improvement to tax revenues for both the state and the city. But such numbers cannot be glossed over and should be based upon serious calculations and benefits to the public.

What the final mix should be on the contributions for infrastructure[9] improvements remains open and will take shape in the unusual process of negotiation which occurs on sports facilities.

No one can say for sure when this project will get its approvals. The process is both public and private. As we've seen in the few weeks since the Red Sox came forward with a real spending plan, much give and take has occurred and will occur in the coming weeks. The Legislature has a responsibility to act prudently so that the Red Sox are treated no better or worse than others who seek public help for their projects.

7. *Tax increment financing* refers to the use of tax increases to finance local projects.
8. *Eminent domain* is the right of the government to take private land if it can prove that its use of the land will benefit the public.

Quickwrite

If you were a taxpayer in Boston, would you approve of paying more taxes in order to fund a new baseball park? Write a paragraph explaining why or why not.

9. *Infrastructure* is the network of public systems that includes roads, telephone wires, water pipes, and other means of public communication, transportation, and operation.

Big Idea Finding Common Ground *Who does the author see as part of the "give and take"?* BI2

Vocabulary

magnitude (mag′ nə to͞od′) *n.* great size, volume, or extent; importance; significance

Teach

BI2 Big Idea

Finding Common Ground
Answer: *The author sees the Red Sox owners, the city of Boston, the fans, and the state of Massachusetts as part of this give and take.* OL

Quickwrite

Encourage students to consider writing two paragraphs; one for each side of the question. Divide the class in half and assign one viewpoint to each group. Invite one student from each group to face off and debate the two positions.

Cultural History

Building Fenway John Taylor, former owner of the Boston Red Sox, built Fenway Park on land he owned. The stadium was built for the team and opened in 1912. AS

English Language Coach

Compound Nouns Explain that a compound word consists of two or more words that may be written as one word, as separate words, or with hyphens. Have students identify and decode compound words in the selection. (Examples: *whirlwind, ballpark, taxpayer, overall)* EL

Differentiated Instruction

Main Ideas and Details Less-proficient readers may find it difficult to recognize the main ideas and details in the selection. Pair students with proficient readers. Have pairs read and discuss the selection one paragraph at a time and identify the main idea and supporting details. BL

Academic Standards

Additional Support activities on pp. 474 and 475 cover the following standards:

Skills Practice: **9.5.4** Write persuasive compositions that…clarify and defend positions with precise and relevant evidence…

English Language Coach: **9.1** [Use] word parts [and] relationships…to determine the meaning of words…

Differentiated Instruction: **9.2** Develop [reading] strategies…

AFTER YOU READ

Assess

1. (a) Answers will vary. (b) Save Fenway: anecdotes about players and the costs of a new stadium. Replace the stadium: concerns about being able to afford to field a good team
2. (a) The team's history in Fenway Park, the Green Monster (b) The atmosphere at Fenway could not be re-created.
3. (a) A new ballpark (b) Red Sox might become a bad team.
4. (a) Naming rights (b) Fans may want a new stadium to be called Fenway Park.
5. Harrington is sincere and promises to keep the Red Sox in Boston. Straus uses real numbers.
6. Harrington addresses fans; Straus's audience may be taxpayers or the Legislature.
7. Harrington's calculations were not accurate and the benefits were not clear.
8. Students should support their responses.

Vocabulary

1. a **2.** b **3.** a **4.** b

COMPARING LITERATURE

AFTER YOU READ

RESPONDING AND THINKING CRITICALLY

Respond

1. (a)Who do you think presented the most persuasive argument about Fenway Park? (b)What evidence persuaded you to choose this argument?

Recall and Interpret

2. (a)Why is Fenway Park so loved by Boston Red Sox fans? (b)What would be the most serious loss if a new stadium were built for the team?
3. (a)According to John L. Harrington, what is essential to the future of the Red Sox? (b)What does he think would be the most negative repercussion if this project is stalled?
4. (a)According to William M. Straus, what is the most obvious source of private funding for a new Red Sox stadium? (b)What might Red Sox fans dislike about this kind of funding?

Analyze and Evaluate

5. Harrington argues that the Yawkey Trust is "not a traditional profit-making enterprise." But Straus refers to the Yawkey Trust as "a private for-profit business enterprise." Whom do you believe, and why?
6. Who is Harrington's audience? Straus's audience? Support your answers with evidence from the text.
7. (a)Straus writes, "But such numbers cannot be glossed over and should be based upon serious calculations and benefits to the public." What does he suggest about the numbers Harrington cites?

Connect

8. **Big Idea** **Finding Common Ground** After reading these opinions and arguments, what ideas do you have about how opposing sides might find common ground?

LITERARY ANALYSIS

Literary Element Rhetorical Devices

Appeals to logic rely on facts and reasoning that can be proven. Appeals to emotion often consist of anecdotes or use ambiguous language. Appeals to ethics emphasize what is morally right and wrong. Appeals to authority use the audience's respect for another person who shares the view of the author.

1. Choose one of the selections and describe a rhetorical device its author uses. What is the intended effect of the device?
2. Which of the authors did you find most trustworthy? Explain your answer in terms of the rhetorical devices the author uses.

Writing About Literature

Respond to Arguments The authors of these selections present several different arguments regarding the fate of Fenway Park. Whose evidence did you find most convincing? Whose use of rhetorical devices did you find most persuasive? Write a one- or two-page essay identifying and responding to three different arguments.

READING AND VOCABULARY

Reading Strategy Identifying Problem and Solution

Sometimes one person's solution can be another person's problem.

1. What two solutions are offered to the problem of Fenway Park?
2. What new problems would these solutions cause for people on the other side of the issue?

Vocabulary Practice

Practice with Synonyms Choose the synonym for each vocabulary word. Use a dictionary or thesaurus if you need help.

1. cathedral	**a.** church	**b.** building
2. nostalgia	**a.** optimism	**b.** wistfulness
3. staggering	**a.** awesome	**b.** primary
4. magnitude	**a.** charge	**b.** immense

LiteratureOnline **Web Activities** For eFlashcards, Selection Quick Checks, and other Web activities, go to www.glencoe.com.

Web Activities Have students access the Web site for interactive activities that will help them assess their understanding of the selection.

Literary Element

1. Answers should describe appeals to logic, emotion, ethics, or authority. Effects might be urgency, trust, desperation, or anger.
2. Answers will vary.

Reading Strategy

1. Renovate Fenway or replace it.
2. People in favor of replacing Fenway say it cannot compete with new stadiums. Those who want to save Fenway say its history cannot be duplicated.

Wrap-Up: Comparing Literature: *Different Viewpoints*

- *Thoughts on Fenway Park* by Various authors
- *Taxpayers Will Get a Return on Investment* by John L. Harrington
- *Other Revenue Sources Should Be Pursued* by William M. Straus

COMPARING THE Big Idea Finding Common Ground

Writing Each of the authors you read makes an attempt to find common ground with the audience. For example, authors may mention ideas or facts that they know will resonate with their audience. Write a brief essay in which you compare the ways that three of the authors seek to establish that they share goals, feelings, or ideas—common ground—with the reader. Cite evidence from the selections to support your ideas.

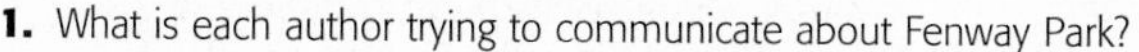

COMPARING Persuasion

Group Activity As an attempt to influence, a persuasive appeal—to logic, emotion, ethics, or authority—can be a very powerful thing. It is important for readers to identify these appeals so that they can draw informed conclusions. The selections that you just read use persuasive appeals to communicate the authors' positions. With a small group, discuss the following questions:

1. What is each author trying to communicate about Fenway Park?
2. What persuasive appeals does each author use to influence the reader?
3. Which of the selections, in your opinion, presents the strongest argument about what should be done with Fenway? Support your answer with passages from the selections.

COMPARING Author's Viewpoint

Speaking and Listening With a partner, research one of the following questions using the resources at the library and on the Internet. Present your findings in an oral presentation to your class.

1. Why did John Harrington sell the Boston Red Sox in 2002?
2. What recent renovations have been made to Fenway Park? Who is paying for these improvements?
3. How has the neighborhood around Fenway Park changed in the past ten years?
4. What issues are Red Sox fans currently debating?

INDIANA ACADEMIC STANDARDS (page 477)

9.2.7 Evaluate an author's argument or defense of a claim...

9.3.2 Compare and contrast the presentation of a similar theme or topic across genres...

9.3.5 Compare works that express a universal theme and provide evidence to support the views expressed in each work.

COMPARING LITERATURE

AFTER YOU READ

Assess

Comparing the Big Idea

Critique student essays on these criteria:

- Do students discuss how the authors establish common ground with their readers?
- Do students support their ideas with evidence from the selections?

Comparing Persuasion

Students should support their answers with details from the text. They should note where authors employed similar persuasive appeals to different ends.

Comparing Author's Viewpoint

Students' presentations should be well-researched and provide facts to answer the question they choose.

CheckPoint

Use the CheckPoint questions on Presentation Plus! to check students' mastery of the selection. These questions can be used with interactive response keypads for immediate student feedback.

Differentiated Instruction

Point/Counterpoint Invite students to work in pairs to write persuasive essays. Partners should take opposing views on the topic.

- Have partners present their essays to the class.
- Have students use a set of criteria for analyzing and evaluating the presenters' arguments. **AL**

Academic Standards

The Additional Support activity on p. 477 covers the following standard:

Differentiated Instruction: **9.5.4** Write persuasive compositions that...address readers' concerns [and] counterclaims...

Focus

BELLRINGER

Bellringer Options
Selection Focus Transparency 27
Daily Language Practice Transparency 45

Or display images of students from the 1940s and 1950s. Show students standing in lines, seated at a school assembly—situations that required students to behave themselves in an orderly and quiet fashion. **Ask:** How might student life today be similar to or different from student life in the 1940s or 1950s? Have students consider as they read what they might have in common with the author.

Author Search To expand students' appreciation of Anna Quindlen, have them access the Web site for additional information and resources.

Put Down the Backpack

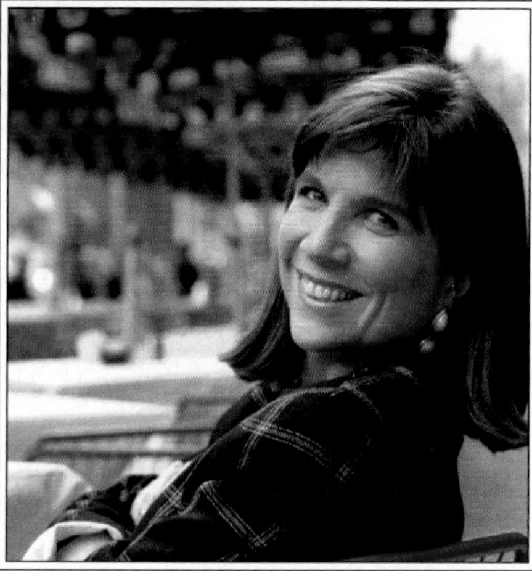

MEET ANNA QUINDLEN

Anna Quindlen knows the power of language. She once said that reading "has made me more human by exposing me to worlds I might never have entered and people I might never meet." Her love of reading and writing led to a successful career as a journalist and fiction writer.

Quindlen was born in Philadelphia. Her parents raised her and her four siblings in a traditional, Catholic household. From an early age, Quindlen knew that she wanted to be a writer. At the age of eighteen, she was working part-time as a reporter for the *New York Post* while attending Barnard College, where she earned a bachelor's degree in English literature. In 1977 she left the *Post* for the *New York Times*.

"There's no greater happiness than doing something every day that you love."

—Anna Quindlen

Trailblazer By 1983 Quindlen was writing editorial columns for the *New York Times*. In spite of her success, however, Quindlen decided she wanted to spend more time with her children. She resigned from the paper but continued to write from home. In 1985 she began writing "Life in the 30s." In the column, Quindlen openly discussed her own childhood, the struggles of parenting, and a variety of political issues. Readers were drawn to the honest nature of her writing.

With her next column, "Public and Private," Quindlen became the third woman in the *New York Times'* history to write a regular column on the prestigious op-ed page. Quindlen made observations about social issues and linked these observations to her personal life. She was awarded a Pulitzer Prize for "Public and Private" in 1992. A collection of Quindlen's essays, *Thinking Out Loud*, was published in 1993.

A Novelist Too Quindlen's first novel, *Object Lessons*, was published in 1991. It was followed by *One True Thing* and the bestselling *Black and Blue*. In her fiction, she explores themes of tragedy, loss, violence, and power. Despite these grave themes, Quindlen's message often is about finding happiness and meaning in life.

Quindlen's successful career as a novelist, social critic, and prize-winning journalist continues today. Currently, she writes for the popular column "The Last Word" in *Newsweek* magazine. She lives in New York with her husband and three children.

Anna Quindlen was born in 1952.

Literature Online **Author Search** For more about Anna Quindlen, go to www.glencoe.com.

Selection Skills

Put Down the Backpack

Literary Elements
- Author's Purpose (SE pp. 479, 481, 483, 486)

Reading Skills
- Evaluating Credibility (SE p. 479–481, 483, 486)

Vocabulary Skills
- Analogy (SE p. 486)

Listening/Speaking/Viewing Skills
- Analyzing Art (SE p. 484; TWE p. 483)

Writing Skills/Grammar
- Respond to Thesis (SE p. 487)
- Juxtaposition (SE p. 487)

Study Skills/Research/Assessment
- Short-Response Questions (TWE p. 486)

LITERATURE PREVIEW

Connecting to the Speech

Anna Quindlen, in her speech to a group of young women at their college graduation, offers some unusual advice regarding imitation and success. Before you read the speech, think about the following questions:

- Which qualities in others do you find yourself imitating most often?
- In what ways do you see yourself as unique or different from other people?

Building Background

Quindlen delivered this speech at Mount Holyoke College in South Hadley, Massachusetts. Mount Holyoke is a women's college, similar to Barnard College, which Quindlen attended. Mount Holyoke was founded in 1837 and Barnard in 1889, both at times when many universities did not admit women. In fact, as recently as the 1970s, nationwide there were fewer choices for women who sought the same quality of education available to men. Women's colleges played an important part in bridging the educational gender gap.

Setting Purposes for Reading

Big Idea Finding Common Ground

As you read, notice how Quindlen establishes common ground with her audience.

Literary Element Author's Purpose

An author writes a speech for a particular occasion and a particular audience. An **author's purpose** might be one or more of the following: to inform, to explain, to entertain, to describe, or to persuade. Being aware of the author's purpose gives the reader a clearer understanding of the meaning and intent of a writer or speaker. As you read, try to determine Quindlen's specific purpose in writing for this particular audience.

- See Literary Terms Handbook, p. R3.

Literature Online **Interactive Literary Elements Handbook** To review or learn more about the literary elements, go to www.glencoe.com.

READING PREVIEW

Reading Strategy Evaluating Credibility

Evaluating credibility means judging how credible, or believable, an author is. Credible authors' claims will be supported by evidence. This evidence might include facts, personal experience, or examples so that readers will trust the information presented.

Reading Tip: Making a Web As you read, keep track of the author's claims and how she supports them. Make a web like the one shown below for each claim to help evaluate whether the author is credible.

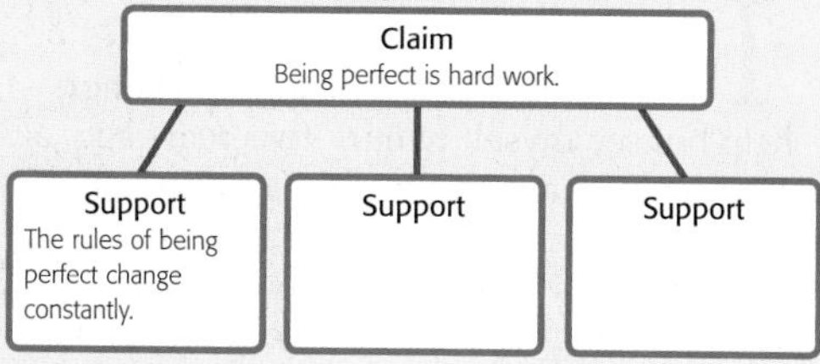

Claim
Being perfect is hard work.
Support
The rules of being perfect change constantly.
Support
Support

Vocabulary

monogrammed (mon′ ə gramd) *adj.* decorated with a design of one or more letters, usually the initials of a name; p. 480 *As a wedding present, they received monogrammed towels.*

template (tem′ plāt) *n.* a pattern that serves as a guide to making something accurately; p. 481 *The teacher asked all students to use a template when drawing their graphic organizers.*

redundant (ri dun′ dənt) *adj.* unnecessarily repetitive; without a purpose; p. 482. *Carla decided that repeating her instructions would be redundant.*

denigrate (den′ ə grāt′) *v.* to criticize or belittle; p. 483 *The coach did not denigrate the kicker for the missed field goal.*

INDIANA ACADEMIC STANDARDS (pages 479–487)

9.2 Develop strategies such as...identifying and analyzing...purpose...

9.3.9 Explain how voice...affect[s]...credibility.

9.5.4 Write persuasive compositions...

9.7.7 Make judgments about...ideas and support those judgments with convincing evidence.

BEFORE YOU READ

Focus

Summary

An author uses her youthful quest for perfection as the topic of a graduation speech. She explains that being perfect in the eyes of the world is hard work, but it is an attainable goal. However, the more difficult task is finding out who you are as an individual. It is also by far the most rewarding task a person can undertake.

V Vocabulary

Vocabulary File **Say:** Add these words and definitions to your vocabulary file. For each word, include a sentence that gives you an example of how to use the word. **OL** Students with English language needs should include the pronunciations of these words in their files. **EL**

Literary Elements Have students access the Web site to improve their understanding of author's purpose.

Selection Resources

Print Materials

- Unit 2 Resources (Fast File), pp. 77–79
- Leveled Vocabulary Development, p. 37
- Selection and Unit Assessments, pp. 81–82
- Selection Quick Checks, p. 41

Transparencies

- Bellringer Options Transparencies: Selection Focus Transparency 27 Daily Language Practice Transparency 45
- Literary Elements Transparency 35

Technology

- TeacherWorks Plus™ CD-ROM
- StudentWorks Plus™ CD-ROM
- Presentation Plus!™ CD-ROM
- Literature Online, glencoe.com
- Online Student Edition, mhln.com
- Exam*View*® Assessment Suite CD-ROM
- Vocabulary PuzzleMaker CD-ROM
- Listening Library, disc 1 track 47

Teach

BI1 **Big Idea**

Finding Common Ground
Answer: *She creates a bond with her audience by showing she was once where they are. This common ground makes it more likely they will listen to what she says and consider her advice.* **OL**

R1 **Reading Strategy**

Evaluating Credibility
Answer: *The admission strengthens the speaker's credibility because it shows that she is humble in willingly disclosing a weakness and therefore more likely to be honest with the audience.* **OL**

★ Writer's Technique

Repetition Writers often repeat sounds, words, or phrases to emphasize an idea. **Ask:** Why does the writer repeat the phrase "to be perfect in every possible way" in the second paragraph? *(To emphasize her goal; it is a mantra in her quest for perfection.)* **AS**

Readability Scores
Dale-Chall: 7.4
DRP: 57
Lexile: 1020

Put Down the Backpack

Anna Quindlen

I look at all of you today and I cannot help but see myself twenty-five years ago, at my own Barnard commencement. I sometimes seem, in my mind, to have as much in common with that girl as I do with any stranger I might pass in the doorway of a coffee shop or in the aisle of an airplane. I cannot remember what she wore or how she felt that day. But I can tell you this about her without question: she was perfect.

★ Let me be very clear what I mean by that. I mean that I got up every day and tried to be perfect in every possible way. If there was a test to be had, I had studied for it; if there was a paper to be written, it was done. I smiled at everyone in the dorm hallways, because it was important to be friendly, and I made fun of them behind their backs because it was important to be witty. And I worked as a residence counselor[1] and sat on housing council. If anyone had ever stopped and asked me why I did those things—well, I'm not sure what I would have said. But I can tell you, today, that I did them to be perfect, in every possible way.

Being perfect was hard work, and the hell of it was, the rules of it changed. So that while I arrived at college in 1970 with a trunk full of perfect pleated kilts and perfect **monogrammed** sweaters, by Christmas vacation I had another perfect uniform: overalls, turtlenecks, and the perfect New York City Barnard College affect[2]—part hyper-intellectual, part ennui.[3] This was very hard work indeed. I had read neither Sartre nor Sappho,[4] and the closest I ever came to being bored and above it all was falling asleep. Finally, it was harder to become perfect because I realized, at Barnard, that I was not the smartest girl in the world. Eventually being perfect day after day, year after year, became like always carrying a backpack filled with bricks on my back. And oh, how I secretly longed to lay my burden down.

So what I want to say to you today is this: if this sounds, in any way, familiar to you, if

1. A *residence counselor* is an older student who lives with and supervises other students in a college dormitory.

2. Here, *affect* (af′ ekt) is a noun meaning "a quality pretended to impress others."

3. *Ennui* (än wē′) is the French word for *boredom*. The word has a connotation of world weariness or boredom brought on by intellectual superiority.

4. *Jean-Paul Sartre* (1905–1980) was a French writer and philosopher. *Sappho* was an ancient Greek poet.

Big Idea Finding Common Ground *Why do you think the author opens her speech with this reference to Barnard?* **BI1**

Reading Strategy Evaluating Credibility *Does this admission strengthen or weaken the author's credibility?* **R1**

Vocabulary

monogrammed (mon′ ə gramd) *adj.* decorated with a design of one or more letters, usually the initials of a name

Additional Support

Academic Standards

The Additional Support activity on p. 480 covers the following standard:

Skills Practice: **9.2.7** Evaluate an author's argument…by examining…the comprehensiveness of evidence…

Skills Practice

READING: Analyzing Arguments
Explain that this selection presents an argument to the reader. The writer may use facts, logic, and emotion to influence the intended audience. Suggest that students use the following steps to analyze arguments in persuasive writing:

- Restate the author's main argument.
- List the facts or reasons the author uses to support his or her argument.
- List the points with which you agree.
- Decide if the argument is fair and reasonable. **OL**

you have been trying to be perfect in one way or another, too, then make today, when for a moment there are no more grades to be gotten, classmates to be met, terrain to be scouted, positioning to be arranged—make **BI2** today the day to put down the backpack. Trying to be perfect may be sort of inevitable for people like us, who are smart and ambitious and interested in the world and in its good opinion. But at one level it's too hard, and at another, it's too cheap and easy. Because it really requires you mainly to read the zeitgeist[5] of wherever and whenever you happen to be, and to assume the masks necessary to be the best of whatever the zeitgeist dictates or requires. Those requirements shapeshift, sure, but when you're clever you can read them and do the imitation required.

But nothing important, or meaningful, or beautiful, or interesting, or great ever came out of imitations. The thing that is really hard, and really amazing, is giving up on being perfect and beginning the work of becoming yourself.

This is more difficult, because there is no zeitgeist to read, no **template** to follow, no mask to wear. Set aside what your friends expect, what your parents demand, what your acquaintances require. Set aside the messages this culture sends, through its advertising, its entertainment, its disdain and its disapproval, about how you should behave.

Set aside the old traditional notion of female as nurturer[6] and male as leader; set aside, too, the new traditional notions of female as superwoman and male as oppressor.[7] Begin with that most terrifying of all things, a clean slate. Then look, every day, at the choices you are making, and when you ask yourself why you are making them, find this answer: for me, for me. Because they are who and what I am, and mean to be.

This is the hard work of your life in the world, to make it all up as you go along, to acknowledge the introvert, the clown, the artist, the reserved, the distraught, the goofball, the thinker. You will have to bend all your will not to march to the music that all of those great "theys" out there pipe on their flutes. They want you to go to professional school, to wear khakis, to pierce your navel, to bare your soul. These are the fashionable ways. The music is tinny, if you listen close enough. Look inside. That way lies dancing to the melodies spun out by your own heart. This is a symphony. All the rest are jingles.[8]

This will always be your struggle whether you are twenty-one or fifty-one. I know this from experience. When I quit the *New York Times* to be a full-time mother, the voices of the world said that I was nuts. When I quit it again to be a full-time novelist, they said I was nuts again. But I am not nuts. I am happy. I am successful on my own terms. Because if your success is not on your own terms, if it looks good to the world but does not feel good in your heart, it is not success at all. Remember the words of Lily Tomlin:[9] If you win the rat race, you're still a rat.

Look at your fingers. Hold them in front of your face. Each one is crowned by an abstract design that is completely different than those of anyone in this crowd, in this country, in this world. They are a metaphor for you. Each of you is as different as your

5. *Zeitgeist* means "the culture of a particular place and time."
6. A *nurturer* is someone who takes care of others.
7. An *oppressor* is someone who dominates others through an unjust use of force or authority.
8. Here, *jingles* refers to the short, catchy songs used in advertising.
9. *Lily Tomlin* (1939–) is a U.S. comedian and actress.

Big Idea Finding Common Ground *What effect might this phrase have on the audience at this point in the speech?* **BI3**

Vocabulary

template (tem′ plāt) *n.* a pattern that serves as a guide to making something accurately

Literary Element Author's Purpose *What is the author's purpose in this paragraph? How can you tell?* **L**

Reading Strategy Evaluating Credibility *What evidence has Quindlen provided to support this claim?* **R2**

Teach

BI2 Big Idea

Finding Common Ground

Ask: What metaphor does Quindlen use to represent the burden of trying to be perfect? *(A heavy backpack)* What suggestion does she make to her audience? *(Stop trying to be perfect; put the backpack down.)* **OL**

BI3 Big Idea

Finding Common Ground

Answer: *By allying herself with her listeners, the speaker increases her chances of convincing them that her message is valid.* **OL**

L Literary Element

Author's Purpose **Answer:** *She wants people to develop themselves as individuals.* **OL**

R2 Reading Strategy

Evaluating Credibility

Answer: *She shares a personal story—quitting her job at the* New York Times, *the first time because she wanted "to be a full-time mother," and the second time because she wanted to write novels.* **OL**

CheckPoint

Use the CheckPoint questions on Presentation Plus! to monitor students' comprehension. These questions can be used with interactive response keypads for immediate student feedback.

Academic Standards

Additional Support activities on p. 481 cover the following standards:

English Language Coach: **9.6** Use appropriate...spelling...

Differentiated Instruction: **9.1.1** Identify and use the literal...meanings of words...

English Language Coach

Spelling New Words It may be problematic for a student to look up a new word in a dictionary when they cannot spell it. Suggest that English language learners keep their vocabulary booklets up to date by carefully entering unfamiliar words as they read. **EL**

Differentiated Instruction

Reviewing Vocabulary Less-proficient readers can benefit from working in small groups to learn the vocabulary words for each selection. Have students make note cards with a vocabulary word on one side and its definition on the reverse. Students can quiz each other on the words. **BL**

Teach

L1 Literary Element

Author's Purpose Ask: Why does the author end the paragraph with a rhetorical question? *(Possible answer: The question helps her transition between two ideas.)* OL

L2 Literary Element

Author's Purpose

Answer: *She uses imperative sentences to persuade her audience to do something. The repetition strengthens the persuasion. She wants the graduates to be as a child is, unaware of others' expectations.* OL

fingerprints. Why in the world should you L1 march to any lockstep?[10]

The lockstep is easier, but here is why you cannot march to it. Because nothing great or even good ever came of it. When young writers write to me about following in the footsteps of those of us who string together nouns and verbs for a living, I tell them this: every story has already been told. Once you've read *Anna Karenina, Bleak House, The Sound and the Fury, To Kill a Mockingbird,* and *A Wrinkle in Time,* you understand that there is really no reason to ever write another novel. Except that each writer brings to the table, if she will let herself, something that no one else in the history of time has ever had. And that is herself, her own personality, her own voice. If she is doing Faulkner[11] imitations, she can stay home. If she is giving readers what she thinks they want instead of what she is, she should stop trying.

But if her books reflect her character, who she really is, then she is giving them a new and wonderful gift. Giving it to herself, too.

And that is true of music and art and teaching and medicine. Someone sent me a T-shirt not long ago that read "Well-Behaved Women Don't Make History." They don't make good lawyers, either, or doctors or businesswomen. Imitations are **redundant.** Yourself is what is wanted.

You already know this. I just need to remind you. Think back. Think back to first or second grade, when you could still hear the sound of your own voice in your head, when you were too young, too unformed, too fantastic[12] to understand that you were supposed to take on the protective coloration of the expectations of those around you. Think of what the writer Catherine Drinker Bowen[13] once wrote, more than half a century ago: "Many a man who has known himself at ten forgets himself utterly between ten and thirty." Many a woman, too.

You are not alone in this. We parents have forgotten our way sometimes, too. I say this as the deeply committed, often flawed mother of three. When you were first born, each of you, our great glory was in thinking you absolutely distinct from every baby who had ever been born before. You were a miracle of singularity, and we knew it in every fiber of our being.

But we are only human, and being a parent is a very difficult job, more difficult than any other, because it requires the shaping of other people, which is an act of extraordinary hubris.[14] Over the years we learned to want for you things that you did not want for yourself. We learned to want the lead in the play, the acceptance to our own college, the straight and narrow path that often leads absolutely nowhere. Sometimes we wanted those things because we were convinced it would make life better, or at least easier for you. Sometimes we had a hard time distinguishing between where you ended and we began.

So that another reason that you must give up on being perfect and take hold of being yourself is because sometime, in the distant future, you may want to be parents, too. If you can bring to your children the self that you truly are, as opposed to some amalgam[15] of manners and mannerisms, expectations and fears that you have acquired as a carapace[16] along the way, you will give them,

10. A *lockstep* is any process or method of doing something that is adhered to strictly and without question or thought. The word comes from a style of marching in which a group march as one, precisely in step and very close together.
11. *William Faulkner* (1897–1962) was a renowned American writer.
12. Here, *fantastic* means "reliant on imagination."

13. *Catherine Drinker Bowen* (1897–1973) was an American writer of what she called "semifictional biographies."
14. *Hubris* means "arrogance or excessive pride."
15. An *amalgam* is a mixture of different elements.
16. A *carapace* is a figurative shell that protects a person, just as the literal shell of a turtle protects it.

Vocabulary

redundant (ri dun ′ dənt) *adj.* unnecessarily repetitive; without a purpose

Literary Element Author's Purpose *What do the writing techniques in this paragraph reveal about the author's purpose? What is unusual about her purpose in this passage?* L2

Additional Support

Skills Practice

READING: Previewing Explain that this selection is about finding our own unique identities. The author urges her audience to quit living a life of false perfection based on other people's expectations. Write the following questions on the board for students to answer as they read:

- What rhetorical devices does the author use to influence the reader?
- How does the author support her arguments?
- How does the author find common ground with the reader? OL

Ciurana, the path, 1917. Joan Miro. Coll. Tappenbeck, Mouzay, France

too, a great gift. You will teach them by example not to be terrorized by the narrow and parsimonious[17] expectations of the world, a world that often likes to color within the lines when a spray of paint, a scrawl of crayon, is what is truly wanted.

Remember yourself, from the days when you were younger and rougher and wilder, more scrawl than straight line. Remember all of yourself, the flaws and faults as well as the many strengths. Carl Jung[18] once said, "If people can be educated to see the lowly side of their own natures, it may be hoped that they will also learn to understand and to love their fellow men better. A little less hypocrisy[19] and a little more tolerance toward oneself can only have good results in respect for our neighbors, for we are all too prone to transfer to our fellows the injustice and violence we inflict upon our own natures."

Most commencement speeches suggest you take up something or other: the challenge of the future, a vision of the twenty-first century. Instead I'd like you to give up. Give up the backpack. Give up the nonsensical and punishing quest for perfection that dogs too many of us through too much of our lives. It is a quest that causes us to doubt and **denigrate** ourselves, our true selves, our quirks and foibles[20] and great leaps into the unknown, and that is bad enough.

17. *Parsimonious* means "stingy or ungenerous."
18. *Carl Jung* (1875–1961) was a Swiss psychiatrist who wrote about the human unconscious.
19. *Hypocrisy* is the act of pretending to have certain values, beliefs, or feelings in order to appear moral or superior to others.

20. *Quirks and foibles* are odd qualities and small weaknesses in a person's character.

Reading Strategy Evaluating Credibility *Why do you think Quindlen included a quote from Carl Jung?* **R**

Literary Element Author's Purpose *How is Quindlen's repetition of the phrase "give up" in this passage related to her purpose?* **L3**

Big Idea Finding Common Ground *Quindlen has established that she has given up the quest for perfection. Why then do you think she uses the pronouns* us *and* our *in this sentence?* **BI**

Vocabulary

denigrate (den′ ə grāt′) *v.* to criticize or belittle

Teach

R Reading Strategy

Evaluating Credibility
Answer: *Because Jung was a psychiatrist and an authority on the human mind and behavior, his words increase Quindlen's credibility.* **OL**

L3 Literary Element

Author's Purpose **Answer:** *Her purpose is to persuade the audience to give up the quest for perfection based on external expectations. Her repetition emphasizes the importance of this message.* **OL**

BI Big Idea

Finding Common Ground
Answer: *She may use* us *and* our *to indicate solidarity with the members of her audience and all people.* **OL**

Viewing the Art

Although he loved his native Spain, Joan Miro (1893–1983) spent a great deal of time in Paris, the artistic hotbed of his time. In Paris, Miro interacted with cutting-edge poets and artists, like Picasso. Miro drew from movements including Fauvism, Surrealism, Cubism, Dadaism, and Abstract art. **AS**

English Language Coach

Pronunciation English learners may be uncertain of the pronunciation of words that do not conform to typical phonetic patterns. Explain how to use the pronunciation guide in a dictionary. Have students list unfamiliar words from the selection. Help them interpret the pronunciation of the words. **EL**

Differentiated Instruction

Research The author quotes William Faulkner, Catherine Drinker Bowen, Carl Jung, and George Eliot in her speech. Ask students to select one person from the list and write a biographical sketch. Have students share their research with the class. **AL**

Academic Standards

Additional Support activities on pp. 482 and 483 cover the following standards:

Skills Practice: **9.2.7** Evaluate an author's argument...by examining...the comprehensiveness of evidence...

English Language Coach: **9.1** Use phonics...and a growing knowledge of English...to...become fluent readers.

Differentiated Instruction: **9.5.1** Write biographical...narratives...that describe with specific details...the characters...

Teach

R1 Reading Strategy

Interpret Ask: How does Eliot's quote apply to you? *(There is no time limit on when a person can take up the task of finding his or her inner self.)* OL

R2 Reading Strategy

Interpret Ask: How might parents discourage their children from finding their unique selves? *(They may encourage a child to pursue goals that are theirs, not their child's.)* OL

★ Viewing the Art

Answer: *In this painting, two women look into a mirror and see one reflection. Quindlen argues that the pursuit of perfection is driven by societal pressure, which cripples creativity. It is our imperfections, she believes, that mark us as individuals.* AS

CheckPoint

Use the CheckPoint questions on Presentation Plus! to check students' mastery of the selection. These questions can be used with interactive response keypads for immediate student feedback.

Two Women and Mirror. Ludvik Glazer-Naude.
Viewing the Art: In what ways does this picture reflect Quindlen's call to "put down the backpack"? ★

But this is worse: that someday, sometime, you will be somewhere, maybe on a day like today—a berm[21] overlooking a pond in Vermont, the lip of the Grand Canyon at sunset. Maybe something bad will have happened: you will have lost someone you loved, or failed at something you wanted to succeed at very much.

And sitting there, you will fall into the center of yourself. You will look for that core to sustain you. If you have been perfect all your life, and have managed to meet all the expectations of your family, your friends, your community, your society, chances are excellent that there will be a black hole where your core ought to be.

Don't take that chance. Begin to say no to the Greek chorus[22] that thinks it knows the parameters of a happy life when all it knows is the homogenization[23] of human experience. Listen to that small voice from inside you, that tells you to go another way. George Eliot[24] wrote, "It is never too late to be what you might have been." It is never too early, either. R1 And it will make all the difference in the world. Take it from someone who has left the backpack full of bricks far behind. Every day feels light as a feather. R2

21. A *berm* is a narrow path along the top or bottom of a hill.

22. A *Greek chorus* is a group of actors in an ancient Greek play who comment in unison on what is happening.

23. *Homogenization* means "making the same."

24. *George Eliot* was the pen name of British novelist Mary Ann Evans (1819–1880).

Additional Support

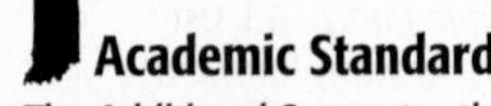

Academic Standards

The Additional Support activity on p. 484 covers the following standard:

Skills Practice: **9.2** Develop [reading] strategies...

Skills Practice

READING: Paraphrasing Explain to students that paraphrasing can help improve their comprehension of the selection.

- Model paraphrasing the first paragraph in the selection with students.
- Have students work in pairs to choose and paraphrase several paragraphs from the selection.
- Have each partner rewrite one of the paragraphs in his or her own words.
- Have students compare their work to the original text. OL

AFTER YOU READ

RESPONDING AND THINKING CRITICALLY

Respond

1. Did Quindlen's speech persuade you to change the way in which you think about success? Explain your answer using examples from the speech.

Recall and Interpret

2. (a)In Quindlen's view, what is the problem with imitation? (b)How does her opinion of imitation relate to her message of "becoming yourself"?
3. (a)According to Quindlen, how must real success be measured? (b)How do her standards compare to the "messages this culture sends, through its advertising, its entertainment, its disdain and its disapproval"?
4. (a)Why does Quindlen urge the members of her audience to remember being children? (b)When might "coloring outside the lines" be beneficial?

Analyze and Evaluate

5. (a)Why might "walking in lockstep" with the rest of the world be preferable for some people? (b)What are the dangers of the "lockstep"?
6. Compare the content and purpose of Quindlen's speech to most commencement speeches.
7. Explain whether you think Quindlen was a good choice as a commencement speaker for the graduating class at Mount Holyoke.

Connect

8. **Big Idea** **Finding Common Ground** Does Quindlen's speech reach out to all types of students? Use examples from the text to explain your answer.

VISUAL LITERACY

Topics and Transitions

In her speech, Quindlen establishes clear topics and then links those topics together with transition sentences. Make a flowchart like the one shown to identify the topics and transitions in Quindlen's speech. First fill in the chart with topics by summarizing Quindlen's main ideas in your own words. Then identify the sentences from the speech that connect Quindlen's ideas to one another. Note which words or phrases connect the transition sentence to the previous topic and the following topic.

1. How does Quindlen help her audience follow the flow of her ideas? Use examples from your flowchart to illustrate your answer.
2. Why does the author of a speech need to make sure that all topics and transitions are clear and easy to follow?

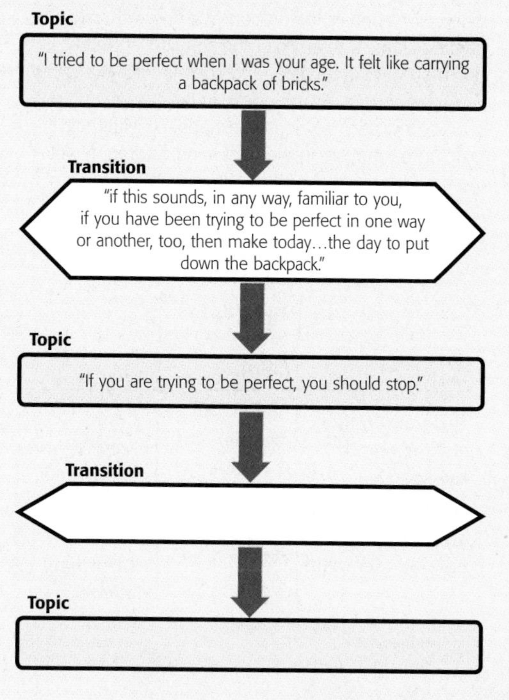
Topic
"I tried to be perfect when I was your age. It felt like carrying a backpack of bricks."
Transition
"if this sounds, in any way, familiar to you, if you have been trying to be perfect in one way or another, too, then make today...the day to put down the backpack."
Topic
"If you are trying to be perfect, you should stop."
Transition
Topic

Visual Literacy

1. She uses transition words such as *this, that*, and *but* to signal a connection or a contrast between ideas. She repeats key words and phrases such as *perfect, imitation*, and *give up* to help the audience follow her ideas.
2. The audience for a speech, unlike readers, cannot follow along on the page or go back to clarify a word or concept.

AFTER YOU READ

Assess

1. Students may be persuaded that success should be measured by internal factors rather than outside forces. Others may say she is unrealistic and success is dictated by factors such as wealth and status.
2. (a) She says "nothing important, or meaningful, or beautiful, or interesting, or great ever came out of imitations." (b) She urges listeners to pursue their own paths.
3. (a) "on your own terms;" feels "good in your heart" (b) Her standards are not the messages transmitted through our culture. One should define success using his or her own parameters.
4. (a) Children are free and do not face expectations from the outside world. (b) When facing a problem or situation that requires original and creative thinking.
5. (a) They would not have to think about what to do. (b) It is easy to forget how to make decisions, and set individual goals.
6. She, too, inspires the audience to do great things. However, she encourages them to reject the expectations of others and fulfill their own needs.
7. Possible answer: Excellent choice—she attended a women's college, became a successful writer, and is a role model for the graduates.
8. Yes, especially those who strive to be perfect. Her speech validates those who have established their own paths.

AFTER YOU READ

Assess

Literary Element

1. She wants graduates to lead fulfilled lives by determining their own success rather than following cultural norms.
2. Students should support their analysis with evidence. Her purpose is persuasion.

Review: Argument

Invite students to share their completed charts with the class. Discuss how the quotations appeal to reason or emotion.

Reading Strategy

1. Perfection, imitation, success, parenting, writing, accepting imperfections, cultural standards
2. She is a Barnard graduate, a successful journalist and novelist, and a parent.

Vocabulary

1. a **2.** b **3.** a **4.** b

Academic Vocabulary

1. Being mediocre and unoriginal, forgetting your true self, feeling empty, and not reaching your potential
2. Our internal voices and our hearts will tell us when we are successful, even if the world disagrees.

LITERARY ANALYSIS

Literary Element Author's Purpose

Frequently an author has more than one **purpose** in a particular piece of writing. A newspaper columnist, for example, may seek to inform, explain, and entertain at the same time. The author of a campaign speech, on the other hand, most likely wants to persuade and defend.

1. Describe Quindlen's possible intent in speaking on this particular topic to this particular audience.
2. Choose one or two paragraphs from "Put Down the Backpack" and analyze Quindlen's purpose(s). Support your analysis with specific examples from the text.

Review: Argument

As you learned on pages 436–437, an **argument** is a type of persuasive writing in which logic and reason, rather than emotion, are used to influence a reader's ideas or actions.

Partner Activity With a classmate, look for places in "Put Down the Backpack" when Quindlen appeals to logic or reason. Then find an equal number of places where she appeals to emotion. Working with your partner, create a three-column chart similar to the one below. Fill in the left-hand column with examples you have chosen from the text. In the middle column, explain how each portion of text appeals either to logic or to emotion. In the right-hand column, rewrite the argumentative text so that it appeals to emotion, and rewrite the emotion-driven text to appeal to reason or logic.

Text	Appeals to Logic/ Emotion	Rewrite
"I cannot help but see myself twenty-five years ago, at my own Barnard commencement."	Logic: The speaker was a student at Barnard, so she can relate to her audience.	"I can imagine your excitement and anticipation at finishing college."

READING AND VOCABULARY

Reading Strategy Evaluating Credibility

In order to establish **credibility** with an audience, an author must be viewed as an authority. Being an authority usually requires varying degrees of education, training, and experience. An author who is credible for some topics may not be credible for others. In those instances, he or she may seek to support certain points with additional information or expert opinions.

1. List the topics Quindlen discusses in her speech that you believe she has the credibility to address.
2. What factors make Quindlen qualified to write and speak about these topics?

Vocabulary Practice

Practice with Analogies Complete each analogy below. Use a dictionary if you need help.

1. **monogrammed : undecorated :: creation :**
   a. destruction **b.** evolution **c.** war
2. **templates : identical :: paupers :**
   a. hungry **b.** poor **c.** unclean
3. **imitation : redundant :: singularity :**
   a. unique **b.** identical **c.** parallel
4. **denigrate : elevate :: move :**
   a. wander **b.** settle **c.** travel

Academic Vocabulary

Here are two words from the vocabulary list on page R80.

submit (səb mit′) *v.* to give in to authority

differentiate (dif′ər en′ shē āt′) *v.* to notice the differences between two or more things

Practice and Apply

1. According to Quindlen, what are the dangers of **submitting** to cultural standards of success?
2. How does Quindlen say that we can **differentiate** between our own standards and the standards of our culture?

Additional Support

Skills Practice

TEST PREPARATION: Short-Response Questions Explain that short-response questions often do not have one correct answer. Instead, an answer is generally judged by its insightfulness and the quality of textual evidence included.

Ask: Which selection in this part was of most interest to you? Explain. Tell students to write a response, using three to five lines. *(Possible answer: "Put Down the Backpack" was the most interesting, because the content was of personal interest to me and the writer's style was engaging.)* OL

WRITING AND EXTENDING

Writing About Literature

Respond to Thesis In "Put Down the Backpack," Quindlen speaks passionately about the importance of being yourself. What experiences have encouraged or discouraged you from discovering who you really are? Write a one- or two-page persuasive speech about the pros or cons of being yourself. Aim your speech at a particular audience, such as students about to graduate from eighth grade.

Before you begin drafting, find quotations in Quindlen's essay that you would like to use in your speech. Authors use quotations for a variety of purposes, including adding insight or supporting a point. Create a diagram like the one below to help organize your ideas:

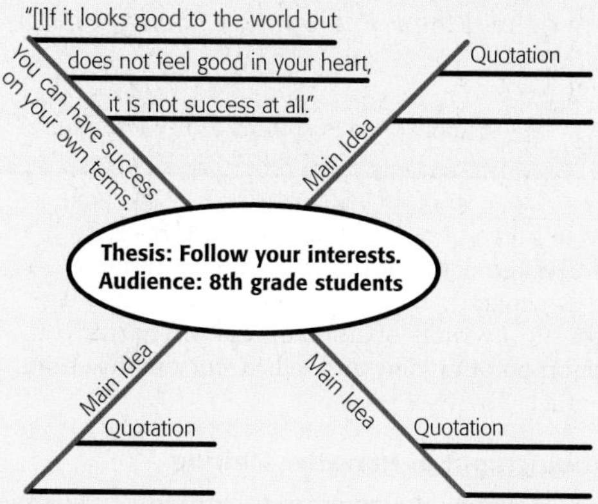

Choose main ideas that you can support with your own experience as well as with quotations from Quindlen's speech. Once you have completed the diagram, begin drafting.

When you have completed the first draft of your speech, meet with a peer reviewer. Edit your speech based on your peer reviewer's suggestions. Make sure that you have correctly cited any quotations you included in your speech.

Performing

Act It Out In groups of three or four students, write and perform skits about self-discovery. Each skit should have a well-defined conflict, such as individuality versus conformity or perfection.

GRAMMAR AND STYLE

Quindlen's Language and Style

Making the Most of Juxtaposition Juxtaposition is the placement of two things next to each other. In writing, this device is often used to accentuate similarities or differences, sometimes both. Throughout "Put Down the Backpack," Quindlen uses juxtaposition of ideas or images to influence her audience.

Quindlen juxtaposes both ideas and images in her speech.

Text	Image or Idea	Effect
"But at one level [trying to be perfect is] too hard, and at another, it's too cheap and easy."	Idea	Suggests to audience that perfection is both impractical (hard) and shameful (cheap and easy). Leads audience toward alternative to perfection.
"I smiled at everyone in the dorm hallways, because it was important to be friendly, and I made fun of them behind their backs, because it was important to be witty."	Image	Illustrates how following cultural standards creates hypocrisy and a false personality.

Activity Read through the speech again and find other examples of juxtaposition. Create your own chart listing the additional juxtapositions you found.

Revising Check

Juxtaposition Using juxtaposition for contrast helps a writer influence the audience's emotions, an important aspect of persuasive writing. With a partner, read through your speech on being yourself. Identify several key points at which an emotional appeal would help influence your audience. Create and insert juxtapositions of images or ideas that will emotionally appeal to your listeners at those key moments.

LiteratureOnline **Web Activities** For eFlashcards, Selection Quick Checks, and other Web activities, go to www.glencoe.com.

English Language Coach

Language Questions Encourage students to focus on the content of their writing and/or responses, not on spelling or grammar. They can concentrate on the mechanics of good writing in the revision and editing stages. Explain that their skills will improve with practice. EL

AFTER YOU READ

Assess

Writing About Literature

Use these criteria when evaluating students' writing:

- Do students correctly cite quotations from Quindlen's essay?
- Do students provide examples from personal experience to support their theses?
- Do students use correct grammar, spelling, and punctuation?

Performing

Ask each group to write a paragraph explaining the conflict in their skit. Invite volunteers to perform their skits for the class.

Quindlen's Language and Style

Encourage students to share with the class the juxtapositions they find in the speech.

Revising Check

Encourage students to compare their speeches with and without justapositions and decide which version is more effective.

Web Activities Have students access the Web site for interactive activities that will help them assess their understanding of the selection.

Academic Standards

Additional Support activities on pp. 486 and 487 cover the following standards:

Skills Practice: **9.5.2** Write responses to literature that demonstrate an awareness of the author's style...

English Language Coach: **9.5.2** Write responses to literature that demonstrate a comprehensive grasp of the significant ideas of literary works...

Focus

BELLRINGER

Display images of events you would be likely to find in a photo album, such as a birthday party, a wedding, a graduation, and a vacation trip. **Ask:** What kinds of events do you include in a photo album? Brainstorm with students to develop a list of events, people, and places they would capture in photographs.

Summary

In this workshop, students will write and present an autobiographical narrative. Students will follow the stages of the writing process, including prewriting, drafting, revising, and editing. In addition, the workshop provides two focus lessons, on developing voice and on pronoun-antecedent agreement.

Writing Models Have students access the Web site for interactive writing models and writing guides.

The Writing Process

In this workshop, you will follow the stages of the writing process. At any stage, you may think of new ideas to include and better ways to express them. Feel free to return to earlier stages as you write.

- **Prewriting**
- **Drafting**
- **Revising**
  -  Focus Lesson: Developing Your Voice
- **Editing and Proofreading**
  - Focus Lesson: Pronoun-Antecedent Agreement
- **Presenting**

Writing Models For models and other writing activities, go to www.glencoe.com.

ACADEMIC STANDARDS (pages 488–495)

9.5.1 Write...autobiographical narratives...

9.4.11 Edit and proofread one's own writing...using an editing checklist with specific examples of corrections of frequent errors.

Writing Workshop

Autobiographical Narrative

Writing About A Memory

"Being an only daughter in a family of six sons forced me by circumstance to spend a lot of time by myself because my brothers felt it beneath them to play with a girl in public. But that aloneness, that loneliness, was good for a would-be writer—it allowed me time to think and think, to imagine, to read and prepare myself."

—Sandra Cisneros, from "Only Daughter"

Connecting to Literature In much of her writing, Sandra Cisneros reflects on growing up in Chicago with her parents and six brothers. Autobiographical narratives generally focus on memories and their significance to the writer. Like most writers of autobiographical narratives, Cisneros uses the first-person point of view and tells a story with setting, characters, theme, and conflict.

Rubric: Features of Autobiographical Narrative Writing

Goals	Strategies
To relate a personally meaningful experience	☑ Choose an experience with some kind of conflict or tension
To use specific details in a narrative	☑ Make a list of details that you remember ☑ Describe the characters, setting, theme, and conflict ☑ Use dialogue
To present your narrative in logical order	☑ Choose an appropriate pattern of organization such as chronological order ☑ Use an outline or flow chart to organize your narrative
To draw conclusions about human experiences from your memories	☑ Point out how your experience helped you understand people, yourself, or a situation

Print Materials
- Unit 2 Resources (Fast File), pp. 80–83
- REAL Success in Writing: Research and Reports
- Writing Constructed Responses, pp. 1–26, 54–60
- Glencoe Literature Library

Transparencies
- Grammar and Language Transparencies 39
- Writing Workshop Transparencies 11–15
- Visual Literacy/Fine Art Transparencies

Technology
- Grammar & Language eWorkbook
- Revising with Style eWorkbook
- Sentence Diagraming eWorkbook
- Spelling Power eWorkbook
- Online Essay Grader, glencoe.com
- Literature Library Exam*View*® Assessment Suite CD-ROM
- Literature Library Vocabulary PuzzleMaker CD-ROM

Assignment

Write an autobiographical narrative in which you explain how a personal experience was meaningful in your life. As you move through the stages of the writing process, keep your audience and purpose in mind.

Audience: peers, classmates, and teacher

Purpose: to relate a personal experience and explain why it was meaningful

Real-World Connection

From ex-presidents to professional baseball players, people often write autobiographical narratives about their experiences. When a friend asks what you did over the weekend, how do you respond? You tell an autobiographical story in which you narrate the events most important to you.

Analyzing a Professional Model

In the following selection, Nobel Prize winner in literature Isaac Bashevis Singer describes a memorable experience from his childhood. As you read the narrative, notice Singer's use of the first-person point of view, concrete words, and dialogue. Pay close attention to the comments in the margin. They point out features that you might want to include in your own autobiographical narrative.

"A Day of Pleasures" from *In My Father's Court*
by Isaac Bashevis Singer ★

When times were good, I would get a two-groschen piece from Father or Mother every day. For me this piece—or kopeck—represented all worldly pleasures. Across the street was Esther's sweetshop, where one could buy chocolates, jelly beans, candy squares, ice cream, caramels, and all sorts of cookies. Since I had begun at an early age to write copy exercises, and had a weakness for drawing and coloring with crayons, which cost money, a kopeck proved not nearly so large a coin as Father and Mother made it out to be. There were times when I was forced to borrow money from a heder classmate, a young usurer who demanded interest—for every four groschen, I paid a groschen a week.

Now imagine the indescribable joy that I felt when I once earned a whole ruble—that is, one hundred kopecks!

I no longer remember exactly how I came to earn that ruble. I think it happened like this: Someone had ordered a pair of kidskin boots from a shoemaker, but upon delivery the boots proved to be either too tight or too loose. The man who had ordered them refused to accept them, and the shoemaker summoned him to a Din Torah. Father sent me to another shoemaker

Introduction

Make the topic clear to your readers and hint at its significance.

Narrative Details

Use specific details to vividly explain your situation and give background information.

First-Person Point of View

Comment on the events in your narrative using the first-person point of view.

Teach

Big Idea

Finding Common Ground

Ask: How might an autobiographical narrative aid people in finding common ground? *(Students may say that in an autobiography an author shares his experiences, ideas, and feelings. This gives the reader the chance to experience what the author has experienced and to find common ground.)* Point out to students that one advantage of an autobiography is that the author, by speaking from a first-person point of view, speaks directly to readers in sharing an experience. **OL**

★ Literary History

Isaac Bashevis Singer

Although he immigrated to the United States in 1935, writer Isaac Bashevis Singer (1904–1991) conjures up the Poland of his childhood in his writings. Poland's Jewish community was destroyed in World War II, so Singer's writings serve as a window to a time, a place, and a culture that have been lost. Singer won the Nobel Prize in Literature in 1978. **AS**

Word Meanings Ask students to define the word *autobiography*. *("the story of a person's life written by that person from a first-person point of view")* Point out that *auto* means "self" and that the root *bio* means "life." **EL**

Word Meanings Ask students to discuss the difference between a biography and an autobiography. *(A biography is the story of someone's life written by someone else; an autobiography is written by that person.)* **BL**

Academic Standards

Additional Support activities on p. 489 cover the following standards:

English Language Coach: **9.1** [Use] word parts…to determine the meaning of words…

Differentiated Instruction: **9.1** [Use] word parts…to determine the meaning of words…

Teach

Writing Skills

Dialogue Invite students to explain who is speaking in this conversation. **Ask:** What effect does adding dialogue at the end have for the reader? *(Students may say that the dialogue breaks up the narration, that it engages the reader, or that it adds humor.)* OL

Writing Skills

Visualization Have students reread the dialogue at the end of Singer's story. **Ask:** Can you describe Singer's expression when he shows the ruble to the driver? *(Students should be able to visualize a look of triumph, satisfaction, or glee on Singer's face from the details given.)*

Point out that having a detailed image in mind when students write will help them create something that the reader can visualize clearly. OL

to ask him to appraise the value of the boots or perhaps even to buy them, since he also dealt in ready-made footwear. It so happened that the second shoemaker had a customer who wanted the boots and was prepared to pay a good price for them. I do not recall all the details, but I remember that I carried a pair of brand-new boots around, and that one of the litigants rewarded me with a ruble.

Conflict
Describe the conflict, or problem, that you had to confront.

I knew that if I stayed home my parents would ruin that ruble. They would buy me something to wear which I would have got in any case, or they would borrow the ruble from me and, though they would never deny the debt, I would never see it again. I therefore took the ruble and decided for once to indulge myself in the pleasures of this world, to enjoy all those good things for which my heart yearned.

Order of Events
Use a logical order or sequence to show the events in the narrative.

I quickly passed through Krochmalna Street. Here everyone knew me too well. Here I could not afford to act the profligate. But on Gnoyna Street I was unknown. I signaled to the driver of a droshky, and he stopped.

Dialogue
Use dialogue to move your story along and bring it to life.

"What do you want?"

"To ride."

"Ride where?"

"To the other streets."

"What other streets?"

"To Nalewki Street."

"That costs forty groschen. Have you got the money to pay?"

Significance
Show why the experience was meaningful in your life.

I showed him the ruble.

The Village Sweet Shop, 1897. Ralph Hedley. Oil on canvas.

Reading–Writing Connection Think about the writing techniques that you have just encountered and try them out in the autobiographical narrative you write.

Additional Support

SPEAKING: Dialogue Encourage students to experiment with dialogue in their autobiographical narratives. Pair students and ask partners to describe to each other a conversation that relates to their narrative. The listener should ask questions to clarify the conversation.

Ask students to write out the dialogue they practiced with their partners. Instruct students to use dialogue techniques, such as ellipses to indicate pauses and dashes to indicate interruptions. OL

Narration

Prewriting

Choose an Experience As you consider subjects to write about, think of experiences that have been meaningful in your life. Also consider what experiences will be interesting to others. Choose an experience you want to share with readers, and one that you remember in detail.

Gather Your Thoughts Use the following criteria to help you choose a meaningful experience to describe.

- **Think About the Experience** Recall the details by asking yourself what happened and when. Try replaying the experience in your mind and talking about it with others who were there. You might have a photo or diary entry that will provide details you have forgotten.
- **Connect to Your Audience** Consider what details will be interesting to your readers. Plan to provide background or narrative details so that your readers can relate to the experience.
- **Be Specific and Concrete** Your readers will feel like participants in the experience if you include specific details and concrete words. Sensory images, dialogue, and your own thoughts about the experience will make it come alive for your readers.

Make a Plan To write an autobiographical narrative, you may want to tell what happened in chronological order. A flow chart or timeline can help you get organized during the prewriting step. Put the events in the sequence in which they happened. Draw arrows to show how one idea flows into the next.

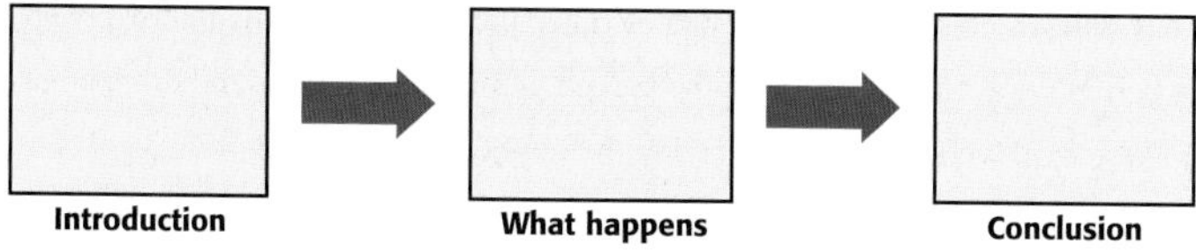

Discuss Your Ideas Before you begin drafting, meet with a partner to talk about the details of your autobiographical narrative. Talking through the experience will help you recall events and specific details that you may not have thought about for a long time. Jot down notes to refer to as you write.

Tell a Story

Remember that a narrative tells a story. Be sure to include the elements of a good narrative. Begin with an exposition, or introduction. Identify the setting, characters, and conflict. Tell what happens as the suspense builds to a high point and then comes to a conclusion.

Test Prep

If you are writing an autobiographical narrative for an essay test during a class, you won't have much time to recall and check the details. Take a few minutes to decide on an experience before you begin writing. Make sure you choose one that is familiar to you and will be meaningful to your readers.

Teach

Writing Skills

Connecting to the Audience Suggest that students ask their peers for feedback if they have trouble settling on an idea. Have students work in pairs to discuss possible subjects. Instruct students to list the ideas that elicit the strongest responses and to choose an idea from this list. OL

Writing Process

Prewriting For many students, choosing a topic to write about is the most challenging part of the writing process. Many students become tense when they are faced with essay choices on a test. Encourage students to approach the brainstorming process as an opportunity to be creative rather than as something stressful. Point out that this is one of the few times when they are encouraged to daydream! OL

College In college, students study celebrated authors. Ask students to research Isaac Bashevis Singer in the library or on the Internet. Suggest that they read more of his biography, excerpts from his other work, and his Nobel Prize acceptance speech. They should share their findings in a class discussion. OL

Outlines Many students fear that they have too little time to create an outline when writing essays during a test. Remind them that they need not write a detailed outline. They should jot down their ideas and then number them in the order in which they will be used. BL

Academic Standards

Additional Support activities on pp. 490 and 491 cover the following standards:

Skills Practice: **9.3.10** Identify and describe the function of dialogue... **9.7.1** Summarize a speaker's purpose and...ask questions concerning the speaker's content... **9.6.1** Identify and correctly use...the mechanics of punctuation, such as... ellipses...

Reading in the Real World: **9.2.4** Synthesize the content from several sources... [and] paraphrase the ideas... **9.7.7** Make judgments about the ideas under discussion and support those judgments with convincing evidence.

Differentiated Instruction: **9.4** Write clear, coherent, and focused paragraphs and essays.

Teach

Writing Process

Drafting At this stage, students should work on obvious errors or solve structural problems. Students must be flexible during the drafting process. They may use ideas from prewriting but can also extend those ideas or explore new ones. OL

Writing Skills

First-Person Point of View **Answer:** *The writer tells about his own life experiences.* OL

Writing Skills

Introduction **Answer:** *It must catch the reader's interest and set the tone for the writing.* OL

Writing Skills

Narrative Details **Answer:** *They help readers feel that they are living through the experience.* OL

Writing Skills

Order of Events **Answer:** *It is organized in chronological order.* OL

Drafting

Put Your Words Down on Paper Using your plan as a guide, begin drafting your autobiographical narrative. However, don't get stuck trying to find the exact words. During the drafting step, you want to put your ideas in writing. Keep in mind that you are writing a narrative, so try to incorporate conflict and suspense. You may find that writing about a memory gives you a fresh understanding of it.

Analyzing a Workshop Model

Here is a final draft of an autobiographical narrative. Read the narrative and answer the questions in the margin. Use the answers to these questions to guide you as you write.

First-Person Point of View
Why is an autobiographical narrative always told from the first-person point of view?

Introduction
Why is your first paragraph important?

Narrative Details
How do specific details make your story vivid and engaging?

Order of Events
How is this essay organized?

Surprise! Surprise!

I should have been more suspicious from the start. A few weeks before my birthday, my mother said casually, "Now that you are in high school, it's time to give up those big parties. You will probably have more fun if you go out for pizza and a movie. You can have birthday money to treat yourself and three friends."

"That sounds like a great idea," I replied. What I didn't know was that she was setting me up. My friends were part of her scheme. I found out later that she had called Jason, Darryl, and Will and sworn them to secrecy.

My dad was sworn to secrecy, too. He gave me a ten-dollar bill and two twenties before we got in the car. Then he picked up my three friends and dropped us off at the mall with the theater showing the movie we all wanted to see. Dad said, "I'll pick you up at the entrance in front of Pat's Pizza Place at 7:30."

Meanwhile, my mom was decorating the backyard with blue and orange streamers and balloons in honor of my favorite football team. My sister made a banner and a sign. She hung the banner between two trees.

Dad picked us up at exactly 7:30. During the drive home, he made comments like, "I bet this was your best birthday celebration ever." His words signaled that the party was over. As we pulled up to the house at quarter to eight, he said, "Why don't you guys come in for an hour. I want to watch a television show at 8:00. Then I'll drive all of you home." My father had successfully set the trap.

As I walked with the guys into the house, my mom said, "Why don't you wait in the backyard so your dad can watch his show uninterrupted?"

Additional Support

WRITING: Point of View **Ask:** Is first-person point of view objective? *(no)* Why might this be an advantage in an autobiography? *(Conveying thoughts and emotions instead of just facts allows an author to share his own feelings.)* Invite students to explore point of view by rewriting one of their paragraphs from a third-person point of view and compare the two drafts.
Ask: How do the drafts differ? *(The first-person draft may express more feelings; the third-person may be more objective.)* Have students consider adding first-person advantages—sensory details or personal observations—in their drafts. OL

When I walked out the patio door, I heard faceless voices yelling, "Surprise! Surprise!" Then suddenly people started popping up from behind the trees and bushes all over the backyard. "Happy Birthday, Andy." I was stunned! At least twenty of my friends from school were in the yard.

I congratulated my parents on their plan to surprise me. Few people are clever enough to throw a surprise party that really is a surprise. I felt like I was getting a double party—the one with a movie and pizza and now this one.

First-Person Point of View
Why is it important to explain how you felt or feel about the events?

The party continued, and the surprises kept coming. As everyone was singing "Happy Birthday," three strangers dressed in black and wearing sunglasses appeared in the backyard. They carried large wire cages draped with black scarves.

Order of Events
Why is chronological order often used in a narrative?

My mom introduced the mysterious guests. She said, "May I have your attention, everybody. I would like to introduce Craig, Tim, and Wanda, a trio of animal trainers from Creepy Crawling Creatures."

Wanda, the head animal trainer, slipped off the black scarves covering the cages. Everyone gasped!

Conflict
How can you create conflict or tension in a narrative?

"Ewwww . . ."

"Oh!"

"Wow!"

"What kind of snakes are they?"

Dialogue
How does dialogue add interest to a narrative?

Craig said, "Each cage holds a huge boa constrictor."

"These snakes are over seven feet long. They are all tame. Don't be afraid," Tim continued.

My friend Darryl asked, "Can we pet them?"

"Yes, if you want," Wanda said.

Darryl was brave enough to let Wanda wrap one of the boa constrictors around his neck like a scarf.

My friend Martha said, on her way out the door at the end of the party, "What a cool surprise party! We surprised you, but those snakes surprised us."

I just smiled. I had learned something new about my parents: Expect the unexpected.

Significance
Why is it important to draw a conclusion to wrap up the story?

Teach

Writing Skills

First-Person Point of View **Answer:** *Your feelings help make the events seem real to the reader.* OL

Writing Skills

Order of Events **Answer:** *It is a clear way to present a memory, and may be the way the writer remembers the events.* OL

Writing Skills

Conflict **Answer:** *Including the unexpected or disagreement among characters can create tension.* OL

Writing Skills

Dialogue **Answer:** *It provides detail and makes the reader feel part of the events.* OL

Writing Skills

Significance **Answer:** *A good conclusion leaves the reader thinking about the story.* OL

Journal Writing Some students may need more practice with autobiographical writing. Encourage them to hone their first-person writing skills by keeping a journal. Instruct students to write in the journal each day and to include both concrete and sensory details in their descriptions. BL

Academic Standards
Additional Support activities on pp. 492 and 493 cover the following standards:
Skills Practice: **9.4** Write clear, coherent, and focused essays.
Differentiated Instruction: **9.5.1** Write… autobiographical narratives…that describe with specific details the sights, sounds, and smells of a scene and the specific actions…

Teach

Writing Process

Revising **Ask:** Why is it helpful to separate the drafting and revising processes? *(Students may say that if they try to revise while they are drafting, they interrupt their writing flow.)* Suggest that if students revise while they write, they may take longer to finish the story. Suggest that they take a break before they revise their work so that they may look at their writing with a fresh perspective. **OL**

Writing Skills

Voice Have students talk with their peer reviewer about voice and see what elements of individual style are noticed by the reviewer. **Ask:** How would you describe your voice? *(Students might note their use of vocabulary or detail.)*

Instruct students to note their strengths and also where they could use improvement. **OL**

Traits of Strong Writing

Follow these traits of strong writing to effectively express your ideas.

Ideas message or theme and the details that develop it

Organization arrangement of main ideas and supporting details

Voice writer's unique way of using tone and style

Word Choice vocabulary a writer uses to convey meaning

Sentence Fluency rhythm and flow of sentences

Conventions correct spelling, grammar, usage, and mechanics

Presentation the way words and design elements look on a page

For more information on using the Traits of Strong Writing, see pages R32–R33 of the Writing Handbook.

Revising

Peer Review Once you complete your draft, exchange papers with a partner. Your partner should note if you have consistently used the first-person point of view, and if you have used details to elaborate. Also, your partner can evaluate how you keep your audience interested by making suggestions for dialogue and for developing a conflict.

Use the rubric below to evaluate your essay.

Rubric: Writing an Autobiographical Narrative

- ☑ Does your introduction create suspense or draw interest?
- ☑ Do you use the first-person point of view?
- ☑ Do you elaborate using narrative details that develop the plot?
- ☑ Do you use chronological order, or another clear organizational pattern?
- ☑ Do you use dialogue to make your narrative more immediate for your audience?
- ☑ Do you effectively communicate the significance of the memory?

Focus Lesson

Developing Your Voice

Your voice is what gives your writing its own style. Your writing should reflect your unique personality. Voice is determined by your use of language, your choice of words, and your tone. Remember that tone is your attitude toward your subject. As you revise your narrative, use vivid words and expressive details to create your own voice. See the revised sentences from the student workshop model below.

Draft:

"That sounds fine," I replied. What I didn't know was her plan. My friends were involved.

Revision:

"That sounds like <u>a great idea</u>,"[1] I replied. What I didn't know was that <u>she was setting me up.</u>[2] My friends were <u>part of her scheme.</u>[3]

1: <u>tone</u> **2:** <u>language (idiom)</u> **3:** <u>word choice</u>

Additional Support

WRITING: Diction Point out that word choice is an important element in the development of a writing voice. Working in pairs, students should review their drafts and list weak word choices. Have students consult a dictionary, a thesaurus, or the Internet to find stronger choices for the words on their lists. Instruct students to pay attention to connotations so that they do not accidentally change the meaning or the tone of the writing. Students should discuss their new word choices with their partners. **OL**

Editing and Proofreading

Get It Right When you have completed the final draft of your autobiographical narrative, proofread it to correct errors in grammar, usage, mechanics, and spelling. Refer to the Language Handbook, pages R45–R59, as a guide.

Focus Lesson

Pronoun-Antecedent Agreement

A pronoun is a word that takes the place of a noun or group of words acting as a noun. It can also take the place of another pronoun. Remember that the antecedent is the word or words the pronoun replaces. Every pronoun refers back to its antecedent. The pronoun must agree with its antecedent in number, gender, and person.

Problem: It is unclear which antecedent the pronoun refers to.

My sister made a banner and a sign. She hung it between two trees.

Solution: To avoid an unclear pronoun reference, revise by using the noun or otherwise making the meaning clear.

My sister made a banner and a sign. She hung the banner between two trees.

Problem: A pronoun does not agree with its antecedent in number.

I found out later that she had called Jason, Darryl, and Will and sworn him to secrecy.

Solution: Use a singular pronoun if the antecedent is singular; use a plural pronoun if the antecedent is plural.

I found out later that she had called Jason, Darryl, and Will and sworn them to secrecy.

Gaining New Insight

Think about your memory and the process of writing about it. What details came back to you as you planned the narrative? How has this memory affected the way you think and act today? What new insight do you have about yourself as a result of writing about this experience?

Presenting

The Right Look Before you turn in your autobiographical narrative, make sure it is neat and presentable. Your narrative should be typed with appropriate margins or neatly handwritten. Be sure to include an interesting title that catches your readers' attention from the start. Check with your teacher for additional presentation guidelines.

Writer's Portfolio

Place a clean copy of your autobiographical narrative in your portfolio to review later.

Teach

Writing Process

Proofreading Remind students that relying on a computer's spell-check program to catch all their errors will not work. Point out that the computer will not find a common typing error such as typing *form* instead of *from* because the word is not spelled incorrectly.
Say: Make sure that you examine spelling, grammar, and overall flow in your final draft before turning in your work. OL

Writing Skills

Test-Taking Tip Point out to students that it is common on standardized tests to have grammar questions about catching and correcting pronoun errors. Suggest that when taking a grammar test, students check to be sure that pronouns match their antecedents in number, gender, and case and that the antecedents are clear. OL

Pronouns Review with students the difference between subjective and objective pronouns.
Write on the board: Subjective: I, you, he, she, they, who. Explain that these pronouns may be used as subjects of sentences or clauses.
Write on the board: Objective: me, you, him, her, them, whom. Explain that these pronouns may be used as objects, usually of verbs or prepositions.
Ask: Do you say *to who* or *to whom*? Why? (To whom; whom *is the object of the preposition* to.) EL

Academic Standards

Additional Support activities on pp. 494 and 495 cover the following standards:
Skills Practice: **9.4.12** Revise writing to improve…the precision of word choice…
English Language Coach: **9.6.2** Demonstrate an understanding of sentence construction…and proper English usage…

Focus

Summary

In this workshop, students will learn techniques for planning, preparing, and gathering props for an autobiographical narrative presentation.

Teach

Speaking Skills

Memorization To some students, the idea of "learning lines" seems daunting. Share the following tips to help them feel more comfortable:

- Memorize the order. Make a list of the events in order and become familiar with it.
- Break the list into sections, such as beginning, middle, and end. Think about the effect each section should have. Is the beginning funny? Sad?
- Memorize one section at time.
- Practice reading through the entire story every day, working on the flow between sections. **OL**

Speaking, Listening, and Viewing Workshop

Narrative Presentation

Delivering a Narrative Presentation

Connecting to Literature Sandra Cisneros is a master storyteller whose work, which often deals with themes of identity and heritage, is emotional and gripping. When you present your autobiographical narrative, it is important to understand the themes and emotions you want to convey to your audience. To present a narrative effectively, use eye contact, facial expressions, and gestures to communicate your message.

Assignment **Create an oral presentation of your autobiographical narrative and present it to an audience.**

Planning Your Presentation

It is time to present your autobiographical narrative to an audience. To get started, reread your narrative, and note places that are funny, poignant, or tense. Think about how your audience will react to those moments. Ask yourself: What can I do to help the audience connect to my story?

- Work with a partner to prepare your presentation. Read your narrative aloud. Have your partner suggest ways to liven up your performance. For example, you can use a loud, exuberant voice for exciting moments and a softer voice for more serious, reflective moments.
- Practice your story until you know it well enough to present it without notes. Make eye contact with your audience and respond to their reactions.
- If you are concerned about forgetting where you are during your presentation, you may want to make note cards to remind you of the order of events. Check with your teacher for guidelines.

Dad asked, "why don't you come in for an hour?"
Mom said, "why don't you go out to the yard?"

Additional Support

LISTENING: Sound Devices Point out that sound devices can create atmosphere and rhythm, and can engage the listener. **Ask:** What sound devices might you use? *(Students may suggest rhythm, repetition, or alliteration.)* How might word repetition affect a story presentation? *(Repetition can link ideas and build tension.)*

Be sure students know what alliteration and onomatopoeia are. Discuss the effect of alliteration and onomatopoeia on the listener. Have students volunteer examples of each and note the reactions of their classmates. **OL**

Gathering Your Props

Storytellers often use objects to make their presentations visual. For example, the writer of "Surprise! Surprise!" might use a stub from a movie theater ticket, balloons, a sign, a banner, and a black scarf. Decide what props you will use and how you will use them during the presentation. You might put them behind the podium and hold them up when you come to that part of the story. Use your imagination. You can brainstorm ideas in a chart like the one below.

What objects are mentioned in my narrative?	Which of these are easy to find and carry around?	How can I display the objects during the presentation?

Getting Prepared

You will need a lot of practice to remember all of the details when you present your narrative in front of an audience. Begin by reviewing the story several times to fix the order of events in your mind. Then invite members of your family to a dress rehearsal where you give your presentation. They may be able to suggest additional details to enhance the story if they remember the event. Ask them to comment on how clearly you are speaking and on the effectiveness of your props.

Use some of the verbal and nonverbal techniques mentioned below.

Hints for Delivering an Effective Presentation

Verbal Techniques	Nonverbal Techniques
☑ **Emphasis** Speak expressively. Stress important words and phrases that help communicate the meaning of the experience.	☑ **Posture** Stand with confidence to show you believe you have a good story to tell.
☑ **Pace** Speak at a moderate speed but vary your rate and use of dramatic pauses.	☑ **Eye Contact** Look at your audience. Relate to them. Make eye contact.
☑ **Tone** Make sure your tone of voice reflects the subject matter.	☑ **Gestures** Use gestures and facial expressions to communicate with your audience.

Time Your Presentation

Your teacher may set a guideline for how long your presentation should take. Use a clock, a watch, or a kitchen timer to make sure your delivery takes the right amount of time.

Record Your Presentation

Use a tape recorder to know how your narrative will sound to your audience. Listen to make sure you are speaking with expression and pronouncing your words clearly.

Make a Videotape

Have someone videotape your presentation of your autobiographical narrative. View it and evaluate your delivery as part of your preparation. Make adjustments based on your evaluation.

ACADEMIC STANDARDS (pages 496–497)

9.7.14 Deliver narrative presentations…

9.7.4 Use props…to enhance the appeal and accuracy of presentations.

9.7.6 Analyze the occasion and the interests of the audience and choose effective verbal and nonverbal techniques…

Teach

Speaking Skills

Using Props Point out that working with props takes practice. If used awkwardly, props can detract from, rather than add to, the story. To avoid prop difficulties, ask students to bring props to class. Have students work in pairs to practice incorporating their props into their presentations. Instruct students to point out to their partners any areas of awkwardness or difficulty in prop use. **OL**

Viewing Skills

Analyzing the Presentation Have students present their stories to partners. Advise the partners to comment on these physical aspects of the presentation:

- Is the speaker wiggling or rocking back and forth?
- Does the speaker use hand movements or arm waving that distracts the audience?
- Is the speaker's gaze on the audience or elsewhere? **OL**

Easing Nervousness Some speakers may feel self-conscious about their speech. Remind them that nervousness often makes people speak too quickly and too softly. Each day have students practice reading aloud at a slow pace and at a clearly audible level. **EL**

Academic Standards

Additional Support activities on pp. 496 and 497 cover the following standards:

Skills Practice: **9.7.10** Assess how language and delivery affect the mood and tone of the oral communication and make an impact on the audience.

English Language Coach: **9.7** [Develop] speaking skills…in conjunction with…strategies…[for] delivery of oral presentations.

INDEPENDENT READING

Focus

Summary

This Independent Reading feature encourages students to read nonfiction by introducing them to the wide variety of subjects and styles that are available.

Teach

Literary History

Douglas Adams British author Douglas Adams (1952–2001) worked in many genres besides nonfiction. For his *Hitchhiker's Guide to the Galaxy* series, he adapted the story for radio, television, novels, a computer game, stage, and most recently film. Adams is known for the unique sense of humor with which he imbues his writing, regardless of genre. AS

Nonfiction and Novels

NONFICTION WRITING RANGES FROM DIARY ENTRIES TO COOKBOOKS. It can tell us how, why, what, and when. Some nonfiction selections look back and reflect on entire lives while others describe just one chapter or experience in a life. For more nonfiction on a range of themes, try the first three suggestions below. For novels that incorporate the Big Ideas of *Looking into Lives*, *Being on the Move*, and *Finding Common Ground*, try the titles from the Glencoe Literature Library on the next page.

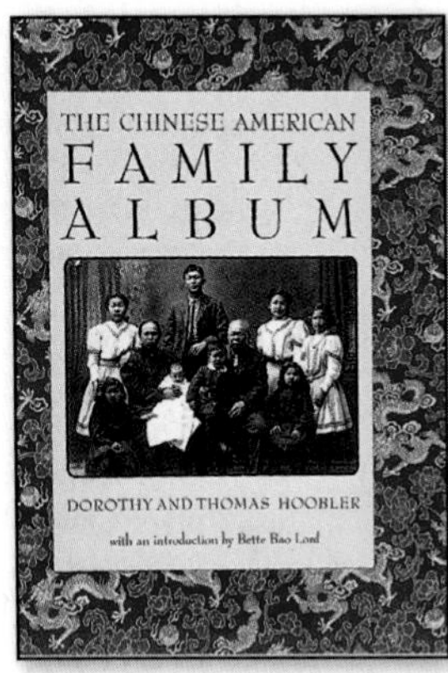

The Chinese American Family Album

Dorothy and Thomas Hoobler

In order to tell the story of Chinese immigration to the United States, the Hooblers gathered photographs, letters, journals, and other firsthand accounts from the people who made the trip from one country to the other. Challenges of the new world, including clashes of culture, are presented in personal, intimate detail. Other topics include the Gold Rush, the construction of the transcontinental railroad, and the establishment of Chinese businesses.

Last Chance to See

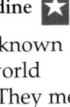

Douglas Adams and Mark Carwardine 

A best-selling author and a well-known zoologist team up to travel the world looking for endangered species. They meet up with exotic species such as the Komodo dragon, the northern white rhinoceros, and the mountain gorilla. Adams and Carwardine retell some of their adventures with sidesplitting humor and flair. At the same time, they describe the heartbreaking plight of the animals that they encounter and make a convincing case for greater awareness and conservation efforts.

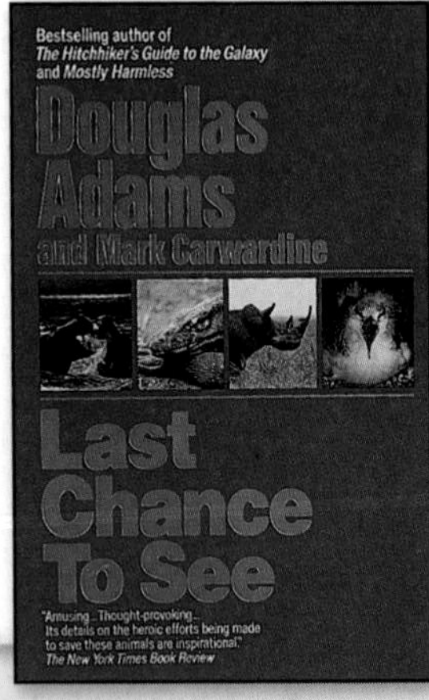

Additional Support

READING: Nonfiction When approaching the nonfiction genre, students imagine dry, boring, informational texts. Point out that nonfiction includes a wide range of topics and styles, such as humorous opinion pieces, magazine articles, and topical essays. Invite students to research the nonfiction genre in the library or on the Internet and create a list of subjects, authors, and styles that interest them. Have them read further on those topics. OL

CRITICS' CORNER

"Sarah and Annie Elizabeth Delany . . . . were taught to participate in history, not just witness it, and they have had the wit to shape their histories with style. . . . And no, I am not saying their memoirs, deftly arranged in alternating chapters by the journalist Amy Hill Hearth, are literature: I am saying that they are literature's living kin."

—Margo Jefferson, the *New York Times*

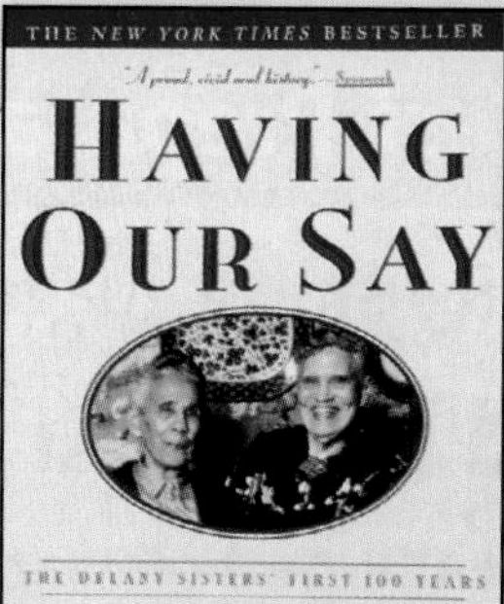

Pedestrians stroll along Lenox Avenue in Harlem.

Having Our Say

Sarah and A. Elizabeth Delany with Amy Hill Hearth ★

This is the remarkable story of two sisters, who were 101 and 103 when they told their stories. Born on a North Carolina farm to a father who had been a slave, the Delany sisters lived through most of the twentieth century and its myriad changes. Both sisters were part of the Great Migration from South to North. Both lived in Harlem. Both were pioneers in their own ways in the era that ended segregation and saw the birth of civil rights. Neither married. Their insights into history and life reflect the wisdom gained over a century.

From the Glencoe Literature Library

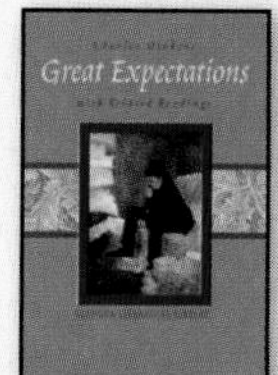

Great Expectations

Charles Dickens

This coming-of-age novel looks into the life of a boy as he becomes a man in Victorian England.

. . . And the Earth Did Not Devour Him

Tomás Rivera

This collection of related stories recounts the struggles, hopes, and dreams of migrant workers on the move.

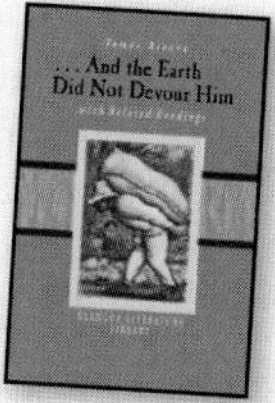

To Kill a Mockingbird

Harper Lee

Set in the rural south of the 1930s, this is a tale of justice and injustice, family, community, and the courage needed to find common ground.

Teach

★ Literary History

Amy Hill Hearth Amy Hill Hearth was a reporter for the *New York Times* when she interviewed Sarah "Sadie" Delany and her sister Annie Elizabeth "Bessie" Delany. From a *New York Times* feature, Hearth worked with the Delany sisters to develop the story into a novel. The story became a sensation, spawning a Broadway play and a television movie and winning several awards. **AS**

Glencoe Literature Library

Glencoe Literature Library offers an extensive collection of hardcover books that help you encourage your students to read independently. Choose among the more than 120 full-length literary works—novels, novellas, plays, and nonfiction. Each book includes related readings from a broad range of genres. Go to glencoe.com for more information.

Reading Nonfiction Point out to students that reading nonfiction is a good way to hone their language skills while learning more about subjects that interest them. Encourage students to bring nonfiction magazine articles to class for discussion. **EL**

Writing Nonfiction Encourage students to try writing nonfiction—anything from a journal entry to an op-ed piece. Instruct students to incorporate one of the Big Ideas from Unit Two in their writing. Encourage students to experiment with tone in their nonfiction writing. **AL**

Academic Standards

Additional Support activities on pp. 498 and 499 cover the following standards:

Skills Practice: **9.2** [Understand] grade-level-appropriate material...

English Language Coach: **9.2.8** Make reasonable statements and draw conclusions about a text, supporting them with accurate examples.

Differentiated Instruction: **9.5.8** Write for different purposes and audiences...

Test Preparation and Practice

English Language Arts

Focus

BELLRINGER

Ask: What is the most challenging part of a test for you? *(Students may say that reading a passage or answering multiple-choice questions is most difficult.)* Discuss students' test-taking fears and challenges; list them on the board. Each time they address one of these challenges in class, cross it off the board.

Test Preparation and Practice

English Language Arts

Indiana Test Practice

READING: Vocabulary, Comprehension, and Analysis

Read the following passage. Then, on a separate sheet of paper, answer the questions on page 502.

from *To Be Young, Gifted and Black* by Lorraine Hansberry

R—O—S—S
This spells Ross
We'll get along at any old cost
With one good Principal
& teachers all so fine
You may search the wide world over
No school like Ross you'll find.

The heartbreaking part was this: It was *not* an old building but, on the contrary, a relatively new and modern one. Its substandard quality had been planned from the drawing board. For from its inception[1] Betsy Ross had been earmarked as a ghetto[2] school, a school for black children and, therefore, one in which as many things as possible might be safely thought of as "expendable." That, after all, was why it existed: *not* to give education but to withhold as much as possible, just as the ghetto itself exists not to give people homes but to cheat them out of as much decent housing as possible.

I was given, during the grade school years, one-half the amount of education prescribed by the Board of Education of my city. This was so because the children of the Chicago ghetto were jammed into a segregated[3] school system. I am a product of that system and one result is that—to this day—I cannot count properly. I do not add, subtract or multiply with ease. Our teachers, devoted and indifferent alike, had to sacrifice something to make the system work at all—and in my case it was arithmetic that got put aside most often. Thus, the mind which was able to grasp university level reading materials in the sixth and seventh grades had not been sufficiently exposed to elementary arithmetic to make even simple change in a grocery store.

This is what is meant when we speak of the scars, the marks that the ghettoized child carries through life. To be imprisoned in the ghetto is to be forgotten—or deliberately cheated of one's birthright—at best.

—

I recall being the only child in my class who did not come from the Rooseveltian[4] atmosphere of the homes of the Thirties. Father ran for Congress as a Republican. He believed in American private enterprise and, among other things which he had done by the time I was old enough to be aware of him, amassed[5]—in the terms of his community—a "fortune," (though actually he had done absolutely nothing of the kind: relative to American society of the Nineteen Thirties and Forties Carl A. Hansberry had simply become a reasonably successful businessman of the middle class). But we are all shaped, are we not, by that particular rim of the

[1]**inception:** beginning point
[2]**ghetto:** section of a city where members of a minority group live because of social discrimination
[3]**segregated:** set apart from others of the same kind or group (In this case, the school system had separate facilities for minority students.)

[4]**Rooseveltian:** during the presidency of Franklin D. Roosevelt, a Democrat
[5]**amassed:** collected; accumulated

Reading

Active Reading When reading actively, students should consciously look for the main idea or theme as well as supporting details. Have students reread the first paragraph of the passage, taking notes as they do. **Ask: What does the first paragraph introduce?** *(Students may say that it introduces them to the theme that children in poor areas are often cheated of a decent education.)* Have students volunteer important details from the first paragraph. *(Students should include the location of the school and that it was located in a ghetto where the students' education was intentionally inadequate.)* **OL**

soup-bowl where we swim, and I have remained throughout the balance of my life a creature formed in a community atmosphere where I was known as—a "rich" girl.

In any case, my mother sent me to kindergarten in white fur in the middle of the depression;[6] the kids beat me up; and I think it was from that moment I became—a rebel. . . .

—

Because it was the largest, most finely wrapped of all the boxes, she had noticed it for days. And when, at last, the morning came and she was allowed to rip asunder the smooth white tissue paper and see what lay inside, the child could do nothing but sit stunned.

The grown-ups ohhhed and ahhhed around her.

They congratulated the mother.

They insisted that the outfit be put, at once, upon the child.

They touched the fur and exclaimed afresh with passion.

And all the while the child sat half ill with the outrage that had been committed against her Christmas. She was compelled to stand up, a small angry mannequin[7] in her pajamas, while the coat was first lovingly shaken and thrust upon her frame and buttoned to her chin quite as if she was about to go out into the cold. Then the muff was placed on her fists, and the scratching little cap on her brow.

Now she was ready and she was made to walk up and down so that the grown-ups could ohh and ahh yet another chorus. At the hall mirror she saw herself and the image in the long panel was even more awful than the imagined one: she looked exactly like one of the enormous stupid rabbits in her silly coloring books. She *hated* those rabbits. Several tears, fat and lush, rose at once and spilled down her cheeks and past her tight lips until they dripped directly onto the ermine[8]. . . .

—

But the ohhs and ahhs prevailed. Swathed in white she was sent to school where the children of the ghetto had promptly set upon her with fist and inkwell,[9] and ever since then she had been antagonistic to the symbols of affluence.[10] In fact, after that day she had chosen her friends with intense fascination from among—her assailants.[11]

Children such as Carmen Smith, who invariably lived in walk-up flats[12] where it was very bare and rugless and one was permitted to eat good-doing bologna sandwiches on white bread with mustard and hold them in the hands so that the bread got moist like cereal while Carmen, with her teensie plaits[13] carefully parted off all over her head, talked to her mother, who lay on a mattress on the floor, with no spring or linen,[14] looking very tired or sick, and who had to tell the girls about the chores that they would have to do when they came home from school because she would be gone to work by then. Children who, above all, had their own door keys: gleaming yellow metal, hung proudly, in her eyes, on a string around the neck! Throughout her childhood she had tried various props in fiercely jealous emulation:[15] her skate key, stray keys found in the streets, any number of things, but make-believe wasn't the same.

Kids like Carmen Smith did more things and laughed harder when they laughed and they got to go to the movies alone on Saturday afternoons without adults and they knew all the secret things that grown-ups did and the secret words to describe them. They had authority and they were loud and bucked their eyes and cursed when their games went badly. *They were like grown-ups*—and she had admired them mightily.

[6]**depression:** the Great Depression (1929–1939), a time of reduced business activity, high unemployment, and low wages

[7]**mannequin:** full-sized model of a human figure used for displaying clothes

[8]**ermine:** white fur of the ermine, a type of weasel

[9]**inkwell:** container for ink (Students at this time used fountains pens, which must be dipped in ink periodically as they are used.)

[10]**affluence:** much material wealth

[11]**assailants:** attackers

[12]**flats:** apartments

[13]**plaits:** braids

[14]**with no spring or linen:** having no coiled springs for support and no sheets

[15]**emulation:** effort to equal or surpass

Test Preparation and Practice

English Language Arts

Teach

Assessment Explain to students that this Test Preparation and Practice lesson is designed to develop test-taking strategies as well as to test their mastery of the skills covered in this unit. The lesson is modeled on tests they will be required to pass to be eligible to receive a high school diploma. Students will read one or two grade-level-appropriate selections and answer vocabulary, comprehension, and literary analysis questions, including multiple-choice, constructed-response, and extended-response items. In other sections, students' ability to use Standard English in their writing is assessed, and they are given an extended-writing prompt. **OL**

Assess

1. **C** is the correct answer. The school was racially segregated.
2. **C** is the correct answer. *Substandard* means "of low quality."
3. **A** is the correct answer. The scars are the long-term effects of prejudice, such as the effects of being poorly educated.
4. Rubric:

   2 points versions of two exemplars

   1 point version of one exemplar

   0 points other

   Exemplars:
   - She admired the fact that children like Carmen Smith were free to do things without grown-up supervision.
   - She admired that they knew what grown-ups did and knew grown-up words.
   - She admired the fact that they had their own door keys.
5. **B** is the correct answer. A community is compared to a soup bowl.
6. **B** is the correct answer. The birthright is a good education.
7. Refer to the Reading Comprehension, Writing Applications, and Language Conventions rubrics provided by the State of Indiana Department of Education.

1 According to Hansberry, what factor led to her attending the kind of school she did?

A family
B politics
C race
D talent

2 Read this sentence from the beginning of the passage.

> Its substandard quality had been planned from the drawing board.

What does *substandard* mean as it is used in this sentence?

A average
B high
C poor
D unusual

3 Read this sentence from the passage.

> This is what is meant when we speak of the scars, the marks that the ghettoized child carries through life.

What does Hansberry refer to when she writes of "scars" in this sentence?

A lasting effects of prejudice
B shame of feeling left out
C suffering caused by poverty
D corruption in public schools

4 Hansberry says that, as a child, she admired children like Carmen Smith, whose family had less money than hers. Give TWO details from the passage that reveal what she admired.

5 In order to explain why she was thought of as a "rich" girl even though her family was middle class, Hansberry says "we are all shaped . . . by that particular rim of the soup-bowl where we swim."

Her words are an example of

A an allusion
B a metaphor
C a simile
D a symbol

6 What does Hansberry mean when she talks about being "cheated of one's birthright"?

A Her parents were not respected enough in the community.
B Many children did not receive the education they deserved.
C Some children suffered terribly during the thirties.
D Her upbringing was unusual for the time.

7 Hansberry states that she tried hard to fit in with the children at her school, even though they perceived her as different. Do you think it is important to try to fit in with peers, or should people just be themselves? Write a letter to your school's newspaper in which you give your opinion and try to persuade others to agree with it. **In your letter, be sure to include at least TWO details or examples from the passage or your own life to support your position.**

Use a separate sheet of paper to plan your writing.

Writing Checklist

The following checklist will help you write your essay. Be sure to

- ❑ brainstorm for ideas and develop a plan before you start writing
- ❑ organize your writing with an introduction, a body, and a conclusion
- ❑ pay attention to your word choice and voice
- ❑ edit for sentence fluency and conventions
- ❑ have a neat and organized presentation

Student essays should include the following:
- a clearly stated and defended position supported by relevant evidence from the passage
- effective voice, word choice, and sentence variety
- effective presentation, with attention to grammar and spelling conventions

WRITING: Writing Process

The following passage is from the first draft of a student's essay. Read the passage and use it to answer questions 8–11 on a separate sheet of paper.

> [1]There is a long history of segregation in American public schools. [2]Prejudice and racism was keeping minorities out of white schools. [3]Even though much progress had been made in Civil Rights <u>during those times</u>, segregation practices continued. [4]In a famous 1896 case, the Supreme Court ruled that "separate but equal" facilities for Whites and African Americans were acceptable. [5]That ruling allowed public school systems to continue segregating students.
>
> [6]The Supreme Court finally changed its position. [7]The Supreme Court held that "separate but equal" was no longer acceptable. [8]While many people applauded this change, others were outraged. [9]Schools throughout the country were segregated in the nineteenth century.

8 Choose the BEST way to revise Sentence 2.

A Prejudice and racism kept minorities out of white schools.
B Prejudice and racism keeps minorities out of white schools.
C Prejudice and racism had kept minorities, out of white schools.
D Prejudice and racism was keeping minorities, out of white schools.

9 The writer wants to replace the underlined phrase in Sentence 3 with a more precise expression. Which of these is the BEST replacement?

A over a long period of time
B since the movement began
C during the nineteenth century
D on a regular basis

10 Choose the BEST way to combine Sentences 6 and 7.

A The Supreme Court finally changed its position, and they also held that "separate but equal" was no longer acceptable.
B The Supreme Court finally changed its position, that "separate but equal" was no longer acceptable.
C The Supreme Court finally changed its position and held that "separate but equal" was no longer acceptable.
D The Supreme Court finally changed its position, and the court held that "separate but equal" was no longer acceptable.

11 Which sentence is not related to the main idea of the second paragraph?

A 6
B 7
C 8
D 9

Literature Online **Unit Assessment** To prepare for the Unit test, go to www.glencoe.com.

Test Preparation and Practice

English Language Arts

8. A is the correct answer. There is an incorrect verb form in the original. No other option corrects this error without introducing further errors.

9. C is the correct answer. "During the nineteenth century" is more precise than the other options.

10. C is the correct answer. It is the simplest rewording and retains the meaning of the two original sentences.

11. D is the correct answer. Segregation in the nineteenth century does not directly relate to the changes that occurred later.

Unit Assessment Have students access the Web site to prepare for the Unit Two test.

Assess

12. **B** is the correct answer. Use a comma to set off conjunctive adverbs (such as *however, moreover,* and *consequently*).
13. **C** is the correct answer. Use a comma after an introductory adverb clause.
14. **A** is the correct answer. The past tense is the best choice.
15. **C** is the correct answer.
16. **B** is the correct answer. The other options contain punctuation or pronoun errors.
17. **D** is the correct answer. Use the past tense to correspond with the other verbs in the sentence.
18. **A** is the correct answer. The name of the U.S. Supreme Court is always capitalized.

WRITING: English Language Conventions

Answer questions 12–18 on a separate sheet of paper.

12 Decide which punctuation mark is needed in the sentence.

However even the Supreme Court could not fully integrate schools.

A .
B ,
C :
D ;

13 Choose the sentence that is punctuated correctly.

A Although the causes of racial separation have changed many believe that the effects are similar.
B Although the causes of racial separation have changed; many believe that the effects are similar.
C Although the causes of racial separation have changed, many believe that the effects are similar.
D Although the causes of racial separation have changed—many believe that the effects are similar.

14 Read this sentence.

Many people once <u>seen</u> school segregation as natural.

Choose the word or group of words that BEST replaces the underlined word.

A saw
B had seen
C were seeing
D had been seen

15 Choose the word that is spelled correctly.

Unlike her _____ classmates, Hansberry was always respectful toward her teachers.

A irreverant
B irreverint
C irreverent
D irreverunt

16 Choose the sentence that is correct and MOST clearly expressed.

A In order to address this problem many cities would have students travel, to other communities, to desegregate its schools.
B In order to address this problem, many cities would have students travel to other communities to desegregate their schools.
C In order to address this problem many cities would have students travel to other communities, to desegregate its schools.
D In order to address this problem, many cities would have students travel to another community to desegregate their schools.

17 Read this sentence.

When they saw the fur coat, the grown-ups clapped their hands in wonder, congratulated the mother, <u>and touching the fur in delight</u>.

Choose the group of words that BEST replaces the underlined part of the sentence.

A to touch the fur in delight
B and were touching the fur in delight
C and touch the fur in delight
D and touched the fur in delight

18 What additional word in the sentence should be capitalized?

In 1954 the United States Supreme court outlawed racial segregation of public education facilities.

A court
B racial
C segregation
D facilities

Grammar

Review Have students examine their English Language Conventions exercises to discover specific grammar points that trouble them. Help students list the kinds of errors they made, such as incorrect use of commas or lack of parallelism. Then have students use the Language Handbook and the Index of Skills at the back of the textbook to find relevant lessons. Ask students to prepare and present short grammar reviews on their trouble spots to the class. **OL**

WRITING: Writing Applications

Complete the writing activity below. Do your planning and writing on separate sheets of paper.

The Common Things of Life

> "It is my belief that to do strong work any writer must stick to the things he truly knows, the simple, common things of life as he has lived them."
>
> —Gene Stratton-Porter (1863–1924)
> author and native of Wabash County, Indiana

Write an essay in response to this quotation, explaining to your teacher your interpretation of its meaning. Support your interpretation with examples and reasons based on your own experiences, observations, and/or readings.

Be sure to include

- five paragraphs, including an introduction, a body, and a conclusion
- an interpretation that completes the assigned task
- examples and reasons to support your interpretation

Use a separate sheet of paper to plan your writing. As you write, keep in mind that your essay will be evaluated for **ideas and content, organization, style, voice,** and **language conventions.**

Writing Checklist

Before you begin writing, be sure to

- ❑ brainstorm for ideas
- ❑ organize your ideas into a logical pattern
- ❑ develop a plan for an introduction, a body, and a conclusion

As you write your essay, be sure to

- ❑ respond to the quotation and clearly state your interpretation
- ❑ provide reasons for your interpretation
- ❑ use language and vocabulary that will help convey a clear and interesting message
- ❑ maintain a tone that is appropriate for your intended audience
- ❑ use correct sentence structure, grammar, and punctuation

Assess

Assessment of writing prompts should focus on four elements:

- **Ideas and Content,** the message or theme and the details that develop it
- **Organization,** the arrangement of main ideas and supporting details
- **Style,** the word choices that a writer uses to convey meaning and the fluency, or rhythm and flow, of sentences
- **Voice,** the writer's unique way of using tone and style

Students' writing should also be assessed for **capitalization, punctuation, spelling, grammar and usage, paragraphing,** and **sentence structure.**

In addition, student essays should:

- fully complete the assigned task
- include complete, thorough, relevant, and logically organized ideas
- exhibit correct word usage
- demonstrate exceptional writing technique
- use language and tone appropriate for the task and audience

Unit at a Glance

About the Unit

Unit Three delves into poetry. Poetry is the most distilled way for writers to express their experiences in words. The form lends itself to beautiful, musical language intended to be read aloud. Poets face the challenge of appealing to the reader's senses while making the work also applicable to the reader's life. In this way, a poem can be larger than the sum of its parts.

Unit Introduction
Building Background
2–3 days

Part 1: Nature Inspires
9–11 days

Part 1 includes poetry inspired by nature, or the environment in which humans live. A chart showing the core skills taught in this Part appears on pages 515A–515D.

SELECTIONS AND FEATURES

Part 2: Life Lessons
6–8 days

Part 2 contains poetry that is about learning. Specifically it is concerned with wisdom gleaned from experiences, family, and nature. A chart showing the core skills taught in this Part appears on pages 573A–573B.

SELECTIONS AND FEATURES

Part 3: The Strength of Family
4–6 days

Part 3 includes poems about what it means to be part of a family. Family members can wound each other, and the same people can also be a source of healing, strength, and inspiration. A chart showing the core skills taught in this Part appears on pages 619A–619B.

SELECTIONS AND FEATURES

End-of-Unit Features
5–6 days

Unit Resources

Glencoe Literature: The Reader's Choice offers a comprehensive package of tools to optimize student learning and the teaching experience. Each resource has been designed to assist students in specific areas and to offer instructional support for teachers. While all of these areas are covered in the core textbook, some students may need extra practice or additional help in specific areas. The resource package is designed so that you, the teacher, can choose which items will best assist your students. You may also use these resources as homework assignments and for assessment purposes. The following are resources recommended for use with Unit Three.

Key for Unit Resource

- Blackline Master
- Workbook
- Supplemental Text
- CD-ROM
- DVD
- Transparency
- Web-based

Essential Instructional Support

FAST FILE UNIT 3 RESOURCES

Reading and Literature

- Unit Introduction, pp. 1–2
- The Big Idea Foldable, pp. 3–4
- The Big Idea School-Home Connection, p. 5
- The Big Idea School-Home Connection (Spanish), p. 6
- Challenge Planner, pp. 7–10
- Academic Vocabulary Development, pp. 11–13
- Comparing Literature Graphic Organizers, pp. 28, 73
- Literary Element, pp. 17, 20, 23, 25, 29, 31, 33, 38, 44, 47, 49, 51, 54, 57, 60, 62, 65, 70, 74, 76, 78, 81
- Reading Strategy, pp. 18, 21, 22, 24, 26, 30, 32, 34, 36, 39, 45, 48, 50, 52, 55, 58, 61, 63, 66, 71, 75, 77, 79, 82, 84
- Active Reading Graphic Organizers, pp. 89–98
- Selection Vocabulary Practice, pp. 19, 27, 35, 40, 46, 53, 56, 59, 64, 72, 80, 83
- Literary Focus, pp. 15, 42, 68

Writing, Grammar, and Spelling

- Spelling Practice, p. 85
- Grammar Workshop, p. 37
- Writing Workshop Graphic Organizer, p. 86

Listening, Speaking, and Viewing

- Listening, Speaking, and Viewing Activities, pp. 87–88

English Language Learners

- English Language Coach Review, pp. 16, 43, 69

DIFFERENTIATED INSTRUCTION

- Active Learning and Note Taking Guide, pp. 78–112
- Leveled Vocabulary Development, pp. 38–49
- Skill Level Up!™ A Language Arts Game
- Listening Library Audio CD, disc 1, tracks 48–80
- Glencoe BookLink 3
- Vocabulary PuzzleMaker
- Literature Library Vocabulary PuzzleMaker

ASSESSMENT

- Selection and Unit Assessments, Unit Three, pp. 83–132, 215–216
- Selection Quick Checks, pp. 42–66
- Selection Quick Checks (Spanish), pp. 42–66
- Assessment by Learning Objectives, pp. 26–40
- Rubrics for Assessing Student Writing, Listening, and Speaking, pp. 10–11, 30–31
- Standardized Test Preparation and Practice
- Glencoe Online Essay Grader
- Interactive Tutor: Self-Assessment
- Exam*View*® Assessment Suite
- Literature Library Exam*View*® Assessment

Additional Instructional Support

LITERATURE AND READING

- Active Learning and Note Taking Guide
- *inTIME* Magazines
- Glencoe Literature Library
- Literature Launchers: Pre-Reading Video
- Literature Classics

WRITING, GRAMMAR, AND SPELLING

- REAL Success in Writing: Research and Reports
- Writing Constructed Responses
- Spelling Power eWorkbook
- Revising with Style eWorkbook
- Sentence Diagraming eWorkbook
- Glencoe Grammar and Composition Handbook
- Grammar and Language Workbook
- Grammar & Language eWorkbook

PROFESSIONAL DEVELOPMENT

- Professional Development Package

TRANSPARENCIES

- Read Aloud, Think Aloud Transparencies 27–28
- Bellringer Options Transparencies
  - Selection Focus Transparencies 28–42
  - Daily Language Practice Transparencies 44–69
- Grammar and Language Transparencies 56, 57, 66
- Writing Workshop Transparencies 16–20
- Visual Literacy/Fine Art Transparencies

ENGLISH LANGUAGE LEARNER

- English Language Coach, Unit Resources (Fast File)
- *inTIME* Magazines (Spanish)
- Spanish Listening Library

TECHNOLOGY

- TeacherWorks Plus™
- StudentWorks Plus™
- Literature Launchers: Pre-Reading Videos
- Vocabulary PuzzleMaker
- Literature Library Vocabulary PuzzleMaker
- Skill Level Up!™ A Language Arts Game
- glencoe.com
- Presentation Plus!™
- Exam*View*® Assessment Suite
- Literature Library Exam*View*® Assessment Suite
- Listening Library Audio CD, disc 1 tracks 48–80
- Interactive Tutor: Self-Assessment
- Glencoe BookLink 3
- Online Student Edition, mhln.com
- Glencoe Online Essay Grader
- Grammar and Language eWorkbook
- Revising with Style eWorkbook
- Sentence Diagraming eWorkbook
- Spelling Power eWorkbook
- Literature Classics
- Spanish Listening Library

Additional Glencoe Resources

Dinah Zike's Foldables™

Foldables™ are three-dimensional, interactive graphic organizers that help students practice basic writing skills, review key vocabulary terms, and answer Big Ideas. Every unit contains a Foldable™ activity. You can find the pattern and directions for the Unit 3 Foldable™ in the Unit 3 Resources Fast Files booklet. You can use the Foldables™ as they are presented or modify them to suit the needs of your students.

For a wealth of online resources that support the instruction in Unit 3, students and teachers can visit our Web site at glencoe.com. Students will find additional learning, practice, and assessment opportunities such as these, which are noted in the student text:

- Author Search
- Big Idea Overview and Activity
- Interactive Literary Elements Handbook
- Study Central
- Unit Assessment
- Web Activities
- Writing Models

Teachers will find planning and instructional tools that include the following:

- Book Lesson Plans
- Web Activity Lesson Plans
- Teacher Forum
- Professional Resources

Go to glencoe.com to see the entire selection of *Glencoe Literature* online resources.

Glencoe's Presentation Plus!™, a multimedia teaching tool, lets you present dynamic lessons that will engage your students. Using Microsoft PowerPoint®, you can customize the presentations to create your own personalized lessons. Use CheckPoint questions with interactive response keypads to get immediate student feedback during lessons, to increase student participation, and to assess student comprehension.

Glencoe Literature Library

The collection of hardcover books include full-length novels, novellas, plays, and works of nonfiction. Each volume consists of at least one complete extended-length reading accompanied by several related readings from a broad range of genres. A separate Study Guide for each *Glencoe Literature Library* book provides teaching notes and reproducible activity pages for students.
Glencoe Literature Library titles that complement this unit include:

- ***High Elk's Treasure with Related Readings*** by Virginia Driving Hawk Sneve
- ***The Chosen with Related Readings*** by Chaim Potok
- ***The Glory Field with Related Readings*** by Walter Dean Myers

GLENCOE BOOKLINK

Use the Glencoe BookLink 3 CD-ROM, a database of more than 26,700 titles, to *create customized reading lists* for your students.

- Search for award-winning titles (e.g., Newbery Award winners, Coretta Scott King Award winners, and Caldecott Medal winners) and for books on several state-recommended reading lists.
- Find Degrees of Reading Power™ (DRP) and Lexile™ readability scores for all selections.
- Organize reading lists by students' reading level, author, genre, theme, or area of interest.
- Get a brief summary of each selection.

You can find recommended leveled readings for this unit with Independent Reading (see pages 672 and 673).

Online Essay Grader

Use Glencoe's online essay grader powered by SkillWriter™ to score your students' writing and to provide individualized feedback to each student automatically.

You and your students can visit glencoe.com to link to the essay grader. *Students* can enter their essays and receive feedback on demand. *You* can manage demographic data, assign tests and generate individual student and aggregated reports. The essay grader can help you

- Save time with automatic scoring and individualized feedback.
- Supplement in-class writing instruction using guided writing practice.

REAL Success: Reading Excellence at All Levels

Glencoe REAL Success is a suite of new reading and language arts products designed to foster reading excellence at all levels.

Look for TWE point-of-use references for these specific products that will help your students succeed in reading this Unit.

- *Jamestown Literature: An Adapted Reader*
- REAL Success in Writing: Research and Reports
- Skill Level Up! A Language Arts Game
- CheckPoint PowerPoint™ slides
- Literature/Reading support at Glencoe Web site

Literature Launchers

Set the scene with Glencoe's Literature Launchers, engaging pre-reading video segments that introduce each unit. Each Unit Launcher brings the literature to life, featuring expert testimony and archival stills and footage from the time.

Insert your Glencoe Literature Launchers into your DVD player. Select the Unit 3 Launcher from the menu to introduce Poetry.

A lively collection of articles drawn from issues of the TIME family of magazines helps students develop the skills they need to interact with informational text in a meaningful way. Each of the news stories, feature articles, reviews, profiles, and essays in the magazine connect to an author, work, or theme in *Glencoe Literature: The Reader's Choice.* See the *inTIME* Teacher's Guide for specific connections to each unit and for reproducible student worksheets designed to develop students' reading and critical thinking skills.

Teacher Wraparound Edition Key

Level Appropriate Code

AL = Activities for students working above grade level

OL = Activities for students working at grade level

BL = Activities for students working below grade level

EL = Activities for English language learners

AS = Information for all students

Teacher Wraparound Prompts

R Reading Skill These activities help you teach reading skills and vocabulary.

V Vocabulary These activities help students comprehend words and incorporate them into reading.

BI Big Idea These activities and questions prompt students to prepare to answer the Big Idea.

L Literary Element These activities and questions help students comprehend selections and learn more about each genre.

★ Enrichment Additional activities and information involving art appreciation and history.

Professional Development Center

From Your Authors:

Douglas Fisher and Jacqueline Jones Royster

Teaching Literary Analysis: Poetry

Start with an Illustration. Note that poetry should create visual images in the reader's mind. Starting with a powerful photograph or illustration and asking students to use words to describe the visual information allows them to consider the reverse–that the words of the poet can be used to create a visual image for the reader. Don't limit the discussion about the visual image to descriptive terms; also invite students to talk about the feelings, instincts, reactions, and emotions that the image evokes. For example, before students read the poem "The Peace of Wild Things" by Wendell Berry, have them examine the painting paired with the poem. Invite them to describe what their reactions and feelings are regarding the painting. After students have read the poem, ask them to discuss what visual images the poem suggests. Have them compare the visual imagery evoked by the poem to the visual information in the painting. Encourage students to use descriptive terms in their comparison.

Connect to the Big Idea. Understanding the theme is an important skill for students to develop as they read literature. The Big Idea can help them understand the overarching theme for the poems in this section. After reading each poem, ask students how they think the poet might respond to the Big Idea. As students read the poems in part 2, for which the Big Idea is "Life Lessons," ask students to discuss how the poems show that "every experience brings a new lesson." For example, as students read "I Was a Skinny Tomboy Kid" by Alma Luz Villanueva, have them describe what lessons the speaker learned based on her experiences in the poem. Then, in part two, have students answer the question presented at the beginning of this part: "What lesson has the speaker learned?"

Maria Eugina Lopez
Martin High School
Laredo, Texas

Teacher to Teacher

In a classroom that has students with diverse ethnic backgrounds, I believe it is important to allow students to connect to, and share their backgrounds with, other students. For example, I share with them traditions from my culture that surround the Halloween season. Rather than wearing costumes and going trick-or-treating, the Hispanic tradition includes a writing form called the calaveras, which means "skull." The calaveras is a humorous limerick that pokes fun at death in a way that we often refer to as a "dig." The poem is also something that individuals write to their friends. The challenge of the limerick is to allude to death without ever mentioning the word. As a unit-opening activity, I have students compose a calaveras that they can share with their friends. I compile these limericks and publish them in an anthology.

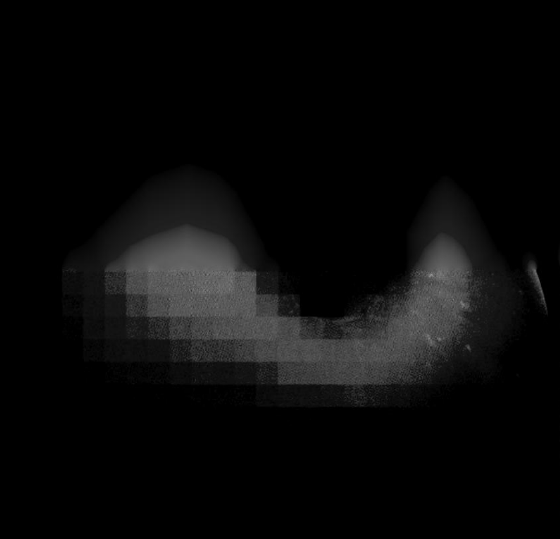

Making Literature Come Alive

Before you begin this unit or sometime during the unit, talk with other teachers about ways they have taught poetry. Have a lunch-time discussion group or an after-school hour for professional development and discuss the following questions and answers from our authors:

How can I show students that images and figurative language create vivid, detailed pictures with words?

- Read poetry aloud to students and ask them to visualize the images evoked by the poem. For example, read "Good Night, Willie Lee, I'll See You in the Morning" by Alice Walker, to students. Ask them to write down the images evoked by the poem, or have them draw pictures of the imagery, as you read the poem. Encourage students to use sensory words to re-create the poem in words or illustrations.
- Ask students to consider a song that they know. How do the words in the song help them "see" what the musician wants them to see?

What coaching tips should I use to help students read poems aloud?

- Students should always be provided time to practice the poem before being asked to read it aloud. Whenever possible, students should practice reading aloud with a partner before reading in front of the whole class.
- Allow students to read poems aloud as a group. You may want to establish a rule that every member of the group has to speak. For example, break students into groups of four. Then ask each student in a group to choose one stanza from "My Mother Combs My Hair" by Chitra Banerjee Divakaruni. Encourage students to practice reading their own stanzas several times. After the groups have practiced, have them read the poem aloud, each student reading his or her assigned stanza.
- Model your expectations for reading aloud with the class. If you want students to enunciate important words, vary their tone, or maintain their rhythm, show them how.

What strategies can I teach students to use to analyze sound devices and their musical effect?

- Students should practice with a partner, and partners should understand how to provide feedback. Have students work with a partner to read "I Wandered Lonely as a Cloud" by William Wordsworth. Have each student take a turn reading the poem while the other student listens and makes note of the reader's use of sound devices in the poem.
- Use popular songs to analyze as a class. Discuss how singers change their voices, place emphasis on specific words, and modify vocal patterns. Remind students that they should pay attention to these qualities while reading poems as well.
- Teach students to make notes about the sound qualities that they need to emphasize when reading poems out loud.

Focus

BELLRINGER

Bellringer Options
Literature Launcher Video
Daily Language Practice Transparency 44
Or tell students that they have been studying poetry, in many forms, since early childhood. Point out to students that nursery rhymes are a form of poetry.
Ask: What is your favorite nursery rhyme from childhood? Engage students in a class discussion of their favorites.
Ask: What other types of poetry do you recall? Have students volunteer poems that they remember and explain why the poems made an impression on them.

Objectives for the Unit Introduction

- To identify and interpret various literary elements used in poetry (SE)
- To analyze the effect that poetic elements have upon the reader (SE)
- To analyze poetry for the ways in which poets inspire the reader to share emotion (SE)

Pollard Willows and Setting Sun, 1888. Vincent van Gogh. Rijksmuseum Kroeller-Mueller, Otterio, The Netherlands. 

506

Unit Introduction Skills

Poetry

Reading Skills
- Reading Poetry (SE pp. 508–509)

Listening/Speaking/Viewing Skills
- Memorize a Stanza (SE p. 514)
- Venn Diagram (SE p. 514)
- Analyzing Art (TWE pp. 506, 511)

Writing Skills/Grammar
- Metaphor and Simile Essay (SE p. 514)
- Concrete and Abstract Nouns (TWE p. 510)
- Journal (TWE p. 514)

Literary Elements
- Form and Structure (SE p. 508)
- Language of Poetry (SE pp. 508–509)
- Sound of Poetry (SE p. 509)
- Literary Analysis (SE pp. 510–511)
- Limericks (TWE p. 512)

UNIT THREE

Poetry

Looking Ahead

According to Nicaraguan poet Daisy Zamora, poetry is "a way of feeling life." But how does poetry help us "feel" life? Poetry captures intense experiences or creative perceptions of the world in a musical language. If prose is like talking, poetry is like singing.

PREVIEW **Big Ideas and Literary Focus**

1	BIG IDEA: Nature Inspires	LITERARY FOCUS: Form and Structure
2	BIG IDEA: Life Lessons	LITERARY FOCUS: Language
3	BIG IDEA: The Strength of Family	LITERARY FOCUS: Sound Devices

INDIANA ACADEMIC STANDARDS (pages 506-513)

9.3.7 Recognize and understand the significance of various literary devices, including figurative language, imagery...and symbolism...

9.3.11 Evaluate the aesthetic qualities of style, including the impact of diction and figurative language on tone, mood, and theme.

Focus

Summary

The unit begins with an introduction to form, structure, language, and sound in poetry. It includes quotes from writers on reading poetry as well as an analysis of "The Charge of the Light Brigade."

Viewing the Art

Pollard Willows and Setting Sun was painted by Vincent van Gogh (1853–1890) in 1888, the year he moved from Paris to Arles in Provence, in the south of France. The light, colors, and landscapes of Provence inspired Van Gogh. During this prolific period, his technique matured, and many of his works were saturated with color, such as his famous *Sunflowers*.

Ask: What poems does the painting remind you of? *(Prompt students to include rhymes, song lyrics, and plays written in verse.)* **AS**

Unit Resources

Classroom Management Tools
- TeacherWorks Plus™ CD-ROM
- StudentWorks Plus™ CD-ROM
- Literature Launchers™: Pre-Reading Videos DVD, Unit Three

Core Instructional Support
- Unit 3 Resources (Fast File)
- Literature Online, glencoe.com
- Presentation Plus!™ CD-ROM, Unit Three

Transparencies
- Literary Elements Transparencies 45, 59, 60, 61, 62, 67, 68, 69, 70, 71, 72, 73, 74
- Bellringer Options Transparencies: Selection Focus Transparencies 28–42 Daily Language Practice Transparencies 44–69

Differentiated Instruction
- Active Learning and Note Taking Guide, pp. 78–112
- Skill Level Up!™ A Language Arts Game

Assessment
- Selection and Unit Assessments, Unit Three, pp. 83–132, 215–216
- Exam*View*® Assessment Suite CD-ROM
- Assessment by Learning Objectives, pp. 26–40

Supplemental Reading
- Glencoe Literature Library
- Glencoe BookLink 3 CD-ROM
- *inTIME* Magazines

Teach

Write on the board:

- Imagery
- Figurative Language
  - Simile
  - Metaphor
  - Hyperbole
- Rhythm and Meter
- Rhyme

Leave space under each heading. As you go through the section, pause at each topic and ask students for examples. List examples under the appropriate headings and have students copy the lists into their notebooks. OL

★ Writer's Technique

Sound Elements The use of sound elements such as rhythm, meter, and rhyme is an integral part of a poet's technique. Shakespeare, for example, is known for his use of iambic pentameter. Edna St. Vincent Millay is noted for her sonnets. AS

Study Central Have students visit the Web site for resources that will help them to review poetry.

Genre Focus: Poetry

What distinguishes poetry from prose?

Mexican poet Octavio Paz believes that "the poem is an original and unique creation, but it is also reading and recitation: participation." Paz's point is that poetry is meant to be read, understood, and *enjoyed.* Literary elements such as figurative language, rhyme, and rhythm help us to enjoy a poem.

The Form and Structure of Poetry

Organization

The **structure** of a poem is its organization of images, ideas, words, and lines. Most poems are divided into **stanzas**—the "paragraphs" of poetry. Each stanza contains a prescribed number of **lines**—rows of words that may or may not form sentences. Some poems have regular stanzas. For example, each stanza of "A Red, Red Rose" has four lines. However, a poem can have stanzas of different lengths.

O, my love is like a red, red rose,
That's newly sprung in June.
O, my love is like the melody,
That's sweetly play'd in tune

—Robert Burns, **from "A Red, Red Rose"**

★ The Language of Poetry

Imagery

Imagery is descriptive language used to represent objects, feelings, and thoughts. Images appeal to one or more of the five senses and are intended to remind readers of something they have seen, heard, tasted, smelled, or touched.

The room is full
of the scent of crushed hibiscus,
my mother's breath.

—Chitra Banerjee Divakaruni, **from "My Mother Combs My Hair"**

Figurative Language

Figurative language is words used differently from their ordinary, literal meanings. Poets use figurative language to bring power, vitality, and freshness to their writing. A **figure of speech** is a word or expression not meant to be taken literally. Simile, metaphor, personification, and hyperbole are all figures of speech.

Literature Online **Study Central** Visit www.glencoe.com to review distinguishing poetry from prose.

Additional Support

Skills Practice

WRITING: Note Taking Suggest that students record their observations about various poems in a notebook for future reference. Have them copy the following headings: **Poem-Speaker; Lines and Stanzas; Rhythm and Meter; Rhyme/ Sound Devices; Imagery; Figures of Speech.** OL

- A **simile** uses the word *like* or *as* to compare two seemingly unlike things.

> How dreary—to be—Somebody!
> How public—like a Frog—
>
> —Emily Dickinson, **from "I'm Nobody! Who are you?"**

- A **metaphor** compares two or more different things by stating or implying that one thing *is* another.

> The sun is a smoldering fire,
> That creeps through the high gray plain,
>
> —Vachel Lindsay, **from "An Indian Summer Day on the Prairie"**

- **Hyperbole** uses exaggeration to express strong emotion, make a point, or evoke humor.

> And I will come again, my love,
> Tho' it were ten thousand mile!
>
> —Robert Burns, **from "A Red, Red Rose"**

The Sound of Poetry

Rhythm and Meter

Rhythm is the pattern of stressed and unstressed syllables in a line of poetry. A poem's rhythm can be regular or irregular. **Meter** is the regular pattern of stressed and unstressed syllables that can establish the rhythm of a poem. The basic unit of measuring meter is the **foot**. A foot usually contains one stressed syllable marked with ´ and one or more unstressed syllables marked with ˘.

> I've heard it in the chillest land—
> And on the strangest Sea—
> Yet, never, in Extremity,
> It asked a crumb—of Me.

> —Emily Dickinson, **from "'Hope' is the thing with feathers—"** L2

Rhyme

Rhyme is the repetition of the same stressed vowel sounds and any succeeding sounds in two or more words. For example, *stop* rhymes with *drop*. **Internal rhyme** occurs when two words in the same line rhyme. **End rhyme** occurs at the end of lines. In this passage, the end rhymes are underlined.

> I know what the caged bird feels, alas!
> When the sun is bright on the upland slopes;
> When the wind stirs soft through the springing grass,
> And the river flows like a stream of glass;
>
> —Paul Laurence Dunbar, **from "Sympathy"**

Teach

L1 Literary Element

Rhythm Have a volunteer read the poem out loud, emphasizing the stressed and unstressed syllables. Have students count the number of stressed and unstressed syllables.

Ask: What is the meter of "'Hope' is the thing with feathers—"? *(There are four feet in the first and third lines and three feet in the second and fourth lines.)* **OL**

L2 Literary Element

Rhyme **Ask:** What is the rhyme scheme of "'Hope'"? *(It is abbb.)* **OL**

English Language Coach

Figurative Language English language learners may have trouble decoding new vocabulary in the context of figurative language. Note the *smoldering fire* metaphor in the lines by Lindsay. Explain that the poem's title is a clue to *smoldering*'s meaning. Point out that *Indian summer* refers to the warm days in late fall. Then read definitions of *smoldering* from a dictionary and thesaurus aloud. Stress the "double meaning" (flames/dying embers) associated with the word and discuss how it captures the particular quality of early autumn. **EL**

Academic Standards

Additional Support activities on pp. 508 and 509 cover the following standards:

Skills Practice: **9.5.2** Write responses to literature that demonstrate an awareness of the author's style and an appreciation of the effects created…

English Language Coach: **9.1.1** Identify and use the literal and figurative meanings of words…

Teach

R Reading Strategy

Reading Poetry **Ask:** How does the poem's rhythm and rhyme affect you? *(Urge students to characterize these elements and explain their personal reactions.)* Suggest that when they read a poem, they should ask themselves the following questions:

- What is the rhythm like—fast, slow, regular, or irregular?
- What sound devices are used?
- What effect do these elements have on the mood and on me? **OL**

★ Writer's Technique

Repetition Note Tennyson's use of repetition. The pounding rhythm of the poem echoes the sound of marching, drumming, hoof beats, and gunfire, bringing the battle to life and drawing the reader into the center of the drama. **AS**

Literary Analysis Model

How do literary elements create meaning in a poem?

In his poem "The Charge of the Light Brigade," Alfred, Lord Tennyson pays tribute to the 673 soldiers who made an ill-advised charge against Russian artillery positions near Sebastopol, Russia, during the Crimean War (1853–1856). Fought largely on the Crimean Peninsula in what is now Ukraine, the war began after Russia tried to expand into the Black Sea region by invading Turkish territory.

APPLYING Literary Elements

 **Rhythm**

The repeated phrases of the first stanza suggest galloping horses. Tennyson maintains this rhythm throughout.

R Rhyme

Notice that the last word in line 12 rhymes with the last word of the fourth line of stanzas 3 and 5 as well as the words *wondered* and *sundered* in stanzas 4 and 6. It also forms a slant rhyme with *hundred* throughout the poem.

The Charge of the Light Brigade

by Alfred, Lord Tennyson

Half a league, half a league,
Half a league, onward
All in the valley of Death
    Rode the six hundred.
"Forward, the Light Brigade!
Charge for the guns!" he said.
Into the valley of Death
    Rode the six hundred.

"Forward, the Light Brigade!"
Was there a man dismayed?
Not though the soldier knew
    Someone had blundered.
Theirs not to make reply,
Theirs not to reason why,
Theirs but to do and die.
Into the valley of Death
    Rode the six hundred.

Cannon to right of them,
Cannon to left of them,
Cannon in front of them,
    Volleyed and thundered;
Stormed at with shot and shell,
Boldly they rode and well,

John Charlton 1889 reproduced in "The Nation's Pictures."

Additional Support

Skills Practice

GRAMMAR AND LANGUAGE: Concrete and Abstract Nouns
Note that abstract nouns name ideas, while concrete nouns name objects recognizable by the senses. Write down *valley* and *Death* on the board and ask students to categorize each noun (*valley*—concrete; *Death*—abstract). Have students locate other examples that link abstract and concrete nouns and explain how the combinations make the poem more vivid. **OL**

Into the jaws of Death,
Into the mouth of hell
Rode the six hundred.
Flashed all their sabers bare,
Flashed as they turned in air
Sabering the gunners there,
Charging an army, while
All the world wondered.
Plunged in the battery smoke
Right through the line they broke;
Cossack and Russian
Reeled from the saber stroke
Shattered and sundered.
Then they rode back, but not,
Not the six hundred.

Cannon to right of them,
Cannon to left of them,
Cannon behind them
Volleyed and thundered;
Stormed at with shot and shell,
While horse and hero fell,
They that had fought so well
Came through the jaws of Death,
Back from the mouth of hell,
All that was left of them,
Left of six hundred.

When can their glory fade?
O the wild charge they made!
All the world wondered.
Honor the charge they made!
Honor the Light Brigade,
Noble six hundred!

Metaphor
Tennyson uses fiercely dramatic metaphors (24 "jaws of death", 25 "mouth of hell") to describe the challenge the soldiers face in the charge.

Imagery
Words like *volleyed* and *thundered* help the reader "hear" the action on the battlefield.

Structure
Tennyson shortened the final stanza in order to emphasize his themes of courage and honor.

Alfred, Lord Tennyson, ca. 1860. Mathew Brady. Photograph.

Reading Check

Interpreting What effect does the repetition of words and lines have on the depiction of the battle?

Teach

Reading Check

Answer: *The repetition re-creates the sounds of battle and evokes a feeling of inevitability and omnipresent danger. The soldiers must do their duty and ride into the fray even though they are surrounded. The relentless rhythm gradually builds a sense of impending doom.*

L Literary Element

Imagery Ask: In addition to *volleyed* and *thundered,* what other words from this stanza evoke strong images? *(Possible answers: "jaws of Death" or "mouth of hell.")* **OL**

Viewing the Photograph

Mathew Brady (1823–1896) is probably best known for his striking Civil War photographs, but he started out as a portrait photographer. He photographed many famous people of his time including politicians and authors. When the Civil War began in 1861, Brady hired a team of photographers to document the war. Although Brady rarely photographed the war himself, the photos are attributed to him because he would not credit them to his staff members. **AS**

English Language Coach

Subject-Verb Order English language learners may need help with sentences that invert subject-verb order. On the board, write: *Into the mouth of hell rode the six hundred.* Have students rephrase the sentence so that the subject precedes the verb, and then have students work in pairs to locate other unusual sentence constructions. Have students rewrite the lines to include missing words and express complete thoughts. **EL**

Academic Standards

Additional Support activities on pp. 510 and 511 cover the following standards:

Skills Practice: **9.6.2** Demonstrate an understanding of…proper English usage…

English Language Coach: **9.6.2** Demonstrate an understanding of sentence construction…

Teach

R Reading Strategy

Reading Poetry Ask: If one way of creating poetry is "inspired" what is the other? *(Students should infer that the other way is through hard work, through process.)*
Ask: Which way do you think Roethke's example of "catchy" poetry came about? Why? *(An argument could be made for either–the rhythm and internal rhymes were probably worked out, but there is also something "mysterious" and inspired about it. Most poems probably involve both.)* OL

★ Literary History

Octavio Paz Mexican poet and essayist Octavio Paz (1914–1998) won the 1990 Nobel Prize in Literature. Paz was a prolific essayist, as well as a poet. His work was influenced by his diplomatic career and covered topics ranging from Mexican identity, history, and politics to art criticism. AS

Writers on Reading

What do writers say about poetry?

Rhythm in Poetry

What do *I* like? Listen:

Hinx, minx, the old witch winks!
The fat begins to fry!
There's nobody home but Jumping Joan,
And father, and mother, and I.

Now what makes that "catchy," to use Mr. Frost's word? For one thing: the rhythm. Five stresses out of a possible six in the first line, though maybe "old" doesn't take quite as strong a stress as the others. And three—keep noticing that magic number—internal rhymes, *hinx, minx, winks*. And notice too the apparent mysteriousness of the action: something happens right away—the old witch winks and she sets events into motion.

R —Theodore Roethke, **from *On the Poet and His Craft***

"Our poems will have failed if our readers are not brought by them beyond the poems."

—Muriel Rukeyser

The Precision of Poetry

The medium of poetry is language, our common property. It belongs to no one and to everyone. Poetry never entirely loses sight of how the language is being used, fulfilled, debased. We ought to speak more often of the precision of poetry, which restores the innocence of language, which makes the language visible again. Language is an impure medium. Speech is public property and words are the soiled products, not of nature, but of society, which circulates and uses them for a thousand different ends. L

—Edward Hirsch, **from *How to Read a Poem***

The Survival of Poetry

How many and what kind of people read poems?—is inevitably bound up with the question of the survival of poetry in the modern world. And that question, in turn, is bound up with one of greater urgency and graver import: the survival of humanity itself. The poem, founded on the fraternity of the elements, forms, and creatures of the universe, is a model of survival. Hugo said it in a magnificent phrase: *Tout cherche tout, sans but, sans trêve, sans repos*—Everything seeks everything, without purpose, without end, without cease. The relationship between man and poetry is as old as our history: it began when human beings began to be human. The first hunters and gatherers looked at themselves in astonishment one day, for an interminable instant, in the still waters of a poem. Since that moment, people have not stopped looking at themselves in this mirror. And they have seen themselves, at one and the same time, as creators of images and as images of their creations. For that reason I can say, with a modicum of certainty, that as long as there are people, there will be poetry.

—Octavio Paz, **from *The Other Voice*** 

The Inspired Poem

Poems come into being in two ways. There are those which are—or used to be—spoken of as *inspired*; poems which seem to appear out of nowhere, complete or very nearly so; which are quickly written without conscious premeditation, taking the writer by surprise. These are often the best poems; at least, a large proportion of those that I have been "given" in this way are the poems I myself prefer and which readers, without knowledge of their history, have singled out for praise. Such poems often seem to have that aura of authority, of the incontrovertible, that air of being mysteriously lit from within their substance, which is exactly what a poet strives to attain in the poems that are hard to write. But

Additional Support

Skills Practice

LITERARY ELEMENT: Limericks
Some students may find poetry intimidating. To show that poetry can be fun, read some limericks from Edward Lear's *Book of Nonsense.* Explain the pattern of a limerick.

Write on the board:
- Five lines
- *aabba* rhyme scheme

Ask volunteers to write examples of this rhyme scheme on the board. *(Possible answers: fine, line, grow, know, mine).*

Student Working at his Desk, ca. 19th century. German school.

though the inspired poem is something any poet naturally feels awed by and grateful for, nevertheless if one wrote only such poems one would have, as it were, no occupation; and so most writers, surely, are glad that some of their work requires the labor for which they are constitutionally fitted. For the artist—every kind of artist, and, I feel sure, not only the artist but everyone engaged in any kind of creative activity—is as enamored of the process of making as of the thing made.

—Denise Levertov, **from *The Poet in the World*** 

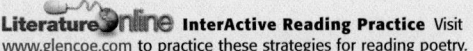

Literature Online **InterActive Reading Practice** Visit www.glencoe.com to practice these strategies for reading poetry.

Reading Check

Responding From your own reading experiences, which passage do you identify with most closely? Explain.

Teach

Reading Check

Answer: *Answers will vary. Make sure students support their responses with reasons.*

L Literary Element

Diction **Ask:** Why is diction so important in poetry? *(Students should note the condensed nature of poetry, making the language choices all the more crucial.)* **OL**

Literary History

Denise Levertov Activism and commitment deeply informed Denise Levertov's (1923–1997) life and poetry. Greatly influenced by William Carlos Williams, Levertov used her simple, clear style to speak out against the Vietnam War and support feminism. **AS**

InterActive Reading Practice Have students access the Web site for more practice with reading strategies.

Brainstorm a list of possible limerick topics for students to use. Invite students to share their limericks with the class. **OL**

Differentiated Instruction

Author's Points Ask volunteers to read each of the quotes aloud. Then, have the class paraphrase each author's point. In a discussion of the various points, urge students to tell why they agree or disagree with each one. **BL**

Academic Standards

Additional Support activities on pp. 512 and 513 cover the following standards:

Skills Practice: **9.4.1** Discuss ideas for writing with classmates, teachers…and develop drafts alone…

Differentiated Instruction: **9.7.7** Make judgments about the ideas under discussion and support those judgments with convincing evidence.

Assess/Close

Guide to Reading Poetry

Suggest to students that they consider the following when reading a poem three times:

- On the first reading consider your overall response to the poem.
- On the second, ask what ideas, emotions, and images the poet is trying to convey.
- On the third, read for structure and language and make notes about the different elements.

Elements of Poetry

Suggest that students make a checklist of all the elements of poetry to reference.

Activities

1. **Speaking/Listening** Suggest that while practicing in front of the mirror, students experiment with tone of voice and hand gestures.
2. **Visual Literacy** Suggest students choose a genre that they really enjoy for their comparison. Have students look for similarities between the two genres.
3. **Writing** Remind students that they can use everyday objects in their metaphors.

Wrap-Up

Guide to Reading Poetry

- Pay attention to the ways a poem may "refresh language" and make it seem new.
- Use your emotions, experiences, and imagination to help you create meaning in a poem.
- Read a poem at least three times: once for enjoyment, once for meaning, and once for structure and language.
- Respond to a poem as a whole before analyzing its details.

Elements of Poetry

- Poems are organized into stanzas. Each **stanza** contains one or more **lines.**
- **Imagery** is descriptive language that appeals to the five senses: sight, sound, smell, touch, taste.
- **Figurative language** is language used for descriptive effect, often to imply ideas indirectly.
- A **figure of speech** is a specific device or kind of figurative language, like a **simile** or a **metaphor.**
- **Rhythm** is the pattern of stressed and unstressed syllables in a line of poetry.
- **Rhyme** and other sound devices repeat certain sounds to create musical effects.

Activities

Use what you learned about reading and analyzing poetry to do one of these activities.

1. **Speaking/Listening** Memorize a stanza of Tennyson's "Charge of the Light Brigade." Practice your delivery in front of a mirror, and then recite your stanza for the class.
2. **Visual Literacy** Create a Venn diagram that compares and contrasts poetry with another literary genre. Use the center section to record elements the two genres have in common.
3. **Writing** Write a brief essay explaining the difference between the terms *metaphor* and *simile.* Write your own examples of each type of figurative language to include.

THREE-POCKET BOOK

Try using this study organizer to keep track of the Big Ideas in this unit.

INDIANA ACADEMIC STANDARDS (page 514)
9.3.2 Compare and contrast the presentation of a similar theme or topic across genres...
9.5.3 Write expository compositions...

Additional Support

Have students make and label the Three-Pocket Book. They can insert their notes on each Big Idea in the pockets.

Skills Practice

WRITING: Journal Urge students to record ideas for poems, practice writing descriptions, and record their questions and reactions to poems in a journal. **OL**

Academic Standards
The Additional Support activity on p. 514 covers the following standard:
Skills Practice: **9.5.8** Write for different purposes..., adjusting tone, style, and voice as appropriate.

Nature Inspires

The Rooster, 1928. Marc Chagall. Fundacion Coleccion Thyssen-Bornemisza, Madrid, Spain.

BIG IDEA

BI Many poets take their subjects from nature. A flower, a bug, a morning, or an entire day—from these natural elements poets draw lessons about the human condition. The poems in Part 1 react to nature in various ways. As you read them, ask yourself: How much of the world around me do I really see?

Analyzing and Extending

BI Big Idea

Nature Inspires **Ask:** When is the last time you saw a sunset? Engage students in a discussion of subjects from the natural world that could inspire them to create art. Suggest students list elements of nature that they see on the way to and from school. Have students share their observations with the class. OL

Viewing the Art

At various points in his career, Russian artist Marc Chagall (1887–1985) was exposed to cubism, the suprematist movement, Fauvism, and surrealism. Rather than joining any one movement, Chagall used elements from each to create his own style. Chagall believed in the idea of the artist as messenger, and this theme can be seen throughout his work.

Ask: How does the artist relate to nature in this painting? *(Students may discuss the subject of the painting or the mood created by the artist toward his subject.)* AS

English Language Coach

Building Background Nonnative language learners may be unfamiliar with the various nature preservation efforts in the United States. Suggest they research the National Park Service and other U.S. conservation efforts. EL

Differentiated Instruction

Visualizing Poetic Effects Visual learners may be inspired by Chagall's unusual use of color. Suggest they create their own painting of a subject from nature in the style of Chagall. Have students discuss their projects in class. BL

Academic Standards

Additional Support activities on p. 515 cover the following standards:

English Language Coach: **9.2.4** Synthesize the content from several sources or works…; paraphrase the ideas and connect them to…related topics…

Differentiated Instruction: **9.7.13** Identify the artistic effects of a media presentation and evaluate the techniques used to create them.

Part 1: Skills Scope and Sequence

Readability Scores Key
Dale-Chall/DRP/Lexile

PACING (DAYS) STANDARD	BLOCK	SELECTIONS AND FEATURES	LITERARY ELEMENTS
2 class sessions	1	"I Wandered Lonely As A Cloud" by William Wordsworth, pp. 518–523	Rhyme and Rhyme Scheme, SE pp. 519, 522 Form and Structure, SE p. 522
		"who are you,little i" by E. E. Cummings, pp. 524–527	Speaker, SE pp. 525, 526, 527
2 class sessions	1	"A Red, Red Rose" by Robert Burns, pp. 528–531	Meter and Rhythm, SE pp. 529, 531
		"A Noiseless Patient Spider" by Walt Whitman, pp. 532–536	Free Verse, SE pp. 533, 534, 535 Tone, SE p. 535
1–2 class sessions	1	TIME magazine, "The Island Within" by Leslie Marshall **7.0/60/1130**, pp. 537–540	
		COMPARING LITERATURE Across Genres "An Indian Summer Day on the Prairie" by Vachel Lindsay, pp. 541–545 "North Shore Mornings" by Patricia Hampl **6.2/62/1140**, pp. 546–549 "Earth Your Dancing Place" by May Swenson, pp. 550–551	Line and Stanza, SE pp. 543, 544, 545
2 class sessions	1	"The Black Snake" by Mary Oliver, pp. 552–555	Parallelism, SE pp. 553, 554, 555
		"The Peace of Wild Things" by Wendell Berry, pp. 556–559	Enjambment, SE pp. 557, 558, 559 Visualizing a Scene, TWE p. 558

About the Part

Part 1 deals with poetry about nature and the environment.

READING AND CRITICAL THINKING	VOCABULARY	WRITING AND GRAMMAR	LISTENING, SPEAKING, AND VIEWING
Previewing, SE pp. 519, 520, 522 Paraphrasing, TWE p. 520	Word Origins, SE pp. 519, 522 Academic Vocabulary, SE p. 522	Analyze Imagery and Mood, SE p. 523 Using Semicolons in Poetry, SE p. 523	Group Activity, SE p. 521 Literature Groups, SE p. 523
Analyzing Style, SE pp. 525, 526, 527		Respond to Theme, SE p. 527	Reading Aloud, TWE p. 526
Making Inferences About the Speaker, SE pp. 529, 530, 531	Academic Vocabulary, SE p. 531	Revise a Traditional Song, TWE p. 530	Interdisciplinary Activity: Music, SE p. 531
Monitoring Comprehension, SE pp. 533, 536	Word Parts, SE pp. 533, 536 Academic Vocabulary, SE p. 536 Researching Word Histories, TWE p. 534	Evaluate Author's Craft, SE p. 536	
Determining Main Idea and Supporting Details, SE p. 537; TWE pp. 538, 539 K-W-L Chart, TWE p. 538		Parenthetical Information, TWE p. 539 Describing, TWE p. 540	
Comparing and Contrasting Imagery, SE pp. 543, 544, 545 Sensory Detail, TWE p. 544	Academic Vocabulary, SE p. 545	Analyze Stanzas, SE p. 545 Essay on Structure, SE p. 551	Analyzing Art, SE p. 549; TWE p. 547 Choral Reading, TWE p. 550 Visual Display, SE p. 551 Group Activity, SE p. 551
Analyzing Mood, SE pp. 553, 554, 555	Academic Vocabulary, SE p. 555	Evaluate Author's Craft, SE p. 555 Connotations, TWE p. 554	Analyzing Art, TWE p. 554
Analyzing Cause-and-Effect Relationships, SE pp. 557, 559	Synonyms, SE pp. 557, 559	Respond to Conflict, SE p. 559	

Part 1: Skills Scope and Sequence (continued)

Readability Scores Key
Dale-Chall/DRP/Lexile

2–3 class sessions	1–2	HISTORICAL PERSPECTIVE on Nature Inspires: "A Mysterious Poetic Effect" from *Devil in the White City* by Erik Larson **12.0/70/1410**, pp. 560–564	
		Grammar Workshop: Making Subjects and Verbs Agree, p. 565	
		"Haiku" by Bashō, Chiyo, Paula Yup, and Katy Peake, pp. 566–571	Haiku, SE pp. 567, 568, 570 Diction, SE p. 570
		Vocabulary Workshop: Using a Thesaurus, p. 572	

Analyzing Cultural and Historical Context, SE p. 560; TWE p. 563 Monitoring Comprehension, TWE p. 562	Conjure, TWE p. 562		Analyzing Art, TWE pp. 561, 563
		Subject-Verb Agreement, SE p. 565	
Interpreting Imagery, SE pp. 567, 568, 570 Making Critical Judgments, TWE p. 568	Analogies, SE pp. 567, 570 Academic Vocabulary, SE p. 570	Analyze Cultural Context, SE p. 571 Using Colons in Poetry, SE p. 571	Group Activity, SE p. 569 Art Activity, SE p. 571
	Using a Thesaurus, SE p. 572		

Focus

BELLRINGER

Bellringer Options

Daily Language Practice Transparency 45

Or build a house of cards. Pull a card out from the foundation. When the house collapses, have students explain the importance of form and structure in architecture. *(The need for a firm foundation and the visual effect of the building)* Note that form and structure are just as crucial in poetry. Discuss how these elements relate to poetry.

Teach

L Literary Element

Form and Structure Ask: Do you have a preference for a particular structure or form in poetry? Why? Discuss why certain elements in poetry appeal to them. OL

Literary Elements Have students access the Web site to improve their understanding of form and structure.

LITERARY FOCUS

Form and Structure

How do form and structure affect meaning in a poem?

L Poets pack a lot into a small space. When you read a poem, you can be sure that each word and phrase was chosen carefully by the poet. Even the organization and appearance of a poem can be important aspects of fully understanding the meaning. Form and structure both address organization in poetry—the order of the ideas presented and the sound and visual patterns created by the poet's choices.

Form

The **form** of a poem is its prescribed pattern, usually involving meter, rhyme, rhyme scheme, and structure.

Stanza The basic unit of form is the **stanza**—a group of lines that create a unit. A **line** of poetry is a word or row of words that may or may not form a complete sentence. Calvin's poem about Hobbes is written in couplets, or sets of two rhyming lines. The chart at right shows several options for stanza length. Poets are not limited by these options, however. For example, some poems have stanzas of varying lengths, and other poems have no stanza divisions at all. Whatever the form, be sure to consider how the poet's choice affects the overall meaning.

Some Common Forms

Type	Lines per stanza
couplet	two
quatrain	four
cinquain	five
sestet	six
octave	eight

Additional Support

Skills Practice

LITERARY ELEMENT: Form and Structure Assign groups of students to research one of the following: ballads, sonnets, quatrains, or couplets. Each group should bring at least three examples to class. Have students explain to the class how the form and structure affects the meaning of the poems. Encourage students to include visual and sound elements and explain their relationship to the poems. OL

Rhythm

Rhythm is the pattern of sound created by the arrangement of stressed and unstressed syllables in a line. Rhythm can be regular or irregular. **Meter** is a regular pattern of stressed and unstressed syllables, which sets the overall rhythm of certain poems. The basic unit of meter is the foot. A foot usually contains two or three syllables with varying patterns of stress.

Scansion The analysis of the meter in a line of poetry is called **scansion.** To scan a line of poetry means to note the stressed (´) and unstressed (˘) syllables and to divide the line into its feet, or rhythmic units. For example, look at the meter in these lines from Robert Burns's poem "A Red, Red Rose":

And fare | thee weel, | my on | ly love,
And fare | thee weel | a while!

—Robert Burns, **from "A Red, Red Rose"**

Rhyme

Rhyme is the repetition of the same stressed vowel sounds and any succeeding sounds in two or more words. For example, *sing* rhymes with *ring*. **End rhyme** is the rhyming of words at the end of a line, while internal rhyme is the rhyming of words within a single line. **Slant rhyme** occurs when the sounds of words are similar but not identical. For example, *soul* and *all* are slant rhymes in this poem by Emily Dickinson.

"HOPE" is the thing with feathers
That perches in the soul,
And sings the tune without the words,
And never stops at all,

—Emily Dickinson, **from "'HOPE' is the Thing with Feathers"**

Rhyme Scheme The **rhyme scheme** is the pattern of end rhyme in a poem. You can mark the rhyme scheme of a poem by using a different letter of the alphabet for each new rhyme. Many types of poems have specific rhyme schemes. Using *a* to denote the first rhyme, *b* the second, and so on, you can see that the poem below follows an *abab* rhyme scheme.

who are you,little i a
(five or six years old) b
peering from some high a
window;at the gold b

—E. E. Cummings, **from "who are you,little i"**

Structure

R

The **structure** of a poem is created through the organization of its images, ideas, words, and lines. They may use rhythm and rhyme to connect ideas. They may use stanzas to separate the poem into distinct parts, in much the same way paragraphs separate the ideas in an essay. Each stanza within a poem may serve a different purpose. For example, one stanza could describe a problem, one stanza could explore its solutions, and one stanza could re-create a time before the problem existed.

Quickwrite

Writing Recall the nursery rhymes you heard as a child, such as "Humpty Dumpty" and "Hickory Dickory Dock." What can you remember about their form and structure? What did their rhythm sound like? What were their rhyme schemes? Write your recollections.

LiteratureOnline Interactive Literary Elements Handbook Go to www.glencoe.com to review or learn more about form and structure.

INDIANA ACADEMIC STANDARDS (pages 516–517)
9.2 Develop strategies such as...identifying and analyzing structure...
9.5.1 Write...autobiographical narratives...
9.5.2 Write responses to literature...

English Language Coach

Slant Rhyme English language learners may find slant rhyme challenging. Have a student read the Dickinson poem aloud. Note the similar but not identical sounds of *soul* and *all.* Ask students to volunteer their own examples of slant rhyme. EL

Differentiated Instruction

Sound Elements Auditory learners will excel at the sound elements of poetry. Challenge them to provide examples of rhyme, end rhyme, and slant rhyme and to write a poem using them. AL

Teach

R Reading Strategy

Reading Poetry Suggest that when analyzing a poem for structure, students first look at the poem as a whole and note anything unusual about the structure. OL

Viewing the Cartoon

Bill Watterson's *Calvin and Hobbes* has run in more than 2,400 papers and is one of the most popular cartoons of all time. The hallmarks of Watterson's style include fine drawing and character-driven humor.

Ask: How do the form and structure of Calvin's poem affect your understanding of it? *(Students may say that the structure makes the poem easy to understand and adds to the humor.)* AS

Assess

Quickwrite

Students' memories will vary. Make sure their written recollections are specific and address various aspects of form and structure.

Academic Standards

Additional Support activities on pp. 516 and 517 cover the following standards:

Skills Practice: **9.7.15** Deliver expository (informational) presentations...

English Language Coach: **9.3.7** Recognize and understand the significance of various literary devices...

Differentiated Instruction: **9.5.8** Write for different purposes and audiences, adjusting tone, style, and voice as appropriate.

BEFORE YOU READ

FOCUS

BELLRINGER

Bellringer Options
Selection Focus Transparency 28
Daily Language Practice Transparency 46
Or display images of nature (flowers, trees, animals in their natural habitats).
Ask: What do you feel when you look at these images? How does nature affect your life? Have students consider as they read how nature affects the poem's speaker.

Author Search To expand students' appreciation of William Wordsworth, have them access the Web site for additional information and resouces.

Use the CheckPoint questions on Presentation Plus! to monitor students' comprehension. These questions can be used with interactive response keypads for immediate student feedback.

BEFORE YOU READ

I Wandered Lonely as a Cloud

MEET WILLIAM WORDSWORTH

English literature in the 1700s was dominated by values of intellect, order, and restraint—values some people found stifling. Then a rebellious young genius came along and revitalized poetry. His name was William Wordsworth.

Exciting Education Wordsworth was born and raised in England's Lake District, an area of breathtaking scenery. His mother died when he was eight, and he and his three brothers were sent to live at a boarding school. There, Wordsworth was free to hike, skate, and explore the countryside. As an adult, he often wrote about these happy times.

"One impulse from a vernal wood
May teach you more of man,
Of moral evil and of good,
Than all the sages can."

—William Wordsworth
from "The Tables Turned"

After completing his studies at Cambridge University, Wordsworth visited France, where he became an ardent supporter of the French Revolution. He wished to stay in France, but a lack of money forced him to return to England. There, unhappiness at not finding suitable employment, and the growing conviction that the revolution had compromised its democratic ideals, brought Wordsworth to the brink of mental collapse.

Pioneer of Poetry In 1795 Wordsworth began to enjoy happier times. He came into enough money to move into a small cottage with his sister Dorothy, who was his close friend and confidante, and soon afterward, he met the poet and critic Samuel Taylor Coleridge. The meeting resulted in what has been called the most significant friendship in English literature. Coleridge inspired new ideas in Wordsworth and encouraged Wordsworth to follow his own path as a writer.

Spontaneity, excess, power, and emotion: These are the traits of Romanticism praised by Wordsworth and Coleridge in a famous book of poems called *Lyrical Ballads.* The two placed a high value on nature and intuition and advocated a poetry that spoke simply and to the heart. Together, the poets championed many ideas that continue to influence literature. For example, Wordsworth argued that the language of literature need not be classical or formal but could be pared down and commonplace. He wrote of rustic, humble people whose feelings were genuine and pure and who lived in communion with nature. To his early readers, this emphasis on ordinary people was radical.

Wordsworth spent most of his life back in the Lake District with his wife, Mary, and his sister. When he died, he was one of the most famous and revered figures in England.

William Wordsworth was born in 1770 and died in 1850.

Literature Online **Author Search** For more about William Wordsworth, go to www.glencoe.com.

Selection Skills

I Wandered Lonely as a Cloud

Literary Elements
- Rhyme and Rhyme Scheme (SE pp. 519, 522)

Reading Skills
- Previewing (SE pp. 519, 520, 522)
- Paraphrasing (TWE p. 520)

Vocabulary Skills
- Word Origins (SE pp. 519, 522)
- Academic Vocabulary (SE p. 522)

Listening/Speaking/Viewing Skills
- Visual Literacy: Photograph (SE p. 521)

Writing Skills/Grammar
- Using Semicolons in Poetry (SE p. 523)
- Analyze Imagery and Mood (SE p. 523)

LITERATURE PREVIEW

Connecting to the Poem

The full meaning of a personal experience often does not become clear until much later. Before you read the poem, think about the following questions:

- What memories comfort you when you are lonely or sad?
- What are the rewards of solitude?

Building Background

The Lake District of northern England is famous for its scenic mountains, hills, and lake-strewn valleys. As an avid student of nature, Wordsworth explored the Lake District on many long walks. The experience that inspired "I Wandered Lonely as a Cloud" occurred on a walk that Wordsworth took in the Lake District countryside on April 15, 1802, with his beloved sister and companion, Dorothy. She was also moved by the experience and recorded it in her journal. Today, thousands of tourists flock each year to the picturesque Lake District, which was incorporated as a national park in 1951.

Setting Purposes for Reading

Big Idea Nature Inspires

As you read, think about how nature's beauty can provide encouragement and joy in times of trouble.

Literary Element Rhyme and Rhyme Scheme

Rhyme is the repetition of the same stressed vowel sounds and any succeeding sounds in two or more words, as in *cat* and *bat.* **End rhyme** occurs at the ends of lines of poetry. **Rhyme scheme** is the pattern that end rhymes form in a stanza or poem. As you read, notice how Wordsworth uses rhyme and rhyme scheme to evoke a particular feeling.

- See Literary Terms Handbook, pp. R14–R15.

LiteratureOnline **Interactive Literary Elements Handbook** To review or learn more about the literary elements, go to www.glencoe.com.

READING PREVIEW

Reading Strategy Previewing

Previewing can help you get more meaning from a text. To preview, first read the title and think about what it may mean. Then look at any accompanying art, such as illustrations, and at how the text is organized. Skim the text to get a sense of what it is about. Then predict what the author's purpose for writing might be. Finally, set a purpose for your reading—a goal that you aim to accomplish while reading.

Reading Tip: Taking Notes Use a chart to record your thoughts as you preview the poem. Then write down your predictions about the poem and your purpose for reading.

My thoughts after . . .

Reading title	
Looking at art	
Skimming poem	

My prediction about poem:

My purpose for reading:

Vocabulary

host (hōst) *n.* a great number; a multitude; p. 520 *We saw a host of animals at the zoo.*

solitude (sol′ ə to͞od′) *n.* isolation; the state of being alone; p. 520 *After a hectic day of working with others, Maria retreated to the solitude of her apartment.*

Vocabulary Tip: Word Origins The origin and history of a word is called its etymology. A dictionary is usually the best place to find the etymology of a particular word.

INDIANA ACADEMIC STANDARDS (pages 519–523)

9.3.11 Evaluate the aesthetic qualities of style, including the impact of diction...on mood...

9.2 Develop strategies such as...identifying and analyzing structure...

9.5.1 Write...autobiographical narratives...

9.5.2 Write responses to literature...

BEFORE YOU READ

Focus

Summary

The poem's speaker recalls taking a walk and seeing a field of yellow daffodils. He does not understand the flowers' impact on him until the memory provides him with pleasure at a later time.

V Vocabulary

Vocabulary File Say: Add these words and definitions to your vocabulary file. For each word, include a sentence that gives you an example of how to use the word. **OL** Students with English language needs should include the pronunciations of these words in their files. **EL**

Literary Elements Have students access the Web site to improve their understanding of rhyme and rhyme scheme.

Selection Resources

Print Materials
- Unit 3 Resources (Fast File), pp. 17–19
- Leveled Vocabulary Development, p. 38
- Selection and Unit Assessments, pp. 83–84
- Selection Quick Checks, p. 42

Transparencies
- Bellringer Options Transparencies: Selection Focus Transparency 28 Daily Language Practice Transparency 46
- Literary Elements Transparency 60

Technology
- TeacherWorks Plus™ CD-ROM
- StudentWorks Plus™ CD-ROM
- Presentation Plus!™ CD-ROM
- Literature Online, glencoe.com
- Online Student Edition, mhln.com
- Exam*View*® Assessment Suite CD-ROM
- Vocabulary PuzzleMaker CD-ROM
- Listening Library, disc 1 track 48

Teach

R Reading Strategy

Previewing Answer: *Students may say the poem will be about loneliness or isolation. They may find the comparison with a cloud intriguing and suggest that the poem will talk about the spirit.*
Say: Look for clues in the text and use your own experiences to make a prediction. As you read, confirm or correct your predictions. OL

BI Big Idea

Nature Inspires Answer: *The speaker compares the daffodils to sprightly dancers.*
Ask: How is the speaker affected by the flowers? *(He feels great pleasure when he remembers them.)* OL

Literary History

The Romantic Movement
In the preface to *Lyrical Ballads,* Wordsworth signaled a momentous cultural change. He called poetry the expression of a "spontaneous overflow of feeling." In stressing feeling over intellect and individuals over society, he helped define Romanticism. This movement embraced folk tradition, explored spirituality, and glorified human struggles. AS

I Wandered Lonely as a Cloud

William Wordsworth

Big Daffodils, 1990. John Newcomb. Casein on canvas. Private Collection.

I wandered lonely as a cloud
That floats on high o'er vales and hills,
When all at once I saw a crowd,
A **host**, of golden daffodils;
Beside the lake, beneath the trees,
Fluttering and dancing in the breeze.

Continuous as the stars that shine
And twinkle on the milky way,
They stretched in never-ending line
Along the margin of a bay:
Ten thousand saw I at a glance,
Tossing their heads in sprightly[1] dance.

The waves beside them danced; but they
Outdid the sparkling waves in glee:
A poet could not but be gay,
In such a jocund[2] company:
I gazed—and gazed—but little thought
What wealth the show to me had brought:

For oft,[3] when on my couch I lie
In vacant or in pensive mood,
They flash upon that inward eye
Which is the bliss of **solitude**;
And then my heart with pleasure fills,
And dances with the daffodils.

1. *Sprightly* (sprīt′ lē) means "lighthearted" or "merry."
2. *Jocund* (jok′ ənd) means "cheerful" or "carefree."
3. *Oft* is an old, poetic form of "often."

Reading Strategy Previewing *After reading the title and first line, what do you think the poem might be about?* R

Big Idea Nature Inspires *To what does the speaker compare the daffodils?* BI

Vocabulary

host (hōst) *n.* a great number; a multitude

solitude (sol′ ə to͞od′) *n.* isolation; the state of being alone

Additional Support

Skills Practice

READING: Paraphrasing Explain that a good way to understand literature—particularly poetry where meaning is not always clear or direct—is to paraphrase it. A paraphrase is a restatement of a text, line for line, in one's own words. Have students work independently or with partners to paraphrase Wordsworth's poem. Ask volunteers to read aloud their paraphrases. Lead a class discussion in which students talk about how paraphrasing did or did not aid in their comprehension of the events described in the poem and of the poem's meaning. OL

RESPONDING AND THINKING CRITICALLY

Respond

1. Which lines from the poem did you find most memorable, powerful, or surprising? Explain.

Recall and Interpret

2. (a)In your own words, describe the scene that the speaker sees. (b)Why does the speaker find the sight so special?
3. (a)What is the "wealth" that the sight brings to the speaker? (b)Why do you think the speaker experiences that "wealth" after the fact, rather than at the moment of his vision?
4. Explain what the speaker means by the "inward eye" in line 21.

Analyze and Evaluate

5. "I Wandered Lonely as a Cloud" is considered by many to be one of Wordsworth's most memorable poems. What do you think makes it memorable?
6. Wordsworth uses personification in this poem, that is, he gives human qualities or characteristics to elements in nature. What does his use of this technique suggest about his response to the scene?

Connect

7. **Big Idea** **Nature Inspires** (a)Why do you think nature brings so much joy to the speaker? (b)The theme of a poem is its overall message about life or human nature. What, in your opinion, is the theme of this poem?

VISUAL LITERACY: PHOTOGRAPH

Finding Inspiration in Nature

Study this photograph of the Lake District of northern England. Notice the details it reveals, such as water, plants, trees, grass, mountains, hills, and the contours of the landscape.

Group Activity Discuss the following questions with classmates. Refer to the poem for evidence to support your answers.

1. What parts of the scene in the photograph could serve as the setting for "I Wandered Lonely as a Cloud"?
2. Does the photograph help you better understand the source of Wordsworth's inspiration? Explain.

England's Lake District

AFTER YOU READ

Assess

1. Students should support answers with text details.
2. (a) The speaker sees a field of daffodils beside a lake; the flowers and water ripple in the wind. (b) The color, movement, and sudden appearance of the view surprise and delight him.
3. (a) The "wealth" is a recurring image of the daffodils, which brings pleasure and lightens his mood. (b) The speaker enjoys many returns; he experiences the vision of the flowers again and again in his memory.
4. The "inward eye" is memory or the mind's eye.
5. Students may say that the poem is memorable because its elements reinforce the happy mood and theme of "bliss of solitude." A harmony of sounds, clear and appealing images, and positive language create a pleasing whole.
6. By making the daffodils dance, the speaker conveys not only the movement of the flowers but his delight in them.
7. (a) Nature brings the speaker so much joy because in the moment, his experience is so fresh, unexpected, and life-affirming. Later, his memory of the moment lifts his spirits. (b) Students may mention the restorative power of nature.

CheckPoint

Use the CheckPoint questions on Presentation Plus! to check students' mastery of the selection. These questions can be used with interactive response keypads for immediate student feedback.

Visual Literacy: Photograph

1. The clouds, the lake, and the shore along the lake could all be part of the setting of the poem.
2. Answers will vary. Students may suggest after viewing the photograph that they understand how Wordsworth could feel so moved by a scene in nature.

Academic Standards

The Additional Support activity on p. 520 covers the following standard:

Skills Practice: **9.5.2** Write responses to literature that demonstrate a comprehensive grasp of the significant ideas of literary works…

AFTER YOU READ

Assess

Literary Element

1. The rhyme scheme may be described as *ababcc*.
2. The rhyme helps create a mood of cheerful harmony, with each stanza's musical rhyme unifying the whole effect.

Reading Strategy

1. Students may say that they thought the poem would be sadder than it turned out to be.
2. Students may say that they predicted the author's purpose would be to make connections with nature, and the subject would be clouds, flowers, or other natural objects.
3. Answers will vary. Students should support their answers. They may say that by previewing the poem, they were prepared to learn about or enjoy one writer's views on nature.

Vocabulary

1. a
2. a

LITERARY ANALYSIS

Literary Element Rhyme and Rhyme Scheme

Wordsworth uses **end rhyme** and a particular **rhyme scheme** in "I Wandered Lonely as a Cloud" to create various effects. For example, the emphasis of certain sounds helps create a mood, or feeling, that reinforces the point of the poem. Rhyme scheme is designated by the assignment of a different letter of the alphabet to each new rhyme. For example, the first four lines of Wordsworth's poem have an *abab* rhyme scheme.

1. What is the rhyme scheme of the entire poem?
2. What is the mood of the poem? Explain how rhyme and rhyme scheme contribute to the mood.

Review: Form and Structure

As you learned on pages 516–517, **form** is the external pattern of a poem—its rhythm, rhyme scheme, and organization by line and stanza. The **structure** of a poem is related to form; it is created through the organization of images, ideas, and words. The writer organizes the form and structure of a work of literature in order to present a unified impression to the reader. Without an organized form and structure, a poem would not be a coherent whole.

Partner Activity Meet with another classmate and discuss the form and structure of "I Wandered Lonely as a Cloud." How do they interact to create a coherent whole? Work with your partner to create a web diagram like the one below. Fill in the diagram with examples of elements that help unify the poem.

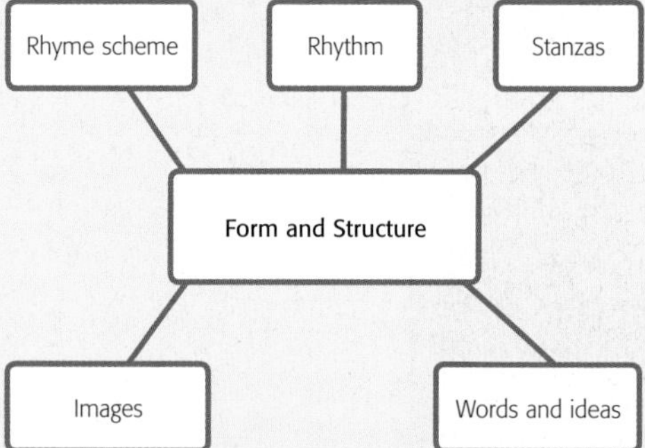

READING AND VOCABULARY

Reading Strategy Previewing

Now that you have previewed and read the poem, you should have enough information to answer the following questions.

1. How did your initial thoughts about the meaning of the title change as you read the poem?
2. What did you predict the author's purpose would be? What did you predict the subject of the poem would be?
3. How did previewing help prepare you for reading?

Vocabulary Practice

Practice with Word Origins The origins of most words can be found in a dictionary. Usually, the language from which the word came reveals something about the word's history. For each vocabulary word below, choose its language of origin. Use a dictionary.

1. host
   a. Middle English **b.** Greek **c.** Sanskrit
2. solitude
   a. Latin **b.** Norse **c.** Greek

Academic Vocabulary

Here are two words from the vocabulary list on page R80. These words will help you think, talk, and write about the selection.

relax (ri laks′) *v.* to become less tense

trigger (trig′ ər) *v.* to start a sequence of events

Practice and Apply

1. What helps the speaker **relax** when he is in a pensive mood?
2. What **triggers** the speaker's change in mood as he walks alone?

Review: Form and Structure

Students' web diagrams should indicate how the parts of the poem interact. Students should see how the stanzas (with regular rhyme scheme and rhythm, and uniform length) and the poet's choice of words help express the idea that nature can be a source of delight and inspiration.

Academic Vocabulary

1. He remembers the daffodil scene.
2. He suddenly sees a lovely field of daffodils beside a lake.

WRITING AND EXTENDING

Writing About Literature

Analyze Imagery and Mood Imagery is descriptive language that appeals to the senses. In a paragraph or two, discuss the imagery in "I Wandered Lonely as a Cloud." How does it help create a strong mood, or feeling, from stanza to stanza? What mood or moods do the images suggest to you? Write a brief essay explaining your answer.

As you write, follow the path shown here to help organize your essay.

Introductory paragraph or statement telling your purpose
↓
Types of imagery and descriptive detail
↓
Types of mood created
↓
Conclusion summarizing your main idea and adding insight

After you complete your draft, meet with a peer reviewer to evaluate each other's work and suggest revisions. Then proofread and edit your draft to correct errors in spelling, grammar, and punctuation.

Literature Groups

Dorothy Wordsworth wrote this description of the daffodils she spotted while walking with her brother:

> [We] saw that there was a long belt of them along the shore, about the breadth of a country turnpike road. I never saw daffodils so beautiful. They grew among the mossy stones about and about them; some rested their heads upon these stones as on a pillow for weariness; and the rest tossed and reeled and danced, and seemed as if they verily laughed with the wind, that blew upon them over the lake; they looked so gay, ever glancing, ever changing.

Using specific details from each account, debate within a small group which writer, Dorothy or her brother, has given the more meaningful description of the same experience.

GRAMMAR AND STYLE

Wordsworth's Language and Style

Using Semicolons in Poetry In "I Wandered Lonely as a Cloud," Wordsworth uses a semicolon to emphasize the contrast between the waves and the daffodils:

> The waves beside them danced; but they
> Outdid the sparkling waves in glee:

The semicolon is a punctuation mark with several uses. It can be used to join independent clauses that are not linked by a coordinating conjunction such as *and* or *but*. It can also be used between items in a series if the items contain commas. It can be used before a coordinating conjunction to join independent clauses that contain commas, or, as in the lines quoted, to emphasize a separation or contrast between the clauses.

Activity Study Wordsworth's use of semicolons in the first and last stanzas of the poem. What is the function of the semicolons? How would emphasis or meaning change if Wordsworth had used another punctuation mark in place of a semicolon?

Revising Check

Semicolons in Poetry Look back at your essay on imagery and mood in "I Wandered Lonely as a Cloud." You probably listed various images and the ways in which they contribute to mood. With a partner, go through your analysis to see if you could have used semicolons to clarify lists with many commas. Would adding a semicolon help you suggest a particular contrast or emphasis? Revise your essay as necessary.

Literature Online **Web Activities** For eFlashcards, Selection Quick Checks, and other Web activities, go to www.glencoe.com.

AFTER YOU READ

Assess

Writing About Literature

Use these criteria when evaluating students' writing:

- The introduction clearly states a purpose or main idea about the poem's mood. It identifies at least one mood.
- The body paragraphs contain details from the poem that support the main point about mood.
- The conclusion restates the main idea and offers insight into the writer's own feelings about the poem.

Wordsworth's Language and Style

In the first stanza, Wordsworth uses a semicolon to reduce the number of commas and to separate phrases separated by commas. To drop the semicolon and use a period would bring the reader to a full stop and disrupt the rhythm. To use a comma would be confusing. In the last stanza, Wordsworth uses a semicolon before the coordinating conjunction *and*. He uses the semicolon to separate the recalled moment from the pensive mood and to heighten the contrast.

Web Activities Have students access the Web site for interactive activities that will help them assess their understanding of the selection.

Literature Groups

Possible response: William Wordsworth is more poetic because he uses rhyme, meter, and a poetic form; he imparts more meaning to the experience than his sister does. Dorothy's account is more straightforward and accessible.

Revising Check

Students may benefit from listing the rules of semicolon use before revising their analysis. Before inserting a semicolon or using one to replace a comma, they should review the rules. Challenge students to use a semicolon at least once and to explain why they used it.

Focus

BELLRINGER

Bellringer Options
Selection Focus Transparency 29
Daily Language Practice Transparency 47
Or display an image of a sunset.
Ask: Have you ever stopped to watch a sunset? What did it make you feel or think? Have students consider as they read the poem how nature affects the speaker.

Author Search To expand students' appreciation of E. E. Cummings, have them access the Web site for additional information and resources.

Use the CheckPoint questions on Presentation Plus! to monitor students' comprehension. These questions can be used with interactive response keypads for immediate student feedback.

BEFORE YOU READ

who are you, little i

MEET E. E. CUMMINGS

In a presentation that was later published as part of a collection titled *i: Six Nonlectures,* E. E. Cummings stated, "Poetry and every other art was and is and forever will be strictly and distinctly a question of individuality. . . ." That "i" was an important theme for this ardent individualist.

A painter, playwright, and novelist, Edward Estlin Cummings was born in Cambridge, Massachusetts, in 1894. His father was a sociology instructor at Harvard University and later a Unitarian minister. Cummings determined very early to become a poet, and his mother made up word games and other activities to nurture her son's creativity. After high school, Cummings went to Harvard. He studied Latin, Greek, and literature, exploring poetry and its traditional forms. He also published poetry in Harvard magazines, which led to his meeting people who would encourage him throughout most of his career.

From War to Writer After receiving his master's degree, Cummings went to New York City to work as a painter and poet. But when World War I began, Cummings volunteered as an ambulance driver in France. There he and a friend were arrested by the French on suspicion of spying. The two were kept with other prisoners in a large room in a detention camp. Cummings's father wrote to President Woodrow Wilson asking for help, and the poet and his friend were soon free. Out of this experience, however, came Cummings's first book, *The Enormous Room,* a witty attack on bureaucracy published in 1922.

"Poetry is being, not doing."

—E. E. Cummings

The "lowercase poet" When Cummings moved back to New York City in 1924, he was already a celebrated writer. John Dos Passos, a friend from Harvard and a successful author himself, had helped Cummings get his first collection of poems, *Tulips and Chimneys,* published in 1923. While living in Greenwich Village, Cummings developed the style of poetry writing for which he became renowned, with its unconventional use of capitalization, punctuation, spacing, and structure. Many people began printing even his name with all lowercase letters, as e. e. cummings.

Honors and awards began to flood in. Cummings was awarded Guggenheim Fellowships in 1933 and 1951. He began to tour the country, reading his poetry to an eager public. In 1958, his final work, *95 Poems,* was published. As both a person and a poet, Cummings was a champion of freedom and of the individual. His fight for individualism and nonconformity was balanced by his sense of wonder about nature and his love of family.

E. E. Cummings was born in 1894 and died in 1962.

Literature Online **Author Search** For more about E. E. Cummings, go to www.glencoe.com.

Selection Skills

who are you,little i

Literary Elements
- Speaker (SE pp. 525, 526, 527)

Reading Skills
- Analyzing Style (SE pp. 525, 526, 527)

Listening/Speaking/Viewing Skills
- Reading Aloud (TWE p. 526)

Writing Skills/Grammar
- Respond to Theme (SE p. 527)

LITERATURE PREVIEW

Connecting to the Poem

Cummings's poem describes a child looking out a window at the end of the day. Before you read, think about the following questions:

- Have you ever looked out a window and taken comfort or pleasure in what you saw?
- If so, what were you looking at? If not, what are some beautiful scenes you think would make you want to look out the window?

Building Background

Unconventional capitalization, punctuation, and spacing are the hallmarks of E. E. Cummings's poetry. They have won the poet both praise and criticism. Cummings also has been known to weave slang, jazzy rhythms, and invented words into his poems. Some of his poems are keenly critical of problems he observed, but many of his poems are joyous celebrations of life, love, and nature. Despite the nontraditional form, Cummings's poems often utilize rhyme and sound patterns.

Setting Purposes for Reading

Big Idea Nature Inspires

As you read "who are you,little i," look for details about nature and the effect it has on the speaker.

Literary Element Speaker

The **speaker** is the person (or animal or thing) that is speaking in a poem, similar to a narrator in a work of prose. Sometimes the speaker's voice is that of the poet, but this is not always the case. As you read "who are you,little i," consider whether you think the speaker is Cummings.

- See Literary Terms Handbook, p. R16.

LiteratureOnline Interactive Literary Elements Handbook To review or learn more about the literary elements, go to www.glencoe.com.

READING PREVIEW

Reading Strategy Analyzing Style

Style is the expressive qualities that distinguish an author's work, including word choice and the length and arrangement of sentences, as well as the use of figurative language and imagery. Cummings's style is highly individual and unconventional. He may capitalize words that usually are not capitalized but more often does not capitalize words that usually are. He uses punctuation such as colons, semicolons, and ampersands (&) in odd places. He may close up space between words or between words and punctuation. He often breaks lines or even words apart.

What Cummings essentially does is break down and then restructure the words and lines of his poems. This style creates a visual pattern that is just as important as the meaning and sound of the words. Therefore, analyzing Cummings's style can help you understand his poetry.

Reading Tip: Read First, Then Analyze Read the poem from beginning to end at least twice. Read it aloud or, if that is not possible, try to hear the words in your head. Ask yourself how the entire poem makes you feel and what it makes you think about. Then you can go back and look at certain pieces and parts of the poem to analyze their use and their effect. You can use a web diagram, like the one below, to help you develop your ideas.

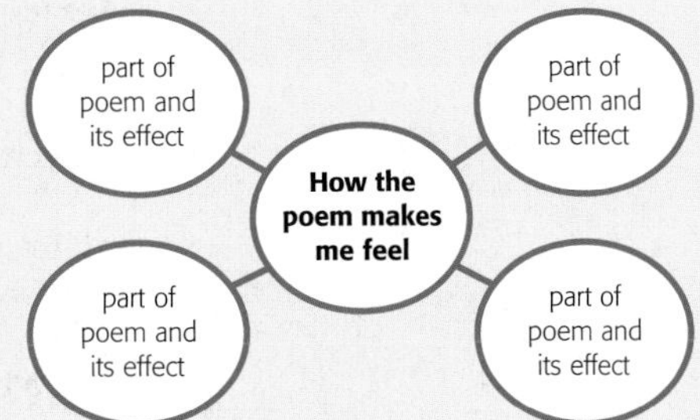

INDIANA ACADEMIC STANDARDS (pages 525-527)

9.3.13 Explain how voice...affect[s] tone...

9.3.11 Evaluate the aesthetic qualities of style, including the impact of diction and figurative language...

9.5.2 Write responses to literature...

BEFORE YOU READ

Focus

Summary

The speaker recalls a moment from childhood when he thoughtfully watched a sunset.

Literary Elements Have students access the Web site to improve their understanding of speaker.

Selection Resources

Print Materials

- Unit 3 Resources (Fast File), pp. 20–21
- Selection and Unit Assessments, pp. 85–86
- Selection Quick Checks, p. 43

Transparencies

- Bellringer Options Transparencies: Selection Focus Transparency 29 Daily Language Practice Transparency 47
- Literary Elements Transparency 21

Technology

- TeacherWorks Plus™ CD-ROM
- StudentWorks Plus™ CD-ROM
- Presentation Plus!™ CD-ROM
- Literature Online, glencoe.com
- Online Student Edition, mhln.com
- Exam*View*® Assessment Suite CD-ROM
- Vocabulary PuzzleMaker CD-ROM
- Listening Library, disc 1 track 49

Teach

L Literary Element

Speaker Explain that the speaker is the person who speaks the words in a poem. **Say:** As you read, look for clues to the speaker's identity, such as age, gender, or experiences. If you cannot find clear clues, the speaker may be the poet. **Answer:** *The speaker, who may be Cummings himself, is an adult looking back at the child he once was.* OL

R Reading Strategy

Analyzing Style Answer: *The semicolon creates a stop, or pause, in the line. Cummings is using punctuation unconventionally. The reader would not normally pause between these two words.* OL

★ Writer's Technique

Parentheses Parentheses usually set off supplemental information in a text. In Cummings' poem, however, some key details are enclosed in parentheses—the age of the young person and the young person's realization. Cummings' technique challenges a reader's expectation of how punctuation is used. AS

Songs of Sunset Series 1. Ashton Hinrichs.

who are you, little i?

E. E. Cummings

who are you,little i

(five or six years old)
peering from some high

window;at the gold

of november sunset

(and feeling:that if day
has to become night

this is a beautiful way) 

Literary Element Speaker *What can you infer about the speaker of this poem? Explain.* L

Reading Strategy Analyzing Style *Why might Cummings have placed a semicolon between the words* window *and* at? R

Additional Support

Use the CheckPoint questions on Presentation Plus! to check students' mastery of the selection. These questions can be used with interactive keypads for immediate feedback.

Skills Practice

SPEAKING: Reading Aloud Note that poems are intended to be read aloud. Ask these questions:

- What does the speaker's voice sound like in your mind?
- Who is the speaker and what is he or she like?
- What is the speaker's tone?

Have students practice reading the poem aloud, using different voice, tone, and expression to make the speaker come alive. Invite volunteers to read the poem aloud to the class. Discuss the different interpretations. OL

AFTER YOU READ

RESPONDING AND THINKING CRITICALLY

Respond

1. What did you like about this poem? Did you like the style better, or the imagery? Explain.

Recall and Interpret

2. (a)What is "little i" doing? (b)What is the relationship between "little i" and the speaker of the poem?
(c)Explain the pun, or play on words, in the name "little i" that is related to what he is doing.
3. (a)What time of day is it in the poem? What time of year? (b)How does the speaker seem to feel about these times?
4. (a)What is the speaker remembering from childhood? (b)Why do you think this event is so memorable?

Analyze and Evaluate

5. What do the time of day and time of year suggest about the speaker?
6. In this poem, an adult reflects on a childhood experience. Based on that, what might be the subtext of the lines: "(and feeling:that if day / has to become night / this is a beautiful way)"?
7. How has reading this poem affected your views of poetry in general? Explain.

Connect

8. **Big Idea** **Nature Inspires** Explain how nature inspires the speaker in "who are you,little i."

LITERARY ANALYSIS

Literary Element Speaker

The **speaker** of a poem is the person "voicing" the words. A poem is told from the perspective of the speaker. The speaker's words communicate a particular tone, or attitude, toward the subject of the poem.

1. If the speaker is the child grown up, why would he ask, "who are you"?
2. What attitude does the speaker seem to have toward the child in the poem? Explain.

Writing About Literature

Respond to Theme Freewrite a journal entry in which you recall a childhood moment when you felt closely connected with nature. Describe the time and place as well as your feelings and thoughts. Did nature calm you? In what ways? Or maybe you witnessed an awesome display of nature's power. Did it frighten you? Why or why not?

LiteratureOnline **Web Activities** For eFlashcards, Selection Quick Checks, and other Web activities, go to www.glencoe.com.

READING AND VOCABULARY

Reading Strategy Analyzing Style

Poets such as Cummings choose their writing style in order to help convey meaning and emotion.

1. How does Cummings's use of lowercase letters affect your understanding of the poem? Explain.
2. How does his use of unconventional punctuation and spacing affect your understanding of the poem? Explain.
3. (a)What is the rhyme scheme used in the poem? (b)Why might Cummings have chosen to break the rhyme scheme and not rhyme two lines?
4. What is the structure of the poem, and how does it help distinguish between the speaker as child and as adult?

Reading Strategy

1. It suggests how small the speaker ("little i") felt as a child looking at nature.
2. They link words to each other and give the poem an eager, youthful rhythm and appearance.
3. (a) *ababcded* (b) The technique jars the ear, shows contrast, and emphasizes the parenthetical nature of the last statement. It stresses endings: *sunset* and *night.*
4. There are two parts; each has 4 lines; in each part, the second and fourth lines rhyme. A space separates the parts. The first part describes the child. The second reveals the adult's understanding of the child's feelings.

AFTER YOU READ

Assess

1. Students should give reasons for their opinions.
2. (a) Peering through a high window (b) They are the same person at different times. (c) The pun refers to the speaker's younger self and to the "little eye" looking out the window.
3. (a) Dusk; November (b) Sadness or nostalgia
4. (a) Watching a sunset from a high window (b) The beauty and drama of the sunset; the memory of dreading nightfall
5. The day and the year are ending; the adult speaker may be contemplating the end of his life.
6. The adult speaker is approaching death (night) in a beautiful way by remembering the joys of youth.
7. Students should cite reasons for their responses.
8. The beauty of the sunset stayed with the speaker and enabled him to connect life with the world around him.

Literary Element

1. He feels that he has lost touch with the child he once was.
2. Affection and respect

Writing About Literature

Journal entries should describe the effect of nature on the student in the childhood moment.

Academic Standards

The Additional Support activity on p. 526 covers the following standards:

Skills Practice: **9.7** [Develop] speaking skills…in conjunction with…strategies…[for] delivery of oral presentations. **9.7.10** Assess how language and delivery affect the mood and tone of the oral communication and make an impact on the audience.

BEFORE YOU READ

Focus

BELLRINGER

Bellringer Options
Selection Focus Transparency 30
Daily Language Practice Transparency 48
Or display images associated with love, such as roses, hearts, and cupids.
Ask: What do these images suggest about the nature of romantic love? Have students consider as they read the poem how the speaker's love is or is not like a flower.

Author Search To expand students' appreciation of Robert Burns, have them access the Web site for additional information and resources.

CheckPoint

Use the CheckPoint questions on Presentation Plus! to monitor students' comprehension. These questions can be used with interactive response keypads for immediate student feedback.

BEFORE YOU READ

A Red, Red Rose

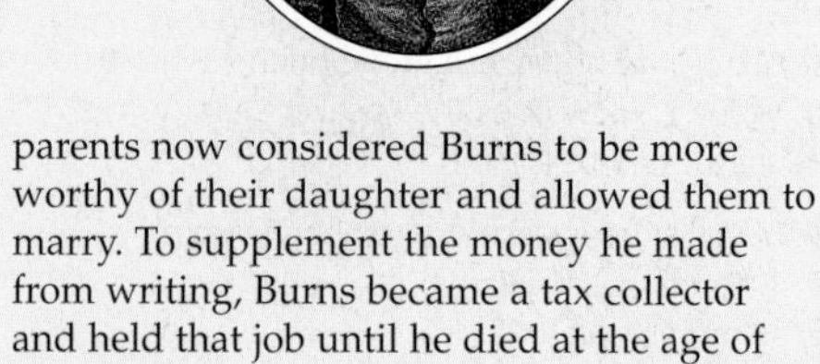

MEET ROBERT BURNS

Robert Burns wrote more than six hundred poems. If you have ever sung "Auld Lang Syne" on New Year's Eve, then you are familiar with one of his most famous works. He is considered the national poet of Scotland, and the critic Raymond Bentman says, "Robert Burns is the first truly modern poet in British literature."

> *"For my own part I never had the least thought or inclination of turning poet till I got once heartily in Love. . . ."*
>
> —Robert Burns

Early Years Burns was born in Alloway, Scotland. His father was a tenant farmer, and Burns worked as a plowboy. However, because his family valued reading and writing, his father tutored Burns and his brothers at home. His father used whatever resources he had to provide additional education for his sons. Burns grew up poor but well-read. He even taught himself to read French. He also began writing poetry in Scottish dialect. As an adult, he was as unsuccessful as his father in making a living at farming and had even less success as a flax weaver.

Unexpected Success In addition to his financial woes, Burns had other problems. He wanted to marry his girlfriend Jean Armour. When her family refused to let them marry, Burns decided to leave Scotland for the West Indies (Jamaica). To raise money for the voyage, he planned to sell a volume of the poems he had written. This book, *Poems, Chiefly in the Scottish Dialect,* was an immediate success and Burns suddenly found himself famous. Jean's parents now considered Burns to be more worthy of their daughter and allowed them to marry. To supplement the money he made from writing, Burns became a tax collector and held that job until he died at the age of thirty-seven.

Style and Form Burns wrote in the standard verse forms for eighteenth-century poets, namely epistles (verse letters), satires, epigrams, and elegies. But perhaps he was shrewd enough to realize that lyric poems would appeal to a wider audience, because during the last ten years of his life he mainly wrote songs in Scottish dialect. These poems express a wide range of emotions, from rapture to despair. Some of the lyrics, such as those in "A Red, Red Rose," are deceptively simple. Burns was also sensitive and caring enough to write many of these poems from a female point of view, often reflecting the perspective of women suffering from betrayal or loss of love. Burns's works have been translated into nearly fifty languages and have remained in print since 1786.

Ian McIntyre, a recent Burns biographer, summed up his appeal: "He does not, all that often, make us think. But he makes us laugh, and he makes us cry, and in doing so, most precious of all poetic gifts, he heightens the sense we have of our common humanity."

Robert Burns was born in 1759 and died in 1796.

LiteratureOnline **Author Search** For more about Robert Burns, go to www.glencoe.com.

Selection Skills

A Red, Red Rose

Literary Elements
- Meter and Rhythm (SE pp. 529, 531)

Reading Skills
- Making Inferences About the Speaker (SE pp. 529, 530, 531)
- Interdisciplinary Activity: Music (SE p. 531)

Writing Skills/Grammar
- Revise a Traditional Song (TWE p. 530)

LITERATURE PREVIEW

Connecting to the Poem

How do people express love? In this poem, the author uses vivid images from nature to voice his feelings. Consider other ways people express their love. Before you read the poem, think about the following questions:

- What images in nature would you use to express love?
- How do your image choices compare with Burns's choices?

Building Background

Burns wrote original songs and collected and expanded upon existing folk song lyrics and tunes. "A Red, Red Rose" is a love song that he modeled after bits and pieces from various Scottish folk songs. However, as the critic Christina Keith says, "Burns has far outstripped all his models." He composed it to the tune of "Major Graham," a song from *Oswald's Companion Book*, published in the mid-1700s.

Setting Purposes for Reading

Big Idea Nature Inspires

As you read, think about how nature can inspire, what it inspires, and how the author uses aspects of nature in this poem.

Literary Element Meter and Rhythm

Rhythm is the pattern of beats created by the arrangement of stressed and unstressed syllables, especially in poetry. Rhythm can be regular, with a predictable pattern, or irregular. When a poem has regular rhythm, the predictable pattern of stressed and unstressed syllables is called **meter.** Being aware of meter and rhythm can help you better appreciate the artistic beauty of a poem or other literary work, as well as help you grasp its purpose and meaning. As you read, pay particular attention to the poem's meter and rhythm and look for ways that they emphasize certain words and help convey meaning.

- See Literary Terms Handbook, pp. R11 and R15.

READING PREVIEW

Reading Strategy Making Inferences About the Speaker

When you infer, you use reason and your experience to decipher the author's implied meaning. **Making inferences about the speaker** helps you determine and understand the author's purpose for writing a work of literature. As you read, pay attention to details about the speaker. Consider what these details suggest about the speaker's tone and attitude, as well as about whom the speaker is addressing.

Reading Tip: Charting Inferences Use a chart to record inferences that you draw about the speaker based on the details presented.

Details	Inferences
"As fair art thou, my bonny lass"	The speaker's identity is male, and he is the lover of the woman he is addressing.

Literature Online Interactive Literary Elements Handbook To review or learn more about the literary elements, go to www.glencoe.com.

INDIANA ACADEMIC STANDARDS (pages 529-531)

9.3.7 Recognize and understand...the significance of various literary devices...

9.3.13 Explain how voice...affect[s] ...tone...

9.2.8 Make reasonable statements and draw conclusions about a text, supporting them with accurate examples.

BEFORE YOU READ

Focus

Summary

The speaker describes his deep love by comparing it to a red rose and a melody. He says his love will last across years and miles.

Literary Elements Have students access the Web site to improve their understanding of meter and rhythm.

Selection Resources

Print Materials

- Unit 3 Resources (Fast File), pp. 23–24
- Selection and Unit Assessments, pp. 87–88
- Selection Quick Checks, p. 44

Transparencies

- Bellringer Options Transparencies: Selection Focus Transparency 30 Daily Language Practice Transparency 48
- Literary Elements Transparencies 45, 61, 62

Technology

- TeacherWorks Plus™ CD-ROM
- StudentWorks Plus™ CD-ROM
- Presentation Plus!™ CD-ROM
- Literature Online, glencoe.com
- Online Student Edition, mhln.com
- Exam*View*® Assessment Suite CD-ROM
- Vocabulary PuzzleMaker CD-ROM
- Listening Library, disc 1 track 50

Teach

BI Big Idea

Nature Inspires **Answer:** *Like the rose, the speaker's love is beautiful, fresh, and vibrant.* **OL**

R Reading Strategy

Making Inferences About the Speaker **Answer:** *The speaker is committed to returning to his love, regardless of the obstacles that stand between them.* **OL**

★ Literary History

From Rebel to Traditionalist As a young man, Robert Burns considered himself a rebel. However, after the publication of his *Poems,* he wished to serve his Scottish people and preserve their songs. He spent the last years of his life collecting, editing, updating, and writing songs and poems in the Scottish tradition. **AS**

CheckPoint

Use the CheckPoint questions on Presentation Plus! to check students' mastery of the selection. These questions can be used with interactive response keypads for immediate student feedback.

A Red, Red Rose

Robert Burns ★

I

O, my love is like a red, red rose,
That's newly sprung in June.
O, my love is like the melody,
That's sweetly play'd in tune.

II

As fair art thou, my bonny lass,[1]
So deep in love am I,
And I will love thee still, my dear,
Till a' the seas gang dry.[2]

III

Till a' the seas gang dry, my dear,
And the rocks melt wi' the sun!
And I will love thee still, my dear,
While the sands o' life shall run.

IV

And fare thee weel,[3] my only love,
And fare thee weel a while!
And I will come again, my love,
Tho' it were ten thousand mile!

Rosa indica cruenta (blood-red Bengal rose), engraved by Langlois, from 'Les Roses', 1817–24. Pierre Joseph Redoute. Coloured Aquatint, 36.8 x 26.7 cm. Private collection.

1. *Bonny lass* means "pretty young woman" or "sweetheart."
2. *[Till a' the seas gang dry]* This line, in Standard English, is "Until all the seas go dry."
3. *Weel* means "well."

Big Idea Nature Inspires *How does nature compare with the speaker's love?* **BI**

Reading Strategy Making Inferences About the Speaker *What can you infer about the speaker's devotion from these lines?* **R**

Additional Support

Web Activities Have students access the Web site for interactive activities that will help them assess their understanding.

Skills Practice

WRITING: Revise a Traditional Song Ask students to think about the cultures that influence their lives and to identify songs that capture the voice or sounds of their traditions. Discuss word choices, images, rhythms, and rhymes in those songs. Then have students work in small groups to revise a song or poem from a particular culture. Encourage them to write appropriate lyrics and to find a suitable melody for their songs. Allow students to practice before they perform or read their songs for the class. **OL**

RESPONDING AND THINKING CRITICALLY

Respond

1. What image in the poem was most memorable or surprising to you? Explain.

Recall and Interpret

2. (a)To what two things does the speaker compare his love in the first stanza? (b)When the speaker says "my love," do you think he refers to the person he loves or to the love that he feels for her? Explain.
3. (a)What does the speaker promise in the second and third stanzas? (b)What imagery does he use in his promise, and why do you think he uses this language?
4. (a)In the last stanza, what event is about to happen? (b)What do you think the speaker is trying to convey by mentioning the number of miles?

Analyze and Evaluate

5. (a)How does the speaker use exaggeration, or overstatement, in the poem? What is its purpose? (b)How effective do you find the use of exaggeration?
6. Literary critic Christina Keith wrote: "Each of Burns's four verses leads on to the next, with love, like a thread of gold, linking them all together. Love is the recurrent motif. Burns has at last realized you cannot have too much of it in a love-song. Or bring it in too soon. Or pitch it too high." What do you think she meant?

Connect

7. **Big Idea** **Nature Inspires** What descriptions from nature does Burns use to describe the power of his love?

LITERARY ANALYSIS

Literary Element Meter and Rhythm

Readers can analyze a poet's use of **meter** and **rhythm** by mapping the rhythm. This type of mapping is called *scansion.* Write out each line of the poem and use stress symbols above each syllable to show the rhythm. Use a ˘ to indicate an unstressed syllable and a ´ to indicate a stressed syllable.

1. Write out the scansion for the first four lines of the poem.
2. How effective did you find Burns's use of meter and rhythm in the poem? Explain.

Interdisciplinary Activity: Music

Work in small groups to research and gather folk songs from other nations and cultures. Listen to them while reading their lyrics, and try to identify the various meters and how they function in the songs. Present your findings to the class.

LiteratureOnline **Web Activities** For eFlashcards, Selection Quick Checks, and other Web activities, go to www.glencoe.com.

READING AND VOCABULARY

Reading Strategy Making Inferences About the Speaker

Use the **inferences** you have made about the speaker to help you answer the following questions.

1. Who is the speaker and to whom is he speaking?
2. What did you infer about the speaker's feelings?
3. What details in the poem suggest the degree of the speaker's feelings?

Academic Vocabulary

Here is a word from the vocabulary list on page R80.

mutual (myōō′ chə wəl) *adj.* shared; having the same feelings

Practice and Apply
Do you think the emotion expressed in this poem is mutual? Explain.

AFTER YOU READ

Assess

1. Students may mention the rose and the melting rocks. They should provide an explanation for their answers.
2. (a) A newly bloomed rose and a pleasing melody (b) He may refer to both the woman's beauty and the depth of his love.
3. (a) to love his beloved his entire life (b) Images of natural forces show his love is strong.
4. (a) He is leaving. (b) He will return no matter what.
5. (a) Examples: "Till a' the seas gang dry" and "rocks melt wi' the sun." These show that his love is deep, long-lasting, and sincere. (b) The exaggerations work well if not interpreted literally; he is not being realistic.
6. Students should understand Keith's point that Burns knew that saturating a poem with love made for good poetry.
7. He uses vivid natural images of a red rose, seas drying, and rocks melting.

Literary Element

1.

´ ˘ ´ ˘ ´ ˘ ´ ´ ´
O, my love is like a red, red rose,
˘ ´ ˘ ´ ˘ ´
That's newly sprung in June.
´ ˘ ´ ˘ ´ ˘ ´ ˘ ˘
O, my love is like the melody,
˘ ´ ˘ ´ ˘ ´
That's sweetly play'd in tune.

2. The meter and rhythm stress key words and ideas.

Interdisciplinary Activity: Music

Students should copy songs onto a sheet of paper and then mark their meters and rhyme schemes.

Academic Vocabulary

It is impossible to know, but since the speaker feels so strongly, the reader might assume it is mutual.

Reading Strategy

1. A lover; the woman he loves
2. His love is sincere but his expression is exaggerated.
3. Seas going dry, rocks melting, sands of life running

Academic Standards

The Additional Support activity on p. 530 covers the following standard:

Skills Practice: **9.5.8** Write for different purposes and audiences, adjusting tone, style, and voice as appropriate.

BEFORE YOU READ

Focus

BELLRINGER

Bellringer Options
Selection Focus Transparency 31
Daily Language Practice Transparency 49
Or display images of spiders.
Ask: What associations might people have with spiders? Have students consider as they read what the spider and its web stand for in the poem.

Author Search To expand students' appreciation of Walt Whitman, have them access the Web site for additional information and resources.

Use the CheckPoint questions on Presentation Plus! to monitor students' comprehension. These questions can be used with interactive response keypads for immediate student feedback.

BEFORE YOU READ

A Noiseless Patient Spider

MEET WALT WHITMAN

When Walt Whitman first published *Leaves of Grass,* a collection of poetry that broke with tradition both in form and content, it caused an uproar. A critic for the *Boston Intelligencer* wrote, "The author should be kicked from all decent society as below the level of brute . . . it seems to us that he must be some escaped lunatic, raving in pitiable delirium."

Whitman, however, refused to give up. After all, not everyone disliked *Leaves of Grass.* Ralph Waldo Emerson, a major figure in American literature, read the book cover to cover, then sent off a congratulatory letter in which he praised the collection of poems as "the most extraordinary piece of wit and wisdom" the United States had yet produced. Today, *Leaves of Grass* is considered one of the most important works in American literature, and Whitman is regarded as one of the first uniquely American poets.

> *"I am as bad as the worst, but thank God I am as good as the best."*
>
> —Walt Whitman

Early Years Walt Whitman was born in Long Island, New York. His family moved to Brooklyn when he was four years old. Unfortunately, the move proved to be financially unsuccessful, and young Walt was forced to leave school. By age twelve, he was working to help support the growing family. Whitman's early departure from school did not prevent him from obtaining an education. While working for a printer, he discovered a love of books and literature, and read everything he could find. When he was seventeen, Whitman became a schoolteacher. He left teaching to pursue his interest in journalism, working as an editor for several New York and Brooklyn newspapers. On his own time, he began to experiment with writing poetry.

Civil War Years Whitman traveled a great deal, chronicling the trials and triumphs in the lives of everyday people. He considered himself a vagabond and felt that America's strength was in its working class. During the Civil War, Whitman went to Virginia to care for his injured brother George. While in Virginia, he published two more collections of poetry, *Drum-Taps* and *Sequel to Drum-Taps.* Two of Whitman's most famous poems, "When Lilacs Last in the Dooryard Bloom'd" and "O Captain! My Captain!" are found in these volumes. Both poems are elegies written for Abraham Lincoln, whom Whitman greatly admired.

Final Years Whitman spent his final years in his modest home in Camden, New Jersey. One year before he died, Whitman wrote an essay in which he looked back upon his life. He ended the essay on a hopeful note, saying, "The strongest and sweetest songs remain yet to be sung."

Walt Whitman was born in 1819 and died in 1892.

Literature Online **Author Search** For more about Walt Whitman, go to www.glencoe.com.

Selection Skills

A Noiseless Patient Spider

Literary Elements
- Free Verse (SE pp. 533, 534, 535)
- Tone (SE p. 538)

Reading Skills
- Monitoring Comprehension (SE pp. 533, 536)

Vocabulary Skills
- Word Parts (SE pp. 536)
- Academic Vocabulary (SE p. 536)

Writing Skills/Grammar
- Evaluate Author's Craft (SE p. 536)

Study Skills/Research/Assessment
- Researching Word Histories (TWE p. 534)

LITERATURE PREVIEW

Connecting to the Poem

In the title of this poem, Whitman uses the adjectives *noiseless* and *patient* to describe a spider. Before you read the poem, think about the following questions:

- What actions or habits of the spider might have led Whitman to use these adjectives to describe it?
- What other adjectives could you use to describe a spider?

Building Background

All spiders spin silky thread. Many spiders use this substance to create complex, sticky webs in which they catch food. Spiders also spin a long thread called a dragline, which can be used like a trapeze, to cross through the air from one point to another. First, the spider spins a ball of thread to form a sticky anchor. Then it swings on the dragline to a new location. Once it lands, it spins a new anchor. The result is a bridge that can be used to scurry back and forth.

Setting Purposes for Reading

Big Idea Nature Inspires

As you read the poem, note how the speaker compares the spider's actions to aspects of human behavior.

Literary Element Free Verse

Free verse is poetry that has no fixed pattern of meter, rhyme, line length, or stanza arrangement. Throughout history, great artists have stretched rules and experimented with new art forms. As you read, think about the effects that Whitman achieves by ignoring meter, rhyme, and traditional poetic structures.

- See Literary Terms Handbook, p. R8.

Literature Online **Interactive Literary Elements Handbook** To review or learn more about the literary elements, go to www.glencoe.com.

READING PREVIEW

Reading Strategy Monitoring Comprehension

A poem can pack a lot into a few lines. Therefore, readers need to pause from time to time to ask questions such as:

- How could I restate these lines?
- Is there another meaning beneath the literal one?
- How can I use my own knowledge and experiences to understand the poet's meaning?

Reading Tip: Paraphrasing As you ask questions to monitor your comprehension, use a chart to restate the poet's thoughts in your own words.

Lines of Poem	Restated
1–2	I saw a quiet, patient spider standing alone on the edge of a rock.

Vocabulary

isolated (ī′ sə lāt′ əd) *adj.* alone, cut off from others; p. 534 *The cabin stood in an isolated clearing, far away from any other structures.*

detached (di tacht′) *adj.* separated, apart; p. 534 *After moving to a new town, I felt detached from my old friends and familiar surroundings.*

ceaselessly (sēs′ lis lē) *adv.* without stopping; continually; p. 534 *The speaker went on and on, ceaselessly stressing his point of view.*

Vocabulary Tip: Word Parts When you encounter unfamiliar words, look for word parts such as prefixes *(un-, re-)* and suffixes *(-ment, -ous).* Then note the base words to which the word parts have been added.

INDIANA ACADEMIC STANDARDS (pages 533-536)

9.2 Develop strategies such as...asking questions [and]...analyzing structure...

9.3.7 Recognize and understand the significance of...imagery...

9.5.3 Write...literary analyses that gather information in support of a thesis...

BEFORE YOU READ

Focus

Summary

The poem's speaker contemplates a spider as it casts its web into a vast open space and suggests that he and the spider share the same destiny.

Literary Elements Have students access the Web site to improve their understanding of free verse.

V Vocabulary

Vocabulary File Say: Add these words and definitions to your vocabulary file. For each word, include a sentence that gives you an example of how to use the word. **OL** Students with English language needs should include the pronunciations of these words in their files. **EL**

Selection Resources

Print Materials

- Unit 3 Resources (Fast File), pp. 25–27
- Leveled Vocabulary Development, p. 39
- Selection and Unit Assessments, pp. 89–90
- Selection Quick Checks, p. 45

Transparencies

- Bellringer Options Transparencies: Selection Focus Transparency 31, Daily Language Practice Transparency 49
- Literary Elements Transparencies 45, 49

Technology

- TeacherWorks Plus™ CD-ROM
- StudentWorks Plus™ CD-ROM
- Presentation Plus!™ CD-ROM
- Literature Online, glencoe.com
- Online Student Edition, mhln.com
- Exam*View*® Assessment Suite CD-ROM
- Vocabulary PuzzleMaker CD-ROM
- Listening Library, disc 1 track 51

Teach

L Literary Element

Free Verse Answer: *The lines are of different lengths; there is no regular meter; there is no rhyme.* OL

BI Big Idea

Nature Inspires Ask: What is the connection between the spider and the speaker's soul? *(The spider's weaving its clinging threads reminds the speaker of his soul's search for meaning.)* **Answer:** *Like the spider launching its threads, the speaker's soul must go out in many directions to seek its destiny.* OL

★ Writer's Technique

Apostrophe and Catalog
Whitman uses two traditional poetic devices in this poem—apostrophe and catalog. Apostrophe is the addressing of a person or object. It often begins with an exclamation, such as *O* or *Oh.* A catalog is a list of people, things, or attributes. In this poem, Whitman addresses his soul ("O my soul") and catalogs its ceaseless activity (musing, venturing, throwing, and seeking). AS

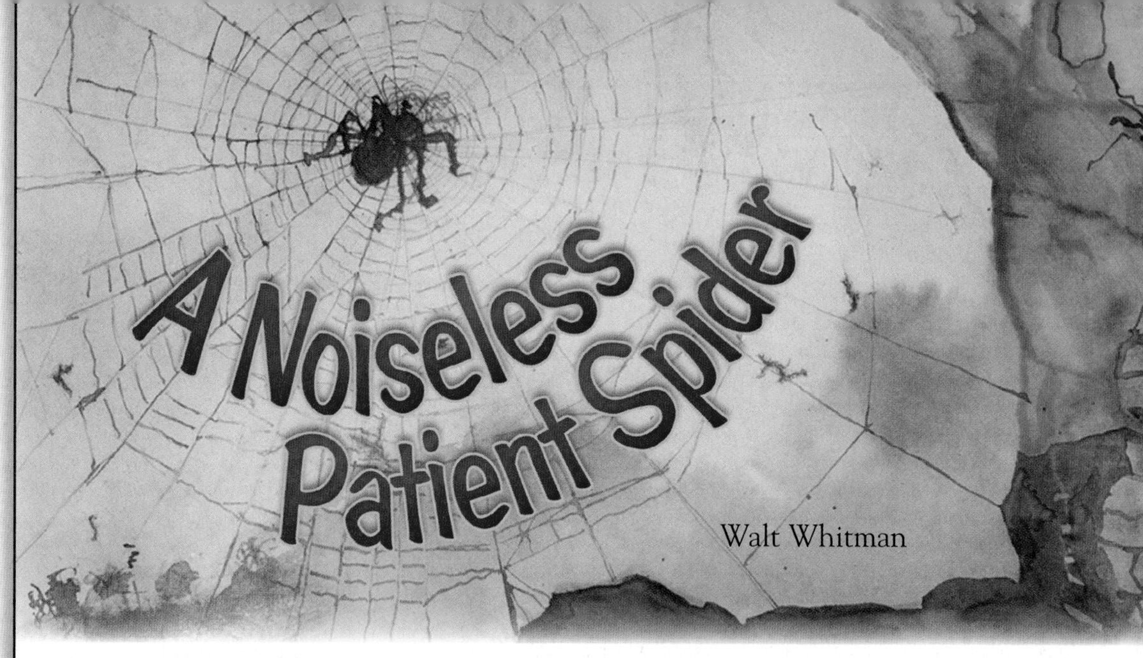

Crossing the Spider Web. Victor Hugo (1802–1885). Musee de la Ville de Paris, France.

A noiseless patient spider,
I mark'd where on a little promontory[1] it stood **isolated,**
Mark'd how to explore the vacant vast surrounding,
It launch'd forth filament,[2] filament, filament, out of itself,
Ever unreeling them, ever tirelessly speeding them.

★ And you O my soul where you stand,
Surrounded, **detached,** in measureless oceans of space,
Ceaselessly musing, venturing, throwing, seeking the spheres[3]
to connect them,
Till the bridge you will need be form'd, till the ductile[4]
anchor hold,
Till the gossamer[5] thread you fling catch somewhere, O my soul.

1. A *promontory* is a high ridge of rock or land, jutting out into a body of water.
2. Here, *filament* refers to the spider's thin thread of silk.
3. The phrase *seeking the spheres* means "seeking the truth about the heavens."
4. Something that is *ductile* (dukt′ əl) is easily molded or shaped.
5. Here, *gossamer* means "light, delicate, filmy."

Literary Element Free Verse *In what ways are lines 3–4 good examples of free verse?* L

Big Idea Nature Inspires *How do the actions of the spider remind the speaker of his own destiny? Explain.* BI

Vocabulary

isolated (ī′ sə lāt′ əd) *adj.* alone, cut off from others
detached (di tacht′) *adj.* separated, apart
ceaselessly (sēs′ lis lē) *adv.* without stopping; continually

Additional Support

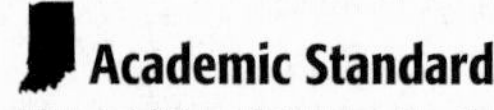

Academic Standards
The Additional Support activity on p. 534 covers the following standard:
Skills Practice: **9.1** Understand the basic features of words: word parts, patterns, relationships, and origins.

Skills Practice

VOCABULARY: Researching Word Histories Whitman uses beautiful, specific, and interesting vocabulary, such as *filament, musing,* and *gossamer.* Have students identify at least five unfamiliar words in the poem. Ask them to research the words to learn their meanings, parts of speech, roots and suffixes, and histories. Have students make a chart of the information they find. Invite volunteers to share their charts and, as a class, formulate a generalization about Whitman's choice of words. OL

AFTER YOU READ

RESPONDING AND THINKING CRITICALLY

Respond

1. What did you like best about this poem? What did you like least? Explain.

Recall and Interpret

2. (a)Where is the spider and what is it doing? (b)What might be the purpose of the spider's actions?
3. (a)What adjectives does the speaker use to describe the spider and its actions? (b)What do those adjectives suggest about his feelings toward the spider?
4. (a)How is the predicament of the speaker's soul like that of the spider? (b)What might the speaker be looking or hoping for?

Analyze and Evaluate

5. (a)How might the speaker be using the words *noiseless* and *patient* to contrast the spider with himself? (b)Do you feel sympathy for the speaker? Explain why or why not.
6. (a)The speaker compares the spider's "filament" with his soul's "gossamer thread." What is the meaning of each term? (b)Do you think the image of a person's "gossamer thread" is effective? Explain.
7. (a)In your own words, summarize the speaker's feelings for the spider. (b)Does this poem make you think about spiders in a different way? Explain why or why not.

Connect

8. **Big Idea** **Nature Inspires** In your opinion, why does this poem fit into the overall theme of "Nature Inspires"?

LITERARY ANALYSIS

Literary Element **Free Verse**

When writing **free verse,** a poet varies meter, rhyme, line length, and stanza arrangement to emphasize an idea or create a tone. Whitman's use of free verse initially shocked critics and readers who thought that he had broken the rules of poetry. However, Whitman's free verse poetry allows him to express ideas and themes in innovative and poignant ways.

1. When free verse was first used, it forced people to redefine poetry. What do you think is poetic about Whitman's work? Provide examples from the text.
2. In "A Noiseless Patient Spider," how is free verse like ordinary speech? How is it different?

Review: Tone

As you learned on page 258, the **tone** of a piece of literature is the author's attitude toward his or her subject matter. Tone is conveyed through elements such as word choice, punctuation, sentence structure, and figures of speech or comparisons. A writer's tone might convey a variety of attitudes, such as sympathy, objectivity, or humor.

Partner Activity Meet with a classmate to discuss and identify the overall tone of "A Noiseless Patient Spider." Use a cluster diagram like the one shown below to provide specific details from the poem—word choice, sentence structure, and figures of speech or comparisons—that support your ideas regarding the tone.

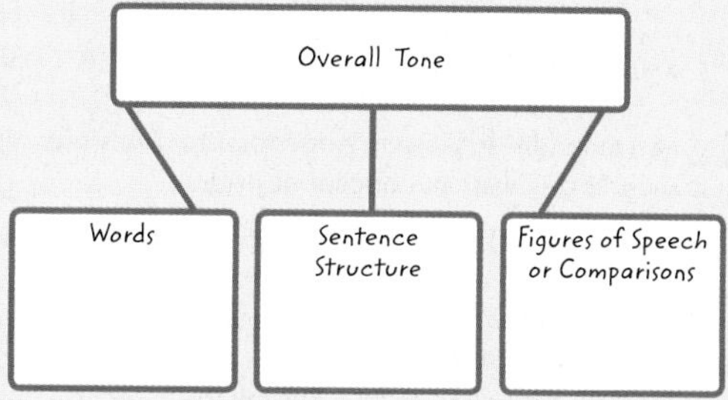

AFTER YOU READ

Assess

1. Students' answers will vary.
2. (a) It stands on a rocky overlook casting out silk strands. (b) It may use the strands to travel to a new location.
3. (a) *Patient, noiseless, isolated, tireless in its efforts* (b) He admires and respects it for its hard work and courage.
4. (a) Both are isolated in empty space and try to find an anchor. (b) The speaker might be seeking answers about life.
5. (a) Unlike the quiet, hardworking spider, the speaker is restless and unsure. (b) Students should support their answers with reasons.
6. (a) The filament is the spider's silky thread. The speaker's gossamer thread is a metaphor for the speaker's searching soul. (b) It is effective because it is visual, tactile, and easy to imagine.
7. (a) He admires the spider's courage and tenacity; he identifies with the difficulty of its task. (b) Some students may have new respect for what spiders do.
8. The speaker is inspired by the spider's actions; the spider has caused him to examine his own feelings, needs, and emotions.

CheckPoint

Use the CheckPoint questions on Presentation Plus! to check students' mastery of the selection. These questions can be used with interactive response keypads for immediate student feedback.

Literary Element

1. Students should support answers with references to the poem.
2. It expresses thoughts in sentences. Some of the language is poetic with a distinct and regular meter or vivid vocabulary—*promontory, filament,* and *gossamer.* The speaker addresses his soul in a poetic manner.

Review: Tone

Students should use graphic organizers to identify specific examples of tone. They may find that the tone is reverent, awed, or searching. Challenge students to explain how their evidence supports their ideas about the poem's tone.

AFTER YOU READ

Assess

Reading Strategy

1. The speaker feels isolated, small, and insignificant in the vast universe.
2. The narrator yearns to be able to cross into a new and meaningful part of his life.
3. The speaker does not know where he will find answers, but yearns to make a connection somewhere.

Vocabulary

1. a **2.** b **3.** c

Academic Vocabulary

1. The speaker's goal is to feel less isolated and to find answers and meaning in life.
2. The two want to fulfill different goals: the spider wants to cross a physical space, and the speaker wants to find meaning in the universe.

Writing About Literature

Students' essays should:

- use the introduction to state their point of view clearly.
- use the body of the essay to support the point of view with specific details from the poem, as well as specific features of free verse.
- use the conclusion to sum up the point of view.

READING AND VOCABULARY

Reading Strategy Monitoring Comprehension

A reader can find deeper meanings by pausing from time to time to ask questions and to rephrase certain lines in his or her own words. Review the chart you created while reading the poem.

1. Reread lines 6–7. What does the speaker mean by "detached, in measureless oceans of space"?
2. Reread lines 9–10. What does the image of building a bridge suggest?
3. In the final line, why might the speaker have chosen to use the vague word "somewhere" rather than identify a specific location?

Vocabulary Practice

Practice with Word Parts Use your knowledge of base words to choose the best definition for each word below. If you need help, use a dictionary.

1. isolation
   a. the condition of being alone
   b. solved **c.** full of sunshine
2. detachment
   a. conjoined **b.** separation **c.** unhinged
3. ceaseless
   a. inferno **b.** extinguisher **c.** unending

Academic Vocabulary

Here are two words from the vocabulary list on page R80. These words will help you think, write, and talk about the selection.

abstract (ab′ strakt) *adj.* not concrete or visible, such as the abstract concept of pride

attain (ə tān′) *v.* to gain through effort; to achieve

Practice and Apply

1. What **abstract** goal does the speaker have in this poem?
2. What is the difference between what the spider and the speaker hope to **attain**?

WRITING AND EXTENDING

Writing About Literature

Evaluate Author's Craft In this lesson, you have learned about free verse, paraphrased lines of the poem, and identified its overall tone. Now use that knowledge to write an essay that answers the following question:

Would Whitman's message and tone have been as effective if he had chosen to write this poem using a strict rhyme scheme and meter?

Follow the writing path shown here to help you organize your essay.

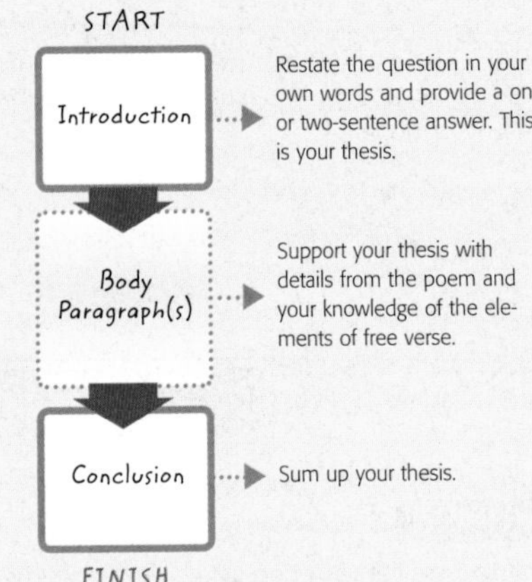

START
Introduction
Restate the question in your own words and provide a one- or two-sentence answer. This is your thesis.
Body Paragraph(s)
Support your thesis with details from the poem and your knowledge of the elements of free verse.
Conclusion
Sum up your thesis.
FINISH

After you complete your draft, have a peer read it and suggest revisions. Then proofread and edit your work to correct errors in spelling, grammar, and punctuation.

Reading Further

You might also enjoy reading the works in these collections:

Selected Poems and Prose, by Walt Whitman, which contains some of Whitman's most famous poems.

Urban Nature: Poems About Wildlife in the City, edited by Laure-Anne Bosselaar, which contains many poems that speak of inspirations watchful people can find in nature even in the most crowded and paved-over environments.

LiteratureOnline Web Activities For eFlashcards, Selection Quick Checks, and other Web activities, go to www.glencoe.com.

Reading Further

Ask students to work individually or with a partner to read additional poetry, analyze the images they find, and present their findings to the class. They may read the poems aloud and explain them or present posters with the poem text and illustrations of its images.

LiteratureOnline

Web Activities Have students access the Web site for interactive activities that will help them assess their understanding of the selection.

Academic Standards

The Additional Support activity on p. 537 covers the following standard:

English Language Coach: **9.5.9** Write or deliver a research report that...uses information from a variety of sources...

Informational Text

Media Link to Nature Inspires

Preview the Article

In "The Island Within," Leslie Marshall describes how she finds refuge in the landscape of Cumberland Island, Georgia.

1. Based on the title, what do you think this article will be about?
2. Scan the article's subheadings. What do you think the writer will describe?

Set a Purpose for Reading

Read to understand how nature and solitude influence the writer's perspective on life.

Reading Strategy

Determining Main Idea and Supporting Details
The main idea of a text is the most important thing that the writer wants to convey about his or her subject. The main idea is not always obvious; you may have to identify it from the details in the text.

As you read, create a graphic organizer to help you organize your thoughts. R

Main Idea:
Detail 1
Detail 2
Detail 3

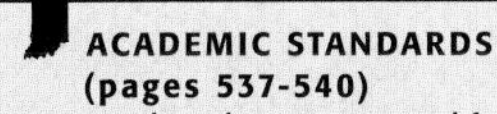

ACADEMIC STANDARDS (pages 537-540)

9.2.1 Analyze the structure and format of reference...documents, including the... headers...

9.2 Develop [reading] strategies...

9.3.2 Compare and contrast...a similar theme or topic across genres...

TIME

The Island Within

On a walk on Cumberland Island, a writer dusts off her sense of wonder—and discovers the healing power of nature.

By LESLIE MARSHALL

Whenever I feel weary, worn out, and bogged down by the complications of my modern life, all I have to do is walk into nature. The moment I step off the path of my daily routine and let myself wander, a transformation begins. For me, a walk just about anywhere will do. But a walk on Cumberland Island, off the coast of Georgia, is as good as it gets. ★

Part of Cumberland's appeal is classic island magic—that mix of adventure and simplicity that comes with geographic isolation. During a visit to this 36,415-acre wilderness, there will be no shopping, no catching a movie or a play, no working out at the gym. There will be only that rare luxury: free time.

Every time I set foot on Cumberland, I experience the fresh sense of arriving on a new stage. It is as if I am shedding my skin. Upon arriving, I am certain that my spirit will be restored by the time I leave. The island will do its work, and so will I.

Stepping Stones to Growth

I have been coming to Cumberland for years; it is a place layered with personal memories. The trips I have made here over time—some alone, some with large groups of friends, some with my husband and three children—form a series of stepping stones that chart a path of self-knowledge and growth. I have experienced some of my most peaceful moments here—and some of the most harrowing. And I have had a few lessons in the art of holding on and letting go.

On this particular trip, I have come alone, leaving my children safe at home on another island, Manhattan. After a long, gray winter in the city, I have come to dust off my sense of wonder. I have no doubt that Cumberland will jump-start my heart, mind, and imagination.

Informational Text TIME

Focus

Summary

After describing how her visits to Cumberland Island refresh her spirit, the writer tells of a recent visit there with a naturalist. Later, as she walks alone, she thinks about life cycles and how life is a gift and a miracle.

Teach

Preview the Article

1. The writer's feelings and thoughts
2. The writer's feelings about the island

R Reading Strategy

Determining Main Idea and Supporting Details In "The Island Within," the writer's main idea is a personal one—her visits to Cumberland Island restore her spirit. She supports the idea by recalling what she learned about herself. OL

★ Cultural History

Cumberland Island Cumberland Island is a barrier island that separates the Atlantic Ocean from the Georgia coast. It is unique because it has three ecological zones—beaches, forests, and saltwater marshes. AS

English Language Coach

Scientific Plant Names Students may have trouble with the scientific plant names in the essay. Have them list difficult or unfamiliar words, such as *live oak, wax myrtle bushes, sea-oat, allelopathic trees,* and *epiphytic trees.* Allow students to work together using library resources or the Internet to find information about the plants. Students who are interested in botany may wish to create a visual or multimedia presentation to illustrate and discuss plants on Cumberland Island. EL

Readability Scores

Dale-Chall: 7.0
DRP: 60
Lexile: 1130

Teach

R1 Reading Strategy

Determining Main Idea and Supporting Details Ask students to read the subheads to predict the writer's thoughts and ideas.
Ask: What do you think Marshall will talk about in the section called "Walking in Wonder"? *(She may recall amazing things she saw on a walk.)* OL

Literary History

Anne Morrow Lindbergh (1906–2001) was the wife of Charles Lindbergh, the first man to fly solo across the Atlantic Ocean. She was an accomplished writer. Like Leslie Marshall, Anne Lindbergh sought refuge in nature. In her book, *Gift from the Sea,* she wonders how women can meet responsibilities and find peace of mind and creative inspiration. AS

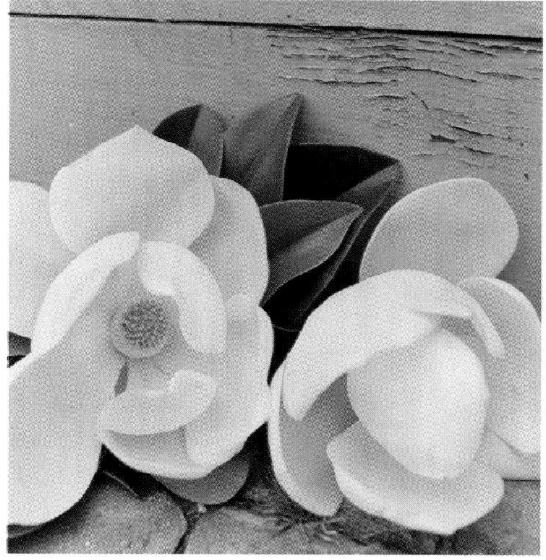
MAGNOLIA PETALS ARE LANDING STRIPS FOR POLLINATING INSECTS.

SALT MARSHES AND BOGS ARE HOMES FOR A DIVERSITY OF WILDLIFE.

Brian Doben

R1 Walking in Wonder

Stacia Hendricks, a naturalist who has lived on Cumberland for 14 years, is sitting beside me at sunrise, softly sharing her understanding of nature. "We are sitting on top of the forest right now," she tells me. "Those are the tops of live oak trees and wax myrtle bushes sticking out of the sand. They are the reason the dunes are here. They anchor the dunes." Her hushed enthusiasm is contagious. "Look at this guy," she exclaims, holding up a sea-oat seed that has sprouted a shoot of green. "Isn't he beautiful?" Stacia explains how over the years the dunes shift in response to wet and dry cycles, in a slow-motion imitation of the sea.

To walk six square feet of forest, dune field, or marsh with Stacia is to invite a lifetime of insights into the complex play of nature, science, history, commerce, and human emotion. After one early-morning inland walk, I rush home and fill several pages of a journal with a quick summary of what I've just learned. I write about allelopathic trees, like the magnolia, whose leaves contain a toxic substance that is drawn out by rain. When they fall and cover the ground, these leaves prevent other plants from growing. I write about epiphytic plants, like the Spanish moss that hangs from the live oaks all over the island. These plants have no roots, but they absorb enough moisture through their fuzzy bodies to get nourishment and thrive.

Reading the Landscape

Walking through the forest, Stacia has shown me the Lyonia plant, which is the first plant to burst into flames as fire approaches. Remarkably enough,

> "How wonderful are islands. . . . The past and the future are cut off; only the present remains. Existence in the present gives island living an extreme vividness and purity. One lives like a child or a saint in the immediacy of the here and now."
> —ANNE MORROW LINDBERGH
> *Gift from the Sea*

Additional Support

See also Active Learning and Note Taking Guide, pp. 92–98.

Skills Practice

READING: K-W-L Chart Leslie Marshall describes her impressions of Cumberland Island. Have students create a K-W-L chart before they read the essay, and then preview the selection. As a class, fill in the first column (what students know about Cumberland Island or the power of nature) and the second column (what students hope to learn). After reading, have students independently complete the third column (what they learned). Ask volunteers to share their ideas. OL

Brian Doben

SOUTHERN RED CEDAR BERRIES IN SPRING

WILD POINSETTIA SEEDS STUDIED UP CLOSE

it is also the first plant to begin growing after a fire (thanks to its nutrient-rich ashes). Stacia also shows me the sensitive (or "shy") plant, a delicate fern-like creation with a bright fuchsia blossom, which folds up its leaves when touched. Then she points out the woolly mullein plant (also known as Hunter's Friend because its leaves make good emergency toilet paper); Lion's Paw (often considered a weed, it actually produces a beautiful orange flower); and the prickly ash, called the toothache tree by Native Americans because chewing its bark numbs the mouth. (I tried it—it works!)

Stacia tells me that Native Americans, Cumberland's first residents, began living here around 2000 B.C. Next came the Spanish, who brought horses to the island. The wild horses that roam everywhere now are descendants of their horses, the work horses kept by plantation owners who came later, and the fancy riding horses imported in the 20th century. Today, most of the island is owned by the National Park Service.

There is so much I haven't yet touched on—the details of animal, fish, and bird life, the sweet symphony of sounds that has begun to sift into recognizable voices. ("Sweet, sweet, I'm so sweet!" calls the yellow-throated warbler.) It is not that I need to know all these things, or care if I get them exactly right. But a nature-walk tutorial from Stacia reminds me of how much is to be read in the activity in the landscape. After spending time with Stacia, I am ready to explore this island alone, and to explore my own inner island. R2

A Solitary Stroll

I am walking in the heat of midmorning around the ruins of Dungeness, a huge mansion that was rebuilt by Thomas and Lucy Carnegie in 1881 and burned down in 1959. (Thomas Carnegie, a steel baron, bought a large part of the island in 1881.) Along the way, I have stopped to tease a few doodlebugs—small insects that hide in the sand and wait to catch unlucky ants. I have picked up a beautiful owl feather and, after admiring the way it tapers off to make owls the quietest fliers, I've tucked it behind my ear. (Airplane designers studied owl feathers, Stacia says.) Even in the morning light, the ivy-covered remains of Dungeness are grand and exotic. "It makes a much more beautiful ruin than it ever did a mansion," the late Lucy Ferguson, granddaughter of Lucy and Thomas Carnegie, is said to have commented. It's impossible to stroll across the former lawns and gardens, now the home of wild horses and pigs, without feeling a rush of nostalgia. Everything passes, everything rots, everything gets recycled, this once grand home seems to say.

On the front lawn, a dead magnolia tree lost to lightning stands against a backdrop of lush, green marsh. The magnolia must no longer be emitting its

Informational Text

TIME

Teach

R2 Reading Strategy

Determining Main Idea and Supporting Details Each paragraph in an essay will have its own main idea.

Ask: What is the main idea of the paragraph that begins "There is so much I haven't yet touched on." *(The writer realizes there is much more to learn from the land.)* **Ask:** What details support this idea? *(She points to all the things she wants to learn about and what her friend has taught her.)* OL

★ Writer's Technique

Parenthetical Information Parentheses provide non-essential but related information in a sentence or paragraph. This parenthetical information adds color and detail to the selection and creates an informal tone. AS

Building Reading Fluency

Reading Aloud Ask student partners to find lines from the essay that contain descriptions of what the author sees as she walks. Then, have students take turns reading aloud the passages they have chosen to improve their fluency. BL

Reading in the Real World

Career Invite interested students to learn about becoming a naturalist. They should use library and Internet resources to read about how one prepares for this career and what the job entails. They should research famous naturalists. Allow students to share their findings. OL

Academic Standards

Additional Support activities on pp. 538 and 539 cover the following standards:

Skills Practice: **9.2** Develop [reading] strategies…

Building Reading Fluency: **9.7** [Develop] speaking skills…in conjunction with…strategies…[for] delivery of oral presentations.

Reading in the Real World: **9.5.9** Write or deliver a research report that has been developed using a systematic research process…

Informational Text

TIME

Assess

1. Nature may comfort or awe with its silence and beauty.
2. (a) Her friends and her family (b) For peace of mind and inspiration
3. (a) Information about the island's plants and settlers (b) She contemplates the source of living things and their end.
4. (a) Nostalgia (b) Yes, the nostalgia comes from prior visits.
5. *Optimistic, open, observant, introspective, and imaginative*
6. (a) "Arriving on a new stage," "as if I'm shedding my skin," "dust off my sense of wonder," and "read in the activity of the landscape" (b) They enhance the writer's style of writing and give her narrative a lyrical tone.
7. Because of the new insights into nature learned from Stacia Hendricks
8. Both the spider and the island are symbols of isolation and forms of inspiration.

For additional assessment, see Selection and Unit Assessment, pp. 91–92.

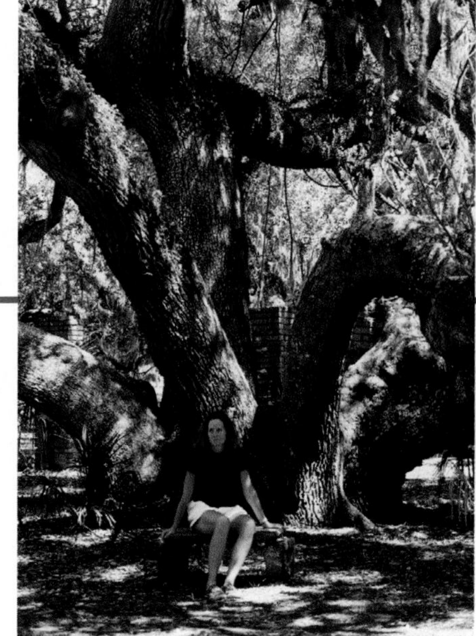
Brian Doben

THE WRITER SITTING UNDER AN ANCIENT OAK ▶

allelopathic poisons, for underneath it, all kinds of ragged plants have sprung up. Lightning is so random and so fierce.

Deeper in the forest now, on a road that leads to a pair of abandoned silos near where Stacia keeps her beehives, I pass a rotting log and a patch of mushrooms. I remember what Stacia has explained about the wonders of bacteria—what a crucial role it plays in the cycles of decay and life. Death as a process is visible everywhere on this island. Cemeteries abound. A big Indian burial mound rises from the flat of the landing field; a plantation-era group of graves lies near the marsh. I pause and listen to the multitoned whisper of the forest. It is then that I come to a realization: The miracle is not that we die, but that we are given a chance to live. Cumberland jams the circuits with evidence of this simple, radical truth; but I remind myself that a walk anywhere, properly conducted, can do the same.

—Updated 2005, from REAL SIMPLE, August 2000

RESPONDING AND THINKING CRITICALLY

Respond

1. In what ways do you think people can find solace in nature?

Recall and Interpret

2. (a)With whom has Marshall made trips to Cumberland Island? (b)Why does she travel there so often?
3. (a)What kinds of information does Stacia Hendricks, the naturalist, share with the writer? (b)How does this knowledge affect Marshall?
4. (a)What feeling does Marshall experience after viewing the Dungeness ruins? (b)Judging by her comment, do you think that she had seen the ruins before?

Analyze and Evaluate

5. What adjectives would you use to describe Marshall's personality?
6. (a)Give examples from the text of figurative language. (b)Do they work well in this context? Why or why not?
7. Of all the trips Marshall has made to Cumberland Island, why do you think she chose to write about this one?

Connect

8. Compare the literary function and purpose of the spider in Walt Whitman's "A Noiseless Patient Spider" with that of the island in Leslie Marshall's "The Island Within."

Additional Support

Academic Standards

The Additional Support activity on p. 540 covers the following standard:

Skills Practice: **9.4.3** Use precise language [and] sensory details...

Skills Practice

WRITING: Describing Marshall uses description to help readers imagine the plants and sights she sees. For example, on p. 539, she describes the sensitive (or shy) plant as "a delicate fern-like creation with a bright fuchsia blossom, which folds up its leaves when touched." Have students use the author's descriptions as a model for writing their own descriptions of three or four natural objects they see every day. Remind students to use language that appeals to the senses. Ask volunteers to share their descriptions with the class. OL

Comparing Literature Across Genres

Connecting to the Reading Selections

You may have heard or read the phrase *communing with nature.* When we commune with nature, we observe it closely, ponder it, and even lose ourselves in it. The three literary works compared here—two poems and a journal entry—celebrate nature and demonstrate how deeply it rewards our close attention.

COMPARING THE Big Idea Nature Inspires

Nature inspires different thoughts in different people. One person may perceive nature as a safe, open place for people to play in. Others may perceive it as a deep mystery. Still others view nature as a school for sharpening the senses.

COMPARING Structure

Literary works can be patterned in different ways. In poems, **structure** is sometimes created with rhythm, rhyme, repetition, or stanzas. In works of prose, there may be a variety of structures at work. For instance, works of prose may be structured by the order of the events they describe or by a simple idea that is methodically elaborated on during the course of the work. Poets Vachel Lindsay and May Swenson use poetic structures to organize their thoughts. Author Patricia Hampl adopts a prose structure to express her ideas in a journal.

COMPARING Authors' Beliefs

The authors featured here have both similar and different beliefs about nature's meaning and value. These beliefs are sometimes stated outright; at other times, they are implied through the details of the works.

Focus

BELLRINGER

Bellringer Options
Daily Language Practice Transparency 50
Or display images of the sky during different seasons or kinds of weather.
Ask: What do you notice about the sun and the sky during your day? How does the sky affect the way you feel?
As students read the selections, ask them to think about how the sun and sky affect the writers.

Connecting to the Reading Selections

Allow students to share their responses to the opening statement. Then have students discuss their experiences of reading the nature writing they have encountered in this unit. Challenge them to list characteristics of nature writing based on their experiences as readers.

Selection Skills

Comparing Literature

Literary Elements
- Line and Stanza (SE pp. 543, 544, 545)

Reading Skills
- Comparing and Contrasting Imagery (SE pp. 543, 544, 545)
- Sensory Detail (TWE p. 544)

Vocabulary Skills
- Academic Vocabulary (SE p. 545)

Listening/Speaking/Viewing Skills
- Analyzing Art (SE p. 549; TWE p. 547)
- Choral Reading (TWE p. 550)

Writing Skills/Grammar
- Analyze Stanzas (SE p. 545)

Study Skills/Research/Assessment
- Using Personal Experience (TWE p. 548)

Focus

BI Big Idea

Nature Inspires Ask: What images and words come to mind when you recall a beautiful sunrise or sunset? Have students consider as they read how the poet uses words and imagery to describe the sun as it appears to move across the sky. OL

Author Search To expand students' appreciation of Vachel Lindsay, have them access the Web site for additional information and resources.

CheckPoint

Use the CheckPoint questions on Presentation Plus! to monitor students' comprehension. These questions can be used with interactive response keypads for immediate student feedback.

An Indian Summer Day on the Prairie

MEET VACHEL LINDSAY

Vachel Lindsay was a unique and talented poet. Born in Springfield, Illinois, in a house associated with Abraham Lincoln's family, Lindsay considered himself to be a Midwesterner through and through. In his work, he attempted to embody the region's love of democracy, faith, and nature. Lindsay's parents hoped their son would become a doctor. To that end, Lindsay studied science at Hiram College. He also studied oratory, or the art of effective public speaking. It was this skill that eventually ensured his fame.

The Troubadour After giving up his scientific studies, Lindsay spent time studying art in both Chicago and New York City. In New York, he lectured on art at a local YMCA. Through the experience, art and public speaking became intertwined in his life. At this time, Lindsay was also writing poems but having little success getting them published.

> *"No one cared for my pictures, no one cared for my verse, and I turned beggar in sheer desperation."*
>
> —Vachel Lindsay

At the age of twenty-seven, Lindsay began what was to become a famous walking trip from Florida to Illinois by way of Georgia, the Carolinas, and Kentucky. To support himself, Lindsay traded lectures and poetry recitals for food and shelter. He became a troubadour, or a wandering artist. It was a role that he would repeat many times in his life.

A Democratic Poet At thirty-four, Lindsay published his first book of poetry, *General William Booth Enters into Heaven and Other Poems.* Although this book did not receive high praise, Lindsay's next book, *The Congo and Other Poems,* thrust the poet into the public eye. In 1914 Lindsay recited his poem "The Congo" at a banquet sponsored by a poetry magazine. Many famous poets, including Carl Sandburg, were in attendance. When Lindsay read his poetry, he swayed, chanted, and shouted out words. Viewers said "he rocked on the balls of his feet—his eyes blazing, his arms pumping like pistons" and "his tone [changed] color in response to the noise and savage imagery of the lines."

Lindsay believed that poetry was an oral art form that all people could appreciate. In order to appeal to a broad audience, Lindsay consciously echoed vaudeville—popular variety shows that were performed before live audiences—in his rhythms and performance style. To this day, his poems are admired for their vivid imagery and persistent, thumping rhythms.

Vachel Lindsay was born in 1879 and died in 1931.

LiteratureOnline **Author Search** For more about Vachel Lindsay, go to www.glencoe.com.

Selection Resources

Print Materials
- Unit 3 Resources (Fast File), pp. 29–30
- Selection and Unit Assessments, pp. 93–94
- Selection Quick Checks, p. 47

Transparencies
- Bellringer Options Transparencies: Daily Language Practice Transparency 50
- Literary Elements Transparencies 45, 59

Technology
- TeacherWorks Plus™ CD-ROM
- StudentWorks Plus™ CD-ROM
- Presentation Plus!™ CD-ROM
- Literature Online, glencoe.com
- Online Student Edition, mhln.com
- Exam*View*® Assessment Suite CD-ROM
- Vocabulary PuzzleMaker CD-ROM
- Listening Library, disc 1 tracks 53–55

LITERATURE PREVIEW

Connecting to the Poem

The following poem describes a fall day in the Midwest. Before you read, think about the following questions:

- What techniques do poets use to describe things?
- How does poetry help readers to share an experience?

Building Background

Vachel Lindsay was known not only as a poet, but also as a performer. He traveled around the country reciting his poems, sometimes adding sound effects with a whistle or tambourine. His performances highlighted the rhythmic quality of his poems. One audience member said, "His reading is almost singing." Dating back to as early as the late 1700s, the term *Indian summer* refers to the warm, dry, hazy days that occur during the autumn months after a killing frost.

Setting Purposes for Reading

Big Idea Nature Inspires

Since ancient times, nature has inspired artists of all kinds to create drawings, paintings, carvings, and songs. As you read the poem, notice the creativity that nature inspires in poet Vachel Lindsay.

Literary Element Line and Stanza

A **line** is a row of words in a poem. A **stanza** is a group of lines that forms a unit in a poem, much like a paragraph forms a unit in a prose selection. Usually stanzas are indicated by lines of space that break up continuous lines of text.

- See Literary Terms Handbook, pp. R10 and R16.

Literature Online **Interactive Literary Elements Handbook** To review or learn more about the literary elements, go to www.glencoe.com.

READING PREVIEW

Reading Strategy Comparing and Contrasting Imagery

Images are the "word pictures" that writers use to evoke an emotional response in readers. For example, the poem "An Indian Summer Day on the Prairie" begins with the image of the sun as a "huntress young." Most images appeal to one or more of the five senses. As you read, ask yourself these questions: What pictures, or images, come into my mind? What ideas or feelings do these images convey? How are the images alike and different?

Reading Tip: Noting Imagery Use a chart to note details that appeal to the five senses.

Image	Sense	Idea or Feeling Suggested by Image
huntress	sight	beauty

Wigeon at Sunrise, 1994. Julian Novorol. Oil on canvas. Private Collection.

INDIANA ACADEMIC STANDARDS (pages 543-545)

9.2 Develop strategies such as...identifying and analyzing structure...

9.3.7 Understand...figurative language [and] imagery...

9.5.3 Write...analytical essays...

COMPARING LITERATURE

BEFORE YOU READ

Focus

Summary

The speaker describes the sun at four times of the day. He compares it to a huntress, a fire, a wounded deer, and an aging eagle.

Literature Online

Literary Elements Have students access the Web site to improve their understanding of line and stanza.

English Language Coach

Indian Summer Have students who have experienced Indian Summer describe it in their own words. Ask them if this weather goes by a different name in other parts of the world. Invite students to share what they know about warm autumn days in their native lands. EL

Differentiated Instruction

Researching Indian Summer

Students may enjoy researching the origin of the phrase *Indian Summer.* Allow them time to consult reference tools and appropriate Web sites to do their research. Ask volunteers to share their findings with the class. Have them cite specific sources. AL

Academic Standards

Additional Support activities on p. 543 cover the following standards:

English Language Coach: **9.1.2** Distinguish between what words mean literally and what they imply and interpret what the words imply.

Differentiated Instruction: **9.7.15** Deliver expository (informational) presentations that convey information and ideas from... sources accurately and coherently...

Teach

L Literary Element

Line and Stanza **Answer:** *Each stanza describes a particular time of day.* OL

R Reading Strategy

Comparing and Contrasting Imagery **Answer:** *Both are metaphors that compare the sun to youth and age.*
Ask: What do all the poem's images have in common? *(All are of living beings, and most suggest heat or color.)* OL

★ Writer's Technique

Rhyme and Rhythm Lindsay's poem uses a rhyme scheme and meter found in many traditional ballads and songs. In each stanza, the second and fourth lines rhyme, and each line contains three beats. AS

CheckPoint

Use the CheckPoint questions on Presentation Plus! to check students' mastery of the selection. These questions can be used with interactive response keypads for immediate student feedback.

COMPARING LITERATURE

An Indian Summer Day on the Prairie

Vachel Lindsay

In the Beginning
The sun is a huntress young,
The sun is red, red joy,
The sun is an Indian girl,
Of the tribe of the Illinois.[1]

Mid-morning
The sun is a smoldering fire,
That creeps through the high gray plain,
And leaves not a bush of cloud
To blossom with flowers of rain.

Noon
The sun is a wounded deer,
That treads pale grass in the skies,
Shaking his golden horns,
Flashing his baleful[2] eyes.

Sunset
The sun is an eagle old;
There in the windless west,
Atop of the spirit-cliffs
He builds him a crimson nest. 

1. The *Illinois,* or Illini, are a tribe of Native Americans who once lived in what is now the state of Illinois. Their descendants maintain headquarters in Miami, Oklahoma.

2. *Baleful* means "threatening" or "deadly."

Literary Element Line and Stanza *What does each stanza describe?* L

Reading Strategy Comparing and Contrasting Imagery *In what way is this image like the one that begins the poem? How is it different?* R

Additional Support

Academic Standards
The Additional Support activity on p. 544 covers the following standard:
Skills Practice: **9.3.7** Recognize and understand the significance of various literary devices, including figurative language, imagery...

Skills Practice

READING: Sensory Detail Writers often choose words that appeal to the senses to help readers visualize the scene. Have students work independently, with partners or in small groups, to identify all the words in the poem that appeal to the senses. Then have students connect the appeal, such as visual images, to other senses that could be contained in that image or idea.
For example, the image of the sun as a smoldering fire is a visual image, but a fire also appeals to the senses of touch (heat) and smell (smoke). OL

AFTER YOU READ

RESPONDING AND THINKING CRITICALLY

Respond

1. In your opinion, which image from the poem most vividly portrays the sun? Explain.

Recall and Interpret

2. (a)What does the speaker compare the sun to at the beginning of each stanza? (b)Why do the comparisons differ?
3. (a)Where is the sun at mid-morning? (b)What does the speaker mean by the last line of the second stanza?
4. (a)Where is the sun at sunset? (b)Why is its nest crimson?

Analyze and Evaluate

5. (a)How are the stanzas ordered? (b)Explain why you think Lindsay organized the poem this way.
6. (a)How would you describe the poem's rhythm? (b)How did it contribute to your enjoyment of the poem? Explain.
7. What do you think of the title of the poem? Explain what details of the poem justify the inclusion of "on the prairie" in the title.

Connect

8. **Big Idea** **Nature Inspires** What kinds of feelings does nature seem to inspire in the speaker of this poem? Explain.

LITERARY ANALYSIS

Literary Element Line and Stanza

Each **line and stanza** in a poem contains distinct ideas that contribute to the poem's overall message or effect.

1. Which lines in the poem did you consider especially vivid or memorable?
2. What key ideas are expressed by each of the stanzas? What impression of the sun do the four stanzas create?

Writing About Literature

Analyze Stanzas Read the poem aloud to yourself, paying particular attention to the rhythm—the pattern of stressed and unstressed syllables—and rhymes. Also notice the analogies, or comparisons, made in each stanza. Then write a brief essay in which you discuss your insights into the rhythm, rhyme, and analogies. How would you describe the rhythm? How might the poem have been different without the rhymes? Why do the analogies vary from stanza to stanza? When you are finished with your draft, exchange it with a partner for review. Then revise your draft to correct errors in grammar, spelling, and punctuation.

LiteratureOnline **Web Activities** For eFlashcards, Selection Quick Checks, and other Web activities, go to www.glencoe.com.

READING AND VOCABULARY

Reading Strategy Comparing and Contrasting Imagery

Images are "word pictures" that appeal to the senses. Review the images in the poem.

1. (a)Which images convey positive or joyful feelings to you? (b)Which images convey power or might? Explain.
2. In your opinion, what do the images in stanzas two and three have in common with one another? How are they different? Explain.

Academic Vocabulary

Here are two words from the vocabulary list on page R80.

cycle (sī′ kəl) *n.* a series of events that keep repeating regularly from beginning to end

transit (tran′ sit) *n.* passage; trip through or across

Practice and Apply

1. What **cycle** does the poem describe?
2. What color is the sun at the beginning and end of its **transit** across the sky?

COMPARING LITERATURE
AFTER YOU READ

Assess

1. Students should use text references to support answers.
2. (a) An Indian girl, a smoldering fire, a wounded deer, an old eagle (b) Each describes the sun at a different time of day.
3. (a) It is rising higher. (b) The sun destroys the clouds and, therefore, the chance of rain.
4. (a) In the west, its light just above the cliff tops (b) The sunset turns everything red.
5. (a) Chronologically (b) The reader can easily follow the sun through its daily course.
6. (a) Possible answers: regular, persistent, driving (b) Possible answer: The rhythm helped make the poem clear.
7. It shows the setting. The Indian, the huntress, the deer, and the eagle might have appeared on prairies.
8. He is captivated or enthralled.

Literary Element

1. Students should cite specific lines and give clear reasons.
2. First: red morning sun; second: hot mid-morning sun; third: noon sun shimmering high in the sky; fourth: red sun losing strength in the west. Together they create a picture of a dazzling, powerful phenomenon of nature.

Academic Vocabulary

1. The poem describes the cycle, or series of events, in a single day.
2. The sun is red when it begins and ends its journey.

Writing About Literature

Students' essays should

- introduce their insights into the poem's rhythm, rhyme, and analogies
- support their ideas, citing specific images from the poem
- summarize the main idea of the essay and offer insight into the poem's overall effect

Reading Strategy

1. (a) Students may say the images in the first two stanzas, when the sun is young and beautiful (b) The sun as a fire and the sun as a young huntress
2. Students may say the deer and the fire both creep slowly and are beautiful.

Focus

Summary

As the author watches a sunrise, she thinks about the landscape, the way she sees color, the view from her kitchen window, and the way a freshly cut flower blooms and fades. At the end, she vows to remember the view of the lake from her cabin in the moment before she dies.

Author Search To expand students' appreciation of Patricia Hampl, have them access the Web site for additional information and resources.

Use the CheckPoint questions on Presentation Plus! to monitor students' comprehension. These questions can be used with interactive response keypads for immediate student feedback.

Readability Scores
Dale-Chall: 6.2
DRP: 62
Lexile: 1140

North Shore Mornings

Patricia Hampl

BEFORE YOU READ

Building Background

Born in St. Paul, Minnesota, in 1946, Patricia Hampl attended the University of Minnesota, where her writing earned her the job of associate editor of the student magazine. Today she is a Regents Professor at the same university.

Hampl won acclaim from the very start of her career. Her earliest publications were memoirs about places and experiences that Hampl says are part of "that world that will never be again." Her book *A Romantic Education* deals with a visit to Prague, where Hampl explored her Czech heritage. Another work describes her "antique education" at a convent school run by French nuns. Hampl begins her writing days by quickly describing what she sees outside her window.

Patricia Hampl was born in 1946.

LiteratureOnline **Author Search** For more about Patricia Hampl, go to www.glencoe.com.

July, August, September 1978–1980

The sun is rising. I've been awake all night and can feel my tiredness, but I can't be bothered. The sky, as it lightens, is becoming a huge shell. The pink, orange, and strange lavenders of a deepwater conch[1] rising, appropriately, out of the lake.

At first, the light arranged itself in a striated[2] band along the horizon, very sleek and oddly modern, only a few undulating[3] lines streaming across that immensity. Now, after an hour or so, the cloud terrain, which is the only landscape out there, has acquired depth and diversity. The simple formalism of bands of color, the replica of a rainbow, is gone.

These full-sun days are the most beautiful at the shore, but not because they are replicas of Italy or the south of France. Those European histories of light go back to the Phoenician sailors and glide through the bright eyes of the crazed nineteenth-century painters. Our light is different.

It is possible, sometimes, to forget the giant forests behind us, forests where even today an old couple can go into a thicket off the fire road to pick blueberries and never come out again, lost in the density of the boundary waters.[4] Sometimes their bodies are found the following spring, or many springs later. There are people who are never found, who lie somewhere in that deep forest with a plastic berry pail knocked over on its side, the blueberries rotted and wormy at the bottom, having been eaten by a bear or disintegrated over the years.

1. A *conch* is a tropical mollusk.
2. *Striated* means "marked with bands of different hues."
3. *Undulating* means "moving in a wavy, or rising and falling, way."
4. Here, *boundary waters* refers to the area of Lake Superior that bounds Minnesota and Canada.

Additional Support

Academic Standards

Additional Support activities on pp. 546 and 547 cover the following standards:

Skills Practice: **9.3.7** Recognize and understand the significance of various literary devices, including…imagery…

Differentiated Instruction: **9.5.7** Use varied and expanded vocabulary, appropriate for specific forms and topics.

Skills Practice

STUDY: Using Graphic Organizers
Students can use a web diagram to organize and keep track of words and images Hampl uses to describe what she sees. Have students create a web for each central image, such as the forest and the flower. As they read the text, they should note descriptive phrases for each. They should write and circle their findings around the central circle for each web. Have students share their web diagrams. **OL**

Above Lake Superior, c. 1922. Lawren Stewart Harris. Oil on canvas, 121.9 x 152.4 cm. Art Gallery of Ontario, Toronto, Canada.

It is possible to forget that immensity behind us, that forest that goes into Canada—that *is* Canada—and is the real, implacable[5] Indian country, the land that has remained so fiercely loyal to the Indian way of life that no other way makes sense or is possible for long in the boundary waters.

BI Facing away from that forest, you can almost forget the immensity of it, the pathless acres of birch and pine, the beaded necklace of lakes thrown casually onto that dark green. You almost forget the wilderness and death. You almost forget because here you look out across the lake, the big water, which seems limitless, but somehow civilized by its shoreline.

This big lake should really be called a sea; it has nothing to do with those small bowls of saltless water that the glacier left behind in great numbers all over the state. But even here, at the edge of the lake that could almost remind you of the Mediterranean and all that swarmy color, the beauty is northern, is empty the way ice is, full of its own transparency and the refracted color of the sun. The light itself does not allow you to forget where you are. North, reaching far north.

It is one of those strange idiosyncrasies[6] of reality that color is most itself in the absence of object and form. It must have space to to be itself—effulgent,[7] gorged with light which is its only content, the only occasion for for its body at all. That is why color and light are most authentic and haunting, most memorable, in the North, not in the South, which has such a reputation for light.

R I've never been to Mexico. I haven't seen the markets at Oaxaca and Cuernavaca or on the Pacific coast which have taught some of my friends all they know about color. The burned-off mantle of light, the absolute glare and intensity, the piled-up pomegranates and the melons like lessons in primary colors, the Indian embroidery, the cheap, gaudy jewelry that only loses its divine, gemlike quality north of the border, the deep color even of human skin there. Or, on the coast in the shrimp markets, the boiled prawns, lying in glass dishes and straw baskets, as big and luscious as rhododendron blossoms. I haven't seen how those white Mexican blouses with the eyelet embroidery zing off the flesh and almost hurt the eye with their blinding flash of white. I've been told there is an orange color that hurts the eye, and I believe the crazy nineteenth-century painters with their cranky lives and their stunned conversion to the light of Arles, of Nice,[8] the sun of the South and its emphatic power.

5. *Implacable* means "unchangeable."
6. *Idiosyncrasies* are odd or unusual mannerisms of individuals.
7. *Effulgent* means "radiant."
8. *Arles and Nice are cities in France.*

Teach

BI Big Idea

Nature Inspires Writers may describe common sights in nature, such as a sunrise or a flower, in a fresh, new way. Invite a volunteer to read aloud the second paragraph in the selection. Discuss how Hampl describes the sunrise as if it were a modern painting. OL

R Reading Strategy

Comparing and Contrasting Imagery Point out how even though the author has never been to Mexico, she imagines the colors there.

Ask: How do the colors of Mexico compare to those the author has seen in Canada? *(Unlike pale milky colors of Canada, Mexico's colors are vivid and bright.)* OL

★ Viewing the Art

Canadian Lawren Stewart Harris (1885–1970) was an original member of the nature-inspired Group of Seven. Over his career, Harris painted Lake Superior, the Rockies, and the Arctic. Harris believed in expressing the spiritual along with the visible in his art.

Ask: In what way does the painting reflect the author's fondness for the North? *(Students may say the painting reflects the colors and austere beauty of the North.)* AS

Differentiated Instruction

Building Vocabulary Some students may find many unfamiliar words in this selection.

Ask students to create a list of words they do not know as they read the selection. Then, working individually or with a partner, they should find and write the definition and part of speech for each word on their list. Ask students to write an essay describing a natural scene, using at least five words from their list. Invite students to read their essays in small groups. BL

Teach

L1 Literary Element

Figurative Language Remind students that a simile is a comparison that uses *like* or *as*. **Ask:** What similes does the author use to describe the rocks and stones? *(She says they look like "a faded tapestry," "wild-birds' eggs," "semiprecious stones," "a chunk of . . . garnet.")* OL

L2 Literary Element

Sensory Details Remind students that sensory details appeal to the senses—sight, hearing, taste, touch, and smell. **Ask:** To which sense does the author's description of the peony mostly appeal? *(The author focuses mostly on how the flower looks; most details appeal to the sense of sight.)* OL

★ Literary History

Hampl and the Memoir Patricia Hampl's two best known works were memoirs about her childhood and her travels. She believes that in telling her own stories, she learns about her place in the universe and is part of something larger. AS

But there is an eye studied[9] only in the labyrinth of pastel. The milkiness of winter is what I mean, the shiver that qualifies northern light, northern sun, even in August. Our light here is like a gauzy streamer flowing first out of the black night before it becomes the light of day. The Milky Way, the blurry auras of the northern lights—this is where the quality of light we know comes from, where it starts. Our light has a birth, a childhood; it has a loving mother (the night and the starry sky). It does not come like a god, blazing, the way the southern sun does. It is silk, spun, given, created, and streaming from the cocoons of night and the smudged, planetary sky.

Therefore, our eyesight is different. We see differently. Here is what I see this moment: the kitchen window divided into rectangles by the pale, chipped green paint of the wooden frame. Then, a strip of grass—rich green and bluish at the top of the wheatlike tassels of the tall grasses. After that, a dip to the band of shore covered with small rocks and stones, which look dusty in the full sun. At first they seem like one indistinct color, like a faded tapestry. But really, they are blues and reds, grays, weed greens; many are mottled and spotted like wild-birds' eggs. Closer to the water, where the waves splash them the rocks have a deeper color; they become more distinct and look like semiprecious stones. Often I've picked up a dark, gleaming stone that looked like a broken chunk of some opaque, unpolished garnet,[10] and brought it into the cabin, and placed it on the windowsill, where I could admire it. It would fade, disappear into a pale, dry nugget, and become a chalky, unremarkable stone. I would keep it there, just because I couldn't bring myself to throw it out. Sometimes there would be 10 or 12 rocks on the windowsill, as if I couldn't learn the lesson. The truth is, each one seemed so permanently beautiful, I couldn't believe it, too, would turn.

Beyond the shore where all the drenched stones are, the real thing begins, the school of the northern eye. Not just the lake—the lake and the sky, the lake-sky-sky-lake. How do you suggest the breathtaking confusion, marriage, whatever it is, of the two elements? I think I come here just to look at it, to watch it perform its magic trick. How many times will I sit exactly here and be completely satisfied: a patch of green by the north shore of Lake Superior, off Highway 61 on the road from Duluth to the border, at Schroeder, Minnesota, in Cabin No. 1 of Gunderson's Modern Cabins (est. 1929)—and look out at this plate of water that is our ocean and which turns into our sky, our arc, our beautiful boundary of light. It is the perfect opened shell, the bivalve[11] of the two parts of life: the air, the water. And I am here, where I should be, in the exact middle. I am here to notice it.

All day the white peony Jim brought home from his walk to the abandoned resort has been opening. He discovered it even before it bloomed; there are several peony bushes over there, as well as roses and bachelor buttons that have been left untended since the resort closed almost ten years ago. Before this flower opened, it looked waxy and deathlike. Now, open, it is as voluptuous[12] as a rose, even more frilled and petaled than a rose, in fact. And white, so white.

The fascinating part is where the flecks of red touch the inner petals. On first glance, just a few of the petals appear to be rimmed with the port color, the way gold leaf glints on the edge of a page in an expensive book. It is remarkable the way that deep, heavy color has been applied in so thin and precise a line at the edge of the petal without somehow smudging or slurring the boundaries of

9. Here, *studied* means "acquired by learning or study."
10. A *garnet* is a semiprecious stone that has a dark red color.
11. A *bivalve* is any shellfish that has two hinged shells, such as a clam or an oyster.
12. *Voluptuous* means "especially pleasing to the senses."

Additional Support

Skills Practice

ASSESSMENT: Using Personal Experience Many state tests pose writing prompts that ask students to support an idea by drawing on their own experiences.

Write on the board: Patricia Hampl says that "we keep thinking, privately, that everything is like us. We are at our best, perhaps, when we do think this way, for it is harder to do harm then. . . ." Do you agree or disagree with Hampl? Have students write an essay in which they draw on their own experiences to support their point of view. Allow students time to prewrite, write, and proofread their essays. OL

L2 dark and pure white. Then, from those first speckles of color, the petals form more tightly in a rigid bundle; at the center of the entire blossom the port is spilled more liberally in splotches of maroon, down the inner sides of the petals in a random, swirled design. A chaotic, gaudy design, but because of the pages and pages of white petals, their superabundance, the effect is silent and deathly. Lovely death. It does seem like lovely death when you look a long time at such a perfect, uncorrupted thing. Even the spots of red are not imperfections, but suggestions of blood. I suppose, the blood we cannot help but feel flows through all living things, irrational as the thought is. If you tear the whitest, sheerest, most watery flower petal, for a moment it is difficult to realize that anything but warm, bright blood will spurt from the cut. We keep thinking, privately, that everything is like us. We are at our best, perhaps, when we do think this way, for it is harder to do harm then, though the method is anthropomorphic[13] and inaccurate.

The peony is full-blown. The heat of the cabin has released its last restraint. Here it is, the white, delicate cabbage, the streaked rose, the flower from the abandoned resort we have taken in, and allowed to die.

Sitting on the rock that juts into the lake by the cabin. The gulls, which sometimes look so piggish and stupid on shore, are silvery and magnificent tonight. One just glided across the water; the movement was so perfect, so unbroken, as if a second, more casual, line had been drawn by the horizon.

The lake is as still as I've ever seen it, shimmering and opalescent[14] at the horizon far back, all the misting of blue and pink, the satisfying complexity of pastel. I remembered how Aldous Huxley[15] helped his wife, Maria, to die, telling her to "let go," to imagine herself going across a calm, wide water.

When I come to die, I will summon every particle of imagination I possess to see this exact picture of water and evening sky. I will try, at the last moment, to fit myself exactly into the subtle mark, the slit of the far horizon that unites the two elements. And I will disappear.

Viewing the Art: How would you describe the mood of this painting? Explain. ★

Discussion Starter

How does Hampl use stories about her life, as well as descriptions of the Minnesota landscape, to express respect for the natural world? Use specific details from the selection to support your responses.

13. *Anthropomorphic* means "giving human qualities to an animal or other nonhuman thing."
14. *Opalescent* means "having a lustrous display of colors."
15. *Aldous Huxley* (1894–1963) was a famous British novelist.

Teach

★ Viewing the Art

Answer: *The mood is one of nocturnal peace and beauty.*

Artist and illustrator Lloyd Birmingham has illustrated numerous books, both fiction and nonfiction. However, his true love is bringing something that only lives in his head into the real world by painting it. AS

Discussion Starter

Students' discussion should identify specific details that suggest the speaker's feelings about nature.

Use the CheckPoint questions on Presentation Plus! to check students' mastery of the selection. These questions can be used with interactive response keypads for immediate student feedback.

Building Reading Fluency

Reading Aloud Getting a sense of the writer's rhythms and cadences will help students understand long sentences. Assign paragraphs from the selection. After they practice, invite students to read their paragraphs aloud. Discuss how the exercise helped comprehension. BL

Differentiated Instruction

Sharing Journal Entries Have students share their own journal entry about some aspect of nature. Or have students write a response to Hampl's entry and read it aloud. Students who do not wish to read their own writing aloud can ask a volunteer to read it for them. BL

Academic Standards

Additional Support activities on pp. 548 and 549 cover the following standards:

Skills Practice: **9.5.1** Write...autobiographical narratives...that...use interior monologue...to show the character's feelings.

Building Reading Fluency: **9.7** [Develop] speaking skills...in conjunction with... strategies...[for] delivery of oral presentations.

Differentiated Instruction: **9.7.14** Deliver narrative presentations that describe with specific details the sights, sounds, and smells of a scene...

Focus

Summary

The speaker calls on readers to live in nature as if they are warriors or actors.

Teach

L Literary Element

Line and Stanza Note that Swenson's poem does not provide punctuation marks. New lines and new thoughts are indicated by a capitalized word. **Ask:** What effect does the absence of punctuation have on the way you read the poem? *(We read quickly without slowing down for each thought.)* OL

Quickwrite

Students' writing should

- identify feelings or ideas suggested by the poem's analogies.
- interpret the analogies in clear language.

Use the CheckPoint questions on Presentation Plus! to monitor students' comprehension. These questions can be used with interactive response keypads for immediate student feedback.

BEFORE YOU READ

Building Background

May Swenson once defined poetry as "a craving to get through the curtains of things as they appear." Swenson wrote playfully experimental poems which used rich detail to evoke the complexities of nature.

Swenson was born in Logan, Utah, into a family of ten children. After working as an editor in New York City, she taught at colleges across the country. She also released many acclaimed volumes of poetry. Critics agree that Swenson had an unusual gift for fresh, sensuous, and musical descriptions of nature. One poet says that in Swenson's poems "the sheer thingness of things is joyfully celebrated" and calls her "the poet par excellence of sights and colors."

May Swenson was born in 1919 and died in 1989.

LiteratureOnline **Author Search** For more about May Swenson, go to www.glencoe.com.

Earth Your Dancing Place

May Swenson

Beneath heaven's vault
remember always walking
through halls of cloud
down aisles of sunlight
or through high hedges
of the green rain
walk in the world
highheeled with swirl of cape
hand at the swordhilt
of your pride
Keep a tall throat
Remain aghast[1] at life

Enter each day
as upon a stage
lighted and waiting
for your step
Crave upward as flame
have keenness in the nostril
Give your eyes
to agony or rapture
Train your hands
as birds to be
brooding[2] or nimble
Move your body
as the horses
sweeping on slender hooves
over crag and prairie
with fleeing manes
and aloofness of their limbs

Take earth for your own large room
and the floor of earth
carpeted with sunlight
and hung round with silver wind
for your dancing place L

Quickwrite

In this poem, Swenson makes several analogies, or comparisons: between the earth and a stage, between people and birds or horses, and between the earth and a large room. What ideas or feelings do these analogies suggest? For instance, do they convey pride, hope, despair, or exuberance? Write a brief paragraph in which you explore these questions.

1. *Aghast* means "shocked" or "terrified."

2. *Brooding* birds sit quietly on top of eggs or chicks.

Additional Support

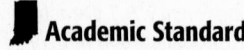

Academic Standards

The Additional Support activity on p. 550 covers the following standards:

Skills Practice: **9.7.6** Analyze the occasion and…choose effective verbal and nonverbal techniques… **9.7.11** Evaluate the clarity, quality, effectiveness…of a speaker's…delivery…

Skills Practice

SPEAKING: Choral Reading Without regular rhythm, rhyme scheme, or punctuation to indicate line endings, Swenson's poem presents a challenge to readers. Have students work in small groups to prepare a choral reading of the poem. Remind them to consider the meanings behind the images and to use their voices, facial expressions, and gestures to stress certain words, images, or ideas. After groups perform the poem, ask listening students to examine the choices the performers made. OL

Wrap-Up: Comparing Literature *Across Genres*

- *An Indian Summer Day on the Prairie* by Vachel Lindsay
- *North Shore Mornings* by Patricia Hampl
- *Earth Your Dancing Place* by May Swenson

COMPARING THE Big Idea Nature Inspires

Visual Display Each one of these writers—Vachel Lindsay, Patricia Hampl, and May Swenson—was inspired by nature to create a work of literature. Their works include vivid images that help readers see and feel details of nature. Create a collage of the images in each work that you find most inspirational or thought-provoking. Begin by reviewing the selections to determine which images you want to capture. Then find visual aids, such as copies of photographs or works of fine art, that contain images of nature similar to the ones evoked by the writers. Assemble the images into three collages and present your collages to the class. Quote the lines from the poems and journal that helped you select your images. What makes these nature images memorable?

Sunset at Sea. Odilon Redon. Private collection.

COMPARING Structure

Writing The **structure** of a literary work gives it coherence and order. Structure allows the reader to perceive relationships and to carefully build an understanding of the work's theme, or central insight. Poems are often organized by rhythm, rhyme, repetition, or stanzas. Works of prose may use a variety of structures to organize their ideas. Look at Hampl's journal entry and either Lindsay's or Swenson's poem. Write a brief essay describing each work's structure—the organization or pattern that helps give coherence to the work. How are the structures similar? How are they different? Are the authors' messages especially suited to the structures they selected? Why or why not? Cite evidence from the selections to support your ideas.

COMPARING Authors' Beliefs

Group Activity An **author's beliefs** are the ideas or convictions that he or she expresses in a work. To draw conclusions about an author's beliefs, closely examine the details of his or her work. In a small group, discuss the beliefs that Lindsay, Hampl, and Swenson express. As you answer the following questions, cite evidence from the selections to support your points.

1. What is the topic or subject of each work? What attitudes or ideas does each author seem to be expressing toward his or her topic?
2. What is each author's opinion of the relationship between humans and the natural world?
3. Which author or authors pay the most attention to the dangers of the natural world? Which author or authors consider nature to be a benevolent, or positive, force?

INDIANA ACADEMIC STANDARDS (page 551)

9.3.2 Compare and contrast the presentation of a similar theme or topic across genres...

9.3.5 Compare works that express a universal theme and provide evidence to support the views...in each work.

Assess

Comparing the Big Idea

Students' collages and presentations should

- show images from each work;
- depict key images;
- identify the source of each image.

Comparing Structure

Students' essays should

- compare and contrast the structure of one poem and the journal entry;
- identify structural patterns in both works;
- explain the relationship between an author's theme and choice of structure;
- include specific details as supporting evidence.

Comparing Author's Beliefs

Students should support their answers with evidence from the texts. Possible answers:

1. Lindsay: changes in the sun during one day; Hampl: color and light on the things around her; Swenson: how we live in nature. The authors appreciate the power and variety of nature and express a sense of awe.
2. Lindsay and Hampl observe nature and take lessons from it. Swenson gives directions on how readers should live life with gusto.
3. Swenson suggests the power and dangers of nature best. The speaker in her poem reminds readers to "remain aghast at life" (l. 12). Hampl is aware of the dangers when she describes the people who wander into the Canadian woods, never to return. Lindsay's poem suggests that nature is potent, positive, and beautiful. The images of the huntress, the fire, the wounded deer, and the eagle are life-affirming.

CheckPoint

Use the CheckPoint questions on Presentation Plus! to check students' mastery of the selection. These questions can be used with interactive response keypads for immediate student feedback.

Focus

BELLRINGER

Bellringer Options
Daily Language Practice Transparency 51
Or display images of snakes—real snakes and snakes that appear in art, logos, and symbols or seals.
Ask: What is your reaction to seeing a snake? What do they often represent in art and in literature? Have students consider as they read how the poem's speaker feels about the snake she encounters.

Author Search To expand students' appreciation of Mary Oliver, have them access the Web site for additional information and resources.

BEFORE YOU READ

The Black Snake

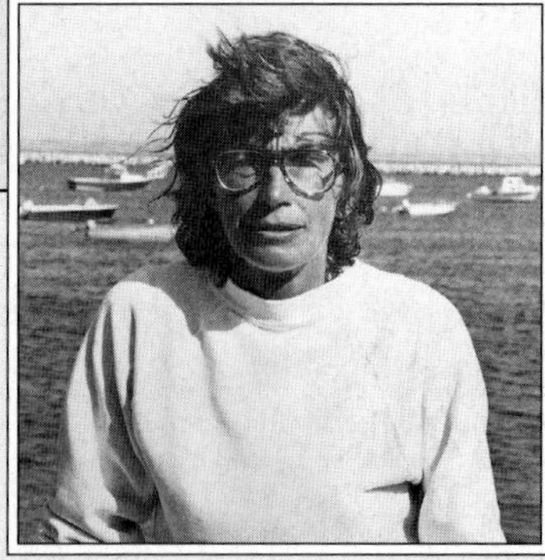

MEET MARY OLIVER

Mary Oliver once told an interviewer, "I don't think I have ever been bored one day in my life." Yet Oliver leads and always has led a relatively quiet life. She was born in Maple Heights, Ohio, in 1935. As a child, she developed the strong bond with the natural world that informs and enlivens her work and serves as a guiding principle in her life.

Learning the Craft Oliver attended college, but never graduated. Nevertheless, she began to hone her craft. As she says, "To keep writing was always a first priority." When she entered the workforce, she remained focused on writing. "I was careful never to take an interesting job. Not an interesting one. I took lots of jobs. But if you take an interesting job, you get interested in it."

> *"I have never felt yet that I've done it right. This is the marvelous thing about language. It can always be done better."*
>
> —Mary Oliver

Oliver's first collection of poems, *No Voyage,* was published in 1963. She acknowledges that her early work is derivative, that is, clearly influenced by the poets she was reading at the time—Robert Frost, William Carlos Williams, Edna St. Vincent Millay, and James Wright, among others. "Every poet learns by imitating other poets," she says, "but there is finally a time when you begin to hear something new and different—something of your own—and that's the part of your work you want then to cherish, to make strong."

Oliver continued to read and write every day, often waking at 4:30 or 5:00 in the morning and writing for several hours before work. Over the years, she developed her distinctive voice. In 1983 she published *American Primitive,* a collection of poetry with one voice throughout—a voice that she says "can, imaginatively, become the reader's inner voice." This book was well received and won the Pulitzer Prize in 1984.

Meticulous Technique Since that time, Oliver has written almost twenty books—mostly poetry and some essays. Writing is not an effortless act of creation for Oliver. She revises extensively, often producing up to sixty drafts. She prefers to use an electric typewriter, pens, and pencils—or, as she calls them, "the old-fashioned stuff."

As her meticulous technique suggests, Oliver examines her subjects in great detail. But it is her ability to translate these details into universal experience that makes her work great poetry.

Today, Mary Oliver lives in Provincetown, Massachusetts, where she teaches, writes, and revels in the natural world. Oliver keeps a notebook with her at all times, so that she can write down immediate impressions. She has a keen appreciation for the natural world, and she has always tried to share that with her readers.

Mary Oliver was born in 1935.

Literature Online **Author Search** For more about Mary Oliver, go to www.glencoe.com.

Selection Skills

The Black Snake

Literary Elements
- Parallelism (SE pp. 553, 554, 555)

Reading Skills
- Analyzing Mood (SE pp. 553, 554, 555)

Vocabulary Skills
- Academic Vocabulary (SE p. 555)

Listening/Speaking/Viewing Skills
- Analyzing Art (TWE p. 554)

Writing Skills/Grammar
- Evaluate Author's Craft (SE p. 555)
- Connotations (TWE p. 554)

LITERATURE PREVIEW

Connecting to the Poem

The subject of the following poem is not only a black snake but also the larger issues of life and death. Before you read, think about the following questions:

- What is the speaker's attitude toward the snake?
- What does the snake represent to the speaker?

Building Background

Of the approximately 2,900 snake species alive today, only about 300 are venomous, and only half of these can inflict a lethal bite. A few venomous snakes—including rattlesnakes and water moccasins, or cottonmouths—live in North America. Snakes have much more reason to fear people, their worst enemies, than people have to fear snakes. In fact, many ancient and modern cultures have considered snakes to be valuable or even sacred. The caduceus, which is the symbol of the physician and the emblem of the U.S. Army Medical Corps, depicts two "healing" snakes entwined around a staff. The Aztecs worshipped the feathered serpent god Quetzalcoatl. In Arizona, Hopi people still perform the snake-antelope dance, a ceremony using live snakes, to plea for rain from the gods.

Setting Purposes for Reading

Big Idea Nature Inspires

As you read this selection, notice how the black snake inspires the poet to contemplate life and death.

Literary Element Parallelism

Parallelism is the use of a series of words, phrases, or sentences that have similar grammatical form. It is a form of repetition that emphasizes the items that are arranged in similar structures. Understanding parallelism will help you to identify ideas the author considers important. As you read the selection, notice examples of parallelism within lines and stanzas.

- See Literary Terms Handbook, pp. R12–R13.

Literature Online Interactive Literary Elements Handbook To review or learn more about the literary elements, go to www.glencoe.com.

READING PREVIEW

Reading Strategy Analyzing Mood

Mood is the feeling or emotional quality of a literary work. The mood can suggest a specific emotion, such as excitement or fear. In a poem, word choice, line length, rhythm, and other elements contribute to its mood. Descriptive language and figures of speech also help establish the mood.

Reading Tip: Noting Mood Words As you read the poem, use a chart to record the words that suggest a particular mood.

Word	Mood Suggested
flashed	excitement

A sculpture of the god Quetzalcoatl, depicted as a plumed serpent, adorns the outside of a temple in his honor, Teotihuacan, Mexico.

INDIANA ACADEMIC STANDARDS (page 551)

9.2 Identif[y] and analyz[e] structure...

9.3.11 Evaluate the aesthetic qualities of style, including the impact of...figurative language on...mood...

9.5.3 Write expository compositions...

BEFORE YOU READ

Focus

Summary

A snake crawls onto a road and is killed by an oncoming truck. The speaker stops her car and moves the snake's body to the side of the road. As she drives off, she thinks about death and how our deepest impulse is to think that we will never die.

Literature Online

Literary Elements Have students access the Web site to improve their understanding of parallelism.

CheckPoint

Use the CheckPoint questions on Presentation Plus! to monitor students' comprehension. These questions can be used with interactive response keypads for immediate student feedback.

Selection Resources

Print Materials
- Unit 3 Resources (Fast File), pp. 31–32
- Selection and Unit Assessments, pp. 95–96
- Selection Quick Checks, p. 48

Transparencies
- Bellringer Options Transparencies: Daily Language Practice Transparency 51
- Literary Elements Transparencies 63, 62

Technology
- TeacherWorks Plus™ CD-ROM
- StudentWorks Plus™ CD-ROM
- Presentation Plus!™ CD-ROM
- Literature Online, glencoe.com
- Online Student Edition, mhln.com
- Exam*View*® Assessment Suite CD-ROM
- Vocabulary PuzzleMaker CD-ROM
- Listening Library, disc 1 track 56

Teach

R Reading Strategy

Analyzing Mood Answer: *Students may say that the mood is melancholy or pensive. The once vital snake is now something to be thrown away.* Explain that mood is a feeling that is evoked by images, sounds, and words.

Ask: Why does the image of the tire evoke such feelings? *(Possible answer: The image of something useless and limp makes readers feel something has been lost or wasted.)* OL

L Literary Element

Parallelism Answer: *The phrase "he is" is followed twice by a pair of adjectives and a simile—"he is as cool and gleaming as a braided whip . . . beautiful and quiet as a dead brother" (ll. 9–11). The snake is compared to both a whip and a dead brother.* OL

★ Viewing the Art

The Lurking Place by Ismael Frigerio (1955–), a Chilean artist, is one of many works by the artist that depict a snake. As an artist and immigrant whose native country has been divided by war and political upheaval, Frigerio fills his works with symbols of exile—boats, body parts, and snakes. AS

The Black Snake

Mary Oliver

The Lurking Place, 1985. Ismael Frigerio. Tempera and acrylic on burlap, 92 x 120 in. Collection of the artist. ★

When the black snake
flashed onto the morning road,
and the truck could not swerve—
death, that is how it happens.

Now he lies looped and useless
as an old bicycle tire.
I stop the car
and carry him into the bushes.

He is as cool and gleaming
as a braided whip, he is as beautiful and quiet
as a dead brother.
I leave him under the leaves

and drive on, thinking
about *death:* its suddenness,
its terrible weight,
its certain coming. Yet under

reason burns a brighter fire, which the bones
have always preferred.
It is the story of endless good fortune.
It says to oblivion:[1] not me!

It is the light at the center of every cell.
It is what sent the snake coiling and flowing forward
happily all spring through the green leaves before
he came to the road.

---

1. *Oblivion* is the state of being entirely forgotten.

Reading Strategy Analyzing Mood *What mood does this comparison convey?* R

Literary Element Parallelism *Identify the parallelism in this sentence. To what unlikely things is the snake being compared?* L

Additional Support

Academic Standards

The Additional Support activity on p. 554 covers the following standard:

Skills Practice: **9.1.2** Distinguish between what words mean literally and what they imply and interpret what the words imply.

Skills Practice

WRITING: Connotations Remind students that words have connotations, or feelings, associated with them as well as definitions. In the poem, for example, the word *useless* evokes feelings of tenderness and sadness. If Oliver had used the word *ugly,* the connotation would be less sympathetic. Have students replace the underlined words in the following excerpts with words of similar meaning but different connotations. "Yet under reason burns a brighter fire;" "It is the story of endless good fortune;" ". . . what sent the snake coiling and flowing forward happily." OL

AFTER YOU READ

RESPONDING AND THINKING CRITICALLY

Respond

1. What was your reaction to the speaker's description of the snake?

Recall and Interpret

2. (a)What does the speaker do with the snake? (b)What does this tell you about the speaker?
3. (a)What image begins and ends the poem? (b)What does the repetition of this image suggest?
4. (a)What is the "brighter fire, which the bones / have always preferred"? (b)Why is the fire brighter?

Analyze and Evaluate

5. (a)Identify words and phrases that describe circles. (b)Why does the author repeat the image of a circle?
6. How does the idea of a "light at the center of every cell" tie in with the speaker's thoughts?
7. The **speaker** in a poem is the voice that communicates with the reader. Why do you suppose Oliver wrote so little about the speaker and so much about the snake?

Connect

8. **Big Idea** **Nature Inspires** What does this poem suggest about the ability of nature to provide inspiration?

LITERARY ANALYSIS

Literary Element Parallelism

Parallelism emphasizes thoughts and ideas and also helps shape the rhythm of a sentence or a line of poetry.

1. How does parallelism underscore the seriousness of death in the poem?
2. How does the author use parallelism to signal a change in mood in stanzas 4–6?

Writing About Literature

Evaluate Author's Craft Oliver uses a series of comparisons to structure this poem: life and death, reason and emotion, the speaker and the snake. Write a brief essay in which you describe one of these comparisons and evaluate how it contributes to the poem. Before you get started, ask yourself the following questions: How are the two elements of the comparison you chose similar? How are they different? What is Oliver's intended effect? Do you think she has succeeded? Provide examples from the poem to support your main points.

LiteratureOnline **Web Activities** For eFlashcards, Selection Quick Checks, and other Web activities, go to www.glencoe.com.

READING AND VOCABULARY

Reading Strategy Analyzing Mood

Often, the **mood** of a work of literature changes as the work progresses. Reread "The Black Snake" and note if and where the mood changes.

1. What is the mood at the beginning of the poem? What words or images help evoke this mood?
2. (a)How does the poem's structure reflect a change in mood? (b)Does the final line of the poem affect the mood? Explain.

Academic Vocabulary

Here are two words from the vocabulary list on page R80.

vehicle (vē′ ə kəl) *n.* a medium through which ideas are expressed

induce (in dōōs′) *v.* to cause something to happen

Practice and Apply

1. What **vehicle** does the author use to talk about life and death?
2. What **induces** the snake to move happily through the leaves?

Reading Strategy

1. sober and reflective; *death, useless, beautiful, quiet, dead brother*
2. (a) The mood moves from mournful to life-affirming. (b) No. It is consistent with the life-affirming mood.

Academic Vocabulary

1. The vehicle or device is a poem.
2. Its innate life force.

AFTER YOU READ

Assess

1. Answers will vary.
2. (a) Places it under the leaves (b) She has respect and sympathy for the snake.
3. (a) The living snake on the road (b) The cycle of life
4. (a) The life force (b) The life force gives the illusion of immortality.
5. (a) *looped, tire, coiling,* (b) It symbolizes the cycle of life and death.
6. It may refer to the will to survive.
7. The snake symbolizes natural forces; the speaker is merely a witness.
8. Despite our knowledge of certain death, humans want to live forever.

Literary Element

1. Lines 14–16: *its suddenness, its terrible weight,* and *its certain coming* stress the reality of death.
2. In stanza 4, Oliver repeats *its* and uses parallel phrases to describe death, creating a somber mood. In stanzas 5 and 6, she repeats *it is* in parallel sentences to describe the will to live, creating a positive mood.

CheckPoint

Use the CheckPoint questions on Presentation Plus! to check students' mastery of the selection. These questions can be used with interactive response keypads for immediate student feedback.

BEFORE YOU READ

Focus

BELLRINGER

Bellringer Options
Daily Language Practice Transparency 52
Or display images of water scenes—ponds, seascapes, and river views.
Ask: How do these scenes make you feel? Why do you think people enjoy spending time near the water? Have students consider as they read the poem how nature soothes the speaker's worries.

Author Search To expand students' appreciation of Wendell Berry, have them access the Web site for additional information and resources.

CheckPoint

Use the CheckPoint questions on Presentation Plus! to monitor students' comprehension. These questions can be used with interactive response keypads for immediate student feedback.

BEFORE YOU READ

The Peace of Wild Things

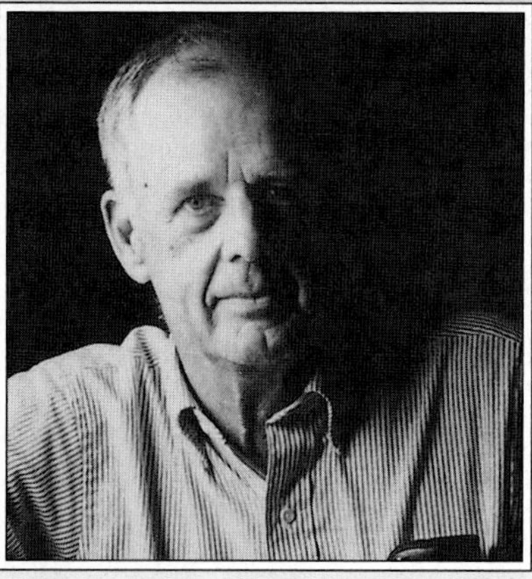

MEET WENDELL BERRY

Wendell Berry is a farmer without a tractor and a writer without a computer. Berry does not believe in modern technology, but he does believe in the importance of sustaining local community life, small farms, and family heritage. Nature and the environment are central to his writing and his work.

Love of the Land Berry was born in New Castle, Kentucky, and grew up on his family's farm. After earning a bachelor's degree and a master's degree in English at the University of Kentucky, Berry taught at Georgetown College from 1957 to 1959. Later, Berry taught at the creative writing center at Stanford University and then at New York University. While at Stanford, Berry wrote his first novel, entitled *Nathan Coulter*. Published in 1960, it was the first in his series of "Port William" novels. The series deals with the themes of family, community, and love of the land.

"My work has been motivated by a desire to make myself responsible at home in this world and in my native and chosen place."

—Wendell Berry

In addition to being a novelist, Berry is also a poet, an essayist, and the author of more than thirty books. His nature writing is often compared with that of William Wordsworth and Henry David Thoreau. Most of his fiction is set in his home state of Kentucky. Farming and community continue to be the focus of his writing.

Organics, Pencils, and Paper Today, Berry lives in the county where he was born, on a 125-acre farm where members of the Berry family have lived since the early 1800s. He and his wife came to the farm for a vacation in 1965 but decided to stay. "It is a real farm," Berry has said, "not a writer-professor's country estate." He farms organically—using no chemical pesticides or herbicides. Berry does not use modern farm equipment, preferring to use draft horses to plow his fields instead of "exhaust-stinking, engine-roaring, gasoline-guzzling tractors."

Berry also refuses to use a computer to write, explaining his reasons in an essay entitled "Why I Am Not Going to Buy a Computer." Berry does not want to use electricity generated by the burning of strip-mined coal and is not convinced that his writing would improve if he used a computer rather than pencil and paper.

In all of his writing, Berry promotes the message that respect and appreciation for nature are essential to human life.

Wendell Berry was born in 1934.

Literature Online **Author Search** For more about Wendell Berry, go to www.glencoe.com.

Selection Skills

The Peace of Wild Things

Literary Elements
- Enjambment (SE pp. 557, 558, 559)

Reading Skills
- Analyzing Cause-and-Effect Relationships (SE pp. 557, 559)

Vocabulary Skills
- Synonyms (SE p. 559)

Listening/Speaking/Viewing Skills
- Listening: Visualizing a Scene (TWE p. 558)

Writing Skills/Grammar
- Respond to Conflict (SE p. 559)

LITERATURE PREVIEW

Connecting to the Poem

The opening lines of the poem "The Peace of Wild Things" mention the speaker's "despair for the world." Before you read, think about the following questions:

- Why might someone feel despair for the world?
- What things make you feel peaceful?

Building Background

The setting of the poem is "still water," that is, a lake, pond, or wetland where waterfowl such as wood ducks and herons stop to feed or nest. The wood drake, or male wood duck, is the most colorful of all North American ducks, marked by bright iridescent green, blue, and purple, as well as a crest extending from the back of its head. The heron is a water bird that wades in shallow water to fish. Its long, curved neck, long legs, and tapered bill equip it for such feeding.

Setting Purposes for Reading

Big Idea Nature Inspires

As you read "The Peace of Wild Things," think about the role that nature plays in the speaker's life.

Literary Element Enjambment

Enjambment is the continuation of a sentence from one line of a poem into the next. Also called a run-on line, enjambment draws the reader's eye to the following line and makes the poem's meter and rhythm flow naturally. Poets use enjambment in both metered and free-verse poetry. When you notice a line of poetry with no punctuation at the end, check to see if the poet is using enjambment. An awareness of the poet's use of punctuation and enjambment will help you read the poem as the poet intended. This will make the poem more enjoyable and easier to understand.

- See Literary Terms Handbook, p. R6.

Literature Online Interactive Literary Elements Handbook To review or learn more about the literary elements, go to www.glencoe.com.

READING PREVIEW

Reading Strategy Analyzing Cause-and-Effect Relationships

When a writer presents a **cause-and-effect relationship,** he or she explains why something happens or shows both an action and its result. Noting causes and their effects as you read can help you determine the writer's intended meaning and understand the purpose of a literary work as a whole. As you read "The Peace of Wild Things," try to identify cause-and-effect relationships. Remember that a single cause may have many effects.

Reading Tip: Noting Cause and Effect Read the poem from beginning to end at least twice. How does the poem make you feel? What does it make you think about? Then identify the cause-and-effect relationships in the poem, and record them in a chart like the one below.

Cause	Effect
Despair and fear	Speaker wakes up in the night

Vocabulary

tax (taks) *v.* to place a heavy burden on; to strain; p. 558 *Studying for long hours without a break can tax your brain.*

forethought (fôr′ thôt′) *n.* thinking or planning beforehand; p. 558 *We had the forethought to make alternate plans in case of rain.*

Vocabulary Tip: Synonyms Synonyms are words that have the same or similar meanings. Note that synonyms are always the same part of speech.

INDIANA ACADEMIC STANDARDS (page 551)
9.2 Identif[y] and analyz[e] structure...
9.3.13 Explain how voice...affect[s]...meaning...
9.5.2 Write responses to literature that...identify and assess the impact of...complexities within the text.

BEFORE YOU READ

Focus

Summary

The speaker tells how, when his worries wake him at night, he goes down to the water to watch the birds and stars and feels comforted.

Literary Elements Have students access the Web site to improve their understanding of enjambment.

V Vocabulary

Vocabulary File Say: Add these words and definitions to your vocabulary file. Include a sentence that gives you an example of how to use the word. **OL** Students with English language needs should include the pronunciations of these words in their files. **EL**

Selection Resources

Print Materials
- Unit 3 Resources (Fast File), pp. 33–35
- Leveled Vocabulary Development, p. 40
- Selection and Unit Assessments, pp. 97–99
- Selection Quick Checks, p. 49

Transparencies
- Bellringer Options Transparencies: Daily Language Practice Transparency 52
- Literary Elements Transparency 65

Technology
- TeacherWorks Plus™ CD-ROM
- StudentWorks Plus™ CD-ROM
- Presentation Plus!™ CD-ROM
- Literature Online, glencoe.com
- Online Student Edition, mhln.com
- Exam*View*® Assessment Suite CD-ROM
- Vocabulary PuzzleMaker CD-ROM
- Listening Library, disc 1 track 57

Teach

L Literary Element

Enjambment Enjambment is often used in free verse. Without the structure of meter and rhyme scheme, poets can break lines where they wish to focus on the visual aspect of the poem or to build suspense. **Answer:** *The thought sounds incomplete; a verb is missing. Students would normally pause after "on the water."* OL

★ Language History

Drake The word *drake* dates back to the thirteenth century. It is derived from a Germanic word *draak, drake,* or *drache.* For medieval Germans, *drake* was part of a compound word *anddrake,* which meant "duck drake." English speakers borrowed the second part, *drake,* to refer to a male duck. AS

CheckPoint

Use the CheckPoint questions on Presentation Plus! to check students' mastery of the selection. These questions can be used with interactive response keypads for immediate student feedback.

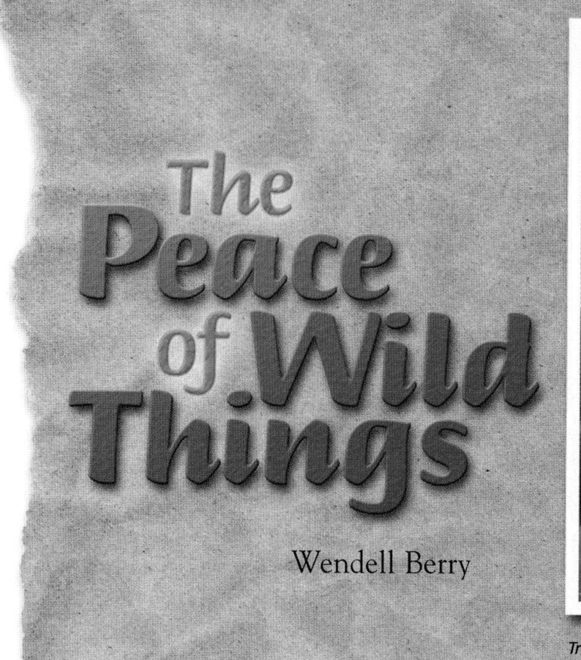

The Peace of Wild Things

Wendell Berry

Tranquility. Nilaus Fristrup. Bourne Gallery, Reigate, Great Britain.

When despair for the world grows in me
and I wake in the night at the least sound
in fear of what my life and my children's lives may be,
I go and lie down where the wood drake ★
rests in his beauty on the water, and the great heron feeds.
I come into the peace of wild things
who do not **tax** their lives with **forethought**
of grief. I come into the presence of still water.
And I feel above me the day-blind stars
waiting with their light. For a time
I rest in the grace of the world, and am free.

Literary Element Enjambment *Why would it sound unnatural to pause at the end of this line? Where is a natural place to pause?* L

Vocabulary

tax (taks) *v.* to place a heavy burden on; to strain
forethought (fôr′ thôt′) *n.* thinking or planning beforehand

Additional Support

Academic Standards

The Additional Support activity on p. 558 covers the following standard:

Skills Practice: **9.7.11** Evaluate the…quality [and] effectiveness…of a speaker's…choice of words, and use of language.

Skills Practice

LISTENING: Visualizing a Scene

Advise students to visualize as they hear the poem to help them understand the mood change the speaker experiences. Read Berry's poem aloud or play a recording at least twice while students draw what they visualize. Read the poem once more while students examine their drawings. Invite them to discuss the feelings or emotions the drawings convey. Ask students if they think Berry's images produce the effect he might have desired. OL

AFTER YOU READ

RESPONDING AND THINKING CRITICALLY

Respond

1. Which lines from this poem did you find most memorable, powerful, or surprising? Explain.

Recall and Interpret

2. (a)What is it that people do that "wild things" do not? (b)What do wild things teach the speaker and reader about living?
3. (a)What does the speaker do when in the frame of mind described in the beginning of the poem? (b)What do his actions suggest about his personal values or philosophy of life?
4. (a)For how long does the experience with nature allow the speaker to be free? (b)What is the nature of this freedom?

Analyze and Evaluate

5. (a)What ironic contrast is presented in the title of the poem? (b)How does the title reflect the poem's content?
6. How well do you think the poem evokes the feeling of peace in nature? Support your answer with details from the poem.
7. (a)What does the phrase "For a time" in line 10 contribute to the mood, or emotional quality, of the poem? (b)Is this choice of words effective?

Connect

8. **Big Idea** **Nature Inspires** (a)Where have you experienced nature, and what importance does nature have in your life? (b)How does your experience with nature compare with the experience described in the poem?

LITERARY ANALYSIS

Literary Element Enjambment

Poetry that has punctuation at the ends of its lines gives a sense of structure and order. Enjambment, on the other hand, can create a sense of disorder.

1. What effect does breaking line 10 after "For a time" have on the flow of the poem? Explain your answer.
2. Identify one other example of enjambment in the poem. What effect does it have?

Writing About Literature

Respond to Conflict Write a journal entry in which you reflect on the speaker's internal conflict. Some questions you might consider and respond to include the following: With what is the speaker in conflict? Do you think this is a common conflict? If so, what are some ways that people deal with it? Have you ever experienced a similar conflict? If so, how did you deal with it?

LiteratureOnline **Web Activities** For eFlashcards, Selection Quick Checks, and other Web activities, go to www.glencoe.com.

READING AND VOCABULARY

Reading Strategy Analyzing Cause-and-Effect Relationships

Cause-and-effect relationships can help you understand why events happen. They can also help you map a speaker's motive.

1. What are the initial feelings that cause the speaker to take action?
2. What action does the speaker take as a result of these feelings, and what is the effect of his action?
3. What effect might a sunrise have on the speaker?

Vocabulary Practice

Practice with Synonyms Choose the best synonym for each word.

1. tax
   - **a.** pay
   - **b.** imitate
   - **c.** strain
   - **d.** relieve
2. forethought
   - **a.** planning
   - **b.** gratitude
   - **c.** omen
   - **d.** sadness

LiteratureOnline

Web Activities Have students access the Web site for interactive activities that will help them assess their understanding of the selection.

AFTER YOU READ

Assess

1. Answers will vary.
2. (a) Worry about the future (b) To live in the present
3. (a) Lies down outdoors in a wild place, near still water (b) He is calmed by nature.
4. (a) Only "for a time" (b) He is free from worry and fear.
5. (a) That wild things provide peace (b)Wild things live without "forethought of grief."
6. Answers will vary.
7. (a) It warns the reader that peace is temporary. (b) It is effective because it is true.
8. Answers will vary.

Literary Element

1. The phrase is emphasized by being suspended.
2. The break after *stars* in line 9 builds suspense.

Reading Strategy

1. Despair and fear for his and his children's future
2. He lies down near water. He gains peace of mind from nature.
3. A return of his anxieties

Writing About Literature

Students' journal entries should note that the speaker is agonizing over what may happen in the future. Their responses will vary as to how they and others deal with similar inner conflict.

Vocabulary

1. c **2.** a

Focus

Summary

This essay describes Frederick Law Olmsted's landscape design for the World's Columbian Exposition in Chicago in 1893. Olmsted's goal was to transform a newly developed tract of city land into a lush garden.

Teach

R Reading Strategy

Analyzing Cultural and Historical Context Before students read, make sure they can distinguish between historical context (the events that happened during a particular time period) and cultural context (the ideas and attitudes of a particular group of people). OL

★ Cultural History

World's Fairs Since 1928, the International Bureau of Expositions has organized the World's Fairs. People gather at the fairs to see exhibits about the world's cultures and new developments in technology and science. AS

A Mysterious Poetic Effect

Erik Larson

Horticulture Building, World's Columbian Exposition, Chicago, 1893. Childe Hassam. Oil on canvas, 18½ x 26¼ in. Terra Foundation, Chicago.

Finalist for the National Book Award

Building Background

Frederick Law Olmsted oversaw the landscape design of the World's Columbian Exposition of 1893, a world's fair that provided international entertainment and exhibits. Olmsted led the transformation of a soggy marsh in Chicago into a series of lagoons and canals, complete with its own islands and passenger ferries. In "A Mysterious Poetic Effect," Erik Larson describes Olmsted's conceptualization of the Exposition's landscape. This excerpt begins at the end of a meeting of the architects who would be designing the fair's buildings.

Set a Purpose for Reading

★ Read to discover Olmsted's vision for the landscape of the World's Columbian Exposition of 1893.

Reading Strategy

Analyzing Cultural and Historical Context

When you **analyze cultural and historical context,** you consider the societal, artistic, and intellectual R forces that influenced the time period a literary work discusses. As you read, think about the historical and cultural context of topics in the selection.

The meeting confirmed Frederick Law Olmsted's[1] growing concern that the architects were losing sight of the nature of the thing they were proposing to build. The shared vision expressed in their drawings struck him as being too sober and monumental. After all, this was a world's fair, and fairs should be fun. Aware of the architects' increasing emphasis on size, Olmsted shortly before the meeting had written to Burnham[2] suggesting ways to enliven the grounds. He wanted the lagoons and canals strewn with waterfowl of all kinds and colors and traversed continually by small boats. Not just any boats, however: *becoming*[3] boats. The subject became an obsession for him. His broad view of what

1. *Frederick Law Olmsted* (1822–1903) was a landscape architect who designed many public parks, beginning with Central Park in New York City.
2. *Daniel H. Burnham* (1846–1912) was the chief of construction for the World's Columbian Exposition of 1893. He was a leader in Chicago commercial architecture in the late nineteenth century.
3. Here, *becoming* means "attractive."

Additional Support

See also Active Learning and Note Taking Guide, pp. 99–104.

Skills Practice

RESEARCH: Columbian Exposition The selection focuses on Frederick Law Olmsted's efforts to plan the landscape of the World's Columbian Exposition. Students may be interested in learning more about the exposition. Have them list questions about the exposition. Then have them consult books, articles, and reference tools to find the answers. Invite students to share their questions and their findings with the class. If time allows, ask students to present their findings in a visual form. OL constituted landscape architecture[4] included **BI** anything that grew, flew, floated, or otherwise entered the scenery he created. Roses produced dabs of red; boats added intimacy and life. But it was crucial to choose the right kind of boat. He dreaded what would happen if the decision were left to one of the fair's many committees. He wanted Burnham to know his views from the start.

"We should try to make the boating feature of the exposition a gay and lively one," he wrote. He loathed the clatter and smoke of steam launches; he wanted electric boats designed specifically for the park, with emphasis on graceful lines and silent operation. It was most important that these boats be constantly but quietly in motion, to provide diversion for the eye, peace for the ear. "What we shall want is a regular service of boats like that of an omnibus[5] line in a city street," he wrote. He also envisioned a fleet of large birchbark canoes paddled by Indians in deerskin and feathers and recommended that various foreign watercraft be moored in the fair's harbor. "I mean such as Malay proas, catamarans, Arab dhows, Chinese

4. *Landscape architecture* is a branch of architecture that takes into consideration the decorative and functional arrangement of land and the structures and plantings on it.

5. Here, *omnibus* means "bus."

Poster advertising transportation to the World's Columbian Exposition in Chicago. 1893. ★

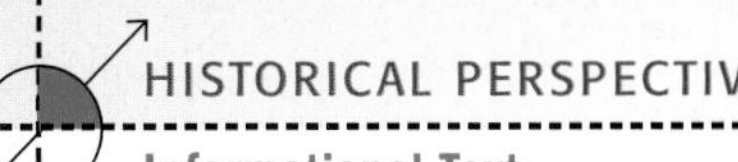

HISTORICAL PERSPECTIVE

Informational Text

Teach

BI Big Idea

Nature Inspires Ask: What is Olmsted's attitude toward the undeveloped land in Chicago and what is his goal? *(He considers it a "desolate" prairie. His goal is to transform it into a rich water landscape.)* **OL**

★ Viewing the Art

The British London & North Western Railway was formed in 1846 by the merger of three railways. The railway system in Victorian England made traveling affordable for large numbers of people for the first time. Those in upper society, like Queen Victoria, had their own special coaches. **AS**

Readability Scores

Dale-Chall: 12.0

DRP: 70

Lexile: 1410

English Language Coach

Vocabulary Journal Have partners preview the selection for unfamiliar vocabulary words and write them down in a log or journal. Challenge them to use their knowledge of context clues and word parts to guess at their meanings before they look up and confirm or correct their answers. **EL**

Differentiated Instruction

Listening and Reading To help less proficient readers with the long sentences in the essay, read the selection aloud or make a recording of it for students to listen to as they read. Remind students to pause after every few paragraphs to summarize what they have heard so far. **BL**

Academic Standards

Additional Support activities on pp. 560 and 561 cover the following standards:

Skills Practice: **9.2.3** Generate relevant questions about…topics… **9.2.4** Synthesize the content from several sources… **9.7.4** Use…visual aids…to enhance… presentations.

English Language Coach: **9.1** [Use] word parts…and…context clues…to determine the meaning of words…

Differentiated Instruction: **9.7** [Respond] to oral communication [with] careful listening and evaluation…

Teach

BI Big Idea

Nature Inspires Point out that Olmsted believes that the artful arrangement of plants adds up to more than "the mere sum of petals and leaves." **Ask:** How would a poet like May Swenson or Walt Whitman respond to that idea? *(The poets might be insulted or offended by the idea that a person could improve upon nature.)* OL

V Vocabulary

Conjure The word *conjure* dates back to the fourteenth century when it had several different meanings. In medieval times, to conjure was to conspire with another or to form a secret pact. The word also meant to give one's word or to beg or entreat another person. A third meaning is the meaning Olmsted uses—to produce or create something, as if by magic. This is the word's primary meaning today. OL

The "Universal Brotherhood" Barge at the World's Columbian Exposition, Chicago, 1893. Thure de Thulstrup. Oil on canvas. Chicago Historical Society, IL.

sampans, Japanese pilot boats, Turkish caiques, Esquimaux kiacks, Alaskan war canoes, the hooded boats of the Swiss Lakes,[6] and so on."

A far more important outcome of the Rookery[7] meeting, however, was Olmsted's recognition that the architects' noble dreams magnified and complicated the already-daunting challenge that faced him in Jackson Park. When he and Calvert Vaux[8] had designed Central Park in New York, they had planned for visual effects that would not be achieved for decades; here he would have just twenty-six months to reshape the desolation of the park into a prairie Venice[9] and plant its shores, islands, terraces, and walks with whatever it took to produce a landscape rich enough to satisfy his vision. What the architects' drawings had shown him, however, was that in reality he would have far fewer than twenty-six months. The portion of his work that would most shape how visitors appraised his landscape—the planting and grooming of the grounds immediately surrounding each building—could only be done *after* the major structures were completed and the grounds cleared of construction equipment, temporary tracks and roads, and other aesthetic impedimenta.[10] Yet the palaces unveiled in

6. Olmsted lists traditional boats from a variety of cultures.
7. *The Rookery,* a building in downtown Chicago, was designed by Daniel Burnham and his partner, J. W. Root, and held their offices. It was the site of the meeting described.
8. *Calvert Vaux* (1824–1895) was a landscape architect who, along with Olmsted, designed New York City's Central Park. They eventually formed an architecture firm together.
9. *Venice* is a major seaport in northern Italy built on a lagoon. People travel around the city by walking or in boats.
10. The *impedimenta* includes all of the equipment, tools, and supplies that will impede, or get in the way, of Olmsted's work on the *aesthetics,* or visual appeal, of the park.

Additional Support

Skills Practice

READING: Monitoring Comprehension When reading an informative essay that has long sentences and unfamiliar vocabulary, it is helpful to stop after reading a few paragraphs to review the information. Have partners read the selection silently, stopping after every few paragraphs to summarize and ask questions. Students should understand what Olmsted's job was, what he worried about, and what he hoped to accomplish. Have partners discuss points they do not understand and list questions to be answered by rereading or in class discussion. OL

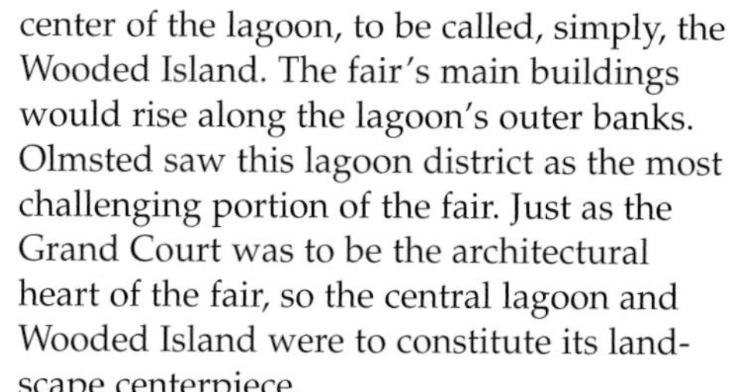

the Rookery were so immense, so detailed, that their construction was likely to consume nearly all the remaining time, leaving little for him.

Soon after the meeting Olmsted composed a strategy for the transformation of Jackson Park. His ten-page memorandum captured the essence of all he had come to believe **V** about the art of landscape architecture and how it should strive to conjure effects greater **BI** than the mere sum of petals and leaves.

He concentrated on the fair's central lagoon, which his dredges[11] soon would begin carving from the Jackson Park shore. The dredges would leave an island at the center of the lagoon, to be called, simply, the Wooded Island. The fair's main buildings would rise along the lagoon's outer banks. Olmsted saw this lagoon district as the most challenging portion of the fair. Just as the Grand Court was to be the architectural heart of the fair, so the central lagoon and Wooded Island were to constitute its landscape centerpiece.

Above all he wanted the exposition landscape to produce an aura of "mysterious poetic effect." Flowers were not to be used as an ordinary gardener would use them. Rather, every flower, shrub, and tree was to be deployed with an eye to how each would act upon the imagination. This was to be accomplished, Olmsted wrote, "through the mingling intricately together of many forms of foliage, the alternation and complicated 

11. A *dredge* is a type of machine used for digging and removing dirt.

World's Columbian Exposition, Chicago, Illinois. View east from the terrace of the Transportation Building across the Lagoon to the south end of the Wooded Island. Painting by H. Bolton Jones c. 1893. 

Teach

R Reading Strategy

Analyzing Cultural and Historical Context Have students carefully read the quotations from Olmsted's memorandum.

Ask: What can you tell about Olmsted from reading his comments? *(Olmsted is well educated but perhaps too flowery in his language.)* **OL**

★ Viewing the Art

American artist H. (Hugh) Bolton Jones (1848–1927) was an acclaimed landscape artist. He and his brother Francis, also an artist, studied in both the United States and Europe to master their techniques. In many of his most acclaimed works, H. Jones often favored painting landscapes of the eastern United States. **AS**

Building Reading Fluency

Pronunciations and Vocabulary Have students look up the meanings and pronunciations of words they do not know. Then have partners practice reading sentences aloud that contain the unfamiliar words. Listening students should help readers pronounce new words correctly. **BL**

Differentiated Instruction

Argument Explain that sound arguments are built on logical reasons and are backed up by examples and facts.

Ask: What persuasive techniques might Olmsted have used to get his views adopted? Have students outline their arguments and share them with the class. **AL**

Academic Standards

Additional Support activities on pp. 562 and 563 cover the following standards:

Skills Practice: **9.2** Develop strategies such as asking questions…

Building Reading Fluency: **9.1** Use phonics, context clues,…and a growing knowledge of English…to determine the meaning of words…

Differentiated Instruction: **9.5.7** Use varied and expanded vocabulary, appropriate for specific forms and topics.

Teach

Language History

Lagoon The word *lagoon* comes from the Italian word *laguna* and originally referred to the waters of Venice, Italy. A lagoon is a large pool or small lake of seawater separated from the ocean by a barrier such as a sandbank. AS

Assess

1. Answers will vary.
2. (a) Vivid specific language (b) Yes; readers can visualize the plants.
3. (a) "of the character of a theatrical scene" (b) The Exposition was like a play that appeals to the five senses.
4. (a) The colors of leaves and plants and the light reflecting on them (b) To visualize the grand landscape plan
5. The procession of boats was to be silent, so as not to distract from people's enjoyment of the scenery. The flowers were to "act upon the imagination" and not "be too obtrusive." He placed plants that people could smell near the terraces.

R crossing of salient[12] leaves and stalks of varying green tints in high lights with other leaves and stalks, behind and under them, and therefore less defined and more shaded, yet partly illumined by light reflected from the water."

He hoped to provide visitors with a banquet of glimpses—the undersides of leaves sparkling with reflected light; flashes of brilliant color between fronds[13] of tall grass waving in the breeze. Nowhere, he wrote, should there be "a display of flowers demanding attention as such. Rather, the flowers to be used for the purpose should have the effect of flecks and glimmers of bright color imperfectly breaking through the general greenery. Anything approaching a gorgeous, garish[14] or gaudy display of flowers is to be avoided."

Sedges and ferns and graceful bulrush would be planted on the banks of the Wooded Island to conjure[15] density and intricacy and "to slightly screen, without hiding, flowers otherwise likely to be too obtrusive." He envisioned large patches of cattails broken by bulrush, iris, and flag[16] and pocketed with blooming plants, such as flame-red cardinal flower and yellow creeping buttercup—planted, if necessary, on slightly raised mounds so as to be just visible among the swaying green spires in the foreground.

On the far shore, below the formal terraces of the buildings, he planned to position fragrant plants such as honeysuckle and summersweet, so that their perfume would rise into the nostrils of visitors pausing on the terraces to view the island and the lagoon. ★

The overall effect, he wrote, "is thus to be in some degree of the character of a theatrical scene, to occupy the Exposition stage for a single summer." ∾

12. *Salient* here means "protruding."
13. *Fronds* are large leaves.
14. *Garish* means "loud and flashy."
15. Here, *conjure* means "evoke" or "bring to mind."
16. Here, *flag* refers to a type of plant with long, bladelike leaves, such as a wild iris.

RESPONDING AND THINKING CRITICALLY

Respond

1. How has your environment, urban or natural, inspired you?

Recall and Interpret

2. (a)What language does Olmsted use to describe his vision? (b)Is it effective? Why or why not?
3. (a)What "overall effect" was Olmsted attempting to create with his landscape design for the Exposition? (b)Why do you think he made this comparison?

Analyze and Evaluate

4. (a)What are examples of sensory details the author uses to describe the grounds of the Exposition? (b)What reaction do you think the author wants from the reader?
5. A landscape architect considers how people will interact with the land and the structures on it. How was Olmsted's design crafted with people in mind?

Connect

6. Recall the poems "I Wandered Lonely as a Cloud," by William Wordsworth and "The Peace of Wild Things" by Wendell Berry. What is similar and different about the opinions of nature held by these poets and by Frederick Law Olmsted?

INDIANA ACADEMIC STANDARDS (pages 560–564)
9.3.12 Analyze the way in which a work of literature is related to the themes and issues of its historical period.
9.3.2 Compare...a similar theme or topic across genres...

6. The poets and Olmsted were both inspired by nature. Olmsted wished to arrange it and create a beautiful effect, while the poets appreciated untouched landscapes.

Use the CheckPoint questions on Presentation Plus! to check students' mastery of the selection. These questions can be used with interactive response keypads for immediate student feedback.

Grammar Workshop

Language Usage

Making Subjects and Verbs Agree

"For a time I rest in the grace of the world, and am free."

—Wendell Berry, "The Peace of Wild Things"

Connecting to Literature When the speaker in Berry's poem says "I rest" and "am free," the verb forms of *to rest* and *to be* agree with the subject *I*. The subject, or person or thing doing the action, and the verb must always agree in number. In other words, if the subject of the sentence is singular (*he, it, book*), then the verb must be singular (*eats, describes, conveys*).

Learn to identify agreement problems and correct them.

Problem 1 A prepositional phrase or other words come between the subject and the verb.
The author of these lines celebrate the peace of wild things.

Solution Make the verb agree with the subject, not the object of the preposition.
The author of these lines celebrates the peace of wild things.

Problem 2 The subject is a compound joined by *and.*
The great heron and the wood drake feeds at the pond.

Solution Be sure to use the plural form of the verb.
The great heron and the wood drake feed at the pond.

Problem 3 A compound subject is joined by *or* or *nor.*
Fear or worries fades away.
Neither the stars nor water destroy the speaker's peace.

Solution Make the verb agree with the subject that is closer to it.
Fear or worries fade away.
Neither the stars nor water destroys the speaker's peace.

Exercise

Revise for Agreement Rewrite these sentences, correcting any agreement problems. If the sentence is correct, write *Correct.*

1. A crowd of golden daffodils catch the speaker's eye.
2. The trees and the lake frames the field of flowers.
3. Along the bay are ten thousand daffodils.
4. Neither the daffodils nor the landscape call out to me.

Grammar Terms

The **subject** of a sentence is the person or thing that does the action or exists; the **verb** is the action or state of being.

Test-Taking Tip

When you write for a test, check for subject-agreement as a separate step in the proofreading process. Look twice at sentences with unexpected word order, compound subjects, and words or phrases between the subject and verb.

Grammar Handbook

For more about verbs, see Language Handbook, p. R50.

eWorkbooks To link to the Grammar and Language eWorkbook, go to www.glencoe.com.

ACADEMIC STANDARDS (page 565)

9.6.2 Demonstrate an understanding of sentence construction...

9.4.10 Revise writing for... mechanics.

Focus

Write this sentence on the board: Many works by this author is nonfiction. Discuss why this sentence is incorrect. Remind students that verbs should agree with the subject of the sentence in person and number and that the subject does not always immediately precede the verb.

Teach

Subject-Verb Agreement Point out that the verb must agree with its subject in number and person. To help eliminate errors in subject-verb agreement, students may identify and mentally place the subject next to the verb. **OL**

Assess

1. A crowd of golden daffodils catches the speaker's eye.
2. The trees and the lake frame the sight of the flowers.
3. Correct
4. Neither the daffodils nor the landscape calls out to me.

eWorkbooks Have students access the Web site for more practice with subject-verb agreement.

English Language Coach

Review Writing Assignments Have students look back at writings they have submitted in this class and others. Ask them to reread their work, circling the subjects in each sentence and underlining the verbs. Have partners check each other's subject-verb agreement. **EL**

Differentiated Instruction

Visual Learning Have students copy the workshop example sentences and then use markers to highlight plural nouns in one color and singular nouns in another. Have them do the same for the verbs. If the colors do not match, ask them to correct the subject-verb agreement. **BL**

Academic Standards

Additional Support activities on p. 565 cover the following standards:

English Language Coach: **9.6.2** Demonstrate an understanding of sentence construction...and proper English usage...

Differentiated Instruction: **9.6.2** Demonstrate an understanding of sentence construction...and proper English usage...

Focus

BELLRINGER

Bellringer Options
Selection Focus Transparency 32
Daily Language Practice Transparency 53
Or display images associated with traditional Japanese culture—cherry trees in blossom, Mount Fuji, kimonos, or Buddhist temples.
Ask: What do these images tell you about the relationship between traditional Japanese culture and nature?
Have students consider as they read how important nature has been to haiku writers.

Literature Online

Author Search To expand students' appreciation of Matsuo Bashō, Kaga no Chiyo, Katy Peake, and Paula Yup, have them access the Web site for additional resources.

CheckPoint

Use the CheckPoint questions on Presentation Plus! to monitor students' comprehension. These questions can be used with interactive response keypads for immediate student feedback.

BEFORE YOU READ

Haiku

Matsuo Bashō

MEET THE AUTHORS

How much can seventeen syllables say? In the form of a haiku, they can express simple yet profound ideas and observations. Here are four haiku writers—two traditional masters from Japan and two modern voices.

Matsuo Bashō For many years, Bashō wandered the Japanese countryside in the Buddhist tradition. He slept in dusty inns and ancient monasteries. He visited famous towns and marveled at natural wonders. Most important, he recorded his thoughts and observations in poetic travel diaries. Bashō is revered as one of Japan's greatest masters of haiku. Born into the samurai class of society, he received an education in Japanese and Chinese classics and began writing at an early age. When he was twelve, he entered the service of a local feudal lord. After his lord's death, Bashō traveled to the capital, Edo (now Tokyo), where he worked for four years as a clerk in the waterworks. However, the life of a civil servant was not for Bashō. He started a school of haiku and soon attracted a group of patrons and students whose support made it possible for him to spend his life traveling, writing, and meditating.

For Bashō, traveling allowed him the freedom to collect imagery for his poetry. At the same time, the hardships he encountered while roaming Japan afforded him an opportunity to discipline his mind. He said, "A poet needs to discipline himself every day." Widely respected in his own lifetime, Bashō's influence continued to grow in the twentieth century.

Matsuo Bashō was born in 1644 and died in 1694.

Chiyo Kihaku, a well-known disciple of Bashō, discovered Chiyo's poetry when she was eighteen years old. Kihaku sought her out and helped to make her famous throughout Japan. Chiyo's poetry was greatly influenced by Bashō's work and shared its emphasis on a "oneness with nature." Nevertheless, Chiyo developed her own voice as an honest observer of nature. For Chiyo, writing poetry was a source of awakening that allowed her to live with simplicity and clarity.

Chiyo was born in 1703 and died in 1775.

Katy Peake Catherine Anne (Katy) Peake was a poet, artist, author of children's stories, and social activist from Santa Barbara, California. Her work includes *The Indian Heart of Carrie Hodges* (1972), *A Four Gathering* (1981), and *Dancing Among Foxes* (1993). She was also a photographer.

Katy Peake was born in 1917 and died in 1995.

Paula Yup Born in Phoenix, Arizona, Chinese American poet Paula Yup spent two years in Japan studying Japanese language and literature. She has published more than seventy poems. In addition to writing poetry, she translates Japanese poems into English.

Paula Yup was born in 1957.

Literature Online **Author Search** For more about the authors, go to www.glencoe.com.

Selection Skills

Haiku

Literary Elements
- Haiku (SE pp. 567, 568, 570)
- Review: Diction (SE p. 570)

Reading Skills
- Interpreting Imagery (SE pp. 567, 568, 570)

Vocabulary Skills
- Analogies (SE pp. 567, 570)
- Academic Vocabulary (SE p. 570)

Study Skills/Research/Assessment
- Making Critical Judgments (TWE p. 568)

Writing Skills/Grammar
- Analyze Cultural Context (SE p. 571)
- Using Colons in Poetry (SE p. 571)
- Interdisciplinary Activity: Art (SE p. 571)

LITERATURE PREVIEW

Connecting to the Poems

Haiku create meaning with only a few words. Before you read the four haiku, think about the following questions:

- Have you ever been inspired by nature?
- Have you ever struggled to find the right words to describe something?

Building Background

The purpose of a haiku—traditionally an untitled, unrhymed, seventeen-syllable poem—is to capture a flash of insight based on a solitary observation of nature. Since nature may change suddenly, the poet's challenge in writing a haiku is to record a fleeting moment in precise language. Traditional haiku contain one *kigo,* or "season word," to suggest the season associated with the moment in the poem. Season words do not simply name the seasons; they may be associated with astronomy, climate, geography, animals, plants, and even human events. For example, the term *kare-hasu,* meaning "withered lotus flower," is a season word associated with winter. *Koromo-gae,* meaning "changing clothes," implies summer. When haiku are translated from Japanese into English (or are written in English), the season word must be carefully implied.

Setting Purposes for Reading

Big Idea Nature Inspires

As you read, think about the image from nature that gave rise to each haiku. Try to determine why that image inspired the poet.

Literary Element Haiku

Haiku is a traditional Japanese form of poetry that has three lines and seventeen syllables. The first and third lines have five syllables each; the middle line has seven syllables. As you read these haiku, note how translation may change the number of syllables but not the essential aim of haiku, which is to capture a single moment in nature.

- See Literary Terms Handbook, p. R8.

READING PREVIEW

Reading Strategy Interpreting Imagery

Imagery describes the "word pictures" that writers create to evoke an emotional response in readers. In creating effective images, writers use sensory details or descriptions that appeal to one or more of the five senses: sight, hearing, touch, taste, and smell. **Interpreting imagery** means deciding how these descriptions create or affect a text's meaning.

Reading Tip: Taking Notes Use a chart to record images and your interpretations.

Image	Interpretation
old pond	represents stillness, maybe old age

Vocabulary

calligraphy (kə lig′ rə fē) *n.* artistic, decorative, or stylized writing or lettering; p. 568 *Written in calligraphy, the message was beautiful but difficult to read.*

twine (twīn) *v.* to coil around; p. 568 *The ivy twined around the chimney, covering it on all sides.*

Vocabulary Tip: Analogies Comparisons that reveal the relationship between two words or ideas are called analogies. In analogy exercises, you are given a pair of words that demonstrates a relationship. You are then asked to indicate the same type of relationship in two other words. To complete such an exercise, decide on the relationship represented by the first two words. Then apply that relationship to the second set of words.

Literature Online Interactive Literary Elements Handbook To review or learn more about the literary elements, go to www.glencoe.com.

INDIANA ACADEMIC STANDARDS (pages 567-571)

9.2 Develop strategies such as identifying and analyzing structure...

9.3.7 Recognize and understand the significance of various literary devices, including...imagery...

9.5.3 Write...analytical essays...that gather evidence in support of a thesis...

BEFORE YOU READ

Focus

Summary

Each haiku conveys an ordinary but beautiful natural event—a frog jumping, a sky clearing, a flower growing, and a butterfly resting.

V Vocabulary

Vocabulary File Say: Add these words and definitions to your vocabulary file. Include a sentence that gives you an example of how to use the word. **OL** Students with English language needs should include the pronunciations of these words in their files. **EL**

Literary Elements Have students access the Web site to improve their understanding of haiku.

Selection Resources

Print Materials

- Unit 3 Resources (Fast File), pp. 38–40
- Leveled Vocabulary Development, p. 41
- Selection and Unit Assessments, pp. 101–102
- Selection Quick Checks, p. 51

Transparencies

- Bellringer Options Transparencies: Selection Focus Transparency 32, Daily Language Practice Transparency 53
- Literary Elements Transparency 48

Technology

- TeacherWorks Plus™ CD-ROM
- StudentWorks Plus™ CD-ROM
- Presentation Plus!™ CD-ROM
- Literature Online, glencoe.com
- Online Student Edition, mhln.com
- Exam*View*® Assessment Suite CD-ROM
- Vocabulary PuzzleMaker CD-ROM
- Listening Library, disc 1 tracks 59–62

Teach

R Reading Strategy

Interpreting Imagery
Answer: *Students may say that the morning glory is receiving water from the bucket or has set roots down in it.* OL

L Literary Element

Haiku **Answer:** *Students may say that the image of the butterfly captures a few seconds in time—butterflies rarely linger and they do not live long.* OL

★ Viewing the Art

Kimonos Although the kimono has long been associated with traditional Japanese culture, it originally came from China. The Chinese wore kimonos until the overthrow of the Ming dynasty. The Japanese adopted the kimono in the eighth century. The long, wide-sleeved robe is secured only with a wide sash called an obi and is traditionally worn by both men and women. AS

Haiku

The old pond;
A frog jumps in:
Sound of water.

Matsuo Bashō
Translated by Robert Hass

a clear sheet of sky
calligraphy of blackbirds
written and erased

Katy Peake

The bottom of the bucket which Lady Chiyo filled has fallen out; the moon has no home in the water, November, 1889. Yoshitoshi.

A morning glory
Twined round the bucket:
I will ask my neighbor for water.

Chiyo
Translated by Yasuko Horioka

Peace

I spy butterfly
In quietly still waters
living for today.

Paula Yup

Reading Strategy Interpreting Imagery *What is the relationship between the morning glory and the bucket?* R

Literary Element Haiku *How well does this haiku capture a single moment?* L

Vocabulary

calligraphy (kə lig′ re fē) *n.* artistic, decorative, or stylized writing or lettering

twine (twīn) *v.* to coil around

Additional Support

Skills Practice

READING: Making Critical Judgments
Have students recall poems they have read in this unit and compare their different forms and techniques—rhyme scheme, meter, free verse, enjambment, and haiku. Ask them to generate a critical judgment about the forms of poetry by answering these questions:

- What makes a good poem?
- What does a poem do that other forms of writing do or cannot?

Have students write their judgment in the form of a journal entry. Ask volunteers to share their judgments with the class. OL

AFTER YOU READ

RESPONDING AND THINKING CRITICALLY

Respond

1. Which of the haiku gives you the clearest image of a specific moment in time in a natural setting? Explain.

Recall and Interpret

2. (a)What does the speaker in Bashō's haiku see and hear? (b)What makes this a fleeting moment?
3. (a)What event in nature does Katy Peake's haiku describe? (b)What human activity does she compare it with?
4. (a)Based on the poem, name two reasons why Chiyo might have noticed the morning glory. (b)Why does the speaker decide to get water from a neighbor?

Analyze and Evaluate

5. Reread Bashō's haiku. In which season do you think this moment took place? Explain your opinion.
6. The speaker in most traditional haiku does not often appear in the poem as "I." Do you think Chiyo's break with tradition makes her haiku more or less effective? Explain.
7. Explain how Paula Yup's poem is both similar to and different from traditional Japanese haiku.
8. As an art form, the haiku has sometimes been compared to the photograph, which can capture a fleeting moment. Do you think this is an appropriate comparison? Explain.

Connect

9. **Big Idea** **Nature Inspires** What image or natural scene would you use in a haiku? Explain.

DAILY LIFE AND CULTURE

Early Japanese Women Writers

During the Heian Period (794–1192), the development of *kana*—a Japanese phonetic syllabary—made writing the native Japanese language much easier. As scholars and government officials, men remained under pressure to use the Chinese language, which was in political favor at the time. Women, however, did not hold such positions at court, and they were able to write privately in *kana*.

In fact, during this time period, many women published prose anthologies or collections that often combined stories, catalogues, and other "bits" of personal nonfiction from diaries. These diaries present historians with a vivid picture of Japanese life and culture from this time period.

Group Activity Work with classmates to discuss and answer the following questions.

1. Why were women uniquely positioned to play an important role in the development of native Japanese culture?
2. (a)What form did the earliest writing by Japanese women take? (b)Why do you think it took this form?
3. What might a diary entry and a haiku have in common?

Matsushima no Tsubone, 1875. Yoshitoshi Taiso. Woodblock print, 14¼ x 9½ in. Private collection.

CheckPoint

Use the CheckPoint questions on Presentation Plus! to check students' mastery of the selection. These questions can be used with interactive response keypads for immediate student feedback.

Daily Life and Culture

1. Women did not have roles at court that required them to use Chinese.
2. (a) diaries and lists (b) Women did not participate in public life. Their work was not meant for publication.
3. Both often include observations about the human experience.

AFTER YOU READ

Assess

1. Students may suggest the image of blackbirds scrawled against the sky or the flower growing around the bucket.
2. (a) The speaker sees a pond and a frog; he hears a splash of water. (b) The movement of the frog is quick. The reader knows that the sound and ripples in the water will fade quickly.
3. (a) A flock of blackbirds flying through the sky (b) handwriting that is quickly erased
4. (a) She needed water from the bucket. The flower is entwined with the bucket. (b) The speaker realizes that picking up the bucket will disturb the flower.
5. The season is probably spring or summer because the pond is not frozen.
6. Students may say the "I" makes the poem more effective because it shows the relationship between the speaker and nature.
7. Similar: It focuses sharply on one natural image at a particular moment and has the traditional line and syllable requirements. Different: It has a title and there is no punctuation separating the final line from the rest of poem.
8. Some students may say that the comparison to a photograph is apt because both capture a fleeting image in the moment.
9. Answers will vary.

Academic Standards

The Additional Support activity on p. 568 covers the following standard:

Skills Practice: **9.3.2** Compare and contrast the presentation of a similar theme or topic across genres...to explain how the selection of genre shapes the theme or topic.

AFTER YOU READ

Assess

Literary Element

1. It shows how patterns are written and erased in the sky. The poem illustrates that nothing is constant.
2. It shows how a morning glory becomes part of a bucket and how a human is affected by this natural occurrence. It illustrates the connection between the human and the natural worlds.
3. The poem suggests silence before the frog jumps and after the sound of the water fades away.

Reading Strategy

1. (a)The water is still, clear, and mirror-like; the butterfly is fluttering and colorful. The butterfly's life is short; the water will last. (b)The butterfly is not conscious of or worried about the passage of time; it simply exists in the moment.
2. A morning glory is a vine-like flower that grows rapidly. The flowers might literally appear in the bucket overnight. Most other flowers, such as tulips or daisies, cannot grow around an object. Also, morning glories are seasonal. The flower may be a *kigo* signifying summer.

Vocabulary

1. a
2. c

LITERARY ANALYSIS

Literary Element Haiku

Most **haiku** use vivid but fleeting images to sketch a scene that usually involves the world of nature and also says something about the human experience. This tradition revolves around some key Buddhist principles about the natural world: that all things change; that all things are interrelated; and that all things suffer. Another Buddhist principle that underlies haiku is a respect or concern for silence.

1. How does Peake's haiku demonstrate that all things change?
2. How does Chiyo's poem show that all things are related to each other?
3. Explain how Bashō's poem is concerned with silence.

Review: Diction

As you learned on page 209, **diction** is a writer's choice of words. Translators are keenly aware of diction. A single word in one language may have many counterparts in another language, and the translator must choose the word that best conveys the meaning of the original text. Conversely, certain words may have no counterpart in another language, so the translator must create phrases that are as close as possible in meaning to the original. As a result, translations of haiku often veer from the traditional haiku syllable pattern.

Partner Activity Meet with a partner to discuss the translated poems. Count the syllables in each line to find places where the poem veers from the traditional syllable pattern. Brainstorm a list of words and phrases that have the same or similar meaning as those in the poem. Using your list or words, write a new version of the haiku that follows the traditional 5-7-5 syllable pattern. Share your haiku with the rest of the class.

Original words	New words
jumps	leaps hops

READING AND VOCABULARY

Reading Strategy Interpreting Imagery

An **image** brings a picture, sound, or other sensory experience to mind, but it may also have some sort of symbolic value. Look back at the chart you created, and think about the deeper meanings of the images in the poems.

1. In Yup's haiku, how do you suppose the appearance of the water compares with that of the butterfly? Why might Yup think that the butterfly is "living for today"?
2. One image in Chiyo's poem is the morning glory. Why do you think she chose this vinelike plant, which grows very fast?

Vocabulary Practice

Practice with Analogies Choose the word that best completes each analogy.

1. **photography : camera :: calligraphy :**

   a. brush **b.** appliance **c.** hoe

2. **broken : split :: twined :**

   a. open **b.** doubled **c.** twisted

Academic Vocabulary

Here are two words from the vocabulary list on page R80. These words will help you think, write, and talk about the selection.

refine (ri fīn′) *v.* to improve or perfect

unify (ū′ na fī′) *v.* to bring together

Practice and Apply

1. How did reading these four poems help **refine** your understanding of the haiku form?
2. Which words help **unify** the images presented in Peake's haiku?

Reviewing: Diction

Students might brainstorm synonyms for these words and use them to write a new version of the haiku with the traditional syllable pattern: *twined, round, bucket, ask, neighbor, water, old, pond, jumps, sound*

Academic Vocabulary

1. Students may say that these poems helped them sharpen, or refine, their understanding of the haiku form.
2. The words related to writing—*calligraphy, sheet, written,* and *erased*—bring together, or unify, the images in the haiku.

WRITING AND EXTENDING

Writing About Literature

Analyze Cultural Context Haiku is a national art form in Japan. At least 700 periodicals and 1,000 books are devoted to haiku and the related tanka form of poetry each year. Haiku is a strict form that celebrates the natural world. This formal and attentive approach to nature is typical of other Japanese art forms. For example, traditional Japanese architecture uses natural wood and subordinates itself to the landscape. The carefully arranged rocks, trees, and raked pebbles in Japanese rock gardens create places for the quiet contemplation of nature. Write an essay in which you explain haiku as a distinctively Japanese art form. Draw on the information presented in this lesson, as well as any outside research you deem necessary.

As you draft, follow an organizational plan like this one:

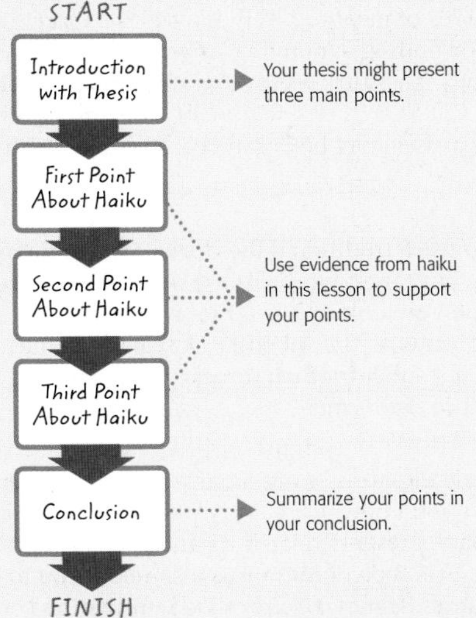

After you complete your draft, have a peer read it and suggest revisions. Then proofread and edit your work to correct errors in spelling, grammar, and punctuation.

Interdisciplinary Activity: Art

Draw or paint an illustration to accompany one of the haiku you just read, an original haiku, or another haiku of your choosing. Use your artwork to convey how you "see" the haiku's main image. Be sure to incorporate the words of the haiku in your illustration.

GRAMMAR AND STYLE

Haiku Language and Style

Using Colons in Poetry Haiku often include a "cutting," or separation, that signals a contrast or change of some kind. In English, cutting is usually marked with punctuation such as a colon or dash. For example, in Bashō's haiku, the translator has used a colon as a cutting device to separate the poet's impressions of the pond before and after the frog jumps in.

The old pond;
A frog jumps in:
Sound of water.

The use of the colon in haiku mirrors one of the four ways writers use colons in everyday writing—to separate words that explain, restate, illustrate, or amplify the words that come before the colon. The colon can also be used in everyday prose to introduce a list or to set off a long, formal quotation. The colon always follows an independent clause (a group of words that can stand on its own as a sentence).

Activity Rewrite each haiku as a single complete sentence that includes a colon. Be sure that an independent clause precedes each colon.

Revising Check

Colons If you have used any colons in your essay about haiku, check to be sure that the words preceding the colon make up an independent clause. If you have not used a colon, look for a place where a colon might help you relate two important ideas.

LiteratureOnline **Web Activities** For eFlashcards, Selection Quick Checks, and other Web activities, go to www.glencoe.com.

AFTER YOU READ

Assess

Writing About Literature

Use these criteria when evaluating students' writing:

- The introduction clearly identifies the characteristics of haiku and explains why it is distinctively Japanese.
- Each body paragraph makes a clear point about a characteristic of haiku and contains details from the poems to support the point.
- The conclusion restates the main idea and offers insight into the form of haiku.

Interdisciplinary Activity: Art

Students' artwork should clearly illustrate or suggest the central image of the haiku and contain the actual words of the poem.

Haiku Language and Style

Possible sentence versions of the haiku include the following:

Basho: The frog jumps in the old pond and makes this sound: splash, plop, and drip.

Chiyo: Because a morning glory is twined around the bucket I must do the following: ask my neighbor for water.

Web Activities Have students access the Web site for interactive activities that will help them assess their understanding of the selection.

Revising Check

Students may benefit from writing the rules for using colons on an index card before revising their essays. Before inserting a colon in a sentence or using one to introduce a list or question, students should review the list of rules and make sure they apply. Challenge students to use a colon at least once in their essays and to explain why they used it.

Focus

The words in the exercise are all verbs or adjectives. Students should find synonyms that are the same part of speech and can be used correctly in the sentences. Have students find two synonyms for each word and write sentences that feature them.

eFlashcards Have students access the Web site for more practice in using a thesaurus.

Assess

1. Possible answers:
   a. swerve—veer, turn
   b. reconcile—reunite, settle
   c. isolated—separated, secluded
   d. vast—huge, giant
   e. vacant—empty, absent
2. Possible sentences:
   a. You have to swerve to avoid the pothole.
   Turn to the right at the stop sign.
   Veer away from the shoulder, or you will skid.
   b. The sisters will reconcile their differences.
   Bob hopes to reunite the arguing brothers.
   Can you settle the differences between those two teams?
   c. The isolated village was far from the highway.
   The secluded house could not be seen from the street.
   The separated children ate lunch at different desks.
   d. The universe is vast.
   The auditorium is huge.
   The servings are enormous.
   e. The apartment is vacant.
   The pot is empty.
   The student was absent from class.

Vocabulary Workshop

Language Resources

▶ **Technology Tip**
Many Internet and CD-ROM thesauruses have extra features such as audio pronunciation and the ability to define a word within an entry.

▶ **Test-Taking Tip**
To decide whether two words are synonyms, first determine what part of speech each word is. Synonyms are always the same part of speech.

▶ **Reading Handbook**
For more about using a thesaurus, see Reading Handbook, p. R19.

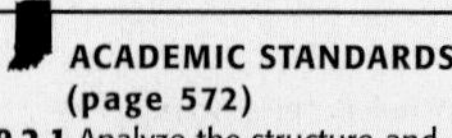

eFlashcards For eFlashcards and other vocabulary activities, go to www.glencoe.com.

ACADEMIC STANDARDS (page 572)
9.2.1 Analyze the structure and format of reference or functional workplace documents...

Using a Thesaurus

"I spy butterfly / in quietly still waters / living for today."

—Paula Yup, "Peace"

Connecting to Literature Some synonyms, such as *twined* and *wound,* are practically interchangeable, while others, such as *quietly* and *still,* can have different meanings. For instance, *still* means "motionless," as well as "quiet." *Still* can also mean "yet." Learning the differences between similar words can help you read better, write more expressively and precisely, and speak and listen more effectively.

Dictionaries sometimes provide a list of synonyms at the end of an entry and explain the different shades of meaning. A thesaurus is a more specialized reference work for finding synonyms, as well as antonyms, words with opposite meanings. Thesauruses (or thesauri) are available in different formats: online, on CD-ROMs, as a feature of word-processing software, and in print. Thesauruses may be organized traditionally or in dictionary order.

Traditional Organization To use a traditional thesaurus, you begin by browsing a category to find your target word. To use other thesauruses that are organized by concept, you look up the target word, such as *remove,* in the index. Then you choose the subentry closest to the meaning you want, such as *subtract.* That subentry then directs you to a list of synonyms under the heading of *subtraction.*

Dictionary Organization Some thesauruses are organized like dictionaries. You simply look up the word you know. Each entry provides the part of speech, and, like a dictionary, presents related meanings in separate, numbered parts of the entry. This type of thesaurus also refers you to synonyms with their own entries. It may also provide information about idioms.

Exercise

1. Using a thesaurus, find two synonyms for each word below. Then look up the definitions of those synonyms in a dictionary to identify the precise meaning of each one.
   a. swerve **b.** reconcile **c.** isolated **d.** vast **e.** vacant
2. Write each word above, as well as each synonym you find, in a sentence. Be sure your sentences reflect the slight differences in meaning for each group of synonyms.

PART 2

Life Lessons

Spectators, 20th century. Andrew Gadd. Oil on canvas, 46.97 x 70.98 in. 

BIG IDEA

BI Perhaps the most important thing life teaches us is that there is always more to learn. Every experience brings a new lesson. The selections in this part explore the wisdom gained from some of life's greatest teachers—love, family, and nature. As you read these poems, ask yourself: What lesson has each speaker learned?

Differentiated Instruction

Discussion Have a student read the blurb aloud. Engage students in a discussion of their greatest teachers.

Ask: What has been your greatest teacher so far: love, family, nature, or something else? Have students explain their answers with specific examples. **BL**

Analyzing and Extending

BI Big Idea

Life Lessons Encourage students to look at the art and discuss who, if anyone, is learning a lesson.

Ask: What is one of the most important life lessons you've learned? *(Answers will vary.)* **OL**

★ Viewing the Art

While English artist Andrew Gadd's (1968–) technique shows classic influences, his subjects are contemporary. Gadd is a figurative painter—he paints real subjects that may not strictly represent what they are—and his work is often allegorical.

Ask: What does this painting literally show? What might this painting represent figuratively? *(The painting literally shows some kids watching something. Answers will vary as to the figurative meaning.)* **AS**

Academic Standards

The Additional Support activity on p. 573 covers the following standard:

Differentiated Instruction: **9.2** Develop [reading] strategies…

Part 2: Skills Scope and Sequence

Readability Scores Key
Dale-Chall/ **DRP**/ Lexile

PACING (DAYS) STANDARD	BLOCK	SELECTIONS AND FEATURES	LITERARY ELEMENTS
1–2 class sessions	1	"How Things Work" by Gary Soto, pp. 576–579	Imagery, SE pp. 577, 579
		"I Was a Skinny Tomboy Kid" by Alma Luz Villanueva, pp. 580–584	Free Verse, SE pp. 581, 582, 584 Character, TWE p. 582
2 class sessions	1	"The World Is Not a Pleasant Place to Be" by Nikki Giovanni, pp. 585–588	Personification, SE pp. 586–588
		"'Hope' is the thing with feathers" and "I'm Nobody! Who are you?" by Emily Dickinson, pp. 589–595	Metaphor, SE pp. 590, 594 Speaker, SE p. 594
1–2 class sessions	1	"Defining the Grateful Gesture" by Yvonne Sapia, pp. 596–599	Metaphor and Simile, SE pp. 597, 598, 599
		"Sympathy" by Paul Laurence Dunbar, pp. 600–603	Symbol, SE pp. 601, 602, 603 Analyzing Symbolism, TWE p. 602
2 class sessions	1	"Remember" by Joy Harjo, pp. 604–607	Repetition, SE pp. 605, 607
		"The Road Not Taken" by Robert Frost, pp. 608–613	Lyric Poetry, SE pp. 609, 612 Rhythm, SE p. 612 Understanding Lyric Poetry, TWE p. 610
		"The Secret" by Denise Levertov, pp. 614–618	Paradox, SE pp. 615–617 Free Verse, SE p. 617

About the Part

Part 2 presents poetry that concerns learning through experiences, family, and nature.

READING AND CRITICAL THINKING	VOCABULARY	WRITING AND GRAMMAR	LISTENING, SPEAKING, AND VIEWING
Analyzing Structure, SE pp. 577, 579 Using a Graphic Organizer, SE p. 577	Context Clues, SE pp. 577, 579	Respond to Voice, SE p. 579 Cause and Effect, TWE p. 578	Analyzing Art, TWE p. 578
Analyzing Sensory Details, SE pp. 581, 582, 584	Academic Vocabulary, SE p. 584	Creating Character, TWE p. 582	Art Activity, SE p. 584
Analyzing Tone, SE pp. 586, 588 Looking for Clues, SE p. 586		Respond to Mood, SE p. 588	Analyzing Art, TWE p. 587
Imagery, SE pp. 590, 592, 594 Taking Notes, SE p. 590	Analogies, SE p. 594 Academic Vocabulary, SE p. 594 Rhythmic and Rhyming Vocabulary, TWE p. 594	Analyze Meter, SE p. 595 Using Dashes in Poetry, SE p. 595 Dashes in Prose, TWE p. 592	Group Activity, SE p. 594
Connecting to Personal Experience, SE pp. 597, 599 Asking Questions Graphic Organizer, SE p. 597	Denotation and Connotation, SE pp. 597, 599 Analyzing Connotations, TWE p. 598	Analyze Imagery, SE p. 599	
Applying Background Knowledge, SE pp. 601, 602, 603 Creating a Web, SE p. 601	Analogies, SE pp. 601, 603	Respond to Theme, SE p. 603	
Drawing Conclusions About Author's Beliefs, SE pp. 605–607	Academic Vocabulary, SE p. 607	Repetition, TWE p. 606	Choral Reading, SE p. 607 Analyzing Art, TWE p. 606
Making Inferences About Theme, SE pp. 609, 610, 612	Context Clues, SE pp. 609, 612 Academic Vocabulary, SE p. 612	Explore Author's Purpose, SE p. 613 Using Inversion in Poetry, SE p. 613 Lyric Poem, TWE p. 612	Group Activity Parody, SE p. 611 Analyzing Art, TWE p. 610
Analyzing Parallelism and Juxtaposition, SE pp. 615, 618 Analyzing Rhetorical Devices, TWE p. 616	Academic Vocabulary, SE p. 618	Analyze Theme, SE p. 618 Analyzing Paradoxes, TWE p. 616 Free Verse, TWE p. 618	Giving a Speech, SE p. 618

Focus

BELLRINGER

Bellringer Options
Daily Language Practice Transparency 54
Or **write on the board:** It was so hot I could have fried an egg on the sidewalk. Point out to students that imagery can be fun and funny. Have students work in groups to complete the following: It was so cold . . . , It rained so hard . . . , The fog was so dense . . .

Invite students to add humorous examples of their own.

Teach

L Literary Element

Language Ask: What are some common examples of a figure of speech? *(If necessary, prompt students with something like "I have a million things to do.")* Note that a figure of speech can evoke a vivid image. As students offer examples, discuss the images they evoke. OL

Literary Elements Have students access the Web site to improve their understanding of the language of poetry.

LITERARY FOCUS

The Language of Poetry

In what distinctive ways does poetry use language?

Imagery

Imagery refers to the word pictures the poet creates that can remind readers of something they have seen, heard, tasted, smelled, or touched. To create an image, the poet uses sensory details—that is, words that appeal to one or more of the five senses.

L Figurative Language

Figurative language is language used for descriptive effect, often to imply meanings indirectly. The words in figurative language suggest more than their ordinary, literal meanings. All writers use figurative language, although it is particularly important to poets, who rely on it to bring power, vitality, and freshness to their writing. Notice the way Yvonne Sapia uses the word *passenger* in this excerpt from "Defining the Grateful Gesture."

but she would eat it
to gain strength
taken from her by long hot days
of working in her mother's house
and helping her father make
candy in the family kitchen.
No idle passenger
Traveling through life was she.

—Yvonne Sapia, **from "Defining the Grateful Gesture"**

Additional Support

Skills Practice

LITERARY ELEMENT: The Language of Poetry Invite students to experiment with the language of poetry.
Write these heads on the board: Hyperbole, Figure of Speech, Simile, Metaphor, Personification

Choose a subject or concept—happiness, for example—and have the class provide examples of poetic language to describe it. OL

Figurative language is based on figures of speech. A **figure of speech** is an expression in which words are used in unusual ways to create vivid or dramatic effects. Simile, metaphor, personification, and hyperbole are all figures of speech.

Simile A **simile** is a comparison of two unlike things that uses the word *like* or *as*. Poets employ similes to help the reader understand an abstraction—to make it easier for the reader to grasp what is being described.

R

He is as cool and gleaming as a braided whip.

—Mary Oliver, **from "The Black Snake"**

The simile comparing a snake to a braided whip helps the reader see the snake in a new way. A simile can also startle the reader and inject fresh life into a familiar idea, as does William Shakespeare's simile, "Death lies on her, like an untimely frost."

Metaphor Like a simile, a **metaphor** is a direct comparison between two unlike things. However, in a metaphor, the comparison is implied rather than stated; there is no use of connective words such as *like* or *as*.

a clear sheet of sky
calligraphy of blackbirds

—Paula Yup, **from "Haiku"**

In her haiku, Paula Yup compares the sky to a clear, or clean, sheet of paper and the appearance of birds as calligraphy, or handwriting, on the paper. In most metaphors, the first object is seen as being or having similar qualities to the second object. Poets use metaphors to enliven language and to help readers see a familiar subject in a new way.

Personification When a writer gives human qualities to nonhuman things, he or she is using **personification**. Poets use personification for the same reasons they use a metaphor: to help the reader see something familiar in a slightly different way.

And then my heart with pleasure fills,
And dances with the daffodils.

—William Wordsworth, **from "I Wandered Lonely as a Cloud"**

Hyperbole This figure of speech uses overstatement or exaggeration for dramatic effect. Poets use hyperbole to add flavor to their writing and bring emphasis to their images:

And you, O my Soul, where you stand,
Surrounded, surrounded, in measureless oceans
of space

—Walt Whitman, **from "A Noiseless Patient Spider"**

Quickwrite

Sensing Winter What sights, smells, or tastes come to mind when you think of winter? Can you smell chestnuts roasting? Can you taste a snowflake on your tongue? Or do you feel the warmth of the sun on your face? Jot down images that would help a reader see, hear, smell, taste, and touch winter.

Literature Online Interactive Literary Elements Handbook Go to www.glencoe.com to review or learn more about imagery and figurative language.

INDIANA ACADEMIC STANDARDS (pages 574-575)

9.3.7 Recognize and understand the significance of various literary devices, including figurative language [and] imagery...

9.4.3 Use...sensory details...

Teach

R Reading Strategy

Understanding Imagery

Have students read each of the poem excerpts aloud. After each excerpt is read, pause and **ask:** What images do you see when you read the poem? Encourage students to be specific. Point out any figurative language the students use as they talk. OL

Viewing the Cartoon

Cartoonist Wiley Miller has received four National Cartoonist Society Reuben Awards for "Non Sequitur." As the title implies, the cartoon is not confined to any specific subject, but ranges from political satire to pure comedy. AS

Assess

Quickwrite

Answers will vary. Make sure students are specific and that their images address all five senses.

Differentiated Instruction

Imagery Students with different learning styles will respond to different aspects of imagery. For example, visual learners will respond to sight, and auditory learners will respond to sound. Encourage students to consider all the senses when investigating imagery, not just the ones that are their strengths. BL

Academic Standards

Additional Support activities on pp. 574 and 575 cover the following standards:

Skills Practice: **9.3.7** Recognize and understand the significance of various literary devices, including figurative language...

Differentiated Instruction: **9.3.7** Recognize and understand the significance of various literary devices, including...imagery...

BEFORE YOU READ

Focus

BELLRINGER

Bellringer Options
Daily Language Practice Transparency 55
Or **say:** Buying, selling, and trading are basic to modern life. What do you buy or trade? How might surfing the Web or downloading information be considered a form of commerce? *(Possible answers: Companies provide information in return for your exposure to their ads; information might be seen as a type of currency.)* Encourage students to discuss how these forms of commerce affect their personal economics.

Literature Online

Author Search To expand students' appreciation of Gary Soto, have them access the Web site for additional information and resources.

Use the CheckPoint questions on Presentation Plus! to monitor students' comprehension. These questions can be used with interactive response keypads for immediate student feedback.

BEFORE YOU READ

How Things Work

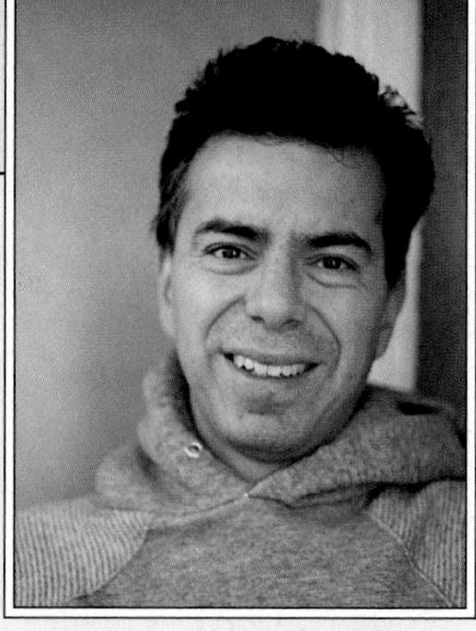

MEET GARY SOTO

Gary Soto first became interested in poetry while procrastinating on a college research paper. Instead of writing, he picked up an anthology of poetry and began leafing through it. Excited by what he found there, Soto decided to write poetry himself.

Handle with Care Soto was born and raised in Fresno, California, in the *barrio,* a working-class Mexican American neighborhood. There were no books in his home, and he was not encouraged to read. Still, he developed an interest in geography and eventually went to college at Fresno State University. There, he enrolled in a writing class where he learned "to handle language with care," under the strict guidance of poet Philip Levine. Soto memorized the poems of English and Chinese authors, because this practice was supposed to help his writing. However, he was more interested in Spanish and Latin American poets.

Soto received his Master of Fine Arts degree in creative writing from the University of California, Irvine. A year later, his first collection of poetry, *The Elements of San Joaquin* (1977), was published. A reviewer for *Western American Literature* called Soto "considerably more than just a good ethnic writer, he is a good poet."

A Writer and a Teacher Since his first book of poems, Soto has written memoirs, novels, plays, films, and an opera libretto. His writing appeals to all age groups and his work has won many awards, including the Academy of American Poets Prize and the Andrew Carnegie Medal. In addition to writing, Soto teaches English and Ethnic Studies at the University of California, Berkeley. He encourages young poets and writers by telling them to look within themselves for inspiration. Since 1993, he has taught part-time in order to devote more time to writing.

"I woke up to poetry and went to bed with poetry."

—Gary Soto

Examining Life Unlike some authors, Soto does not begin writing with a particular audience in mind. As a result, his work often appeals to adults and young adults alike. His writing encourages readers to recall the details of their own childhoods. His memoir *Living Up the Street* is a collection of twenty-one anecdotes about his life growing up in the *barrio.* In one chapter, he writes about struggling to make his world like the one he sees on 1950s television by trying to get his rowdy siblings to dress for dinner as they do in "Leave It to Beaver."

Most of Soto's work describes the pain and promise of growing up. In his poem "That Girl," for example, he reveals the way in which discovering girls in seventh grade caused him to lose interest in his schoolwork.

Gary Soto was born in 1952.

Literature Online **Author Search** For more about Gary Soto, go to www.glencoe.com.

Selection Skills

How Things Work

Literary Elements
- Imagery (SE pp. 577, 579)

Reading Skills
- Analyzing Structure (SE pp. 577, 579)
- Using a Graphic Organizer (SE p. 577)

Vocabulary Skills
- Context Clues (SE pp. 577, 579)

Writing Skills/Grammar
- Respond to Voice (SE p. 579)
- Cause and Effect (TWE p. 578)

Listening/Speaking/Viewing Skills
- Analyzing Art (TWE pp. 573, 578)

LITERATURE PREVIEW

Connecting to the Poem

"How Things Work" describes a chain of events set off by one person's routine purchases. Before you read the poem, think about the following questions:

- What routine purchases do you and your family make?
- Do you think anyone's life might change if you were to stop spending money on those things? Why or why not?

Building Background

In 1982, the United States suffered a recession that was the worst economic downturn since the Great Depression of the 1930s. Businesses failed, farms went bankrupt, and many were jobless. By 1985, when Gary Soto published the poem "How Things Work," the U.S. economy was beginning to turn around and the mood was more hopeful.

Setting Purposes for Reading

Big Idea Life Lessons

As you read "How Things Work," try to decide what lesson the speaker might be encouraging his daughter to learn.

Literary Element Imagery

Imagery refers to the "word pictures" that writers create to evoke an emotional response in the reader. In creating effective images, writers use sensory details—descriptions that appeal to one or more of the five senses. Recognizing imagery will improve your understanding of a poem's meaning. As you read this poem, notice which of Soto's words and phrases create imagery and an emotional response.

- See Literary Terms Handbook, p. R9.

LiteratureOnline Interactive Literary Elements Handbook To review or learn more about the literary elements, go to www.glencoe.com.

READING PREVIEW

Reading Strategy Analyzing Structure

The **structure** of a poem is created through the organization of images, ideas, and words. The writer uses the structure of a work of literature in order to present a unified impression to the reader. Without organized structure, a poem, or any other piece of writing, would not be a coherent whole. As you read, notice the structure Soto uses. Try to make connections between the structural choices he makes and the meaning of the poem.

Reading Tip: Rereading Read the poem thoroughly, thinking only about what the words mean. Then read it again, concentrating on its structure. As you reread the poem, think about the ways Soto is able to make the poem relevant to his readers while structuring it in his own unique way.

Structure	Purpose
short sentences	emphasize a point

Vocabulary

rosin (roz′ in) *n.* a resin made from the sap of various pine trees used to increase sliding friction on the bows of certain stringed instruments; p. 578 *New violin students have to learn when and where to use rosin on the bow.*

belligerent (be lij′ ər ənt) *adj.* inclined or eager to fight; p. 578 *The opposing team's belligerent coach screamed and kicked dirt when the umpire made a questionable call.*

Vocabulary Tip: Context Clues When you encounter an unfamiliar word, consider the surrounding words and phrases. Using this strategy, you can often find good clues about the word's meaning.

INDIANA ACADEMIC STANDARDS (pages 577-579)

9.3.7 Recognize and understand the significance of various literary devices, including...imagery...

9.2 Develop strategies such as...analyzing structure...

9.5.2 Write responses to literature...

BEFORE YOU READ

Focus

Summary

The speaker first describes how he spends his 20 dollars. Then he theorizes how the people who received the money will use it. He explains to his daughter that by purchasing something, he indirectly helps others buy things of their own. But he admits some uncertainty about whether this is true or not.

V Vocabulary

Vocabulary File Say: Add these words and definitions to your vocabulary file. For each word, include a sentence that gives you an example of how to use the word. **OL** Students with English language needs should include the pronunciations of these words in their files. **EL**

Literary Elements Have students access the Web site to improve their understanding of imagery.

Selection Resources

Print Materials

- Unit 3 Resources (Fast File), pp. 44–46
- Leveled Vocabulary Development, p. 42
- Selection and Unit Assessments, pp. 103–104
- Selection Quick Checks, p. 52

Transparencies

- Bellringer Options Transparencies: Daily Language Practice Transparency 55
- Literary Elements Transparency 71

Technology

- TeacherWorks Plus™ CD-ROM
- StudentWorks Plus™ CD-ROM
- Presentation Plus!™ CD-ROM
- Literature Online, glencoe.com
- Online Student Edition, mhln.com
- Exam*View*® Assessment Suite CD-ROM
- Vocabulary PuzzleMaker CD-ROM
- Listening Library, disc 1 track 63

Teach

BI **Big Idea**

Life Lessons **Answer:** *To admit his uncertainty*

Ask: How does this admission affect the reader? *(Students may say that it makes him seem honest and human; rather than claiming to be all knowing, he questions his own wisdom. By establishing the persona of a "regular guy," he encourages readers to identify with him.)* **OL**

Viewing the Art

The influence of Impressionism and Cubism can clearly be seen in French artist Robert Delaunay's (1885–1941) unique painting style. Delaunay often collaborated with his wife, artist Sonia Terk. **AS**

CheckPoint

Use the CheckPoint questions on Presentation Plus! to check students' mastery. These questions can be used with interactive response keypads for immediate student feedback.

How Things Work

Gary Soto

Menage de Cochon or Menage Electrique. Robert Delaunay. Musee National d'Art Moderne, Centre Georges Pompidou, Paris, France.

Today it's going to cost us thirty-five dollars
To live. Six for a softball. Eight for a book,
A handful of ones for coffee and two sweet rolls,
Bus fare, **rosin** for your mother's violin.
We're completing our task. The tip I left
For the waitress filters down
Like rain, wetting the new roots of a child
Perhaps, a **belligerent** cat that won't let go
Of a balled sock until there's chicken to eat.
As far as I can tell, daughter, it works like this:
You buy crayons from a stationer, a bag of apples
From the farmer's market, and what dollars
Are passed on help others buy pencils, a guitar,
Tickets to a matinee movie.
If we buy a goldfish, someone tries on a hat.
If we buy crayons, someone walks home with a broom.
A tip, a small purchase here and there,
And things just keep going. I guess.

Big Idea Life Lessons *Why might the speaker start his lesson with this phrase? Explain.* **BI**

Vocabulary

rosin (roz′ in) *n.* a resin made from the sap of various pine trees used to increase sliding friction on the bows of certain stringed instruments

belligerent (be lij′ ər ənt) *adj.* inclined or eager to fight

Additional Support

Academic Standards

The Additional Support activity on p. 578 covers the following standard:

Skills Practice: **9.5.1** Write…short stories that describe a sequence of events and communicate the significance of the events to the audience…

Skills Practice

WRITING: Cause and Effect Have students experiment with cause and effect by writing about an incidental encounter. Discuss the various types of people that students bump into during their day. For example, do they ever stop at a store after school? If so, how do they interact with the clerk?

Ask: How might your encounter affect this other person? Have students suggest a possible scenario in the form of a short story. **OL** Have students write the story from the other person's point of view. **AL**

AFTER YOU READ

RESPONDING AND THINKING CRITICALLY

Respond

1. Do you agree with the speaker's interpretation of how things work? Explain.

Recall and Interpret

2. (a)What does the speaker say it will cost today to live? (b)What do you think "to live" means in the context of the poem?
3. (a)What happens if the characters "buy a goldfish"? (b)What does the speaker mean by this?
4. (a)What words and phrases express uncertainty? (b)Why might the speaker be uncertain?

Analyze and Evaluate

5. What might the speaker mean by "We're completing our task"? Explain.
6. What emotion does the image in line 7 evoke in the reader?
7. How appropriate or effective do you think the poem's title is?

Connect

8. **Big Idea** **Life Lessons** What does the speaker of the poem seem to be teaching his daughter about money and life?

LITERARY ANALYSIS

Literary Element Imagery

Poets and other writers use **imagery** to communicate what they see, hear, feel, taste, and smell. Appealing to the senses draws readers into the writing and encourages them to develop a personal relationship with the text. Soto relies on imagery throughout his poem to help readers understand his ideas.

1. Identify two examples of imagery in this poem.
2. Why do you think Soto chose not to create images of the father or the daughter in the poem?

Writing About Literature

Respond to Voice Voice is the way the author uses language to convey his personality or the personality of the speaker to the reader. Word choice and style affect the voice of a piece of writing. The voice, in turn, often determines the tone. Write a short essay in which you respond to the voice in "How Things Work." What is Soto's attitude toward his subject? How can you tell? Are you comfortable with his voice? Do you find it effective? Why or why not? Use evidence from the poem to support your position.

LiteratureOnline **Web Activities** For eFlashcards, Selection Quick Checks, and other Web activities, go to www.glencoe.com.

READING AND VOCABULARY

Reading Strategy Analyzing Structure

The **structure** of a poem includes the organization of images, ideas, words, and lines. The structure of a poem is sometimes created through the use of rhythm, rhyme, repetition, or stanzas. With many options from which to choose, a poet's final decision about the structure a poem takes will help reveal the meaning.

1. Find two lines in the poem that end in enjambment, or the breaking of a sentence where there is not a natural pause.
2. What is the effect of these enjambments?

Vocabulary Practice

Practice with Context Clues Read each of the following sentences and identify the word or words that provide a context clue for the meaning of the word in bold.

1. The baseball player used **rosin** on his hands to keep them from getting slippery.
   a. baseball player **b.** keep them from getting slippery
2. As usual, the **belligerent** coach became aggressive when arguing with the referee and was thrown out of the game.
   a. aggressive **b.** referee

LiteratureOnline

Web Activities Have students access the Web site for interactive activities that will help them assess their understanding of the selection.

Reading Strategy

1. 1, 5, 8, 12
2. The line breaks add emphasis to the words that follow the break.

Vocabulary

1. b
2. a

AFTER YOU READ

Assess

1. Possible answers: No, his examples prove him wrong. Yes, the world is too complex to reduce to this simple cause-and-effect cycle.
2. (a) Thirty-five dollars (b) "To live" means to buy what is needed to sustain their daily routines. Some may argue that the literal cost of living is much higher; explain that the small dollar amount points to Soto's meaning.
3. (a) Someone may try on a hat. (b) This sale paid for the hat.
4. (a) "Perhaps," "as far as I can tell," and "I guess" (b) Although most adults take this cause-and-effect idea for granted, he seems to wonder if it might be too simplistic.
5. They are doing their duty by contributing to the economy.
6. Tender or caring; the flow of money may be seen as contributing to child raising.
7. Students should support their answers.
8. He suggests that because this cycle sustains daily life, we have a duty to participate; yet he also questions the truth of this idea.

Literary Element

1. "Filters down like rain"; "someone walks home with a broom"
2. His focus is on a political and philosophical statement about consumer society, not characters.

Writing About Literature

Students should use textual examples to support their opinions.

BEFORE YOU READ

Focus

BELLRINGER

Bellringer Options
Selection Focus Transparency 33
Daily Language Practice Transparency 56
Or **write on the board:** Are you a rebel? Discuss which societal and cultural rules students conform to. Then ask which restrictions they rebel against. Point out that the word *rebellious* can have negative connotations.
Ask: Do you think being rebellious is a bad thing? Explain.

Literature Online

Author Search To expand students' appreciation of Alma Luz Villanueva, have them access the Web site for additional information and resources.

BEFORE YOU READ

I Was a Skinny Tomboy Kid

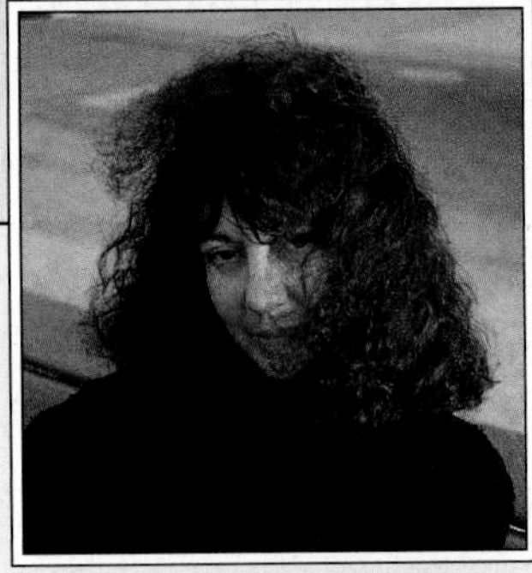

MEET ALMA LUZ VILLANUEVA

Alma Luz Villanueva writes about the struggles and joys of life in a personal voice that suggests universal feelings and experiences. Her writing explores the roles of women and her Mexican American, or Chicana, culture. Her works incorporate the themes of identity, love, and nature.

One with Nature Born in Lompoc, California, and raised in the Mission District of San Francisco, Villanueva never knew her German father. Her grandmother, a native of Mexico's Yaqui tribe, taught Villanueva about Mexican culture as well as her German heritage. Her grandmother also told her stories and myths of the Yaqui people. When Villanueva was eleven years old, her grandmother died. Later, Villanueva would heal the pain of her loss through writing.

Villanueva left high school in tenth grade. She married young, and while her husband was overseas with the U.S. Marines, Villanueva worked two jobs to support herself and the first of their three children. Her marriage ended, and Villanueva left San Francisco to live in the Sierra Nevada Mountains. In these untamed surroundings, she felt at ease. She enjoyed the peace and the gentle sounds of nature.

Villanueva returned to school to receive her high school diploma and then went on to earn a degree in creative writing. She married a Chicano artist, Wilfredo Castaño. Not until she was thirty years old was she able to write on a regular basis. Through her writing, she began to explore themes of nature and her own difficult childhood. In 1977 her first book, *Bloodroot,* was published. In *Bloodroot,* Villanueva develops the connection between humans and nature, a theme she had heard in her grandmother's stories.

Illuminated Self In 1978 Villanueva's second book, *Mother, May I?,* was published. It is a long autobiographical poem in which she reflects upon the death of her grandmother, the struggles of growing up poor, and the alienation she felt as a tomboy in a culture that values femininity. The book symbolizes Villanueva's survival and hope. The poem contains many sensory images steeped in emotion that illuminate the trials in her life.

> *"Almost daily I will sit down to my poetry first and see what it has to tell me."*
>
> —Alma Luz Villanueva

Life Span, a book of poems written in the isolation of the mountains, was published in 1985. In writing these poems, Villanueva relied on her traditional Chicana background and the ancient wisdom she learned from her grandmother. Villanueva has gone on to publish a novel and short stories that, like her poetry, explore the unique experiences of her life. Her style leads readers to see the world in new and fascinating ways. Her description of the environment and the sense of self in her writing send the message that everyone is brought together by nature and emotion.

Alma Luz Villanueva was born in 1944.

Literature Online **Author Search** For more about Alma Luz Villanueva, go to www.glencoe.com.

Selection Skills

I Was a Skinny Tomboy Kid

Literary Elements
- Free Verse (SE pp. 581, 582, 584)

Reading Skills
- Analyzing Sensory Details (SE pp. 581, 582, 584)

Vocabulary Skills
- Academic Vocabulary (SE p. 584)

Writing Skills/Grammar
- Creating Character (TWE p. 582)

Listening/Speaking/Viewing Skills
- Viewing the Art (SE p. 583)

Connecting to the Poem

In the poem that follows, Villanueva shares the details of a childhood spent defying society's expectations for girls. Before you read, think about the following questions:

- What societal rules or expectations keep you from expressing who you really are?
- What activities make you feel free?

Building Background

In many societies and during different times in history, girls and women have been expected to fulfill certain roles and behave in particular ways. The English language itself reveals that our different expectations for men and women are even older than our country. In the 1400s, the word *tomboy* meant "a rude, boisterous, or forward boy"; by the late 1500s, it meant "a bold or immodest woman." Modern British and U.S. definitions of *tomboy*—"a wild romping girl who behaves like a boy," "a girl who enjoys those activities and interests that are usually considered to be preferred by boys"—continue to imply that there are distinct codes of female behavior, and that girls' interests should be different from those of boys.

Setting Purposes for Reading

Big Idea Life Lessons

As you read "I Was a Skinny Tomboy Kid," notice what life lessons the speaker of the poem has learned since she was a child.

Literary Element Free Verse

Free verse is poetry that has no fixed pattern of meter, rhyme, line length, or stanza arrangement. Although poets who write free verse often do not follow traditional rules of form, meter, and rhyme, they use other techniques to create unique patterns. As you read the poem, identify the techniques Villanueva uses and the patterns she creates.

- See Literary Terms Handbook, p. R8.

Reading Strategy Analyzing Sensory Details

Sensory details are the words or phrases in a work of literature that appeal to one or more of the five senses: sight, hearing, touch, smell, and taste. Paying close attention to these details can direct you to the author's theme or message. While reading this poem, notice where Villanueva uses sensory images and think about the effect they are meant to have on the reader.

Reading Tip: Making a Chart As you read, use a chart like the one below to categorize the sensory details Villanueva uses.

Detail	Sense	Effect
"my fists clenched into / tight balls"	Touch Sight	Helps the reader identify physically with the speaker of the poem; when you read it, it might make you clench your fists too.

Literature Online Interactive Literary Elements Handbook To review or learn more about the literary elements, go to www.glencoe.com.

INDIANA ACADEMIC STANDARDS (pages 581-584)

9.2 Develop strategies such as identifying and analyzing structure...

9.3.11 Evaluate the aesthetic qualities of style...

Focus

Summary

Poet Alma Luz Villanueva describes growing up as a tomboy. Activities such as walking along rooftops and fishing made her feel victorious and independent. Fearful of becoming like her mother, whom she saw as helpless, she invented a heroic self-image. Only as an adult did she realize how strong her mother was. Sometimes, she reexperiences the old fear and anger and has to comfort the child inside her.

Literature Online

Literary Elements Have students access the Web site to improve their understanding of free verse.

Selection Resources

Print Materials

- Unit 3 Resources (Fast File), pp. 47–48
- Selection and Unit Assessments, pp. 105–106
- Selection Quick Checks, p. 53

Transparencies

- Bellringer Options Transparencies: Selection Focus Transparency 33; Daily Language Practice Transparency 56
- Literary Elements Transparency 49

Technology

- TeacherWorks Plus™ CD-ROM
- StudentWorks Plus™ CD-ROM
- Presentation Plus!™ CD-ROM
- Literature Online, glencoe.com
- Online Student Edition, mhln.com
- Exam*View*® Assessment Suite CD-ROM
- Vocabulary PuzzleMaker CD-ROM
- Listening Library, disc 1 track 64

Teach

L Literary Element

Free Verse Answer: *She probably isolated the words "tight balls" at the far right to emphasize them. This line breaks the rhythm, jolting the reader in a way that echoes the sudden tensing of her clenched fists.* OL

R1 Reading Strategy

Analyzing Sensory Details
Answer: *It appeals to the sense of touch.* OL

BI1 Big Idea

Life Lessons Ask: What does the speaker learn about herself from the feeling inspired by walking on the rooftops? *(The line "I liked the edge of almost not making it" suggests she enjoys danger.)* OL

CheckPoint

Use the CheckPoint questions on Presentation Plus! to monitor students' comprehension. These questions can be used with interactive response keypads for immediate student feedback.

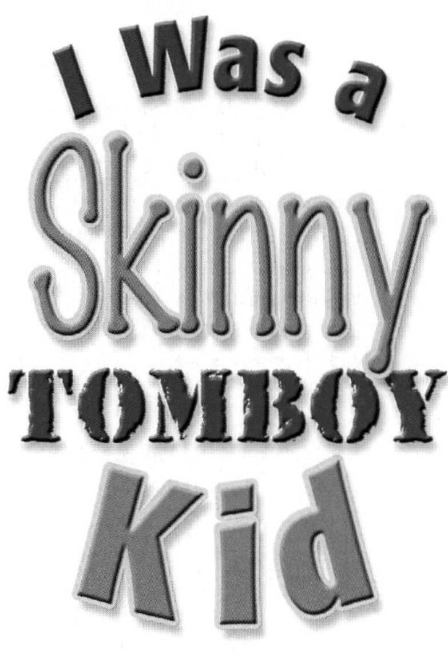

Alma Luz Villanueva

I was a skinny tomboy kid
who walked down the streets
with my fists clenched into
tight balls.
I knew all the roofs
and back yard fences,
I liked traveling that way
sometimes
not touching
the sidewalks
for blocks and blocks
it made
me feel

victorious
somehow
over the streets.
I liked to fly
from roof
to roof
the gravel
falling
away
beneath my feet,
I liked
the edge
of almost
not making it.
And the freedom
of riding
my bike
to the ocean
and smelling it
long before
I could see it,

Literary Element Free Verse *Why do you think Villanueva chose to make this line look this way?* L

Reading Strategy Analyzing Sensory Details *To which of the five senses does this detail appeal?* R1

Additional Support

Skills Practice

LITERARY CONCEPTS: Character
Ask students to imagine themselves as legendary heroes. What character traits and other qualities would they have? List the students' suggestions on the board. Instruct students to write a magazine interview with their legendary selves, revealing their talents, character traits, and powers, and telling how possessing these attributes makes them feel. OL Have students write their self-descriptions as a poem. AL

and I traveled disguised
as a boy
(I thought)
in an old army jacket
carrying my
fishing tackle
to the piers, and
bumming bait
and a couple of cokes
and catching crabs
sometimes and
selling them
to some Chinese guys
and I'd give
the fish away,
I didn't like fish
I just liked to fish—
and I vowed
to never
grow up
to be a woman
and be helpless
like my mother,
but then I didn't realize
the kind of guts
it often took
for her to just keep
standing
where she was.
I grew like a thin, stubborn weed
watering myself whatever way I could
believing in my own myth
transforming my reality
and creating a
legendary/self
every once in a while

late at night
in the deep
darkness of my sleep
I wake
with a tenseness
in my arms
and I follow
it from my elbow to
my wrist
and realize
my fists are tightly clenched
and the streets come grinning
and I forget who I'm protecting
and I coil up
in a self/mothering fashion
and tell myself
it's o.k.

R2

Big Idea Life Lessons *What has the speaker of the poem learned about her childhood view of her mother as helpless?* **BI2**

Teach

BI2 Big Idea

Life Lessons Answer: *Villanueva saw her mother as weak for not rebelling against her role, but then realized she actually showed strength and courage by fulfilling it.* **OL**

R2 Reading Strategy

Clarify Have students paraphrase what happens at the end of the poem. Ask what the speaker's action reveals about herself? *(She still feels at odds with the world and alone; she needs solace and mothering.)* **OL**

CheckPoint

Use the CheckPoint questions on Presentation Plus! to check students' mastery of the selection. These questions can be used with interactive response keypads for immediate student feedback.

Reading in the Real World

Citizenship Have students find magazine articles about peers involved in nontraditional pursuits. A girl playing football or a boy running a baby-sitting service could be used as examples. Ask students to share their examples with the class. **OL**

Building Reading Fluency

Rhythm Explain that focusing on the rhythm of a poem can help students improve their reading fluency and comprehension. Have them practice reading the poem aloud, first pausing at the end of each line, then pausing only where punctuation indicates. **BL**

Academic Standards

Additional Support activities on pp. 582 and 583 cover the following standards:

Skills Practice: **9.5.8** Write for different purposes and audiences, adjusting tone, style, and voice as appropriate.

Reading in the Real World: **9.7.15** Deliver expository (informational) presentations that convey information and ideas from… sources accurately and coherently…

Building Reading Fluency: **9.7** [Develop] speaking skills…in conjunction with… strategies…[for] delivery of oral presentations.

AFTER YOU READ

Assess

1. Accept reasonable answers.
2. (a) Flying from roof to roof, almost not making it; riding her bike to the ocean; fishing (b) She craved thrills, challenges, and freedom.
3. (a) Victorious over the streets (b) So she could feel in charge.
4. (a) Line 74 (b) She is now an adult looking back.
5. A woman remembering her tomboy phase; tense shift in line 74 and *was* in the title
6. (a) To rebel against the image of girls as helpless (b) By inventing a heroic self-image
7. (a) It reflects her circular journey back home. (b) Possible answers: It conveys a long, convoluted life journey; its rhythm is tedious; the syntax, confusing.
8. She can be herself without rejecting her femaleness.

Literary Element

1. In line 7, the indentation implies traveling; lines 14 and 15 are isolated, "being above it all"; lines 17–23 mimic the speaker's action.
2. The sense of free exploration might be lost.

Web Activities Have students access the Web site for interactive activities that will help them assess their understanding of the selection.

AFTER YOU READ

RESPONDING AND THINKING CRITICALLY

Respond

1. In what ways can you relate to the speaker of this poem?

Recall and Interpret

2. (a)What does the speaker of the poem say she liked as a girl? (b)What can you tell about her from these details?
3. (a)How did "not touching the sidewalks / for blocks and blocks" make the speaker of the poem feel? (b)Why was it important for her to feel this way?
4. (a)Identify the point in the poem where the verb tense changes. (b)What does this change indicate?

Analyze and Evaluate

5. Who is the speaker of this poem? Use clues from the text to support your answer.
6. (a)Why does the speaker of the poem want to disguise herself as a boy? (b)In what other ways does the speaker disguise herself?
7. (a)One sentence in this poem runs from line 28 to line 63. What might have been the author's purpose in making this sentence so long? (b)In your opinion, how successful is the author's strategy?

Connect

8. **Big Idea** **Life Lessons** What lessons has the speaker of the poem learned about being female?

LITERARY ANALYSIS

Literary Element Free Verse

Before the twentieth century, most poets used regular meter and rhyme. Modern poets, rebelling against tradition, began writing in **free verse,** creating their own patterns with irregular meter and form.

1. Identify two places in "I Was a Skinny Tomboy Kid" where Villanueva uses the poem's form to emphasize the content of the poem.
2. How would "I Was a Skinny Tomboy Kid" differ if Villanueva had written it using regular meter and rhyme rather than free verse?

Interdisciplinary Activity: Art

Create a portrait of the speaker of the poem as a "skinny tomboy kid" in the form of a collage or in another medium, such as watercolor, pastels, or pen and ink.

LiteratureOnline Web Activities For eFlashcards, Selection Quick Checks, and other Web activities, go to www.glencoe.com.

READING AND VOCABULARY

Reading Strategy Analyzing Sensory Details

Many authors depend heavily on **sensory details** to help readers imagine the characters, the setting, and the action in a piece of writing.

1. What types of sensory details does Villanueva use most often in her poem? Support your answer with examples from the text.
2. Which of the sensory details in the poem do you find most striking or effective? Explain.

Academic Vocabulary

Here are two words from the vocabulary list on page R80.

tense (tens) *adj.* held tight and stiff; in a state of mental agitation

assure (ə shoor′) *v.* to cause to feel sure; to comfort

Practice and Apply

1. What made the speaker of "I Was a Skinny Tomboy Kid" **tense** as a child?
2. Why does the speaker need to **assure** herself at the end of the poem?

Reading Strategy

1. Sight, touch, smell, and taste
2. Accept reasonable answers.

Academic Vocabulary

1. Society's views of girls and rejection of her true self
2. To assure herself that she is okay; To reassure herself against the old anger and frustration

The World Is Not a Pleasant Place to Be

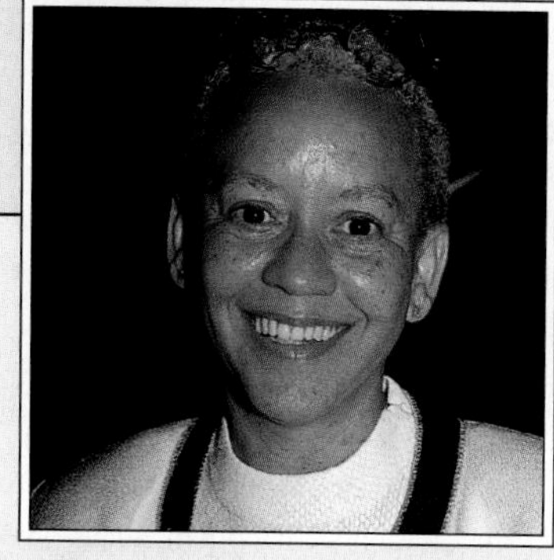

MEET NIKKI GIOVANNI

In the early 1960s, Nikki Giovanni's sister was one of the first African American students to attend a previously all-white high school in Cincinnati, Ohio. Giovanni herself, however, chose to continue her education in the all-black schools she had always attended.

Giovanni was born Yolande Cornelia Giovanni Jr. in Knoxville, Tennessee. When she was still an infant, the family moved to Cincinnati, where her parents were employed as teachers. At that time, many neighborhoods had restrictive policies that prevented non-whites from buying property in them, so Giovanni's parents bought a house in Lincoln Heights, an all-black suburb. Sometime before Yolande turned three, she acquired the nickname Nikki.

Early Protests During high school, Giovanni returned to Knoxville to live with her grandparents and attend the school where her grandfather taught Latin. It was in Knoxville that she began accompanying her grandmother to rallies protesting racial inequality. As the end of high school neared, Giovanni applied and was accepted to Fisk University, an all-black college. But when she openly voiced her contempt for the school's rules during her first semester, Giovanni was expelled. Three years later, a new dean of students invited her to return to Fisk, where she eventually graduated with honors in history.

A Passion for Poetry Giovanni began writing poetry when she was a teen. After the death of her grandmother, she used her writing more and more as a refuge from emotional pain. During that period, she also met members of the civil rights movement. The assassination of Malcolm X in February 1965 and the rise of the Black Panthers (a militant African American civil rights group) had a radical effect on Giovanni's poetry. It was at this time that Giovanni became involved in the Black Arts movement.

In 1968, using borrowed money, Giovanni self-published her first book, *Black Feeling, Black Talk.* Most of the poems were the ones she had written while in mourning for her grandmother. That same year, with the profits from her first book and an arts grant, Giovanni published her second book, *Black Judgement*. By that time, Giovanni was being invited to speak and read her poetry regularly.

> *"Life, I believe is not only a journey, it is an adventure. Every day there is something new and wonderful about life."*
>
> —Nikki Giovanni

Woman of the Year In 1970, *Ebony* magazine named Giovanni "Woman of the Year." Although her writing continued to reflect a radical point of view, the mainstream magazine *Mademoiselle* named her "Woman of the Year" in 1971. Her activism led to national and international honors and awards.

Nikki Giovanni was born in 1943.

Literature Online **Author Search** For more about Nikki Giovanni, go to www.glencoe.com.

Focus

BELLRINGER

Bellringer Options
Selection Focus Transparency 34
Daily Language Practice Transparency 57
Or **write on the board:** "Ah, look at all the lonely people." Ask students if they recognize this line from the Beatles' song "Eleanor Rigby." See how many "lonely" references they can recall from songs, movies, or books. Discuss why loneliness is such a popular theme.

Literature Online

Author Search To expand students' appreciation of Nikki Giovanni, have them access the Web site for additional information and resources.

Selection Skills

The World Is Not a Pleasant Place to Be

Literary Elements
- Personification (SE pp. 586, 587, 588)

Reading Skills
- Analyzing Tone (SE pp. 586, 588)
- Looking for Clues (SE p. 586)

Writing Skills/Grammar
- Respond to Mood (SE p. 588)

Listening/Speaking/Viewing Skills
- Analyzing Art (TWE p. 587)

BEFORE YOU READ

Focus

Summary

The poem describes and communicates the deep pain of loneliness. The speaker's overwhelming need to connect is reflected in humanized images of the natural world.

Literary Elements Have students access the Web site to improve their understanding of personification.

LITERATURE PREVIEW

Connecting to the Poem

The following poem expresses Giovanni's feelings about the importance of companionship. Before you read the poem, think about the following questions:

- Why is it important to have a friend or family member who cares about you?
- How does friendship or family support affect you when life seems difficult?

Building Background

Many of Nikki Giovanni's early poems focus on social and political issues, including black pride and black solidarity. The themes of her later poetry turned increasingly to such personal subjects as family, love, and loneliness. "The World Is Not a Pleasant Place to Be" appears in the book of poems *My House,* which was first published in 1972. Giovanni has often emphasized the importance of family love in her life. An often-quoted line from her poem "Nikki-Rosa" is "Black love is Black wealth."

Setting Purposes for Reading

Big Idea Life Lessons

As you read, think about what life lessons might have led Giovanni to write this poem.

Literary Element Personification

Personification is a figure of speech in which an animal, object, force of nature, or idea is given human characteristics. Personification provides insight into the thoughts and feelings a thing might have if it were human. Through the use of personification, readers experience the emotions as well as hear the words of entities that would never otherwise have a voice. This literary device often generates and facilitates shifts in perspective. As you read, try to identify examples of personification in the poem.

- See Literary Terms Handbook, p. R13.

Literature Online Interactive Literary Elements Handbook To review or learn more about the literary elements, go to www.glencoe.com.

READING PREVIEW

Reading Strategy Analyzing Tone

An author's **tone** reflects his or her feelings about the subject matter. One piece of writing can contain several different tones—humorous, sarcastic, serious, regretful, and so on. As you read "The World Is Not a Pleasant Place to Be," try to identify Giovanni's tone.

Reading Tip: Looking for Clues As you read the poem, look for clues that will help identify the author's tone. These clues may include word choice, the rhythm of a line, and line breaks or other organizational choices. Record your list of clues and the conclusions you draw from them in a chart like the one below.

Clues to Author's Tone	Conclusion About Clue
not a pleasant place to be	mournful, sad

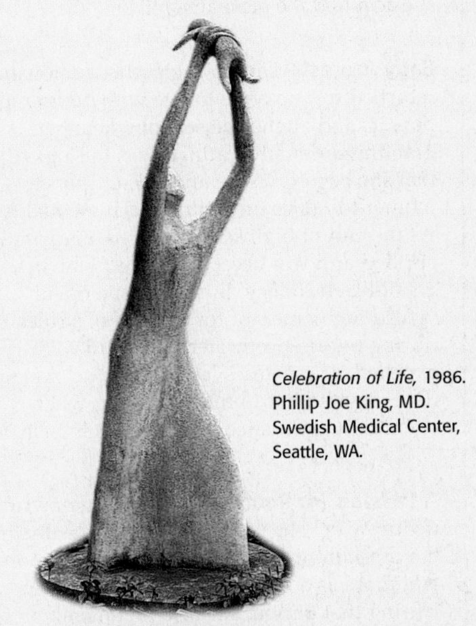

Celebration of Life, 1986. Phillip Joe King, MD. Swedish Medical Center, Seattle, WA.

INDIANA ACADEMIC STANDARDS (pages 586-588)

9.3.7 Recognize and understand...figurative language...

9.3.13 Explain...tone and meaning...

9.5.2 Write responses to literature that demonstrate a...grasp of the significant ideas of literary works...

Selection Resources

Print Materials
- Unit 3 Resources (Fast File), pp. 49–50
- Selection and Unit Assessments, pp. 107–108
- Selection Quick Checks, p. 54

Transparencies
- Bellringer Options Transparencies: Selection Focus Transparency 34, Daily Language Practice Transparency 57
- Literary Elements Transparencies 67, 70

Technology
- TeacherWorks Plus™ CD-ROM
- StudentWorks Plus™ CD-ROM
- Presentation Plus!™ CD-ROM
- Literature Online, glencoe.com
- Online Student Edition, mhln.com
- Exam*View*® Assessment Suite CD-ROM
- Vocabulary PuzzleMaker CD-ROM
- Listening Library, disc 1 track 65

The World Is Not a Pleasant Place to Be

Nikki Giovanni

the world is not a pleasant place
to be without
someone to hold and be held by

a river would stop
its flow if only
a stream were there
to receive it

an ocean would never laugh
if clouds weren't there
to kiss her tears

the world is not
a pleasant place to be without
someone

Big Idea Life Lessons *What kinds of life experiences do you think the speaker of this poem has had?* **BI**

Literary Element Personification *Why does Giovanni describe the ocean as laughing?* **L**

Seated Figure, 1979. Elizabeth Catlett. Mahogany, 22 x 13½ x 15¾ in. Collection of the artist.

Teach

BI Big Idea

Life Lessons Answer: *Students may say that her life has been difficult and lonely. She seems to have been deprived of love and protection. Others may say that the speaker once had love and lost it.* **OL**

L Literary Element

Personification Answer: *She is showing how natural and universal the desire for connection is by suggesting the ocean delights in its relationship with the sky.* **OL**

Viewing the Art

Sculptor, graphic artist, and teacher Elizabeth Catlett (1919–) has worked tirelessly for racial equality and social change. The first recipient of a master's degree in sculpture from the University of Iowa, she later became director of the sculpture department at the National University of Mexico.
Ask: How does this sculpture reflect the tone of the poem? *(Its mournful expression and posture reflect the tone.)* **AS**

Reading in the Real World

Community Ask students which groups in their community might feel the most alienated and lonely. *(Students may suggest homeless or elderly people.)* Have students research one of these groups at a library or on the Internet and discuss their results in class. Divide the class into small groups. Have students design community service projects that address the needs of their chosen group. Have students design an action plan for implementing their ideas. **OL**

Academic Standards

The Additional Support activity on p. 587 covers the following standard:

Reading in the Real World: **9.4.6** Synthesize information from multiple sources…

AFTER YOU READ

Assess

1. Accept reasonable answers.
2. (a) Loneliness, lack of love (b) A strong sense of connection with others is a basic human need.
3. (a) stream receiving a river; clouds kissing the ocean's tears (b) The example should relate to the theme.
4. (a) No (b) The negative expressions suggest there is no one in her life.
5. (a) To emphasize the need for a companion (b) It creates a sense of desolation.
6. (a) Vaporization and precipitation are personified. (b) To convey that love makes the difference between sorrow and joy
7. Possible answers: provocative, arouses curiosity; repetitive with lines in the poem
8. Accept reasonable answers.

Literary Element

1. Laughing ocean, clouds kissing tears, stream receiving the river
2. Emphasizes that the need for love is universal.

Writing About Literature

Remind students to explain their responses with examples.

AFTER YOU READ

RESPONDING AND THINKING CRITICALLY

Respond

1. Which of your friends, family members, or acquaintances would you like to read this poem? Explain.

Recall and Interpret

2. (a)According to this poem, what makes the world unpleasant? (b)Why might it make the world unpleasant?
3. (a)What does the speaker say about the river in stanza 2? (b)How does this stanza connect to the main idea expressed in the first and last stanzas?
4. (a)Does the speaker ever state that he or she is alone? (b)What evidence do you have that the speaker is or is not alone?

Analyze and Evaluate

5. (a)In your opinion, why did Giovanni repeat the first stanza in the last stanza but leave out the last few words? (b)What is the effect?
6. (a)How does the third stanza express a scientific fact in a poetic way? (b)In your opinion, why does the poet make a connection between laughter and tears in the stanza?
7. Do you think the title of this poem is appropriate and effective? Explain.

Connect

8. **Big Idea** **Life Lessons** What lesson does the author share about loneliness?

LITERARY ANALYSIS

Literary Element Personification

Many authors use **personification** in their works. While readers recognize that nonhuman characters do not literally exhibit human qualities, personification can help readers see and feel the author's point more vividly.

1. List two examples of personification in the poem.
2. What purpose does personification serve in Giovanni's poem?

Writing About Literature

Respond to Mood In literature, mood refers to the emotional quality of a literary work. The author uses a whole range of elements in order to evoke the intended mood, including tone, language, subject matter, setting, rhetorical devices, and sound devices.

How would you describe the mood of "The World Is Not a Pleasant Place to Be"? Write a brief personal response in which you describe your feelings toward the speaker, the mood, and the message of the poem.

READING AND VOCABULARY

Reading Strategy Analyzing Tone

Analyzing tone means determining an author's attitude toward the subject matter. Tone often informs and shapes the meaning of a story, essay, or poem. For example, two essays on the same topic might have very different tones: one might have a sober tone, while the other might have a sarcastic tone.

1. What is Giovanni's tone in this poem? What specific clues led you to your conclusion?
2. How does the use of all lowercase letters in the poem affect its tone?
3. How do Giovanni's organizational choices affect the tone of the poem?

LiteratureOnline **Web Activities** For eFlashcards, Selection Quick Checks, and other Web activities, go to www.glencoe.com.

Reading Strategy

1. Sad, forsaken; "not pleasant," "if only," "never laugh," "tears"
2. They suggest a small, muted childlike voice.
3. The lines ending "without," "if only," "never laughs," and "tears" emphasize sadness. The lone word at the end suggests the speaker's isolation and the primacy of the longed-for companion.

LiteratureOnline

Web Activities Have students access the Web site for interactive activities that will help them assess their understanding of the selection.

"Hope" is the thing with feathers— I'm Nobody! Who are you?

MEET EMILY DICKINSON

Few people who lived in Amherst, Massachusetts, in the mid-1800s probably suspected that their neighbor Emily Dickinson would come to be known as one of the greatest poets in American literature. Dickinson appeared proper and shy to her neighbors, but as a writer she was bold, daringly experimental, and spontaneous. Her poems broke conventions and spoke in a fresh, unique voice. Even today, her poems are recognizable as her own and no one else's.

"I find ecstasy in living."

—Emily Dickinson

Experiences Common and Unique Dickinson came from a family that encouraged learning. Her grandfather founded Amherst College, and her father was a lawyer and treasurer of the college. Her home was filled with books. Among Emily's favorite authors were William Shakespeare, Ralph Waldo Emerson, Emily Brontë, and English Romantic poets such as John Keats.

Dickinson did not begin writing poems until she was twenty years old. Her early years in Amherst were typical for a young woman of her time. She attended Mount Holyoke Female Seminary from 1847 to 1848. There, religious education and growth were just as important as intellectual development. Unlike most of her classmates, Dickinson remained a skeptic. Nevertheless, her poems often touch on religious themes.

Several of her letters express longing for a character named "Master," but it is unclear who he was. It seems, though, that Dickinson was disappointed in love. As time went by, she became a recluse. She walked often—but only on her father's property. Even though nature is a strong theme in her poetry, her own yard seemed to provide all the inspiration she needed.

A Prolific Poet Dickinson wrote about 1,775 poems and just as many letters. She wrote most of her poems on scraps of paper and kept them in her apron pocket along with a small pencil. She saved the poems in bureau drawers. Only seven of her poems were published during her lifetime. Her sister discovered the rest after Dickinson's death.

The first volume of Dickinson's poetry was published in 1890, four years after her death. The book was organized into five sections—Life, Love, Nature, Time, and Eternity. The volume was an immediate success. Many editions followed, but it was not until the 1950s that her poems were published exactly as she had written them, complete with all her dashes and capitalizations. It was then that people began to appreciate her work anew.

Emily Dickinson was born in 1830 and died in 1886.

LiteratureOnline **Author Search** For more about Emily Dickinson, go to www.glencoe.com.

Focus

BELLRINGER

Bellringer Options
Daily Language Practice Transparency 58
Or **write on the board:** How do you know when your work is ready for public scrutiny? Note that many celebrated artists, such as Dickinson and Van Gogh, received recognition only after their death. Brainstorm innovative methods of presenting work to the public, such as blogging and posting photos and art on Web sites.

Author Search To expand students' appreciation of Emily Dickinson, have them access the Web site for additional information and resources.

Selection Skills

"Hope" is the thing with feathers/ I'm Nobody! Who are you?

Literary Elements
- Metaphor (SE pp. 590, 594; TWE p. 591)

Reading Skills
- Interpreting Imagery (SE pp. 590, 592, 594)
- Taking Notes (SE p. 590)

Vocabulary Skills
- Analogies (SE p. 594)
- Rhythmic and Rhyming Vocabulary (TWE p. 594)

Listening/Speaking/Viewing Skills
- Speaker Group Activity (SE p. 594)

Writing Skills/Grammar
- Analyzing Meter (SE p. 595)
- Using Dashes in Poetry (SE p. 595)
- Dashes in Prose (TWE p. 592)

Study Skills/Research/Assessment
- Comparing Viewpoints (SE p. 593)

BEFORE YOU READ

Focus

Summary

In "'Hope' is the thing with feathers–," Emily Dickinson uses bird imagery to describe the nature of hope. In "I'm Nobody! Who are you?" Dickinson invites another "nobody" to join forces with her. She compares being "somebody" to a frog constantly singing its own praises to its admirers.

V Vocabulary

Vocabulary File **Say:** Add these words and definitions to your vocabulary file. For each word, include a sentence that gives you an example of how to use the word. **OL** Students with English language needs should include the pronunciations of these words in their files. **EL**

Literary Elements Have students access the Web site to improve their understanding of metaphor.

LITERATURE PREVIEW

Connecting to the Poems

The natural world offers valuable insights into life if we are open to its lessons. Before you read the poems, think about the following questions:

- Where do you go for inspiration when you are trying to understand your life or resolve personal problems?
- How can observing nature suggest new ways to look at issues that are important to us?

Building Background

Emily Dickinson's poetry is full of unusual capitalization and dashes. The capitalization puts extra emphasis on certain words. The dashes serve as interrupters, breaking up text, slowing the reader down, and usually adding emphasis. Although just a few of Dickinson's poems were published during her lifetime, editors, who perhaps thought her work a bit strange, often changed them and eliminated the very things that made her poems unique–such as the dashes.

Setting Purposes for Reading

Big Idea Life Lessons

As you read Dickinson's poems, think about how everyday sights can illustrate abstract concepts.

Literary Element Metaphor

A **metaphor** is a figure of speech that compares or equates two seemingly unlike things. Unlike a simile, a metaphor does not use the words *like* or *as;* instead, the comparison is implied. An extended metaphor compares two unlike things in various ways throughout a paragraph, a stanza, or an entire selection. Metaphors can help you better grasp what the author wishes to communicate about his or her subject. As you read, note where Dickinson uses these techniques.

- See Literary Terms Handbook, pp. R10–R11.

 **Interactive Literary Elements Handbook** To review or learn more about the literary elements, go to www.glencoe.com.

READING PREVIEW

Reading Strategy Interpreting Imagery

Imagery is the "word pictures" that writers create to evoke an emotional response in their readers. These images can involve any of the five senses. As you read, pay attention to the sensory details Dickinson uses. Note the natural associations and meanings that you draw from these details.

Reading Tip: Taking Notes Use a chart to help organize your ideas.

"Hope" is the thing with feathers—

Image	Associations	Possible meaning
a bird singing an endless song	bird: freedom, flight; song: joy; endless song: eternity, constancy	

Vocabulary

gale (gāl) *n.* a very strong wind; p. 591 *The gale blew the lawn chairs down the street.*

abash (ə bash′) *v.* to make ashamed or uneasy; to embarrass; p. 591 *Jean was abashed when her sister insulted her in front of her friends.*

dreary (drēr′ ē) *adj.* sad; depressing; dull; uninteresting; p. 592 *The rain and dark clouds made the day seem dreary.*

livelong (liv′ lông′) *adj.* complete; whole; used to emphasize the length of a period of time; p. 592 *That year it seemed to snow throughout the livelong winter.*

bog (bog) *n.* a wetland ecosystem where shrubs and peat moss grow and various animals live; p. 592 *They pulled on tall rubber boots before heading into the bog.*

INDIANA ACADEMIC STANDARDS (pages 590-595)
9.3.11 Evaluate...the impact of...figurative language...
9.3.7 Recognize and understand the significance of...imagery...
9.5.3 Write...analytical essays......that...use technical terms and notations accurately.

Selection Resources

Print Materials
- Unit 3 Resources (Fast File), pp. 51–53
- Leveled Vocabulary Development, p. 43
- Selection and Unit Assessments, pp. 109–110
- Selection Quick Checks, p. 55

Transparencies
- Bellringer Options Transparencies: Daily Language Practice Transparency 58
- Literary Elements Transparency 69

Technology
- TeacherWorks Plus™ CD-ROM
- StudentWorks Plus™ CD-ROM
- Presentation Plus!™ CD-ROM
- Literature Online, glencoe.com
- Online Student Edition, mhln.com
- Exam*View*® Assessment Suite CD-ROM
- Vocabulary PuzzleMaker CD-ROM
- Listening Library, disc 1 tracks 66, 67

"Hope" is the thing with feathers—

Emily Dickinson

"Hope" is the thing with feathers—
That perches in the soul—
And sings the tune without the words—
And never stops—at all— **L**

And sweetest—in the **Gale**—is heard—
And sore[1] must be the storm—
That could **abash** the little Bird
That kept so many warm—

I've heard it in the chillest land—
And on the strangest Sea—
Yet, never, in Extremity,[2]
It asked a crumb—of Me. **R**

1. Here, *sore* means "dreadful" or "terrible."
2. Here, *extremity* means "great danger" or "distress."

Big Idea Life Lessons *What does the bird teach us about the nature of hope?* **BI**

Vocabulary

gale (gāl) *n.* a very strong wind

abash (ə bash′) *v.* to make ashamed or uneasy; to embarrass

Teach

L Literary Element

Dash Ask: What is the effect of the final dashes in the first stanza? *(It may suggest an unfinished thought or introduce the next element.)*

Ask: What other punctuation might substitute for the dash? *(An ellipsis for an unfinished thought; a period to suggest a complete thought; an exclamation point to emphasize the thought)* **OL**

BI Big Idea

Life Lessons Answer: *Hope is a gift available to everyone and costs nothing. It resides in the soul and can endure all but the most brutal trials.* **OL**

R Reading Strategy

Interpreting Imagery Ask: What might you infer about the speaker from the poem's images? *(Some may see the speaker as an optimist; others, as embattled based on the last stanza.)* **OL**

Use the CheckPoint questions on Presentation Plus! to monitor students' comprehension. These questions can be used with interactive response keypads for immediate student feedback.

Differentiated Instruction

Metaphors Visual learners may benefit from actualizing the metaphors of the bird from "'Hope' is the thing with feathers—" and the frog from "I'm Nobody! Who are you?" Instruct students to design either the "hope bird" or the "somebody frog." Students should incorporate the speaker's tone into their pieces. Have students share the results with the class. **OL**

Academic Standards

The Additional Support activity on p. 591 covers the following standard:

Differentiated Instruction: **9.3.7** Recognize and understand the significance of various literary devices, including figurative language...

Teach

BI Big Idea

Life Lessons **Ask:** What does the "Nobody" teach us about being a "Somebody"? *(Being a somebody is overrated. Somebodies are loud, self-aggrandizing, and trite.)* OL

R Reading Strategy

Interpreting Imagery
Answer: *Frogs are green and slimy and have protruding eyes and bulging throats. These features suggest a comical, grotesque, and puffed-up creature. Their loud croaking might be considered offensive. The poet seems to suggest that self-important people are similarly obnoxious and repulsive.* OL

L Literary Element

Metaphor **Ask:** What is the bog a metaphor for? *(The general public or any undiscerning audience)* OL

I'm Nobody! Who are you?

Emily Dickinson

Sun Shower, 1995. Diana Ong. Computer graphics, 5 x 4 in. Chrome.

I'm Nobody! Who are you?
Are you—Nobody—Too?
Then there's a pair of us!
Don't tell! they'd advertise—you know! BI

How **dreary**—to be—Somebody!
How public—like a Frog—
To tell one's name—the **livelong** June—
To an admiring **Bog**! L

Reading Strategy Interpreting Imagery *What characteristics do you associate with a frog? What meanings do these associations convey?* R

Vocabulary

dreary (drēr′ ē) *adj.* sad; depressing; dull; uninteresting

livelong (liv′ lông′) *adj.* complete; whole; used to emphasize the length of a period of time

bog (bog) *n.* a wetland ecosystem where shrubs and peat moss grow and various animals live

Additional Support

Academic Standards

The Additional Support activity on p. 592 covers the following standard:

Skills Practice: **9.6.1** Identify and correctly use…the mechanics of punctuation…

Skills Practice

GRAMMAR AND LANGUAGE: Dashes in Prose **Ask:** Where are dashes used in prose? *(In dialogue, to replace commas or parentheses, for an aside)* Stress that before students experiment as Dickinson did, they should learn traditional usage. Mention that if the information between the dashes can be deleted without changing the sense, the dashes are probably correct.

Write on the board: The Grand Canyon, one of the wonders of the American West, is in Arizona.

Ask: Where might dashes be used? *(In place of the commas)* Note that dashes can indicate a change in thought.

AFTER YOU READ

RESPONDING AND THINKING CRITICALLY

Respond

1. Which of the Dickinson poems did you prefer? Explain.

Recall and Interpret

2. (a)In "'Hope' is the thing with feathers–," where does hope perch? (b)Why do you think Dickinson uses the verb *perches*?
3. (a)Where does the speaker say she has heard the bird singing? (b)Are these figurative or literal places?
4. (a)In "I'm Nobody! Who are you?" what does the speaker say will happen if people discover a pair of nobodies? (b)What is the speaker's tone or attitude?
5. (a)In the second poem, what adjective does Dickinson use to describe the bog? (b)What does the bog represent? Explain.

Analyze and Evaluate

6. (a)How are the metaphors in the two poems similar? (b)How effective are these metaphors, considering the subject matter of the poems? Explain.
7. Why might Dickinson have chosen to capitalize words in the middle or at the end of a sentence? Use specific examples from the two poems to support your answer.
8. (a)In "I'm Nobody! Who are you?" how does the speaker feel about being "Nobody"? Explain. (b)Why do you suppose she feels this way?

Connect

9. **Big Idea** **Life Lessons** What do these poems reveal about Emily Dickinson and her values? Explain.

YOU'RE THE CRITIC: Different Viewpoints

Her Own Style

When Dickinson's first volume of poetry appeared in 1890, it received mixed critical reviews. Most of the poets of the time wrote traditionally, meaning that they used language, meter, rhyme, and punctuation in predetermined and predictable ways. Arlo Bates, a Boston critic, and William Dean Howells, a novelist and editor of the *Atlantic Monthly* magazine, agreed that Dickinson's poetry was like nothing they had ever seen before. As you read the two excerpts below, note how each writer interprets Dickinson's nontraditional techniques somewhat differently.

> *"[Her poetry is] so wholly without the pale of conventional criticism, that it is necessary at the start to declare the grounds upon which it is to be judged as if it were a new species of art."*
>
> —Arlo Bates

> *"[I]f nothing else had come out of our life but this strange poetry we should feel that in the work of Emily Dickinson America, or New England rather, had made a distinctive addition to the literature of the world."*
>
> —William Dean Howells

Group Activity With one or two other students, gather evidence from Dickinson's poems to demonstrate how her writing style was innovative. Then consider the following questions.

1. What aspects of Dickinson's poetry may have surprised Arlo Bates?
2. Why might William Dean Howells recommend poetry he describes as "strange"?
3. What aspects of Dickinson's poems are nontraditional or experimental? What effects do these techniques have on the subjects she chooses?

You're the Critic

1. Broken meter created by dashes, capitalization, unconventional metaphors
2. *Strange* can suggest originality and a sense of wonder and fascination. Great art often challenges or breaks traditional rules.
3. Her use of capitalization and punctuation and the meter of her poems seem untraditional. For example, in "I'm Nobody! Who are you?" the rhyme scheme is *aabc defe.* The effect of such irregularity is that the subject matter is made new and surprising.

AFTER YOU READ

Assess

1. Students should support their answers with specific reasons.
2. (a) In the soul (b) She strengthens the bird metaphor; *perches* suggest that hope, like a bird, can easily come and go.
3. (a) "In the chillest land / And on the strangest Sea" (b) Figurative; hope does not literally sing.
4. (a) "They'd advertise." (b) Intimate
5. (a) Admiring (b) The public; she imagines the admiring public as a gross, undifferentiated mass.
6. (a) Both use animals to represent abstract characteristics. (b) Accept reasonable answers.
7. Possible answers: "'Hope' . . ." capitalizes *Gale, Bird, Sea, Extremity,* and *Me* to emphasize those words; "I'm Nobody!" *Nobody, Too, Somebody, Frog, Bog*
8. (a) The exclamation point suggests that the speaker is happy or proud to be Nobody and content to be ignored. (b) She enjoys her privacy and disdains public opinion.
9. She is thoughtful, positive, and ironically humorous and values humility and privacy.

CheckPoint

Use the CheckPoint questions on Presentation Plus! to check students' mastery of the selection. These questions can be used with interactive response keypads for immediate student feedback.

AFTER YOU READ

Assess

Literary Element

1. "'Hope' is the thing with feathers—" begins with a comparison of hope to a bird ("thing with feathers") and continues with words associated with birds *(perches, sings, crumb)*.
2. She uses concrete images of everyday life—a bird, a frog—to help readers grasp the idea of hope as a natural human endowment and to compare the relative merits of privacy and fame.

Review: Speaker

Students should incorporate Dickinson's characteristic style and voice into their responses.

Reading Strategy

1. Possible answers: feathers, bird, birdsong, gale, storm, cold, sea, frog, June, bog
2. Responses should include an analysis of how the poet uses the detail.

Vocabulary

1. a **2.** c **3.** c **4.** a **5.** b

Academic Vocabulary

Only the worst upheavals can still the voice of hope.

LITERARY ANALYSIS

Literary Element Metaphor

Some poems contain one or more short **metaphors,** while others feature an extended metaphor that runs from the beginning to the end of the poem.

1. Which of these two poems contains an extended metaphor? Explain.
2. How does the use of metaphors help Dickinson explain her ideas?

Review: Speaker

As you learned on page 525, the **speaker** of a poem is similar to the narrator of a story. It is the voice that describes what is happening in a poem. Sometimes the speaker's voice is that of the poet, and sometimes it is the voice of a fictional person or even an object. The speaker's words communicate a particular tone, or attitude, toward the subject of the poem.

Partner Activity Meet with a classmate and discuss the speaker in each of the Dickinson poems. Working with your partner, brainstorm a list of at least five questions you would like to ask Emily Dickinson about these poems. Discuss the questions and narrow your list down to the three questions you would most like answered. Then work together to craft a response to these questions, writing them as you believe Emily Dickinson would have responded to an interviewer.

Reed marsh, 1921. Max Pechstein. Coll. Henri Nannen, Emden, Germany.

READING AND VOCABULARY

Reading Strategy Interpreting Imagery

Imagery is an important component of both "'Hope' is the thing with feathers—" and "I'm Nobody! Who are you?" Dickinson often used sensory details from the natural world in her poems.

1. List three sensory details from "'Hope' is the thing with feathers—" and/or "I'm Nobody! Who are you?" that have to do with nature.
2. Choose one of these details and explain how Dickinson uses it to create a certain effect.

Vocabulary Practice

Practice with Analogies An analogy shows the relationships between words. The symbol : means "is to," and the symbol :: means "as." Find the word that completes each of the analogies below.

1. **abash : humiliate :: understand :**
   a. comprehend **b.** confuse **c.** tolerate
2. **gale : storm :: field :**
   a. tractor **b.** corn **c.** farm
3. **dreary : exciting :: perfect :**
   a. interesting **b.** lifeless **c.** flawed
4. **livelong : whole :: chilly :**
   a. cold **b.** shivering **c.** icy
5. **peat moss : bog :: seaweed :**
   a. mountain **b.** ocean **c.** valley

Academic Vocabulary

Here is a word from the vocabulary list on page R80.

cease (sēs) *v.* to stop; to come to an end

Practice and Apply
What causes hope to **cease** according to "'Hope' is the thing with feathers—"?

Additional Support

Skills Practice

LANGUAGE: Rhythm and Rhyme
Have students practice using rhyme and rhythm while learning their vocabulary words. Instruct students to create a rhyme for each of their vocabulary words. The rhyme should contain context clues that help the student learn the word. Instruct students to use iambic pentameter and to turn each vocabulary word into a rhyming couplet. Challenge students to use the vocabulary to create a poem with a specific rhythmic pattern. OL

WRITING AND EXTENDING

Writing About Literature

Analyze Meter Emily Dickinson's unconventional style is evident even in the rhythm of her poems. Write a brief essay analyzing the meter in the first two stanzas of either "'Hope' is the thing with feathers–" or "I'm Nobody! Who are you?" Identify whether any regular meter exists in the stanzas. Discuss why Dickinson might have chosen the meter she did.

Before you begin drafting, scan the stanzas you will be analyzing. To scan a line of poetry means to note stressed and unstressed syllables. Typically, stressed syllables are marked with ´ and unstressed syllables with ˘. The sample scansion below is from William Wordsworth's "I Wandered Lonely as a Cloud."

˘ ´ ˘ ´ ˘ ´ ˘ ´
I wandered lonely as a cloud

˘ ´ ˘ ´ ˘ ´ ˘ ´
That floats on high o'er vales and hills.

Once you have scanned the Dickinson stanzas, begin drafting your essay.

When you have completed your draft, meet with a peer reviewer to evaluate each other's work. Suggest revisions that would make the essay more clear or precise. Then make changes to your draft. Finally, proofread and edit your draft to correct errors in spelling, grammar, and punctuation.

Internet Connection

With a partner, survey Web sites and online comments to create a list of the most popular Emily Dickinson poems. Read through the poems and choose a personal favorite. Discuss with your partner which poem you have chosen. Then write a short oral report to deliver to the class about why you like the poem.

LiteratureOnline **Web Activities** For eFlashcards, Selection Quick Checks, and other Web activities, go to www.glencoe.com.

GRAMMAR AND STYLE

Dickinson's Language and Style

Using Dashes in Poetry One of the most noticeable ways in which Emily Dickinson's poetry differs from that of most other poets is her use of the dash. When a reader sees a dash, he or she cannot help but pause. Consider the visual difference between the following stanzas, one with dashes and one without:

I'm Nobody! Who are you?–
Are you–Nobody–Too?
Then there's a pair of us!
Don't tell! they'd advertise–you know!

I'm Nobody! Who are you?
Are you Nobody Too?
Then there's a pair of us!
Don't tell! they'd advertise you know!

Activity Read the Dickinson poems aloud into an audio recorder, making sure to pause when a dash appears. Then reread the poems without pausing for the dashes. Play the recordings and listen closely to the differences in the poems. Discuss with a partner whether or not the dashes seem to be necessary.

Revising Check

Dashes You can use dashes in your own writing to set off and emphasize supplemental information or parenthetical comments. For example, the parentheses in this sentence could be changed to dashes: *The shiny new car (the first he had ever owned) was his most prized possession.* As with parentheses, you should be careful not to overuse dashes in your writing. With a partner, go through your essay on meter in Dickinson's poetry and note one place where you might use a dash or dashes.

AFTER YOU READ

Assess

Writing About Literature

Before students begin drafting, have them read each line of their chosen stanzas aloud, slowly and distinctly pronouncing each syllable of every word. Encourage them to exaggerate accented syllables.

Students' essays should include

- an analysis of the meter in one of the selections.
- possible reasons the poet chose that type of meter.

Internet Connection

Accept all reasonable responses.

Dickinson's Language and Style

Encourage students to suggest alternative punctuation for the poem's dashes. Discuss how the dashes affect the way one reads and interprets the poem.

Revising Check

Have students compare and contrast sentences with dashes and those without in their essays.

LiteratureOnline

Web Activities Have students access the Web site for interactive activities that will help them assess their understanding of the selection.

Academic Standards

Additional Support activities on pp. 594 and 595 cover the following standards:

Skills Practice: **9.1** Use...context clues, and a growing knowledge of English...to determine the meaning of words... **9.5.7** Use varied and expanded vocabulary, appropriate for specific forms and topics.

Differentiated Instruction: **9.5.2** Write responses to literature that demonstrate a comprehensive grasp of the significant ideas of literary works...

Differentiated Instruction

Advanced Learners Encourage gifted and talented students to explore poetry through their own writing. Review Dickinson's use of extended metaphor in "'Hope' is the thing with feathers–."

Say: Name some other things you think might work well as extended metaphors. List students' ideas on the board and have them write poems based on one of the ideas. **AL**

Focus

BELLRINGER

Bellringer Options
Daily Language Practice Transparency 59
Or **write on the board:** Family Dinner. Invite volunteers to share their descriptions of a typical family meal. Is it a loud and boisterous gathering or a more solemn affair? What happens when the meal includes extended family? Are certain traditions or foods included? Invite students to compare and contrast their family mealtime traditions.

Author Search To expand students' appreciation of Yvonne Sapia, have them access the Web site for additional information and resources.

BEFORE YOU READ

Defining the Grateful Gesture

MEET YVONNE SAPIA

Poet Yvonne Sapia counts among her influences Robert Frost and Mother Goose, whose rhymes she describes as "funny, sad, and inspiring." Sapia was born in 1946 in New York City to parents who had emigrated from Puerto Rico during the 1920s. Her father was a barber, and her mother was a homemaker. Her father became wealthy during the 1920s but lost his fortune as a result of the stock market crash in 1929. He was known in his neighborhood in the Bronx for having cut the hair of silent film star Rudolph Valentino. Sapia swept the floor of her father's shop when she was a girl. As a result, she said, "I learned at an early age the value of work."

> *"Reading poetry is cool stuff. It always provides a solution and then years later it provides a new solution because we change."*
>
> —Yvonne Sapia

Mourning and Imagination As a young woman, Sapia left New York and went to Florida to attend college. She graduated from Florida Atlantic University in Boca Raton. Sapia then entered the working world as a newspaper reporter and a writer of technical books on horticulture, the science of cultivating plants. Sapia wanted to write poetry and novels, so she returned to college to earn a Master of Fine Arts degree in creative writing from the University of Florida in Gainesville. In 1976 she became a poet-in-residence and English professor at Lake City Community College in Lake City, Florida, where she still writes and teaches today.

In 1983 Sapia published her first collection of poetry, *Fertile Crescent,* which won the Florida Chapbook Award. She titled her second book after her poem "Valentino's Hair," which tells the story of a Puerto Rican barber in New York City during the 1920s. The poem is a tribute to Sapia's father, who died when she was nineteen. The book *Valentino's Hair* won the Samuel French Morse Prize for poetry in 1987, and the title poem was included in the *Best American Poetry* anthology.

Moment of Discovery Sapia has been writing and teaching for many years at Lake City Community College. She loves the moment when students discover that they, too, can draw on their own thoughts and experiences in order to write poetry. Sapia hopes that her poetry will serve as a legacy and inspiration for her students. She describes her poems as a reflection of "being a Puerto Rican American woman in the late 20th century. . . . They convey what this Latina thought at this point in time. I see students as books, a story waiting to be shared, written. Everyone has a human experience to share."

Yvonne Sapia was born in 1946.

LiteratureOnline **Author Search** For more about Yvonne Sapia, go to www.glencoe.com.

Selection Skills

Defining the Grateful Gesture

Literary Elements
- Metaphor and Simile (SE pp. 597, 598, 599)

Reading Skills
- Connecting to Personal Experience (SE pp. 597, 599)
- Asking Questions Graphic Organizer (SE p. 597)

Vocabulary Skills
- Denotation and Connotation (SE pp. 597, 599; TWE p. 598)

Writing Skills/Grammar
- Analysis of Imagery (SE p. 599)

LITERATURE PREVIEW

Connecting to the Poem

Sapia's poem explores the desire of parents to instill gratitude in their children. Before you read the poem, think about the following questions:

- What do you feel especially grateful for in your own life?
- What are some of the things you have that your parents or grandparents did not have when they were your age?

Building Background

The childhood home of the mother in "Defining the Grateful Gesture" is Puerto Rico, a small, resource-poor island that has long suffered the effects of overpopulation. Its population density is more than one thousand people per square mile. By comparison, the average for the United States is about seventy people per square mile. By U.S. standards, Puerto Rico has a high rate of unemployment and poverty.

The situation today, however, is much better than it was in the past. In the 1940s, a self-help program called "Operation Bootstrap" was launched to promote social welfare and stimulate economic growth by developing manufacturing and service industries. Tourism, in particular, grew tremendously. The program helped ease much of the dire poverty on the island.

Setting Purposes for Reading

Big Idea Life Lessons

As you read "Defining the Grateful Gesture," notice how Sapia portrays gratitude as an important life lesson.

Literary Element Metaphor and Simile

A **simile** is a figure of speech that uses *like* or *as* to compare seemingly unlike things. A **metaphor** also compares two seemingly unlike things, but implies the comparison instead of stating it directly. Identifying metaphors and similes will help you understand the poet's meaning. As you read, notice how Sapia uses metaphors and similes to emphasize the mother's lesson.

- See Literary Terms Handbook, pp. R10–R11 and R15–R16.

READING PREVIEW

Reading Strategy Connecting to Personal Experience

Connecting to personal experience can make a literary work more real to you and help you understand its meaning. While reading this poem, make connections between the lives of the children and their mother's childhood and your own experiences.

Reading Tip: Asking Questions As you read, use a chart to record your personal connections to the poem.

Line from Poem	Personal Experience
and helping her father make candy in the family kitchen.	I help my father in his carpentry shop.

Vocabulary

reverent (rev′ ər ənt) *adj.* feeling or expressing respect or courtesy; p. 598 *Faye was always reverent in the presence of her teachers.*

archetypal (är′ kə tī′ pəl) *adj.* serving as an ideal model or perfect example; p. 598 *Achilles is the archetypal hero with only one weakness—his heel.*

supplicant (sup′ lə kənt) *n.* one who asks humbly and earnestly; p. 598 *The supplicants begged the king to grant their requests.*

Vocabulary Tip: Denotation and Connotation Denotation is the literal meaning of a word. Connotation is the suggested or implied meaning associated with a word. The denotation of the word *flower* is "the blossom of a plant." Connotations of the word *flower* include "beauty" and "perfume."

Literature Online **Interactive Literary Elements Handbook** To review or learn more about the literary elements, go to www.glencoe.com.

INDIANA ACADEMIC STANDARDS (pages 597-599)

9.3.7 Recognize and understand...figurative language [and] imagery...

9.2 Develop [reading] strategies...

9.5.3 Write...analytical essays...

BEFORE YOU READ

Focus

Summary

Yvonne Sapia recalls a typical family dinner. Her mother would lecture Sapia and her brother about appreciating their food and contrast her children's lives with her own poor, hardworking childhood. The children tried to seem sufficiently grateful to please their mother, but always fell short.

V Vocabulary

Vocabulary File Say: Add these words and definitions to your vocabulary file. For each word, include a sentence that gives you an example of how to use the word. **OL** Students with English language needs should include the pronunciations of these words in their files. **EL**

Literary Elements Have students access the Web site to improve their understanding of metaphor and simile.

Selection Resources

Print Materials
- Unit 3 Resources (Fast File), pp. 54–56
- Leveled Vocabulary Development, p. 44
- Selection and Unit Assessments, pp. 111–112
- Selection Quick Checks, p. 56

Transparencies
- Bellringer Options Transparencies: Daily Language Practice Transparency 59
- Literary Elements Transparencies 68, 69

Technology
- TeacherWorks Plus™ CD-ROM
- StudentWorks Plus™ CD-ROM
- Presentation Plus!™ CD-ROM
- Literature Online, glencoe.com
- Online Student Edition, mhln.com
- Exam*View*® Assessment Suite CD-ROM
- Vocabulary PuzzleMaker CD-ROM
- Listening Library, disc 1 track 68

Teach

L Literary Element

Metaphor and Simile
Answer: *Metaphor; students should recognize that the mother was not a lazy or passive person.* OL

BI Big Idea

Life Lessons **Answer:** *To teach gratitude for their food and the hard work that brought it to them* OL **Ask:** What can you infer about the mother's attitude toward her children from the lesson she is teaching? *(Students may say that by taking the time to reinforce this lesson, the mother shows she cares about her children and does not want them to be spoiled.)* OL

Use the CheckPoint questions on Presentation Plus! to check students' mastery of the selection. These questions can be used with interactive response keypads for immediate student feedback.

Defining the Grateful Gesture

Yvonne Sapia

According to our mother,
when she was a child
what was placed before her
for dinner was not a feast,
but she would eat it
to gain back the strength
taken from her by long hot days
of working in her mother's house
and helping her father make
candy in the family kitchen.
No idle passenger
traveling through life was she.

And that's why she resolved
to tell stories about
the appreciation for satisfied hunger.
When we would sit down
for our evening meal
of arroz con pollo[1]
or frijoles negros con plátanos[2]
she would expect us
to be **reverent** to the sources
of our undeserved nourishment
and to strike a thankful pose
before each lift of the fork
or swirl of the spoon.

For the dishes she prepared,
we were ungrateful,
she would say, and repeat
her **archetypal** tale about the Pérez
brothers who stumbled over themselves
with health in her girlhood town
of Ponce,[3] looking like ripe mangoes,
their cheeks rosed despite poverty.

My mother would then tell us about
the day
she saw Mrs. Pérez searching
the neighborhood garbage,
picking out with a missionary's care
the edible potato peels, the plantain
skins,
the shafts of old celery to take
home to her muchachos[4]
who required more food
than she could afford.

Although my brothers and I
never quite mastered the ritual
of obedience our mother craved,
and as **supplicants** failed
to feed her with our worthiness,
we'd sit like solemn loaves of bread,
sighing over the white plates
with a sense of realization, or relief,
guilty about possessing appetite.

1. *Arroz con pollo* (ä rōs′ kōn pō′ yō) is Spanish for "rice with chicken."
2. *Frijoles negros con plátanos* (frē hō′ les neg′ rōs′ kōn plä′ tä nōs) are black beans with plantains (plant′ ənz). Plantain is a banana-like fruit that is starchy and eaten cooked.
3. *Ponce* (pōn′ sā) is a city in Puerto Rico.
4. *Muchachos* (mo͞o chä′ chōs) means "boys" in Spanish.

Literary Element Metaphor and Simile *What figure of speech is this and what does it mean?* L

Big Idea Life Lessons *What does the mother hope to accomplish by sharing this tale with her children?* BI

Vocabulary

reverent (rev′ ər ənt) *adj.* feeling or expressing respect or courtesy

Vocabulary

archetypal (är′ kə tī′ pəl) *adj.* serving as an ideal model or perfect example

supplicant (sup′ lə kənt) *n.* one who asks humbly and earnestly

Additional Support

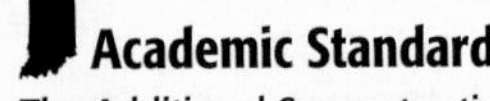

Academic Standards

The Additional Support activity on p. 598 covers the following standard:

Skills Practice: **9.1.2** Distinguish between what words mean literally and what they imply and interpret what the words imply.

Skills Practice

Analyzing Connotations Explain that grasping the connotations—the unspoken meanings and associations—of words can help students appreciate a poet's use of language and gain an awareness of the various layers of meaning in poetry. Play a game of word association using words from the poem. Have students choose a word, consider its context, and discuss its associations. Note, for instance, how the connotations of virtue and purity associated with *white* ("white plates") deepen the poem's religious overtones. EL

AFTER YOU READ

RESPONDING AND THINKING CRITICALLY

Respond

1. How do the mother's stories make you feel about showing thanks? Explain.

Recall and Interpret

2. (a)How did the mother help her family when she was young? (b)What is significant about this detail?
3. (a)What does the speaker mean by the children's "undeserved nourishment"? (b)How does their situation compare with their mother's childhood experiences?
4. (a)What does the speaker of the poem see Mrs. Pérez doing? (b)What is the significance of the "missionary's care" with which Mrs. Pérez goes about her task?

Analyze and Evaluate

5. (a)What do mangos represent in the poem? With what do they contrast? (b)How is this contrast related to the poem's theme?
6. Why does the author include the story about the Pérez family in her poem?
7. What words and phrases does the author use to convey a religious, or spiritual, tone? Why might she have used this tone?

Connect

8. **Big Idea** Life Lessons Have the children learned the lesson their mother was trying to teach them? Explain.

LITERARY ANALYSIS

Literary Element Metaphor and Simile

Metaphor and **simile** are two of the strongest tools a writer has at his or her disposal. A poet uses these figurative devices to create powerful images and to imply meaning, rather than state it directly.

1. How are the speaker and her brothers like "solemn loaves of bread"? Is this a suitable simile for this poem? Explain.
2. The speaker says that she and her brothers "failed to feed" their mother with their worthiness. Is this an appropriate metaphor for this poem? Explain.

Writing About Literature

Analyze Imagery Sapia uses powerful images in the final stanza. Why do you think she ends the poem with these particular images? How do they relate to the theme of the poem? Write a one- or two-page essay in which you analyze the imagery of this final stanza and discuss how it connects to the theme of the poem. Use evidence from the poem to support your answers.

LiteratureOnline **Web Activities** For eFlashcards, Selection Quick Checks, and other Web activities, go to www.glencoe.com.

READING AND VOCABULARY

Reading Strategy Connecting to Personal Experience

Authors often share **personal experiences** that are unique to their lives. But the content, theme, and details of these experiences may remind readers of episodes in their own lives. In Sapia's poem, for instance, the narrator's mother tells a story about the Pérez family. Many of us may have been told similar stories in order to change our attitudes about something.

1. What elements of this poem are unfamiliar to you?
2. What elements of the poem can you connect to your own life?

Vocabulary Practice

Practice with Denotation and Connotation
Decide whether the definition of each word is a denotation or connotation.

1. reverent: expressing respect
   a. denotation **b.** connotation
2. archetypal: intellectual; high-minded
   a. denotation **b.** connotation
3. supplicant: inferior
   a. denotation **b.** connotation

LiteratureOnline

Web Activities Have students access the Web site for interactive activities that will help them assess their understanding of the selection.

Reading Strategy

1. Students should support their answers.
2. Accept reasonable answers.

Vocabulary

1. a **2.** b **3.** b

AFTER YOU READ

Assess

1. Students should support their answers.
2. (a) She helped her mother with housework and helped her father make candy. (b) The candy connects with the food motif.
3. (a) They don't work for their food. (b) They take food for granted; she earned hers and ate whatever was served to regain her strength.
4. (a) Scavenging for scraps from the garbage (b) She dedicates herself to her task as if it were a sacred duty.
5. (a) The health of the Pérez boys; their poverty (b) The image suggests that the children's health depended on their mother's labor and sacrifice.
6. It enables the mother to show her children the difficulty of feeding one's family and how lucky they are.
7. *Reverent, thankful missionary's, ritual, supplicants,* and *solemn loaves of bread*; it emphasizes the idea of food as a blessing and of the devotion of mothers.
8. They do not express the degree of gratitude their mother desires.

Literary Element

1. They are supposed to "feed" their mother. It fits the food motif.
2. Students should support their answers.

Writing About Literature

Remind students to include textual support for their analysis.

BEFORE YOU READ

Focus

BELLRINGER

Bellringer Options
Selection Focus Transparency 35
Daily Language Practice Transparency 60
Or **ask:** Can an individual be free while imprisoned? Are there other kinds of prisons besides jail? Discuss how a person might be free in mind and spirit while physically incarcerated. Then ask students to consider how a person who is literally free might feel psychologically or spiritually imprisoned by society's rules and prejudices.

Literature Online

Author Search To expand students' appreciation of Paul Laurence Dunbar, have them access the Web site for additional information and resources.

Use the CheckPoint questions on Presentation Plus! to monitor students' comprehension. These questions can be used with interactive response keypads for immediate student feedback.

BEFORE YOU READ

Sympathy

MEET PAUL LAURENCE DUNBAR

The only African American in his high school class in Dayton, Ohio, Paul Laurence Dunbar was class president, editor of the school newspaper, and president of the literary society. While still in school, he also edited an African American newspaper funded by the Wright brothers, the *Dayton Tattler,* and published poems in the *Dayton Herald.* As a young man, Dunbar wrote that his ambition was to "be able to interpret my own people through song and story, and to prove to the many that after all we are more human than African."

Although Dunbar grew up in the post–Civil War North, both of his parents had been enslaved. When he graduated from high school in 1891, despite the excellence he had achieved, racism in society limited his prospects. Dunbar was only able to obtain work as an elevator operator in Dayton's Callahan Building. During downtime on the job, the young Dunbar wrote poetry, including a first draft of the poem that would become his most well known: "Sympathy."

"With our short sight we affect to take a comprehensive view of eternity. Our horizon is the universe."

—Paul Laurence Dunbar

Early Acclaim and Continued Success Dunbar found a publisher for his first book of poems, *Oak and Ivy,* and published it in 1892. To pay off his debt to the publisher, Dunbar sold copies of his book to people who rode the elevator that he operated. As word of the young "elevator boy poet" got around, several respected writers and critics began applauding his work. His friend Frederick Douglass introduced Dunbar to other African American writers. Author and literary critic William Dean Howells praised Dunbar's work in a national magazine.

Dunbar also branched out into other forms of writing. At the height of his career, he contributed songs to the first full-length African American musical on Broadway, *In Dahomey* (1902). He also published several novels and a well-received collection of short stories, *The Strength of Gideon and Other Stories* (1900).

Diverse Styles Like other popular poets of the time, Dunbar wrote in Standard English and imitated classical verse. He also found inspiration in John Whitcomb Riley's nostalgic poems, which were largely written in dialect and described ordinary people. Some of Dunbar's most highly praised poems were written in an authentic dialect form that imitated the conventions of plantation life.

Paul Laurence Dunbar was the first African American poet to gain national recognition. He died at the age of thirty-three after several years of suffering from tuberculosis.

Paul Laurence Dunbar was born in 1872 and died in 1906.

Literature Online **Author Search** For more about Paul Laurence Dunbar, go to www.glencoe.com.

Selection Skills

Sympathy

Literary Elements
- Symbol (SE pp. 601, 602, 603; TWE p. 602)

Reading Skills
- Applying Background Knowledge (SE pp. 601, 602, 603)
- Create a Web (SE p. 601)

Vocabulary Skills
- Analogies (SE pp. 601, 603)

Writing Skills/Grammar
- Respond to Theme (SE p. 603)

LITERATURE PREVIEW

Connecting to the Poem

In the following poem, Dunbar expresses an understanding of the feelings and actions of a caged bird. Before you read, think about how you might feel if your freedoms were taken away and you could not do the things you wanted to do.

Building Background

In 1863, during the Civil War, President Abraham Lincoln banned slavery in the states that had seceded from the Union. Many enslaved people rejoiced, but their fight against discrimination and persecution was far from over. African American men were given the right to vote with the passage of the Fifteenth Amendment in 1870, and some African American men were elected to public office. However, most African Americans still worked as farmers and manual laborers. Reconstruction in the South ended in 1877, and southern states regained control of their state governments. Shortly after, they enacted Jim Crow laws to restrict the rights of African Americans. In 1896 the federal government supported Jim Crow laws with the Supreme Court's ruling in *Plessy v. Ferguson,* which held that "separate but equal" public facilities were legal.

Setting Purposes for Reading

Big Idea Life Lessons

As you read "Sympathy," consider the types of obstacles Dunbar and others might have faced. How might he have wanted his poem to affect those who were not confronted with so many obstacles?

Literary Element Symbol

A **symbol** is any object, person, or place that has meaning in itself but also stands for something else, usually on an abstract level. In a poem, symbols are used to convey meaning and feelings or to show something that is not easily defined in a literal way. Recognizing an author's use of symbols can help you understand the intended meaning or theme of a literary work. As you read, examine how Dunbar uses the image of the bird to symbolize something deeper.

- See Literary Terms Handbook, p. R17.

READING PREVIEW

Reading Strategy Applying Background Knowledge

A reader can use the strategy of **applying background knowledge** to understand an author's point of view. Knowing the perspective from which an author writes can help you evaluate and more deeply understand a literary work. As you read, determine how events in Dunbar's life might be reflected in the theme of the poem.

Reading Tip: Creating a Web Use a graphic organizer like the one below to record experiences in Dunbar's life that would lead him to sympathize with a caged bird.

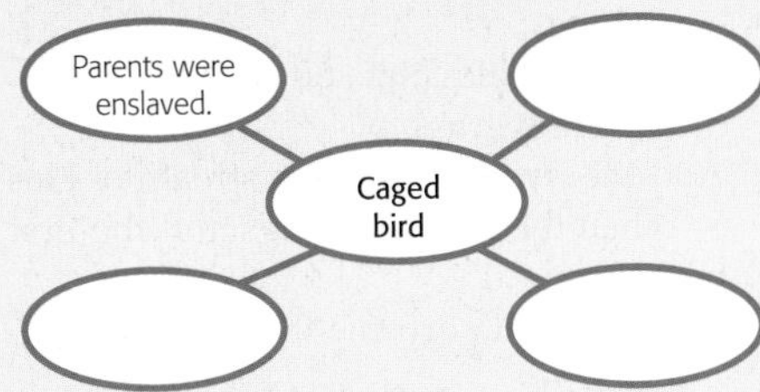

Vocabulary

chalice (chal′ is) *n.* drinking cup; a cup-shaped interior of a flower; p. 602 *The bee nestled in the chalice of the flower.*

keen (kēn) *adj.* sharp; intense; p. 602 *She hurt her friend's feelings with her keen sarcasm.*

Vocabulary Tip: Analogies An analogy conveys a relationship between words or ideas. A pair of words that are antonyms may be, for example, related to another pair of words simply because they are also antonyms.

LiteratureOnline Interactive Literary Elements Handbook To review or learn more about the literary elements, go to www.glencoe.com.

INDIANA ACADEMIC STANDARDS (pages 601-603)

9.3.7 Recognize and understand...symbolism...

9.2 Develop [reading] strategies...

9.3.7 Write responses to literature that...demonstrate an awareness of the author's style and...the effects created.

BEFORE YOU READ

Focus

Summary

Paul Laurence Dunbar uses the suffering of a caged bird as a metaphor for his own feelings of imprisonment. In the first stanza, he relates to how the bird feels looking out from its cage. In the second, he relates to its struggle against confinement. In the final stanza, he compares the bird's singing to a prayer.

V Vocabulary

Vocabulary File Say: Add these words and definitions to your vocabulary file. For each word, include a sentence that gives you an example of how to use the word. **OL** Students with English language needs should include the pronunciations of these words in their files. **EL**

Literary Elements Have students access the Web site to improve their understanding of symbol.

Selection Resources

Print Materials

- Unit 3 Resources (Fast File), pp. 57–59
- Leveled Vocabulary Development, p. 45
- Selection and Unit Assessments, pp. 113–114
- Selection Quick Checks, p. 57

Transparencies

- Bellringer Options Transparencies: Selection Focus Transparency 35, Daily Language Practice Transparency 60
- Literary Elements Transparency 20

Technology

- TeacherWorks Plus™ CD-ROM
- StudentWorks Plus™ CD-ROM
- Presentation Plus!™ CD-ROM
- Literature Online, glencoe.com
- Online Student Edition, mhln.com
- Exam*View*® Assessment Suite CD-ROM
- Vocabulary PuzzleMaker CD-ROM
- Listening Library, disc 1 track 69

Teach

R Reading Strategy

Applying Background Knowledge Answer: *Dunbar's identification with the bird may be rooted in the pain that resulted from knowing the terrible hardships his parents faced as enslaved people and from the racial prejudice that he experienced.* OL

L Literary Element

Symbol Answer: *Obstacles such as racism and lack of economic opportunity* OL

Use the CheckPoint questions on Presentation Plus! to check students' mastery of the selection. These questions can be used with interactive response keypads for immediate student feedback.

Sympathy

Parrot outside his cage. Cornelis Biltius. Private Collection.

Paul Laurence Dunbar

I know what the caged bird feels, alas!
When the sun is bright on the upland slopes;
When the wind stirs soft through the springing grass,
And the river flows like a stream of glass;
When the first bird sings and the first bud opes,[1]
And the faint perfume from its **chalice** steals—
I know what the caged bird feels!

I know why the caged bird beats his wing
Till its blood is red on the cruel bars;
For he must fly back to his perch and cling
When he fain[2] would be on the bough a-swing;[3]
And a pain still throbs in the old, old scars
And they pulse again with a **keener** sting—
I know why he beats his wing!

I know why the caged bird sings, ah me,
When his wing is bruised and his bosom sore,—
When he beats his bars and he would be free;
It is not a carol of joy or glee,
But a prayer that he sends from his heart's deep core,
But a plea, that upward to Heaven he flings—
I know why the caged bird sings!

1. *Opes* means "opens."
2. *Fain* means "gladly" or "preferably."
3. *A-swing* means "swinging."

Reading Strategy Applying Background Knowledge *Why might Dunbar identify with the caged bird's throbbing pain and old scars?* R

Literary Element Symbol *What kind of "bars" did Dunbar run up against?* L

Vocabulary

chalice (chal′ is) *n.* drinking cup; a cup-shaped interior of a flower

keen (kēn) *adj.* sharp; intense

Additional Support

Academic Standards

The Additional Support activity on p. 602 covers the following standard:

Skills Practice: **9.3.7** Recognize and understand the significance of various literary devices, including...symbolism...and explain their appeal.

Skills Practice

Analyzing Symbolism At the end of each stanza, pause and discuss the following:

- What is the literal meaning of this stanza?
- How might the stanza be interpreted symbolically?
- What specific symbols can be found in the stanza?

Discuss with students what they think the author's overall intention was and what impression he wanted to leave with the reader. OL

AFTER YOU READ

RESPONDING AND THINKING CRITICALLY

Respond

1. How does the bird's life help you understand the lives of the oppressed?

Recall and Interpret

2. (a)What images from nature does Dunbar use in the first stanza? (b)In what ways does Dunbar create a sense of freedom with his words?
3. (a)What causes the bird in the poem to bleed? (b)What conclusion do you think Dunbar wanted the reader to draw from this image?
4. (a)According to Dunbar, why do the caged bird's scars "pulse again with a keener sting"? (b)Why do you think Dunbar emphasizes that the bird's singing is not a joyful or gleeful carol?

Analyze and Evaluate

5. (a)What passages most focus your attention on the idea of sympathy? (b)Is Dunbar's use of the bird as a symbol of this idea effective? Explain.
6. Why do you think Dunbar uses the same rhyming sound for the final couplets in the second and third stanzas?
7. (a)Do you think the poem's title is appropriate? Explain. (b)How might the title detract from what the author intended?

Connect

8. **Big Idea** **Life Lessons** Dunbar struggled against discrimination to become a writer and poet. What circumstances might lead a person today to write a poem like "Sympathy"?

LITERARY ANALYSIS

Literary Element Symbol

A traditional **symbol** may be recognized by most people and usually is met with a predictable response. For example, a thorn on a rose might symbolize both good and bad existing together. Sometimes an author will select an original symbol, for which the meaning is not as easily recognized and requires further analysis.

1. What type of symbols does Dunbar use: traditional symbols or original ones? Why?
2. How effectively do you think Dunbar uses symbols to represent abstract concepts?

Writing About Literature

Respond to Theme Imagine that the song the bird in "Sympathy" sings includes lyrics that humans could understand. Write the words of the caged bird's song. Use a structure and rhyme scheme similar to Dunbar's. Reflect on the bird's past experiences, as well as on its hopes for the future.

LiteratureOnline **Web Activities** For eFlashcards, Selection Quick Checks, and other Web activities, go to www.glencoe.com.

READING AND VOCABULARY

Reading Strategy Applying Background Knowledge

Writers often write about experiences from their own lives, and knowing something about an author's background can give the reader insight into the theme(s) of a particular work.

1. Using what you know about the poet's life, what do you think is the theme of "Sympathy"?
2. List three details from Dunbar's life that correspond to the theme of the poem.

Vocabulary Practice

Practice with Analogies Choose the word that best completes the analogy.

1. ladle : spoon :: chalice :
   a. flower **c.** throne
   b. cup **d.** gilded
2. inspired : bland :: keen :
   a. moderate **c.** dull
   b. vivid **d.** moved

LiteratureOnline

Have students access the Web site for interactive activities that will help them assess their understanding of the selection.

Reading Strategy

1. The pain caused by barriers to freedom and fulfillment
2. His enslaved parents, his battle with racism, his rejection by critics

Vocabulary

1. b **2.** c

AFTER YOU READ

Assess

1. Accept reasonable answers.
2. (a) Shining sun, wind softly blowing, springing grass, river flowing, flowers opening
   (b) The vowel sounds and the one-syllable words lend a sense of serenity, ease, and freedom.
3. (a) Repeatedly running into the same barriers brings back the pain of imprisonment and intensifies it (b) to emphasize the pain caused by these constraints
4. (a) The hope for freedom is renewed despite the pain.
   (b) To contradict comforting assumptions and alert people to suffering
5. (a) "Till its blood is red on the cruel bars"; "he fain would be on the bough a-swing"; "When his wing is bruised"
   (b) Students should support their answers.
6. Possible answers: To achieve a songlike effect; for emphasis
7. (a) Accept reasonable answers. (b) Students should support their answers.
8. Members of minorities, political prisoners, or the physically disabled might write on this theme.

Literary Element

1. Traditional symbols; accept reasonable answers.
2. Accept reasonable answers.

Writing About Literature

Remind students to base their poem's structure and content on Dunbar's poem.

BEFORE YOU READ

Focus

BELLRINGER

Bellringer Options
Selection Focus Transparency 36
Daily Language Practice Transparency 61
Or **write on the board:** What is your definition of family? Ask students to quickly jot down the names of their family members. Now ask them to reconsider their lists. Did they include any pets? Any distant or deceased relatives? Any friends? What about plants? Urge students to broaden their definition of *family* and consider to whom and what they are truly connected.

Literature Online

Author Search To expand students' appreciation of Joy Harjo, have them access the Web site for additional information and resources.

CheckPoint

Use the CheckPoint questions on Presentation Plus! to monitor students' comprehension. These questions can be used with interactive response keypads for immediate student feedback.

BEFORE YOU READ

Remember

MEET JOY HARJO

"I read a lot as a child," says poet Joy Harjo, "but I always felt that to read poetry I had to change *myself* to be inside the work. I had to think like a European or a white American."

An enrolled member of the Muscogee Creek Indian Tribe, Joy Harjo was born in Tulsa, Oklahoma. She embraced her American Indian heritage early in life. Harjo had family members who were painters, and they inspired her to study the visual arts. She left home at sixteen to attend the Institute of American Indian Arts in Arizona. She then attended the University of New Mexico, where she focused on painting and theater.

The Road to Poetry As a student at the University of New Mexico, Harjo attended a reading by the poet Simon Ortiz. Listening to Ortiz's poetry, Harjo realized that "poetry can include the experience of a person of the Southwest." This experience led her to seek out American Indian, African American, and Latin American writers. It also spurred her to begin writing poetry herself. In 1978, she earned a master's degree in creative writing from the University of Iowa. Harjo returned to the Institute of American Indian Arts as a creative writing instructor in 1978. Since then, she has taught at several universities, including the University of New Mexico, where she was a professor of creative writing.

Women Warriors Survival and gender play important roles in Harjo's depiction of the American Indian experience. "I believe those so-called 'womanly' traits are traits of the warrior," Harjo remarks. "They've been brave—not in the national headlines, but they've been true to themselves, and who they are, and to their families. Their act of bravery could have been to feed their children, to more than survive."

> *"We are inventing our own poetic forms and these should take place alongside traditional European forms in the study of literature."*
>
> —Joy Harjo

Harjo's artistic goals focus on spreading awareness of the historical conditions in which Native Americans have lived. She urges her readers to examine their own worlds and to become aware of realities they may never have considered before. Her techniques reflect her intention to preserve memory. By repeating an idea or word, she guides the reader to focus on it.

Poetic Justice Harjo's mother composed songs of heartache, and Harjo has followed in her musical footsteps. Her poems often turn into lyrics for her band, Joy Harjo and Poetic Justice. Their sound is described as a blend of tribal, jazz, and reggae.

Joy Harjo was born in 1951.

Literature Online **Author Search** For more about Joy Harjo, go to www.glencoe.com.

Selection Skills

Remember

Literary Elements
- Repetition (SE pp. 605, 607)

Writing Skills/Grammar
- Repetition (TWE p. 606)

Reading Skills
- Drawing Conclusions About Author's Beliefs (SE pp. 605, 606, 607)
- Paying Attention to Details (SE p. 605)

Listening/Speaking/Viewing Skills
- Choral Reading (SE p. 607)
- Viewing the Art (TWE p. 606)

LITERATURE PREVIEW

Connecting to the Text

The following poem celebrates life and its origins. Before you read, think about the following questions:

- What about your family and heritage is most important to you?
- How does your life affect other living beings and even the Earth itself?

Building Background

From earliest times, American Indian cultures have believed in a deep spiritual connection between humans, animals, and forces of nature. Respect—for the past, for social traditions, and for the various processes of all life—is deeply embedded in American Indian cultural heritage.

Harjo is part of the Muscogee Creek Indians. This American Indian group lived in the upper flatlands of Alabama and Georgia. Between 1813 and 1814, the Creek Indians were at war with the United States. When they lost, they were forced off their homelands and had to relocate farther west. When Oklahoma was made a state in 1907, some of the land was given to American Indians. For this reason, about twenty thousand Creek Indians now live in Oklahoma, while a small group, about five hundred, call southwestern Alabama home.

Setting Purposes for Reading

Big Idea Life Lessons

As you read, think about what life lesson Harjo might want you to take away from this poem.

Literary Element Repetition

Repetition is the recurrence of sounds, words, phrases, lines, or stanzas in a speech or literary work. Repetition increases the sense of unity in a work and can call attention to particular ideas. As you read "Remember," try to determine the purpose behind Harjo's use of repetition.

- See Literary Terms Handbook, p. R14.

READING PREVIEW

Reading Strategy Drawing Conclusions About Author's Beliefs

Literature can often provide you with clues to an **author's beliefs.** In most works, you will need to piece together clues from the writing to identify those beliefs. While reading this poem, see what you can learn about Harjo's beliefs through the content, tone, and organization of her poem.

Reading Tip: Paying Attention to Details When you read, remember that authors add details only when those details serve a particular purpose. Watching for details and making connections between them will help you determine what an author believes. Use a chart to organize the conclusions you draw from details in the poem.

Details	Conclusion
Harjo refers to the moon as "she"	Harjo gives nature human attributes

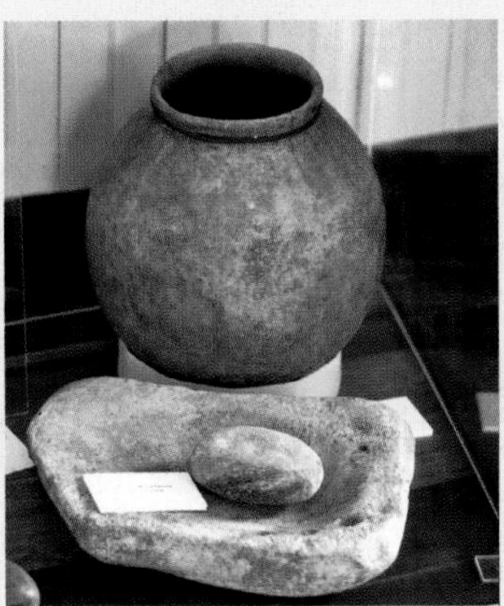

Muscogee Creek pottery jar and mano with pestle grinding rock.

Literature Online **Interactive Literary Elements Handbook** To review or learn more about the literary elements, go to www.glencoe.com.

INDIANA ACADEMIC STANDARDS (pages 605-607)

9.3.11 Evaluate the aesthetic qualities of style...

9.2.8 Draw conclusions about a text, supporting them with accurate examples.

9.7.6 Choose effective verbal...techniques...

BEFORE YOU READ

Focus

Summary

Joy Harjo urges readers to remember that they are part of nature. She stresses the unity of and interdependence of all peoples and cultures and suggests that the natural world is also a work of art.

Literary Elements Have students access the Web site to improve their understanding of repetition.

Selection Resources

Print Materials

- Unit 3 Resources (Fast File), pp. 60–61
- Selection and Unit Assessments, pp. 115–116
- Selection Quick Checks, p. 58

Transparencies

- Bellringer Options Transparencies:
  Selection Focus Transparency 36
  Daily Language Practice Transparency 61
- Literary Elements Transparency 64

Technology

- TeacherWorks Plus™ CD-ROM
- StudentWorks Plus™ CD-ROM
- Presentation Plus!™ CD-ROM
- Literature Online, glencoe.com
- Online Student Edition, mhln.com
- Exam*View*® Assessment Suite CD-ROM
- Vocabulary PuzzleMaker CD-ROM
- Listening Library, disc 1 track 70

Teach

BI Big Idea

Life Lessons Answer: *All generations are connected, and appreciating that connection is important to understanding one's heritage. Students may also note the importance of respecting one's mother.* **OL**

R Reading Strategy

Drawing Conclusions About Author's Beliefs

Answer: *She believes that all things in nature, including various peoples, are connected and are part of a whole.* **OL**

★ Viewing the Art

Native American artist Tim Nicola (1954–) considered becoming a painter but found that sculpture provided a better avenue for his artistic vision.

Say: A three-dimensional sculpture can often be appreciated through touch as well as sight. Consider how texture contributes to the mood of the work. How does this sculpture relate to the poem? *(Students may mention the sculpture's title or notice how the smooth curving shape suggests a sense of wholeness.)* **AS**

Remember

Joy Harjo

Remember the sky that you were born under,
know each of the star's stories.
Remember the moon, know who she is.
Remember the sun's birth at dawn, that is the
strongest point of time. Remember sundown
and the giving away to night.
Remember your birth, how your mother struggled
to give you form and breath. You are evidence of
her life, and her mother's, and hers.
Remember your father. He is your life, also.
Remember the earth whose skin you are:
red earth, black earth, yellow earth, white earth
brown earth, we are earth.
Remember the plants, trees, animal life who all have their
tribes, their families, their histories, too. Talk to them,
listen to them. They are alive poems.
Remember the wind. Remember her voice. She knows the
origin of this universe.
Remember you are all people and all people
are you.
Remember you are this universe and this
universe is you.
Remember all is in motion, is growing, is you.
Remember language comes from this.
Remember the dance language is, that life is.
Remember.

In the Wind. Tim Nicola. Utah alabaster, height: 19 in. Artistic Gallery, Santa Fe, New Mexico. ★

Big Idea Life Lessons *What lesson about heritage does Harjo want you to learn from this passage?* **BI**

Reading Strategy Drawing Conclusions About Auhor's Beliefs *What can you conclude about Harjo's beliefs from these two lines?* **R**

Skills Practice

WRITING: Repetition Since students are often cautioned against repetition in their prose, they may have trouble grasping its value in poetry. Discuss the effects repetition can achieve. Note that by repeating *remember,* Harjo both reinforces her point and actually helps the reader to remember. Encourage students to practice using repetition in their own poetry. Have them choose an idea or a theme and use repetition to reinforce it. **OL**

Academic Standards

The Additional Support activity on p. 606 covers the following standard:

Skills Practice: **9.5.8** Write for different purposes and audiences, adjusting tone, style, and voice as appropriate.

AFTER YOU READ

RESPONDING AND THINKING CRITICALLY

Respond

1. How did you feel after reading this poem? What did you find yourself thinking about? Explain.

Recall and Interpret

2. (a)Give five examples of elements in nature and in the universe that the speaker urges readers to remember. (b)Why might she want readers to remember these things?
3. (a)According to the speaker, what does the wind know? (b)What does she mean by this statement?
4. (a)Where does the speaker say language comes from? (b)Why does she call language "a dance"?

Analyze and Evaluate

5. Personification is giving human qualities or characteristics to an object, animal, force of nature, or idea. How does Harjo use personification in this poem?
6. (a)Harjo urges readers to remember "the plants, trees, animal life" because "they are alive poems." What does this statement mean? (b)Is it possible to learn from these parts of nature? Explain.
7. (a)In lines 19–22, what idea is Harjo trying to express? (b)Do you agree with this idea? Explain.

Connect

8. **Big Idea** **Life Lessons** (a)What lesson does Harjo want you to remember? (b)How do you think she learned this lesson?

LITERARY ANALYSIS

Literary Element Repetition

Repetition increases the sense of unity in a work and can call attention to particular ideas. It also establishes a sense of rhythm in a speech or literary work. Repetition can also be a useful mnemonic, or memory, device.

1. What are two examples of repetition used in the poem?
2. What is the effect of these instances of repetition?

Listening and Speaking

With a group, prepare a choral reading of this poem. Experiment with different ways of reading the poem aloud. For example, you might try reading the poem in unison. Or you might decide to read around a circle, taking turns reading the poem aloud one line or group of lines at a time. Try to increase your fluency, or ease with which you read, each time you read the poem. You may wish to record your practice readings. Then, play them back and evaluate the results. When you are satisfied with your reading, present it to the class.

LiteratureOnline **Web Activities** For eFlashcards, Selection Quick Checks, and other Web activities, go to www.glencoe.com.

READING AND VOCABULARY

Reading Strategy Drawing Conclusions About Author's Beliefs

Even when the speaker of a poem or story is different from the author, you can sometimes still tell something about the **author's beliefs** from the tone, content, and point of view of the writing.

1. Based on this poem and the background knowledge you have of the poet, what do you think Harjo believes about people's relationships with one another and with the earth?
2. In support of your opinion, list three details from the poem.

Academic Vocabulary

Here is a word from the vocabulary list on page R80.

reinforce (rē′in fôrs′) *v.* to make stronger

Practice and Apply
What idea does Harjo **reinforce** in her poem?

AFTER YOU READ

Assess

1. Answers should focus on family connections and origins.
2. (a) Sky, stars, moon, sun, sundown, night, birth, parents, ancestors, earth, and so forth (b) To consider their lives within a broader perspective
3. (a) The "origin of the universe" (b) It was part of the world forever.
4. (a) "Remember all is in motion, is growing, is you." Language is the result of all that is in and around us. (b) Language sets things in motion and connects people as a dance does.
5. The stars having stories, the plants and animals having families and histories, and the wind having a voice
6. (a) Possible answer: They are living works of art with their own stories to tell. (b) Students should support their ideas.
7. (a) Our heritage and the essence of our being are shaped by everyone and everything around us. (b) Students should support their answers.
8. (a) That all lives are interconnected and united as part of the universe (b) Possibly from her family, Native Americans who revered their ancestors, nature, and the great mysteries of the universe

LiteratureOnline

Web Activities Have students access the Web site for interactive activities that will help them assess their understanding of the selection.

Reading Strategy

1. She believes all life forms have equal value.
2. Students should support their answers with appropriate details.

Academic Vocabulary

The importance of one's heritage

Literary Element

1. "Remember" and "earth"
2. Rhythm and emphasis

Listening and Speaking

Encourage each group to be creative in presenting the poem to the class.

BEFORE YOU READ

Focus

BELLRINGER

Bellringer Options
Selection Focus Transparency 37
Daily Language Practice Transparency 62
Or **ask:** How might you experience the road not taken? Suggest students jot down their regular, daily routines. Brainstorm ways they might deviate, such as taking a different way to class or eating lunch at a different table. Have them implement the changes and report on the results. Discuss what they've learned.

Author Search To expand students' appreciation of Robert Frost, have them access the Web site for additional information and resources.

Use the CheckPoint questions on Presentation Plus! to monitor students' comprehension. These questions can be used with interactive response keypads for immediate student feedback.

BEFORE YOU READ

The Road Not Taken

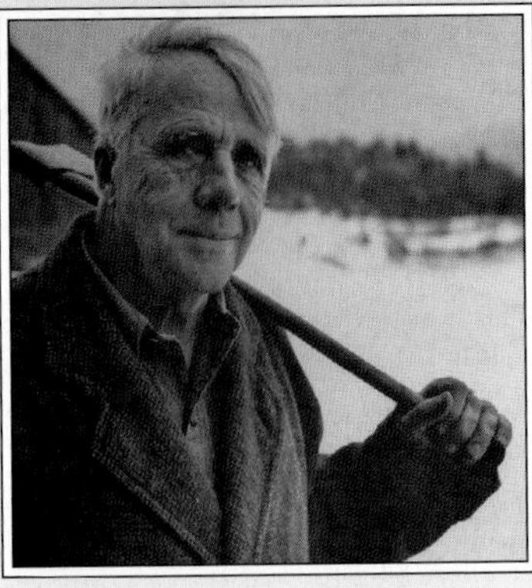

MEET ROBERT FROST

According to poet Robert Frost, a good poem "begins in delight, and ends in wisdom." Frost is one of the most popular American poets of the twentieth century. He used both traditional and modern forms in his poems, which perhaps accounts for the wide appeal of his writing. Throughout more than fifty years of outstanding achievements, Frost received numerous awards and honors, including four Pulitzer Prizes for Literature.

A Rich Heritage Robert Frost was born in San Francisco, where his father was establishing a career in journalism. When Frost was eleven years old, his father died, and his mother moved the family back to New England, where Frost would spend much of his adult life. From his boyhood until his later years, Frost enjoyed long walks in the woods, a practice that fed his curiosity about the natural world. Not surprisingly, references to nature and New England settings and speech patterns abound in Frost's poetry.

> *"[T]he ear does it. The ear is the only true writer and the only true reader."*
>
> —Robert Frost

Frost began writing poetry while in high school, a passion he shared with his co-valedictorian and future wife, Elinor Miriam White. After spending a year at college and marrying Elinor, Frost went to work as a teacher. He also worked as a factory laborer, a newspaper editor, and a lecturer at Amherst College and several other universities throughout his life.

A New England Poet In 1900 Frost and his family moved to a farm in Derry, New Hampshire. While Frost was ultimately unsuccessful as a farmer, he did write many of the poems during those years that would make up his first books. *A Boy's Will* (1913) and *North of Boston* (1914) were published by a London publishing house while Frost and his family were living in England. While in England, Frost wrote "The Road Not Taken," which would appear as the first selection in his third book of poems, *Mountain Interval* (1916).

Frost's first three books of poetry were well received by both critics and the public. His fourth book, *New Hampshire,* won a Pulitzer Prize in 1924. As a successful poet, Frost spent much of his time reading his poems to audiences around the country. He developed the speaking style, appearance, and mannerisms associated with New England, which made him even more appealing to the public.

Frost's middle years were plagued by tragedy. Between 1934 and 1940, he lost his daughter Marjorie; his wife, Elinor; and his son Carol. In 1942 he published a book of poems titled *A Witness Tree,* which explored the themes of loss and sorrow.

Robert Frost was born in 1874 and died in 1963.

LiteratureOnline **Author Search** For more about Robert Frost, go to www.glencoe.com.

Selection Skills

The Road Not Taken

Literary Elements
- Lyric Poetry (SE pp. 609, 612)
- Rhythm (SE p. 612)

Reading Skills
- Making Inferences About Theme (SE pp. 609, 610, 612)

Vocabulary Skills
- Context Clues (SE pp. 609, 612)

Writing Skills/Grammar
- Author's Purpose Essay (SE p. 613)
- Using Inversion in Poetry (SE p. 613)
- Writing a Lyric Poem (TWE p. 612)

Listening/Speaking/Viewing Skills
- Parody (SE p. 611)
- Connect to Lyric Poetry (TWE p. 610)

Study Skills/Research/Assessment
- Taking Notes (SE p. 609)

LITERATURE PREVIEW

Connecting to the Poem

In the following poem, Frost explores the dilemma of questioning decisions made in the past. He contemplates, as many people do, the opportunities presented but not chosen, the roads not traveled. Before you read the poem, think about the following questions:

- What kinds of decisions are most difficult to make?
- Do you have regrets about a decision you made in the past?

Building Background

"The Road Not Taken" is one of Frost's most famous poems. Although Frost was a voice of the Modern period of American literature, much of his poetry takes place in rural settings typical of the previous Romantic era. "The Road Not Taken" is one such poem, a musing upon a seemingly small choice made while walking through a forest. On the surface, this poem was meant as a friendly jest toward Frost's British friend, Edward Thomas, who used to guide Frost on walks in the countryside. Thomas often complained that the well-worn path was not the best way to go. The poem's deeper meaning as a metaphor for choices determining our destinies has universal significance and appeal.

Setting Purposes for Reading

Big Idea Life Lessons

As you read "The Road Not Taken," notice how Frost links making decisions and having second thoughts to the theme of life lessons.

Literary Element Lyric Poetry

A **lyric poem** expresses a speaker's personal thoughts and feelings. The ability to distinguish a lyric poem from other kinds of poetry will help you understand a poet's goals. As you read, pay close attention to how the speaker expresses his thoughts and feelings.

- See Literary Terms Handbook, p. R10.

Literature Online **Interactive Literary Elements Handbook** To review or learn more about the literary elements, go to www.glencoe.com.

READING PREVIEW

Reading Strategy Making Inferences About Theme

A **theme** in fiction, poetry, or drama is the work's main idea or message. A literary work may have more than one theme. Some themes are universal, meaning that they are widely held ideas about life. Sometimes, the reader has to **infer** the author's theme, or use reason and his or her experience to deduce a work's implied meaning. Learning to make inferences about theme will help you find deeper meaning in works of literature. As you read "The Road Not Taken," make inferences about the poem's theme.

Reading Tip: Taking Notes As you read, record your inferences about the theme.

Detail	Inference
"sorry I could not travel both"	I think the speaker is expressing regret here.

Vocabulary

diverge (di vurj′) *v.* to lead in different directions away from a common starting point; p. 610 *The path diverged at the edge of the water and led in two directions around the lake.*

want (wont) *v.* to fail to possess; to lack; p. 610 *The old station wagon wanted a proper paint job.*

Vocabulary Tip: Context Clues Context clues are hints within the text that help you figure out the meaning of a word. In the sentence, *The hallway diverged after the third door and led to a stairway to the left and a living room to the right,* the context clues for *diverged* are *led* and the two different places. You can use *led* to figure out that to *diverge* is to lead somewhere. *Stairway* and *living room* tell you that to *diverge* is to go to different places or in different directions.

INDIANA ACADEMIC STANDARDS (pages 609-613)

9.2 Develop strategies such as...identifying and analyzing...structure...and purpose...

9.3 [Identify]...elements such as...theme...

9.3.8 Interpret and evaluate the impact of ambiguities...

9.5.3 Write...analytical essays...

BEFORE YOU READ

Focus

Summary

The speaker describes a day when he was walking in the woods and came to a fork in the path. He chose the less-traveled path. Though he wonders about the other path, he states that taking the less traveled path has defined his life.

V Vocabulary

Vocabulary File **Say:** Add these words and definitions to your vocabulary file. For each word, include a sentence that gives you an example of how to use the word. **OL** Students with English language needs should include the pronunciations of these words in their files. **EL**

Literary Elements Have students access the Web site to improve their understanding of lyric poetry.

Selection Resources

Print Materials
- Unit 3 Resources (Fast File), pp. 62–64
- Leveled Vocabulary Development, p. 46
- Selection and Unit Assessments, pp. 117–118
- Selection Quick Checks, p. 59

Transparencies
- Bellringer Options Transparencies: Selection Focus Transparency 37 Daily Language Practice Transparency 62
- Literary Elements Transparency 52

Technology
- TeacherWorks Plus™ CD-ROM
- StudentWorks Plus™ CD-ROM
- Presentation Plus!™ CD-ROM
- Literature Online, glencoe.com
- Online Student Edition, mhln.com
- Exam*View*® Assessment Suite CD-ROM
- Vocabulary PuzzleMaker CD-ROM
- Listening Library, disc 1 track 71

Teach

R Reading Strategy

Making Inferences About Theme **Answer:** *Students may suggest that the speaker wants to know where both roads lead.* OL

BI Big Idea

Life Lessons **Answer:** *It suggests how one choice leads to another, gradually defining a person's life and making it harder to turn back or change direction.*
Ask: What life lesson is Frost sharing with the reader? *(He seems to suggest that a person can take pride in making an unusual or less popular choice.)* OL

★ Viewing the Art

Claude Monet (1840–1926) was the leader of the Impressionist movement in painting. A central goal of Impressionism was to realistically portray the colors and forms of objects in nature, rejecting the muted colors and conventional forms traditionally used in painting. Monet's many landscape paintings showcase this technique. **Ask:** Do you think the colors and forms in this painting display a realistic setting? *(Accept reasonable responses.)* AS

The Road Not Taken

Robert Frost

Sous-Bois, 1876. Claude Monet. Oil on canvas, 73 x 54 cm. London, Sotheby's. Lot 3, 28/6/99. ★

Two roads **diverged** in a yellow wood,
And sorry I could not travel both
And be one traveler, long I stood
And looked down one as far as I could
To where it bent in the undergrowth;

Then took the other, as just as fair,
And having perhaps the better claim,
Because it was grassy and **wanted** wear;
Though as for that the passing there
Had worn them really about the same,

And both that morning equally lay
In leaves no step had trodden black.
Oh, I kept the first for another day!
Yet knowing how way leads on to way,
I doubted if I should ever come back.

I shall be telling this with a sigh
Somewhere ages and ages hence:
Two roads diverged in a wood, and I—
I took the one less traveled by,
And that has made all the difference.

Reading Strategy Making Inferences About Theme *Why might the speaker want to travel both roads?* R

Vocabulary

diverge (di vurj′) *v.* to lead in different directions away from a common starting point

want (wont) *v.* to fail to possess; to lack

Big Idea Life Lessons *What does Frost mean by this line?* BI

Additional Support

Skills Practice

LITERARY ELEMENT: Lyric Poetry
Ask: What does the word *lyric* call to mind? *(Most students will say music.)* Explain that one definition of *lyric* is "songlike style."
Say: Lyric poetry uses many of the same techniques, such as repetition and striking imagery, as songs do to move an audience. Imagine setting this poem to music. What style of song would it be: country, opera, rock? Have students choose music and read the poem with the music playing. Ask students to explain their choices. OL

AFTER YOU READ

RESPONDING AND THINKING CRITICALLY

Respond

1. (a)Which road would you have taken? (b)Does one road seem better than the other?

Recall and Interpret

2. (a)What clues tell you the season during which the poem takes place? (b)How is the season related to the theme?
3. (a)What time of day is it? (b)Why do you think Frost chose this time of day for the poem?
4. (a)Does the speaker think that he will ever return to the fork in the road? (b)Do you think that he wants to return? Explain.

Analyze and Evaluate

5. Frost uses contradiction, or opposing thoughts and ideas, in this poem. Explain how the descriptions of the two paths include a contradiction. What does this contradiction show about the speaker?
6. How does Frost communicate the speaker's self-doubt? Give examples.
7. (a)What techniques does Frost use to create an emotional impact at the end of the poem? (b)Do you find these techniques effective? Explain.

Connect

8. **Big Idea** **Life Lessons** Is the speaker happy or regretful at the end of the poem? Explain.

VISUAL LITERACY: Cartoon

Parody

A **parody** is a humorous imitation of a literary work that often aims to point out the work's shortcomings. A parody may imitate the plot, characters, or style of a work. As you read the cartoon below, think about which aspects of Frost's poem it is parodying.

Group Activity Discuss the following questions with classmates.

1. What does the cartoonist use in place of Frost's two roads?
2. How does this comic strip trivialize, or lessen the importance of, the emotions felt by the speaker in Frost's poem?

AFTER YOU READ

Assess

1. (a) Accept reasonable answers. (b) Students should support their answers.
2. (a) The yellow wood and leaves on the ground suggest autumn. (b) Autumn suggests a later stage of life, times when people look back and reflect on their choices.
3. (a) Morning (b) Morning symbolizes the beginning of life, the opportunity to make fresh choices.
4. (a) The speaker doubts that he will ever return. (b) Students should support their answers with details from the text. Possible answer: "With a sigh" suggests regret.
5. They are described the same in terms of wear, but then one is described as less worn. It suggests that a person's memory of past circumstances may be inaccurate.
6. The speaker hesitates at the fork, wavers, and wonders about the forsaken path.
7. (a) Repetition of *I* in the last stanza evokes emotion: regret in the first line, faltering hesitation in the third line. The ambiguity of the final line lets readers draw their own conclusions. (b) Students should support their answers.
8. Students should support their answers.

CheckPoint

Use the CheckPoint questions on Presentation Plus! to check students' mastery of the selection. These questions can be used with interactive response keypads for immediate student feedback.

Visual Literacy

1. The cartoonist uses two slugs in place of Frost's roads.
2. Possible answer: The comic makes the speaker's dilemma seem silly—that a person's life-changing decisions amount to no more than a cat's dilemma about which slug to eat.

Academic Standards

The Additional Support activity on p. 610 covers the following standard:

Skills Practice: **9.3.7** Recognize and understand the significance of various literary devices, including...imagery...

AFTER YOU READ

Assess

Literary Element

1. Second stanza: *cdccd;* third stanza: *efeef;* fourth stanza: *ghggh;* yes
2. Doubt, curiosity, pride; possible answers: musical flow conveys changing emotions and suggests a life journey; rigid rhyme scheme suggests conventionality and counters the speaker's claim to individuality

Review: Rhythm

Possible answer:

Line: And sor/ry I could/ not trav/el both
Rhythm: Irregular
Effect: Stresses the speaker's sense of regret

Line: And be/ one travel/er, long/ I stood
Rhythm: Irregular
Effect: Emphasizes that the speaker is only "one" person and can only take one road

Line: And looked/ down one/ as far/ as I could
Rhythm: Irregular
Effect: Continues to stress the idea of one person, one choice, one road

Line: To where/ it bent/ in the un/dergrowth;
Rhythm: Irregular
Effect: Sound enhances the image of a bending and obscured road

LITERARY ANALYSIS

Literary Element Lyric Poetry

A **lyric poem** is a short, musical poem that has a concrete meter and rhyme scheme. It is generally an expression of the author's thoughts and feelings. Determining the rhyme scheme can help the reader better hear a poem's musical quality.

The standard method used to indicate a poem's rhyme scheme is to assign the same letter of the alphabet to the words at the ends of lines that rhyme. In the first stanza, the lines that end with *wood, stood,* and *could* can be labeled *a;* the lines that end with *both* and *growth* can be labeled *b.* Thus, the rhyme scheme in the first stanza is *abaab.*

1. Using this standard poetic notation, identify the rhyme schemes of the second, third, and fourth stanzas of "The Road Not Taken." Is the rhyme scheme identical in each stanza?
2. What thoughts and feelings are expressed in this poem? How does the structure help express them?

Review: Rhythm

As you learned on page 529, **rhythm** is the pattern of beats created by the arrangement of stressed and unstressed syllables. Rhythm gives poetry a musical quality, adds emphasis to certain words, and may help convey the poem's meaning. Rhythm can be regular—with a predictable pattern or meter—or irregular.

Partner Activity With a classmate, analyze the rhythm of "The Road Not Taken." Working with your partner, create a graphic organizer similar to the one below. First mark the scansion for each line in the first stanza. Then fill in the boxes with the type of rhythm—regular or irregular—and the effect of the rhythm. Then mark the scansion of each line in the stanza provided.

Line	Rhythm	Effect
Two roads diverged in a yellow wood,	Irregular	Stresses the image of two roads, or two choices

READING AND VOCABULARY

Reading Strategy Making Inferences About Theme

Some works have a **stated theme,** which is expressed directly. More often, works have an **implied theme,** which is revealed gradually through events, dialogue, or description. Sometimes, the reader has to make an inference about the theme by using reason and experience to deduce what is said indirectly.

1. What do you think is the primary theme in "The Road Not Taken"?
2. Is the theme stated directly or implied? Explain.

Vocabulary Practice

Practice with Context Clues Choose the word or phrase that is a context clue for the boldfaced word.

1. Two roads **diverged** in a yellow wood,
   And sorry I could not travel both
   a. in a yellow wood
   b. could not travel both
2. Then took the other, as just as fair,
   And having perhaps the better claim,
   Because it was grassy and **wanted** wear
   a. as just as fair
   b. Because it was grassy

Academic Vocabulary

Here are two words from the vocabulary list on page R80.

route (ro͞ot) *n.* a traveled way, such as a road; a course of travel to a particular destination

commence (kə mens′) *v.* to begin; to make a start

Practice and Apply

1. How does the speaker feel about the **route** he did not choose?
2. What is symbolized by the speaker's **commencing** his journey on the road?

Reading Strategy

1. Possible answer: the finality of a life-altering choice
2. Implied; it can be inferred from metaphor: the paths represent the choices; the contrast between morning and autumn represent the beginning and later stage of life.

Vocabulary

1. b 2. b

Academic Vocabulary

1. The speaker wonders about the alternative choice.
2. The commencing stands for the beginning of his path in life.

WRITING AND EXTENDING

Writing About Literature

Explore Author's Purpose Robert Frost once confided, "Sometimes I have my doubts about words altogether. . . . They are worse than nothing unless they do something, unless they amount to deeds." How do you think this expression of reservations about his chosen profession relates to the theme of "The Road Not Taken"? Why do you think Frost might have believed that this theme was important enough to write about? State your opinions in a one- to two-page written analysis of "The Road Not Taken." Use the quote from Frost and evidence from the poem to support your arguments.

Before you begin drafting, take notes on the parts of the poem that support your opinions. Jot down phrases that relate to the poem's theme, as well as any images that are particularly striking. Use a cluster diagram to help organize your ideas. The finished cluster will list the thesis of your essay, a statement describing what you believe is the theme of the poem, and the supporting details.

After completing a first draft of your analysis, meet with a peer reviewer to evaluate each other's essays and suggest changes and improvements. Then proofread and edit your essay to correct errors in spelling, grammar, and punctuation.

Learning for Life

What path might you choose in life? Where would you look for information on career possibilities? Use the Internet and the library to put together a source list on a career or on how to choose a career. Present your findings in a chart or poster and share it with the class.

Literature Online **Web Activities** For eFlashcards, Selection Quick Checks, and other Web activities, go to www.glencoe.com.

GRAMMAR AND STYLE

Frost's Language and Style

Using Inversion in Poetry In "The Road Not Taken," Frost uses inversion—the reversal of word order—to maintain rhyme scheme and meter and to emphasize certain words. For example, Frost sometimes swaps nouns and verbs or verbs and adverbs. Study the inversion Frost uses in the examples below:

Example	What Is Inverted
"long I stood"	verb and adverb
"both that morning equally lay"	verb and adverb

Think about how the two examples above would look if written in a more typical word order: *I stood long; both that morning lay equally.* Read the poem with the rewritten lines. Is the poem as lyrical, or musical, without the inverted language?

Activity Create a chart of your own, listing other examples of inversion in the poem and which words are inverted. Then rewrite each phrase to reflect a more typical word order.

Revising Check

Inversion in Prose Word order is important to consider when revising your own writing. With a partner, go through your analysis of Frost's choice of theme in "The Road Not Taken" and make sure that you have used the correct word order in your sentences. If you invert any words, be sure there is a good reason, such as emphasizing a word or idea. Revise your draft as needed.

AFTER YOU READ

Assess

Writing About Literature

Students' essays should

- provide a reaction to the poem's theme and the author's quotation.
- examine the author's purpose.
- exhibit correct grammar, punctuation, and spelling.

Learning for Life

Encourage students to focus on the "paths" to and from the careers they research: the path in preparation for the career, and the path of the career itself.

Frost's Language and Style

Example revisions: I stood for a long time; both were equally covered with leaves

Revising Check

Students should make sure that inversion is used properly and not overused in their drafts.

Web Activities Have students access the Web site for interactive activities that will help them assess their understanding of the selection.

English Language Coach

Word Order English word order may confuse nonnative speakers. Discuss the inversion exercises to ensure students understand Frost's reasons for using this technique. Have students reread the poem line by line, noting inversions. Then, have them reorder the words according to English conventions. Discuss the differences between the standard and the inverted versions. EL

Academic Standards

The Additional Support activity on p. 613 covers the following standard:

English Language Coach: **9.6.2** Demonstrate an understanding of sentence construction…and proper English usage…

BEFORE YOU READ

Focus

BELLRINGER

Bellringer Options
Selection Focus Transparency 38
Daily Language Practice Transparency 63
Or **write on the board:** Are songs the poems of the modern age? Discuss how song lyrics can inspire people now in the same way that poetry has throughout history. What are the similarities and differences? Invite students to share song lyrics they find inspiring.

Author Search To expand students' appreciation of Denise Levertov, have them access the Web site for additional information and resources.

CheckPoint

Use the CheckPoint questions on Presentation Plus! to monitor students' comprehension. These questions can be used with interactive response keypads for immediate student feedback.

BEFORE YOU READ

The Secret

MEET DENISE LEVERTOV

Poet Kenneth Rexroth once said that Denise Levertov was "the most subtly skillful poet of her generation, the most profound, the most modest, the most moving." Poet, educator, essayist, and political activist—Levertov has a voice that brims with imagination and vision.

Born in London, Levertov was raised by religious and artistic parents. Her mother home-schooled Levertov, who studied painting and ballet and read books by authors such as Leo Tolstoy and Joseph Conrad. When she decided to become a writer at age twelve, she sent some of her poems to writer T. S. Eliot. He responded with a letter encouraging Levertov to keep writing. At age seventeen, she was working as a World War II nurse in London when her work appeared in *Poetry Quarterly*. In 1946, her first book of poetry, *The Double Image*, was published.

Influences and Style After Levertov married American writer Mitchell Goodman, the two moved to New York. There she met the Black Mountain Poets—Robert Creeley, Charles Olson, and Robert Duncan. They introduced Levertov to open verse poetry that used direct description of nature, feeling, and human experience. Her poetry moved away from the formal structure of Romantic poetry and focused more on creating an emotional tone. Her second and third books of poetry, *Here and Now* (1957) and *Overland to the Islands* (1958), represented her change in style.

Social Consciousness Levertov wrote her first political poetry during the Vietnam War. In the 1960s, Levertov was caught up with the anti-war movement and began writing poetry that reflected her beliefs. She also organized a group called the Writers' and Artists' Protest Against the War in Vietnam. In the 1970s, Levertov's style shifted again. She moved away from political concerns to explore private thoughts and experiences.

> *"For me revelation in poetry always concerns the movement of the mind as it thinks and feels. . . . For a poet, the thinking-feeling process is not merely immediately transposed into language. Rather, it takes place in language."*
>
> —Denise Levertov

From 1981 to 1994, Levertov taught at Stanford University. She published more than twenty volumes of poetry and won the Governor's Award from the Washington Commission for the Humanities. As Robert Creeley wrote after her death, "[Levertov] always had a vivid emotional response and also a completely dedicated sense of political and social need."

Denise Levertov was born in 1923 and died in 1997.

LiteratureOnline **Author Search** For more about Denise Levertov, go to www.glencoe.com.

Selection Skills

The Secret

Literary Elements
- Paradox (SE pp. 615, 616, 617)
- Free Verse (SE p. 617)

Reading Skills
- Analyzing Parallelism and Juxtaposition (SE pp. 615, 618)

Vocabulary Skills
- Academic Vocabulary (SE p. 618)

Listening/Speaking/Viewing Skills
- Giving a Speech (SE p. 618)

Writing Skills/Grammar
- Analyzing Theme Essay (SE p. 618)
- Writing Paradoxes (TWE p. 616)
- Writing Free Verse (TWE p. 618)

Study Skills/Research/Assessment
- Graphic Organizer (SE p. 615)

LITERATURE PREVIEW

Connecting to the Poem

The following poem describes the profound effect a single line of poetry can have on a reader. Levertov shows that beauty can be locked away or hidden, just waiting to inspire the right person at the right time. Before you read the poem, think about the following questions:

- How does reading affect your life?
- What is your favorite poem or line of poetry? Why?

Building Background

Since ancient times, people around the world have enjoyed and respected poetry as a special form of communication. In times and places where many people did not know how to read, memorizing, reciting, and teaching poetry offered a way to pass along knowledge and ideas from one generation to another. Today poetry remains a popular art form. By reading, writing, and reciting poetry, combining it with visual arts, music, and drama, and even posting it on the Internet, people of all ages continue to demonstrate their love of poetic expression.

Setting Purposes for Reading

Big Idea Life Lessons

As you read "The Secret," think about how poetry can be a form of communication with the power to change people's lives.

Literary Element Paradox

A **paradox** is a situation or statement that seems to be impossible or contradictory but is nevertheless true, literally or figuratively. Learning how to identify a paradox will help you understand hidden meanings. As you read, watch for paradoxes within the text.

- See Literary Terms Handbook, p. R12.

LiteratureOnline Interactive Literary Elements Handbook To review or learn more about the literary elements, go to www.glencoe.com.

READING PREVIEW

Reading Strategy Analyzing Parallelism and Juxtaposition

Parallelism uses a series of words, phrases, or sentences that have similar grammatical structures to show the relationship between ideas and help emphasize thoughts. **Juxtaposition** is the placement of two or more distinct things side by side in order to contrast or compare them. Both of these techniques are used by writers of all genres. Recognizing an author's use of parallelism and juxtaposition will help you understand the meaning of a literary work. While reading this poem, notice Levertov's use of these devices.

Reading Tip: Charting Style Use a chart like the one below to identify and record examples of parallelism and juxtaposition in Levertov's poem.

Examples of Parallelism	Examples of Juxtaposition
the secret, the line, the name of the poem	

In the 1950s, poets belonging to the Beat Movement began reciting their works in coffeehouses. The practice continues today.

INDIANA ACADEMIC STANDARDS (pages 615-618)

9.3.8 Interpret and evaluate the impact of...contradictions...in a text.

9.2 Develop strategies such as...identifying and analyzing structure...

9.5.3 Write...analytical essays...

BEFORE YOU READ

Focus

Summary

Denise Levertov writes of two girls who claim they found the secret of life in a line of her poetry. She herself has no idea what the secret was. She suspects that the girls will forget everything about the secret, but that they will continue to find meaning in other writing. Levertov loves them for searching for truth and for finding it in poetry.

Literary Elements Have students access the Web site to improve their understanding of paradox.

Selection Resources

Print Materials

- Unit 3 Resources (Fast File), pp. 65–66
- Selection and Unit Assessments, pp. 119–120
- Selection Quick Checks, p. 60

Transparencies

- Bellringer Options Transparencies: Daily Language Practice Transparency 63
- Literary Elements Transparency 96

Technology

- TeacherWorks Plus™ CD-ROM
- StudentWorks Plus™ CD-ROM
- Presentation Plus!™ CD-ROM
- Literature Online, glencoe.com
- Online Student Edition, mhln.com
- Exam*View*® Assessment Suite CD-ROM
- Vocabulary PuzzleMaker CD-ROM
- Listening Library, disc 1 track 72

Teach

L Literary Element

Paradox **Answer:** *The speaker wrote the line of poetry but does not know the secret the girls found in the line.*
Ask: How does this paradox contribute to the tone? *(Students may find the line ironic or say that it contributes to the poem's tone of affectionate humor.)* OL

R Reading Strategy

Analyzing Rhetorical Devices **Ask:** What are some examples of repetition? *(The words* secret *and* line *are repeated.)* OL

BI Big Idea

Life Lessons **Answer:** *She feels that it is important to believe that there is a purpose or meaning in life.*
Ask: How does the speaker feel about the girls' discovering the secret? *(Students should point to the line "I love them.")* OL

Use the CheckPoint questions on Presentation Plus! to check students' mastery of the selection. These questions can be used with interactive response keypads for immediate student feedback.

The Secret

Denise Levertov

Two Girls at a Window, 1937. Georg Schrimpf. Oil on canvas, 78.5 x 73 cm. Inv. A IV 92. Nationalgalerie, Staatliche Museen zu Berlin, Germany.

Two girls discover
the secret of life
in a sudden line of
poetry.

I who don't know the
secret wrote
the line. They
told me

(through a third person)
they had found it
but not what it was
not even

what line it was. No doubt
by now, more than a week
later, they have forgotten
the secret,

the line, the name of
the poem. I love them
for finding what
I can't find,

and for loving me
for the line I wrote, R
and for forgetting it
so that

a thousand times, till death
finds them, they may
discover it again, in other
lines

in other
happenings. And for
wanting to know it,
for

assuming there is
such a secret, yes,
for that
most of all.

Literary Element Paradox *How is this sentence paradoxical?* L

Big Idea Life Lessons *Why does the speaker consider it so important to assume there is such a secret?* BI

Additional Support

Skills Practice

WRITING: Analyzing Paradoxes Have pairs of students work together to write paradoxical statements. Stress that although the statements should be contradictory, they must be true.

Write this example on the board: I love you, but you make me crazy. Discuss how such statements can add irony and complexity to writing. Invite volunteers to share their statements with the class. Have the class evaluate the statements for validity and contradiction. OL

AFTER YOU READ

RESPONDING AND THINKING CRITICALLY

Respond

1. Do you think the author knows, or will ever discover, the secret? Explain.

Recall and Interpret

2. (a)In the first stanza, what adjective does Levertov use to describe the line of poetry? (b)Why do you think Levertov chose this particular word?
3. (a)Why can't the girls tell the poet what the secret was? (b)What does this say about the nature of the secret?
4. (a)The girls approach the secret in several different ways. For which approach does the poet most love the girls? (b)What is the metaphorical meaning of the word *secret* in this poem?

Analyze and Evaluate

5. What is the poet's tone, or attitude, toward her readers, and how does she convey this tone?
6. How does Levertov make the secret seem mysterious?
7. Does this poem make you want to read more poetry? Why or why not?

Connect

8. **Big Idea** **Life Lessons** What do you think Levertov wants the reader to learn about poetry and life from this poem?

LITERARY ANALYSIS

Literary Element Paradox

Although a **paradox** seems contradictory, it is true. It can be either literally true or figuratively true. Some writers use paradox to express conflicting ideas or emotions that work together to create a greater truth.

1. Is the paradox in lines 18–20 literally or figuratively true? Explain.
2. How could Levertov write the line but not know the secret?

Toroni-Nagy, 1969. Victor Vasarely. Private Collection, U.S.A.

Review: Free Verse

Poetry is often written to follow a specific form. This form may include a well-defined rhyme scheme, highly metered lines, a prescribed line length, and a predetermined stanza arrangement. As you learned on page 581, **free verse** is poetry that has no fixed pattern of meter, rhyme, line length, or stanza arrangement. Free verse often imitates natural forms of speech and can be used to emphasize the relationship between form and meaning in a poem. Although poets who write free verse do not follow traditional rules of form, they use techniques such as repetition and alliteration to create musical patterns in their poems.

Partner Activity Pair up with a classmate and read lines 1–13 aloud. Then answer the questions below.

1. How would you describe the rhythm of these lines?
2. What tone does Levertov convey in these lines?

Literary Element

1. Figurative; the girls have not found the secret either.
2. She cannot know exactly what meaning the girls saw in the poem.

Review: Free Verse

1. Natural, not regular
2. Playful, a bit rueful

AFTER YOU READ

Assess

1. Possible answers: She has discovered the secret before because she says it can be repeatedly forgotten and rediscovered; or, she has never found it because she says, "I love them for finding what I can't find."
2. (a) *Sudden* (b) It is surprising in this context and therefore imparts a sense of discovery.
3. (a) They forget the secret and even its location. (b) It is elusive and ever changing.
4. (a) For assuming there is meaning to be found in poetry and in life (b) It refers to meaning, purpose, or truth.
5. She loves her readers for engaging with her poetry. The overall tone is gentle, conversational, and direct. Simple words, short lines, and commas help create the conversational tone.
6. She talks about how and where it can be found, how it can be forgotten, and the importance of believing that it exists, but she never says what it is.
7. Students should support their answers.
8. Students should support their answers.

Academic Standards

The Additional Support activity on p. 616 covers the following standard:

Skills Practice: **9.4.1** Discuss ideas for writing with classmates…and develop drafts…collaboratively.

Assess

Reading Strategy

1. Juxtaposing all they have forgotten (the secret, which line, which poem) highlights the difficulty of finding where the truth lies.
2. It unifies the poem.

Academic Vocabulary

1. They can derive meaning from other writing and other experiences.
2. She passed the secret along through her poetry.

Writing About Literature

Students should

- make a list of points they wish to make in their essay.
- find quotes for support.
- order the points and the correlating quotes as they will appear in the essay.

Learning for Life

Remind students to incorporate parallelism and juxtaposition into their speeches.

Web Activities Have students access the Web site for interactive activities that will help them assess their understanding of the selection.

READING AND VOCABULARY

Reading Strategy Analyzing Parallelism and Juxtaposition

A writer may use parallelism or juxtaposition to achieve a number of different effects. **Parallelism** is often used to unify a section of a literary work. **Juxtaposition** can be used to show similarities in or differences between two or more things. Juxtaposition is also commonly used to evoke an emotional response in the reader.

1. In lines 15–18, "they have forgotten / the secret, // the line, the name of / the poem," Levertov juxtaposes the secret, the line, and the name of the poem. Why does she list the juxtaposed terms in this particular order?
2. Levertov uses parallel structure in lines 18–36. Read these lines aloud, emphasizing the parallel structures. What effect does this parallelism have on the poem?

Academic Vocabulary

Here are two words from the vocabulary list on page R80. These words will help you think, write, and talk about the selection.

extract (ek′ strakt) *v.* to remove; to draw or pull out

transmit (trans mit′) *v.* to send from one thing to another

Practice and Apply

1. Where else will the two girls be able to **extract** the secret?
2. How did Levertov **transmit** the secret?

WRITING AND EXTENDING

Writing About Literature

Analyze Theme A literary work can have many themes, but there is usually one main theme that the author wants to emphasize. Based on Levertov's theme in "The Secret," how do you think she would define poetry? What would she say is the purpose of poetry? Write a one- or two-page analysis of how Levertov defines poetry and how she uses it. Use evidence from "The Secret" to defend your position.

Before you begin drafting, take notes on the main theme of "The Secret" and what Levertov says and implies about poetry through this theme. Include quotes from the poem related to the theme and Levertov's views, as well as any impressions or ideas that strike you as you read. Once you have finished taking notes, begin drafting.

After completing your draft, meet with a peer reviewer to evaluate each other's work and suggest revisions. Then proofread and edit your draft to correct errors in spelling, grammar, and punctuation.

Learning for Life

Write a speech about a personal interest, passion, or hobby. Before drafting your speech, answer the following questions:

1. What is the interest or hobby you will be talking about?
2. For how long have you pursued this interest or hobby?
3. How would you describe it to someone who had never heard of it before?

After you have answered these questions, list some strategies for how you will pursue and develop this interest over the course of your life. When you have finished taking notes, write your speech, keeping in mind the literary devices you have learned about in this lesson: parallelism and juxtaposition. Practice delivering the speech to a classmate and have him or her suggest revisions to the speech or changes in your delivery. Once you are satisfied with your speech, deliver it to the class.

Literature Online **Web Activities** For eFlashcards, Selection Quick Checks, and other Web activities, go to www.glencoe.com.

Additional Support

Skills Practice

WRITING: Connect Note that the focus of Levertov's poetry changed over time. Have students outline the stages of their lives so far. Have them think about their major concerns at different points. For example, was a favorite toy their focus in kindergarten? Ask students to consider what holds their attention now. Have them choose one such concern and explore it in a free verse poem. **OL**

PART 3

The Strength of Family

Circle of Love, 1996. Michael Escoffery. Private Collection. ★

BIG IDEA

BI Family members sometimes seem to give one another endless grief, but the real truth about families lies in their healing power. The poems in Part 3 explore the strength of families. As you read the poems, ask yourself: What about my family might others find inspiring?

Analyzing and Extending

BI Big Idea

The Strength of Family
Discuss what qualities lend a family strength.
Ask: How do you define *family?* Note that the concept of family can be broadened to include anyone who is close to them. Discuss what strengths these extended family members lend. **OL**

★ Viewing the Art

Originally from Kingston, Jamaica, Michael Escoffery came to the U.S. in his 20s. His work focuses on the strength of women in African American culture and often highlights the beauty of the female form. He has won many awards but says "awards are just icing on the cake. They point the direction I should go and remind me of where I've been." **AS**

Differentiated Instruction

Discussion Ask a student volunteer to read the "Big Idea" blurb aloud. Ask students what they think the author means by the "strength" and "healing power" of family. Have students use specific examples. Instruct students to look for these themes as they read the poems in this part. **BL**

Academic Standards

Additional Support activities on pp. 618 and 619 cover the following standards:

Skills Practice: **9.5.1** Write...autobiographical narratives...that describe with specific details the sights, sounds, and smells of a scene and the specific actions, movements, gestures, and feelings of the characters...

Differentiated Instruction: **9.7.1** Summarize a speaker's purpose and point of view...

Part 3: Skills Scope and Sequence

Readability Scores Key
Dale-Chall/DRP/Lexile

PACING (DAYS) STANDARD	BLOCK	SELECTIONS AND FEATURES	LITERARY ELEMENTS
2–3 class sessions	1–2	"Grape Sherbet" by Rita Dove, pp. 622–626	Assonance and Consonance, SE pp. 623–625 Metaphor, SE p. 625 Exact Rhyme and Slant Rhyme, TWE p. 624
		COMPARING LITERATURE Across Genres "Good Night, Willie Lee, I'll See You in the Morning" by Alice Walker, pp. 627–631 "Beyond the Bedroom Wall" by Larry Woiwode **9.2/57/990**, pp. 632–637 "In Praise of Grandfathers" by Rudolfo A. Anaya, pp. 638–642	Epiphany, SE pp. 629, 631
2–3 class sessions	1–2	"Elena" by Pat Mora, pp. 643–647	Free Verse, SE pp. 644, 646 Diction, SE p. 646
		"My Mother Combs My Hair" by Chitra Banerjee Divakaruni, pp. 648–654	Simile, SE pp. 649, 651, 653 Structure, SE p. 653
		VISUAL PERSPECTIVE on The Strength of Family: from *Bone: Out from Boneville* by Jeff Smith, pp. 655–657	
		"Lineage" by Margaret Walker, pp. 658–661	Alliteration, SE pp. 659, 661
2–3 class sessions	1	Writing Workshop: Reflective Essay, pp. 662–669	
1 class session		Speaking, Listening, and Viewing Workshop: Reflective Presentation, pp. 670–671	
2 class sessions		Test Preparation and Practice, pp. 674–679	

About the Part

Part 3 includes poems about what it means to be part of a family.

READING AND CRITICAL THINKING	VOCABULARY	WRITING AND GRAMMAR	LISTENING, SPEAKING, AND VIEWING
Making Inferences About Setting, SE pp. 623, 624, 626	Analogy, SE pp. 623, 626 Academic Vocabulary, SE p. 626	Respond to Form, SE p. 626	
Making Generalizations, SE pp. 629, 631 Monitoring Comprehension, TWE p. 634 Multiple Meaning Words, TWE p. 636 Comparing Authors' Purposes, TWE p. 638	Academic Vocabulary, SE p. 631 Word Roots, TWE p. 630	Compare and Contrast Tone, SE p. 631 Sentence Structure, TWE p. 632 Irregular Verbs, TWE p. 640	Group Activity, SE p. 642 Oral Interpretation, SE p. 642 Analyzing Art, TWE p. 634
Responding to the Speaker, SE pp. 644, 645, 647	Academic Vocabulary, SE p. 647	Poem, SE p. 647	Performing, SE p. 647 Analyzing Art, TWE p. 645
Visualizing, SE pp. 649, 653	Analogies, SE pp. 649, 653 Academic Vocabulary, SE p. 653	Essay, SE p. 654 Literary Criticism, SE p. 654 Using Italics, SE p. 654	Role-Playing, TWE p. 650 Analyzing Art, TWE p. 650
Interpreting Graphic Forms of Literature, SE p. 655; TWE p. 656 Comparison and Contrast, TWE p. 656			
Analyzing Rhythm, SE pp. 659, 661	Synonyms, SE pp. 659, 661	Essay, SE p. 661 Description, TWE p. 660	Analyzing Art, TWE p. 660
Reading Aloud, TWE p. 665		Reflecting on an Experience, SE pp. 662–669 Show Versus Tell, TWE p. 664	Getting Feedback, TWE p. 668
			Delivering a Reflective Presentation, SE pp. 670–671 Speaking Effectively, TWE p. 670
Visualizing, TWE p. 674		Using Semicolons, TWE p. 678	

LITERARY FOCUS

Focus

BELLRINGER

Bellringer Options
Daily Language Practice Transparency 64
Or write a random letter on the board and give students 30 seconds to come up with as many words as they can string together that begin with that letter and still make sense.
Write on the board as an example: L—lovely lemon lollypop.

Teach

L Literary Element

Sound Devices Point out to students that sound devices can be used to make poems jarring and dissonant.
Ask: How could you use sound devices to create an unsettling mood? *(Answers will vary.)* OL

Literary Elements Have students access the Web site to improve their understanding of sound devices.

LITERARY FOCUS

Sound Devices

What does sound contribute to poetry?

L A poem's impact depends not only on what it says but on how it sounds. Read this poem aloud or, if that is impractical, read each word so you hear it in your head.

from *The Bells*

by Edgar Allan Poe

R
Hear the sledges with the bells—
Silver bells!
What a world of merriment their melody foretells!
How they tinkle, tinkle, tinkle,
In the icy air of night!
While the stars that oversprinkle
All the heavens, seem to twinkle
With a crystalline delight;
Keeping time, time, time,
In a sort of Runic rhyme,
To the tintinnabulation that so musically wells
From the bells, bells, bells, bells,
Bells, bells, bells—
From the jingling and the tinkling of the bells.

Jingle Bells. George Harlow White. ★

Additional Support

Academic Standards

The Additional Support activity on p. 620 covers the following standard:

Skills Practice: **9.3.7** Recognize and understand the significance of various literary devices...

Skills Practice

LITERARY ELEMENT: Sound Devices Challenge students to a sound device competition. Have categories such as Awesome Alliteration where students create their own examples for alliteration and vote on which examples are best. Include categories for assonance, consonance, onomatopoeia, repetition, and one for best overall sound device usage. OL

Sound Devices

Sound devices are the elements in poetry that appeal to the ear. Poets use them to establish mood, create rhythm, reinforce meaning, or add a musical quality. Examples of sound devices include alliteration, assonance, consonance, and onomatopoeia.

Alliteration The repetition of consonant sounds at the beginnings of words is called **alliteration.** Poets use alliteration as a way of emphasizing important words in the poem. Note the alliteration Poe uses in "The Bells":

> What a world of merriment their melody foretells!
>
> —Edgar Allan Poe, **from "The Bells"**

Assonance The repetition of similar vowel sounds within non-rhyming words is called **assonance.** Assonance is often used in place of end rhyme, especially in ballads and free verse. Like all sound devices, assonance helps unify a poem and emphasize important ideas.

> They followed plows and bent to toil.
> They moved through fields sowing seed.
>
> —Margaret Walker, **from "Lineage"**

Consonance When two words have different vowel sounds but share a single consonant sound —such as *brick* and *clock*—they are said to have **consonance.** Like assonance, consonance can be used in place of rhyme or to supplement rhyme.

> Pain—has an Element of Blank—
> It cannot recollect
>
> —Emily Dickinson, **from "Pain—has an Element of Blank—"**

Onomatopoeia Words such as "ping," "splash," and "knock" are examples of another sound device. **Onomatopoeia** is the use of words that imitate the sound of what they describe. Poe uses onomatopoeia in "The Bells":

> From the jingling and the tinkling of the bells.
>
> —Edgar Allan Poe, **from "The Bells"**

Repetition The **repetition** of a sound, word, phrase, line, or even an entire stanza is another frequently used poetic sound device. Repetition can occur anywhere in a poem, including within lines and from one stanza to another. Among other things, poets use repetition to create unity and mood and to enhance meaning. Notice how repetition affects the sound of the lines below:

> They followed plows and bent to toil.
> They moved through fields sowing seed.
> They touched earth and grain grew.
>
> —Margaret Walker, **from "Lineage"**

Quickwrite

Writing Sounds Think about the sounds you hear in a given location, such as in a crowded room, on a bus or train, during a sporting event, or in the woods. Make a list of the sounds. How many examples of onomatopoeia can you use in your list? Write a short paragraph using words that capture the sounds in your chosen location.

LiteratureOnline Interactive Literary Elements Handbook Go to www.glencoe.com to review or learn more about sound devices.

INDIANA ACADEMIC STANDARDS (pages 620-621)

9.3.11 Evaluate the aesthetic qualities of style...

9.4.3 Use precise language...[and] sensory details...

Building Reading Fluency

Sound Devices Explain that it's helpful to hear sound devices read aloud. Have partners take turns reading Edgar Allan Poe's "The Bells" aloud to each other. As one student reads, the other should note which sound devices stand out. Afterward, partners can compare notes. BL

Teach

R Reading Strategy

Test-Taking Tip In a testing situation, it isn't appropriate for students to read aloud or even whisper as they read. Suggest to students that they get into the habit of "hearing" the words as they read to themselves. **Ask:** What does the speaker in your head sound like? Does your speaker have an accent? Is your speaker male or female? Have students experiment with "hearing" different kinds of speakers as they read. OL

Viewing the Art

George Harlow White (1817–1887) came to Canada from England in the 1870s. He was known for his drawings and watercolors of Canadian pioneer life. He returned to England in 1878.
Ask: Is the scene in this painting similar to what you envision when you read the excerpt from Poe's poem? Explain. *(Answers will vary.)* AS

Assess

Quickwrite

Answers will vary. Make sure students choose locations that lend themselves to onomatopoeic sounds.

Academic Standards

The Additional Support activity on p. 621 covers the following standard:

Building Reading Fluency: **9.7** [Respond] to oral communication [with] careful listening and evaluation of content...

Focus

BELLRINGER

Bellringer Options
Daily Language Practice Transparency 65
Or display images associated with Memorial Day, such as a military cemetery with identical headstones, a veteran selling red paper poppies, parades, or picnics with flags and red, white, and blue bunting.
Ask: Has your family participated in any of these activities? How does your family celebrate Memorial Day?
Ask students to compare their Memorial Day practices with that described in this poem.

Author Search To expand students' appreciation of Rita Dove, have them access the Web site for additional information and resources.

Use the CheckPoint questions on Presentation Plus! to monitor students' comprehension. These questions can be used with interactive response keypads for immediate student feedback.

Grape Sherbet

MEET RITA DOVE

Perhaps you think of a poet as a person with his or her head buried in a notebook all day, struggling to create the perfect phrase. Not Rita Dove. "If you don't have a life, then I don't see where you're going to write your poems from," she has said. Dove is serious about poetry, but she also finds joy in classical voice training, ballroom dancing, and playing the viola de gamba—a seventeenth-century instrument similar to the cello.

An Unfamiliar Path Dove was born in Akron, Ohio, to a middle-class family. Her father was the first African American research chemist at Goodyear Tire, and he instilled in his children a desire to excel in all areas of life. Dove began writing at an early age, but as a child, she never thought of writing as a possible career; her father wanted her to become a doctor or a lawyer. "[Poetry] simply wasn't in the stars," Dove has said. "It wasn't anything anyone I knew had ever done." Luckily, she had a high-school English teacher who noticed her talent and took her to a writer's conference. Soon Dove began to think of herself as a real writer. She went on to study poetry at the highly esteemed University of Iowa Writer's Workshop, where she met her husband, the German writer Fred Viebahn.

> *"One can be a poet, but you have to have a life."*
>
> —Rita Dove

Family and Fame "Grape Sherbet" comes from a series of poems written about Dove's father, entitled "My Father's Telescope." She wrote these poems to better understand her brilliant but sometimes distant father. Many of Dove's poems seek an understanding of history, family, and a sense of place in the ever-changing landscape of America. Her most famous work, *Thomas and Beulah,* is a re-creation of her grandparents' lives from the 1920s to the 1960s. The book earned Dove the Pulitzer Prize in 1987, one of the highest honors a writer can achieve. Dove was the second African American poet to win the award, after Gwendolyn Brooks in 1950.

Dove's achievement as a poet includes making poetry a more visible art form. From 1993 to 1995, she acted as Poet Laureate of the United States and used the distinguished platform to incorporate poetry into language-arts classrooms in elementary schools. Dove's fame has allowed her to enter unusual worlds—she has read her poetry at a White House state dinner and has appeared on *Sesame Street.* In 1999 she published *On the Bus with Rosa Parks*, a collection in which several poems explore the life of civil-rights icon Rosa Parks. Dove currently teaches at the University of Virginia in Charlottesville.

Rita Dove was born in 1952.

LiteratureOnline **Author Search** For more about Rita Dove, go to www.glencoe.com.

Selection Skills

Grape Sherbet

Literary Elements
- Assonance and Consonance (SE pp. 623–625)
- Metaphor (SE p. 625)
- Exact Rhyme and Slant Rhyme (TWE p. 624)

Reading Skills
- Making Inferences About Setting (SE pp. 623, 624, 626)

Vocabulary Skills
- Analogy (SE p. 623, 626)
- Academic Vocabulary (SE p. 626)

Writing Skills/Grammar
- Analysis of Form (SE p. 626)

Study Skills/Research/Assessment
- Internet Connection (SE p. 626)

LITERATURE PREVIEW

Connecting to the Poem

"Grape Sherbet" takes place on Memorial Day, an American holiday created to remember those who died while serving their country in the armed forces. People often spend the holiday visiting with family and friends. Before you read the poem, think about the following questions:

- Does your family have a traditional way of celebrating Memorial Day?
- What childhood memories do you have of holidays spent with parents or guardians?

Building Background

In 1868 General John Logan, the leader of a group of former Civil War soldiers, declared, "The 30th of May, 1868, is designated for the purpose of strewing with flowers, or otherwise decorating the graves of comrades who died in defense of their country during the late rebellion, and whose bodies now lie in almost every city, village, and hamlet churchyard in the land." Memorial Day was traditionally observed on May 30 but is now observed on the last Monday in May.

Setting Purposes for Reading

Big Idea The Strength of Family

As you read "Grape Sherbet," notice how Dove describes her father and what this description tells you about their relationship.

Literary Element Assonance and Consonance

Assonance is the repetition of the same or similar vowel sounds in poetry or other writing. **Consonance** is the repetition of consonant sounds, typically at the end of nonrhyming words and preceded by different vowel sounds. As you read "Grape Sherbet," note instances of assonance and consonance.

- See Literary Terms Handbook, pp. R2 and R5.

Literature Online **Interactive Literary Elements Handbook** To review or learn more about the literary elements, go to www.glencoe.com.

READING PREVIEW

Reading Strategy Making Inferences About Setting

Setting is the time and place in which the events of a literary work occur. You can often determine the setting even if it is not directly stated. Look for clues in "Grape Sherbet" from which you can infer the setting.

Reading Tip: Noting Details Create a chart like the one below to help you list and categorize details that define the setting in "Grape Sherbet."

Detail	What it tells about setting
The day? Memorial.	The events take place on Memorial Day.

Vocabulary

gelled (jeld) *adj.* in a semisolid state after having been liquid; p. 624 *The treat was made of gelled lemonade.*

dollop (dol′ əp) *n.* a glob of a soft, mushy substance; p. 624 *He spooned a dollop of whipped cream onto his pie.*

Vocabulary Tip: Analogies Analogies are one way to show relationships between words that might not usually be thought of as similar. To finish an analogy, decide what relationship exists between the first two things or ideas. Then apply that relationship to another pair of words and see if it is the same.

INDIANA ACADEMIC STANDARDS (pages 623-626)

9.3.11 Evaluate the aesthetic qualities of style...

9.2 Develop [reading] strategies...

9.5.2 Write responses to literature that...demonstrate an awareness of the author's style and an appreciation of the effects created...

BEFORE YOU READ

Focus

Summary

The speaker describes memories of her family's Memorial Day celebration, a day in which they visit a cemetery and her father makes a special dessert.

V Vocabulary

Vocabulary File **Say:** Add these words and definitions to your vocabulary file. For each word, include a sentence that gives you an example of how to use the word. **OL** Students with English language needs should include the pronunciations of these words in their files. **EL**

Literary Elements Have students access the Web site to improve their understanding of assonance and consonance.

Selection Resources

Print Materials

- Unit 3 Resources (Fast File), pp. 70–72
- Leveled Vocabulary Development, p. 47
- Selection and Unit Assessments, pp. 121–122
- Selection Quick Checks, p. 61

Transparencies

- Bellringer Options Transparencies: Daily Language Practice Transparency 65
- Literary Elements Transparency 73, 74

Technology

- TeacherWorks Plus™ CD-ROM
- StudentWorks Plus™ CD-ROM
- Presentation Plus!™ CD-ROM
- Literature Online, glencoe.com
- Online Student Edition, mhln.com
- Exam*View*® Assessment Suite CD-ROM
- Vocabulary PuzzleMaker CD-ROM
- Listening Library, disc 1 track 73

Teach

R Reading Strategy

Making Inferences About Setting **Answer:** *She is describing a cemetery.* **OL**

L Literary Element

Assonance and Consonance **Answer:** *The words* I've *and* trying *create assonance by repeating the long* i *sound, and* it *and* exist *repeat the short* i *sound. The words* taste, but, it, doesn't, *and* exist *all contain the* t *sound, which creates consonance.* **OL**

Use the CheckPoint questions on Presentation Plus! to check students' mastery of the selection. These questions can be used with interactive response keypads for immediate student feedback.

GRAPE

SHERBET

Rita Dove

The day? Memorial.
After the grill
Dad appears with his masterpiece—
swirled snow, **gelled** light.
We cheer. The recipe's
a secret, and he fights
a smile, his cap turned up
so the bib[1] resembles a duck.

That morning we galloped
through the grassed-over mounds
and named each stone
for a lost milk tooth.[2] Each **dollop**
of sherbet, later,
is a miracle,
like salt on a melon that makes it sweeter.

Everyone agrees—it's wonderful!
It's just how we imagined lavender
would taste. The diabetic[3] grandmother
stares from the porch, a torch
of pure refusal.

We thought no one was lying
there under our feet,
we thought it
was a joke. I've been trying
to remember the taste,
but it doesn't exist.
Now I see why
you bothered,
father.

1. Here, *bib* means "the bill or visor of a cap."
2. *Milk tooth* is another term for a baby tooth that falls out during childhood and is replaced by a permanent tooth.

Reading Strategy Making Inferences About Setting
What place is the speaker describing in these lines? **R**

Vocabulary

gelled (jeld) *adj.* in a semisolid state after having been liquid

dollop (dol′ əp) *n.* a glob of a soft, mushy substance

3. *Diabetic* means "affected by diabetes, a disease which prevents the body from metabolizing sugar properly."

Literary Element Assonance and Consonance
Which words in these lines create assonance? Which create consonance? **L**

Additional Support

Skills Practice

LITERARY ELEMENT: Exact Rhyme and Slant Rhyme *Rhyme* refers to the sounds that are repeated at the ends of two or more words. *Slant rhyme* refers to words at the ends of lines whose sounds are similar but are not quite exact rhymes. Sometimes the vowel sounds are slightly different, as in *sweeter* and *better.* Sometimes the consonant sounds are slightly different, as in *lights* and *bright* or *pack* and *lacked.*

In "Grape Sherbet," Rita Dove uses exact rhyme and slant rhyme. Have students identify the rhymes in each stanza, stating whether they are exact rhymes or slant rhymes. **OL**

AFTER YOU READ

RESPONDING AND THINKING CRITICALLY

Respond

1. How are the speaker's Memorial Day experiences the same as or different from your own?

Recall and Interpret

2. (a)What is the masterpiece of the speaker's father? (b)How do you know?
3. (a)List two ways the speaker describes the grape sherbet. (b)What do you think is so special about this treat?
4. (a)What did the speaker of the poem do that morning? (b)Why does that experience make the sherbet seem like "a miracle"?

Analyze and Evaluate

5. In the first line of the poem, the speaker describes the day as "Memorial." Explain at least two different meanings the word might have within the context of the poem. Use a dictionary if you need help.
6. (a)What does line 2, "After the grill," mean? (b)Why does the poet use so few words to describe what is happening?
7. (a)Who is the speaker of this poem? Explain how you know. (b)To whom is she referring when she uses the pronoun *we*?

Connect

8. **Big Idea** **The Strength of Family** The last three lines of the poem read "Now I see why / you bothered, / father." What do those lines mean?

LITERARY ANALYSIS

Literary Element Assonance and Consonance

A poem that lacks regular meter or rhyme can be unified using other techniques, such as **assonance** and **consonance.** Words that do not quite rhyme but contain some variation of assonance or consonance—such as *owl* and *power,* or *jackal* and *buckle*—are called *slant rhymes.*

1. Identify three places in the first, second, or fourth stanzas of the poem where Dove uses slant rhyme.
2. Read through the third stanza of "Grape Sherbet." Focusing on the last word in each line, describe how assonance and consonance work to unify this stanza.

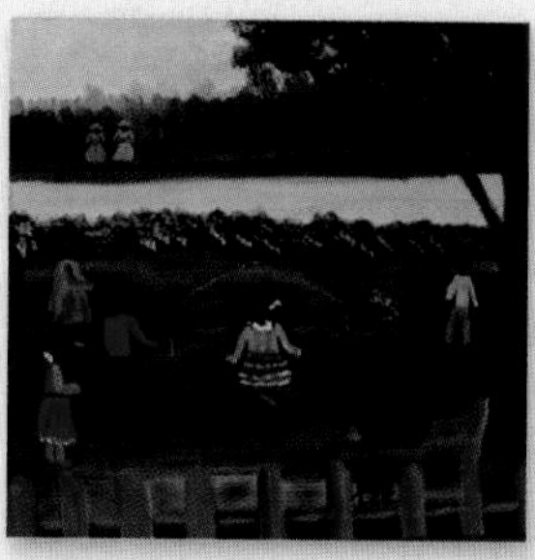

Game We Played, 1992 (detail). Anna Belle Lee Washington. Oil on canvas.

Review: Metaphor

As you learned on page 590, **metaphor** is a figure of speech that compares or equates two seemingly unlike things. In contrast to a simile, a metaphor implies the comparison rather than stating it directly, so there is no use of connective words such as *like* or *as.* Poet Carl Sandburg once used the metaphor: "The past is a bucket of ashes."

Partner Activity Pair up with a classmate and identify the metaphors in "Grape Sherbet." Create a chart similar to the one below and fill in the left column with the poem's metaphors and the right column with the effect each one has on the reader.

Metaphor	Effect on the Reader
Dad appears with his masterpiece—/ swirled snow, gelled light.	The sherbet seems almost magical, as though made from snow or light.

Literary Element

1. Possible answers: *up* and *duck; lavender* and *grandmother; bothered* and *father*
2. The consonance between *wonderful* and *refusal,* which end the first and last lines of the stanza, tie the stanza together. There is assonance and consonance between *lavender* and *grandmother* and rhyme between *porch* and *torch.*

Review: Metaphor

Check that the passages students identify are in fact metaphors and that their explanations of the metaphors' effects are plausible.

AFTER YOU READ

Assess

1. Students' answers will vary.
2. (a) The grape sherbet (b) Clues are the title of the poem and lines 12–14: "Each dollop / of sherbet, later, / is a miracle."
3. (a) "swirled snow, gelled light"; "a miracle" (b) The father makes it just for this holiday; it tastes different from anything else.
4. (a) The speaker played in the cemetery. (b) Eating the sherbet makes everyone glad to be alive, in contrast to the dead lying in the cemetery.
5. The literal meaning is the holiday set aside to remember the war dead. *Memorial* also means "a reminder of a person or of somebody's life and work."
6. (a) It means "after the meal prepared on the grill." (b) To suggest flashes of images or memories
7. (a) The speaker is an adult looking back on a childhood memory. The poem is in the present tense, as if the speaker were still a child, but in the last stanza we realize she is an adult because of the shift to past tense. (b) Everybody, as in lines 5 and 17, or the speaker and other children, as in lines 9 and 21
8. Students may say the lines refer to the father making the sherbet, because a day set aside to remember the dead calls for something to remind people of the joys of living.

Academic Standards

The Additional Support activity on p. 624 covers the following standard:

Skills Practice: **9.3.7** Recognize and understand the significance of various literary devices…

AFTER YOU READ

Assess

Reading Strategy

1. The opening line, "The day? Memorial," tells us it is Memorial Day. "After the grill" indicates a cookout. The setting shifts to an earlier time and place when the speaker says, "That morning we galloped / through the grassed-over mounds / and named each stone / for a lost milk tooth." These lines reveal that the setting is a graveyard.
2. Students may infer that the Memorial Day cookout is an annual family event, that it is important for the adults to remember their deceased loved ones by visiting the cemetery, and that it is a custom for the children to play there.

Vocabulary

1. b **2.** b **3.** a

Academic Vocabulary

1. It seems that her father doesn't make it often, probably once a year for this cookout.
2. The poet creates a contrast between the setting of the cookout and the cemetery, a contrast that depends on the cemetery.

Web Activities Have students access the Web site for interactive activities that will help them assess their understanding of the selection.

READING AND VOCABULARY

Reading Strategy Making Inferences About Setting

Setting includes not only the physical surroundings, but also the ideas, customs, values, and beliefs of a particular time and place. Setting can help create an atmosphere or mood in a literary work.

1. Compare the different settings in "Grape Sherbet." Describe each setting using details from the poem.
2. What can you infer about the speaker's family customs, values, and beliefs from the settings in "Grape Sherbet"?

Vocabulary Practice

Practice with Analogies Choose the word that best completes each analogy.

1. **masterpiece : art :: summit :**
   a. success **b.** mountain **c.** valley
2. **liquid : gelled :: rainy :**
   a. stormy **b.** snowy **c.** sunny
3. **dollop : spoonful :: expansion :**
   a. growth **b.** contraction **c.** size

Academic Vocabulary

Here are two words from the vocabulary list on page R80. These words will help you think, write, and talk about the selection.

plus (plus) *n.* something favorable or beneficial

integral (in′ tə grəl) *adj.* an essential or necessary part of something

Practice and Apply

1. What makes the grape sherbet a **plus** to the speaker of the poem?
2. Why is the cemetery an **integral** part of the poem "Grape Sherbet"?

LiteratureOnline Web Activities For eFlashcards, Selection Quick Checks, and other Web activities, go to www.glencoe.com.

WRITING AND EXTENDING

Writing About Literature

Respond to Form "Grape Sherbet" is a lyric poem, a poem that expresses a personal experience or emotional state. Do you think free verse is the best form for this poem, or would the subject have been better served by the use of regular rhyme and meter? Write a one- to two-page analysis in which you defend or critique Rita Dove's use of free verse in "Grape Sherbet."

Before you begin a draft of your analysis, read through "Grape Sherbet" again and list the pros and cons of free verse in relation to this poem. Use a diagram like the one below to help organize your thoughts.

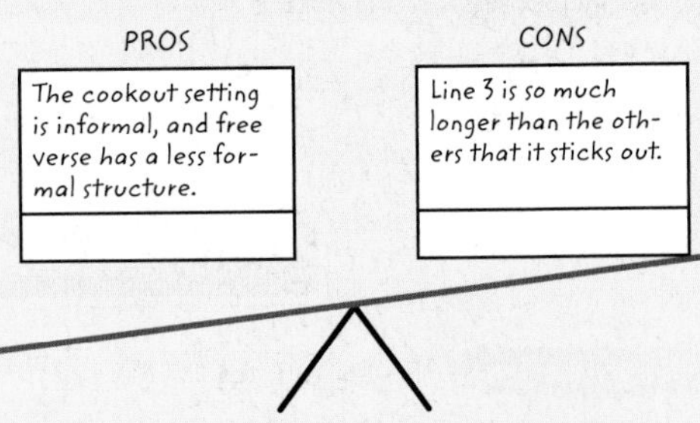

PROS
CONS
The cookout setting is informal, and free verse has a less formal structure.
Line 3 is so much longer than the others that it sticks out.

When you have generated as many pros and cons as you can, look at the relative length of your lists. The longer list is the one that will determine your argument. For example, if you listed more pros of free verse than cons, you should argue that free verse is the appropriate form for this poem.

When you have completed a draft, meet with a classmate for peer review. Exchange essays, evaluate each other's work, and suggest revisions. After making revisions, proofread your draft to correct errors in spelling, punctuation, and grammar.

Internet Connection

Use a search engine to find Rita Dove's homepage on the Internet. Write a review that addresses the following questions, using specific descriptions of her Web site:

1. How user-friendly is the site?
2. What are the site's strengths?
3. What could be improved?

Writing About Literature

Use these criteria when evaluating students' writing:

- Does the introduction contain a clear statement of the position being argued?
- Does the body contain specific reasons for the position?
- Does the conclusion include a final summary or thought about the position?

Internet Connection

Student reviews should include the following:

- features that make the site easy or difficult to navigate
- specific features that the writer considers useful or appealing
- specific suggestions for improvement

Comparing Literature *Across Genres*

Connecting to the Reading Selections

What does it feel like to lose someone you love? The three writers compared here—Alice Walker, Larry Woiwode, and Rudolfo A. Anaya—express their thoughts and feelings about the loss of a loved one.

COMPARING THE Big Idea The Strength of Family

Some of life's greatest lessons can come from one's family. Alice Walker, Larry Woiwode, and Rudolfo A. Anaya use different genres to explore these lessons.

COMPARING Sound Devices

Writers try to make their words sing on the page. To achieve that effect, they use sound devices such as assonance, consonance, and alliteration. As you read, notice these sound devices and consider their effects.

COMPARING Author's Purpose

Although they treat a similar subject, Walker, Woiwode, and Anaya have different reasons for writing. The choice of genre and the elements in a literary work—for example, the details included—provide clues about the author's purpose.

Focus

BELLRINGER

Bellringer Options
Selection Focus Transparency 39
Daily Language Practice Transparency 66
Or display images of a funeral.
Say: After a loved one's death, survivors often reflect on their feelings about that person.
Ask: What feelings might someone have after the death of a family member or close friend? How might a loved one's death cause a change of feelings about that person?
Encourage students to keep these questions in mind as they read the following selections.

Connecting to the Reading Selections

Allow students to share their responses to the opening question. Then have students discuss what they already know about Alice Walker, Larry Woiwode, and Steve Martin.

Selection Skills

Comparing Literature

Literary Elements
- Epiphany (SE pp. 629, 631)

Reading Skills
- Making Generalizations (SE pp. 629, 631)
- Monitoring Comprehension (TWE p. 634)
- Multiple-Meaning Words (TWE p. 636)
- Comparing Authors' Purposes (TWE p. 638)

Vocabulary Skills
- Word Roots (TWE p. 630)

Writing Skills/Grammar
- Sentence Structure (TWE p. 632)
- Irregular Verbs (TWE p. 640)

Listening/Speaking/Viewing Skills
- Discussion (SE p. 642)
- Oral Interpretation (SE p. 642)

Focus

Author Search To expand students' appreciation of Alice Walker, have them access the Web site for additional information and resources.

Use the CheckPoint questions on Presentation Plus! to monitor students' comprehension. These questions can be used with interactive response keypads for immediate student feedback.

"Good Night, Willie Lee, I'll See You in the Morning"

MEET ALICE WALKER

When Alice Walker was eight, her brother accidentally shot her with a BB gun, blinding her in the right eye. Had this misfortune not occurred, Walker might never have become an internationally acclaimed writer. Believing that the scar tissue in her eye disfigured her, Walker became self-conscious and withdrawn. She began to spend much of her time alone, reading and writing poems. By the time she was fourteen and had undergone eye surgery to improve her appearance, she was hooked on literature. Her youthful passion for the written word would blossom into an impressive body of creative works.

> *"Not enough credit has been given to the black woman, who has been oppressed beyond recognition."*
>
> —Alice Walker

Early Years Born near Eatonton, Georgia, Walker grew up in rural poverty. Her parents were poor sharecroppers who raised a family of eight children. Walker left home to attend Spelman College in Atlanta, thus ending a troubled relationship with her father. After traveling to Africa, she attended Sarah Lawrence College in New York, graduating in 1965. During and after college, Walker actively participated in the civil rights movement.

In 1970 Walker discovered the works of Zora Neale Hurston, a deceased and neglected Harlem Renaissance writer. Deeply moved by Hurston's books, especially *Mules and Men* (1935) and *Their Eyes Were Watching God* (1937), Walker dedicated herself to promoting Hurston's works, ensuring that they would receive the credit they deserved.

Walker's poetry, fiction, and essays explore African American history and culture. Much of her work focuses on personal and family relationships, portraying black women whose strength of spirit enables them to triumph over racism and other forms of oppression.

Literary Acclaim Walker is a prolific writer, adept in all genres. Her collections of poetry include *Once* (1968), which relates her experiences working in the civil rights movement and living in Africa, and *Good Night, Willie Lee, I'll See You in the Morning* (1979). Her short stories about black women appear in the collections *In Love and Trouble* (1973) and *You Can't Keep a Good Woman Down* (1981). Walker's most famous work is *The Color Purple* (1982). This highly acclaimed novel won both the Pulitzer Prize and the American Book Award. It was adapted into a successful movie and later into a Broadway musical.

Alice Walker was born in 1944.

Literature Online **Author Search** For more about Alice Walker, go to www.glencoe.com.

Selection Resources

Print Materials
- Unit 3 Resources (Fast File), pp. 74–75
- Selection and Unit Assessments, pp. 123–124
- Selection Quick Checks, p. 62

Transparencies
- Bellringer Options Transparencies: Selection Focus Transparency 39 Daily Language Practice Transparency 66
- Literary Elements Transparency 110

Technology
- TeacherWorks Plus™ CD-ROM
- StudentWorks Plus™ CD-ROM
- Presentation Plus!™ CD-ROM
- Literature Online, glencoe.com
- Online Student Edition, mhln.com
- Exam*View*® Assessment Suite CD-ROM
- Vocabulary PuzzleMaker CD-ROM
- Listening Library, disc 1 tracks 74–76

LITERATURE PREVIEW

Connecting to the Poem

Civility means "politeness." Sometimes people choose to be civil when, in truth, they do not feel like it. Before you read this poem, think about the following questions:

- Have you ever felt forced to be polite?
- Have you ever decided to be civil as a courtesy?

Building Background

Alice Walker and her father, whose name was Willie Lee, were often at odds. What Walker regrets most about their relationship is that "it did not improve until after his death." In an essay titled "Father," Walker wrote that her father "was one of the leading supporters of the local one-room black school, and according to everyone who knew him then, including my older brothers and sisters, believed in education above all else."

In addition to writing essays and poems about him, Walker has drawn on her father's experience in her novels. She states, "Writing about people helps us understand them, and understanding them helps us understand ourselves."

Setting Purposes for Reading

Big Idea The Strength of Family

As you read, consider what the poem reveals about the source of a family's strength.

Literary Element Epiphany

An **epiphany,** or "showing forth," is a moment of sudden revelation of the true meaning of a situation, person, or object. In a moment of epiphany, a character sees something in a new light. The character often gains insight into the essential meaning or nature of that thing as a result. As you read, consider the speaker's epiphany and what it suggests.

- See Literary Terms Handbook, p. R6.

LiteratureOnline **Interactive Literary Elements Handbook** To review or learn more about the literary elements, go to www.glencoe.com.

READING PREVIEW

Reading Strategy Making Generalizations

You **make generalizations** when you formulate a broad statement that is supported by details in a work. For example, after reading a certain literary work, you might make a generalization that true heroes control their fears instead of giving in to them.

Reading Tip: Taking Notes On a chart like the one below, write a generalization about death. Then, after reading the poem by Alice Walker, write a generalization supported by the poem.

Before Reading	After Reading
Grieving people long to relive good times with the deceased.	

Relatives Embracing. Jim Dandy.

INDIANA ACADEMIC STANDARDS (pages 629-631)

9.3.7 Recognize and understand...various literary devices...

9.2.8 Make reasonable statements...about a text...

9.5.3 Write...literary analyses...

9.3.11 Evaluate the aesthetic qualities of...tone...

COMPARING LITERATURE

BEFORE YOU READ

Focus

Summary

In "Good Night, Willie Lee, I'll See You in the Morning," the speaker reflects on the death of her father and on her mother's response to his death. Even though her mother seems to have no emotional response to his death, she treats him with "civility" in her last goodbye. The speaker recognizes that old wounds can be healed through forgiveness.

LiteratureOnline

Literary Elements Have students access the Web site to improve their understanding of epiphany.

English Language Coach

Making Inferences English language learners may have difficulty understanding the poem. Help them analyze the following lines from the next page and answer the questions:

- lines 1–2: What can you tell about the setting or location? *(Help students see that "Looking down into my father's / dead face" probably means that the mother is standing over a casket.)*
- lines 4–6: Which words tell you how the mother feels about the father's death? *(Direct students' attention to the phrases "without / tears, without smiles / without regrets." She does not seem to feel great loss or sadness.)* EL

Academic Standards

The Additional Support activity on p. 629 covers the following standard:

English Language Coach: **9.3** [Identify] story elements such as character...and setting...

Teach

BI Big Idea

The Strength of Family
Answer: *It suggests that the mother and Willie Lee had a stronger bond and were better able to share their feelings.*
Ask: On the basis of these words, do you think the mother has forgiven the father? Explain. *(She seems to have forgiven him, since she says that she will see him "in the morning.")* OL

L Literary Element

Epiphany Ask: According to this line, when does the speaker's epiphany take place? *(The epiphany takes place when the mother speaks the words, "Good night, Willie Lee, I'll see you in the morning.")* OL

CheckPoint

Use the CheckPoint questions on Presentation Plus! to check students' mastery of the selection. These questions can be used with interactive response keypads for immediate student feedback.

Serenity, 1901. Alphonse Osbert. Oil on canvas, 22.5 x 51 cm. Private collection.

"Good Night, Willie Lee, I'll See You in the Morning"

Alice Walker

Looking down into my father's
dead face
for the last time
my mother said without
tears, without smiles
without regrets
but with *civility*
"Good night, Willie Lee, I'll see you
in the morning."

And it was then I knew that the healing L
of all our wounds
is forgiveness
that permits a promise
of our return
at the end.

Big Idea The Strength of Family *The mother speaks to Willie Lee, but the speaker does not. What does this suggest about their respective relationships to Willie Lee?* BI

Additional Support

Academic Standards

The Additional Support activity on p. 630 covers the following standard:

Skills Practice: **9.1** [Use] word parts...to determine the meaning of words...

Skills Practice

VOCABULARY: Word Roots Tell students that a root is a word part that conveys a basic meaning. A key word in this poem is *civility.* It contains the Latin word *civ,* meaning "citizen." This root is found in many other English words.

All of the following terms contain the root *civis.* Have students locate them in a dictionary and write their definitions. Then have students explain how each is related to the meaning of *civis.*

- civil rights
- civics
- civilization
- civil war
- civilized OL

AFTER YOU READ

RESPONDING AND THINKING CRITICALLY

Respond

1. What questions would you like to ask the speaker of this poem?

Recall and Interpret

2. (a)What happens in this poem? (b)Where might the events be taking place?
3. (a)What is missing when the mother looks at her husband's face and speaks? (b)In your opinion, what does the absence of these things convey?
4. (a)What might be going through the mother's mind as she says, "Good night, Willie Lee, I'll see you / in the morning"? (b)Why might she say "good night" rather than "good-bye," and what might "morning" refer to?

Analyze and Evaluate

5. In your opinion, why did Walker write the word *civility* in italics?
6. Describe your reactions to the mother's words. What does her statement make you think or feel about her?
7. (a)What kind of relationship do you imagine the speaker's mother had with her husband? (b)What kind of relationship do you imagine the speaker had with her father? Give evidence from the poem to support your interpretations.

Connect

8. **Big Idea** **The Strength of Family** How does forgiveness promote spiritual and emotional healing in families?

LITERARY ANALYSIS

Literary Element Epiphany

The word *epiphany* comes from the Greek *epiphania*, which means "manifestation." The word was first applied to literature by the Irish writer James Joyce, who used it to describe a sudden, new understanding of something commonplace. In addition to revealing new meaning, an epiphany often marks a change in a speaker or character.

1. What life lesson does the speaker learn from her mother's words?
2. Explain how lines 10–15 support your interpretation.

Writing About Literature

Compare and Contrast Tone In a brief essay, describe the tone of voice that you imagine the mother might use in lines 8–9 of this poem. Compare and contrast that tone with the speaker's tone in the rest of the poem. Point to specific words and phrases from the poem to support your opinions.

LiteratureOnline **Web Activities** For eFlashcards, Selection Quick Checks, and other Web activities, go to www.glencoe.com.

READING AND VOCABULARY

Reading Strategy Making Generalizations

Review the chart you made on page 629, and then answer the following questions.

1. What generalization can you make about the parents' relationship in this poem?
2. Based on the poem, what generalization can you make about the healing power of forgiveness?

Academic Vocabulary

Here is a word from the vocabulary list on page R80.

protocol (prō′ tə kôl′) *n.* a code of predescribed conduct

Practice and Apply
What **protocols** are usually observed in situations such as the one Walker describes?

Literary Element

1. Restraint, kindness, and forgiveness are necessary to a long-term relationship between human beings.
2. The speaker realizes that her parents hurt each other but also forgave each other, strengthening their relationship.

Reading Strategy

1. The relationship was conflicted but had its redeeming qualities.
2. The healing power of forgiveness brings people together, in life and in death.

Academic Vocabulary

The final viewing of the deceased and the last goodbye are observed.

AFTER YOU READ

Assess

1. Students' answers will vary.
2. (a) A wife says goodbye to her husband before he is buried. (b) In a funeral home
3. (a) The mother does not cry, smile, or show regret. (b) Her calm and dignity suggest that acceptance and faith keep her on an even keel.
4. (a) That she forgives her late husband and that she will see him in heaven (b) Her belief that they are not parted for good but will be reunited when she dies. "Morning" refers to heaven.
5. Possible answer: to emphasize the speaker's surprise
6. She is a woman of great dignity and faith, and she has great emotional strength.
7. (a) "Wounds" suggests that the marriage was stormy at times. (b) Because the speaker is just learning about the healing power of forgiveness, she may not have forgiven her father for problems in their relationship.
8. Students may say that forgiveness allows families to put aside injuries and renew their loving commitment.

Writing About Literature

Students' essays should compare and contrast the mother's and the speaker's tones, using the poem's words and phrases to support their opinions.

LiteratureOnline

Web Activities Have students access the Web site for interactive activities that will help them assess their understanding of the selection.

Focus

Summary

In "Beyond the Bedroom Wall," the narrator recalls his childhood move from North Dakota to a small town in Illinois, followed by his mother's unhappiness and gradual fading. One night, his mother is taken away by ambulance. He never sees her again. After this event, he is afraid of the dark.

Author Search To expand students' appreciation of Larry Woiwode, have them access the Web site for additional information and resources.

Readability Scores
Dale-Chall: 9.2
DRP: 57
Lexile: 990

Beyond the Bedroom Wall

Larry Woiwode

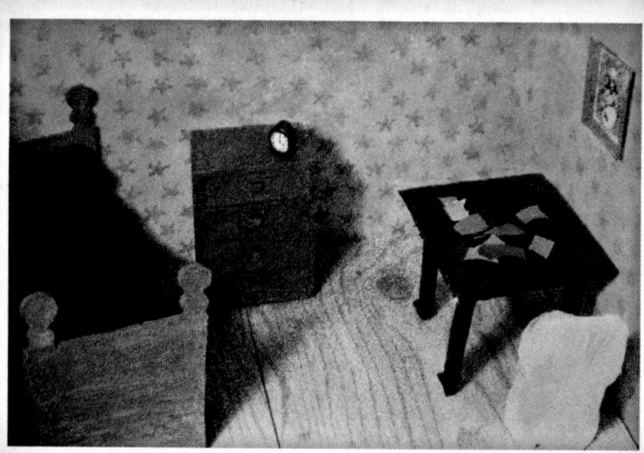

BEFORE YOU READ

Building Background

Award-winning author Larry Woiwode was born in Carrington, North Dakota, in 1941. His parents were both schoolteachers, and his father was also a school superintendent. When Woiwode was nine, his father moved the family to Illinois. A year later, his mother died from kidney disease, and her loss deeply marked the young Woiwode. At the age of eighteen, he started attending the University of Illinois, where he published his first short story. Woiwode soon moved to New York City and devoted himself to writing. He returned to live in North Dakota in 1978.

The story "Beyond the Bedroom Wall" originally appeared in *The New Yorker* magazine, which published many of Woiwode's early stories. Characters from this story also appeared in Woiwode's widely admired novel of the same name, published in 1975. Both works of fiction are semiautobiographical, drawing upon Woiwode's early experiences.

Literature Online **Author Search** For more about Larry Woiwode, go to www.glencoe.com.

At the age of nine I wasn't afraid of the dark. When I ran down a deserted street at night, I knew the chilling pursuer I felt at my back was put there by my own act of running, and would disappear—like any creature of the imagination when put to a test—the second I slowed to a walk. The gray hands that reached for me as I lay in bed were of my own creation, too, and once I had proved my power to summon them up, for the sake of a safe, enjoyable scare, I could destroy them.

When the change came, it seemed to come in a moment, but I believe I was being prepared for it. I believe it began one morning when my father read a letter at the breakfast table. The letter was from his father, a prosperous contractor[1] in Illinois; a new school district was being formed in the town he lived in, and they were looking for a high-school principal. For the large and muscular, leathery-faced man my father was—strong-minded about his beliefs, uncompromising in carrying out school policies—he was surprisingly unaggressive when it came to

1. Here, *contractor* means "one who agrees to perform work on buildings."

Additional Support

Skills Practice

GRAMMAR: Sentence Structure
Write this sentence on the board:

Setting aside his usual calm and reserve, he went at the place with such a passion that I was inspired; I learned to use a hammer like a man and started to have at the old house, too.

Point out the semicolon, explaining that it is used to join two independent clauses. Have students replace the semicolon with a comma followed by *and*, then read the sentence aloud. Discuss whether this change makes a difference in the sound of the sentence. **OL** family matters. He seemed to dread the possibility of making the wrong decision. He turned to my mother.

Wasn't he satisfied with the job he had, she wanted to know. Of course, but there wasn't much chance of getting ahead in North Dakota. Wasn't he the superintendent of a high school now? Yes, that was true, he said, speaking as calmly and as reasonably as she did. And didn't he make enough to keep them happy? More than enough. Then would it be wise to give up the job he had, and sell the house, and move to Illinois, where it was so hot and so humid, when a job hadn't actually been promised to him yet? Didn't she like Illinois? Not especially. Well, they had only been there in the summer, and he imagined that was why. His father hadn't liked it at first, either, but now he called it God's country. Then why did he so often come back to North Dakota? Well, probably because North Dakota was his home state. And wasn't it theirs? Yes, but his father had done so well for himself down there, and maybe he could, too. Wouldn't she like a nicer house? This was the house she had always wanted—how could there be a better one? Well, his only reason for considering the idea at all was that his father was getting old and wanted the family reunited. She knew that, didn't
BI she? Yes, she said, and leaned to him and kissed him. He took both her hands in his. Wouldn't she like it if they were in a bigger town where he could make more money and she could have more friends? She
R bowed her head, as she did only when she was sad or very ashamed.

And so, in the early summer of that year, we moved from North Dakota to the small town in central Illinois where my grandfather lived. While my father was waiting to hear about the appointment, he bought and started remodeling a duplex[2] that had originally been a gasoline station. He ripped up the twelve-inch baseboards and tore stucco off the inside walls, knocked down a small enclosure in one corner of the living room (what it was, no one knew), sawed a long rectangular hole in the kitchen floor and put up a partition in front of it, creating a new stairway to the basement, and converted the concrete island that had once held the gasoline pumps, a car's breadth from the front door, into a flower planter. Setting aside his usual calm and reserve, he went at the place with such a passion that I was inspired; I learned to use a hammer like a man and started to have at the old house, too.

The bedroom I was given had no window. It was a small upstairs room with a ceiling that took its sharp slant from the pitch[3] of the roof. There wasn't any floor in the rest of the attic, so the room was surrounded by bare ceiling joists,[4] and felt as isolated as I did in this place we had moved to. There was no daylight and no light fixture in the room, no smell but the smell of dust and old lumber (the previous owner had used it as a storeroom), no color, no company; the seasons outside were merely changes in temperature. When my father first showed me the room, he said he would add a dormer[5] and fill it with daylight as soon as he finished remodeling the downstairs, but, for the time being, all he did was move a dresser into the room and set up a narrow cot against one wall.

Lying on the cot, I learned the secrets of the dark. A wooden catwalk[6] with a banister ran from the door of the bedroom to the head of the stairs. If I got out of bed, feeling my way to the steps, and went down them, I entered a house deep in sleep. A low hallway (I could hear it!) led from the foot of the stairs in one direction, to the left, past the bathroom, and ended at the living room.

2. A *duplex* is a building divided into two homes.

3. *Pitch* is the amount of slope or inclination of something.
4. *Joists* are wood, steel, or concrete beams arranged in a parallel series to support a ceiling or floor.
5. A *dormer* is a window projecting from a sloping roof.
6. A *catwalk* is a narrow walkway.

COMPARING LITERATURE

Teach

BI Big Idea

The Strength of Family
Ask: What family strength does the give-and-take between husband and wife emphasize? *(Students may suggest that it emphasizes the willingness to discuss important decisions.)* OL

R Reading Strategy

Making Inferences Ask: Is the narrator's mother happy with the decision to move to Illinois? Explain. *(Students may suggest that she is not happy with the decision. She argues against it, and when the decision is finally made to move, she bows her head as if she is sad.)* OL

CheckPoint

Use the CheckPoint questions on Presentation Plus! to monitor students' comprehension. These questions can be used with interactive response keypads for immediate student feedback.

Differentiated Instruction

Dialogue Explain that in the first paragraph above, a third person (the narrator) is reporting a conversation between two people. Read the paragraph aloud, identifying the speaker of each line.

Have students work in pairs to rewrite the paragraph in dialogue form, adding quotation marks, changing the sentences to present tense, and using identifying words such as "she asked" or "he answered," as necessary. Demonstrate with the first sentence: "Aren't you satisfied with the job you have?" she asked. Have students read their completed paragraphs to the class. BL

Academic Standards

Additional Support activities on pp. 632 and 633 cover the following standards:

Skills Practice: **9.6.1** Identify and correctly use clauses…and the mechanics of punctuation, such as semicolons…

Differentiated Instruction: **9.6.4** Apply appropriate manuscript conventions… by…using direct quotations…

Teach

L1 Literary Element

Personification Tell students that personification attributes human characteristics to an animal, object, or idea.
Ask: What is being personified in this passage? What human qualities are attributed to this object? *(The air is being personified. The qualities attributed to it are anger and agitation.)* OL

Viewing the Art

Grace Cossington Smith (1892–1984) painted what she knew best–the streets of Sydney, Australia; landscapes around her home at Turamumurra; still lifes of flowers; and interior scenes, such as *The Sock Knitter.* This painting captures the still, solitary activity of knitting. Smith's sister Charlotte posed for the painting. In 1915, when Smith made this painting, many Australian women were knitting socks for soldiers fighting in World War I. AS

If I snapped the wall switch, the whole living room was caught off guard—the windows blinked, rugs stretched out flat, and chair backs straightened. To my right, in the far wall of the living room, the door of my parents' bedroom guarded their sleep; to my left, an arch leading to the kitchen—a high, wide arch—yawned. Utensils on the stove and the glass knobs on the doors and drawers of the cabinets, picking up the light from the living room, were like half-opened, protesting eyes.

Back in bed, hearing the whole house creak and sigh in its heavy sleep, I also learned about the one element that stays awake: the air. Long after the house was asleep, and long after I should have been, the dark air was alive with excitement. Because there was never any light in the room, from the sun or the moon, the air was my gauge of time and events. A disturbance outside—a passing train, a car, the lashing of a tree—caused it to ripple. When the sun rose, the air became angry, agitated, and some nights, for a reason I could never understand, it thickened and pressed against me. L1

Before the state of Illinois officially certified my father as a teacher, all the administrative and even the teaching positions in the new school district were filled. He had to start working for my grandfather, as a carpenter. My father wasn't one to go back on a promise or leave a job unfinished, but his remodeling of the house slowed to a stop; gray rock lath rose to shoulder height, and above that the bare studs, black with dirt and age, stood exposed. My room remained without a window.

My mother did not like the house we were living in, and was troubled that my father had to give up teaching, the profession he loved, and become a common laborer. She was also in her last months of pregnancy. She became silent and secretive, and kept her eyes lowered. My father watched her from the time he came home from work until he went to bed. How was she feeling today? Fine. Was there anything he could do? No. Would she like to go out—to a movie or somewhere? No. When her answers turned from single words to shrugs, and when his smile and his

The Sock Knitter, 1915. Grace Cossington Smith. Oil on canvas, 61.6 x 50.7 cm. Art Gallery of New South Wales, Sydney, Australia.

Additional Support

Skills Practice

READING: Monitoring Comprehension Explain that monitoring comprehension is essential when reading prose that contains long, complex sentences or complex imagery. After each long, difficult sentence, a reader might ask, What is the main idea of the sentence? How can I restate this sentence? How can I relate this description or image to a personal experience?

Have students work in pairs to read aloud pages 634 and 635. Have them stop to monitor their comprehension. Encourage them to break down long sentences into main clauses and dependent clauses and phrases. OL time-honored burlesque of the schottische,[7] with the broom as his partner, failed to cheer her up, he became silent, too.

One afternoon I stood near the top of a stepladder and nailed lath to the partition in the kitchen. My mother sat at the table, paying little attention to the noise I made, and embroidered on a dish towel. Once when I missed the nail completely, and the stud, too, sending a circular hole through the rock lath with the head of the hammer, I cursed. Still she didn't look up. When I had first started using foul language, she had washed my mouth out with soap. I had never heard my father swear, and now she was letting me get away with it. I felt manly and arrogant, and made even more noise.

But then I realized how much she must have changed, to ignore what she had once disapproved of, and I studied her from the top of the stepladder. Her face had lost all its beauty. It was dry and chapped, and her dark-brown hair, which usually hung loose, was pinned back behind her ears. At her temples, just above her eyebrows, I could see the bones of her skull. She had paused in her sewing, and was looking at her hand—first the palm, then the back.

"Mom? Are you okay?"

Without looking up, she said, "Yes," and quickly continued sewing, as if I'd caught her at something. "Don't worry about me," she said. "Do your job."

Her manner upset me. I came down from the stepladder, marked a piece of lath, and cut across it with the razor knife, shakily curving off in the wrong direction a couple of times. I snapped the lath across my knee, broke off the hinged endpiece, and started up the ladder, when an emotion spread from her and pressed on me like a hand. I stopped, my eyes on the grooves of one of the steps, and tried to figure out what she was feeling. Then I turned to look at her, and the grooves seemed to lift with my eyes, stretch through the air, and link us. She raised her face and I felt weak; I'd never been so close to her. At any other time she might have smiled, or told me, with a blush, to quit staring, but now she stared at me until I was the one who blushed, and so badly I had to start hammering again.

"Don't," she said.

"Don't what?"

I turned to her and she was running her fingertips over the embroidery.

"Don't work anymore."

"The hammering bothers you?"

"No. I don't want you to work."

"Why not?"

She wouldn't look at me. "Go and play."

"Who with?" I took a nail out of my mouth and pounded it in place. "Dad told me to do this wall."

"I don't want you to work with your hands! You're too young to work."

"No, I'm not!"

"Don't argue. Go outside."

With her head lowered, her voice didn't seem a part of her. I came down the ladder angrily, determined to make her look at me, and saw that the length and breadth of her cheeks were wet with tears.

I went out the back door and sat on the steps. It wasn't right of her to go against my father's word, and she never had. She was even going against her own! She wouldn't talk to you, and when she did she wouldn't look at you, and then she cried. If something was wrong and she didn't want me to know what it was, I wished she would simply leave me alone. Then I remembered the long, unguarded look she had held me with.

One January night I woke, for no apparent reason, and felt the air above my cot had thickened. It was denser than it was when the sun rose, and some sound was trying to make its way through the denseness. I listened so intently my eyes joined in the effort, searching the volume of dark air, and then I heard (coming from the ground floor? from somewhere above the roof?) a sound like the breathy creak

7. Here, *burlesque* means a "mocking imitation," and the *schottische* is a Scottish dance.

Teach

L2 Literary Element

Sound Devices **Ask:** What sound device does the author use here? What words are involved? *(The author uses alliteration. The words beginning with an* s *sound are* stud, sending, *and* circular; *words beginning with an* h *sound are* hole, head, *and* hammer.*)* **OL**

R Reading Strategy

Author's Purpose **Ask:** What is the author's purpose in describing the intense exchange of looks between the narrator and his mother? *(The author may want to show the strong connection between the narrator and his mother.)* Why is it important to show this connection? *(Showing this close connection helps the reader understand how deeply the mother affects the boy.)* **OL**

Reading in the Real World

Career In this selection, the narrator's father moves his family to Illinois in hopes of getting an administrative position or a teaching job. Tell students that each state has its own requirements for certifying public school teachers and administrators. A teacher cannot simply move to another state and automatically get a job without fulfilling the certification requirements. You might share your personal experiences with students.

Suggest that students use the Internet to research the requirements for certification in their state. Then have them report to the class on their findings. **OL**

Academic Standards

Additional Support activities on pp. 634 and 635 cover the following standards:

Skills Practice: **9.2** Develop [reading] strategies...

Reading in the Real World: **9.7.15** Deliver expository (informational) presentations that convey information and ideas from... sources accurately and coherently...

Teach

R1 Reading Strategy

Author's Purpose **Ask:** Why do you think the narrator says that he thinks he did something wrong? *(Students may suggest that the author wants to convey the boy's fear and pain.)* OL

★ Cultural History

Kidney Disease This story is semiautobiographical and reflects the author's experience with his mother's kidney disease. Little could be done to treat kidney disease at the time this story is set. The first artificial kidney used for hemodialysis—or purifying the blood—was developed during World War II, but it could be used only for temporary kidney disorders. In 1960, advances in technology allowed for regular hemodialysis treatment for kidney patients. Prior to this new technology, kidney disease meant certain death for most patients. AS

COMPARING LITERATURE

of a pigeon's wings, rising and falling, reaching for me and then falling away again. I rolled over and my shoulder struck the wall.

Light switches clicked downstairs, there were footsteps, the telephone jingled as it was cranked, and I felt the heavy throb of my father's bass voice. After a number of throbs, punctuated by silences that seemed humming question marks in the dark air, the receiver slapped into its holder, my father's footsteps crossed the kitchen, and another switch clicked. A white rectangle, its top end bent up against the foot of the wall, gripped the floor; he had turned on the light in the hallway downstairs. He made several quick trips from the bathroom to their bedroom and back again. I went to the banister, looked down the stairwell, and saw his shadow cross the bottom steps.

"Dad?"

After a silence, a pause in the footsteps, his head appeared around the corner. "What are you doing up at this hour?"

"Nothing."

"You'd better go back to bed."

"Who were you talking to on the phone?"

"The doctor. Do you realize it's three o'clock?"

"Is somebody sick?"

He stared up at me, and finally said, "Go to bed. Please."

I did, but I couldn't sleep. The birdlike sounds rose up again, his footsteps crossed the house, in long strides this time, and the jingling of the telephone was harsh. I got out of bed and was nearly to the bottom of the stairs when I heard my father's voice: ". . . realize it's practically a half hour since I called? You can't be more than a block away, and . . . *What?* How in the world can a man read at a time like this? . . . Well, I don't give a damn about your—your *damn* family doctor's book! . . ."

The profanity, so wrong on my father's tongue, scared me. And his voice was usually under control; I had never heard it like this. I went to the kitchen doorway and saw that he was trembling, holding on to the wooden box of the wall telephone to steady himself. "Are you listening? You get over here this minute or I'll come and get you!"

He hooked the receiver into its metal cradle, leaned a shoulder against the wall, and whispered, "Oh, God! What next?" Then he gathered himself and drew his body erect, and when he turned his face to me it wasn't my father's face. It was so white it looked as if his day's growth of beard had caved it in, and his large eyes were glazed.

"I thought I told you to go to bed."

"Are you sick?"

"What are you *doing* down here?"

"I have to go to the bathroom."

He bowed his head, gripped the bridge of his nose, and let out a moan of someone deathly ill. "Go," he said.

"What's the matter?"

"Do as you're told."

I decided I would go to their bedroom before I went back upstairs, to find out from my mother what was wrong, but when I stepped out of the bathroom he stood blocking the hall.

"Hurry up," he said. "I'll turn out the light."

"I want to see Mom."

"Not now. Not tonight."

"Why not?"

"She's too sick." ★

"Let me *see* her!"

"Maybe tomorrow. Go now."

"She's sick?"

He nodded his head with such finality I wasn't able to ask anything else, or disobey—run past him to their bedroom—but as I climbed the stairs I was sure I had done something wrong. Because I didn't know what it was, and at the same time realized it was my *mother* who was ill, I started to tremble, and when I settled into bed and the rectangle on the wall vanished, darkness pressed on me as it never had before. It took my entire imagination, and closed eyes, to keep it away, and just as I heard strange voices—several of them, it seemed—I gave in to the dark. R1

Additional Support

Skills Practice

READING: Multiple-Meaning Words Refer students to the word *cradle* on page 636. Explain that the word has several meanings. In order to determine its meaning here, students should look at the context surrounding the word. Ask a volunteer to read aloud the paragraph preceding the paragraph with *cradle.* **Ask:** What is happening in this paragraph? *(The father is talking on the phone.)* Then have students read the sentence in which *cradle* appears. Help students recognize that *receiver* refers to a telephone receiver. Then ask students to give their own definition of *cradle.* OL

White Wall, 1964–65. George Tooker. Egg tempera on gesso panel. Delaware Art Museum, Wilmington, USA.

I dreamed I was walking with my mother through a department store. The walls and ceiling were white, and the floor of white marble, with low display cases set at great distances from one another. My mother held my hand in a firm grip. She wanted to go upstairs, and I wanted to stay where we were, on the ground floor, and look in the display cases. I pulled away from her and ran to one. *Don't. Don't look!* she called after me, and her voice echoed through the empty store.

R2 The case was filled with blue china figurines. There was a blue swan, similar to the one in our kitchen, with a hole in its back, so that it could be used as a flowerpot, blue angels, and small blue busts of children. My mother put her hand on my shoulder and said, *Come away.* I turned to say no and couldn't breathe. She stood far above me, taller than she had ever been, her face made of blue china and her eyes alive and staring at me as they had in the kitchen. She pulled her coat close around her throat, turned and walked away, and when I tried to run after her, my feet wouldn't move.

I woke to darkness, twisted in the blankets, my heart beating hard against the cot. I had to see my mother. I started to get out of bed and struck the wall. I was stupefied; the wall was on the other side of the cot. I tried again. I knew there was no wall there, and not all the logic in the world, or the wall itself, could convince me otherwise. Nothing as simple as getting reversed in bed occurred to me. I tried again and again, and finally fell back onto the cot, and my left arm extended into open space. If there was a wall where I was convinced there was none, I couldn't imagine what waited for me in that emptiness where the wall should be. I pulled my arm back and held it over my chest, afraid to move, afraid of the dark.

In the morning, without having to be told, I knew my mother was gone. My father, who had had no sleep, said she had been taken by ambulance to the hospital. Without being able to confide in him, or in anyone (once the sun has risen, the dark seems partly our imagination), I knew I would never see my mother again, and started preparing myself for her death. ~

Quickwrite

Write a paragraph explaining what the narrator's dream suggests about his relationship with his mother. Use details from the story to support your interpretations.

COMPARING LITERATURE

Teach

R2 Reading Strategy

Making Inferences **Ask:** What ideas might be associated with the color blue and with angels? *(Students may suggest heaven or the afterlife.)* What do you think is the significance of the mother's walking away and the boy's being unable to follow? *(This suggests that the mother has gone somewhere he cannot go; perhaps that she has died.)* **OL**

Quickwrite

Students' answers should

- consist of complete sentences
- explain the connection between the narrator's dream and the loss of his mother
- provide details from the story as supporting evidence

Use the CheckPoint questions on Presentation Plus! to check students' mastery of the selection. These questions can be used with interactive response keypads for immediate student feedback.

Differentiated Instruction

Connect Help students understand the events in the paragraph beginning "I woke to darkness . . ." by pointing out that the boy has turned around in bed, so that his head is at the opposite end from where he had started. When he reaches out with his left arm, he expects to feel the wall, but instead feels empty space. Remind students that his room is completely dark, with no light and no window. Ask students to share times when they awoke in the darkness and were confused by unfamiliar or unexpected surroundings. **BL**

Academic Standards

Additional Support activities on pp. 636 and 637 cover the following standards:

Skills Practice: **9.1** Use...context clues, and a growing knowledge of English... to determine the meaning of words...

Differentiated Instruction: **9.2** Develop [reading] strategies...

Focus

Summary

In this essay, the author reflects on the importance of respecting the elderly. He uses his grandfather as an example. His grandfather was a hardworking farmer in New Mexico who taught his family simple but powerful lessons about life. In his final years, his family returned the favor by taking care of him when he was no longer able to take care of himself.

Author Search To expand students' appreciation of Rudolfo A. Anaya, have them access the Web site for additional information and resources.

COMPARING LITERATURE

In Praise of Grandfathers

Peasants, 1947. Diego Rivera. Oil on panel, 64 x 98 cm. Museu de Arte, Sao Paulo, Brazil.

Rudolfo A. Anaya

BEFORE YOU READ

Building Background

Rudolfo Anaya's best-known work is his novel *Bless Me, Ultima.* Ultima, a wise old woman, is a friend of the narrator's family and a medicine woman—she helps cure people's illnesses through her knowledge of herbs and traditional remedies.

In this essay, Anaya describes Puerto de Luna, the village in which his grandfather lived. There, community and a deep sense of respect for elders, or *ancianos,* are important parts of the culture. These and other values are passed from generation to generation "so the string of life would not be broken."

Literature Online Author Search For more about Rudolfo A. Anaya, go to www.glencoe.com.

My grandfather was a plain man, a farmer from Puerto de Luna on the Pecos River. He was probably a descendent of those people who spilled over the mountain from Taos, following the Pecos River in search of farmland. There in that river valley he settled and raised a large family.

Bearded and walrus-mustached, he stood five feet tall, but to me as a child he was a giant. I remember him most for his silence. In the summers my parents sent me to live with him on his farm, for I was to learn the ways of a farmer. My uncles also lived in that valley, the valley called Puerto de Luna, there where only the flow of the river and the whispering of the wind marked time. For me it was a magical place.

I remember once, while out hoeing the field, I came upon an anthill, and before I knew it I was badly bitten. After he had covered my welts with the cool mud from the irrigation ditch, my grandfather calmly said: "Know where you stand." That is the way he spoke, in short phrases, to the point.

One very dry summer, the river dried to a trickle, there was no water for the fields. The young plants withered and died. In my sadness and with the impulses of youth I said, "I wish it would rain!" My grandfather touched me, looked up into the sky and whispered, "Pray for rain." In his language there was a difference. He felt connected to the cycles that brought the rain or kept it from us. His prayer was a meaningful action,

Additional Support

Skills Practice

READING: Comparing Authors' Purposes Ask students why they think Anaya wrote "In Praise of Grandfathers." Guide them to recognize that the author's main purpose is to urge readers to take good care of older family members. Then ask students why an author might write a short story such as "Beyond the Bedroom Wall."

Have students make a two-column chart in which they note differences between the essay and the short story. Point out that they can begin with the heading "Purpose," then move on to categories such as "Organization," "Point of View," and "Use of Dialogue." OL because he was a participant with the forces that filled our world, he was not a bystander.

A young man died at the village one summer. A very tragic death. He was dragged by his horse. When he was found I cried, for the boy was my friend. I did not understand why death had come to one so young. My grandfather took me aside and said: "Think of the death of the trees and the fields in the fall. The leaves fall, and everything rests, as if dead. But they bloom again in the spring. Death is only this small transformation in life."

These are the things I remember, these fleeting images, few words.

I remember him driving his horse-drawn wagon into Santa Rosa in the fall when he brought his harvest produce to sell in the town. What a tower of strength seemed to come in that small man huddled on the seat of the giant wagon. One click of his tongue and the horses obeyed, stopped or turned as he wished. He never raised his whip. How unlike today when so much teaching is done with loud words and threatening hands.

A new time did come, a new time is here.

I would run to greet the wagon, and the wagon would stop. "Buenos días le de Dios, abuelo,"[1] I would say. This was the prescribed greeting of esteem and respect. Only after the greeting was given could we approach these venerable old people. "Buenos días te de Dios, mi hijo,"[2] he would answer and smile, and then I could jump up on the wagon and sit at his side. Then I, too, became a king as I rode next to the old man who smelled of earth and sweat and the other deep aromas from the orchards and fields of Puerto de Luna.

We were all sons and daughters to him. But today the sons and daughters are breaking with the past, putting aside los abuelitos. The old values are threatened, and threatened most where it comes to these relationships with the old people. If we don't take the time to watch and feel the years of their final transformation, a part of our humanity will be lessened.

I grew up speaking Spanish, and oh! how difficult it was to learn English. Sometimes I would give up and cry out that I couldn't learn. Then he would say, "Ten paciencia." Have patience. *Paciencia,* a word with the strength of centuries, a word that said that someday we would overcome. *Paciencia,* how soothing a word coming from this old man who could still sling hundred-pound bags over his shoulder, chop wood for hours on end, and hitch up his own horses and ride to town and back in one day.

"You have to learn the language of the Americanos,"[3] he said. "Me, I will live my last days in my valley. You will live in a new time, the time of the gringos."[4]

A new time did come, a new time is here. How will we form it so it is fruitful? We need to know where we stand. We need to speak softly and respect others, and to share what we have. We need to pray not for material gain, but for rain for the fields, for the sun to nurture growth, for nights in which we can sleep in peace, and for a harvest in which everyone can share. Simple lessons from a simple man. These lessons he learned from his past which was as deep and strong as the currents of the river of life, a life which could be stronger than death.

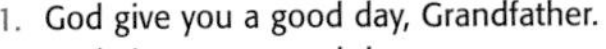

1. God give you a good day, Grandfather.
2. God give you a good day, my son.
3. Americans
4. Here, *gringos* refers to non-Hispanic people.

English Language Coach

Polite Expressions Anaya mentions the polite expression *Buenos días le de Dios, abuelo* on this page. Encourage students to share similar polite expressions from their native languages and to determine the English equivalents. EL

Differentiated Instruction

Listing The essay includes several quotations from the author's grandfather that can be considered words of advice. Have students list these quotations, and then ask them how these words of advice could be applied to situations in their own lives. BL

COMPARING LITERATURE

Teach

Political History

New Mexico The events described in Anaya's essay take place in New Mexico. According to the 2000 Census, Latinos make up 42 percent of the population of New Mexico. This is a higher percentage than in any other state. New Mexico has produced a number of notable political leaders of Latino ancestry. In 1917, Ezequiel Cabeza de Baca became the nation's first governor of Latino ancestry. In 1928, Octaviano Larrazolo became the first Latino to be elected to the U.S. Senate. Manuel Lujan Jr. served as U.S. secretary of the interior from 1989 to 1993. AS

CheckPoint

Use the CheckPoint questions on Presentation Plus! to monitor students' comprehension. These questions can be used with interactive response keypads for immediate student feedback.

Academic Standards

Additional Support activities on pp. 638 and 639 cover the following standards:

Skills Practice: **9.3.2** Compare and contrast the presentation of a similar theme or topic across genres…

English Language Coach: **9.1.2** Distinguish between what words mean literally and what they imply…

Differentiated Instruction: **9.3.6** Analyze and trace an author's development of time and sequence, including the use of…flashbacks… **9.5.8** Write for different purposes…

Teach

L Literary Element

Author's Purpose In this paragraph, Anaya includes four sentences describing his grandfather's accomplishments as a young man. **Ask:** Why might the author list so many accomplishments in this one paragraph? *(to draw a contrast with the grandfather's weakness during the final years of his life; to show the value of his life)* OL

★ Viewing the Art

Liz Wright (1950–) is an English artist who attended art school in London and Bristol. She identifies the most important element in her work as "the spirit of life." She has traveled widely and seeks to capture the "essence of a place" in her work.

Ask: Would you say this depiction of a tree in autumn is a realistic work or a work of the imagination? *(Students may point out that many leaves are falling at the same time, which does not seem realistic.)*

Fire Colours of Autumn, 1981. Liz Wright. Gouache. Private collection. 

He was a man; he died. Not in his valley, but nevertheless cared for by his sons and daughters and flocks of grandchildren. At the end, I would enter his room which carried the smell of medications and Vicks, the faint pungent odor of urine, and cigarette smoke. Gone were the aroma of the fields, the strength of his young manhood. Gone also was his patience in the face of crippling old age. Small things bothered him; he shouted or turned sour when his expectations were not met. It was because he could not care for himself, because he was returning to that state of childhood, and all those wishes and desires were now wrapped in a crumbling old body.

"Ten paciencia," I once said to him, and he smiled. "I didn't know I would grow this old," he said. "Now, I can't even roll my own cigarettes." I rolled a cigarette for him, placed it in his mouth and lit it. I asked him why he smoked, the doctor had said it was bad for him. "I like to see the smoke rise," he said. He would smoke and doze, and his quilt was spotted with little burns where the cigarettes dropped. One of us had to sit and watch to make sure a fire didn't start.

L I would sit and look at him and remember what was said of him when he was a young man. He could mount a wild horse and break it,[5] and he could ride as far as any man. He could dance all night at a dance, then work the acequia[6] the following day. He helped neighbors, they helped him. He married, raised children. Small legends, the kind that make up everyman's life.

He was 94 when he died. Family, neighbors, and friends gathered; they all agreed he had led a rich life. I remembered the last years, the years he spent in bed. And as I remember now, I am reminded that it is too easy to romanticize old age. Sometimes we forget the pain of the transformation into old age, we forget the natural breaking down of the body. Not all go gentle into the last years, some go crying and cursing, forgetting the names of those they loved the most, withdrawing into an internal anguish few of us can know. May we be granted the patience and care to deal with our ancianos.

For some time we haven't looked at these changes and needs of the old ones. The

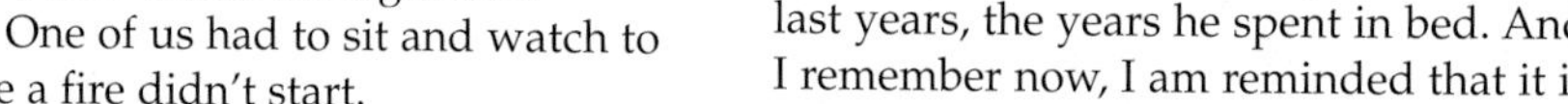

5. To break a horse is to train it to be ridden.
6. An *acequia* is an irrigation ditch.

Additional Support

Skills Practice

GRAMMAR: Irregular Verbs Remind students that an irregular verb does not form its past tense and past participle by adding *-d* or *-ed.* Instead, the principal parts of the verb change spelling. Tell students that they must memorize the principal parts of irregular verbs. Write the following word forms on the board:

Present: *go, say*
Past: *went, said*
Past Participle: *gone, said*

Have students review page 640 and find other examples of irregular verbs *(break, ride, lead, forget).* Then have them list the present, past, and past participle forms of each verb. OL

American image created by the mass media is R an image of youth, not of old age. It is the beautiful and the young who are praised in this society. If analyzed carefully, we see that same damaging thought has crept into the way society views the old. In response to the old, the mass media have just created old people who act like the young. It is only the healthy, pink-cheeked outgoing, older persons we are shown in the media. And they are always selling something, as if an entire generation of old people were salesmen in their lives. Commercials show very lively old men, who must always be in excellent health according to the new myth, selling insurance policies or real estate as they are out golfing; older women selling coffee or toilet paper to those just married. That image does not illustrate the real life of the old ones.

Real life takes into account the natural cycle of growth and change. My grandfather pointed to the leaves falling from the tree. So time brings with its transformation the often painful, wearing-down process. Vision blurs, health wanes; even the act of walking carries with it the painful reminder of the autumn of life. But this process is something to be faced, not something to be hidden away by false images. Yes, the old can be young at heart, but in their own way, with their own dignity. They do not have to copy the always-young image of the Hollywood star.

My grandfather wanted to return to his valley to die. But by then the families of the valley had left in search of a better future. It is only now that there seems to be a return to the valley, a revival. The new generation seeks its roots, that value of love for the land moves us to return to the place where our ancianos formed the culture.

I returned to Puerto de Luna last summer, to join the community in a celebration of the founding of the church. I drove by my grandfather's home, my uncles' ranches, the neglected adobe[7] washing down into the earth from whence it came. And I wondered, how might the values of my grandfather's generation live in our own? What can we retain to see us through these hard times? I was to become a farmer, and I became a writer. As I plow and plant my words, do I nurture as my grandfather did in his fields and orchards? The answers are not simple.

"They don't make men like that anymore" is a phrase we hear when one does honor to a man. I am glad I knew my grandfather. I am glad there are still times when I can see him in my dreams, hear him in my reverie.[8] Sometimes I think I catch a whiff of that earthy aroma that was his smell, just as in the lonely times sometimes I catch the fragrance of Ultima's herbs. Then I smile. How strong these people were to leave such a lasting impression.

"They don't make men like that anymore . . .

So, as I would greet my abuelo long ago, it would help us all to greet the old ones we know with this kind and respectful greeting: "Buenos días le de Dios."

Quickwrite

Anaya's grandfather views death as part of the cycle of nature and tells Anaya, "Death is only this small transformation in life." Write a paragraph explaining why you agree or disagree with this statement.

7. *Adobe* is a building material made from sun-dried clay.
8. A *reverie* is a daydream or a moment during which one is lost in thought.

Teach

R Reading Strategy

Evaluating Opinions Have students consider the statement "It is the beautiful and the young who are praised in this society." **Ask:** What are some examples you can give in support of this statement? *(Many television shows and magazines that focus on young movie stars and recording artists are very successful.)* Which people who are not young and beautiful also receive a great deal of praise? *(some government officials and leaders of humanitarian groups)*

Quickwrite

Students' answers will vary but should

- be composed of complete sentences
- indicate agreement or disagreement with the statement
- provide support for the opinion

CheckPoint

Use the CheckPoint questions on Presentation Plus! to check students' mastery of the selection. These questions can be used with interactive response keypads for immediate student feedback.

Academic Standards

Additional Support activities on pp. 640 and 641 cover the following standards:

Skills Practice: **9.6.2** Demonstrate an understanding of...proper English usage, including the use of...verb tenses.

Building Reading Fluency: **9.7** [Develop] speaking skills...in conjunction with... strategies...[for] delivery of oral presentations.

9.7.17 Deliver oral responses to literature that support important ideas and viewpoints through accurate and detailed references to the text...

Building Reading Fluency

Paraphrasing Have partners take turns reading the last three paragraphs of the selection. After each paragraph, the student who is not reading should try to paraphrase the main idea of the paragraph.

When students have finished, ask volunteers to share their main ideas. **Ask:** What would be an appropriate tone of voice to use when reading this type of material aloud? *(Some students may suggest a measured, thoughtful tone; others may suggest a warm, emotional tone.)* BL

Assess

Comparing the Big Idea

Students may say that the speaker in "Good Night, Willie Lee, I'll See You in the Morning" learns about the importance of forgiveness in family life, the narrator in "Beyond the Bedroom Wall" learns about the darkness of spirit brought about by the loss of a loved one, and Rudolfo Anaya learns about the wisdom of older people.

Comparing Sound Devices

Possible examples of sound devices:

Walker:
Assonance—line 8, "Willie Lee, I'll see"
Consonance—line 6, "without regrets"
Alliteration—line 13, "permits a promise"

Woiwode:
Assonance—page 633, second column, line 25, "no color, no company"
Consonance—page 635, first column, lines 10–11, "lath with"
Alliteration—page 632, first column, line 11, "sake of a safe, enjoyable scare"

Anaya:
Assonance—page 639, fifth paragraph, line 4, "greeting of esteem"
Consonance—page 640, fourth paragraph, line 12, "into an internal anguish"
Alliteration—page 638, second paragraph, line 9, "whispering of the wind"

Comparing Author's Purpose

Students should use tone of voice to convey the emotions expressed in the poem and the story.

Use the CheckPoint questions on Presentation Plus! to check students' mastery of the selection. These questions can be used with interactive response keypads for immediate student feedback.

Wrap-Up: Comparing Literature Across Genres

- *Good Night, Willie Lee, I'll See You in the Morning* by Alice Walker
- *Beyond the Bedroom Wall* by Larry Woiwode
- *In Praise of Grandfathers* by Rudolfo A. Anaya

COMPARING THE Big Idea The Strength of Family

Partner Activity With a partner, review the following quotations. Then discuss the lessons about life that each person learns from his or her family. Cite evidence from the selections to support your interpretations.

*"And it was then I knew that the healing
of all our wounds
is forgiveness"*

—Walker, "Good Night, Willie Lee, I'll See You in the Morning"

"Without being able to confide in him, or in anyone (once the sun has risen, the dark seems partly our imagination), I knew I would never see my mother again, and started preparing myself for her death."

—Woiwode, "Beyond the Bedroom Wall"

"These lessons he learned from his past which was as deep and strong as the currents of the river of life, a life which could be stronger than death."

—Anaya, "In Praise of Grandfathers"

The Family, Henri Rousseau.

COMPARING Sound Devices

Group Activity Walker, Woiwode, and Anaya use sound devices such as assonance, consonance, and alliteration to create rhythmic effects. With a small group, discuss how these sound devices are used in all three genres: poetry, short story, and essay. Follow these steps:

1. Define each sound device.
2. Find examples of each sound device in the three selections.
3. Discuss the effects that particular sound devices create.
4. Choose a spokesperson to present your group's conclusions to the rest of the class.

COMPARING Author's Purpose

Speaking and Listening Prepare an oral interpretation of Walker's poem and selected passages from Woiwode's short story and Anaya's essay. Then indicate what the poem and the passages reveal about each writer's reason for writing.

INDIANA ACADEMIC STANDARDS (page 642)
9.3.2 Compare and contrast the presentation of a similar theme or topic across genres...

BEFORE YOU READ

Elena

MEET PAT MORA

Pat Mora would likely agree with the saying: "Blood is thicker than water." For Mora, family—blood ties—is where it all begins. "Being Mexican American, I come from a culture in which family is very important, and the metaphor of family is very important to me, our family in this country, our family on the planet," she says.

Mora writes poems, short stories, and essays that reflect the love of her family and her years growing up near the Mexico-United States border, in El Paso, Texas. Mora is interested in the ways families preserve their heritage—their language and traditions. She sees herself as a teacher and a "child at heart" who wants to help young people understand what is unique about their own families and about themselves.

Love for the Written Word Mora's love for writing goes back to her love for reading. One of her aunts loved to tell stories, which inspired Mora to become a storyteller herself. When Mora graduated from eighth grade, her parents gave her a typewriter. She remembers waiting for everyone to leave her graduation party so that she could use her new typewriter to write rhyming poems.

Over the years, Mora worked in jobs that restricted the amount of time she could spend writing. Finally, she thought, "My life is soon going to be half over, and I want writing to be part of it." For inspiration, she taped a quote from Spanish author Miguel Cervantes on her kitchen cabinet so that she could see it often as she cooked. The quote read, "By the Street of By and By you arrive at the House of Never." It was a way to remind herself that if she kept putting off writing, she would never be a writer. She began taking an hour a day to write, then two hours, and soon she was doing what she loves best—telling stories through the written word.

> *"I love words and their power to move us, to entertain us, to make us laugh, to comfort us."*
>
> —Pat Mora

Encouraging Literacy Since she began publishing books in the 1980s, Mora has written numerous poems, picture books, short stories, and essays. While some of her works are for adults, many are written for young people and children. As an award-winning author, Mora also travels frequently and speaks about her life as a writer.

In 1997 Mora began a family literacy program called *El día de los niños/El día de los libros*—Children's Day/Book Day. April 30 is designated as a celebration that encourages families to read together.

Pat Mora was born in 1942.

Literature Online **Author Search** For more about Pat Mora, go to www.glencoe.com.

BEFORE YOU READ

Focus

BELLRINGER

Bellringer Options
Selection Focus Transparency 40
Daily Language Practice Transparency 67
Or draw a two-column chart on the board. Write as the title "Moving to a New Country." Label the left column "Advantages" and the right column "Disadvantages." Have students brainstorm advantages and disadvantages, and list their responses in the chart. Engage students in a discussion about how moving to a new country affects families.

Literature Online

Author Search To expand students' appreciation of Pat Mora, have them access the Web site for additional information and resources.

CheckPoint

Use the CheckPoint questions on Presentation Plus! to monitor students' comprehension. These questions can be used with interactive response keypads for immediate student feedback.

Selection Skills

Elena

Literary Elements
- Free Verse (SE pp. 644, 646)
- Diction (SE p. 646)

Reading Skills
- Responding to the Speaker (SE pp. 644, 645, 647)

Listening/Speaking/Viewing Skills
- Oral Reading (SE p. 647)
- Analyzing Art (TWE p. 645)

Writing Skills/Grammar
- Poem (SE p. 647)

BEFORE YOU READ

Focus

Summary

In "Elena," the speaker describes her feelings of fear and isolation as she watches her children learn to speak English fluently. Meanwhile, she, a native Spanish speaker, struggles to learn the language. Her greatest fear is that as her children grow, she will no longer be able to communicate with them.

Literary Elements Have students access the Web site to improve their understanding of free verse.

LITERATURE PREVIEW

Connecting to the Poem

This poem is about a mother's efforts to communicate with her children and feel close to them. As you read "Elena," think about the following questions:

- What are some events or activities that draw family members closer together?
- When have you felt alone or left out because you did not understand something?

Building Background

People who are bilingual can speak a foreign language as fluently as they speak their native language. Sometimes children learn two languages simultaneously—one at home and another at school. Young children are generally able to learn a new language quickly and easily, but adults acquire new language skills much more slowly and are often frustrated by the learning process. Researchers believe that young children may process new linguistic information more easily because their brains and cognitive functions are still developing.

Setting Purposes for Reading

Big Idea The Strength of Family

Sometimes, despite a parent's best intentions, a family drifts apart over time. Obstacles that may push family members apart include generational conflicts, as well as everyday concerns such as growing up and moving away. As you read "Elena," notice the speaker's concerns that her family may be growing apart.

Literary Element Free Verse

Free verse is poetry that has no fixed pattern of meter, rhyme, or line length. Though poets who write in free verse disregard the traditional rules of meter, they often create rhythm through the use of other literary devices, such as alliteration. Recognizing that a poem is written in free verse can help you to appreciate the author's unique style. As you read "Elena," notice how the author uses free verse to express her intimate thoughts and feelings.

- See Literary Terms Handbook, p. R8.

READING PREVIEW

Reading Strategy Responding to the Speaker

The **speaker** is the narrator or person whose voice you hear when you read a poem. The speaker and the author are not always the same. For example, in "Elena," Mora is not the speaker. Determining who the speaker of a poem is can help you better understand the author's intended meaning. As you read, think about what the speaker may be feeling or experiencing.

Reading Tip: Using Your Imagination Use a chart like the one below to record details about the feelings and characteristics of the speaker. Suggest reasons for these feelings and characteristics.

Feelings or Characteristics	Reason
dumb	She doesn't speak English and can't understand what her children are saying.

Literature Online Interactive Literary Elements Handbook To review or learn more about the literary elements, go to www.glencoe.com.

INDIANA ACADEMIC STANDARDS (pages 644-647)

9.2 Develop strategies such as...identifying and analyzing structure...

9.3.13 Explain how voice [and] persona...affect...tone...

9.5.1 Write...autobiographical narratives...that describe a sequence of events and communicate the significance of the events to the audience...

Selection Resources

Print Materials
- Unit 3 Resources (Fast File), pp. 76–77
- Selection and Unit Assessments, pp. 125–126
- Selection Quick Checks, p. 63

Transparencies
- Bellringer Options Transparencies: Selection Focus Transparency 40 Daily Language Practice Transparency 67
- Literary Elements Transparency 49

Technology
- TeacherWorks Plus™ CD-ROM
- StudentWorks Plus™ CD-ROM
- Presentation Plus!™ CD-ROM
- Literature Online, glencoe.com
- Online Student Edition, mhln.com
- Exam*View*® Assessment Suite CD-ROM
- Vocabulary PuzzleMaker CD-ROM
- Listening Library, disc 1 track 77

La Cocinera, 1922. Leopoldo Romanach. Oil on canvas, 90.2 x 122 cm. Private collection. 

Elena

Pat Mora

My Spanish isn't enough.
I remember how I'd smile
listening to my little ones,
understanding every word they'd say,
their jokes, their songs, their plots.
Vamos a pedirle dulces a mamá. Vamos.[1]
But that was in Mexico.
Now my children go to American high schools.
They speak English. At night they sit around
the kitchen table, laugh with one another.
I stand by the stove and feel dumb, alone.
I bought a book to learn English.
My husband frowned, drank more beer.
My oldest said, "*Mamá,* he doesn't want you
to be smarter than he is." I'm forty,
embarrassed at mispronouncing words,
embarrassed at the laughter of my children,
the grocer, the mailman. Sometimes I take
my English book and lock myself in the bathroom,
say the thick words softly,
for if I stop trying, I will be deaf
when my children need my help.

1. Let's ask Mama for some candy. Let's go.

Big Idea The Strength of Family *What do these lines tell you about the speaker's relationship with her children?* **BI**

Reading Strategy Responding to the Speaker *How do you feel about the speaker after reading this line?* **R**

English Language Coach

Discussing Feelings This poem might have special meaning for English language learners and give Spanish speakers a chance to shine. Encourage students to meet in small groups to discuss feelings they have had that are similar to those expressed in the poem. For example, have they ever felt alone when in a group of English-only speakers? Have they ever been embarrassed by their mispronunciation of words? If there are Spanish speakers in the class, encourage them to translate line 6 for the class. Have them discuss specific language problems Spanish speakers might face when learning English. **EL**

Teach

BI Big Idea

The Strength of Family

Answer: *The speaker fondly remembers past times, ones that make her smile when thinking of her children. The poet suggests that the good relationship she and her children once enjoyed no longer exists. She does not understand "every word" they say.* **OL**

R Reading Strategy

Responding to the Speaker

Answer: *Students may say that they feel sympathetic toward the speaker because the line shows her loneliness and difficulties in learning English.* **OL**

Viewing the Art

Leopoldo Romanach (1862–1951) was an influential Cuban painter and art professor. He is noted for his use of live models and his promotion of Naturalist painting.
Ask: In what ways is this a Naturalist painting? *(Answers will vary.)* **AS**

CheckPoint

Use the CheckPoint questions on Presentation Plus! to check students' mastery of the selection. These questions can be used with interactive response keypads for immediate student feedback.

Academic Standards

The Additional Support activity on p. 645 covers the following standards:

English Language Coach: **9.2** Develop [reading] strategies... **9.7.7** Make judgments about the ideas under discussion and support those judgments with convincing evidence.

AFTER YOU READ

Assess

1. Students may have felt compassion for the mother, who feels left out.
2. (a) She is a Mexican woman, who speaks only Spanish and now lives in an English-speaking country. (b) She was happier in Mexico because she could understand her children.
3. (a) She is isolated by her inability to communicate in the "new" language. (b) In the past, she could understand her children, which made life easier.
4. (a) The mother attempts to learn English, while the father withdraws. (b) The mother is tough and resilient, while the father is stubborn. In their relationship, the mother looks after the children, and the father does not want her to become smarter than he.
5. (a) She knows that she must understand her children in order to help them. (b) She feels that the closeness she once shared with them may be changing.
6. The Spanish sentence offers a glimpse into the everyday world of Elena's life in Mexico.
7. (a) Elena speaks in a direct manner, describing how she feels and acts. (b) Students' answers will vary.
8. She hopes to learn English.

AFTER YOU READ

RESPONDING AND THINKING CRITICALLY

Respond

1. What feelings or thoughts did you experience while reading this poem?

Recall and Interpret

2. (a)Who is the speaker in "Elena"? (b)What do the speaker's memories of Mexico reveal about her?
3. (a)How has the speaker's life changed since she left Mexico? (b)Why do you think she is now thinking about the way life used to be?
4. (a)How does each parent in the poem react to the changes in the family's life? (b)What do their reactions suggest about each of them and about their relationship with each other?

Analyze and Evaluate

5. (a)What motivates the speaker in "Elena"? (b)How does she feel about her relationship with her children?
6. What is the effect of Mora's inclusion of Spanish words in this English poem?
7. (a)How does the voice in this poem convey Elena's character? (b)How would you characterize her personality?

Connect

8. **Big Idea** **The Strength of Family** What is the speaker hoping to do to strengthen her family?

LITERARY ANALYSIS

Literary Element Free Verse

Writers often use **free verse** to emphasize the relationship between form and meaning in a poem. On the first reading, a free verse poem may appear to have no regular form at all. However, analysis usually reveals one or more poetic techniques that help to make the poem memorable and give it meaning.

"Elena" has no fixed meter, fixed line lengths, or formal stanza structures. It does, however, make use of natural speech rhythms as well as enjambment, the continuation of a sentence from one line in a poem to the next.

1. How does the use of free verse affect the overall feel of this poem?
2. Reread lines 14 and 15. What is the effect of breaking line 14 where there is no natural pause?

Review: Diction

As you learned on page 209, **diction** refers to a writer's choice of words and the arrangement of those words in phrases, sentences, or lines of a poem. Poets generally consider the meanings of their words very carefully. They consider the sounds and associations of the words and are also careful about the arrangement of words on a page. Each word in a poem is carefully chosen to create the intended mood and meaning.

Partner Activity With a classmate, discuss Mora's use of diction in "Elena." Work together to create a chart similar to the one below. In the left column, list diction elements used in the poem, and in the right column, explain the effect that they have on the poem as a whole.

Diction Element	Effect
Simple words	Conversational tone

Literary Element

1. The free verse gives the poem natural rhythms of human speech.
2. Students may say the line break emphasizes the phrase "doesn't want you."

Review: Diction

Student charts should indicate words that show a conversational tone, a sense of sadness *(dumb, alone)*, and a sense of discomfort *(embarrassed, lock, deaf)*.

READING AND VOCABULARY

Reading Strategy Responding to the Speaker

The **speaker** in a poem can be the poet, a fictional character, or even an object. The speaker's character is developed by the feelings he or she expresses and the way he or she portrays settings and events. The speaker creates the particular tone or attitude of the poem through the way that he or she tells the story.

1. Which lines of this poem reveal the most about Elena's character?
2. What attitude or tone does the speaker in "Elena" create?

Academic Vocabulary

Here are two words from the vocabulary list on page R80.

priority (prī ôr′ ə tē) *n.* having precedence; superiority in rank, position, or privilege

precede (pri sēd′) *v.* to go before

Practice and Apply

1. What does the speaker in "Elena" consider to be her chief **priority**?
2. What is the effect of the speaker's descriptions of events that **precede** her current situation?

La Cocinera, 1922 (detail).

Literature Online **Web Activities** For eFlashcards, Selection Quick Checks, and other Web activities, go to www.glencoe.com.

WRITING AND EXTENDING

Writing About Literature

Apply Theme Family members often have trouble communicating with one another and feel that they are misunderstood. Have you been in situations when you had trouble communicating with members of your family? How do your experiences compare with those of the speaker in "Elena"? Write a poem, song lyrics, or a rap about the problems teens face when trying to communicate with their families.

Before you begin writing, think about how you want to present your poem and who your intended audience is. Use a web diagram like the one below to help you organize the ideas and details that you will include in your poem.

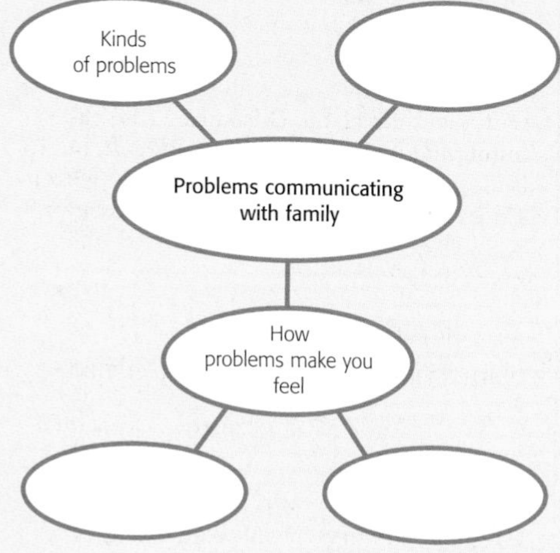

After completing your draft, meet with a peer reviewer to evaluate each other's work and to suggest improvements. Then proofread and edit your poem to correct errors in spelling, grammar, and punctuation.

Performing

Perform a reading of "Elena" in front of the class or record it on video. Rehearse by reading the poem aloud to yourself, experimenting with rhythm and the tone and pitch of your voice. Try to bring the poem and the experiences of the speaker to life as much as possible.

AFTER YOU READ

Assess

Reading Strategy

1. Students may mention the lines describing her loneliness and her purchase of an English book or the lines about locking herself in the bathroom to practice English.
2. Students may say that the speaker gives the poem a direct, honest tone. They may say that the speaker's attitude is one of determination but also one of longing.

Academic Vocabulary

1. Elena considers understanding and helping her children to be her chief priority.
2. Students may say that this gives the reader a better understanding of Elena's present life by showing what she misses about Mexico.

Writing About Literature

Use these criteria when evaluating students' writing:

- Does the poem or song focus on problems of communicating with family?
- Does the poem or song have a pleasing rhythm and fresh imagery?
- Does the poem or song's diction reinforce its content?

Web Activities Have students access the Web site for interactive activities that will help them assess their understanding of the selection.

Performing

Before they make their presentations, encourage students to practice reading in front of a mirror. They might also practice in front of friends or family members, and ask for feedback and suggestions.

Encourage students to continue practicing until they can read the poem fluently, without stuttering or stumbling. As they read, encourage them to make brief eye contact with the audience or camera, looking at the text only when necessary.

Focus

BELLRINGER

Bellringer Options
Selection Focus Transparency 41
Daily Language Practice Transparency 68
Or show images of mothers and adult children. **Ask:** How do you think the relationship between mothers and their children changes as children mature? What behaviors remain the same? Discuss with students how their relationships with their parents are changing.

Author Search To expand students' appreciation of Chitra Banerjee Divakaruni, have them access the Web site for additional information and resources.

Use the CheckPoint questions on Presentation Plus! to monitor students' comprehension. These questions can be used with interactive response keypads for immediate student feedback.

My Mother Combs My Hair

MEET CHITRA BANERJEE DIVAKARUNI

Imagine stepping off a plane to live in a land where the traditions and values are very different from anything you have ever known. That is what it was like for Chitra Banerjee Divakaruni. In 1976 she left her home in Calcutta, India, to live in the United States. She was nineteen years old.

Since then, Divakaruni has straddled two worlds. As a poet and fiction writer, she gives a voice to immigrants who, like herself, struggle to create a new life while maintaining ties with their homeland. Divakaruni says the immigrant experience is often difficult, but it is also a source of inspiration: "We draw from a dual culture, with two sets of worldviews."

> *"To me, the art of dissolving boundaries is what living is all about."*
>
> —Chitra Banerjee Divakaruni

Poetic Beginnings Divakaruni did not start out as a writer. When she first came to the United States, she worked odd jobs—as a salesclerk, a babysitter, and a bread-slicer in a bakery—to earn money for college. Eventually, she earned a master's degree, and a Ph.D. Divakaruni studied literature, but she did not write her own works until after her grandfather died. "I felt like I was forgetting things, forgetting him, and how things were in India and how people thought," she says. She joined a writing group, and by 1990, she had published her first book of poems, *The Reason for Nasturtiums*.

Divakaruni's first poems were deeply personal. Soon she found additional inspiration. While working as a volunteer in a women's center, she witnessed firsthand the plight of battered women. To help these women, Divakaruni founded a nonprofit group for Southeast Asian women called Maitri. The women of Maitri inspired Divakaruni, and soon she was writing short stories based on her experiences with them. Her first collection, *Arranged Marriages*, was published in 1995. It won the American Book Award.

Creating a New Tradition Divakaruni followed her early poems and short stories with a novel, *The Mistress of Spices*. It tells the story of a mystical figure who must choose between her heritage and her love for a non-Indian. The novel was included in the *New York Times* list of best books of 1997. Since then, Divakaruni has published numerous novels, short stories, and poems. Like the characters in these works, Divakaruni often crosses boundaries. She blends poetry and prose, fable and fiction, to bring together different traditions.

Divakaruni has also helped create a new tradition in the classroom. She teaches creative writing at the University of Houston. As the editor of *Multitude*, a cross-cultural anthology designed for writing classes, Divakaruni brings together diverse perspectives for a new vision of the American experience.

Chitra Banerjee Divakaruni was born in 1956.

Literature Online **Author Search** For more about Chitra Banerjee Divakaruni, go to www.glencoe.com.

Selection Skills

My Mother Combs My Hair

Literary Elements
- Simile (SE pp. 649, 651, 653)
- Structure (SE p. 653)

Reading Skills
- Visualizing (SE pp. 649, 653)

Vocabulary Skills
- Analogies (SE pp. 649, 653)

Listening/Speaking/Viewing Skills
- Role-Playing (TWE p. 650)
- Analyzing Art (TWE p. 650)

Writing Skills/Grammar
- Essay (SE p. 654)
- Literary Criticism (SE p. 654)
- Using Italics (SE p. 654)

LITERATURE PREVIEW

Connecting to the Poem

The poem "My Mother Combs My Hair" explores the relationship between a mother and daughter and their disagreement over family traditions. Before you read the poem, think about the following questions:

- What traditions does your family have?
- How would you tell your family that you had plans for your future that did not coincide with their traditions or plans for you?

Building Background

In India, many marriages are arranged by parents for their children, and sometimes the bride and groom do not meet each other until their wedding day. As part of a marriage agreement, the women's family provides a *dowry,* a payment in money or property, to the husband. Today, traditions are relaxing, but some families still follow these traditions.

In India and in other South Asian cultures, long hair is a symbol of beauty. Long hair is often braided and decorated with flowers and jewelry. Among those who cling to certain traditions, Indian women are not considered to have equal status with men intellectually. In these traditions, feminine beauty becomes a source of status and power.

Setting Purposes for Reading

Big Idea The Strength of Family

As you read the poem, notice how the relationship between the mother and daughter is revealed as the mother combs the daughter's hair.

Literary Element Simile

A **simile** is a figure of speech that uses *like* or *as* to compare things that do not seem alike. As you read, notice how Divakaruni uses similes for comparisons.

- See Literary Terms Handbook, pp. R15–R16.

LiteratureOnline Interactive Literary Elements Handbook To review or learn more about the literary elements, go to www.glencoe.com.

READING PREVIEW

Reading Strategy Visualizing

To **visualize** means to use your imagination to form mental pictures of the setting, characters, and action based on the details you read. When you visualize, you should ask yourself such basic questions as how does this setting, character, or object look? Who is in this scene? Where are the characters in relation to one another and their surroundings? By visualizing, you can immerse yourself in the action that takes place. As you read, use the descriptions and sensory details in the poem to form a mental picture of the mother and daughter as well as of the setting.

Reading Tip: Noting Descriptive Details
Descriptive details can help you visualize what is being described in writing. As you read, pick out phrases and similes from the selection. Use a chart like the one below to help you organize your details.

Descriptive Words	Item Described
scent of crushed hibiscus	room, hair

Vocabulary

plait (plāt) *n.* a braid of material or hair; p. 651 *The woman's long hair was worked into an elaborate plait.*

brocade (brō kād′) *n.* a silk fabric with raised patterns embroidered on it; p. 651 *The shiny, patterned jacket was made of a luxurious brocade.*

Vocabulary Tip: Analogies Analogies are comparisons based on the relationships between things or ideas. To complete an analogy, you must first decide what relationship exists in a pair of words. Then choose the word that creates the same relationship in a second pair of words.

INDIANA ACADEMIC STANDARDS (pages 649-654)
9.3.7 Recognize and understand the significance of...figurative language...[and] symbolism...
9.2. Develop [reading] strategies...
9.5.3 Write...literary analyses that gather evidence in support of a thesis...

BEFORE YOU READ

Focus

Summary

"My Mother Combs My Hair" describes an incident involving a grown daughter and her mother, in which the mother combs and braids the daughter's hair. During the course of the poem, the relationship between the mother and the daughter is revealed, along with the values that the mother holds.

V Vocabulary

Vocabulary File Say: Add these words and definitions to your vocabulary file. For each word, include a sentence that gives you an example of how to use the word. **OL** Students with English language needs should include the pronunciations of these words in their files. **EL**

Literary Elements Have students access the Web site to improve their understanding of simile.

Selection Resources

Print Materials
- Unit 3 Resources (Fast File), pp. 78–80
- Leveled Vocabulary Development, p. 48
- Selection and Unit Assessments, pp. 127–128
- Selection Quick Checks, p. 64

Transparencies
- Bellringer Options Transparencies: Selection Focus Transparency 41 Daily Language Practice Transparency 68
- Literary Elements Transparency 68

Technology
- TeacherWorks Plus™ CD-ROM
- StudentWorks Plus™ CD-ROM
- Presentation Plus!™ CD-ROM
- Literature Online, glencoe.com
- Online Student Edition, mhln.com
- Exam*View*® Assessment Suite CD-ROM
- Vocabulary PuzzleMaker CD-ROM
- Listening Library, disc 1 track 78

Viewing the Art

The woman in this image displays the traditional ornaments worn by Indian women for centuries. The arm bangles she wears could be made of gold, silver, glass, or other materials. Bangles are worn on important occasions and are considered a sign of good luck. The woman also wears anklets and toe rings. Silver beads are attached to the anklets, so that the tinkling sound of beads is heard as the woman walks. Toe rings, usually made of silver, are customary in some Hindu communities. In North India, toe rings symbolize marriage. The rings are placed on the bride's toes by the bridegroom during the wedding ceremony. Today, toe rings have become fashionable ornaments for women in other parts of the world. **AS**

My Mother Combs My Hair

Chitra Banerjee Divakaruni

Woman Dressing Her Hair, 18th century India. Private collection. 

Additional Support

Skills Practice

LISTENING AND SPEAKING: Role-Playing Before introducing the activity, discuss ways to make characters come alive during role-playing. List the following ideas on the board:

- Use tone of voice or special phrases to give the character personality.
- Use facial expressions and gestures.
- Stay in character.

"My Mother Combs My Hair" deals with a family activity. Have students work in pairs or small groups to role-play family situations, such as conversing at dinnertime, going to the movies, or visiting a relative. Let each group present its family scene. **OL**

The room is full
of the scent of crushed hibiscus,[1]
my mother's breath.
Our positions are of childhood,
I kneeling on the floor,
she crosslegged
on the chair behind.
She works the comb
through permed strands
rough as dry seaweed.
I can read regret in her fingers
untangling snarls,
rubbing red *jabakusum*[2] oil
into brittle ends.

When she was my age,
her hair reached her knees,
fell in a thick black rush
beyond the edges
of old photographs. In one,
my father has daringly
covered her hand with his
and made her smile.
At their marriage, she told me,
because of her hair
he did not ask for a dowry.

This afternoon I wait
for the old comments,
how you've ruined your hair,
this ***plait's*** *like a lizard's tail,*
or, *if you don't take better care*
of it, you'll never get married.
But the braiding is done,
each strand
in its neat place, shining,
the comb put away.

I turn to her, to the gray
snaking in at the temples,
the cracks growing
at the edges of her eyes
since father left.
We hold the silence
tight between us
like a live wire,
like a strip of gold
torn from a wedding **brocade**.

1. *Hibiscus* (hī bis′ kəs) is a showy red flower that grows in India and in many tropical climates.
2. *Jabakusum* is the brand name of expensive scented oil from the hibiscus flower.

Big Idea The Strength of Family *How does this line reflect the relationship between the mother and daughter?* **BI**

Literary Element Simile *Why does the poet use these images to describe the silence?* **L**

Vocabulary

plait (plāt) *n.* a braid of material or hair

brocade (brō kād′) *n.* a silk fabric with raised patterns embroidered on it

Teach

BI Big Idea

The Strength of Family

Answer: *The girl kneels on the floor in front of her mother, who sits in a chair. Their positions suggest the mother's elevated status over her daughter as well as the daughter's duty to be respectful to her mother.* **OL**

L Literary Element

Simile **Answer:** *The silence, like "a live wire" and "a strip of gold," is difficult to ignore, but the two women ignore it, although they hold it between them. A live wire is dangerous if you touch it, and by comparing the silence to such a wire, the author creates tension between the women. The comparison between the silence and the strip of brocade suggests a wedding gone wrong, which creates tension between the mother and daughter.* **OL**

CheckPoint

Use the CheckPoint questions on Presentation Plus! to check students' mastery of the selection. These questions can be used with interactive response keypads for immediate student feedback.

Differentiated Instruction

Planning and Designing When planning a family gathering, one must take many factors into consideration, from where the event will be held to how much food will be needed. Have students work in small groups to plan family gatherings, such as reunions or birthday parties. Let the groups decide if the events will include just immediate family or extended family. Have students outline the decisions needed and make plans for them. Encourage them to estimate how much things such as food or decorations will cost. Have groups present their plans to other groups. **AL**

Academic Standards

Additional Support activities on pp. 650 and 651 cover the following standards:

Skills Practice: **9.7.6** Analyze the occasion and the interests of the audience and choose effective verbal and nonverbal techniques (including voice, gestures, and eye contact) for presentations.

Differentiated Instruction: **9.7.15** Deliver expository (informational) presentations that convey information and ideas…[and] make distinctions between the relative value and significance of specific data, facts, and ideas…

AFTER YOU READ

Assess

1. Students' answers will vary.
2. (a) She permed it. (b) Students may say the daughter permed her hair to rebel against family tradition.
3. (a) The speaker's hair is damaged and rough, whereas the mother's was thick and long. (b) For the mother, long hair symbolizes beauty and power. For the daughter, hair symbolizes the freedom to do as she likes.
4. (a) She usually says that the daughter has ruined her hair and that if she doesn't take better care of it, she'll never get married. (b) They have argued in the past, but the mother wants to avoid an argument this time.
5. (a) The mother's hair has become gray, and wrinkles have appeared around her eyes. (b) Time and sadness over the loss of her husband have aged her.
6. The mother believes that beautiful hair shows respect for traditional values. The daughter's modern hairstyle is symbolic of her desire for independence.
7. Students may say that the speaker is a single young woman at the age when traditionally she should be married. She is independent and probably lives on her own and supports herself.
8. (a) Answers will vary. (b) Similes help the reader visualize the scene. Divakaruni wants readers to use their senses and imagination.
9. Students may say that the relationship seems fairly typical. Mothers and daughters routinely have conflicts.

AFTER YOU READ

RESPONDING AND THINKING CRITICALLY

Respond

1. Which lines from this poem did you find most memorable? Explain.

Recall and Interpret

2. (a)What did the daughter do to her hair that causes the mother's regret? (b)Why did the daughter do it?
3. (a)How does the speaker's hair compare with the hair of her mother at the same age? (b)What does hair symbolize for the mother and daughter?
4. (a)What comments does the mother usually make about the speaker's hair? (b)What does the description of these comments tell you about the relationship between the mother and daughter?
5. (a)What changes does the daughter notice in her mother? (b)Why have these changes occurred?

Analyze and Evaluate

6. Why has the daughter's hair been a source of conflict between the daughter and mother?
7. How would you describe the speaker in this poem? Consider her age and where she might live.
8. (a)In your opinion, what is the most effective simile in the poem? (b)Why do you think the author uses similes in the poem?

Connect

9. **Big Idea** **The Strength of Family** Is the relationship between the mother and daughter in the poem a typical mother-daughter relationship? Explain.

DAILY LIFE AND CULTURE

Life in India Today

A generation gap has occurred in India and within Indian American families. As recently as ten years ago, many girls were not educated in science, and marriages were arranged by parents. Boys, too, were limited by educational and economic opportunities. Today, India's youth are affected by the improvements in the country's economy and by the Internet and other technological advances.

Western television and products have affected the youth culture in India as well. While the older generation in India tends to follow traditions, members of the younger generation are pursuing careers in technology and engineering and mixing Indian culture with Western traditions. Indian youth today more often select their own spouses but continue to ask for their parents' approval. In addition, women earn more money and have more independence than ever before.

1. How do you think a parent or grandparent would feel about traditions changing?
2. Why would young people want traditions to change?

A woman in Bangalore, India, uses a hand-held computer.

Daily Life and Culture

1. A parent or grandparent may be worried about traditions changing or disappearing. They may be angry that their children do not respect their heritage.
2. Young people may not agree with the way their parents do things. Some traditions may be obstacles to pursuing careers and opportunities.

LITERARY ANALYSIS

Literary Element Simile

A **simile** can be concrete or abstract. A concrete simile uses *like* or *as* to describe two tangible objects, such as "The wind was like a bulldozer." An abstract simile uses a tangible object to describe a concept or idea, for example, "Freedom was like a surprise gift."

1. Which image in "My Mother Combs My Hair" is an abstract simile?
2. How does this simile make the abstract concept concrete?
3. How well does the poet's use of the abstract simile convey the mother's and daughter's feelings? Explain.

Review: Structure

As you learned on pages 516–517, **structure** is the order or pattern a writer uses to present ideas. In poetry, free verse has no particular pattern of meter, rhyme, line length, or stanza arrangement. Free verse is often arranged in verse paragraphs that, unlike stanzas, have no set number of lines. While poems written before the twentieth century usually contain stanzas, many contemporary poems are made up of verse paragraphs, which help organize a poem into thoughts, in much the same way that paragraphs help organize prose.

Partner Activity Meet with a classmate and discuss the use of free verse and verse paragraphs in "My Mother Combs My Hair." Working with your partner, rewrite the poem in stanzas with a regular rhyme scheme. Determine the effect this new structure has on the sound and theme of the poem. Use a chart like the one below to list your ideas.

	Original Poem	Rewritten Poem
Sound		
Theme		

READING AND VOCABULARY

Reading Strategy Visualizing

A poet will sometimes use descriptions or comparisons to help a reader form a mental image of a character. A poet may use similes, symbols, and deliberate word choice to help the reader **visualize** characters. Look back at the chart you made of descriptive details in the poem.

1. Which details help you visualize what the mother looked like in her youth? Which details help you imagine what she looks like now?
2. Which details help you see the mother in the poem combing the daughter's hair?

Vocabulary Practice

Practice with Analogies Choose the word that best completes each analogy.

1. ring : jewelry :: plait :
   a. curl **c.** hairstyle
   b. dish **d.** necklace
2. yarn : sweater :: brocade :
   a. pattern **c.** dress
   b. silk **d.** suit

Academic Vocabulary

Here are two words from the vocabulary list on page R80.

passive (pas′ iv) *adj.* not taking an active part; enduring without resistance

commodity (kə′ mod ə tē) *n.* something that is useful or valued

Practice and Apply

1. Why is the daughter **passive** while her mother combs her hair?
2. Why does the mother consider long hair an important **commodity**?

AFTER YOU READ

Assess

Literary Element

1. An abstract simile is "silence / tight between us / like a live wire."
2. Comparing silence to a live wire gives the impression that the mother and daughter want to speak to each other but are afraid of the tense current that runs between them.
3. Answers will vary.

Review: Structure

Students' poems may change words to regularize rhythm and add rhyme. However, their poems should include the same main ideas and maintain the same tone.

Reading Strategy

1. In her youth, the mother's hair "reached her knees." It "fell in a thick black rush / beyond the edges / of old photographs." The author also describes her smiling in a photo. Now, the mother has "gray / snaking in at the temples" and "cracks growing / at the edges of her eyes." There is no further mention of a smile.
2. The poet shows the speaker "kneeling on the floor" and the mother "crosslegged / on the chair behind." We can see the mother working the comb through the snarls in the daughter's hair and smell the flowery scent of the oil she applies to the hair's brittle ends.

Vocabulary

1. c **2.** c

Academic Vocabulary

1. The daughter is thrown back into her childhood role when her mother combs her hair.
2. Long hair is a symbol of beauty in traditional Indian culture. In order to attract a suitable husband, women use their beauty as a bargaining tool.

AFTER YOU READ

Assess

Writing About Literature

Use these criteria when evaluating students' writing:

- Does the introduction include a clear thesis that states the writer's interpretation?
- Do the body paragraphs include appropriate details to support the thesis?
- Does the conclusion include a summary of the main idea and a final thought on the topic?

Literary Criticism

Offer students these suggestions as they write their literary criticism:

- Focus on one or two aspects of the poem.
- Make sure your comments are concrete. Include one or two specific examples from the poem to support your comments.
- Include a mention of the larger issue of how the use of free verse, style, or characters reveals the author's attitudes toward women, relationships, or Indian culture.

WRITING AND EXTENDING

Writing About Literature

Evaluate Author's Craft In "My Mother Combs My Hair," the poet uses hair as a symbol. Write a short essay evaluating the use of the symbol in the poem and what it represents to both the mother and the daughter. Use examples from the poem and your personal experience to support your main points.

Follow the writing path shown here to help you organize your essay and keep you on track.

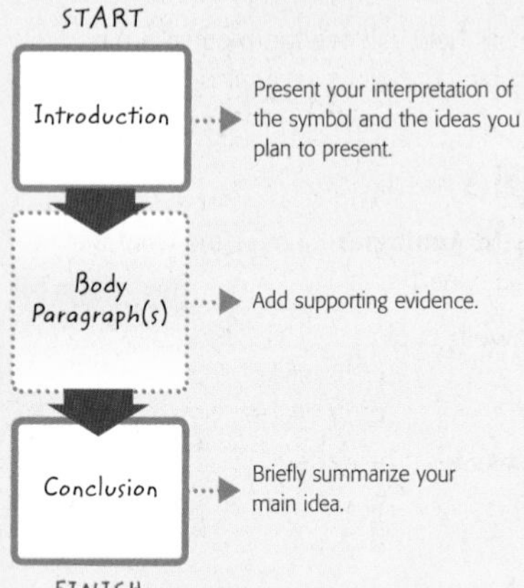
START
Introduction
Present your interpretation of the symbol and the ideas you plan to present.
Body Paragraph(s)
Add supporting evidence.
Conclusion
Briefly summarize your main idea.
FINISH

After completing your draft, meet with a peer reviewer to evaluate each other's work and to suggest revisions. Then proofread and edit your draft to correct errors in spelling, grammar, and punctuation.

Literary Criticism

Read the following criticism of Chitra Banerjee Divakaruni's work.

"Divakaruni's books, which are set in both India and America, feature Indian-born women torn between Old and New World values. She gives laser-like insight and skilled use of story, plot, and lyrical description to give readers a many-layered look at her characters and their respective worlds, which are filled with fear, hope, and discovery."

—Doubleday

Write your own literary criticism of "My Mother Combs My Hair." You may select any aspect of the poem to criticize, such as author's style or use of free verse.

GRAMMAR AND STYLE

Divakaruni's Language and Style

Using Italics Italic type is a special type that slants upward and to the right. Italics are used for several reasons, including emphasis. In her poem, Divakaruni uses italics in two instances. In line 13, she uses it to indicate a word from a different language, *jabakusum*. In lines 28–31, she uses italics to indicate her mother's unspoken comments.

You will benefit from knowing how to use italics properly, especially when writing book reviews and research papers. (Note that when writing by hand, you can indicate italics by underlining.) Here are some words and phrases that should be italicized:

titles of books, long poems, plays, films, and television series	*The Invisible Man* [novel] *Leaves of Grass* [long poem]
titles of newspapers and magazines	*St. Louis Post-Dispatch* [newspaper] *Psychology Today* [magazine]
foreign words and expressions that are not frequently used in English	James writes *hasta la vista* at the end of his letters to me.

Activity Rewrite the following sentences correctly, underlining the words and letters that should be italicized.

1. Toni Morrison's novel Beloved won a Pulitzer Prize for fiction in 1988.
2. In 1984, Haing S. Ngor won an Academy Award for his role in the film The Killing Fields.
3. The chef Julia Child used the expression Mangez bien during her television broadcasts.

Revising Check

Italics Use italics for emphasis only when it is absolutely necessary. Review the essay you wrote about Divakaruni's use of hair as a symbol. Are there words or phrases in your essay that should be italicized?

LiteratureOnline **Web Activities** For eFlashcards, Selection Quick Checks, and other Web activities, go to www.glencoe.com.

Divakaruni's Language and Style

1. Toni Morrison's novel <u>Beloved</u> won a Pulitzer Prize for fiction in 1988.
2. In 1984, Haing S. Ngor won an Academy Award for his role in the film <u>The Killing Fields</u>.
3. The chef Julia Child used the expression <u>Mangez bien</u> during her television broadcasts.

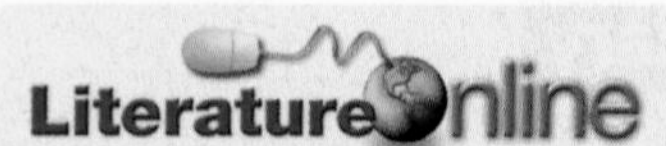
LiteratureOnline

Web Activities Have students access the Web site for interactive activities that will help them assess their understanding of the selection.

Winner of the Eisner Award

Jeff Smith

Focus

Summary

In searching for his cousins, Fone Bone nearly steps on Ted the bug. Fone Bone inadvertently offends Ted by telling him he looks like a leaf, so Ted calls his big brother, who is far bigger than Fone Bone. Big Brother lets Fone Bone go without harm but warns him to move quickly so he doesn't become trapped by impending winter. Ted takes Fone Bone to Thorn, who is very knowledgeable and may help Fone Bone find his cousins.

Building Background

You may enjoy reading comic books or comic strips in newspapers. A graphic novel is a longer form of a comic book, often with more complex plot lines and aimed at a more mature audience. The graphic novel *Maus* (1986) by Art Spiegelman, for example, tells the story of the Holocaust with characters depicted as mice and cats.

One of the most popular series of graphic novels in recent years is Jeff Smith's *Bone,* which appeared from 1991 to 2004. Smith has observed that his series, whose hero is an amiable Everyman character named Fone Bone, focuses on the theme of "growing up and leaving home for the first time." The story begins when Fone Bone and his two cousins are expelled from their hometown, Boneville. The three soon become separated in an uncharted desert, and each eventually finds his way into a forested valley filled with strange, menacing creatures. In the following excerpt from *Bone: Out from Boneville,* Fone Bone, just arrived in the valley, encounters two of its inhabitants.

Set a Purpose for Reading

As you read, think about how Fone Bone's adventures relate to the Big Idea. How do Ted and his big brother show strength of family?

Reading Strategy Interpreting Graphic Forms of Literature

How is reading a graphic novel different from reading a conventional novel? The writer of a literary work uses imagery, or "word pictures," to evoke an emotional response in the reader. A graphic novelist can use actual pictures, along with words.

Here are a few guidelines for reading and interpreting graphic forms of literature:

- Pay attention to visual details of characters, such as facial expressions, which are shown rather than described in words.
- Look for visual indications about the setting. Is the action taking place outdoors? Indoors? In the past?
- Typography cues show the emotions, speed, and sound level of dialogue. Capitalization, for example, usually means that the character is shouting. Boldfaced type means that a word is being stressed. Tiny type often indicates whispering.
- Scan the background of each panel. Artists sometimes like to insert clues or hidden details for the reader to discover.

Differentiated Instruction

Creating a Cartoon Tell students that cartoonists often use their characters to comment on life or relationships. Ask them to create their own cartoon to make a statement about an idea, feeling, or situation that is important to them. Students should first decide on the message that they want to convey. Then they should develop their cartoon characters and decide how those characters can convey their message. Have students display their completed cartoons in class. **AL**

Academic Standards

The Additional Support activity on p. 655 covers the following standard:

Differentiated Instruction: **9.5.1** Write… short stories that describe a sequence of events and communicate the significance of the events to the audience; describe with specific details the sights, sounds, and smells of a scene and the specific actions, movements, gestures, and feelings of the characters…

Teach

R Reading Strategy

Interpreting Graphic Forms of Literature Have student volunteers read the different roles aloud once for comprehension. Then have the volunteers read the parts again, this time including some characterization. Encourage students to use the punctuation and the font type and size to help them in their readings. Encourage students to play with regional dialect or accent to add to the characterizations. OL

R

Additional Support

Skills Practice

READING: Comparison and Contrast Discuss with students the most important feature of a cartoon—its ability to tell a story with pictures as well as words. Ask students how different the cartoon on page 656 would be if it were presented as a short story, using only text. Would it have the same impact? Would it be funny? What would take the place of the pictures?

Have pairs or small groups of students write paragraphs telling the story shown in the *Bone* cartoon. Invite volunteers to read their paragraphs aloud. Ask them what problems they encountered as they wrote. OL

RESPONDING AND THINKING CRITICALLY

Respond

1. Have you ever been in a situation where a mistaken first impression got you in trouble? Explain.

Recall and Interpret

2. (a)How does Ted react when Bone mistakes him for a leaf? (b)What is the effect of this reaction?
3. (a)How does Bone respond when Ted calls for his big brother? (b)Why does Bone react this way?

Analyze and Evaluate

4. (a)How do family ties shape this episode from *Bone*? (b)How are these family ties presented?
5. (a)What is the difference between the way Ted's big brother is presented in the first panels in which he appears and in the last panel in which he appears? (b)What is the effect of this last panel?

Connect

6. What other works have you read that remind you of *Bone*? What similarities do you see?

ACADEMIC STANDARDS (pages 655-657)
9.2 Develop strategies such as...identifying and analyzing structure, organization, perspective, and purpose...
9.3.5 Compare works that express a universal theme...

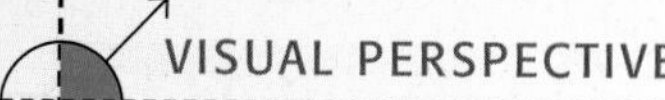

Assess

1. Most students will have had an experience in which a mistaken impression led to an unfortunate remark.
2. (a) Ted becomes furious. (b) The effect is humorous because Ted is so tiny.
3. (a) Bone cannot imagine that Ted's big brother could pose any threat. (b) Because he assumes that Ted's big brother will be another tiny insect
4. (a) Bone is searching for his lost cousins; Ted calls in his big brother to punish Bone for his "insulting" remark. (b) These family ties are presented as strong, binding, and protective.
5. (a) In the first panels, Ted's big brother is presented from the side and seems huge and monstrous; in the final panel, he is presented in silhouette from the rear and appears delicate. (b) The effect is both odd and funny.
6. Students might mention *Peanuts.* Both Smith's graphic depiction of Bone and the character's child-like personality are similar to Charles Schulz's Charlie Brown.

English Language Coach

Following the Cartoon Students may need some guidance in following the cartoon. Point out that the dialogue "bubbles" show the words that each character is speaking. You may wish to have a small group of students work together to read the parts of each character. EL

Differentiated Instruction

Visual Learners Students with exceptional visual interpretation abilities might be interested in sharing some of their favorite cartoons with the class. Encourage these students to bring their favorite cartoon strips to class. Have them describe the characters and tell what they like about the cartoons. AL

Academic Standards

Additional Support activities on pp. 656 and 657 cover the following standards:

Skills Practice: **9.3.2** Compare and contrast the presentation of a similar theme or topic across genres...

English Language Coach: **9.2.1** Analyze the structure and format of...documents...

Differentiated Instruction: **9.7.17** Deliver oral responses to literature that...[demonstrate] a comprehensive understanding of the significant ideas...

BEFORE YOU READ

Focus

BELLRINGER

Bellringer Options
Selection Focus Transparency 42
Daily Language Practice Transparency 69
Or display images of elderly women at work. **Say:** Think about how you remember or think about your grandmother. What qualities do you associate with her? What qualities does or did your grandmother possess that you wish you had?

Author Search To expand students' appreciation of Margaret Walker, have them access the Web site for additional information and resources.

Use the CheckPoint questions on Presentation Plus! to monitor students' comprehension. These questions can be used with interactive response keypads for immediate student feedback.

BEFORE YOU READ

Lineage

MEET MARGARET WALKER

Margaret Walker was born in Birmingham, Alabama, the daughter of a minister and a music teacher. The home was a nurturing environment full of poetry, philosophy, and music. Walker went to high school in New Orleans, and then attended New Orleans University (now Dillard University) for two years. During college, she met the renowned poet Langston Hughes at a reading. Hughes recognized her talent and urged her to study and hone her craft in the North. Walker transferred to Northwestern University in Illinois, where she received a bachelor's degree in English at the age of nineteen.

"Let a people loving freedom come to growth."

—Margaret Walker, from "For My People"

A Witness to History In 1936 Walker began work with the Federal Writers' Project in Chicago, funded by Franklin D. Roosevelt's Works Project Administration (WPA). There she forged a lasting friendship and working relationship with Richard Wright, the novelist and short-story writer best known for his novel *Native Son* (1940) and his autobiography *Black Boy* (1945). Walker would soon become Wright's confidante, as well as researcher and editor for many of his works. Involvement in the Writers' Project provided Walker with firsthand knowledge of the Great Migration, a period of American history that resulted in hard times and broken dreams for many Southern blacks who moved north during the first half of the twentieth century.

After completing her tenure with the WPA in 1939, Walker returned to school, entering the creative writing program at the University of Iowa, where she earned a master's degree and a Ph.D. From 1949 to 1979 she taught English at Jackson State University in Mississippi.

Her Published Works In 1937 "For My People" appeared in *Poetry* magazine. It was Walker's first published poem and became the work for which she is best known. Walker's first book of poetry appeared in 1942. The volume, which began as her master's thesis, garnered Walker the Yale Younger Poets Award. Her other creative works include *Jubilee* (1968), which was her first published novel, *Prophets for a New Day* (1970), and *October Journey* (1973). In 1988 Walker wrote *Richard Wright, Daemonic Genius: A Portrait of the Man, a Critical Look at His Work.* The book chronicled her friendship and professional collaboration with the great African American writer.

Throughout Walker's life, the art of writing was an integral part of her identity. A gifted poet and determined woman, Walker became a successful writer and scholar at a time when few African American women had the opportunity to pursue a college education.

Margaret Walker was born in 1915 and died in 1998.

LiteratureOnline **Author Search** For more about Margaret Walker, go to www.glencoe.com.

Selection Skills

Lineage

Literary Elements
- Alliteration (SE pp. 659, 661)

Reading Skills
- Analyzing Rhythm (SE pp. 659–661)

Vocabulary Skills
- Synonyms (SE pp. 659, 661)

Writing Skills/Grammar
- Essay (SE p. 661)
- Description (TWE p. 660)

LITERATURE PREVIEW

Connecting to the Poem

The speaker of Walker's poem describes the strength and resilience of her hardworking grandmothers. Before you read, think about the following questions:

- What traits do you associate with your ancestors?
- How does your life today compare with the lives of your grandparents when they were your age?

Building Background

Margaret Walker lived in Mississippi during a time of great inequality, when African Americans were seen as second-class citizens and treated with little or no respect. Segregation was still enforced through Jim Crow laws. These laws forbade many forms of interaction between blacks and whites, and people could be severely punished if they broke the law.

For example, by law black and white children had to go to separate schools, and marriage between a white person and a black person was forbidden. It was even forbidden for a black person to be buried in a white cemetery. The civil rights movement that began in the 1950s fought against these and many other unjust laws.

Setting Purposes for Reading

Big Idea The Strength of Family

As you read this poem, note the traits that the speaker associates with her grandmothers.

Literary Element Alliteration

Alliteration is the repetition of consonant sounds at the beginnings of words. It can be used to reinforce meaning or create a musical effect. Recognizing alliteration in poetry helps the reader both see and hear the songlike quality of the piece. The phrase "the wild, wild West" is an example of alliteration. As you read "Lineage," look for examples of alliteration.

- See Literary Terms Handbook, p. R1.

LiteratureOnline Interactive Literary Elements Handbook To review or learn more about the literary elements, go to www.glencoe.com.

READING PREVIEW

Reading Strategy Analyzing Rhythm

Rhythm is the pattern of beats created by the arrangement of stressed and unstressed syllables in poetry. Rhythm can be regular, with a predictable pattern or meter, or irregular. Being alert to rhythm can help you recognize how a poet evokes an emotional response.

Reading Tip: Reading Aloud You may want to read this poem aloud to get a stronger impression of its rhythmic emphasis and structure. As you read, use a chart like the one below to keep track of how rhythmic elements are used.

Place in the Poem	How Rhythm Is Used
First line	Simple sentence that gives rhythmic emphasis to the last word, "strong."

Vocabulary

toil (toil) *v.* to work very hard or for long hours; p. 660 *After the flood, we toiled for days trying to clean the grime out of the basement.*

sow (sō) *v.* to plant by scattering seeds; p. 660 *In the spring, the gardener will sow the seeds, walking the length of the garden several times as she scatters them.*

Vocabulary Tip: Synonyms Synonyms are words that have the same or similar meanings. For example, *love* and *adore* are synonyms. Note that synonyms are always the same part of speech.

INDIANA ACADEMIC STANDARDS (pages 659-661)

9.3.7 Recognize and understand...figurative language...
9.2 Develop [reading] strategies...
9.5.3 Write...analytical essays...
9.3.11 Evaluate the...impact of diction...on...theme.

BEFORE YOU READ

Focus

Summary

In this poem, the speaker describes the qualities that her grandmothers possessed and her memories of them. She ends by wondering why she does not possess the same qualities.

V Vocabulary

Vocabulary File Say: Add these words and definitions to your vocabulary file. For each word, include a sentence that gives you an example of how to use the word. **OL** Students with English language needs should include the pronunciations of these words in their files. **EL**

Literary Elements Have students access the Web site to improve their understanding of alliteration.

Selection Resources

Print Materials

- Unit 3 Resources (Fast File), pp. 81–83
- Leveled Vocabulary Development, p. 49
- Selection and Unit Assessments, pp. 131–132
- Selection Quick Checks, p. 66

Transparencies

- Bellringer Options Transparencies: Selection Focus Transparency 42, Daily Language Practice Transparency 69
- Literary Elements Transparency 72

Technology

- TeacherWorks Plus™ CD-ROM
- StudentWorks Plus™ CD-ROM
- Presentation Plus!™ CD-ROM
- Literature Online, glencoe.com
- Online Student Edition, mhln.com
- Exam*View*® Assessment Suite CD-ROM
- Vocabulary PuzzleMaker CD-ROM
- Listening Library, disc 1 track 80

Teach

R Reading Strategy

Analyzing Rhythm Answer: *The line gives an impression of balance, solidity, and finality. The series of lines ending with periods creates a rhythm that reflects the sequence of planting a crop.* OL

Use the CheckPoint questions on Presentation Plus! to check students' mastery of the selection. These questions can be used with interactive response keypads for immediate student feedback.

Woman Sowing. Robert Gwathmet (1903–1988). Watercolor and ink, 13⅞ x 15⅝ in. Gift of International Business Machines Corporation. Smithsonian American Art Museum, Washington, DC.

Lineage

Margaret Walker

My grandmothers were strong.
They followed plows and bent to **toil.**
They moved through fields **sowing** seed.
They touched earth and grain grew.
They were full of sturdiness and singing.
My grandmothers were strong.

My grandmothers are full of memories
Smelling of soap and onions and wet clay
With veins rolling roughly over quick hands
They have many clean words to say.
My grandmothers were strong.
Why am I not as they?

Reading Strategy Analyzing Rhythm *What effect does the rhythm of this line have, both as one line and in the context of its stanza?* R

Vocabulary

toil (toil) *v.* to work very hard or for long hours

sow (sō) *v.* to plant by scattering seeds

Additional Support

Academic Standards

The Additional Support activity on p. 660 covers the following standard:

Skills Practice: **9.5.1** Write biographical… narratives…that describe with specific details…the characters…

Skills Practice

WRITING: Description Point out the vivid images the poet uses to describe the grandmothers, particularly in lines 7–9.

Have students think about people whom they admire. Have them write poems or paragraphs describing these people, using a few well-chosen vivid details to convey a sense of the people. Encourage students to share their descriptions with the rest of the class. OL

AFTER YOU READ

RESPONDING AND THINKING CRITICALLY

Respond

1. Which sensory image from the poem appeals to you most? Why?

Recall and Interpret

2. (a)What kind of work does the speaker say her grandmothers did? (b)What do the details suggest to you about the grandmothers?
3. (a)How are the verb tenses different in the first and second stanzas of this poem? (b)What does this change in verb tense suggest about the speaker's grandmothers?
4. (a)How would you describe the speaker's attitude toward her grandmothers? (b)What details from the poem reveal this attitude?

Analyze and Evaluate

5. Why might the speaker describe herself as different from her grandmothers?
6. (a)What does the title of this poem mean? (b)Why might Walker have chosen this title?
7. How do you think the speaker defines strength? Support your opinion with evidence from the poem.

Connect

8. **Big Idea** **The Strength of Family** (a)What kind of relationship do you think the speaker has with her grandmothers? Cite evidence from the poem. (b)What are some ways the speaker might feel connected to her grandmothers?

LITERARY ANALYSIS

Literary Element Alliteration

Alliteration is often used in poetry, where it helps to emphasize particular words or phrases, create specific images, and establish an appealing sound and rhythm. Alliteration may also help us to remember lines or phrases.

1. In lines 3 and 4, how does the emphasis created by alliteration support the meaning?
2. Identify another instance of alliteration. Why do you think the author chose to use it there?

Writing About Literature

Analyze Repetition In "Lineage," Margaret Walker makes frequent use of repetition–the recurrence of sounds, words, phrases, lines, or stanzas. How does this technique help develop the themes in the poem? What is the effect of repeating a line? What is the effect of repeating and contrasting the pronouns *they* and *my*? Write a short essay in which you analyze Walker's use of repetition in "Lineage."

LiteratureOnline **Web Activities** For eFlashcards, Selection Quick Checks, and other Web activities, go to www.glencoe.com.

READING AND VOCABULARY

Reading Strategy Analyzing Rhythm

Rhythm gives a musical quality to poetry. It can add emphasis to certain words and help to convey the poem's meaning. It can also be used to highlight structural elements and reinforce the poem's most important ideas.

1. (a)How does the rhythm in the first stanza differ from the rhythm in the second? (b)How does this difference reinforce the meaning of the poem?
2. What rhythmic effect does the poet's repetition of the line "My grandmothers were strong" have on the poem?

Vocabulary Practice

Practice with Synonyms Choose the best synonym for each vocabulary word.

1. toil
   - **a.** job
   - **b.** labor
   - **c.** study
   - **d.** release
2. sow
   - **a.** plant
   - **b.** sadden
   - **c.** mend
   - **d.** reap

Literary Element

1. It draws attention to the cause/effect and time relationship described.
2. The *r* sounds in "rolling roughly" parallel the image of distended veins moving on quick hands.

Reading Strategy

1. (a) First-stanza lines have a regular meter; the others do not. (b) The first stanza mimics the rhythm of field labor; the second implies that the grandmothers are now free to tell of their memories.
2. It frames the first stanza.

AFTER YOU READ

Assess

1. Students' answers will vary.
2. (a) They plowed and planted fields of grain by hand. (b) They were strong, hard-working, capable women.
3. (a) In the first stanza, the verbs are in the past tense. In the second, most are in the present tense. (b) It suggests that the grandmothers are no longer working in the fields. They are now "full of memories."
4. (a) She admires them for their ability to draw life from the earth. (b) "Sturdiness and singing" and "clean words"
5. She may not have experienced hard labor or lived in touch with the earth.
6. (a) *Lineage* means "ancestry." (b) She wants to emphasize the speaker's roots.
7. The first stanza focuses on the grandmothers' physical strength. The second emphasizes their mental and spiritual strength.
8. (a) "They have many clean words to say" suggests that the grandmothers talk frequently to the speaker. (b) She is an African American woman who is connected to them by blood and the family memories they have shared.

Vocabulary

1. b **2.** a

LiteratureOnline

Web Activities Have students access the Web site for interactive activities that will help them assess their understanding of the selection.

Focus

BELLRINGER

Display images of daily life, such as photographs depicting work, family life, or recreation. **Ask:** What feelings or thoughts do these images evoke? Ask students to reflect on an important activity in their own life as a first step in writing a reflective essay.

Summary

The process of writing a reflective essay is presented in stages, beginning with prewriting activities such as brainstorming. Students are guided through drafting, revising, and editing their essays. Instruction on precise adjectives and dangling participles is included. Students will also present reflections orally.

Writing Models Have students access the Web site for interactive writing models and writing guides.

The Writing Process

In this workshop, you will follow the stages of the writing process. At any stage, you may think of new ideas to include and better ways to express them. Feel free to return to earlier stages as you write.

- **Prewriting**
- **Drafting**
- **Revising**
  - 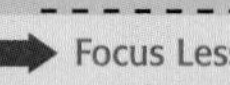 Focus Lesson: Using Precise Adjectives
- **Editing and Proofreading**
  -  Focus Lesson: Correcting Dangling Participles
- **Presenting**

Writing Models For models and other writing activities, go to www.glencoe.com.

ACADEMIC STANDARDS (pages 662–669)

9.5.1 Write…autobiographical narratives…

9.4.3 Use precise language…

9.6.1 Identify and correctly use … phrases, including… participial…

Writing Workshop

Reflective Essay

Reflecting on an Experience

who are you,little i

(five or six years old)
peering from some high

window;at the gold

of november sunset

(and feeling:that if day
has to become night

this is a beautiful way)

—E. E. Cummings, "who are you,little i"

Connecting to Literature In "who are you,little i," E. E. Cummings reflects on looking out a window at a November sunset as a child. Poets contemplate many experiences, from observations of nature to the meaning of life and death. Similarly, writers of essays reflect on their experiences. When you write a reflective essay, you describe something you observed or experienced and how it affected you. The purpose is to communicate your thoughts to others. To write a successful essay, follow the goals and strategies of reflective essay writing.

Rubric: Features of Reflective Essays

Goals	Strategies
To use details to describe an experience	☑ List descriptive details and sensory images you recall from the experience
To express the meaning of the experience	☑ Explain the significance of the experience in your life ☑ Show the meaning of the experience to your readers
To order your details effectively	☑ Let one thought flow into another ☑ End by drawing a conclusion
To communicate with an audience	☑ Use a casual style of writing ☑ Express what happened in everyday language

Workshop Resources

Print Materials
- Unit 3 Resources (Fast File), pp. 85–88
- REAL Success in Writing: Research and Reports
- Writing Constructed Responses, pp. 1–26, 54, 55–60
- Glencoe Literature Library

Transparencies
- Grammar and Language Transparencies 10, 14
- Writing Workshop Transparencies 16–20
- Visual Literacy/Fine Art Transparencies

Technology
- Grammar & Language eWorkbook
- Revising with Style eWorkbook
- Sentence Diagraming eWorkbook
- Spelling Power eWorkbook
- Online Essay Grading, glencoe.com
- Literature Library Exam*View*® Assessment Suite CD-ROM
- Literature Library Vocabulary PuzzleMaker CD-ROM

Assignment

Write a reflective essay about a meaningful experience you had or an observation you made. As you move through the stages of the writing process, keep your audience and purpose in mind.

Audience: peers, classmates, and teacher

Purpose: create a vivid and memorable impression of your experience for others

Real-World Connection

Although reflective essays can be about unusual or dramatic events, they usually are about ordinary events or common situations. Writers look around them, observe people and places, and think about the meaning of what they see. BI

Analyzing a Professional Model

Donald Hall is a noted poet whose work expresses his reflections about the world. He has also written more than twenty collections of essays. In the selection below, look for his observations about the pride New Englanders take in their bad weather. Pay close attention to the comments in the margin. They point out features that you might want to include in your own reflective essay.

"Good Use for Bad Weather" by Donald Hall

My grandparents nailed two thermometers side by side on the porch of their New Hampshire farmhouse. One registered ten degrees cold, the other ten degrees hot, so that there was always something to brag about. Every morning when my grandmother sat in the rocker under Christopher the canary, writing three postcards to three daughters, she could say, "Thirty below this morning. Seems like it might get cold." Or, "Ninety already and the sun's not over the mountain."

In New England we take pride in our weather because it provides us with pain and suffering, necessities for the spirit, like food and clothing for the body. We never brag about good weather. Let Tucson display self-esteem over eighty-three days without rain. Let Sarasota newspapers go free for the asking when the sun doesn't shine. We smirk in the murk, superior. It's true that we have good weather; we just don't pay it any mind. When summer people flock north to the lakes and the mountains, they do not gather to enjoy our foggy rain. If they're from Boston, they don't come *for* bright sun

Introduction

Introduce the setting and subject with an interesting anecdote.

Quote

Exact words make your writing come alive. Quotes should be enclosed in quotation marks.

Point of View

Use the first-person point of view in a reflective essay. Plural pronouns, such as *we, us,* and *our,* identify the writer as part of a group.

Elaboration

Comparing and contrasting can help develop your ideas.

Teach

Big Idea

Life Lessons Explain that in reflective essays writers gather their thoughts on a subject and, in the process, derive insights about life and human nature. Often, everyday events and experiences serve as their starting point.

Ask: What are some typical everyday activities? *(Students may mention school, jobs, hobbies, sports, recreation, commuting and doing chores.)* OL

Literary History

Michel de Montaigne

One of the great thinkers of the Renaissance, Michel de Montaigne (1533–1592) pioneered the reflective essay in a series of personal observations renowned for their wit, skepticism, and disarming honesty. Montaigne's *Essays* explores his own experiences and the customs and beliefs of his contemporaries to arrive at universal truths. AS

Differentiated Instruction

Descriptive Details Challenge gifted and talented students to enliven their writing with specific concrete details. Note, for instance, how much more effectively the reader's senses are engaged when the word *garments* is replaced by the phrase *rustling red silk robes.* Encourage students to consider the kinds of details that will engage their target audience. AL

Academic Standards

The Additional Support activity on p. 663 covers the following standard:

Differentiated Instruction: **9.4.3** Use precise language, action verbs, sensory details, and appropriate modifiers.

Teach

Writing Skills

Using Anecdotes **Ask:** What does the anecdote in the first paragraph show us about Hall's grandparents? *(They are rugged country people who like to show how tough they are.)* What makes the anecdote humorous? *(They make light of bad weather, but in fact the weather is never really so bad as their broken thermometers indicate.)* **OL**

★ Political History

New Hampshire On June 21, 1788, New Hampshire became the ninth state to ratify the Constitution. The proud motto "Live Free or Die," stamped on the state's license plates, was penned by the Revolutionary War general John Stark, hero of the Battle of Bennington. Robert Frost, who worked as a farmer and schoolteacher in Derry, celebrated New Hampshire's picturesque rural landscape in many of his poems. **AS**

Descriptive Details
Use sensory details that show how things look, sound, feel, smell, and taste.

Tone
A casual, conversational style shows how language is spoken in a particular region.

Narrative Details
Details about time and clue words of time order, such as *then,* show the chronological order of the story.

Descriptive Details
Use details to describe people and places.

Significance
Explain your thoughts and feelings about what you have observed.

and cool dry air; they migrate north *against* the soup-kettle mugginess of home. It seems more decent.

In good weather—apple days of October, brilliant noons and cool evenings of August—we remain comfortable despite our pleasure by talking about pleasure's brevity, forecasting what we're in for as soon as the good spell is done with. Winter is best for bragging. For a week or two in March, mud is almost as good. (Mud is weather as much as snow is; leaves are landscape.) "Tried to get the Buick up New Canada this morning. Have to wait for a dry spell to pull it out, I suppose. Of course, we'll have to dig to find it, first."

Black ice is first rate, but most of us who cherish difficulty will settle for a good ten feet of snow. We get up about five-fifteen, make the coffee, check the thermometer: ten degrees above. The warmth must account for the snow. Highway department plows blunder down Route 4 in the dark outside. We get dressed, dragging on flannel-lined chinos, flannel shirt, sweater, down jacket, and boots. Then we broom one car, headlights and taillights, gun it in reverse over the hump of snow Forrest's plow left, swing it up Forrest's alley, and swoop it down to the road, scattering ridges of snow.

Only two miles to the store. It's not adventurous driving, but it pays to be attentive, to start slowing for a turn a hundred yards early. The store opens at six. Because this is New Hampshire, somebody's bound to be there by five-forty-five. ★ We park with the motor running and the heater on—it'll get warm while we pick up the *Globe*—to go inside. Bob's there with his cup of coffee, and Bill who owns garage and store, and Judy the manager who makes coffee and change. We grin at each other as I stamp my boots and slip my paper out of the pile. We say things like, "Nice weather!" "Bit of snow out there!" "Hear we're getting two feet more!" but what we're really saying is *It takes more than a couple of feet of snow to slow us down!*

Reading-Writing Connection Think about the writing techniques that you have just encountered and try them out in your own reflective essay.

Additional Support

Skills Practice

WRITING: Show Versus Tell **Say:** Reread the last paragraph. Note Hall's use of specific details and actions to *show* the hardiness of New Hampshire natives. Instead of simply stating that they are resilient, he paints a picture with words. Ask students to identify examples. *(They drive to the store in thick snow, rise early, arrive even before the store opens, and make jokes about the cold.)* **OL**

Prewriting

Gather Ideas To reflect means to think. When you write a reflective essay, you describe what happened or what you observed. You also tell or imply how you think or feel about your experience or observation.

Choose a Subject Below are some hints for choosing a subject that is important to you and will be meaningful to your readers.

- **Find a familiar subject.** Ask yourself questions such as the following: How do I feel about this place? What do I notice about the people who live in my neighborhood? What do I think about what happens here every morning/afternoon/evening?
- **Select a subject that is meaningful to others.** Choose a subject that others will find meaningful, either because it is familiar to them or because it gives them new insight. Ask yourself: Why do I think people are interested in this subject? How can I describe it so that it is meaningful to others?
- **Use a cluster diagram.** To gather your ideas before you begin to write, jot them down in an organizer. You might, for example, put "Things That Happened Last Year" in the center. Then add notes to help you decide on a memorable experience for your essay.

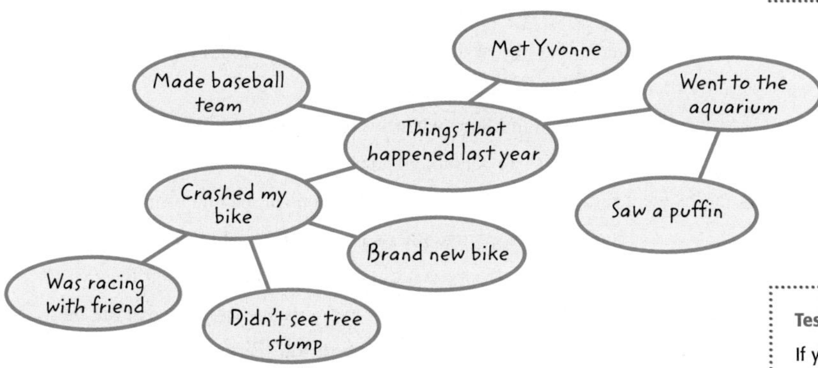

Reflect on Your Subject Before you begin drafting, think about why this event was important in your life and why others will want to read about it. Consider what you learned or how it changed your life.

Talk About Your Ideas To help develop your writing voice, describe your reflections to a partner. Ask your partner to suggest where you might add narrative details to help develop the story or sensory details to help your readers experience what you went through. Listen to your partner's reflections too. Ask questions to help your partner recall the details and conversations that took place.

Explore Sensory Details

Record sensory details about your experience or observation. Make a list of images. Describing one image may help you remember others.

bright orange beak
loud, growling calls
sturdy webbed feet
fake rocks
painted blue sky
plastic bucket

Test Prep

If you know you will be writing a reflective essay for a timed test in class, prepare ahead of time by listing possible subjects. Consider how you think or feel about them. Then you will be able to plan quickly during the test and spend most of your time writing.

Teach

Writing Process

Prewriting Allow students time for brainstorming, and ask them to recall examples of meaningful people, places, or activities. Ask them to visualize and record as many memories, details, and impressions as possible. **OL**

Writing Skills

Observation Hall brought his essay to life through close observations of his subjects. Tell students to imagine watching their subjects in a movie or looking at them in photographs. Challenge them to capture these pictures in words, so that an audience can "see" them, too. **OL**

Building Reading Fluency

Reading Aloud Read a paragraph of the essay aloud to help students grasp the rhythm and expressiveness of fluent reading. Pay special attention to enunciation, pacing, tone of voice, and emphasis. Guide students to recognize the techniques you used to make the meaning of the passage clearer. Invite volunteers to read aloud, using these techniques. **BL**

Academic Standards

Additional Support activities on pp. 664 and 665 cover the following standards:

Skills Practice: **9.3.11** Evaluate the aesthetic qualities of style, including the impact of diction and figurative language on tone, mood, and theme.

Building Reading Fluency: **9.7** [Respond] to oral communication [with] careful listening and evaluation of content…

Teach

Writing Process

Drafting Encourage students to explore their hunches and inspirations in the early stages of writing. Stress the importance of generating a flow of ideas rather than struggling with word choices or sentence construction. Urge them to jot down ideas and then review them for unexpected insights or a fresh angle on their subject. Remind students that they can revise later. **OL**

Writing Skills

Introduction: Answer: *The "close-up" description of the puffin* **OL**

Writing Skills

Point of View Answer: *First person* **OL**

Writing Skills

Narrative Details Answer: *They provide the narrative structure, or "story," of the essay.* **OL**

Writing Skills

Descriptive Details Answer: *The details about the puffins' calls and appearance make the experience seem real.* **OL**

Drafting

Put Your Thoughts and Feelings into Words Using your plan as a guide, begin drafting your reflective essay. Write a topic sentence to state the main idea of each paragraph. Remember that your goal in this step is to let your ideas flow without being concerned about grammar and mechanics. Leave the evaluation of your writing for later.

Analyzing a Workshop Model

Here is a final draft of a reflective essay. Read the essay and answer the questions in the margin. Use the answers to these questions to guide you as you write.

Introduction
What draws you into this essay?

Point of View
From what point of view is a reflective essay told?

Narrative Details
What do narrative details add to an essay?

Descriptive Details
How do sensory images help you visualize an experience?

Elaboration
Why might a writer choose to include a different but similar experience?

Watching a Puffin Through Glass

I stood in front of the aquarium glass and watched a puffin. Not two inches away from my nose, the puffin gazed earnestly back at me. I thought, "How wonderful to be so close." I could see every detail of the feathers. I watched the sturdy webbed feet paddle beneath the water. For a long time, I had hoped to see a puffin up close.

Yet this was not quite what I expected. As I looked around at the fake rocks and painted blue sky of the tiny place where it lived, I remembered my first experience with puffins.

It was on a vacation in Maine when I was six years old. My parents took me on a "puffin watch," an Audubon-sponsored boat trip to an island where puffins were being reintroduced. I can still remember leaning over the rail of the boat and looking through my father's binoculars to find the three or four real puffins among the decoys set to attract them. I remember their loud, growling calls and bright orange beaks. It was amazing to see in real life the birds that I had seen only in pictures. That boat trip sparked my interest in studying nature.

Since then, I have looked for activities that put me in touch with nature. The summer before my sophomore year, I took part in a program with other teenagers to help a biologist with her field research. We traveled around the lakes of New Hampshire for two weeks to record the behavior of loons. I was fascinated by the actions of these graceful birds. It was well worth the challenge of paddling across a large lake to watch a family of loons with two newborn chicks.

Writing Skills

Elaboration Answer: *To show how and why the experience was meaningful* **OL**

Looking through the aquarium glass, I realized that I was missing the satisfaction of observing puffins in their own habitat. I felt I got to know the loons better from fifty feet away than I could possibly get to know this puffin in its tiny enclosure. The puffin turned away from looking at me to take a morsel of food that a worker handed it from a plastic bucket. As I walked away from the puffin, I saw tanks of fish. The fish were swimming in endless circles. At that point I knew that I wanted to study animals in their natural habitats.

Tone

Why is tone, or attitude toward something, important in a reflective essay?

Significance

Why should a writer explain the significance of an experience?

Teach

Writing Skills

Tone **Answer:** *To convey the writer's attitude toward the topic* OL

Writing Skills

Significance **Answer:** *To share the meaning of the experience* OL

Writing Process

Elaboration Explain that writing an effective reflective essay requires showing how a particular subject is relevant to your audience by elaborating, or expanding, on your main ideas. Stress the value of making connections between the main subject and related topics to flesh out an essay. OL

English Language Coach

Conversational Tone Developing an ear for tone can be challenging for English language learners. Reading their essays aloud will provide practice in listening and speaking and will build confidence. Meet independently with students who need to work on gaining fluency. EL

Academic Standards

The Additional Support activity on p. 667 covers the following standard:

English Language Coach: **9.7** [Develop] speaking skills…in conjunction with… strategies…[for] delivery of oral presentations.

Teach

Writing Process

Revising Feedback from partners can provide students with a starting point for their revisions. You may want to have peer readers focus particularly on issues of clarity and completeness. **Ask:** Did any sections seem unclear? Are there any points or details you'd like to know more about? Encourage students to refer to the "Writing an Effective Reflective Essay" rubric to help them evaluate their partners' work. OL

Writing Skills

Punctuation Many students will have trouble punctuating quotations. **Write on the board:** I thought, "How wonderful to be so close." Note the placement of the comma after *thought,* which introduces the quotation. Point out that *How* is capitalized, even though it comes after a comma. Stress that in American English, periods and commas always go inside quotation marks. OL

Revising

Traits of Strong Writing

Use these traits of strong writing to express your ideas effectively.

Ideas message or theme and the details that develop it

Organization arrangement of main ideas and supporting details

Voice writer's unique way of using tone and style

Word Choice vocabulary a writer uses to convey meaning

Sentence Fluency rhythm and flow of sentences

Conventions correct spelling, grammar, usage, and mechanics

Presentation the way words and design elements look on a page

For more information on using the Traits of Strong Writing, see pages R32–R33 of the Writing Handbook.

Peer Review Once you complete your draft, exchange papers with a partner. Evaluate each other's narrative and descriptive details. Discuss your tone, or attitude, as shown by your word choice. Is it the tone you want to communicate? You can refer to the traits of strong writing.

Rubric: Writing an Effective Reflective Essay

- ☑ Do you describe an observation about the world or an experience that was meaningful to you?
- ☑ Do you use words that reflect your attitude or feeling?
- ☑ Do you use narrative details to hold your reader's interest?
- ☑ Do you use descriptive details to make your words come alive?
- ☑ Do you put thoughts and spoken comments in quotation marks?
- ☑ Do you leave your readers with a clear idea of the significance of your reflection?

Focus Lesson

Using Precise Adjectives

Your essay will be more memorable if you use descriptive adjectives. Remember that adjectives modify nouns and pronouns by telling what kind, how many, which one, or how much. Phrases and clauses can act as adjectives. Adjectives, adjective phrases, and adjective clauses make your writing more vivid and precise.

Draft:

The puffin turned away from looking at me to take a morsel.

Revision:

The puffin turned away from looking at me to take a morsel of food[1] that a worker handed it[2] from a plastic[3] bucket.

1: Adjective phrase describing morsel

2: Adjective clause telling which morsel of food

3: Adjective telling what kind of bucket

Additional Support

Skills Practice

LISTENING AND SPEAKING: Getting Feedback Writers may want to ask peer reviewers to consider specific questions such as the following:

- Which descriptive details are most powerful?
- What is the main point of the essay?
- Which parts of the essay are the most interesting?

Emphasize that writers need not accept every suggested change. They should use the comments as a basis for making improvements. OL

Editing and Proofreading

Get It Right When you have completed the final draft of your essay, proofread for errors in grammar, usage, mechanics, and spelling. Refer to the Language Handbook, pages R45–R59, as a guide.

Focus Lesson

Correcting Dangling Participles

A participle is the form of a verb used to modify a noun or pronoun—for example, *diving* puffin. A participial phrase is made up of a participle and its objects and modifiers: All puffins *viewed on the tour* were part of an experiment. A participial phrase needs to be connected to the word it modifies. If it has no referent, it is called a dangling participle and the sentence should be revised. Below is an example of a dangling participle from the Workshop Model. Note the two ways to correct this problem.

Problem: Dangling Participle

Looking through the aquarium glass, the satisfaction of observing puffins in their own habitat was missing.

Solution A: To avoid a dangling participle, make sure that the participial phrase and the word it modifies appear next to each other.

Looking through the aquarium glass, I realized that I was missing the satisfaction of observing puffins in their own habitat.

Solution B: Rewrite the sentence.

I realized that I was missing the satisfaction of observing puffins in their own habitat because I was looking at them through the aquarium glass.

Effective Communication

It is easy to misplace a word or phrase when you write. Your reader, however, might misread the sentence and not understand your meaning. That is why it is important to make sure modifiers are near the words they modify. Try reading your paper aloud to a partner. Your partner can tell you if something does not make sense.

Presenting ★

Checking Details Before you submit your essay for others to read, you should check all the details. Make sure you have followed the assignment guidelines for placement of your title and name. Whether you type or handwrite your paper, it should have a neat appearance.

Writer's Portfolio

Place a clean copy of your reflective essay in your portfolio to review later.

Teach

Writing Skills

Correcting Dangling Participles Students sometimes misplace modifiers in their sentences, resulting in unclear or inaccurate statements. Explain that in participles and participial phrases, verbs can act as adjectives: a *diving* puffin, all puffins *viewed on the tour.* Read the example sentences on page 669. Note that the meaning of the problem sentence is less clear than that of the two correct alternatives. **OL**

★ Writer's Technique

Blogs These days, one of the easiest and most popular ways of sharing personal reflections is through a Web log or "blog." Blogs can take the form of journals, editorials, informal essays, or any possible combination of these and other kinds of information. Often blogs focus on writers' major interests, such as movies, music, sports, or politics. **AS**

Reading in the Real World

Career Discuss how strategies for writing a reflective essay can be applied to writing a personal statement for a job application. Begin by developing a list of jobs. Each student should then choose one and write a personal statement that would be appropriate for an application for that position. Direct students to the rubric on page 662, "Features of Reflective Essays." **OL**

Academic Standards

Additional Support activities on pp. 668 and 669 cover the following standards:

Skills Practice: **9.4.11** Edit and proofread one's own writing, as well as that of others, using an editing checklist with specific examples of corrections of frequent errors.

Reading in the Real World: **9.5.5** Write documents related to career development…that present information purposefully and in brief to meet the needs of the intended audience…

Focus

Summary

Students will plan and develop a reflection and will learn techniques for presenting it to an audience.

Teach

Speaking Skills

Addressing an Audience

Some students will find the prospect of addressing an audience daunting. Explain that learning and practicing specific skills, such as preparing note cards and rehearsing their delivery, will build their confidence. Stress the importance of speaking slowly and clearly and of modulating their expression appropriately. Emphasize that these techniques will make it easier for listeners to process the content of their speeches. OL

Speaking, Listening, and Viewing Workshop

Reflective Presentation

Delivering a Reflective Presentation

Connecting to Literature Poet E. E. Cummings also wrote essays and a novel. The novel was based on his experiences in prison in France during World War I. As a young man, he joined an ambulance corps and served in France, but he and a friend were mistakenly held in a detention camp for about three months. After returning home, he wrote his first and only novel, *The Enormous Room,* a witty attack on bureaucracy based on his experiences in prison. The novel was published in 1922.

In this workshop, you will learn to present your reflections on an observation or experience.

Assignment **Plan and present a reflection.**

Planning Your Presentation

When you wrote your reflective essay, you focused on descriptive details and sensory images. You expressed why an experience was meaningful to you, and you communicated with your reader by using a conversational style and everyday language. Keep these strategies in mind as you prepare your reflective presentation.

- You can use your essay as a starting point, or you can choose another experience or observation.
- Discuss your options with a partner and choose one of them for your presentation.
- Write down descriptive details and sensory images to include.
- Write concise notes on cards to use in your presentation. Be sure to include a note about why the experience was meaningful in your life.

gnarled old stump
wind rushing past my face
sound of dogs barking

Additional Support

Skills Practice

SPEAKING, LISTENING, AND VIEWING: Speaking Effectively Remind students that an effective presentation involves more than reciting words. Successful speakers use many of the skills that actors employ, such as eye contact, expression, gestures, and body language. Have students watch a videotape of a famous speech, such as John F. Kennedy's inaugural address, noting the techniques they observe. OL

Developing Your Presentation

As you work on your presentation, choose an organizational model that makes sense for the subject you have chosen. You might order your presentation chronologically, by comparison and contrast, by cause and effect, or by order of importance. Include an introduction to grab your listeners' interest, a body in which you tell what happened, and a conclusion in which you explain the meaning of what happened. Remember that quotations or an anecdote will enliven your presentation.

Communicating with an Audience

While presenting your reflection, connect with your audience. Speak to them, not at them. Make eye contact. Use gestures and facial expressions to communicate meaning. Vary the speed of your delivery to match the events you describe. Use everyday words and a conversational manner to create a friendly tone.

Techniques for Presenting a Reflection

Verbal Techniques	Nonverbal Techniques
☑ **Volume** Speak loudly enough to be heard by everyone in your audience.	☑ **Eye Contact** Look from person to person in your audience, but focus on one individual at a time. Respond to the expressions you see.
☑ **Pace** Pause at appropriate places in your presentation to let your audience reflect on your words.	☑ **Body Language** Gesture with your hands to make important points. Use facial expressions to help communicate joy, sadness, surprise, fear, and other emotions.
☑ **Tone** Match your tone to the content. Some reflections are humorous, but others require a serious tone of voice.	☑ **Visuals** Consider how to display any photographs or other illustrations you plan to use.
☑ **Pronunciation** Speak clearly, pronouncing all words.	☑ **Posture** Stand up tall with your head straight.

Choose Carefully

When you are presenting a reflection to others, you will want to choose a subject you are comfortable talking about and a subject that will be meaningful to others.

Speaking Effectively

Think about comedians and how they respond to their audiences. As a presenter, you will be more effective if you speak directly to your audience rather than reading to them from note cards.

Practice Makes Perfect

It helps to rehearse your presentation beforehand. Meet with two or three others who are also making presentations. Practice your presentations. Ask for comments that will help you improve your delivery.

ACADEMIC STANDARDS (pages 670–671)

9.7.14 Deliver narrative presentations that...describe... sights, sounds, and smells...

9.7.6 Choose effective verbal and nonverbal techniques (including voice, gestures, and eye contact) for presentations.

Differentiated Instruction

Speech Practice To build students' confidence before they give their presentations, encourage them to participate actively in class discussions. Encourage less proficient readers and learning-disabled students to tape-record rehearsals of their presentations. Have students work with partners or in small groups to listen to, analyze, and critique the presentations. **BL**

Teach

Speaking Skills

Voice Remind students of the importance of using their voice effectively when making a presentation. Point out that audiences become bored when they speak in a monotone. Encourage students to do the following:

- Practice changing pitch and tone to communicate emotions.
- Speak loudly enough so that every person in the room can hear clearly.
- Eliminate expressions such as *uh, um, you know,* and *okay.* **OL**

Listening Skills

Assessing a Presentation Encourage active listening by having students assess one another's speeches. Tell them to base their evaluations on the following questions:

- What feelings and ideas did the presentation reflect?
- What descriptive details do you remember?
- Did the presentation explain why the subject was important to the speaker? **OL**

Academic Standards

Additional Support activities on pp. 670 and 671 cover the following standards:

Skills Practice: **9.7.10** Assess how...delivery affect[s] the mood and tone of the oral communication and makes an impact on the audience.

Differentiated Instruction: **9.7** [Develop] speaking skills...in conjunction with... strategies...[for] delivery of oral presentations. **9.7.11** Evaluate the clarity, quality, effectiveness, and general coherence of a speaker's...delivery...

Focus

Summary

Students are encouraged to explore a variety of poems and novels covering a range of themes, including the inspiring beauty of nature, life's lessons, and the value of family.

Teach

Literary History

Favorite Poem Project
Started in 1997 by former poet laureate Robert Pinsky, the Favorite Poem Project is a series of print anthologies and documentaries in which Americans from every walk of life present their favorite poems. In its first year, 18,000 people volunteered. The videos became a popular feature on PBS's *The News Hour with Jim Lehrer* and can be viewed online at www.favoritepoem.org. AS

INDEPENDENT READING

Poetry and Novels

As you have seen in this unit, poems do everything from asking questions of identity to celebrating nature. They can be short, playful, and sassy or long, measured, and serious. They can take you deeper inside yourself or well beyond the world you know. For more poetry on a range of themes, try the first three suggestions below. For novels that address the Big Ideas of *Nature Inspires, Life Lessons,* and *The Strength of Family,* try the titles from the Glencoe Literature Library on the next page.

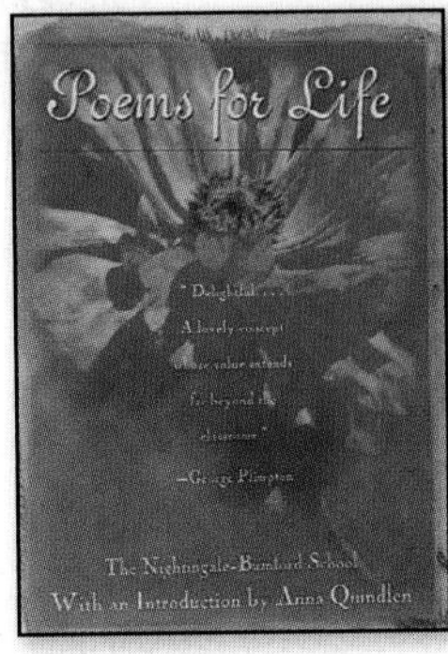

Poems for Life: Famous People Select Their Favorite Poem and Say Why It Inspires Them

compiled by the Grade 5 Classes from the Nightingale-Bamford School

Determined to raise money for a good cause, a group of students in New York City mailed letters to a host of famous people. "We were wondering if you would like to send us a copy of your favorite poem with an explanation of why you chose it," they wrote. Fifty renowned writers, musicians, politicians, actors, and television personalities responded. The result is this fascinating collection.

This Same Sky: A Collection of Poems from Around the World

selected by Naomi Shihab Nye

Nearly every culture has a poetic tradition, and, as this anthology reflects, all over the world, poets adress similar subjects: childhood, family, and the beauty of the natural world. In addition to these topics, some poems in *This Same Sky* treat the nature of poetry. Others explore political topics. As a whole, this collection of 129 poets from sixty-eight countries celebrates both the diversity of their origins and the similarity of their feelings and aspirations.

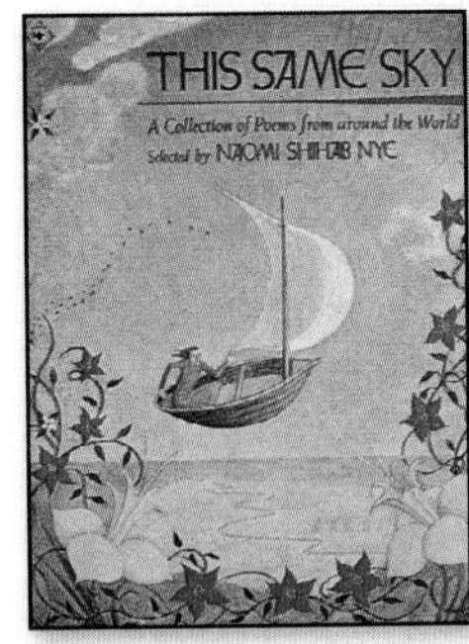

Additional Support

Skills Practice

READING: Understanding Poetic Form Ask students to memorize a short poem and to recite it aloud in class. The two processes will help students understand and internalize the use of rhythm, syntax, and other techniques in poetry while also improving reading fluency. OL

CRITICS' CORNER

"[W]hat Ogden Nash does is take words apart to see what makes them tick, and put them together so that they click. And not necessarily in the condition in which he found them. [Nash] demonstrates that our mother tongue can be made to behave in a manner hardly becoming a mother, but irreproachably amusing. [In his work] the English language is not only flexible; it is double jointed, ambidextrous, telescopic, kaleidoscopic, and slightly demented."

—Lisle Bell, *New York Herald Tribune Books*

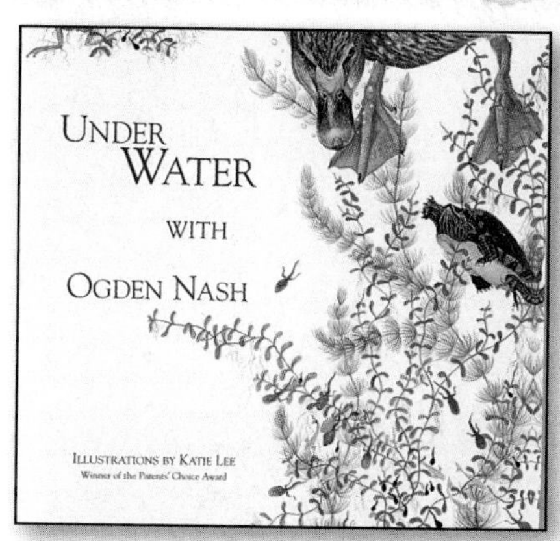

Under Water with Ogden Nash ★

by Ogden Nash

In this collection of twenty-six delightfully humorous poems, Ogden Nash writes about sea creatures such as the turtle, the jellyfish, the squid, and the shark. Each poem is sweetly surprising, slightly laughable, and utterly original. Detailed color drawings by award-winning zoological illustrator Katie Lee are paired with the poems.

From the Glencoe Literature Library

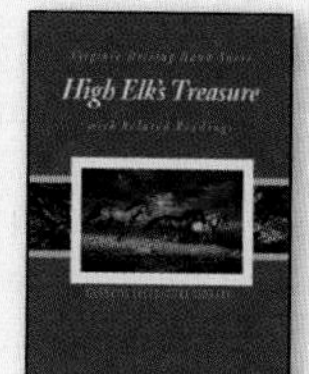

High Elk's Treasure

by Virginia Driving Hawk Sneve

Nature inspires Joe as his love of horses leads him to a new understanding of the Lakota people.

The Chosen

by Chaim Potok

Two young Jewish men form an enduring friendship as they learn lessons for life.

The Glory Field

by Walter Dean Myers

Over 241 years, a family's strength is tested as they journey away from and back to a small plot of land.

Teach

★ Literary History

Ogden Nash Nash (1902–1971) was brought up in Savannah, Georgia, and several other eastern cities. He began his career as a book editor and children's author before going on to become one of the twentieth century's masters of light verse. Known for their whimsy and clever word play, his poems achieved great popular success. AS

Glencoe Literature Library

Glencoe Literature Library offers an extensive collection of hardcover books that help you encourage your students to read independently. Choose among the more than 120 full-length literary works—novels, novellas, plays, and nonfiction. Each book includes related readings from a broad range of genres. Go to www.Glencoe.com for more information.

English Language Coach

Understanding Idioms Students who have trouble interpreting idiomatic language are likely to miss out on the distinctive flavor of a text. Explain that "taking language apart" involves looking under the surface of the words for their unspoken meanings and associations.

Then, ask students to "dissect" the following idioms:

- what makes them tick
- mother tongue
- in a manner hardly becoming a mother EL

Academic Standards

Additional Support activities on pp. 672 and 673 cover the following standards:

Skills Practice: **9.7** [Develop] speaking skills…in conjunction with…strategies…[for] delivery of oral presentations.

English Language Coach: **9.1** [Use] relationships…and a growing knowledge of English…to determine the meaning of words…

Focus

BELLRINGER

Say: Test-taking strategies can be helpful on standardized tests, such as the SAT, or on subject-matter tests administered by your teachers. Learning test-taking strategies and applying them to any test that you encounter will help you be a more successful test taker. Have students discuss tests they have taken recently and the different test-taking strategies they have used to improve their scores.

Test Preparation and Practice

English Language Arts

Indiana Test Practice

READING: Vocabulary, Comprehension, and Analysis

Read the following passages. Then, on a separate sheet of paper, answer the questions on page 676.

"Possum Crossing" by Nikki Giovanni

Backing out the driveway
the car lights cast an eerie[1] glow
in the morning fog centering
on movement in the rain slick street

Hitting brakes I anticipate a squirrel or a cat or sometimes
a little raccoon
I once braked for a blind little mole[2] who try though he did
could not escape the cat toying with his life
Mother-to-be possum occasionally lopes[3] home . . . being
naturally . . . slow her condition makes her even more ginger[4]

We need a sign POSSUM CROSSING to warn coffee-gurgling neighbors:
we share the streets with more than trucks and vans and
railroad crossings

All birds being the living kin of dinosaurs
think themselves invincible and pay no heed
to the rolling wheels while they dine
on an unlucky rabbit

I hit brakes for the flutter of the lights hoping it's not a deer
or a skunk or a groundhog
coffee splashes over the cup which I quickly put away from me
and into the empty passenger seat
I look . . .
relieved and exasperated . . .
to discover I have just missed a big wet leaf
struggling . . . to lift itself into the wind
and live

---

[1]**eerie:** strange
[2]**mole:** a small mammal
[3]**lope:** to move in long, easy steps
[4]**ginger:** cautious

Reading

Visualizing As students read the selections, encourage them to form mental pictures of the scenes, animals, and events described by Giovanni and Twain. Tell them to focus on the details and descriptions the authors give them.

Ask: According to the text and your imagination, what is the setting like? What do the animals look like? What do they do? If students can visualize what they read, selections will be more interesting, and the imagery in the poems will become clearer. **OL**

from "The Laborious Ant" by Mark Twain

Now and then, while we rested, we watched the laborious[1] ant at his work. I found nothing new in him—certainly nothing to change my opinion of him. It seems to me that in the matter of intellect the ant must be a strangely overrated bird. During many summers, now, I have watched him, when I ought to have been in better business, and I have not yet come across a living ant that seemed to have any more sense than a dead one. I refer to the ordinary ant, of course; I have had no experience of those wonderful Swiss and African ones which vote, keep drilled armies, and dispute about religion. Those particular ants may be all that the naturalist paints them, but I am persuaded that the average ant is a sham. I admit his industry, of course; he is the hardest working creature in the world—when anybody is looking—but his leather-headedness is the point I make against him. He goes out foraging,[2] he makes a capture, and then what does he do? Go home? No—he goes anywhere but home. He doesn't know where home is. His home may be only three feet away—no matter, he can't find it. He makes his capture, as I have said; it is generally something which can be of no sort of use to himself or anybody else; it is usually seven times bigger than it ought to be; he hunts out the awkwardest place to take hold of it; he lifts it bodily up in the air by main force, and starts: not toward home, but in the opposite direction; not calmly and wisely, but with a frantic haste which is wasteful of his strength; he fetches up against a pebble, and instead of going around it, he climbs over it backwards, dragging his booty[3] after him, tumbles down on the other side, jumps up in a passion, kicks the dust off his clothes, moistens his hands, grabs his property viciously, yanks it this way then that, shoves it ahead of him a moment, turns tail and lugs it after him another moment, gets madder and madder, then presently hoists it into the air and goes tearing away in an entirely new direction; comes to a weed; it never occurs to him to go around it; no, he must climb it; and he does climb it, dragging his worthless property to the top—which is as bright a thing to do as it would be for me to carry a sack of flour from Heidelberg to Paris by way of Strasburg steeple;[4] when he gets up there he finds that that is not the place; takes a cursory[5] glance at the scenery and either climbs down again or tumbles down, and starts off once more—as usual, in a new direction. At the end of half an hour, he fetches up within six inches of the place he started from and lays his burden down; meantime he has been over all the ground for two yards around, and climbed all the weeds and pebbles he came across.

[1]**laborious:** industrious; hardworking
[2]**foraging:** hunting for food
[3]**booty:** prize; loot
[4]**Strasburg steeple:** the pointed top of the church tower at Strasbourg (France) cathedral, which was one of the world's tallest buildings during Twain's time
[5]**cursory:** hasty

Test Preparation and Practice

English Language Arts

Teach

Assessment Explain to students that this Test Preparation and Practice lesson is designed to develop test-taking strategies as well as to test their mastery of the skills covered in this unit. The lesson is modeled on tests they will be required to pass to be eligible to receive a high school diploma. Students will read one or two grade-level-appropriate selections and answer vocabulary, comprehension, and literary analysis questions, including multiple-choice, constructed-response, and extended-response items. In other sections, students' ability to use Standard English in their writing is assessed, and they are given an extended-writing prompt. **OL**

Assess

1. **B** is the correct answer. The other options do not convey sensory experiences.
2. Rubric:
   2 points versions of two exemplars
   1 point version of one exemplar
   0 points other
   Exemplars:
   - The speaker backs the car carefully out of the driveway to avoid hitting animals.
   - The speaker brakes for animals.
   - The speaker thinks there should be signs to warn drivers of possums crossing the street.
3. **C** is the correct answer. Twain disparages ants.
4. **C** is the correct answer.
5. **C** is the correct answer. Twain is making fun of scholars who ascribe human characteristics to creatures such as ants.
6. **B** is the correct answer. Twain does not state the need to protect nature, as Giovanni does.
7. Refer to the Reading Comprehension, Writing Applications, and Language Conventions rubrics provided by the State of Indiana Department of Education.

Numbers 1 and 2 are based on "Possum Crossing."

1 Sensory details are used to help readers experience what is being described. Which line from the poem is the BEST example of a sensory detail?

A Backing out the driveway
B the car lights cast an eerie glow
C All birds being the living kin of dinosaurs
D think themselves invincible and pay no heed

2 Give TWO examples from the poem that demonstrate the speaker's concern for living things.

Numbers 3 through 5 are based on "The Laborious Ant."

3 What is the overall tone of this passage?

A sad
B comic
C sarcastic
D respectful

4 Read this sentence from the selection.

> **I have had no experience of those wonderful Swiss and African [ants] which vote, keep drilled armies, and dispute about religion.**

What does *drilled* mean as it is used in this sentence?

A beaten
B thrown
C trained
D burrowed

5 Which statement BEST summarizes the main idea of this selection?

A Ants are the most fascinating of all creatures.
B Life is a constant struggle between humankind and nature.
C Ant behavior can seem ridiculous when judged by human standards.
D People are really no more important than small creatures, such as ants.

Number 6 and 7 are based on both selections.

6 According to the selections, what belief about nature do Giovanni and Twain MOST LIKELY share?

A Nature should be tamed.
B Nature is worth observing.
C Nature needs to be protected.
D Nature is violent and unforgiving.

7 Both of these selections deal with the theme of humankind's fascination with the natural world. The authors seem to suggest that studying the natural world can offer insights into human nature. **Write an essay in which you explain why you agree or disagree with this idea. Try to present your readers with a persuasive argument. Be sure to include at least TWO specific details or examples from the passages to support your position.**

Use a separate sheet of paper to plan your writing.

Writing Checklist

The following checklist will help you write your essay. Be sure to

- ❑ brainstorm for ideas and develop a plan before you start writing
- ❑ organize your writing with an introduction, a body, and a conclusion
- ❑ pay attention to your word choice and voice
- ❑ edit for sentence fluency and conventions
- ❑ have a neat and organized presentation

Student essays should include the following:

- a clearly stated and defended position supported by relevant evidence from the passage
- effective voice, word choice, and sentence variety
- effective presentation, with attention to grammar and spelling conventions

WRITING: Writing Process

The following passage is from the first draft of a student's essay. Read the passage and use it to answer numbers 8–11 on a separate sheet of paper.

> [1]I often think how much easier life might be if I were my dog. [2]My dog has very few cares in life. [3]A full bowl of food, an open dog door, and to nap in a warm place are all it takes to make her happy. [4]Life must be much simpler if that was all we needed. [5]Hurrying from one <u>thing we have to do</u> to another, we often miss out on the little things.

8 Choose the BEST way to combine Sentences 1 and 2.

A I often think how much easier life might be if I were my dog because my dog has very few cares in life.
B I often think how much easier life might be if I were my dog, who has very few cares in life.
C I often think how much easier life might be if I had very few cares in life, as does my dog.
D I often think how much easier life might be if my dog, who has very few cares in life, and I were alike.

9 Choose the BEST way to revise Sentence 3.

A A full bowl of food, a dog door that is open, and napping in a warm place are all it takes to make her happy.
B A full bowl of food, an open dog door, and a warm place to nap are all it takes to make her happy.
C Eating a full bowl of food, an open dog door, and a warm place to nap are all it takes to make her happy.
D All it takes to make her happy are to eat a full bowl of food, to have an open dog door, and a warm place to nap.

10 Choose the BEST way to revise Sentence 4.

A Life would be much simpler, if that was all we needed.
B Life is much simpler, if that is all we need.
C Life could be much simpler if that was all we needed.
D Life would be much simpler if that were all we needed.

11 The writer wants to replace the underlined phrase in Sentence 5 with a more formal expression. Which of these is the BEST replacement?

A burden
B obligation
C alternative
D arrangement

Literature Online Unit Assessment To prepare for the Unit test, go to www.glencoe.com.

Test Preparation and Practice

English Language Arts

8. **B** is the correct answer. The other options contain awkward wording.
9. **B** is the correct answer. The three items in the compound subject should be in parallel form.
10. **D** is the correct answer. The subjunctive mood of the verb is needed when a supposition or a hypothetical case is expressed.
11. **B** is the correct answer. *Obligation* means "that by which one is bound, as a promise or duty or responsibility."

Unit Assessment Have students access the Web site to prepare for the Unit Three test.

Assess

12. C is the correct answer. No comma is needed when an adverb clause follows a main clause.

13. D is the correct answer. All nouns should be capitalized in titles.

14. A is the correct answer. Use a semicolon to separate two main clauses.

15. D is the correct answer. The singular antecedent "each owner" should be followed by a singular pronoun.

16. B is the correct answer. All verbs in the compound subject should be in parallel form.

17. C is the correct answer.

18. B is the correct answer. The quotation marks are misplaced or missing in the other options.

WRITING: English Language Conventions

Answer numbers 12–18 on a separate sheet of paper.

12 Choose the sentence that is punctuated correctly.

A Wouldn't it be nice, if everyone was so happy to see you.
B Wouldn't it be nice if everyone was so happy to see you.
C Wouldn't it be nice if everyone was so happy to see you?
D Wouldn't it be nice, if everyone was so happy to see you?

13 What additional word in the sentence should be capitalized?

A good title for an essay about saving animals might be "The importance of Pet Rescue."

A title
B essay
C animals
D importance

14 Decide which punctuation mark is needed in the sentence.

Dogs have no pressures of work and paying bills in that case, we might all be able to give unconditional love.

A ;
B :
C . . .
D ,

15 What type of an error has the writer of this sentence made?

Before purchasing a dog from a breeder or shelter, each owner should decide which breed best suits their personality.

A spelling
B capitalization
C run-on sentence construction
D pronoun-antecedent agreement

16 Read this sentence.

Choosing the appropriate dog breed for your family, finding dog breeders who are reliable, and locate shelters with puppies for sale all take considerable time and effort.

Choose the word or group of words that BEST replaces the underlined part of the sentence.

A located
B locating
C in locating
D to locate

17 Choose the word that is spelled correctly.

After working at the busy animal shelter, Ana felt that everything at home was _____ and lacking in excitement.

A dreery
B drerry
C dreary
D drearie

18 Read this sentence.

I see her Jon called to Eli when he spotted the lost dog at the far end of the park.

Choose the correct way to punctuate the underlined part of the sentence.

A I see her, Jon called to Eli,
B "I see her," Jon called to Eli,
C "I see her, Jon," called to Eli
D "I see her, Jon called to Eli,"

Writing

Using Semicolons Remind students that the semicolon has these main uses:

- to separate main clauses that are not joined by a coordinating conjunction *(and, but, or, nor, yet, for)*
- to separate main clauses joined by a conjunctive adverb (such as *however, therefore, nevertheless*) or by an expression such as *for example* or *that is*
- to separate the items in a series when the items contain commas **OL**

WRITING: Writing Applications

Complete the writing activity below. Do your planning and writing on separate sheets of paper.

Help Save the Environment

Read the writing prompt below and complete the writing activity.

> Your class has come up with the following ideas for activities to help preserve the environment:
>
> - Pick up litter in an empty lot near the school.
> - Start a program at your school for recycling paper.
> - Eliminate the use of pesticides or other harmful chemicals on school grounds.
> - Hold a bake sale to raise money to help save the world's rainforests.
>
> Choose one of these ideas and write an essay to persuade your classmates that your choice is the activity the class should do first. In your persuasive essay, be sure to include convincing reasons that will persuade readers that your choice is the best one.

Be sure to include

- a statement of your opinion on the subject
- an explanation of why you think as you do
- detailed examples to support your argument
- an introduction, a body, and a conclusion to your essay

Use a separate sheet of paper to plan your writing. As you write, keep in mind that your essay will be evaluated for **ideas and content, organization, style, voice,** and **language conventions.**

Writing Checklist

Before you begin writing, be sure to

- ❑ brainstorm for ideas
- ❑ organize your ideas into a logical pattern
- ❑ develop a plan for an introduction, a body, and a conclusion

As you write your essay, be sure to

- ❑ describe the issue and clearly state your opinion
- ❑ provide reasons for your opinion
- ❑ discuss alternative opinions and show why you disagree with them
- ❑ end with a conclusion that restates your opinion

Assess

Assessment of writing prompts should focus on four elements:

- **Ideas and Content,** the message or theme and the details that develop it
- **Organization,** the arrangement of main ideas and supporting details
- **Style,** the word choices that a writer uses to convey meaning and the fluency, or rhythm and flow, of sentences
- **Voice,** the writer's unique way of using tone and style

Students' writing should also be assessed for correct **capitalization, punctuation, spelling, grammar and usage, paragraphing,** and **sentence structure.**

In addition, student essays should:

- fully complete the assigned task
- include complete, thorough, relevant, and logically organized ideas
- exhibit correct word usage
- demonstrate exceptional writing technique
- use language and tone appropriate for the task and audience

Unit at a Glance

Drama

About the Unit

Unit Four includes several plays, or stories told through actions. The unique elements of the theater are called into question, and students will investigate how elements like dialogue, stage directions, acts, and scenes serve their purposes in everything from tragedies to comedies.

Unit Introduction
Building Background
2–3 days

Part 1: The Power of Love
8–12 days

Part 1 includes William Shakespeare's "Romeo and Juliet," which illustrates the intense passion of two young lovers. A chart showing the core skills taught in this Part appears on pages 689A–689B.

SELECTIONS AND FEATURES

Part 2: Awkward Encounters
8–10 days

Part 2 is about awkward encounters in drama. The characters in these plays face difficult situations that propel each story. Elements of drama, comedy, and irony are closely examined in this section. A chart showing the core skills taught in this Part appears on pages 819A–819B.

SELECTIONS AND FEATURES

End-of-Unit Features
5–6 Days

Unit Resources

Glencoe Literature: The Reader's Choice offers a comprehensive package of tools to optimize student learning and the teaching experience. Each resource has been designed to assist students in specific areas and to offer instructional support for teachers. While all of these areas are covered in the core textbook, some students may need extra practice or additional help in specific areas. The resource package is designed so that you, the teacher, can choose which items will best assist your students. You may also use these resources as homework assignments and for assessment purposes. The following are resources recommended for use with Unit Four.

Key for Unit Resource

- Blackline Master
- Workbook
- Supplemental Text
- CD-ROM
- DVD
- Transparency
- Web-based

Essential Instructional Support

FAST FILE UNIT 4 RESOURCES

Reading and Literature

- Unit Introduction, pp. 1–2
- The Big Idea Foldable, pp. 3–4
- The Big Idea School-Home Connection, p. 5
- The Big Idea School-Home Connection (Spanish), p. 6
- Challenge Planner, pp. 7–10
- Academic Vocabulary Development, pp. 11–12
- Literary History, pp. 16–17
- Comparing Literature Graphic Organizers, pp. 35, 42
- Literary Element, pp. 18, 21, 24, 27, 30, 39, 43, 46, 49, 53, 56, 59
- Reading Strategy, pp. 19, 22, 25, 28, 31, 33, 40, 44, 47, 50, 52, 54, 57, 60
- Active Reading Graphic Organizers, pp. 66–75
- Selection Vocabulary Practice, pp. 20, 23, 26, 29, 32, 41, 45, 48, 51, 55, 58, 61
- Literary Focus, pp. 14, 37

Writing, Grammar, and Spelling

- Spelling Practice, p. 62
- Grammar Workshop, p. 34
- Writing Workshop Graphic Organizer, p. 63

Speaking, Listening, and Viewing

- Speaking, Listening, and Viewing Activities, pp. 64–65

English Language Learners

- English Language Coach Review, pp. 15, 38

DIFFERENTIATED INSTRUCTION

- Active Learning and Note Taking Guide, pp. 113–147
- Leveled Vocabulary Development, pp. 50–61
- Skill Level Up!™ A Language Arts Game
- Listening Library Audio CD, disc 2, tracks 1–19
- Glencoe BookLink 3
- Vocabulary PuzzleMaker
- Literature Library Vocabulary PuzzleMaker

ASSESSMENT

- Selection and Unit Assessments, pp. 133–162, 217–218
- Selection Quick Checks, pp. 67–81
- Selection Quick Checks (Spanish), pp. 67–81
- Assessment by Learning Objectives, pp. 41–47
- Rubrics for Assessing Student Writing, Listening, and Speaking, pp. 12–13, 32–33
- Standardized Test Preparation and Practice
- Glencoe Online Essay Grader
- Interactive Tutor: Self-Assessment
- Exam*View*® Assessment Suite
- Literature Library Exam*View*® Assessment

Additional Instructional Support

LITERATURE AND READING

- Active Learning and Note Taking Guide, pp. 113–147
- *inTIME* Magazines
- Glencoe Literature Library
- Literature Launchers: Pre-Reading Videos
- Literature Classics

WRITING, GRAMMAR, AND SPELLING

- REAL Success in Writing: Research and Reports
- Writing Constructed Responses
- Spelling Power eWorkbook
- Revising with Style eWorkbook
- Sentence Diagraming eWorkbook
- Glencoe Grammar and Composition Handbook
- Grammar and Language Workbook
- Grammar & Language eWorkbook

PROFESSIONAL DEVELOPMENT

- Professional Development Package

TRANSPARENCIES

- Read Aloud, Think Aloud Transparencies 29–43
- Bellringer Options Transparencies
  - Selection Focus Transparencies 43
  - Daily Language Practice Transparencies 70–80
- Grammar and Language Transparencies 21
- Writing Workshop Transparencies 21–25
- Visual Literacy/Fine Art Transparencies

ENGLISH LANGUAGE LEARNER

- English Language Coach
- *inTIME* Magazines (Spanish)
- Spanish Listening Library

TECHNOLOGY

- TeacherWorks Plus™
- StudentWorks Plus™
- Literature Launchers: Pre-Reading Videos
- Vocabulary PuzzleMaker
- Literature Library Vocabulary PuzzleMaker
- Skill Level Up!™ A Language Arts Game
- glencoe.com
- Presentation Plus!™
- Exam*View*® Assessment Suite
- Literature Library Exam*View*® Assessment Suite
- Listening Library Audio CD, disc 2, tracks 1–19
- Interactive Tutor: Self-Assessment
- Glencoe BookLink 3
- Online Student Edition, mhln.com
- Glencoe Online Essay Grader
- Grammar and Language eWorkbook
- Revising with Style eWorkbook
- Sentence Diagraming eWorkbook
- Spelling Power eWorkbook
- Literature Classics
- Spanish Listening Library

Additional Glencoe Resources

Dinah Zike's Foldables™

Foldables™ are three-dimensional, interactive graphic organizers that help students practice basic writing skills, review key vocabulary terms, and answer Big Ideas. Every unit contains a Foldable™ activity. You can find the pattern and directions for the Unit 4 Foldable™ in the Unit 4 Resources Fast File booklet. You can use the Foldables™ as they are presented or modify them to suit the needs of your students.

For a wealth of online resources that support the instruction in Unit 4, students and teachers can visit our Web site at glencoe.com. Students will find additional learning, practice, and assessment opportunities such as these, which are noted in the student text:

- Author Search
- Big Idea Overview and Activity
- Interactive Literary Elements Handbook
- Study Central
- Unit Assessment
- Web Activities
- Writing Models

Teachers will find planning and instructional tools that include the following:

- Book Lesson Plans
- Web Activity Lesson Plans
- Teacher Forum
- Professional Resources

Go to glencoe.com to see the entire selection of *Glencoe Literature* online resources.

Glencoe's Presentation Plus!™, a multimedia teaching tool, lets you present dynamic lessons that will engage your students. Using Microsoft PowerPoint®, you can customize the presentations to create your own personalized lessons. Use CheckPoint questions with interactive response keypads to get immediate student feedback during lessons, to increase student participation, and to assess student comprehension.

Glencoe Literature Library

The collection of hardcover books includes full-length novels, novellas, plays, and works of nonfiction. Each volume consists of at least one complete extended-length reading accompanied by several related readings from a broad range of genres. A separate Study Guide for each *Glencoe Literature Library* book provides teaching notes and reproducible activity pages for students. Glencoe Literature Library titles that complement this unit include:

- ***Missing May with Related Readings*** by Cynthia Rylant
- ***Heart of Darkness with Related Readings*** by Joseph Conrad

GLENCOE BOOKLINK

Use the Glencoe **BookLink 3** CD-ROM, a database of more than 26,700 titles, to *create customized reading lists* for your students.

- Search for award-winning titles (e.g., Newbery Award winners, Coretta Scott King Award winners, and Caldecott Medal winners) and for books on several state recommended reading lists.
- Find Degrees of Reading Power™ (DRP) and Lexile™ readability scores for all selections.
- Organize reading lists by students' reading level, author, genre, theme, or area of interest.
- Get a brief summary of each selection.

You can find recommended leveled readings for this unit with Independent Reading (see pages 936 and 937).

Online Essay Grader

Use Glencoe's online essay grader powered by SkillWriter™ to score your students' writing and to provide individualized feedback to each student automatically.

You and your students can visit glencoe.com to link to the essay grader. *Students* can enter their essays and receive feedback on demand. *You* can manage demographic data, assign tests, and generate individual student and aggregated reports. The essay grader can help you

- Save time with automatic scoring and individualized feedback.
- Supplement in-class writing instruction using guided writing practice.

REAL Success: Reading Excellence at All Levels

Glencoe REAL Success is a suite of new reading and language arts products designed to foster reading excellence at all levels.

Look for TWE point-of-use references for these specific products that will help your students succeed in reading this Unit.

- *Jamestown Literature: An Adapted Reader*
- REAL Success in Writing: Research and Reports
- Skill Level Up!™ A Language Arts Game
- CheckPoint PowerPoint™ slides
- Literature/Reading support at Glencoe Web site

Literature Launchers

Set the scene with Glencoe's Literature Launchers, engaging pre-reading video segments that introduce each unit. Each Unit Launcher brings the literature to life, featuring expert testimony and archival stills and footage from the time.

Insert your Glencoe Literature Launchers into your DVD player. Select the Unit 4 Launcher from the menu to introduce Drama.

A lively collection of articles drawn from issues of the TIME family of magazines helps students develop the skills they need to interact with informational text in a meaningful way. Each of the news stories, feature articles, reviews, profiles, and essays in the magazine connects to an author, work, or theme in *Glencoe Literature: The Reader's Choice.* See the *inTIME* Teacher's Guide for specific connections to each unit and for reproducible student worksheets designed to develop students' reading and critical thinking skills.

Teacher Wraparound Edition Key

Level Appropriate Code

AL = Activities for students working above grade level

OL = Activities for students working at grade level

BL = Activities for students working below grade level

EL = Activities for English language learners

AS = Information for all students

Teacher Wraparound Prompts

R Reading Skill These activities help you teach reading skills and vocabulary.

V Vocabulary These activities help students comprehend words and incorporate them into reading.

BI Big Idea These activities and questions prompt students to explore the Big Idea.

L Literary Element These activities and questions help students comprehend selections and learn more about each genre.

★ Enrichment Additional activities and information involving art appreciation and history.

Professional Development Center

From Your Authors:

Beverly Chin and Jeffrey D. Wilhelm

Teaching Literary Analysis: Drama

Build Background Quickwrites are commonly used in the English classroom to focus students on the topic and to activate their thinking about the subject being studied. Carefully crafted quickwrites provide students an opportunity to think as they write. Crafting a number of quickwrites during the unit on drama will help students focus on the plays, the characters in the plays, and how the study of these pieces of literature relates to their own lives. As students read *Romeo and Juliet* by William Shakespeare, have students complete a quickwrite before each act using the following topics:

- Act 1: Quickwrite should describe thoughts and feelings about the power of love
- Act 2: Quickwrite should describe different attitudes people have towards love
- Act 3: Quickwrite should describe how love is affected by society's expectations
- Act 4: Quickwrite should describe if love can sometimes rob people of good judgment
- Act 5: Quickwrite should describe if people can love too much and the possible consequences of doing so

Make Media Connections Ask students to compare a book they have read with its movie version. Which did they like better? Were there things from the book that were difficult to portray in the movie? Were there opportunities in the movie to provide visual information that was not emphasized in the book? While reading *Romeo and Juliet,* ask students to think about how they would "produce" the play. They may want to pause periodically to discuss "production values" and how they think that the drama might best be presented on the stage or in film. Then show students one or two film versions of the play. Ask students to compare and contrast the film(s) to the drama and describe why they preferred one media form to the other.

Susan Rech
Jefferson High School
Tampa, Florida

Teacher to Teacher

I like my students to understand that drama is more than a literary piece; it is a presentation that requires teamwork. I ask students to form groups of six to seven people. First, they form a circle with every other student facing outward. Then I physically manipulate their hands so they are intertwined—in essence, forming a human knot. I then tell the students to turn their knot back into a unified circle without letting go of one another's hands. This activity forces them into a cooperative effort, and they learn about one another while they are getting untangled.

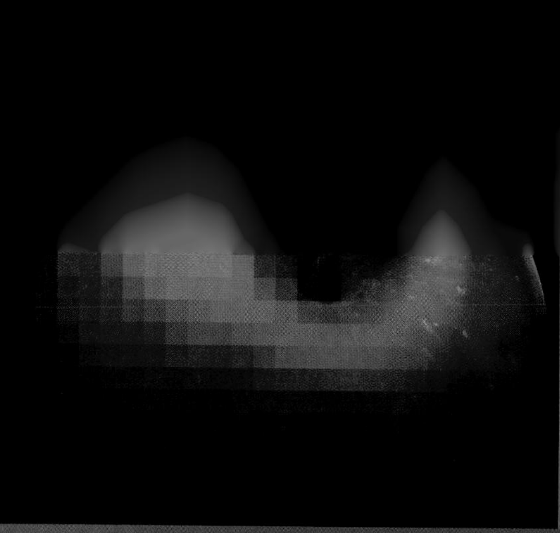

Making Literature Come Alive

Before you begin this unit or sometime during the unit, talk with other teachers about ways they have taught drama. Have a lunch-time discussion group or an after-school hour for professional development and discuss the following questions and answers from our authors:

How can I help students imagine a staged performance of a play as they read?

- Show students script notes from a TV show or movie to help them understand how the director constructs the scenes using dialogue and movement.
- Focus on visualization skills. Discuss with students the ways in which visualization helps the reader to understand the movement in a scene or the energy of an interaction between characters.
- Remember that we learn by doing. Periodically, as students read the plays in this section, they should be encouraged to perform. Divide the class into drama groups and have them perform scenes from *Romeo and Juliet* or one act plays like *The Bear* by Anton Chekhov.

What are some effective strategies that help all students appreciate the language of Shakespearean dramas?

- Discuss the history of the language and how language has evolved over time.
- Discuss the ways that Shakespeare uses language that often has multiple meanings for its ironic or humorous effect.
- Acknowledge that the language is difficult, but reading and understanding the rich language that Shakespeare employs is worth the effort.

How can I make literature about the social and cultural life of Elizabethan England accessible to students?

- Provide students with visual images and artwork from this time period. Discuss the images and ask students to consider the daily life of the people who lived at this time.
- Visit the library to research the daily life of people during the Elizabethan period. Ask students to compare these experiences with the experiences of people in other periods.
- Ask students to describe Europe today. For those who have visited Europe, what did they see there that reminded them of the Elizabethan period?

How can students better understand why many plays are organized into acts and scenes?

- Discuss the placement of commercials in TV shows and the role of chapters in books. Ask students to think about how different kinds of writers decide where to pause the story line. Ask students how this is similar to or different from the organization of plays by acts and scenes.
- Invite students to create a storyboard for a play that they would like to write. What are the major scenes they would have? How would these scenes combine to form acts? How would the acts combine to create a cohesive whole?

Focus

BELLRINGER

Bellringer Options
Literature Launcher Video
Daily Language Practice Transparency 70
Or **ask:** What was the first role you played? Prompt students to remember plays they did in kindergarten or skits they did as children with their friends.
Ask: If you could play any character, who would it be? Why?

Objectives for the Unit Introduction

- To understand characteristics of different types of drama (SE)
- To identify and explore literary elements significant to drama (SE)
- To analyze the effect that literary elements in drama have upon the reader (SE)

Comedia dell'Arte, 1991. Andre Rouillard. Acrylic on canvas, 73 x 100 cm. Private Collection.

680

Unit Introduction Skills

Looking Ahead

Literary Elements
- Drama (SE pp. 682–683)
- Literary Analysis (SE pp. 684–685)
- Comedy (TWE p. 684)

Listening/Speaking/Viewing Skills
- Play Discussion (SE p. 688)
- Irony Chart (SE p. 688)
- Staged Reading (TWE p. 682)

Writing Skills/Grammar
- Dialogue (SE p. 688)
- Critical Review (TWE p. 688)

Reading Skills
- Reading Drama (SE pp. 686–687, TWE p. 686)
- Guide to Reading Drama (SE p. 688)

UNIT FOUR

Drama

Looking Ahead

What do horror movies, soap operas, sitcoms, and *Romeo and Juliet* have in common? They are all examples of drama—stories told mainly through dialogue and the actions of the characters. Drama differs from other genres in that it is written to be performed by actors in front of an audience. Although it shares some literary elements with other genres, it also has its own unique elements, including comedy, tragedy, and dramatic conventions such as stage directions, acts, and scenes.

PREVIEW **Big Ideas and Literary Focus**

	BIG IDEA:	LITERARY FOCUS:
1	The Power of Love	Tragedy
2	Awkward Encounters	Comedy and Modern Drama

INDIANA ACADEMIC STANDARDS (pages 680–687)

9.3.1 Explain the relationship between the purposes and the characteristics of different forms of dramatic literature (including comedy, tragedy, and dramatic monologue).

9.3.10 Identify and describe the function of dialogue, soliloquies, asides, character foils, and stage designs in dramatic literature.

Focus

Summary

The unit discusses acts and scenes, dialogue, stage directions, tragedy, chorus, comedy, and irony in drama. It includes quotes from writers on reading drama as well as a literary analysis of *The Importance of Being Earnest*.

Viewing the Art

Commedia dell'arte originated in Renaissance Italy, where roving bands of actors improvised performances for the public. The costumed figures in Rouillard's painting suggest the stereotyped roles that characterized this form of drama.

Ask: What emotions are expressed in this painting? *(Sadness, rapture, excitement, longing)*

Ask: What do you think the figures represent? *(Roles such as the clown, the damsel, and the melancholy youth)*

Ask: What do you think each plane of space (the two "walls" and the floor) represents? *(The horizontal plane may be the stage, the right vertical plane may be a curtain, and the left may be the "window on the world" that drama represents.)* AS

Unit Resources

Classroom Management
- TeacherWorks Plus™ CD-ROM
- StudentWorks Plus™ CD-ROM
- Literature Launchers™: Pre-Reading Videos DVD, Unit Four

Core Instructional Support
- Unit 4 Resources (Fast File)
- Literature Online, glencoe.com
- Presentation Plus!™ CD-ROM, Unit Four

Transparencies
- Literary Elements Transparencies 1, 8, 9, 13, 18, 67, 75–81, 90
- Bellringer Options Transparencies: Selection Focus Transparency 43 Daily Language Practice Transparencies 70–80

Differentiated Instruction
- Active Learning and Note Taking Guide, pp. 113–147
- Skill Level Up!™ A Language Arts Game

Assessment
- Selection and Unit Assessments, pp. 133–162, 217–218
- Exam*View*® Assessment Suite CD-ROM
- Assessment by Learning Objectives, pp. 41–47

Supplemental Reading
- Glencoe Literature Library
- Glencoe BookLink 3 CD-ROM
- *inTIME* Magazines

Teach

L1 Literary Element

Dialogue Have students experiment with dialogue. **Ask:** What do you notice about the Chekhov dialogue? *(Students should note the simple language, the emphasis on particular words, and the alternating questions and exclamations.)* Have students read the dialogue aloud, using the punctuation as a guide. **Ask:** Do you think Popóva is telling the truth? Have students read the dialogue once as if she is, and once as if she isn't, and then discuss the readings. OL

★ Cultural History

Greek Drama Greek drama evolved out of the choral odes in religious festivals. Early Greek plots and characters were drawn from the Greek myths. Unlike modern theater, Greek drama was a core public activity, not a business enterprise. AS

Genre Focus: Drama

How does drama differ from other genres of literature?

As you have learned, prose, such as short stories and essays, is structured in paragraphs. Longer works of prose are often divided into chapters. Similarly, poems are structured by line and stanza. In plays, **acts** and **scenes** are the major divisions.

Most plays have two or more acts, but short plays often have only one act. Acts are often further divided into scenes. Scene changes often signal a new setting.

Acts and Scene

Dialogue

The conversation between characters, called **dialogue,** provides the substance of a play. Among other things, dialogue can further the plot, provide clues about character or theme, and heighten the overall dramatic effect.

POPÓVA. What can I do? I don't *have* the money!
SMÍRNOFF. That means you won't pay me?
POPÓVA. It means I *can't* pay you!
SMÍRNOFF. I see. Is that your final word?
POPÓVA. That is my final word.

—Anton Chekhov, **from *The Bear*** L1

Stage Directions

The written instructions that explain how to perform a play, including how the characters should look, speak, move, and behave, are called **stage directions.** Stage directions can also specify details of the setting and scenery.

FORTESCUE. [*Offering chocolates out of enormous satin-lined candy box, requiring both hands to handle. Ladies choose, cooing.*] Desmond? The liquid cherries are in the fourteenth row—balcony.

—Eudora Welty, **from *Bye-Bye Brevoort***

Tragedy

Tragedy

Tragedy is drama in which the main character, called the **tragic hero,** suffers a fall from good fortune. This usually occurs because of some **tragic flaw,** such as pride or indecisiveness. Well known tragedies include Sophocles' *Oedipus Rex* and William Shakespeare's *Hamlet* and *Macbeth*. In *Romeo and Juliet*, Friar Lawrence identifies Romeo's tragic flaw—irrationality and impulsive behavior.

FRIAR. Hold thy desperate hand.
Art thou a man? Thy form cries out thou art;
Thy tears are womanish, thy wild acts denote
The unreasonable fury of a beast.
Unseemly woman in a seeming man,
And ill-beseeming beast in seeming both.

—William Shakespeare, **from *Romeo and Juliet* Act 3, Scene 3**

Additional Support

Skills Practice

LISTENING/SPEAKING/VIEWING:

Staged Reading Have groups of students choose poems from Unit 3. Instruct students to design and perform a staged reading of their poem, including stage directions, costumes, and music. Students should write lines for a chorus as well as for individual speakers. OL

Chorus

★ The tragedy originated in Greece. The earliest productions included choral groups that sang hymns in praise of the gods. Soon Greek dramatists emerged and introduced other actors, as well as dialogue in early plays. As plays evolved, the actors became more significant to the plot than the chorus. During the Elizabethan era in England, the **chorus** was portrayed by one actor, who often spoke the prologue and epilogue to the play. Unlike the other actors, who engaged in dialogue, the chorus spoke directly to the audience.

[The Chorus enters and addresses the audience] L2

CHORUS. Now old desire doth in his deathbed lie,
And young affection gapes to be his heir;
That fair for which love groan'd for and would die,
With tender Juliet match'd, is now not fair.

—William Shakespeare, **from *Romeo and Juliet*** R
Act 2, Prologue

Comedy and Modern Drama

Comedy

Comedy is drama that deals with light and amusing subjects or with serious subjects in a light, familiar, or satirical manner. A **satire** is a kind of comedy that ridicules people, practices, or institutions in order to reveal their failings. A **farce** is a kind of comedy that places flat, one-dimensional characters in ridiculous situations.

ANNOUNCER. The leader's coming. He approaches. He's bending. He's unbending. . . . Ah . . . ! He's signing autographs. The leader is stroking a hedgehog, a superb hedgehog! The crowd applauds. He's dancing, with the hedgehog in his hand. He's embracing his dancer. Hurrah! Hurrah!

—Eugène Ionesco, **from *The Leader***

Irony

Irony is a contrast between appearance and reality. There are three types of irony.

1. **Situational Irony** The outcome of a situation is the opposite of what is expected.
2. **Verbal Irony** A person says one thing but means another.
3. **Dramatic Irony** The reader or audience knows something the characters do not.

At the beginning of *Romeo and Juliet*, a heartsick Romeo laments the end of his relationship with Rosaline. Later, while Mercutio and Benvolio are looking for Romeo, Mercutio teasingly says he can make the lovesick boy appear merely by describing Rosaline. At this point in the play, the audience knows that Romeo is no longer pining for Rosaline, but rather for Juliet, creating dramatic irony.

MERCUTIO. I conjure thee by Rosaline's bright eyes,
By her high forehead and her scarlet lip,
That in thy likeness thou appear to us!

—William Shakespeare, **from *Romeo and Juliet***
Act 2, Scene 1

Literature Online **Study Central** Visit www.glencoe.com to review drama.

Teach

L2 Literary Element

Stage Directions Discourage students from glossing over or skipping the stage directions when reading a play. Remind them that stage directions often contain crucial information and will help them visualize the action. OL

R Reading Strategy

Choral Reading Guide the class in a choral reading. First, have one student read the Shakespeare chorus excerpt, then have the class read it as a group.

Ask: How does having a group instead of an individual read affect the audience? Discuss the differences between the two readings. OL

Study Central Have students visit the Web site for resources that will help them to review drama.

Differentiated Instruction

Oral Interpretation Auditory learners will benefit from hearing choral readings. Invite students to read the chorus excerpt several times, experimenting with volume, intensity, and the number of people reading each line. Discuss the effect of the different readings. BL

Academic Standards

Additional Support activities on pp. 682 and 683 cover the following standards:

Skills Practice: **9.5** Become proficient at...writing...**9.7.6** Analyze the occasion... and choose effective verbal and nonverbal techniques...

Differentiated Instruction: **9.7** [Develop] speaking skills...in conjunction with... strategies...[for] delivery of oral presentations. **9.7.10** Assess how language and delivery affect the mood and tone of the oral communication and make an impact on the audience.

Teach

R Reading Strategy

Reading Satire Have a student read the blurb at the beginning of the excerpt aloud. **Ask:** How does this information help prepare you to read the excerpt? *(It gives the background for the scene and the characters and reveals that the play is a satirical farce.)* OL

★ Writer's Technique

Oscar Wilde Wilde's brilliant use of situational irony is a sly way of bringing the audience around to his way of thinking. His characters are so ridiculous that the audience can only concur that they are deserving of mockery. AS

Literary Analysis Model

How do literary elements create meaning in a play?

R In *The Importance of Being Earnest,* a young Victorian man named Jack—supposedly a pillar of his community—falls in love with Gwendolen, a somewhat shallow and pretentious young woman. Over the course of the play, both characters find out that the other is not what he or she seems. This scene is a conversation between Jack and Gwendolen's mother, Lady Bracknell. R

Oscar Wilde, or Fingal O'Flahertie Wills, 1854–1900, Irish writer, poet, and playwright based in England, ca. 19th century.

from *The Importance of Being Earnest*

by Oscar Wilde ★

CHARACTERS:

LADY BRACKNELL She is an elderly English woman who is neither deep nor subtle. Her ideas about what makes a suitable husband are extremely rigid.

JACK Jack Worthing is superficial, flippant, flirtatious, dishonest, witty, charming, and entirely self-serving.

SITUATION: In this satirical farce, Wilde ridicules the social attitudes of nineteenth-century England. The action takes place in a fashionable apartment in London. Lady Bracknell interviews Jack for the position of son-in-law.

APPLYING Literary Elements

Farce

Through Lady Bracknell and her pompous pronouncements, Wilde is able to mock the social attitudes of Victorian England.

LADY BRACKNELL. Now to minor matters. Are your parents living?

JACK. I have lost both my parents.

LADY BRACKNELL. To lose one parent, Mr. Worthing, may be regarded as a misfortune; to lose both looks like carelessness. Who was your father? He was evidently a man of some wealth. Was he born in what the Radical papers call the purple of commerce, or did he rise from the ranks of the aristocracy?

JACK. I am afraid I really don't know. The fact is, Lady Bracknell, I said I had lost my parents. It would be nearer the truth to say that my parents seem to have lost me . . . I don't actually know who I am by birth. I was . . . well, I was found.

LADY BRACKNELL. Found!

JACK. The late Mr. Thomas Cardew, an old gentleman of a very charitable and kindly disposition, found me, and gave me the name Worthing, because he happened to have a first-class ticket for Worthing in his pocket at the time. Worthing is a place in Sussex. It is a seaside resort.

Additional Support

Skills Practice

LITERARY ELEMENT: Comedy
Ask: What does the term *sitcom* mean? *(Situation comedy)* Note that a comic situation involves the complications that arise from a character's awkward dilemma. Have groups of students create characters and a predicament for a sitcom. Suggest that students write a scene for their sitcom and perform it for the class. Discuss which elements of the scenes and pitches worked best and why. OL

Rupert Everett as Jack and Judi Dench as Lady Bracknell

LADY BRACKNELL. Where did the charitable gentleman who had a first-class ticket for this seaside resort find you?

JACK. [*Gravely.*] In a handbag.

LADY BRACKNELL. A handbag?

JACK. [*Very seriously.*] Yes, Lady Bracknell. I was in a handbag—a somewhat large, black leather handbag, with handles to it—an ordinary handbag, in fact.

LADY BRACKNELL. In what locality did this Mr. James, or Thomas, Cardew come across this ordinary handbag?

JACK. In the cloakroom at Victoria Station. It was given to him in mistake for his own.

LADY BRACKNELL. The cloakroom at Victoria Station?

JACK. Yes. The Brighton line.

LADY BRACKNELL. The line is immaterial. Mr. Worthing, I confess I feel somewhat bewildered by what you have just told me. To be born, or at any rate bred, in a handbag, whether it had handles or not, seems to me to display a contempt for the ordinary decencies of family life that remind one of the worst excesses of the French Revolution. And I presume you know what that unfortunate movement led to? As for the particular locality in which the handbag was found, a cloakroom at a railway station might serve to conceal a social indiscretion—has probably, indeed, been used for that purpose before now—but, it could hardly be regarded as an assured basis for a recognized position in good society.

Irony
In this example of situational irony, the audience sees what the characters do not: that Lady Bracknell is a pompous fool.

JACK. May I ask you then what you would advise me to do? I need hardly say I would do anything in the world to ensure Gwendolen's happiness.

LADY BRACKNELL. I would strongly advise you, Mr. Worthing, to try and acquire some relations as soon as possible, and make a definite effort to produce at any rate one parent, of either sex, before the season is quite over.

JACK. Well, I don't see how I could possibly manage to do that. I can produce the handbag at any moment. It is in my dressing room at home. I really think that should satisfy you, Lady Bracknell.

LADY BRACKNELL. Me, sir! What has it to do with me? You can hardly imagine that I and Lord Bracknell would dream of allowing our daughter—a girl brought up with the utmost care—to marry into a cloakroom, and form an alliance with a parcel? Good morning, Mr. Worthing! [*Lady Bracknell sweeps out in majestic indignation.*]

Stage Directions
Stage directions can describe clues about a character's tone, giving his or her state of mind.

JACK. Good morning!

Reading Check

Interpreting What literary elements does Wilde use to create comic effect in this scene from *The Importance of Being Earnest*?

Teach

Reading Check

Answer: *Wilde uses situational irony, farce, and satire.*

L Literary Element

Farce Ask: How is the character of Lady Bracknell farcical? *(She is a "one note" character in the ridiculous situation of interviewing a son-in-law.)* OL

Cultural History

Victorian England

Nineteenth-century English society in the era of Queen Victoria was characterized by concern with status, morality, manners, and hard work. Wilde's plays defied the rigid conventions of his time by pushing the limits of what was deemed acceptable. AS

Differentiated Instruction

Character Traits To emphasize the various character traits of farcical characters, suggest that students use exaggerated voices that fit the character. For example, have students read the part of Lady Bracknell in a highly pompous voice. Have students suggest appropriate voices for Jack. BL

Academic Standards

Additional Support activities on pp. 684 and 685 cover the following standards:

Skills Practice: **9.7.10** Assess how language and delivery affect the mood and tone of the oral communication and make an impact on the audience.

Differentiated Instruction: **9.7.6** Analyze the occasion and the interests of the audience and choose effective verbal…techniques (including voice…) for presentations.

Teach

R1 Reading Strategy

Reading Drama Have a volunteer read each piece of advice aloud. After each piece, write the author's name on the board and have the class outline the author's reading strategies. Discuss which pieces of advice are most helpful. Have students copy the notes into their notebooks. OL

★ Literary History

Robertson Davies

Robertson Davies (1913–1995) was a notable Canadian playwright and novelist whose works often commented on Canadian society. Early in his career, he garnered acclaim for his satirical plays *Eros at Breakfast* (1949) and *At My Heart's Core* (1950). Later, he became most well known for his brilliantly witty trilogies of novels—the Salterton trilogy and the famous Deptford trilogy, which focuses on small-town Canadian life. AS

Writers on Reading

What do writers say about drama?

R1 The Law of Imagination

You can train yourself to read plays so that they will give you keen enjoyment. The directions are few. First, you must give the play a fair chance; it is not a novel, and it should not be read in scraps; try to complete it in an evening. Second, always read it in a theatrical framework; it was written for the stage, and you must, to the best of your ability, visualize it as a stage production. This takes some doing, for you may not have a strong theatrical imagination. When a play is well performed in the theater, a crowd of experts have all worked to give you pleasure; you will not at first trial provide in your mind a director, a designer, and a cast of talented actors. Do not be disappointed if your early attempts seem a little heavy. If you persist, the art will come, in a sufficient measure, for it is the law of imagination that the more you want, the more it will provide. Persist, and the reading of plays can become a splendid private indulgence.

—Robertson Davies, **from** *A Voice from the Attic* 

Shakespeare reading his works to Queen Elizabeth and others, ca. 19th century.

"Drama is life with the dull bits cut out."

—Alfred Hitchcock

Reading Shakespeare

Shakespeare, whose art is so rich, is also the master of ellipsis, the art of leaving things out. In *Antony and Cleopatra* we do not see the imperial lovers alone together; we have to imagine how they are to one another when their onstage audience of followers and retainers are not present. *King Lear* is a play in which the prime villain, Edmund, and Lear never speak to one another. Shakespeare wants us to surmise why it would be unfeasible for them to communicate. In *Hamlet*, there is an extraordinary difference between the Prince in Acts 1 through 4, where he is perhaps seventeen or eighteen, and the mature figure of Act 5, who is at least thirty, though the lapsed time depicted in the play seems no more than three or four months.

Reading Shakespeare's plays, you learn to meditate upon what is left out. That is one of the many advantages that a reader has over a theatergoer in regard to Shakespeare. Ideally, one should read a Shakespearean play, watch a good performance of it, and then read it again.

—Harold Bloom, **from** *How to Read and Why*

LiteratureOnline **InterActive Reading Practice** Visit www.glencoe.com to practice these strategies for reading drama.

Additional Support

Skills Practice

READING: Drama Note that many popular movies started out as plays. **Ask:** What are some examples of movies that were originally plays? Make a list of these movies on the board. Assign students to research plays that have become movies. Have students pick an example, then research the differences and similarities between the movie and stage versions and present their findings to the class. OL

Stage design for the ballet *The Midnight Sun* by Rimski-Korsakov, from the opera *Snow Maiden,* 1915. Mikhali Larionov. Watercolor. Private collection.

Characters on Stage

Before I write down one word, I have to have the character in mind through and through. I must penetrate into the last wrinkle of his soul. I always proceed from the individual; the stage setting, the dramatic ensemble, all of that comes naturally and does not cause me any worry, as soon as I am certain of the individual in every aspect of his humanity. But I have to have his exterior in mind also, down to the last button, how he stands and walks, how he conducts himself, what his voice sounds like. Then I do not let him go until his fate is fulfilled.

—Henrik Ibsen

What *is* so different about the stage is that you're just *there,* stuck—there are your characters stuck on the stage, you've got to live with them and deal with them.

—Harold Pinter, **from *Writer at Work***

The Relevance of Plays

More than any other art, theater asks for relevance. A play that convinces us that "this is the way it is now" can be excused many shortcomings. At any one moment there is a particular quality of feeling which dominates in human intercourse, a tonality which marks the present from the past, and when this tone is struck on the stage, the theater seems necessary again, like self-knowledge. Lacking this real or apparent contemporaneity, many well-written plays pass quickly into oblivion, their other virtues powerless to convince us of their importance. **R2**

—Arthur Miller, **from "What Makes Plays Endure?"** 

Reading Check

Responding From your own reading experiences, which passage do you identify with most closely? Explain.

Teach

Reading Check

Answers will vary. Make sure students support their responses with reasons.

R2 Reading Strategy

Connect Ask: What does Miller mean by "theater asks for relevance?" *(No matter when they were written, good plays have themes to which the audience can relate.)* Discuss the kinds of themes that are relevant today. Ask whether students feel these themes will be relevant in the future. **OL**

Literary History

Arthur Miller Arthur Miller (1915–2005) took the relevance of theater very seriously, responding to the most controversial issues of his day with dramas such as *The Crucible,* a searing indictment of the McCarthy communist witch hunts. **AS**

InterActive Reading Practice Have students access the Web site for more practice with reading strategies

English Language Coach

Reading Aloud Ask a student to paraphrase Miller's quote. Explain that universally relevant themes by definition transcend language and cultural barriers. Suggest to English language learners that as they read the plays, they try to relate their themes to ideas and messages in the literature of their native culture. **EL**

Academic Standards

Additional Support activities on pp. 686 and 687 cover the following standards:

Skills Practice: **9.7.8** Compare and contrast the ways in which media genres…cover the same event.

English Language Coach: **9.3.5** Compare works that express a universal theme…

Assess/Close

Guide to Reading Drama

Stress that students should take time to note visual details as well as other sensory details, such as sounds and smells.

Elements of Drama

Suggest students keep notes on which elements of each play they find most appealing. Do they relate to the characters or get wrapped up in the suspenseful plot? Is the dialogue insightful or witty?

Activities

1. **Speaking/Listening** If students feel that Wilde is making an important point, they should clearly state that point and how he makes it.
2. **Visual Literacy** Suggest students work in groups and have them compare their completed charts.
3. **Writing** Have students consider what theme their dialogue expresses and why it is meaningful to them.

FOLDABLES™ Study Organizer

Have students jot down notes on each literary element in the sections of their organizer.

Wrap-Up

Guide to Reading Drama

- Plays should not be read a few pages at a time, as you might read a novel. Try to read a play in its entirety in one sitting.
- Because drama is meant to be performed, you will need to use your imagination to visualize what is happening in each scene.
- Focus your attention on plot and character. Think about theme only after you finish reading.
- Read the stage directions and then try to visualize what the set stage would look like.

Elements of Drama

- **Drama** is written to be performed by actors in front of an audience.
- Written drama is mostly **dialogue** and **stage directions.**
- Most plays are divided into **acts** and **scenes.**
- In a **tragedy,** the **tragic hero** suffers a reversal of fortune.
- In a **monologue** or **soliloquy,** the character reveals important thoughts and feelings about the action.
- In an **aside,** a character says something to the audience that the other characters are unable to hear.
- There are three types of **irony** that can contribute to humor: **verbal, situational,** and **dramatic.**

Activities

Use what you have learned about reading drama to complete one of these activities.

1. **Speaking/Listening** Discuss with a small group your opinion of the excerpt from *The Importance of Being Earnest.* Begin by reviewing Wilde's characters. Does Wilde successfully make a point in this scene? Why or why not?
2. **Visual Literacy** Create a four-column chart that you can use to compare and contrast the three types of irony: verbal, situational, and dramatic. Use the fourth column to note examples from the unit.
3. **Writing** Write out a bit of dialogue from your favorite movie or television show. Then write a brief explanation of what elements in the dialogue make it memorable.

THREE-TAB BOOK

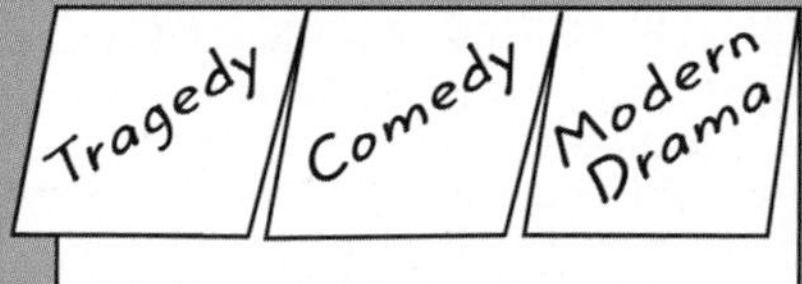

Try using this study organizer to keep track of the literary elements you learn in this unit.

INDIANA ACADEMIC STANDARDS (page 688)
9.7.7 Make judgments about the ideas under discussion…
9.3.8 Interpret and evaluate the impact of…ironies in a text.
9.3.10 Identify and describe the function of dialogue…in dramatic literature.

Additional Support

Academic Standards

The Additional Support activity on p. 688 covers the following standard:
Skills Practice: **9.2.8** Make reasonable statements and draw conclusions about a text…

Skills Practice

WRITING: Critical Review Have the class design a checklist based on the elements of drama and use it to write a critique of a play or movie. Include the following:

- Is the dialogue effective?
- Do the scenes flow smoothly?
- Is there a tragic hero?
- Is there irony?

Have students add elements to the checklist, then write their reviews. **OL**

PART 1

The Power of Love

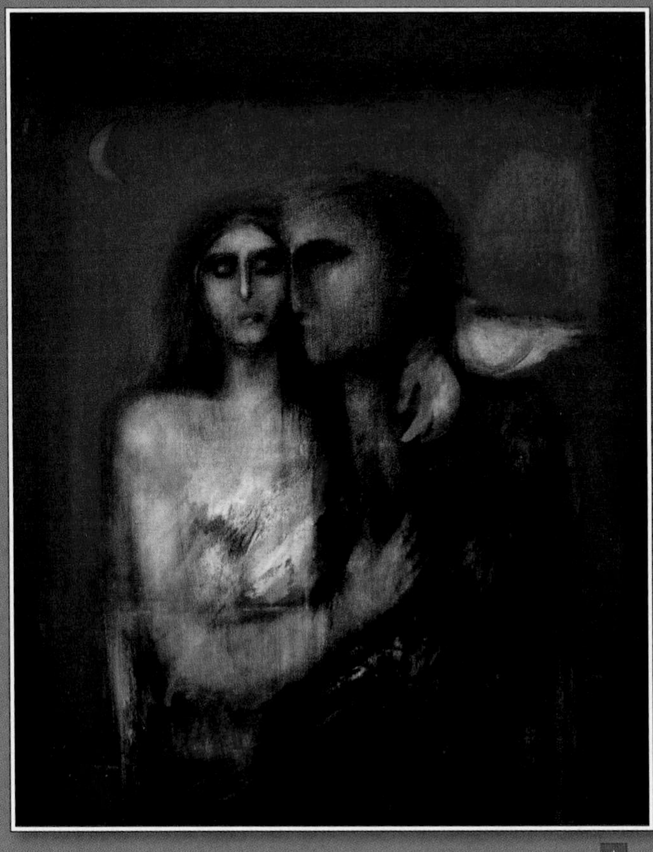

Couple with a Dove, 2001. Suad Al-Attar. Oil on canvas, 24.02 x 18.11 in. ★

BIG IDEA

BI Throughout history young lovers have spoken of the strength of their love and pledged that it would last forever. The selections in Part 1 focus on this universal subject. As you read the selections, ask yourself: What makes love so powerful? How does it drive the action of these works?

Analyzing and Extending

BI Big Idea

The Power of Love **Ask:** What is powerful about love? *(Answers will vary.)* Discuss the various ways love can motivate people. Have students cite examples of the power of love in literature, music, movies, and other arts. **OL**

★ Viewing the Art

Suad Al-Attar (1942–) held the first solo exhibition by a female artist in Baghdad. She has degrees from universities in California, Baghdad, and London and has exhibited her work all over the world. **Ask:** How does this painting reflect the power of love? *(Students may note how the two people relate to each other or to the dove, or mention the expressive colors.)* **AS**

English Language Coach

Building Background Discuss the various definitions of love with English language learners and how each type of love might be considered powerful. **EL**

Differentiated Instruction

Responding to Artwork Visual learners will respond to the strong colors in the artwork. Have students discuss the different kinds of love found in the painting. *(Students may note the love of the artist for painting or the love of the people for the dove.)* **BL**

Academic Standards

Additional Support activities on pp. 688 and 689 cover the following standards:

Skills Practice: **9.5.3** Write expository compositions, including analytical essays…, that gather evidence in support of a thesis…[and] make distinctions between the relative value and significance of…ideas…

English Language Coach: **9.2** Develop [reading] strategies…

Differentiated Instruction: **9.7.13** Identify the artistic effects of a media presentation and…the techniques used to create them…

UNIT FOUR

Part 1: Skills Scope and Sequence

Readability Scores Key
Dale-Chall/**DRP**/Lexile

PACING (DAYS) STANDARD	BLOCK	SELECTIONS AND FEATURES	LITERARY ELEMENTS
1–2 class sessions	1	LITERARY HISTORY: Shakespearean Drama, pp. 692–693	
		Romeo and Juliet Act 1 by William Shakespeare pp. 694–721	Foil, SE pp. 695–721
2–3 class sessions	1–2	*Romeo and Juliet* Act 2 by William Shakespeare pp. 722–745	Figurative Language, SE pp. 722–745
		Romeo and Juliet Act 3 by William Shakespeare pp. 746–773	Monologue, Soliloquy, and Aside, SE pp. 746–773 Pun, TWE pp. 749, 755 Irony, TWE p. 770
2–3 class sessions	1–2	*Romeo and Juliet* Act 4 by William Shakespeare pp. 774–789	Irony, SE pp. 774–789 Tone, TWE p. 781
		Romeo and Juliet Act 5 by William Shakespeare pp. 790–807	Tragedy, SE pp. 790–806 Style, SE p. 806 Critical Perspectives, TWE p. 802
3–4 class sessions	2–3	TIME magazine, "A Long-Overdue Encore" by Barry Hillenbrand 8.7/**64**/1170, pp. 808–811	
		Grammar Workshop: Language Usage, p. 812	
		COMPARING LITERATURE Across Genres *The Tragedy of Romeo and Juliet* by William Shakespeare, pp. 696–807 "The Taxi" by Amy Lowell, pp. 813–814 "Counting the Beats" by Robert Graves, p. 815 "The Princess and All the Kingdom" by Pär Lagerkvist 7.0/**54**/910, pp. 816–818	Comparing Theme, SE pp. 813, 818 Mood, TWE p. 815

About the Part

Part 1 deals with plays and how certain elements of the theater are able to function in both comedies and tragedies

READING AND CRITICAL THINKING	VOCABULARY	WRITING AND GRAMMAR	LISTENING, SPEAKING, AND VIEWING
Previewing, SE p. 692		Researching Historical Context, TWE p. 692	
Summarizing, SE pp. 695–721 Using Graphic Aids, TWE pp. 696, 702 Monitoring Comprehension, TWE p. 710	Synonyms, SE pp. 695, 721	Respond to Character, SE p. 721 Possessives, TWE p. 698 Parallelism, TWE p. 704	Analyzing Art, SE pp. 699, 704, 718 Comic vs. Dramatic Speeches, TWE p. 700
Making Inferences About Characters, SE pp. 722–745 Inferring, TWE p. 726	Context Clues, SE pp. 722, 745	Correlative Conjunctions, TWE p. 724 Similes, TWE p. 728	Analyzing Art, SE pp. 732, 737, 741; TWE pp. 726, 744 Literature Groups, SE p. 745
Comparing and Contrasting Scenes, SE pp. 746–773 Previewing, TWE p. 748 Researching, TWE p. 750	Analogies, SE pp. 746, 773	Compare and Contrast Mood, SE p. 773 Reports, TWE p. 752 Hyperbole, TWE p. 754	Analyzing Art, SE pp. 751, 754; TWE p. 766 Oral Communication Strategies, TWE p. 762
Interpreting Imagery, SE pp. 774–789; Monitoring Comprehension, TWE p. 778 Listening, TWE p. 784	Context Clues, SE pp. 774, 789 Multiple Meanings, TWE p. 780	Respond to Character and Plot, SE p. 789 Active Voice, TWE p. 776 Prepositions, TWE p. 780	Analyzing Art, SE pp. 777, 783, 786 Oral Interpretation, TWE p. 786
Making Inferences About Theme, SE pp. 790–806 Setting a Purpose for Reading, TWE p. 792	Word Parts, SE pp. 790, 806 Academic Vocabulary, SE p. 806	Using Apostrophes, SE p. 807 Author's Craft, SE p. 807 Descriptive Paragraph, TWE p. 796	Analyzing Art, SE pp. 796, 800, 804 Reader's Theater, SE p. 807 Oral Reading, TWE p. 798
Identifying Sequence, SE p. 808 Previewing and Outlining, TWE p. 808 Recognizing Sequence, TWE p. 810			
		Sequence of Tenses, TWE p. 812	
Comparing Author's Beliefs, SE pp. 813, 818		Quickwrite, SE pp. 814, 817 Compare-and-Contrast Essay, SE p. 818	Discussion Starter, SE p. 815 Group Activity, SE p. 818

LITERARY FOCUS

Focus

BELLRINGER

Bellringer Options
Daily Language Practice Transparency 71
Or note that people use the word *tragedy* in reference to both major and minor catastrophes as well as to unfortunate circumstances that involve comic or absurd elements. **Write on the board:** Major, Minor, Tragicomic. Ask what constitutes a major tragedy *(Death, war, natural disasters),* a minor tragedy *(flat tire),* and a comic tragedy *(fools who continually make the same mistakes),* and list the results on the board. Discuss how these notions of tragedy compare with the definition of classical tragic drama.

Teach

L Literary Element

Tragedy Ask: If tragedies are about bad things happening to good people, why does the audience enjoy them? Introduce students to the concept of catharsis—a purifying release of tension and emotion through art. OL

LITERARY FOCUS

Tragedy

What are the elements that define a tragedy?

L According to the ancient Greek philosopher Aristotle, a tragedy is a play about a person of high social standing (a hero or a king) who suffers a fall from good fortune. Aristotole also outlined the Six Elements of Drama which many playwrights have used as a guide throughout history.

Aristotle's Six Elements	
Element	**Definition**
Plot	What happens in a play
Diction/ Language/ Dialogue	The playwright's word choices and the actors' enunciation while delivering their lines
Music/ Rhythm	Not music as we think of it, but rather the sound, rhythm, and melody of the speeches
Theme	What a play means, as opposed to what happens
Spectacle	The scenery, costumes, and special effects in a play
Character	The person an actor represents in a play

In *Romeo and Juliet,* the plot centers on the young Romeo and Juliet, who fall in love at first sight at a masked ball. Since they belong to rival families—the Montagues and the Capulets—Romeo and Juliet must keep their love a secret. The rivalry of the Montague and Capulet families soon erupts into violence. In the following scene, Tybalt, a Capulet, vows revenge on Romeo.

TYBALT. This, by his voice, should be a Montague.
Fetch me my rapier, boy. What! Dares the slave
Come hither, cover'd with an antic face,
To fleer and scorn at our solemnity?
Now, by the stock and honor of my kin,
To strike him dead I hold it not a sin.

—from Act 1, Scene 5

Aristotle's elements of diction/language/dialogue and music/rhythm are apparent in Shakespeare's *Romeo and Juliet,* as most of his characters often speak in **blank verse,** or unrhymed iambic pentameter. (**Iambic pentameter** means that there are ten syllables per line, and every second syllable is stressed.) In order to deliver lines from Shakespearean text, an actor must develop an ear for the rhythm and musicality of the text, as well as be able to enunciate Shakespeare's often tongue-twisting phrases.

Tragic mask from a mosaic in the House of the Fawn in Pompeii by Gustavo Tomsich.

The elements of theme and spectacle also appear in Shakespearean tragedy. As you read the play, you will discover the main ideas that Shakespeare wants to convey to his audiences. In viewing the play, an audience member would witness such spectacles as sword fights, a masked ball, a secret exchange upon a balcony, and a tragic death scene.

Additional Support

Academic Standards

The Additional Support activity on p. 690 covers the following standard:

Skills Practice: **9.3.10** Identify and describe the function of...soliloquies [and] asides... in dramatic literature.

Skills Practice

LITERARY ELEMENT: Tragedy Have students research modern tragedies. Students should use Aristotle's six elements as a guideline for their analyses. Provide questions as an additional reference: Does the play have a tragic hero? What makes this person tragic and heroic? What dramatic devices are included—are there monologues, soliloquies, or asides? How does the play differ from a Greek tragedy? Have students create a graphic organizer to illustrate their written analysis. OL

The final Aristotelian element is character. Characters' actions and words define their personalities. There are often many characters in plays, including the **protagonist,** or the central character; the **antagonist,** or the character who opposes the protagonist; and a number of supporting and minor characters. The protagonist is often a tragic hero.

Tragic Hero

The most important character in a tragedy is its **tragic hero.** He or she is a person born into nobility and responsible for his or her own fate. A tragic hero has the potential for greatness but is doomed to make one or more serious errors in judgment. In most cases, these errors are the result of a **tragic flaw** in the hero's character. Romeo's tragic flaw is that he is blinded by his love for Juliet; therefore, he behaves rashly. In these lines, he wills to lose his life for his love.

ROMEO. Let me be ta'en, let me put to death.
I am content, so thou wilt have it so.

—from Act 3, Scene 5

In most tragedies, the tragic hero eventually realizes his mistake and faces death with great honor and dignity.

R Dramatic Devices

Playwrights cannot comment directly upon how a character is thinking or feeling, so they rely on three dramatic devices. The first is **monologue,** in which the character speaks directly to another character or to himself or herself. In a **soliloquy** a character speaks his or her innermost thoughts when no other characters are on stage. For example, in Act 1, Scene 4, of *Romeo and Juliet,* Mercutio, Romeo's best friend, in a monologue refers to Queen Mab, a mythological queen of fairies who takes the form of an evil spirit. Mercutio uses the metaphor to express his cynicism about love.

MERCUTIO. O, then I see Queen Mab hath been with you.
She is the fairies' midwife, and she comes
In shape no bigger than an agate stone
On the forefinger of an alderman. . . .

—from Act 1, Scene 4

The third device playwrights rely on for revealing a character's thoughts or feelings is the **aside.** In an aside, a character says something to the audience that the other characters are not supposed to hear.

JULIET. O Romeo, Romeo! Wherefore art thou Romeo?
Deny thy father and refuse thy name;
Or, if thou wilt not, be but sworn my love,
And I'll no longer be a Capulet.

ROMEO. [*Aside.*] Shall I hear more, or shall I speak at this?

—from Act 2, Scene 2

Literature Online Interactive Literary Elements Handbook Go to www.glencoe.com to review or learn more about tragedy.

Quickwrite

Defining Tragedy Take fifteen minutes to complete a quickwrite in which you answer the question, "What is your definition of a tragedy?" Your answer should be specific to you and can include examples, personal experiences, feelings, and reactions.

INDIANA ACADEMIC STANDARDS (pages 690–691)

9.3.1 Explain the relationship between the purposes and the characteristics of different forms of dramatic literature (including comedy, tragedy, and dramatic monologue).

9.3.10 Identify and describe the function of dialogue, soliloquies, asides, character foils, and stage designs in dramatic literature.

Teach

R Reading Strategy

Analyzing Plays Encourage students to jot down their first impressions of a play immediately after their initial reading. Then, they can go back to analyze the play for elements such as plot or dramatic devices. **OL**

Viewing the Art

When drama was born in Greece, all actors were male. These actors played multiple roles, including those of women. There were only two types of plays—comedy and tragedy—so the two types of masks allowed actors to easily slip between multiple roles. Eventually the comedy and tragedy masks became the symbol of the theater. **AS**

Quickwrite

Answers will vary. Make sure students support their definitions with reasons and examples.

Literary Elements Have students access the Web site to improve their understanding of tragedy.

Differentiated Instruction

Theater Masks Have the class choose a tragic play or movie. Assign students to create masks for each of the characters. Instruct them to consider elements such as composition, color, and expression. Also caution students to keep in mind that the masks need to be functional. **AL**

Academic Standards

The Additional Support activity on p. 691 covers the following standard:

Differentiated Instruction: **9.3** [Identify] story elements such as character…

Focus

BELLRINGER

Bellringer Options
Daily Language Practice Transparency 72
Or note that in live theater the use of special effects is far more limited than in movies. **Ask:** Do you think a stage play could ever be as exciting as one of today's movies? Encourage students who have seen live theater to participate in the discussion. Point out how compelling plots, dialogue, and characters can engage the imagination of the audience.

Teach

R Reading Strategy

Preview Have students review the subheads and the illustrations on pages 692 and 693. Then read the introductory quotation and the first paragraph of the essay aloud. Encourage students to list any questions they have about the Elizabethan era. OL

Literary History Have students access the Web site for a summary, bibliography, and other online resources to enhance their understanding of Shakespearean drama.

Shakespearean Drama

> *"Theater in Elizabeth's day took the place now filled by the novel, the short story, the drama, the newspaper, motion pictures, radio, and television."*
>
> —Vera Mowry Roberts, *On Stage*

William Shakespeare, 1564–1616.

★ IT IS A SUMMER AFTERNOON IN LONDON, ENGLAND, near the end of the reign of Queen Elizabeth I. People from all classes of London society—from laborers to the nobility—have crossed the Thames River to the suburb of Southwark to see a play. Groups of excited playgoers are arriving at a large round building—William Shakespeare's Globe Theatre. A fanfare of trumpets signals that the performance will soon begin. Because a black flag flies over the theater, everyone knows that today's play is a tragedy. The playgoers take their seats in the galleries, except for those "groundlings" who stand in the open courtyard around the stage. The actors are about to perform *The Tragedy of Romeo and Juliet,* an early play of Shakespeare's that has remained a great favorite with Elizabethan audiences.

R The Age of Shakespeare

Shakespeare was fortunate to begin his career in the late 1500s, when English theater was going through major changes. Professional actors had been performing in England for centuries. Called "players," they traveled from town to town, setting up makeshift stages in public halls, marketplaces, and the courtyards of inns. Often they met hostility from local authorities, who believed that crowds of playgoers were a magnet for crime and also contributed to the spread of disease.

Actor James Burbage built England's first permanent playhouse in 1576. Other open-air theaters sprang up during the next few decades. These playhouses were all located in the suburbs rather than in London, which had strict laws governing entertainment. In 1599 Shakespeare's acting company, the Lord Chamberlain's Men, built their own playhouse, the Globe. This roughly circular building had three levels of covered galleries. A platform stage about forty feet wide projected out into the open courtyard, where people who paid the lowest admission price could stand and watch the play. Admission to the gallery benches cost about twice as much. Wealthy people paid sixpence (what a skilled laborer earned in a day) to sit in the "lords' room," the part of the gallery directly over the stage. In all, Shakespeare's Globe could accommodate about 3,000 spectators. Toward the end of his career, his company acquired a fully-enclosed theater in London for the winter season.

Additional Support

See also Active Learning and Note Taking Guide, pp. 127–130.

Skills Practice

WRITING: Researching Historical Context The original Globe Theatre opened in 1599 and closed in 1642. In June 1997, a new Globe Theatre was completed. The restoration faithfully replicated the original theater's materials and design. Tell groups of students to research the old and new Globe Theatres and have them compare their findings in class. OL

Shakespeare's Stagecraft

The stage at the Globe had trapdoors for the entrance and exit of actors playing ghosts or other supernatural characters. At the back of the main stage was a small, curtained inner stage used for indoor scenes. Above this stood a two-tiered gallery. The first tier was used to stage balcony and bedroom scenes; the second to house musicians. Sound effects, such as the booming of thunder, were produced in a hut on top of the stage roof.

BI All performances took place in the afternoon because there was no artificial lighting. The stage was mostly bare. There were few props and no movable scenery. Instead of relying on scenery, Shakespeare used descriptive language to help audiences visualize the settings of his plays. For example, his long descriptions of the moon are more than just beautiful writing—they reminded Elizabethan audiences that the characters were meeting at night.

What the Elizabethan stage lacked in scenery, it made up for in costumes. Shakespeare's audiences considered clothing an important indication of social rank, so they demanded extravagant—if not always historically accurate—costuming. Along with its playbooks, an elaborate wardrobe was an Elizabethan theater company's biggest expense and most important asset.

Boy actors had an important function in Elizabethan theater. Because it was considered immoral for women to appear onstage, adolescent males played the female parts. They used wigs, costumes, and their voices to create this illusion. Very popular with Elizabethan theatergoers, these boy actors must have been highly skilled performers who created convincing and moving portrayals of Shakespeare's great female roles, from Lady Macbeth and Cleopatra to Rosalind and Juliet.

Even though Shakespeare was a very popular dramatist in his time, the audiences at the Globe would have been surprised to learn that their era would be best known for his work. Shakespeare's contemporary Ben Jonson saw far into the future when he described his great rival as "not of an age, but for all time."

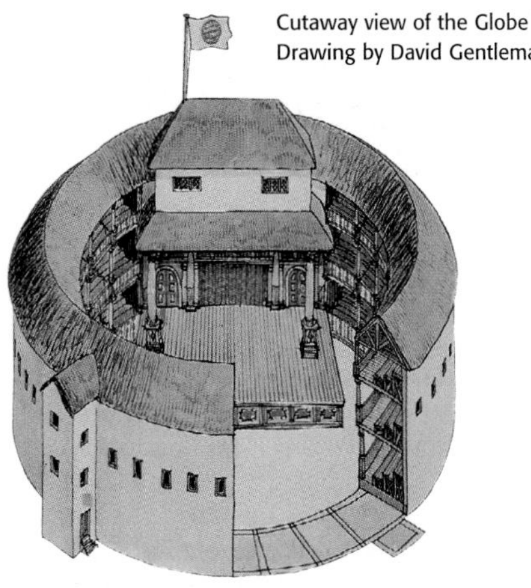
Cutaway view of the Globe Theatre. Drawing by David Gentleman.

LiteratureOnline **Literary History** For more about Shakespearean drama, go to www.glencoe.com.

RESPONDING AND THINKING CRITICALLY

1. If you had been a member of the audience at the Globe, what feature of the theater do you think would have most held your attention? Explain.
2. What event during Shakespeare's lifetime probably helped his career as a dramatist?
3. How do today's productions of Shakespeare's plays differ from productions during his lifetime? Consider the use of scenery and props.

INDIANA ACADEMIC STANDARDS (pages 692–693)
9.3.12 Analyze the way in which a work of literature is related to the themes and issues of its historical period.

Teach

BI Big Idea

The Power of Love **Ask:** How might the stage at the Globe lend itself to expressing a powerful love story like that of Romeo and Juliet? *(The size of the stage lends itself to bold expression of emotion. The semicircular seating allows the audience to see all the action and connect closely with the play. Also, the lack of scenery puts the focus strongly on the actors and the play.)* OL

Cultural History

The Elizabethan Era
Queen Elizabeth I (1558–1603) was a notable writer, orator, and patron of the arts who loved theater. Through patronage and protection of theater companies, she helped support the great flowering of drama during her time. AS

Assess

1. Students may mention the elaborate costuming.
2. The construction of England's first permanent theaters
3. Women act in today's productions; today's theaters have elaborate props and can achieve dramatic effects with lighting.

English Language Coach

Compound Nouns Write these words on the board: *playbooks, theatergoers, playhouse.* Explain that a compound noun consists of two or more nouns that are written as one word or as separate or hyphenated words. Encourage English language learners to enter compound nouns and their definitions in their vocabulary notebooks as they read. EL

Academic Standards
Additional Support activities on pp. 692 and 693 cover the following standards:
Skills Practice: **9.5.3** Write expository compositions…that communicate information and ideas from…sources accurately…
English Language Coach: **9.1** [Use] word parts…to determine the meaning of words…

BEFORE YOU READ

Focus

BELLRINGER

Bellringer Options
Selection Focus Transparency 43
Daily Language Practice Transparency 73
Or students may have read stories about people who accomplished extraordinary feats on behalf of loved ones. **Ask:** What examples can you think of that illustrate the remarkable power of love? **Say:** Jot down some case studies. For example, how might love overcome hatred? Defeat prejudice? Strengthen—or shatter—the will to live?

Author Search To expand students' appreciation of William Shakespeare, have them access the Web site for additional information and resources.

BEFORE YOU READ

Romeo and Juliet

MEET WILLIAM SHAKESPEARE

Few authors have proven as timeless as William Shakespeare. Nearly four centuries after his death, his plays are still read and performed around the world. Shakespeare's appeal is profound. Poet Maya Angelou summed up the feelings of many people toward Shakespeare when she said, "I know it was written for me."

> *"All the world's a stage,*
> *And all the men and women*
> *merely players:*
> *They have their exits and their entrances."*
>
> —William Shakespeare

From Stratford to London Shakespeare was born in Stratford-upon-Avon, a market town about one hundred miles from London. His father was a glove maker, tradesman, and bailiff (the equivalent of a mayor). His mother came from a prosperous farming family. Because of his family's status, Shakespeare almost certainly attended the town's grammar school, considered one of the best in England. There he would have learned Latin and read classical literature.

At eighteen, he married Anne Hathaway. The couple had a daughter, Susanna, and twins, Judith and Hamnet. Sometime between 1585 and the early 1590s, Shakespeare moved to London to pursue a career in theater. He worked as an actor and playwright, quickly gaining attention for his comedies and historical plays.

By 1594 he had joined a theater group called the Lord Chamberlain's Men (renamed the King's Men during the reign of James I). This remained his professional home for the rest of his career. Although playwrights of that time were not well-compensated, Shakespeare made substantial earnings from his share in the company's profits. He bought a large estate for his family in Stratford, retiring there in 1610. He died in 1616. Seven years later, a group of friends published a collected edition of his works, ensuring their preservation for future generations.

A Master of His Craft Shakespeare wrote thirty-seven plays, including such tragic masterpieces as *Hamlet, Othello, Macbeth, King Lear,* and *Romeo and Juliet.* Shakespeare's plays are rich, complex, and full of beautifully poetic language. Shakespeare's friend and rival playwright Ben Jonson declared that Shakespeare was "not of an age, but for all time," and Shakespeare continues to inspire writers, filmmakers, and other artists.

Of *Romeo and Juliet,* celebrated critic William Hazlitt wrote, "[Shakespeare] has given a picture of human life, such as it is in the order of nature." The play is praised for its portrayal of the various stages of life—youth, middle age, and old age—and for its captivating dramatization of young love.

William Shakespeare was born in 1564 and died in 1616.

Literature Online **Author Search** For more about William Shakespeare, go to www.glencoe.com.

Selection Skills

The Tragedy of Romeo and Juliet, Act I

Literary Elements
- Foil (SE pp. 695–721)

Reading Skills
- Summarizing (SE pp. 695–721)
- Paraphrasing (TWE p. 706)

Vocabulary Skills
- Synonyms (SE pp. 695, 721)

Listening/Speaking/Viewing Skills
- Analyzing Art (SE pp. 699, 704, 718)
- Comic/Dramatic Speeches (TWE p. 700)
- Oral Interpretation (TWE p. 718)

Writing Skills/Grammar
- Respond to Character (SE p. 721)
- Possessives (TWE p. 698)
- Parallelism (TWE p. 704)
- Subject-Verb Order (TWE p. 708)
- Vivid Description (TWE p. 714)
- Complements (TWE p. 720)

LITERATURE PREVIEW

Connecting to the Drama

"I can't stop thinking about him." "She's the most perfect girl in the world . . ." Have you ever heard or expressed such feelings? Before you read Act 1, think about the following questions:

- Do you believe that young teenagers can fall as deeply in love as adults can?
- How would you help a friend who was depressed as a result of unrequited love?

Building Background

Shakespeare borrowed the Romeo and Juliet story from an old tale. The events in the play take place during the summer in Verona and Mantua, two cities in northern Italy, in the 1300s. The characters Romeo and Juliet come from two distinguished families who are embroiled in a bitter feud. In Italy during the 1300s, such feuds between families were common. Italian families were extended to include brothers, sisters, aunts, uncles, nieces, nephews, cousins, and even servants. All these members of a family might become involved in a *vendetta,* a feud between two families often ignited by a murder and perpetuated by acts of revenge.

Setting Purposes for Reading

Big Idea The Power of Love

As you read Act 1, compare and contrast the characters' differing attitudes toward love.

Literary Element Foil

A **foil** is a character who provides a strong contrast to another character. A foil may emphasize another character's distinctive traits or may make another character look better by comparison. For example, in *Romeo and Juliet* Mercutio serves as a foil to Romeo.

- See Literary Terms Handbook, p. R7.

LiteratureOnline **Interactive Literary Elements Handbook** To review or learn more about the literary elements, go to www.glencoe.com.

READING PREVIEW

Reading Strategy Summarizing

Summarizing means stating the main ideas of a work or passage in your own words and in a logical sequence. A summary is much shorter than the original. Summarizing can help you focus your understanding and remember what you have read.

Reading Tip: Answering the 5 Ws When reading a Shakespeare play, it is helpful to summarize eventful or difficult passages. For each passage you summarize, make a list answering *who, what, when, where,* and *why* questions about the passage. Use the list to help create your summary.

Vocabulary

pernicious (pər nish′ əs) *adj.* destructive; deadly; p. 701 *The false rumor had a pernicious effect on our friendship.*

posterity (pos ter′ ə tē) *n.* future generations; p. 705 *We must protect the environment for posterity.*

anguish (ang′ gwish) *n.* extreme suffering; agony; p. 707 *The hurricane victim described the anguish of losing everything he owned.*

profane (prō fān′) *v.* to degrade or disrespect something holy or important; p. 719 *Do not profane the sanctuary with loud noise.*

Vocabulary Tip: Synonyms Synonyms are words that have the same, or nearly the same, meaning. The words *enemy* and *adversary,* for example, are synonyms. Note that synonyms are always the same part of speech.

INDIANA ACADEMIC STANDARDS (pages 695–721)

9.3.10 Identify and describe the function of...character foils...in dramatic literature.

9.2 Develop [reading] strategies...

9.5.2 Write responses to literature...

BEFORE YOU READ

Focus

Summary

Two prominent families, the Montagues and the Capulets, are locked in a bitter feud. After a street fight between their servants, the Prince of Verona bans further violence. That night, the Capulet patriarch holds a ball, where his teenaged daughter Juliet meets a young stranger in disguise, unaware that he is Romeo, the son of her father's sworn enemy. Romeo is forced to flee the ball to avoid a skirmish with Juliet's cousin, Tybalt. When Romeo and Juliet learn each other's identity, both feel torn between romantic attraction and family loyalty.

V Vocabulary

Vocabulary File Say: Add these words and definitions to your vocabulary file. For each word, include a sentence that gives you an example of how to use the word. **OL** Students with English language needs should include the pronunciation of these words in their files. **EL**

Literary Elements Have students access the Web site to improve their understanding of foil.

Selection Resources

Print Materials
- Unit 4 Resources (Fast File), pp. 18–32
- Leveled Vocabulary Development, pp. 50–54
- Selection and Unit Assessments, pp. 135–144
- Selection Quick Checks, pp. 67–71

Transparencies
- Bellringer Options Transparencies: Selection Focus Transparency 43; Daily Language Practice Transparency 73
- Literary Elements Transparencies 8, 67, 78, 79, 80

Technology
- TeacherWorks Plus™ CD-ROM
- StudentWorks Plus™ CD-ROM
- Presentation Plus!™ CD-ROM
- Literature Online, glencoe.com
- Online Student Edition, mhln.com
- Exam*View*® Assessment Suite CD-ROM
- Vocabulary PuzzleMaker CD-ROM
- Listening Library, disc 2 tracks 2–6

Teach

Big Idea

The Power of Love **Say:** Keep these questions in mind as you read: How does Shakespeare juxtapose loyalty and love with conflict in Act I? *(By alternating between themes of love and conflict in the dialogue)* What is the effect of this technique? *(It creates contrast and builds dramatic tension.)* **OL**

Viewing the Art

Although created in the twentieth century, *Juliet on the Balcony* recalls the illuminated manuscripts popular during the Middle Ages and the Renaissance. Illumination is the art of embellishing parchment book pages with ornately drawn letters and designs using colored inks and gold leaf. **AS**

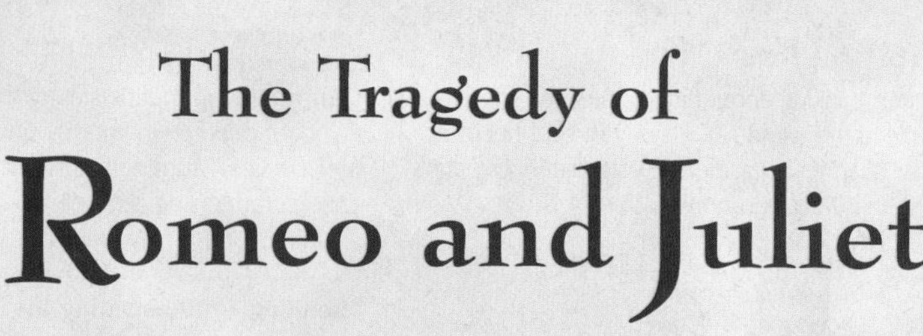

The Tragedy of Romeo and Juliet

William Shakespeare

Juliet on the Balcony. Illumination from text *The Tragedy of Romeo and Juliet,* 1920. Sangorski and Sutcliffe, binders, calligraphers, and illuminators. Private collection.

Additional Support

Leveled Reading An adapted version of this selection is available on page 146 of *Jamestown Literature: An Adapted Reader* for grade 9.

Skills Practice

READING: Using Graphic Aids Note the value of previewing illustrations before reading a text. Artwork can set the mood and provide clues to the tone, content, and theme. Review the artwork in the selection and discuss students' impressions. Then have them write a paragraph about their expectations of the play. **OL**

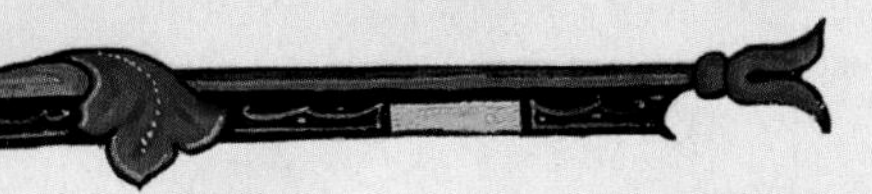

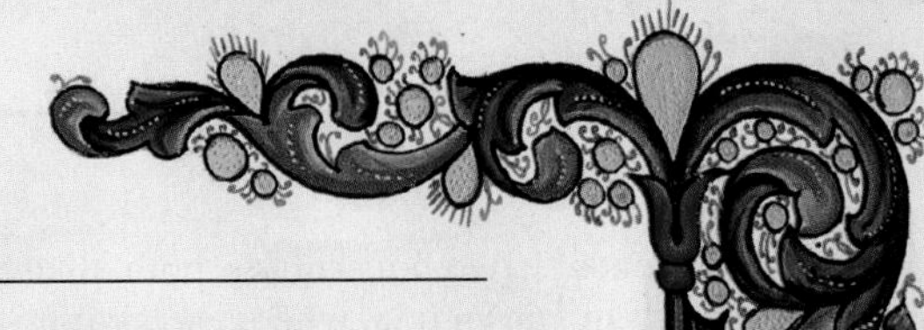

CHARACTERS

The Montagues

LORD MONTAGUE: wealthy nobleman of Verona and enemy to Lord Capulet

LADY MONTAGUE: his wife

ROMEO: their son

BENVOLIO: Lord Montague's nephew, Romeo's cousin and friend

BALTHASAR: Romeo's servant

ABRAM: a servant

The Capulets

LORD CAPULET: wealthy nobleman of Verona and enemy to Lord Montague

LADY CAPULET: his wife

JULIET: their daughter, who is thirteen years old

TYBALT: Lady Capulet's nephew, Juliet's cousin

OLD MAN: elderly relative of the family

NURSE: servant who has cared for Juliet since infancy

PETER: the Nurse's servant

SAMPSON: servant

GREGORY: servant

Others

★ CHORUS: actor who speaks directly to the audience to introduce the play

PRINCE ESCALUS: ruler of Verona

COUNT PARIS: relative of the Prince and suitor to Juliet

MERCUTIO: relative of the Prince and Romeo's friend

FRIAR LAWRENCE: Catholic priest of the order of Franciscans and a pharmacist

APOTHECARY: pharmacist in Mantua

FRIAR JOHN: Franciscan priest

PAGE: servant to Paris

OFFICERS AND CITIZENS OF VERONA, RELATIVES OF BOTH FAMILIES, MASKERS, OFFICERS, GUARDS, WATCHMEN, SERVANTS, AND ATTENDANTS

SETTING

R SCENE: *Italy—the cities of Verona and Mantua. The fourteenth century.*

Teach

R Reading Strategy

Visualize Discuss what fourteenth-century Verona and Mantua might have looked like. Encourage students to picture the buildings, streets, and methods of transportation. Have them describe the appearance of the cities' inhabitants. OL

★ Cultural History

Theatrical Chorus The chorus has its roots in ancient Greek tragedy. Groups of twelve to fifteen performers would chant an entrance song and then sing and dance during the play. The group's leader would engage in dialogue with the characters. In Shakespeare's plays, the chorus is usually one individual whose role ranges from introducing the play to helping the audience visualize the unfolding drama. AS

English Language Coach

Words No Longer in Use Explain to English language learners that many words and expressions common in Shakespeare's day are now obsolete or have changed in meaning. The word *doth,* for instance, is a shortened form of *doeth,* and both words are archaic forms of the verb *do.* Pair nonnative English speakers with native English speakers. Have partners work together to identify other examples and then write pairs of sentences illustrating archaic and modern usage. EL

Academic Standards

Additional Support activities on pp. 696 and 697 cover the following standards:

Skills Practice: **9.2** Develop [reading] strategies ...

English Language Coach: **9.1** [Use] origins...and a growing knowledge of English...to determine the meaning of words...

Teach

R1 Reading Strategy

Summarizing **Ask:** Why do you think Shakespeare begins the play with a rowdy, action-packed street fight? *(To capture the audience's attention and to introduce the main conflict)* **OL**

L Literary Element

Foil **Answer:** *Sampson seems rash and eager to fight the Montagues. Gregory pokes fun at his friend's boasts to steer him away from a confrontation.* **OL**

★ Writer's Technique

The Prologue is in the form of a fourteen-line sonnet with the following rhyme scheme: *abab, cdcd, efef, gg.* Shakespeare often uses sonnets and rhymed couplets to emphasize crucial speeches. **AS**

CheckPoint

Use CheckPoint questions on Presentation Plus! to monitor students' comprehension. These questions can be used with interactive response keypads for immediate student feedback.

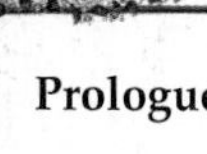

Act 1

Prologue

CHORUS.° Two households, both alike in dignity,°
In fair Verona, where we lay our scene,
From ancient grudge break to new mutiny,°
Where civil blood makes civil hands unclean.°
From forth the fatal° loins of these two foes
A pair of star-cross'd° lovers take their life;
★ Whose misadventur'd° piteous overthrows°
Doth with their death bury their parents' strife.
The fearful passage of their death-mark'd love,
And the continuance of their parents' rage,
Which, but° their children's end, nought could remove,
Is now the two hours' traffic of our stage;°
The which if you with patient ears attend,
What here shall miss, our toil shall strive to mend.°

[*The* CHORUS *exits.*]

1 **Chorus:** Elizabethan dramatists sometimes used a figure known as the chorus to comment on a play's action and describe events not shown on stage. In this prologue, or introduction, the chorus explains what the play is about. **dignity:** social status.
3 **mutiny** (mū′ tə nē): violence.
4 **civil blood . . . unclean:** citizens soil their hands with each other's blood.
5 **fatal:** ill-fated.
6 **star-cross'd:** doomed because of the positions of the planets when they were born.
7 **misadventur'd:** unfortunate. **overthrows:** ruin.
11 **but:** except for.
12 **two hours' . . . stage:** subject of our play.
14 **What here . . . mend:** We will try to clarify in our performance whatever is unclear in this prologue.

SCENE 1. Early morning. A public square in Verona.

R1 [*SAMPSON and GREGORY, servants of the Capulets, enter. Because of the feud between the powerful Capulet and Montague families, they are armed with swords and bucklers, or small shields.*]

SAMPSON. Gregory, on my word, we'll not carry coals.°

GREGORY. No, for then we should be colliers.°

SAMPSON. I mean, and we be in choler, we'll draw.°

GREGORY. Ay, while you live, draw your neck out of collar.°

SAMPSON. I strike quickly,° being mov'd.°

GREGORY. But thou art not quickly° mov'd to strike.

SAMPSON. A dog of the house of Montague moves me.

GREGORY. To move is to stir, and to be valiant is to stand. Therefore, if thou art mov'd, thou run'st away.

SAMPSON. A dog of that house shall move me to stand. I will take the wall° of any man or maid of Montague's.

GREGORY. That shows thee a weak slave, for the weakest goes to the wall.°

SAMPSON. 'Tis true, and therefore women, being the weaker vessels, are ever thrust to the wall;° therefore I will push Montague's men from the wall, and thrust his maids to the wall.

GREGORY. The quarrel is between our masters and us their men.

1 **carry coals:** put up with insults (an Elizabethan expression).
2 **colliers** (kol′ yərz): coal vendors.
3 **and . . . draw:** if we are angry, or **in choler** (kol′ ər), we will draw our swords.
4 **collar:** the hangman's noose. (Gregory extends the pun with *collier* and *choler.*)
5 **quickly:** vigorously. **mov'd:** roused.
6 **quickly:** speedily.
11 **take the wall:** walk on the side of the path closest to the walls of houses. (Since this was the cleaner side, Sampson is asserting his superiority over any of the Montague servants.)
12–13 **weakest . . . wall:** the weakest are pushed to the rear.
15 **thrust to the wall:** assaulted.

Literary Element Foil *What contrasts do you see between Gregory and Sampson?* **L**

Additional Support

Skills Practice

LANGUAGE: Exceptional Possessives **Write on the board:** *the heads of the maids.* **Ask:** How else could you say this? *(the maids' heads)* Point out "or maid of Montague's" in line 11. **Ask:** Is this possessive form an error? *(No, when one of several is implied, this usage is fine. Note that we typically say "a friend of mine" (possessive pronoun) as opposed to "a friend of me.")* **Write on the board:** *(a) Romeo and Juliet's love and (b) Romeo's and Juliet's love.* **Ask:** Which is right? *(a; When something is possessed equally by two closely linked nouns, only the second noun takes the possessive form.)* **OL**

Camera degli Sposi (The Wedding Chamber), 1474 (detail). Andrea Mantegna. Fresco. Palazzo Ducale, Mantua, Italy.
Viewing the Art: Which details in this fresco help you visualize what life was like in northern Italy in the fourteenth and fifteenth centuries? ★

SAMPSON. 'Tis all one.° I will show myself a tyrant. When I have fought with the men, I will be civil with the maids; I will cut off their heads.

GREGORY. The heads of the maids?

SAMPSON. Ay, the heads of the maids, or their maidenheads, take it in what sense thou wilt.

GREGORY. They must take it in sense° that feel it.

SAMPSON. Me they shall feel while I am able to stand, and 'tis known I am a pretty piece of flesh.

GREGORY. 'Tis well thou art not fish; if thou hadst, thou hadst been poor-John.° Draw thy tool,° here comes two of the house of Montagues.

[*ABRAM and BALTHASAR, servants of the Montagues, enter.*]

SAMPSON. My naked weapon is out. Quarrel! I will back thee.

GREGORY. How? Turn thy back and run?

SAMPSON. Fear me not.

GREGORY. No, marry.° I fear thee!

SAMPSON. Let us take the law of our sides; let them begin.°

19 **one:** the same.

25 Gregory plays on two meanings of **sense,** "feeling" and "meaning."

29 **poor-John:** salted fish (considered a poor man's dish). **tool:** sword.

34 **marry:** by the Virgin Mary (a mild oath similar to *indeed*).

35 **Let us . . . begin:** Sampson wants to let them begin the fight so that he and Gregory can claim to have fought in self-defense.

Reading Strategy Summarizing *What have you learned so far about the grudge between the Capulets and Montagues?* R2

Teach

R2 Reading Strategy

Summarizing Answer: *The long-standing hostility between the families is so intense and unyielding that even their servants are at war.*

Have students review the dialogue between Sampson and Gregory and describe its subject, mood, and language. *(Their crude talk about their master's feud is alternately hostile and jesting.)* OL

★ Viewing the Art

Answer: *Clothing shows nobles' lavish lifestyle; ornate carvings and domed arches show architectural style; figure groupings suggest sexes didn't mingle as freely as today.*

This detail from The *Wedding Chamber* by Andrea Mantegna (1431–1506) is a small segment of a famous *trompe l'oeil* (French for "trick of the eye") fresco. Painted on the walls and ceiling of a tiny windowless room, the mural's masterly use of perspective creates the illusion of a pavilion topped with a dome opening to the sky. AS

Differentiated Instruction

Character Movement To help students struggling to understand the play's language to envision the action, discuss the stage directions accompanying the dialogue. Invite volunteers to pantomime a summary of the scene, while classmates direct them in appropriate movements. Other volunteers can write and read a summary of the action. BL

Academic Standards

Additional Support activities on pp. 698 and 699 cover the following standards:

Skills Practice: **9.6.2** Demonstrate an understanding of...proper English usage...

Differentiated Instruction: **9.3.3** Analyze interactions between characters...and explain the way those interactions affect the plot.

Teach

R Reading Strategy

Summarizing **Answer:** *The Capulets' servants Gregory and Sampson encounter Abram and Balthasar, Montague servants. After Sampson and Gregory banter about whether to pick a fight, Sampson goads their enemies into a skirmish.*
Say: Shakespeare doesn't reveal the cause of the feud. What do you think it might be? *(Students may propose issues serious enough to cause deep and lasting hatred. Note that the omission of a specific cause might also imply that the feud's origin is too trivial to recall.)* OL

★ Writer's Technique

Puns The puns exemplified in the clever wordplay between Gregory and Sampson were sure-fire crowd pleasers in Shakespeare's day. Also known as paronomasias, puns often employ homophones—words that sound alike but have different meanings—for humorous or ironic effect. AS

GREGORY. I will frown as I pass by, and let them take it as they list.°

SAMPSON. Nay, as they dare. I will bite my thumb° at them, which is disgrace to them if they bear it.

ABRAM. Do you bite your thumb at us, sir?

SAMPSON. I do bite my thumb, sir.

ABRAM. Do you bite your thumb at us, sir?

SAMPSON. [*Aside to* GREGORY.] Is the law of our side if I say ay?

GREGORY. [*Aside to* SAMPSON.] No.

SAMPSON. No, sir, I do not bite my thumb at you, sir; but I bite my thumb, sir.

GREGORY. Do you quarrel, sir?

ABRAM. Quarrel, sir? No, sir.

SAMPSON. But if you do, sir, I am for you.° I serve as good a man as you.

ABRAM. No better?

SAMPSON. Well, sir.

[*Enter* BENVOLIO, LORD MONTAGUE'S *nephew.*]

GREGORY. Say "better." Here comes one of my master's kinsmen.

SAMPSON. Yes, better, sir.

ABRAM. You lie.

SAMPSON. Draw, if you be men. Gregory, remember thy washing° blow.

[*They fight.*]

BENVOLIO. Part, fools!
Put up your swords. You know not what you do. [*Beats down their swords.*]

[TYBALT, LADY CAPULET'S *nephew, enters with his sword drawn. He speaks first to* BENVOLIO.]

TYBALT. What, art thou drawn among these heartless hinds?°
Turn thee, Benvolio; look upon thy death.

BENVOLIO. I do but keep the peace. Put up thy sword,
Or manage it to part these men with me.

37 **list:** please.

38 **bite my thumb:** an insulting gesture.

49 **I am for you:** I accept your challenge.

58 **washing:** slashing.

61 **heartless hinds:** cowardly servants. Tybalt, assuming that Benvolio is involved in the servants' quarrel, challenges him to fight someone of his own rank.

Reading Strategy Summarizing *Summarize what has happened thus far in Scene 1.* R

Additional Support

Skills Practice

LISTENING/SPEAKING: Comic vs. Dramatic Speeches This scene jumps from comic wordplay into violent action. An oral interpretation will enable students to experience this dramatic shift firsthand. Assign segments of dialogue from the first and second halves of the scene to groups of students. Discuss character and motivation to determine each speaker's tone of voice, gestures, and body language before each group performs before the class. OL

TYBALT. What, drawn, and talk of peace? I hate the word
As I hate hell, all Montagues, and thee.
Have at thee, coward!

[*BENVOLIO and TYBALT fight as men of both families enter and join the brawl. Then an OFFICER of the town and several CITIZENS enter. They carry clubs, battle-axes (bills), and spears (partisans).*]

CITIZENS. Clubs, bills and partisans! Strike! Beat them down!
Down with the Capulets! Down with the Montagues!

[*LORD CAPULET, in his dressing gown, and LADY CAPULET enter.*]

CAPULET. What noise is this? Give me my long sword, ho!

LADY CAPULET. A crutch, a crutch! Why call you for a sword?

CAPULET. My sword, I say! Old Montague is come
And flourishes his blade in spite° of me.

[*LORD MONTAGUE and LADY MONTAGUE enter. LADY MONTAGUE tries to hold back her husband.*]

MONTAGUE. Thou villain Capulet!—Hold me not; let me go.

LADY MONTAGUE. Thou shalt not stir one foot to seek a foe.

[*PRINCE ESCALUS enters with his TRAIN.*]

PRINCE. Rebellious subjects, enemies to peace,
Profaners of this neighbor-stained steel°—
Will they not hear? What, ho! You men, you beasts,
That quench the fire of your **pernicious** rage
With purple fountains issuing from your veins!
On pain of torture, from those bloody hands
Throw your mistemper'd° weapons to the ground
And hear the sentence of your moved° prince.
Three civil brawls, bred of an airy word
By thee, old Capulet, and Montague,
Have thrice disturb'd the quiet of our streets
And made Verona's ancient citizens
Cast by their grave beseeming ornaments°
To wield old partisans, in hands as old,
Cank'red with peace,° to part your cank'red hate.°
If ever you disturb our streets again,
Your lives shall pay the forfeit of the peace.°
For this time all the rest depart away.
You, Capulet, shall go along with me;
And, Montague, come you this afternoon,

73 **spite:** defiance.

77 **Profaners . . . steel:** Those who disrespect the law by staining their weapons with neighbors' blood.

82 **mistemper'd:** "poorly made" or "put to bad use."
83 **moved:** angry.

88 **Cast by . . . ornaments:** put aside the dignified clothing appropriate for their age.

90 **Cank'red with peace:** rusty from disuse. **cank'red hate:** dangerous feud.

92 **Your lives . . . peace:** You will pay with your lives for disturbing the peace.

Literary Element Foil *What does this comment indicate about the difference between Benvolio and Tybalt?* **L**

Vocabulary

pernicious (pər nish′ əs) *adj.* destructive; deadly

Teach

L Literary Element

Foil **Answer:** *Benvolio is more restrained and conciliatory than the hotheaded Tybalt.* **OL**

Literary History

Shakespeare's 37 plays comprise 104,000 lines. About 28 percent of his work is prose; 7 percent, rhyming verse; and 65 percent, blank verse (unrhymed poetry with 10 syllables per lines, 5 stressed and 5 unstressed). *Romeo and Juliet* deviates from this pattern, consisting of about 17 percent rhymed verse. **AS**

Building Reading Fluency

Reading Aloud Closer study of Shakespeare's use of punctuation in long passages such as the prince's speech may be helpful. Have students reread the passage silently, noting pauses, line endings, and apostrophes. Point out that the passage resembles a poem and remind students that a line break does not necessarily indicate the end of a sentence. Partners should then take turns reading the speech aloud and paraphrasing its meaning. **BL**

Academic Standards

Additional Support activities on pp. 700 and 701 cover the following standards:

Skills Practice: **9.7.6** Analyze the occasion and...choose effective verbal and nonverbal techniques (including voice, gestures, and eye contact) for presentations.

Building Reading Fluency: **9.7.17** Deliver oral responses to literature that demonstrate awareness of the author's writing style and an appreciation of the effects created...

Teach

R1 Reading Strategy

Summarizing Answer: *He condemns the families for disturbing the peace, bans further fighting, and warns that violators will be executed.* OL

★ Cultural History

Melancholy In sixteenth-century England, four cardinal "humors," or fluids—choler, phlegm, blood, and melancholy—were thought to control personality, mood, and health. An imbalance in these humors was believed to cause sickness or even death. *The Anatomy of Melancholy,* a famous treatise on depression published by Robert Burton in 1621, recognized the melancholy of lovers, such as that suffered by Romeo, as a serious disease. AS

To know our farther pleasure in this case,
To old Freetown, our common judgment place.
Once more, on pain of death, all men depart.

[*Everyone leaves except* MONTAGUE, LADY MONTAGUE, *and their nephew* BENVOLIO.]

MONTAGUE. Who set this ancient quarrel new abroach?°
Speak, nephew, were you by when it began?

BENVOLIO. Here were the servants of your adversary
And yours, close fighting ere I did approach.
I drew to part them. In the instant came
The fiery Tybalt, with his sword prepar'd;
Which, as he breath'd° defiance to my ears,
He swung about his head and cut the winds,
Who, nothing hurt withal,° hiss'd him in scorn.
While we were interchanging thrusts and blows,
Came more and more, and fought on part and part,°
Till the Prince came, who parted either part.

LADY MONTAGUE. O, where is Romeo? Saw you him today?
Right glad I am he was not at this fray.

BENVOLIO. Madam, an hour before the worship'd sun
Peer'd forth° the golden window of the east,
A troubl'd mind drive° me to walk abroad;
Where, underneath the grove of sycamore
That westward rooteth from° this city side,
So early walking did I see your son.
Towards him I made, but he was ware° of me
And stole into the covert of the wood.°
I, measuring his affections,° by my own,
Which then most sought where most might not be found,°
Being one too many by my weary self,
★ Pursued my humor not pursuing his,°
And gladly shunn'd who gladly fled from me.

MONTAGUE. Many a morning hath he there been seen,
With tears augmenting the fresh morning's dew,
Adding to clouds more clouds with his deep sighs;
But all so soon as the all-cheering sun
Should in the farthest east begin to draw
The shady curtains from Aurora's° bed,
Away from light steals home my heavy° son
And private in his chamber pens himself,
Shuts up his windows, locks fair daylight out,
And makes himself an artificial night.

99 **Who . . . abroach:** Who reopened this old feud?

105 **breath'd:** uttered.

107 **nothing hurt withal:** not hurt by this.

109 **Came more . . . part:** More and more men arrived and fought on one side or the other.

114 **forth:** out from.

115 **drive:** drove.

117 **westward rooteth from:** grows to the west of.

119 **ware:** aware.

120 **covert of the wood:** concealment of the forest.

121 **affections:** feelings.

122 **most sought . . . found:** wanted to find a solitary place.

124 **Pursued my . . . his:** followed my own mood **(humor)** by not following him.

131 **Aurora** (ə rôr′ ə): the goddess of the dawn in classical mythology.

132 **heavy:** sad.

Reading Strategy Summarizing *Summarize the prince's words to the crowd. What is his attitude toward the brawls between the Capulets and Montagues?* R1

Additional Support

Skills Practice

READING: Constructing a Flow Chart Have students create a flow chart to map the progression of the plot. Suggest that they arrange events in either sequential or cause-and-effect order. Encourage interested students to draw parallel charts, diagramming (1) the conflict between the Capulets and Montagues and (2) Romeo and Juliet's dilemma. Challenge them to connect the charts when the events overlap. OL

Black and portentous must this humor prove
Unless good counsel may the cause remove.°

BENVOLIO. My noble uncle, do you know the cause?

MONTAGUE. I neither know it nor can learn of him.

BENVOLIO. Have you importun'd° him by any means?

MONTAGUE. Both by myself and many other friends;
But he, his own affections' counselor,
Is to himself—I will not say how true°—
But to himself so secret and so close,°
So far from sounding and discovery,°
As is the bud bit with an envious worm
Ere he can spread his sweet leaves to the air
Or dedicate his beauty to the sun.°
Could we but learn from whence his sorrows grow,
We would as willingly give cure as know.

[*ROMEO enters. He appears distracted and does not notice the others on stage.*]

BENVOLIO. See where he comes. So please you step aside;
I'll know his grievance, or be much denied.

MONTAGUE. I would thou wert so happy by thy stay
To hear true shrift.° Come, madam, let's away.

[*MONTAGUE and LADY MONTAGUE leave.*]

BENVOLIO. Good morrow,° cousin.

ROMEO. Is the day so young?

BENVOLIO. But new° struck nine.

ROMEO. Ay me! Sad hours seem long.
Was that my father that went hence so fast?

BENVOLIO. It was. What sadness lengthens Romeo's hours?

ROMEO. Not having that which having makes them short.

BENVOLIO. In love?

ROMEO. Out—

BENVOLIO. Of love?

ROMEO. Out of her favor where I am in love.

BENVOLIO. Alas that love, so gentle in his view,
Should be so tyrannous and rough in proof!°

136–137 **Black and . . . remove:** Montague fears that this mood will lead to trouble if allowed to continue.

140 **importun'd:** questioned.

143 **how true:** how trustworthy (a counselor Romeo is to himself).
144 **close:** secretive, reticent.
145 **far from . . . discovery:** unwilling to let others question and come to understand him.

146–148 **As is the bud . . . the sun:** Montague compares Romeo to a bud that is destroyed by a malicious caterpillar before it can open its petals.

153–154 **I would . . . shrift:** I hope that by waiting (for Romeo) you will be lucky enough to hear a true confession.

155 **morrow:** morning.

156 **But new:** only just.

164–165 **love . . . proof:** love appears so gentle but proves to be a rough tyrant.

Big Idea The Power of Love *From Montague's description of Romeo's behavior, what ideas are you forming about Romeo?* **BI**

Reading Strategy Summarizing *What information has Benvolio just extracted from Romeo?* **R2**

Teach

BI Big Idea

The Power of Love Answer: *Students may say that Romeo seems romantic, emotional, or impulsive.* **OL** Invite two volunteers to read the parts of Benvolio and Montague (lines 113–139) aloud. **Ask:** Why might Benvolio have decided not to pursue Romeo into the woods? *(Perhaps he sensed Romeo's desire to be alone or had too much on his mind to deal with Romeo's distress.)* **OL**

L Literary Element

Rhymed Couplets Have students read Benvolio's and Montague's speeches aloud. Explain that each speech comprises a couplet—a pair of lines that rhyme. Then have students read aloud the speeches of Benvolio and Romeo. Note that one character speaks the first half of a line; and another, the second half. Together, the four lines form a couplet, with the near rhyme (or off rhyme) *young* and *long.* **OL**

R2 Reading Strategy

Summarizing Answer: *Romeo is in love, but his love is not returned.* **OL**

Differentiated Instruction

Prereading Vocabulary Students may find checking definitions in the side column as they read distracting. Suggest that instead of plunging into the main text, they begin each page by reviewing the side-column information. Have them locate the sentence in which the word or phrase appears, review the definition, and then read the sentence. This preparation will not only improve their comprehension but also increase their enjoyment of the play. **BL**

Academic Standards

Additional Support activities on pp. 702 and 703 cover the following standards:

Skills Practice: **9.3.6** Analyze and trace an author's development of time and sequence...

Differentiated Instruction: **9.2** Develop [reading] strategies...

Teach

BI1 Big Idea

The Power of Love **Answer:** *Love is blind ("love, whose view is muffled still"); love of family can lead to feuds ("O brawling love, O loving hate").* **OL**

L Literary Element

Oxymoron Remind students that an oxymoron combines opposite or contradictory terms. Invite a volunteer to identify the oxymorons in Romeo's speech and explain in what sense they are true. *(Example: "brawling love . . . loving hate." Family loyalty demands that Montagues hate Capulets; Romeo loves, but his love has not brought happiness.)* **OL**

BI2 Big Idea

The Power of Love **Answer:** *He is distressed to see his good friend so depressed.* **OL**

★ Viewing the Art

Answer: *His fine clothes suggest a young aristocratic hero. His expression is pensive, suggesting Romeo's melancholy.*

Known for religious paintings, Italian painter Biagio d'Antonio (1446–1516) assisted with work on the Sistine Chapel. **AS**

Portrait of a Young Man, ca. 1470. Biagio d'Antonio.
Viewing the Art: In what ways does the young man in the painting remind you of Romeo? ★

ROMEO. Alas that love, whose view is muffled still,
Should without eyes see pathways to his will!°
Where shall we dine? O me! What fray was here?°
Yet tell me not, for I have heard it all.
Here's much to do with hate, but more with love.
Why then, O brawling love, O loving hate,
O any thing, of nothing first create!°
O heavy lightness, serious vanity,
Misshapen chaos of well-seeming forms,
Feather of lead, bright smoke, cold fire, sick health,
Still-waking sleep, that is not what it is!°
This love feel I, that feel no love in this.°
Dost thou not laugh?

BENVOLIO. No, coz,° I rather weep.

ROMEO. Good heart, at what?

BENVOLIO. At thy good heart's oppression.

ROMEO. Why, such is love's transgression.
Griefs of mine own lie heavy in my breast,
Which thou wilt propagate, to have it press'd
With more of thine.° This love that thou hast shown

166–167 **Alas that . . . will:** Romeo regrets that love, although blind, is still able to hit its target. (Cupid, the god of love, is often portrayed wearing a blindfold.)

168 **What fray was here:** Romeo only now notices blood or some other sign of the fighting.

172 **of nothing first create:** Romeo refers to the idea that God created the universe from nothing.

170–176 **Here's much . . . it is:** Romeo says that the feud involves love (of fighting and devotion to family) as well as hatred. He then suggests the paradoxical nature of love.

177 **that feel no love in this:** who feels no happiness from this sort of love.

178 **coz:** cousin. (Any relative might be addressed as cousin.)

182–183 **Which thou . . . thine:** Your concern over my grief only increases the burden of my sorrow.

Big Idea The Power of Love *What details in Romeo's dialogue help illustrate love's power?* **BI1**

Big Idea The Power of Love *Why is Benvolio upset?* **BI2**

Additional Support

Skills Practice

WRITING: Related Ideas Within Sentences Have students read lines 170–177: Write contrasting word pairs on the board:

brawling	loving
love	hate

Note how the use of parallel construction—using two participles with opposite meanings to modify two nouns with opposite meanings—weighs one idea against the other in a way that is pleasing to the ear.

Have students write sentences that balance related ideas. **OL**

Doth add more grief to too much of mine own.
Love is a smoke made with the fume of sighs;
Being purg'd,° a fire sparkling in lovers' eyes;
Being vex'd, a sea nourish'd with loving tears.
What is it else? A madness most discreet,°
A choking gall,° and a preserving sweet.
Farewell, my coz.

BENVOLIO. Soft!° I will go along.
And if you leave me so, you do me wrong.

ROMEO. Tut! I have lost myself; I am not here;
This is not Romeo, he's some other where.

BENVOLIO. Tell me in sadness,° who is that you love?

ROMEO. What, shall I groan and tell thee?

BENVOLIO. Groan? Why, no;
But sadly tell me who.

ROMEO. Bid a sick man in sadness make his will.
A word ill urg'd to one that is so ill!
In sadness, cousin, I do love a woman.

BENVOLIO. I aim'd so near when I suppos'd you lov'd.

ROMEO. A right good markman. And she's fair I love.

BENVOLIO. A right fair mark,° fair coz, is soonest hit.

ROMEO. Well, in that hit you miss. She'll not be hit
With Cupid's arrow. She hath Dian's wit,°
And, in strong proof° of chastity well arm'd,
From Love's weak childish bow she lives uncharm'd.
★ She will not stay the siege of loving terms,°
Nor bide° th' encounter of assailing eyes,
Nor ope her lap to saint-seducing gold.°
O, she is rich in beauty; only poor
That, when she dies, with beauty dies her store.°

BENVOLIO. Then she hath sworn that she will still° live chaste?

ROMEO. She hath, and in that sparing makes huge waste;
For beauty starv'd with her severity
Cuts beauty off from all **posterity.**°
She is too fair,° too wise, wisely too fair,
To merit bliss° by making me despair.
She hath forsworn to° love, and in that vow
Do I live dead that live to tell it now.

BENVOLIO. Be ruled by me; forget to think of her.

186 **Being purg'd:** when the smoke has cleared.

188 **discreet:** discriminating.

189 **gall:** bitterness.

190 **Soft:** Wait a minute!

194 **in sadness:** seriously.

202 **right fair mark:** easily seen target.

204 **Dian's wit:** the cleverness of Diana, Roman goddess of chastity.

205 **proof:** armor.

207 **stay . . . terms:** submit to courtship.

208 **bide:** tolerate.

209 **Nor ope . . . gold:** Nor can she be seduced by expensive gifts.

211 **when she . . . store:** When she dies, all her wealth will die with her beauty (because she will have no children to inherit her beauty).

212 **still:** always.

213–215 **In that sparing . . . posterity:** Romeo says that her thriftiness is really wasteful, because no children will be born to perpetuate her beauty.

216 **fair:** "beautiful" or "just."

217 **To merit bliss:** to win heavenly bliss.

218 **forsworn to:** sworn not to.

Reading Strategy Summarizing *What do we learn about the woman Romeo loves in this speech?* **R**

Vocabulary

posterity (pos ter′ ə tē) *n.* future generations

Teach

R Reading Strategy

Summarizing **Answer:** *She vows to remain chaste, refuses to be courted, and accepts no presents.* **OL**

★ Cultural History

Women's Place In Shakespeare's time, marriage and childbearing were considered a woman's destiny. While Elizabeth I managed to remain unmarried without damaging her immense popularity, single women were generally regarded with suspicion. The choice of a mate was usually dictated by a woman's father and generally involved complicated negotiations in pursuit of financial or political gain or to cement alliances. **AS**

Differentiated Instruction

Interpersonal Learning Invite volunteers to describe how they might counsel a friend about a relationship. Ask them to explain what Benvolio senses about Romeo's predicament and to evaluate his strategy for helping Romeo.

Have partners write a letter that a modern-day Romeo might send to an advice columnist. Then ask pairs to exchange letters, with each partner writing a reply. Have partners read their letters to the class and discuss them. **BL**

Academic Standards

Additional Support activities on pp. 704 and 705 cover the following standards:

Skills Practice: **9.6.2** Demonstrate an understanding of sentence construction, including parallel structure…

Differentiated Instruction: **9.5.8** Write for different purposes and audiences, adjusting tone, style, and voice as appropriate.

Teach

R Reading Strategy

Summarizing Answer: *Romeo claims that nothing can cure him of his love. Benvolio vows to keep trying.* **OL**

★ Cultural History

Velvet Masks Women of the Elizabethan era often carried or wore black velvet masks that covered their entire faces to protect their complexions from the sun. Sometimes viewed as an expression of modesty, the mask would also hide women's faces from undesirable acquaintances. **AS**

ROMEO. O, teach me how I should forget to think!

BENVOLIO. By giving liberty unto thine eyes.
Examine other beauties.

ROMEO. 'Tis the way
To call hers, exquisite, in question more.°
★ These happy° masks° that kiss fair ladies' brows,
Being black puts us in mind they hide the fair.
He that is strucken blind cannot forget
The precious treasure of his eyesight lost.
Show me a mistress that is passing° fair:
What doth her beauty serve but as a note
Where I may read who pass'd° that passing fair?
Farewell. Thou canst not teach me to forget.

BENVOLIO. I'll pay that doctrine, or else die in debt.°

[*They exit.*]

223–224 **'Tis . . . more:** Examining other women will only make me dwell more upon her exquisite beauty.
225 **happy:** fortunate. **masks:** worn by fashionable Elizabethan women to protect fair complexions from the sun.

229 **passing:** surpassingly.

231 **pass'd:** surpassed.

233 **I'll pay . . . debt:** I'll teach you to forget, or never give up trying until I die.

SCENE 2. Later that afternoon. A street near CAPULET's house in Verona.

[*CAPULET enters with COUNT PARIS, a young relative of the PRINCE, and with a SERVANT.*]

CAPULET. But Montague is bound as well as I,
In penalty alike; and 'tis not hard, I think,
For men so old as we to keep the peace.

PARIS. Of honorable reckoning° are you both,
And pity 'tis you liv'd at odds so long.
But now, my lord, what say you to my suit?

CAPULET. But saying o'er what I have said before:
My child is yet a stranger in the world,
She hath not seen the change of fourteen years;
Let two more summers wither in their pride
Ere we may think her ripe to be a bride.

PARIS. Younger than she are happy mothers made.

CAPULET. And too soon marr'd are those so early made.
Earth hath swallowed all my hopes but she;°
She is the hopeful lady of my earth.°
But woo her, gentle Paris, get her heart;
My will to her consent is but a part.
And she agreed within her scope of choice
Lies my consent and fair according voice.°
This night I hold an old accustom'd° feast,
Whereto I have invited many a guest,
Such as I love; and you among the store,

4 **reckoning:** reputation.

14 **Earth hath . . . she:** She is my only surviving child.
15 **She is . . . earth:** "She will inherit all my property," or "she is the woman in whom all my hopes lie."

18–19 **And she . . . voice:** As long as she chooses appropriately, I will let her marry whomever she chooses.
20 **old accustom'd:** long established.

Reading Strategy Summarizing *How would you summarize Romeo and Benvolio's conversation?* **R**

Additional Support

Skills Practice

READING: Paraphrasing Note that paraphrasing means restating an author's words in one's own. Explain that the ability to paraphrase will be essential to understanding this play.

Have volunteers read aloud passages such as Capulet's speech (lines 13–34, Scene 2). Pause to read explanatory notes. Then invite several volunteers to paraphrase the passage, and ask the class to critique each version to arrive at the correct meaning. **OL**

One more, most welcome, makes my number more.
At my poor house look to behold this night
Earth-treading stars° that make dark heaven light.
Such comfort as do lusty young men feel
When well-apparel'd April on the heel
Of limping Winter treads, even such delight
Among fresh fennel buds shall you this night
Inherit at my house.° Hear all, all see,
And like her most whose merit most shall be;
Which, on more view of many, mine, being one,
May stand in number, though in reck'ning none.°
Come, go with me.

[*CAPULET speaks to his SERVANT and hands him a piece of paper that contains the names of the people he is inviting to his party.*]

Go, sirrah,° trudge about
Through fair Verona; find those persons out
Whose names are written there, and to them say
My house and welcome on their pleasure stay.°

[*CAPULET and PARIS exit. The SERVANT, who cannot read, looks at the paper.*]

SERVANT. Find them out whose names are written here! It is written that the shoemaker should meddle with his yard and the tailor with his last, the fisher with his pencil and the painter with his nets; but I am sent to find those persons whose names are here writ, and can never find what names the writing person hath here writ.° I must to the learned. In good time!°

[*ROMEO and BENVOLIO enter, still talking about ROMEO's unhappiness in love.*]

BENVOLIO. Tut, man, one fire burns out another's burning;
One pain is less'ned by another's **anguish;**
Turn giddy, and be holp by backward turning;°
One desperate grief cures with another's languish.
Take thou some new infection to thy eye,
And the rank poison of the old will die.

ROMEO. Your plantan° leaf is excellent for that.

BENVOLIO. For what, I pray thee?

ROMEO. For your broken° shin.

25 **Earth-treading stars:** young women.

26–30 **Such comfort . . . house:** Tonight the pleasure you will take at my house is like the joy that young men feel when spring replaces winter.

30–33 **Hear all . . . none:** Capulet suggests that after Paris has compared Juliet to the others, she may strike him as merely one woman among many, not worth special consideration.

34 **sirrah** (sir′ ə): a term of address used when speaking to someone inferior in rank.

37 **stay:** wait.

38–43 **Find them . . . writ:** The illiterate servant means to say that people should stick to what they know how to do, but he comically mixes up the types of workers and their tools.

43 **In good time:** Just in time! (He sees men who appear to be educated.)

47 **Turn giddy . . . turning:** Become dizzy, and be helped by turning in the opposite direction.

51 **plantan:** plantain (a type of leaf used to stop bleeding).

52 **broken:** scraped.

Literary Element Foil *How does the character of the servant provide contrast to the characters who have just been talking?* **L**

Big Idea The Power of Love *What cure does Benvolio suggest for Romeo's lovesickness?* **BI**

Vocabulary

anguish (ang′ gwish) n. extreme suffering; agony

Teach

L Literary Element

Foil **Answer:** *The servant provides contrast in that he is from a lower class, is less knowledgeable, and provides comic relief.* **OL**

BI Big Idea

The Power of Love **Answer:** *Exposing Romeo to other beautiful women will extinguish his excessive love.* **OL** Invite a volunteer to read aloud lines 45–50. **Ask:** What point is Benvolio trying to make in this passage? *(He is trying to convince Romeo that there is a way out of his lovesickness, only if he would be willing to listen and consider what Benvolio has to say.)* **OL**

Reading in the Real World

Citizenship Instruct students to consult an almanac for statistics about the average age at which couples marry today and factors that affect this statistic. Invite volunteers to discuss their research and to compare and contrast Romeo and Juliet's situation with that of today's brides and grooms. **OL**

Academic Standards

Additional Support activities on pp. 706 and 707 cover the following standards:

Skills Practice: **9.7.7** Make judgments about the ideas under discussion and support those judgments with convincing evidence.

Reading in the Real World: **9.2.4** Synthesize the content from several sources or works...; paraphrase the ideas and connect them to...related topics...

Teach

BI1 Big Idea

The Power of Love Say: Explain Romeo's metaphor in line 55 when he says, "Shut up in prison, kept without my food." *(The prison is his own lovesick heart, and his food—which he lacks—is Rosaline's love.)* **OL**

R Reading Strategy

Summarizing Answer: *They learn that the Capulets are holding a big party. Since Rosaline will be there, Benvolio proposes that he and Romeo attend the party so Romeo can see that other women there are as fair as Rosaline.* **OL**

BI2 Big Idea

The Power of Love Have students identify and analyze the comparison Romeo makes here.
Ask: How does the comparison characterize Romeo? *(Romeo's lofty, extravagant comparison of love to a fiercely demanding religion suggests an impetuous nature and a highly romantic view of love.)* **OL**

BENVOLIO. Why, Romeo, art thou mad?

ROMEO. Not mad, but bound more than a madman is;
BI1 Shut up in prison, kept without my food,
Whipt and tormented and—God-den,° good fellow.

SERVANT. God gi'° god-den. I pray, sir, can you read?

ROMEO. Ay, mine own fortune in my misery.

SERVANT. Perhaps you have learn'd it without book.
But, I pray, can you read anything you see?

ROMEO. Ay, if I know the letters and the language.

SERVANT. Ye say honestly. Rest you merry.°

ROMEO. Stay, fellow; I can read. [*He reads.*]
"Signior Martino and his wife and daughters; County° Anselm and his beauteous sisters; the lady widow of Vitruvio; Signior Placentio and his lovely nieces; Mercutio and his brother Valentine; mine uncle Capulet, his wife and daughters; my fair niece Rosaline; Livia; Signior Valentio and his cousin Tybalt; Lucio and the lively Helena."
A fair assembly. Whither should they come?

SERVANT. Up.

ROMEO. Whither? To supper?

SERVANT. To our house.

ROMEO. Whose house?

SERVANT. My master's.

ROMEO. Indeed I should have ask'd thee that before.

SERVANT. Now I'll tell you without asking. My master is the great rich Capulet; and if you be not of the house of Montagues, I pray come and crush a cup° of wine. Rest you merry.

[*The* SERVANT *exits.*]

BENVOLIO. At this same ancient° feast of Capulet's
Sups the fair Rosaline whom thou so loves;
With all the admired beauties of Verona.
Go thither,° and with unattainted° eye
Compare her face with some that I shall show,
And I will make thee think thy swan a crow.

BI2 ROMEO. When the devout religion of mine eye
Maintains such falsehood, then turn tears to fires;
And these, who, often drown'd, could never die,
Transparent heretics,° be burnt for liars!°

56 **God-den:** good afternoon; good evening.
57 **God gi':** God give you.

62 **Rest you merry:** The servant misunderstands Romeo's reply and bids him farewell.
64 **County:** Count.

79 **crush a cup:** have a drink.

81 **ancient:** traditional.

84 **thither:** there. **unattainted:** impartial.

87–90 **When the . . . liars:** Romeo says that if he accepted such a falsehood, his tearful eyes would be heretics for having broken faith with Rosaline, and he would wish the tears turned to fire so that his eyes could be burned like heretics.
90 **heretics:** People who maintain a religious belief contrary to accepted doctrine.

Reading Strategy Summarizing *What do Benvolio and Romeo learn from the servant? What does Benvolio propose to do with the information?* **R**

Additional Support

Skills Practice

GRAMMAR: Subject-Verb Order
In most English sentences, the subject precedes the verb, but in verse this order is sometimes reversed (e.g., lines 81–82). Have students reverse the subject-verb order in each sentence. Point out the following sentences on page 709:

1. ". . . in that crystal scales let there be weigh'd / Your lady's love against some other maid." (lines 95 and 96) *((You) Let your lady's love be weighed . . . in that crystal scale.)*
2. "Come Lammas Eve at night shall she be fourteen." (line 17) *(She shall be fourteen come . . . night.)* **OL**

One fairer than my love? The all-seeing sun
Ne'er saw her match since first the world begun.

BENVOLIO. Tut! you saw her fair, none else being by,
Herself pois'd° with herself in either eye;
But in that crystal scales° let there be weigh'd
Your lady's love against some other maid
That I will show you shining at this feast,
And she shall scant show well that now seems best.

ROMEO. I'll go along, no such sight to be shown,
But to rejoice in splendor of mine own.°

[*They exit.*]

94 **pois'd:** weighed; compared.

95 **crystal scales:** That is, Romeo's eyes.

100 **in splendor of mine own:** in the splendor of my own lady (Rosaline).

SCENE 3. Later that evening, before the party. A room in CAPULET's house.

[*LADY CAPULET and the Capulets' NURSE enter.*]

LADY CAPULET. Nurse, where's my daughter? Call her forth
to me.

NURSE. Now by my maidenhead at twelve year old,
I bade her come. What, lamb! What, ladybird!
God forbid! Where's this girl? What, Juliet!

[*JULIET enters.*]

JULIET. How now? Who calls?

NURSE. Your mother.

JULIET. Madam, I am here.
What is your will?

LADY CAPULET. This is the matter—Nurse, give leave° awhile;
We must talk in secret. Nurse, come back again.
I have remember'd me; thou's hear our counsel.°
Thou knowest my daughter's of a pretty age.

NURSE. Faith, I can tell her age unto an hour.

LADY CAPULET. She's not fourteen.

NURSE. I'll lay fourteen of my teeth—
And yet, to my teen° be it spoken, I have but four—
She's not fourteen. How long is it now
To Lammastide?°

LADY CAPULET. A fortnight and odd days.°

NURSE. Even or odd, of all days in the year,
Come Lammas Eve at night shall she be fourteen.
Susan and she (God rest all Christian souls!)
Were of an age.° Well, Susan is with God;
She was too good for me. But, as I said,

8 **give leave:** leave us alone.

9 **thou's hear our counsel:** You shall hear our conversation.

13 **teen:** sorrow.

15 **Lammastide:** August 1, a religious feast day. **A fortnight and odd days:** two weeks plus a few days.

19 **of an age:** the same age. (The Nurse's daughter, now dead, was born around the same time as Juliet.)

Teach

Writer's Technique

Greek and Roman Influences Shakespeare used a wide variety of sources for the plots of his plays. Foremost among these were the history, mythology, and literature of ancient Greece and Rome. He was probably introduced to the comedies of the Roman playwright Plautus as well as to Ovid's *Metamorphoses* while studying Latin in school. The *Chronicles* of Rafael Holingshed was the source of many of his English history plays. **AS**

Differentiated Instruction

Read-Along Below-level readers may benefit from reading while listening to either a recording of the play or a dramatized reading by other members of the class. Select one scene for students to read along with an audiotape or dramatized reading. After students have finished reading, have them work in groups to complete a chart showing who was in the scene, what happened, when it happened, and why it happened. **BL**

Academic Standards

Additional Support activities on pp. 708 and 709 cover the following standards:

Skills Practice: **9.6.2** Demonstrate an understanding of sentence construction... and proper English usage...

Differentiated Instruction: **9.3** [Identify] story elements such as character,...plot, and setting...

Teach

L1 Literary Element

Foil Answer: *One is the biological mother; the other, the foster mother. The coarse Nurse is warm and intimate with Juliet. Lady Capulet is refined and reserved.*
Ask: How does Shakespeare temper the humor of the dialogue and engage our sympathy for the Nurse? *(In lines 18–20, the Nurse remembers her dead daughter, who would now be Juliet's age had she lived.)* OL

L2 Literary Element

Foil Answer: *She seems stiff and unamused.* AL Note that this long speech establishes the Nurse as a fully rounded character: humorous, affectionate, self-aware, and observant. **Ask:** Why do you think Shakespeare features the Nurse so prominently in the scene that introduces Juliet? *(Because the Nurse serves as a surrogate mother to Juliet, it's possible she'll play an important role in the relationship between Romeo and Juliet.)* OL

On Lammas Eve at night shall she be fourteen;
That shall she, marry;° I remember it well.
'Tis since the earthquake now eleven years;
And she was wean'd—I shall never forget it—
Of all the days of the year, upon that day;
For I had then laid wormwood° to my dug,°
Sitting in the sun under the dove-house wall.
My lord and you were then at Mantua—
Nay, I do bear a brain°—but as I said,
When it did taste the wormwood on the nipple
Of my dug and felt it bitter, pretty fool,
To see it teachy° and fall out wi' th' dug!
Shake, quoth the dove-house;° 'twas no need, I trow,
To bid me trudge.°
And since that time it is eleven years,
For then she could stand high-lone;° nay, by th' rood,°
She could have run and waddled all about;
For even the day before, she broke her brow,
And then my husband—God be with his soul!
'A° was a merry man—took up the child.
"Yea," quoth he, "dost thou fall upon thy face?
Thou wilt fall backward when thou hast more wit,°
Wilt thou not, Jule?" and by my holidam,°
The pretty wretch left crying and said, "Ay."
To see now how a jest shall come about!
I warrant, and I should live a thousand years,
I never should forget it: "Wilt thou not, Jule?" quoth he;
And, pretty fool, it stinted° and said, "Ay."

LADY CAPULET. Enough of this, I pray thee hold thy peace.

NURSE. Yes, madam, yet I cannot choose but laugh
To think it should leave crying and say, "Ay."
And yet I warrant it had upon its brow
A bump as big as a young cock'rel's stone—
A perilous knock—and it cried bitterly.
"Yea," quoth my husband, "fall'st upon thy face?
Thou wilt fall backward when thou comest to age,
Wilt thou not, Jule?" It stinted and said, "Ay."

JULIET. And stint thou too, I pray thee, nurse, say I.

NURSE. Peace, I have done. God mark thee to his grace!
Thou wast the prettiest babe that e'er I nurs'd.
And I might live to see thee married once,
I have my wish.

22 **marry:** indeed.

26 **wormwood:** a bitter oil from the leaves of a plant. **dug:** breast.

29 **I do bear a brain:** My mind is still sharp.

32 **teachy:** tetchy; irritably or peevishly sensitive.
33 **Shake . . . dove-house:** The dove-house began to shake from the earthquake.
34–35 **'twas . . . trudge:** I didn't need any urging to get away.
37 **high-lone:** upright without support. **rood:** cross.

40 **'A:** he.

42 **wit:** knowledge.
43 **by my holidam:** by my holiness (an oath).

48 **stinted:** stopped.

Literary Element Foil *How do the Nurse and Lady Capulet differ? How do their characters contrast?* L1

Literary Element Foil *How would you characterize Lady Capulet's response to the Nurse's funny story?* L2

Additional Support

Skills Practice

READING: Monitoring Comprehension Note that an awareness of the play's structure—its organization into acts and scenes with stage directions and labeled dialogue—will make it easier for students to follow the action. Suggest that students resolve confusion by reviewing elements such as character descriptions and the main events of the previous scene. Encourage them to jot down any unresolved questions in their notebooks. OL

LADY CAPULET. Marry, that "marry" is the very theme
I came to talk of. Tell me, daughter Juliet,
How stands your disposition to be married?

JULIET. It is an honor that I dream not of.

NURSE. An honor! were not I thine only nurse,
I would say thou hadst suck'd wisdom from thy teat.

LADY CAPULET. Well, think of marriage now. Younger than you,
Here in Verona, ladies of esteem,
Are made already mothers. By my count,
I was your mother much upon these years°
That you are now a maid. Thus then in brief:
The valiant Paris seeks you for his love.

NURSE. A man, young lady! Lady, such a man
As all the world—Why, he's a man of wax.°

LADY CAPULET. Verona's summer hath not such a flower.

NURSE. Nay, he's a flower, in faith—a very flower.

LADY CAPULET. What say you? Can you love the gentleman?
This night you shall behold him at our feast.
Read o'er the volume° of young Paris' face,
And find delight writ there with beauty's pen;
Examine every married lineament,°
And see how one another lends content;
And what obscur'd in this fair volume lies
Find written in the margent° of his eyes.
This precious book of love, this unbound lover,
To beautify him only lacks a cover.°
The fish lives in the sea, and 'tis much pride
For fair without the fair within to hide.°
That book in many's eyes doth share the glory,
That in gold clasps locks in the golden story;
So shall you share all that he doth possess,
By having him making yourself no less.

★ NURSE. No less! nay, bigger: women grow° by men.

LADY CAPULET. Speak briefly, can you like of Paris' love?

JULIET. I'll look to like, if looking liking move;
But no more deep will I endart mine eye
Than your consent gives strength to make it fly.°

72 **much upon these years:** at about the same age.

76 **man of wax:** a model man, as perfect as a wax statue.

81 **volume:** book. (This metaphor is extended in lines 82–92.)

83 **every married lineament** (lin′ ē ə mənt): all the harmonious features of his face.

86 **margent** (mär′ jənt): margin (which, like the marginal notes in a book, reveal whatever is not clear in the rest of his face).

88 **cover:** binding (that is, a wife).

89–90 **The fish . . . hide:** The fair sea is made even more beautiful by the fair fish hiding within it.

95 **grow:** become pregnant.

97–99 **I'll look . . . fly:** I am prepared to look favorably on him, if looking can persuade me, but I won't give him encouraging glances beyond your approval.

Literary Element Foil *Compare and contrast the reactions of the Nurse and Lady Capulet in this scene. What is the focus and principal concern of each character?* L3

Reading Strategy Summarizing *Summarize Lady Capulet's attempt to persuade her daughter. How does Juliet respond?* R

Teach

L3 Literary Element

Foil **Answer:** *Although both women approve of the match, the Nurse's emphasis on the physical aspects of marriage contrasts with Lady Capulet's focus on wealth and status. The Nurse seems concerned primarily with Juliet's happiness, while the more distant Lady Capulet wants to ensure Juliet's financial security and social position.* OL

R Reading Strategy

Summarizing **Answer:** *She notes Paris's good looks and fine character as well as the economic advantages to be gained. Juliet seems neutral on the proposal but dutifully agrees to consider it.* OL

★ Cultural History

Men in Women's Roles
Because English law barred Elizabethan women from appearing onstage, male actors played all the female roles. Most scholars believe that the majority of these actors were teenagers who, because of the less nutritious diet of those times, tended to be frailer and less physically mature than today's adolescents. AS

Differentiated Instruction

Evaluating Reason Ask logical-type, mathematical learners what persuasive techniques they'd use to get a friend to agree to a blind date. What evidence would they provide to support their arguments? Have students list and evaluate the reasons the Nurse and Lady Capulet give for accepting Paris's proposal.
Ask: Are they based on logic or emotion? What arguments might work better? AL

Academic Standards

Additional Support activities on pp. 710 and 711 cover the following standards:
Skills Practice: **9.2** Develop [reading] strategies…
Differentiated Instruction: **9.2.7** Evaluate an author's argument…by examining…the comprehensiveness of evidence…

Teach

L1 Literary Element

Rhyming Couplet **Ask:** How does Shakespeare end Scene 3? *(He ends it with a pair of rhyming couplets.)* OL

R Reading Strategy

Connect **Ask:** What are Benvolio and Mercutio doing in the opening of Scene 4? *(Students should note that Romeo is being morose and his friends, Benvolio and Mercutio, are trying to shake him out of his bad mood.)* OL

[*A* SERVANT *enters.*]

SERVINGMAN. Madam, the guests are come, supper served up, you call'd, my young lady ask'd for, the nurse curs'd° in the pantry, and everything in extremity. I must hence to wait. I beseech you follow straight.°

[*The* SERVANT *exits.*]

LADY CAPULET. We follow thee. Juliet, the County stays.°

NURSE. Go, girl, seek happy nights to happy days.

[*They exit.*]

SCENE 4. Later that night. A street in Verona.

[*ROMEO enters with his friends MERCUTIO and BENVOLIO. They are on their way to CAPULET's party; they wear masks to conceal their identities because ROMEO and BENVOLIO are Montagues. Several other MASKERS and TORCHBEARERS accompany them.*]

ROMEO. What, shall this speech be spoke for our excuse?
Or shall we on without apology?°

BENVOLIO. The date is out of such prolixity:°
We'll have no Cupid hoodwink'd° with a scarf,
Bearing a Tartar's painted bow of lath,°
Scaring the ladies like a crow-keeper,°
Nor no without-book prologue,° faintly spoke
After the prompter, for our entrance;
But let them measure us by what they will,
We'll measure them a measure° and be gone.

ROMEO. Give me a torch. I am not for this ambling.
Being but heavy,° I will bear the light.

MERCUTIO. Nay, gentle Romeo, we must have you dance.

ROMEO. Not I, believe me. You have dancing shoes
With nimble soles; I have a soul of lead
So stakes me to the ground I cannot move.

MERCUTIO. You are a lover. Borrow Cupid's wings
And soar with them above a common bound.°

ROMEO. I am too sore enpierced with his shaft°
To soar with his light feathers; and so bound
I cannot bound a pitch° above dull woe.
Under love's heavy burden do I sink.

MERCUTIO. And, to sink in it, should you burden love—
Too great oppression for a tender thing.

ROMEO. Is love a tender thing? It is too rough,
Too rude, too boist'rous and it pricks like thorn.

101 **curs'd:** The Nurse is cursed because she is not helping.

103 **straight:** immediately.

104 **the County stays:** Count Paris is waiting.

1–2 **What, shall . . . apology:** Maskers would arrive uninvited to a festival or celebration and expect hospitality. Romeo wonders if they should deliver a customary speech greeting the host and apologizing for their intrusion.
3 **The date . . . prolixity:** Such wordiness is out of fashion.
4 **hoodwink'd:** blindfolded.
5 **Tartar's . . . lath:** a short bow made of thin wood.
6 **crow-keeper:** scarecrow holding a bow.
7 **without-book prologue:** memorized speech.
10 **measure them a measure:** stay for a dance.
12 **heavy:** sad.

18 **bound:** leap (in a dance).

19 **enpierced . . . shaft:** wounded with Cupid's arrow.

21 **a pitch:** any height.

Additional Support

Skills Practice

READING: Literary Response
Encourage students to express their reactions to the play in a journal as they read. Provide these questions as a starting point:

- What impresses you about the drama?
- What bothers you about it?
- What questions, if any, do you have about it?

Encourage students to support their views with examples from the text. Invite volunteers to share their journals in a class discussion. OL

Italian Palace, 1623. Hendrik Steenwyck the Younger. Oil on copper, 54.5 x 80 cm. Hermitage, St. Petersburg, Russia. ★

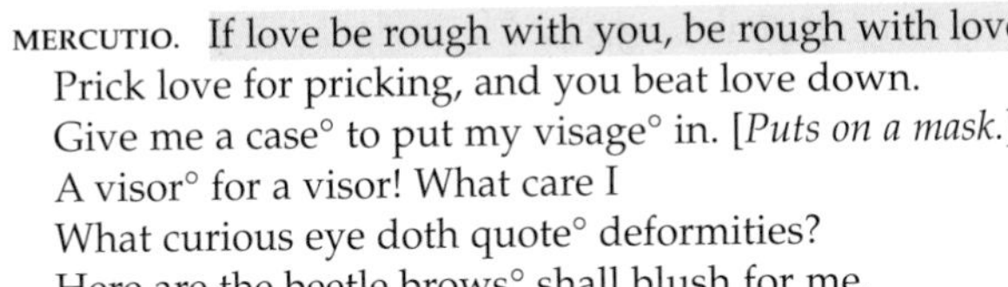

MERCUTIO. If love be rough with you, be rough with love.
Prick love for pricking, and you beat love down.
Give me a case° to put my visage° in. [*Puts on a mask.*]
A visor° for a visor! What care I
What curious eye doth quote° deformities?
Here are the beetle brows° shall blush for me.

BENVOLIO. Come, knock and enter; and no sooner in
But every man betake him to his legs.°

ROMEO. A torch for me! Let wantons light of heart
Tickle the senseless rushes° with their heels;
For I am proverb'd with a grandsire phrase,°
I'll be a candleholder° and look on;
The game was ne'er so fair, and I am done.

MERCUTIO. Tut, dun's the mouse,° the constable's own word.
If thou art Dun, we'll draw thee from the mire
Of this sir-reverence° love, wherein thou stickest
Up to the ears. Come, we burn daylight,° ho!

ROMEO. Nay, that's not so.

29 **case:** cover. **visage:** face.

30 **visor:** mask.

31 **quote:** make note of.

32 **beetle brows:** bushy eyebrows.

34 **betake . . . legs:** begin to dance.

36 **rushes:** straw floor covering.

37 **proverb'd . . . phrase:** guided by an old saying.

38 **candleholder:** spectator. The proverb advises leaving a gambling table when you are ahead.

40 **dun's the mouse:** an expression meaning, "Keep quiet and hidden." (Mercutio plays off the word *done* with *dun,* meaning "dark.")

42 **sir-reverence:** an apologetic expression used to introduce something thought indecent (but Mercutio ironically uses it to introduce the word *love*).

43 **burn daylight:** waste time.

Literary Element Foil *How does Mercutio's attitude and energy level differ from Romeo's? What does the contrast between the two characters lend to the scene?* L2

Teach

L2 Literary Element

Foil Answer: *Mercutio is energetic and upbeat. Romeo is weary and morose because of unrequited love. The contrast lends drama and humor to the scene.*

Point out that Mercutio is trying to cajole Romeo out of his bleak mood. Invite two volunteers to assume the parts of Romeo and Mercutio and read lines 11–26 aloud. Encourage them to express the mood of each character through voice inflection. OL

★ Viewing the Art

Flemish painter Hendrik Steenwyck the Younger (1580–1649) and his father, the Elder, specialized in painting architectural views. Both the Younger and the Elder are known for their paintings of churches. AS

Differentiated Instruction

Musical Performance Four centuries ago, lovesick suitors wrote poems; today, they write songs. Encourage musical learners to brainstorm ideas for songs about romantic disappointment. Discuss possible lyrics, melodies, and musical styles. Have students write lyrics for a song about Romeo's state of mind and then set them to original or existing music. Students should rehearse and then perform their songs. AL

Academic Standards

Additional Support activities on pp. 712 and 713 cover the following standards:

Skills Practice: **9.5.2** Write responses to literature that demonstrate a comprehensive grasp of the significant ideas of literary works [and] support statements with evidence from the text...

Differentiated Instruction: **9.5.8** Write for different purposes and audiences, adjusting tone, style, and voice as appropriate.

Teach

R1 Reading Strategy

Summarizing Answer: *Mercutio encourages Romeo to go to the party. Romeo insists he has wearied of love and the enjoyments of youth. Mercutio makes light of Romeo's lovesickness and urges him to cheer up and have fun.*
Ask: What does Romeo's persistent refusal to join in the fun suggest about his personality? *(He seems stubborn and self-involved, preferring to wallow in his suffering.)* OL

R2 Reading Strategy

Visualize Note that the Queen Mab speech is famous for its inventive language. Have students describe the impressions created by its images and details. Have students compare this speech with the Nurse's in Scene 3 and describe what each speech reveals about the speaker. *(Nurse: bumbling, affectionate, talkative; Mercutio clever, imaginative, cynical about women.)* OL

MERCUTIO. I mean, sir, in delay
We waste our lights in vain, like lights by day!
Take our good meaning, for our judgment sits
Five times in that ere once in our five wits.°

ROMEO. And we mean well in going to this mask,
But 'tis no wit to go.

MERCUTIO. Why, may one ask?

ROMEO. I dreamt a dream tonight.°

MERCUTIO. And so did I.

ROMEO. Well, what was yours?

MERCUTIO. That dreamers often lie.

ROMEO. In bed asleep, while they do dream things true.

[As ROMEO speaks with his friends, the MASKERS and TORCHBEARERS march about the stage. MERCUTIO continues trying to cheer ROMEO.]

MERCUTIO. O, then I see Queen Mab° hath been with you.
She is the fairies' midwife,° and she comes
In shape no bigger than an agate stone°
On the forefinger of an alderman,
Drawn with a team of little atomi°
Over men's noses as they lie asleep;
Her chariot is an empty hazelnut,
Made by the joiner° squirrel or old grub,
Time out o' mind the fairies' coachmakers.
Her wagon spokes made of long spinners'° legs,
The cover, of the wings of grasshoppers;
Her traces,° of the smallest spider web;
Her collars, of the moonshine's wat'ry beams;
Her whip, of cricket's bone; the lash, of film;°
Her wagoner,° a small gray-coated gnat,
Not half so big as a round little worm
Pricked from the lazy finger of a maid;°
And in this state° she gallops night by night
Through lovers' brains, and then they dream of love;
O'er courtiers' knees, that dream on curtsies straight;°
O'er lawyers' fingers, who straight dream on fees;
O'er ladies' lips, who straight on kisses dream,
Which oft the angry Mab with blisters plagues,
Because their breath with sweetmeats° tainted are.
Sometime she gallops o'er a courtier's nose,
And then dreams he of smelling out a suit;°
And sometime comes she with a tithe pig's° tail
Tickling a parson's nose as 'a lies asleep,

46–47 **Take our . . . wits:** Accept our intended **(good)** meaning, for true understanding is five times as likely to be found there as in cleverness.

50 **tonight:** last night.

53 **Queen Mab:** queen of the fairies.

54 **fairies' midwife:** the fairy who helps sleepers give birth to dreams.

55 **agate stone:** gem set in a ring.

57 **little atomi:** tiny creatures.

60 **joiner:** carpenter.

62 **spinners':** spiders'.

64 **traces:** harnesses.

66 **film:** cobweb.

67 **wagoner:** driver.

68–69 **worm . . . maid:** Worms were said to grow in the fingers of lazy maids.

70 **state:** majestic style.

72 **that dream . . . straight:** who immediately dream of respectful bows.

76 **sweetmeats:** sweets.

78 **smelling out a suit:** having someone pay him for his influence with the king.

79 **tithe** (tīth) **pig:** a pig that a parishioner gives to a parson as a customary contribution to the church.

Reading Strategy Summarizing *Reread lines 35–47. Also read the margin notes. How would you summarize this exchange?* R1

Additional Support

Skills Practice

WRITING: Vivid Description Stress the importance of specific concrete details in writing. **Write these sentences on the board:**

- *She drives around in a nutshell with an insect for a driver.*
- *Her chariot is an empty hazelnut, her wagoner, a small, gray-coated gnat.*

Ask students to compare the specificity of the nouns and adjectives. Discuss how these words paint a picture and create a mood. Have students write a vivid description of a natural setting. OL

Then he dreams of another benefice.°
Sometime she driveth o'er a soldier's neck,
And then dreams he of cutting foreign throats,
Of breaches, ambuscadoes,° Spanish blades,
Of healths° five fathom deep; and then anon°
Drums in his ear, at which he starts and wakes,
And being thus frighted, swears a prayer or two
And sleeps again. This is that very Mab
That plats° the manes of horses in the night,
And bakes the elf-locks° in foul sluttish hairs,
Which, once untangled, much misfortune bodes.
This is the hag, when maids lie on their backs,
That presses them and learns them first to bear,
Making them women of good carriage.
This is she—

ROMEO. Peace, peace Mercutio, peace!
Thou talk'st of nothing.

MERCUTIO. True, I talk of dreams;
Which are the children of an idle brain,
Begot of nothing but vain fantasy;
Which is as thin of substance as the air,
And more inconstant° than the wind, who woos
Even now the frozen bosom of the north
And, being anger'd, puffs away from thence,
Turning his side to the dew-dropping south.

BENVOLIO. This wind you talk of blows us from ourselves.
Supper is done, and we shall come too late.

ROMEO. I fear, too early; for my mind misgives
Some consequence yet hanging in the stars
Shall bitterly begin his fearful date
With this night's revels and expire the term
Of a despised life, clos'd in my breast,
By some vile forfeit of untimely death.°
But He that hath the steerage of my course
Direct my sail! On, lusty gentlemen!

BENVOLIO. Strike, drum.

[*They march about the stage and exit.*]

81 **benefice** (ben′ ə fis): church appointment with an assured income.

84 **ambuscadoes** (am′ bus kä′ dōz): ambushes.

85 **healths:** drinking toasts. **anon:** at once.

89 **plats:** tangles.

90 **elf-locks:** hair that is matted from lack of grooming.

100 **inconstant:** fickle, changing.

106–111 **I fear . . . death:** Romeo says that he has a premonition that some event (**consequence**) being worked out by fate will occur at the festivities and lead to his premature death, like a loan that comes due early.

Reading Strategy Summarizing *Briefly summarize Mercutio's dialogue here. In your opinion, what effect was Shakespeare attempting to create with this dialogue?* R3

Big Idea The Power of Love *What connection is Mercutio making here between dreams and Romeo's love?* BI

Reading Strategy Summarizing *What does Romeo reveal in lines 106–110?* R4

Teach

R3 Reading Strategy

Summarizing Answer: *Mercutio describes the dreams and nightmares created by Queen Mab. Students may say that Shakespeare was representing the dreamlike quality of romance or foreshadowing the dream romance of Romeo and Juliet turning into a nightmare.* OL

BI Big Idea

The Power of Love Answer: *Romeo's love is as unreal and insubstantial as his dreams.* OL

L Literary Element

Figurative Language Ask: What examples of simile, metaphor, and personification do you find in Mercutio's speech in lines 98–103? *(Metaphor: dreams are the "children of an idle brain"; Simile: fantasy "as thin of substance as the air"; Personification: "the wind, who woos . . . puffs away from thence.")* OL

R4 Reading Strategy

Summarizing Answer: *Romeo reveals his premonition that an event at the festivities will lead to his premature death.* OL

Reading in the Real World

Careers Costuming is an essential element of stagecraft. Explain that costume designers must study a play and its era in order to create authentic costumes. Encourage interested students to research Renaissance clothing styles and design a historically accurate ball costume for Romeo or Juliet. Have them present their designs to the class. OL

Academic Standards

Additional Support activities on pp. 714 and 715 cover the following standards:

Skills Practice: **9.4.3** Use precise language...sensory details, and appropriate modifiers.

Reading in the Real World: **9.2.4** Synthesize the content from several sources or works...and connect...to...related topics...

Teach

★ Cultural History

Renaissance Dance
Dancing was a popular pastime among the privileged classes of the Renaissance. Capulet's guests probably engaged in a simple line or circle dance rather than a more complex type led by dance masters. Because of constrictive clothing styles, most dances of that period relied more on footwork than on upper body movement. **AS**

SCENE 5. Immediately following the previous scene. A hall in CAPULET's house.

[*SERVANTS enter carrying napkins. They are clearing away the tables from dinner and making the hall ready for dancing.*]

FIRST SERVINGMAN. Where's Potpan, that he helps not to take away?° He shift a trencher!° He scrape a trencher!

SECOND SERVINGMAN. When good manners° shall lie all in one or two men's hands, and they unwash'd too, 'tis a foul thing.

FIRST SERVINGMAN. Away with the join-stools,° remove the court cupboard,° look to the plate.° Good thou, save me a piece of marchpane,° and, as thou loves me, let the porter let in Susan Grindstone and Nell. Anthony, and Potpan!

[*ANTHONY and POTPAN enter. SECOND SERVANT exits.*]

ANTHONY. Ay, boy, ready.

FIRST SERVINGMAN. You are look'd for and call'd for, ask'd for and sought for, in the great chamber.

POTPAN. We cannot be here and there too. Cheerly, boys! Be brisk awhile, and the longer liver take all.°

[*The SERVANTS retire to the back. CAPULET enters with LADY CAPULET, JULIET, TYBALT, and other CAPULETS, the NURSE, and all the GUESTS. The MASKERS join the group.*]

CAPULET. Welcome, gentlemen! Ladies that have their toes
Unplagu'd with corns will walk a bout° with you.
Ah, my mistresses, which of you all
Will now deny to dance? She that makes dainty,°
She I'll swear hath corns. Am I come near ye now?°

[*CAPULET notices the MASKERS and speaks to them.*]

Welcome, gentlemen! I have seen the day
That I have worn a visor and could tell
A whispering tale in a fair lady's ear,
Such as would please. 'Tis gone, 'tis gone, 'tis gone.
You are welcome, gentlemen! Come, musicians, play.

★ [*Music plays, and the GUESTS dance.*]

A hall, a hall! Give room!° And foot it, girls.
More light, you knaves, and turn the tables up,
And quench the fire; the room is grown too hot.
Ah, sirrah, this unlook'd-for sport° comes well.
Nay, sit; nay, sit, good cousin Capulet;
For you and I are past our dancing days.
How long is't now since last yourself and I
Were in a mask?

SECOND CAPULET. By'r Lady, thirty years.

CAPULET. What, man? 'Tis not so much, 'tis not so much;
'Tis since the nuptial° of Lucentio,

1–2 **take away:** clean up after dinner.

2 **trencher:** wooden platter.

3 **manners:** a pun on the Latin root for "hands."

5 **join-stools:** sturdy stools made by a joiner, or carpenter.

6 **court cupboard:** cabinet that holds linen, silver, and china. **plate:** silverware.

7 **marchpane:** marzipan, a sweet made of sugar and almonds.

13 **the longer . . . all:** The one who outlives the rest of us takes everything.

15 **walk a bout:** dance.

17 **makes dainty:** coyly hesitates.

18 **Am I . . . now:** Have I struck close to home?

24 **A hall . . . room:** Clear the hall and make room for dancing!

27 **unlook'd-for sport:** unexpected entertainment (referring to the arrival of the maskers).

33 **nuptial** (nup′ shəl): wedding.

Additional Support

Skills Practice

READING: Setting a Purpose for Reading Remind students that establishing a goal for their reading will improve their focus and help them grasp the material. Note that Scene 5 culminates in the meeting of Romeo and Juliet. Have students write down questions they hope to answer by reading Scene 5. When they've finished reading the text and answering their questions, have them summarize the scene. **OL**

Come Pentecost° as quickly as it will,
Some five-and-twenty years, and then we mask'd.

SECOND CAPULET. 'Tis more, 'tis more. His son is elder, sir;
His son is thirty.

CAPULET. Will you tell me that?
His son was but a ward° two years ago.

[*ROMEO has been watching JULIET and stops a SERVANT to ask about her.*]

ROMEO. [*To a SERVINGMAN.*] What lady's that which doth enrich the hand
Of yonder knight?

SERVINGMAN. I know not, sir.

ROMEO. O, she doth teach the torches to burn bright!
It seems she hangs upon the cheek of night
As a rich jewel in an Ethiop's ear—
Beauty too rich for use, for earth too dear!
So shows° a snowy dove trooping with crows
As yonder lady o'er her fellows shows.
The measure done, I'll watch her place of stand°
And, touching hers, make blessed my rude° hand.
Did my heart love till now? Forswear° it, sight!
For I ne'er saw true beauty till this night.

R2

TYBALT. This, by his voice, should be a Montague.
Fetch me my rapier,° boy. What! Dares the slave
Come hither, cover'd with an antic face,°
To fleer and scorn at our solemnity?°
Now, by the stock and honor of my kin,
To strike him dead I hold it not a sin.

CAPULET. Why, how now, kinsman? Wherefore° storm you so?

TYBALT. Uncle, this is a Montague, our foe,
A villain, that is hither come in spite
To scorn at our solemnity this night.

CAPULET. Young Romeo is it?

TYBALT. 'Tis he, that villain Romeo.

CAPULET. Content thee, gentle coz,° let him alone.
'A bears him like a portly gentleman,°
And, to say truth, Verona brags of him
To be a virtuous and well-govern'd youth.
I would not for the wealth of all this town
Here in my house do him disparagement.°
Therefore be patient; take no note of him.

34 **Pentecost** (pen′ tə kôst): seventh Sunday after Easter.

38 **but a ward:** only a minor (under twenty-one).

46 **shows:** appears.

48 **The measure . . . stand:** After this dance I will see where she goes to stand.

49 **rude:** "rough" or "unmannerly."

50 **Forswear:** deny.

53 **rapier** (rā′ pē ər): sword.

54 **antic face:** grotesque mask.

55 **fleer . . . solemnity:** mock our celebration.

58 **Wherefore:** why.

63 **Content . . . coz:** Be calm, noble cousin.

64 **'A bears . . . gentleman:** He bears himself like a well-mannered gentleman.

68 **do him disparagement:** insult him.

Reading Strategy Summarizing *Summarize the dialogue in lines 14–37.* **R1**

Big Idea The Power of Love *What has just happened? From this speech, how would you characterize Romeo?* **BI**

Teach

R1 Reading Strategy

Summarizing Answer: *Capulet welcomes his guests and urges the women to dance. He sees the masked guests and welcomes them, remembering the days when he and his friends wore masks and crashed parties. He and his cousin disagree about when they last did this.* **OL**

BI Big Idea

The Power of Love Answer: *Romeo is awed by Juliet's beauty; his dramatic shift in mood and his immediate infatuation with Juliet make him seem fickle and impetuous.* **OL**

R2 Reading Strategy

Summarizing Ask: What is the purpose of Tybalt's speech? *(It reminds the audience that the feud poses a dangerous obstacle to the young lovers.)* **OL**

Differentiated Instruction

Visualizing Have students visualize the placement of characters as the ball swirls around onstage. Draw a stage on the board and have students place the characters (Capulet, Tybalt, the serving man, Romeo, and Juliet) in locations where they might appear at different points in the action. Discuss how the movement of the characters changes the focus of the audience's attention as the scene unfolds. **BL**

Academic Standards

Additional Support activities on pp. 716 and 717 cover the following standards:

Skills Practice: **9.2** Develop strategies such as asking questions...and identifying... purpose...

Differentiated Instruction: **9.3.10** Identify and describe the function of...stage designs in dramatic literature...

Teach

L Literary Element

Foil **Answer:** *Proud and impulsive, the youthful Tybalt is fiercely eager to defend the family honor. Capulet refuses to see his guests treated rudely. He is a mature gentleman who values courtesy and respects Romeo's good reputation.* OL

R Reading Strategy

Summarizing **Answer:** *Capulet and Tybalt argue about whether to evict the maskers, and while the guests remain oblivious, the audience senses that violence could erupt.* OL

★ Viewing the Art

Answer: *They're alone in a hushed and intimate world away from the festive whirl. The lines of their bodies seem to fit together.*

The work of English illustrator and painter Sir Frank Dicksee (1853–1928) combines poetic sentiment with realistic detail. *Gouache*—an opaque watercolor paint—and a technique for achieving varied tones known as *en grisaille* were used to create this intricately detailed scene. AS

The Ball Scene from Romeo and Juliet, 1882. Sir Frank Dicksee. Gouache, en grisaille. Private collection.

Viewing the Art: What does this painting suggest about Romeo and Juliet at the ball? Consider their body language, facial expressions, and relationship to the rest of the people at the ball. ★

It is my will, the which if thou respect,
Show a fair presence and put off these frowns,
An ill-beseeming semblance° for a feast.

TYBALT. It fits when such a villain is a guest.
I'll not endure him.

CAPULET. He shall be endured.
What, goodman boy! I say he shall. Go to!°
Am I the master here, or you? Go to!
You'll not endure him, God shall mend my soul!°
You'll make a mutiny among my guests!
You will set cock-a-hoop!° You'll be the man!

TYBALT. Why, uncle, 'tis a shame.

CAPULET. Go to, go to!
You are a saucy boy. Is't so, indeed?
This trick may chance to scathe you.° I know what.
You must contrary me! Marry, 'tis time—
Well said, my hearts°—You are a princox°—go!
Be quiet, or—More light, more light!—For shame!
I'll make you quiet. What!—Cheerly, my hearts!

72 **ill-beseeming semblance:** inappropriate appearance.

75 **Go to:** an expression of impatience. Capulet rebukes Tybalt by calling him a boy and using a term of address **(goodman)** appropriate for someone below the rank of gentleman.

77 **God . . . soul:** God save me!

79 **set cock-a-hoop:** abandon all restraint.

82 **This trick . . . you:** This mischief may come to harm you.

84 **Well said, my hearts:** Well done, my friends (addressed to the dancers). **princox:** conceited youngster.

Literary Element Foil *What differences in attitude and tone do you see between Tybalt and Capulet? Why do they respond so differently to the maskers?* L

Reading Strategy Summarizing *What is happening in this scene? What makes this scene suspenseful?* R

Additional Support

Skills Practice

LISTENING AND SPEAKING: Oral Interpretation Have pairs of students present oral interpretations of dialogues between Tybalt and Romeo or Romeo and Juliet. Provide the following guidelines:

- Decide where pauses go.
- Vary pitch and tone appropriately.
- Experiment with phrasings and emphases.
- Rehearse until confident. OL

TYBALT. Patience perforce° with willful choler° meeting
Makes my flesh tremble in their different greeting.°
I will withdraw; but this intrusion shall,
Now seeming sweet, convert to bitt'rest gall.

[*Trembling with anger,* TYBALT *exits. At the same time,* ROMEO *walks over to* JULIET *and speaks to her.*]

★ ROMEO. If I **profane** with my unworthiest hand
This holy shrine,° the gentle sin is this:
My lips, two blushing pilgrims, ready stand
To smooth that rough touch with a tender kiss.

JULIET. Good pilgrim, you do wrong your hand too much,
Which mannerly devotion shows in this;
For saints° have hands that pilgrims' hands do touch,
And palm to palm is holy palmers'° kiss.

ROMEO. Have not saints lips, and holy palmers too?

JULIET. Ay, pilgrim, lips that they must use in pray'r.

ROMEO. O, then, dear saint, let lips do what hands do!
They pray; grant thou, lest faith turn to despair.

JULIET. Saints do not move, though grant for prayers' sake.°

ROMEO. Then move not while my prayer's effect I take.
Thus from my lips, by thine my sin is purg'd.

[*He kisses her.*]

JULIET. Then have my lips the sin that they have took.

ROMEO. Sin from my lips? O trespass sweetly urg'd!°
Give me my sin again.

[*He kisses her again.*]

JULIET. You kiss by th' book.°

[*The* NURSE *joins* JULIET.]

NURSE. Madam, your mother craves a word with you.

[JULIET *goes to speak with her mother.*]

ROMEO. What is her mother?

NURSE. Marry, bachelor,°
Her mother is the lady of the house,
And a good lady, and a wise and virtuous.
I nurs'd her daughter that you talk'd withal.°
I tell you, he that can lay hold of her
Shall have the chinks.°

87 **Patience perforce:** enforced restraint.
choler (kol′ ər): anger.
88 **different greeting:** opposition.

92 **holy shrine:** referring to Juliet's hand, which Romeo has taken.

97 **saints:** statues of saints.

98 **palmers:** pilgrims who visited the Holy Sepulcher in Jerusalem. (The term is derived from their practice of wearing palm leaves as a sign of devotion.)

103 **Saints . . . sake:** Statues of saints cannot move, although saints may help people if they are moved by prayer.

107 **urg'd:** argued.

108 **kiss by th' book:** "kiss as if you've studied books of etiquette" or "use poetry and rhetoric to gain kisses from me."

111 **bachelor:** young man.

113 **withal:** with.

115 **the chinks:** plenty of money.

Big Idea The Power of Love *What is your response to this interchange?* **BI**

Vocabulary

profane (prō fān′) *v.* to degrade or disrespect something holy or important

Teach

BI Big Idea

The Power of Love Answer: *Students may express anticipation or dread about the situation of two people from feuding families falling in love.* **OL**

★ Writer's Technique

Sonnet In his sonnets, Shakespeare uses an *abab, cdcd* (*cbcb,* here), *efef, gg* rhyme scheme, and his meter is iambic pentameter. The three quatrains usually present three examples or restatements of an idea, followed by a concluding couplet. In lines 91–104, Shakespeare skillfully weaves Romeo and Juliet's conversation into a sonnet. **AS**

Differentiated Instruction

Focused Reading Help below-level readers focus on the scene by listening to an audiotape while reading along in their books. Then suggest that students listen again and try to think of a gesture that complements each speech (e.g., a clenched fist, a hand on a cheek). **BL**

Academic Standards

Additional Support activities on pp. 718 and 719 cover the following standards:

Skills Practice: **9.7.6** Analyze the occasion… and choose effective verbal…techniques (including voice…) for presentations.

Differentiated Instruction: **9.7.6** Choose effective…nonverbal techniques (including…gestures…) for presentations.

Teach

BI1 Big Idea

The Power of Love Answer: *Her love for Romeo is the only love she has ever experienced, but it is connected to her only hate, her hate for his family.* OL

BI2 Big Idea

The Power of Love Ask: How does love affect Romeo throughout Act 1? *(Romeo is incapacitated by love, just as one can be incapacitated by an illness.)* Have students evaluate the connection of love and violence in the play.

Ask: Which seems more powerful? *(Accept thoughtful and well-supported answers.)* OL

CheckPoint

Use the CheckPoint questions on Presentation Plus! to check students' mastery of the selection. These questions can be used with interactive response keypads for immediate student feedback.

Web Activities Have students access the Web site for interactive activities that will help them assess their understanding of the selection.

ROMEO. Is she a Capulet?
O dear account! My life is my foe's debt.°

BENVOLIO. Away, be gone; the sport is at the best.°

ROMEO. Ay, so I fear; the more is my unrest.

CAPULET. Nay, gentlemen, prepare not to be gone;
We have a trifling foolish banquet towards.°
[They whisper in his ear.]
Is it e'en so?° Why then, I thank you all.
I thank you, honest gentlemen. Good night.
More torches here! Come on then; let's to bed.
Ah, sirrah, by my fay,° it waxes° late;
I'll to my rest.

[JULIET returns to the NURSE as everyone else starts to leave. JULIET disguises her interest in ROMEO by asking about other men first.]

JULIET. Come hither, nurse. What is yond gentleman?

NURSE. The son and heir of old Tiberio.

JULIET. What's he that now is going out of door?

NURSE. Marry, that, I think, be young Petruchio.

JULIET. What's he that follows here, that would not dance?

NURSE. I know not.

JULIET. Go ask his name.

[The NURSE goes to ask ROMEO'S name.]

—If he be married,
My grave is like to be my wedding bed.

[The NURSE returns.]

NURSE. His name is Romeo, and a Montague,
The only son of your great enemy.

JULIET. My only love, sprung from my only hate!
Too early seen unknown, and known too late!
Prodigious° birth of love it is to me
That I must love a loathed enemy.

NURSE. What's this? What's this?

JULIET. A rhyme I learnt even now
Of one I danc'd withal.

[Someone calls from another room, "Juliet."]

NURSE. Anon,° anon!
Come, let's away; the strangers all are gone.

BI2 *[They exit.]*

116 **O dear . . . debt:** O costly transaction! My life now belongs to my enemy.

117 **the sport is at the best:** The fun has already reached its peak.

120 **banquet towards:** light refreshment in preparation.

121 **Is it e'en so:** Do you insist (on leaving)?

124 **fay:** faith. **waxes:** grows.

138 **Prodigious** (prə dij′ əs): unnatural and ominous.

141 **Anon:** at once.

Big Idea The Power of Love *What is the meaning of Juliet's remark?* BI1

Additional Support

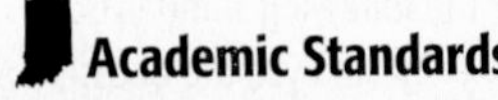

Academic Standards

The Additional Support activity on p. 720 covers the following standard:

Skills Practice: **9.6.2** Demonstrate an understanding of sentence construction... and proper English usage...

Skills Practice BI1

GRAMMAR: Complements Write the following sentences on the board:

1. *Your mother craves a word with you.*
2. *Is she a Capulet?*

Say: In the first sentence, *word* is a direct object; it tells what the mother craves. In the second, *Capulet* is a subject complement renaming the subject *she.* Have students identify other examples of each kind of complement in the selection. OL

AFTER YOU READ

RESPONDING AND THINKING CRITICALLY

Respond

1. What are your thoughts about the first encounter between Romeo and Juliet?

Recall and Interpret

2. (a)What causes members of the Capulet and Montague households to fight in the streets of Verona? (b)What might the quarrel reveal about Verona's society?
3. (a)Why is Romeo depressed at the beginning of the play? (b)How would you characterize Benvolio's attitude toward Romeo?
4. (a)What does Paris seek from Capulet? (b)From his response to Paris, what do you infer about the kind of father Capulet is?
5. (a)Describe the circumstances that lead to Romeo meeting Juliet. (b)What seems to be the basis for their attraction to each other?

Analyze and Evaluate

6. (a)How do Benvolio and Mercutio propose to cure Romeo of his lovesickness over Rosaline? (b)Were you in agreement with their advice? Explain.
7. (a)What do the Nurse and Lady Capulet have in common? How are they different? (b)Which character do you prefer? Explain your response.

Connect

8. **Big Idea** The Power of Love How would you feel about being asked to marry at age thirteen? Explain.

LITERARY ANALYSIS

Literary Element Foil

In drama, the purpose of a **foil** is to highlight the particular qualities of another character.

1. Which character serves as a foil to Lady Capulet? Explain the contrast between the two characters.
2. Which character serves as a foil to Tybalt? What does the contrast between the two characters tell you about each of them?

Writing About Literature

Respond to Character Imagine that Juliet speaks to Rosaline after the party. Write a scene in which they discuss what they think of Romeo. Feel free to invent details, but make sure that your dialogue for Juliet is consistent with her character in the play. Base Rosaline's dialogue on Romeo's descriptions of her attitude toward him.

LiteratureOnline **Web Activities** For eFlashcards, Selection Quick Checks, and other Web activities, go to www.glencoe.com.

READING AND VOCABULARY

Reading Strategy Summarizing

A **summary** is a brief restatement of the main ideas and events in a literary work.

1. (a)How would you summarize Juliet's discussion with Lady Capulet and the Nurse? (b)What did you learn about their relationships with each other?
2. (a)Briefly summarize the main events of Act 1. (b)What questions did you have as the act closed?

Vocabulary Practice

Practice with Synonyms For each boldfaced vocabulary word, choose the correct synonym.

1. Do not **profane** the church.
   a. dishonor **b.** redesign **c.** destroy
2. She tore at her clothes in **anguish.**
   a. anger **b.** determination **c.** grief
3. A **pernicious** virus threatened the city.
   a. deadly **b.** unusual **c.** new
4. I make scrapbooks for **posterity.**
   a. future **b.** relatives **c.** fun

AFTER YOU READ

Assess

1. Accept reasonable answers.
2. (a) A Capulet servant makes a rude gesture at the Montague servants. (b) Servants' identities are closely tied to their masters'.
3. (a) Rosaline has rejected him. (b) Concerned
4. (a) Juliet's hand in marriage (b) He is attached to his child.
5. (a) Her father's ball (b) Her beauty; his gallant manner
6. (a) By showing him girls more beautiful (b) Answers will vary.
7. (a) Both love Juliet; Nurse is closer to Juliet than the mother. (b) Students should explain their answers.
8. Accept reasonable answers.

Literary Element

1. The Nurse offsets Lady Capulet's refinement with her bawdy humor.
2. Benvolio serves as the foil to Tybalt. Tybalt is ruled by his temper, which leads to his downfall. Benvolio controls his temper and is much happier. The contrast shows the dangers of an unruly temper and the benefits of moderation.

Reading Strategy

1. (a) Juliet agrees to consider Paris's proposal but seems indifferent. (b) She respects her mother but confides in the Nurse. The mother seems ambivalent toward the Nurse; she's condescending but close to Juliet.
2. (a) Prince bans brawling between feuding Montagues and Capulets. Romeo and his friends crash Lord Capulet's ball. Romeo spots Juliet; it's love at first sight. Capulet defuses a quarrel. Romeo and Juliet learn each other's true identities. (b) Accept reasonable answers.

Vocabulary

1. a **2.** c **3.** a **4.** a

Writing About Literature

Remind students to make their dialogue consistent with details from the text.

BEFORE YOU READ

Focus

Summary

Romeo and Juliet declare their love and make plans to meet secretly and marry. Romeo's spiritual advisor, Friar Lawrence, agrees to marry them, hoping the union will end the feud between the families.

V Vocabulary

Vocabulary File Say: Add these words and definitions to your vocabulary file. For each word, include a sentence that gives you an example of how to use the word. **OL** Students with English language needs should include the pronunciation of these words in their files. **EL**

Literary Elements Have students access the Web site to improve their understanding of figurative language.

BEFORE YOU READ *Romeo and Juliet*, Act 2

LITERATURE PREVIEW

Connecting to the Drama

In this play, the relationship of two people in love is complicated by the opinions of their families. Before you read Act 2, think about the following questions:

- What do individuals owe to their families?
- In the present day and time, to what groups or ideals are people expected to show loyalty?

Building Background

During the Renaissance, young people needed permission from their parents or guardians to get married. In practice, parents from upper-class households frequently chose partners for their children. Such arranged marriages usually required the bride's consent. Girls could legally marry at age twelve, but fifteen or sixteen was a more customary age. Juliet, at age thirteen, would have been considered a young bride.

Setting Purposes for Reading

Big Idea The Power of Love

As you read Act 2, notice what actions Romeo and Juliet take because of love.

Literary Element Figurative Language

Figurative language helps us see and understand the world by describing it in a way that is imaginative but not literally true. As you read Act 2, notice the following types of figurative language.

- **Similes** compare seemingly unlike things using the word *like* or *as* (as in *Her eyes are like jewels*).
- **Metaphors** compare seemingly unlike things without using the word *like* or *as* (as in *Her eyes are jewels*).
- **Personification** gives human characteristics to an animal, object, force of nature, or idea (as in *A cool breeze blew mercifully*).

- See Literary Terms Handbook, pp. R7, R10–R11, R13, and R15–R16.

LiteratureOnline Interactive Literary Elements Handbook To review or learn more about the literary elements, go to www.glencoe.com.

READING PREVIEW

Reading Strategy Making Inferences About Characters

A character's motivations, or reasons for acting in a certain way, are not always clear. To find out what drives characters to think, act, or speak the way they do, we often have to **make inferences,** or use reason and our knowledge of the situation to form our own ideas of characters' motivations.

Reading Tip: Examining the Evidence Use a chart like the one below to record details about characters and the inferences you make based on those details.

I know	I infer
Juliet tells Romeo, "I'll no longer be a Capulet."	Juliet wishes to reassure Romeo that her primary loyalty is to him, not to her family.

Vocabulary

adjacent (ə jā′ sənt) *adj.* next to or close to; neighboring; p. 724 *His office is adjacent to mine, so I know who visits him.*

retain (ri tān′) *v.* to keep possession of; p. 726 *The children retain good memories of the holidays.*

perverse (pər vurs′) *adj.* deliberately unreasonable or wrong; stubborn; p. 728 *She seems to take a perverse delight in teasing me.*

rancor (rang′ kər) *n.* bitter resentment against someone; long-lasting spite; p. 734 *There was rancor between the feuding families.*

Vocabulary Tip: Context Clues When you come across an unfamiliar word, use context clues—the words and phrases surrounding the word—to determine the word's definition.

INDIANA ACADEMIC STANDARDS (pages 722–745)

9.3.7 Recognize and understand...figurative language...

9.3.3 Analyze interactions between characters...

9.1.2 Distinguish between what words mean literally and what they imply and interpret what the words imply.

Selection Skills

The Tragedy of Romeo and Juliet, Act 2

Literary Elements
- Figurative Language (SE pp. 722–745)

Reading Skills
- Making Inferences About Characters (SE pp. 722–745; TWE p. 726)

Vocabulary Skills
- Context Clues (SE pp. 722, 745)

Listening/Speaking/Viewing Skills
- Analyzing Art (SE pp. 732, 737, 741; TWE pp. 726, 744)

Writing Skills/Grammar
- Correlative Conjunctions (TWE p. 724)
- Similes (TWE p. 728)
- Intensive Pronouns (TWE p. 732)
- Persuasive Writing (TWE p. 736)
- Interjections (TWE p. 740)
- Clauses (TWE p. 742)

Act 2

Prologue

[*The* CHORUS *enters and addresses the audience.*]

CHORUS. Now old desire° doth in his deathbed lie,
And young affection gapes° to be his heir;
That fair° for which love groan'd for and would die,
With tender Juliet match'd, is now not fair.
Now Romeo is belov'd and loves again,°
Alike bewitched by the charm of looks;
But to his foe suppos'd he must complain,°
And she steal love's sweet bait from fearful hooks.
Being held a foe, he may not have access
To breathe such vows as lovers use° to swear,
And she as much in love, her means much less
To meet her new beloved anywhere;
But passion lends them power, time means, to meet,
Temp'ring extremities with extreme sweet.°

[*The* CHORUS *exits.*]

1 **old desire:** Romeo's love for Rosaline.

2 **young affection gapes:** new love is eager.

5 **is belov'd . . . again:** is loved and loves in return.

7 **to his foe . . . complain:** he must express his love to a supposed enemy.

10 **use:** are accustomed.

14 **Temp'ring . . . sweet:** mixing difficulties with great delights.

SCENE 1. Later the same night. Outside the wall that surrounds CAPULET's orchard.

[ROMEO *enters. He is walking alone after the party.*]

ROMEO. Can I go forward when my heart is here?
Turn back, dull earth,° and find thy center° out.

[BENVOLIO *and* MERCUTIO *enter; they are looking for* ROMEO. *Because he wishes to remain near* JULIET *and because he prefers to be alone,* ROMEO *avoids his friends and climbs the wall into* CAPULET'S *orchard.*] **L**

BENVOLIO. Romeo! My cousin Romeo! Romeo!

MERCUTIO. He is wise
And, on my life, hath stol'n him home to bed.

BENVOLIO. He ran this way and leapt this orchard wall.
Call, good Mercutio.

MERCUTIO. Nay, I'll conjure° too.
Romeo! Humors! Madman! Passion! Lover!
Appear thou in the likeness of a sigh;
Speak but one rhyme, and I am satisfied!
Cry but "Ay me!" pronounce but "love" and "dove."
Speak to my gossip Venus one fair word,
One nickname for her purblind° son and heir,

2 **dull earth:** Romeo's body. **center:** heart (that is, Juliet).

6 **conjure** (kon′ jər): summon a spirit. (In the conjuring that follows, Mercutio mocks Romeo's lovesickness.)

12 **purblind:** completely blind.

Big Idea The Power of Love *How would you restate what the Chorus explains here?* **BI**

Reading Strategy Making Inferences About Characters *What is Mercutio's attitude toward Romeo's lovesickness?* **R**

Teach

BI Big Idea

The Power of Love Answer: *Romeo's love for Rosaline has died; he is now in love with Juliet, and Juliet returns his love. Though their love is made difficult by the feud, the difficulties are tempered by the sweetness of love; they will still attempt to meet.* **OL**

L Literary Element

Stage Directions Point out that stage directions are an important component of a play's text. Stage directions provide information about the setting and about the movements, appearance, gestures, and motivation of the characters.
Ask: What do we learn from the stage directions here about Romeo's motivation? *(He avoids his friends and does not want to reveal his new love interest.)* **OL**

R Reading Strategy

Making Inferences About Characters Answer: *He finds Romeo's lovesickness foolish and amusing. He does not take love so seriously.* **OL**

English Language Coach

Summarizing Plot Explain to English language learners that summarizing passages can help them understand and remember what they've read. To summarize effectively, they should omit details and condense main events and ideas. A summary gives a general idea of action, theme, and mood. Have students write a short summary of Act 2, Scene 1. **EL**

Academic Standards

The Additional Support activity on p. 723 covers the following standard:

English Language Coach: **9.5.3** Write expository compositions, including... summaries...that communicate information and ideas...accurately and coherently...

Teach

L1 Literary Element

Figurative Language
Answer: *The wound of love, inflicted by Cupid's arrow* OL

Cultural History

Cupid Shakespeare's plays contain numerous allusions to Greek and Roman mythology and history. Here, the reference to Cupid is to the god of love, son of the goddess Venus. Cupid was often depicted as a mischievous boy who used arrows to incite the pangs of love. AS

Young Abraham Cupid, he that shot so trim
When King Cophetua lov'd the beggar-maid!°
He heareth not, he stirreth not, he moveth not;
The ape is dead,° and I must conjure him.
I conjure thee by Rosaline's bright eyes,
By her high forehead and her scarlet lip,
By her fine foot, straight leg, and quivering thigh,
And the demesnes° that there **adjacent** lie,
That in thy likeness thou appear to us!

BENVOLIO. And if he hear thee, thou wilt anger him.

MERCUTIO. This cannot anger him; 'twould anger him
To raise a spirit in his mistress' circle,
Of some strange nature, letting it there stand
Till she had laid it and conjur'd it down.°
That were° some spite. My invocation
Is fair and honest:° in his mistress' name,
I conjure only but to raise up him.

BENVOLIO. Come, he hath hid himself among these trees
To be consorted with° the humorous° night.
Blind is his love and best befits the dark.

MERCUTIO. If love be blind, love cannot hit the mark.
Now will he sit under a medlar tree,
And wish his mistress were that kind of fruit
As maids call medlars, when they laugh alone.
O, Romeo, that she were, O that she were
An open-arse, thou a pop'rin pear!
Romeo, good night. I'll to my truckle bed;°
This field bed° is too cold for me to sleep.
Come, shall we go?

BENVOLIO. Go then, for 'tis in vain
To seek him here that means not to be found.

[*They exit.*]

SCENE 2. Immediately following the previous scene. CAPULET'S **orchard.**

[*ROMEO, alone, comments on MERCUTIO's joking.*]

ROMEO. He jests at scars that never felt a wound.

[*JULIET enters at a window above and stands on a balcony. She does not know that ROMEO is nearby.*]

13–14 **Young . . . beggar-maid:** Mercutio refers to an old ballad about a king who falls in love with a beggar maid after being wounded by Cupid's arrow.
16 **The ape is dead:** Romeo is playing dead, like a trained ape.

20 **demesnes** (di mānz′): regions.

23–26 **This . . . down:** Mercutio says that his conjuring would anger Romeo only if it led to someone else romancing Rosaline.
27 **were:** would be.
28 **honest:** honorable.

31 **consorted with:** in the company of. **humorous:** damp.

39 **truckle bed:** a small rollaway bed for a child or servant.
40 **field bed:** portable bed used by soldiers during a campaign.

Literary Element Figurative Language *What "wound" does Romeo suggest that Mercutio has never felt?* L1

Vocabulary

adjacent (ə jā′ sənt) *adj.* next to or close to; neighboring

Additional Support

Skills Practice

GRAMMAR AND LANGUAGE: Correlative Conjunctions Explain that correlative conjunctions *(both/and, either/or, neither/nor, not only/but also)* join pairs of words to frame parallel terms. Have students write sentences about relationships between pairs of characters, such as Romeo and Benvolio or Benvolio and Mercutio, using correlative conjunctions. Then have partners exchange papers and evaluate each other's use of parallel terms. OL

But soft!° What light through yonder window breaks?
It is the East, and Juliet is the sun!
Arise, fair sun, and kill the envious moon,
Who is already sick and pale with grief
That thou her maid art far more fair than she.
Be not her maid, since she is envious.
Her vestal livery is but sick and green,
And none but fools do wear it. Cast it off.°
It is my lady! O, it is my love!
O, that she knew she were!
She speaks, yet she says nothing. What of that?
Her eye discourses; I will answer it.
I am too bold; 'tis not to me she speaks.
Two of the fairest stars in all the heaven,
Having some business, do entreat her eyes
To twinkle in their spheres till they return.
What if her eyes were there, they in her head?
The brightness of her cheek would shame those stars
As daylight doth a lamp; her eyes in heaven
Would through the airy region stream so bright°
That birds would sing and think it were not night.
See how she leans her cheek upon her hand!
O, that I were a glove upon that hand,
That I might touch that cheek!

JULIET. Ay me!

ROMEO. [*Aside.*] She speaks.
O, speak again, bright angel, for thou art
As glorious to this night, being o'er my head,
As is a winged messenger of heaven
Unto the white-upturned wond'ring eyes
Of mortals that fall back to gaze on him
When he bestrides the lazy puffing clouds
And sails upon the bosom of the air.

JULIET. O Romeo, Romeo! Wherefore art thou Romeo?°
Deny thy father and refuse thy name;
Or, if thou wilt not, be but sworn my love,
And I'll no longer be a Capulet.

ROMEO. [*Aside.*] Shall I hear more, or shall I speak at this?

JULIET. 'Tis but thy name that is my enemy.
Thou art thyself, though not° a Montague.
What's Montague? It is nor hand, nor foot,°
Nor arm, nor face, nor any other part
Belonging to a man. O, be some other name!
What's in a name? That which we call a rose

2 **soft:** wait!

4–9 **Arise . . . off:** The moon is associated with Diana, Roman goddess of chastity. Romeo urges Juliet to cast off the virginal uniform (**vestal livery**) she wears as one of the moon's maids, since the moon is envious of her beauty.

21 **stream so bright:** shine so brightly.

33 **Wherefore . . . Romeo:** Why are you Romeo (a Montague)?

39 **though not:** even if you were not.

40 **nor hand, nor foot:** neither hand nor foot.

Literary Element Figurative Language *What figure of speech is Romeo using here? Explain.* L2

Teach

R Reading Strategy

Interpret Have students compare these lines to Romeo's speech about Rosaline in Act 1, Scene 2, lines 86–91.
Ask: What do these two speeches suggest about Romeo? *(Comparing both girls to the sun suggests he sees them as idealized images rather than as individuals.)* OL

L2 Literary Element

Figurative Language
Answer: *Personification; he suggests Juliet's eyes are capable of speech.* OL

L3 Literary Element

Figurative Language **Say:** Romeo compares Juliet's eyes to stars. Why might Shakespeare use heavenly bodies to express passion here? *(Stars suggest the otherworldly idealism of Romeo's devotion. Juliet's perfection and the joy and lightness of spirit she brings Romeo make their love heavenly in his eyes.)* OL

CheckPoint

Use CheckPoint questions on Presentation Plus! to monitor students' comprehension. These questions can be used with interactive response keypads for immediate student feedback.

English Language Coach

Dated Language English language learners may have trouble with dated language. Note that dictionaries label such words and definitions as archaic. Have students list unfamiliar words from Scene 2. Then have small groups of native and nonnative speakers define the words, using context clues and dictionaries. Have them note which words are obsolete, which words have changed meaning, and which words haven't changed. EL

Academic Standards

Additional Support activities on pp. 724 and 725 cover the following standards:

Skills Practice: **9.6.2** Demonstrate an understanding of sentence construction, including parallel structure...

English Language Coach: **9.1** Use... context clues, and a growing knowledge of English...to determine the meaning of words...

Teach

Viewing the Art

Emphasizing the importance of technique, German artist Anselm Feuerbach (1829–1880) painted in a classic style reminiscent of the style favored in ancient Greek and Roman art. **AS**

Romeo and Juliet, 1864. Anselm Feuerbach. Oil on canvas, 200 x 115 cm. Thueringer Museum, Eisenach, Germany.

By any other word would smell as sweet.
So Romeo would, were he not Romeo call'd,
Retain that dear perfection which he owes°
Without that title. Romeo, doff° thy name;
And for thy name, which is no part of thee,
Take all myself.

[*ROMEO speaks aloud so that JULIET can hear him for the first time.*]

ROMEO. I take thee at thy word.
Call me but love, and I'll be new baptiz'd;°
Henceforth I never will be Romeo.

JULIET. What man art thou, that, thus bescreen'd° in night,
So stumblest on my counsel?°

46 **owes:** owns.

47 **doff:** remove.

50 **Call . . . baptiz'd:** Romeo says that if she only calls him her love, he will take *love* for his new name (as infants are given their Christian names when they are baptized).

52 **bescreen'd:** hidden.

53 **counsel:** secret thoughts.

Vocabulary

retain (ri tān′) *v.* to keep possession of

Additional Support

Skills Practice

READING: Inferring Explain that authors build their characters detail by detail. Each detail is a clue to the character's personality. For example, Mercutio's words in Acts 1 and 2 suggest that he is a cynic in regard to romantic love. Divide the class into groups and assign each a character from the play. Groups should list their characters' actions and statements and then write a description of the character's personality. **OL**

ROMEO. By a name
I know not how to tell thee who I am.
My name, dear saint, is hateful to myself
Because it is an enemy to thee.
Had I it written, I would tear the word.

JULIET. My ears have yet not drunk a hundred words
Of thy tongue's uttering, yet I know the sound.
Art thou not Romeo, and a Montague?

ROMEO. Neither, fair maid, if either thee dislike.

JULIET. How camest thou hither, tell me, and wherefore?
The orchard walls are high and hard to climb,
And the place death, considering who thou art,
If any of my kinsmen find thee here.

ROMEO. With love's light wings did I o'erperch° these walls;
For stony limits cannot hold love out,
And what love can do, that dares love attempt.
Therefore thy kinsmen are no stop° to me.

JULIET. If they do see thee, they will murder thee.

ROMEO. Alack, there lies more peril in thine eye
Than twenty of their swords! Look thou but sweet,
And I am proof against° their enmity.

JULIET. I would not for the world they saw thee here.

ROMEO. I have night's cloak to hide me from their eyes;
And but° thou love me, let them find me here.
My life were better ended by their hate
Than death prorogued,° wanting of° thy love.

JULIET. By whose direction foundst thou out this place?

ROMEO. By love, that first did prompt me to inquire.
He lent me counsel,° and I lent him eyes.
I am no pilot; yet, wert thou as far
As that vast shore wash'd with the farthest sea,
I should adventure° for such merchandise.

JULIET. Thou knowest the mask of night is on my face;
Else would a maiden blush bepaint my cheek
For that which thou hast heard me speak tonight.
Fain would I dwell on form°—fain, fain deny
What I have spoke; but farewell compliment!°
Dost thou love me? I know thou wilt say "Ay";

66 **o'erperch:** fly over.

69 **stop:** obstacle.

73 **proof against:** protected from.

76 **but:** unless.

78 **prorogued** (prō rōgd'): postponed. **wanting of:** lacking.

81 **counsel:** advice.

84 **adventure:** risk a journey.

88 **Fain . . . form:** Gladly would I show concern for decorum.
89 **compliment:** formal manners.

Reading Strategy Making Inferences About Characters *Why does Romeo say this? What does it suggest about his attitude toward the feud between the Capulets and Montagues?* **R**

Literary Element Figurative Language *What figure of speech does Juliet use here? What words does Shakespeare use to suggest the strength of Juliet's love?* **L1**

Teach

R Reading Strategy

Making Inferences About Characters **Answer:** *He tries to reassure Juliet that his love for her matters far more than the feud. He would rather not be a Montague than lose Juliet.* **OL**

L1 Literary Element

Figurative Language **Answer:** *Personification; "My ears have not yet drunk" suggests an emotional thirst in her.* **OL**

BI Big Idea

The Power of Love Invite volunteers to read the dialogue of Romeo and Juliet on this page. Note that despite the risks Romeo has taken to see her, Juliet hesitates to promise her love to Romeo.
Ask: What else does she ask of Romeo? *(She wants him to swear he loves her faithfully.)* **OL**

L2 Literary Element

Characterization **Ask:** What does this speech reveal about Juliet's character? *(She is intelligent and thoughtful and seems more mature and cautious than Romeo but remains vulnerable to Romeo's attentions.)* **OL**

Differentiated Instruction

Keeping a Sketchbook Encourage students to visualize by sketching their impressions of events, objects, and characters from the play in a notebook as they read. Suggest they include captions and the page number of the passage that inspired each image. Invite students to share their work with the class. **BL**

Academic Standards

Additional Support activities on pp. 726 and 727 cover the following standards:

Skills Practice: **9.3.4** Determine characters' traits by what the characters say about themselves in narration, dialogue, and soliloquy…

Differentiated Instruction: **9.2** Develop [reading] strategies…

Teach

R1 Reading Strategy

Making Inferences About Characters **Answer:** *She worries that she might seem too easily won and that their feelings arose too suddenly to last.* OL

L1 Literary Element

Figurative Language **Answer:** *She worries that their love is like lightning, which comes and goes in a flash. The metaphor of the flower expresses a wish that their love will grow and blossom.* OL

★ Cultural History

West Side Story In this modern (1957) musical adaptation of *Romeo and Juliet,* the main characters, Tony and Maria, are affiliated with rival gangs in New York City. Their love blooms amid ethnic tensions that lead to a deadly rumble. In *West Side Story,* the balcony scene occurs on the fire escape of Maria's apartment. AS

And I will take thy word. Yet, if thou swear'st,
Thou mayst prove false. At lovers' perjuries,
They say Jove° laughs. O gentle Romeo,
If thou dost love, pronounce it faithfully.
Or if thou thinkest I am too quickly won,
I'll frown and be **perverse** and say thee nay,
So thou wilt woo;° but else,° not for the world.
In truth, fair Montague, I am too fond,°
And therefore thou mayst think my behavior light;°
But trust me, gentleman, I'll prove more true
Than those that have more coying to be strange.°
I should have been more strange, I must confess,
But that thou overheard'st, ere I was ware,°
My truelove passion. Therefore pardon me,
And not impute this yielding° to light love,
Which the dark night hath so discovered.°

ROMEO. Lady, by yonder blessed moon I vow,
That tips with silver all these fruit-tree tops—

JULIET. O, swear not by the moon, th' inconstant moon,
That monthly changes in her circle orb,
Lest that thy love prove likewise variable.

ROMEO. What shall I swear by?

JULIET. Do not swear at all;
Or if thou wilt, swear by thy gracious self,
Which is the god of my idolatry,°
And I'll believe thee.

ROMEO. If my heart's dear love—

JULIET. Well, do not swear. Although I joy in thee,
I have no joy of this contract° tonight.
It is too rash, too unadvis'd, too sudden;
Too like the lightning, which doth cease to be
Ere one can say it lightens. Sweet, good night!
This bud of love, by summer's ripening breath,
May prove a beauteous flow'r when next we meet.
Good night, good night! As sweet repose and rest
Come to thy heart as that within my breast!

93 **Jove:** the most powerful god in Roman mythology.

97 **So thou wilt woo:** so you will have to woo me. **else:** otherwise.
98 **fond:** loving, infatuated.
99 **light:** frivolous, unmaidenly.

101 **coying to be strange:** ability to appear distant.

103 **ere I was ware:** before I was aware (of your presence).

105 **not impute this yielding:** do not attribute this giving in so easily.
106 **discovered:** revealed.

114 **idolatry** (ī dol′ ə trē): blind devotion.

117 **contract:** exchange of vows.

Reading Strategy Making Inferences About Characters *In this passage, what worries does Juliet express?* R1

Literary Element Figurative Language *Why does Juliet compare her and Romeo's declarations of love to lightning in lines 119–120? What is the point of the metaphor in lines 121–122?* L1

Vocabulary

perverse (pər vurs′) *adj.* deliberately unreasonable or wrong; stubborn

Additional Support

Skills Practice

WRITING: Similes in Character Description Juliet calls her love "as boundless as the sea." Note that with just a few words, this simile vividly conveys the idea of a love that is vast, overwhelming, and all-encompassing. After students have finished reading the scene, have them skim it for two other similes and describe the impression each creates. (*Possible answers: [1] page 725, lines 26–28—"for thou art . . . as is a winged messenger of heaven"; [2] page 730, lines 165–166—"How silver-sweet . . . night, / Like softest music to attending ears!"*) OL

ROMEO. O, wilt thou leave me so unsatisfied?

JULIET. What satisfaction canst thou have tonight?

ROMEO. Th' exchange of thy love's faithful vow for mine.

JULIET. I gave thee mine before thou didst request it;
And yet I would it were to give again.°

ROMEO. Wouldst thou withdraw it? For what purpose, love?

JULIET. But to be frank° and give it thee again.
And yet I wish but for the thing I have.
My bounty is as boundless as the sea,
My love as deep; the more I give to thee,
The more I have, for both are infinite. [*The* NURSE *calls from within the house.*]
I hear some noise within. Dear love, adieu!
Anon,° good nurse! Sweet Montague, be true.
Stay but a little, I will come again.

[*JULIET goes into the house.*]

L2

ROMEO. O blessed, blessed night! I am afeard,
Being in night, all this is but a dream,
Too flattering-sweet to be substantial.°

[*JULIET reappears on the balcony.*]

JULIET. Three words, dear Romeo, and good night indeed.
If that thy bent° of love be honorable,
Thy purpose marriage, send me word tomorrow,
By one that I'll procure° to come to thee,
Where and what time thou wilt perform the rite;°
And all my fortunes at thy foot I'll lay
And follow thee my lord throughout the world.

NURSE. [*She calls from within the house.*] Madam!

JULIET. [*To the* NURSE.] I come anon. [*To* ROMEO.]—But if thou meanest not well,
I do beseech° thee—

NURSE. [*From within again.*] Madam!

JULIET. [*To the* NURSE.] By and by° I come.—
[*To* ROMEO.] To cease thy strife° and leave me to my grief.
Tomorrow will I send.

ROMEO. So thrive my soul—

JULIET. A thousand times good night!

[*JULIET goes into the house.*]

129 **I would . . . again:** I wish I had it back.

131 **frank:** generous.

137 **Anon:** right away.

141 **substantial:** real.

143 **bent:** intention.

145 **procure** (prə kyoor'): obtain.

146 **rite:** marriage ceremony.

151 **beseech** (bi sēch'): beg. **By and by:** in a moment.

152 **strife:** efforts.

Reading Strategy Making Inferences About Characters *Why do you think Juliet wants to marry Romeo?* R2

Teach

R2 Reading Strategy

Making Inferences About Characters **Answer:** *She wants him to prove his love is true and honorable. She may also think that once they're married they'll be safe from the interference of their families.* OL

L2 Literary Element

Figurative Language Ask students to characterize the tone of Romeo's and Juliet's speeches. (*Joyous, loving*) **Ask:** How does Shakespeare communicate this tone? *(With imagery involving vast surroundings—the sea and the sky—and exclamations and vows.)* OL

Differentiated Instruction

Graphing Emotions Have mathematically inclined students graph the lovers' shifting emotions, using the scene's events (e.g., the ball, the balcony scene) as the *x*-axis and a "barometer" of emotions (e.g., joy, anxiety) as the *y*-axis. They should graph each character's emotions separately. AL

Academic Standards

Additional Support activities on pp. 728 and 729 cover the following standards:

Skills Practice: **9.3.7** Recognize and understand the significance of various literary devices, including figurative language…

Differentiated Instruction: **9.3** [Identify] story elements such as character…

Teach

L1 Literary Element

Figurative Language Answer: *The simile conveys the reluctance of lovers to part. People in love rush as eagerly toward their beloved as children rush out of school and part as reluctantly as children drag into class.* **OL**

L2 Literary Element

Figurative Language Answer: *It suggests she wants to nurture and protect him, while at the same time implying that her possessiveness might "smother" a creature that by nature wants freedom.*

Students should appreciate the ironic truth in Juliet's "sweet sorrow." (line 184) **Ask:** How is this phrase appropriate to the lovers' dilemma? *(It suggests that joy and sorrow in love are closely connected and foreshadows the tragedy to come.)* **OL**

ROMEO. A thousand times the worse, to want° thy light!
Love goes toward love as schoolboys from their books;
But love from love, toward school with heavy looks.

[*JULIET returns to the balcony.*]

JULIET. Hist! Romeo, hist! O for a falc'ner's voice
To lure this tassel gentle back again!°
Bondage is hoarse and may not speak aloud,°
Else would I tear the cave where Echo° lies
And make her airy tongue more hoarse than mine
With repetition of my Romeo's name. Romeo!

ROMEO. It is my soul that calls upon my name.
How silver-sweet sound lovers' tongues by night,
Like softest music to attending ears!

JULIET. Romeo!

ROMEO. My niesse?°

JULIET. What o'clock tomorrow
Shall I send to thee?

ROMEO. By the hour of nine.

JULIET. I will not fail. 'Tis twenty year till then.
I have forgot why I did call thee back.

ROMEO. Let me stand here till thou remember it.

JULIET. I shall forget, to have thee still stand there,
Rememb'ring how I love thy company.

ROMEO. And I'll still stay, to have thee still forget,
Forgetting any other home but this.

JULIET. 'Tis almost morning. I would have thee gone—
And yet no farther than a wanton's° bird,
That lets it hop a little from his hand,
Like a poor prisoner in his twisted gyves,°
And with a silken thread plucks it back again,
So loving-jealous of his liberty.

ROMEO. I would I were thy bird.

JULIET. Sweet, so would I.
Yet I should kill thee with much cherishing.
Good night, good night! Parting is such sweet sorrow
That I shall say good night till it be morrow.

[*JULIET goes into the house.*]

155 **want:** be deprived of.

158–159 **Hist! . . . again:** Juliet refers to the special call that a falcon master **(falc'ner)** uses to lure back a male falcon **(tassel gentle)**.

160 **Bondage . . . aloud:** Juliet compares being under her family's control to hoarseness, since it prevents her from speaking loudly.

161 **Echo:** a wood nymph in classical mythology. After being rejected in love, she retired to a cave and wasted away until only her voice was left.

167 **niesse** (nē esʹ): a young hawk ready to leave the nest.

177 **wanton's:** spoiled child's.

179 **gyves** (jīvz): shackles.

Literary Element Figurative Language *What idea is communicated by the simile in lines 156–157? Restate it in your own words.* **L1**

Literary Element Figurative Language *In an extended metaphor, Juliet compares Romeo to a bird. What idea about her love is communicated by this comparison?* **L2**

Additional Support

Skills Practice

READING: Monitoring Comprehension Explain that stopping after each scene to review the plot developments and jot down notes will improve comprehension. Have partners work together to summarize events, revelations about character or motive, and ideas that contribute to theme in each scene. Encourage students to discuss points of confusion and to list questions to be answered by rereading. **OL**

ROMEO. Sleep dwell upon thine eyes, peace in thy breast!
Would I were sleep and peace, so sweet to rest!
Hence will I to my ghostly sire's° close cell,°
His help to crave and my dear hap° to tell.

[*ROMEO exits to find the FRIAR.*]

188 **ghostly sire's:** spiritual advisor's. **close cell:** small private room.
189 **hap:** good fortune.

SCENE 3. Early the next morning. FRIAR LAWRENCE's cell.

★ [*FRIAR LAWRENCE, ROMEO's spiritual advisor, enters alone carrying a basket full of herbs.*]

FRIAR. The gray-ey'd morn smiles on the frowning night,
Check'ring the eastern clouds with streaks of light;
And flecked° darkness like a drunkard reels
From forth day's path and Titan's fiery wheels.°
Now, ere the sun advance his burning eye
The day to cheer and night's dank dew to dry,
I must upfill this osier cage° of ours
With baleful° weeds and precious-juiced flowers.
The earth that's nature's mother is her tomb;
What is her burying grave, that is her womb;
And from her womb children of divers° kind
We sucking on her natural bosom find:
Many for many virtues° excellent,
None but for some,° and yet all different.
O, mickle° is the powerful grace° that lies
In plants, herbs, stones, and their true qualities;
For naught° so vile that on the earth doth live
But to the earth some special good doth give;
Nor aught so good but, strained from that fair use,°
Revolts from true birth, stumbling on abuse.°
Virtue itself turns vice, being misapplied,
And vice sometime by action dignified.

[*ROMEO enters. The FRIAR does not see him and continues speaking until ROMEO interrupts him.*]

Within the infant rind° of this weak flower
Poison hath residence and medicine power;°
For this, being smelt, with that part cheers each part;
Being tasted, stays all senses with the heart.°
Two such opposed kings encamp them still
In man as well as herbs—grace and rude will;°
And where the worser is predominant,
Full soon the canker° death eats up that plant.

ROMEO. Good morrow, father.

FRIAR. *Benedicite!*°
What early tongue so sweet saluteth me?

3 **flecked:** spotted.
4 **From . . . wheels:** out of the path of the sun god (who was said to drive a fiery chariot across the sky).
7 **upfill this osier cage:** fill up this willow basket.
8 **baleful:** harmful.
11 **divers** (dī′ vərz): varied.
13 **virtues:** healing properties.
14 **None but for some:** None that are not good for some use.
15 **mickle:** great. **grace:** divine goodness.
17 **naught** (nôt): there is nothing.
19 **strained from that fair use:** diverted from its proper use.
20 **Revolts . . . abuse:** rebels against its natural state and becomes harmful.
23 **infant rind:** tender skin.
24 **Poison . . . power:** there dwells poison and medicinal power.
25–26 **For this . . . heart:** When the flower is smelled, it stimulates every part of the body, but when tasted it causes the heart to stop beating.
27–28 **Two such . . . will:** Two such opposing qualities are always present in man as well as in herbs–goodness and a tendency toward violence.
30 **canker:** cankerworm, a larva that feeds on buds.
31 ***Benedicite*** (ben′ ə dis′ ə tē): God bless you!

Literary Element Figurative Language *In lines 7–30, how does the Friar describe herbs and their nature? How are people like herbs?* L3

Teach

L3 Literary Element

Figurative Language Answer: *Herbs are diverse, and people are as well. None are so bad that they are worthless, and none are so good that they can't be put to bad use if they deviate from their true nature.* OL

★ Cultural History

Friars Friars (from *frater,* the Latin word for "brother") of Shakespeare's time spent much of their time traveling from town to town, preaching to the poor. Pledged to a strict vow of poverty, they survived on charity and lived and served in the secular world rather than secluded in monasteries. AS

Building Reading Fluency

Oral Presentation To improve reading fluency, invite volunteers to recite Friar's opening speech (lines 1–30). Have each one read four lines, pausing only where punctuation indicates a break in the flow. After these individual readings, organize a choral reading to reinforce students' understanding of the rhythm of Shakespeare's verse. BL

Academic Standards

Additional Support activities on pp. 730 and 731 cover the following standards:

Skills Practice: **9.2** Develop [reading] strategies…

Building Reading Fluency: **9.7** [Develop] speaking skills in…conjunction with…strategies…[for] delivery of oral presentations.

Teach

R1 Reading Strategy

Making Inferences About Characters **Answer:** *Friar Lawrence is wise and kindly; he has a fatherly attitude toward Romeo.* OL

★ Viewing the Art

Answer: *Romeo confides in the Friar and seeks his help. The young man looks earnest and troubled. The older man's compassionate expression and upraised hands suggest he's sympathetic while advising Romeo to be careful.*

One of the most influential artists of the Italian Renaissance, Raphael (1483–1520) was famed for his portraits and use of perspective. AS

Studies of the Heads of Two Men, 1517. Raphael (Raffaello Sanzio). Chalk on gray paper. Ashmolean Museum, Oxford, England.
Viewing the Art: What attitudes and emotions are conveyed by the facial expressions and hand gestures of these men? What parallels can you draw between these men and Romeo and the Friar? ★

Young son, it argues a distempered head°
So soon to bid good morrow to thy bed.
Care keeps his watch in every old man's eye,
And where care lodges, sleep will never lie;
But where unbruised youth with unstuff'd brain
Doth couch° his limbs, there golden sleep doth reign.
Therefore thy earliness doth me assure
Thou art uprous'd with some distemp'rature;°
Or if not so, then here I hit it right—
Our Romeo hath not been in bed tonight.

ROMEO. That last is true. The sweeter rest was mine.

FRIAR. God pardon sin! Wast thou with Rosaline?

ROMEO. With Rosaline, my ghostly father? No.
I have forgot that name and that name's woe.

FRIAR. That's my good son! But where hast thou been then?

ROMEO. I'll tell thee ere thou ask it me again.
I have been feasting with mine enemy,

33 **argues a distempered head:** suggests a disturbed mind.

38 **couch:** lay down.

40 **uprous'd . . . distemp'rature:** awakened by some emotional or mental disturbance.

Reading Strategy Making Inferences About Characters *What can you infer about Friar Lawrence's character and his attitude toward Romeo from these lines?* R1

Additional Support

Skills Practice

GRAMMAR: Intensive Pronouns

Write on the board: *Virtue itself turns vice.* Note that *itself* is placed right after the noun *virtue* to emphasize it. When the pronoun *himself, herself, themselves,* or *itself* is used this way, it is called an intensive pronoun. Have students add an intensive pronoun to each of these sentences. (Answers appear in parentheses.)

1. Romeo (*himself*) visited the Friar to arrange the wedding.
2. The lovers (*themselves*) cannot change their destiny.
3. I find the story (*itself*) sad but fascinating. OL

Where on a sudden one hath wounded° me
That's by me wounded. Both our remedies
Within thy help and holy physic° lies.
I bear no hatred, blessed man, for, lo,
My intercession° likewise steads° my foe.

FRIAR. Be plain, good son, and homely in thy drift.
Riddling confession finds but riddling shrift.°

ROMEO. Then plainly know my heart's dear love is set
On the fair daughter of rich Capulet;
As mine on hers, so hers is set on mine,
And all combin'd,° save what thou must combine
By holy marriage. When and where and how
We met, we wooed, and made exchange of vow,
I'll tell thee as we pass; but this I pray,
That thou consent to marry us today.

FRIAR. Holy Saint Francis! What a change is here!
Is Rosaline, that thou didst love so dear,
So soon forsaken? Young men's love then lies
Not truly in their hearts, but in their eyes.
Jesu Maria! What a deal of brine°
Hath washed thy sallow° cheeks for Rosaline!
How much salt water thrown away in waste
To season love, that of it doth not taste!
The sun not yet thy sighs from heaven clears,
Thy old groans yet ringing in mine ancient ears.
Lo, here upon thy cheek the stain doth sit
Of an old tear that is not wash'd off yet.
If e'er thou wast thyself, and these woes thine,
Thou and these woes were all for Rosaline.
And art thou chang'd? Pronounce this sentence° then:
Women may fall when there's no strength in men.°

ROMEO. Thou chidst° me oft for loving Rosaline.

FRIAR. For doting, not for loving, pupil mine.

ROMEO. And badst me° bury love.

FRIAR. Not in a grave
To lay one in, another out to have.

ROMEO. I pray thee chide me not. Her I love now
Doth grace for grace and love for love allow.°
The other did not so.

50 **wounded:** That is, wounded with Cupid's arrow.

52 **physic:** medicine; healing power.

54 **intercession:** petition. **steads:** benefits.

55–56 **Be plain . . . shrift:** Speak plainly and directly. A confusing confession only leads to confusing forgiveness.

60 **all combin'd:** We are completely united.

69 **brine:** salt water (tears).

70 **sallow:** sickly yellow.

79 **sentence:** saying; general truth.

80 **Women . . . men:** Women can be expected to be unfaithful when men are so fickle.

81 **chidst** (chĭdst): scolded.

83 **badst** (bădst) **me:** urged me to.

85–86 **Her I love . . . allow:** I love her because she gives back or exchanges favor for favor and love for love.

Big Idea The Power of Love *What ironic comment is the friar making about the love of "young men"?* **BI1**

Big Idea The Power of Love *This section of the play permits the audience to hear an adult's view of Romeo and his passions. How does this help to show Romeo in a new light? Explain.* **BI2**

Teach

BI1 Big Idea

The Power of Love **Answer:** *They are fickle and shallow: a young man weeps bitterly over a woman, only to forget all about her when another catches his eye.* **OL**

BI2 Big Idea

The Power of Love **Answer:** *From the Friar's perspective, Romeo appears rash and immature and does not really understand the difference between infatuation and love.* **OL**

R2 Reading Strategy

Interpret Friar Lawrence's reactions to Romeo provide an adult's insights into his character.

Ask: Why might Shakespeare have chosen to insert the Friar's viewpoint here? *(It deepens the audience's understanding of Romeo, highlighting the tragic flaw of youthful impetuousness that will lead to his downfall.)* **OL**

Differentiated Instruction

Storytelling Guide verbally proficient students to use storytelling skills to enhance other students' enjoyment and comprehension of the play. Organize several small groups, including a student with strong verbal skills in each one. Have students summarize and list the key events so far in Act 2. Then invite a student to retell the events as a story. **AL**

Academic Standards

Additional Support activities on pp. 732 and 733 cover the following standards:

Skills Practice: **9.6.2** Demonstrate an understanding of sentence construction... and proper English usage...

Differentiated Instruction: **9.7.17** Deliver oral responses to literature that...[demonstrate] a comprehensive understanding of the significant ideas of works...

Teach

R1 Reading Strategy

Making Inferences About Characters Answer: *He believes their marriage might end the feud.* OL

R2 Reading Strategy

Making Inferences About Characters Ask: What do Mercutio's words suggest about his attitude toward romantic love? *(Love weakens a man and will prove to be his downfall.)* OL

FRIAR. O, she knew well
Thy love did read by rote, that could not spell.°
But come, young waverer, come go with me.
In one respect I'll thy assistant be;
For this alliance may so happy prove
To turn your households' **rancor** to pure love.

ROMEO. O, let us hence! I stand° on sudden haste.

FRIAR. Wisely and slow. They stumble that run fast.

[*They exit.*]

SCENE 4. Approximately nine o'clock in the morning, the time at which JULIET was to send a messenger to ROMEO. A street in Verona.

[*BENVOLIO and MERCUTIO enter; they are still concerned about ROMEO's disappearance the night before.*]

MERCUTIO. Where the devil should this Romeo be?
Came he not home tonight?

BENVOLIO. Not to his father's. I spoke with his man.

MERCUTIO. Why, that same pale hardhearted wench, that Rosaline,
Torments him so that he will sure run mad.

BENVOLIO. Tybalt, the kinsman to old Capulet,
Hath sent a letter to his father's house.

MERCUTIO. A challenge, on my life.

BENVOLIO. Romeo will answer it.°

MERCUTIO. Any man that can write may answer a letter.

BENVOLIO. Nay, he will answer the letter's master, how he dares, being dared.

R2 MERCUTIO. Alas, poor Romeo, he is already dead: stabbed with a white wench's black eye; run through the ear with a love song; the very pin° of his heart cleft with the blind bow-boy's butt-shaft;° and is he a man to encounter Tybalt?

BENVOLIO. Why, what is Tybalt?

MERCUTIO. More than Prince of Cats.° O, he's the courageous captain of compliments.° He fights as you sing prick-song,° keeps time, distance, and proportion;° he rests his minim rests,° one, two, and the third in your bosom: the very

88 **read . . . spell:** read by memorizing words, without understanding their meaning.

93 **stand:** insist.

10 **answer it:** accept the challenge to a duel.

16 **pin:** peg in the center of an archery target.

16–17 **blind . . . shaft:** Cupid's blunt practice arrow.

19 **Prince of Cats:** a pun on Tybalt's name. In a popular fable, the Prince of Cats was called Tybert.

20 **captain of compliments:** master of all the formal rules of dueling. **prick-song:** from printed music (as opposed to the less accurate singing from memory).

21 **proportion:** rhythm.

21–22 **minim rests:** shortest possible musical pauses.

Reading Strategy Making Inferences About Characters *Why is the Friar motivated to help Romeo?* R1

Vocabulary

rancor (rang′ kər) *n.* bitter resentment against someone; long-lasting spite

Additional Support

Skills Practice

READING: Elaborating Explain that elaboration develops and supports an important point in the text. For example, the many details about Tybalt's skill as a duelist emphasize that he poses a real threat to Romeo. Have partners compose a general statement about Romeo's character; for example, "Romeo acts without thinking about the consequences." Then have students locate and list details that elaborate on this point of character. OL butcher of a silk button, a duelist, a duelist! A gentleman of the very first house,° of the first and second cause.° Ah, the immortal *passado!*° The *punto reverso!*° The *hay!*°

BENVOLIO. The what?

MERCUTIO. The pox of such antic, lisping, affecting phantasimes, these new tuners of accent! "By Jesu, a very good blade! a very tall man! a very good whore!" Why, is not this a lamentable thing, grand-sire, that we should be thus afflicted with these strange flies, these fashion-mongers, these pardon-me's who stand so much on the new form, that they cannot sit at ease on the old bench? O, their bones, their bones!°

[*ROMEO enters. He seems much happier than he was at the beginning of the play.*]

BENVOLIO. Here comes Romeo! Here comes Romeo!

MERCUTIO. Without his roe,° like a dried herring: O flesh, flesh, how art thou fishified! Now is he for the numbers° that Petrarch° flow'd in. Laura° to his lady was a kitchen wench (marry, she had a better love to berhyme her), Dido a dowdy, Cleopatra a gipsy, Helen and Hero hildings and harlots, Thisby a gray eye or so, but not to the purpose.° Signior Romeo, *bonjour!* there's a French salutation to your French slop!° You gave us the counterfeit° fairly last night.

ROMEO. Good morrow to you both. What counterfeit did I give you?

MERCUTIO. The slip, sir, the slip. Can you not conceive?°

ROMEO. Pardon, good Mercutio. My business was great, and in such a case as mine a man may strain courtesy.

MERCUTIO. That's as much as to say, such a case as yours constrains a man to bow in the hams.

ROMEO. Meaning to cur'sy.°

MERCUTIO. Thou hast most kindly hit it.°

ROMEO. A most courteous exposition.

MERCUTIO. Nay, I am the very pink° of courtesy.

ROMEO. Pink for flower.

MERCUTIO. Right.

ROMEO. Why then is my pump° well flower'd.°

MERCUTIO. Sure wit! Follow me this jest now, till thou hast worn out thy pump, that when the single sole of it is worn, the jest may remain, after the wearing, soly singular.

23–24 **very first house:** best fencing school.
24 **cause:** excuse for challenging a man to a duel.
25 ***passado*** (pə sä′ dō): forward sword thrust. ***punto reverso*** (poon′ tō rə ver′ sō): back-handed thrust. ***hay:*** a fencing term signaling a hit.

27–34 **The pox . . . bones:** Mercutio mimics an old traditionalist complaining about the younger fencers who use newfangled and foreign terminology.

36 **roe:** fish eggs. Mercutio makes a pun on Romeo's name (without "Ro" he is all sighs—"meo" or "oh me!").
37 **numbers:** verses; poems.
38 **Petrarch** (pē′ trärk): an influential Italian poet who composed love sonnets to his chaste love, **Laura.**
38–41 **Laura . . . purpose:** Mercutio refers to famous women from classical mythology and ancient history. He suggests these women are good-for-nothings **(hildings)** and not worth mentioning **(to the purpose)** in Romeo's eyes.
43 **French slop:** loose breeches, or pants. **counterfeit:** A counterfeit coin was called a *slip*, a word that also means "escape."

46 **conceive:** understand (my pun).

51 **cur'sy:** curtsy, a slight lowering of the body with bending of the knees, usually done by women.
52 **most kindly hit it:** put it most graciously.

54 **pink:** perfection.
55–57 **Pink . . . flower'd:** Romeo plays on two other meanings of *pink:* "flower" and "decorative perforations," which might be found on a shoe **(pump).**
58–61 **Sure . . . singleness:** Mercutio and Romeo play on the words **sole** ("solitary" or "bottom of a shoe"), **soly** ("only" or "uniquely"), **single-sol'd** ("shoddy"), **singular** ("unique"), and **singleness** ("silliness").

Reading Strategy Making Inferences About Characters ***What points does Mercutio make about Tybalt's skill at dueling? Why does Mercutio make these points?*** **R3**

Teach

R3 Reading Strategy

Making Inferences About Characters Answer: *Tybalt is an experienced duelist, and Mercutio seems concerned that Romeo is in no shape to face him in a fight.* **OL**

★ Cultural History

Cleopatra and Helen Mercutio refers to two famously bewitching but faithless women whose great loves ended in disaster. Cleopatra, queen of Egypt from 51 to 30 B.C., killed herself when a plan to help Marc Antony regain control of Rome failed. Helen of Troy, wife to Menelaus of Sparta, fell in love with her abductor, Paris, sparking the Trojan War. **AS**

English Language Coach

Interpret Text Students from other cultures may be puzzled by the exchange between Romeo and Mercutio. Invite English-speaking volunteers to illustrate banter (good-natured teasing and joking). Ask English language learners to describe how friends in their culture might use wordplay. Have small groups including proficient English speakers interpret Romeo and Mercutio's wordplay. **EL**

Academic Standards

Additional Support activities on pp. 734 and 735 cover the following standards:

Skills Practice: **9.3** [Identify] story elements such as character…

English Language Coach: **9.3.3** Analyze interactions between characters…

Teach

R1 Reading Strategy

Making Inferences About Characters **Answer:** *Romeo and Mercutio tease each other and compete in witty wordplay in the same way two brothers might.* OL

L Literary Element

Figurative Language **Answer:** *Romeo maintains a playful mood, joking about the servants' clothing, suggesting they are comically overdressed.* OL

ROMEO. O single-sol'd jest, soly singular for the singleness!°

MERCUTIO. Come between us, good Benvolio, my wits faints.

ROMEO. Swits and spurs,° swits and spurs, or I'll cry a match.°

MERCUTIO. Nay, if our wits run the wild-goose chase,° I am done; for thou hast more of the wild goose° in one of thy wits than, I am sure, I have in my whole five. Was I with you° there for the goose?°

ROMEO. Thou wast never with me for any thing when thou wast not there for the goose.

MERCUTIO. I will bite thee by the ear for that jest.

ROMEO. Nay, good goose, bite not.

MERCUTIO. Thy wit is a very bitter sweeting, it is a most sharp sauce.

ROMEO. And is it not then well serv'd in to a sweet goose?°

MERCUTIO. O, here's a wit of cheverel,° that stretches from an inch narrow to an ell° broad!

ROMEO. I stretch it out for that word "broad,"° which, added to the goose, proves thee far and wide a broad goose.

MERCUTIO. Why, is not this better now than groaning for love? Now art thou sociable, now art thou Romeo; now art thou what thou art, by art as well as by nature, for this drivelling love is like a great natural that runs lolling up and down to hide his bable in a hole.°

BENVOLIO. Stop there, stop there.

MERCUTIO. Thou desirest me to stop in my tale against the hair.

BENVOLIO. Thou wouldst else have made thy tale large.

MERCUTIO. O, thou art deceiv'd; I would have made it short, for I was come to the whole depth of my tale and meant indeed to occupy the argument no longer.

ROMEO. Here's goodly gear!°

[*The* NURSE *enters with* PETER, *a servant.*]

A sail,° a sail!

MERCUTIO. Two, two! A shirt and a smock.°

NURSE. Peter!

PETER. Anon.

NURSE. My fan, Peter.

63 **Swits and spurs:** spur on your horse (keep going). **cry a match:** claim victory.
64 **wild-goose chase:** a game of "follow the leader" on horseback.
65 **goose:** fool.

67 **with you:** even with you. **for the goose:** to chase women.

74 **is it not . . . goose:** doesn't my wit (a sharp sauce) go well with you (its sweet victim).
75 **cheverel** (shev′ ər el′): kid leather (which stretches easily).
76 **ell:** forty-five inches.
77 **broad:** "obvious" or "indecent."

80–83 **Now art . . . hole:** Mercutio compares love to a drooling idiot **(natural)** running around with his fool's wand **(bable),** a stick with an inflated bladder, or balloon, on one end.

90 **goodly gear:** fine stuff (an inappropriate reference to the Nurse's appearance or outfit that is meant to be funny).
91 **A sail:** an expression used when a sailor sees another ship.
92 **A shirt and a smock:** a man and a woman.

Reading Strategy Making Inferences About Characters *From their banter, what inferences can you make about the relationship between Romeo and Mercutio?* R1

Literary Element Figurative Language *Why does Romeo compare the sight of the Nurse and Peter to the sight of ships coming into view?* L

Additional Support

Skills Practice

WRITING: Persuasive Writing
Explain that persuasive writing tries to influence readers to accept an idea, adopt a position, or take a particular action. Have students write an essay that persuades readers to accept their view of romantic love. Have one half of the class write the essay from Romeo's point of view; and the other, from Mercutio's. Remind them to support their claims with evidence from the text. OL

A Capriccio with Figures Conversing Under an Archway, a Courtyard Beyond. Francesco Guardi (1712–1793). Oil on canvas, 24.2 x 17.7 cm. Private collection.
Viewing the Art: Does the scene depicted in this painting correspond with your impression of the setting of Act 2, Scene 4? Explain. ★

MERCUTIO. Good Peter, to hide her face; for her fan's the fairer face.

NURSE. God ye° good morrow, gentlemen.

MERCUTIO. God ye good den,° fair gentlewoman.

NURSE. Is it good den?

MERCUTIO. 'Tis no less, I tell ye, for the bawdy hand of the dial is now upon the prick° of noon.

NURSE. Out upon you, what a man are you?

ROMEO. One, gentlewoman, that God hath made, himself to mar.°

NURSE. By my troth, it is well said; "for himself to mar," quoth 'a! Gentlemen, can any of you tell me where I may find the young Romeo?

ROMEO. I can tell you; but young Romeo will be older when you have found him than he was when you sought him. I am the youngest of that name, for fault of a worse.°

98 **God ye:** God give you.

99 **good den:** good afternoon.

102 **prick:** mark on a clock.

103–105 **Out upon . . . mar:** The Nurse indignantly asks Mercutio what sort of a man he is. Romeo responds that Mercutio was made in God's image but marred by himself.

111 **fault of a worse:** Romeo plays on the expression "for want of a better." **fault:** lack.

Teach

R2 Reading Strategy

Making Inferences About Characters Invite volunteers to read the parts of Mercutio and the Nurse. **Ask:** Which phrases in Mercutio's speech demonstrate his rudeness? *("Hide her face; for her fan's the fairer face." ". . . for the bawdy hand of the dial . . .")* **OL**

★ Viewing the Art

Answer: *The close figure groupings suggest intimate conversations such as those that occur in the scene.*

The sunny, romantic scenes of Venice painted by Francesco Guardi (1712–1793) typically display sparkling colors and intricate details. **AS**

Differentiated Instruction

Dialogue with Wordplay Discuss the techniques Shakespeare uses to make his dialogue lively and revealing. Invite students to give examples of ways they use wordplay with friends. Have partners write a skit about two friends discussing a conflict. They should first write a summary of the situation. Their dialogue should use wordplay to reveal personality traits. Invite partners to perform their skits for the class. **AL**

Academic Standards

Additional Support activities on pp. 736 and 737 cover the following standards:

Skills Practice: **9.5.4** Write persuasive compositions that...clarify and defend positions with precise and relevant evidence...

Differentiated Instruction: **9.5.8** Write for different purposes and audiences, adjusting tone, style, and voice as appropriate.

Teach

R1 Reading Strategy

Making Inferences About Characters **Answer:** *She probably brings a message from Juliet.* **OL**

R2 Reading Strategy

Making Inferences About Characters **Answer:** *Romeo behaves with courtesy and gentleness. Students may infer that he is decent and kind.* **OL**

★ Language History

Scurvy Knave The derivations of *scurvy* and *knave* shed light on the Nurse's insults. The Middle English word *skurfr* referred to scaly skin or dandruff; *scurfy* meant "vile, contemptible." *Knave*, spelled *knaue* in Middle English, originally meant "serving boy" but came to mean "a low deceitful person." **AS**

NURSE. You say well.

MERCUTIO. Yea, is the worst well? Very well took, i' faith! Wisely, wisely.

NURSE. If you be he, sir, I desire some confidence with you.

BENVOLIO. She will indite him to some supper.°

MERCUTIO. A bawd, a bawd, a bawd! So ho!°

ROMEO. What hast thou found?

MERCUTIO. No hare, sir, unless a hare, sir, in a lenten pie, that is something stale and hoar° ere it be spent.°

[*MERCUTIO walks by them and sings.*]

An old hare hoar,
And an old hare hoar,
Is very good meat in Lent;
But a hare that is hoar
Is too much for a score,
When it hoars ere it be spent.

Romeo, will you come to your father's? We'll to dinner thither.

ROMEO. I will follow you.

MERCUTIO. Farewell, ancient lady. Farewell. [*Singing.*] "lady, lady, lady."

[*BENVOLIO and MERCUTIO exit.*]

NURSE. I pray you, sir, what saucy merchant° was this that was so full of his ropery?°

ROMEO. A gentleman, nurse, that loves to hear himself talk and will speak more in a minute than he will stand to° in a month.

NURSE. And 'a° speak anything against me, I'll take him down, and 'a were lustier than he is, and twenty such Jacks; and if I cannot, I'll find those that shall. ★ Scurvy knave, I am none of his flirt-gills,° I am none of his skains-mates.° [*She turns to PETER, her man.*] And thou must stand by too and suffer every knave to use me at his pleasure!

PETER. I saw no man use you at his pleasure; if I had, my weapon should quickly have been out. I warrant you, I dare draw as soon as another man, if I see occasion in a good quarrel, and the law on my side.

115–116 **If you . . . supper:** Benvolio deliberately misuses **indite** to mean "invite" as a way of mocking the Nurse's use of **confidence** to mean "private conversation."

117 **So ho:** The cry a hunter makes upon spotting prey.

119–120 **No hare . . . spent:** Mercutio compares the Nurse to meat hidden in a pie for Lent (when it is forbidden to eat meat) and kept long after it has become stale and moldy.

120 **hoar:** gray or white from age.

132 **saucy merchant:** rude fellow.

133 **ropery:** lewd jesting.

135 **stand to:** carry out.

137 **And 'a:** if he.

140 **flirt-gills:** loose women. **skains-mates:** cutthroats' companions.

Reading Strategy Making Inferences About Characters *What can you guess about the Nurse's reasons for looking for Romeo?* **R1**

Reading Strategy Making Inferences About Characters *Mercutio teased and mocked the Nurse. In contrast, how does Romeo behave toward her? What do you infer about Romeo?* **R2**

Additional Support

Skills Practice

READING: Readers Theater Explain that readers theater involves speaking the characters' lines without physically performing the parts. Note that effective interpretation requires a careful study of the script. Readers must imagine the characters' feelings and use tone of voice, facial expressions, body language, and gestures to communicate meaning. Invite volunteers to interpret Romeo's exchange with the Nurse. **OL**

NURSE. Now, afore God, I am so vex'd that every part about me quivers. Scurvy Knave! Pray you, sir, a word; and, as I told you, my young lady bid me inquire you out. What she bid me say, I will keep to myself; but first let me tell ye, if ye should lead her in a fool's paradise, as they say, it were a very gross kind of behavior, as they say; for the gentlewoman is young; and therefore, if you should deal double with her, truly it were an ill thing to be off'red to any gentlewoman, and very weak° dealing.

ROMEO. Nurse, commend me° to thy lady and mistress.
I protest° unto thee—

NURSE. Good heart, and i' faith I will tell her as much. Lord, Lord, she will be a joyful woman.

ROMEO. What wilt thou tell her, nurse? Thou dost not mark° me.

NURSE. I will tell her, sir, that you do protest, which, as I take it, is a gentlemanlike offer.

ROMEO. Bid her devise
Some means to come to shrift° this afternoon;
And there she shall at Friar Lawrence' cell
Be shriv'd° and married. Here is for thy pains.

[*He puts money into her hand.*]

NURSE. No, truly, sir; not a penny.

ROMEO. Go to! I say you shall.

NURSE. This afternoon, sir? Well, she shall be there.

ROMEO. And stay, good nurse, behind the abbey wall.
Within this hour my man shall be with thee
And bring thee cords made like a tackled stair,°
Which to the high topgallant° of my joy
Must be my convoy° in the secret night.
Farewell. Be trusty, and I'll quit thy pains.°
Farewell. Commend me to thy mistress.

NURSE. Now God in heaven bless thee! Hark you, sir.

ROMEO. What say'st thou, my dear nurse?

NURSE. Is your man secret? Did you ne'er hear say,
"Two may keep counsel, putting one away?"°

ROMEO. Warrant thee my man's as true as steel.

NURSE. Well, sir, my mistress is the sweetest lady. Lord, Lord! When 'twas a little prating° thing—O, there is a nobleman in town, one Paris, that would fain lay knife aboard;° but she, good soul, had as lieve° see a toad, a very toad, as see

155 **weak:** contemptible.

156 **commend me:** send my regards.

157 **protest:** swear.

161 **mark:** pay attention to.

165 **shrift:** confession.

167 **shriv'd:** forgiven of her sins.

173 **tackled stair:** rope ladder.

174 **topgallant:** a platform atop a ship's mast.

175 **convoy:** means of conveyance.

176 **quit thy pains:** reward your trouble.

181 **Two . . . away:** A secret cannot be kept by more than one person.

184 **prating:** chattering.

185 **lay knife aboard:** claim her for himself.

186 **had as lieve** (lēv): would as willingly.

Reading Strategy Making Inferences About Characters *What concern does the Nurse express here? Why?* **R3**

Teach

R3 Reading Strategy

Making Inferences About Characters Answer: *She worries that Romeo might take advantage of Juliet's innocence and abandon her. She fears he will break her heart.* **OL**

Differentiated Instruction

Cartoon Easily distracted students may benefit from shorter reading times and extra motivation. Inform them that they will be expected to re-create a scene in pictures. Divide scenes into segments and have students read them aloud. Pause throughout and encourage students to describe the events. Then have them draw a comic strip summarizing a scene in Act 2, with speech balloons containing paraphrases of important dialogue. **BL**

Academic Standards

Additional Support activities on pp. 738 and 739 cover the following standards:

Skills Practice: **9.7** [Develop] speaking skills...in conjunction with...strategies...[for] delivery of oral presentations.

Differentiated Instruction: **9.3** [Identify] story elements such as character,...plot, and setting...

Teach

R Reading Strategy

Making Inferences About Characters **Answer:** *She seems to be looking after Juliet's interests, enhancing Juliet's value in Romeo's eyes by revealing that she's sought after and implying he may have to fight for her affections.* OL

L Literary Element

Foil **Ask:** How do the Nurse and Mercutio function as foils to Juliet and Romeo? *(The Nurse and Mercutio, in refusing to take Romeo and Juliet as seriously as they take themselves, provide the audience with a realistic view of the lovers' immaturity and impetuosity.)* OL

him. I anger her sometimes, and tell her that Paris is the properer man; but I'll warrant you, when I say so, she looks as pale as any clout in the versal world.° Doth not rosemary and Romeo begin both with a letter?°

ROMEO. Ay, nurse; what of that? Both with an *R.*

NURSE. Ah, mocker! That's the dog's name.° *R* is for the—No; I know it begins with some other letter; and she hath the prettiest sententious° of it, of you and rosemary, that it would do you good to hear it.

ROMEO. Commend me to thy lady.

NURSE. Ay, a thousand times. [*ROMEO exits.*] Peter!

PETER. Anon.

NURSE. Before, and apace.°

L [*PETER exits, followed by the NURSE.*]

SCENE 5. Later that day. CAPULET's orchard.

[*JULIET, waiting for the NURSE to return from the meeting with ROMEO, paces impatiently.*]

JULIET. The clock struck nine when I did send the nurse;
In half an hour she promised to return.
Perchance she cannot meet him. That's not so.
O, she is lame! Love's heralds should be thoughts,
Which ten times faster glides than the sun's beams
Driving back shadows over low'ring° hills.
Therefore do nimble-pinion'd doves draw Love,°
And therefore hath the wind-swift Cupid wings.
Now is the sun upon the highmost hill
Of this day's journey, and from nine till twelve
Is three long hours; yet she is not come.
Had she affections and warm youthful blood,
She would be as swift in motion as a ball;
My words would bandy° her to my sweet love,
And his to me.
But old folks, many feign as they were dead—
Unwieldy, slow, heavy and pale as lead.

[*The NURSE enters, with PETER.*]

O God, she comes! O honey nurse, what news?
Hast thou met with him? Send thy man away.

NURSE. Peter, stay at the gate. [*PETER exits.*]

JULIET. Now, good sweet nurse—O Lord, why lookest thou sad?
Though news be sad, yet tell them merrily;

189 **any clout in the versal world:** any cloth in the whole world.
190 **a letter:** the same letter.

192 **dog's name:** The letter *R* sounds like a dog's growl.

194 **sententious** (sen ten′ shəs): The Nurse means to say *sentences,* or "pithy sayings."

199 **Before, and apace:** Go before me, and hurry.

6 **low'ring:** dark, threatening.

7 **Therefore . . . Love:** Venus, the goddess of love, was often portrayed riding a chariot drawn by nimble-winged **(nimble-pinion'd)** doves.

14 **bandy:** toss back and forth.

Reading Strategy Making Inferences About Characters *Why does the Nurse give Romeo this information?* R

Additional Support

Skills Practice

GRAMMAR AND LANGUAGE: Interjections Explain that interjections—words or phrases that express emotion—emphasize a character's reaction. Ask for examples. *(Wow! No kidding! Hey!)* Have students find interjections in the dialogue on pages 740 and 741 and suggest modern expressions to replace them. *(Fie: Oh man!; Jesu, what haste: Slow down! Cool it!; I' faith: Really)* OL

If good, thou shamest the music of sweet news
By playing it to me with so sour a face.

NURSE. I am aweary, give me leave° awhile.
Fie, how my bones ache! What a jaunce° have I!

JULIET. I would thou hadst my bones, and I thy news.
Nay, come, I pray thee speak. Good, good nurse, speak.

NURSE. Jesu, what haste! Can you not stay awhile?
Do you not see that I am out of breath?

JULIET. How art thou out of breath when thou hast breath
To say to me that thou art out of breath?
The excuse that thou dost make in this delay
Is longer than the tale thou dost excuse.

25 **give me leave:** let me alone.

26 **jaunce** (jôns): rough walk.

Juliet and her Nurse, John Roddam Spencer Stanhope. Oil on canvas. Private collection. 
Viewing the Art: Which lines in this scene fit the mood of this painting?

Teach

Viewing the Art

Answer: *Lines 38–44 seem to fit the painting best, in which the Nurse looks earnest and Juliet looks distracted.*

English painter John Roddam Spencer Stanhope (1829–1908) was a captain in the militia before becoming an artist. Known for his use of color, Stanhope tended to paint allegorical and mythical subjects. He moved to Florence in 1880 to help cure his asthma. **AS**

Differentiated Instruction

Pantomime Students attuned to movement and body language can demonstrate their understanding of mood and action in the play through pantomimes. Have partners create pantomimes of Romeo's actions and emotions in Scene 4 and those of Juliet in Scenes 5 and 6. After rehearsing, students should perform their pantomimes for the class. Invite audience members to assess each performance. **BL**

Academic Standards

Additional Support activities on pp. 740 and 741 cover the following standards:

Skills Practice: **9.6.1** Identify and correctly use…phrases…

Differentiated Instruction: **9.7.6** Analyze the occasion and the interests of the audience and choose effective…nonverbal techniques (including…gestures, and eye contact) for presentations.

Teach

R1 Reading Strategy

Making Inferences About Characters **Answer:** *She complains of weariness. She seems to enjoy teasing Juliet, perhaps to heighten the excitement of the moment or to prolong her own pleasure in the power she enjoys as the messenger of such important news.* OL

Is thy news good or bad? Answer to that.
Say either, and I'll stay the circumstance.°
Let me be satisfied, is't good or bad?

NURSE. Well, you have made a simple° choice; you know not how to choose a man. Romeo? No, not he. Though his face be better than any man's, yet his leg excels all men's; and for a hand and a foot, and a body, though they be not to be talk'd on,° yet they are past compare. He is not the flower of courtesy, but, I'll warrant him, as gentle as a lamb. Go thy ways,° wench; serve God. What, have you din'd at home?

JULIET. No, no. But all this did I know before.
What says he of our marriage? What of that?

NURSE. Lord, how my head aches! What a head have I!
It beats as it would fall in twenty pieces.
My back a t'other side—ah, my back, my back!
Beshrew° your heart for sending me about
To catch my death with jauncing up and down!

JULIET. I'faith, I am sorry that thou art not well.
Sweet, sweet, sweet nurse, tell me, what says my love?

NURSE. Your love says, like an honest° gentleman,
And a courteous, and a kind, and a handsome,
And, I warrant, a virtuous— Where is your mother?

JULIET. Where is my mother? Why, she is within.
Where should she be? How oddly thou repliest!
"Your love says, like an honest gentleman,
'Where is your mother?'"

NURSE. O God's Lady dear!
Are you so hot?° Marry come up, I trow.°
Is this the poultice for my aching bones?
Henceforward do your messages yourself.

JULIET. Here's such a coil!° Come, what says Romeo?

NURSE. Have you got leave to go to shrift today?

JULIET. I have.

NURSE. Then hie you hence° to Friar Lawrence' cell;
There stays a husband to make you a wife.
Now comes the wanton° blood up in your cheeks:
They'll be in scarlet straight° at any news.
Hie you to church; I must another way,
To fetch a ladder, by the which your love
Must climb a bird's nest soon when it is dark.
I am the drudge, and toil in your delight;

36 **stay the circumstance:** wait for the details.

38 **simple:** foolish.

41–42 **not to be talk'd on:** not worth mentioning.

43–44 **Go thy ways:** off you go.

50 **Beshrew:** curse.

54 **honest:** honorable.

61 **hot:** impatient. **Marry . . . trow:** Come on now, I declare.

64 **coil:** fuss.

67 **hie you hence:** hurry from here.

69 **wanton** (wont′ ən): unrestrained.

70 **They'll . . . straight:** They will turn red immediately.

Reading Strategy Making Inferences About Characters *What details suggest that the Nurse is deliberately delaying the telling of her message? Why is she doing this?* R1

Additional Support

Skills Practice

GRAMMAR AND LANGUAGE: Clauses Explain that a main clause is independent because it expresses a complete thought. It may be accompanied by a subordinate clause, which cannot stand alone.

Have students compose two sentences about Juliet with main and subordinate clauses. OL

But you shall bear the burthen soon at night.
Go; I'll to dinner; hie you to the cell.

JULIET. Hie to high fortune! Honest nurse, farewell.

[They exit in separate directions.]

★ SCENE 6. Later that afternoon. FRIAR LAWRENCE's cell.

[ROMEO and FRIAR LAWRENCE are waiting for JULIET so that the wedding can take place.]

FRIAR. So smile the heavens upon this holy act
That after hours with sorrow chide us not!°

ROMEO. Amen, amen! But come what sorrow can,
It cannot countervail the exchange of joy°
That one short minute gives me in her sight.
Do thou but close our hands with holy words,
Then love-devouring death do what he dare—
It is enough I may but call her mine.

FRIAR. These violent delights have violent ends
And, in their triumph die, like fire and powder,
Which, as they kiss, consume.° The sweetest honey
Is loathsome in his own deliciousness
And in the taste confounds the appetite.°
Therefore love moderately: long love doth so;
Too swift arrives as tardy as too slow.

[JULIET enters.]

Here comes the lady. O, so light a foot
Will ne'er wear out the everlasting flint.°
A lover may bestride the gossamers°
That idles in the wanton° summer air,
And yet not fall; so light is vanity.°

JULIET. Good even to my ghostly confessor.

FRIAR. Romeo shall thank thee, daughter, for us both.

JULIET. As much to° him, else is his thanks too much.

ROMEO. Ah, Juliet, if the measure of thy joy
Be heap'd like mine, and that thy skill be more
To blazon it,° then sweeten with thy breath
This neighbor air, and let rich music's tongue

2 **That after . . . not:** and not punish us for it later.

4 **countervail the exchange of joy:** outweigh the joy I receive.

9–11 **These violent . . . consume:** Like lighted gunpowder, these extreme joys destroy themselves as they reach their high point.

12–13 **Is loathsome . . . appetite:** becomes cloying and destroys our appetite for it.

16–17 **Here . . . flint:** In observing Juliet's light footsteps, the Friar alludes to a saying that small drops of water can wear away stones.

18 **bestride the gossamers:** walk on the cobwebs.

19 **wanton:** Here, it means "playful."

20 **vanity:** the temporary pleasures of this world.

23 **As much to:** the same to.

25–26 **that thy . . . blazon it:** if you are better able to proclaim it.

Reading Strategy Making Inferences About Characters *What would you say are the Nurse's true feelings about the situation in which she is playing a part?* **R2**

Big Idea The Power of Love *What wish does the friar express?* **BI**

Literary Element Figurative Language *Identify the simile in the Friar's warning. What does this simile add to the drama of the scene?* **L**

Teach

R2 Reading Strategy

Making Influences About Characters **Answer:** *She's thoroughly caught up in their romance and seems to be reliving the excitement of young love vicariously through Juliet while at the same time experiencing a mother's mixed feelings of joy and concern for her daughter.* **OL**

BI Big Idea

The Power of Love **Answer:** *The Friar hopes that God will allow the wedding and marriage to go favorably, and not punish anyone for it later.* **OL**

L Literary Element

Figurative Language **Answer:** *He compares Juliet and Romeo's love to fire touched to gunpowder—consuming one another as they unite. This simile injects a note of volatility and danger into the atmosphere.* **OL**

★ Cultural History

Monks' Cells In keeping with a Franciscan monk's vow of poverty, Friar Lawrence's cell would have been a tiny, unadorned room or cubicle in a larger building or a free-standing mud hut. **AS**

Differentiated Instruction

Visual Interpretation Challenge students to interpret the wedding scene. Assign students to provide a visual representation of Scene 6. Instruct students to consider:

- what the friar's cell looks like
- what the characters are wearing
- the expressions on the characters' faces

Remind students to use color and style elements to reflect the mood of the scene. Have students share their projects with the class. **AL**

Academic Standards

Additional Support activities on pp. 742 and 743 cover the following standards:

Skills Practice: **9.6.1** Identify and correctly use clauses, both main and subordinate...

Differentiated Instruction: **9.7.14** Deliver narrative presentations that describe with specific details...a scene...and the... characters...

Teach

BI Big Idea

The Power of Love Answer: *The mood is solemn, reflecting the irrevocable nature of what Romeo and Juliet are doing.* OL

★ Viewing the Art

The Footsbarn Traveling Theatre is an international company based in France, which tours the world, like the wandering storytellers of old. The multinational group has performed on all six continents. The company repertoire tends toward classics such as plays by Shakespeare and Molière. AS

Use the CheckPoint questions on Presentation Plus! to check students' mastery of the selection. These questions can be used with interactive response keypads for immediate student feedback.

Romeo and Juliet silhouette from Shakespeare's play as performed by the Footsbarn Traveling Theatre at Brighton on 07/05/93. ★

Unfold the imagin'd happiness that both
Receive in either by this dear encounter.

JULIET. Conceit, more rich in matter than in words,
Brags of his substance, not of ornament.°
They are but beggars that can count their worth;
But my true love is grown to such excess
I cannot sum up sum of° half my wealth.

FRIAR. Come, come with me, and we will make short work;
For, by your leaves, you shall not stay alone
Till Holy Church incorporate two in one.

[*They exit to perform the wedding ceremony.*]

30–31 Conceit . . . ornament: True understanding does not need to be elaborated in words.

34 sum up sum of: add up the total of.

Big Idea The Power of Love *How would you describe the mood, or feeling, of this scene? Why did Shakespeare create such a mood?* BI

Additional Support

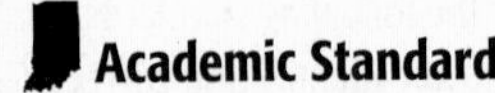

Academic Standards

The Additional Support activity on p. 744 covers the following standard:

Skills Practice: **9.5.8** Write for different purposes and audiences, adjusting tone, style, and voice as appropriate.

Skills Practice

WRITING: Rewriting Challenge students to rewrite the wedding scene as a journal entry from the Friar's point of view. Have students answer these questions:

- How does the Friar feel about the marriage?
- How does he feel about Romeo and Juliet?
- How does he feel about the role he's playing? OL

AFTER YOU READ

RESPONDING AND THINKING CRITICALLY

Respond

1. Do you approve of Romeo and Juliet's quick actions? Why or why not?

Recall and Interpret

2. (a)Why does Mercutio make fun of Romeo after they leave the party? (b)What makes this incident ironic?
3. (a)How does Romeo find out that Juliet shares his feelings? (b)What does Juliet seem most concerned about during the balcony scene?
4. (a)How do Romeo and Juliet carry out their plan to marry? (b)Why do they want to act so quickly?

Analyze and Evaluate

5. (a)Contrast how Romeo and Juliet respond to their sudden love. (b)Who seems more mature to you, Romeo or Juliet? Why?
6. Which moments in this act did you consider especially amusing or humorous? Why?

Connect

7. **Big Idea** **The Power of Love** In this act, Shakespeare presents several different views of love. With which view do you most identify? Explain.

LITERARY ANALYSIS

Literary Element Figurative Language

At times, Shakespeare may extend a metaphor over several lines, elaborating on its meaning.

1. To what does Romeo compare Juliet when he first sees her on the balcony in Scene 2? How does he extend this metaphor?
2. Identify the figurative language used by Juliet in Scene 5, lines 1–17. What do these lines convey?

Literature Groups

A **pun** is a humorous play on different meanings of a word or on words that sound alike but have different meanings. For example, when Benvolio says that Romeo will answer Tybalt's challenge in Scene 4, Mercutio responds, "Any man that can write may answer a letter." His pun plays on two meanings of *answer*: "accept a challenge to duel" and "reply in writing."

1. Find a pun in Act 2, Scene 4, that plays on different meanings of a word. Explain.
2. Find a pun in Act 1, Scene 1, that plays on words that sound alike but have different meanings.

LiteratureOnline **Web Activities** For eFlashcards, Selection Quick Checks, and other Web activities, go to www.glencoe.com.

READING AND VOCABULARY

Reading Strategy Making Inferences About Characters

A character's motivations are his or her reasons for acting in a certain way.

1. (a)Why is Tybalt eager to fight Romeo? (b)Why does Mercutio want Romeo to fall out of love?
2. (a)In your opinion, what motivates the Nurse and Friar Lawrence to help Romeo and Juliet? (b)Are these characters wise, irresponsible, or a mixture of the two? Explain.

Vocabulary Practice

Practice with Context Clues For each boldfaced word, choose the best definition.

1. My friend's classroom is **adjacent** to mine; it is a short walk.
   a. equidistant **b.** near **c.** subordinate
2. To deliberately not study is **perverse.**
   a. unreasonable **b.** daring **c.** sensible
3. Ana's **rancor** toward her enemy is great.
   a. generosity **b.** resentment **c.** violence
4. Give me one book, but **retain** the other.
   a. sell **b.** keep **c.** copy

LiteratureOnline

Web Activities Have students access the Web site for interactive activities that will help them assess their understanding of the selection.

Reading Strategy

1. (a) Tybalt is aggressive, hot-tempered, and obsessed with the feud.
   (b) Mercutio thinks his friend is behaving like a fool.
2. (a) They both genuinely care about the lovers; they get caught up in the secrecy and excitement. The friar also hopes to end the feud. (b) Students should explain their answers.

AFTER YOU READ

Assess

1. Accept reasonable answers.
2. (a) He thinks Romeo is silly for mooning over Rosaline. (b) Romeo has forgotten about Rosaline.
3. (a) From her speech on the balcony (b) Romeo's safety
4. (a) Juliet pretends she's going to confession and meets Romeo in the friar's cell. (b) Passion and fear of discovery
5. (a) Romeo is totally carried away, while Juliet worries about the suddenness of it, Romeo's sincerity, and family complications. (b) Juliet is more mature in considering the realities of their situation.
6. Students should support their answers.
7. Accept reasonable answers.

Literary Element

1. To the sun; asks her to rise and kill her mistress, the moon
2. Juliet wishes the news from Romeo would come faster—rushing to her in the winged chariot of the goddess of love. She compares the Nurse to lead—heavy, cold, and slow. A younger messenger would bounce between the lovers like a ball. The lines convey impatience.

Literature Groups

1. *slip* (2.4.43–46), *pink* (54–57), *single* and *sole* (58–61), *goose* (64–69)
2. *collier, collar,* and *choler* (2.1.1–4)

Vocabulary

1. b **2.** a **3.** b **4.** b

BEFORE YOU READ

Focus

Summary

Tybalt challenges Romeo to a duel. Mercutio fights Tybalt and is killed. Enraged, Romeo kills Tybalt and is banished. The friar urges Romeo to wait in Mantua until the situation cools down. Although horrified by Romeo's crime, Juliet remains loyal to her new husband, and they spend the night together before Romeo leaves. Juliet's father commands her to wed Paris.

V Vocabulary

Vocabulary File Say: Add these words and definitions to your vocabulary file. For each word, include a sentence that gives you an example of how to use the word. **OL** Students with English language needs should include the pronunciation of these words in their files. **EL**

Literary Elements Have students access the Web site to improve their understanding of monologue, soliloquy, and aside.

LITERATURE PREVIEW

Connecting to the Drama

Where do you look for help when life is hard? Before you read Act 3, think about the following questions:

- Why is it sometimes difficult to communicate your feelings to elders?
- How is your attitude toward the world different from that of adults you know and trust?

Building Background

Seven hundred years ago Italy was not the unified country that it is today. The north of the peninsula was a patchwork of independent city-states, which had their own governments and frequently went to war with each other. Two such city-states were Verona and Mantua in the northeast of the country. Only twenty-four miles apart, they were completely independent of each other, akin to independent countries in our own time.

Setting Purposes for Reading

Big Idea The Power of Love

As you read, think about how societal expectations affect the love between friends or family members.

Literary Element Monologue, Soliloquy, and Aside

In a play, a **monologue** is a long speech by a character. A **soliloquy** is a special type of monologue delivered by a character who is alone onstage. An **aside** is a comment made by a character that is heard by the audience or another character but is not heard by the other characters onstage. Both soliloquies and asides are used to provide information to the audience and to reveal the private thoughts of characters.

- See Literary Terms Handbook, pp. R2, R11, and R16.

Literature Online **Interactive Literary Elements Handbook** To review or learn more about the literary elements, go to www.glencoe.com.

READING PREVIEW

Reading Strategy Comparing and Contrasting Scenes

Playwrights carefully craft the scenes within an act to further plot and to create artful parallels and contrasts. As you read Act 3, compare each scene with the ones that come after and/or before. Notice how an expert dramatist such as Shakespeare uses each scene to deepen characterizations and to add further dimensions to situations or events.

Reading Tip: Making a Web Diagram Use web diagrams like the one below to record pertinent details of each scene. Then review your web diagrams to compare and contrast the details.

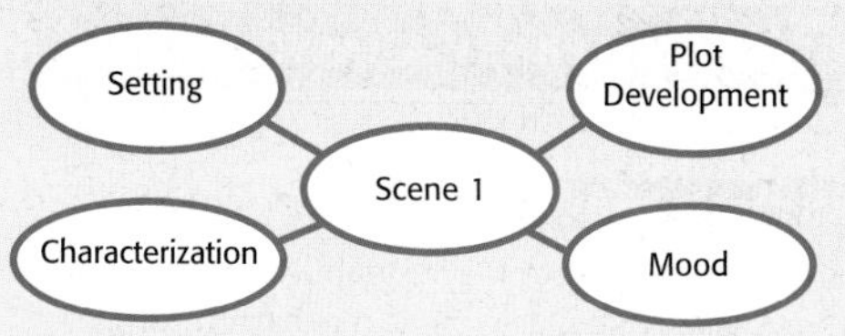

Vocabulary

eloquence (el′ ə kwəns) *n.* the quality of persuasive, inspirational speech; p. 754 *The defense lawyer's eloquence brought tears to the jurors' eyes.*

adversity (ad vur′ sə tē) *n.* hardship; p. 759 *She is upbeat despite adversity.*

predicament (pri dik′ ə mənt) *n.* a difficult or tricky situation; p. 760 *When a skunk started a family in our cellar, we were in quite a predicament.*

fickle (fik′ əl) *adj.* given to frequent changes of thought or mood; unreliable; inconstant; p. 767 *The ups and downs of life prove that fate is fickle.*

Vocabulary Tip: Analogies Analogies express the relationship between two words or sets of words.

INDIANA ACADEMIC STANDARDS (pages 746–773)

9.3.10 Identify and describe the function of...soliloquies [and] asides...in dramatic literature.

9.2 Develop [reading] strategies...

9.5.3 Write...literary analyses...

Selection Skills

The Tragedy of Romeo and Juliet, Act 3

Literary Elements
- Monologue, Soliloquy, and Aside (SE pp. 746–773)

Reading Skills
- Comparing and Contrasting Scenes (SE pp. 746–773)

Vocabulary Skills
- Analogies (SE pp. 746, 773)

Listening/Speaking/Viewing Skills
- Analyzing Art (SE pp. 750, 754, 761; TWE p. 766)

Writing Skills/Grammar
- Writing Reports (TWE p. 752)
- Hyperbole (TWE p. 754)
- Appositives (TWE p. 756)
- Persuasion (TWE p. 764)
- Compound-Complex Sentences (TWE p. 766)
- Using Aphorisms (TWE p. 768)

Act 3

SCENE 1. The same afternoon. A street in Verona.

[BENVOLIO and MERCUTIO enter with some of their SERVANTS.]

R2

BENVOLIO. I pray thee, good Mercutio, let's retire.
The day is hot, the Capels° are abroad,
And, if we meet, we shall not 'scape a brawl,
For now, these hot days, is the mad blood stirring.

MERCUTIO. Thou art like one of these fellows that, when he enters the confines of a tavern, claps me his sword upon the table and says, "God send me no need of thee!" and by the operation of the second cup draws him on the drawer,° when indeed there is no need.

BENVOLIO. Am I like such a fellow?

MERCUTIO. Come, come, thou art as hot a Jack° in thy mood as any in Italy; and as soon mov'd to be moody, and as soon moody to be mov'd.°

BENVOLIO. And what to?

L

MERCUTIO. Nay, and° there were two such, we should have none shortly, for one would kill the other. Thou! Why, thou wilt quarrel with a man that hath a hair more or a hair less in his beard than thou hast. Thou wilt quarrel with a man for cracking nuts, having no other reason but because thou hast hazel eyes. What eye but such an eye would spy out such a quarrel? Thy head is as full of quarrels as an egg is full of meat;° and yet thy head hath been beaten as addle° as an egg for quarreling. Thou hast quarreled with a man for coughing in the street, because he hath wakened thy dog that hath lain asleep in the sun. Didst thou not fall out with a tailor for wearing his new doublet° before Easter? With another for tying his new shoes with old riband?° And yet thou wilt tutor me from quarreling!°

BENVOLIO. And I were so apt to quarrel as thou art, any man should buy the fee simple of my life for an hour and a quarter.°

MERCUTIO. The fee simple? O simple!°

[TYBALT, JULIET's cousin, enters with other CAPULETS. He has not been able to find ROMEO since sending him a challenge earlier that day.]

BENVOLIO. By my head, here comes the Capulets.

MERCUTIO. By my heel, I care not.

2 **Capels:** Capulets.

7–8 **by the . . . drawer:** when the second cup has had its effect, draws his sword on the waiter.

11 **Jack:** fellow.

12–13 **and as soon mov'd . . . mov'd:** as easily provoked to be angry as you are angry at being provoked.

15 **and:** if.

22 **meat:** food. **addle:** confused; rotten.

26 **doublet:** jacket. (New fashions were traditionally not supposed to be worn before Easter.)

27 **riband:** ribbon.

28 **tutor me from quarreling:** teach me not to quarrel.

31 **buy . . . quarter:** buy complete ownership of my life for a fraction of its value (since I would not live long).

32 **O simple:** Oh, how stupid!

Reading Strategy Comparing and Contrasting Scenes *What new information about Benvolio does the audience learn here?* R1

Teach

R1 Reading Strategy

Comparing and Contrasting Scenes **Answer:** *The audience learns that he has a quick temper.* OL

R2 Reading Strategy

Predicting Have students read Benvolio's first lines and recall the challenge Tybalt sent to Romeo. **Ask:** What do you predict might happen? *(Benvolio's words establish that the time is ripe for a confrontation. Students know that Tybalt is looking for one. There may be a duel.)* OL

L Literary Element

Tone Point out that Mercutio's speech mingles a number of different tones: humorous wordplay; ironic teasing; and hyperbole, or exaggeration. **Ask:** What makes Mercutio a round character? *(He has a mixture of conflicting, believable personality traits, which are revealed in his dialogue.)* OL

Differentiated Instruction

Mapping Information Flow Encourage students who have trouble following plot developments to create diagrams or flowcharts that show how a given piece of information moves through the scene or across scenes. Encourage students to stop and model this flow (or patterns of character interaction) throughout the play as they read. BL

Academic Standards

The Additional Support activity on p. 747 covers the following standard:

Differentiated Instruction: **9.3** [Identify] story elements such as...plot...

Teach

R1 Reading Strategy

Interpreting Have students describe Tybalt's character. **Ask:** What effect do you imagine Tybalt and Mercutio have on each other? With what result? *(Mercutio's biting wit and Tybalt's temper are likely to clash.)* OL

R2 Reading Strategy

Comparing and Contrasting Scenes **Answer:** *Mercutio, Tybalt, and Benvolio have encountered one another and seem on the verge of fighting.* OL

L1 Literary Element

Foil Note that compared with Romeo and Mercutio, Tybalt is a flat character. Tybalt's driving motivation is resentment toward the Montagues. Under the circumstances, Romeo shows considerable restraint, counting Tybalt a relative by marriage now that Romeo is married to Juliet—although, ironically, Romeo cannot reveal this fact. OL

BI Big Idea

The Power of Love **Answer:** *Romeo alludes to his marriage to Tybalt's kinswoman, Juliet.* OL

TYBALT. [*To his companions.*] Follow me close, for I will speak to them. [*To BENVOLIO and MERCUTIO.*] Gentlemen, good-den. A word with one of you.

MERCUTIO. And but one word with one of us? Couple it with something; make it a word and a blow.

R1 TYBALT. You shall find me apt enough to that, sir, and you will give me occasion.

MERCUTIO. Could you not take some occasion without giving?

TYBALT. Mercutio, thou consortest with Romeo.

MERCUTIO. Consort? What, dost thou make us minstrels?°
And thou make minstrels of us, look to hear nothing but discords. [*He places his hand on the hilt of his sword.*] Here's my fiddlestick;° here's that shall make you dance. 'Zounds,° consort!

BENVOLIO. We talk here in the public haunt of men.
Either withdraw unto some private place,
Or reason coldly of your grievances,
Or else depart. Here all eyes gaze on us.

MERCUTIO. Men's eyes were made to look, and let them gaze.
I will not budge for no man's pleasure, I.

[*ROMEO enters. He is calm and happy after his secret marriage to JULIET.*]

TYBALT. Well, peace be with you, sir. Here comes my man.°

MERCUTIO. But I'll be hang'd, sir, if he wear your livery.°
Marry, go before to field,° he'll be your follower!°
Your worship in that sense may call him man.

TYBALT. Romeo, the love I bear thee can afford
No better term than this: thou art a villain.

L ROMEO. Tybalt, the reason that I have to love thee
Doth much excuse the appertaining rage°
To such a greeting. Villain am I none.
Therefore farewell. I see thou knowest me not.

TYBALT. Boy, this shall not excuse the injuries
That thou hast done me; therefore turn and draw.

ROMEO. I do protest I never injured thee,
But love thee better than thou canst devise°
Till thou shalt know the reason of my love;
And so, good Capulet, which name I tender°
As dearly as mine own, be satisfied.

43–44 **Mercutio . . . minstrels:** Mercutio plays on the word consort, which can refer to a group of musicians (minstrels). Here, consortest means "keep company."

47 **fiddlestick:** violin bow. **'Zounds:** an exclamation of surprise or anger.

55 **my man:** the man I am looking for.

56 **But . . . livery:** Mercutio then plays on another meaning of my man, which is "servant," declaring that Romeo shall never wear the servant's uniform (**livery**) of Tybalt's household.

57 **field:** dueling field. **follower:** servant (but Mercutio means that Romeo will follow him to fight).

62 **the appertaining rage:** the appropriate angry response.

68 **devise:** imagine.

70 **tender:** value.

Reading Strategy Comparing and Contrasting Scenes *What plot complications are developing in this scene?* R2

Big Idea The Power of Love *To what does Romeo allude in line 61?* BI

Additional Support

Skills Practice

READING: Previewing Ask students how they preview a chapter *(flip through it quickly, noting headings and important words)*. Explain that they can also preview a scene or act of a drama by glancing through it to identify changes in setting, characters who interact, and illustrations. Have students scan the dialogue tags, stage directions, and illustrations on pages 750, 761, and 766, noting who interacts in the scene and how. Ask students to formulate three questions they think the scene will answer. OL

MERCUTIO. O calm, dishonorable, vile submission!
Alla stoccata° carries it away.

[*MERCUTIO, upset at TYBALT's insults and at ROMEO's refusal to fight, draws his sword.*]

Tybalt, you ratcatcher, will you walk?°

TYBALT. What wouldst thou have with me?

MERCUTIO. Good King of Cats, nothing but one of your nine lives. That I mean to make bold withal,° and, as you shall use me hereafter, dry-beat the rest of the eight.° Will you pluck your sword out of his pilcher° by the ears?° Make haste, lest mine be about your ears ere it be out.

TYBALT. I am for you. [*TYBALT draws his sword.*]

ROMEO. Gentle Mercutio, put thy rapier up.

MERCUTIO. Come sir, your *passado!*°

[*MERCUTIO and TYBALT fight. ROMEO, trying to stop the fight, turns to BENVOLIO for help.*]

ROMEO. Draw, Benvolio; beat down their weapons.
Gentlemen, for shame! Forbear this outrage!
Tybalt, Mercutio, the Prince expressly hath
Forbid this bandying in Verona streets.
Hold, Tybalt! Good Mercutio!

[*ROMEO, trying to separate the two men, steps between them and blocks MERCUTIO's sword arm. At that moment TYBALT thrusts his sword under ROMEO's arm and stabs MERCUTIO. TYBALT flees with his followers.*]

MERCUTIO. I am hurt.
A plague a' both houses!° I am sped.°
Is he gone and hath nothing?

BENVOLIO. What, art thou hurt?

MERCUTIO. Ay, ay, a scratch, a scratch. Marry, 'tis enough.
Where is my page? Go, villain, fetch a surgeon.

[*The PAGE, a servant, exits.*]

ROMEO. Courage, man. The hurt cannot be much.

MERCUTIO. No, 'tis not so deep as a well, nor so wide as a church door; but 'tis enough, 'twill serve. Ask for me tomorrow, and you shall find me a grave° man. I am pepper'd,° I warrant, for this world. A plague a' both your houses! 'Zounds, a dog, a rat, a mouse, a cat, to scratch a man to death! A braggart, a rogue, a villain, that fights

73 ***Alla stoccata*** (ä' lä stə kä' tə): Italian fencing term that means "at the thrust." Mercutio may be using this as a contemptuous nickname for Tybalt, or he may mean that his sword thrust will erase Romeo's "vile submission."
74 **walk:** withdraw (to fight).

77 **make bold withal:** take.
77–78 **as you shall . . . eight:** According to how you treat me from now on, I will either spare your other lives or thrash them.
79 **pilcher:** scabbard, sheath. **by the ears:** as one would pull out a coward from hiding.

83 ***passado:*** Italian fencing term meaning "pass" or "lunge."

89 **a' both houses:** on the Montagues and Capulets. **sped:** done for.

96 **grave:** "serious" or "dead."
97 **pepper'd:** finished.

Reading Strategy Comparing and Contrasting Scenes *How does the mood, or feeling, suddenly shift as the scene progresses?* R4

Teach

R3 Reading Strategy

Listening Ask students to imagine the emotions of Tybalt, Mercutio, and Romeo in this situation. What tone of voice does each character use? What volume? Invite volunteers to demonstrate by reading selected lines of each character aloud. OL

R4 Reading Strategy

Comparing and Contrasting Scenes **Answer:** *As the fight escalated, the scene was tense, exciting, and full of action. Now that Mercutio has been stabbed, the mood becomes intensely poignant and tragic.* OL

L2 Literary Element

Pun Point out that Mercutio puns with his dying breath. Have students explain the pun. (*Grave means both "serious" and "a place for the dead." Mercutio is being dead serious: he will soon be in the grave.*) OL

Differentiated Instruction

Visualizing the Action A live-action display will bring the swordfight scene alive for below-level readers struggling to grasp Shakespeare's language. Enlist students who express concepts best through body movement to analyze the fight scenes and have them work with small groups to stage the two fencing scenarios (lines 66–93 and 114–134). Group members should be prepared to explain how they determined the placement and movements of each character. BL

Academic Standards

Additional Support activities on pp. 748 and 749 cover the following standards:

Skills Practice: **9.2** Develop strategies such as. . .making predictions. . .

Differentiated Instruction: **9.7.14** Deliver narrative presentations that describe with specific details. . .the specific actions, movements, gestures, and feelings of characters. . .

Teach

L Literary Element

Monologue, Soliloquy, and Aside **Answer:** *Romeo laments that Mercutio died protecting Romeo's honor from Tybalt's slurs. Romeo regrets that because he was softened toward Tybalt by Juliet's love, he tried to intervene in the duel, inadvertently giving Tybalt a fatal advantage.* OL

★ Viewing the Art

Answer: *The dress, architecture, and fierce, angry energy of the fight scene are true to Scene 1. While the painting shows many people involved in the melee, only Tybalt and Mercutio fight in the play, with Romeo trying to separate them.*

Sir Frank Dicksee (1853–1928) was an English painter and illustrator renowned for expressing poetic sentiments in a realistic style. AS

Rival Factions from Romeo & Juliet, 1882. Sir Frank Dicksee. Gouache, en grisaille. Private collection.

Viewing the Art: Does this painting fit your image of the fight scene? Why or why not? ★

by the book of arithmetic!° Why the devil came you
between us? I was hurt under your arm.

ROMEO. I thought all for the best.

MERCUTIO. Help me into some house, Benvolio.
Or I shall faint. A plague a' both your houses!
They have made worms' meat of me. I have it,
And soundly too. Your houses!

[*MERCUTIO exits, supported by BENVOLIO and his men.*]

ROMEO. This gentleman, the Prince's near ally,°
My very friend, hath got this mortal hurt
In my behalf—my reputation stain'd
With Tybalt's slander—Tybalt, that an hour
Hath been my cousin. O sweet Juliet,
Thy beauty hath made me effeminate
And in my temper soft'ned valor's steel!°

[*BENVOLIO returns.*]

BENVOLIO. O Romeo, Romeo, brave Mercutio is dead!
That gallant spirit hath aspir'd° the clouds,
Which too untimely here did scorn the earth.

ROMEO. This day's black fate on moe days doth depend;°
This but begins the woe others must end.

[*TYBALT returns.*]

100 **book of arithmetic:** fencing manual.

107 **near ally:** close relative.

113 **in my . . . steel:** softened the courage in my character.

115 **aspir'd** (əs pīrd′): risen to.

117 **This day's . . . depend:** Today's fatal event will darken future days.

Literary Element Monologue, Soliloquy, and Aside *What inner thoughts does Romeo reveal in this soliloquy?* L

Additional Support

Academic Standards

The Additional Support activity on p. 750 covers the following standard:

Skills Practice: **9.5.3** Write expository compositions...that make distinctions between the...significance of specific data, facts, and ideas [and] include visual aids...

Skills Practice

READING: Researching Note that sword fights such as the one at the beginning of Act 3 added excitement to many Shakespearean plays and were a popular attraction of his productions. Have students research various types of swords used during Shakespeare's time, including rapiers, broadswords, and épées. Students should begin by learning the shapes and dimensions of the weapons and then include other interesting facts about their histories and uses. Encourage them to illustrate their reports. OL

BENVOLIO. Here comes the furious Tybalt back again.

ROMEO. He gone in triumph, and Mercutio slain?
Away to heaven, respective lenity,°
And fire-ey'd fury be my conduct° now!
Now, Tybalt, take the "villain" back again
That late thou gavest me; for Mercutio's soul
Is but a little way above our heads,
Staying for thine to keep him company.
Either thou or I, or both, must go with him.

TYBALT. Thou, wretched boy, that didst consort him here,
Shalt with him hence.

ROMEO. This shall determine that.

[ROMEO draws his sword; TYBALT draws his in response. They fight until ROMEO stabs TYBALT, who falls.]

BENVOLIO. Romeo, away, be gone!
The citizens are up, and Tybalt slain.
Stand not amazed. The Prince will doom thee death
If thou art taken. Hence, be gone, away!

ROMEO. O, I am fortune's fool!

BENVOLIO. Why dost thou stay?

[ROMEO flees just before a group of angry CITIZENS enters.]

CITIZEN. Which way ran he that kill'd Mercutio?
Tybalt, that murderer, which way ran he?

BENVOLIO. There lies that Tybalt.

CITIZEN. Up, sir, go with me.
I charge thee in the Prince's name obey.

[PRINCE ESCALUS, LORD MONTAGUE, LADY MONTAGUE, LORD CAPULET, and LADY CAPULET enter with various followers.]

PRINCE. Where are the vile beginners of this fray?

BENVOLIO. O noble Prince, I can discover° all
The unlucky manage° of this fatal brawl.
There lies the man, slain by young Romeo,
That slew thy kinsman, brave Mercutio.

LADY CAPULET. Tybalt, my cousin! O my brother's child!
O Prince! O husband! O, the blood is spill'd
Of my dear kinsman! Prince, as thou art true,
For blood of ours shed blood of Montague.
O cousin, cousin!

121 **respective lenity** (len′ə tē): careful leniency.
122 **conduct:** guide.

140 **discover:** disclose.
141 **manage:** course.

Reading Strategy Comparing and Contrasting Scenes *How does this scene compare with the last one in which the Prince appeared?* R2

Big Idea The Power of Love *From this scene, what do you infer about common beliefs about love, obligation, and revenge in Italy in the 1300s?* BI

English Language Coach

Western Art English language learners may be unfamiliar with the Western style of art in the selection. The artwork by Dicksee on page 750, for example, uses color and line to re-create a violent scene from this play. Note that as an artist in Victorian England, Dicksee employed subject matter and a style that are representative of a particular time and place in the history of Western art. Have students research an artwork that reflects an example of the artistic traditions of their native culture. EL

Teach

R1 Reading Strategy

Connecting Mercutio and Romeo were the best of friends. Have students consider how they would respond to Mercutio's death if they were Romeo. OL

R2 Reading Strategy

Comparing and Contrasting Scenes **Answer:** *The Prince enters after a street fight, as he did in Act 1. This time, however, there have been two deaths.* OL

BI Big Idea

The Power of Love **Answer:** *Family obligations seem paramount. Any insult to the family required an immediate forceful response.* OL

★ Cultural History

Revenge In Shakespeare's time, intense friendships between men were considered a higher form of love than the romantic bond between men and women. Mercutio fights Tybalt to defend Romeo's honor, and Romeo puts aside his feelings for Juliet to avenge his friend's death. Although complicated by Christianity's emphasis on forgiveness, Elizabethan attitudes toward revenge included the expectation that men were honor-bound to avenge the murder of a friend or relative. AS

Academic Standards

The Additional Support activity on p. 751 covers the following standard:

English Language Coach: **9.5.3** Write expository compositions, including… descriptive pieces…that communicate information and ideas from…sources accurately and coherently…

Teach

R1 Reading Strategy

Comparing and Contrasting Scenes

Answer: *He seems to suggest that a person's perception of a situation is colored by his or her prejudices. Benvolio neglects to mention that Mercutio started the swordplay with Tybalt. Students may not agree with Lady Capulet's idea that the murder of a family member requires revenge.* **OL**

PRINCE. Benvolio, who began this bloody fray?

BENVOLIO. Tybalt, here slain, whom Romeo's hand did slay.
Romeo, that spoke him fair, bid him bethink
How nice the quarrel was, and urg'd withal
Your high displeasure.° All this—uttered
With gentle breath, calm look, knees humbly bowed—
Could not take truce with the unruly spleen
Of Tybalt deaf to peace, but that he tilts°
With piercing steel at bold Mercutio's breast;
Who, all as hot,° turns deadly point to point,
And, with a martial scorn, with one hand beats
Cold death aside and with the other sends
It back to Tybalt, whose dexterity
Retorts it.° Romeo he cries aloud,
"Hold, friends! Friends, part!" and swifter than his tongue,
His agile arm beats down their fatal points,
And 'twixt them rushes; underneath whose arm
An envious° thrust from Tybalt hit the life
Of stout Mercutio, and then Tybalt fled;
But by and by comes back to Romeo,
Who had but newly entertain'd revenge,
And to't they go like lightning; for, ere I
Could draw to part them, was stout Tybalt slain;
And, as he fell, did Romeo turn and fly.
This is the truth, or let Benvolio die.

LADY CAPULET. He is a kinsman to the Montague;
Affection makes him false, he speaks not true.
Some twenty of them fought in this black strife,
And all those twenty could but kill one life.
I beg for justice, which thou, Prince, must give.
Romeo slew Tybalt; Romeo must not live.

PRINCE. Romeo slew him; he slew Mercutio.
Who now the price of his dear blood doth owe?

MONTAGUE. Not Romeo, Prince; he was Mercutio's friend;
His fault concludes but what the law should end,
The life of Tybalt.°

PRINCE. And for that offense
Immediately we do exile him hence.
I have an interest in your heart's proceeding,
My blood° for your rude brawls doth lie a-bleeding;
But I'll amerce° you with so strong a fine
That you shall all repent the loss of mine.
I will be deaf to pleading and excuses;
Nor tears nor prayers shall purchase out abuses.°

151–153 **Romeo . . . displeasure:** Romeo, who spoke courteously to him, asked him to consider how trivial the quarrel was, and also argued that it would greatly displease you.
156 **tilts:** points.

158 **all as hot:** just as angry.

159–162 **And, with . . . Retorts it:** This description suggests that both Mercutio and Tybalt ward off the other's jabs with a dagger held in one hand and return **(Retorts)** the jabs with a sword held in the other hand.
166 **envious** (en′ vē əs): hateful.

183–184 **His fault . . . Tybalt:** His only offense was that he killed Tybalt, which the law should have done anyway.

187 **blood:** relative.

188 **amerce** (ə murs′): penalize.

191 **purchase out abuses:** buy forgiveness for crimes.

Reading Strategy Comparing and Contrasting Scenes *Consider what Shakespeare is suggesting about human nature. Is Benvolio's version of the fight completely truthful? Is Lady Capulet's argument valid?* **R1**

Additional Support

Skills Practice

WRITING: Developing a Report

In response to escalating violence in public schools, many local governments have started in-school programs aimed at peaceful resolution of conflicts. Have each student work with a partner to research such programs. Suggest that the students speak with members of the school's counseling department, identify Internet resources, and interview local police officers. Student reports on their findings should include a strategy for peacefully resolving the feud in Verona. **OL**

Therefore use none. Let Romeo hence in haste,
Else, when he is found, that hour is his last.
Bear hence this body and attend our will.°
Mercy but murders, pardoning those that kill.

[*They all exit.*]

SCENE 2. Later that day. CAPULET'**s orchard.**

[*JULIET, unaware of what has happened, waits impatiently for the night so that she can see* ROMEO *again.*]

JULIET. Gallop apace, you fiery-footed steeds,
Towards Phoebus' lodging! Such a wagoner
As Phaëton would whip you to the west
And bring in cloudy night immediately.°
Spread thy close° curtain, love-performing night,
That th' runaway's eyes may wink,° and Romeo
Leap to these arms untalk'd of and unseen!
Lovers can see to do their amorous rites
By their own beauties, or, if love be blind,
It best agrees with night. Come, civil° night,
Thou sober-suited matron all in black,
And learn me how to lose a winning match,
Play'd for a pair of stainless maidenhoods.
Hood my unmann'd blood, bating in my cheeks,
With thy black mantle; till strange love grows bold,
Think true love acted simple modesty.°
Come, night, come, Romeo, come, thou day in night,
For thou wilt lie upon the wings of night,
Whiter than new snow upon a raven's back.
Come, gentle night; come, loving, black-brow'd night;
Give me my Romeo; and, when I shall die,
Take him and cut him out in little stars,
And he will make the face of heaven so fine
That all the world will be in love with night
And pay no worship to the garish sun.
O, I have bought the mansion of a love,
But not possess'd it, and though I am sold,
Not yet enjoy'd. So tedious is this day
As is the night before some festival
To an impatient child that hath new robes
And may not wear them. O, here comes my nurse,

194 **attend our will:** obey my wishes.

1–4 **Gallop . . . immediately:** Juliet urges the horses that drive **Phoebus** (fē′ bus) the sun god's chariot across the sky to hurry home. **Phaëton** (fā′ət ən), a son of the sun god, was known for recklessly driving the chariot.
5 **close:** concealing.
6 **That . . . wink:** so that the eyes of wandering observers may close.
10 **civil:** solemn.

14–16 **Hood . . . modesty:** Falconers would place a hood on an untamed **(unmanned)** falcon to prevent it from fluttering **(bating)** its wings. Juliet asks the night to conceal her blushing until she overcomes her innocent modesty.

Reading Strategy Comparing and Contrasting Scenes *How does the situation of Scene 2 contrast with that of Scene 1? What is the effect?* R2

Literary Element Monologue, Soliloquy, and Aside *What emotions and concerns does Juliet reveal here?* L2

Literary Element Monologue, Soliloquy, and Aside *What makes Juliet's impatience particularly touching?* L3

Differentiated Instruction

Classical Allusions Encourage gifted students to delve deeper into the play's allusions to Greek mythology. Have them find the meaning of the names *Phoebus* and *Phaëton* in a dictionary *("shining" and "bright one," respectively)*. Direct them to research Phoebus and Phaëton at the library or on the Internet. Then have them summarize their findings for the class and explain why Juliet's allusion foreshadows calamity. *(Phaëton's recklessness almost set the world on fire.)* **AL**

Teach

L1 Literary Element

Characterization Discuss the major personality traits of Benvolio, the Prince, Lady Capulet, and Lord Montague. Note that the Prince becomes the fulcrum of their interaction by demanding an explanation for the fray. **Ask:** What traits does the Prince display? *(Sternness, sorrow over bloodshed, moderation in determining Romeo's punishment by death)* **OL**

R2 Reading Strategy

Comparing and Contrasting Scenes **Answer:** *Juliet's happy anticipation of her reunion with Romeo poses a jarring contrast to the fatal fight in the previous scene. Her obliviousness to the disastrous complications in Scene 1 is poignant.* **OL**

L2 Literary Element

Monologue, Soliloquy, and Aside **Answer:** *Juliet anticipates but also worries about her first night with her husband.* **OL**

L3 Literary Element

Monologue, Soliloquy, and Aside **Answer:** *Her ignorance of Romeo's banishment for the murder of her cousin makes her eagerness to see him particularly touching.* **OL**

Academic Standards

Additional Support activities on pp. 752 and 753 cover the following standards:

Skills Practice: **9.5.3** Write expository compositions...that communicate information and ideas from primary and secondary sources accurately and coherently...

Differentiated Instruction: **9.3.7** Recognize and understand the significance of various literary devices...

Teach

R Reading Strategy

Connecting Students will be able to empathize with Juliet's impatience and the perception that time is creeping. Have them recall a meeting, date, or event they looked forward to anxiously and describe how their anticipation affected their mood and perception of time. **OL**

★ Viewing the Art

Answer: *Responses will vary. Students may point out that although the painting reflects the romance of the play, Romeo and Juliet would not be able to take a romantic walk in public like the couple in the painting.*

Italian painter Francesco Zuccarelli (1702–1788) was one of the most popular landscape painters of his time. His landscapes focus more on lyricism than realism. **AS**

Verona, Italy, ca. 1722–1788. Francesco Zuccarelli.
Viewing the Art: Is this how you visualize the setting of this play? Explain. ★

[*The* NURSE *enters carrying a rope ladder.*]

And she brings news; and every tongue that speaks
But Romeo's name speaks heavenly **eloquence.**
Now, nurse, what news? What hast thou there, the cords
That Romeo bid thee fetch?

NURSE. Ay, ay, the cords.

[*She throws down the ladder.*]

JULIET. Ay me! What news? Why dost thou wring thy hands?

NURSE. Ah, weraday!° He's dead, he's dead, he's dead!
We are undone, lady, we are undone!
Alack the day! He's gone, he's kill'd, he's dead!

37 **weraday:** welladay (alas!).

Vocabulary

eloquence (el′ ə kwəns) *n.* the quality of persuasive, inspirational speech

Additional Support

Skills Practice

WRITING: Using Exaggeration for Effect Discuss the effect of using hyperbole—extravagant, overstated language—in Juliet's soliloquy to describe her mood and emotions. Note how her words help the reader imagine the thrill of a teenager's first love. Have students write about a personal experience that inspired overwhelming excitement (e.g., seeing their favorite singer perform, winning a big game), using extravagant figures of speech. **OL**

JULIET. Can heaven be so envious?

NURSE. Romeo can,
Though heaven cannot. O Romeo, Romeo!
Who ever would have thought it? Romeo!

JULIET. What devil art thou that dost torment me thus?
This torture should be roar'd in dismal hell.
Hath Romeo slain himself? Say thou but ay,
And that bare vowel *I* shall poison more
Than the death-darting eye of cockatrice.°
I am not I, if there be such an ay,
Or those eyes shut, that makes thee answer ay.
If he be slain, say ay, or if not, no.
Brief sounds determine my weal° or woe.

NURSE. I saw the wound, I saw it with mine eyes,
(God save the mark!)° here on his manly breast.

47 **cockatrice** (kok′ə tris′): a mythical serpent that was thought to kill with a glance.

51 **weal:** happiness.

53 **God save the mark:** an expression uttered to ward off bad luck when something unpleasant is mentioned.

Teach

L Literary Element

Pun Have students identify Juliet's pun. *(*I *and* eye *sound like* ay, *which means "yes.")* Juliet now has the sinking feeling that her self, which now is defined by her relationship to Romeo, is taken from her. **OL**

English Language Coach

Deciphering Speech Help English language learners to decipher Juliet's speech by working line by line. Have student volunteers read a line aloud, then have the class paraphrase the line. Ask students to point out words that give them clues as to how Juliet is feeling. **EL**

Academic Standards

Additional Support activities on pp. 754 and 755 cover the following standards:

Skills Practice: **9.3.7** Recognize and understand the significance of various literary devices, including figurative language... **9.5.1** Write...autobiographical narratives...that describe a sequence of events...

English Language Coach: **9.3.3** Analyze interactions between characters...and explain the way those interactions affect the plot.

Teach

L1 Literary Element

Monologue, Soliloquy, and Aside **Answer:** *Juliet expresses outrage at Romeo's deceit. He appeared to be "beautiful" and "divine," but was in fact a "villain" and "vile."* **OL**

L2 Literary Element

Oxymoron Have students locate the oxymorons—abruptly paradoxical or contradictory phrases or statements—that Juliet uses in this speech. *(beautiful tyrant, fiend angelical, damned saint, honorable villain)*
Ask: Why does she combine these opposites to describe Romeo? *(To express the conflict she feels and the two conflicting images of her husband: gentle lover and raging murderer)* **OL**

A piteous corse, a bloody piteous corse;°
Pale, pale as ashes, all bedaub'd in blood,
All in gore-blood. I sounded° at the sight.

JULIET. O, break, my heart! Poor bankrout,° break at once!
To prison, eyes; ne'er look on liberty!
Vile earth, to earth resign;° end motion here,
And thou and Romeo press one heavy bier!°

NURSE. O Tybalt, Tybalt, the best friend I had!
O courteous Tybalt! Honest gentleman!
That ever I should live to see thee dead!

JULIET. What storm is this that blows so contrary?
Is Romeo slaught'red, and is Tybalt dead?
My dearest cousin, and my dearer lord?
Then, dreadful trumpet, sound the general doom!
For who is living, if those two are gone?

NURSE. Tybalt is gone, and Romeo banished;
Romeo that kill'd him, he is banished.

JULIET. O God! Did Romeo's hand shed Tybalt's blood?

NURSE. It did, it did! Alas the day, it did!

JULIET. O serpent heart, hid with a flow'ring face!°
Did ever dragon keep° so fair a cave?
Beautiful tyrant! fiend angelical!
Dove-feather'd raven! wolvish ravening lamb!
Despised substance of divinest show!°
Just opposite to what thou justly seem'st,
A damned saint, an honorable villain!
O nature, what hadst thou to do in hell
When thou didst bower° the spirit of a fiend
In mortal paradise of such sweet flesh?
Was ever book containing such vile matter
So fairly bound? O, that deceit should dwell
In such a gorgeous palace!

NURSE. There's no trust,
No faith, no honesty in men; all perjur'd,
All forsworn, all naught,° all dissemblers.°
Ah, where's my man? Give me some aqua vitae.°
These griefs, these woes, these sorrows make me old.
Shame come to Romeo!

JULIET. Blister'd be thy tongue
For such a wish! He was not born to shame.
Upon his brow shame is asham'd to sit;
For 'tis a throne where honor may be crown'd

54 **corse:** corpse.

56 **sounded:** swooned, fainted.

57 **bankrout:** bankrupt (because it has lost everything it values).

59 **Vile earth, to earth resign:** Miserable body, give yourself back to the earth.
60 **bier** (bēr): a platform on which corpses are displayed before burial.

73 **hid with a flow'ring face:** hidden by a flower-like face. (Similar images throughout this speech express Juliet's shock that evil can dwell within one she finds so attractive.)
74 **keep:** guard.
77 **show:** appearance.

81 **bower:** enclose, conceal.

87 **naught:** wicked. **dissemblers:** liars.

88 **aqua vitae** (ak′ wə vī′ tē): brandy.

Literary Element Monologue, Soliloquy, and Aside *How would you describe the emotions Juliet expresses over the course of this monologue?* **L1**

Additional Support

Skills Practice

GRAMMAR AND LANGUAGE: Appositive Phrases Explain that an appositive is a noun or pronoun that follows and identifies another noun or pronoun. An appositive phrase includes the appositive and its modifiers, as in line 99: "When I, thy three-hours wife, have mangled it?" An appositive phrase not essential to a sentence's meaning is set off by commas. Have students correctly punctuate and underline the appositive phrase in each sentence.

1. The Prince, a kinsman of Mercutio, must pass judgment on Romeo.
2. Juliet grieves for Tybalt, her dear cousin. **OL**

Sole monarch of the universal earth.
O, what a beast was I to chide at him!

NURSE. Will you speak well of him that kill'd your cousin?

JULIET. Shall I speak ill of him that is my husband?
Ah, poor my lord, what tongue shall smooth° thy name
When I, thy three-hours wife, have mangled it?
But wherefore, villain, didst thou kill my cousin?
That villain cousin would have kill'd my husband.
Back, foolish tears, back to your native spring!
Your tributary drops° belong to woe,
Which you, mistaking, offer up to joy.
My husband lives, that Tybalt would have slain;
And Tybalt's dead, that would have slain my husband.
All this is comfort; wherefore weep I then?
Some word there was, worser than Tybalt's death,
That murd'red me. I would forget it fain;°
But O, it presses to my memory
Like damned guilty deeds to sinners' minds!
"Tybalt is dead, and Romeo—banished."
That "banished," that one word "banished,"
Hath slain ten thousand Tybalts. Tybalt's death
Was woe enough, if it had ended there;
Or, if sour woe delights in fellowship
And needly will be rank'd with° other griefs,
Why followed not, when she said "Tybalt's dead,"
Thy father, or thy mother, nay, or both,
Which modern lamentation might have moved?°
But with a rearward° following Tybalt's death,
"Romeo is banished"—to speak that word
Is father, mother, Tybalt, Romeo, Juliet,
All slain, all dead. "Romeo is banished"—
There is no end, no limit, measure, bound,
In that word's death; no words can that woe sound.°
Where is my father and my mother, nurse?

NURSE. Weeping and wailing over Tybalt's corse.
Will you go to them? I will bring you thither.

JULIET. Wash they his wounds with tears? Mine shall be spent,
When theirs are dry, for Romeo's banishment.
Take up those cords. Poor ropes, you are beguil'd,°
Both you and I, for Romeo is exil'd.

98 **smooth:** speak well of.

103 **Your tributary drops:** the drops you have contributed.

109 **fain:** gladly.

117 **needly . . . with:** must be accompanied by.

120 **modern . . . moved:** might have roused ordinary grief.

121 **rearward:** rear guard.

126 **no words can that woe sound:** no words can express the depth of that misery.

132 **beguil'd:** cheated.

Big Idea The Power of Love *Describe the rapid changes Juliet's ideas undergo as she comes to understand the situation. Why does she say, ". . . wherefore weep I then"?* **BI**

Literary Element Monologue, Soliloquy, and Aside *At the time and place of the story, a young woman such as Juliet had no power to go where she wanted. How does this affect Juliet's reaction to Romeo's banishment?* **L3**

Teach

BI Big Idea

The Power of Love Answer: *As Juliet reflects, she remembers her love for her husband and that Tybalt wanted to kill him. Her anger toward Romeo rapidly changes to despair over his banishment.* **OL**

L3 Literary Element

Monologue, Soliloquy, and Aside Answer: *She falls into despair because Romeo's banishment to another city is tantamount to a permanent separation from him.* **OL**

★ Writer's Technique

Metaphor Shakespeare is famous for his use of the extended metaphor. Here he refers to "native spring" and "tributary drops." Both the spring and the tributary are parts of a river. In this case, Shakespeare is using the terminology of an actual river to refer to the flow of Juliet's "river" of tears. **AS**

English Language Coach

Exaggeration for Effect English language learners may be confused by Shakespeare's use of hyperbole. Ask students to recall stories that included exaggerations. How did they react to these overstatements? Note that exaggeration can be used humorously, but it can also dramatize the intensity of feelings. Discuss how slowly time seems to be passing for Juliet. Ask students to use similes or exaggeration to emphasize the intensity of Juliet's longing. **EL**

Academic Standards

Additional Support activities on pp. 756 and 757 cover the following standards:

Skills Practice: **9.6.1** Identify and correctly use...phrases...

English Language Coach: **9.3.7** Recognize and understand the significance of various literary devices, including figurative language...

Teach

R Reading Strategy

Comparing and Contrasting Scenes **Answer:** *Since Scene 1, many fresh obstacles to Romeo and Juliet's happiness have developed. Tybalt and Mercutio have been killed, and Romeo has been banished.* OL

BI Big Idea

The Power of Love **Answer:** *Some students may say that because of his immaturity, impetuousness, and passion for Juliet, Romeo overreacts to the Friar's sensible advice, although as adolescents, some may sympathize and recall experiencing similar feelings.* OL

He made you for a highway to my bed,
But I, a maid, die maiden-widowed.
Come, cords, come, nurse, I'll to my wedding-bed,
And death, not Romeo, take my maidenhead!

NURSE. Hie to your chamber. I'll find Romeo
To comfort you. I wot° well where he is.
Hark ye, your Romeo will be here at night.
I'll to him; he is hid at Lawrence' cell.

JULIET. O, find him! Give this ring to my true knight
And bid him come to take his last farewell.

[*They exit.*]

139 **wot:** know.

SCENE 3. Later. FRIAR LAWRENCE**'s cell.**

[*FRIAR LAWRENCE enters and notices that ROMEO is hiding in the room.*]

FRIAR. Romeo, come forth; come forth, thou fearful man.
Affliction is enamor'd of thy parts,°
And thou art wedded to calamity.

2 **Affliction . . . parts:** Misfortune has fallen in love with your attractive qualities.

[*ROMEO steps forward.*]

ROMEO. Father, what news? What is the Prince's doom?°
What sorrow craves acquaintance at my hand
That I yet know not?

4 **doom:** judgment.

FRIAR. Too familiar
Is my dear son with such sour company.
I bring thee tidings of the Prince's doom.

ROMEO. What less than doomsday° is the Prince's doom?

9 **doomsday:** my death.

FRIAR. A gentler judgment vanish'd° from his lips—
Not body's death, but body's banishment.

10 **vanish'd:** escaped.

ROMEO. Ha, banishment? Be merciful, say "death";
For exile hath more terror in his look,
Much more than death. Do not say "banishment."

FRIAR. Here from Verona art thou banished.
Be patient, for the world is broad and wide.

ROMEO. There is no world without° Verona walls,
But purgatory, torture, hell itself.
Hence "banished" is banish'd from the world,
And world's exile is death. Then "banished"
Is death misterm'd. Calling death "banished,"
Thou cut'st my head off with a golden ax
And smilest upon the stroke that murders me.

17 **without:** outside.

Reading Strategy Comparing and Contrasting Scenes *How have events developed since Scene 1?* R

Big Idea The Power of Love *How would you evaluate Romeo's claim that the Friar is downplaying the severity of banishment?* BI

Additional Support

Skills Practice

LISTENING AND SPEAKING: Point of View In her speech about banishment, Juliet speaks from the point of view of a young woman with almost no power to act independently. Have students write a poem or journal entry describing how Juliet feels and why. They may use a logical explanation or expressive language to communicate their understanding. OL

FRIAR. O deadly sin! O rude unthankfulness!
Thy fault our law calls death;° but the kind Prince,
Taking thy part, hath rush'd° aside the law,
And turn'd that black word "death" to "banishment."
This is dear° mercy, and thou seest it not.

ROMEO. 'Tis torture, and not mercy. Heaven is here,
Where Juliet lives; and every cat and dog
And little mouse, every unworthy thing,
Live here in heaven and may look on her;
But Romeo may not. More validity,°
More honorable state, more courtship lives
In carrion flies than Romeo. They may seize
On the white wonder of dear Juliet's hand
And steal immortal blessing from her lips.
Who, even in pure and vestal° modesty,
Still° blush, as thinking their own kisses sin;°
But Romeo may not, he is banished.
Flies may do this but I from this must fly;
They are free men, but I am banished.
And sayest thou yet that exile is not death?
Hadst thou no poison mix'd, no sharp-ground knife,
No sudden mean° of death, though ne'er so mean,°
But "banished" to kill me—"banished"?
★ O friar, the damned use that word in hell;
Howling attends it! How hast thou the heart,
Being a divine, a ghostly confessor,
A sin-absolver, and my friend profess'd,
To mangle me with that word "banished"?

FRIAR. Thou fond° mad man, hear me a little speak.

ROMEO. O, thou wilt speak again of banishment.

FRIAR. I'll give thee armor to keep off that word;
Adversity's sweet milk, philosophy,
To comfort thee, though thou art banished.

ROMEO. Yet "banished"? Hang up° philosophy!
Unless philosophy can make a Juliet,
Displant° a town, reverse a prince's doom,
It helps not, it prevails not. Talk no more.

FRIAR. O, then I see that madmen have no ears.

ROMEO. How should they, when that wise men have no eyes?

25 **our law calls death:** is punishable by death.
26 **rush'd:** brushed.
28 **dear:** uncommon.
33 **validity:** value.
38 **vestal** (vest′əl): virginal.
39 **Still:** always. **thinking . . . sin:** believing it is sinful for them to touch when her mouth closes.
45 **mean:** means. **mean:** lowly.
52 **fond:** foolish.
57 **Hang up:** forget about.
59 **Displant:** transplant.

Literary Element Monologue, Soliloquy, and Aside *What details in this monologue suggest Romeo's youth?* L

Vocabulary

adversity (ad vur′ sə tē) *n.* hardship

Teach

L Literary Element

Monologue, Soliloquy, and Aside **Answer:** *His extreme descriptions of his situation and his melodramatic assertions of his own doom suggest that he is juvenile, inexperienced, and out of control.* OL

★ Cultural History

Christian Hell Explain that to Renaissance Christians, hell represented a state or place to which the spirits of unrepentant sinners were condemned to suffer for eternity after death. Purgatory was the state or place in which those who had died in a state of God's grace atoned by suffering. Hell was permanent; purgatory was temporary. AS

Differentiated Instruction

Less Proficient Readers Before students read each scene, read a prose summary of it aloud. (Charles and Mary Lamb's *Tales from Shakespeare*, available on the Internet, contains a prose version of *Romeo and Juliet.*) After students finish reading silently, read selected passages aloud, explaining language and clarifying meaning. Encourage students to take time after reading each scene to record notes in a journal on events, characters' reactions, and personal thoughts. BL

Academic Standards

Additional Support activities on pp. 758 and 759 cover the following standards:

Skills Practice: **9.5.2** Write responses to literature that demonstrate a comprehensive grasp of the significant ideas of literary works…

Differentiated Instruction: **9.5.2** Write responses to literature that demonstrate a comprehensive grasp of the significant ideas of literary works…

Teach

R Reading Strategy

Comparing and Contrasting Scenes **Answer:** *In both cases, young people turn to adults for help.* OL

L Literary Element

Suspense Note how Shakespeare capitalizes on the suspense created by the Nurse's knocking. **Ask:** How would you describe the effect when the Nurse finally enters? *(Anticlimactic, humorous)* OL

FRIAR. Let me dispute with thee of thy estate.°

ROMEO. Thou canst not speak of that thou dost not feel.
Wert thou as young as I, Juliet thy love,
An hour but married, Tybalt murdered,
Doting like me,° and like me banished,
Then mightst thou speak, then mightst thou tear thy hair,
And fall upon the ground, as I do now,

[ROMEO throws himself on the floor.]

Taking the measure of an unmade grave.°

[There is a knock at the door to the cell.]

FRIAR. Arise, one knocks. Good Romeo, hide thyself.

ROMEO. Not I; unless the breath of heartsick groans
Mistlike infold me° from the search of eyes.

[Another knock.]

FRIAR. Hark, how they knock! Who's there? Romeo, arise;
Thou wilt be taken.—Stay° awhile!—Stand up;

[The knocking continues more loudly than before.]

Run to my study.—By and by!°—God's will,
What simpleness° is this.—I come, I come!

[There is a very loud knock. The FRIAR goes to the door.]

Who knocks so hard? Whence come you? What's your will?

NURSE. Let me come in, and you shall know my errand.
I come from Lady Juliet.

FRIAR. Welcome then.

[The NURSE enters.]

NURSE. O holy friar, O, tell me, holy friar,
Where is my lady's lord, where's Romeo?

FRIAR. There on the ground, with his own tears made drunk.

NURSE. O, he is even in my mistress' case,°
Just in her case! O woeful sympathy!
Piteous **predicament!** Even so lies she,
Blubb'ring and weeping, weeping and blubb'ring.
Stand up, stand up! Stand, and you be a man.
For Juliet's sake, for her sake, rise and stand!
Why should you fall into so deep an O?°

63 **dispute . . . estate:** discuss your situation with you.

67 **Doting like me:** as obsessively in love as I am.

69–70 **And fall . . . grave:** Romeo makes his gesture of throwing himself to the ground even more melodramatic by suggesting that he is seeing how large a grave he will need.

73 **Mistlike infold me:** forms a mist to hide me.

75 **Stay:** wait.

76 **By and by:** in a moment. The Friar interrupts his pleading with Romeo to address the person knocking at the door.

77 **simpleness:** foolishness.

84 **even in my mistress' case:** exactly in Juliet's condition.

90 **so deep an O:** so heavy a cry of grief.

Reading Strategy Comparing and Contrasting Scenes *What echoes do you see between this conversation and Juliet's conversation with the Nurse in Scene 2?* R

Vocabulary

predicament (pri dik′ ə mənt) *n.* a difficult or tricky situation

Additional Support

Skills Practice

READING: Steps in a Process
Explain that Shakespeare reveals the changes in Juliet's attitude toward Romeo through her dialogue. By studying what she says about him, we can infer the steps in the process that move her from blaming and condemning him to defending him. Have students use a graphic organizer to summarize the steps through which Juliet comes to accept what Romeo has done. OL

Romeo in Friar Laurence's Cell, Illustration to "Romeo and Juliet" Act III, Scene 3. William Hatherell. Watercolor over pencil on board, 37.1 x 27 cm. Birmingham Museums and Art Gallery, UK.

Viewing the Art: What words would you use to describe the emotions displayed by Romeo, the friar, and the Nurse in this painting? ★

ROMEO. [*He rises.*] Nurse—

NURSE. Ah sir, ah sir! Death's the end of all.

ROMEO. Spakest thou of Juliet? How is it with her?
Doth not she think me an old° murderer,
Now I have stain'd the childhood of our joy
With blood removed but little from her own?
Where is she? And how doth she! And what says
My conceal'd lady° to our cancel'd° love?

NURSE. O, she says nothing, sir, but weeps and weeps;
And now falls on her bed, and then starts up,
And Tybalt calls; and then on Romeo cries,
And then down falls again.

94 **old:** hardened.

98 **conceal'd lady:** secret bride. **cancel'd:** nullified.

Big Idea The Power of Love *Why does Romeo ask these questions?* BI

Teach

BI Big Idea

The Power of Love Answer: *Knowing that Juliet has probably heard that he killed Tybalt, Romeo is anxious to know if Juliet is well and if she still loves him.* OL

★ Viewing the Art

Answer: *Students may say that the Friar and the Nurse look frightened or concerned. Romeo looks distraught, heartbroken, or exhausted.*

This picture is one of twenty-two watercolors that illustrator and painter William Hatherell (1855–1928) created for *Romeo and Juliet.* Hatherell worked as an illustrator for numerous Victorian magazines and had a reputation for refusing to rush his work. AS

Differentiated Instruction

Analyzing the Painting Challenge visual learners to write an interpretive analysis of the painting in relation to the scene. Have students interpret the following:

- color
- positioning of the characters
- setting
- facial expressions

Ask students to read their interpetations to the class. Hold a class discussion comparing the various analyses. AL

Academic Standards

Additional Support activities on pp. 760 and 761 cover the following standards:

Skills Practice: **9.3.3** Analyze interactions between characters...and explain the way those interactions affect the plot.

Differentiated Instruction: **9.5.3** Write expository compositions, including analytical essays...that communicate information and ideas...accurately and coherently...

Teach

L1 Literary Element

Tragedy Note that in tragedies, the main characters, though admirable in many ways, have one or more tragic flaws that bring about their downfall. Have a student read aloud the Friar's speech (lines 109–121).
Ask: What tragic flaws does the Friar see in Romeo? *(He is too emotional and impetuous; he fails to consider the consequences of his actions.)* **OL**

L2 Literary Element

Monologue, Soliloquy, and Aside **Answer:** *The repetition has an upbeat rhythm and a persuasive effect. The Friar reminds Romeo that he has many reasons to be grateful: Juliet is still alive; Tybalt is dead and no longer a threat; and Romeo has been allowed to live.* **OL**

ROMEO. As if that name,
Shot from the deadly level of a gun,
Did murder her; as that name's cursed hand
Murder'd her kinsman. O, tell me, friar, tell me,
In what vile part of this anatomy
Doth my name lodge? Tell me, that I may sack°
The hateful mansion.

[*ROMEO takes out his dagger and offers to stab himself. The NURSE snatches the dagger away.*]

FRIAR. Hold thy desperate hand.
Art thou a man? Thy form cries out thou art;
Thy tears are womanish, thy wild acts denote
The unreasonable fury of a beast.
Unseemly woman in a seeming man,
And ill-beseeming beast in seeming both,°
Thou hast amaz'd me. By my holy order,
I thought thy disposition better temper'd.
Hast thou slain Tybalt? Wilt thou slay thyself?
And slay thy lady that in thy life lives,
By doing damned hate upon thyself?
Why railest thou on° thy birth? the heaven and earth?
Since birth,° and heaven,° and earth,° all three do meet
In thee at once, which thou at once wouldst lose.
Fie, fie, thou shamest thy shape, thy love, thy wit,
Which like a usurer abound'st in all,
And usest none in that true use indeed
Which should bedeck thy shape, thy love, thy wit.°
Thy noble shape is but a form of wax,
Digressing from the valor of a man;°
Thy dear love sworn but hollow perjury,
Killing that love which thou hast vow'd to cherish;
Thy wit, that ornament to shape and love,
Misshapen in the conduct° of them both,
Like powder in a skilless soldier's flask,
Is set afire by thine own ignorance,
And thou dismemb'red with thine own defense.°
What, rouse thee, man! Thy Juliet is alive,
For whose dear sake thou wast but lately dead.°
There art thou happy. Tybalt would kill thee,
But thou slewest Tybalt. There art thou happy.
The law, that threat'ned death, becomes thy friend
And turns it to exile. There art thou happy.
A pack of blessings light° upon thy back;
Happiness courts thee in her best array;°

107 **sack:** plunder.

110–113 **Thy tears . . . both:** The Friar scolds Romeo for grieving like a woman and expressing fury inappropriate **(ill-beseeming)** even for a beast.

119 **Why railest thou on:** why do you complain bitterly about.
120 **birth:** family origin. **heaven:** soul. **earth:** body.

122–125 **thou shamest . . . thy wit:** Like a moneylender who misuses his wealth, you are misusing the appearance **(shape)**, love, and intelligence **(wit)** you have been blessed with.
126–127 **Thy noble . . . man:** You are nothing but a waxwork figure, straying from a real man's courage.

131 **Misshapen in the conduct:** badly flawed in the guidance.

132–134 **Like powder . . . defense:** Just as a clumsy soldier might accidentally set off his container of gunpowder, you have ignored good reason and let yourself be blown apart by your intelligence, which should have been your defense.
136 **but lately dead:** only just now declaring yourself dead.

141 **light:** alight, set down lightly.

142 **array** (ə rā′): outfit.

Literary Element Monologue, Soliloquy, and Aside *Consider the effect of the repeated sentence "There art thou happy." How does the Friar try to reassure Romeo?* **L2**

Additional Support

Skills Practice

LISTENING AND SPEAKING: Expressing State of Mind Through Tone Discuss the Friar's state of mind in Scene 3. *(Concerned, reasonable, and impatient)* Invite volunteers to suggest how each character would speak, move, and gesture to convey these feelings.

Have volunteers read portions of the Friar's speech from line 109 to line 158 in Scene 3. Encourage students to use various tones to communicate states of mind. **OL**

But, like a mishaved° and sullen wench,
Thou pouts upon thy fortune and thy love.
Take heed, take heed, for such die miserable.
Go get thee to thy love, as was decreed,
Ascend her chamber, hence and comfort her.
But look thou stay not till the watch be set,°
For then thou canst not pass to Mantua,
Where thou shalt live till we can find a time
To blaze° your marriage, reconcile your friends,
Beg pardon of the Prince, and call thee back
With twenty hundred thousand times more joy
Than thou went'st forth in lamentation.°
Go before, nurse. Commend me to thy lady,
And bid her hasten all the house to bed,
Which heavy sorrow makes them apt unto.°
Romeo is coming.

NURSE. O Lord, I could have stay'd here all the night
To hear good counsel. O, what learning is!
My lord, I'll tell my lady you will come.

ROMEO. Do so, and bid my sweet prepare to chide.°

L3 [*The* NURSE *begins to exit but turns again to* ROMEO *handing him a ring.*]

NURSE. Here, sir, a ring she bid me give you, sir.
Hie you,° make haste, for it grows very late.

ROMEO. How well my comfort is reviv'd by this!

[NURSE *exits.*]

L4

FRIAR. Go hence; good night; and here stands all your state:°
Either be gone before the watch be set,
Or by the break of day disguis'd from hence.
Sojourn in Mantua. I'll find out your man,
And he shall signify from time to time
Every good hap to you that chances here.°
Give me thy hand. 'Tis late. Farewell; good night.

ROMEO. But that a joy past joy calls out on me,
It were a grief so brief to part with thee.
Farewell.

[ROMEO *and* FRIAR LAWRENCE *clasp hands and then exit in opposite directions.*]

SCENE 4. Late that night. A room in CAPULET's house.

[PARIS, LORD CAPULET, *and* LADY CAPULET *enter.*]

CAPULET. Things have fall'n out, sir, so unluckily
That we have had no time to move° our daughter.
Look you, she lov'd her kinsman Tybalt dearly,
And so did I. Well, we were born to die.
'Tis very late; she'll not come down tonight.

143 **mishaved:** misbehaved.

148 **look . . . set:** See that you do not remain with her until the watchmen go on duty at the city gates.

151 **blaze:** make public.

154 **lamentation:** sorrowful outcry.

157 **apt unto:** inclined to.

162 **prepare to chide:** to be ready to scold.

164 **Hie you:** hurry.

166 **here . . . state:** this is your situation.

169–171 **Sojourn . . . here:** The Friar asks Romeo to stay temporarily **(sojourn)** in Mantua, a city near Verona. He will send Romeo's servant there occasionally to bring news of favorable events.

2 **move:** persuade.

Teach

L3 Literary Element

Symbol Ask: What might the ring the Nurse hands Romeo symbolize? ***(Love, the lovers' wedding, or their eternal devotion to one another)*** OL

L4 Literary Element

Atmosphere Ask: What is the atmosphere at the end of this scene? Ask students to support their interpretations with references to the text. ***(The mood at the end of the scene is hopeful. Romeo has agreed to the Friar's plan. The ring from Juliet raises Romeo's spirits.)*** OL

Reading in the Real World

Careers Note that planning a career will require students to gather information, assess their interests and skills, and make a plan. Discuss the Friar's plan for Romeo and Juliet. Invite volunteers to summarize the steps and evaluate the plan. Have students suggest alternative plans. Encourage students to plan for a personal goal. Suggest that they create a chart listing the steps toward their goal and fill in the results after completing each step. OL

Academic Standards

Additional Support activities on pp. 762 and 763 cover the following standards:

Skills Practice: **9.7** [Develop] speaking skills...in conjunction with...strategies... [for] delivery of oral presentations.

Reading in the Real World: **9.7.7** Make judgments about the ideas under discussion and support those judgments with evidence. **9.5.8** Write for different purposes...

Teach

BI1 Big Idea

The Power of Love Answer: *Students may say that Capulet thinks marriage will comfort his grieving daughter. They may also say that his own grief causes Capulet to hastily push for a joyous event within the family. The audience knows that Juliet is married, but Capulet does not.* **OL**

L1 Literary Element

Conflict Ask: What conflict will Juliet have with her parents soon as a result of this action? *(Juliet cannot marry Paris because she's already married to Romeo.)* **OL**

R1 Reading Strategy

Comparing and Contrasting Scenes Answer: *In this scene, Romeo and Juliet share loving and hopeful conversation. They are completely unaware of the new obstacles to their union presented in the previous scene. The contrast evokes tension and sadness.* **OL**

I promise you, but for your company,
I would have been abed an hour ago.

PARIS. These times of woe afford no times to woo.
Madam, good night. Commend me to your daughter.

LADY. I will, and know her mind early tomorrow;
Tonight she's mewed up to her heaviness.°

CAPULET. Sir Paris, I will make a desperate tender°
Of my child's love. I think she will be rul'd
In all respects by me; nay more, I doubt it not.
Wife, go you to her ere you go to bed;
Acquaint her here of my son Paris' love
And bid her (mark you me?) on Wednesday next—
But soft! What day is this?

PARIS. Monday, my lord.

CAPULET. Monday! Ha, ha! Well, Wednesday is too soon.
A'° Thursday let it be—a' Thursday, tell her,
She shall be married to this noble earl.
Will you be ready? Do you like this haste?
We'll keep no great ado°—a friend or two;
For hark you, Tybalt being slain so late,
It may be thought we held him carelessly,°
Being our kinsman, if we revel much.
Therefore we'll have some half a dozen friends,
And there an end. But what say you to Thursday?

PARIS. My lord, I would that Thursday were tomorrow.

CAPULET. Well, get you gone. A' Thursday be it then.
[*To his wife.*] Go you to Juliet ere you go to bed;
Prepare her, wife, against° this wedding day.
Farewell, my lord.—Light to my chamber, ho!
Afore me,° it is so very late that we
May call it early by and by. Good night.

[*They exit.*]

SCENE 5. Later that night, just before daybreak. CAPULET's orchard and, above, JULIET's room and balcony.

[*ROMEO and JULIET are on the balcony. The rope ladder hangs down from the balcony into the garden.*]

11 **mewed up to her heaviness:** confined to her sadness. (Hawks were housed in structures called *mews.*)

12 **desperate tender:** bold offer.

20 **A':** on.

23 **keep no great ado:** not make a big fuss.

25 **held him carelessly:** had little regard for him.

32 **against:** for.

34 **Afore me:** indeed.

Big Idea **The Power of Love** *Earlier, Capulet seemed reluctant to let his daughter become engaged at so young an age. How would you explain his seeming change of heart? What information does the audience possess that Capulet lacks?* **BI1**

Reading Strategy **Comparing and Contrasting Scenes** *How does this scene contrast with the one that comes before? Taken together, what mood or feeling do the scenes evoke?* **R1**

Additional Support

Academic Standards

The Additional Support activity on p. 764 covers the following standard:

Skills Practice: **9.5.4** Write persuasive compositions that…use specific rhetorical devices to support assertions…

Skills Practice

WRITING: Using Evidence to Persuade Remind students that persuasion requires arguments and evidence as support. Have students summarize the arguments the Friar uses to convince Romeo not to end his life. *(His conduct is unmanly, he has been spared death, and he and Juliet can be reunited.)* Have students write a letter to the Prince, urging him to pardon Romeo by using arguments that appeal to logic and feelings and by presenting evidence. **OL**

JULIET. Wilt thou be gone? It is not yet near day.
It was the nightingale, and not the lark,
That pierc'd the fearful hollow of thine ear.
Nightly she sings on yond pomegranate tree.
Believe me, love, it was the nightingale.

ROMEO. It was the lark, the herald of the morn;
No nightingale. Look, love, what envious streaks
Do lace the severing° clouds in yonder east.
Night's candles° are burnt out, and jocund° day
Stands tiptoe on the misty mountaintops.
I must be gone and live, or stay and die.

JULIET. Yond light is not daylight; I know it, I.
It is some meteor° that the sun exhal'd
To be to thee this night a torchbearer
And light thee on thy way to Mantua.
Therefore stay yet; thou need'st not to be gone.

ROMEO. Let me be ta'en, let me be put to death.
I am content, so thou wilt have it so.
I'll say yon gray is not the morning's eye,°
'Tis but the pale reflex° of Cynthia's brow;°
Nor that is not the lark whose notes do beat
The vaulty heaven so high above our heads.
I have more care to stay than will to go.
Come, death, and welcome! Juliet wills it so.
How is't, my soul! Let's talk; it is not day.

R3

JULIET. It is, it is! Hie hence, be gone, away!
It is the lark that sings so out of tune,
Straining harsh discords and unpleasing sharps.°
Some say the lark makes sweet division;°
This doth not so, for she divideth us.
Some say the lark and loathed toad change° eyes;
O, now I would they had chang'd voices too,
Since arm from arm that voice doth us affray,°
Hunting thee hence with hunt's-up° to the day.
O, now be gone! More light and light it grows.

L2 ROMEO. More light and light—more dark and dark our woes.

[*The* NURSE *enters* JULIET*'s room.*]

NURSE. Madam!

JULIET. Nurse?

8 **severing:** dispersing.

9 **Night's candles:** the stars. **jocund** (jok′ənd): cheerful.

13 **meteor:** thought to be gasses that the sun ignited.

19 **morning's eye:** sunrise.

20 **reflex:** reflection. **Cynthia's brow:** the forehead of Cynthia, the moon goddess.

28 **Straining . . . sharps:** singing harsh sounds and unpleasant high notes.

29 **division:** melody.

31 **change:** exchange. (The lark has a beautiful body and ugly eyes, while the toad has an ugly body and beautiful eyes.)

33 **affray:** frighten.

34 **hunt's-up:** a morning song to awaken hunters.

Reading Strategy Comparing and Contrasting Scenes *How do Scenes 4 and 5 contrast in terms of characters and setting? What points are reinforced by the contrast?* R2

Big Idea The Power of Love *How does Romeo show his love for Juliet?* BI2

Differentiated Instruction

Social Studies Marriages in some countries—such as India, Pakistan, and Japan—are still arranged by parents. Discuss arranged marriages versus love matches. Have students list questions they would like answered about arranged marriages and search the Internet and other sources to find answers. Ask students to write a paragraph explaining if and how their research has changed their opinion about arranged marriage. BL

Teach

R2 Reading Strategy

Comparing and Contrasting Scenes **Answer:** *In Scene 4, Capulet, Lady Capulet, and Paris converse in the Capulet house. In Scene 5, Romeo and Juliet converse on Juliet's balcony. In the same house, quite different scenes are being played out. The contrast helps to create tension and to reinforce the dangerous nature of the arrangements the characters are making.* OL

BI2 Big Idea

The Power of Love **Answer:** *Romeo's remark implies that he is willing to die for Juliet's sake.* OL

R3 Reading Strategy

Listening Discuss how Romeo and Juliet must feel as their night together draws to a close. Students should be sensitive to the mood changes both undergo throughout this scene. OL

L2 Literary Element

Imagery **Ask:** How have the mood and meaning of Shakespeare's light and dark imagery changed over the course of the play? *(At the start of the play the love scenes included images of stars, the sun, and heavenly light. Here, light is dim (pre-dawn), and darkness has become a heavy gloom, blotting out the lovers' happiness.)* OL

Academic Standards

The Additional Support activity on p. 765 covers the following standard:

Differentiated Instruction: **9.4.4** Use writing to formulate clear research questions and to compile information from…secondary print or Internet sources.

Teach

★ Viewing the Art

Early in his career, English artist Sir Frank Dicksee (1853–1928) illustrated books and magazines. With his painting *Harmony,* Dicksee became a noted painter, known for using figures from history and legend as subjects. Dicksee is also famous for his portraits of beautiful women. **AS**

Romeo and Juliet, 1884. Frank Dicksee. Oil on canvas. Southampton City Art Gallery, Hampshire, UK. 

Additional Support

Skills Practice

GRAMMAR AND LANGUAGE: Compound-Complex Sentences

Ask students to locate the main and subordinate clauses in this sentence: *I'll find out your man, and he shall signify from time to time every good hap to you* **that chances here.** (*main clauses;* **subordinate clause**) Point out that a sentence that contains at least two main clauses and one or more subordinate clauses is called a compound-complex sentence. Have students locate another compound-complex sentence and copy it. Ask them to identify its main clauses and subordinate clause(s) and underline each subject and verb. **OL**

NURSE. Your lady mother is coming to your chamber.
The day is broke; be wary, look about.

[*She exits.*]

JULIET. Then, window, let day in, and let life out.

ROMEO. Farewell, farewell! One kiss, and I'll descend.

[*They kiss. Then* ROMEO *climbs down the rope ladder to the garden below.*]

JULIET. Art thou gone so, love, lord, ay husband, friend?
I must hear from thee every day in the hour,
For in a minute there are many days.
O, by this count I shall be much in years
Ere I again behold my Romeo!

ROMEO. Farewell!
I will omit no opportunity
That may convey my greetings, love, to thee.

JULIET. O, think'st thou we shall ever meet again?

ROMEO. I doubt it not; and all these woes shall serve
For sweet discourses° in our times to come.

JULIET. O God, I have an ill-divining soul!°
Methinks I see thee, now thou art so low,
As one dead in the bottom of a tomb.
Either my eyesight fails, or thou lookest pale.

ROMEO. And trust me, love, in my eye so do you.
Dry° sorrow drinks our blood. Adieu, adieu!

[ROMEO *leaves.*]

JULIET. O Fortune, Fortune! All men call thee **fickle.**
If thou art fickle, what dost thou with him
That is renown'd for faith?° Be fickle, Fortune,
For then I hope thou wilt not keep him long
But send him back.

[LADY CAPULET *enters* JULIET'*s room.*]

LADY CAPULET. Ho, daughter! Are you up?

JULIET. Who is't that calls? It is my lady mother.
Is she not down° so late, or up so early?
What unaccustom'd cause procures her hither?°

53 **discourses:** conversations.

54 **ill-divining soul:** soul that foresees misfortune.

59 **Dry:** thirsty. (Romeo refers to a belief that each sigh draws a drop of blood from the heart.)

61–62 **If thou . . . faith:** If you are unfaithful, why are you involved with a man known for his faithfulness?

66 **down:** going to bed.

67 **What . . . hither:** What unusual reason brings her here?

Reading Strategy Comparing and Contrasting Scenes *In this act, Shakespeare develops the plot rapidly, raising the conflict level along several fronts. As tension rises and falls and the mood changes from moment to moment, what responses do you have?* **R**

Vocabulary

fickle (fik′ əl) *adj.* given to frequent changes of thought or mood; unreliable; inconstant

Teach

R Reading Strategy

Comparing and Contrasting Scenes **Answer:** *Students should support their answers.* **OL**

Differentiated Instruction

Tracking Action Students must keep track of characters' movements to and from several settings in Act 3. Students will benefit by diagramming the locations and movements of characters in each scene. Have them create a diagram of each scene, label the setting, and place the characters onstage when they first appear. Suggest that students then use color coding and numbers to show which characters interact and in what order. Below the diagram, students should write a phrase summarizing the action for each number. **BL**

Academic Standards

Additional Support activities on pp. 766 and 767 cover the following standards:

Skills Practice: **9.6.1** Identify and correctly use clauses, both main and subordinate…

Differentiated Instruction: **9.3** [Identify] story elements such as character,…plot, and setting…

Teach

R1 Reading Strategy

Drawing Conclusions Ask: What does Lady Capulet conclude causes Juliet's distress? *(The loss of her well-loved cousin)* What conclusion can you draw about Juliet's reaction to her mother's conclusion? *(Juliet tries to sustain it to keep the real reason a secret from her parents.)* OL

R2 Reading Strategy

Comparing and Contrasting Scenes Answer: *Some grief can be traced to love and is understandable. Some grief, however, shows a lack of judgment or good sense and thus is problematic. Older characters are more cynical and less emotional about romantic love than the young people are.* OL

L Literary Element

Monologue, Soliloquy, and Aside Answer: *It alerts the audience to Juliet's true feelings about Romeo. She does not consider him a villain.* OL

[*JULIET returns to her room from the balcony.*]

LADY CAPULET. Why, how now, Juliet?

JULIET. Madam, I am not well.

LADY CAPULET. Evermore weeping for your cousin's death?
What, wilt thou wash him from his grave with tears?
And if thou couldst, thou couldst not make him live.
Therefore have done. Some grief shows much of love;
But much of grief shows still some want of wit.°

JULIET. Yet let me weep for such a feeling loss.

LADY CAPULET. So shall you feel the loss, but not the friend°
Which you weep for.

JULIET. Feeling so the loss,
I cannot choose but ever weep the friend.

LADY CAPULET. Well, girl, thou weep'st not so much for his death
As that the villain lives which slaughter'd him.

JULIET. What villain, madam?

LADY CAPULET. That same villain Romeo.

JULIET. [*Aside.*] Villain and he be many miles asunder.°—
[*To LADY CAPULET.*] God pardon him! I do, with all my heart;
And yet no man like he doth grieve my heart.

LADY CAPULET. That is because the traitor murderer lives.

JULIET. Ay, madam, from the reach of these my hands.
Would none but I might venge my cousin's death!

LADY CAPULET. We will have vengeance for it, fear thou not.
Then weep no more. I'll send to one in Mantua,
Where that same banish'd runagate° doth live,
Shall give him such an unaccustom'd dram°
That he shall soon keep Tybalt company;
And then I hope thou wilt be satisfied.

JULIET. Indeed I never shall be satisfied
With Romeo till I behold him—dead°—
Is my poor heart so for a kinsman vex'd.
Madam, if you could find out but a man
To bear a poison, I would temper° it;
That Romeo should, upon receipt thereof,
Soon sleep in quiet. O, how my heart abhors
To hear him nam'd and cannot come to him,

73 **shows . . . wit:** always shows lack of judgment.

75 **friend:** "cousin" or "lover."

81 **asunder:** apart.

89 **runagate:** renegade; runaway.

90 **unaccustom'd dram:** unexpected dose (of poison).

94 Here, as elsewhere in this dialogue, Juliet communicates one thing to her mother and something else to the audience. The word ***dead*** can be understood to complete this line ("till I behold him dead") or to begin the next line ("Dead is my poor heart").

97 **temper:** "mix" or "dilute."

Reading Strategy Comparing and Contrasting Scenes *Restate Lady Capulet's remark in your own words. Throughout this act, what contrast do you see between the ideas of older and younger characters?* R2

Literary Element Monologue, Soliloquy, and Aside *Why does Shakespeare include this aside?* L

Additional Support

Skills Practice

WRITING: Using Aphorisms to Make a Point An aphorism is a succinctly worded statement of a principle. For example, Lady Capulet scolds Juliet for what she sees as an overreaction to Tybalt's death (page 768, lines 72–73).

Have students brainstorm other sayings that could apply to Romeo and Juliet's situation. Then ask them to choose one and write a paragraph showing how it applies. OL

To wreak° the love I bore my cousin
Upon his body that hath slaughter'd him!

LADY CAPULET. Find thou the means, and I'll find such a man.
But now I'll tell thee joyful tidings, girl.

JULIET. And joy comes well in such a needy time.
What are they, beseech your ladyship?

LADY CAPULET. Well, well, thou hast a careful° father, child;
One who, to put thee from thy heaviness,°
Hath sorted out° a sudden day of joy
That thou expects not nor I look'd not for.

JULIET. Madam, in happy time! What day is that?

LADY CAPULET. Marry, my child, early next Thursday morn
The gallant, young, and noble gentleman,
The County Paris, at Saint Peter's Church,
Shall happily make thee there a joyful bride.

JULIET. Now by Saint Peter's Church, and Peter too,
He shall not make me there a joyful bride!
I wonder at this haste, that I must wed
Ere he that should be husband comes to woo.
I pray you tell my lord and father, madam,
I will not marry yet; and when I do, I swear
It shall be Romeo, whom you know I hate,
Rather than Paris. These are news indeed!

LADY CAPULET. Here comes your father. Tell him so yourself,
And see how he will take it at your hands.

[*CAPULET and the NURSE enter.*]

CAPULET. When the sun sets the earth doth drizzle dew,
But for the sunset of my brother's son
It rains downright.
How now? A conduit,° girl? What, still in tears?
Evermore show'ring? In one little body
Thou counterfeits° a bark,° a sea, a wind:
For still thy eyes, which I may call the sea,
Do ebb and flow with tears; the bark thy body is,
Sailing in this salt flood; the winds, thy sighs,
Who, raging with thy tears and they with them,
Without a sudden calm will overset°
Thy tempest-tossed body. How now, wife?
Have you delivered to her our decree?

101 **wreak** (rēk): "avenge" or "express."

107 **careful:** considerate.

108 **put . . . heaviness:** remove you from sorrow.

109 **sorted out:** chosen.

129 **conduit** (kon′ do͞o it): fountain.

131 **counterfeits:** resemble. **bark:** small sailing vessel.

136 **overset:** upset, capsize.

Big Idea The Power of Love *What double meaning can be read into lines 93–102?* **BI**

Reading Strategy Comparing and Contrasting Scenes *How has Juliet's attitude toward Paris changed since the first conversation she and her mother had about him?* **R3**

Teach

BI Big Idea

The Power of Love **Answer:** *Juliet's words suggest that she will never be happy until she sees Romeo dead, but the audience realizes she means that she will never be happy until she sees Romeo. She would like to "wreak" the love she bore her cousin upon Romeo's body; the audience realizes that these words imply love for Romeo.* **OL**

R3 Reading Strategy

Comparing and Contrasting Scenes **Answer:** *In Act 1, Scene 3, Juliet appears open to taking her mother's advice regarding Paris. Now she is resolutely against marriage to him.* **OL**

Historical Note

Mantua, Italy Considered one of the great Renaissance Court cities, Mantua was the city to which Romeo was exiled. At the time *Romeo and Juliet* was written, Mantua was under the control of the powerful Gonzaga family, who ruled from 1328 to 1707. **AS**

English Language Coach

Word Meanings Direct students' attention to the marginal notes giving meanings for the words *careful, heaviness,* and *sorted out* in lines 107–110. Remind students that some words in Shakespeare's time had different meanings from their meanings today. Have students look up these words in a dictionary and copy down the current meanings for each word. **EL**

Academic Standards

Additional Support activities on pp. 768 and 769 cover the following standards:

Skills Practice: **9.3.7** Recognize and understand the significance of various literary devices…

English Language Coach: **9.1** Use… a growing knowledge of English… to determine the meaning of words…

Teach

L1 Literary Element

Irony Note that in line 140, Lady Capulet out of impatience wishes her daughter dead. Ironically, her wish will soon come true—twice. OL

BI1 Big Idea

The Power of Love **Answer:** *She is deferential toward them and grateful in spite of their hateful words, because the words stem from an action intended as loving.* OL

★ Historical Note

St. Peter's The most famous St. Peter's Church is St. Peter's Basilica. Located in Vatican City, within the city of Rome, the basilica was named for the apostle Peter. Verona, however, had its own saint named Peter. St. Peter of Verona (1206–1252) was canonized in 1253. AS

LADY CAPULET. Ay, sir; but she will none, she gives you thanks.
L1 I would the fool were married to her grave!

CAPULET. Soft! Take me with you, take me with you,° wife.
How? Will she none? Doth she not give us thanks?
Is she not proud? Doth she not count her blest,
Unworthy as she is, that we have wrought°
So worthy a gentleman to be her bride?°

JULIET. Not proud you have, but thankful that you have.
Proud can I never be of what I hate,
But thankful even for hate that is meant love.

CAPULET. How, how, how, how, chopp'd-logic?° What is this?
"Proud"—and "I thank you"—and "I thank you not"—
And yet "not proud"? Mistress minion° you,
Thank me no thankings, nor proud me no prouds,
But fettle your fine joints 'gainst° Thursday next
★ To go with Paris to Saint Peter's Church,
Or I will drag thee on a hurdle° thither.
Out, you green-sickness carrion!° Out, you baggage!°
You tallow-face!°

LADY CAPULET. [*To* CAPULET.] Fie, fie! What, are you mad?

JULIET. [*She kneels before her father.*] Good father, I beseech
you on my knees,
Hear me with patience but to speak a word.

CAPULET. Hang thee, young baggage! Disobedient wretch!
I tell thee what—get thee to church a' Thursday
Or never after look me in the face.
Speak not, reply not, do not answer me!
My fingers itch. Wife, we scarce thought us blest
That God had lent us but this only child;
But now I see this one is one too much,
And that we have a curse in having her.
Out on her, hilding!°

NURSE. God in heaven bless her!
You are to blame, my lord, to rate° her so.

CAPULET. And why, my Lady Wisdom? Hold your tongue,
Good Prudence. Smatter with your gossips, go!°

NURSE. I speak no treason.°

CAPULET. O, God-i-god-en!°

NURSE. May not one speak?

141 **Soft! . . . you:** Wait, let me understand you.

144 **wrought** (rôt): arranged for.

145 **bride:** bridegroom.

149 **chopp'd-logic:** clever but false argument.

151 **Mistress minion:** spoiled miss.

153 **fettle your fine joints 'gainst:** prepare your fine limbs for.

155 **hurdle:** a sled used to bring prisoners to their executions.

156 **green-sickness carrion:** anemic flesh. **baggage:** shameless girl.

157 **tallow-face:** pale face.

168 **hilding:** worthless person.

169 **rate:** scold angrily.

171 **Smatter with your gossips, go:** Go chatter with your old pals.

172 **treason:** disloyalty. **God-i-god-en:** God give you good evening (used here as a mild oath).

Big Idea The Power of Love *From this remark, how would you describe Juliet's treatment of her parents?* BI1

Additional Support

Skills Practice

READING: Sequencing Point out that the plot develops rapidly in Act 3. This would be a good time to assess students' grasp of the plot by having them create a timeline. Have partners first list the events that occur from the end of Act 2 (Scene 5) to the end of Act 3. Then have them place each event in order of occurrence on a timeline. Encourage students to compare their work with the work of other students, and discuss any discrepancies. OL

CAPULET. Peace, you mumbling fool!
Utter your gravity° o'er a gossip's bowl,°
For here we need it not.

LADY CAPULET. You are too hot.

CAPULET. God's bread! It makes me mad. Day, night; work, play;
Alone, in company; still my care hath been
To have her match'd; and having now provided
A gentleman of noble parentage,
Of fair demesnes,° youthful, and nobly lien'd,°
Stuff'd, as they say, with honorable parts,°
Proportion'd as one's thought would wish a man—
And then to have a wretched puling° fool,
A whining mammet,° in her fortune's tender,°
To answer, "I'll not wed, I cannot love;
I am too young, I pray you pardon me"!
But, and° you will not wed, I'll pardon you!°
Graze where you will, you shall not house with me.
Look to't, think on't; I do not use° to jest.
Thursday is near; lay hand on heart, advise:°
And you be mine, I'll give you to my friend;
And you be not, hang, beg, starve, die in the streets,
For, by my soul, I'll ne'er acknowledge thee,
Nor what is mine shall never do thee good.°
Trust to't. Bethink you. I'll not be forsworn.°

[*CAPULET exits. JULIET rises and speaks to her mother.*]

JULIET. Is there no pity sitting in the clouds
That sees into the bottom of my grief?
O sweet my mother, cast me not away!
Delay this marriage for a month, a week;
Or if you do not, make the bridal bed
In that dim monument where Tybalt lies.

LADY CAPULET. Talk not to me, for I'll not speak a word.
Do as thou wilt, for I have done with thee.

[*LADY CAPULET exits.*]

JULIET. O God!—O nurse, how shall this be prevented?
My husband is on earth, my faith in heaven.°

174 **gravity:** wisdom. **gossip's bowl:** cup of hot punch.

180 **demesnes** (di mānz′): property. **lien'd:** descended.
181 **parts:** qualities.

183 **puling** (pūl′ ing): whimpering.

184 **mammet:** puppet. **in her fortune's tender:** when good fortune is offered her.

187 **and:** if. **pardon you:** excuse you (from this house).

189 **I do not use:** it is not my custom.

190 **advise:** consider.

193–194 **I'll ne'er . . . good:** Capulet threatens to disown Juliet and cut off any family support.
195 **be forsworn:** break my vow.

205 **my faith in heaven:** my marriage vow is recorded in heaven.

Reading Strategy Comparing and Contrasting Scenes *Are you surprised by the way characters are behaving in this scene? Why or why not?* **R**

Literary Element Monologue, Soliloquy, and Aside *Why is this passage in quotation marks? How might Capulet say these lines?* **L2**

Big Idea The Power of Love *Why does Capulet make this threat?* **BI2**

Teach

R Reading Strategy

Comparing and Contrasting Scenes **Answer:** *Students may be surprised at the change in Capulet's behavior. Previously, he seemed gentle, sympathetic, and civilized. He now seems brutal and unjust.* **OL**

L2 Literary Element

Monologue, Soliloquy, and Aside **Answer:** *The words are in quotation marks because Capulet is quoting Juliet's words to him. He might mimic her voice as he says her words.* **OL**

BI2 Big Idea

The Power of Love **Answer:** *Some students may consider Capulet a tyrant. Others may point out that his fury results from great love. Juliet is his only daughter, and Paris is a perfect match. He is baffled by her disobedience.* **OL**

Differentiated Instruction

Character Details Kinesthetic learners will benefit from staging the scene and exploring the relationships between characters. Have students write detailed descriptions of Juliet, the Nurse, Lady Capulet, and Lord Capulet. Then have students use these details in staging the scene. Encourage students to incorporate body positioning, facial expressions, and gestures into the subtext of the scene. **BL**

Academic Standards

Additional Support activities on pp. 770 and 771 cover the following standards:

Skills Practice: **9.3** [Identify] story elements such as…plot…

Differentiated Instruction: **9.5.3** Write expository compositions, including… descriptive pieces…

Teach

L Literary Element

Monologue, Soliloquy, and Aside **Answer:** *She expresses determination and unwillingness to obey her father.* OL

Use the CheckPoint questions on Presentation Plus! to check students' mastery of the selection. These questions can be used with interactive response keypads for immediate student feedback.

Web Activities Have students access the Web site for interactive activities that will help them assess their understanding of the selection.

How shall that faith return again to earth
Unless that husband send it me from heaven
By leaving earth?° Comfort me, counsel me.
Alack, alack, that heaven should practice stratagems°
Upon so soft a subject as myself!
What say'st thou? Hast thou not a word of joy?
Some comfort, nurse.

NURSE. Faith, here it is.
Romeo is banished; and all the world to nothing
That he dares ne'er come back to challenge you;°
Or if he do, it needs must be by stealth.
Then, since the case so stands as now it doth,
I think it best you married with the County.
O, he's a lovely gentleman!
Romeo's a dishclout to him.° An eagle, madam,
Hath not so green, so quick, so fair an eye
As Paris hath. Beshrew° my very heart,
I think you are happy in this second match,
For it excels your first; or if it did not,
Your first is dead—or 'twere as good he were
As living here and you no use of him.

JULIET. Speak'st thou from thy heart?

NURSE. And from my soul too; else beshrew them both.

JULIET. Amen!

NURSE. What?

JULIET. Well, thou has comforted me marvelous much.
Go in; and tell my lady I am gone,
Having displeas'd my father, to Lawrence' cell,
To make confession and to be absolv'd.°

NURSE. Marry, I will; and this is wisely done.

[*The* NURSE *exits to find* LADY CAPULET.]

JULIET. Ancient damnation!° O most wicked fiend!
Is it more sin to wish me thus forsworn,
Or to dispraise my lord with that same tongue
Which she hath prais'd him with above compare
So many thousand times? Go, counselor!
Thou and my bosom henceforth shall be twain.°
I'll to the friar to know his remedy.
If all else fail, myself have power to die.

[*JULIET exits.*]

206–208 **How . . . earth:** How can I be free to pledge myself again unless by Romeo's death?
209 **stratagems** (strat′ ə jəmz): tricks.

213–214 **all the world . . . you:** The odds are greatly against his ever coming back to claim you.

219 **dishclout to him:** dish cloth compared to him.

221 **Beshrew** (bi shro͞o′): curse (used in mild oaths).

233 **absolv'd:** forgiven.

235 **Ancient damnation:** wicked old woman.

240 **Thou and . . . twain:** From now on I'll keep my secrets from you.

Literary Element Monologue, Soliloquy, and Aside *In this soliloquy, what mood does Juliet express?* L

Additional Support

Skills Practice

READING: Verifying Predictions
Have students compare their predictions about Juliet's response to her parents with the action in this scene. Were they surprised? Why or why not? Have students write a paragraph explaining their reaction to Juliet's response. Students should give reasons why they were surprised by Juliet's behavior (or felt it was natural, given her character). Have students exchange papers, compare responses, and discuss differences of opinion. OL

AFTER YOU READ

RESPONDING AND THINKING CRITICALLY

Respond

1. What would you do if you were Juliet?

Recall and Interpret

2. (a)How does Romeo respond to Tybalt's challenge? (b)Why does Mercutio decide to fight in Romeo's place?
3. (a)How does Romeo accidentally help cause Mercutio's death? (b)How do you interpret Romeo's description of himself as "fortune's fool"?
4. In Scene 3, what plan for the future does the Friar propose to Romeo?
5. (a)What excuse does Juliet use to leave her house? (b)How would you describe her state of mind at this point?

Analyze and Evaluate

6. (a)Explain why Friar Lawrence and Romeo argue in Scene 3. (b)Defend one side or the other.
7. (a)How does the character of Capulet develop during this act? (b)What insight or truth might Shakespeare be expressing through this character?
8. (a)How does Juliet's relationship with the Nurse change during this act? (b)How do you think this change affects Juliet's state of mind and faith in her plan?

Connect

9. **Big Idea** **The Power of Love** How does Act 3 of *Romeo and Juliet* suggest a dark side to love?

LITERARY ANALYSIS

Literary Element Monologue, Soliloquy, and Aside

A **monologue** may be addressed to other characters, or it may take the form of a **soliloquy**, spoken privately by a character alone on stage. An **aside** is a brief remark that only the audience or another selected character is meant to hear.

1. Find a soliloquy in Act 3. What thoughts or feelings does it reveal?
2. What was your favorite monologue in Act 3? Explain.

Writing About Literature

Compare and Contrast Mood Mood is the emotional quality or atmosphere of a literary work. A writer creates mood through language, subject matter, setting, and tone. What is the mood of Act 2? How does the mood change over the course of Act 3? Write a brief essay explaining the shifts in mood in Acts 2 and 3. In your essay, use passages and examples from the text that support your conclusions.

LiteratureOnline **Web Activities** For eFlashcards, Selection Quick Checks, and other Web activities, go to www.glencoe.com.

READING AND VOCABULARY

Reading Strategy Comparing and Contrasting Scenes

By **comparing and contrasting scenes** within this play, you will gain a deeper appreciation for Shakespeare's skill at suggesting emotions and ideas.

1. By varying setting, mood, and characters from scene to scene, what effects does Shakespeare create in Act 3? Explain.
2. Explain how your understanding of one character is enriched over the course of Act 3.

Vocabulary Practice

Practice with Analogies Find the word that best completes each analogy.

1. speech : eloquence :: appearance : _____
   a. persuasion b. laughter c. beauty
2. wealth : riches :: adversity : _____
   a. hardship b. happiness c. health
3. sad : tragedy :: difficult : _____
   a. documentary b. truimph c. predicament
4. fickle : reliable :: satisfaction : _____
   a. displeasure b. changeable c. amused

Writing About Literature

Students should support their main ideas with specific examples from the text.

Reading Strategy

1. The mood varies from gentle love scenes between Romeo and Juliet to violence between Tybalt, Mercutio, and Romeo. There are also various complications involving the Friar, the Nurse, and the Capulets. These shifting moods increase the suspense.
2. Students should support their answers.

Vocabulary

1. c **2.** a **3.** c **4.** a

AFTER YOU READ

Assess

1. Accept reasonable answers.
2. (a) He refuses to accept Tybalt's challenge to fight because the two are now related by the secret marriage. (b) To avenge Romeo's honor
3. (a) By trying to step between them, blocking Mercutio's sword arm (b) Fate has tricked him into making fatal mistakes.
4. For Romeo to go to Mantua until the Friar can work things out with the Prince
5. (a) Going to confession (b) She is desperate.
6. (a) Romeo despairs, and the Friar thinks he's overreacting. (b) Students should support their answers.
7. (a) He loses patience and becomes enraged by Juliet's disobedience. (b) The inevitability of conflict between the generations.
8. (a) She feels betrayed when the Nurse advises her to marry Paris. (b) The loss of her one confidante increases her desperation; the plan seems like her only hope.
9. Their ideal love is now tainted by family conflict, exile, and death.

Literary Element

1. Example: Scene 2, lines 1–31; Juliet expresses longing and impatience to see Romeo.
2. Example: Scene 3, lines 29–51; Romeo despairs over his exile.

Academic Standards

The Additional Support activity on p. 772 covers the following standard:

Skills Practice: **9.5.2** Write responses to literature that…demonstrate a comprehensive grasp of the significant ideas of literary works…

BEFORE YOU READ

Focus

Summary

Friar Lawrence learns from Paris of the intended wedding. He advises Juliet to take a potion that will simulate death on the night before the ceremony. When she revives in forty-two hours, Romeo and the Friar will rescue her from the Capulet vault. Despite misgivings, she drinks the potion and is borne to the vault by her grieving parents.

V Vocabulary

Vocabulary File **Say:** Add these words and definitions to your vocabulary file. For each word, include a sentence that gives you an example of how to use the word. **OL** Students with English language needs should include the pronunciation of these words in their files. **EL**

Literary Elements Have students access the Web site to improve their understanding of irony.

LITERATURE PREVIEW

Connecting to the Drama

When circumstances are really horrific, people will act in ways they would not normally consider. Before you read about the desperate situation confronting Juliet in Act 4, think about the following questions:

- Under what circumstances would you risk your life?
- What situations have you heard about in which people have taken desperate measures?

Building Background

In fifteenth-century Italy, the evergreen herb called *rosemary* was regarded as a symbol of immortality. It was also prized for its fragrance. When a person died, he or she was often strewn with rosemary, which was also carried by mourners.

Setting Purposes for Reading

Big Idea The Power of Love

Can love make us act in ways that are reckless or even unethical? As you read this act, consider whether love robs the characters of good judgment.

Literary Element Irony

Irony refers to a contrast or discrepancy between appearance and reality. There are three main types of irony.

- **Situational irony** exists when an occurrence is the opposite of what is expected. For example, in trying to stop Tybalt and Mercutio from dueling, Romeo causes Mercutio's death.
- **Verbal irony** occurs when a person says one thing and means another.
- **Dramatic irony** exists when the reader or audience knows something that a character does not know. For example, Juliet dreams of her future with Romeo when we know that he has been banished.

- See Literary Terms Handbook, p. R9.

Literature Online **Interactive Literary Elements Handbook** To review or learn more about the literary elements, go to www.glencoe.com.

READING PREVIEW

Reading Strategy Interpreting Imagery

The word pictures in a work of literature are called **imagery.** In creating effective imagery, writers use sensory details, or descriptions that appeal to one or more of the five senses: sight, sound, touch, taste, or smell. Imagery is used to suggest ideas and to evoke an emotional response in the reader.

Reading Tip: Taking Notes Keep a record of your responses to Shakespeare's imagery on a chart like the one below.

Image	My Response
Scene 1, line 29: Juliet's face is "much abused with tears."	Her eyes must be red and swollen. She's miserable.

Vocabulary

lurk (lurk) *v.* to conceal oneself; to move about in a sneaky manner; p. 778 *Foxes lurk in the woods, awaiting their prey.*

stifle (stī′ fəl) *v.* to smother for lack of air; to prevent from developing properly; p. 782 *We felt stifled by the obstacles in our path.*

revive (ri vīv′) *v.* to bring back to life; to give new strength; p. 784 *A bit of fresh air will revive me.*

lament (lə ment′) *v.* to express deep sorrow; p. 787 *Many old friends gathered at the funeral to lament his passing.*

Vocabulary Tip: Context Clues The context in which an unfamiliar word appears often provides clues to its meaning.

INDIANA ACADEMIC STANDARDS (pages 774–789)

9.3.8 Interpret and evaluate...ironies in a text.

9.3.7 Recognize and understand the significance of...imagery...

9.5.2 Write responses to literature...

Selection Skills

The Tragedy of Romeo and Juliet, Act 4

Literary Elements
- Irony (SE pp. 774–789)

Reading Skills
- Interpreting Imagery (SE pp. 774–789)

Vocabulary Skills
- Context Clues (SE pp. 774, 789)

Listening/Speaking/Viewing Skills
- Oral Interpretation (TWE p. 786)
- Sound Devices (TWE p. 788)
- Analyzing Art (SE pp. 777, 783, 786)

Writing Skills/Grammar
- Respond to Character and Plot (SE p. 789)
- Active and Passive Voices (TWE p. 776)
- Prepositions (TWE p. 780)
- Researching (TWE p. 782)
- Response to Literature (TWE p. 784)

Act 4

SCENE 1. Later that morning. FRIAR LAWRENCE'S **cell.**

[*FRIAR LAWRENCE and PARIS enter. PARIS has just explained to the confused FRIAR that he will marry JULIET.*]

FRIAR. On Thursday, sir? The time is very short.

PARIS. My father° Capulet will have it so,
And I am nothing slow to slack his haste.°

FRIAR. You say you do not know the lady's mind.
Uneven is the course;° I like it not.

PARIS. Immoderately she weeps for Tybalt's death,
And therefore have I little talk'd of love;
For Venus smiles not in a house of tears.
Now, sir, her father counts it dangerous
That she do give her sorrow so much sway,
And in his wisdom hastes our marriage
To stop the inundation of her tears,
Which, too much minded° by herself alone,
May be put from her by society.
Now do you know the reason of this haste.

FRIAR. [*Aside.*] I would I knew not why it should be slowed.—
Look, sir, here comes the lady toward my cell.

R [*JULIET enters. Surprised to see PARIS there, she pretends to be in good spirits.*]

PARIS. Happily met, my lady and my wife!

JULIET. That may be, sir, when I may be a wife.

PARIS. That "may be" must be, love, on Thursday next.

JULIET. What must be shall be.

FRIAR. That's a certain text.°

PARIS. Come you to make confession to this father?

JULIET. To answer that, I should confess to you.

PARIS. Do not deny to him that you love me.

JULIET. I will confess to you that I love him.

PARIS. So will ye, I am sure, that you love me.

JULIET. If I do so, it will be of more price,°
Being spoke behind your back, than to your face.

PARIS. Poor soul, thy face is much abus'd with tears.

JULIET. The tears have got small victory by that,
For it was bad enough before their spite.°

PARIS. Thou wrong'st it more than tears with that report.

2 **father:** father-in-law.

3 **I am . . . haste:** I will not delay him.

5 **Uneven is the course:** The plan is irregular.

13 **minded:** brooded over.

21 **That's a certain text:** That's an indisputable saying.

27 **price:** value.

31 **it was . . . spite:** my face was bad enough before the tears marred it.

Literary Element Irony *What is ironic about this situation?* **L**

Teach

R Reading Strategy

Predicting Have students read the setting details and stage directions on page 775 and name the characters brought together. Ask them to predict what Juliet and Paris will say to each other.

Ask: What problem does Juliet have as she greets Paris? *(She has to pretend that she is content to marry Paris, and not show her grief and concern about Romeo.)* **OL**

L Literary Element

Irony Answer: *Juliet has come to the Friar's cell to discuss her reunion with Romeo, but Paris believes that Juliet will soon be his wife.* **OL**

English Language Coach

Students from some cultures will be unfamiliar with the Roman Catholic practice of confession. Invite volunteers to describe the ritual and its meaning. Have partners find the meanings of *confession* in a dictionary and decide which one applies ironically to Juliet's situation *(an admission of the truth)*. Ask partners to write a short paragraph explaining the dual meaning. Have students who are more proficient in English help answer questions about vocabulary or grammar. **EL**

Academic Standards

The Additional Support activity on p. 775 covers the following standard:

English Language Coach: **9.3.8** Interpret and evaluate the impact of...ironies in a text.

Teach

R1 Reading Strategy

Interpreting Have students examine Juliet's responses to Paris and explain the double meaning.

Ask: How does she avoid lying? *("What must be shall be" [page 775, line 21] could refer to the wedding, but in fact refers to her joining Romeo or dying. She uses words that introduce doubt without contradicting Paris ["If I do so"–page 775, line 27]. She says her face is not [her] own [page 776, line 36]–meaning she shows Paris a false face, which is true.)* **OL**

L Literary Element

Irony **Answer:** *Juliet does not wish to confess to the Friar; she wishes instead to discuss her plans for reuniting with Romeo.* **OL**

R2 Reading Strategy

Interpreting Imagery
Answer: *Now Romeo's wife, Juliet would sooner kill herself and Paris than marry him.* **OL**

R1

JULIET. That is no slander, sir, which is a truth;
And what I spake, I spake it to my face.°

PARIS. Thy face is mine, and thou hast sland'red it.

JULIET. It may be so, for it is not mine own.°
[*To* FRIAR LAWRENCE.] Are you at leisure, holy father, now,
Or shall I come to you at evening mass?

FRIAR. My leisure serves me, pensive daughter, now.
[*To* PARIS.] My lord, we must entreat the time alone.

PARIS. God shield I should disturb devotion!
Juliet, on Thursday early will I rouse ye.
Till then, adieu, and keep this holy kiss.

[PARIS *exits.*]

JULIET. O, shut the door, and when thou hast done so,
Come weep with me—past hope, past cure, past help!

FRIAR. O Juliet, I already know thy grief;
It strains me past the compass of my wits.°
I hear thou must, and nothing may prorogue° it,
On Thursday next be married to this County.

JULIET. Tell me not, friar, that thou hearest of this,
Unless thou tell me how I may prevent it.
If in thy wisdom thou canst give no help,
Do thou but call my resolution wise
And with this knife I'll help it presently.°
God join'd my heart and Romeo's, thou our hands;
And ere this hand, by thee to Romeo's seal'd,
Shall be the label to another deed,°
Or my true heart with treacherous revolt
Turn to another, this shall slay them both.
Therefore, out of thy long-experienc'd time,
Give me some present counsel;° or, behold,
'Twixt my extremes and me this bloody knife
Shall play the umpire, arbitrating that
Which the commission of thy years and art
Could to no issue of true honor bring.°
Be not so long to speak. I long to die
If what thou speak'st speak not of remedy.

FRIAR. Hold, daughter. I do spy a kind of hope,
Which craves° as desperate an execution°
As that is desperate which we would prevent.
If, rather than to marry County Paris,

34 **to my face:** openly (not behind my back).

36 **It may . . . own:** Juliet's reply suggests that her face belongs to Romeo or that she is presenting a false face to Paris.

47 **strains me past the compass of my wits:** forces me beyond the limits of my understanding.
48 **prorogue** (prō rōg′): postpone.

53–54 **Do thou . . . presently:** Juliet asks the Friar to approve of her resolution to kill herself, a mortal sin.

57 **be the . . . deed:** confirm another marriage.

61 **present counsel:** immediate advice.
62–65 **'Twixt my . . . bring:** Juliet threatens that her knife will settle the dispute between herself and her great difficulties, which the Friar's wisdom and learning could not bring to an honorable outcome.

69 **craves:** requires. **execution:** act.

Literary Element Irony *What information about this private meeting is known to the audience, but not to Paris?* **L**

Reading Strategy Interpreting Imagery *How do you interpret the imagery in lines 55–59?* **R2**

Additional Support

Skills Practice

WRITING: Active Voice Note that writers may frame sentences so that the subject performs the action: Romeo *married* Juliet (active voice) or so that the action is performed on the subject: They *were married* by the Friar (passive voice). The active voice is generally preferable. Have students write a paragraph about Romeo and Juliet's misfortunes thus far, using the active voice as much as possible. **OL**

Friar Lawrence and Juliet, exhibited 1874. John Pettie. Oil on canvas, 110.5 x 76.5 cm. Royal Shakespeare Theatre Collection, Stratford-upon-Avon, England.

Viewing the Art: Does this portrayal of Friar Lawrence match your own image of him? Why or why not? ★

Teach

★ Viewing the Art

Answer: *Some may say he looks kind, comforting, and compassionate, as they imagined. Others may imagine the Friar as younger and less stern looking.*

The work of Scottish artist John Pettie (1839–1893) focuses on historical scenes and themes. He is best known for his scenes of the English Civil Wars (1642–1651) and the Jacobite Rebellion (1689). **AS**

English Language Coach

Write on the board:

This is *a pitiful case.*
Never was seen *so black a day.*

In the first example, *is* links a noun in the predicate with a pronoun in the subject. Explain that *was seen* is a verb phrase using *was* as an auxiliary, or helping, verb. Have students underline and identify the verbs as linking verbs or verb phrases.

1. Everyone in the Capulet household is grieving for Juliet. *(verb phrase)*
2. The musicians are opportunists. *(linking verb)*
3. Peter's puns and wisecracks are crass under the circumstances. *(linking verb)* **EL**

Academic Standards

Additional Support activities on pp. 776 and 777 cover the following standards:

Skills Practice: **9.6.2** Demonstrate an understanding of sentence construction…

English Language Coach: **9.6.2** Demonstrate an understanding of…proper English usage…

Teach

R1 Reading Strategy

Interpreting Imagery
Answer: *They appeal to all five senses and emphasize her willingness to sacrifice for Romeo and her fidelity to him.* OL

L1 Literary Element

Irony Note that while Juliet is making a point about her determination to remain faithful to Romeo, she is also describing an ordeal like the one she will have to endure. OL

R2 Reading Strategy

Interpreting Imagery
Answer: *The disturbing images create a grim, desperate mood.* OL

Thou hast the strength of will to slay thyself,
Then is it likely thou wilt undertake
A thing like death to chide away this shame,
That cop'st with death himself to scape from it;°
And, if thou darest, I'll give thee remedy.

JULIET. O, bid me leap, rather than marry Paris,
From off the battlements of any tower,
Or walk in thievish ways,° or bid me **lurk**
Where serpents are; chain me with roaring bears,
Or hide me nightly in a charnel house,°
O'ercover'd quite with dead men's rattling bones,
With reeky shanks° and yellow chapless° skulls;
Or bid me go into a new-made grave
And hide me with a dead man in his shroud—
Things that, to hear them told, have made me tremble—
And I will do it without fear or doubt,
To live an unstain'd wife to my sweet love.

FRIAR. Hold, then. Go home, be merry, give consent
To marry Paris. Wednesday is tomorrow.
Tomorrow night look that thou lie alone;
Let not the nurse lie with thee in thy chamber.
Take thou this vial, being then in bed,
And this distilling liquor° drink thou off;
When presently through all thy veins shall run
A cold and drowsy humor;° for no pulse
Shall keep his native progress,° but surcease;°
No warmth, no breath, shall testify thou livest;
The roses in thy lips and cheeks shall fade
To wanny ashes,° thy eyes' windows° fall
Like death when he shuts up the day of life;
Each part, depriv'd of supple government,°
Shall, stiff and stark and cold, appear like death;
And in this borrowed likeness of shrunk death
Thou shalt continue two-and-forty hours,
And then awake as from a pleasant sleep.
Now, when the bridegroom in the morning comes
To rouse thee from thy bed, there art thou dead.
Then, as the manner of our country is,
In thy best robes uncovered on the bier
Thou shalt be borne to that same ancient vault

71–75 **If, rather . . . from it:** The Friar says that since Juliet is willing to face **(cop'st)** death itself to avoid the shame of marrying Paris, then she probably would go through something similar to death to achieve the same result.
79 **in thievish ways:** on roads where thieves lurk.

81 **charnel** (chärn′ əl) **house:** a vault where skulls and bones were stored.

83 **reeky shanks:** foul-smelling limbs. **chapless:** jawless.

94 **distilling liquor:** liquid medicine that permeates the body.

96 **cold and drowsy humor:** a fluid that will make your body cold and put you to sleep.
97 **his native progress:** its natural movement. **surcease:** stop.

100 **To wanny ashes:** to the paleness of ashes. **eyes' windows:** eyelids.

102 **supple government:** the ability to move.

Reading Strategy Interpreting Imagery *To what senses do the details in this passage appeal? What do the images help Juliet to convey?* R1

Reading Strategy Interpreting Imagery *What mood does Shakespeare establish with this imagery?* R2

Vocabulary
lurk (lurk) *v.* to conceal oneself; to move about in a sneaky manner

Additional Support

Skills Practice

READING: Monitoring Comprehension Explain that readers can monitor their comprehension by summarizing, asking questions, and noting how and why their understanding of a subject has changed. Have students recall major events of Act 4 and discuss the effect of each one on the main characters. Students should organize their thoughts on events and characters in Act 4 in a chart. OL

Where all the kindred of the Capulets lie.
In the meantime, against° thou shalt awake,
Shall Romeo by my letters know our drift;°
And hither shall he come; and he and I
Will watch thy waking, and that very night
Shall Romeo bear thee hence to Mantua.
And this shall free thee from this present shame,
If no inconstant toy° nor womanish fear
Abate thy valor° in the acting it.

[*JULIET takes the vial.*]

JULIET. Give me, give me! O, tell not me of fear!

FRIAR. Hold! Get you gone, be strong and prosperous°
In this resolve. I'll send a friar with speed
To Mantua, with my letters to thy lord.

JULIET. Love give me strength, and strength shall help afford.°
Farewell, dear father.

[*They exit.*]

113 **against:** in preparation for when.

114 **drift:** intentions.

119 **inconstant toy:** whim.

120 **Abate thy valor:** lessen your courage.

122 **prosperous:** successful.

125 **afford:** carry out.

SCENE 2. Later that day. A hall in CAPULET's house.

[*LORD CAPULET, LADY CAPULET, and the NURSE enter with several SERVANTS. They are making arrangements for the wedding that will be held in just two days.*]

L2

CAPULET. So many guests invite as here are writ.

[*CAPULET hands a SERVANT a guest list, and the SERVANT exits to invite the wedding guests.*]

Sirrah, go hire me twenty cunning° cooks.

SERVINGMAN. You shall have none ill, sir; for I'll try° if they
can lick their fingers.

CAPULET. How canst thou try them so?

SERVINGMAN. Marry, sir, 'tis an ill cook that cannot lick his
own fingers.° Therefore he that cannot lick his fingers goes
not with me.

[*The second SERVANT exits to hire more cooks.*]

CAPULET. Go begone.
We shall be much unfurnish'd° for this time.
What, is my daughter gone to Friar Lawrence?

NURSE. Ay, forsooth.°

CAPULET. Well, he may chance to do some good on her.
A peevish self-will'd harlotry it is.°

[*JULIET enters, returning from FRIAR LAWRENCE's cell.*]

2 **cunning:** skilled.

3 **try:** test.

6–7 **'tis an ill . . . fingers:** a proverbial expression for cooks who lack faith in their cooking.

10 **unfurnish'd:** unprepared.

12 **forsooth:** in truth.

14 **A peevish . . . is:** She is a quarrelsome, stubborn good-for-nothing.

Big Idea The Power of Love *How would you summarize the Friar's plan to save Juliet from marrying Paris?* **BI**

Teach

BI Big Idea

The Power of Love

Answer: *To avoid marrying Paris, Juliet will fake her death by taking a sleeping potion. Her family will bury her in the vault. In the meantime, the Friar will notify Romeo of the plan. When Juliet revives, Romeo will rescue her from the vault and take her to Mantua.* **OL**

L2 Literary Element

Comic Relief **Ask:** How would you describe the change in mood and tone in the opening lines of Scene 2? *(This bustling, comical scene contrasts sharply with the dark mood of the previous one.)* Explain that dramatists often inject a note of comic relief after a particularly draining episode. **OL**

Differentiated Instruction

Less Proficient Readers Acting out the meanings of words can help less proficient readers absorb and remember difficult vocabulary. Have students look up and define the following words: *headstrong, prostrate, disobedient, beseech, opposition,* and *modesty.* Ask pairs of students to locate each word in the scene and discuss which meaning applies. Then have them stage a very brief skit that illustrates the meaning of the word in context. **BL**

Academic Standards

Additional Support activities on pp. 778 and 779 cover the following standards:

Skills Practice: **9.3.3** Analyze interactions between characters...and explain the way those interactions affect the plot.

Differentiated Instruction: **9.1** Use...context clues and a growing knowledge of English...to determine the meaning of words...

Teach

R1 Reading Strategy

Interpreting In this speech, Juliet comes nearer to outright lying than at any other point. **Ask:** Is she justified in pretending to repent? Why or why not? *(Encourage students to support their opinions with reasons.)* OL

BI1 Big Idea

The Power of Love **Answer:** *His decision throws the Friar's plan off schedule. Juliet will awaken from her induced sleep sooner than anticipated.* OL

L1 Literary Element

Irony **Answer:** *Capulet is relieved that Juliet's future is settled, unaware that she has agreed to a dangerous plan to avoid marrying Paris.* OL

V Vocabulary

Multiple Meanings Direct students' attention to the following words in this passage: *stir, warrant, deck, forth,* and *light.* Note that they all have multiple meanings. Have small groups of students look up the words in a dictionary and then determine the correct meaning for the context. OL

NURSE. See where she comes from shrift with merry look.

CAPULET. How now, my headstrong? Where have you been
gadding?

JULIET. Where I have learnt me to repent the sin
Of disobedient opposition
To you and your behests,° and am enjoin'd° R1
By holy Lawrence to fall prostrate° here
To beg your pardon.

[*She kneels before her father.*]

Pardon, I beseech you!
Henceforward I am ever rul'd by you.

CAPULET. Send for the County. Go tell him of this.
I'll have this knot knit up tomorrow morning.°

JULIET. I met the youthful lord at Lawrence' cell
And gave him what becomed° love I might,
Not stepping o'er the bounds of modesty.

CAPULET. Why, I am glad on't. This is well. Stand up.

[*JULIET rises.*]

This is as't should be. Let me see the County.
Ay, marry, go, I say, and fetch him hither.
Now, afore God, this reverend holy friar,
All our whole city is much bound° to him.

JULIET. Nurse, will you go with me into my closet°
To help me sort such needful ornaments°
As you think fit to furnish me tomorrow?

LADY CAPULET. No, not till Thursday. There is time enough.

CAPULET. Go, nurse, go with her. We'll to church tomorrow.

[*JULIET and the NURSE exit.*]

LADY CAPULET. We shall be short in our provision.
'Tis now near night.

CAPULET. Tush, I will stir about,
And all things shall be well, I warrant thee, wife.
Go thou to Juliet, help to deck up her.° V
I'll not to bed tonight; let me alone.
I'll play the housewife for this once. What, ho!
They are all forth; well, I will walk myself°
To County Paris, to prepare up him

19 **behests** (bi hests′): requests. **enjoin'd:** directed.
20 **fall prostrate:** kneel down in humility.

23–24 **Send for . . . morning:** Juliet's apparent change of heart moves Capulet to change the wedding day to Wednesday.

26 **becomed:** becoming; proper.

32 **bound:** indebted.

33 **closet:** private room.

34 **sort such needful ornaments:** select the necessary clothing.

41 **deck up her:** dress her.

43–44 **I'll play . . . walk myself:** Capulet calls for a servant but realizes that he has already sent them all on errands.

Big Idea The Power of Love *Capulet decides to move the wedding from Thursday to Wednesday. What problems could this cause for Juliet and the Friar?* BI1

Literary Element Irony *Why is Capulet's statement ironic?* L1

Additional Support

Academic Standards

The Additional Support activity on p. 780 covers the following standard:

Skills Practice: **9.6.1** Identify and correctly use…phrases…

Skills Practice

GRAMMAR: Prepositions Explain that a preposition shows the relationship of a noun or pronoun to another word in the sentence. Note this example in line 25: "I met the youthful lord at Lawrence' cell."

Have students underline the prepositional phrases and circle the prepositions in this passage (pages 778–779):

Now, when the bridegroom in the morning comes / To rouse thee from thy bed, there art thou dead. / Then, as the manner of our country is, / In thy best robes uncovered on the bier / Thou shalt be borne to that same ancient vault / Where all the kindred of the Capulets lie. OL

V Against tomorrow. My heart is wondrous light,
Since this same wayward girl is so reclaim'd.

L2 [*CAPULET and LADY CAPULET exit.*]

SCENE 3. The evening of the same day, the night before the wedding. JULIET's room.

[*JULIET and the NURSE have been preparing JULIET's clothing for the wedding.*]

JULIET. Ay, those attires are best; but, gentle nurse,
I pray thee leave me to myself tonight;
For I have need of many orisons°
To move the heavens to smile upon my state,
Which, well thou knowest, is cross° and full of sin.

[*LADY CAPULET enters.*]

LADY CAPULET. What, are you busy, ho? Need you my help?

JULIET. No, madam; we have cull'd° such necessaries
As are behoveful for our state° tomorrow.
So please you, let me now be left alone,
And let the nurse this night sit up with you;
For I am sure you have your hands full all
In this so sudden business.

LADY CAPULET. Good night.
Get thee to bed, and rest; for thou hast need.

[*LADY CAPULET and the NURSE exit.*]

JULIET. Farewell! God knows when we shall meet again.
I have a faint cold fear thrills through my veins
That almost freezes up the heat of life.
I'll call them back again to comfort me.
Nurse!—What should she do here?
My dismal scene I needs must act alone.
Come, vial.
What if this mixture do not work at all?
Shall I be married then tomorrow morning?
No, no! This shall forbid it. Lie thou there.

R2 [*She places a dagger beside the bed.*]

What if it be a poison which the friar
Subtly hath minist'red to have me dead,
Lest in this marriage he should be dishonor'd
Because he married me before to Romeo?
I fear it is; and yet methinks it should not,
For he hath still been tried° a holy man.
How if, when I am laid into the tomb,
I wake before the time that Romeo

3 **orisons** (ôr′ i zənz): prayers.

5 **cross:** wrong; perverse.

7 **cull'd:** selected.

8 **behoveful for our state:** appropriate for our ceremony.

29 **still been tried:** always proven to be.

Big Idea The Power of Love *What is Juliet's state of mind? Why does she want to call the Nurse back?* BI2

Teach

L2 Literary Element

Tone Have students discuss the overall tone of Scene 2. Note that the scene contains some complex ironies; for example, Capulet's fussy attention to detail, his ignorance of Friar Lawrence's true role, and Juliet's feigned submission. **Ask:** How might these elements affect a live audience? *(The audience would probably laugh uneasily because of the tension from knowing the situation is not what it seems.)* OL

BI2 Big Idea

The Power of Love **Answer:** *Juliet is anxious and frightened and feels a sense of foreboding. She's fearful of the Friar's position and is gathering her courage to go ahead with the plan. She starts to call the Nurse back for comfort.* OL

R2 Reading Strategy

Making Inferences Ask students if they are surprised that Juliet has a knife in her bedroom. Have them recall preceding scenes and decide when and how Juliet might have armed herself. You may wish to share the following model for drawing inferences.

MODEL: Right after her parents insist she marry Paris, Juliet says, "If all else fail, myself have power to die." In the next scene, she says, "'Twixt me and my extremes this bloody knife shall . . ." I can infer from these remarks that she's been considering suicide as an option. OL

Differentiated Instruction

Paraphrasing Invite students to share helpful techniques for understanding Shakespeare's language. Stress that paraphrasing, or putting a passage into one's own words, can help them monitor their comprehension. Have partners write paraphrases of the conversation between Capulet, Lady Capulet, and Juliet in Scene 2 and then read them aloud. BL

Academic Standards

The Additional Support activity on p. 781 covers the following standard:

Differentiated Instruction: **9.5.2** Write responses to literature…

Teach

R Reading Strategy

Interpreting Imagery

Answer: *Juliet imagines the burial vault to be a ghoulish, nightmarish place. Students may react with dismay at the thought of her waking up there.* OL

★ Cultural Note

Shakespeare has Juliet become so agitated by her gruesome fantasies that she drinks the potion in a rush, out of sheer terror. He did this not only to help the audience imagine the grim vault where Juliet lies but also to make her extreme act plausible. The Elizabethan audience would otherwise doubt that a young girl could be so bold and resolute, which were considered exclusively masculine qualities at that time. AS

Come to redeem° me? There's a fearful point!
Shall I not then be **stifled** in the vault,
To whose foul mouth no healthsome air breathes in,
And there die strangled ere my Romeo comes?
Or, if I live, is it not very like°
The horrible conceit° of death and night,
Together with the terror of the place—
As in a vault, an ancient receptacle
Where for this many hundred years the bones
Of all my buried ancestors are pack'd;
Where bloody Tybalt, yet but green in earth,°
Lies fest'ring° in his shroud; where, as they say,
At some hours in the night spirits resort°—
Alack, alack, is it not like that I,
So early waking—what with loathsome smells,
And shrieks like mandrakes° torn out of the earth,
That living mortals, hearing them, run mad—
O, if I wake, shall I not be distraught,°
Environed° with all these hideous fears,
And madly play with my forefathers' joints,
And pluck the mangled Tybalt from his shroud,
And, in this rage, with some great kinsman's bone
As with a club dash out my desp'rate brains?
O, look! Methinks I see my cousin's ghost
Seeking out Romeo, that did spit° his body
Upon a rapier's point. Stay,° Tybalt, stay!
Romeo, Romeo, Romeo! Here's drink—I drink to thee.

★ [*JULIET drinks the contents of the vial and falls onto her bed, which is surrounded with curtains.*]

32 **redeem:** rescue.

36 **like:** likely.

37 **conceit:** thought.

42 **green in earth:** newly buried.

43 **fest'ring:** decaying.

44 **resort:** gather.

47 **mandrakes:** plants with thick forked roots. (Many people in Shakespeare's time believed that mandrakes shrieked when pulled up and that anyone who heard the sound would become insane.)

49 **distraught** (dis trôt′): crazed.

50 **Environed:** surrounded.

56 **spit:** impale.

57 **Stay:** Remain where you are.

SCENE 4. During the night. A hall in CAPULET's house.

[*Preparations for the wedding continue. LADY CAPULET and the NURSE enter.*]

LADY CAPULET. Hold, take these keys and fetch more spices, nurse.

NURSE. They call for dates and quinces° in the pastry.°

[*LORD CAPULET enters.*]

CAPULET. Come, stir, stir, stir! The second cock hath crowed,
The curfew bell° hath rung, 'tis three o'clock.
Look to the bak'd meats, good Angelica;
Spare not for cost.

2 **quinces** (kwin′ səz): a golden, apple-shaped fruit. **pastry:** place where baking is done.

4 **curfew bell:** rung in the morning at daybreak as well as in the evening.

Reading Strategy Interpreting Imagery *How does Juliet imagine the burial vault? How does the imagery in this passage make you feel about Juliet waking up in such a place?* R

Vocabulary

stifle (stī′ fəl) *v.* to smother for lack of air; to prevent from developing properly

Additional Support

Skills Practice

WRITING: Researching Cultural Context Direct students to a library or the Internet to research reports on wedding celebrations in either Elizabethan England or Renaissance Italy. Students should include information on wedding attire, food served, and other customs. Encourage them to present their data creatively—for example, as an exposé in news magazine format, or as a skit performed by parents of the bride. OL

Story of Alatiel Tavoli (detail), 15th century. Master of Jarves Cassoni. Tempera on panel. Museo Correr, Venice.
Viewing the Art: How might Juliet react if she were to see the preparations for her wedding? How might Paris react? ★

NURSE. Go, you cotquean,° go,
Get you to bed! Faith, you'll be sick tomorrow
For this night's watching.°

CAPULET. No, not a whit. What, I have watch'd ere now
All night for lesser cause, and ne'er been sick.

LADY CAPULET. Ay, you have been a mouse hunt° in your time;
But I will watch you from such watching now.

[*LADY CAPULET and the NURSE exit.*]

CAPULET. A jealous hood,° a jealous hood!

[*Several SERVANTS enter with spits, logs, and baskets for preparing the wedding feast.*]

Now, fellow, what is there?

FIRST FELLOW. Things for the cook, sir; but I know not what.

CAPULET. Make haste, make haste.

[*One SERVANT exits.*]

Sirrah, fetch drier logs.
Call Peter; he will show thee where they are.

SECOND FELLOW. I have a head, sir, that will find out logs
And never trouble Peter for the matter.

CAPULET. Mass,° and well said; a merry whoreson,° ha!
Thou shalt be loggerhead.°

[*The SERVANTS exit.*]

Good faith, 'tis day.
The County will be here with music straight,°
For so he said he would.

6 **cotquean** (kät′ kwēn): a man who does housework.

8 **watching:** staying awake.

11 **mouse hunt:** woman chaser.

13 **jealous hood:** "jealousy" or "jealous woman."

20 **Mass:** by the mass (a mild oath). **whoreson** (hōr′ sən): rascal.
21 **loggerhead:** blockhead.

22 **straight:** immediately.

Literary Element Irony *What ironies do you see in this scene?* L

Teach

L Literary Element

Irony Answer: *The family happily fusses over preparations for a wedding that the audience knows will never happen. Students may feel a sense of impending doom that conflicts with Capulet's joy.* OL

★ Viewing the Art

Answer: *Although probably filled with dread, Juliet would have to act excited. Paris would be delighted.*

Tempera, a fast-drying paint that contains egg yolk and water, dates back to ancient times. Much of the panel painting done between the twelfth and fifteenth centuries was done in tempera, which allows the artist to use extremely delicate brushwork to show fine detail. AS

Differentiated Instruction

Making Connections Students with strong emotional responses can help others in the class relate their own feelings and experiences to Juliet's terrifying predicament. Have students write a poem or journal entry about Juliet's fear. Encourage them to consider her anxiety in the context of their own personal fears. Invite volunteers to share their work with the class. AL

Academic Standards

Additional Support activities on pp. 782 and 783 cover the following standards:

Skills Practice: **9.5.3** Write expository compositions…that communicate information and ideas from…secondary sources accurately and coherently…

Differentiated Instruction: **9.5.2** Write responses to literature that demonstrate an awareness of the author's style and an appreciation of the effects created…

each

Literary Element

Irony Answer: *The audience knows Juliet is only sleeping; the Nurse does not. This may help to create suspense about what reaction the Nurse will have to Juliet's state.* OL

Reading Strategy

Listening Say: Describe how the Nurse delivers these lines. Have students read lines 1–16 aloud, noting how phrasing suits the situation. *(The speech consists of abrupt, exclamatory verse, spoken in a loud voice and interrupted often by pauses. Its uneven, jarring rhythm suits the emotional bomb about to go off.)* OL

[*Music plays from offstage.* PARIS *is outside the house with musicians.*]

I hear him near.
Nurse! Wife! What, ho! What, nurse, I say!

[*The* NURSE *enters.*]

Go waken Juliet; go and trim her up.
I'll go and chat with Paris. Hie, make haste,
Make haste! The bridegroom he is come already:
Make haste, I say.

[*They exit.*]

SCENE 5. Immediately after the previous scene. JULIET's room.

[JULIET *is behind the curtain that surrounds her bed. The* NURSE *enters.*]

NURSE. Mistress! What, mistress! Juliet! Fast,° I warrant her, she.
Why, lamb! Why, lady! Fie, you slugabed.
Why, love, I say! Madam; Sweetheart! Why, bride!
What, not a word? You take your pennyworths° now;
Sleep for a week, for the next night, I warrant,
The County Paris hath set up his rest°
That you shall rest but little, God forgive me!
Marry and amen! How sound is she asleep!
I needs must wake her. Madam, madam, madam!
Ay, let the County take you° in your bed,
He'll fright you up, i' faith. Will it not be?

[*The* NURSE *pulls open the bed curtain.*]

What, dress'd, and in your clothes, and down again?°
I must needs wake you. Lady! Lady! Lady!
Alas, alas! Help, help! My lady's dead!
O weraday that ever I was born!
Some aqua vitae, ho! My lord! My lady!

[LADY CAPULET *enters.*]

LADY CAPULET. What noise is here?

NURSE. O lamentable day!

LADY CAPULET. What is the matter?

NURSE. Look, look! O heavy day!

LADY CAPULET. O me, O me! My child, my only life!
Revive, look up, or I will die with thee!
Help, help! Call help.

[LORD CAPULET *enters.*]

1 **Fast:** fast asleep.

4 **pennyworths:** small amounts (of rest).

6 **set up his rest:** resolved.

10 **take you:** catch you.

12 **down again:** gone back to bed.

Literary Element Irony *What information does the audience have that the Nurse lacks? How does this irony help to create tension?* L1

Vocabulary

revive (ri vīv') *v.* to bring back to life; to give new strength

Additional Support

Skills Practice

WRITING: Personal Response to Literature Explain that writing about one's response to a work of literature creates a lasting tribute that gives personal meaning to the work. Ask students to decide which character they most identify with in *Romeo and Juliet,* and have them write a letter to that character. The letter should express and explain the sympathy or other emotion prompted by the character's situation or actions. OL

CAPULET. For sha[illegible] [illegible]uliet forth; her lord is come.

NURSE. She's dead, [illegible] [illegible]e's dead, alack the day!

LADY CAPULET. Alack the [illegible] [illegible]dead, she's dead, she's dead!

CAPULET. Ha! Let me see her. [illegible] She's cold,
Her blood is settled, and her [illegible] stiff;
Life and these lips have long be[illegible] [illegible]ated.
Death lies on her like an untimely [illegible]
Upon the sweetest flower of all the fi[illegible]

NURSE. O lamentable day!

LADY CAPULET. O woeful time!

CAPULET. Death, that hath ta'en her hence to make [illegible] wail,
Ties up my tongue and will not let me speak.

[*FRIAR LAWRENCE and PARIS enter.*]

FRIAR. Come, is the bride ready to go to church?

CAPULET. Ready to go, but never to return.
O son, the night before thy wedding day
Hath Death lain with thy wife. There she lies,
Flower as she was, deflowered by him.
Death is my son-in-law, Death is my heir;
My daughter he hath wedded. I will die
And leave him all. Life, living, all is Death's.

PARIS. Have I thought long to see this morning's face,
And doth it give me such a sight as this?

LADY CAPULET. Accurs'd, unhappy, wretched, hateful day!
Most miserable hour that e'er time saw
In lasting labor of his pilgrimage!
But one, poor one, one poor and loving child,
But one thing to rejoice and solace° in,
And cruel Death hath catch'd it from my sight.

NURSE. O woe! O woeful, woeful, woeful day!
Most lamentable day, most woeful day
That ever ever I did yet behold!
O day, O day, O day! O hateful day!
Never was seen so black a day as this.
O woeful day! O woeful day!

PARIS. Beguil'd,° divorced, wronged, spited, slain!
Most detestable Death, by thee beguil'd,

47 **solace** (sol′ is): take comfort.

55 **Beguil'd** (bi gild′): cheated.

Reading Strategy Interpreting Imagery *Why does Capulet compare death to an "untimely frost" and Juliet to "the sweetest flower of all the field"?* R2

Big Idea The Power of Love *What details in this scene reveal how much Capulet, Lady Capulet, and the Nurse love Juliet?* BI

Teach

R2 Reading Strategy

Interpreting Imagery
Answer: *The comparison expresses his feeling that Juliet was beautiful and precious, and that death has taken her too soon.* OL

L2 Literary Element

Figurative Language Have students identify the similes and metaphors Capulet uses for death. *(Death as killing frost on a flower; as bridegroom and heir)*
Ask: What makes them apt? *(Frost kills delicate young plants. In place of all that Capulet hoped to achieve—his daughter's marriage, a son-in-law, grandchildren—there is only death.)* OL

BI Big Idea

The Power of Love **Answer:** *Their dramatic exclamations of grief: "all is death's"; "wretched, hateful day!"; "O woe!"* OL

English Language Coach

Exclamation Points English language learners may be surprised at the heavy use of exclamation points in lines 1–16. Note that while writers today are often cautioned against their overuse, Shakespeare's style was in keeping with the standards of his time. Discuss the emotions these exclamations convey. *(The Nurse's speech first expresses excitement over the wedding, then shock and anguish over the apparent death.)*

Have partners write dialogue between two friends in a heated argument. Remind them to reserve exclamation points for lines that express the strongest feelings. EL

Academic Standards

Additional Support activities on pp. 784 and 785 cover the following standards:

Skills Practice: **9.5.2** Write responses to literature that demonstrate a comprehensive grasp of the significant ideas of literary works; demonstrate an awareness of the author's style and an appreciation of the effects created…

English Language Coach: **9.6.1** Identify and correctly use…the mechanics of punctuation…

each

BI1 Big Idea

The Power of Love Note that Shakespeare portrays Romeo and Juliet's love as sincere and beautiful. At the same time, he shows how passion leads both characters into acts that violate the rules of their families and society and put themselves at risk. Have students summarize these acts. Discuss the paradoxical nature of love in the play. OL

★ Viewing the Art

Answer: *Students may say that the emotions shown by the people in the painting seem more restrained and decorous than the emotions expressed by the characters in the text.*

Frederick Leighton (1830–1896) was known for works with classical themes. His earlier works, like the one on this page, reflect the influence of the Florentine masters. AS

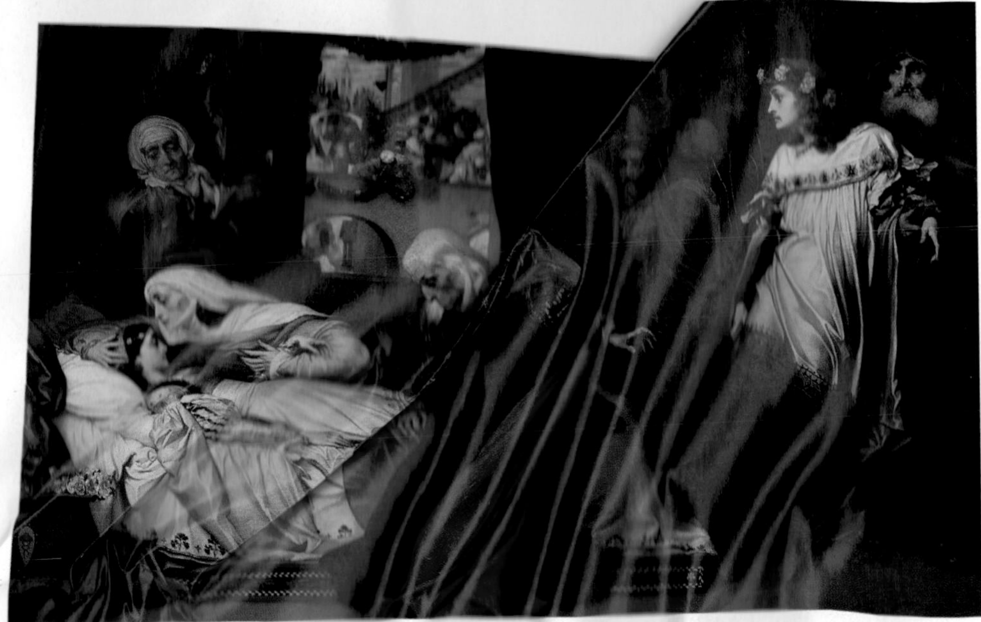

The Feigned Death of Juliet, c. 1856–1858. Frederick Leighton. Oil on canvas, 44 x 68 in. Art Gallery of South Australia, Adelaide.

Viewing the Art: In your opinion, do the emotions portrayed in the painting reflect the emotions of this scene? Explain. ★

BI1

By cruel, cruel thee quite overthrown.
O love! O life!—not life, but love in death!

CAPULET. Despis'd, distressed, hated, martyr'd, kill'd!
Uncomfortable° time, why cam'st thou now
To murder, murder our solemnity?°
O child, O child! My soul, and not my child!
Dead art thou—alack, my child is dead,
And with my child my joys are buried!

FRIAR. Peace, ho, for shame! Confusion's cure lives not
In these confusions.° Heaven and yourself
Had part° in this fair maid—now heaven hath all,
And all the better is it for the maid.
Your part° in her you could not keep from death,
But heaven keeps his part in eternal life.
The most you sought was her promotion,°
For 'twas your heaven she should be advanc'd;°
And weep ye now, seeing she is advanc'd
Above the clouds, as high as heaven itself?
O, in this love, you love your child so ill

60 **Uncomfortable:** bringing no comfort.
61 **solemnity** (sə lem′ nə tē): celebration.

65–66 **Confusion's . . . confusions:** The healing of this calamity does not lie in your uncontrolled outbursts.
67 **Had part:** shared.
69 **Your part:** that is, Juliet's mortal self.

71 **promotion:** social advancement (from marrying Paris).
72 **For 'twas . . . advanc'd:** For the greatest joy you could imagine was to see her elevated to a higher station in life.

Additional Support

Skills Practice

LISTENING AND SPEAKING: Oral Interpretation Acting out their favorite scenes will encourage students to become actively engaged in the play while improving both reading comprehension and oral presentation skills. Keep the sessions relaxed and fun. Urge students who are reluctant to participate to take on nonspeaking parts. OL

That you run mad, seeing that she is well.°
She's not well married that lives married long,
But she's best married that dies married young.
Dry up your tears and stick your rosemary°
On this fair corse, and, as the custom is,
And in her best array bear her to church;
For though fond nature bids us all **lament**,
Yet nature's tears are reason's merriment.°

CAPULET. All things that we ordained festival°
Turn from their office° to black funeral—
Our instruments to melancholy bells,
Our wedding cheer to a sad burial feast;
Our solemn hymns to sullen dirges° change;
Our bridal flowers serve for a buried corse;
And all things change them to the contrary.

FRIAR. Sir, go you in; and, madam, go with him;
And go, Sir Paris. Everyone prepare
To follow this fair corse unto her grave.
The heavens do low'r° upon you for some ill;°
★ Move them no more by crossing their high will.

[*They all cast rosemary leaves on* JULIET. *All but the* NURSE *and the* MUSICIANS *exit.*]

FIRST MUSICIAN. Faith, we may put up our pipes and be gone.

NURSE. Honest good fellows, ah, put up, put up,
For well you know this is a pitiful case.°

[NURSE *exits.*]

FIRST MUSICIAN. Ay, by my troth, the case° may be amended.°

[PETER *enters.*]

PETER. Musicians, O musicians, "Heart's ease,"° "Heart's
ease"! O, and you will have me live, play "Heart's ease."

FIRST MUSICIAN. Why "Heart's ease"?

PETER. O musicians, because my heart itself plays "My heart
is full." O, play me some merry dump° to comfort me.

FIRST MUSICIAN. Not a dump we, 'tis no time to play now.

PETER. You will not then?

76 **well:** in heaven.

79 **rosemary:** an herb used in funerals as a symbol of remembrance.

82–83 **For though . . . merriment:** Although foolish human nature commands us to grieve, reason finds cause for rejoicing (because Juliet is in heaven).

84 **ordained festival:** ordered for festive purposes.

85 **office:** function.

88 **sullen dirges** (dur′ jəz): gloomy funeral music.

94 **low'r:** frown. **ill:** sin.

98 **case:** situation.

99 **the case:** my instrument's case. **amended:** repaired. (This may be a pun, or the First Musician might have misunderstood the Nurse.)

100 **"Heart's ease":** a popular song.

104 **dump:** sad tune.

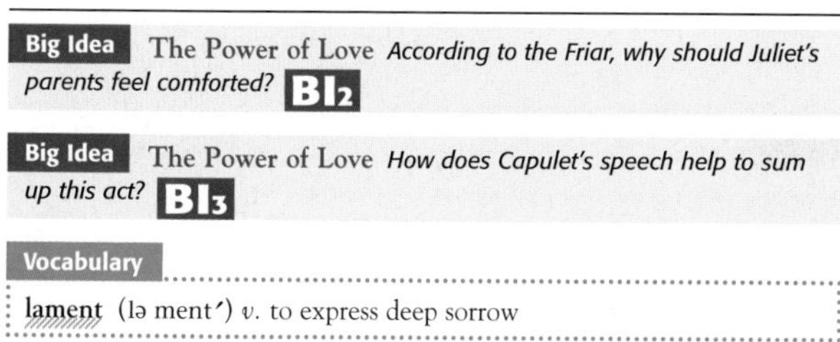

Big Idea The Power of Love *According to the Friar, why should Juliet's parents feel comforted?* **BI2**

Big Idea The Power of Love *How does Capulet's speech help to sum up this act?* **BI3**

Vocabulary

lament (lə ment′) *v.* to express deep sorrow

Teach

BI2 Big Idea

The Power of Love Answer: *Juliet is in heaven.* **OL**

BI3 Big Idea

The Power of Love Answer: *Capulet recounts the journey the family has taken from celebration at the upcoming wedding to mourning at a funeral.* **OL**

★ Writer's Technique

Irony Note that although the Friar offers religious consolation as if Juliet were dead, in fact he knows she is only sleeping. Ask students to reconsider this passage when they read the final scene of the play, in which the Friar does not invoke religion, although both Romeo and Juliet are, in fact, dead. **AS**

English Language Coach

Antonyms Explain that words with opposite meanings are called antonyms. List several pairs from the play on the board: *love/hate, melancholy/joyous, light/dark.* Have English language learners define each word and supply other comparable pairs. Have groups of students locate other antonyms in the play, define them, and explain their importance to the plot or theme. **EL**

Academic Standards

Additional Support activities on pp. 786 and 787 cover the following standards:

Skills Practice: **9.7.6** Analyze the occasion and the interests of the audience and choose effective verbal and nonverbal techniques...for presentations.

English Language Coach: **9.1** [Use] relationships...and a growing knowledge of English...to determine the meaning of words...

each

BI Big Idea

The Power of Love Answer: *The hired musicians are indifferent to the family's grief and focused on their own pleasures. This glimpse into human nature shows how grief and gaiety, sorrow and self-interest are intermingled in life.* **OL**

Cultural History

Minstrel Wandering minstrels and troubadours provided the precursors to modern drama. Performers would travel, sharing songs, stories, and news. Eventually, stable groups formed, sponsored by wealthy patrons or by the towns. Even the Catholic Church sometimes used minstrels to spread stories from the Bible as plays. **AS**

CheckPoint

Use the CheckPoint questions on Presentation Plus! to check students' mastery of the selection. These questions can be used with interactive response keypads for immediate student feedback.

FIRST MUSICIAN. No.

PETER. I will then give it you soundly.°

FIRST MUSICIAN. What will you give us?

PETER. No money, on my faith, but the gleek;° I will give you the minstrel.°

FIRST MUSICIAN. Then will I give you the serving-creature.

PETER. Then will I lay the serving-creature's dagger on your pate.° I will carry° no crotchets,° I'll *re*° you, I'll *fa*° you. Do you note° me?

FIRST MUSICIAN. And you *re* us and *fa* us, you note us.

SECOND MUSICIAN. Pray you put up your dagger, and put out° your wit.

PETER. Then have at you with my wit! I will drybeat° you with an iron wit, and put up my iron dagger. Answer me like men:

"When griping° griefs the heart doth wound,
And doleful dumps the mind oppress,
Then music with her silver sound"—

why "silver sound"? Why "music with her silver sound"? What say you, Simon Catling?°

FIRST MUSICIAN. Marry, sir, because silver hath a sweet sound.

PETER. Pretty! What say you, Hugh Rebeck?°

SECOND MUSICIAN. I say, "silver sound," because musicians sound° for silver.

PETER. Pretty too! What say you, James Soundpost?°

THIRD MUSICIAN. Faith, I know not what to say.

PETER. O, I cry you mercy, you are the singer;° I will say for you; it is "music with her silver sound," because musicians have no gold for sounding:

"Then music with her silver sound
With speedy help doth lend redress."

[*PETER exits.*]

FIRST MUSICIAN. What a pestilent knave is this same!

SECOND MUSICIAN. Hang him, Jack! Come, we'll in here, tarry for the mourners, and stay° dinner.

[*MUSICIANS exit.*]

108 **give it you soundly:** let you have it thoroughly.

110–111 **gleek:** insulting jest. **give you the minstrel:** call you a minstrel (an insult).

114 **pate:** head. **carry:** put up with. **crotchets** (kroch′ itz): "whims" or "quarter notes in music." **Re** and **fa** are musical notes, which Peter uses threateningly.

115 **note:** understand.

117 **put out:** display.

119 **drybeat:** thrash.

122 **griping:** distressing. (Peter is reciting lines from a poem.)

126 **Catling** (kat′ ling): a lute string.

128 **Rebeck** (rē′ bek): a three-stringed fiddle.

130 **sound:** play.

131 **Soundpost:** a small peg beneath the bridge of a stringed instrument.

133 **you are the singer:** that is, you can only sing, not say.

140 **stay:** wait for.

Big Idea The Power of Love *What does this final dialogue suggest about human nature?* **BI**

Additional Support

Academic Standards

The Additional Support activity on p. 788 covers the following standard:

Skills Practice: **9.7.10** Assess how language and delivery affect the mood and tone of the oral communication and make an impact on the audience.

Skills Practice

LISTENING AND SPEAKING: Sound Devices Shakespeare uses repetition, alliteration (the repetition of initial consonant sounds), and assonance (the repetition of internal vowel sounds) to emphasize the characters' grief. Have students view a videotape or listen to an audiotape of Scene 5. Ask students to listen for sound devices that help express grief in the characters' speeches: for example, the repeated long *o* sound in the Nurse's speech. **OL**

AFTER YOU READ

RESPONDING AND THINKING CRITICALLY

Respond

1. What do you think of Friar Lawrence's plan and its consequences?

Recall and Interpret

2. (a)What plan does the Friar suggest to Juliet? (b)Why does he suggest this plan?
3. (a)What does Capulet decide when Juliet agrees to marry Paris? (b)Why do you think he makes this decision, and how might it cause problems for Juliet?
4. (a)What does Juliet fear most about carrying out the Friar's plan? (b)What does her resolution to go ahead with the plan indicate about her?

Analyze and Evaluate

5. Do you think the Friar's plan is realistic? Why or why not?
6. (a)How does Capulet respond after Juliet's body is found? (b)Do you think he regrets his earlier harshness toward her? Why or why not?

Connect

7. **Big Idea** **The Power of Love** What would you have done if you had been in Juliet's situation? Explain.

LITERARY ANALYSIS

Literary Element Irony

Irony is a contrast between appearance and reality.

1. What is one example of situational irony in Act 4? What effect does it help create? Explain.
2. What is one example of dramatic irony? Explain.

Writing About Literature

Respond to Character and Plot Imagine that you are either Friar Lawrence or the Nurse–characters who have been entrusted with the secret of Romeo and Juliet's marriage. Write a diary entry about the events in Act 4. Discuss the young lovers' dilemma, the advice you have offered, and your hopes and fears about their future. Include specific details from the play in your diary entry.

Literature Online **Web Activities** For eFlashcards, Selection Quick Checks, and other Web activities, go to www.glencoe.com.

READING AND VOCABULARY

Reading Strategy Interpreting Imagery

In creating effective **imagery,** writers use descriptions that appeal to the senses–sight, sound, touch, taste, and smell.

1. Which image in this act struck you as the most vivid or effective? Explain.
2. Find two other examples of imagery in Act 4. (a)What senses do they appeal to? (b)What effect do they have on you?

Vocabulary Practice

Practice with Context Clues For each boldfaced vocabulary word, choose the best definition.

1. His mourners will **lament** Chris's death.
   a. disbelieve **b.** confront **c.** regret
2. Paramedics **revive** victims of heat exhaustion.
   a. bring back to life **c.** carry
   b. bring to a doctor
3. Do not **lurk** in shadow; you will startle someone.
   a. move in concealment **c.** depart
   b. rest
4. **Stifle** your discomfort and sing aloud for me.
   a. remember **b.** explain **c.** smother

Literature Online

Web Activities Have students access the Web site for interactive activities that will help them assess their understanding of the selection.

Reading Strategy

1. Students should support their answers.
2. Students should support their answers.

Vocabulary

1. c **2.** a **3.** a **4.** c

AFTER YOU READ

Assess

1. Accept well-reasoned answers.
2. (a) He gives her a potion that will make her appear dead for forty-two hours. Romeo can then be summoned to rescue her from the burial vault. (b) Juliet has spoken of suicide so desperate measures seem justified.
3. (a) He moves the wedding up a day, hoping to dispel the gloom caused by Tybalt's death. (b) There may not be time to summon Romeo back to Verona.
4. (a) Wakening alone in the gruesome tomb (b) Desperation to be with Romeo
5. Accept reasonable answers.
6. (a) He is devastated and feels that his joy in life will be buried with Juliet. (b) He does not mention regret, but perhaps his guilt is too painful to acknowledge.
7. Accept reasonable answers.

Literary Element

1. Capulet's decision to have the wedding sooner so Juliet will be safely and happily married is a situational irony. Although his intentions are good, his act causes the lovers' plan to go awry. The irony creates tension and arouses pity for Capulet.
2. The Capulets' grief over Juliet's apparent death is a dramatic irony because the audience knows she's alive.

Writing About Literature

Remind students that their diary entries should be written in the first person and based on evidence from the text.

EFORE YOU READ

ocus

Summary

Balthasar reports to Romeo that Juliet is dead. Romeo decides to join her and persuades a pharmacist to sell him poison. Paris confronts Romeo; they fight and Romeo kills Paris. Romeo takes the poison and dies just before the arrival of Friar Lawrence, who has learned that his letter never reached Romeo. Juliet wakes and refuses to leave; the Friar flees, and Juliet stabs herself with Romeo's dagger. The various witnesses confess to the Prince, and Montague and Capulet express remorse.

V Vocabulary

Vocabulary File Say: Add these words and definitions to your vocabulary file. For each word, include a sentence that gives you an example of how to use the word. **OL** Students with English language needs should include the pronunciation of these words in their files. **EL**

Literary Elements Have students access the Web site to improve their understanding of tragedy.

LITERATURE PREVIEW

Connecting to the Drama

Do children wind up paying a price for the ill deeds of their parents? Before you read this act, think about the following questions:

- Does aggression hurt the aggressor as much as it hurts the victim?
- What is one example of people suffering due to the foolish actions of previous generations?

Building Background

In this act, one character is prevented from delivering a message because he is suspected by the authorities of having been exposed to infectious disease. Called the Black Death, the bubonic plague was among the most feared diseases in Europe. Dirt and overcrowding in cities encouraged rats, which carried fleas infected with the disease. It has been estimated that one-quarter of the population of Europe died from plague during the epidemic.

Setting Purposes for Reading

Big Idea The Power of Love

As you read, think about whether Romeo and Juliet's misfortunes are due to an excess of love, or whether they are due to the failures of other people.

Literary Element Tragedy

A **tragedy** is a play in which a main character, called the tragic hero, suffers a downfall. The downfall may result from outside forces or from a weakness within the character, which is known as a tragic flaw. *Romeo and Juliet* is an unusual tragedy because it has two tragic heroes.

- See Literary Terms Handbook, p. R18.

Literature Online **Interactive Literary Elements Handbook** To review or learn more about the literary elements, go to www.glencoe.com.

READING PREVIEW

Reading Strategy Making Inferences About Theme

The **theme** of a piece of literature is a dominant idea—often a universal message about life—that the writer communicates to the reader. A work may have more than one theme. **Make inferences,** or reasonable guesses, about the theme or themes of *Romeo and Juliet* by thinking about what insights Shakespeare is expressing through plot and dialogue.

Reading Tip: Taking Notes Use a chart to record the inferences you draw from the details presented by Shakespeare in Act 5. Model your chart on the one shown below for Act 3.

Detail	Inference About Theme
Romeo accidentally causes Mercutio's death.	The source of one's death is fated, yet cannot be predicted.

Vocabulary

misadventure (mis′ əd ven′ chər) *n.* a mishap; an unfortunate event; p. 791 *Mark had a misadventure with a flat bike tire.*

haughty (hô′ tē) *adj.* very proud and scornful of others; p. 795 *Maria talked down to people and acted rudely; I thought she was haughty.*

unsavory (un sā′ vər ē) *adj.* unpleasant in character; disagreeable to the taste; p. 798 *Because of dishonest dealings, Greg has an unsavory reputation.*

tedious (tē′ dē əs) *adj.* tiresome; boring; p. 802 *I found the long bus ride tedious and uncomfortable.*

Vocabulary Tip: Word Parts Knowing the meanings of prefixes, suffixes, and root words can help you figure out the meanings of new vocabulary words.

INDIANA ACADEMIC STANDARDS (pages 790–807)

9.3.1 Explain the...purposes and characteristics of...tragedy...

9.3 [Identify] story elements such as...theme...

9.5.3 Write expository compositions...

Selection Skills

The Tragedy of Romeo and Juliet, Act 5

Literary Elements
- Tragedy (SE pp. 790–806)
- Style (SE p. 806)

Reading Skills
- Making Inferences About Theme (SE pp. 790–806)

Vocabulary Skills
- Word Parts (SE pp. 790, 806)
- Academic Vocabulary (SE p. 806)

Listening/Speaking/Viewing Skills
- Reader's Theater (SE p. 807)
- Oral Reading (TWE p. 798)
- Analyzing Art (SE pp. 796, 800, 804)

Writing Skills/Grammar
- Author's Craft (SE p. 807)
- Pronouns (TWE p. 794)
- Descriptive Paragraph (TWE p. 796)
- Subject-Verb Agreement (TWE p. 800)
- Indefinite Pronouns (TWE p. 804)

Act 5

SCENE 1. The next day. A street in Mantua, the city where ROMEO lives in exile.

[ROMEO enters; he is waiting for his servant, BALTHASAR, to return from Verona with news of JULIET.]

ROMEO. If I may trust the flattering truth of sleep,
My dreams presage,° some joyful news at hand.
My bosom's lord° sits lightly in his throne,
And all this day an unaccustom'd spirit
Lifts me above the ground with cheerful thoughts.
I dreamt my lady came and found me dead
(Strange dream that gives a dead man leave to think!)
And breath'd such life with kisses in my lips
That I reviv'd and was an emperor.
Ah me! How sweet is love itself possess'd,
When but love's shadows° are so rich in joy!

[ROMEO's servant, BALTHASAR, enters.]

News from Verona! How now, Balthasar?
Dost thou not bring me letters from the friar?
How doth my lady? Is my father well?
How fares my Juliet? That I ask again,
For nothing can be ill if she be well.

BALTHASAR. Then she is well, and nothing can be ill.
Her body sleeps in Capel's monument,°
And her immortal part with angels lives.
I saw her laid low in her kindred's vault
And presently took post° to tell it you.
O, pardon me for bringing these ill news,
Since you did leave it for my office,° sir.

ROMEO. Is it e'en so? Then I defy you, stars!
Thou knowest my lodging. Get me ink and paper
And hire post horses. I will hence° tonight.

BALTHASAR. I do beseech you, sir, have patience.
Your looks are pale and wild and do import
Some **misadventure.**°

ROMEO. Tush, thou art deceiv'd.
Leave me and do the thing I bid thee do.
Hast thou no letters to me from the friar?

BALTHASAR. No, my good lord.

2 **presage** (pres′ ij): predict.
3 **bosom's lord:** heart.

11 **but love's shadows:** only dreams of love.

18 **Capel's monument:** the Capulet tomb.

21 **presently took post:** immediately set out on post horses.

23 **office:** duty.

26 **hence:** leave here.

28–29 **and do . . . misadventure:** suggest that some misfortune will occur.

Literary Element Tragedy *Why does Romeo decide to return to Verona? What is your response to his decision?* **L**

Vocabulary

misadventure (mis′ əd ven′ chər) n. a mishap; an unfortunate event

Teach

R Reading Strategy

Interpret How would students describe Romeo's mood after reading this opening soliloquy in Act 5? *(He has had a strange dream about being brought back to life by the kisses of his beloved. He takes it as a positive sign that joyful news is on its way, and he is hopeful and excited.)* **OL**

L Literary Element

Tragedy **Answer:** *Romeo decides to return to Verona because he believes Juliet is dead. Students may consider Romeo's decision to be a rash one.* **OL**

English Language Coach

Mastering Pronunciation and Meaning English language learners may need extra practice with pronunciation and vocabulary. Make English dictionaries available, and be sure students understand how to use the pronunciation key. Have groups of students choose a scene, discuss the meanings of unfamiliar vocabulary and phrases in the scene, and work together to look up pronunciations. Encourage students to question each other about unclear passages. **EL**

Academic Standards

The Additional Support activity on p. 791 covers the following standards:

English Language Coach: **9.2.1** Analyze the structure and format of reference… documents… **9.1** Use phonics, context clues, and a growing knowledge of English…to determine the meaning of words…

Teach

L1 Literary Element

Tragedy Answer: *Balthasar, like Friar Lawrence, urges Romeo to stop and think, but Romeo is ruled by impatience.* OL

L2 Literary Element

Tragedy With this decision, the final stage of the tragedy is set in motion. Romeo and Juliet must die, as we have known from the prologue. This miscommunication, though well intended, is deadly. Encourage students to consider Romeo's response to the news.

Ask: What evidence of unthinking behavior do you see in his response? *(He never asks what happened or how it happened. He also neglects to wonder much that the Friar did not inform him, simply saying "No matter." All of this points to unreasonable impulsiveness.)* OL

★ Cultural History

Known as the Black Death, the bubonic plague was among the most feared diseases in Europe. An estimated one third to one half of Europe's population died from the disease during the Middle Ages and the Renaissance. AS

ROMEO. No matter. Get thee gone.
And hire those horses. I'll be with thee straight.

[*BALTHASAR exits. ROMEO, grief stricken, begins to walk aimlessly.*]

Well, Juliet, I will lie with thee tonight.
L2 Let's see for means. O mischief, thou art swift
To enter in the thoughts of desperate men!
I do remember an apothecary,°
And hereabouts 'a dwells, which late I noted
In tatt'red weeds,° with overwhelming° brows,
Culling of simples.° Meager were his looks,
Sharp misery had worn him to the bones;
And in his needy shop a tortoise hung,
An alligator stuff'd, and other skins
Of ill-shap'd fishes; and about his shelves
A beggarly account° of empty boxes,
Green earthen pots, bladders, and musty seeds.
Remnants of packthread,° and old cakes of roses°
Were thinly scattered, to make up a show.
Noting this penury,° to myself I said,
"An' if a man did need a poison now
Whose sale is present death° in Mantua,
Here lives a caitiff ° wretch would sell it him."
O, this same thought did but forerun my need,
And this same needy man must sell it me.
As I remember, this should be the house.
Being holiday, the beggar's shop is shut.
What, ho! Apothecary!

[*APOTHECARY enters.*]

APOTHECARY. Who calls so loud?

ROMEO. Come hither, man. I see that thou art poor.
Hold, there is forty ducats.° Let me have
A dram of poison, such soon-speeding gear°
As will disperse itself through all the veins
That the life-weary taker may fall dead.
And that the trunk° may be discharg'd of breath
As violently as hasty powder fir'd
Doth hurry from the fatal cannon's womb.

APOTHECARY. Such mortal° drugs I have; but Mantua's law
Is death to any he that utters° them.

ROMEO. Art thou so bare and full of wretchedness
And fearest to die? Famine is in thy cheeks,
Need and oppression starveth in thy eyes,
Contempt and beggary hangs upon thy back:

37 **apothecary** (ə poth′ ə ker′ ē): one who prepares and sells drugs.

39 **tatt'red weeds:** torn clothing. **overwhelming:** overhanging.

40 **Culling of simples:** sorting medicinal herbs.

45 **beggarly account:** small number.

47 **packthread:** twine for tying packages. **cakes of roses:** rose petals pressed into cakes and used for perfume.

49 **penury** (pen′ yər ē): poverty.

51 **Whose sale . . . death:** the sale of which is punishable by immediate execution.

52 **caitiff** (kā′ tif): miserable.

59 **ducats** (duk′ ətz): gold coins.

60 **soon-speeding gear:** fast-working stuff.

63 **trunk:** body.

66 **mortal:** deadly.

67 **any he that utters:** any man who dispenses.

Literary Element Tragedy *Think about Balthasar's caution and Romeo's response. What consistent flaw in Romeo is revealed again here?* L1

Additional Support

Skills Practice

READING: Setting a Purpose for Reading Remind students to set a purpose for reading. Have them describe Romeo's state of mind in Act 5, Scene 1. Suggest that they jot down their ideas about his reactions and their potential consequences as the play proceeds. Have students write brief journal responses as they read Scene 3, revising their predictions as needed and noting their reactions and associations. OL

The world is not thy friend, nor the world's law;
The world affords no law to make thee rich;
Then be not poor, but break it and take this.

APOTHECARY. My poverty but not my will consents.

ROMEO. I pay thy poverty and not thy will.

APOTHECARY. Put this in any liquid thing you will
And drink it off, and if you had the strength
Of twenty men, it would dispatch you straight.

ROMEO. There is thy gold—worse poison to men's souls,
Doing more murder in this loathsome world,
Than these poor compounds that thou mayst not sell.
I sell thee poison; thou hast sold me none.
Farewell. Buy food and get thyself in flesh.

[*APOTHECARY exits.*]

Come, cordial° and not poison, go with me
To Juliet's grave; for there must I use thee.

[*ROMEO exits.*]

85 **cordial** (kôr′ jəl): tonic, restoring drink.

SCENE 2. The same afternoon. FRIAR LAWRENCE's cell in Verona.

[*FRIAR JOHN enters. Sent by FRIAR LAWRENCE to Mantua with a letter for ROMEO, he has just returned.*]

JOHN. Holy Franciscan friar, brother, ho!

[*FRIAR LAWRENCE enters.*]

LAWRENCE. This same should be the voice of Friar John.
Welcome from Mantua. What says Romeo?
Or, if his mind be writ,° give me his letter.

JOHN. Going to find a barefoot brother° out,
One of our order, to associate° me
Here in this city visiting the sick,
And finding him, the searchers° of the town,
Suspecting that we both were in a house
Where the infectious pestilence° did reign,
Seal'd up the doors, and would not let us forth,
So that my speed to Mantua there was stay'd.°

LAWRENCE. Who bare° my letter, then, to Romeo?

JOHN. I could not send it—here it is again—
Nor get a messenger to bring it thee,
So fearful were they of infection.

LAWRENCE. Unhappy fortune! By my brotherhood,
The letter was not nice, but full of charge,°
Of dear import;° and the neglecting it

4 **if his mind be writ:** if his message is written.
5 **barefoot brother:** Franciscan friar.
6 **associate:** accompany.
8 **searchers:** health officials who searched houses for victims of the plague and quarantined, or isolated, them.
10 **infectious pestilence:** plague.
12 **stay'd:** stopped.
13 **bare:** bore; carried.
18 **not nice, but full of charge:** not trivial, but full of importance.
19 **dear import:** serious consequence.

Reading Strategy Making Inferences About Theme *Why did Romeo not receive Friar Lawrence's letter? What do these repeated misfortunes suggest about destiny or fate?* R

Teach

L3 Literary Element

Irony Ask students to explain the irony of Romeo's lines. *(To Romeo, the poison is like medicine that will cure his longing because it allows him to rejoin Juliet.)* Have students scan Act 2, Scene 3 (page 731, lines 23–24) to recall words that foreshadow this action. ("Within the infant rind of this weak flower / Poison hath residence and medicine power.") *(The point is that even a good thing taken to an extreme is harmful; here the extreme has become the only remedy for Romeo.)* OL

L4 Literary Element

Theme Once again, unforeseeable bad luck thwarts the lovers. Have students relate this incident to the prologue's statement about "star-cross'd" lovers bound for "misadventur'd piteous" ruin. *(They might have been reunited if the letter had arrived on time, but a chance incident prevents the letter from being delivered.)* OL

R Reading Strategy

Making Inferences About Theme **Answer:** *The courier was quarantined because of possible exposure to the plague. Romeo's repeated misfortunes suggest that a person's destiny is fixed.* OL

English Language Coach

Prefixes and Suffixes Write *unaccustomed, joyful, misadventure, discharged,* and *wretchedness* on the board. Explain that the underlined letters are prefixes and suffixes added to words to change their form and meaning. Help English language learners use dictionaries to analyze the affix meanings and how they alter the words to which they are added.

Have students list common suffixes and prefixes and their meanings in their vocabulary notebooks. Suggest that students scan the play for additional examples. EL

Academic Standards

Additional Support activities on pp. 792 and 793 cover the following standards:

Skills Practice: **9.2** Develop strategies such as...making predictions; and identifying...purpose...

English Language Coach: **9.1** [Use] word parts...to determine the meaning of words...

Teach

BI1 Big Idea

The Power of Love Answer: *The scene reveals Paris's love for Juliet.* **OL**

May do much danger. Friar John, go hence,
Get me an iron crow° and bring it straight
Unto my cell.

JOHN. Brother, I'll go and bring it thee.

[*FRIAR JOHN exits.*]

LAWRENCE. Now must I to the monument alone.
Within this three hours will fair Juliet wake.
She will beshrew° me much that Romeo
Hath had no notice of these accidents,°
But I will write again to Mantua,
And keep her at my cell till Romeo come—
Poor living corse, clos'd in a dead man's tomb!

[*He exits.*]

21 **crow:** crowbar.

25 **beshrew:** blame; scold.

26 **accidents:** occurrences.

SCENE 3. Late that night. The churchyard that contains the Capulets' tomb.

[*PARIS enters with his PAGE who carries a torch and flowers.*]

PARIS. Give me thy torch, boy. Hence, and stand aloof.
Yet put it out, for I would not be seen.
Under yond yew trees lay thee all along,°
Holding thy ear close to the hollow ground.
So shall no foot upon the churchyard tread
(Being loose, unfirm, with digging up of graves)
But thou shalt hear it. Whistle then to me,
As signal that thou hearest something approach.
Give me those flowers. Do as I bid thee, go.

PAGE. [*Aside.*] I am almost afraid to stand alone
Here in the churchyard; yet I will adventure.°

[*The PAGE retires to a watching place while PARIS sprinkles the tomb with flowers.*]

PARIS. Sweet flower, with flowers thy bridal bed I strew
(O woe! thy canopy is dust and stones)
Which with sweet° water nightly I will dew;°
Or, wanting that, with tears distill'd by moans.
The obsequies° that I for thee will keep
Nightly shall be to strew thy grave and weep.

[*The PAGE whistles, his signal that someone is coming.*]

The boy gives warning something doth approach.
What cursed foot wanders this way tonight
To cross° my obsequies and true love's rite?
What, with a torch? Muffle° me, night, awhile.

[*PARIS hides as ROMEO and BALTHASAR enter.*]

3 **lay thee all along:** lie flat on the ground.

11 **adventure:** risk it.

14 **sweet:** perfumed. **dew:** sprinkle.

16 **obsequies** (ob′ sə kwēz): funeral rites.

20 **cross:** interrupt.

21 **Muffle:** hide.

Big Idea The Power of Love *What does Shakespeare reveal about Paris in this scene?* **BI1**

Additional Support

Skills Practice

GRAMMAR: Pronouns Pronouns are used in place of nouns. Review the following:

Personal: singular—*I, me, you, he, him, she, her, it;* **plural**—*we, us, you, they, them*
Possessive: singular—*my, mine, your, yours, his, her, hers, its;* **plural**—*our, ours, your, yours, their, theirs*

Have students explain what Elizabethan pronouns replace *you* and *your* in Shakespeare's work. *(thee, thou, thy)* Have students scan Scene 3 to identify at least one example of each personal and possessive pronoun on the list and to name its antecedent. **OL**

ROMEO. Give me that mattock° and the wrenching iron.°
Hold, take this letter. Early in the morning
See thou deliver it to my lord and father.
Give me the light. Upon thy life I charge° thee,
Whate'er thou hearest or seest, stand all aloof
And do not interrupt me in my course.
Why I descend into this bed of death
Is partly to behold my lady's face,
But chiefly to take thence from her dead finger
A precious ring—a ring that I must use
In dear employment.° Therefore hence, be gone.
But if thou, jealous,° dost return to pry
In what I farther shall intend to do,
By heaven, I will tear thee joint by joint
And strew this hungry churchyard with thy limbs.
The time and my intents are savage-wild,
More fierce and more inexorable far°
Than empty° tigers or the roaring sea.

BALTHASAR. I will be gone, sir, and not trouble ye.

ROMEO. So shalt thou show me friendship. Take thou that.

[He hands BALTHASAR money.]

Live, and be prosperous; and farewell, good fellow.

BALTHASAR. [*Aside.*] For all this same, I'll hide me hereabout.
His looks I fear, and his intents I doubt.

[BALTHASAR hides.]

ROMEO. Thou detestable maw,° thou womb of death,
Gorg'd° with the dearest morsel of the earth,
Thus I enforce thy rotten jaws to open,
And in despite° I'll cram thee with more food.

[As ROMEO forces open the tomb, PARIS watches from his hiding place.]

PARIS. This is that banish'd **haughty** Montague
That murd'red my love's cousin—with which grief
It is supposed the fair creature died—
And here is come to do some villainous shame
To the dead bodies. I will apprehend° him.

[PARIS comes forward and speaks to ROMEO.]

22 **mattock** (mat′ək): pickaxe.
wrenching iron: crowbar.

25 **charge:** command.

32 **In dear employment:** for an important purpose.
33 **jealous:** suspicious.

38 **More . . . far:** far more fierce and determined.
39 **empty:** hungry.

45 **maw:** the mouth, jaws, or stomach of a flesh-eating animal.
46 **Gorg'd** (gôrjd): stuffed.

48 **in despite:** to spite you.

53 **apprehend:** arrest.

Big Idea The Power of Love *Why does Shakespeare put such harsh and angry words in Romeo's mouth?* **BI2**

Literary Element Tragedy *Shakespeare is bringing together characters who are in extreme emotional turmoil. What do you think will happen next?* **L**

Vocabulary

haughty (hô′ tē) *adj.* very proud and scornful of others

Teach

BI2 Big Idea

The Power of Love **Answer:** *The angry words suggest Romeo's grim determination to die.* **OL**

L Literary Element

Tragedy **Answer:** *Students may anticipate that something bad is about to happen.* **OL**

Differentiated Instruction

Improving Comprehension The final scene moves rapidly and involves a great deal of action. Students who process knowledge through body movement will grasp the significance of the actions more easily if they act them out. Have students visualize the movements of characters in each part of the scene. Invite volunteers to pantomime segments as other classmates summarize the action. **BL**

Academic Standards

Additional Support activities on pp. 794 and 795 cover the following standards:
Skills Practice: **9.6.2** Demonstrate an understanding of...proper English usage...
Differentiated Instruction: **9.7.6** Analyze the occasion...and choose effective... nonverbal techniques...for presentations.

Teach

R1 Reading Strategy

Making Inferences About Theme **Answer:** *Romeo has wearied of the pain and death caused by the feud.* OL

R2 Reading Strategy

Drawing Conclusions Using the following model, guide students to compare and contrast Romeo and Paris, noting how Romeo has grown as a character.

MODEL: Romeo and Paris are both young men of the same class and background who love Juliet. Romeo is the one whose love is returned. Juliet's love opens Romeo's heart, enabling him to look beyond the feud. Paris, however, remains stuck in the world of the feud and views Romeo only as his enemy. When they meet, only Paris wants vengeance. Paris lacks the deeper perspective on life that Romeo has gained through love. OL

★ Viewing the Art

Answer: *Juliet, although presumed dead, remains the only light of their lives. She is the central figure.*

Swiss-born Henry Fuseli (1741–1825), a leading painter of the Romantic Movement, emulated the grand style of Renaissance master Michelangelo. AS

Romeo Slaying Paris at the Bier of Juliet, 1809. Henry Fuseli. Folger Shakespeare Library, Washington, DC.

Viewing the Art: Why might only the figure of Juliet seem to radiate light? What does that tell you about Juliet's importance in this scene? 

Stop thy unhallowed° toil, vile Montague!
Can vengeance be pursued further than death?
Condemned villain, I do apprehend thee.
Obey, and go with me; for thou must die.

ROMEO. I must indeed; and therefore came I hither.
Good gentle youth, tempt not a desp'rate man.
Fly hence and leave me. Think upon these gone;
Let them affright thee. I beseech thee, youth,
Put not another sin upon my head
By urging me to fury. O, be gone!
By heaven, I love thee better than myself,
For I come hither arm'd against myself.
Stay not, be gone. Live, and hereafter say
A madman's mercy bid thee run away.

R2 PARIS. I do defy thy conjurations.°
And apprehend thee for a felon here.

ROMEO. Wilt thou provoke me? Then have at thee, boy!

[*They draw swords and fight.*]

PAGE. O Lord, they fight! I will go call the watch.

54 **unhallowed:** unholy.

68 **conjurations:** appeals.

Reading Strategy Making Inferences About Theme *Why is Romeo so reluctant to fight Paris?* R1

Additional Support

Skills Practice

WRITING: Descriptive Paragraph Invite students to recall a piece of vivid descriptive writing and describe the dominant mood it communicates. Encourage them to explain how the writer created this impression. *(Specific, concrete details that appeal to the senses)*

Provide these guidelines for writing descriptions:

- Decide what overall impression to create.
- List details that contribute to the impression.
- Organize details so that the eye moves logically over the scene or object. OL

[*The* PAGE *runs off to call the* WATCHMEN. PARIS *is wounded and falls.*]

PARIS. O, I am slain! If thou be merciful,
Open the tomb, lay me with Juliet.

[PARIS *dies.*]

ROMEO. In faith, I will. Let me peruse° this face.
Mercutio's kinsman, noble County Paris!
What said my man when my betossed° soul
Did not attend° him as we rode? I think
He told me Paris should have married Juliet.
Said he not so, or did I dream it so?
Or am I mad, hearing him talk of Juliet,
To think it was so? O, give me thy hand,
One writ with me in sour misfortune's book!
I'll bury thee in a triumphant grave.
A grave? O, no, a lanthorn,° slaught'red youth,
For here lies Juliet, and her beauty makes
This vault a feasting presence,° full of light.
Death, lie thou there, by a dead man interr'd.

[ROMEO *carries* PARIS *into the tomb and lays him there. Then he walks to* JULIET'S *body.*]

How oft when men are at the point of death
Have they been merry! Which their keepers call
A lightning before death.° O, how may I
Call this a lightning? O my love, my wife!
Death, that hath suck'd the honey of thy breath,
Hath had no power yet upon thy beauty.
Thou art not conquer'd. Beauty's ensign° yet
Is crimson in thy lips and in thy cheeks,
And death's pale flag is not advanced there.
Tybalt, liest thou there in thy bloody sheet?
O, what more favor can I do to thee
Than with that hand that cut thy youth in twain
To sunder his that was° thine enemy?
Forgive me, cousin! Ah, dear Juliet,
Why art thou yet so fair? Shall I believe
That unsubstantial° Death is amorous,°
And that the lean abhorred monster keeps
Thee here in dark to be his paramour?°
For fear of that I still will stay with thee
And never from his pallet° of dim night
Depart again. Here, here will I remain
With worms that are thy chambermaids. O, here
Will I set up my everlasting rest

74 **peruse** (pə ro͞oz′): examine.

76 **betossed:** upset.

77 **attend:** pay attention to.

84 **lanthorn** (lan′ tərn): a dome with windows that let sunlight into a church or palace.

86 **feasting presence:** a hall lit brightly for celebration.

90 **lightning before death:** a proverbial phrase based on the idea that people's spirits revive just before death.

94 **ensign** (en′ sīn): flag.

100 **sunder his that was:** cut off the youth of the man who was.

103 **unsubstantial:** without a body. **amorous:** in love.

105 **paramour** (par′ə moor′): mistress.

107 **pallet:** bed.

Literary Element Tragedy *How does Romeo's speech heighten the audience's sense of tragedy and of suspense?* **L**

Teach

L Literary Element

Tragedy Answer: *The suffering Romeo expresses as he mourns for Juliet and ponders suicide seems unbearably tragic because it rests on the mistaken idea that Juliet is dead. The audience is gripped by suspense because they know that all is lost unless Juliet awakens in time.* **OL**

Differentiated Instruction

Less Proficient Readers Writing about the text will reinforce students' reading skills, and it will enable you to monitor their comprehension. Have students review Act 5 and write down lines of dialogue that reveal joy, anger, fear, or despair. Tell them to identify the emotion each line expresses. **BL**

Academic Standards

Additional Support activities on pp. 796 and 797 cover the following standards:

Skills Practice: **9.5.3** Write expository compositions, including descriptive pieces...

Differentiated Instruction: **9.3.10** Identify and describe the function of dialogue...in dramatic literature.

Teach

★ Cultural Note

St. Francis Founder of the Franciscan Order of monks, St. Francis of Assisi (1181 or 1182–1226) is the Catholic patron saint of animals and the environment. St. Francis followed the Bible literally, doing as Jesus said and emulating Jesus as much as possible. St. Francis was canonized in 1228. **AS**

And shake the yoke of inauspicious stars°
From this world-wearied flesh. Eyes, look your last!
Arms, take your last embrace! And, lips, O you
The doors of breath, seal with a righteous kiss
A dateless° bargain to engrossing death!°
Come, bitter conduct; come, **unsavory** guide!
Thou desperate pilot, now at once run on
The dashing rocks thy seasick weary bark!°
Here's to my love!

[*He takes out the poison and drinks it.*]

O true apothecary!
Thy drugs are quick. Thus with a kiss I die.

[*ROMEO kisses JULIET and falls. Outside the tomb, FRIAR LAWRENCE enters the churchyard carrying a lantern, crowbar, and spade.*]

★ FRIAR. Saint Francis be my speed! How oft tonight
Have my old feet stumbled at graves! Who's there?

[*BALTHASAR steps out from his hiding place.*]

BALTHASAR. Here's one, a friend, and one that knows you well.

FRIAR. Bliss be upon you! Tell me, good my friend,
What torch is yond that vainly lends his light
To grubs° and eyeless skulls? As I discern,°
It burneth in the Capels' monument.

BALTHASAR. It doth so, holy sir; and there's my master,
One that you love.

FRIAR. Who is it?

BALTHASAR. Romeo.

FRIAR. How long hath he been there?

BALTHASAR. Full half an hour.

FRIAR. Go with me to the vault.

BALTHASAR. I dare not, sir.
My master knows not but I am gone hence,
And fearfully° did menace me with death
If I did stay to look on his intents.

FRIAR. Stay then; I'll go alone. Fear comes upon me.
O, much I fear some ill unthrifty° thing.

BALTHASAR. As I did sleep under this yew tree here,
I dreamt my master and another fought,
And that my master slew him.

111 **inauspicious** (in′ ôs pish′ əs) **stars:** ill fate.

115 **dateless:** eternal. **engrossing death:** death who buys up everything.

116–118 **Come . . . bark:** Romeo addresses the poison as a guide **(conduct)** who, like a navigator that runs a ship **(bark)** into the rocks, will lead him to destruction.

126 **grubs:** worms. **discern:** make out.

133 **fearfully:** fearsomely.

136 **unthrifty:** unfortunate.

Vocabulary

unsavory (un sā′ vər ē) *adj.* unpleasant in character; disagreeable to the taste

Additional Support

Skills Practice

LISTENING AND SPEAKING: Oral Reading Lines 74–119 convey Romeo's anguished struggle with guilt and despair. Play the audiotape of these lines, pausing to discuss how Romeo's tone of voice helps listeners understand his meaning. Have groups of four to six students take turns reading this speech aloud, using tone, pace, and expression to communicate their view of his state of mind. Ask students to evaluate one other's interpretations and summarize what they learned from them. **OL**

FRIAR. Romeo!
Alack, alack, what blood is this which stains
The stony entrance of this sepulcher?
What mean these masterless and gory swords
To lie discolor'd by this place of peace?

[*He enters the tomb.*]

Romeo! O, pale! Who else? What, Paris too?
And steep'd in blood? Ah, what an unkind hour
Is guilty of this lamentable chance!°
The lady stirs.

[*JULIET wakes.*]

JULIET. O comfortable friar! Where is my lord?
I do remember well where I should be,
And there I am. Where is my Romeo?

FRIAR. I hear some noise. Lady, come from that nest
Of death, contagion, and unnatural sleep.
A greater power than we can contradict
Hath thwarted our intents.° Come, come away.
Thy husband in thy bosom there lies dead;
And Paris too. Come, I'll dispose of thee
Among a sisterhood of holy nuns.
Stay not to question, for the watch is coming.
Come, go, good Juliet. I dare no longer stay.

JULIET. Go, get thee hence, for I will not away.

[*Hearing the approaching* WATCHMAN, FRIAR LAWRENCE *hurries off.*]

What's here? A cup, clos'd in my true love's hand?
Poison, I see, hath been his timeless° end.
O churl!° Drunk all, and left no friendly drop
To help me after? I will kiss thy lips.
Haply° some poison yet doth hang on them
To make me die with a restorative.°

[*She kisses* ROMEO'*s lips.*]

Thy lips are warm!

CHIEF WATCHMAN. [*He calls from off stage.*]
Lead, boy. Which way?

JULIET. Yea, noise? Then I'll be brief. O happy dagger!

[*She snatches* ROMEO'*s dagger.*]

This is thy sheath; there rust, and let me die.

146 **chance:** event.

154 **thwarted our intents:** ruined our plans.

162 **timeless:** untimely.

163 **churl:** miser.

165 **Haply:** perhaps.

166 **restorative:** a medicine or other substance that restores health or consciousness. (However, Juliet wants the kiss to restore her to Romeo by killing her.)

Reading Strategy Making Inferences About Theme *What power has thwarted Romeo and Juliet, in your opinion?* **R**

Teach

R Reading Strategy

Making Inferences About Theme Answer: *Students may put the blame on fate, the characters' own natures, the feud, or a combination of circumstances.* **OL**

Reading in the Real World

Citizenship Discuss Balthasar's dream of a fight between Romeo and Paris. Note that modern research indicates that external sounds are often incorporated into our dreams.

Ask: How might this fact explain Balthasar's dream? *(His sleeping mind may have heard the fight.)* Discuss the implications of this detail. Do students think it suggests that Shakespeare was keenly observant of how the dreaming mind functions? Have students research theories about dreaming and write a report on their findings. **OL**

Academic Standards

Additional Support activities on pp. 798 and 799 cover the following standards:

Skills Practice: **9.7** [Develop] speaking skills…in conjunction with…strategies…[for] delivery of oral presentations. **9.7.10** Assess how…delivery affects…the mood and tone…

Reading in the Real World: **9.5.9** Write…a research report that…demonstrates that information that has been gathered has been summarized…and that conclusions have been drawn from synthesizing information…

[T]each

Literary Element

[T]ragedy Answer: *Juliet is naïve and impulsive and subject to extremes of emotion.* **OL**

★ Viewing the Art

Answer: *She appears agitated and desperate as she reacts to both the discovery of her husband's corpse and the sounds of the approaching watchmen.*

This work by Joseph Wright (1734–1797) reflects the English Romantic painter's skill as a portraitist as well as his fascination with the effects of light and atmosphere. **AS**

Romeo and Juliet: The Tomb Scene, exhibited 1790. Joseph Wright of Derby. Oil on canvas, 177.8 x 241 cm. Derby Museum & Art Gallery, England.
Viewing the Art: How would you describe what Juliet is feeling at this moment? 

[She stabs herself, falls, and dies. PARIS' PAGE *enters the churchyard with a troop of* WATCHMEN.*]*

PAGE. This is the place. There, where the torch doth burn.

CHIEF WATCHMAN. The ground is bloody. Search about the churchyard.
Go, some of you; whoe'er you find attach.°

[Some of the WATCHMEN *exit to search the churchyard. The remainder of the* WATCHMEN, *with the* PAGE, *enter the tomb.]*

Pitiful sight! Here lies the County slain;
And Juliet bleeding, warm, and newly dead,
Who here hath lain this two days buried.
Go, tell the Prince; run to the Capulets;
Raise up the Montagues; some others search.

[Other WATCHMEN *exit.]*

We see the ground° whereon these woes do lie,
But the true ground of all these piteous woes
We cannot without circumstance descry.°

[Some WATCHMEN *return with* BALTHASAR.*]*

SECOND WATCHMAN. Here's Romeo's man. We found him in the churchyard.

173 **attach:** arrest.

179 **ground:** cause.

181 **without circumstance descry** (di skrī'): understand without more information.

Literary Element Tragedy *What common human traits and weaknesses are displayed by Juliet?* **L**

Additional Support

Skills Practice

GRAMMAR: Subject-Verb Agreement Stress that subjects and verbs must agree in number. Discuss how to determine agreement in verb phrases such as the ones below.

1. Her body sleeps in Capel's monument, and her immortal part with angels (live, *lives*).
2. My poverty but not my will (*consents,* consent).
3. A greater power than we can contradict (*has,* have) thwarted our intents. **OL**

CHIEF WATCHMAN. Hold him in safety till the Prince come hither.

[*Another* WATCHMAN *returns with* FRIAR LAWRENCE.]

THIRD WATCHMAN. Here is a friar that trembles, sighs, and weeps.
We took this mattock and this spade from him
As he was coming from this churchyard's side.

CHIEF WATCHMAN. A great suspicion! Stay the friar too.

[PRINCE ESCALUS *enters with his* ATTENDANTS.]

PRINCE. What misadventure is so early up,
That calls our person from our morning rest?

[LORD CAPULET *and* LADY CAPULET *enter with others.*]

CAPULET. What should it be, that is so shriek'd abroad?

LADY CAPULET. O, the people in the street cry "Romeo,"
Some "Juliet," and some "Paris"; and all run
With open outcry toward our monument.

PRINCE. What fear is this which startles in your ears?

CHIEF WATCHMAN. Sovereign,

[*He calls them to the entrance of the tomb.*]

here lies the County Paris slain;
And Romeo dead; and Juliet, dead before,
Warm and new kill'd.

PRINCE. Search, seek, and know how this foul murder comes.

CHIEF WATCHMAN. Here is a friar, and slaughter'd Romeo's man,
With instruments upon them fit to open
These dead men's tombs.

CAPULET. O heavens! O wife, look how our daughter bleeds!
This dagger hath mista'en,° for, lo, his house°
Is empty on the back of Montague,
And it missheathed in my daughter's bosom!

LADY CAPULET. O me, this sight of death is as a bell
That warns° my old age to a sepulcher.

[LORD MONTAGUE *enters with others. The* PRINCE *calls them to the entrance of the tomb.*]

PRINCE. Come, Montague; for thou art early up
To see thy son and heir now early down.

MONTAGUE. Alas, my liege,° my wife is dead tonight!
Grief of my son's exile hath stopp'd her breath.
What further woe conspires against mine age?

203 **mista'en:** missed its proper target. **his house:** its sheath.

207 **warns:** summons; calls.

210 **liege** (lēj): lord.

Reading Strategy Making Inferences About Theme *Lady Capulet predicts her coming death. How are this prediction and the murders and suicides in this scene related to the feud?* **R**

Teach

R Reading Strategy

Making Inferences About Theme **Answer:** *The feud is the original source of all the misfortunes and misunderstandings that ultimately lead to these deaths.* **OL**

Differentiated Instruction

Mapping Information Note that a play's action builds to a climax and must then be resolved. Thus, the surviving characters must discover and respond to the climactic events and grasp whatever truth can be learned from the tragedy. Have students create a graphic organizer to map the events that resolve the action. They should include the following:

- Who provides what information to the Prince
- Which characters have died and why
- How the survivors react **BL**

Academic Standards

Additional Support activities on pp. 800 and 801 cover the following standards:

Skills Practice: **9.6.2** Demonstrate an understanding of sentence construction… and proper English usage…

Differentiated Instruction: **9.3** [Identify] story elements such as…plot…

ach

Literary Element

agedy Answer: *The Prince's remark suggests that Montague has been blind to the consequences of the feud. He wants Montague to open his eyes to the high price of hatred and violence.* **OL**

R Reading Strategy

Evaluating Ask: Why might Shakespeare have inserted this summary even though the audience already knows this information? *(The passage serves to inform the remaining characters and also to provide the vehicle for their remorse and reconciliation.)* Have students note how economically the lines summarize the complex plot. **OL**

★ Cultural Note

Herbal Medicine
Historically, the science and art of herbal medicine was often the province of monks. In Europe, writings about herbs by Catholic monks date to the eighth century. Monks tended to be well educated and were able to translate older herbal texts from Latin and Greek and then to build on that knowledge. **AS**

PRINCE. Look, and thou shalt see.

MONTAGUE. O thou untaught!° What manners is in this,
To press before thy father to a grave?

PRINCE. Seal up the mouth of outrage° for a while,
Till we can clear these ambiguities°
And know their spring,° their head, their true descent;
And then will I be general of your woes°
And lead you even to death. Meantime forbear,
And let mischance be slave to patience.°
Bring forth the parties of suspicion.

FRIAR. I am the greatest,° able to do least,
Yet most suspected, as the time and place
Doth make against me, of this direful murder;
And here I stand, both to impeach and purge°
Myself condemned and myself excus'd.

PRINCE. Then say at once what thou dost know in this.

FRIAR. I will be brief, for my short date of breath°
Is not so long as is a **tedious** tale.
Romeo, there dead, was husband to that Juliet;
And she, there dead, that's Romeo's faithful wife.
I married them; and their stol'n marriage day
Was Tybalt's doomsday, whose untimely death
Banish'd the new-made bridegroom from this city;
For whom, and not for Tybalt, Juliet pin'd.
You, to remove that siege of grief from her,
Betroth'd and would have married her perforce°
To County Paris. Then comes she to me
And with wild looks bid me devise some mean
To rid her from this second marriage,
Or in my cell there would she kill herself.
Then gave I her (so tutor'd by my art)°
A sleeping potion; which so took effect
As I intended, for it wrought on her
The form of death. Meantime I writ to Romeo
That he should hither come as this° dire night
To help to take her from her borrowed° grave,
Being the time the potion's force should cease.
But he which bore my letter, Friar John,
Was stayed by accident,° and yesternight
Return'd my letter back. Then all alone

214 **untaught:** one who is unschooled in manners.

216 **Seal up the mouth of outrage:** hold off your emotional outcry.

217 **ambiguities:** mysteries.

218 **spring:** source.

219 **general of your woes:** chief mourner.

221 **let mischance be slave to patience:** let your response to misfortune be governed by restraint.

223 **greatest:** most suspect.

226 **impeach and purge:** blame and clear from blame.

229 **date of breath:** time I have left to live.

238 **perforce:** forcibly.

243 **so tutor'd by my art:** which I learned to do from my studies.

247 **as this:** this.

248 **borrowed:** temporary.

251 **stayed by accident:** prevented from going by circumstances.

Literary Element Tragedy *Why does the Prince say this? What might he be helping Montague to understand?* **L1**

Vocabulary

tedious (tē′ dē əs) *adj.* tiresome; boring

Additional Support

Skills Practice

RESEARCH: Critical Perspectives
Note that the meaning of *Romeo and Juliet* has been debated for more than 400 years.
Ask: What main ideas can you identify in this play? List students' responses on the board. Have students look in a library or on the Internet for critical essays about *Romeo and Juliet.* Tell them to write an essay comparing their own view of the play's main ideas with one or more of these critical perspectives. **OL**

R

At the prefixed hour of her waking
Came I to take her from her kindred's vault;
Meaning to keep her closely° at my cell
Till I conveniently could send to Romeo.
But when I came, some minute ere the time
Of her awakening, here untimely lay
The noble Paris and true Romeo dead.
She wakes; and I entreated her come forth
And bear this work of heaven with patience;
But then a noise did scare me from the tomb,
And she, too desperate, would not go with me,
But, as it seems, did violence on herself.
All this I know, and to the marriage
Her nurse is privy;° and if aught in this
Miscarried by my fault, let my old life
Be sacrific'd some hour before his time
Unto the rigor of severest law.

PRINCE. We still° have known thee for a holy man.
Where's Romeo's man? What can he say to this?

BALTHASAR. I brought my master news of Juliet's death;
And then in post he came from Mantua
To this same place, to this same monument.
This letter he early bid me give his father,
And threat'ned me with death, going in the vault,
If I departed not and left him there.

PRINCE. Give me the letter. I will look on it.

[*BALTHASAR hands the letter to the PRINCE.*]

Where is the County's page that rais'd the watch?
Sirrah, what made your master in this place?°

PAGE. He came with flowers to strew his lady's grave;
And bid me stand aloof, and so I did.
Anon° comes one with light to ope the tomb;
And by and by my master drew on him;
And then I ran away to call the watch.

PRINCE. [*He is reading ROMEO's letter.*] This letter doth make
good the friar's words,
Their course of love, the tidings of her death;
And here he writes that he did buy a poison
Of a poor pothecary and therewithal°
Came to this vault to die and lie with Juliet.
Where be these enemies? Capulet, Montague,
See what a scourge is laid upon your hate,

255 **closely:** secretly.

266 **is privy:** shares the secret.

270 **still:** always.

280 **what . . . place:** What was your master doing here?

283 **Anon:** shortly.

289 **therewithal:** with this.

Literary Element Tragedy *In your opinion, how much blame does Friar Lawrence deserve for the deaths of Romeo and Juliet?* **L2**

Teach

L2 Literary Element

Tragedy Answer: *Some students may argue that he has been a loyal and resourceful friend to the young lovers. Others may point out that he has been reckless and weak when put to the test.* **OL**

Differentiated Instruction

Less Proficient Readers Students with special needs may need help tying the play's many plot strands together. Read aloud lines 229–269, pausing every few lines to have students pinpoint the act and scene in which each event took place. Have groups of students collaborate on one of the following projects:

- Captioned illustrations of the play's highlights
- A multimedia presentation on the play's themes **BL**

Academic Standards

Additional Support activities on pp. 802 and 803 cover the following standards:

Skills Practice: **9.5.3** Write expository compositions, including analytical essays... that make distinctions between the relative value and significance of...ideas...

Differentiated Instruction: **9.3** [Identify] story elements such as...theme, plot...

ach

Literary Element

Tragedy Answer: *He regrets not dealing more severely with the warring families. If he had taken stronger measures, Romeo and Juliet might still be alive.* **OL**

R Reading Strategy

Making Inferences About Theme Answer: *Violence and hatred don't pay off for anybody. A person who acts violently winds up experiencing violence.* **OL**

★ Viewing the Art

Answer: *He is probably overcome with remorse and regret that his plan has ended in tragedy. Students may imagine similar feelings.*

Frederick Leighton (1830–1896) tended to lose the freshness of his sketches and studies in the elaboration of the finished piece. **AS**

The Reconciliation of the Montagues and Capulets Over the Dead Bodies of Romeo and Juliet, 1853–1855. Frederick Leighton. Oil on canvas, 70 x 91 in. Agnes Scott College, Decatur, GA.

Viewing the Art: What do you suppose the Friar is thinking? What would you be thinking? 

That heaven finds means to kill your joys with love.
And I, for winking at your discords too,
Have lost a brace of kinsmen.° All are punish'd.

CAPULET. O brother Montague, give me thy hand.
This is my daughter's jointure,° for no more
Can I demand.

MONTAGUE. But I can give thee more;
For I will raise her statue in pure gold,
That whiles Verona by that name is known,
There shall no figure at such rate° be set
As that of true and faithful Juliet.

CAPULET. As rich shall Romeo's by his lady's lie—
Poor sacrifices of our enmity!

PRINCE. A glooming° peace this morning with it brings.
The sun for sorrow will not show his head.
Go hence, to have more talk of these sad things;
Some shall be pardon'd, and some punished;
For never was a story of more woe
Than this of Juliet and her Romeo.

[*Everyone exits.*]

295 **brace of kinsmen:** pair of relatives (Mercutio and Paris).

297 **jointure** (join′ chər): marriage settlement.

301 **rate:** value.

305 **glooming:** cloudy; gloomy.

Literary Element Tragedy *What does the Prince mean when he tells Capulet and Montague, "See what a scourge is laid upon your hate"? Why does the Prince regret "winking" at their discords?* **L**

Reading Strategy Making Inferences About Theme *What did Capulet and Montague learn from their childrens' deaths?* **R**

Additional Support

Academic Standards

The Additional Support activity on p. 804 covers the following standard:

Skills Practice: **9.6.2** Demonstrate an understanding of…proper English usage…

Skills Practice

GRAMMAR: Indefinite Pronouns

Explain that indefinite pronouns such as *one* and *all* refer to people or things in a general way. Ask students to make a list of other indefinite pronouns.

Activity Have students find examples of indefinite pronouns in the play, referring as necessary to the list they made. **OL**

RESPONDING AND THINKING CRITICALLY

Respond

1. What was your reaction to the end of the play?

Recall and Interpret

2. (a)While in Mantua, what news does Romeo hear about Juliet? (b)What plan does Romeo make when he hears the news? (c)Why does he choose such a drastic course of action?
3. (a)What prevents Romeo from finding out the truth about Juliet? (b)What happens when he arrives at the Capulet's tomb?
4. (a)As a result of events at the tomb, what do Capulet, Montague, and the Prince say they will do? (b)What is the mood, or feeling of the scene, in lines 229–310? Explain.

Analyze and Evaluate

5. The Prince said that if Romeo returned to Verona, he would be punished by death. When Paris tries to apprehend Romeo at the tomb, why does Romeo refuse to surrender to Paris and accept his punishment? Explain.
6. (a)How can the causes of the deaths of Romeo and Juliet be traced back to the feud between their families? (b)How does Romeo and Juliet's need for secrecy shape the action of the play?

Connect

7. **Big Idea** **The Power of Love** What proves to be the real power of love in this play? Do the deaths of Romeo and Juliet prove or disprove that love is powerful? Explain.

DAILY LIFE AND CULTURE

The Two Worlds of the Renaissance

What was life like in Verona in the 1300s, when the Italian Renaissance was at its height? For some, it was a time and place of luxury. Paintings from the period show beautifully clothed men and women in grand palaces. For the noble and the very wealthy, life sometimes resembled these images. The ruling families of Italian city-states could afford expensive decorations and many servants.

But just outside the doors of the nobility was a world of poverty. Cities were disorganized, dirty, and densely crowded. People and animals jostled for space on narrow, unpaved roads. Open ditches reeked with the smell of garbage. A poor family typically slept in one room. At a time when half the population did not live to the age of thirty, there were few gray hairs among the poor.

1. (a)What evidence do you see in the play of the poverty suffered by many in Italy in the 1300s? (b)What examples do you see of the great wealth of the Italian nobility?
2. (a)What insights do you gain about the lives of servants through this play? (b)Do you think Shakespeare portrayed servants and other commoners sympathetically? Explain.

The Benevolence of St. Elizabeth, 1529. Nikolaus Glockendon. Painting. Collection of Kassel, Murhard'sche und landesbibliothek.

Daily Life and Culture

1. (a) Mention of the plague; the poverty of the apothecary (b) The families have servants and hold lavish celebrations.
2. (a) The servants' lives are controlled by their masters; their masters' interests and loyalties dictate their own. (b) Accept reasonable answers.

AFTER YOU READ

Assess

1. Students should explain their reactions.
2. (a) Juliet is dead. (b) He buys poison to commit suicide. (c) He can't bear living without her.
3. (a) The Friar's courier is delayed, and Romeo never learns that Juliet is alive. (b) Romeo kills Paris, takes the poison, and dies just before Friar Lawrence appears. Juliet awakens and refuses to leave with the Friar. She stabs herself with Romeo's knife as watchmen approach.
4. (a) They will make peace and erect statues to the lovers. (b) The sorrowful mood is balanced by a sense of harmony and resolution.
5. He wants to control his own destiny; he can't wait to join Juliet.
6. (a) If there had been no feud, all of the complications and misunderstandings that led to their deaths would've been avoided. They would not have had to scheme to be together. (b) It leads to fatal misunderstandings; the characters act on the basis of wrong or incomplete information.
7. Students should explain their answers.

CheckPoint

Use the CheckPoint questions on Presentation Plus! to check students' mastery of the selection. These questions can be used with interactive response keypads for immediate student feedback.

AFTER YOU READ

Assess

Literary Element

1. Romeo and Juliet share the tragic flaw of allowing themselves to be ruled by passion and despair, which causes them both to act impetuously. The uncompromising quality of their love is itself a tragic flaw—it results in their suicides.
2. They are doomed by a combination of bad luck, social and family circumstances, and their own youthful impetuousness and passion.

Review: Style

Make sure students' webs contain examples of figurative language, imagery, sound devices, and wordplay.

Reading Strategy

1. Love is a powerful force that can make people act without reason or fear.
2. Examples: Romeo and Juliet show courage in defying the feud and engaging in a risky plot to be together. At the same time their passion causes them to act rashly and results in a double suicide. Shakespeare seems to emphasize that the power of love can be as dark and deadly as it is beautiful and redemptive.

LITERARY ANALYSIS

Literary Element Tragedy

A **tragedy** is a drama that ends in the downfall of a main character. The main character, or tragic hero, who suffers this fate is usually a high-ranking or respected person whose personality is marred by a fatal weakness or tragic flaw. Fate or bad luck may work against this tragic hero, but usually his or her downfall is also brought about by an error or character flaw. Even if flawed, most tragic heroes are admirable individuals, and the audience regrets their loss.

1. Does Romeo have a tragic flaw? Does Juliet? If so, what are they?
2. Do you think that Romeo and Juliet are destroyed by fate, by their own character flaws, by the flaws of others, or by a combination of factors? Explain your answer.

Review: Style

As you learned on page 270, **style** is the distinctive way in which an author uses language. Elements that are important to Shakespeare's style include:

- **figurative language,** descriptive language used to imply ideas, including metaphor, simile, and personification.
- **imagery,** "word pictures" that appeal to the five senses.
- **sound devices,** elements that appeal to the ear, enhance rhythm, and create a musical quality.
- **wordplay,** puns or other instances of language that rely on double meanings.

Group Activity In a small group choose a favorite scene or passage from the play and discuss how Shakespeare uses the elements listed above. Create a web diagram like the one below to record examples of Shakespeare's style that you find striking.

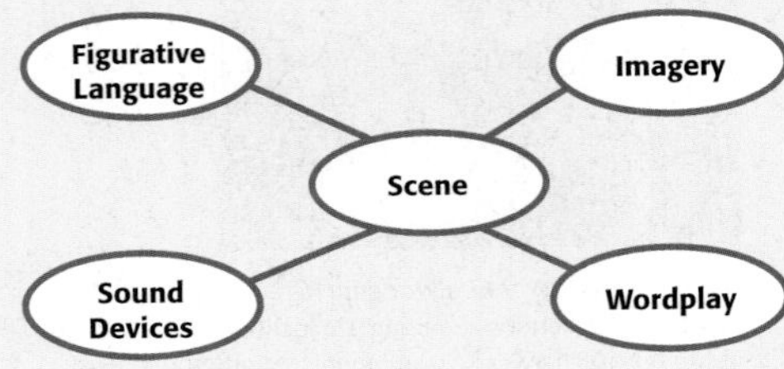

READING AND VOCABULARY

Reading Strategy Making Inferences About Theme

The **theme** of a work is its central message or insight about life. A work may have more than one theme. Consider the plot, characters, and dialogue of *Romeo and Juliet.* What insight do they express about family, society, or human nature?

1. How would you state one important theme of *Romeo and Juliet?*
2. To support your theme, list three important details from the play and the inferences about theme that you drew from them.

Vocabulary Practice

Practice with Word Parts Use your knowledge of prefixes, suffixes, and root words to choose the best definition for each boldfaced word.

1. Missing the tour bus was a **misadventure.**
   a. great adventure
   b. bad happening
   c. omen
2. His attempts to cheat me were **unsavory.**
   a. distasteful
   b. obvious
   c. unsuccessful
3. Romeo came from a **prosperous** family.
   a. famous
   b. rigid
   c. wealthy

Academic Vocabulary

Here are two words from the vocabulary list on page R80.

valid (val′ id) *adj.* based on reliable facts or evidence

restrict (ri strikt′) *v.* to keep within limits

Practice and Apply

1. In your opinion, is it **valid** to argue that Romeo's love for Rosaline equals his love for Juliet? Explain.
2. How does Capulet attempt to **restrict** Juliet's freedom?

Vocabulary

1. b **2.** a **3.** c

Academic Vocabulary

1. This is not a sound argument, given that Romeo forgets Rosaline in an instant and ultimately dies for love of Juliet.
2. He limited her freedom by insisting she marry Paris.

WRITING AND EXTENDING

Writing About Literature

Evaluate Author's Craft Comic relief occurs when a short, funny episode interrupts an otherwise serious or tragic work. Such an episode can serve a variety of functions. For example, it may break the tension after a particularly intense scene, it may provide a bitterly humorous twist on the work's theme, or it may emphasize an unfolding tragedy. Write a brief essay in which you evaluate, or judge, Shakespeare's use of comic relief, irony, and wordplay in *Romeo and Juliet.* Which episodes and characters provide comic relief? Is the comic relief effective? Which puns did you find especially humorous?

After you complete your draft, meet with a partner to evaluate each other's work and to suggest revisions. Then proofread and edit your draft to correct errors in spelling, grammar, and punctuation.

Performing

Reader's Theater In reader's theater, actors read their lines from a script instead of speaking them from memory. They use their voices and facial expressions to convey emotion. With a small group, choose a scene from *Romeo and Juliet* and prepare a reader's theater performance of it. Decide who will play what role, and rehearse the scene, referring to the tips below. Then perform your scene for the class.

- Read the script silently several times. Take note of how the characters relate to one another.
- Read your lines aloud, making sure you understand—and can pronounce—each word.
- Use the tone and pitch of your voice to express what your character feels.
- Decide whether to stand or sit during your performance.

GRAMMAR AND STYLE

Shakespeare's Language and Style

Using Apostrophes Apostrophes turn nouns into possessives (as in *the nobleman's daughter* and *the servants' quarters*). They also mark omitted letters in contractions (as in *he won't forgive me*). Shakespeare uses apostrophes throughout *Romeo and Juliet.* For instance, in the play's opening scene, Capulet's servant Sampson says, "I will take the wall of any man or maid of Montague's." After the deaths of Romeo and Juliet, Friar Lawrence explains to the Prince, ". . . their stol'n marriage day / Was Tybalt's doomsday. . . ." And the Prince, speaking of the catastrophe that has befallen the Montagues and Capulets, says, "All are punish'd."

Examples of Proper Use of Apostrophes

no one's business
the child's toy
Peru's mountains
The duchess's problem
The teachers' cafeteria
The children's surprise
My father and mother's house
Julio's and Betty's test scores
Two hours' drive
I'd, can't

Activity Read the first two pages of Act 1, Scene 1, and list the other words with apostrophes. For each word, tell whether it is a contraction or a possessive.

Revising Check

Apostrophes In writing, a misplaced or missing apostrophe stands out. Always review your writing to make sure your use of apostrophes is correct. Review your essay evaluating Shakespeare's use of comic relief in *Romeo and Juliet.* Check to make sure you have used apostrophes correctly.

LiteratureOnline Web Activities For eFlashcards, Selection Quick Checks, and other Web activities, go to www.glencoe.com.

AFTER YOU READ

Assess

Writing About Literature

Remind students to include examples of comic elements from the text in their essays.

Performing

Make sure students do the following as they read their scenes:

- speak slowly and clearly
- use tone and pitch to suggest characters' feelings
- use facial expressions and gestures that convey characters' emotions

Shakespeare's Language and Style

star-cross'd (contraction); misadventur'd (contraction); death-mark'd (contraction); parents' (possessive); children's (possessive); hours' (possessive); we'll (contraction); mov'd (contraction); run'st (contraction); Montague's (possessive); 'Tis (contraction)

LiteratureOnline

Web Activities Have students access the Web site for interactive activities that will help them assess their understanding of the selection.

ational Text

ocus

Summary

This article describes the construction of a replica of Shakespeare's Globe Theatre in London, England. The new theater stages the plays to resemble the productions of the original 1599 playhouse.

Teach

R Reading Strategy

Identifying Sequence Note that a sequence of information should be logical. Three common forms of sequencing are chronological order, spatial order, and order of importance. OL

Readability Scores

Dale-Chall: 8.7
DRP: 64
Lexile: 1170

Informational Text

Media Link to William Shakespeare

Preview the Article

In "A Long-Overdue Encore," Barry Hillenbrand tells the story of the Globe Theatre in London, England.

1. Skim the first three paragraphs. What part of the Globe Theatre's history do you think this article focuses on?
2. Scan the article's subheadings. What topics do you think this article will discuss?

Set a Purpose for Reading

Read to learn about the history of the Globe Theatre in London and its audiences.

Reading Strategy

Identifying Sequence

R Identifying sequence involves recognizing the order in which thoughts are arranged. Identifying sequence will help you remember ideas better. As you read "A Long-Overdue Encore," take notes on the sequence of events. Use a graphic organizer like the one below.

ACADEMIC STANDARDS (pages 808–811)

9.2.1 Analyze the...format of... documents, including...headers...

9.2.6 Critique the logic of functional documents...by examining the sequence of information...

9.2.7 Evaluate...the way in which the author's intent affects the structure...

TIME

A LONG-OVERDUE ENCORE

In a reproduction of the theater where Shakespeare's plays were first performed, actors put on shows the way they were done in the Bard's day.

By BARRY HILLENBRAND

THE OPENING LINES OF WILLIAM SHAKESPEARE'S *HENRY V* have a seductive charm. Using the humble voice of the narrator, the playwright asks the audience to suspend disbelief. It is a bit much to ask, he admits, but might the audience transform "this unworthy scaffold" of the stage into the "vasty fields of France? Or may we cram / Within this wooden O the very casques / That did affright the air at Agincourt?" For nearly four centuries, audiences have readily joined in this theatrical pretense. After all, who can refuse the Bard a favor?

When those famous lines were spoken at the opening of a contemporary London production of *Henry V,* they were more irresistible—and relevant—than ever before. For they were delivered from the stage of Shakespeare's Globe Theatre, a remarkably faithful reconstruction of Shakespeare's original "wooden *O.*" The first Globe, which Shakespeare called a "wooden *O*" because it was an open-air, round building, was built in 1599. Shakespeare worked there for many years, and wrote many of his greatest plays for its company of actors. In 1613, a cannon used in a production of *Henry VIII* set the thatched roof on fire, and the theater burned to the ground. A new playhouse was built on the original foundation and continued to operate until 1642, when the Puritans closed down all theaters. Two years later, the Globe was torn down, and more than 350 years passed before the new Globe opened its doors in 1997.

Located on the south bank of the River Thames and only a stone's throw from where the original once stood, the new Globe Theatre is an accurate replica of Shakespeare's playhouse. The structure has a brick foundation and oak beams, and its roof is open to the sky in the center, letting in sunshine or rain just as the original Globe did. But the new Globe is more

Additional Support

See also Active Learning and Note Taking Guide, pp. 131–136.

Skills Practice

READING: Previewing and Outlining Have students preview the text by reading the title and introductory notes and scanning for headings, pictures, marked text, and quotations. Students should then write a skeleton outline:

I. Historical Overview
II. To Build or Not to Build
III. Close to the Action

As students read, they should add major details under each heading. OL

Richard Kalina

THE PLAY'S THE THING
A group of students at the Globe.

than the ultimate theme park for Shakespeare fanatics: It is also the arena for a fresh and fascinating style of Shakespearean performances.

To Build or Not To Build

Much to the dismay of some tradition-minded British theater fans, the new Globe owes its existence to a U.S. actor named ★ Sam Wanamaker, who came to England in 1949 to shoot a movie. During his stay, he learned that a government committee led by U.S. Senator Joseph McCarthy was investigating him for his leftist political views. Like many others in the movie industry, Wanamaker was blacklisted. No longer able to work in Hollywood, he decided to pursue a stage career in England. It would be years before his film career took off again. **BI**

When Wanamaker first arrived in London, he searched for the site of Shakespeare's playhouse. He was shocked to discover that the only acknowledgment of the original Globe was a plaque attached to the front of a brewery. In 1970, he began a long and difficult campaign to build a modern version of the theater. There were many ups and downs along the way, and sometimes it seemed as if the new Globe would never get built. But Wanamaker was a determined man, and by 1993, after 23 years of fund-raising, he had squeezed enough money ($20.5 million) from corporations and individual donors to start construction. First, however, he and his building team had to struggle to come up with the right design.

Few details about the original theater had survived, but the team found designs for two other theaters, the Rose and the Fortune, that had stood near the old Globe. Since both theaters were built by the same master carpenter who constructed the Globe, the building team relied on those designs to guide them. But many of the most basic questions remained unanswered. For example, no one could agree on how many sides the polygon structure should have. In 1992, a group

Informational Text
TIME

Teach

BI Big Idea

The Power of Love **Ask:** What might have motivated Sam Wanamaker to spend more than twenty years on this project? *(His love of theater and history)* **OL**

★ Cultural Note

Sam Wanamaker
Wanamaker's parents came to the United States in 1905 from Russia. His early encounters with anti-Semitic persecution prompted him to consider a career as a boxer, but he settled instead on law and later went on to pursue his true passion, acting, at Chicago's Goodman Theatre School. His distinguished career has also included television and movie acting. **AS**

English Language Coach

Breaking Down the Article Help English language learners understand the features of the magazine article. Note that the headings break the article into smaller sections, making text easier to navigate. Have students read the headings and first sentence in each section. Then, have them predict the section's topic. Read the article aloud, pausing after each section to check students' predictions. **EL**

Academic Standards

Additional Support activities on pp. 808 and 809 cover the following standards:

Skills Practice: **9.2** Develop [reading] strategies…

English Language Coach: **9.2.1** Analyze the structure and format of…documents, including the…headers, and explain how authors use the features to achieve their purposes.

…each

BI **Big Idea**

The Power of Love **Ask:** Why do you think Shakespeare's works have stood the test of time? *(Students may note his eloquent language and his timeless, powerful themes.)* Is it possible for people to love something like the Globe Theatre? *(Students may say that if someone's time, energy, and life are put into a place, they may grow to love it. Others may say that most people do not love something inanimate such as a building.)* **OL**

★ Cultural History

Today's Globe Since the Globe Theatre is open air, plays are performed there only from May to September. The theater also stages modern dramas and works by other Elizabethan playwrights. **AS**

of experts met to settle the controversy. The scholars voted—14 to 6—for 20 sides.

Workmen used traditional building methods and materials. "I am proud that the general way we constructed the whole structure is entirely consistent with the practices of 1595," says Peter McCurdy, the meticulous master carpenter who directed the construction project. Still, some compromises had to be made. For example, goat hair had to be used to give body to the plaster because no cow hair of the proper—and authentic—length could be found.

FOUNDER Wanamaker, who died in 1993, views a design model in 1986.

Kaveh Golestan

Close to the Action **BI**

Wanamaker died in 1993, too soon to see the completion of his grand project. He would not have been surprised that the Globe's productions reveal a style of Shakespearean performances different from what is offered in the darkened theaters of the modern world. For one thing, performances take place during the day, in natural light. Sometimes women's roles are played by men, as they were in Shakespeare's day. And because the 900 seats curve around the stage in tiered galleries, everyone in the audience sees the action from a different angle. Some views are blocked by pillars, but the sense of intimacy makes up for any obstructions. No audience member is farther than 50 feet from the stage. In fact, some of the hundreds of people who stand in the central yard, where the "groundlings" stood in Shakespeare's day, even rest their arms on the edge of the stage. They may have to stand, but many of these modern-day groundlings say they have the best "seats" in the house. They're close to the stage, and the atmosphere in the yard is casual and fun.

"I was so close I felt I was part of the action," says Katie Marshall, a U.S. college student who stood during a performance of *The Winter's Tale.* As in Elizabethan times, audience members tend to be vocal, and some even join in the proceedings. Mentions of the French are often hissed,

Additional Support

Skills Practice

READING: Recognizing Sequence Explain the three major types of sequential order: chronological, or time, order; spatial order, or describing an object by moving from one detail to the next; and order of importance, or arranging details from most important to least or vice versa. Ask which type of order is used in this article. **OL**

The Granger Collection

Drawing of William Shakespeare

and when a French officer in *Henry V* proclaimed that "England shall couch down in fear and yield," an English patriot in the audience shouted back, "Never!"

Still, performances of Shakespeare's plays at the Globe are not for everyone. Purists are annoyed by the distractions during performances: small children who sometimes roam around in the central yard, vendors who circulate selling drinks and sandwiches, and elderly tourists defeated by the hard seats who flee in the middle of an act. "This is nothing like the film [starring Kenneth Branagh]," complained a disappointed woman from New York City after viewing a performance of *Henry V.* But that, of course, is exactly the point. Seeing Shakespeare's works at the Globe is not like seeing them anywhere else in the world.

—Updated 2005, from TIME, June 23, 1997

RESPONDING AND THINKING CRITICALLY

Respond

1. Would you like to visit the Globe Theatre? Why or why not?

Recall and Interpret

2. (a)What is the purpose of the opening lines of *Henry V*? (b)Why do you think Shakespeare used this device?
3. (a)What makes the performances in the modern Globe Theatre similar to those in Shakespeare's day? (b)Do you think the Globe audiences are disrespectful to the actors on stage? Why or why not?
4. (a)How is the Globe Theatre shaped? (b)How does this affect the audience's experience of a play?

Analyze and Evaluate

5. Consider the article's organization. What details does the writer use to maintain the reader's interest?
6. (a)What is Hillenbrand's opinion of his subject? (b)How does his opinion influence his tone?
7. Is this article an example of an informative essay or a persuasive essay? Explain.

Connect

8. Recall the ball scene from *Romeo and Juliet,* Act 1, Scene 5. How would you stage this scene at the Globe Theatre?

Informational Text
TIME

Assess

1. Students should explain their answers.
2. (a) The purpose is to tell the audience that an imaginative work is going to take place. (b) Shakespeare used this device to suggest how the audience should view the play.
3. (a) Performances take place in the daytime; some audience members stand near the stage; male actors sometimes play female roles; there are vendors; the audience tends to be boisterous. (b) Students should explain their answers. Some may feel that the theater encourages boisterous behavior. Others may feel that audiences should always be quiet when watching a theatrical performance.
4. (a) The theater is a polygon with 20 sides. (b) Everyone sees the show from a different angle; pillars sometimes block the view.
5. Hillenbrand begins with a comment on *Henry V.* He then tells an anecdote about a cannon destroying the original theater and the story of Wanamaker's blacklisting. To maintain interest, he mentions the plaque on the brewery where the original theater stood, describes details about the workmanship, and includes quotes from audience.
6. (a) He is enthusiastic about Shakespeare and the story of the Globe. (b) His tone is engaging because he is excited about his subject.
7. Students may suggest that the article seems more persuasive than informative. However, the primary purpose is to be informative. While statements such as "seeing Shakespeare's works at the Globe is not like seeing it anywhere else in the world" reflect the bias of the author, the article's main purpose is to provide a history of the project.
8. Accept reasonable answers.

Academic Standards

The Additional Support activity on p. 810 covers the following standard:

Skills Practice: **9.3.6** Analyze and trace an author's development of time and sequence...

…ocus

…Jsing Correct Verb Tenses
Write this sentence on the board: The Capulets and Montagues have fighted each other for a long time.

Discuss what makes this sentence incorrect. Remind students that incorrect verb tense is a common mistake that can adversely affect their writing.

Teach

Using Verbs Ask students to explain how to use verbs to show time. Review rules for forming the simple tenses, and have students list the tenses of several irregular verbs. Also remind students that when two or more verbs in a sentence describe events that occur at the same time, the verbs must be parallel. **OL**

Assess

1. A feud had gone on for a long time.
2. One night, Capulet gave a ball.
3. Romeo saw Juliet there.
4. Soon, she had stolen his heart.
5. She drove all other thoughts from his mind.

Grammar Workshop

Language Usage

Forming Verb Tenses

Regular verbs form the **past tense** and **past participle** by adding *-ed;* for example, *love* becomes *loved.* **Irregular verbs** form the past tense and past participle in irregular ways; for example, *write* becomes *wrote* in the past tense and *written* in the past participle.

Test-Taking Tip

Always check your writing for correct verb usage as a separate step in proofreading. Ask yourself what form of the verb the sentence requires; then ask yourself if the verb you used is regular or irregular and whether it is in the correct tense and form.

Language Handbook

For more on verb tenses, see Language Handbook, p. R50.

Literature Online
eWorkbooks To link to the Grammar and Language eWorkbook, go to www.glencoe.com.

ACADEMIC STANDARDS (page 812)
9.6.2 Demonstrate an understanding of…consistent verb tenses.
9.4.10 Revise writing for… clarity…

Using Correct Verb Tenses

"For I ne'er saw true beauty till this night."

—William Shakespeare, from *Romeo and Juliet*

Connecting to Literature Both the poetry and perfection of Shakespeare's line would have been lost had he written, "For I never seen true beauty till this night." Instead, Shakespeare used the correct form of the verb *see* by selecting the past tense (saw) rather than the past participle (seen).

Check your sentences for the correct forms and tenses of verbs.

Problem 1 The sentence uses an incorrect form of an irregular verb.
Romeo and Juliet falled deeply in love.

Solution Remember that some verbs do not form the past tense and past participle by adding *-ed*.
Romeo and Juliet fell deeply in love.

Problem 2 The sentence uses the past tense when the past participle is needed.
What light has broke through the window?

Solution Use the past participle, not the past tense, in a sentence with any form of the helping, or auxiliary, verbs *have* or *be*.
What light has broken through the window?

Problem 3 The past participle is used incorrectly.
Romeo taken a potion.

Solution A Add a helping or auxiliary verb.
Romeo had taken a potion.

Solution B Replace the past participle with the past tense of the verb.
Romeo took a potion.

Exercise

Revise for Clarity Rewrite each sentence correctly, using either the past tense or past participle form of the verb.

1. A feud had went on for a long time.
2. One night, Capulet gived a ball.
3. Romeo seen Juliet there.
4. Soon, she had stole his heart.
5. She drived all other thoughts from his mind.

Additional Support

Academic Standards

The Additional Support activity on p. 812 covers the following standard:

Skills Practice: **9.6.2** Demonstrate an understanding of…proper English usage…

Skills Practice

WRITING: Sequence of Tenses
Discuss the sequence of tenses:
Juliet woke, but Romeo had already killed himself. *(The action in the dependent clause occurred **before** the action in the independent clause, so its verb is in the **past perfect** tense.)*

When the Capulets saw Juliet, they wept. *(The actions are simultaneous; both verbs are in the **simple past**.)* Have students correct the following:

1. Juliet *(had)* already threatened to kill herself when the Friar suggested the potion.
2. Because Romeo *(had)* killed Tybalt, he had been *(was)* banished. **OL**

Comparing Literature Across Genres

Connecting to the Reading Selections

Literature of every age and culture abounds with love stories. Throughout the centuries, works of poetry and prose describe the happiness, heartache, worry, and delight of love. The following works explore the many sides of love, an all-consuming emotion that has the power to depress and the power to elate.

COMPARING THE Big Idea The Power of Love

Love is unpredictable. It can come upon us suddenly, and it can change our lives in ways we never anticipated. The authors featured here explore different facets of love's power.

COMPARING Theme

What difficulties does love bring? The **theme** of a literary work is its central insight or message. Each of these selections expresses an insight about the dark or difficult side of love.

COMPARING Author's Beliefs

When reading a literary work, you may make inferences about the ideas or beliefs of the author. As you read, make inferences about the beliefs of William Shakespeare, Amy Lowell, Robert Graves, and Pär Lagerkvist.

Focus

BELLRINGER

Bellringer Options
Daily Language Practice Transparency 74
Or display images of loving couples of different ages and from a variety of cultures.
Ask: What do you think these people are feeling? How do people generally show that they are in love? What effects can lost love have on a person?

Connecting to the Reading Selections

Allow students to share responses to the opening statements about love. Then have students discuss what they already know about William Shakespeare, Amy Lowell, Robert Graves, and Pär Lagerkvist.

Selection Skills

Comparing Literature

Reading Skills
- Comparing Author's Beliefs (SE pp. 813, 818)
- Identifying Main Ideas and Supporting Details (TWE p. 816)

Literary Elements
- Comparing Theme (SE pp. 813, 818)

Listening/Speaking/Viewing Skills
- Discussion Starter (SE p. 815)

Writing Skills/Grammar
- Quickwrite (SE pp. 814, 817)
- Compare-and-Contrast Essay (SE p. 818)
- Recognizing Voice (TWE p. 818)

ocus

ummary

This poem is about the speaker's sadness over parting with someone he or she loves.

Teach

Quickwrite

Students may say that the drum and the shout appeal to hearing, the stars and the lamps appeal to sight, and wedging and wounding appeal to touch.

Literature Online

Author Search To expand students' appreciation of Amy Lowell, have them access the Web site for additional information and resources.

CheckPoint

Use the CheckPoint questions on Presentation Plus! to check students' mastery. These questions can be used with interactive response keypads for immediate student feedback.

BEFORE YOU READ

Building Background

Amy Lowell was a controversial, uncompromising woman, and one of the most important poets of the Imagist movement. She was born in 1874 into a wealthy and socially prominent family in Brookline, Massachusetts, and spent her first twenty-eight years like most women of her social set. She traveled, was educated in private schools in Boston, and considered prospects for marriage. However, in 1902, Lowell chose a new path and dedicated her life to poetry.

Lowell connected immediately to the Imagist style. The Imagists were a group of American poets in the early twentieth century whose goal was to produce poems that create vivid pictures in the reader's mind. Imagist poetry uses straightforward, everyday language and makes a radical break with traditional poetic rhythms. Lowell is known for both her literary contributions and her promotion of Imagism.

Literature Online **Author Search** For more about Amy Lowell, go to www.glencoe.com.

When I go away from you
The world beats dead
Like a slackened drum.
I call out for you against the jutted stars
And shout into the ridges of the wind.
Streets coming fast,
One after the other,
Wedge you away from me,
And the lamps of the city prick my eyes
So that I can no longer see your face.
Why should I leave you,
To wound myself upon the sharp edges of the night?

Quickwrite

What senses does Lowell appeal to in this poem? Write a paragraph describing details that appeal to your senses of sight, sound, smell, taste, and/or touch.

Selection Resources

Print Materials

- Unit 4 Resources (Fast File), p. 35
- Selection and Unit Assessments, pp. 145–146
- Selection Quick Checks, p. 73

Transparencies

- Bellringer Options Transparencies: Daily Language Practice Transparency 74
- Literary Elements Transparency 18

Technology

- TeacherWorks Plus™ CD-ROM
- StudentWorks Plus™ CD-ROM
- Presentation Plus!™ CD-ROM
- Literature Online, glencoe.com
- Online Student Edition, mhln.com
- Exam*View*® Assessment Suite CD-ROM
- Vocabulary PuzzleMaker CD-ROM
- Listening Library, disc 2 tracks 8–10

Counting the Beats

Robert Graves

BEFORE YOU READ

Building Background

Robert Graves was a classical scholar. One of his best-known works is the historical novel *I, Claudius,* which is narrated in the first person by an ancient Roman emperor. Published in 1934, this novel remains an enduring work of English literature. Although he achieved fame as a writer of prose, Graves thought of himself as a poet.

Graves was fifteen when he decided to become a poet. Picked on by bullies at an English boarding school called Charterhouse, he took refuge in poetry. At the suggestion of a friend, he also took up boxing, which he found to be more effective in warding off his tormentors. In addition to boxing, Graves further demonstrated his physical prowess when he became a mountain climber.

In Graves's life, as well as in his poetry, romantic love was of vital importance. He regarded the women he loved as muses who inspired him.

LiteratureOnline **Author Search** For more about Robert Graves, go to www.glencoe.com.

L

You, love, and I,
(He whispers) you and I,
And if no more than only you and I
What care you or I?

Counting the beats,
Counting the slow heart beats,
The bleeding to death of time in slow
heart beats,
Wakeful they lie.

Cloudless day,
Night, and a cloudless day,
Yet the huge storm will burst upon
their heads one day
From a bitter sky.

Where shall we be,
(She whispers) where shall we be,
When death strikes home, O where
then shall we be
Who were you and I?

Not there but here,
(He whispers) only here,
As we are, here, together, now and
here,
Always you and I.

Counting the beats,
Counting the slow heart beats,
The bleeding to death of time in slow
heart beats,
Wakeful they lie.

Discussion Starter

Robert Graves once said that he wrote about "the practical impossibility, transcended only by a belief in miracle, of absolute love between man and woman." Discuss how this quotation applies to "Counting the Beats."

Differentiated Instruction

Reading Aloud Encourage less proficient readers to read through the poem several times. First have them read the poem silently. Then have students take turns reading aloud to a partner.

Ask: What does the punctuation tell you? *(When to pause)* What sound devices does the poet use? *(Assonance, consonance, alliteration)* **BL**

Focus

Summary

This poem is about two people who believe that their love can be ended only by death.

Teach

L Literary Element

Mood Have students read the first two stanzas and describe the mood.

Ask: Which words and connotations help build this feeling? *(The man's whisper and the slow heartbeats build a mood of intimacy; the couple's wakefulness and the comparison of heartbeats as time "bleeding to death" tinge it with dread.)* **OL**

LiteratureOnline

Author Search To expand students' appreciation of Robert Graves, have them access the Web site for additional information and resources.

CheckPoint

Use the CheckPoint questions on Presentation Plus! to monitor students' comprehension and to check students' mastery. These questions can be used with interactive response keypads for immediate student feedback.

Academic Standards

The Additional Support activity on p. 815 covers the following standards:

Differentiated Instruction: **9.7** [Develop] speaking skills…in conjunction with…strategies…[for] delivery of oral presentations. **9.3.7** Recognize…various literary devices…

CUS

ummary

his fable is about a prince who conquers a kingdom to win the love of the beautiful princess. The chancellor of the kingdom informs the prince, much to the prince's dismay, that he has not only won the princess but also the responsibilities of king.

Teach

BI1 Big Idea

The Power of Love Ask: How does the prince prove his love for the princess? *(He fights bravely and risks his life.)* Why would the prince suffer for his love? *(His desire for the princess is so strong that he would endure any trial to win her love.)* OL

CheckPoint

Use the CheckPoint questions on Presentation Plus! to monitor students' comprehension. These questions can be used with interactive response keypads for immediate student feedback.

Readability Scores
Dale-Chall: 7.0
DRP: 54
Lexile: 910

BEFORE YOU READ

Building Background

Swedish-born Pär Lagerkvist wrote for more than three decades before achieving international fame. A writer of poetry, novels, and plays, his works are beloved for their striking simplicity of imagery and expression. In 1951, Lagerkvist was awarded the Nobel Prize for literature.

Born in 1891, Lagerkvist made a decision to become a writer at an early age. The son of a railroad stationmaster, he did something people in his town rarely did—he left to study at a university. He stayed there only one year before moving to Paris at age 22.

Lagerkvist may be best remembered as one of the creators of Swedish Expressionism, which emphasized the use of experimental styles of writing. The works of Expressionists, whether in painting, drama, or poetry, frequently contain dark and terrifying images that evoke a dreamlike state. Lagerkvist said that as a writer, he was interested in "the enigma of our life which makes human destiny at once so great and so hard."

Literature Online Author Search For more about Pär Lagerkvist, go to www.glencoe.com.

Pär Lagerkvist
Translated by Alan Blair

Once upon a time there was a prince, who went out to fight in order to win the princess whose beauty was greater than all others' and whom he loved above everything. He dared his life, he battled his way step by step through the country, ravaging it; nothing BI1 could stop him.

Additional Support

Literature Online

Author Search To expand students' appreciation of Pär Lagerkvist, have them access the Web site for additional information and resources.

Skills Practice

READING: Identifying Main Ideas and Supporting Details Have students reread this fable to find the main ideas and the major supporting details. Remind them that fictional works often have several main ideas. Suggest that they take notes on the selection using an outline like the one below.

I. Prince fights to win the princess.
   A. He ravages the country.
   B. He fights brave noblemen.
   C. He rides as a conqueror. OL

He bled from his wounds but merely cast himself from one fight to the next, the most valiant nobleman to be seen and with a shield as pure as his own young features. At last he stood outside the city where the princess lived in her royal castle. It could not hold out against him and had to beg for mercy. The gates were thrown open; he rode in as conqueror.

When the princess saw how proud and handsome he was and thought of how he had dared his life for her sake, she could not withstand his power but gave him her hand. He knelt and covered it with ardent kisses. "Look, my bride, now I have won you!" he exclaimed, radiant with happiness. "Look, everything I have fought for, now I have won it!"

And he commanded that their wedding should take place this same day. The whole city decked itself out for the festival and the wedding was celebrated with rejoicing, pomp, and splendor.

When in the evening he went to enter the princess's bedchamber, he was met outside by the aged chancellor, a venerable man. Bowing his snow-white head, he tendered the keys of the kingdom and the crown of gold and precious stones to the young conqueror.

"Lord, here are the keys of the kingdom which open the treasuries where everything that now belongs to you is kept."

The prince frowned.

"What is that you say, old man? I do not want your keys. I have not fought for sordid gain. I have fought merely to win her whom I love, to win that which for me is the only costly thing on earth."

The old man replied, "This, too, you have won, lord. And you cannot set it aside. Now you must administer and look after it."

"Do you not understand what I say? Do you not understand that one can fight, can conquer, without asking any reward other than one's happiness—not fame and gold, not land and power on earth? Well, then, I have conquered but ask for nothing, only to live happily with what, for me, is the only thing of value in life."

"Yes, lord, you have conquered. You have fought your way forward as the bravest of the brave, you have shrunk from nothing, the land lies ravaged where you have passed by. You have won your happiness. But, lord, others have been robbed of theirs. You have conquered, and therefore everything now belongs to you. It is a big land, fertile and impoverished, mighty and laid waste, full of riches and need, full of joy and sorrow, and all is now yours. For he who has won the princess and happiness, to him also belongs this land where she was born; he shall govern and cherish it."

The prince stood there glowering and fingering the hilt of his sword uneasily.

"I am the prince of happiness, nothing else!" he burst out. "Don't want to be anything else. If you get in my way, then I have my trusty sword."

But the old man put out his hand soothingly and the young man's arm sank. He looked at him searchingly, with a wise man's calm.

BI2

"Lord, you are no longer a prince," he said gently. "You are a king."

And lifting the crown with his aged hands, he put it on the other's head.

When the young ruler felt it on his brow he stood silent and moved, more erect than before. And gravely, with his head crowned for power on earth, he went in to his beloved to share her bed. ☙

Quickwrite

What difficulties does the prince suffer in his effort to reach the princess? What surprises occur when he reaches his destination? How does the mood, or feeling, of the story shift as the story progresses? Write a paragraph in which you address these questions.

Teach

BI2 Big Idea

The Power of Love **Ask:** Why is the prince angry about having the responsibility of king? *(His desire was only for love, not responsibility.)* Why does the prince accept the responsibility of king in the end? *(Out of love for the princess)* **OL**

Quickwrite

Students should mention that the prince has to fight battles and has to lay siege to a castle. Students may be surprised that the prince at first refuses the land's riches. The mood shifts as the prince realizes that he is responsible for the land and not just the princess.

CheckPoint

Use the CheckPoint questions on Presentation Plus! to check students' mastery of the selection. These questions can be used with interactive keypads for immediate student feedback.

Differentiated Instruction

Creating Symbolic Art Have gifted and talented students create artwork that represents one of the main ideas in this fable, such as the relationship between love and responsibility. Have students share their artwork with the rest of the class and explain what their work symbolizes. **AL**

Academic Standards

Additional Support activities on pp. 816 and 817 cover the following standards:

Skills Practice: **9.3** [Identify] story elements such as…theme, plot…

Differentiated Instruction: **9.7.4** Use…visual aids…to enhance the appeal and accuracy of presentations.

ssess

Vriting

Remind students to support their arguments with details from the selections.

Group Activity

Student discussions should focus on the nature of the problems or hardships love poses in each of the selections as well as on the outcome of the various complications that ensue.

Partner Activity

Students' charts should include examples of imagery, dialogue, and plot events that reveal the authors' beliefs about love.

Wrap-Up: Comparing Literature *Across Genres*

- ***The Tragedy of Romeo and Juliet*** by William Shakespeare
- ***The Taxi*** by Amy Lowell
- ***Counting the Beats*** by Robert Graves
- ***The Princess and All the Kingdom*** by Pär Lagerkvist

COMPARING THE Big Idea The Power of Love

Writing How does love affect a person? In "The Taxi" and "Counting the Beats," the speakers are dramatically affected by love. In *Romeo and Juliet* and "The Princess and All the Kingdom," the main characters are strongly influenced by love. Write a short-response essay comparing and contrasting the way the four selections represent love's power over a person.

COMPARING Theme

Group Activity In each of these selections, love's dark or difficult side comes into focus. With a group of classmates, answer the following questions as you compare and contrast the messages about love, responsibility, and parting that these works convey.

1. What is similar about the themes of the four works?
2. How do the themes differ?
3. In your opinion, which work conveys its theme or themes most effectively? Why do you think so?

COMPARING Author's Beliefs

Partner Activity What do Shakespeare, Lowell, Graves, and Lagerkvist believe about love's role in a person's life? How can you tell? With a partner, go back through the selections and look for details that may reveal what each author believes about love. Think about which aspects of love each author seems to consider especially important. Compile your thoughts in a chart like the one below. Then, share your ideas with the class.

Author	Beliefs About Love
Shakespeare	
Lowell	
Graves	
Lagerkvist	

INDIANA ACADEMIC STANDARDS (page 818)

9.3.2 Compare and contrast...theme...across genres...

9.3.5 Compare works that express a universal theme and provide evidence to support the views expressed in each work.

Additional Support

Skills Practice

WRITING: Recognizing Voice Note that the first-person perspective in the line "When I go away from you" from "The Taxi" emphasizes the speaker's personal feelings. Note that the lines "You, love, and I, / (He whispers) you and I" from "Counting the Beats" are in third person. Ask students to write a paragraph that discusses how the choice of perspective affects the mood and meaning of the poem. OL

PART 2

Awkward Encounters

Midsummer's Dream, 1986. Charles Bell. ★

BIG IDEA

BI Being asked a question you do not know the answer to, slipping and falling in front of a group of friends, having to lead your class in a song—any of these moments may make you feel awkward. The plays in Part 2 present characters who face awkward moments. As you read these selections, ask yourself: How would I handle these awkward moments?

Analyzing and Extending

BI Big Idea

Awkward Encounters

Ask: How do you react in an awkward situation? Discuss various strategies. Do students walk away, try to be diplomatic, or ignore the situation? Have them point out any correlations between how they react and how the characters in the painting are reacting. OL

★ Viewing the Art

American photorealist Charles Bell (1935–1995) painted ordinary objects such as toys and gumball machines in exacting detail. Photorealism reacted against the fantastical elements of surrealism and Pop Art with paintings of mundane subjects that resembled photographic images.

Ask: What is awkward about this painting? *(Students may note the awkward way the characters are posed, their positions in relation to one another, and the expressions on their faces.)* AS

English Language Coach

Building Background Nonnative speakers often find adjusting to new cultural norms a challenge. Invite them to share their encounters with awkward situations. Suggest ways to turn such experiences into positive learning experiences. EL

Differentiated Instruction

Dramatizing a Mood Invite students to create a story that explains the awkward positioning in the painting. Tell them to include all the characters in the painting in their stories. AL

Academic Standards

Additional Support activities on pp. 818 and 819 cover the following standards:

Skills Practice: **9.3.9** Explain how voice and the choice of a narrator affect…the tone [and] plot… **9.5.2** Write responses to literature that demonstrate an awareness of the author's style…

English Language Coach: **9.2** Develop [reading] strategies…

Differentiated Instruction: **9.5.1** Write…short stories that describe with specific details the sights [and] sounds…and the specific actions…of the characters…

Part 2: Skills Scope and Sequence

Readability Scores Key
Dale–Chall/DRP/Lexile

PACING (DAYS) STANDARD	BLOCK	SELECTIONS AND FEATURES	LITERARY ELEMENTS
2–3 class sessions	1–2	*The Bear* by Anton Chekhov pp. 822–836	Farce, SE pp. 823–835 Dialogue, SE p. 835
		COMPARING LITERATURE Across Genres *A Sunny Morning* by Serafín and Joaquín Álvarez Quintero, pp. 837–850 "About Two Nice People" by Shirley Jackson **7.1/61/1220**, pp. 851–861 "Simile" by N. Scott Momaday, pp. 862–863	Stage Directions, SE pp. 839–850 Genre Elements, SE p. 850 Major and Minor Characters, TWE p. 842 Understanding Theme, TWE p. 848 Point of View, TWE p. 856
1–2 class sessions	1	*Bye-Bye Brevoort* by Eudora Welty, pp. 864–874	High Comedy, SE pp. 865, 869, 872, 874 Analyze Setting, SE p. 874
		Vocabulary Workshop: Denotation and Connotation, p. 875	
2 class sessions	1	*The Leader* by Eugène Ionesco, pp. 876–885	Satire, SE pp. 877, 879, 882, 884 Farce, SE p. 884
		HISTORICAL PERSPECTIVE on Eugène Ionesco: "How I Came to the Theater" by Claude Bonnefoy pp. 886–889	
3 class sessions	1–2	*Marty* Act 1 by Paddy Chayefsky, pp. 890–903	Plot, SE pp. 891, 894, 898, 903 Setting, TWE p. 893
		Marty Act 2 by Paddy Chayefsky, pp. 904–915	Characterization, TWE p. 908
		Marty Act 3 by Paddy Chayefsky, pp. 916–925	Character, SE pp. 916–924 Stage Directions, SE p. 924
2–3 class sessions	2–3	Writing Workshop: Literary Analysis Essay, pp. 926–933	
1 class session		Speaking, Listening, and Viewing Workshop: Literary Analysis, pp. 934–935	
2 class sessions		Test Preparation and Practice, pp. 938–943	

About the Part

Part 2 deals with difficult situations faced by the characters in a play and how conflict propels the story forward.

READING AND CRITICAL THINKING	VOCABULARY	WRITING AND GRAMMAR	LISTENING, SPEAKING, AND VIEWING
Analyzing Cause-and-Effect Relationships, SE pp. 823–835	Antonyms, SE pp. 823, 835 Academic Vocabulary, SE p. 835	Respond to Characters, SE p. 836	Literature Groups, SE p. 836
Making and Verifying Predictions About Plot, SE pp. 839, 842, 844, 845, 847, 849, 850 Outlining, TWE p. 840 Questioning, TWE p. 846 Comparing Characters, TWE p. 854	Word Origins, SE pp. 839, 850	Analyze Genre Elements, SE p. 850 Quickwrite, SE p. 862 Compare-and-Contrast Essay, SE p. 863 Graphing a Plot, TWE p. 844	Analyzing Art, SE pp. 846, 848, 855, 857, 859 Discussion Starter, SE p. 861 Collage, SE p. 863 Presenting Arguments, TWE p. 858
Questioning, SE pp. 865–874	Analogies, SE pp. 865, 874 Connotation, TWE p. 868	Analyze Setting, SE p. 874 Character Sketch, TWE p. 872	
	Using a Semantic Chart, SE p. 875		
Drawing Conclusions About Author's Meaning, SE pp. 877–885	Context Clues, SE pp. 877, 885 Academic Vocabulary, SE p. 885	Evaluate Contemporary Relevance, SE p. 885	Performing, SE p. 885 Vocal Clues, TWE p. 878
Identifying Assumptions and Ambiguities, SE p. 886; TWE pp. 887, 888			
Analyzing Dialogue, SE pp. 891, 894–903	Antonyms, SE pp. 891, 903	Respond to Conflict, SE p. 903	Movie Discussion, SE p. 925 Analyzing Art, SE p. 896, 899
	Context Clues, SE pp. 904, 915	*Who* and *Whom,* TWE p. 906	Analyzing Art, SE p. 906; TWE p. 912
Analyzing Characterization, SE pp. 917, 920, 921, 922, 924	Word Origins, SE pp. 916, 924 Academic Vocabulary, SE p. 924	Analyze Genre Elements, SE p. 925	Analyzing Art, SE p. 919 Group Activity, SE p. 823
Supporting Examples, TWE p. 928		Literary Analysis, SE pp. 926–933	Getting Feedback, TWE p. 932
			Literary Analysis, SE pp. 934–935
		Book Titles, TWE p. 942	Functional Material, TWE p. 938

ARY FOCUS

us

LLRINGER

ellringer Options
Daily Language Practice Transparency 75
Or list students' favorite movies on the board. Sort them by category into drama and comedy. Discuss what makes these movies special and memorable.

Teach

L Literary Element

Comedy and Modern Drama **Ask:** What makes the scene from *Marty* comedic? How is it dramatic? *(Students should cite specific lines from the excerpt.)* OL

Literature Online

Literary Elements Have students access the Web site to improve their understanding of modern drama and comedy.

LITERARY FOCUS

Comedy and Modern Drama

How can you use the elements of drama to help you read a play?

In *Marty*, the title character is a thirty-six-year-old man living in an Italian American neighborhood in the borough of the Bronx in New York City. His mother pressures him to get married. At the beginning of the play, Marty says, "I been looking for a girl every Saturday night of my life." In this scene, a young man wants to leave a dance without the woman he brought and asks Marty to take her home.

MARTY. You say something to me?

YOUNG MAN. Yeah. I was just asking you if you was here stag or with a girl.

MARTY. I'm stag.

YOUNG MAN. Well, I'll tell you. I got stuck onna blind date with a dog, and I just picked up a nice chick, and I was wondering how I'm gonna get ridda the dog. Somebody to take her home, you know what I mean? I be glad to pay you five bucks if you take the dog home for me.

MARTY. [*A little confused.*] What?

YOUNG MAN. I'll take you over, and I'll introduce you as an old army buddy of mine, and then I'll cut out. Because I got this chick waiting for me out by the hat-check, and I'll pay you five bucks.

MARTY. [*Stares at the young man.*] Are you kidding?

YOUNG MAN. No, I'm not kidding.

MARTY. You can't just walk off onna girl like that.

—Paddy Chayefsky, **from *Marty*, Act 2** 

People Dancing. Mark di Vincenzo. 

Additional Support

Skills Practice

GRAMMAR AND LANGUAGE: Dialogue **Ask:** What does the slang in the dialogue from the *Marty* excerpt add to the scene? *(It gives the dialogue a regional flavor, adds realism, and helps develop character.)* Invite students to write a scene using colloquial dialogue. Brainstorm situations, locations, and characters. Have students work in groups to write the dialogue. When the scenes are finished, have the groups present them to the class. OL

Elements of Drama

Acts and Scenes Plays usually contain two or more acts, which are major divisions in the action. In some plays, acts are further divided into scenes. Usually, an act or scene change means that the characters and setting will change.

Dialogue Dialogue is the conversation between characters in a play or other literary work. Dialogue reveals the personalities, feelings, and thoughts of the characters. It also advances the plot.

Stage Directions Stage directions are the written instructions that explain how to perform the play, including how the characters should look, speak, move, and behave. Stage directions are also used to establish the time and place of the play, as well as the sets, costumes, lighting, props, and sound effects.

DON GONZALO. [*Muttering to himself, he sits at the extreme end of Doña Laura's bench and looks at her indignantly. Touches his hat as he greets her.*] Good morning.

—Serafín and Joaquín Alvarez Quintero, **from *A Sunny Morning***

Elements of Comedy

Comedy is a type of drama that deals with light and amusing subjects—or with serious subjects in a light or satirical manner. Comedies typically have happy endings, and they entertain audiences with verbal wit, physical humor, ridicule, or irony.

Irony

Irony is a contrast between what appears to be and what really is. Playwrights use three types of irony as the basis for humor in a comedy:

- **Situational irony** exists when the outcome of the situation is the opposite of what is expected.
- **Dramatic irony** occurs when the audience knows something that the characters do not. While watching Eugène Ionesco's *The Leader,* the audience realizes there is nothing truly exceptional about the Leader, yet all of the characters onstage cheer for him.

ANNOUNCER. [*To the* ADMIRERS.] Quiet, you two! Calm down! You're spoiling everything! [*Then, once more looking up-stage, with the* ADMIRERS *silenced.*] Long live the leader! [*Wildly enthusiastic.*] Hurrah! Hurrah! He's changing his shirt. He disappears behind a red screen. He reappears! [*The applause intensifies.*] Bravo! Bravo!

—Eugène Ionesco, **from *The Leader***

- **Verbal irony** occurs when a character says one thing and means another. Sarcasm, hyperbole, and understatement are forms of verbal irony.

SMÍRNOFF. What kind of logic is that? Here's a man so desperate for money he's ready to hang himself, and she can't pay him because—excuse me very much—she's "in no condition to talk about money." Talk about petticoat logic! This is why I don't like women and hate talking to them. I'd rather light a campfire on a powder keg than talk to a woman.

—Anton Chekhov, **from *The Bear*** **R**

Tone

Tone expresses an author's attitude toward the subject of a literary work. The tone of a comedy may be bawdy, satirical, or lighthearted.

Quickwrite

Defining Comedy Write for two to three minutes finishing this statement: "For comedy to be funny, it should . . ." Support your opinion with examples from movies and plays you have seen.

LiteratureOnline Interactive Literary Elements Handbook Go to www.glencoe.com to review or learn more about comedy and modern drama.

INDIANA ACADEMIC STANDARDS (pages 820–821)

9.3.1 Explain the relationship between the purposes and the characteristics of different forms of dramatic literature…

9.3.8 Interpret and evaluate the impact of…ironies in a text.

9.3.9 Explain how voice…affect[s]…tone…

Teach

R Reading Strategy

Identifying Elements Invite volunteers to read the excerpts aloud. Ask students what stands out about each of the excerpts. Is there important information in the stage directions? Is the dialogue humorous? Instruct students to read the descriptions of the elements of comedy and drama. Discuss how focusing on these new elements improved their comprehension. **OL**

Viewing the Art

Mark di Vincenzo (1955–) has art studios in Brooklyn and Buffalo in New York and has received both corporate and public commissions. **Ask:** What dramatic elements do you see in this painting? *(Students may mention the swirling lines and movements of the people.)* **AS**

Quickwrite

Answers will vary. Make sure students support their responses.

English Language Coach

Understanding Slang English language learners may find the slang in the *Marty* excerpt confusing. Have them work in groups to rewrite the sentences in standard English. Have students share their rewrites with the class. **EL**

Differentiated Instruction

Thinking of Tone Auditory learners may find it useful to think of tone in musical terms. Suggest they think of the writer's words as his or her instrument for expressing attitudes and emotions and creating moods. **BL**

Academic Standards

Additional Support activities on pp. 820 and 821 cover the following standards:

Skills Practice: **9.5.8** Write for different purposes and audiences, adjusting tone, style, and voice as appropriate.

English Language Coach: **9.1** Use…context clues and a growing knowledge of English to determine the meaning of words…

Differentiated Instruction: **9.3.11** Evaluate the aesthetic qualities of style, including the impact of diction…on tone…

Focus

BELLRINGER

Bellringer Options
Daily Language Practice Transparency 76
Or have students brainstorm a list of promises people often make. Write their ideas on the board. Ask students to consider which of these promises are usually kept and which are generally broken.
Say: The drama you are about to read is about a woman who makes a promise she plans to keep for the rest of her life. As students read, have them predict if Popóva will keep her promise.

Author Search To expand students' appreciation of Anton Chekhov, have them access the Web site for additional information and resources.

BEFORE YOU READ

The Bear

MEET ANTON CHEKHOV

In 1886 in Moscow, Russia, a young doctor and writer wrote, "All my hope is pinned to the future. I am only twenty-six. Perhaps I shall succeed in achieving something, though time flies fast." Little did that writer, Anton Chekhov, know that one day he would be considered the father of the modern short story and the modern drama.

A Russian Childhood Anton Pavlovich Chekhov was born in Taganrog, a Russian seaport near the Black Sea, in 1860. Chekhov had very few positive things to say about his childhood. He was particularly critical of his father, Pavel, who was a grocer. His mother, Yevgeniya, however, taught Chekhov how to read and write. She was an excellent storyteller and passed that gift on to her son. The Chekhov family faced many financial difficulties. In 1875, his father's store failed. The family left Taganrog, but Chekhov stayed behind to finish his schooling.

"It is time for writers, particularly artists, to confess that in this world you cannot make head or tail of anything."

—Anton Chekhov

Chekhov started writing as a way to earn money, not for artistic expression. While studying medicine at Moscow University, Chekhov published many short sketches, humorous stories, jokes, and trivia in popular magazines. After graduating from medical school in 1884, Chekhov continued to write. By 1886, he had become a well-known writer in more prestigious magazines and journals.

Gaining Momentum Between 1888 and 1893, Chekhov began writing longer narratives. He included contrasting themes, such as life and death and beauty and ugliness. Many of his characters were challenged by isolation, missed opportunities, and class barriers. During this time, Chekhov also produced several one-act plays, such as *The Bear,* as well as full-length dramas.

The years between 1894 and 1904 proved to be the most artistically productive for Chekhov. In this period, his short stories began to have more complex plots. He also wrote some of his more acclaimed plays during this period, including *Uncle Vanya, The Three Sisters,* and *The Cherry Orchard.*

Chekhov first noticed signs of tuberculosis in 1884. However, the disease went largely untreated, an irony given his medical background. He finally agreed to treatment in 1897, but, in 1904, he died of the disease.

Because of his focus on mood rather than action, and on a broken rather than straightforward plot line, Chekhov transformed short story and drama writing.

Anton Chekhov was born in 1860 and died in 1904.

Literature Online **Author Search** For more about Anton Chekhov, go to www.glencoe.com.

Selection Skills

The Bear

Literary Elements
- Farce (SE pp. 823–835)
- Dialogue (SE p. 835)

Reading Skills
- Analyzing Cause-and-Effect Relationships (SE pp. 823–835)

Vocabulary Skills
- Antonyms (SE pp. 823, 835)
- Academic Vocabulary (SE p. 835)

Listening/Speaking/Viewing Skills
- Analyzing Art (SE p. 829)
- Acting (TWE p. 830)

Writing Skills/Grammar
- Respond to Characters (SE p. 836)
- Different Sentence Types (SE p. 836)
- Summarizing (TWE p. 828)

LITERATURE PREVIEW

Connecting to the Play

The following drama tells the story of a woman who has made a promise to herself that she intends to keep until the day she dies. Before you read, consider the following questions:

- What kinds of promises have you made to yourself or to other people?
- Have you ever had trouble keeping a promise?

Building Background

In the second half of the 1880s, great changes and cultural advances were being made across the globe. It was in this atmosphere that some of the best known and most highly acclaimed works of Russian literature were written.

This time was known as the modern period in Russian literary history and it gave rise to a different kind of literature. Very early Russian literature usually was religious in content; later, influences from western Europe helped to shape Russian literature. But by the 1800s, Russian writers had developed a tradition that was uniquely their own. During the later part of the modern period, writers like Aleksandr Pushkin, Leo Tolstoy, and Fyodor Dostoyevsky, along with Anton Chekhov, were becoming recognized as some of the best-known and most respected writers of any generation.

Setting Purposes for Reading

Big Idea Awkward Encounters

As you read *The Bear,* think about how the characters' actions and reactions create awkward moments.

Literary Element Farce

Farce is a type of comedy that incorporates ridiculous situations, characters, or events. Most farce incorporates exaggerated speech and action.

- See Literary Terms Handbook, p. R7.

Literature Online **Interactive Literary Elements Handbook** To review or learn more about the literary elements, go to www.glencoe.com.

READING PREVIEW

Reading Strategy Analyzing Cause-and-Effect Relationships

A **cause** is an event that makes something happen, and the **effect** is the result of the cause. You can see the **cause-and-effect relationship** in a work of literature by noting what happens in a story or a drama and then identifying what leads to the event. As you read *The Bear,* look for cause-and-effect relationships.

Reading Tip: Taking Notes As you read *The Bear,* take careful notes on the play's action. Use a cause-and-effect chart like the one below to record your thoughts.

Cause and Effect

Vocabulary

mourn (môrn) *v.* to feel or express grief or sorrow; p. 824 *She needed to mourn after experiencing such a great loss.*

logic (loj′ ik) *n.* a method of reasoning; p. 827 *To solve the problem, you must use logic.*

pretentious (pri ten′ shəs) *adj.* expressing exaggerated importance or worth; p. 829 *At first they thought she seemed pretentious, but later they realized she had just been nervous.*

monopoly (mə nop′ ə lē) *n.* exclusive possession or control; p. 829 *He has a monopoly on good restaurants in our town.*

Vocabulary Tip: Antonyms Antonyms are words with opposite meanings. *Hot* and *cold* are antonyms, as are *happy* and *sad.* A word can have more than one antonym. Sometimes you can form a word's antonym by adding a prefix like *un-* to the beginning of the word.

INDIANA ACADEMIC STANDARDS (pages 823–836)

9.3.1 Explain the relationship between the purposes and the characteristics of different forms of dramatic literature...

9.2 Develop [reading] strategies...

9.5.2 Write responses to literature that...support statements with evidence from the text.

9.3.3 Analyze interactions between characters...

BEFORE YOU READ

Focus

Summary

After the death of her husband, Yeléna Ivánovna Popóva vows to wear black and remain inside her house until she dies. When Smírnoff shows up to collect on a debt owed by Popóva's late husband, Popóva tells him she cannot pay until the day after tomorrow. The two argue until Smírnoff falls in love with Popóva.

V Vocabulary

Vocabulary File **Say:** Add these words and definitions to your vocabulary file. For each word, include a sentence that gives you an example of how to use the word. **OL** Students with English language needs should include the pronunciations of these words in their files. **EL**

Literary Elements Have students access the Web site to improve their understanding of farce.

Selection Resources

Print Materials

- Unit 4 Resources (Fast File), pp. 39–41
- Selection and Unit Assessments, pp. 147–148
- Selection Quick Checks, p. 74

Transparencies

- Bellringer Options Transparencies: Daily Language Practice Transparency 76
- Literary Elements Transparency 77

Technology

- TeacherWorks Plus™ CD-ROM
- StudentWorks Plus™ CD-ROM
- Presentation Plus!™ CD-ROM
- Literature Online, glencoe.com
- Online Student Edition, mhln.com
- Exam*View*® Assessment Suite CD-ROM
- Vocabulary PuzzleMaker CD-ROM
- Listening Library, disc 2 track 11

Teach

L1 Literary Element

Farce Answer: *The drama will probably not be realistic since a person would not spend a whole year in the house. There will probably be other exaggerations.* OL

BI Big Idea

Awkward Encounters Ask: Why is the exchange between Popóva and Luká awkward? *(Luká is a servant and would not speak to his mistress this way.)* Ask students to find additional dialogue that creates an awkward encounter. OL

★ Viewing the Art

British painter Edmund Blair Leighton (1853–1922) was the son of a professional painter. After he completed his studies at the Royal Academy Schools, he painted primarily historical people and scenes. At first, he focused on medieval scenes. Later, many of his paintings, such as *Olivia*, depicted elegant, upper-class women. **Ask:** What qualities and details in the painting create a sense of richness? *(Students might note the ornate gold-colored background or the woman's dress.)* AS

Olivia. Edmund Blair Leighton. ★

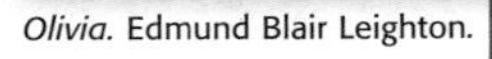

The Bear

A Comic Sketch in One Act

Anton Chekhov

CHARACTERS

YELÉNA IVÁNOVNA POPÓVA: a widow with dimples and a large estate

GRIGÓRY STEPÁNOVICH SMÍRNOFF: landowner, in his thirties

LUKÁ: an elderly servant

The action takes place in Popóva's living room.

POPÓVA's living room. POPÓVA, dressed completely in black, sits staring at a photograph. LUKÁ, her old servant, tries to talk sense to her.

LUKÁ. It's just not right, missus. You're letting yourself fall to pieces. Cook and the maid have gone berry picking, every living thing is out enjoying the sunshine, even your cat, now, he's out there trying to catch himself a bird, and here you sit, shut up in the house all day long, like some kind of nun. That's no fun. You listen to what I'm saying, now! It's been a whole year since you left the house! L1

BI POPÓVA. I shall never leave this house. Why should I? My life is over. He's dead and buried, and so am I, buried here within these four walls. We're both dead.

LUKÁ. I never heard the like! Your husband's dead. Well, God rest him, he's not coming back. You **mourned** him good and proper; now it's time to move on. You can't sit here wearing black and crying for the rest of your life. I lost my old woman, too, a while back, I cried for a month, and that was that. No need to sit around for years singing hymns; she wasn't worth it. [*Sighs.*] You haven't seen your neighbors in months, you don't go out, and you tell us not to let anybody in. We're all living like spiders in the dark here, if BI

Literary Element Farce *From Luká's comments, how realistic do you think this drama will be? Explain.* L1

Vocabulary

mourn (môrn) *v.* to feel or express grief or sorrow

Additional Support

Skills Practice

READING: Summarizing To help students understand and remember what they read, ask them to summarize what happens on each page after they have read it. Have them write the number of the first text page for this selection at the top of a sheet of paper. Tell students to read page 824 silently. Then have them discuss with a partner what occurs on that page. Finally, ask them to write a brief summary of the page on their paper. Ask them to do the same for each page as they complete it. OL you'll excuse the expression. My livery jacket's[1] got moth holes. Fine, if there was nobody around worth seeing, but the whole country's crawling with eligible young men. There's a regiment in the next town, all those good-looking officers, melt in your mouth, most of them, and they have a dance every Friday night, and the band gives a concert every afternoon. Oh, missus, take a look at yourself—you're still a juicy young thing, you're still beautiful, you can go out and enjoy life. But a beautiful face won't last forever, you know. You wait—ten years from now you're going to want to go swanning[2] after those officers, and it'll be too late.

BI

POPÓVA. [*Firmly.*] I must ask you never to talk to me like this again! When my husband died, life lost all meaning for me. You know that. I may look like I'm alive, but I'm not. I swore I'd wear black and shut myself up here until the day I die, didn't I? And I will. He'll see how much I loved him. . . . Oh, I know he treated me badly—I don't have to tell you about it. He was mean and . . . and even unfaithful. But I intend to be faithful to the grave and show him *what* real love means.

LUKÁ. That's just a lot of talk. You'd do better to go out and take a walk, or have me hitch up Toby and go visit the neighbors.

POPÓVA. Oh! [*Bursts into hysterical tears.*]

LUKÁ. Missus! What is it? For God's sake, what's the matter?

POPÓVA. Toby! He used to love Toby so! He'd ride all over the neighborhood on him. What a horseman! Remember how grand he looked in the saddle? Oh, Toby, Toby! Go tell them he gets extra oats today.

LUKÁ. [*Sighs.*] Don't worry, I will.

[*The doorbell rings. And keeps ringing.*]

POPÓVA. [*Exasperated.*] Now who's that? Go tell whoever it is I am not at home! To anyone!

LUKÁ. Whatever you say, missus. [*Goes out.*]

POPÓVA. [*To the photograph.*] You see what real love means, Nicky? My love will last as long as I do, right to my last heartbeat. [*Laughs, almost crying.*] And I hope you're ashamed of yourself! You see what a good girl I am, what a faithful wife? I locked myself up here and will be faithful to you till the day I die, while you . . . I hope you're ashamed, you little pig. You were mean to me, you cheated on me, you left me alone for weeks at a time—

[*Enter* LUKÁ; *he's upset.*]

LUKÁ. Missus, there's someone wants to see you. Says it can't wait.

POPÓVA. Didn't you tell him that my husband is dead and that I see no one?

LUKÁ. I did, but he doesn't want to listen, says it's very important.

POPÓVA. And I said I see no one!

LUKÁ. That's what I told him, but he's . . . he's kind of a wild man—he started shouting and pushed his way into the house. He's in the dining room right now.

POPÓVA. All right, all right, tell him all right. Really! The nerve of some people!

[LUKÁ *goes out.*]

Why must people be so difficult? Why can't they just leave me alone? [*Sighs.*] Oh, I may have to go join a nunnery[3] after all. [*Thinks.*] I wonder what kind of nun I'd make. . . .

[*Enter* SMÍRNOFF, *trailed by* LUKÁ.]

SMÍRNOFF. [*To* LUKÁ.] You dingbat, stop trying to talk me out of here! Idiot! [*Sees* POPÓVA; *suddenly very dignified.*] Ah, madam. Let me introduce myself: Grigóry Stepánovich

---

1. *Livery* is the feeding, stabling, and care of horses for pay. Here, Luká refers to the jacket he wears when he drives Popóva in a horse carriage.
2. Here, *swanning* means wandering aimlessly or idly.
3. A *nunnery* is a convent of nuns.

Reading Strategy Analyzing Cause-and-Effect Relationships *What causes Popóva to imprison herself at home?* R

Literary Element Farce *How does Smírnoff's language help define the play as farce?* L2

Teach

R Reading Strategy

Analyzing Cause-and-Effect Relationships **Answer:** *She wants to show she is more faithful than her late husband was during their marriage by remaining in a state of mourning.* OL

L2 Literary Element

Farce **Answer:** *His language is silly and exaggerated, which creates an atmosphere in which ridiculous things might be possible.*
Ask: Why is it ridiculous for Popóva to say she will join a nunnery? *(This is an extreme measure for her to take.)* OL

CheckPoint

Use the CheckPoint questions on Presentation Plus! to monitor students' comprehension. These questions can be used with interactive response keypads for immediate student feedback.

English Language Coach

Understanding Farce Remind English learners that farce puts characters in ridiculous situations by using exaggerated speech and actions.
Ask: What unreasonable promise does Popóva make? *(She promises to mourn forever and never leave her house.)* How is Smírnoff's behavior ridiculous? *(His language is extreme for the context.)* In what ways is Luká absurd? *(He speaks improperly to Popóva.)* EL

Academic Standards

Additional Support activities on pp. 824 and 825 cover the following standards:

Skills Practice: **9.5.2** Write responses to literature that demonstrate a comprehensive grasp of the significant ideas of literary works…

English Language Coach: **9.3.1** Explain… the characteristics of different forms of dramatic literature…

Teach

BI Big Idea

Awkward Encounters
Answer: *He has intruded upon her and won't take "No" for an answer.*
Ask: Why is this awkward? *(It was customary at that time to greet a person with a handshake.)* OL

L1 Literary Element

Repetition Have two students read the dialogue in the first column between Popóva and Smírnoff. **Ask:** What effect does the repetition of the two characters' positions have on the audience? *(Students may feel it creates an absurd circular argument that stresses the farcical quality of the scene.)* OL

R1 Reading Strategy

Analyzing Cause-and-Effect Relationships **Answer:** *He thinks her reasoning is poor and that she does not understand his situation and is self-absorbed.*
Ask: Why can't Popóva pay Smírnoff? *(Her manager is out of town, and she has no money.)* OL

Smírnoff, Field Artillery,[4] retired. I own a place over in the next county. Sorry to disturb you, but this is important—

POPÓVA. [*Doesn't offer him her hand.*] What can I do for you?

SMÍRNOFF. I had the pleasure of knowing your late husband, and as it happens, he left me two IOUs—the total comes to twelve hundred rubles.[5] Now, I have a mortgage[6] payment due tomorrow, so I have to ask you, madam, to pay up. And I'm afraid I need the money today.

POPÓVA. Twelve hundred? What did my husband owe you the money for?

SMÍRNOFF. I sold him a couple of loads of oats.

POPÓVA. [*With a sigh, to* LUKÁ.] Now don't forget what I told you, Luká. You make sure Toby gets his extra oats.

[*LUKÁ goes out.*]

[*To* SMÍRNOFF.] If my husband owed you the money, then of course I'll pay it, but you'll have to excuse me—I don't have any cash on me today. My manager will be back from town the day after tomorrow, and he'll see that you get paid. But today, I'm afraid, I cannot help you. It's exactly seven months today that my husband died, and I'm in a sad mood. I'm in no condition to talk about money.

SMÍRNOFF. [*Annoyed.*] And I'm in a sad mood too, because if I don't meet my mortgage payment tomorrow, they'll foreclose[7] on my property! I'll lose my shirt!

L1 POPÓVA. You'll have your money the day after tomorrow.

SMÍRNOFF. I need the money today, not the day after tomorrow.

POPÓVA. Excuse me; I've already said I cannot pay you today.

SMÍRNOFF. And I've already said I can't wait till the day after tomorrow.

POPÓVA. What can I do? I don't *have* the money!

SMÍRNOFF. That means you won't pay me? L1

POPÓVA. It means *I can't* pay you!

SMÍRNOFF. I see. Is that your final word?

POPÓVA. That is my final word.

SMÍRNOFF. You've made up your mind?

POPÓVA. I've made up my mind.

SMÍRNOFF. Thank you very much. I won't forget this. [*Shrugs.*] Am I supposed to take all this lying down? On my way here, I met my accountant. "Why are you always so down in the dumps?" he asks me. Well, excuse me, he should know! I'm desperate for money! I got up at dawn yesterday and rode around to everyone I know who owes me money, and not a one of them came across! I ran in more circles than a hunting dog, spent the night in some godforsaken fleabag[8] hotel, and finally I get here, fifty miles from home, expect to get paid, and what do I get? "A sad mood"! What kind of mood do you think that puts *me* in?

POPÓVA. I think I made myself perfectly clear: I'll pay you as soon as my manager gets back from town.

SMÍRNOFF. I came to see you, not your manager! What the hell—excuse my language—do I want with your manager?

POPÓVA. My dear sir, I will not have such language in my house, nor will I tolerate that tone of voice! I refuse to listen to any more of this! [*Storms out.*]

SMÍRNOFF. I don't believe this! "It's seven months today my husband died, and I'm in a sad mood. . . ." What's that got to do with

---

4. *Artillery* refers to firearms or guns.
5. A *ruble* is Russian currency.
6. A *mortgage* is a lien, or claim, against property.
7. To *foreclose* is to deal with or close (such as a loan or a mortgage) in advance. In other words, if Smírnoff misses his mortgage payment, he will lose ownership of his property.
8. A *fleabag* is an inferior hotel or rooming house.

Big Idea Awkward Encounters *Why does Popóva refuse to shake his hand?* BI

Reading Strategy Analyzing Cause-and-Effect Relationships *Why does Popóva's explanation provoke Smírnoff?* R1

Additional Support

Skills Practice

LITERARY ELEMENT: Comedy This drama is a comedy. Comedies often deal with light and amusing subjects and typically have happy endings. They entertain through the use of verbal wit, physical humor, ridicule, or irony.
Ask: What did you find most amusing in this drama? *(Students may point to the duel.)* Discuss examples of verbal wit, physical humor, ridicule, and irony. *(Verbal wit is used when the characters make outrageous statements. Physical humor is present in the exaggerated actions of Smírnoff and Luká. Ridicule is present in the names the characters call each other.)* OL

me? I have to make a mortgage payment! Fine, your husband's dead, your manager's gone to town, you're in a mood or whatever—what do you expect me to do? Flap my wings and fly away from my creditors?[9] Run around banging my head into a brick wall? I go see Grúzdeff, he's not home. I go see Yarosévich, he hides. I go see Kurítsyn, we get into a fight; I nearly threw him out his own window. I go see Mazútov, he's sick. And now this one has "a sad mood." Not a one of them paid me! What a bunch of deadbeats![10] And it's all because I'm such a soft touch, I'm a sucker for a hard-luck story! I'm too nice for my own good! Well, it's time to get a little tough. Nobody's going to fool around with me like this! I'm not moving; I'm staying put until she pays up! Oh, boy, am I mad! Look at me—I'm quivering mad! Mad through and through! Mad enough to get nasty! [*Shouts.*] Hey, you!

[*Enter* LUKÁ.]

LUKÁ. What do you want?

SMÍRNOFF. A glass of water. Or better yet, a beer.

[LUKÁ *goes out.*]

What kind of **logic** is that? Here's a man so desperate for money he's ready to hang himself, and she can't pay him because—excuse me very much—she's "in no condition to talk about money." Talk about petticoat logic! This is why I don't like women and hate talking to them. I'd rather light a campfire on a powder keg[11] than talk to a woman. Makes my skin crawl, they make me so mad! All I have to do is see one of those romantic creatures coming, my leg muscles start cramping up. I want to start shouting for help.

[*Enter* LUKÁ.]

LUKÁ. [*Brings* SMÍRNOFF *a glass of water.*] The missus is sick; she says she can't see anybody!

SMÍRNOFF. Get out of here!

[LUKÁ *goes out.*]

She's sick and she can't see anybody! That's fine; she doesn't have to see me. I'll just stay right here until I get my money, that's all. She stays sick for a week, I stay here for a week. She's sick for a year, I stay here for a year. I want my money, lady! Your black dress and your dimples don't impress me. I've seen plenty of dimples before! [*Goes to the window and shouts.*] Hey, Semyón, unhitch the horses! We're not leaving just yet! I'm staying right here! Tell them in the stable to give my horses some oats! And watch it, you nitwit—you've got the trace horse[12] tangled again! You just wait till I get . . . oh, forget it. [*Moves away from the window.*] What a mess. Hottest day of the year, nobody wants to pay me, couldn't sleep the whole night, and now I've got to deal with some wacky widow and her moods. It's enough to give a man a headache. I need a drink, that's what I need. [*Yells.*] Hey, you!

[*Enter* LUKÁ.]

LUKÁ. What do you want?

SMÍRNOFF. A shot of vodka!

[LUKÁ *goes out;* SMÍRNOFF *falls into a chair and looks himself over.*]

Oof, I'm a mess. Dirt, mud on my boots, I need a shave, my hair needs combing, straw sticking out of my pockets. The lady must have thought I was out to rob her. [*Yawns.*] Not too polite, I guess, showing up like this, but what the hell . . . I'm not a guest, I'm a bill collector; nobody says I have to dress right. . . .

9. *Creditors* are people to whom money is owed.
10. A *deadbeat* is someone who does not pay his or her debts.
11. A *powder keg* is a small, usually metal, cask for holding gunpowder or blasting powder.

12. A *trace horse* is a horse that is harnessed for pulling a load or a wagon.

Vocabulary

logic (loj′ ik) *n.* a method of reasoning

Literary Element Farce *Is the play humorous at this point? Why or why not?* L2

Reading Strategy Analyzing Cause-and-Effect Relationships *Why does Smírnoff think Popóva might have suspected he was a robber?* R2

Teach

L2 Literary Element

Farce Answer: *Some students will find the situation comical, based on the language and Smírnoff's exaggerated reaction. Others may say the situation is frightening.* OL

R2 Reading Strategy

Analyzing Cause-and-Effect Relationships Answer: *Smírnoff notices his rough appearance. He needs a shave, his hair is uncombed, and he has dirt on his boots.* OL

Differentiated Instruction

Performing Drama Emphasize that drama is intended to be performed rather than read. Ask gifted and talented students to act out the play for the class. Assign parts, and allow students time to rehearse and to create a set. Advise students to use their voices and body language to create a humorous tone in their performance. AL

Academic Standards

Additional Support activities on pp. 826 and 827 cover the following standards:

Skills Practice: **9.3.1** Explain...the characteristics of different forms of dramatic literature...

Differentiated Instruction: **9.7.6** Analyze the occasion and the interests of the audience and choose effective verbal and nonverbal techniques (including voice, gestures, and eye contact) for presentations.

Teach

L1 Literary Element

Farce Ask: How do Smírnoff's actions add to the farce? *(Smírnoff's silly and exaggerated fake lisp and fake bow, as well as his use of French expressions, add to the humor.)* OL

BI Big Idea

Awkward Encounters
Answer: *She and Smírnoff may be flirting, so it is possible that she is enjoying the conversation.* OL

[*Enter* LUKÁ; *he gives* SMÍRNOFF *a glass of vodka.*]

LUKÁ. You take too many liberties, you know that . . . ?

SMÍRNOFF. [*Angry.*] What?

LUKÁ. Oh, nothing. I just . . . Nothing.

SMÍRNOFF. Who do you think you're talking to? Just shut up, will you?

LUKÁ. [*Aside, as he goes out.*] How're we going to get rid of him. . . ?

SMÍRNOFF. Oh, I'm mad! I am so mad! Mad enough to blow up the world! Mad enough to get nasty! [*Shouts.*] Hey, you!

[*Enter* POPÓVA.]

POPÓVA. [*Not looking at him.*] My dear sir, I have lived so long in retirement I have grown unused to the human voice. I cannot stand shouting. I must earnestly beg you to respect my solitude.[13]

SMÍRNOFF. Pay me my money and I'll go.

POPÓVA. I have told you in no uncertain terms that I have no money here at the moment and you will have to wait until the day after tomorrow.

SMÍRNOFF. And I also told you in no uncertain terms that I need the money today, not the day after tomorrow. If you don't pay me today, I might as well hang myself by the day after tomorrow.

POPÓVA. But what can I do, since I don't have the money?

SMÍRNOFF. You mean you're not going to pay me? Is that what you mean?

POPÓVA. I can't!

SMÍRNOFF. In that case, I stay right here until I get it. [*Sits down.*] You're going to pay me the day after tomorrow? Fine. I'll be sitting right here! [*Jumps up.*] Look, don't you believe I have a mortgage payment due tomorrow? You think I'm joking?

POPÓVA. I asked you not to shout! You're not in a stable.

13. *Solitude* refers to being alone.

SMÍRNOFF. I didn't ask you about a stable! What I asked you was, Don't you believe I have a mortgage payment due tomorrow?

POPÓVA. You haven't the faintest idea of how to behave in a lady's presence.

SMÍRNOFF. I do so know how to behave in a lady's presence!

POPÓVA. No, you do not! You are ill-mannered and vulgar![14] No gentleman would speak like this in front of a lady!

SMÍRNOFF. Oh, well, excuse me! Just how would he speak in front of a lady? In French? [*With a nasty lisp.*] *Madame, je vous prie* . . . How charmed I am to know that you reject to pay me my money! Ah, *pardon,* I seem to be upsetting you! Lovely weather we're having! And my, my, don't you look lovely in black! [*Makes a fake bow.*] L1

POPÓVA. You're being very stupid and not funny.

SMÍRNOFF. [*Mocking.*] Stupid and not funny! I don't know how to behave in a lady's presence! Woman, I have seen more ladies in my time than you have seen sparrows in yours! I have fought three duels[15] because of ladies, I have walked out on twelve ladies, and nine ladies have walked out on me! So there! Oh, I used to be an idiot, got crushes on them, sweet-talked, cast my pearls before— Well . . . Bow, click my heels, fall in love, suffer, sigh in the moonlight, freeze up, melt into puddles—I did it all. I could rattle on for hours about women's rights: I spent half my life hanging around women, but not anymore! No, thank you very much! No more wool over my eyes! I've had it! Dark eyes, red lips, dimples in the cheeks, moonlight, sighs—no, sir, I wouldn't give you two cents for any of it now. Present company excepted, of course,

14. *Vulgar* means "lacking in cultivation, perception, or taste."
15. *Duels* are combats between two persons, usually men, using pistols or swords.

Big Idea Awkward Encounters *Do you think Popóva is enjoying her conversation with Smírnoff at this point? Explain.* BI

Additional Support

Skills Practice

WRITING: Summarizing When students write a summary, they use three skills. They identify the main ideas of a selection, put the ideas in a logical sequence, and write them in their own words. A good summary includes the main ideas but does not include insignificant details. Ask students to summarize what they have read so far in *The Bear.* Have them trade summaries with a partner and answer the following questions about their partner's summary: Does this summary include all the main ideas? Does it answer *who, what, where, why,* and *when*? OL but all women are **pretentious**, affected,[16] gossipy, hateful, liars to the marrow[17] of their bones, vain,[18] petty,[19] merciless, they can't think straight, and as for this part here [*Slaps his forehead.*] . . . well—excuse my frankness—a sparrow has ten times more brains than any philosopher in skirts. Take a good look at anyone of these romantic creatures: petticoats and hot air, divine transports, the whole works; then take a look at her soul. Pure crocodile. [*Grabs the back of a chair; the chair cracks and breaks.*] And the worst part is, this crocodile thinks she has a **monopoly** on the tender emotion of love! Has any woman ever known how to love anything except her lapdog? She's in love, all she can do is snivel[20] and whine. A man in love, now, he suffers and sacrifices, but a woman, her love shows up how? She swishes her skirt and gets a firm grip on your nose. You're a woman, unfortunately, but at least you know what I mean, what woman's nature is like. Tell me honestly: have you ever seen a woman who was faithful and true? No, you haven't! The only honest and faithful women are old or ugly.

POPÓVA. Excuse me, but would you mind telling me just who you think *is* faithful and true? Men?

SMÍRNOFF. Well, of course, men.

16. Here, *affected* means "fake" or "cultivated."
17. *Marrow* is the tissue that fills the inner hollow part of most bones.
18. *Vain* means "having no real value."
19. *Petty* means "small-minded."
20. To *snivel* is to speak or act in a whining, sniffling, tearful, or overly emotional manner.

Literary Element Farce *How does this stage direction add to the element of farce in this play?* L2

Vocabulary

pretentious (pri ten′ shəs) *adj.* expressing exaggerated importance or worth

monopoly (mə nop′ ə lē) *n.* exclusive possession or control

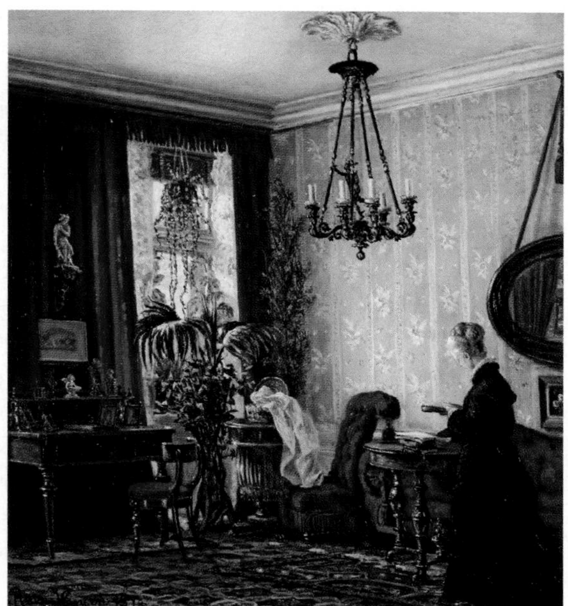

A Woman In An Interior, c. 1878. Luisa Rovn Hansen. Oil on canvas.
Viewing the Art: What similarities might the woman in this painting have with Popóva? Explain. ★

POPÓVA. Men! [*A mean laugh.*] Men are faithful and true in love! Well, spread the good news! [*Hotly.*] How dare you say that? Men faithful and true? Let me tell you a thing or two! Of all the men I know or have ever known, my dear departed husband was the best. I loved him passionately, with all my heart and soul, the way only a young and sensitive girl can love; I gave him my youth, my happiness, my life, my money; I lived and breathed for him, I worshiped him, he was my idol, and . . . and what do you think he did? This best of all possible men betrayed me in the worst possible way: he cheated on me every chance he got. After he died I found boxes and boxes of love letters in his desk! And when he was alive he'd leave me alone for weeks on end. And he flirted with other women right in front of me, he deceived me, he spent all my money, he laughed at me when I objected.

Reading Strategy Analyzing Cause-and-Effect Relationships *Why does Popóva doubt Smírnoff's statement about the faithfulness of men?* R

Teach

L2 Literary Element

Farce Answer: *This detail is funny and ridiculous. The chair breaking reminds the audience that this play is taking place in an exaggerated version of reality.* OL

R Reading Strategy

Analyzing Cause-and-Effect Relationships Answer: *She experienced her husband's unfaithfulness.*
Ask: What evidence does Popóva give to support her claim that men are not faithful? *(She says that she loved her husband, but he cheated on her, left her for weeks at a time, flirted with other women in front of her, and spent all of her money.)* OL

★ Viewing the Art

Answer: *Students may point out that the woman pictured seems to be of roughly the same class as Popóva and that the room's furnishings are similar to those that might be found in Popóva's house. Also the woman in the painting seems contemplative, as Popóva may have been before being interrupted by Smírnoff.* AS

Building Reading Fluency

Reading the Drama Divide students into groups of three. In each group, assign students to read the parts of Popóva, Smírnoff, and Luká. Have them practice reading the drama aloud. Encourage them to use the tone of their voices to create a humorous mood. After the groups have read through the entire play, read the play together as a class. Start with one group reading the drama out loud. Then after a page or so, ask a second group to pick up where the first group left off. Move from group to group until everyone has had a chance to read aloud. BL

Academic Standards

Additional Support activities on pp. 828 and 829 cover the following standards:

Skills Practice: **9.5.2** Write responses to literature that demonstrate a comprehensive grasp of the significant ideas of literary works… **9.4.10** Review [and] evaluate… writing for meaning, clarity, [and] content…

Building Reading Fluency: **9.7** [Develop] speaking skills…in conjunction with… strategies…[for] delivery of oral presentations.

Teach

L1 Literary Element

Farce Answer: *The language, especially the phrase "tossed salad," exaggerates Smírnoff's behavior. The words show his frustration, but are humorous in nature.*

Ask: How does Luká's response to Smírnoff add to the farce? *(Luká's heart attack is greatly exaggerated and ridiculous. His reaction is more comical than realistic.)* OL

★ Writer's Technique

Writing a Farce Chekhov said about writing that "only he is an emancipated thinker who is not afraid to write foolish things." Discuss what Chekhov might have meant by this statement.

Ask: How does this statement relate to *The Bear*? *(Students might note that Chekhov may consider himself a free thinker since this drama is foolish.)* AS

And despite everything, I loved him, and I will be faithful to his memory. Even though he's dead, I am faithful and unshakable. I have buried myself within these four walls, where I shall mourn him forever. I shall wear black until the day I die.

SMÍRNOFF. [*A sneering laugh.*] Black? Don't make me laugh! How dumb do you think I am? I know exactly why you go around in that Mardi Gras[21] outfit and why you've buried yourself within these walls! Of course! It's all so romantic, so mysterious! You're waiting for some shavetail[22] army lieutenant to come riding by, or some sentimental schoolboy with a bad complexion, and he'll look up at your window and think: Ah! There dwells the mysterious Tamara, who loved her husband so much she buried herself within four walls. . . . I know all about your little games.

POPÓVA. [*Flares up.*] What? How dare you even suggest anything of the kind!

SMÍRNOFF. You buried yourself alive, but you didn't forget to powder your nose!

POPÓVA. How dare you!! How dare you speak to me like this!

SMÍRNOFF. Don't yell at me—I'm not your manager. But I'm a man, not a woman, and I'm used to calling a spade a spade. And please stop shouting.

POPÓVA. I'm not shouting—you are! Will you please go away and leave me alone!

SMÍRNOFF. Pay me my money and I'll go!

POPÓVA. I will not give you any money!

SMÍRNOFF. You will too!

POPÓVA. I will not! You won't get one red cent from me! Now please go away!

SMÍRNOFF. I do not have the pleasure of being either your husband or your fiancé,[23] so please stop making scenes for my benefit. [*Sits down.*] I hate that.

POPÓVA. [*Snorting with anger.*] You dare sit down?

SMÍRNOFF. Exactly.

POPÓVA. Will you please go!

SMÍRNOFF. Just give me my money! [*Aside.*] Oh, am I mad! Am I *mad*!

POPÓVA. Of all the nerve! I want nothing more to do with you! Please leave!

[*Pause.*]

You're still here? You haven't left?

SMÍRNOFF. No.

POPÓVA. No?

SMÍRNOFF. No.

POPÓVA. All right! [*Rings.*] ★

[*Enter* LUKÁ.]

Luká, will you please show this gentleman out?

LUKÁ. [*Goes over to* SMÍRNOFF.] Please leave, sir. The lady asked you to. She doesn't want you here.

SMÍRNOFF. [*Leaps to his feet.*] And you shut up! Who do you think you're talking to? I'll make a tossed salad out of you!

LUKÁ. [*Clutches his heart.*] Oh, my God! Oh, mother of God! [*Falls into an armchair.*] I'm dying! I'm dying! I can't breathe!

POPÓVA. Dásha! Where's Dásha? [*Screams.*] Dásha! Pelégea! Dásha! [*Rings frantically.*]

LUKÁ. They all went off berry picking. There's nobody else in the house! Oh, I'm dying! Water!

POPÓVA. Will you get out of here?

SMÍRNOFF. Can't you be a little more polite?

POPÓVA. [*Makes a fist and stamps her foot.*] You peasant! You bear! You vulgar bear! Monster! You . . . *radical!*

SMÍRNOFF. What? What did you call me?

21. *Mardi Gras* is a festival of carnivals, masquerade balls, costumes, and revelry that culminates on Shrove Tuesday (the day before Ash Wednesday) on the Christian calendar.
22. A *shavetail* is a pack mule. Here, it is used to mean a second lieutenant.
23. *Fiancé* is a man engaged to be married.

Literary Element Farce *How does the word choice here communicate an element of farce?* L1

Additional Support

Skills Practice

LISTENING/SPEAKING/VIEWING: Acting Brainstorm ways in which students can bring the drama alive. Encourage them to use the stage directions in parentheses to help them act out a scene in the play. In addition, their pitch, tone of voice, eye contact, and posture should contribute to their portrayal of the characters. Invite students to form groups of three members, and choose to portray Popóva, Smírnoff, or Luká. Ask each group to rehearse the part of the drama starting with the line, "Luká, will you please show this

POPÓVA. I said you were a bear!

SMÍRNOFF. [*Moves toward her.*] And just who said you could insult me like that?

POPÓVA. You're right, I am insulting you! What about it? You think I'm afraid of you?

SMÍRNOFF. You think, just because you're some kind of romantic heroine, that gives you the right to insult me with impunity?[24] Is that it? Oh, no! This is a matter for the field of honor!

LUKÁ. Oh, my God! Oh, my God! Water!

SMÍRNOFF. Time to choose weapons!

POPÓVA. And just because you've got big fists and a bull neck, you think I'm afraid of you? You . . . you bear!

SMÍRNOFF. To the field of honor! Nobody insults me like that, not even a woman!

POPÓVA. [*Trying to shout him down.*] Bear! Bear! Bear!

SMÍRNOFF. It's about time we got rid of old prejudices about only men needing to defend themselves on the field of honor! If it's equality you want, then it's equality you get! I challenge you to a duel!

POPÓVA. You want to fight a duel! Good! Let's fight!

SMÍRNOFF. Right this minute!

POPÓVA. Right this minute! My husband had a set of pistols; wait here, I'll go get them. [*Starts out and immediately returns.*] You have no idea what a pleasure it will be for me to put a bullet through your thick head! [*Goes out.*]

SMÍRNOFF. I'll shoot her like a sitting duck! I'm not a schoolboy anymore, I'm no sentimental puppy—I don't care if she *is* the weaker sex!

LUKÁ. Oh, please, sir! [*Falls to his knees.*] Please don't do this, please just leave, please. I'm an old man, my heart won't stand all the excitement! Please don't shoot her!

24. *Impunity* is freedom from punishment, harm, or loss.

Literary Element Farce *What makes Smírnoff's remark here ridiculous?* L2

SMÍRNOFF. [*Pays no attention to him.*] I'll shoot her—that's real equality; that'll emancipate her! Equality of the sexes at last! But what a woman! [*Imitates her.*] "You have no idea what a pleasure it will be to put a bullet through your thick head!" Yes, what a woman! She got all flushed; her eyes were flashing fire; she accepted my challenge without even thinking! That's the first time this has ever happened to me!

LUKÁ. Oh, please, sir, please go! Just go away!

SMÍRNOFF. Now, that's a woman I understand! That's a real woman! She's not one of your sissies, nothing wishy-washy about her; she's all flint and firepower! I'm almost sorry to have to kill her!

LUKÁ. [*Cries.*] Please, sir, please, just go! Please!

SMÍRNOFF. I definitely like this woman! Definitely! So she has dimples—I still like her. I'm almost ready to tell her to forget about the money. And I'm not mad anymore. . . . What an astonishing woman!

[*Enter* POPÓVA; *she carries a pair of dueling pistols.*]

POPÓVA. Here's the pistols. But before we have our duel, will you please show me how to use the things? I've never even touched one before.

LUKÁ. Oh, God have mercy on us all! I'm going to get the gardener and the coachman. . . . Why did this have to happen to us. . . ? [*Goes out.*]

SMÍRNOFF. [*Looks over the pistols with a professional eye.*] You see, there are several different makes of weapon. You've got your Mortimer,[25] now—that's a special dueling pistol, percussion[26] action. But what you have here are Smith and Wesson revolvers,

25. *Mortimer* and *Smith and Wesson* are manufacturers of firearms.

26. *Percussion* is the striking of a cap in a way to set off the charge in a firearm.

Reading Strategy Analyzing Cause-and-Effect Relationships *How does Smírnoff react to Popóva's acceptance to a duel?* R

Teach

L2 Literary Element

Farce Answer: *He is suggesting that equal rights for women means the right to die in a duel, as men do. But fighting does not really signify equality. Smírnoff does not seem to understand the concept of equality between men and women. He thinks women are weaker than men are.* OL

R Reading Strategy

Analyzing Cause-and-Effect Relationships Answer: *At first, he seems happy to kill her and calls her the weaker sex, but then he realizes that he is attracted to her. The irony is that it is Popóva's strength and personality that Smírnoff is attracted to, not her alleged "weakness."* OL

gentleman out?" and ending with, "My husband had a set of pistols; wait here, I'll go get them." Tell each group to perform the scene for the rest of the class. Discuss how each group made the scene unique or humorous. OL

Reading in the Real World

Citizenship Have students read about the Russian government, under the czars or communism. Ask them to focus on how the Russian government differs from U.S. government. Have students share their findings in a class discussion comparing the governments. OL

Academic Standards

Additional Support activities on pp. 830 and 831 cover the following standards:

Skills Practice: **9.7.6** Analyze the occasion and the interests of the audience and choose effective verbal and nonverbal techniques (including voice, gestures, and eye contact) for presentations.

Reading in the Real World: **9.7.15** Deliver expository (informational) presentations that convey information and ideas from… sources accurately and coherently…

Teach

R1 Reading Strategy

Analyzing Cause-and-Effect Relationships **Answer:** *He wants to end the proposed duel with Popóva. He no longer wants to harm her.*
Ask: What has caused Smírnoff to change his attitude toward Popóva? *(He likes her bravery in accepting his challenge.)* OL

Awkward Encounters
Answer: *His feelings for Popóva are changing and he is tongue-tied. He hesitates to admit his new feelings.*
Ask: How might Smírnoff's words, tone, and actions make the situation more awkward? *(Smírnoff is stuttering, shouting, and breaking furniture, which might cause Popóva to feel more uncomfortable.)* OL

★ Viewing the Art

One of the most influential painters of his time, Jean Louis André Théodore Géricault was a key figure in the nineteenth century Romantic movement. Romanticism was a reaction against Classicism. It emphasized emotion over reason and celebrated the beauty of nature. AS

Anglo-Arabian Stallion In The Imperial Stables At Versailles. ★
Theodore Gericault.

triple action, with an extractor[27] and central sights. Beautiful pieces! Must have cost at least ninety rubles the pair. Now look, you hold the pistol like this. . . . [*Aside.*] What amazing eyes she's got! What a little spitfire!

POPÓVA. Like this?

SMÍRNOFF. That's it, that's the way. Next you cock the piece, like this . . . and you take aim. . . . Move your head back a little. Stretch out your arm . . . that's the way. Then you press your finger on this little thing here, and that's all there is to it. Main thing is, keep your cool and take slow, careful aim. Try not to let your hand shake.

POPÓVA. Right. . . . We shouldn't shoot indoors—let's go outside.

SMÍRNOFF. All right, let's go outside. Only I warn you, I intend to shoot into the air.

POPÓVA. Oh, that's the last straw! Why?

SMÍRNOFF. Because . . . because . . . It's none of your business why!

POPÓVA. Are you getting scared? Is that it? Aha, that's it! Oh no, you won't get out of this so easily! Come on, we're going outside! I won't rest until I put a bullet through that head of yours—that head I hate so! What's the matter, are you a coward?

SMÍRNOFF. That's it, I'm a coward.

POPÓVA. You're lying! Why don't you want to fight?

SMÍRNOFF. Because . . . because . . . because I like you.

POPÓVA. [*Sarcastic laugh.*] He likes me! He dares to tell me he likes me! [*Points to the door.*] Just go.

SMÍRNOFF. [*Puts down the pistol in silence, takes his hat, and starts out; at the door, he stops and turns. They look at each other in silence for a moment; then he goes hesitantly toward* POPÓVA.] Listen . . . are you still mad? I was crazy myself until just a minute ago, but you know . . . how can I put it? Well, the fact is, I . . . you see, the fact is, nothing like this ever happened to me before. . . . [*Shouts.*] Well, is it my fault I like you? [*Grabs a chair behind his*

27. The *extractor* is the mechanism in a firearm that dislodges a used cartridge from the chamber.

Reading Strategy Analyzing Cause-and-Effect Relationships *What result does Smírnoff hope to achieve by saying he's a coward?* R1

Big Idea Awkward Encounters *Why do you think Smírnoff is having trouble expressing himself?* BI

Additional Support

Skills Practice

READING: Making Predictions The drama's ending hints that Popóva and Smírnoff have fallen in love. Ask students to predict what will happen to the couple in the future. They should write down their predictions and support them with examples and quotations from the drama. Tell students to form small groups to discuss their conclusions. Each group should choose one prediction to discuss with the rest of the class. OL *back; the chair cracks and breaks.*] Why do you have such fragile furniture! I like you! You understand? I . . . I think I'm in love with you!

POPÓVA. Get away from me! I hate you!

SMÍRNOFF. What a woman! I've never seen anything like her in my entire life! I'm done for! I'm caught in her mousetrap!

POPÓVA. Get away from me, or I'll shoot!

SMÍRNOFF. Go ahead, shoot! You don't know how happy that will make me, to die with your beautiful eyes upon me, die from a gun in your silky little hand. . . . Oh, I'm out of my mind! Look, you'd better think this over fast and decide right away. Once I leave here, we'll never see each other again. Make up your mind. I own a lot of land, I'm from a good family, I've got an income of ten thousand a year. . . . I can put a bullet through a coin in the air at twenty paces. . . . I've got the best horses you'll ever see. . . . Will you marry me?

POPÓVA. [*Angry, she waves the pistol.*] Marry you? I intend to shoot you! On the field of honor!

SMÍRNOFF. I'm out of my mind! I don't understand what's happening. . . .

POPÓVA. On the field of honor!

SMÍRNOFF. I'm out of my mind! I'm in love! I'm behaving like an idiot schoolboy! [*Grabs her hand; she shrieks with pain.*] I love you! [*Falls to his knees.*] I love you, the way I've never loved anyone before! I walked out on twelve women, nine walked out on me, but I never loved one of them the way I do you! My mind has turned to jelly, my joints have turned to sugar, I'm on my knees like a dope, and I'm asking for your hand. . . . Oh, the shame, the shame! I haven't been in love for six years, I swore I never would again, and all of a sudden I'm head over heels! I'm asking you to marry me! Yes or no? Will you? Yes or no? No? Fine! [*Gets up and heads quickly toward the door.*]

POPÓVA. Wait a minute . . .

SMÍRNOFF. [*Stops.*] Well?

POPÓVA. Nothing, just go! No, I mean, wait. . . . No, go away! Go away! I hate you! I mean, no, don't go! Oh, you make me so mad! [*Throws the pistol on the floor.*] My finger's all swollen up from that thing! [*Starts tearing her handkerchief.*] Well, what are you waiting for? Just get out of here!

SMÍRNOFF. All right then. Good-bye.

POPÓVA. Yes, yes, just go! [*Screams.*] Where are you going? Wait a minute. . . . Oh, come on back. Oh, I'm so mad! Stay away from me! Stay away from me!

SMÍRNOFF. [*Crosses to her.*] *You're* mad? *I'm* mad. I fell in love like a schoolboy, got down on my knees, I even got goose bumps. . . . [*Roughly.*] I love you! That's all I needed, to fall in love with you! Tomorrow I've got to pay the mortgage, start cutting hay, and now you— [*Grabs her around the waist.*] I'll never forgive myself for this—

POPÓVA. Get away from me! Get your hands off me! I . . . I hate you! I want to fight the d-d-duel!

[*A long kiss. Enter* LUKÁ *with a shovel, the gardener with a rake, the coachman with a pitchfork, some farmworkers with sticks.*]

LUKÁ. [*Sees the couple kissing.*] Oh, my. . . .

[*Pause.*]

POPÓVA. [*Shyly.*] Luká, go out to the stable and tell them Toby doesn't get extra oats anymore.

CURTAIN.

Literary Element Farce *Would you interpret Smírnoff's comments literally? Explain.* **L**

Reading Strategy Analyzing Cause-and-Effect Relationships *Why does Popóva change her mind about feeding Toby the extra oats?* **R2**

Differentiated Instruction

Examining the Play in Parts Help less proficient readers understand what is happening in the text by breaking the play into short sections. After students read a section, have them pause to clarify the action that has taken place. Ask students to identify and take notes on elements of farce, cause-and-effect relationships, and awkward encounters in what they have just read. Invite volunteers to read the section aloud and then incorporate actions. **BL**

Teach

L Literary Element

Farce Answer: *It is not a literal statement. It is exaggerated. Smírnoff thinks that because of Popóva's temperament, a romance might be challenging. Yet, her spark is attractive.*
Ask: What aspects of this scene add to the farce? *(The indecisiveness of Popóva, her exaggerated distress over what Smírnoff is saying and doing, and his list of things to do the next day make the scene ridiculous.)* **OL**

R2 Reading Strategy

Analyzing Cause-and-Effect Relationships Answer: *Feeding Toby extra oats was meant to show loyalty to her late husband. Her loyalty to him is replaced with her feelings for Smírnoff.*
Ask: What causes Popóva to change her mind about Smírnoff? *(Students may say the kiss did, but others may say Popóva was lonely and did not really want to mourn her dead husband for the rest of her life.)* **OL**

Use the CheckPoint questions on Presentation Plus! to check students' mastery of the selection. These questions can be used with interactive response keypads for immediate student feedback.

Academic Standards

Additional Support activities on pp. 832 and 833 cover the following standards:

Skills Practice: **9.2** Develop strategies such as...making predictions...

Differentiated Instruction: **9.2** Develop [reading] strategies...

AFTER YOU READ

Assess

1. (a) Answers will vary and may reflect students' difficulty in comprehending the story at the first reading. (b) Students may conclude that Popóva or Smírnoff surprised them in the course of the play's events.
2. (a) He thinks she has mourned long enough and encourages her to begin socializing again. (b) He feels she has a chance at new love before she ages.
3. (a) He shouts and pushes his way in. (b) She is put off by his forceful and loud behavior.
4. (a) He wants her to repay her husband's debt to him. (b) He will lose his property.
5. In the beginning, he is angry with her and dislikes her; at the end, he is in love with her.
6. Students may respond that he has had difficulty getting money from other people. Students may offer the opinion that Smírnoff is by nature impatient and demanding. They may conclude that Smírnoff thinks force will produce quick results.
7. Her quick change of heart reveals that she was not sincerely sorrowful. She was mourning to prove a point.
8. Students should identify a personal story about an awkward encounter.

Academic Standards

The Additional Support activity on p. 835 covers the following standards:

Differentiated Instruction: **9.5.9** Write or deliver a research report that has been developed using a systematic research process… **9.7.4** Use…electronic media to enhance the appeal and accuracy of presentations.

AFTER YOU READ

RESPONDING AND THINKING CRITICALLY

Respond

1. (a)What was your first reaction to *The Bear*? (b)How do the characters' actions over the course of the play verify or challenge your initial reaction?

Recall and Interpret

2. (a)What does Luká encourage Popóva to do at the beginning of the play? (b)What is his reasoning?
3. (a)What tactics does Smírnoff use to get into the house? (b)How do these tactics influence the way Popóva views him?
4. (a)Why is Smírnoff eager to see Popóva? (b)What will happen if he cannot accomplish his goal?

Analyze and Evaluate

5. How do Smírnoff's feelings for Popóva change over the course of the play? Explain.
6. Why do you think Smírnoff initially approaches Popóva in an aggressive manner?
7. What does Popóva's change of heart toward Smírnoff reveal about her period of mourning?

Connect

8. **Big Idea** **Awkward Encounters** Describe a similar awkward encounter you have experienced or heard about. Identify some ways in which it was similar to the encounter described in *The Bear.*

YOU'RE THE CRITIC: Different Viewpoints

Chekhov as Humorist

In *The Bear* we see two people who are very different. Yet in some ways, they are very much alike. Read the two excerpts below, which offer perspectives about Chekhov and *The Bear.* As you read, look for ways that these two opinions are similar and ways that they are different.

> "The Bear *condenses so much of human nature into this short, comical, bizarre, and ultimately triumphant act. Chekhov demonstrates how close (at times) is the relationship between anger and passion, and how strange and wonderful is the human condition.*"
>
> —Jack Coulehan

> *"What happens in the course of the Chekhov play is that the characters are shown responding and reacting to one another on the emotional level: Chekhov creates among them what may be called an emotional network, in which it is not the interplay of character but the interplay of emotion that holds the attention of the audience."*
>
> —Harvey Pitcher

Group Activity Discuss the following questions with classmates. Refer to the excerpts and cite evidence from *The Bear* for support.

1. Chekhov chose to write *The Bear* as a play rather than as a short story, another literary genre at which he was adept. According to Pitcher, what dramatic elements or effects does Chekhov master in his plays? Would these elements or effects be possible in the short story genre? Explain.
2. How do Coulehan's statements show that *The Bear* employs both farce and realism to good effect?

From the Antaeus Company production of Chekhov X 4. Dawn Didawick as Yeléna Popóva, Jeremy Lawrence as Luká, Harry Groener as Smírnoff in *The Bear.*

You're The Critic

1. Pitcher says that it is the immediacy and interplay of emotion that holds the attention of the audience. Short stories usually rely more on character development than drama does. Answers will vary as to whether this immediacy could be replicated in the short story form.
2. Coulehan praises Chekhov's ability to realistically display the relationship between anger and passion. He also implies that without the "comical, bizarre," and "strange and wonderful" aspects—in short, its farcical elements—the play would be less lively, less a triumph.

LITERARY ANALYSIS

Literary Element Farce

A comedy is a type of play that is humorous and that often has a happy ending. A **farce** is a specific type of comedy. In a farce, you can expect to find situations, characters, or events that are absurd or ridiculous, as well as funny. *The Bear* is an example of a farce.

1. In a play, the characters' words and actions tell you about the story. Identify the first line of dialogue in *The Bear* that tells you the play might be a farce.
2. Why do you think Chekhov might have written *The Bear* as a farce?

Review: Dialogue

As you learned on pages 820–821, **dialogue** is the conversation between two characters in a literary work. Dialogue can help to create mood, develop the plot, and convey theme. It is also an excellent way for a writer to reveal a character's personality.

Partner Activity Use a graphic organizer like the one below to help you think about how the characters in *The Bear* are developed through dialogue. Then pair up with a classmate and write one page of dialogue that Smírnoff and Popóva might speak after the play's end. Present the dialogue to the rest of the class and give a brief analysis of how the dialogue shows that Smírnoff and Popóva have either changed or stayed the same.

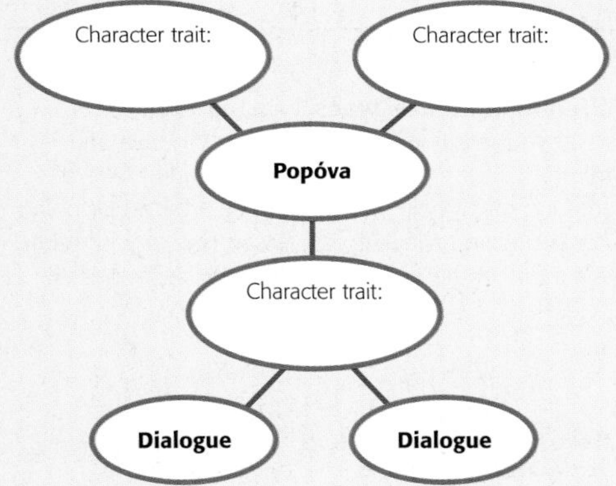

READING AND VOCABULARY

Reading Strategy Analyzing Cause-and-Effect Relationships

In a story or drama there may be several **cause-and-effect relationships.** Think about how these relationships in *The Bear* affect the sequence of events. Note how Chekhov uses cause-and-effect relationships to reveal the personalities of the characters and to develop the play as a farce.

1. Identify one cause-and-effect relationship in *The Bear* that happens before the final cause-and-effect event.
2. Much of the action of the play is the result of an unpaid debt. If Smírnoff's visit had been a social call rather than a business request, how might the play have been different?

Vocabulary Practice

Practice with Antonyms Select the best antonym for each of the following vocabulary words.

1. pretentious	a. humble	b. overbearing
2. mourn	a. celebrate	b. weep
3. logic	a. reason	b. nonsense
4. monopoly	a. community	b. company

Academic Vocabulary

Here are two words from the vocabulary list on page R80. These words will help you think, talk, and write about the selection.

status (stā′təs) *n.* the condition of a person or thing

fund (fund) *n.* a sum of money or other resources set apart for a specific purpose

Practice and Apply

1. Explain Popóva's **status** at the beginning of the play.
2. Why did Smírnoff need to increase his **funds**?

AFTER YOU READ

Assess

Literary Element

1. Possible answer might be, "He was mean and . . . and even unfaithful. But I intend to be faithful to the grave and show him what real love means."
2. Answers should indicate that by creating a farce, Chekhov could make statements about high society and about members of the military, as well as about male-female relationships and customs of the times.

Review: Dialogue

Responses should indicate students' understanding of the way in which dialogue helps to create characters and enables the audience to understand the action and the play's intent.

Reading Strategy

1. A possible citation may be: "And I'm in a sad mood too, because if I don't meet my mortgage payment tomorrow, they'll foreclose on my property! I'll lose my shirt!"
2. Without the business request to pay a debt, the initial tension of the play would be lost. The main characters may not have argued and probably would not have connected romantically.

Vocabulary

1. a **2.** a **3.** b **4.** b

Academic Vocabulary

1. She was unmarried because her husband was dead.
2. He needed money to make a mortgage payment.

Differentiated Instruction

Research Interested students can research more about Russian culture and history. Encourage students to conduct their research in a variety of sources including, but not limited to, the Internet. Remind students that the reliability of Internet information varies a great deal. They should evaluate Web sites carefully and find at least one additional source to verify each point researched on any given site. Allow time for students to share their findings. Challenge students to use their research to create a multimedia presentation. **AL**

AFTER YOU READ

Assess

Writing About Literature

Essays should convey the idea that Smírnoff and Popóva may have a stormy relationship; we may guess this because of the evidence of their fiery personalities.

Literature Groups

Popóva's traits may include: overly dramatic; flighty; changeable; quick to make decisions; ready to prove her ability as a woman; quick to love.

Answers should include the idea that stereotypes emphasize the traits of a group of people; therefore, stereotypical characters allow an author to criticize groups or classes of individuals. Creating stereotypical characters can be a type of "shorthand" in that audiences recognize what the author is trying to say without requiring a lengthy and complex explanation.

Web Activities Have students access the Web site for interactive activities that will help them assess their understanding of the selection.

WRITING AND EXTENDING

Writing About Literature

Respond to Characters In *The Bear,* the characters Smírnoff and Popóva have an awkward first encounter. By the end of the play, they have fallen in love and are planning to marry. Use what you know about these characters to write a brief essay describing what will happen to them after the play is over. Think about what a marriage between Smírnoff and Popóva would be like. Are these two characters suited to each other? How might the servants react to them? Would they be happy? Use examples from the text to support your ideas.

Before you begin drafting, use a graphic organizer like the one below to decide how you will introduce, develop, and conclude your essay.

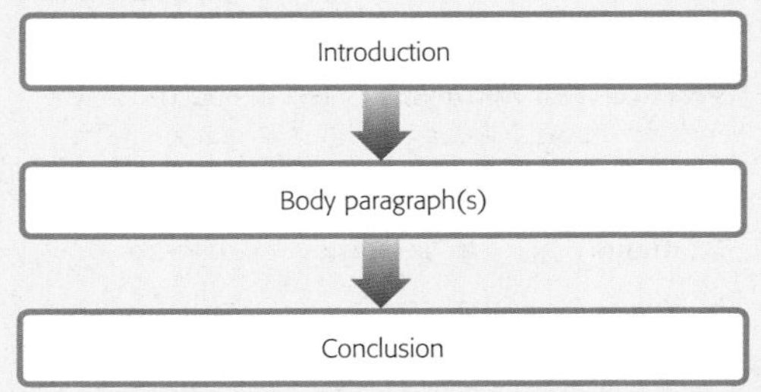

After you complete your draft, exchange essays with a peer reviewer. Review each other's work and suggest revisions. Remember to proofread and edit your work for errors in spelling, grammar, and punctuation.

Literature Groups

Often in literature you will find characters that are stereotypes. A stereotype is a character who is not individually unique, but instead represents traits and characteristics that are supposedly shared by all members of a particular group. In *The Bear,* Popóva may be viewed as a stereotypical character. She represents a beautiful woman of the upper class as well as a tragic widow.

With a partner, review *The Bear.* Look for details that tell you about the character of Popóva. Then write a short paragraph to explain why you think Chekhov might have used stereotypes when creating characters for *The Bear.*

GRAMMAR AND STYLE

Chekhov's Language and Style

Using Different Sentence Types In *The Bear,* Chekhov creates an atmosphere of excitement and action. His use of different types of sentences helps to achieve this effect. Notice that Chekhov uses each of these types of sentences:

- Declarative (statements)
- Exclamatory (statements with emphasis, such as shouts, usually marked with an exclamation point)
- Imperative (statements that give direction to another person or character)
- Interrogative (questions)

The chart below shows examples of each kind of sentence from *The Bear.*

Declarative	Exclamatory	Imperative	Interrogative
I shall never leave this house.	I never heard the like!	Go tell them he gets extra oats today.	Why must people be so difficult?

Activity Use a chart like the one above to record additional examples of each type of sentence in *The Bear.*

Revising Check

Different Sentence Types With a peer reviewer, reread your essay about the future of Popóva and Smírnoff. Are there places where a different type of sentence might help you emphasize a particular point? After you have reviewed your essay, review your partner's essay in the same way. Then revise your essay as needed.

LiteratureOnline Web Activities For eFlashcards, Selection Quick Checks, and other Web activities, go to www.glencoe.com.

Chekhov's Language and Style

Declarative Possible answer: You'll have your money the day after tomorrow.

Exclamatory Possible answer: I don't have the money!

Imperative Possible answer: Get out of here!

Interrogative Possible answer: What do you want?

Comparing Literature *Across Genres*

Connecting to the Reading Selections

Have you ever felt uncomfortable, or strange, around a certain person? In the three selections compared here, playwrights Serafín and Joaquín Álvarez Quintero, fiction writer Shirley Jackson, and poet N. Scott Momaday describe the uneasy—and sometimes surprising—circumstances surrounding relationships.

COMPARING THE Big Idea Awkward Encounters

People often have awkward encounters with people they barely know or with people around whom they feel uncomfortable. Each of the following three selections describes such an encounter.

COMPARING Conflict

Conflict is the central struggle between two opposing forces in a work of literature. Conflict creates the tension that makes a play, story, or poem interesting to read. Without conflict, there is no compelling story.

COMPARING Authors' Cultures

Details of an author's culture are often evident in his or her work. The authors featured here each reflect the times and places in which they live. Through their writing, they also transmit the traditional values and belief systems of their cultures.

Focus

BELLRINGER

Bellringer Options
Daily Language Practice Transparency 77
Or display images of people meeting in public. Show different numbers and combinations of people, including large and small groups, adults and children, men and women.
Ask: What emotions do you think the people in these images are feeling?

Connecting to the Reading Selections

Allow students to share their responses to the opening question. Then have students discuss what they already know about awkward encounters found in different types of literature.

Selection Skills

Comparing Literature

Reading Skills
- Making and Verifying Predictions About Plot (SE pp. 839–850)
- Outlining (TWE p. 840)
- Questioning (TWE p. 846)
- Comparing Characters (TWE p. 854)
- Main Ideas and Supporting Details (TWE p. 856)
- Relating to the Poem (TWE p. 862)

Literary Elements
- Stage Directions (SE pp. 839–850)
- Genre Elements (SE p. 850)
- Major and Minor Characters (TWE p. 842)
- Understanding Theme (TWE p. 848)

Listening/Speaking/Viewing Skills
- Analyzing Art (SE pp. 846, 855, 859)

Writing Skills/Grammar
- Genre Analysis (SE pp. 850)

Focus

Big Idea

Awkward Encounters
Ask: What awkward encounters have you experienced? Have students consider as they read what factors may make a meeting uncomfortable. They should recognize how the history of the two main characters contributes to the awkwardness. OL

Author Search To expand students' appreciation of Serafín and Joaquín Álvarez Quintero, have them access the Web site for additional information and resources.

COMPARING LITERATURE
BEFORE YOU READ

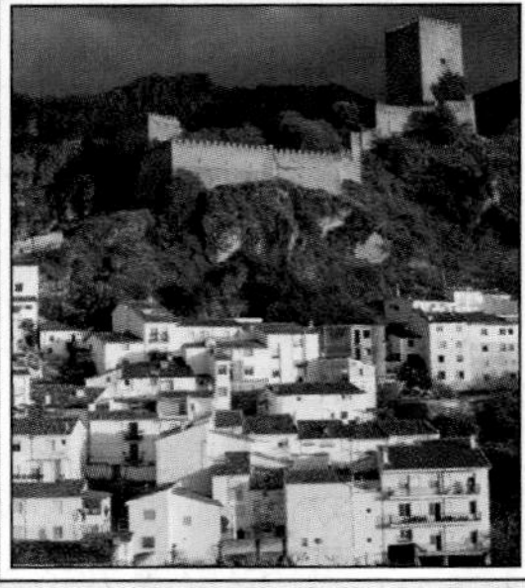

A Sunny Morning

MEET SERAFÍN AND JOAQUÍN ÁLVAREZ QUINTERO

Many people may have an image of an older and younger brother as a rough-and-tumble pair of rivals, but one famous pair of siblings worked together their entire lives. Over the course of fifty years, brothers Serafín and Joaquín Álvarez Quintero wrote approximately two hundred plays together, captivating audiences throughout Spain and around the world.

Young Playwrights Serafín was born in 1871 and his brother Joaquín in 1873. They grew up in Utrera, a small town near Seville in the region of Spain called Andalusia. They began writing for the theater at a young age. Their first play, *Esgrima y amor (Love and Fencing),* was produced in 1888, when they were only teenagers.

The brothers enjoyed early success with a *zarzuela* (musical comedy) called *La buena sombra (Charm).* They wrote mostly one-act *zarzuelas* or short plays called *sainetes,* which sometimes included music. These plays described the local life and customs of Andalusia in a romantic rather than a realistic way. *Mañana de sol (A Sunny Morning),* first published in 1905, was the sort of play for which the brothers became famous.

The Álvarez Quintero brothers chose topics for their plays that would be familiar to their audiences in Madrid and throughout Spain. Their stories interpreted popular folk songs or poems and often included humorous sketches about love and relationships. *A Sunny Morning* is based on a *dolora,* a type of sentimental and philosophical poem, created by Ramón de Campoamor. However, the brothers wrote many farces too.

A farce is a comedy written for the stage that amuses the audience by creating ridiculous situations. Common elements of farce include exaggerated characters, unlikely plots, and silly physical humor. *Fortunato* is one of the Álvarez Quinteros' best-known farces. They were not usually concerned with serious moral or social issues, but their play *Malvaloca* was a serious drama that received the prize of the Spanish Royal Academy in 1912. It was later made into a film.

Widespread Popularity The Álvarez Quinteros were popular outside Spain as well, and more than one hundred of their plays were translated into other languages. A number of these plays were produced in London and New York during the 1920s and 1930s, with famous stage actors playing the lead roles.

The complete collection of plays written by Serafín and Joaquín Álvarez Quintero was published in seven volumes as *Obras Completas* in the early 1950s. The brothers lived their last years in Madrid, where their careers as playwrights had begun. Serafín died in 1938 during the Spanish Civil War. After his death, Joaquín continued to write plays, using both their names.

Serafín Álvarez Quintero was born in 1871 and died in 1938. Joaquín Álvarez Quintero was born in 1873 and died in 1944.

LiteratureOnline **Author Search** For more about Serafín and Joaquín Álvarez Quintero, go to www.glencoe.com.

Selection Resources

Print Materials
- Unit 4 Resources (Fast File), pp. 43–45
- Selection and Unit Assessments, pp. 149–150
- Selection Quick Checks, p. 75

Transparencies
- Bellringer Options Transparencies: Daily Language Practice Transparency 77
- Literary Elements Transparency 81

Technology
- TeacherWorks Plus™ CD-ROM
- StudentWorks Plus™ CD-ROM
- Presentation Plus!™ CD-ROM
- Literature Online, glencoe.com
- Online Student Edition, mhln.com
- Exam*View*® Assessment Suite CD-ROM
- Vocabulary PuzzleMaker CD-ROM
- Listening Library, disc 2 tracks 12–14

LITERATURE PREVIEW

READING PREVIEW

Connecting to the Play

A Sunny Morning tells the story of an unexpected meeting between two people who seem to have nothing in common. Before you read, think about the following questions:

- How might your expectations influence the way you interact with others?
- How have unexpected encounters in your life sometimes turned out to be rewarding? Why?

Building Background

During the early part of the twentieth century, when Serafín and Joaquín Álvarez Quintero wrote some of their best-loved plays, the world of the theater was undergoing change around the globe. Political and social transformations were reflected in the kinds of plays offered to the public. Movements for reform and revolution sprang up, and people looked for practical answers to their problems. These ideas were reflected in the theater, preparing the way for the realism movement in literature.

Setting Purposes for Reading

Big Idea Awkward Encounters

As you read *A Sunny Morning,* watch for details that may remind you of an awkward encounter you have experienced.

Literary Element Stage Directions

Stage directions are instructions written by a playwright to describe the appearance, actions, and thoughts of characters. Stage directions can also describe the sets, costumes, and type of lighting the author has intended for the play. Another use of stage directions is to indicate asides. An aside is a character's comment that is directed to the audience but is not heard by the other characters on the stage. Some asides provide information that is crucial for the audience to comprehend the action or themes of the play. As you read *A Sunny Morning,* look for stage directions and asides that convey important bits of information.

- See Literary Terms Handbook, p. R16.

Literature Online Interactive Literary Elements Handbook To review or learn more about the literary elements, go to www.glencoe.com.

Reading Strategy Making and Verifying Predictions About Plot

When reading a play, you can use what you read about characters to **make and verify predictions about the plot.** Sometimes your predictions turn out to be accurate. At other times, the plot takes an unexpected turn and surprises you. Then you may find that your predictions were incorrect. In both cases, making and verifying predictions can help you become a more intuitive thinker. As you read, consider outcomes that you predict will take place. After you have finished reading the selection, decide if your predictions matched what actually took place.

Reading Tip: Taking Notes As you read, use a chart to document and verify your predictions.

Prediction	What Happened
Don Gonzalo and Doña Laura will meet.	They meet when Don Gonzalo disturbs the birds that Doña Laura feeds.

Vocabulary

parasol (par′ ə sôl) *n.* small, decorative umbrella used for protection from the sun; p. 840 *Women protected their faces from sunburn by carrying parasols as they walked along the boardwalk.*

glutton (glut′ ən) *n.* someone who eats greedily; p. 841 *The dog was a glutton; it quickly ate everything in sight.*

philosopher (fi los′ ə fər) *n.* thinker; p. 841 *Lily was always seeking wisdom, so she made a good philosopher.*

Vocabulary Tip: Word Origins As you read, you may encounter unfamiliar words. Learning the origin of a word can often help you understand its meaning.

English Language Coach

Remind English language learners that understanding the stage directions will help them with their overall comprehension of a scene. Tell students that stage directions provide insight into the feelings and motives of characters and can also provide important plot information. Suggest that students keep a running list indicating the page of the stage direction, whom it applies to, and what bits of information it provides. EL

COMPARING LITERATURE

BEFORE YOU READ

Focus

Summary

An elderly man and woman meet on a sunny morning in the park. Despite the awkward beginnings of their meeting, they sit together on a bench and discuss their youth. They discover that they were in love long ago but will not admit who they are because they have grown old. They agree to meet the next morning.

V Vocabulary

Vocabulary File Say: Add these words and definitions to your vocabulary file. For each word, include a sentence that gives you an example of how to use the word. OL Students with English language needs should include the pronunciations of these words in their files. EL

Literature Online

Literary Elements Have students access the Web site to improve their understanding of stage directions.

Academic Standards

The Additional Support activity on p. 839 covers the following standard:

English Language Coach: **9.3.10** Identify and describe the function of…stage designs in dramatic literature…

Teach

Big Idea

Awkward Encounters

As students read the first pages of the play, have them consider these questions.

Ask: What makes the encounter awkward in the beginning? *(The man is gruff and inconsiderate; the woman is outspoken about what she thinks.)* What helps to ease the awkwardness between the two characters? *(They share a fondness for snuff.)* **OL**

★ Cultural History

Geography of Spain

Spain shares the Iberian Peninsula with Portugal and is part of the European continent. Due to its location, Spain has historically connected Africa and Europe and has been influenced by many different cultures. **AS**

COMPARING LITERATURE

A Sunny Morning

by Serafín and Joaquín Álvarez Quintero

translated by Lucretia Xavier Floyd

CHARACTERS

DON GONZALO [gan za′ lō]

JUANITO [hwän ē′ tō]: his servant

DOÑA LAURA

PETRA [pā′ tra]: her maid

★ Scene: A park in Madrid[1]

Time: The present

[A sunny morning in a retired corner of a park in Madrid. Autumn. A bench at right. DOÑA[2] LAURA, *a handsome, white-haired old lady of about seventy, refined in appearance, her bright eyes and entire manner giving evidence that despite her age her mental faculties are unimpaired, enters leaning upon the arm of her maid,* PETRA. *In her free hand she carries a* **parasol,** *which serves also as a cane.]*

DOÑA LAURA. I am so glad to be here. I feared my seat would be occupied. What a beautiful morning!

PETRA. The sun is hot.

DOÑA LAURA. Yes, you are only twenty. [*She sits down on the bench.*] Oh, I feel more tired

1. *Madrid* is the capital of Spain.
2. *Doña* means "lady" or "madam" in Spanish.

Vocabulary

parasol (par′ ə sôl) *n.* small, decorative umbrella used for protection from the sun

The Red Parasol. From Public Gardens. Right panel of triptych. 1894. Edouard Vuillard. Musee d'Orsay, Paris, France.

Additional Support

Skills Practice

READING: Outlining As they read, have students outline the text to improve understanding. Tell them to take notes on the setting, the characters, and the main points of the plot. Remind them to record any transitions in the plot. Model this sample outline:

I. Doña Laura arrives in the park.
  A. She is an alert, elderly lady.
  B. Her maid leaves her alone to feed the birds.

II. Don Gonzalo arrives.
  A. He is old and impatient.
  B. He frightens the birds. **OL**

today than usual. [*Noticing* PETRA, *who seems impatient.*] Go, if you wish to chat with your guard.

PETRA. He is not mine, señora;[3] he belongs to the park.

DOÑA LAURA. He belongs more to you than he does to the park. Go find him, but remain within calling distance.

PETRA. I see him over there waiting for me.

DOÑA LAURA. Do not remain more than ten minutes.

PETRA. Very well, señora. [*Walks toward right.*]

DOÑA LAURA. Wait a moment.

PETRA. What does the señora wish?

DOÑA LAURA. Give me the bread crumbs.

PETRA. I don't know what is the matter with me.

DOÑA LAURA. [*Smiling.*] I do. Your head is where your heart is—with the guard.

PETRA. Here, señora. [*She hands* DOÑA LAURA *a small bag. Exit* PETRA *by right.*]

DOÑA LAURA. Adiós. [*Glances toward trees at right.*] Here they come! They know just when to expect me. [*She rises, walks toward right, and throws three handfuls of bread crumbs.*] These are for the spryest, these for the **gluttons**, and these for the little ones which are the most persistent. [*Laughs. She returns to her seat and watches, with a pleased expression, the pigeons feeding.*] There, that big one is always first! I know him by his big head. Now one, now another, now two, now three— That little fellow is the least timid. I believe he would eat from my hand. That one takes his piece and flies up to that branch alone. He is a **philosopher**. But where do they all come from? It seems as if the news had spread. Ha, ha! Don't quarrel. There is enough for all. I'll bring more tomorrow.

[*Enter* DON GONZALO *and* JUANITO *from left center.* DON GONZALO *is an old gentleman of seventy, gouty*[4] *and impatient. He leans upon* JUANITO'S *arm and drags his feet somewhat as he walks.*]

DON GONZALO. Idling their time away! They should be saying Mass.[5]

JUANITO. You can sit here, señor. There is only a lady. [DOÑA LAURA *turns her head and listens.*]

DON GONZALO. I won't, Juanito. I want a bench to myself.

JUANITO. But there is none.

DON GONZALO. That one over there is mine.

JUANITO. There are three priests sitting there.

DON GONZALO. Rout them out.[6] Have they gone?

JUANITO. No, indeed. They are talking.

DON GONZALO. Just as if they were glued to the seat. No hope of their leaving. Come this way, Juanito. [*They walk toward the birds, right.*]

DOÑA LAURA. [*Indignantly.*] Look out!

DON GONZALO. Are you speaking to me, señora?

DOÑA LAURA. Yes, to you.

DON GONZALO. What do you wish?

DOÑA LAURA. You have scared away the birds who were feeding on my crumbs.

3. *Señora* means "ma'am" in Spanish; it is used to address married women. *Señorita* is the term used to address unmarried women, and *señor* is used to address men.

4. *Gouty* means "suffering from gout." Gout is a disease that causes pain and swelling in the joints, especially in the feet and toes.

5. *Mass* is a religious celebration held regularly in the Roman Catholic Church.

6. *Rout out* means "to drive away."

Literary Element Stage Directions *Why do you think these stage directions have been included?* **L**

Vocabulary

glutton (glut′ ən) *n.* someone who eats greedily

philosopher (fi los′ ə fər) *n.* thinker

Teach

L Literary Element

Stage Directions Answer: *Students may say the stage directions enable the reader to visualize and understand why the characters do what they do. Without them, parts of the dialogue might not make sense.* **OL**

Use the CheckPoint questions on Presentation Plus! to monitor students' comprehension. These questions can be used with interactive response keypads for immediate student feedback.

English Language Coach

Titles Explain to English language learners that the titles Don and Doña are used similarly to the titles Mr., Mrs., Ms., and Miss. Clarify the difference between the female titles. ("Mrs." is for married women, "Miss" is for single women, and "Ms." is for women who do not wish to designate their marital status.) Have students tell about titles in their native countries. **EL**

Academic Standards

Additional Support activities on pp. 840 and 841 cover the following standards:

Skills Practice: **9.2** Develop strategies such as [outlining]…

English Language Coach: **9.1** Use…a growing knowledge of English and other languages to determine the meaning of words…

Teach

BI1 Big Idea

Awkward Encounters
Answer: *Yes, because Don Gonzalo insults Doña Laura by chiding her for talking to him.* OL

R Reading Strategy

Making and Verifying Predictions About Plot
Answer: *Students may suggest that the two will fight. Others may suggest that they will begin talking and find something in common.*
Ask: What details lead you to believe that they will fight? *(Don Gonzalo is rough and ornery, and he has already irritated Doña Laura by scaring the birds.)* What details lead you to believe that they will find something in common? *(They seem to be about the same age and they both like sitting in the park when it's sunny.)* OL

★ Viewing the Art

Lesser Ury (1861–1931) was part of the Berlin Secession movement. The Secession was created by artists as an alternative to existing exhibition options.
Answer: *The painting depicts a sunny morning, as does the play.* AS

COMPARING LITERATURE

The Tiergarten Park, Berlin. Im Tiergarten, Berlin. Lesser Ury. Oil on canvas.
Viewing the Art: How does the mood in this painting compare with the mood in the play? ★

DON GONZALO. What do I care about the birds?

DOÑA LAURA. But I do.

DON GONZALO. This is a public park.

DOÑA LAURA. Then why do you complain that the priests have taken your bench?

DON GONZALO. Señora, we have not met. I cannot imagine why you take the liberty of addressing me. Come, Juanito. [*Both go out right.*]

DOÑA LAURA. What an ill-natured old man! Why must people get so fussy and cross when they reach a certain age? [*Looking toward right.*] I am glad. He lost that bench, too. Serves him right for scaring the birds. He is furious. Yes, yes; find a seat if you can. Poor man! He is wiping the perspiration from his face. Here he comes. A carriage would not raise more dust than his feet.

[*Enter* DON GONZALO *and* JUANITO *by right and walk toward left.*]

DON GONZALO. Have the priests gone yet, Juanito?

JUANITO. No, indeed, señor. They are still there.

DON GONZALO. The authorities should place more benches here for these sunny mornings. Well, I suppose I must resign myself and sit on the bench with the old lady. [*Muttering to himself, he sits at the extreme end of* DOÑA LAURA'S *bench and looks at her indignantly. Touches his hat as he greets her.*] Good morning.

Big Idea Awkward Encounters *Would you describe this encounter as awkward? Explain.* BI1

Reading Strategy Making and Verifying Predictions About Plot *What do you predict will happen when Don Gonzalo sits on the bench with Doña Laura?* R

Additional Support

Skills Practice

LITERARY ELEMENT: Major and Minor Characters Explain that every narrative has major, or important, characters, and minor, or less significant, characters. Have students examine the roles of Doña Laura, Petra, Don Gonzalo, and Juanito and complete a chart to compare and contrast them. The chart should describe appearance and personality traits and interactions with other characters. Based on these notes, students should indicate whether each character plays a major or minor role in the drama. OL

DOÑA LAURA. What, you here again?

DON GONZALO. I repeat that we have not met.

DOÑA LAURA. I was responding to your salute.

DON GONZALO. "Good morning" should be answered by "good morning," and that is all you should have said.

DOÑA LAURA. You should have asked permission to sit on this bench, which is mine.

DON GONZALO. The benches here are public property.

DOÑA LAURA. Why, you said the one the priests have was yours.

DON GONZALO. Very well, very well. I have nothing more to say. [*Between his teeth.*] Senile old lady! She ought to be at home knitting and counting her beads.[7]

DOÑA LAURA. Don't grumble any more. I'm not going to leave just to please you.

DON GONZALO. [*Brushing the dust from his shoes with his handkerchief.*] If the ground were sprinkled a little it would be an improvement.

DOÑA LAURA. Do you use your handkerchief as a shoe brush?

DON GONZALO. Why not?

DOÑA LAURA. Do you use a shoe brush as a handkerchief?

DON GONZALO. What right have you to criticize my actions?

DOÑA LAURA. A neighbor's right.

DON GONZALO. Juanito, my book. I do not care to listen to nonsense.

DOÑA LAURA. You are very polite.

DON GONZALO. Pardon me, señora, but never interfere with what does not concern you.

DOÑA LAURA. I generally say what I think.

DON GONZALO. And more to the same effect. Give me the book, Juanito.

JUANITO. Here, señor. [*JUANITO takes a book from his pocket, hands it to DON GONZALO, then exits by right. DON GONZALO, casting indignant glances at DOÑA LAURA, puts on an enormous pair of glasses, takes from his pocket a reading-glass, adjusts both to suit him, and opens his book.*] **L**

DOÑA LAURA. I thought you were taking out a telescope.

DON GONZALO. Was that you?

DOÑA LAURA. Your sight must be keen.

DON GONZALO. Keener than yours is.

DOÑA LAURA. Yes, evidently.

DON GONZALO. Ask the hares and partridges.[8]

DOÑA LAURA. Ah! Do you hunt?

DON GONZALO. I did, and even now—

DOÑA LAURA. Oh, yes, of course!

DON GONZALO. Yes, señora. Every Sunday I take my gun and dog, you understand, and go to one of my estates near Aravaca[9] and kill time.

DOÑA LAURA. Yes, kill time. That is all you kill.

DON GONZALO. Do you think so? I could show you a wild boar's head in my study—

DOÑA LAURA. Yes, and I could show you a tiger's skin in my boudoir.[10] What does that prove?

DON GONZALO. Very well, señora, please allow me to read. Enough conversation.

DOÑA LAURA. Well, you subside, then.

DON GONZALO. But first I shall take a pinch of snuff.[11] [*Takes out snuff box.*] Will you have some? [*Offers box to DOÑA LAURA.*]

7. *Counting her beads* is a reference to the rosary, a string of beads used by Roman Catholics to count prayers. Don Gonzalo is saying Doña Laura should be at home praying.

8. *Hares and partridges* are both small game, or small animals that are frequently hunted.

9. *Aravaca* is a village near Madrid.

10. A *boudoir* is a woman's bedroom.

11. *Snuff* is powdered tobacco. The use of snuff is no longer common.

Big Idea Awkward Encounters *What do Doña Laura's comments tell about how she feels about Don Gonzalo?* **BI2**

Teach

BI2 Big Idea

Awkward Encounters
Answer: *Doña Laura's comments may indicate that she is not altogether put off by the prospect of talking with Don Gonzalo and that he does not intimidate her.*
Ask: What is Doña Laura's tone in this scene? *(Students may say she is having fun teasing Don Gonzalo or she is mocking him because of his impolite behavior.)* What do you think is the motive for each of the characters to continue sitting together and talking? *(Students may say that although they are outwardly argumentative with each other, the two characters want to talk and visit with someone, perhaps because they are lonely.)* **OL**

L Literary Element

Stage Directions **Ask:** What tone do these stage directions create? *(These directions create a comedic tone as readers picture Don Gonzalo with his huge glasses and reading glass.)* **OL**

Differentiated Instruction

Stage Directions Help less proficient readers visualize stage directions. Read the play aloud with them and discuss how the stage directions help characterize Doña Laura, Don Gonzalo, Petra, and Juanito. Help students act out the stage directions so they can visualize the action. **BL**

Academic Standards

Additional Support activities on pp. 842 and 843 cover the following standards:

Skills Practice: **9.3** [Identify] story elements such as character…

Differentiated Instruction: **9.3.10** Identify and describe the function of…stage designs in dramatic literature…

Teach

BI Big Idea

Awkward Encounters **Ask:** What is the significance of this scene? *(The two find they have something in common and the awkwardness between them begins to fade.)* OL

R1 Reading Strategy

Making and Verifying Predictions About Plot
Answer: *(This scene verifies students who predicted the characters would find something in common.)* OL

L Literary Element

Stage Directions **Answer:** *We learn that she is fooling Don Gonzalo to make him think she does not need glasses to read.* OL

★ Writer's Technique

Historical References
The Quintero brothers make historical references to Columbus, caravels, and Isabella and Ferdinand.
Ask: Why do you think they included these references? *(The historical references support the comedic tone of the play. Doña Laura now playfully teases Don Gonzalo about being old.)* AS

DOÑA LAURA. If it is good.

DON GONZALO. It is of the finest. You will like it.

DOÑA LAURA. [*Taking pinch of snuff.*] It clears my head.

DON GONZALO. And mine.

DOÑA LAURA. Do you sneeze?

DON GONZALO. Yes, señora, three times.

BI DOÑA LAURA. And so do I. What a coincidence!

[*After taking the snuff, they await the sneezes, both anxiously, and sneeze alternately three times each.*]

DON GONZALO. There, I feel better.

DOÑA LAURA. So do I. [*Aside.*] The snuff has made peace between us.

DON GONZALO. You will excuse me if I read aloud?

DOÑA LAURA. Read as loud as you please; you will not disturb me.

DON GONZALO. [*Reading.*] "All love is sad, but sad as it is, it is the best thing that we know." That is from Campoamor.[12]

DOÑA LAURA. Ah!

DON GONZALO. [*Reading.*] "The daughters of the mothers I once loved kiss me now as they would a graven[13] image." Those lines, I take it, are in a humorous vein.

DOÑA LAURA. [*Laughing.*] I take them so, too.

DON GONZALO. There are some beautiful poems in this book. Here. "Twenty years pass. He returns."

DOÑA LAURA. You cannot imagine how it affects me to see you reading with all those glasses.

DON GONZALO. Can you read without any?

DOÑA LAURA. Certainly.

DON GONZALO. At your age? You're jesting.

DOÑA LAURA. Pass me the book, then. [*Takes book; reads aloud.*]

"Twenty years pass. He returns.
And each, beholding the other, exclaims—
Can it be that this is he?
Heavens, is it she?"

[*DOÑA LAURA returns the book to DON GONZALO.*]

DON GONZALO. Indeed, I envy you your wonderful eyesight.

DOÑA LAURA. [*Aside.*] I know every word by heart.

DON GONZALO. I am very fond of good verses, very fond. I even composed some in my youth.

DOÑA LAURA. Good ones?

DON GONZALO. Of all kinds. I was a great friend of Espronceda, Zorrilla, Bécquer,[14] and others. I first met Zorrilla in America.

DOÑA LAURA. Why, have you been in America?

DON GONZALO. Several times. The first time I went I was only six years old.

DOÑA LAURA. You must have gone with Columbus in one of his caravels![15]

DON GONZALO. [*Laughing.*] Not quite as bad as that. I am old, I admit, but I did not know Ferdinand and Isabella.[16] [*They both laugh.*] I was also a great friend of Campoamor. I met him in Valencia.[17] I am a native of that city. ★

DOÑA LAURA. You are?

12. *Campoamor* refers to Spanish poet Ramón de Campoamor (1817–1901).
13. *Graven* means "carved."
14. *José de Espronceda* (1808–1842), *José Zorrilla* (1817–1893), and *Gustavo Adolfo Bécquer* (1836–1870) were Spanish poets.
15. *Caravels* are ships built in Spain and Portugal in the fifteenth century. Two of Christopher Columbus's ships were caravels.
16. *Ferdinand and Isabella* were the king and queen of Spain who financed Christopher Columbus's voyage across the Atlantic Ocean in the late 1400s.
17. *Valencia* is a city on the eastern coast of Spain.

Reading Strategy Making and Verifying Predictions About Plot *Was your earlier prediction about Doña Laura and Don Gonzalo accurate?* R1

Literary Element Stage Directions *How does this aside help us understand Doña Laura's actions?* L

Additional Support

Skills Practice

WRITING: Graphing a Plot The plot is the sequence of events in a narrative. Students may use a plot graph to show how the plot grows and changes and to remember major events of a story. Have students create a plot graph about what they have already read. They should add to the graph as they read. OL

A Sunny Morning

Doña Laura feeds the birds. Don Gonzalo scares them away. → Doña Laura and Don Gonzalo sit on a bench and trade insults. → Doña Laura and Don Gonzalo share his snuff and find something they have in common.

The Bench, 1873. Claude Monet. 

DON GONZALO. I was brought up there and there I spent my early youth. Have you ever visited that city?

DOÑA LAURA. Yes, señor. Not far from Valencia there was a villa that, if still there, should retain memories of me. I spent several seasons there. It was many, many years ago. It was near the sea, hidden away among lemon and orange trees. They called it—let me see, what did they call it—Maricela.

DON GONZALO. [*Startled.*] Maricela?

DOÑA LAURA. Maricela. Is the name familiar to you?

DON GONZALO. Yes, very familiar. If my memory serves me right, for we forget as we grow old, there lived in that villa the most beautiful woman I have ever seen, and I assure you I have seen many. Let me see—what was her name? Laura—Laura—Laura Llorente.

DOÑA LAURA. [*Startled.*] Laura Llorente?

DON GONZALO. Yes. [*They look at each other intently.*]

DOÑA LAURA. [*Recovering herself.*] Nothing. You reminded me of my best friend.

DON GONZALO. How strange!

DOÑA LAURA. It is strange. She was called "The Silver Maiden."

DON GONZALO. Precisely, "The Silver Maiden." By that name she was known in that locality. I seem to see her as if she were before me now, at that window with the red roses. Do you remember that window?

Reading Strategy Making and Verifying Predictions About Plot *What prediction can you make about the plot by reading this line?* **R2**

Teach

R2 Reading Strategy

Making and Verifying Predictions About Plot

Answer: *The characters may have something in common. They might have visited the same city or have friends or relatives there.* **OL**

★ Viewing the Art

Claude Monet (1840–1926) is best known as a creator of the French Impressionist movement. In his artwork, Monet sought to capture the fleeting effects of light in natural settings. He created many landscape series in which he painted the same subject at different times of day or year in order to show the changes in light and color. **AS**

Building Reading Fluency

Reading in Groups Divide students into groups of four and assign each student a part. Have the groups read the first half of the play aloud; then, members should switch roles and read the rest of the play so that all students in a group have the chance to be a main character. Remind students to maintain a comedic tone as they read. **BL**

Academic Standards

Additional Support activities on pp. 844 and 845 cover the following standards:

Skills Practice: **9.3** [Identify] story elements such as...plot...

Building Reading Fluency: **9.7** [Develop] speaking skills...in conjunction with...strategies...[for] delivery of oral presentations.

Teach

L1 Literary Element

Stage Directions **Answer:** *They probably wanted to maintain the suspense of the plot while letting the audience and readers know that Doña Laura recognizes Don Gonzalo.*

Ask: Why is the use of asides important in this passage? *(The asides reveal the previous relationship of Doña Laura and Don Gonzalo to the audience, but the two characters do not admit what they know to each other.)* OL

★ Viewing the Art

During his time at Arles, Vincent Van Gogh (1853–1890) painted outdoors, capturing the landscape in single, long sessions. The Arles paintings are characterized by intensely saturated color and showcase Van Gogh's maturing technique.

Answer: *They are a man and a woman sharing each other's company in a park.* AS

Couple in the park, Arles, 1888. Vincent Van Gogh.
Viewing the Art: How are the people pictured in this painting similar to characters in the play? ★

DOÑA LAURA. Yes, I remember. It was the window of her room.

DON GONZALO. She spent many hours there. I mean in my day.

DOÑA LAURA. [*Sighing.*] And in mine, too.

DON GONZALO. She was ideal. Fair as a lily, jet black hair and black eyes, with an uncommonly sweet expression. She seemed to cast a radiance wherever she was. Her figure was beautiful, perfect. "What forms of sovereign[18] beauty God models in human clay!" She was a dream.

DOÑA LAURA. [*Aside.*] If you but knew that dream was now by your side, you would realize what dreams come to. [*Aloud.*] She was very unfortunate and had a sad love affair.

DON GONZALO. Very sad. [*They look at each other.*]

DOÑA LAURA. Did you hear of it?

DON GONZALO. Yes.

DOÑA LAURA. The ways of Providence[19] are strange. [*Aside.*] Gonzalo!

DON GONZALO. The gallant lover, in the same affair—

18. Here, *sovereign* means "outstanding" or "excellent."

19. *Providence* means "a force that determines human fate, often attributed to God."

Literary Element Stage Directions *Why do you think the authors chose to use an aside here instead of making it part of the dialogue?* L1

Additional Support

Skills Practice

READING: Questioning Some students may need to clarify the conversation about the couple's love affair. Discuss the tactics the characters use to get information from each other. Help students understand the use of asides and the couple's deception by asking these questions:

1. How did Doña Laura and Don Gonzalo know each other in the past?
2. How do Doña Laura and Don Gonzalo claim to know the love story of Laura and Gonzalo? Why do they say this? OL

DOÑA LAURA. Ah, the duel!

DON GONZALO. Precisely, the duel. The gallant lover was—my cousin, of whom I was very fond.

DOÑA LAURA. Oh, yes, a cousin? My friend told me in one of her letters the story of that affair, which was truly romantic. He, your cousin, passed by on horseback every morning down the rose path under her window, and tossed up to her balcony a bouquet of flowers which she caught.

DON GONZALO. And later in the afternoon the gallant horseman would return by the same path, and catch the bouquet of flowers she would toss him. Am I right?

DOÑA LAURA. Yes. They wanted to marry her to a merchant whom she would not have.

DON GONZALO. And one night, when my cousin waited under her window to hear her sing, this other person presented himself unexpectedly.

DOÑA LAURA. And insulted your cousin.

DON GONZALO. There was a quarrel.

DOÑA LAURA. And later a duel.

DON GONZALO. Yes, at sunrise, on the beach, and the merchant was badly wounded. My cousin had to conceal himself for a few days and later to fly.

DOÑA LAURA. You seem to know the story well.

DON GONZALO. And so do you.

DOÑA LAURA. I have explained that a friend repeated it to me.

DON GONZALO. As my cousin did to me. [*Aside.*] This is Laura!

DOÑA LAURA. [*Aside.*] Why tell him? He does not suspect.

DON GONZALO. [*Aside.*] She is entirely innocent.

DOÑA LAURA. And was it you, by any chance, who advised your cousin to forget Laura?

DON GONZALO. Why, my cousin never forgot her!

DOÑA LAURA. How do you account, then, for his conduct?

DON GONZALO. I will tell you. The young man took refuge in my house, fearful of the consequences of a duel with a person highly regarded in that locality. From my home he went to Seville,[20] then came to Madrid. He wrote Laura many letters, some of them in verse. But undoubtedly they were intercepted by her parents, for she never answered at all. Gonzalo then, in despair, believing his love lost to him forever, joined the army, went to Africa, and there, in a trench, met a glorious death, grasping the flag of Spain and whispering the name of his beloved Laura—

DOÑA LAURA. [*Aside.*] What an atrocious lie!

DON GONZALO. [*Aside.*] I could not have killed myself more gloriously.

DOÑA LAURA. You must have been prostrated[21] by the calamity.

DON GONZALO. Yes, indeed, señora. As if he were my brother. I presume, though, on the contrary, that Laura in a short time was chasing butterflies in her garden, indifferent to regret.

DOÑA LAURA. No señor, no!

DON GONZALO. It is woman's way.

DOÑA LAURA. Even if it were woman's way, "The Silver Maiden" was not of that disposition. My friend awaited news for days, months, a year, and no letter came. One afternoon, just at sunset, as the first stars were appearing, she was seen to leave the house, and with quickening steps wend her way

Reading Strategy Making and Verifying Predictions About Plot *Can you guess the real identities of the lovers in this story from the past?* **R**

Big Idea Awkward Encounters *How has the source of the awkwardness of this unexpected meeting shifted?* **BI**

20. *Seville* is a city in southern Spain.
21. *Prostrated* means "flattened."

Literary Element Stage Directions *What does this aside reveal about Don Gonzalo?* **L2**

Teach

R Reading Strategy

Making and Verifying Predictions About Plot
Answer: *Most students will say that they can guess that the lovers in the story are really Doña Laura and Don Gonzalo.* **OL**

BI Big Idea

Awkward Encounters
Answer: *Before it was awkward because the two seemed to clash. Now it is awkward because they both realize they know each other, yet choose to keep the information secret.*
Ask: Why do you think Doña Laura and Don Gonzalo will not reveal their true identities to each other? *(Students may say that the two fear rejection because they are now old, or that their earlier relationship ended badly.)* **OL**

L2 Literary Element

Stage Directions **Answer:** *He is the Gonzalo in the story.* **OL**

Reading in the Real World

Citizenship Have students research on the Internet and in a library to discover some famous duels that took place in this country and share their findings. Ask students to find out about different ways in which disputes are settled today. Discuss the advantages of today's methods. **OL**

Academic Standards

Additional Support activities on pp. 846 and 847 cover the following standards:

Skills Practice: **9.3.10** Identify and describe the function of...asides...in dramatic literature. **9.2** Develop strategies such as asking questions...

Reading in the Real World: **9.4.6** Synthesize information from multiple sources... **9.7.7** Make judgments about the ideas under discussion and support those judgments with convincing evidence.

Teach

BI1 **Big Idea**

Awkward Encounters
Answer: *He probably expected the conversation to be extremely brief and unpleasant.* **OL**

Viewing the Art

Pierre Henri de Valenciennes (1750–1819) fought for respect for landscape painting. Rather than just sketching nature, he painted it in oil. He painted outside and encouraged other artists to do the same. His open-air work influenced future artists, such as the Barbizon painters and the Impressionists. **AS**

COMPARING LITERATURE

At the Villa Farnese: Houses Among the Trees.
Pierre Henri de Valenciennes. Oil on paper on cardboard. Louvre, Paris, France. 

toward the beach, the beach where her beloved had risked his life. She wrote his name on the sand, then sat down upon a rock, her gaze fixed upon the horizon. The waves murmured their eternal threnody[22] and slowly crept up to the rock where the maiden sat. The tide rose with a boom and swept her out to sea.

DON GONZALO. Good heavens!

DOÑA LAURA. The fishermen of that shore who often tell the story affirm that it was a long time before the waves washed away that name written on the sand. [*Aside.*] You will not get ahead of me in decorating my own funeral.

DON GONZALO. [*Aside.*] She lies worse than I do.

DOÑA LAURA. Poor Laura!

DON GONZALO. Poor Gonzalo!

DOÑA LAURA. [*Aside.*] I will not tell him that I married two years later.

DON GONZALO. [*Aside.*] In three months I ran off to Paris with a ballet dancer.

DOÑA LAURA. Fate is curious. Here are you and I, complete strangers, met by chance, discussing the romance of old friends of long ago! We have been conversing as if we were old friends.

DON GONZALO. Yes, it is curious, considering the ill-natured prelude to our conversation.

DOÑA LAURA. You scared away the birds.

DON GONZALO. I was unreasonable, perhaps.

22. *Threnody* is a song of lament for the dead.

Big Idea Awkward Encounters *Based on these comments, how do you think Don Gonzalo expected his conversation with Doña Laura to conclude?* **BI1**

Additional Support

Skills Practice

LITERARY ELEMENT: Understanding Theme The theme of a literary work is the main idea or message. It is not the subject of the work but rather an insight about life or human nature. The theme may be directly stated or implied. Help students clarify their understanding of the play's theme by answering these questions:

- What is the theme of this play?
- What details establish this theme?
- Is the theme directly stated or implied? Explain using evidence from the play. **OL**

DOÑA LAURA. Yes, that was evident. [*Sweetly.*] Are you coming again tomorrow?

DON GONZALO. Most certainly, if it is a sunny morning. And not only will I not scare away the birds, but I will bring a few crumbs.

DOÑA LAURA. Thank you very much. Birds are grateful and repay attention. I wonder where my maid is? Petra! [*Signals for her maid.*]

DON GONZALO. [*Aside, looking at* LAURA, *whose back is turned.*] No, no, I will not reveal myself. I am grotesque now. Better that she recall the gallant horseman who passed daily beneath her window tossing flowers.

DOÑA LAURA. Here she comes.

DON GONZALO. That Juanito! He plays havoc with the nursemaids. [*Looks right and signals with his hand.*]

DOÑA LAURA. [*Aside, looking at* GONZALO, *whose back is turned.*] No, I am too sadly changed. It is better he should remember me as the black-eyed girl tossing flowers as he passed among the roses in the garden.

[*JUANITO enters by right, PETRA by left. She has a bunch of violets in her hand.*]

DOÑA LAURA. Well, Petra! At last!

DON GONZALO. Juanito, you are late.

PETRA. [*To DOÑA LAURA.*] The guard gave me these violets for you, señora.

DOÑA LAURA. How very nice! Thank him for me. They are fragrant. [*As she takes the violets from her maid a few loose ones fall to the ground.*]

BI2 DON GONZALO. My dear lady, this has been a great honor and a great pleasure.

DOÑA LAURA. It has also been a pleasure to me.

DON GONZALO. Good-bye until tomorrow.

DOÑA LAURA. Until tomorrow.

DON GONZALO. If it is sunny.

DOÑA LAURA. A sunny morning. Will you go to your bench? BI2

DON GONZALO. No, I will come to this—if you do not object?

DOÑA LAURA. This bench is at your disposal.

DON GONZALO. And I will surely bring the crumbs.

DOÑA LAURA. Tomorrow, then?

DON GONZALO. Tomorrow!

[*LAURA walks away toward right, supported by her MAID. GONZALO, before leaving with JUANITO, trembling and with a great effort, stoops to pick up the violets LAURA dropped. Just then LAURA turns her head and surprises him picking up the flowers.*]

JUANITO. What are you doing, señor?

DON GONZALO. Juanito, wait—

DOÑA LAURA. [*Aside.*] Yes, it is he!

DON GONZALO. [*Aside.*] It is she, and no mistake. [*DOÑA LAURA and DON GONZALO wave farewell.*]

DOÑA LAURA. "Can it be that this is he?"

DON GONZALO. "Heavens, is it she?" [*They smile once more, as if she were again at the window and he below in the rose garden, and then disappear upon the arms of their servants.*]

Reading Strategy Making and Verifying Predictions About Plot *What purpose do you think this question serves, given that it appears so near the end of the scene?* **R**

Literary Element Stage Directions *Why do you think the authors include stage directions for dropping and picking up the flowers?* **L**

Differentiated Instruction

Forming an Acting Company Have gifted and talented students form an acting company to put on a performance of *A Sunny Morning.* The company should have a director, a set designer, a costume coordinator, a program writer, and at least two actors and two actresses. Provide advice and feedback to the students as they perform their jobs, and give students time to fulfill their tasks. Plan a theatrical event at school and invite other classes to see a performance of the play. **AL**

Teach

R Reading Strategy

Making and Verifying Predictions About Plot

Answer: *It shows that Doña Laura now likes Don Gonzalo, and readers and viewers can reasonably predict that a lost love might blossom again.* **OL**

BI2 Big Idea

Awkward Encounters **Ask:** How has this awkward encounter turned out to be a good experience for the characters? *(The Don and Doña have found each other after many years apart.)* **OL**

L Literary Element

Stage Directions **Answer:** *Students may say that Don Gonzalo's act of picking up the flowers reveals his feelings for her and refers back to his receiving the flowers she threw from her balcony many years ago.* **OL**

CheckPoint

Use the CheckPoint questions on Presentation Plus! to check students' mastery of the selection. These questions can be used with interactive response keypads for immediate student feedback.

Academic Standards

Additional Support activities on pp. 848 and 849 cover the following standards:

Skills Practice: **9.3** [Identify] story elements such as…theme…

Differentiated Instruction: **9.7.17** Deliver oral responses to literature that demonstrate awareness of the author's writing style and an appreciation of the effects created; identify and assess the impact of ambiguities, nuances, and complexities within the text.

Assess

1. Answers should reflect understanding of the text.
2. (a) "Good morning" should be answered with "Good morning . . . and that is all." (b) He did not want to talk with her.
3. (a) He thinks she should be at home knitting and "counting her beads." (b) Don Gonzalo may be insulting her because she speaks her mind in a culture that may not have tolerated it.
4. (a) She was known as "The Silver Maiden." (b) The name implies that she had beauty and good character.
5. (a) Each wanted the other to remember them as they were in younger days. (b) The information is revealed mostly through asides.
6. Students may say "no" because they both formed other relationships; others may say "yes" because they each held out hope to renew ties.
7. They like each other more at the end than at the beginning.
8. Answers should reflect students' understanding of the play and of the concept of an awkward encounter.

RESPONDING AND THINKING CRITICALLY

Respond

1. What was your reaction to the outcome of the conversation between Don Gonzalo and Doña Laura?

Recall and Interpret

2. (a)According to Don Gonzalo, how should the greeting "Good morning" be answered? (b)Why do you think Don Gonzalo mentions this to Doña Laura?
3. (a)In an aside that appears after Don Gonzalo sits, where does he say that Doña Laura should be? (b)What does this tell you about Don Gonzalo's impression of Doña Laura?
4. (a)Identify the title by which Doña Laura was known in earlier times. (b)Explain what this title implies about Doña Laura.

Analyze and Evaluate

5. (a)Why do neither Doña Laura nor Don Gonzalo reveal their true identities? (b)How is this information revealed?
6. Do you think that the earlier relationship between Doña Laura and Don Gonzalo was a strong and serious one? Explain.
7. How do Doña Laura and Don Gonzalo feel about each other by the end of the play?

Connect

8. **Big Idea** **Awkward Encounters** Do you think it was wise for Doña Laura and Don Gonzalo to keep their identities secret? How might their secrets affect future meetings?

LITERARY ANALYSIS

Literary Element Stage Directions

Stage directions are an important component of a play. When you watch a play being performed, you hear only the dialogue, or the words the characters say. Through stage directions, a reader of a play can learn how the playwright wanted those words to be spoken.

Partner Activity Review the play and note each instance of the use of asides. Read the asides aloud, and discuss how each one advances the plot or gives the audience new information.

Writing About Literature

Analyze Genre Elements The play *A Sunny Morning* is a comedy, a type of drama that is humorous and usually has a happy ending. Write an essay that explains how one of the two main characters is portrayed in a comic fashion. Use details from the play to support your statements.

LiteratureOnline **Web Activities** For eFlashcards, Selection Quick Checks, and other Web activities, go to www.glencoe.com.

READING AND VOCABULARY

Reading Strategy Making and Verifying Predictions About Plot

As you read, you make predictions about the plot of a story or play. After reading, you may want to verify your predictions.

1. Did this play end in the way you predicted? Explain.
2. What do you predict will happen in the next meeting between Doña Laura and Don Gonzalo?

Vocabulary Practice

Practice with Word Origins Use a dictionary to help you choose the word whose origin is similar to that of the vocabulary word.

1. parasol	**a.** parrot	**b.** solar
2. philosopher	**a.** phobia	**b.** sophomore
3. glutton	**a.** gullet	**b.** gluten

LiteratureOnline

Web Activities Have students access the Web site for interactive activities that will help them assess their understanding of the selection.

Literary Element

Have students work in small groups to read and discuss asides.

Writing About Literature

Remind students to look for absurd situations, physical comedy, and exaggeration.

Reading Strategy

1. Students may be surprised that the characters intend to meet again.
2. Answers should reflect students' understanding of the characters.

Vocabulary

1. b **2.** b **3.** a

COMPARING LITERATURE

BEFORE YOU READ

Building Background

Shirley Jackson (1919–1965) is best known for disturbing stories such as "The Lottery," in which seemingly normal situations are revealed as sinister and "ordinary" people turn out to be cruel conformists. Jackson did, however, have a lighter side. Although she claimed that her humorous stories had little literary value, critics describe her child-rearing memoirs, *Life Among the Savages* (1953) and *Raising Demons* (1957), as part of "a major branch of American women's humor and a mirror of post–World War II culture." Critic Joan Wylie Hall writes, "Whether the genre is domestic comedy, gothic horror, or realistic narrative, Jackson pulls the rug from under her precariously balanced housewives and career women." "About Two Nice People" was first published in *Ladies' Home Journal* magazine in 1951.

LiteratureOnline **Author Search** For more about Shirley Jackson, go to www.glencoe.com.

About Two Nice People

Shirley Jackson

A problem of some importance, certainly, these days, is that of anger. When one half of the world is angry at the other half, or one half of a nation is angry at the rest, or one side of town feuds with the other side, it is hardly surprising, when you stop to think about it, that so many people lose their tempers with so many other people. Even if, as in this case, they are two people not usually angry, two people whose lives are obscure[1] and whose emotions are gentle, whose smiles are amiable[2] and whose voices are more apt to be cheerful than raised in fury. Two people, in other words, who would much rather be friends than not and who yet, for some reason, perhaps chemical or sociological[3] or environmental, enter upon a mutual feeling of dislike so intense that only a very drastic means can bring them out of it.

Take two such people:

Ellen Webster was what is referred to among her friends as a "sweet" girl. She had pretty, soft hair and dark, soft eyes, and she

1. Here, *obscure* means "not well known."
2. *Amiable* means "friendly."
3. *Sociological* reasons are those having to do with the structure and rules of a society and the behavior of people within that society.

Focus

Summary

This narrative describes the relationship of Walter and Ellen, who are neighbors. Although both are nice and have much in common, Walter and Ellen start off on the wrong foot. They terrorize each other by playing mean practical jokes on each other until Walter's aunt unintentionally brings them together.

LiteratureOnline

Author Search To expand students' appreciation of Shirley Jackson, have them access the Web site for additional information and resources.

CheckPoint

Use the CheckPoint questions on Presentation Plus! to monitor students' comprehension. These questions can be used with interactive response keypads for immediate student feedback.

Readability Scores

Dale-Chall: 7.1
DRP: 61
Lexile: 1220

Differentiated Instruction

Contrasting Dramas and Short Stories Examine the major differences between a drama and a short story. A drama consists of dialogue and stage directions. A short story may or may not have dialogue and contains descriptive passages. A drama requires the reader to interpret what characters think and feel based on dialogue and stage directions. A short story describes what people say, think, do, and feel. After students read "About Two Nice People," encourage them to contrast this short story with the drama "A Sunny Morning." BL

Academic Standards

The Additional Support activity on p. 851 covers the following standard:

Differentiated Instruction: **9.3.2** Compare and contrast the presentation of a similar theme...across genres...to explain how the selection of genre shapes the theme...

Teach

R Reading Strategy

Making and Verifying Predictions About Plot

Ask: What does the reader learn about Ellen in the first paragraph on page 852? *(Students may say that she is very nice.)* Based on this description and the title, what do you predict will happen in this story? *(Students may predict that something will happen between Ellen and another person like her.)* OL

COMPARING LITERATURE

Hand Picking up Telephone. Hillary Younglove.

dressed in soft colors and wore frequently a lovely old-fashioned brooch[4] which had belonged to her grandmother. Ellen thought of herself as a very happy and very lucky person, because she had a good job, was able to buy herself a fair number of soft-colored dresses and skirts and sweaters and coats and hats; she had, by working hard at it evenings, transformed her one-room apartment from a bare, neat place into a charming little refuge with her sewing basket on the table and a canary at the window; she had a reasonable conviction that someday, perhaps soon, she would fall in love with a nice young man and they would be married and Ellen would devote herself wholeheartedly to children and baking cakes and mending socks. This not-very-unusual situation, with its perfectly ordinary state of mind, was a source of great happiness to Ellen. She was, in a word, not one of those who rail against their fate, who live in sullen hatred of the world. She was—her friends were right—a sweet girl.

On the other hand, even if you would not have called Walter Nesmith sweet, you would very readily have thought of him as a "nice" fellow, or an "agreeable" person, or even—if you happened to be a little old white-haired lady—a "dear boy." There was a subtle resemblance between Ellen Webster and Walter Nesmith. Both of them were the first resort of their friends in trouble, for instance. Walter's ambitions, which included the rest of his life, were refreshingly similar to

4. A *brooch* is a decorative pin.

Additional Support

Skills Practice

LISTENING/SPEAKING/VIEWING: Telling Stories Point out that telling a story is different from presenting a drama. In a story, the narrator provides the tone of the selection. Divide the story into sections so that each student has a part of the story to read. Allow students to practice reading their part aloud. Then ask students to read their part at the appropriate time. Remind students to use their tone of voice to create the appropriate mood. OL

Ellen's: Walter thought that someday he might meet some sweet girl, and would then devote himself wholeheartedly to coming home of an evening to read his paper and perhaps work in the garden on Sundays.

Walter thought that he would like to have two children, a boy and a girl. Ellen thought that she would like to have three children, a boy and two girls. Walter was very fond of cherry pie, Ellen preferred Boston cream. Ellen enjoyed romantic movies, Walter preferred Westerns. They read almost exactly the same books.

In the ordinary course of events, the friction between Ellen and Walter would have been very slight. But—and what could cause a thing like this?—the ordinary course of events was shattered by a trifle like a telephone call.

The ordinary course of events was shattered by a trifle like a telephone call.

Ellen's telephone number was 3–4126. Walter's telephone number was 3–4216. Ellen lived in apartment 3–A and Walter lived in apartment 3–B; these apartments were across the hall from each other and very often Ellen, opening her door at precisely quarter of nine in the morning and going toward the elevator, met Walter, who opened *his* door at precisely quarter of nine in the morning and went toward the elevator. On these occasions Ellen customarily said "Good morning" and looked steadfastly[5] the other way, Walter usually answered "Good morning," and avoided looking in her direction. Ellen thought that a girl who allowed herself to be informal with strangers created a bad impression, and Walter thought that a man who took advantage of living in the same building to strike up an acquaintance with a girl was a man of little principle. One particularly fine morning, he said to Ellen in the elevator, "Lovely day," and she replied, "Yes, isn't it?" and both of them felt scarcely that they had been bold. How this mutual respect for each other's dignity could have degenerated[6] into fury is a mystery not easily understood.

It happened that one evening—and, to do her strict justice, Ellen had had a hard day, she was coming down with a cold, it had rained steadily for a week, her stockings were unwashed, and she had broken a fingernail—the phone which had the number 3–4126 rang. Ellen had been opening a can of chicken soup in the kitchenette, and she had her hands full; she said, "Darn," and managed to drop and break a cup in her hurry to answer the phone.

"Hello?" she said, thinking, *This is going to be something cheerful.*

"Hello, is Walter there?"

"Walter?"

"Walter Nesmith. I want to speak to Walter, please."

"This is the wrong number," Ellen said thinking with the self-pity that comes with the first stages of a head cold that no one ever called *her.*

"Is this three—four two one six?"

"This is three—four one two six," Ellen said, and hung up.

At that time, although she knew that the person in the apartment across the hall was named Walter Nesmith, she could not have told the color of his hair or even of the outside of his apartment door. She went back to her soup and had a match in her hand to light the stove when the phone rang again.

"Hello?" Ellen said without enthusiasm; this *could* be someone cheerful, she was thinking.

"Hello, is Walter there?"

L

5. *Steadfastly* means "without wavering."

6. *Degenerated* means "worsened" or "degraded."

Teach

L Literary Element

Repetition Have volunteers read aloud the parts of the narrator, Ellen, and the callers on page 853.

Ask: What is the effect of the repeated calls for Walter and Ellen's attempts to clarify the difference between the two almost identical phone numbers? *(Students may say the situation is humorous, or that it allows the reader to see Ellen's building frustration, which leads to her uncharacteristic behavior in confronting Walter.)* **OL**

Differentiated Instruction

Connect with Characters Help less proficient readers connect to the characters in this story. Have students reread pages 851 to 853. To clarify their understanding of Walter and Ellen, tell them to respond to the following:

1. Describe Ellen's physical characteristics.
2. Describe Walter's physical characteristics.
3. List Ellen's personality traits.
4. List Walter's personality traits.
5. Would Ellen or Walter be a good friend? Explain your answer. **BL**

Academic Standards

Additional Support activities on pp. 852 and 853 cover the following standards:

Skills Practice: **9.7.6** Analyze the occasion… and choose effective verbal…techniques (including voice…) for presentations.

Differentiated Instruction: **9.3** [Identify] story elements such as character…

Teach

R1 Reading Strategy

Making and Verifying Predictions About Plot

Ask: What do you predict will happen next? *(Ellen and Walter may have a confrontation or a conversation.)* What details support this prediction? *(The author's hints about gentle people losing their tempers, and the description of Ellen's state of mind may lead students to believe the two will have a confrontation.)* OL

BI1 Big Idea

Awkward Encounters

Ask: How does Walter's state of mind contribute to the awkward encounter at his door? *(He, too, has had a bad day and is not feeling well. Ellen's tone of voice causes him to respond in kind.)* OL

COMPARING LITERATURE

"This is the wrong number again," Ellen said; if she had not been such a very sweet girl she might have let more irritation show in her voice.

"I *want* to *speak* to Walter Nesmith, *please*."

"This is three—four one two six again," Ellen said patiently. "You want three—four two one six."

"What?" said the voice.

"This," said Ellen, "is number three—four one two six. The number you want is three—four two one six." Like anyone who has tried to say a series of numbers several times, she found her anger growing. Surely anyone of *normal* intelligence, she was thinking, surely anyone *ought* to be able to dial a phone, anyone who can't dial a phone shouldn't be allowed to have a nickel.

She had got all the way back into the kitchenette and was reaching out for the can of soup before the phone rang again. This time when she answered she said "Hello?" rather sharply for Ellen, and with no illusions about who it was going to be.

> "Hello, may I please speak to Walter?"

"Hello, may I please speak to Walter?"

R1 At that point it started. Ellen had a headache and it was raining and she was tired and she was apparently not going to get any chicken soup until this annoyance was stopped.

"Just a minute," she said into the phone.

She put the phone down with an understandable bang on the table, and she marched, without taking time to think, out of her apartment and up to the door across the hall. "Walter Nesmith" said a small card at the doorbell. Ellen rang the doorbell with what was, for her, a vicious poke. When the door opened she said immediately, without looking at him:

"Are you Walter Nesmith?"

Now Walter had had a hard day, too, and *he* was coming down with a cold, and *he* had been trying ineffectually[7] to make himself a cup of hot tea in which he intended to put a spoonful of honey to ease his throat, that being the remedy his aunt had always recommended for the first onslaught[8] of a cold. If there had been one fraction less irritation in Ellen's voice, or if Walter had not taken off his shoes when he came home that night, it might very probably have turned out to be a pleasant introduction, with Walter and Ellen dining together on chicken soup and hot tea, and perhaps even sharing a bottle of cough medicine. But when Walter opened the door and heard Ellen's voice, he was unable to answer her cordially, and so he said briefly: BI1

"I am. Why?"

"Will you please come and answer my phone?" said Ellen, too annoyed to realize that this request might perhaps bewilder Walter.

"Answer your phone?" said Walter stupidly.

"Answer my phone," said Ellen firmly. She turned and went back across the hall, and Walter, wondering briefly if they allowed harmless lunatics to live alone as though they were just like other people, hesitated for an instant and then followed her, on the theory that it would be wiser to do what she said when she seemed so cross, and reassuring himself that he could leave the door open and yell for help if necessary. Ellen stamped into her apartment and pointed at the phone where it lay on the table. "There. Answer it."

Eyeing her sideways, Walter edged over to the phone and picked it up. "Hello," he said

7. *Ineffectually* means "without success."
8. An *onslaught* is an attack.

Additional Support

Skills Practice

READING: Comparing Characters Jackson repeatedly compares Ellen Webster and Walter Nesmith. As students read the story, have them take notes on how Walter and Ellen are alike. Tell students to organize their notes in a two-column chart. Have them label each column with one of the character's names. *(Possible traits: **Walter** – "nice," "agreeable," wants two children, a boy and a girl; **Ellen** – "sweet," has pretty, soft hair and dark, soft eyes, wants three children, a boy and two girls)* OL

Interior with Woman at the Table. Natalia Goncharova. Russian State Museum, St. Petersburg, Russia. ★
Viewing the Art: What personality traits might the woman in the painting share with Ellen? Explain.

R2 nervously. Then, "Hello? Hello?" Looking at her over the top of the phone, he said, "What do you want me to do now?"

"Do you mean to say," said Ellen ominously,[9] "that that terrible terrible person has hung up?"

"I guess so," said Walter, and fled back to his apartment.

The door had only just closed behind him when the phone rang again, and Ellen, answering it, heard, "May I speak to Walter, please?"

BI2 Not a very serious mischance,[10] surely. But the next morning Walter pointedly avoided going down in the elevator with Ellen, and sometime during that day the deliveryman left a package addressed to Ellen at Walter's door.

When Walter found the package he took it manfully under his arm and went boldly across the hall and rang Ellen's doorbell. When Ellen opened her door she thought at first—and she may have been justified—that Walter had come to apologize for the phone

9. When persons speak *ominously* about an event, they suggest that something bad is about to happen.

10. A *mischance* is something that happens as a result of bad luck.

Teach

R2 Reading Strategy

Making and Verifying Predictions About Plot

Ask: What predictions does this passage verify? *(It verifies that the two characters would clash.)* How do you think Walter and Ellen will relate after their negative encounter? *(Students may say that Walter and Ellen will avoid each other or have a confrontation.)* OL

BI2 Big Idea

Awkward Encounters

Ask: Why would it be difficult to have an awkward encounter with a neighbor? *(Students may say that a person cannot avoid contact with a neighbor, which would make an awkward encounter worse.)* OL

★ Viewing the Art

Natalia Goncharova (1881–1962) was an important member of the Russian avant-garde movement. In addition to her paintings, Goncharova collaborated with impresario Sergei Diaghilev, creating stage design for his Ballets Russes in Paris.

Answer: *The woman in the painting might live alone and be a little lonely.* AS

Building Reading Fluency

Partner Activity This selection contains long, complex sentences. Reading complicated passages out loud will give students the chance to hear the rhythm and tempo of Jackson's writing. Have students take turns reading paragraphs aloud with a partner. After each reading, have students work together to clarify meaning and understand the tone of the story. BL

Academic Standards

Additional Support activities on pp. 854 and 855 cover the following standards:

Skills Practice: **9.3** [Identify] story elements such as character…

Building Reading Fluency: **9.7** [Respond] to oral communication [with] careful listening and evaluation of content…

Teach

L Literary Element

Point of View This story uses a third-person omniscient, or all-knowing, point of view. The narrator is not a character in the story and knows everything about the characters, including what they think.
Ask: Is Walter's opinion that Ellen is "a very odd girl" justified at this point in the story? Why or why not? *(Most students may say yes, because she has acted strangely in dragging him into her apartment to answer her phone, and in behaving as though he was giving her a gift when he returned her package.)* OL

BI1 Big Idea

Awkward Encounters
Ask: Does anger sometimes play a part in causing an awkward encounter? *(Students may say that angry people sometimes do not think before they act or speak, which can lead to an uncomfortable encounter.)* OL

call the evening before, and she even thought that the package under his arm might contain something delightfully unexpected, like a box of candy. They lost another chance then; if Walter had not held out the package and said "Here," Ellen would not have gone on thinking that he was trying to apologize in his own shy way, and she would certainly not have smiled warmly, and said, "You *shouldn't* have bothered."

Walter, who regarded transporting a misdelivered parcel across the hall as relatively little bother, said blankly, "No bother at all," and Ellen, still deceived, said, "But it really wasn't *that* important."

L Walter went back into his own apartment convinced that this was a very odd girl indeed, and Ellen, finding that the package had been mailed to her and contained a wool scarf knitted by a cousin, was as much angry as embarrassed because, once having imagined that an apology is forthcoming, it is very annoying not to have one after all, and particularly to have a wool scarf instead of a box of candy.

BI1 How this situation disintegrated[11] into the white-hot fury which rose between these two is a puzzle, except for the basic fact that when once a series of misadventures has begun between two people, everything tends to contribute further to a state of misunderstanding. Thus, Ellen opened a letter of Walter's by mistake, and Walter dropped a bottle of milk—he was still trying to cure his cold, and thought that perhaps milk toast[12] was the thing—directly outside Ellen's door, so that even after his nervous attempts to clear it up, the floor was still littered with fragments of glass, and puddled with milk.

Then Ellen—who believed by now that Walter had thrown the bottle of milk against her door—allowed herself to become so far confused by this succession of small annoyances that she actually wrote and mailed a letter to Walter, asking politely that he try to turn down his radio a little in the late evenings. Walter replied with a frigid letter to the effect that certainly if he had known that she was bothered by his radio, he should surely never have dreamed—

That evening, perhaps by accident, his radio was so loud that Ellen's canary woke up and chirped hysterically, and Ellen, pacing her floor in incoherent[13] fury, might have been heard—if there had been anyone to hear her, and if Walter's radio had not been so loud—to say, "I'll get even with him!" A phrase, it must be said, which Ellen had never used before in her life.

Ellen made her preparation with a sort of loving care that might well have been lavished on some more worthy object. When the alarm went off she turned in her sleep and smiled before quite waking up, and, once awake and the alarm turned off, she almost laughed out loud. In her slippers and gown, the clock in her hand, she went across her small apartment to the phone; the number was one she was not soon apt to forget. The dial tone sounded amazingly loud, and for a minute she was almost frightened out of her resolution. Then, setting her teeth, she dialed the number, her hand steady. After a second's interminable[14] wait, the ringing began. The phone at the other end rang three times, four times, with what seemed interminable waits between, as though even the mechanical phone system hesitated at this act. Then, at last, there was an irritable crash at the other end of the line, and a voice said, "Wah?"

"Good morning," said Ellen brightly. "I called to tell you that my clock has stopped—"

"Wah?"

"This is Ellen Webster," said Ellen still brightly. "I called to tell you that my clock has stopped—"

"Wah?"

11. *Disintegrated* means "fell apart."
12. *Milk toast* is buttered cinnamon toast soaked and eaten in warm milk.
13. *Incoherent* means "unable to be expressed clearly or logically."
14. *Interminable* means "seemingly endless."

Additional Support

Skills Practice

READING: Main Ideas and Supporting Details Ask students to reread part of the story beginning on page 855 with "When Walter found the package" through the paragraph on page 856 beginning with "That evening, perhaps by accident." Working with a partner, students should write the main idea and the major supporting details of each paragraph. To model notes on the first paragraph, write on the board: main idea—Ellen and Walter have another misunderstanding; supporting details—Walter returns the package, Ellen thinks he has come to apologize. OL

Mr. Cooper, 1992. Rosemary Morrison. Gouache.

She felt fairly certain that he would not call her back, but she sat on her bed and giggled a little before she went back to sleep.

Walter's response to this was miserably weak: he contacted a neighboring delicatessen a day or so later, and had an assortment of evil-smelling cheese left in Ellen's apartment while she was out. This, which required persuading the superintendent to open Ellen's apartment so that the package might be left inside, was a poor revenge but a monstrous exercise of imagination upon Walter's part, so that, in one sense, Ellen was already bringing out in him qualities he never knew he had. The cheese, it turned out, more than evened the score: the apartment was small, the day was warm, and Ellen did not get home until late, and long after most of the other tenants on the floor had gone to the superintendent with their complaints about something dead in the woodwork. BI2

"—and I wonder if you could tell me what time it is?"

There was a short pause at the other end of the line. Then after a minute, his voice came back: "Tenny minna fah."

"I beg your pardon?"

There was another short pause at the other end of the line, as of someone opening his eyes with a shock. "Twenty minutes after four," he said. *"Twenty minutes after four."*

"The reason I thought of asking you," Ellen said sweetly, "was that you were so *very* obliging before. About the radio, I mean."

"—calling a person at—"

"Thanks so much," said Ellen. "Good-bye."

Since breaking and entering had thus become one of the rules of their game, Ellen felt privileged to retaliate[15] in kind upon Walter. It was with great joy, some evenings later, that Ellen, sitting in her odorous apartment, heard Walter's scream of pure terror when he put his feet into his slippers and found a raw egg in each.

Walter had another weapon, however, which he had been so far reluctant to use; it was a howitzer[16] of such proportions that

15. To *retaliate* is to harm someone as revenge for something that person has done.
16. A *howitzer* is a type of cannon used in warfare. Here, the word is used figuratively to mean a "serious weapon."

Teach

BI2 Big Idea

Awkward Encounters

Ask: How does Walter and Ellen's feud escalate? *(Students may say that as the characters continue to misunderstand each other their retaliations grow more extreme.)* How do the characters avoid face-to-face encounters? *(Ellen calls Walter in the middle of the night; Walter has smelly cheese put into Ellen's apartment while she is at work.)* OL

Viewing the Art

Rosemary Morrison painted this picture using *gouache* (pronounced *gwash*). The word *gouache* comes from the Italian *aguazzo* for "mud." Invented in Europe, gouache is a heavy, wet, opaque (mud-like) watercolor paint that produces stronger colors than regular watercolor. AS

Differentiated Instruction

Writing a Play Have gifted and talented students collaborate to rewrite "About Two Nice People" as a play. Encourage students to include Jackson's comparison of Walter and Ellen and the humor of the escalating tricks in her short story. They may include dialogue from the story in their work. Allow students time to rehearse the completed drama and then enact the story for another class. AL

Academic Standards

Additional Support activities on pp. 856 and 857 cover the following standards:

Skills Practice: **9.5.8** Write for different purposes...

Differentiated Instruction: **9.5.2** Write responses to literature that...demonstrate a comprehensive grasp of the significant ideas of literary works; demonstrate an awareness of the author's style and an appreciation of the effects created... **9.6.4** Apply appropriate manuscript conventions...

Teach

R Reading Strategy

Making and Verifying Predictions About Plot

Ask: Why is Walter's aunt in Ellen's apartment? *(Walter may have sent her to intimidate Ellen.)* OL

BI Big Idea

Awkward Encounters

Ask: How does Ellen's encounter with Walter's aunt begin awkwardly? *(Students may say that finding a stranger in Ellen's home is awkward and the aunt is intimidating.)*

Ask: How does Walter's aunt make the awkwardness between Walter and Ellen worse? *(Students may say she embarrasses them both by accusing Ellen of scheming to marry Walter.)* OL

★ Literary History

Just an Ordinary Day

The story "About Two Nice People" was republished in an anthology of 54 short stories entitled *Just an Ordinary Day.* The collection was put together by two of Jackson's children after her death, when some of her manuscripts were discovered in a barn. AS

★ Walter felt its use would end warfare utterly. After the raw eggs he felt no compunction whatever in bringing out his heavy artillery.

It seemed to Ellen, at first, as though peace had been declared. For almost a week things went along smoothly; Walter kept his radio tuned down almost to inaudibility, so that Ellen got plenty of sleep. She was over her cold, the sun had come out, and on Saturday morning she spent three hours shopping, and found exactly the dress she wanted at less than she expected to pay.

About Saturday noon she stepped out of the elevator, her packages under her arm, and walked briskly down the hall to her apartment, making, as usual, a wide half circle to avoid coming into contact with the area around Walter's door.

Her apartment door, to her surprise, was open, but before she had time to phrase a question in her own mind, she had stepped inside and come face to face with a lady who—not to make any more mysteries—was Walter Nesmith's aunt, and a wicked old lady in her own way, possessing none of Walter's timidity and none of his tact.

"Who?" said Ellen weakly, standing in the doorway.

R "Come in and close the door," said the old lady darkly. "I don't think you'll want your neighbors to hear what I have to say. I," she continued as Ellen obeyed mechanically, "am Mrs. Harold Vongarten Nesmith. Walter Nesmith, young woman, is my nephew."

"Then you are in the wrong apartment," said Ellen, quite politely considering the reaction which Walter Nesmith's name was beginning by now to arouse in her. "You want Apartment Three–B, across the hall."

BI "I do *not,*" said the old lady firmly. "I came here to see the designing young woman who has been shamelessly pursuing my nephew, and to warn her"—the old lady shook her gloves menacingly—"to warn her that *not one cent* shall she have from me if she marries Walter Nesmith."

"Marries?" said Ellen, thoughts too great for words in her heart.

"It has long been my opinion that some young woman would be after Walter Nesmith for his money," said Walter's aunt with satisfaction.

"Believe me," said Ellen wholeheartedly, "there is not that much money in the world."

"You deny it?" The old lady leaned back and smiled triumphantly. "I expected something of the sort. Walter," she called suddenly, and then, putting her head back and howling. "Wal-l-l-l-l-ter."

"Sh-h-h," said Ellen fearfully. "They'll hear you all over."

"I expect them to," said the old lady. "Wal-l-l-l-l—Oh, there you are."

Ellen turned and saw Walter Nesmith, with triumph in his eyes, peering around the edge of the door. "Did it work?" he asked.

"She denies everything," said his aunt.

"About the eggs?" Walter said, confused. "You mean, she denies about the eggs and the phone call and—"

"Look," Ellen said to Walter, stamping across the floor to look him straight in the eye, "of all the insufferable, conceited, rude, self-satisfied—"

"What?" said Walter.

"I wouldn't want to marry you," said Ellen, "if—if—" She stopped for a word, helpless.

"If he were the last man on earth," Walter's aunt supplied obligingly. "I think she's really after your *money,* Walter."

> "Not one cent shall she have from me if she marries Walter Nesmith."

Additional Support

Skills Practice

LISTENING/SPEAKING/VIEWING:

Presenting Arguments Have students imagine that Walter and Ellen have taken their dispute to a court of law. Divide students into two groups. Ask one group to write an argument for Ellen's case while the other group presents Walter's perspective. Both groups must use details from the story to support their arguments. One student from each group presents the argument. The remaining students become the jury who must decide who is at fault. OL

Auntie. Bernard Fleetwood-Walker. Royal Academy of Arts, London, UK.
Viewing the Art: How would you describe the woman's attitude? Look at her posture, her facial expression, and her overall appearance. 

COMPARING LITERATURE

Teach

★ Viewing the Art

English painter and draughtsman Bernard Fleetwood-Walker (1893–1965) was famous for his figures and portraits. Despite being wounded and gassed in World War I, he continued to paint, draw, and teach.
Answer: *She appears calm and dignified.* AS

English Language Coach

Understanding Dialogue To help English learners understand what is happening on page 858, have them work in groups of three. In each group, assign one person to read the part of the aunt, another, the part of Ellen, and the third, the part of Walter. Encourage students to read the scene through once, pausing as needed to clarify words or ideas that are confusing. Then have students read the scene through a second time without pausing and let the dialogue flow more naturally. As a class, discuss how the dialogue affected their understanding. EL

Academic Standards

Additional Support activities on pp. 858 and 859 cover the following standards:

Skills Practice: **9.7.18** Deliver persuasive arguments…that structure ideas and arguments in a coherent, logical fashion… **9.7.12** Analyze the types of arguments used by the speaker…

English Language Coach: **9.7** [Respond] to oral communication [with] careful listening and evaluation of content…

Teach

R1 Reading Strategy

Making and Verifying Predictions About Plot

Ask: Are the aunt's appearance and her statements predictable or surprising? Explain. *(Students may say her presence was probably at Walter's request and she is part of his next act of revenge; the aunt's statements will surprise most students who expect her to intimidate Ellen but not to accuse her of wanting to marry Walter.)* OL

L Literary Element

Climax The climax is the point of greatest emotional intensity or suspense in the plot. It typically comes at the turning point in the story.

Ask: How does the ringing of the telephone signal the climax of the story? *(Students may point out that Ellen is angrily sending Walter away as the phone rings. At that point, the emotional tension breaks, the original misunderstanding and ensuing conflict is resolved, and Ellen and Walter revert to their natural warm and gentle personalities.)* OL

COMPARING LITERATURE

Walter stared at his aunt. "I didn't tell you to tell her—" he began. He gasped, and tried again. "I mean," he said, "I never thought—" He appealed to Ellen. "I don't want to marry you, either," he said, and then gasped again, and said, "I mean, I told my aunt to come and tell you—"

"If this is a proposal," Ellen said coldly, "I decline."

"All I wanted her to do was scare you," Walter said finally.

"It's a good way," his aunt said complacently.[17] "Turned out to be the only way with your Uncle Charles and a Hungarian adventuress."

"I mean," Walter said desperately to Ellen, "she owns the building. I mean, I wanted her to tell you that if you didn't stop—I mean, I wanted her to scare you—"

"Apartments are too hard to get these days," his aunt said. "That would have been *too* unkind."

"That's how I got my apartment at all, you see," Walter said to Ellen, still under the impression he was explaining something Ellen wanted to understand.

"Since you have an apartment," Ellen said with restraint, "may I suggest that you take your aunt and the both of you—"

The phone rang.

"Excuse me," said Ellen mechanically, moving to answer it. "Hello?" she said.

"Hello, may I speak to Walter, please?"

Ellen smiled rather in the manner that Lady Macbeth[18] might have smiled if she found a run in her stocking.

"It's for you," she said, holding the phone out to Walter.

"For me?" he said, surprised. "Who is it?"

"I really could not say," said Ellen sweetly. "Since you have so many friends that one phone is not adequate to answer all their calls—"

Since Walter made no move to take the phone, she put it gently back on the hook.

"They'll call again," she assured him, still smiling in that terrible fashion.

"I ought to turn you both out," said Walter's aunt. She turned to Ellen. "Young woman," she said, "do you deny that all this nonsense with eggs and telephone calls is an attempt to entangle my nephew into matrimony?"

"Certainly not," Ellen said, "I mean, I *do* deny it."

"Walter Nesmith," said his aunt, "do you admit that all your finagling with cheeses and radios is an attempt to strike up an acquaintance with this young woman?"

"Certainly," said Walter. "I mean, I do *not* admit it."

"Good," said Walter's aunt. "You are precisely the pair of silly fools I would have picked out for each other." She rose with great dignity, motioned Walter away from her, and started for the door. "Remember," she said, shaking her gloves again at Ellen, "not one cent."

She opened the door and started down the hall, her handkerchief over her eyes, and—a sorry thing in such an old lady—laughing until she had to stop and lean against the wall near the elevator.

"I'm sorry," Walter was saying to Ellen, almost babbling, "I'm *really* sorry this time—please believe me, I had *no* idea—I wouldn't for the world—nothing but the most profound respect—a joke, you know—hope you didn't really think—"

"I understand perfectly," Ellen said icily. "It is all perfectly clear. It only goes to show what I have always believed about young men who think that all they have to do is—"

"All I wanted her to do was scare you."

17. *Complacently* means "in a self-satisfied manner."
18. *Lady Macbeth* is an evil and merciless character who plots to murder the king in Shakespeare's play *Macbeth*.

Additional Support

Skills Practice

WRITING: Summarizing By writing a summary, students can improve their understanding of a selection. Remind students that a summary should include only the main ideas and important details of a literary work. Have students write a summary of "About Two Nice People." They should include the main idea that two nice people become angry and seek revenge on each other because of a misunderstanding. Students should not include insignificant details. Have students share their summaries with a partner. OL

Countryside home on a sunny day. Christopher Zacharow.

The phone rang.

Ellen waited a minute before she spoke. Then she said, "You might as well answer it."

"I'm *terribly* sorry," Walter said, not moving toward the phone. "I mean, I'm *terribly* sorry." He waved his hands in the air. "About what she said about what she thought about what you wanted me to do—" His voice trailed off miserably.

BI Suddenly Ellen began to giggle.

Anger is certainly a problem that will bear much analysis. It is hardly surprising that one person may be angry at another, particularly if these are two people who are gentle, usually, and rarely angry, whose emotions tend to be mild and who would rather be friends with everyone than be enemies with anyone. Such an anger argues a situation so acute that only the most drastic readjustment can remedy it. BI

Either Walter Nesmith or Ellen Webster could have moved, of course. But, as Walter's aunt had pointed out, apartments are not that easy to come by, and their motives and their telephone numbers were by now so inextricably[19] mixed that on the whole it seemed more reasonable not to bother.

Moreover, Walter's aunt, who still snickers when her nephew's name is mentioned, did not keep them long in suspense, after all. She was not lavish, certainly, but she wrote them a letter which both of them found completely confusing and which enclosed a check adequate for a down payment on the extremely modest house in the country they decided upon without disagreement. They even compromised and had four children—two boys and two girls. R2

Discussion Starter

What circumstances lead Ellen and Walter to become angry with each other? Discuss this question in a small group. In your discussion, refer to personal experiences of frustration or failed communication. Support your opinions with specific details from the story. Then share your conclusions with the class.

19. Things that are *inextricably* mixed can no longer be untangled or separated.

COMPARING LITERATURE

Teach

BI Big Idea

Awkward Encounters

Ask: How is the awkward encounter between Walter and Ellen finally resolved? *(Possible answers: The aunt's trick allows the two to interact and begin to develop a relationship; the ringing phone and Ellen's response finally clarify the initial misunderstanding; the main characters' kindness finally reemerges.)* **OL**

R2 Reading Strategy

Making and Verifying Predictions About Plot

Ask: Was it predictable or surprising that Walter and Ellen end up together? *(Some students may say that once their differences were resolved, Walter and Ellen would realize they were made for each other.)* **OL**

Discussion Starter

Discussions should reflect students' understanding that circumstances and misunderstandings led to Ellen and Walter's feud. Students should compare their responses to frustrating circumstances with the reactions of the characters.

Differentiated Instruction

Understanding Inferences Help less proficient readers understand what Walter's aunt has done. Clarify that in seeming to make false accusations, she has forced Walter and Ellen to come together, talk, and overcome their differences. Explain that the aunt first introduces the idea of marriage and then gives them money for their first home. **BL**

Academic Standards

Additional Support activities on pp. 860 and 861 cover the following standards:

Skills Practice: **9.5.1** Write…narratives…that describe a sequence of events and communicate the significance of the events to the audience.

Differentiated Instruction: **9.3.3** Analyze interactions between characters…

Focus

Summary

In this poem two people who have had an awkward encounter are compared to deer.

Teach

Quickwrite

Students should compare people and animals. The subject should be a familiar feeling.

Author Search To expand students' appreciation of N. Scott Momaday, have them access the Web site for additional information and resources.

Use the CheckPoint questions on Presentation Plus! to check students' mastery of the selection. These questions can be used with interactive response keypads for immediate student feedback.

BEFORE YOU READ

Building Background

Navarre Scott Momaday was born in 1934 and grew up on reservations in the American Southwest, where he was influenced by his Kiowa heritage. Momaday's first novel, *House Made of Dawn,* won the Pulitzer Prize for Fiction in 1969. The award stunned the literary world, since Momaday was virtually unknown as a writer at the time. Much of Momaday's writing reflects the Native American belief that there is, as he puts it, "harmony in the universe."

Literature Online **Author Search** For more about N. Scott Momaday, go to www.glencoe.com.

SIMILE

N. Scott Momaday

What did we say to each other
that now we are as the deer
who walk in single file
with heads high
with ears forward
with eyes watchful
with hooves always placed on firm ground
in whose limbs there is latent[1] flight

1. Something that is *latent* is unseen or undeveloped but capable of bursting into full activity under certain conditions.

Quickwrite

How do the descriptions of the deer in this poem help illustrate a truth about people? Write a poem or paragraph in which you make your own comparison between people and animals.

Additional Support

Skills Practice

READING: Relating to the Poem
Help students understand and relate to the poem by connecting it to their own experiences.
Ask: When you have had an awkward encounter with someone, how do you behave when you next meet that person?

Give the class time to discuss their answers. Brainstorm a list of words that describe students' feelings in such a situation. Create a list of similes and metaphors that make these feelings clear to others. OL

Wrap-Up: Comparing Literature *Across Genres*

- ***A Sunny Morning*** by Serafín and Joaquín Álvarez Quintero
- ***About Two Nice People*** by Shirley Jackson
- ***Simile*** by N. Scott Momaday

COMPARING THE Big Idea Awkward Encounters

Writing Activity Write a brief essay explaining which of these selections describes the most interesting encounter. Remember to include an introduction and a conclusion in your essay, and at least three reasons for your choice. After you finish writing, review your essay for grammar, punctuation, and spelling errors. Then exchange papers with a classmate for a final review.

COMPARING Conflict

Partner Activity Use a graphic organizer like the one shown here to write your thoughts about the conflict in each of the three selections you have read. Compare your chart with a classmate's. Are there differences? What might account for those differences? Review the selections once more and make a final chart that you and your partner can share with the rest of the class.

Title of Selection	Characters Involved in Conflict	Reason for Conflict
A Sunny Morning		
About Two Nice People		
Simile		

COMPARING Authors' Culture

Visual Display Review the selections once more, noting details that tell you something about the author's culture. Begin by looking at the setting for each selection. The setting can reveal much about the time and place in which the author lived and wrote. Use details from the selections to create a three-panel collage of images—one panel for each selection—that illustrates the culture of each author. Include passages from the selections with the images in your display.

INDIANA ACADEMIC STANDARDS (page 818)

9.3.2 Compare and contrast...a similar theme or topic across genres...

9.7.4 Use...visual aids...to enhance the appeal and accuracy of presentations.

Assess

Comparing the Big Idea

Critique students' essays on these criteria:

- Do students present three clear reasons for their choice?
- Do students support their reasons with examples from the selection?

Comparing Conflict

In "A Sunny Morning," the characters are Doña Laura and Don Gonzalo; the conflict is over sharing a park bench.
In "About Two Nice People," the characters are Walter and Ellen; the conflict begins when Ellen gets repeated calls meant for Walter.
In "Simile," the characters are the narrator and an unnamed person; the conflict is about something that was said.

Comparing Authors' Cultures

Collages should include specific examples from the selections about where the author lived, when the author lived, and the author's status in society.

Differentiated Instruction

Compare and Contrast Help less proficient readers see the similarities and differences in these three selections by completing a chart. They should place the title of each selection in a row in the first column, then briefly tell the main idea of the selection in the second column, and the conflict and its resolution in the third column. Have students meet in small groups to compare their completed charts. **BL**

Academic Standards

Additional Support activities on pp. 862 and 863 cover the following standards:

Skills Practice: **9.2** Develop [reading] strategies...

Differentiated Instruction: **9.3.2** Compare and contrast the presentation of a similar theme or topic across genres...

BEFORE YOU READ

Focus

BELLRINGER

Bellringer Options
Daily Language Practice Transparency 78
Or show images from television sitcoms or movies in which humor is partially based on a character who seems clueless about the reality of his or her situation. **Ask:** What makes these characters humorous?

As they read, students should consider how Welty's characters and play are similar to modern sitcoms. OL

Author Search To expand students' appreciation of Eudora Welty, have them access the Web site for additional information and resources.

BEFORE YOU READ

Bye-Bye Brevoort

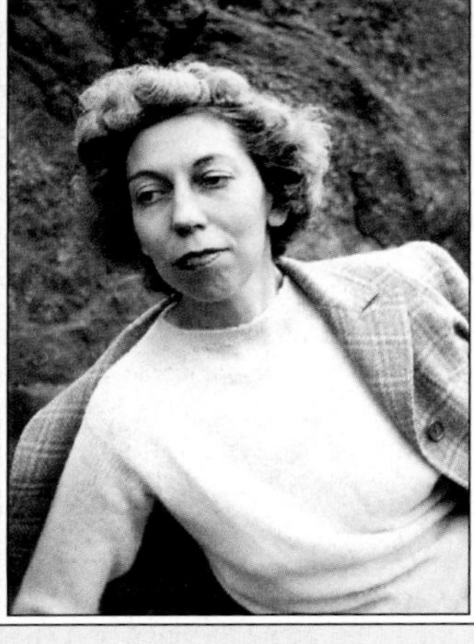

MEET EUDORA WELTY

Eudora Welty reportedly spoke her last words to a doctor who leaned over her bed and asked if there was anything he could do for her. "No," she said, "but thank you so much for inviting me to the party."

Those who knew Welty said she was as gracious on her deathbed as she had been during her ninety-two years of life. "Yet," according to one critic, "her writing revealed an entirely different person: the tough-minded woman with a shrewd eye and perfect ear whose always memorable, often violent stories helped change how non-southerners saw the American South."

Home and Away Eudora Welty was born in Jackson, Mississippi, where she lived most of her life. From the time she was a small girl, she loved books and would read and listen to stories for hours. Welty's fine listening skills are evident in her writing.

"Long before I wrote stories, I listened for stories."

—Eudora Welty

In 1925 Welty left Mississippi to attend college, first in Wisconsin and later in New York. She returned in 1931 when her father became seriously ill. Welty remained in Jackson after her father died, working at a radio station and a newspaper. In 1935 Welty became a photographer for President Franklin Roosevelt's Works Progress Administration (WPA). She traveled to rural areas in all of the counties of Mississippi and documented the development projects that provided work for the poor and unemployed. These photos showed the poverty and determination of the people she met. In 1936 she displayed a collection of her photographs in New York City. She later published several volumes of photographs.

The Writing Life Welty's career as a writer took off in 1936, with the publication of her first short story, "Death of a Traveling Salesman." The story later appeared in Welty's first book, *A Curtain of Green and Other Stories.* This collection displays Welty's fine understanding of comedy, even when her writing explores serious topics.

Welty followed *A Curtain of Green and Other Stories* with many novels, collections of short stories and essays, an autobiography, and the one-act play *Bye-Bye Brevoort*. But in the early 1950s, she stopped writing almost completely in order to care for her sick mother and brothers. It was not until 1966, after their deaths, that she began writing regularly again. In 1973 she was awarded the Pulitzer Prize for her novel *The Optimist's Daughter.*

Eudora Welty was born in 1909 and died in 2001.

LiteratureOnline **Author Search** For more about Eudora Welty, go to www.glencoe.com.

Selection Skills

Bye-Bye Brevoort

Literary Elements
- High Comedy (SE pp. 865, 869, 872, 874)

Reading Skills
- Questioning (SE pp. 865–874)
- Previewing (TWE p. 866)

Vocabulary Skills
- Analogies (SE pp. 865, 874)
- Connotation (TWE p. 868)

Writing Skills/Grammar
- Setting Analysis (SE p. 874)
- Character Sketch (TWE p. 872)

LITERATURE PREVIEW

Connecting to the Play

The following one-act play is a comic look at a group of friends who enjoy each other's company while ignoring obvious signs that something is not quite right. Before you read the play, think about the following questions:

- With whom do you most enjoy spending time? Why?
- Have you ever deliberately ignored negative circumstances? Explain.

Building Background

Brevoort House was a hotel located near Washington Square in Greenwich Village, a section of Manhattan, in New York City. It was first built as a home for the Brevoorts, a Dutch family, in 1834. In 1851 it was converted to a hotel. During the late 1800s, many wealthy travelers stayed at Brevoort House when visiting New York. The basement café at the Brevoort was also an occasional gathering place for writers and artists, including Edgar Allan Poe, Edith Wharton, Mark Twain, and, later, Jack Kerouac and Allen Ginsberg. In 1954 the Brevoort House was demolished to make way for the nineteen-story Brevoort apartment building.

Setting Purposes for Reading

Big Idea Awkward Encounters

As you read *Bye-Bye Brevoort,* notice how the last inhabitants respond to their awkward encounter with the wrecking crew.

Literary Element High Comedy

Comedy refers to a drama that is humorous and often has a happy ending. **High comedy** is a type of comedy that uses sophisticated humor, often to make fun of the upper classes. As you read, note the type of humor found in *Bye-Bye Brevoort.*

- See Literary Terms Handbook, p. R8.

Literature Online **Interactive Literary Elements Handbook** To review or learn more about the literary elements, go to www.glencoe.com.

READING PREVIEW

Reading Strategy Questioning

Questioning can help deepen your understanding of a text. When a detail of setting, a bit of dialogue, or even a vocabulary word puzzles you while reading, ask questions about what it means. Responding to your own questions in multiple ways can help you find an answer that makes sense.

Reading Tip: Making a List When a specific stage direction or bit of dialogue strikes you as interesting or odd, ask what it might reveal about the characters or the themes of the play.

Question	Possible Answers
Why do the set directions require a painting "which can fall"?	The painting will probably fall during the course of the play.

Vocabulary

dismantling (dis mant′ əl ing) *v.* taking apart; tearing down; p. 866 *They began dismantling the children's playhouse when snow was forecast.*

furled (furld) *adj.* rolled up and secured; p. 867 *The first mate stowed the furled sails after the ship reached shore.*

tiered (tērd) *adj.* arranged in layers or levels; p. 868 *The auditorium was tiered, containing both lower and upper balconies.*

sanction (sangk′ shən) *v.* to give official approval or permission; p. 870 *The debate coach asked the principal to sanction the team's attendance at an out-of-town tournament.*

Vocabulary Tip: Analogies Analogies illustrate similar relationships between sets of dissimilar words.

INDIANA ACADEMIC STANDARDS (pages 865–874)

9.3.8 Interpret and evaluate the impact of...ironies in a text.
9.2 Develop [reading] strategies...
9.5.3 Write...analytical essays...
9.3.10 Describe the function of...stage designs...

BEFORE YOU READ

Focus

Summary

In this short play, three friends enjoy an afternoon of cards and conversation in anticipation of four o'clock high tea. The three ladies of genteel breeding await the arrival of tea cakes, via the maid, and a dear friend, Desmond Dupree. Their world is so insulated from reality that they are unaware that their building is being demolished.

V Vocabulary

Vocabulary File Say: Add these words and definitions to your vocabulary file. For each word, include a sentence that gives you an example of how to use the word. **OL** Students with English language needs should include the pronunciations of these words in their files. **EL**

Literature Online

Literary Elements Have students access the Web site to improve their understanding of high comedy.

Selection Resources

Print Materials
- Unit 4 Resources (Fast File), pp. 46–48
- Selection and Unit Assessments, pp. 151–152
- Selection Quick Checks, p. 76

Transparencies
- Bellringer Options Transparencies: Daily Language Practice Transparency 78
- Literary Elements Transparency 76

Technology
- TeacherWorks Plus™ CD-ROM
- StudentWorks Plus™ CD-ROM
- Presentation Plus!™ CD-ROM
- Literature Online, glencoe.com
- Online Student Edition, mhln.com
- Exam*View*® Assessment Suite CD-ROM
- Vocabulary PuzzleMaker CD-ROM
- Listening Library, disc 2 track 15

Teach

L1 Literary Element

Characterization **Ask:** Why does Welty portray the three women as hard of hearing? *(She wants the misinterpretation of the demolition sounds to be believable.)* OL

★ Writer's Technique

Setting The time and place in which the events in a story or play occur is the setting. The setting helps create an atmosphere or mood. It includes more than physical features; it presents the ideas, customs, values, and beliefs of a time and place. Have students find details that Welty uses to describe the play's setting. AS

Bye-Bye Brevoort

Eudora Welty

Explosion of Red on Green, 1910. Gerardo Dottori. Oil on Canvas. 49.2 x 69.5 cm. Tate Gallery, London.

CHARACTERS

MILLICENT FORTESCUE
VIOLET WHICHAWAY
AGATHA CHROME
EVANS: Miss Fortescue's maid
DESMOND DUPREE
FIRST WRECKER
SECOND WRECKER
THIRD WRECKER

★ *[MISS FORTESCUE'S sitting room in the Brevoort, a room not yet reached by wreckers* ***dismantling*** *the building and obviously occupied by her.*

Set marked off perhaps by one collapsible wall and one folding screen. A window, heavily looped with curtains. A large dark oil painting of a lady ancestor in ornate frame, which can fall. Crowded and abundant Victorian furnishings, two scrolled wicker high-backed chairs and a wicker settee,[1] *a tea table down front big enough to load with china and service and fixed so as to shudder or shimmy with every crash outside as the Brevoort is being torn down, so that some dishes and a flower vase eventually fall off. Right, a stand with an old-fashioned telephone on it, a big seashell, and a large silver dish with a mountain of calling cards*[2]

Vocabulary

dismantling (dis mant′ əl ing) *v.* taking apart; tearing down

1. A *settee* is a cushioned seat for two people.
2. *Calling cards* are cards containing a person's name, address, and telephone number, given out to social or business contacts.

Additional Support

Skills Practice

READING: Previewing Explain that this play is about finding humor in an awkward situation. The audience witnesses the discomfort of a group of privileged people as they gradually come face to face with an unpleasant reality—the demolition of the building that is their home. Have students consider these questions as they read:

- What do Fortescue, Chrome, and Whichaway have in common?
- What is Evans's function? OL

in it. In rear, a dumbwaiter.[3] *Other things might be stacked albums, a fishnet full of postcards and Valentines, at least one musical instrument. Plant stands with luxuriant growth appropriately placed. Door, down left.*

Curtain rises to show FORTESCUE, WHICHAWAY, *and* CHROME, *three old Brevoort relics, in* FORTESCUE'S *sitting room, each playing her own game of solitaire—one on the as yet unlaid tea table, the other two perhaps on checkerboards on their knees.*

The old ladies are dressed de rigueur.[4] *Suggest* FORTESCUE *in lace,* CHROME *in velvet or in floral silk,* WHICHAWAY *in tweeds with white shoes and stockings. A lace parasol will be available for* FORTESCUE. *All wear hearing aids, though* L1 WHICHAWAY *may prefer the trumpet.*[5] CHROME *and* WHICHAWAY, *who come from across the hall, may wear their hats throughout.* EVANS *will wear an elaborate maid's uniform, starched and winged, with frilled cotton drawers as seen.* DESMOND DUPREE, *for whom the extra chair waits, is an old sport in a chesterfield,*[6] *with a* **furled** *umbrella (as he goes out to the park) and yellow gloves.*

The moment before curtain rise, a few bangs and a dull thud. The wreckers dismantling the building are coming closer and closer as skit proceeds. Noises come intermittently,[7] *sometimes a hoarse shout. The ladies do not hear, or else they ignore these crude sounds. But a moment after curtain rise: A faint tinkle. Ladies all hear that. They sit bolt upright in polite, pleased anticipation. All speak up in high, carrying voices.*]

FORTESCUE. [*Waving her battery*[8] *gaily.*] Tea time![9] Tea time! Four o'clock! Did you notice I'd had an alarm put in my hearing aid? Tiffany's[10] sent a man down. To work by the hour, my dears.

WHICHAWAY. *Et tu,* Tiffany.[11]

FORTESCUE. [*Calling out.*] Tea, Evans! Isn't Evans back?

CHROME. [*As crash, off, dies away. Without flinching.*] I haven't heard even a little mouse.

FORTESCUE. I sent her to Charles's—for petit fours.[12] Desmond's coming, with his appetite.

CHROME. Our Thursday Tiger!

WHICHAWAY. Desmond! Shall we go back to our rooms for our hats?

FORTESCUE. You have on *something,* dear.

WHICHAWAY. [*Touching up top.*] Chances are it hasn't been removed since *yesterday's* tea. Simpler. [*Tinkle again, from hearing aid.*]

FORTESCUE. There goes the second bell. If Evans isn't back soon, I'll telephone down and have the Brevoort search Sixth Avenue.

[*Enter* EVANS, *from door left, in cape, parcel in both hands and purse swinging from teeth. She is riding a bicycle. They don't turn to see her.*] 

EVANS. [*Speaking through teeth.*] The cheese straws from Charles's, mum.

FORTESCUE. Evans: don't—hiss.

3. A *dumbwaiter* is a small elevator used to carry food and other items from one floor of a building to another.
4. *De rigueur* is a French term meaning "according to convention."
5. *Trumpet* here refers to an old-fashioned hearing aid, a cone held up to the ear to amplify sound.
6. A *chesterfield* is a type of overcoat, often featuring hidden buttons and a velvet collar.
7. *Intermittently* means "from time to time."

Reading Strategy Questioning *Why do you think the women respond to the faint sound of tinkling when none of them seem to hear loud crashes?* R1

Vocabulary

furled (furld) *adj.* rolled up and secured

8. Early *battery*-operated hearing aids relied on a large battery that had to be carried in a separate box.
9. *Tea time* refers to the largely British custom of gathering together for tea and a snack in the late afternoon or early evening. At high tea, a meal is served along with cakes and tea.
10. *Tiffany's* refers to Tiffany & Co., the famous New York City store that sells expensive jewelry and watches.
11. "Et tu, *Tiffany*" means "Even you, Tiffany." It parodies a famous line from Shakespeare's play *Julius Caesar.* Caesar speaks the Latin phrase *"Et tu, Brute?"* when he recognizes his friend Brutus among the men who are assassinating him. The expression is used to communicate a feeling of betrayal.
12. *Petit fours* are bite-size layer cakes.

Reading Strategy Questioning *Why do you suppose the author chose to have Miss Fortescue respond to the hissing in Evans's speech but not her entrance by bicycle?* R2

Teach

R1 Reading Strategy

Questioning **Answer:** *Answers will vary. Students might say that the ladies are anticipating and looking forward to whatever is signified by the tinkling, but they've grown so accustomed to the crashes that they don't notice them anymore.* OL

L2 Literary Element

Stage Directions Have students describe Evans as she enters. *(She rides a bicycle in the building, carrying a parcel in her hands and her purse in her mouth.)* **Ask:** How do you know what she does? *(The stage directions describe her actions and her appearance.)* OL

R2 Reading Strategy

Questioning **Answer:** *Students may say that Fortescue and her friends notice only what they wish to see; manners are of primary importance to her. The ladies are in denial, and ignoring Evans's entrance illustrates that.* OL

CheckPoint

Use the CheckPoint questions on Presentation Plus! to monitor students' comprehension. These questions can be used with interactive response keypads for immediate student feedback.

English Language Coach

Building Background Explain the divisions between the wealthy and working classes in the United States in the late nineteenth century. This will help students better understand the behavior of the three women, Dupree, Evans, and the workmen. EL

Differentiated Instruction

Sketching the Scene Students with spatial abilities may improve comprehension by sketching pictures of the setting.

- Have students sketch the setting before they read the dialogue.
- Allow students to create additional sketches of the scene and characters. BL

Academic Standards

Additional Support activities on pp. 866 and 867 cover the following standards:

Skills Practice: **9.2** Develop [reading] strategies...

English Language Coach: **9.3.12** Analyze the way in which a work...is related to...issues of its historical period.

Differentiated Instruction: **9.3** [Identify] story elements such as...setting...

Teach

L1 Literary Element

Characterization Ask: How would you describe Chrome's character, based on her words and actions? *(Possible answer: She is overly dramatic and possibly a hypochondriac.)* **OL**

V Vocabulary

Connotation Ask: What is the connotation of the word *scorching* as used in the dialogue spoken by Fortescue? *(The word might be used to mean moving very fast or speeding.)* **OL**

R1 Reading Strategy

Questioning Answer: *Students might say that Desmond will look like a man who was once handsome but now is disheveled and that he will act much like the women, in an overly refined manner.* **OL**

[EVANS dismounts. With faint clicking sound as she walks, goes with burdens behind screen, comes out in her elaborate apron, and begins business of setting the tea table for high tea. Brings from behind screen a linen cloth and napkins, elaborate tea service, which seems to overflow the whole set, covered dishes, several pots, silver and china, cake stand with half a tiered cake. Whenever the pounding or a crash occurs off, all this shakes.]

L1 CHROME. *[Sharply clapping her hand to her back as if shot by an arrow.]* Oh! There's a draft! It struck me!

WHICHAWAY. For thirty-nine years I've said the Brevoort had a draft. And have mentioned it Downstairs. *[Meaningly.]* They know it.

FORTESCUE. We should simply *avoid* the *corridors.*

EVANS. *[In normal voice, since they won't hear. As she bends over to set a bud vase with rose and fern on tea table, as final touch.]* Draft, they call it. We're living in a fool's Swiss cheese.

FORTESCUE. *Evans!*

EVANS. *[Bending over, arrested motion.]* Mum?

FORTESCUE. You've come in with your bicycle clips[13] on. *How* did you come through the lobby?

EVANS. *[Proudly.]* Sidesaddle.

FORTESCUE. *[To others.]* And *yesterday,* she came in on skates!

EVANS. *One* skate.

CHROME. Millicent—is *Evans* slipping—or the *Brevoort?* *[A large crash, off.]*

EVANS. *[Sitting down hard, with the rose.]* We'll go down together.

V FORTESCUE. And as you came scorching through the lobby, Evans, tell me—did anyone budge?

13. *Bicycle clips* are bands that are worn around the calf to prevent clothing from getting caught in the bicycle's chain.

Vocabulary

tiered (tērd) *adj.* arranged in layers or levels

EVANS. No one saw me downstairs, mum, except some persons with axes and the persons with dynamite to blow up the building.

FORTESCUE. No one with lorgnettes?[14] Then thank your lucky stars.

CHROME. Must we wait for Desmond?

FORTESCUE. Dear Desmond! So dashing! Such a wreck!

CHROME. Mr. Knickerbocker says, nothing keeps Desmond in one piece but penicillin and *passe-partout.*[15]

WHICHAWAY. Nonsense, he's always looked that way. It's only from wincing.[16]

CHROME. He insists on going *out,* you know.

FORTESCUE. There's something gallant about him. Shine or shine, he goes forth and strolls in the park. *[They all shake their heads over it.]* And I understand the elevator isn't running past our floor. Some sort of obstruction in the passage!

EVANS. It's got the hiccups. *[Knock at door.]*

EVANS. *[Going to door and opening.]* Hold that tiger.

DUPREE. *[Entering, with EVANS behind.]* Hullo, old things.

LADIES. *[All together, gladly. All kissing.]* Desmond dear! Desmond, you're looking *shattered!*

DUPREE. *[EVANS trying to take his coat. Does so.]* Difficult time getting through again. Odd thing in the corridor: persons all about sawing the walls. Didn't look too savory. Can't help noticing—thing like that during *Lent.*[17]

14. *Lorgnettes* are eye glasses or opera glasses with a handle on the side.
15. In French *passe-partout* means literally "to pass everywhere." The phrase suggests the freedom and ability to go anywhere one pleases.
16. In this context, *wincing* means "making a facial expression reflecting pain as a result of seeing something unpleasant."
17. *Lent* is a period of penitence and prayer leading up to Easter that is observed by many Christian denominations.

Reading Strategy Questioning *Why might Fortescue describe Desmond Dupree this way? How do you expect him to look and act?* **R1**

Additional Support

Skills Practice

READING: Monitoring Comprehension Some students may have difficulty with the format of the play. Explain how reading a play differs from reading a story. Give students some tools for monitoring their comprehension. Suggest that students stop reading when they are not certain about what is happening.

Have students write questions such as: What do the character's words mean? Why did the character do or say what he or she did? Then tell students to reread to answer their questions. **OL**

CHROME. [*Gives him a pat of comfort.*] Riffraff.[18] Best not to notice them.

DUPREE. [*Sinking into chair, offhand.*] They must be looking for treasure.

WHICHAWAY. Yes. Millicent, didn't you once lose an old Carolina moonstone?[19]

FORTESCUE. [*Coldly.*] *Not* in the *corridor.*

[*EVANS, busy with tea, now brings it in. As she bends over tea table, DUPREE stares.*]

DUPREE. Aluminum garters?[20] Daresay it was bound to come.

FORTESCUE. Dear Desmond. You're looking frightfully crepey.[21]

DUPREE. Thanks, old thing. Shall we feed?

FORTESCUE. Evans!

[*EVANS skips, dropping napkins in everybody's lap and DUPREE's on the floor, as in drop-the-handkerchief.*[22] *Goes to FORTESCUE's side.*]

Telephone down, Evans. Ask room service for an earthen jug of *hotter and fresher water.* Pouring, dears! [*FORTESCUE begins to pour. All the dishes start to hobble and shake as bangs and thuds begin coming louder. They bravely ignore. They call a little more loudly and at higher pitch to one another to make themselves heard. Drink tea, eat cake.*]

CHROME. Modern times! The noise of the city is frightful. The vehicles!

WHICHAWAY. Yes. Rat-a-tat—rat-a-tat.

FORTESCUE. I cawn't think why they don't make vehicles go *around* the island![23]

DUPREE. This cake has a marvelous texture—marvelous crumb, Millicent. Wherever did you get it?

EVANS. [*Over her shoulder. She is still at the phone, which doesn't answer.*] Hearn's, and I didn't say Hicks's.

FORTESCUE. No answer below, Evans?

EVANS. No, mum. The last we was in communication with the outside world was a week ago Saturday. A copy of the *Villager*[24] was thrown through the window. R2

CHROME. [*As crash comes.*] I think they're trying it again.

[*All shudder.*]

FORTESCUE. Keep listening, Evans. I cawn't think they'd have given *me* a telephone without the other end. Thirty-nine years in the Brevoort—why, the phone should ring incessantly by this time. [*Decides.*] Hang up, and let them call us.

EVANS. [*Hanging up.*] I'd rather skate across the street and fill my earthen jug at the King Cole Room.

FORTESCUE. [*Offering chocolates out of enormous satin-lined candy box, requiring both hands to handle. Ladies choose, cooing.*] Desmond? The liquid cherries are in the fourteenth row—balcony.

DUPREE. [*Cramming.*] Teddibly good of you. Any quail sandwiches, or do I presume?

EVANS. [*Carrying long, old-fashioned flintlock*[25] *across stage and standing it in corner.*] You presume. It's Lent—remember?

CHROME. [*Gaily.*] That last time we had a bird! Do you recall, Millicent?

FORTESCUE. [*A short scream.*] Oh! Indelibly. That was the afternoon Raymond Duncan[26] came to tea.

18. *Riffraff* means "people who are disreputable or worthless."
19. A *moonstone* is a bluish-white gemstone made from the mineral feldspar.
20. Dupree is mistaking Evans's bicycle clips for *garters,* which are clips attached to a band used to hold up socks or stockings.
21. *Crepey* [krā′ pē] means "wrinkled, like crepe fabric," which has a crinkled surface.
22. *Drop-the-handkerchief* is a children's circle game.
23. *The island* means Manhattan Island, the part of New York City where Greenwich Village and the Brevoort are located.
24. The *Villager* is a Greenwich Village newspaper published since 1933.
25. A *flintlock* is an old-fashioned type of gun that uses a type of rock called flint to ignite the gunpowder.
26. *Raymond Duncan,* the brother of the famous modern dancer Isadora Duncan, was an artist who, among other things, designed clothes and created his own fabrics.

Literary Element High Comedy *How is the author making fun of Miss Fortescue and her class here?* L2

Teach

R2 Reading Strategy

Questioning Ask: Which character seems most in tune with reality? Explain. *(Possible answer: Evans does not live in the sheltered world of her wealthy employer or her employer's friends.)* OL

L2 Literary Element

High Comedy Answer: *Miss Fortescue is so used to privilege she can't believe her phone doesn't work. She ignores the fact that the building is being demolished and the phones are disconnected.* OL

English Language Coach

Oral Presentation English learners may gain confidence by acting out part of the play. Be sure to keep the sessions relaxed so students will feel comfortable taking part. Allow students to choose the role they play. EL

Differentiated Instruction

Character Biography Actors sometimes create a biography of a character's life before the time of the story to provide a history of the character. Invite students to select one character and write his or her biography. Ask students to share their work. AL

Academic Standards

Additional Support activities on pp. 868 and 869 cover the following standards:

Skills Practice: **9.2** Develop [reading] strategies...

English Language Coach: **9.7.17** Deliver oral responses to literature that...[demonstrate] a comprehensive understanding of the significant ideas of...passages [and] demonstrate awareness of the author's writing style and an appreciation of the effects created...

Differentiated Instruction: **9.5.1** Write biographical...narratives... that describe a sequence of events and communicate the significance of the events to the audience...

Teach

R1 Reading Strategy

Questioning **Answer:** *She implies that the Waldorf, where Raymond Duncan lives, allows goats, while the Brevoort does not. Thus, the Brevoort is the superior hotel.* OL

R2 Reading Strategy

Drawing Conclusions **Ask:** Why does Fortescue explain Evans's behavior and who Aunt Emmeline is? *(To help readers understand the maid's actions and how Aunt Emmeline fits into the story)* OL

BI Big Idea

Awkward Encounters
Answer: *The poems are about ships sinking. Desmond, like the ladies, has been ignoring the demolition, but here he realizes they are in danger.* OL

★ Viewing the Art

Answer: *Both the painting and the play feature tea scenes. However, the painting shows a calm still life, while the play takes place during a noisy, chaotic time.* AS

Still Life With Dishes, 1909. Vasilij Vasilevic Rozdestvenskij. Oil on canvas. Museum of Art, Kazan, Russia.
Viewing the Art: How is the scene pictured similar to and different from the scene in the play? ★

WHICHAWAY. Threading his way down from the Waldorf.[27]

CHROME. Bringing his weaving.

FORTESCUE. Saint Valentine's Day! . . . And he took the bones home in his pocket.—He *had* pockets, hadn't he?

CHROME. For the goats. The Brevoort, of course, doesn't **sanction** goats.

WHICHAWAY. [*Calling over noises off.*] Sanction who?

ALL THE OTHERS, WITH EVANS. Goats!

[*The portrait falls off the wall at this extra clamor.*]

EVANS. [*Gesture of announcement.*] E-o-leven! [*Then rehangs portrait. On second thought, turns it face to the wall.*]

FORTESCUE. [*Explaining to* DUPREE.] Evans is keeping count of the times Aunt Emmeline falls—*excellent* count. [*Fuller explanation.*] This was *her* home, you know. R2

WHICHAWAY. [*Broodingly.*] There are moments when I seem to notice something over and beyond the noise of traffic and falling portraits.

FORTESCUE. You hear the seashell, dear. Evans, hold up the seashell for Miss Whichaway.

[EVANS *holds it up, and it vibrates and jerks in her hands as the noises sound. She shudders.*]

FORTESCUE. See, dear? It makes Evans shudder.—That will *do,* Evans.

EVANS. [*Gesturing with seashell aloft, reciting.*]
"It was the schooner Hesperus
That sailed the wintry sea—"[28]

FORTESCUE. More tea? Let's all have more hot tea. [*She begins to pour.*]

EVANS. [*Reciting with shell.*]
"We are lost, the Captain shouted
as he staggered down the stair."[29]

[*This makes* DESMOND'S *hand shake; his cup falls and breaks.*]

DUPREE. Seems to me at times *china* isn't lasting much better than *we* are.

[EVANS *is immediately bringing him another cup.*]

EVANS. Ooh, don't talk that way—Mr. Wedgewood![30]

FIRST WRECKER. [*Off.*] That's it! Hook a chain around her middle and drag her down!

27. The *Waldorf* refers to the Waldorf-Astoria, a famous New York City hotel that opened in 1931 known for its luxurious accommodations.

28. *"It was the schooner Hesperus / That sailed the wintry sea—"* are lines from the poem "The Wreck of the Hesperus" by Henry Wadsworth Longfellow (1807–1882), which tells the story of a shipwreck in a winter storm.

29. *"We are lost, the Captain shouted / as he staggered down the stairs"* are lines from the poem "The Tempest" by James T. Fields (1817–1881), which tells the story of a ship that made it to safety through a winter storm.

30. *Mr. Wedgewood* refers to Josiah Wedgwood, a British potter who created the famous Wedgwood china.

Reading Strategy Questioning *Read both sentences of Chrome's dialogue here. What does her comment mean, exactly? What does it suggest about the Waldorf?* R1

Vocabulary
sanction (sangk′ shən) *v.* to give official approval or permission

Big Idea Awkward Encounters *Why does Evans's recitation upset Desmond?* BI

Additional Support

Skills Practice

RESEARCH: Literary Reference
Have students pick either the Longfellow or the Fields poem referenced in the story. Have students obtain a copy of the poem they have chosen. Then have them write an analysis of the poem, including an interpretation and explanation of how it relates to the story. After students write their analyses, assign them to work in groups to present readings of the two poems. After the readings, discuss how the poems relate to the story. OL

CHROME. Did you speak, Desmond?

FORTESCUE. I think that was someone in the corridor, dealing with a maid.

EVANS. Doing it with chains now, are they? [*A large crash, off.*]

SECOND WRECKER. [*Off.*] Crack her open—ah! Chock full of termites!

R3 WHICHAWAY. Do you feel that life's quite the same, since traffic? I say, a disrespectful element is creeping in.

CHROME. The Brevoort should do away with the taxi stand.

DUPREE. It's worse than that. I'd meant to keep it from you—but the skaters in Washington Square of late are heavily bearded.

FORTESCUE. I *do* think we should alarm the Brevoort. Evans, will you telephone below? Inform the desk that out there *bullies* are *skating*.

[*EVANS goes to phone, jiggles it. A pounding right at door.*]

CHROME. [*Crossing to EVANS, graciously.*] Here, Evans. Let me try. I'm awfully good with a telephone. My father played chess for years with Mr. Bell.[31] [*Takes phone, jiggles.*] Hello? Hello? . . . There seem to be *mice* at the other end. [*She hangs up.*]

[*Pounding at the door.*]

FORTESCUE. Often I console myself by pretending the traffic noises are simply pistol shots—the riffraff *murdering* one another.

DUPREE. [*Touched. Kissing her ear.*] Dear Millicent!

FIRST WRECKER. [*Just outside door.*] This door's locked! My God, whose *bicycle?*

[*Crash and bicycle bell ringing.*]

CHROME. The traffic seems curiously active for St. Swithin's Day.[32]

31. *Mr. Bell* refers to Alexander Graham Bell (1847–1922), who is credited with inventing the telephone.

32. *St. Swithin* was an English bishop in the Catholic church, and is the patron saint of weather. July 15 is set aside to honor him. If the play takes place during Lent, it cannnot be St. Swithin's day.

EVANS. I'm holding out for St. Vitus's Day.[33] [*The WRECKERS break down the door and enter. EVANS steps to the door as it falls. To the WRECKERS:*] You knocked?

FORTESCUE. Evans, we are not at home.

FIRST WRECKER. Anudder nest of 'em. You can't smoke 'em out.

SECOND WRECKER. Want to use the block and tackle on these, boss?

FIRST WRECKER. Foist we'll see if dey won't come out nice. [*Pounding outside keeps on, WRECKERS galvanized at sight of the tea table shimmying. WRECKER speaks in wheedling voice:*] Folks—how about coming outside in de nice . . . sunshine?

[*They all rise, reel, give little cries, and cling together.*]

THIRD WRECKER. [*Unwinding ropes and chains and creeping up at DUPREE.*] Ya see? Ya never loin, Leonard.

FIRST WRECKER. [*Trying again. Smiling.*] Would youse boys and goils like to come out and see my great, big, shiny—*bulldozer?*

[*They cry out again.*]

CHROME. Bulldozers, or any other kind, are not mentioned in the Brevoort Hotel.

[*THIRD WRECKER holds up a square rule.*]

FORTESCUE. I *beg* your pardon. I think you people are looking for Klein's on the Square.[34]

[*A carrier pigeon flies in window, bringing a note to FORTESCUE.*]

33. *St. Vitus's Day*, June 15, is a Catholic feast day set aside to honor Vitus, a Christian martyr who lived in Sicily during the fourth century AD. He is known as the patron saint of dancers, dogs, and protection against wild beasts.

34. *Klein's on the Square* was a discount department store on Union Square in a working-class area of New York City.

Literary Element High Comedy *What makes this line humorous?* L1

Reading Strategy Questioning *What might this line indicate about the wreckers and the people who lived in the Brevoort?* R

Teach

R3 Reading Strategy

Drawing Conclusions Ask: What does the conversation about traffic and disrespectful elements indicate? *(Perhaps the friends hear the workmen but continue to deny their lives are about to change.)* OL

English Language Coach

Multiple-Meaning Words When English learners encounter a familiar word used in an unexpected way, they should use context clues or a dictionary to figure out the meaning. Write on the board:

WHICHAWAY. Threading his way down from the Waldorf.

FORTESCUE I *do* think we should alarm the Brevoort.

Ask: What do the underlined words mean? Have students substitute a similar word in the sentence. EL

Academic Standards

Additional Support activities on pp. 870 and 871 cover the following standards:

Skills Practice: **9.2.4** Synthesize the content from several sources or works… **9.5.2** Write responses to literature…

English Language Coach: **9.1** Use…context clues…to determine the meaning of words…

Teach

L1 Literary Element

High Comedy Answer: *This line is spoken as if someone were politely knocking; however, the wreckers have actually broken down the door. Miss Fortescue is more concerned about her tea party being interrupted than the demolition of her home.* OL

R Reading Strategy

Questioning Answer: *The wrecker's speech shows he is of a lower class than the ladies. These ladies are not the only ones the wreckers have found still in the building.* OL

L2 Literary Element

High Comedy Answer: *Welty implies that the upper classes live in a dream world rather than in the real world. Miss Fortescue is working hard to ignore the fact that the wreckers have arrived and are taking her things. The act of having tea makes her feel untouchable by the "riffraff."* OL

Demolition, 1936. Mario Mafai. Oil on canvas. Calleria Narciso, Turin, Italy. 

FORTESCUE. [*Explaining brightly to* WRECKERS.] Oh, the mail. There you are, my pretty. [*Pokes cake crumb at pigeon, which flies back out window. Prettily, to* WRECKERS.] We much prefer pigeons to the government. Always on time—and in the end, of course, they can be eaten.

WHICHAWAY. Open your letter. Maybe it's from the Metropolitan Museum[35] again—insisting that we take care of ourselves.

FORTESCUE. [*Opens note, reads, gasps.*] Oh! Listen to this! [*Reads aloud.*] "The management-in-exile of the Hotel Brevoort hereby notifies you that Wreckers are on their way to your suite. You will please receive them and carry out their wishes."

[*Horrified pause.*]

DUPREE. [*Manfully.*] *Where's* that pigeon?

EVANS. [*Pensively.*] Their wishes?

FIRST WRECKER. Okay, boys.

[*They begin moving stuff out of the room, the plant stands, musical instruments, etc. But leave the group at tea table for moment.*]

35. The *Metropolitan Museum* is a New York City art museum established in 1870.

FORTESCUE. [*Brightly.*] Tea's what we need, my dears. Fresh tea! Do sit down. [*Flutters at tea table.*]

[WHICHAWAY *sits, extends cup.*]

CHROME. [*Sitting.*] One must be impervious[36] to the riffraff. Two lumps.

DUPREE. [*Remains standing, thoughtfully.*] Yes. But still, I cawn't think too highly of those old women knitting on the roof of Wanamaker's.[37]

FORTESCUE. Desmond, dear—room service! You can get them. Tell them *fresh hot tea* on the dumbwaiter instantly.

[*Dumbwaiter signals.*]

Why, here it is! Evans—tea!

[WRECKERS *still carrying out.* EVANS *goes through them to dumbwaiter. Lifts tray and turns to room, showing it loaded with lighted dynamite sticks.*]

36. *Impervious* means "incapable of being affected."
37. *Wanamaker's* was the first department store, created by John Wanamaker in Philadelphia in 1876. He opened a second Wanamaker's in New York City in 1896.

Literary Element High Comedy *What does Welty's joke here say about Miss Fortescue and her friends? How does the joke play on class issues?* L2

Additional Support

Skills Practice

WRITING: Character Sketch The stage directions on pages 872–873 describe how the characters in the play retain their well-bred manners even as they are being carried out of the building. They refuse to acknowledge the reality of their situation and remain snobbishly aloof to the very end.

Ask students to write a short scene in which they depict a person they know, such as a friend or a family member. Tell them to include stage directions that describe

- the character's name, age, and distinguishing physical features;

EVANS. [*Taking dashing position, with crossed feet.*] TNT is served, mum.

FORTESCUE. [*Grandly.*] Bring it on!

[*EVANS brings tray forward and sets it down on the tea table, DESMOND absentmindedly tucking in his napkin, and they all sit there grandly. FIRST and SECOND WRECKERS swoop down on WHICHAWAY in her wicker chair and carry her off. She snatches her solitaire pack and deliberately plays the first card, up in the air.*]

L3 WHICHAWAY. I insist there's a draft. [*WRECKERS return and pick up CHROME in her chair.*]

CHROME. Will you dip in Suite Two for my tippet?[38]

[*They bear her away. Return for FORTESCUE, who is on the settee. She takes up her lace parasol and opens it over her head. Rides out with it over her, as in a howdah.*[39]]

MILLICENT. [*Aloft.*] Shall I tell you what I think about Life, all? I think there's something of *elegance* gone.

[*She is borne off. EVANS jumps up on the back of the remaining WRECKER and rides out piggyback, showing her bicycle clips attached to her long drawers. She prods him in the back.*]

EVANS. What wishes?

[*WRECKERS return and surround DUPREE. A fusillade of crashes, off.*]

DUPREE. [*Stiffly.*] I can go unaided, thank you.

[*He opens his collar and bares his throat, as one going to the guillotine. Suffers the WRECKERS to light his cigarette, or a long cheroot, for him with a dynamite stick. To sounds of wrecking, mingled with a strain of the "Marseillaise,"*[40] *he goes nobly out ahead of WRECKERS. Last WRECKER out lifts Aunt Emmeline's portrait and carries it under his arm. Aunt Emmeline's fingers are in her ears. Explosion and walls collapse as curtain falls.*]

38. A *tippet* is a shawl or cape, often made of fur.
39. A *howdah* is a canopied seat that sits on the back of an elephant.
40. The *Marseillaise* is the French national anthem. It was written in 1792 during the French revolution, which was an uprising of the lower classes. Many members of the nobility were beheaded by guillotine during this time.

Big Idea Awkward Encounters *How does Desmond Dupree respond to his encounter with the wreckers?* BI

Teach

L3 Literary Element

Stage Directions Remind students that stage directions provide important information to readers. **Ask:** How does the contrast between the dialogue and the action add to the humor of the play? *(The characters attempt to maintain their superior airs even as they are carried from the room.)* OL

BI Big Idea

Awkward Encounters

Answer: *He responds with pride, as though he is a French noble surrounded by working-class members of the revolution.* OL

CheckPoint

Use the CheckPoint questions on Presentation Plus! to check students' mastery of the selection. These questions can be used with interactive response keypads for immediate student feedback.

Viewing the Art

Mario Mafai (1902–1965) was one of a group of painters known as the Roman School. Point out how the painting's bright colors contrast with its subject matter. AS

- a location in which the scene occurs;
- an object or prop that reveals something about the character's personality.

Have students read their scenes aloud to the class. OL

Differentiated Instruction

Stage Directions Have a student volunteer read the stage directions aloud. Hold a class discussion about what the stage directions reveal about the individual characters. Have students discuss how the characters' exits reinforce the characteristics they've displayed throughout the story. BL

Academic Standards

Additional Support activities on pp. 872 and 873 cover the following standards:

Skills Practice: **9.5.1** Write biographical… narratives… **9.6.4** Apply appropriate manuscript conventions…

Differentiated Instruction: **9.3.11** Identify and describe the function of…stage designs in dramatic literature.

AFTER YOU READ

Assess

1. Students may focus on a specific character or joke.
2. (a) Evans is Miss Fortescue's maid. (b) Miss Fortescue must be wealthy.
3. (a) He is "Our Thursday Tiger," "So dashing!" "Such a wreck!" "gallant," "shattered," and "frightfully creepy." (b) From going "out" and mixing with riffraff.
4. (a) She says they come from the seashell. (b) Evans seems loyal to Miss Fortescue.
5. (a) They do not respond to the noises, but hear the hearing aid alarm. (b) They have hearing aids and don't flinch when dishes shake.
6. (a) Miss Fortescue and her friends speak formally, while the wreckers speak roughly. (b) To contrast the groups
7. Evans is a foil for the ladies. She shows how the working class makes possible the life of the wealthy.
8. They don't ever go *out,* for fear of mixing with the riffraff.

Literary Element

1. The play depends on dialogue. It pokes fun at the upper class.
2. Welty shows the upper class's inability to cope with the real world, and its attitude toward the working class.

AFTER YOU READ

RESPONDING AND THINKING CRITICALLY

Respond

1. Which scene or aspect of this play did you find most humorous? Explain.

Recall and Interpret

2. (a)Who is Evans? (b)What does her description in the cast of characters tell you about Miss Fortescue?
3. (a)How do the women describe Desmond Dupree? (b)Upon what do they blame his condition?
4. (a)According to Miss Fortescue, where are the loud sounds "over and beyond the noise of traffic and falling portraits" coming from? (b)Why do you think Evans plays along?

Analyze and Evaluate

5. (a)What evidence in the play supports the idea that Miss Fortescue and her friends are ignoring the sounds of the demolition? (b)What evidence supports the idea that they do not hear the sounds at all?
6. (a)Compare and contrast the dialogue between Miss Fortescue and her friends with the dialogue between the wreckers. (b)What is the author's purpose in creating such a contrast?
7. In your opinion, what is the function of the character of Evans in this play?

Connect

8. **Big Idea** **Awkward Encounters** Why do Miss Fortescue and her friends respond the way they do when the First Wrecker says, "Folks—how about coming outside in de nice . . . sunshine?"

LITERARY ANALYSIS

Literary Element High Comedy

High comedy often uses wit, irony, or sarcasm to comment on social customs and institutions. High comedy depends heavily on verbal humor. In contrast, low comedy often depends on physical humor.

1. What characteristics define *Bye-Bye Brevoort* as high comedy?
2. What social customs or institutions is the author critiquing in this play? Cite examples from the play to support your answer.

Writing About Literature

Analyze Setting How does Eudora Welty help create a sense of a real hotel in *Bye-Bye Brevoort*? How do the sets, props, and dialogue of the play help create a sense of time, place, and culture? What kind of atmosphere does the setting create? Write a one- or two-page analysis of the play's setting. Use examples from the play to support your ideas.

LiteratureOnline **Web Activities** For eFlashcards, Selection Quick Checks, and other Web activities, go to www.glencoe.com.

READING AND VOCABULARY

Reading Strategy Questioning

Asking questions about an author's choices in setting, characters, and tone can help you draw conclusions about the themes of a literary work.

1. Why do you think Welty set her play in the Brevoort, an actual hotel with an actual history?
2. What is the theme of *Bye-Bye Brevoort*? What questions led you to this conclusion?

Vocabulary Practice

Practice with Analogies Choose the word that best completes each analogy.

1. dismantling : building :: leaving :
   a. hiking b. going c. staying
2. furled : sleeping bag :: spun :
   a. web b. story c. home
3. tiered : flat :: textured :
   a. jagged b. smooth c. round
4. sanction : approve :: hoodwink :
   a. flaunt b. enthrall c. fool

LiteratureOnline

Web Activities Have students access the Web site for interactive activities that will help them assess their understanding of the selection.

Writing About Literature

Students should cite details from the play in their analyses.

Reading Strategy

1. Students may say the setting shows the end of the old class order.
2. Themes: the comfort of ritual; the nature of class distinctions; and the effects of progress on society. Questions: "What did interactions between Evans and Miss Fortescue show?" or "Why are the women scornful of 'the riffraff'?"

Vocabulary

1. c **2.** a **3.** b **4.** c

Vocabulary Workshop

Denotation and Connotation

Using a Semantic Chart

"Modern times! The noise of the city is frightful! The vehicles!"

—Eudora Welty, *Bye-Bye Brevoort*

Connecting to Literature When Agatha Chrome utters these words, the reader can hear her sense of civilized outrage. This is accomplished, in part, through **connotation**—the ideas, images, or feelings suggested by the words she uses. For example, Agatha Chrome calls the noise of the city "frightful." She might also have called it "awful" or "unspeakable." All these words are similar in **denotation,** or their dictionary definition, but they do not convey precisely the same feelings and associations.

A semantic chart like the one below can help you closely examine the differences in similar words. Follow these instructions to complete the chart:

- Write the words you will analyze in the first column of the chart.
- Use a dictionary to find the definition of each word. Record each definition in the denotation column.
- In the third column of the chart, record each word's connotations: ideas, images, or feelings that you associate with each word. For example, you might associate *frightful* with events in a horror movie, as well as with the screeching sound some people make when something frightful occurs.

	Denotation	Connotation
frightful		
awful		
unspeakable		

Exercise

1. Draw the chart above on a separate sheet of paper and complete it. Discuss the denotations and connotations of the three words. Decide why Welty chose *frightful* instead of *awful* or *unspeakable.* Explain.
2. Find another word in *Bye-Bye Brevoort* or another selection in Unit 4, Part 2, for which you can name two or three additional synonyms or closely related words. Explain how the connotations of the words help the author suggest particular shades of meaning.

▸ **Vocabulary Terms**

The **denotation** of a word is its literal meaning; the **connotation** of a word is its implied meanings and associations.

▸ **Test-Taking Tip**

If a test asks you for a word's denotation, do your best to supply its dictionary definition. If a test asks you for connotations, think of your own associations with the word, especially positive and negative feelings. Also consider situations in which you might use the word and images the word brings to mind.

▸ **Reading Handbook**

For more about denotation and connotation, see Reading Handbook, p. R19.

Literature Online

eFlashcards For eFlashcards and other vocabulary activities, go to www.glencoe.com.

ACADEMIC STANDARDS (page 875)
9.1.2 Distinguish between what words mean literally and what they imply...

Focus

Brainstorm a list of words that carry an association beyond their definition. Have students list synonyms for the noun *smell (scent, odor, stench, fragrance, stink,* and *aroma).* Discuss the connotation of each word.

Teach

Denotation and Connotation Remind students that a denotation indicates the exact meaning of a word. Connotation refers to an underlying emotion or value beyond a word's dictionary meaning.

Assess

Exercise

1. Students might say that Welty chose *frightful* because the sound of traffic was like a horror movie to Agatha Chrome and her friends. They were terrified to experience the sounds of the "riffraff." It wasn't unspeakable: Chrome and the others could easily talk about it, and it wasn't awful in the sense of being repulsive. It was, however, a frightful issue in their lives.
2. From *The Bear,* students might take the word *beauty* and compare it with *attractiveness* or *gorgeousness*; they might also take *weep* and compare it with *cry* and *lament.* Students' responses should accurately state denotations and suggest a variety of connotations.

eFlashcards Have students access the Web site for more practice with denotation and connotation.

BEFORE YOU READ

Focus

BELLRINGER

Bellringer Options
Daily Language Practice Transparency 79
Or display images of fans at a sports event or pep rally and images of people rioting.
Ask: How are these scenes alike and how are they different?

As they read, students should think about how people lose control of their behavior when drawn into emotionally charged situations.

Author Search To expand students' appreciation of Eugène Ionesco, have them access the Web site for additional information and resources.

BEFORE YOU READ

The Leader

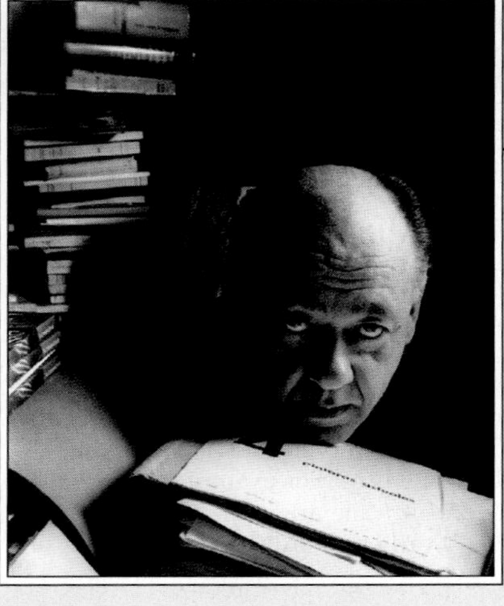

MEET EUGÈNE IONESCO

Eugène Ionesco's first play, *The Bald Soprano* (1949), sprang from an idea he had while learning English. The English language textbook he was reading featured empty clichés and pointless dialogue. With this type of language, he wondered how people managed to communicate at all. In *The Bald Soprano*, conversation between characters becomes more and more meaningless as they continue to talk.

This was like no comedy ever written before. Audiences used to traditional drama booed the actors on stage. Audiences for Ionesco's second play, *The Lesson*, chased the lead actor off the stage and demanded their money back. Even though most theater critics also ridiculed Ionesco's early work, *The Bald Soprano* and *The Lesson* established Ionesco as an avant-garde artist.

> *"It's not a certain society that seems ridiculous to me, it's mankind."*
>
> —Eugène Ionesco

Trouble at Home Eugène Ionesco was born in Slatina, Romania. His father was Romanian and his mother was French, and in 1911, his family moved to Paris. His parents were not happy together and his father soon returned to Romania. Some of Ionesco's fondest childhood memories were of attending a boarding school in the French village of La Chapelle-Anthenaise with his younger sister.

In 1925, Ionesco's mother returned to Bucharest, Romania, to reunite with her husband. When she arrived, she found that he had secretly divorced her, remarried, and gained custody of the children. From then on Ionesco lived unhappily with his father, whom he described as controlling and violent. Ionesco escaped his troubled home when he went to college. There he studied literature and French and began writing poems and literary criticism.

Stampeding Rhinoceroses Once Ionesco began to write plays, he wrote many of them in the space of just a few years. His first popular success came with the play *Rhinoceros* (1959), which contains the following exchange between an elderly man and a logician, a person with special training in logic:

> LOGICIAN [to the Old Gentleman]: Here is an example of a syllogism. The cat has four paws. Isidore and Fricot both have four paws. Therefore Isidore and Fricot are cats.
>
> OLD GENTLEMAN [to the Logician]: My dog has got four paws.
>
> LOGICIAN [to the Old Gentleman]: Then it's a cat.

Such is the humor and wit of Ionesco.

Eugène Ionesco was born in 1909 and died in 1994.

Literature Online **Author Search** For more about Eugène Ionesco, go to www.glencoe.com.

Selection Skills

The Leader

Literary Elements
- Satire (SE pp. 877, 879, 882, 884)
- Farce (SE p. 884)

Reading Skills
- Drawing Conclusions About Author's Meaning (SE pp. 877–885)

Vocabulary Skills
- Context Clues (SE pp. 877, 885)
- Academic Vocabulary (SE p. 885)

Listening/Speaking/Viewing Skills
- Performing (SE p. 885)
- Vocal Clues (TWE p. 878)

Writing Skills/Grammar
- Evaluating Contemporary Relevance (SE p. 885)
- Interjections (TWE p. 880)

LITERATURE PREVIEW

Connecting to the Drama

In the following play, Ionesco comments on conformity in society. Before you read the play, think about the following questions:

- When do you think it is important to conform to the rules of society? When do you feel it is important to go your own way?
- Have you ever found yourself going along with something even though you thought it was silly or even wrong?

Building Background

The Leader and Ionesco's other plays are classified as theater of the absurd, a style of drama that first appeared in the 1950s. Theater of the absurd does not tell a story but instead presents a series of scenes in which the characters, confused and anxious, seem to exist in a meaningless world. Plays of this style include ridiculous and even surreal settings. Nevertheless, the characters illuminate the profound nonsense of human action and interaction. Ionesco himself preferred the terms *theater of derision* and *anti-play.* He wanted to emphasize the way in which his plays mocked human behavior and the way they rejected the form and style of realistic drama.

Setting Purposes for Reading

Big Idea Awkward Encounters

As you read *The Leader,* think about why Ionesco creates awkward encounters between his characters.

Literary Element Satire

Satire is writing that comments, sometimes humorously, on human flaws, ideas, social customs, or institutions. Satire aims to reform through ridicule, while comedy aims simply to amuse.

- See Literary Terms Handbook, p. R15.

Interactive Literary Elements Handbook To review or learn more about the literary elements, go to www.glencoe.com.

READING PREVIEW

Reading Strategy Drawing Conclusions About Author's Meaning

In plays, poems, and fiction, an author's meaning is usually implied rather than stated directly. You **draw conclusions about an author's meaning** when you form an opinion based on evidence from the text.

Reading Tip: Creating a Chart As you read, use a chart like the one below to collect details found in dialogue and in set and scene descriptions that strike you as important or compelling. When you have finished reading, identify details that seem to support the same idea or meaning.

Compelling Detail	Underlying Idea

Vocabulary

riveted (riv′ it əd) *adj.* fixed or secured firmly; p. 878 *In his fear, he felt as though his feet were riveted to the floor.*

itinerary (ī tin′ ər er′ ē) *n.* the planned route for a journey; p. 880 *Using the map, they planned the itinerary for their cross-country vacation.*

exalted (eg′ zôl təd) *adj.* noble; exaggerated; p. 880 *The scientist had an exalted commitment to finding a cure for cancer.*

vanquished (vang′ kwishd) *n.* people who have been defeated in battle; p. 881 *The vanquished surrendered their arms.*

apparition (ap′ ə rish′ ən) *n.* an unexpected or unusual sight; p. 883 *When bubbles appeared to be coming from the magician's hand, the audience gasped at the apparition.*

Vocabulary Tip: Practice with Context Clues Context clues are words that provide clues to an unfamiliar word's meaning.

INDIANA ACADEMIC STANDARDS (pages 877–885)

9.3.8 Interpret and evaluate the impact of...ironies...
9.2.8 Draw conclusions about a text...
9.5.2 Write responses to literature...
9.3.12 [Relate] a work...to...its historical period.

BEFORE YOU READ

Focus

Summary

The characters in this play are citizens anxiously awaiting the arrival of their leader. They are encouraged and admonished by the announcer, who is the only one able to see the approaching leader. The announcer gives a running commentary on the leader's activities until the leader finally arrives on stage. The characters are shocked and then accept the fact that their leader has no head.

V Vocabulary

Vocabulary File Say: Add these words and definitions to your vocabulary file. For each word, include a sentence that gives you an example of how to use the word. **OL** Students with English language needs should include the pronunciations of these words in their files. **EL**

Literary Elements Have students access the Web site to improve their understanding of satire.

Selection Resources

Print Materials
- Unit 4 Resources (Fast File), pp. 49–51
- Selection and Unit Assessments, pp. 153–154
- Selection Quick Checks, p. 77

Transparencies
- Bellringer Options Transparencies: Daily Language Practice Transparency 79
- Literary Elements Transparency 90

Technology
- TeacherWorks Plus™ CD-ROM
- StudentWorks Plus™ CD-ROM
- Presentation Plus!™ CD-ROM
- Literature Online, glencoe.com
- Online Student Edition, mhln.com
- Exam*View*® Assessment Suite CD-ROM
- Vocabulary PuzzleMaker CD-ROM
- Listening Library, disc 2 track 16

Teach

BI1 Big Idea

Awkward Encounters Have students keep these questions in mind as they read.

Ask: Why does Ionesco have the announcer give a running commentary on the leader's actions? *(In a society, few people have direct contact with their leaders. They must rely on the observations of others, such as news reporters.)* Why are the characters willing to accept a headless leader? *(Ionesco sees most people as mindless members of a group, capable only of a "herd" mentality.)* **OL**

BI2 Big Idea

Awkward Encounters

Answer: *They comply immediately. The announcer is in charge of the situation. The admirers do as he says, even though what he is telling them does not make sense.* **OL**

French Print of a Man in an Overcoat, 1811.

The Leader

Eugène Ionesco

CHARACTERS		
THE ANNOUNCER	THE FEMALE ADMIRER	THE GIRLFRIEND
THE MALE ADMIRER	THE BOYFRIEND	THE LEADER

BI1 [*Standing with his back to the public, center-stage, and with his eyes fixed on the up-stage exit, the* ANNOUNCER *waits for the arrival of the* LEADER. *To right and left,* **riveted** *to the walls, two of the* LEADER'S ADMIRERS, *a man and a woman, also wait for his arrival.*]

ANNOUNCER. [*After a few tense moments in the same position.*] There he is! There he is! At the end of the street! [*Shouts of "Hurrah!" etc., are heard.*] There's the leader! He's coming, he's coming nearer! [*Cries of acclaim and applause are heard from the wings.*] It's better if he doesn't see us . . . [*The* TWO ADMIRERS *hug the wall even closer.*] Watch out! [*The* ANNOUNCER *gives vent to a brief display of enthusiasm.*] Hurrah! Hurrah! The leader! The leader! Long live the leader! [*The* TWO ADMIRERS, *with their bodies rigid and flattened against the wall, thrust their necks and heads as far forward as they can to get a glimpse of the* LEADER.] The leader! The leader! [*The* TWO ADMIRERS *in unison:*] Hurrah! Hurrah! [*Other "Hurrahs!" mingled with "Hurrah! Bravo!" come from the wings and gradually die down.*] Hurrah! Bravo!

[*The* ANNOUNCER *takes a step up-stage, stops, then up-stage, followed by the* TWO ADMIRERS, *saying as he goes: "Ah! Too bad! He's going*

Vocabulary

riveted (riv′ it əd) *adj.* fixed or secured firmly

Big Idea Awkward Encounters *How do the admirers respond to the announcer's command? What does their response tell you about the relationship between the admirers and the announcer?* **BI2**

Additional Support

Academic Standards

The Additional Support activity on p. 878 covers the following standard:

Skills Practice: **9.3.10** Identify and describe the function of dialogue in dramatic literature…

Skills Practice

LISTENING AND SPEAKING: Vocal Clues Actors give clues when they speak. For example, on page 878, the announcer says, "There he is! There he is! At the end of the street!" The stage directions don't tell if the character shouts his dialogue or speaks softly. The audience must rely on the actor to interpret the words.

- Have students think of situations in which their voices convey meaning, such as winning a prize or apologizing.
- Have students write dialogue to go with each situation and read their lines to a partner. **OL**

away! He's going away! Follow me quickly! After him!" The ANNOUNCER *and the* TWO ADMIRERS *leave, crying: "Leader! Leeeeader! Lee-ee-eader!" (This last "Lee-ee-eader!" echoes in the wings like a bleating cry.)*] **R**

[*Silence. The stage is empty for a few brief moments. The* BOYFRIEND *enters right, and his* GIRLFRIEND *left; they meet center-stage.*]

BOYFRIEND. Forgive me, Madame, or should I say Mademoiselle?

GIRLFRIEND. I beg your pardon, I'm afraid I don't happen to know you!

BOYFRIEND. And I'm afraid I don't know you either!

GIRLFRIEND. Then neither of us knows each other.

BOYFRIEND. Exactly. We have something in common. It means that between us there is a basis of understanding on which we can build the edifice[1] of our future.

GIRLFRIEND. That leaves me cold, I'm afraid.

[*She makes as if to go.*]

BOYFRIEND. Oh, my darling, I adore you.

GIRLFRIEND. Darling, so do I!

[*They embrace.*]

BOYFRIEND. I'm taking you with me, darling. We'll get married straightaway.

[*They leave left. The stage is empty for a brief moment.*]

ANNOUNCER. [*Enters up-stage followed by the* TWO ADMIRERS.] But the leader swore that he'd be passing here.

MALE ADMIRER. Are you absolutely sure of that?

ANNOUNCER. Yes, yes, of course.

FEMALE ADMIRER. Was it really on his way?

1. An *edifice* is a building or a complex structure of ideas.

Big Idea Awkward Encounters *How does the boyfriend respond to his awkward encounter with the girlfriend?* **BI3**

Literary Element Satire *What is the author poking fun at here? What comment is he making about it?* **L1**

ANNOUNCER. Yes, yes. He should have passed by here, it was marked on the Festival program . . .

MALE ADMIRER. Did you actually see it yourself and hear it with your own eyes and ears?

ANNOUNCER. He told someone. Someone else!

MALE ADMIRER. But who? Who was this someone else?

FEMALE ADMIRER. Was it a reliable person? A friend of yours?

ANNOUNCER. A friend of mine who I know very well. [*Suddenly in the background one hears renewed cries of "Hurrah!" and "Long live the leader!"*] That's him now! There he is! Hip! Hip! Hurrah! There he is! Hide yourselves. Hide yourselves!

[*The* TWO ADMIRERS *flatten themselves as before against the wall, stretching their necks out towards the wings from where the shouts of acclamation come; the* ANNOUNCER *watches fixedly up-stage his back to the public.*]

ANNOUNCER. The leader's coming. He approaches. He's bending. He's unbending. [*At each of the* ANNOUNCER'S *words, the* ADMIRERS *give a start and stretch their necks even farther; they shudder.*] He's jumping. He's crossed the river. They're shaking his hand. He sticks out his thumb. Can you hear? They're laughing. [*The* ANNOUNCER *and the* TWO ADMIRERS *also laugh.*] Ah . . . ! they're giving him a box of tools. What's he going to do with them? Ah . . . ! he's signing autographs. The leader is stroking a hedgehog, a superb hedgehog! The crowd applauds. He's dancing, with the hedgehog in his hand. He's embracing his dancer. Hurrah! Hurrah! [*Cries are heard in the wings.*] He's being photographed, with his dancer on one hand and the hedgehog on the other . . . He greets the crowd . . . He spits a tremendous distance.

FEMALE ADMIRER. Is he coming past here? Is he coming in our direction?

Literary Element Satire *What subject is satirized in the announcer's speech?* **L2**

Teach

R Reading Strategy

Interpret **Ask:** What does the stage direction, "echoes . . . like a bleating cry" tell you about the author's purpose? *(Ionesco may want the audience to associate his characters with sheep.)* **OL**

BI3 Big Idea

Awkward Encounters
Answer: *He finds common ground on which to build a future in the fact that they are strangers.* **OL**

L1 Literary Element

Satire **Answer:** *He is making fun of falling in love. People fall in love easily, without any real reason, and with complete strangers.* **OL**

L2 Literary Element

Satire **Answer:** *It satirizes how the public admires without question anything a leader does, even trivial things, such as moving from one position to another.* **OL**

CheckPoint

Use the CheckPoint questions on Presentation Plus! to monitor students' comprehension. These questions can be used with interactive response keypads for immediate student feedback.

English Language Coach

Reading Dialogue English learners may find Ionesco's dialogue confusing when it is interrupted with stage directions for actors on and off the stage. Allow students to hear the dialogue read aloud by offstage actors out of view of the audience. **EL**

Differentiated Instruction

Peer Reading Ionesco's style of writing may challenge less proficient readers. Pair students with proficient readers. As partners read, have them stop to discuss the dialogue and clarify anything they do not understand. **BL**

Academic Standards

Additional Support activities on p. 879 cover the following standards:

English Language Coach: **9.7** [Respond] to oral communication [with] careful listening…

Differentiated Instruction: **9.7.1** Ask questions concerning the speaker's content…

Teach

L Literary Element

Satire Ask: What is being satirized in this dialogue? *(The author is satirizing how some people praise their leader regardless of the leader's actions.)* OL

R1 Reading Strategy

Drawing Conclusions About Author's Meaning

Answer: *The author uses repetition here. The admirers repeat what the announcer has said about the leader embracing the little girl. Conclusions will vary but might include the fact that the repetition seems hypnotic and that the author is drawing attention to the way in which people are hypnotized into following a leader, whether or not he or she is worthy of admiration.* OL

R2 Reading Strategy

Drawing Conclusions About Author's Meaning

Ask: Why are the admirers obedient to the announcer? *(They have accepted the idea that following his advice against their own judgment is the only way to see the leader.)* OL

MALE ADMIRER. Are we really on his route?

ANNOUNCER. [*Turns his head to the* TWO ADMIRERS.] Quiet, and don't move, you're spoiling everything . . .

FEMALE ADMIRER. But even so . . .

ANNOUNCER. Keep quiet, I tell you! Didn't I tell you he'd promised, that he had fixed his **itinerary** himself. . . . [*He turns back up-stage and cries.*] Hurrah! Hurrah! Long live the leader! [*Silence.*] Long live, long live, the leader! [*Silence.*] Long live, long live, long live the lead-er! [*The* TWO ADMIRERS, *unable to contain themselves, also give a sudden cry of:*] Hurrah! Long live the leader!

ANNOUNCER. [*to the* ADMIRERS] Quiet, you two! Calm down! You're spoiling everything! [*Then, once more looking up-stage, with the* ADMIRERS *silenced.*] Long live the leader! [*Wildly enthusiastic.*] Hurrah! Hurrah! He's changing his shirt. He disappears behind a red screen. He reappears! [*The applause intensifies.*] Bravo! Bravo! [*The* ADMIRERS *also long to cry "Bravo" and applaud; they put their hands to their mouths to stop themselves.*] He's putting his tie on! He's reading his newspaper and drinking his morning coffee! He's still got his hedgehog . . . He's leaning on the edge of the parapet.[2] The parapet breaks. He gets up . . . he gets up unaided! [*Applause, shouts of "Hurrah!"*] Bravo! Well done! He brushes his soiled clothes. L

TWO ADMIRERS. [*Stamping their feet.*] Oh! Ah! Oh! Oh! Ah! Ah!

ANNOUNCER. He's mounting the stool! He's climbing piggy-back, they're offering him a thin-ended wedge, he knows it's meant as a joke, and he doesn't mind, he's laughing.

[*Applause and enormous acclaim.*]

MALE ADMIRER. [*To the* FEMALE ADMIRER.] You hear that? You hear? Oh! If I were king . . .

2. A *parapet* is a low wall or railing.

Vocabulary

itinerary (ī tin′ ər er′ ē) *n.* the planned route for a journey

FEMALE ADMIRER. Ah . . . ! the leader! [*This is said in an* **exalted** *tone.*]

ANNOUNCER. [*Still with his back to the public.*] He's mounting the stool. No. He's getting down. A little girl offers him a bouquet of flowers . . . What's he going to do? He takes the flowers . . . He embraces the little girl . . . calls her "my child" . . .

MALE ADMIRER. He embraces the little girl . . . calls her "my child" . . .

FEMALE ADMIRER. He embraces the little girl . . . calls her "my child" . . .

ANNOUNCER. He gives her the hedgehog. The little girl's crying . . . Long live the leader! Long live the leead-er!

MALE ADMIRER. Is he coming past here?

FEMALE ADMIRER. Is he coming past here?

ANNOUNCER. [*With a sudden run, dashes out up-stage.*] He's going away! Hurry! Come on!

[*He disappears, followed by the* TWO ADMIRERS, *all crying "Hurrah! Hurrah!"*] R2

[*The stage is empty for a few moments. The* BOYFRIEND *and* GIRLFRIEND *enter, entwined*[3] *in an embrace; they halt center-stage and separate; she carries a basket on her arm.*]

GIRLFRIEND. Let's go to the market and get some eggs!

BOYFRIEND. Oh! I love them as much as you do!

[*She takes his arm. From the right the* ANNOUNCER *arrives running, quickly regaining his place, back to the public, followed closely by the* TWO ADMIRERS, *arriving one from the left and the other from the right; the* TWO ADMIRERS *knock into the* BOYFRIEND *and* GIRLFRIEND *who were about to leave right.*]

3. *Entwined* means "coiled or twisted together."

Reading Strategy Drawing Conclusions About Author's Meaning *What technique does the author use in this and the previous few lines? What conclusions can you draw about the author's meaning?* R1

Vocabulary

exalted (eg′ zôl təd) *adj.* noble; exaggerated

Additional Support

Skills Practice

GRAMMAR: Interjections An interjection is a word or phrase that expresses emotion. It has no grammatical connection to other words in a sentence. Point out the interjections in these examples:

Ha! That is a funny story.
Oh, look at the sky!
Great! You are on time for once.

Have students complete each statement with an interjection.

1. ____, the cake is ruined.
2. ____! Stop that.
3. ____, what happened?
4. ____! I lost my wallet. OL

MALE ADMIRER. Sorry!

BOYFRIEND. Oh! Sorry!

FEMALE ADMIRER. Sorry! Oh! Sorry!

GIRLFRIEND. Oh! Sorry, sorry, sorry, so sorry!

MALE ADMIRER. Sorry, sorry, sorry, oh! sorry, sorry, so sorry!

BOYFRIEND. Oh, oh, oh, oh, oh, oh! So sorry, everyone!

GIRLFRIEND. [*To her* BOYFRIEND.] Come along, Adolphe! [*To the* TWO ADMIRERS:] No harm done!

R3 [*She leaves, leading her* BOYFRIEND *by the hand.*]

ANNOUNCER. [*Watching up-stage.*] The leader is being pressed forward, and pressed back, and now they're pressing[4] his trousers! [*The* TWO ADMIRERS *regain their places.*] The leader is smiling. Whilst they're pressing his trousers, he walks about. He tastes the flowers and the fruits growing in the stream. He's also tasting the roots of the trees. He suffers the little children to come unto him. He has confidence in everybody. He inaugurates the police force. He pays tribute to justice. He salutes the great victors and the great **vanquished.** Finally he recites a poem. The people are very moved.

TWO ADMIRERS. Bravo! Bravo! [*Then, sobbing:*] Boo! Boo! Boo!

ANNOUNCER. All the people are weeping. [*Loud cries are heard from the wings; the* ANNOUNCER *and the* ADMIRERS *also start to bellow.*] Silence! [*The* TWO ADMIRERS *fall silent; and there is silence from the wings.*] They've given the leader's trousers back. The leader puts them on. He looks happy. Hurrah! [*"Bravos," and acclaim from the wings. The* TWO ADMIRERS *also shout their acclaim, jump about, without being able to see anything of what is presumed to be happening in the wings.*] The leader's sucking his thumb! [*To the* TWO ADMIRERS:] Back, back to your places, you two, don't move, behave yourselves and shout: "Long live the leader!"

TWO ADMIRERS. [*Flattened against the wall, shouting.*] Long live, long live the leader!

ANNOUNCER. Be quiet, I tell you, you'll spoil everything! Look out, the leader's coming!

MALE ADMIRER. [*In the same position.*] The leader's coming!

FEMALE ADMIRER. The leader's coming!

ANNOUNCER. Watch out! And keep quiet! Oh! The leader's going away! Follow him! Follow me!

[*The* ANNOUNCER *goes out up-stage, running; the* TWO ADMIRERS *leave right and left, whilst in the wings the acclaim mounts, then fades. The stage is momentarily empty. The* BOYFRIEND, *followed by his* GIRLFRIEND, *appear left running across the stage right.*]

Expectation (Erwartung). 1935–36. Richard Oelze. Oil on canvas, 32 1/8 x 39 5/8 in. The Museum of Modern Art, New York. ★

4. Here, *pressing* means "ironing."

Reading Strategy Drawing Conclusions About Author's Meaning *From this monologue, what conclusion can you draw about the author's attitude toward the leader's actions?* R4

Vocabulary

vanquished (vang′ kwishd) *n.* people who have been defeated in battle

Teach

R3 Reading Strategy

Interpret Ask: How can the boyfriend and girlfriend be oblivious of the excitement surrounding them? *(They are so in love that they are unaware of anything else.)* OL

R4 Reading Strategy

Drawing Conclusions About Author's Meaning

Answer: *The author is showing how the leader's image is delivered to the public. The announcer helps with this delivery. According to this image, the leader is a man in tune with nature, children, and the public. He cares about people and is sensitive. Because the author's tone is ironic, we know that the author does not really believe the leader embodies these traits.* OL

★ Viewing the Art

Expectation is perhaps the best-known work by German painter and draughtsman Richard Oelze (1900–1980). During the period *Expectation* was painted, Oelze was living in Paris, where he was immersed in the Surrealist movement. *Expectation* reflects the anxious climate of pre–World War II Europe. AS

English Language Coach

Idioms English language learners are often challenged by idioms. Have students work in pairs with proficient English speakers to decode these idioms.

1. GIRLFRIEND: That leaves me cold, I'm afraid. *(disinterested)*
2. ANNOUNCER: You're spoiling everything! *(disrupting the situation)*
3. ANNOUNCER: The people are very moved. *(Their emotions are engaged.)* EL

Academic Standards

Additional Support activities on pp. 880 and 881 cover the following standards:

Skills Practice: **9.6.2** Demonstrate an understanding of...proper English usage...

English Language Coach: **9.1** Use...context clues, and a growing knowledge of English...to determine the meaning of words...

Teach

R1 Reading Strategy

Interpret **Ask:** Why is the boyfriend running from the girlfriend? *(The author is reversing traditional courtship roles to add to the absurdity of the dramatic action.)* OL

BI1 Big Idea

Awkward Encounters
Answer: *They have missed the leader. The admirers blame bad luck, but the announcer blames them. When they refuse to take the blame, he assumes they are blaming him.* OL

L Literary Element

Satire **Answer:** *He is comparing the children's game Follow the Leader to the action of the play. This comparison makes the process of following the leader in this play even more ridiculous.* OL

★ Viewing the Art

Ilja Efimovic Repin (1844–1930) was a famous Russian artist. He created realistic paintings that often criticized faults he saw in society.
Answer: *The people in the painting show a variety of expressions including awe, rapture, sternness, and boredom.* AS

Procession of the Cross in the Kursk Region (detail), 1880–83. Ilja Efimovic Repin. Oil on canvas. Tretykov Gallery, Moscow, Russia.
Viewing the Art: How would you describe the expressions on the faces of the people in this painting? ★

BOYFRIEND. [*Running.*] You won't catch me! You won't catch me!

[*Goes out.*]

GIRLFRIEND. [*Running.*] Wait a moment! Wait a moment!

[*She goes out. The stage is empty for a moment; then once more the* BOYFRIEND *and* GIRLFRIEND *cross the stage at a run, and leave.*]

R1 BOYFRIEND. You won't catch me!

GIRLFRIEND. Wait a moment!

[*They leave right. The stage is empty. The* ANNOUNCER *reappears up-stage, the* MALE ADMIRER *from the right, the* FEMALE ADMIRER *from the left. They meet center.*]

MALE ADMIRER. We missed him!

FEMALE ADMIRER. Rotten luck!

ANNOUNCER. It was your fault!

MALE ADMIRER. That's not true!

FEMALE ADMIRER. No, that's not true!

ANNOUNCER. Are you suggesting it was mine?

MALE ADMIRER. No, we didn't mean that!

FEMALE ADMIRER. No, we didn't mean that!

[*Noise of acclaim and "Hurrahs" from the wings.*]

ANNOUNCER. Hurrah!

FEMALE ADMIRER. It's from over there! [*She points up-stage.*]

MALE ADMIRER. Yes, it's from over there! [*He points left.*]

ANNOUNCER. Very well. Follow me! Long live the leader!

[*He runs out right, followed by the* TWO ADMIRERS, *also shouting.*]

TWO ADMIRERS. Long live the leader!

[*They leave. The stage is empty for a moment. The* BOYFRIEND *and his* GIRLFRIEND *appear left; the* BOYFRIEND *exits up-stage; the* GIRLFRIEND, *after saying "I'll get you!", runs out right. The* ANNOUNCER *and the* TWO ADMIRERS *appear from up-stage. The* ANNOUNCER *says to the* ADMIRERS:] Long live the leader! [*This is repeated by the* ADMIRERS. *Then, still talking to the* ADMIRERS, *he says:*] Follow me! Follow the leader! [*He leaves up-stage, still running and shouting:*] Follow him!

[*The* MALE ADMIRER *exits right, the* FEMALE ADMIRER *left into the wings. During the whole of this, the acclaim is heard louder or fainter according to the rhythm of the stage action; the stage is empty for a moment, then the*

Big Idea Awkward Encounters *Why is the conversation here between the admirers and the announcer so awkward?* BI1

Literary Element Satire *What satiric comparison is the author making here?* L

Additional Support

Academic Standards
The Additional Support activity on p. 882 covers the following standard:
Skills Practice: **9.2.8** Make reasonable statements and draw conclusions about a text, supporting them with accurate examples.

Skills Practice

READING: Identifying Author's Purpose Give examples of ways in which students can determine author's purpose:

- Locate a direct statement.
- Infer from tone.
- Compare the work with other work by the same author.

After students have read the play, have them summarize its message and explain how they arrived at their conclusions. Students should refer to the author's background and his opinions and analysis of society. OL

BOYFRIEND and GIRLFRIEND appear from right and left, crying:]

BOYFRIEND. I'll get you!

GIRLFRIEND. You won't get me!

R2 *[They leave at a run, shouting:]* Long live the leader! *[The ANNOUNCER and the TWO ADMIRERS emerge from up-stage, also shouting: "Long live the leader", followed by the BOYFRIEND and GIRLFRIEND. They all leave right, in single file, crying as they run: "The leader! Long live the leader! We'll get him! It's from over here! You won't get me!"]*

[They enter and leave, employing all the exits; finally, entering from left, from right, and from up-stage they all meet center, whilst the acclaim and the applause from the wings becomes a fearful din.[5] *They embrace each other feverishly, crying at the tops of their voices:]* Long live the leader! Long live the leader! Long live the leader!

[Then, abruptly, silence falls.]

ANNOUNCER. The leader is arriving. Here's the leader. To your places! Attention!

[The MALE ADMIRER and the GIRLFRIEND flatten themselves against the wall right; the FEMALE ADMIRER and the BOYFRIEND against the wall left; the two couples are in each other's arms, embracing.]

MALE ADMIRER AND GIRLFRIEND. My dear, my darling!

FEMALE ADMIRER AND BOYFRIEND. My dear, my darling!

[Meanwhile the ANNOUNCER has taken up his place, back to the audience, looking fixedly upstage; a lull in the applause.]

ANNOUNCER. Silence. The leader has eaten his soup. He is coming. He is nigh.[6]

[The acclaim redoubles its intensity; the TWO ADMIRERS and the BOYFRIEND and GIRLFRIEND shout:]

ALL. Hurrah! Hurrah! Long live the leader!

[They throw confetti before he arrives. Then the ANNOUNCER hurls himself suddenly to one side to allow the LEADER to pass; the other four characters freeze with outstretched arms holding confetti; but still say:] Hurrah! *[The LEADER enters from up-stage, advances downstage to center; to the footlights, hesitates, makes a step to left, then takes a decision and leaves with great, energetic strides by right, to the enthusiastic "Hurrahs!" of the ANNOUNCER and the feeble, somewhat astonished "Hurrahs!" of the other four; these, in fact, have some reason to be surprised, as the LEADER is headless, though wearing a hat. This is simple to effect: the actor playing the LEADER needing only to wear an overcoat with the collar turned up round his forehead and topped with a hat. The-man-in-an-overcoat-with-a-hat-without-a-head is a somewhat surprising* ***apparition*** *and will doubtless produce a certain sensation. After the LEADER'S disappearance, the FEMALE ADMIRER says:]*

FEMALE ADMIRER. But . . . but . . . the leader hasn't got a head!

ANNOUNCER. What's he need a head for when he's got genius!

BOYFRIEND. That's true! *[To the GIRLFRIEND:]* What's your name?

[The BOYFRIEND to the FEMALE ADMIRER, the FEMALE ADMIRER to the ANNOUNCER, the ANNOUNCER to the GIRLFRIEND, the GIRLFRIEND to the BOYFRIEND:] What's yours? What's yours? What's yours? *[Then, all together, one to the other:]* What's your name? ~

Big Idea Awkward Encounters *Consider Ionesco's attitude toward his subject so far. How do you think the Admirers and the Boyfriend and Girlfriend will react to their encounter with the headless leader?* BI2

Reading Strategy Drawing Conclusions About Author's Meaning *What theme does the end of the play convey? Why do you think Ionesco chose to end the play this way?* R3

Vocabulary

apparition (ap′ ə rish′ ən) *n.* an unexpected or unusual sight

5. *Din* means "a jumble of loud, confused sounds."
6. *Nigh* means "near."

Teach

R2 Reading Strategy

Drawing Conclusions About Author's Purpose

Ask: What is the author's purpose for these stage directions? *(The author shows how the boyfriend and the girlfriend, previously unaware of the leader, are drawn into the general excitement; they begin shouting because everyone else is.)* OL

BI2 Big Idea

Awkward Encounters

Answer: *Evidence in the play supports conformity. The characters will still find the leader "admirable."* OL

R3 Reading Strategy

Drawing Conclusions About Author's Meaning

Answer: *The theme is that people—even people in love—are anonymous or unidentifiable to each other. Leaders, as well as lovers, are interchangeable and do not need to be present to be admired. People project leadership traits onto a leader, rather than finding out who the leader actually is.* OL

CheckPoint

Use the CheckPoint questions on Presentation Plus! to check students' mastery of the selection. These questions can be used with interactive response keypads for immediate student feedback.

English Language Coach

Choral Reading English learners may benefit from taking part in choral reading. It helps students understand the relationship between the written and spoken word. Choral reading can help foster self-confidence, develop vocabulary, improve pronunciation, and motivate students to read.

Assign students to read sections of the play together. At first, read a section of the play aloud as students follow along silently. Later, have students join in as you read aloud. Make the most of the dramatic elements of the play. EL

Academic Standards

The Additional Support activity on p. 883 covers the following standard:

English Language Coach: **9.7** [Develop] speaking skills...in conjunction with...strategies...[for] delivery of oral presentations.

AFTER YOU READ

Assess

1. Many students will find the play humorous.
2. (a) He tells them to follow him, to be quiet, and to stand still or hide. (b) He will take them to the leader if they obey him.
3. (a) The leader falls down, signs autographs, dances with a hedgehog, and recites a poem. (b) To show how we dramatize trivial activities of powerful people
4. (a) He says, "What's he need a head for when he's got genius?" (b) That people may follow a leader because others do, not because they have informed opinions.
5. The effect is rhythmic and hypnotic.
6. (a) At first, they are strangers, but they quickly declare their love. (b) They shift their affections to the admirers.
7. (a) It is humorous, with a bit of anxiety. (b) Details: Descriptions of the leader's activities, and the lines of the boyfriend and girlfriend are humorous. The announcer's bullying creates anxiety.
8. (a) Students may mention the leader without his trousers and the boyfriend and girlfriend embracing the admirers. (b) People behave inappropriately, but are unaware of this.

AFTER YOU READ

RESPONDING AND THINKING CRITICALLY

Respond

1. What was your overall reaction to the play? Explain.

Recall and Interpret

2. (a)What does the announcer repeatedly instruct the admirers to do? (b)Why do they follow his directions?
3. (a)What types of activities is the leader involved in throughout the play? (b)Why does the announcer narrate these activities?
4. (a)How does the announcer respond when the female admirer points out that the leader has no head? (b)What theme is the author emphasizing here?

Analyze and Evaluate

5. The sentence "Long live the leader!" appears many times in Ionesco's play. What is the effect of such repetition on the audience?
6. (a)How does the relationship of the boyfriend and girlfriend change as the play progresses? (b)Evaluate the significance of their relationship at the end of the play.
7. (a)Describe the atmosphere the play conveys. (b)List three details that help to create this atmosphere.

Connect

8. **Big Idea** **Awkward Encounters** (a)Describe a scene in the play in which you would have felt awkward but the characters did not seem to. (b)What comment about human behavior is the author making?

LITERARY ANALYSIS

Literary Element Satire

Satire often uses an ironic tone and ridicule to communicate its themes. An ironic tone is one that conveys the feeling that the author's attitude is opposite that of his characters. Ridicule is a type of humor that mocks its subject scornfully.

1. Describe a scene in which Ionesco creates an ironic tone.
2. In your opinion, what purpose does ridicule serve in *The Leader*?

Review: Farce

As you learned on page 823, **farce** is a type of comedy that uses ridiculous situations, characters, or events. Often in farce, ordinary people are affected by extraordinary events.

Partner Activity Where do the characteristics of farce and satire overlap? Pair up with a classmate and discuss which aspects of *The Leader* could be categorized as farcical. Create a Venn diagram similar to the one below. In the left-hand circle, write words and phrases that describe the play as farcical. In the right-hand circle, write words and phrases that describe the play as satirical. In the place where the two circles intersect, write words and phrases that describe *The Leader* as both farce and satire.

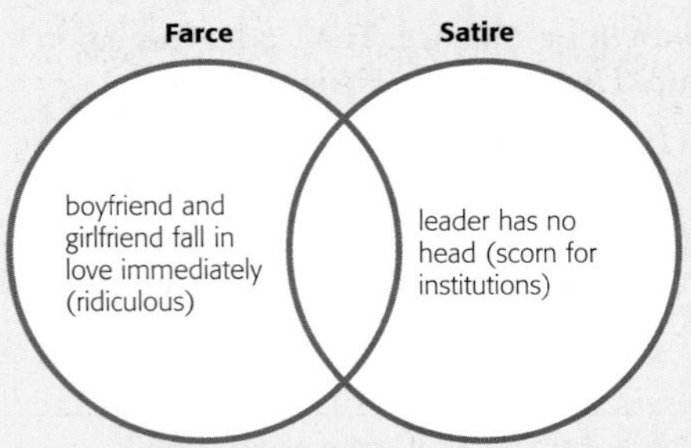

Literary Element

1. Any scene in which the announcer describes the leader has an ironic tone.
2. Ionesco uses ridicule to urge audience members to think before following a leader.

Review: Farce

Farce: Boyfriend and girlfriend fall in love immediately; characters run around the stage; characters have exaggerated characteristics
Both Use humor and irony
Satire: Leader has no head; ridicules love; equates characters' actions with the game Follow the Leader

Academic Standards

The Additional Support activity on p. 885 covers the following standard:

English Language Coach: **9.3.3** Analyze interactions between characters…and explain the way those interactions affect the plot.

READING AND VOCABULARY

Reading Strategy Drawing Conclusions About Author's Meaning

Drawing conclusions about an author's meaning involves gathering evidence from the writing and using it to support general ideas suggested by the work as a whole.

1. What conclusions about the nature of leadership can you support with evidence from Ionesco's play?
2. How are your conclusions related to the author's meaning?

Vocabulary Practice

Practice with Context Clues Identify the word or phrase that helps define each vocabulary word from *The Leader.*

1. She couldn't move; her feet felt **riveted** to the floor.
   a. couldn't move **b.** her feet
2. According to the **itinerary,** their route would take them through the grotto.
   a. through **b.** route
3. They praised the leader in **exalted** tones.
   a. praised **b.** leader
4. At the end of the game, Don's team was the winner; the opponents were the **vanquished.**
   a. Don's team **b.** the opponents
5. The headless leader is an **apparition** that will doubtless produce surprise in the audience.
   a. doubtless **b.** surprise

Academic Vocabulary

Here are two words from the vocabulary list on page R80.

identical (ī den′ ti kəl) *adj.* exactly the same as something else

sphere (sfēr) *n.* an area of control or influence

Practice and Apply
1. Why does Ionesco give different characters **identical** lines of dialogue in *The Leader*?
2. How large do you think the leader's **sphere** is?

WRITING AND EXTENDING

Writing About Literature

Evaluate Contemporary Relevance In *The Leader,* Ionesco illuminates the problems inherent in the relationship between leaders and followers. Are the issues Ionesco tackled in the 1950s still relevant today? Which of the problems from *The Leader* do you think we face in our culture today? Write an essay evaluating a current problem you see in the relationship between a leader and a group of followers. Use examples from Ionesco's play, current events, and personal experience to support your main ideas.

Before you begin drafting, use a chart like the one below to take notes on the similarities between the relationship described in Ionesco's play and in the situation you have chosen to analyze.

Relationship in The Leader	Relationship in Contemporary Situation

After completing your draft, meet with a peer reviewer to evaluate each other's work and suggest revisions. Then proofread and edit your draft to correct errors in spelling, grammar, and punctuation.

Performing

With a group of classmates, choose a favorite section of Ionesco's *The Leader* and stage it for your class, following the stage directions exactly. While practicing your scene, discuss how the physical movement of the actors can reinforce the theme of the play. Incorporate appropriate movements into your performance.

Literature Online **Web Activities** For eFlashcards, Selection Quick Checks, and other Web activities, go to www.glencoe.com.

AFTER YOU READ

Assess

Reading Strategy

1. Leadership creates a following. Some people want to be leaders but end up exalting leaders instead of trying to lead. Most people are followers who do not question why they believe in certain leaders.
2. The author believes that people must be prodded into examining their reasons for following a leader. He wants people to think for themselves rather than depend on leaders who lack brains and judgment.

Vocabulary

1. a **2.** b **3.** a **4.** b **5.** b

Academic Vocabulary

1. The identical lines give the impression that they all have identical beliefs and that they are all following the same leader.
2. His activities seemed both local and global. The locals think of him as their leader, but since he is not seen often locally, he is probably a country or world leader.

Writing About Literature

Students should include specific details about the situation and from the play in their analyses.

Performing

Students should follow the stage directions and explain how the movements reinforce the play's theme.

English Language Coach

Evaluate Encourage English language learners to discuss how the characters relate to each other and the Leader. Ask how the behavior of the characters toward their Leader compares with how people in their homeland act toward their leader. EL

Web Activities Have students access the Web site for interactive activities that will help them assess their understanding of the selection.

Focus

Summary

During his conversation with Eugène Ionesco, Claude Bonnefoy asks Ionesco to share a personal analysis of his writing. The author shares his experiences as a poet, novelist, and playwright.

Teach

R1 Reading Strategy

Identifying Assumptions and Ambiguities Before students read the excerpt, tell them that Bonnefoy makes assumptions about Ionesco's work and motivation. Ionesco's responses reflect an honest ambiguity as he tries to analyze himself and his work. OL

Readability Scores
Dale-Chall: 9.2
DRP: interview format not scorable
Lexile: 1000

How I Came *to the* THEATER

Claude Bonnefoy

Building Background

Eugène Ionesco's plays are categorized as part of the theater of the absurd, a style of drama that emphasizes the absurdity of humanity. Absurdists often use unrealistic, illogical play structure. Dialogue may include repetition, plays on words, and a random sequence of ideas. In this excerpt from *Conversations with Eugène Ionesco,* Claude Bonnefoy and Ionesco discuss Ionesco's viewpoint on his own writing.

Set a Purpose for Reading

Read to discover contrasting ideas about Eugène Ionesco and his plays.

Reading Strategy

Identifying Assumptions and Ambiguities

Identifying assumptions involves looking at assumptions an author makes based on his or her experiences, observations, and knowledge. Recognizing these assumptions can help you understand why an author has drawn certain conclusions. **Identifying ambiguities** involves looking at how a text can support two or more contrasting interpretations. R1 Ambiguity may be used to state complex ideas that may even be contradictory. As you read, take notes on assumptions and ambiguities in the text. Use graphic organizers like the ones below.

Assumption or Ambiguity	Interpretation

CLAUDE BONNEFOY. I can't help wondering how and why you happened to become a playwright.

EUGÈNE IONESCO. It puzzles me as well. You'd do better to ask a psychologist about it. Why *did* I write my first play? Perhaps it was to prove that nothing had any real importance, that everything was unlivable—literature, drama, life, human values, they were all unlivable.

C.B. But you could have chosen to express this in another literary form—a poem, a novel, or an essay. Certain of your plays like *The Killer, Victims of Duty, Rhinoceros,* and *A Stroll in the Air* were originally short stories that you've now published in a single volume called *The Colonel's Photograph.* Wasn't your vocation originally more that of a storyteller?

E.I. I started by writing literary criticism. And poems, very bad poems.

C.B. Should I contradict you?

E.I. Oh, they're really pitiful, full of a primitive anthropomorphism:[1] flowers weeping and bleeding and dreaming of meadows and springtime and heaven knows what else. I was only seventeen. It wasn't all my fault,

1. *Anthropomorphism* means "the assigning of human characteristics or behavior to inanimate objects, animals, or nature."

Additional Support

See also Active Learning and Note Taking Guide, pp. 141–147.

Skills Practice

READING: Summarizing Have students reread the conversation between Ionesco and Bonnefoy. Note that Bonnefoy limits himself to comments and questions, while Ionesco replies at length. Have students write Bonnefoy's remarks on a sheet of paper, leaving space between each for a summary of Ionesco's responses. OL

R2 Maeterlinck[2] and Francis Jammes[3] were partly to blame. Anyway, after I'd written some very bad poems, I started writing extremely harsh criticism, as though I was trying to punish myself by punishing other people. After that, I tried to write a novel. It was all a long, long time ago.

C.B. What was the novel about?

E.I. About me, of course.

C.B. So you started out in the classic adolescent way by writing poems?

E.I. No, I'd already written some plays before that.

C.B. Already?

R3 E.I. Well, let me see . . . first of all, when I was about ten or eleven, I started to write my *Memoirs.* I wrote two pages, but I've now lost them both. I can still remember the first page, the first sentences. I described how I'd had my photograph taken at the age of three. Now, of course, I've forgotten what it was like having my photo taken at the age of three. I can only remember being ten and writing down what it was like. And when I was eleven, I wrote poetry and some patriotic plays. *French* patriotic plays. When I was thirteen, I moved to Romania and learned Romanian, and when I was fourteen, I translated my patriotic play and turned it into a Romanian patriotic play.

C.B. One could say you were doubly patriotic.

R4 E.I. Actually, I was very confused as a child. At primary school, in France, I'd been taught that French—which was my language—was the most beautiful language in the world, that the French were the bravest people in the world, that they'd always defeated their enemies, that if they had on occasion been defeated themselves, it was because the odds had been ten-to-one against them or because of a few individuals like Grouchy at Waterloo[4] and Bazaine in the Franco-Prussian War.[5] When I got to Bucharest, my teachers explained that my language was Romanian, that the most beautiful language in the world was not French but Romanian, that the Romanians had always defeated their enemies, that if they hadn't always been victorious it was because they'd had people like Grouchy and Bazaine—I can't even remember their names—on their side. So I learned that it was not the French but the Romanians who were the best people, superior to everyone else. It's a good thing I didn't move to Japan the year after that. . . . So, I began by writing a patriotic play. And I also wrote a comic play at the same time.

C.B. You were always drawn towards comedy, then?

E.I. Yes. But my memory of the play is very hazy. I was eleven or twelve years old at the time and it was set in Paris, on the Rue de l'Avre. A child, one of my schoolfriends, had told me that he could make a film because he had a camera, which in fact wasn't true. He was a little mythomaniac. He's asked me to write a script for him. What I do remember is that it ended with the characters smashing everything in the house. Seven or eight children were sitting having their tea together, and afterwards they smashed their cups, they smashed all the crockery, they smashed up all the furniture, and threw their parents out of the windows.

C.B. I suppose it couldn't have ended with an atom bomb, like *Anger.*[6] But it's curious

2. *Maurice Maeterlinck* (1862–1949) was a Belgian poet, playwright, and essayist who was awarded the 1911 Nobel Prize for Literature. His work, written in French, was considered part of the symbolist movement, which used symbols and myth to convey universal truths.
3. *Francis Jammes* (1868–1938) was a French poet and novelist. His work was categorized as Naturism, which emphasized nature and simplicity.
4. *Grouchy at Waterloo* refers to Emmanuel Grouchy, one of Napoléon's marshals during the Battle of Waterloo in 1815. Grouchy's leadership was considered weak.
5. *Bazaine in the Franco-Prussian War* refers to Achille Bazaine (1811–1888), a French marshal sentenced to death for withdrawing his forces in battle on October 27, 1870, during the Franco-Prussian War. His sentence was reduced to twenty years of imprisonment.
6. Ionesco's play *Anger*, published in 1963, casts a scene of an ordinary day with three happy couples sitting down to eat dinner. Tension ensues, and the husbands and wives attack one another.

Teach

R2 Reading Strategy

Interpreting Ask: Why does Ionesco blame Maeterlinck and Jammes for his work? *(Both men influenced the literary style of their time and, therefore, Ionesco's writing.)* OL

R3 Reading Strategy

Sequence Ask: What sequence of events does Ionesco describe in this passage? *(He describes the stages of his growth as a writer from the age of ten until he was fourteen.)* OL

R4 Reading Strategy

Identifying Assumptions and Ambiguities Ask: Which statement is an assumption? Which statement is ambiguous? *(Bonnefoy's statement is an assumption. Ionesco's statement is ambiguous because it is contradictory.)* OL

English Language Coach

Conditional Sentences Conditional sentences present two events linked by a cause-effect relationship. If A occurs, then B will follow. It may begin with the word *if, when,* or *whenever.* Ask students to find examples of conditional sentences in the selection. EL

Building Reading Fluency

Oral Presentation Have students work in pairs to prepare an oral presentation of the interview. Ask students to practice tone, volume, and expression. Allow time for students to present their interviews to the class. BL

Academic Standards

Additional Support activities on pp. 886 and 887 cover the following standards:

Skills Practice: **9.5.3** Write expository compositions, including...summaries...that communicate information and ideas...accurately and coherently...

English Language Coach: **9.6.2** Demonstrate an understanding of sentence construction...

Building Reading Fluency: **9.7** [Develop] speaking skills...in conjunction with...strategies...[for] delivery of oral presentations.

Teach

R1 Reading Strategy

Identifying Assumptions and Ambiguities **Ask:** Is Bonnefoy's statement an assumption or an ambiguity? *(An assumption)* OL

R2 Reading Strategy

Interpret **Ask:** What is Ionesco's concern about the analyses of his writing by others? *(People assume that his writing is an expression of his innermost thoughts. He does not believe that is necessarily the case.)* OL

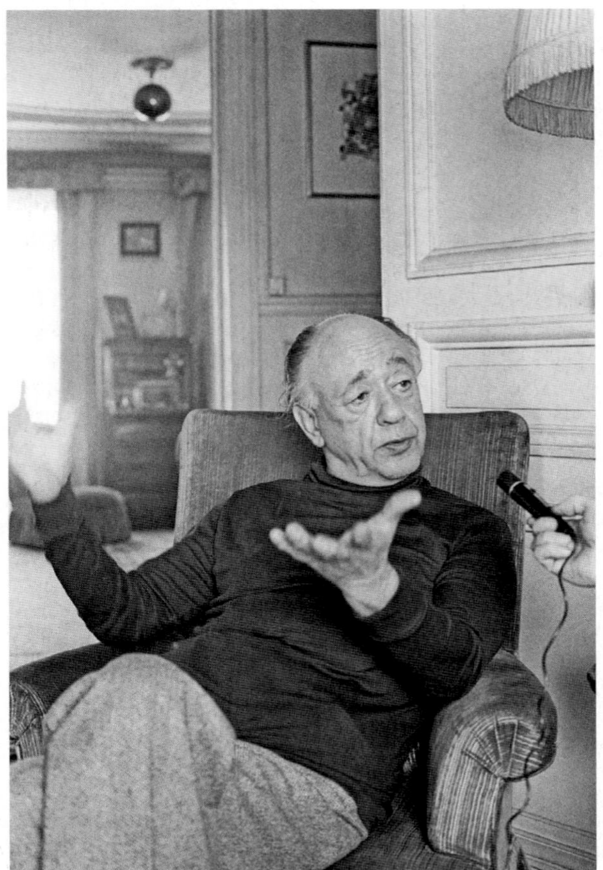

Romanian-born French playwright Eugène Ionesco speaks to an interviewer at home. Ionesco was elected to the Académie Française in 1970.

to discover in this childhood script the same patterns and themes that one finds in *Anger:* acceleration, proliferation, and destruction.

E.I. Perhaps I've always thought along the same lines. You get the same thing in Feydeau[7] too, the same acceleration and proliferation; maybe it goes back to his childhood as well. Acceleration and proliferation are probably a part of my personal rhythm, of the way I see things.

C.B. Were they also present in the novel that you'd started?

E.I. No. Definitely not.

C.B. Was it a fear of exposing yourself, a fear of being recognized that made you stop work on this novel, whose subject, you say, was yourself?

E.I. Possibly.

C.B. In the theater, on the other hand, because of the characters, you can wear a mask even when you're talking about yourself. R1

E.I. What irritates me is that, increasingly, when I write anything new, everyone—academics, psychologists and so on—ferrets[8] about to find evidence that it's me who's talking. Every day it's brought home to me more and more clearly that my plays can be seen as a series of confessions in which I give voice to my most unspeakable thoughts. People send me doctoral theses,[9] they send me unpublished books about myself and I am absolutely terrified. Did I really have all these hidden meanings? Did I really hope that people wouldn't understand or that they'd put all the blame on my characters? I also realize that I've said certain things without intending to. And it's other people who discover all the things that I wasn't really aware of: it's insane. R2 For the sake of clarity, I ought to say that my characters are not always "alter-egos"; they're other people, as well, imaginary people; they're also caricatures of myself, of what I've been frightened of becoming, of what I could have—but fortunately didn't—become; or

7. *Georges Feydeau* (1862–1921) was a French playwright of popular farces during World War I, many of which are still performed today.

8. Here, *ferrets* means "hunts or searches."

9. *Doctoral theses* are lengthy and formal treatises written by graduate students at a university.

Additional Support

Academic Standards

Additional Support activities on pp. 888 and 889 cover the following standards:

Skills Practice: **9.2.8** Make reasonable statements and draw conclusions…

Differentiated Instruction: **9.2** Develop [reading] strategies…

Skills Practice

READING: Identifying Main Idea and Supporting Details Remind students that the main idea is the most important idea contained in a piece of writing. **Ask:** What are supporting details? *(Information that supports or tells about the main idea)* Have students synthesize the main idea of the selection and summarize the supporting details. Then have students identify how the supporting details are organized. OL else they're simply enlargements of different facets of myself; or else—and I'm repeating myself deliberately—they're other people, people I pity, people I laugh at, people I hate or love; sometimes, but more rarely, they are people I should have liked to be. They are also the personifications of a kind of anguish. And quite often, too, they are characters from my dreams.

C.B. If writing was a way of liberating yourself from certain things, didn't it upset you to rediscover these things in the distorting mirrors of other people's criticism?

E.I. Yes, it did.

C.B. So there's the danger that what starts out as a liberation can cease to be one as a result of this mirror of criticism.

E.I. Yes, in fact, you could say that everything shared this danger, but only if everyone were a poet or an artist, or else a psychiatrist or a priest. But as most people have the mentality of a concierge,[10] or else are society people, which is to say, simply concierges further up the social ladder, literature is constantly being undressed. The whole of literary history as we know it is just back-stairs snooping. Journalists and readers don't understand what a man says in the same way an artist would, or a priest, or a doctor or a psychologist. They don't see the meaning of these confessions, they don't understand the deepest or most universal truth of an individual confession. What interests them isn't the universal truth but the personal confession—looking through the keyhole, in other words. What interests people is not what's universal or general in a writer's work, but knowing about his private life. In other words, everything but the work itself. Of course, it's interesting to study sources, but it's more interesting to study the work itself. A work is more than the sum of its causes, it goes beyond them.

C.B. What I find interesting is the reverse—I want to find out how and why you came to put on the mask of playwright.

E.I. How I came to the theater? Quite simply, I don't know.

10. Here, *concierge* means "a person who lives in a building and acts as its janitor, especially in France."

RESPONDING AND THINKING CRITICALLY

Respond

1. Why do you think Ionesco does not give clear-cut answers to Bonnefoy's questions?

Recall and Interpret

2. (a)In what genre does Ionesco say he began writing? (b)How does he contradict himself when answering questions about the genre of his early writings?
3. (a)What does Bonnefoy say that writing characters allows Ionesco to do? (b)What is Bonnefoy assuming?

Analyze and Evaluate

4. (a)Ionesco says his characters are many things. Why do you think he does not make one specific statement about his characters? (b)What would be two possible interpretations of the purpose of Ionesco's characters?
5. Ionesco says that "a work is more than the sum of its causes, it goes beyond them." What do you think he means by this statement?

Connect

6. Ionesco says that "acceleration," which is the act of increasing speed, and "proliferation," which is the act of rapid growth, might be part of his "personal rhythm." How does he use acceleration and proliferation in *The Leader*?

INDIANA ACADEMIC STANDARDS (pages 886–889)

9.3.8 Interpret and evaluate the impact of ambiguities...in a text.

9.3.11 Evaluate the aesthetic qualities of style, including the impact of diction...on tone, mood, and theme.

Differentiated Instruction

Reading Selections in Parts To facilitate comprehension for less-proficient readers, suggest they break the selection into smaller parts, such as one question and its response. Have students paraphrase the main idea of each section. Students may benefit from working in pairs with more proficient readers. BL

HISTORICAL PERSPECTIVE

Informational Text

AFTER YOU READ

Assess

1. Responses will vary. Some students may think that Ionesco avoids giving an answer because he feels it is up to readers to interpret his work. Others may say that Ionesco is trying to answer Bonnefoy's questions, but in the end, he realizes that he doesn't know why.
2. (a) Literary criticism and poetry (b) At first, he says he wrote poetry, criticism, and a novel. Then, he says that when he was eleven, he wrote a memoir, poetry, and a play.
3. (a) He says it allows Ionesco to wear a mask. (b) He assumes that Ionesco writes about himself.
4. (a) It would limit readers' interpretations of his characters. (b) Some may say his characters are comic exaggerations, as well as images of true humanity. Others may say that his characters are surreal, as well as realistic.
5. He means that a work comments on more than its writer, the time period when it was written, and its subject matter. The work makes a broader statement about the human condition.
6. Dialogue happens in short, quick bursts. The characters enter and exit many times. Growth occurs when all the characters are entering and exiting the stage at the same time. There is the climax of the Leader entering without a head. The play accelerates again with all the characters asking, "What's your name?"

BEFORE YOU READ

Focus

BELLRINGER

Bellringer Options
Daily Language Practice Transparency 80
Or display images of people socializing in malls, large restaurants, or parks. Have students discuss the social customs that affect how men and women interact with each other in social situations.

Author Search To expand students' appreciation of Paddy Chayefsky, have them access the Web site for additional information and resources.

BEFORE YOU READ

Marty

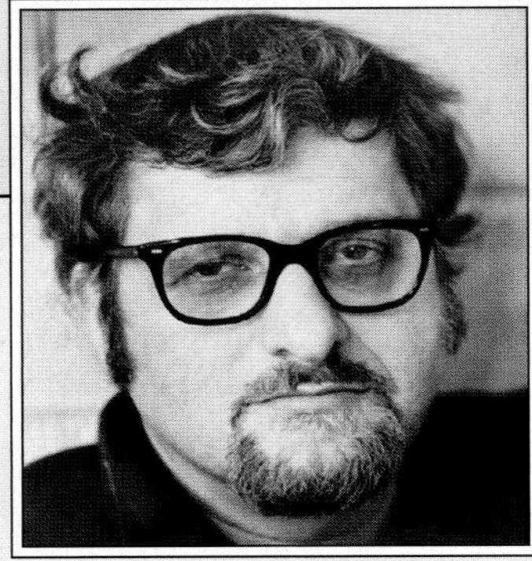

MEET PADDY CHAYEFSKY

How does the son of Russian Jewish immigrants come to be called by the Irish nickname Paddy? As a young draftee in the United States Army during World War II, Sidney Chayefsky was summoned one day for KP (kitchen police), an undesirable assignment. He fibbed to his duty officer that he needed to be excused from KP in order to attend Catholic religious service. The officer reminded Chayefsky that the day before he had claimed to be Jewish. Chayefsky replied, "Yes, but my mother is Irish." The officer said, "OK, Paddy," giving him the nickname by which he was known forever afterward.

Success in Screenwriting Paddy Chayefsky was born in New York City. After graduating from City College of New York, he was drafted into the Army. While serving his country, he stepped on a German land mine, was wounded, and received a Purple Heart. Because of the humorous manner with which Chayefsky dealt with his injury, he was assigned to the Special Service Division, where his creative talents were put to work. He wrote and produced a short musical comedy entitled "No T.O. [Table of Organization] for Love." In January 1945, the play was performed at a number of Army camps in England and also opened at the Scala Theatre in London.

After the war, Chayefsky continued to pursue his new craft. He began writing live television dramas, including *Marty, The Catered Affair,* and *The Bachelor Party*. Over the next three decades, Chayefsky became a successful writer in three media: theater, television, and film. During his career as a screenwriter, he won three Academy Awards for his work on the films *Marty* (1955), *The Hospital* (1971), and *Network* (1976). He also wrote a novel, *Altered States.*

A Critical Eye on Culture In the early 1950s, Chayefsky was described as "a poet of the streets" because of the characters he created. He did not write about the rich and famous or the beautiful; he wrote about common people, those just trying to get along in life. He was a master craftsman with dialogue, and he filled his scripts with provocative language.

> *"Characters caught in the decline of their society—that's the essence of almost everything I write."*
>
> —Paddy Chayefsky

Chayefsky cast a critical eye on American society and culture, as much of his work reflects. He was particularly critical of television—although, ironically, he enjoyed much success there. The film *Network* is a caustic portrayal of television networks whose only goal is high ratings. Chayefsky objected to the way television news reported grisly stories meant to shock their audiences. He said, "That is the basic problem of television. We've lost our sense of shock, our sense of humanity."

Paddy Chayefsky was born in 1923 and died in 1981.

LiteratureOnline **Author Search** For more about Paddy Chayefsky, go to www.glencoe.com.

Selection Skills

Marty, Act One

Literary Elements
- Plot (SE pp. 891, 894, 898, 901–903)
- Conflict (TWE p. 892)

Reading Skills
- Analyzing Dialogue (SE pp. 891, 893–903)
- Monitoring Comprehension (TWE p. 894)
- Cause and Effect (TWE p. 900)

Vocabulary Skills
- Antonyms (SE pp. 891, 903)

Listening/Speaking/Viewing Skills
- Analyze Art (SE p. 896; TWE p. 899)
- Expressing Emotion (TWE p. 898)
- Readers Theater (TWE p. 902)

Writing Skills/Grammar
- Response to Conflict (SE p. 903)

LITERATURE PREVIEW

Connecting to the Play

This play begins with an ordinary man looking for love. He is troubled by what he perceives as his own unattractiveness and pressures from others to find a wife. Before you read, think about the following questions:

- Have you ever wanted something that seemed out of reach?
- How do you feel when your family or friends try to push you into something?

Building Background

The 1950s were a time of new beginnings and social changes. After the hardships of World War II, people wanted to settle down and enjoy life. One of the major inventions that affected people's lives was the television. Although television technology had been developed some years earlier, broadcasting was suspended during the war. It was not until the 1950s that television viewing became widely popular. *Marty* aired in 1953.

Setting Purposes for Reading

Big Idea Awkward Encounters

Awkward encounters are uncomfortable because they reveal an underlying problem or conflict. As you read Act 1, notice how the characters react during awkward encounters with other characters.

Literary Element Plot

Plot is the sequence of events in a literary work. Most plots develop around a conflict—a struggle between opposing forces. Keeping track of unfolding events helps the reader identify the conflict, its development, and resolution. As you read, try to discover the underlying conflict Marty is experiencing.

- See Literary Terms Handbook, p. R13.

LiteratureOnline Interactive Literary Elements Handbook To review or learn more about the literary elements, go to www.glencoe.com.

READING PREVIEW

Reading Strategy Analyzing Dialogue

Dialogue is the conversation between characters in a literary work. As you read the play, ask yourself the following questions: What are the differences in the ways the characters express themselves? How is the plot developed through dialogue? How do the characters interact with each other?

Reading Tip: Asking Questions Use a chart like the one below to organize your impressions of the characters as revealed by their dialogue.

Character	Dialogue	What It Reveals
Marty	"You're next right now, Missus Canduso."	Marty is patient and friendly.

Vocabulary

amiability (ā′ mē ə bil′ə tē) *n.* the state of being friendly, sociable, and generally agreeable; p. 893 *His amiability and easygoing manner won him the admiration of many.*

baleful (bāl′ fəl) *adj.* threatening evil or intending harm; p. 894 *The police officer on the subway cast a baleful look at the rowdy passengers.*

contrive (kən trīv′) *v.* to plan creatively; to bring about by scheming; p. 895 *After many attempts, they contrived to set up the tent in the dark.*

effusive (i fū′ siv) *adj.* showing feeling freely; p. 897 *Her mother's effusive greetings to her friends were a bit embarrassing.*

Vocabulary Tip: Antonyms Antonyms are words with opposite meanings. Note that antonyms are always the same part of speech.

INDIANA ACADEMIC STANDARDS (pages 891–903)
9.3 [Identify] story elements such as…plot…
9.3.10 Identify and describe the function of dialogue…
9.5.3 Write…analytical essays…

BEFORE YOU READ

Focus

Summary

The time is the 1950s. The place is an Italian neighborhood in New York City. The events take place in a 36-hour period in the life of Marty Pilletti, a 36-year-old butcher. Marty is not a handsome man. He is single and has been unsuccessful in dating. His mother and just about everyone else in his neighborhood keep asking him when he is going to get married. Marty feels he is destined to remain a bachelor.

V Vocabulary

Vocabulary File Say: Add these words to your vocabulary file. For each word, include a sentence that gives you an example of how to use the word. **OL** Students with English language needs should include the pronunciations of these words in their files. **EL**

Literary Elements Have students access the Web site to improve their understanding of plot.

Selection Resources

Print Materials
- Unit 4 Resources (Fast File), pp. 53–61
- Selection and Unit Assessments, pp. 157–162
- Selection Quick Checks, pp. 79–81

Transparencies
- Bellringer Options Transparencies: Daily Language Practice Transparency 80
- Literary Elements Transparencies 1, 9, 13

Technology
- TeacherWorks Plus™ CD-ROM
- StudentWorks Plus™ CD-ROM
- Presentation Plus!™ CD-ROM
- Literature Online, glencoe.com
- Online Student Edition, mhln.com
- Exam*View*® Assessment Suite CD-ROM
- Vocabulary PuzzleMaker CD-ROM
- Listening Library, disc 2 tracks 17–19

Teach

Big Idea

Awkward Encounters
Have students consider these questions as they read.
Ask: Why does the author begin with a discussion of Marty's siblings? *(So the reader knows he comes from a large family and is the only one not yet married)* What does Marty's response to people's efforts to find him a wife reveal about his temperament? *(He has a pleasant, patient temperament.)* **OL**

Additional Support

Skills Practice

LITERARY ELEMENT: Conflict
External conflict, or a struggle between a character and his or her environment, is an important element of plot. Characters also experience conflict within themselves, or internal conflict.

Have students identify the external and internal conflict experienced by Marty. *(External conflict: He is constantly pressured by his mother and friends to get married. Internal conflict: Marty wants to get married but has been unsuccessful in finding someone.)* **OL**

CHARACTERS

MARTY PILLETTI	ITALIAN WOMAN	YOUNG MOTHER
ANGIE	BARTENDER	MOTHER
THOMAS	VIRGINIA	SHORT GIRL
YOUNG MAN	STAG	GIRL / CLARA DAVIS
AUNT CATHERINE	CRITIC	TWENTY-YEAR-OLD
FORTY-YEAR-OLD		

Act One

L [*Fade In:*[1] *A butcher shop in the Italian district of New York City. Actually, we fade in on a close-up of a butcher's saw being carefully worked through a side of beef, and we dolly*[2] *back to show the butcher at work, and then the whole shop. The butcher is a mild-mannered, stout, short, balding young man of thirty-six. His charm lies in an almost indestructible good-natured* ***amiability.***

The shop contains three women customers. One is a YOUNG MOTHER *with a baby carriage. She is chatting with a second woman of about forty at the door. The customer being waited on at the moment is a stout, elderly* ITALIAN WOMAN *who is standing on tiptoe, peering over the white display counter, checking the butcher as he saws away.*]

ITALIAN WOMAN. Your kid brother got married last Sunday, eh, Marty?

MARTY. [*Absorbed in his work.*] That's right, Missus Fusari. It was a very nice affair.

ITALIAN WOMAN. That's the big tall one, the fellow with the mustache.

MARTY. [*Sawing away.*] No, that's my other brother, Freddie. My other brother, Freddie, he's been married four years already. He lives down on Quincy Street. The one who got married Saturday, that was my little brother, Nickie.

ITALIAN WOMAN. I thought he was a big, tall, fat fellow. Didn't I meet him here one time? Big, tall, fat fellow, he tried to sell me life insurance?

MARTY. [*Sets the cut of meat on the scale, watches its weight register.*] No, that's my sister Margaret's husband, Frank. My sister Margaret, she's married to the insurance salesman. My sister Rose, she married a contractor. They moved to Detroit last year. And my other sister, Frances, she got married about two-and-a-half years ago in Saint John's Church on Adams Boulevard. Oh, that was a big affair. Well, Missus Fusari, that'll be three dollars, ninety-four cents. How's that with you? R

[*The* ITALIAN WOMAN *produces an old leather change purse from her pocketbook and painfully extracts three single dollar bills and ninety-four cents to the penny and lays the money piece by piece on the counter.*]

YOUNG MOTHER. [*Calling from the door.*] Hey, Marty, I'm inna hurry.

1. To *fade in* is to go from a dark screen to a full picture in a few seconds.
2. To *dolly* is to shoot with a camera that is moving on a dolly, or wheeled platform.

Vocabulary

amiability (ā′ mē ə bil′ə tē) *n.* the state of being friendly, sociable, and generally agreeable

Teach

L Literary Element

Setting Ask: How do the setting and stage direction in a screenplay differ from setting and direction in a stage play? *(Possible answer: The screenwriter has to consider how to use the camera to tell the story and engage the audience. In a play, the author relies on the actors, props, and sound effects to tell the story.)* OL

R Reading Strategy

Analyzing Dialogue Ask: Why does Marty name all of his siblings and give a brief update on their lives? *(Possible answer: The information provides background about Marty's family; Marty knows that Mrs. Fusari will persist in her questioning until she can make her point that he should be ashamed that he is not yet married.)* OL

CheckPoint

Use the CheckPoint questions on Presentation Plus! to monitor students' comprehension. These questions can be used with interactive response keypads for immediate student feedback.

English Language Coach

Dialect Dialect is a variation of standard language spoken by a group of people who live in a particular region. Explain that dialect affects sentence structure, vocabulary, and pronunciation. The characters in *Marty* speak a dialect that was common in the Italian section of New York City in the 1950s. Have students choose several lines of dialogue and rewrite the dialect as Standard English. Example: Dialect: *Watsa matta wi' you?* Standard English: What is the matter with you? EL

Academic Standards

Additional Support activities on pp. 892 and 893 cover the following standards:

Skills Practice: **9.3** [Identify] story elements such as…plot…

English Language Coach: **9.5.2** Write responses to literature that demonstrate an awareness of the author's style…

Teach

L1 Literary Element

Plot Answer: *Finding a wife for Marty probably will be a major focus of the plot.* OL

R1 Reading Strategy

Analyzing Dialogue Answer: *She is fixated on Marty's marital status and thinks that shaming him is a good way to influence him.* OL

L2 Literary Element

Tone Ask: What does Marty's reaction to the young mother's comments reveal about his feelings? *(Possible answer: Marty is losing patience with all the comments.)* OL

L3 Literary Element

Plot Answer: *Like Marty, he wants a date. If Marty joins him, it will make it easier for both of them.* OL

MARTY. [*Wrapping the meat, calls amiably back.*] You're next right now, Missus Canduso.

[*The old* ITALIAN WOMAN *has been regarding Marty with a* ***baleful*** *scowl.*]

ITALIAN WOMAN. Well, Marty, when you gonna get married? You should be ashamed. All your brothers and sisters, they all younger than you, and they married, and they got children. I just saw your mother inna fruit shop, and she says to me: "Hey, you know a nice girl for my boy Marty?" Watsa matter with you? That's no way. Watsa matter with you? Now, you get married, you hear me what I say?

MARTY. [*Amiably.*] I hear you, Missus Fusari.

[*The old lady takes her parcel of meat, but apparently feels she still hasn't quite made her point.*]

ITALIAN WOMAN. My son Frank, he was married when he was nineteen years old. Watsa matter with you?

MARTY. Missus Fusari, Missus Canduso over there, she's inna big hurry, and . . .

ITALIAN WOMAN. You be ashamed of yourself.

[*She takes her package of meat, turns, and shuffles to the door and exits.* MARTY *gathers up the money on the counter, turns to the cash register behind him to ring up the sale.*]

YOUNG MOTHER. Marty, I want a nice big fat pullet, about four pounds. I hear your kid brother got married last Sunday.

MARTY. Yeah, it was a very nice affair, Missus Canduso.

YOUNG MOTHER. Marty, you oughtta be ashamed. All your kid brothers and sisters, married and have children. When you gonna get married?

[*Close-up:* MARTY *He sends a glance of weary exasperation up to the ceiling. With a gesture of mild irritation, he pushes the plunger of the cash register. It makes a sharp ping.* L2

Dissolve[3] *to: Close-up of television set. A baseball game is in progress. Camera pulls back to show we are in a typical neighborhood bar—red leatherette booths, a jukebox, some phone booths. About half the bar stools are occupied by neighborhood folk.* MARTY *enters, pads amiably to one of the booths where a young man of about thirty-odd already sits. This is* ANGIE. MARTY *slides into the booth across from* ANGIE. ANGIE *is a little wasp of a fellow. He has a newspaper spread out before him to the sports pages.* MARTY *reaches over and pulls one of the pages over for himself to read. For a moment the two friends sit across from each other, reading the sports pages. Then* ANGIE, *without looking up, speaks.*]

ANGIE. Well, what do you feel like doing tonight?

MARTY. I don't know, Angie. What do you feel like doing?

ANGIE. Well, we oughtta do something. It's Saturday night. I don't wanna go bowling like last Saturday. How about calling up that big girl we picked up inna movies about a month ago in the RKO Chester?[4]

MARTY. [*Not very interested.*] Which one was that?

ANGIE. That big girl that was sitting in front of us with the skinny friend.

MARTY. Oh, yeah.

ANGIE. We took them home alla way out in Brooklyn. Her name was Mary Feeney. What do you say? You think I oughtta give her a ring? I'll take the skinny one.

Literary Element Plot *What idea does this give you about where the plot of the play might lead?* L1

Reading Strategy Analyzing Dialogue *What impression do you get about this woman as she keeps repeating this sentence?* R1

Vocabulary

baleful (bāl′ fəl) *adj.* threatening evil or intending harm

3. To *dissolve* is to overlap the end of one scene with the beginning of another.
4. The *RKO Chester* was a movie theater in the Bronx.

Literary Element Plot *Why do you think Angie is making this suggestion?* L3

Additional Support

Skills Practice

READING: Monitoring Comprehension Writers use dialogue to reveal character, define conflict, and advance plot. Focusing on important dialogue will help students understand key ideas.

- Have students make a chart with three headings: Character, Conflict, Theme. As they read, they should copy important phrases or sentences under each heading.
- Have students include the name of the character speaking and the page where the dialogue appears.
- Students should add to their charts as they read each act. OL

MARTY. It's five o'clock already, Angie. She's probably got a date by now.

ANGIE. Well, let's call her up. What can we lose?

MARTY. I didn't like her, Angie. I don't feel like calling her up.

ANGIE. Well, what do you feel like doing tonight?

MARTY. I don't know. What do you feel like doing?

ANGIE. Well, we're back to that, huh? I say to you: "What do you feel like doing tonight?" And you say to me: "I don't know, what do you feel like doing?" And then we wind up sitting around your house, watching Sid ★ Caesar[5] on television. Well, I tell you what I feel like doing. I feel like calling up this Mary Feeney. She likes you.

[*MARTY looks up quickly at this.*]

MARTY. What makes you say that?

ANGIE. I could see she likes you.

MARTY. Yeah, sure.

ANGIE. [*Half rising in his seat.*] I'll call her up.

MARTY. You call her up for yourself, Angie. I don't feel like calling her up.

[*ANGIE sits down again. They both return to reading the paper for a moment. Then ANGIE looks up again.*]

ANGIE. Boy, you're getting to be a real drag, you know that?

MARTY. Angie, I'm thirty-six years old. I been looking for a girl every Saturday night of my life. I'm a little, short, fat fellow, and girls don't go for me, that's all. I'm not like you. I mean, you joke around, and they laugh at you, and you get along fine. I just stand around like a bug. What's the sense of kidding myself? Everybody's always telling me to get married. Get married. Get married. Don't you think I wanna get married? I wanna get married. They drive me crazy. Now, I don't want to wreck your Saturday night for you, Angie. You wanna go somewhere, you go ahead. I don't wanna go.

ANGIE. Boy, they drive me crazy too. My old lady, every word outta her mouth, when you gonna get married?

MARTY. My mother, boy, she drives me crazy.

[*ANGIE leans back in his seat, scowls at the paper napkin container. MARTY returns to the sports page. For a moment a silence hangs between them. Then . . .*]

ANGIE. So what do you feel like doing tonight?

MARTY. [*Without looking up.*] I don't know. What do you feel like doing?

[*They both just sit, ANGIE frowning at the napkin container, MARTY at the sports page.*

The camera slowly moves away from the booth, looks down the length of the bar, up the wall, past the clock—which reads ten to five—and over to the television screen, where the baseball game is still going on.

*Dissolve slowly to: The television screen, now blank. The clock now reads a quarter to six. Back in the booth, MARTY now sits alone. He is sitting there, his face expressionless, but his eyes troubled. Then he pushes himself slowly out of the booth and shuffles to the phone booth; he goes inside, closing the booth door carefully after him. For a moment MARTY just sits squatly. Then with some exertion—due to the cramped quarters—he **contrives** to get a small address book out of his rear pants pocket. He slowly flips through it, finds the page he wants, and studies it, scowling; then he takes a dime, plunks it into the proper slot, waits for a dial tone . . . then carefully dials a number. . . . he waits. He is beginning to sweat a bit in* R3

5. *Sid Caesar* is a comic writer and actor who hosted several television comedy shows in the 1950s and 1960s.

Reading Strategy Analyzing Dialogue *How does this line reflect Marty's attitude during this conversation?* R2

Big Idea Awkward Encounters *How does Marty feel about himself?* BI

Vocabulary

contrive (kən trīv′) *v.* to plan creatively; to bring about by scheming

Teach

R2 Reading Strategy

Analyzing Dialogue
Answer: *Marty seems uninspired and passive. This conversation is probably one they have had many times before.* OL

BI Big Idea

Awkward Encounters
Answer: *He views himself as insignificant and unnoticed, like a bug. He thinks his situation is hopeless.* OL

R3 Reading Strategy

Draw a Conclusion **Ask:** Why does Marty begin to sweat? *(Possible answer: He is nervous. He is probably going to call the girl Angie mentioned earlier.)* OL

★ Cultural History

Television The 1950s are often referred to as the Golden Age of Television. Most programs were variety shows, formatted in the style of vaudeville reviews—live performances that included singing, dancing, and comedy. "Your Show of Shows" featured a versatile comedian named Sid Caesar. His range and talented ensemble made the program a big hit.

English Language Coach

Specialized Vocabulary Have students find terms in the screenplay that might be confusing or unfamiliar to them, such as *fade in, fade out, close up, dissolve* (to black), *pan* (left or right). Discuss the meanings of the terms. EL

Differentiated Instruction

Pantomime Ask students to show their understanding of mood and action in the teleplay through pantomime. Have students work in pairs to create and perform a pantomime that shows the movements of Marty and Angie in the bar as they discuss their evening plans. BL

Academic Standards

Additional Support activities on pp. 894 and 895 cover the following standards:

Skills Practice: **9.3.10** Identify and describe the function of dialogue…in dramatic literature.

English Language Coach: **9.1.1** Identify…the literal and figurative meanings of words…

Differentiated Instruction: **9.7.6** Analyze the occasion and…choose effective…nonverbal techniques (including…gestures…) for presentations.

Teach

BI Big Idea

Awkward Encounters

Answer: *After Angie said the girl liked Marty, and he finally worked up the courage to call, he must have felt terrible when she didn't remember him.*

Ask: How do you know how Marty feels after the phone conversation with Mary Feeney? *(Possible answer: His body language shows his sadness and depression.)* OL

★ Viewing the Art

Ted Blackall is a contemporary Australian artist well known for his oil paintings. In addition to painting and teaching, Blackall works as a color and design consultant for major corporations.

Answer: *The painting has a mood of excitement and frenzy. The painting conveys a much higher level of activity than the play so far.* AS

The Bride and Groom. 1983. Ted Blackall. Oil on canvas, 121.9 x 121.9 cm. Private Collection.

Viewing the Art: How would you describe the mood of this painting? How does it compare with the mood of the play so far? ★

the hot little booth, and his chest begins to rise and fall deeply.]

MARTY. [*With a vague pretense at good diction.*] Hello, is this Mary Feeney? . . . Could I please speak to Miss Mary Feeney? . . . Just tell her an old friend . . .

[*He waits again. With his free hand he wipes the gathering sweat from his brow.*]

. . . Oh, hello there, is this Mary Feeney? Hello there, this is Marty Pilletti. I wonder if you recall me . . . Well, I'm kind of a stocky guy. The last time we met was inna movies, the RKO Chester. You was with another girl, and I was with a friend of mine name Angie. This was about a month ago . . .

[*The girl apparently doesn't remember him. A sort of panic begins to seize* MARTY. *His voice rises a little.*]

The RKO Chester on Payne Boulevard. You was sitting in front of us, and we was annoying you, and you got mad and . . . I'm the fellow who works inna butcher shop . . . come on. You know who I am! . . . That's right, we went to Howard Johnson's and we had hamburgers. You hadda milk shake . . . Yeah, that's right. I'm the stocky one, the heavy-set fellow . . . Well, I'm glad you recall

Big Idea **Awkward Encounters** *Why do you suppose this bothers Marty so much?* BI

Additional Support

Skills Practice

READING: Previewing Ask students to discuss how they preview a chapter in a book before they read. *(flip through pages, look at headings and important terms)* Tell students that they can preview a scene by noting changes in setting and characters. As they scan, students should keep in mind what they know about the characters and predict how they may act. Tell students to scan the script and staging directions to note which characters interact. Have students write three questions they think the scene will answer. OL me, because I hadda swell time that night, and I was just wondering how everything was with you. How's everything? . . . That's swell . . . Yeah, well, I'll tell you why I called . . . I was figuring on taking in a movie tonight, and I was wondering if you and your friend would care to see a movie tonight with me and my friend . . . [*His eyes are closed now.*] Yeah, tonight. I know it's pretty late to call for a date, but I didn't know myself till . . . Yeah, I know, well how about . . . Yeah, I know, well maybe next Saturday night. You free next Saturday night? . . . Well, how about the Saturday after that? . . . Yeah, I know . . . Yeah . . . Yeah . . . Oh, I understand, I mean . . .

[*He just sits now, his eyes closed, not really listening. After a moment, he returns the receiver to its cradle and sits, his shoulders slack, his hands resting listlessly in the lap of his spotted white apron. . . . Then he opens his eyes, straightens himself, pushes the booth door open, and advances out into the bar. He perches on a stool across the bar from the* BARTENDER, *who looks up from his magazine.*]

BARTENDER. I hear your kid brother got married last week, Marty.

MARTY. [*Looking down at his hands on the bar.*] Yeah, it was a very nice affair.

BARTENDER. Well, Marty, when you gonna get married?

[MARTY *tenders the* BARTENDER *a quick scowl, gets off his perch, and starts for the door—untying his apron as he goes.*]

MARTY. If my mother calls up, Lou, tell her I'm on my way home.

[*Dissolve to:* MARTY'S MOTHER, *and a young couple sitting around the table in the dining room of* MARTY'S *home. The young couple—we will soon find out—are* THOMAS, MARTY'S *cousin, and his wife,* VIRGINIA. *They have apparently just been telling the mother some sad news, and the three are sitting around frowning.*

The dining room is a crowded room filled with chairs and lamps, pictures and little statues, perhaps even a small grotto of little vigil lamps.[6] *To the right of the dining room is the kitchen, old-fashioned, Italian, steaming, and overcrowded. To the left of the dining room is the living room, furnished in same fashion as the dining room. Just off the living room is a small bedroom, which is* MARTY'S. *This bedroom and the living room have windows looking out on front. The dining room has windows looking out to side alleyway. A stairway in the dining room leads to the second floor.*

The MOTHER *is a round, dark,* **effusive** *little woman.*]

MOTHER. [*After a pause.*] Well, Thomas, I knew sooner or later this was gonna happen. I told Marty, I said: "Marty, you watch. There's gonna be real trouble over there in your cousin Thomas' house." Because your mother was here, Thomas, you know?

THOMAS. When was this, Aunt Theresa?

MOTHER. This was one, two, three days ago. Wednesday. Because I went to the fruit shop on Wednesday, and I came home. And I come arounna back, and there's your mother sitting onna steps onna porch. And I said: "Catherine, my sister, wadda you doing here?" And she look uppa me, and she beganna cry.

THOMAS. [*To his wife.*] Wednesday. That was the day you threw the milk bottle.

MOTHER. That's right. Because I said to her: "Catherine, watsa matter?" And she said to me: "Theresa, my daughter-in-law, Virginia, she just threw the milk bottle at me."

VIRGINIA. Well, you see what happen, Aunt Theresa . . .

MOTHER. I know, I know . . .

VIRGINIA. She comes inna kitchen, and she begins poking her head over my shoulder

---

Reading Strategy Analyzing Dialogue *What is the effect of Marty's repetition of this line?* **R**

6. A *grotto of little vigil lamps* is a shrine with prayer candles.

Vocabulary

effusive (i fū′ siv) *adj.* showing feeling freely

Teach

R Reading Strategy

Analyzing Dialogue

Answer: *It shows that people bring up this event often, perhaps as a way of prodding him about getting married. Marty is always ready with a stock reply.* **OL**

English Language Coach

Historical Context Explain to English learners that it was customary among Italian Americans in the 1950s to live together as extended families. This tradition began to change when women began to work outside the home. **EL**

Differentiated Instruction

Character Interaction Ask students to explain how information travels from one character to another in the teleplay. Have students make a flowchart to show how Catherine finds out her son and daughter-in-law want her to move out of their home. **BL**

Academic Standards

Additional Support activities on pp. 896 and 897 cover the following standards:

Skills Practice: **9.2** Develop strategies such as...making predictions...

English Language Coach: **9.3.12** Analyze the way in which a work...is related to...issues of its historical period.

Differentiated Instruction: **9.3.3** Analyze interactions between characters in a literary text and explain the way those interactions affect the plot.

Teach

R Reading Strategy

Analyzing Dialogue **Answer:** *Virginia and her mother-in-law, Marty's Aunt Catherine, do not get along. They have difficulty being in the same room.* OL

L1 Literary Element

Plot **Ask:** What new issue involving Marty does the author introduce on page 898? *(Marty's cousin Thomas and his wife, Virginia, want Catherine to move into the house Marty shares with his mother.)* OL

BI Big Idea

Awkward Encounters
Answer: *Besides Aunt Catherine's bossiness, the young couple has no privacy.* OL

L2 Literary Element

Plot **Answer:** *Students may say that family conflicts are not so easily resolved and new problems may result. Others may say that this change may be a good idea.* OL

here and poking her head over my shoulder there . . .

MOTHER. I know, I know . . .

VIRGINIA. And she begins complaining about this, and she begins complaining about that. And she got me so nervous, I spilled some milk I was making for the baby. You see, I was making some food for the baby, and . . .

MOTHER. So I said to her, "Catherine . . ."

VIRGINIA. So, she got me so nervous I spilled some milk. So she said: "You're spilling the milk." She says: "Milks costs twenty-four cents a bottle. Wadda you, a banker?" So I said, "Mama, leave me alone, please. You're making me nervous. Go on in the other room and turn on the television set." So then she began telling me how I waste money, and how I can't cook, and how I'm raising my baby all wrong, and she kept talking about these couple of drops of milk I spilt, and I got so mad, I said: "Mama, you wanna see me really spill some milk?" So I took the bottle and threw it against the door. I didn't throw it at her. That's just something she made up. I didn't throw it anywheres near her. Well, of course, alla milk went all over the floor. The whole twenty-four cents. Well, I was sorry right away, you know, but she ran outta the house.

[*Pause.*]

MOTHER. Well, I don't know what you want me to do, Virginia. If you want me, I'll go talk to her tonight.

[*THOMAS and VIRGINIA suddenly frown and look down at their hands as if of one mind.*]

THOMAS. Well, I'll tell you, Aunt Theresa . . .

VIRGINIA. Lemme tell it, Tommy.

THOMAS. Okay.

VIRGINIA. [*Leaning forward to the MOTHER.*] We want you to do a very big favor for us, Aunt Theresa.

MOTHER. Sure.

VIRGINIA. Aunt Theresa, you got this big house here. You got four bedrooms upstairs. I mean, you got this big house just for you and Marty. All your other kids are married and got their own homes. And I thought maybe Tommy's mother could come here and live with you and Marty. L1

MOTHER. Well . . .

VIRGINIA. She's miserable living with Tommy and me and you're the only one that gets along with her. Because I called up Tommy's brother, Joe, and I said: "Joe, she's driving me crazy. Why don't you take her for a couple of years?" And he said: "Oh, no!" I know I sound like a terrible woman . . .

MOTHER. No, Virginia, I know how you feel. My husband, may God bless his memory, his mother, she lived with us for a long time, and I know how you feel.

VIRGINIA. [*Practically on the verge of tears.*] I just can't stand it no more! Every minute of the day! Do this! Do that! I don't have ten minutes alone with my husband! We can't even have a fight! We don't have no privacy! Everybody's miserable in our house!

THOMAS. All right, Ginnie, don't get so excited.

MOTHER. She's right. She's right. Young husband and wife, they should have their own home. And my sister, Catherine, she's my sister, but I gotta admit, she's an old goat. And plenny-a times in my life I felt like throwing the milk bottle at her myself. And I tell you now, as far as I'm concerned, if Catherine wantsa come and live here with me and Marty, it's all right with me.

[*VIRGINIA promptly bursts into tears.*]

THOMAS. [*Not far from tears himself, lowers his face.*] That's very nice-a you, Aunt Theresa.

Reading Strategy Analyzing Dialogue *What does this bit of dialogue tell you about the relationship between Virginia and her mother-in-law?* R

Big Idea Awkward Encounters *Why is life so awkward at Thomas and Virginia's home?* BI

Literary Element Plot *Do you think this will resolve the conflicts in the family?* L2

Additional Support

Skills Practice

LISTENING AND SPEAKING: Expressing Emotion Discuss the emotional state of Thomas, Virginia, and Mother. *(Thomas is agitated; Virginia is tense, emotional; Mother is concerned.)* Ask students to suggest how each character might speak, move, or gesture to convey these feelings. Have students work in groups of three to read the parts of Thomas, Virginia, and Mother. Encourage them to use tone of voice and pacing to communicate each character's state of mind. After each reading, have listeners respond to the interpretations. OL

Bride and Groom (The Couple). 1915–1916. Amedeo Modigliani. Metropolitan Museum of Art, New York, USA.

Teach

Viewing the Art

Italian Amedeo Modigliani (1884–1920) was a sculptor and painter. His sculptures reflect simple, elongated forms. In his paintings, Modigliani kept the graceful, elongated forms and added distorted figures and big, flat areas of color. AS

English Language Coach

Slang Explain to English language learners that slang is informal language that may express a new idea in a new way. Slang often uses colorful metaphors and can be witty. Caution students that some slang words can also be flippant, irreverent, and insulting. EL

Differentiated Instruction

Using a Storyboard Some students may find long selections difficult to comprehend. Introduce the idea of a storyboard—a series of pictures and notes that depict one scene in a play. Have students create storyboards and review them before reading a new scene. BL

Academic Standards

Additional Support activities on pp. 898 and 899 cover the following standards:

Skills Practice: **9.7.6** Analyze the occasion and the interests of the audience and choose effective verbal and nonverbal techniques (including voice, gestures, and eye contact) for presentations. **9.7.10** Assess how…delivery affect[s] the mood and tone of the oral communication and makes an impact on the audience.

English Language Coach: **9.1.2** Distinguish between what words mean literally and what they imply and interpret what the words imply.

Differentiated Instruction: **9.3** [Identify] story elements such as character,…plot, and setting…

Teach

R1 Reading Strategy

Analyzing Dialogue **Answer:** *Students may say she wants him to be happy, or she may feel like a failure if her son does not marry. It could also be a cultural norm; most younger people in their family and neighborhood are married with families.* **OL**

L1 Literary Element

Figure of Speech **Ask:** What does Thomas mean by the Waverly Ballroom being "loaded with tomatoes"? *(During that era, attractive young women were referred to in slang as "tomatoes.")* **OL**

R2 Reading Strategy

Analyzing Dialogue
Answer: *She knows her sister well and understands the difficulties in living with her. By describing Catherine as someone "nobody wants," she makes it difficult for Marty to say no.*
Ask: What does Marty's response tell you about him? *(Possible answer: He is easy-going and generous.)* **OL**

MOTHER. We gotta ask Marty, of course, because this is his house too. But he's gonna come home any minute now.

VIRGINIA. [*Having mastered her tears.*] That's very nice-a you, Aunt Theresa.

MOTHER. [*Rising.*] Now, you just sit here. I'm just gonna turn onna small fire under the food.

[*She exits into the kitchen.*]

VIRGINIA. [*Calling after her.*] We gotta go right away because I promised the baby sitter we'd be home by six, and it's after six now . . .

[*She kind of fades out. A moment of silence.*]

THOMAS. [*Calling to his aunt in the kitchen.*] How's Marty been lately, Aunt Theresa?

MOTHER. [Off in kitchen.] Oh, he's fine. You know a nice girl he can marry?

[*She comes back into the dining room, wiping her hands on a kitchen towel.*]

I'm worried about him, you know? He's thirty-six years old, gonna be thirty-seven in January.

THOMAS. Oh, he'll get married, don't worry, Aunt Theresa.

MOTHER. [*Sitting down again.*] Well, I don't know. You know a place where he can go where he can find a bride?

THOMAS. The Waverly Ballroom. That's a good place to meet girls, Aunt Theresa. That's a kind of big dance hall, Aunt Theresa. Every Saturday night, it's just loaded with girls. It's a nice place to go. You pay seventy-seven cents. It used to be seventy-seven cents. It must be about a buck and a half now. And you go in and you ask some girl to dance. That's how I met Virginia. Nice, respectable place to meet girls. You tell Marty, Aunt Theresa, you tell
L1 him: "Go to the Waverly Ballroom. It's loaded with tomatoes."[7]

MOTHER. [*Committing the line to memory.*] The Waverly Ballroom. It's loaded with tomatoes.

THOMAS. Right.

VIRGINIA. You tell him, go to the Waverly Ballroom.

[*There is the sound of a door being unlatched off through the kitchen. The* MOTHER *promptly rises.*]

MOTHER. He's here.

[*She hurries into the kitchen. At the porch entrance to the kitchen,* MARTY *has just come in. He is closing the door behind him. He carries his butcher's apron in a bundle under his arm.*]

MARTY. Hello, Ma.

[*She comes up to him, lowers her voice to a whisper.*]

MOTHER. [*Whispers.*] Marty, Thomas and Virginia are here. They had another big fight with your Aunt Catherine. So they ask me, would it be all right if Catherine come to live with us. So I said, all right with me, but we have to ask you. Marty, she's a lonely old lady. Nobody wants her. Everybody's throwing her outta their house . . .

MARTY. Sure Ma, it's okay with me. [*The* MOTHER'S *face breaks into a fond smile. She reaches up and pats his cheek with genuine affection.*]

MOTHER. You gotta good heart. [*Turning and leading the way back to the dining room.* THOMAS *has risen.*] He says okay, it's all right Catherine comes here.

THOMAS. Oh, Marty, thanks a lot. That really takes a load offa my mind.

MARTY. Oh, we got plenny-a room here.

MOTHER. Sure! Sure! It's gonna be nice! It's gonna be nice! I'll come over tonight to your house, and I talk to Catherine, and you see, everything is gonna work out all right.

7. *Tomatoes* is outdated slang for attractive young women.

Reading Strategy Analyzing Dialogue *Why do you think Marty's mother wants him to get married?* **R1**

Reading Strategy Analyzing Dialogue *What does the way she describes her sister say about Marty's mother?* **R2**

Additional Support

Skills Practice

READING: Cause and Effect Cause-and-effect relationships play a role in moving the teleplay from scene to scene. Example: Thomas and Virginia come to the mother with their request. She agrees on the condition that Marty also agrees. Marty does agree, so Aunt Catherine will move into his home. Have students list causes and effects that occur in the first act. Discuss how these relationships connect the events and interactions in the story and allow the audience to predict what may happen next. **OL**

THOMAS. I just wanna thank you people again because the situation was just becoming impossible.

MOTHER. Siddown, Thomas, siddown. All right, Marty, siddown . . .

[She exits into the kitchen. MARTY has taken his seat at the head of the table and is waiting to be served. THOMAS takes a seat around the corner of the table from him and leans across to him.]

THOMAS. You see, Marty, the kinda thing that's been happening in our house is Virginia was inna kitchen making some food for the baby. Well, my mother comes in, and she gets Virginia so nervous, she spills a couple-a drops...

VIRGINIA. *[Tugging at her husband.]* Tommy, we gotta go. I promise the baby sitter six o'clock.

THOMAS. *[Rising without interrupting his narrative.]* So she starts yelling at Virginia, waddaya spilling the milk for. So Virginia gets mad . . .

[His wife is slowly pulling him to the kitchen door.]

She says, "You wanna really see me spill milk?" So Virginia takes the bottle and she throws it against the wall. She's got a real Italian temper, my wife, you know that . . .

[He has been tugged to the kitchen door by now.]

VIRGINIA. Marty, I don't have to tell you how much we appreciate what your mother and you are doing for us.

THOMAS. All right, Marty, I'll see you some other time . . . I'll tell you all about it.

MARTY. I'll see you, Tommy.

[THOMAS disappears into the kitchen after his wife.]

VIRGINIA. *[Off, calling.]* Good-bye, Marty!

MARTY. Good-bye, Virginia! See you soon!

Literary Element Plot *What do you think will be the result of Marty's and his mother's decision?* L2

[He folds his hands on the table before him and waits to be served.

The MOTHER enters from the kitchen. She sets the meat plate down in front of him and herself takes a chair around the corner of the table from him. MARTY without a word takes up his knife and fork and attacks the mountain of food in front of him. His mother sits quietly, her hands a little nervous on the table before her, watching him eat. Then . . .]

MOTHER. So what are you going to do tonight, Marty?

MARTY. I don't know, Ma. I'm all knocked out. I may just hang arounna house.

[The MOTHER nods a couple of times. There is a moment of silence. Then . . .]

MOTHER. Why don't you go to the Waverly Ballroom?

[This gives MARTY a pause. He looks up.]

MARTY. What?

MOTHER. I say, why don't you go to the Waverly Ballroom? It's loaded with tomatoes.

[MARTY regards his mother for a moment.]

MARTY. It's loaded with what?

MOTHER. Tomatoes.

MARTY. *[Snorts.]* Ha! Who told you about the Waverly Ballroom?

MOTHER. Thomas, he told me it was a very nice place.

MARTY. Oh, Thomas. Ma, it's just a big dance hall, and that's all it is. I been there a hundred times. Loaded with tomatoes. Boy, you're funny, Ma. ★

MOTHER. Marty, I don't want you hang arounna house tonight. I want you to go take a shave and go out and dance.

MARTY. Ma, when are you gonna give up? You gotta bachelor on your hands. I ain't never gonna get married.

MOTHER. You gonna get married.

Reading Strategy Analyzing Dialogue *What tone does this sentence have now that it is Marty's mother who is saying it?* R3

Teach

L2 Literary Element

Plot **Answer:** *Students may think this will solve Virginia's and Thomas's problem while creating a new one for Marty and his mother.* OL

R3 Reading Strategy

Analyzing Dialogue
Answer: *It may sound whiny and nagging—or it may simply be amusing because of her use of slang ("tomatoes").* OL

★ Cultural Note

As early as the late nineteenth century, dance halls were a social gathering place for singles. By 1953, when *Marty* is set, rock and roll was becoming popular and the paired-dancing days of the dance hall were disappearing in favor of nonpartnered dances. AS

English Language Coach

Culture and Customs Ask students to share information about the marriage customs in their homelands. Discuss how Marty's bachelorhood at the age of 36 would be perceived in their home culture. EL

Academic Standards
Additional Support activities on pp. 900 and 901 cover the following standards:
Skills Practice: **9.3.3** Analyze interactions between characters...and explain the way those interactions affect the plot.
English Language Coach: **9.3** [Identify] story elements such as...theme...

Teach

BI Big Idea

Awkward Encounters

Answer: *Although up until now he has been mild and good-natured, his frustration and anger come through clearly here.* OL

R Reading Strategy

Analyzing Dialogue

Answer: *Students may suggest that Marty, although frustrated, is still able to find humor in the way his mother phrased her suggestion. He has calmed down.* OL

MARTY. Sooner or later, there comes a point in a man's life when he gotta face some facts, and one fact I gotta face is that whatever it is that women like, I ain't got it. I chased enough girls in my life. I went to enough dances. I got hurt enough. I don't wanna get hurt no more. I just called a girl this afternoon, and I got a real brushoff, boy. I figured I was past the point of being hurt, but that hurt. Some stupid woman who I didn't even wanna call up. She gave me the brush. That's the history of my life. I don't wanna go to the Waverly Ballroom because all that ever happened to me there was girls made me feel like I was a bug. I got feelings, you know. I had enough pain. No, thank you.

MOTHER. Marty . . .

MARTY. Ma, I'm gonna stay home and watch Sid Caesar.

MOTHER. You gonna die without a son.

MARTY. So I'll die without a son.

MOTHER. Put on your blue suit . . .

MARTY. Blue suit, gray suit, I'm still a fat little man. A fat little ugly man.

MOTHER. You not ugly.

MARTY. [*His voice rising.*] I'm ugly . . . I'm ugly! . . . I'm UGLY!

MOTHER. Marty . . .

MARTY. [*Crying aloud, more in anguish than in anger.*] Ma! Leave me alone! . . .

[*He stands abruptly, his face pained and drawn. He makes half-formed gestures to his mother, but he can't find words at the moment. He turns and marches a few paces away, turns to his mother again.*]

MARTY. Ma, waddaya want from me?! Waddaya want from me?! I'm miserable enough as it is! Leave me alone! I'll go to the Waverly Ballroom! I'll put onna blue suit and I'll go! And you know what I'm gonna get for my trouble? Heartache! A big night of heartache!

[*He sullenly marches back to his seat, sits down, picks up his fork, plunges it into the lasagna, and stuffs a mouthful into his mouth; he chews vigorously for a moment. It is impossible to remain angry for long. After a while he is shaking his head and muttering.*]

MARTY. Loaded with tomatoes . . . boy, that's rich . . .

[*He plunges his fork in again. Camera pulls slowly away from him and his mother, who is seated—watching him.*]

Fade out.[8]

8. To *fade out* is to go from a full picture to black in a few seconds.

Big Idea Awkward Encounters *How does this response from Marty affect your perception of him?* BI

Reading Strategy Analyzing Dialogue *What does this bit of dialogue reveal about Marty's mood at this point?* R

Additional Support

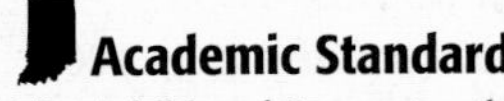

Academic Standards

The Additional Support activity on p. 902 covers the following standard:

Skills Practice: **9.7.6** Analyze the occasion and...choose effective verbal and nonverbal techniques (including voice, gestures, and eye contact) for presentations.

Skills Practice

LISTENING AND SPEAKING: Readers Theater Explain that in Readers Theater, actors read their lines from a script and use their voices and facial expressions to convey emotion. The actors may sit in a semicircle of chairs in front of an audience, or they may walk through the stage directions, using body language to help make the words come alive. Have pairs of students give a Readers Theater performance of the scene between Marty and his mother at the end of Act 1. To prepare for their performance, tell students to read the script silently several times, practice reading the lines aloud, and try to feel what the characters feel. OL

AFTER YOU READ

RESPONDING AND THINKING CRITICALLY

Respond

1. How do you feel about Marty so far? Explain your reasoning.

Recall and Interpret

2. (a)What does Angie suggest that he and Marty do on Saturday night? (b)Why do you think Marty is so unenthusiastic?
3. (a)What is at the root of the conflict between Virginia and Aunt Catherine? (b)What does this tell you about the two women's attitudes toward their roles in the family?
4. (a)How do Marty's responses to the people telling him to get married change over the course of Act 1? (b)What does this reveal about his character?

Analyze and Evaluate

5. How is the first scene in the butcher shop important in establishing the play's characters and plot?
6. What do you think Marty actually thinks about marriage? Support your answer with examples from the text.
7. How would you describe the relationship between Marty and his mother? Base your answer on examples from Act 1.

Connect

8. **Big Idea** **Awkward Encounters** What do you predict will happen in the rest of the play?

LITERARY ANALYSIS

Literary Element Plot

Plots have a general structure. The plot begins with exposition, which introduces the story's characters, setting, and conflicts, or problems. The rising action adds complications that lead to the climax, or turning point. The falling action follows the climax. The resolution, sometimes called the *denouement,* presents the final outcome.

1. What conflicts are introduced in Act 1?
2. Where does the climax of this act occur? What makes this moment so emotional?

Writing About Literature

Respond to Conflict An external conflict is a struggle between a character and an outside force, while an internal conflict takes place within the mind of a character. Write a one- to two-page essay in which you discuss the conflicts that arise in the first act of this play. Are the conflicts external, internal, or both?

LiteratureOnline **Web Activities** For eFlashcards, Selection Quick Checks, and other Web activities, go to www.glencoe.com.

READING AND VOCABULARY

Reading Strategy Analyzing Dialogue

Plays are made up almost entirely of **dialogue.** The conversations between the characters advance the plot, develop theme and characterization, and help create the mood of the work.

1. Identify a point in Act 1 where the dialogue is especially important for the development of characterization. Explain why you chose that point.
2. What mood does the dialogue in Act 1 create?

Vocabulary Practice

Practice with Antonyms Find the antonym for each vocabulary word. Use a dictionary or a thesaurus if you need help.

1. amiability
   a. unfriendliness **b.** pleasantness
2. baleful
   a. threatening **b.** benign
3. contrive
   a. repair **b.** fail
4. effusive
   a. reserved **b.** hysterical

LiteratureOnline

Web Activities Have students access the Web site for interactive activities that will help them assess their understanding of the selection.

Reading Strategy

1. Examples include Marty and Angie in the bar, Marty's phone call, Marty and his mother discussing the Waverly Ballroom.
2. Students may say the dialogue creates a mood of intimacy. The characters argue passionately, creating a tense mood at times.

AFTER YOU READ

Assess

1. Students may feel sympathy for Marty because everyone is pressuring him to marry.
2. (a) Angie suggests that they invite two young women to see a movie. (b) Marty doesn't like the girl, and his dates never work out.
3. (a) Both want to control the household. (b) Both are competing for control.
4. (a) He begins with amiable replies, moves to indifferent shrugs, and finally to an angry outburst at his mother. (b) He is slow to anger.
5. It shows the close-knit community, the cultural concern about marriage, and Marty's patience.
6. He longs to marry ("I wanna get married"). He thinks it is beyond his reach ("whatever it is that women like, I ain't got it").
7. They are close. He wants to tell his mother he is on the way home.
8. Students may predict that Marty will have an awkward encounter on a date.

Literary Element

1. Conflicts: his mother and others pressure him to marry; Aunt Catherine and her daughter-in-law are fighting.
2. Marty's outburst to his mother in which he finally reveals his pain.

Writing About Literature

Remind students to support ideas with text references.

Vocabulary

1. a **2.** b **3.** b **4.** a

BEFORE YOU READ

Focus

Summary

Marty finds himself at the Waverly Ballroom. He has gone there to placate his mother, but he enters into the spirit of the evening. His perseverance pays off when he meets Clara Davis, and they find they share a lot in common.

V Vocabulary

Vocabulary File **Say:** Add these words to your vocabulary file. For each word, include a sentence that gives you an example of how to use the word. **OL** Students with English language needs should include the pronunciations of these words in their files. **EL**

Literary Elements Have students access the Web site to improve their understanding of setting.

CheckPoint

Use the CheckPoint questions on Presentation Plus! to monitor students' comprehension. These questions can be used with interactive response keypads for immediate student feedback.

BEFORE YOU READ *Marty, Act 2*

LITERATURE PREVIEW

Connecting to the Play

Marty's compassion for a young woman in an awkward situation brings him a new friend. Before you read, think about the following questions:

- Have you ever made a good friend in an unexpected situation?
- When you feel hurt or unhappy, does this make you more sensitive toward others who feel the same way?

Building Background

Dancing was very popular with young people during the 1950s. Dances were a common social function, and many new types of dances developed during this decade. The jitterbug, which begins the dance scene in *Marty,* began to be popular in the 1940s. Part of its widespread popularity was due to the simplicity of the step, but teenagers in the 1950s took the dance to new levels of sophistication. The jitterbug, also referred to as the East Coast swing, is danced in pairs to swing music.

One of the most popular group dances during the 1950s was the hand jive. This dance was distinctive because of its various hand movements, which involved slapping the thighs, crossing the palms, pounding the fists, and touching the elbows.

Setting Purposes for Reading

Big Idea Awkward Encounters

As you read, notice the many awkward encounters in Act 2 and how they help move the plot along.

Literary Element Setting

Setting is the time and place in which the events of a literary work occur. The setting also includes the ideas, customs, beliefs, and values of the time and place. As you read Act 2, think about the customs and values that are an important part of this play's setting.

- See Literary Terms Handbook, p. R15.

Literature Online **Interactive Literary Elements Handbook** To review or learn more about the literary elements, go to www.glencoe.com.

READING PREVIEW

Reading Strategy Analyzing Cultural Context

The **cultural context** of a work includes the normal behavior and attitudes of people in a given time and place. In drama, stage directions give information about the setting, characters, and action. This information, combined with details in the dialogue and action of the play, can reveal much about the work's cultural context.

Reading Tip: Taking Notes As you read Act 2, note details about the cultural context of the play.

Detail	What It Reveals
Marty knows his customers.	It is a close-knit Italian community.

Vocabulary

diffidence (dif′ə dəns) *n.* shyness; p. 905 *His natural diffidence made him uneasy about speaking in front of the class.*

nonchalant (non′shə länt′) *adj.* having an air of easy unconcern or indifference; p. 905 *She was nonchalant about losing the election and moved on to the next challenge.*

blatantly (blāt′ ənt lē) *adv.* obviously or conspicuously; p. 907 *The dog barked blatantly in an effort to attract attention.*

imperious (im pēr′ ē əs) *adj.* commanding, dominant; p. 908 *The queen's imperious manner showed that she expected to be obeyed.*

solicitude (sə lis′ ə to͞od′) *n.* care or concern; p. 908 *His solicitude for his friend's health led him to visit her often.*

Vocabulary Tip: Context Clues Look at the information around an unfamiliar word for clues that can help you figure out its meaning.

INDIANA ACADEMIC STANDARDS (pages 904–915)
9.3 [Identify] story elements such as...setting...
9.3.12 [Relate] a work to its historical period.
9.4.6 Synthesize information from multiple sources...

Selection Skills

Marty, Act Two

Literary Elements
- Setting (SE pp. 904–915)
- Characterization (TWE p. 908)

Vocabulary Skills
- Context Clues (SE pp. 904, 915)

Reading Skills
- Analyzing Cultural Context (SE pp. 904–915)
- Sequence (TWE p. 910)
- Author's Purpose (TWE p. 912)

Listening/Speaking/Viewing Skills
- Analyzing Art (SE p. 906; TWE pp. 909, 912)

Writing Skills/Grammar
- Pamphlet (SE p. 915)
- Using *Who* and *Whom* (TWE p. 906)

Study Skills/Research/Assessment
- Short Response (TWE p. 914)

Act Two

[*Fade in: Exterior, three-story building. Pan*[1] *up to second floor . . . bright neon lights reading "Waverly Ballroom". . . The large, dirty windows are open; and the sound of a fair-to-middling swing band whooping it up comes out.*

Dissolve to: Interior, Waverly Ballroom—large dance floor crowded with jitterbugging couples, eight-piece combination hitting a loud kick. Ballroom is vaguely dark, made so by papier-mâché over the chandeliers to create alleged romantic effect. The walls are lined with stags[2] *and waiting girls, singly and in small murmuring groups. Noise and mumble and drone.*

Dissolve to: Live shot—a row of stags along a wall. Camera is looking lengthwise down the row. Camera dollies slowly past each face, each staring out at the ★ *dance floor, watching in his own manner of hungry eagerness. Short, fat, tall, thin stags. Some pretend* ***diffidence****. Some exhibit patent hunger.*

Near the end of the line, we find MARTY *and* ANGIE *freshly shaved and groomed. They are leaning against the wall, watching their more fortunate brethren out on the floor.*]

ANGIE. Not a bad crowd tonight, you know?

MARTY. There was one nice-looking one there in a black dress and beads, but she was a little tall for me.

ANGIE. [*Looking down past* MARTY *along the wall right into the camera.*] There's a nice-looking little short one for you right now.

MARTY. [*Following his gaze.*] Where?

ANGIE. Down there. That little one there.

[*The camera cuts*[3] *about eight faces down, to where the girls are now standing. Two are against the wall. One is facing them, with her back to the dance floor. This last is the one* ANGIE *has in mind. She is a cute little kid, about twenty, and she has a bright smile on—as if the other two girls are just amusing her to death.*]

MARTY. Yeah, she looks all right from here.

ANGIE. Well, go on over and ask her. You don't hurry up, somebody else'll grab her.

[MARTY *scowls, shrugs.*]

MARTY. Okay, let's go.

[*They slouch along past the eight stags, a picture of* ***nonchalant*** *unconcern. The three girls, aware of their approach, stiffen, and their chatter comes to a halt.* ANGIE *advances to one of the girls along the wall.*]

ANGIE. Waddaya say, you wanna dance?

[*The girl looks surprised—as if this were an extraordinary invitation to receive in this place—looks confounded at her two friends, shrugs, detaches herself from the group, moves to the outer fringe of the pack of dancers, raises her hand languidly to dancing position, and awaits* ANGIE *with ineffable*[4] *boredom.* MARTY, *smiling shyly, addresses the short girl.*]

MARTY. Excuse me, would you care for this dance?

[*The short girl gives* MARTY *a quick glance of appraisal,*[5] *then looks quickly at her remaining friend.*]

1. To *pan* is to move a camera so as to get a sweeping view or follow a moving subject.
2. Here, a *stag* is a single man without a companion.
3. To *cut* is to change scenes without using an optical effect, such as a dissolve or fade.
4. *Ineffable* means "incapable of being expressed in words."
5. *Appraisal* means "judgment" or "evaluation."

Literary Element Setting *What atmosphere is created by this description?* **L**

Reading Strategy Analyzing Cultural Context *Why might the girl respond in this way?* **R**

Vocabulary

diffidence (dif′ə dəns) *n.* shyness

Vocabulary

nonchalant (non′shə länt′) *adj.* having an air of easy unconcern or indifference

Teach

L Literary Element

Setting Answer: *Although the ballroom sounds like a depressing place, the people who are there make it seem lively and more attractive.* **OL**

R Reading Strategy

Analyzing Cultural Context
Answer: *The girl may not have been impressed with Angie's casual tone, or she may have wanted to act as if it didn't matter. She may also have wanted to show her friends that she is not interested in Angie and is only dancing with him because he asked her.* **OL**

★ Writer's Technique

Setting The author creates emotional tension in the ballroom without having the characters use any dialogue. He uses the camera to take close-up shots of the young men. Each face shows an emotion—eagerness, hunger, anticipation, or seeming indifference. **AS**

English Language Coach

Cultural Context Explain the social purpose of a place like the Waverly Ballroom in the context of the 1950s culture in the United States. Ask students to share how young single people meet in their homeland's culture. **EL**

Building Reading Fluency

Dramatic Reading Discuss with students how tone of voice can enrich the meaning of spoken words. Have students work in small groups to prepare a dramatic reading of Act 2. Allow time for students to present their interpretations to the class. **BL**

Academic Standards

Additional Support activities on p. 905 cover the following standards:

English Language Coach: **9.3** [Identify] story elements such as…theme…

Building Reading Fluency: **9.7.6** Analyze the occasion and the interests of the audience and choose effective verbal…techniques (including voice…) for presentations.

Teach

R1 Reading Strategy

Analyzing Dialogue **Ask:** What is the young man's problem? *(Possible answer: He met an attractive girl, and he wants to get rid of his current date because she is not as pretty.)* OL

★ Viewing the Art

Scottish painter and printmaker Willie Rodger (1930–) uses techniques such as woodcut and linocut (using linoleum instead of wood) to make his prints. In addition to his printmaking, Rodger teaches, illustrates, designs stained glass, and works in pen, ink, and oil. His work is often characterized by humor. **Answer:** *The ballroom in the play is dark whereas the one in the painting is brightly lit. In the play, the dance floor is crowded with dancing couples, whereas in the painting, more people are standing along the edges than dancing.* AS

I Remember My First School Dance. Willie Rodger. Oil on board, 76.2 x 76.2 cm. Private collection.

Viewing the Art: How is the scene pictured here similar to and different from the one described in the play? ★

SHORT GIRL. [*Not unpleasantly.*] Sorry. I just don't feel like dancing just yet.

MARTY. Sure.

[*He turns and moves back past the eight stags, all of whom have covertly watched his attempt. He finds his old niche by the wall, leans there. A moment later he looks guardedly down to where the short girl and her friend are. A young, dapper boy is approaching the short girl. He asks her to dance. The short girl smiles, excuses herself to her friend, and follows the boy out onto the floor.* MARTY *turns back to watching the dancers bleakly. A moment later he is aware that someone on his right is talking to him. . . . He turns his head. It is a young man of about twenty-eight.*]

MARTY. You say something to me?

YOUNG MAN. Yeah. I was just asking you if you was here stag or with a girl.

MARTY. I'm stag.

YOUNG MAN. Well, I'll tell you. I got stuck onna blind date with a dog, and I just picked up a nice chick, and I was wondering how I'm gonna get ridda the dog. Somebody to take her home, you know what I mean? I be glad to pay you five bucks if you take the dog home for me. R1

MARTY. [*A little confused.*] What?

YOUNG MAN. I'll take you over, and I'll introduce you as an old army buddy of mine, and then I'll cut out. Because I got this chick waiting for me out by the hatcheck, and I'll pay you five bucks.

Additional Support

Skills Practice

GRAMMAR AND LANGUAGE:

Using *Who* and *Whom* Clarify that *who* is the subject of a sentence or clause; *whom* is an object. Write these sentences on the board and discuss the answers.

1. (Who, Whom) did the young man want to leave at the dance? *(Whom)*
2. (Who, Whom) follows the girl out onto the fire escape? *(Who)*
3. With (who, whom) is Marty dancing? *(whom)*
4. (Who, Whom) is asking to speak with Catherine? *(Who)*

Ask students to use *who* and *whom* in four new sentences. Have students check each other's work. OL

MARTY. [*Stares at the* YOUNG MAN.] Are you kidding?

YOUNG MAN. No, I'm not kidding.

MARTY. You can't just walk off onna girl like that.

[*The* YOUNG MAN *grimaces impatiently and moves down the line of stags. . . .* MARTY *watches him, still a little shocked at the proposition. About two stags down, the* YOUNG MAN *broaches his plan to another* STAG. *This* STAG, *frowning and pursing his lips, seems more receptive to the idea. . . . The* YOUNG MAN *takes out a wallet and gives the* STAG *a five-dollar bill. The* STAG *detaches himself from the wall and, a little ill at ease, follows the* YOUNG MAN *back past* MARTY *and into the lounge.* MARTY *pauses a moment and then, concerned, walks to the archway that separates the lounge from the ballroom and looks in.*

The lounge is a narrow room with a bar and booths. In contrast to the ballroom, it is brightly lighted—causing MARTY *to squint.*

In the second booth from the archway sits a GIRL, *about twenty-eight. Despite the careful grooming that she has put into her cosmetics, she is* ***blatantly*** *plain. The* YOUNG MAN *and the* STAG *are standing, talking to her. She is looking up at the* YOUNG MAN, *her hands nervously gripping her Coca-Cola glass. We cannot hear what the* YOUNG MAN *is saying, but it is apparent that he is introducing his new-found army buddy and is going through some cock-and-bull story about being called away on an emergency. The* STAG *is presented as her escort-to-be, who will see to it that she gets home safely. The* GIRL *apparently is not taken in at all by this, though she is trying hard not to seem affected.*

R2

She politely rejects the STAG'S *company and will get home by herself, thanks for asking anyway. The* YOUNG MAN *makes a few mild protestations and then he and the* STAG *leave the booth and come back to the archway from where* MARTY *has been watching the scene. As they pass* MARTY, *we overhear a snatch of dialogue.*]

YOUNG MAN. . . . In that case, as long as she's going home alone, give me the five bucks back . . .

STAG. . . . Look, Mac, you paid me five bucks. I was willing. It's my five bucks . . .

[*They pass on.* MARTY *returns his attention to the* GIRL. *She is still sitting as she was, gripping and ungripping the glass of soda in front of her. Her eyes are closed. Then, with a little nervous shake of her head, she gets out of the booth and stands—momentarily at a loss for what to do next. The open fire doors leading out onto the large fire escape catch her eye. She crosses to the fire escape, nervous, frowning, and disappears outside.* R3

MARTY *stares after her, then slowly shuffles to the open fire-escape doorway. It is a large fire escape, almost the size of a small balcony. The* GIRL *is standing by the railing, her back to the doorway, her head sunk on her bosom. For a moment* MARTY *is unaware that she is crying. Then he notices the shivering tremors running through her body and the quivering shoulders. He moves a step onto the fire escape. He tries to think of something to say.*]

MARTY. Excuse me, Miss. Would you care to dance?

[*The* GIRL *slowly turns to him, her face streaked with tears, her lip trembling. Then, in one of those peculiar moments of simultaneous impulse, she lurches to* MARTY *with a sob, and* MARTY *takes her to him. For a moment they stand in an awkward embrace,* MARTY *a little embarrassed, looking out through the doors to the lounge, wondering if anybody is seeing them. Reaching back with one hand, he closes the fire doors, and then, replacing the hand around her shoulder, he stands stiffly, allowing her to cry on his chest.*

Big Idea Awkward Encounters *What does this encounter tell you about Marty?* **BI1**

Vocabulary

blatantly (blāt′ ənt lē) *adv.* obviously or conspicuously

Big Idea Awkward Encounters *Do you think Marty says the right thing to the young woman?* **BI2**

Teach

BI1 Big Idea

Awkward Encounters
Answer: *He is a gentleman and has a code of conduct about how to treat a woman properly.* **OL**

R2 Reading Strategy

Evaluate Ask: What is your reaction to the way the girl handles the situation? *(Some students may think she made the better choice by saying she would be able to get home on her own rather than going with a stranger.)* **OL**

R3 Reading Strategy

Make an Inference Ask: Why does the girl go out onto the fire escape? *(Possible answers: She is upset about being abandoned by her date; she feels embarrassed and wants to get away from the people in the ballroom; she needs time to be alone to calm down.)* **OL**

BI2 Big Idea

Awkward Encounters
Answer: *Answers will vary but students may agree that Marty said the right thing in order not to come on as trying to invade her privacy.* **OL**

English Language Coach

Building Vocabulary Help English language learners determine the meanings of unfamiliar words from context clues. Have students work with a fluent English speaker to find the meaning of *proposition, broaches, pursing,* and *protestation.* **EL**

Differentiated Instruction

Understanding Characterization Students may achieve a deeper understanding of the selection by identifying words that describe the traits of each character. Have students create a list of characters in Act 2. Have students write down words that they associate with each character. **BL**

Academic Standards

Additional Support activities on pp. 906 and 907 cover the following standards:

Skills Practice: **9.6.2** Demonstrate an understanding of...proper English usage...

English Language Coach: **9.1** Use...context clues...to determine the meaning of words...

Differentiated Instruction: **9.3** [Identify] story elements such as character...

Teach

R1 Reading Strategy

Analyzing Cultural Context **Answer:** *It shows that Virginia will make an effort to give the grandmother a sense of importance, and that even though she doesn't want to live with her, she respects her and doesn't want to hurt her feelings. The fact that she asks the mother to speak to Aunt Catherine shows that the two of them are close.* OL

R2 Reading Strategy

Predict **Ask:** Do you think the mother will have an easy time convincing Catherine to move out of Thomas's house? *(Possible answer: It will not be easy because Catherine is tough and embittered about life.)* OL

R3 Reading Strategy

Making Inferences **Ask:** Why might Catherine be suspicious of Virginia's solicitude? *(Possible answer: They have been arguing and generally do not get along.)* OL

L Literary Element

Setting **Answer:** *It calls attention to how out of place Aunt Catherine is. The heavy, old-fashioned chair that is her place is at odds with the rest of the modern apartment.* OL

Dissolve to: Exterior, apartment door. The MOTHER *is standing, in a black coat and a hat with a little feather, waiting for her ring to be answered. The door opens.* VIRGINIA *stands framed in the doorway.*]

VIRGINIA. Hello, Aunt Theresa, come in.

[*The* MOTHER *goes into the small foyer.* VIRGINIA *closes the door.*]

MOTHER. [*In a low voice, as she pulls her coat off.*] Is Catherine here?

VIRGINIA. [*Helps her off with coat, nods—also in a low voice.*] We didn't tell her nothing yet. We thought we'd leave it to you. We thought you'd put it like how you were lonely, and why don't she come to live with you. Because that way it looks like she's doing you a favor, insteada we're throwing her out, and it won't be so cruel on her. Thomas is downstairs with the neighbors . . . I'll go call him.

MOTHER. You go downstairs to the neighbors and stay there with Thomas.

VIRGINIA. Wouldn't it be better if we were here?

MOTHER. You go downstairs. I talk to
R2 Catherine alone. Otherwise, she's gonna start a fight with you.

[*A shrill,* **imperious** *woman's voice from an offstage room suddenly breaks into the muttered conference in the foyer.*]

AUNT. [*Off.*] Who's there?! Who's there?!

[*The* MOTHER *heads up the foyer to the living room, followed by* VIRGINIA, *holding the* MOTHER'S *coat.*]

MOTHER. [*Calls back.*] It's me, Catherine! How you feel?

[*At the end of the foyer, the two sisters meet. The* AUNT *is a spare, gaunt woman with a face carved out of granite. Tough, embittered, deeply hurt type of face.*]

AUNT. Hey! What are you doing here? R3

MOTHER. I came to see you. [*The two sisters quickly embrace and release each other.*] How you feel?

AUNT. I gotta pain in my left side, and my leg throbs like a drum.

MOTHER. I been getting pains in my shoulder.

AUNT. I got pains in my shoulder, too. I have a pain in my hip, and my right arm aches so much I can't sleep. It's a curse to be old. How you feel?

MOTHER. I feel fine.

AUNT. That's nice.

[*Now that the standard greetings are over,* AUNT CATHERINE *abruptly turns and goes back to her chair. It is obviously her chair. It is an old, heavy oaken chair with thick armrests. The rest of the apartment is furnished in what is known as "modern"—a piece from* House Beautiful *here, a piece from* Better Homes and Gardens *there.* AUNT CATHERINE *sits, erect and forbidding, in her chair. The* MOTHER *seats herself with a sigh in a neighboring chair.* VIRGINIA, *having hung the* MOTHER'S *coat, now turns to the two older women. A pause.*]

VIRGINIA. I'm going downstairs to the Cappacini's. I'll be up inna little while.

[AUNT CATHERINE *nods expressionlessly.* VIRGINIA *looks at her for a moment, then impulsively crosses to her mother-in-law.*]

VIRGINIA. You feel all right?

[*The old lady looks up warily, suspicious of this sudden* **solicitude**.]

AUNT. I'm all right.

[VIRGINIA *nods and goes off to the foyer. The two old sisters sit, unmoving, waiting for*

Reading Strategy Analyzing Cultural Context *What does this suggestion say about the family members' relationships with one another?* R1

Vocabulary

imperious (im pēr′ ē əs) *adj.* commanding, dominant

Literary Element Setting *How do the contrasts in this setting mirror the situation in the house?* L

Vocabulary

solicitude (sə lis′ ə to͞od′) *n.* care or concern

Additional Support

Skills Practice

LITERARY ELEMENT: Characterization The author reveals several aspects of the mother's personality through dialogue and stage directions. She can be loving, smothering, concerned, and fearful. Ask students to create a chart to show the mother's positive and negative traits. Students should be prepared to support their opinions with evidence from the teleplay. Then tell students to write a character description based on their charts. OL *the door to close behind* VIRGINIA. *Then the* MOTHER *addresses herself to* AUNT CATHERINE.]

MOTHER. We gotta post card from my son, Nickie, and his bride this morning. They're in Florida inna big hotel. Everything is very nice.

AUNT. That's nice.

MOTHER. Catherine, I want you come live with me in my house with Marty and me. In my house, you have your own room. You don't have to sleep onna couch inna living room like here.

[*The* AUNT *looks slowly and directly at the* MOTHER.]

Catherine, your son is married. He got his own home. Leave him in peace. He wants to be alone with his wife. They don't want no old lady sitting inna balcony. Come and live with me. We will cook in the kitchen and talk like when we were girls. You are dear to me, and you are dear to Marty. We are pleased for you to come.

AUNT. Did they come to see you?

MOTHER. Yes.

AUNT. Did my son Thomas come with her?

MOTHER. Your son Thomas was there.

AUNT. Did he also say he wishes to cast his mother from his house?

MOTHER. Catherine, don't make an opera outta this. The three-a you anna baby live in three skinny rooms. You are an old goat, and she has an Italian temper. She is a good girl, but you drive her crazy. Leave them alone. They have their own life.

[*The old* AUNT *turns her head slowly and looks her sister square in the face. Then she rises slowly from her chair.*]

AUNT. [*Coldly.*] Get outta here. This is my son's house. This is where I live. I am not to be cast out inna street like a newspaper.

Reading Strategy Analyzing Cultural Context *What does this tell you about where widows with grown children usually live in this community?* **R4**

[*The* MOTHER *likewise rises. The two old women face each other directly.*]

MOTHER. Catherine, you are very dear to me. We have cried many times together. When my husband died, I would have gone insane if it were not for you. I ask you to come to my house because I can make you happy. Please come to my house.

[*The two sisters regard each other. Then* AUNT CATHERINE *sits again in her oaken chair, and the* MOTHER *returns to her seat. The hardened muscles in the old* AUNT'S *face suddenly slacken, and she turns to her sister.*]

AUNT. Theresa, what shall become of me?

MOTHER. Catherine . . .

AUNT. It's gonna happen to you. Mark it well. These terrible years. I'm afraida look inna mirror. I'm afraid I'm gonna see an old lady with white hair, like the old ladies inna park, little bundles inna black shawl, waiting for the coffin. I'm fifty-six years old. What

Man and Woman Dancing. Sandra Speidel. 

Teach

R4 Reading Strategy

Analyzing Cultural Context

Answer: *Aunt Catherine's reaction shows that she would expect to live with her son and his family for the rest of her life. She is very hurt by the idea that he could wish his own mother out of the house.* **OL**

Viewing the Art

Sandra Speidel is a contemporary artist who has always loved to draw. When she was a child, she filled the pages of the scribble pads that her mother gave her. As an adult, Speidel went to art school, where she studied illustration, drawing, and painting. For more than fifteen years, she has worked as an illustrator. She has illustrated children's books and has created advertisements for several different companies. **AS**

English Language Coach

Writing for Many Cultures Have small groups explore ideas about how literature can speak to readers of many cultures.

Ask: What cultures and generations are represented in this play? What universal themes are presented? **EL**

Building Reading Fluency

Dramatic Reading Have students work in small groups to prepare a dramatic reading of Act 2. Allow time for students to present their interpretations to the class. **BL**

Academic Standards

Additional Support activities on pp. 908 and 909 cover the following standards:

Skills Practice: **9.3** [Identify] story elements such as character… **9.5.2** Write responses to literature that demonstrate a comprehensive grasp of the significant ideas of literary works…

English Language Coach: **9.7.17** Deliver oral responses to literature that support…ideas and viewpoints through…references to the text and to other works…

Building Reading Fluency: **9.7** [Develop] speaking skills…in conjunction with…strategies…[for] delivery of oral presentations.

Teach

R1 Reading Strategy

Analyzing Cultural Context
Answer: *This statement reflects an old-fashioned attitude of a time when a woman's usefulness was often defined by keeping house and caring for children.* OL

BI1 Big Idea

Awkward Encounters
Answer: *Despite all her nagging for him to get married, it is something she secretly dreads because she fears being alone and would be in the same situation as Aunt Catherine.* OL

R2 Reading Strategy

Analyzing Cultural Context
Answer: *The girl sits passively, waiting to be asked to dance, and she feels miserable because no one asks her. Meanwhile, Marty has to go around and ask girls who usually refuse. It seems to always be the man who asks the woman to dance, although in this case, both feel rejected.* OL

BI2 Big Idea

Awkward Encounters
Answer: *They both are having a good time and feel comfortable with each other.* OL

am I to do with myself? I have strength in my hands. I wanna cook. I wanna clean. I wanna make dinner for my children. I wanna be of use to somebody. Am I an old dog to lie in fronta the fire till my eyes close? These are terrible years, Theresa! Terrible years!

MOTHER. Catherine, my sister . . . [The old *AUNT* stares, distraught, at the *MOTHER*.]

AUNT. It's gonna happen to you! It's gonna happen to you! What will you do if Marty gets married?! What will you cook?! What happen to alla children tumbling in alla rooms?! Where is the noise?! It is a curse to be a widow! A curse! What will you do if Marty gets married?! What will you do?!

[*She stares at the MOTHER—her deep, gaunt, eyes haggard and pained. The MOTHER stares back for a moment, then her own eyes close. The AUNT has hit home. The AUNT sinks back onto her chair, sitting stiffly, her arms on the thick armrests. The MOTHER sits hunched a little forward, her hands nervously folded in her lap.*]

AUNT. [*Quietly.*] I will put my clothes inna bag and I will come to you tomorrow.

[*The camera slowly dollies back from the two somber sisters.*

Slow fade out.

Cut to: Close-up, intimate. MARTY and the GIRL dancing cheek to cheek. Occasionally, the heads of other couples slowly waft across the camera view, temporarily blocking out view of MARTY and the GIRL. Camera stays with them as the slow dance carries them around the floor. Tender scene.]

GIRL. . . . The last time I was here, the same sort of thing happened.

MARTY. Yeah?

GIRL. Well, not exactly the same thing. The last time I was up here about four months ago. Do you see that girl in the gray dress sitting over there?

MARTY. Yeah.

GIRL. That's where I sat. I sat there for an hour and a half without moving a muscle. Now and then, some fellow would sort of walk up to me and then change his mind. I just sat there, my hands in my lap. Well, about ten o'clock, a bunch of kids came in swaggering. They weren't more than seventeen, eighteen years old. Well, they swaggered down along the wall, leering at all the girls. I thought they were kind of cute . . . and as they passed me, I smiled at them. One of the kids looked at me and said: "Forget it, ugly, you ain't gotta chance." I burst out crying. I'm a big crier, you know.

MARTY. So am I.

GIRL. And another time when I was in college . . .

MARTY. I cry alla time. Any little thing. I can recognize pain a mile away. My brothers, my brother-in-laws, they're always telling me what a good-hearted guy I am. Well, you don't get good-hearted by accident. You get kicked around long enough you get to be a real professor of pain. I know exactly how you feel. And I also want you to know I'm having a very good time with you now and really enjoying myself. So you see, you're not such a dog as you think you are.

GIRL. I'm having a very good time too.

MARTY. So there you are. So I guess I'm not such a dog as I think I am.

Reading Strategy Analyzing Cultural Context *How does Aunt Catherine's statement reflect the time in which the play was written?* R1

Big Idea Awkward Encounters *What feelings does the mother's reaction reveal?* BI1

Reading Strategy Analyzing Cultural Context *Compare and contrast the young woman's experience at dances with Marty's.* R2

Big Idea Awkward Encounters *How is this awkward encounter different from earlier ones for both characters?* BI2

Additional Support

Skills Practice

READING: Sequence The play moves between a main storyline and a subplot, signaled by stage directions and setting. Some students may find the transitions confusing. Ask students to draw a sequencing chart that has a line for the main plot: "Marty's Search for Love," and a line for the subplot: "What To Do About Aunt Catherine." Have students add to the sequence of events in each storyline, beginning with Act 1, continuing into Act 2, and ending with Act 3. OL

GIRL. You're a very nice guy, and I don't know why some girl hasn't grabbed you off long ago.

MARTY. I don't know either. I think I'm a very nice guy. I also think I'm a pretty smart guy in my own way.

GIRL. I think you are.

MARTY. I'll tell you some of my wisdom which I thunk up on those nights when I got stood up, and nights like that, and you walk home thinking: "Watsa matter with me? I can't be that ugly." Well, I figure, two people get married, and they gonna live together forty, fifty years. So it's just gotta be more than whether they're good-looking or not. My father was a real ugly man, but my mother adored him. She told me that she used to get so miserable sometimes, like everybody, you know? And she says my father always tried to understand. I used to see them sometimes when I was a kid, sitting in the living room, talking and talking, and I used to adore my old man because he was so kind. That's one of the most beautiful things I have in my life, the way my father and my mother were. And my father was a real ugly man. So it don't matter if you look like a gorilla. So you see, dogs like us, we ain't such dogs as we think we are. **L1**

[They dance silently for a moment, cheeks pressed against each other. Close-ups of each face.]

GIRL. I'm twenty-nine years old. How old are you?

MARTY. Thirty-six.

[They dance silently, closely. Occasionally the heads of other couples sway in front of the camera, blocking our view of MARTY and the GIRL. Slow, sweet dissolve.

Dissolve to: Interior, kitchen. MARTY'S home. Later that night. It is dark. Nobody is home. The rear porch door now opens, and the silhouettes of MARTY and the GIRL appear—blocking up the doorway.]

MARTY. Wait a minute. Lemme find the light.

[He finds the light. The kitchen is suddenly brightly lit. The two of them stand squinting to adjust to the sudden glare.]

MARTY. I guess my mother ain't home yet. I figure my cousin Thomas and Virginia musta gone to the movies, so they won't get back till one o'clock, at least.

[The GIRL has advanced into the kitchen, a little ill at ease, and is looking around. MARTY closes the porch door.]

MARTY. This is the kitchen.

GIRL. Yes, I know.

[MARTY leads the way into the dining room.]

MARTY. Come on inna dining room. *[He turns on the light in there as he goes. The GIRL follows him in.]* Siddown, take off your coat. You want something to eat? We gotta whole halfa chicken left over from yesterday.

GIRL. *[Perching tentatively on the edge of a chair.]* No, thank you. I don't think I should stay very long.

MARTY. Sure. Just take off your coat a minute.

[He helps her off with her coat and stands for a moment behind her, looking down at her. Conscious of his scrutiny, she sits uncomfortably. MARTY takes her coat into the dark living room. The GIRL sits patiently, nervously. MARTY comes back, sits down on another chair. Awkward silence.]

MARTY. So I was telling you, my kid brother Nickie got married last Sunday . . . That was a very nice affair. And they had this statue of some woman. I never saw anything so grand in my life. *[The silence falls between them again.]* And watta meal. I'm a butcher, so I know a good hunka steak when I see one. That was choice fillet, right off the toppa the chuck. A buck-eighty a pound. Of course, if you wanna cheaper cut, get rib steak. That

Literary Element Setting *How does the change in light emphasize the change in setting?* **L2**

Reading Strategy Analyzing Cultural Context *Why do you think the young woman seems a bit uneasy at this point?* **R3**

Teach

L1 Literary Element

Setting Ask: What is the effect of Marty's description of this scene? *(Possible answers: His memory of his parents adds tenderness; it gives insight into Marty and what he values in relationships.)* **OL**

L2 Literary Element

Setting Answer: *The sudden brightness is a metaphor for bringing their relationship out of the dreamy darkness of the ballroom and into the harsh light of the kitchen.* **OL**

R3 Reading Strategy

Analyzing Cultural Context
Answer: *She finds herself alone in the home of a single man she has just met. Such a situation was considered socially improper at that time.* **OL**

English Language Coach

Formal Versus Informal English
Write *Formal English* and *Informal English* on the board, and ask English learners to suggest examples for each category. The two categories roughly correspond to written English (formal) and spoken English (informal). Understanding the slang, jargon, and idioms of informal English may be challenging. Review the informal English found in Act 2. Have students list each example and use it in a sentence. Suggest students add other words and phrases to their lists as they read. **EL**

Academic Standards
Additional Support activities on pp. 910 and 911 cover the following standards:

Skills Practice: **9.3.6** Analyze and trace an author's development of time and sequence...

English Language Coach: **9.1.2** Distinguish between what words mean literally and what they imply and interpret what the words imply.

Teach

Viewing the Art

Nicolai N. Yakovenko (1920–) is a Russian-born painter. **Ask:** How would you describe the young woman in this painting? Explain. *(Most students will say the woman is happy and excited. Her smile, posture, and the glowing colors all support this answer.)* **AS**

The Dance, 1954. Nicolai N. Yakovenko. Oil on canvas, 36.1 x 34.6 cm. Springville Museum of Art, Utah.

gotta lotta waste on it, but it comes to about a buck and a quarter a pound, if it's trimmed. Listen, Clara, make yourself comfortable. You're all tense.

GIRL. Oh, I'm fine.

MARTY. You want me to take you home, I'll take you home.

GIRL. Maybe that would be a good idea.

[She stands. He stands, frowning, a little angry—turns sullenly and goes back into the living room for her coat. She stands unhappily. He comes back and wordlessly starts to help her into her coat. He stands behind her, his hands on her shoulders. He suddenly seizes her, begins kissing her on the neck. Camera comes up quickly to intensely intimate close-up, nothing but the heads. The dialogue drops to quick, hushed whispers.]

GIRL. No, Marty, please . . .

MARTY. I like you, I like you, I been telling you all night I like you…

GIRL. Marty…

MARTY. I just wanna kiss, that's all…

[He tries to turn her face to him. She resists.]

GIRL. No . . .

MARTY. Please . . .

GIRL. No . . .

MARTY. Please . . .

GIRL. Marty . . .

[He suddenly releases her, turns away violently.]

MARTY. *[Crying out.]* All right! I'll take you home! All right! *[He marches a few angry paces away, deeply disturbed. Turns to her.]* All I wanted was a lousy kiss! What am I, a leper or something?!

Additional Support

Skills Practice

READING: Author's Purpose Have students reread the close of Act 2. Discuss the mother's physical reaction to the realization of what Marty's marrying might mean to her. *(She remains standing, her body is rigid; her eyes are open wide and she is staring straight ahead; there is fear in her eyes.)*

Ask: What might be the author's purpose for ending Act 2 in this manner? *(It creates dramatic tension. The mother has been prodding Marty to get married, but now the thought frightens her because she does not want to be left alone.)* **OL**

[*He turns and goes off into the living room to hide the flush of hot tears threatening to fill his eyes. The* GIRL *stands, herself on the verge of tears.*]

GIRL. [*Mutters, more to herself than to him.*] I just didn't feel like it, that's all.

[*She moves slowly to the archway leading to the living room.* MARTY *is sitting on the couch, hands in his lap, looking straight ahead. The room is dark except for the overcast of the dining-room light reaching in. The* GIRL *goes to the couch, perches on the edge beside him. He doesn't look at her.*]

MARTY. Well, that's the history of my life. I'm a little short, fat, ugly guy. Comes New Year's Eve, everybody starts arranging parties, I'm the guy they gotta dig up a date for. I'm old enough to know better. I'll take you home.

[*He starts to rise but doesn't . . . sinks back into the couch, looking straight ahead. The* GIRL *looks at him, her face peculiarly soft and compassionate.*]

GIRL. I'd like to see you again, very much. The reason I didn't let you kiss me was because I just didn't know how to handle the situation. You're the kindest man I ever met. The reason I tell you this is because I want to see you again very much. Maybe, I'm just so desperate to fall in love that I'm trying too hard. But I know that when you take me home, I'm going to just lie on my bed and think about you. I want very much to see you again.

[MARTY *stares down at his hands in his lap.*]

MARTY. [*Without looking at her.*] Waddaya doing tomorrow night?

GIRL. Nothing.

MARTY. I'll call you up tomorrow morning. Maybe we'll go see a movie.

GIRL. I'd like that very much.

MARTY. The reason I can't be definite about it now is my Aunt Catherine is probably coming over tomorrow, and I may have to help out.

GIRL. I'll wait for your call.

MARTY. We better get started to your house because the buses only run about one an hour now.

GIRL. All right.

[*She stands. They start to walk to the dining room. In the archway,* MARTY *pauses, turns to the* GIRL.]

MARTY. Waddaya doing New Year's Eve?

GIRL. Nothing.

[*They quietly slip into each other's arms and kiss. Slowly their faces part, and* MARTY'S *head sinks down upon her shoulder. He is crying. His shoulders shake slightly. The* GIRL *presses her cheek against the back of his head. They stand. . . . There is the sound of the rear porch door being unlatched. They both start from their embrace. A moment later the* MOTHER'S *voice is heard off in the kitchen.*]

MOTHER. Hallo! Hallo, Marty? [*She comes into the dining room, stops at the sight of the* GIRL.] Hallo, Marty, when you come home?

MARTY. We just got here about fifteen minutes ago, Ma. Ma, I want you to meet Miss Clara Davis. She's a graduate of New York University. She teaches history in Benjamin Franklin High School.

[*This seems to impress the* MOTHER.]

MOTHER. Siddown, siddown. You want some chicken? We got some chicken in the icebox.

GIRL. No, Mrs. Pilletti, we were just going home. Thank you very much anyway.

MOTHER. Well, siddown a minute. I just come inna house. I'll take off my coat. Siddown a minute.

[*She pulls her coat off.*]

Big Idea Awkward Encounters *Why do you think both Marty and Clara are upset?* **BI**

Literary Element Setting *How does the setting mirror the mood of the scene at this point?* **L**

Reading Strategy Analyzing Cultural Context *Why do you think Marty shares these details?* **R**

Teach

BI Big Idea

Awkward Encounters

Answer: *Students may say that they both seem to like each other and want the evening to go well and are bothered by the fact that they want different things at this moment. Marty is hurt that the girl doesn't want to kiss him, while she is upset that he has misunderstood her refusal to do so.* **OL**

L Literary Element

Setting **Answer:** *The darkness and the awkward positioning of the characters call attention to their estrangement at this moment and create a somewhat melancholy mood.* **OL**

R Reading Strategy

Analyzing Cultural Context

Possible answer: *He wants his mother to be impressed with Clara because he likes her.* **OL**

English Language Coach

Cultural Context Ask English language learners to discuss their reactions to Clara's discomfort at being alone with Marty. Ask students to share dating and courtship customs in their homeland. **EL**

Differentiated Instruction

Character Conflict Explore the interactions of the mother and Clara as the characters discuss Aunt Catherine's situation. Ask students to consider these questions in their discussion. What are the conflicting perspectives? Why do the two women view this situation differently? **AL**

Academic Standards

Additional Support activities on pp. 912 and 913 cover the following standards:

Skills Practice: **9.2.8** Make reasonable statements and draw conclusions about a text, supporting them with accurate examples.

English Language Coach: **9.3** [Identify] story elements such as character…

Differentiated Instruction: **9.3.3** Analyze interactions between characters…and explain the way those interactions affect the plot.

Teach

BI Big Idea

Awkward Encounters

Answer: *After encouraging the prospective daughter-in-law to stay and chat, Mother realizes that she is a prospective mother-in-law. She may be displaced herself one day.* OL

R Reading Strategy

Analyzing Cultural Context

Answer: *The younger characters are not as concerned with tradition. They want to go their own ways in life without being bound so much to their older relatives.* OL

MARTY. How'd you come home, Ma? Thomas give you a ride?

[*The* MOTHER *nods.*]

MOTHER. Oh, it's a sad business, a sad business.

[*She sits down on a dining-room chair, holding her coat in her lap. She turns to the* GIRL, *who likewise sits.*]

MOTHER. My sister Catherine, she don't get along with her daughter-in-law, so she's gonna come live with us.

MARTY. Oh, she's coming, eh, Ma?

MOTHER. Oh, sure. [*To the* GIRL.] It's a very sad thing. A woman, fifty-six years old, all her life, she had her own home. Now, she's just an old lady, sleeping on her daughter-in-law's couch. It's a curse to be a mother, I tell you. Your children grow up, and then what is left for you to do? What is a mother's life but her children? It is a very cruel thing when your son has no place for you in his home.

GIRL. Couldn't she find some sort of hobby to fill out her time?

MOTHER. Hobby! What can she do? She cooks and she cleans. You gotta have a house to clean. You gotta have children to cook for. These are the terrible years for a woman, the terrible years.

GIRL. You mustn't feel too harshly against her daughter-in-law. She also wants to have a house to clean and a family to cook for.

[*The* MOTHER *darts a quick, sharp look at the* GIRL*—then looks back to her hands, which are beginning to twist nervously.*]

MOTHER. You don't think my sister Catherine should live in her daughter-in-law's house?

GIRL. Well, I don't know the people, of course, but, as a rule, I don't think a mother-in-law should live with a young couple.

MOTHER. Where do you think a mother-in-law should go?

GIRL. I don't think a mother should depend so much upon her children for her rewards in life.

MOTHER. That what it says in the book in New York University. You wait till you are a mother. It don't work out that way.

GIRL. Well, it's silly for me to argue about it. I don't know the people involved.

MARTY. Ma, I'm gonna take her home now. It's getting late, and the buses only run about one an hour.

MOTHER. [*Standing.*] Sure.

[*The* GIRL *stands.*]

GIRL. It was very nice meeting you, Mrs. Pilletti. I hope I'll see you again.

MOTHER. Sure.

[*MARTY and the* GIRL *move to the kitchen.*]

MARTY. All right, Ma. I'll be back in about an hour.

MOTHER. Sure.

GIRL. Good night, Mrs. Pilletti.

MOTHER. Good night.

[*MARTY and the* GIRL *exit into the kitchen. The* MOTHER *stands, expressionless, by her chair watching them go. She remains standing rigidly even after the porch door can be heard being opened and shut. The camera moves up to a close-up of the* MOTHER. *Her eyes are wide. She is staring straight ahead. There is fear in her eyes.*

Fade out.]

Big Idea Awkward Encounters *How has this conversation suddenly taken an uncomfortable turn for Marty's mother?* BI

Reading Strategy Analyzing Cultural Context *What tension has been set up between the younger and older characters in the play?* R

Additional Support

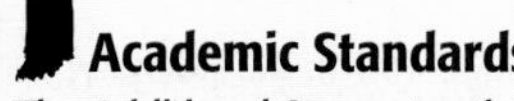

Academic Standards

The Additional Support activity on p. 914 covers the following standard:

Skills Practice: **9.5.2** Write responses to literature that support statements with evidence from the text…

Skills Practice

TEST PREPARATION: Short Response Short-response questions may require a response in which the writer must take a position.

Ask: What would be your reaction to having Aunt Catherine move in with you? Ask students to write their answers using 3–5 lines. *(Possible positions: I would not want her to live in my home. She likes to be in charge and complains a lot. She would cause a lot of tension and unpleasantness. OR Catherine has nowhere else to go. I'm not home much so I might allow her to move in. She would be better off with me than in her son's home.)* OL

AFTER YOU READ

RESPONDING AND THINKING CRITICALLY

Respond

1. What is your response to the developments in Act 2? Have your feelings toward any of the characters changed? Explain.

Recall and Interpret

2. (a)What is Marty's response when the man says he will pay him five dollars to take his date home? (b)Why do you think Marty decides to follow the man?
3. (a)What does Aunt Catherine decide to do after her talk with Marty's mother? (b)Why do you think she finally makes this choice?
4. (a)How does Marty's mother's attitude toward Clara change over the course of the last scene? (b)What does this tell you about her expectations?

Analyze and Evaluate

5. (a)How would you describe the way Marty's mother talks to Aunt Catherine about moving in with her? (b)What does this reveal about their relationship?
6. (a)How do Marty and Clara interact at the dance? (b)How is this different from the way that most other people interact there?
7. Based on what he says in this act, what does Marty consider most important in a relationship?

Connect

8. **Big Idea** **Awkward Encounters** What do you think is at the root of the awkwardness between Marty and Clara when he takes her to his house?

LITERARY ANALYSIS

Literary Element Setting

The **setting** of a literary work often helps create a specific mood, or emotional quality.

1. Give several details from one of the settings in this act and tell how they help create a mood.
2. When Clara steps out on the fire escape at the Waverly Ballroom, how does the new setting reflect her feelings?

Learning for Life

Research situations and cultures in which parents and their adult children live together, as in *Marty.* Prepare a pamphlet in which you list the advantages and disadvantages of such arrangements. Cite expert sources in your pamphlet.

Literature Online **Web Activities** For eFlashcards, Selection Quick Checks, and other Web activities, go to www.glencoe.com.

READING AND VOCABULARY

Reading Strategy Analyzing Cultural Context

The **cultural context** of a literary work is reflected not only in the setting but also in the way the characters speak, act, and think.

1. How does knowing the time period in which *Marty* takes place affect the way you think about the play?
2. How might a play written today on the same subject be different?

Vocabulary Practice

Practice with Context Clues Use context clues to determine the meaning of each boldfaced word.

1. He made an effort to appear **nonchalant** and act as if the news did not bother him.
   a. unconcerned **b.** pleased **c.** brave
2. By dyeing her hair pink, she **blatantly** attempted to stand out.
   a. commonly **b.** obviously **c.** futilely
3. His **solicitude** for her well-being was heightened by his regard for her.
   a. concern **b.** involvement **c.** difficulty

AFTER YOU READ

Assess

1. The mother and aunt may be more sympathetic characters. Students should explain why their feelings have changed.
2. (a) He is horrified and refuses to go along with it. (b) He feels compassion for the girl because of his similar situation.
3. (a) She agrees to move. (b) Perhaps she feels a bond with her sister and thinks she will be better off living with someone in a similar situation.
4. (a) The mother is friendly at first but becomes cool. (b) She fears Marty might marry the girl, and her own life may change.
5. (a) She is direct and tells her sister the situation as she sees it. (b) They have been through a lot together; they express their opinions freely.
6. (a) They are sincere; they have a serious and honest conversation. (b) The others flirt and play games.
7. He values the compassion and understanding his father showed his mother.
8. Neither has much experience dating, so each is unsure.

Literary Element

1. Students may refer to the ballroom scenes or the scenes at Marty's home. They should support their choice with details that establish mood.
2. She is alone on the fire escape; this reflects her loneliness.

Learning for Life

Encourage students to use at least three sources on the Internet and in the library for their research.

Reading Strategy

1. It provides insight into the characters and their actions.
2. Contrasts between the culture then and now would affect the story.

Vocabulary

1. a **2.** b **3.** a

Literature Online

Web Activities Have students access the Web site for interactive activities that will help them assess their understanding of the selection.

BEFORE YOU READ

Focus

Summary

Marty is feeling pleased with himself after meeting Clara. He plans to call her again. One by one, his mother and his friends critique her and find her lacking. Marty is in danger of caving in to their criticism until he realizes Clara means a lot to him. He follows his heart and gives her a call.

V Vocabulary

Vocabulary File **Say:** Add these words to your vocabulary file. For each word, include a sentence that gives you an example of how to use the word. **OL** Students with English language needs should include the pronunciations of these words in their files. **EL**

Literary Elements Have students access the Web site to improve their understanding of character.

BEFORE YOU READ *Marty, Act 3*

LITERATURE PREVIEW

Connecting to the Play

Marty's joy over the young woman he has met causes him to act differently, and he begins to see certain aspects of his life in a new way. Before you read, think about a positive interaction or relationship that has given you a new perspective on life.

- How do you feel after a job well done?
- What moment in your life could be seen as an important turning point?

Building Background

In the 1950s, literature reflected post-World War II optimism, as well as anxiety about Communism and new conflicts. As advances were made in science and technology, science fiction enjoyed a boom in the 1950s.

Mickey Spillane, the writer discussed in this act of *Marty,* was one of the most popular fiction writers of the decade. He wrote thriller detective novels featuring Mike Hammer, a tough, patriotic detective that many Americans found compelling and comforting in an age of uncertainty.

Setting Purposes for Reading

Big Idea Awkward Encounters

As you read, notice the awkwardness that the characters experience when their expectations for each other clash.

Literary Element Character

A **character** is a person portrayed in a literary work. A main character is central to the story and is usually fully developed. Minor characters generally display fewer personality traits and are used to help drive the plot.

- See Literary Terms Handbook, p. R3.

LiteratureOnline **Interactive Literary Elements Handbook** To review or learn more about the literary elements, go to www.glencoe.com.

READING PREVIEW

Reading Strategy Analyzing Characterization

Characterization is the methods the writer uses to reveal the personality of a character. One method is to create a character foil, a character whose traits contrast with those of another character, usually a main character. By using a foil, a writer calls attention to the strengths or weaknesses of a main character. As you read Act 3, notice how Chayefsky uses Angie as a foil for Marty. Are there any other foils in the play?

Reading Tip: Taking Notes Use a chart to record details about the use of foils in Act 3.

Character	Foil	Details
Marty	Angie	disagree about Clara

Vocabulary

conspiratorial (kən spir′ ə tôr′ ē əl) *adj.* suggesting a secret plot or plan; p. 917 *The spies hatched their conspiratorial plan to overthrow the government the night before the president took office.*

ebulliently (i bul′ yent lē) *adv.* with overflowing enthusiasm; p. 918 *The hostess ebulliently greeted the guests, hugging everyone and smiling warmly.*

résumé (rez′ oo mā′) *n.* a listing of one's accomplishments; a summary; p. 919 *In his oral presentation, Jonas gave a résumé of all the events in the film.*

Vocabulary Tip: Word Origins Many words in English have their origins in other languages, such as Greek or Latin. For example, the word *drama* comes from the Greek *dran,* meaning "to do" or "to act." Knowing the origins of words can help you figure out the meanings of unfamiliar words that have similar word parts.

INDIANA ACADEMIC STANDARDS (pages 916–925)

9.3.3 Analyze interactions between characters…
9.3.4 Determine characters' traits by…dialogue…
9.7.8 Compare and contrast…media genres…
9.5.3 Write…analytical essays…

Selection Skills

Marty, Act Three

Literary Elements
- Character (SE pp. 916–924)
- Stage Directions (SE p. 924)

Reading Skills
- Analyzing Characterization (SE pp. 916–924)

Vocabulary Skills
- Word Origins (SE pp. 916, 924)
- Academic Vocabulary (SE p. 924)

Listening/Speaking/Viewing Skills
- Analyzing Art (SE p. 919; TWE p. 921)
- Visual Literacy (SE p. 923)

Writing Skills/Grammar
- Analysis of Genre Elements (SE p. 925)
- Using Dialect (SE p. 925)
- Plot Summary (TWE p. 920)

Study Skills/Research/Assessment
- Historical Context (TWE p. 918)
- Short Response (TWE p. 922)

ACT THREE

L1 [*Fade in: Film—close-up of church bells clanging away. Pan down church to see typical Sunday morning, people going up the steps of a church and entering. It is a beautiful June morning.*

Dissolve to: Interior, MARTY'S *bedroom—sun fairly streaming through the curtains.* MARTY *is standing in front of his bureau, slipping his arms into a clean, white shirt. He is freshly shaved and groomed. Through the doorway of his bedroom we can see the* MOTHER *in the dining room, in coat and hat, all set to go to Mass,*[1] *taking the last breakfast plates away and carrying them into the kitchen. The camera moves across the living room into the dining room. The* MOTHER *comes out of the kitchen with a paper napkin and begins crumbing the table.*

There is knock on the rear porch door. The MOTHER *leaves her crumbing and goes into the kitchen. Camera goes with her. She opens the rear door to admit* AUNT CATHERINE, *holding a worn old European carpetbag. The* AUNT *starts to go deeper into the kitchen, but the* MOTHER *stays her with her hand.*]

MOTHER. [*In low,* ***conspiratorial*** *voice.*] Hey, I come home from your house last night, Marty was here with a girl.

AUNT. Who?

MOTHER. Marty.

AUNT. Your son Marty?

MOTHER. Well, what Marty you think is gonna be here in this house with a girl?

AUNT. Were the lights on?

MOTHER. Oh, sure. [*Frowns suddenly at her sister.*] The girl is a college graduate.

AUNT. They're the worst. College girls are one step from the streets. They smoke like men inna saloon.

[*The* AUNT *puts her carpetbag down and sits on one of the wooden kitchen chairs. The* MOTHER *sits on another.*]

MOTHER. That's the first time Marty ever brought a girl to this house. She seems like a nice girl. I think he has a feeling for this girl.

[*At this moment a burst of spirited whistling emanates from* MARTY'S *bedroom. Cut to:* MARTY'S *bedroom—*MARTY *standing in front of his mirror, buttoning his shirt or adjusting his tie, whistling a gay tune.*

Cut back to: The two sisters, both their faces turned in the direction of the whistling. The whistling abruptly stops. The two sisters look at each other. The AUNT *shrugs.*]

MOTHER. He been whistling like that all morning.

[*The* AUNT *nods bleakly.*]

AUNT. He is bewitched. You will see. Today, tomorrow, inna week, he's gonna say to you: "Hey, Ma, it's no good being a single man. I'm tired running around." Then he's gonna say: "Hey, Ma, wadda we need this old house? Why don't we sell this old house, move into a nicer parta town? A nice little apartment?"

MOTHER. I don't sell this house, I tell you that. This is my husband's house, and I had six children in this house.

AUNT. You will see. A couple-a months, you gonna be an old lady, sleeping onna couch in your daughter-in-law's house.

MOTHER. Catherine, you are a blanket of gloom. Wherever you go, the rain follows.

---

1. *Mass* is a Catholic church service.

Literary Element Character *What does this question tell you about what Aunt Catherine thinks of Marty?* L2

Vocabulary

conspiratorial (kən spir′ ə tôr′ ē əl) *adj.* suggesting a secret plot or plan

Reading Strategy Analyzing Characterization *Why do you think Chayefsky consistently portrays Aunt Catherine as gloomy?* R

Teach

L1 Literary Element

Setting Ask: How does the author use setting to establish day and time? *(Possible answer: The camera shows people entering a church, and bells are ringing. Students may assume it is a Sunday morning.)* OL

L2 Literary Element

Character Answer: *She considers it very much out of character for him to bring a date to the house.* OL

R Reading Strategy

Analyzing Characterization
Answer: *Students may say Catherine is portrayed as a "blanket of gloom" as a foil for Marty's mother—or to warn her of what she may become.* OL

CheckPoint

Use the CheckPoint questions on Presentation Plus! to monitor students' comprehension. These questions can be used with interactive response keypads for immediate student feedback.

English Language Coach

Dialects Over the years, technological advances such as the telephone, radio, television, and personal computer have reduced the differences in dialects across the country. Invite students to examine regional differences in American English. Ask them to provide examples of words that are pronounced differently in various regions of the United States. Have students share their findings. EL

Academic Standards

The Additional Support activity on p. 917 covers the following standard:

English Language Coach: **9.7.15** Deliver expository presentations that convey information and ideas from…sources accurately and coherently…

Teach

L1 Literary Element

Character Answer: *Marty's energetic, optimistic tone is completely different from the discouraged and insecure attitude he had before he met Clara.* OL

BI Big Idea

Awkward Encounters

Answer: *No. She has been influenced by her sister's situation. She now realizes that she may lose her home if Marty marries.* OL

Some day, you gonna smile, and we gonna declare a holiday.

[*Another burst of spirited whistling comes from* MARTY, *off. It comes closer, and* MARTY *now enters in splendid spirits, whistling away. He is slipping into his jacket.*]

MARTY. [*Ebulliently.*] Hello, Aunt Catherine! How are you? You going to Mass with us?

AUNT. I was at Mass two hours ago.

MARTY. Well, make yourself at home. The refrigerator is loaded with food. Go upstairs, take any room you want. It's beautiful outside, aint' it?

AUNT. There's a chill. Watch out, you catch a good cold and pneumonia.

MOTHER. My sister Catherine, she can't even admit it's a beautiful day.

[MARTY*—now at the sink, getting himself a glass of water—is examining a piece of plaster that has fallen from the ceiling.*]

MARTY. [*Examining the chunk of plaster in his palm.*] Boy, this place is really coming to pieces. [*Turns to* MOTHER.] You know, Ma, I think, sometime we oughtta sell this place. The plumbing is rusty—everything. I'm gonna have to replaster that whole ceiling now. I think we oughtta get a little apartment somewheres in a nicer parta town . . . You all set, Ma?

MOTHER. I'm all set.

[*She starts for the porch door. She slowly turns and looks at* MARTY, *and then at* AUNT CATHERINE*—who returns her look.* MOTHER *and* MARTY *exit.*

Literary Element Character *How does Marty's behavior here compare with his behavior earlier in the play?* L1

Vocabulary

ebulliently (i bul′ yent lē) *adv.* with overflowing enthusiasm

Dissolve to: Church. The MOTHER *comes out of the doors and down a few steps to where* MARTY *is standing, enjoying the clearness of the June morning.*]

MOTHER. In a couple-a minutes nine o'clock Mass is gonna start—in a couple-a minutes . . . [*To passers-by off.*] hallo, hallo . . . [*To* MARTY.] Well, that was a nice girl last night, Marty. That was a nice girl.

MARTY. Yeah.

MOTHER. She wasn't a very good-looking girl, but she look like a nice girl. I said, she wasn't a very good-looking girl, not very pretty.

MARTY. I heard you, Ma.

MOTHER. She look a little old for you, about thirty-five, forty years old?

MARTY. She's twenny-nine, Ma.

MOTHER. She's more than twenny-nine years old, Marty. That's what she tells you. She looks thirty-five, forty. She didn't look Italian to me. I said, is she an Italian girl?

MARTY. I don't know. I don't think so.

MOTHER. She don't look like Italian to me. What kinda family she come from? There was something about her I don't like. It seems funny, the first time you meet her she comes to your empty house alone. These college girls, they all one step from the streets.

[MARTY *turns, frowning, to his* MOTHER.]

MARTY. What are you talkin' about? She's a nice girl.

MOTHER. I don't like her.

MARTY. You don't like her? You only met her for two minutes.

MOTHER. Don't bring her to the house no more.

MARTY. What didn't you like about her?

Big Idea Awkward Encounter *Would Marty's mother have said this in Act 1? If not, what has changed?* BI

Additional Support

Skills Practice

RESEARCH: Historical Context

Students may better understand *Marty* if they are familiar with the culture and customs of Italian families living in Little Italy in New York City in the 1950s. Have students check the school library and Internet sites to learn background information about Italian and Italian-American culture. Have them compare what they learn to the customs and behavior of the characters in *Marty.* OL

The Butcher's Shop, Chulmleigh, 2000. Valerie Barden. Oil on board. 30.5 x 45.7 cm. Private collection.
Viewing the Art: How do the colors in this painting affect its mood? Does the mood of the painting match the mood of Act 3? Explain. ★

MOTHER. I don't know! She don't look like Italian to me, plenty nice Italian girls around.

MARTY. Well, let's not get into a fight about it, Ma. I just met the girl. I probably won't see her again. [*MARTY leaves frame.*[2]]

MOTHER. Eh, I'm no better than my sister Catherine.

[*Dissolve to: Interior, the bar . . . about an hour later. The after-Mass crowd is there, about six men ranging from twenty to forty. A couple of women in the booths. One woman is gently rocking a baby carriage.*

Sitting in the booth of Act 1 are ANGIE and three other fellows, ages twenty, thirty-two, and forty. One of the fellows, aged thirty-two, is giving a critical **résumé** *of a recent work of literature by Mickey Spillane.*]

CRITIC. . . . So the whole book winds up, Mike Hammer, he's inna room there with this doll.[3] So he says: "You rat, you are the murderer." So she begins to con him, you know? She tells him how she loves him. And then Bam! He shoots her in the stomach. So she's laying there, gasping for breath, and she says: "How could you do that?" And he says: "It was easy."

2. The *frame* is the part of the scene shown by the camera at a particular moment.

3. Here, *doll* is slang for woman.

Literary Element Character *What does this admission tell you about the mother's conscience?* L2

Vocabulary

résumé (rez′ oo mā′) *n.* a listing of one's accomplishments; a summary

Teach

L2 Literary Element

Character Answer: *She realizes she is acting out of fear for her future rather than in Marty's best interest.* OL

★ Viewing the Art

Contemporary English artist Valerie Barden's work is characterized by rich use of color contrasted with mundane surroundings, such as everyday street scenes.

Answer: *The bright colors in the painting convey a happy mood, which is the prevailing sentiment expressed by Marty in this part of the play.* AS

Building Reading Fluency

Small-Group Activity Encourage groups to prepare a dramatic reading of the scene that takes place in the barroom. Have groups practice reading their parts so they are comfortable with the dialect and can read the dialogue with proper expression. BL

Differentiated Instruction

Reading Focus Give students a question to answer as they read. This will strengthen their ability to focus on specific aspects of the selection. They may also improve their general comprehension of the work. BL

Academic Standards

Additional Support activities on pp. 918 and 919 cover the following standards:

Skills Practice: **9.2.4** Synthesize the content from several sources or works. . . **9.3.12** Analyze the way in which a work. . . is related to. . . issues of its historical period.

Building Reading Fluency: **9.7** [Develop] speaking skills. . . in conjunction with. . . strategies. . . [for] delivery of oral presentations.

Differentiated Instruction: **9.2** Develop strategies such as asking questions. . .

Teach

R1 Reading Strategy

Make an Inference Ask: Why is Angie keeping a watchful eye out for Marty? *(Possible answer: Visiting the neighborhood bar after Mass might be a routine activity for the friends.)* OL

L1 Literary Element

Character Ask: What does Angie's remark reveal about his feelings? *(He may sense that Marty is changing; he may be worried that Marty has new interests that don't include him.)* OL

R2 Reading Strategy

Analyzing Characterization

Answer: *Students may say that this description is accurate because Marty and Angie bond through their mutual loneliness. They spend every weekend together trying to think of something to do.* OL

L2 Literary Element

Character Answer: *He adds to the conflict by suggesting that he couldn't stand to marry an ugly girl. His comment, on top of the discouragement Marty gets from the other characters, emphasizes how everyone—even the most minor character—opposes him on the subject of Clara.* OL

TWENTY-YEAR-OLD. Boy, that Mickey Spillane. Boy, he can write.

ANGIE. [*Leaning out of the booth and looking down the length of the bar, says with some* R1 *irritation.*] What's keeping Marty?

CRITIC. What I like about Mickey Spillane is he knows how to handle women. In one book, he picks up a tomato who gets hit with a car, and she throws a pass[4] at him. And then he meets two beautiful twins, and they throw passes at him. And then he meets some beautiful society leader, and she throws a pass at him, and . . .

TWENTY-YEAR-OLD. Boy, that Mickey Spillane, he sure can write . . .

ANGIE. [*Looking out, down the bar again.*] I L1 don't know watsa matter with Marty.

FORTY-YEAR-OLD. Boy, Angie, what would you do if Marty ever died? You'd die right with him. A couple-a old bachelors hanging to each other like barnacles.[5] There's Marty now.

[*ANGIE leans out of the booth.*]

ANGIE. [*Calling out.*] Hello, Marty, where you been?

[*Cut to: Front end of the bar. MARTY has just come in. He waves back to ANGIE, acknowledges another hello from a man by the bar, goes over to the bar, and gets the bartender's attention.*]

MARTY. Hello, Lou, gimme change of a half and put a dime in it for a telephone call.

[*The BARTENDER takes the half dollar, reaches into his apron pocket for the change.*]

BARTENDER. I hear you was at the Waverly Ballroom last night.

MARTY. Yeah. Angie tell you?

BARTENDER. [*Picking out change from palm full of silver.*] Yeah, I hear you really got stuck with a dog.

[*MARTY looks at him.*]

MARTY. She wasn't so bad.

BARTENDER. [*Extending the change.*] Angie says she was a real scrawny-looking thing. Well, you can't have good luck alla time.

[*MARTY takes the change slowly and frowns down at it. He moves down the bar and would make for the telephone booth, but ANGIE hails him from the booth.*]

ANGIE. Who you gonna call, Marty?

MARTY. I was gonna call that girl from last night, take her to a movie tonight.

ANGIE. Are you kidding?

MARTY. She was a nice girl. I kinda liked her.

ANGIE. [*Indicating the spot in the booth vacated by the FORTY-YEAR-OLD.*] Siddown. You can call her later.

[*MARTY pauses, frowning, and then shuffles to the booth where ANGIE and the other two sit. The CRITIC moves over for MARTY. There is an exchange of hellos.*]

TWENTY-YEAR-OLD. I gotta girl, she's always asking me to marry her. So I look at that face, and I say to myself: "Could I stand looking at that face for the resta my life?"

CRITIC. Hey, Marty, you ever read a book called *I, the Jury* by Mickey Spillane?

MARTY. No.

ANGIE. Listen, Marty, I gotta good place for us to go tonight. The kid here, he says, he was downna bazaar at Our Lady of Angels last night and . . .

MARTY. I don't feel like going to the bazaar, Angie. I thought I'd take this girl to a movie.

ANGIE. Boy, you really musta made out good last night.

---

4. Here, *throws a pass* is slang for "makes a suggestive proposal."
5. *Barnacles* are marine crustaceans that cling tightly to rocks, boat hulls, driftwood, other objects, seaweed, or the bodies of large sea creatures, such as whales.

Reading Strategy Analyzing Characterization *Do you agree with this description of Marty and Angie? Why or why not?* R2

Literary Element Character *What purpose does this minor character serve in this scene?* L2

Additional Support

Skills Practice

WRITING: Plot Summary Have students review the main plot, subplot, and the main characters in Acts 1 and 2. Ask them to recall the main ideas and supporting details. Tell students to write a plot summary of the play so far. They should assume their summaries will be read by someone unfamiliar with *Marty.* Remind students to pay attention to verb tenses and transition words in their summaries to ensure that readers know the sequence in which events occurred. OL

Couple, 1982. Harold Stevenson. Mixed Media. Chisholm Gallery, West Palm Beach, Florida. 

MARTY. We just talked.

ANGIE. Boy, she must be some talker. She musta been about fifty years old.

CRITIC. I always figger a guy oughtta marry a girl who's twenny years younger than he is, so that when he's forty, his wife is a real nice-looking doll.

TWENTY-YEAR-OLD. That means he'd have to marry the girl when she was one year old.

CRITIC. I never thoughta that.

MARTY. I didn't think she was so bad-looking.

ANGIE. She musta kept you inna shadows all night.

CRITIC. Marty, you don't wanna hang around with dogs. It gives you a bad reputation.

ANGIE. Marty, let's go downna bazaar.

MARTY. I told this dog I was gonna call her today.

ANGIE. Brush her.

[*MARTY looks questioningly at ANGIE.*]

MARTY. You didn't like her at all?

ANGIE. A nothing. A real nothing. [*MARTY looks down at the dime he has been nervously turning between two fingers and then, frowning, he slips it into his jacket pocket. He lowers his face and looks down, scowling at his thoughts. Around him, the voices clip along.*] R4

Reading Strategy Characterization *How is Angie used as a foil to Marty here?* R3

Big Idea Awkward Encounters *What thoughts might Marty be struggling with at this moment?* BI

Teach

R3 Reading Strategy

Analyzing Characterization

Answer: *Angie appears superficial throughout this scene. His reaction to Clara serves as a contrast to Marty's more sensitive perspective.* OL

R4 Reading Strategy

Analyzing Characterization

Ask: Why might Angie make cruel remarks about Clara? *(Possible answer: He wants to find out how much Marty likes her; he is envious of his friend's good fortune; he does not want to lose Marty's companionship.)* OL

BI Big Idea

Awkward Encounters

Answer: *Marty may be debating what to do. He may be disturbed that his friends are so negative about Clara based on her appearance.* OL

Viewing the Art

Oklahoma-born artist Harold Stevenson (1929–) has been challenging the art world with his provocative figures for five decades. Stevenson meshes many styles to create his artwork. AS

English Language Coach

Interpreting Dialogue English learners may better follow the scene if they review the dialogue as they read. Pair English language learners with English speakers. Ask them to answer these questions:

- What are the young men discussing? *(how a man should choose a bride and why she should be younger than the groom)*
- What is the purpose of the conversation between Marty and Angie? *(Angie makes Marty hesitate before he tries to see Clara again.)* EL

Academic Standards

Additional Support activities on pp. 920 and 921 cover the following standards:

Skills Practice: **9.5.2** Write responses to literature that demonstrate a comprehensive grasp of the significant ideas of literary works [and] support statements with evidence from the text…

English Language Coach: **9.2.8** Make reasonable statements and draw conclusions about a text, supporting them with accurate examples.

Teach

L Literary Element

Character **Answer:** *Marty shows more passion and decisiveness here than he has throughout the play. His friends' derision has helped him realize that his values are different from theirs.* OL

R Reading Strategy

Analyzing Characterization
Answer: *Marty teases Angie with the same comments he heard in the butcher shop. Students may say that they see a new side of Marty because he can now make jokes and is hopeful about his new relationship.* OL

CheckPoint

Use the CheckPoint questions on Presentation Plus! to check students' mastery of the selection. These questions can be used with interactive response keypads for immediate student feedback.

CRITIC. What's playing on Fordham Road? I think there's a good picture in the Loew's Paradise.

ANGIE. Let's go down to Forty-second Street and walk around. We're sure to wind up with something.

[*Slowly* MARTY *begins to look up again. He looks from face to face as each speaks.*]

CRITIC. I'll never forgive LaGuardia[6] for cutting burlesque outta New York City.

TWENTY-YEAR-OLD. There's burlesque over in Union City. Let's go to Union City . . .

ANGIE. Ah, they're always crowded on Sunday night.

CRITIC. So wadda you figure on doing tonight, Angie?

ANGIE. I don't know. Wadda you figure on doing?

CRITIC. I don't know [Turns to the *TWENTY-YEAR-OLD.*] Wadda you figure on doing?

[*The* TWENTY-YEAR-OLD *shrugs. Suddenly* MARTY *brings his fist down on the booth table with a crash. The others turn, startled, toward him.* MARTY *rises in his seat.*]

MARTY. "What are you doing tonight?" "I don't know, what are you doing?" Burlesque! Loew's Paradise! Miserable and lonely! Miserable and lonely and stupid! What am I, crazy or something?! I got something good! What am I hanging around with you guys for?!

[*He has said this in tones so loud that it attracts the attention of everyone in the bar. A little embarrassed,* MARTY *turns and moves quickly to the phone booth, pausing outside the door to find his dime again.* ANGIE *is out of his seat immediately and hurries after him.*]

ANGIE. [*A little shocked at* MARTY'S *outburst.*] Watsa matter with you?

MARTY. [*In a low, intense voice.*] You don't like her. My mother don't like her. She's a dog, and I'm a fat, ugly little man. All I know is, I had a good time last night. I'm gonna have a good time tonight. If we have enough good times together, I'm going down on my knees and beg that girl to marry me. If we make a party again this New Year's, I gotta date for the party. You don't like her, that's too bad. [*He moves into the booth, sits, turns again to* ANGIE, *smiles.*]

When you gonna get married, Angie? You're thirty-four years old. All your kid brothers are married. You oughtta be ashamed of yourself.

[*Still smiling at his private joke, he puts the dime into the slot and then—with a determined finger—he begins to dial.*

Fade out.]

6. *Fiorello LaGuardia,* mayor of New York City from 1934 to 1945, vowed when elected to "clean house and clean it thoroughly."

Literary Element Character *How does this outburst reveal a change in Marty?* L

Reading Strategy Analyzing Characterization *How does this echo the opening scene of the play? Does this reveal a new side of Marty?* R

Additional Support

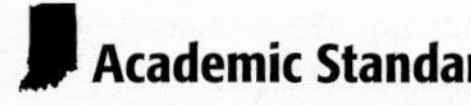

Academic Standards

The Additional Support activity on p. 922 covers the following standard:

Skills Practice: **9.5.2** Write responses to literature that demonstrate a comprehensive grasp of the significant ideas of literary works…

Skills Practice

TEST PREPARATION: Short Response
Explain that short-response questions often do not have one correct answer. An answer is judged by its insight and the quality of textual evidence.
Write on the board: Explain how and why the Mother and Angie respond to the news that Marty has met a girl. Ask students to write their answers using 3–5 lines. *(Possible answer: They find fault with her and urge Marty not to pursue the relationship. Mother is afraid she will be forced out of her home. Angie is afraid he will lose Marty's friendship.)* OL

AFTER YOU READ

RESPONDING AND THINKING CRITICALLY

Respond

1. Did you find the ending of the play satisfying? Why or why not?

Recall and Interpret

2. (a)What does Marty say to his mother that is exactly what Aunt Catherine predicted he would say? (b)How does this affect his mother and Aunt Catherine?
3. (a)How does Marty's mother speak about Clara when she talks with Marty after church? (b)Why do you think she has this attitude toward the young woman?
4. (a)How does Marty react to his friends when they try to discourage him from seeing Clara again? (b)What do you think is the main reason behind this reaction?

Analyze and Evaluate

5. What elements of the setting at the beginning of this act reflect a change in the mood, or emotional quality, of the play?
6. (a)What actions of Marty's friends during the scene in the bar affect your impression of them? (b)Did those actions make you see them in a different way from before?
7. How does Marty change over the course of the play?

Connect

8. **Big Idea** **Awkward Encounters** Which encounter in this act strikes you as the most awkward? Why?

VISUAL LITERACY: Graphic Organizer

Character Development

For each main character in the play, create a web diagram to show how his or her character develops over the course of the play. Begin by writing the character's name in the center of the page. In circles around the name, write ways in which his or her character develops throughout the three acts. In the outermost circles, provide reasons why each development occurs. The example shows a web that has been started for Marty.

Group Activity Discuss the following questions with classmates. Cite evidence from *Marty* for support.

1. Which character in the play changes the most? Explain.
2. What is an example of a way in which one character influences another to change in this play?

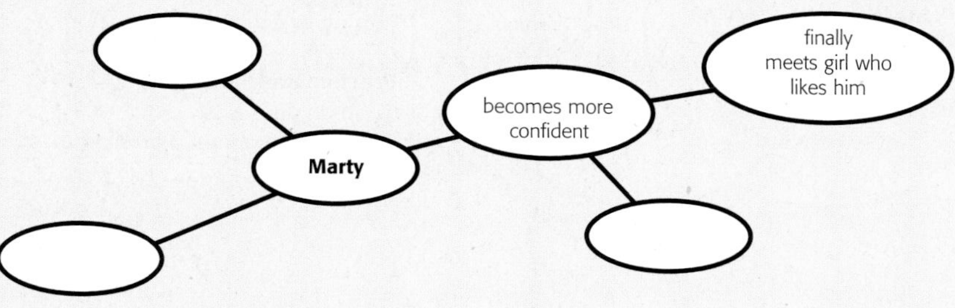

Visual Literacy

1. Students may say Marty, his mother, or Clara changes most. They should support answers with examples from the text.
2. Students may say Marty and Clara build each other's self-confidence, Marty's mother convinces Aunt Catherine to get over her resentment toward her daughter-in-law and come live with her, or the aunt causes the mother to be negative about Marty's new relationship.

AFTER YOU READ

Assess

1. Some students may find it satisfying because Marty decides to pursue his relationship with Clara with new confidence. Others may wonder what conflicts will arise with his mother and Aunt Catherine.
2. (a) He says they should sell the house and move to an apartment. (b) It confirms their fears about the future if Marty marries Clara.
3. (a) She criticizes Clara's looks, age, and that she is not Italian. (b) She fears she will be forced from her home as her sister has been if Marty marries Clara.
4. (a) He is angry and confused. (b) He is frustrated because he has finally found someone he likes, and they discourage him.
5. The beautiful June morning and streaming sun reflect Marty's happiness.
6. (a) Students may say that they appear superficial when they focus solely on looks. (b) Some students may say they always seemed superficial; others may say that they had seemed benign.
7. Students may say that at first, he is insecure, frustrated, and resigned to being single. Clara gives him confidence and makes him feel that the time with his friends is unfulfilling.
8. Possibilities include Marty's mother's rejection of Clara and Marty's outburst at the bar. Students should explain what makes the encounter awkward.

AFTER YOU READ

Assess

Literary Element

1. Marty, Mother, and Clara are round characters. Marty, for example, is both rough and sensitive.
2. Examples include Aunt Catherine, Virginia, and Angie. Students should use text evidence to support their answers.

Review: Stage Directions

TV: camera directions—fade in and out; dissolves; close-ups
Both: actors' movements and expressions; set and actor descriptions
Play: limited setting changes within an act; actions that can be seen by an audience

Reading Strategy

1. Students may point out the stage directions where he describes the traits of a character, such as the first time Marty is introduced, or the descriptions of Aunt Catherine. They may also cite the characters' words and actions.
2. Answers will vary. Students may mention the characterization of Aunt Catherine by Marty's mother, Thomas, and Virginia. These characters give an unflattering picture of her.

LITERARY ANALYSIS

Literary Element Character

You know about main **characters,** minor characters, and foils. There are other types of characters as well. A round character shows varied and sometimes contradictory traits. A flat character reveals only one personality trait. A dynamic character grows and changes during the story. A static character remains the same throughout.

1. Who is an example of a round character in *Marty*? What contradictory traits does this character have?
2. Who is an example of a static character in this play? How does he or she remain the same?

Review: Stage Directions

As you learned on page 839, **stage directions** are instructions written by a dramatist to describe the actions and appearance of characters as well as the sets, props, sound effects, costumes, and lighting for a play.

Partner Activity With a classmate, look over the stage directions for *Marty,* which was written for television. Discuss the function the directions serve and what aspects Chayefsky wanted to make particularly clear about the staging or setting. Also think about how these directions for a television production differ from those for a live play in a theater. Create a Venn diagram in which you compare and contrast the stage directions used in television movies and plays.

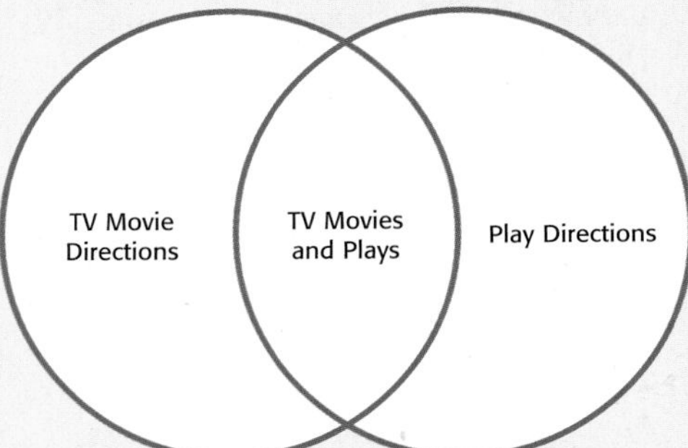

READING AND VOCABULARY

Reading Strategy Analyzing Characterization

In **direct characterization,** a writer makes explicit statements about a character's personality. In **indirect characterization,** the writer reveals a character's personality through his or her words, thoughts, and actions, as well as through what other characters think and say about the character.

1. Where does Chayefsky use direct characterization in this play?
2. Give an example of a character who is developed by what other characters say about him or her. What impression do they give of the character?

Vocabulary Practice

Practice with Word Origins Use a dictionary to find the language of origin for each vocabulary word.

1. conspire
   a. Latin **b.** Greek **c.** Sanskrit
2. ebullient
   a. Latin **b.** French **c.** Greek
3. résumé
   a. Latin **b.** French **c.** Norse

Academic Vocabulary

Here are two words from the vocabulary list on page R80.

integrity (in teg′ rə tē) *n.* firm adherence to a code of morals or values

dominate (dom′ ə nāt′) *v.* to exert the determining or guiding influence on

Practice and Apply
1. When does Marty demonstrate his **integrity**?
2. What kind of mood **dominates** Act 3?

Vocabulary

1. a **2.** a **3.** b

Academic Vocabulary

1. Students may say he shows integrity when he refuses to accept money to escort Clara home.
2. Students may say a joyful or hopeful mood dominates Act 3.

WRITING AND EXTENDING

Writing About Literature

Analyze Genre Elements Although *Marty* was written for television, it fits into the genre of drama because it is a work to be performed by actors. What elements help bring the play to life? Are there parts that strike you as unique? Are there any comic or tragic elements? Write a short essay in which you analyze Chayefsky's work within the dramatic form.

Before you begin writing, take some notes about how the elements of drama are presented in *Marty.* Make a list of elements that strike you as typical and a list of elements that strike you as special or unusual. Explain why you think the elements fit into their particular lists.

When you have completed a draft of your paper, meet with a peer reviewer to read and discuss each other's work. Then proofread and edit your draft to correct errors in spelling, grammar, and punctuation.

Film still from the movie *Marty* in 1955.

Listening and Speaking

Watch the 1955 Oscar-winning film adaptation of *Marty.* Discuss your thoughts in a small group. Remember that Paddy Chayefsky also won an Oscar for Best Screenplay for his work. Compare and contrast the film with the television play. Present your review as an oral report to the class.

Literature Online Web Activities For eFlashcards, Selection Quick Checks, and other Web activities, go to www.glencoe.com.

GRAMMAR AND STYLE

Chayefsky's Language and Style

Using Dialect Dialect is a variation of a language or manner of speaking specific to a particular region or group of people. Chayefsky uses dialect throughout *Marty* in order to portray how people speak in Marty's working-class Italian neighborhood. As a result, the dialogue is colloquial and realistic. Consider the following examples.

Speaker	Dialect	Standard
woman in butcher shop	"Watsa matter with you? Now, you get married, you hear me what I say?"	"What's the matter with you? You should get married. Do you hear what I'm saying?"
Virginia	"We don't have no privacy."	"We don't have any privacy."

How would this play be different if it had been written in Standard English? How does the use of dialect affect your impression of the characters?

Activity Make your own chart in which you examine the use of dialect in the play. In the first column, list the speaker, in the second column, list examples of dialect, and in the third column, rewrite it in Standard English. Note in which scenes or segments of dialogue the use of dialect strikes you as particularly important and explain why.

Revising Check

Dialect In your essay about the dramatic genre elements of *Marty,* did you discuss dialect? Read over your essay and think about how you could incorporate dialect as an important dramatic element. Revise as necessary.

AFTER YOU READ

Assess

Writing About Literature

Use these criteria to evaluate students' analyses:

- Do students identify unique parts of the drama and explain their choices?
- Do students identify comic and tragic elements?

Listening and Speaking

Use these criteria to assess students' movie reviews and presentations:

- Does the student discuss plot, tone, characterization, setting, and dialogue?
- Does the review compare and contrast specific elements of the movie and television production?
- Is the presentation well-organized and engaging?

Chayefsky's Language and Style

Students may say the play would be darker. In Standard English, the dialogue becomes harsh, insulting, and almost cruel. The dialect softens the content, making the characters less menacing.

Revising Check

Students should realize that the dialect impacts the characters, setting, and tone of the play.

English Language Coach

English language learners may find the Listening and Speaking activity difficult because of the use of dialect. Be sure to play back the related scenes as part of any discussion or question-answer process. EL

Web Activities Have students access the Web site for interactive activities that will help them assess their understanding of the selection.

Academic Standards

The Additional Support activity on p. 925 covers the following standard:

English Language Coach: **9.3.2** Compare and contrast the presentation of a…topic across genres…to explain how the selection of genre shapes the…topic.

Focus

BELLRINGER

Write on the board: revenge, justice, friendship, love

Go around the room and ask students which of these four words they find most powerful.

Ask: Which do you think would make the best subject for

- a play or a story?
- a reflective essay?
- an analytical essay about Shakespeare's *Romeo and Juliet?*

Summary

In this workshop, students will write and present a literary analysis essay. Students will follow the stages of the writing process, including prewriting, drafting, revising, and editing. In addition, the workshop includes two focus lessons, on supporting a thesis statement and quoting from a play.

Writing Models Have students access the Web site for interactive writing models and writing guides.

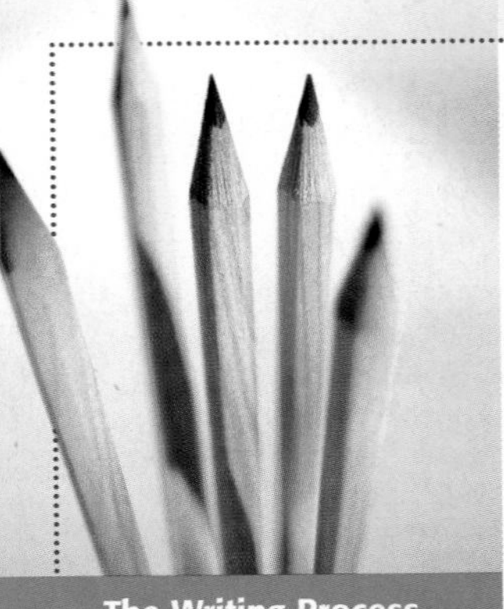

The Writing Process

In this workshop, you will follow the stages of the writing process. At any stage, you may think of new ideas to include and better ways to express them. Feel free to return to earlier stages as you write.

- **Prewriting**
- **Drafting**
- **Revising**
  - 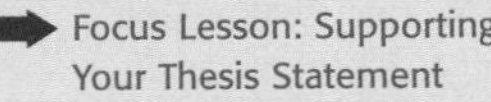
- **Editing and Proofreading**
  - 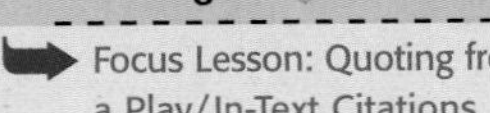
- **Presenting**

Writing Models For models and other writing activities, go to www.glencoe.com.

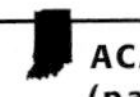

ACADEMIC STANDARDS (pages 926–933)

9.4.2 Establish a coherent thesis…

9.5.3 Write…literary analyses that gather evidence in support of a thesis…

Writing Workshop

Literary Analysis Essay

Analyzing Drama

"My only love, sprung from my only hate!
Too early seen unknown, and known too late!
Prodigious birth of love it is to me
That I must love a loathed enemy."

—William Shakespeare, from *Romeo and Juliet*, Act 1, Scene 5

Connecting to Literature William Shakespeare's dramas have stood the test of time because they are about universal themes that are still relevant today, hundreds of years after they were written. Shakespeare develops many themes in his dramas, from revenge and justice to friendship and love. A literary analysis essay about *Romeo and Juliet* would discuss and evaluate one or more elements in the play. The focus might be the characters, plot, setting, or theme. For example, Shakespeare's portrayal of romantic love would be a good topic for an essay.

Features of Literary Analysis Essays

Goals	Strategies
To analyze a drama	☑ Examine the elements of the drama ☑ Provide the title, author's name, and necessary background information
To state a thesis	☑ Take a position on the function of an element in the drama ☑ Write a clear thesis statement
To support the thesis	☑ Present examples and direct quotations (with citations) to support your thesis
To analyze a drama in a logical order	☑ Summarize your evidence and final analysis ☑ Conclude by restating your position

Additional Support

Workshop Resources

Print Materials

- Unit 4 Resources (Fast File), pp. 18–61
- REAL Success in Writing: Research and Reports
- Writing Constructed Responses, pp. 1–26, 36–41, 54
- Glencoe Literature Library

Transparencies

- Grammar and Language Transparencies 4
- Writing Workshop Transparencies 21–25
- Visual Literacy/Fine Art Transparencies

Technology

- Grammar & Language eWorkbook
- Revising with Style eWorkbook
- Sentence Diagraming eWorkbook
- Spelling Power eWorkbook
- Online Essay Grading, glencoe.com
- Literature Library Exam*View*® Assessment Suite CD-ROM
- Literature Library Vocabulary PuzzleMaker CD-ROM

Exposition

Assignment

Write a literary analysis essay in which you support your thesis about a drama. As you move through the stages of the writing process, keep your audience and purpose in mind.

Audience: your classmates and teacher

Purpose: to analyze a drama by presenting a viewpoint and supporting it with examples and quotations

Real-World Connection

Movies are a form of drama, and you probably analyze them all the time. Think about what makes a movie special. Good screenwriters use techniques similar to the ones Shakespeare used so successfully. They tell a good story, make characters come alive, and often combine comedy and tragedy.

Analyzing a Professional Model

In the following selection, literary historian and biographer Marchette Chute analyzes *Romeo and Juliet* by showing how William Shakespeare took an ordinary plot and used it to create a remarkable play, one of the most beloved dramas ever written. As you read, note the quoted lines from the poem on which Shakespeare's story is based. Pay close attention to the comments in the margin. They point out features that you might want to include in your literary analysis essay.

From *An Introduction to Shakespeare* by Marchette Chute

It is part of Shakespeare's great strength as a writer that he never felt superior to anyone, and he kept a gentle courtesy in his point of view even towards fools.

This same gentleness on Shakespeare's part shows in his attitude towards the earlier writers from whom he took the plots of some of his plays. He could pick up a rather foolish play or poem, read it with great care, ignore its foolishness for the little of value there might be in it, and then transform it into a masterpiece.

For instance, at about this time [before he wrote *The Tragedy of Romeo and Juliet*], Shakespeare read a popular poem by Arthur Brooke on the tragedy of two young lovers named Romeus and Juliet. Brooke was retelling an old Italian story, and he used an extraordinary style. This, according to Brooke, is Juliet's behavior in the potion scene:

Her dainty tender parts gan shiver all for dread,
Her golden hairs did stand upright upon her chillish head . . .

Introduction

Introduce your subject in an interesting way and provide a bit of background.

Thesis Statement

Include a statement that presents your position or makes an argument.

Quotation

A quotation is one form of support that strengthens your argument. Note that when you quote a play, you should include a citation that lists the act number, the scene number, and, if available, the line number.

Teach

Big Idea

The Power of Love *Romeo and Juliet* is one of the most famous love stories of all time. **Ask:** What do you think it is that makes this play such a popular love story? What does the play say about the power of love? *(Students may say that Romeo and Juliet's struggle to be together constitutes a powerful drama. The failure of their love to triumph over circumstances—even though Romeo and Juliet are willing to sacrifice everything for it—is profoundly moving.)* **OL**

Cultural History

Film Adaptations A famous film adaptation of *Romeo and Juliet* was made in 1968 by the Italian director Franco Zeffirelli. Shot on location in northern Italy's medieval villages, it was the first movie version to cast teenagers—Leonard Whiting and Olivia Hussey—in the title roles. A more recent adaptation, Baz Luhrmann's 1996 *Romeo + Juliet,* stars Leonardo DiCaprio and Claire Danes. **AS**

Differentiated Instruction

Sight and Sound Students who have trouble reading Shakespeare's language may benefit from seeing and hearing the play performed. Encourage them to watch a film version of the play. Note that a film's visual elements—costumes, close-ups, set designs—help shape the audience's reactions to the story. Similarly, a film's musical score gives the viewer important clues about the story's turning points and the characters' emotions. **AL**

Academic Standards

The Additional Support activities on pp. 927 covers the following standard:

Differentiated Instruction: **9.3.2** Compare and contrast the presentation of a...topic across genres...to explain how the selection of genre shapes the...topic.

Teach

Writing Skills

Introducing a Thesis

Refer students to Chute's essay. **Ask:** How would you paraphrase this essay's thesis statement? *(Shakespeare could transform another writer's inferior work into a masterpiece.)* Explain how Chute's thesis grows out of two introductory sentences. First Chute argues that Shakespeare "never felt superior to anyone." Then she shows how this generous view of others allowed Shakespeare to find value even in inferior literature. **OL**

Shakespeare's Sources

Although Shakespeare was one of the most original and gifted dramatists of all time, he rarely invented the plots of his plays. Instead, he often adapted well-known stories by writers such as Giovanni Boccaccio or historical writings by authors such as Plutarch or Holinshed. What makes Shakespeare a genius is the way he transformed these stories into something wholly his own. **AS**

Example
Support your thesis statement with examples.

Elaboration
Explain and clarify your example. The writer explains that Shakespeare made *Romeo and Juliet* a story of "haste" to provide a reason for the tragedy.

Shakespeare took Brooke's stuffed characters and transformed them into real people, he took the pretentious verse and transmuted it into golden poetry, and he made *Romeo and Juliet* into one of the most loved plays ever written. Brooke's tragedy was meaningless because there was no special reason why it should have happened, but Shakespeare made it into a tragedy of haste. He emphasizes the sense of hurry by making Juliet younger than she was in the original version and condensing the action into less than a week. Even the weather is hot, and an atmosphere of quick-flowering beauty and early death is the background that is created for the story of the immortal and tragic lovers. ★

Example
Additional examples further support your thesis statement.

Comparison and Contrast
Compare and contrast characters to explain the dramatist's technique.

Conclusion
End with a brief summary that draws a conclusion.

A lesser writer than Shakespeare might have tried to keep the play to a single note of lyric love. But Shakespeare, who had thrust a weaver into fairyland, had no hesitation about putting a couple of cheerful realists into *Romeo and Juliet*. Mercutio and Juliet's nurse do not weaken the tragedy; they enrich it, in the usual astonishing fashion of Shakespeare's comedians. Mercutio is a humorist by intention; he is a subtle and intelligent young man who knows exactly how entertaining he is, and the fact that he "loves to hear himself talk" is only proof of his good judgment. The Nurse, on the other hand, does not mean to be funny. She feels she is a very sober, sensible, practical woman and she has no idea what actually happens every time she opens her mouth. Shakespeare had no objection to laughter in his tragedies. The two elements combine in real life and they were free to combine in his plays also.

Reading-Writing Connection Think about the writing techniques that you have just encountered and try them out in the literary analysis essay you write.

Additional Support

Skills Practice

READING: Supporting Examples

In her second-to-last paragraph, Chute uses examples and elaboration to support her claim that Shakespeare transformed Brooke's mediocre poem into a masterpiece. Have students reread the paragraph. **Ask:** In what ways did Shakespeare improve on Brooke? *(He created more realistic characters and better poetry, added haste as a factor in the tragedy, made Juliet younger, compressed the action, and intensified the dramatic atmosphere by introducing hot weather.)* **OL**

Exposition

Romeo and Mercutio, however, do share similar views about the powerful bonds of love and loyalty between friends and family. In Act 3, Scene 1, the strength of their friendship is put to the test. Tybalt challenges Romeo to a duel, but Romeo refuses to fight him. Tybalt does not know that Romeo has just secretly married Juliet and thus has become Tybalt's cousin by marriage. Mercutio, seeing Romeo's refusal to fight as a threat to Romeo's reputation, feels compelled to save Romeo's honor and fights Tybalt in Romeo's place. As Romeo tries to stop the duel, Tybalt stabs and kills Mercutio. Romeo declares, "My very friend, hath got this mortal hurt / In my behalf—my reputation stain'd / With Tybalt's slander. . . . " (3.1.106–108). Romeo then rises to defend Mercutio's honor by slaying Tybalt. This scene shows how both Romeo and Mercutio are willing to sacrifice their lives for the sake of their friendship.

Example

What is the purpose of including more than one example in support of a thesis?

Out of love for Juliet, Romeo tries to end the feud between his family, the Montagues, and Juliet's family, the Capulets. Initially, he responds to Tybalt's challenge with love. When Tybalt challenges Romeo in Act 3, Romeo says to him, "[I] love thee better than thou canst devise" (3.1.67). This shows that love can conquer hatred and bring about peace. However, love can also be destructive. Out of love for Romeo and loyalty to him, Mercutio insists on fighting Tybalt, but Mercutio's duel with Tybalt only intensifies the conflict between the feuding families and leads to a series of senseless deaths.

In-Text Citation

Why is it important to tell readers exactly where in the play a quotation comes from?

The idea of love in *Romeo and Juliet* is more complicated than it first appears. As one might expect in a love story, love is shown to be a powerful, wonderful thing, but also something that can encourage destructive behavior. The differences and similarities between Romeo's and Mercutio's attitudes toward love serve a dramatic purpose. The views and actions of these two friends help develop a major theme of the play—that love can be both a constructive and a destructive force.

Conclusion

How does it help to summarize and restate the thesis in the conclusion?

Teach

Writing Skills

Paragraphs One of the difficulties students face in constructing an essay is deciding how to organize it in paragraphs. Referring to the workshop model essay, ask students to identify the central or unifying idea of paragraphs 3–6. Direct them to look for cues in the opening sentence of each paragraph. OL

Writing Skills

Example **Answer:** *Multiple examples provide more firm support for the thesis.* OL

Writing Skills

In-Text Citation **Answer:** *It allows readers to verify the quotation and its context.* OL

Writing Skills

Conclusion **Answer:** *It sums up all that has been written in the essay and reminds readers of the thesis.* OL

English Language Coach

Transitional Expressions Students new to the English language may struggle with the formal vocabulary used in essays, particularly transitional expressions. Go over the workshop model essay, defining words and phrases such as *for example, in contrast,* and *however.* Explain that their function is to connect ideas in an essay and to create a sense of flow. EL

Academic Standards

Additional Support activities on pp. 930 and 931 cover the following standards:

Skills Practice: **9.4** Write clear, coherent, and focused paragraphs and essays. **9.7.10** Assess how language…affect[s]… oral communication…

English Language Coach: **9.1** Use…context clues, and a growing knowledge of English to determine the meaning of words…

Teach

Writing Skills

Support As students revise their drafts, have them go back to make sure their arguments are supported properly. If their arguments are weak, students may need to elaborate on their ideas.

Say: Supporting information must be related to your main idea. As you elaborate on the points in your arguments, make sure that the information you have added truly explains, clarifies, or extends your points instead of making new points. **OL**

★ Writer's Technique

Revising Revising is a way of enhancing and clarifying the arguments made in an essay. Referring to the rubric "Writing an Effective Literary Analysis Essay" on page 932, point out to students that the goal of an essay is to communicate as clearly as possible.

Say: When answering the questions, remember that your essay is addressed to another person. Would they share your viewpoint? **AS**

Traits of Strong Writing

Follow these traits of strong writing to effectively express your ideas.

Ideas message or theme and the details that develop it

Organization arrangement of main ideas and supporting details

Voice writer's unique way of using tone and style

Word Choice vocabulary a writer uses to convey meaning

Sentence Fluency rhythm and flow of sentences

Conventions correct spelling, grammar, usage, and mechanics

Presentation the way words and design elements look on a page

For more information on using the Traits of Strong Writing, see pages R32–R33 of the Writing Handbook.

Revising

Peer Review Exchange your finished draft with that of a partner. Use this rubric to evaluate your writing.

Rubric: Writing an Effective Literary Analysis Essay ★

- ☑ Do you state a clear thesis?
- ☑ Do you use examples to support your position?
- ☑ Do you use direct quotations as evidence and include in-text citations?
- ☑ Do you summarize your evidence and final analysis?
- ☑ Do you conclude by restating your position?

Focus Lesson

Supporting Your Thesis Statement

The effectiveness of your literary analysis essay depends on strong support for your thesis statement. As you decide on a thesis and begin drafting a statement, review the drama to find specific examples to illustrate your argument. See the example below.

Draft:

Shakespeare's portrayal of the friends' differences and similarities helps develop a major theme of the play—the constructive and destructive forces of love.

Revision:

Shakespeare's portrayal of the friends' differences and similarities helps develop a major theme of the play—the constructive and destructive forces of love.

From the very beginning of the play, love is Romeo's entire motivation and the source of both his happiness and his suffering.[1] For example, before Romeo meets Juliet at the beginning of the play, he tells Mercutio about his lovesickness[2] for a young lady named Rosaline. . . . In contrast, Mercutio has a more practical attitude toward romantic love.[3]

1: Description of Romeo's attitude toward romantic love **2:** Example shows Romeo's attitude **3:** Explanation of how Mercutio's attitude differs

Additional Support

Skills Practice

LISTENING AND SPEAKING: Getting Feedback If students read each other's essays, they may want to consider specific questions, such as,

- Which evidence is most convincing?
- What further evidence could I add?
- Are there opposing arguments that I should address?

Emphasize that writers do not have to accept every suggested change. They should listen to all comments and choose the ideas they think will improve their essays. **OL**

Editing and Proofreading

Get It Right When you have completed the final draft of your essay, proofread for errors in grammar, usage, mechanics, and spelling. Refer to the Language Handbook, pages R45–R59, as a guide.

Focus Lesson

Quoting from a Play/In-Text Citations

Quotations from the drama provide clear, convincing support for your thesis. Any time you include the exact words from a play, these words should be enclosed in quotation marks. If the play is written in lines in the form of poetry, as Shakespeare's plays are, line breaks should be indicated by slashes (/). Cite the location of the words in the play by listing the act number, scene number, and, if available, line number(s) so that your readers can look up and read the quotation in context.

Problem: Quotation marks and slashes are omitted in quoting lines from a play. The location of the quotation in the text is not identified.

Is love a tender thing? It is too rough, Too rude, too boist'rous and it pricks like thorn

Solution: Enclose the exact words from a play in quotation marks and use slashes to show line breaks. Use an in-text citation to identify where the quote occurs in the play.

"Is love a tender thing? It is too rough, / Too rude, too boist'rous and it pricks like thorn" (1.4.25–26)

Use the Third Person

A literary analysis essay is a type of formal writing usually written from the third-person point of view. This means that the writer is an outside observer who evaluates and comments on the literary work. Avoid using first-person pronouns such as *I, me, we,* and *us.* Also avoid the second-person pronoun *you.*

Give Credit

When you write a literary analysis essay, identify your sources. This is true whether the source is the literary work itself or a comment about it by another writer. Cite your sources in footnotes and a bibliography, or use in-text citations, as on pages 930 and 931.

Presenting

Check It Twice Your use of grammar, capitalization, punctuation, and spelling is crucial in a literary analysis essay because it affects your readers' response to your argument and influences your grade. After you correct errors, make sure your paper looks neat. If possible, type it. Double-check that you have followed your teacher's general guidelines regarding length, spacing, font size, and margins.

Writer's Portfolio

Place a clean copy of your literary analysis essay in your portfolio to review later.

Writing Workshop

Literary Analysis Essay

Teach

Writing Skills

Quoting/In-Text Citations Many students have difficulty remembering the proper mechanics when using quotations. Help students practice by writing on the board a few quotations from *Romeo and Juliet,* leaving out the punctuation and citation information. Then ask students to come up to the board and fill in the missing details. OL

Writer's Technique

Presentation The first impression an essay makes has nothing to do with its ideas or the way they're supported. A reader's first response is to the physical appearance of the essay. Emphasize the importance of a neat manuscript, free of typographical errors and sloppy writing. AS

English Language Coach

Editing and Proofreading English language learners may have special difficulties with grammar and usage. It may be helpful to set aside extra time to meet with them independently to proofread their papers. Alternatively, these students can be given the opportunity to submit an extra draft, either before or after the final drafts for the entire class are due. EL

Academic Standards

Additional Support activities on pp. 932 and 933 cover the following standards:

Skills Practice: **9.4.10** Review [and] evaluate writing…for meaning, clarity, [and] content… **9.7.7** Make judgments about the ideas under discussion and support those judgments with evidence.

English Language Coach: **9.4.11** Edit and proofread…one's own writing…

Focus

Summary

In this workshop, students will learn techniques for planning, rehearsing, presenting, and listening to a literary analysis.

Teach

Speaking Skills

Reciting Passages One of the challenges of presenting a literary analysis is reciting quotations from a play or other source. As practice, choose a few of the most famous or important speeches from *Romeo and Juliet* and ask students to recite them. It may spark enthusiasm to turn this into a contest, having a series of students recite the same passage and then polling the class about whose performance was best. OL

Speaking, Listening, and Viewing Workshop

Literary Analysis

Select Passages

To support your literary analysis of a drama, choose lines from the play to illustrate the points you want to make. Make sure the lines accurately represent the context in which they appear. To capture the attention of your audience, look for dramatic quotes and familiar passages with universal meaning.

Presenting a Literary Analysis

Connecting to Literature Marchette Chute retold thirty-six of William Shakespeare's plays as narratives. Although her book of retellings was first published almost fifty years ago, it is still available and widely used today. Chute is known for her critical analyses of the works of some of the best-loved English writers, including Shakespeare.

Literary critics often present their ideas by speaking to large or small groups. When you present your literary analysis, you can increase the effectiveness of any quotations you include in support of your argument by saying them as an actor would before an audience. In this workshop, you will learn to present your literary analysis of a drama. Keep in mind that before you make a presentation in front of an audience, you need to prepare what you will say.

Assignment Plan and present a literary analysis.

Planning Your Presentation

In your literary analysis essay, you expressed your position about an element in a drama and presented evidence to convince your readers. You wrote a thesis statement and provided examples to support it. These examples included quotations. As you prepare your literary analysis for presentation, keep the following strategies in mind:

Use your essay as a starting point, but adapt it for your oral presentation. Discuss your essay with a partner and decide what ideas to include in your presentation.

"Under love's heavy burden do I sink"
Romeo, Act 1, Scene 4

Additional Support

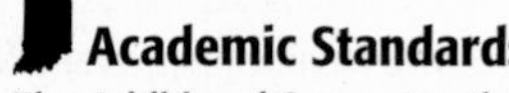

Academic Standards

The Additional Support activity on p. 934 covers the following standard:

Skills Practice: **9.7.10** Assess how language and delivery affect…the mood and tone of the oral communication and make an impact on the audience.

Skills Practice

LISTENING AND VIEWING: Analyzing a Performance For further practice in understanding Shakespearean language, show students a few scenes from a film version of the play.

Ask: What kinds of emotions do the actors convey? Direct them to pay close attention to the actors' speaking styles, pacing, gestures, and body language.

Ask: Which scene did you like best? Why? OL

Record the main ideas on note cards to use when you present. Remember to include direct quotations from the drama. Copy these exactly so you can quote them verbatim.

Communicating Your Ideas

When you give a presentation with quotes from a drama, use your voice to communicate the meaning of the lines. The examples and quotations you use for support will capture your listeners' attention if they are spoken expressively rather than in a monotone. If possible, memorize quotations so that you can make eye contact with your audience while speaking.

Rehearsing

With a partner, practice saying each quotation as you would for an audience. Give your partner constructive suggestions for using tone of voice, pitch, and volume. Listen to your partner's ideas for your interpretation and incorporate the suggestions to make your presentation stronger.

Techniques for Presenting a Literary Analysis

Verbal Techniques	Nonverbal Techniques
☑ **Volume** Use the loudness or softness of your voice to express the meaning of the quotations you use in support of your argument.	☑ **Facial Expressions** Use facial expressions to emphasize the feelings of the characters you quote.
☑ **Pitch** Use the level of your voice to communicate meaning. In other words, speak in a high or low voice when appropriate.	☑ **Gestures** Use hand motions and other gestures to highlight the drama in the lines you quote or examples you provide.
☑ **Tone** Adjust your tone to reflect your attitude toward the drama, or to reflect the attitude of a character you are quoting.	☑ **Posture** Maintain straight (but not stiff) posture. Modify your posture as necessary to reveal the mood or personality of the characters when quoting them.
☑ **Enunciation** Pronounce your words clearly. This is especially important when lines quoted from the drama are in a regional dialect or include words that are no longer common.	☑ **Eye Contact** As you speak, make eye contact with your audience. Adjust the intensity of your eye contact to reveal the emotions of the characters being quoted.

Organizing

Organize your presentation with an introduction, body, and conclusion. State your thesis clearly at the start. In the body of your presentation, clarify your argument and provide examples and quotations to support it. Briefly summarize by restating your thesis and final analysis in your conclusion.

Use the Model to Practice

Consider the following two quotations. How would you say each line in order to show the contrast between Romeo's attitude toward romantic love and that of Mercutio?

(1) "Under love's heavy burden do I sink" (Romeo, Act 1, Scene 4, line 22).

(2) "If love be rough with you, be rough with love" (Mercutio, Act 1, Scene 4, line 27).

ACADEMIC STANDARDS (pages 934–935)

9.7.15 Deliver expository… presentations that provide evidence in support of a thesis…

9.7.2 [Develop] the introduction and conclusion in a speech, including the use of literary quotations…

Differentiated Instruction

Speech Practice Provide less proficient readers and learning disabled students with extra time to practice giving their speeches. Suggest that they use a tape recorder to record themselves. Have students work with partners or in small groups to listen to, analyze, and critique their presentations. **BL**

Teach

Speaking Skills

Addressing an Audience As students rehearse their presentations, remind them that it is important to remember the audience. Encourage students to

- speak at an appropriate pace and not rush
- make eye contact with individuals in the audience to make a stronger connection
- enunciate clearly and speak loudly enough for all to hear **OL**

Listening Skills

Paying Attention Remind students that listening to a presentation is not passive but requires active engagement with the speaker. As they listen to the presentations of other students, encourage students to

- make a mental note of what each speaker's thesis is
- assess how the speaker's argument is supported
- look for patterns in the presentation
- reflect on the speaker's conclusion **OL**

Academic Standards

The Additional Support activity on p. 935 covers the following standards:

Differentiated Instruction: **9.7.6** Analyze the occasion and the interests of the audience and choose effective verbal and nonverbal techniques…for presentations. **9.7.11** Evaluate the clarity, quality, effectiveness, and general coherence of a speaker's important points, arguments, evidence, organization of ideas, delivery, choice of words, and use of language.

Focus

Summary

In this section, students will read summaries of dramas from a variety of cultures and time periods. They will also be introduced to two novels that address the themes of the power of love and awkward encounters.

Teach

★ Literary History

Gary Soto Born in Fresno, California, in 1952, Gary Soto is recognized as one of the most important voices in Mexican American literature. Acclaimed as a poet, essayist, and fiction writer, Soto was a finalist for the National Book Award for his *New and Selected Poems* (1995). His memoir *Living up the Street* (1985) won the American Book Award. Soto lives in Northern California. **AS**

INDEPENDENT READING

Drama and Novels

DRAMA IS THE ONE TYPE OF LITERATURE THAT IS ALWAYS WRITTEN to be performed rather than just read. More than any other genre, drama requires a reader to see, hear, and feel the action. Therefore, readers who want to experience the life and impact of drama should pay careful attention to stage directions. For more drama on a range of themes, try the first three suggestions below. For novels that address the Big Ideas of the *Power of Love* and *Awkward Encounters,* try the titles from the Glencoe Literature Library on the next page.

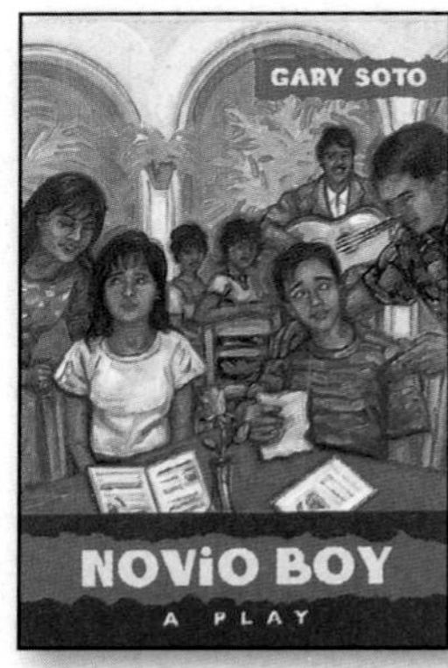

Novio Boy: A Play

by Gary Soto ★

This play begins with Rudy asking his friend Alex for advice about girls. Rudy, a ninth grader, has finally gotten a date with Patricia, who is two years older than he is. He eventually takes her to a restaurant in their Mexican American community. When Rudy's best friend, his "crazy" guitar-playing uncle, and his mother show up, he worries that they might embarrass him and pretends not to know them. The play includes performance notes, a Spanish-English glossary, and plenty of humor.

Plays of America from American Folklore

by L. E. McCullough

The ten plays that form this collection draw on subjects ranging from Native American myths to traditional European, African, and Asian stories and include pioneer-era heroes as well as more recent cultural figures such as Elvis Presley. Each play includes notes about the setting, as well as tips on costumes, casting, and special effects. Many plays have contemporary narrators, even though they deal with past events.

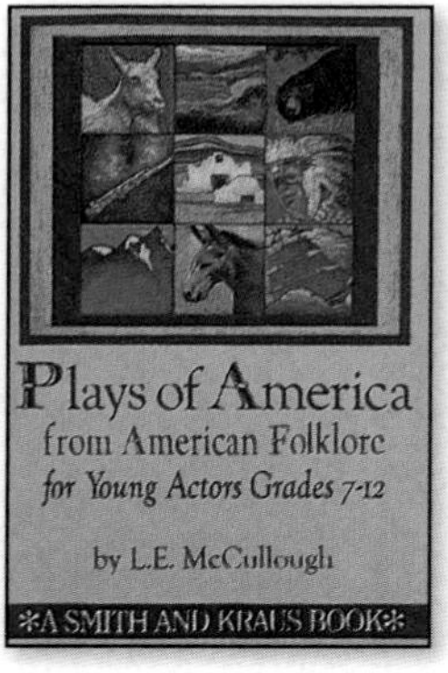

Additional Support

Reading in the Real World

College In many college courses, professors recommend additional reading to supplement the required texts. Explain to students that the purpose of supplemental reading is to broaden their frame of reference. One practical benefit of this is that they will accumulate a reservoir of general knowledge from which they can draw ideas and examples for their writing. **OL**

CRITICS' CORNER

"*Our Town* is popular, in part at least, because it is not tragic. The American public has approved of it because of its charming, folksy presentation of simple, 'good' people, its sentimentally idealized account of the small town. It projects a vision of a time and place which have vanished from the American scene, which never existed in fact. . . ."

—George D. Stephens, from *Modern Drama*

Thornton Wilder

Our Town

by Thornton Wilder ★

In Grover's Corners, New Hampshire, in the first days of the twentieth century, two neighbor children fall in love and grow up. The town is meant to represent a typical American town; the characters are meant to be typical middle-class Americans. Each of the play's three acts takes place at a different point in the characters' lives, providing snapshots of life and death in a small town. Generations of readers have been moved by this Pulitzer Prize–winning play, which includes one of the most famous final acts in American theater.

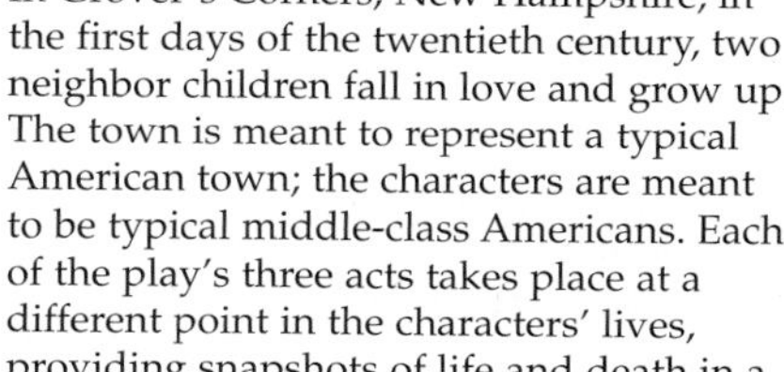

From the Glencoe Literature Library

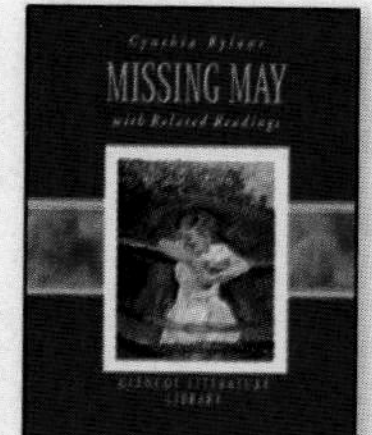

Missing May

by Cynthia Rylant

This is a touching story of change, loss, and the power of love.

Heart of Darkness

by Joseph Conrad

The interior of Africa is the setting for this tale of psychological unraveling and a disturbing and awkward encounter.

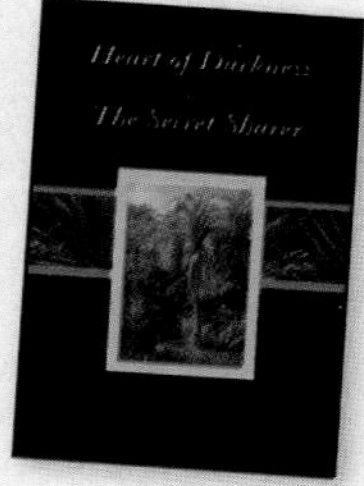

Teach

★ Literary History

Thornton Wilder
American playwright and novelist Thornton Wilder (1897–1975) spent his early years in China, where his father was a diplomat. His most famous play, *Our Town,* won a Pulitzer Prize. **AS**

Glencoe Literature Library

Glencoe Literature Library offers an extensive collection of hardcover books that help you encourage your students to read independently. Choose among the more than 120 full-length literary works—novels, novellas, plays, and nonfiction. Each book includes related readings from a broad range of genres. Go to www.Glencoe.com for more information.

Differentiated Instruction

Responding to Other Eras Gifted and talented students may enjoy investigating literary works from other eras. Challenge them to read books such as Conrad's *Heart of Darkness.* Have them consider such questions as,

- How does the writer's language differ from contemporary American English?
- What ideas and themes are presented in the book?
- What does the book teach you about life in its time period? **AL**

Academic Standards

Additional Support activities on pp. 936 and 937 cover the following standards:

Reading in the Real World: **9.3** [Respond] to grade-level-appropriate material…

Differentiated Instruction: **9.3.12** Analyze the way in which a work of literature is related to…themes and issues of its historical period.

Focus

BELLRINGER

Say: Some of you may experience stress and anxiety when faced with a test. Knowing and using test-taking strategies will help to minimize that stress. Have half the students brainstorm reasons why taking a test might cause anxiety and have the other half brainstorm strategies to reduce test anxiety.

Test Preparation and Practice

English Language Arts

Indiana Test Practice

READING: Vocabulary, Comprehension, and Analysis

Read the following passages. Then, on a separate sheet of paper, answer the questions on page 940.

from *In the Bear's House* by N. Scott Momaday

One: You are, Urset. I AM, Yahweh

[Undefined space. Two chairs under a light, perhaps a street lamp or a Chinese lantern in a tree. YAHWEH, *the Creator, is slouched in one of the chairs, dozing. Enter* URSET, *the bear, very softly, warily. He stands for a moment beside the empty chair, tentative, ill at ease. He sits.]*

URSET. Ah, ahem. Pardon, Great Mystery. Beg pardon.

[YAHWEH *stirs, stretches, looks up.]*

It is only I, Urset.

YAHWEH. Yes? What? Oh, yes, it is you, Urset. How are you?

URSET. Do you know me, then?

YAHWEH. Know you? How could I not know you, Urset. I created you.

URSET. Yes, yes, I have dreamed of that. I have dreamed that I came very small from your hands.

YAHWEH. So small. You were scarcely larger than a rat. I thought, when I saw you in your new corporeal[1] being, that I had made some mistake, for I meant you to be formidable, and there you were, a wet rat. And yes, you did indeed come from these hands. These very fingers, these palms, the heels of these hands. I made a little ball of fur, wet fur—from something floating on the waters, as I recall—a knot of hair, a bit of drift. It was you! And, behold, you became formidable. I don't mind telling you, Urset, you are one of my showpieces. I am proud of you.

(pause)

But there is something on your mind, Urset. Why do you come to me?

URSET. I cannot easily speak of it. Had I words . . .

YAHWEH. Words, language, speech. That old, old matter of words. Yes, I might have known.

In the beginning was the word, you know, and I was there. I *was* the word. We are indivisible, the word and I. *I Am* is my name, and Jehovah[2] and God and the Supreme Being and the Great Mystery. I hope that you will speak to me from your heart, Urset. And I hope that you will express your heart in fine, beautiful language.

I would hear your voice, Urset, as I would hear rolling thunder, as I would hear the waves of the ocean crashing against the Cliffs of Moher, as I would hear the Fifth Symphony,[3] as I would hear Charles Laughton[4] reading from my story of Job[5] or that of Shadrach, Meshach, and Abednego,[6] as I would hear the lines of

[1]**corporeal:** material; capable of being touched

[2]**Jehovah:** the name of God in ancient Hebrew literature (derived from *Yahweh*)

[3]**Fifth Symphony:** Ludwig van Beethoven's Symphony No. 5 in C Minor, a well-known classical music composition

[4]**Charles Laughton:** English stage and film actor (1899–1962)

[5]**Job:** in the Bible, a rich man who endures many hardships with fortitude and faith

[6]**Shadrach, Meshach, and Abednego:** in the Bible, three friends who refuse to worship a golden idol and are thrown into a fiery furnace; miraculously, they are unharmed

Listening

Functional Material Explain to students that instructors often give test directions orally. Ask students to listen carefully as you read aloud the test directions at the top of the page. Ask students who clearly understand the directions to restate them. Tell students that restating or paraphrasing information is a listening strategy for checking comprehension. OL

Homer, in which are sung the Trojan Wars.[7] I would hear of it in words that play upon the sunrise, that resound in the caverns of the Malpais, that roll on the winds of the desert at first light. I would hear of it in words, Urset, in words that soothe and strike, that console and devastate, in words that descend into the blackness of the ocean depths and soar in the terrible brilliance of the sun. I would be astonished by your words.

URSET. *(after a long pause, humbled)* As I am by yours, Great Mystery. To tell you the truth, all words confound[8] me. The word "rock" confounds me. "Tree" confounds me. "Child" confounds me. The word "sorrow" staggers me. The word "love" drops me to my knees. And yet silence resonates among all these words, and silence disturbs me most of all.

YAHWEH. I see that you are well enough, Urset. With these hands I placed you in the elements of earth, air, fire, water, and language—and silence. You can talk to me, Urset. You may confide in me, and you may know that you exist in your name and in the words that tell your story, as I exist in my name and in the story in which all other stories have origin and being from the beginning to the end of time.

[7]**Trojan Wars:** legendary wars waged against the city of Troy in Asia Minor (modern-day Turkey) by the Achaeans, as recounted in the *Iliad* by Homer

[8]**confound:** bewilder; confuse

"The Traveling Bear" by Amy Lowell

Grass-blades push up between the cobblestones[9]
And catch the sun on their flat sides
Shooting it back,
Gold and emerald,
In the eyes of passers-by.

And over the cobblestones,
Square-footed and heavy,
Dances the trained bear.
The cobbles cut his feet,
And he has a ring in his nose
Which hurts him;
But still he dances,
For the keeper pricks[10] him with a sharp stick,
Under his fur.

Now the crowd gapes and chuckles,
And boys and young women shuffle their feet in time to the dancing bear.
They see him wobbling
Against a dust of emerald and gold,
And they are greatly delighted.

The legs of the bear shake with fatigue,
And his back aches,
And the shining grass-blades dazzle and confuse him.
But still he dances,
Because of the little, pointed stick.

[9]**cobblestones:** naturally rounded stones, used in paving a street

[10]**pricks:** pierces slightly with a sharp point

Teach

Assessment Explain to students that this Test Preparation and Practice lesson is designed to develop test-taking strategies as well as to test their mastery of the skills covered in this unit. The lesson is modeled on tests they will be required to pass to be eligible to receive a high school diploma. Students will read one or two grade-level-appropriate selections and answer vocabulary, comprehension, and literary analysis questions, including multiple-choice, constructed-response, and extended-response items. In other sections, students' ability to use Standard English in their writing is assessed, and they are given an extended-writing prompt. **OL**

Assess

1. **B** is the correct answer. The stage directions describe the manner in which Urset enters the area where Yahweh is sleeping as *softly, warily*, and *tentatively*.
2. **C** is the correct answer. The word is contrasted with something insignificant. No other option makes sense in this context.
3. Rubric:
   2 points versions of two exemplars
   1 point version of one exemplar
   0 points other
   Exemplars:
   - Yahweh is glad to speak with Urset, even though he had been sleeping.
   - Yahweh says that Urset is one of his showpieces, and he is proud of his handiwork.
   - Yahweh urges Urset to speak from his heart and confide in him.
4. **D** is the correct answer. A stick is used to urge the bear to dance.
5. **C** is the correct answer. The poem deals with a painfully serious subject.
6. **B** is the correct answer. Both selections explore the feelings of animals.
7. Refer to the Reading Comprehension, Writing Applications, and Language Conventions rubrics provided by the State of Indiana Department of Education.

Questions 1 through 3 are based on *In the Bear's House.*

1 What can you infer from the stage directions at the beginning of *In the Bear's House*?

A Urset is bold.
B Urset respects Yahweh.
C Yahweh knows Urset well.
D Yahweh is unhappy with Urset.

2 Read these lines from the dialogue.

> **I thought, when I first saw you in your new corporeal being, that I had made some mistake, for I meant you to be formidable, and there you were, a wet rat.**

Which of these BEST defines *formidable* as it is used in these lines?

A frightful
B beautiful
C impressive
D complicated

3 Give TWO examples from *In the Bear's House* that demonstrate Yahweh's consideration for Urset.

Questions 4 and 5 are based on "The Traveling Bear."

4 Why does the bear in the poem dance?

A He is afraid.
B He is hungry.
C He is popular.
D He is prodded.

5 The overall mood of the poem "The Traveling Bear" is

A comic
B hopeful
C somber
D mysterious

Questions 6 and 7 are based on both selections.

6 Which of the following themes do *In the Bear's House* and "The Traveling Bear" share?

A Animals are spiritual.
B Animals have feelings.
C Animals are mysterious.
D Animals are treated badly.

7 Suppose that your town's council is thinking of building an animal shelter. The shelter will be a home for stray animals and provide services such as dog training, pet adoption, and spaying and neutering of pets. Some people in the community think the money could be spent to build something of greater benefit to people. Write a persuasive essay in which you explain your position on this issue. **Include at least TWO details or examples from one or both of the passages to support your position.**

Use a separate sheet of paper to plan your writing.

Writing Checklist

The following checklist will help you write your essay. Be sure to

- ❑ brainstorm for ideas and develop a plan before you start writing
- ❑ organize your writing with an introduction, a body, and a conclusion
- ❑ pay attention to your word choice and voice
- ❑ edit for sentence fluency and conventions
- ❑ have a neat and organized presentation

Student essays should include the following:
- a clearly stated and defended position supported by relevant evidence from the passage
- effective voice, word choice, and sentence variety
- effective presentation, with attention to grammar and spelling conventions

WRITING: Writing Process

The following passage is from the first draft of a student's essay. Read the passage and use it to answer questions 8–11 on a separate sheet of paper.

> [1]The constellation Ursa Major has long fascinated people. [2]It has been an object of interest since the dawn of time. [3]Many cultures have noticed Ursa Major, also known as the "Great Bear," and have attached great significance to it. [4]The bear has been associated with the constellation since the Classical Age. [5]Polaris is often referred to as the North Star. [6]Throughout the ages, the Great Bear connected with the gods and royalty.

8 Choose the BEST way to combine Sentences 1 and 2.

- **A** The constellation Ursa Major has long fascinated people since the dawn of time.
- **B** The constellation Ursa Major, an object of interest since the dawn of time, has long fascinated people.
- **C** The constellation Ursa Major has fascinated people since the dawn of time.
- **D** An object of interest since the dawn of time, the constellation Ursa Major has long fascinated people.

9 Which sentence is not related to the main idea of the paragraph?

- **A** Sentence 3
- **B** Sentence 4
- **C** Sentence 5
- **D** Sentence 6

10 Choose the BEST way to revise Sentence 6.

- **A** Throughout the ages, the Great Bear is connected with the gods and royalty.
- **B** Throughout the ages, the Great Bear connects with the gods and royalty.
- **C** Throughout the ages, the Great Bear will connect with the gods and royalty.
- **D** Throughout the ages, the Great Bear has been connected with the gods and royalty.

11 The Modern Library Association (MLA) recommends these guidelines for citing works used for reference.

1. List entries by author name. Write the author's last name first.
2. Underline the title of a book.
3. Place a colon between the place of publication and the name of the publisher.
4. Include the year of publication last.

The student who wrote about Ursa Major found the information in a book about constellations. According to the MLA recommendations above, which is the correct way for the student to cite this source?

- **A** Winters, Gerald R. Looking at the Night Sky. Covington Press—San Diego, 2005.
- **B** Winters, Gerald R. Looking at the Night Sky. San Diego: Covington Press, 2005.
- **C** Winters, Gerald R. Looking at the Night Sky. 2005: Covington Press, San Diego.
- **D** Gerald R. Winters. Looking at the Night Sky. San Diego: Covington Press, 2005.

Literature Online Unit Assessment To prepare for the Unit test, go to www.glencoe.com.

Test Preparation and Practice

English Language Arts

8. C is the correct answer. The other options contain redundancies.

9. C is the correct answer. The paragraph is concerned with the relationship between Ursa Major and the figure of a bear. The specific name of one of the stars in the constellation is extraneous information.

10. D is the correct answer. The present perfect tense of the verb is used when expressing an action or condition that occurred at some indefinite time in the past.

11. B is the correct answer. It is the only option that meets all four requirements.

Unit Assessment Have students access the Web site to prepare for the Unit Four test.

Assess

12. **B** is the correct answer. The nonessential appositive "king of the gods" should be set off with commas.
13. **C** is the correct answer. A comma is needed after the introductory prepositional clause and before the nonessential appositive "a follower of the goddess Artemis."
14. **C** is the correct answer. Dangling modifiers do not logically modify any word in the sentence.
15. **C** is the correct answer. The past tense is the best choice.
16. **A** is the correct answer. Commas should be used to set off the nonessential adjective clause.
17. **D** is the correct answer.
18. **B** is the correct answer. All nouns should be capitalized in a book title.

WRITING: English Language Conventions

Answer questions 12–18 on a separate sheet of paper.

12 Decide which punctuation mark is needed in the sentence.

Zeus, king of the gods fell in love with Callisto, and they had a child named Arcas.

A .
B ,
C :
D ;

13 Choose the sentence that is punctuated correctly.

A To the ancient Greeks Ursa Major represented Callisto a follower of the goddess Artemis.
B To the ancient Greeks, Ursa Major represented Callisto a follower of the goddess Artemis.
C To the ancient Greeks, Ursa Major represented Callisto, a follower of the goddess Artemis.
D To the ancient Greeks, Ursa Major represented Callisto, a follower of the goddess, Artemis.

14 What type of an error has the writer of this sentence made?

Looking at the night sky, Ursa Major contains the group of stars commonly known as the Big Dipper.

A spelling
B capitalization
C dangling modifier
D parallelism

15 Read this sentence.

Zeus, seeing what was about to happen, would turn Arcas into a small bear.

Choose the word or group of words that BEST replaces the underlined part of the sentence.

A will turn
B is turning
C turned
D has turned

16 Read this sentence.

Some North American tribes including the Algonquin and Iroquois also associated the constellation with a gigantic bear.

Choose the correct way to punctuate the underlined part of the sentence.

A Some North American tribes, including the Algonquin and Iroquois,
B Some North American tribes, including the Algonquin and Iroquois
C Some North American tribes—including the Algonquin and Iroquois
D Some North American tribes, including the Algonquin and Iroquois;

17 Choose the word that is spelled correctly.

Confident and experienced, the bear trainer exhibited a _____ attitude toward what seemed like a dangerous activity.

A nonshalant
B nonchalent
C nonchelant
D nonchalant

18 Read this sentence.

In Gentle Giants: The black bears of British Columbia, author Michael Winthrop explores the lives of these intelligent mammals.

Which of the following is the BEST way to capitalize the underlined group of words?

A Gentle Giants: the Black bears of British Columbia
B Gentle Giants: The Black Bears of British Columbia
C Gentle giants: the Black Bears of British Columbia
D Gentle Giants: The Black Bears Of British Columbia

Writing

Book Titles Remind students that they will need to know how to capitalize the titles of books when they compile bibliographies for research reports. The usual practice is to capitalize the first and last words of the title, all nouns, pronouns, verbs, adverbs, and adjectives, as well as all prepositions of more than four letters. Do not capitalize articles, coordinating conjunctions, or prepositions of fewer than five letters unless they appear as the first word of the title. **OL**

WRITING: Writing Applications

Complete the writing activity below. Do your planning and writing on separate sheets of paper.

Word Power

"A word has power in and of itself. It comes from nothing into sound and meaning; it gives origin to all things. By means of words can a man deal with the world on equal terms. And the word is sacred."

—N. Scott Momaday
American author

Do you agree or disagree with this quotation? Write an essay in which you explain to your teacher your ideas about the quotation. Support your viewpoint with examples and reasons based on your own experiences, observations, and/or readings.

Be sure to include

- five paragraphs, including an introduction, a body, and a conclusion to your essay
- a viewpoint based on the assigned task
- examples and reasons to support your viewpoint

Use a separate sheet of paper to plan your writing. As you write, keep in mind that your essay will be evaluated for **ideas and content, organization, style, voice,** and **language conventions.**

Writing Checklist

Before you begin writing, be sure to

- ❑ brainstorm for ideas
- ❑ organize your ideas into a logical pattern
- ❑ develop a plan for an introduction, a body, and a conclusion

As you write your essay, be sure to

- ❑ respond to the quotation and clearly state your interpretation
- ❑ provide reasons for your interpretation
- ❑ use language and vocabulary that will help convey a clear and interesting message
- ❑ maintain a tone that is appropriate for your intended audience
- ❑ use correct sentence structure, grammar, and punctuation

Assess

Assessment of writing prompts should focus on four elements:

- **Ideas and Content,** the message or theme and the details that develop it
- **Organization,** the arrangement of main ideas and supporting details
- **Style,** the word choices that a writer uses to convey meaning and the fluency, or rhythm and flow, of sentences
- **Voice,** the writer's unique way of using tone and style

Students' writing should also be assessed for correct **capitalization, punctuation, spelling, grammar and usage, paragraphing,** and **sentence structure.**

In addition, student essays should:

- fully complete the assigned task
- include complete, thorough, relevant, and logically organized ideas
- exhibit correct word usage
- demonstrate exceptional writing technique
- use language and tone appropriate for the task and audience

Unit at a Glance
Epic and Myth

About the Unit

Unit 5 charts the voyages of epic and mythic characters. These stories have universal qualities that make them just as applicable in modern times as when they were written. Epics and myths tell large, dramatic stories with grand flourishes; although, individual examples vary in a number of ways. As presented in this unit, the form can range from a hero's journey to a tale of humans interacting with gods.

Unit Introduction
Building Background
2–3 days

Part 1: Journeys
8–12 days

Part 1 covers mythic and epic literature in which the main character embarks on a journey. Specifically, this part includes the story of the hero Odysseus. A chart showing the core skills taught in this Part appears on pages 953A–953B.

SELECTIONS AND FEATURES

Part 2: Courage and Cleverness
4–6 days

Part 2 presents archetypal literature in which characters triumph over supernatural powers. A chart showing the core skills taught in this Part appears on pages 1053A–1053B.

SELECTIONS AND FEATURES

End-of-Unit Features
6–8 Days

Unit Resources

Glencoe Literature: The Reader's Choice offers a comprehensive package of tools to optimize student learning and the teaching experience. Each resource has been designed to assist students in specific areas and to offer instructional support for teachers. While all of these areas are covered in the core textbook, some students may need extra practice or additional help in specific areas. The resource package is designed so that you, the teacher, can choose which items will best assist your students. You may also use these resources as homework assignments and for assessment purposes. The following are resources recommended for use with Unit 5.

Key for Unit Resource

- Blackline Master
- Workbook
- Supplemental Text
- CD-ROM
- DVD
- Transparency
- Web-based

Essential Instructional Support

FAST FILE UNIT 5 RESOURCES

Reading and Literature

- Unit Introduction, pp. 1–2
- The Big Idea Foldable, pp. 3–4
- The Big Idea School-Home Connection, p. 5
- The Big Idea School-Home Connection (Spanish), p. 6
- Challenge Planner, pp. 7–10
- Academic Vocabulary Development, pp. 11–12
- Literary History, pp. 16–17
- Comparing Literature Graphic Organizer, p. 30
- Literary Element, pp. 18, 21, 24, 27, 30, 32, 39, 42, 45, 47, 51
- Reading Strategy, pp. 19, 22, 25, 28, 31, 33, 35, 40, 43, 46, 48, 52
- Active Reading Graphic Organizers, pp. 57–66
- Selection Vocabulary Practice, pp. 20, 23, 26, 29, 34, 41, 44, 49
- Literary Focus, pp. 14, 37

Writing, Grammar, and Spelling

- Spelling Practice, p. 53
- Grammar Workshop, p. 50
- Writing Workshop Graphic Organizer, p. 54

Speaking, Listening, and Viewing

- Speaking, Listening, and Viewing Activities, pp. 55–56

English Language Learners

- English Language Coach Review, pp. 15, 38

DIFFERENTIATED INSTRUCTION

- Active Learning and Note Taking Guide, pp. 148–178
- Leveled Vocabulary Development, pp. 62–69
- Skill Level Up!™ A Language Arts Game
- Listening Library Audio CD, disc 2, tracks 20–33
- Glencoe BookLink 3
- Vocabulary PuzzleMaker
- Literature Library Vocabulary PuzzleMaker

ASSESSMENT

- Selection and Unit Assessments, pp. 163–188, 219–220
- Selection Quick Checks, pp. 82–94
- Selection Quick Checks (Spanish), pp. 82–94
- Assessment by Learning Objectives, pp. 48–56
- Rubrics for Assessing Student Writing, Listening and Speaking, pp. 14–15, 34–35
- Standardized Test Preparation and Practice
- Glencoe Online Essay Grader
- Interactive Tutor: Self-Assessment
- Exam*View*® Assessment Suite
- Literature Library Exam*View*® Assessment

Additional Instructional Support

LITERATURE AND READING

- Active Learning and Note Taking Guide, pp. 148–178
- *inTIME* Magazines
- Glencoe Literature Library
- Literature Launchers: Pre-Reading Videos
- Literature Classics

WRITING, GRAMMAR, AND SPELLING

- REAL Success in Writing: Research and Reports
- Writing Constructed Responses
- Spelling Power eWorkbook
- Revising with Style eWorkbook
- Sentence Diagraming eWorkbook
- Glencoe Grammar & Composition Handbook
- Grammar and Language Workbook
- Grammar & Language eWorkbook

PROFESSIONAL DEVELOPMENT

- Professional Development Package

TRANSPARENCIES

- Read Aloud, Think Aloud Transparencies 44–49
- Bellringer Options Transparencies
  - Selection Focus Transparencies 44–48
  - Daily Language Practice Transparencies 81–92
- Grammar and Language Transparencies 3, 5
- Writing Workshop Transparencies 26–30
- Visual Literacy/Fine Art Transparencies

ENGLISH LANGUAGE LEARNER

- English Language Coach, Unit Resources (Fast File)
- *inTIME* Magazines (Spanish)
- Spanish Listening Library

TECHNOLOGY

- TeacherWorks Plus™
- StudentWorks Plus™
- Literature Launchers: Pre-Reading Videos
- Vocabulary PuzzleMaker
- Literature Library Vocabulary PuzzleMaker
- Skill Level Up!™ A Language Arts Game
- glencoe.com
- Presentation Plus!™
- Exam*View*® Assessment Suite
- Literature Library Exam*View*® Assessment Suite
- Listening Library
- Interactive Tutor: Self-Assessment
- Glencoe BookLink 3
- Online Student Edition, mhln.com
- Glencoe Online Essay Grader
- Grammar and Language eWorkbook
- Revising with Style eWorkbook
- Sentence Diagraming eWorkbook
- Spelling Power eWorkbook
- Literature Classics
- Spanish Listening Library

Additional Glencoe Resources

Dinah Zike's Foldables™

Foldables™ are three-dimensional, interactive graphic organizers that help students practice basic writing skills, review key vocabulary terms, and answer Big Ideas. Every unit contains a Foldable™ activity. You can find the pattern and directions for the Unit 5 Foldable™ in the Unit 5 Resources Fast File booklet. You can use the Foldables™ as they are presented or modify them to suit the needs of your students.

LiteratureOnline

For a wealth of online resources that support the instruction in Unit 5, students and teachers can visit our Web site at glencoe.com. Students will find additional learning, practice, and assessment opportunities such as these, which are noted in the student text:

- Author Search
- Big Idea Overview and Activity
- Interactive Literary Elements Handbook
- Study Central
- Unit Assessment
- Web Activities
- Writing Models

Teachers will find planning and instructional tools that include the following:

- Book Lesson Plans
- Web Activity Lesson Plans
- Teacher Forum
- Professional Resources

Go to glencoe.com to see the entire selection of *Glencoe Literature* online resources.

Glencoe's Presentation Plus!™, a multimedia teaching tool, lets you present dynamic lessons that will engage your students. Using Microsoft PowerPoint®, you can customize the presentations to create your own personalized lessons. Use CheckPoint questions with interactive response keypads to get immediate student feedback during lessons, to increase student participation, and to assess student comprehension.

Glencoe Literature Library

The collection of hardcover books includes full-length novels, novellas, plays, and works of nonfiction. Each volume consists of at least one complete extended-length reading accompanied by several related readings from a broad range of genres. A separate Study Guide for each *Glencoe Literature Library* book provides teaching notes and reproducible activity pages for students. Glencoe Literature Library titles that complement this unit include:

- ***Call of the Wild with Related Readings*** by Jack London
- ***The Adventures of Tom Sawyer with Related Readings*** by Mark Twain

GLENCOE BOOKLINK

Use the Glencoe BookLink 3 CD-ROM, a database of more than 26,700 titles, to *create customized reading lists* for your students.

- Search for award-winning titles (e.g., Newbery Award winners, Coretta Scott King Award winners, and Caldecott Medal winners) and for books on several state recommended reading lists.
- Find Degrees of Reading Power™ (DRP) and Lexile™ readability scores for all selections.
- Organize reading lists by students' reading level, author, genre, theme, or area of interest.
- Get a brief summary of each selection.

You can find recommended leveled readings for this unit with Independent Reading (see pages 1104 and 1105).

Online Essay Grader

Use Glencoe's online essay grader powered by SkillWriter™ to score your students' writing and to provide individualized feedback to each student automatically.

You and your students can visit glencoe.com to link to the essay grader. *Students* can enter their essays and receive feedback on demand. *You* can manage demographic data, assign tests and generate individual student and aggregated reports. The essay grader can help you

- Save time with automatic scoring and individualized feedback.
- Supplement in-class writing instruction using guided writing practice.

REAL Success: Reading Excellence at All Levels

Glencoe REAL Success is a suite of new reading and language arts products designed to foster reading excellence at all levels.

Look for TWE point-of-use references for these specific products that will help your students succeed in reading this Unit.

- *Jamestown Literature: An Adapted Reader*
- REAL Success in Writing: Research and Reports
- Skill Level Up!™ A Language Arts Game
- CheckPoint PowerPoint™ slides
- Literature/Reading support at Glencoe Web site

Literature Launchers

Set the scene with Glencoe's Literature Launchers, engaging pre-reading video segments that introduce each unit. Each Unit Launcher brings the literature to life, featuring expert testimony and archival stills and footage from the time.

Insert your Glencoe Literature Launchers into your DVD player. Select the Unit 5 Launcher from the menu to introduce Epic and Myth.

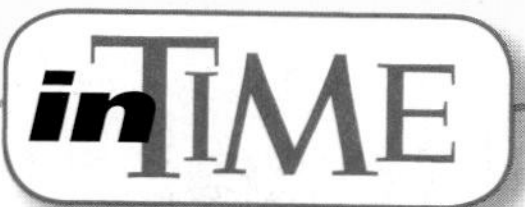

A lively collection of articles drawn from issues of the TIME family of magazines helps students develop the skills they need to interact with informational text in a meaningful way. Each of the news stories, feature articles, reviews, profiles, and essays in the magazine connect to an author, work, or theme in *Glencoe Literature: The Reader's Choice.* See the *inTIME* Teacher's Guide for specific connections to each unit and for reproducible student worksheets designed to develop students' reading and critical thinking skills.

Teacher Wraparound Edition Key

Level Appropriate Code

AL = Activities for students working above grade level

OL = Activities for students working at grade level

BL = Activities for students working below grade level

EL = Activities for English language learners

AS = Information for all students

Teacher Wraparound Prompts

R Reading Skill These activities help you teach reading skills and vocabulary.

V Vocabulary These activities help students comprehend words and incorporate them into reading.

BI Big Idea These activities and questions prompt students to explore the Big Idea.

L Literary Element These activities and questions help students comprehend selections and learn more about each genre.

★ Enrichment Additional activities and information involving art appreciation and history.

Professional Development Center

From Your Authors:

Teaching Literary Analysis: Epic and Myth

Connect to Today Talking with students about the universal nature of myths can help them to understand why myths are still relevant today. Discuss with students the origins of myths. Ask them to think about what the various myths explain about the world. Ask students to consider how similar myths emerge in different cultures, showing how their themes are universal. Discuss how the myths from the past become part of the culture today. After students have read "Perseus" by Edith Hamilton, "The Fenris Wolf" by Olivia Coolidge, and "Coyote and Crow" by Ella Clark, ask them to create a three-column chart to compare the three myths. In their charts, have students recount the origins of these stories, tell what these stories explain about the world, describe their universal nature, and explain how these myths are a part of our culture today.

Douglas Fisher and Beverly Chin

Make Personal Connections As students read the epics and myths in this chapter, ask them to make connections to their own lives. Have they ever gone on a journey? Where did they go? What did they hope to gain from the experience? Ask students why they think characters in myths often go on long journeys. Before students read the *Odyssey* by Homer, ask the above questions to activate students' prior knowledge and increase their interest in the text. As students read, keep the idea of going on a journey fresh in their minds by referring back to these questions occasionally.

Teacher to Teacher

Manuel (Manny) Galvan
Pueblo Magnet High School
Tucson, Arizona

As a unit-opening exercise, I lead my students on their own epic journeys using guided imagery in which they close their eyes and picture images from their lives. This is usually a journey through their past where they visit safe, familiar places and loved ones. Throughout the journey, I constantly reassure them of their complete safety and concentrate on the positive aspects of their past. I always have them meet a loved one who gives them an heirloom of some kind, either tangible or intangible. When they return from the journey, I ask them to write about their experiences by answering questions: "Where did you go? What did you see? Who was there and what happened?" I have found the writing that comes out of this experience is powerful and profound.

Making Literature Come Alive

Before you begin this unit or sometime during the unit, talk with other teachers about ways they have taught epic and myth. Have a lunch-time discussion group or an after-school hour for professional development and discuss the following questions and answers from our authors:

How can I help students learn about heroism from reading epics and myths?

- Ask students to pay attention to the actions of the hero or heroine and to determine what constitutes a heroic action. What are the essential features of a hero?
- Discuss why heroes often go on a journey. Is it the person or the opportunity that makes one a hero?
- Discuss the motivation that heroes have. What is the driving force for the heroes and heroines in these stories? Can anyone be a hero? What does it take? As students read each section of the excerpt from the *Odyssey,* ask them what motivates Odysseus.

If the oral tradition in literature is a foreign subject for students, how can I help them experience it?

- Teachers should read aloud and provide students listening opportunities to hear from expert readers.
- Students can play the "telephone game" in which a long message is started on one side of the room and whispered person to person until it gets across the room. This can reinforce the difficulty in maintaining the original message and why storytellers work so hard to provide their listeners with an authentic experience.
- Students should be invited to retell, orally, the information they have read. They should practice retelling the main ideas from the myth or epic to their peers. They should use lots of descriptive language, but not the exact language from the text in their retellings. After students have read "Vasilisa of the Golden Braid and Ivan the Pea" by Elizabeth Ann Warner, have students retell the events of the story. Have one student begin by describing the opening of the story. Once that student has described the first event, move to another student to pick up where the first student left off. Continue randomly allowing students to share the next event in the story until they have retold the entire myth.

How can reading myths help students understand cause-and-effect relationships?

- Many myths have a message or theme for the listener that involves a cause-and-effect relationship. For example, in the myth "Coyote and Crow" retold by Ella Clark, we learn that if you are prideful and enjoy flattery, then you may behave foolishly. Analyzing these messages helps students understand relationships between causes and effects.
- Students should be taught to use a "cause-and-effect" graphic organizer as part of their note taking when reading myths.

Focus

BELLRINGER

Bellringer Options
Literature Launcher Video
Daily Language Practice Transparency 81
Or **write on the board:** Name as many modern epics as you can. *(Possible answers could include* The Lord of the Rings, Star Wars, *and the Harry Potter books.)* Encourage students to consider multiple media, including movies, TV, books, and computer and video games. Discuss what makes these stories epic.

Objectives for the Unit Introduction

- To understand characteristics of epics and myths (SE)
- To identify and explore literary elements significant to epics and myths (SE)
- To analyze the effect that literary elements have upon the reader (SE)

The Burning of Troy, 1606. Pieter Schoubroeck. ★

944

Unit Introduction Skills

Epic and Myth

Reading Skills
- Reading the Epic (SE pp. 950–951)

Listening/Speaking/Viewing Skills
- Epic Ad Presentation (TWE p. 952)

Literary Elements
- The Epic (SE p. 946)
- Structure (SE p. 946)
- Myth and Archetype (SE p. 947)
- Symbol (SE p. 947)
- Literary Analysis (SE pp. 948–949)

Writing Skills/Grammar
- Write Your Own Adventure (TWE p. 946)
- Graphic Novel (TWE p. 948)
- Critique (TWE p. 950)

Epic and Myth

Looking Ahead

Many centuries ago, before books, magazines, paper, and pencils were invented, people recited their stories. Some of the stories they told offered explanations of natural phenomena, such as thunder and lightning, or the culture's customs or beliefs. Other stories were meant for entertainment. Taken together, these stories—these myths, epics, and legends—tell a history of loyalty and betrayal, heroism and cowardice, love and rejection. In this unit, you will explore the literary elements that make them unique.

PREVIEW **Big Ideas and Literary Focus**

	BIG IDEA:	LITERARY FOCUS:
1	Journeys	Hero
2	Courage and Cleverness	Archetype

INDIANA ACADEMIC STANDARDS (pages 944-951)

9.3 [Identify] story elements such as character, theme, plot, and setting...

9.3.7 Recognize and understand the significance of various literary devices, including figurative language, imagery, allegory...and symbolism...

Focus

Summary

The unit defines literary structure, myth, archetype, and symbol and gives examples of their use in epics and myths. Quotes from writers on reading Homer and an analysis of "The Wedding" from the Hindu epic *The Ramayana* are included.

Viewing the Art

Dutch artist Pieter Schoubroeck (c. 1570–1607) belonged to the Flemish school of painting, a style that arose in the Middle Ages in Flanders, an area now divided between Belgium, the Netherlands, and France. The influence of manuscript illumination on the Flemish style is visible in the painstaking attention to detail, rich colors, and highly developed technique of artists such as Schoubroeck. **AS**

Unit Resources

Classroom Management
- TeacherWorks Plus™ CD-ROM
- StudentWorks Plus™ CD-ROM
- Literature Launchers™: Pre-Reading Videos DVD, Unit Five

Core Instructional Support
- Unit 5 Resources (Fast Files)
- Literature Online, glencoe.com
- Presentation Plus!™ CD-ROM, Unit Five

Transparencies
- Literary Elements Transparencies 1, 3, 13, 15, 18, 19, 20, 45, 59, 80, 82, 86, 87
- Bellringer Options Transparencies: Selection Focus Transparencies 44–48 Daily Language Practice Transparencies 81–92

Differentiated Instruction
- Active Learning and Note Taking Guide, pp. 148–178
- Skill Level Up!™ A Language Arts Game

Assessment
- Selection and Unit Assessments, pp. 163–188, 219–220
- Exam*View*® Assessment Suite CD-ROM
- Assessment by Learning Objectives, pp. 48–56

Supplemental Reading
- Glencoe Literature Library
- Glencoe BookLink 3 CD-ROM
- *inTIME* Magazines

Teach

R Reading Strategy

Connecting Have a student read aloud the paragraph at the top of the page.
Ask: Do you agree with Jung that in order for us to understand ourselves today, we must understand the past? Have students consider the impact of the past on their lives. What beliefs, knowledge, or traditions have their families handed down through the generations? How have they been affected by various historical events? Instruct students to keep this interconnectedness in mind while reading. OL

★ Cultural History

Poseidon The god Poseidon was believed by the Greeks to be the cause of violent, unpredictable movement. He ruled over the sea, earthquakes, and horses and was the son of Gaia (Earth) and Kronos (Time), brother to Zeus, Hera, Hades, and Demeter. The equivalent Roman god was called Neptune. His symbol is the trident, a three-pronged fishing spear. AS

Genre Focus: Epic and Myth

What is unique about epics and myths?

R Why do we read stories from the distant past? Why should we care about heroes and villains long dead? About cities and palaces that were destroyed centuries before our time? The noted psychologist and psychiatrist Carl Jung thought he knew the answer. He thought that in order for us to understand the people we are today, we have to learn about those who came before us. One way to do that, Jung believed, was to read the myths and epics of long ago. R

Epic

Epics often include descriptions of huge battles or wars.

The Epic

An **epic** is a long narrative poem about a serious subject. Its action centers on the **epic hero,** whose primary goal is usually to save his nation or its people during a time of crisis. The purpose of an epic poem is threefold: to entertain, to teach, and to inspire with examples of how people can succeed against great odds.

Epic Tales and Their Gods In epics, gods may take part in the action or at least take an interest in what happens, sometimes intervening to affect the course of events.

> Yet all the gods had pitied Lord Odysseus,
> all but Poseidon, raging cold and rough 
> against the brave king till he came ashore
> at last on his own land.
>
> —Homer, **from the *Odyssey***

Structure The way an author organizes images, ideas, words, and lines is called **structure.** Like many epics, the *Odyssey* begins with an **invocation,** a request to a muse to provide inspiration. In Greek mythology, the **muses** are nine goddesses who preside over the arts and sciences and inspire those who show talent in these areas.

> Sing in me, Muse, and through me tell the story
> of that man skilled in all ways of contending,
> the wanderer, harried for years on end,
> after he plundered the stronghold
> on the proud height of Troy.
>
> —Homer, **from the *Odyssey***

Additional Support

Skills Practice

WRITING: Choose Your Own Adventure Have students sharpen their writing skills by creating an adventure. Have the class work together to develop a hero, a setting, and a tricky situation. Then, split the class into groups. Invite each one to solve how the hero handles the situation and wins the day. Have each group present its finished story to the class. Then, have the class vote on the best adventure. OL

Myth and the Archetype

Myth

A **myth** is a traditional story of anonymous origin. Many myths are about the creation of earth; others are about love, adventure, trickery, or revenge. In many myths, human action is controlled or guided by gods, goddesses, and other supernatural beings.

For a time she kept his birth secret from her father, but it became increasingly difficult to do so in the narrow limits of that bronze house and finally one day the little boy—his name was Perseus—was discovered by his grandfather. "Your child!" Acrisius cried in great anger. "Who is his father?" But when Danaë answered proudly, "Zeus," he would not believe her.

—Edith Hamilton, **from "Perseus"**

L Archetype

An **archetype** is a thing, person, or pattern of circumstances that appears repeatedly in literature. Most ancient myths, folktales, fables, ballads, and legends contain archetypal characters, such as the evil villain, the lovesick suitor, and the fool. They also may contain archetypal themes, such as the hidden treasure or the rite of passage.

When the gods first saw the Fenris Wolf, he was so young that they thought they could tame him. They took him to Asgard, therefore, and brave Tyr undertook to feed and train him. Presently, however, the black monster grew so enormous that his open jaws would stretch from heaven to earth, showing teeth as large as the trunks of oak trees and as sharply pointed as knives.

—Olivia Coolidge, **from "The Fenris Wolf"**

Symbol

A **symbol** is an object, person, place, or event that has a literal meaning and a figurative meaning. For example, a heart is often used as a symbol of love, while a book might be used as a symbol of knowledge. Some symbols have more than one figurative meaning, and their meanings may change or evolve through a literary work.

I thought, as I wiped my eyes on the corner
   of my apron:
Penelope did this too.
And more than once: you can't keep
   weaving all day
And undoing it all through the night . . .

—Edna St. Vincent Milay, **from "An Ancient Gesture"**

LiteratureOnline **Study Central** Visit www.glencoe.com to review epics and myths.

Teach

L Literary Element

Archetype Note that the character of the evil villain is a familiar example of an archetype.

Ask: Who would you consider to be an archetypal villain in modern films? *(Possible answers: Sauron from* Lord of the Rings, *Voldemort from the Harry Potter books, Darth Vader from* Star Wars*)* OL

Study Central Have students visit the Web site for resources that will help them to review epic and myth.

Differentiated Instruction

Myth Making Suggest that creative and gifted students try their hand at creating a myth. Instruct them to begin with an outline that includes:

- plot events
- characterization of their hero, including background and character traits
- archetypes and symbols

Encourage students to include drawings, paintings, or collages of their settings and characters to illustrate their stories. Have them share their work with the class. AL

Academic Standards

Additional Support activities on pp. 946 and 947 cover the following standards:

Skills Practice: **9.4.1** Discuss ideas for writing with classmates...and develop drafts...collaboratively.

Differentiated Instruction: **9.5.1** Write... short stories that describe a sequence of events and communicate the significance of the events to the audience [and] describe with specific details...the specific actions, movements, gestures, and feelings of the characters...

Teach

R Reading Strategy

Setting a Purpose Remind students that setting a purpose before reading a passage will improve their reading speed and comprehension. Suggest that students read with the purpose of being able to summarize the plot concisely. After they've read the story, have them write a one-paragraph summary and then compare it with their classmates' to determine if they missed any important plot points or characters. OL

★ Cultural History

Mount Meru The reference to "Mount Meru, which churned the Ocean of Milk," refers to a Hindu myth in which the god Vishnu restored equilibrium between the forces of light and darkness by enlisting them to use Meru as a churning stick to churn a cosmic sea of milk for the nectar of immortality. AS

Literary Analysis Model

How do literary elements help us enjoy epics and myths?

R The *Ramayana*, which was written by a man named Maharishi Valmiki, is a Hindu epic of 24,000 verses divided into seven chapters, or books. It tells the story of Prince Rama of Ayodhya (an ancient city of India), his wife, Sita, and his close companion and brother, Lakshmana. The *Ramayana* is thought to contain the teachings of ancient Hindu sages.

APPLYING Literary Elements

Symbol

Here, as in many myths and epics, the bow is a symbol of war and vengeance. This bow belonged to Shira, a Hindu god also known as the "Destroyer."

Style

Most epics are written in a grand or elevated style. Language is formal, and descriptions can be extensive.

The Wedding from the *Ramayana*

translated by R. K. Narayan

King Janaka had in his possession an enormous bow which at one time belonged to Shiva, who had abandoned it and left it in the custody of an early ancestor of Janaka's, and it had remained an heirloom. Sita, as a baby girl, was a gift of Mother Earth to Janaka, being found in a furrow when a field was ploughed. Janaka adopted the child, tended her, and she grew up into a beauty, so much so that several princes who considered themselves eligible thronged Janaka's palace and contended for Sita's hand. Unable to favor anyone in particular, and in order to ward them off, King Janaka made it a condition that whoever could lift, bend, and string Shiva's bow would be considered fit to become Sita's husband. When her suitors took a look at the bow, they realized that it was a hopeless and unacceptable condition. They left in a rage, and later returned with their armies, prepared to win Sita by force. But Janaka resisted their aggression, and ultimately the suitors withdrew. As time passed Janaka became anxious whether he would ever see his daughter married and settled—since the condition once made could not be withdrawn. No one on earth seemed worthy of approaching Shiva's bow. Janaka sighed. "I tremble when I think of Sita's future, and question my own judgment in linking her fate with this mighty, divine heirloom in our house."

"Do not despair," said Viswamithra soothingly. "How do you know it was not a divine inspiration that gave you the thought?"

"In all the worlds, is there anyone who can tackle this bow, the very sight of which in Shiva's hand made erring gods and godlings tremble and collapse—until Shiva put it away and renounced its use?"

"With your permission, may we see it?"

Janaka said, "I'll have it brought here. It has lain in its shed too long. . . . Who knows, moving it out may change all our fates." He called on his attendants to fetch the bow. . . .

The bow was placed in a carriage on eight pairs of wheels and arrived drawn by a vast number of men. During its passage from its shed through the streets, a crowd followed it. It was so huge that no one could comprehend it at one glance. "Is this a bow or that mountain called Meru, which churned the Ocean of Milk in ancient times?" people marveled. "What ★

Additional Support

Skills Practice

WRITING: Graphic Novel Challenge students to create a graphic novel of *The Wedding.* Assign groups of students various sections of the story. Remind them to include plot, dialogue, and characters. Students may use clippings from magazines or their own drawings for visuals. When all the sections have been combined, have students review the novel for completeness. OL

The marriage of Rama and his brothers from the Sangri Ramayana, ca. 1760–65. Pahari School. National Museum, New Delhi, India.

target is there to receive the arrow shot out of this bow, even if someone lifts and strings it!" wondered some. "If Janaka meant seriously to find a son-in-law, he should have waived this condition. How unwise of him!"

Rama looked at his master. Viswamithra nodded as if to say, "Try it." As Rama approached the bow with slow dignity, the onlookers held their breath and watched. Some prayed silently for him. Some commented, "How cruel! This supposed sage is not ashamed to put the delicate, marvelous youth to this harsh trial!" "The King is perverse and cruel to place this godlike youth in this predicament. . . . If he was serious about it, he should have just placed Sita's hand in his instead of demanding all this acrobatic feat. . . ." "The King's aim is to keep Sita with him forever—this is one way of never facing separation!"

Archetype The handsome suitor forced to earn the trust and admiration of the bride's father is a thematic archetype.

L While they were speculating thus, Rama approached the bow. Some of the onlookers, unable to bear the suspense, closed their eyes and prayed for his success, saying, "If he fails to bring the ends of this bow together, what is to happen to the maiden?" What they missed, because they had shut their eyes, was to note how swiftly Rama picked up the bow, tugged the string taut, and brought the tips together. They were startled when they heard a deafening report, caused by the cracking of the bow at its arch, which could not stand the pressure of Rama's grip.

The atmosphere was suddenly relaxed. The gods showered down flowers and blessings, clouds parted and precipitated rains, the oceans tossed up in the air all the rare treasures from their depths. The sages cried, "Janaka's tribulations and trials are ended." Music filled the air.

Epic  Gods, goddesses, and other supernatural beings are important characters in most myths and epics.

Reading Check

Interpreting Why does Janaka worry that his daughter, Sita, will never be married?

Teach

Reading Check

Answer: *The task he set for the suitors proved too difficult.*

L Literary Element

Hero Ask: Who is the hero in this story? How do you know he is the hero? *(Rama; He faces a difficult challenge and overcomes it against great odds.)* OL

★ Writer's Technique

Epic Style The grand writing style characteristic of epics is evident in the formal tone of the dialogue in *The Wedding.* The highly proper language sharply contrasts with the colloquial style that modern readers expect in realistic dialogue. AS

Differentiated Instruction

Identifying Characters Learning disabled students may find the unusual names overwhelming. Have students keep a list in their reading journals with the following heads:

- Name
- Description and character traits
- Role (include who the person is related to and how; for example, Viswamithra is Rama's master) BL

Academic Standards

Additional Support activities on pp. 948 and 949 cover the following standards:

Skills Practice: **9.5.2** Write responses to literature that demonstrate a comprehensive grasp of the significant ideas of literary works [and] demonstrate an awareness of the author's style and an appreciation of the effects created…

Differentiated Instruction: **9.3** [Identify] story elements such as character…

Teach

R Reading Strategy

Connect Instruct students to read the quotes.
Ask: Which quote do you find the most interesting? Why? Go through each quote with the students and guide them to identify the salient points. OL

★ Viewing the Art

Flemish painter Joos van Ghent (active 1460–1480) was also known as Joos van Wassenhove and Giusto da Guanto (Justus of Ghent). Although there are many paintings attributed to Joos, the only documented painting is his *Communion of the Apostles*, which helped bring the Flemish oil-painting technique to Italy. AS

InterActive Reading Practice
Have students access the Web site for more practice with reading strategies.

Writers on Reading

What do writers say about epics and myths?

R Homer's Naturalness

What has made Homer for three thousand years the greatest poet in the world is his naturalness. We love each other as in Homer. We hate each other as in Homer. We are perpetually being interfered with as in Homer by chance and fate and necessity, by invisible influences for good and by invisible influences for evil.

—John Cowper Powys, **from *Homer and the Aether***

Homer, Joos van Ghent. Mid-15th century. Painting. Galleria Nazionale delle Marche, Urbino, Italy. ★

Literature Online **InterActive Reading Practice**
Visit www.glencoe.com to practice these strategies for reading the epic.

Homer's Authenticity

Few men can be sailors, soldiers, and naturalists. Yet this Homer was neither land-lubber nor stay-at-home nor ninny. He wrote for audiences to whom adventures were daily life and the sea their universal neighbor. So he dared not err.

—T. E. Shaw ("Lawrence of Arabia"), **from *The Odyssey of Homer***

Homer's Style

The best-known piece of lore about Homer is that he was blind, and it does not really matter whether this was literally so or was a story that developed as a metaphor for an eye that turned inward. The main thing is that his sense of the world was the work of his imagination. What the rest of us take for granted as daylight reality was for the poet the basis of a new envisaging. "We must shut our eyes," said the Irish poet Patrick Kavanagh, "to see our way to heaven," but since Homer's eyes were closed already, what he had to envisage were the ways of earth, and this accounts for the unique fullness with which ordinary things and routine activities are endowed in his poetry. The famous directness of his style is a natural consequence of his inner lucidity, his need for images of immediate phenomenal presence, of an almost cinematic speed and focus.

—Seamus Heaney, **from the Introduction to the *Odyssey***

Odysseus's Realism

There is no one else remotely like Odysseus in the Homeric poems, no one else so mature, worldly, intellectually curious, or as we now might say, so realistic. . . . No hero ever has been so little doom-eager as Homer's Odysseus. Self-controlled, pragmatic, he is the paradigm of the will-to-live, and teaches us survival through cunning and endurance.

—Harold Bloom, **from *Odysseus/Ulysses***

Additional Support

Skills Practice

WRITING: Critique Brainstorm a list of epics. Have students choose one as the subject of a one-page critique explaining what makes the story so effective. Suggest students review their essays for a passage that can be used as a pull-out quote, like the ones in the Writers on Reading section. Have students read their quotes aloud and discuss their effectiveness with the class. OL

(above) *A Reading from Homer,* 1885. Lawrence Alma-Tadema. Oil on canvas, 91.8 X 183.5 cm. Philadelphia Museum of Art, Pennsylvania. ★

(right) *Muse Reading a Scroll,* Klugmann painter, late 5th century B.C. Red figure vase, Louvre, Paris.

Odysseus's Cunning

L That Odysseus is a hoaxer is already known before the *Odyssey.* Wasn't it he who thought up the great swindle of the wooden horse? And at the beginning of the *Odyssey* the first recollections of his character are two flashbacks to the Trojan War . . . two tales of trickery.

—Italo Calvino, **from** ***The Uses of Literature***

Odysseus's Humanity

Organization, coolness, tact, cunning. These qualities are all to be found in Odysseus, and to them we can add various endearing imperfections of character. . . . When Helen is carried off to Troy he tries to evade his obligations by pretending to be mad. Still, once launched on the expedition he proves wise and cunning in counsel and prudently brave in war. He is more likeable than Achilles and Ajax and Aeneas; he is more human. . . .

—Anthony Burgess, **from** ***Odysseus/Ulysses***

Reading Check

Responding From your own reading experiences, which passage do you identify with most closely? Explain.

Teach

Reading Check

Answer: *Answers will vary. Make sure students support their responses.*

L Literary Element

Hero Ask: What character traits can you infer about the hero Odysseus from Calvino's quote? *(He makes good use of trickery and is a seasoned warrior.)* **OL**

★ Viewing the Art

Sir Lawrence Alma-Tadema (1836–1912) was one of the most successful artists of the Victorian era. Lawrence emigrated from Holland to England, where he was knighted in 1899. His artwork features idealized ancient settings, elaborate detail, and beautiful people. **AS**

English Language Coach

Vocabulary Help English language learners may find some of the vocabulary in the quotes troublesome. Invite volunteers to write unfamiliar words on the board. Instruct partners to use a dictionary to find the definition of a word and then generate a list of synonyms. Have students share their results with the class. Instruct students to add synonyms from their classmates' lists to their own lists. **EL**

Academic Standards

Additional Support activities on pp. 950 and 951 cover the following standards:

Skills Practice: **9.5.3** Write expository compositions, including analytical essays...that communicate information and ideas...accurately and coherently...

English Language Coach: **9.1** Use... a growing knowledge of English... to determine the meaning of words...

Assess/Close

Guide to Reading Epics and Myths

Suggest that students take notes on these points:

- What insight into human nature does the story provide?
- What emotions are explored?

Elements of Epics and Myths

Suggest that students create a chart that includes *myth, epic hero, symbol,* and *archetype*. As they read, have students add specifics to their charts.

Activities

1. **Visual Literacy** Suggest that students use color coding to help them with organization.
2. **Speaking/Listening** Have students consider whether they wish to use formal or colloquial language.
3. **Writing** Have students brainstorm a list of epics and myths to use as examples.

FOLDABLES™ Study Organizer

Have students make and label the Tab Book. Their notes on people, places, and events can be written on each tab.

Wrap-Up

Guide to Reading Epics and Myths

- Epics and myths give us insight into human nature.
- Most epics and myths explore a range of human emotions, including anger, love, jealousy, rage, and vengeance.
- Epics and myths are timeless because they have the characteristics of a good story. They are imaginative, interesting, inspiring, and completely authentic.

Elements of Epics and Myths

- An **epic** is a long narrative poem written about a serious subject.
- A **myth** is a traditional story of anonymous origin that deals with gods, goddesses, heroes, and supernatural events.
- The **epic hero** is the central character in an epic. He is driven by his desire to save his country or its people during a time of crisis.
- An **archetype** is a thing, person, or pattern of circumstances that appears repeatedly in literature.

Activities

Use what you have learned about reading epics and myths to complete one of these activities.

1. **Visual Literacy** Develop a story frame or sequence organizer that explores the major events in a myth or epic you have read.
2. **Speaking/Listening** With a partner, invent a conversation between two characters mentioned in the Unit Introduction. Write your dialogue, rehearse it, and then present it to the class.
3. **Writing** Create a bulleted list that details the characteristics of a myth and another that details the characteristics of an epic. Use your lists to write a brief compare-and-contrast essay about the two genres.

TAB BOOK

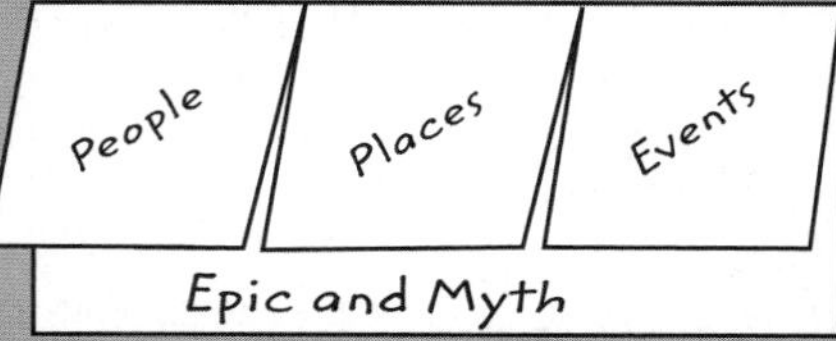

Try using this study organizer to take notes on the people, places, and events you read about in this unit.

INDIANA ACADEMIC STANDARDS (page 952)

9.3.6 Analyze and trace an author's development of time and sequence...

9.7.17 Deliver oral responses to literature...

9.3.2 Compare and contrast...genres...

Additional Support

Skills Practice

LISTENING/SPEAKING/VIEWING: Epic Ad Presentation Invite students to create an ad for the *Odyssey*. Divide the class into groups. Have them decide on a form for the epic, such as a novel, movie, or TV miniseries. Instruct them to use elements from the Introduction, such as quotes and adjectives, to help them "sell" their concepts. Stress the importance of including strong visuals. Have students present their completed projects to the class. OL

PART 1

Journeys

Captain Desse of Bordeaux saves the crew of the Dutch ship "Columbus", ca. 19th century. J. A. Theodore Gudin. Musée des Beaux-Arts, Bordeaux, France.

BIG IDEA

BI Journeys have long been important in literature and in history. Travelers encounter new cultures, new sights, new experiences, and sometimes grave dangers. The literature in Part 1 includes the epic tale of a legendary hero of ancient Greece, Odysseus. As you read the epic, ask yourself: What actions or traits make a person heroic?

Analyzing and Extending

BI Big Idea

Journeys Encourage students to connect with the idea of the journey by considering their own travels.

Write on the board: Sights, Experiences, Challenges. Have students recall a trip and list their impressions under each category. Invite students to share their impressions. OL

Viewing the Art

French painter Jean-Antoine Theodore Gudin (1802–1880) was renowned for his marine paintings. French King Louis-Philippe commissioned Gudin to paint pictures of the French navy for the palace of Versailles. AS

Differentiated Instruction

Building Background Explain that journeys can be both literal and figurative. While a story may be about an actual journey, the author may also be writing about the emotional or spiritual journeys of the characters. As they read, have students look for the different kinds of journeys. BL

Academic Standards

Additional Support activities on pp. 952 and 953 cover the following standards:

Skills Practice: **9.5.7** Use varied and expanded vocabulary, appropriate for specific forms and topics. **9.7.4** Use…visual aids…to enhance the appeal and accuracy of presentations.

Differentiated Instruction: **9.3.5** Compare works that express a universal theme…

Part 1: Skills Scope and Sequence

Readability Scores Key
Dale-Chall/**DRP**/Lexile

PACING (DAYS) STANDARD	BLOCK	SELECTIONS AND FEATURES	LITERARY ELEMENTS
1–2 class sessions	1	LITERARY HISTORY: Homer and the Epic, pp. 956–957	
		from *The Odyssey* Part 1 by Homer **7.9/61/NA**, pp. 958–979	Epic and Epic Hero, SE pp. 959, 963, 967–970, 972, 974, 976, 977, 979 Irony, TWE p. 975
2–3 class sessions	1	from *The Odyssey* Part 2 by Homer **7.9/61/NA**, pp. 980–993	Conflict, SE pp. 980, 983–985, 989, 990, 993 Similes, TWE p. 991
		from *The Odyssey* Part 3 by Homer **7.9/61/NA**, pp. 994–1007	Characterization, SE pp. 994, 996, 997, 999, 1000, 1003, 1005, 1007
2 class sessions	1	from *The Odyssey* Part 4 by Homer **7.9/61/NA**, pp. 1008–1021	Plot, SE pp. 1008, 1009, 1012, 1013, 1015, 1017, 1020 Narrator, SE p. 1020 Character, TWE p. 1014
		Vocabulary Workshop: Word Origins, p. 1022	
2–3 class sessions	1	COMPARING LITERATURE Across Genres "Odyssey" by Homer, pp. 958–1021 "Ithaca" by C.P. Cavafy, pp. 1024–1025 "An Ancient Gesture" by Edna St. Vincent Millay, p. 1026 "Waiting" from *The Penelopiad* by Margaret Atwood **7.9/59/510**, pp. 1027–1028	Comparing Theme, SE pp. 1023, 1029 Symbolism, TWE p. 1026
		TIME magazine, "Leaving It All Behind" by Susan Jakes **7.9/58/920**, pp. 1030–1034	
1–2 class sessions	1	"Over Hill and Under Hill" from *The Hobbit* by J.R.R Tolkien **7.3/59/1080**, pp. 1035–1047	Motif, SE pp. 1036, 1038, 1040–1044, 1046 Narrator, SE p. 1046
		VISUAL PERSPECTIVE on *The Hobbit:* from *The Hobbit* by Charles Dixon and David Wenzel, pp. 1048–1052	Dialogue, TWE pp. 1048, 1050 Motif, TWE pp. 1049, 1050

About the Part

Part 1 deals with physical journeys and quests as well as characters' personal journeys through life and how their decisions affect the outcome.

READING AND CRITICAL THINKING	VOCABULARY	WRITING AND GRAMMAR	LISTENING, SPEAKING, AND VIEWING
Preview, TWE p. 956 Researching Oral Literature, TWE p. 956			
Analyzing Figurative Language, SE pp. 959, 963, 970, 972, 975, 978, 979	Synonyms, SE pp. 959, 979 Context Clues, TWE p. 971	Appositives, TWE p. 967 Using Spatial Order, TWE p. 968	Analyzing Art, SE pp. 974; TWE pp. 964, 966, 973, 976 Literature Groups, SE p. 979
Identifying Sequence, SE pp. 982, 986, 988, 989, 992, 993 Problem and Solution, TWE p. 982	Context Clues, SE pp. 980, 993	Analyze Description, SE p. 993 Monologue Using Jargon, TWE p. 984	Analyzing Art, SE p. 987; TWE pp. 983, 985, 992 Oral Interpretation, TWE p. 988
Determining Main Idea and Supporting Details, SE pp. 994, 996, 997, 1000, 1002, 1005, 1007	Analogies, SE pp. 994, 1007	Poetry, TWE p. 996 Verb Tenses, TWE p. 1000 Explanations, TWE p. 1004	Analyzing Art, SE p. 1006; TWE pp. 998, 1001, 1003 Literature Groups, SE p. 1007
Analyzing Cause-and-Effect Relationships, SE pp. 1008–1020	Word Origins, SE pp. 1008, 1020 Academic Vocabulary, SE p. 1020	Analyze Character, SE p. 1021 Using Compound Adjectives, SE p. 1021	Analyzing Art, SE p. 1010; TWE pp. 1015, 1018 Geography Activity, SE p. 1021
	Examining Words from Greek and Roman Myth, SE p. 1022		
Predict, TWE p. 1026 Analyzing Cause and Effect, TWE p. 1028 Perspective, TWE p. 1028		Quickwrites, SE pp. 1025, 1026, 1028 Essay, SE p. 1029 Writing from Alternate Point of View, TWE p. 1028	Comparing Author's Meaning, SE p. 1029 Using Visuals, TWE p. 1027
Responding to Events, SE p. 1030; TWE pp. 1032, 1033		Connecting, TWE p. 1032	
Comparing Contrasting Characters, SE pp. 1036, 1038, 1039, 1042, 1046 Character Chart, SE p. 1036	Context Clues, SE pp. 1036, 1046 Academic Vocabulary, SE p. 1046	Respond to Voice, SE p. 1047 Gerunds, SE p. 1047 Parentheses, TWE p. 1038 Rewriting, TWE p. 1044	Visual Image, SE p. 1045 Analyzing Art, SE p. 1039 Class Discussion, TWE p. 1042
Comparing and Contrasting Versions of a Story, SE p. 1048		Graphic Novel, TWE p. 1048	

LITERARY FOCUS

Focus

BELLRINGER

Bellringer Options
Daily Language Practice Transparency 82
Or **write on the board:** How many heroes and heroines can you think of? List the examples on the board and prompt students to consider other categories of heroes they had overlooked, such as real-life or imaginary heroes. Discuss what makes a character heroic.

Teach

L1 Literary Element

Hero **Ask:** What qualities do you consider heroic? *(Students may mention courage, honesty, or compassion.)* OL

Viewing the Art

The choice of figures from medieval legends as subject matter by Pre-Raphaelite painter Charles Ernest Butler (1864–c. 1918) was typical of artists of that movement. His painting of King Arthur idealizes a major hero of Celtic mythology. AS

LITERARY FOCUS

Hero

L1 What qualities make a hero?

In this passage from Margaret Atwood's *The Penelopiad,* Odysseus's wife, Penelope, tells how she learned of her husband's exploits while he was away at war. Minstrels sang ballads that passed history from one man to the next and one town to the next, tailoring their performance to each audience. Penelope hears only the tales that make her husband seem heroic. Does this make him a hero to her?

> They always sang the noblest versions in my presence—the ones in which Odysseus was clever, brave, and resourceful, and battling supernatural monsters, and beloved of goddesses. The only reason he hadn't come back home was that a god—the sea-god Poseidon, according to some—was against him, because a Cyclops crippled by Odysseus was his son.

King Arthur, 1903. Charles Ernest Butler. Oil on canvas, 123.2 x 73.7 cm. Private Collection. 

Heroes

The hero is the main character in a literary work. His or her admirable character or noble actions arouse the admiration of the reader. While epic heroes are traditionally male, women can also be heroes. At one time, female heroes were called heroines, but today *hero* is used for both men and women who exhibit admirable qualities. Heroes appear not just in epic literature, but also in other genres of literature and in film as well. Modern heroes include comic book superheroes such as Superman.

> At that he woke up with a horrible start, and found that part of his dream was true. A crack had opened at the back of the cave, and was already a wide passage. He was just in time to see the last of the ponies' tails disappearing into it. Of course he gave a very loud yell, as loud a yell as a hobbit can give, which is surprising for their size.
>
> —J. R. R. Tolkien, from *The Hobbit*

Additional Support

Skills Practice

LITERARY ELEMENT: Hero Have students work in groups to create their own hero or heroine. Students should create a list of character traits that make their characters heroic. Students should write a short adventure detailing an exploit of their heroic character. The adventure should show how the character demonstrates the heroic traits. Invite students to create a visual representation of their character in the medium of their choice. OL

The Tragic Hero

As you learned in Unit 4, a tragic hero is a person of great ability who often comes to grief because of a fault within his or her character. This fault, the tragic flaw, is often a characteristic that has helped him or her achieve success: pride, ambition, jealousy, self-doubt, or anger. Sometimes the human weakness that defeats the hero is an excess of virtue, such as the love of honor or the pursuit of duty.

The Epic Hero

An epic is a long narrative poem that recounts the actions, adventures, and travels of a heroic figure, called the epic hero. The epic hero—whose typical goal is to save his nation or its people—embarks on a journey over the expanse of continents or even the entire universe. Along the way, natural and supernatural beings test the hero's bravery, wits, and battle skills.

Characteristics of Most Myths

- Written in the style of a long poem
- Language is formal, lofty
- Mood is serious
- Protagonist undergoes many adventures
- Gods and monsters intervene in action
- Poet uses extended similes, called epic similes
- Poem begins in the middle of the action *(in medias res)*

The traditional epic hero is a strong, courageous, noble, and confident man with a thirst for glory. Most epic heroes, Odysseus included, are known for their intelligence, quick thinking, and tremendous self-confidence.

L2 I am Laertes' son, Odysseus.
Men hold me
formidable for guile in peace and war:
this fame has gone abroad to the sky's rim.

—Homer, **from the *Odyssey***

Literature Online **Interactive Literary Elements Handbook** Go to www.glencoe.com to review or learn more about heroes.

As a result of their keen intelligence, most epic heroes are articulate speakers and can win over an audience with ease. They are deeply admired for their ability to use both brains and brawn to defeat an enemy or to deal with any other challenge that arises.

Odysseus in one motion strung the bow.
Then slid his right hand down the cord and
plucked it,
so the taut gut vibrating hummed and sang
a swallow's note.

—Homer, **from the *Odyssey***

Gods and Monsters Epics often feature gods and monsters that hold power over the human world. Monsters like Typhon with its one hundred heads kill without mercy and wreak general havoc. Gods have the power to create and destroy, and they use that power at will. Often it is the task of the epic hero to subdue a monster or appease the gods. Perseus does this, as does Odysseus.

I happened to glance aft at ship and oarsmen and caught sight of their arms and legs, dangling high over head. Voices came down to me in anguish, calling my name for the last time. . . . [Scylla] ate them as they shrieked there, in her den.

—Homer, **from the *Odyssey***

Quickwrite

Describing Monsters If you could create an epic monster, would it have seventy eyes, wings made of fire, or a voice so beautiful it could lure humans to their deaths? Write a description of your monster and what it could do. Then ask a partner to read your description and draw a picture of your monster.

INDIANA ACADEMIC STANDARDS (pages 954-955)

9.3.4 Determine characters' traits...
9.3.1 Explain...the characteristics of...tragedy...
9.3.5 Compare works that express a universal theme...
9.5.3 Write...descriptive pieces...

LITERARY FOCUS

Teach

L2 Literary Element

Character Have volunteers read each section aloud. Pause after each section and ask students for examples of the type of character described. OL

Assess

Quickwrite

Students' descriptions should include features that are frightening, grotesque, and dangerous.

Literary Elements Have students access the Web site to improve their understanding of hero.

English Language Coach

Study Skills Instruct students to copy the headings *tragic hero, epic, epic hero, gods,* and *monsters* into their notebooks. Have students make a list of characteristics under each heading for use as a reference as they read. EL

Differentiated Instruction

Improving Comprehension Instruct students to copy the characteristics of an epic into their notebooks. Have them refer to the list as they read the *Odyssey.* Instruct students to write examples under each item on the list as they read. BL

Academic Standards

Additional Support activities on pp. 954 and 955 cover the following standards:

Skills Practice: **9.5.1** Write...short stories that describe a sequence of events and... the specific actions, movements, gestures, and feelings of the characters...

English Language Coach: **9.2** Develop [reading] strategies...

Differentiated Instruction: **9.2** Develop [reading] strategies...

Focus

BELLRINGER

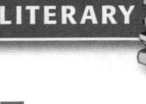

Bellringer Options
Daily Language Practice Transparency 83
Or **have students discuss this question:** What personal challenges have you faced that you were unsure that you could meet? How did you manage to meet the challenge?

Teach

R1 Reading Strategy

Preview Have students examine the subheads and the illustrations on pages 956–957. Then read aloud the introductory quotation and the first paragraph of the essay. Explain that American scholar Milman Parry pioneered the field of oral literature studies in the 1920s and 1930s. Parry's research proved that Homer's epics were intended to be presented orally. OL

Literary History Have students access the Web site for a summary, bibliography, and other online resources to enhance their understanding of Homeric epic.

LITERARY HISTORY

Homer and the Epic

R1

> *"We will have Demodocus to sing to us; for there is no bard like him whatever he may choose to sing about."*
>
> —Homer, the *Odyssey*

★ Like the fictional bard Demodocus in the *Odyssey,* ancient Greek oral poets composed narratives and chanted them to musical accompaniment. The greatest of these Greek oral poets was Homer. Little is certain about him—even his name. We know that his works include two of the earliest surviving epic poems—the *Iliad* and the *Odyssey*. The precise dates are unknown, but most experts believe that Homer composed his epics around 750 B.C.

The Art of the Bard

How did an oral poet such as Homer compose his poems? In some ways, he was like a jazz musician who starts with a well-known tune and plays different variations on it every time he performs. Just as a musician plays to a steady rhythm, so Homer had a steady rhythm in his words. The Greek singers recited their poems so that long syllables and short syllables alternated in a regular pattern.

Composing poetry in front of an audience without hesitating or "drawing a blank" may sound like an impossible task, but the fact that Homer performed to a rhythm simplified the job. It meant that certain phrases worked better than others because they would fit rhythmically into a line of poetry. So Homer used them again and again. When describing people or things, he often used verbal "formulas." For example, he repeatedly refers to the goddess Athena as "gray-eyed Athena," and mentions dawn's "fingertips of rose." Homer would also recycle longer passages of description. These passages often concerned routine actions, such as a character's way of entering a room, putting on his armor, going to bed, or saying good-bye to his host.

This use of repetition helped Homer and pleased his audience. The poet did not have to memorize or make up every word. Most of his story was a little different each time it was told, but the repeated phrases remained like handles for the poet to grip. Homer's audience looked forward to these repetitions, as listeners look forward to the repeated chorus of a song.

A book illustration depicts Homer reciting one of his epic poems.

Epic Poetry

Homer's most famous compositions, the *Iliad* and the *Odyssey*, have been read for centuries as **epic poems.** Since Homer's time, epic poetry has been considered a genre, or type of literature,

Additional Support

See also Active Learning and Note Taking Guide, pp. 162–165.

Skills Practice

READING: Researching Oral Literature Point out that in addition to the epic, there are many other types of oral literature. These include riddles, folk tales, myths, legends, ballads, nursery rhymes, hymns, and spirituals.

Have students select an oral form of literature (other than epic) and use encyclopedias and Internet resources to research and write a short report. Students' reports should include the characteristics of the form, the specific ways in which this oral tradition conveys the content from generation to generation, and geographic regions in which this particular oral form has flourished. OL just as nonfiction, fiction, and drama are genres. The epic poem has the following characteristics:

R2

- It is a long narrative poem.
- The speaker is a narrator who tells a story.
- The setting is expansive. It may be a sea, a region, the world, or a universe.
- There is a main character, who is a hero or is capable of being heroic.
- The action includes extraordinary or superhuman deeds. Typically, the epic hero has a goal and has embarked upon a long journey. In this journey, he struggles with natural and supernatural obstacles and antagonists—gods, monsters, and humans—which test his bravery, wits, and physical prowess.
- Gods or supernatural beings take a part, or an interest, in the action.
- The purpose of an epic poem is not only to entertain but also to teach and inspire the listener or reader with examples of how people can strive and succeed against great odds.

Epic Narration

An epic poem is narrated in predictable ways:

- In an invocation, the poet-narrator begins by stating the tale's subject and asking for poetic inspiration from a guiding spirit.
- The narrator begins telling the tale in the "middle of things," describing what is happening after certain important events have already occurred.

Hercules fighting Cerberus, the monsterous three-headed dog that guards the entrance to Hades. 530–525 B.C. Terra-cotta. Louvre Museum, Paris.

R2

- The narrative includes speeches by principal characters—including gods and antagonists of the epic hero—which reveal their personalities.
- The narrative's tone and style are formal rather than conversational.
- The use of figurative language makes the narrative vivid and exciting for listeners and readers.

The epic you are about to read, the *Odyssey*, is a celebration of the human spirit and of ordinary life. It is for this timeless appeal to our common humanity that the *Odyssey* is still read and enjoyed nearly three thousand years after its creation.

LiteratureOnline **Literary History** For more about Homer and the epic, go to www.glencoe.com.

RESPONDING AND THINKING CRITICALLY

1. Why do you think the works of Homer are still enjoyed today?
2. How does the composition method of ancient Greek oral poets resemble that of a jazz musician?
3. What different purposes did Homer's epics serve for the ancient Greeks?

INDIANA ACADEMIC STANDARDS (pages 956-957)

9.3.9 Explain how…the choice of a narrator affect[s]…plot…

9.3.12 Analyze the way in which a work of literature is related to the themes and issues of its historical period.

English Language Coach

Epics in Other Cultures Ask English language learners to name some of the epic poets in their cultures and to talk about the subjects and sources of their poems. Make sure students understand that the term "epic poetry" is applied to an entire genre of literature and that epic poems were originally long oral stories—hence the use of formulas and repetition.

Have English language learners compare the list of characteristics on page 957 to epic poems in their native languages. EL

Teach

R2 Reading Strategy

Monitoring Comprehension Prepare a checklist of the elements in epic poetry and epic narration, and give each student a copy. Have students check off each element as they identify it in the *Odyssey.* Next to each element, leave a space in which students can write the example. OL

Literary History

Translations of Homer Since the English Renaissance in the 1500s, every age has produced distinctive translations of Homer's epics. The first notable translation in English was by George Chapman (c. 1559–1634). Robert Fitzgerald was widely praised for his version of the *Odyssey.* AS

Assess

1. They tell exciting stories and provide a glimpse into ancient life.
2. Like a jazz musician, the ancient Greek poets took a familiar theme and used it as the basis for improvisation.
3. His epics provided entertainment and instruction.

Academic Standards

Additional Support activities on pp. 956 and 957 cover the following standards:

Skills Practice: **9.5.9** Write…a research report that uses information from a variety of sources…

English Language Coach: **9.3.5** Compare works that express a universal theme…

Focus

BELLRINGER

Bellringer Options
Selection Focus Transparency 44
Daily Language Practice Transparency 84
Or tell students that in reading these selections from the *Odyssey,* they will meet a man who journeys through lands and seas of mythical proportions to get to that most elusive destination of all—home. Students will also meet a woman who represents another facet of travel—learning how to plan and how to wait.
Ask: Is there a place you dream of visiting? What do you hope to find there? What obstacles might you encounter along the way?

Author Search To expand students' appreciation of Homer, have them access the Web site for additional information and resources.

BEFORE YOU READ

from the Odyssey

MEET HOMER

> *"Where shall a man find sweetness to surpass his own home and his parents?"*
>
> —Homer, from the *Odyssey*

Homer is one of the great mysteries of literature. His poems are among the most famous in the world, but it is unlikely that he ever "wrote" a word. His name is as well known as Shakespeare's, but no one has found any convincing evidence to indicate who he was or exactly when and where he lived. Legend has it that he was a blind man who lived on the rocky Greek island of Chios, but legends are impossible to prove. Although Homer was one of the greatest poets of the ancient world, he composed his works orally and recited or sang them aloud. Like most people in his day, Homer could probably neither read nor write.

The Few Facts What we do know for certain is that Homer's works include two of the earliest surviving epic poems, the *Iliad* and the *Odyssey.* Although the precise dates are uncertain, most experts believe that Homer composed and recited his poems over 2,700 years ago, sometime before the year 700 B.C. This was the period when speakers of Greek were emerging from illiteracy—developing an alphabet and learning the benefits of recording things on a kind of paper called papyrus. However, in those days people were still accustomed to hearing, rather than reading, their literature. Homer's great poems were written down only long after his death.

Homer's poetic tales describe famous people and events from history as well as from legends, myths, and folktales—characters and events that people had been describing for centuries. The *Iliad* and the *Odyssey,* which are set during and after the siege of Troy, include all of these ingredients. To this mix of fact and fiction, Homer added his insights into human experience, his imaginative plots, and his expert storytelling style.

Action and Adventure Homer's audience was especially fascinated by tales of the Mycenaean era of 500 years earlier. People said the huge stones of ruined Mycenaean walls had been toppled by a race of giants known as the Cyclopes. People thought palaces had been grander and cities larger in those days, that men had been braver, women more alluring, and monsters more terrifying. Homer and his fellow poets brought this ancient world to life.

Homer's repertoire probably included hundreds of tales by the time he was a mature artist. Audiences would call for certain ones—the "action-adventure" stories of the day—again and again: the legend of Theseus, Jason and the Golden Fleece, the twelve labors of Hercules, and the many love affairs of Zeus. Homer's audiences believed the stories were true. To appreciate Homer's gift, modern readers must suspend their disbelief.

Homer lived sometime before the year 700 B.C.

Literature Online **Author Search** For more about Homer, go to www.glencoe.com.

Selection Skills

from the Odyssey, Part 1

Literary Elements
- Epic (SE pp. 959–979)

Reading Skills
- Analyzing Figurative Language (SE pp. 959–979)
- Using Pronunciation Guides (TWE p. 962)

Vocabulary Skills
- Synonyms (SE pp. 959, 979)

Listening/Speaking/Viewing Skills
- Analyzing Art (SE p. 974)
- Listening (TWE p. 966)
- Storytelling (TWE p. 972)

Writing Skills/Grammar
- Using Spatial Order (TWE p. 968)
- Dashes (TWE p. 970)
- Simple and Compound Sentences (TWE p. 978)

Study Skills/Research/Assessment
- Research (TWE p. 965)

LITERATURE PREVIEW

Connecting to the Poem

Like people today, the ancient Greeks enjoyed a good horror story. Before you read, think about the following questions:

- What is it about horror stories that people find fascinating?
- Why do people love hearing about the exploits of a hero?

Building Background

The *Odyssey* describes the wanderings of the Greek general Odysseus on his return from the city of Troy in what is now northwest Turkey to his home island of Ithaca (ith′ ə kə), off the west coast of Greece. The events take place shortly before the year 1200 B.C. The events in another one of Homer's epic poems, the *Iliad*, take place during the Trojan War, which was well known to Homer's audience. This great siege, which the poet claimed lasted ten years, ended with the destruction of the city of Troy by a huge Greek army. The mastermind behind the army's success was a Greek general known for his bravery, but even more for his cunning: Odysseus, hero of the *Odyssey*.

Setting Purposes for Reading

Big Idea Journeys

As you read Part 1, notice how Homer crafts Odysseus's journey home as a great adventure with many thrilling stops along the way.

Literary Element Epic and Epic Hero

An **epic** is a long narrative poem that traces the adventures of a larger-than-life hero, called an **epic hero.** Epics intertwine myths, legends, and history, reflecting the values of the societies in which they originate. As you read, look for elements of poetry, fiction, and drama.

- See Literary Terms Handbook, p. R6.

LiteratureOnline Interactive Literary Elements Handbook To review or learn more about the literary elements, go to www.glencoe.com.

READING PREVIEW

Reading Strategy Analyzing Figurative Language

Figurative language is language or expressions that are not literally true but reveal some truth beyond the literal level. Figurative language is especially common in poetry. Like most poets, Homer intensifies his images and descriptions by using metaphors, similes, personification, and other figures of speech. An **epic simile** (also called a Homeric simile) extends a comparison with elaborate descriptive details that can fill several lines of verse.

Reading Tip: Taking Notes Use a chart to record striking figures of speech in Part 1.

Figure of Speech	Analysis
lines 82–83 "but he seemed rather a shaggy mountain reared in solitude"	metaphor capturing the size, roughness, and antisocial behavior of the Cyclops

Vocabulary

plunder (plun′ dər) *v.* to take (property) by force, especially in warfare; p. 963 *The victorious army plundered the defenseless city.*

valor (val′ ər) *n.* great courage, especially in battle; p. 963 *The medal was awarded to the soldier for valor in combat.*

guile (gīl) *n.* slyness; craftiness; skillful deception; p. 965 *The con man relied on quick thinking and guile to fool his clients.*

ponderous (pon′ dər əs) *adj.* having great weight or bulk; heavy; p. 970 *The workers tried to lift the ponderous stone with their hands but finally had to use a pulley.*

Vocabulary Tip: Synonyms Synonyms are words that have the same, or almost the same, meaning. For example, "furious" is a synonym for "angry."

INDIANA ACADEMIC STANDARDS (pages 959-979)

9.3.4 Determine characters' traits...

9.2 Develop strategies such as...identifying and analyzing...purpose...

9.3.11 Evaluate...the impact of...figurative language on tone, mood, and theme.

BEFORE YOU READ

Focus

Summary

In the invocation, the poet summarizes some of Odysseus's major adventures. Odysseus begins recounting his travels to the Phaeacian king, Alcinous. In the land of the Cyclopes, Odysseus and twelve of his men explore the cave of Polyphemus and become trapped. The giant eats six of Odysseus's men before the hero contrives an escape plan. They get the giant drunk, and when he falls asleep, they blind him with a sharpened tree trunk. In the morning, the adventurers tie themselves to the bellies of sheep and escape.

V Vocabulary

Vocabulary File Say: Add these words and definitions to your vocabulary file. For each word, include a sentence that gives you an example of how to use the word. **OL** Students with English language needs should include the pronunciations of these words in their files. **EL**

Literary Elements Have students access the Web site to improve their understanding of epic and epic hero.

Selection Resources

Print Materials
- Unit 5 Resources (Fast File), pp. 18–29
- Leveled Vocabulary Development, pp. 62–65
- Selection and Unit Assessments, pp. 165–172
- Selection Quick Checks, pp. 82–85

Transparencies
- Bellringer Options Transparencies: Selection Focus Transparency 44, Daily Language Practice Transparency 84
- Literary Elements Transparencies 1, 3, 15, 82

Technology
- TeacherWorks Plus™ CD-ROM
- StudentWorks Plus™ CD-ROM
- Presentation Plus!™ CD-ROM
- Literature Online, glencoe.com
- Online Student Edition, mhln.com
- Exam*View*® Assessment Suite CD-ROM
- Vocabulary PuzzleMaker CD-ROM
- Listening Library, disc 2 tracks 20–23

Teach

Big Idea

Journeys Say: Look at the photograph on pages 960–961, and then imagine spending many months on a sailboat on the open sea.
Ask: How would you feel, knowing that you would be out on the ocean for many months before returning home? *(Students' responses will vary but should reflect some of the fears and joys associated with a long journey.)* How might the natural elements affect you? *(Students may suggest feelings of insignificance and helplessness against such powerful forces.)* OL

from the Odyssey

Homer

Translated by Robert Fitzgerald

Additional Support

Leveled Reading An adapted version of this selection is available on page 170 of *Jamestown Literature: An Adapted Reader,* grade 9.

Skills Practice

READING: Character Chart Have students begin a chart of characters and their actions.

Characters	Actions

Tell students to make an entry on their chart each time they come across a new character whose actions are important to the plot. Point out that they may need to list several items in the "Actions" column for each character. Explain that the completed chart will provide a plot outline. OL

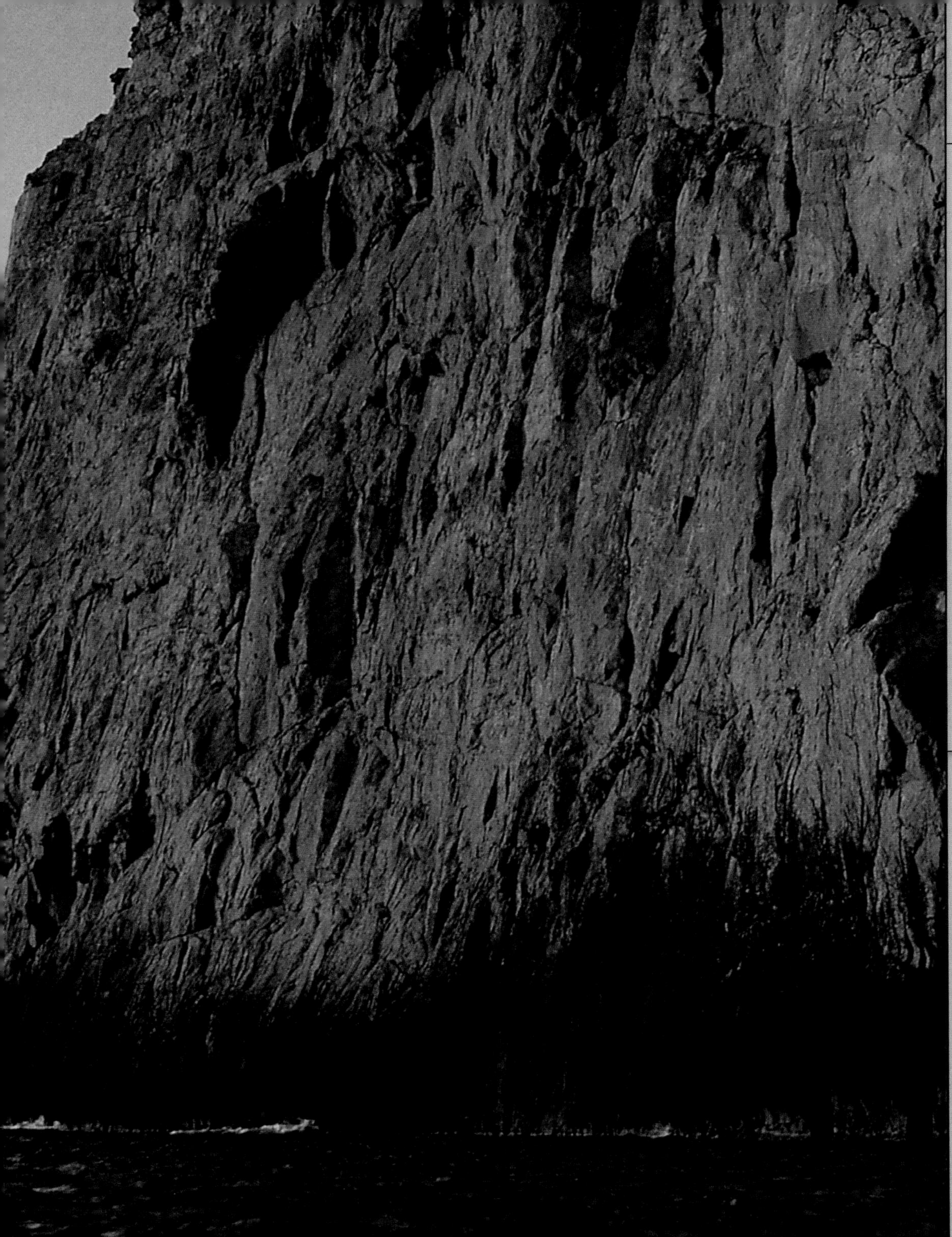

Teach

★ Cultural History

Ancient Greece The geography of Ancient Greece caused people to be isolated. The sea and the mountainous terrain hindered travel between communities. The simple, herding lifestyle and the warlike characteristics of the Achaeans prevented alliances between city-states, which began developing in the seventh century B.C.

Ancient Greece never became a united nation. Ancient Greeks felt loyalty only to their cities, whose populations were tiny by today's standards. Only Athens, the largest city-state, had more than 20,000 inhabitants. **AS**

English Language Coach

Mythology Encourage students with little knowledge of Greek mythology to refer to handbooks of mythology as they read.

Have English language learners research Zeus, Calypso, Helios, Poseidon, and other figures they encounter as they read these excerpts from the *Odyssey.* Encourage students to keep a list of the divinities, jotting down descriptive attributes or drawing illustrations to accompany each one. **EL**

Academic Standards

Additional Support activities on pp. 960 and 961 cover the following standards:

Skills Practice: **9.3.3** Analyze interactions between characters...and explain the way those interactions affect the plot.

English Language Coach: **9.2.4** Synthesize the content from several sources or works...; paraphrase the ideas and connect them to...related topics to demonstrate comprehension.

Teach

L1 Literary Element

Epic Explain that the *Odyssey* is an epic poem, with elements that may remind students of poetry, fiction, and drama. It uses meter and poetic devices, but it also tells an adventure story, filled with dramatic action and graphic details. The list of characters serves the same purpose as that preceding a play: It helps the reader keep the many characters and their relationships straight. OL

PRINCIPAL CHARACTERS IN THE ODYSSEY L1

HUMANS

AGAMEMNON (ag′ ə mem′ non): king and leader of Greek forces during the Trojan war

ALCINOUS (al sin′ ō əs): king of the Phaeacians and person to whom Odysseus relates his story

AMPHINOMUS (am fin′ ə məs): one of Penelope's suitors

ANTINOUS (an tin′ ō əs): rudest of Penelope's suitors

EUMAEUS (yoo mē′ əs): Odysseus's loyal swineherd

EURYCLEIA (yoó ri klē′ ə): Odysseus's faithful old nurse

EURYLOCHUS (yoo ril′ ə kəs): one of Odysseus's crew

EURYMACHUS (yoo rim′ ə kəs): one of Penelope's suitors

EURYNOME (yoo rin′ ə mē): Penelope's housekeeper

LAERTES (lā ur′ tēz): Odysseus's father

MARON (mār′ on): priest of Apollo who gives Odysseus a gift of powerful wine

ODYSSEUS (ō dis′ ē əs): king of Ithaca and hero of the Trojan war

PENELOPE (pə nel′ ə pē): Odysseus's wife

PERIMEDES (per′ i mē′ dēz): one of Odysseus's crew

TELEMACHUS (tə lem′ ə kəs): Odysseus and Penelope's son

TIRESIAS (tī rē′ sē əs): blind prophet from the underworld

GODS AND IMMORTALS

APOLLO (ə pol′ ō): god of sunlight, music, poetry, medicine, law, and the tending of flocks and herds

ATHENA (ə thē′ nə): daughter of Zeus and goddess of wisdom, skills, and warfare who helps her chosen heroes

CALYPSO (kə lip′ sō): immortal sea nymph who holds Odysseus captive for many years

CHARYBDIS (kə rib′ dis): dangerous whirlpool personified as a female monster

CIRCE (sur′ sē): enchantress who lives on the island of Aeaea

CYCLOPES (sī klō′ pēz): race of one-eyed giants; an individual member of the race is a Cyclops (sī′ klops)

HELIOS (hē′ lē os′): god of the sun; another name for Apollo

LOTUS (lō′ təs) EATERS: inhabitants of a land visited by Odysseus and his crew

POLYPHEMUS (pol′ i fē′ məs): a Cyclops and son of Poseidon

POSEIDON (pə sīd′ ən): god of the sea and earthquakes

SCYLLA (sil′ ə): six-headed female sea monster

SIRENS (sī′ rənz): sea nymphs who sing songs that lure men to their death

ZEUS (zo͞os): king of the gods

Additional Support

Skills Practice

READING: Using Pronunciation Guides Explain to students that they will become more comfortable with the unfamiliar Greek names if they can pronounce them properly. Before students read through the list of names, review pronunciation clues, such as stress marks and vowel marks.

To help students with the correct pronunciations of the names, have them work with a partner to read through the lists of humans and gods and immortals. Tell students to read the names aloud with their partners. Then ask volunteers to read the names aloud to the class. Correct pronunciations as needed. OL

Part I

An Invocation

R1

Poets in Homer's day believed that the gods inspired their storytelling and singing. According to custom, Homer begins his performance with an invocation, calling upon the Muse, the goddess of epic poetry, for help and inspiration. The invocation serves a second purpose: to capture the audience's attention with highlights of heroic adventures that the poet will later describe in detail.

Sing in me, Muse, and through me tell the story
of that man skilled in all ways of contending,°
the wanderer, harried° for years on end,
after he **plundered** the stronghold
on the proud height of Troy.

He saw the townlands
and learned the minds of many distant men,
and weathered° many bitter nights and days
in his deep heart at sea, while he fought only
to save his life, to bring his shipmates home.
But not by will nor **valor** could he save them,
for their own recklessness destroyed them all—
children and fools, they killed and feasted on
the cattle of Lord Helios,° the Sun,
and he who moves all day through heaven
took from their eyes the dawn of their return.

Of these adventures, Muse, daughter of Zeus,°
tell us in our time, lift the great song again.
Begin when all the rest who left behind them
headlong death in battle or at sea
had long ago returned, while he alone still hungered
for home and wife. Her ladyship Calypso°
clung to him in her sea-hollowed caves—
a nymph,° immortal° and most beautiful,
who craved him for her own.

And when long years and seasons
wheeling brought around that point of time

2 **contending:** fighting or dealing with difficulty.
3 **harried:** constantly tormented or troubled.

8 **weathered:** got through safely; survived.

14 **Helios** (hē′ lē os′): the god of the sun.

17 **Zeus** (zo͞os): The most powerful of the gods, Zeus is the father of countless major and minor gods.

22 **Calypso** (kə lip′ sō)

24 **nymph:** a young, beautiful spirit, or minor goddess, representing the divine power of a place or of something in nature, such as a tree, cave, or body of water. **immortal:** living forever; eternal.

Literary Element Epic and Epic Hero *How does the reader quickly learn that the story about to unfold recounts the deeds of an epic hero?* L2

Reading Strategy Analyzing Figurative Language *Why might the poet have used the verb* wheeling *to describe the passing of years and seasons?* R2

Vocabulary

plunder (plun′ dər) *v.* to take (property) by force, especially in warfare

valor (val′ ər) *n.* great courage, especially in battle

Teach

R1 Reading Strategy

Clarify Point out that the paragraphs in italics give essential background or summarize omitted sections of the epic. After students read the paragraph, ask them to explain the significance of the invocation. *(It honors the gods and creates interest in the audience.)* OL

L2 Literary Element

Epic and Epic Hero Answer: *The reader immediately learns that Odysseus has triumphed over many hardships after leaving Troy and is determined to make it home. This opening passage establishes that his adventures are intertwined with history and mythology.* OL

R2 Reading Strategy

Analyzing Figurative Language Answer: *By describing the passage of time as "wheeling," Homer draws attention to the fact that a year is like a circle, always coming back to where it started.* OL

CheckPoint

Use the CheckPoint questions on Presentation Plus! to monitor students' comprehension. These questions can be used with interactive response keypads for immediate student feedback.

English Language Coach

Word Meanings Tell students that many English words are derived from Latin. The word *invocation,* for example, comes from the Latin verb *invocare,* meaning "to call on." Ask students to tell whom Homer is calling on. *(the Muse, the goddess of epic poetry)* Having some background in Latin, Greek, or Anglo-Saxon roots can be a useful vocabulary tool. Help students to understand that knowing root words in other languages—including their own—can help them determine meanings in English. EL

Academic Standards

Additional Support activities on pp. 962 and 963 cover the following standards:

Skills Practice: **9.2.1** Analyze the structure and format of reference…documents…and…use the features to achieve their purposes.

English Language Coach: **9.1** [Use] word parts…and origins…to determine the meaning of words…

Teach

R1 Reading Strategy

Clarify Explain to students that the paraphrased summary in italics covers the first eight books of the original epic (which contains 24 books in all). Also, be sure students understand the handling of time. Odysseus is entertaining his hosts, the Phaeacians, by telling the story of his earlier adventures at sea. In fact, "the present" is ten years after Odysseus set out from Troy. **OL**

★ Viewing the Art

In Greek mythology, Calliope was the muse of epic poetry. As in this sculpture, Calliope is usually depicted with a tablet for writing. **Ask:** Why might Greek mythology include a character whose primary purpose is to help writers find inspiration? *(Students may note that the Greek epics were long inspiring stories and anyone setting out to write an epic must have felt a desire for help from the gods.)* **AS**

ordained° for him to make his passage homeward,
trials and dangers, even so, attended him
even in Ithaca, near those he loved.
Yet all the gods had pitied Lord Odysseus,
all but Poseidon, raging cold and rough°
against the brave king° till he came ashore
at last on his own land.

28 **ordained:** set or determined by an authority—in this case, fate, or the gods.

31–33 **Odysseus** (ō dis′ ē əs) . . . **the brave king:** Odysseus is the king of Ithaca.

32 **Poseidon** (pə sīd′ ən), **raging cold and rough:** Poseidon, brother of Zeus, governs the oceans as well as earthquakes. In the next section, you will find clues to his anger at Odysseus.

New Coasts and Poseidon's Son

The gods are worried. Nearly ten years have passed since the end of the war against Troy, but one of the greatest Greek generals has not yet returned home. Odysseus has encountered a series of disasters on his voyage and is now the prisoner of a nymph named Calypso. He has also angered Poseidon, who has prevented him from returning to his wife, Penelope (pə nel′ ə pē), *and his son, Telemachus* (tə lem′ ə kəs), *on the island of Ithaca. But Poseidon is visiting Africa, and the other gods agree to act behind his back.*

The poet now tells of Odysseus, who is miserable after seven years on his island prison. Calypso loves her handsome captive and will not let him go, but she is forced to reconsider her position when she receives a strongly worded order from Mount Olympus. Giving in, Calypso helps Odysseus make a raft, and he thankfully departs. But he does not have smooth sailing. Poseidon, returning from Africa, spots his old enemy at sea and shipwrecks him in an instant with a fierce storm. **R1**

Zeus's daughter Athena intervenes. She casts Odysseus, naked and near death, ashore on the island of Phaeacia (fē ā′ shə). *There a beautiful princess discovers him and takes him home to the palace of her father, King Alcinous* (al sin′ ō əs). *The Phaeacians treat Odysseus as a noble guest and urge him to reveal his identity. At last he relents and uncertainly begins to tell his gripping story.*

★ *Calliope,* Muse of epic poetry. Marble. Ludovisi collection.

Additional Support

Skills Practice

READING: Identifying Author's Purpose Explain some ways to determine an author's purpose: (1) locate a direct statement of purpose; (2) infer from the tone and indirect statements; (3) recall similar readings and their purposes.

After students read the invocation, ask them to summarize the speaker's purpose for telling the *Odyssey* and explain how they determined it. (*Students should use methods 1 and 2 to decide that the purpose is to describe the adventures of Odysseus and to inspire listeners with his feats and the interactions of gods with men.*) **OL**

"What shall I
say first? What shall I keep until the end?
The gods have tried° me in a thousand ways.
But first my name: let that be known to you,
and if I pull away from pitiless death,
friendship will bind us, though my land lies far.
I am Laertes' son, Odysseus.
Men hold° me
formidable° for **guile** in peace and war:
this fame has gone abroad to the sky's rim.
My home is on the peaked sea-mark of Ithaca
under Mount Neion's° wind-blown robe of leaves,
in sight of other islands—Dulichium,°
Same,° wooded Zacynthus°—Ithaca
being most lofty in that coastal sea,
and northwest, while the rest lie east and south.
A rocky isle, but good for a boy's training;
I shall not see on earth a place more dear,
though I have been detained long by Calypso,
loveliest among goddesses, who held me
in her smooth caves, to be her heart's delight,
as Circe of Aeaea, the enchantress,°
desired me, and detained me in her hall.
But in my heart I never gave consent.
Where shall a man find sweetness to surpass
his own home and his parents? In far lands
he shall not, though he find a house of gold.
What of my sailing, then, from Troy?
What of those years
of rough adventure, weathered under Zeus?"°

3 **tried:** tested.

8 **hold:** regard; consider.

9 **formidable:** causing fear, dread, awe, or admiration as a result of size, strength, power, or some other impressive quality.

12 **Neion** (nē′ on)

13 **Dulichium** (doo lik′ ē əm)

14 **Same** (sā′ mē). **Zacynthus** (zə sin′ thəs)

22 **Circe** (sur′ sē). . . **the enchantress:** Circe is a goddess capable of enchanting, or working magic upon, men. **Aeaea** (ē ē′ ə) is her island.

30 **weathered under Zeus:** Odysseus uses words craftily. Here, he appears to give respectful credit to Zeus for getting him safely through danger; but he also is making a pun on the word *weathered.* Zeus governs the heavens and the weather and is well known for sending people storms, lightning, and thunder when he is displeased.

Odysseus relates his first adventure. He and his fleet of twelve ships attacked and plundered the coastal settlement of the Cicones (si kō′ nēz). *The raid was a success, but the overconfident men became drunk and mutinous (unresponsive to Odysseus's orders to retreat). The Cicones's army surprised Odysseus and his men at dawn, and drove them back to sea with heavy losses.*

"I might have made it safely home, that time,
but as I came round Malea° the current
took me out to sea, and from the north
a fresh gale drove me on, past Cythera.°
Nine days I drifted on the teeming sea
before dangerous high winds. Upon the tenth

32 **Malea** (mə lē′ ə)

34 **Cythera** (sith′ ə rə)

Big Idea Journeys *How has Odysseus proved to his audience that he is determined to achieve his journey's end?* **BI**

Vocabulary

guile (gīl) *n.* slyness; craftiness; skillful deception

Teach

R2 Reading Strategy

Evaluate Ask: How would you describe Odysseus's feelings about Ithaca, his home? *(He calls it "lofty," indicating that he has fond feelings for Ithaca. He cherishes it, as expressed in the line "I shall not see on earth a place more dear.")* **OL**

BI Big Idea

Journeys Answer: *Even the love of two beautiful goddesses has failed to tempt him from his objective of reaching home. Odysseus is eager to return to his home and parents, whose sweetness cannot be surpassed by far lands, even those where he finds a house of gold.* **OL**

Differentiated Instruction

Research Students can use the library and the Internet to learn more about some of the places referred to in the *Odyssey.* They might research some of the places mentioned up to this point, such as Troy and Ithaca. If students find information on the Internet, have them evaluate the source. Emphasize that not everything on the Internet comes from a reputable and authoritative source. have students compare the information they find. Then encourage students to give oral presentations on their findings. **AL**

Academic Standards

Additional Support activities on pp. 964 and 965 cover the following standards:

Skills Practice: **9.2** Develop strategies such as...identifying...[author's] purpose...

Differentiated Instruction: **9.5.9** Write or deliver a research report that has been developed using a systematic research process (defines the topic, gathers information, determines credibility, reports findings)...

Teach

R Reading Strategy

Draw Conclusions

Odysseus's perspective and behavior allow students to recognize some traits that set him apart from his men. **Say:** Odysseus reports that the Lotus Eaters did not coerce his men and that the lotus is sweet and drains one of desire for real action and real life. I think that the sailors easily gave in to temptation, but Odysseus did not. **Ask:** What can you tell about Odysseus's character from the way he treats his men? *(Since Odysseus drove his men back to the ship, I can conclude that he looked on them as weaker beings for whom he was responsible.)* OL

★ Viewing the Art

Swiss-born artist Francois-Louis Schmied (1873–1941) was an engraver well-known for his collaborations with binders and publishers on illustrated books. His style reflects the art Deco movement of the period, which emphasized "modernity" in art, expressed with angular, geometric figures and drawing on the new technology of the period. AS

we came to the coastline of the Lotus Eaters,
who live upon that flower. We landed there
to take on water. All ships' companies
mustered° alongside for the mid-day meal.
Then I sent out two picked men and a runner
to learn what race of men that land sustained.°
They fell in, soon enough, with Lotus Eaters,
who showed no will to do us harm, only
offering the sweet Lotus to our friends—
but those who ate this honeyed plant, the Lotus,
never cared to report, nor to return:
they longed to stay forever, browsing on
that native bloom, forgetful of their homeland.
I drove them, all three wailing, to the ships,

40 **mustered:** gathered together.

42 **sustained:** kept alive; supported.

The Ship of Odysseus with Oars and a Furled Sail, 1930–1933. Francois-Louis Schmied. Stapleton Collection. ★

Additional Support

Skills Practice

LISTENING: Listening Techniques

Explain that most listeners remember only a fraction of what they hear. Discuss techniques that can help students become better listeners:

1. Listen actively and think about what you hear.
2. Jot down important ideas.
3. Concentrate on the speaker.

Have students close their books and listen as you read aloud part of the passage on pages 966–967. Then ask them to list what they remember on a sheet of paper. After you finish reading, have them check their lists against the text. OL

tied them down under their rowing benches,
and called the rest: 'All hands aboard;
come, clear the beach and no one taste
the Lotus, or you lose your hope of home.'
Filing in to their places by the rowlocks
my oarsmen dipped their long oars in the surf,
and we moved out again on our sea faring.

In the next land we found were Cyclopes,°
giants, louts,° without a law to bless them.
In ignorance leaving the fruitage of the earth in mystery
to the immortal gods, they neither plow
nor sow by hand, nor till the ground, though grain—
wild wheat and barley—grows untended, and
wine-grapes, in clusters, ripen in heaven's rain.
Cyclopes have no muster and no meeting,
no consultation or old tribal ways,
but each one dwells in his own mountain cave
dealing out rough justice to wife and child,
indifferent to what the others do."

58 **Cyclopes** (sī klō′ pēz): a race of one-eyed giants.
59 **louts:** stupid beings.

Just offshore from the land of the Cyclopes is a deserted island with a fine natural harbor. Odysseus and his men spend two comfortable nights there. On the second day, overcome by curiosity, Odysseus sails with one ship and a crew to the mainland. He wants to see just what sort of creatures these Cyclopes are.

"As we rowed on, and nearer to the mainland,
at one end of the bay, we saw a cavern
yawning above the water, screened with laurel,°
and many rams and goats about the place
inside a sheepfold°—made from slabs of stone
earthfast between tall trunks of pine and rugged
towering oak trees.
A prodigious° man
slept in this cave alone, and took his flocks
to graze afield—remote from all companions,
knowing none but savage ways, a brute
so huge, he seemed no man at all of those
who eat good wheaten bread; but he seemed rather
a shaggy mountain reared in solitude.
We beached there, and I told the crew
to stand by and keep watch over the ship;
as for myself I took my twelve best fighters
and went ahead. I had a goatskin full

72 **screened with laurel:** partly hidden behind laurel trees.

74 **sheepfold:** an enclosure, or pen, for holding sheep.

77 **prodigious:** huge; enormous.

Literary Element Epic and Epic Hero *What traits does Odysseus reveal in this episode that set him apart from his men?* **L1**

Big Idea Journeys *Why is Odysseus making this expedition? What does this side trip suggest about epic journeys?* **BI**

Teach

L1 Literary Element

Epic and Epic Hero Answer: *In making his men return to their ships, he proves that he is a true leader, responsible for the welfare of his crew and determined to attain his goal.* **OL**

L2 Literary Element

Figurative Language Have students explain the metaphor here and explain why it is appropriate to the Cyclops. *(The giant is compared to a "shaggy mountain": the comparison accurately captures his size, roughness, and antisocial behavior.)* **OL**

BI Big Idea

Journeys Answer: *He is curious to find out more about the people who live on these islands. Students may conclude that epic journeys are rarely direct; they often include other travels and adventures.* **OL**

Differentiated Instruction

Appositives Remind students that appositives are nouns placed next to other nouns or pronouns to identify or give more information. **Write on the board:** I had a goatskin full of that sweet liquor that Euanthes' son, Maron, had given me. Explain that *Maron* is an appositive identifying *Euanthes' son.* Tell students to find three other examples of appositives in the text so far. Then ask students to write three original sentences that contain appositives. **BL**

Academic Standards

Additional Support activities on pp. 966 and 967 cover the following standards:

Skills Practice: **9.7** [Respond] to oral communication [with] careful listening and evaluation of content…

Differentiated Instruction: **9.6.2** Demonstrate an understanding of sentence construction…and proper English usage…

Teach

R1 Reading Strategy

Visualize Ask students to describe their impressions of the Cyclops's cave—how it looks, sounds, smells, and feels. Encourage students to use vivid, concrete details. **OL**

L1 Literary Element

Epic and Epic Hero Answer: *He is admitting that staying in the cave was a mistake. This suggests that an epic hero can have human failings, as well as the humility to acknowledge them.* **OL**

of that sweet liquor that Euanthes' son,
Maron, had given me. He kept Apollo's
holy grove at Ismarus;° for kindness
we showed him there, and showed his wife and child,
he gave me seven shining golden talents°
perfectly formed, a solid silver winebowl,
and then this liquor—twelve two-handled jars
of brandy, pure and fiery. Not a slave
in Maron's household knew this drink; only
he, his wife and the storeroom mistress knew;
and they would put one cupful—ruby-colored,
honey-smooth—in twenty more of water,
but still the sweet scent hovered like a fume
over the winebowl. No man turned away
when cups of this came round.
                                        A wineskin full
I brought along, and victuals° in a bag,
for in my bones I knew some towering brute
would be upon us soon—all outward power,
a wild man, ignorant of civility.°

We climbed, then, briskly to the cave. But Cyclops°
had gone afield, to pasture his fat sheep,
so we looked round at everything inside:
a drying rack that sagged with cheeses, pens
crowded with lambs and kids, each in its class:
firstlings apart from middlings, and the 'dewdrops,'
or newborn lambkins, penned apart from both.°
And vessels full of whey° were brimming there—
bowls of earthenware and pails for milking.
My men came pressing round me, pleading:
                                        'Why not
take these cheeses, get them stowed, come back,
throw open all the pens, and make a run for it?
We'll drive the kids and lambs aboard. We say
put out again on good salt water!'
                                        Ah,
how sound° that was! Yet I refused. I wished
to see the caveman, what he had to offer—
no pretty sight, it turned out, for my friends.
We lit a fire, burnt an offering,°
and took some cheese to eat; then sat in silence
around the embers, waiting. When he came
he had a load of dry boughs on his shoulder
to stoke his fire at suppertime. He dumped it

88–90 **Euanthes'** (yoo an′ thēz) **son, . . . Ismarus** (iz mār′ əs): In ancient Greece, worshippers of certain gods built shrines to them, surrounded by woods, or "groves," that were considered sacred sanctuaries. Priests oversaw the planting and tending of the groves. **Maron** (mār′ on) is a priest of **Apollo** (ə pol′ ō), an important god associated with music, medicine, law, and the tending of flocks and herds.

92 **talents:** bars of gold used as money in ancient Greece.

104 **victuals** (vit′ əls): food

107 **civility:** polite and courteous behavior.

108 **Cyclops** (sī′ klops): Note the different spelling and pronunciation of this reference to a single one-eyed giant.

111–114 **pens . . . both:** The lambs are grouped by age.

115 **whey:** the watery part of milk that separates from the curd, or solid part, during the cheese-making process.

124 **sound:** sensible.

127 **burnt an offering:** The men burned some food as a gift to the gods in the hope of winning their support.

Literary Element Epic and Epic Hero *What is Odysseus admitting here? What do we learn about the traits of an epic hero from this decision?* **L1**

Additional Support

Skills Practice

WRITING: Using Spatial Order

Refer students to lines 110–117 on page 968 and discuss how the cave is probably arranged. *(May be right-to-left or near-to-far spatial description, with cheeses drying near cave opening, pens in back, and vessels to left)* Point out that when describing a place, writers often use spatial order to describe things in a sequence that the eye would follow.

Have students write a paragraph describing a room at home. They should use spatial order to organize the description. Remind them to try to establish an overall impression of the place through their word choices. **OL**

with a great crash into that hollow cave,
and we all scattered fast to the far wall.
Then over the broad cavern floor he ushered
the ewes he meant to milk. He left his rams
and he-goats in the yard outside, and swung
high overhead a slab of solid rock
to close the cave. Two dozen four-wheeled wagons,
with heaving wagon teams, could not have stirred
the tonnage of that rock from where he wedged it
over the doorsill. Next he took his seat
and milked his bleating ewes. A practiced job
he made of it, giving each ewe her suckling;
thickened his milk, then, into curds and whey,
sieved out the curds to drip in withy baskets,°
and poured the whey to stand in bowls
cooling until he drank it for his supper.
When all these chores were done, he poked the fire,
heaping on brushwood. In the glare he saw us.

'Strangers,' he said, 'who are you? And where from?
What brings you here by sea ways—a fair traffic?
Or are you wandering rogues, who cast your lives
like dice, and ravage other folk by sea?'°

We felt a pressure on our hearts, in dread
of that deep rumble and that mighty man.
But all the same I spoke up in reply:

'We are from Troy, Achaeans,° blown off course
by shifting gales on the Great South Sea;
homeward bound, but taking routes and ways
uncommon; so the will of Zeus would have it.
We served under Agamemnon, son of Atreus°—
the whole world knows what city
he laid waste, what armies he destroyed.
It was our luck to come here; here we stand,
beholden for your help, or any gifts
you give—as custom is to honor strangers.
We would entreat you, great Sir, have a care
for the gods' courtesy; Zeus will avenge
the unoffending guest.'°

He answered this
from his brute chest, unmoved:

'You are a ninny,°

144–145 **thickened . . . baskets:** The milk is curdled (**thickened**) by adding fig juice, and the whey is drained off through wicker (**withy**) baskets.

151–153 **What brings . . . by sea:** What brings you here from the sea—honest trade? Or are you wandering scoundrels who carelessly risk your lives and steal from others?

157 **Achaeans** (ə kē′ əns): Greeks.

161 **Agamemnon** (ag′ ə mem′ non), **son of Atreus** (ā′ trē əs): king of Argos, in southern Greece, who led the war against Troy.

167–169 **We would . . . guest:** Odysseus earnestly asks or begs (**entreat**) for the Cyclops's hospitality and warns him that Zeus punishes anyone who mistreats a harmless guest.

172 **ninny:** fool.

Literary Element Epic and Epic Hero *Epics include a mixture of the everyday and the supernatural. How does the Cyclops embody both of these states?* **L2**

Big Idea Journeys *What is Odysseus suggesting about misfortunes that occur on a journey?* **BI**

Teach

L2 Literary Element

Epic and Epic Hero Answer: *The Cyclops is an enormous, supernatural creature. He also carries on the domestic tasks of shepherding and milking.* **OL**

R2 Reading Strategy

Question Odysseus hopes to lessen the giant's anger as he introduces himself and his men. **Ask:** What are three pieces of information that Odysseus gives in order to accomplish his purpose? *(He says that they are able soldiers; he reminds the Cyclops of the code of hospitality; and he warns of Zeus's anger.)* What has Odysseus assumed about the Cyclops's beliefs? *(that he respects soldiers, honors societal codes, and fears the gods)* **OL**

BI Big Idea

Journeys Answer: *He is suggesting that misfortunes are orchestrated by the gods.* **OL**

Differentiated Instruction

Less Proficient Readers The language in the *Odyssey* may present obstacles for students who lack strong reading skills. Explain to students that the side notes are aids to comprehension: the degree symbol (°) in the text indicates a corresponding note in the margin, defining difficult words or paraphrasing difficult passages.

As they read, students should use a dictionary and jot down additional definitions of challenging words or phrases. Tell them to note the corresponding line numbers for each entry. **BL**

Academic Standards

Additional Support activities on pp. 968 and 969 cover the following standard:

Skills Practice: **9.5.3** Write expository compositions, including…descriptive pieces…

Differentiated Instruction: **9.2** Develop [reading] strategies…

Teach

L Literary Element

Epic and Epic Hero **Answer:** *He displays cunning. He is proud of this quality, as it was the chief trait he named in introducing himself to the Phaeacians.* OL

R Reading Strategy

Analyzing Figurative Language **Answer:** *The Cyclops caught two men "like squirming puppies." Then he made a meal of them, crunching "like a mountain lion."* OL

★ Cultural History

Greek Ships The ancient Greeks were primarily seafaring people, relying on their ships for trade, warfare, and food. When winds were contrary, ships were propelled by physical labor, and so they were equipped with oars and benches for twenty rowers on either side. Gear and supplies were stored beneath the benches. AS

or else you come from the other end of nowhere,
telling me, mind the gods! We Cyclopes
care not a whistle for your thundering Zeus
or all the gods in bliss; we have more force by far.
I would not let you go for fear of Zeus—
you or your friends—unless I had a whim to.
Tell me, where was it, now, you left your ship—
around the point, or down the shore, I wonder?'

He thought he'd find out, but I saw through this,
and answered with a ready lie:

★ 'My ship?
Poseidon Lord, who sets the earth a-tremble,
broke it up on the rocks at your land's end.
A wind from seaward served him, drove us there.
We are survivors, these good men and I.'

Neither reply nor pity came from him,
but in one stride he clutched at my companions
and caught two in his hands like squirming puppies
to beat their brains out, spattering the floor.
Then he dismembered them and made his meal,
gaping and crunching like a mountain lion—
everything: innards, flesh, and marrow bones.
We cried aloud, lifting our hands to Zeus,
powerless, looking on at this, appalled;°
but Cyclops went on filling up his belly
with manflesh and great gulps of whey,
then lay down like a mast among his sheep.
My heart beat high now at the chance of action,
and drawing the sharp sword from my hip I went
along his flank to stab him where the midriff
holds the liver. I had touched the spot
when sudden fear stayed me: if I killed him
we perished there as well, for we could never
move his **ponderous** doorway slab aside.
So we were left to groan and wait for morning.

When the young Dawn with fingertips of rose
lit up the world, the Cyclops built a fire

196 **appalled:** horrified; shocked; terrified.

Literary Element Epic and Epic Hero *What character trait does Odysseus display here?* L

Reading Strategy Analyzing Figurative Language *The poet uses two similes in this grisly description of the Cyclops's dinner. What are they?* R

Vocabulary

ponderous (pon′ dər əs) *adj.* having great weight or bulk; heavy

Additional Support

Skills Practice

GRAMMAR AND LANGUAGE: Dashes Point out the dashes on pages 970–971. Explain that dashes signal an abrupt break or change of thought or set off information added to a thought. For example, in line 193, the dash sets off added information.

Have students explain why dashes are used in the following places and the effect on meaning:

1. line 215 *(To signal a break; suggesting first hope at the door's opening, then disappointment at its closing)*
2. lines 239–240 *(Added information; it emphasizes why Odysseus would have chosen the men.)* OL

and milked his handsome ewes, all in due order,
putting the sucklings to the mothers. Then,
his chores being all dispatched,° he caught
another brace° of men to make his breakfast,
and whisked away his great door slab
to let his sheep go through—but he, behind,
reset the stone as one would cap a quiver.°
There was a din of whistling as the Cyclops
rounded his flock to higher ground, then stillness.
And now I pondered how to hurt him worst,
if but Athena° granted what I prayed for.
Here are the means I thought would serve my turn:

a club, or staff, lay there along the fold—
an olive tree, felled green and left to season
for Cyclops's hand. And it was like a mast
a lugger of twenty oars, broad in the beam—
a deep-sea-going craft—might carry:°
so long, so big around, it seemed. Now I
chopped out a six foot section of this pole
and set it down before my men, who scraped it;
and when they had it smooth, I hewed° again
to make a stake with pointed end. I held this
in the fire's heart and turned it, toughening it,
then hid it, well back in the cavern, under
V one of the dung piles in profusion there.
Now came the time to toss for it: who ventured
along with me? whose hand could bear to thrust
and grind that spike in Cyclops's eye, when mild
sleep had mastered him? As luck would have it,
the men I would have chosen won the toss—
four strong men, and I made five as captain.

At evening came the shepherd with his flock,
his woolly flock. The rams as well, this time,
entered the cave: by some sheep-herding whim—
or a god's bidding—none were left outside.
He hefted his great boulder into place
and sat him down to milk the bleating ewes
in proper order, put the lambs to suck,
and swiftly ran through all his evening chores.
Then he caught two more men and feasted on them.
My moment was at hand, and I went forward
holding an ivy bowl of my dark drink,°
looking up, saying:

'Cyclops, try some wine.
Here's liquor to wash down your scraps of men.

212 **dispatched:** finished.

213 **brace:** pair.

216 **cap a quiver:** put the cap on a case for holding arrows.

220 **Athena:** Odysseus prays for the support of Athena, his patron goddess who guides and protects him. Among other things, Athena is a warrior goddess who directly helps her chosen heroes.

221–226 **Here are . . . carry:** Odysseus spies the trunk of an olive tree, which the Cyclops cut down **(felled)** when the wood was green and left to dry **(season)** before carving it into a club or staff. Odysseus compares its size to that of a mast on a seafaring ship **(lugger)** that is wide in the middle **(broad in the beam)**.

230 **hewed:** chopped or hacked.

251 **dark drink:** This is the liquor Odysseus described in lines 94–102.

Big Idea **Journeys** *What hint is Odysseus dropping here about the future of his journey?* **BI**

Teach

V Vocabulary

Context Clues Ask: What details about the cave suggest that *profusion* in line 234 means "abundance"? *(Homer has described the many sheep in the cave. It is logical to assume that their droppings would be everywhere.)* **OL**

BI Big Idea

Journeys Answer: *He is alerting his audience to the importance of the Cyclops's rams in this adventure. He is also suggesting that a god may be taking an interest in the hero's journey.* **OL**

Differentiated Instruction

Logical-Mathematical Odysseus approaches the problem of escaping from the Cyclops's cave by carrying out a series of steps. Guide students through Odysseus's thinking process.

1. Decide how to impair the giant without diminishing his strength.
2. Find raw materials for the spear.
3. Set up a way and a time to make the spear without being seen.
4. Think of a way to dull the giant's senses and make him sleep soundly.

Have students work in small groups to solve a problem—such as how to help someone anonymously. **AL**

Academic Standards

Additional Support activities on pp. 970 and 971 cover the following standards:

Skills Practice: **9.6.1** Identify…the mechanics of punctuation…

Differentiated Instruction: **9.7.1** Summarize a speaker's purpose and…ask questions concerning the speaker's content…

Teach

L Literary Element

Epic and Epic Hero Answer: *Students should understand that Odysseus almost certainly has a trick in mind. He knows his own limitations and tries to outwit his opponents when he lacks the physical strength to overcome them.* **OL**

R Reading Strategy

Analyzing Figurative Language Answer: *He compares driving the stake into the Cyclops's eye to boring a hole with a shipwright's drill. This action was most likely a familiar image to Homer's audience.* **OL**

★ Cultural History

Ambrosia In Greek mythology, ambrosia, which means "immortal," was the food of the gods; nectar was their drink, which was brought by the cupbearer Ganymede. **AS**

Taste it, and see the kind of drink we carried
under our planks. I meant it for an offering
if you would help us home. But you are mad,
unbearable, a bloody monster! After this,
will any other traveler come to see you?'

He seized and drained the bowl, and it went down
so fiery and smooth he called for more:

'Give me another, thank you kindly. Tell me,
how are you called? I'll make a gift will please you.
Even Cyclopes know the wine-grapes grow
out of grassland and loam in heaven's rain,
★ but here's a bit of nectar and ambrosia!'°

Three bowls I brought him, and he poured them down.
I saw the fuddle and flush° cover over him,
then I sang out in cordial tones:

'Cyclops,
you ask my honorable name? Remember
the gift you promised me, and I shall tell you.
My name is Nohbdy: mother, father, and friends,
everyone calls me Nohbdy.'

And he said:
'Nohbdy's my meat, then, after I eat his friends.
Others come first. There's a noble gift, now.'

Even as he spoke, he reeled and tumbled backward,
his great head lolling to one side; and sleep
took him like any creature. Drunk, hiccuping,
he dribbled streams of liquor and bits of men.

Now, by the gods, I drove my big hand spike
deep in the embers, charring it again,
and cheered my men along with battle talk
to keep their courage up: no quitting now.
The pike of olive,° green though it had been,
reddened and glowed as if about to catch.
I drew it from the coals and my four fellows
gave me a hand, lugging it near the Cyclops
as more than natural force nerved them; straight
forward they sprinted, lifted it, and rammed it
deep in his crater eye, and I leaned on it
turning it as a shipwright turns a drill
in planking, having men below to swing

266 **nectar and ambrosia:** the foods of the gods, causing immortality. The Cyclops suggests that any wine is a gift from heaven, but this one is like the gods' own drink.

268 **fuddle and flush:** the confused mental state and reddish complexion caused by drinking alcohol.

286 **pike of olive:** the sharpened stake made from the olive tree.

Literary Element Epic and Epic Hero *What do you think Odysseus has in mind? What does it confirm about his character?* **L**

Reading Strategy Analyzing Figurative Language *To what action does Homer compare the blinding of the Cyclops? Why might he have chosen this comparison?* **R**

Additional Support

Skills Practice

SPEAKING AND LISTENING: Storytelling Point out that Homer uses imagery and concrete language to bring action to life. Point out the simple syntax he uses for reporting what happens (for example, "straight forward they sprinted, lifted it, and rammed it deep in his crater eye"). He focuses on sight, touch, and hearing. Point out that simple language and vivid details are vital to good storytelling.

Have partners make up a story about Polyphemus fighting a monstrous beast. Students should practice telling their stories, focusing on creating vivid pictures in listeners' minds. **OL**

Teach

Viewing the Art

Alessandro Allori (1535–1607) painted in late sixteenth century Florence. On a visit to Rome, Allori was influenced by the artwork of Michelangelo. He returned to Florence, where he painted for the ruling Medici family. In the mid-1570s, Allori became director of the Florentine tapestry workshop. In his painting, Allori depicted the human body in complicated twisting poses. **AS**

Ulysses and Polyphemos, 1560 (detail). Alessandro Allori. Fresco. Collection of Banca Toscana (Palazzo Salviati), Florence, Italy.

the two-handled strap that spins it in the groove.
So with our brand° we bored that great eye socket
while blood ran out around the red hot bar.
Eyelid and lash were seared; the pierced ball
hissed broiling, and the roots popped.
In a smithy
one sees a white-hot axehead or an adze°
plunged and wrung in a cold tub, screeching steam—
the way they make soft iron hale° and hard—:
just so that eyeball hissed around the spike.
The Cyclops bellowed and the rock roared round him,
and we fell back in fear. Clawing his face
he tugged the bloody spike out of his eye,
threw it away, and his wild hands went groping;
then he set up a howl for Cyclopes
who lived in caves on windy peaks nearby.
Some heard him; and they came by divers° ways
to clump around outside and call:
'What ails you,
Polyphemus?° Why do you cry so sore
in the starry night? You will not let us sleep.

296 **brand:** the piece of burning hot wood.

301 **adze:** an axe-like tool with a curved blade.

303 **hale:** strong.

311 **divers:** several different; various.

314 **Polyphemus** (pol′ i fē′ məs): the blinded Cyclops's name.

English Language Coach

Diction Explain that translations of the Odyssey often use words that are difficult or use words in unusual ways. Even native English-speaking readers find the translation difficult to read sometimes.

Have English language learners identify difficult words on this page. Then, have them write what they think the words mean by studying the context. Have them look up each word in the dictionary to clarify meaning. **EL**

Academic Standards

Additional Support activities on pp. 972 and 973 cover the following standards:

Skills Practice: **9.7.14** Deliver narrative presentations that narrate a sequence of events [and]...describe with specific details the sights, sounds, and smells of a scene and the specific actions, movements, gestures, and feelings of characters...

English Language Coach: **9.1** Use... context clues and a growing knowledge of English...to determine the meaning of words...

Teach

L1 Literary Element

Epic and Epic Hero Answer: *Odysseus uses a false name to deceive the Cyclops's neighbors into thinking that nobody has hurt him. Odysseus's plan has served him well, but he will find that he has made a powerful enemy in Poseidon, Polyphemus's father.* OL

Viewing the Art

Answer: *Students may say they would fear being discovered or falling off the ram. They may say the ram is experiencing intense pain. The Cyclops is as determined to destroy the men as they are to escape.*

Jacob Jordaens (1593–1678) was a Flemish painter who was famous for large canvases, often featuring scenes of revelry. *Odysseus* is typical in its sensuous use of color, deep red tones, and focus on a dramatic moment. AS

Odysseus. Jacob Jordaens (1593–1678). Oil on canvas, 61 × 97 cm. Pushkin Museum, Moscow.

Viewing the Art: Imagine that you are the man beneath the ram on the left. What is going through your mind? What might the Cyclops be thinking and feeling in this scene? 

Sure no man's driving off your flock? No man
has tricked you, ruined you?'
Out of the cave
the mammoth Polyphemus roared in answer:
'Nohbdy, Nohbdy's tricked me, Nohbdy's ruined me!'
To this rough shout they made a sage° reply:
'Ah well, if nobody has played you foul
there in your lonely bed, we are no use in pain
given by great Zeus. Let it be your father,
Poseidon Lord, to whom you pray.'
So saying
they trailed away. And I was filled with laughter
to see how like a charm the name deceived them.
Now Cyclops, wheezing as the pain came on him,
fumbled to wrench away the great doorstone
and squatted in the breach° with arms thrown wide
for any silly beast or man who bolted°—
hoping somehow I might be such a fool.

321 **sage:** wise.

331 **breach:** a gap or opening.

332 **bolted:** broke away.

Literary Element Epic and Epic Hero *Why did Odysseus tell the Cyclops his name was Nohbdy? How well has Odysseus's plan worked?* L1

Additional Support

Skills Practice

READING: Identifying Cause-and-Effect Relationships Ask students to recall what happened because Odysseus wanted to see the Cyclops. *(He and his men were trapped in the cave; some men were devoured.)* Point out that Odysseus's impulsive actions cause some of his troubles. Have students use a form like the following to show cause-and-effect relationships. OL

Cause	Effect
Odysseus taunts Cyclops.	Boat nearly washed ashore
Odysseus gives his real name.	Allows Cyclops to curse him

But I kept thinking how to win the game:
death sat there huge; how could we slip away?
I drew on all my wits, and ran through tactics,
reasoning as a man will for dear life,
until a trick came—and it pleased me well.
The Cyclops' rams were handsome, fat, with heavy
fleeces, a dark violet.
Three abreast
I tied them silently together, twining
cords of willow from the ogre's° bed;
then slung a man under each middle one
to ride there safely, shielded left and right.
So three sheep could convey each man. I took
the woolliest ram, the choicest of the flock,
and hung myself under his kinky belly,
pulled up tight, with fingers twisted deep
in sheepskin ringlets for an iron grip.
So, breathing hard, we waited until morning.

When Dawn spread out her fingertips of rose
the rams began to stir, moving for pasture,
and peals of bleating echoed round the pens
where dams with udders full called for a milking.
Blinded, and sick with pain from his head wound,
the master stroked each ram, then let it pass,
but my men riding on the pectoral fleece°
the giant's blind hands blundering never found.
Last of them all my ram, the leader, came,
weighted by wool and me with my meditations.
The Cyclops patted him, and then he said:

'Sweet cousin ram, why lag behind the rest
in the night cave? You never linger so,
but graze before them all, and go afar
to crop sweet grass, and take your stately way
leading along the streams, until at evening
you run to be the first one in the fold.
Why, now, so far behind? Can you be grieving
over your Master's eye? That carrion° rogue
and his accurst companions burnt it out
when he had conquered all my wits with wine.
Nohbdy will not get out alive, I swear.
Oh, had you brain and voice to tell
where he may be now, dodging all my fury!
Bashed by this hand and bashed on this rock wall

343 **ogre:** monster; fearsome giant.

358 **pectoral fleece:** the wool on the rams' chests.

370 **carrion:** rotten, filthy.

Reading Strategy Analyzing Figurative Language *Why do you think the poet chose to personify death in this passage?* **R**

Teach

R Reading Strategy

Analyzing Figurative Language **Answer:** *Death is made human to emphasize the life-and-death struggle. Homer describes it as a game Odysseus is playing with the personified character "Death," with wit and courage as his tools.* **OL**

L2 Literary Element

Irony Remind students that a situation is ironic when its outcome is the opposite of what is expected to happen. Invite a volunteer to explain the irony of Polyphemus's words in this passage. *(He thinks the ram lags behind out of grief for the Cyclops's eye and that the animal would tell its master where Odysseus is if it could speak. In fact, the ram is giving Odysseus a way out.)* **OL**

Differentiated Instruction

Clarifying The vivid descriptions and suspenseful action will motivate students who may be struggling with the reading. Play the audiotape as students read along. Pause to answer students' questions and to have them paraphrase the action. Use dramatic activities to reinforce students' comprehension.

Play the audiotape of students' favorite scenes a second time, having volunteers pantomime actions, such as tying the men under the rams, and character reactions, such as Odysseus's fury and exhilaration after he escapes. **BL**

Academic Standards

Additional Support activities on pp. 974 and 975 cover the following standards:

Skills Practice: **9.3** [Identify] story elements such as…plot…

Differentiated Instruction: **9.7** [Respond] to oral communication [with] careful listening and evaluation of content…

Teach

L1 Literary Element

Epic and Epic Hero **Answer:** *The Cyclops expresses self-pity and rage. Odysseus, in contrast, is always using his intelligence and cunning.* **OL**

R Reading Strategy

Oral Reading **Ask:** What is Odysseus feeling after the narrow escape? Have students suggest the tone with which Odysseus delivers these lines. Invite students to read them aloud with suitable expressions and gestures. **OL**

L2 Literary Element

Epic and Epic Hero **Answer:** *Odysseus is furious with the Cyclops and proud that his trick has worked. Students may point out that he is drawing attention to himself, exactly what he had told his men* not to do *a few moments earlier.* **OL**

★ Viewing the Art

Ask: In your opinion, how well does this picture illustrate the scene described in lines 395–401? Explain. *(Students my say the picture accurately shows the events but lacks emotion.)* **AS**

his brains would strew the floor, and I should have
rest from the outrage Nohbdy worked upon me.'

He sent us into the open, then. Close by,
I dropped and rolled clear of the ram's belly,
going this way and that to untie the men.
With many glances back, we rounded up
his fat, stiff-legged sheep to take aboard,
and drove them down to where the good ship lay.
We saw, as we came near, our fellows' faces
shining; then we saw them turn to grief
tallying those who had not fled from death.
I hushed them, jerking head and eyebrows up,
and in a low voice told them: 'Load this herd;
move fast, and put the ship's head toward the breakers.'°
They all pitched in at loading, then embarked°
and struck their oars into the sea. Far out,
as far off shore as shouted words would carry,
I sent a few back to the adversary:

R
'O Cyclops! Would you feast on my companions?
Puny, am I, in a Caveman's hands?
How do you like the beating that we gave you,
you damned cannibal? Eater of guests
under your roof! Zeus and the gods have paid you!'

The blind thing in his doubled fury broke
a hilltop in his hands and heaved it after us.
Ahead of our black prow it struck and sank
whelmed in a spuming geyser, a giant wave
that washed the ship stern foremost back to shore.
I got the longest boathook out and stood
fending us off, with furious nods to all
to put their backs into a racing stroke—
row, row, or perish. So the long oars bent
kicking the foam sternward, making head
until we drew away, and twice as far.°
Now when I cupped my hands I heard the crew
in low voices protesting:

'Godsake, Captain!
Why bait the beast again? Let him alone!'
'That tidal wave he made on the first throw
all but beached us.'

'All but stove us in!'

'Give him our bearing with your trumpeting,
he'll get the range and lob a boulder.'°

Literary Element Epic and Epic Hero *What emotions does the Cyclops express in this passage? Contrast his character with that of Odysseus.* **L1**

Literary Element Epic and Epic Hero *Why does Odysseus behave in this way?* **L2**

390 **put . . . breakers:** turn the ship around, toward the open sea.
391 **embarked:** got on board.

Odysseus and Polyphem, 1910. After L. du Bois-Reymond. Color print. Collection of Karl Becker, Sagen des klassischen Altertums, Berlin (Verlag Jugendhort). ★

402–410 **Ahead . . . twice as far:** The sinking hilltop creates a wave at the ship's front end **(prow)** that washes the boat backwards **(stern foremost)** to the shore.
415–419 **That tidal . . . boulder:** The men complain, reasonably enough, that Polyphemus nearly smashed the ship **(All but stove us in)** and that Odysseus's shouting will give away their position **(bearing)**.

Additional Support

Skills Practice

RESEARCH: Causes of Earthquakes The ancient Greeks explained earthquakes as the handiwork of the god Poseidon. Today, geologists believe that earthquake tremors result from the shifting tectonic plates on which the continents of Earth's crust ride.

Have students use an earth science text, encyclopedia, or the Internet to learn more about the causes of earthquakes and the technology used to monitor and measure them. Suggest that students add illustrations and graphic organizers to clarify their notes. Have students break into groups and share their findings. **OL**

'Aye
He'll smash our timbers and our heads together!'
I would not heed them in my glorying spirit,
but let my anger flare and yelled:

'Cyclops,
if ever mortal man inquire
how you were put to shame and blinded, tell him
Odysseus, raider of cities, took your eye:
Laertes' son, whose home's on Ithaca!'
At this he gave a mighty sob and rumbled:
'Now comes the weird° upon me, spoken of old.
A wizard, grand and wondrous, lived here—Telemus,°
a son of Eurymus;° great length of days
he had in wizardry among the Cyclopes,
and these things he foretold for time to come:
my great eye lost, and at Odysseus' hands.
Always I had in mind some giant, armed
in giant force, would come against me here.
But this, but you—small, pitiful and twiggy—
you put me down with wine, you blinded me.
Come back, Odysseus, and I'll treat you well,
praying the god of earthquake° to befriend you—
his son I am, for he by his avowal
fathered me, and, if he will, he may
heal me of this black wound—he and no other
of all the happy gods or mortal men.'
Few words I shouted in reply to him:
'If I could take your life I would and take
your time away, and hurl you down to hell!
The god of earthquake could not heal you there!'
At this he stretched his hands out in his darkness
toward the sky of stars, and prayed Poseidon:
'O hear me, lord, blue girdler of the islands,
if I am thine indeed, and thou art father:
grant that Odysseus, raider of cities, never
see his home: Laertes' son, I mean,
who kept his hall on Ithaca. Should destiny
intend that he shall see his roof again
among his family in his father land,
far be that day, and dark the years between.
Let him lose all companions, and return
under strange sail to bitter days at home.'°

L4

Literary Element Epic and Epic Hero *How would you characterize Odysseus's judgment?* L3

430 **the weird:** the strange fate.

431 **Telemus** (tel′ ə məs)

432 **Eurymus** (yoo ri′ məs)

441 **god of earthquake:** Poseidon

452–461 **O hear . . . home:** In ancient cultures, curses were neither made nor taken lightly. Homer's audience would have believed in their power. In his curse upon Odysseus, Polyphemus begs Poseidon to make his enemy suffer, using every detail he knows about Odysseus to make sure the god's punishment will be directed toward the right person.

Teach

L3 Literary Element

Epic and Epic Hero **Answer:** *Odysseus's judgment is clouded by his pride and his desire for fame. He reveals who he is and where he lives, allowing the Cyclops to have him pursued and punished.* OL

L4 Literary Element

Foreshadowing Explain that foreshadowing is planting clues to suggest future events.
Ask: What do you think lines 456–461 foreshadow for Odysseus? *(That Poseidon will try to destroy Odysseus's men and delay his return home—perhaps through storms at sea or earthquakes.)* OL

CheckPoint

Use the CheckPoint questions on Presentation Plus! to check students' mastery of the selection. These questions can be used with interactive response keypads for immediate student feedback.

English Language Coach

Pronoun Reference Extensive use of pronouns in the selection may prove confusing for English language learners, expecially for students who have difficulty with the *he/she* distinction.

As students read the selection, ask them to pause to identify the noun referents for the pronouns, including subject and object pronouns, possessives, and indefinite pronouns such as *one*. Remind students that *it* does not always have a noun referent. EL

Academic Standards

Additional Support activities on pp. 976 and 977 cover the following standards:

Skills Practice: **9.4.6** Synthesize information from multiple sources...

English Language Coach: **9.6.2** Demonstrate an understanding of sentence construction...and proper English usage...

Teach

BI1 Big Idea

Journeys Answer: *This passage suggests that Odysseus's journey home will be long and difficult.* **OL**

BI2 Big Idea

Journeys Ask students to name other stories they know that tell of a hero's adventures while on a journey. How is this story similar to and different from the *Odyssey?* **OL**

R Reading Strategy

Analyzing Figurative Language Answer: *It also appears in lines 208 and 352. Note that repetition aids the memory of both poet and audience. Also, each mention of the dawn signals the arrival of a new day, so each reference serves as a transition.* **OL**

Web Activities Have students access the Web site for interactive activities that will help them assess their understanding of the selection.

In these words he prayed, and the god heard him.
Now he laid hands upon a bigger stone
and wheeled around, titanic for the cast,°
to let it fly in the black-prowed vessel's track.
But it fell short, just aft° the steering oar,
and whelming seas rose giant above the stone
to bear us onward toward the island.°

There
as we ran in we saw the squadron waiting,
the trim° ships drawn up side by side, and all
our troubled friends who waited, looking seaward.
We beached her, grinding keel in the soft sand,
and waded in, ourselves, on the sandy beach.
Then we unloaded all the Cyclops's flock
to make division, share and share alike,
only my fighters voted that my ram,
the prize of all, should go to me. I slew him
by the seaside and burnt his long thighbones
to Zeus beyond the stormcloud, Cronus's° son,
who rules the world. But Zeus disdained° my offering;
destruction for my ships he had in store
and death for those who sailed them, my companions.
Now all day long until the sun went down
we made our feast on mutton and sweet wine,
till after sunset in the gathering dark
we went to sleep above the wash of ripples.

BI2 When the young Dawn with fingertips of rose
touched the world, I roused the men, gave orders
to man the ships, cast off the mooring lines;
and filing in to sit beside the rowlocks
oarsmen in line dipped oars in the gray sea.
So we moved out, sad in the vast offing,°
having our precious lives, but not our friends."

464 **titanic for the cast:** drawing upon his great size and strength in preparation for the throw.
466 **aft:** behind.

468 **the island:** the deserted island where the other eleven ships and their crews have remained while Odysseus and his handpicked men explored the Cyclops's mainland.
471 **trim:** in good condition and ready to sail.

480 **Cronus** (krō′ nəs): Heaven and Earth, the first gods, had been dethroned by their son Cronus, who was in turn overthrown by his son Zeus.
481 **disdained:** rejected.

493 **vast offing:** the visible expanse of open sea.

Big Idea Journeys *What does this passage suggest about Odysseus's return journey to Ithaca?* **BI1**

Reading Strategy Analyzing Figurative Language *Where have you encountered this figure of speech before? Why might the poet have repeated it?* **R**

Additional Support

Academic Standards

The Additional Support activity on p. 978 covers the following standard:

Skills Practice: **9.6.2** Demonstrate an understanding of sentence construction…

Skills Practice

GRAMMAR: Simple and Compound Sentences Write on the board:

In these words he prayed, and the god heard him.
We beached her, grinding keel in the soft sand, and waded in.

Explain that the first item is a compound sentence, and the second is a simple sentence with two verbs. Have students identify subjects and verbs and label the sentence below as simple or compound.

He raged at Polyphemus, and the giant nearly beached their boat. *(compound)* **OL**

AFTER YOU READ

RESPONDING AND THINKING CRITICALLY

Respond

1. How did you respond to Part 1? Explain.

Recall and Interpret

2. (a)What happens to the men who go ashore in the land of the Lotus Eaters? (b)Why might Odysseus be so opposed to the eating of lotus?
3. (a)Summarize what happens inside the Cyclops's cave. (b)What personality traits does Odysseus reveal in leading his men to safety?
4. (a)Describe an instance of Odysseus acting against the advice of his men. (b)In your opinion, why does Odysseus decide not to listen to them?

Analyze and Evaluate

5. (a)Explain why Odysseus might have commented on the Cyclopes's way of life before describing his adventures in their land. (b)Were you influenced by his description? Why or why not?
6. (a)How does the Cyclops's treatment of Odysseus's men differ from his treatment of his animals? (b)Do you feel any sympathy for the Cyclops? Why or why not?
7. (a)Find supporting evidence for the following statement: "There are two distinct sides to Odysseus's personality." (b)How do you think his crew regards him, given these aspects of his personality?

Connect

8. **Big Idea** **Journeys** The Invocation reveals what happens to Odysseus and his men. How did knowing the outcome affect your reading of Part 1?

LITERARY ANALYSIS

Literary Element Epic and Epic Hero

An **epic** is no ordinary adventure story. It is big in every way—in length, in action, and in setting. Even its purpose is large. Epics were not intended simply to entertain their listeners but to inspire and instruct them as well. The **epic hero** is also larger than life, but he or she has recognizable human characteristics—including human faults.

1. What is extraordinary about Odysseus? What is ordinary about him? Give an example of each quality.
2. How could the *Odyssey* serve to entertain, to inspire, and to teach? Explain.

Literature Groups

With your group, discuss Odysseus's actions as a leader: When does he make mistakes, and when does he act wisely? Together, make a list of "good moves" and "bad moves" that might have had a better result. Compare your list with those of other groups.

LiteratureOnline **Web Activities** For eFlashcards, Selection Quick Checks, and other Web activities, go to www.glencoe.com.

READING AND VOCABULARY

Reading Strategy Analyzing Figurative Language

An epic simile extends a comparison with elaborate descriptive details that can fill several lines of verse.

1. The scene describing the blinding of the Cyclops contains two epic similes. Identify the lines of each simile and tell what is being compared.
2. In your opinion, why might Homer have used more than one epic simile to describe this event?

Vocabulary Practice

Practice with Synonyms For each vocabulary word, choose the synonym.

1. plunder
   a. seize **b.** donate
2. valor
   a. bravery **b.** strength
3. guile
   a. foolishness **b.** craftiness
4. ponderous
   a. light **b.** heavy

AFTER YOU READ

Assess

1. Answers will vary.
2. (a) They lose all desire to leave the island. (b) Odysseus is determined to reach his home.
3. (a) The Cyclops eats six men. Odysseus and his men get the giant drunk and blind him. They tie themselves beneath sheep to escape. (b) Courage and cunning
4. (a) He taunts the Cyclops from the boat. (b) He is impulsive and self-confident.
5. (a) By criticizing their crude way of life, he builds up tension. (b) Odysseus's remarks about the Cyclopes give clues to the kind of behavior to expect from Polyphemus.
6. (a) The Cyclops treats the men like animals, but he treats animals like humans. (b) Some students may pity the Cyclops's situation. However, his brutality makes it difficult to feel sympathy for him.
7. (a) Odysseus is both a strong, caring leader and a reckless adventurer. (b) The crew respects and trusts Odysseus, but may feel that his inconsistent behavior puts them at risk.
8. The story's appeal lies in what happens along the way, not in how the journey ends.

Literary Element

1. Odysseus is clever at solving problems. His pride and anger make him ordinary.
2. The fight with the Cyclops is entertaining. Odysseus's love of his home is inspirational. His leadership in escaping from the Lotus Eaters is instructive.

Reading Strategy

1. Lines 293–295: Boring the spike into the eye is like a shipbuilder drilling into a plank. Lines 300–304: The hissing of the eyeball is like the sound of hot metal plunged into a tub of cold water.
2. The emphasis is appropriate, as the act avenges the deaths of Odysseus's men.

Vocabulary

1. a **2.** a **3.** b **4.** b

Literature Groups

Encourage students to support their evaluations with evidence from the epic.

BEFORE YOU READ

Focus

Summary

Odysseus and his crew set sail from Circe's island. Odysseus uses wax to plug his men's ears so that they cannot hear the irresistible song of the Sirens, and he tells the men to tie him to the mast. As they pass Scylla and Charybdis, Scylla devours six men. They travel near Helios's island, and Odysseus lets the men go ashore. The desperate crew members kill some cattle for food. In revenge, Zeus sends a squall to destroy the ship. Odysseus is the only man to survive, and after nine days adrift, he lands on the island of Ogygia, where the nymph Calypso detains him.

V Vocabulary

Vocabulary File **Say:** Add these words and definitions to your vocabulary file. For each word, include a sentence that gives you an example of how to use the word. **OL** Students with English language needs should include the pronunciations of these words in their files. **EL**

Literary Elements Have students access the Web site to improve their understanding of conflict.

BEFORE YOU READ *Odyssey, Part 2*

LITERATURE PREVIEW

Connecting to the Poem

Have you ever heard the expression "between a rock and a hard place?" It means whichever choice you make is going to be difficult or risky. Before you read Part 2, think about the following questions:

- When have you had to choose between two equally unpleasant alternatives?
- How did you make your decision, and how did it work out?

Building Background

To the ancient Greeks, the gods were a common yet important part of everyday life. Some were associated with abstract ideas, such as wisdom, while others presided over particular activities, such as warfare. All Greek deities had magical powers and were immortal, but they also possessed various human foibles and failings. The gods often held grudges and behaved vengefully toward humans or toward other gods. The Greeks frequently attributed disaster or good fortune to the influence of the gods.

Setting Purposes for Reading

Big Idea Journeys

As you read, think about the stages of Odysseus's journey. What tests must he pass as he makes his way home?

Literary Element Conflict

Conflict is the central struggle between two opposing forces in a story. External conflict exists when a character struggles against some outside force, such as another person, nature, society, or fate. An internal conflict takes place within the mind of a character. Look for conflict as you read Part 2 of the *Odyssey*.

- See Literary Terms Handbook, p. R4.

Literature Online **Interactive Literary Elements Handbook** To review or learn more about the literary elements, go to www.glencoe.com.

READING PREVIEW

Reading Strategy Identifying Sequence

The *Odyssey* is a series of vivid adventures that happen so rapidly that identifying the **sequence** of the events, or understanding their correct order, can become confusing. Stopping to summarize the story periodically—using words such as *then, next, later,* and *finally*—is one way to identify sequence.

Reading Tip: Taking Notes Use a graphic organizer to keep a visual record of the sequence of events.

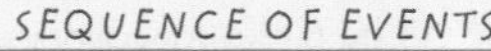

SEQUENCE OF EVENTS

Odysseus and men leave Circe's island.

↓

Odysseus is lashed to mast. Only he can hear Sirens.

↓

Ship sails between Scylla and Charybdis. Six men are lost.

Vocabulary

shun (shun) *v.* to keep away from; avoid; p. 982 *Do not shun people for their ideas.*

ardor (är′ dər) *n.* passion; intensity of emotion; enthusiasm; p. 982 *Jon's ardor for video games waned as he grew interested in skiing.*

tumult (to͞o′ məlt) *n.* commotion; uproar; p. 983 *The escaped horse caused a scene of tumult on the crowded city street.*

shroud (shroud) *v.* to cover, as with a veil or burial cloth; conceal; p. 988 *The contents of the will were shrouded in secrecy.*

Vocabulary Tip: Context Clues Often you can unlock the meaning of unfamiliar words by examining context clues, the phrases and sentences surrounding them.

INDIANA ACADEMIC STANDARDS (pages 980–993)

9.3.3 Analyze interactions between characters…
9.3.6 Analyze development of…sequence…
9.5.3 Write…analytical essays…

Selection Skills

***from the* Odyssey, Part 2**

Literary Elements
- Conflict (SE pp. 980–993)

Reading Skills
- Identifying Sequence (SE pp. 980–993)
- Problem and Solution (TWE p. 982)
- Sequence of Events (TWE p. 990)

Vocabulary Skills
- Context Clues (SE pp. 980, 993)

Listening/Speaking/Viewing Skills
- Analyzing Art (SE p. 987; TWE pp. 983, 985, 992)
- Oral Interpretation (TWE p. 988)

Writing Skills/Grammar
- Analyze Description (SE p. 993)
- Monologue Using Jargon (TWE p. 984)
- Adverb Clauses (TWE p. 986)
- Participles and Participial Phrases (TWE p. 992)

Part 2

Sea Perils and Defeat

Odysseus and his men traveled to the floating islands of Aeolus (ē′ ə ləs), god of the winds, who then gave Odysseus a bag containing all of the unfavorable winds. With only the good west wind behind them, Odysseus and his crew made rapid progress. Odysseus fell asleep when Ithaca was in sight, but his men, believing that Odysseus was not sharing valuable treasures with them, opened the bag. Instantly, the winds rushed out, blowing them back to Aeolus, who refused to help them a second time.

After several days back at sea, they reached the land of the Laestrygonians, monstrous cannibals. Only Odysseus's ship and crew escaped destruction.

Next stop: a thickly forested island. When Odysseus sent half of his remaining men to explore the interior, only a single breathless survivor returned. He told Odysseus that the goddess Circe had lured the rest of the men to her house with food and wine and then turned them into pigs. Odysseus rescued them, forcing Circe to restore his men to their original forms with a magical herb provided by the messenger god Hermes.

Before Circe allowed Odysseus to leave a year later, he had to journey to the land of the dead. There he learned from the blind prophet, Tiresias, that he would eventually return home, but that he must not injure the cattle of the sun god Helios. Upon Odysseus's return from the land of the dead, Circe repeated this warning and described the dangers that Odysseus would encounter. First, he'd meet the sirens, who lure sailors to their deaths with a beautiful song; then, the many-headed Scylla, who lurks in a cave on a high cliff above a ship-devouring whirlpool named Charybdis. She instructed him to steer toward Scylla and not try to fight back. **R**

Odysseus continues telling his host about his adventures.

"As Circe spoke, Dawn mounted her golden throne, **L**
and on the first rays Circe left me, taking
her way like a great goddess up the island.
I made straight for the ship, roused up the men
to get aboard and cast off at the stern.
They scrambled to their places by the rowlocks
and all in line dipped oars in the gray sea.
But soon an off-shore breeze blew to our liking—
a canvas-bellying breeze, a lusty shipmate
sent by the singing nymph with sunbright hair.°
So we made fast the braces,° and we rested,
letting the wind and steersman work the ship.

8–10 **But soon . . . hair:** The goddess Calypso has sent the breeze.

11 **made fast the braces:** tied down the ropes used to maneuver the sails.

Big Idea Journeys *Assess how Odysseus's men must be feeling at the beginning of this journey. Why might Odysseus feel differently?* **BI**

Teach

R Reading Strategy

Review Have students read the interpolation and note Odysseus's problems with his crew and with the gods. **Ask:** Why might the gods and goddesses inform Odysseus of what is ahead and warn him about certain actions? *(They mean to test him, not to kill him.)* **OL**

L Literary Element

Personification Remind students that personification is a figure of speech in which human qualities are given to something inanimate. Ask students to identify the personification in line 1 on page 981. *(Dawn is a queen rising to her throne.)* **OL**

BI Big Idea

Journeys **Answer:** *The men feel delighted to be starting for home again after a year of captivity. Odysseus must feel less cheerful, knowing that there are serious hardships ahead.* **OL**

Use the CheckPoint questions on Presentation Plus! to monitor students' comprehension. These questions can be used with interactive response keypads for immediate student feedback.

English Language Coach

Greek Mythology Because English language learners may be unfamiliar with the Greek myths, provide brief introductions to Circe, the Sirens, Helios, Scylla, and Charybdis, who figure in this part of the *Odyssey.* Students may enjoy describing similar mythic figures with which they are familiar.

Have pairs of students select one of the gods or monsters in the *Odyssey* and read further stories and summaries about it. Have students report their findings to the class. **EL**

Academic Standards

The Additional Support activity on p. 981 covers the following standard:

English Language Coach: **9.7** [Respond] to oral communication [with] careful listening and evaluation of content…

Teach

R1 Reading Strategy

Evaluate **Ask:** Is this a sound plan? What danger is there in leaving Odysseus's ears unplugged? *(With his powerful, persuasive ability, Odysseus might convince the men to untie him; a crewman might unplug his ears and succumb to the Sirens' voices.)* What is implied by his being the only man to hear the Sirens' song? *(As a hero, Odysseus is made of stronger stuff than his men, and he should experience adventures to the fullest.)* **OL**

R2 Reading Strategy

Identifying Sequence
Answer: *The wind has suddenly fallen still. The men stow the sail and begin to row.* **OL**

★ Cultural History

Sirens The Sirens were three sea nymphs, part bird and part woman, whose singing was so seductive that sailors were either lured to their deaths on rocky coasts or forgot to eat and starved. According to myth, when the Sirens failed to lure Odysseus, they threw themselves into the sea and perished. **AS**

The crew being now silent before me, I
addressed them, sore at heart:
'Dear friends,
more than one man, or two, should know those things
Circe foresaw for us and shared with me,
so let me tell her forecast: then we die
with our eyes open, if we are going to die,
★ or know what death we baffle if we can. Sirens
weaving a haunting song over the sea
we are to **shun**, she said, and their green shore
all sweet with clover; yet she urged that I
alone should listen to their song. Therefore
R1 you are to tie me up, tight as a splint,
erect along the mast, lashed to the mast,
and if I shout and beg to be untied,
take more turns of the rope to muffle me.'

I rather dwelt on this part of the forecast,
while our good ship made time, bound outward down
the wind for the strange island of Sirens.
Then all at once the wind fell, and a calm
came over all the sea, as though some power
lulled the swell.
The crew were on their feet
briskly, to furl the sail, and stow it; then,
each in place, they poised the smooth oar blades
and sent the white foam scudding° by. I carved
a massive cake of beeswax into bits
and rolled them in my hands until they softened—
no long task, for a burning heat came down
from Helios, lord of high noon. Going forward
I carried wax along the line, and laid it
thick on their ears. They tied me up, then, plumb
amidships,° back to the mast, lashed to the mast,
and took themselves again to rowing. Soon,
as we came smartly° within hailing distance,°
the two Sirens, noting our fast ship
off their point, made ready, and they sang. . . .

The lovely voices in **ardor** appealing over the water
made me crave to listen, and I tried to say
'Untie me!' to the crew, jerking my brows;

38 **scudding:** moving swiftly.

44–45 **plumb amidships:** at the exact center of the ship.

47 **smartly:** proudly; insultingly. **hailing distance:** earshot.

Reading Strategy Identifying Sequence *How has a change in the weather influenced the actions of the men?* **R2**

Vocabulary

shun (shun) *v.* to keep away from; avoid
ardor (är′ dər) *n.* passion; intensity of emotion; enthusiasm

Additional Support

Skills Practice

READING: Problem and Solution Odysseus faces many problems and is clever at solving most of them. Point out that problem solving requires the ability to carry out several tasks:

1. To define the problem clearly
2. To analyze options and select the best option
3. To plan steps and carry them out

Have small groups discuss Odysseus's problem-solving strategy for getting by the Sirens. What steps does it involve? Have groups suggest another way he might have solved the problem. **OL**

Ulysses and the Sirens, 1891. John William Waterhouse. Oil on canvas, 100 x 201.7 cm. Collection of National Gallery of Victoria, Melbourne, Australia. 

but they bent steady to the oars. Then Perimedes°
got to his feet, he and Eurylochus,°
and passed more line about, to hold me still.
So all rowed on, until the Sirens
dropped under the sea rim,° and their singing
dwindled° away.
My faithful company
rested on their oars now, peeling off
the wax that I had laid thick on their ears;
then set me free.
But scarcely had that island
faded in blue air than I saw smoke
and white water, with sound of waves in **tumult**—
a sound the men heard, and it terrified them.
Oars flew from their hands; the blades went knocking
wild alongside till the ship lost way,
with no oarblades to drive her through the water.
Well, I walked up and down from bow to stern,
trying to put heart into them, standing over

53 **Perimedes** (per′ i mē′ dēz)

54 **Eurylochus** (yoo ril′ ə kəs)

57 **sea rim:** horizon.

58 **dwindled:** gradually lessened; diminished.

Literary Element Conflict *Why are the men disobeying Odysseus? What would happen if they obeyed him?* **L**

Vocabulary

tumult (to͞o′ məlt) *n.* commotion; uproar

Teach

L Literary Element

Conflict Answer: *They disobey him here in order to obey his prior order. Otherwise, their ship would be destroyed.* **OL**

Viewing the Art

English painter John William Waterhouse (1849–1917) was influenced by the Pre-Raphaelites but used paint in his own unique, rich way. *Ulysses and the Sirens* reflects Waterhouse's shift in the 1880s from Greek and Roman pictures to literary subjects, using a romantic style. **AS**

Differentiated Instruction

Creating Storyboards The vivid descriptions and action in this part may hold the attention of students who have difficulty focusing. Discuss how they would direct the scenes with the sirens for a film.

Have students prepare storyboards for a film summary of a scene. Explain that the product should look like a comic book, with an abbreviated version of what happens and what is said. Ask students to present their materials as if to persuade a producer to finance the film. **BL**

Academic Standards

Additional Support activities on pp. 982 and 983 cover the following standards:

Skills Practice: **9.3** [Identify] story elements such as...plot...

Differentiated Instruction: **9.7.18** Deliver persuasive arguments...that structure ideas and arguments in a coherent, logical fashion...[and] clarify and defend positions with precise and relevant evidence...

Teach

R Reading Strategy

Connect Have students reread lines 73–91, in which Odysseus gives heart to the panicked crew. Students may be able to relate to the leader's urgency and tone of voice through their own experience. Ask a volunteer to describe the manner in which a coach delivers a pep talk to players or to describe another similar situation with which they are familiar. **OL**

L1 Literary Element

Conflict Answer: *Odysseus is avoiding having his men disobey orders. Students may argue that Odysseus knows his men well enough to predict how they will behave.* **OL**

every oarsman, saying gently,
'Friends,
have we never been in danger before this?
More fearsome, is it now, than when the Cyclops
penned us in his cave? What power he had!
Did I not keep my nerve, and use my wits
to find a way out for us?
Now I say
by hook or crook this peril° too shall be
something that we remember.
Heads up, lads!
We must obey the orders as I give them.
Get the oarshafts in your hands, and lay back
hard on your benches; hit these breaking seas.
Zeus help us pull away before we founder.
You at the tiller, listen, and take in
all that I say—the rudders are your duty;
keep her out of the combers and the smoke;
steer for that headland; watch the drift, or we
fetch up in the smother, and you drown us.'

That was all, and it brought them round to action.
But as I sent them on toward Scylla,° I
told them nothing, as they could do nothing.
They would have dropped their oars again, in panic,
to roll for cover under the decking. Circe's
bidding against arms had slipped my mind,
so I tied on my cuirass° and took up
two heavy spears, then made my way along
to the foredeck—thinking to see her first from there,
the monster of the gray rock, harboring
torment for my friends. I strained my eyes
upon that cliffside veiled in cloud, but nowhere
could I catch sight of her.
And all this time,
in travail,° sobbing, gaining on the current,
we rowed into the strait—Scylla to port
and on our starboard beam Charybdis, dire
gorge of the salt sea tide. By heaven! when she
vomited, all the sea was like a cauldron
seething over intense fire, when the mixture
suddenly heaves and rises.
The shot spume
soared to the landside heights, and fell like rain.°

But when she swallowed the sea water down
we saw the funnel of the maelstrom,° heard

80 **peril:** danger; risk; something that may cause injury or destruction.

93 **Scylla** (sil′ ə): an immortal monster with twelve tentacled arms, six heads, and three rows of teeth in each of her six mouths.

98 **cuirass:** armor.

106 **travail:** exhausting, painful labor.

107–114 **we rowed . . . rain:** The ship enters a narrow channel **(strait)** between Scylla on the left and **Charybdis** (kə rib′ dis) on the right. Rising and falling with the surge of tidal currents, the whirlpool sucks water down her dreadful throat **(dire gorge),** then spews it into the air as a geyser.

116 **maelstrom:** violent whirlpool.

Literary Element Conflict *What potential conflict is Odysseus trying to avoid here? Do you think he is being wise?* **L1**

Additional Support

Skills Practice

WRITING: Monologue Using Jargon Odysseus's speech to the sailors in lines 73–91 is filled with sailing jargon. Explain that jargon is the special vocabulary of a group or profession. Ask students who play a sport to explain some of its jargon. Point out that jargon makes prose sound more realistic.

Form small groups of students who have knowledge of a specific hobby or sport. Have them write a brief monologue that uses jargon. Volunteers can take turns delivering their monologue to the class. **OL**

Scylla Devours Odysseus' Companions, undated. Peter Connolly. Watercolor. ★

the rock bellowing all around, and dark
sand raged on the bottom far below.
My men all blanched° against the gloom, our eyes
were fixed upon that yawning mouth in fear
of being devoured.
Then Scylla made her strike,
whisking six of my best men from the ship.
I happened to glance aft at ship and oarsmen
and caught sight of their arms and legs, dangling
high overhead. Voices came down to me
in anguish, calling my name for the last time.

A man surfcasting on a point of rock
for bass or mackerel, whipping his long rod

119 **blanched:** turned pale.

Literary Element Conflict *The men are in conflict with both Scylla and Charybdis. Why are the two a particularly dangerous combination?* L2

Teach

L2 Literary Element

Conflict **Answer:** *One is a monster that can kill six men at a time. The other is a whirlpool that can destroy the whole ship.* OL

★ Viewing the Art

Contemporary author and artist Peter Connolly has written many books about the ancient world, including a set of paintings depicting the story of Odysseus. AS

Reading in the Real World

Career Discuss skills that students have noticed in a good leader. *(Possible responses: Understands the people with whom he/she works; knows when and how much information to give; is a good listener; sees the big picture and the larger goal).*

Group students and have them evaluate Odysseus's leadership in this episode. They might use a graph like the following to record their observations. OL

Odysseus's Leadership Skill Rating							
low							high
1	2	3	4	5	6	7	8

Academic Standards

Additional Support activities on pp. 984 and 985 cover the following standards:

Skills Practice: **9.5.7** Use varied and expanded vocabulary, appropriate for specific forms and topics.

Reading in the Real World: **9.3** [Identify] story elements such as character…

Teach

R1 Reading Strategy

Identifying Sequence
Answer: *Odysseus and his men are rowing on, leaving behind the rocks, Scylla, and Charybdis.* OL

R2 Reading Strategy

Making Judgments Students should note that these lines provide further evidence that Odysseus is made of tougher stuff than his crew. You may want to discuss the implications of a saga in which a mortal reaches godlike stature and gods stoop to human behavior. OL

★ Cultural History

Scylla Myth has it that Circe fell in love with a god who loved Scylla. To get rid of her rival, Circe poisoned the waters where Scylla bathed. This changed Scylla into a frightful monster, and she threw herself into the sea. She was changed into rocks, which still bear her name and continue to pose danger to sailors. AS

to drop the sinker and the bait far out,
will hook a fish and rip it from the surface
to dangle wriggling through the air:
so these
were borne aloft in spasms° toward the cliff.
She ate them as they shrieked there, in her den,
in the dire grapple,° reaching still for me—
and deathly pity ran me through
at that sight—far the worst I ever suffered,
questing° the passes of the strange sea.
We rowed on.
★ The Rocks were now behind; Charybdis, too,
and Scylla dropped astern.
Then we were coasting
the noble island of the god, where grazed
those cattle with wide brows, and bounteous flocks
of Helios,° lord of noon, who rides high heaven.

From the black ship, far still at sea, I heard
the lowing of the cattle winding home
and sheep bleating; and heard, too, in my heart
the words of blind Tiresias of Thebes
and Circe of Aeaea: both forbade me
the island of the world's delight, the Sun.
So I spoke out in gloom to my companions:

'Shipmates, grieving and weary though you are,
listen: I had forewarning from Tiresias
and Circe, too; both told me I must shun
this island of the Sun, the world's delight.
Nothing but fatal trouble shall we find here.
Pull away, then, and put the land astern.'
That strained them to the breaking point, and, cursing,
Eurylochus cried out in bitterness:

R2 'Are you flesh and blood, Odysseus, to endure
more than a man can? Do you never tire?
God, look at you, iron is what you're made of.
Here we all are, half dead with weariness,
falling asleep over the oars, and you
say "No landing"—no firm island earth
where we could make a quiet supper. No:
R3 pull out to sea, you say, with night upon us—
just as before, but wandering now, and lost.
Sudden storms can rise at night and swamp
ships without a trace.

134 **borne aloft in spasms:** carried high while struggling furiously.

136 **dire grapple:** desperate struggle.

139 **questing:** seeking; searching or pursuing in order to find something or achieve a goal.

146 **Helios:** the Greek god of the sun. Odysseus's ship is nearing the island where Helios lives.

Reading Strategy Identifying Sequence *How can you tell that Odysseus's ship has successfully navigated Scylla and Charybdis?* R1

Additional Support

Skills Practice

GRAMMAR: Adverb Clauses Remind students that a subordinate clause must be joined to a main clause because it cannot stand alone.

Give students this sentence: *More fearsome, is it now, than when the Cyclops penned us in his cave?* Explain that the underlined clause functions as an adverb telling when.

Write this sentence on the board. Have students underline the adverb clause and identify its subject and verb.

When **she** vomited, all the sea was like a cauldron seething . . . OL

The Companions of Ulysses Slaying the Cattle of the Sun God Helios, 16th century. Pellegrino Tibaldi. Fresco. Palazzo Poggi, Bologna, Italy.

Viewing the Art: What does the facial expression and body language of the man in the lower left corner of the painting suggest to you? Consider the warning Odysseus has given his crew. 

Where is your shelter
if some stiff gale blows up from south or west—
the winds that break up shipping every time
when seamen flout° the lord gods' will? I say
do as the hour demands and go ashore
before black night comes down.
We'll make our supper
alongside, and at dawn put out to sea.'
Now when the rest said 'Aye' to this, I saw
the power of destiny devising ill.
Sharply I answered, without hesitation:
'Eurylochus, they are with you to a man.
I am alone, outmatched.
Let this whole company
swear me a great oath: Any herd of cattle
or flock of sheep here found shall go unharmed;
no one shall slaughter out of wantonness°
ram or heifer; all shall be content

176 **flout:** defy; ignore; scoff at.

189 **wantonness:** recklessness or lack of restraint.

Big Idea Journeys *What does this passage suggest about sea journeys in Homer's time?* 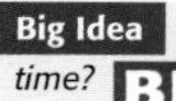

Teach

R3 Reading Strategy

Evaluate Eurylochus wants to persuade Odysseus to land the ship for the night. Help students evaluate his argument.

Say: First, Eurylochus points out two undeniable facts. The men are exhausted and unfit to cope with a night storm. Without food and rest, they face death at sea. Second, he suggests that they will stay only one night. He also suggests that Odysseus is heartless, reminding him of what he owes to the men. The argument is persuasive. **OL**

BI Big Idea

Journeys **Answer:** *It was unusual to sail at night.* **OL**

★ Viewing the Art

Answer: *It suggests both terror and desperation. The men fear for their lives, but since they are starving, they will risk the wrath of Helios.*

Pellegrino Tibaldi (1527–1596) is noted for his "inspired" work. His use of color and bold perspectives added a sense of three-dimensionality, a quality that earlier art had lacked. **AS**

Differentiated Instruction

Examining Etymologies Explain that a word's history can provide clues to its meaning. Provide this history for the word *supplication:* Latin *supplicare* to kneel down, pray < *sub-* under, below + *plicare,* to fold, double up. Point out that the word originally described the posture of someone "folded up" in prayer. Explain how this word relates to *supplicant* (names a person) and *pliable* (something foldable).

Have students use a dictionary to learn about the following word: **insidious.** *(Latin* insidiae, *an ambush, plot* < insidere *to sit in or on, lie in wait for* < in- *in* + sidere *to sit)* **AL**

Academic Standards

Additional Support activities on pp. 986 and 987 cover the following standards:

Skills Practice: **9.6.1** Identify and correctly use clauses, both main and subordinate…

Differentiated Instruction: **9.1** [Use] word parts…and origins…to determine the meaning of words…

Teach

L1 Literary Element

Personification Ask: How are hunger and thirst given human qualities? *(They are compared to besiegers.)* Why is this comparison appropriate? *(The men are fighters. To them, hunger and thirst are enemies who have threatened the men just as human besiegers would have.)* OL

R1 Reading Strategy

Identifying Sequence
Answer: *They eat and drink.* OL

★ Literary History

Helios Helios belonged to the race of Titans. Ancient Greek artists pictured him as a vigorous young man with a beardless face, his head crowned by sunbeams, racing his chariot from India to the Atlantic Ocean. At the close of each day, he was thought to return to a large bowl, from which he would rise again the next morning. AS

with what the goddess Circe put aboard.'

They fell at once to swearing as I ordered,
and when the round of oaths had ceased, we found
a halfmoon bay to beach and moor the ship in,
with a fresh spring nearby. All hands ashore
went about skillfully getting up a meal.
Then, after thirst and hunger, those besiegers,
were turned away, they mourned for their companions
plucked from the ship by Scylla and devoured,
and sleep came soft upon them as they mourned.

In the small hours of the third watch, when stars
that shone out in the first dusk of evening
had gone down to their setting, a giant wind
blew from heaven, and clouds driven by Zeus
shrouded land and sea in a night of storm;
so, just as Dawn with fingertips of rose
touched the windy world, we dragged our ship
to cover in a grotto, a sea cave
where nymphs had chairs of rock and sanded floors.
I mustered all the crew and said:

'Old shipmates,
our stores are in the ship's hold, food and drink;
the cattle here are not for our provision,
or we pay dearly for it.

Fierce the god is
who cherishes these heifers and these sheep:
Helios; and no man avoids his eye.'

To this my fighters nodded. Yes. But now
we had a month of onshore gales, blowing
day in, day out—south winds, or south by east.
As long as bread and good red wine remained
to keep the men up, and appease their craving,
they would not touch the cattle. But in the end,
when all the barley in the ship was gone,
hunger drove them to scour the wild shore
with angling hooks, for fishes and sea fowl,
whatever fell into their hands; and lean days
wore their bellies thin.

The storms continued.
So one day I withdrew to the interior

Reading Strategy Indentifying Sequence *What do the men do before mourning their dead companions?* R1

Vocabulary

shroud (shroud) *v.* to cover, as with a veil or burial cloth; conceal

Additional Support

Skills Practice

SPEAKING AND LISTENING: Oral Interpretation Present these guidelines for oral interpretation:

1. Use posture, gestures, and movements to suggest mood and character.
2. Vary expression and use stress and pauses to convey meaning and mood.

Have students work in small groups to prepare an oral interpretation of one section of the *Odyssey.* After assigning roles, have students practice several times before delivering their presentations. OL

to pray the gods in solitude, for hope
that one might show me some way of salvation.
Slipping away, I struck across the island
to a sheltered spot, out of the driving gale.
I washed my hands there, and made supplication
to the gods who own Olympus, all the gods—
but they, for answer, only closed my eyes
under slow drops of sleep.
Now on the shore Eurylochus
made his insidious° plea:
'Comrades,' he said,
'You've gone through everything; listen to what I say.
All deaths are hateful to us, mortal wretches,
but famine is the most pitiful, the worst
end that a man can come to.
Will you fight it?
Come, we'll cut out the noblest of these cattle
for sacrifice to the gods who own the sky;
and once at home, in the old country of Ithaca,
if ever that day comes—
we'll build a costly temple and adorn° it
with every beauty for the Lord of Noon.
But if he flares up over his heifers lost,
wishing our ship destroyed, and if the gods
make cause with him, why, then I say: Better
open your lungs to a big sea once for all
than waste to skin and bones on a lonely island!'

Thus Eurylochus; and they murmured 'Aye!'
trooping away at once to round up heifers.
Now, that day tranquil cattle with broad brows
were grazing near, and soon the men drew up
around their chosen beasts in ceremony.
They plucked the leaves that shone on a tall oak—
having no barley meal—to strew the victims,°
performed the prayers and ritual, knifed the kine°
and flayed° each carcass, cutting thighbones free
to wrap in double folds of fat. These offerings,
with strips of meat, were laid upon the fire.
Then, as they had no wine, they made libation°

240 **insidious:** slyly treacherous or deceitful; scheming.

251 **adorn:** to decorate; add beauty, honor, or distinction.

263–264 **They . . . victims:** Usually, in preparing a burnt offering, fruit or grain was spread over and around the animal's carcass.
265 **kine:** cattle.
266 **flayed:** stripped off the skin of.

269 **libation:** a ritual pouring of wine or another liquid as part of an offering.

Reading Strategy Identifying Sequence *What sequence of events is described in lines 218–232?* **R2**

Literary Element Conflict *With whom, or what, are Eurylochus and the other men in conflict?* **L2**

Big Idea Journeys *Why would Eurylochus rather drown than starve?* **BI**

Teach

R2 Reading Strategy

Identifying Sequence

Answer: *The men experience a month of wind storms, during which they eat bread and drink red wine. After they eat all the barley, the men fish and hunt. Many men become thin. Then Odysseus prays to the gods for help.* **OL**

L2 Literary Element

Conflict **Answer:** *There is a conflict between what Odysseus has told them—not to kill Helios's cattle—and their own natures, which tell them to do anything to survive.* **OL**

BI Big Idea

Journeys **Answer:** *Eurylochus would rather die in action, attempting to reach home, than starve to death.* **OL**

Differentiated Instruction

Connecting Intrapersonal learners have a capacity for self-knowledge and understanding. They are able to accurately assess their feelings, motivations, and needs.

Ask students to imagine that they are members of Odysseus's crew. Have them choose one of the incidents described in the *Odyssey* so far and write a paragraph in which they examine how they would react in that situation. What would they do? How would their actions differ from those of Odysseus? How would they feel? What strengths do they have that would help them? **BL**

Academic Standards

Additional Support activities on pp. 988 and 989 cover the following standards:

Skills Practice: **9.7.6** Analyze the occasion and the interests of the audience and choose effective verbal and nonverbal techniques (including voice, gestures, and eye contact) for presentations.

Differentiated Instruction: **9.5.2** Write responses to literature that demonstrate a comprehensive grasp of the significant ideas of literary works…

Teach

R1 Reading Strategy

Respond **Ask:** Do you agree with Odysseus? Have the bad weather and his sleep been caused by the gods to force Odysseus's men to kill the cattle? *(Students should recall Poseidon's fury against Odysseus and Polyphemus's prayer that Odysseus be doomed to wander long and alone.)* OL

L1 Literary Element

Conflict **Answer:** *Helios has threatened to stop shining on the earth if Odysseus and his men are not punished. Zeus is not personally angry with Odysseus but agrees to Helios's demand in order to keep the sun in the sky.* OL

R2 Reading Strategy

Visualize Call attention to the grim picture of the dead cattle being reanimated. This is not only horrifying to the men but also a ghostly foreboding that they will pay with their lives. OL

with clear spring water, broiling the entrails° first;
and when the bones were burnt and tripes° shared,
they spitted° the carved meat.
Just then my slumber
left me in a rush, my eyes opened,
and I went down the seaward path. No sooner
had I caught sight of our black hull, than savory
odors of burnt fat eddied° around me;
grief took hold of me, and I cried aloud:

R1
'O Father Zeus and gods in bliss forever,
you made me sleep away this day of mischief!
O cruel drowsing, in the evil hour!
Here they sat, and a great work they contrived.'°

Lampetia° in her long gown meanwhile
had borne swift word to the Overlord of Noon:

'They have killed your kine.'

And the Lord Helios
burst into angry speech amid the immortals:

'O Father Zeus and gods in bliss forever,
punish Odysseus' men! So overweening,°
now they have killed my peaceful kine, my joy
at morning when I climbed the sky of stars,
and evening, when I bore westward from heaven.
Restitution or penalty they shall pay—
and pay in full—or I go down forever
to light the dead men in the underworld.'°

Then Zeus who drives the stormcloud made reply:

'Peace, Helios: shine on among the gods,
shine over mortals in the fields of grain.
Let me throw down one white-hot bolt, and make
splinters of their ship in the winedark sea.'°

—Calypso later told me of this exchange,
as she declared that Hermes° had told her.
Well, when I reached the sea cave and the ship,
I faced each man, and had it out;° but where
could any remedy be found? There was none.
The silken beeves° of Helios were dead.
R2
The gods, moreover, made queer signs appear:
cowhides began to crawl, and beef, both raw
and roasted, lowed like kine upon the spits.

Now six full days my gallant crew could feast
upon the prime beef they had marked for slaughter
from Helios' herd; and Zeus, the son of Cronus,
added one fine morning.

270–271 **entrails, tripes:** internal organs.

272 **spitted:** threaded pieces onto a spit, or rod, for roasting over a fire.

276 **eddied:** swirled.

281 **contrived:** schemed; plotted.

282 **Lampetia** (lam pē′ shə): a guardian of the island and animals. Her father is Helios; her mother is a human woman.

288 **overweening:** arrogant; self-important; not humble enough.

292–294 **Restitution . . . underworld:** Helios threatens to abandon the sky and shine, instead, on the land of the dead if the gods do not punish Odysseus's men.

296–299 **Peace . . . winedark sea:** Zeus coolly silences Helios, offering to set matters straight with a single thunderbolt.

301 **Hermes** (hur′ mēz): the messenger god.

303 **I faced each man, and had it out:** Odysseus confronts each crewman.

305 **beeves:** cattle.

Literary Element Conflict *Why has Zeus entered the conflict?* L1

Additional Support

Skills Practice

READING: Sequence of Events and Summarizing Epics are action-driven. Assess students' comprehension of Part 2 with a reviewing exercise. Have students summarize the main events that have occurred up to this point.

Have students close their books and list, in chronological order, the events they can recall from Part 2. Ask volunteers to read their lists as you compile a master list on the board. Then have students check the text for forgotten or out-of-order incidents. OL

All the gales
had ceased, blown out, and with an offshore breeze
we launched again stepping° the mast and sail,
to make for the open sea. Astern of us
the island coastline faded, and no land
showed anywhere, but only sea and heaven,
when Zeus Cronion° piled a thunderhead
above the ship, while gloom spread on the ocean.
We held our course, but briefly. Then the squall
struck whining from the west, with gale force, breaking
both forestays,° and the mast came toppling aft
along the ship's length, so the running rigging°
showered into the bilge.°
On the afterdeck
the mast had hit the steersman a slant blow
bashing the skull in, knocking him overside,
as the brave soul fled the body, like a diver.
With crack on crack of thunder, Zeus let fly
a bolt against the ship, a direct hit,
so that she bucked, in reeking fumes of sulphur,
and all the men were flung into the sea.
They came up 'round the wreck, bobbing awhile
L2 like petrels° on the waves.
No more seafaring
homeward for these, no sweet day of return;
the god had turned his face from them.
I clambered
fore and aft my hulk until a comber
split her, keel from ribs, and the big timber
floated free; the mast, too, broke away.
A backstay floated dangling from it, stout
rawhide rope, and I used this for lashing
mast and keel together. These I straddled,
riding the frightful storm.°
Nor had I yet
seen the worst of it: for now the west wind
dropped, and a southeast gale came on—one more
twist of the knife—taking me north again,
straight for Charybdis. All that night I drifted,
and in the sunrise, sure enough, I lay
off Scylla mountain and Charybdis deep.
L3 There, as the whirlpool drank the tide, a billow°
tossed me, and I sprang for the great fig tree,
catching on like a bat under a bough.
Nowhere had I to stand, no way of climbing,
the root and bole° being far below, and far
above my head the branches and their leaves,

315 **stepping:** fixing into position.

319 **Cronion:** a name that identifies Zeus as Cronus's son.

323 **forestays:** the ropes that support the main mast.

324 **running rigging:** the ropes that support all masts and sails.

325 **bilge:** the lowest interior part of a ship.

335 **petrels:** sea birds.

339–346 **I clambered . . . storm:** Before the ship is broken in two by a long breaking wave **(comber)**, Odysseus scrambles from front to back **(fore and aft)**; afterwards, he grabs a mast rope **(backstay)** and pieces together a crude raft.

354 **billow:** a great, swelling wave.

358 **bole:** trunk.

Big Idea **Journeys** *Is Zeus's action just? Why or why not?* **BI**

Teach

L2 Literary Element

Similes As students read this page, tell them to look for comparisons. *(Example: The doomed men bob in the ocean "like petrels on the waves" at line 335.)* **Ask:** How does this simile make the men appear? *(They are reduced to helpless animals, fighting for survival.)* **OL**

BI Big Idea

Journeys **Answer:** *Since the men were forewarned, Zeus's action is just. Or students may say that the gods made it impossible to leave the island, thereby practically assuring the slaughter of the cattle. This manipulation is not really fair.* **OL**

L3 Literary Element

Personification Have students note the personification of the whirlpool. **Ask:** What is the effect of giving it the human capacity to drink the tide? *(It seems more terrifying, as if it were striving with an evil intent.)* **OL**

Differentiated Instruction

Research Point out that one of Odysseus's most impressive skills is his tactful adaptability to almost any situation. Encourage advanced learners to research the skills and duties of diplomats.

Challenge students to research a topic related to the subject of diplomacy. They might choose an ambassador and learn about his or her background, qualifications, and duties. They could find out what skills are required to become a diplomat. They could interview someone who works at a consulate. They might also research the written and unwritten rules of diplomacy. Have students report their results to the class. **AL**

Academic Standards

Additional Support activities on pp. 990 and 991 cover the following standards:

Skills Practice: **9.3.6** Analyze and trace an author's development of time and sequence…

Differentiated Instruction: **9.7.15** Deliver expository (informational) presentations that convey information and ideas from primary and secondary sources accurately and coherently…

Teach

R Reading Strategy

Identifying Sequence
Answer: *After the Invocation, all of Parts 1 and 2 have been a retelling.* OL

★ Viewing the Art

Ask: How does this relief of Scylla differ from the painting on page 985? In your opinion, which piece of art gives a better sense of Scylla? Why? *(The painting, though not true to the description of Scylla, gives a greater sense of horror and monstrosity.)* AS

CheckPoint

Use the CheckPoint questions on Presentation Plus! to check students' mastery of the selection. These questions can be used with interactive response keypads for immediate student feedback.

massed, overshadowing Charybdis pool.
But I clung grimly, thinking my mast and keel
would come back to the surface when she spouted.
And ah! how long, with what desire, I waited!
till, at the twilight hour, when one who hears
and judges pleas in the marketplace all day
between contentious men, goes home to supper,
the long poles at last reared from the sea.

Now I let go with hands and feet, plunging
straight into the foam beside the timbers,
pulled astride, and rowed hard with my hands
to pass by Scylla. Never could I have passed her
had not the Father of gods and men, this time,
kept me from her eyes. Once through the strait,
nine days I drifted in the open sea
before I made shore, buoyed up by the gods,
upon Ogygia° Isle. The dangerous nymph
Calypso lives and sings there, in her beauty,
and she received me, loved me.

But why tell
the same tale that I told last night in hall
to you and to your lady? Those adventures
made a long evening, and I do not hold
with° tiresome repetition of a story." ∾

376 **Ogygia** (ō gij′ yə)

382–383 **hold with:** approve of; have patience for.

Reading Strategy Identifying Sequence *Odysseus has been telling his story to the Phaeacians. When did this narrative begin?* R

Scylla. 5th century B.C. Melos, Greece. Terra-cotta relief. British Museum, London. ★

Additional Support

Academic Standards

The Additional Support activity on p. 992 covers the following standard:
Skills Practice: **9.6.1** Identify and correctly use...phrases, including...participial...

Skills Practice

GRAMMAR: Participles and Participial Phrases Explain that a participle is an *-ing* or *-ed* verb form used as an adjective. Point out these examples: *These I straddled, riding the frightful storm* (lines 345–346). Point out that *riding the frightful storm* is a participial phrase describing the subject.

Ask students to find two other participial phrases on pages 991 and 992.

1. I sprang for the great fig tree, *catching on like a bat under a bough.* (lines 355–356)
2. Now I let go with hands and feet, *plunging straight into the foam . . .* (lines 368–369) OL

AFTER YOU READ

RESPONDING AND THINKING CRITICALLY

Respond

1. At the end of Part 2, is Odysseus very lucky, very unlucky, or a combination of both? Explain.

Recall and Interpret

2. (a)How does Odysseus protect his men from the song of the Sirens? (b)How do his men protect him?
3. (a)What are Scylla and Charybdis? (b)Why does Odysseus not tell his men about Scylla?
4. (a)Why do Odysseus and his men stay longer than planned on the island of Helios, and what are the consequences of this delay? (b)Why does Eurylochus prove to be a more persuasive leader in this episode than Odysseus?

Analyze and Evaluate

5. (a)Describe the relationship Odysseus has with his men. (b)What, if anything, might Odysseus have done to improve this relationship?
6. (a)What character traits do the events in Part 2 expose in Odysseus and his men? (b)Do you find these traits believable? Why or why not?
7. (a)In your opinion, is Zeus or Odysseus responsible for Odysseus's survival? (b)What is your opinion of Zeus's character?

Connect

8. **Big Idea** **Journeys** Which circumstances of Odysseus's journey so far might happen on real-life journeys? Explain.

LITERARY ANALYSIS

Literary Element Conflict

As in most adventure stories, external **conflict** takes center stage in the *Odyssey*. Look a little closer, however, and you will also see evidence of internal conflict, the struggle that occurs within a person's mind.

1. (a)Identify three examples of external conflict in Part 2. (b)What did these conflicts reveal about the characters involved in them?
2. (a)What is an example of an internal conflict in Part 2? (b)What did this internal conflict suggest about life or about human nature?

Writing About Literature

Analyze Description A description is a detailed portrayal of a person, place, thing, or event. Descriptive details help readers see, hear, smell, taste, or feel the subject of the description. Review Odysseus's encounters with the Sirens, Scylla and Charybdis, Helios's cattle, and Zeus's wrath. List the details that are most important in each episode. Then write a paragraph explaining how the descriptive details in the episode make the action more vivid or exciting.

READING AND VOCABULARY

Reading Strategy Identifying Sequence

Writers often use signal words and phrases to show the order of events. Examples are *then, next, at the same time, immediately, a few months later,* and *finally.*

1. List four different sequence signal words or phrases used in Part 2. What did they help signal?
2. Summarize the events on Helios's island. Use a different signal word for each event.

Vocabulary Practice

Practice with Context Clues For each boldfaced vocabulary word, select the best definition.

1. We had to **shroud** our plans in secrecy.
   a. form **b.** cover **c.** revise
2. The patriots felt **ardor** for their cause.
   a. enthusiasm **b.** repulsion **c.** concern
3. **Shun** the outdoors during an ice storm.
   a. visit **b.** examine **c.** avoid
4. The school yard is full of **tumult** during recess.
   a. silence **b.** uproar **c.** cooperation

Writing About Literature

Encourage students to identify the mood created by the descriptions.

Reading Strategy

1. Examples: But *soon* an off-shore breeze blew to our liking (line 8); *Then all at once* the wind fell (line 32); *Then, after* thirst and hunger, those besiegers were turned away (lines 197–198); *All that night* I drifted (line 351).
2. Example: *First,* the men moored the ship; *then* they prepared a meal; *next,* they mourned for their companions. *At last,* they slept.

Vocabulary

1. b **2.** a **3.** c **4.** b

AFTER YOU READ

Assess

1. Odysseus is unlucky in that he has lost all of his men. He is lucky in that his life has been spared.
2. (a) Plugs their ears with wax (b) Tie him to the mast
3. (a) Scylla is a six-headed monster that lives in a cliff. Charybdis is a whirlpool. (b) He knows that they will be terrified.
4. (a) A month of fierce gales prevents them from leaving. When supplies run out, the men kill some of Helios's cattle. (b) Starvation makes the men want to do as Eurylochus says.
5. (a) Like a stern father (b) Be honest
6. (a) Desire and weakness are exposed. (b) These are believable human responses.
7. (a) Odysseus (b) Some students may find Zeus guilty of unjust punishment. Others may argue that he must keep the sun happy.
8. Any journey can have delays caused by weather and equipment failures.

Literary Element

1. (a) Getting past the sirens and Scylla and Charybdis are both external conflicts as is Odysseus's attempts at keeping his men from killing the sun god's cattle. (b) Odysseus seems stronger than his men and more able to resist temptation.
2. (a) Odysseus's men know that killing the cattle will lead to punishment, but they can see no other way to survive. (b) That humans have a conscience

BEFORE YOU READ

Focus

Summary

Odysseus reveals his identity to Telemachus. Then, disguised as a beggar, Odysseus returns to the manor. Penelope sends for the beggar to discover if he has news of Odysseus. She reveals problems she has had during her husband's absence. She sets the suitors to a test and promises to marry the winner. When the beggar succeeds, his identity is revealed.

V Vocabulary

Vocabulary File **Say:** Add these words and definitions to your vocabulary file. For each word, include a sentence that gives you an example of how to use the word. **OL** Students with English language needs should include the pronunciations of these words in their files. **EL**

Literary Elements Have students access the Web site to improve their understanding of characterization.

BEFORE YOU READ *Odyssey, Part 3*

LITERATURE PREVIEW

Connecting to the Poem

Meeting someone you love after a long absence is often surprising and not always easy. Before you read Part 3 of the *Odyssey*, think about the following questions:

- How have you changed over the last five years?
- Recall an occasion when you met someone after a long absence. What did you notice? What surprised you?

Building Background

Strangers were important figures in Greek culture during Homer's time. In a society divided into tiny kingdoms that were often at war, a stranger was a potential threat. On the other hand, kindness to strangers could lead to valuable alliances. And what if a stranger was a god, wandering the earth in disguise? Strangers expected—and generally received—hospitality.

Think back to Part 1, when Odysseus wondered what gift the Cyclops would give him on his arrival. As you read Part 3, notice how the arrival of a stranger plays a major role in the developing drama.

Setting Purposes for Reading

Big Idea Journeys

At the beginning of Part 3, Odysseus arrives on the shores of Ithaca after an absence of twenty years. Read to find out if his troubles are over.

Literary Element Characterization

Characterization refers to the methods a writer uses to reveal the personality of a character. In direct characterization, explicit statements are made about a character. In indirect characterization, the writer reveals a character's personality through his or her words, thoughts, and actions and through what other characters think and say about that individual.

- See Literary Terms Handbook, p. R4.

Literature Online **Interactive Literary Elements Handbook** To review or learn more about the literary elements, go to www.glencoe.com.

READING PREVIEW

Reading Strategy Determining Main Idea and Supporting Details

Epic poems, like the *Odyssey*, are so rich with descriptive language that it is sometimes hard to distinguish the **main idea** from the **supporting details.** As you read, ask yourself: What is the point of this scene? Then ask yourself: How is Homer making his point? The answer to the first question will provide the main idea; the second question relates to the details.

Reading Tip: Taking Notes Use an organizer to record main ideas and supporting details as you read.

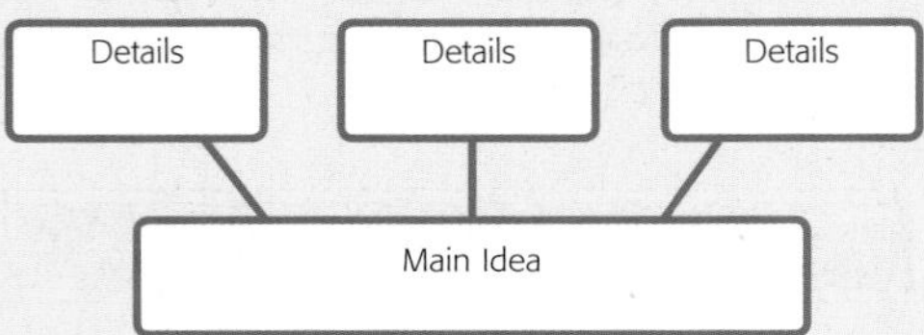

Vocabulary

cower (kou′ ər) *v.* to crouch or shrink back, as in fear or shame; p. 995 *The mouse cowered in the corner as the cat moved toward it.*

impudence (im′ pyə dəns) *n.* speech or behavior that is aggressively forward or rude; p. 999 *We were amazed at our guests' impudence in requesting special privileges.*

guise (gīz) *n.* outward appearance; false appearance; p. 1000 *He worked for his own interests under the guise of compassion toward others.*

renowned (ri nound′) *adj.* famous; widely known; p. 1002 *Many people attended the talk by the renowned scientist.*

Vocabulary Tip: Analogies Analogies are comparisons based on the relationships between ideas.

INDIANA ACADEMIC STANDARDS (pages 994-1007)

9.3.4 Determine characters' traits by what the characters say about themselves in…dialogue…

9.2 Develop [reading] strategies…

9.7.3 Recognize and use elements of…debate.

Selection Skills

from the Odyssey, Part 3

Literary Elements
- Characterization (SE pp. 994–1007)

Reading Skills
- Determining Main Idea and Details (SE pp. 994–1007)
- Steps in a Process (TWE p. 998)

Vocabulary Skills
- Analogies (SE pp. 994, 1007)

Listening/Speaking/Viewing Skills
- Analyzing Art (SE p. 1006)
- Interviewing (TWE p. 1002)

Writing Skills/Grammar
- Poetry (TWE p. 996)
- Exposition (TWE p. 1004)
- Compound Predicates (TWE p. 1006)

Study Skills/Research/Assessment
- Legacy of Greek Heroes and Gods (TWE p. 1003)

Part 3

Father and Son

R *The kindly Phaeacians load Odysseus with gifts and take him home, leaving him fast asleep on the shores of Ithaca. On their return journey, Poseidon turns their ship into a lump of stone for daring to assist Odysseus.*

Odysseus is disoriented after twenty years away from home, but the goddess Athena meets him and tells him what happened: during his long absence, a number of young men from Ithaca and neighboring islands have moved into Odysseus's great house. Thinking Odysseus is dead, the suitors, as they are called, eat his food, drink his wine, and insist that Odysseus's wife Penelope choose one of them as her husband. Penelope, who still loves Odysseus and prays for his safe return, has put off a decision as long as she can, but the situation has become very tense.

Athena disguises Odysseus as an old beggar and promises to help him. She tells him to seek shelter with a swineherd named Eumaeus (yoo mē′ əs). Meanwhile, Odysseus's son, Telemachus (tə lem′ ə kəs), who had set out on a journey to discover the fate of his father, escapes an ambush planned by the suitors and secretly lands on Ithaca. Following Athena's instructions, he also goes to Eumaeus's hut. While the loyal swineherd is informing Penelope of her son's return, Athena appears to the disguised Odysseus.

Statue of Athena, 340–330 BC Bronze. National Archaeological Museum, Athens.

From the air
she walked, taking the form of a tall woman,
handsome and clever at her craft, and stood
beyond the gate in plain sight of Odysseus,
unseen, though, by Telemachus, unguessed,
for not to everyone will gods appear.°
Odysseus noticed her; so did the dogs,
who **cowered** whimpering away from her. She only
nodded, signing to him with her brows,
a sign he recognized. Crossing the yard,
he passed out through the gate in the stockade
to face the goddess. There she said to him:

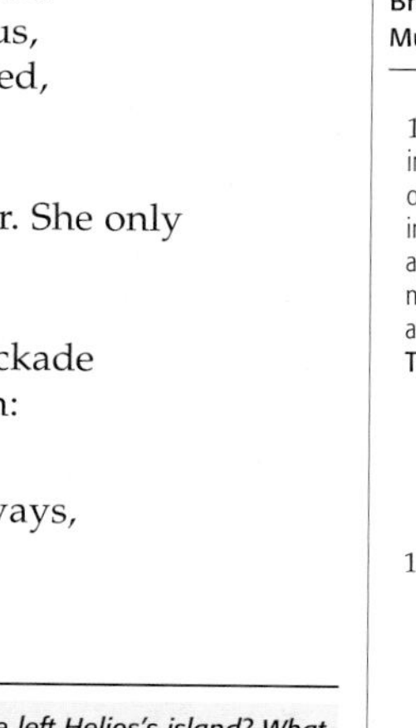

"Son of Laertes and the gods of old,
Odysseus, master of land ways and sea ways,
dissemble° to your son no longer now.

1–6 **From . . . appear:** Athena's "craft" includes the ability to disguise herself or others and to make herself visible or invisible. She has already made Odysseus appear to be an old beggar. Now she makes herself visible to Odysseus and, at the same time, invisible to his son **Telemachus.**

15 **dissemble:** pretend.

Big Idea Journeys *What has happened to Odysseus since he left Helios's island? What is happening now?* BI

Vocabulary

cower (kou′ ər) *v.* to crouch or shrink back, as in fear or shame

Teach

R Reading Strategy

Respond After students read the interpolation, have them discuss how Odysseus feels about the suitors. **Ask:** How have they betrayed him? *(They intend to take his wife and squander his assets.)* OL

BI Big Idea

Journeys **Answer:** *Odysseus was pursued by the gods and helpless among strangers. Now he is back in Ithaca, reunited with his son and befriended by a powerful goddess.* OL

CheckPoint

Use the CheckPoint questions on Presentation Plus! to monitor students' comprehension. These questions can be used with interactive response keypads for immediate student feedback.

English Language Coach

Precise Description Ask English language learners to brainstorm a list of traits that describe Athena *(intelligent, clever, powerful).* Then have students work with partners or in small groups to identify possible synonyms for the words using a thesaurus, an English dictionary, or a bilingual dictionary. Discuss the way each of these sources can be used to find synonyms. Make sure that students are aware that synonyms must be the same part of speech. EL

Academic Standards

The Additional Support activity on p. 995 covers the following standard:

English Language Coach: **9.1** [Use] relationships...and a growing knowledge of English...to determine the meaning of words...

Teach

R1 Reading Strategy

Determining Main Idea and Supporting Details
Answer: *Her aim is to make him a father Telemachus can be proud of.* OL

L1 Literary Element

Characterization **Answer:** *Odysseus is emotional and loving.* OL

★ Writer's Technique

Abstract vs. Concrete Language Help students identify language that communicates the emotion of this scene and also reminds readers of the involvement of the gods. The passage combines concrete descriptions with abstract emotion. For example, the abstract word *thunderstruck* reminds us of Zeus, while "looked down and away" creates an image of fear and humility. Encourage students to note how instances of abstract and concrete language support each other. AS

The time has come: tell him how you together
will bring doom on the suitors in the town.
I shall not be far distant then, for I
myself desire battle."
Saying no more,
she tipped her golden wand upon the man,
making his cloak pure white, and the knit tunic
fresh around him. Lithe and young she made him,
ruddy° with sun, his jawline clean, the beard
no longer gray upon his chin. And she
withdrew when she had done.
Then Lord Odysseus
reappeared—and his son was thunderstruck.°
Fear in his eyes, he looked down and away
as though it were a god, and whispered:
"Stranger,
you are no longer what you were just now!
Your cloak is new; even your skin! You are
one of the gods who rule the sweep of heaven!
Be kind to us, we'll make you fair oblation°
and gifts of hammered gold. Have mercy on us!"

The noble and enduring man replied:

"No god. Why take me for a god? No, no.
I am that father whom your boyhood lacked
and suffered pain for lack of. I am he."

Held back too long, the tears ran down his cheeks
as he embraced his son.
Only Telemachus,
uncomprehending,° wild
with incredulity,° cried out:
"You cannot
be my father Odysseus! Meddling spirits
conceived this trick to twist the knife in me!°
No man of woman born could work these wonders
by his own craft, unless a god came into it
with ease to turn him young or old at will.
I swear you were in rags and old,
and here you stand like one of the immortals!"°

Odysseus brought his ranging mind to bear°
and said:

24 **ruddy:** tanned.

28 **thunderstruck:** astonished. The word is carefully chosen for its additional association with the works of one of the gods (Zeus).

35 **make you fair oblation:** offer you good sacrifices and proper worship.

44 **uncomprehending:** not understanding.
45 **incredulity:** disbelief.

47–48 **Meddling . . . me:** Telemachus assumes that interfering gods **(Meddling spirits)** thought up **(conceived)** this astonishing transformation to intensify his pain **(twist the knife)** over his father's long absence and possible death.

53 **the immortals:** a common reference to the gods, who never die.
54 **Odysseus . . . bear:** Odysseus focuses his thoughts.

Reading Strategy Determining Main Idea and Supporting Details *What is the purpose of Athena's transformations of Odysseus?* R1

Literary Element Characterization *What do you learn about Odysseus here?* L1

Additional Support

Skills Practice

WRITING: Poetry Explain that lyric poems use images, sound effects, and other devices to express feelings about a personal subject. Ask volunteers to recall lines from favorite poems, noting poetic uses of language (such as rhyme, metaphor, and personification). Have students freewrite for ten minutes on the subject of returning home after a long absence. Then have them choose images from their notes and draft a poem about homecoming. Encourage students to revise their poems and add illustrations. Prepare a class display. OL

"This is not princely, to be swept
away by wonder at your father's presence.
No other Odysseus will ever come,
for he and I are one, the same; his bitter
fortune and his wanderings are mine.
Twenty years gone, and I am back again
on my own island.
As for my change of skin,
that is a charm Athena, Hope of Soldiers,°
uses as she will; she has the knack
to make me seem a beggar man sometimes
and sometimes young, with finer clothes about me.
It is no hard thing for the gods of heaven
to glorify a man or bring him low."°

L2

When he had spoken, down he sat.
Then, throwing
his arms around this marvel of a father
Telemachus began to weep. Salt tears
rose from the wells of longing in both men,
and cries burst from both as keen and fluttering
as those of the great taloned hawk,
whose nestlings farmers take before they fly.
So helplessly they cried, pouring out tears,
and might have gone on weeping so till sundown,
had not Telemachus said:
"Dear father! Tell me
what kind of vessel put you here ashore
on Ithaca? Your sailors, who were they?
I doubt you made it, walking on the sea!"
Then said Odysseus, who had borne the barren sea:°
"Only plain truth shall I tell you, child.
Great seafarers, the Phaeacians, gave me passage
as they give other wanderers. By night
over the open ocean, while I slept,
they brought me in their cutter,° set me down
on Ithaca, with gifts of bronze and gold
and stores of woven things. By the gods' will
these lie all hidden in a cave. I came
to this wild place, directed by Athena,
so that we might lay plans to kill our enemies.
Count up the suitors for me, let me know

64 **Hope of Soldiers:** When she chooses to be, Athena is a fierce battle-goddess, defending Greece—and favored Greeks—from outside enemies.

68–69 **It is . . . low:** It is not difficult for the gods to make a man appear great or humble.

85 **borne the barren sea:** endured the hardships of the sea.

90 **cutter:** a single-masted sailboat.

Literary Element Characterization *Why did Telemachus not believe his father at first? What are your impressions of Telemachus?* L3

Reading Strategy Determining Main Idea and Supporting Details *Why does Homer include these details?* R2

Teach

L2 Literary Element

Characterization Ask students to find details in this scene that reveal Telemachus's character. *(He is at first disbelieving and then weeps for joy, suggesting that he steels himself against further disappointment and has strong feelings about his father.)* Tell students to look for the further development of Telemachus and Penelope. OL

L3 Literary Element

Characterization **Answer:** *Telemachus has not seen his father since he was a little boy and did not recognize him or trust him. Telemachus has strong feelings for Odysseus but wants to shield himself against disappointment.* OL

R2 Reading Strategy

Determining Main Idea and Supporting Details
Answer: *Homer wants to share the great emotion that Odysseus and Telemachus feel when they find each other. He uses the simile of hawks whose young have been taken. The details support and intensify the main idea of the father-son reunion.* OL

Differentiated Instruction

Oral Reading Consider reading key speeches, explanations, and descriptions aloud or playing the audiotape for students who are struggling with the reading.

As you read a speech aloud (or play a segment of the tape), have students read along. You may also have students make notes on their reactions to each scene. After completing the part as a group, students can reread it on their own and complete the questions and activities at the end. BL

Academic Standards

Additional Support activities on pp. 996 and 997 cover the following standards:

Skills Practice: **9.5** [Demonstrate] an awareness of the audience...and purpose for writing.

Differentiated Instruction: **9.7** [Respond] to oral communication [with] careful listening and evaluation of content...

Teach

BI Big Idea

Journeys Answer: *Although he is home, Odysseus's journey is far from over. He now faces the huge task of ridding his halls of the suitors.* OL

R Reading Strategy

Logical Reasoning After students read the interpolation, have them consider the logic behind not telling Penelope about Odysseus's return.
Say: The situation at the manor is treacherous. There are many suitors; they have ill intentions (they intend to consume or take everything) and willingness to kill (they plotted against Telemachus). It is logical that they would try to kill the king and prince if forewarned. These two need the element of surprise if they are to succeed. It might be impossible for Penelope to hide her feelings if she knew her husband had returned. Therefore, Odysseus and Telemachus must keep their secret for now. OL

Viewing the Art

Francois-Louis Schmied (1873–1941) is considered one of the finest wood-block engravers of the early 1900s. He was known for his meticulous attention to detail. AS

Odysseus, title page of "Homer: The Odyssey," 1830–33. Francois-Louis Schmied. Color lithograph. Private collection. ★

what men at arms are there, how many men.
I must put all my mind to it, to see
if we two by ourselves can take them on
or if we should look round for help."

The Beggar at the Manor

R *The next morning Telemachus returns home and tells Penelope about his travels but not about his father's homecoming. Odysseus, disguised again as a beggar, also returns to his own house. No one recognizes him except his faithful old dog, which lifts up its head, wags its tail, and dies. In the great hall, Telemachus permits the "beggar" to ask for food. The suitors give him bread and meat, as is the custom, but one of their leaders, a man named Antinous* (an tin′ ō əs), *is particularly insulting. He refuses to offer any food, and while Odysseus is talking, he angrily interrupts.*

But here Antinous broke in, shouting:
"God!

Big Idea Journeys *In what sense is Odysseus's journey far from over?* BI

Additional Support

Skills Practice

READING: Steps in a Process Point out that authors often describe steps in a process. Ask students to reread lines 37–100 and outline the steps in the process through which Telemachus accepts that Odysseus has returned. *(1. He thinks the stranger is a trick of the gods. 2. He hears and accepts the explanation. 3. He expresses grief, love, and relief. 4. He asks for details and plans to defeat the suitors.)*

Have students select an episode in which Odysseus takes steps to escape a dangerous situation (such as the Cyclops's cave or passing the Sirens). Then have them outline the steps. OL

What evil wind blew in this pest?
Get over,
stand in the passage! Nudge my table, will you?
Egyptian whips are sweet
to what you'll come to here, you nosing rat,
making your pitch to everyone!
These men have bread to throw away on you
because it is not theirs. Who cares? Who spares
another's food, when he has more than plenty?"

With guile Odysseus drew away,° then said:

"A pity that you have more looks than heart.
You'd grudge a pinch of salt from your own larder
to your own handy man. You sit here, fat
on others' meat, and cannot bring yourself
to rummage out a crust of bread for me!"

Then anger made Antinous' heart beat hard,
and, glowering° under his brows, he answered:
"Now!
You think you'll shuffle off and get away
after that **impudence?** Oh, no you don't!"

The stool he let fly hit the man's right shoulder
on the packed muscle under the shoulder blade—
like solid rock, for all the effect one saw.
Odysseus only shook his head, containing
thoughts of bloody work,° as he walked on,
then sat, and dropped his loaded bag again
upon the door sill. Facing the whole crowd
he said, and eyed them all:
"One word only,
my lords, and suitors of the famous queen.
One thing I have to say.
There is no pain, no burden for the heart
when blows come to a man, and he defending
his own cattle—his own cows and lambs.
Here it was otherwise. Antinous
hit me for being driven on by hunger—
how many bitter seas men cross for hunger!
If beggars interest the gods, if there are Furies

12 **With guile . . . away:** Odysseus is slyly provoking Antinous.

19 **glowering:** scowling; looking at angrily.

26–27 **containing thoughts of bloody work:** keeping murderous thoughts under control. Odysseus imagines killing Antinous, but holds his temper.

Literary Element Characterization *What have you learned about Antinous so far?* L

Vocabulary

impudence (im′pyə dəns) *n.* speech or behavior that is aggressively forward or rude

Teach

L Literary Element

Characterization Answer: *Antinous is arrogant, selfish, and cruel.* OL

★ Cultural History

Hospitality The ancient Greeks revered the tradition of hospitality. In fact, they took it so seriously that Zeus was considered to be the protector of strangers, as well as the defender of oaths and the patron of suppliants. Thus, Antinous's violation of hospitality is particularly shocking. Students may compare the Cyclops's behavior in Part 1, in which the monster rejects Odysseus's argument that strangers should be given a hospitable reception. AS

Differentiated Instruction

Illustrating Characters The scene involving Odysseus, Telemachus, Antinous, and the other suitors involves tensions and subtle, hidden emotions. Students may enjoy creating pictures that communicate the emotions simmering under the surface.

Have students draw a picture that reveals the reactions of the following characters to the violence of Antinous and the eloquence of Odysseus:

1. Odysseus
2. Telemachus
3. Antinous
4. the mortified suitors BL

Academic Standards

Additional Support activities on pp. 998 and 999 cover the following standards:

Skills Practice: **9.3** [Identify] story elements such as...plot...

Differentiated Instruction: **9.3.3** Analyze interactions between characters...and explain the way those interactions affect the plot.

Teach

R1 Reading Strategy

Determining Main Idea and Supporting Details **Answer:** *Odysseus's main point is that Antinous is completely lacking in compassion, as evidenced by his attacking a hungry beggar.* OL

R2 Reading Strategy

Clarifying Odysseus's words to Antinous are powerful and dignified. Their rhythm illustrates the meter of epic verse. Have a strong reader read aloud Odysseus's response in lines 31–42. **Ask:** Why do the suitors suspect they are not dealing with a simple beggar? *(Odysseus has shown strength, eloquence, poise, and dignity—qualities that all suggest nobility.)* OL

L Literary Element

Characterization **Answer:** *She seems kind because she chastises Antinous for his treatment of the beggar. Homer describes her as gentle. From her speech, it is clear that she has strong opinions about the suitors, especially Antinous.* OL

pent in the dark to avenge a poor man's wrong, then may
Antinous meet his death before his wedding day!"°
Then said Eupeithes'° son, Antinous:
"Enough.
Eat and be quiet where you are, or shamble elsewhere,
unless you want these lads to stop your mouth
pulling you by the heels, or hands and feet,
over the whole floor, till your back is peeled!"

But now the rest were mortified,° and someone
spoke from the crowd of young bucks to rebuke° him:
"A poor show, that—hitting this famished tramp—
bad business, if he happened to be a god.
You know they go in foreign **guise**, the gods do,
looking like strangers, turning up
in towns and settlements to keep an eye
on manners, good or bad." **R2**
But at this notion
Antinous only shrugged.
Telemachus,
after the blow his father bore, sat still
without a tear, though his heart felt the blow.
Slowly he shook his head from side to side,
containing murderous thoughts.
Penelope
on the higher level of her room had heard
the blow, and knew who gave it. Now she murmured:
"Would god you could be hit yourself, Antinous—
hit by Apollo's bowshot!"°
And Eurynome°
her housekeeper, put in:
"He and no other?
If all we pray for came to pass, not one
would live till dawn!"
Her gentle mistress said:
"Oh, Nan, they are a bad lot; they intend
ruin for all of us; but Antinous
appears a blacker-hearted hound than any.

34–42 **There is . . . wedding day:** A man is not really hurt, the beggar says, when he is injured defending his property; but when he is attacked for being hungry, that's another matter. Odysseus's curse upon Antinous calls upon the **Furies**—three female spirits who punish wrongdoers—to bring about his death.
43 **Eupeithes** (yoo pē′ thēz)

49 **mortified:** deeply embarrassed, shamed, or humiliated.
50 **rebuke:** to scold sharply; criticize.

68 **Apollo's bowshot:** Among other things, Apollo is the archer god and the god of truth. His sacred silver bow can kill literally with an arrow and figuratively with the truth.
69 **Eurynome** (yoo rin′ ə mē)

Reading Strategy Determining Main Idea and Supporting Details *What is Odysseus's main point about Antinous's behavior?* **R1**

Literary Element Characterization *From what you have read so far, how would you describe Penelope?* **L**

Vocabulary

guise (gīz) *n.* outward appearance; false appearance

Additional Support

Skills Practice

GRAMMAR: Compatibility of Verb Tenses Have students note the verb tenses in lines 1–12. *(As storyteller, Odysseus uses past tense. As characters speak and bring the past to life, present tense is used.)* Point out that within each kind of narrative, the tense is consistent. Write on the board: *With guile Odysseus drew away, then says . . .* Point out that in this sentence past and present tenses are combined.

Have students make the tenses in the following sentence consistent.

Odysseus soon hatches a plan and disguised himself as a beggar again. *(hatched or disguises)* OL

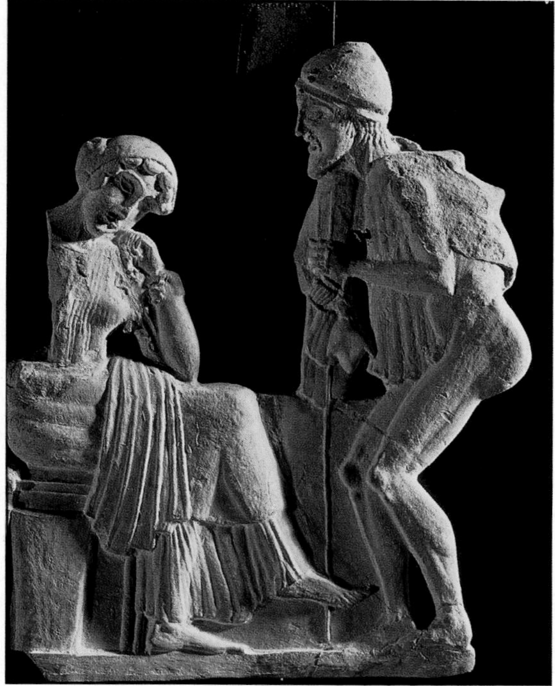

Odysseus Reunited with Penelope. Terra-cotta relief. Louvre Museum, Paris.

Here is a poor man come, a wanderer,
driven by want to beg his bread, and everyone
in hall gave bits, to cram his bag—only
Antinous threw a stool, and banged his shoulder!"

So she described it, sitting in her chamber
among her maids—while her true lord was eating.
Then she called in the forester and said:
"Go to that man on my behalf, Eumaeus,°
and send him here, so I can greet and question him.
Abroad in the great world, he may have heard
rumors about Odysseus—may have known him!"

85 **Eumaeus** (yoo mē′ əs)

Lively action continues in the great hall, where another beggar attempts to bully Odysseus. Antinous mockingly arranges a boxing match between the two, which Odysseus wins. Telemachus orders the disorderly crowd to leave for the evening. Surprised by his authority, the suitors obey, giving Odysseus and Telemachus time to remove all weapons from the hall as part of their preparation for battle. Then Odysseus goes to meet his wife for the first time in nearly twenty years.

Carefully Penelope began:
"Friend, let me ask you first of all:
who are you, where do you come from, of what nation
and parents were you born?"

Teach

Viewing the Art

Ask: On the basis of this relief, what is your impression of the relationship between Odysseus and Penelope? Explain. *(Students may say Penelope looks shy or coy. Odysseus's bent knees indicate a gentleness in his approach, as if he were talking to a small child.)* **AS**

Building Reading Fluency

Performing The dialogue in lines 51–88 presents an opportunity for students to act out the scene. Encourage interested groups of students to study the scene, cast parts, and prepare oral interpretations. After rehearsing, students can perform their dialogues for the class as a whole. **BL**

Academic Standards

Additional Support activities on pp. 1000 and 1001 cover the following standards:

Skills Practice: **9.6.2** Demonstrate an understanding of...proper English usage, including the use of consistent verb tenses.

Building Reading Fluency: **9.7** [Develop] speaking skills...in conjunction with...strategies...[for] delivery of oral presentations.

Teach

L1 Literary Element

Simile Make sure that students understand the basis for comparison in this extended simile. *(The disguised Odysseus compares Penelope to a good king, whose justice and benevolent rule result in prosperity for his kingdom.)* Point out that the simile, in some respects, inverts the situation. In actuality, it is Odysseus who is the "good king" and Penelope who is his consort. Is he hinting at his own identity by using this comparison? Ask students to speculate. **OL**

R Reading Strategy

Determining Main Idea and Supporting Details

Answer: *The interview is difficult because Odysseus is happy to be home but is not ready to reveal his identity to Penelope. He is not willing to answer her questions about his parents, because that would let her know his true identity.* **OL**

And he replied:
"My lady, never a man in the wide world
should have a fault to find with you. Your name
has gone out under heaven like the sweet
honor of some god-fearing king, who rules
in equity° over the strong: his black lands bear
both wheat and barley, fruit trees laden bright,
new lambs at lambing time—and the deep sea
gives great hauls of fish by his good strategy,
so that his folk fare well.
O my dear lady,
this being so, let it suffice° to ask me
of other matters—not my blood, my homeland.
Do not enforce me to recall my pain.
My heart is sore; but I must not be found
sitting in tears here, in another's house:
it is not well forever to be grieving.
One of the maids might say—or you might think—
I had got maudlin° over cups of wine."
And Penelope replied:
"Stranger, my looks,
my face, my carriage,° were soon lost or faded
when the Achaeans crossed the sea to Troy,
Odysseus my lord among the rest.
If he returned, if he were here to care for me,
I might be happily **renowned!**
But grief instead heaven sent me—years of pain.
Sons of the noblest families on the islands,
Dulichium, Same, wooded Zacynthus,
with native Ithacans, are here to court me,
against my wish; and they consume this house.
Can I give proper heed to guest or suppliant°
or herald° on the realm's affairs?
How could I?
wasted with longing for Odysseus, while here
they press for marriage.
Ruses° served my turn
to draw the time out—first a close-grained web
I had the happy thought to set up weaving
on my big loom in hall. I said, that day:
'Young men—my suitors, now my lord is dead,
let me finish my weaving before I marry,
or else my thread will have been spun in vain.

98 **equity:** fairness and justice.

104 **suffice:** be enough.

111 **maudlin:** excessively and foolishly emotional.

114 **carriage:** manner of moving or holding the head and body.

124 **suppliant** (sup′ lē ənt): one who humbly begs or requests something.
125 **herald:** court messenger.

129 **Ruses:** tricks; schemes.

Reading Strategy Determining Main Idea and Supporting Details *Why is this a particularly difficult interview for Odysseus?* **R**

Vocabulary

renowned (ri nound′) *adj.* famous; widely known

Additional Support

Skills Practice

SPEAKING AND LISTENING: Interviewing Point out that one way to get inside a character is to conduct an imaginary interview. Have students role-play—one taking the role of a character and another taking the role of the interviewer.

Pair students and have them choose roles. Have the interviewee take the role of Penelope or Odysseus and review what they know about the character. Interviews should address the hardships the character has faced and focus on what it was like to meet his or her partner after twenty years. Have students practice and then present their interviews "live." **OL**

Scenes From the Odyssey, ca. 1509. Bernardino Pintoricchio. National Gallery Collection, London, U.K. ★

It is a shroud I weave for Lord Laertes°
when cold Death comes to lay him on his bier.°
The country wives would hold me in dishonor
if he, with all his fortune, lay unshrouded.' **L2**
I reached their hearts that way, and they agreed.
So every day I wove on the great loom,
but every night by torchlight I unwove it;
and so for three years I deceived the Achaeans.
But when the seasons brought a fourth year on,
as long months waned,° and the long days were spent,
through impudent folly in the slinking maids
they caught me—clamored up to me at night;°
I had no choice then but to finish it.

136 **It is . . . Laertes:** Penelope has claimed to be weaving a burial cloth **(shroud)** for Odysseus's father.
137 **bier:** a platform on which a corpse or coffin is placed before burial.

145 **waned:** drew to an end.

146–147 **through . . . night:** After outwitting the suitors for more than three years, Penelope is finally betrayed by some of her own sneaky **(slinking)** maids, who crept into her room at night and caught her in the act of undoing her weaving.

Literary Element Characterization *What characteristic do Odysseus and Penelope share?* **L3**

Teach

L2 Literary Element

Characterization Continue to have students analyze Penelope's actions in order to add to their portrait of her character. What new traits appear? What traits are further developed? *(She speaks honestly and without fear. She has set a task that requires her potential future husband to be the equal of Odysseus. Her intelligence and dignity are further developed.)* **OL**

L3 Literary Element

Characterization Answer: *They are both crafty, using their wits to defeat their opponents.* **OL**

★ Viewing the Art

Bernardino Pintoricchio (1454–1513), also known as Bernardino di Betto, was a prolific painter. He worked for five popes and several cardinals. Pintoricchio was one of the artists who worked on the scenes in the Sistine Chapel. The Metropolitan Museum of Art in New York City owns several of his paintings that represent mythological scenes. The National Gallery in Washington, D.C., has several of his religious paintings. **AS**

Differentiated Instruction

Legacy of Greek Heroes and Gods Point out that the *Odyssey* and the Greek gods it features have had lasting effects on Western thought and culture. Write on the board, "caught between Scylla and Charybdis." **Ask:** What is the meaning of this phrase today? What is its origin? Have students research and report on language, customs, and concepts that derive from Greek mythology or from the *Odyssey.* Encourage students to supply illustrations to enliven their reports. **AL**

Academic Standards

Additional Support activities on pp. 1002 and 1003 cover the following standards:

Skills Practice: **9.7.16** Apply appropriate interviewing techniques...

Differentiated Instruction: **9.5.9** Write...a research report that...demonstrates that information that has been gathered has been summarized...and that conclusions have been drawn from synthesizing information...

Teach

BI Big Idea

Journeys Answer: *Penelope has run out of time. A few days later, and she might have remarried.* OL

R1 Reading Strategy

Evaluate Guide students in evaluating Penelope's choice of contest. Remind them that they will need to review her history with the suitors. OL

R2 Reading Strategy

Identifying Bias Ask: What slanted thinking does the suitors' reaction show? *(Students should deduce from their laughter and sarcasm that the suitors look down on the beggar and dismiss him as a threat. Their class bias is so great that they do not even consider the fact that the "beggar" has already shown great strength and prowess.)* OL

And now, as matters stand at last,
I have no strength left to evade a marriage,
cannot find any further way; my parents
urge it upon me, and my son
will not stand by while they eat up his property.
He comprehends it, being a man full grown,
able to oversee the kind of house
Zeus would endow° with honor.

156 **endow:** provide or equip.

The Test of the Bow

Resigned to ending the suitors' reign over her home, Penelope cries herself to sleep that night, dreaming of the husband she believes is lost forever. The next day the suitors return to the hall, more unruly than ever. Penelope appears, carrying the huge bow that belongs to Odysseus. Her maids follow, bearing twelve iron ax heads. Penelope has a proposition for the suitors.

"My lords, hear me:
suitors indeed, you commandeered° this house
to feast and drink in, day and night, my husband
being long gone, long out of mind. You found
no justification° for yourselves—none
except your lust to marry me. Stand up, then:
we now declare a contest for that prize.
Here is my lord Odysseus' hunting bow.
Bend and string it if you can. Who sends an arrow
through iron axe-helve sockets, twelve in line?°
I join my life with his, and leave this place, my home,
my rich and beautiful bridal house, forever
to be remembered, though I dream it only."

2 **commandeered:** seized by force or threats.

5 **justification:** a reason for an action that shows it to be just, right, or reasonable.

9–10 **Bend . . . line:** The challenge has two parts: First, a suitor must bend and string the heavy bow—a task requiring strength and skill. Second, he must shoot an arrow through the narrow holes of twelve ax-heads set in a row.

One by one the suitors try to string the bow, and all fail. Only Antinous delays his attempt. In the meantime, Odysseus steps outside with the swineherd Eumaeus and Philoetius (fi loi′ tē əs), *another faithful herdsman, and reveals his identity to them. Odysseus returns to the hall and asks to try his hand at stringing the bow. Antinous sneers at this idea, but Penelope and Telemachus both insist he proceed. Telemachus orders the women to leave, Philoetius locks the gates of the hall, and Eumaeus presents to Odysseus the great bow he has not held for twenty years.*

And Odysseus took his time,
turning the bow, tapping it, every inch,
for borings that termites might have made
while the master of the weapon was abroad.
The suitors were now watching him, and some
jested among themselves:

14–25 **And Odysseus . . . old buzzard:** As Odysseus examines the old bow for termite holes **(borings)** that might have weakened the wood since he last used it, the suitors take the chance to make fun of the "beggar."

Big Idea Journeys *Why was this the perfect time for Odysseus to arrive home?* BI

Additional Support

Skills Practice

WRITING: How-To Explanation If they had been given specific directions by Odysseus, perhaps the suitors could have strung the bow. Explain that a key to writing clear explanations for a process is to break the process down into steps and include all the information a novice will need. Ask students to think of a task and write a paragraph explaining how to carry out the process. Students should define unfamiliar terms and make explanations of each step as simple as possible. Remind them to be as clear and complete as possible. Have students read their papers aloud and demonstrate the task. OL

"A bow lover!"
"Dealer in old bows!"
"Maybe he has one like it
at home!"
"Or has an itch to make one for himself."
"See how he handles it, the sly old buzzard!"
And one disdainful suitor added this:
"May his fortune grow an inch for every inch he bends it!"
But the man skilled in all ways of contending,
satisfied by the great bow's look and heft,°
like a musician, like a harper, when
with quiet hand upon his instrument
he draws between his thumb and forefinger
a sweet new string upon a peg: so effortlessly
Odysseus in one motion strung the bow.
Then slid his right hand down the cord and plucked it,
so the taut gut° vibrating hummed and sang
a swallow's note.
In the hushed hall it smote° the suitors
and all their faces changed. Then Zeus thundered
overhead, one loud crack for a sign.
And Odysseus laughed within him that the son
of crooked-minded Cronus had flung that omen° down.°
He picked one ready arrow from his table
where it lay bare: the rest were waiting still
in the quiver for the young men's turn to come.°
He nocked it,° let it rest across the handgrip,
and drew the string and grooved butt of the arrow,
aiming from where he sat upon the stool.
Now flashed
arrow from twanging bow clean as a whistle
through every socket ring, and grazed° not one,
to thud with heavy brazen head° beyond.
Then quietly
Odysseus said:
"Telemachus, the stranger
you welcomed in your hall has not disgraced you.
I did not miss, neither did I take all day
stringing the bow. My hand and eye are sound,

29 **heft:** weight.

36 **taut gut:** tightly drawn bowstring (made of animal "gut" or intestine).

38 **smote:** struck, as though from a hard blow; affected suddenly with a powerful and unexpected feeling, such as fear.

39–42 **Then Zeus . . . down:** Odysseus recognizes the crack of thunder as a sign that Zeus is on his side.

42 **omen:** a sign or event thought to foretell good or bad fortune; forewarning.

44–45 **the rest . . . come:** The remaining arrows will be used by the contestants who follow Odysseus.

46 **nocked it:** fitted the nock, or notched end, of the arrow into the string.

51 **grazed:** touched.

52 **brazen head:** brass arrowhead.

Reading Strategy Determining Main Idea and Supporting Details *How does the inclusion of this line among the taunts and jeers of the suitors relate to the main idea presented in this scene?* **R3**

Literary Element Characterization *To what is Homer comparing Odysseus in lines 28–34? What do these comparisons contribute to his characterization?* **L**

Teach

R3 Reading Strategy

Determining Main Idea and Supporting Details

Answer: *The suitors are blinded by pride. The inclusion of this line indicates that they are beginning to see that this man might present a threat. Because of their sense of superiority over the disguised Odysseus, they have failed to notice his strength and intelligence.* **OL**

L Literary Element

Characterization **Answer:** *Odysseus is compared to a poet and musician. He handles the bow like a musical instrument. These comparisons emphasize his skill—almost an artistic talent—at warfare.* **OL**

Reading in the Real World

Career **Ask:** Does the art in this selection enhance your understanding of the text? If so, how? If not, why not? Have students bring to class a business or technical magazine article or a printout of a corporate Web site's home page. Discuss how the images, graphics, headers, and other visual elements help the authors achieve their goals. **OL**

Academic Standards

Additional Support activities on pp. 1004 and 1005 cover the following standards:

Skills Practice: **9.5.6** Write technical documents…that report information and express ideas logically and correctly…

Reading in the Real World: **9.7.13** Identify the artistic effects of a media presentation and evaluate the techniques used to create them…

Teach

BI Big Idea

Journeys Answer: *Odysseus's journey—a long, exhausting, and trying adventure designed by the gods to test him—has ended, but his struggles have not.*
Ask: How has his struggle changed? Why is his homecoming incomplete and his metaphoric "journey" not over? OL

Viewing the Art

Answer: *Odysseus may be thinking that he must make the shot so that he can win the contest.*

The art appears on a skyphos, an ancient Greek drinking vessel. A skyphos had a deep body, a flat bottom, and two horizontal handles near the rim. AS

CheckPoint

Use the CheckPoint questions on Presentation Plus! to check students' mastery of the selection. These questions can be used with interactive response keypads for immediate student feedback.

Odysseus Competes with the Suitors (detail). 5th century bc, Greek. Attic red-figured skyphos. Staatliche Museum, Antikensammlung, Berlin, Germany.
Viewing the Art: What do you suppose Odysseus is thinking as he takes aim?

not so contemptible as the young men say.
The hour has come to cook their lordships' mutton°—
supper by daylight. Other amusements later,
with song and harping that adorn a feast."
He dropped his eyes and nodded, and the prince
Telemachus, true son of King Odysseus,
belted his sword on, clapped hand to his spear,
and with a clink and glitter of keen bronze
stood by his chair, in the forefront near his father.

60 **cook their lordships' mutton:** literally, cook their sheep meat. But Odysseus is using a phrase that Telemachus can take metaphorically, like the phrase *cook their goose* ("get even").

Big Idea Journeys *Do you think that Odysseus's long journey is finally over? Why or why not?* BI

Additional Support

Academic Standards

The Additional Support activity on p. 1006 covers the following standard:

Skills Practice: **9.6.2** Demonstrate an understanding of sentence construction... and proper English usage...

Skills Practice

GRAMMAR: Compound Predicates

Explain that a compound predicate has two or more verbs joined by a conjunction. The verbs share the same subject. Write the following sentence on the board, and have students identify each verb: *He notched it, let it rest against the handgrip, and drew the string.* (Verbs are underlined.)

Have students scan the rest of page 1006 for other examples and write each compound predicate they identify.

1. dropped . . . and nodded (line 63)
2. belted . . . clapped . . . stood (lines 65–67) OL

AFTER YOU READ

RESPONDING AND THINKING CRITICALLY

Respond

1. Did any aspects of Odysseus's behavior surprise you in Part 3? Explain, telling what you might have done if you were in his place.

Recall and Interpret

2. (a)What role does Athena play in reuniting Odysseus with his son, Telemachus? (b)Give two reasons why Telemachus might have trouble identifying his father at first.
3. (a)Why does Penelope summon the beggar? (b)How does Odysseus behave, and what does this say about his character?
4. (a)What is "the test of the bow"? (b)Why might Penelope have given it?

Analyze and Evaluate

5. (a)Compare the behavior of Odysseus and Telemachus during the recognition scene. (b)In your opinion, is this scene believable? Why or why not?
6. (a)What is Antinous like, and how does he stand apart from the rest of the suitors? (b)Why do you think Homer develops Antinous's character in this way?
7. (a)Which scene in this part did you consider the most interesting or effective? (b)What does the scene suggest about Greek culture and values? Explain.

Connect

8. **Big Idea** **Journeys** What do you think might happen next? Explain.

LITERARY ANALYSIS

Literary Element Characterization

Authors do not have to restrict themselves to one form of **characterization.** They may describe their characters directly but also allow them to reveal their personalities through words and actions.

1. What method of characterization does Homer use to reveal Penelope's personality? Support your ideas with examples.
2. For another character in Part 3, find an action, a line or two of dialogue, or another clue to that character's personality. Explain what insight the detail gave you about the character.

Literature Groups

Odysseus is planning to make the suitors pay for their behavior—but do they all deserve the same fate? What do you predict will happen? What do you want to happen? Discuss these questions in your group. Then discuss the advantages and disadvantages of two opposite courses of action available to Odysseus and Telemachus. Call one "Let 'em have it" and the other "Let's be reasonable." Vote on which course of action you prefer. Share your results with the class.

READING AND VOCABULARY

Reading Strategy Determining Main Idea and Supporting Details

The main idea of a piece of writing may be directly stated or implied.

1. Review Penelope's speech in lines 141–151. Where does she express the main idea in this passage?
2. Examine the last five lines of Part 3. What idea does Homer indirectly state in this description of Telemachus?

Vocabulary Practice

Practice with Analogies Complete each analogy.

1. **guise : mask :: omen :**
   a. prayer **b.** forewarning **c.** gift
2. **cower : fear :: cringe :**
   a. happiness **b.** sadness **c.** embarrassment
3. **healthful : unwholesome :: renowned :**
   a. unknown **b.** knowing **c.** unknowable
4. **impudence : politeness :: reluctance :**
   a. cheerfulness **b.** eagerness **c.** intelligence

Literary Element

1. Odysseus's words about her "sweet honor" directly reveal her virtue and beauty. She indirectly reveals both compassion and cunning when she talks to the "beggar."
2. Answers will vary. One example is Antinous. He rants and throws a stool at the beggar. He shows bad temper and contempt. He reveals these qualities through his actions.

Reading Strategy

1. In the last sentence of this passage
2. Telemachus is a grown man, ready to stand by his father.

AFTER YOU READ

Assess

1. Students may be surprised at his tears, his keeping his identity secret from his wife, and his boasting.
2. (a) Athena directs both men to Eumaeus's hut. She first disguises Odysseus as a beggar but then transforms him so he can convince his son of his identity.
   (b) Telemachus had not seen his father since he was young; a beggar looks nothing like a king.
3. (a) She hopes the beggar has some word of Odysseus.
   (b) He shows self-restraint and inner strength.
4. (a) The winner must string Odysseus's bow and shoot an arrow through twelve axe-helve sockets. (b) In creating a test that none of the suitors is likely to pass, she has found an effective delaying tactic.
5. (a) Odysseus weeps for joy, but Telemachus is more cautious. (b) The scene is believable. Students should provide support for their opinions.
6. (a) Antinous is arrogant, selfish, and cruel. The other suitors are shocked by his behavior. (b) To show that he deserves Odysseus's revenge
7. Students' responses will vary.
8. Students' responses will vary.

Vocabulary

1. b **2.** c **3.** a **4.** b

Literature Groups

Encourage students to empathize with Odysseus and Telemachus as they discuss these issues.

BEFORE YOU READ

Focus

Summary

Odysseus kills Antinous with an arrow. The suitors react angrily. Odysseus insists on revenge; the suitors decide to "go down fighting." Odysseus, Telemachus and two herdsmen kill all the suitors. Penelope sets a secret test for Odysseus. When he proves that he is Odysseus, the two are joyfully reunited.

V Vocabulary

Vocabulary File Say: Add these words and definitions to your vocabulary file. For each word, include a sentence that gives you an example of how to use the word. **OL** Students with English language needs should include the pronunciations of these words in their files. **EL**

Literature Online

Literary Elements Have students access the Web site to improve their understanding of plot.

LITERATURE PREVIEW

Connecting to the Poem

Home is a word rich in associations. Before you read Part 4, think about the following questions:

- What does *home* mean to you?
- What do you miss most when you are away from home?

Building Background

Although Homer probably composed the *Odyssey* between 750 and 700 B.C., the epic is set during the Mycenaean period, a much earlier time in Greek history. Archaeologists have discovered that from about 1600 B.C. to 1200 B.C., a remarkable civilization grew up around the city of Mycenae. This culture built massive palaces and forts. Skilled artisans created exquisitely decorated tools, including weapons and drinking vessels in bronze and silver. There was a form of writing.

But the Mycenaean culture came tumbling down swiftly and mysteriously. By about 1100 B.C., its palaces were in ruins, its artists scattered, and the secret of its writing lost. In Part 4, as in much of the *Odyssey,* Homer offers his audience glimpses of the government, social classes, customs, architecture, and values of Mycenaean culture, which he collected from the myths and legends that had been passed on orally from that time.

Setting Purposes for Reading

Big Idea Journeys

As you read Part 4, notice how Homer resolves questions about Odysseus's homecoming.

Literary Element Plot

The sequence of events in a narrative work is its **plot.** The point of greatest emotional intensity, interest, or suspense is the plot's climax. Try to identify this point in the plot as you read Part 4.

- See Literary Terms Handbook, p. R13.

Literature Online Interactive Literary Elements Handbook To review or learn more about the literary elements, go to www.glencoe.com.

READING PREVIEW

Reading Strategy Analyzing Cause-and-Effect Relationships

One event frequently causes another. For example, Odysseus offends Poseidon (cause) and spends much of the poem paying for his behavior (effect). Analyzing **cause-and-effect relationships** in a work of literature will help you better understand the work's plot.

Reading Tip: Taking Notes Use a graphic organizer to help you visualize cause-and-effect relationships.

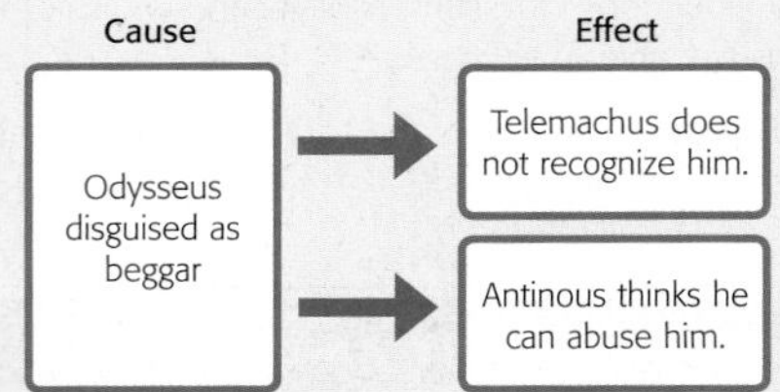
Cause
Effect
Odysseus disguised as beggar
Telemachus does not recognize him.
Antinous thinks he can abuse him.

Vocabulary

jostle (jos′əl) *v.* to bump, push, or shove roughly, as with elbows in a crowd; p. 1009 *I was jostled in the crowd.*

implacable (im plak′ə bəl) *adj.* impossible to satisfy or soothe; unyielding; p. 1011 *The general was implacable and refused to admit defeat.*

lavish (lav′ish) *v.* to give generously; provide in abundance; p. 1016 *Ben's grandparents lavished gifts upon him when he graduated.*

aloof (ə lo͞of′) *adj.* emotionally distant; uninvolved; disinterested; standoffish; p. 1016 *Rather than interfere, I tried to remain aloof.*

Vocabulary Tip: Word Origins It is not always obvious how the history of a word is tied to its present-day meaning. Use a dictionary to research the etymologies of everyday words.

INDIANA ACADEMIC STANDARDS (pages 1008-1021)

9.3 [Identify] story elements such as...plot...
9.2 Develop [reading] strategies...
9.5.3 Write...analytical essays...
9.3.3 Analyze...and explain...plot.

Selection Skills

***from the* Odyssey, Part 4**

Literary Elements
- Plot (SE pp. 1008–1020)
- Character (TWE p. 1014)
- Parody (TWE p. 1016)

Reading Skills
- Analyzing Cause-and-Effect Relationships (SE pp. 1008–1020)

Vocabulary Skills
- Word Origins (SE pp. 1008, 1020)
- Academic Vocabulary (SE p. 1020)

Listening/Speaking/Viewing Skills
- Analyzing Art (SE p. 1010; TWE pp. 1015, 1018)
- Inflection (TWE p. 1012)

Writing Skills/Grammar
- Analyze Character (SE p. 1021)
- Compound Adjectives (SE p. 1021)
- Noun Clauses (TWE p. 1018)

Study Skills/Research/Assessment
- Geography (SE p. 1021)

Part 4

Death in the Great Hall

Now shrugging off his rags the wiliest fighter of the islands
leapt and stood on the broad door sill, his own bow in his hand.
He poured out at his feet a rain of arrows from the quiver
and spoke to the crowd:

"So much for that. Your clean-cut game is over.
Now watch me hit a target that no man has hit before,
if I can make this shot. Help me, Apollo."

BI

He drew to his fist the cruel head of an arrow for Antinous
just as the young man leaned to lift his beautiful drinking cup,
embossed,° two-handled, golden: the cup was in his fingers:
the wine was even at his lips: and did he dream of death?
How could he? In that revelry° amid his throng of friends
who would imagine a single foe—though a strong foe indeed—
could dare to bring death's pain on him and darkness on his
eyes?
Odysseus' arrow hit him under the chin
and punched up to the feathers° through his throat.

Backward and down he went, letting the winecup fall
from his shocked hand. Like pipes his nostrils jetted
crimson runnels,° a river of mortal red,
and one last kick upset his table
knocking the bread and meat to soak in dusty blood.
Now as they craned to see their champion where he lay
the suitors **jostled** in uproar down the hall,
everyone on his feet. Wildly they turned and scanned
the walls in the long room for arms; but not a shield,
not a good ashen spear was there for a man to take and throw.°
All they could do was yell in outrage at Odysseus:

"Foul! to shoot at a man! That was your last shot!"

"Your own throat will be slit for this!"

"Our finest lad is down!
You killed the best on Ithaca."

"Buzzards will tear your eyes out!"

For they imagined as they wished—that it was a wild shot,

10 **embossed:** decorated with designs that are slightly raised from the surface.

12 **revelry:** noisy festivity; merrymaking.

16 **punched up to the feathers:** The arrow goes clear through the throat so that only the arrow's feathers remain visible in front.

19 **runnels:** streams.

24–26 **Wildly . . . throw:** Odysseus and Telemachus had removed all weapons and armor from the room on the previous night.

Literary Element Plot *How would you describe the level of suspense at this point in the story? Explain.* **L**

Vocabulary

jostle (jos′ əl) *v.* to bump, push, or shove roughly, as with elbows in a crowd

Teach

L Literary Element

Plot Answer: *Most students will agree that Odysseus will take his bloody revenge on the suitors. Any suspense lies in exactly when and how this will happen.* **OL**

BI Big Idea

Journeys Ask: Do you think it was inevitable that Odysseus's journey led to his confrontation with Antinous? *(Answers will vary. Some will feel that Antinous's behavior combined with Odysseus's personality made the conflict inevitable. Others may feel that regardless of Antinous's behavior, Odysseus could have chosen a different path.)* **OL**

Use the CheckPoint questions on Presentation Plus! to monitor students' comprehension. These questions can be used with interactive response keypads for immediate student feedback.

English Language Coach

Compound Words Learning the meanings of compound words can be difficult for English language learners. Have students use a dictionary to find the following compound words in Part 4. They can add the words and definitions to their notebooks.

- hereafter (in the future)
- countryside (rural region)
- ringleader (one who leads opposition to authority)

Encourage students to continue to add compound words from Part 4 to this list. **EL**

Academic Standards

The Additional Support activity on p. 1009 covers the following standard:

English Language Coach: **9.1** [Use] word parts...to determine the meaning of words...

Teach

R1 Reading Strategy

Analyzing Cause-and-Effect Relationships **Answer:** *Odysseus is enraged by what has gone on in his own house while he was away.*
Ask: Why does Eurymachus request that Odysseus spare the other suitors? *(Antinous was the leader and chief instigator of the suitors. With the leader dead, Eurymachus reasons that the rest of the suitors will disband. He also offers restitution.)* OL

Viewing the Art

Answer: *Odysseus is larger than life and stands alone. The men cower behind their shields. Odysseus is feared and respected for his strength and skill in battle.*

Odysseus and his bow are alone on the left side. They are balanced against the group of men who are huddled and appear to be hiding more than attacking. Point out that contrasting posture, bearing, and lines give Odysseus power while diminishing the others. AS

Odysseus Slaying the Suitors.

Viewing the Art: What does this image suggest to you about Odysseus's standing among other men? ★

an unintended killing—fools, not to comprehend
they were already in the grip of death.°
But glaring under his brows Odysseus answered:

"You yellow dogs, you thought I'd never make it
home from the land of Troy. You took my house to plunder,
twisted my maids to serve your beds. You dared
bid for my wife while I was still alive.
Contempt was all you had for the gods who rule wide heaven,
contempt for what men say of you hereafter.
Your last hour has come. You die in blood."

As they all took this in, sickly green fear
pulled at their entrails, and their eyes flickered
looking for some hatch or hideaway from death.
Eurymachus alone could speak. He said:

"If you are Odysseus of Ithaca come back,
all that you say these men have done is true.
Rash actions, many here, more in the countryside.
But here he lies, the man who caused them all.
Antinous was the ringleader, he whipped us on°
to do these things. He cared less for a marriage

33–35 **For they . . . death:** The suitors still do not realize that their opponent is Odysseus and that he has killed Antinous intentionally.

52 **whipped us on:** encouraged us; drove us.

Reading Strategy Analyzing Cause-and-Effect Relationships *What has caused Odysseus to decide to kill the suitors? Explain.* R1

Additional Support

Skills Practice

WRITING: Predictions Have students list their predictions for the battle. After they finish reading "Death in the Great Hall," have students create a chart to compare predictions with actual events. Suggest that students draw conclusions about what they learned from the unexpected. OL

Actions of	Predicted	Actual
Odysseus		
Telemachus		
Suitors		

Conclusions: ____________________

than for the power Cronion° has denied him
as king of Ithaca. For that
he tried to trap your son and would have killed him.
He is dead now and has his portion.° Spare
your own people. As for ourselves, we'll make
restitution of wine and meat consumed,
and add, each one, a tithe° of twenty oxen
with gifts of bronze and gold to warm your heart.
Meanwhile we cannot blame you for your anger."

Odysseus glowered under his black brows
and said:

"Not for the whole treasure of your fathers,
all you enjoy, lands, flocks, or any gold
put up by others, would I hold my hand.
There will be killing till the score is paid.
You forced yourselves upon this house. Fight your way out,
or run for it, if you think you'll escape death.
I doubt one man of you skins by."°

They felt their knees fail, and their hearts—but heard
Eurymachus for the last time rallying them.

"Friends," he said, "the man is **implacable**.
Now that he's got his hands on bow and quiver
he'll shoot from the big door stone there
until he kills us to the last man.

Fight, I say,
let's remember the joy of it. Swords out!
Hold up your tables to deflect° his arrows.
After me, everyone: rush him where he stands.
If we can budge him from the door, if we can pass
into the town, we'll call out men to chase him.
This fellow with his bow will shoot no more."

He drew his own sword as he spoke, a broadsword of fine
bronze,
honed like a razor on either edge. Then crying hoarse and loud
he hurled himself at Odysseus. But the kingly man let fly
an arrow at that instant, and the quivering feathered butt°
sprang to the nipple of his breast as the barb° stuck in his liver.

54 **Cronion:** Zeus.

57 **his portion:** what he deserved; what fate had in store for him.

60 **tithe** (tīth): payment; tax.

71 **skins by:** gets out alive.

80 **deflect:** to cause to go off course; turn aside.

88 **butt:** end.

89 **barb:** arrowhead; point.

Reading Strategy Analyzing Cause-and-Effect Relationships *The suitors vastly outnumber Odysseus and Telemachus. Why are they so alarmed?* **R2**

Vocabulary

implacable (im plak′ ə bəl) *adj.* impossible to satisfy or soothe; unyielding

Teach

BI Big Idea

Journeys Ask: How do the suitors choose to face the end of their lives' journeys? *(Students should point to Eurymachus encouraging the suitors to remember the joy of fighting. Some may say the suitors are brave, while others may feel that they are desperate.)* **OL**

R2 Reading Strategy

Analyzing Cause-and-Effect Relationships Answer: *The suitors have seen Odysseus's extraordinary skill with the bow, they have no armor or heavy weapons themselves, and Odysseus and Telemachus are blocking the door.* **OL**

English Language Coach

Following the Action Nonnative speakers may find the unusual phrasing difficult to follow. Students may have trouble following the action in a fight scene. Have students map out the suitors' battle plan. Then have them go through, line by line, and act out the fight scene in slow motion. Appoint one student to be the narrator, and divide the rest of the students into the remaining parts. As the narrator reads the scene, have students walk through the action. **EL**

Academic Standards

Additional Support activities on pp. 1010 and 1011 cover the following standards:

Skills Practice: **9.5.2** Write responses to literature that demonstrate a comprehensive grasp of the significant ideas of literary works…

English Language Coach: **9.3** [Identify] story elements such as…plot…

Teach

L1 Literary Element

Plot Answer: *This is the high point of tension in the scene. Negotiation has failed. The battle has begun in earnest; the characters must kill or be killed.* **OL**

R1 Reading Strategy

Analyzing Cause-and-Effect Relationships Ask: When Telemachus slays Amphinomus and saves Odysseus, how does this differ from the typical father-son relationship? *(Students should note that typically it is the father who protects the son. In this case, it is the son who is protecting the father.)* **OL**

BI Big Idea

Journeys Answer: *He is aiding Odysseus as an equal in battle.* **OL**

L2 Literary Element

Plot Ask: Why does Telemachus leave the battle? *(to get spears, shields, and helmets to aid Odysseus)* Do you think this was an act of bravery? *(Some may feel that Telemachus is being brave in volunteering to fetch the armor by himself. Others may feel he shouldn't leave Odysseus's side.)* **OL**

The bright broadsword clanged down. He lurched and fell aside,
pitching across his table. His cup, his bread and meat,
were spilt and scattered far and wide, and his head slammed on the ground.
Revulsion,° anguish in his heart, with both feet kicking out,
he downed his chair, while the shrouding wave of mist° closed on his eyes.

Amphinomus° now came running at Odysseus,
broadsword naked in his hand. He thought to make
the great soldier give way at the door.
But with a spear throw from behind Telemachus hit him
between the shoulders, and the lancehead drove
clear through his chest. He left his feet and fell
forward, thudding, forehead against the ground.
Telemachus swerved around him, leaving the long dark spear
planted in Amphinomus. If he paused to yank it out
someone might jump him from behind or cut him down with a sword
at the moment he bent over. So he ran—ran from the tables
to his father's side and halted, panting, saying:

"Father let me bring you a shield and spear,
a pair of spears, a helmet.
I can arm on the run myself; I'll give
outfits to Eumaeus and this cowherd.
Better to have equipment."

Said Odysseus:

"Run then, while I hold them off with arrows
as long as the arrows last. When all are gone
if I'm alone they can dislodge° me."

Quick
upon his father's word Telemachus
ran to the room where spears and armor lay.
He caught up four light shields, four pairs of spears,
four helms of war high-plumed with flowing manes,°
and ran back, loaded down, to his father's side.
He was the first to pull a helmet on
and slide his bare arm in a buckler strap.°
The servants armed themselves, and all three took their stand
beside the master of battle.°

While he had arrows

93 **revulsion:** intense dislike, disgust, or horror.
94 **shrouding wave of mist:** death.

95 **Amphinomus** (am fin′ ə məs)

115 **dislodge:** force back; kill.

120 **helms . . . manes:** war helmets decorated from front to back with a crest or ridge of long feathers resembling horses' manes.
123 **slide . . . strap:** The Greeks' small, round shield **(buckler)** had a strap in back through which the warrior slid his arm.
125 **master of battle:** Odysseus.

Literary Element Plot *Is tension rising or falling at this point? Explain.* **L1**

Big Idea Journeys *How is Telemachus responding to the challenges of the fight?* **BI**

Additional Support

Skills Practice

SPEAKING: Inflection Point out that the tone, volume, and pitch of a person's voice, as well as his or her gestures and facial expressions, affect the meaning of what the person says. Demonstrate by saying "Close the door" in different ways (for example: pleasantly, curtly, wearily, secretively). Then ask students how the meaning of the sentence changes each time. Have students choose one of Odysseus's speeches and one of Eurymachus's speeches and decide what tone, volume, pitch, gestures, and expressions they would use. **OL**

he aimed and shot, and every shot brought down
one of his huddling enemies.
But when all barbs had flown from the bowman's fist,
he leaned his bow in the bright entry way
beside the door, and armed: a four-ply shield
hard on his shoulder, and a crested helm,
horsetailed, nodding stormy upon his head,
then took his tough and bronze-shod spears.

Odysseus and Telemachus, along with their two allies, cut down all the suitors. Athena also makes an appearance, rallying their spirits and ensuring that none of her favorites is injured. Finally the great hall is quiet.

In blood and dust
he saw that crowd all fallen, many and many slain.
Think of a catch that fishermen haul in to a halfmoon bay
in a fine-meshed net from the whitecaps of the sea:
how all are poured out on the sand, in throes for° the salt sea,
twitching their cold lives away in Helios' fiery air:
so lay the suitors heaped on one another.

139 **in throes for:** in pain or struggle to return to.

The Trunk of the Olive Tree

Penelope's old nurse hurries upstairs to tell her mistress that Odysseus has returned and that all the suitors are dead. Penelope is amazed but refuses to admit that the stranger could be her husband. Instead, she believes that he must be a god.

The old nurse sighed:
"How queer, the way you talk!
Here he is, large as life, by his own fire,
and you deny he ever will get home!
Child, you always were mistrustful!
But there is one sure mark that I can tell you:
that scar left by the boar's tusk long ago.
I recognized it when I bathed his feet
and would have told you, but he stopped my mouth,
forbade me, in his craftiness.
Come down,
I stake my life on it, he's here!
Let me die in agony if I lie!"
Penelope said:

Statuette of Ulysses. Roman. Bronze. Bibliotheque Nationale, Paris.

Literary Element Plot *How does Odysseus perform as a fighter?* **L3**

Reading Strategy Analyzing Cause-and-Effect Relationships *What causes and effects did you notice in this scene?* **R2**

Teach

L3 Literary Element

Plot Answer: *He is superior to all of his opponents.*

Ask: If the outcome of the battle is a foregone conclusion, is the battle truly climactic? *(Some students may feel that the battle is so intense and action-packed that it concludes a portion of Odysseus's journey, and therefore it is climactic. Others may say that knowing the outcome makes the battle anticlimactic.)* **OL**

R2 Reading Strategy

Analyzing Cause-and-Effect Relationships Answer: *Eurymachus encourages the suitors to fight; then he draws his sword and hurls himself toward Odysseus. That action causes Odysseus to shoot an arrow at Eurymachus. Amphinomus runs toward Odysseus, causing Odysseus to throw a spear at him. That action causes Telemachus to help his father. After Telemachus brings weapons to his father, Odysseus, Telemachus, and their allies kill all the suitors.* **OL**

Differentiated Instruction

Mood Music Encourage students with musical abilities to compose rhythms and melodies appropriate to the different moods of Part 4. Have students work in small groups to create musical motifs, such as drum rhythms and melodic lines, to represent differing moods and actions in Part 4. After they have practiced, groups can present their music, live or recorded, as background to a reading from Part 4. Encourage students to research Greek music and incorporate Greek instruments, rhythms, and musical motifs into their compositions. **AL**

Academic Standards

Additional Support activities on pp. 1012 and 1013 cover the following standards:

Skills Practice: **9.7.6** Analyze the occasion and the interests of the audience and choose effective verbal and nonverbal techniques (including voice, gestures, and eye contact) for presentations.

Differentiated Instruction: **9.3** [Identify] story elements… **9.7.10** Assess how… delivery affect[s] the mood…of the oral communication and makes an impact on the audience.

Teach

BI Big Idea

Journeys **Answer:** *She still suspects that the stranger might be a trick played by the gods. She is not ready to let her guard down and accept him.* **Ask:** If you were Penelope, what criteria would you set to satisfy yourself that the beggar is Odysseus? Have students brainstorm a list of criteria. Write the list on the board. Include criteria that the beggar has already passed, such as his being able to string Odysseus's bow, something no one else could do. As students read, have them compare what they read to what they have listed on the board. OL

L1 Literary Element

Plot **Ask:** Why does Odysseus smile when he hears Penelope's speech? *(Penelope needs proof, and he realizes he can give it. He also knows that he'll be more recognizable when he's clean.)* OL

"Nurse dear, though you have your wits about you,
still it is hard not to be taken in
by the immortals. Let us join my son, though,
and see the dead and that strange one who killed them."
She turned then to descend the stair, her heart
in tumult. Had she better keep her distance
and question him, her husband? Should she run
up to him, take his hands, kiss him now?°
Crossing the door sill she sat down at once
in firelight, against the nearest wall,
across the room from the lord Odysseus.
There
leaning against a pillar, sat the man
and never lifted up his eyes, but only waited
for what his wife would say when she had seen him.
And she, for a long time, sat deathly still
in wonderment—for sometimes as she gazed
she found him—yes, clearly—like her husband,
but sometimes blood and rags were all she saw.°
Telemachus's voice came to her ears:
"Mother,
cruel mother, do you feel nothing,
drawing yourself apart this way from Father?
Will you not sit with him and talk and question him?
What other woman could remain so cold?
Who shuns her lord, and he come back to her
from wars and wandering, after twenty years?
Your heart is hard as flint and never changes!"

Penelope answered:
"I am stunned, child.
I cannot speak to him. I cannot question him.
I cannot keep my eyes upon his face.
If really he is Odysseus, truly home,
beyond all doubt we two shall know each other
better than you or anyone. There are
secret signs we know, we two."°
A smile
L1 came now to the lips of the patient hero, Odysseus,
who turned to Telemachus and said:

"Peace: let your mother test me at her leisure.
Before long she will see and know me best.
These tatters, dirt—all that I'm caked with now—
make her look hard at me and doubt me still.
As to this massacre, we must see the end.
Whoever kills one citizen, you know,

19–22 **She turned . . . now:** Penelope's thoughts reveal that she is not so uncertain of "that strange one" as she has let on.

33 **blood . . . saw:** Odysseus is again disguised as the old beggar.

50 **secret . . . two:** Eurynome has already said that she recognized Odysseus's scar; but Penelope is thinking of signs that are a secret strictly between her and Odysseus.

Big Idea Journeys *Why does Penelope hesitate to accept her husband?* BI

Additional Support

Skills Practice

LITERARY ELEMENT: Character Discuss with students the traits that Homer gives to Odysseus and whether Homer considers Odysseus the ideal Greek man. Then discuss the traits that Homer gives to Penelope and whether Homer considers her to be the ideal Greek woman. Have students write a brief comparison of Odysseus and Penelope. How do the two characters demonstrate the ideals of Greek manhood and womanhood, and how do they differ? Remind students to support their opinions with evidence from the poem. OL

and has no force of armed men at his back,
had better take himself abroad by night
and leave his kin. Well, we cut down the flower of Ithaca,
the mainstay of the town. Consider that."

Telemachus replied respectfully:

"Dear
Father,
enough that you yourself study the danger,
foresighted in combat as you are,
they say you have no rival.

We three
stand
ready to follow you and fight. I say
for what our strength avails,° we have the courage."

And the great tactician,° Odysseus, answered:

"Good.
Here is our best maneuver, as I see it:
bathe, you three,° and put fresh clothing on,
order the women to adorn themselves,
and let our admirable harper choose a tune
for dancing, some lighthearted air, and strum it.
Anyone going by, or any neighbor,
will think it is a wedding feast he hears.
These deaths must not be cried about the town
till we can slip away to our own woods. We'll see
what weapon, then, Zeus puts into our hands."°

They listened attentively, and did his bidding,
bathed and dressed afresh; and all the maids
adorned themselves. Then Phemius° the harper
took his polished shell° and plucked the strings,
moving the company to desire
for singing, for the sway and beat of dancing,
until they made the manor hall resound
with gaiety of men and grace of women.
Anyone passing on the road would say:

"Married at last, I see—the queen so many courted.
Sly, cattish wife! She would not keep—not she!—
the lord's estate until he came."

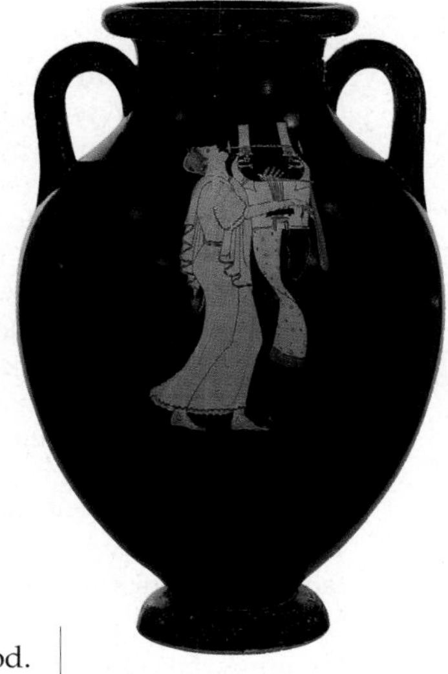

Youth Singing and Playing the Kithara, c. 490 B.C. Terra-cotta, height: 16⅜ in. The Metropolitan Museum of Art, New York. 

71 **avails:** is worth; helps.
72 **tactician:** one skilled in forming and carrying out (military) tactics or plans.
75 **you three:** Telemachus, Eumaeus, and Philoetius.

74–83 **Here . . . hands:** Odysseus's plan is this: First, stall for time by making people think that Penelope's wedding feast is in progress. Then escape to the woods, and trust in Zeus.
86 **Phemius** (fē′ mē əs)
87 **polished shell:** harp.

Reading Strategy Analyzing Cause-and-Effect Relationships *What does Odysseus fear will be the effect of his slaughter of the suitors?* 

Literary Element Plot *How is Homer introducing rising tension?* L2

Teach

R Reading Strategy

Analyzing Cause-and-Effect Relationships **Answer:** *He fears that he must once again leave home when the people of Ithaca come to avenge the loss of the suitors.* OL

L2 Literary Element

Plot **Answer:** *A battle is looming between Odysseus and the families and friends of the slaughtered suitors.* OL

★ Viewing the Art

The kithara was a musical instrument of the lyre family with two hollow arms, a wooden box, seven strings, and often a flat base. Larger than a typical lyre, the kithara was held by a standing musician who strummed the strings to produce music. AS

Differentiated Instruction

Reading Aloud Read aloud this part of the *Odyssey* or play a recording while students follow along. A combination of oral and visual stimuli will help students stay focused. Invite volunteers to act out the characters' parts while the final segment is read aloud. Encourage actors to use facial expression, posture, and gesture. Freeze the action at appropriate points, and have viewers tell what a given character may be thinking or feeling. BL

Academic Standards

Additional Support activities on pp. 1014 and 1015 cover the following standards:

Skills Practice: **9.3.4** Determine characters' traits by what the characters say about themselves in dialogue…

Differentiated Instruction: **9.7.6** Analyze the occasion and the interests of the audience and choose effective verbal and nonverbal techniques…for presentations.

Teach

BI1 Big Idea

Journeys Ask: How might Odysseus's appearance have changed since the last time Penelope saw him? *(Twenty years have past since Penelope last saw Odysseus. Students may say that he will be older. They may also say that he will be hardened from his adventures and possibly scarred from battle.)* **OL**

R1 Reading Strategy

Analyzing Cause-and-Effect Relationships Answer: *Athena is having Odysseus bathed and clothed in hopes that Penelope might finally recognize him as the husband she last saw twenty years earlier.* **OL**

R2 Reading Strategy

Analyzing Cause-and-Effect Relationships Ask: How do you think Penelope's unwillingness to accept Odysseus reflects on her character? *(Students may say that Penelope is a reflection of the Greek ideal of womanhood. She's exceedingly loyal to her husband and very careful not to betray that loyalty.)* **OL**

So travelers'
thoughts might run—but no one guessed the truth.
Greathearted Odysseus, home at last,
was being bathed now by Eurynome
and rubbed with golden oil, and clothed again
in a fresh tunic and a cloak. Athena
lent him beauty, head to foot. She made him
taller, and massive, too, with crisping hair
in curls like petals of wild hyacinth
but all red-golden. Think of gold infused **BI1**
on silver by a craftsman, whose fine art
Hephaestus° taught him, or Athena:° one
whose work moves to delight: just so she **lavished**
beauty over Odysseus' head and shoulders.
He sat then in the same chair by the pillar,
facing his silent wife, and said:

"Strange woman,
the immortals of Olympus made you hard,
harder than any. Who else in the world
would keep **aloof** as you do from her husband
if he returned to her from years of trouble,
cast on his own land in the twentieth year?°

Nurse, make up a bed for me to sleep on.
Her heart is iron in her breast."

Penelope
spoke to Odysseus now. She said:

"Strange man,
if man you are . . . This is no pride on my part
nor scorn for you—not even wonder, merely.
I know so well how you—how he—appeared **R2**
boarding the ship for Troy. But all the same . . .

Make up his bed for him, Eurycleia.°
Place it outside the bedchamber my lord
built with his own hands. Pile the big bed
with fleeces, rugs, and sheets of purest linen."°

With this she tried him to the breaking point,
and he turned on her in a flash raging:

"Woman, by heaven you've stung me now!
Who dared to move my bed?

107 **Hephaestus** (hi fes′ təs): the god of fire and metalworking. **Athena:** in addition to all her other roles, she was the goddess of arts and crafts.

112–117 **Strange . . . year:** Finally, after all his other battles have been won, Odysseus must win back his wife. Now he questions and criticizes her with uncharacteristic directness.

127 **Eurycleia** (yoo′ ri klē′ ə)

127–130 **Make up . . . linen:** Sounding sweetly hospitable, Penelope now tests the man who says he is her husband. She proposes that her maid move Odysseus's big bed out of the bedchamber and make it up.

Reading Strategy Analyzing Cause-and-Effect Relationships *What is Athena doing? Why?* **R1**

Vocabulary

lavish (lav′ ish) *v.* to give generously; provide in abundance

aloof (ə lo͞of′) *adj.* emotionally distant; uninvolved; disinterested; standoffish

Additional Support

Skills Practice

LITERARY ELEMENT: Parody Ask: What is a parody? *(A work that imitates another work in a satirical or humorous manner.)* Invite students to write a parody of Part 4 of the *Odyssey.* Divide students into groups. Assign each group a different section of Part 4. Instruct students to write their parodies as if they were mini-plays. After students rehearse, have each group perform their section for the class. Encourage students to consider the use of costumes and props to add to the comedy of their parodies. **OL**

No builder had the skill for that—unless
a god came down to turn the trick. No mortal
in his best days could budge it with a crowbar.
There is our pact and pledge, our secret sign,
built into that bed—my handiwork
and no one else's!
An old trunk of olive
grew like a pillar on the building plot,
and I laid out our bedroom round that tree,
lined up the stone walls, built the walls and roof,
gave it a doorway and smooth-fitting doors.
Then I lopped off the silvery leaves and branches,
hewed and shaped that stump from the roots up
into a bedpost, drilled it, let it serve
as model for the rest. I planed them all,
inlaid them all with silver, gold and ivory,
and stretched a bed between—a pliant web
of oxhide thongs dyed crimson.
There's our sign!
I know no more. Could someone else's hand
have sawn that trunk and dragged the frame away?"°

Their secret! as she heard it told, her knees
grew tremulous° and weak, her heart failed her.
With eyes brimming tears she ran to him,
throwing her arms around his neck, and kissed him,
murmuring:
"Do not rage at me, Odysseus!
No one ever matched your caution! Think
what difficulty the gods gave: they denied us
life together in our prime and flowering years,
kept us from crossing into age together.
Forgive me, don't be angry. I could not
welcome you with love on sight! I armed myself
long ago against the frauds of men,
impostors who might come—and all those many
whose underhanded ways bring evil on! . . .
But here and now, what sign could be so clear
as this of our own bed?
No other man has ever laid eyes on it—
only my own slave, Actoris,° that my father
sent with me as a gift—she kept our door.
You make my stiff heart know that I am yours."

133–155 **Woman, . . . away:** The original bed could not be moved. One bedpost was a tree trunk rooted in the ground, a secret known only by Penelope, a servant, and Odysseus, who built the bed with his own hands. Furious and hurt, Odysseus thinks Penelope has allowed someone to saw the bed frame from the tree.

157 **tremulous:** characterized by trembling; shaky.

174 **Actoris** (ak tôr′ is)

Literary Element Plot *How does Odysseus respond to Penelope's suggestion that the maid move the bed outside the bedchamber?* **L**

Big Idea Journeys *How has Penelope's tone shifted? Why?* **BI2**

Teach

L Literary Element

Plot Answer: *Odysseus is outraged that Penelope would have his bed moved outside their bedchamber.*

Ask: How is this scene climactic? *(Students should recognize that tension is at its height while Odysseus waits for Penelope to recognize him. He is home, yet his home and wife are still being denied to him. When he explodes against Penelope, it shows his distress and the action takes a new turn.)* **OL**

BI2 Big Idea

Journeys Answer: *She is passionate now, where before she had been guarded; she expresses joy and relief from long suffering.* **OL**

Differentiated Instruction

Understanding Emotions Students who are sensitive to others' moods and motivations will be good at reading between the lines in the final scene between Penelope and Odysseus. What seems cold-hearted is wisely cautious. Encourage students to explain how Penelope hides her reactions and thought processes beneath her formality. Have students write a journal entry from Penelope's point of view about her internal conflicts as she keeps "aloof" from Odysseus. Students might write their entries in the form of dialogue between her head and her heart. **AL**

Academic Standards

Additional Support activities on pp. 1016 and 1017 cover the following standards:

Skills Practice: **9.5.8** Write for different purposes and audiences, adjusting tone, style, and voice as appropriate.

Differentiated Instruction: **9.5.2** Write responses to literature…

Teach

BI Big Idea

Journeys At last Odysseus's homecoming is complete. **Ask:** What do you think the future holds for Odysseus, Penelope, and Telemachus? What role might his past journeys play in Odysseus's future? Do you believe he is home for good? *(Students' answers will vary. They should support their answers with details from the text.)* OL

★ Viewing the Art

This picture has also been called *The Meeting of Ulysses and Penelope.* When the Romans told the story of the Trojan War, they referred to Odysseus as Ulysses. "Ulysses" is a Latin form of Odysseus's name. AS

CheckPoint

Use the CheckPoint questions on Presentation Plus! to check students' mastery of the selection. These questions can be used with interactive response keypads for immediate student feedback.

Ulysses and Penelope Embracing. ★

Now from his breast into his eyes the ache
of longing mounted, and he wept at last,
his dear wife, clear and faithful, in his arms,
longed for
as the sunwarmed earth is longed for by a swimmer
spent in rough water where his ship went down
under Poseidon's blows, gale winds and tons of sea.
Few men can keep alive through a big surf
to crawl, clotted with brine, on kindly beaches
in joy, in joy, knowing the abyss behind:°
and so she too rejoiced, her gaze upon her husband,
her white arms round him pressed as though forever.

181–186 **a swimmer . . . behind:** Odysseus is compared to someone who swims to shore after a shipwreck. Coated with sea salt **(clotted with brine)**, he rejoices that his wife is in his arms and his hellish experience **(the abyss)** is over.

BI *The next day, Odysseus is reunited with his father, Laertes, as news of the death of the suitors passes through town. Families go to Odysseus's manor to gather the bodies for burial. There, Antinous's father rallies the families to avenge the deaths of their sons and brothers. As battle begins, however, Athena appears and calls the island to peace.*

Additional Support

Academic Standards

The Additional Support activity on p. 1018 covers the following standard:

Skills Practice: **9.6.1** Identify and correctly use clauses…

Skills Practice

GRAMMAR: Noun Clauses Explain to students that a clause (a word group with a subject and verb) can act as a noun. As an example, write on the board: Odysseus values whatever shows respect for the gods. Identify the underlined words as a clause; have students replace it with a single noun, such as *honor.* Explain that like *honor*, the clause *whatever shows respect for the gods* is a direct object telling what Odysseus values. Have students identify two noun clauses in Part 4 and tell how they function, as object of a preposition, subject, or direct object. OL

AFTER YOU READ

RESPONDING AND THINKING CRITICALLY

Respond

1. What do you think of the way in which Odysseus deals with the suitors?

Recall and Interpret

2. (a)How does Eurymachus attempt to avert bloodshed? (b)How does Odysseus respond?
3. (a)How do the nurse and Telemachus try to convince Penelope that the stranger is Odysseus? (b)Why might Penelope be unclear about what to do?
4. (a)How is proving himself to his wife different from the other challenges Odysseus has faced? (b)What enables him to meet this challenge?

Analyze and Evaluate

5. (a)Compare Eurymachus's first speech to Odysseus with his second plea to the suitors. (b)Which do you think represents the "real" Eurymachus?
6. (a)What kind of person is Telemachus? (b)How does he compare with his father?
7. Do you believe that Odysseus's desire for revenge is a moral flaw? Explain.

Connect

8. **Big Idea** **Journeys** How have Odysseus's adventures shaped his character?

DAILY LIFE AND CULTURE

Ancient Greek Society and Family Roles

The geography of ancient Greece created isolation. The sea and the mountainous terrain hindered travel between city-states. The simple herding lifestyle and warlike character of the Achaeans (who comprise the characters of the *Odyssey*), as well as their local pride and jealousies, prevented permanent alliances between the independent city-states. Although the *Iliad* tells how Greeks from many city-states joined to fight a common foe, ancient Greece never became a united nation. Citizens felt loyalty only to their city or kingdom.

At the center of their societies were the households of the aristocratic families. These did not consist simply of a nobleman, his wife, and their offspring but also included members of the extended family, along with servants and slaves. All men, including the noblemen, were familiar with the physical tasks of daily life, including plowing and caring for animals. An important chieftain such as Odysseus, however, would have rarely spent time in such lowly occupations.

The wife in a great household had status, but women in ancient Greece were not equal to men. Marriages were arranged by men for political or social reasons. A woman had little say in the matter. A noblewoman might spend her days managing her household or working at crafts such as weaving or embroidery.

Discuss the following questions with your classmates.

1. Why might the geographical and political isolation of ancient Greece have made a journey like Odysseus's particularly difficult?
2. What evidence do you find in the *Odyssey* to confirm that women were not considered of equal status to men?

Daily Life and Culture

1. Many of the people on islands and in the cities might never have heard of his homeland or might have been at war with it. As a result, people might send a traveler in the wrong direction or hinder his return.
2. Although Penelope is an important woman—the wife of a king—there is no question that she must marry one of the suitors. She does not have the power simply to refuse.

AFTER YOU READ

Assess

1. Some students will think it savage; others will think it just.
2. (a) Eurymachus asks Odysseus to spare his people. (b) Odysseus feels that their crimes cannot be repaid with material wealth; he is determined to even the score.
3. (a) The nurse sees a familiar scar. Telemachus urges Penelope to talk with him to be convinced. (b) After so many years, it is hard for her to accept him as real; she thinks the gods are meddling.
4. (a) He cannot use strength or cunning to win her. He must earn her trust. (b) Remembering the secret of how their bedpost was rooted in the ground
5. (a) His first speech is diplomatic, reasonable; he pledges to reimburse Odysseus. His second speech urges the suitors to join him in attacking Odysseus. (b) Most students will say that the second plea represents the "real" Eurymachus.
6. (a) He is a young man who has grown up without a father and is eager to please him. (b) He is a brave fighter, but he has a long way to go before acquiring Odysseus's abilities.
7. Many will say that the desire for revenge is a moral flaw. Some may find revenge through the legal system to be less of a moral problem.
8. He proves to be a courageous, curious, cunning, and resourceful survivor.

AFTER YOU READ

Assess

Literary Element

1. "Death in the Great Hall": line 85, when the battle begins in earnest; "The Trunk of the Olive Tree": line 133, when Odysseus rages against Penelope
2. The conflict that results in Odysseus's acceptance by Penelope and brings the whole epic to a successful close, for it restores home and hearth—the things he sought and has come to value most.

Reading Strategy

Possible responses are given:

1. Cause: Odysseus blinds Polyphemus, angering Zeus.

   Effect: Odysseus grows through suffering.
2. Cause: The men begin to starve.

   Effect: Zeus destroys their ship and kills them.
3. Cause: She doesn't want to marry any of the suitors.

   Effect: She postpones having to choose a husband.
4. Cause: Odysseus baits Antinous.

   Effect: Observers fault Antinous.

LITERARY ANALYSIS

Literary Element Plot

In a story or epic narrative, the climax is the moment when the events of the **plot** reach an emotional high point and the action takes a new turn. Very often this is also the moment of greatest interest or excitement for the reader. In a long work such as the *Odyssey,* there may be more than one climax. Odysseus's encounter with Polyphemus, for example, is a self-contained tale within the epic—and the moment when Odysseus blinds the Cyclops is its climax.

1. What is the climax of "Death in the Great Hall"? What is the climax of "The Trunk of the Olive Tree"?
2. Which of these climaxes could be considered the climax of the epic as a whole? Explain your answer.

Review: Narrator

As you learned on pages 206–207, a **narrator** is the person who tells a story. An epic poem is narrated in predictable ways. For example, a poet-narrator may start out with an invocation that states the tale's subject and asks for inspiration from a guiding spirit. The narration may begin in the "middle of things," describing what is happening after certain important events have already occurred. The *Odyssey* has two principal narrators: Odysseus and the poet.

Partner Activity Meet with a classmate and go through the text to decide which events are narrated by Odysseus and which by the poet. Then designate one of you to be Odysseus and one to be the poet. Take turns narrating the sections assigned to you in your own words. Use note cards to help you recall details. Remember that if you are Odysseus, you should narrate your part of the story in the first person, using *I*. If you are the poet, use the third person.

Episode: the Sirens
Narrator: Odysseus

warned by Circe
sea goes calm
beeswax for ears
begs to be released
men tie him tighter

READING AND VOCABULARY

Reading Strategy Analyzing Cause-and-Effect Relationships

Writers often try to show their readers why things happen as they do. The ancient Greeks believed that gods caused many of life's mysteries: thunder, war, particular storms at sea. How a person behaved mattered too. Good and bad actions led to rewards and punishments. The *Odyssey* is full of examples of cause and effect. Decide whether each event listed below is a cause, an effect, or both. If the event is a cause, write down one effect, and vice versa. If it is both, include a cause and an effect.

1. Odysseus suffers a series of misfortunes at sea.
2. Odysseus's men kill the cattle of Helios.
3. Each night Penelope unravels the shroud she is weaving.
4. Antinous throws a stool at Odysseus.

Vocabulary Practice

Practice with Word Origins For each boldfaced word, use a dictionary to find the word's origin.

1. **jostle**
   a. Middle English **b.** Greek **c.** other
2. **implacable**
   a. German **b.** Latin **c.** Greek
3. **lavish**
   a. German **b.** Latin **c.** French
4. **aloof**
   a. German **b.** Latin **c.** other

Academic Vocabulary

Here are two words from the vocabulary list on page R80.

encounter (en koun′tər) *v.* to come across; meet

decade (dek′ād) *n.* a period of ten years

Practice and Apply

1. Where in the *Odyssey* do you **encounter** graphic descriptions of fighting?
2. For how many **decades** is Odysseus absent from Ithaca?

Review: Narrator

Challenge students to explore how the passages spoken by Odysseus differ in tone from those retold by the narrator.

Vocabulary

1. a **2.** b **3.** c **4.** c

Academic Vocabulary

1. "Death in the Great Hall" includes graphic descriptions of fighting.
2. Odysseus spends two decades away from home.

Assess

Writing About Literature

Students' character analyses should:

- begin with a thesis that explains Penelope's actions.
- outline her reactions to Odysseus and explain what these reactions reveal about her character.
- tell how Penelope's reaction affects students' responses to this part of the *Odyssey.*

Interdisciplinary Activity

Remind students to use both print and online resources and to review basic design principles before planning their travel brochures. Exhibit finished products in an *Odyssey* "gallery showing."

WRITING AND EXTENDING

Writing About Literature

Analyze Character Reread the section in which Odysseus's identity is revealed to Penelope. Why does Penelope not immediately accept her long-lost husband? What does her hesitation say about her character and about her twenty-year ordeal? In a few paragraphs, explain why Penelope acts the way she does. Explore how her reaction affects your own response to this part of the *Odyssey*.

Prepare for your essay with flow charts like the ones below. Use the flow charts to list Penelope's actions and the motivations for those actions.

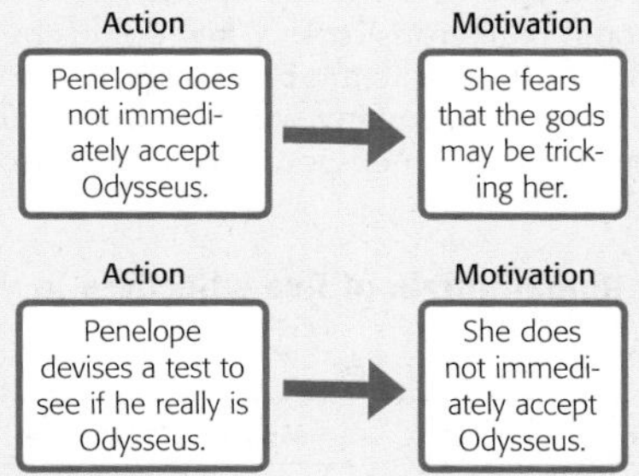

Action
Penelope does not immediately accept Odysseus.
Motivation
She fears that the gods may be tricking her.
Action
Penelope devises a test to see if he really is Odysseus.
Motivation
She does not immediately accept Odysseus.

After you complete your draft, meet with a peer reviewer to evaluate each other's work and to suggest revisions. Then proofread and edit your draft to correct errors in spelling, grammar, and punctuation.

Interdisciplinary Activity: Geography

Did Homer have real places in mind when he plotted Odysseus's fantastic voyage? Over the centuries, many scholars have tried to show that Odysseus did follow an actual geographical route. Some theorists think he sailed as far away as Iceland. Others think he simply circled the island of Sicily. Many of Homer's geographical descriptions are hazy, confusing, or even contradictory, making it difficult to pinpoint the route he describes with precision. Research some of the places that scholars have associated with Odysseus's journey. Choose one of these sites and find out what it is like today. Create a travel brochure describing the place.

GRAMMAR AND STYLE

Homer's Language and Style

Using Compound Adjectives What do the following phrases from the *Odyssey* have in common?

sea-hollowed caves

black-prowed vessel

canvas-bellying breeze

Each is a compound adjective made up of two words joined by a hyphen. Such compounds have the effect of shortening and simplifying a descriptive passage. They also allow a poet to change the sound and rhythm of a line to make it more effective.

Remember that Homer's words were written down long ago. The translator, Robert Fitzgerald, has tried to capture the flavor and rhythm of Homer's spoken language. For example, instead of "the sea was as dark as wine," Fitzgerald's Greek translation includes "the winedark sea"—the same meaning but with a more concentrated and direct effect. Instead of talking of "Cronus, who had a crooked mind," he refers to "crooked-minded Cronus." Note that a compound adjective often includes one word that is not normally an adjective at all. For example, *black-prowed* turns a noun *(prow)* into an adjective *(prowed).*

Activity Rewrite the following phrases so that they contain compound adjectives.

1. a jar with two handles
2. a ship with long oars
3. a bolt that is white with heat
4. a bow that is made well
5. a sheep with stiff legs

Revising Check

Compound Adjectives Compound adjectives can add to the liveliness of your own writing. With a partner, go through your character analysis of Penelope and note places where compound adjectives would make your writing more vivid. Revise your draft as needed.

LiteratureOnline **Web Activities** For eFlashcards, Selection Quick Checks, and other Web activities, go to www.glencoe.com.

Homer's Language and Style

1. a two-handled jar
2. a long-oared ship
3. a white-hot bolt
4. a well-made bow
5. a stiff-legged sheep

Web Activities Have students access the Web site for interactive activities that will help them assess their understanding of the selection.

Focus

Write on the board: Word: Siren; Word Origin: Sirens of Greek myth; Meaning Today: alarm. Ask students to consider how the Sirens of Greek mythology evolved into today's meaning.

Teach

Word Origins Have students add the word-origin chart on page 1022 to their vocabulary lists. Suggest that students organize all their *Odyssey* vocabulary in this manner. OL

Assess

1. muse—museum, music; Olympus—Olympics, Olympian; Chronus—chronology, chronometer
2. **a.** atlas—a bound book of maps; from Atlas, a Titan, who supports the world on his shoulders
   b. cereal—a grain; from Ceres, the Roman goddess of agriculture
   c. mentor—coach or tutor; from Mentor, Odysseus's friend who was to educate his son, Telemachus

Vocabulary Workshop

Word Origins

▶ **Vocabulary Terms** A word's *etymology* is its origin. Etymologies can usually be found in brackets in a word's dictionary entry.

▶ **Test-Taking Tip** Always apply your knowledge of word history when you encounter unfamiliar words while reading passages or when you have to choose a correct meaning on a multiple-choice test.

▶ **Reading Handbook** For more about word origins, see Reading Handbook, p. R19.

Examining Words from Greek and Roman Mythology

"Soon
as we came smartly within hailing distance,
the two Sirens, noting our fast ship
off their point, made ready, and they sang . . ."

—Homer, the *Odyssey*

Connecting to Literature In Homer's story, the Sirens are creatures who lure sailors off their course and onto dangerous rocks. They do this by singing. Today, we use the word *siren* to refer to a type of alarm. Although its meaning has changed, the word *siren,* like many words in the English language, originated in Greek myth. Many other words come to us from Roman myth.

This chart shows the Greek or Roman origin of five adjectives in the English language.

Word	Origin	Meaning Today
jovial	from Jove or Jupiter, the Roman god of light, the sky, and weather	good humored; jolly
martial	from Mars, the Roman god of war	warlike; relating to war
mercurial	from Mercury, the Roman god of business and travel, known for shrewdness	characterized by unpredictable and quickly changing moods
narcissistic	from Narcissus, the Greek youth who fell in love with his reflection	self-loving; egocentric
volcanic	from Vulcan, the Roman god of fire and metalworking	relating to or produced by a volcano

LiteratureOnline
eFlashcards For eFlashcards and other vocabulary activities, go to www.glencoe.com.

Exercise

1. Write one modern English word that comes from or is related to each of the following words from the *Odyssey: muse, Olympus, Chronus*. Use a dictionary if you need help.
2. Find the etymology for each of these words from Greek or Roman myth. Write the word's meaning and its origin.
   a. atlas
   b. cereal
   c. mentor

ACADEMIC STANDARDS (page 1022)
9.1.1 Understand the origins of words.
9.1.3 Use knowledge of mythology (Greek, Roman, and other mythologies) to understand the origin and meaning of new words.

Additional Support

Academic Standards
The Additional Support activity on p. 1022 covers the following standard:
Skills Practice: **9.4.6** Synthesize information from multiple sources…

Skills Practice

RESEARCH AND STUDY SKILLS: Gods Assign students to research the Roman and Greek gods. Have students create a graphic organizer with the name of the Greek god or goddess in one column, the Roman name in a second column, and in the third column, that god's attributes and associations. Have students create a fourth column in which they add vocabulary that relates to that god or goddess. OL

Comparing Literature *Across Genres*

Connecting to the Reading Selections

Have you ever found a character or setting from a literary work particularly inspiring? C. P. Cavafy, Edna St. Vincent Millay, and Margaret Atwood use characters and settings from Homer's classic epic, the *Odyssey,* in their works. As you read, notice the different aspects of the *Odyssey* that have inspired these writers. Note as well how the authors give their own twist to this classic story.

COMPARING THE **Big Idea** Journeys

Journeys are an important element in each of these works. Two of the selections present the journey from the viewpoint of the traveler, while the other two relate to the person awaiting the traveler's return.

COMPARING Theme

Although the writers of the following selections draw their subject matter from the same source, each work has its own theme. As you read, notice how each writer illustrates his or her understanding of life.

COMPARING Author's Meaning

As you read, consider the underlying meaning behind each author's references to the *Odyssey.* In the selections that follow, C. P. Cavafy, Edna St. Vincent Millay, and Margaret Atwood allude to the characters, places, and events in the *Odyssey.*

Focus

BELLRINGER

Bellringer Options
Selection Focus Transparency 48
Daily Language Practice Transparency 85
Or **write on the board:** Do you think it's harder to be the person who leaves for a journey or the person who is left behind? Discuss times when students have been away from home and what it felt like to leave. Then, discuss what it was like to stay when someone they knew left. Prompt students to consider the benefits and drawbacks of both experiences.

Connecting to the Reading Selections

Allow students to share their responses to the opening question. Then have students discuss what they already know about C. P. Cavafy, Edna St. Vincent Millay, and Margaret Atwood.

Selection Skills

Comparing Literature

Literary Elements
- Comparing Theme (SE pp. 1023, 1029)
- Symbolism (TWE p. 1026)
- Allusion (TWE p. 1027)

Reading Skills
- Perspective (TWE p. 1028)
- Analyzing Cause and Effect (TWE p. 1028)

Listening/Speaking/Viewing Skills
- Discuss Author's Meaning (SE p. 1029)

Writing Skills/Grammar
- Analyze Symbols (SE p. 1025)
- Analyze Gestures (SE p. 1026)
- Analyze Point of View (SE p. 1028)
- Comparing the Journeys (SE p. 1029)

Teach

Journeys Ask: If the journey to Ithaca is a metaphor, what journey might it represent? *(Answers will vary. Students may say that it's about enjoying the larger journey of life and not focusing just on the end goal.)* **OL**

Literature Online

Author Search To expand students' appreciation of C. P. Cavafy, have them access the Web site for additional information and resources.

CheckPoint

Use the CheckPoint questions on Presentation Plus! to check students' mastery of the selection. These questions can be used with interactive response keypads for immediate student feedback.

ITHACA

C. P. Cavafy

Translated by Rae Dalven

Ulysses Returns Chryseis to Her Father. Claude Lorrain. Collection of Louvre, Paris, France.

BEFORE YOU READ

Building Background

Constantine Cavafy (1863–1933) was a Greek poet who spent most of his life in the Egyptian city of Alexandria, where he was born. During his lifetime he published few poems and received little literary acclaim, but he is now regarded as the finest Greek poet of the twentieth century. In his writing, Cavafy reintroduced literary forms that had rarely been used since the time of the ancient Greeks. With its classical themes and subjects, much of Cavafy's poetry reflects his interest in ancient Greek and Roman culture.

The city in which Cavafy lived also plays an important role in his work. Cavafy was proud of the fact that Alexandria, built by Alexander the Great, was known for centuries as a city vital to trade and scholarship. European visitors to Alexandria reported that Cavafy had an extraordinary gift for bringing history to life in conversation, and they said that he would gossip about historical figures as if they were alive and living in contemporary Alexandria.

Literature Online **Author Search** For more about C. P. Cavafy, go to www.glencoe.com.

Selection Resources

Print Materials
- Unit 5 Resources (Fast File), p. 30
- Selection and Unit Assessments, p. 171
- Selection Quick Checks, p. 86

Transparencies
- Bellringer Options Transparencies: Selection Focus Transparency 48 Daily Language Practice Transparency 85
- Literary Elements Transparency 18

Technology
- TeacherWorks Plus™ CD-ROM
- StudentWorks Plus™ CD-ROM
- Presentation Plus!™ CD-ROM
- Literature Online, glencoe.com
- Online Student Edition, mhln.com
- Exam*View*® Assessment Suite CD-ROM
- Vocabulary PuzzleMaker CD-ROM
- Listening Library, disc 2 tracks 24–26

When you start on your journey to Ithaca,
then pray that the road is long,
full of adventure, full of knowledge.
Do not fear the Lestrygonians
and the Cyclopes and the angry Poseidon.
You will never meet such as these on your path,
if your thoughts remain lofty, if a fine
emotion touches your body and your spirit.
You will never meet the Lestrygonians,
the Cyclopes and the fierce Poseidon,
if you do not carry them within your soul,
if your soul does not raise them up before you.

Then pray that the road is long.
That the summer mornings are many,
that you will enter ports seen for the first time
with such pleasure, with such joy!
Stop at Phoenician markets,
and purchase fine merchandise,
mother-of-pearl and corals, amber and ebony,
and pleasurable perfumes of all kinds,
buy as many pleasurable perfumes as you can;
visit hosts of Egyptian cities,
to learn and learn from those who have knowledge.

Always keep Ithaca fixed in your mind.
To arrive there is your ultimate goal.
But do not hurry the voyage at all.
It is better to let it last for long years;
and even to anchor at the isle when you are old,
rich with all that you have gained on the way,
not expecting that Ithaca will offer you riches.

Ithaca has given you the beautiful voyage.
Without her you would never have taken the road.
But she has nothing more to give you.

And if you find her poor, Ithaca has not defrauded you.
With the great wisdom you have gained, with so much experience,
you must surely have understood by then what Ithacas mean.

Quickwrite

Cavafy uses many symbols in this poem. Symbols are objects, places, or experiences that represent something other than what they mean literally. Write a paragraph in which you discuss the symbols you find most important in the poem. What do you think they stand for? How do they contribute to the overall message of the poem?

Teach

L Literary Element

Allusion **Ask:** What do the allusions to the "journey to Ithaca" and to the giants and god of the sea bring to mind? *(Odysseus's disastrous encounters with beings and gods)* **Ask:** How do they affect the view of the journey the speaker describes? *(They suggest that difficulty will come to those who stop appreciating the beauty life offers or whose thoughts do not "remain lofty.")* OL

★ Cultural History

Phoenicians The Phoenicians had a large impact on many societies. The Phoenicians were traders and sailors who dominated the Mediterranean area for centuries. Although most of their writings were lost when they were conquered, the Phoenicians were responsible for creation of the modern alphabet. AS

Quickwrite

Students should discuss two or more symbols from "Ithaca." Students might discuss how Cavafy gives the Lestrygonians, the Cyclopes, and Poseidon new meaning by indicating that they are symbols of internal enemies, enemies in a person's soul.

Differentiated Instruction

Monitoring Comprehension
Learning disabled students may feel overwhelmed by the passages in the Comparing Literature section. Help students to maintain focus by breaking each passage into smaller goals:

- Preview the passage and set a purpose for their reading.
- Read the passage once to get an overall impression.
- Reread the passage and summarize each stanza.
- Review what they've learned to see if they've accomplished their purpose. BL

Academic Standards

The Additional Support activity on p. 1025 covers the following standard:
Differentiated Instruction: **9.2** Develop [reading] strategies…

Teach

R Reading Strategy

Predict Have students read the first two lines of the poem. Ask them to predict what they think the poem will be about. Discuss with students how the allusion to Penelope influences their predictions. OL

Quickwrite

Students' responses should demonstrate an understanding of the concept of gestures as physical movements that communicate meaning or emotion.

Author Search To expand students' appreciation of Edna St. Vincent Millay, have them access the Web site for additional information and resources.

Use the CheckPoint questions on Presentation Plus! to check students' mastery of the selection. These questions can be used with interactive response keypads for immediate student feedback.

BEFORE YOU READ

Building Background

Like Penelope in the *Odyssey*, Edna St. Vincent Millay held off many suitors, preferring her independence and writing career to marriage and domestic life. Through her poetry and her life, she came to represent the rebellious, independent, youthful spirit of the 1920s. At age thirty-one, however, she married a man who supported her dedication to her writing and assumed all domestic responsibilities in order to give her time for her literary pursuits.

Literature Online **Author Search** For more about Edna St. Vincent Millay, go to www.glencoe.com.

Edna St. Vincent Millay

R I thought, as I wiped my eyes on the corner of my apron:
Penelope did this too.
And more than once: you can't keep weaving all day
And undoing it all through the night;
Your arms get tired, and the back of your neck gets tight;
And along towards morning, when you think it will never be light,
And your husband has been gone, and you don't know where, for years,
Suddenly you burst into tears;
There is simply nothing else to do.

And I thought, as I wiped my eyes on the corner of my apron:
This is an ancient gesture, authentic, antique,
In the very best tradition, classic, Greek;
Ulysses[1] did this too.
But only as a gesture,—a gesture which implied
To the assembled throng that he was much too moved to speak.
He learned it from Penelope . . .
Penelope, who really cried.

1. Ulysses (ū lis′ ēz) was the Roman name for the Greek hero Odysseus.

Quickwrite

Think of a gesture or other action that has special significance for you. Write a paragraph describing this gesture and its meanings and associations.

Additional Support

Skills Practice

LITERARY ELEMENT: Symbolism Point out that common objects often have a great deal of symbolism. Ask students to give the definition of the word "apron." Broaden the discussion to include any symbolic associations the apron may represent (domesticity, women being tied to the home). Have students work in pairs to find other common words that have deeper symbolic meanings. Hold a class discussion to share the students' findings. Discuss with students how the symbolism affects the connotation of the words. OL

WAITING
from
The Penelopiad

Margaret Atwood

Penelope. Sir Frank Dicksee. Watercolour on paper. Private collection.

BEFORE YOU READ

Building Background

Poet and novelist Margaret Atwood says that spending a large part of her childhood in the Canadian wilderness aided her development as a writer. With "no theaters, movies, parades, or very functional radios," she had plenty of time for meditation and reading. She produced her first award-winning book of poems, *The Circle Game,* while still in her twenties.

In *The Penelopiad*, Atwood tells the story of the *Odyssey* from Penelope's point of view. Atwood writes, "Homer's *Odyssey* is not the only version of the story." The tale of Odysseus, she explains, came out of Greek oral tradition, which means that the myth would have been told differently by different storytellers. She takes on the role of storyteller and provides a new version of the tale.

Literature Online **Author Search** For more about Margaret Atwood, go to www.glencoe.com.

What can I tell you about the next ten years? Odysseus sailed away to Troy. I stayed in Ithaca. The sun rose, traveled across the sky, set. Only sometimes did I think of it as the flaming chariot of Helios.[1] The moon did the same, changing from phase to phase. Only sometimes did I think of it as the silver boat of Artemis.[2] Spring, summer, fall, and winter followed one another in their appointed rounds. Quite often the wind blew. Telemachus grew from year to year, eating a lot of meat, indulged by all.

We had news of how the war with Troy was going: sometimes well, sometimes badly. Minstrels sang songs about the notable heroes—Achilles, Ajax, Agamemnon, Menelaus, Hector, Aeneas,[3] and the rest. I didn't care about them: I waited only for news of Odysseus. When would he come back and relieve my boredom? He too

1. *Helios* is the Greek god of the sun.
2. *Artemis* is the Greek goddess of the Moon.
3. These men were the heroes of Homer's *Iliad*, his account of the battle of Troy.

COMPARING LITERATURE

Teach

L Literary Element

Allusion The speaker alludes to the chariot of Helios and the silver boat of Artemis. **Ask:** What does the speaker reveal about herself with these allusions? *(Answers will vary, but students should note that the speaker believes in Greek mythology and probably lives in a time and place where that belief was prevalent.)* OL

CheckPoint

Use the CheckPoint questions on Presentation Plus! to check students' mastery of the selection. These questions can be used with interactive response keypads for immediate student feedback.

Readability Scores

Dale-Chall: 7.9
DRP: 59
Lexile: 910

English Language Coach

Greek Mythology English language learners may find the allusions to Greek mythology confusing. Point out that Greek myths, like many religions, were an attempt by the ancient Greeks to explain the world around them. Have students keep this in mind as they decode these references. EL

Author Search To expand students' appreciation of Margaret Atwood, have them access the Web site for additional information and resources.

Academic Standards

Additional Support activities on pp. 1026 and 1027 cover the following standards:
Skills Practice: **9.3.7** Recognize and understand the significance of various literary devices, including...symbolism...
English Language Coach: **9.2** Develop [reading] strategies...

Teach

BI Big Idea

Journeys **Ask:** How does the speaker handle the rumors about what has been delaying Odysseus? *(The speaker points out the contradictions in the rumors. She makes humorous asides. Students should infer that she doesn't take any of the rumors very seriously.)* OL

R Reading Strategy

Analyzing Cause-and-Effect Relationships Instruct students to read the last sentence of the story. **Ask:** What effect has Odysseus's absence had on the speaker? *(Students may say that despite the humor, the speaker despairs because of Odysseus's absence. Others may feel that she has grown stronger as a result of his absence.)* OL

Quickwrite

Students should cite the differences in the story of the *Odyssey* as told from different viewpoints. For example, when told with Odysseus as the central figure, the story is an epic tale of heroism. When told from Penelope's point of view, Odysseus's adventures can be exaggerated to make them seem dangerous.

COMPARING LITERATURE

appeared in the songs, and I relished those moments. There he was making an inspiring speech, there he was uniting the quarreling factions,[4] there he was inventing an astonishing falsehood, there he was delivering sage advice, there he was disguising himself as a runaway slave and sneaking into Troy and speaking with Helen[5] herself, who—the song proclaimed—had bathed him and anointed him with her very own hands.

I wasn't so fond of that part.

Finally, there he was, concocting the stratagem of the wooden horse filled with soldiers.[6] And then—the news flashed from beacon to beacon—Troy had fallen. There were reports of a great slaughtering and looting in the city. The streets ran red with blood, the sky above the palace turned to fire; innocent boy children were thrown off a cliff, and the Trojan women were parceled out as plunder, King Priam's daughters among them. And then, finally, the hoped-for news arrived: the Greek ships had set sail for home.

And then, nothing.

Day after day I would climb up to the top floor of the palace and look out over the harbor. Day after day there was no sign. Sometimes there were ships, but never the ship I longed to see.

Rumors came, carried by other ships. Odysseus and his men had got drunk at their first port of call and the men had mutinied, said some; no, said others, they'd eaten a magic plant that had caused them to lose their memories, and Odysseus had saved them by having them tied up and carried onto the ships. Odysseus had been in a fight with a giant one-eyed Cyclops, said some; no, it was only a one-eyed tavern keeper, said another, and the fight was over non-payment of the bill. Some of the men had been eaten by cannibals, said some; no, it was just a brawl of the usual kind, said others, with ear-bitings and nosebleeds and stabbings and eviscerations.[7] Odysseus was the guest of a goddess on an enchanted isle, said some; she'd turned his men into pigs—not a hard job in my view—but had turned them back into men because she'd fallen in love with him and was feeding him unheard-of delicacies prepared by her own immortal hands; no, said others, he was sponging off[8] the woman.

Needless to say, the minstrels took up these themes and embroidered them considerably. They always sang the noblest versions in my presence—the ones in which Odysseus was clever, brave, and resourceful, and battling supernatural monsters, and beloved of goddesses. The only reason he hadn't come back home was that a god—the sea-god Poseidon, according to some—was against him, because a Cyclops crippled by Odysseus was his son. Or several gods were against him. Or the Fates. Or something. For surely—the minstrels implied, by way of praising me—only a strong divine power could keep my husband from rushing back as quickly as possible into my loving—and lovely—wifely arms. BI

The more thickly they laid it on, the more costly were the gifts they expected from me. I always complied. Even an obvious fabrication[9] is some comfort when you have few others. R

4. A *faction* is a small group within a larger group.
5. *Helen* refers to Helen of Troy, who was, according to myth, the most beautiful woman in Greece and the cause of the Trojan war.
6. The *wooden horse* refers to Odysseus's successful plan to get inside the fortress at Troy by building a gigantic wooden horse and offering it as a gift of peace. The Trojans accepted the gift, not knowing that Greek soldiers were hiding inside it.
7. *Evisceration* means "the removal of internal organs."
8. Here, *sponging off* means "living at the expense of."
9. A *fabrication* is a lie or a made-up story.

Quickwrite

What impression do you have of Penelope's character after reading this selection? Write a paragraph addressing how Atwood's version of Penelope's point of view affects your impression of the events and characters in the *Odyssey*.

Additional Support

Skills Practice

READING: Perspective **Ask:** Have you ever been away from home? Prompt students to consider everything from sleepovers to going to camp.

Ask: Who was waiting for you to return? Prompt students to consider the experience of the people who were waiting. Were they eagerly anticipating students' return? What did they do while students were gone? Have students write journal entries from those people's point of view. OL

Wrap-Up: Comparing Literature *Across Genres*

- from the *Odyssey* by Homer
- *Ithaca* by C. P. Cavafy
- *An Ancient Gesture* by Edna St. Vincent Millay
- *Waiting* from *The Penelopiad* by Margaret Atwood

COMPARING THE Big Idea Journeys

Writing What role do journeys play in each of these selections? In what ways are the journeys similar? In what ways are they different? Create a chart to organize your ideas about the ways journeys are important to each of these selections. Then write a short essay comparing and contrasting the role of the Big Idea in the selections.

Selection	Who Is Traveling	Purpose of Journey	Speaker's Attitude
Odyssey	Odysseus	to return home	
Ithaca			
An Ancient Gesture			
Waiting			

COMPARING Theme

Partner Activity With a partner, discuss the themes of each of these selections. What attitudes about life and human nature do each of these works convey? How are these attitudes similar or different? In your discussion, address the following questions, referring to specific places in the texts to support your answers.

COMPARING Author's Meaning

Group Activity In a small group, discuss the author's overall meaning in each selection. Then work separately, each looking closely at the action or actions of one character in one of the selections. What do you think the author means to tell the reader by describing this action in the way he or she does? Meet with your group to share your ideas.

Julia at Start Point, Devon, 1992. Robert O'Rorke. Oil on canvas, 17 × 21 in. London.

INDIANA ACADEMIC STANDARDS (page 1029)

9.3.2 Compare and contrast the presentation of a similar theme or topic across genres...

9.3.5 Compare works that express a universal theme and provide evidence to support the views...in each work.

COMPARING LITERATURE

AFTER YOU READ

Assess

Comparing the Big Idea

Possible student answers: "Ithaca"—Who: reader; Purpose: self-discovery; Attitude: welcoming. "An Ancient Gesture"—Who: wife's husband; Purpose: fame and recognition; Attitude: sorrowful, lonely. "Waiting"—Who: Odysseus; Purpose: to get home; Attitude: skeptical, doubtful.

Comparing Theme

The theme of "Ithaca" is that life is an exciting journey and should be enjoyed, since much of our fate is shaped by our own decisions. The message of "An Ancient Gesture" is that a common expressive gesture in times of hardship draws people together in an ancient tradition. A theme of "Waiting" is that those long anticipating a traveler's return accept tall tales and false comfort to escape boredom and worry.

Comparing Author's Meaning

Cavafy develops the symbolic journey in the poem and imbues it with vivid historical associations. Millay bestows a sense of timelessness and expressive power upon a traditional feminine gesture. Atwood brings to life the world of the *Odyssey* from Penelope's point of view. As students examine one character, they should support their conclusions with examples.

Academic Standards

The Additional Support activity on p. 1028 covers the following standard:

Skills Practice: **9.2** Develop [reading] strategies...

Informational Text

TIME

Focus

Summary

Susan Jakes tells the story of a Chinese country girl immigrating to the city. Seventeen-year-old Mo wants to find a factory job in the city of Shenzhen. However, she is overwhelmed by the number of factories. Finally, she takes a job as a waitress. As soon as she gets paid, Mo plans to go home and work two jobs.

Teach

R Reading Strategy

Responding to Events
Author Susan Jakes says Mo leaned against her suitcase "as if for support." **Ask:** What can you infer about Mo from this? *(Students may say that she's nervous.)* How does this detail help you relate to her? *(Students may say that knowing Mo is nervous helps them feel empathy for her right from the beginning.)* OL

See also Active Learning and Note Taking Guide, pp. 166–174.

Readability Scores
Dale-Chall: 7.9
DRP: 58
Lexile: 920

Informational Text

Media Link to the *Odyssey*

Preview the Article

In "Leaving It All Behind," journalist Susan Jakes tracks Mo Yunxiu, a seventeen-year-old girl from rural China who hopes to build a new life in the city of Shenzhen.

1. Read the *deck*, or the sentence in large type that appears next to the title. What do you predict the outcome of this article will be?
2. Scan the captions to the photographs. In your opinion, what do they say about the girl in the photographs?

Set a Purpose for Reading

Read to discover the purpose and outcome of Mo Yunxiu's journey to Shenzhen.

Reading Strategy

Responding to Events
Responding to events involves telling what you like, dislike, or find interesting or surprising about the events in a selection. Reacting in a personal way to what you read helps you enjoy and remember the selection. As you read "Leaving It All Behind," take notes on the events that occur and how you respond to them. Use a graphic organizer like the one below.

Events	Response

ACADEMIC STANDARDS (pages 1030–1034)
9.2.1 Analyze the structure and format of...functional...documents, including the graphics and headers, and explain how authors use the features to achieve their purposes.
9.2 Develop strategies such as...identifying and analyzing...purpose...

TIME

Leaving It All Behind

With $100 in her pocket, a teenage girl bids farewell to life in rural China and heads to the big city in search of work.

By SUSAN JAKES

FOR THE FIRST 20 MINUTES OF HER NEW LIFE IN Shenzhen, Mo Yunxiu stood perfectly still. Behind her, sleeper coaches rolled, groaning into the city's crowded bus depot. Ahead stretched a tangle of freeways, already teeming at 10 a.m. on a Sunday. A plastic bag containing a package of sour plums, a water bottle, and the remains of a loaf of sliced bread—snacks left over from the overnight ride—hung from her left wrist. Her right hand gripped the handle of a small suitcase on wheels, and she leaned against it stiffly, as if for support. R

The Promise of the City

Mo said nothing, but it was clear that she had a lot on her mind. She was 17 years old, and farther from her farm in Guangxi province than she'd ever been. She knew no one in Shenzhen, and had nowhere specific to go. This was a place she'd dreamed about. She had seen pictures of Shenzhen's high-tech factories on television, and she pictured herself working in one, wearing a smart uniform and making a good salary. But her dream had left out the scenes between the arrival of her bus and her arrival in paradise.

At last, for no discernible reason, Mo moved. She walked uncertainly, and very quietly asked a policeman for directions to the nearest bus stop. There, she stood silently again for 20 minutes, looking at the buses come and go. Finally, she asked a stranger where to find a cheap place to stay. Within minutes Mo was back on a bus, pressing her face to the window, watching the sprawl of her new home slip by. Our arrival in Shenzhen had been fraught with anticipation: for Mo because she had so much riding on this journey; for me because I was writing about what would happen to her.

I'd told Chinese friends that I wanted to find a country girl lured from her home by the promise of the city. Mo had been introduced to me by her cousin, a tour guide in Yangshuo, a vacation spot on the Li River

Additional Support

Skills Practice

READING: Predicting After reading the beginning of the article, have students jot down their predictions about Mo's journey. Tell students to list what they know about Mo so far, and then have them predict how she will change because of her journey. Next, have students write what they know so far about Mo's journey. Have students make predictions about what else Mo will encounter along the way. When students have finished reading, have them compare their predictions with the actual events. OL

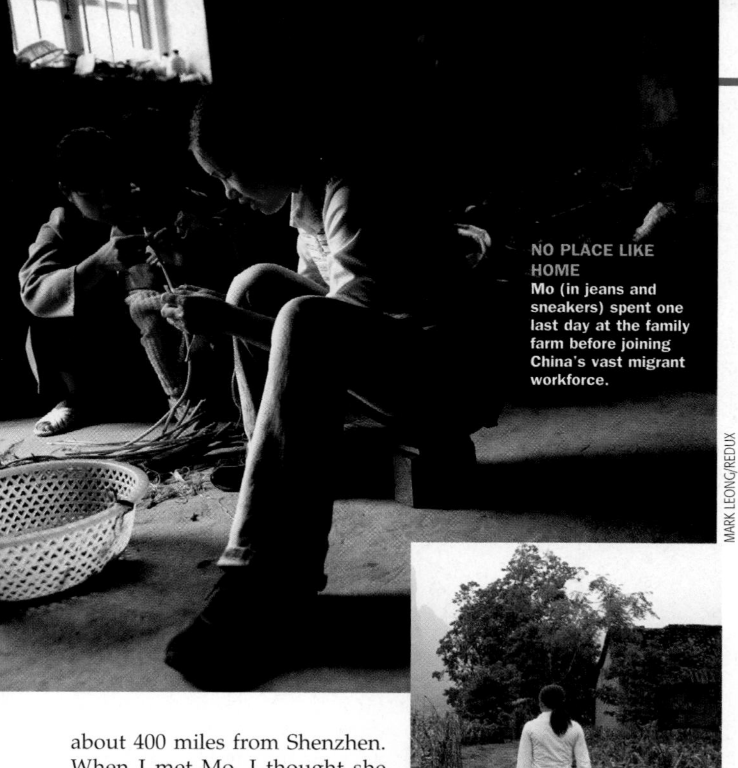

NO PLACE LIKE HOME
Mo (in jeans and sneakers) spent one last day at the family farm before joining China's vast migrant workforce.

MARK LEONG/REDUX

about 400 miles from Shenzhen. When I met Mo, I thought she was all wrong. I wanted a typical migrant—whatever that meant—and Mo had tinted hair and stylish, bleach-striped jeans. After a three-month stay with her cousin, she already seemed a bit worldly.

Mo had been one of the best students in her middle school, but high school cost $500 a year—nearly seven times her farmer family's annual income. If she got a decent job in Shenzhen, she figured, she could save enough money in a year or two to attend a vocational school and learn a skill, like computer programming or English, which in turn could get her a better job. She wanted to build a new house for her parents and treat herself to "one of those tape recorders, the kind with the earphones that you can listen to in bed before you fall asleep." She believed Shenzhen had the power to change her life.

MARK LEONG/REDUX

I was impressed by Mo's determination—and by her courage. She had only $100 when she boarded the bus in Yangshuo. It seemed to me an incredibly risky proposition, but when I'd pressed her to tell me how she would manage, she just shrugged her shoulders. She'd work it out when she got there. "Bu yaojin," Mo would often say: "It's not serious." **BI**

But now that she'd arrived in Shenzhen, it all felt very serious. I started to worry that the trip had been a mistake. Mark Leong, the photographer, and I had agreed to try our best to observe Mo without interfering in her decisions; we'd agreed to intercede only if we thought she was putting herself in danger. Now we wondered if we'd been irresponsible to put so much faith in the dreams of a 17-year-old who'd never been more than three hours away from home.

Saying Good-bye

Two days before leaving Yangshuo for Shenzhen, Mo had returned to her parents' farm to say good-bye. Mo's father, Li Simin, had come to the village of Matou in 1972 to marry. His wife's family had lived in Matou, a village of about 50 households, for generations. Neither of Mo's parents had ever traveled outside Guangxi province. "Being a farmer is relatively difficult," Li told me, but he sounded modestly satisfied with what he'd achieved. The family ate the rice he grew, raised pigs, and grew oranges and pomelos for cash—about $75 most years—and could now afford to eat meat a few times a month.

The mud-brick house was comfortably cool and airy. Its four rooms were clean and furnished with the barest of necessities. The only decorations were some calendars tacked to one wall, and a row of Mo's certificates of academic merit hung neatly on another. In the corner sat a television the family bought for about $120 in 2000, its edges still cushioned in blocks of Styrofoam.

Li clearly had a soft spot for his only daughter. But he had no reservations about her decision to move to Shenzhen. "I couldn't leave," he explained, "I didn't have the right requirements. But now things are better. If kids want to go, they can just go." Besides, he added with a small laugh, Mo was stubborn. When

Informational Text

TIME

Teach

BI Big Idea

Journeys **Ask:** Do you think Mo's decision to leave home with only $100 was brave? Why or why not? *(Some students will say that Mo is from a poor area and this was all she could afford, so she was brave. Others will feel she was foolish not to save more money before attempting such a journey.)* **OL**

★ Cultural History

Shenzhen Shenzhen is located in the Guangdong province in China and borders Hong Kong. In 1979, Shenzhen gained prefecture status, allowing it to be directly governed by the province. This paved the way for the 1980 promotion to China's first "special economic zone (SEZ)." SEZ status allows a province to have different economic laws than are typical for the country. As a result, Shenzhen has become a thriving economic hub. **AS**

English Language Coach

Alienation Students who are struggling to grasp the English language may respond to Mo's feelings of alienation. Discuss the parts of Mo's story that ring true for them. Encourage students to note how they've overcome their own challenges. **EL**

Differentiated Instruction

Charting the Details Learning disabled students may struggle to follow Mo's approach to her job search. Instruct students to create a flow chart that follows Mo's progress. Have students start with her leaving her home in Matou, and then add details as they read. **BL**

Academic Standards

Additional Support activities on pp. 1030 and 1031 cover the following standards:

Skills Practice: **9.2** Develop strategies such as...making predictions...

English Language Coach: **9.2** Develop [reading] strategies...

Differentiated Instruction: **9.3.6** Analyze and trace an author's development of time and sequence...

Informational Text

TIME

Teach

R1 Reading Strategy

Responding to Events The author includes the detail (on page 1033) that Mo's nightgown has a teddy bear on it. **Ask:** How do you think this detail is intended to help you to relate to Mo? *(Students may say that the teddy bear reinforces that Mo is young and makes her seem vulnerable, eliciting sympathy from the reader. Students may also note that this detail reminds them that Mo is near their own age.)* OL

she was little she'd once refused to go to school for a whole year.

In the afternoon, Mo took a walk through the fields, showing off the rosebush and the two geraniums she had planted when she was a student. Ever since she could remember, Mo said, she had been told that she lived in one of the world's most beautiful places. Not having ever seen other places, she had been skeptical. But the grandeur of the landscape was unmistakable. The expanse of limestone hills and rice fields made me wonder if she would feel bereft when she left it behind.

Now it was time to leave. I expected an emotional farewell. Instead, Mo simply told her parents that she was leaving, tousled her young niece's hair, and walked toward the road without looking back.

The Job Search

The local Shenzhen bus dropped us off close to the center of downtown. The buildings were more than 20 stories high. When an alley plastered with signs for boardinghouses came into view, I heaved a sigh of relief. The neighborhood looked promising: crowded and poor, but not seedy. Mo's eyes were fixed on the ground. There were people all around, but Mo didn't ask anyone for advice. Once or twice I asked her where she was going: she said she didn't know. Eventually we wound up where we had begun. Mo slipped into the first boardinghouse we'd seen and emerged a few minutes later with her first smile of the day. She'd found a room. It was just big enough to hold a single bed, an electric fan, and a plastic basin for washing clothes. It looked safe. It cost $3 a night.

After lunch, Mo started to look for work. We walked all afternoon along wide roads lined with skyscrapers. I recognized them as luxury apartments, and could tell that we wouldn't find factories in this neighborhood. But Mo couldn't discern this, and I reminded myself that people aren't born with an understanding of how cities work.

> "People aren't born with an understanding of how cities work."

Even here, though, Shenzhen revealed itself as a city thriving on migrant labor. At one intersection, we came across a bulletin board full of job announcements, mostly for hotel workers and security guards. The salaries were high—up to $200 per month—and most employers wanted applicants under the age of 30. While Mo studied the board, a couple of men walked up and offered unsolicited advice. "Don't believe these ads," they told her. "They're fakes. They trick you into paying deposits, and then they disappear."

That night, Mo washed one of her three sets of clothes and hung them in my room to dry—hers was too small. "Tomorrow," she said, spreading a Shenzhen map on my bed, "we'll go to Longhua." Earlier this year, a woman from her village had come home and said that she'd worked in a factory in this industrial, Shenzhen satellite town, but that was all Mo knew. "I think Longhua has a lot of

INTO THE URBAN JUNGLE
After arriving in Shenzhen, Mo wandered its streets seeking a cheap but safe place to live.

MARK LEONG/REDUX

Additional Support

Skills Practice

WRITING: Connecting Suggest that students connect with Mo's adventure by creating one of their own. Have students write a story about visiting a city in search of a job. Have students include specific details, such as:

- What kind of job are you pursuing?
- Why are you looking in this city?
- How will you get there and where will you stay?
- What kind of resources will you have? Money? Clothes?
- How would you feel on this journey?

Invite students to share their stories with the class. OL

factories," said Mo, "but I guess they don't put them on the map." She was wearing a nightgown with a teddy bear on it, and she R1 looked exhausted and very young.

The next morning, Mo got on the wrong bus and found herself heading in the opposite direction from Longhua. She had wasted a 3-yuan fare, about 40¢. We crossed the street, paid another fare, and Mo spent the hour-long ride with her head in her hands, feeling carsick. At the Longhua stop, Mo squatted on the sidewalk for nearly half an hour. Behind her was a giant sign for the Star River Talent Market, an employment agency. For a long R2 time she seemed not to see it.

The Star River office had a giant bulletin board cluttered with hand-painted and computer-printed job listings. Mo wrote down the address of a factory looking for "ordinary workers," and we tried to find it. The search for the Meiyu Electric Works ate up the rest of the day. First we walked, passing factory upon factory with signs on their doors advertising vacancies. Then we took a bus in the wrong direction. We reached Meiyu four hours later on motorcycle taxis. By the time we arrived, the job Mo wanted had been filled.

> "I thought it would be smaller and the factories would be easier to find. It's a bad place."
>
> —MO YUNXIU, 17-year-old migrant worker

Looking for the bus stop to get back to Shenzhen, Mo got lost again. Eventually, in desperation, she overcame her aversion to asking directions, and we boarded our last bus of the day. By then Mo had spent more than $2 on bus fares. She hadn't had lunch. "Longhua isn't what I'd expected," she said. "I thought it would be smaller and the factories would be easier to find. It's a bad place." Tomorrow, she said, she would stay closer to her base. "There was a moment today," she whispered, "when I didn't think I'd find my way back."

That night, I left Mo and went to find an Internet café. When I called the boardinghouse to say I was on my way back, Mo sounded giddy: "Can I tell you something? While you were out, I found a job." The next morning, she bounced in her chair as she related the story. On the bus back from Longhua, she had spotted a restaurant with a "Help Wanted" sign in the window. Later, she retraced the route, found the restaurant, and waited an hour for the manager. He offered her a waitressing job on the spot. The salary was only 500 yuan, or $60, a month, but the job came with free room and board. "I was so happy last night," said Mo, "I thought I was going to die."

JOB SEARCH
Mo visited an employment agency, took a motorcycle taxi to a factory, and got lost on buses.

MARK LEONG/REDUX

Working Girl

I walked with her to the restaurant, which was on a bustling, tree-lined street. While Mo went inside to put down a 260-yuan ($30) deposit for her uniform, I noticed that the restaurant was open 24 hours a day. There were grandparents playing with babies right outside, and the neighborhood seemed safe. A cab driver said the restaurant was known for 24-hour dim sum, a brunch or light meal.

Mo emerged a few hours later with a shiny tag stamped with her employee number—and an enormous smile. That afternoon, we shopped for necessities. Mo weighed each purchase heavily. She bought a ceramic mug for 3 yuan instead of a 5-yuan plastic mug with a cartoon character.

Informational Text
TIME

Teach

R2 Reading Strategy

Responding to Events
Ask: Why do you think that Mo doesn't see the Star River Talent Market sign? *(Students may say that Mo is too carsick, frightened, or overwhelmed to see what's going on around her.)* OL

Reading in the Real World

Career Ask students how Mo's story might inspire them to approach their own career goals. Have students work in groups and use the Internet or the library to research different career paths. Have groups research options, such as vocational schools, two- and four-year colleges, and co-op education. Have the groups present their results to the class, including an assessment of the advantages and drawbacks of their paths. OL

Academic Standards
Additional Support activities on pp. 1032 and 1033 cover the following standards:

Skills Practice: **9.5.1** Write...narratives or short stories that describe a sequence of events and communicate the significance of the events to the audience...

Reading in the Real World: **9.5.9** Write or deliver a research report that has been developed using a systematic research process...

Informational Text

TIME

Teach

BI Big Idea

Journeys Ask: What is the result of Mo's journey? *(She gets a job as a waitress but doesn't get paid. She plans to go home.)* **OL**

Assess

1. Answers will vary. Some will think it was a good choice.
2. (a) Mo saw the sign for the job from the bus. She went back and applied. (b) She is determined and resourceful.
3. (a) She never asked for directions. (b) She could have learned more about the layout of the city.
4. (a) She still had not been paid. (b) She did not know how to stand up for herself.
5. (a) She has some preconceptions about how they are supposed to behave. (b) Some may feel the author made Mo sound naïve. Others may feel she was objective.

After buying a towel to use as a blanket (22 yuan), she decided she could live without a pillow. A blue plastic bowl to wash her clothes cost 4 yuan—twice as much as it would have been at home, she said. Her one extravagance was a fork. It cost more than a pair of chopsticks, but for some reason she wanted it badly. Her bill for the day came to $5—the most money Mo had ever spent.

After her first day at the restaurant, Mo and I parted ways. A week later, I returned to watch her on the job. She was working up to 11 hours a day, seven days a week. Her feet were sore from standing in the flimsy cloth shoes she had to wear with her uniform; her wrists ached from carrying heavy trays. The older waitresses didn't talk to her except to order her around. She was tired, but it wasn't serious, she said.

As the weeks wore on, her stamina grew but her enthusiasm dimmed. After a solid month of work, she still hadn't received a cent of her salary. She'd decided she wanted to work elsewhere, or just head back to Yangshuo. But, to prevent her leaving, her boss wouldn't pay her and refused to refund the 260-yuan deposit she'd paid him for her uniform. She had no contract. She was trapped.

LANDING ON HER FEET
After only two days of searching, Mo found a job—waitressing in a 24-hour dim-sum restaurant.

MARK LEONG/REDUX

Just before the end of her second month, we met again. I was shocked at how different Mo looked. Her smile was just as broad, but the ruddiness in her cheeks had gone. She was so pale that her skin had an almost greenish cast. She was now on the night shift, walking the empty streets with a friend after she finished work at 2:30 a.m., then sleeping during the day. But she had a new plan. Her boss—who still had yet to pay her salary—told her he wasn't letting her quit because she was a hard worker. Flattered, Mo reckoned she could take it a little longer until he found someone to replace her. With her usual optimism, she assured me the money would come eventually and that for now she was fine without it. As soon as she was paid, she'd decided, she would head home. **BI**

No Place Like Home

"I've figured it out," she told me exuberantly. "I'll go back to Yangshuo and work two jobs. At night I'll waitress at a café and practice speaking English with the customers, and during the day I'll try to find people to let me be their tour guide." The money, she admitted, might not be as good but at least she would be near her family. She could always return to Shenzhen if she changed her mind, knowing now that she could make it on her own. "Shenzhen was fine," she said, "but home will be better."

—Updated 2005, from TIME Asia, July 26/August 2, 2004

RESPONDING AND THINKING CRITICALLY

Respond

1. How do you feel about the journalist Susan Jakes's decision to follow Mo and observe her life?

Recall and Interpret

2. (a)How did Mo get the job at the restaurant? (b)What does this say about her character?
3. (a)Why did Mo get lost so often? (b)How might she have better prepared for her journey?
4. (a)What happened at Mo's job after two months? (b)Why do you think she reacted the way she did?

Analyze and Evaluate

5. (a)What preconceptions did the writer have about migrant workers? (b)Do you think her preconceptions of migrants interfered with her portrayal of Mo? Why or why not?
6. What details does the writer use to illustrate Mo's youthful and energetic demeanor?

Connect

7. Jakes wrote that Mo "believed Shenzhen had the power to change her life." Based on the outcome of the article, what do you think Mo may have learned from her journey?

6. She describes Mo's reaction to getting a job as "giddy." She writes that Mo considered buying a "plastic mug with a cartoon character."
7. She may have learned that when you set out to do something, there are a number of unexpected factors that may get in the way of success. She learned the importance of family and that city life may not be for everyone.

For additional assessment, see Selection and Unit Assessments, pp. 175–176.

BEFORE YOU READ

Over Hill and Under Hill from *The Hobbit*

MEET J. R. R. TOLKIEN

The Lord of the Rings is probably the most well-known fantasy story ever written and undoubtedly the most important. Even before the award-winning movies were produced, the popular trilogy sold millions of copies. *The Lord of the Rings* trilogy, however, is a sequel to one of J. R. R. Tolkien's most successful works, *The Hobbit*. Indeed, *The Hobbit* is the starting place for the fantasy world that has been embraced by readers, viewers, and video gamers worldwide.

A Young Orphan Born in South Africa, Tolkien returned to his parents' birthplace, England, when he was three and a half years old. Tolkien was four when his father died. His mother died a few years later, and a Roman Catholic priest became Tolkien's guardian.

As a young student, Tolkien developed a passion for languages. He studied Latin and Greek and taught himself Welsh, Old and Middle English, Old Norse, Gothic, and Finnish. Eventually, Tolkien became a professor of language and literature at Oxford University. His knowledge and love of languages would help to inspire all of his work. Drawing upon his familiarity with various Northern European and other ancient literatures, he invented entire languages and used them in his stories. In fact, he created a complete world of his own, with a distinctive history and a variety of civilizations.

A Hobbit Is Born The story of how *The Hobbit* was born is well known to Tolkien fans. One hot summer day while Tolkien was correcting papers at Oxford, his mind began to wander. Soon, he was scribbling in an examination book. He wrote: "In a hole in the ground there lived a hobbit." In Tolkien's imagination, the hobbit was a little creature, reminiscent of a rustic human being, but much smaller, and very fond of his or her comforts and meals.

"I always in writing start with a name. Give me a name and it produces a story, not the other way about normally."

—J. R. R. Tolkien

Fame and Fortune The name *hobbit* went on to inspire first, the imaginary creature, and later, the adventures. Tolkien developed his ideas about the hobbit into a book, which he published in 1937. At first it was popular among children, but Tolkien insisted that children were not the intended audience. Seventeen years later, he published the first volume of *The Lord of the Rings.* By the late 1960s, his fame was widespread. Tolkien fan clubs sprang up all over America and elsewhere.

Tolkien was also an important scholar and translator. But he acknowledged that he would be remembered most of all as the author of *The Lord of the Rings.*

J. R. R. Tolkien was born in 1892 and died in 1973.

LiteratureOnline **Author Search** For more about J. R. R. Tolkien, go to www.glencoe.com.

BEFORE YOU READ

Focus

BELLRINGER

Bellringer Options
Daily Language Practice Transparency 86
Or **ask:** If you could live in a fictional world, where would you live? Prompt students to consider multiple fictional settings, such as the *Star Wars* and Harry Potter universes. Have students discuss what the allure is of these places and why they chose their particular setting.

Author Search To expand students' appreciation of J. R. R. Tolkien, have them access the Web site for additional information and resources.

Selection Skills

Over Hill and Under Hill

Literary Elements
- Motif (SE pp. 1036, 1038, 1040–1044, 1046)
- Narrator (SE p. 1046)
- Character (TWE p. 1040)

Reading Skills
- Comparing and Contrasting Characters (SE pp. 1036, 1038–1039, 1042, 1046)

Vocabulary Skills
- Context Clues (SE pp. 1036, 1046)
- Academic Vocabulary (SE p. 1046)

Listening/Speaking/Viewing Skills
- Analyzing Art (SE p. 1039)
- Visual Literacy (SE p. 1045)
- Class Discussion (TWE p. 1040)

Writing Skills/Grammar
- Respond to Voice (SE p. 1047)
- Gerunds (SE p. 1047)
- Parentheses (TWE p. 1038)
- Rewriting (TWE p. 1044)

BEFORE YOU READ

Focus

Summary

Bilbo the hobbit is traveling with Gandalf the wizard and some dwarves on a quest to retrieve treasure from a dragon. While sheltering in a mountain cave from a massive storm, Bilbo and company are captured by goblins. Gandalf escapes capture and rescues the company, killing the Great Goblin in the process. As they retreat through the goblin tunnels, the company is overtaken by more goblins. Bilbo falls, hits his head, and blacks out.

V Vocabulary

Vocabulary File Say: Add these words and definitions to your vocabulary file. For each word, include a sentence that gives you an example of how to use the word. **OL** Students with English language needs should include the pronunciations of these words in their files. **EL**

Literary Elements Have students access the Web site to improve their understanding of motif.

LITERATURE PREVIEW

Connecting to the Story

You are about to enter a world inhabited by dwarves, wizards, goblins, and other fantastic creatures. Before you read this excerpt from *The Hobbit,* think about the following questions:

- Why do you think artists create fantastical, imaginary worlds?
- How do you deal with hardships and other obstacles?

Building Background

Bilbo Baggins is a hobbit: a small, human-like creature who lives in a hobbit hole. One day, Gandalf, a wise old wizard, asks Bilbo to join him and thirteen dwarves on a great adventure to reclaim the dwarves' treasure. Bilbo, an unlikely hero, does not want to leave his comfortable home, but he sets out with the group on a long journey that involves encounters with trolls, giants, goblins, elves, wargs, and even humans. In this excerpt, which occurs early in the novel, the group has just left Elrond, the leader of the elves at Rivendell. Elrond has given the group ponies and helpful advice.

Setting Purposes for Reading

Big Idea Journeys

As you read, think about how a journey can be an adventure into the unknown, as well as a kind of test.

Literary Element Motif

A **motif** is a significant word, phrase, image, idea, or other element repeated throughout a literary work and related to the theme. Common motifs in hero stories include good and evil, light and darkness, and awareness and deception. As you read the excerpt from *The Hobbit,* note how each character and place is described. Are any characters or places associated with light or darkness? Good or evil?

- See Literary Terms Handbook, p. R11.

LiteratureOnline Interactive Literary Elements Handbook To review or learn more about the literary elements, go to www.glencoe.com.

READING PREVIEW

Reading Strategy Comparing and Contrasting Characters

When you **compare and contrast characters,** you look for similarities and differences in the way characters think, look, and act. You even look for similarities and differences in the way that characters are presented. For example, you can compare and contrast main characters that are described in great detail with minor characters that are described in only a few words.

Reading Tip: Making a Chart As you read, use a chart to record the names of main characters and minor characters.

Main Characters	Minor Characters
Gandalf	Elrond

Vocabulary

uncanny (un kan′ ē) *adj.* not normal or natural; seemingly supernatural in origin; p. 1037 *Ruth could predict the outcome of every football game with uncanny precision.*

paraphernalia (par′ ə fər nāl′ yə) *n.* personal items or equipment; p. 1040 *Amanda laid out all her hiking and climbing paraphernalia before deciding what to pack for the expedition.*

ingenious (in jēn′ yəs) *adj.* especially clever, inventive, or original; p. 1041 *His solution to their problem was ingenious.*

horde (hôrd) *n.* crowd, throng, or swarm; p. 1044 *The horde of angry Vikings swept through the English town, pillaging and destroying houses.*

Vocabulary Tip: Context Clues Context clues are words, phrases, and sentences that surround an unfamiliar word and hint at its meaning. Context clues can take many forms, including synonyms, antonyms, restatements, definitions, and examples.

INDIANA ACADEMIC STANDARDS (pages 1036-1047)

9.3.7 Recognize and understand...various literary devices, including...imagery...

9.3.4 Determine characters' traits...

9.5.3 Write expository compositions...

9.3.13 Explain how voice...and the choice of narrator affect...tone...

Selection Resources

Print Materials

- Unit 5 Resources (Fast File), pp. 32–34
- Leveled Vocabulary Development, p. 66
- Selection and Unit Assessments, pp. 175–176
- Selection Quick Checks, p. 88

Transparencies

- Bellringer Options Transparencies: Daily Language Practice Transparency 86
- Literary Elements Transparency 19

Technology

- TeacherWorks Plus™ CD-ROM
- StudentWorks Plus™ CD-ROM
- Presentation Plus!™ CD-ROM
- Literature Online, glencoe.com
- Online Student Edition, mhln.com
- Exam*View*® Assessment Suite CD-ROM
- Vocabulary PuzzleMaker CD-ROM
- Listening Library, disc 2 track 28

Over Hill and Under Hill

from The Hobbit

J. R. R. Tolkien

There were many paths that led up into those mountains, and many passes over them. But most of the paths were cheats and deceptions and led nowhere or to bad ends; and most of the passes were infested by evil things and dreadful dangers. The dwarves and the hobbit, helped by the wise advice of Elrond and the knowledge and memory of Gandalf, took the right road to the right pass.

Long days after they had climbed out of the valley and left the Last Homely House[1] miles behind, they were still going up and up and up. It was a hard path and a dangerous path, a crooked way and a lonely and a long. Now they could look back over the lands they had left, laid out behind them far below. Far, far away in the West, where things were blue and faint, Bilbo knew there lay his own country of safe and comfortable things, and his little hobbit-hole. He shivered. It was getting bitter cold up here, and the wind came shrill among the rocks. Boulders, too, at times came galloping down the mountain-sides, let loose by mid-day sun upon the snow, and passed among them (which was lucky), or over their heads (which was alarming). The nights were comfortless and chill, and they did not dare to sing or talk too loud, for the echoes were **uncanny,** and the silence seemed to dislike being broken—except by the noise of water and the wail of wind and the crack of stone.

"The summer is getting on down below," thought Bilbo, "and haymaking is going on and picnics. They will be harvesting and

1. The *Last Homely House* is the name of Elrond's home in Rivendell.

Big Idea Journeys *How would you describe this journey?* **BI**

Vocabulary

uncanny (un kan′ ē) *adj.* not normal or natural; seemingly supernatural in origin

Teach

BI Big Idea

Journeys **Answer:** *The journey is long, dangerous, and confusing. It is guided by Gandalf's memory and Elrond's advice.*

Ask: Do you think the journey will be successful? *(Students may feel that the ominous imagery bodes ill for the journey. Others will feel that with Gandalf and Elrond aiding the company, they will succeed.)* **OL**

CheckPoint

Use the CheckPoint questions on Presentation Plus! to monitor students' comprehension. These questions can be used with interactive response keypads for immediate student feedback.

Readability Scores

Dale-Chall: 7.3

DRP: 59

Lexile: 1080

English Language Coach

Reading Aloud English language learners may find the dense language difficult to follow. Assign one student to read each paragraph aloud. Pause periodically to discuss any questions students may have and to clarify any ambiguous references. **EL**

Differentiated Instruction

Breaking Down a Passage Less-proficient readers may benefit from breaking the passage into smaller, discrete sections. As students finish each section, have students paraphrase it. As a class, have students compare their paraphrases to make sure they don't miss any important details. **BL**

Academic Standards

Additional Support activities on p. 1037 cover the following standards:

English Language Coach: **9.7** [Respond] to oral communication [with] careful listening and evaluation of content…

Differentiated Instruction: **9.2.8** Make reasonable statements and draw conclusions about a text, supporting them with accurate examples.

Teach

R1 Reading Strategy

Comparing and Contrasting Characters **Answer:** *Gandalf is aware of the dangers and difficulties that lie ahead. He has traveled through the Wild and seen its evil firsthand. The dwarves have not traveled that way for a long time. Both Bilbo and the dwarves are more optimistic and think that the journey might be easy.* OL

L Literary Element

Motif **Answer:** *The darkness and the storm are frightening and foreboding. The storm, which is compared to war, causes the rocks to shiver. The darkness threatens to overwhelm the company. Even the lightning only illuminates the vicious giants below.* OL

R2 Reading Strategy

Comparing and Contrasting Characters **Ask:** How do the giants react to the storm as compared to Bilbo and his friends? *(The storm makes Bilbo and his friends terrified and miserable. The giants are laughing.)* OL

blackberrying, before we even begin to go down the other side at this rate." And the others were thinking equally gloomy thoughts, although when they had said good-bye to Elrond in the high hope of a midsummer morning, they had spoken gaily of the passage of the mountains, and of riding swift across the lands beyond. They had thought of coming to the secret door in the Lonely Mountain,[2] perhaps that very next first moon of Autumn—"and perhaps it will be Durin's Day"[3] they had said. Only Gandalf had shaken his head and said nothing. Dwarves had not passed that way for many years, but Gandalf had, and he knew how evil and danger had grown and thriven[4] in the Wild, since the dragons had driven men from the lands, and the goblins had spread in secret after the battle of the Mines of Moria.[5] Even the good plans of wise wizards like Gandalf and of good friends like Elrond go astray sometimes when you are off on dangerous adventures over the Edge of the Wild; and Gandalf was a wise enough wizard to know it. R1

He knew that something unexpected might happen, and he hardly dared to hope that they would pass without fearful adventure over those great tall mountains with lonely peaks and valleys where no king ruled. They did not. All was well, until one day they met a thunderstorm—more than a thunderstorm, a thunder-battle. You know how terrific a really big thunderstorm can be down in the land and in a river-valley; especially at times when two great thunderstorms meet and clash. More terrible still are thunder and lightning in the mountains at night, when storms come up from East and West and make war. The lightning splinters on the peaks, and rocks shiver, and great crashes split the air and go rolling and tumbling into every cave and hollow; and the darkness is filled with overwhelming noise and sudden light. L

Bilbo had never seen or imagined anything of the kind. They were high up in a narrow place, with a dreadful fall into a dim valley at one side of them. There they were sheltering under a hanging rock for the night, and he lay beneath a blanket and shook from head to toe. When he peeped out in the lightning-flashes, he saw that across the valley the stone-giants were out, and were hurling rocks at one another for a game, and catching them, and tossing them down into the darkness where they smashed among the trees far below, or splintered into little bits with a bang. Then came a wind and a rain, and the wind whipped the rain and the hail about in every direction, so that an overhanging rock was no protection at all. Soon they were getting drenched and their ponies were standing with their heads down and their tails between their legs, and some of them were whinnying with fright. They could hear the giants guffawing[6] and shouting all over the mountainsides. R2

"This won't do at all!" said Thorin, "If we don't get blown off, or drowned, or struck by lightning, we shall be picked up by some giant and kicked sky-high for a football."

"Well, if you know of anywhere better, take us there!" said Gandalf, who was feeling very grumpy, and was far from happy about the giants himself.

The end of their argument was that they sent Fili and Kili to look for a better shelter. They had very sharp eyes, and being the youngest of the dwarves by some fifty years they usually got these sort of jobs (when everybody could see that it was absolutely no use sending Bilbo). There is nothing like looking, if you want to find something (or so Thorin said to the young dwarves). You

2. *Lonely Mountain* is the dwarves' ultimate destination.
3. *Durin's Day* is the dwarf new year.
4. *Thriven* means "prospered" or "increased."
5. The battle at the *Mines of Moria* occurred before *The Hobbit* begins and involved the ancestors of Thorin, the dwarf who is leading the journey described here.
6. *Guffawing* means "laughing loudly."

Reading Strategy Comparing and Contrasting Characters *How does Gandalf's knowledge of what lies ahead compare with Bilbo's and the dwarves' knowledge?* R1

Literary Element Motif *How does this description of the dark thunderstorm help illustrate the danger that surrounds Bilbo and his friends?* L

Additional Support

Academic Standards

The Additional Support activity on p. 1038 covers the following standard:

Skills Practice: **9.6.1** Identify and correctly use…the mechanics of punctuation…

Skills Practice

WRITING: Parentheses Point out that Tolkien uses parentheses in his writing.

Ask: What is the proper use of parentheses?

Write the following rules on the board:

- Parentheses set off supplemental material.
- If the parentheses contain a sentence, the sentence does not need to be capitalized and does not need a period.
- If the parentheses contain a sentence that requires a question mark or exclamation point, the punctuation goes inside the parentheses.

Mountain Landscape with Firtrees in the Torrent, after 1591. Joos de Momper. Oil on oak, 53 × 71.5 cm. Collection of Gemäldegalerie, Alte Meister, Dresden, Germany.

Viewing the Art: How does the journey pictured here compare with the journey Bilbo, Gandalf, and the dwarves are on? 

certainly usually find something, if you look, but it is not always quite the something you were after. So it proved on this occasion. **BI**

Soon Fili and Kili came crawling back, holding on to the rocks in the wind. "We have found a dry cave," they said, "not far round the next corner; and ponies and all could get inside."

"Have you *thoroughly* explored it?" said the wizard, who knew that caves up in the mountains were seldom unoccupied.

"Yes, yes!" they said, though everybody knew they could not have been long about it; they had come back too quick. "It isn't all that big, and it does not go far back."

That, of course, is the dangerous part about caves: you don't know how far they go back, sometimes, or where a passage behind may lead to, or what is waiting for you inside. But now Fili and Kili's news seemed good enough. So they all got up and prepared to move. The wind was howling and the thunder still growling, and they had a business getting themselves and their ponies along. Still it was not very far to go, and before long they came to a big rock standing out into the path. If you stepped behind, you found a low arch in the side of the mountain. There was just room to get the ponies through with a squeeze, when they had been unpacked and unsaddled. As they passed under the arch, it was good to hear the wind and the rain outside instead of all about them, and to feel safe from the giants

Reading Strategy Comparing and Contrasting Characters *Do either Fili or Kili exhibit character traits that set them apart from each other or the other dwarves? Explain.* **R3**

Teach

BI Big Idea

Journeys Ask: How does the comment "So it proved on this occasion" foreshadow the next part of the journey? *(Students may say that the line foreshadows that the journey is about to take an unexpected turn.)* **OL**

R3 Reading Strategy

Comparing and Contrasting Characters Answer: *Fili and Kili are the youngest dwarves. Neither exhibits any trait that would distinguish him from the other or from the other dwarves.* **Ask:** How are Fili and Kili different from Gandalf? *(Students may say that Fili and Kili are dwarves, whereas Gandalf is a wizard. Fili and Kili are young and seem eager to go to the cave, whereas Gandalf is older and more cautious about entering the cave.)* **OL**

Viewing the Art

Answer: *The journey appears equally long and dangerous, but the weather is clear in the painting.*

Belgian painter Joos de Momper (1564–1635) was a pioneer in landscape painting. His work is marked by the use of dark colors in the foreground and blue or green for mountains and background. **AS**

Have students go through the selection and point out examples for each rule. Invite students to write one example of each rule. Have students compare their examples for accuracy. **OL**

Building Reading Fluency

Reading Aloud To keep students focused on the text, assign students to read each of the characters. Have the remaining students take turns reading the part of the narrator. Encourage students to vary their tone and volume to reflect the emotions of the characters and the events taking place. **BL**

Academic Standards

The Additional Support activity on p. 1039 covers the following standard:

Building Reading Fluency: **9.7.6** Analyze the occasion and the interests of the audience and choose effective verbal...techniques (including voice...) for presentations.

Teach

L1 Literary Element

Motif Answer: *Light is equated with knowledge. Gandalf uses his wand to light the cave. The light allows the company to investigate the cave and to see their surroundings.* OL

BI1 Big Idea

Journeys Ask: How do you think being captured by goblins will affect Bilbo's journey? *(Students may feel that he will be sidetracked but not deterred from his ultimate goal. Others may point out that overcoming such a big challenge will help Bilbo to grow and succeed on many levels.)* OL

L2 Literary Element

Motif Answer: *The image of lightning or light is repeated here.* **Ask:** How does this reinforce the motif of good versus evil? *(Students may say that the lightning flash allows Gandalf to escape the goblins, allowing good to triumph over evil.)* OL

and their rocks. But the wizard was taking no risks. He lit up his wand—as he did that day in Bilbo's dining-room that seemed so long ago, if you remember—and by its light they explored the cave from end to end.

It seemed quite a fair size, but not too large and mysterious. It had a dry floor and some comfortable nooks.[7] At one end there was room for the ponies; and there they stood (mighty glad of the change) steaming, and champing in their nosebags. Oin and Gloin wanted to light a fire at the door to dry their clothes, but Gandalf would not hear of it. So they spread out their wet things on the floor, and got dry ones out of their bundles; then they made their blankets comfortable, got out their pipes and blew smoke rings, which Gandalf turned into different colors and set dancing up by the roof to amuse them. They talked and talked, and forgot about the storm, and discussed what each would do with his share of the treasure (when they got it, which at the moment did not seem so impossible); and so they dropped off to sleep one by one. And that was the last time that they used the ponies, packages, baggages, tools, and paraphernalia that they had brought with them.

> "When he did sleep, he had very nasty dreams . . ."

It turned out a good thing that night that they had brought little Bilbo with them, after all. For, somehow, he could not go to sleep for a long while; and when he did sleep, he had very nasty dreams. He dreamed that a crack in the wall at the back of the cave got bigger and bigger, and opened wider and wider, and he was very afraid but could not call out or do anything but lie and look. Then he dreamed that the floor of the cave was giving way, and he was slipping—beginning to fall down, down, goodness knows where to.

At that he woke up with a horrible start, and found that part of his dream was true. A crack had opened at the back of the cave, and was already a wide passage. He was just in time to see the last of the ponies' tails disappearing into it. Of course he gave a very loud yell, as loud a yell as a hobbit can give, which is surprising for their size.

Out jumped the goblins, big goblins, great ugly-looking goblins, lots of goblins, before you could say *rocks and blocks*. There were six to each dwarf, at least, and two even for Bilbo; and they were all grabbed and carried through the crack, before you could say *tinder and flint*. But not Gandalf. Bilbo's yell had done that much good. It had wakened him up wide in a splintered second, and when goblins came to grab him, there was a terrific flash like lightning in the cave, a smell like gunpowder, and several of them fell dead. BI1

The crack closed with a snap, and Bilbo and the dwarves were on the wrong side of it! Where was Gandalf? Of that neither they nor the goblins had any idea, and the goblins did not wait to find out. They seized Bilbo and the dwarves and hurried them along. It was deep, deep, dark, such as only goblins that have taken to living in the heart of the mountains can see through. The passages there were crossed and tangled in all directions, but the goblins knew their way, as well as you do to the nearest post-office; and the way went down and down, and it was most horribly stuffy. The goblins were very rough, and pinched unmercifully, and chuckled and laughed in their horrible stony voices; and Bilbo was more unhappy even than when the troll had picked

7. *Nooks* are small areas of a room.

Literary Element Motif *How is the cave lit? What is the connection between light and awareness in this passage?* L1

Vocabulary

paraphernalia (par′ə fər nāl′ yə) *n.* personal items or equipment

Literary Element Motif *What image or motif is repeated here?* L2

Additional Support

Skills Practice

LITERARY ELEMENT: Character
Have students review their character charts. So far, they should have columns for Main and Minor characters. Have the class brainstorm column headings that would be useful additions to their charts, such as type of creature (elf, dwarf, etc.), physical characteristics, and good guy or bad guy. Make a list of the column headings that the class agrees on. Instruct students to add these columns to their charts and to update them as they continue to read. OL

him up by his toes. He wished again and again for his nice bright hobbit-hole. Not for the last time.

Now there came a glimmer of a red light before them. The goblins began to sing, or croak, keeping time with the flap of their flat feet on the stone, and shaking their prisoners as well.

Clap! Snap! the black crack!
Grip, grab! Pinch, nab!
And down down to Goblin-town
You go, my lad!

Clash, crash! Crush, smash!
Hammer and tongs! Knocker and gongs!
Pound, pound, far underground!
Ho, ho! my lad!

Swish, smack! Whip crack!
Batter and beat! Yammer and bleat![8]
Work, work! Nor dare to shirk,[9]
While Goblins quaff,[10] *and Goblins laugh,*
Round and round far underground
Below, my lad!

It sounded truly terrifying. The walls echoed to the *clap, snap!* and the *crush, smash!* and to the ugly laughter of their *ho, ho! my lad!* The general meaning of the song was only too plain; for now the goblins took out whips and whipped them with a *swish, smack!*, and set them running as fast as they could in front of them; and more than one of the dwarves were already yammering and bleating like anything, when they stumbled into a big cavern.

It was lit by a great red fire in the middle, and by torches along the walls, and it was full of goblins. They all laughed and stamped and clapped their hands, when the dwarves (with poor little Bilbo at the back and nearest to the whips) came running in, while the goblin-drivers whooped and cracked their whips behind. The ponies were already there huddled in a corner; and there were all the baggages and packages lying broken open, and being rummaged by goblins, and smelt by goblins, and fingered by goblins, and quarreled over by goblins.

I am afraid that was the last they ever saw of those excellent little ponies, including a jolly sturdy little white fellow that Elrond had lent to Gandalf, since his horse was not suitable for the mountain-paths. For goblins eat horses and ponies and donkeys (and other much more dreadful things), and they are always hungry. Just now, however, the prisoners were thinking only of themselves. The goblins chained their hands behind their backs and linked them all together in a line, and dragged them to the far end of the cavern with little Bilbo tugging at the end of the row.

There in the shadows on a large flat stone sat a tremendous goblin with a huge head, and armed goblins were standing round him carrying the axes and the bent swords that they use. Now goblins are cruel, wicked, and bad-hearted. They make no beautiful things, but they make many clever ones. They can tunnel and mine as well as any but the most skilled dwarves, when they take the trouble, though they are usually untidy and dirty. Hammers, axes, swords, daggers, pickaxes, tongs, and also instruments of torture, they make very well, or get other people to make to their design, prisoners and slaves that have to work till they die for want of air and light. It is not unlikely that they invented some of the machines that have since troubled the world, especially the **ingenious** devices for killing large numbers of people at once, for wheels and engines and explosions always delighted them, and also not working with their own hands more than they could help; but in those days and those wild parts they had not advanced (as it is

8. To *yammer* is to talk loudly on and on. To *bleat* is to cry out in complaint.
9. To *shirk* is to avoid responsibility for a task.
10. To *quaff* is to drink deeply.

Big Idea Journeys *Gandalf chose Bilbo to join this journey. Based on what you have read here, do you think it was a good choice? Explain.* **BI2**

Literary Element Motif *How does this light differ from Gandalf's light?* **L3**

Vocabulary

ingenious (in jēn′ yəs) *adj.* especially clever, inventive, or original

Teach

BI2 Big Idea

Journeys **Answer:** *Bilbo is a reluctant traveler. This is the second time he has wished for his hobbit-hole. At this point, students who are unfamiliar with the story may say Bilbo was a bad choice because his heart is not in the journey.* Point out that the narrator says this isn't the last time Bilbo wishes for his hobbit-hole. **Ask:** What does that foretell about the rest of his journey? *(Students may say that the journey will continue to be filled with danger and that Bilbo will remain a reluctant traveler.)* How does the foreshadowing of danger encourage the reader? *(By alerting the reader to further drama and adventure, Tolkien entices the reader to continue on.)* **OL**

L3 Literary Element

Motif **Answer:** *Gandalf's light is generally white or blue rather than red. His light defends or helps the travelers, while this light reveals the threatening goblins.* **OL**

Differentiated Instruction

Creating Fantasy Realms Advanced learners will benefit from the opportunity to express their creativity. Ask students to create their own fantasy realms using Tolkien's method of starting with a name. Have students first decide the names of the creatures and places about which they are going to write. Instruct students to fill in as many specific details as possible. Have students design and deliver a presentation for the class as if they were travel agents trying to convince the class to visit their worlds. Encourage students to include visual aids and sound effects. **AL**

Academic Standards

Additional Support activities on pp. 1040 and 1041 cover the following standards:

Skills Practice: **9.3** [Identify] story elements such as character…

Differentiated Instruction: **9.7.19** Deliver descriptive presentations…

Teach

L1 Literary Element

Motif **Answer:** *The goblins come secretly in the darkness and seize Bilbo and the dwarves. They live deep underground, where there is little air or light. They are associated with shadows; they need torches and a "great red fire" to light their world. The goblins represent evil and deception; they make instruments of torture, take joy in hurting others, capture people secretly, and enslave them.* **OL**

R1 Reading Strategy

Comparing and Contrasting Characters **Answer:** *Thorin is the leader of the dwarves. He is not a fully developed character, but he is presented in much greater detail than the other dwarves. Some of Thorin's inner thoughts are revealed by the narrator.* **OL**

R2 Reading Strategy

Comparing and Contrasting Characters **Answer:** *Gandalf knows what is going on; he takes action to protect the dwarves and to fight evil. The Great Goblin is unaware; even at the moment of his death, he does not know what is happening.* **OL**

called) so far. They did not hate dwarves especially, no more than they hated everybody and everything, and particularly the orderly and prosperous; in some parts wicked dwarves had even made alliances with them. But they had a special grudge against Thorin's people, because of the war which you have heard mentioned, but which does not come into this tale; and anyway goblins don't care who they catch, as long as it is done smart and secret, and the prisoners are not able to defend themselves.

"Who are these miserable persons?" said the Great Goblin.

"Dwarves, and this!" said one of the drivers, pulling at Bilbo's chain so that he fell forward onto his knees. "We found them sheltering in our Front Porch."

"What do you mean by it?" said the Great Goblin turning to Thorin. "Up to no good, I'll warrant![11] Spying on the private business of my people, I guess! Thieves, I shouldn't be surprised to learn! Murderers and friends of Elves, not unlikely! Come! What have you got to say?"

"Thorin the dwarf at your service!" he replied—it was merely a polite nothing. "Of the things which you suspect and imagine we had no idea at all. We sheltered from a storm in what seemed a convenient cave and unused; nothing was further from our thoughts than inconveniencing goblins in any way whatever." That was true enough!

"Um!" said the Great Goblin. "So you say! Might I ask what you were doing up in the mountains at all, and where you were coming from, and where you were going to? In fact I should like to know all about you. Not that it will do you much good, Thorin Oakenshield, I know too much about your folk already; but let's have the truth, or I will prepare something particularly uncomfortable for you!"

"We were on a journey to visit our relatives, our nephews and nieces, and first, second, and third cousins, and the other descendants of our grandfathers, who live on the East side of these truly hospitable mountains," said Thorin, not quite knowing what to say all at once in a moment, when obviously the exact truth would not do at all.

"He is a liar, O truly tremendous one!" said one of the drivers. "Several of our people were struck by lightning in the cave, when we invited these creatures to come below; and they are as dead as stones. Also he has not explained this!" He held out the sword which Thorin had worn, the sword which came from the Trolls' lair.[12]

The Great Goblin gave a truly awful howl of rage when he looked at it, and all his soldiers gnashed their teeth, clashed their shields, and stamped. They knew the sword at once. It had killed hundreds of goblins in its time, when the fair elves of Gondolin hunted them in the hills or did battle before their walls. They had called it Orcrist, Goblin-cleaver, but the goblins called it simply Biter. They hated it and hated worse any one that carried it.

"Murderers and elf-friends!" the Great Goblin shouted. "Slash them! Beat them! Bite them! Gnash them! Take them away to dark holes full of snakes, and never let them see the light again!" He was in such a rage that he jumped off his seat and himself rushed at Thorin with his mouth open.

Just at that moment all the lights in the cavern went out, and the great fire went off poof! into a tower of blue glowing smoke, right up to the roof, that scattered piercing white sparks all among the goblins.

11. Here, *warrant* means "declare."

12. In an earlier chapter, hungry trolls capture the group, but Gandalf tricks the trolls, and they are turned to stone. Gandalf and Thorin take their magic swords.

Literary Element Motif *In what ways are the goblins associated with darkness? How do the goblins represent deception and evil?* **L1**

Reading Strategy Comparing and Contrasting Characters *How is Thorin presented differently from the other dwarves?* **R1**

Reading Strategy Comparing and Contrasting Characters *How does the leader of the goblins compare with Gandalf?* **R2**

Additional Support

Skills Practice

LISTENING, SPEAKING, AND VIEWING: Class Discussion Engage students in a class discussion about which characters they identify with and why. Have students cite specific examples from the story. Invite students to write a journal entry from the point of view of their favorite character. Instruct students to consider and include sensory details, such as what the caves smell like and whether they are cold and achy from the rain. Have students include an internal monologue of how the character feels about the events that are unfolding. Are they frightened? Excited? Instruct students to be descriptive and specific. **OL**

The Posillipo Cave at Naples. Hubert Robert. Oil on canvas. Collection of Musée Jeanne d'Aboville, La Fere, France.

quiet; and before Bilbo understood what had happened he was trotting along again, as fast as he could trot, at the end of the line, down more dark passages with the yells of the goblin-hall growing fainter behind him. A pale light was leading them on.

"Quicker, quicker!" said the voice. "The torches will soon be relit."

"Half a minute!" said Dori, who was at the back next to Bilbo, and a decent fellow. He made the hobbit scramble on his shoulders as best he could with his tied hands, and then off they all went at a run, with a clink-clink of chains, and many a stumble, since they had no hands to steady themselves with. Not for a long while did they stop, and by that time they must have been right down in the very mountain's heart.

Then Gandalf lit up his wand. Of course it was Gandalf; but just then they were too busy to ask how he got there. He took out his sword again, and again it flashed in the dark by itself. It burned with a rage that made it gleam if goblins were about; now it was bright as blue flame for delight in the killing of the great lord of the cave. It made no trouble whatever of cutting through the goblin-chains and setting all the prisoners free as quickly as possible. This sword's name was Glamdring the Foe-hammer, if you remember.[13] The goblins just called it Beater, and hated it worse than Biter if possible. Orcrist, too, had been saved; for Gandalf had brought it along as well, snatching it from one of the terrified

The yells and yammering, croaking, jibbering and jabbering; howls, growls and curses; shrieking and skriking, that followed were beyond description. Several hundred wild cats and wolves being roasted slowly alive together would not have compared with it. The sparks were burning holes in the goblins, and the smoke that now fell from the roof made the air too thick for even their eyes to see through. Soon they were falling over one another and rolling in heaps on the floor, biting and kicking and fighting as if they had all gone mad.

Suddenly a sword flashed in its own light. Bilbo saw it go right through the Great Goblin as he stood dumbfounded in the middle of his rage. He fell dead, and the goblin soldiers fled before the sword shrieking into the darkness.

The sword went back into its sheath. "Follow me quick!" said a voice fierce and

13. Elrond explains the history of *Glamdring* to Gandalf in a previous chapter.

Literary Element Motif *How does this image relate to the group's dangerous position?* **L2**

Teach

L2 Literary Element

Motif Answer: *The companions are following a pale light, but they are still surrounded by darkness. There is hope of escape from the goblins, but they are not yet safe.* **OL**

Differentiated Instruction

Three-Dimensional Representation Spatial learners may have an easier time relating to the events if they can see them unfold. Split the story into sections: the mountainside, the cave, the Great Goblin's room, and the underground passages. Have each group design a three-dimensional representation of one section. Instruct students to include some representation of the characters. Students can use anything from cardboard cutouts to game pieces from a board game. Tell students to consider the mood their pieces will create. **BL**

Academic Standards

Additional Support activities on pp. 1042 and 1043 cover the following standards:

Skills Practice: **9.5.1** Write...narratives...that describe with specific details the sights, sounds, and smells of a scene and the specific actions, movements, gestures, and feelings of the characters;...use interior monologue to show the character's feelings.

Differentiated Instruction: **9.3** [Identify] story elements such as character,...plot, and setting...

Teach

L Literary Element

Motif Answer: *Gandalf "thought of most things"; he knows what to do to protect and save the dwarves. He also knows enough to save the sword, which will probably be needed later. He is also the source of "safe" light throughout the story.* **OL**

BI1 Big Idea

Journeys Answer: *The struggle between good and evil is ongoing; different characters play their parts, and while the journey eventually ends for everyone, the fight continues.* **OL**

BI2 Big Idea

Journeys Ask: How might you relate the ups and downs of Bilbo's journey with life's journey? *(Answers will vary. Students may say that real life is filled with dangers and unexpected events, just like Bilbo's journey.)* **OL**

CheckPoint

Use the CheckPoint questions on Presentation Plus! to check students' mastery of the selection. These questions can be used with interactive response keypads for immediate student feedback.

guards. Gandalf thought of most things; and though he could not do everything, he could do a great deal for friends in a tight corner.

"Are we all here?" said he, handing his sword back to Thorin with a bow. "Let me see: one—that's Thorin; two, three, four, five, six, seven, eight, nine, ten, eleven; where are Fili and Kili? Here they are! twelve, thirteen—and here's Mr. Baggins:[14] fourteen! Well, well! it might be worse, and then again it might be a good deal better. No ponies, and no food, and no knowing quite where we are, and **hordes** of angry goblins just behind! On we go!"

On they went. Gandalf was quite right: they began to hear goblin noises and horrible cries far behind in the passages they had come through. That sent them on faster than ever, and as poor Bilbo could not possibly go half as fast—for dwarves can roll along at a tremendous pace, I can tell you, when they have to—they took it in turn to carry him on their backs.

Still goblins go faster than dwarves, and these goblins knew the way better (they had made the paths themselves), and were madly angry; so that do what they could the dwarves heard the cries and howls getting closer and closer. Soon they could hear even the flap of the goblin feet, many many feet which seemed only just round the last corner. The blink of red torches could be seen behind them in the tunnel they were following; and they were getting deadly tired.

"Why, O why did I ever leave my hobbit-hole!" said poor Mr. Baggins bumping up and down on Bombur's back.

"Why, O why did I ever bring a wretched little hobbit on a treasure hunt!" said poor Bombur, who was fat, and staggered along with the sweat dripping down his nose in his heat and terror.

At this point Gandalf fell behind, and Thorin with him. They turned a sharp corner. "About turn!"[15] he shouted. "Draw your sword Thorin!"

There was nothing else to be done; and the goblins did not like it. They came scurrying round the corner in full cry, and found Goblin-cleaver, and Foe-hammer shining cold and bright right in their astonished eyes. The ones in front dropped their torches and gave one yell before they were killed. The ones behind yelled still more, and leaped back knocking over those that were running after them. "Biter and Beater!" they shrieked; and soon they were all in confusion, and most of them were hustling back the way they had come.

It was quite a long while before any of them dared to turn that corner. By that time the dwarves had gone on again, a long, long, way on into the dark tunnels of the goblins' realm.[16] When the goblins discovered that, they put out their torches and they slipped on soft shoes, and they chose out their very quickest runners with the sharpest ears and eyes. These ran forward, as swift as weasels in the dark, and with hardly any more noise than bats.

That is why neither Bilbo, nor the dwarves, nor even Gandalf heard them coming. Nor did they see them. But they were seen by the goblins that ran silently up behind, for Gandalf was letting his wand give out a faint light to help the dwarves as they went along.

Quite suddenly Dori, now at the back again carrying Bilbo, was grabbed from behind in the dark. He shouted and fell; and the hobbit rolled off his shoulders into the blackness, bumped his head on hard rock, and remembered nothing more. **BI2**

14. *Mr. Baggins* is Bilbo.

15. *About turn* is a command meaning "turn around 180 degrees" or "about face."

16. Here, *realm* means "domain" or "own area."

Literary Element Motif *How does Gandalf represent awareness?* **L**

Vocabulary

horde (hôrd) *n.* crowd, throng, or swarm

Big Idea Journeys *The goblins know the ancient history surrounding Biter and Beater. What does this say about the struggle between good and evil?* **BI1**

Additional Support

Skills Practice

WRITING: Rewriting Have students rewrite the story of the goblin raid from the point of view of one of the goblins who captured Bilbo and company. Have students consider the following questions:

- What was the goblin's day like before the raid?
- How did the goblin feel when the Great Goblin was slain?
- What was the goblin's reaction to seeing Biter and Beater?
- Was their goblin one who continued chasing Bilbo and company, or did their goblin do something else? **OL**

AFTER YOU READ

RESPONDING AND THINKING CRITICALLY

Respond

1. What do you think is the most otherworldly or fantastical element of this story? Explain.

Recall and Interpret

2. (a)Who is traveling on this adventure? (b)Describe the setting of this story in your own words.
3. (a)How do the goblins capture the adventurers? (b)How does Tolkien characterize the goblins?
4. (a)What happens to the captured companions? (b)What happens to Bilbo at the end of the excerpt? (c)Based on what you read in this excerpt, what do you predict will happen next?

Analyze and Evaluate

5. Bilbo and his companions' journey is full of twists and turns. How is the plot of this excerpt full of ups and downs?
6. (a)What is Gandalf's role in this story? (b)How would you describe Gandalf? Cite examples to support your analysis.
7. Do you think Bilbo is a hero? Explain.

Connect

8. **Big Idea** **Journeys** How would you describe this journey? Jot down three words that you think characterize this adventure. Support each of your choices with an example from the text.

VISUAL LITERACY: Fine Art

Illustrating Bilbo

In his novels, Tolkien creates an entirely new world populated with bizarre and distinctive creatures. Generations of readers, filmmakers, and other artists have enjoyed visualizing and re-creating *The Hobbit*. In fact, the first artist to illustrate the world of *The Hobbit* was Tolkien himself, who did so for the 1937 British edition.

One of the many great visual delights and challenges for artists and illustrators has been capturing the appearance and personality of each of the many characters.

Group Activity Study the illustration of Bilbo on his pony by Mikhail Belomlinsky. Discuss the following questions with your classmates.

1. How well does this illustration reflect Bilbo's appearance as he is described in this excerpt from *The Hobbit*? How well does it capture Bilbo's personality? Cite details from the text and the illustration that support your opinion.
2. What does the artist bring to the illustration that is not mentioned in the story?

AFTER YOU READ

Assess

1. Students' responses will vary.
2. (a) Bilbo Baggins, Gandalf the wizard, Thorin the dwarf leader, and twelve other dwarves (six other dwarves are given names). (b) Mountains with dangerous paths, rolling boulders, treacherous thunderstorms, and dark caverns
3. (a) While everyone is sleeping, they open a crack at the back of the cave. (b) They live deep underground in the darkness; they do evil things.
4. (a) They are about to be killed when Gandalf kills the Great Goblin and rescues them. (b) Bilbo falls and blacks out. (c) Gandalf will rescue Bilbo.
5. They face the dangers of the mountains in a thunderstorm; they finally find shelter and are attacked by goblins; Gandalf rescues them; the goblins attack again and hurt Bilbo.
6. (a) The leader (b) He is wise and brave. Example of his wisdom: the dwarves take the right road because of Gandalf's memory. He demonstrates courage when he saves the others.
7. Students cannot call Bilbo a hero based on the information in this excerpt.
8. Students' answers will vary. Possible answers: *perilous, unpredictable, fantastic, determined,* and *adventurous.*

Visual Literacy

1. Answers will vary. Students may say that the illustration captures Bilbo's physical likeness. Students may say the expression captures Bilbo's sweetness.
2. Answers will vary. Students may point to Bilbo's thinning hair in the illustration, which the artist uses to show age.

Academic Standards

The Additional Support activity on p. 1044 covers the following standard:

Skills Practice: **9.5.2** Write responses to literature that demonstrate a comprehensive grasp of the significant ideas of literary works...

AFTER YOU READ

Assess

Literary Element

1. The most obvious use is the thunderstorm.
2. (a) The dwarves, Bilbo, and especially Gandalf (b) The goblins (c) Students' responses may vary. Examples may include the Goblin's dark cavernous home and Gandalf's lighted sword.

Review: Narrator

1. (a) The reader (b) No
2. (a) Third-person point of view: the narrator is outside the story. (b) The narrator comments on events.
3. Examples include: "Even the good plans of wise wizards . . . the Wild" and "The sword's name was . . . if you remember."

Reading Strategy

1. (a) The Great Goblin is a stock character; he embodies the "evil villain" archetype. (b) Gandalf is not strictly a stock character, but he embodies "the wise wizard" archetype. (c) The Great Goblin represents evil and Gandalf represents good.
2. (a) Bilbo is not a stock character. He is the most fully developed character in the story. (b) Bilbo is an individual character. The goblins are stock characters.

Vocabulary

1. b **2.** a **3.** c **4.** a

Academic Vocabulary

1. The goblins have developed clever devices that "have troubled the world," including machines for killing large numbers of people at once.
2. Bilbo first dreams about it, then, upon waking, he sees it.

LITERARY ANALYSIS

Literary Element Motif

Good and evil, light and darkness, and awareness and deception can all be viewed as two sides of the same idea. In *The Hobbit,* Tolkien uses these **motifs** to advance the plot, foreshadow events, create suspense, reveal character traits, and convey themes.

1. Explain how Tolkien uses one or more of these motifs to create suspense. Cite specific passages.
2. (a)Which characters are associated with goodness and awareness? (b)Which characters are associated with evil and deception? (c)How does Tolkien's use of light and dark imagery support your observations? Cite specific examples in your response.

Review: Narrator

As you learned on pages 206–207, the **narrator** is the person who tells a story. If the narrator is a character inside the story then the story is told from the first-person point of view. If the narrator is outside the story then the story is told from the third-person point of view. Sometimes a story is told by an **intrusive narrator**—a narrator who openly comments on and evaluates characters, decisions, and actions in a story.

Partner Activity Meet with a partner to study the following passage and determine whether the narrator is inside or outside the story.

> "You certainly usually find something, if you look, but it is not always quite the something you were after. So it proved on this occasion."

1. (a)In this passage, who is the narrator addressing? (b)Does the narrator take part in the action of the story?
2. (a)Is the story told from the first-person or third-person point of view? Explain. (b)Describe the narrator's role in telling the story.
3. Find two more examples in the story where the narrator intrudes, or comments upon the story itself.

READING AND VOCABULARY

Reading Strategy Comparing and Contrasting Characters

Stock characters are flat characters who embody stereotypes. Stock characters are familiar characters that reappear in literature, such as the "evil villain," the "beautiful princess," and the "hard-boiled detective."

1. (a)Do you think the Great Goblin is a stock character? Explain. (b)Do you think Gandalf is a stock character? Explain. (c)Compare and contrast the Great Goblin and Gandalf.
2. (a)Do you think Bilbo is a stock character? Explain. (b)Compare and contrast Bilbo with the goblins.

Vocabulary Practice

Practice with Context Clues Read each of the following sentences and then decide which word is closest in meaning to the boldfaced word.

1. Fred's ability to predict the weather without instruments or data is **uncanny.**
   a. familiar **b.** eerie **c.** crazy
2. That store sells tons of **paraphernalia** and other things for camera buffs.
   a. items **b.** film **c.** education
3. The **ingenious** plan involved reusing old cans as conductors.
   a. costly **b.** simple **c.** clever
4. The **horde** was made up of thousands of fans.
   a. crowd **b.** team **c.** auditorium

Academic Vocabulary

Here are two words from the vocabulary list on page R80.

device (di vīs′) *n.* piece of equipment or mechanism for a special purpose

detect (di tekt′) *v.* to discover the presence, existence, or fact of

Practice and Apply

1. What **devices** have the goblins developed?
2. How does Bilbo **detect** the crack in the cave?

WRITING AND EXTENDING

Writing About Literature

Respond to Voice How would you characterize the narrator's voice in this excerpt from *The Hobbit*? Is it formal, knowing, enthusiastic, or something else? Write an essay in which you rate, on a scale of 1 to 10, Tolkien's use of diction, tone, and one other element that contributes to voice, such as description or point of view.

Begin your essay with a general statement that describes the voice used in *The Hobbit.* Also, in your introduction, be sure to provide a statement that explains the three aspects of voice that you intend to discuss. This will help you to organize your essay. In separate paragraphs, rate each facet of the voice. Be sure to include one or more examples from the text in each body paragraph, and clearly explain your examples and rating. When you draft, follow a plan like this one:

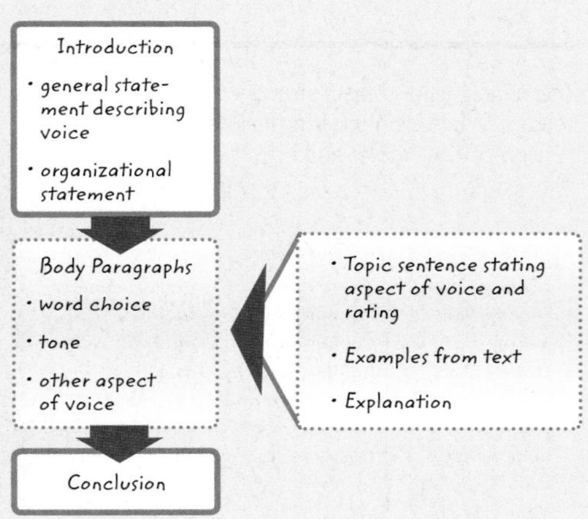

After completing your draft, have a peer reviewer read it and suggest revisions. Then proofread and edit your work to correct errors in spelling, grammar, and punctuation.

GRAMMAR AND STYLE

Tolkien's Language and Style

Using Gerunds One way that Tolkien brings the goblins and their world of darkness to life is by using gerunds—verb forms that end in *-ing* and that function as nouns in a sentence. While gerunds look like verbs and other verb forms called participles, they are always either subjects or objects. Tolkien uses gerunds to create suspense and a sense of continuing action. Note how each gerund functions as a noun in this sentence:

> The yells and yammering, croaking, jibbering and jabbering; howls, growls and curses; shrieking and skriking, that followed were beyond description.

Tolkien is a very careful and crafty writer; the gerunds in this sentence allow you to hear the terrifying sounds the goblins make. His language is both descriptive and immediate. Notice how the gerund is a stronger, more active and interesting choice in these sentences:

> Haymaking was going on in the valley below.
> (instead of *They were making hay in the valley below.*)
>
> "Fighting dragons is good exercise," the hero glibly said.
> (instead of *"To fight dragons is good exercise," the hero glibly said.*)

Activity Find three more examples of gerunds in this story. Be careful not to confuse them with other verb forms ending in *-ing*: remember, gerunds function as nouns (that is, subjects or objects) in a sentence. For each gerund you identify, think of a different noun or phrase that Tolkien might have used instead.

Revising Check

Gerunds Try adding gerunds to your evaluative essay about voice. Remember that many verbs drop the silent *e* before adding *-ing (skate, skating)* or double the final consonant *(swim, swimming).*

LiteratureOnline Web Activities For eFlashcards, Selection Quick Checks, and other Web activities, go to www.glencoe.com.

AFTER YOU READ

Assess

Writing About Literature

Remind students that their essays should tie together the various elements that make up voice.

For advanced writers, point out that after restating the elements of the narrator's voice, they can draw a broader conclusion rather than just simply summarizing. While this doesn't introduce new information, it can broaden the scope of the essay, leaving the reader with something to ponder.

Tolkien's Language and Style

Suggest to students that if they have any confusion as to whether the gerund is a noun or verb, they should consider the following:

- Is the word a person, place, or thing?
- Where is the word located in the sentence?
- Is the word the subject of the sentence or phrase?
- Is the word the object of a verb or preposition?

Web Activities Have students access the Web site for interactive activities that will help them assess their understanding of the selection.

English Language Coach

Gerunds Nonnative speakers may find gerunds confusing. Remind students that a gerund acts as a noun. Therefore, if the word ends in *-ing* and is a person, place, or thing, it's a gerund. If the word ends in *-ing* and is an action word, it is a verb, not a gerund. EL

Differentiated Instruction

Working with Gerunds Work with gerunds as a class exercise. Working page by page, have students find examples of gerunds from the story. Have the class vote as to whether the example is actually a gerund or a verb, and clarify any confusion. Make a list of the gerunds on the board. BL

Academic Standards
Additional Support activities on p. 1047 cover the following standards:
English Language Coach: **9.6.1** Identify… phrases, including gerund…
Differentiated Instruction: **9.6.1** Identify and correctly use…phrases, including gerund…

Focus

Summary

While resting in a cave on their journey trhough the mountains, Bilbo and a company of dwarves are captured by goblins. Gandalf the wizard escapes capture. The Goblin King is infuriated by Thorin the dwarf's sword Orcrist, the goblin-cleaver. As he sentences the company to torment, Gandalf appears to rescue them. A battle ensues and the company flees.

Teach

L1 Literary Element

Dialogue Engage students in a classroom discussion of the graphic novel dialogue. Have them note such elements as length, diction, punctuation, and dialect. Discuss whether students find the dialogue realistic and effective. OL

from The Hobbit

Adapted by Charles Dixon
Illustrated by David Wenzel

Building Background

Graphic novels are longer versions of comic books and are more complex and literary in nature. Will Eisner, who wrote what is considered to be the first modern graphic novel in 1978, popularized the term "graphic novel." In 1992 Art Spiegelman received the Pulitzer Prize for his graphic novel, *Maus: A Survivor's Tale*. Other graphic novels that have achieved success include *Ghost World* by Daniel Clowes and *American Splendor* by Harvey Pekar; both have been adapted into films. In this graphic novel version of *The Hobbit*, Charles Dixon uses dialogue and David Wenzel illustrates the characters from the novel by J. R. R. Tolkien.

Set a Purpose for Reading

L1 Read to discover the similarities and differences between the graphic novel version of *The Hobbit* and the original text.

Reading Strategy

Comparing and Contrasting Versions of a Story

When you **compare and contrast,** you identify the similarities and differences between two works of literature. Many elements of different works can be compared and contrasted, including theme, imagery, use of language, characterization, and setting. As you read, take notes on the images in the graphic novel version of *The Hobbit* and how they are similar to or different from images evoked by the original text.

Images	Similarities	Differences
"There in the shadows on a large flat stone sat a tremendous goblin with a huge head, and armed goblins were standing round him carrying axes and the bent swords that they use."	There is one large goblin. Goblins are holding axes and swords, and they surround the dwarves.	More defined facial characteristics of goblins in the graphic novel. Dialogue is also different from the original.

Additional Support

Skills Practice

WRITING: Graphic Novel Challenge students to create their own graphic novel version of a popular work. Brainstorm with the class to create a list of stories from which they can choose. Have students work in groups to create a one-page graphic representation of the story. Encourage students to work in a variety of mediums. Have students use their graphic novel to create a parody. Encourage students to include elements of humor in their visual and written designs. OL

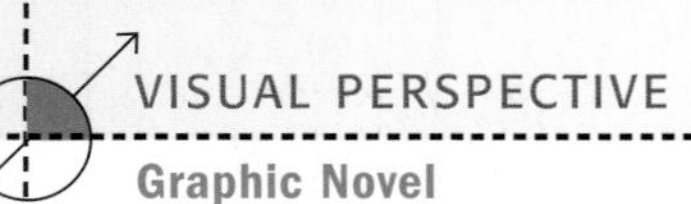

Teach

L2 Literary Element

Motif Ask: How does the graphic representation of the goblins and dwarves reflect the motif of darkness and light, and good and evil? *(Answers will vary. Students may point to the color palette used by the artist or the repulsive appearance of the goblins as examples of darkness and evil. They should contrast the dwarves' appearance as more representative of the light and good.)* **OL**

English Language Coach

Connotation and Denotation Point out to English language learners that graphic novels are a good way to learn connotations and denotations. The story told by the pictures shows what the words mean. The expressions and body language of the characters provide connotation. **EL**

Differentiated Instruction

Critique Graphic Novel Visual learners will respond strongly to the graphic representation of the story. Have students engage in a classroom critique of the graphic novel. Have students point out what they would do differently and why. Include discussion of color, character, and storyline. **BL**

Academic Standards

Additional Support activities on pp. 1048 and 1049 cover the following standards:

Skills Practice: **9.5** [Demonstrate] an awareness of the audience…and purpose for writing.

English Language Coach: **9.1.2** Distinguish between what words mean literally and what they imply and interpret what the words imply.

Differentiated Instruction: **9.7.13** Identify the artistic effects of a media presentation and evaluate the techniques used to create them…

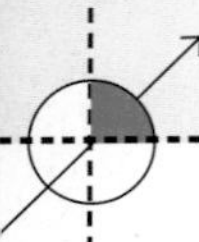

Teach

L Literary Element

Motif Ask: How does the artist visually express that Thorin and Orcrist are forces of good? *(Students should note the use of color, specifically of white for purity and truth. They may also note that the dwarf and the sword are prettier than their surroundings.)* OL

R1 Reading Strategy

Interpreting Meaning Have students look at the pictures of the goblins. **Ask:** How would you describe the Goblin King's expression? *(Students may note the anger, disgust, and hatred.)* Point out to students the importance of incorporating the visual information when reading the dialogue. OL

THORIN THE DWARF AT YOUR SERVICE!
WE SHELTERED FROM A STORM IN WHAT SEEMED A CONVENIENT CAVE AND UNUSED; NOTHING WAS FURTHER FROM OUR THOUGHTS THAN INCON-VENIENCING GOBLINS IN ANY WAY WHATEVER.
UM! SO YOU *SAY!*
MIGHT I ASK WHAT YOU WERE DOING UP IN THE MOUNTAINS AT ALL, AND WHERE YOU WERE COMING FROM, AND WHERE YOU WERE GOING TO?
IN FACT I SHOULD LIKE TO KNOW ALL ABOUT YOU, *THORIN OAKENSHIELD!*
I KNOW TOO MUCH ABOUT YOUR FOLK ALREADY; BUT LET'S HAVE THE TRUTH, OR I WILL PREPARE SOME-THING PARTICULARLY UNCOMFORTABLE FOR YOU!
WE WERE ON A JOURNEY TO VISIT OUR RELATIVES WHO LIVE ON THE EAST SIDE OF THESE TRULY HOSPITABLE MOUNTAINS.
HE IS A *LIAR,* O TRULY TREMENDOUS ONE!
SEVERAL OF OUR PEOPLE WERE STRUCK BY LIGHT-NING IN THE CAVE WHEN WE *INVITED* THESE CREATURES TO COME BELOW; AND THEY ARE DEAD AS STONES.
ALSO HE HAS NOT EXPLAINED *THIS!*
ORCRIST! THE GOBLIN-CLEAVER! BITER!
THE *THRICE* CURSED SWORD OF THE ELVES OF *GONDOLIN!*
MURDERERS AND ELF-FRIENDS!
Artwork © 2006 David Thom Wenzel

L R1

Additional Support

Skills Practice

Dialogue Discuss with students the impact of the dialogue used in the graphic novel. Have students point out characteristics of the dialogue. *(informality; the use of bold and italics)* Challenge students to rewrite the dialogue in a more formal, epic style. Remind students that the epic style adheres to proper language rules. Assign groups of students to rewrite one page. Have students perform their new dialogue aloud. Discuss the differences between the two dialogue styles and how each affects the interpretation of the story. OL

VISUAL PERSPECTIVE
Graphic Novel

Teach

R2 Reading Strategy

Sound Effects **Ask:** How does the author use sound to illustrate plot? *(Students should note the use of the words* foosh, pfff, *and* kroooshh *to indicate actions that are taking place.)* Point out to students that the use of sound to indicate action and plot is a common attribute of the comic book and graphic novel. **BL**

English Language Coach

Interpreting Art Point out to students that on a graphic novel page where the dialogue is scant, they have an opportunity to really study the images. Encourage students to infer as much as possible about plot and characterization from the artwork. **EL**

Differentiated Instruction

Sounds Auditory learners may relate well to the use of sound words such as "pfff." Invite students to point out instances of these words in the graphic novel. Invite students to suggest their own sound word substitutions to illustrate the action in the novel. **BL**

Academic Standards

Additional Support activities on pp. 1050 and 1051 cover the following standards:

Skills Practice: **9.5.8** Write for different purposes and audiences, adjusting tone, style, and voice as appropriate. **9.3.2** Compare and contrast the presentation of a...topic across genres...to explain how the...genre shapes the...topic.

English Language Coach: **9.3** [Identify] story elements such as character...[and] plot...

Differentiated Instruction: **9.3.7** Recognize and understand the significance of various literary devices...

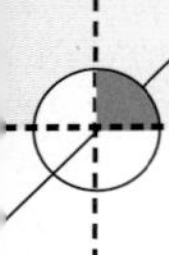

Assess

1. Answers will vary.
2. (a) They are surrounded by goblins and accused of being murderers and the friends of elves. (b) The dwarves represent peace, and the goblins represent unrest.
3. (a) The illustrations show the physical characteristics of goblins, who appear lizard and rat-like in nature. They are also dark to emphasize the idea of darkness and evil. (b) The illustrations stress that the goblins are dark and evil.
4. (a) Students may say that he wanted to make the dialogue more active. (b) Many students will say that adaptation is a way to pass stories on in a variety of artistic and literary mediums.
5. Dialogue changes the tone of the piece into more of an action-adventure than a tale.
6. Answers will vary. Some may argue that it is exciting to create your own images of what you read. Others may feel the graphic novel helps them understand the plot more easily.

RESPONDING AND THINKING CRITICALLY

Respond

1. Does the graphic novel version of *The Hobbit* enhance your understanding of the original text? Why or why not?

Recall and Interpret

2. (a)What happens to the dwarves in this selection? (b)What do you think the dwarves and the goblins represent?
3. (a)What aspects of direct characterization, or statements about character, do Wenzel's illustrations convey? (b)Are the illustrations effective? Why or why not?

Analyze and Evaluate

4. (a)Why do you think Dixon did not use direct quotes from the original text of *The Hobbit*? (b)Do you think there is value in adapting literary works to other mediums? Why or why not?
5. Why do you think Dixon used dialogue instead of narration for his adaptation of *The Hobbit*?

Connect

6. Which do you prefer, imagining the characters from *The Hobbit*, or seeing illustrations of them? Why?

INDIANA ACADEMIC STANDARDS (pages 1048-1052)

9.3.2 Compare and contrast the presentation of a similar theme or topic across genres...to explain how the selection of genre shapes the theme or topic.

Additional Support

For additional assessment, see Selection and Unit Assessments, pp. 179–180.

Skills Practice

LITERARY ELEMENT: Setting
Discuss with students the effect of the setting on the story. Ask students to explain how the story would change if the setting wasn't the cave. Ask students how a new setting would change the graphic novel representation. **OL**

PART 2

Courage and Cleverness

Siegfried killing Fafner, illustration from "Puissances Secretes," c.1935. S. Schroeter. Color lithograph. ★

BIG IDEA

BI Almost every culture has its stories of humans who triumph over fate, the gods, or natural disaster. They do so not always by great strength, but often by their personal attributes, which may include courage or cleverness. The selections in Part 2 relate some of these tales. As you read them, ask yourself: Why do these stories remain popular through time?

Differentiated Instruction

Building Background **Ask:** What do you consider an act of courage? An act of cleverness? Make a list on the board. Discuss with students why they feel each item qualifies to be on the list. Prompt students to consider grand heroic acts as well as small personal acts. **BL**

Analyzing and Extending

BI Big Idea

Courage and Cleverness
Ask: How do you define *courage* and *cleverness*? *(Answers will vary.)* Discuss with students how the painting shows courage and cleverness. *(Students may find the act of fighting courageous or the means of fighting clever.)* **OL**

★ Viewing the Art

"Siegfried Killing Fafner" is a reference to Richard Wagner's (1813–1883) Ring Cycle, which consists of four operas: *Das Rheingold (The Rhinegold), Die Walküre (The Valkyrie), Siegfried,* and *Götterdämmerung (Twilight of the Gods).* In the opera *Siegfried,* the character of Siegfried is the hero. **AS**

Academic Standards

Additional Support activities on pp. 1052 and 1053 cover the following standards:

Skills Practice: **9.3** [Identify] story elements such as…setting…

Differentiated Instruction: **9.2** Develop [reading] strategies…

Part 2: Skills Scope and Sequence

Readability Scores Key
Dale-Chall/DRP/Lexile

PACING (DAYS) STANDARD	BLOCK	SELECTIONS AND FEATURES	LITERARY ELEMENTS
2–3 class sessions	1–2	"Perseus" by Edith Hamilton **6.9/54/1030**, pp. 1056–1066	Plot Pattern Archetype, SE pp. 1057–1065 Hero, SE p. 1065
		"The Fenris Wolf" by Olivia Coolidge **9.4/57/1120**, pp. 1067–1072	Image Archetype, SE pp. 1068–1072
		Vocabulary Workshop: Word Origins, p. 1073	
2–3 class sessions	1–2	"Coyote and Crow" by Ella Clark **3.8/42/510**, pp. 1074–1077	Character Archetype, SE pp. 1075–1077
		"Vasilisa of the Golden Braid and Ivan the Pea" by Elizabeth Warner **6.9/56/1010**, pp. 1078–1086	Theme Archetype, SE pp. 1079–1085 Image Archetype, SE p. 1085
		Grammar Workshop: Coherence, p. 1087	
		"Sweet Betsy from Pike" by anonymous, pp. 1088–1091	Ballad, SE pp. 1088–1090 Meter and Rhythm, SE p. 1090
3–5 class sessions	2–3	Writing Workshop: Research Paper, pp. 1092–1101	
1 class session	2	Speaking, Listening, and Viewing Workshop: Expository Presentation, pp. 1102–1103	
2 class sessions		Test Preparation and Practice, pp. 1106–1111	

About the Part

Part 2 explores the different ways in which courage and cleverness can be used and looks at what other qualities separate the heroic characters from the evil ones.

READING AND CRITICAL THINKING	VOCABULARY	WRITING AND GRAMMAR	LISTENING, SPEAKING, AND VIEWING
Identifying Genre, SE pp. 1057–1065 Predicting, TWE p. 1058	Antonyms, SE pp. 1057, 1065 Academic Vocabulary, SE p. 1065	Evaluate Contemporary Relevance, SE p. 1066 Using Active Voice, SE p. 1066	Analyzing Art, SE p. 1063, 1064; TWE p. 1058 Interviewing, TWE p. 1062
Interpreting Imagery, SE pp. 1068, 1072	Context Clues, SE pp. 1068, 1072	Analyze Plot, SE p. 1072	Analyzing Art, SE p. 1071 Oral Interpretation, TWE p. 1070
	Examining Words from Norse Mythology, SE p. 1073		
Activating Prior Knowledge, SE pp. 1075–1077	Word Origins, SE pp. 1079, 1086	Respond to Character, SE p. 1077	Telling a Tale, TWE p. 1076
Connecting to Personal Experience, SE pp. 1079–1086 Setting a Purpose for Reading, TWE p. 1080	Word Origins, SE pp. 1079, 1086 Academic Vocabulary, SE p. 1086	Compare and Contrast Characters, SE p. 1086 Modern Fairy Tale, TWE p. 1082	Analyzing Art, SE p. 1084; TWE p. 1080 Performing, SE p. 1086
		Using Transitional Expressions, SE p. 1087	
Analyzing Archetypes, SE pp. 1088–1091	Academic Vocabulary, SE p. 1091	Apply Form, SE p. 1091	Music Activity, SE p. 1091
Gathering Information, TWE p. 1094	Verb Tense, TWE p. 1098	Effective Introductions, TWE p. 1096 Using Details, TWE p. 1100	
			Studying a Presentation, TWE p. 1102
Establishing a Purpose for Reading, TWE p. 1106		Varying Sentence Length, TWE p. 1110	

LITERARY FOCUS

Focus

BELLRINGER

Bellringer Options
Daily Language Practice Transparency 87
Or **write on the board:** What are your favorite myths? List examples on the board. Then have students point out the heroes, villains, and other characters associated with each myth. Discuss what makes these myths and characters memorable.

Teach

L1 Literary Element

Characteristics of Myth
Ask: Why do you think the myth of Perseus has stood the test of time? *(Students may mention Perseus's heroic acts and the inclusion of a monster in the myth.)* OL

★ Viewing the Art

Ask: What kinds of archetypes do you see in this image? (Students may mention the heroic knight or the terrifying monster.) AS

LITERARY FOCUS

Archetypes

What kinds of stories endure over thousands of years?

In the myth of Perseus, Danaë gives birth to the god Zeus's son, Perseus. Danaë's father, King Acrisus of Argos, wants to be rid of Danaë and her son. Acrisus places the two in a great chest and casts them adrift at sea. They drift ashore on a little island where a kind fisherman, Dictys, discovers them and takes them in. They live with him for years as Perseus grows to manhood. Dictys's brother, Polydectes, ruler of the island, falls in love with Danaë, but he wants to get rid of Perseus. To do so, Polydectes convinces Perseus to bring him the head of a Gorgon.

L1
Medusa was one of the Gorgons,
And they are three, the Gorgons, each with wings
And snaky hair, most horrible to mortals.
Whom no man shall behold and draw again
The breath of life,
for the reason that whoever looked at them turned instantly into stone. It seemed that Perseus had been led by his angry pride into making an empty boast. No man unaided could kill Medusa.

—Edith Hamilton, **from "Perseus"**

Knight on Horse Battling Dragon ★

Archetypes

An **archetype** is a character, thing, or pattern of events that appears repeatedly in myth, folk tales, and other literature and is something that has concerned humans deeply throughout history. For example, you may have noticed several familiar character types in the summary of the Perseus myth, such as the brave young hero, the villainous king, and the hideous monster.

The Perseus myth also involves some familiar situations: The innocents—Danaë and the child Perseus—are exposed to mortal danger. The hero undertakes a seemingly impossible task. Not all familiar characters and situations, however, are archetypes.

Additional Support

Skills Practice

RESEARCH: Myths Invite students to connect to mythology by researching a myth of their choosing. Students' reports should include the following:

- A summary of the myth
- Character synopses
- A chart showing how the characters are related to one another
- Illustrations

Have students present their reports in class. Encourage them to talk about retellings of the myth over time (e.g., the myth of Helen of Troy has been used in books, poetry, and movies). OL

Stock Characters

A **stock character** is a common character type, such as the tough-guy detective, the faithful friend of the hero, or the damsel in distress whom the hero rescues. Stock characters do not have the same universal quality as archetypes, however. They may be limited to a specific culture or time period.

L2 After a time he heard a fearful whistling: it was the dragon. His horse came galloping through the sky like an arrow shot from a bow, fire snorting from its nostrils. The dragon had the head of a serpent but the body of a man. Usually, as he approached, the palace would begin to revolve on its single pillar, even when he was many miles distant.

—Elizabeth Warner, **from "Vasilisa of the Golden Braid and Ivan the Pea"**

Symbol

A **symbol** is an object, person, place, or event that is literal but also represents something other than itself. Writers often use symbols to make abstract ideas or concepts concrete. For example, water represents the force of life in this Russian myth.

Next Ivan found where the magic water, the Water of Life and Death, was hidden and sprinkled some over the corpses of his brothers. They stood up, rubbing their eyes as if they had just woken from a long sleep.

—Elizabeth Warner, **from "Vasilisa of the Golden Braid and Ivan the Pea"**

Archetypes can be used to symbolize something else. For example, the tale of the hero defeating the monster can remind people that they too can triumph over adversity.

Myth

The word *myth* comes from the Greek *mythos,* meaning "word" or "story." As you know, ancient people told one another stories to interpret natural events and to explain the nature of the universe and humanity. These stories, which have been passed down from one generation to another for thousands of years, are today's myths. Virtually all ancient cultures had myths that were particular to that culture, although many of these stories had certain elements in common.

Characteristics of Most Myths

- Sought to explain things people could not otherwise understand
- Served to bind a group of people together
- Were used to set examples for both virtuous behavior and flawed behavior
- Contain supernatural elements

Ballad

A **ballad** is a song or poem that tells a story. Most ballads focus on action and dialogue rather than narration and description. Folk ballads, which typically tell the saga of thrilling, dramatic—and often catastrophic—events, were passed on by word of mouth for generations before being written down. As such, the style and structure of a ballad are usually quite simple.

Quickwrite

Writing a Description Choose one of these thematic archetypes: the quest, the task, the loss of innocence. Write a description of who and what comes to mind when you think about your chosen archetype. If you can, give a modern example of your chosen archetype. (For example, *the hero*: Superman.)

Literature Online Interactive Literary Elements Handbook Go to www.glencoe.com to review or learn more about archetypes.

INDIANA ACADEMIC STANDARDS (pages 1054-1055)
9.3.12 Analyze the way in which a work of literature is related to the themes and issues of its historical period.
9.3.7 Recognize and understand the significance of... symbolism...

Teach

L2 Literary Element

Characteristics of Myth

Have volunteers read the descriptions and quotations aloud. After each quote is read, **ask:** How is this quote a good example? Discuss how the quotes relate to the section topic. OL

Assess

Quickwrite

Descriptions and examples of the chosen archetype should reflect an understanding of its universal significance.

Literary Elements Have students access the Web site to improve their understanding of archetypes.

English Language Coach

Understanding Archetypes Note that archetypes are universal characters, plots, or themes that transcend language barriers. Have the class read the other Literary Focus topics and discuss how identifying these elements will help with reading comprehension. EL

Academic Standards

Additional Support activities on pp. 1054 and 1055 cover the following standards:

Skills Practice: **9.5.9** Write or deliver a research report that has been developed using a systematic research process...

English Language Coach: **9.3** [Identify] story elements such as character, theme, plot...

Focus

BELLRINGER

Bellringer Options
Daily Language Practice Transparency 88
Or display images of characters from ancient Greek mythology.
Ask: What do you know about the ancient Greeks? Why do you think their myths and stories are still studied today? Ask students to consider as they read what the story of Perseus has to teach modern readers.

Author Search To expand students' appreciation of Edith Hamilton, have them access the Web site for additional information and resources.

BEFORE YOU READ

Perseus

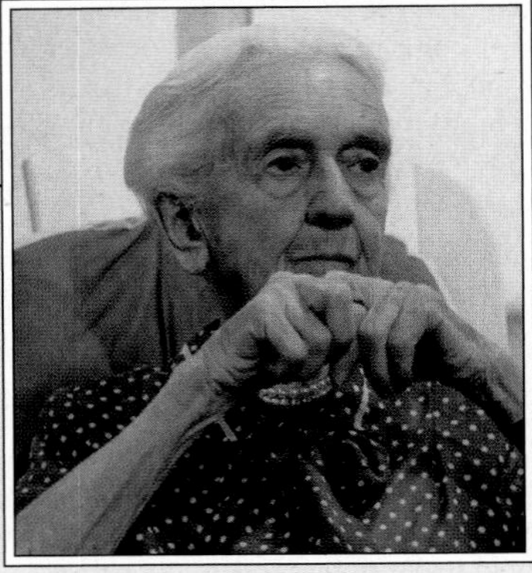

MEET EDITH HAMILTON

Students who enjoy reading Greek and Roman mythology as part of their English classes have Edith Hamilton to thank. At the age of sixty-three, Hamilton began a second career retelling the ancient myths of Greece and Rome. Hamilton's scholarly work single-handedly renewed an interest in the classical world in American schools.

Edith Hamilton was born in 1867 in Dresden, Germany. Her father, Montgomery Hamilton, was the son of a prominent Fort Wayne, Indiana, family, and her mother, Gertrude Pond Hamilton, was the daughter of a Confederate sympathizer who moved to Europe during the Civil War. Montgomery and Gertrude eventually moved their family back to Fort Wayne, where Edith and her three sisters grew up.

A Classical Education As girls, Hamilton and her sisters were educated at home by their parents and private tutors. From 1884 to 1886, Hamilton attended Miss Porter's School for Young Ladies in Connecticut. In 1891 she entered Bryn Mawr College, where she studied Greek and Latin languages and literature.

Headmistress In 1896 Hamilton accepted an offer from M. Carey Thomas, the President of Bryn Mawr College, to head Bryn Mawr School. It was the first private high school that focused on college preparation for young women. Hamilton's theories of education were based on the Greek ideals of individualism, academic freedom, and intellectual exploration. She encouraged her students to develop their own individual talents. Students at Bryn Mawr School admired Hamilton's intellect, her high expectations, and her sense of humor. She remained headmistress at Bryn Mawr School for twenty-six years.

The Greek Way After her retirement, Hamilton turned to writing about her favorite subject: the Greek and Roman classics. In 1930 she published her first book, *The Greek Way*. Several other books followed, including her most famous work, *Mythology* (1942).

> *"Ideals have tremendous power. When ideals are low they fade out and are forgotten; great ideals have had power of persistent life."*
>
> —Edith Hamilton

In her books, Hamilton made ancient cultures accessible to a wide range of readers. She also idealized Greek culture over all others. In *Mythology* she wrote, "In Greece man first realized what mankind was." She believed that the Greeks maintained a balance of mind, body, and spirit superior to other cultures. Some critics have called her portrayal of the Greeks simplistic. However, her work in classical studies proved instrumental in reviving the study of the classics in America in the mid-twentieth century.

Edith Hamilton was born in 1867 and died in 1963.

LiteratureOnline **Author Search** For more about Edith Hamilton, go to www.glencoe.com.

Selection Skills

Perseus

Literary Elements
- Plot Pattern Archetype (SE pp. 1057–1065)
- Hero (SE p. 1065)

Reading Skills
- Identifying Genre (SE pp. 1057–1065)
- Predicting (TWE p. 1058)

Vocabulary Skills
- Antonyms (SE pp. 1057, 1065)
- Academic Vocabulary (SE p. 1065)

Listening/Speaking/Viewing Skills
- Analyzing Art (SE pp. 1063, 1064; TWE p. 1058)

Writing Skills/Grammar
- Evaluate Contemporary Relevance (SE p. 1066)
- Using Active Voice (SE p. 1066)

LITERATURE PREVIEW

Connecting to the Myth

The following myth is about a hero who goes to great lengths to complete a quest. Before you read, think about the following questions:

- What does the word *hero* mean to you?
- Who are your personal heroes?

Building Background

In the story of Perseus, as in other Greek myths, humans interact with gods, goddesses, and other fantastic beings. Hermes and Athena both play major roles in the story of Perseus. Hermes was the son of Zeus, the ruler of the gods. Hermes was known as the messenger god and the bringer of good fortune and was also thought to offer protection to travelers. Athena, Zeus's daughter, had no mother but sprang fully formed from her father's head. She was therefore identified with wisdom. Athena was also described as an expert in war and strategy.

Medusa was one of the monstrous Gorgons: creatures with snakes for hair, whose stare turned any living creature into stone. According to myths, the flying horse Pegasus arose from Medusa's blood after she was beheaded.

Setting Purposes for Reading

Big Idea Courage and Cleverness

As you read this myth, look for examples of Perseus's bravery and intelligence.

Literary Element Plot Pattern Archetype

An **archetype** is an image or symbol used repeatedly in art or literature. A **plot pattern archetype** is a sequence of events that is familiar because it appears repeatedly in stories told across cultures, all over the world. One plot pattern archetype, for example, involves a hero guided by magical beings or gods. As you read, see how many different plot pattern archetypes you can identify in this story.

- See Literary Terms Handbook, p. R13.

READING PREVIEW

Reading Strategy Identifying Genre

Genre refers to a category of literature. Each genre has its own conventions, or standards, that give readers certain expectations. When reading a story categorized as a mystery, for example, the reader expects a mysterious event to occur. The reader also expects a suspenseful tone, twists and turns in the plot, and a final resolution in which the mystery is solved. "Perseus" is a myth. As you read, try to identify the characteristics of the myth genre.

Reading Tip: Listing Characteristics As you read, it may help you to list the characteristics that make "Perseus" different from contemporary realistic fiction—fiction that describes everyday life in the present. Compare the characteristics of myth and contemporary realistic fiction in a chart like the one below.

Myth	Contemporary Realistic Fiction
Set in the distant past	Set in the present

Vocabulary

kindred (kin′drid) *n.* people who are related; family; p. 1058 *My brothers, parents, aunts, and uncles are my kindred.*

shrill (shril) *adj.* loud; piercing; p. 1059 *The shrill cry of the neighbor's cat keeps us up at night.*

withered (with′ərd) *adj.* shriveled or dried up; p. 1061 *He looked out on his withered fields and cursed the drought.*

Vocabulary Tip: Antonyms Words that have opposite meanings are called antonyms. *Little* and *big* are antonyms, as are *night* and *day*.

LiteratureOnline Interactive Literary Elements Handbook To review or learn more about the literary elements, go to www.glencoe.com.

INDIANA ACADEMIC STANDARDS (pages 1057-1066)

9.3 [Identify] story elements such as...plot...and [make] connections and comparisons across texts...

9.2 Develop [reading] strategies...

9.5.2 Write responses to literature...

BEFORE YOU READ

Focus

Summary

A prophecy foretells the killing of King Acrisius by his grandson. After his daughter gives birth to Perseus, the king tries to kill the mother and child, but both survive. As a young man, Perseus offers to kill the monster Medusa for King Polydectes. With the help of the gods Hermes and Athena, he accomplishes his quest.

V Vocabulary

Vocabulary File Say: Add these words and definitions to your vocabulary file. For each word, include a sentence that gives you an example of how to use the word. **OL** Students with English language needs should include the pronunciations of these words in their files. **EL**

Literary Elements Have students access the Web site to improve their understanding of plot pattern archetypes.

Selection Resources

Print Materials

- Unit 5 Resources (Fast File), pp. 39–41
- Leveled Vocabulary Development, p. 67
- Selection and Unit Assessments, pp. 179–180
- Selection Quick Checks, p. 90

Transparencies

- Bellringer Options Transparencies: Daily Language Practice Transparency 88
- Literary Elements Transparency 87

Technology

- TeacherWorks Plus™ CD-ROM
- StudentWorks Plus™ CD-ROM
- Presentation Plus!™ CD-ROM
- Literature Online, glencoe.com
- Online Student Edition, mhln.com
- Exam*View*® Assessment Suite CD-ROM
- Vocabulary PuzzleMaker CD-ROM
- Listening Library, disc 2 track 30

Teach

R Reading Strategy

Identifying Genre **Answer:** *It is common in myth for humans to consult gods.*
Say: Another convention of myth is for humans to try to avoid their fates. Ask students to predict how the king will respond to the news. OL

L1 Literary Element

Plot Pattern Archetype
Note that many folk and fairy tales use elements of myths.
Possible answers: *"Rapunzel," "Rumplestiltskin"* OL

★ Viewing the Art

Xavier Cortada was born in New York in 1964 but was raised in Miami. He is well known for his public art projects, including several murals, and has been commissioned to create works for the White House and many cultural institutions. AS

Readability Scores
Dale-Chall: 6.9
DRP: 54
Lexile: 1030

Perseus, 1998. Xavier Cortada. Acrylic on canvas, 121.9 3 91.4 cm. Private Collection. ★

Perseus

Edith Hamilton

King Acrisius of Argos[1] had only one child, a daughter, Danaë. She was beautiful above all the other women of the land, but this was small comfort to the King for not having a son. He journeyed to Delphi[2] to ask the god if there was any hope that some day he would be the father of a boy. The priestess told him no, and added what was far worse: that his daughter would have a son who would kill him.

The only sure way to escape that fate was for the King to have Danaë instantly put to death—taking no chances, but seeing to it himself. This Acrisius would not do. His fatherly affection was not strong, as events proved, but his fear of the gods was. They visited with terrible punishment those who shed the blood of **kindred**. Acrisius did not dare slay his daughter. Instead, he had a house built all of bronze and sunk underground, but with part of the roof open to the sky so that light and air could come through. Here he shut her up and guarded her.

1. *Argos* was a powerful city in southeastern Greece during the seventh century b.c.
2. *Delphi* was an ancient Greek town to the south of Mount Parnassus. It was the site of an oracle, or shrine, where a priestess supposedly channeled predictions of the god Apollo.

Reading Strategy Identifying Genre *What do the details of the story so far tell you about the characteristics of myth?* R

Literary Element Plot Pattern Archetype *What other stories, fairy tales, or myths do you know that include a woman shut up alone?* L1

Vocabulary
kindred (kin′ drid) *n.* people who are related; family

Additional Support

Skills Practice

READING: Predicting Note that even in myths, characters usually behave in predictably human ways. Engage students' interest in the story by having them predict the outcome of its major events. Invite volunteers to read sections of the story aloud. After each major event, stop and discuss what happened. Ask the class what they think will happen next. At the end of the story, discuss the accuracy of students' predictions. OL

So Danaë endured, the beautiful,
To change the glad daylight for brass-bound walls,
And in that chamber secret as the grave
She lived a prisoner. Yet to her came
★ Zeus in the golden rain.

As she sat there through the long days and hours with nothing to do, nothing to see except the clouds moving by overhead, a mysterious thing happened, a shower of gold fell from the sky and filled her chamber. How it was revealed to her that it was Zeus who had visited her in this shape we are not told, but she knew that the child she bore was his son.

For a time she kept his birth secret from her father, but it became increasingly difficult to do so in the narrow limits of that bronze house and finally one day the little boy—his name was Perseus—was discovered by his grandfather. "Your child!" Acrisius cried in great anger. "Who is his father?" But when Danaë answered proudly, "Zeus," he would not believe her. One thing only he was sure of, that the boy's life was a terrible danger to his own. He was afraid to kill him for the same reason that had kept him from killing her, fear of Zeus and the Furies[3] who pursue such murderers. But if he could not kill them outright, he could put them in the way of tolerably certain death. He had a great chest made, and the two placed in it. Then it was taken out to sea and cast into the water.

In that strange boat Danaë sat with her little son. The daylight faded and she was alone on the sea.

When in the carven chest the winds and waves
Struck fear into her heart she put her arms,
Not without tears, round Perseus tenderly
She said, "O son, what grief is mine.
But you sleep softly, little child,
Sunk deep in rest within your cheerless home,
Only a box, brass-bound. The night, this darkness visible,
The scudding[4] waves so near to your soft curls,
The shrill voice of the wind, you do not heed,
Nestled in your red cloak, fair little face."

Through the night in the tossing chest she listened to the waters that seemed always about to wash over them. The dawn came, but with no comfort to her for she could not see it. Neither could she see that around them there were islands rising high above the sea, many islands. All she knew was that presently a wave seemed to lift them and carry them swiftly on and then, retreating, leave them on something solid and motionless. They had made land; they were safe from the sea, but they were still in the chest with no way to get out.

Fate willed it—or perhaps Zeus, who up to now had done little for his love and his child—that they should be discovered by a good man, a fisherman named Dictys. He came upon the great box and broke it open and took the pitiful cargo home to his wife who was as kind as he. They had no children and they cared for Danaë and Perseus as if they were their own. The two lived there many years, Danaë content to let her son follow the fisherman's humble trade, out of harm's way. But in the end more trouble came. Polydectes, the ruler of the little island, was the brother of Dictys, but he was a cruel and ruthless man. He seems to have taken no notice of the mother and son for a long time, but at last Danaë attracted his attention. She was still radiantly beautiful even though Perseus by now was full grown,

3. The *Furies* were female snake-haired goddesses who carried out revenge on humans for their wrongdoings.

4. *Scudding* means "moving along at a fast pace."

Literary Element Plot Pattern Archetype *Does this turn of events seem familiar or surprising to you? Explain.* L2

Vocabulary

shrill (shril) *adj.* loud; piercing

Teach

L2 Literary Element

Plot Pattern Archetype
Answer: *Students may say that mythical characters often are placed in dangerous situations with little hope of survival.* Ask students for examples of other stories (including film and television shows) in which characters are in similar situations. OL

★ Literary History

Zeus and Cronus Like Perseus, Zeus was fated to kill his father, Cronus. Cronus, too, tried to kill his children, but his wife escaped with Zeus, who later replaced Cronus as king of the gods. AS

CheckPoint

Use the CheckPoint questions on Presentation Plus! to monitor students' comprehension. These questions can be used with interactive response keypads for immediate student feedback.

English Language Coach

Character Chart Students may have trouble keeping track of all the different characters. Have them list the names of the characters as they read. Next to each character's name, students should jot down basic characterizations, such as Acrisius: *king, bad*; or Danaë: *princess, good.* EL

Differentiated Instruction

Reading Verse Less proficient readers may have trouble with the verse sections of the story. Remind them that the punctuation indicates when to pause in a sentence. Ask a proficient reader to read the verse parts aloud for the class. Then ask volunteers to paraphrase them. BL

Academic Standards

Additional Support activities on pp. 1058 and 1059 cover the following standards:

Skills Practice: **9.2** Develop strategies such as…making predictions…

English Language Coach: **9.3** [Identify] story elements such as character…

Differentiated Instruction: **9.7** [Develop] speaking skills…in conjunction with…strategies…[for] delivery of oral presentations. **9.7.1** Summarize a speaker's purpose and point of view…

Teach

BI Big Idea

Courage and Cleverness
Answer: *Although he knows that the Gorgons are fierce monsters, he goes after them anyway in order to keep his promise.*
Remind students that ancient Greek culture celebrated individuals with courage and intelligence. OL

R1 Reading Strategy

Identifying Genre **Answer:** *The presence of the gods indicates that the story is a myth, which generally includes supernatural forces like gods and goddesses. The god or goddess aiding a mortal is also a common myth archetype.* OL

★ Literary History

The Quest A hero's quest, or attempt to claim a prize or meet a challenge, is one of the most common plot patterns in mythology and literature. The hero's encounters with daunting obstacles make quest stories exciting and suspenseful. Readers identify with the hero as he or she rises to each task required. AS

and Polydectes fell in love with her. He wanted her, but he did not want her son, and he set himself to think out a way of getting rid of him.

There were some fearsome monsters called Gorgons who lived on an island and were known far and wide because of their deadly power. Polydectes evidently talked to Perseus about them; he probably told him that he would rather have the head of one of them than anything else in the world. This seems practically certain from the plan he devised for killing Perseus. He announced that he was about to be married and he called his friends together for a celebration, including Perseus in the invitation. Each guest, as was customary, brought a gift for the bride-to-be, except Perseus alone. He had nothing he could give. He was young and proud and keenly mortified. He stood up before them all and did exactly what the King had hoped he would do, declared that he would give him a present better than any there. He would go off and kill ★ Medusa and bring back her head as his gift. Nothing could have suited the King better. No one in his senses would have made such a proposal. Medusa was one of the Gorgons,

> And they are three, the Gorgons, each
> with wings
> And snaky hair, most horrible to
> mortals.
> Whom no man shall behold and draw
> again
> The breath of life,

for the reason that whoever looked at them was turned instantly into stone. It seemed that Perseus had been led by his angry pride into making an empty boast. No man unaided could kill Medusa.

But Perseus was saved from his folly. Two great gods were watching over him. He took ship as soon as he left the King's hall, not daring to see his mother first and tell her what he intended, and he sailed to Greece to learn where the three monsters were to be found. He went to Delphi, but all the priestess would say was to bid him seek the land where men eat not Demeter's golden grain,[5] but only acorns. So he went to Dodona,[6] in the land of oak trees, where the talking oaks were which declared Zeus's will and where the Selli[7] lived who made their bread from acorns. They could tell him, however, no more than this, that he was under the protection of the gods. They did not know where the Gorgons lived.

When and how Hermes and Athena came to his help is not told in any story, but he must have known despair before they did so. At last, however, as he wandered on, he met a strange and beautiful person. We know what he looked like from many a poem, a young man with the first down upon his cheek when youth is loveliest, carrying, as no other young man ever did, a wand of gold with wings at one end, wearing a winged hat, too, and winged sandals. At sight of him hope must have entered Perseus' heart, for he would know that this could be none other than Hermes, the guide and the giver of good.

This radiant personage[8] told him that before he attacked Medusa he must first be properly equipped, and that what he needed was in the possession of the nymphs[9] of the North. To find the nymphs' abode,[10] they must go to the Gray Women who alone could tell them the way. These women dwelt in a land where all was dim and shrouded in twilight. No ray of sun looked ever on that country, nor the moon by night. In that gray

5. *Demeter's golden grain* refers to Demeter, the Greek goddess of agriculture.
6. *Dodona*, in northwestern Greece, was the site of an oracle dedicated to Zeus.
7. The *Selli* were a tribe of people who lived in the northwestern part of ancient Greece.
8. *Personage* means "an important person."
9. *Nymphs* are female nature spirits in Greek mythology.
10. An *abode* is a home or place of residence.

Big Idea Courage and Cleverness *Does Perseus show courage here? Why or why not?* BI

Reading Strategy Identifying Genre *Why do you think the Greeks created this and other stories about humans aided by gods?* R1

Additional Support

Skills Practice

ASSESSMENT: Making Connections Across Texts Standardized tests often ask students to trace a particular plot pattern through several literary works. To help students practice writing a response, provide the following prompt: *Identify two works of literature with plots based on the quest archetype and compare and contrast the development of the archetype in your two examples.* Divide the class into small groups to discuss how to prepare an answer to the writing prompt. OL

★ place the three women lived, all gray themselves and **withered** as in extreme old age. They were strange creatures, indeed, most of all because they had but one eye for the three, which it was their custom to take turns with, each removing it from her forehead when she had had it for a time and handing it to another.

All this Hermes told Perseus and then he unfolded his plan. He would himself guide Perseus to them. Once there Perseus must keep hidden until he saw one of them take the eye out of her forehead to pass it on. At that moment, when none of the three could see, he must rush forward and seize the eye and refuse to give it back until they told him how to reach the nymphs of the North.

> They were strange creatures, indeed . . .

He himself, Hermes said, would give him a sword to attack Medusa with—which could not be bent or broken by the Gorgon's scales, no matter how hard they were. This was a wonderful gift, no doubt, and yet of what use was a sword when the creature to be struck by it could turn the swordsman into stone before he was within striking distance? But another great deity[11] was at hand to help. Pallas[12] Athena stood beside Perseus. She took off the shield of polished bronze which covered her breast and held it out to him. "Look into this when you attack the Gorgon," she said. "You will be able to see her in it as in a mirror, and so avoid her deadly power."

Now, indeed, Perseus had good reason to hope. The journey to the twilight land was long, over the stream of Ocean and on to the very border of the black country where the Cimmerians[13] dwell, but Hermes was his guide and he could not go astray. They found the Gray Women at last, looking in the wavering light like gray birds, for they had the shape of swans. But their heads were human and beneath their wings they had arms and hands. Perseus did just as Hermes had said, he held back until he saw one of them take the eye out of her forehead. Then before she could give it to her sister, he snatched it out of her hand. It was a moment or two before the three realized they had lost it. Each thought one of the others had it. But Perseus spoke out and told them he had taken it and that it would be theirs again only when they showed him how to find the nymphs of the North. They gave him full directions at once; they would have done anything to get their eye back. He returned it to them and went on the way they had pointed out to him. He was bound, although he did not know it, to the blessed country of the Hyperboreans,[14] at the back of the North Wind, of which it is said: "Neither by ship nor yet by land shall one find the wondrous road to the gathering place of the Hyperboreans." But Perseus had Hermes with him, so that the road lay open to him, and he reached that host of happy people who are always banqueting and holding joyful revelry.[15] They showed him great kindness: they welcomed him to their feast, and the maidens dancing to the sound of flute and lyre[16] paused to get for

11. A *deity* is a god or goddess.
12. *Pallas* is another name for Athena and is sometimes used as part of her regular name. One myth claims Pallas was a friend of Athena's whom she killed accidentally. She added his name to her own so that he would not be forgotten.

13. *Cimmerians* were a race of people living in what is now Russia and Ukraine.
14. *Hyperboreans* were a mythical group of people living in the northern parts of Asia and Europe. Their land was supposed to be perfect.
15. *Revelry* means "loud, boisterous celebrating."
16. A *lyre* is a stringed instrument similar to a harp.

Reading Strategy Identifying Genre *How does the description of this sword fit the characteristics of a myth?* **R2**

Vocabulary

withered (wi*th*′ərd) *adj.* shriveled or dried up

Teach

R2 Reading Strategy

Identifying Genre **Answer:** *Magical elements like this sword are common in myth. This sword is magical or fantastic because it cannot be bent or broken. In some cases, swords can represent an archetype.* **OL**

★ Literary History

Mythical Sisters According to the ancient Greek poet Hesiod, the Gray Women, or Graiae, and the Gorgons were sisters. They were all children of the sea deities Phorcys and Ceto. Images of these fearsome creatures were believed capable of warding off evil spirits. **AS**

Building Reading Fluency

Reading Aloud Reading passages aloud will give students a sense of the rhythm of Hamilton's prose. Have partners take turns reading the same paragraph aloud. After each has read, have students summarize what has happened. **BL**

Differentiated Instruction

Mythological Relationships Advanced readers may enjoy researching the Greek pantheon in a library or on the Internet. Have them use their findings to create a family tree or other graphic organizer that can be shared with the class. **AL**

Academic Standards

Additional Support activities on pp. 1060 and 1061 cover the following standards:

Skills Practice: **9.3.5** Compare works that express a universal theme and provide evidence to support the views expressed in each work.

Building Reading Fluency: **9.7** [Develop] speaking skills…in conjunction with…strategies…[for] delivery of oral presentations. **9.7.1** Summarize a speaker's purpose and point of view…

Differentiated Instruction: **9.2.4** Synthesize the content from several sources…

Teach

R Reading Strategy

Identifying Genre **Answer:** *No; in a realistic story set in the present, people do not rely on magic or supernatural powers to solve their problems.* OL

BI1 Big Idea

Courage and Cleverness
Answer: *Because Medusa could turn a person to stone with one look, Perseus cleverly avoids her gaze.*
Ask: Do you think the fact that Athena helped Perseus makes him less clever or brave? *(Encourage students to support their opinions with logical arguments.)* OL

BI2 Big Idea

Courage and Cleverness
Say: Quest myths always circle back to the place or the conflict that started the quest.
Ask: How is Perseus better equipped to realize his destiny after defeating the Gorgons? *(He has completed his quest. He has not only done the impossible, but also has the tools to kill his enemies.)* OL

him the gifts he sought. These were three: winged sandals, a magic wallet[17] which would always become the right size for whatever was to be carried in it, and, most important of all, a cap which made the wearer invisible. With these and Athena's shield and Hermes' sword Perseus was ready for the Gorgons. Hermes knew where they lived, and leaving the happy land the two flew back across Ocean and over the sea to the Terrible Sisters' island.

By great good fortune they were all asleep when Perseus found them. In the mirror of the bright shield he could see them clearly, creatures with great wings and bodies covered with golden scales and hair a mass of twisting snakes. Athena was beside him now as well as Hermes. They told him which one was Medusa and that was important, for she alone of the three could be killed; the other two were immortal. Perseus on his winged sandals hovered above them, looking, however, only at the shield. Then he aimed a stroke down at Medusa's throat and Athena guided his hand. With a single sweep of his sword he cut through her neck and, his eyes still fixed on the shield with never a glance at her, he swooped low enough to seize the head. He dropped it into the wallet which closed around it. He had nothing to fear from it now. But the two other Gorgons had awakened and, horrified at the sight of their sister slain, tried to pursue the slayer. Perseus was safe; he had on the cap of darkness and they could not find him.

> So over the sea rich-haired Danaë's son,
> Perseus, on his winged sandals sped,
> Flying swift as thought.
> In a wallet of silver,
> A wonder to behold,
> He bore the head of the monster,
> While Hermes, the son of Maia,
> The messenger of Zeus,
> Kept ever at his side.

On his way back he came to Ethiopia[18] and alighted there. By this time Hermes had left him. Perseus found, as Hercules was later to find, that a lovely maiden had been given up to be devoured by a horrible sea serpent. Her name was Andromeda and she was the daughter of a silly vain woman,

> That starred Ethiop queen who strove
> To set her beauty's praise above
> The sea-nymphs, and their power
> offended.

She had boasted that she was more beautiful than the daughters of Nereus, the Sea-god. An absolutely certain way in those days to draw down on one a wretched fate was to claim superiority in anything over any deity; nevertheless people were perpetually doing so. In this case the punishment for the arrogance the gods detested fell not on Queen Cassiopeia, Andromeda's mother, but on her daughter. The Ethiopians were being devoured in numbers by the serpent; and, learning from the oracle that they could be freed from the pest only if Andromeda were offered up to it, they forced Cepheus, her father, to consent. When Perseus arrived the maiden was on a rocky ledge by the sea, chained there to wait for the coming of the monster. Perseus saw her and on the instant loved her. He waited beside her until the great snake came for its prey; then he cut its head off just as he had the Gorgon's. The headless body dropped back into the water; Perseus took Andromeda to her parents and asked for her hand, which they gladly gave him.

With her he sailed back to the island and his mother, but in the house where he had lived so long he found no one. The fisherman Dictys' wife was long since dead, and the two others, Danaë and the man who had been like a father to Perseus, had had to fly and hide themselves from Polydectes, who was furious at Danaë's refusal to marry him. They had BI2

17. Here, *wallet* is used in its Middle English sense and means "knapsack."

18. *Ethiopia* is a coastal country in northeastern Africa.

Reading Strategy Identifying Genre *Would these three items be found in a realistic story set in the present? Explain.* R

Big Idea Courage and Cleverness *What is clever about Perseus's method of killing Medusa?* BI1

Additional Support

Skills Practice

SPEAKING AND LISTENING: Interviewing Guide the class to role-play an interview with Perseus and Athena to improve their understanding of mythological characters. Invite two volunteers to play the hero and the goddess. Tell the class to imagine they are the audience at a talk show with the two characters as guests. Offer an example of questions they might ask about the characters' attitudes and feelings. For instance, **ask:** Athena, why did you decide to help Perseus? OL

Perseus assisted by Minerva, presents the head of Medusa to Phineus and his companions. Jean Marc Nattier. Musee des Beaux-Arts, Tours, France.

Viewing the Art: What adjectives would you use to describe this scene? ★

taken refuge in a temple, Perseus was told. He learned also that the King was holding a banquet in the palace and all the men who favored him were gathered there. Perseus instantly saw his opportunity. He went straight to the palace and entered the hall. As he stood at the entrance, Athena's shining buckler[19] on his breast, the silver wallet at his side, he drew the eyes of every man there. Then before any could look away he held up the Gorgon's head; and at the sight one and all, the cruel King and his servile courtiers,[20] were turned into stone. There they sat, a row of statues, each, as it were, frozen stiff in the attitude he had struck when he first saw Perseus.

When the islanders knew themselves freed from the tyrant it was easy for Perseus to find Danaë and Dictys. He made Dictys king of the island, but he and his mother decided that they would go back with Andromeda to Greece and try to be reconciled to Acrisius, to see if the many years that had passed since he had put them in the chest had not softened him so that he would be glad to receive his daughter and grandson. When they reached Argos, however, they found that Acrisius had been driven away from the city, and where he was no one could say. It happened that soon after their arrival Perseus heard that the King of Larissa,[21] in the North, was holding a great athletic contest, and he journeyed there to take part. In the discus-throwing[22] when his turn came and he hurled the heavy missile, it swerved and fell among the spectators. Acrisius was there on a visit to the King, and the discus struck him. The blow was fatal and he died at once.

So Apollo's[23] oracle was again proved true. If Perseus felt any grief, at least he knew that his grandfather had done his best to kill him and his mother. With his death their troubles came to an end. Perseus and Andromeda lived happily ever after. Their son, Electryon, was the grandfather of Hercules.[24]

Medusa's head was given to Athena, who bore it always upon the aegis, Zeus's shield, which she carried for him.

19. A *buckler* is a type of shield.
20. The term *servile courtiers* refers to the submissive people who advised the king.

21. *Larissa* is a city in eastern Greece.
22. A *discus* is a heavy round disk that is thrown in track and field competitions.
23. *Apollo* is a Greek god known for healing, prophesy, and music.
24. *Hercules* is the Roman name for the Greek hero Heracles, who was the son of Zeus and a human woman named Alcemene. Hercules successfully completed twelve tasks in order to become a god.

Literary Element Plot Pattern Archetype *How does this event complete one archetypal pattern in the story?* L

Teach

L Literary Element

Plot Pattern Archetype

Answer: *With this event, the prophesy is fulfilled. Even though Acrisius does everything possible to stop the prophecy from coming true, he fails. Perseus kills him just as was prophesied, but by accident rather than intent.*

Ask: Did the story of Perseus end the way you expected? Why or why not? *(Students may say that they knew that in Greek myths, the fates never lie.)* OL

★ Viewing the Art

Answer: *Student's answers will vary. Responses may include the following adjectives:* violent, courageous, victorious, gruesome, heroic. AS

Use the CheckPoint questions on Presentation Plus! to check students' mastery of the selection. These questions can be used with interactive response keypads for immediate student feedback.

English Language Coach

Multiple-Meaning Words Tell students that *missile* as used in this myth means "an object thrown at a target," and does not refer to a weapon or ballistic missile. Explain that this is a good example of a situation where context clues can help you determine meaning.

Ask students to find other examples of multiple-meaning words in the selection. *(Students might identify* oracle, *which in this case means the response of a prophetic person. Another example is* bore, *which here means "wore" and not "gave birth to.")* EL

Academic Standards

Additional Support activities on pp. 1062 and 1063 cover the following standards:

Skills Practice: **9.7.16** Apply appropriate interviewing techniques...

English Language Coach: **9.1** Use...context clues...to determine the meaning of words...

AFTER YOU READ

Assess

1. Accept reasonable answers.
2. (a) He sets them adrift in the sea. (b) A prophecy said his daughter's son would kill him. (c) He loves himself more than he loves his family and stubbornly rebels against fate.
3. (a) Hermes helps him find his way. Both Athena and Hermes give him magical tools. (b) They consider him worthy; he is Zeus's son—and their brother.
4. (a) He pulls out Medusa's head, and her stare turns Polydectes to stone. (b) Polydectes was a threat to Perseus's mother; also, Polydectes tricked Perseus into going on a deadly quest.
5. (a) By trying to save himself, he began the chain of events that resulted in his death. Although Perseus causes his death, he wanted to reconcile. (b) Fate is unchangeable.
6. Both Andromeda and Perseus were placed in life-threatening situations by their family members.
7. His relationship with her shows his bravery and also allows him to become an adult with a family of his own.
8. Students should support their answers.

AFTER YOU READ

RESPONDING AND THINKING CRITICALLY

Respond

1. What event in the story surprised you the most? Why?

Recall and Interpret

2. (a)What does King Acrisius do to Danaë and Perseus? (b)Why does Acrisius take such drastic measures? (c)What does this tell you about his character?
3. (a)How do the gods help Perseus achieve his goal of killing Medusa and cutting off her head? (b)Why are they willing to help him?
4. (a)How does Perseus kill Polydectes? (b)Why does he kill him?

Analyze and Evaluate

5. **Irony** occurs when there is a discrepancy between appearance and reality. (a)How is Acrisius's death ironic? (b)What does his death in this myth reveal about the Ancient Greeks' beliefs about fate?
6. How are Andromeda and Perseus similar? Consider the nature of the situations they find themselves in.
7. Why is Perseus's relationship with Andromeda important to the story?

Connect

8. **Big Idea** **Courage and Cleverness** How courageous and clever is Perseus? Support your answer with scenes and details from the story.

VISUAL LITERACY: Graphic Organizer

Flowchart of Events

Perseus Freeing Andromeda, 1515. Piero di Cosimo. Oil on wood, 70 × 123cm. Galleria degli Uffizi, Florence.

Viewing the Art: What gives Perseus the ability to fly? Is this how you would expect to see him as he flew? Explain. ★

Sometimes when you are reading, it can be helpful to create a flowchart showing what is happening in the plot. The flowchart allows you to define the major plot events and character decisions in a story. Use the flowchart shown as the beginning of your own flowchart, charting the major events of the myth of Perseus.

Partner Activity When you have completed your flowchart, meet with a classmate to answer the following questions.

1. At what point does Perseus decide to kill Medusa? Why does he make this decision?
2. At what point in the story do the gods intervene and help Perseus?

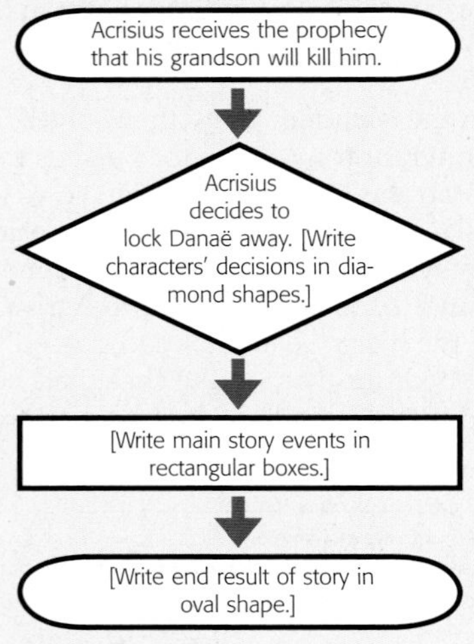
Acrisius receives the prophecy that his grandson will kill him.
Acrisius decides to lock Danaë away. [Write characters' decisions in diamond shapes.]
[Write main story events in rectangular boxes.]
[Write end result of story in oval shape.]

Visual Literacy

Students' charts should summarize the main events and decisions.

1. At the wedding announcement dinner of Polydectes and Danaë; To make up for the embarrassment of having no gift
2. The text states that it is not known when they came to his aid, but suggests that it was after he became discouraged.

★ Viewing the Art

Answer: *The Gray Women told Perseus where to find winged sandals that allowed him to fly. Students' responses will vary.*

LITERARY ANALYSIS

Literary Element Plot Pattern Archetype

Certain plot patterns are characterized as archetypal when they are common across cultures. Most cultures, for example, have created myths about how Earth and its people were created. Similarly, many cultures have stories in which humans are helped by gods.

1. List some plot patterns from this story that you have come across in other stories, books, plays, or movies.
2. Choose one plot pattern from this story and explain why it might be meaningful to readers around the world.

Review: Hero

As you learned on pages 954–955, the **hero** in a literary work is the main character. In myths, the hero usually has traits or abilities that exceed those of a normal person. These traits or abilities allow the hero to accomplish great deeds.

Partner Activity With a partner, create a chart like the one below listing the actions and personality traits that make Perseus a hero. In the second column of your chart, explain why each element demonstrates heroism.

Heroic Action or Trait	Heroic Explanation
Perseus does not give up his quest even before the gods help him.	His actions show that he is willing to persevere even when things look hopeless.

READING AND VOCABULARY

Reading Strategy Identifying Genre

Knowing a story's genre can help you understand what to expect. Myths like "Perseus" are traditional stories that involve gods, goddesses, heroes, and supernatural forces. Myths may explain beliefs, customs, or forces of nature.

1. What elements of "Perseus" fit the description of a myth?
2. How do supernatural events in a story affect your expectations as a reader?

Vocabulary Practice

Practice with Antonyms For each vocabulary word below, choose the best antonym. Consult a dictionary or thesaurus if you need help.

1. kindred
   a. relatives **c.** people
   b. strangers **d.** friends
2. shrill
   a. quiet **c.** cacophonous
   b. piercing **d.** bright
3. withered
   a. blooming **c.** fresh
   b. dried up **d.** shriveled

Academic Vocabulary

Here are two words from the vocabulary list on page R80. The words will help you think, talk, and write about the selection.

voluntary (vol´ən ter´ ē) *adj.* done by choice

method (meth´ əd) *n.* a way of accomplishing something

Practice and Apply

1. Why does Perseus go on his **voluntary** quest?
2. What **methods** of help do the gods provide for Perseus?

AFTER YOU READ

Assess

Literary Element

1. Students' answers should refer to patterns from quest stories, such as a hero slaying monsters or winning a beautiful maiden; they may also refer to stories in which evil parents try to kill their heirs or in which fate triumphs.
2. People enjoy the suspense and adventure of a quest story. Tales of people meeting seemingly impossible challenges are instructive and uplifting.

Review: Hero

Remind students that while heroes need not be perfect, they possess qualities that are considered extraordinary. Stress the importance of including specific evidence from the text in their charts.

Reading Strategy

1. Inclusion of supernatural elements, prophecy, and fate; involvement of heroes and rulers
2. The reader knows that anything can happen. The laws of science do not apply.

Vocabulary

1. b **2.** a **3.** a

Academic Vocabulary

1. He agrees to go because he wants to make a good impression on Polydectes.
2. The way the gods help is to offer guidance and tools.

AFTER YOU READ

Assess

Writing About Literature

Students' essays should identify one or more modern heroes, compare and contrast the actions of modern heroes with those of ancient ones, and provide insight about life and human nature today. Students should cite the text for support.

Hamilton's Language and Style

Sample answers:
Original passive: (p. 1059) "Then it was taken out to sea and cast into the water."
Active: Then men took it out to sea and cast it into the water. (The revision tells who took the chest.)
Original passive: (p. 1062) "The Ethiopians were being devoured in numbers by the serpent."
Active: The serpent was devouring the Ethiopians in numbers. (The revision emphasizes the serpent.)

Internet Connection

Students should list the common plot elements found in the different versions of the story and incorporate their findings in a Venn diagram or other graphic organizer that clearly illustrates points of contrast.

WRITING AND EXTENDING

Writing About Literature

Evaluate Contemporary Relevance Although the story of Perseus dates back to ancient Greece, stories of heroes are timeless. Who are our modern heroes? How do their actions compare to those of ancient heroes like Perseus? What do the stories about modern heroes say about life and human nature today? Answer these questions in a short essay. Use evidence from the story to support your position.

Before you start writing, brainstorm a list of heroes and reasons they are considered heroic. Use a chart like the one below.

Modern Hero	Reasons
Firefighters	They bravely risk their lives to save others.

When you are finished writing, exchange papers with a partner. Read your partner's paper once all the way through. Then go back through the paper and make suggestions for improvement. Be sure to proofread and edit your essay to correct any errors in spelling, punctuation, and grammar.

Internet Connection

Edith Hamilton's version of the story of Perseus is only one example of this myth. Using the Internet, find two other versions of the Perseus story. Read through the alternate versions and create a chart comparing the most common story elements in all three versions.

Head of Medusa. Gian Lorenzo Bernini

GRAMMAR AND STYLE

Hamilton's Language and Style

Using Active Voice Edith Hamilton tells the story of Perseus using active voice. Active voice involves the use of active verbs rather than linking verbs. With active voice, the subject of the sentence engages in an activity. For example, the sentence "Bob lost the money," is written in active voice: *Bob* is the subject and he performs the action of losing.

The opposite of active voice is passive voice. In passive voice sentences, the subject of the sentence is acted upon. For example, the sentence "The money was lost by Bob" is written in passive voice. In most writing, active voice is preferred over passive voice.

Passive Voice	Active Voice
A gift was brought by each guest, as was customary, except by Perseus.	"Each guest, as was customary, brought a gift for the bride-to-be, except Perseus alone."

Activity Following the example in the chart above, reread the story and find several sentences written in passive voice. Rewrite the sentences using active voice. Explain in a sentence or two why the active voice is more engaging in each example.

Revising Check

Active Voice Reread the essay you wrote about modern heroes, looking for sentences written in passive voice. Rewrite as many of these sentences as possible in active voice.

LiteratureOnline **Web Activities** For eFlashcards, Selection Quick Checks, and other Web activities, go to www.glencoe.com.

Revising Check

Remind students to avoid the passive voice. Challenge them to change every example they find in their writing to the active voice.

Web Activities Have students access the Web site for interactive activities that will help them assess their understanding of the selection.

The Fenris Wolf

MEET OLIVIA COOLIDGE

Nothing interests Olivia Coolidge like history, biography, ancient legends, and myths—and when Coolidge is interested in something, she explores it thoroughly. She has written about the Trojan War, imperial Romans, Revolutionary War heroes, the British, Mahatma Gandhi, Abraham Lincoln, and the struggle for women's rights. She has retold myths and tales from a variety of cultures.

An Early Interest in Stories Coolidge was born in England, the daughter of Sir Robert Charles Kirkwood, a journalist and historian who taught at Oxford University. She grew up in a house without gas, electricity, central heating, or a hot-water system. Stories were an early amusement, and she and her sister spent hours creating fairy tales to tell each other before bedtime.

When she was older, Coolidge attended Oxford and went on to become a teacher. She moved to the United States just before World War II, and her experiences as a teacher in American schools inspired her to write her first book for young adults, a collection called *Greek Myths.* Soon after, she published *Legends of the North,* which includes "The Fenris Wolf." Since then, Coolidge has published more than two dozen other works.

The Norse god, Thor, with a hammer, statuette found in Iceland. Bronze. National Museum of Iceland, Reykjavik, Iceland.

Her Own Voice Coolidge is a voracious reader and a stylish writer. In her work, she provides fascinating insights into the minds of characters. Above all, she believes that it is important for young people to read work that excites and entertains them.

> *"A good book should excite, amuse and interest. It should give a sense of seeing as a movie does."*
>
> —Olivia Coolidge

Coolidge explains that she focuses on history, biography, and legends because she is interested in "values that always have been of concern to people." According to her, the experiences of the past have a lot to teach people of the present day about their own humanity. Many experiences, emotions, and values are universal, known to all cultures and eras.

Recent Work One recent book of Coolidge's tells the story of a colonial businessman in Maine at the time of the American Revolution. In this work, she invites readers into a world of lumber camps, immigrants, and harsh winters. Coolidge remains best known, however, for mythological retellings based on careful research and for her extraordinary ability to bring more well-known chapters of the past to life. Her work teaches valuable lessons to people of all ages.

Olivia Coolidge was born in 1908.

Literature Online **Author Search** For more about Olivia Coolidge, go to www.glencoe.com.

BEFORE YOU READ

Focus

BELLRINGER

Bellringer Options
Daily Language Practice Transparency 89
Or display photographs and other images of wolves.
Ask: What characteristics do you associate with wolves? Why do you think they are often portrayed as villains? Encourage students to consider the relationship between people and wolves as they read.

Author Search To expand students' appreciation of Olivia Coolidge, have them access the Web site for additional information and resources.

Selection Skills

The Fenris Wolf

Literary Elements
- Image Archetype (SE pp. 1068, 1070, 1071, 1072)

Reading Skills
- Interpreting Imagery (SE pp. 1068, 1070, 1072)

Vocabulary Skills
- Context Clues (SE pp. 1068, 1072)

Listening/Speaking/Viewing Skills
- Analyzing Art (SE p. 1071)
- Oral Interpretation (TWE p. 1070)

Writing Skills/Grammar
- Analyze Plot (SE p. 1072)

BEFORE YOU READ

Focus

Summary

The Fenris Wolf is the offspring of Loki, the fire god, and a giantess. Odin and the other gods think they can tame the young wolf, but it soon grows out of control. The gods forge two chains, but the wolf breaks free. Then the gods tie the wolf with a magical thread, and it holds—but only until the end of the world.

V Vocabulary

Vocabulary File Say: Add these words and definitions to your vocabulary file. For each word, include a sentence that gives you an example of how to use the word. **OL** Students with English language needs should include the pronunciations of these words in their files. **EL**

Literature Online

Literary Elements Have students access the Web site to improve their understanding of image archetypes.

LITERATURE PREVIEW

Connecting to the Myth

"The Fenris Wolf" is the story of an evil beast, courage, and fate. As you read the myth, think about the following questions:

- How is the Fenris Wolf like or unlike other evil beasts you have encountered in myths or other tales?
- What makes this myth different from other myths and tales about good and evil that you have read?

Building Background

"The Fenris Wolf" is a Norse tale, or a tale that comes from the pre-Christian religion of the Danish, Icelandic, Norwegian, and Swedish peoples. According to Norse mythology, Asgard was the home of the warrior gods, including Odin, who was the chief of all gods. Loki, Tyr, and Thor were other great gods. Thor, the son of Odin, was one of the most popular. He was both the god of thunder and a blacksmith. Smiths are often powerful figures in myths and tales because they can control fire and make tools, chains, and weapons out of metal.

Setting Purposes for Reading

Big Idea Courage and Cleverness

As you read, notice the wolf's cleverness and Tyr's courage.

Literary Element Image Archetype

An **archetype** is a pattern, image, theme, character type, or plot type that occurs in literature and folklore across many cultures. **Common image archetypes** include the snake or serpent, which when shown eating its own tail represents the life cycle; the chain, which holds back, ties up, or restrains; and the wolf, which represents devouring. As you read "The Fenris Wolf," think about your response to the archetypal images of the snake, the wolf, and the chain.

- See Literary Terms Handbook, p. R9.

Literature Online Interactive Literary Elements Handbook To review or learn more about the literary elements, go to www.glencoe.com.

READING PREVIEW

Reading Strategy Interpreting Imagery

To **interpret imagery,** notice details in the text that appeal to your senses. Analyze how these details affect your emotions and influence your understanding of the text.

Reading Tip: Taking Notes As you read, make a list of images and record your emotional responses to them.

Image	My Emotional Response
Huge serpent that completely encircles the earth so that its head meets its tail.	This image seems horrifying and repulsive to me.

Vocabulary

brood (bro͞od) *n.* the young of a family; p. 1069 *The cat gave birth to a large brood of kittens.*

fetter (fet′ər) *v.* to chain; p. 1070 *The animal control officer fettered the dangerous animal.*

forge (fôrj) *v.* to form or make, especially by heating or hammering; p. 1070 *The smith forged a large metal tool over the fire.*

writhe (rīth) *v.* to twist in pain; p. 1071 *The wounded elephant was writhing in pain when the explorers discovered him.*

Vocabulary Tip: Context Clues Context clues are words, phrases, and sentences that surround an unfamiliar word and give clues to its meaning.

INDIANA ACADEMIC STANDARDS (pages 1068-1072)

9.3 [Identify] story elements such as character, theme, [and] plot...and [make] connections and comparisons across texts...

9.3.1 Recognize and understand...imagery...

9.5.3 Write...analytical essays...

Selection Resources

Print Materials
- Unit 5 Resources (Fast File), pp. 42–44
- Leveled Vocabulary Development, p. 68
- Selection and Unit Assessments, pp. 181–182
- Selection Quick Checks, p. 91

Transparencies
- Bellringer Options Transparencies: Daily Language Practice Transparency 89
- Literary Elements Transparency 87

Technology
- TeacherWorks Plus™ CD-ROM
- StudentWorks Plus™ CD-ROM
- Presentation Plus!™ CD-ROM
- Literature Online, glencoe.com
- Online Student Edition, mhln.com
- Exam*View*® Assessment Suite CD-ROM
- Vocabulary PuzzleMaker CD-ROM
- Listening Library, disc 2 track 31

The Fenris Wolf

Retold by Olivia Coolidge

Three standing figures identified as Odin, Thor and Frey. From a Viking tapestry, 12th c. Statens Historiska Museet, Stockholm, Sweden.

Though Loki, the fire god, was handsome and ready-witted, his nature was really evil. He was, indeed, the cause of most of the misfortunes which befell the gods. He was constantly in trouble, yet often forgiven because the gods valued his cleverness. It was he who found ways out of difficulty for them, so that for a long time they felt that they could not do without him.

In the early days Loki, though a god, had wedded a monstrous giantess, and the union of these two evil beings produced a fearful **brood.** BI The first was the great world serpent, whom Odin cast into the sea, and ★ who became so large that he completely encircled the earth, his tail touching his mouth. The second was Hel, the grisly goddess of the underworld, who reigned in the

Vocabulary

brood (bro͞od) *n.* the young of a family

Teach

BI Big Idea

Courage and Cleverness
Ask: Why are the gods so afraid of the brood? *(The serpent encircles the earth, Hel rules the underworld, and the wolf is huge and ferocious.)* **OL**

★ Literary History

Odin Odin, the king of the Norse gods, was the god of sky, wind, and war. Scholars believe that his name meant "wild or furious." Norse mythology tells stories of his triumphs over frost giants and his fall during an ending of the world. Odin could also take human form, appearing in our world as an old, one-eyed man wearing a floppy hat. **AS**

CheckPoint

Use the CheckPoint questions on Presentation Plus! to monitor students' comprehension. These questions can be used with interactive response keypads for immediate student feedback.

Readability Scores

Dale-Chall: 9.4
DRP: 57
Lexile: 1120

English Language Coach

Connotations Have English language learners discuss the connotations of the words used to describe the Fenris Wolf on page 1070. **Ask:** What do words such as *howl, beast, dreadful,* and *violently* suggest about the wolf? **EL**

Differentiated Instruction

Visualization Encourage students with a strong visual sense to create illustrations for the story's most dramatic images and present them in class. Discuss how students' visual interpretations differ. **AL**

Academic Standards

Additional Support activities on p. 1069 cover the following standards:

English Language Coach: **9.1.2** Distinguish between what words mean literally and what they imply and interpret what they imply.

Differentiated Instruction: **9.3.7** Recognize and understand the significance of various literary devices, including…imagery…

Teach

L1 Literary Element

Image Archetype Answer: *Students may mention howling wolves in horror films; students will probably suggest that a wolf's howl sounds ominous.* Remind students that the Fenris Wolf is both an animal and a symbol of destructive impulses. OL

R Reading Strategy

Interpreting Imagery
Answer: *Students should recognize that these unusual items could only be acquired and used in a magical world by magical beings.*
Ask: What quality is suggested by each of the rope's ingredients? *(They all are immaterial and insubstantial, suggesting a spiritual quality.)* OL

horrible land of the dead. The third was the most dreadful of all, a huge monster called the Fenris Wolf.

When the gods first saw the Fenris Wolf, he was so young that they thought they could tame him. They took him to Asgard, therefore, and brave Tyr undertook to feed and train him. Presently, however, the black monster grew so enormous that his open jaws would stretch from heaven to earth, showing teeth as large as the trunks of oak trees and as sharply pointed as knives. The howls of the beast were so dreadful as he tore his vast meals of raw meat that the gods, save for Tyr, dared not go near him, lest[1] he devour them.

At last all were agreed that the Fenris Wolf must be **fettered** if they were to save their very lives, for the monster grew more ferocious towards them every day. They **forged** a huge chain, but since none was strong enough to bind him, they challenged him to a trial of strength. "Let us tie you with this to see if you can snap the links," said they.

The Fenris Wolf took a look at the chain and showed all his huge white teeth in a dreadful grin. "Bind me if you wish," he growled, and he actually shut his eyes as he lay down at ease to let them put it on.

The gods stepped back, and the wolf gave a little shake. There was a loud cracking sound, and the heavy links lay scattered around him in pieces. The wolf howled in triumph until the sun and moon in heaven trembled at the noise.

Thor, the smith, called other gods to his aid, and they labored day and night at the second chain. This was half as strong again[2] as the first, and so heavy that no one of the gods could drag it across the ground. "This is by far the largest chain that was ever made," said they. "Even the Fenris Wolf will not be able to snap fetters such as these."

Once more they brought the chain to the wolf, and he let them put it on, though this time it was clear that he somewhat doubted his strength. When they had chained him, he shook himself violently, but the fetters held. His great, red eyes burned with fury, the black hair bristled[3] on his back, and he gnashed his teeth until the foam flew. He strained heavily against the iron until the vast links flattened and lengthened, but did not break. Finally with a great bound and a howl he dashed himself against the ground, and suddenly the chain sprang apart so violently that broken pieces were hurled about the heads of the watching gods.

Now the gods realized in despair that all their strength and skill would not avail[4] to bind the wolf. Therefore Odin sent a messenger to the dwarf people under the earth, bidding them forge him a chain. The messenger returned with a little rope, smooth and soft as a silken string, which was hammered on dwarfish anvils[5] out of strange materials which have never been seen or heard. The sound of a cat's footfall, the breath of a fish, the flowing beard of a woman, and the roots of a mountain made the metal from which it was forged.

The gods took the tiny rope to the Fenris Wolf. "See what an easy task we have for you this time," they said.

1. Here, *lest* means "for fear that."

Literary Element Image Archetype *Where else have you seen the image of a wolf howling? What feeling does it evoke?* L1

Vocabulary

fetter (fet′ər) *v.* to chain

forge (fôrj) *v.* to form or make, especially by heating or hammering

2. *Half as strong again* means one and one-half times as strong.
3. Here, *bristle* means "to raise the hairs on the back, as in fear, anger, or excitement."
4. Here, *avail* means "be sufficient."
5. *Anvils* are blocks on which blacksmiths pound hot metal into shapes.

Reading Strategy Interpreting Imagery *What do these images suggest about the chain and the dwarves who made it?* R

Additional Support

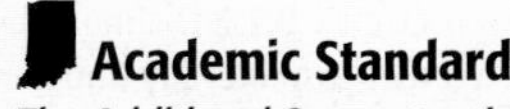

Academic Standards
The Additional Support activity on p. 1070 covers the following standard:
Skills Practice: **9.7.6** Analyze the occasion…and choose effective verbal…techniques (including voice…) for presentations.

Skills Practice

SPEAKING: Oral Interpretation
Have students analyze how Coolidge's use of imagery and concrete and figurative language bring the myth to life. Assign pairs of students to prepare an oral interpretation of various paragraphs in the selection. Stress the importance of using tone of voice and expression to reflect the content and the mood of the text. Students should rehearse before presenting to the class. OL

The Norse god Tyr losing his hand to the bound wolf, Fenrir. Manuscript. Royal Library, Copenhagen, Denmark.

Viewing the Art: In what ways does this illustration correspond with or differ from your mental image of the Fenris Wolf and Tyr? ★

"Why should I bother myself with a silken string?" asked the wolf sullenly. "I have broken your mightiest chain. What use is this foolish thing?"

"The rope is stronger than it looks," answered they. "We are not able to break it, but it will be a small matter to you."

"If this rope is strong by enchantment," said the wolf in slow suspicion, "how can I tell that you will loosen me if I cannot snap it after all? On one condition you may bind me: You must give me a hostage from among yourselves."

"How can we do this?" they asked.

The Fenris Wolf stretched himself and yawned until the sun hid behind clouds at the sight of his great, red throat. "I will let you bind me with this rope," he said, "if one of you gods will hold his hand between my teeth while I do it."

The gods looked at one another in silence. The wolf grinned from ear to ear. Without a word Tyr walked forward and laid his bare hand inside the open mouth.

The gods bound the great wolf, and he stretched himself and heaved as before. This time, however, he did not break his bonds. He gnashed his jaws together, and Tyr cried out in pain as he lost his hand. Nevertheless, the great black wolf lay howling and **writhing** and helplessly biting the ground. There he lay in the bonds of the silken rope as long as the reign of Odin endured. The Fates declared, however, that in the last days, when the demons of ice and fire should come marching against the gods to the battlefield, the great sea would give up the serpent, and the Fenris Wolf would break his bonds. The wolf would swallow Odin, and the gods would go down in defeat. Sun and moon would be devoured, and the whole earth would perish utterly. ∾

Big Idea Courage and Cleverness *How is the Fenris Wolf clever?* **BI**

Literary Element Image Archetype *What image archetypes appear in this paragraph?* **L2**

Vocabulary

writhe (rīth) *v.* to twist in pain

Teach

BI Big Idea

Courage and Cleverness

Answer: *He senses the magical power of the rope and tries to protect himself by demanding a terrible sacrifice.* **Ask:** Why does the wolf become suspicious? *(The clever wolf realizes that the tiny rope must have special powers or the gods would not use it.)* **OL**

L2 Literary Element

Image Archetype **Answer:** *Students should mention the serpent rising out of the sea, which completes the "life cycle" of Odin's reign and the wolf devouring the god Odin. They may also mention the sea, sun, and moon, as well as the end of Earth.* **Say:** Image archetypes grab readers on some level, reminding them of something symbolic. **OL**

★ Viewing the Art

Answer: *Students' answers will vary. Many will have imagined Fenris Wolf as more fearsome.*

CheckPoint

Use the CheckPoint questions on Presentation Plus! to check students' mastery of the selection. These questions can be used with interactive response keypads for immediate student feedback.

Differentiated Instruction

Prose into a Poem Invite gifted and talented students to write a poem about the wolf, based on Coolidge's story. The poems can be about their reactions to reading the story, or they can retell the story in verse from the wolf's or Tyr's point of view. Remind students that they can use traditional poetic forms (meter, rhyme scheme), free verse, or a mixture of the two. **AL**

Academic Standards

The Additional Support activity on p. 1071 covers the following standard:

Differentiated Instruction: **9.5.8** Write for different purposes and audiences, adjusting tone, style, and voice as appropriate.

AFTER YOU READ

Assess

1. Accept reasonable answers.
2. (a) He is born of Loki and a giantess. (b) All are monsters or associated with misfortune or death.
3. (a) He is huge and destructive. (b) They try to tame and fetter him. (c) He is too strong.
4. (a) The underground dwarves (b) He turns to tiny beings to solve a problem too big for the gods; the solution is an insubstantial rope.
5. He is crafty, powerful, and destructive.
6. (a) Courage, self-sacrifice, and restraint (b) They recognize the need for restraint and order. The culture seems fatalistic, realizing that the wolf will finally break free.
7. (a) Accept reasonable answers. (b) Accept reasonable answers.
8. (a) Tyr's courage allows a temporary solution. (b) He is bound despite his cleverness.

Literary Element

1. The wolf is devouring and cruel. He bites the god who cares for him.
2. (a) The wolf it controls can cause destruction. (b) Order and restraint, or connections between people

Writing About Literature

Remind students to provide examples.

Vocabulary

1. b **2.** a **3.** c **4.** a

AFTER YOU READ

RESPONDING AND THINKING CRITICALLY

Respond

1. What did you find most fearful about the Fenris Wolf? Explain.

Recall and Interpret

2. (a)How does the Fenris Wolf come to be? (b)What is evil about the Fenris Wolf's family?
3. (a)Why do the gods feel that they must control the Fenris Wolf? (b)How do they attempt to control the Fenris Wolf? (c) Why are the gods unsuccessful at first?
4. (a)To whom does Odin turn for help in defeating the Fenris Wolf? (b)What is surprising about his solution to the problem?

Analyze and Evaluate

5. What characteristics does the Fenris Wolf display?
6. (a)What qualities or character traits does this tale seem to promote? (b)After reading this tale, what insights do you have into the Norse gods and culture?
7. (a)Do you think that Tyr and the gods betray the Fenris Wolf? (b)Do you think that the Fenris Wolf betrays Tyr?

Connect

8. **Big Idea** **Courage and Cleverness** (a)How does Tyr's courage affect the outcome of this story? (b)Does the Fenris Wolf's cleverness change the outcome of this story? Explain.

LITERARY ANALYSIS

Literary Element Image Archetype

An **image archetype** is an image that occurs in literature and folklore across many cultures. These archetypes are powerful and mysterious.

1. How does the Fenris Wolf symbolize evil? Cite examples from the text to support your opinion.
2. (a)In this story, how might the breaking of the chain or rope represent chaos? (b)The chain often represents binding, but it can also represent other things. What other things might a chain represent?

Writing About Literature

Analyze Plot The plot structure of "The Fenris Wolf" may be familiar to you. For example, it pits good against evil and contains three distinct tests—the trials undergone by the Fenris Wolf. Do these elements seem like **plot archetypes**—elements of plot that may recur in the stories of other cultures and eras? Write an essay in which you identify possible plot archetypes in this tale. Link these elements to other stories and tales you have encountered.

LiteratureOnline Web Activities For eFlashcards, Selection Quick Checks, and other Web activities, go to www.glencoe.com.

READING AND VOCABULARY

Reading Strategy Interpreting Imagery

Images help the reader to visualize and understand various aspects of a story.

1. List three or more images that demonstrate the enormous strength and power of the Fenris Wolf. Explain how each image appeals to your senses.
2. Name one image that shows the Fenris Wolf's cleverness.

Vocabulary Practice

Practice with Context Clues For each boldfaced vocabulary word, use context clues to determine the word's meaning.

1. The mother hen is followed by her **brood.**
   a. father **b.** young **c.** feathers
2. Please **fetter** the mean dog to the shed.
   a. chain **b.** pull **c.** invite
3. The woman **forges** strong tools from hot iron.
   a. copies **b.** analyzes **c.** makes
4. The sick animals **writhe** in pain.
   a. twist **b.** give up **c.** cry out

Reading Strategy

1. Possible answer: Tearing "vast meals of raw meat" (visual); "teeth as large as oak trees" (visual); growling and gnashing (auditory)
2. Proposing that one of the gods hold his hand between the wolf's teeth

Web Activities Have students access the Web site for interactive activities that will help them assess their understanding of the selection.

Vocabulary Workshop

Word Origins

Examining Words from Norse Mythology

"They took him to Asgard, therefore, and brave Tyr undertook to feed and train him."

—Olivia Coolidge, "The Fenris Wolf"

Connecting to Literature In Norse mythology, Tyr, who took on the job of feeding the Fenris Wolf, is the bravest and noblest of gods—which may be one reason why we have a day of the week named after him. The personality of Tyr, whose name can also be spelled *Tiu,* may be the source of our word *Tuesday.* Many words from Old Norse are difficult to trace, however, because the Old Norse language was so similar to another source of our language, Old English.

This chart shows the origins of the names of three other days of the week.

Day of the Week	Origin
Wednesday	From the greatest of the Norse gods, Odin, + *daeg,* or "day" (Odin's Day)
Thursday	From the Norse god Thor, or from the Old English word *thunor* (both meaning "thunder"), + *daeg,* or "day" (Thor's Day)
Friday	From Old English or from the Norse goddess Frigga, wife of Odin, + *daeg,* or "day" (Frigga's Day)

Exercise

1. There are approximately nine hundred words of Scandinavian origin in the English language. Several of them have just one syllable and begin with *sk.* Use a dictionary to find one of them.
2. Identify the words, other than *Tyr* and *Fenris Wolf,* that come from Old Norse in each of the following sentences. Use a dictionary for help.
   - **a.** Loki was the husband of a monstrous giantess.
   - **b.** Good gods, such as Tyr, knew right from wrong and acted to preserve the world.
   - **c.** The teeth of the Fenris Wolf were sharper than a knife.
   - **d.** No chain, rule, or law could bind the powerful Fenris Wolf.
   - **e.** Where could the gods get something strong enough to hold him?

▶ **Test-Taking Tip**

Always apply your knowledge of word history when you encounter unfamiliar words in reading passages or have to choose a correct meaning on a multiple-choice test.

▶ **Reading Handbook**

For more about word origins, see Reading Handbook, p. R19.

Literature Online

eFlashcards For eFlashcards and other vocabulary activities, go to www.glencoe.com.

ACADEMIC STANDARDS (page 1073)

9.1.3 Use knowledge of mythology…to understand the origin and meaning of new words.

9.1.1 Understand the origins of words.

Focus

Explain that letter combinations can serve as a clue to a word's origin. Words of Old Norse origin tend to sound harsh because they include combined consonants, such as *g* and *t.* Have students look for short words with combined consonants as they complete the second activity.

Teach

Old Norse Old Norse is the medieval language in which the literature of Norway, Iceland, Denmark, and Sweden was first recorded. It is a North Germanic language. The Norwegian and Icelandic languages spoken today come from Old Norse.

Assess

1. Possible answers: *sky, skirt, skin*
2. (a) husband, (b) wrong, (c) knife, (d) law, (e) get

Literature Online

eFlashcards Have students access the Web site for more practice with word origins.

Differentiated Instruction

RESEARCH: Indo-European Languages Explain that modern English and Old Norse both fall into the broader category of Indo-European languages. Encourage advanced learners and other interested students to look in a library or on the Internet to learn more about this language family and its influence on English. Have groups of students consolidate their findings and present them to the class. **AL**

Academic Standards

The Additional Support activity on p. 1073 covers the following standard:

Differentiated Instruction: **9.7.15** Deliver expository (informational) presentations…

BEFORE YOU READ

Focus

BELLRINGER

Bellringer Options
Daily Language Practice Transparency 90
Or display photos and other images of coyotes and crows.
Ask: What characteristics do we often associate with these animals? Why do you think people attribute human characteristics to animals? Have students consider as they read how the coyote and the crow illustrate human strengths and weaknesses.

Author Search To expand students' appreciation of Ella Clark, have them access the Web site for additional information and resources.

BEFORE YOU READ

Coyote and Crow

MEET ELLA CLARK

Ella Clark taught English for most of her life; however, once Native American literature and culture captured her attention, she devoted herself to preserving its legacy in myth and folktale collections.

English Teacher Ella Clark's teaching career began in 1917, and she continued teaching high school English and dramatics while completing a bachelor's degree at Northwestern University.

From 1927 to 1961, Clark taught in the English department at Washington State University in Pullman, Washington. There she taught writing courses and wrote about diverse subjects such as poetry, botany, Native American mythology, and firefighting in the national forests.

In the 1930s, Clark began to travel around the Pacific Northwest, Alaska, and Canada. While living in Washington state, she began to collect Native American myths and stories, laying the foundation for her later books.

Fire Lookout During World War II, Clark served as a fire lookout for the United States Forest Service in the Cascade Mountains. During her service there, her interest in Native American stories developed into a book entitled *Indian Legends of the Pacific Northwest* (1953). As she collected material for the book, Clark developed clear goals. She writes, "My two criteria in the consideration of each tale have been inseparable: Is it authentic? And is it interesting?"

Clark's first collection of Native American stories is diverse in its sources—she found bits and pieces from government documents, anthropological reports, manuscripts of pioneers, old periodicals, and published histories. Clark also included interviews with Native Americans. Using these varied sources, she produced a written history of what was once an exclusively oral tradition. Some of the stories she included had not previously been published.

Sacagawea

> *"Until modern civilization changed family life, the telling of stories was one of the most satisfying pastimes for the entire family."*
>
> —Ella Clark

Storyteller While she aimed to collect authentic materials, Clark did not consider herself an anthropologist or sociologist. She considered herself an anthologist of literature. "Collecting myths and legends that the general reader will enjoy either as entertainment or as information about an American way of living strange to him."

In 1979 Clark co-authored the book *Sacagawea of the Lewis and Clark Expedition* with Margo Edmonds. This work stands as one of the first attempts at a realistic biography of Sacagawea.

Ella Clark died in San Diego County, California. She left behind a rich collection of Native American stories and myths, now considered an integral part of American literature.

Ella Clark was born in 1896 and died in 1984.

LiteratureOnline **Author Search** For more about Ella Clark, go to www.glencoe.com.

Selection Skills

Coyote and Crow

Literary Elements
- Character Archetype (SE pp. 1075, 1076, 1077)

Reading Skills
- Activating Prior Knowledge (SE pp. 1075, 1076, 1077)

Listening/Speaking/Viewing Skills
- Telling a Tale (TWE p. 1076)

Writing Skills/Grammar
- Respond to Character (SE p. 1077)

LITERATURE PREVIEW

Connecting to the Story

In Native American legends, animals often exhibit human characteristics. In the following story, one animal schemes to get something from the other. Before you read the story, think about the following questions:

- Have you ever been nice to someone only because you wanted something in return?
- When someone gives you a compliment, do you always believe it?

Building Background

"Coyote and Crow" is a Yakama legend. The Yakama were part of a larger group of Native Americans known as the Sahaptians, who lived in the northwestern part of the United States. The Yakama made their homes along the rivers of central Washington. Like most of the Sahaptians, the Yakama lived mainly by fishing for salmon. They believed in the existence of guardian spirits and viewed their shamans (medicine men) as leaders.

Setting Purposes for Reading

Big Idea Courage and Cleverness

As you read this selection, watch for examples of cleverness in the main characters.

Literary Element Character Archetype

A **character archetype** is a type of character who appears repeatedly in literature across cultures. Some character archetypes include the hero, the poor person who wishes to be rich, and the mysterious stranger. As you read, try to identify the character archetype being used in this story.

- See Literary Terms Handbook, p. R4.

Literature Online Interactive Literary Elements Handbook To review or learn more about the literary elements, go to www.glencoe.com.

READING PREVIEW

Reading Strategy Activating Prior Knowledge

When you read a story or other text for the first time, you **activate prior knowledge** to make sense of the information. Prior knowledge is what you already know. It includes ideas and information you have learned from reading, listening, observing, or acting. Prior knowledge influences how you understand the material you read. While reading this story, notice details that seem familiar or that spark connections in your mind.

Reading Tip: Brainstorming From the title of the story you are about to read, you know that it will include at least two characters: a coyote and a crow. Like many other animals, coyotes and crows represent common character traits. For example, owls and elephants are often associated with wisdom. Before you read "Coyote and Crow," use your prior knowledge of these animals to make a list of the characteristics you associate with them. Create a chart like the one below to help you organize your ideas.

Coyote Characteristics	Crow Characteristics
Swift	Loud

Native American ceremonial dance regalia

INDIANA ACADEMIC STANDARDS (pages 1075-1077)

9.3 [Identify] story elements such as character...

9.2 Develop [reading] strategies...

9.5.2 Write responses to literature that...support statements with evidence from the text...

BEFORE YOU READ

Focus

Summary

After traveling across the country, Coyote is hungry when he meets Crow, who has a mouthful of food. Coyote flatters Crow into singing, and Crow drops the food. Coyote eats the food and tells Crow he is foolish.

Literary Elements Have students access the Web site to improve their understanding of character archetypes.

Selection Resources

Print Materials

- Unit 5 Resources (Fast File), pp. 45–46
- Selection and Unit Assessments, pp. 183–184
- Selection Quick Checks, p. 92

Transparencies

- Bellringer Options Transparencies: Daily Language Practice Transparency 90
- Literary Elements Transparency 13, 87

Technology

- TeacherWorks Plus™ CD-ROM
- StudentWorks Plus™ CD-ROM
- Presentation Plus!™ CD-ROM
- Literature Online, glencoe.com
- Online Student Edition, mhln.com
- Exam*View*® Assessment Suite CD-ROM
- Vocabulary PuzzleMaker CD-ROM
- Listening Library, disc 2 track 32

Teach

R Reading Strategy

Activating Prior Knowledge
Answer: *Coyote will probably figure out how to get the deer fat from Crow, because coyotes are considered cunning.* Have students read and summarize the first paragraph.
Ask: Does this story sound familiar to you? What other tales does it remind you of? *(Students may suggest that the story sounds like other folktales or trickster tales they have read.)* OL

L Literary Element

Character Archetype **Answer:** *Coyote: cunning, tricky, sly; Crow: foolish, gullible, proud* OL

★ Literary History

Coyote The Coyote is an important figure in the mythology of North American Indians. In many tales of the Native Americans of the Great Plains, California, and the Southwest, Coyote is a creature who introduces humans to fire and daylight. AS

Readability Scores
Dale-Chall: 3.8
DRP: 42
Lexile: 510

Coyote and Crow

Retold by Ella Clark

★ Coyote traveled through the country, fighting monsters and making the world ready for the people who were to follow. He crossed the Cascade Mountains[1] and came into the Puget Sound[2] country. He was hungry, very hungry.

He saw Crow sitting on the peak of a high cliff, with a ball of deer fat in his mouth. Coyote looked at Crow with this fat and thought how good it would taste. Becoming hungrier and hungrier, he wondered how he could get the fat for himself. He thought hard. Then he laughed.

"I know what to do. I know how I can get the fat from Crow."

Then Coyote came close to the base of the cliff and called, "Oh, Chief! I hear that you can make a good noise, a pleasing noise with your voice. You are a big chief, I know. You are a wise chief, I have heard. Let me hear your voice, Chief. I want to hear you, Chief Crow."

Crow was pleased to be called chief. So he answered, "Caw!"

"Oh, Chief Crow," called Coyote, "that wasn't much. You can sing better than that. Sing a good song for me, Chief. I want to hear you sing loud."

Crow was pleased again. So he opened his mouth wide and called from the cliff in a loud voice, "C-a-a-w!"

Of course the ball of deer fat fell down from Crow's open mouth.

Coyote grabbed it quickly. Then he laughed.

"You are not a wise chief," said Coyote. "You are not a chief at all. I called you 'Chief' just to fool you. I wanted your deer fat. I am hungry. Now you can go hungry because of your foolishness." ∾

1. The *Cascade Mountains* cut across Oregon, Washington, and northern California.
2. *Puget Sound* is a large bay off the Pacific Ocean. It is located in northwestern Washington state.

Reading Strategy Activating Prior Knowledge *Make a prediction about what will happen in the story based on your prior knowledge of such tales.* R

Literary Element Character Archetype *What adjectives would you use to describe Coyote and Crow?* L

Additional Support

Academic Standards
The Additional Support activity on p. 1076 covers the following standard:
Skills Practice: **9.7.14** Deliver narrative presentations…

Skills Practice

SPEAKING: Telling a Tale Students may enjoy creating and telling their own version of a trickster tale. Have pairs of students devise a trickster character, a situation, and an outcome. They may use "Coyote and Crow" as a model or read other trickster tales for more background. Their tricksters should be animals with human traits. Invite volunteers to tell their stories to the class. OL

AFTER YOU READ

RESPONDING AND THINKING CRITICALLY

Respond

1. What is your opinion of Coyote? Explain.

Recall and Interpret

2. (a)What was Coyote doing before he encountered Crow? (b)Why is this information important to the story?
3. (a)What does Coyote want from Crow? (b)Why must Coyote trick Crow in order to get what he wants from him?
4. (a)What does Coyote call Crow in order to trick him? (b)In your opinion, what is the significance of this particular name?

Analyze and Evaluate

5. (a)In your own words, describe Coyote's plan to get the deer fat from Crow. (b)Use what you know about both of these animals to determine why Coyote is confident that his plan will work.
6. (a)How would you describe the personalities of Coyote and Crow? (b)Have you encountered characters like them in other stories? Explain.
7. (a)Why does Coyote say Crow is foolish? (b)Do you think Crow behaved foolishly? Explain.

Connect

8. **Big Idea** **Courage and Cleverness** Was Coyote clever in the story? Explain.

LITERARY ANALYSIS

Literary Element Character Archetype

In this story, one of the **character archetypes** is the trickster. A trickster is a mischievous character. He or she deceives or plays pranks on other characters. Readers usually like trickster characters because they are entertaining.

1. Which character is the trickster in this story?
2. Support your answer with two examples from the story.

Writing About Literature

Respond to Character Trickster characters have appeared in stories told in many different cultures for thousands of years. Tricksters may be portrayed as heroes, fools, or cunning predators, but they all share a disregard for accepted standards of behavior. However, in many cultures, tricksters are respected and admired even though they often deceive others. What is your opinion of the trickster? Do you find the trickster entertaining or annoying? Clever or cruel? In a short essay, discuss your response to this popular archetype. Remember to use specific examples from the story to support your ideas.

READING AND VOCABULARY

Reading Strategy Activating Prior Knowledge

When you began to read "Coyote and Crow," the story may have seemed familiar or predictable to you. You may have had some preconceived ideas about how the characters would behave. These ideas were based on your **prior knowledge** of the character types and story pattern. In fact, you may have been surprised by how accurate your initial thoughts about the characters turned out to be. When you draw on your personal background and prior knowledge, combining it with words on a page, you create meaning in a selection.

1. Before you read the story, what role did you think the Coyote would play? Explain.
2. Were your initial ideas about Crow's character correct? Explain.

LiteratureOnline **Web Activities** For eFlashcards, Selection Quick Checks, and other Web activities, go to www.glencoe.com.

Literary Element

1. Coyote is the trickster.
2. Coyote gets what he wants without having to work hard, and he outsmarts Crow.

Writing About Literature

Stress that students should explain why they responded negatively or positively to the archetype portrayed in the text.

Reading Strategy

1. Students should explain their answers.
2. Students should explain their answers.

AFTER YOU READ

Assess

1. Students should explain their answers.
2. (a) He was killing monsters and making the world safe for people. (b) It shows that Coyote is the hero of the story.
3. (a) The deer fat in Crow's mouth (b) Coyote cannot reach the top of a cliff where Crow sits.
4. (a) Chief (b) It suggests a respected leader, and this appeals to Crow's vanity.
5. (a) Coyote asks Crow to sing so he will drop the deer fat. (b) The wily Coyote knows the vain Crow will fall for his flattery.
6. (a) Coyote is smart and tricky; Crow is foolishly vain. (b) Students should explain their answers.
7. (a) It was obvious what would happen when Crow opened his mouth. (b) Students should support their answers.
8. Yes; he showed keen insight into Crow's nature.

CheckPoint

Use the CheckPoint questions on Presentation Plus! to check students' mastery of the selection. These questions can be used with interactive response keypads for immediate student feedback.

LiteratureOnline

Web Activities Have students access the Web site for interactive activities that will help them assess their understanding of the selection.

BEFORE YOU READ

Focus

BELLRINGER

Bellringer Options
Daily Language Practice Transparency 91
Or **ask:** Why do stories of princes and princesses still fascinate modern readers and listeners? What do these tales tell us about ourselves?
Have students consider as they read what feelings or ideas the story of Vasilisa and Ivan the Pea inspires.

Author Search To expand students' appreciation of Elizabeth Ann Warner, have them access the Web site for additional information and resources.

BEFORE YOU READ

Vasilisa of the Golden Braid and Ivan the Pea

MEET ELIZABETH ANN WARNER

As a young person growing up in England, scholar and translator Elizabeth Ann Warner became fascinated with the melody of the Russian language. She began to learn it as a voluntary lunchtime activity, and, determined to read Russia's great literature in its original language, she went on to study at Edinburgh University, one of the only universities at that time to offer a course on Russian folklore. Thanks to Warner's passionate pursuit of Russian, today readers of English are able to sample the richness and strangeness of ancient Russian culture.

Hooked on Russia During her studies at Edinburgh, Warner discovered aspects of traditional Russian culture such as folk tales, heroic epics and songs, rituals and customs which accompany funerals and weddings, and beliefs in supernatural beings such as the house spirit. Warner says, "I was hooked from then on and the study of Russian folklore and the way of life of its tradition bearers became my only research interest." Warner embarked on a career as a scholar and translator of Russian folklore.

> *"Now I can hear for myself, from the people who created them, the songs [and] folk tales . . . about which I could only read in historical archives before."*
>
> —Elizabeth Ann Warner

On Location For most of her adult life, Warner has visited Russia regularly, often several times a year. But before the collapse of the Soviet Union at the beginning of the 1990s, she was not permitted to visit the remote areas of the country where elements of Russia's traditional folk culture still survive. Since the opening of these areas to foreigners, Warner has joined Russian friends and colleagues on their yearly expeditions to Vologda province in the northwestern part of the country. There she can experience the colorfulness of Russia's traditional folk culture firsthand.

Bird of Paradise (Jar-Ptiza), 20th Century. Russian School. Colour lithograph. Bibliotheque des Arts Decoratifs, Paris, France.

Sharing a Legacy Warner is the author of many books and articles in both Russian and English, including *Heroes, Monsters and Other Worlds from Russian Mythology,* which contains stories that originated in Kiev such as the one you are about to read. In the ninth to thirteenth centuries, Kiev was the center of Russian civilization. Stories from Kiev include tales of heroes and their adventures, wonder tales of "pure fantasy," and tales of the supernatural and the dead. For example, tales from Kiev give special powers to the cold winds that sweep across the flat open steppe. All Russian tales reflect the geographical and political world in which their original tellers lived. Because forests and rivers abound in the Russian countryside, tales are often filled with fantastic beings like wood demons and water nymphs.

Elizabeth Ann Warner was born in 1940.

LiteratureOnline **Author Search** For more about Elizabeth Ann Warner, go to www.glencoe.com.

Selection Skills

Vasilisa of the Golden Braid and Ivan the Pea

Literary Elements
- Theme Archetype (SE pp. 1079, 1082, 1083, 1085)

Reading Skills
- Connecting to Personal Experience (SE pp. 1079–1086)

Vocabulary Skills
- Word Origins (SE pp. 1079, 1086)
- Academic Vocabulary (SE p. 1086)

Listening/Speaking/Viewing Skills
- Analyzing Art (SE p. 1084; TWE p. 1080)
- Performing (SE p. 1086)

Writing Skills/Grammar
- Compare and Contrast Characters (SE p. 1086)
- Writing a Fairy Tale (TWE p. 1082)

LITERATURE PREVIEW

Connecting to the Story

For every culture and in every era, people form their own ideas about beauty, bravery, and loyalty. Before you read the story, think about the following questions:

- Which people do you consider especially smart, kind, or brave?
- What good qualities are most important for a person to have?

Building Background

You are about to read a "wonder tale," a type of Russian fantasy story. Wonder tales often explain bad weather by tracing it to the actions of dragons or other supernatural forces. The main hero of these stories is often called Ivan, a common name in Russia. The character Ivan may be the son of a tsar (or Russian ruler), the son of a soldier, or even the son of an animal. Regardless, the hero Ivan is always brave and humane. In this tale, Ivan is the son of a tsar; he is born magically after his mother swallows a pea.

Setting Purposes for Reading

Big Idea Courage and Cleverness

As you read this story, think about which characters demonstrate courage and cleverness.

Literary Element Theme Archetype

A **theme** is a literary work's central idea or message about life or human nature. A **theme archetype** is a theme that recurs in myths, stories, and tales all over the world. Examples of theme archetypes include the victory of good over evil, the importance of courage and family loyalty, and the triumph of the unlikely hero. As you read this story, think about the theme archetypes it may contain.

- See Literary Terms Handbook, p. R18.

Literature Online **Interactive Literary Elements Handbook** To review or learn more about the literary elements, go to www.glencoe.com.

READING PREVIEW

Reading Strategy Connecting to Personal Experience

Connecting to personal experience is using your own knowledge and experience of life and people to deepen your understanding of a work of literature. You can connect to this text by recognizing familiar archetypes in the story, such as a beautiful girl who is desired by many suitors.

Reading Tip: Making a Chart Use a chart to record details from the story that strike you as familiar.

Detail	Why It Is Familiar to Me
Vasilisa lives in a high tower for twenty years.	This reminds me of "Rumpelstiltskin" and other fairy tales. Maybe a prince will try to rescue Vasilisa.

Vocabulary

chamber (chām′ bər) *n.* a room, especially a bedroom; p. 1080 *No one entered the princess's chamber except her personal maid.*

suitor (sōō′ tər) *n.* a man who courts a woman in hope of marrying her; p. 1080 *The suitor, who adored Keisha, called her every night.*

staff (staf) *n.* a long stick used for assistance with walking or as a weapon; p. 1081 *The weary woman leaned heavily on her staff.*

stead (sted) *n.* place; p. 1084 *When the quarterback was injured, Tim played in his stead.*

Vocabulary Tip: Word Origins The origin of a word is its history. You can find a word's origin in a dictionary.

INDIANA ACADEMIC STANDARDS (pages 1079-1086)

9.3 [Identify] story elements such as...theme...
9.2 Develop [reading] strategies...
9.5.3 Write...analytical essays...that gather evidence in support of a thesis...

BEFORE YOU READ

Focus

Summary

After being locked in a tower for twenty years, a young princess goes outside and is carried away by a dragon disguised as a whirlwind. When her two brothers attempt a rescue, the dragon kills them. Their little brother, Ivan the Pea, defeats the dragon with a magic staff and resurrects the two dead brothers.

V Vocabulary

Vocabulary File **Say:** Add these words and definitions to your vocabulary file. For each word, include a sentence that gives you an example of how to use the word. **OL** Students with English language needs should include the pronunciations of these words in their files. **EL**

Literature Online

Literary Element Have students access the Web site to improve their understanding of theme archetypes.

Selection Resources

Print Materials

- Unit 5 Resources (Fast File), pp. 47–49
- Leveled Vocabulary Development
- Selection and Unit Assessments, pp. 185–186
- Selection Quick Checks, p. 93

Transparencies

- Bellringer Options Transparencies: Daily Language Practice Transparency 91
- Literary Elements Transparency 18, 87

Technology

- TeacherWorks Plus™ CD-ROM
- StudentWorks Plus™ CD-ROM
- Presentation Plus!™ CD-ROM
- Literature Online, glencoe.com
- Online Student Edition, mhln.com
- Exam*View*® Assessment Suite CD-ROM
- Vocabulary PuzzleMaker CD-ROM
- Listening Library, disc 2 track 33

Teach

R1 Reading Strategy

Connecting to Personal Experience Say: Most fairy tales begin with the phrase "Once there was" or "Once upon a time."
Ask: What do you expect from such stories? *(Students may say that they expect to read about magical or fantastical events and a happy ending.)* OL

R2 Reading Strategy

Connecting to Personal Experience Answer: *Stories such as "Rapunzel" deal with a princess locked in a tower. Princesses often have long, golden hair and get into trouble by breaking a rule.* OL

★ Viewing the Art

Pierre-Auguste Renoir (1841–1919) was an influential Impressionist painter. Unlike many painters of the Impressionist movement who mainly painted landscapes, Renoir painted many portraits, especially of women.
Ask: What similarities does this girl have with Vasilisa? *(Long, golden hair)* AS

Readability Scores
Dale-Chall: 6.9
DRP: 56
Lexile: 1010

Vasilisa of the Golden Braid and Ivan the Pea

retold by
Elizabeth Ann Warner

Blonde girl combing her hair, 1894. Pierre Auguste Renoir. Oil on canvas. Metropolitan Museum of Art, New York, USA. ★

Once there reigned a tsar[1] called R1 Svetozar who had two sons and a beautiful daughter. For twenty years the girl lived in her **chamber** at the top of a high tower and although she had the company of her maids and ladies-in-waiting she was never allowed outside and no prince or knight was allowed to set eyes on her. People called her Vasilisa of the Golden Braid because she had long, silky hair the color of gold, wound into a single braid which reached to her ankles.

Soon the fame of Vasilisa's beauty spread and kings from far-off lands sent ambassadors to ask for her hand in marriage. The tsar, her father, was in no hurry. When the time came, he himself sent out messengers to say that Vasilisa would choose a husband, inviting royal **suitors** to a great feast at his palace.

When Vasilisa heard about this she was very pleased but she longed more than ever to see the green grass and flowers outside the palace. She begged her father to let her out just once and at last he agreed.

1. A *tsar* was a Russian ruler, much like a king. The *tsarevna* is his daughter, the *tsaritsa* is his wife, and the *tsarevich* is his son.

Vocabulary

chamber (chām′ bər) *n.* a room, especially a bedroom

Reading Strategy Connecting to Personal Experience
How does this situation remind you of situations you have seen in movies and fairy tales? R2

Vocabulary

suitor (so͞o′ tər) *n.* a man who courts a woman in hope of marrying her

Additional Support

Skills Practice

READING: Setting a Purpose for Reading After students read the first paragraph of the story, discuss why fairy tales are still read today and what we can learn from them. Before students continue reading, ask them to jot down their purposes for reading. They may say to be entertained or to learn about theme archetypes. After students finish reading the story, discuss whether they fulfilled their purpose for reading. OL

For a while the tsarevna picked the pretty, blue flowers in a big green meadow at the foot of a steep hill covered with leafy trees. She grew a little careless, however, and moved away from her ladies-in-waiting and for the first time her beauty was uncovered, her face unveiled and visible for all to see. Suddenly, out of nowhere, a great, whirling gust of wind blew up, a wind stronger than anyone could remember before and which sent everything spinning before it. In a moment it had lifted the tsarevna from the ground and made off with her. Her attendants screamed and ran about, flapping their arms, but all in vain. The whirlwind carried the tsarevna away, over many lands and deep rivers. Through three kingdoms they passed and into a fourth, which was the home of a fierce dragon.

Vasilisa's parents were heartbroken and her two brothers, seeing their parents' tears, asked their blessing to go and look for their lost sister. "We will search the whole world over," they said, "and we will surely find her."

The brothers traveled for a whole year and then another. They passed through three kingdoms until they could see in the distance a range of high mountains, with stretches of sandy desert in between. This was the land of the fierce dragon.

The brothers began to ask passersby if they had heard or seen anything of Vasilisa of the Golden Braid but nobody knew anything about her. As they drew near a great city, they noticed a feeble old man standing at the roadside, begging for alms. He was lame and blind in one eye and carried a **staff**. The brothers threw him a silver coin and asked him, too, if he had seen their sister. "Well now," replied the old man, "it is clear you are strangers here. Our master is a fierce dragon and he has forbidden us to talk to strangers or to tell anyone how, one day, a whirlwind blew a beautiful tsarevna over the mountains and into our kingdom."

From this the brothers guessed that their sister was not far away and they spurred on their high-spirited horses. Next they came to a golden palace. It was a strange building, standing on one silver pillar. Over it hung a canopy studded with precious stones and on either side was a staircase of mother-of-pearl, which from time to time rose and fell, like a pair of wings.

As they approached, Vasilisa was peeping through the gilded[2] bars at the window of her room and she cried out with joy when she recognized her brothers in the distance. She sent her servant to bring them secretly into the palace for the fierce dragon was not at home.

No sooner had the brothers set foot in the palace than the pillar upon which it stood began to creak, the staircases were suddenly raised, the stones on the roof began to glow and the whole palace began to revolve and change its position. "Hide yourselves, brothers," cried the tsarevna, for she knew this meant the dragon was on his way back.

In flew the dragon. He gave a loud whistle and called out at the top of his voice: "I smell a living creature. Is it a man?"

Fearing nothing the brothers spoke up. "Yes," they said. "We have come to fetch our sister home."

"Two young heroes I see," said the dragon, flapping his wings. "Only not very big ones." With that he picked up one brother with his wing and dashed him against the other brother, killing them both. Then he summoned his servants to take away the bodies and had them thrown into a deep pit.

The tsarevna burst into tears. For some days she would neither eat nor drink, then she decided that she did not want to die but

Reading Strategy Connecting to Personal Experience *What is familiar to you about the plot so far?* R3

Vocabulary

staff (staf) *n.* a long stick used for assistance with walking or as a weapon

2. *Gilded* means "covered in a thin layer of gold."

Teach

R3 Reading Strategy

Connecting to Personal Experience **Answer:** *Students may note it is a familiar plot device for harm to befall a beautiful princess. They may cite "Snow White" or "Sleeping Beauty."* OL

★ Cultural History

Dragons Most of the world's cultures have stories about dragons. Dragons and snakes often serve as symbols of evil, but there are exceptions. Ancient Greeks and Romans considered snakes and dragons to be wise and powerful. In Asian cultures, the dragon is a powerful symbol of goodness. AS

CheckPoint

Use the CheckPoint questions on Presentation Plus! to monitor students' comprehension. These questions can be used with interactive response keypads for immediate student feedback.

English Language Coach

Unfamiliar Words Students may have trouble with Russian names and words. Suggest that as they read, they jot these down. Encourage them to consult footnotes and a dictionary. If time allows, ask them to write sentences, using the words. EL

Differentiated Instruction

Fairy-Tale Checklist Remind less proficient readers that while the details of fairy tales may vary, most conform to the same structure. Review the familiar elements: a setting in the distant past, magical powers, a happy ending. Have students list these elements and check them off as they read. BL

Academic Standards

Additional Support activities on pp. 1080 and 1081 cover the following standards:

Skills Practice: **9.2** Develop strategies such as...identifying...purpose...

English Language Coach: **9.1** Use...a growing knowledge of English and other languages to determine the meaning of words and become fluent readers.

Differentiated Instruction: **9.3** [Identify] story elements...and [make] connections... across texts...

Teach

BI1 Big Idea

Courage and Cleverness
Answer: *She wants to fool him into letting his guard down so she can escape.* **Ask:** Referring to what you know of other fairy tales, what do you think will happen next in the story? *(The princess will trick the dragon into freeing her, or another hero will try to rescue her.)* OL

L1 Literary Element

Theme Archetype **Answer:** *He was born from a pea and resembles one. At 10 years of age, he is already a powerful knight. It is written that he will defeat the dragon.*
Ask: What do these clues suggest about Ivan? *(He seems an unlikely hero, but his magical birth and the prophecy about him suggest he has special powers.)* OL

★ Cultural History

Baba Yaga Although a benevolent character, the old woman in the story borrows elements from the famous evil witch of Russian folklore, Baba Yaga (or Baba-jaga), who lives in a house atop a pair of chicken legs. She guards the water of life and feeds on the souls of murdered children. AS

would try to escape from the dragon. She began to speak kindly to him.

"Dear dragon," she said, "you are so big and strong and you fly so well, I am sure no-one could get the better of you."

"It is written," replied the dragon, "that the only person who could beat me is Ivan the Pea. But that won't be for some time yet," he laughed.

The dragon was only joking. He did not believe there could be any such person. But his joke turned out to be true.

Vasilisa's mother, the tsaritsa, had been left without any news of her children and she was very sad. One day she went walking in the garden with the ladies of the court. It was a hot day and the tsaritsa became thirsty. A stream of clear spring water flowed down the hillside into the garden. A marble well had been built over it and the tsaritsa filled a golden cup with the pure water and drank. At the bottom of the cup was a little pea which she swallowed.

The pea began to swell in the tsaritsa's stomach and she grew fatter and fatter and heavier and heavier. After a while she gave birth to a son, whom she called Ivan the Pea.

Ivan the Pea grew very, very fast and was smooth and round, just like a pea! He was very jolly too and jumped and rolled about all over the place. As he grew he became very strong, so that by the age of ten he was a powerful *bogatyr.*[3] One day he asked his parents if he had any brothers or sisters and he learned the sad story.

"Mother and father," said Ivan, "give me your blessing to go in search of them."

At first his parents did not want to let him go for he was too young and inexperienced, but he begged and begged until they agreed.

Ivan rode for a day and then another. Towards evening on the second day he came to a dark forest. In the forest he found a little wooden house on chickens' legs. The house revolved when the wind blew and Ivan went up to it and blew hard, saying, "Little house, little house, turn your back to the trees and your face towards me."

Buff earthenware tile, depicting a fantastic dragon, c. 1882–88. William de Morgan. Fitzwilliam Museum, University of Cambridge, England.

The house turned towards him and there, at a little window, sat a gray-haired crone.[4] ★

Ivan bowed and asked, "Granny, have you seen a whirlwind pass over here?"

The old woman coughed and said, "Dear lad, I know all about that whirlwind. He gave me such a fright I haven't left this house for one hundred and twenty years. But he isn't really a whirlwind. He is a fierce dragon who will gobble you up."

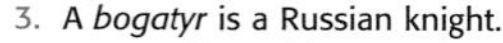

3. A *bogatyr* is a Russian knight.
4. A *crone* is an old woman.

Big Idea Courage and Cleverness *Why does the princess say kind and flattering things to the dragon?* BI1

Literary Element Theme Archetype *What do you know about Ivan so far? Do you think his search will be successful?* L1

Additional Support

Skills Practice

WRITING: A Modern Fairy Tale
Encourage students to use this tale as the basis for a modern fairy tale. Challenge them to write a version of the tale that preserves some aspects of a traditional fairy tale (the events occurring in threes) but updating others (such as the helplessness of the heroine). OL

"Tell me how to find him," pleaded Ivan.

"Very well," mumbled the old woman through her toothless gums, "but first promise to bring me some of the magic water he keeps in his palace. It makes people young again."

Ivan gave his word of honor and the old woman told him to follow the direction of the sun until he came to the Bald Mountain. There he should ask again where the dragon lived.

After a long journey, Ivan found himself at the gate of the dragon's city, where he met the lame and blind beggar. He gave him a coin and from the replies to his questions guessed, just as his brothers had done, that his sister was near.

Just then Vasilisa was looking out of her window and she noticed the young knight approaching. She was curious to know who he was and sent out a messenger to discover if, by chance, he had been sent by her parents. When she learned that he was her youngest brother, she begged him with tears to run away quickly before the dragon flew home and destroyed him.

"Dear sister," said Ivan, "I do not fear the dragon nor his strength."

"Is it possible," asked Vasilisa, "that you are Ivan the Pea, the only man who can defeat the dragon?"

"Before you start asking questions," said Ivan, "bring me something to drink, for I am tired and hot and thirsty after a long journey. Bring me some sweet honey-mead." He drank a whole bucketful of ★ mead at a single gulp and then asked for a second.

Vasilisa watched in amazement. "I see now that you are indeed Ivan the Pea," she exclaimed. She drew up a strong chair for her brother to rest on but the chair collapsed under his weight. The servants brought another, bound with iron, but that, too, began to creak and bend.

"Oh dear," cried Vasilisa, "that was the fierce dragon's chair."

"That's all right then," laughed Ivan. "That means I am heavier than he!"

Ivan left the palace and went to the smithy, where he asked the court smith, who was old and skilled in his craft, to forge[5] a heavy iron staff, five hundred *poods*[6] in weight. Day and night the smith and his assistants labored to make the iron staff, while the hammers thundered and the sparks flew. In forty hours the staff was ready. It took fifty men to lift it, but Ivan the Pea picked it up in one hand and tossed it up into the air. It rose like a clap of thunder, higher than the clouds, and disappeared from sight.

Everyone ran away, terrified of what would happen when the staff landed. If it fell in the town it would surely knock all the houses down and kill people but if it fell in the sea it would make such a splash they would all be drowned.

Ivan the Pea was quite unconcerned. He strolled back into the palace and asked to be informed when the staff came back to earth. People kept peeping out from behind their windows and under their gates to see if there was any sign of the staff. An hour passed, then another. The third hour had begun when, trembling with fear, a messenger ran to tell Ivan the Pea that the staff had been sighted. Ivan jumped out into the middle of the square, stuck out his hand and caught the staff as it fell. The impact had no effect on Ivan but the staff bent a little so he laid it across his knee and pulled it back into shape. Then he returned to the palace.

After a time he heard a fearful whistling: it was the dragon. His horse came galloping through the sky like an arrow shot from a

5. A *smithy* or *smith* makes, or *forges*, iron objects over a fire.
6. A *pood* is thirty-six pounds; therefore, the staff weighs 18,000 pounds.

Literary Element Theme Archetype *What do Vasilisa's concerns and Ivan's reply reveal about their relationship?* **L2**

Big Idea Courage and Cleverness *From this episode, what ideas are you forming about Ivan?* **BI2**

Teach

L2 Literary Element

Theme Archetype **Answer:** *Although they have just met, Vasilisa and her brother immediately feel a strong family bond. Ivan refuses to run away. He will do anything for his sister.* **Ask:** What theme archetype is being set up here with the arrival of Ivan? *(Students may suggest the archetype of the triumph of the unlikely hero.)* **OL**

BI2 Big Idea

Courage and Cleverness
Answer: *Ivan is clever as well as courageous.* **OL**

★ Language History

Mead Mead (pronounced "meed") is an ancient drink made of fermented honey and water. Historians believe that it was made almost everywhere in ancient Europe and Asia and was traditionally the drink of warriors. **AS**

Reading in the Real World

College Note that psychologists think that fairy tales reflect our culture's fears and concerns. Fairy tales illustrate the challenges young people face as they grow up. Invite advanced students to read the introduction to Bruno Bettelheim's *The Uses of Enchantment* (1976) and report on it to the class. **OL**

Differentiated Instruction

Sketching the Scene Encourage visual learners to sketch or draw vividly detailed scenes from the story. Have them tell the class why certain images inspired them. **BL**

Academic Standards

Additional Support activities on pp. 1082 and 1083 cover the following standards:

Skills Practice: **9.5** [Demonstrate] an awareness of the audience…and purpose for writing.

Reading in the Real World: **9.7.15** Deliver expository (informational) presentations…

Differentiated Instruction: **9.3** [Identify] story elements such as…setting…

Teach

R Reading Strategy

Connecting to Personal Experience Answer: *Students may mention family events such as holiday celebrations, weddings, or reunions with loved ones.* OL

★ Viewing the Art

Answer: *Accept reasonable answers. Students may contrast the dragons' different forms.* AS

Use the CheckPoint questions on Presentation Plus! to check students' mastery of the selection. These questions can be used with interactive response keypads for immediate student feedback.

Battle with the Dragon, 1912. Nikolai Konstantinovich Rerikh. Gouache on paper, 66.5 × 86 cm. Art Museum of Ryasan, Russia.

Viewing the Art: Compare and contrast the battle scene depicted here with the battle between Ivan the Pea and the dragon in this story. ★

bow, fire snorting from its nostrils. The dragon had the head of a serpent but the body of a man. Usually, as he approached, the palace would begin to revolve on its single pillar, even when he was many miles distant. But this time it had not moved and the dragon knew someone very heavy must be inside.

The horse shook its black mane, flapped its great wings and dived straight at the palace again. But still the palace did not stir.

"Aha!" roared the dragon. "I see I have a worthy opponent. Can it be that Ivan the Pea has come visiting?"

When Ivan the Pea appeared, the dragon sneered and said he would sit him on the palm of one hand and clap the other hand down on top so that Ivan would be crushed to nothing.

"We'll see about that," said Ivan, raising his staff. "Out of my way!"

"Out of *my* way," yelled the dragon, flying at him with his lance. But he missed! Ivan the Pea had jumped to one side.

"Now it is my turn," cried Ivan and threw his staff at the dragon. The dragon was smashed into tiny pieces, while the staff went straight through the ground and came out two kingdoms away.

All the people threw their hats in the air and wanted to make Ivan their tsar. But Ivan, remembering how well the staff had done its job, called the clever blacksmith and told the people he would rule over them.

Next Ivan found where the magic water, the Water of Life and Death, was hidden and sprinkled some over the corpses of his brothers. They stood up, rubbing their eyes as if they had just woken from a long sleep.

"Dear brothers, if it hadn't been for me," said Ivan, "you would have slept forever." And he embraced them.

Together with their sister, the three brothers boarded a ship and sailed back to their own land, not forgetting to take some of the magic water with them for the old woman in the hut on chickens' legs.

When they arrived home, Ivan's father and mother ran out to meet them. They sent out messengers over all the land with the glad tidings that Vasilisa of the Golden Braid had been found. All the bells in the city rang out, the band played and cannons roared. Vasilisa found a husband and Tsarevich Ivan a wife and the two weddings were celebrated together. After his father's death, Ivan the Pea became tsar in his **stead** and ruled his people well.

Reading Strategy Connecting to Personal Experience
What experience in your own life helps you understand this joyous celebration? R

Vocabulary

stead (sted) n. place

Additional Support

Skills Practice

RESEARCH: Historical Context Be sure that students understand the importance of the blacksmith in the story. Explain that blacksmiths have shaped metals for thousands of years. Have students research methods of metalworking. Ask them to create an illustrated explanation of the craft. OL

AFTER YOU READ

RESPONDING AND THINKING CRITICALLY

Respond

1. What do you think is the most exciting or entertaining part of this story?

Recall and Interpret

2. (a)What events lead to Vasilisa's being captured by the dragon? (b)Explain the connection between the whirlwind and the dragon.
3. (a)Who first tries to rescue Vasilisa? (b)Why is the attempt unsuccessful?
4. (a)Who is Ivan the Pea? (b)What role does he play in the rescue of Vasilisa? Explain.

Analyze and Evaluate

5. This Russian tale contains characters that recur in many folk tales, such as a lame beggar and an old woman. (a)What role do they play in the story? (b)Why are these characters important despite their seeming infirmity or weakness?
6. (a)What role does the blacksmith play in this story? (b)How is he rewarded at the end of the story? (c)What lesson might this suggest?
7. Why do you think generations of Russians have enjoyed retelling the story of Ivan the Pea?

Connect

8. **Big Idea** **Courage and Cleverness** In your opinion, does Ivan use courage or cleverness—or a mix of both—to rescue his sister? Explain.

LITERARY ANALYSIS

Literary Element Theme Archetype

The same basic **theme archetypes** appear in myths and tales from all over the world. Time, setting, and character may vary, but the main ideas and lessons are repeated from place to place, people to people, and age to age. You may have detected several theme archetypes in "Vasilisa of the Golden Braid and Ivan the Pea." It is a distinctively Russian version of a story known all over the world.

1. (a)In this story, who represents good? (b)Who represents evil? (c)In what sense can the theme of the victory of good over evil be called an archetype?
2. Arguably, one theme archetype in this story is the importance of family loyalty. Explain how both the characters and the plot reflect this theme.
3. Another possible theme archetype in this story is the triumph of an unlikely hero over a powerful villain. In your opinion, why do so many stories share this theme?

Review: Image Archetype

As you learned on page 1068, an **image archetype** is an image that occurs in literature and folklore across many cultures. What images in this story are familiar to you?

Partner Activity With a partner, go back through the story and list images that could qualify as image archetypes. Using a chart like the one below, record your thoughts about why these archetypes are common across cultures.

Image Archetype	Why Image Is Common
dragon	Dragons are frightening but also fascinating. They may help a culture imagine evil.

AFTER YOU READ

Assess

1. Accept reasonable answers.
2. (a) Vasilisa goes outside, revealing her beauty, and is taken by a whirlwind. (b) The whirlwind carries her to the dragon's kingdom.
3. (a) Her two brothers; (b) They rely on courage alone and have no plan.
4. (a) Ivan is Vasilisa's little brother born after the first two brothers are killed. (b) He rescues her.
5. (a) They help Vasilisa's brothers find the dragon and his castle. (b) Their qualities of perception help the main characters.
6. (a) He makes the staff that Ivan uses to kill the dragon. (b) He becomes the tsar of the fourth kingdom. (c) It suggests the importance of intelligence and skill in overcoming obstacles.
7. The themes of defeating evil and of family loyalty are appealing.
8. Both; it took bravery to face the dragon and cleverness to devise his plan.

Literary Element

1. (a) The family (b) The dragon (c) Stories in every culture deal with the battle against evil.
2. The brothers face death to save their sister; the major events center on the family.
3. People typically like to root for the underdog. Such heroes suggest that unlikely people can turn out to be heroes.

Review: Image Archetype

Remind students that archetypes function as patterns for ideas and characters that recur across cultures and over time.

Academic Standards

The Additional Support activity on p. 1084 covers the following standard:

Skills Practice: **9.3.12** Analyze the way in which a work…is related to…issues of its historical period.

AFTER YOU READ

Assess

Reading Strategy

1. In real life, children often beg to do what older siblings do until their parents give in.
2. Possible answers: girl sheltered by her parents, the wise old woman who helps a young person

Vocabulary

1. a **2.** a **3.** b **4.** a

Academic Vocabulary

It is unusual because it revolves when the wind blows, and it stands on chicken legs.

Writing About Literature

Remind students to include two or more points of comparison or contrast and support them with textual evidence.

Performing

Remind students to incorporate the key events and dialogue from the story into the script.

READING AND VOCABULARY

Reading Strategy Connecting to Personal Experience

Vasilisa, like the princess Rapunzel, is kept locked in a tower and has extremely long hair. Think about all the other details in the story that are familiar to you from myths, tales, or everyday experience.

1. Ivan the Pea is the youngest child. What is familiar to you about his request to follow his brothers, his parents' first response to that request, and his getting permission to go?
2. List two other details in the story to which you connected through personal experience.

Vocabulary Practice

Practice with Word Origins Using a dictionary, determine the origin of the following words.

1. chamber
   - **a.** from Greek for "vault"
   - **b.** from French for "tower"
2. suitor
   - **a.** from Latin for "to follow"
   - **b.** from Sanskrit for "husband"
3. staff
   - **a.** from Greek for "they reach"
   - **b.** from Sanskrit for "he supports"
4. stead
   - **a.** from Old English for "stand"
   - **b.** from Latin for "power"

Academic Vocabulary

Here is a word from the vocabulary list on page R80.

odd (äd) *adj.* irregular, unexpected, unplanned; different from others

Practice and Apply
What is **odd** about the old woman's house?

WRITING AND EXTENDING

Writing About Literature

Compare and Contrast Characters How is Vasilisa similar to or different from other characters you have read about or seen in movies or on television? How is Ivan similar to or different from other heroes you have encountered? Write an essay in which you compare and contrast one of these characters with another character you know well.

Brainstorm by listing details about each character in a Venn diagram like the one below. Consider their actions, appearances, and relationships to other characters.

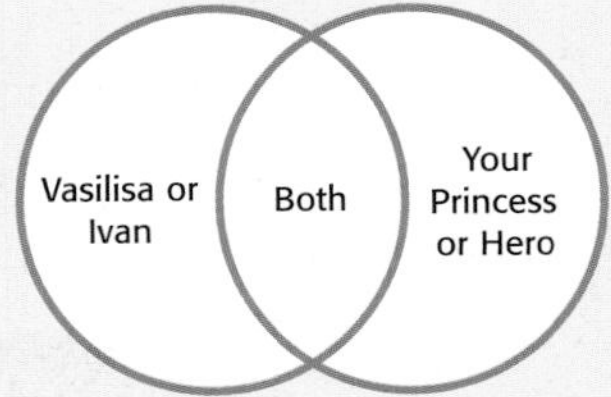

Use your diagram to develop a thesis that states two or more main points of comparison or contrast between the characters. Use body paragraphs to explain the points of comparison and contrast, citing details from the works in question. Conclude your essay by restating your thesis in a fresh way and summing up your main points.

When your draft is complete, meet with a peer reviewer to evaluate each other's work and suggest revisions. Then proofread and edit your draft to correct errors in spelling, grammar, and punctuation.

Performing

Work with a small group to rework a section from "Vasilisa of the Golden Braid and Ivan the Pea" into a script complete with stage directions. Then assign roles and practice reading through your script, revising as necessary. Perform your one-act play for the class.

LiteratureOnline Web Activities For eFlashcards, Selection Quick Checks, and other Web activities, go to www.glencoe.com.

LiteratureOnline

Web Activities Have students access the Web site for interactive activities that will help them assess their understanding of the selection.

Grammar Workshop

Coherence

Using Transitional Expressions

"At first his parents did not want to let him go for he was too young and inexperienced, but he begged and begged and they agreed."

—Elizabeth Ann Warner, "Vasilisa of the Golden Braid and Ivan the Pea"

Connecting to Literature In Elizabeth Ann Warner's retelling of the story of Vasilisa and Ivan the Pea, transitions function as they do in every good story: they are the bits of glue that hold sentences, paragraphs, and story parts together and help them all make sense to the reader. In the example above, the transitional words and phrases include *at first*, which tells when; *for*, which tells why; *but*, which shows contrast; and *and*, which connects similar sentence elements.

Transitional words and phrases show how ideas are related. This chart shows only some of these relationships and transitions.

Relationship	Transitional Words and Phrases
Time	*after, before, finally, meanwhile, then, today, when*
Location	*above, along, beneath, inside, next to, throughout*
Importance	*above all, first, in fact, mainly, to begin with*
Contrast	*although, but, in spite of, nevertheless, on the other hand, yet*
Cause and Effect	*as a result, because, for, so, so that, therefore*

Examples

- After a long journey, Ivan reached the dragon's city.
  [*After* shows a time relationship.]
- The messenger was trembling because the staff was about to fall.
  [*Because* shows a cause-and-effect relationship.]

Exercise

Revise for Clarity Add a transitional word or phrase to show a relationship between each pair of sentences. Underline the transition and tell what relationship it shows.

1. Vasilisa's parents had always kept her in a tower. One day they let her out.
2. The dragon had special powers. It took a special opponent to triumph over him.
3. Vasilisa showed courage and cleverness. She asked the dragon if anyone could get the better of him.

Test-Taking Tip
When you are taking a writing test, check your work for transitions. Transitions are especially important when you switch from one main idea to the next or from one paragraph to the next.

Literature Online
eWorkbooks To link to the Grammar and Language eWorkbook, go to www.glencoe.com.

ACADEMIC STANDARDS (page 1087)
9.4.13 Establish coherence… through effective transitions…
9.4.12 Revise writing to improve…the precision of word choice…

Focus

On the board, write: Many princes wished to marry the princess, but the king was in no hurry. When the time was right, the king sent out messengers. Discuss with students what purpose the underlined word and phrase are serving.

Teach

Transitional Expressions
Explain that transitional expressions show the relationship between ideas in sentences. OL

Assess

Note that there is more than one possible answer to each item in the exercise.

Possible rewrites:

1. Vasilisa's parents had always kept her in a tower, but one day they let her out. *(Contrast)*
2. The dragon had special powers; therefore it took a special opponent to triumph over him. *(Cause and effect)*
3. Vasilisa showed courage and cleverness when she asked the dragon if anyone could get the better of him. *(Time)*

English Language Coach

Classifying Transitional Expressions Help English learners classify transitional expressions by creating a four-column chart. Label the columns as follows: *Location, Importance, Contrast, Cause and Effect.* Guide students to write the transitional words and phrases under the appropriate headings. EL

Differentiated Instruction

Reinforcing the Lesson Students who need extra reinforcement to process the instruction may benefit from writing transitional words and phrases on individual self-stick notes. As they complete the exercise, they can place the right transitions on the page and see how they "fit." BL

Academic Standards
Additional Support activities on p. 1087 cover the following standards:
English Language Coach: **9.6.2** Demonstrate an understanding of sentence construction…and proper English usage…
Differentiated Instruction: **9.5.8** Write for different purposes…

BEFORE YOU READ

Focus

BELLRINGER

Bellringer Options
Daily Language Practice Transparency 92
Or display images of the Old West. **Ask:** Why do tales about people who sought a new life in the West remain fascinating today?

Summary

The ballad describes Betsy and Ike's long and perilous journey to California. As they cross deserts and mountains, they face hunger, thirst, and deep discouragement.

Literary Elements Have students access the Web site to improve their understanding of ballads.

BEFORE YOU READ *Sweet Betsy from Pike*

LITERATURE PREVIEW

Connecting to the Ballad

The ballad "Sweet Betsy from Pike" tells the story of two people on a long and difficult journey. Before you read, think about the following questions:

- Do you have a goal that you would travel a long way and overcome many obstacles to reach?
- What types of characters would you expect to meet along the way?

Building Background

During the 1800s the desire for gold, land, adventure, and greater opportunity led women and men to undertake the dangerous journey westward across the United States. Several overland routes existed at the time. Each one presented challenges for travelers. Mountains, rivers, harsh weather, and disease were only some of the obstacles encountered by these determined adventurers. Written accounts offer evidence of the hardships they faced. In such conditions, it may have seemed to the struggling men and women that only a "superhero" could successfully complete the trip. The anonymous ballad "Sweet Betsy from Pike" originated on one of these overland trails.

Setting Purposes for Reading

Big Idea Courage and Cleverness

As you read "Sweet Betsy from Pike," notice how the characters use courage and cleverness to deal with their circumstances.

Literary Element Ballad

A **ballad** is a narrative song or poem, which means it is a song or poem that tells a story. As you read, think about how "Sweet Betsy from Pike" may have sounded to the people who heard it first.

- See Literary Terms Handbook, p. R3.

Literature Online Interactive Literary Elements Handbook To review or learn more about the literary elements, go to www.glencoe.com.

READING PREVIEW

Reading Strategy Analyzing Archetypes

An **archetype** is a model, or a perfect example of something. Archetypal characters are often found in literature. An archetypal hero, for example, has all the characteristics readers would expect a hero to have: bravery, intelligence, strength, and wit. As you read "Sweet Betsy from Pike," try to determine what archetypes the characters are based on.

Reading Tip: Creating Character Webs As you read, use a character web to describe the main character in "Sweet Betsy from Pike."

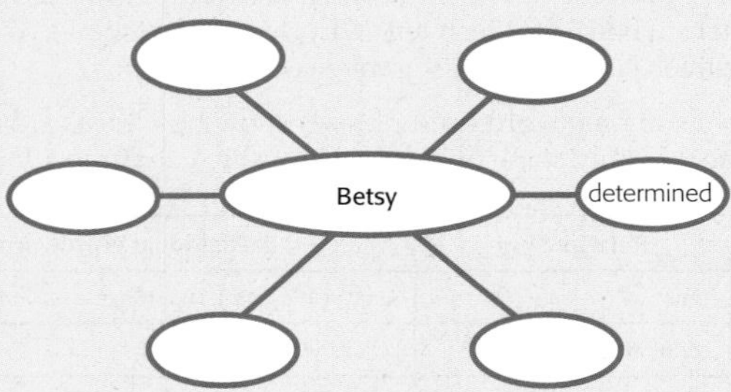

The Oregon Trail, 1869. Albert Bierstadt. Oil on canvas, 78.7 × 124.5 cm. Butler Institute of American Art, Youngstown, OH.

INDIANA ACADEMIC STANDARDS (pages 1088-1091)

9.2 Develop strategies such as...identifying and analyzing structure...

9.3 [Identify] story elements such as character...

9.5.8 Write for different purposes and audiences, adjusting tone, style, and voice as appropriate.

Selection Skills

Sweet Betsy from Pike

Literary Elements
- Ballad (SE pp. 1088, 1090)
- Meter and Rhythm (SE p. 1090)

Reading Skills
- Analyzing Archetypes (SE pp. 1088, 1089, 1091)

Vocabulary Skills
- Academic Vocabulary (SE p. 1091)

Listening/Speaking/Viewing Skills
- Listening to Music for Creative Inspiration (SE p. 1091)

Writing Skills/Grammar
- Writing a Ballad (SE p. 1091)

Encampment in the Valley of the Sacramento (from *California: Its Past, Present & Future.*). 1850. Newberry Library, Chicago. ★

Oh, do you remember sweet Betsy from Pike,
Who crossed the wide prairies with her hus-
band Ike?
With two yoke[1] of oxen, a big yaller dog,
A tall Shanghai rooster,[2] and one spotted hog.

Chorus:
Hoodle dang, fol dee dye do,
Hoodle dang, fol dee day.

The rooster ran off and the oxen all died;
The last piece of bacon that morning was
fried.
Poor Ike got discouraged and Betsy got mad;
The dog wagged his tail and looked wonder-
fully sad.

Chorus

The alkali[3] desert was burning and hot,
And Ike, he decided to leave on the spot:
"My dear old Pike County, I'll go back to you."
Said Betsy, "You'll go by yourself if you do."

Chorus

They swam the wide rivers, they crossed the
tall peaks,
They camped out on prairies for weeks and
for weeks,
Fought off starvation and big storms of dust,
Determined to reach California or bust.

Chorus

They passed the Sierras[4] through mountains
of snow,
'Til old California was sighted below.
Sweet Betsy, she hollered, and Ike gave a
cheer,
Said, "Betsy, my darlin', I'm a made mil-
lioneer."

Chorus

1. A *yoke* is a pair of animals joined together for working.
2. A *Shanghai rooster* is a breed of rooster that originated in East Asia. *Shanghai* is an ancient city in China.
3. Here, *alkali* means "composed of soil that contains a mineral salt that prevents or stunts plant growth."
4. The *Sierras* refers to the Sierra Nevada Mountains, a mountain range in the western United States.

Reading Strategy Analyzing Archetypes *What characteristics of Betsy's seem familiar? Explain.* **R**

Teach

R Reading Strategy

Analyzing Archetypes

Answer: Her determination and toughness are reminiscent of the archetypal pioneer. **OL**

★ Cultural History

California Gold Rush

After a sawmill builder discovered gold near Sacramento in 1848, thousands of prospectors flooded into the region. By 1853, more than a quarter of a million people had moved to California in search of wealth, and the value of the gold mined from its rivers and hills amounted to almost $2 billion. **AS**

CheckPoint

Use the CheckPoint questions provided on Presentation Plus! to check students' mastery of the selection. These questions can be used with interactive response keypads for immediate student feedback.

Selection Resources

Print Materials
- Unit 5 Resources (Fast File), pp. 51–52
- Selection and Unit Assessments, pp. 187–188
- Selection Quick Checks, p. 94

Transparencies
- Bellringer Options Transparencies: Daily Language Practice Transparency 92
- Literary Elements Transparency 53, 54, 61, 62

Technology
- TeacherWorks Plus™ CD-ROM
- StudentWorks Plus™ CD-ROM
- Presentation Plus!™ CD-ROM
- Literature Online, glencoe.com
- Online Student Edition, mhln.com
- Exam*View*® Assessment Suite CD-ROM
- Vocabulary PuzzleMaker CD-ROM
- Listening Library, disc 2 track 34

AFTER YOU READ

Assess

1. (a) Answers should show an understanding of that era's challenges. (b) Students should include their view of today's challenges.
2. (a) Seven (b) Their journey took them through isolated territory with few places to get provisions.
3. (a)The rooster runs off, the oxen dies, and the food runs out. (b) Everything has gone wrong, and the journey looks hopeless.
4. (a) Home to Pike County (b) She's going to California with or without him.
5. (a) They are adventurous, courageous, clever, and determined. (b) Accept reasonable answers.
6. Accept reasonable answers.
7. The regular rhythm and rhyme scheme make the ballad easy to remember.
8. Betsy seems representative of the many strong, resourceful women who journeyed west in those times.

Web Activities Have students access the Web site for interactive activities that will help them assess their understanding of the selection.

AFTER YOU READ

RESPONDING AND THINKING CRITICALLY

Respond

1. (a)Do you think Betsy would have been a good role model for people in the 1800s? Explain. (b)Describe a fictional character who you think would be a good role model for people today.

Recall and Interpret

2. (a)How many animals do Betsy and Ike take with them on their trip? (b)What does the fact that Betsy and Ike are traveling with these animals tell you about their journey?
3. (a)What happens on the day the last piece of bacon is fried? (b)Explain why Ike may become discouraged at that time.
4. (a)To what place does Ike want to return? (b)Explain what Betsy means by saying, "You'll go by yourself if you do."

Analyze and Evaluate

5. (a)What qualities do Betsy and Ike exhibit that would make them successful in the present day? (b)What do you think Betsy and Ike would be doing if they were living in the present day?
6. Which of the two characters—Betsy or Ike—is more memorable? Why?
7. Would this ballad be easy or difficult to memorize? Explain.

Connect

8. **Big Idea** **Courage and Cleverness** Why do you think a woman is the central character in this ballad about courage and cleverness?

LITERARY ANALYSIS

Literary Element Ballad

A **ballad** may be either a folk ballad or a literary ballad. A **folk ballad** usually tells of an exciting or dramatic event. Folk ballads have no known author and were passed along orally—usually as songs—from generation to generation before being written down. In contrast, a **literary ballad** is written in imitation of a folk ballad and has at least one known author. Most ballads tell their stories primarily through characters' action and dialogue.

1. Is "Sweet Betsy from Pike" a folk ballad or a literary ballad? How do you know?
2. What is the main action taking place in "Sweet Betsy from Pike"? How does the main action help define it as a ballad?
3. What feature or features of this ballad tell you that it may have originated as a song?

Review: Meter and Rhythm

As you learned on page 529, meter and rhythm are elements in poetic expression. **Meter** is a regular pattern of stressed and unstressed syllables that gives a line of poetry or a song a predictable rhythm. **Rhythm** is the sound pattern created by the arrangement of stressed and unstressed syllables that gives poetry a musical quality. You can analyze the rhythm in poetry by scanning it. To scan a line, write out the words and use symbols to indicate stressed and unstressed syllables. A ˘ above a syllable indicates that it is unstressed, and a ´ indicates that it is stressed. An example is given below.

Ĭ wándĕrĕd lónelў́ ás ă clóud
Thăt flóats ŏn hígh o'ĕr vales ănd hílls.

Partner Activity With a classmate, discuss the meter and rhythm in "Sweet Betsy from Pike." Scan the lines in the first verse to determine the number of beats in each line and to decide which syllables are stressed.

Literary Element

1. Folk ballad; no author is listed; the song is labeled "Traditional."
2. The ballad tells of Betsy and Ike's journey to California. The events constitute a story, or narrative.
3. Its rhythm and a rhyme scheme, the chorus

Review: Meter and Rhythm

Students should indicate four beats in each line with the following syllables stressed:

˘ ´ ˘ ˘ ´ ˘ ˘ ´ ˘
(Oh, do you remember sweet Betsy
˘ ´
from Pike,
˘ ´ ˘ ˘ ´ ˘ ˘
Who, crossed the wide prairies with
´ ˘ ˘ ´
her husband Ike?

READING AND VOCABULARY

Reading Strategy Analyzing Archetypes

Archetypal characters occur often in folklore—the traditional beliefs, customs, stories, and songs belonging to a culture that are passed down by word of mouth. These characters are universally recognized "types," such as heroes or villains. The stubborn wife and henpecked husband on a quest for riches while battling hunger and the elements are character archetypes typical to folklore.

1. Describe Betsy and Ike. Why might Betsy be considered an archetypal wife?
2. Do you think the journey of Betsy and Ike could be considered archetypal? Explain.

Academic Vocabulary

Here are two words from the vocabulary list on page R80.

challenge (cha′ lənj) *n.* something that makes demands upon one's talents and interests

abandon (ə ban′ dən) *v.* to give up

Practice and Apply

1. What might have been the greatest **challenge** for the characters in "Sweet Betsy from Pike"?
2. Do you think Betsy or Ike wanted to **abandon** their goals at any time? Explain.

A wagoner drives his horses along the eastern section of the Union Pacific Railroad.

WRITING AND EXTENDING

Writing About Literature

Apply Form Have you ever read about or participated in an experience that you thought should be immortalized in song? Use what you know about the ballad form and archetypal characters to write a ballad about an exciting or memorable event. Like "Sweet Betsy from Pike," your ballad should have a regular meter, a rhyme scheme, and at least four verses.

As you create your characters and decide on the plot and setting for your ballad, use a chart like the one below to help you generate rhyming words.

	Rhyming Words
Event: Family reunion	softball game, lame, fame, blame, name, same barbecue, do, new, you
Setting:	
Archetypal Characters:	

After completing your draft, meet with a peer reviewer. Evaluate each other's work and suggest revisions. Then proofread and edit your draft to correct errors in spelling, grammar, and punctuation.

Interdisciplinary Activity: Music

Travelers on the overland trails headed for California entertained and comforted themselves by singing. Listen to a recording of "Sweet Betsy from Pike" and other songs popular in the United States in the mid-1800s. As you listen, draw an illustration for the song or create a journal entry as though you were traveling with Betsy and Ike.

LiteratureOnline **Web Activities** For eFlashcards, Selection Quick Checks, and other Web activities, go to www.glencoe.com.

AFTER YOU READ

Assess

Reading Strategy

1. Betsy is tougher than her discouraged husband. She is ready to go on without him if she has to. She is the archetype of the stubborn wife who pushes her husband for the sake of her own goals.
2. It seems typical of stories about pursuing a goal. There is usually a point in such journeys when the long, hard struggle seems hopeless.

Academic Vocabulary

1. The greatest challenge is the lack of food and water.
2. Yes, at one point Ike wants to give up and go back to Pike County.

Writing About Literature

Students' ballads should feature

- Regular meter and rhyme scheme
- Characters with familiar traits
- An exciting event

Interdisciplinary Activity: Music

Students' illustrations or journal entries should reflect the content of the song.

English Language Coach

Historical Context English language learners may need some historical background. Have them research the Oregon Trail and report their findings in class. They should be able to trace the approximate route on a map and describe some of the hazards the trail presented. EL

Differentiated Instruction

Illustrating the Song Invite visual learners to illustrate the ballad and present their work to the class. Discuss how they decided which details to include and how the tone of the ballad informed their style. AL

Academic Standards

Additional Support activities on p. 1091 cover the following standards:

English Language Coach: **9.3.12** Analyze the way in which a work…is related to…issues of its historical period.

Differentiated Instruction: **9.3** Identify story elements such as…plot [and tone]…

Focus

BELLRINGER

Display pictures showing different kinds of heroes, including celebrities, such as athletes, and noncelebrities, such as firemen. **Ask:** What makes these people heroes? Which one do you find most heroic? Is it possible to be a hero without being famous?

Have students freewrite about aspects of heroism that interest them or about people they have known who have acted heroically.

Summary

In this workshop, students will write a research paper and give an expository presentation of it. Students will follow the stages of the writing process, including prewriting, drafting, revising, and editing. In addition, the workshop includes two focus lessons, on building paragraph unity and using quotation marks correctly.

Writing Models Have students access the Web site for interactive writing models and writing guides.

The Writing Process

In this workshop, you will follow the stages of the writing process. At any stage, you may think of new ideas to include and better ways to express them. Feel free to return to earlier stages as you write.

- **Prewriting**
- **Drafting**
- **Revising**
  - Focus Lesson: Building Paragraph Unity
- **Editing and Proofreading**
  - Focus Lesson: Using Quotation Marks Correctly
- **Presenting**

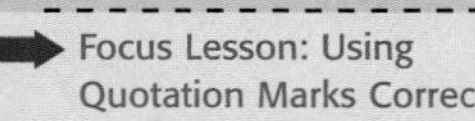

Writing Models For models and other writing activities, go to www.glencoe.com.

ACADEMIC STANDARDS (pages 1092–1101)

9.5.9 Write...a research report that has been developed using a systematic research process...

9.4.8 Use appropriate conventions for documentation in...bibliographies...

Writing Workshop

Research Paper

Writing a Research Paper

"Cyclops,
if ever mortal man inquire
how you were put to shame and blinded, tell him
Odysseus, raider of cities, took your eye.
Laertes' son, whose home's on Ithaca!"

—Homer, from the *Odyssey*

Connecting to Literature In the *Odyssey*, the epic hero Odysseus makes a ten-year journey home to Ithaca after the Trojan War. Odysseus is strong, courageous, and able to conquer monsters with nearly superhuman power. Although he is often tested, he lives according to a strict code of honor and never shrinks from danger or duty. Ordinary people often share some of these same traits. For example, during World War II, women were called on to do jobs they had never done before, and they responded eagerly. They made weapons, built airplanes, and drove trucks. They became heroes in the war effort.

Features of a Research Paper

Goals	Strategies
To choose a research topic and narrow the focus	☑ Explore ideas ☑ Refine and shape your topic
To gather information	☑ Generate questions to research ☑ Look for both primary and secondary sources
To organize information	☑ Take notes and make an outline ☑ Present information in a logical, effective order
To write a paper with a thesis supported by facts and details	☑ Write a clear thesis statement ☑ Develop topic sentences and paragraphs to support the thesis

Workshop Resources

Print Materials

- Unit 5 Resources (Fast File), pp. 53–56
- REAL Success in Writing: Research and Reports
- Writing Constructed Responses, pp. 1–26, 54, 67–72
- Glencoe Literature Library

Transparencies

- Grammar and Language Transparencies 4
- Writing Workshop Transparencies 26–30

Technology

- Grammar & Language eWorkbook
- Revising with Style eWorkbook
- Sentence Diagraming eWorkbook
- Spelling Power eWorkbook
- Online Essay Grader, glencoe.com
- Literature Library Exam*View*® Assessment Suite CD-ROM
- Literature Library Vocabulary PuzzleMaker CD-ROM

Assignment

Write a research paper showing how an everyday hero has character **BI** traits similar to those of an epic hero. As you move through the stages of the writing process, keep your audience and purpose in mind.

Audience: classmates and teacher

Purpose: to research a topic and present your conclusions supported by evidence

Prewriting

Explore Your Ideas Think about heroic qualities. How do ordinary people demonstrate these qualities in their everyday lives?

▶ **Ask Questions** Questions like these may help you find a topic for your research paper.

- Who are some everyday heroes?
- What character traits make them heroic?
- How are everyday heroes like epic heroes?

▶ **Choose a Topic and Narrow the Focus** Do investigative research to refine and shape your topic. If your topic is too narrow, you will not be able to find the information you need. If it is too broad, you will have difficulty organizing the details and making a clear point. The chart shows examples of topics that are too broad, too narrow, and just right.

Too Broad	Too Narrow	Just Right
The soldiers in World War II, Red Cross workers, and Rosie the Riveter are heroes who share character traits with epic heroes.	Rosie Bonavita was a real riveter who fastened a record number of rivets in six hours.	Rosie the Riveter symbolizes the American women who became everyday heroes during World War II.

Gather Information Begin by writing four or five questions for research. It may help you to think of a reporter's questions—*who, what, why, when, where,* and *how.* Look for answers on reliable Web sites and in encyclopedias, books, and magazines. Try to use primary sources such as letters, diaries, and interviews as well as books and articles about the topic.

Student Model

Who was Rosie the Riveter?

What kind of work did women do during World War II?

When and where did women start working?

Real-World Connection

If you listen to television or radio newscasts, you are familiar with reports. Reporters do research on nearly anything that may interest their viewers or listeners—from defective toys to the latest advances in health care. A good report includes information from multiple sources, presents the information objectively, and identifies the sources of information. ★

Quote Versus Paraphrase

The exact words from a reliable authority give credibility to research, so you will want to include direct quotes in your paper. On the other hand, when the exact words from another source are not memorable, it is better to put the idea in your own words, or paraphrase. Paraphrasing helps you maintain the flow of your writing.

Teach

BI Big Idea

Courage and Cleverness

At first glance, students may be puzzled by the idea of "everyday" heroics. Remind them that even in everyday life we have opportunities to display our courage and our cleverness. **Ask:** What are some examples of courage or cleverness that you remember from your own life? What are some examples that you've heard of from the news? *(In answer to the second question, students may mention humanitarian relief workers, rescue workers, or other vivid "human interest" stories.)* **OL**

★ Cultural History

Edward R. Murrow After a distinguished career as a radio reporter during World War II, Edward R. Murrow (1908–1965) and his associate Fred Friendly became pioneers of TV reporting with their show *See It Now.* Murrow loved stories about ordinary Americans and their quiet heroism. Known also as an effective political and social commentator, Murrow was the subject of George Clooney's 2005 film *Good Night, and Good Luck.* **AS**

English Language Coach

Finding and Recording Information Encourage English language learners to select a hero from their native culture. They may be able to research resources in their native language. After they organize information, pair them with a more proficient English speaker to help translate notes into English. **EL**

Differentiated Instruction

Using Resources Less proficient readers may be intimidated by the prospect of doing research. Encourage them to take advantage of school and public librarians, who are very willing to help with research projects; students should not feel shy in asking questions. **BL**

Academic Standards

Additional Support activities on p. 1093 cover the following standards:

English Language Coach: **9.4.6** Synthesize information from multiple sources…

Differentiated Instruction: **9.7.1** Summarize a speaker's purpose and…ask questions concerning the speaker's content…

Teach

Writing Skills

Narrowing Focus Use the chart on page 1093 to help students understand how to determine the proper scope of a topic. **Ask:** Why is the example cited under the first subhead too broad? *(Each of the three examples could be the subject of a whole essay on their own.)* Why is the example cited under the second subhead too narrow? *(This statement is a detail that could best be used to support a more general thesis.)* **OL**

★ Political History

Rosie the Riveter Memorial Dedicated in October of 2000, the Rosie the Riveter Memorial is a large outdoor sculpture set in the former Kaiser Shipyards of Richmond, California, where many women worked to assemble ships used in World War II. The large stainless steel structure was designed by visual artist Susan Schwartzberg and landscape architect/environmental sculptor Cheryl Barton. It commemorates the important labor done by women during the war. **AS**

Take Notes As you find sources, take notes on index cards. Keep track of your sources as you research so you can list them on a Works Cited page at the end of your paper. Copy direct quotations if you think you will be able to use them to support your thesis. Other information can be paraphrased, or put into your own words.

▶ Bibliography Note Card

Online interview	
Source number	4
Author	Harvey, Sheridan.
Title	"Rosie the Riveter: Real Women Workers in World War II."
Web site information	Rosie the Riveter Transcript (Journeys and Crossings)
Sponsoring organization	Library of Congress Digital Reference Team.
Date of access	Dec. 19, 2005
URL	http://www.loc.gov/rr/program/journey/rosie—transcript.

▶ Paraphrase Note Card

Norman Rockwell's Rosie 3

Rosie the Riveter appears on a cover that Norman Rockwell illustrated for the Saturday Evening Post in May 1943. She is a big, strong woman, and she has a smudge on her face. Rosie wears overalls, loafers, and a leather strap around her arm. There is a riveter gun in her lap. ★

▶ Direct Quotation Note Card

Norman Rockwell's Rosie 2

"Rosie is powerful, competent, and womanly. But there are contradictions in the image. She's masculine: look at the size of her arms, which are a real focus of the cover. . . . Yet she's feminine: She's wearing rouge and lipstick. Makeup is essential to women's mental health, according to some articles of the time. Her compact and handkerchief peek out of her pocket; she has nail polish on; her curly red hair and upturned nose feminize her; her visor almost looks like a halo, providing an angelic side to this strong woman."

Primary Sources

Research papers require sources, and it is good to include primary sources when you can find them. Primary sources are the recorded words and thoughts of a person involved in the event or an eyewitness. Examples of primary sources include letters, interviews, autobiographies, and diaries.

Additional Support

Skills Practice

READING: Gathering Information One of the challenges of researching a paper is deciding what information is worth including. As students begin to research their papers, offer them the following advice:

- Choose source material that you can understand, neither too technical nor too complex.
- Start with a general source that will give you just the basics, such as an encyclopedia or a reliable Web site.
- Read for big ideas, rather than details. **OL**

Organize Your Information An outline is an excellent way to organize the data you collect from various sources. Begin with a working outline that you can revise as you draft your paper. Below are some tips.

- **Groupings** Group note cards and use the groupings to develop the main topics in your outline.
- **Topic Groups** Form subtopics in the main topic groups and use these as secondary heads in your outline.
- **Order** Put your main topics in the most logical order.

Secondary Sources

Secondary sources are words written by someone who has researched or interpreted primary sources. Encyclopedia articles, biographies, and book reviews are secondary sources.

Sample Outline

Rosie the Riveter: A Symbol for Everyday Heroes During World War II
I. Posters of Rosie the Riveter
  A. Famous in the 1940s
    1. A made-up character
    2. Based on a real woman, maybe Rosie Bonavita
  B. All women with men's jobs came to be known as Rosie the Riveter
II. Men left jobs to join the military
  A. Workers needed to keep the country running
  B. OWI created in 1942
    1. Ran advertising campaign
    2. Posters challenged women to join the war effort

Develop Your Thesis Statement After you have chosen the main ideas, draft a thesis statement that covers them. You may revise the statement as you write, but it helps to get something down on paper.

Sample Thesis Statement

During World War II, Rosie the Riveter was a symbol for the women who became everyday heroes when they accepted the challenge and showed strength and courage in doing jobs that they had never done before.

Teach

Writing Skills

Taking Notes To help students take effective notes while researching their papers, emphasize the following strategies:

- Make sure that the information is relevant to your topic.
- For each subject, use a separate note card.
- Be sure to carefully note your sources for your bibliography.
- When you're finished taking notes, organize your note cards according to subject. OL

Writing Skills

Creating an Outline Tell students that all of the information they have gathered in their research should fit somewhere in their outline. If something doesn't fit, students should consider whether to eliminate the bit of information or adapt any of the topics or subtopics to incorporate it. Creating an outline may also bring to light any gaps in the gathered information, and more research may be required. OL

Differentiated Instruction

Organization Students who reason logically will excel at organizing their note cards and preparing their outlines. Have students bring their note cards to class. After students have divided their cards into subtopics, discuss logical ways to organize them.

- Chronological order is a good way to describe the sequence of an event or process.
- Cause-and-effect order works best for historical information. AL

Academic Standards

Additional Support activities on pp. 1094 and 1095 cover the following standards:

Skills Practice: **9.2.3** Generate relevant questions about readings on...topics that can be researched.

Differentiated Instruction: **9.5.9** Write... a research report...that...organizes information by...categorizing...and sequencing...

Teach

Writing Skills

Introduce Subject Answer: *The subject is Rosie the Riveter.* **OL**

Writing Skills

Thesis Statement Answer: *During World War II, Rosie the Riveter symbolized the possibility that women can do jobs they have never done before and become everyday heroes.* **OL**

Writing Skills

Main Idea Answer: *Right away the reader understands that the idea of Rosie the Riveter and what she symbolized was well-known.* **OL**

Writing Skills

Supporting Details Answer: *The details present facts and information about the woman upon whom the poster character is believed to be based, reinforcing the message that women can be everyday heroes.* **OL**

Drafting

Getting Started As with any writing, it is best to start writing your research paper immediately even if you feel like putting it off until you have more information. Begin with the ideas in your notes and outline. As you draft, keep your thesis in mind, and do not stray too far from it. Be sure to include examples and details to support your topic sentences and main ideas. Always remember that you can revise at any point.

Analyzing a Workshop Model

Here is a final draft of a research paper. Read the paper and pay close attention to the comments in the margin. They point out features that you might want to include in your own paper. Answer the questions in the margin, and use the answers to guide you as you write your own draft.

Introduce Subject
Begin by letting your readers know the subject. What will this research paper be about?

Thesis Statement
State your point of view in a thesis statement. What viewpoint will be presented?

Main Idea
Use the main ideas from your outline to develop your paper. Why is this a good main idea to put at the beginning?

Supporting Details
Use facts, examples, statistics, quotations, and reasons to support your main idea. How do these details support the main idea of the paragraph?

Rosie the Riveter: Symbol of Women Who Were Everyday Heroes

If you had been alive during World War II, you would have seen posters on the walls of banks, post offices, and other public places of a young American woman wearing overalls and carrying a wrench or a rivet gun in her hand. Who was this woman, and why was her image all over town? The woman in the posters was known as Rosie the Riveter. During World War II, Rosie the Riveter was a symbol for all of the women who became everyday heroes when they accepted the challenge and showed strength and courage in doing jobs that they had never done before.

Rosie the Riveter was one of the most famous women in the United States in the early 1940s. She was a made-up character, but she may have been based on a real woman named Rosina D. Bonavita who, in one shift with her partner, drove a record 3,345 rivets to assemble the wing of a torpedo bomber (Ambrose 42). Even though the Rosie in the posters was not a real person, she set a powerful example for women during the war. She called on them to serve their country by doing jobs they had never done before.

Millions of men left their jobs to fight in World War II. While they were away, somebody had to fill their jobs to keep the country running. Who could do peacetime jobs such as driving buses? Who could do wartime jobs such as making weapons? Around 1942, although the exact date is not known, an artist named J. Howard Miller worked for a company that probably wanted to encourage women to work there. According to Library of

Additional Support

Skills Practice

WRITING: Effective Introductions
Say: Your introduction should grab the reader's attention. **List the following ideas on the board:**

- Begin with an unusual fact or detail.
- Ask a question that the paper will answer.
- State your thesis.
- Begin with an anecdote.

Have students choose at least two ideas with which to experiment and draft the introductions. Then have them exchange papers with a partner, who will determine which is the strongest. **OL**

Congress women's studies specialist Sheridan Harvey, Miller created an image of a woman rolling up her sleeve as if getting ready to work. The poster is titled "We Can Do It!" However, Rosie was not connected to this poster (Harvey 1).

Then, on May 29, 1943, Norman Rockwell's picture of a confident woman in overalls and loafers illustrated the cover of the *Saturday Evening Post*. She wears goggles and a leather strap around her arm. One hand rests on a lunch box that is labeled "Rosie" and the other holds a ham sandwich. A huge riveter lies across her lap.

> Rosie is powerful, competent, and womanly. But there are contradictions in the image. She's masculine: look at the size of her arms, which are a real focus of the cover. . . . Yet she's feminine: She's wearing rouge and lipstick. Makeup is essential to women's mental health, according to some articles of the time. Her compact and handkerchief peek out of her pocket; she has nail polish on; her curly red hair and upturned nose feminize her; her visor almost looks like a halo, providing an angelic side to this strong woman (Harvey 2).

The country needed women to go to work, and that is where Rosie and the Office of War Information, or OWI, came in. The OWI was created in 1942, and it was an important U.S. government agency during World War II. One of the OWI's many tasks was to run an advertising campaign. They were not selling a product, though. They were selling an idea: All able-bodied citizens, including women, should go to work in jobs that would help the war effort. Until then, some women had worked but not in jobs usually held by men. For example, they worked in clothing factories (Appleby, Brinkley, and McPherson 308–09). Posters of Rosie that were created by the OWI challenged women to do their patriotic duty and play an important part in the war effort. They helped convince women that they could do men's work, and they could do it well.

More than six million women met the challenge and joined the workforce (Colman 16). Women worked in factories and shipyards. They served in the military or worked as nurses in hospitals overseas. Some were farmworkers. Others drove trucks, taxis, and buses. Women learned many new skills, such as welding, hammering, and—

Long Direct Quotation
Use direct quotations to keep the exact words of your sources. If a quotation is long, indent it and do not use quotation marks. Why do you think the writer used this long quotation?

Paraphrase
Put information in your own words but be sure to identify your source. Why are there no quotation marks with this information even though a source is cited?

Facts and Examples
Statistics and specific details support your argument. How do these facts and examples support the idea that women met the challenge and joined the workforce?

Teach

Writing Skills

Long Direct Quotation

Answer: *The quotation supports the idea that women were strong and capable of filling what were traditionally men's roles at home while the men were fighting for our country.* **OL**

Writing Skills

Paraphrase

Answer: *Paraphrased information is not a direct quotation, so quotation marks are unnecessary.* **OL**

Writing Skills

Facts and Examples

Answer: *The facts and examples provide specific information about the kinds of work women did.* **OL**

Writing Skills

Quoting and Paraphrasing

Review with students the mechanics of using quotations and paraphrases. Short quotations can be inserted directly into paragraphs. Longer quotations should be treated as extracts visually set off by indentation, without quotation marks. Similarly, remind students that quotation marks are not used when paraphrasing. In all cases, students should cite source information directly after the quote or paraphrase. **OL**

English Language Coach

Diction English learners may have trouble distinguishing high and low diction. Although a research paper uses relatively formal language, remind students that a simple, friendly style is best. Challenge students to point out sentences in the model essay that use clear, simple language. **EL**

Academic Standards

Additional Support activities on pp. 1096 and 1097 cover the following standards:

Skills Practice: **9.4.10** Review [and] evaluate writing...for meaning, clarity, [and] content...

English Language Coach: **9.3.11** Evaluate the aesthetic qualities of style, including the impact of diction...

Teach

Writing Skills

Primary Sources *The quotations come from women who actually filled men's roles during the war.* OL

Writing Skills

Secondary Sources *Encyclopedias compile information from many primary sources to provide general background and factual information.* OL

Writing Skills

Restate Thesis *Restating the thesis reinforces its impact.* OL

Writing Skills

Draw Conclusions *Rosie the Riveter not only was a symbol during World War II but remains an inspiration for women to join the work force.* OL

of course—riveting. Posters let them know they could help the war effort by working as typists, waitresses, salespeople, elevator operators, and conductors ("Powers").

Joining the workforce during the war changed many women's lives. One of these women, Jane Ward Mayta, said, "I learned a lot in those years. . . . I learned to look for a job. I learned to get along with and mingle with people from totally different backgrounds. We were all in little pockets before then" (Wise and Wise 12). Many women have donated their stories and photographs to the National Park Service's collection center for memories of the World War II years. One of these women, Helyn A. Potter, wrote "War changes everything. I was a welder and now a riveter in an all-woman workforce. Five years earlier, I was studying ballet, planning to become a ballerina. As we supported the War Effort, the collective soul of women changed" ("Rosie").

Primary Sources

Try to include the words of someone who experienced the event. What makes this quotation a primary source?

On October 19, 1942, *Time* magazine reported on the "striking evidence" of the social changes brought by World War II. The reason given was that women were working in new occupations. "Northwest lumber yards now have 4,000 women whistle punks, talleymen, flunkies, bull cooks. . . . In Marshfield, Ore., gaffers watched incredulously as a woman maneuvered a State Highway Commission steam roller down the main street" ("Women").

In 1945 World War II came to an end, and men who returned from the war expected to return to their old jobs. As a result, many women had to leave their wartime jobs. The work opportunities for women closed when the war ended. Many women were not happy to be out of work, but most of them returned to lives focused on homemaking and raising children. By 1960 fewer women were employed as professionals than in 1930 ("Feminism").

Secondary Sources

A secondary source is the interpretation of someone who studied primary sources. Why is an encyclopedia a secondary source?

Yet the example set by Rosie the Riveter would continue to inspire women in the years that followed. Her name remained a symbol for women's strength, courage, and ability to perform a variety of jobs. Women now had a real choice about whether they would work outside the home. They also had more choices about the kinds of work they would do, since more jobs were open to them. As summarized in an article in *Prologue* magazine, social change resulted because women took over men's jobs during World War II. It was "a turning point in the evolution of women's roles and rights in American culture" (Fried). To this day, the symbol of Rosie the Riveter hard at work remains a real inspiration for generations of women.

Restate Thesis

Restate your viewpoint. Why is it a good idea to restate your thesis in your conclusion?

Draw Conclusions

End by drawing your own conclusions from the information presented. What idea does this writer want to leave with readers?

Additional Support

Skills Practice

GRAMMAR: Verb Tense Many students have trouble remaining in the past tense when writing an essay about an historical event. **Write the following two sentences on the board:** Women work in lumberyards and on highways. They prove that in a time of crisis people can do extraordinary things. Have students rewrite the sentences in the past tense. *(Women worked in lumberyards and on highways. They proved that in a time of crisis people could do extraordinary things.)* OL

We Can Do It!

Works Cited

Ambrose, Stephen E. The Good Fight: How World War II Was Won. New York: Atheneum, 2001.

Appleby, Joyce Oldham, Alan Brinkley, and James M. McPherson. The American Journey. New York: Glencoe/McGraw-Hill, 2003.

Colman, Penny. Rosie the Riveter: Women Working on the Home Front in World War II. New York: Crown, 1995.

"Feminism." Encyclopaedia Britannica Online. 2005. Encyclopaedia Britannica Premium Service. 19 Dec. 2005. <http://www.britannica.com/eb/article-216009>

Fried, Ellen. "From Pearl Harbor to Elvis: Images That Endure." Prologue 36.4, Winter 2004.

Harvey, Sheridan. "Rosie the Riveter: Real Women Workers in World War II." Journeys and Crossings, Library of Congress, Transcript. <http://www.loc.gov/rr/program/journey/rosie-transcript.html>

"Powers of Persuasion: Poster Art from World War II." National Archives. <http://www.archives.gov/exhibits/powers_of_persuasion/its_a_womans_war_too/its_a_womans_war_too.html>

"Rosie the Riveter: Women Working During World War II."<http://www.nps.gov/pwro/collection/website/rosie.htm>

Wise, Nancy Baker and Christy Wise. A Mouthful of Rivets: Women at Work in World War II. San Francisco: Jossey-Bass, 1994.

"Women, Women Everywhere." Time Archive Online. XL.16, October 19, 1942. <http://www.time.com/time/archive/preview/0,10987,850057,00.html>

Citing Sources

Books and textbooks are usually reliable sources. What information should be included in the citation for a book?

Reliable Sources

Web sites often have interviews or documents that are primary sources. Why do you have to be careful when you use the Internet as a resource?

Internet Research

Back issues of some magazines are found in archives on the Internet. Why might you want to use information from an old magazine article?

Teach

Writing Skills

Citing Sources *The information included in a book citation is the author, article title (if there is one), book title, publisher and its location, and publication year.* **OL**

Writing Skills

Reliable Sources *Internet sources are not always reliable. It's a good idea to check two or three sources to be sure Internet information is accurate.* **OL**

Writing Skills

Internet Research *Issues of old magazines can provide interesting and appropriate historical or background information that may be difficult to find in other sources or otherwise unavailable.* **OL**

Building Reading Fluency

Reading for Comprehension Some students will have limited stamina when reading a long essay, such as the workshop model, and may lose the thrust of the argument. In order to help them stay focused, go around the room and ask students to read the essay aloud, one paragraph at a time. Instruct them to pay close attention to pronunciation, tone, pacing, and emphasis—all indicators of how well a student understands what they are reading. Some students may need to read a passage more than once in order to get it right. **BL**

Academic Standards

Additional Support activities on pp. 1098 and 1099 cover the following standards:

Skills Practice: **9.6.2** Demonstrate an understanding of...proper English usage, including the use of consistent verb tenses.

Building Reading Fluency: **9.7** [Develop] speaking skills...in conjunction with...strategies...[for] delivery of oral presentations.

Teach

Writing Skills

Paragraph Unity Explain that the sentences in a paragraph work like a team: Each sentence is a "player" contributing to the overall good. Refer to the focus lesson. **Ask:** Why should the sentence about Norman Rockwell be omitted? *(Because the paragraph is about women joining the workforce, not about Norman Rockwell.)* How does adding the phrase "such as welding, hammering, and—of course—riveting" strengthen the sentence about women learning new skills? *(It makes the sentence more vivid, giving a clearer idea of what kind of new skills women learned.)* OL

★ Writer's Technique

Gurganus on Revision
The novelist Allan Gurganus (1947–) wrote, "The first impulse in writing is to flood it out, let as much run freely as you possibly can. Then to take a walk or go to the bank . . . and come back in a day or six months later. To read it with a cold eye and say, 'This is good. This is not. That sentence works. This is magical. This is crummy.'" AS

Revising

Traits of Strong Writing

Follow these traits of strong writing to express your ideas effectively.

Ideas message or theme and the details that develop it

Organization arrangement of main ideas and supporting details

Voice writer's unique way of using tone and style

Word Choice vocabulary a writer uses to convey meaning

Sentence Fluency rhythm and flow of sentences

Conventions correct spelling, grammar, usage, and mechanics

Presentation the way words and design elements look on a page

For more information on using the Traits of Strong Writing, see pages R32–R33 of the Writing Handbook.

Peer Review Exchange drafts with a partner. Check for a strong, clear thesis statement. Also make sure main ideas are supported with facts and examples. Note problems in the organization or the lack of a conclusion. Use the rubric below to evaluate and strengthen your essay. ★

Rubric: Writing a Research Paper

- ☑ Do you introduce your subject?
- ☑ Do you state your thesis and use main ideas to develop it?
- ☑ Do you include supporting details from a variety of sources?
- ☑ Do you use direct quotations and paraphrasing and cite your sources correctly?
- ☑ Do you draw your own conclusion in the end?

Focus Lesson

Building Paragraph Unity

A good paragraph has one main idea. To build paragraph unity, use a topic sentence with related supporting details. The topic sentence is often the first sentence, although it can be anywhere in the paragraph. See the example below.

Draft:

Women worked in factories and shipyards. They served in the military or worked as nurses in hospitals overseas. Some were farmworkers. In the 1940s, Norman Rockwell was a popular illustrator. Others drove trucks, taxis, and buses. Women learned many new skills. Posters let them know they could help the war effort by working as typists, waitresses, salespeople, elevator operators, and conductors.

Revision:

More than six million women met the challenge and joined the workforce[1] (Colman 16). Women worked in factories and shipyards. They served in the military or worked as nurses in hospitals overseas. Some were farmworkers. ~~In the 1940s, Norman Rockwell was a popular illustrator.~~[2] Others drove trucks, taxis, and buses. Women learned many new skills, such as welding, hammering, and—of course—riveting.[3] Posters let them know they could help the war effort by working as typists, waitresses, salespeople, elevator operators, and conductors.

1: Begin with a topic sentence. **2: Omit sentences that do not relate to the topic.**
3: Add specific details.

Additional Support

Skills Practice

WRITING: Using Details Remind students that using vivid details supports the reader's understanding of a topic. Refer to the focus lesson. **Ask:** What details in this paragraph support the topic that many women joined the work force? *(Details of the specific kinds of work women did support the topic.)* Have partners exchange drafts and take turns identifying the topics of several paragraphs and their supporting details. Ask students to suggest to their partners how the details could more clearly or strongly support the paragraph topics. OL

Editing and Proofreading

Get It Right When you have completed the final draft of your research paper, proofread for errors in grammar, usage, mechanics, and spelling. Refer to the Language Handbook, pages R45–R59, as a guide.

Focus Lesson

Using Quotation Marks Correctly

When you quote the exact words from a source, use double quotation marks. Open-quotation marks come before the first word you quote, and close-quotation marks follow the last word. Begin the quotation with a capital letter unless you begin in the middle of a sentence or quote only a word or two. A comma or period belongs inside the quotation marks. An exception is a long quotation, which is indented and needs no quotation marks. When you paraphrase from a source, do not use quotation marks, but do cite your source.

Original: Quoted information is not in quotation marks.

Helyn A. Potter wrote, war changes everything. I was a welder and now a riveter in an all-woman workforce. Five years earlier, I was studying ballet, planning to become a ballerina. As we supported the War Effort, the collective soul of women changed.

Improvement: Add a capital letter and quotation marks.

Helyn A. Potter wrote, "War changes everything. I was a welder and now a riveter in an all-woman workforce. Five years earlier, I was studying ballet, planning to become a ballerina. As we supported the War Effort, the collective soul of women changed."

Original: Quotation marks are used with words that are paraphrased.

"By 1960 fewer women were employed as professionals than in 1930" ("Feminism").

Improved: Omit the quotation marks.

By 1960 fewer women were employed as professionals than in 1930 ("Feminism").

Using Ellipses

Use ellipsis points (. . .) to show that a word or words are omitted from an original quotation.

Works Cited

In the body of your paper, use parentheses to credit your sources briefly by giving the last name of the author or first word in the title and the page reference. Internet sources often do not have page references. Include a separate page, titled Works Cited, at the end of your paper to give a full description of each source.

Works Cited Style

List your sources alphabetically by the last name of the author. If an article has no author, list it by title. Put the first line of a citation flush left and indent any lines that follow. Remember that book titles can be shown in *italic type* or by underscoring. The important thing is to be consistent.

Presenting

Finishing your Research Paper You want your research paper to be perfect, but you will need to finish it before the due date. Before you turn the paper in, make sure it is neat. Review the assignment guidelines to see if you have forgotten anything. Check your use of quotation marks, identification of sources, and Works Cited page for accuracy and format.

Writer's Portfolio

Place a clean copy of your research paper in your portfolio to review later.

Teach

Writing Process

Editing and Proofreading

After students proofread their own papers, have them exchange papers with a partner, each of them proofreading the other's. Instruct them to pay special attention to quotations and citations. Have them keep these questions in mind as they work:

- Is the punctuation correct?
- Are all the sources cited?

Remind students to be respectful while proofreading their partners' manuscripts. **OL**

Writing Skill

Using Quotation Marks

Students are often confused by the mechanics of quotations. As practice, write on the board some sample quotations, such as the ones in the focus lesson, leaving out the quotation marks and punctuation. Ask students to come up to the board and correct the mistakes. Review the placement of quotation marks, commas, and periods, as well as the rules for capitalization. **OL**

Differentiated Instruction

Editing and Proofreading Less proficient students may need extra time editing and proofreading their papers. Pair them with proficient students and have the pairs work together throughout the editing and proofreading process. Have the proficient students check papers for spelling, grammar, and usage problems. Encourage students to reread the workshop model as needed for clues about how to construct an effective research paper. **BL**

Academic Standards

Additional Support activities on pp. 1100 and 1101 cover the following standards:

Skills Practice: **9.4.10** Review [and] evaluate writing…for meaning, clarity, [and] content…

Differentiated Instruction: **9.4.11** Edit and proofread one's own writing, as well as that of others…

Focus

Summary

In this workshop, students will learn techniques for planning, rehearsing, delivering, and listening to an expository presentation.

Teach

Speaking Skills

Preparation Emphasize to students that careful preparation is the key to giving an effective presentation. **Say:** The more you prepare, the more confident you will feel when giving your presentation. Give students these tips on preparation:

- Organize your notes.
- Rehearse your presentation aloud.
- Get feedback from a parent or another student.
- Know your material well.

Remind students that eye contact is very important in public speaking. **OL**

Speaking, Listening, and Viewing Workshop

Expository Presentation

Delivering an Expository Presentation

Connecting to Literature Did Homer create the *Odyssey* by himself? The ancient Greeks believed he did. Later, some scholars challenged this theory and suggested that more than one person played a role. Today, most researchers again believe the *Odyssey* is the work of one poet. Scholars often give lectures to express their strong viewpoints on subjects such as the *Odyssey*. They explain their theories and back them up with documented examples. In this workshop, you will learn how to deliver an expository presentation with evidence in support of a thesis.

Assignment **Plan and deliver an expository presentation on the subject of your research paper.**

Planning Your Presentation

In your research paper, you presented a thesis, developed main ideas related to the thesis, and supported them with documentation. For your expository presentation, you will follow a similar process. Below are some tips to help you plan.

- Introduce your subject with an attention-grabbing sentence. Then state your thesis.
- In the body of your presentation, include the main ideas that relate to your thesis. Provide source information to back up these ideas. Develop the most important main ideas from your research paper.
- Presentations that use visuals are effective. You might use a poster, a bar graph, or a line graph.
- Finish with your conclusion. Explain how you arrived at your opinion.

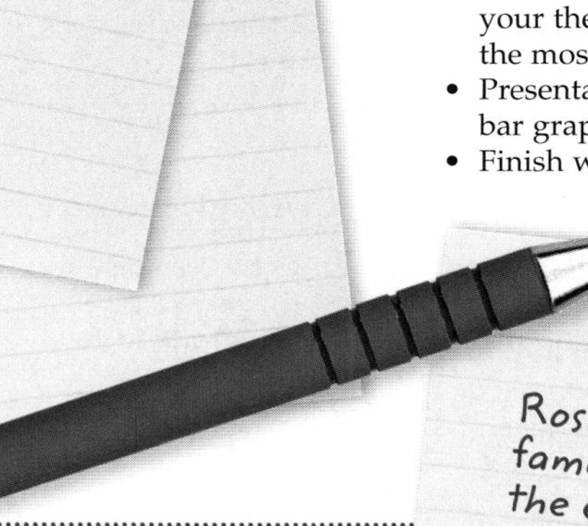

Rosie the Riveter was one of the most famous women in the United States in the early 1940s.

Additional Support

Skills Practice

VIEWING: Studying a Presentation Before students begin preparing their own presentations, show them a brief instructional or documentary film. Have them pay careful attention to how the film uses not only words but also images, music, and visual displays to get its points across. **Ask:** What is the main goal of this film? What kinds of arguments does it make? How does it support those arguments? It may be helpful to watch the film a second time after this discussion. **OL**

Developing Your Presentation

Choose an Introduction Ask yourself how you can grab your audience's attention. Try asking a question or making a dramatic statement.

Choose Several Main Ideas Review your research paper. List your main ideas. Then star the ones that you think best summarize your thesis.

Support Each Main Idea Your paper and the outline you prepared before writing should provide specific details. You will want to credit your sources as part of the presentation. Do this by giving the author's name and the title of the work as you explain how the information supports a main idea.

Create a Visual How could you illustrate the thesis that Rosie the Riveter was a symbol for all of the women who became everyday heroes when they accepted the challenge and showed strength and courage in doing jobs that they had never before done? Here are a few examples:

- Draw a line graph to show how the number of women in the work force increased from 1942 until 1945 and then declined after 1945.
- Draw a bar graph to compare the number of women working in 1930, 1945, and 1960.
- Use one of the titles of the posters done by the Office of War Information and create your own drawing to illustrate it.

Decide How to End Review the conclusion of your research paper for ideas on how to end your presentation. What ideas does your paper suggest for your presentation? Remember, you want to draw your own conclusion based on the evidence you have presented.

Delivering Your Presentation

Techniques for Delivering a Presentation

Verbal Techniques	Nonverbal Techniques
☑ **Volume** Speak loudly enough so everyone can hear you.	☑ **Eye Contact** Make eye contact with your audience.
☑ **Pace** Speak at a moderate speed but vary the rate and use pauses.	☑ **Facial Expressions** Vary your facial expressions to reflect what you are saying.
☑ **Tone** Speak with confidence.	☑ **Posture** Stand up tall with your head straight.
☑ **Emphasis** Stress important words and ideas.	☑ **Visual Aids** Use charts or other visual aids to enhance your presentation.

Speaking Effectively

If you express your ideas confidently and with authority, they are likely to be taken seriously by your audience. The best way to build confidence is to know your subject well. During your presentation, stand tall and look at your audience, including those in the back of the room.

Using Software

Publishing software can help you prepare an expository presentation. Some programs allow users to paste sections of a written research paper into the software. In addition, graphs and illustrations can be scanned onto paper that can be shown on overhead visuals when the presentation is delivered.

ACADEMIC STANDARDS (pages 1102–1103)

9.7.15 Deliver expository (informational) presentations that...include visual aids...

9.7.2 Choose appropriate techniques for developing the introduction and conclusion in a speech...

Teach

Speaking Skills

Addressing an Audience

Before students deliver their presentations, give them the following tips on keeping an audience's attention:

- Begin with an attention-grabbing sentence.
- Use clear and effective visuals to illustrate your ideas.
- Speak clearly and with confidence.
- Make eye contact.
- Emphasize key points with your tone of voice and by pausing afterwards. **OL**

Listening Skills

Evaluating Remind students that when they are not making their own presentations, they should listen actively to their fellow students. Have them make a chart for each presentation in which they answer the following questions:

- What are the speaker's key points?
- What evidence does the speaker give to support these points?
- How does the speaker use visuals to illustrate his or her ideas? **OL**

Differentiated Instruction

Using Visuals Not all students will have equal proficiency using software and computers, so some may need extra time to develop their presentations. Work with the school librarian, an AV specialist, or a student who is computer proficient to arrange a demonstration of presentation software such as PowerPoint. In addition, take time to point out the uses of charts, graphs, and other visual aids. Have small groups work together to determine what kinds of information can be adapted as a visual aid. **BL**

Academic Standards

Additional Support activities on pp. 1102 and 1103 cover the following standards:

Skills Practice: **9.7.13** Identify the artistic effects of a media presentation and evaluate the techniques used to create them.

Differentiated Instruction: **9.7.8** Compare and contrast the ways in which media genres...cover the same event.

Focus

Summary

In this section, students will be introduced to epics and myths from cultures around the world, as well as two novels related to the Big Ideas of journeys and courage and cleverness. Encourage students to read these works, which are related to the themes they learned about in this unit.

Teach

★ Literary History

Edith Hamilton The author of many popular books on ancient Greece and Rome, Edith Hamilton (1867–1963) grew up in Fort Wayne, Indiana. After graduating from Bryn Mawr College, she and her sister Alice went on to further studies at universities in Leipzig and Munich, Germany. Hamilton then spent 26 years as the headmistress of a school for girls, before retiring in 1922 to devote herself to classical studies. In honor of her achievements, the city of Athens, Greece, made her an honorary citizen in 1957. AS

INDEPENDENT READING

Epics, Myths, and Novels

EPICS AND MYTHS ARE TRADITIONAL TALES. WHILE MYTHS OFTEN feature creatures whose traits are linked to supernatural powers, epics usually feature human or superhuman heroes. Both epics and myths take place long ago and far away and are told in a dignified, grave, or awe-filled tone. For more epics and myths covering a range of themes, try the first three suggestions below. For novels that treat the Big Ideas of *Journeys* and *Courage and Cleverness,* try the titles from the Glencoe Literature Library on the next page.

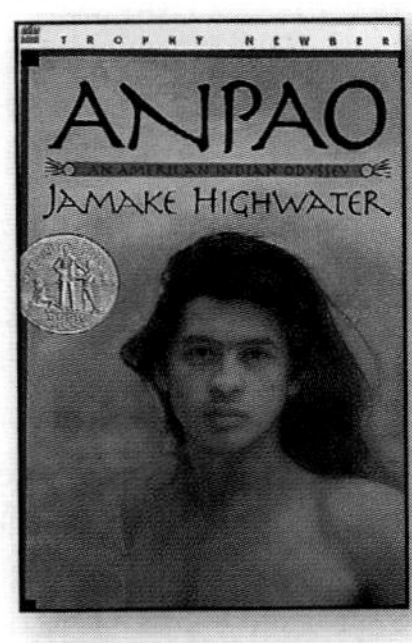

Anpao: An American Indian Odyssey

by Jamake Highwater

This book incorporates the folklore of Plains and Southwest Indians to tell the story of Anpao, a poor but brave young man who falls in love with the daughter of a chief. She agrees to marry him, but only after he gets the permission of the Sun. Anpao undertakes a dramatic journey across mountains, deserts, and prairies to reach back in time to the dawn of the world. He must relive his own creation and do battle with mythological forces before he can achieve his goal.

Mythology

by Edith Hamilton 

Zeus and Odysseus, Cupid and Psyche, Hercules and the Titans—these and other Greek gods and heroes have inspired, frightened, enlightened, and entertained generations of readers around the world. This collection includes the stories that are an important part of Western culture. For example, in one story, Midas turns everything to gold. In another, Arachne is turned into a spider for being too proud.

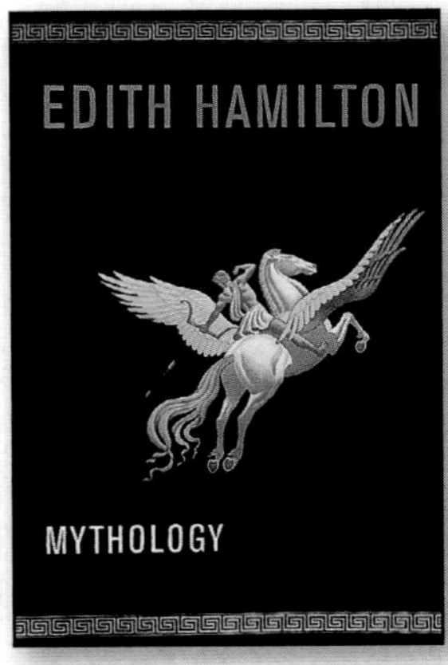

Additional Support

Skills Practice

SPEAKING: Presenting a Book Review Students interested in the recommended literature can be encouraged to present book reviews. Such a presentation would include

- a brief summary or overview of the book
- a description of notable highlights
- opinions on the writer's style and technique
- a recommendation to read the book (or not), supported by sound reasons

OL

CRITICS' CORNER

"Seasons of Splendour *simply and playfully reveals to the Western reader the heart and soul of traditional Indian society, where order and continuity are still preferred to the pursuit of [illusory] progress. . . . In all these stories the surfaces ripple, shimmer, change, but the center holds.*"

—Barbara Thompson, *The New York Times Book Review*

Hindu god Ganesh

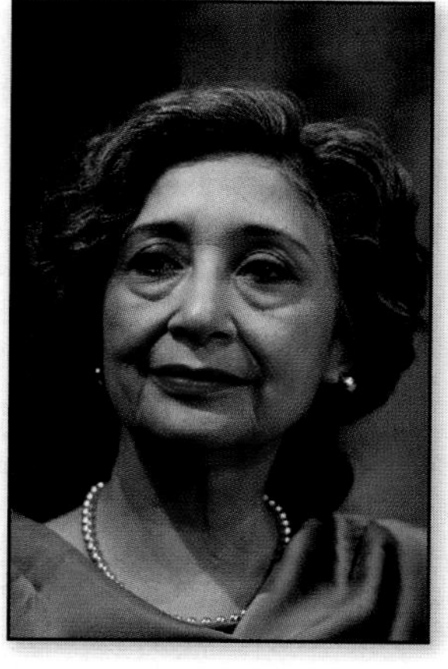

Seasons of Splendour: Tales, Myths, and Legends of India

by Madhur Jaffrey ★

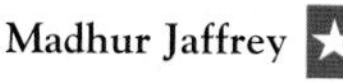

This collection of myths and folklore from India is arranged in chronological sequence, starting with tales that might be told at the beginning of the Hindu calendar year in April. The author introduces each tale with a recollection from her childhood. Many of the stories come from Hindu epics. There are stories from the life of Krishna and episodes in Ram's defeat over the demon king Ravan. There are also origin tales, such as how Ganesh got his elephant's head.

From the Glencoe Literature Library

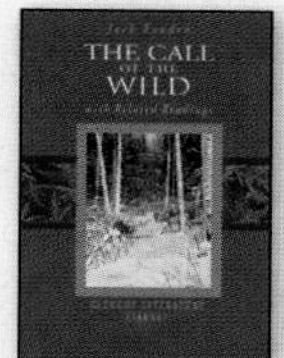

The Call of the Wild

by Jack London

Told from the perspective of a dog, this journey of change and discovery has universal meaning.

The Adventures of Tom Sawyer

by Mark Twain

The clever pranks and narrow escapes of a boy growing up along the Mississippi River in the 1840s have entertained generations of readers.

★ Cultural History

Madhur Jaffrey Born in Delhi, India, Madhur Jaffrey later emigrated to England, where she embarked on a multifaceted career. As a screen actress, she has made notable appearances in such films as *Shakespeare Wallah* (1965) and *Heat and Dust* (1983). In 1973, her book *An Invitation to Indian Cooking* made her famous around the world as an authority on Indian cooking, leading to a well-received TV series on the BBC. Subsequent books have included everything from children's books to a memoir, *Climbing the Mango Trees* (2006). **AS**

Glencoe Literature Library

Glencoe Literature Library offers an extensive collection of hardcover books that help you encourage your students to read independently. Choose among the more than 120 full-length literary works—novels, novellas, plays, and nonfiction. Each book includes related readings from a broad range of genres. Go to glencoe.com for more information.

Reading in the Real World

Citizenship Reading literature from other cultures develops our understanding of those cultures. Ask students what they think are some of the benefits of reading the epics and myths of another culture. **Ask:** Do you think literature can help build a bridge between different cultures? **OL**

Academic Standards

Additional Support activities on pp. 1104 and 1105 cover the following standards:

Skills Practice: **9.7.17** Deliver oral responses to literature that support important ideas and viewpoints through accurate… references to the text…

Reading in the Real World: **9.2** Develop [reading] strategies…

Focus

BELLRINGER

Say: A multiple-choice test like this one is different from essay tests and short answer tests. In a multiple-choice test, each answer is provided for you along with several incorrect answer choices. To identify the correct answer, you sometimes need to identify the incorrect answers first. Have students discuss which type of test they prefer and why.

Test Preparation and Practice

English Language Arts

Indiana Test Practice

READING: Vocabulary, Comprehension, and Analysis

Read the following passages. Then, on a separate sheet of paper, answer the questions on page 1108.

from "The Trojan War" by Thomas Bulfinch

Minerva was the goddess of wisdom, but on one occasion she did a very foolish thing; she entered into competition with Juno[1] and Venus[2] for the prize of beauty. It happened thus: At the nuptials[3] of Peleus and Thetis all the gods were invited with the exception of Eris, or Discord. Enraged at her exclusion, the goddess threw a golden apple among the guests, with the inscription, "For the fairest." Thereupon Juno, Venus, and Minerva each claimed the apple. Jupiter,[4] not willing to decide in so delicate a matter, sent the goddesses to Mount Ida, where the beautiful shepherd Paris was tending his flocks, and to him was committed the decision. The goddesses accordingly appeared before him. Juno promised him power and riches, Minerva glory and renown in war, and Venus the fairest of women for his wife, each attempting to bias his decision in her own favor. Paris decided in favor of Venus and gave her the golden apple, thus making the two other goddesses his enemies. Under the protection of Venus, Paris sailed to Greece, and was hospitably received by Menelaus, king of Sparta.

Now Helen, the wife of Menelaus, was the very woman whom Venus had destined for Paris, the fairest of her sex. She had been sought as a bride by numerous suitors, and before her decision was made known, they all, at the suggestion of Ulysses, one of their number, took an oath that they would defend her from all injury and avenge her cause if necessary. She chose Menelaus, and was living with him happily when Paris became their guest. Paris, aided by Venus, persuaded her to elope[5] with him, and carried her to Troy, whence arose the famous Trojan War, the theme of the greatest poems of antiquity, those of Homer[6] and Virgil.[7]

Menelaus called upon his brother chieftains of Greece to fulfill their pledge, and join him in his efforts to recover his wife. Priam was king of Troy, and Paris, the shepherd and seducer of Helen, was his son. Paris had been brought up in obscurity,[8] because there were certain ominous forebodings[9] connected with him from his infancy that he would be the ruin of the state. These forebodings seemed at length likely to be realized, for the Grecian armament[10] now in preparation was the greatest that had ever been fitted out. Agamemnon, king of Mycenae, and brother of the injured Menelaus, was chosen commander-in-chief. Achilles was their most

[1] **Juno:** queen of the gods
[2] **Venus:** goddess of beauty
[3] **nuptials:** wedding
[4] **Jupiter:** king of the gods

[5] **elope:** run away to get married
[6] **Homer:** Greek poet (lived sometime before the year 700 B.C.), author of the epic poems the *Iliad* and the *Odyssey*
[7] **Virgil:** Roman poet (70–19 B.C.), author of the epic poem the *Aeneid*
[8] **brought up in obscurity:** As an infant, Paris was sent to live with a herdsman to conceal his whereabouts.
[9] **forebodings:** feelings that something evil is going to happen
[10] **armament:** military forces, equipment, and supplies

Reading

Establishing a Purpose for Reading For this Test Preparation and Practice, students will be reading two different types of text. When students are reading from varied types of materials, it is important that they establish a purpose for reading to get the greatest benefit from the material. Have students preview the selections. **Ask: What do you think is your purpose for reading each selection?** *(Students may say that the purpose for reading the first selection is to enjoy or interpret; the second selection, to find information or discover.)* **OL**

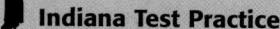

illustrious warrior. After him ranked Ajax, gigantic in size and of great courage, but dull of intellect; Diomede, second only to Achilles in all the qualities of a hero; Ulysses, famous for his sagacity[11]; and Nestor, the oldest of the Grecian chiefs, and one to whom they all looked up for counsel.[12]

[11]**sagacity:** wisdom
[12]**counsel:** advice

After two years of preparation the Greek fleet and army assembled in the port of Aulis in Boeotia. The wind now proving fair the fleet made sail and brought the forces to the coast of Troy.

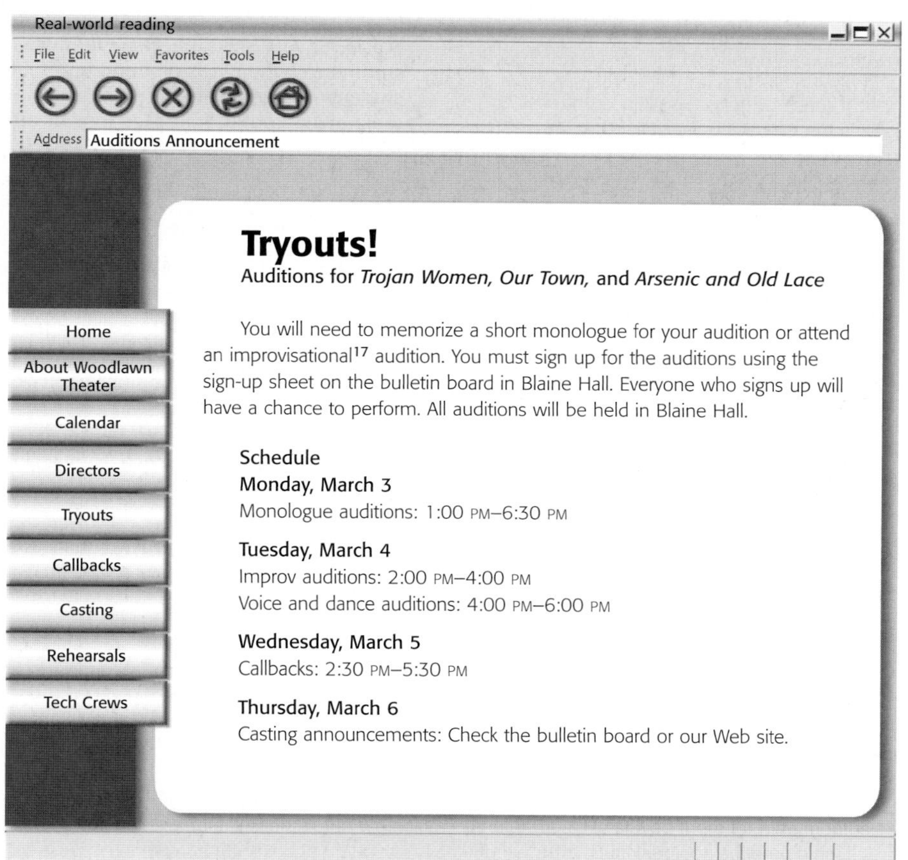

Tryouts!

Auditions for *Trojan Women, Our Town,* and *Arsenic and Old Lace*

You will need to memorize a short monologue for your audition or attend an improvisational[17] audition. You must sign up for the auditions using the sign-up sheet on the bulletin board in Blaine Hall. Everyone who signs up will have a chance to perform. All auditions will be held in Blaine Hall.

Schedule

Monday, March 3
Monologue auditions: 1:00 PM–6:30 PM

Tuesday, March 4
Improv auditions: 2:00 PM–4:00 PM
Voice and dance auditions: 4:00 PM–6:00 PM

Wednesday, March 5
Callbacks: 2:30 PM–5:30 PM

Thursday, March 6
Casting announcements: Check the bulletin board or our Web site.

[17]**improvisational:** produced without preparation

Test Preparation and Practice

English Language Arts

Teach

Assessment Explain to students that this Test Preparation and Practice lesson is designed to develop test-taking strategies as well as to test their mastery of the skills covered in this unit. The lesson is modeled on tests they will be required to pass to be eligible to receive a high school diploma. Students will read one or two grade-level-appropriate selections and answer vocabulary, comprehension, and literary analysis questions, including multiple-choice, constructed-response, and extended-response items. In other sections, students' ability to use Standard English in their writing is assessed, and they are given an extended-writing prompt. **OL**

Assess

1. **C** is the correct answer. The competition among the goddesses leads Paris to Helen, which eventually sets off the Trojan War.
2. **D** is the correct answer.
3. **B** is the correct answer. The order of events is C, A, D, B.
4. **A** is the correct answer. A myth is a traditional story that deals with gods, goddesses, heroes, and supernatural forces.
5. **C** is the correct answer. Those auditioning will learn the results when the casting is posted.
6. Rubric:
   2 points versions of two exemplars
   1 point version of one exemplar
   0 points other
   Exemplars:
   - Memorize a short monologue or attend an improvisational audition.
   - Sign up for an audition on the sign-up sheet on the bulletin board in Blaine Hall.
7. Refer to the Reading Comprehension, Writing Applications, and Language Conventions rubrics provided by the State of Indiana Department of Education.

Numbers 1 through 4 are based on "The Trojan War."

1 What is the MAIN purpose of the first paragraph?

A to describe the setting of the passage
B to introduce the history of gods and goddesses
C to tell the story that brought together Paris and Helen
D to explain why Minerva, Juno, and Venus were enemies

2 Read this sentence from the passage.

> **The wind now proving fair the fleet made sail and brought the forces to the coast of Troy.**

Which of these dictionary definitions of *proving* BEST fits the way the word is used in the sentence?

A showing convincingly
B testing the truth of
C challenging the courage of
D demonstrating a particular quality

3 Which happens LAST in the lives of the characters?

A Eris throws a golden apple among the wedding guests.
B Paris chooses Venus as the fairest.
C Eris is not invited to the wedding.
D Juno, Venus, and Minerva each claim the apple.

4 Which of these elements identifies this selection as a myth?

A The characters include gods and goddesses.
B The action takes place in ancient Greece.
C Helen's suitors take an oath to protect her.
D The Greeks take two years to prepare for war.

Numbers 5 and 6 are based on "Tryouts!"

5 According to the auditions announcement, when will those who audition learn whether they were chosen for a role?

A Tuesday
B Wednesday
C Thursday
D Friday

6 What TWO things must students do to audition for the plays?

7 Suppose that you are putting on a play based on the excerpt from "The Trojan War." **Write an article for your school newspaper that summarizes the play's plot and urges students to participate. Be sure to include main ideas from the passage in your article.**

Use a separate sheet of paper to plan your writing.

Writing Checklist

The following checklist will help you write your essay. Make sure to

- ❑ brainstorm for ideas and develop a plan before you start writing
- ❑ organize your writing with an introduction, a body, and a conclusion
- ❑ pay attention to your word choice and voice edit for sentence fluency and conventions
- ❑ have a neat and organized presentation

Student essays should include the following:

- clearly stated main ideas supported by quotations, examples, and details from the passage
- effective voice, word choice, and sentence variety
- effective presentation, with attention to grammar and spelling conventions

WRITING: Writing Process

The following passage is from the first draft of a student's essay. Read the passage and use it to answer questions 8–11 on a separate sheet of paper.

> [1]The *Iliad* and the *Odyssey*, two of the greatest epic poems ever written. [2]They are extremely long works involving many characters and tales. [3]Homer is credited with writing both of these poems by most scholars. [4]However, there was a period when many of them questioned this. [5]In the nineteenth century, people discussed both sides of this "Homeric question": was he really the author of both of these works, and did he write them alone?

8 Choose the BEST way to combine Sentences 1 and 2.

A The *Iliad* and the *Odyssey* are two of the greatest epic poems ever written because they are extremely long works involving many characters and tales.

B The *Iliad* and the *Odyssey*, two of the greatest epic poems ever written, are extremely long works involving many characters and tales.

C Two of the greatest epic poems ever written are extremely long works involving many characters and tales, the *Iliad* and the *Odyssey*.

D The *Iliad* and the *Odyssey* are two of the greatest epic poems ever written, and they are extremely long works involving many characters and tales.

9 Choose the BEST way to revise Sentence 3.

A Most scholars credit Homer with the writing of both of these poems.

B Both of these poems were written by Homer, most scholars credit.

C Homer is credited by most scholars with writing both of these poems.

D The writing of both of these poems is credited to Homer by most scholars.

Literature Online **Unit Assessment** To prepare for the Unit test, go to www.glencoe.com.

10 The writer wants to replace the underlined phrase in Sentence 5 with a more formal expression. Which of these is the BEST replacement?

A lectured on
B pondered
C chatted about
D debated

11 The Modern Language Association (MLA) recommends these guidelines for citing works used for reference.

1. Alphabetize unsigned articles according to the first major word of the title.
2. Underline the title of a book.
3. Use quotation marks to indicate the title of an essay, chapter, or article.
4. Include publishing information last.

The student who wrote the paragraph about Homer found the information in an unsigned essay in a book. According to the MLA recommendations above, which is the correct way for the student to cite this source?

A "Who Wrote the Classics?" A Guide to Classical Literature. Chicago: Sanderson, 2004.

B A Guide to Classical Literature. Chicago: Sanderson, 2004. "Who Wrote the Classics?"

C Chicago: Sanderson, 2004. "Who Wrote the Classics?" from A Guide to Classical Literature.

D Who Wrote the Classics? from "A Guide to Classical Literature," Chicago: Sanderson, 2004.

Test Preparation and Practice

English Language Arts

Assess

8. B is the correct answer. The other options are too wordy.

9. C is the correct answer. The other options contain awkward phrasing.

10. D is the correct answer. To debate is to discuss or argue a matter by giving opposing viewpoints.

11. A is the correct answer. It is the only option that meets all four requirements.

Unit Assessment Have students access the Web site to prepare for the Unit Five test.

Assess

12. **B** is the correct answer.
13. **A** is the correct answer. The nonessential clause "not written by Homer" should be set off with commas.
14. **C** is the correct answer. Option A contains a misplaced modifier.
15. **D** is the correct answer. All verbs should be in the past tense.
16. **B** is the correct answer. Use a comma to set off conjunctive adverbs (such as *however, moreover,* and *consequently*).
17. **A** is the correct answer. Two main clauses need punctuation between them, such as a semicolon or period.
18. **C** is the correct answer. Capitalize the first word of a book title.

WRITING: English Language Conventions

Answer numbers 12–18 on a separate sheet of paper.

12 Choose the word that is spelled correctly.

Under the ____ of darkness, the Greek fleet arrived at the coast of Troy.

A guys
B guise
C gise
D gaze

13 Choose the sentence that is punctuated correctly.

A These works, not written by Homer, tell many of the same tales.
B These works not written by Homer, tell many of the same tales.
C These works, not written by Homer tell many of the same tales.
D These, works not written by Homer, tell many of the same tales.

14 Choose the sentence that is correct and MOST clearly expressed.

A Analyzing the *Iliad* carefully, the great poem was written by one author, the professor finally determined.
B The *Iliad,* analyzed carefully by the professor, finally determined that the great poem was written by one author.
C Analyzing the *Iliad* carefully, the professor finally determined that the great poem was written by one author.
D Analyzed carefully, the great poem was finally determined by the professor to be written by one author.

15 Read this sentence.

Priam had been a wise prince and had strengthened the state, but by the time he reached old age, he <u>is willing to rely</u> on Hector for advice.

Choose the word or group of words that BEST replaces the underlined part of the sentence.

A had been willing to rely
B will be willing to rely
C willingly relies
D was willing to rely

16 Decide which punctuation mark is needed in the sentence.

Moreover considerable historical evidence suggests that a poet named Homer did actually live before 700 B.C.

A .
B ,
C ;
D :

17 What type of an error has the writer of this sentence made?

Homer deserves his legendary reputation after all, he produced two of the greatest works of literature in the history of civilization.

A run-on sentence
B incorrect verb tense
C pronoun-antecedent agreement
D sentence fragment

18 What additional word in the sentence should be capitalized?

Kerry wrote a book report on *the Nymphs: Nature's Maidens of Mythology* by Sara Blevins.

A book
B report
C the
D by

Writing

Varying Sentence Length Remind students about the use of main and subordinate clauses.
Say: The use of main and subordinate clauses to vary the length of sentences is an important part of a well-written essay. Have students write a brief firsthand account of a birthday or another celebration. Encourage students to use a variety of sentence lengths and structures to engage the reader. Students should read their drafts aloud and help classmates check their essays for a variety of sentence styles. **OL**

WRITING: Writing Applications

Complete the writing activity below. Do your planning and writing on separate sheets of paper.

Music: Free or Fee?

Read the writing prompt below and complete the writing activity.

> Recording artists have lost hundreds of thousands of dollars in royalties on copyrighted songs that have been downloaded from the Internet. The music industry wants users who download music to pay a fee. Music lovers say they should be able to copy the music for free if it's available on the Internet.
>
> Decide how you feel about paying to download music from the Internet. Write a letter to the editor of the local newspaper in which you either defend the music industry's movement to charge a fee for downloading music or oppose such a fee. Clearly state your position. Be sure to provide well-developed supporting arguments to convince readers of the paper to agree with you.

Be sure to include

- your position on the issue
- an explanation of why you feel as you do
- specific details to support your ideas
- an introduction, a body, and a conclusion to your essay

Use a separate sheet of paper to plan your writing. As you write, keep in mind that your essay will be evaluated for **ideas and content, organization, style, voice,** and **language conventions.**

Writing Checklist

Before you begin writing, make sure to

- ❑ brainstorm for ideas
- ❑ organize your ideas into a logical pattern
- ❑ develop a plan for an introduction, a body, and a conclusion

As you write your essay, be sure to

- ❑ describe the issue and clearly state your opinion about it
- ❑ provide reasons for your opinion
- ❑ discuss alternative opinions and show why you disagree with them
- ❑ end with a conclusion that restates your opinion

Assess

Assessment of writing prompts should focus on four elements:

- **Ideas and Content,** the message or theme and the details that develop it
- **Organization,** the arrangement of main ideas and supporting details
- **Style,** the word choices that a writer uses to convey meaning and the fluency, or rhythm and flow, of sentences
- **Voice,** the writer's unique way of using tone and style

Students' writing should also be assessed for correct **capitalization, punctuation, spelling, grammar and usage, paragraphing,** and **sentence structure.**

In addition, student essays should:

- fully complete the assigned task
- include complete, thorough, relevant, and logically organized ideas
- exhibit correct word usage
- demonstrate exceptional writing technique
- use language and tone appropriate for the task and audience

Unit at a Glance

Genre Fiction

About the Unit

Unit Six includes fiction that falls within the category of Genre Fiction. This broad selection of literature includes genres such as romance, mystery, and science fiction. These genres are easily recognizable by their stylistic conventions. For example, science fiction is either futuristic or other-worldly in its setting. Elements of literature learned thus far, such as description, imagery, suspense, and tone can all be seen in Genre Fiction.

Unit Introduction
Building Background
2–3 days

Featured Unit Art/Looking Ahead
pp. 1112–1113

Genre Focus: Genre Fiction
pp. 1114–1115

Literary Analysis Model: Isaac Asimov, from *Buy Jupiter*
pp. 1116–1117

Writers on Reading
pp. 1118–1119

Unit Introduction Wrap-Up
p. 1120

Part 1: Our World and Beyond
7–9 days

Part 1 covers the fantasy and science fiction genres. In these genres, writers are able to accomplish the unconventional, as time and space are in flux. A chart showing the core skills taught in this Part appears on pages 1121A–1121B.

SELECTIONS AND FEATURES

LITERARY FOCUS: Description pp. 1122–1123

Arthur C. Clarke, "The Sentinel" pp. 1124–1137

HISTORICAL PERSPECTIVE on **"The Sentinel":**
Roger Ebert, review of "2001: A Space Odyssey"
pp. 1138–1140

Grammar Workshop, Commas p. 1141

Shinichi Hoshi, "He–y, Come on Ou–t" pp. 1142–1149

Ursula K. Le Guin, "The Rule of Names" pp. 1150–1163

Comparing Literature Across Genres
Nancy Kress, "In Memoriam"
Naomi Long Madgett, "Purchase"
Alan Lightman, "World Without Memory"
pp. 1164–1177

Ray Bradbury, "The Golden Kite, the Silver Wind"
pp. 1178–1185

Vocabulary Workshop: Denotation and Connotation p. 1186

Part 2: Revealing the Concealed
4–6 days

Part 2 deals with the genre of mystery writing. Writers in this genre must be aware of pacing and revealing enough information to entertain the reader with puzzles. A chart showing the core skills taught in this Part appears on pages 1187A–1187B.

SELECTIONS AND FEATURES

LITERARY FOCUS: Style and Tone pp. 1188–1189

Agatha Christie, "The Mystery of Hunter's Lodge" pp. 1190–1202

Ellery Queen, "The Adventure of the President's Half Disme" pp. 1203–1223

TIME magazine, "Lost Apes of the Congo" pp. 1224–1226

Sir Arthur Conan Doyle, "The Red-Headed League" pp. 1227–1247

Bret Harte, "The Stolen Cigar Case" pp. 1248–1257

End-of-Unit Features
5–6 days

Writing Workshop: Editorial pp. 1258–1265

Speaking, Listening, and Viewing Workshop: Persuasive Presentation pp. 1266–1267

INDEPENDENT READING pp. 1268–1269

Test Preparation and Practice pp. 1270–1275

Unit Resources

Glencoe Literature: The Reader's Choice offers a comprehensive package of tools to optimize student learning and the teaching experience. Each resource has been designed to assist students in specific areas and to offer instructional support for teachers. While all of these areas are covered in the core textbook, some students may need extra practice or additional help in specific areas. The resource package is designed so that you, the teacher, can choose which items will best assist your students. You may also use these resources as homework assignments and for assessment purposes. The following are resources recommended for use with Unit 6.

Key for Unit Resource

- Blackline Master
- Workbook
- Supplemental Text
- CD-ROM
- DVD
- Transparency
- Web-based

Essential Instructional Support

FAST FILE UNIT 6 RESOURCES

Reading and Literature

- Unit Introduction, pp. 1–2
- The Big Idea Foldable, pp. 3–4
- The Big Idea School-Home Connection, p. 5
- The Big Idea School-Home Connection (Spanish), p. 6
- Challenge Planner, pp. 7–10
- Academic Vocabulary Development, pp. 11–12
- Comparing Literature Graphic Organizer, p. 27
- Literary Element, pp. 16, 21, 24, 28, 31, 37, 40, 44, 47
- Reading Strategy, pp. 17, 19, 22, 25, 29, 32, 38, 41, 43, 45, 48
- Active Reading Graphic Organizers, pp. 54–63
- Selection Vocabulary Practice, pp. 18, 23, 26, 30, 33, 39, 42, 46, 49
- Literary Focus, pp. 14, 35

Writing, Grammar, and Spelling

- Spelling Practice, p. 50
- Grammar Workshop, p. 20
- Writing Workshop Graphic Organizer, p. 51

Speaking, Listening, and Viewing

- Speaking, Listening, and Viewing Activities, pp. 52–53

English Language Learners

- English Language Coach Review, pp. 15, 36

DIFFERENTIATED INSTRUCTION

- Active Learning and Note Taking Guide, pp. 179–207
- Leveled Vocabulary Development, pp. 70–79
- Skill Level Up!™ A Language Arts Game
- Listening Library Audio CD, disc 2, tracks 33–47
- Glencoe BookLink 3
- Vocabulary PuzzleMaker
- Literature Library Vocabulary PuzzleMaker

ASSESSMENT

- Selection and Unit Assessments, pp. 189–210, 221–222
- Selection Quick Checks, pp. 95–105
- Selection Quick Checks (Spanish), pp. 95–105
- Assessment by Learning Objectives, pp. 57–66
- Rubrics for Assessing Student Writing, Listening, and Speaking, pp. 18–19, 40–41
- Standardized Test Preparation and Practice
- Glencoe Online Essay Grader
- Interactive Tutor: Self-Assessment
- Exam*View*® Assessment Suite
- Literature Library Exam*View*® Assessment

Additional Instructional Support

LITERATURE AND READING

- Active Learning and Note Taking Guide, pp. 179–207
- *inTIME* Magazines
- Glencoe Literature Library
- Literature Launchers: Pre-Reading Videos
- Literature Classics

WRITING, GRAMMAR, AND SPELLING

- REAL Success in Writing: Research and Reports
- Writing Constructed Responses
- Spelling Power eWorkbook
- Revising with Style eWorkbook
- Sentence Diagraming eWorkbook
- Glencoe Grammar and Composition Handbook
- Grammar and Language Workbook
- Grammar & Language eWorkbook

PROFESSIONAL DEVELOPMENT

- Professional Development Package

TRANSPARENCIES

- Read Aloud, Think Aloud Transparencies 50–76
- Bellringer Options Transparencies
  - Selection Focus Transparencies 49–50
  - Daily Language Practice Transparencies 93–104
- Grammar and Language Transparencies 25
- Writing Workshop Transparencies 31–35
- Visual Literacy/Fine Art Transparencies

ENGLISH LANGUAGE LEARNER

- English Language Coach, Unit Resources (Fast File)
- Fluency Practice and Assessment
- *inTIME* Magazines (Spanish)
- Spanish Listening Library

TECHNOLOGY

- TeacherWorks Plus™
- StudentWorks Plus™
- Literature Launchers: Pre-Reading Videos
- Vocabulary PuzzleMaker
- Literature Library Vocabulary PuzzleMaker
- Skill Level Up!™ A Language Arts Game
- glencoe.com
- Presentation Plus!™
- Exam*View*® Assessment Suite
- Literature Library Exam*View*® Assessment Suite
- Listening Library
- Interactive Tutor: Self-Assessment
- Glencoe BookLink 3
- Online Student Edition, mhln.com
- Glencoe Online Essay Grader
- Grammar and Language eWorkbook
- Revising with Style eWorkbook
- Sentence Diagraming eWorkbook
- Spelling Power eWorkbook
- Literature Classics
- Spanish Listening Library

Additional Glencoe Resources

Dinah Zike's Foldables™

Foldables™ are three-dimensional, interactive graphic organizers that help students practice basic writing skills, review key vocabulary terms, and answer Big Ideas. Every unit contains a Foldable™ activity. You can find the pattern and directions for the Unit 6 Foldable™ in the Unit 6 Resources Fast File booklet. You can use the Foldables™ as they are presented or modify them to suit the needs of your students.

Literature Online

For a wealth of online resources that support the instruction in Unit 6, students and teachers can visit our Web site at glencoe.com. Students will find additional learning, practice, and assessment opportunities such as these, which are noted in the student text:

- Author Search
- Big Idea Overview and Activity
- Interactive Literary Elements Handbook
- Study Central
- Unit Assessment
- Web Activities
- Writing Models

Teachers will find planning and instructional tools that include the following:

- Book Lesson Plans
- Web Activity Lesson Plans
- Teacher Forum
- Professional Resources

  Go to glencoe.com to see the entire selection of *Glencoe Literature* online resources.

Glencoe's Presentation Plus!™, a multimedia teaching tool, lets you present dynamic lessons that will engage your students. Using Microsoft PowerPoint®, you can customize the presentations to create your own personalized lessons. Use CheckPoint questions with interactive response keypads to get immediate student feedback during lessons, to increase student participation, and to assess student comprehension.

Glencoe Literature Library

The collection of hardcover books includes full-length novels, novellas, plays, and works of nonfiction. Each volume consists of at least one complete extended-length reading accompanied by several related readings from a broad range of genres. A separate Study Guide for each *Glencoe Literature Library* book provides teaching notes and reproducible activity pages for students. Glencoe Literature Library titles that complement this unit include:

- ***Animal Farm with Related Readings*** by George Orwell
- ***Frankenstein with Related Readings*** by Mary Shelley

Glencoe BookLink

Use the Glencoe BookLink 3 CD-ROM, a database of more than 26,700 titles, to *create customized reading lists* for your students.

- Search for award-winning titles (e.g., Newbery Award winners, Coretta Scott King Award winners, and Caldecott Medal winners) and for books on several state-recommended reading lists.
- Find Degrees of Reading Power™ (DRP) and Lexile™ readability scores for all selections.
- Organize reading lists by students' reading level, author, genre, theme, or area of interest.
- Get a brief summary of each selection.

You can find recommended leveled readings for this unit with Independent Reading (see pages 1268 and 1269).

Online Essay Grader

Use Glencoe's online essay grader powered by SkillWriter™ to score your students' writing and to provide individualized feedback to each student automatically.

You and your students can visit glencoe.com to link to the essay grader. *Students* can enter their essays and receive feedback on demand. *You* can manage demographic data, assign tests, and generate individual student and aggregated reports. The essay grader can help you

- Save time with automatic scoring and individualized feedback.
- Supplement in-class writing instruction using guided writing practice.

REAL Success: Reading Excellence at All Levels

Glencoe REAL Success is a suite of new reading and language arts products designed to foster reading excellence at all levels.

Look for TWE point-of-use references for these specific products that will help your students succeed in reading this Unit.

- *Jamestown Literature: An Adapted Reader*
- REAL Success in Writing: Research and Reports
- Skill Level Up!™ A Language Arts Game
- CheckPoint PowerPoint™ slides
- Literature/Reading support at Glencoe Web site

Literature Launchers

Set the scene with Glencoe's Literature Launchers, engaging pre-reading video segments that introduce each unit. Each Unit Launcher brings the literature to life, featuring expert testimony and archival stills and footage from the time.

Insert your Glencoe Literature Launchers into your DVD player. Select the Unit 6 Launcher from the menu to introduce Genre Fiction.

A lively collection of articles drawn from issues of the TIME family of magazines helps students develop the skills they need to interact with informational text in a meaningful way. Each of the news stories, feature articles, reviews, profiles, and essays in the magazine connect to an author, work, or theme in *Glencoe Literature: The Reader's Choice.* See the *inTIME* Teacher's Guide for specific connections to each unit and for reproducible student worksheets designed to develop students' reading and critical thinking skills.

Teacher Wraparound Edition Key

Level Appropriate Code

AL = Activities for students working above grade level

OL = Activities for students working at grade level

BL = Activities for students working below grade level

EL = Activities for English language learners

AS = Information for all students

Teacher Wraparound Prompts

R Reading Skill These activities help you teach reading skills and vocabulary.

V Vocabulary These activities help students comprehend words and incorporate them into reading.

BI Big Idea These activities and questions prompt students to explore the Big Idea.

L Literary Element These activities and questions help students comprehend selections and learn more about each genre.

★ Enrichment Additional activities and information involving art appreciation and history.

Professional Development Center

From Your Authors:

Teaching Literary Analysis: Mystery and Science Fiction

Make Media Connections Ask students to discuss the ways in which the media portrays the genre of mystery and the genre of science fiction. What sound effects are common in mysteries? In science fiction? What types of visual images are used for these two genres? Ask students to think about particular movies or television shows they have seen that represent these two genres. Then have students use the same questions to compare two short stories from these genres. After students have read "The Sentinel" by Arthur C. Clarke and "The Mystery of Hunter's Lodge" by Agatha Christie, ask them to create a T chart. What makes these two genres unique? How do you know that you are reading a mystery? When do you know you are reading a work of science fiction? Do the genres share any qualities? Have students answer the questions in their chart to see the similarities and differences between the two stories.

Jeffrey D. Wilhelm and Jacqueline Jones Royster

Start with an Illustration Using a series of illustrations or photos, ask students to classify the visual information as mystery, science fiction, or other. How do they know which category to place each illustration in? Ask students to discuss the visual information. Develop a list of vocabulary terms that they might find in each of these genres, such as "mysterious" or "futuristic." Students will likely use a number of terms in their discussions that are common to the genres themselves. Then, have students examine the artwork presented with "He-y, Come on Ou-t!" by Shinichi Hoshi and the painting presented in "The Adventures of the President's Half Disme" by Ellery Queen. Ask students to explain how the two pieces represent the two different genres.

Bradley Wallace
Benedictine Military School
Savannah, Georgia

Teacher to Teacher

A useful activity for opening a unit on science fiction and fantasy is to begin with a general discussion of how living things, such as penguins, beavers, camels, and so on, adapt to their environments. I point out that science fiction is often merely an adaptation of what we see through our own experiences and tends to mirror the strangest of realities. Students then form groups and are instructed to create their own fantastical creatures. First, they must define the environment in which the creature exists and then visually illustrate how the creature adapts to its environment. Further discussion involves this question: "What in your experience mimics what writers create in science fiction and fantasy?" After we draw some comparisons, students take their creatures, give them names, and put them into science-fiction stories of their own making.

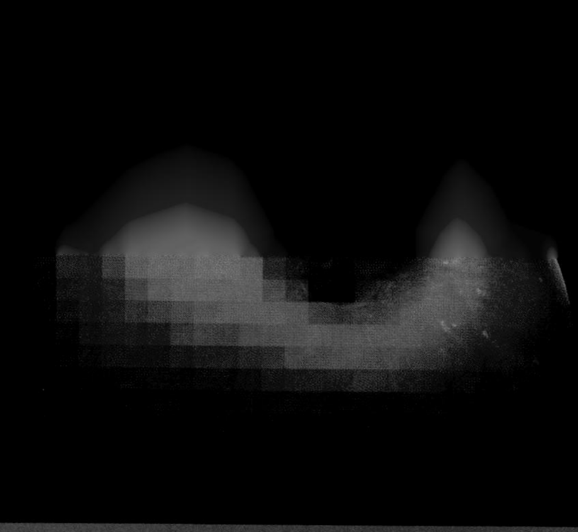

Making Literature Come Alive

Before you begin this unit or sometime during the unit, talk with other teachers about ways they have taught mystery and science fiction. Have a lunch-time discussion group or an after-school hour for professional development and discuss the following questions and answers from our authors:

How can reading mysteries build students' skills in making predictions?

- Mysteries provide students an excellent opportunity to focus on making and revising predictions. The key to learning to predict lies in learning from wrong predictions and reviewing the text for missed clues. As students read "The Red-Headed League," have them pause after every other page to write down their predictions of what will happen next. As students continue to read, have them revise their predictions to make them more accurate.
- Provide students with a simple definition of deductive and inductive logic and ask them to analyze their thinking as they read. Helping students understand the way their mind works builds their metacognitive skills. As students read "The Stolen Cigar Case" by Bret Harte, ask students to be aware of and take notes on their thinking process as they read.

What thinking skills can students learn from fictional detectives?

- Problem solving
- Using evidence
- Persevering
- Maintaining integrity

After reading Agatha Christie's "The Mystery of Hunter's Lodge," ask students to write about what they have learned from Hercule Poirot and Captain Hastings. Have students explain how these two characters display the characteristics listed above.

How can reading science fiction help enhance students' knowledge of technology?

- Science fiction is known for its unique applications of technology to solve problems. Consider showing your students clips from the original *Star Trek* series. Discuss the range of technology now available that was barely thinkable at the time the show was written.
- Invite students to keep a log of the technology used in science fiction that was not available at the time of the writing of the text. Ask them to analyze their list and determine how much technology has evolved. Have students keep a technology log as they read "The Sentinel" by Arthur C. Clarke and "2001: Space Odyssey" by Roger Ebert. After reading both, lead students in a discussion of how technology has evolved since these selections were written.
- Discuss the future of technology. How might science fiction contribute to the development of new technology? Discuss the idea that this field of literature has had a profound impact on technology research and development.

Focus

BELLRINGER

Bellringer Options
Literature Launcher Video
Daily Language Practice Transparency 93
Or **write on the board:** What is your favorite movie genre? Literary genre? Would you rather read a newspaper or watch a television newscast? Discuss with students why a genre appeals to them more in one medium than in another.

Objectives for the Unit Introduction

- To understand characteristics of mystery, modern fable, and science fiction/fantasy
- To identify and explore literary elements significant to the genres
- To analyze the effect that these literary elements have upon the reader

Government Office, George Tooker. Metropolitan Museum of Art, New York.

1112

Unit Introduction Skills

Genre Fiction

Literary Elements
- Genre Fiction (SE pp. 1114–1115)
- Description and Imagery (SE p. 1115)
- Style and Tone (SE p. 1115)

Reading Skills
- Literary Analysis Model (SE pp. 1116–1117)
- Reading Check (SE pp. 1117, 1119)

Listening/Speaking/Viewing Skills
- Create Your Own Genre (TWE p. 1114)

Writing Skills/Grammar
- Alternate Point of View (TWE p. 1116)
- Imagery (TWE p. 1120)

Study Skills/Research/Assessment
- Foldables (SE p. 1120)

Genre Fiction

Looking Ahead

Genre fiction is a flexible term used to group works of fiction that have similar characters, plots, or settings. Bookstores and libraries often shelve their fiction by genre categories—such as romance, mystery, science fiction, and fantasy—for the convenience of readers who prefer particular kinds of stories. You know the conventions—the requirements of character, plot, or setting—that distinguish many genres of fiction. Westerns, for example, have a particular setting—the U.S. frontier during the second half of the 1800s—and often particular character types—rugged, individualistic cowboys—as heroes. You have been studying genres, or types, of literature. This unit presents a few genres specific to fiction.

PREVIEW **Big Ideas and Literary Focus**

	BIG IDEA:	LITERARY FOCUS:
1	Our World and Beyond	Description
2	Revealing the Concealed	Style and Tone

INDIANA ACADEMIC STANDARDS (pages 1112–1119)

9.3.2 Compare and contrast...genres (different types of writing) to explain how the selection of genre shapes the theme or topic.

9.3.7 Recognize and understand the significance of various literary devices...

9.3.11 Evaluate the aesthetic qualities of style...

Focus

Summary

The unit introduction begins with the Genre Focus, which identifies the characteristics of science fiction, fantasy, modern fable, and mystery. An analysis of a science fiction story, *Buy Jupiter,* is provided. The introduction ends with quotations from writers on reading various genres of fiction.

Viewing the Art

Brooklyn-born artist George Tooker (1920–) often paints figures that reflect the alienation and disaffection of Americans in the Cold War era. His paintings combine elements of stark realism with an unsettling surreal quality. AS

Unit Resources

Classroom Management
- TeacherWorks Plus™ CD-ROM
- StudentWorks Plus™ CD-ROM
- Literature Launchers™: Pre-Reading Videos DVD, Unit Six

Core Instructional Support
- Unit 6 Resources (Fast File)
- Literature Online, glencoe.com
- Presentation Plus!™ CD-ROM, Unit Six

Transparencies
- Literary Elements Transparencies 1, 6, 7, 16, 17, 89, 91, 92, 109
- Bellringer Options Transparencies: Selection Focus Transparencies 49–50 Daily Language Practice Transparencies 93–104

Differentiated Instruction
- Active Learning and Note Taking Guide, pp. 179–207
- Skill Level Up!™ A Language Arts Game

Assessment
- Selection and Unit Assessments, pp. 189–210, 221–222
- Exam*View*® Assessment Suite CD-ROM
- Assessment by Learning Objectives, pp. 57–66

Supplemental Reading
- Glencoe Literature Library
- Glencoe BookLink 3 CD-ROM
- *inTIME* Magazines

Teach

R Reading Strategy

Summarizing Instruct students to copy the column headings on this page in their notebooks. Under each heading, have them write brief notes summarizing the elements of the different genres. OL

★ Cultural History

Aesop One famous fable writer is Aesop. While Aesop's exact birthplace remains a matter of debate, historians believe he was born a slave in the sixth century B.C. After earning his freedom, he traveled and became involved in public affairs. King Croesus was so impressed by Aesop that he gave him a position in his court. AS

Genre Focus: Genre Fiction

What are some genres of fiction?

This unit includes several kinds, or genres, of fiction: fantasy, mysteries, modern fables, and science fiction. In each genre, the world can be as familiar as a city street at twilight or as strange as an island that speaks to its inhabitants. Part of the fun in reading these types of fiction is discovering what these wonderful worlds are like and understanding the elements the author used to create them.

Science Fiction, Fantasy, and Fable

R Science Fiction

A setting in the future or away from Earth is often a major element of **science fiction.** Writers of the genre also address the impact of science and technology—real or imagined—on society and on individuals. Many critics argue that the best science fiction reveals an underlying truth about our own world. These truths are uncovered by reflecting on common themes in uncommon settings.

We had begun our journey early in the slow lunar dawn, and still had almost a week of Earth-time before nightfall. Half a dozen times a day we would leave our vehicle and go outside in the space suits to hunt for interesting minerals, or to place markers for the guidance of future travelers. It was an uneventful routine.

—Arthur C. Clarke, **from "The Sentinel"**

Fantasy

Like science fiction, **fantasy** fiction is generally set in an unfamiliar setting. Unlike science fiction, however, fantasy stories commonly take place in imaginary worlds and may include gnomes, elves, or other fantastical beings and forces. The use of some type of magic is common in fantasy stories.

He was all the little island had in the way of a wizard, and so deserved respect—but how could you respect a little man of fifty who waddled along with his toes turned in, breathing steam and smiling?

—Ursula K. Le Guin, **from "The Rule of Names"**

Modern Fable

★ A **fable** is a brief, usually simple story intended to teach a lesson about human behavior or to give advice about how to behave. Modern fables also focus on themes relating to human behavior, with little development of individual characters. In "The Golden Kite, The Silver Wind," Ray Bradbury tells a simple tale that points out the destructiveness of political rivalry.

"I have called you here," said the Mandarin aloud, "because our city is shaped like an orange, and the vile city of Kwan-Si has this day shaped theirs like a ravenous pig—"

—Ray Bradbury, **from "The Golden Kite, The Silver Wind"**

Additional Support

Skills Practice

WRITING: Genre Instruct groups of students to combine several existing literary genres to create a new one. Students should prepare illustrated reports explaining what kind of characters, imagery, style, and tone typify their genre and how it differs from other genres with similar elements. Have students present their reports to the class. OL

Description and Imagery

L In fiction set in unfamiliar places or imaginary worlds, description becomes especially important. **Description** is a detailed portrayal of a person, place, thing, or event. Good description allows a reader to understand what he or she has never encountered.

> Once a couple of boys, thinking the wizard was over on the West Shore curing Mrs. Ruuna's sick donkey, brought a crowbar and a hatchet up there, but at the first whack of the hatchet on the door there came a roar of wrath from inside, and a cloud of purple steam.
>
> —Ursula K. Le Guin, **from "The Rule of Names"**

Imagery is descriptive language that appeals to one or more of the five senses (sight, hearing, touch, taste, and smell). The use of these sensory details helps to create an emotional response in the reader.

> All those memories: the shade of blue of a dress worn fifty years ago, the tilt of the head of someone long dead, the sudden sharp smell of a grandmother's cabbage soup mingled with the dusty scent of an apartment razed for two decades.
>
> —Nancy Kress, **from "In Memoriam"**

Mystery

Mystery

Mysteries or detective stories follow a particular plot pattern: a crime is committed and a detective gathers clues to identify the criminal. The detective may be a tough, street-smart character—often called the hard-boiled detective—or a brilliant eccentric with keen powers of observation and reasoning, like Sherlock Holmes.

> "Beyond the obvious facts that he has at some time done manual labor, that he takes snuff, that he is a Freemason, that he has been in China, and that he has done a considerable amount of writing lately, I can deduce nothing else."
>
> —Sir Arthur Conan Doyle, **from "The Red-Headed League"**

Style and Tone

Style is the expresssive qualities that distinguish an author's work, including word choice, sentence structure, and figures of speech. **Tone** is the author's attitude toward the audience or the subject of the work. Style and tone help create the mood of a story, such as the suspenseful mood common in mystery stories.

> "Havering has one or two shady incidents in his past. When he was a boy at Oxford there was some funny business about the signature on one of his father's checks. All hushed up of course. . . ."
>
> —Agatha Christie, **from "The Mystery of Hunter's Lodge"**

LiteratureOnline Study Central
Visit www.glencoe.com to review genre fiction.

Differentiated Instruction

Visual Learners Explain to visual learners that like artwork, each literary genre has a style, theme, tone, and imagery specific to it. The more students allow these elements to help them visualize works in a genre, the more easily they will comprehend the author's meaning. BL

Teach

L Literary Element

Description and Imagery

Suggest students organize their notes on description and imagery by listing images under the appropriate senses. Have them write the heads "Seeing," "Hearing," "Tasting," "Touching," and "Smelling" in their notebooks and add examples to the categories as they read. OL

Study Central Have students visit the Web site for resources that will help them to review genre fiction.

Academic Standards

Additional Support activities on pp. 1114 and 1115 cover the following standards:

Skills Practice: **9.5.6** Write technical documents…that report information and express ideas logically and correctly; offer detailed and accurate specifications; include scenarios, definitions, and examples to aid comprehension; [and] anticipate readers' problems, mistakes, and misunderstandings.

Differentiated Instruction: **9.2** Develop [reading] strategies…

Teach

R Reading Strategy

Setting a Purpose Have a volunteer read the introductory paragraph aloud. Instruct students to consider the goals of the science fiction writer as they read the excerpt from *Buy Jupiter.*

- Does the story entertain?
- Does it inspire wonder?
- Does the story force the reader to ask "What if?" OL

Viewing the Photo

Contemporary photographer Douglas Kirkland has photographed icons including Marilyn Monroe and Elizabeth Taylor. In addition to his work on more than 100 movies, Kirkland also has exhibited fine art photography and published several books. AS

Literary Analysis Model

How do literary elements impact genre fiction?

R The Russian-born American biochemist and writer Isaac Asimov (1920–1992) wrote close to five hundred books, many of which were science fiction. The imaginary worlds he created in his stories and novels greatly influenced other writers of science fiction. In many of the books he published, Asimov met the goals of the science fiction writer: to entertain, to awe, and to force the reader to ask, "What if . . . ?" In his short story, "Buy Jupiter," Asimov describes an encounter between a simulacron, representing the people of Mizzarett, and government officials on Earth. The Mizzarett people want to buy Jupiter, which is on their new trade route. The simulacron is secretive and keen on concealing the deal from the Lamberj people, which arouses the suspicion of some Earth officials. Are the two peoples at war? In this scene, Earth's Secretary of Science reveals the truth about the Mizzarett people's plans.

APPLYING Literary Elements

Description
The description of how the Secretary *looks* clues us in to how he *feels.*

Suspense
The Secretary of Defense's distrust of the simulacron heightens the reader's worries that something is not quite right with this deal.

from *Buy Jupiter*

by Isaac Asimov

The Secretary of Science emerged, mopping his forehead and looking ten years younger. He said softly, "I told him his people could have it as soon as I obtained the President's formal approval. I don't think he'll object, or Congress, either. Good Lord, gentlemen, think of it; free power at our fingertips in return for a planet we could never use in any case."

The Secretary of Defense, growing purplish with objection, said, "But we had agreed that only a Mizzarett-Lamberj war could explain their need for Jupiter. Under those circumstances, and comparing their military potential with ours, a strict neutrality is essential."

"But there is no war, sir," said the Secretary of Science, "The simulacron presented an alternate explanation of their need for Jupiter so rational and plausible that I accepted at once. I think the President will agree with me, and you gentlemen, too, when you understand. In fact, I have here their plans for the new Jupiter, as it will soon appear."

The others rose from their seats, clamoring. "A new Jupiter?" gasped the Secretary of Defense.

"Not so different from the old, gentlemen," said the Secretary of Science. "Here are the sketches provided in form suitable for observation by matter beings such as ourselves."

He laid them down. The familiar banded planet was there before them on one of the sketches: yellow, pale green, and light brown with curled white streaks here and there and all against the speckled velvet background of space. But across

Author and scientist Isaac Asimov, ca. 1989. Douglas Kirkland. 

Additional Support

Skills Practice

LITERARY ELEMENT: Point of View
Ask: Do you think the simulacron in the story was telling the truth about the reason for buying Jupiter? Have students rewrite *Buy Jupiter* from the simulacron's point of view. Suggest they consider the following:

- What kind of ethics would an advanced race have?
- What alternative motives might they have for buying Jupiter?
- How might an advanced race like the Mizzaretts view humanity? OL

Flying Saucers, September 6, 2001. Tim Bird.

the bands were streaks of blackness as velvet as the background, arranged in a curious pattern.

"That," said the Secretary of Science, "is the day side of the planet. The night side is shown in this sketch." (There,  Jupiter was a thin crescent enclosing darkness, and within that darkness were the same thin streaks arranged in similar pattern, but in a phosphorescent glowing orange this time.)

"The marks," said the Secretary of Science, "are a purely optical phenomenon, I am told, which will not rotate with the planet, but will remain static in its atmospheric fringe."

"But what is it?" asked the Secretary of Commerce.

"You see," said the Secretary of Science, "our solar system is now on one of their major trade routes. As many as seven of their ships pass within a few hundred million miles of the system in a single day, and each ship has the major planets under telescopic observation as they pass. Tourist curiosity, you know. Solid planets of any size are a marvel to them."

"What has that to do with these marks?"

"That is one form of their writing. Translated, those marks read: 'Use Mizzarett Ergone Vertices For Health and Glowing Heat.'"

"You mean Jupiter is to be an advertising billboard?" exploded the Secretary of Defense. **L**

"Right. The Lamberj people, it seems, produce a competing ergone tablet, which accounts for the Mizzarett anxiety to establish full legal ownership of Jupiter—in case of Lamberj lawsuits. Fortunately, the Mizzaretts are novices at the advertising game, it appears."

"Why do you say that?" asked the Secretary of the Interior.

"Why, they neglected to set up a series of options on the other planets. The Jupiter billboard will be advertising our system, as well as their own product. And when the competing Lamberj people come storming in to check on the Mizzarett title to Jupiter, we will have Saturn to sell to *them. With* its rings. As we will be easily able to explain to them, the rings will make Saturn much the better spectacle."

"And therefore," said the Secretary of the Treasury, suddenly beaming, "worth a *much* better price."

And they all suddenly looked very cheerful.

Description
This comparison to velvet helps the reader "see" and even "touch" the absolute darkness of the streaks on the bands.

Tone
The Secretary of Science projects a calm, objective tone, which makes him sound reliable and authoritative.

Style
Asimov uses italics to indicate emphasized words in dialogue.

Reading Check

Interpreting Why is the committee pleased with the Secretary of Science's deal with the simulacron?

Teach

Reading Check

Answer: *They will be able to use the Jupiter billboard to advertise their own system.*

L Literary Element

Description **Ask:** How does the author characterize the Secretary of Defense? Does this characterization make him seem more or less reliable than the Secretary of Science? *(Words such as "gasped" and "exploding" suggest the Secretary of Defense is overly emotional and therefore less reliable than the calm Secretary of Science.)* **OL**

★ Writer's Technique

Description By using description strategically and sparingly, Asimov encourages readers to use their own imagination to infer details. **AS**

English Language Coach

Visualization English language learners may feel overwhelmed by the odd names and places in *Buy Jupiter.* Explain that this difficulty is not a language issue. Since the names and places are imaginary, all readers have to visualize them from the writer's description. Assign the roles, including a narrator, to student volunteers and have them read the story aloud. To help them interpret the characters, have students imitate the facial expressions and hand gestures indicated by Asimov. **EL**

Academic Standards

Additional Support activities on pp. 1116 and 1117 cover the following standards:

Skills Practice: **9.5.8** Write for different purposes and audiences, adjusting tone, style, and voice as appropriate.

English Language Coach: **9.7.6** Analyze the occasion and...choose effective... nonverbal techniques (including... gestures...) for presentations.

Teach

R1 Reading Strategy

Connect Ask students which of the authors quoted they are familiar with. Discuss how knowledge of the authors and their works can help them to better connect with the quotes. OL

Viewing the Art

Contemporary American artist Max Ferguson combines a background in animation with the influence of seventeenth-century Dutch paintings to create his realistic paintings. AS

Writers on Reading

What do writers say about genre fiction? R1

Realizing a Fantasy World

R1 Anyone inheriting the fantastic device of human language can say *the green sun*. Many can then imagine or picture it. But that is not enough—though it may already be a more potent thing than many a "thumbnail sketch" or "transcript of life" that receives literary praise.

To make a Secondary World inside which the green sun will be credible, commanding Secondary Belief, will probably require labor and thought, and will certainly demand a special skill, a kind of elvish craft. Few attempt such difficult tasks. But when they are attempted and in any degree accomplished then we have a rare achievement of Art: indeed narrative art, story-making in its primary and most potent mode.

—J. R. R. Tolkien, **from** ***The Letters of J. R. R. Tolkien***

Take the A Train, 1983. Max Ferguson. Oil on panel, 29.53 x 44.09 in. 

Additional Support

Skills Practice

RESEARCH: Genre History Have the class brainstorm fiction genres and list them in their notebooks. Assign groups of students genres to research. Have them consider these questions:

- When did the genre first emerge?
- What media (print, film, TV) are associated with the genre?
- What authors and works are associated with the genre?

Groups should include timelines in their histories and present the reports in class. OL

On Messages

What you get out of a story, in the way of understanding or perception or emotion, is partly up to me—because, of course, the story is passionately meaningful to me (even if I only find out what it's about after I've told it). But it's also up to you, the reader. Reading is a passionate act. If you read a story not just with your head, but also with your body and feelings and soul, the way you dance or listen to music, then it becomes your story. And it can mean infinitely more than any message. It can offer beauty. It can take you through pain. It can signify freedom. And it can mean something different every time you reread it. . . .

R2

I wish, instead of looking for a message when we read a story, we could think, "Here's a door opening on a new world: what will I find there?"

—Ursula K. Le Guin, **from "A Message about Messages"**

> *"Science fiction writers foresee the inevitable."*
>
> —Isaac Asimov

Montage Painting of Spacemen, ca. 20th century. Anton Brzezinski. ★

The Triumph of the Mystery Story

There will always be those who claim that a fascination with the murder story is unhealthy, and that the success of the genre rests on ghoulishness. No doubt there are and always will be some bloodthirsty readers. But the beauty of the mystery story, and what, when well done, gives it its power and raises it to the level of "serious" fiction, is how it reveals human weakness. Tough guys crack wise and entertain, but the emotional center of good mysteries is weakness of character and such failures of courage or surrenders to temptation as can turn reasonably good men or women into criminals and at worst, murderers. (The "psycho," the monster whose motivations are incomprehensible, is for that reason one of the most boring characters in popular literature.) Whether seen as crimes or sins, the acts that drive the plots of mysteries and the emotions behind them rivet our attention.

—Bruce F. Murphy, **from** *The Encyclopedia of Murder and Mystery*

Literature Online **InterActive Reading Practice**
Visit www.glencoe.com to practice these strategies for reading genre fiction.

Reading Check

Responding From your own reading experiences, which passage do you identify with most closely? Explain.

Teach

Reading Check

Answer: *Students' responses should include an explanation of why the passage was chosen.*

R2 Reading Strategy

Ask: How does Ursula LeGuin characterize reading? *(She calls it an active, passionate act. She sees the reader as being as important as the writer in storytelling.)* Discuss how students can become more active readers. *(predicting, questioning, imagining themselves in a character's role, making connections)* OL

★ Viewing the Art

Contemporary American artist Anton Brzezinski specializes in science fiction and fantasy art. In this painting, Brzezinski reproduces images from the *Buck Rogers* comic strip of the 1930s. AS

Literature Online

InterActive Reading Have students access the Web site for more practice with reading strategies.

English Language Coach

Role-Play Suggest that English language learners imagine that the authors of the quotations are speaking directly to them. Have pairs of students take turns assuming the role of the author of a quotation and answering questions put to them by their partners. EL

Academic Standards

Additional Support activities on pp. 1118 and 1119 cover the following standards:

Skills Practice: **9.5.9** Write or deliver a research report that has been developed using a systematic research process…

English Language Coach: **9.7.17** Deliver oral responses to literature…

Assess/Close

Guide to Genre Fiction

Go through each bullet point with the class. **Ask:** What elements of this genre entertain you?

Elements of Genre Fiction

Go through each bullet point with the class and have them volunteer examples. To demonstrate diction, have several different students describe the same thing, noting how the various word choices of the students result in different styles.

Activities

1. **Visual Literacy** Suggest that students make note of word choices that catch their attention.
2. **Writing** Remind students that similes contain *like* or *as* and that metaphors do not.
3. **Speaking/Listening** Encourage students to include sounds, such as footsteps or traffic.

FOLDABLES™ Study Organizer

Have students make the Bound Book. Their notes on the literary elements can be written on the pages.

Wrap-Up

Guide to Genre Fiction

- Like all fiction, **genre fiction** is usually meant to teach, to entertain, or to do both.
- **Mystery** deals with the unknown. Thrillers, horror stories, and detective stories are types of mysteries.
- **Fables** teach a lesson, or moral, about human behavior.
- **Science fiction** frequently deals with the interplay between science or technology and human nature.
- **Fantasy** fiction is usually set in an imaginary world and includes supernatural creatures and forces.

Elements of Genre Fiction

- **Description** makes readers feel that they are part of the action.
- **Imagery** makes description more vivid by appealing to the reader's five senses.
- **Suspense** heightens a reader's interest and strengthens his or her desire to continue reading.
- **Figurative language** compares unlike things in imaginative ways.
- **Style** is the distinctive way an author uses language. **Diction** and **word choice** contribute to a writer's style.
- **Tone** is the writer's attitude toward the subject or the audience.

Activities

Use what you have learned about reading genre fiction to do one of these actvities.

1. **Visual Literacy** Create a three-column chart that you can use to compare and contrast the tone and style of three different selections from the unit.
2. **Writing** Write a one-paragraph description of an imaginary world. Use a simile, a metaphor, or imagery if you can.
3. **Speaking/Listening** In a small group, prepare a dramatic reading of an important scene from one of the stories in the unit. Pretend your reading is being recorded for a radio program. Assign one student in the group to provide background music for the show.

BOUND BOOK

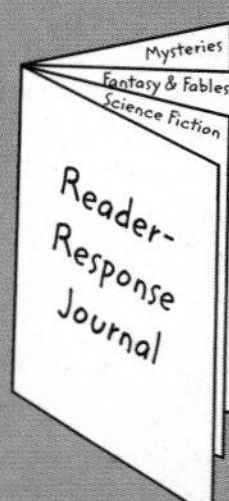

You might try using this study organizer to explore your personal response to genre fiction you read in this unit.

INDIANA ACADEMIC STANDARDS (page 1120)

9.3 [Identify] story elements...
9.3.11 Evaluate...the impact of diction...on tone...
9.5.3 Write...descriptive pieces...
9.7.4 Use...electronic media to enhance the appeal and accuracy of presentations.

Additional Support

Skills Practice

LITERARY ELEMENT: Imagery Have students practice identifying and using imagery. Have them use "Hearing," "Seeing," "Smelling," "Tasting," and "Touching" as column headers. Then have them pick a person, place, or thing to describe. Alternatively, assign one subject to the class and have students write one metaphor, simile, or other image describing the subject under each column heading. Invite students to share some of their descriptions with the class. **OL**

Our World and Beyond

The Rimfall, 20th century. Jonathan Barry. Oil on canvas.

BIG IDEA

BI Imagine that time can move backward, that space has more than three dimensions, or that fantastic creatures share the universe with us. The stories in Part 1 will engage your imagination. As you read them, ask yourself: What can we gain from thinking about realities different from our own?

Analyzing and Extending

BI Big Idea

Ask: What is your definition of "reality"? What makes something "real"? Discuss differences between fantasy and reality and examples of fantasies of the past, for instance space travel, that have become realities. OL

Viewing the Art

Contemporary Irish artist and illustrator Jonathan Barry specializes in painting scenes from literature, including such classics as *Alice in Wonderland*, *The Wind in the Willows*, and *Peter Pan*. "Rimfall" is a reference to author Terry Pratchett's Discworld series of books. AS

Differentiated Instruction

Visualizing Visual learners will benefit from engaging with the artwork. Have students view the picture and then read the Big Idea sentences.

Ask: In what ways is the picture different from our usual view of reality? Have students interpret the figures and other elements in the picture. BL

Academic Standards

Additional Support activities on pp. 1120 and 1121 cover the following standards:

Skills Practice: **9.3.7** Recognize and understand the significance of various literary devices, including...imagery...

Differentiated Instruction: **9.2** Develop [reading] strategies...

Part 1: Skills Scope and Sequence

Readability Scores Key
Dale–Chall/DRP/Lexile

PACING (DAYS) STANDARD	BLOCK	SELECTIONS AND FEATURES	LITERARY ELEMENTS
2–3 class sessions	1	"The Sentinel" by Arthur C. Clark **8.3/63/1240**, pp. 1124–1137	Suspense, SE pp. 1125–1136 Description, SE p. 1136
		HISTORICAL PERSPECTIVE on *The Sentinel*: Film Review "2001: A Space Odyssey" by Roger Ebert **6.8/62/940**, pp. 1138–1140	Conversational Tone, TWE p. 1139
		Grammar Workshop: Commas, p. 1141	
2 class sessions	1	"He–y, Come on Ou–t!" by Shinichi Hoshi **7.7/55/890**, pp. 1142–1149	Moral, SE pp. 1143, 1146, 1147, 1148 Character, SE p. 1148
		"The Rule of Names" by Ursula K. Le Guin **7.3/60/1050**, pp. 1150–1163	Humor, SE pp. 1151, 1156, 1158–1160, 1162 Dialect, SE p. 1162
2 class sessions	1	COMPARING LITERATURE Across Genres "In Memoriam" by Nancy Kress **4.8/54/650**, pp. 1164–1173 "Purchase" by Naomi Long Madgett, p. 1174 "World Without Memory" from *Einstein's Dreams* by Alan Lightman **6.8/58/1090**, pp. 1175–1177	Dialogue, SE pp. 1166, 1168, 1169, 1172, 1173
1–2 class sessions	1	"The Golden Kite, the Silver Wind" by Ray Bradbury **7.1/55/1030**, pp. 1178–1185	Allegory, SE pp. 1179, 1180, 1182–1184 Moral, SE p. 1184
		Vocabulary Workshop: Denotation and Connotation, SE p. 1186	

About the Part

Part 1 deals with the human desire to explore new worlds through imaginative and fantastic stories.

READING AND CRITICAL THINKING	VOCABULARY	WRITING AND GRAMMAR	LISTENING, SPEAKING, AND VIEWING
Identifying Assumptions, SE pp. 1125–1136 Identifying Author's Purpose, TWE p. 1126	Analogies, SE pp. 1125, 1136 Academic Vocabulary, SE p. 1136 Words with Prefixes, TWE p. 1130	Explore Author's Purpose, SE p. 1137 Using Infinitives and Infinitive Phrases, SE p. 1137 Literary Criticism, SE p. 1137	Analyzing Art, SE pp. 1127, 1132; TWE p. 1129 Graphic Organizer, SE p. 1135 Telling a Suspenseful Story, TWE p. 1130
Evaluating Argument, SE p. 1138			Reviewing, TWE p. 1138 Analyzing a Photograph, TWE p. 1139
		Using Commas in a Series, SE p. 1141	
Connecting to Contemporary Issues, SE pp. 1143, 1145, 1146, 1149 Parables, TWE p. 1144	Antonyms, SE pp. 1143, 1149 Academic Vocabulary, SE p. 1149	Analyze Satire, SE p. 1149	Analyzing Art, SE p. 1147; TWE p. 1144 Imagine Alternate Ending, SE p. 1149
Analyzing Sensory Details, SE pp. 1151–1162	Word Origins, SE pp. 1151, 1162 Academic Vocabulary, SE p. 1162	Apply Description, SE p. 1163 Using Idioms, SE p. 1163	Analyzing Art, SE p. 1155; TWE pp. 1158, 1160 Illustrations, SE p. 1161
Comparing and Connecting to the Story, TWE p. 1168 Rereading, TWE p. 1170 Summarizing, TWE p. 1172 Making Comparisons, TWE p. 1176	Context Clues, SE p. 1173	Evaluate Contemporary Relevance, SE p. 1173 Quickwrite, SE p. 1174 Comparison Essay, SE p. 1177 Descriptive Writing, TWE p. 1174	Analyzing Art, SE p. 1171; TWE pp. 1174, 1175 Discussion Starter, SE p. 1176 Group Activity, SE p. 1177 Reading Dialogue, TWE p. 1171
Evaluating Figures of Speech, SE pp. 1179, 1181, 1182, 1185 Drawing Conclusions, TWE p. 1180 Problem and Solution, TWE p. 1182	Synonyms, SE pp. 1179, 1185 Academic Vocabulary, SE p. 1185	Analyze Comic Devices, SE p. 1185	Analyzing Art, SE p. 1183; TWE p. 1180 Literature Groups, SE p. 1185
	Identifying Word Relationships, TWE p. 1186		

LITERARY FOCUS

Focus

BELLRINGER

Bellringer Options
Daily Language Practice Transparency 94
Or **ask:** Did anyone have an imaginary friend as a child?
Say: Suppose that you have an imaginary friend now. Instruct students to write a detailed description of this friend. Encourage them to include as many sensory details as possible. Have them share their descriptions with the class.

Teach

L Literary Element

Description Instruct students to describe a common object, such as an orange. Write the descriptions on the board.
Ask: What's missing? Have students add sensory details and figurative language to the descriptions. OL

★ Viewing the Art

Russian painter Konstantin Yuon (1875–1958) was strongly influenced by Impressionism's distinctive use of light and color. In later works, his emphasis shifted to social realism. AS

LITERARY FOCUS

Description

How do writers describe fantastic places and creatures?

Writers of fantasy and science fiction sometimes face the challenge of describing something that no one has ever seen or heard of. Good description can help a reader see, hear, smell, taste, or feel a **L** person, place, creature, or object. There are many literary techniques a writer can use to describe something. Figurative language and imagery are two. In "The Sentinel," Arthur C. Clarke describes the observations of a team of lunar explorers on the Mare Crisium, a large walled plain on the moon.

The New Planet, 1921. Konstantin Yuon. Tretyakov Gallery, Moscow, Russia. ★

I said just now that there was nothing exciting about lunar exploration, but of course that isn't true. One could never grow tired of those incredible mountains, so much more rugged than the gentle hills of Earth. We never knew, as we rounded the capes and promontories of that vanished sea, what new splendors would be revealed to us. The whole southern curve of the Mare Crisium is a vast delta where a score of rivers once found their way into the ocean, fed perhaps by the torrential rains that must have lashed the mountains in the brief volcanic age when the Moon was young.

—Arthur C. Clarke, **from "The Sentinel"**

Additional Support

See also Active Learning and Note Taking Guide, pp. 189–192.

Skills Practice

SPEAKING AND LISTENING:
Description Divide the class into two groups. Assign each group several objects to describe. Have one group begin by asking the other a question about the object, such as "What color is it?" or "What does it smell like?" Each group may ask only one question per sense in each round. If students haven't guessed the object by the fifth sense, they start over again by asking another question in the category of the first sense (for example, if they started with a visual question, they can now ask

R Figurative Language

Figurative language in literature often implies ideas indirectly. Figurative expressions are not literally true but express some truth beyond the literal level. In science fiction and fantasy, authors can use figurative language to describe the unfamiliar. A **figure of speech** is a specific device or kind of figurative language such as simile, metaphor, and personification.

Simile A figure of speech that uses *like* or *as* to compare seemingly unlike things is a **simile.** A good simile can help the reader see something familiar in a brand new way. In science fiction and fantasy, similes allow a writer to introduce something imaginary by comparing it to something the reader knows.

> The crows' feet at the corners of his eyes were still tentative, like lines scratched in soft sand.
>
> —Nancy Kress, **from "In Memoriam"**

Metaphor A figure of speech that compares or equates two or more things that have something in common is a **metaphor.** Unlike a simile, a metaphor does not use *like* or *as.*

> Without his Book of Life, a person is a snapshot, a two-dimensional image, a ghost.
>
> —Alan Lightman, **from "A World Without Memory"**

In the passage above, Lightman's metaphor gives the reader a sense of the limitations of living without memory.

LiteratureOnline Interactive Literary Elements Handbook Go to www.glencoe.com to review or learn more about description.

Personification A figure of speech that gives human qualities to an animal, an object, a force of nature, or an idea is **personification.** Writers use personification to explain, expand, and create vivid images.

> The waters were retreating down the flanks of those stupendous cliffs, retreating into the empty heart of the Moon.
>
> —Arthur C. Clarke, **from "The Sentinel"**

Imagery

Writing that portrays people, places, things, and events with vivid details that help the reader create a mental picture is called descriptive writing. Good descriptive writing uses imagery—language that appeals to one or more of the five senses: sight, hearing, touch, taste, and smell. In creating new worlds, writers use imagery to help create effective description that will engage the reader.

> Palani, a plump, pretty girl of twenty, made a charming picture there in the wintry sunlight, sheep and children around her, a leafless oak above her, and behind her dunes and sea and clear, pale sky.
>
> —Ursula Le Guin, **from "The Rule of Names"**

Quickwrite

Describing a Process Write a journal entry describing a real or imagined time you prepared a special food. For example, you might tell about the time you made a birthday cake or the time you created a feast for the birds outside your window. Describe the steps involved in the process and what you saw, heard, smelled, tasted, and touched as you worked.

INDIANA ACADEMIC STANDARDS (pages 1122-1123)

9.3.7 Recognize and understand the significance of various literary devices, including figurative language [and] imagery...

9.5.8 Write for different purposes and audiences, adjusting tone, style, and voice as appropriate.

Teach

R Reading Strategy

Visualizing Explain that the purpose of description is to help the reader "see" the writer's world. Have students read each displayed quotation aloud.
Ask: What does the description make you see? OL

Quickwrite

Students' descriptions should include details from each of the five senses.

Literary Elements Have students access the Web site to improve their understanding of description.

another visual question). The groups continue asking questions using each sense until they guess the object. The group to guess the most objects with the fewest questions wins. OL

Differentiated Instruction

Description Visual learners will benefit from clearly "seeing" the descriptions. Invite them to illustrate the quotations. Instruct students to use the author's description to imagine as many details as possible, and then to translate those details into an image. AL

Academic Standards

Additional Support activities on pp. 1122 and 1123 cover the following standards:

Skills Practice: **9.7.1** Summarize a speaker's purpose and...ask questions concerning the speaker's content...

Differentiated Instruction: **9.3.7** Recognize and understand the significance of various literary devices, including...imagery...

BEFORE YOU READ

Focus

BELLRINGER

Bellringer Options
Selection Focus Transparency 49
Daily Language Practice Transparency 95
Or display images of outer space and space travel.
Ask: Why do people dream of exploring the stars? What do people hope to discover in space?
As they read, tell students to consider what the story says about the human desire to explore the universe.

Literature Online

Author Search To expand students' appreciation of Arthur C. Clarke, have them access the Web site for additional information and resources.

BEFORE YOU READ

The Sentinel

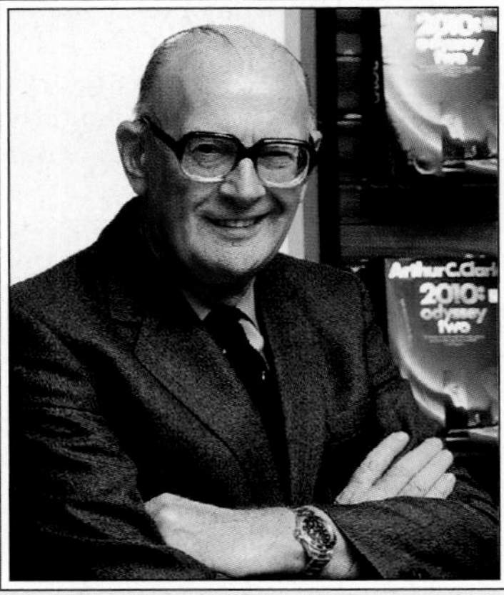

MEET ARTHUR C. CLARKE

Unlike many science fiction authors, Arthur C. Clarke is truly a scientist. In fact, in 1945, when he was only twenty-eight years old, he developed the idea for orbital communication satellites, which are indispensable to global communications today.

Imagining the Future Arthur C. Clarke was born in the seaside town of Minehead, England. He was the son of an English farming family and attended schools in his home county until moving to London at the age of nineteen. In London, Clarke pursued his interest in space sciences by joining the British Interplanetary Society and beginning to write science fiction. When World War II started in 1939, Clarke joined the Royal Air Force, eventually becoming an officer in charge of the first radar talk-down equipment, which was used to help pilots land.

In 1945 Clarke initiated a new era of communication when he published a technical paper entitled "Extra-terrestrial Relays" in the British magazine *Wireless World*. The paper introduced his idea of orbital communication satellites. That same year, Clarke also wrote the short story "Rescue Party," which appeared in *Astounding Science* in May 1946.

Milestones in Science Fiction After the war, Clarke resumed his formal studies, obtaining a Fellowship at King's College London. He began publishing stories, and his career blossomed. He quickly emerged as a prolific and renowned science fiction writer. His works have been credited with inspiring space exploration and missions such as NASA's Apollo moon landings. His short story "The Sentinel" inspired legendary filmmaker Stanley Kubrick, and the two men worked together to expand the story into the screenplay for the film *2001: A Space Odyssey*. The movie stands as a milestone in science fiction filmmaking and earned Clarke and Kubrick Academy Award nominations.

> *"I've seen far more than I ever imagined would happen. I mean, I never dreamed we would have explored the solar system as we have."*
>
> —Arthur C. Clarke

The Future Is Now Clarke has written more than eighty science fiction books, many of which describe "fantastic" elements that have since become realities, such as lunar landings, orbiting space stations, and computers with artificial intelligence. He has received numerous honors for his work, including a nomination for the Nobel Peace Prize. Since 1956 Clarke has lived in Sri Lanka, keeping in touch with his international friends and colleagues by satellite, fax, and e-mail, all of which he predicted in his early science fiction.

Arthur C. Clarke was born in 1917.

Literature Online **Author Search** For more about Arthur C. Clarke, go to www.glencoe.com.

Selection Skills

The Sentinel

Literary Elements
- Suspense (SE pp. 1125–1136)
- Description (SE p. 1136)

Reading Skills
- Identifying Assumptions (SE pp. 1125–1136)

Vocabulary Skills
- Analogies (SE pp. 1125, 1136)
- Academic Vocabulary (SE p. 1136)

Listening/Speaking/Viewing Skills
- Analyzing Art (SE pp. 1127, 1132; TWE p. 1129)
- Visual Literacy (SE p. 1135)

Writing Skills/Grammar
- Explore Author's Purpose (SE p. 1137)
- Using Infinitives and Infinitive Phrases (SE p. 1137)
- Literary Criticism (SE p. 1137)

LITERATURE PREVIEW

Connecting to the Story

In Clarke's short story, the main character makes a startling discovery thanks to his good instincts. Before you read, think about the following questions:

- Have you ever decided to do something based on your own instincts or intuition?
- Describe a time when you took a risk and were surprised by the outcome.

Building Background

First published in 1951, "The Sentinel" looks ahead to the "future." It takes place on the surface of the moon during the late summer of 1996. Like most of Clarke's fiction, the story presents several science-based concepts that at the time were conjecture—that is, ideas based on incomplete information. Some of the elements of Clarke's fiction, such as space travel and lunar exploration, eventually became realities. The story's ideas about ancient water formations and basic life are similar to some currently developing hypotheses about the surface of Mars.

A sentinel is a person or object stationed to guard against and warn of danger.

Setting Purposes for Reading

Big Idea Our World and Beyond

As you read, notice how the narrator compares living on the Moon with living on Earth.

Literary Element Suspense

Suspense is the growing interest and excitement readers experience while reading a work of literature. To build suspense, a writer may provide just enough information to keep the reader wondering: "What will happen next?"

- See Literary Terms Handbook, p. R17.

LiteratureOnline Interactive Literary Elements Handbook To review or learn more about the literary elements, go to www.glencoe.com.

READING PREVIEW

Reading Strategy Identifying Assumptions

Just as people do in real life, fictional narrators and characters often make assumptions based on their observations, experience, and knowledge. **Identifying assumptions** in a work of literature can help you understand characters and their actions.

Reading Tip: Taking Notes Use a chart to record assumptions made by characters in the story.

Assumption	Why
Narrator assumes he has spotted something worth exploring.	He saw a metallic glitter.

Vocabulary

tantalize (tant′ əl īz′) *v.* to torment or tease by tempting with something and then withholding it; p. 1129 *She tantalized the horse by keeping its hay just out of reach.*

enigma (i nig′ mə) *n.* a mystery; a baffling person or thing; p. 1129 *The stranger kept to himself and remained an enigma to everyone.*

ebb (eb) *v.* to become less or weaker; decline; fail; p. 1131 *As the battery died, the device's power slowly ebbed.*

irrevocably (i rev′ ə kə blē) *adv.* in a way that cannot be revoked or undone; p. 1133 *As a result of the fire, the church was irrevocably damaged.*

Vocabulary Tip: Analogies Analogies are comparisons based on relationships between ideas. On a test, you may be asked to determine the relationship between a pair of words and then show that relationship in a second pair of words.

INDIANA ACADEMIC STANDARDS (pages 1125–1137)

9.3.6 Analyze and trace an author's development of time and sequence, including the use of…foreshadowing…

9.2 Develop [reading] strategies…

9.5.3 Write expository compositions…

9.3 [Identify] story elements such as character [and] setting…

BEFORE YOU READ

Focus

Summary

The story is set in 1996. A team of scientists is living on and exploring the surface of the moon. One morning, the narrator sees a bright metallic flash on the horizon, and he and a fellow scientist go in search of its source. What they find is a mysterious structure that changes their ideas about the moon, the human race, and the universe.

V Vocabulary

Vocabulary File Say: Add these words and definitions to your vocabulary file. For each word, include a sentence that gives you an example of how to use the word. **OL** Students with English language needs should include the pronunciations of these words in their files. **EL**

Literary Elements Have students access the Web site to improve their understanding of suspense.

Selection Resources

Print Materials

- Unit 6 Resources (Fast File), pp. 16–18
- Leveled Vocabulary Development, p. 70
- Selection and Unit Assessments, pp. 189–190
- Selection Quick Checks, p. 95

Transparencies

- Bellringer Options Transparencies: Daily Language Practice Transparency 95
- Literary Elements Transparency 7

Technology

- TeacherWorks Plus™ CD-ROM
- StudentWorks Plus™ CD-ROM
- Presentation Plus!™ CD-ROM
- Literature Online, glencoe.com
- Online Student Edition, mhln.com
- Exam*View*® Assessment Suite CD-ROM
- Vocabulary PuzzleMaker CD-ROM
- Listening Library, disc 2 track 37

Teach

BI **Big Idea**

Our World and Beyond
Answer: *Clarke begins by looking at the moon from far away and then zooms in to the moon's surface, where the action begins.*

Remind students that the story was written in 1951, when space travel and exploration were still a distant possibility. For Clarke's original readers, moon exploration was an idea possible only in stories. **OL**

Readability Scores
Dale-Chall: 8.3
DRP: 63
Lexile: 1240

The Sentinel

Arthur C. Clarke

The next time you see the full moon high in the south, look carefully at its right-hand edge and let your eye travel upward along the curve of the disk. Round about two o'clock you will notice a small, dark oval: anyone with normal eyesight can find it quite easily. It is the great walled plain, one of the finest on the Moon, known as the Mare Crisium[1]—the Sea of Crises. Three hundred miles in diameter, and almost completely surrounded by a ring of magnificent mountains, it had never been explored until we entered it in the late summer of 1996.

Our expedition was a large one. We had two heavy freighters which had flown our supplies and equipment from the main lunar base in the Mare Serenitatis,[2] five hundred miles away. There were also three small rockets which were intended for short-range transport over regions which our surface vehicles couldn't cross. Luckily, most of the Mare Crisium is very flat. There are none of the great crevasses[3] so common and so dangerous elsewhere, and very few craters or mountains of any size. As far as we could tell, our powerful caterpillar tractors would have no difficulty in taking us wherever we wished to go.

I was geologist—or selenologist, if you want to be pedantic[4]—in charge of the group exploring the southern region of the Mare. We had crossed a hundred miles of it in a week, skirting the foothills of the mountains along the shore of what was once the ancient sea, some thousand million years before. When life was beginning on Earth, it was already dying here. The waters were retreating down the flanks of those stupendous cliffs, retreating into the empty heart of the Moon. Over the land which we were crossing, the tideless ocean had once been half a mile deep, and now the only trace of moisture was the hoarfrost one could sometimes find in caves which the searing sunlight never penetrated.

We had begun our journey early in the slow lunar dawn, and still had almost a week of Earth-time before nightfall. Half a dozen times a day we would leave our vehicle and go outside in the space suits to hunt for interesting minerals, or to place markers for the guidance of future travelers. It was an uneventful routine. There is nothing hazardous or even particularly exciting about lunar exploration. We could live comfortably for a month in our pressurized tractors, and if we ran into trouble, we could always radio for help and sit tight until one of the spaceships came to our rescue.

---

1. *[Mare Crisium]* In 1609, when Italian scientist Galileo Galilei first viewed the moon's dark patches through an early telescope, he called them "seas." *Mare* (mär′ ā) is Latin for "sea." Today, these dark areas are known to be broad, lowland plains, but the Latin names given them in the 1600s are still used.
2. *[Mare Serenitatis]* In the early 1970s, Apollo astronauts landed near the Sea of Serenity ("calmness").
3. A *crevasse* (kri vas′) is a deep narrow crack.
4. One who is *pedantic* (pi dan′ tik) pays excessive attention to minor details and formal rules. Such a person would insist that a *geologist* studies the structure and history of Earth, while a *selenologist* studies the Moon.

Big Idea Our World and Beyond *How does this opening paragraph create the effect of transporting the reader to the moon?* **BI**

Additional Support

Skills Practice

READING: Identifying Author's Purpose Most fiction is meant to entertain readers. Science fiction writers, however, may have other purposes in mind. One thing many science fiction writers try to do is answer questions that are beyond the scope of human knowledge.

Ask students what purpose, besides entertaining his readers, Clarke may have had as he wrote the story. As students read, ask them to look for clues that suggest Clarke's purpose. Challenge students to write a statement explaining Clarke's purpose or purposes. **OL**

Man Gazing at a Dark Moon. Paul Anderson.
Viewing the Art: What do you think the man pictured is thinking? Why?

I said just now that there was nothing exciting about lunar exploration, but of course that isn't true. One could never grow tired of those incredible mountains, so much more rugged than the gentle hills of Earth. We never knew, as we rounded the capes and promontories[5] of that vanished sea, what new splendors would be revealed to us. The whole southern curve of the Mare Crisium is a vast delta where a score of rivers once found their way into the ocean, fed perhaps by the torrential rains that must have lashed the mountains in the brief volcanic age when the Moon was young. Each of these ancient valleys was an invitation, challenging us to climb into the unknown uplands beyond. But we had a hundred miles still to cover, and could only look longingly at the heights which others must scale.

5. Points of land that project out into a body of water, *capes* are usually low and flat, whereas *promontories* are elevated.

Teach

Viewing the Art

Answer: *Answers will vary. Students may note the prominence of the planet and the sky and conclude that the figure is dreaming about space.*

In addition to his artwork, Paul Anderson creates historical, news, sports, and entertainment photographs. Anderson's artwork is often characterized by a dreamlike quality. AS

CheckPoint

Use the CheckPoint questions on Presentation Plus! to monitor students' comprehension. These questions can be used with interactive response keypads for immediate student feedback.

English Language Coach

Scientific Terms The first readers of Clarke's story would have struggled with the astronomical and scientific terms. Have students preview the story for words that are unfamiliar and create a log. Refer them to the story's footnotes and a dictionary to learn the words. EL

Differentiated Instruction

Character Traits Suggest that less proficient readers pretend they are casting a movie of the story. Encourage them to form a well-rounded mental image of the characters' appearances and personalities. Then have them think of actors and actresses who might play the characters in a film version of the story. BL

Academic Standards

Additional Support activities on pp. 1126 and 1127 cover the following standards:

Skills Practice: **9.2** Develop strategies such as...identifying and analyzing... purpose...

English Language Coach: **9.1** Use phonics, context clues, and a growing knowledge of English...to determine the meaning of words...

Differentiated Instruction: **9.3.4** Determine characters' traits by what the characters say about themselves in narration...

Teach

BI Big Idea

Our World and Beyond
Answer: *Students may say that the explorers find comfort in a daily routine kept on an Earth timetable.* Point out Clarke's realism here—explorers and settlers always bring their culture and traditions with them when they go to new places. OL

L1 Literary Element

Suspense **Answer:** *He points out a moment he still remembers. Readers don't yet know what happened. This creates suspense.*
Say: Authors may build suspense by emphasizing the normal and then disrupting it. OL

R Reading Strategy

Identifying Assumptions
Answer: *He assumes that the metallic light is from a rock, because he believes that no one has been to the moon before his group; the object must be a natural object.*
Ask: What do you think may be the source of the glitter? *(Students may say a spacecraft that the men do not know about.)* OL

We kept Earth-time aboard the tractor, and precisely at 2200 hours the final radio message would be sent out to Base and we would close down for the day. Outside, the rocks would still be burning beneath the almost vertical sun, but to us it would be night until we awoke again eight hours later. Then one of us would prepare breakfast, there would be a great buzzing of electric razors, and someone would switch on the shortwave radio from Earth. Indeed, when the smell of frying sausages began to fill the cabin, it was sometimes hard to believe that we were not back on our own world—everything was so normal and homely, apart from the feeling of decreased weight and the unnatural slowness with which objects fell.

It was my turn to prepare breakfast in the corner of the main cabin that served as a galley. I can remember that moment quite vividly after all these years, for the radio had just played one of my favorite melodies, the old Welsh air "David of the White Rock." Our driver was already outside in his space suit, inspecting our caterpillar treads. My assistant, Louis Garnett, was up forward in the control position, making some belated entries in yesterday's log.

As I stood by the frying pan, waiting, like any terrestrial[6] housewife, for the sausages to brown, I let my gaze wander idly over the mountain walls which covered the whole of the southern horizon, marching out of sight to east and west below the curve of the Moon. They seemed only a mile or two from the tractor, but I knew that the nearest was twenty miles away. On the Moon, of course, there is no loss of detail with distance—none of that almost imperceptible[7] haziness which softens and sometimes transfigures[8] all far-off things on Earth.

Those mountains were ten thousand feet high, and they climbed steeply out of the plain as if ages ago some subterranean eruption had smashed them skyward through the molten crust. The base of even the nearest was hidden from sight by a steeply curving surface of the plain, for the Moon is a very little world, and from where I was standing the horizon was only two miles away.

I lifted my eyes toward the peaks which no man had ever climbed, the peaks which, before the coming of terrestrial life, had watched the retreating oceans sink sullenly into their graves, taking with them the hope and the morning promise of a world. The sunlight was beating against those ramparts[9] with a glare that hurt the eyes, yet only a little way above them the stars were shining steadily in a sky blacker than a winter midnight on Earth.

I was turning away when my eye caught a metallic glitter high on the ridge of a great promontory thrusting out into the sea thirty miles to the west. It was a dimensionless point of light, as if a star had been clawed from the sky by one of those cruel peaks, and I imagined that some smooth rock surface was catching the sunlight and heliographing[10] it straight into my eyes. Such things were not uncommon.

On the Moon, of course, there is no loss of detail with distance . . .

6. *Terrestrial* means "of the earth; earthly."
7. *Imperceptible* means "not noticeable."
8. To *transfigure* a thing is to change its outward appearance, often into something glorious.
9. *Ramparts* are walls or embankments built for protection, as around a castle. Here, metaphorically, the ramparts are the mountain walls.
10. Here, *heliographing* means "reflecting." A *heliograph* is a signaling device that uses mirrors to reflect light from the sun.

Big Idea Our World and Beyond *Why do you think the lunar explorers live much as they would on Earth?* BI

Literary Element Suspense *What does this comment suggest about the moment the narrator is about to describe?* L1

Reading Strategy Identifying Assumptions *What assumption does the narrator make? Why does he make this assumption?* R

Additional Support

Skills Practice

WRITING: Comparing and Contrasting Explain that because the story was written before astronauts actually explored space, Clarke was free to imagine space explorers' daily routines. Students may be interested in learning about how real astronauts eat, cook, groom themselves, and exercise. Suggest that students use the Internet and other reference sources to find out about astronauts' routines. Then have students write about their findings in a brief compare-and-contrast essay. OL

A group of lunar mountains stand on the surface of the moon, creating the ideal lunar landscape. ★

When the Moon is in her second quarter, observers on Earth can sometimes see the great ranges in the Oceanus Procellarum[11] burning with a blue-white iridescence[12] as the sunlight flashes from their slopes and leaps again from world to world. But I was curious to know what kind of rock could be shining so brightly up there, and I climbed into the observation turret and swung our four-inch telescope round to the west.

I could see just enough to **tantalize** me. Clear and sharp in the field of vision, the mountain peaks seemed only half a mile away, but whatever was catching the sunlight was still too small to be resolved.[13] Yet it seemed to have an elusive[14] symmetry, and the summit upon which it rested was curiously flat. I stared for a long time at the glittering **enigma**, straining my eyes into space, until presently a smell of burning from the galley told me that our breakfast sausages had made their quarter-million-mile journey in vain.

11. *Oceanis Procellarum* is the (waterless) Ocean of Storms.
12. *Iridescence* is a display of shimmering and changing colors.

13. Here, *resolved* means "made clearly visible."
14. The precise shape of the object was difficult to identify or grasp (*elusive*).

Literary Element Suspense *What descriptive phrases in this passage help build suspense?* L2

Vocabulary

tantalize (tant′ əl īz′) *v.* to torment or tease by tempting with something and then withholding it

Vocabulary

enigma (i nig′ mə) *n.* a mystery; a baffling person or thing

Teach

L2 Literary Element

Suspense Answer: *Students may suggest these phrases:* elusive symmetry, curiously flat, *and* glittering enigma.
Say: The writer builds suspense and then undercuts it with humor when the narrator lets breakfast burn. OL

★ Viewing the Art

Lunar mountains, also called mons or montes, can be viewed from Earth with simple telescopes. By measuring the shadows of the mountains, their heights can be determined. AS

Differentiated Instruction

Solving Math Problems Students who have strong math and logic skills may enjoy solving math problems related to the story. Have them complete the following calculations. **Ask:** If the mountain is 12,000 feet high and the narrator can scale it in twenty hours, how many feet will he climb per hour? *(600)*

Ask: If a person's weight on the moon is one-sixth of his or her normal weight on earth, how much would a 120-pound man weigh on the moon? *(20 pounds)* Challenge students to create their own story-related math problems and share them with the class. AL

Academic Standards

Additional Support activities on pp. 1128 and 1129 cover the following standards:
Skills Practice: **9.4.4** Use writing to… compile information from primary and secondary print or Internet sources.
Differentiated Instruction: **9.5.8** Write for different purposes…

Teach

R Reading Strategy

Identifying Assumptions

Answer: *He assumes that there has never been any life on the moon except for a few plants. He thinks that sometimes scientists make discoveries when they're not afraid to do foolish things.*

Say: The reader has to trust the narrator because he is a scientist and explorer, and yet, it is clear that the narrator does not know everything. OL

V Vocabulary

Words with Prefixes

Remind students that the prefixes *un-* and *in-* mean "not" or "the reverse of." Point out several words on pages 1130 and 1131 that contain these prefixes—*unscalable, unaccustomed, incorruptible, unchanging,* and *unusual.* The narrator's choice of words suggests that he is succinct. OL

★ Language History

Goose Chase The origin of the expression "a wild goose chase" is unknown, but it first appeared in print in Shakespeare's 1592 tragedy *Romeo and Juliet.* The expression is a vivid one that connotes a foolish and unproductive pursuit. AS

All that morning we argued our way across the Mare Crisium while the western mountains reared higher in the sky. Even when we were out prospecting in the space suits, the discussion would continue over the radio. It was absolutely certain, my companions argued, that there had never been any form of intelligent life on the Moon. The only living things that had ever existed there were a few primitive plants and their slightly less degenerate[15] ancestors. I knew that as well as anyone, but there are times when a scientist must not be afraid to make a fool of himself.

"Listen," I said at last, "I'm going up there, if only for my own peace of mind. That mountain's less than twelve thousand feet high—that's only two thousand under Earth gravity—and I can make the trip in twenty hours at the outside. I've always wanted to go up into those hills, anyway, and this gives me an excellent excuse."

"If you don't break your neck," said Garnett, "you'll be the laughingstock of the expedition when we get back to Base. That mountain will probably be called Wilson's Folly from now on."

"I won't break my neck," I said firmly. "Who was the first man to climb Pico and Helicon?"[16]

"But weren't you rather younger in those days?" asked Louis gently.

15. Here, *degenerate* (di jen′ er it) means "having sunk below a former condition." The idea is that as water vanished, the moon's plant life gradually deteriorated in quality and finally died out.

16. Moon mountains are commonly named after Earth mountains. *Pico* is a mountain in the Azores, a group of islands in the northern Atlantic, and *Helicon* is a peak in Greece.

Reading Strategy Identifying Assumptions *What assumptions does the narrator make about what he has seen and about how discoveries are made?* R

"That," I said with great dignity, "is as good a reason as any for going."

We went to bed early that night, after driving the tractor to within half a mile of the promontory. Garnett was coming with me in the morning; he was a good climber, and had often been with me on such exploits[17] before. Our driver was only too glad to be left in charge of the machine.

At first sight, those cliffs seemed completely unscalable, but to anyone with a good head for heights, climbing is easy on a world where all weights are only a sixth of their normal value. The real danger in lunar mountaineering lies in overconfidence; a six-hundred-foot drop on the Moon can kill you just as thoroughly as a hundred-foot fall on Earth. V

> The real danger in lunar mountaineering lies in overconfidence.

We made our first halt on a wide ledge about four thousand feet above the plain. Climbing had not been very difficult, but my limbs were stiff with the unaccustomed effort, and I was glad of the rest. We could still see the tractor as a tiny metal insect far down at the foot of the cliff, and we reported our progress to the driver before starting on the next ascent.

Inside our suits it was comfortably cool, for the refrigeration units were fighting the sun and carrying away the body heat of our exertions. We seldom spoke to each other, except to pass climbing instructions and to discuss our best plan of ascent. I do not know what Garnett was thinking, probably that this was the craziest goose chase he had ever embarked upon. I more than half agreed with him, but the joy of climbing, the knowledge that no man had ever gone this way before, and the exhilaration of the steadily widening landscape gave me all the reward I needed. ★

I don't think I was particularly excited when I saw in front of us the wall of rock

17. An *exploit* is a bold, daring deed.

Additional Support

Skills Practice

SPEAKING AND LISTENING: Telling a Suspenseful Story Explain that Clarke uses several techniques to create suspense. He piques readers' interest by giving just enough information to keep them guessing what will happen next. He also uses foreshadowing to give clues about future events. Have students use these techniques in their own storytelling. Ask each student to think of a story and tell it to a classmate. Students should use foreshadowing and reveal only enough information to keep listeners interested. Afterwards, listeners should tell storytellers whether their stories were effective. OL

I had first inspected through the telescope from thirty miles away. It would level off about fifty feet above our heads, and there on the plateau would be the thing that had lured me over these barren wastes. It would be, almost certainly, nothing more than a boulder splintered ages ago by a falling meteor, and with its cleavage planes[18] still fresh and bright in this incorruptible, unchanging silence.

There were no handholds on the rock face, and we had to use a grapnel. My tired arms seemed to gain new strength as I swung the three-pronged metal anchor round my head and sent it sailing up toward the stars. The first time it broke loose and came falling slowly back when we pulled the rope. On the third attempt, the prongs gripped firmly and our combined weights could not shift it.

Garnett looked at me anxiously. I could tell that he wanted to go first, but I smiled back at him through the glass of my helmet and shook my head. Slowly, taking my time, I began the final ascent.

Even with my space suit, I weighed only forty pounds here, so I pulled myself up hand over hand without bothering to use my feet. At the rim I paused and waved to my companion, then I scrambled over the edge and stood upright, staring ahead of me.

You must understand that until this very moment I had been almost completely convinced that there could be nothing strange or unusual for me to find here. Almost, but not quite; it was that haunting doubt that had driven me forward. Well, it was a doubt no longer, but the haunting had scarcely begun.

. . . the haunting had scarcely begun.

I was standing on a plateau perhaps a hundred feet across. It had once been smooth—too smooth to be natural—but falling meteors had pitted and scored its surface through immeasurable eons.[19] It had been leveled to support a glittering, roughly pyramidal structure, twice as high as a man, that was set in the rock like a gigantic, many-faceted jewel.

Probably no emotion at all filled my head in those first few seconds. Then I felt a great lifting of my heart, and a strange, inexpressible joy. For I loved the Moon, and now I knew that the creeping moss of Aristarchus and Eratosthenes[20] was not the only life she had brought forth in her youth. The old, discredited dream of the first explorers was true. There had, after all, been a lunar civilization—and I was the first to find it. That I had come perhaps a hundred million years too late did not distress me; it was enough to have come at all.

My mind was beginning to function normally, to analyze and to ask questions. Was this a building, a shrine—or something for which my language had no name? If a building, then why was it erected in so uniquely inaccessible a spot? I wondered if it might be a temple, and I could picture the adepts[21] of some strange priesthood calling on their gods to preserve them as the life of the Moon **ebbed** with the dying oceans, and calling on their gods in vain.

18. Here, *planes* are rock surfaces, exposed as a result of the boulder's splitting, or *cleavage*.

19. An *eon* (ē′ ən) is an indefinitely long period of time.

20. Most moon craters are named for scientists and philosophers, such as these Greek astronomers of the third century B.C. *Aristarchus* was among the first to say that Earth moves around the Sun; *Eratosthenes* accurately calculated Earth's circumference.

21. *Adepts* are experts; here, they are priests.

Literary Element Suspense *How does the narrator's uncertainty help build suspense as he climbs toward the plateau?* **L**

Big Idea Our World and Beyond *Why do you think the narrator is thrilled to have made this discovery?* **BI**

Vocabulary

ebb (eb) *v.* to become less or weaker; decline; fail

Teach

L Literary Element

Suspense **Answer:** *The narrator doesn't know what he is about to discover, and neither does the reader.* **OL**

BI Big Idea

Our World and Beyond

Answer: *He is the first person to make the discovery. Also, humans have long wondered about life elsewhere in the universe; this discovery supports that hypothesis.* **OL**

★ Literary History

Eratosthenes A poet, librarian, and astronomer, Eratosthenes (276–194 B.C.) calculated Earth's circumference and the tilt of its axis. His calculations were not accurate by modern standards, but his work was groundbreaking. **AS**

English Language Coach

Making Discoveries Like the scientists in the story, students from different cultures make discoveries. Ask groups of students with diverse backgrounds to discuss a topic, such as holidays or music. After students discuss the topic, ask them to share one discovery they have made. **EL**

Differentiated Instruction

Latin Invite advanced students to learn more about the Latin words used in the names of the lunar landmarks. Ask students to make a list of the Latin words that appear in the story and research them. Challenge students to find other common words we use today that are derived from Latin roots. **AL**

Academic Standards

Additional Support activities on pp. 1130 and 1131 cover the following standards:

Skills Practice: **9.7.14** Deliver narrative presentations that time the presentation of actions to accommodate time or mood changes.

English Language Coach: **9.7.15** Deliver expository (informational) presentations that anticipate and address the listeners' potential misunderstandings, biases, and expectations…

Differentiated Instruction: **9.1** Use… knowledge of English and other languages to determine the meaning of words…

Teach

R1 Reading Strategy

Identifying Assumptions

Answer: *Because the object is small, it must have been made by people less advanced than humans.*

Ask: Are the narrator's assumptions correct? Why or why not? *(Students may say that beings greater than humans may be responsible.)* OL

★ Viewing the Art

Answer: *The image on page 1129 more closely reflects the setting and mood of the story.*

Georgia O'Keeffe (1887–1986) was inspired by the landscape of the American Southwest. Many of her paintings capture the wide-open feeling of that part of the country. She also made many large-scale, abstract paintings of flowers. AS

Misti Again–A Memory, 1957. Georgia O'Keeffe. Oil on canvas, 10 x 20 in. Collection of the Georgia O'Keeffe Museum, Santa Fe, New Mexico.
Viewing the Art: Compare the mountain and the overall setting and mood in this painting with those of the image on page 1129. Which image more closely reflects the setting and mood of this story? 

I took a dozen steps forward to examine the thing more closely, but some sense of caution kept me from going too near. I knew a little of archaeology, and tried to guess the cultural level of the civilization that must have smoothed this mountain and raised the glittering mirror surfaces that still dazzled my eyes.

The Egyptians could have done it, I thought, if their workmen had possessed whatever strange materials these far more ancient architects had used. Because of the thing's smallness, it did not occur to me that I might be looking at the handiwork of a race more advanced than my own. The idea that the Moon had possessed intelligence at all was still almost too tremendous to grasp, and my pride would not let me take the final, humiliating plunge.

And then I noticed something that set the scalp crawling at the back of my neck—something so trivial and so innocent that many would never have noticed it at all. I have said that the plateau was scarred by meteors; it was also coated inches deep with the cosmic dust that is always filtering down upon the surface of any world where there are no winds to disturb it. Yet the dust and the meteor scratches ended quite abruptly in a wide circle enclosing the little pyramid, as though an invisible wall was protecting it from the ravages of time and the slow but ceaseless bombardment from space.

There was someone shouting in my earphones, and I realized that Garnett had been calling me for some time. I walked unsteadily to the edge of the cliff and signaled him to join me, not trusting myself to speak. Then I went back toward the circle in the dust. I picked up a fragment of splintered rock and tossed it gently toward the shining enigma. If the pebble had vanished at that invisible barrier, I should not have been surprised, but it seemed to hit a smooth, hemispheric surface and slide gently to the ground.

Reading Strategy Identifying Assumptions *What assumption does the narrator make about the civilization that created the structure?* R1

Additional Support

Skills Practice

RESEARCH: Investigating Radiation Explain that a nuclear reactor throws off both radioactive neutrons and gamma rays. Therefore, a reactor must be surrounded by a shield that absorbs the radiation and protects the people who work with it, as well as those who live near it. Have students research a topic related to radiation, such as how nuclear reactors work, how nuclear waste is created and disposed of, or the dangers that radioactivity poses to humans. Have students prepare a brief report in which they share their findings. OL

I knew then that I was looking at nothing that could be matched in the antiquity of my own race. This was not a building, but a machine, protecting itself with forces that had challenged Eternity. Those forces, whatever they might be, were still operating, and perhaps I had already come too close. I thought of all the radiations man had trapped and tamed in the past century. For all I knew, I might be as **irrevocably** doomed as if I had stepped into the deadly, silent aura of an unshielded atomic pile.[22]

I remember turning then toward Garnett, who had joined me and was now standing motionless at my side. He seemed quite oblivious to me, so I did not disturb him but walked to the edge of the cliff in an effort to marshal my thoughts.[23] There below me lay the Mare Crisium—Sea of Crises, indeed—strange and weird to most men, but reassuringly familiar to me. I lifted my eyes toward the crescent Earth, lying in her cradle of stars, and I wondered what her clouds had covered when these unknown builders had finished their work. Was it the steaming jungle of the Carboniferous,[24] the bleak shoreline over which the first amphibians must crawl to conquer the land—or, earlier still, the long loneliness before the coming of life?

Do not ask me why I did not guess the truth sooner—the truth that seems so obvious now. In the first excitement of my discovery, I had assumed without question that this crystalline apparition[25] had been built by some race belonging to the Moon's remote past, but suddenly, and with overwhelming force, the belief came to me that it was as alien to the Moon as I myself.

In twenty years we had found no trace of life but a few degenerate plants. No lunar civilization, whatever its doom, could have left but a single token of its existence.

I looked at the shining pyramid again, and the more I looked, the more remote it seemed from anything that had to do with the Moon. And suddenly I felt myself shaking with a foolish, hysterical laughter, brought on by excitement and overexertion: For I had imagined that the little pyramid was speaking to me and was saying, "Sorry, I'm a stranger here myself."

It has taken us twenty years to crack that invisible shield and reach the machine inside those crystal walls. What we could not understand, we broke at last with the savage might of atomic power and now I have seen the fragments of the lovely, glittering thing I found up there on the mountain.

They are meaningless. The mechanisms—if indeed they are mechanisms—of the pyramid belong to a technology that lies far beyond our horizon, perhaps to the technology of paraphysical forces.[26] ★

The mystery haunts us all the more now that the other planets have been reached and we know that only Earth has ever been the home of intelligent life in our Universe. Nor could any lost civilization of our own world have built that machine, for the thickness of the meteoric dust on the plateau has enabled us to measure its age. It was set there upon

22. *Atomic pile* is another term for a nuclear reactor.
23. Garnett seemed *oblivious to,* or unaware of, the narrator. *To marshal one's thoughts* is to organize and make sense of them.
24. In geologic time, earth's *Carboniferous* (kär′ bə nif′ ər əs) Period was between 280 million and 345 million years ago, when land was covered with lush vegetation and swamps.

25. An *apparition* is a ghost or ghostly vision.
26. *Paraphysical forces* produce ordinary physical effects without using recognizable physical causes. Such effects might include the ability to float in midair, to materialize and dematerialize, and to move objects with the mind.

Big Idea Our World and Beyond *What questions do you have about the narrator's discovery?* **BI**

Literary Element Suspense *How is suspense built in this passage?* **L**

Vocabulary

irrevocably (i rev′ə kə blē) *adv.* in a way that cannot be revoked or undone

Reading Strategy Identifying Assumptions *What assumption does the narrator finally dismiss?* **R2**

Teach

BI Big Idea

Our World and Beyond
Answer: *Student questions should reflect the clues given by the narrator.* **OL**

L Literary Element

Suspense **Answer:** *The narrator's own fear helps build suspense.*
Ask: What techniques does the narrator use to build suspense? *(He withholds information and uses foreshadowing.)* **OL**

R2 Reading Strategy

Identifying Assumptions
Answer: *He dismisses his assumption that the pyramid was created by an ancient lunar civilization.* **OL**

★ Writer's Technique

Sentence Variety Point out that most of the sentences in the story are long, often compound or complex, with interrupters or asides. Then direct students to the three-word sentence "They are meaningless." Stylistically, the sentence is like hitting the brakes. After paragraphs of long, winding sentences, the sentence pulls readers up short and makes them pay attention. **AS**

Reading in the Real World

Career Clarke wrote about astronauts long before real astronauts went into outer space. Students may be curious to learn about the requirements that astronauts must meet in order to pursue an aeronautical career. Invite students to research Web sites and other resources to find out about becoming an astronaut. **OL**

Building Reading Fluency

Reading Aloud The story contains several descriptions of the lunar landscape. Have students work in pairs and choose a favorite passage from the story to share and read aloud. Remind students to use their voices to convey emotion and to build suspense. **BL**

Academic Standards

Additional Support activities on pp. 1132 and 1133 cover the following standards:

Skills Practice: **9.5.9** Write or deliver a research report…

Reading in the Real World: **9.4.6** Synthesize information from multiple sources…

Building Reading Fluency: **9.7** [Develop] speaking skills…in conjunction with…strategies…[for] delivery of oral presentations.

Teach

BI Big Idea

Our World and Beyond
Answer: *Answers will vary. Based on the title of the story, students may predict that the machine was created to watch for something.* OL

L Literary Element

Suspense Answer: *He implies that a major event involving the aliens will happen soon.*
Ask: How does this last sentence make you feel? *(Students may say that the ending is not reassuring; they may feel uneasy or worried.)*
Ask: Is the ending appropriate to what you expected in a science fiction story? *(Students may say that they do not expect a science fiction story to have such an open or ominous ending.)* OL

CheckPoint

Use the CheckPoint questions on Presentation Plus! to check students' mastery of the selection. These questions can be used with interactive response keypads for immediate student feedback.

its mountain before life had emerged from the seas of Earth.

When our world was half its present age, *something* from the stars swept through the Solar System, left this token of its passage, and went again upon its way. Until we destroyed it, that machine was still fulfilling the purpose of its builders; and as to that purpose, here is my guess.

Nearly a hundred thousand million stars are turning in the circle of the Milky Way, and long ago other races on the worlds of other suns must have scaled and passed the heights that we have reached. Think of such civilizations, far back in time against the fading afterglow of Creation, masters of a universe so young that life as yet had come only to a handful of worlds. Theirs would have been a loneliness we cannot imagine, the loneliness of gods looking out across infinity and finding none to share their thoughts.

They must have searched the star clusters as we have searched the planets. Everywhere there would be worlds, but they would be empty or peopled with crawling, mindless things. Such was our own Earth, the smoke of the great volcanoes still staining the skies, when that first ship of the peoples of the dawn came sliding in from the abyss[27] beyond Pluto. It passed the frozen outer worlds, knowing that life could play no part in their destinies. It came to rest among the inner planets, warming themselves around the fire of the Sun and waiting for their stories to begin.

Those wanderers must have looked on Earth, circling safely in the narrow zone between fire and ice, and must have guessed that it was the favorite of the Sun's children. Here, in the distant future, would be intelligence; but there were countless stars before them still, and they might never come this way again.

So they left a sentinel, one of millions they scattered throughout the Universe, watching over all worlds with the promise of life. It was a beacon that down the ages patiently signaled the fact that no one had discovered it.

Perhaps you understand now why that crystal pyramid was set upon the Moon instead of on the Earth. Its builders were not concerned with races still struggling up from savagery. They would be interested in our civilization only if we proved our fitness to survive—by crossing space and so escaping from the Earth, our cradle. That is the challenge that all intelligent races must meet, sooner or later. It is a double challenge, for it depends in turn upon the conquest of atomic energy and the last choice between life and death.

. . . we have set off the fire alarm . . .

Once we had passed that crisis, it was only a matter of time before we found the pyramid and forced it open. Now its signals have ceased, and those whose duty it is will be turning their minds upon Earth. Perhaps they wish to help our infant civilization. But they must be very, very old, and the old are often insanely jealous of the young.

I can never look now at the Milky Way without wondering from which of those banked clouds of stars the emissaries[28] are coming. If you will pardon so commonplace a simile, we have set off the fire alarm and have nothing to do but wait.

I do not think we will have to wait for long. ∾

27. Here, *abyss* (ə bis′) refers to the immeasurably vast reaches of space.

28. An *emissary* is a person or agent sent, often in secret, on an official mission.

Big Idea Our World and Beyond *What purpose do you think the machine was fulfilling?* BI

Literary Element Suspense *Why does Clarke end the story on a suspenseful note?* L

Additional Support

Skills Practice

SPEAKING AND LISTENING: Discussion Group Have students find newspaper, magazine, or online articles about space exploration. Divide the class into small groups to discuss the articles. Students should answer questions such as these: *What is the topic of the article? What problems are addressed? What discoveries have been made?* Students should notice similarities and differences in the ways scientific topics are reported. Ask volunteers to summarize the discussions. OL

AFTER YOU READ

RESPONDING AND THINKING CRITICALLY

Respond

1. If you could leave something on a distant world to be found by an alien civilization, what would it be?

Recall and Interpret

2. (a)Describe the setting of the story. Include details about daily life, as well as about people's ideas and values at the time. (b)What can you infer about life on the Moon from the setting's details?
3. (a)When the narrator makes breakfast, what does he see out the window? How do he and his crew members react? (b)"A scientist must not be afraid to make a fool of himself," says the narrator. How does this sentiment set him apart from his crew members?
4. (a)Why did the narrator experience "a strange, inexpressible joy" upon making his discovery? (b)Early in the story, the narrator states, "There is nothing hazardous or even particularly exciting about lunar exploration." Given the outcome of the story, what do you make of this statement?

Analyze and Evaluate

5. In your opinion, why did the scientists try for twenty years to crack the shield surrounding the machine?
6. Why do you think Clarke chose not to give any definitive answers about the machine's origins or purpose?
7. In your opinion, was the use of atomic power against "the sentinel" appropriate, or should the scientists have left it intact? Explain.

Connect

8. **Big Idea** **Our World and Beyond** A hypothesis is a theory or educated guess about something. If this story were true, would you find its hypothesis reasonable—that "wanderers" from other worlds left sentinels to watch over all worlds that hold the promise of life? Explain.

VISUAL LITERACY: Graphic Organizer

Timeline of a Mystery

As the mystery of "The Sentinel" unfolds, we slowly learn the narrator's hypothesis about the origin and purpose of the machine. The narrator describes his hypothesis in relationship to events in Earth's history. The timeline below marks events as described in the story. After studying the timeline, answer the following questions.

1. Roughly how much time passed between the formation of the earth and the aliens leaving "the sentinel" on the moon?
2. In what year do humans discover "the sentinel"?
3. The sentinel is eventually destroyed by curious humans. If you were going to add the date of the destruction of "the sentinel" to this timeline, where would you place it? Explain.

Story Timeline

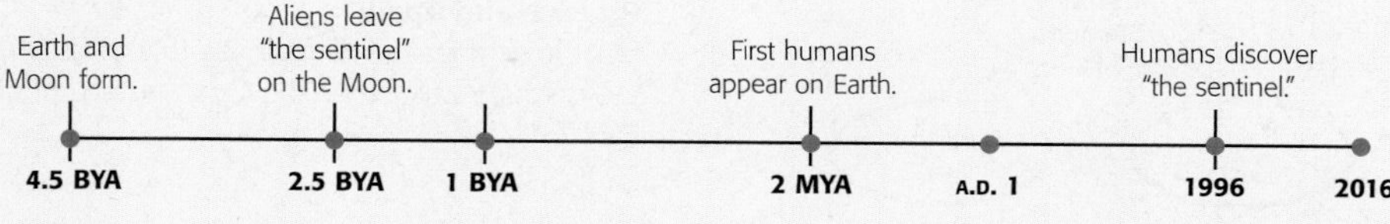

Earth and Moon form.
Aliens leave "the sentinel" on the Moon.
First humans appear on Earth.
Humans discover "the sentinel."
4.5 BYA
2.5 BYA
1 BYA
2 MYA
A.D. 1
1996
2016

BYA = billion years ago
MYA = million years ago

Visual Literacy

1. About two billion years passed between the formation of Earth and the aliens' leaving of "the sentinel" on the Moon.
2. Humans discovered the sentinel in 1996.
3. Students' answers will vary.

AFTER YOU READ

Assess

1. Students should explain their choices.
2. (a) The story is set in an imaginary 1996 on the Moon. It is daytime and will remain light for "almost a week of Earth-time." The scientists assume that earthlings are the only intelligent beings there. When not exploring the Moon's surface, they live in their tractor. (b) The Moon seems silent, bleak, and lifeless.
3. (a) The narrator sees a mysterious glittering object high up on a ridge. The other crew members are not interested in finding the object, but he is intrigued. (b) Unlike his crew members, the narrator is not afraid to take risks.
4. (a) He loves the Moon and is glad it hosted an earlier civilization. He is happy to be the first to discover that fact. (b) Something exciting happens to a man who felt lunar exploration was unexciting.
5. They thought that by cracking the shield, they would release the machine's mysteries.
6. It adds to the mystery of the story and allows readers to use their own imaginations.
7. Students may think the use of atomic power was destructive and cowardly or that it was an appropriate action.
8. Students should provide support for their opinions.

Academic Standards

The Additional Support activity on p. 1134 covers the following standards:

Skills Practice: **9.4.6** Synthesize information from multiple sources… **9.7.1** Summarize a speaker's purpose and point of view…

AFTER YOU READ

Assess

Literary Element

1. Students' answers may include that the narrator says the glitter captivated him so thoroughly that he let breakfast burn.
2. The narrator's belief that he will find nothing makes the actual discovery more exciting. The fact that the narrator pursues his search despite his beliefs also builds suspense. His actions cause readers to ask, "What is going to happen?"

Review: Description

Students should fill their web diagrams with details from the story. Encourage students to select appropriate details and quotations from the story.

Reading Strategy

1. Garnett assumes that they will find nothing atop the mountain and that the narrator's efforts will amount to nothing.
2. The narrator assumes that the destruction of the object will sound an alarm on the planet from which it came. In response to this alarm, the creators will come to Earth.

LITERARY ANALYSIS

Literary Element Suspense

Authors use a variety of techniques to create **suspense** in their work. One technique is the use of foreshadowing, which provides clues to future events and allows readers to make guesses about the outcome.

1. The narrator is cooking breakfast on the morning of his discovery. What specific events and details in this scene add to the suspense of the story?
2. Several times in the story, the narrator says that he and others believed that nothing "strange or unusual" would be found on top of the mountain and that intelligent life had never existed on the Moon. Why might these statements be considered foreshadowing of discoveries to come? What do they add to the overall suspensefulness of the story?

Review: Description

As you learned on pages 1122–1123, **description** is writing that helps readers picture settings, events, and characters. In "The Sentinel" Clarke provides vivid descriptions of elements such as the moonscape, the mysterious pyramid, and the actions of the astronauts. Strong description is especially important in science fiction and fantasy, which may have characters, settings, and actions that are totally unfamiliar to the reader.

Partner Activity Meet with a classmate and choose a story element that Clarke describes in detail, such as the machine he finds. Create a web diagram like the one below, and use it to record the details Clarke uses to describe the element.

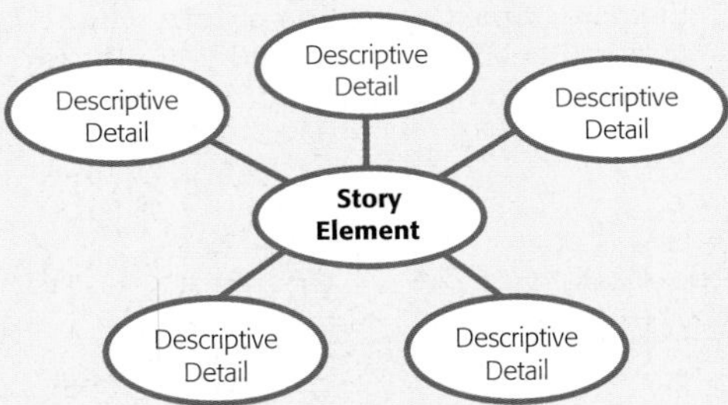

READING AND VOCABULARY

Reading Strategy Identifying Assumptions

The narrator and his colleagues assume that there has never been intelligent life on the Moon. Later in the story, they are shocked to learn otherwise. Explain the assumptions that led characters to make the following conclusions.

1. Garnett concludes that the narrator will be the laughingstock of the expedition following their exploration of the mountain.
2. The narrator concludes that the aliens will come to Earth in the near future.

Vocabulary Practice

Practice with Analogies Choose the word that best completes each analogy.

1. tantalize : discourage :: pull :
   a. yank **b.** drop **c.** push
2. enigma : mystery :: answer :
   a. question **b.** solution **c.** maybe
3. work : relax :: ebb :
   a. flatten **b.** struggle **c.** increase
4. irrevocably : firmly :: similarly :
   a. identically **b.** differently **c.** closely

Academic Vocabulary

Here are two words from the vocabulary list on page R80.

logic (loj′ ik) *n.* a mode of reasoning; valid reasoning

panel (pan′ əl) *n.* a flat, usually rectangular piece forming a raised, recessed, or framed part of the surface in which it is set

Practice and Apply
What **logic** does the narrator use to explain why the machine was left on the Moon instead of on Earth?

Vocabulary

1. c **2.** b **3.** c **4.** a

Academic Vocabulary

He reasons that the aliens would only want to contact a species that was capable of space travel. Therefore, they placed the sentinel on the Moon, where humans could not reach it until they found a way to travel in space.

WRITING AND EXTENDING

Writing About Literature

Explore Author's Purpose The author's purpose is the author's reason for creating a literary work. When exploring the author's purpose, it is useful to examine the reasons for specific choices the writer made. For example, in "The Sentinel," Clarke chose to use a scientist as the narrator and to set the story on the Moon. Exploring why Clarke made these choices can help you determine his purpose in writing the story. Write a brief essay that explores the reasons behind Clarke's choices of setting and character. Be sure to explain how these choices support his overall purpose for writing.

Before you begin writing, organize your ideas using a Venn diagram. Use the circles to list the author's reasons for the following creative choices: using a scientist as narrator and setting the story on the Moon. In the overlapping area, list any purposes that both choices serve.

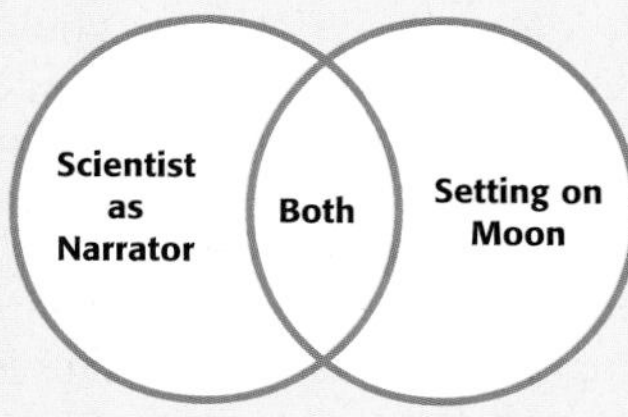

After you complete your draft, meet with a partner to evaluate each other's work and to suggest revisions. Then proofread and edit your draft to correct errors in spelling, grammar, and punctuation.

Literary Criticism

In his introduction to "The Sentinel" in the story collection *Science Fiction: Masters of Today,* Arthur Liebman writes that this story "did more to enhance the popularity of science fiction than perhaps any other short story of recent times. It remains 'must' reading for all science fiction fans." Write a critical review of "The Sentinel" in which you explain why the story might have made science fiction so popular, and why you agree or disagree with Liebman's opinion that it is "must" reading.

GRAMMAR AND STYLE

Clarke's Language and Style

Using Infinitives and Infinitive Phrases An infinitive is a verb form that begins with the word *to* and functions as a noun, an adjective, or an adverb. The most common use of an infinitive is as a noun, as in the three examples below.

An infinitive can come at the end of a sentence. Here, it is being used as an object:

> The astronauts were curious and decided to investigate.

Alternatively, an infinitive can come at the beginning of a sentence. Here, it is being used as a subject:

> To leave was not an option for the lunar explorers.

An infinitive phrase includes the infinitive and any complements and modifiers. In this example, the phrase is used as a noun:

> Wilson and Garnett decided to climb the mountain.

Activity In "The Sentinel," find three examples of sentences containing an infinitive or infinitive phrase used as a noun. Copy the sentences and underline the infinitive or infinitive phrase in each one.

Revising Check

Infinitives and Infinitive Phrases Review your essay about the author's purpose. Are all of the infinitives or infinitive phrases used properly? Correct any sentences that require revision. If you have not used any infinitives or infinitive phrases in your essay, try rewriting one or two sentences to include an infinitive or infinitive phrase where appropriate.

LiteratureOnline Web Activities For eFlashcards, Selection Quick Checks, and other Web activities, go to www.glencoe.com.

AFTER YOU READ

Assess

Writing About Literature

Each student essay should include

- a thesis statement that expresses an opinion clearly and concisely
- brief, well-reasoned explanations for why Clarke made these choices
- a discussion of how the choices support the author's purpose
- examples from the text that support the argument
- a conclusion that convincingly restates the opinion

Clarke's Language and Style

Answers may include the following:

- Indeed, when the smell of frying sausages began to fill the cabin, it was sometimes hard to believe that we were not back on our own world. (p. 1128)
- That I had come perhaps a hundred million years too late did not distress me; it was enough to have come at all. (p. 1131)

LiteratureOnline

Web Activities Have students access the Web site for interactive activities that will help them assess their understanding of the selection.

Literary Criticism

Each critical review should include

- a statement of agreement or disagreement about whether the story is a "must" read
- an explanation of why the story made science fiction popular
- evidence that supports the explanation and the opinion

Focus

Summary

Roger Ebert reviews Stanley Kubrick's 1968 film *2001: A Space Odyssey.* Ebert considers the film's visual style, lack of action, and message.

Teach

R Reading Strategy

Evaluating Argument

Recall that an effective argument expresses an opinion and then supports it with reasons and evidence. Review the different kinds of evidence—facts, statistics, anecdotes, and personal experiences. OL

★ Cultural History

Stanley Kubrick American filmmaker Stanley Kubrick (1928–1999) focused on detail and portrayed an ironic view. His films included political satire, works of literature, and antiwar statements. AS

Readability Scores
Dale-Chall: 6.8
DRP: 62
Lexile: 940

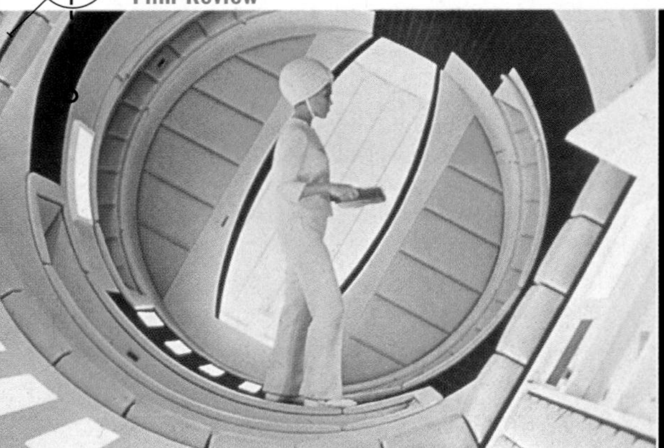

2001: A Space Odyssey

Roger Ebert

Pulitzer Prize Winner

Building Background

The innovative film director Stanley Kubrick began his career as a photographer. In 1953 he entered feature filmmaking. Kubrick based many of his films on literary works. The screenplay for his movie *2001: A Space Odyssey,* was based on Arthur C. Clarke's short story "The Sentinel." In fact, Kubrick collaborated with the science fiction writer on the project. The following selection is a review of the film by Roger Ebert.

Set a Purpose for Reading

Read to discover how Roger Ebert supports his opinion of the film *2001: A Space Odyssey.*

Reading Strategy

Evaluating Argument

Evaluating argument requires you to make a judgment about an author's opinion and how it is supported. Consider the evidence used by the author to support his or her opinion, as well as the author's chain of reasoning. Are the author's claims fully supported? Do you agree? As you read, take notes on Ebert's opinions and the support he provides for them. Use a graphic organizer like the one below. R

Opinion	Support
the space ships are "out of scale with human concerns."	Ebert says the focus is on machines, not people.

Chicago Sun-Times

April 12, 1968

It was e. e. cummings, the poet, who said he'd rather learn from one bird how to sing than teach 10,000 stars how not to dance. I imagine cummings would not have enjoyed Stanley Kubrick's *2001: A Space Odyssey,* in which stars dance but birds do not sing. ★ The fascinating thing about this film is that it fails on the human level but succeeds magnificently on a cosmic scale.

Kubrick's universe, and the space ships he constructed to explore it, are simply out of scale with human concerns. The ships are perfect, impersonal machines which venture from one planet to another, and if men are tucked away somewhere inside them, then they get there too.

But the achievement belongs to the machine. And Kubrick's actors seem to sense this; they are lifelike but without emotion, like figures in a wax museum. Yet the machines are necessary because man himself is so helpless in the face of the universe.

Kubrick begins his film with a sequence in which one tribe of apes discovers how splendid it is to be able to hit the members of another tribe over the head. Thus do man's ancestors become tool-using animals.

Additional Support

See also Active Learning and Note Taking Guide, pp. 193–197.

Skills Practice

VIEWING: Reviewing *2001: A Space Odyssey* If students are not familiar with Kubrick's film *2001: A Space Odyssey,* they may benefit from viewing scenes that are described in Ebert's review. Show students excerpts from the film, including the scene of the apes as they encounter the monolith and a scene that highlights the movie's special effects, such as the final sequence. Invite students to jot down their responses. In a class discussion, have them compare their reactions to Ebert's. OL

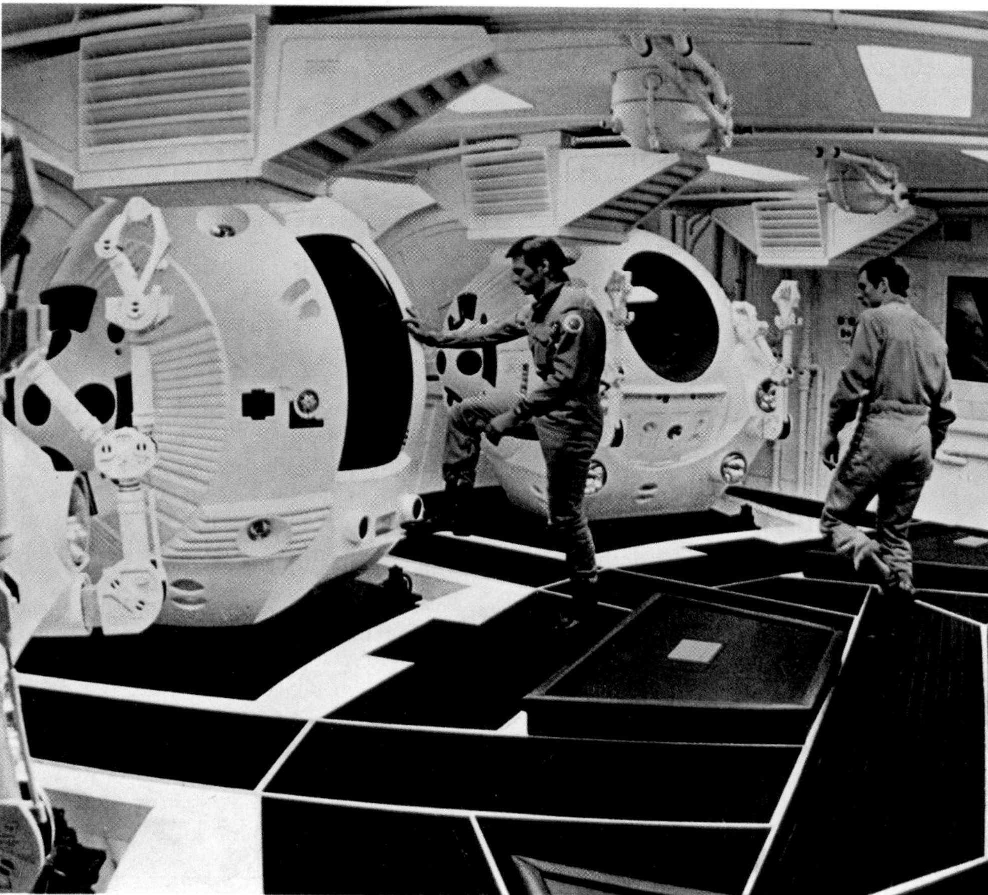

Scene from the film: *2001: A Space Odyssey.* 

At the same time, a strange monolith[1] appears on Earth. Until this moment in the film, we have seen only natural shapes: earth and sky and arms and legs. The shock of the monolith's straight edges and square corners among the weathered rocks is one of the most effective moments in the film. Here, you see, is perfection. The apes circle it warily, reaching out to touch, then jerking away. In a million years, man will reach for the stars with the same tentative motion.

Who put the monolith there? Kubrick never answers, for which I suppose we must be thankful. The action advances to the year 2001, when explorers on the moon find another of the monoliths. This one beams signals toward Jupiter. And man, confident of his machines, brashly follows the trail. **L**

Only at this point does a plot develop. The ship is manned by two pilots, Keir Dullea and Gary Lockwood. Three scientists are put on board in suspended animation to conserve supplies. The pilots grow suspicious of the computer, "Hal," which runs the ship. But

1. *Monolith* means a large stone block.

Teach

L Literary Element

Tone Point out that Ebert writes in a conversational tone. Draw students' attention to the second paragraph on page 1139, which begins with a question. Discuss how Ebert writes almost as if he's having a conversation with the reader. This highly readable style engages readers and is especially effective for a movie critic, whose job is not only to give opinions but also to inform readers about the content of the movie. **OL**

★ Viewing the Photograph

Stanley Kubrick's 1968 film *2001: A Space Odyssey* was loosely based upon Arthur C. Clarke's short story "The Sentinel." The movie was a collaboration between Kubrick and Clarke; Kubrick wrote the screenplay as Clarke wrote the novel *2001*. **AS**

Differentiated Instruction

Identifying Main Ideas Ebert's discursive style and cultural references may confuse less proficient readers. Students may benefit from working in pairs or small groups to identify the main idea in each paragraph of the review. Ask students to paraphrase the main ideas and to share their paraphrases with the class. **BL**

Academic Standards

Additional Support activities on pp. 1138 and 1139 cover the following standards:

Skills Practice: **9.7.13** Identify the artistic effects of a media presentation...

Differentiated Instruction: **9.2** Develop strategies such as...identifying and analyzing structure, organization, perspective, and purpose...

Assess

1. Students' answers will vary. Some may say that the review makes the film sound unappealing. Others may be interested in seeing how Clarke's short story was made into a film.
2. (a) Ebert thinks that the movie lacks character development and suspense but keeps viewer's interest with fantastic special effects.
(b) He supports his opinion by describing the dull way in which the characters speak and the convincing special effects: "The stars look like stars and outer space is bold and bleak."
3. (a) Ebert does not see any significance in the monolith.
(b) He may be unfamiliar with the story. The monolith in the story was a pyramid that may have been built by intelligent life forms other than human beings.
4. The introductory paragraph is effective because Ebert captures the reader's attention with an intriguing quotation from e. e. cummings and ends the paragraph with a mix of criticism and praise.

they behave so strangely—talking in monotones like characters from *Dragnet*[2]—that we're hardly interested.

There is hardly any character development in the plot, then, and as a result little suspense. What remains fascinating is the fanatic care with which Kubrick has built his machines and achieved his special effects. There is not a single moment, in this long film, when the audience can see through the props. The stars look like stars and outer space is bold and bleak.

Man will eventually outgrow his machines . . .

Some of Kubrick's effects have been criticized as tedious. Perhaps they are, but I can understand his motives. If his space vehicles move with agonizing precision, wouldn't we have laughed if they'd zipped around like props on *Captain Video*?[3] This is how it would really be, you find yourself believing.

In any event, all the machines and computers are forgotten in the astonishing last half-hour of this film, and man somehow comes back into his own. Another monolith is found beyond Jupiter, pointing to the stars. It apparently draws the spaceship into a universe where time and space are twisted.

What Kubrick is saying, in the final sequence, apparently, is that man will eventually outgrow his machines, or be drawn beyond them by some cosmic awareness. He will then become a child again, but a child of an infinitely more advanced, more ancient race, just as apes once became, to their own dismay, the infant stage of man.

And the monoliths? Just road markers, I suppose, each one pointing to a destination so awesome that the traveler cannot imagine it without being transfigured. Or as cummings wrote on another occasion, "listen—there's a good universe next door; let's go." ❧

2. *Dragnet* was a television police drama that aired from 1952 to 1959, and received high television ratings. The actors read from a teleprompter, contributing to their terse speech.
3. *Captain Video* is credited with being the first science fiction program aired on television. The series aired from 1949 to 1955.

RESPONDING AND THINKING CRITICALLY

Respond

1. After reading this review, are you interested in seeing the film *2001: A Space Odyssey*? Why or why not?

Recall and Interpret

2. (a)How does Ebert feel about the interest level of the film? (b)Does he support his opinion well? Explain.
3. (a)What does Ebert think of the monolith? (b)Do you think Ebert understood the context provided by Clarke's short story "The Sentinel"? Explain.

Analyze and Evaluate

4. Is Ebert's introductory paragraph effective? Explain.
5. Ebert wrote his review in 1968. Do you think his opinion of the film would be different today?

Connect

6. Ebert says that there is "little suspense" in the film. Why might the use of suspense have been more effective in the story than in the film? Explain.

INDIANA ACADEMIC STANDARDS (pages 1138–1140)
9.2.7 Evaluate an author's argument...
9.2.6 Critique the logic of functional documents...

For additional assessment, see Selection and Unit Assessments, pp. 191–192.

5. Ebert says that "Kubrick's universe, and the space ships he constructed to explore it, are simply out of scale with human concerns." Today there are space stations. Ebert might now applaud Kubrick's imagination.
6. When Clarke wrote "The Sentinel," he wanted to captivate readers with the element of suspense, and so he wrote the story in such a way that readers would want to keep reading. Kubrick, on the other hand, was more interested in special effects than character development, and so he wasn't concerned with creating a suspenseful movie.

Grammar Workshop

Commas

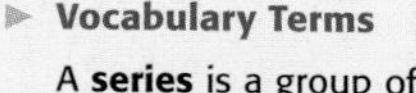

Using Commas in a Series

"When our world was half its present age, something from the stars swept through the Solar System, left this token of its passage, and went again upon its way."

—Arthur C. Clarke, "The Sentinel"

Connecting to Literature In the sentence above, "swept through the Solar System," "left this token of its passage," and "went again upon its way" are items in a series. Each item in this series is a verb phrase: a verb followed by a direct object and/or prepositional phrases. Notice how a comma follows each phrase; the comma separates one phrase in the series from the next. A series can consist of single words, phrases like the verb phrases shown above, or clauses.

Read these problems with commas in a series and their solutions.

Problem 1 There are no commas separating words in a series.
The narrator is curious daring and energetic.

Solution Use a comma after each word in the series that precedes the coordinating conjunction.
The narrator is curious, daring, and energetic.

Problem 2 There are no commas separating clauses in a series.
Each morning the lunar explorers awake at 0600 hours they prepare breakfast and they switch on the shortwave radio.

Solution Use a comma after each clause in the series that precedes the coordinating conjunction.
Each morning the lunar explorers awake at 0600 hours, they prepare breakfast, and they switch on the shortwave radio.

Exercise

Revise for Clarity Rewrite each sentence, adding commas and conjunctions as needed.

1. The freighters had flown supplies equipment and personnel to the Mare Crisium.
2. The explorers left their vehicle to examine the landscape to hunt for interesting minerals and to place markers for future travelers.
3. The narrator was inquisitive he was brave and he was unprepared for what he discovered.

► **Vocabulary Terms**
A **series** is a group of parallel items, such as three adjectives, four infinitive phrases, or three independent clauses in a row.

► **Test-Taking Tip**
When proofreading your writing on a test, check for commas that separate items in a series. If these commas are missing, the sentence may be unclear to your reader.

► **Language Handbook**
For more about commas, see Language Handbook, pp. R53–R54.

Literature Online
eWorkbooks To link to the Grammar and Language eWorkbook, go to www.glencoe.com.

ACADEMIC STANDARDS (page 1141)
9.6.1 Identify and correctly use…the mechanics of punctuation…
9.4.10 Revise writing for…clarity [and] mechanics.

English Language Coach

Writing Descriptions Write the following sentence on the board: *It had been leveled to support a glittering, pyramidal structure, twice as high as a man, that was set in the rock like a gigantic, many-faceted jewel.* Ask students to point out which commas separate words in a series. *(glittering, pyramidal structure; gigantic, many-faceted jewel)* Then have students write a short descriptive paragraph about a place, an object, or a person, using a series of vivid adjectives or adverbs. Have students read their descriptions aloud. EL

Focus

Write the following sentence on the board: The narrator sees the shiny glittering object decides to discover it and reaches a disturbing conclusion. Discuss why the lack of commas makes the sentence hard to understand.

Teach

Using Commas in a Series Offer this strategy for placing commas.
Say: Try saying *and* between words, phrases, or clauses in a series. If the word *and* makes sense, then insert a comma between the words, phrases, or clauses. OL

Assess

1. The freighters had flown supplies, equipment, and personnel to the Mare Crisium.
2. The explorers left their vehicle to examine the landscape, to hunt for interesting minerals, and to place markers for future travelers.
3. The narrator was inquisitive, he was brave, and he was unprepared for what he discovered.

Literature Online
eWorkbooks Have students access the Web site for more practice with commas.

Academic Standards
The Additional Support activity on p. 1141 covers the following standard:
English Language Coach: **9.4.3** Use precise language,…sensory details, and appropriate modifiers.

BEFORE YOU READ

Focus

BELLRINGER

Bellringer Options
Selection Focus Transparency 50
Daily Language Practice Transparency 96
Or show images of trash (such as trash bins or landfills).
Say: Each generation hopes that the following generation will solve the problem of how to get rid of waste.
Ask: How do you think your generation will solve problems it inherits, such as landfills and nuclear waste?
As they read, have students consider whether the people in the village make the right decision about the hole.

Literature Online

Author Search To expand students' appreciation of Shinichi Hoshi, have them access the Web site for additional information and resources.

BEFORE YOU READ

He—y, Come on Ou—t!

MEET SHINICHI HOSHI

Shinichi Hoshi is considered the grandfather of Japanese science fiction. As a result of the U.S. post–World War II occupation of Japan, American science fiction paperbacks circulated throughout Japan. By the time Hoshi graduated from Tokyo University in the late 1940s, the genre was amazingly popular. However, while there were numerous translations of writers such as Isaac Asimov and Fredric Brown, there was a noticeable lack of original Japanese science fiction. When Hoshi began publishing his short stories in the late 1950s, he helped usher in a new era of original Japanese science fiction.

> *"Everyone disliked thinking about the eventual consequences."*
>
> —Shinichi Hoshi
> from "He—y, Come on Ou—t!"

Short-Short Stories Hoshi was born in Tokyo and grew up in the house of his grandparents, Koganei Yoshikiyo, an anthropologist, and Kimiko. He studied agricultural chemistry at Tokyo University, and at the age of twenty-three, took over as president of his family's pharmaceutical company when his father died. After selling the company, Hoshi joined the Japan Flying Saucer Research Club and began writing science fiction. Hoshi published his first story in 1957, when "Sekisutora" was selected for inclusion in the magazine *Hôseki* (The Jewel). At the time, this magazine published mystery stories; original Japanese science fiction was so rare that the genre did not yet have its own magazine.

Hoshi focused on writing short-short stories and made them his specialty. His distinctive short-shorts were usually more abstract, focusing mainly on the story line and minimizing description. His prose has been described as uniquely Japanese and his stories have been likened to haiku—sparse, simple, and indispensable. Hoshi soon emerged as one of the most popular short story writers of postwar Japan. His work became known for combining a deep human understanding and social criticism with strange, surprising, and twisting tales.

1,001 Tales His first collection, *Jinzô bijîn* (An Artificial Beauty, 1961) was nominated for the Naoki Prize, and his collection *Môsô ginkô* (The Delusion Bank, 1968) won the Japan Mystery Writers Award. After finishing his 1,001st story in 1983, Hoshi put down his pen, saying, "One thousand and one stories are enough."

In addition to his one thousand and one stories, Hoshi also wrote several highly regarded longer works. These included the science fiction novel *Koe no ami* (A Net of Voices, 1971) and the biographies *Jinmin wa yowashi, kanri wa tsuyoshi* (The People Are Weak, Bureaucracy Is Strong, 1968), about Hoshi's father, and *Sôfu: Koganei Yoshikiyo no ki* (My Grandfather: An Account of Koganei Yoshikiyo, 1975).

Shinichi Hoshi was born in 1926 and died in 1997.

Literature Online **Author Search** For more about Shinichi Hoshi, go to www.glencoe.com.

Selection Skills

He–y, Come on Ou–t!

Literary Elements
- Moral (SE pp. 1143, 1146, 1147, 1148)
- Character (SE p. 1148)

Reading Skills
- Connecting to Contemporary Issues (SE pp. 1143, 1145, 1146, 1149)

Vocabulary Skills
- Antonyms (SE pp. 1143, 1149)
- Academic Vocabulary (SE p. 1149)

Listening/Speaking/Viewing Skills
- Analyzing Art (SE p. 1147; TWE p. 1144)

Writing Skills/Grammar
- Analyze Satire (SE p. 1149)

Study Skills/Research/Assessment
- Tracking Society's Waste (TWE p. 1146)

LITERATURE PREVIEW

Connecting to the Story

In the story you are about to read, villagers discover a mysterious hole. Before you read the story, think about the following questions:

- What is usually your first reaction when you encounter something that you know nothing about?
- Have you ever discovered that a solution you thought was perfect only caused more problems?

Building Background

The story "He–y, Come on Ou–t!" provides a unique perspective on a growing environmental problem throughout the world: the disposal of waste materials. In the United States alone, people generate more than 200 million tons of trash each year. Unrecyclable solid wastes are incinerated (burned), buried in landfills, or sometimes illegally dumped in oceans or rivers. All of these disposal methods, however, contribute to air, water, and soil pollution, and many landfills are nearing their capacity. In addition, no safe method has ever been found for the disposal of nuclear waste.

Setting Purposes for Reading

Big Idea Our World and Beyond

As you read this story, distinguish its realistic elements from its fantastic elements.

Literary Element Moral

A **moral** is a practical lesson about right and wrong conduct, often found in fables and parables. A **parable** is a simple story that is intended to teach a lesson about human behavior or society. Science fiction tales such as the one you are about to read are sometimes parables. As you read, look for the smaller moral lessons or social commentary within the story that support the larger or overall moral.

- See Literary Terms Handbook, p. R11.

Literature Online Interactive Literary Elements Handbook To review or learn more about the literary elements, go to www.glencoe.com.

READING PREVIEW

Reading Strategy Connecting to Contemporary Issues

Connecting the story to events and issues in today's world can help you understand the author's message. Particularly when reading works that have an unusual or unfamiliar setting, it is important to consider how the events in the story relate to issues in the real world today.

Reading Tip: Making the Link The first step in connecting a story to contemporary issues is to identify the significant issues in the story. As you read, record at least three significant issues or problems that the story raises. After finishing the story, note issues from today's world that relate to each issue in the story.

Vocabulary

plausible (plô′ zə bəl) *adj.* apparently true or acceptable; likely; p. 1145 *The scientist had the most experience and his explanation was the most plausible.*

disperse (dis purs′) *v.* to go off in different directions; to scatter; p. 1145 *When the police arrived, the unruly crowd began to disperse.*

cohort (kō′ hôrt) *n.* a companion, associate, or member of the same group; p. 1146 *Even if it meant that she would be caught and sent to jail, Evelyn promised that she wouldn't leave her cohort behind.*

reverie (rev′ ər ē) *n.* fanciful thinking, especially of pleasant things; a daydream; p. 1147 *He tried to get her attention, but she was lost in reverie.*

Vocabulary Tip: Antonyms Antonyms are words with opposite meanings. *Hot* and *cold* are antonyms, as are *happy* and *sad.*

INDIANA ACADEMIC STANDARDS (pages 1143–1149)

9.3.8 Evaluate the impact of...subtleties...in a text.
9.2 Develop [reading] strategies...
9.5.3 Write...analytical essays...
9.4.2 Establish a coherent thesis that conveys a clear perspective on the subject and maintain a consistent tone and focus throughout the piece of writing.

BEFORE YOU READ

Focus

Summary

In the aftermath of a typhoon, the people of a small Japanese village discover a mysterious hole at the site of a destroyed shrine. The hole seems endlessly deep, and the people decide to use it for waste disposal—a decision they will live to regret.

V Vocabulary

Vocabulary File **Say:** Add these words and definitions to your vocabulary file. For each word, include a sentence that gives you an example of how to use the word. **OL** Students with English language needs should include pronunciations of these words in their files. **EL**

Literary Elements Have students access the Web site to improve their understanding of moral.

Selection Resources

Print Materials
- Unit 6 Resources (Fast File), pp. 21–23
- Leveled Vocabulary Development, p. 71
- Selection and Unit Assessments, pp. 193–194
- Selection Quick Checks, p. 97

Transparencies
- Bellringer Options Transparencies: Daily Language Practice Transparency 96
- Literary Elements Transparency 89

Technology
- TeacherWorks Plus™ CD-ROM
- StudentWorks Plus™ CD-ROM
- Presentation Plus!™ CD-ROM
- Literature Online, glencoe.com
- Online Student Edition, mhln.com
- Exam*View*® Assessment Suite CD-ROM
- Vocabulary PuzzleMaker CD-ROM
- Listening Library, disc 2 track 39

Teach

BI **Big Idea**

Our World and Beyond
Answer: *The story is set in a village in modern times, but the mysterious hole seems to come from another world.*
Say: Science fiction is often set in the real world, but the events that take place would be impossible in the world as we know it. OL

★ Viewing the Art

This illustration is by Ralph B. Fuller, a frequent contributor to *Judge* magazine and co-creator of the comic *Oaky Doaks* with writer Bill McCleery. *Judge,* a national magazine with humor, satire, and cartoons, was published in the early 20th century. AS

Readability Scores
Dale-Chall: 7.7
DRP: 55
Lexile: 890

The professor splits the atom with devastating results. ★

He—y, Come on Ou—t!

Shinichi Hoshi
translated by Stanleigh H. Jones

The typhoon had passed and the sky was a gorgeous blue. Even a certain village not far from the city had suffered damage. A little distance from the village and near the mountains, a small shrine[1] had been swept away by a landslide.

"I wonder how long that shrine's been here."

"Well, in any case, it must have been here since an awfully long time ago."

"We've got to rebuild it right away."

While the villagers exchanged views, several more of their number came over.

"It sure was wrecked."

"I think it used to be right here."

"No, looks like it was a little more over there."

Just then one of them raised his voice. "Hey, what in the world is this hole?"

Where they had all gathered there was a hole about a meter in diameter. They peered in, but it was so dark nothing could be seen. However, it gave one the feeling that it was so deep it went clear through to the center of the earth.

There was even one person who said, "I wonder if it's a fox's hole."

"He—y, come on ou—t!" shouted a young man into the hole. There was no echo from the bottom. Next he picked up a pebble and was about to throw it in.

"You might bring down a curse on us. Lay off," warned an old man, but the younger one energetically threw the pebble in. As before, however, there was no answering response from the bottom. The villagers cut

1. A *shrine* is any site or structure used in worship or devotion.

Big Idea Our World and Beyond *What does the setting of this story have in common with the world you know? What is different?* BI

Additional Support

Skills Practice

READING: Parables Explain that this selection is a parable, a story that was written to teach a lesson about human behavior. Ask students to name other parables they have read. List the parables on the board, and have students briefly describe the plot and the moral of each one. Tell students that as they read, they should think about how the author teaches a moral and whether his method is effective. OL down some trees, tied them with rope and made a fence which they put around the hole. Then they repaired[2] to the village.

"What do you suppose we ought to do?"

"Shouldn't we build the shrine up just as it was over the hole?"

A day passed with no agreement. The news traveled fast, and a car from the newspaper company rushed over. In no time a scientist came out, and with an all-knowing expression on his face he went over to the hole. Next, a bunch of gawking curiosity seekers showed up; one could also pick out here and there men of shifty glances who appeared to be concessionaires.[3] Concerned that someone might fall into the hole, a policeman from the local substation kept a careful watch.

One newspaper reporter tied a weight to the end of a long cord and lowered it into the hole. A long way down it went. The cord ran out, however, and he tried to pull it out, but it would not come back up. Two or three people helped out, but when they all pulled too hard, the cord parted at the edge of the hole. Another reporter, a camera in hand, who had been watching all of this, quietly untied a stout rope that had been wound around his waist.

The scientist contacted people at his laboratory and had them bring out a high-powered bullhorn, with which he was going to check out the echo from the hole's bottom. He tried switching through various sounds, but there was no echo. The scientist was puzzled, but he could not very well give up with everyone watching him so intently. He put the bullhorn right up to the hole, turned it to its highest volume, and let it sound continuously for a long time. It was a noise that would have carried several dozen kilometers above ground. But the hole just calmly swallowed up the sound.

Visual Vocabulary
A *bullhorn* is a handheld microphone combined with a speaker that is used to communicate to a large group of people.

In his own mind the scientist was at a loss, but with a look of apparent composure he cut off the sound and, in a manner suggesting that the whole thing had a perfectly **plausible** explanation, said simply, "Fill it in."

Safer to get rid of something one didn't understand.

The onlookers, disappointed that this was all that was going to happen, prepared to **disperse.** Just then one of the concessionaires, having broken through the throng and come forward, made a proposal.

"Let me have that hole. I'll fill it in for you."

"We'd be grateful to you for filling it in," replied the mayor of the village, "but we can't very well give you the hole. We have to build a shrine there."

"If it's a shrine you want, I'll build you a fine one later. Shall I make it with an attached meeting hall?"

Before the mayor could answer, the people of the village all shouted out.

"Really? Well, in that case, we ought to have it closer to the village."

"It's just an old hole. We'll give it to you!"

So it was settled. And the mayor, of course, had no objection.

The concessionaire was true to his promise. It was small, but closer to the village he did build for them a shrine and an attached meeting hall.

About the time the autumn festival was held at the new shrine, the hole-filling company established by the concessionaire

2. In this context, *repaired* means simply "went."
3. *Concessionaires* (kən sesh′ ə nārz′) are business owners or operators.

Reading Strategy Connecting to Contemporary Issues *In what ways does this paragraph reflect how modern events unfold in the real world?* R

Vocabulary

plausible (plô′ zə bəl) *adj.* apparently true or acceptable; likely

disperse (dis purs′) *v.* to go off in different directions; to scatter

Teach

R Reading Strategy

Connecting to Contemporary Issues **Answer:** *News spreads quickly in the modern world; just one day after the discovery of the hole, the media arrived, as well as a scientist and a group of curiosity seekers.* OL

Writer's Technique

Understatement Hoshi's subtle use of detail and understatement creates humor. The first part of the paragraph shows how people discover that the hole is extremely deep and that objects cannot be retrieved from it. The last detail of a reporter removing a rope from his waist implies that he has changed his mind about being lowered into the hole. AS

CheckPoint

Use the CheckPoint questions on Presentation Plus! to monitor students' comprehension. These questions can be used with interactive response keypads for immediate student feedback.

English Language Coach

Making Discoveries Write the words *scientists, officials, functionaries, authorities, concessionaires, mayor, citizens, police officers, vagrants, students,* and *criminals* on the board. While some of these words will be familiar to English language learners, others will not. Tell students to list the words in their vocabulary notebooks. Then with partners, they can discuss the words and create a working definition of each one. As they read the story, students should look for the words and write down the sentences in which the words first appear. EL

Academic Standards

Additional Support activities on pp. 1144 and 1145 cover the following standards:

Skills Practice: **9.3.5** Compare works that express a universal theme and provide evidence to support the views expressed in each work.

English Language Coach: **9.1** Use phonics, context clues, and a growing knowledge of English…to determine the meaning of words and become fluent readers.

Teach

L1 Literary Element

Moral **Answer:** *Students may be surprised by the concessionaire's decision to get rid of nuclear waste at a site so close to a shrine.* OL

R1 Reading Strategy

Connecting to Contemporary Issues **Answer:** *Students may say that without complete study of the hole and the consequences of dumping waste in it, the decision is shortsighted and motivated by greed.*

Ask: Why do the local people agree to the plan? *(The locals are told that there will be no safety issues and that they will profit.)* OL

R2 Reading Strategy

Connecting to Contemporary Issues **Answer:** *The hole provides the perfect answer to the community's waste disposal problems. Landfills play a similar role in the real world. Garbage is put in landfills and forgotten. People don't think about garbage once it has been dumped.* OL

hung out its small shingle at a shack near the hole.

The concessionaire had his **cohorts** mount a loud campaign in the city. "We've got a fabulously deep hole! Scientists say it's at least five thousand meters deep! Perfect for the disposal of such things as waste from nuclear reactors."

Government authorities granted permission. Nuclear power plants fought for contracts. The people of the village were a bit worried about this, but they consented when it was explained that there would be absolutely no above-ground contamination for several thousand years and that they would share in the profits. Into the bargain, very shortly a magnificent road was built from the city to the village.

Trucks rolled in over the road, transporting lead boxes. Above the hole the lids were opened, and the wastes from nuclear reactors tumbled away into the hole.

From the Foreign Ministry and the Defense Agency boxes of unnecessary classified documents were brought for disposal. Officials who came to supervise the disposal held discussions on golf. The lesser functionaries,[4] as they threw in the papers, chatted about pinball.

The hole showed no signs of filling up. It was awfully deep, thought some; or else it might be very spacious at the bottom. Little by little the hole-filling company expanded its business.

Bodies of animals used in contagious disease experiments at the universities were brought out, and to these were added the unclaimed corpses of vagrants.[5] Better than dumping all of its garbage in the ocean, went the thinking in the city, and plans were made for a long pipe to carry it to the hole.

The hole gave peace of mind to the dwellers of the city. They concentrated solely on producing one thing after another. Everyone disliked thinking about the eventual consequences. People wanted only to work for production companies and sales corporations; they had no interest in becoming junk dealers. But, it was thought, these problems too would gradually be resolved by the hole.

Young girls whose betrothals[6] had been arranged discarded old diaries in the hole. There were also those who were inaugurating new love affairs and threw into the hole old photographs of themselves taken with former sweethearts. The police felt comforted as they used the hole to get rid of accumulations of expertly done counterfeit bills. Criminals breathed easier after throwing material evidence[7] into the hole.

Whatever one wished to discard, the hole accepted it all. The hole cleansed the city of its filth; the sea and sky seemed to have become a bit clearer than before.

Aiming at the heavens, new buildings went on being constructed one after the other.

One day, atop the high steel frame of a new building under construction, a workman was taking a break. Above his head he heard a voice shout:

"He—y, come on ou—t!"

4. *Functionaries* are also officials.

5. *Vagrants* (vā′ grənts) are people who, whether by choice or by circumstance, are without homes and jobs and who wander from place to place, often supporting themselves by begging.

6. Their parents had arranged the girls' *betrothals* (bi trō′ thəlz), or engagements to be married.

7. *Material evidence* would be any object that could directly connect a criminal to a crime.

Literary Element Moral *Is this how you expected the concessionaire to fill the hole? Explain.* L1

Reading Strategy Connecting to Contemporary Issues *Do you think that this is a practical approach toward pollution? Explain.* R1

Vocabulary

cohort (kō′ hôrt) *n.* a companion, associate, or member of the same group

Reading Strategy Connecting to Contemporary Issues *What role does the hole come to play in this community? What plays a similar role in the real world?* R2

Additional Support

Skills Practice

RESEARCH: Tracking Society's Waste Students may be interested in learning more about the garbage their community makes and throws out. Encourage students to use a search engine to find information on waste-related Web sites by typing in the word *garbage, trash,* or *waste.* Challenge students to use the sites and other sources of information to find out more about where local waste products and trash go. Ask students to share their findings in an oral report or visual presentation. OL

The Messenger. René Magritte. Private collection.

Viewing the Art: What might the objects in this sphere represent? In light of this story, what might the sphere itself symbolize? What connection can you draw between the title of the painting and the story's ending? ★

But, in the sky to which he lifted his gaze there was nothing at all. A clear blue sky merely spread over all. He thought it must be his imagination. Then, as he resumed his former position, from the direction where the voice had come, a small pebble skimmed by him and fell on past.

Big Idea Our World and Beyond *This passage bends the rules of reality. Following the logic of this passage, what do you think will happen next?* **BI**

The man, however, was gazing in idle[8] **reverie** at the city's skyline growing ever more beautiful, and he failed to notice. ~

8. Here, *idle* means "useless."

Literary Element Moral *How might this ending be seen as a warning?* **L2**

Vocabulary

reverie (rev′ ər ē) *n.* fanciful thinking, especially of pleasant things; a daydream

Teach

BI Big Idea

Our World and Beyond

Answer: *If later events mirror the earlier events, the cord with a weight will fall, and so will the nuclear waste and pollution dumped into the hole.* **OL**

L2 Literary Element

Moral **Answer:** *It warns that actions have consequences that will force us to take notice eventually.* **OL**

★ Viewing the Art

Answer: *The objects might represent society's garbage. The sphere might symbolize the earth buried in trash. Both might warn about controlling our wastes. The garbage sphere is like the pebble in the story's ending.*

René Magritte (1898–1967) was a prominent Surrealist painter. His art blends fantasy, horror, humor, and danger. **AS**

CheckPoint

Use the CheckPoint questions on Presentation Plus! to check students' mastery of the selection. These questions can be used with interactive response keypads for immediate student feedback.

English Language Coach

Bureaucracy Discuss how students' communities make decisions. Help students draw a flow chart that shows who influences decisions in the village. Compare how decisions are made in the story and the real world. **EL**

Differentiated Instruction

Tracking Story Events Students may benefit from listing, in order, the things that are thrown into the hole. Suggest that students use the list to get a sense of the sequence in which things were thrown into the hole. At the end of the story, ask students to consult their list to predict what may happen next. **BL**

Academic Standards

Additional Support activities on pp. 1146 and 1147 cover the following standards:

Skills Practice: **9.4.4** Compile information from…print or Internet sources.

English Language Coach: **9.7.4** Use…visual aids…

Differentiated Instruction: **9.3.6** Analyze and trace an author's development of time and sequence…

AFTER YOU READ

Assess

1. Most students will be surprised by the shout and the pebble falling from the sky.
2. (a) They are afraid and want to fill it in or fence it off. (b) They want to know more about the hole.
3. (a) He conducts inconclusive echo tests. (b) To fill in the hole (c) His pride won't let him admit that he can't figure out the hole. He'd rather get rid of it.
4. (a) He promises them a new shrine and meeting hall. (b) He knows the hole will be more valuable than the shrine.
5. The pebble is the first thing thrown into the hole and the first to fall from the sky at the end. Its appearance at the end recalls the old man's warning at the start.
6. Students may not have expected the pebble to fall out of the sky; the hole defies the laws of physics.
7. People from all walks of life put things into the hole.
8. The setting helps connect the story's problems to the real-world problem of waste.

AFTER YOU READ

RESPONDING AND THINKING CRITICALLY

Respond

1. Were you surprised by the ending? Why or why not?

Recall and Interpret

2. (a)What is the villagers' first reaction to the hole? (b)Why do the villagers try to measure the hole?
3. (a)How does the scientist try to measure the hole, and what does he learn about it? (b)What does he then tell people to do? (c)Considering what he learned, why does he give instructions to the villagers?
4. (a)How does the concessionaire convince the villagers to let him have the hole? (b)Why is the concessionaire willing to make this offer?

Analyze and Evaluate

5. How does Hoshi use the pebble to connect the beginning of the story to the end of the story?
6. How effective is Hoshi in creating unexpected twists in the story? Explain.
7. How does Hoshi show us that all of society is responsible for what happened to the hole?

Connect

8. **Big Idea** **Our World and Beyond** Why do you think Hoshi chose to place the story in a contemporary setting instead of a more unusual science fiction setting?

LITERARY ANALYSIS

Literary Element Moral

Sometimes the **moral** of a story is explicitly stated, as in the well-known fable by Aesop, "The Hare and the Tortoise," which ends with the moral "Slow and steady wins the race." In other stories, however, the moral is implied rather than directly stated. In science fiction parables such as "He–y, Come on Ou–t!" the moral of the story is usually implied.

1. In your opinion, what is the implied moral of "He–y, Come on Ou–t!"?
2. What smaller lessons and details lead the reader to the final moral of the story?
3. Do you think the moral is a worthwhile one, or one people should listen to? Explain.

Review: Character

As you learned on pages 106–107, a **character** is a person portrayed in a literary work. A main character is central to the story and is usually fully developed. A minor character usually displays few personality traits. In general, Hoshi does not use proper nouns in his writing. He does this for a reason. In fables and parables, characters are typically flat or one-dimensional because they are intended to represent a type of person or part of society.

Partner Activity With a partner, identify the characters in the story. Together, examine what part of society each character might represent. Using a chart like the one below, record the characters and what part of society they represent.

Character	Part of Society

Literary Element

1. There are no easy answers; every action has a consequence.
2. At the end of the story it appears that the garbage put into the hole will come back.
3. Students may say yes; people must make careful decisions; actions taken now affect the future world.

Review: Character

young man, old man, worker	ordinary citizens
scientist and reporter	educated authorities
concessionaire	money maker
mayor	local authority

READING AND VOCABULARY

Reading Strategy Connecting to Contemporary Issues

After identifying the **contemporary issues connected** to the story, you can determine what the author's message is in regard to those issues. The author usually reveals his or her criticism or opinion through the events of the story. For example, if a story about people and technology ends with the technology saving the people, the author probably thinks that technology is good for society.

1. In "He–y, Come on Ou–t!" the pebble does not drop from the sky until long after it is thrown into the hole. (a)What is Hoshi's criticism in regard to waste disposal and protecting the environment? (b)Do you agree or disagree with Hoshi's commentary?
2. Based on what happens in the story, what action do you think Hoshi would want us to take in order to prevent the catastrophe created by the villagers in the story?

Vocabulary Practice

Practice with Antonyms Select the best antonym for the following vocabulary words.

1. plausible	**a.** conceivable	**b.** unlikely
2. disperse	**a.** gather	**b.** dissolve
3. cohort	**a.** enemy	**b.** comrade
4. reverie	**a.** fantasy	**b.** nightmare

Academic Vocabulary

Here is a word from the vocabulary list on page R80. This word will help you think, write, and talk about the selection.

transport (trans pôrt′) *v.* to carry from one place to another; convey.

Practice and Apply
Do you think the villagers should have suspected that the hole would **transport** its contents somewhere else? Explain.

WRITING AND EXTENDING

Writing About Literature

Analyze Satire Satire is a form of writing that ridicules people, practices, or institutions in order to reveal their failings. Satire usually incorporates familiar elements from a society or situation, but portrays them in a comic or hyperbolic way. Write a brief essay explaining why Hoshi's story may be considered a satire. Discuss how the details of the items and the people dumping those items help to build the satire.

Before you begin writing, make a list of the societal flaws that Hoshi points out and a list of elements from the story that are familiar to you. Finally, organize your ideas using a flowchart like the one below.

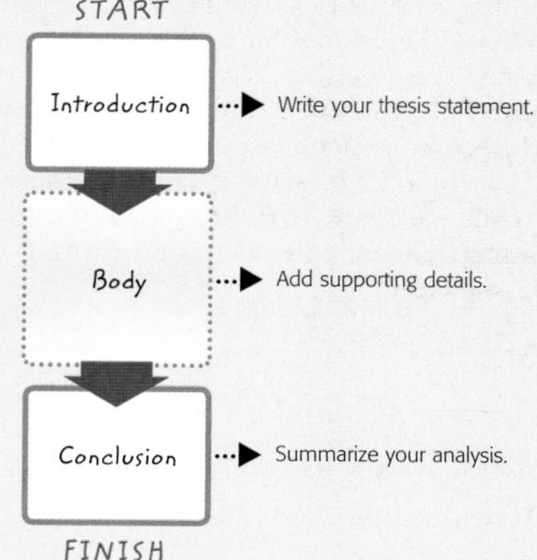

START
Introduction
Write your thesis statement.
Body
Add supporting details.
Conclusion
Summarize your analysis.
FINISH

After you complete your draft, meet with a partner to review each other's work and to suggest revisions. Then proofread and edit your draft to correct errors in spelling, grammar, and punctuation.

Listening and Speaking

Imagine that the construction worker does *not* fail to notice the amazing occurrence at the end of the story. Instead, he reports to a scientist exactly what happened. As the scientist, develop a theory about what happened and explain it to the class.

LiteratureOnline **Web Activities** For eFlashcards, Selection Quick Checks, and other Web activities, go to www.glencoe.com.

AFTER YOU READ

Assess

Reading Strategy

1. (a) We should be cautious because we may not know what consequences will result from things we do now. (b) Students' responses should be based on their understanding of real events.
2. People today should produce less waste and learn more about the effects of the waste that we are disposing.

Vocabulary

1. b **2.** a **3.** a **4.** b

Writing About Literature

Each essay should
- include a main idea that tells why the story is a satire
- provide details from the text that support the main idea
- summarize the argument in the conclusion

Web Activities Have students access the Web site for interactive activities that will help them assess their understanding of the selection.

Academic Vocabulary

Students' answers should suggest that they suspected that the hole's contents would have been carried somewhere else.

Listening and Speaking

Students' theories should
- be based on the text
- incorporate details from the story
- provide plausible explanations
- use clear and understandable language

Focus

BELLRINGER

Bellringer Options
Daily Language Practice Transparency 97
Or **begin a discussion by asking:** Why are names important? What do names and nicknames tell us about people? As they read, have students consider why the people on the island are cautious about sharing their real names.

Literature Online

Author Search To expand students' appreciation of Ursula K. Le Guin, have them access the Web site for additional information and resources.

BEFORE YOU READ

The Rule of Names

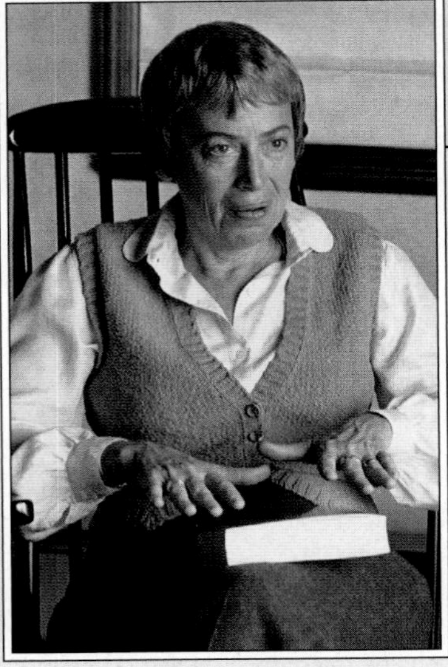

MEET URSULA K. LE GUIN

Ursula K. Le Guin remembers high school as "a living death," but she always loved reading books and writing. For her, "Stopping at the library on my way home saved me."

Le Guin was born Ursula Kroeber in 1929. Her father, Alfred Kroeber, an anthropologist, and her mother, Theodora Covel Brown, a writer, encouraged their daughter to think independently and creatively. Le Guin graduated from Radcliffe College in 1951, and earned her master's degree in French and Italian literature from Columbia University in 1952. The next year, while studying in France on a Fulbright scholarship, she met and married historian Charles Le Guin.

> *"We writers all stand on each other's shoulders, we all use each other's ideas and skills and plots and secrets."*
>
> —Ursula Le Guin

An Offbeat Quality Le Guin spent the next decade balancing writing and child rearing. Between 1953 and 1964, she had two daughters and a son. She also wrote several short stories and five novels. She categorized her early stories as "fairy tales in space suits." Because of her unusual style, Le Guin had a difficult time finding a publisher for her work. But when she began sending her work to science fiction and fantasy publishers, she found success. Le Guin says, "I was always writing about things with an offbeat quality, things that were out of the ordinary. So I sort of drifted into science fiction because they would buy my stuff."

A Communal Enterprise In 1968 Le Guin published the first of a four-book series for young adults, *A Wizard of Earthsea*. The world she created, Earthsea, has been favorably compared with J. R. R. Tolkien's Middle Earth and C. S. Lewis's Narnia.

Le Guin's fiction has been influenced by Native American tales, mythology, and Taoism, which is an ancient Chinese religion. In 1997 Le Guin published her translation of the important Tao book *Tao Te Ching*. As a female writer in the 1970s, she was also affected by the women's movement, and her writing often focuses on a female protagonist. A voracious reader, she calls herself an "absolute fiction addict."

In addition to her science fiction and fantasy writing, Le Guin has also published children's picture books, volumes of poetry, and essays on writing. In her advice to aspiring writers, she is pragmatic: "Well, the secret to writing is writing. . . . Writing is how you be a writer."

Ursula K. Le Guin was born in 1929.

Literature Online **Author Search** For more about Ursula K. Le Guin, go to www.glencoe.com.

Selection Skills

The Rule of Names

Literary Elements
- Humor (SE pp. 1151–1162)
- Dialect (SE p. 1162)

Reading Skills
- Analyzing Sensory Details (SE pp. 1151–1162)

Vocabulary Skills
- Word Origins (SE pp. 1151, 1162)
- Academic Vocabulary (SE p. 1162)

Listening/Speaking/Viewing Skills
- Analyzing Art (SE p. 1155; TWE pp. 1158, 1160)
- Visual Literacy (SE p. 1161)

Writing Skills/Grammar
- Apply Description (SE p. 1163)
- Using Idioms (SE p. 1163)

Study Skills/Research/Assessment
- Internet Connection (SE p. 1163)

LITERATURE PREVIEW

Connecting to the Story

The following story describes a character who does not seem very good at his chosen profession. Before you read the story, think about the following questions:

- When have you done less than your best at a task? Why did you do it that way?
- What skills do you wish you could improve or perfect?

Building Background

Fantasy literature is a genre defined by its use of imaginary worlds and incredible characters and events. Stories containing such elements as monsters, fairies, and heroes with magical powers have existed orally for thousands of years, across cultures, in mythology, folklore, and fairy tales. Contemporary fantasy writers, including Le Guin, transplant the character and plot archetypes of these oral traditions to alternate realities in order to explore timeless issues such as heroism, power, and the nature of evil.

"The Rule of Names" (1964) is set in the imaginary realm of Earthsea. Le Guin continues the story of Earthsea in the novels *A Wizard of Earthsea* (1968), *The Tombs of Atuan* (1972), *The Farthest Shore* (1974), *Tehanu: The Last Book of Earthsea* (1990), and the short story collection *The Other Wind* (2001).

Setting Purposes for Reading

Big Idea Our World and Beyond

As you read "The Rule of Names," notice how Sattins Island is similar to and different from our world.

Literary Element Humor

Humor is the quality of a literary work that makes the characters and their situations seem funny, amusing, or ridiculous. As you read "The Rule of Names," notice when and how Le Guin makes you smile or laugh.

- See Literary Terms Handbook, p. R8.

LiteratureOnline Interactive Literary Elements Handbook To review or learn more about the literary elements, go to www.glencoe.com.

READING PREVIEW

Reading Strategy Analyzing Sensory Details

Sensory details are the words, phrases, and passages in a text that appeal to the five senses. When you **analyze sensory details,** you ask what the details suggest and why the author might have used them.

Reading Tip: Listing Details Use a chart to record the most striking sensory details from the story.

Sight	Hearing	Smell	Taste	Touch
p. 1152 Each breath shot out of his nostrils as a double puff of steam, snow-white in the morning sunshine.				

Vocabulary

elixir (i lik′ sər) *n.* magical cure; p. 1152 *After she broke her leg, Jill found herself wishing there were an elixir for both broken bones and boredom.*

literate (lit′ ər it) *adj.* able to read and write; p. 1153 *Many ancient cultures were not literate but passed their histories down orally.*

spew (spū) *v.* to emerge forcefully, in a stream; p. 1159 *She thought he had turned the water off, but when she unscrewed the faucet, water spewed out.*

cataract (kat′ ə rakt′) *n.* a waterfall; p. 1159 *Well upstream from the cataract, the scouts planned to get out and carry the canoe.*

Vocabulary Tip: Word Origins Learning the origin of a word can lead to a deeper understanding of how that word is used in English today.

INDIANA ACADEMIC STANDARDS (pages 1151–1163)

9.3.8 Interpret and evaluate the impact of…ironies…

9.3.11 Evaluate the aesthetic qualities of style, including the impact of…diction on theme.

9.5.1 Write…short stories that…describe with specific details the sights, sounds, and smells of a scene…

9.4.3 Use…sensory details…

BEFORE YOU READ

Focus

Summary

Mr. Underhill is an ineffective wizard on a small island. No one knows his real name; the Rule of Names forbids anyone to share or learn another person's true name. One day, a bearded stranger arrives. People suspect he is a wizard. He is in search of his stolen treasure. The stranger and Mr. Underhill engage in a battle that yields a great surprise for the islanders.

V Vocabulary

Vocabulary File **Say:** Add these words and definitions to your vocabulary file. For each word, include a sentence that gives you an example of how to use the word. **OL** Students with English language needs should include pronunciations of these words in their files. **EL**

Literary Elements Have students access the Web site to improve their understanding of humor.

Selection Resources

Print Materials

- Unit 6 Resources (Fast File), pp. 24–26
- Leveled Vocabulary Development, p. 72
- Selection and Unit Assessments, pp. 195–196
- Selection Quick Checks, p. 98

Transparencies

- Bellringer Options Transparencies: Daily Language Practice Transparency 97
- Literary Elements Transparency 109

Technology

- TeacherWorks Plus™ CD-ROM
- StudentWorks Plus™ CD-ROM
- Presentation Plus!™ CD-ROM
- Literature Online, glencoe.com
- Online Student Edition, mhln.com
- Exam*View*® Assessment Suite CD-ROM
- Vocabulary PuzzleMaker CD-ROM
- Listening Library, disc 2 track 41–43

Teach

BI1 Big Idea

Our World and Beyond
Ask: What is your first clue that the story will not be realistic? *(Students may say the clues are that Mr. Underhill breathes out snow-white steam, it is bad luck to say good morning, or an adjective could change the weather.)* OL

L Literary Element

Humor Say: Mr. Underhill's ineffectiveness as a wizard is a source of humor in the story. **Ask:** How does the description of Mr. Underhill's ineffectiveness affect your understanding of his character? *(Students may suggest that they do not expect much of him. He sounds weak and strange.)* OL

Readability Scores
Dale-Chall: 7.3
DRP: 60
Lexile: 1050

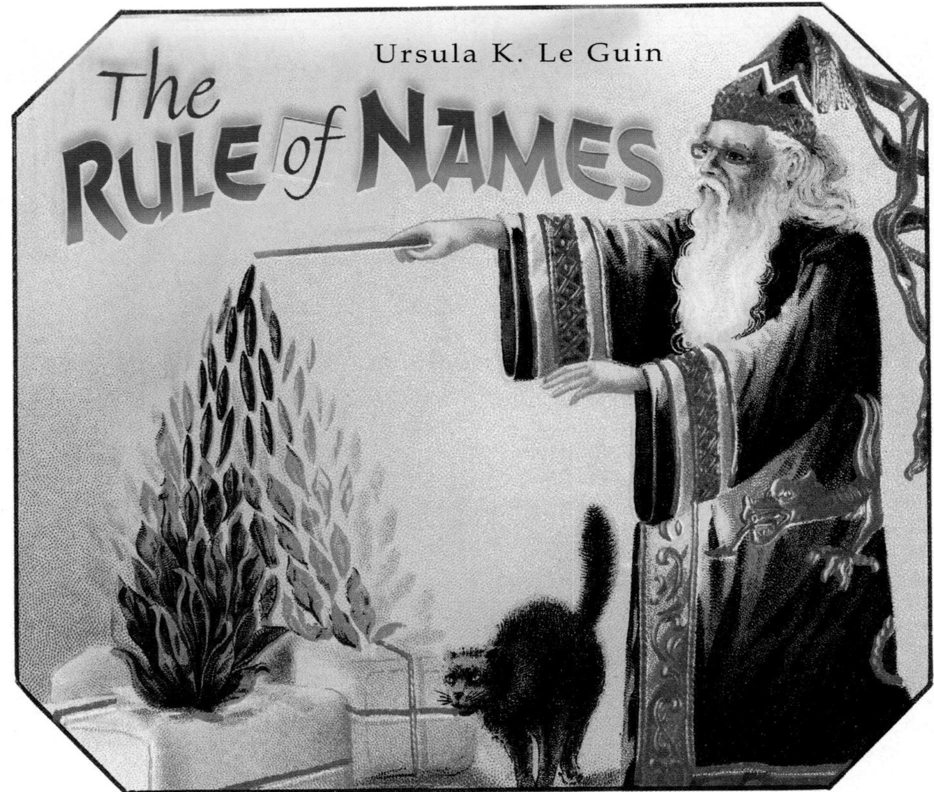

Mr. Underhill came out from under his hill, smiling and breathing hard. Each breath shot out of his nostrils as a double puff of steam, snow-white in the morning sunshine. Mr. Underhill looked up at the bright December sky and smiled wider than ever, showing snow-white teeth. Then he went down to the village.

BI1 "Morning, Mr. Underhill," said the villagers as he passed them in the narrow street between houses with conical, overhanging roofs like the fat red caps of toadstools. "Morning, morning!" he replied to each. (It was of course bad luck to wish anyone a *good* morning; a simple statement of the time of day was quite enough, in a place so permeated[1] with Influences as Sattins Island, where a careless adjective might change the weather for a week.) All of them spoke to him, some with affection, some with affectionate disdain. He was all the little island had in the way of a wizard, and so deserved respect—but how could you respect a little fat man of fifty who waddled along with his toes turned in, breathing steam and smiling? He was no great shakes as a workman either. His fireworks were fairly elaborate but his **elixirs** were weak. Warts he charmed off frequently reappeared after three days; tomatoes he enchanted grew no bigger than cantaloupes; and those rare times when a strange ship stopped at

1. *Permeated* means "filled in every pore."

Vocabulary
elixir (i lik′ sər) n. magical cure

Additional Support

Skills Practice

READING: Monitoring Comprehension Explain that good readers are constantly monitoring, or checking, their comprehension as they read. They reread parts they do not understand. They ask and answer questions about characters and events. Tell students to set up a two-column chart in which they record the events in "The Rule of Names" and their reactions to those events. What do the events tell students about the characters and the world they live in? OL

Sattins Harbor, Mr. Underhill always stayed under his hill—for fear, he explained, of the evil eye.[2] He was, in other words, a wizard the way walleyed[3] Gan was a carpenter: by default. The villagers made do with badly-hung doors and inefficient spells, for this generation, and relieved their annoyance by treating Mr. Underhill quite familiarly, as a mere fellow-villager. They even asked him to dinner. Once he asked some of them to dinner, and served a splendid repast, with silver, crystal, damask,[4] roast goose, and plum pudding with hard sauce;[5] but he was so nervous all through the meal that it took the joy out of it, and besides, everybody was hungry again half an hour afterward. He did not like anyone to visit his cave, not even the anteroom,[6] beyond which in fact nobody had ever got. When he saw people approaching the hill he always came trotting out to meet them. "Let's sit out here under the pine trees!" he would say, smiling and waving towards the fir grove, or if it was raining, "Let's go to the inn, eh?"

Some of the village children, teased by that locked cave, poked and pried and made raids while Mr. Underhill was away; but the small door that led into the inner chamber was spell-shut, and it seemed for once to be an effective spell. Once a couple of boys, thinking the wizard was over on the West Shore curing Mrs. Ruuna's sick donkey, brought a crowbar and a hatchet up there, but at the first whack of the hatchet on the door there came a roar of wrath from inside, and a cloud of purple steam. Mr. Underhill had got home early. The boys fled. He did not come out, and the boys came to no harm, though they said you couldn't believe what a huge hooting howling hissing horrible bellow that little fat man could make unless you'd heard it.

His business in town this day was three dozen fresh eggs and a pound of liver; also a stop at Seacaptain Fogeno's cottage to renew the seeing-charm on the old man's eyes (quite useless when applied to a case of detached retina, but Mr. Underhill kept trying), and finally a chat with old Goody Guld, the concertina-maker's[7] widow. Mr. Underhill's friends were mostly old people. He was timid with the strong young men of the village, and the girls were shy of him. "He makes me nervous, he smiles so much," they all said, pouting, twisting silky ringlets round a finger. "Nervous" was a newfangled word, and their mothers all replied grimly, "Nervous my foot, silliness is the word for it. Mr. Underhill is a very respectable wizard!"

After leaving Goody Guld, Mr. Underhill passed by the school, which was being held this day out on the common.[8] Since no one on Sattins Island was **literate**, there were no books to learn to read from and no desks to carve initials on and no blackboards to erase, and in fact no schoolhouse. On rainy days the children met in the loft of the Communal Barn, and got hay in their pants; on sunny days the schoolteacher, Palani, took them anywhere she felt like. Today, surrounded by thirty interested children under twelve and forty uninterested sheep under five, she was teaching an important item on the curriculum:[9] the Rules of Names. Mr. Underhill, smiling

2. *The evil eye* refers to a superstition that certain people can bring bad luck to others simply by looking at them.
3. *Walleyed* means "suffering a condition of the eye that turns the cornea white."
4. The meal, or *repast,* is served on a *damask,* a woven tablecloth made of heavy cotton, linen, or silk.
5. *Hard sauce* is an uncooked mixture of butter, sugar, and flavorings, used as a topping.
6. An *anteroom* is a small room that opens onto another room, often used as a waiting area.
7. A *concertina* is a handheld musical instrument that resembles an accordion, with buttonlike keys on both ends.
8. Here, *common* means "an area set aside for public use or animal grazing."
9. *Curriculum* means "the list of and guidelines for what is taught at a particular educational institution."

Big Idea Our World and Beyond *Which details in the story so far tell you that it is not taking place in our world?* **BI2**

Reading Strategy Analyzing Sensory Details *To what senses does this passage appeal? Of what does this detail remind you?* **R**

Vocabulary

literate (lit′ ər it) *adj.* able to read and write

Teach

BI2 Big Idea

Our World and Beyond

Answer: *The references to spells and wizards indicate that the story is set in a magical world.* **OL**

R Reading Strategy

Analyzing Sensory Details

Answer: *The passage appeals to the sense of sound. Students might say that the sounds emanating from Mr. Underhill are like those of an animal.* **OL**

Use the CheckPoint questions on Presentation Plus! to monitor students' comprehension. These questions can be used with interactive response keypads for immediate student feedback.

English Language Coach

Setting and Character Students may need help understanding the magical world of this story. Have them create a two-column chart with the headings *setting* and *characters,* and jot down details that will help them picture the place and its people. **EL**

Differentiated Instruction

Visualizing Place and Character
Many of the story's details appeal to the sense of sight. Invite students to make sketches of characters or scenes. Challenge students to identify lines from the story to serve as captions for their sketches. Ask volunteers to share their artwork with the class. **BL**

Academic Standards

Additional Support activities on pp. 1152 and 1153 cover the following standards:

Skills Practice: **9.2** Develop strategies such as asking questions…

English Language Coach: **9.3** [Identify] story elements such as character…and setting…

Differentiated Instruction: **9.3.4** Determine characters' traits by what the characters say about themselves in narration [and] dialogue…

Teach

R Reading Strategy

Analyzing Sensory Details

Answer: *The visual details–the plump, pretty girl; the children and sheep; the backdrop of sky–give the impression that Mr. Underhill likes Palani.* OL

BI1 Big Idea

Our World and Beyond

Answer: *The wind, waves, and boat in this passage all seem familiar. Students see these things in their world, too. The people of Sattins Island speak as we do, and eat similar foods (fish, eggs, liver).* OL

★ Writer's Technique

Capitalization for Effect

Le Guin uses capitalization to show that certain ideas or terms are important to her characters. Examples include *Influences, Rules of Names, Mage, White Magicians,* and *Greenstone.* AS

shyly, paused to listen and watch. Palani, a plump, pretty girl of twenty, made a charming picture there in the wintry sunlight, sheep and children around her, a leafless oak above her, and behind her the dunes and sea and clear, pale sky. She spoke earnestly, her face flushed pink by wind and words. "Now ★ you know the Rules of Names already, children. There are two, and they're the same on every island in the world. What's one of them?"

"It ain't polite to ask anybody what his name is," shouted a fat, quick boy, interrupted by a little girl shrieking, "You can't never tell your own name to nobody my ma says!"

"Yes, Suba. Yes, Popi dear, don't screech. That's right. You never ask anybody his name. You never tell your own. Now think about that a minute and then tell me why we call our wizard Mr. Underhill." She smiled across the curly heads and the woolly backs at Mr. Underhill, who beamed, and nervously clutched his sack of eggs.

"'Cause he lives under a hill!" said half the children.

"But is it his truename?"

"No!" said the fat boy, echoed by little Popi shrieking, "No!"

"How do you know it's not?"

"'Cause he came here all alone and so there wasn't anybody knew his truename so they couldn't tell us, and *he* couldn't—"

"Very good, Suba. Popi, don't shout. That's right. Even a wizard can't tell his truename. When you children are through school and go through the Passage, you'll leave your childnames behind and keep only your truenames, which you must never ask for and never give away. Why is that the rule?"

The children were silent. The sheep bleated gently. Mr. Underhill answered the question: "Because the name is the thing," he said in his shy, soft, husky voice, "and the truename is the true thing. To speak the name is to control the thing. Am I right, Schoolmistress?"

She smiled and curtseyed, evidently a little embarrassed by his participation. And he trotted off towards his hill, clutching his eggs to his bosom. Somehow the minute spent watching Palani and the children had made him very hungry. He locked his inner door behind him with a hasty incantation[10] but there must have been a leak or two in the spell, for soon the bare anteroom of the cave was rich with the smell of frying eggs and sizzling liver.

The wind that day was light and fresh out of the west, and on it at noon a little boat came skimming the bright waves into Sattins Harbor. Even as it rounded the point a sharp-eyed boy spotted it, and knowing, like every child on the island, every sail and spar of the forty boats of the fishing fleet, he ran down the street calling out, "A foreign boat, a foreign boat!" Very seldom was the lonely isle visited by a boat from some equally lonely isle of the East Reach, or an adventurous trader from the Archipelago.[11] By the time the boat was at the pier half the village was there to greet it, and fishermen were following it homewards, and cowherds and clam-diggers and herb-hunters were puffing up and down all the rocky hills, heading towards the harbor.

But Mr. Underhill's door stayed shut.

There was only one man aboard the boat. Old Seacaptain Fogeno, when they told him that, drew down a bristle of white brows over his unseeing eyes. "There's only one kind of man," he said, "that sails the Outer Reach alone. A wizard, or a warlock, or a Mage . . ."

10. Here, an incantation is the words recited of a magical spell.

11. Here, *reach* means "an open stretch of water." Sattins Island is located in the *East Reach*, a body of water located south and east of the largest bodies of land in Earthsea, the Archipelago. An *archipelago* is a large group of islands.

Reading Strategy Analyzing Sensory Details *What do the sensory details in this sentence tell you about how Mr. Underhill feels about Palani?* R

Big Idea Our World and Beyond *In what ways is life on Sattins Island similar to life in our world?* BI1

Additional Support

Skills Practice

VIEWING: Comparing and Contrasting Worlds Le Guin's work is often compared to that of J.R.R. Tolkien, the author of *The Lord of the Rings* series. Bring in one of the film versions of Tolkien's books, and show scenes that depict life in a Hobbit village. Ask students to look for details that are similar to and different from those in Le Guin's story. Ask students to compare and contrast the setting and characters in a class discussion. OL

Fort Utrecht, Java coast in Strait of Bali. Thomas Baines.
Viewing the Art: This painting depicts a real place. Compare and contrast it with the depiction of the fictional Earthsea in the story. ★

So the villagers were breathless hoping to see for once in their lives a Mage, one of the mighty White Magicians of the rich, towered, **V** crowded inner islands of the Archipelago. They were disappointed, for the voyager was quite young, a handsome black-bearded fellow who hailed them cheerfully from his boat, and leaped ashore like any sailor glad to have made port. He introduced himself at once as a sea-peddlar. But when they told Seacaptain Fogeno that he carried an oaken walking-stick around with him, the old man nodded. "Two wizards in one town," he said. "Bad!" And his mouth snapped shut like an old carp's.

As the stranger could not give them his name, they gave him one right away: Blackbeard. And they gave him plenty of attention. He had a small mixed cargo of cloth and sandals and piswi feathers for trimming cloaks and cheap incense and levity stones and fine herbs and great glass beads from Venway—the usual peddlar's lot. Everyone on Sattins Island came to look, to chat with the voyager, and perhaps to buy something—"Just to remember him by!" cackled Goody Guld, who like all the women and girls of the village was smitten with Blackbeard's bold good looks. All the boys hung round him too, to hear him tell of his voyages to far, strange islands of the Reach or describe the great rich islands of the Archipelago, the Inner Lanes, the roadsteads white with ships, and the golden roofs of Havnor. The men willingly listened to his tales; but some of them wondered why a trader should sail alone, and kept their eyes thoughtfully upon his oaken staff.

Big Idea Our World and Beyond *How are the people of Earthsea similar to people you know?* **BI2**

Teach

V Vocabulary

Word Origins Explain that *archipelago,* which means "groups of islands," has its origins in Greek. The root *arch-* means "chief or main," and *pelagos* is a Greek word for the Aegean Sea, which is home to many small islands. **OL**

BI2 Big Idea

Our World and Beyond
Answer: *The people of Earthsea are curious and cautious about strangers.* **OL**

★ Viewing the Art

Answer: *Both are islands with boats and houses, but the village houses have conical red overhanging roofs.*

English painter John Thomas Baines (1820–1875) spent most of his life traveling through the lands that Great Britain held as colonies at the time. His work reflects his travels, often depicting scenes from Australia or the South Pacific. **AS**

English Language Coach

Dialect People with a specific background may speak with certain variations. The children in the story use *ain't* for *isn't* and say *'cause* instead of *because.* Have English learners find other examples of dialect. Ask students to use Standard English to rewrite the sentences. **EL**

Differentiated Instruction

Reader's Log Advanced readers familiar with fantasy/science fiction know that characters may not be what they seem. Ask students to keep a reader's log in which they track their reactions and suspicions. After they read the story, have them summarize their logs. **AL**

Academic Standards

Additional Support activities on pp. 1154 and 1155 cover the following standards:

Skills Practice: **9.3.2** Compare and contrast the presentation of a similar theme or topic across genres... **9.7.13** Identify the artistic effects of a media presentation...

English Language Coach: **9.3.11** Evaluate the aesthetic qualities of style, including the impact of diction...

Differentiated Instruction: **9.5.8** Write for different purposes...

Teach

R1 Reading Strategy

Analyzing Sensory Details

Answer: *Birt's blushing and spilling his tea show that he feels nervous. He speaks negatively about Mr. Underhill, which suggests that he lacks respect for Mr. Underhill's skill as a wizard.*

Say: The narrator says that Birt loves the schoolmistress and seems to be setting up a conflict between Birt and Mr. Underhill. OL

L Literary Element

Humor **Answer:** *It is humorous to think of a wizard using his powers for something as mundane as curing a cat's mange. It is ironic that he could not even do that small task correctly: the cat's fur grew in a different color.* OL

★ Writer's Technique

Indirect Characterization The author uses indirect characterization to tell about Mr. Underhill. Instead of having the narrator describe Mr. Underhill's background, the author has Goody Guld tell it in her own way with her own voice. Goody Guld is a comic character, and her telling adds humor to the story. AS

But all this time Mr. Underhill stayed under his hill.

"This is the first island I've ever seen that had no wizard," said Blackbeard one evening to Goody Guld, who had invited him and her nephew and Palani in for a cup of rushwash tea. "What do you do when you get a toothache, or the cow goes dry?"

"Why, we've got Mr. Underhill!" said the old woman.

"For what that's worth," muttered her nephew Birt, and then blushed purple and spilled his tea. Birt was a fisherman, a large, brave, wordless young man. He loved the schoolmistress, but the nearest he had come to telling her of his love was to give baskets of fresh mackerel to her father's cook.

"Oh, you do have a wizard?" Blackbeard asked. "Is he invisible?"

"No, he's just very shy," said Palani. "You've only been here a week, you know, and we see so few strangers here. . . ." She also blushed a little, but did not spill her tea.

> "WHY, WE'VE GOT MR. UNDERHILL!"

Blackbeard smiled at her. "He's a good Sattinsman, then, eh?"

"No," said Goody Guld, "no more than you are. Another cup, nevvy? keep it in the cup this time. No, my dear, he came in a little bit of a boat, four years ago was it? just a day after the end of the shad[12] run, I recall, for they was taking up the nets over in East Creek, and Pondi Cowherd broke his leg that very morning—five years ago it must be. No, four. No, five it is, 'twas the year the garlic didn't sprout. So he sails in on a bit of a sloop loaded full up with great chests and boxes and says to Seacaptain Fogeno, who wasn't blind then, though old enough goodness knows to be blind twice over, 'I hear tell,' he says, 'you've got no wizard nor warlock at all, might you be wanting one?' 'Indeed, if the magic's white!' says the Captain, and before you could say cuttlefish Mr. Underhill had settled down in the cave under the hill and was charming the mange[13] off Goody Beltow's cat. Though the fur grew in gray, and 'twas an orange cat. Queer-looking thing it was after that. It died last winter in the cold spell. Good Beltow took on so at that cat's death, poor thing, worse than when her man was drowned on the Long Banks, the year of the long herring-runs, when nevvy Birt here was but a babe in petticoats." Here Birt spilled his tea again, and Blackbeard grinned, but Goody Guld proceeded undismayed, and talked on till nightfall. ★

Next day Blackbeard was down at the pier, seeing after the sprung board in his boat which he seemed to take a long time fixing, and as usual drawing the taciturn[14] Sattinsmen into talk. "Now which of these is your wizard's craft?" he asked. "Or has he got one of those the Mages fold up into a walnut shell when they're not using it?"

"Nay," said a stolid[15] fisherman. "She's oop in his cave, under hill."

"He carried the boat he came in up to his cave?"

"Aye. Clear oop. I helped. Heavier as lead she was. Full oop with great boxes, and they full oop with books o' spells, he says. Heavier as lead she was." And the stolid fisherman turned his back, sighing stolidly. Goody Guld's nephew, mending a net nearby, looked up from his work and asked with equal stolidity, "Would ye like to meet Mr. Underhill, maybe?"

12. *Shad* are a type of game fish of the herring family, found in the coastal waters of Europe and North America.

13. *Mange* is a contagious skin disease that affects domestic animals. It is caused by a mite and marked by scaly pimples and loss of hair.

14. *Taciturn* means "uncommunicative" or "reserved."

15. *Stolid* means "showing little emotion."

Reading Strategy Analyzing Sensory Details *What do the sensory details in this sentence tell you about Birt? What do they say about Birt's feelings toward Mr. Underhill?* R1

Literary Element Humor *What is funny about Goody Guld's description of Mr. Underhill and his magic?* L

Additional Support

Academic Standards

The Additional Support activity on p. 1156 covers the following standard:

Skills Practice: **9.7.1** Summarize a speaker's... content...

Skills Practice

LISTENING AND SPEAKING: Active Listening Techniques Explain to students that most listeners remember only a fraction of what they hear. Discuss techniques that can help students remember more of what they hear. Have students close their books as you read aloud Goody Guld's explanation (page 1156) of Mr. Underhill's past. Then ask students to list what they remember on a sheet of paper. Have them check their lists against the text. Discuss which details they forgot and what techniques would help them remember. OL

Blackbeard returned Birt's look. Clever black eyes met candid blue ones for a long moment; then Blackbeard smiled and said, "Yes. Will you take me up to the hill, Birt?"

"Aye, when I'm done with this," said the fisherman. And when the net was mended, he and the Archipelagan set off up the village street towards the high green hill above it. But as they crossed the common Blackbeard said, "Hold on a while, friend Birt. I have a tale to tell you, before we meet your wizard."

"Tell away," says Birt, sitting down in the shade of a live-oak.

"It's a story that started a hundred years ago, and isn't finished yet—though it soon will be, very soon. . . . In the very heart of the Archipelago, where the islands crowd thick as flies on honey, there's a little isle called Pendor. The sealords of Pendor were mighty men, in the old days of war before the League. Loot and ransom and tribute came pouring into Pendor, and they gathered a great treasure there, long ago. Then from somewhere away out in the West Reach, where dragons breed on the lava isles, came one day a very mighty dragon. Not one of those overgrown lizards most of you Outer Reach folk call dragons, but a big, black, winged, wise, cunning monster, full of strength and subtlety, and like all dragons loving gold and precious stones above all things. He killed the Sealord and his soldiers, and the people of Pendor fled in their ships by night. They all fled away and left the dragon coiled up in Pendor Towers. And there he stayed for a hundred years, dragging his scaly belly over the emeralds and sapphires and coins of gold, coming forth only once in a year or two when he must eat. He'd raid nearby islands for his food. You know what dragons eat?"

"YOU KNOW WHAT DRAGONS EAT?"

Birt nodded and said in a whisper, "Maidens."

"Right," said Blackbeard. "Well, that couldn't be endured forever, nor the thought of him sitting on all that treasure. So after the League grew strong, and the Archipelago wasn't so busy with wars and piracy, it was decided to attack Pendor, drive out the dragon, and get the gold and jewels for the treasury of the League. They're forever wanting money, the League is. So a huge fleet gathered from fifty islands, and seven Mages stood in the prows of the seven strongest ships, and they sailed towards Pendor. . . . They got there. They landed. Nothing stirred. The houses all stood empty, the dishes on the tables full of a hundred years' dust. The bones of the old Sealord and his men lay about in the castle courts and on the stairs. And the Tower rooms reeked of dragon. But there was no dragon. And no treasure, not a diamond the size of a poppyseed, not a single silver bead . . . Knowing that he couldn't stand up to seven Mages, the dragon had skipped out. They tracked him, and found he'd flown to a deserted island up north called Udrath; they followed his trail there, and what did they find? Bones again. His bones—the dragon's. But no treasure. A wizard, some unknown wizard from somewhere, must have met him single-handed, and defeated him—and then made off with the treasure, right under the League's nose!"

The fisherman listened, attentive and expressionless.

"Now that must have been a powerful wizard and a clever one, first to kill a dragon, and second to get off without leaving a trace. The lords and Mages of the Archipelago

Big Idea Our World and Beyond *Compare the story Blackbeard is telling with the stories we tell in our world.* BI

Reading Strategy Analyzing Sensory Details *To which of the five senses does this detail appeal? Why do you think the author chose to use this detail at this point in the story?* R2

Teach

BI Big Idea

Our World and Beyond
Answer: *Students may say that we tell similar stories in our world about dragons and treasure, but Blackbeard is telling it as history or truth, rather than as entertainment. In Blackbeard's world, dragons are real.* OL

R2 Reading Strategy

Analyzing Sensory Details
Answer: *This detail appeals to the sense of smell. The author probably used this detail to provide the reader with a vivid description of an unpleasant odor. The detail gives readers a clear sense of how long ago the event took place.* OL

★ Cultural History

Blackbeard There really was a Blackbeard who was associated with lost treasure. Blackbeard was the nickname of Edward Teach or Thatch, a young Briton who became a pirate in the early seventeen hundreds. Blackbeard sailed along the coast of colonial America and harassed passing ships for tolls and booty. He was said to have hidden a great treasure, but no one has ever found it. AS

English Language Coach

Building Vocabulary Give English learners practice with pronunciation and vocabulary. Make English dictionaries available and be sure students know how to use the pronunciation keys. Have groups identify difficult words in the story and look up meanings and pronunciations. EL

Differentiated Instruction

Reading Aloud Ask students who can express shades of meaning to read aloud passages of the story. Assign sections of the story to students, and give them time to prepare. Tape-record or videotape the readings, so that the audience can evaluate the effectiveness of each reading. BL

Academic Standards

Additional Support activities on p. 1157 cover the following standards:

English Language Coach: **9.1** Use phonics, context clues, and a growing knowledge of English…to determine the meaning of words…

Differentiated Instruction: **9.7** [Develop] speaking skills, such as phrasing, pitch, and tone…

Teach

L1 Literary Element

Humor **Answer:** *Blackbeard is suggesting that Mr. Underhill is a powerful wizard who stole his family treasure. He has never seen or met Mr. Underhill, however. Since readers know what Mr. Underhill is like, they find Blackbeard's expectations funny. It is difficult to believe that Mr. Underhill is what Blackbeard says he is.* OL

★ Viewing the Art

Contemporary American illustrator Wayne Anderson is best known for his depictions of fantastic subjects like fairies, elves, and dragons. He frequently illustrates children's books. AS

Sleeping Dragon on Gold Hoard, 20th Century. Wayne Anderson. Pencil and colored crayon on paper. Private collection. 

couldn't track him at all, neither where he'd come from nor where he'd made off to. They were about to give up. That was last spring; I'd been off on a three-year voyage up in the North Reach, and got back about that time. And they asked me to help them find the unknown wizard. That was clever of them. Because I'm not only a wizard myself, as I think some of the oafs[16] here have guessed, but I am also a descendant of the Lords of Pendor. That treasure is mine. It's mine, and knows that it's mine. Those fools of the League couldn't find it, because it's not theirs. It belongs to the House of Pendor, and the great emerald, the star of the hoard, Inalkil the Greenstone, knows its master. Behold!" Blackbeard raised his oaken staff and cried aloud, "Inalkil!" The tip of the staff began to glow green, a fiery green radiance, a dazzling haze the color of April grass, and at the same moment the staff tipped in the wizard's hand, leaning, slanting till it pointed straight at the side of the hill above them.

"It wasn't so bright a glow, far away in Havnor," Blackbeard murmured, "but the staff pointed true. Inalkil answered when I called. The jewel knows its master. And I know the thief, and I shall conquer him. He's a mighty wizard, who could overcome a dragon. But I am mightier. Do you want to know why, oaf? Because I know his name!"

As Blackbeard's tone got more arrogant, Birt had looked duller and duller, blanker and blanker; but at this he gave a twitch, shut his mouth, and stared at the Archipelagan. "How did you . . . learn it?" he asked very slowly.

Blackbeard grinned, and did not answer.

"Black magic?"

16. *Oafs* are clumsy or unintelligent people.

Literary Element Humor *What suggestion is Blackbeard making about Mr. Underhill? How is this humorous?* L1

Additional Support

Skills Practice

WRITING: Mr. Underhill's Perspective There are two stories within the story of "The Rule of Names." Goody Guld and Blackbeard tell tales about events that they have witnessed and provide background to the main story. Have students write their own back-story, or history, of Mr. Underhill from his perspective. Students should provide information that explains his behavior. They should develop a voice that sounds like the character. Have students share their stories with the class. OL

"How else?"

Birt looked pale, and said nothing.

"I am the Sealord of Pendor, oaf, and I will have the gold my fathers won, and the jewels my mothers wore, and the Greenstone! For they are mine. —Now, you can tell your village idiots the whole story after I have defeated this wizard and gone. Wait here. Or you can come and watch, if you're not afraid. You'll never get the chance again to see a great wizard in all his power." Blackbeard turned, and without a backward glance strode off up the hill towards the entrance to the cave.

Very slowly, Birt followed. A good distance from the cave he stopped, sat down under a hawthorn tree, and watched. The Archipelagan had stopped; a stiff, dark figure alone on the green swell of the hill before the gaping cave-mouth, he stood perfectly still. All at once he swung his staff up over his head, and the emerald radiance shone about him as he shouted, "Thief, thief of the Hoard of Pendor, come forth!"

There was a crash, as of dropped crockery, from inside the cave, and a lot of dust came **spewing** out. Scared, Birt ducked. When he looked again he saw Blackbeard still standing motionless, and at the mouth of the cave, dusty and disheveled,[17] stood Mr. Underhill. He looked small and pitiful, with his toes turned in as usual, and his little bowlegs in black tights, and no staff—he never had had one, Birt suddenly thought. Mr. Underhill spoke. "Who are you?" he said in his husky little voice.

"I am the Sealord of Pendor, thief, come to claim my treasure!"

At that, Mr. Underhill slowly turned pink, as he always did when people were rude to him. But he then turned something else. He turned yellow. His hair bristled out, he gave a coughing roar—and was a yellow lion leaping down the hill at Blackbeard, white fangs gleaming.

But Blackbeard no longer stood there. A gigantic tiger, color of night and lightning, bounded to meet the lion. . . . ★

The lion was gone. Below the cave all of a sudden stood a high grove of trees, black in the winter sunshine. The tiger, checking himself in mid-leap just before he entered the shadow of the trees, caught fire in the air, became a tongue of flame lashing out at the dry black branches. . . .

But where the trees had stood a sudden **cataract** leaped from the hillside, an arch of silvery crashing water, thundering down upon the fire. But the fire was gone. . . .

For just a moment before the fisherman's staring eyes two hills rose—the green one he knew, and a new one, a bare, brown hillock ready to drink up the rushing waterfall. That passed so quickly it made Birt blink, and after blinking he blinked again, and moaned, for what he saw now was a great deal worse. Where the cataract had been there hovered a dragon. Black wings darkened all the hill, steel claws reached groping, and from the dark, scaly, gaping lips fire and steam shot out.

Beneath the monstrous creature stood Blackbeard, laughing.

"Take any shape you please, little Mr. Underhill!" he taunted. "I can match you. But the game grows tiresome. I want to look upon my treasure, upon Inalkil. Now, big dragon, little wizard, take your true shape. I command you by the power of your true name—Yevaud!"

Birt could not move at all, not even to blink. He cowered, staring whether he would or not. He saw the black dragon hang there in the air above Blackbeard. He saw the fire lick like many tongues from the scaly mouth, the steam jet from the red nostrils.

17. *Disheveled* means "with clothes and hair in disarray."

Literary Element Humor *Do you find this description of Mr. Underhill humorous? Why or why not?* L2

Vocabulary

spew (spū) *v.* to emerge forcefully, in a stream

Vocabulary

cataract (kat′ ə rakt′) *n.* a waterfall

Teach

L2 Literary Element

Humor Answer: *The image of Mr. Underhill is humorous because Blackbeard was expecting a mighty wizard. Students might feel sorry for Mr. Underhill because he may be killed or hurt.*

Ask: What do you think will happen next? *(Students may predict a fight or that Mr. Underhill will be killed.)* OL

★ Writer's Technique

Ellipses The author uses ellipses to separate actions in the fight. Usually, ellipses indicate words that are omitted from a quotation or show a pause in dialogue. Here they link one action sequence to the next. They suggest that more action is coming. AS

English Language Coach

Transition Words Transition words help link events in stories. Have students write the following words, with space between them: *first, second, then, after,* and *finally.* Ask partners to fill in details from Blackbeard's story. EL

Differentiated Instruction

Multiple Timelines Have less proficient readers work in pairs to create timelines of the events in Goody Guld's and Blackbeard's stories. As a class, create a third timeline that shows the events in "The Rule of Names." Make sure students notice any overlap in events. BL

Academic Standards

Additional Support activities on pp. 1158 and 1159 cover the following standards:

Skills Practice: **9.5.1** Write…narratives or short stories that locate scenes and incidents in specific places…

English Language Coach: **9.1** Use…context clues and a growing knowledge of English to determine the meaning of words…

Differentiated Instruction: **9.3.6** Analyze and trace the author's development of time and sequence…

Teach

L Literary Element

Humor **Answer:** *Students are used to thinking of Mr. Underhill as a comical figure, so when he reveals himself as a dragon, the contrast between appearance and reality is humorous. Also, it is humorous to see Blackbeard outsmarted.* OL

R Reading Strategy

Analyzing Sensory Details
Answer: *The image of Mr. Underhill with "double puffs of steam" coming from his nostrils; the way the young women felt nervous around him; how Mr. Underhill becomes hungry after watching Palani; and the "huge hooting howling hissing horrible bellow" the vandals hear.* OL

★ Viewing the Art

Japanese artist Hashimoto Sadahide (1807–ca. 1878) painted during the period when Japan—long closed to outside trade, travel, and influences—once again allowed contact with the world. His paintings often reflect the new sights that came with this new openness. AS

A Dragon and Two Tigers. Sadahide. 

He saw Blackbeard's face grow white, white as chalk, and the beard-fringed lips trembling.

"Your name is Yevaud!"

"Yes," said a great, husky, hissing voice. "My truename is Yevaud, and my true shape is this shape."

"But the dragon was killed—they found dragon-bones on Udrath Island—"

"That was another dragon," said the dragon, and then stooped like a hawk, talons outstretched. And Birt shut his eyes.

When he opened them the sky was clear, the hillside empty, except for a reddish-blackish trampled spot, and a few talon-marks in the grass.

Birt the fisherman got to his feet and ran. He ran across the common, scattering sheep to right and left, and straight down the village street to Palani's father's house. Palani was out in the garden weeding the nasturtiums.[18] "Come with me!" Birt gasped. She stared. He grabbed her wrist and dragged her with him. She screeched a little, but did not resist. He ran with her straight to the pier, pushed her into his fishing-sloop the *Queenie,* untied the painter,[19] took up the oars and set off rowing like a demon. The last that Sattins Island saw of him and Palani was the *Queenie*'s sail vanishing in the direction of the nearest island westward.

The villagers thought they would never stop talking about it, how Goody Guld's nephew Birt had lost his mind and sailed off with the schoolmistress on the very same day that the peddlar Blackbeard disappeared without a trace, leaving all his feathers and beads behind. But they did stop talking about it, three days later. They had other things to talk about, when Mr. Underhill finally came out of his cave.

Mr. Underhill had decided that since his truename was no longer a secret, he might as well drop his disguise. Walking was a lot harder than flying, and besides, it was a long, long time since he had had a real meal. ∾

18. *Nasturtiums* are flowers with large orange, yellow, or red flowers. The leaves, flowers, and seeds of the plant can be eaten.

19. Here, a *painter* is a rope attached to the bow of a boat for tying it to something.

Literary Element Humor *How does this scene make the whole story ironic?* L

Reading Strategy Analyzing Sensory Details *Now that you know Mr. Underhill's true identity, what specific sensory details do you remember that foreshadow his true form?* R

Additional Support

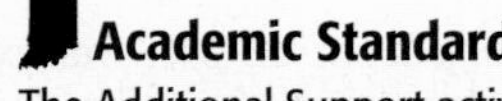

Academic Standards

The Additional Support activity on p. 1160 covers the following standard:

Skills Practice: **9.1** Use phonics, context clues, and a growing knowledge of English...to determine the meaning of words...

Skills Practice

VOCABULARY: Paraphrasing Word Meanings Tell students to look up the definitions and pronunciations of unfamiliar words. Then have partners read aloud the sections from the story that contain the unfamiliar words and then paraphrase them. Have students read aloud a sentence several times if they have trouble with a word's pronunciation. OL

AFTER YOU READ

RESPONDING AND THINKING CRITICALLY

Respond

1. Do you like stories set in alternate worlds? Explain.

Recall and Interpret

2. (a)How do the people on Sattins Island feel about Mr. Underhill? (b)Why do they think he is living on Sattins Island?
3. (a)What are "the rules of names"? (b)What is the consequence if one of these rules is broken?
4. (a)When Birt asks Blackbeard how he learned Mr. Underhill's truename, what is Blackbeard's explanation? (b)Why does Birt react the way he does at the end of the story?

Analyze and Evaluate

5. On page 1152 Le Guin describes Sattins Island as "so permeated with Influences" that "a careless adjective might change the weather for a week." What do you think she means by that? Why do you think the word *influences* is capitalized?
6. Compare the uses of white and black magic as they are described in the story.
7. (a)Why do you think Mr. Underhill disguises himself the way he does? (b)How does your impression of him change over the course of the story?
8. What do you think will happen on Sattins Island after this story ends? Support your answer with evidence from the story.

Connect

9. **Big Idea** **Our World and Beyond** What themes from "The Rule of Names" connect our world with Le Guin's Earthsea?

VISUAL LITERACY: ILLUSTRATIONS

All Dragons Are Not Created Equal

Dragons have appeared in folk and fairy tales for thousands of years. While it is generally agreed that dragons have four legs, sharp talons, and powerful bodies covered in scales, dragons have not played the same role in folklore worldwide. In many Asian cultures, dragons are respected as gods and are often thought to bring power and good luck to humankind. In contrast, Western cultures usually portray dragons as evil creatures that can take any shape at will.

1. How are the pictured dragons similar in appearance? How are they different?
2. Which of the dragons pictured is more like the dragon in the story? Explain.

Visual Literacy

1. Both dragons have long tails and claw feet. The dragon on the left has large wings while the dragon on the right has horns.
2. The dragon on the left is more like the dragon in the story. The dragon in the story is described as hovering above Blackbeard on "black wings." The dragon in the picture on the left is the one with wings.

AFTER YOU READ

Assess

1. Some students like to read about fantasy worlds. Others might prefer realistic stories.
2. (a) They put up with him, although he is not a good wizard. Some speak to him "with affection, some with affectionate disdain."
(b) They think he was driven off his former island by a better wizard.
3. (a) Never ask anyone's name, and never tell your own truename. (b) Someone can use your truename to control you.
4. (a) Black magic (b) Dragons eat maidens, so Birt takes Palani away.
5. Words have power on Sattins Island. "Influences" is capitalized to emphasize it; it is a synonym for *magic.*
6. Wizards use white magic to heal the sick. Black magic is for evil, such as controlling people.
7. (a) In human form, he can hide more easily. (b) At first, he seemed like a shy, ineffective wizard. At the end, he was a scary dragon.
8. The dragon will scare the inhabitants and eat some maidens because he wants a "real meal."
9. The power of language and the illusion of appearances

CheckPoint

Use the CheckPoint questions on Presentation Plus! to check students' mastery of the selection. These questions can be used with interactive response keypads for immediate student feedback.

AFTER YOU READ

Assess

Literary Element

1. Irony; She presents characters in one way and then reverses them.
2. She describes how the "villagers made do with badly-hung doors and inefficient spells," and she has Birt spill his tea twice.

Review: Dialect

Additional sample answers:

- Goody Guld: ". . . I recall, for they was taking up the nets . . ." Grammar: they were
- Stolid Fisherman: "Nay, she's oop in his cave, under hill." Vocabulary: nay = no; Grammar: under hill = under the hill; Pronunciation: oop = up

Reading Strategy

1. Sights: She describes how Mr. Underhill and Blackbeard look. Hearing: She describes sounds from Mr. Underhill's cave, and the characters' voices as they tell stories. The fight scene appeals to both sight and hearing.
2. Appearances can be deceiving. Neither Mr. Underhill nor Blackbeard is who he appears to be. What people say does not always reflect what they think or who they really are.

LITERARY ANALYSIS

Literary Element Humor

Humor often points out human failings. Humorous language might include sarcasm, exaggeration, puns, and verbal irony. Verbal irony occurs when the meaning of a statement is the opposite of what is meant.

1. Which method or methods does Le Guin use to create humor in "The Rule of Names"? Explain.
2. When does Le Guin use humor to point out human failings? Provide two or three examples.

Review: Dialect

As you learned on page 68, **dialect** is a variation of language spoken by people of a particular region or class. Dialects may differ from the standard form of a language in vocabulary, pronunciation, or grammatical form.

Partner Activity With a classmate, identify examples of dialogue in "The Rule of Names" that differ markedly from Standard English. Take turns reading the dialogue aloud. Then create a chart similar to the one below to help analyze the English dialect on Sattins Island. In the left-hand column copy the dialogue. In the right-hand column check which elements of dialect exist in the example and list specific words or phrases.

Dialogue	Analysis of Dialect
"Another cup, nevvy?"	☑ Vocabulary: nevvy = nephew ☐ Punctuation ☐ Grammar

READING AND VOCABULARY

Reading Strategy Analyzing Sensory Details

Analyzing sensory details can help draw out the themes of a story.

1. Which sense or senses do you feel Le Guin was emphasizing in "The Rule of Names"? Explain.
2. What theme or themes was Le Guin building through her emphasis on certain sensory details?

Vocabulary Practice

Practice with Word Origins Choose the word origin for each vocabulary word. Use a dictionary if you need help.

1. elixir
   - **a.** a Greek word for "powder for wounds"
   - **b.** an Old French word meaning "to drown"
2. literate
   - **a.** a Latin word meaning "lit up"
   - **b.** a Latin word for "letters"
3. spew
   - **a.** an Old High German word for "spitting"
   - **b.** an Old French word for "dancing"
4. cataract
   - **a.** a Latin word for "tied wood"
   - **b.** a Greek word for "down-rushing"

Academic Vocabulary

Here are two words from the vocabulary list on page R80. These words will help you think, write, and talk about the selection.

contradict (kon′ trə dikt′) *v.* to suggest that the opposite of something is true

scenario (si nār′ ē ō′) *n.* an imagined sequence of events

Practice and Apply

1. How did Mr. Underhill's awkward appearance **contradict** his true nature?
2. What **scenario** might have resulted if Birt had not taken Palani away from Sattins Island?

Vocabulary

1. a **2.** b **3.** a **4.** b

Academic Vocabulary

1. Mr. Underhill seemed like a shy, inept wizard, but he was actually a shape-shifting dragon.
2. Mr. Underhill, the dragon, might have eaten the maiden Palani.

WRITING AND EXTENDING

Writing About Literature

Apply Description Like many characters in myth and folklore, the dragon in "The Rule of Names" is a shapeshifter, a creature that can change its form at will. The shapeshifter is a character archetype that appears often in myth, folklore, and fantasy stories. Use your prior knowledge of this archetype and your imagination to write a fantasy story in which a shapeshifter plays a central role. Create an original setting for your story, one that differs from our world in distinct ways. Consult "The Rule of Names" as a model for writing sensory descriptions in your story.

Use a chart like the one below to create an outline of your plot.

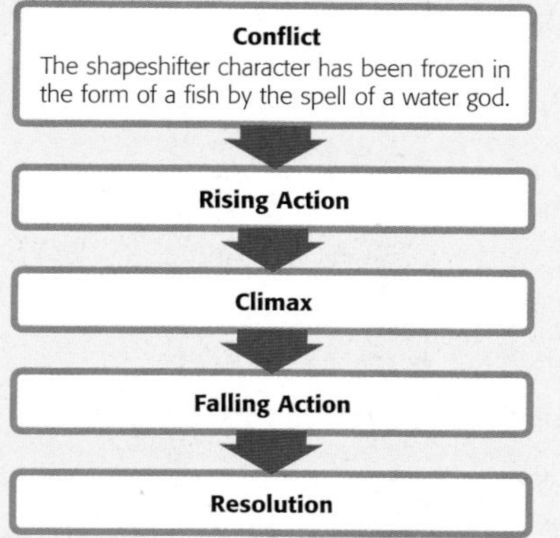

When you have completed the diagram, begin drafting your story. Exchange drafts with a peer, and discuss ways to make each other's work more vivid and engaging for the reader. Then proofread and edit your story to correct errors in spelling, grammar, and punctuation.

Internet Connection

In fantasy literature, the idea that names are sacred is a common theme. Research the meaning of your own name using the Internet, and then share the meaning with the rest of the class. You may also choose a secret name or "truename" that you feel reflects your nature.

GRAMMAR AND STYLE

Le Guin's Language and Style

Using Idioms In "The Rule of Names," Le Guin uses idioms to make her narration and dialogue vivid and lively. Idioms are expressions that are not literally true but that express certain ideas. Idioms are common in casual conversation. For example, when you say you are "sick to death" of something, you are neither sick nor near death, but the expression communicates the idea that you are very tired of a certain subject. Consider how the tone of Le Guin's writing would change if it did not contain the following idioms:

"He was *no great shakes* as a workman either." (p. 1152)

"[T]heir mothers all replied grimly, 'Nervous *my foot,* silliness is the word for it.'" (p. 1153)

"'Indeed, if the magic's white!' says the Captain, and *before you could say cuttlefish* Mr. Underhill had settled down in the cave under the hill . . ." (p. 1156)

"Knowing that he couldn't stand up to seven Mages, the dragon had *skipped out.*" (p. 1157)

Activity With a partner, make a list of familiar idioms. Read through "The Rule of Names" and find places where you can substitute your idioms for some of the more straightforward phrases. Share your substitutions with the class.

Revising Check

Idioms Using the list of idioms you created with your partner, revisit your shapeshifter story and find places where idioms might liven up the description and dialogue. For example, have a certain character use idioms repeatedly to distinguish that character from your other characters.

LiteratureOnline **Web Activities** For eFlashcards, Selection Quick Checks, and other Web activities, go to www.glencoe.com.

AFTER YOU READ

Assess

Writing About Literature

Each story should include
- a vivid setting and characters, one of which is a shape shifter
- a plot that contains a clear conflict and rising action, climax, falling action, and resolution

Le Guin's Language and Style

Students' lists of idioms will vary. Allow students to use a dictionary of idioms to compile their lists.

Students might suggest the following revisions:
- *Mr. Underhill's friends were mostly old fogies* instead of "Mr. Underhill's friends were mostly old people." (p. 1153)
- *By the time the boat was at the pier half the village had turned out with bells on* instead of "By the time the boat was at the pier half the village was there to greet it." (p. 1154)
- *Next day Blackbeard was down at the pier, seeing after the sprung board in his boat which he seemed to be as slow as molasses fixing* instead of "Next day Blackbeard was down at the pier, seeing after the sprung board in his boat which he seemed to take a long time fixing . . . (p. 1156)"

Internet Connection

Students should conduct an online search for the meaning of their given names. Then they should use their imagination to devise a "truename."

Web Activities Have students access the Web site for interactive activities that will help them assess their understanding of the selection.

Focus

BELLRINGER

Bellringer Options
Daily Language Practice Transparency 98
Or **ask:** What are some of the biggest changes you have gone through? How did you feel about these changes? How do these changes affect your future? Tell students that the characters in the following selections face changes in their lives. As students read, encourage them to compare their feelings about change with those of the characters in the selections.

Connecting to the Reading Selections

Allow students to share their responses to the opening questions. Then have students discuss what they already know about Nancy Kress, Naomi Long Madgett, and Alan Lightman.

Comparing Literature Across Genres

Connecting to the Reading Selections

Do you ever feel a desire to look toward the future and not think about the past? What kinds of new beginnings do you find the most exciting? Most of the characters in the three works compared here leave the past behind and focus on the present or the future. As you read, notice the attitudes about novelty and change in each of these selections.

COMPARING THE Big Idea Our World and Beyond

New possibilities are important in each of these selections, whether the characters are living in a world we find familiar or a world with different rules.

COMPARING Description

Description is an author's portrayal of characters, places, objects, or events. Good descriptive writing helps the reader imagine what the characters are experiencing in a story or poem. The sensory images in the works by Madgett, Kress, and Lightman create new worlds for the reader to explore.

COMPARING Authors' Beliefs

It is often possible to infer authors' beliefs about a subject by analyzing their approach to their subject. Clues to an author's beliefs can be found in the tone, mood, and theme. As you read "In Memoriam," "Purchase," and "World Without Memory," identify and compare these authors' beliefs about memory and time.

Additional Support

Academic Standards
The Additional Support activity on p. 1164 covers the following standard:
Skills Practice: **9.4.6** Synthesize information from multiple sources…

Skills Practice

STUDY SKILLS: Graphic Organizer
Help students develop a graphic organizer to aid in comparing the selections. They should make a chart with four columns labeled as follows: *Selection Title, Familiar or Different World, Description,* and *Beliefs.* Have them put the selection titles in the rows of the first column. Invite students to suggest additional columns they think might be helpful. Instruct them to include specific details in their organizers and page numbers for reference. **OL**

BEFORE YOU READ

In Memoriam

MEET NANCY KRESS

Nancy Kress never read science fiction as a child or even took high school chemistry. But when she decided to pick up writing as a hobby, "it came out science fiction."

A shy child, Kress loved reading, telling stories, and playing in the woods near her family's home in East Aurora, New York. As a teenager, she read Nancy Drew, Zane Grey, and Jane Austen, who would later influence her writing style. Kress chose teaching as a profession. She taught fourth grade for several years before leaving the profession to marry and raise children.

From Fantasy to Sci-Fi While at home with her sons during the day, Kress turned to writing as a way to relax and "explore reality." Her first novel, *Prince of the Morning Bells* (1981), was a lighthearted fantasy about a young princess and an enchanted dog. Kress never gave up trying to find a publisher for her manuscript, even though five years passed before it was accepted for publication.

By 1990 Kress was working full-time as a writer. Her first major success was the novella *Beggars in Spain* (1991), which explores a world of genetically modified humans who never need sleep. According to Kress, who requires nine hours of sleep a night, the idea for the book came from her "sheer jealousy" of people who get by on much less. Later, Kress expanded the novella into a novel and then into a trilogy that includes the novels *Beggars and Choosers* (1994) and *Beggars Ride* (1996).

Making Her Mark For the novella *Beggars in Spain,* Kress won a Nebula Award and a Hugo Award. These awards honor groundbreaking work in science fiction and fantasy. She has also won two Nebula awards for short fiction in 1985 and 1997. Kress remains one of the leading science fiction writers of the day. The topics of her novels and stories include genetic engineering, biological weapons, poverty, and alien life forms. She also writes guidebooks for writers containing advice on how to keep readers engaged from beginning to end.

> *"[In science fiction,] the setting can be specifically chosen to throw into sharp relief those aspects of human nature which concern the writer."*
>
> —Nancy Kress

In 2002, Kress lost her second husband, fellow science fiction writer Charles Sheffield. She moved back to Rochester, New York, to live near her grown children. When she is not writing fiction, she writes a monthly fiction column for *Writer's Digest* magazine and teaches at the Clarion Science Fiction and Fantasy Writers' Workshop at Michigan State University.

Nancy Kress was born in 1948.

LiteratureOnline **Author Search** For more about Nancy Kress, go to www.glencoe.com.

NANCY KRESS 1165

COMPARING LITERATURE

BEFORE YOU READ

Focus

Writer's Technique

Kress's Hobby Kress began writing as a hobby because she was not good at needlework. Even though her writing began as a hobby, it turned into a highly successful career. Kress has more than 70 short stories and 18 books to her credit. AS

LiteratureOnline

Author Search To expand students' appreciation of Nancy Kress, have them access the Web site for additional information and resources.

Selection Skills

Comparing Literature

Literary Elements
- Dialogue (SE pp. 1166, 1168–1169, 1172–1173)

Reading Skills
- Comparing and Contrasting Characters (SE pp. 1166, 1170, 1172–1173)

Vocabulary Skills
- Context Clues (SE pp. 1173)

Listening/Speaking/Viewing Skills
- Analyzing Art (SE pp. 1171; TWE pp. 1174, 1175)

Writing Skills/Grammar
- Writing About Literature (SE p. 1173)
- Descriptive Writing (TWE p. 1174)

Focus

Summary

This story is set in the future, at a time when people's memories can be wiped away so that they can live longer. Mrs. Kinnian argues with her son Aaron because he wants her to have her memory erased so that she will not die. Mrs. Kinnian believes that having her memory wiped would be a death in itself. Aaron plans to have his own memory wiped so that he can continue living.

V Vocabulary

Vocabulary File **Say:** Add these words and definitions to your vocabulary file. For each word, include a sentence that gives you an example of how to use the word. OL Students with English language needs should include the pronunciations of these words in their files. EL

Literary Elements Have students access the Web site to improve their understanding of dialogue.

LITERATURE PREVIEW

Connecting to the Story

This science fiction story is set in a future in which technology allows people to live longer than they do today. The story raises many questions about memory, life, death, and aging. Before you read, think about the following questions:

- How much does your past define who you are?
- What are some of your favorite memories?

Building Background

The phrase *in memoriam* means "in memory of." It is a phrase often found on gravestones. Long before Spanish explorer Juan Ponce de León searched for an elusive "fountain of youth" in the 1500s, people longed to extend their lives. Myths from many cultures tell stories of quests to be rejuvenated, or made youthful and vigorous again. The quest was never fulfilled, but research continues today for processes and products that will slow the signs and effects of aging. In the future, rejuvenation of some type may be possible through stem cells, biochemical repair, or nanotechnology.

Setting Purposes for Reading

Big Idea Our World and Beyond

As you read, notice the ways in which the future world of this story is different from the world as we know it today.

Literary Element Dialogue

Dialogue is the conversation between characters in a literary work. It can contribute to characterization, create a mood, advance the plot, and develop the theme. Pay attention to what the dialogue reveals about each character and his or her relationships with the other characters.

- See Literary Terms Handbook, p. R5.

Literature Online **Interactive Literary Elements Handbook** To review or learn more about the literary elements, go to www.glencoe.com.

READING PREVIEW

Reading Strategy Comparing and Contrasting Characters

Characters are the people who appear in a literary work. A main character is central to the work, while a minor character may appear only to help develop the story or act as a contrast to the main characters. All characters help develop plot, conflict, and theme.

Reading Tip: Taking Notes Use a Venn diagram to help you recognize important similarities and differences between the characters in this story.

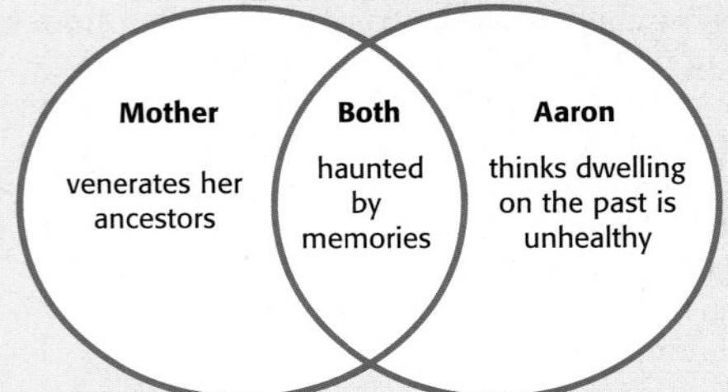

Vocabulary

acquiescence (ak′ wē es′ əns) *n.* passive acceptance; compliance; p. 1168 *Although she did not agree with the plan, she announced her acquiescence without arguing.*

meticulous (mi tik′ yə ləs) *adj.* characterized by extreme or excessive care in the treatment of details; p. 1169 *He was meticulous about the organization of his books, arranging them by date.*

repulsive (ri pul′ siv) *adj.* arousing aversion or disgust; p. 1170 *Her mother considered rats repulsive and would not let her keep one as a pet.*

bewildered (bi wil′ dərd) *adj.* perplexed or confused; p. 1172 *The hikers became bewildered when they discovered they had taken the wrong path.*

INDIANA ACADEMIC STANDARDS (pages 1166–1173)

9.3.4 Determine characters' traits by what the characters say about themselves in…dialogue…

9.3.3 Analyze interactions between characters…

9.5.3 Write…analytical essays…

Selection Resources

Print Materials

- Unit 6 Resources (Fast File), pp. 28–30
- Leveled Vocabulary Development, p. 73
- Selection and Unit Assessments, pp. 197–198
- Selection Quick Checks, p. 99

Transparencies

- Bellringer Options Transparencies: Daily Language Practice Transparency 98
- Literary Elements Transparency 17

Technology

- TeacherWorks Plus™ CD-ROM
- StudentWorks Plus™ CD-ROM
- Presentation Plus!™ CD-ROM
- Literature Online, glencoe.com
- Online Student Edition, mhln.com
- Exam*View*® Assessment Suite CD-ROM
- Vocabulary PuzzleMaker CD-ROM
- Listening Library, disc 2 track 41

In Memoriam

Nancy Kress

As soon as Aaron followed me into the garden, I knew he was angry. He pursed his mouth, that sweet exaggerated fullness of lips that hadn't changed since he was two years old and that looked silly on the middle-aged man he had become. But he said nothing—in itself a sign of trouble. Oh, I knew him through and through. As well as I knew his father, as well as his father had known me.

Aaron closed the door behind us and walked to the lawn chairs, skirting the tiny shrine as if it weren't there. He lowered himself gingerly into a chair.

"Be careful," I said, pointlessly. "Your back again?"

He waved this remark away; even as a little boy he had hated to have attention called to any physical problem. A skinned knee, a stiff neck, a broken wrist. I remembered. I remembered everything.

"Coffee? A splash?"

"Coffee. Come closer, I don't want to shout. You don't have your hearing field on, do you?"

I didn't. I poured him his coffee from the lawn bar and floated my chair close enough to hand it to him. Next door, Todd came out of his house, dressed in shorts and carrying a trowel. He waved cheerfully.

"I know you don't want to hear this," Aaron began—he had never been one for small talk, never one for subtlety—"but I have to say it one more time. Listen to Dr. Lorsky about the operation."

"Sugar?"

Big Idea Our World and Beyond *What impression do you have so far about the kind of world these characters live in?* **BI**

Teach

BI Big Idea

Our World and Beyond

Answer: *The characters live in the future, at a time when new inventions and technologies have been created to make life easier.*

Ask: How do the details of this world differ from our own? *(Our world does not have floating chairs or lawn bars in people's homes.)* As students continue reading, encourage them to look for additional details that make the world in the story different from our own world. **OL**

CheckPoint

Use the CheckPoint questions on Presentation Plus! to monitor students' comprehension. These questions can be used with interactive response keypads for immediate student feedback.

Readability Scores

Dale-Chall: 4.8
DRP: 54
Lexile: 650

Differentiated Instruction

Creating Diagrams Less proficient readers will increase their comprehension by recording information about the characters, setting, and plot in a chart or diagram. Demonstrate how to create cluster diagrams for recording basic information about the literary elements of character, plot, and setting. Tell students to add information to their diagrams as they read through the story. Suggest that they use a separate sheet of paper for each cluster. **BL**

Academic Standards

The Additional Support activity on p. 1167 covers the following standards:

Differentiated Instruction: **9.4.4** Use writing to…compile information…
9.3 Identify story elements such as character,…plot, and setting…

Teach

L1 Literary Element

Dialogue **Answer:** *He has strong feelings, but he is logical and methodical. He tries to appeal to his mother's sense of reason to convince her to see things his way.* OL

BI1 Big Idea

Our World and Beyond
Answer: *A wirehead may be a device worn on the head and used for viewing images. The author is emphasizing the fact that these characters live in a different world from ours, where things are possible that we have not even imagined.* OL

L2 Literary Element

Dialogue **Ask:** Why does Aaron ask his mother what she does? *(Students may say that he does not want the conversation to move toward what the shrine means to his mother, perhaps because it makes him feel uncomfortable or simply because he does not want to be diverted from his argument.)* OL

COMPARING LITERATURE

"Black. Mom—"

"Be quiet," I said, and he looked startled enough, but his surprise wasn't followed by a scowl. Aaron, who always reacted to a direct order as if to assault. I sat up straighter and peered at him. No scowl.

He took a long, deliberate sip of coffee, which was too hot for long sips. "Is there a reason you won't listen to Dr. Lorsky? A real, rational reason?" He didn't look at the shrine.

"You know the reason," I said. Thirty feet away in his side yard, Todd began to weed his flower beds, digging out the most stubborn weeds with the trowel, pulling the rest by hand. He never used a power hoe. The flowers, snapdragons and yarrow and azaleas and lemondrop marigolds, crowded together in the brief hot riot of midsummer.

Aaron waggled his fingers at the shrine he still wouldn't see. "That's not a reason!"

He was right, of course—the shrine was effect, not cause. I smiled at his perceptiveness, unable to help the sly, silly glow of a maternal pride thirty years out of date. But Aaron took the smile for something else: **acquiescence,** perhaps, or weakening. He put his cup on the grass and leaned forward. Earnestly[1]—he had been such an earnest little boy, unsmiling in the face of jokes he didn't understand, putting his toys away in the exact same spots each night, presenting his teenage demands in carefully numbered lists, lecturing the other boys on their routine childish brutality.

A prig,[2] actually.

"That's not a reason!"

"Mom, listen to me. I'm asking you to reconsider. That's all. For three reasons. First, because it's getting dangerous for you to live out here all alone. Despite the electronic surveillance. What if you were robbed?"

"Robbed," I said dryly. Aaron didn't catch it; I didn't really expect him to. He knew why I had bought this house, why I stayed in it. I said gently, "Your coffee's getting cold." He ignored me, pressing doggedly on, his hands gripping the arms of his chair. On the back of the left hand were two liver spots. When had that happened?

"*Second,* this business of ancestor worship or whatever it's supposed to be. This shrine. You never believed in this nonsense before. You raised me to think rationally, without superstition, and here you are planting flowers to your dead forebears unto the nth generation and meditating to them like you were some teenaged wirehead split-brain."

"We used to meditate a lot when I was a girl, before wireheads were invented," I said, to annoy him. His intensity was scaring me. "But Aaron, darling, that's not what I do here."

"What do you do?" he said, and immediately, I could see, regretted it. The shrine shone lustrous in the sunlight. It was a triptych[3] of black slabs two feet high. In the late afternoon heat, the black neo-nitonol[4] had softened into featurelessness, but when night fell, the names would again spring into L2

1. *Earnestly* means "in a very serious manner."
2. A *prig* is someone who is irritatingly proper.

3. A *triptych* is a painting or altar made up of three hinged panels.
4. *Nitonol* is a metal made of titanium and nickel.

Vocabulary

acquiescence (ak′ wē es′ əns) *n.* passive acceptance; compliance

Literary Element Dialogue *What does Aaron's dialogue reveal about his character?* L1

Big Idea Our World and Beyond *What do you think a wirehead is? Why does the author use it without explanation?* BI1

Additional Support

Skills Practice

READING: Connecting to the Story
Encourage students to try connecting to a character in this story on a personal level. They might ask themselves if a certain exchange of dialogue reminds them of their own lives. Also, they might try to put themselves into a character's shoes and imagine what they would do in that character's situation. As students read, have them consider this question: *Is there some aspect of Mrs. Kinnian and Aaron's relationship that reminds you of your relationship with one of your parents? If so, what is it?* OL

hard-etched clarity. Hundreds of tiny names, engraved close together in **meticulous** script, linked with the lines of generation. At the base of the triptych bloomed low flowers: violets and forget-me-nots and rosemary.

"'There's rosemary, that's for remembrance,'" I said, but Aaron, being Aaron, didn't recognize Ophelia's line.[5] Not a reader, my Aaron. Bytes not books. Oh, I remembered.

In the other yard, Todd's trowel clunked as it hit a buried stone.

"It isn't healthy," Aaron said. "Shrines. Ancestor worship! And in the third place, time is running out for you to have the operation. I spoke to Dr. Lorsky yesterday—"

It is our memories that kill us.

"You spoke to my doctor without my permission—"

"—and he said your temporal lobes[6] still scan well but he can't say how much longer that will be true. There's that cut-off point where the body just can't handle it anymore. And then the brain wipe wouldn't do you any good. It would be too late. Mom—you *know.*"

I knew. The sheer weight of memory reached some critical mass. All those memories: the shade of blue of a dress worn fifty years ago, the tilt of the head of someone long dead, the sudden sharp smell of a grandmother's cabbage soup mingled with the dusty scent of an apartment razed for two decades. And each memory bringing on others, a rush of them, till the grandmother was there before you, whole. The burden and bulk of all those minute sensations over days and years and decades, triggering chemical changes in the brain which in turn trigger cellular changes, until the body cannot bear any more and breakdown accelerates. The cut-off point. It is our memories that kill us.

Aaron groped with one hand for his coffee cup, beside his chair on the grass. The crows' feet at the corners of his eyes were still tentative, like lines scratched in soft sand. He ducked his head and mumbled. "I just . . . I just don't want you to die, Mom."

I looked away. It is always, somehow, a surprise to find that an adult child still loves you.

Next door, Todd straightened from one flower bed and moved to the next. He pulled his shirt over his head and tossed it to the ground. Sweat gleamed on the muscles of his back, still hard and taut in his mid-thirties body. The shirt made a dark patch on the bright grass.

A bee buzzed up from the flowers around the black triptych and circled by my ear. Glad of the distraction, I waved it away.

"Aaron . . . I *can't.* I just can't. Be wiped."

"Even if you die for it? What point is there to that?"

I stayed silent. We had discussed it before, all of it, the whole dreary topic. But Aaron had never before looked like that. And he had never begged.

"Please, Mom. Please. You already get confused. Last week you thought that woman in the park was your dead sister. I know you're going to say it was just for a second, but that's the way it starts. Just for a

5. *Ophelia* is a character in William Shakespeare's *The Tragedy of Macbeth.*

6. The *temporal lobes* are the sensory part of the brain.

Literary Element Dialogue *What does this comment tell you about Aaron's attitude toward his mother and toward the past?* **L3**

Vocabulary

meticulous (mi tik′ yə ləs) *adj.* characterized by extreme or excessive care in the treatment of details

Big Idea Our World and Beyond *What effect do you think this would have on the way people see themselves and think about the world?* **BI2**

COMPARING LITERATURE

Teach

L3 Literary Element

Dialogue **Answer:** *Aaron seems to have no use for the past; he fears and scorns it. He seems to think it is a sign of his mother's approaching senility that she values her memory.* **OL**

BI2 Big Idea

Our World and Beyond
Answer: *People would fear memory and try to forget the past as much as possible. These people might try to see the world as if it existed solely in the present, and not consider their past as part of their identity.* **OL**

Differentiated Instruction

Group Discussion Write on the board the following rules for effective group discussion:

1. Listen to other group members as they speak. Don't interrupt.
2. Help members stay on track if the discussion starts to wander.
3. Challenge ideas, not people.
4. Accept criticism gracefully.
5. Encourage quiet members to participate.

Ask: If our society discovered that memories kill us, what effect would that knowledge have on the way we live? **AL**

Academic Standards

Additional Support activities on pp. 1168 and 1169 cover the following standards:

Skills Practice: Determine characters' traits by what the characters say about themselves in narration, dialogue, and soliloquy...

Differentiated Instruction: **9.7.11** Evaluate the clarity, quality, effectiveness, and general coherence of a speaker's important points, arguments, evidence, organization of ideas, delivery, choice of words, and use of language.

Teach

BI Big Idea

Our World and Beyond
Answer: *Students should explain their varied opinions.* OL

R1 Reading Strategy

Comparing and Contrasting Characters **Answer:** *Aaron prefers wiping his memory clean to growing old and dying. However, his mother sees the loss of memory as far too great a sacrifice to make simply in order to live longer.* OL

R2 Reading Strategy

Comparing and Contrasting Characters **Answer:** *Aaron wishes he could forget his memories, but the fact that he cannot shows that they are very powerful for him. He makes his memories sound like a disease that will kill him in the end if he does not get rid of them.* OL

COMPARING LITERATURE

second, then more and more, and then it's too late for the wipe. You say you wouldn't be 'you' anymore with a wipe—but if your memory goes and the body follows it, are you 'you' anyway? Feeble and senile? Are you still 'you' if you're dead?"

"That isn't the point," I began, but he must have seen on my face something which he thought was a softening, a wavering. He reached for my hand. His fingers were dry and hot.

"It *is* the point! Death is the point! Your body can't be made any younger, but it doesn't have to become any older. You *don't*. And you have the bodily strength, still, you have the money—it isn't as if you would be a vegetable. You'd still remember language, routines—and you'd make new memories, start over. A new life. *Life*, not death!"

I said nothing to that. Aaron could see the years of my life stretching behind me, years he wanted me to cut off as casually as paring a fingernail. He could not see the other, greater loss.

"You're wrong," I said, as gently as I could, and took my fingers from his. "I'm not refusing the wipe because I want death. I'm refusing it because too much of me has already died."

He stared at me with incomprehension. The bee I had waved away buzzed around his left ear. I saw his blue eyes flick to it and then back to me, refusing to be distracted. Linear thinking, always: was it growing up with all those computers? Such blue eyes, such a handsome man, still.

Next door Todd began to whistle. Aaron stiffened and half-turned to look for the first time over his shoulder; he had not realized Todd was there. He looked back at me. His eyes shadowed and dropped, and in that tiny sideways slide—not at all linear—I knew. I suddenly knew.

He saw it. "Mom . . . Mother . . ."

"You're going to have the wipe."

He raised the coffee cup to his mouth and drank: an automatic covering gesture, the coffee must have been cold. **Repulsive.** Cold coffee is repulsive.

I folded my arms across my belly and leaned forward.

He said quietly, "My back is getting worse. The migraines are back, once or twice every week. Lorsky says I'm an old forty-two, you know how much people vary. I'm not the easy-living type who forgets easily. I take things hard, I don't forget, and I don't want to die."

I said nothing.

"Mom?"

I said nothing.

"Please understand . . . please." It came out in a whisper. I said nothing. Aaron put his cup on the table and eased himself from the chair, leaning heavily on its arm and webbed back. The movement attracted Todd's attention. I saw, past the bulk of Aaron's body, the moment Todd decided to walk over and be neighborly.

"Hello, Mrs. Kinnian. Aaron."

I watched Aaron's face clench. He turned slowly.

Todd said, "Hot, isn't it? I was away for a week and my weeds just ambushed everything."

"Sailing," Aaron said carefully.

"Yes, sailing." Todd said, faintly surprised. He wiped the sweat from his eyes. "Do you sail?" R3

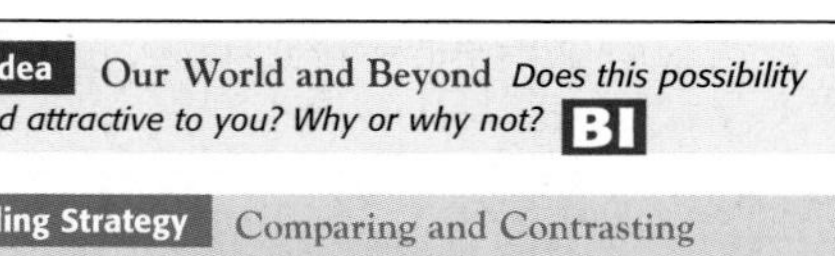

Big Idea Our World and Beyond *Does this possibility sound attractive to you? Why or why not?* BI

Reading Strategy Comparing and Contrasting Characters *What fundamental difference between the characters becomes apparent here?* R1

Reading Strategy Comparing and Contrasting Characters *What is Aaron's attitude toward his own memories?* R2

Vocabulary

repulsive (ri pul′ siv) *adj.* arousing aversion or disgust

Additional Support

Skills Practice

READING: Rereading Tell students that rereading a passage like the paragraphs in the first column on this page will help them clarify meaning. Suggest that students write down any words or terms with which they are unfamiliar. Then tell them to refer to a dictionary to look up these words and terms. For example, students might want to clarify the meaning of the term "linear thinking." Suggest that students use the Internet if they cannot find any words or terms in a dictionary. OL

Song from a Distant Land. Ferdinand Hodler. Oil on canvas, 180 x 125 cm. Collection of Hamburger Kunsthalle, Hamburg, Germany.

Viewing the Art: How would you describe the attitude of the woman pictured? In what ways is she like the narrator of the story? ★

COMPARING LITERATURE

Teach

R3 Reading Strategy

Predicting **Ask:** What role do you think Todd may play in this story? Support your prediction with clues from the text on page 1170. *(Some students may guess that Todd is a family member by references to both men's blue eyes and sailing and from Aaron's reaction when he notices Todd. Students may not realize Todd is Aaron's father because he seems younger than Aaron.)* **OL**

★ Viewing the Art

Answer: *The woman in the painting appears to be self-confident and in control of her body and mind. Like the narrator, she is in control of herself.*

Ferdinand Hodler (1853–1918) was a Swiss painter who started out painting realistic landscapes and portraits. He later was influenced by symbolism and art nouveau. Hodler called his style Parallelism, which mainly consisted of groups of figures arranged in dance-like poses. **AS**

Differentiated Instruction

Reading Dialogue Some gifted and talented students excel at dramatic reading. Allow students to form pairs and read the dialogue between Mrs. Kinnian and Aaron (page 1170) aloud. Assign speaking parts or let students choose their roles. Encourage students to read only the words of the characters and use nonverbal communication to convey underlying meanings. Give students time to prepare. When they are ready, invite students to present their dramatic reading to the class. **AL**

Academic Standards

Additional Support activities on pp. 1170 and 1171 cover the following standards:

Skills Practice: **9.1.1** Identify and use the literal and figurative meaning of words and understand the origins of words.

Differentiated Instruction: **9.7.17** Deliver oral responses to literature that demonstrate awareness of the author's writing style and an appreciation of the effects created...

Teach

L Literary Element

Dialogue **Answer:** *The mother's comment implies that she will be deeply affected by her son's choice to erase her from his memory. Aaron's answer emphasizes his concern for himself and the present, not acknowledging that his past is intertwined with others.* OL

R Reading Strategy

Comparing and Contrasting Characters **Answer:** *The mother's comment implies that if Aaron had been less caught up in abstract things, he would not be afraid of death or eager to erase his memories.* OL

BI Big Idea

Our World and Beyond
Answer: *The fervor with which these old people hold on to their memories* OL

"I did. Once. When I was a kid. My father used to take me."

"You should have kept it up. Great sport. Mrs. Kinnian, can I weed those flowers for you?"

He pointed to the black triptych. I said, "No, thank you, Todd. The gardener will be around tomorrow."

"Well, if you . . . all right. Take care."

He smiled at us: a handsome blue-eyed man in his prime, ruddy with health and exercise, his face as open and clear as a child's. Beside him, Aaron looked puffy, stiff, out of shape. The skin at the back of Aaron's neck formed ridges that worked up and down above his collar.

"Take care," I said to Todd. He walked back to his weeding. Aaron turned to me. I saw his eyes.

"I'm sorry, Mom. I am . . . sorry. But I'm going to have the wipe. I'm going to do it."

"To me."

"For me."

After that there was nothing else to say. I watched Aaron walk around the flowered shrine, open the door to the house, disappear in the cool interior. There was a brief hum from the air conditioner, cut off the moment the door closed. A second door slammed; Todd, too, had gone inside his house.

I realized that I had not asked Aaron when Dr. Lorsky would do the wipe. He might not have told me. He had already been stretched as far as he would go, pulled off center by emotion and imagination, neither of which he wanted. He had never been an imaginative child, only a practical one. Coming to me in the garden with his math homework, worried about fractions, unconcerned with the flowers blooming and dying around him. I remembered.

But *he* would not.

Todd came back outside, carrying a cold drink, and returned to weeding. I watched him a while. I watched him an hour, two. I watched him after he had left and dusk began to fall over the garden. Then I struggled out of my chair—everything ached, I had been sitting too long—and picked some snapdragons. Purple, deepened by the shadows. I laid them in front of the black triptych.

When Todd and I had been married, I had carried roses: white with pink undertones at the tips of the petals, deep pink at the heart. I hadn't seen such roses in years. Maybe the strain wasn't grown anymore.

The script on the shrine had sprung out clear and hard. I touched it with one finger, tracing the names. Then I went into the house to watch TV. A brain-wipe clinic had been bombed. Elderly activists crowded in front of the camera, yelling and waving gnarled fists. They were led away by police, strong youthful men and women trying to get the old people to *behave* like old people. The unlined faces beneath their helmets looked **bewildered**. They *were* bewildered. Misunderstanding everything; believing that remembrance is death; getting it all backwards. Trying to make us go away as if we didn't exist. As if we never had. ❧

Literary Element Dialogue *What does this simple exchange reveal about the different viewpoints of these characters?* L

Reading Strategy Comparing and Contrasting Characters *What is the significance of Aaron's indifference to the flowers?* R

Big Idea Our World and Beyond *What is it that these young police officers cannot understand?* BI

Vocabulary

bewildered (bi wil′ dərd) *adj.* perplexed or confused

Additional Support

Academic Standards

The Additional Support activity on p. 1172 covers the following standard:

Skills Practice: **9.3** [Identify] story elements such as character, theme, plot, and setting…

Skills Practice

READING: Summarizing Tell students that summarizing a short story can help ensure comprehension. Ask students to summarize the events in "In Memoriam." Remind them to answer who, what, where, when, and why questions in their summaries. OL

CheckPoint

Use the CheckPoint questions on Presentation Plus! to check students' mastery of the selection. These questions can be used with interactive response keypads for immediate student feedback.

AFTER YOU READ

RESPONDING AND THINKING CRITICALLY

Respond

1. Do you find the idea of a "memory wipe" that would prolong your life exciting or disturbing? Explain.

Recall and Interpret

2. (a)What does Aaron want to convince his mother to do? (b)What are his motivations for wanting her to do it?
3. (a)What is Aaron's response to his mother's shrine? (b)Why do you suppose it affects him in this way?
4. (a)Who is Todd and how has he changed? (b)What effect do you think Todd's presence has had on the narrator of the story?

Analyze and Evaluate

5. (a)How does Aaron's reaction to Todd's presence compare with his mother's reaction? (b)What do their reactions reveal about their attitudes toward life?
6. What effect does the mother's description and characterization of Aaron and Todd have on the story?
7. At the end of the story, the mother comments that people like her son live their lives "believing that remembrance is death; getting it all backwards." How does this comment explain her choice not to have the brain wipe?

Connect

8. **Big Idea** **Our World and Beyond** (a)How would you feel if someone you loved decided to have a brain wipe? (b)How do you think the existence of such a possibility would affect our society?

LITERARY ANALYSIS

Literary Element Dialogue

Dialogue reveals characters' personalities through their words. It can also serve to increase the drama of a story and call attention to important themes.

1. What impression do you get of Aaron from his dialogue? How does this impression compare with the way he is described by his mother?
2. At what point in the story does the dialogue create a moment of drama or high tension? Explain.

Writing About Literature

Evaluate Contemporary Relevance What attitudes do people today tend to have toward growing old? What is the relationship between who we are and what we remember? Write an essay in which you discuss contemporary attitudes toward aging and memory, and how they compare with the attitudes presented in this story.

LiteratureOnline **Web Activities** For eFlashcards, Selection Quick Checks, and other Web activities, go to www.glencoe.com.

READING AND VOCABULARY

Reading Strategy Comparing and Contrasting Characters

Characters with contrasting viewpoints are important to the development of a story, but there are usually similarities even between characters who are very different, adding a layer of complexity.

1. What do Aaron and his mother have in common?
2. How do the characters' ways of expressing themselves differ?

Vocabulary Practice

Practice with Context Clues Use context clues to determine the meaning of each boldfaced word.

1. He nodded to indicate his **acquiescence.**
   a. impatience **b.** agreement **c.** understanding
2. Curt was **meticulous** in putting everything back exactly where it belonged.
   a. slow **b.** irritated **c.** careful
3. Kim found the idea of dissecting a frog **repulsive,** and shuddered at the thought.
   a. disgusting **b.** ridiculous **c.** unnecessary

Reading Strategy

1. They know memory is powerful.
2. He is direct; she tries to avoid the discussion. Aaron's urgent tone reflects his underlying fear; she appears wise.

Vocabulary

1. b **2.** c **3.** a

LiteratureOnline

Web Activities Have students access the Web site for interactive activities that will help them assess their understanding of the selection.

COMPARING LITERATURE

AFTER YOU READ

Assess

1. Students should explain the reasons behind their choices.
2. (a) To have a "memory wipe" (b) He does not want her to die.
3. (a) He avoids looking at it; it makes him uncomfortable. (b) He wants to escape the past.
4. (a) Todd, Aaron's father, has had a memory wipe. (b) Todd's action may have influenced her decision.
5. (a) Aaron is uneasy in Todd's presence, while his mother accepts him as a neighbor. (b) Aaron's awkwardness reflects his discomfort towards his life. She is resigned to the fact that her husband is gone.
6. They emphasize the power of the past.
7. To her, memory is life in that people live in others' memories.
8. (a) Students might feel grief. (b) People would become more isolated and self-centered.

Literary Element

1. Aaron seems stubborn and logical. She makes him seem more human.
2. Students should refer to story details and dialogue.

Writing About Literature

Students' essays should

- define attitudes toward aging and memory in the story
- define contemporary attitudes toward aging and memory
- use specific details from the story and from their own experiences

Focus

Summary

The poem's narrator tells how new clothes make her feel like a new person because no memories are connected with them.

Teach

★ Viewing the Art

Contemporary artist Caroline Burrows paints mainly in acrylics, using a stylized technique. **AS**

Quickwrite

Ask volunteers to read aloud their paragraphs. Discuss different attitudes toward change and why some people like changes while others fear them.

Literature Online

Author Search To expand students' appreciation of Naomi Long Madgett, have them access the Web site for additional information and resources.

COMPARING LITERATURE

BEFORE YOU READ

Building Background

Naomi Long Madgett is a teacher, writer, poet, and editor. She began writing at an early age and says, "I do not recall any time in my life when I was not involved with poetry." She had trouble getting her first book of poetry published, but "was determined to keep writing in my voice."

She became a teacher in the Detroit public schools, and soon began to make a name for herself as a poet and teacher. To help other African American writers, she founded Lotus Press, Inc. In 1993 she received an American Book Award for her work as an editor and publisher.

Literature Online **Author Search** For more about Naomi Long Madgett, go to www.glencoe.com.

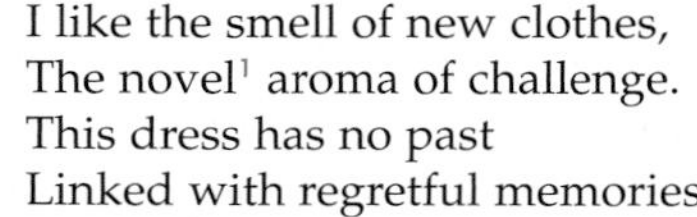

Naomi Long Madgett

I like the smell of new clothes,
The novel[1] aroma of challenge.
This dress has no past
Linked with regretful memories
To taint[2] it,
Only a future as hopeful
As my own.
I can say of an old garment
Laid away in a trunk:
"This lace I wore on that day when. . . ."
But I prefer the new scent
Of a garment unworn,
Untainted like the new self
That I become
When I first wear it.

1. Here, *novel* means "new."
2. To *taint* something is to spoil it.

Do you do anything special to mark new beginnings in your life? Write a paragraph in which you describe the significance of an object or activity that you associate with change and new opportunities.

Additional Support

Skills Practice

WRITING: Descriptive Writing
Engage students' imagination by asking them to try on an accessory or an article of clothing that you bring to class, such as a scarf, gloves, shirt, or hat. Have students describe the feel of the new clothes and explain what they like about the items. Then read "Purchase" aloud. Have small groups discuss how what people wear reflects their personalities and outlooks. Ask students to write a paragraph describing one article of clothing and the "inner me" it reflects. **OL**

World Without Memory

★ Alan Lightman

BEFORE YOU READ

Building Background

Alan Lightman is a writer, physicist, and educator. He has always been interested in both science and writing, and began writing poetry in high school. He started publishing poetry in literary magazines at the same time that he was studying astrophysics. His work explores the worlds of science and art, and often examines their conflicting viewpoints.

Lightman's novel *Einstein's Dreams,* from which "World Without Memory" is taken, was an international bestseller. *Einstein's Dreams* has also been used as the basis for several theatrical and musical productions.

Literature Online **Author Search** For more about Alan Lightman, go to www.glencoe.com.

20 MAY 1905

A glance along the crowded booths on Spitalgasse[1] tells the story. The shoppers walk hesitantly from one stall to the next, discovering what each shop sells. Here is tobacco, but where is mustard seed? Here are sugar beets, but where is cod? Here is goat's milk, but where is sassafras?[2] These are not tourists in Bern on their first visit. These are the citizens of Bern. Not a man can remember that two days back he bought a chocolate at a shop named Ferdinand's, at no. 17, or beef at the Hof delicatessen, at no. 36. Each shop and its specialty must be found anew. Many walk with maps, directing the map-holders from one arcade[3] to the next in the city they have lived in all their lives, in the street they have traveled for years. Many walk with notebooks to record what they have learned while it is briefly in their heads. For in this world, people have no memories.

When it is time to return home at the end of the day, each person consults his address book to learn where he lives. The butcher, who has made some unattractive cuts in his one day of butchery, discovers that his home

1. Lightman mentions four streets in Bern, Switzerland. They are *Spitalgasse, Nägeligasse, Bundesgasse,* and *Brunngasshalde.* In German, which is the language spoken in Bern, *Gasse* means "alley" or "small street."
2. *Sassafras* is a type of tree, the roots of which have been traditionally used as a flavoring or an ingredient in medicine.
3. Here, *arcade* means a row of shops.

Differentiated Instruction

Writing Books of Life Help less proficient readers connect to the story and have a better understanding of what a world without memory would be like. Ask students to write a page describing their day so far. Remind students that they must include every detail that they want to remember because their books are the only things they have to help them remember that day. BL

COMPARING LITERATURE

Focus

Summary

This story describes a world where people have no memory. People record their days in Books of Life.

★ Viewing the Art

The works of American artist Edward Hopper (1882–1967) reveal the truth in daily life. His images often reflect loneliness through his blunt angles and stark use of light and shadow. AS

Literature Online

Author Search To expand students' appreciation of Alan Lightman, have them access the Web site for additional information and resources.

CheckPoint

Use the CheckPoint questions on Presentation Plus! to monitor students' comprehension. These questions can be used with interactive response keypads for immediate student feedback.

Readability Scores

Dale-Chall: 6.8
DRP: 58
Lexile: 1090

Academic Standards

Additional Support activities on pp. 1174 and 1175 cover the following standards:

Skills Practice: **9.5.3** Write expository compositions…

Differentiated Instruction: **9.5.1** Write… autobiographical narratives…

Teach

BI Big Idea

Our World and Beyond

Ask: How would you feel about living in a world without memory? *(Some may say the world would be hopeless and isolating; others may say each day would be a fresh start.)* Do the Books of Life work well? *(Some may say they do, but others may say people must choose which parts of their lives to remember.)*

Discussion Starter

Discuss who would benefit from a lack of memory. Ask students to consider the effect on how doctors, teachers, or pilots could do their jobs. OL

CheckPoint

Use the CheckPoint questions on Presentation Plus! to check students' mastery of the selection. These questions can be used with interactive response keypads for immediate student feedback.

COMPARING LITERATURE

is no. 29 Nägeligasse. The stockbroker, whose short-term memory of the market has produced some excellent investments, reads that he now lives at no. 89 Bundesgasse. Arriving home, each man finds a woman and children waiting at the door, introduces himself, helps with the evening meal, reads stories to his children. Likewise, each woman returning from her job meets a husband, children, sofas, lamps, wallpaper, china patterns. Late at night, the wife and husband do not linger at the table to discuss the day's activities, their children's school, the bank account.

A world without memory is a world of the present. The past exists only in books, in documents. In order to know himself, each person carries his own Book of Life, which is filled with the history of his life. By reading its pages daily, he can relearn the identity of his parents, whether he was born high or born low, whether he did well or did poorly in school, whether he has accomplished anything in his life. Without his Book of Life, a person is a snapshot, a two-dimensional image, a ghost. In the leafy cafés on the Brunngasshalde, one hears anguished shrieking from a man who just read that he once killed another man, sighs from a woman who just discovered she was courted by a prince, sudden boasting from a woman who has learned that she received top honors from her university ten years prior. Some pass the twilight hours at their tables reading from their Books of Life; others frantically fill its extra pages with the day's events.

> A world without memory is a world of the present.

With time, each person's Book of Life thickens until it cannot be read in its entirety. Then comes a choice. Elderly men and women may read the early pages, to know themselves as youths; or they may read the end, to know themselves in later years. BI

Some have stopped reading altogether. They have abandoned the past. They have decided that it matters not if yesterday they were rich or poor, educated or ignorant, proud or humble, in love or empty-hearted—no more than it matters how a soft wind gets into their hair. Such people look you directly in the eye and grip your hand firmly. Such people walk with the limber stride of their youth. Such people have learned how to live in a world without memory.

Discussion Starter

Are there advantages to a world without memory? In what ways would this circumstance make life difficult? How do you think living in a world where no one had memories would affect what people consider important? Discuss these or other aspects of living without memory in your group.

Additional Support

Skills Practice

READING: Making Comparisons

In "World Without Memory," Lightman describes a new and different world where people have no memories. Ask students to compare Lightman's imagined world to their own world by creating a chart like the example below. OL

World Without Memory	My World
Citizens of Berne have to rediscover their marketplace.	In my supermarket, I know where to find milk, etc.
People carry maps of the marketplace.	Supermarkets do not have or need maps.

Wrap-Up: Comparing Literature *Across Genres*

- ***In Memoriam***
  by Nancy Kress
- ***Purchase***
  by Naomi Long Madgett
- ***World Without Memory***
  by Alan Lightman

COMPARING THE Big Idea Our World and Beyond

Writing How would you characterize the worlds presented in these selections? Are they mundane, extraordinary, or both? What elements in these selections do you find familiar? What elements are very different from those of your world? Write a brief essay exploring the worlds in the selections. Before you begin writing, make a chart like the one below to organize your ideas.

Selection	Familiar Aspects	Unfamiliar Aspects
In Memoriam		
Purchase		
World Without Memory		

COMPARING Description

Visual Display Kress describes the garden setting in her story "In Memoriam" as a "hot riot of midsummer." Vivid description also helps us imagine the worlds of Madgett's "Purchase" and Lightman's "World Without Memory." Create a triptych, or three related panels, of collages or paintings based on the descriptions in each of these three works. Each of the three artworks should reflect the world as it is described in the story or poem.

COMPARING Authors' Beliefs

Group Activity Kress, Madgett, and Lightman all explore the subjects of time and memory but from highly individual standpoints. Discuss the following questions with a small group. Support your answers with specific evidence from the texts.

1. What attitudes do the characters in "In Memoriam," "Purchase," and "World Without Memory" have toward time and memory?
2. How is each author's tone similar to or different from the characters' tone on the subject of time and memory?
3. In your opinion, what does each author believe about time and memory?

INDIANA ACADEMIC STANDARDS (page 1177)

9.3.2 Compare and contrast the presentation of a similar theme or topic across genres...

9.3.5 Compare works that express a universal theme and provide evidence to support the views...

3. Each of the authors believes that time is a problem because it carries us closer to death. Kress seems to want others to learn that our identity is inseparable from our memory. Madgett seems gently critical of the speaker of her poem, who has the naive belief that new clothes will create a new beginning. Lightman's beliefs about time and memory are difficult to pin down because he seems to want only to explore a premise to its logical conclusion.

Assess

Comparing the Big Idea

Students' essays should

- show an understanding of the concepts in the selections
- show an ability to compare and contrast fictional and realistic aspects of the worlds in the selections

Comparing Description

Provide students with a wide variety of materials, and encourage them to bring materials from home. Create an exhibit of the finished work.

Comparing Authors' Beliefs

1. In "In Memoriam," Aaron wants a brain wipe. His mother feels that the wipe would be a form of suicide. In "Purchase," the speaker prefers to put the past aside. In "World Without Memory," the characters cannot remember, and the past exists only in what they read.
2. The tone of "In Memoriam" is bittersweet. The story is in first-person point of view and focuses on the mother's viewpoint. The tone of "Purchase" is determined. The speaker wants a new start. The author seems to know that a garment is "tainted" with memories once worn. The tone of "World Without Memory" is dreamlike. The author seems to be the dreamer. He records without judging.

Academic Standards

The Additional Support activity on p. 1176 covers the following standard:

Skills Practice: **9.3.2** Compare and contrast the presentation of a similar theme...

Focus

BELLRINGER

Bellringer Options
Daily Language Practice Transparency 99
Or display images of Chinese culture (such as parades, landscapes, villages, and the Great Wall).
Ask: What seems familiar in these pictures? How is this culture similar to our own? How is this culture different?
Say: The story you will read takes place in two fictional Chinese cities a long time ago.
As they read, have students think about how life in the story is similar to and different from their own.

Author Search To expand students' appreciation of Ray Bradbury, have them access the Web site for additional information and resources.

BEFORE YOU READ

The Golden Kite, the Silver Wind

MEET RAY BRADBURY

"I've never doubted myself," celebrated author Ray Bradbury remarked on his eighty-second birthday. He added that he always knew "writing was in itself the only way to live." A childhood spent attending movies and magic shows, as well as reading the magazine *Amazing Stories,* fired his imagination. At age eleven, he wrote his first stories on butcher paper.

A Fantasy Writer Bradbury, who had no formal education beyond high school, did not follow any formulas for writing success. Instead, he simply wrote and wrote—and then wrote some more. He had written many stories before *The Martian Chronicles* was published in 1950, but that was the book that made his reputation. Many of Bradbury's signature themes appear in it. They include the longing for a simpler world and the fear of nuclear war.

> *"The act of writing is, for me, like a fever—something I must do."*
>
> —Ray Bradbury

The novel *Fahrenheit 451,* often hailed as Bradbury's greatest work, was published in 1953. Set in a future world where firefighters are considered heroes for burning books, *Fahrenheit 451* is Bradbury's only science fiction work—at least according to the author. Bradbury says all his other work is fantasy, because fantasy is about things that cannot happen. Science fiction, he explains, is about things that can happen.

In addition to fantasy, Bradbury has written horror stories. In the 1950s he wrote for two television series, *Alfred Hitchcock* and *The Twilight Zone.* He also adapted many stories for his namesake television show, *Ray Bradbury Theater.* His work includes plays, nonfiction, and children's stories. In addition, he has been a creative consultant on many projects, including the United States Pavilion at the 1964 World's Fair.

Economical Style "The Golden Kite, the Silver Wind" was first published in 1953. In a 2002 interview, Bradbury explained that he had gotten the idea for the story when he was thirteen years old. At the time, he "hung around" various movie studios. There he saw sets being built and destroyed in a seemingly endless cycle. When he was twenty-six, he wrote the story based on the destruction of those sets, he said, "and they were metaphorically representative of the world."

Many writers, including Stephen King, acknowledge Bradbury as an important influence. Bradbury has received many awards, including the O. Henry Memorial Award, the 1988 Nebula Grand Master Award, and the 1989 Bram Stoker Award. In 2004 he was awarded the National Medal of the Arts. Perhaps his most meaningful award, however, was having a crater on the moon, Dandelion Crater, named in honor of his book *Dandelion Wine.*

Ray Bradbury was born in 1920.

LiteratureOnline **Author Search** For more about Ray Bradbury, go to www.glencoe.com.

Selection Skills

The Golden Kite, the Silver Wind

Literary Elements
- Allegory (SE pp. 1179–1180, 1182–1184)

Vocabulary Skills
- Synonyms (SE pp. 1179, 1185)
- Academic Vocabulary (SE p. 1185)

Listening/Speaking/Viewing Skills
- Analyzing Art (SE p. 1183; TWE p. 1180)

Writing Skills/Grammar
- Analyze Comic Devices (SE p. 1185)

Reading Skills
- Evaluating Figures of Speech (SE pp. 1179, 1181–1182, 1185)
- Drawing Conclusions (TWE p. 1180)
- Problem and Solution (TWE p. 1182)

LITERATURE PREVIEW

Connecting to the Story

In "The Golden Kite, the Silver Wind," competition leads only to misery. Before you read the story, think about the following questions:

- Have you ever known of a competition that got out of hand?
- How was the competition resolved?

Building Background

"The Golden Kite, the Silver Wind" is set in an unspecified but long-ago time in China. In this fictional world, Bradbury creates two walled cities: one is called Kwan-Si, and the other is never named. Mandarins, or public officials, rule autocratically, and walls are built laboriously by hand, at the whim of the ruler. In this world, women have no official power. Therefore, the major female character in this story, the daughter of one of the mandarins, dares to give advice to her father only from behind a screen. Her father does not publicly acknowledge its source, yet he repeats her advice exactly. Reflecting the cultural values of his time and place, the mandarin also acknowledges the wisdom of the advice by crediting his daughter with thinking like a son.

Setting Purposes for Reading

Big Idea Our World and Beyond

As you read this story, distinguish its realistic elements from its fantastic elements.

Literary Element Allegory

An **allegory** is a literary work in which all or most of the characters, settings, and events stand for ideas, qualities, or figures beyond themselves. The overall purpose of an allegory is to teach a moral lesson. As you read "The Golden Kite, the Silver Wind," ask yourself what lesson the story conveys about competition and cooperation.

- See Literary Terms Handbook, p. R1.

Literature Online **Interactive Literary Elements Handbook** To review or learn more about the literary elements, go to www.glencoe.com.

READING PREVIEW

Reading Strategy Evaluating Figures of Speech

Figurative language is language or expressions that are not literally true but convey some truth beyond the literal level. **Evaluating figures of speech** is making judgments about the originality and expressive effect of the various similes, metaphors, and personifications in a literary work.

Reading Tip: Taking Notes As you read, use a chart to record how well figures of speech convey ideas or emotions.

Figure of speech	Evaluation
p. 1180 "Death swam in the wetness of an eye"	effectively shows how horrible some "symbols and omens" can be

Vocabulary

portent (pôr′ tent) *n.* something that foreshadows a coming event; p. 1180 *The problems with the car turned out to be a portent of the miserable evening ahead.*

ravenous (rav′ ə nəs) *adj.* extremely hungry; p. 1181 *The ravenous dog had not eaten for two days.*

spurn (spurn) *v.* to reject with disdain or contempt; p. 1181 *Today, the fashion model spurns the same clothes she wore only one year ago.*

monotony (mə not′ ən ē) *n.* undesirable sameness; p. 1183 *Sara hated the monotony of eating the same lunch every day of the week.*

Vocabulary Tip: Synonyms Synonyms are words with the same or similar meanings. Note that synonyms are always the same part of speech.

INDIANA ACADEMIC STANDARDS (pages 1179–1185)

9.3.7 Recognize and understand...allegory...

9.3.11 Evaluate...figurative language...

9.5.3 Write...analytical essays...that gather evidence in support of a thesis...

9.3.8 Interpret and evaluate the impact of...ironies...

BEFORE YOU READ

Focus

Summary

This story tells of two cities that compete with one another by rebuilding their walls over and over again. They do nothing but rebuild their walls until the people are almost dead. Finally, at the advice of the Mandarin's daughter, one city's wall is built like the wind and the other city's wall is built like a kite so that instead of competing, they support and sustain each other.

V Vocabulary

Vocabulary File **Say:** Add these words and definitions to your vocabulary file. For each word, include a sentence that gives you an example of how to use the word. **OL** Students with English language needs should include the pronunciations of these words in their files. **EL**

Literary Elements Have students access the Web site to improve their understanding of allegory.

Selection Resources

Print Materials

- Unit 6 Resources (Fast File), pp. 31–33
- Leveled Vocabulary Development, p. 74
- Selection and Unit Assessments, pp. 199–200
- Selection Quick Checks, p. 100

Transparencies

- Bellringer Options Transparencies: Daily Language Practice Transparency 99
- Literary Elements Transparency 92

Technology

- TeacherWorks Plus™ CD-ROM
- StudentWorks Plus™ CD-ROM
- Presentation Plus!™ CD-ROM
- Literature Online, glencoe.com
- Online Student Edition, mhln.com
- Exam*View*® Assessment Suite CD-ROM
- Vocabulary PuzzleMaker CD-ROM
- Listening Library, disc 2 track 44

Teach

L Literary Element

Allegory Answer: *The shape of the wall represents the strength or character of each city.* OL

Viewing the Art

Giandomenico Tiepolo (1727–1802) was born into an artistic Venetian family, and he took up the family occupation in his youth. His art depicts Venetian street scenes of his time, as well as exotic images of foreign places. AS

Readability Scores
Dale-Chall: 7.1
DRP: 55
Lexile: 1030

The Golden Kite, the Silver Wind

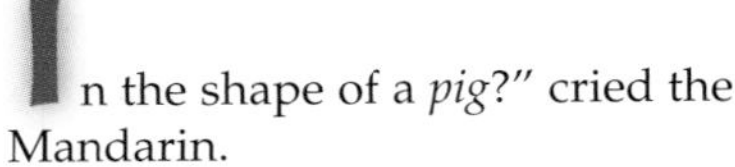

Ray Bradbury

The Walk of the Mandarins. Giandomenico Tiepolo. Villa Valmarana, Vicenza, Italy.

"In the shape of a *pig*?" cried the Mandarin.

"In the shape of a pig," said the messenger, and departed.

"Oh, what an evil day in an evil year," cried the Mandarin. "The town of Kwan-Si, beyond the hill, was very small in my childhood. Now it has grown so large that at last they are building a wall."

"But why should a wall two miles away make my good father sad and angry all within the hour?" asked his daughter quietly.

"They build their wall," said the Mandarin, "in the shape of a pig! Do you see? Our own city wall is built in the shape of an orange. That pig will devour us, greedily!"

"Ah."

They both sat thinking.

Life was full of symbols and omens. Demons lurked everywhere. Death swam in the wetness of an eye, the turn of a gull's wing meant rain, a fan held *so,* the tilt of a roof, and, yes, even a city wall was of immense importance. Travelers and tourists, caravans, musicians, artists, coming upon these two towns, equally judging the **portents,** would say, "The city shaped like an orange? No! I will enter the city shaped like a pig and prosper, eating all, growing fat with good luck and prosperity!"

The Mandarin wept. "All is lost! These symbols and signs terrify. Our city will come on evil days."

"Then," said the daughter, "call in your stonemasons and temple builders. I will whisper from behind the silken screen[1] and you will know the words."

The old man clapped his hands despairingly. "Ho,[2] stonemasons! Ho, builders of towns and palaces!"

Literary Element Allegory *The city walls are more than just walls in this story. What do you think they might represent?* L

1. Movable wall-like *screens* often provide privacy in Chinese and other homes.
2. *Ho* is an interjection used to get somebody's attention.

Vocabulary
portent (pôr′ tent) *n.* something that foreshadows a coming event

Additional Support

Skills Practice

READING: Drawing Conclusions

Explain to students that drawing conclusions is basic to reading text: readers reach decisions or opinions, or draw conclusions, based on the facts and details the author gives. Have students list the details from the story that can be used to draw the following conclusions.

1. The Mandarin will do whatever his daughter suggests.
2. The people of the city will keep rebuilding their wall into different shapes. OL

The men who knew marble and granite and onyx and quartz came quickly. The Mandarin faced them most uneasily, himself waiting for a whisper from the silken screen behind his throne. At last the whisper came.

"I have called you here," said the whisper.

"I have called you here," said the Mandarin aloud, "because our city is shaped like an orange, and the vile city of Kwan-Si has this day shaped theirs like a **ravenous** pig—"

Here the stonemasons groaned and wept. Death rattled his cane in the outer courtyard. Poverty made a sound like a wet cough in the shadows of the room.

"And so," said the whisper, said the Mandarin, "you raisers of walls must go bearing trowels and rocks and change the shape of *our* city!"

The architects and masons gasped. The Mandarin himself gasped at what he had said. The whisper whispered. The Mandarin went on: "And you will change our walls into a club which may beat the pig and drive it off!"

The stonemasons rose up, shouting. Even the Mandarin, delighted at the words from his mouth, applauded, stood down from his throne. "Quick!" he cried. "To work!"

When his men had gone, smiling and bustling, the Mandarin turned with great love to the silken screen. "Daughter," he whispered, "I will embrace you." There was no reply. He stepped around the screen, and she was gone.

Such modesty, he thought. She has slipped away and left me with a triumph, as if it were mine.

Reading Strategy Evaluating Figures of Speech *Is this an effective description of poverty? Why or why not?* **R1**

Big Idea Our World and Beyond *How are the Mandarin and his followers similar to leaders and followers everywhere?* **BI**

Vocabulary

ravenous (rav′ ə nəs) *adj.* extremely hungry

The news spread through the city; the Mandarin was acclaimed. Everyone carried stone to the walls. Fireworks were set off and the demons of death and poverty did not linger, as all worked together. At the end of the month the wall had been changed. It was now a mighty bludgeon[3] with which to drive pigs, boars, even lions, far away. The Mandarin slept like a happy fox every night.

"I would like to see the Mandarin of Kwan-Si when the news is learned. Such pandemonium and hysteria; he will likely throw himself from a mountain! A little more of that wine, oh Daughter-who-thinks-like-a-son."

But the pleasure was like a winter flower; it died swiftly. That very afternoon the messenger rushed into the courtroom. "Oh, Mandarin, disease, early sorrow, avalanches, grasshopper plagues, and poisoned well water!"

The Mandarin trembled.

"The town of Kwan-Si," said the messenger, "which was built like a pig and which animal we drove away by changing our walls to a mighty stick, has now turned triumph to winter ashes. They have built their city's walls like a great bonfire to burn our stick!"

The Mandarin's heart sickened within him, like an autumn fruit upon an ancient tree. "Oh, gods! Travelers will **spurn** us. Tradesmen, reading the symbols, will turn from the stick, so easily destroyed, to the fire, which conquers all!"

"No," said a whisper like a snowflake from behind the silken screen.

"No," said the startled Mandarin.

"Tell my stonemasons," said the whisper that was a falling drop of rain, "to build our walls in the shape of a shining lake."

3. A *bludgeon* is a short stick used as a weapon.

Reading Strategy Evaluating Figures of Speech *Why is the simile in this sentence particularly effective?* **R2**

Vocabulary

spurn (spurn) *v.* to reject with disdain or contempt

Teach

R1 Reading Strategy

Evaluating Figures of Speech **Answer:** *Most students will say* yes. *Poverty is personified as someone who can only cough in the shadows. The sound of poverty is also the sound of illness: a wet cough.* **OL**

BI Big Idea

Our World and Beyond **Answer:** *Even when a leader asks for something absurd, there will always be those who applaud the leader for his or her wisdom.* **OL**

R2 Reading Strategy

Evaluating Figures of Speech **Answer:** *A fox is typically regarded as a sly animal. In this case, the Mandarin feels as if he has just done something clever and has solved his problems at the same time, so he sleeps as contentedly as a sly fox.* **OL**

CheckPoint

Use the CheckPoint questions on Presentation Plus! to monitor students' comprehension. These questions can be used with interactive response keypads for immediate student feedback.

English Language Coach

Words That Set the Tone Point out to English language learners that the author uses several descriptive words to emphasize a tone of fantasy. On the board, write the words *omens, demons, symbols,* and *signs.* Discuss what part of speech each is and how the words help set the tone of the story. As students read, ask them to look for additional examples of words and ideas that set the tone for this fantasy. Have students add the new words to their vocabulary notebooks. **EL**

Academic Standards

Additional Support activities on pp. 1180 and 1181 cover the following standards:

Skills Practice: **9.2.8** Make reasonable statements and draw conclusions about a text, supporting them with accurate examples.

English Language Coach: **9.3.11** Evaluate the aesthetic qualities of style, including the impact of diction and figurative language on tone...

Teach

L1 Literary Element

Allegory Answer: *Students may say it represents the desire to outdo or overcome the rival city once and for all.* OL

BI Big Idea

Our World and Beyond

Answer: *Students may answer generally that peasants, slaves, and other laborers have often been worked to death for the grand aims of rulers. They may cite the Egyptian pyramids or the Great Wall of China as examples.* OL

R Reading Strategy

Evaluating Figures of Speech Answer: *The mandarins are "very ill and withered away," so their breath is like the winter wind, that is, cold like death. The wind flutters, as if the mandarins can just barely breathe. The descriptive language is expressive of their near-death state.* OL

The Mandarin said this aloud, his heart warmed.

"And with this lake of water," said the whisper and the old man, "we will quench the fire and put it out forever!"

The city turned out in joy to learn that once again they had been saved by the magnificent Emperor of ideas. They ran to the walls and built them nearer to this new vision, singing, not as loudly as before, of course, for they were tired, and not as quickly, for since it had taken a month to build the wall the first time, they had had to neglect business and crops and therefore were somewhat weaker and poorer.

There then followed a succession of horrible and wonderful days, one in another like a nest of frightening boxes.

"Oh, Emperor," cried the messenger, "Kwan-Si has rebuilt their walls to resemble a mouth with which to drink all our lake!"

"Then," said the Emperor, standing very close to his silken screen, "build our walls like a needle to sew up that mouth!"

"Emperor!" screamed the messenger. "They make their walls like a sword to break your needle!"

The Emperor held, trembling, to the silken screen. "Then shift the stones to form a scabbard to sheathe that sword!"

"Mercy," wept the messenger the following morn, "they have worked all night and shaped the walls like lightning which will explode and destroy that sheath!"

Sickness spread in the city like a pack of evil dogs. Shops closed. The population, working now steadily for endless months upon the changing of the walls, resembled Death himself, clattering his white bones like musical instruments in the wind. Funerals began to appear in the streets, though it was the middle of summer, a time when all should be tending and harvesting. The Mandarin fell so ill that he had his bed drawn up by the silken screen and there he lay, miserably giving his architectural orders. The voice behind the screen was weak now, too, and faint, like the wind in the eaves.

"Kwan-Si is an eagle. Then our walls must be a net for that eagle. They are a sun to burn our net. Then we build a moon to eclipse their sun!"

Like a rusted machine, the city ground to a halt.

At last the whisper behind the screen cried out:

"In the name of the gods, send for Kwan-Si!"

Upon the last day of summer the Mandarin Kwan-Si, very ill and withered away, was carried into our Mandarin's courtroom by four starving footmen. The two mandarins were propped up, facing each other. Their breaths fluttered like winter winds in their mouths. A voice said:

"Let us put an end to this."

The old men nodded.

"This cannot go on," said the faint voice. "Our people do nothing but rebuild our cities to a different shape every day, every hour. They have no time to hunt, to fish, to love, to be good to their ancestors and their ancestors' children."

"This I admit," said the mandarins of the towns of the Cage, the Moon, the Spear, the Fire, the Sword and this, that, and other things.

"Carry us into the sunlight," said the voice.

The old men were borne out under the sun and up a little hill. In the late summer breeze a few very thin children were flying dragon kites in all the colors of the sun, and frogs and grass, the color of the sea and the color of coins and wheat.

The first Mandarin's daughter stood by his bed.

"See," she said.

Literary Element Allegory *In your opinion, what does this desire to "quench the fire" and "put it out forever" represent?* L1

Big Idea Our World and Beyond *How does this outcome echo political events in world history?* BI

Reading Strategy Evaluating Figures of Speech *How well does descriptive language capture the condition of the two mandarins?* R

Additional Support

Skills Practice

READING: Problem and Solution
Explain that one strategy for reading stories is to think of them as a series of problems and solutions. A character has a problem, the character tries different solutions to the problem, and the problem may or may not be solved. Have small groups of students write three problems and solutions from the story, indicating whether the solutions worked. Have the groups take turns offering their problems and solutions. Compile a list of students' answers that follows the sequence of events in the story. OL

"Those are nothing but kites," said the two old men.

"But what is a kite on the ground?" she said. "It is nothing. What does it need to sustain it and make it beautiful and truly spiritual?"

"The wind, of course!" said the others.

"And what do the sky and the wind need to make *them* beautiful?"

"A kite, of course—many kites, to break the **monotony**, the sameness of the sky. Colored kites, flying!"

"So," said the Mandarin's daughter. "You, Kwan-Si, will make a last rebuilding of your town to resemble nothing more nor less than the wind. And we shall build like a golden kite. The wind will beautify the kite and carry it to wondrous heights. And the kite will break the sameness of the wind's existence and give it purpose and meaning. One without the other is nothing. Together, all will be beauty and cooperation and a long and enduring life."

Tea manufacture, Ming dynasty. Vase decoration. Collection of Golestan Palace, Tehran, Iran.

Viewing the Art: The people shown in this image are hard at work. In what ways are they similar to and different from the villagers in the story? 

Whereupon the two mandarins were so overjoyed that they took their first nourishment in days, momentarily were given strength, embraced, and lavished praise upon each other, called the Mandarin's daughter a boy, a man, a stone pillar, a warrior, and a true and unforgettable son. Almost immediately they parted and hurried to their towns, calling out and singing, weakly but happily.

And so, in time, the towns became the Town of the Golden Kite and the Town of the Silver Wind. And harvestings were harvested and business tended again, and the flesh returned, and disease ran off like a frightened jackal.[5] And on every night of the year the inhabitants in the Town of the Kite could hear the good clear wind sustaining them. And those in the Town of the Wind could hear the kite singing, whispering, rising, and beautifying them.

"So be it," said the Mandarin in front of his silken screen.

Literary Element Allegory *What do the golden kite and the silver wind represent?* **L2**

Vocabulary

monotony (mə not′ ən ē) *n.* undesirable sameness

5. A *jackal* is a small doglike animal. The jackal has long been connected with superstitions about death and evil spirits.

Teach

L2 Literary Element

Allegory **Answer:** *Together they represent harmony, beauty, and a natural order marked by cooperation rather than competition.* **OL**

Viewing the Art

Answer: *Like the villagers, the people in the image work hard and are doing construction tasks. Unlike the story characters, they look happy, healthy, content, and rested.*

The Chinese first drank tea more than 5,000 years ago. The first book about tea, written in A.D. 800, described how ancient China grew and prepared it. Tea is made by processing the leaves of the flowering plant *Camellia Sinensis.* **AS**

CheckPoint

Use the CheckPoint questions on Presentation Plus! to check students' mastery of the selection. These questions can be used with interactive response keypads for immediate student feedback.

Building Reading Fluency

Reading Dialogue The dialogue in this short story is crucial to understanding the selection. An oral interpretation will encourage students to practice reading aloud. Ask students to discuss what they know about the characters and plot of the story. Divide students into groups of three and have each student in a group take the part of the Mandarin, the Mandarin's daughter, or the messenger/Kwan-Si Mandarin. After the small groups have practiced reading their parts silently, have them read the dialogue aloud. **BL**

Academic Standards

Additional Support activities on pp. 1182 and 1183 cover the following standards:

Skills Practice: **9.3** [Identify] story elements such as character [and]...plot...

Building Reading Fluency: **9.7.6** Choose effective verbal and nonverbal techniques (including voice, gestures, and eye contact) for presentations.

AFTER YOU READ

Assess

1. Students may say that they like the clever daughter or that they dislike the excessive figurative language.
2. (a) Kwan-Si has built its walls in the shape of a pig. (b) This gives Kwan-Si greater symbolic power: the pig shape over the orange shape.
3. (a) His daughter (b) He never acknowledges her role, but he values her advice.
4. (a) A lake, a needle, a scabbard, a net, and a moon (b) The people grow exhausted, neglect business and crops, and become sick.
5. (a) Each city wants to be more powerful than its neighbor. (b) Bradbury clearly shows how groups compete at great cost.
6. Competition carried to extremes is destructive; cooperation is positive.
7. (a) She makes the Mandarin look more foolish, for he cannot think for himself. (b) The story would have lacked as many problems and a solution.
8. Competition can still lead to destruction, while cooperation can be a good solution.

AFTER YOU READ

RESPONDING AND THINKING CRITICALLY

Respond

1. What did you like best or least about this story? Explain.

Recall and Interpret

2. (a)What news does the Mandarin learn about Kwan-Si at the beginning of the story? (b)Why is this bad news?
3. (a)Who advises the Mandarin to rebuild his city walls in the shape of a club? (b)Describe the relationship between the Mandarin and his advisor.
4. (a)After the city changes its walls to the shape of a club, it makes other changes to the walls before it decides on the final shape. Name at least three of the changes that precede the final shape. (b)Explain the overall effect of these changes on the city.

Analyze and Evaluate

5. (a)Why does each city keep rebuilding its walls? (b)How well does this wall-building activity represent the competition that has occurred throughout history between city-states, nations, or political alliances?
6. What message does the story express about competition? About cooperation?
7. (a)Why do you think the daughter is a character in the story? (b)Explain what the story would have lacked without her.

Connect

8. **Big Idea** **Our World and Beyond** Bradbury has said that he did not write this story as a political fable. However, are there lessons in the story for leaders of the modern world? Explain your answer.

LITERARY ANALYSIS

Literary Element Allegory

An **allegory** has two levels of meaning. There is a literal level, which is the story, or the events of the plot. There is also a symbolic level, which is what the events mean. In an allegory, the story is less important than the message it conveys.

1. What happens on the literal level of this story? In other words, summarize the main events of the plot.
2. What happens on the symbolic level of the story? In other words, tell what the major events of the plot symbolize or represent.
3. The Mandarin worries that tourists will go to his rival's city because it appears more prosperous. Do modern cities have symbols of prosperity that might sway tourists? Explain.

Review: Moral

As you learned on page 1143, a **moral** is a practical lesson about right and wrong conduct. Morals often are stated at the end of a fable. In most stories, however, the moral is not stated directly. The reader must infer the moral by thinking about the events of the story and by examining what the characters do, say, and think.

Partner Activity Work with a partner to identify the moral in "The Golden Kite, the Silver Wind." Complete an organizer like the one below to show how story events support the moral.

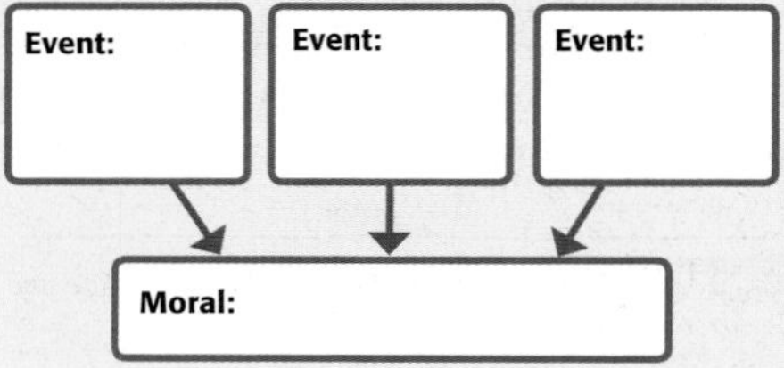

Literary Element

1. Cities rebuild walls to outdo each other. When people die, each city builds its wall to complement the other's.
2. The rebuilding represents a drive for supremacy. The final walls represent harmony and cooperation.
3. Students may cite stadiums, theme parks, and other attractions.

Review: Moral

Students may list these story events:

- Wall building is repeated.
- People grow weak from overwork.
- Prosperity returns when people cooperate.

Students might write this moral:
It is wiser to cooperate than to compete.

READING AND VOCABULARY

Reading Strategy Evaluating Figures of Speech

Bradbury is known for his poetic and figurative language. In "The Golden Kite, the Silver Wind," readers get the first taste of descriptive language in the title and encounter additional examples in nearly every paragraph.

1. What is descriptive about the story's title? Explain how the title conveys ideas and emotions. Consider connotations as well as images. How well does the title fit the story?
2. Return to the chart you created as you read the story. Choose two of the most effective uses of figurative language that you recorded. Explain what makes each of them memorably descriptive or aptly expressive of the emotion in the story.

Vocabulary Practice

Practice with Synonyms Choose the best synonym for each word below. Use a dictionary or thesaurus if you need help.

1. portent	**a.** portable	**b.** sign
2. ravenous	**a.** starving	**b.** diseased
3. spurn	**a.** scorn	**b.** stress
4. monotony	**a.** difficulty	**b.** sameness

Academic Vocabulary

Here are two words from the vocabulary list on page R80. These words will help you think, write, and talk about the selection.

offset (ôf set′) *v.* to balance or counterbalance; to compensate for

radical (rad′ i kəl) *adj.* departing from the usual or traditional; extreme

Practice and Apply

1. How does each city's actions **offset** the other city's actions?
2. Why is the suggestion of the kite and wind shapes a **radical** idea?

WRITING AND EXTENDING

Writing About Literature

Analyze Comic Devices Bradbury's story contains several comic elements. Among these are hyperbole, or deliberate exaggeration, and irony, a contrast between what is expected to happen and what actually happens. Write an essay in which you analyze the use of hyperbole and irony in the story.

Prewrite by listing examples of hyperbole and irony; you will use these examples as evidence in your paper. Then study the examples to decide how they affect the story. For example, do they increase the sense that this is not a realistic story? Craft your thesis before you begin your draft.

Follow the writing plan below to organize your paper and your body paragraphs.

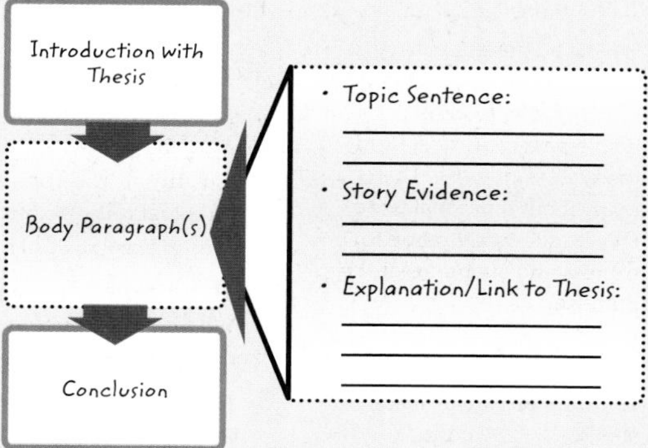

When your draft is complete, meet with a peer reviewer to evaluate each other's work and suggest revisions. Then proofread and edit your draft to correct errors in spelling, grammar, and punctuation.

Literature Groups

Work with a small group to decide whether the daughter in this story is a character archetype, or model, of the wise daughter common to many fables. Also discuss whether her role in the story is strengthened or undermined by the traditional Chinese focus that boys are more valuable than girls.

LiteratureOnline Web Activities For eFlashcards, Selection Quick Checks, and other Web activities, go to www.glencoe.com.

AFTER YOU READ

Assess

Reading Strategy

1. The gold and silver suggest precious things; the two objects suggest two things balanced in harmony. The title fits the ending of the story, in which balance and beauty are achieved through cooperation.
2. Students may include "a whisper like a snowflake," which suggests the softness and gentleness of the daughter's voice; or "disease ran off like a frightened jackal," which provides a strong visual image of how quickly disease disappears and helps convey the mood of harmony at the end of the story.

Vocabulary

1. b **2.** a **3.** a **4.** b

Academic Vocabulary

1. Each time one city changes its wall, the other city responds by changing its wall.
2. The kite and the wind are radical because they are meant to represent cooperation.

Web Activities Have students access the Web site for interactive activities that will help them assess their understanding of the selection.

Writing About Literature

Essay should

- State a thesis that presents an effect of the use of hyperbole and irony in the story
- Use evidence from the story to support the thesis
- Contain a clear introduction, body, and conclusion

Literature Groups

Encourage students to take a personal stance and defend it even if other students do not agree.

Focus

Write this sentence on the board: The basketball player towers over his teammates.

Say: Towers are tall structures, but the word connotes an awesome height that can be intimidating. What would change if instead you say "The boy is tall"? How does the word *tower* affect the sentence? *(Students may say that someone who towers over others shows strength and power as well as great height.)*

Teach

Denotation and Connotation **Say:** The literal meaning of a word is its *denotation.* A word may also have another meaning associated with it, called its *connotation.* For example, you may describe someone as *slim* or *skinny.* The first has a positive connotation and the second a negative one. Both have the denotation "thin." **OL**

Assess

1. b **2.** c **3.** a **4.** b

Vocabulary Workshop

Denotation and Connotation

▶ **Vocabulary Terms**

Loaded words express strong opinions or emotions. Some reveal **bias,** or prejudice. Others express **hyperbole,** or exaggeration. Some are used as **propaganda,** or language that distorts the truth for persuasive purposes.

▶ **Test-Taking Tip**

When you are asked to uncover bias, propaganda, or hyperbole, read the whole passage first to learn the writer's purpose. Then think about individual word choices the writer made to express and support that purpose.

▶ **Reading Handbook**

For more about vocabulary, see Reading Handbook, p. R19.

Literature Online

eFlashcards For eFlashcards and other vocabulary activities, go to www.glencoe.com.

ACADEMIC STANDARDS (page 1186)

9.1.2 Distinguish between what words mean literally and what they imply...

9.7.10 Assess how language... make[s] an impact on the audience.

9.4.12 Revise writing to improve the...precision of word choice...

Recognizing Loaded Words

"They have built their city's walls like a great bonfire to burn our stick!"

—Ray Bradbury, from "The Golden Kite, the Silver Wind"

Connecting to Literature In Bradbury's story, when a messenger utters these words to the Mandarin, the Mandarin's heart sinks. What he responds to are the loaded words in the message. First, the term *great bonfire* makes the fire sound like no ordinary flame, but a huge conflagration. On the other hand, the word *stick* makes the wall, previously referred to as a *club*, seem like less than it is—puny, insignificant, and easily burned. Loaded words like these, which are powerful tools in the art of fiction, can also be used to drive home a point in persuasive writing.

There are different kinds of loaded words.

- **Bias** is language that demonstrates a prejudice—or a prejudgment about people and events that is not necessarily accurate or truthful. Try substituting *avoid* for *spurn* in the sentence below. Notice how *spurn* reflects an especially negative bias or prejudgment about what will occur.
  Travelers will spurn us.
- **Hyperbole** is exaggerated language that is used to make a point.
  We will face disease, early sorrow, avalanches, grasshopper plagues, and poisoned well water.
- **Propaganda** uses language that distorts the truth in order to influence the public.
  The evil Kwan-Si will destroy our city if you don't change the shape of our walls today.

Exercise

From the words and phrases listed below, select those that reflect the greatest bias or hyperbole.

As the greatest, **1.** ______ nation on earth, only we have the right to **2.** ______ space. If life exists in space, it can only be **3.** ______ or degenerate. We will be the explorers who challenge **4.** ______ itself: that is our mighty nation's destiny.

1. a. biggest **b.** most powerful **c.** friendliest
2. a. visit **b.** explore **c.** colonize
3. a. primitive **b.** unimportant **c.** small
4. a. space **b.** eternity **c.** purpose

Additional Support

eFlashcards Have students access the Web site for more practice with recognizing loaded words.

Skills Practice

VOCABULARY: Identifying Word Relationships To help students better understand the relationships of words to each other, play a game of Word Clues. Each player chooses a word that has been used in class recently and coins a nonsense word to represent it. Player One writes a sentence on the board, using the nonsense word in an appropriate context. Others try to identify the word in its context. If others cannot identify the word, Player One supplies a synonym or antonym. Continue the game with other students' sentences. **OL**

PART 2

Revealing the Concealed

See Past and Future with Eyes in Back of Head, ca. 20th Century. Ellen Schuster. ★

BIG IDEA

BI Trying to outwit the mastermind detective is part of the fun of reading mysteries. Collect the clues and listen to the suspects, and you might solve the crime before the writer reveals the solution. The stories in Part 2 tell of puzzling cases and the great literary detectives who solve them. As you read the mysteries in Part 2, ask yourself: What details do I notice that the characters miss?

Analyzing and Extending

BI Big Idea

Suggest that as students read, they make a game of trying to solve the mysteries before the author reveals the solution. Have them keep a running list of details that are revealed as they read. Students should offer a solution before finishing each story and see how close they come to the right answer. OL

★ Viewing the Art

Contemporary American artist Ellen Schuster combines her talents as a photographer, computer illustrator, and graphic artist to create her unique artwork. AS

English Language Coach

Building Background Poll the class to see what kind of exposure they have to the mystery genre. Have students discuss their favorite books, films, or radio or TV shows in this genre. Invite students to tell who their favorite detectives are and why. EL

Differentiated Instruction

Interpreting the Art Have students study the artwork.

Ask: What does this picture reveal? What remains concealed? Discuss what students think the images represent and what questions the picture brings to mind, but leaves unanswered. BL

Academic Standards

Additional Support activities on pp. 1186 and 1187 cover the following standards:

Skills Practice: **9.1** [Use] relationships, and...context clues...to determine the meaning of words...

English Language Coach: **9.7.8** Compare and contrast the ways in which media genres...cover the same event.

Differentiated Instruction: **9.7.13** Identify the artistic effects of a media presentation...

UNIT SIX

Part 2: Skills Scope and Sequence

Readability Scores Key
Dale-Chall/ DRP/ Lexile

PACING STANDARD	(DAYS) BLOCK	SELECTIONS AND FEATURES	LITERARY ELEMENTS
2–3 class sessions	1–2	"The Mystery of Hunter's Lodge" by Agatha Christie **6.1/54/940**, pp. 1190–1202	Motivation, SE pp. 1191, 1194, 1197–1199, 1201 Style, SE p. 1201
		"The Adventure of the President's Half Disme" by Ellery Queen **8.1/60/910**, pp. 1203–1223	Suspense, TWE p. 1205 Plot, SE pp. 1204, 1206, 1209, 1213, 1215, 1218, 1220, 1222 Tone, SE p. 1222
2–3 class sessions	1	TIME, "Lost Apes of the Congo" by Stephan Faris **8.8/61/1020**, pp. 1224–1226	
		"The Red-Headed League" by Sir Arthur Conan Doyle **7.2/61/1110**, pp. 1227–1247	Foreshadowing, SE pp. 1228–1246 Character Archetype, SE p. 1246
		"The Stolen Cigar Case" by Bret Harte **9.4/58/1020**, pp. 1248–1257	Parody, SE pp. 1249–1252, 1254, 1255, 1257
2–3 class sessions	2–3	Writing Workshop: Editorial, pp. 1258–1265	Description, TWE p. 1260
1 class session		Speaking, Listening, and Viewing Workshop: Persuasive Presentation, pp. 1267–1268	
2 class sessions		Test Preparation and Practice, pp. 1270–1275	

About the Part

Part 2 deals with the genre of mystery writing. Writers of this genre must pay particular attention to suspense and foreshadowing.

READING AND CRITICAL THINKING	VOCABULARY	WRITING AND GRAMMAR	LISTENING, SPEAKING, AND VIEWING
Analyzing Details, SE pp. 1191, 1193, 1195, 1198 Analyzing Plot, TWE p. 1192	Word Origins, SE pp. 1191, 1202 Academic Vocabulary, SE p. 1202	Analyze Character, SE p. 1202	Analyzing Art, SE p. 1197; TWE p. 1194 Debating the Case, TWE p. 1200
Reviewing and Summarizing, SE pp. 1204, 1206, 1208, 1210, 1214, 1216, 1219, 1222	Analogies, SE p. 1222 Academic Vocabulary, SE p. 1222	Analyze Sound Devices, SE p. 1223 Using Ellipses, SE p. 1223	Group Activity, SE p. 1221 Performing, SE p. 1223 Analyzing Art, SE p. 1211; TWE pp. 1208, 1217, 1220
Evaluating Credibility, SE p. 1224; TWE p. 1225	Context Clues, TWE p. 1225		
Making Inferences About Characters, SE pp. 1228–1246 Critical Thinking, TWE p. 1230 Paraphrasing, TWE p. 1232	Synonyms, SE pp. 1228, 1246 Academic Vocabulary, SE p. 1246	Analyze Genre Elements, SE p. 1247 Using Formal Language, SE p. 1247	Group Activity, SE p. 1245 Analyzing Art, SE p. 1235; TWE p. 1237
Recognizing Author's Purpose, SE pp. 1249, 1251, 1252, 1255–1257 Previewing, TWE p. 1250 Monitoring Comprehension, TWE p. 1252	Connotation and Denotation, SE pp. 1249, 1257 Vocabulary for Precise Descriptions, TWE p. 1255	Apply Style, SE p. 1257 Interjections, TWE p. 1254	Analyzing Art, SE p. 1253; TWE p. 1256
		Counterarguments, TWE p. 1262	Getting Feedback, TWE p. 1264
			Persuasive Appeals, TWE p. 1266
		Punctuating Dialogue, TWE p. 1270 Outlining, TWE p. 1274	

Focus

BELLRINGER

Bellringer Options
Daily Language Practice Transparency 100
Or invite students to do some detective work by playing a game of "wink." Have students sit in a circle. Secretly select one person to be the villain. The villain should wink at as many people as possible without getting caught. Each student who is winked at should wait a few seconds and then fall over. The game ends when someone identifies the villain.

Teach

L Literary Element

Style and Tone Ask students who their favorite authors are, and list these on the board. Then invite students to discuss each author's style and tone and how these elements make the author's work appealing. OL

LITERARY FOCUS

Style and Tone

How do style and tone contribute to a sense of mystery?

L An author's style and tone contribute strongly to many mysteries. Some mystery writers develop a no-nonsense tone or create a sense of danger through their choice of words.

In his detective stories, Sir Arthur Conan Doyle uses a precise style and a logical tone to create Dr. Watson's moderately acute sense of observation.

I did not gain very much, however, by my inspection. Our visitor bore every mark of being an average, commonplace British tradesman, obese, pompous, and slow. He wore rather baggy gray shepherd's check trousers, a not overclean black frock coat, unbuttoned in the front, and a drab waistcoat with a heavy, brassy Albert chain, and a square pierced bit of metal dangling down as an ornament. A frayed top hat and a faded brown overcoat with a wrinkled velvet collar lay upon a chair beside him. Altogether, look as I would, there was nothing remarkable about the man save his blazing red head, and the expression of extreme chagrin and discontent upon his features.

—Sir Arthur Conan Doyle, from "The Red-Headed League"

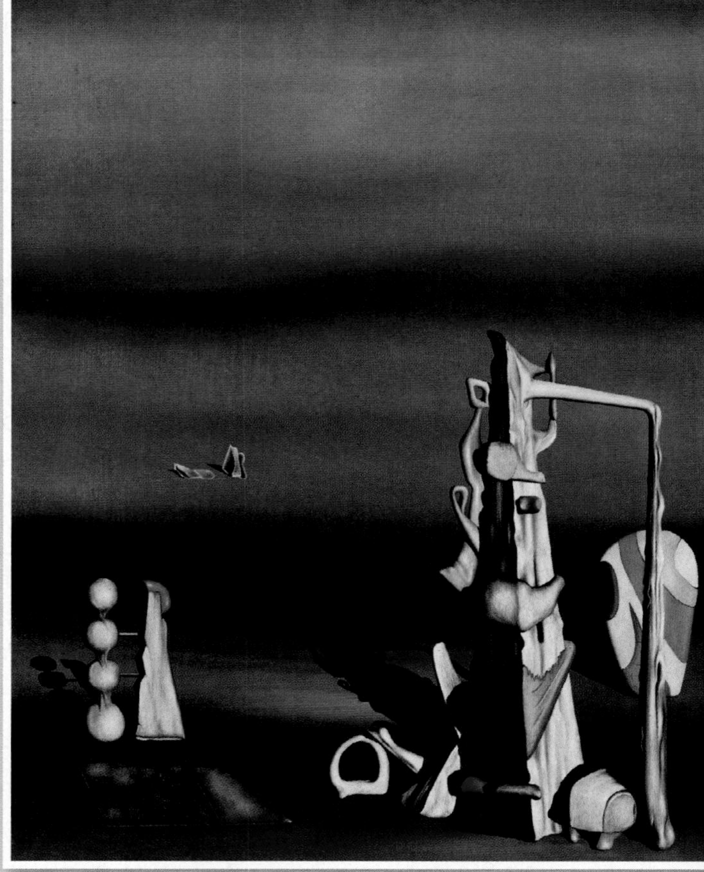

Instead of Fear, 1941. Yves Tanguy. Oil on canvas, 51 x 41 cm. Private collection. 

Interactive Literary Elements Handbook Go to www.glencoe.com to review or learn more about style and tone.

Additional Support

Skills Practice

READING: Mood Ask students to name various elements of a mystery, such as a crime scene, suspects, and detectives, and list them on the board. Brainstorm examples of moods and list them on the board. Have students pick one of the elements and one of the moods and then write a brief description of the element that reflects the chosen mood. Students should then rewrite their descriptions in a contrasting mood. OL

Style

The distinctive way a writer uses language is called **style.** Word choice, diction, use of literary devices, and tone all contribute to an author's style.

Diction and Word Choice The words a writer chooses and the arrangement of those words into phrases and sentences is **diction. Word choice** conveys meaning, suggests attitude, and creates images. The better the word and diction choices a writer makes, the easier it is for the reader to "see" the bullet hole in the wall, "hear" the mysterious footsteps on the stairs, or "feel" the chill on a fog-shrouded moor.

In this excerpt, the author chooses precise language and unique descriptions to create a portrait of a detective concentrating on a case.

R

> Mr. Queen prowled about the Clarke acres for the remainder of the day, his nose at a low altitude. He spent some time in the barn. He devoted at least twenty minutes to each of the twelve holes in the earth. He reinspected the oaken wreckage of his axework like a paleontologist examining an ancient petrifaction for the impression of a dinosaur foot. He measured off the distance between the holes; and, for a moment, a faint tremor of emotion shook him.
>
> —Ellery Queen, **from "The Adventure of the President's Half Disme"**

Mood The feeling or atmosphere of a story is called its **mood.** Often, a writer will establish mood through setting. Bret Harte has the main character in his parody "The Stolen Cigar Case" notice what is surrounding him in Hemlock Jones's study. Harte increases the comic mood by describing the odd items that Jones collects.

Tone

A writer's attitude toward the audience or the subject of the work is called **tone.** Writers communicate tone through words and details that create emotions in the reader. This, in turn, can help the reader feel engaged with the plot and sympathetic toward the characters.

> I was left to undertake my investigation alone.
>
> I may as well confess at once that they were rather disappointing. In detective novels clues abound, but here I could find nothing that struck me as out of the ordinary except a large bloodstain on the carpet where I judge the dead man had fallen. . . . No, I had seen all that Hunter's Lodge had to show me.
>
> —Agatha Christie, **from "The Mystery of Hunter's Lodge"**

Writers also use word choice to establish mood. Words such as *gray, melancholy, jagged, dim,* and *vague* might convey an eerie mood; *drifting, dozing,* and *silky* might create a peaceful mood.

Suspense The growing interest and excitement readers experience while awaiting a climax or resolution in a work of literature is **suspense.** To build suspense, an author may use **foreshadowing**—clues to what will happen next. In this excerpt, the farmer Simeon Clarke observes a man with a sword—a clue that helps unravel a mystery.

> Craning, the farmer saw within the coach a very large, great-nosed gentleman clad in a black velvet suit and a black cloak faced with gold; there was a cocked hat on his wigged head and a great sword in a white leather scabbard at his side.
>
> —Ellery Queen, **from "The Adventure of the President's Half Disme"**

Quickwrite

Creating a Mystery Make up a very basic story with the title "The Mystery of the Tunnel Beneath the School." Then share your ideas in groups of four. What do your group's stories have in common?

INDIANA ACADEMIC STANDARDS (pages 1188–1189)

9.3.11 Evaluate the aesthetic qualities of style, including the impact of diction...on tone, mood, and theme.

9.3.6 Analyze and trace an author's development of time and sequence, including the use of...foreshadowing...

English Language Coach

Word Detectives The meaning of several words and phrases in the Queen passage may pose a mystery for English language learners. Urge students to pretend they are detectives figuring out clues to the author's meaning. Have them study context (the reference to dinosaur footprints, for instance, helps explain *paleontologist*) and look up unfamiliar words (e.g., *altitude*) in a dictionary. For phrases such as "his nose at low altitude," have a volunteer portray the action described. **EL**

Teach

R Reading Strategy

Compare and Contrast

Have students study the Queen and Christie passages.

Ask: How are the two writers' styles alike and different? *(Both report physical details of the scene, but Queen's images are more exact and complex than Christie's. Queen's tone is ironic—"his nose at a low altitude"—while Christie is low-key and understated—"nothing that struck me.")* **OL**

Quickwrite

Students' stories should share elements and conventions of the genre, such as suspense, clues, and suspects.

Viewing the Art

French-born American Surrealist painter Yves Tanguy (1900–1955) spent several years as a merchant marine before pursuing a career as an artist. **AS**

Academic Standards

Additional Support activities on pp. 1188 and 1189 cover the following standards:

Skills Practice: **9.3.11** Evaluate the aesthetic qualities of style, including the impact of diction and figurative language on... mood...

English Language Coach: **9.1** Use...context clues, and a growing knowledge of English...to determine the meaning of words...

Focus

BELLRINGER

Bellringer Options
Daily Language Practice Transparency 101
Or **ask:** When you think of mystery stories, what comes to mind? *(Students may mention Sherlock Holmes or other famous detectives.)* What do you like most about mystery stories? *(Guide the discussion to touch on some of the conventions of mysteries, such as plot twists.)* Note that one such pleasure is the challenge of trying to solve the mystery before the detective does.

Literature Online

Author Search To expand students' appreciation of Agatha Christie, have them access the Web site for additional information and resources.

BEFORE YOU READ

The Mystery of Hunter's Lodge

MEET AGATHA CHRISTIE

During her career as a writer of detective stories, Agatha Christie never struggled with writer's block. She authored eighty-four novels, nearly one hundred fifty short stories, four nonfiction books, and nineteen plays. Her work has been translated into more than one hundred languages and has sold over two billion copies. When reflecting on the sheer output of her work, she referred to herself as "an incredible sausage machine."

Dared to Write Agatha Christie was born Agatha Miller in Torquay, England, to a wealthy family. She did not attend public school but taught herself how to read at a young age. She became an avid reader and began writing stories. She published a poem at age eleven.

In 1914 she met and married Archibald Christie, a fighter pilot. During World War I, while Archibald was away at war, Agatha worked in a local hospital. During this time, on a dare from her sister, she began to piece together the plot and characters for a detective story. The story would eventually become *The Mysterious Affair at Styles*, published in 1920. Christie followed up the success of her first novel with the 1926 publication of *The Murder of Roger Ackroyd*. The book confirmed her talent for creating intriguing mystery plots. During the next four decades, she published prolifically.

Queen of the Puzzle What thrilled Christie's readers was her technique of creating clever, perplexing puzzles in her stories. Many of her plots direct readers' attention away from the most important clues in solving the crime. More often than not, the reader is surprised when the villain is revealed. One biographer wrote, "Friend and foe alike bow to the queen of the puzzle."

> *"All I needed was a steady table and a typewriter."*
>
> —Agatha Christie

Christie's readers also love her characters. Two of her more famous and affable characters appear repeatedly in her novels and stories: Hercule Poirot and Miss Jane Marple. Poirot is a short, pompous Belgian detective with a tidy moustache. In spite of his own eccentricities, Poirot always manages to solve the crime. Miss Marple, on the other hand, is an elderly, unmarried woman and an amateur sleuth. She relies on her intuition and blatant nosiness to solve her crimes.

Christie was modest about her talents as a writer, but it was apparent to critics and readers alike that she had single-handedly created the standard for modern mystery writing. Indeed, her literary legacy to crime literature is still playing out.

Agatha Christie was born in 1890 and died in 1976.

Literature Online **Author Search** For more about Agatha Christie, go to www.glencoe.com.

Selection Skills

The Mystery of Hunter's Lodge

Literary Elements
- Motivation (SE pp. 1191–1201)
- Style (SE p. 1207)

Reading Skills
- Analyzing Details (SE pp. 1191–1202)

Vocabulary Skills
- Word Origins (SE pp. 1191, 1202)
- Academic Vocabulary (SE p. 1202)

Listening/Speaking/Viewing Skills
- Analyzing Art (SE p. 1197)

Writing Skills/Grammar
- Character Analysis (SE p. 1202)

LITERATURE PREVIEW

Connecting to the Story

The following story showcases the talents of one of Agatha Christie's star detectives, Hercule Poirot. Poirot is known for his ability to solve seemingly unsolvable mysteries. Before you read the story, think about the following questions:

- What do you like about mysteries? What do you dislike?
- Have you ever answered a question that at first seemed unanswerable? Explain.

Building Background

Hercule Poirot is considered one of the finest detectives in mystery fiction. A retired Belgian police officer, he is a self-proclaimed wonder of humanity who can spot criminals from a mile away and solve a crime without ever having visited the crime scene. In his first appearance, in Christie's 1920 novel *The Mysterious Affair at Styles,* Poirot is described as a short man, barely 5 feet 4 inches tall, with a precisely groomed moustache and an egg-shaped head. He dresses impeccably and is stately in manner and speech. Many of Christie's Poirot stories, including "The Mystery of Hunter's Lodge," are narrated by Poirot's assistant, Captain Hastings.

Setting Purposes for Reading

Big Idea Revealing the Concealed

As you read, pay close attention to new information as it is revealed in the narrative. Remember, even the smallest detail might be a clue.

Literary Element Motivation

Motivation is the stated or implied reason or cause for a character's actions. As you read, try to determine what motivation each suspect might have had to commit the crime.

- See Literary Terms Handbook, p. R11.

Literature Online Interactive Literary Elements Handbook To review or learn more about the literary elements, go to www.glencoe.com.

READING PREVIEW

Reading Strategy Analyzing Details

In mystery stories, it is important to pay close attention to details, because the solution to the mystery may be revealed by a seemingly unimportant detail. **Analyzing details** in a story means looking carefully at each element of plot, character, and setting, and asking why the author might have chosen those particular details.

Reading Tip: Gathering Evidence As you read, gather evidence from the story. Which details seem important? What do you know about the crime? What motivation might the criminal have?

Detail/Evidence	Significance
Poirot has the flu.	His detective skills may be hurt by his illness.

Vocabulary

implicitly (im plis′ it lē) *adv.* without question or reservation; p. 1193 *The sailors knew they could not question their captain's orders—they had to trust in his ability implicitly.*

prodigal (prod′ i gəl) *adj.* dangerously extravagant; wasteful; p. 1193 *Ana spent prodigal sums of money on a new wardrobe for college.*

veritably (ver′ i tə blē) *adv.* truly; p. 1199 *Pollution is veritably an epidemic in big cities such as Bangkok and Mexico City.*

pretext (prē′ tekst′) *n.* a claimed purpose, usually given to hide another purpose; p. 1200 *Sally asked Craig about the homework assignment as a pretext for asking him out on a date.*

Vocabulary Tip: Word Origins Knowing the origin of a word can help you understand its meaning.

INDIANA ACADEMIC STANDARDS (pages 1191–1202)

9.3.4 Determine characters' traits by what the characters say about themselves in narration [and] dialogue...

9.3 [Identify]...elements such as character,...plot, and setting...

9.5.3 Write...analytical essays...that gather evidence in support of a thesis...

BEFORE YOU READ

Focus

Summary

Roger Havering asks Detective Poirot to find out who murdered his uncle, Harrington Pace. Poirot, who is in bed with the flu, sends his assistant to investigate. While convalescing, Poirot uses the notes and pictures sent by his assistant to solve the mystery.

V Vocabulary

Vocabulary File Say: Add these words and definitions to your vocabulary file. For each word, include a sentence that gives you an example of how to use the word. **OL** Students with English language needs should include the pronunciations of these words in their files. **EL**

Literary Elements Have students access the Web site to improve their understanding of motivation.

Selection Resources

Print Materials
- Unit 6 Resources (Fast File), pp. 37–39
- Leveled Vocabulary Development, p. 75
- Selection and Unit Assessments, pp. 201–202
- Selection Quick Checks, p. 101

Transparencies
- Bellringer Options Transparencies: Daily Language Practice Transparency 101
- Literary Elements Transparency 16

Technology
- TeacherWorks Plus™ CD-ROM
- StudentWorks Plus™ CD-ROM
- Presentation Plus!™ CD-ROM
- Literature Online, glencoe.com
- Online Student Edition, mhln.com
- Exam*View*® Assessment Suite CD-ROM
- Vocabulary PuzzleMaker CD-ROM
- Listening Library, disc 2 track 45

Teach

BI Big Idea

Revealing the Concealed
Ask: What does this passage suggest about Poirot? *(It suggests he's celebrated and popular in high society.)* OL

Literary History

Queen of Crime Agatha Christie has been acknowledged in the *Guinness Book of Records* as the all-time best-selling fiction writer. Only the Bible and the works of Shakespeare have sold better than Christie's writing. Christie's native country honored her in 1971 by giving her the Order of Dame Commander, the highest British honor. AS

Readability Scores
Dale-Chall: 6.1
DRP: 54
Lexile: 940

The Mystery of Hunter's Lodge

Agatha Christie

"After all," murmured Poirot, "it is possible that I shall not die this time."

Coming from a convalescent[1] influenza patient, I hailed the remark as showing a beneficial optimism. I myself had been the first sufferer from the disease. Poirot in his turn had gone down. He was now sitting up in bed, propped up with pillows, his head muffled in a woollen shawl, and was slowly sipping a particularly noxious *tisane*[2] which I had prepared according to his directions. His eye rested with pleasure upon a neatly graduated row of medicine bottles which adorned the mantelpiece.

"Yes, yes," my little friend continued. "Once more shall I be myself again, the great Hercule Poirot, the terror of evildoers! Figure to yourself, *mon ami*,[3] that I have a little paragraph to myself in *Society Gossip*. But yes! Here it is: 'Go it—criminals—all out! Hercule Poirot—and believe me, girls, he's some Hercules!—our own pet society detective can't get a grip on you. 'Cause why? 'Cause he's got *la grippe*[4] himself!' "

I laughed.

"Good for you, Poirot. You are becoming quite a public character. And fortunately you haven't missed anything of particular interest during this time."

"That is true. The few cases I have had to decline did not fill me with any regret."

Our landlady stuck her head in at the door.

"There's a gentleman downstairs. Says he must see Monsieur Poirot or you, Captain.

1. *Convalescent* means "recovering from an illness."
2. A *tisane* (ti′ zän′) is an herbal beverage used for medicinal effects.
3. *Mon ami* (mon ə mē) is French for "my friend."
4. *La grippe* (lä grip) is the French term for influenza, commonly known as the flu.

Additional Support

Skills Practice

READING: Analyzing Plot Explain to students that a mystery's plot entails a series of clues that lead to the resolution of the case. Suggest that as students read, they jot down plot events that strike them as significant. As they review the clues every few pages, they should try to infer the solution. OL

Seeing as he was in a great to-do—and with all that quite the gentleman—I brought up 'is card."

She handed me the bit of pasteboard. "Mr. Roger Havering," I read.

Poirot motioned with his head towards the bookcase, and I obediently pulled forth *Who's Who*.[5] Poirot took it from me and scanned the pages rapidly.

"Second son of fifth Baron Windsor. Married 1913 Zoe, fourth daughter of William Crabb."

"H'm!" I said. "I rather fancy that's the girl who used to act at the Frivolity—only she called herself Zoe Carrisbrook. I remember she married some young man about town just before the War."

"Would it interest you, Hastings, to go down and hear what our visitor's particular little trouble is? Make him all my excuses."

Roger Havering was a man of about forty, well set up and of smart appearance. His face, however, was haggard, and he was evidently laboring under great agitation.

"Captain Hastings? You are Monsieur Poirot's partner, I understand. It is imperative that he should come with me to Derbyshire[6] today."

"I'm afraid that's impossible," I replied. "Poirot is ill in bed—influenza."

His face fell.

"Dear me, that is a great blow to me."

"The matter on which you want to consult him is serious?"

"My God, yes! My uncle, the best friend I have in the world, was foully murdered last night."

"Here in London?"

"No, in Derbyshire. I was in town and received a telegram from my wife this morning. Immediately upon its receipt I determined to come round and beg Monsieur Poirot to undertake the case."

5. *Who's Who* is a reference book that lists important people.
6. *Derbyshire* is the name of a county in north-central England.

Reading Strategy Analyzing Details *Why might this information be important?* **R**

"If you will excuse me a minute," I said, struck by a sudden idea.

I rushed upstairs, and in a few brief words acquainted Poirot with the situation. He took any further words out of my mouth.

"I see. I see. You want to go yourself, is it not so? Well, why not? You should know my methods by now. All I ask is that you should report to me fully every day, and follow **implicitly** any instructions I may wire[7] you."

To this I willingly agreed.

An hour later I was sitting opposite Mr. Havering in a first-class carriage on the Midland Railway, speeding rapidly away from London.

"To begin with, Captain Hastings, you must understand that Hunter's Lodge, where we are going, and where the tragedy took place, is only a small shooting-box in the heart of the Derbyshire moors.[8] Our real home is near Newmarket, and we usually rent a flat[9] in town for the season. Hunter's Lodge is looked after by a housekeeper who is quite capable of doing all we need when we run down for an occasional weekend. Of course, during the shooting season, we take down some of our own servants from Newmarket. My uncle, Mr. Harrington Pace (as you may know, my mother was a Miss Pace of New York), has, for the last three years, made his home with us. He never got on well with my father, or my elder brother, and I suspect that my being somewhat of a **prodigal** son myself rather increased than diminished his affection towards me. Of course I am a poor man, and my uncle was a rich one—in other words, he paid the piper![10]

7. To *wire* is to send a telegram.
8. *Moors* are expanses of open land that often contain marshy areas due to poor drainage.
9. *Flat* is the British term for "apartment."
10. To *pay the piper* usually means to accept the unpleasant results of something you have done. In this case, the uncle has covered the debts of his nephew.

Vocabulary

implicitly (im plis′ it lē) *adv.* without question or reservation

prodigal (prod′ i gəl) *adj.* dangerously extravagant; wasteful

Teach

R Reading Strategy

Analyzing Details Answer: *The second son in an aristocratic family would not inherit his father's title or property; his wife appears to be a commoner. These facts suggest Havering is in an unfavorable position in his family and may not have much money.* **OL**

Use the CheckPoint questions on Presentation Plus! to monitor students' comprehension. These questions can be used with interactive response keypads for immediate student feedback.

Differentiated Instruction

Drawing a Timeline A timeline may help less proficient or learning-disabled students understand and remember the story. Suggest students title their timelines "Murder Mystery." Tell them to mark important events on the timeline in the order in which they happen. For example, students might begin with Roger Havering's request for Poirot's help. Encourage them to review their timelines periodically for clues to the mystery. **BL**

Academic Standards

Additional Support activities on pp. 1192 and 1193 cover the following standards:

Skills Practice: **9.3** [Identify] story elements such as…plot…

Differentiated Instruction: **9.3.6** Analyze and trace an author's development of time and sequence…

Teach

L1 Literary Element

Motivation Answer: *He probably wanted to prevent any further expensive partying.* OL

L2 Literary Element

Motivation Answer: *He gives the impression he would no longer be able to enjoy the place where his uncle was killed.* **Say:** As you learn new information about each character, make note of how the new information might change what you think about that character's motivation. OL

★ Viewing the Art

English artist Sir William Nicholson (1872–1949) painted portraits, still lifes, and landscapes. Nicholson also designed for the theater, made engravings and color woodcuts, and produced posters with his brother-in-law James Pryde. AS

The Library at Hardwick Hall, Derbyshire, 1891. William Nicholson. Watercolor, 38.1 x 55.9 cm. Private collection. ★

But, though exacting in many ways, he was not really hard to get on with, and we all three lived very harmoniously together. Two days ago my uncle, rather wearied with some recent gaieties of ours in town, suggested that we should run down to Derbyshire for a day or two. My wife telegraphed to Mrs. Middleton, the housekeeper, and we went down that same afternoon. Yesterday evening I was forced to return to town, but my wife and my uncle remained on. This morning I received this telegram." He handed it over to me:

COME AT ONCE UNCLE HARRINGTON MURDERED LAST NIGHT BRING GOOD DETECTIVE IF YOU CAN BUT DO COME—ZOE.

"Then, as yet you know no details?"

"No, I suppose it will be in the evening papers. Without doubt the police are in charge."

It was about three o'clock when we arrived at the little station of Elmer's Dale. From there a five-mile drive brought us to a small gray stone building in the midst of the rugged moors.

"A lonely place," I observed with a shiver.

Havering nodded.

"I shall try and get rid of it. I could never live here again."

We unlatched the gate and were walking up the narrow path to the oak door when a familiar figure emerged and came to meet us.

"Japp!" I ejaculated.

Literary Element Motivation *Why might Mr. Pace have wished to go to Derbyshire for a few days?* L1

Literary Element Motivation *What is Mr. Havering's motivation to sell the cabin?* L2

Additional Support

Skills Practice

READING: Questioning Urge students to play detective by questioning vague or ambiguous statements. For instance, What does Havering mean when he calls his uncle "exacting"? What "forced" him to return to town? Note that the clues to a mystery are often found "between the lines." OL

The Scotland Yard[11] inspector grinned at me in a friendly fashion before addressing my companion.

"Mr. Havering, I think? I've been sent down from London to take charge of this case, and I'd like a word with you, if I may, sir."

"My wife—"

"I've seen your good lady, sir—and the housekeeper. I won't keep you a moment, but I'm anxious to get back to the village now that I've seen all there is to see here."

"I know nothing as yet as to what—"

"Ex-actly," said Japp soothingly. "But there are just one or two little points I'd like your opinion about all the same. Captain Hastings here, he knows me, and he'll go on up to the house and tell them you're coming. What have you done with the little man, by the way, Captain Hastings?"

"He's ill in bed with influenza."

"Is he now? I'm sorry to hear that. Rather the case of the cart without the horse, your being here without him, isn't it?"

And on his rather ill-timed jest I went on to the house. I rang the bell, as Japp had closed the door behind him. After some moments it was opened to me by a middle-aged woman in black.

"Mr. Havering will be here in a moment," I explained. "He has been detained by the inspector. I have come down with him from London to look into the case. Perhaps you can tell me briefly what occurred last night."

"Come inside, sir." She closed the door behind me, and we stood in the dimly-lighted hall. "It was after dinner last night, sir, that the man came. He asked to see Mr. Pace, sir, and, seeing that he spoke the same way, I thought it was an American gentleman friend of Mr. Pace's and I showed him into the gun-room, and then went to tell Mr. Pace. He wouldn't give any name, which, of course, was a bit odd, now I come to think of it. I told Mr. Pace, and he seemed puzzled like, but he said to the mistress: 'Excuse me, Zoe, while I just see what this fellow wants.' He went off to the gun-room, and I went back to the kitchen, but after a while I heard loud voices, as if they were quarreling, and I came out into the hall. At the same time, the mistress she comes out too, and just then there was a shot and then a dreadful silence. We both ran to the gun-room door, but it was locked and we had to go round to the window. It was open, and there inside was Mr. Pace, all shot and bleeding."

"What became of the man?"

"He must have got away through the window, sir, before we got to it."

"And then?"

"Mrs. Havering sent me to fetch the police. Five miles to walk it was. They came back with me, and the constable he stayed all night, and this morning the police gentleman from London arrived."

"What was this man like who called to see Mr. Pace?"

The housekeeper reflected.

"He had a black beard, sir, and was about middle-aged, and had on a light overcoat. Beyond the fact that he spoke like an American I didn't notice much about him."

"I see. Now I wonder if I can see Mrs. Havering?"

"She's upstairs, sir. Shall I tell her?"

"If you please. Tell her that Mr. Havering is outside with Inspector Japp, and that the gentleman he has brought back with him from London is anxious to speak to her as soon as possible."

"Very good, sir."

I was in a fever of impatience to get at all the facts. Japp had two or three hours' start of me, and his anxiety to be gone made me keen to be close at his heels.

Mrs. Havering did not keep me waiting long. In a few minutes I heard a light step descending the stairs, and looked up to see a very handsome young woman coming towards me. She wore a flame-colored

11. *Scotland Yard* is the detective division of the British metropolitan police force.

Reading Strategy Analyzing Details *Which details about the crime, as described by the housekeeper, might be important?* **R**

Teach

R Reading Strategy

Analyzing Details Answer: *An unidentified American man came to see Pace. The housekeeper took him to the gun-room before announcing him to Pace. The housekeeper heard shouting in the gun-room. She and Mrs. Havering were in the hall outside the room when they heard a gunshot. The door to the room was locked. The window was open—apparently the killer escaped that way.* **OL**

Differentiated Instruction

Keeping a Journal Gifted and talented students may enjoy keeping a journal of the details of the case. Note that one way to begin making sense of confusing details is to write them down. Tell students to imagine themselves as Captain Hastings when they write their entries. Suggest that they list what they've learned about the case from the nephew, his wife, and the housekeeper, as well as from details of the crime scene. **AL**

Academic Standards

Additional Support activities on pp. 1194 and 1195 cover the following standards:

Skills Practice: **9.2** Develop strategies such as asking questions…

Differentiated Instruction: **9.5.8** Write for different purposes and audiences, adjusting tone, style, and voice as appropriate.

Teach

BI1 Big Idea

Revealing the Concealed
Answer: *This reveals the probable murder weapon, but the reader wonders what happened to the second revolver.* OL

★ Writer's Technique

Developing Characters
Throughout her career, Christie created many detectives with intricately detailed biographies. She even developed an entire life story for Poirot's foil, Captain Hastings, who narrates this story. He first encounters Poirot shortly after having been wounded in World War I. Although Hastings lives in Argentina with his wife and four children, he frequently returns to England to visit Poirot and help solve crimes. AS

jumper,[12] that set off the slender boyishness of her figure. On her dark head was a little hat of flame-colored leather. Even the present tragedy could not dim the vitality of her personality.

I introduced myself, and she nodded in quick comprehension.

"Of course I have often heard of you and your colleague, Monsieur Poirot. You have done some wonderful things together, haven't you? It was very clever of my husband to get you so promptly. Now will you ask me questions? That is the easiest way, isn't it, of getting to know all you want to about this dreadful affair?"

"Thank you, Mrs. Havering. Now what time was it that this man arrived?"

"It must have been just before nine o'clock. We had finished dinner, and were sitting over our coffee."

"Your husband had already left for London?"

"Yes, he went up by the 6:15."

"Did he go by car to the station, or did he walk?"

"Our own car isn't down here. One came out from the garage in Elmer's Dale to fetch him in time for the train."

"Was Mr. Pace quite his usual self?"

"Absolutely. Most normal in every way."

"Now, can you describe this visitor at all?"

"I'm afraid not. I didn't see him. Mrs. Middleton showed him straight into the gun-room and then came to tell my uncle."

"What did your uncle say?"

"He seemed rather annoyed, but went off at once. It was about five minutes later that I heard the sound of raised voices. I ran out into the hall and almost collided with Mrs. Middleton. Then we heard the shot. The gun-room door was locked on the inside, and we had to go right round the house to the window. Of course that took some time, and the murderer had been able to get well away. My poor uncle"—her voice faltered—"had been shot through the head. I saw at once that he was dead. I sent Mrs. Middleton for the police. I was careful to touch nothing in the room but to leave it exactly as I found it."

I nodded approval.

"Now, as to the weapon?"

"Well, I can make a guess at it, Captain Hastings. A pair of revolvers of my husband's were mounted upon the wall. One of them is missing. I pointed this out to the police, and they took the other one away with them. When they have extracted the bullet, I suppose they will know for certain." ★

"May I go to the gun-room?"

"Certainly. The police have finished with it. But the body has been removed."

She accompanied me to the scene of the crime. At that moment Havering entered the hall, and with a quick apology his wife ran to him. I was left to undertake my investigations alone.

I may as well confess at once that they were rather disappointing. In detective novels clues abound, but here I could find nothing that struck me as out of the ordinary except a large blood-stain on the carpet where I judged the dead man had fallen. I examined everything with painstaking care and took a couple of pictures of the room with my little camera which I had brought with me. I also examined the ground outside the window, but it appeared to have been so heavily trampled underfoot that I judged it was useless to waste time over it. No, I had seen all that Hunter's Lodge had to show me. I must go back to Elmer's Dale and get into touch with Japp. Accordingly I took leave of the Haverings, and was driven off in the car that had brought us up from the station.

I found Japp at the Matlock Arms and he took me forthwith[13] to see the body. Harrington Pace was a small, spare, clean-shaven man, typically American in

12. *Jumper* is the British term for "sweater."

13. *Forthwith* means "immediately."

Big Idea Revealing the Concealed *How does this detail about the revolvers both reveal information and complicate the mystery?* BI1

Additional Support

Skills Practice

READING: Analyzing Characters
Have students imagine that they are Poirot, evaluating the information provided by Hastings. Ask them to create a three-column chart in their notebooks with the following heads: "Characters," "Description," and "Motivation." As students read, they should record details from the text in their charts. OL

appearance. He had been shot through the back of the head, and the revolver had been discharged at close quarters.

"Turned away for a moment," remarked Japp, "and the other fellow snatched up a revolver and shot him. The one Mrs. Havering handed over to us was fully loaded and I suppose the other one was also. Curious what darn fool things people do. Fancy keeping two loaded revolvers hanging up on your wall."

"What do you think of the case?" I asked, as we left the gruesome chamber behind us.

"Well, I'd got my eye on Havering to begin with. Oh, yes!"—noting my exclamation of astonishment. "Havering has one or two shady incidents in his past. When he was a boy at Oxford there was some funny business about the signature on one of his father's checks. All hushed up of course. Then, he's pretty heavily in debt now, and they're the kind of debts he wouldn't like to go to his uncle about, whereas you may be sure the uncle's will would be in his favor. Yes, I'd got my eye on him, and that's why I wanted to speak to him before he saw his wife, but their statements dovetail[14] all right, and I've been to the station and there's no doubt whatever that he left by the 6:15. That gets up to London about 10:30. He went straight to his club, he says, and if that's confirmed all right—why, he couldn't have been shooting his uncle here at nine o'clock in a black beard!"

"Ah, yes, I was going to ask you what you thought about that beard?"

Japp winked.

"I think it grew pretty fast—grew in the five miles from Elmer's Dale to Hunter's Lodge. Americans that I've met are mostly clean-shaven. Yes, it's amongst Mr. Pace's

14. When things *dovetail,* they fit neatly together.

Big Idea Revealing the Concealed *What does this detail suggest about Mr. Pace's murder?* **BI2**

Literary Element Motivation *Based on this information, do you think Mr. Havering had a reason to kill Mr. Pace? Explain.* **L**

Luxurious Air-conditioned *Portland Rose* Club Car, 1931.
Viewing the Art: Is this how you imagine Mr. Havering's train ride to London? Explain.

American associates that we'll have to look for the murderer. I questioned the housekeeper first, and then her mistress, and their stories agree all right, but I'm sorry Mrs. Havering didn't get a look at the fellow. She's a smart woman, and she might have noticed something that would set us on the track."

I sat down and wrote a minute[15] and lengthy account to Poirot. I was able to add various further items of information before I posted the letter.

The bullet had been extracted and was proved to have been fired from a revolver identical with the one held by the police. Furthermore, Mr. Havering's movements on the night in question had been checked and verified, and it was proved beyond a doubt that he had actually arrived in London by the

15. Here, *minute* (mī no͞ot′) means "detailed."

Teach

BI2 Big Idea

Revealing the Concealed
Answer: *If he was shot in the back of the head, he was either completely surprised or was running away.* **OL**

L Literary Element

Motivation **Answer:** *Most students will say yes. Havering might want to get his uncle's money to pay off some debts.* **OL**

Viewing the Art

Answer: *Students should infer that Havering could probably not afford such luxurious travel.*

The *Portland Rose* was the state of the art in first-class train travel in the United States when it began running in 1930. Its lavishly appointed club car had its own rose-motif china pattern and provided the services of maids and valets. Passengers who wanted to arrive at their destination looking fresh could even take a bath and have their hair cut or styled on the train. **AS**

Reading in the Real World

Career Encourage interested students to research the training required for police detectives or private investigators. Suggest they try to answer the following questions:

1. What type of education is required?
2. What duties are involved?
3. How are officers promoted?

Have students share their findings with the rest of the class. **OL**

Academic Standards

Additional Support activities on pp. 1196 and 1197 cover the following standards:

Skills Practice: **9.3** [Identify] story elements such as character, theme, plot, and setting...

Reading in the Real World: **9.4.4** Use writing to formulate clear research questions and to compile information from primary and secondary print or Internet sources...

Teach

R Reading Strategy

Analyzing Details Answer: *It suggests that the gun is the murder weapon and that the killer escaped on the train.* OL

L1 Literary Element

Motivation Answer: *Students may speculate that she quarreled with him or was hired by the Haverings to kill him.* OL

BI Big Idea

Revealing the Concealed Answer: *The housekeeper may be something other than she seems.* OL

★ Cultural History

Ealing Ealing is both a borough and a city within the borough, located in western London. The word Ealing is derived from the Saxon place-name *Gillingas.* Archaeological evidence shows that Ealing has been occupied for about 7,000 years. Ealing became a part of greater London in 1912. AS

train in question. And, thirdly, a sensational development had occurred. A city gentleman, living at Ealing, on crossing Haven Green to get to the District Railway Station that morning, had observed a brown-paper parcel stuck between the railings. Opening it, he found that it contained a revolver. He handed the parcel over to the local police station, and before night it was proved to be the one we were in search of, the fellow[16] to that given us by Mrs. Havering. One bullet had been fired from it.

All this I added to my report. A wire from Poirot arrived while I was at breakfast the following morning:

OF COURSE BLACK-BEARDED MAN WAS NOT HAVERING ONLY YOU OR JAPP WOULD HAVE SUCH AN IDEA WIRE ME DESCRIPTION OF HOUSEKEEPER AND WHAT CLOTHES SHE WORE THIS MORNING SAME OF MRS. HAVERING DO NOT WASTE TIME TAKING PHOTOGRAPHS OF INTERIORS THEY ARE UNDEREXPOSED AND NOT IN THE LEAST ARTISTIC.

It seemed to me that Poirot's style was unnecessarily facetious.[17] I also fancied he was a shade jealous of my position on the spot with full facilities for handling the case. His request for a description of the clothes worn by the two women appeared to me to be simply ridiculous, but I complied as well as I, a mere man, was able to.

At eleven a reply wire came from Poirot:

ADVISE JAPP ARREST HOUSEKEEPER BEFORE IT IS TOO LATE.

Dumbfounded, I took the wire to Japp. He swore softly under his breath.

"He's the goods, Monsieur Poirot! If he says so, there's something in it. And I hardly noticed the woman. I don't know that I can go so far as arresting her, but I'll have her watched. We'll go up right away, and take another look at her."

But it was too late. Mrs. Middleton, that quiet middle-aged woman, who had appeared so normal and respectable, had vanished into thin air. Her box had been left behind. It contained only ordinary wearing apparel. There was no clue in it to her identity, or as to her whereabouts.

From Mrs. Havering we elicited all the facts we could:

"I engaged her about three weeks ago when Mrs. Emery, our former housekeeper, left. She came to me from Mrs. Selbourne's Agency in Mount Street—a very well-known place. I get all my servants from there. They sent several women to see me, but this Mrs. Middleton seemed much the nicest, and had splendid references. I engaged her on the spot, and notified the Agency of the fact. I can't believe that there was anything wrong with her. She was such a nice quiet woman."

The thing was certainly a mystery. While it was clear that the woman herself could not have committed the crime, since at the moment the shot was fired Mrs. Havering was with her in the hall, nevertheless she must have some connection with the murder, or why should she suddenly take to her heels and bolt?

I wired the latest development to Poirot and suggested returning to London and making inquiries at Selbourne's Agency.

Poirot's reply was prompt:

USELESS TO INQUIRE AT AGENCY THEY WILL NEVER HAVE HEARD OF HER FIND OUT WHAT VEHICLE TOOK HER UP TO HUNTERS LODGE WHEN SHE FIRST ARRIVED THERE.

16. Here, *fellow* means "one of a pair" or "mate."
17. *Facetious* (fə sē′ shəs) means "humorous" or "sarcastic."

Reading Strategy Analyzing Details *What does this detail suggest?* R

Literary Element Motivation *If Poirot is correct, what reason might the housekeeper have had to kill Mr. Pace?* L1

Big Idea Revealing the Concealed *What do the details in this paragraph tell you about the housekeeper?* BI

Additional Support

Skills Practice

READING: Analyzing Cause-and-Effect Relationships Have students practice writing using transitions such as *because, therefore, so, as a result of,* and *consequently* to link cause and effect. Then, have students write an original sentence showing another cause-and-effect relationship in the selection.

1. Captain Hastings took the case ____ Poirot was ill. *(because)*
2. The murder happened at the lodge; ____, the murderer must have taken the train. *(therefore, consequently)*
3. Poirot can't leave his bed, ____ the flu. *(as a result of, due to, because of)* OL

Though mystified, I was obedient. The means of transport in Elmer's Dale were limited. The local garage had two battered Ford cars, and there were two station flies.[18] None of these had been requisitioned on the date in question. Questioned, Mrs. Havering explained that she had given the woman the money for her fare down to Derbyshire and sufficient to hire a car or fly to take her up to Hunter's Lodge. There was usually one of the Fords at the station on the chance of its being required. Taking into consideration the further fact that nobody at the station had noticed the arrival of a stranger, black-bearded or otherwise, on the fatal evening, everything seemed to point to the conclusion that the murderer had come to the spot in a car, which had been waiting near at hand to aid his escape, and that the same car had brought the mysterious housekeeper to her new post. I may mention that inquiries at the Agency in London bore out Poirot's prognostication.[19] No such woman as "Mrs. Middleton" had ever been on their books. They had received the Hon.[20] Mrs. Havering's application for a housekeeper, and had sent her various applicants for the post. When she sent them the engagement fee, she omitted to mention which woman she had selected.

Somewhat crestfallen, I returned to London. I found Poirot established in an armchair by the fire in a garish,[21] silk dressing gown. He greeted me with much affection.

"*Mon ami* Hastings! But how glad I am to see you. **Veritably** I have for you a great affection! And you have enjoyed yourself? You have run to and fro with the good Japp? You have interrogated and investigated to your heart's content?"

"Poirot," I cried, "the thing's a dark mystery! It will never be solved."

"It is true that we are not likely to cover ourselves with glory over it."

"No, indeed. It's a hard nut to crack."

"Oh, as far as that goes, I am very good at cracking the nuts! A veritable squirrel! It is not that which embarrasses me. I know well enough who killed Mr. Harrington Pace."

"You know? How did you find out?"

"Your illuminating answers to my wires supplied me with the truth. See here, Hastings, let us examine the facts methodically and in order. Mr. Harrington Pace is a man with a considerable fortune which at his death will doubtless pass to his nephew. Point No. 1. His nephew is known to be desperately hard up. Point No. 2. His nephew is also known to be—shall we say a man of rather loose moral fiber? Point No. 3."

"But Roger Havering is proved to have journeyed straight up to London."

"*Précisément*[22]—and therefore, as Mr. Havering left Elmer's Dale at 6:15, and since Mr. Pace cannot have been killed before he left, or the doctor would have spotted the time of the crime as being given wrongly when he examined the body, we conclude quite rightly, that Mr. Havering did *not* shoot his uncle. But there is a Mrs. Havering, Hastings."

"Impossible! The housekeeper was with her when the shot was fired."

"Ah, yes, the housekeeper. But she has disappeared."

"She will be found."

"I think not. There is something peculiarly elusive about that housekeeper, don't you think so, Hastings? It struck me at once."

"She played her part, I suppose, and then got out in the nick of time."

18. Here, *fly* means "a carriage drawn by a single horse."
19. *Prognostication* means "prediction."
20. *Hon.* is short for "Honorable," a form of address used in speaking to or of certain government officials or members of nobility. Because Roger Havering is the son of a baron, he and his wife are referred to in this way.
21. *Garish* means "gaudy" or "excessively ornamented."
22. *Précisément* (prā sēz′ ā môn′) is French for "precisely."

Vocabulary

veritably (ver′ i tə blē) *adv.* truly

Literary Element Motivation *Based on Poirot's conjectures about Mr. Havering, what might be Mrs. Havering's motivation?* L3

Teach

L2 Literary Element

Motivation Say: Poirot plainly outlines Roger Havering's motives for killing his uncle. What are they? *(Pace was a wealthy man, who had probably willed his fortune to his nephew. Havering was in debt.)* How do you think Havering could be a part of the crime even if he was in London? *(Students may suggest a conspiracy involving the housekeeper, the wife, or the stranger.)* OL

L3 Literary Element

Motivation Answer: *She would also benefit if her husband inherited the money.* OL

Building Reading Fluency

Expressiveness The concluding dialogue between Poirot and Hastings outlines the mystery's solution. Have pairs of students read the dialogue aloud to the class, starting with Hastings's return to London on page 1199. Urge readers to vary the tone and volume of their voices to clarify meaning. BL

Academic Standards

Additional Support activities on pp. 1198 and 1199 cover the following standards:

Skills Practice: **9.3.3** Analyze interactions between characters in a literary text and explain the way those interactions affect the plot. **9.6.2** Demonstrate an understanding of sentence construction…

Building Reading Fluency: **9.7.6** Analyze the occasion…and choose effective verbal…techniques (including voice…) for presentations.

Teach

BI1 Big Idea

Revealing the Concealed

Answer: *He implies that Mrs. Middleton was really Mrs. Havering in disguise.* OL

BI2 Big Idea

Revealing the Concealed

Ask: How does Poirot explain the gun that was found in Ealing? *(Havering stashed that gun at Ealing while his wife used the other gun to shoot Pace.)* Did you suspect this outcome to the mystery? Encourage students to recall clues that pointed to the Haverings' guilt. OL

CheckPoint

Use the CheckPoint questions on Presentation Plus! to check students' mastery of the selection. These questions can be used with interactive response keypads for immediate student feedback.

"And what was her part?"

"Well, presumably to admit her confederate, the black-bearded man."

"Oh, no, that was not her part! Her part was what you have just mentioned, to provide an alibi for Mrs. Havering at the moment the shot was fired. And no one will ever find her, *mon ami,* because she does not exist! 'There's no sech person,' as your so great Shakespeare says."

"It was Dickens," I murmured, unable to suppress a smile. "But what do you mean, Poirot?"

"I mean that Zoe Havering was an actress before her marriage, that you and Japp only saw the housekeeper in a dark hall, a dim middle-aged figure in black with a faint subdued voice, and finally that neither you nor Japp, nor the local police whom the housekeeper fetched, ever saw Mrs. Middleton and her mistress at one and the same time. It was child's play for that clever and daring woman. On the **pretext** of summoning her mistress, she runs upstairs, slips on a bright jumper and a hat with black curls attached which she jams down over the gray transformation. A few deft touches, and the make-up is removed, a slight dusting of rouge, and the brilliant Zoe Havering comes down with her clear ringing voice. Nobody looks particularly at the housekeeper. Why should they? There is nothing to connect her with the crime. She, too, has an alibi."

BI2 "But the revolver that was found at Ealing? Mrs. Havering could not have placed it there?"

"No, that was Roger Havering's job—but it was a mistake on their part. It put me on the right track. A man who has committed murder with a revolver which he found on the spot would fling it away at once, he would not carry it up to London with him. No, the motive was clear, the criminals wished to focus the interest of the police on a spot far removed from Derbyshire, they were anxious to get the police away as soon as possible from the vicinity of Hunter's Lodge. Of course the revolver found at Ealing was not the one with which Mr. Pace was shot. Roger Havering discharged one shot from it, brought it up to London, went straight to his club to establish his alibi, then went quickly out to Ealing by the District, a matter of about twenty minutes only, placed the parcel where it was found and so back to town. That charming creature, his wife, quietly shoots Mr. Pace after dinner—you remember he was shot from behind? Another significant point, that!—reloads the revolver and puts it back in its place, and then starts off with her desperate little comedy."

"It's incredible," I murmured, fascinated, "and yet—"

"And yet it is true. *Bien sûr,*[23] my friend, it is true. But to bring that precious pair to justice, that is another matter. Well, Japp must do what he can—I have written him fully—but I very much fear, Hastings, that we shall be obliged to leave them to Fate, or *le bon Dieu,*[24] whichever you prefer."

"The wicked flourish like a green bay tree,"[25] I reminded him.

"But at a price, Hastings, always at a price, *croyez-moi!*"[26]

Poirot's forebodings were confirmed. Japp, though convinced of the truth of his theory, was unable to get together the necessary evidence to ensure a conviction.

Mr. Pace's huge fortune passed into the hands of his murderers. Nevertheless, Nemesis[27] did overtake them, and when I read in the paper that the Hon. Roger and Mrs. Havering were amongst those killed in the crashing of the Air Mail to Paris I knew that Justice was satisfied.

Big Idea Revealing the Concealed *What is Poirot implying here?* BI1

Vocabulary

pretext (prē′ tekst′) *n.* a claimed purpose, usually given to hide another purpose

23. *Bien sûr* (bē ən syōōr) basically means "of course" in French.
24. *Le bon Dieu* (lə bon dyə) is French for "the good God."
25. Hastings is quoting a psalm from the Bible.
26. *Croyez-moi* (kroy ā mwä) means "believe me" in French.
27. *Nemesis* is the Greek goddess of punishment.

Additional Support

Skills Practice

LISTENING/SPEAKING/VIEWING: Debating the Case Divide the class into two debate teams. One will argue for Poirot's theory of the crime; the other, against it. Review the basics of persuasive language, reasoning, and proof, and remind students to use details from the story to support their arguments. Have each team meet to prepare its case and practice its presentation. OL

AFTER YOU READ

RESPONDING AND THINKING CRITICALLY

Respond

1. Were you surprised by the twist involving Mrs. Havering and Mrs. Middleton? Explain.

Recall and Interpret

2. (a)Why is Poirot not physically present during most of the story? (b)Why do you think Christie chose to exclude him in this way?
3. (a)According to Mrs. Havering, where was Mrs. Middleton when Mr. Pace was shot? (b)What makes Mrs. Middleton's location at the time of the murder important?
4. (a)Upon whom do the Haverings blame the murder? (b)How and why do you think the Haverings chose this particular nationality for the suspect?

Analyze and Evaluate

5. How does Christie use humor to enliven "The Mystery of Hunter's Lodge"?
6. How is Havering's decision to hire Poirot both a wise and a poor choice?
7. (a)Evaluate Christie's decision to make Mrs. Havering and Mrs. Middleton the same person. (b)Do you think Mrs. Havering would really be able to fool Captain Hastings and Inspector Japp? Explain.

Connect

8. **Big Idea** **Revealing the Concealed** Christie's Poirot is a master detective known for his incredible ability to solve mysteries with a bare minimum of evidence. Do you believe he would be able to solve this mystery from far away and with only the notes provided by Hastings? Explain.

LITERARY ANALYSIS

Literary Element Motivation

Character **motivation** is especially important in mystery stories because it can point to the culprit and the solution to the mystery. Motivation can be revealed through a character's speech or actions, or through suggestions made by the narrator.

1. What is the Haverings' motivation for committing the murder?
2. When and by whom is the actual motivation first suggested?
3. How does this first suggestion complicate the mystery?

Review: Style

As you learned on pages 1188–1189, **style** refers to the expressive qualities that distinguish an author's work. This includes word choice and the length and arrangement of sentences, as well as the use of figurative language and imagery. Style can reveal an author's attitude and purpose for writing. Christie makes her characters more realistic by using different sentence structure and diction for each character.

Partner Activity With a classmate, discuss the sentence structure and diction of the characters' dialogue in "The Mystery of Hunter's Lodge." Create a chart similar to the one below. Fill in the left-hand column with examples from the text that demonstrate a particular sentence structure or type of diction. In the right-hand column, label each example with the character's name and what the example reveals about his or her character.

Example	Character
"I brought up 'is card."	Poirot's landlady

AFTER YOU READ

Assess

1. Students should explain their answers.
2. (a) He is sick in bed. (b) This device highlights his ability to solve crimes using clever reasoning and keen insight.
3. (a) The hallway (b) Her presence there would support Mrs. Havering's alibi.
4. (a) An unknown American (b) To be convincing the "stranger" needed to have identifiable characteristics, such as an accent; the police would think he'd left the country and be thrown off the Haverings' trail.
5. Poirot cracks jokes and sends sarcastic telegrams. Japp teases Hastings about investigating without Poirot.
6. It suggests Havering really wants to find the culprit, but is ultimately foolish because it underestimates Poirot's ability to solve the case.
7. (a) Students should support their answers. (b) Students should support their answers with logic or details from the text; e.g., it's too far-fetched to work; her acting talent and the dim lighting might enable Mrs. Havering to carry off the deception.
8. Students should support their answers.

Literary Analysis

1. They need Mr. Pace's fortune to pay off debts.
2. On the train to Derbyshire, Havering notes his uncle must "pay the piper."
3. Most readers wouldn't expect the killer to reveal his own motive at the story's start.

Review: Style

Remind students to focus on the distinctive aspects—accent, level of formality and vocabulary, and so on—of each character's speech.

Academic Standards

The Additional Support activity on p. 1200 covers the following standard:

Skills Practice: **9.7.18** Deliver persuasive arguments...that clarify and defend positions with precise and relevant evidence...[and] anticipate and address the listener's concerns and counterarguments.

AFTER YOU READ

Assess

Reading Strategy

1. At the end when Poirot sums up the mystery
2. It serves as a final twist, reinforcing Poirot's skill at outwitting clever criminals.

Vocabulary

1. a **2.** b **3.** a **4.** b

Academic Vocabulary

1. The main events transpire over a few days, but there is no mention of how much time has passed when the killers meet their end.
2. The timetable of arrivals and departures supports Havering's account of his whereabouts.

Writing About Literature

Students should also offer examples of Poirot's dignity, politeness, wit, and perceptiveness. Students' essays should include:

- their general impressions of Poirot's character.
- evidence, including quotations, from the text to support their observations.

READING AND VOCABULARY

Reading Strategy Analyzing Details

Details are vital components of a mystery story. A mystery author uses certain details to lead the reader astray and other details to put the reader on the right track. Often the most subtle details end up being the most significant and incriminating evidence.

1. At what point does Christie reveal the true murder weapon?
2. What reason might Christie have for waiting to reveal the murder weapon?

Vocabulary Practice

Practice with Word Origins Select the vocabulary word best described by the word root. Use a dictionary if you need help.

1. The root of this word comes from the Latin word meaning "a show."
   a. pretext **b.** veritably
2. The root of this word comes from the Old French word for "true."
   a. pretext **b.** veritably
3. The root of this word comes from the Latin word meaning "to connect closely."
   a. implicitly **b.** prodigal
4. The root of this word comes from the Latin word meaning "wasteful."
   a. pretext **b.** prodigal

Academic Vocabulary

Here are two words from the vocabulary list on page R80.

duration (doo rā′ shən) *n.* the length of something, in terms of time

schedule (skej′ o͞ol) *n.* a plan that indicates what is to occur at certain times

Practice and Apply
1. What is the story's **duration**?
2. How is a train **schedule** a vital element of one character's alibi?

WRITING AND EXTENDING

Writing About Literature

Analyze Character In addition to his skills as a detective, Poirot has a well-defined and robust personality. This personality is evident in his rhetoric—how he speaks to and treats others—and in how he carries himself. Write a one- or two-page analysis of Poirot's character as it is depicted in "The Mystery of Hunter's Lodge." Use evidence from the story to support your analysis.

Before you begin drafting, gather evidence about several of Poirot's character traits, recording your evidence in a chart like the one below.

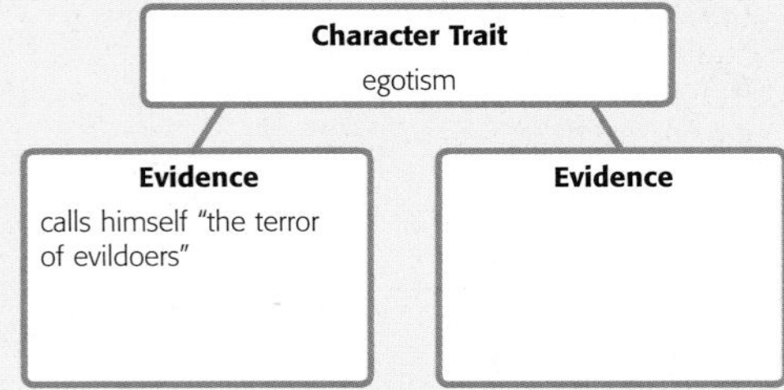

Include quotes from the story related to Poirot's character, as well as any impressions or ideas that strike you as you read. Once you have completed the chart, begin drafting your analysis.

After completing your first draft, meet with a peer reviewer to assess each other's work and to provide constructive criticism. Then proofread and edit your essay to correct errors in spelling, grammar, and punctuation.

Reading Further

If you were impressed by Poirot's performance in "The Mystery of Hunter's Lodge," you may also enjoy Agatha Christie's other Poirot stories and novels, such as *Poirot Investigates, Death on the Nile,* and *Murder on the Orient Express.*

LiteratureOnline Web Activities For eFlashcards, Selection Quick Checks, and other Web activities, go to www.glencoe.com.

LiteratureOnline

Web Activities Have students access the Web site for interactive activities that will help them assess their understanding of the selection.

BEFORE YOU READ

The Adventure of the President's Half Disme

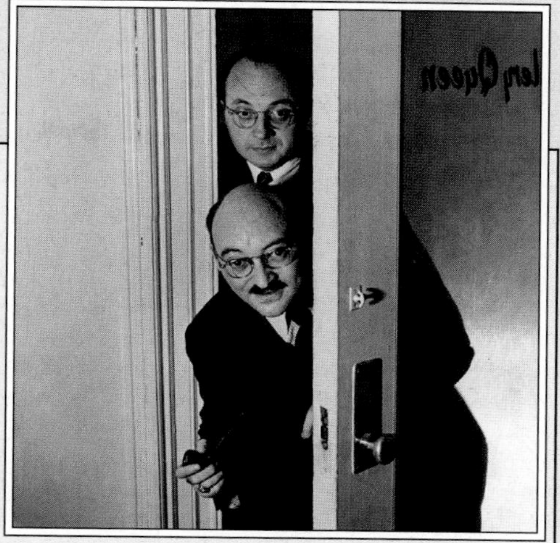

MEET ELLERY QUEEN

With a love for mysteries and a passion for truth, Ellery Queen is one of the most popular detectives and mystery writers of all time—or he would be, if he were real. Ellery Queen is actually the pen name under which two cousins, Manfred B. Lee and Frederic Dannay, wrote detective fiction from the 1920s until the 1970s. Their legacy is still evident in detective fiction today.

Who Is Ellery Queen? Cousins Manford Lepofsky and Daniel Nathan were born in Brooklyn, New York, in 1905. Manford had a fiery spirit, and Daniel was a quiet, shy boy, but their personalities seemed to complement one another. As they grew up, they were such good friends that they became known as Manny and Danny. As young men, they changed their names to Manfred B. Lee and Frederic Dannay.

> *"Our books are as much a canvas of their time as the books by Proust were of his time."*
>
> —Frederic Dannay

Their writing partnership began in 1929, the first year of the Great Depression. Dannay and Lee entered a contest sponsored by *McClure's* magazine. A cash prize of $7,500 was offered for the best novel submitted. The cousins decided to write a detective story. As both their pseudonym and the name of their detective, they chose the name Ellery Queen.

Dannay and Lee's novel, *The Roman Hat Mystery,* won the *McClure's* contest. But *McClure's* went bankrupt, and the cousins never received their prize. However, publisher Frederick A. Stokes bought the book from Dannay and Lee, and it sold well. The career of Ellery Queen, brilliant detective and writer, was off to a promising start.

Whodunit? As Ellery Queen, Dannay and Lee described how the detective investigated various crimes, often asking his father, a police inspector, for advice. Readers were invited to join him as he gathered evidence and tried to solve the crime. Each story contained many clues for readers to puzzle over.

Once Ellery Queen was successfully established in print, Dannay and Lee experimented with other media. From 1939 to 1948 the pair wrote a popular radio mystery show, *The Adventures of Ellery Queen,* which later made its way to television and movies. Another project, *Ellery Queen's Mystery Magazine,* made history by becoming the largest-selling mystery magazine in the world. The magazine represented the cutting edge of crime and mystery fiction and is still published today.

Manfred B. Lee was born in 1905 and died in 1971. Frederic Dannay was born in 1905 and died in 1982.

Literature Online **Author Search** For more about Ellery Queen, go to www.glencoe.com.

BEFORE YOU READ

Focus

BELLRINGER

Bellringer Options
Daily Language Practice Transparency 102
Or display images of popular detectives or detective programs.
Ask: Why do you think detective shows are so popular?
Have students consider as they read how Ellery Queen uses his powers of deduction to solve the mystery of the buried artifacts.

Author Search To expand students' appreciation of Ellery Queen, have them access the Web site for additional information and resources.

Selection Skills

The Adventure of the President's Half Disme

Literary Elements
- Plot (SE pp. 1204, 1206, 1209, 1213, 1215, 1218, 1220, 1222)
- Tone (SE p. 1222)

Vocabulary Skills
- Analogies (SE p. 1222)

Reading Skills
- Reviewing and Summarizing (SE pp. 1204, 1206, 1208, 1210, 1214, 1216, 1219, 1222)
- Previewing (TWE p. 1206)

Listening/Speaking/Viewing Skills
- Analyzing Art (SE p. 1211; TWE pp. 1208, 1217, 1220)

Writing Skills/Grammar
- Analyze Sound Devices (SE p. 1223)
- Using Ellipses (SE p. 1223)
- News Report (TWE p. 1216)
- Confusing Word Pairs (TWE p. 1214)
- Using Dashes (TWE p. 1218)
- Interjections (TWE p. 1220)

BEFORE YOU READ

Focus

Summary

An antiquarian, a coin collector, and a rare book dealer appear at the home of detective Ellery Queen. Soon after, Martha Clarke, the attractive young woman who has summoned them arrives and explains her dilemma. Her only hope of saving the family farm from foreclosure is to sell some valuable artifacts buried on the property by George Washington. She appeals to the experts to find the hidden treasure.

V Vocabulary

Vocabulary File Say: Add these words and definitions to your vocabulary file. For each word, include a sentence that gives you an example of how to use the word. **OL** Students with English language needs should include the pronunciations of these words in their files. **EL**

Literary Elements Have students access the Web site to improve their understanding of plot.

LITERATURE PREVIEW

Connecting to the Story

In the following story, detective Ellery Queen goes on a treasure hunt of sorts in order to solve a historical mystery. Think about the following questions:

- Have you ever searched for a hidden treasure?
- What historical figures or events have influenced your neighborhood, city, or state?

Building Background

George Washington is best known as the first president of the United States. Legend says that young Washington once cut down a cherry tree outside his home. When his father asked him angrily who had cut down the tree, the youth admitted his guilt. This tale, generally agreed to be fictional, is meant to symbolize Washington's honesty.

The United States Mint began operation while Washington was president. It was and remains responsible for the manufacture of official monetary coins for use in the United States, including the half disme, a five-cent coin no longer in circulation. *Disme* (dīm) is the origin of the word *dime.*

Setting Purposes for Reading

Big Idea Revealing the Concealed

As you read this story, notice how the author slowly reveals what has been cleverly concealed.

Literary Element Plot

Plot is the sequence of events in a short story, novel, or drama. A story's plot is broken down into segments, usually beginning with the exposition, which reveals the characters, the setting, and the situation. A plot is sometimes interrupted by a flashback, which relates an earlier event. As you read, notice how Queen develops the plot, through exposition and flashback.

- See Literary Terms Handbook, p. R13.

LiteratureOnline Interactive Literary Elements Handbook To review or learn more about the literary elements, go to www.glencoe.com.

READING PREVIEW

Reading Strategy Reviewing and Summarizing

Detective stories tend to rely on complex plots and extensive details. **Reviewing and summarizing** what happens on the page can help you keep track of details and understand the story. While reading this mystery, try to solve it using the clues Queen uncovers.

Reading Tip: Taking Notes Use a chart to help you summarize as you read.

Beginning of Selection	Summary
"Ellery was in his study that morning of the nineteenth of February . . ."	Three visitors with identical telegrams show up at Ellery's home.

Vocabulary

engrossed (in grōst′) *adj.* completely drawn in; absorbed; p. 1206 *The audience was engrossed by the suspenseful movie.*

expedient (ik spē′ dē ənt) *adj.* fulfilling a specific need in a pressing situation; serving as a means to an end; p. 1207 *When the basement flooded, grabbing a bucket seemed the most expedient action.*

cadaverous (kə dav′ ər əs) *adj.* resembling a corpse in appearance; pale and thin; p. 1209 *The cadaverous witches in* Macbeth *scared Rena.*

perfidious (pər fi′ dē əs) *adj.* characterized by or related to betrayal; treacherous; p. 1214 *Benedict Arnold is known as one of the most perfidious figures of the American Revolution.*

prowess (prau′ əs) *n.* incredible or superior talent or ability; p. 1215 *The archer showed his prowess when he hit five consecutive bull's-eyes.*

INDIANA ACADEMIC STANDARDS (pages 1204–1223)

9.3 [Identify] story elements such as...plot...

9.3.6 Analyze...complex literary devices, such as...flashbacks...

9.2 Develop [reading] strategies...

9.5.3 Write...analytical essays...

9.3.11 Evaluate the aesthetic qualities of style...

Selection Resources

Print Materials

- Unit 6 Resources (Fast File), pp. 40–42
- Leveled Vocabulary Development, p. 76
- Selection and Unit Assessments, pp. 203–204
- Selection Quick Checks, p. 102

Transparencies

- Bellringer Options Transparencies: Daily Language Practice Transparency 102
- Literary Elements Transparency 1

Technology

- TeacherWorks Plus™ CD-ROM
- StudentWorks Plus™ CD-ROM
- Presentation Plus!™ CD-ROM
- Literature Online, glencoe.com
- Online Student Edition, mhln.com
- Exam*View*® Assessment Suite CD-ROM
- Vocabulary PuzzleMaker CD-ROM
- Listening Library, disk 2 track 46

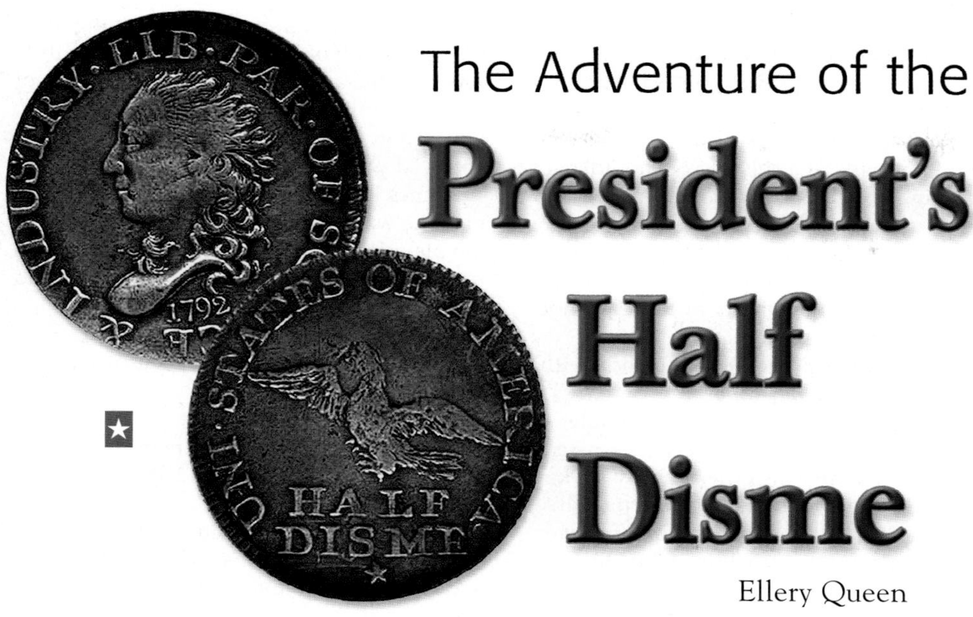

The Adventure of the President's Half Disme

Ellery Queen

Those few curious men who have chosen to turn off the humdrum highway to hunt for their pleasure along the back trails expect—indeed, they look confidently forward to—many strange encounters; and it is the dull stalk which does not turn up at least a hippogriff.[1] But it remained for Ellery Queen to experience the ultimate excitement. On one of his prowls he collided with a President of the United States.

This would have been joy enough if it had occurred as you might imagine: by chance, on a dark night, in some back street of Washington, D.C., with Secret Service men closing in on the delighted Mr. Queen to question his motives by way of his pockets while a large black bullet-proof limousine rushed up to spirit the President away. But mere imagination fails in this instance. What is required is the power of fancy, for the truth is fantastic. Ellery's encounter with the President of the United States took place, not on a dark night, but in the unromantic light of several days (although the night played its role, too). Nor was it by chance: the meeting was arranged by a farmer's daughter. And it was not in Washington, D.C., for this President presided over the affairs of the nation from a different city altogether. Not that the meeting took place in that city, either; it did not take place in a city at all, but on a farm some miles south of Philadelphia. Oddest of all, there was no limousine to spirit the Chief Executive away, for while the President was a man of great wealth, he was still too poor to possess an automobile, and what is more, not all the resources of his Government—indeed, not

1. A *hippogriff* is a mythical creature with the talons, wings, and head of a griffin (a mythical, birdlike creature) and the body of a horse.

Teach

L Literary Element

Suspense **Ask:** What is the effect of the story's opening paragraphs? *(They invoke an atmosphere of suspense. The reader anticipates a strange story and wonders how the circumstances will be explained.)* OL

★ Political History

Half Dismes The 1792 half dismes shown in the photo are the smallest silver coin issued by the fledgling U.S. mint. The mint's limited supply of silver—worth only about $100 in silver bullion—was a personal gift from George Washington. The President even threw in the family silver. A champion of the new nation's republican ideals, he rejected the idea of having his portrait on the coin as too reminiscent of European monarchs. AS

Readability Scores

Dale-Chall: 8.1
DRP: 60
Lexile: 910

English Language Coach

Background Newcomers to the United States may need an introduction to colonial history. Provide a brief overview that touches on George Washington, Philadelphia, the 13 colonies, and other period references. EL

Differentiated Instruction

Listening Hearing an audio recording of the story will improve understanding for less proficient readers and visually impaired students, while sharpening others' listening skills. Students should jot down questions as they listen. BL

Academic Standards

Additional Support activities on p. 1205 cover the following standards:

English Language Coach: **9.3.12** Analyze the way in which a work of literature is related to the themes and issues of its historical period.

Differentiated Instruction: **9.7.1** Ask questions concerning the speaker's content…

Teach

L1 Literary Element

Plot Answer: *It tells you who will be involved (Ellery Queen; George Washington); what the action will consist of (Ellery Queen matching wits with the Father of Our Country); and where the action will take place (on a farm south of Philadelphia).* OL

R1 Reading Strategy

Reviewing and Summarizing Answer: *Ellery Queen, Nikki, and James Ezekiel Patch have been introduced.* OL

R2 Reading Strategy

Making Inferences About Characters Ask: What does this comment imply about Ellery Queen? *(He can be rude and impatient if interrupted.)* OL

★ Political History

George Washington

On April 30, 1789, George Washington (1732–1799) became the first president of the United States. Raised as a Virginia gentleman, Washington served in the military, eventually becoming Commander in Chief of the Continental Army in the American Revolution. AS

all the riches of the world—could have provided one for him.

There are even more curious facets[2] to this jewel of paradox.[3] This was an encounter in the purest sense, and yet, physically, it did not occur at all. The President in question was dead. And while there are those who would not blink at a rubbing of shoulders or a clasping of hands even though one of the parties was in his grave, and to such persons the thought might occur that the meeting took place on a psychic plane—alas, Ellery Queen is not of their company. He does not believe in ghosts, consequently he never encounters them. So he did not collide with the President's shade, either.

And yet their meeting was as palpable[4] as, say, the meeting between two chess masters, one in London and the other in New York, who never leave their respective armchairs and still play a game to a decision. It is even more wonderful than that, for while the chess players merely annihilate space, Ellery and the father of his country annihilated time—a century and a half of it.

★ In fine, this is the story of how Ellery Queen matched wits with George Washington.

Those who are finicky about their fashions complain that the arms of coincidence are too long; but in this case the Designer might say that He cut to measure. Or, to put it another way, an event often brews its own mood. Whatever the cause, the fact is The Adventure of the President's Half Disme, which was to concern itself with the events surrounding President Washington's fifty-ninth birthday, actually first **engrossed** Ellery on February the nineteenth and culminated three days later.

Ellery was in his study that morning of the nineteenth of February, wrestling with several reluctant victims of violence, none of them quite flesh and blood, since his novel was still in the planning stage. So he was annoyed when Nikki[5] came in with a card.

"James Ezekiel Patch," growled the great man; he was never in his best humor during the planning stage. "I don't know any James Ezekiel Patch, Nikki. Toss the fellow out and get back to transcribing those notes on Possible Motives—"

"Why Ellery," said Nikki. "This isn't like you at all."

"What isn't like me?"

"To renege[6] on an appointment."

"Appointment? Does this Patch character claim—"

"He doesn't merely claim it. He proves it."

"Someone's balmy,"[7] snarled Mr. Queen; and he strode into the living room to contend with James Ezekiel Patch. This, he perceived as soon as James Ezekiel Patch rose from the Queen fireside chair, was likely to be a heroic project. Mr. Patch, notwithstanding his mild, even studious eyes, seemed to rise indefinitely; he was a large, a very large, man.

"Now what's all this, what's all this?" demanded Ellery fiercely; for after all Nikki was there. R2

"That's what I'd like to know," said the large man amiably. "What did you want with me, Mr. Queen?"

"What did I want with you! What did you want with me?"

"I find this very strange, Mr. Queen."

"Now see here, Mr. Patch, I happen to be extremely busy this morning—"

2. A *facet* is an aspect of something, or a single side of a cut jewel.
3. A *paradox* is a statement or situation that seems contradictory.
4. *Palpable* means "observable."

Literary Element Plot *How does the exposition leading up to this sentence help introduce the plot?* L1

Vocabulary

engrossed (in grōst′) *adj.* completely drawn in; absorbed

5. *Nikki* refers to Nikki Porter, Ellery Queen's friend and assistant.
6. To *renege* is to break a commitment or promise.
7. Here, *balmy* is a slang term meaning "irrational" or "lacking good sense."

Reading Strategy Reviewing and Summarizing *Which characters have been introduced so far?* R1

Additional Support

Skills Practice

READING: Previewing Review the elements of classic mystery tales seen in this story: strangers brought together under peculiar circumstances; a series of interrelated mysteries connected to the main conflict; and a brilliant detective. Write this question on the board for students to answer as they read: How is this story like a guessing game? Remind students to note the clues Ellery uses to solve the mystery. OL

"So am I." Mr. Patch's large thick neck was reddening and his tone was no longer amiable. Ellery took a cautious step backward as his visitor lumbered forward to thrust a slip of yellow paper under his nose. "Did you send me this wire, or didn't you?"

Ellery considered it tactically **expedient** to take the telegram, although for strategic reasons he did so with a bellicose[8] scowl.

IMPERATIVE YOU CALL AT MY HOME TOMORROW FEBRUARY NINETEEN PROMPTLY TEN A.M. SIGNED

ELLERY QUEEN

"Well, sir?" thundered Mr. Patch. "Do you have something on Washington for me, or don't you?"

"Washington?" said Ellery absently, studying the telegram.

"*George* Washington, Mr. Queen! I'm Patch the antiquarian. I *collect* Washington. I'm an *authority* on Washington. I have a large fortune and I spend it all on Washington! I'd never have wasted my time this morning if your name hadn't been signed to this wire! This is my busiest week of the year. I have engagements to speak on Washington—"

"Desist, Mr. Patch," said Ellery. "This is either a practical joke, or—"

"The Baroness Tchek," announced Nikki clearly. "With another telegram." And then she added: "And Professor John Cecil Shaw, ditto."

The three telegrams were identical.

"Of course I didn't send them," said Ellery thoughtfully, regarding his three visitors. Baroness Tchek was a short, powerful woman, resembling a dumpling with gray hair; an angry dumpling. Professor Shaw was lank and long-jawed, wearing a sack suit[9] which hung in some places and failed in its purpose by inches at the extremities. Along with Mr. Patch, they constituted as deliciously queer a trio as had ever congregated in the Queen apartment. Their host suddenly determined not to let go of them. "On the other hand someone obviously did, using my name . . ."

"Then there's nothing more to be said," snapped the Baroness, snapping her bag for emphasis.

"I should think there's a great deal more to be said," began Professor Shaw in a troubled way. "Wasting people's time this way—"

"It's not going to waste any more of *my* time," growled the large Mr. Patch. "Washington's Birthday only three days off—!"

"Exactly," smiled Ellery. "Won't you sit down? There's more in this than meets the eye . . . Baroness Tchek, if I'm not mistaken, you're the one who brought that fabulous collection of rare coins into the United States just before Hitler invaded Czechoslovakia? You're in the rare-coin business in New York now?"

"Unfortunately," said the Baroness coldly, "one must eat."

"And you, sir? I seem to know you."

"Rare books," said the Professor in the same troubled way.

"Of course. John Cecil Shaw, the rare-book collector. We've met at Mim's and other places. I abandon my first theory. There's a pattern here, distinctly unhumorous. An antiquarian, a coin-dealer, and a collector of rare books—Nikki? Whom have you out there this time?"

R3 "If this one collects anything," muttered Nikki into her employer's ear, "I'll bet it has two legs and hair on its chest. A darned pretty girl—"

"Named Martha Clarke," said a cool voice; and Ellery turned to find himself

8. *Bellicose* means "hostile in manner or mood."

9. A *sack suit* is a type of men's business suit that first came into fashion in the 1850s.

Big Idea Revealing the Concealed *Why does the author isolate this sentence in its own paragraph?* **BI**

Vocabulary

expedient (ik spē′ dē ənt) *adj.* fulfilling a specific need in a pressing situation; serving as a means to an end

Teach

L2 Literary Element

Plot **Ask:** What effect does the wording of the telegram have on the plot? *(Possible answer: It heightens the suspense.)* **OL**

BI Big Idea

Revealing the Concealed
Answer: *It highlights the strangeness of the telegrams and the situation.* **OL**

R3 Reading Strategy

Making Inferences **Ask:** What can you infer about the new visitor from Nikki's comment? *(The visitor must be a pretty woman; the overall tone of the comment and the word* muttered *suggest Nikki may be jealous.)* **OL**

Use the CheckPoint questions on Presentation Plus! to monitor students' comprehension. These questions can be used with interactive response keypads for immediate student feedback.

English Language Coach

Setting English language learners may become confused about the story's setting as it shifts between the past and the present. Have partners make two-column charts headed "Present" and "Past." As students read, they should list major events in the appropriate columns. When the charts are complete, ask students how the two sets of events are related. **EL**

Academic Standards

Additional Support activities on pp. 1206 and 1207 cover the following standards:

Skills Practice: **9.2** Develop [reading] strategies...

English Language Coach: **9.3** [Identify] story elements such as...setting... **9.3.6** Analyze and trace an author's development of time and sequence, including...flashbacks...

Teach

R Reading Strategy

Reviewing and Summarizing **Answer:** *An antiquarian, a coin dealer, and a rare book collector have been summoned to the home of Ellery Queen by a desperate young woman.* OL

L1 Literary Element

Figure of Speech **Ask:** What does the girl mean by saying she'll "make it snappy"? *(She will get right to the point.)* OL

★ Viewing the Art

One of France's most influential painters, Eugene Delacroix (1798–1863) was a painter from the Romantic school. His use of color influenced the development of Impressionism. Delacroix emphasized the importance of imagination and was inspired by literature, history, and his visit to Morocco. AS

The Fireplace, 1824. Eugene Delacroix, Philadelphia Museum of Art. 

regarding one of the most satisfying sights in the world.

"Ah, I take it, Miss Clarke, you also received one of these wires signed with my name?"

"Oh, no," said the pretty girl. "I'm the one who sent them." R

There was something about the comely Miss Clarke which inspired, if not confidence, at least an openness of mind. Perhaps it was the self-possessed manner in which she sat all of them, including Ellery, down in Ellery's living-room while she waited on the hearth-rug, like a conductor on the podium, for them to settle in their chairs. And it was the measure of Miss Clarke's assurance that none of them was indignant, only curious.

"I'll make it snappy," said Martha Clarke briskly. "I did what I did the way I did it because, first, I had to make sure I could see Mr. Patch, Baroness Tchek, and Professor Shaw today. Second, because I may need a detective before I'm through . . . Third," she added, almost absently, "because I'm pretty desperate. L1

"My name is Martha Clarke. My father Tobias is a farmer. Our farm lies just south of Philadelphia; it was built by a Clarke in 1761, and it's been in our family ever since. I won't go gooey on you. We're broke and there's a mortgage. Unless Papa and I can raise six thousand dollars in the next couple of weeks we lose the old homestead."

Reading Strategy Reviewing and Summarizing *Review what has happened since the first visitor was announced at the Queen residence.* R

Additional Support

Skills Practice

READING: Making Critical Judgments Explain that making critical judgments requires evaluating a selection in depth. Divide the class into groups of six. Assign one of six story elements—characterization, setting, plot, theme, dialogue, and imagery—to each group member. After students have written critiques of the elements, the groups should integrate them into a report to be shared in class. OL

Professor Shaw looked vague. But the Baroness said: "Deplorable, Miss Clarke. Now if I'm to run my auction this afternoon—"

And James Ezekiel Patch grumbled: "If it's money you want, young woman—"

"Certainly it's money I want. But I have something to sell."

"Ah!" said the Baroness.

"Oh?" said the Professor.

"Hm," said the antiquarian.

Mr. Queen said nothing, and Miss Porter jealously chewed the end of her pencil.

"The other day while I was cleaning out the attic, I found an old book."

"Well, now," said Professor Shaw indulgently. "An old book, eh?"

"It's called *The Diary of Simeon Clarke.* Simeon Clarke was Papa's great-great-great-something or other. His *Diary* was privately printed in 1792 in Philadelphia, Professor, by a second cousin of his, Jonathan, who was in the printing business there."

"Jonathan Clarke. *The Diary of Simeon Clarke,*" mumbled the **cadaverous** book collector. "I don't believe I know either, Miss Clarke. Have you . . . ?"

Martha Clarke carefully unclasped a large manila envelope and drew forth a single yellowed sheet of badly printed paper. "The title page was loose, so I brought it along."

Professor Shaw silently examined Miss Clarke's exhibit, and Ellery got up to squint at it. "Of course," said the Professor after a long scrutiny, in which he held the sheet up to the light, peered apparently at individual characters, and performed other mysterious rites, "mere age doesn't connote rarity, nor does rarity of itself constitute value. And while this page looks genuine for the purported[10] period and is rare enough to be unknown to me, still . . ."

"Suppose I told you," said Miss Martha Clarke, "that the chief purpose of the *Diary*—which I have at home—is to tell the story of how George Washington visited Simeon Clarke's farm in the winter of 1791—"

"Clarke's farm? 1791?" exclaimed James Ezekiel Patch. "Preposterous. There's no record of—"

"And of what George Washington buried there," the farmer's daughter concluded. By executive order, the Queen telephone was taken off its hook, the door was bolted, the shades were drawn, and the long interrogation began. By the middle of the afternoon, the unknown chapter in the life of the Father of His country was fairly sketched.

Early on an icy gray February morning in 1791, Farmer Clarke had looked up from the fence he was mending to observe a splendid cortège[11] galloping down on him from the direction of the City of Philadelphia. Outriders thundered in the van,[12] followed by a considerable company of gentlemen on horseback and several great coaches-and-six.[13] To Simeon Clarke's astonishment, the entire equipage[14] stopped before his farmhouse. He began to run. He could hear the creak of springs and the snorting of sleek and sweating horses. Gentlemen and lackeys[15] were leaping to the frozen ground and, by the time Simeon had reached the farmhouse, all were elbowing about the first coach, a magnificent affair bearing a coat of arms. Craning, the farmer saw within the coach a very large, great-nosed gentleman clad in a black velvet suit and a black cloak

10. *Purported* means "alleged" or "supposed."
11. A *cortège* is a procession of attendants.
12. *Outriders* are horse-riders that escort a vehicle (such as a carriage). The *van* is the *vanguard*, or the leading group of escorts.
13. *Coaches-and-six* refers to several carriages, each drawn by six horses.
14. An *equipage* is a horse-drawn carriage and its attendants.
15. *Lackeys* are servants, such as footmen.

Big Idea Revealing the Concealed *The reason the book collector was called in has been revealed. What interest do you think the other two people will have in the story Miss Clarke is telling?* **BI**

Vocabulary

cadaverous (kə dav′ ər əs) *adj.* resembling a corpse in appearance; pale and thin

Literary Element Plot *How do you know that this section of the story is a flashback?* **L2**

Teach

BI Big Idea

Revealing the Concealed
Answer: *The things Martha Clarke wants to sell include a historical relic and a coin.* **OL**

L2 Literary Element

Plot **Answer:** *It begins with the sentence "Early on an icy gray February morning in 1791. . . ."* **OL**

English Language Coach

Unusual Meanings This story features some unusual word usage that may confuse English language learners. For instance, the terms *rites* and *executive order,* on page 1209, are used in an ironic, rather than a literal, sense. Have students label a three-column chart with the heads *"Word," "Familiar Meaning,"* and *"Meaning in Context"* and work with a native English speaker to fill in the columns. **EL**

Academic Standards

Additional Support activities on pp. 1208 and 1209 cover the following standards:

Skills Practice: **9.3** [Identify] story elements such as character, theme, plot, and setting... **9.3.7** Recognize and understand the significance of various literary devices, including...imagery...

English Language Coach: **9.1.1** Identify... the literal...meanings of words. **9.1.2** Distinguish between what words mean literally and what they imply and interpret what the words imply.

Teach

R1 Reading Strategy

Reviewing and Summarizing **Answer:** *In 1791, George Washington and his entourage stopped at the Clarke's farm with a sick woman.* OL

R2 Reading Strategy

Reviewing and Summarizing **Answer:** *In gratitude for the Clarkes' hospitality, Washington will plant a grove of oak saplings and, beneath one tree, bury two personal possessions.* OL

BI Big Idea

Revealing the Concealed **Answer:** *They belonged to George Washington.* OL

faced with gold; there was a cocked hat[16] on his wigged head and a great sword in a white leather scabbard at his side. This personage was on one knee, leaning with an expression of considerable anxiety over a chubby lady of middle age, swathed in furs, who was half-sitting, half-lying on the upholstered seat, her eyes closed and her cheeks waxen under the rouge. Another gentleman, soberly attired, was stooping over the lady, his fingers on one pale wrist.

"I fear," he was saying with great gravity to the kneeling man, "that it would be imprudent to proceed another yard in this weather, Your Excellency. Lady Washington requires physicking[17] and a warm bed immediately."

Lady Washington! Then the large, richly dressed gentleman was the President! Simeon Clarke pushed excitedly through the throng.

"Your Mightiness! Sir!" he cried. "I am Simeon Clarke. This is my farm. We have warm beds, Sarah and I!"

The President considered Simeon briefly. "I thank you, Farmer Clarke. No, no, Dr. Craik. I shall assist Lady Washington myself."

And George Washington carried Martha Washington into the little Pennsylvania farmhouse of Simeon and Sarah Clarke. An aide informed the Clarkes that President Washington had been on his way to Virginia to celebrate his fifty-ninth birthday in the privacy of Mount Vernon.

Instead, he passed his birthday on the Clarke farm, for the physician insisted that the President's lady could not be moved, even back to the nearby Capital, without risking complications. On His Excellency's order, the entire incident was kept secret. "It would give needless alarm to the people," he said. But he did not leave Martha's bedside for three days and three nights.

Presumably during those seventy-two hours, while his lady recovered from her indisposition, the President devoted some thought to his hosts, for on the fourth morning he sent Christopher, his body-servant, to summon the Clarkes. They found George Washington by the kitchen fire, shaven and powdered and in immaculate dress, his stern features composed.

"I am told, Farmer Clarke, that you and your good wife refuse reimbursement for the livestock you have slaughtered in the accommodation of our large company."

"You're my President, Sir," said Simeon. "I wouldn't take money."

"We—we wouldn't take money, Your Worship," stammered Sarah.

"Nevertheless, Lady Washington and I would acknowledge your hospitality in some kind. If you give me leave, I shall plant with my own hands a grove of oak saplings behind your house. And beneath one of the saplings I propose to bury two of my personal possessions." Washington's eyes twinkled ever so slightly. "It is my birthday—I feel a venturesome spirit. Come, Farmer Clarke and Mistress Clarke, would you like that?"

"What—what were they?" choked James Ezekiel Patch, the Washington collector. He was pale.

Martha Clarke replied: "The sword at Washington's side, in its white leather scabbard, and a silver coin the President carried in a secret pocket."

"Silver *coin?*" breathed Baroness Tchek, the rare-coin dealer. "What kind of coin, Miss Clarke?"

"The *Diary* calls it 'a half disme,' with an *s*," replied Martha Clarke, frowning. "I guess that's the way they spelled dime in those days. The book's full of queer spellings."

16. A *cocked hat* is a hat with the brim turned up.
17. *Physicking* is an old-fashioned word meaning "a doctor's care."

Reading Strategy Reviewing and Summarizing *Briefly summarize the events so far in the flashback.* R1

Reading Strategy Reviewing and Summarizing *What has President Washington proposed and why?* R2

Big Idea Revealing the Concealed *What makes these personal possessions so valuable?* BI

Additional Support

Skills Practice

READING: Summarizing Ask students to explain what a summary is. *(A brief statement of the main points of a paragraph or longer piece of writing)* Explain that summarizing requires stating a text's main ideas in your own words. Note that summaries are helpful when reviewing material for a test. Invite volunteers to summarize the role that each of the various characters has played in the story so far. OL

Oak in Winter, ca. 1860s. Edward Fox. Stapleton Collection.
Viewing the Art: How does the tree in the foreground of this photograph affect the overall mood of the image? Explain. 

"A United States of America half disme?" asked the Baroness in a very odd way.

"That's what it says, Baroness."

"And this was in 1791?"

"Yes."

The Baroness snorted, beginning to rise. "I thought your story was too impossibly romantic, young woman. The United States Mint didn't begin to strike off half dismes until 1792!"

"Half dismes or any other U.S. coinage, I believe," said Ellery. "How come, Miss Clarke?"

"It was an experimental coin," said Miss Clarke coolly. "The *Diary* isn't clear as to whether it was the Mint which struck it off, or some private agency—maybe Washington himself didn't tell Simeon—but the President did say to Simeon that the half disme in his pocket had been coined from silver he himself had furnished and had been presented to him as a keepsake."

"There's a half disme with a story like that behind it in the possession of The American Numismatic[18] Society," muttered the Baroness, "but it's definitely called one of the earliest coins struck off by the Mint. It's possible I suppose, that in 1791, the preceding year, some specimen coins may have been struck off—"

"Possible my foot," said Miss Clarke. "It's so. The *Diary* says so. I imagine President Washington was pretty interested in the coins to be issued by the new country he was head of."

18. *Numismatics* is the collection or study of coins and money.

Teach

Viewing the Photograph

Answer: *The tree's bare limbs create an ominous mood because they symbolize lifelessness. The black-and-white format of the photograph contributes to this mood.*

Edward Fox (1823–1899) was a photographer mainly in the Brighton area of England. He specialized in landscape and architectural photography. His father, Edward Fox Sr., was a landscape painter and artist. AS

Differentiated Instruction

Sequence of Events The flashbacks in the story may make it difficult for learning disabled students to sort out the sequence of events. Have partners create a sequence-of-events chart, by listing and numbering the events in the order in which they occurred and by transferring the data to the chart. BL

Academic Standards

Additional Support activities on pp. 1210 and 1211 cover the following standards:

Skills Practice: **9.3.3** Analyze interactions between characters in a literary text and explain the way those interactions affect the plot.

Differentiated Instruction: **9.3.6** Analyze and trace an author's development of time and sequence, including…flashbacks…

Teach

BI1 Big Idea

Revealing the Concealed

Answer: *She will present the mystery, revealing that the location of the sword and the coin is unknown.* OL

BI2 Big Idea

Revealing the Concealed

Answer: *She seems to dislike or distrust Martha Clarke, perhaps viewing her as a rival or sensing something shady about her scheme.* OL

"Miss Clarke, I—I want that half disme. I mean—I'd like to buy it from you," said the Baroness.

"And I," said Mr. Patch carefully, "would like to ah . . . purchase Washington's sword."

"The *Diary*," moaned Professor Shaw. "I'll buy *The Diary of Simeon Clarke* from you, Miss Clarke!"

"I'll be happy to sell it to you, Professor Shaw—as I said, I found it in the attic, and I have it locked up in a highboy[19] in the parlor at home. But as for the other two things . . ." Martha Clarke paused, and Ellery looked delighted. He thought he knew what was coming. "I'll sell you the sword, Mr. Patch, and you the half disme, Baroness Tchek, provided"—and now Miss Clarke turned her clear eyes on Ellery—"provided you, Mr. Queen, will be kind enough to find them."

And there was the farmhouse in the frosty Pennsylvania morning, set in the barren winter acres, and looking as bleak as only a little Revolutionary house with a mortgage on its head can look in the month of February.

"There's an apple orchard over there," said Nikki as they got out of Ellery's car. "But where's the grove of oaks? I don't see any!" And then she added sweetly: "Do you, Ellery?"

Ellery's lips tightened. They tightened further when his solo on the front-door knocker brought no response.

"Let's go around," he said briefly; and Nikki preceded him with cheerful step.

Behind the house there was a barn; and beyond the barn there was comfort, at least for Ellery. For beyond the barn there were twelve ugly holes in the earth, and beside each hole lay either a freshly felled oak tree and its stump, or an ancient stump by itself, freshly uprooted. On one of the stumps sat an old man in earth-stained blue jeans.

"Tobias Clarke?" asked Ellery.

"Yump."

"I'm Ellery Queen. This is Miss Porter. Your daughter visited me in New York yesterday—"

"Know all about it."

"May I ask where Martha is?"

"Station. Meetin' them there other folks." Tobias Clarke spat and looked away—at the holes. "Don't know what ye're all comin' down here for. Wasn't nothin' under them oaks. Dug 'em all up t'other day. Trees that were standin' and the stumps of the ones that'd fallen years back. Look at them holes. Hired hand and me dug down most to China. Washin'ton's Grove, always been called. Now look at it. Firewood—for someone else, I guess." There was iron bitterness in his tone. "We're losin' this farm, Mister, unless . . ." And Tobias Clarke stopped. "Well, maybe we won't," he said. "There's always that there book Martha found."

"Professor Shaw, the rare-book collector, offered your daughter two thousand dollars for it if he's satisfied with it, Mr. Clarke," said Nikki.

"So she told me last night when she got back from New York," said Tobias Clarke. "Two thousand—and we need six." He grinned, and he spat again.

"Well," said Nikki sadly to Ellery, "that's that." She hoped Ellery would immediately get into the car and drive back to New York—immediately.

But Ellery showed no disposition to be sensible. "Perhaps, Mr. Clarke, some trees died in the course of time and just disappeared, stumps, roots, and all. Martha"—Martha!—"said the *Diary* doesn't mention the exact number Washington planted here."

"Look at them holes. Twelve of 'em, ain't there? In a triangle. Man plants trees in a triangle, he plants trees in a triangle. Ye don't see no place between holes big enough for another tree, do ye? Anyways, there was the

19. A *highboy* is a type of tall dresser.

Big Idea Revealing the Concealed *What do you think is coming?* BI1

Big Idea Revealing the Concealed *Why does Nikki want to leave so quickly?* BI2

Additional Support

Skills Practice

READING: Sequence Remind students that the sequence of a story is the order in which plot events occur. Because this story contains flashbacks, the plot comprises two alternating sequences of events. Have students show the sequence of events in the main story and in the background story on separate timelines, and then create a third timeline with all the events from the first two timelines arranged chronologically. OL same distance between all the trees. No, sir, Mister, twelve was all there was ever; and I looked under all twelve."

"What's the extra tree doing in the center of the triangle? You haven't uprooted that one, Mr. Clarke."

Tobias Clarke spat once more. "Don't know much about trees, do ye? That's a cherry saplin' I set in myself six years ago. Ain't got nothin' to do with George Washington."

Nikki tittered.

"If you'd sift the earth in those holes—"

"I sifted it. Look, Mister, either somebody dug that stuff up a hundred years ago or the whole yarn's a Saturday night whopper.[20] Which it most likely is. There's Martha now with them other folks." And Tobias Clarke added, spitting for the fourth time: "Don't let me be keepin' ye."

"It reveals Washington rather er . . . out of character," said James Ezekiel Patch that evening. They were sitting about the fire in the parlor, as heavy with gloom as with Miss Clarke's dinner; and that, at least in Miss Porter's view, was heavy indeed. L2 Baroness Tchek wore the expression of one who is trapped in a cave; there was no further train until morning, and she had not yet resigned herself to a night in a farmhouse bed. The better part of the day had been spent poring over *The Diary of Simeon Clarke,* searching for a clue to the buried Washingtonia. But there was no clue; the pertinent passage referred merely to "a Triangle of Oake Trees behinde the red Barn, which His Excellency the President did plant with his own Hands, as he had promis'd me, and then did burie his Sworde and the Half Disme for his Pleasure in a Case of copper beneathe one of the Oakes, the which, he said (the Case), had been fashion'd by Mr. Revere of Boston who is experimenting with this Mettle in his Furnasses."

"How out of character, Mr. Patch?" asked Ellery. He had been staring into the fire for a long time, scarcely listening.

"Washington wasn't given to romanticism," said the large man dryly. "No folderol[21] about him. I don't know of anything in his life which prepares us for such a yarn as this. I'm beginning to think—"

"But Professor Shaw himself says the *Diary* is no forgery!" cried Martha Clarke.

"Oh, the book's authentic enough." Professor Shaw seemed unhappy. "But it may simply be a literary hoax, Miss Clarke. The woods are full of them. I'm afraid that unless the story is confirmed by the discovery of that copper case with its contents . . ."

"Oh, dear," said Nikki impulsively; and for a moment she was sorry for Martha Clarke, she really was.

But Ellery said: "I believe it. Pennsylvania farmers in 1791 weren't given to literary hoaxes, Professor Shaw. As for Washington, Mr. Patch—no man can be so rigidly consistent. And with his wife just recovering from an illness—on his own birthday . . ." And Ellery fell silent again.

Almost immediately he leaped from his chair. "Mr. Clarke!"

Tobias stirred from his dark corner. "What?"

"Did you ever hear your father, or grandfather—anyone in your family—talk of *another barn behind the house?"*

Martha stared at him. Then she cried: "Papa, that's it! It was a different barn, in a different place, and the original Washington's Grove was cut down, or died—"

"Nope," said Tobias Clarke. "Never was but this one barn. Still got some of its original timbers. Ye can see the date burned into the cross-tree—1761."

Nikki was up early. A steady *hack-hack-hack* borne on the frosty air woke her. She peered out of her back window, the coverlet up to

20. A *Saturday night whopper* is a huge hoax or lie.

21. *Folderol* is foolishness or nonsense.

Literary Element Plot *How does this complicate the plot?* 

Literary Element Plot *What is Shaw implying here?* L3

Teach

L1 Literary Element

Plot Answer: *If the objects even exist, they will be much harder to find than everyone thought.* OL

L2 Literary Element

Characterization Ask: How would you characterize the baroness based on this description? *(Possible answer: The Baroness does not care for the plain surroundings and wants to return to her comfortable life in the city.)* OL

L3 Literary Element

Plot Answer: *The story in the diary may be fiction. Unless the story is verified by the discovery of the antiques, the diary is worthless.* OL

English Language Coach

End Marks Write on the board:
What day of the week is it?
That's a great idea!
Today is pizza day in the cafeteria.

Use the sentences to illustrate the proper use of a question mark (after a question), exclamation point (after a sentence that expresses strong emotion), and a period (after a statement). Discuss how questions, exclamations, and statements are punctuated in students' native languages. Have students write examples of each kind of sentence in English. EL

Academic Standards

Additional Support activities on pp. 1212 and 1213 cover the following standards:

Skills Practice: **9.3.6** Analyze and trace an author's development of time and sequence, including...flashbacks...

English Language Coach: **9.6.1** Identify and correctly use...the mechanics of punctuation...

Teach

R1 Reading Strategy

Drawing Conclusions Ask: Why does Nikki think Ellery is working hard to find the buried chest? *(Possible answer: She believes he's romantically interested in Martha Clarke.)* OL

R2 Reading Strategy

Reviewing and Summarizing Answer: *Nikki awakens to the sound of Ellery chopping wood. They discuss how the tree roots may have grown around the copper case and that it may be hidden within the tree stumps. Ellery chops for hours.* OL

R3 Reading Strategy

Making Inferences About Characters Ask: Why is Nikki horrified by Martha's tears? *(She figures tears will win Queen's sympathy and persuade him to do her bidding.)* OL

BI1 Big Idea

Revealing the Concealed
Answer: *He loves a challenge and probably wants to impress Martha.* OL

her nose, to see Mr. Ellery Queen against the dawn, like a pioneer, wielding an axe powerfully.

Nikki dressed quickly, shivering, flung her mink-dyed muskrat over her shoulders, and ran downstairs, out of the house, and around it past the barn.

"Ellery! What do you think you're doing? It's practically the middle of the night!"

"Chopping," said Ellery, chopping.

R1 "There's *mountains* of firewood stacked against the barn," said Nikki. "Really, Ellery, I think this is carrying a flirtation too far." Ellery did not reply. "And, anyway, there's something—something gruesome and indecent about chopping up trees George Washington planted. It's vandalism."

"Just a thought," panted Ellery, pausing for a moment. "A hundred and fifty-odd years is a long time, Nikki. Lots of queer things could happen, even to a tree, in that time. For instance—"

"The copper case," breathed Nikki, visibly. "The roots grew *around* it. It's *in* one of these stumps!"

"Now you're functioning," said Ellery, and he raised the axe again.

He was still at it two hours later, when Martha Clarke announced breakfast.

At 11:30 A.M. Nikki returned from driving the Professor, the Baroness, and James Ezekiel Patch to the railroad station. She found Mr. Queen seated before the fire in the kitchen in his undershirt, while Martha Clarke caressed his naked right arm.

"Oh!" said Nikki faintly. "I *beg* your pardon."

"Where are you going, Nikki?" said Ellery irritably. "Come in. Martha's rubbing liniment[22] into my biceps."

"He's not very accustomed to chopping wood, is he?" asked Martha Clarke in a cheerful voice.

"Reduced those foul 'oakes' to splinters," groaned Ellery. "Martha, ouch!"

"I should think you'd be satisfied *now*," said Nikki coldly. "I suggest we imitate Patch, Shaw, and the Baroness, Ellery—there's a 3:05. We can't impose on Miss Clarke's hospitality forever."

To Nikki's horror, Martha Clarke chose this moment to burst into tears.

"Martha!" R3

Nikki felt like leaping upon her and shaking the cool look back into her **perfidious** eyes.

"Here—here, now, Martha." That's right, thought Nikki contemptuously. Embrace her in front of me! "It's those three rats. Running out that way! Don't worry—I'll find that sword and half disme for you yet."

"You'll never find them," sobbed Martha, wetting Ellery's undershirt. "Because they're not here. They *never* were here. When you s-stop to think of it . . . *burying* that coin, his sword . . . if the story were true, he'd have given them to Simeon and Sarah . . ."

"Not necessarily, not necessarily," said Ellery with a hateful haste. "The old boy had a sense of history, Martha. They all did in those days. They knew they were men of destiny and that the eyes of posterity were upon them. Burying 'em is *just* what Washington would have done!"

"Do you really th-think so?"

Oh . . . *pfui.*

"But even if he did bury them," Martha sniffled, "it doesn't stand to reason Simeon and Sarah would have let them *stay* buried. They'd have dug that copper box up like rabbits the minute G-George turned his back."

"Two simple countryfolk?" cried Ellery. "Salt of the earth? The new American earth? Disregard the wishes of His Mightiness, George Washington, First President of the

22. *Liniment* is a pain-relieving liquid that is rubbed into the skin.

Reading Strategy Reviewing and Summarizing *Summarize what has happened since Nikki woke up.* R2

Big Idea Revealing the Concealed *Why is Ellery so eager to help Martha?* BI1

Vocabulary
perfidious (pər fi′ dē əs) *adj.* characterized by or related to betrayal; treacherous

Additional Support

Skills Practice

GRAMMAR AND LANGUAGE: Confusing Word Pairs Write on the board: The cat is lying near the fireplace. Lay the keys on the table.

Note that the verb *lie* means "to recline" or "to be positioned" and does not take a direct object. *Lay* means "to place" and takes a direct object *(keys).*

Review the principal parts of both words. Then, have students add the correct verb to each of the following sentences:

Go *(lie)* on the couch for a while.
The builder will start *(laying)* bricks today.
She *(lay)* down and went to sleep.
OL

United States? Are you out of your mind? And anyway, what would Simeon do with a dress-sword?"

Beat it into a ploughshare,[23] thought Nikki spitefully—*that's* what he'd do.

"And that half disme. How much could it have been worth in 1791? Martha, they're here under your farm somewhere. You wait and see—"

"I wish I could b-believe it . . . Ellery."

"Shucks, child. Now stop crying—"

From the door Miss Porter said stiffly: "You might put your shirt back on, Superman, before you catch pneumonia."

Mr. Queen prowled about the Clarke acres for the remainder of that day, his nose at a low altitude. He spent some time in the barn. He devoted at least twenty minutes to each of the twelve holes in the earth. He reinspected the oaken wreckage of his axe-work like a palaeontologist examining an ancient petrifaction for the impression of a dinosaur foot. He measured off the distance between the holes; and, for a moment, a faint tremor of emotion shook him. George Washington had been a surveyor in his youth; here was evidence that his passion for exactitude had not wearied with the years. As far as Ellery could make out, the twelve oaks had been set into the earth at exactly equal distances, in an equilateral triangle.

It was at this point that Ellery had seated himself upon the seat of a cultivator behind the barn, wondering at his suddenly accelerated circulation. Little memories were knocking at the door. And as he opened to admit them, it was as if he were admitting a personality. It was, of course, at this time that the sense of personal conflict first obtruded. He had merely to shut his eyes in order to materialize a tall, large-featured man carefully pacing off the distances between twelve points—pacing them off in a sort of objective challenge to the unborn future. George Washington . . .

The man Washington had from the beginning possessed an affinity[24] for numbers. It had remained with him all his life. To count things, not so much for the sake of the things, perhaps, as for the counting, had been of the utmost importance to him. As a boy in Mr. William's school in Westmorland, he excelled in arithmetic, long division, subtraction, weights and measures—to calculate cords of wood and pecks of peas, pints and gallons and avoirdupois[25]—young George delighted in these as other boys delighted in horseplay. As a man, he merely directed his passion into the channel of his possessions. Through his possessions he apparently satisfied his curious need for enumeration. He was not content simply to keep accounts of the acreage he owned, its yield, his slaves, his pounds and pence. Ellery recalled the extraordinary case of Washington and the seed. He once calculated the number of seeds in a pound troy weight[26] of red clover. Not appeased by the statistics on red clover, Washington then went to work on a pound of timothy seed. His conclusions were: 71,000 and 298,000. His appetite unsatisfied, he thereupon fell upon the problem of New River grass. Here he tackled a calculation worthy of his **prowess:** his mathematical labors produced the great, pacifying figure of 844,800.

This man was so obsessed with numbers, Ellery thought, staring at the ruins of Washington's Grove, that he counted the windows in each house of his Mount Vernon

23. To *beat a sword into a ploughshare* is to turn a weapon into the blade of a farming plow, meaning that a tool of destruction is transformed into a tool of creation. It is a reference to Isaiah 2:4 in the Bible.

24. An *affinity* is a great liking or interest.

25. *Avoirdupois* in French means "goods of weight." It is the name of the American system of weights measured in pounds.

26. *Troy weight* is a system of weights based on a twelve-ounce pound.

Literary Element Plot *Why might this flashback be important to the story?* L

Vocabulary

prowess (prau′ əs) *n.* incredible or superior talent or ability

Teach

BI2 Big Idea

Revealing the Concealed **Ask:** What facts about Washington help reveal his thinking to Ellery? *(His work as a surveyor; his talent with numbers.)* OL

R4 Reading Strategy

Author's Purpose **Ask:** How is the reader given clues in this passage? *(Queen recites relevant facts about Washington.)* OL

L Literary Element

Plot **Answer:** *Washington's fascination with numbers could be the key to the mystery.* OL

Political History

The U.S. Mint Thomas Jefferson was the driving force behind the first U.S. mint. Our decimal coin system was also his idea. The Mint Act of 1792, authored by Treasury Secretary Alexander Hamilton, named Philadelphia as the site of the mint. The variety of currency—local and foreign coins, wampum, crops, and livestock—that Americans used to do business before the country standardized the monetary system hampered economic growth. AS

Building Reading Fluency

Tone of Voice Discuss how tone of voice can enrich the meaning of spoken words. Have students work in small groups to prepare dramatic readings of the dialogue on pages 1214 and 1215. Explain that determining the correct tone for the dialogue will require insight into the characters and their motivations. Encourage students to discuss the relationship between Nikki, Ellery, and Martha before rehearsing the parts. Allow time for students to present their interpretations to the class. BL

Academic Standards

Additional Support activities on pp. 1214 and 1215 cover the following standards:

Skills Practice: **9.6.2** Demonstrate an understanding of sentence construction... and proper English usage...

Building Reading Fluency: **9.7** [Develop] speaking skills, such as...tone...

Teach

R1 Reading Strategy

Reviewing and Summarizing **Answer:** *He was meticulous and precise.* OL

R2 Reading Strategy

Predict **Say:** Make a prediction about the copper case based on what you have read. *(Possible answers: The case was dug up by the Clarkes many years ago; Ellery is going to link the clues together and find the case.)* OL

BI Big Idea

Revealing the Concealed **Answer:** *He is trying to get into Washington's head to figure out where Washington would have buried the copper case.* OL

★ Language History

Equilateral An equilateral triangle (also called an acute or equiangular triangle) is a three-sided figure where all the sides are the same length and the interior angles are all the same. The "equi" part of "equilateral" comes from the Latin *aequus* for "even" or "level." AS

estate and the number of "Paynes" in each window of each house, and then triumphantly recorded the exact number of each in his own handwriting.

It was like a hunger, requiring periodic appeasement. In 1747, as a boy of fifteen, George Washington drew "A Plan of Major Law: Washington's Turnip Field as Survey'd by me." In 1786, at the age of fifty-four, General Washington, the most famous man in the world, occupied himself with determining the exact elevation of his piazza above the Potomac's high-water mark. No doubt he experienced a warmer satisfaction thereafter for knowing that when he sat upon his piazza looking down upon the river he was sitting exactly 124 feet 10½ inches above it.

R2 And in 1791, as President of the United States, Ellery mused, he was striding about right here, setting saplings into the ground, twelve of them in an equilateral triangle, and beneath one of them he buried a copper case containing his sword and the half disme coined from his own silver. Beneath one of them . . . But it was not beneath one of them. Or had it been? And had long ago been dug up by a Clarke? But the story had apparently died with Simeon and Sarah. On the other hand . . .

Ellery found himself irrationally reluctant to conclude the obvious. George Washington's lifelong absorption with figures kept intruding. ★ Twelve trees, equidistant, in an equilateral triangle.

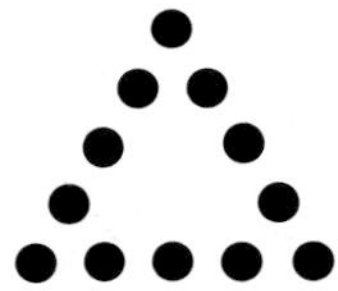

"What is it?" he kept asking himself, almost angrily. "Why isn't it satisfying me?"

And then, in the gathering dusk, a very odd explanation insinuated[27] itself. *Because it wouldn't have satisfied him!*

That's silly, Ellery said to himself abruptly. It has all the earmarks of a satisfying experience. There is no more satisfying figure in all geometry than an equilateral triangle. It is closed, symmetrical, definite, a whole and balanced and finished thing.

But it wouldn't have satisfied George Washington . . . for all its symmetry and perfection.

Then perhaps there is a symmetry and perfection beyond the cold beauty of figures?

At this point, Ellery began to question his own postulates[28] . . . lost in the dark and to his time . . .

They found him at ten-thirty, crouched on the cultivator seat, numb and staring.

He permitted himself to be led into the house, he suffered Nikki to subject him to the indignity of having his shoes and socks stripped off and his frozen feet rubbed to life, he ate Martha Clarke's dinner—all with a detachment and indifference which alarmed the girls and even made old Tobias look uneasy.

"If it's going to have this effect on him," began Martha, and then she said: "Ellery, give it up. Forget it." But she had to shake him before he heard her.

He shook his head. "They're there."

"Where?" cried the girls simultaneously.

"In Washington's Grove."

"Ye found 'em?" croaked Tobias Clarke, half-rising.

"No."

The Clarkes and Nikki exchanged glances.

"Then how can you be so certain they're buried there, Ellery?" asked Nikki gently.

Ellery looked bewildered. "Darned if I know *how* I know," he said, and he even laughed a little. "Maybe George Washington

27. *Insinuated* means "inserted" or "made known."
28. *Postulates* are ideas one assumes are true.

Reading Strategy Reviewing and Summarizing *Based on this section, how would you summarize Washington's personality?* R1

Big Idea Revealing the Concealed *What is Ellery trying to do?* BI

Additional Support

Skills Practice

WRITING: News Report Have students write a news report about one of the following events:

- Washington Visits Local Farm
- Ellery Queen Finds Buried Treasure

Explain that journalists must answer the questions *Who? What? When? Where?* and *Why?* in their reports. Suggest that students begin by deciding whether their report is for a magazine, newspaper, or television broadcast. Invite volunteers to present their reports to the class. OL

Portrait of George Washington. James the Elder Peale. Oil on canvas. Private collection. 

Teach

★ Viewing the Art

American artist James Peale (1749–1831) studied painting under his famous older brother, Charles Willson Peale, until he joined the military to fight in the American Revolution. James later returned to art, painting portraits, still lifes, landscapes, and historical paintings, and working as a portrait miniaturist. **AS**

Differentiated Instruction

Television News Program Have groups of students prepare a script for a news broadcast at the Clarke farm. Have students create dialogue for interviews with the characters in the story. Suggest that students use props and other graphics to help the audience visualize the farm, the people, and the artifacts. Have students present their news programs live or on videotape. **AL**

Academic Standards

Additional Support activities on pp. 1216 and 1217 cover the following standards:

Skills Practice: **9.5.8** Write for different purposes and audiences, adjusting tone, style, and voice as appropriate.

Differentiated Instruction: **9.7.4** Use props [and] visual aids…to enhance the appeal and accuracy of presentations. **9.7.17** Deliver oral responses to literature that demonstrate awareness of the author's writing style and an appreciation of the effects created…

Teach

L1 Literary Element

Figurative Language Ask: What figure of speech does Ellery use to describe his search for clues? *(Metaphor; "wrestling" with Washington)* OL

L2 Literary Element

Plot Answer: *Ellery needs to figure out Washington's thinking to find the copper case.* OL

R1 Reading Strategy

Making Inferences Ask: What does Nikki mean by the "Revolutionary walls" of her bedroom? *(She is referring to the era when the farmhouse was built.)* OL

★ Cultural History

Almanac The first almanacs were yearly calendars that included weather predictions, sunrise and sunset times, and other astronomical data. Today's almanacs often feature political news and commentary. The first issue of *The Old Farmer's Almanac* was published in 1792. Its motto has always been "Our main endeavor is to be useful, but with a pleasant degree of humour." AS

told me." Then he stopped laughing and went into the firelit parlor and—pointedly—slid the doors shut.

At ten minutes past midnight Martha Clarke gave up the contest.

"Isn't he ever going to come out of there?" she said, yawning.

"You never can tell what Ellery will do," replied Nikki.

"Well, I can't keep my eyes open another minute."

"Funny," said Nikki. "I'm not in the least bit sleepy."

"You city girls."

"You country girls."

They laughed. Then they stopped laughing, and for a moment there was no sound in the kitchen but the patient sentry-walk of the grandfather clock and the snores of Tobias assaulting the ceiling from above.

"Well," said Martha. Then she said: "I just *can't*. Are you staying up, Nikki?"

"For a little while. You go to bed, Martha."

"Yes. Well. Good night."

"Good night, Martha."

At the door Martha turned suddenly: "Did he say *George Washington told him?*"

"Yes."

Martha went rather quickly up the stairs.

Nikki waited fifteen minutes. Then she tiptoed to the foot of the stairs and listened. She heard Tobias snuffling and snorting as he turned over in his bed, and an uneasy moan from the direction of Martha's bedroom. Nikki set her jaw grimly and went to the parlor doors and slid them open.

Ellery was on his knees before the fire. His elbows were resting on the floor. His face was propped in his hands. In this attitude[29] his posterior was considerably higher than his head.

"Ellery!"

"Huh?"

"Ellery, what on earth—?"

"Nikki. I thought you'd gone to bed long ago." In the firelight his face was haggard.

"But what have you been *doing?* You looked exhausted?"

"I am. I've been wrestling with a man who could bend a horseshoe with his naked hands. A very strong man. In more ways than one." L1

"What are you talking about? Who?"

"George Washington. Go to bed, Nikki."

"George . . . Washington?"

"Go to bed."

". . . *Wrestling* with him?"

"Trying to break through his defenses. Get into his mind. It's not an easy mind to get into. He's been dead such a long time—that makes the difference. The dead are stubborn, Nikki. Aren't you going to bed?"

Nikki backed out shivering.

The house *was* icy.

It was even icier when an inhuman bellow accompanied by a thunder that shook the Revolutionary walls of her bedroom brought Nikki out of bed with a yelping leap. R1

But it was only Ellery.

He was somewhere up the hall, in the first glacial light of dawn, hammering on Martha Clarke's door.

"Martha. *Martha!* Wake up and tell me where I can find a book in this house! A biography of Washington—a history of the United States—an almanac . . . *anything!*" ★

The parlor fire had long since given up the ghost. Nikki and Martha in wrappers,[30] and Tobias Clarke in an ancient bathrobe over his marbled long underwear, stood around shivering and bewildered as a disheveled,[31] daemonic Ellery leafed eagerly through a 1921 edition of *The Farmer's Fact Book and Complete Compendium.*

"Here it is!" The words shot out of his mouth like bullets, leaving puffs of smoke.

"What is it, Ellery?"

"What on earth are you looking for?"

"He's loony, I tell ye!"

29. Here, *attitude* means "position or orientation of the body."

30. Here, *wrappers* means "loose-fitting robes."

31. *Disheveled* means "with rumpled hair and clothing."

Literary Element Plot *What conflict must be resolved before the plot reaches its conclusion?* L2

Additional Support

Skills Practice

GRAMMAR AND LANGUAGE:

Using Dashes Dashes set off supplemental information and material that interrupts the flow of the text. Have students find dashes in the story and explain what the author wanted to achieve by interrupting the text. Example: "Ellery and the father of his country annihilated time—a century and a half of it." *(The break suggests an interval of time and emphasizes that the amount of time is quite large.)* OL

Ellery turned with a look of ineffable[32] peace, closing the book.

"That's it," he said. "That's it."

"What's it?"

"Vermont. The State of Vermont."

"Vermont . . . ?"

"*Vermont?*"

"Vermont. What in the crawlin' creepers's Vermont got to do with—"

"Vermont," said Ellery with a tired smile, "did not enter the Union until March fourth, 1791. So that proves it, don't you see?"

"Proves *what?*" shrieked Nikki.

"Where George Washington buried his sword and half disme."

"Because," said Ellery in the rapidly lightening dawn behind the barn, "Vermont was the fourteenth State to do so. The *fourteenth.* Tobias, would you get me an axe, please?"

"An axe," mumbled Tobias. He shuffled away, shaking his head.

"Come on, Ellery, I'm d-dying of c-cold!" chattered Nikki, dancing up and down before the cultivator.

"Ellery," said Martha Clarke piteously, "I don't understand *any* of this."

"It's very simple, Martha—oh, thank you, Tobias—as simple," said Ellery, "as simple arithmetic. Numbers, my dears—numbers tell this remarkable story. Numbers and their influence on our first President who was, above all things, a number-man. That was my key. I merely had to discover the lock to fit it into. Vermont was the lock. And the door's open."

Nikki seated herself on the cultivator. You had to give Ellery his head[33] in a situation like this; you couldn't drive him for beans. Well, she thought grudgingly, seeing how pale and how tired-looking he was after a night's wrestling with George Washington, he's earned it.

"The number was wrong," said Ellery solemnly, leaning on Tobias's axe. "Twelve trees. Washington apparently planted twelve trees—Simeon Clarke's *Diary* never did mention the number twelve, but the evidence seemed unquestionable—there were twelve oaks in an equilateral triangle, each one an equal distance from its neighbor.

"And yet . . . I felt that *twelve* oaks couldn't be, perfect as the triangle was. Not if they were planted by George Washington. Not on February the twenty-second, New Style, in the year 1791. BI2

"Because on February the twenty-second, 1791—in fact, until March the fourth, when Vermont entered the Union to swell its original number by one—there was *another* number in the United States so important, so revered, so much a part of the common speech and the common living—and dying—that it was more than a number; it was a solemn and sacred thing; almost not a number at all. It overshadowed other numbers like the still-unborn Paul Bunyan. It was memorialized on the New American flag in the number of its stars and the number of its stripes. It was a number of which George Washington was the standard-bearer!—the head and only recently the strong right arm of the new Republic which had been born out of the blood and muscle of its integers. It was a number which was in the hearts and minds and mouths of all Americans.

"No. If George Washington, who was not merely the living symbol of all this but carried with him that extraordinary compulsion toward numbers which characterized his whole temperament besides, had wished to plant a number of oak trees to commemorate a birthday visit in the year 1791 . . . he would have, he could have, selected only one number out of all the mathematical trillions at his command—*the number thirteen.*"

The sun was looking over the edge of Pennsylvania at Washington's Grove.

32. *Ineffable* means "inexpressible."

33. *To give Ellery his head* refers to allowing a horse to run without reining it in.

Big Idea Revealing the Concealed *What do you think Vermont has to do with the location of the buried items?* BI1

Reading Strategy Reviewing and Summarizing *What does the number thirteen represent?* R2

Teach

BI1 Big Idea

Revealing the Concealed
Answer: *Remembering Vermont as the fourteenth state reminds Ellery of the first thirteen. He deduces that the number thirteen must have been important to Washington.* OL

BI2 Big Idea

Revealing the Concealed
Ask: What does Ellery reveal when he gives the date February 22, 1791? *(The final clue he needed to solve the mystery)* OL

R2 Reading Strategy

Reviewing and Summarizing **Answer:** *Thirteen is the number of original colonies of the United States.* OL

English Language Coach

Using a Dictionary Pronunciation guides may require skills that take an English language learner time to acquire. It may be more helpful for students to hear how words sound. Have students list unfamiliar words from the story and use a dictionary to find the meaning of each word. Pair them with an English-proficient partner to practice pronouncing each word and to discuss its meaning. EL

Academic Standards

Additional Support activities on pp. 1218 and 1219 cover the following standards:

Skills Practice: **9.6.1** Identify and correctly use...the mechanics of punctuation...

English Language Coach: **9.1** Use phonics, context clues, and a growing knowledge of English...to determine the meaning of words and become fluent readers.

Teach

R1 Reading Strategy

Reviewing and Summarizing **Ask:** How do the authors help readers keep up with the plot? *(Queen summarizes what has happened up to this point.)* **OL**

R2 Reading Strategy

Making Inferences About Characters **Ask:** Why does Queen "glance tenderly" at the cherry sapling? *(He may be remembering the story of George Washington cutting down a cherry tree as a child.)* **OL**

L Literary Element

Plot **Answer:** *Answers may include: "an encounter in the purest sense, and yet, physically, it did not occur at all"; "their meeting was . . . palpable"; and "Ellery and the father of his country annihilated time."* **OL**

★ Viewing the Art

This somber rural landscape by Vincent van Gogh (1853–1890) reflects the influence of the Hague School, a group of nineteenth-century artists who revived the style of the seventeenth-century Dutch masters. **AS**

Sunrise, 1883. Vincent van Gogh. ★

R1 "George Washington planted thirteen trees here that day, and under one of them he buried Paul Revere's copper case. Twelve of the trees he arranged in an equilateral triangle, and we know that the historic treasure was not under any of the twelve. Therefore he must have buried the case under the thirteenth—a thirteenth oak sapling which grew to oakhood and, some time during the past century and a half, withered and died and vanished, vanished so utterly that it left no trace, not even its roots.

"Where would Washington have planted that thirteenth oak? Because beneath the spot where it once stood—there lies the copper case containing his sword and the first coin to be struck off in the new United States."

R2 And Ellery glanced tenderly at the cherry sapling which Tobias Clarke had set into the earth in the middle of Washington's Grove six years before.

"Washington the surveyor, the geometer, the man whose mind cried out for integral symmetries? Obviously, in only one place: *In the center of the triangle.* Any other place would be unthinkable."

And Ellery hefted Tobias's axe and strode toward the six-year-old tree. He raised the axe.

But suddenly he lowered it, and turned, and said in a rather startled way: "See here! Isn't today . . . ?"

"Washington's Birthday," said Nikki.

Ellery grinned and began to chop down the cherry tree. ❧

Literary Element Plot *Look back to the beginning of the story. What statements in the exposition hint at this ending?* **L**

Additional Support

Academic Standards

The Additional Support activity on p. 1220 covers the following standard:

Skills Practice: **9.6.2** Demonstrate an understanding of…proper English usage…

Skills Practice

GRAMMAR AND LANGUAGE: Interjections Note that an interjection is an exclamation with no grammatical connection to the rest of the sentence. Discuss these interjections:

Hi! I'm here.

Oh, look at the flowers!

Have students complete each statement with an interjection.

1. ______, the bride is lovely.
2. ______! quit doing that.
3. ______, what is that?

OL

AFTER YOU READ

RESPONDING AND THINKING CRITICALLY

Respond

1. (a)Were you surprised when you learned where the sword and half disme were buried? (b)Where did you think they were buried?

Recall and Interpret

2. (a)Who sent the telegrams to Ellery Queen's unexpected visitors? (b)Why were the telegrams sent?
3. (a)When does Ellery refer to the antiquarian, the coin dealer, and the rare book collector as "rats"? (b)Why might Martha Clarke have such a profound effect on Ellery?
4. (a)Which U.S. state does Ellery claim as proof of the antiques' location? (b)How does this state constitute proof?

Analyze and Evaluate

5. Do you think the long exposition at the beginning of the story is necessary? Why or why not?
6. What is the effect on the reader of each new idea that Ellery has about the location of the lost items?
7. What role does Nikki Porter play in the story?

Connect

8. **Big Idea** **Revealing the Concealed** Many detective stories hint at the solution to the mystery early on in the narrative. What clues does Queen give to the location of the sword and half disme?

YOU'RE THE CRITIC: Different Viewpoints

The American Mystery

Read the following quotations about Ellery Queen. The first is from an article in the *National Review* about Dannay and Lee. The second is from a critique of *The Tragedy of Y*, an Ellery Queen novel.

> *Like a police investigator, Queen arrived at his solutions through meticulous logical deduction from emperical evidence, rather than intuition or psychological insights. Dannay created the genre's most complex puzzles and fairly presented all the clues, even stating explicitly when Ellery and the reader had enough information to solve the riddle.*
>
> —S. T. Karnick

> *Although rooted in a genre that has traditionally been oriented to reason, order, and optimism,* [The Tragedy of Y] *evokes depths of tragic despair that are virtually without parallel in the history of crime fiction.*
>
> —Francis Nevins Jr.

Group Activity Discuss the following questions with classmates. Refer to the quotations and cite evidence from the story for support.

1. According to these quotations, what makes the Ellery Queen stories different from other mystery stories?
2. How do these quotations apply to "The Adventure of the President's Half Disme"? Explain.

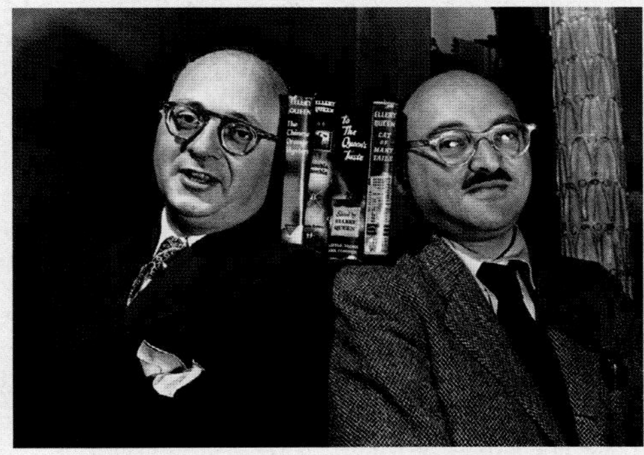

You're the Critic

1. Karnick notes that the mysteries are solved by logic rather than psychological insight. Nevins refers to the dark notes of despair in the stories.
2. Ellery Queen uses logic to piece together the historical clues and solve the puzzle. While this story seems rather light-hearted, descriptions of the "iron-bitterness" of Tobias and his grim farmhouse add a strain of bleak reality.

AFTER YOU READ

Assess

1. (a) Accept reasonable answers. (b) Students should explain their answers.
2. (a) Martha Clarke (b) She needed the help of the people she contacted to get money to pay the mortgage on her family's farm.
3. (a) After the three have returned home, and Martha has burst into tears (b) The idea of a beautiful, seductive woman seeking his help probably appeals to his ego and makes him feel heroic.
4. (a) Vermont (b) Vermont had not yet become a state at the time of Washington's visit. Queen concludes that the number 13—the number of states in the winter of 1791—probably had a special significance for Washington.
5. Students should explain their answers.
6. Each time one of his theories proves false, the tension and suspense increase.
7. Nikki might be regarded as Martha Clarke's foil. Although clearly attracted to Ellery, she deals with him much more straightforwardly than the slyly flirtatious Martha does. Unlike Martha, she seems skeptical of his ability to solve the mystery.
8. His question to Tobias about the cherry tree; the diary never says how many trees were planted.

CheckPoint

Use the CheckPoint questions on Presentation Plus! to check students' mastery of the selection. These questions can be used with interactive response keypads for immediate student feedback.

AFTER YOU READ

Assess

Literary Element

1. The conflict—the effort to find Washington's relics to save the Clarkes' farm—is external.
2. The flashbacks tell how the relics were buried on the Clarke farm. These episodes bring the central mystery to life and make the effort to find the buried relics seem worthwhile.
3. Digging up the tree stumps and roots reveals nothing. Ellery's first few theories turn up nothing.

Reading Strategy

1. Reviewing and summarizing the clues revealed in the story helps the reader determine possible solutions. Ellery's review of the diary and of what he knows about Washington leads to the solution.
2. Washington was obsessed with numbers. The trees were planted in an equilateral triangle. His visit occurred when the country had 13 states, hinting that he might've planted 13 trees.

LITERARY ANALYSIS

Literary Element Plot

Most **plots** develop around a conflict, a struggle between opposing forces. An external conflict is a struggle between a character and an outside force, such as another character, society, nature, or fate. An internal conflict takes place within the mind of a character who struggles with opposing feelings.

1. What is the central conflict in "The Adventure of the President's Half Disme"? Is it an internal or external conflict?
2. How does the use of flashback help develop the conflict in the story?
3. What events add complications to the conflict?

Review: Tone

As you learned on pages 1188–1189, **tone** is the reflection of a writer's attitude toward his or her subject matter, as conveyed through word choice, punctuation, sentence structure, and figures of speech.

Partner Activity With a classmate, discuss the tone of "The Adventure of the President's Half Disme." Working with your partner, create a two-column chart like the one below. Fill in the first column with examples from the text that demonstrate a particular tone. In the second column, label each example with an adjective that describes the tone.

Example	Tone
"and it is the dull stalk which does not turn up at least a hippogriff"	humorous

READING AND VOCABULARY

Reading Strategy Reviewing and Summarizing

When reading a mystery, **reviewing** what you have read can help you keep track of important details and understand the events and characters in the story.

1. How is reviewing both an important reading strategy and an important theme in this story?
2. **Summarize** Ellery's final explanation for the location of the antiques.

Vocabulary Practice

Practice with Analogies To complete an analogy, first determine the relationship between a pair of words. Then choose the word that creates the same relationship between the second pair of words. For each item below, choose the word that best completes the analogy.

1. **engrossed : involved :: changed :**
   a. transformed **b.** similar **c.** unmoved
2. **expedient : inappropriate :: grave :**
   a. serious **b.** humorless **c.** unimportant
3. **cadaverous : dead :: winged :**
   a. flying **b.** earthbound **c.** alive
4. **perfidious : betrayer :: loyal :**
   a. friend **b.** joker **c.** villain
5. **prowess : skilled :: saving :**
   a. prosperous **b.** extravagant **c.** thrifty

Academic Vocabulary

Here are two words from the vocabulary list on page R80.

contrary (kän′ trer ē) *adj.* opposite of what is presented

somewhat (səm′ wət) *adv.* to some degree

Practice and Apply

1. Which characters offer viewpoints or evidence **contrary** to Ellery's conjectures?
2. Which character gets **somewhat** flustered with Ellery's methods?

Review: Tone

Make sure students' charts include both examples and adjectives.

Vocabulary

1. a **2.** c **3.** a **4.** a **5.** c

Academic Vocabulary

1. Tobias and Martha Clarke and Nikki
2. Nikki

WRITING AND EXTENDING

Writing About Literature

Analyze Sound Devices Sound devices lend musical and rhythmic qualities to a literary work and help the writer emphasize important words and phrases. Alliteration, consonance, assonance, and rhythm are some of the tools a writer has at his or her disposal. Write a one- or two-page analysis of Queen's use of sound devices in "The Adventure of the President's Half Disme." Use examples from the story to build and illustrate your argument.

Before you begin drafting, take notes on Queen's use of sound devices in a chart like the one below.

Example	Sound Device
"'James Ezekiel Patch,' growled the great man"	alliteration

Include quotes from the story that exemplify sound devices, as well as related impressions or ideas that strike you as you read. When you have completed the chart, begin drafting.

After completing your draft, meet with a peer reviewer to evaluate each other's work and to offer constructive criticism. Then proofread and edit your draft to correct errors in spelling, grammar, and punctuation.

Performing

In a small group, choose a scene from "The Adventure of the President's Half Disme" to produce as a live or recorded performance. Rewrite the scene as a script, concentrating on dialogue, stage directions, and pacing. If possible, design costumes, sound effects, and lighting. Perform the scene for the class, or record the scene and present the video to the class.

LiteratureOnline **Web Activities** For eFlashcards, Selection Quick Checks, and other Web activities, go to www.glencoe.com.

GRAMMAR AND STYLE

Ellery Queen's Language and Style

Using Ellipses Ellipsis points (. . .) are the type of punctuation used to indicate the omission of words within a text. The most common use of an ellipsis is to show that words have been omitted from a quotation. Another use of an ellipsis is to imply a thought or idea a character either does not want to express aloud or cannot put into words. For example, in "The Adventure of the President's Half Disme," Queen uses ellipsis points when dialogue or thoughts trail off.

The chart below shows several examples of Queen's use of ellipsis points in the story. It also shows the implication, or what is implied, by each use of ellipsis points.

Example	Implication
"Second, because I may need a detective before I'm through . . . Third," she added, almost absently, "because I'm pretty desperate."	Martha Clarke is worried and distracted by her problem.
"Jonathan Clarke. *The Diary of Simeon Clarke*," mumbled the cadaverous book-collector. "I don't believe I know either, Miss Clarke. Have you . . . ?"	Shaw is asking to see the book.
"It reveals Washington rather er . . . out of character," said James Ezekiel Patch that evening.	Patch is trying to be polite about how much he doubts Martha's story.

Activity Find two more examples of ellipses in the story. Then rewrite each sentence, removing the ellipsis points and filling in the gap with what you think the character might have said.

Revising Check

Ellipses The use of ellipses is important to consider when revising your own writing. With a partner, go through your analysis of sound devices and note places where an ellipsis might help you shorten a lengthy quoted passage. Note that the use of ellipses for effect should generally be limited to creative and informal writing.

AFTER YOU READ

Assess

Writing About Literature

Students' essays should include:

- quotes that illustrate the authors' use of sound devices, such as alliteration, assonance, and consonance
- an analysis of how these devices contribute to the quality of the writing

Performing

Use the following criteria to evaluate students' scripts:

- Is the dialogue appropriate to the setting?
- Do the stage directions enhance the scene?
- Do the sound effects add to the drama?

Ellery Queen's Language and Style

Possible answers: When you s-stop to think of it . . . burying that coin, his sword . . . *(When you stop to think of it doesn't it seem strange that he'd bury that coin and his sword?)*
On the other hand . . . *(On the other hand, maybe the story was true.)*

Web Activities Have students access the Web site for interactive activities that will help them assess their understanding of the selection.

Revising Check

Emphasize that when using an ellipsis to replace words in quotations, students should be careful not to change the passage's original meaning.

Informational Text

TIME

Focus

Summary

The writer presents both sides of a debate between scientists regarding a mysterious primate living in the jungles of the Congo. Is it a chimpanzee? A gorilla? An entirely new species? The article offers observations and opinions but no conclusions, leaving readers to consider the evidence and decide for themselves.

Teach

R1 Reading Strategy

Evaluating Credibility Point out that students should keep track of the writer's sources as they read the article so that they can determine how credible the information in the article is. OL

Readability Scores
Dale-Chall: 8.8
DRP: 61
Lexile: 1020

Informational Text

Media Link to Revealing the Concealed

Preview the Article

In "Lost Apes of the Congo," Stephan Faris presents the debate among researchers about whether a certain primate found in the jungles of Bili in the Democratic Republic of the Congo is a new species.

1. Scan the article's title and its subheadings. What do you think it is going to be about?
2. Read the *deck*, or the sentence in large type that appears next to the title. What tone do you think the article might have?

Set a Purpose for Reading

Read to learn about the debate over a primate species in the jungles of the Democratic Republic of the Congo.

Reading Strategy

R1 **Evaluating Credibility**
Evaluating is making a judgment or forming an opinion about something. When you **evaluate the credibility of a text,** you must consider who wrote it, if the sources referenced are reliable, and if the publication in which the article appears is a valid one. To examine the credibility of "Lost Apes of the Congo," take notes about the writer.

Writer: Stephan Faris
Credible?
Why or why not?

ACADEMIC STANDARDS (pages 1224–1226)

9.3.9 Explain how voice…affect[s]… credibility of a text.

9.2.7 Evaluate an author's argument or defense of a claim by examining the… comprehensiveness of evidence, and the way in which the author's intent affects the structure and tone of the text.

TIME

Lost Apes of the Congo

A TIME reporter travels deep into the African jungle in search of a mysterious chimp called "the lion killer."

By STEPHAN FARIS

Ron Pontier was flying light and low above the northern wilds of the Democratic Republic of the Congo when he saw a dark shape racing between two patches of tropical forest. "It was huge," says Pontier, a pilot. "It was black. The skin was kind of bouncing up and down on it." From its bulk and color, Pontier thought it was a buffalo until he circled down for another look. "I saw it again just before it went into the forest," he says. "It was an ape—and a big one." Not buffalo size, but big.

What Pontier saw is a piece of a primate puzzle; it is another splinter of evidence for a mysterious ape with characteristics of gorillas and chimpanzees. It is an animal that has scientists in a furious debate over what it might be.

Bili is a geographic region in Congo's far north, where deep tropical forests break up into patches of savanna, or flat, treeless grasslands. Civil war and neglect have left the region nearly untouched by humans. Overgrown dirt roads with bridges of roughly-cut logs string together thatched-roofed villages. Nearly all goods are carried in by bicycle. Local residents hunt with homemade shotguns and crossbows that seem to be based on 16th-century Portuguese designs. "This area is the last part of Africa where there are still wild animals," says Pontier, who grew up in the region. "It's not a game park. It's not a reserve. The animals are really wild."

A Surprising Animal

When Karl Ammann, a Swiss photographer who works to stop the killing of wild animals for meat, first visited the region in 1996, he was looking for gorillas. He had hoped that the great apes still roamed its jungles. What he found surprised him. Locals had two names for the apes in their forests: the "tree beaters" and the "lion killers." The tree beaters stayed safe in

Additional Support

See also Active Learning and Note Taking Guide, pp. 202–207.

Skills Practice

READING: Main Idea and Supporting Details Have students analyze the first paragraph to determine the main idea. *(A pilot flying over the Congolese jungle spots an unusual ape-like animal.)*

Ask: What details support the main idea? *(The animal's huge size, black fur, and loose skin at first suggest a buffalo. A closer look suggests an ape.)* OL the tree branches. The lion killers were bigger, darker, and so strong that they were unaffected by the poison arrows used by local hunters.

BI Ammann discovered a strange skull with the dimensions of a chimpanzee's but with an odd, prominent crest like a gorilla's. Motion-detecting cameras in the forest caught images of what looked like huge chimpanzees, and a photograph bought from hunters showed the men posing with an animal estimated to be twice the size of an ordinary chimp. Ammann measured an animal dropping three times as large as a chimp's and footprints as large as, or larger than, a gorilla's.

Most unusual were the gorilla-like ground nests found in the swamps. Chimps normally make their nests in the high safety of trees. Why would they build their beds of branches and shoots on the ground? And why here, of all places? At night Cleve Hicks, 32, a graduate student who observes the animals, regularly hears the laughs of hyenas and the low, throaty cries of leopards. Recently, his trackers filmed the footprints of a lion crossing a river. But the apes here—at least some of them—pulled together branches and shoots to make beds on the ground. "We know [the apes] are a perfect target for leopards," says Hicks. "So how can they get away with that?"

A New Species?

The first scientist to see the Bili apes was Shelly Williams, a gorilla expert who visited the region in the summers of 2002 and 2003. She says that she documented separate groups of relatives of East and West African chimpanzees and what she calls the "mystery ape." The larger animal turned gray early in life and had a much flatter face and a straight-across brow like a gorilla. Two or three would nest on the ground, with others low in nearby branches. They made a distinct sound like a howl and were louder when the full moon rose and set. "The unique characteristics they exhibit just don't fit into the other groups of great apes," says Williams. The apes, she argues, could be a new species unknown to science. They might be a new close relative of the chimpanzee, or a cross between the gorilla and the chimp. "At the very least, we have a unique, isolated chimp culture that's unlike any that's been studied," she says.

R2 That last, least dramatic theory is the one which most scientists who have visited the region believe, including Harvard ape expert Richard Wrangham. He thinks that the ground nests are built by chimps looking to escape dampness during the day.

R3 When Hicks and Ammann describe the animal that they are studying, they use the term "mystery ape" only with irony. Ammann is worried that Williams's incredible ideas have brought ridicule to his project. "If there's scientific data, that's one thing," he says. But he believes that there isn't enough proof yet. Recently, Ammann was emailed pictures of a chimp

Karl Ammann

CAUGHT ON FILM A rare shot of the elusive ape taken from a camera trap near the bamboo-lined track to Bili (top).

Informational Text
TIME

Teach

BI Big Idea

Revealing the Concealed **Ask:** What proof of the animals' existence did Ammann gather? *(A strange skull; an image from a motion-detecting camera; a photo taken by hunters; droppings; ground nests)* OL

R2 Reading Strategy

Interpreting **Ask:** Which of Shelly Williams's theories are most scientists who visited the area willing to accept? *(The animals may belong to a previously unobserved chimp culture.)* OL

R3 Reading Strategy

Evaluating Credibility **Ask:** Which observer would you consider least credible? *(Possible answer: Ammann—he isn't a scientist.)* OL

English Language Coach

Context Clues Explain that context clues are the information surrounding an unfamiliar word that suggests what that word means. **Write on the board:** "If there's scientific data, that's one thing." Note that readers who don't know what *data* means could scan the paragraph for hints. The next sentence states, "there isn't enough proof," and the rest of the paragraph talks about various scientific studies needed to provide proof. These clues hint that the word *data* relates to the results of such studies. EL

Academic Standards

Additional Support activities on pp. 1224 and 1225 cover the following standards:

Skills Practice: **9.2.8** Make reasonable statements and draw conclusions about a text, supporting them with accurate examples.

English Language Coach: **9.1** Use...context clues...to determine the meaning of words and become fluent readers.

Assess

1. To deepen scientists' understanding of genes, evolution, and/or animal behavior.
2. Large size, flat face, straight-across eyebrow, black fur that turns gray early
3. (a) She believes they may be a new species. (b) No; the animal's DNA suggests she is wrong.
4. (a) He believes they differ mostly in behavior. (b) The time he's spent observing the animals adds credibility, but he isn't yet fully qualified as a scientist.
5. No; he discusses both sides in neutral language.
6. The initial sighting of the creature, mention of the "strange" skull, introducing evidence in the form of clues, and his closing statement
7. To see the importance of preserving wild species and their habitats
8. Hicks: points to the animals' ground nests and use of tools as evidence of behavioral, rather than biological, difference; Williams: offers theories unsupported by evidence

For additional assessment, see Selection and Unit Assessments, pp. 205–206.

with a pug-dog's head and a seal with a gorilla's face. "Clearly, someone thinks we're a joke," he says. A study of hairs found in the ground nests identified their mitochondrial DNA (mtDNA) as that of the East African chimpanzee. Williams has three arguments concerning that finding: The DNA could have been contaminated, the use of human genetic markers might hide differences, and mtDNA would not show variation in the paternal line. "Until we know the father's lineage, we can't say if it's a new species or not," Williams insists. Williams says she will return to the area in March to set up her own project.

What's in the Forest?

"I think people are going to be disappointed with the yeti in the forest," warns Hicks, referring to the rumored oversize mix of human and ape. Hicks says that the apes that he has seen are clearly chimps, although some are strangely oversize. "The evidence doesn't point to [a new species]." Hicks thinks that more attention has to be paid to the differences in how the apes and chimps live. In addition to building ground nests, the apes fish for ants with tools that are several times longer than those used by other chimps. For now, Hicks is concentrating on living near the animals, getting them used to the noisy, nosy presence of researchers. The science—and the videotapes—will come later.

"Genetically, they're not even a subspecies," says Hicks. But he thinks that behaviorally, they may be different. "We could actually be catching evolution in the act. That is, if they're allowed to survive."

That's an open question. The forests here have been hit hard by commercial hunting. Machine gun-carrying hunters stage raids from the Central African Republic and central Congo. Pontier, the pilot, used to see herds of a hundred elephants when he first flew over the region in 1983. Now seeing three together is a rare sighting. And with the big animals disappearing, Ammann, who has set up a conservation project in the area, says that the illegal hunters are turning to hogs, antelopes, monkeys, and chimpanzees. "The pressure on smaller game is increasing now that the elephants are gone," he says.

If there's one thing that all the scientists can agree on, it's that if this part of the Congo goes the way of other African wild lands, the great apes could soon disappear. All that will be left of the Bili ape will be the mystery.

—From TIME, January 17, 2005

RESPONDING AND THINKING CRITICALLY

Respond

1. Why is it important for researchers to understand the Bili ape?

Recall and Interpret

2. What are some physical characteristics of the Bili apes?
3. (a)What does Shelly Williams, a gorilla expert, believe to be true about the Bili apes? (b)Does she have substantial evidence to support her theory? Why or why not?
4. (a)What does Cleve Hicks, a graduate student and animal observer, believe to be the prime difference between the Bili apes and other chimpanzees? (b)Is he a reliable source? Explain.

Analyze and Evaluate

5. Is the writer's opinion about whether the Bili apes are a new species evident in the article? Explain.
6. How does the writer use the idea of mystery to capture the reader's interest?
7. Faris closes the article by saying that "If there's one thing that all the scientists can agree on, it's that if this part of the Congo goes the way of other African wild lands, the great apes could soon disappear. All that will be left of the Bili ape will be the mystery." What overall reaction to the article do you think Faris wants the reader to have?

Connect

8. Cleve Hicks and Shelly Williams have differing opinions about the species of the Bili apes. Who has more actual clues to support his or her opinion? Explain.

Additional Support

Academic Standards

The Additional Support activity on p. 1226 covers the following standard:
Skills Practice: **9.2** Develop [reading] strategies…

Skills Practice

READING: Rereading Tell students that rereading a text will help them identify its main idea and supporting details, an author's tone and purpose for writing, and any rhetorical or literary devices used to inform, persuade, or entertain.

Write the following headings on the board: Main Ideas, Supporting Details, Tone, Author's Purpose, Rhetorical and Literary Devices. Have students copy them in their notebooks to guide their note taking as they reread the article. OL

The Red-Headed League

MEET SIR ARTHUR CONAN DOYLE

What if you were a doctor with little money but plenty of free time due to a shortage of patients? That is what happened to Arthur Conan Doyle, a Scottish physician. His medical training, however, did not go to waste. While a student at Edinburgh University, Doyle was impressed with one of his medical school instructors, Dr. Bell, who combined keen observations with brilliant deductions to help diagnose diseases. Doyle modeled his fictional detective Sherlock Holmes on Dr. Bell.

Early Career In 1886 Doyle wrote a mystery novel featuring Sherlock Holmes and his colleague John H. Watson. At first, few readers seemed to like it. About a year later, however, the story began to stir interest, prompting an American editor to ask Doyle to write another novel featuring the same detective. Doyle responded by writing *The Sign of Four.* Doyle then wrote six more Sherlock Holmes stories for a magazine, and his life was never the same. The public demanded more and more stories, and Doyle could barely keep up.

> *"Letters of abuse . . . showered upon me when it was thought that I had killed [Holmes]. 'You brute!' was the promising opening of one lady's epistle."*
>
> —Sir Arthur Conan Doyle

Killing Off His Detective Doyle never dreamed that writing mysteries would be his talent. He prided himself on both his nonfiction writing and his historical fiction. With readers clamoring for more Sherlock Holmes stories, however, Doyle could not interest editors in publishing anything else. Frustrated, in 1893 Doyle killed off Holmes, along with his archrival, Professor Moriarty, in a short story called "The Final Solution." Doyle's readers were outraged. Clearly, the author had underestimated Holmes's astounding popularity.

Withstanding the criticism, Doyle went on to write other books on different topics. In 1901, however, after a friend related the story of a ghostly hound, Doyle began writing the mystery that would become *The Hound of the Baskervilles* and resurrect Sherlock Holmes.

Sir Arthur Doyle was knighted in 1902 for his pamphlet defending the British during the Boer War in South Africa. Still, the creation of Sherlock Holmes was Doyle's crowning achievement. To this day, the Baker Street Irregulars, an organization of avid readers of Sherlock Holmes stories, meet regularly to honor the world's best-known detective.

Sir Arthur Conan Doyle was born in 1859 and died in 1930.

LiteratureOnline **Author Search** For more about Sir Arthur Conan Doyle, go to www.glencoe.com.

Focus

BELLRINGER

Bellringer Options
Daily Language Practice Transparency 103
Or display images of the classic fictional detectives, such as Sherlock Holmes, Charlie Chan, Hercule Poirot, and Ellery Queen. Discuss how these sleuths solved crimes through the power of their intellect.
Ask: What do these detectives have in common? How do they compare with today's fictional detectives? Have students consider as they read how Conan Doyle reveals the deductive reasoning powers that are the signature talent of Holmes.

Author Search To expand students' appreciation of Sir Arthur Conan Doyle, have them access the Web site for additional information and resources.

Selection Skills

The Red-Headed League

Literary Elements
- Foreshadowing (SE pp. 1228–1246)
- Character Archetype (SE p. 1246)

Reading Skills
- Making Inferences About Characters (SE pp. 1228–1246)

Vocabulary Skills
- Synonyms (SE pp. 1228, 1246)
- Academic Vocabulary (SE p. 1246)

Listening/Speaking/Viewing Skills
- Analyzing Art (SE p. 1235; TWE p. 1237)

Writing Skills/Grammar
- Analyze Genre Elements (SE p. 1247)
- Using Formal Language (SE p. 1247)

BEFORE YOU READ

Focus

Summary

Jabez Wilson, a London pawnbroker, goes to work for an employer that hires only redheads. When the employer mysteriously vanishes, Wilson consults Holmes and Watson. Holmes's investigation uncovers a serious crime masterminded by the infamous John Clay.

V Vocabulary

Vocabulary File **Say:** Add these words and definitions to your vocabulary file. For each word, include a sentence that gives you an example of how to use the word. **OL** Students with English language needs should include the pronunciations of these words in their files. **EL**

Literary Elements Have students access the Web site to improve their understanding of foreshadowing.

LITERATURE PREVIEW

Connecting to the Story

In this story, Sherlock Holmes must unravel an intriguing mystery. Before you read, think about the following questions:

- Who are your favorite detectives in movies and on television?
- Why do you think people enjoy reading mystery stories?

Building Background

"The Red-Headed League" is told from the first-person point of view. The narrator is Dr. Watson, whom Holmes refers to as his "partner" and "helper." Always one step behind Holmes—if not several—Watson takes the reader's place in the story. In addition to being at Holmes's beck and call, Watson comments on Holmes's observational and deductive powers, thereby shedding light on the detective's character.

Setting Purposes for Reading

Big Idea Revealing the Concealed

As you read, consider what is at first hidden and later revealed in this story.

Literary Element Foreshadowing

Foreshadowing is an author's use of clues to prepare readers for later developments in the plot. This technique involves a reader more fully in a story by generating a feeling of suspense, dread, or eager anticipation. Foreshadowing allows readers to predict what will happen in a story. In doing so, it also spurs readers to read further to see if their predictions are correct. As you read this mystery, look for clues that foreshadow events in the story.

- See Literary Terms Handbook, p. R8.

Literature Online **Interactive Literary Elements Handbook** To review or learn more about the literary elements, go to www.glencoe.com.

READING PREVIEW

Reading Strategy Making Inferences About Characters

Making inferences involves using your reason and your experience to make educated guesses based on what an author implies or suggests. Because writers do not always directly state what they want readers to know, you often must infer a character's motivations, relationships, and personality traits.

Reading Tip: Taking Notes As you read, use a chart to record your inferences about the characters in this story.

Details	Inferences
Holmes deduces facts about Mr. Wilson.	Holmes is very observant and has excellent powers of reasoning and deduction.

Vocabulary

singular (sing′ gyə lər) *adj.* unusual or out of the ordinary; odd; p. 1230 *Jenna remembered the suspect because of his singular appearance.*

nominal (nom′ ən əl) *adj.* insignificant; p. 1231 *Unlike writing an essay, composing an e-mail message often requires only nominal effort.*

languid (lang′ gwid) *adj.* drooping; weak and listless; p. 1239 *He was feeling languid after a day of heavy physical work.*

formidable (fôr′ mi də bəl) *adj.* impressive; awe-inspiring; p. 1240 *The tennis champion was a formidable opponent to the other players in the tournament.*

Vocabulary Tip: Synonyms Synonyms are words that have the same or nearly the same meaning. For example, the words *arid* and *dry* are synonyms.

INDIANA ACADEMIC STANDARDS (pages 1228–1247)

9.3.6 Analyze and trace an author's development of time and sequence, including...foreshadowing...

9.2 Develop [reading] strategies...

9.5.3 Write...analytical essays...that gather evidence in support of a thesis...

Selection Resources

Print Materials
- Unit 6 Resources (Fast File), pp. 44–46
- Leveled Vocabulary Development, p. 77
- Selection and Unit Assessments, pp. 207–208
- Selection Quick Checks, p. 104

Transparencies
- Bellringer Options Transparencies: Daily Language Practice Transparency 103
- Literary Elements Transparency 6

Technology
- TeacherWorks Plus™ CD-ROM
- StudentWorks Plus™ CD-ROM
- Presentation Plus!™ CD-ROM
- Literature Online, glencoe.com
- Online Student Edition, mhln.com
- Exam*View*® Assessment Suite CD-ROM
- Vocabulary PuzzleMaker CD-ROM
- Listening Library, disc 2 track 48

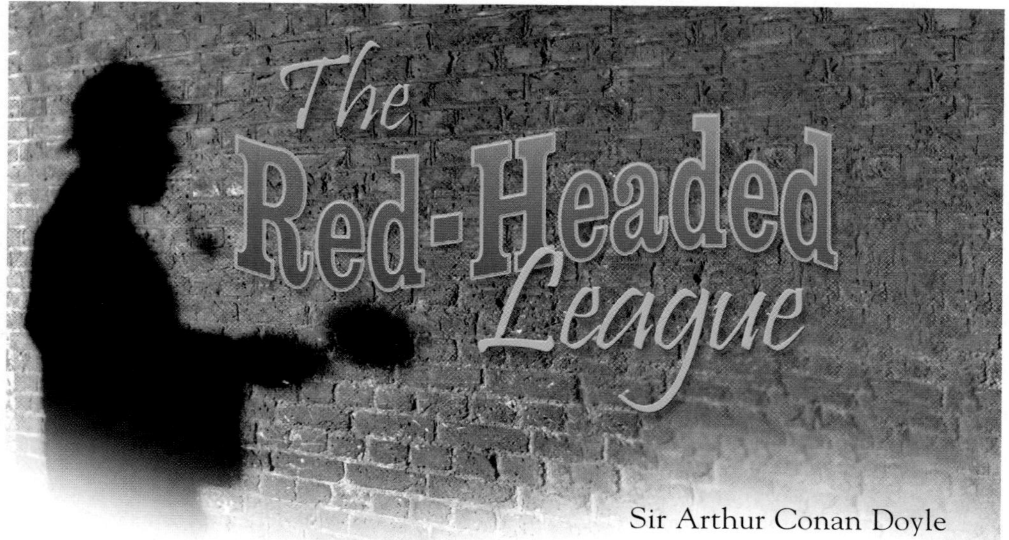

The Red-Headed League
Sir Arthur Conan Doyle

I had called upon my friend, Mr. Sherlock Holmes, one day in the autumn of last year, and found him in deep conversation with a very stout, florid-faced, elderly gentleman, with fiery red hair. With an apology for my intrusion, I was about to withdraw, when Holmes pulled me abruptly into the room and closed the door behind me. "You could not possibly have come at a better time, my dear Watson," he said, cordially.

"I was afraid that you were engaged."

"So I am. Very much so."

"Then I can wait in the next room."

"Not at all, Watson. Mr. Wilson, I would like you to meet Dr. Watson, my partner, friend, and helper in many of my most successful cases."

The stout gentleman half rose from his chair and gave a bob of greeting, with a quick, little, questioning glance from his small, fat-encircled eyes.

"Try the settee,"[1] said Holmes, relapsing into his armchair, and putting his finger tips together, as was his custom when in judicial moods. "I know, my dear Watson, that you share my love of all that is bizarre and outside the conventions and humdrum routine of everyday life. You have shown your relish for it by the enthusiasm which has prompted you to chronicle, and, if you will excuse my saying so, somewhat to embellish so many of my own little adventures."

"Your cases have indeed been of the greatest interest to me," I observed.

"You will remember that I remarked the other day, just before we went into the very simple problem presented by Miss Mary Sutherland, that for strange effects and extraordinary combinations we must go to life itself, which is always far more daring than any effort of the imagination."

"A proposition which I took the liberty of doubting."

Reading Strategy Making Inferences About Characters *Based on what you have read so far, how would you describe Watson's relationship with Holmes?* **R**

1. A *settee* (se tē′) is a medium-sized sofa.

Literary Element Foreshadowing *What might Holmes's remark foreshadow about Wilson's case?* **L**

Teach

R Reading Strategy

Making Inferences About Characters **Answer:** *They are close friends with shared interests and mutual respect, as well as a good professional team.* **OL**

L Literary Element

Foreshadowing **Answer:** *Holmes's remark that life is more extraordinary than imagination suggests that Wilson's case will be unusual.* **OL**

Use the CheckPoint questions on Presentation Plus! to monitor students' comprehension. These questions can be used with interactive response keypads for immediate student feedback.

Readability Scores
Dale-Chall: 7.2
DRP: 61
Lexile: 1110

English Language Coach

Tracking Dialogue English language learners sometimes have trouble identifying who is speaking in passages without dialogue tags. Pair English language learners with native English speakers. Direct them to find all the passages without dialogue tags in the selection and to identify the speakers. Encourage students to explain how they identified each speaker. **EL**

Academic Standards

The Additional Support activity on p. 1229 covers the following standards:

English Language Coach: **9.3.10** Identify and explain the function of dialogue… **9.3.4** Determine characters' traits by what the characters say about themselves in…dialogue...

Teach

L Literary Element

Foreshadowing Answer: *It is another hint that the case will be strange and makes the reader want to find out more about it.* OL

★ Cultural History

Freemasons An international secret society that espouses brotherhood and charity, the Freemasons is thought to have roots in the trade guilds of medieval Europe. (The term *freemason* originally referred to a master stonemason, who was privileged to work where he wanted unrestrained by the guild.) As the Freemasons evolved over the centuries, its members were often subjected to persecution. Even today the organization remains a favorite target of conspiracy theorists—as it was in Conan Doyle's time. AS

"You did, doctor, but nonetheless you must come round to my view, for otherwise I shall keep on piling fact upon fact on you, until your reason breaks down under them and acknowledges me to be right. Now, Mr. Jabez[2] Wilson here has been good enough to call upon me this morning, and to begin a narrative which promises to be one of the most **singular** which I have listened to for some time. You have heard me remark that the strangest and most unique things are very often connected not with the larger but with the smaller crimes, and occasionally, indeed, where there is room for doubt whether any positive crime has been committed. As far as I have heard, it is impossible for me to say whether the present case is an instance of crime or not, but the course of events is certainly among the most singular that I have ever listened to. Perhaps, Mr. Wilson, you would have the great kindness to recommence your narrative. I ask you, not merely because my friend, Dr. Watson, has not heard the opening part, but also because the peculiar nature of the story makes me anxious to have every possible detail from your lips. As a rule, when I have heard some slight indication of the course of events, I am able to guide myself by the thousands of other similar cases, which occur to my memory. In the present instance I am forced to admit that the facts are, to the best of my belief, unique."

The portly client puffed out his chest with an appearance of some little pride, and pulled a dirty and wrinkled newspaper from the inside pocket of his greatcoat. As he glanced down the advertisement column, with his head thrust forward, and the paper flattened out upon his knee, I took a good look at the man, and endeavored, after the fashion of my companion, to read the indications which might be presented by his dress or appearance.

I did not gain very much, however, by my inspection. Our visitor bore every mark of being an average, commonplace British tradesman, obese, pompous, and slow. He wore rather baggy gray shepherd's check trousers, a not overclean black frock coat, unbuttoned in the front, and a drab waistcoat with a heavy, brassy Albert chain,[3] and a square pierced bit of metal dangling down as an ornament. A frayed top hat and a faded brown overcoat with a wrinkled velvet collar lay upon a chair beside him. Altogether, look as I would, there was nothing remarkable about the man save his blazing red head, and the expression of extreme chagrin[4] and discontent upon his features.

Sherlock Holmes's quick eye took in my occupation, and he shook his head with a smile as he noticed my questioning glances. "Beyond the obvious facts that he has at some time done manual labor, that he takes snuff, that he is a Freemason,[5] that he has been in China, and that he has done a considerable amount of writing lately, I can deduce nothing else." ★

Mr. Jabez Wilson started up in his chair, with his forefinger upon the paper, but with his eyes upon my companion. "How, in the name of good fortune, did you know all that, Mr. Holmes?" he asked. "How did you know, for example, that I did manual labor? It's as true as gospel, for I began as a ship's carpenter."

"Your hands, my dear sir. Your right hand is quite a size larger than your left. You have worked with it, and the muscles are more developed."

"Well, the snuff, then, and the Freemasonry?"

"I won't insult your intelligence by telling you how I read that, especially as, rather

2. *Jabez* (jā′ bez) is Wilson's first name.

Literary Element Foreshadowing *How does this statement build suspense?* L

Vocabulary

singular (sing′ gyə lər) *adj.* unusual or out of the ordinary; odd

3. An *Albert chain* is a watch chain named after Prince Albert (1819–1861), the husband of England's Queen Victoria (1819–1901).
4. *Chagrin* is distress caused by disappointment.
5. A *Freemason* is a member of a secret fraternal order. The emblem of the group is the arc and compass, which, as Holmes notes, should always be concealed.

Additional Support

Skills Practice

READING: Critical Thinking Note that Holmes and Watson draw very different inferences about Wilson based on the same evidence. Ask students to evaluate the logic of Holmes's assumptions about Wilson. For instance, might there be other equally valid reasons for the difference in hand sizes? *(The discrepancy might be congenital or the result of injury.)* Urge students to question Holmes's assumptions—and their own—as they read. OL

Mr. Jabez Wilson, Mr. Sherlock Holmes, and Dr. John Watson. Sidney Paget.

against the strict rules of your order, you use an arc-and-compass breastpin."

"Ah, of course, I forgot that. But the writing?"

"What else can be indicated by that right cuff so very shiny for five inches, and the left one with the smooth patch near the elbow where you rest it upon the desk?"

"Well, but China?"

"The fish that you have tattooed immediately above your right wrist could only have been done in China. I have made a small study of tattoo marks, and have even contributed to the literature of the subject. That trick of staining the fishes' scales of a delicate pink is quite peculiar to China. When, in addition, I see a Chinese coin hanging from your watch chain, the matter becomes even more simple."

Mr. Jabez Wilson laughed heavily. "Well, I never!" said he. "I thought at first that you had done something clever, but I see that there was nothing in it, after all."

"I begin to think, Watson," said Holmes, "that I make a mistake in explaining. *'Omne ignotum pro magnifico,'*[6] you know, and my poor little reputation, such as it is, will suffer shipwreck if I am so candid. Can you not find the advertisement, Mr. Wilson?"

"Yes, I have got it now," he answered, with his thick, red finger planted halfway down the column. "Here it is. This is what began it all. You just read it for yourself, sir."

I took the paper from him, and read as follows:

> To the Red-Headed League:
>
> On account of the bequest[7] of the late Ezekiah[8] Hopkins, of Lebanon, Pa., U.S.A., there is now another vacancy open which entitles a member of the League to a salary of four pounds a week for purely **nominal** services. All red-headed men who are sound in body and mind, and above the age of twenty-one years, are eligible. Apply in person on Monday, at eleven o'clock, to Duncan Ross, at the offices of the League, 7 Pope's Court, Fleet Street.

"What on earth does this mean?" I ejaculated, after I had twice read over the extraordinary announcement.

Holmes chuckled, and wriggled in his chair, as was his habit when in high spirits. "It is a little off the beaten track, isn't it?" said he. "And now, Mr. Wilson, off you go at scratch,[9] and tell us all about yourself, your household, and the effect which this advertisement had upon your fortunes. You will first make a note, doctor, of the paper and the date."

"It is *The Morning Chronicle* of April 27, 1890. Just two months ago."

6. *Omne ignotum pro magnifico* is Latin for "Every mysterious thing seems greater than it really is."
7. A *bequest* is something given in a will.
8. *Ezekiah* (ez′ ə kī′ ə) is a first name that was more common in the 1800s than it is now.
9. *At scratch* means "from the beginning."

Reading Strategy Making Inferences About Characters *What are your impressions of Mr. Wilson?* **R1**

Reading Strategy Making Inferences About Characters *How would you contrast Watson and Holmes?* **R2**

Vocabulary

nominal (nom′ ən əl) *adj.* insignificant

Teach

R1 Reading Strategy

Making Inferences About Characters **Answer:** *He seems too dense to appreciate Holmes's intelligence.* **OL**

R2 Reading Strategy

Making Inferences About Characters **Answer:** *Watson is confused, but Holmes's behavior conveys his amusement and suggests that he has already begun to solve the case.* **OL**

English Language Coach

Tales of Suspense Note that Conan Doyle's stories are often filled with suspense. Ask English language learners to share examples of suspenseful stories in the literature of their first language. **EL**

Building Reading Fluency

Dramatic Reading Note that effective oral reading requires more than reciting words. As students practice reading scenes from the story, urge them to focus on pacing and expressiveness. **BL**

Academic Standards

Additional Support activities on pp. 1230 and 1231 cover the following standards:

Skills Practice: **9.2.8** Make reasonable statements and draw conclusions about a text, supporting them with accurate examples.

English Language Coach: **9.7.14** Deliver narrative presentations that narrate a sequence of events and communicate their significance to the audience…

Building Reading Fluency: **9.7** [Develop] speaking skills, such as phrasing, pitch, and tone…

Teach

L1 Literary Element

Foreshadowing **Answer:** *It might foreshadow that Spaulding's real motive is to gain access to Wilson's shop.* OL

R1 Reading Strategy

Making Inferences About Characters **Answer:** *He is not very curious about or engaged in the world.* OL

R2 Reading Strategy

Analyzing Dialogue
Ask: Based on its context in the paragraph, what do you think the expression "prick up my ears" means? *(To pay close attention to what has been said)* Why was Wilson so interested in the league? *(It was an easy way to make money.)* OL

"Very good. Now, Mr. Wilson?"

"Well it is just as I have been telling you, Mr. Sherlock Holmes," said Jabez Wilson, mopping his forehead; "I have a small pawnbroker's business at Coburg Square, near the City.[10] It's not a very large affair, and of late years it has not done more than just give me a living. I used to be able to keep two assistants, but now I only keep one; and I would have a job to pay him, but that he is willing to come for half wages, so as to learn the business."

"What is the name of this obliging youth?" asked Sherlock Holmes.

"His name is Vincent Spaulding, and he's not such a youth, either. It's hard to say his age. I should not wish a smarter assistant, Mr. Holmes; and I know very well that he could better himself, and earn twice what I am able to give him. But, after all, if he is satisfied, why should I put ideas in his head?"

"Why indeed? You seem most fortunate in having an employee who comes under the full market price. It is not a common experience among employers in this age. I don't know that your assistant is not as remarkable as your advertisement."

"Oh, he has his faults, too," said Mr. Wilson. "Never was such a fellow for photography. Snapping away with a camera when he ought to be improving his mind, and then diving down into the cellar like a rabbit into its hole to develop his pictures. That is his main fault; but, on the whole, he's a good worker. There's no vice in him."

"He is still with you, I presume?"

"Yes, sir. He and a girl of fourteen, who does a bit of simple cooking, and keeps the place clean—that's all I have in the house, for I am a widower, and never had any family. We live very quietly, sir, the three of us; and we keep a roof over our heads, and pay our debts, if we do nothing more.

"The first thing that put us out was that advertisement. Spaulding, he came down into the office just this day eight weeks, with this very paper in his hand, and he says:

"'I wish to the Lord, Mr. Wilson, that I was a red-headed man.'

"'Why that?' I asks.

"'Why,' says he, 'here's another vacancy on the League of the Red-Headed Men. It's worth quite a little fortune to any man who gets it, and I understand that there are more vacancies than there are men, so that the trustees are at their wits' end what to do with the money. If my hair would only change color, here's a nice little crib[11] all ready for me to step into.'

"'Why, what is it, then?' I asked. You see, Mr. Holmes, I am a very stay-at-home man, and as my business came to me instead of my having to go to it, I was often weeks on end without putting my foot over the door-mat. In that way I didn't know much of what was going on outside, and I was always glad of a bit of news.

"'Have you never heard of the League of the Red-Headed Men?' he asked, with his eyes open.

"'Never.'

"'Why, I wonder at that, for you are eligible yourself for one of the vacancies.'

"'And what are they worth?' I asked.

"'Oh, merely a couple of hundred a year, but the work is slight, and it need not interfere very much with one's other occupations.'

"Well, you can easily think that that made me prick up my ears, for the business has not been over-good for some years, and an extra couple of hundred would have been very handy. R2

"'Tell me all about it,' said I.

"'Well,' said he, showing me the advertisement, 'you can see for yourself that the League has a vacancy, and there is the address where you should apply for particulars. As far as I can make out, the League

10. The *City* refers to the center of downtown London.

11. A *crib* is an easy job or position.

Literary Element Foreshadowing *What might Spaulding's willingness to work for half wages foreshadow?* L1

Reading Strategy Making Inferences About Characters *What does Wilson's admission suggest about him?* R1

Additional Support

Skills Practice

READING: Paraphrasing Remind students that paraphrasing is restating a passage using different words to convey the same meaning. Paraphrasing can help students review the plot of a story and check their comprehension. Instruct them to write a paragraph paraphrasing the events so far and then exchange papers with a partner for evaluation. OL was founded by an American millionaire, Ezekiah Hopkins, who was very peculiar in his ways. He was himself red-headed, and he had a great sympathy for all red-headed men; so, when he died, it was found that he had left his enormous fortune in the hands of trustees, with instructions to apply the interest to the providing of easy berths to men whose hair is of that color. From all I hear it is splendid pay, and very little to do.'

"'But,' said I, 'there would be millions of red-headed men who would apply.'

"'Not so many as you might think,' he answered. 'You see it is really confined to Londoners, and to grown men. This American had started from London when he was young, and he wanted to do the old town a good turn. Then, again, I have heard it is no use applying if your hair is light red, or dark red, or anything but real bright, blazing, fiery red. Now, if you cared to apply, Mr. Wilson, you would just walk in; but perhaps it would hardly be worth your while to put yourself out of the way for the sake of a few hundred pounds.'

"Now, it is a fact, gentlemen, as you may see for yourself, that my hair is of a very full and rich tint, so that it seemed to me that, if there was to be any competition in the matter, I stood as good a chance as any man that I had ever met. Vincent Spaulding seemed to know so much about it that I thought he might prove useful, so I ordered him to put up the shutters for the day, and to come right away with me. He was very willing to have a holiday, so we shut the business up, and started off for the address that was given us in the advertisement.

"I never hope to see such a sight as that again, Mr. Holmes. From north, south, east, and west every man who had a shade of red in his hair had tramped into the City to ★ answer the advertisement. Fleet Street was choked with red-headed folk, and Pope's Court looked like a coster's orange barrow.[12] I should not have thought there were so many in the whole country as were brought together by that single advertisement. Every shade of color they were—straw, lemon, orange, brick, Irish setter, liver, clay; but, as Spaulding said there were not many who had the real vivid flame-colored tint. When I saw how many were waiting I would have given it up in despair; but Spaulding would not hear of it. How he did it I could not imagine, but he pushed and pulled and butted until he got me through the crowd, and right up the steps which led to the office. There was a double stream upon the stair, some going up in hope, and some coming back dejected; but we wedged in as well as we could, and soon found ourselves in the office."

"Your experience has been a most entertaining one," remarked Holmes, as his client paused and refreshed his memory with a huge pinch of snuff. "Pray continue your very interesting statement."

"There was nothing in the office but a couple of wooden chairs and a deal table, behind which sat a small man, with a head that was even redder than mine. He said a few words to each candidate as he came up, and then he always managed to find some fault in them which would disqualify them. Getting a vacancy did not seem to be such a very easy matter, after all. However, when our turn came, the little man was much more favorable to me than to any of the others, and he closed the door as we entered, so that he might have a private word with us.

"'This is Mr. Jabez Wilson,' said my assistant, 'and he is willing to fill a vacancy in the League.'

"'And he is admirably suited for it,' the other answered. 'He has every requirement. I cannot recall when I have seen anything so fine.' He took a step backward, cocked his head on one side, and gazed at my hair until I felt quite bashful. Then suddenly he

Reading Strategy Making Inferences About Characters *Why do you think it is so important to Spaulding to see Wilson get through the crowd?* **R3**

Literary Element Foreshadowing *What details in this paragraph hint that things are not what they seem?* **L2**

12. A *coster's orange barrow* is a fruit vendor's bin of oranges.

Teach

R3 Reading Strategy

Making Inferences About Characters **Answer:** *Spaulding's determination to get Wilson through the crowd is a clue that the assistant has an interest in making sure Wilson joins the league.* **OL**

L2 Literary Element

Foreshadowing **Answer:** *The "office" contains little furniture, as though it had recently been set up, and each candidate before Wilson is disqualified on the basis of "some fault."* **OL**

★ Literary History

Fleet Street Fleet Street was the journalistic center of London for more than 250 years. The first London daily newspaper, *The Courant,* came from Fleet Street in 1702. Fleet Street also attracted numerous literary figures, including Shakespeare. Fleet Street is named for the Fleet River, which runs under London. **AS**

English Language Coach

Interpretation English language learners may have difficulty with the British usage of English in Conan Doyle's writing. Instruct students to jot down confusing words and phrases. Have them work with native English speakers to find the definitions in a dictionary or on the Internet. **EL**

Academic Standards

Additional Support activities on pp. 1232 and 1233 cover the following standards:

Skills Practice: **9.3** [Identify] story elements such as...plot...

English Language Coach: **9.1.1** Identify and use the literal...meanings of words and understand the origins of words.

Teach

R1 Reading Strategy

Reviewing and Summarizing

Say: In spite of not having a family, Wilson is accepted into the league. **Ask:** Why do you think an exception was made? *(Possible answer: They may have some reason besides his hair for wanting to hire him.)* OL

L Literary Element

Foreshadowing **Answer:** *It adds to the aura of strangeness and mystery surrounding the unusual job.* OL

BI Big Idea

Revealing the Concealed

Answer: *Wilson must copy the* Encyclopedia Britannica, *though no reason is given for this task. He must remain in the office for a set time every day. It does not matter how much Wilson accomplishes or how well he does his "busy work."* OL

plunged forward, wrung my hand, and congratulated me warmly on my success.

"'It would be injustice to hesitate,' said he. 'You will, however, I am sure, excuse me for taking an obvious precaution.' With that he seized my hair in both his hands, and tugged until I yelled with the pain. 'There is water in your eyes,' said he, as he released me, 'I perceive that all is as it should be. But we have to be careful, for we have twice been deceived by wigs and once by paint. I could tell you tales of cobbler's wax[13] which would disgust you with human nature.'

"He stepped over to the window, and shouted through it at the top of his voice that the vacancy was filled. A groan of disappointment came up from below, and the folk all trooped away in different directions, until there was not a red head to be seen except my own and that of the manager.

"'My name,' said he, 'is Mr. Duncan Ross, and I am myself one of the pensioners upon the fund left by our noble benefactor. Are you a married man, Mr. Wilson? Have you a family?'

"I answered that I had not.

"His face fell immediately.

"'Dear me!' he said, gravely, 'that is very serious indeed! I am sorry to hear you say that. The fund was, of course, for the propagation and spread of the redheads as well as for their maintenance. It is exceedingly unfortunate that you should be a bachelor.'

"My face lengthened at this, Mr. Holmes, for I thought that I was not to have the vacancy after all; but, after thinking it over for a few minutes, he said that it would be all right.

"'In the case of another,' said he, 'the objection might be fatal, but we must stretch a point in favor of a man with such a head of hair as yours. When shall you be able to enter upon your new duties?'

"'Well, it is a little awkward, for I have a business already,' said I.

"'Oh, never mind about that, Mr. Wilson!' said Vincent Spaulding. 'I shall be able to look after that for you.'

13. *Cobbler's wax* is a sticky substance with which shoemakers treat thread.

"'What would be the hours?' I asked.

"'Ten to two.'

"Now a pawnbroker's business is mostly done of an evening, Mr. Holmes, especially Thursday and Friday evenings, which is just before payday, so it would suit me very well to earn a little in the mornings. Besides, I knew that my assistant was a good man, and that he would see to anything that turned up.

"'That would suit me very well,' said I. 'And the pay?'

"'Is four pounds a week.'

"'And the work?'

"'Is purely nominal.'

"'What do you call purely nominal?'

"'Well, you have to be in the office, or at least in the building, the whole time. If you leave, you forfeit your whole position forever. The will is very clear upon that point. You don't comply with the conditions if you budge from the office during that time.'

"'It's only four hours a day, and I should not think of leaving,' said I.

"'No excuse will avail,' said Mr. Duncan Ross. 'Neither sickness nor business nor anything else. There you must stay, or you lose your billet.'[14]

"'And the work?'

"'Is to copy out the *Encyclopedia Britannica.* There is the first volume of it in that press.[15] You must find your own ink, pens, and chair. Will you be ready tomorrow?'

"'Certainly,' I answered.

"'Then, good-bye, Mr. Jabez Wilson, and let me congratulate you once more on the important position which you have been fortunate enough to gain.' He bowed me out of the room, and I went home with my assistant, hardly knowing what to say or do, I was so pleased at my own good fortune.

14. A *billet* is a job.
15. A *press* is a cupboard.

Literary Element Foreshadowing *What effect does Ross's emphatic order create?* L

Big Idea Revealing the Concealed *What unusual details about this position does Mr. Wilson overlook?* BI

Additional Support

Skills Practice

READING: Making Critical Judgments Students may lack confidence in their critical judgments about literary elements. Stress that careful reading of the text will help them find support for their critiques. Remind them that in addition to evidence from the text, they can use personal experiences and observations to support their opinions. Have students analyze how Conan Doyle uses foreshadowing to (a) give clues to the mystery being solved by Holmes, and (b) engage the reader. OL

"Well, I thought over the matter all day, and by evening I was in low spirits again for I had quite persuaded myself that the whole affair must be some great hoax or fraud, though what its object might be I could not imagine. It seemed altogether past belief that anyone could make such a will, or that they would pay such a sum for doing anything so simple as copying out the *Encyclopedia Britannica.* Vincent Spaulding did what he could to cheer me up, but by bedtime I had reasoned myself out of the whole thing. However, in the morning I determined to have a look at it anyhow, so I bought a penny bottle of ink, and with a quill pen and seven sheets of foolscap paper,[16] I started off for Pope's Court.

"Well, to my surprise and delight, everything was as right as possible. The table was set out ready for me, and Mr. Duncan Ross was there to see that I got fairly to work. He started me off upon the letter A, then he left me; but he would drop in from time to time to see that all was right with me. At two o'clock he bade me good-day, complimented me upon the amount that I had written, and locked the door of the office after me.

"This went on day after day, Mr. Holmes, and on Saturday the manager came in and planked down four golden sovereigns[17] for my week's work. It was the same next week, and the same the week after. Every morning I was there at ten, and every afternoon I left at two. By degrees Mr. Duncan Ross took to coming in only once of a morning, and then, after a time, he did not come in at all. Still, of course, I never dared to leave the room for an instant, for I was not sure when he might come, and the billet was such a good one, and suited me so well, that I would not risk the loss of it.

"Eight weeks passed away like this, and I had written about Abbots and Archery and Armor and Architecture and Attica, and

Mr. Jabez Wilson reading a sign that says, "THE RED-HEADED LEAGUE IS DISSOLVED OCTOBER 9, 1890." Sidney Paget.

Viewing the Art: How does the man's posture in this illustration reveal his attitude at the moment? 

hoped with diligence that I might get on to the B's before very long. It cost me something in foolscap, and I had pretty nearly filled a shelf with my writings. And then suddenly the whole business came to an end."

"To an end?"

"Yes, sir. And no later than this morning. I went to my work as usual at ten o'clock, but the door was shut and locked, with a little square of cardboard hammered on to the middle of the panel with a tack. Here it is, and you can read for yourself."

He held up a piece of white cardboard about the size of a sheet of note paper. It read in this fashion:

THE RED-HEADED LEAGUE
IS DISSOLVED
OCTOBER 9, 1890

16. *Foolscap paper* is writing paper.
17. *Sovereigns* (sov′ rənz) are gold coins worth one pound each at the time of the story.

Reading Strategy Making Inferences About Characters *What can you infer about Mr. Wilson?* **R2**

Teach

R2 Reading Strategy

Making Inferences About Characters **Answer:** *Wilson is not only gullible but also mercenary. He would rather be paid well than question the value of his work.* **OL**

★ Viewing the Art

Answer: *Answers will vary. Students may note that the man's posture looks tentative, as if he's prepared to leave quickly.*

English illustrator Sidney Paget (1860–1908) illustrated Conan Doyle's Sherlock Holmes series that appeared in the *Strand Magazine.* **AS**

Differentiated Instruction

Attention and Memory Students with learning challenges may have trouble answering questions about the selection because of its length, vocabulary, and complex sentence structure. Have them work in small groups and take turns rereading the story aloud column by column. Urge students to pause whenever a word or passage is puzzling and to work as a group to find answers. **BL**

Academic Standards

Additional Support activities on pp. 1234 and 1235 cover the following standards:

Skills Practice: **9.3.6** Analyze and trace an author's development of time and sequence, including the use of complex literary devices, such as foreshadowing…

Differentiated Instruction: **9.2** Develop [reading] strategies…

Teach

BI Big Idea

Revealing the Concealed
Answer: *The sign does not disclose why the league was dissolved or whom to contact for further information.* OL

R1 Reading Strategy

Predicting Ask: What do you think Mr. Wilson will find out? *(That the league is a fraud)* OL

R2 Reading Strategy

Drawing Conclusions Ask: Do you agree with the assistant's advice to Wilson? *(Possible answer: No; Wilson has been too passive and trusting; by now he should realize something suspicious is going on.)* OL

R3 Reading Strategy

Making Inferences About Characters Ask: What does this remark reveal about Mr. Wilson? *(His only interest seems to be money.)* OL

Sherlock Holmes and I surveyed this curt[18] announcement and the rueful[19] face behind it, until the comical side of the affair so completely overtopped every other consideration that we both burst out into a roar of laughter.

"I cannot see that there is anything very funny," cried our client, flushing up to the roots of his flaming head. "If you can do nothing better than laugh at me, I can go elsewhere."

"No, no," cried Holmes, shoving him back into the chair from which he had half risen. "I really wouldn't miss your case for the world. It is most refreshingly unusual. But there is, if you will excuse my saying so, something just a little funny about it. Pray, what steps did you take when you found the card upon the door?"

"I was staggered, sir. I did not know what to do. Then I called at the offices round, but none of them seemed to know anything about it. Finally, I went to the landlord, who is an accountant living on the ground floor, and I asked him if he could tell me what had become of the Red-Headed League. He said that he had never heard of any such body. Then I asked him who Mr. Duncan Ross was. He answered that the name was new to him.

"'Well,' said I, 'the gentleman at No. 4.'

"'What, the red-headed man?'

"'Yes.'

"'Oh,' said he, 'his name was William Morris. He was a solicitor,[20] and was using my room as a temporary convenience until his new premises were ready. He moved out yesterday.'

"'Where could I find him?'

"'Oh, at his new offices. He did tell me the address. Yes, 17 King Edward Street, near St. Paul's.'[21]

"I started off, Mr. Holmes, but when I got to that address it was a manufactory of artificial kneecaps, and no one in it had ever heard of either Mr. William Morris or Mr. Duncan Ross." R1

"And what did you do then?" asked Holmes.

"I went home to Saxe-Coburg Square, and I took the advice of my assistant. But he could not help me in any way. He could only say that if I waited I should hear by post. R2 But that was not quite good enough, Mr. Holmes. I did not wish to lose such a place without a struggle; so, as I have heard that you were good enough to give advice to poor folk who were in need of it, I came right away to you."

"And you did very wisely," said Holmes. "Your case is an exceedingly remarkable one, and I shall be happy to look into it. From what you have told me I think that it is possible that graver issues hang from it than might at first sight appear."

"Grave enough!" said Mr. Jabez Wilson. "Why I have lost four pounds a week." R3

"As far as you are personally concerned," remarked Holmes, "I do not see that you have any grievance against this remarkable league. On the contrary, you are, as I understand, richer by some thirty pounds, to say nothing of the minute[22] knowledge which you have gained on every subject that comes under the letter A. You have lost nothing by them."

"No, sir. But I want to find out about them, and who they are, and what their object was in playing this prank—if it was a prank—upon me. It was a pretty expensive joke for them, for it cost them two-and-thirty pounds."

"We shall endeavor to clear up these points for you. And, first, one or two questions, Mr. Wilson. This assistant of yours who first called your attention to the advertisement—how long had he been with you?"

"About a month then."

"How did he come?"

"In answer to an advertisement."

18. *Curt* means "so short as to seem impolite."
19. *Rueful* refers to Wilson's pitiably disappointed face.
20. *Solicitor* is the British term for an attorney who handles legal matters but does not appear in court.
21. *St. Paul's* is a famous cathedral in London.

Big Idea Revealing the Concealed *What does the sign leave to the imagination?* BI

22. Here, *minute* (mī no͞ot′) means "detailed."

Additional Support

Skills Practice

GRAMMAR AND LANGUAGE:

Personal Pronouns Remind students that personal pronouns refer to specific persons or things and indicate the person speaking (first person), the person being addressed (second person), or any other person or thing being discussed (third person). Note that this story is told in the first person by Dr. Watson. Tell students to rewrite the story's first paragraph, changing the point of view from first person to third person and adjusting the personal pronouns accordingly. Discuss the effects of changing from first- to third-person point of view. OL

"Was he the only applicant?"

"No, I had a dozen."

"Why did you pick him?"

"Because he was handy, and would come cheap."

"At half wages, in fact?"

"Yes."

"What is he like, this Vincent Spaulding?"

"Small, stout-built, very quick in his ways, no hair on his face, though he's not short of thirty. Has a white splash of acid upon his forehead."

Holmes sat up in his chair in considerable excitement. "I thought as much," said he. "Have you ever observed that his ears are pierced for earrings?"

"Yes sir. He told me that a gypsy had done it for him when he was a lad."

"Hum!" said Holmes, sinking back in deep thought. "He is still with you?"

"Oh, yes, sir; I have only just left him."

"And has your business been attended to in your absence?"

"Nothing to complain of, sir. There's never very much to do of a morning."

"That will do, Mr. Wilson. I shall be happy to give you an opinion upon the subject in the course of a day or two. Today is Saturday, and I hope that by Monday we may come to a conclusion."

"Well, Watson," said Holmes, when our visitor had left us, "what do you make of it all?"

"I make nothing of it," I answered, frankly. "It is a most mysterious business."

"As a rule," said Holmes, "the more bizarre a thing is, the less mysterious it proves to be. It is your commonplace, featureless crimes which are really puzzling, just as a commonplace face is the most difficult to identify. But I must be prompt over this matter."

"What are you going to do, then?" I asked.

"To smoke," he answered. "It is quite a three-pipe problem, and I beg that you won't speak to me for fifty minutes." He curled himself up in his chair, with his thin knees drawn up to his hawk-like nose, and there he sat with his eyes closed and his black clay pipe thrusting out like the bill of some strange bird. I had come to the conclusion that he had dropped asleep, and indeed was nodding myself, when he suddenly sprang out of his chair with the gesture of a man who has made up his mind, and put his pipe down upon the mantelpiece.

"Sarasate[23] plays at the St. James's Hall this afternoon," he remarked. "What do you think, Watson? Could your patients spare you for a few hours?"

"I have nothing to do today. My practice is never very absorbing."

"Then put on your hat and come. I am going through the City first, and we can

Sherlock Holmes deep in thought. Sidney Paget. 

23. *Sarasate* (sa′ rə sa′ tē) is Pablo de Sarasate (1844–1908), a Spanish violinist.

Reading Strategy Making Inferences About Characters *What can you conclude about Holmes?* **R4**

Reading Strategy Making Inferences About Characters *What was Holmes really doing instead of resting?* **R5**

Teach

R4 Reading Strategy

Making Inferences About Characters Answer: *Holmes observes keenly and has excellent recall of details. He surmises Vincent Spaulding's real identity.* **OL**

R5 Reading Strategy

Making Inferences About Characters Answer: *He is contemplating the evidence.* **OL**

★ Viewing the Art

Artist Sidney Paget (1860–1908) seems to have gotten the job of illustrating the Holmes stories by accident. The job was supposed to go to his brother Walter, a more famous illustrator. Instead, Sidney created the first visual images of Holmes and his illustrations increased the popularity of the stories. Paget's drawing of Holmes is supposedly based on his brother. Conan Doyle is said to have complained that Paget made Holmes too handsome. **AS**

Differentiated Instruction

Guided Review Students who have trouble understanding or remembering the story will benefit from meeting periodically to summarize plot events. Stress that summaries consist of main ideas and very few details. Guide the discussion with questions such as the following: What event begins the story? *(Watson presents Wilson's case to Holmes.)* What is Wilson's problem? *(Locating his vanished employer)* **BL**

Academic Standards

Additional Support activities on pp. 1236 and 1237 cover the following standards:

Skills Practice: **9.6.2** Demonstrate an understanding of…proper English usage… **9.3.13** Explain how…choice of narrator affect[s] the mood, tone, and meaning of text.

Differentiated Instruction: **9.3** [Identify] story elements such as…plot…

Teach

R1 Reading Strategy

Visualizing **Ask:** How do you visualize the neighborhood based on the writer's description? *(It is a seedy but respectable neighborhood, where the smoky air makes everything look dirty.)* OL

BI Big Idea

Revealing the Concealed
Answer: *He is checking whether the area beneath the pavement is solid or hollow.* OL

R2 Reading Strategy

Predicting Ask students what they think Holmes has deduced from this clue. Have them revisit their predictions as more information is revealed. OL

★ Cultural History

Underground The world's first underground railway opened in London in 1863. Today, Londoners refer to it as "the Tube." The original Tube covered about 4 miles underground and ran between Paddington (Bishop's Road) and Farrington Street. Currently, the Tube covers about 253 miles, serving 275 stations. AS

have some lunch on the way. I observe that there is a good deal of German music on the program, which is rather more to my taste than Italian or French. It is introspective,[24] and I want to introspect. Come along!"

★ We traveled by the Underground[25] as far as Aldersgate; and a short walk took us to Saxe-Coburg Square, the scene of the singular story which we had listened to in the morning. It was a poky, little, shabby-genteel place, where four lines of dingy, two-storied brick houses looked out into a small railed-in enclosure, where a lawn of weedy grass and a few clumps of faded laurel-bushes made a hard fight against a smoke-laden and uncongenial atmosphere. [R1] Three gilt balls[26] and a brown board with JABEZ WILSON in white letters, upon a corner house, announced the place where our red-headed client carried on his business. Sherlock Holmes stopped in front of it with his head on one side, and looked it all over, with his eyes shining brightly between puckered lids. Then he walked slowly up the street, and then down again to the corner, still looking keenly at the houses. Finally he returned to the pawnbroker's, and, having thumped vigorously upon the pavement with his stick two or three times, he went up to the door and knocked. It was instantly opened by a bright-looking, clean-shaven young fellow, who asked him to step in.

"Thank you," said Holmes, "I only wished to ask you how you would go from here to the Strand."[27]

"Third right, fourth left," answered the assistant, promptly, closing the door. "Smart fellow, that," observed Holmes, as we walked away. "He is, in my judgment, the fourth smartest man in London, and for daring, I am not sure that he has not a claim to be third. I have known something of him before."

"Evidently," said I, "Mr. Wilson's assistant counts for a good deal in this mystery of the Red-Headed League. I am sure that you inquired your way merely in order that you might see him."

"Not him."

"What then?"

"The knees of his trousers." R2

"And what did you see?"

"What I expected to see."

"Why did you beat the pavement?"

"My dear doctor, this is a time for observation, not for talk. We are spies in an enemy's country. We know something of Saxe-Coburg Square. Let us now explore the parts which lie behind it."

> "We are spies in an enemy's country."

The road in which we found ourselves as we turned round the corner from the retired Saxe-Coburg Square presented as great a contrast to it as the front of a picture does to the back. It was one of the main arteries which convey the traffic of the City to the north and west. The roadway was blocked with the immense stream of commerce flowing in a double tide inward and outward, while the footpaths were black with the hurrying swarm of pedestrians. It was difficult to realize, as we looked at the line of fine shops and stately business premises, that they really abutted[28] on the other side upon the faded and stagnant square which we had just quitted.

"Let me see," said Holmes, standing at the corner, and glancing along the line, "I should like just to remember the order of the houses here. It is a hobby of mine to have an exact knowledge of London. There is Mortimer's,

24. *Introspective* means "inward looking."
25. The *Underground* is the London subway system.
26. *Three gilt,* or gold-colored, *balls* signify a pawnbroker's shop.
27. *The Strand* is a major London street.

Big Idea Revealing the Concealed *Why might Holmes do such an odd thing?* BI

28. Here, *abutted* means "bordered."

Additional Support

Skills Practice

GRAMMAR AND LANGUAGE: **Recognizing Nouns** Note that nouns may be the subjects of sentences, the objects of prepositions, direct or indirect objects, objects of infinitives, or predicate nominatives. Have students identify the role of each noun in this passage: "Let me see," said Holmes, standing at the corner, and glancing along the line, "I should like just to remember the order of the houses here." *(Holmes: subject; corner: object of preposition; line: object of preposition; order: direct object; houses: object of preposition)* OL the tobacconist, the little newspaper shop, the Coburg branch of the City and Suburban Bank, the Vegetarian Restaurant, and McFarlane's carriage-building depot. That carries us right on to the other block. And now, doctor, we've done our work, so it's time we had some play. A sandwich and a cup of coffee, and then off to violinland, where all is sweetness and delicacy and harmony, and there are no red-headed clients to vex us with their conundrums."[29]

My friend was an enthusiastic musician, being himself not only a very capable performer, but a composer of no ordinary merit. All the afternoon he sat in the stalls[30] wrapped in the most perfect happiness, gently waving his long, thin fingers in time to the music, while his gently smiling face and his **languid,** dreamy eyes were as unlike those of Holmes, the sleuth-hound, Holmes, the relentless, keen-witted, ready-handed criminal agent, as it was possible to conceive. In his singular character the dual nature alternately asserted itself, and his extreme exactness and astuteness represented, as I have often thought, the reaction against the poetic and contemplative mood which occasionally predominated in him. The swing of his nature took him from extreme languor to devouring energy; and, as I knew well, he was never so truly formidable as when, for days on end, he had been lounging in his armchair amid his improvisations and his black-letter editions. Then it was that the lust of the chase would suddenly come upon him, and that his brilliant reasoning power would rise to the level of intuition, until those who were unacquainted with his methods would look askance at him as on a man whose knowledge was not that of other mortals. When I saw him that afternoon so enwrapped in the music at St. James's Hall, I felt that an evil time might be coming upon those whom he had set himself to hunt down.

"You want to go home, no doubt, doctor," he remarked, as we emerged.

"Yes, it would be as well."

"And I have some business to do which will take some hours. This business at Coburg Square is serious."

"Why serious?"

"A considerable crime is in contemplation.[31] I have every reason to believe that we shall be in time to stop it. But today being Saturday rather complicates matters. I shall want your help tonight."

"At what time?"

"Ten will be early enough."

"I shall be at Baker Street[32] at ten."

"Very well. And, I say, doctor, there may be some little danger, so kindly put your army revolver in your pocket." He waved his hand, turned on his heel, and disappeared in an instant among the crowd.

I trust that I am not more dense than my neighbors, but I was always oppressed with a sense of my own stupidity in my dealings with Sherlock Holmes. Here I had heard what he had heard, I had seen what he had seen, and yet from his words it was evident that he saw clearly not only what had happened, but what was about to happen, while to me the whole business was still confused and grotesque. As I drove home to my house in Kensington I thought over it all from the extraordinary story of the red-headed copier of the *Encyclopedia* down to the visit to Saxe-Coburg Square, and the ominous words with

29. *Conundrums* are puzzling problems.
30. Here, *stalls* are theater seats located on the ground floor close to the stage.
31. *In contemplation* means "being planned."
32. *Baker Street* is the London street where Holmes lives.

Literary Element Foreshadowing *What does Holmes's attention to detail suggest about the street?* L1

Vocabulary

languid (lang′ gwid) *adj.* drooping; weak and listless

Reading Strategy Making Inferences About Characters *What effect does Watson's view of Holmes have on the reader?* R3

Literary Element Foreshadowing *How does this request build suspense?* L2

Teach

L1 Literary Element

Foreshadowing **Answer:** *The street will play an important role in the solution to the mystery.* OL

R3 Reading Strategy

Making Inferences About Characters **Answer:** *His remark bolsters the reader's admiration for and confidence in the detective's abilities.* OL

L2 Literary Element

Foreshadowing **Answer:** *His request hints that there may be serious danger ahead.* OL

Differentiated Instruction

Active Listening Less proficient readers often benefit from following the text while it is read aloud. Have proficient readers read portions of the story aloud to small groups of students. The group should pause periodically to review the events, characters, and literary elements, such as foreshadowing. BL

Academic Standards

Additional Support activities on pp. 1238 and 1239 cover the following standards:

Skills Practice: **9.6.2** Demonstrate an understanding of sentence construction… and proper English usage…

Differentiated Instruction: **9.7.1** Summarize a speaker's purpose and point of view and ask questions concerning the speaker's content…

Teach

R1 Reading Strategy

Making Inferences About Characters **Ask:** Based on Watson's description, what kind of personality would this character most likely have? *(He sounds gloomy, uptight, and conventional.)* **OL**

R2 Reading Strategy

Making Inferences About Characters **Answer:** *Mr. Merryweather probably has a lot of money or may be a bank official because his "stake" in the events is so high.* **OL**

R3 Reading Strategy

Analyzing Dialogue **Ask:** What does Holmes mean? *(He has had dealings with the criminal and acknowledges that the man is clever.)* **OL**

★ Cultural History

Scotland Yard Scotland Yard is officially known as the Metropolitan Police Service. When British Home Secretary Sir Robert Peel founded the police force in 1829, the first police headquarters opened onto a courtyard that was once owned by the Kings of Scotland. Thus, came the name Scotland Yard. **AS**

which he had parted from me. What was this nocturnal expedition, and why should I go armed? Where were we going, and what were we to do? I had the hint from Holmes that this smooth-faced pawnbroker's assistant was a **formidable** man—a man who might play a deep game. I tried to puzzle it out, but gave it up in despair, and set the matter aside until night should bring an explanation.

It was a quarter past nine when I started from home and made my way across the Park, and so through Oxford Street to Baker Street. Two hansoms[33] were standing at the door, and, as I entered the passage, I heard the sound of voices from above. On entering his room I found Holmes in animated conversation with two men, one of whom I recognized as Peter Jones, the official police agent, while the other was a long, thin, sad-faced man, with a very shiny hat and oppressively respectable frock coat. **R1**

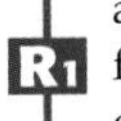
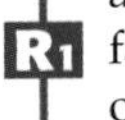
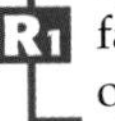
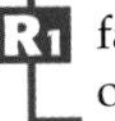

"Ha! our party is complete," said Holmes, buttoning up his pea jacket, and taking his heavy hunting crop from the rack. "Watson, I think you know Mr. Jones, of Scotland Yard?[34] Let me introduce you to Mr. Merryweather, who is to be our companion in tonight's adventure." ★

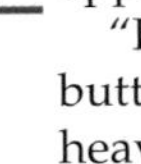
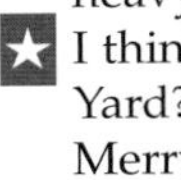

"We're hunting in couples again, doctor, you see," said Jones, in his consequential way. "Our friend here is a wonderful man for starting a chase. All he wants is an old dog to help him do the running down."

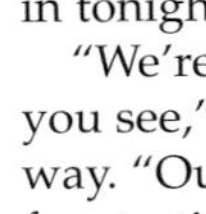

"I hope a wild goose may not prove to be the end of our chase," observed Mr. Merryweather, gloomily.

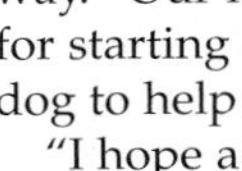
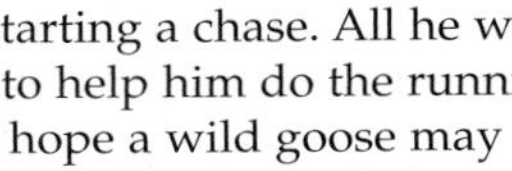

"You may place considerable confidence in Mr. Holmes, sir," said the police agent, loftily. "He has his own little methods, which are, if he won't mind my saying so, just a little too theoretical and fantastic, but he has the makings of a detective in him. It is not too much to say that once or twice, as in that business of the Sholto murder and the Agra treasure,[35] he has been more nearly correct than the official force."

"Oh, if you say so, Mr. Jones, it is all right," said the stranger, with deference. "Still, I confess that I miss my bridge games. It is the first Saturday night for seven-and-twenty years that I have not had my bridge."

"I think you will find," said Sherlock Holmes, "that you will play for a higher stake tonight than you have ever done yet, and that the play will be more exciting. For you, Mr. Merryweather, the stake will be some thirty thousand pounds; and for you, Jones, it will be the man upon whom you wish to lay your hands."

"John Clay, the murderer, thief, smasher,[36] and forger. He's a young man, Mr. Merryweather, but he is at the head of his profession, and I would rather have my bracelets[37] on him than on any criminal in London. He's a remarkable man, is young John Clay. His grandfather was a royal duke, and he himself has been to Eton and Oxford.[38] His brain is as cunning as his fingers, and though we meet signs of him at every turn, we never know where to find the man himself. He'll crack a crib[39] in Scotland one week, and be raising money to build an orphanage in Cornwall the next. I've been on his track for years, and have never set eyes on him yet."

"I hope that I may have the pleasure of introducing you tonight. I've had one or two little turns also with Mr. John Clay, and I agree with you that he is at the head of his profession. It is past ten, however, and quite time that we started. If you two will take the **R3**

33. *Hansoms* are two-wheeled horse carriages.
34. *Scotland Yard* is the headquarters of the London police.
35. *The Sholto murder and the Agra treasure* are references to an earlier Holmes novel, *The Sign of Four.*
36. A *smasher* is a person who passes counterfeit money.
37. Here, *bracelets* are handcuffs.
38. *Eton* is an exclusive private preparatory school near London; *Oxford* is one of England's most famous universities.
39. To *crack a crib* is to break into a building.

Vocabulary

formidable (fôr′ mi də bəl) *adj.* impressive; awe-inspiring

Reading Strategy Making Inferences About Characters *What can you infer about Mr. Merryweather?* **R2**

Additional Support

Skills Practice

READING: Clarifying, Imagining, Interpreting Remind students that interacting with a text—asking and answering questions, imagining themselves in a character's situation, and thinking about the meaning of themes and ideas—will deepen their understanding of literature. Have students write a personal response to the character of Holmes using at least one of these active reading strategies. **OL**

first hansom, Watson and I will follow in the second."

Sherlock Holmes was not very communicative during the long drive, and lay back in the cab humming the tunes which he had heard in the afternoon. We rattled through an endless labyrinth[40] of gas-lit streets until we emerged into Farringdon Street.

"We are close there now," my friend remarked. "This fellow Merryweather is a bank director, and personally interested in the matter. I thought it as well to have Jones with us also. He is not a bad fellow, though an absolute imbecile in his profession. He has one positive virtue. He is as brave as a bulldog, and as tenacious as a lobster if he gets his claws upon anyone. Here we are, and they are waiting for us."

We had reached the same crowded thoroughfare in which we had found ourselves in the morning. Our cabs were dismissed, and, following the guidance of Mr. Merryweather, we passed down a narrow passage and through a side door, which he opened for us. Within, there was a small corridor, which ended in a very massive iron gate. This also was opened, and led down a flight of winding stone steps, which terminated at another formidable gate. Mr. Merryweather stopped to light a lantern, and then conducted us down a dark, earth-smelling passage, and so, after opening a third door, into a huge vault, or cellar, which was piled all round with crates and massive boxes.

"You are not very vulnerable from above," Holmes remarked, as he held up the lantern and gazed about him.

"Nor from below," said Mr. Merryweather, striking his stick upon the flags which lined the floor. "Why, dear me, it sounds quite hollow!" he remarked, looking up in surprise.

"I must really ask you to be a little more quiet," said Holmes, severely. "You have already imperiled the whole success of our expedition. Might I beg that you would have the goodness to sit down upon one of those boxes, and not to interfere?"

The solemn Mr. Merryweather perched himself upon a crate, with a very injured expression upon his face, while Holmes fell upon his knees upon the floor, and, with the lantern and a magnifying lens, began to examine minutely the cracks between the stones. A few seconds sufficed to satisfy him, for he sprang to his feet again, and put his glass in his pocket.

"We have at least an hour before us," he remarked; "for they can hardly take any steps until the good pawnbroker is safely in bed. Then they will not lose a minute, for the sooner they do their work the longer time they will have for their escape. We are at present, doctor—as no doubt you have divined[41]—in the cellar of the City branch of one of the principal London banks. Mr. Merryweather is the chairman of directors, and he will explain to you that there are reasons why the more daring criminals of London should take a considerable interest in this cellar at present." R4

"Why, dear me, it sounds quite hollow!"

"It is our French gold," whispered the director. "We have had several warnings that an attempt might be made upon it."

"Your French gold?"

"Yes. We had occasion some months ago to strengthen our resources and borrowed, for that purpose, thirty thousand napoleons[42] from the Bank of France. It has become known that we have never had occasion to unpack the money, and that it is still lying in our cellar. The crate upon which I sit contains

40. Here, a *labyrinth* suggests an area of winding, twisting streets.

Literary Element Foreshadowing *What might Holmes's decision to bring Jones along foreshadow?* L

41. Here, to *divine* means "to perceive."

42. *Napoleons* are French gold coins; thirty thousand napoleons are worth about $1,200,000 today.

Teach

L Literary Element

Foreshadowing Answer: *His decision to bring someone who is "brave as a bulldog" and "tenacious as a lobster" suggests that catching and holding the culprit will be dangerous and difficult.* OL

R4 Reading Strategy

Drawing Conclusions Ask: What has been the ultimate goal of the criminals who devised the ruse of the Red-Headed League? *(To rob a London bank)* OL

English Language Coach

Vocabulary Resources Books Many English language learners will find that a traditional thesaurus does not provide enough information to help them use words correctly. Explain that in addition to listing synonyms, some regular English dictionaries, most English ASL dictionaries, and dictionaries of synonyms may include their connotations and example sentences. Often, unabridged dictionaries offer substantial guidance on synonyms. EL

Academic Standards

Additional Support activities on pp. 1240 and 1241 cover the following standards:

Skills Practice: **9.2** Develop strategies such as asking questions... **9.5.2** Write responses to literature that demonstrate a comprehensive grasp of the significant ideas of literary works...

English Language Coach: **9.2.1** Analyze the structure and format of reference... documents... **9.1.2** Distinguish between what words mean literally and what they imply and interpret what the words imply.

Teach

L Literary Element

Foreshadowing Answer: *It suggests that the criminals are armed and desperate and ready to kill for the money.* OL

R1 Reading Strategy

Interpreting Ask: Who is speaking? What does he feel? *(Watson is speaking; he feels great anxiety about what might happen.)* OL

BI Big Idea

Revealing the Concealed
Answer: *One of the criminals is about to enter the vault through the underground tunnel.* OL

R2 Reading Strategy

Predicting Ask: What do you think will happen next? *(Possible answer: Once the criminals climb out of the hole, Holmes will spring his trap and capture them.)* OL

two thousand napoleons packed between layers of lead foil. Our reserve of bullion[43] is much larger at present than is usually kept in a single branch office, and the directors have had misgivings upon the subject."

"Which were very well justified," observed Holmes. "And now it is time that we arranged our little plans. I expect that within an hour matters will come to a head. In the meantime, Mr. Merryweather, we must put the screen over that dark lantern."

"And sit in the dark?"

"I am afraid so. I had brought a pack of cards in my pocket, and I thought that, as we were a *partie carrée,*[44] you might have your bridge games after all. But I see that the enemy's preparations have gone so far that we cannot risk the presence of a light. And, first of all, we must choose our positions. These are daring men, and though we shall take them at a disadvantage, they may do us some harm unless we are careful. I shall stand behind this crate, and do you conceal yourself behind those. Then when I flash a light upon them, close in swiftly. If they fire, Watson, have no compunction about shooting them down."

I placed my revolver, cocked, upon the top of the wooden case behind which I crouched. Holmes shot the slide across the front of his lantern, and left us in pitch darkness—such an absolute darkness as I have never before experienced. The smell of hot metal remained to assure us that the light was still there, ready to flash out at a moment's notice. To me, with my nerves worked up to a pitch of expectancy, there was something depressing and subduing in the sudden gloom, and in the cold, dank air of the vault. R1

"They have but one retreat," whispered Holmes. "That is back through the house into Saxe-Coburg Square. I hope that you have done what I asked you, Jones?"

"I have an inspector and two officers waiting at the front door."

"Then we have stopped all the holes. And now we must be silent and wait."

What a time it seemed! From comparing notes afterwards it was but an hour and a quarter, yet it appeared to me that the night must have almost gone, and the dawn be breaking above us. My limbs were weary and stiff, for I feared to change my position; yet my nerves were worked up to the highest pitch of tension, and my hearing was so acute that I could not only hear the gentle breathing of my companions, but I could distinguish the deeper, heavier in-breath of the bulky Jones from the thin, sighing note of the bank director. From my position I could look over the case in the direction of the floor. Suddenly my eyes caught the glint of a light.

At first it was but a lurid spark upon the stone pavement. Then it lengthened out until it became a yellow line, and then, without any warning or sound, a gash seemed to open and a hand appeared; a white, almost womanly hand, which felt about in the center of the little area of light. For a minute or more the hand, with its writhing fingers, protruded out of the floor. Then it was withdrawn as suddenly as it appeared, and all was dark again save the single lurid spark which marked a chink between the stones.

Its disappearance, however, was but momentary. With a rending, tearing sound, one of the broad, white stones turned over upon its side, and left a square, gaping hole, through which streamed the light of a lantern. R2 Over the edge there peeped a clean-cut, boyish face, which looked keenly about it, and then, with a hand on either side of the aperture,[45] drew itself shoulder-high and waist-high, until one knee rested upon the edge. In another instant he stood at the side of the hole, and was hauling after him a companion,

43. Here, *bullion* is gold.
44. *Partie carrée* (pär tē′ ka rā′) is French for "party of four," the number needed to play some card games.
45. An *aperture* is an opening.

Literary Element Foreshadowing *How does this comment build suspense?* L

Big Idea Revealing the Concealed *What is about to be revealed?* BI

Additional Support

Skills Practice

GRAMMAR AND LANGUAGE:
Irregular Verbs Remind students that regular verbs form the past tense by adding *-ed* to the base form. Irregular verbs form the past tense in other ways.

Have students look for past tense verbs in the selection. Then have them determine whether the verb is a regular or an irregular verb. OL lithe and small like himself, with a pale face and a shock of very red hair.

"It's all clear," he whispered. "Have you ★ the chisel and the bags? Great Scott! Jump, Archie, jump, and I'll swing for it!"

Sherlock Holmes had sprung out and seized the intruder by the collar. The other dived down the hole, and I heard the sound of rending cloth as Jones clutched at his skirts.[46] The light flashed upon the barrel of a revolver, but Holmes's hunting crop came down on the man's wrist, and the pistol clinked upon the stone floor.

"It's no use, John Clay," said Holmes blandly. "You have no chance at all."

"So I see," the other answered, with the utmost coolness. "I fancy that my pal is all right, though I see you have got his coattails."

"There are three men waiting for him at the door," said Holmes.

"Oh, indeed! You seem to have done the thing very completely. I must compliment you."

"And I you," Holmes answered. "Your red-headed idea was very new and effective."

"You'll see your pal again presently," said Jones. "He's quicker at climbing down holes than I am. Just hold out while I fix the derbies."[47]

"I beg that you will not touch me with your filthy hands," remarked our prisoner, as the handcuffs clattered upon his wrists. "You may not be aware that I have royal blood in my veins. Have the goodness, also, when you address me always to say 'sir' and 'please.'"

"All right," said Jones, with a stare and a snigger. "Well, would you please, sir, march upstairs, where we can get a cab to carry your highness to the police station?"

"That is better," said John Clay, serenely. He made a sweeping bow to the three of us, and walked quietly off in the custody of the detective.

"Really, Mr. Holmes," said Mr. Merryweather, as we followed them from the cellar, "I do not know how the bank can thank you or repay you. There is no doubt that you have detected and defeated in the most complete manner one of the most determined attempts at bank robbery that has ever come within my experience."

"I have had one or two little scores of my own to settle with Mr. John Clay," said Holmes. "I have been at some small expense over this matter, which I shall expect the bank to refund, but beyond that I am amply repaid by having had an experience which is in many ways unique, and by hearing the very remarkable narrative of the Red-Headed League."

"Great Scott! Jump, Archie, jump, and I'll swing for it!"

"You see, Watson," he explained, in the early hours of the morning, "it was perfectly obvious from the first that the only possible object of this rather fantastic business of the advertisement of the League, and the copying of the *Encyclopedia,* must be to get this not over-bright pawnbroker out of the way for a number of hours every day. It was a curious way of managing it, but, really, it would be difficult to suggest a better. The method was no doubt suggested to Clay's ingenious mind by the color of his accomplice's hair. The four pounds a week was a lure which must draw him, and what was it to them, who were playing for thousands? They put in the advertisement, one rogue[48] has the temporary office, the other rogue incites the man to apply for it, and together they

46. Here, *skirts* refers to any clothing that hangs freely below the waist.

47. *Derbies* are handcuffs.

48. Here, a *rogue* is a dishonest or worthless person.

Reading Strategy Making Inferences About Characters *What are your impressions of Clay?* R3

Teach

R3 Reading Strategy

Making Inferences About Characters **Answer:** *He seems sophisticated, gentlemanly and well bred, even giving credit to Holmes for his skill. On the surface, he is similar to Holmes.* OL

★ Language History

Great Scott The origin of "Great Scott" is under some debate. One popular theory is that it refers to an actual person: American General Winfield Scott (1786–1866). His heroism in the Mexican War in addition to his 300-pound weight later in life make him a good candidate for the expression's origin, figuratively and literally. AS

Differentiated Instruction

Imagine Encourage struggling readers to imagine a new movie adaptation of "The Red-Headed League." What actors would they cast in the various roles? Would they modernize the story or change the setting? Have students create posters and advertising slogans *(Example: The Red-Headed League: Who Are They? And Why Do They Want Jabez Wilson?)* for their version of the movie and present them in class. BL

Academic Standards

Additional Support activities on pp. 1242 and 1243 cover the following standards:

Skills Practice: **9.6.2** Demonstrate an understanding of…proper English usage, including the use of consistent verb tenses.

Differentiated Instruction: **9.7.4** Use…visual aids…to enhance the appeal and accuracy of presentations.

Teach

R1 Reading Strategy

Making Inferences About Characters **Answer:** *Holmes makes deductions about people based on his insights into human nature.* OL

R2 Reading Strategy

Making Inferences About Characters **Answer:** *Watson is clearly impressed by Holmes's reasoning abilities. He seems to regard him as infallible.* OL

manage to secure his absence every morning in the week. From the time that I heard of the assistant having come for half wages, it was obvious to me that he had some strong motive for securing the situation."

"But how could you guess what the motive was?"

"Had there been women in the house, I should have suspected a mere vulgar intrigue. That, however, was out of the question. The man's business was a small one, and there was nothing in his house which could account for such elaborate preparations and such an expenditure as they were at. It must, then, be something out of the house. What could it be? I thought of the assistant's fondness for photography, and his trick of vanishing into the cellar. The cellar! There was the end of this tangled clue. Then I made inquiries as to this mysterious assistant, and found that I had to deal with one of the coolest and most daring criminals in London. He was doing something in the cellar—something which took many hours a day for months on end. What could it be, once more? I could think of nothing save that he was running a tunnel to some other building.

"So far I had got when we went to visit the scene of action. I surprised you by beating upon the pavement with my stick. I was ascertaining whether the cellar stretched out in front or behind. It was not in front. Then I rang the bell, and, as I hoped, the assistant answered it. We have had some skirmishes, but we had never set eyes upon each other before. I hardly looked at his face. His knees were what I wished to see. You must yourself have remarked how worn, wrinkled, and stained they were. They spoke of those hours of burrowing. The only remaining point was what they were burrowing for. I walked round the corner, saw the City and Suburban Bank abutted on our friend's premises, and felt that I had solved my problem. When you drove home after the concert, I called upon Scotland Yard, and upon the chairman of the bank directors, with the result that you have seen."

"And how could you tell that they would make their attempt tonight?"

"Well, when they closed their League offices, that was a sign that they cared no longer about Mr. Jabez Wilson's presence—in other words, that they had completed their tunnel. But it was essential that they should use it soon, as it might be discovered, or the bullion might be removed. Saturday would suit them better than any other day, as it would give them two days for their escape. For all these reasons I expected them to come tonight."

"You reasoned it out beautifully," I exclaimed, in unfeigned admiration. "It is so long a chain, and yet every link rings true."

> "The cellar! There was the end of this tangled clue."

"It saved me from ennui,"[49] he answered, yawning. "Alas! I already feel it closing in upon me. My life is spent in one long effort to escape from the commonplaces of existence. These little problems help me to do so."

"And you are a benefactor of the race," said I.

He shrugged his shoulders. "Well, perhaps, after all, it is of some little use," he remarked. "'*L'homme c'est rien—l'oeuvre c'est tout,*'[50] as Gustave Flaubert wrote to George Sand."[51]

49. *Ennui* (än wē′) is boredom.
50. *L'homme . . . tout* (lôm sā rē en′ loov′ rə sā too) is French for "Man is nothing; his work is everything."
51. *Gustave Flaubert* (goos täv flō bār′) (1821–1880) and *George Sand* (1804–1876) were French novelists.

Reading Strategy Making Inferences About Characters *What does this explanation reveal about Holmes?* R1

Reading Strategy Making Inferences About Characters *How does Watson regard Holmes?* R2

Additional Support

Academic Standards

The Additional Support activity on p. 1244 covers the following standard:

Skills Practice: **9.5.8** Write for different purposes and audiences, adjusting tone, style, and voice as appropriate.

Skills Practice

WRITING: Dramatizing a Scene Have students work in small groups to dramatize the capture of John Clay. After reading aloud the scene that occurs in the bank's basement, instruct them to work together creating dialogue and stage directions. Remind them that the best way to make a scene believable is to have the characters reveal themselves through their words and actions. OL

AFTER YOU READ

RESPONDING AND THINKING CRITICALLY

Respond

1. If you were to meet Sherlock Holmes, do you think you would like him? Explain why or why not.

Recall and Interpret

2. (a)What conclusions does Holmes draw about Jabez Wilson's past activities? Upon what evidence does Holmes base these conclusions? (b)What evidence supports Holmes's conclusion that Wilson is "none too bright"?
3. (a)What does Wilson think the Red-Headed League is? (b)What does it turn out to be?
4. (a)List the clues that enable Holmes to solve the mystery. (b)What does Holmes do to foil the bank robbers' plan?

Analyze and Evaluate

5. Why is Holmes a better observer than Watson? In what other ways are they different?
6. Would you have liked the story better if Holmes had explained his reasoning at each stage of the investigation? Why or why not?
7. Why do you think Sherlock Holmes became so enormously popular with readers? Use evidence from this story to support your answer.

Connect

8. **Big Idea** **Revealing the Concealed** How clever is John Clay in concealing his motives? How clever is Sherlock Holmes in detecting them? Explain.

YOU'RE THE CRITIC: Different Viewpoints

Doyle: A Nearly Perfect Storyteller?

Read the two excerpts of literary criticism below. As you read, notice the difference in emphasis between the two critics.

"Doyle was a master storyteller. Even his weaker fictional efforts hold reader interest; when his plots are hackneyed and contain no real surprises—which is sometimes the case, even though Doyle prided himself on his ability to devise ingenious plots—the reader is carried away by the sheer power of the storyteller's art."

—*Contemporary Authors Online*

"In the stories the logic can sometimes be found wanting; occasionally the end hardly lives up to the beginning; we are not invariably given the clues Holmes has seen. . . . But none of these matter. Doyle's gifts for storytelling . . . sweep away all criticism."

—H. R. F. Keating

Group Activity Discuss the following questions with your classmates. Refer to the quotations and cite evidence from "The Red-Headed League" to support your responses.

1. Does the comment that some of Doyle's stories "contain no real surprises" apply to "The Red-Headed League"? Explain.
2. Are the flaws that Keating notices in some of Doyle's stories also found in "The Red-Headed League"? Explain.

AFTER YOU READ

Assess

1. Students should explain their answers.
2. (a) He's a Freemason, has been to China, has done manual labor and, recently, much writing. He has a Freemason's pin, a fish tattoo, a muscular right hand, and a shiny cuff. (b) He accepts the obviously bizarre and shady circumstances of his employment at face value.
3. (a) A real organization sympathetic to redheads (b) A ruse to get Wilson out of his shop
4. (a) Wilson's gullibility, the league's sudden dissolution, and the description of Spaulding (b) He hides in the vault with Watson, Jones, and Merryweather and catches Clay.
5. Holmes notes the smallest details. He's more learned, imaginative, and sophisticated.
6. Students should explain their answers.
7. Students should support their answers.
8. Students should confirm the cleverness of Clay's elaborate scheme. In recognizing Clay, discerning his plan, and foiling his robbery attempt, Holmes seems almost unbelievably clever.

CheckPoint

Use the CheckPoint questions on Presentation Plus! to check students' mastery of the selection. These questions can be used with interactive response keypads for immediate student feedback.

You're the Critic

1. Possible answer: No; the league's true purpose would probably surprise most readers.
2. Possible answer: Holmes's logic is portrayed as impeccable, but his inferences about Wilson seem elaborately contrived by the author. The details of his appearance could have simpler explanations. There aren't enough clues to identify Clay. The answers are less strange and intriguing than the puzzle at the outset.

AFTER YOU READ

Assess

Literary Element

1. The absurd requirements for membership in the league suggest it is a trick or front. Wilson is too easily hired, as if he were singled out ahead of time, foreshadowing the forthcoming sinister plan.
2. He works for half wages, snaps pictures and then goes into the cellar to develop them, and seems overly interested in the ad. These details foreshadow Spaulding's hidden motives and his involvement in a plot.

Review: Character Archetype

Encourage students to recall other fictional detectives. What qualities do they and Holmes share?

Reading Strategy

1. To get Wilson off the premises so that he can dig a tunnel from the shop to the bank vault
2. To see why criminals might be interested in the area and to check out Spaulding
3. Possible answers: Loyalty to Holmes, curiosity

LITERARY ANALYSIS

Literary Element Foreshadowing

Foreshadowing can take the form of minor incidents or statements that suggest later developments. Foreshadowing increases the reader's involvement in any story, but it is particularly effective in a mystery like "The Red-Headed League." Such clues enable the alert reader to feel like the detective who eventually solves the mystery.

1. What is unusual about the Red-Headed League? How do its requirements for the open position foreshadow a strange outcome? How does Wilson's interview with "Mr. Duncan Ross" provide foreshadowing?
2. What is suspicious about Vincent Spaulding as a worker? About his interest in the ad for the Red-Headed League? What do these details foreshadow?

Review: Character Archetype

As you learned on page 1075, a **character archetype** is the prime or foremost example of a type of character that recurs in different times and places. Sherlock Holmes is the archetype of the detective hero who uses his wits and keen powers of observation to foil criminals.

Partner Activity Meet with a classmate to discuss your ideas about Holmes as the archetypal detective. Working with your partner, create a web like the one below and fill it in with details for each category listed.

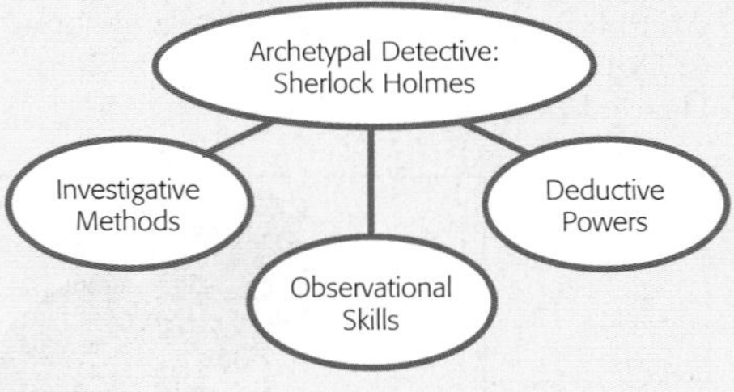

READING AND VOCABULARY

Reading Strategy Making Inferences About Characters

Doyle does not directly state the reason characters in this story act as they do. Instead, he provides clues that the reader must use to **make inferences about characters** and their motives.

1. What motivates Vincent Spaulding in his dealings with Mr. Wilson?
2. What motivates Holmes to examine the area surrounding Wilson's shop and then to knock at Wilson's door?
3. What motivates Watson to accompany Holmes on the Saturday night excursion?

Vocabulary Practice

Practice with Synonyms Choose the synonym for each vocabulary word. Use a dictionary or thesaurus if you need help.

1. singular
   a. normal **b.** unusual **c.** definite
2. nominal
   a. slight **b.** needless **c.** huge
3. languid
   a. contrite **b.** weak **c.** irate
4. formidable
   a. strong **b.** feeble **c.** easy

Academic Vocabulary

Here are two words from the vocabulary list on page R80.

option (op′ shən) *n.* choice or alternative

involve (in volv′) *v.* to include; to relate to closely

Practice and Apply
1. What were Wilson's **options** before hiring Spaulding?
2. How did Spaulding's plan **involve** the use of the pawnbroker's shop?

Vocabulary

1. b **2.** a **3.** b **4.** a

Academic Vocabulary

1. Wilson could have hired a worker at the going rate instead of someone willing to work for half wages.
2. The plan entailed digging a tunnel from the pawnshop cellar to the bank vault.

WRITING AND EXTENDING

Writing About Literature

Analyze Genre Elements What makes "The Red-Headed League" a classic mystery? Write an essay in which you explain how this story reflects the elements of the mystery genre: a strange event that triggers the plot, a series of clues or puzzling events, an exciting climax, and a skillful detective who unravels the mystery and captures the villain.

Before you write, use a chart like the one below to organize your ideas.

Mystery Genre Element	Example
series of clues	Mr. Wilson must copy by hand the *Encyclopedia Britannica*.

When you draft, write an introduction in which you clearly state your thesis. Then write one or more body paragraphs that provide specific examples from the story to support your thesis. In your conclusion, restate your thesis in different words, and, if you like, provide a final insight.

After you complete your draft, meet with a peer reviewer to evaluate each other's work and to suggest revisions. Then proofread and edit your draft to correct errors in spelling, grammar, and punctuation.

Learning for Life

Mysteries are among the most popular novels. Are you a mystery reader or writer, or would you like to become one? Explain why or why not. State your answer, and then list the reasons that support or explain it. Share your reasons with a small group of classmates.

LiteratureOnline Web Activities For eFlashcards, Selection Quick Checks, and other Web activities, go to www.glencoe.com.

GRAMMAR AND STYLE

Doyle's Language and Style

Using Formal Language The language of "The Red-Headed League" may seem formal to the readers of today. One reason is that Doyle, a British author, wrote the story more than one hundred years ago when literary styles were different from what they are now. Another reason is that the language suits the characters in the story who, for the most part, are well-educated and sophisticated. The formality of the language is reflected both in the diction, or word choice, and the syntax, or the order of words.

Doyle's Formal Language: "With an apology for my intrusion, I was about to withdraw, when Holmes pulled me abruptly into the room and closed the door behind me."

Informal Language: I was sorry for barging in. I was about to leave when Holmes pulled me inside fast and closed the door.

Notice the formality of some of these phrases:

Formal Language	Informal Language
"Try the settee."	Sit down on the sofa.
"A proposition which I took the liberty of doubting."	I doubted that statement.
"I did not gain anything much, however, by my inspection."	I did not see anything new.

Activity With a partner, identify additional examples of formal language in the story. Discuss the effect that this kind of language creates.

Revising Check

Formal Language With a partner, review your essay analyzing elements of the mystery genre in "The Red-Headed League." Note places where using formal language would make your writing clearer or more elegant. That does not mean you should use language from Doyle's time or lofty word choices, but you should use correct grammar and omit slang expressions and contractions. Revise your draft accordingly.

AFTER YOU READ

Assess

Writing About Literature

Students' essays should

- discuss the elements of mystery stories.
- identify examples of those elements in the selection.
- end with a formal conclusion.

Learning for Life

Students should clearly state whether they enjoy reading mysteries and whether they aspire to become mystery writers, supporting their positions with logical reasons. Students who have read mysteries that have been made into TV shows or movies might enjoy discussing these with their group.

Doyle's Language and Style

Possible answers: "We traveled by Underground as far as Aldersgate." (We took the Underground to Aldersgate.) and "I should like just to remember the order of the houses here." (I want to remember the order of the houses here.) Students should note that in everyday speech people do not use such ornate sentences or phrases such as "should like."

LiteratureOnline

Web Activities Have students access the Web site for interactive activities that will help them assess their understanding of the selection.

BEFORE YOU READ

Focus

BELLRINGER

Bellringer Options
Daily Language Practice Transparency 104
Or display images of Peter Sellers as Inspector Clouseau or of Tony Shaloub as Adrian Monk. If students are unfamiliar with these characters, explain that both are detectives with comic foibles: Clouseau is bumbling; Monk has an obsessive-compulsive personality.
Ask: Why might Sherlock Holmes be a good subject for parody? *(He's never wrong and seems rather full of himself.)* Have students consider as they read how Harte's characters and plot parallel Doyle's.

Author Search To expand students' appreciation of Bret Harte, have them access the Web site for additional information and resources.

BEFORE YOU READ

The Stolen Cigar Case

MEET BRET HARTE

Bret Harte grew up in the eastern United States, but in his stories, he effortlessly captured the sights and sounds of places all over the world. Harte was a pioneer of the local color movement—a movement of writers who used vivid details to create portrayals of the customs and speech of particular places.

From New York to California Harte was born in Albany, New York, but ventured west in 1854, when he was only eighteen. In California he tried prospecting, rode "shotgun" on a stagecoach, and then found work in journalism, first as a typesetter, then as an editor, and finally as a writer.

In the 1850s California was a booming, turbulent, and exciting frontier. The discovery of gold in 1848 had drawn prospectors and adventurers from all over the United States and the rest of the world. Mining towns had sprung up; small towns had turned into cities; fortunes had been made and lost; and people from all walks of life had been thrown together in rough, sometimes violent circumstances. History was being made, and a whole new way of life was being forged. The colorful incidents of western life and vivid anecdotes of "old-timers" fired Harte's imagination, and he began to turn this material into fiction.

> *"One big vice in a man is apt to keep out a great many smaller ones."*
>
> —Bret Harte

Literary Fame While serving as the editor of a literary magazine, Harte began writing stories that made him famous all over the United States. His fame soon spread to Great Britain, where readers were eager for Harte's descriptions of California and the Wild West. Harte became acquainted with many of the leading writers of his day. In his short stories, he parodied some of them, including Sir Arthur Conan Doyle, with great wit.

Among Harte's friends was celebrated American humorist Mark Twain. Harte helped mentor the young Twain, who later acknowledged his help. Twain said that Harte had changed him from "an awkward utterer of coarse grotesqueness to a writer of paragraphs and chapters."

Harte spent many of his last years abroad, in Germany, Scotland, and England, continuing to write and working as a diplomat. When Harte died, he was nearly penniless, and Doyle and others joined forces to create a small income for Harte's widow. Nevertheless, Harte's legacy is his stories. Many of his characters, such as John Oakhurst, an outlaw with nerves of steel, have become fixtures in American literature.

Bret Harte was born in 1836 and died in 1902.

Literature Online **Author Search** For more about Bret Harte, go to www.glencoe.com.

Selection Skills

The Stolen Cigar Case

Literary Elements
- Parody (SE pp. 1249–1252, 1254, 1255, 1257)

Reading Skills
- Recognizing Author's Purpose (SE pp. 1249, 1251, 1252, 1255–1257)
- Previewing (TWE p. 1250)

Vocabulary Skills
- Connotation and Denotation (SE pp. 1249, 1257)

Listening/Speaking/Viewing Skills
- Analyzing Art (SE p. 1253; TWE p. 1256)

Writing Skills/Grammar
- Apply Style (SE p. 1257)
- Interjections (TWE p. 1254)

Study Skills/Research/Assessment
- Short Response (TWE p. 1256)

LITERATURE PREVIEW

Connecting to the Story

"Anyone who takes himself too seriously always runs the risk of looking ridiculous," author Vaclav Havel once wrote. Before you read the story, ask yourself the following questions:

- What human foibles do you find most amusing?
- What errors in logic or reasoning do you notice yourself and others making?

Building Background

In the story you are about to read, Bret Harte evokes the Sherlock Holmes stories of Sir Arthur Conan Doyle. In "The Stolen Cigar Case," Doyle's heroic and ingenious detective, Sherlock Holmes, has been transformed into the detective Hemlock Jones. The narrator of Harte's story is modeled after Watson, the doctor who is Holmes's sidekick, ardent admirer, and the narrator of the Sherlock Holmes stories.

Setting Purposes for Reading

Big Idea Revealing the Concealed

Detective stories usually revolve around a deep mystery that requires skill to unravel. As you read, notice how this story reverses the conventions of most detective stories.

Literary Element Parody

A **parody** is a work that imitates the style of some other work in a satirical or humorous way. "The Stolen Cigar Case" is a parody of the Sherlock Holmes stories. As you read, ask yourself: How do the characters and events in this story resemble those in a Sherlock Holmes story? How does the style in which it is written resemble that of Sir Arthur Conan Doyle? Also notice how Harte's use of exaggeration helps create a comic effect.

- See Literary Terms Handbook, p. R13.

Literature Online **Interactive Literary Elements Handbook** To review or learn more about the literary elements, go to www.glencoe.com.

READING PREVIEW

Reading Strategy Recognizing Author's Purpose

The **author's purpose** is the author's reason for creating a work. An author may write to persuade, to inform, to explain, to entertain, or to describe. As you read, make inferences about Harte's purpose in imitating a Sherlock Holmes story.

Reading Tip: Taking Notes As you read, list details from the story. Then record your inferences about the purpose of these details.

Detail	Author's Purpose
p. 1250 Jones has "super-human insight" and "powerful intellect"	The author gives the narrator exaggerated ideas about Jones's mental abilities. The effect is comic.

Vocabulary

inscrutable (in skro͞o′ tə bəl) *adj.* not readily understood or interpreted; p. 1250 *Mr. Serkin was a quiet man who kept his intentions to himself; I found him inscrutable.*

trifle (trī′ fəl) *n.* something of little value or importance; p. 1251 *Parents are satisfied with trifles, but children hope for generous gifts.*

perspicacity (pur′ spə kas′ ə tē) *n.* acute mental powers or perception; p. 1252 *The detective's perspicacity resulted in a swift solution to the crime.*

infallibility (in fal′ ə bil′ ə tē) *n.* state of being incapable of error; p. 1256 *Do not credit experts with infallibility; they too can make mistakes.*

Vocabulary Tip: Connotation and Denotation A word's denotation is its dictionary meaning. Its connotations are ideas and meanings associated with the word.

INDIANA ACADEMIC STANDARDS (pages 1249–1257)

9.3.2 Compare…a similar theme…across genres…
9.2 Develop strategies such as…identifying…purpose…
9.5.1 Write…short stories…
9.5.7 Use…vocabulary, appropriate for specific forms…

BEFORE YOU READ

Focus

Summary

The faithful and adoring sidekick of detective Hemlock Jones joins forces with his friend in the hunt for a stolen cigar case. Jones is a paranoid narcissist whose bizarrely convoluted logic makes him the perfect takeoff on Sherlock Holmes.

V Vocabulary

Vocabulary File **Say:** Add these words and definitions to your vocabulary file. For each word, include a sentence that gives you an example of how to use the word. **OL** Students with English language needs should include the pronunciations of these words in their files. **EL**

Literary Elements Have students access the Web site to improve their understanding of parody.

Selection Resources

Print Materials

- Unit 6 Resources (Fast File), pp. 47–49
- Leveled Vocabulary Development, pp. 78–79
- Selection and Unit Assessments, pp. 209–210
- Selection Quick Checks, p. 105

Transparencies

- Bellringer Options Transparencies: Daily Language Practice Transparency 104
- Literary Elements Transparency 91

Technology

- TeacherWorks Plus™ CD-ROM
- StudentWorks Plus™ CD-ROM
- Presentation Plus!™ CD-ROM
- Literature Online, glencoe.com
- Online Student Edition, mhln.com
- Exam*View*® Assessment Suite CD-ROM
- Vocabulary PuzzleMaker CD-ROM
- Listening Library, disc 2 track 49

Teach

L1 Literary Element

Parody **Answer:** *The narrator's slavish worship of Jones and his exaggerated ideas about Jones's brilliance* OL

Readability Scores
Dale-Chall: 9.4
DRP: 58
Lexile: 1020

The Stolen Cigar Case

Bret Harte

I found Hemlock Jones in the old Brook Street lodgings, musing before the fire. With the freedom of an old friend I at once threw myself in my usual familiar attitude at his feet, and gently caressed his boot. I was induced to do this for two reasons: one, that it enabled me to get a good look at his bent, concentrated face, and the other, that it seemed to indicate my reverence for his superhuman insight. So absorbed was he even then, in tracking some mysterious clue, that he did not seem to notice me. But therein I was wrong—as I always was in my attempt to understand that powerful intellect.

"It is raining," he said, without lifting his head.

"You have been out, then?" I said quickly.

Literary Element Parody *What qualities of the narrator's are exaggerated or humorous?* L1

"No. But I see that your umbrella is wet, and that your overcoat has drops of water on it."

I sat aghast at his penetration. After a pause he said carelessly, as if dismissing the subject: "Besides, I hear the rain on the window. Listen."

I listened. I could scarcely credit my ears, but there was the soft pattering of drops on the panes. It was evident there was no deceiving this man!

"Have you been busy lately?" I asked, changing the subject. "What new problem—given up by Scotland Yard[1] as **inscrutable**—has occupied that gigantic intellect?"

1. *Scotland Yard* is the detective division of the British metropolitan police force.

Vocabulary

inscrutable (in skrōō′ tə bəl) *adj.* not readily understood or interpreted

Additional Support

Skills Practice

READING: Previewing Remind students that this story pokes fun at the archetypal brilliant detective (Holmes) and his faithful companion (Watson). Have them use the following questions as a guide to previewing the story: *Who are the main characters? What is their relationship? How do the characters in this story parallel Holmes and Watson? How do they differ?* OL

He drew back his foot slightly, and seemed to hesitate ere he returned it to its original position. Then he answered wearily: "Mere **trifles**—nothing to speak of. The Prince Kupoli has been here to get my advice regarding the disappearance of certain rubies from the Kremlin; the Rajah of Pootibad, after vainly beheading his entire bodyguard, has been obliged to seek my assistance to recover a jeweled sword. The Grand Duchess of Pretzel-Brauntswig is desirous of discovering where her husband was on the night of February 14; and last night"—he lowered his voice slightly—"a lodger in this very house, meeting me on the stairs, wanted to know why they didn't answer his bell."

I could not help smiling—until I saw a frown gathering on his inscrutable forehead.

"Pray remember," he said coldly, "that it was through such an apparently trivial question that I found out Why Paul Ferroll Killed His Wife, and What Happened to Jones!"

I became dumb[2] at once. He paused for a moment, and then suddenly changing back to his usual pitiless, analytical style, he said: "When I say these are trifles, they are so in comparison to an affair that is now before me. A crime has been committed—and, singularly enough, against myself. You start," he said. "You wonder who would have dared to attempt it. So did I; nevertheless, it has been done. *I* have been *robbed!*"

"*You* robbed! You, Hemlock Jones, the Terror of Peculators!"[3] I gasped in amazement, arising and gripping the table as I faced him.

"Yes! Listen. I would confess it to no other. But *you* who have followed my career, who know my methods; you, for whom I have partly lifted the veil that conceals my plans from ordinary humanity,—you, who have for years rapturously accepted my confidences, passionately admired my inductions and inferences, placed yourself at my beck and call, become my slave, groveled at my feet, given up your practice except those few unremunerative and rapidly decreasing patients to whom, in moments of abstraction over *my* problems, you have administered strychnine for quinine and arsenic for Epsom salts;[4] you, who have sacrificed anything and everybody to me—*you* I make my confidant!"

I arose and embraced him warmly, yet he was already so engrossed in thought that at the same moment he mechanically placed his hand upon his watch chain as if to consult the time. "Sit down," he said. "Have a cigar?"

"I have given up cigar smoking," I said.

"Why?" he asked.

I hesitated, and perhaps colored. I had really given it up because, with my diminished practice, it was too expensive. I could afford only a pipe. "I prefer a pipe," I said laughingly. "But tell me of this robbery. What have you lost?"

He arose, and planting himself before the fire with his hands under his coat-tails, looked down upon me reflectively for a moment. "Do you remember the cigar case presented to me by the Turkish Ambassador for discovering the missing favorite of the Grand Vizier[5] in the fifth chorus girl at the Hilarity Theater? It was that one. I mean the cigar case. It was incrusted with diamonds."

"And the largest one had been supplanted by paste,"[6] I said.

"Ah," he said, with a reflective smile, "you know that?"

"You told me yourself. I remember considering it a proof of your extraordinary perception. But, by Jove, you don't mean to say you have lost it?"

2. Here, *dumb* means "speechless."
3. *Peculator* is a term for an embezzler.
4. A doctor who administers *strychnine for quinine and arsenic for Epsom salts* would kill his or her patients.
5. A *Grand Vizier* is a high-ranking political adviser.
6. Here, *paste* refers to a type of fake gemstone.

Reading Strategy Recognizing Author's Purpose *What is the effect of the capitalized words in this passage?* **R**

Vocabulary

trifle (trī′ fəl) *n.* something of little value or importance

Literary Element Parody *What has happened to the narrator as a result of his devotion to Jones?* **L2**

Teach

R Reading Strategy

Recognizing Author's Purpose **Answer:** *The caps suggest a momentous discovery. They make Jones sound very pompous.* **OL**

L2 Literary Element

Parody **Answer:** *Apparently he has lost everything.* **OL**

CheckPoint

Use the CheckPoint questions on Presentation Plus! to monitor students' comprehension. These questions can be used with interactive response keypads for immediate student feedback.

Differentiated Instruction

Parody Mention examples of popular parodies, such as the *Scary Movie* films, *Monty Python and the Holy Grail*, and *Saturday Night Live* newscasts. Ask students to provide others and discuss why they find them enjoyable. Have advanced students create their own parodies based on a subject of their choosing and share them in class. **AL**

Academic Standards

Additional Support activities on pp. 1250 and 1251 cover the following standards:

Skills Practice: **9.3.3** Analyze interactions between characters in a literary text and explain the ways those interactions affect the plot. **9.3.5** Compare works that express a universal theme and provide evidence to support the views expressed in each work.

Differentiated Instruction: **9.3.2** Compare and contrast the presentation of a similar theme or topic across genres...

9.7.13 Identify the artistic effects of a media presentation...

Teach

L Literary Element

Parody **Answer:** *Holmes often solicits ideas and advice from his sidekick Watson.* OL

R1 Reading Strategy

Recognizing Author's Purpose **Ask:** Why does Harte have Jones nod with an inscrutable face? *(Jones maintains an aura of mystery; everything has a secret or double meaning for him. He likes to imply he knows more than he's willing to reveal.)* OL

R2 Reading Strategy

Recognizing Author's Purpose **Answer:** *These details make Jones seem ridiculous.* OL

He was silent for a moment. "No; it has been stolen, it is true, but I shall still find it. And by myself alone! In your profession, my dear fellow, when a member is seriously ill, he does not prescribe for himself, but calls in a brother doctor. Therein we differ. I shall take this matter in my own hands."

"And where could you find better?" I said enthusiastically. "I should say the cigar case is as good as recovered already."

"I shall remind you of that again," he said lightly. "And now, to show you my confidence in your judgment, in spite of my determination to pursue this alone, I am willing to listen to any suggestions from you."

He drew a memorandum book from his pocket and, with a grave smile, took up his pencil.

I could scarcely believe my senses. He, the great Hemlock Jones, accepting suggestions from a humble individual like myself! I kissed his hand reverently, and began in a joyous tone:

"First, I should advertise, offering a reward; I should give the same intimation in hand-bills, distributed at the pubs and the pastry-cooks'. I should next visit the different pawnbrokers; I should give notice at the police station. I should examine the servants. I should thoroughly search the house and my own pockets. I speak relatively," I added, with a laugh. "Of course I mean *your* own."

He gravely made an entry of these details.

"Perhaps," I added, "you have already done this?"

"Perhaps," he returned enigmatically. "Now, my dear friend," he continued, putting the notebook in his pocket and rising, "would you excuse me for a few moments? Make yourself perfectly at home until I return; there may be some things," he added with a sweep of his hand toward his heterogeneously[7] filled shelves, "that may interest you and wile away the time. There are pipes and tobacco in that corner."

Then nodding to me with the same inscrutable face he left the room. R1 I was too well accustomed to his methods to think much of his unceremonious withdrawal, and made no doubt he was off to investigate some clue which had suddenly occurred to his active intelligence.

Left to myself I cast a cursory glance over his shelves. There were a number of small glass jars containing earthy substances, labeled "Pavement and Road Sweepings," from the principal thoroughfares and suburbs of London, with the sub-directions "for identifying foot-tracks." There were several other jars, labeled "Fluff from Omnibus[8] and Road Car Seats," "Cocoanut Fibre and Rope Strands from Mattings in Public Places," "Cigarette Stumps and Match Ends from Floor of Palace Theater, Row A, 1 to 50." Everywhere were evidences of this wonderful man's system and **perspicacity**.

I was thus engaged when I heard the slight creaking of a door, and I looked up as a stranger entered. He was a rough-looking man, with a shabby overcoat and a still more disreputable muffler around his throat and the lower part of his face. Considerably annoyed at his intrusion, I turned upon him rather sharply, when, with a mumbled, growling apology for mistaking the room, he shuffled out again and closed the door. I followed him quickly to the landing and saw that he disappeared down the stairs. With my mind full of the robbery, the incident made a singular impression upon me. I knew my friend's habit of hasty absences from his room in his moments of deep inspiration; it was only too probable that, with his

7. Jones's *heterogeneously* filled shelves include a wide variety of items.

8. *Omnibus* is a term for *bus* that is no longer in use.

Literary Element Parody *What elements in this passage resemble the elements of a Sherlock Holmes story?* L

Reading Strategy Recognizing Author's Purpose *What do these details imply about Jones?* R2

Vocabulary

perspicacity (pur′ spə kas′ ə tē) *n.* acute mental powers or perception

Additional Support

Skills Practice

READING: Monitoring Comprehension Remind students to stop periodically to review plot events and other important information and to jot down any questions they might have. Have students work in pairs to summarize plot developments and revelations about characters or motives. Encourage them to discuss points of confusion and to reread passages to clarify information. OL powerful intellect and magnificent perceptive genius concentrated on one subject, he should be careless of his own belongings, and no doubt even forget to take the ordinary precaution of locking up his drawers. I tried one or two and found that I was right, although for some reason I was unable to open one to its fullest extent. The handles were sticky, as if some one had opened them with dirty fingers. Knowing Hemlock's fastidious[9] cleanliness, I resolved to inform him of this circumstance, but I forgot it, alas! until—but I am anticipating my story.

His absence was strangely prolonged. I at last seated myself by the fire, and lulled by warmth and the patter of the rain on the window, I fell asleep. I may have dreamt, for during my sleep I had a vague semi-consciousness as of hands being softly pressed on my pockets—no doubt induced by the story of the robbery. When I came fully to my senses, I found Hemlock Jones sitting on the other side of the hearth, his deeply concentrated gaze fixed on the fire.

"I found you so comfortably asleep that I could not bear to awaken you," he said, with a smile.

I rubbed my eyes. "And what news?" I asked. "How have you succeeded?"

"Better than I expected," he said, "and I think," he added, tapping his notebook. "I owe much to *you.*"

Deeply gratified, I awaited more. But in vain. I ought to have remembered that in his moods Hemlock Jones was reticence itself, I told him simply of the strange intrusion, but he only laughed.

Later, when I arose to go, he looked at me playfully.

"If you were a married man," he said, "I would advise you not to go home until you had brushed your sleeve. There are a few

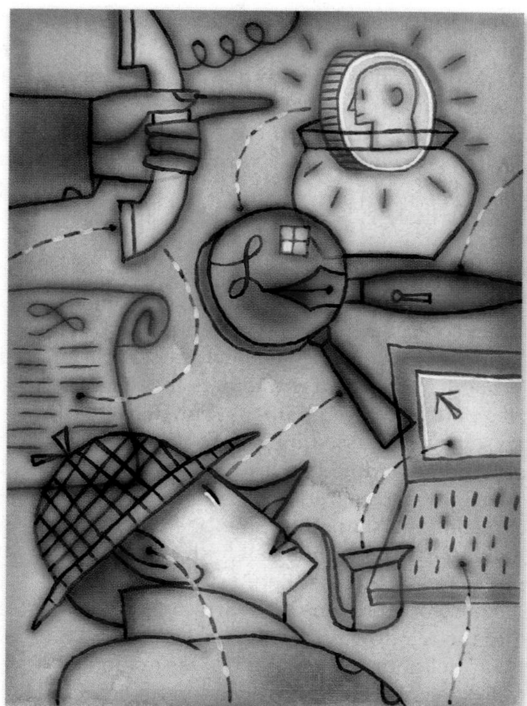

Detective Looking for Clues. Todd Davidson.
Viewing the Art: In your opinion, does this illustration capture the mood of a parody? Why or why not? 

short brown sealskin hairs on the inner side of your forearm, just where they would have adhered if your arm had encircled a sealskin coat with some pressure!"

"For once you are at fault," I said triumphantly; "the hair is my own, as you will perceive; I have just had it cut at the hairdresser's, and no doubt this arm projected beyond the apron."

He frowned slightly, yet, nevertheless, on my turning to go he embraced me warmly—a rare exhibition in that man of ice. He even helped me on with my overcoat and pulled out and smoothed down the flaps of my pockets. He was particular, too, in fitting my arm in my overcoat sleeve, shaking the sleeve down from the armhole to the cuff with his deft fingers. "Come again soon!" he said, clapping me on the back.

9. *Fastidious* means "excessively careful" or "difficult to please."

Big Idea Revealing the Concealed *What new complications to the mystery are introduced in this passage?* **BI**

Teach

BI Big Idea

Revealing the Concealed

Answer: *A mysterious intruder enters Jones's apartment. The narrator notices a strange stickiness in one of Jones's drawers. The narrator hints at exciting events to come.* **OL**

Viewing the Art

Answer: *Answers will vary. Some students may say that the cartoon-like feel of the picture captures the mood of a parody. Others may feel that the picture isn't comic enough to capture the mood of a parody.* **AS**

English Language Coach

Descriptive Words The use of British English in this story may challenge English language learners.

Encourage students to create word bank files by listing troublesome words from the story. Model how to use context clues to decipher the words. Remind students to verify their definitions in a dictionary. **EL**

Academic Standards

Additional Support activities on pp. 1252 and 1253 cover the following standards:

Skills Practice: **9.2** Develop strategies such as asking questions... **9.3** [Identify] story elements such as character, theme, [and] plot...

English Language Coach: **9.1** Use...context clues...to determine the meaning of words and become fluent readers.

Teach

L1 Literary Element

Parody **Answer:** *Jones is presented as a master detective like Holmes, and the twists and turns of the mystery resemble the complications in Doyle's stories. Through exaggeration and bizarre details, Harte makes the characters and their situation seem absurd.* OL

B1 Big Idea

Revealing the Concealed
Answer: *Students should support their answers with examples from the text.* OL

★ Cultural History

The East End "The East End" is a popular designation for the area of London roughly east of the City of London, south of the Thames, and bordered by the River Lea. Historically a poor section of London, the East End is home to the Tower of London and was often visited by Jack the Ripper. AS

"At any and all times," I said enthusiastically; "I only ask ten minutes twice a day to eat a crust at my office, and four hours' sleep at night, and the rest of my time is devoted to you always, as you know."

"It is indeed," he said, with his impenetrable smile.

Nevertheless, I did not find him at home when I next called. One afternoon, when nearing my own home, I met him in one of his favorite disguises—a long blue swallow-tailed coat, striped cotton trousers, large turn-over collar, and white hat, carrying a tambourine. Of course to others the disguise was perfect, although it was known to myself, and I passed him—according to an old understanding between us—without the slightest recognition, trusting to a later explanation. At another time, as I was making a professional visit to the wife of a ★ publican[10] at the East End, I saw him, in the disguise of a broken-down artisan, looking into the window of an adjacent pawnshop. I was delighted to see that he was evidently following my suggestions, and in my joy I ventured to tip him a wink; it was abstractedly returned.

Two days later I received a note appointing a meeting at his lodgings that night. That meeting, alas! was the one memorable occurrence of my life, and the last meeting I ever had with Hemlock Jones! I will try to set it down calmly, though my pulses still throb with the recollection of it.

I found him standing before the fire, with that look upon his face which I had seen only once or twice in our acquaintance—a look which I may call an absolute concatenation of inductive and deductive ratiocination[11]—from which all that was human, tender, or sympathetic was absolutely discharged. He was simply an icy algebraic symbol! Indeed, his whole being was concentrated to that extent that his clothes fitted loosely, and his head was absolutely so much reduced in size by his mental compression that his hat tipped back from his forehead and literally hung on his massive ears.

After I had entered he locked the doors, fastened the windows, and even placed a chair before the chimney. As I watched these significant precautions with absorbing interest, he suddenly drew a revolver and, presenting it to my temple, said in low, icy tones:

"Hand over that cigar case!"

Even in my bewilderment my reply was truthful, spontaneous, and involuntary.

"I haven't got it," I said.

He smiled bitterly, and threw down his revolver. "I expected that reply! Then let me now confront you with something more awful, more deadly, more relentless and convincing than that mere lethal weapon—the damning inductive and deductive proofs of your guilt!" He drew from his pocket a roll of paper and a notebook.

"But surely," I gasped, "you are joking! You could not for a moment believe"—

"Silence! Sit down!" I obeyed.

"You have condemned yourself," he went on pitilessly. "Condemned yourself on my processes—processes familiar to you, applauded by you, accepted by you for years! We will go back to the time when you first saw the cigar case. Your expressions," he said in cold, deliberate tones, consulting his paper, "were, 'How beautiful! I wish it were mine.' This was your first step in crime—and my first indication. From 'I *wish* it were mine' to 'I *will* have it mine,' and the mere detail, '*How can* I make it mine?' the advance was obvious. Silence! But as in my methods it was necessary that there should be an overwhelming inducement to the crime, that unholy admiration of yours for the mere trinket itself was not enough. You are a smoker of cigars."

10. A *publican* is the operator of a British public house, or pub.
11. A *concatenation* is a series of things linked together in a chain. *Ratiocination* is reasoning.

Literary Element Parody *So far, how has this story resembled a Sherlock Holmes mystery story? How has it differed, and what is the effect of the difference?* L1

Big Idea Revealing the Concealed *Are you surprised by this development? Why or why not?* B1

Additional Support

Skills Practice

GRAMMAR AND LANGUAGE: Interjections Remind students that writers use interjections—words or phrases that express emotion—to show a character's reaction. Ask for examples *(Wow! Hurrah! Hey!)* and note how Harte uses interjections to enliven the dialogue. Have students identify interjections used in the selection and explain what emotions they express. OL

"But," I burst out passionately, "I told you I had given up smoking cigars."

"Fool!" he said coldly, "that is the *second* time you have committed yourself. Of course you told me! What more natural than for you to blazon forth that prepared and unsolicited statement to *prevent* accusation. Yet, as I said before, even that wretched attempt to cover up your tracks was not enough. I still had to find that overwhelming, impelling motive necessary to affect a man like you. That motive I found in the strongest of all impulses—Love, I suppose you would call it," he added bitterly, "that night you called! You had brought the most conclusive proofs of it on your sleeve."

"But—" I almost screamed.

"Silence!" he thundered. "I know what you would say. You would say that even if you had embraced some Young Person in a sealskin coat, what had that to do with the robbery? Let me tell you, then, that that sealskin coat represented the quality and character of your fatal entanglement! You bartered your honor for it—that stolen cigar case was the purchaser of the sealskin coat!

"Silence! Having thoroughly established your motive, I now proceed to the commission of the crime itself. Ordinary people would have begun with that—with an attempt to discover the whereabouts of the missing object. These are not *my* methods."

So overpowering was his penetration that, although I knew myself innocent, I licked my lips with avidity to hear the further details of this lucid exposition of my crime.

"You committed that theft the night I showed you the cigar case, and after I had carelessly thrown it in that drawer. You were sitting in that chair, and I had arisen to take something from that shelf. In that instant you secured your booty without rising. Silence! Do you remember when I helped you on with your overcoat the other night? I was particular about fitting your arm in. While doing so I measured your arms with a spring tape measure, from the shoulder to the cuff. A later visit to your tailor confirmed that measurement. It proved to be *the exact distance between your chair and that drawer!"*

I sat stunned.

"The rest are mere corroborative details! You were again tampering with the drawer when I discovered you doing so! Do not start! The stranger that blundered into the room with a muffler on—was myself! More, I had placed a little soap on the drawer handles when I purposely left you alone. The soap was on your hand when I shook it at parting. I softly felt your pockets, when you were asleep, for further developments. I embraced you when you left—that I might feel if you had the cigar case or any other articles hidden on your body. This confirmed me in the belief that you had already disposed of it in the manner and for the purpose I have shown you. As I still believed you capable of remorse and confession, I twice allowed you to see I was on your track: once in the garb of an itinerant minstrel, and the second time as a workman looking in the window of the pawnshop where you pledged your booty."

"But," I burst out, "if you had asked the pawnbroker, you would have seen how unjust"—

"Fool!" he hissed, "that was one of *your* suggestions—to search the pawnshops! Do you suppose I followed any of your suggestions, the suggestions of the thief? On the contrary, they told me what to avoid."

"And I suppose," I said bitterly, "you have not even searched your drawer?"

"No," he said calmly.

I was for the first time really vexed. I went to the nearest drawer and pulled it out sharply. It stuck as it had before, leaving a part of the drawer unopened. By working it, however, I discovered that it was impeded by some obstacle that had slipped to the

Reading Strategy Recognizing Author's Purpose *How does Harte portray the narrator and Jones? Why do you think he portrays them as he does?* **R**

Literary Element Parody *What is your response to this passage?* **L2**

Teach

R Reading Strategy

Recognizing Author's Purpose **Answer:** *Jones is self-absorbed, arrogant, and so lost in analysis and theory that he misses the obvious. The narrator is pathetically worshipful toward Jones. The author's intent is to amuse readers.* **OL**

L2 Literary Element

Parody **Answer:** *Students should support their answers with examples from the selection.* **OL**

Use the CheckPoint questions on Presentation Plus! to check students' mastery of the selection. These questions can be used with interactive response keypads for immediate student feedback.

English Language Coach

Vocabulary for Precise Descriptions Ask English language learners to brainstorm a list of traits that describe Jones. Then have them work with partners to identify synonyms for the words using a thesaurus, English dictionary, or bilingual dictionary. **EL**

Differentiated Instruction

Identifying Comic Effects Hearing Harte's prose read aloud may make it easier for less proficient readers to appreciate his skillful use of exaggeration and absurd details to parody the detective genre. Assign readers for the parts of the narrator and Jones. **BL**

Academic Standards

Additional Support activities on pp. 1254 and 1255 cover the following standards:

Skills Practice: **9.6.2** Demonstrate an understanding of…proper English usage…

English Language Coach: **9.3.4** Determine characters' traits by what the characters say about themselves in narration [and] dialogue…

Differentiated Instruction: **9.7** [Develop] speaking skills, such as phrasing, pitch, and tone…

Teach

BI Big Idea

Revealing the Concealed
Answer: *The answer was obvious. The box was in Jones's drawer.* OL

R Reading Strategy

Recognizing Author's Purpose **Answer:** *Jones cannot even throw someone out of his house on the first try. This makes him seem even more silly and incompetent.* OL

★ Viewing the Art

Contemporary illustrator Bob Commander has illustrated for corporations, ad agencies, publishers, and design firms. Commander combines drawing and painting with oil, acrylic, and watercolor with computer design using programs such as Photoshop, Illustrator, Flash, and 3D animation. AS

Web Activities Have students access the Web site for interactive activities that will help them assess their understanding of the selection.

Eye With Magnifying Glass. Bob Commander. 

upper part of the drawer, and held it firmly fast. Inserting my hand, I pulled out the impeding object. It was the missing cigar case! I turned to him with a cry of joy.

But I was appalled at his expression. A look of contempt was now added to his acute, penetrating gaze. "I have been mistaken," he said slowly; "I had not allowed for your weakness and cowardice! I thought too highly of you even in your guilt! But I see now why you tampered with that drawer the other night. By some inexplicable means—possibly another theft—you took the cigar case out of pawn and, like a whipped hound, restored it to me in this feeble, clumsy fashion. You thought to deceive me, Hemlock Jones! More, you thought to destroy my **infallibility**. Go! I give you your liberty. I shall not summon the three policemen who wait in the adjoining room—but out of my sight forever!"

As I stood once more dazed and petrified, he took me firmly by the ear and led me into the hall, closing the door behind him. This reopened presently, wide enough to permit him to thrust out my hat, overcoat, umbrella, and overshoes, and then closed against me forever!

I never saw him again. I am bound to say, however, that thereafter my business increased, I recovered much of my old practice, and a few of my patients recovered also. I became rich. I had a brougham and a house in the West End.[12] But I often wondered, pondering on that wonderful man's penetration and insight, if, in some lapse of consciousness, I had not really stolen his cigar case! ❧

Big Idea Revealing the Concealed *How hidden was the answer to the mystery? Explain.* BI

12. A *brougham* is a horse-drawn carriage with a driver. At the time of the story, the *West End* was a fashionable residential area of London.

Reading Strategy Recognizing Author's Purpose *What is the effect of this last detail? Why might Harte have included it?* R

Vocabulary

infallibility (in fal′ ə bil′ ə tē) *n.* state of being incapable of error

Additional Support

The Additional Support activity on p. 1256 covers the following standard:

Skills Practice: **9.5.3** Write expository compositions…that gather evidence in support of a thesis…

Skills Practice

TEST PREPARATION: Short Response Explain that short-response questions often do not have one correct answer. Instead, an answer is generally judged by its insightfulness and the quality of textual evidence included.

Ask: Which of the following authors did you enjoy most: Queen, Conan Doyle, or Harte? Ask students to write their answers using 3–5 lines. Remind students to give examples to support their answers whenever possible. OL

AFTER YOU READ

RESPONDING AND THINKING CRITICALLY

Respond

1. What did you enjoy most about "The Stolen Cigar Case"?

Recall and Interpret

2. (a)What mystery does Hemlock Jones set out to solve? (b)What advice does the narrator provide? What does Jones think of this advice?
3. (a)How would you describe the personalities of the narrator and Jones? (b)As the story progresses, what impressions do you gain of their relationship?
4. (a)What steps does Jones take to solve the mystery? (b)How successful are Jones's methods and way of thinking?
5. (a)How is the mystery solved? (b)How do the narrator and Jones respond to the solution of the mystery? What do their responses reveal about them?

Analyze and Evaluate

6. Irony is a contrast or discrepancy between appearance and reality, or between what is expected and what actually happens. How does the use of irony add humor to this story? Explain.
7. On a humor scale of one to ten, evaluate the level of humor of this story. Explain your evaluation.

Connect

8. **Big Idea** **Revealing the Concealed** (a)In what way does the ending of the story reverse the usual conclusion to a detective story? (b)Were you surprised by the ending? Explain.

LITERARY ANALYSIS

Literary Element Parody

Parody imitates the style of another work or author in a humorous way.

1. How does Harte hold up the conventions of detective stories for ridicule? Include details from the story in your answer.
2. What details make Jones and the narrator especially funny or ridiculous? Explain.

Writing About Literature

Apply Style Write your own parody in the style of a familiar genre, such as a detective story, or of a favorite author. First, think of a theme and subject for your parody. Then approach your subject in a humorous manner while maintaining the style and characteristics of the genre or author you are parodying. Proofread and edit your parody to correct errors in grammar, spelling, and punctuation.

LiteratureOnline **Web Activities** For eFlashcards, Selection Quick Checks, and other Web activities, go to www.glencoe.com.

READING AND VOCABULARY

Reading Strategy Recognizing Author's Purpose

The **author's purpose** is the author's goals or intentions in creating a work.

1. What was Harte's purpose in writing this story? Cite evidence from the story in your answer.
2. Why do you think Harte includes the final details about the narrator's life after Jones?

Vocabulary Practice

Practice with Connotation and Denotation Complete each sentence below.

1. A denotation of **inscrutable** is ___.
   a. undesirable b. impenetrable
2. A connotation of **trifle** is ___.
   a. minor b. important
3. A connotation of **perspicacity** is ___.
   a. distance b. shrewdness
4. A connotation of **infallibility** is ___.
   a. perfection b. desirability

Writing About Literature

Urge students to choose a genre or author they know well. A successful parody begins with a strong grasp of its subject's conventions.

Reading Strategy

1. To amuse; Students should note various humorous details from the story.
2. The narrator thrives after his friend exiles him yet he still trusts his friend's crazy logic more than the obvious truth. His endearing gullibility ends the story on an absurd note.

AFTER YOU READ

Assess

1. Students should support their answers.
2. (a) To find his missing cigar case (b) To post notices, call police and check pawnbrokers, the help and his house; He thinks it's worthless.
3. (a) Narrator: idolizes Jones; Jones: conceited, affected, illogical (b) Jones exploits his loyal, gullible friend.
4. (a) Jones accuses the narrator. He tries to search the narrator's clothes and to trap him into revealing his guilt. (b) They are unsuccessful.
5. (a) The narrator finds the cigar case in Jones's drawer. (b) He's delighted until Jones renews his accusation. Both fail to learn from experience.
6. The huge gap between Jones and the archetypal sleuth is what makes this story funny.
7. Students should support their answers.
8. (a) The sidekick solves the mystery. Both the mystery and its solution are mundane. (b) Students should support their answers.

Literary Element

1. (a) Most detective stories hinge on a serious crime and feature a brilliantly logical sleuth; Harte's story revolves around a misplaced cigar box and involves a detective who's wrong about everything.
2. Students should support their answers.

Vocabulary

1. b **2.** a **3.** b **4.** a

Focus

BELLRINGER

Have the class brainstorm aspects of space exploration and list their ideas on the board. **Ask:** What are some benefits of exploring space? Do you think governments should spend money on space programs, or on education, health care, the environment, or other issues? Why? Have students freewrite on questions related to space exploration.

Summary

In this workshop, students will write and present an editorial. Students will follow the stages of the writing process, including prewriting, drafting, revising, and editing. In addition, the workshop includes two focus lessons, on using a reasonable tone and parallelism.

Writing Models Have students access the Web site for interactive writing models and writing guides.

The Writing Process

In this workshop, you will follow the stages of the writing process. At any stage, you may think of new ideas to include and better ways to express them. Feel free to return to earlier stages as you write.

- **Prewriting**
- **Drafting**
- **Revising**
  - Focus Lesson: Using a Reasonable Tone
- **Editing and Proofreading**
  - Focus Lesson: Parallelism
- **Presenting**

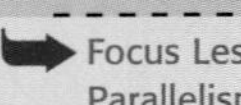

Writing Models For models and other writing activities, go to www.glencoe.com.

ACADEMIC STANDARDS (pages 1258–1265)
9.5.4 Write persuasive compositions that…clarify and defend positions with precise and relevant evidence, including facts, expert opinions…and reasoning…

Writing Workshop

Editorial

Supporting an Opinion

"There had, after all, been a lunar civilization—and I was the first to find it. That I had come perhaps a hundred million years too late did not distress me; it was enough to have come at all."

—Arthur C. Clarke, from "The Sentinel"

Connecting to Literature As a science fiction writer, Arthur C. Clarke has made startling proposals about the future. He wrote "The Sentinel" in 1948, and although experts of the time dismissed space travel as impossible, Neil Armstrong and Buzz Aldrin set foot on the moon in 1969—just over twenty years later. In "The Sentinel," the main character makes a discovery that has enormous implications for the future of people on Earth. Whether or not humans *should* explore space is still a matter of debate. Is space exploration worth the cost in money and possible danger to human lives? Issues such as these are the subjects of editorials.

Rubric: Features of an Editorial

Goals	Strategies
To express an opinion on a current news event or issue	☑ Describe the issue and state your position on it
To convince others of your viewpoint	☑ Provide the reason for your opinion ☑ List facts and examples to support it
To defend your opinion against alternative viewpoints	☑ Describe other points of view ☑ Discuss why you disagree with other points of view
To propose a solution	☑ Restate your opinion ☑ Use evidence to show why your solution is the best one

Additional Support

Workshop Resources

Print Materials
- Unit 6 Resources (Fast File), pp. 50–53
- REAL Success in Writing: Research and Reports
- Writing Constructed Responses, pp. 1–26, 54, 61–66
- Glencoe Literature Library

Transparencies
- Grammar and Language Transparencies 11, 12
- Writing Workshop Transparencies 31–35
- Visual Literacy/Fine Art Transparencies

Technology
- Grammar & Language eWorkbook
- Revising with Style eWorkbook
- Sentence Diagraming eWorkbook
- Spelling Power eWorkbook
- Online Essay Grader, glencoe.com
- Literature Library Exam*View*® Assessment Suite CD-ROM
- Literature Library Vocabulary PuzzleMaker CD-ROM

Assignment

Write an editorial supporting your opinion about an issue affecting the future of the world. As you move through the stages of the writing process, keep your audience and purpose in mind.

Audience: peers, classmates, and teacher

Purpose: present an opinion, acknowledge alternative viewpoints, and provide reasons and support for your opinion

Analyzing a Professional Model

In the following selection, Scott Sheppard, a scientist who studies solar systems, argues that robots should be used to explore space in the future. Pay close attention to the comments in the margin. They point out features that you might want to include in your own editorial.

from *"Decision Time for Space Exploration"*

by Scott Sheppard
San Francisco Chronicle, October 10, 2005

The human space programs of the world are stuck in low Earth orbit. Even the existence of NASA, the agency built in the Cold War to lead America to the Moon, has come into question. Ever since the race to the Moon ended, the question of where to send humans next has yet to be answered. The plan now is to slowly build out, by completing the International Space Station and then going back to the Moon and eventually on to Mars. There is an explanation as to why this has been the general plan for more than 30 years but yet very little has been done to make it reality.

The simple fact is that there is no real reason to do any of this. There is no Cold War to propel us to the Moon again, and even if the space race with China heats up it will not last. There is no major economic benefit for humans going to the Moon or any of the inhospitable planets. Space tourism may one day find a niche, but unlike air travel, there are no major capitalistic reasons to have human space travel, and it seems very unlikely to ever become a major enterprise. What little there is to do in space is far easier and cheaper to do with robotic spacecraft. . . .

Real-World Connection

Daily newspapers have an editorial page where the opinions of the newspaper's editorial board are presented. In addition, letters from readers express opinions on subjects that range from how tax dollars should be spent to the problems created when land is overdeveloped.

School Newspapers

Your school may have a newspaper, and you may at some time feel strongly about an issue and want to express your opinion by submitting a letter to the editor. For example, you might oppose the administration's decision to cancel an event.

Background

Provide background on the subject as preparation for your opinion/argument.

Reasons

Your audience is more likely to consider your opinion if you provide logical reasons for it.

Opinion

State your opinion clearly and concisely.

Teach

Big Idea

Our World and Beyond Help students make a connection between the editorial and issues affecting our planet. Explain that in editorials writers express their views about important issues, from politics to humanity's place in the cosmos. **Ask:** What are some issues that may affect the future of the world? *(Students may mention war, infectious diseases, climate change, energy supplies, or other issues.)* OL

Cultural History

NASA After the Soviet Union launched the Sputnik satellite in 1957, the U.S. government established the National Aeronautics and Space Administration, or NASA. Its mission is to research and develop technologies for space exploration, to broaden our understanding of space, and to establish a human presence there. Famous achievements include the Apollo moon mission, the space shuttle, and the Hubble Space Telescope. AS

Building Reading Fluency

Reading Editorials Editorials are intended to influence or persuade readers to share the writer's perspective. Bring in editorials from the local and major newspapers and magazines. Have students read them aloud, paying attention to pacing, pronunciation, and tone of voice. BL

English Language Coach

Pronunciation English language learners may understand the meaning of words but still struggle with pronunciation. Show students how to use the pronunciation guide in a dictionary, using words from the model, such as *inhospitable* and *niche.* EL

Academic Standards

Additional Support activities on p. 1259 cover the following standards:

Building Reading Fluency: **9.7** [Develop] speaking skills, such as phrasing, pitch, and tone…

English Language Coach: **9.2.1** Analyze the structure and format of reference… documents…and explain how authors use the features to achieve their purposes.

Teach

BI Big Idea

Our World and Beyond
Ask: What does the author feel would be the best motive for human exploration of space? *(The author feels that economic benefit is the best motivator.)* OL

L Literary Element

Description Ask: Do you feel the author does a good job of describing the challenges of purely scientific space exploration? Why or why not? *(Some students may feel that the author presents a succinct description that clarifies the argument. Other students may feel that more concrete descriptive examples would better the argument.)* OL

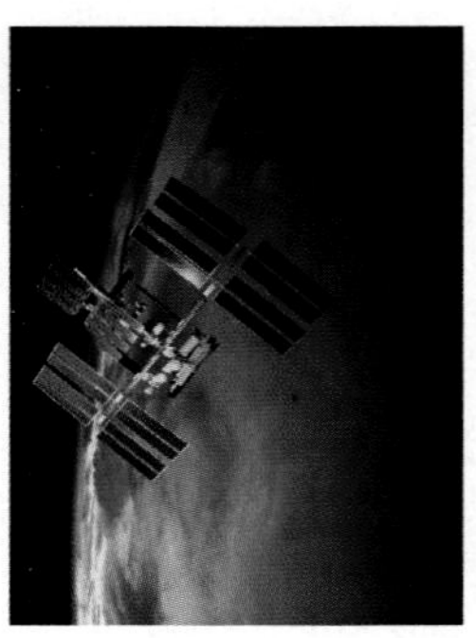

Address other Viewpoints
Anticipate your readers' concerns and their possible objections to your opinion.

Challenge Viewpoint
Point out the problems of any alternative viewpoints. Here the question brings readers back to the focus of the editorial.

Proposal
Suggest the solution you believe will work best.

Facts
Use facts to support your opinion. A fact is a statement that can be proven.

Conclusion
In your conclusion, restate your opinion on the issue and your proposed solution.

Imagine if there were a habitable planet or moon in our Solar System. If Mars, Venus, our Moon, or even one of Jupiter's larger moons could host tenants, the question of where do we go next would not be debatable. We would be on the verge of colonizing these places right now. Imagine what that would do for our technology. It would be similar to the discovery of the Americas by the Europeans in the fifteenth century.

A place that has value and economic benefit would drive our capitalistic society forward with such thrust that no questions would be asked; we would just act. A flood of new technology would be obtained and improved upon as we slowly learned how best to get to such distant places. We would be a true human-spaceflight society that would make space travel commonplace and marketable. . . . BI

Unfortunately, we don't have these habitable areas anywhere near us. Our exploration through curiosity will continue to drive us scientifically, but with no real economic benefits to our society from humans being in space, it will be a much slower process. It is hoped that conditions for civilization on the Earth will improve with increasing technology, but our expansion into outer space is now stunted, because there is no obvious answer to the question "Where do we send humans next?" . . .

Robotic, instead of human, space missions should be used to satisfy our curiosity. The new mobile robots unveiled at the NASA Ames research center last week are a step in the right direction. Robotic exploration is a much cheaper and more productive way to explore our hostile space environment. Robotic spacecraft will soon be able to accomplish most of the science a human would on the Moon or Mars.

Robotic exploration of these environments would cost a few billion dollars, whereas human exploration is expected to cost a few hundred billion dollars. The human Moon-Mars initiative was not proposed or even backed by the vast majority of scientists, because they understand that more science for our money is obtained through robotic missions. It's time our space program put its money where it counts—in the robotic spacecraft that are rolling around right under our noses. L

Reading-Writing Connection Think about the writing techniques that you have just encountered and try them out in the editorial you write.

Additional Support

Skills Practice

RESEARCH: Asking Questions
Writing questions related to the points they want to make in their editorials can help students clarify their ideas and focus their research. Have students use their graphic organizers as the basis for this exercise. Encourage them to write questions they have about the topic, all the viewpoints, and the ideas they have for a solution. When they are finished, have partners exchange papers and make suggestions. Students should use library resources and the Internet to do their research. OL

Prewriting

Read Published Editorials Read a newspaper published in your city or area, paying attention to the different subjects of the editorials over a period of several days. How do you respond to the different issues raised?

Consider Editorial Issues Reading editorials may give you ideas for a subject for your assignment. A few suggestions for editorials about issues affecting the future are space exploration, the environment, and technology.

Choose an Issue Choose an issue about which you feel strongly. If you are invested in your subject, then you will likely communicate your enthusiasm and effectively express your opinion.

Use a Graphic Organizer Create an organizer like the one shown to help you plan your editorial.

Issue or Problem
Destruction of rain forests

My Opinion
We must stop destroying rain forests because they provide many benefits and treasures, including medicines, foods, and animal life.

Other Viewpoints
Timber from rain forests is needed for building new homes and burning as fuel.

My Proposed Solution
Avoid using paper products made from trees. Conserve energy and fuel.

Discuss Your Ideas Meet with a partner to express ideas about your issue. Explain your opinion, talk about other viewpoints, and provide support for your conclusion. Ask your partner for suggestions on how to improve your writing style.

- ▶ Remember, your style should sound natural but professional.
- ▶ Keep your tone calm and reasonable.
- ▶ Finally, have your partner restate your opinion. This will test whether or not you have presented it clearly.

Tips for Editorials

- Include a discussion of various sides of the issue.
- Defend your opinion with confidence.
- Make sure the facts and examples you give are accurate.
- Show your feelings about the issue but keep your tone reasonable.

Test Prep

During tests, be sure to use your time well. Sketch a simple graphic organizer to plan your opinion statement, presentation of other views, and proposed solution. Develop your strongest points and keep your argument focused. Allow enough time to write a strong conclusion.

Teach

Writing Process

Prewriting Remind students to keep an open mind during the prewriting phase of their editorials. Tell them to keep in mind these questions as they work:

- Why does this subject interest me?
- What facts will I need to support my position?
- Based on my research, do I need to modify my opinions?
- What is the most effective way to convince others? OL

Writing Skill

Using a Graphic Organizer The graphic organizer on page 1261 provides an effective template for students to use in constructing their editorials. Tell students to focus on these four points as they develop their essays. Information that does not fit easily under these four headings may be irrelevant. Remind students to be sure that the last three headings are supported by evidence. OL

Differentiated Instruction

Essay Structure Some students may have difficulty organizing their thoughts in a logical structure for their essays. Have students exchange graphic organizers at an early stage in the process and offer each other feedback. Students should check the following criteria:

- The writer's opinion should be clearly stated.
- Each argument should be well supported.
- The information in each rectangle should be related to the topic in the label. BL

Academic Standards

Additional Support activities on pp. 1260 and 1261 cover the following standards:

Skills Practice: **9.4.4** Use writing to formulate clear research questions and to compile information…

Differentiated Instruction: **9.4.1** Discuss ideas for writing with classmates, teachers, and other writers and develop drafts alone and collaboratively.

Teach

Writing Skills

Background Answer: *The writer poses questions about discoveries that might result from exploring other worlds.* **OL**

Writing Skills

Reason Answer: *The editorial will probably be about the benefits of the rain forest.* **OL**

Writing Skills

Opinion Answer: *Stating your opinion early sets the tone and tells the reader the subject.* **OL**

Writing Skills

Examples Answer: *The examples show why the issue has become a problem.* **OL**

Writing Skills

Address Other Viewpoints Answer: *Acknowledging more than one side shows you are fair and logical, and it provides a stronger basis for your argument.* **OL**

Drafting

Get Going Using your graphic organizer as a guide, begin drafting your editorial. Remember to start with some background information about your issue. State your opinion clearly, address other viewpoints, and include strong support for your opinion and proposed solution. While you are writing, make sure you are following your plan. You can revise your plan at any time in the process, so if your research turns up a new example or fact, add it in the appropriate place.

Analyzing a Workshop Model

Here is a final draft of an editorial. Read it and answer the questions in the margin. Use the answers to these questions to guide you as you write.

Background
What technique does this writer use to provide background on the subject?

Reason
What reason is suggested for writing this editorial?

Opinion
Why is it important to state your opinion early in the editorial?

Examples
How do these examples help the audience understand the issue?

Address Other Viewpoints
Why give an opposing view?

The Future of the Rain Forest

Do you ever wonder what incredible discoveries might result from exploring other worlds? Are there miraculous cures for healing the sick? Are there delicious foods that could improve our diets? Are there animals too beautiful to imagine? You don't have to travel through outer space to find this promising but unknown world—it's right here on Earth. It's the rain forest: a warm, lush, and soggy region located mostly in countries near the equator.

We have only begun to uncover the treasure of the rain forest and to recognize its many benefits. The problem is that the rain forests of the world are being destroyed rapidly, and it is necessary to take action now to ensure that these benefits will not disappear in the future.

Let's take a look at how rain forests are being destroyed and what we can do today to save them. Trees are being cut down for a number of purposes. Trees supply wood, fuel, and products made from paper. Burning forests creates land that can be used for subsistence farming by people who have no other way to grow the food they need for survival. Population growth has led some cities to take over land that once was rain forest.

Some argue that homes are needed because of the growth in population, and wood is needed for new construction. Timber is used for fuel to heat the new homes and to make products that people are demanding in today's world. Moreover, logging companies provide jobs and help the economy.

Additional Support

Skills Practice

WRITING: Counterarguments To help students anticipate counterarguments to their opinions, suggest that they work with partners who will review their graphic organizers. Reading partners will have objective viewpoints and can help provide ideas for counterarguments that the writers might miss. Have partners work together to come up with ideas that can be substantiated. Encourage writers to make notes during this meeting, and then address the rebuttals in their essays. **AL**

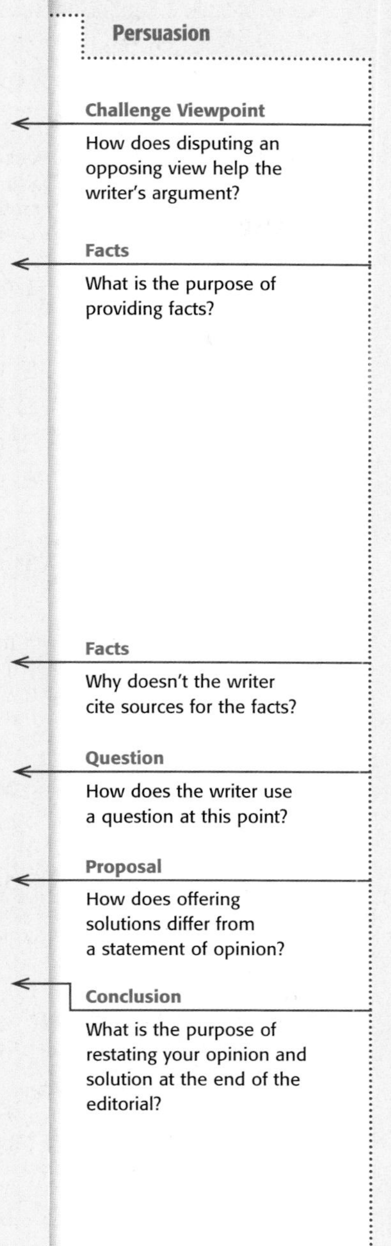

Yet these reasons don't justify the long-term consequences of destroying rain forests. First, we know that many rain-forest plants provide substances helpful in treating illnesses. For example, the bark of a plant found in Latin America contains a chemical used to treat illnesses, such as multiple sclerosis and Parkinson's disease. This same chemical has painkilling qualities, making it a good drug to use during certain kinds of surgery.

Second, we know that the rain forest is a source of countless foods that taste great or help keep you healthy. Favorite snack foods containing ingredients originally from the rain forest include chocolate, popcorn, peanuts, cashews, cola drinks, and salsa. Fruits from the rain forest include bananas, pineapples, lemons, coconuts, and avocados.

Finally, we know that as many as 50 million different kinds of animals live in various rain forests. Millions of these animals have no names because scientists haven't identified them yet. This number includes animals so tiny you can see them only with a microscope. Brilliantly colored butterflies and birds, jaguars, gorillas, and boas are just some of the animals you would see if you explored rain forests around the world.

What can be done to save the treasures of the rain forest? For one thing, it is impractical not to reduce the amount of paper we use and throw away. We can all avoid or cut back on using products made from trees, such as paper plates and cups. Most of us can sometimes walk or ride a bike, but we often choose the easy way and ride in cars, resulting in wasted fuel. Cutting back on electricity also helps.

Saving the rain forest is crucial—to the people who live in and near rain forests as well as everyone in the world who needs to rely on the resources of rain forests in the future.

Challenge Viewpoint
How does disputing an opposing view help the writer's argument?

Facts
What is the purpose of providing facts?

Facts
Why doesn't the writer cite sources for the facts?

Question
How does the writer use a question at this point?

Proposal
How does offering solutions differ from a statement of opinion?

Conclusion
What is the purpose of restating your opinion and solution at the end of the editorial?

Teach

Writing Skills

Challenge Viewpoint **Answer:** *Showing the weaknesses of other arguments strengthens the writer's argument.* OL

Writing Skills

Facts **Answer:** *Facts provide evidence for your opinion.* OL

Writing Skills

Facts **Answer:** *Because editorials don't focus on researched data, a formal bibliography isn't necessary. Sources of quotations should, however, be identified.* OL

Writing Skills

Question **Answer:** *The question opens the discussion of the writer's proposed solutions.* OL

Writing Skills

Proposal **Answer:** *An opinion expresses a belief, but proposing solutions suggests actions for resolving a problem.* OL

Writing Skills

Conclusion **Answer:** *Restating your opinion and solution summarizes the argument and leaves readers with the main point of the editorial.* OL

Building Reading Fluency

Read Aloud Students can both build reading fluency and glean valuable feedback by reading their essay drafts aloud to partners. Have listening partners provide suggestions for improving the essays' organization, flow, and strength of argument. BL

English Language Coach

Editorial Models on the Internet Encourage English language learners to find editorials in their native languages on the Internet. Have them identify the writers' positions on the topics and list reasons, facts, examples, and other evidence the writers give as support. EL

Academic Standards

Additional Support activities on pp. 1262 and 1263 cover the following standards:

Skills Practice: **9.5.4** Write persuasive compositions that address readers' concerns [and] counterclaims…

Building Reading Fluency: **9.7** [Develop] speaking skills…

English Language Coach: **9.4.6** Synthesize information from multiple sources, including…Internet sources.

Teach

Writing Process

Revising Remind students that all writers must constantly revise their work to

- say what they really mean
- present their messages in the most effective way

After students exchange papers and critique each other's work, refer them to the "Writing an Editorial" rubric. Challenge them to take another look at their essays and find at least one or two ways to improve them. **OL**

Writing Skill

Using a Reasonable Tone A calm, rational tone gives a dignified quality to an editorial. Explain to students that a rational argument is more difficult to refute than an emotional one. Refer to the focus lesson. **Ask:** Why is it more effective to say "We can all avoid products made of paper" than it is to say "Only greedy, careless people use products made from trees"? *(The first statement is hard to refute, while the second statement sounds extremist. Since most people use products made from trees, the second statement is insulting. This will alienate the audience, rather than win them over.)* **OL**

Revising

Traits of Strong Writing

Include these traits of strong writing to express your ideas effectively.

Ideas message or theme and the details that develop it

Organization arrangement of main ideas and supporting details

Voice writer's unique way of using tone and style

Word Choice vocabulary a writer uses to convey meaning

Sentence Fluency rhythm and flow of sentences

Conventions correct spelling, grammar, usage, and mechanics

Presentation the way words and design elements look on a page

For more information on using the Traits of Strong Writing, see pages R32–R33 of the Writing Handbook.

Peer Review Exchange completed drafts with a partner. Ask your partner to find your opinion statement and evaluate how effectively your editorial convinces others to support your proposed solution. Use the rubric below to evaluate and strengthen each other's editorials.

Rubric: Writing an Editorial

- ☑ Do you describe the issue and clearly state your opinion about it?
- ☑ Do you provide reasons for your opinion?
- ☑ Do you discuss alternative opinions and show why you disagree?
- ☑ Do you propose a solution and provide facts to support it?
- ☑ Do you conclude your editorial effectively?

Focus Lesson

Using a Reasonable Tone

Tone is the writer's attitude toward the subject of the written work. It is communicated through the choice of words and details. You want your tone to create an emotional response in the reader. But you should use a reasonable, unbiased tone to convince readers that your argument is fair, logical, and worth considering.

Draft:

It is insane not to reduce the amount of paper we use and throw away. Only greedy, careless people use products made from trees, such as paper plates and cups. Absolutely everyone can ride a bike or walk, but lazy people choose the easy way and ride in cars.

Revision:

It is impractical[1] not to reduce the amount of paper we use and throw away. We can all avoid or cut back on using products made of paper,[2] such as paper plates and cups. Most of us can sometimes walk or ride a bike, but we often choose the easy way and ride in cars, resulting in wasted fuel.[3]

1: Avoid emotionally charged words, such as *insane*.
2: Soften your language so that you do not insult your readers.
3: Do not make sweeping statements that may not be true.

Additional Support

Skills Practice

LISTENING AND SPEAKING: Getting Feedback Have peer reviewers consider specific questions, such as the following:

- Which evidence is most convincing?
- What additional evidence could be included?
- Are there opposing arguments that should be challenged?

Emphasize that writers need not accept every suggested change, only ideas they think will improve their editorials. **OL**

Editing and Proofreading

Get It Right When you have completed the final draft of your editorial, proofread for errors in grammar, usage, mechanics, and spelling. Refer to the Language Handbook, pages R45–R59, as a guide.

Focus Lesson

Parallelism

Parallelism is created by a series of words, phrases, or sentences that have a similar grammatical structure. Using parallel structures creates unity in writing, emphasizes certain ideas, and gives rhythm to the words.

Original: The grammatical structure is not the same in both phrases.

We have only begun to uncover the treasure of the rain forest and recognizing its many benefits.

Improved: To avoid nonparallel structure, make both phrases grammatically alike.

We have only begun to uncover the treasure of the rain forest and to recognize its many benefits.

Original: The sentences are unconnected and choppy.

Are there miraculous cures for healing the sick? Our diets could be improved by delicious foods. Imagine beautiful animals!

Improved: Repeat the same grammatical structure to create rhythm and add emphasis.

Are there miraculous cures for healing the sick? Are there delicious foods that could improve our diets? Are there animals too beautiful to imagine?

Looking Back

Did explaining your opinion as you wrote your editorial cause you to change your views in any way? Often your thoughts take you in a slightly different direction as you put your ideas into words, and you might even change your opinion! Writing is one of the best ways to think through an issue and come to a final conclusion.

Presenting

Make a Good Impression The purpose of an editorial is to convince others to take a side on an issue. Making a good case includes making a good impression by taking care with the writing you present. Do not forget to double-check the length of your editorial. Ask yourself if it is the correct number of words for the assignment or an appropriate length to be printed in a newspaper.

Writer's Portfolio

Place a clean copy of your editorial in your portfolio to review later.

Teach

Writing Skill

Parallelism Parallelism is a way of giving coherence and flow to a passage of writing. Refer to the focus lesson. **Say:** The problem with the first example is the verbs "to uncover" and "recognizing." To improve the sentence, make the verbs match: Either use "to uncover" and "to recognize," or use "uncovering" and "recognizing." Point out that the original sentence is confusing to read, as if the writer were saying "We have only begun to recognizing its benefits." **OL**

Writing Process

Presenting Small errors in grammar, punctuation, usage, mechanics, and spelling make a negative impression on the reader. Write on the board a few examples of opening sentences that contain errors of this kind and point out the way these errors cause the reader to mistrust the author. It may be helpful to have students switch papers with partners in order to proofread each other's work. **OL**

English Language Coach

Recognizing Tone Some students will struggle to hear and identify different tones in writing. Bring in samples of different forms of writing, such as an op-ed piece from a newspaper, an editorial written by a scholar or an expert, and a magazine article directed to teenagers. Have students read these different kinds of writing and discuss their effects. Ask them to identify words and phrases that convey particular tones. It may be helpful for students to read the articles aloud. **EL**

Academic Standards

Additional Support activities on pp. 1264 and 1265 cover the following standards:

Skills Practice: **9.7.7** Make judgments about the ideas under discussion and support those judgments with evidence. **9.4.10** Review, evaluate, and revise writing for meaning, clarity, content, and mechanics.

English Language Coach: **9.3.11** Evaluate the aesthetic qualities of style, including the impact of diction on…tone…

Focus

Summary

In this workshop, students will learn techniques for planning, developing, and delivering a persuasive presentation in the form of a radio or television broadcast.

Teach

Speaking Skills

Voice and Tone Students will know from radio and television what an important role an anchorperson or deejay plays in capturing an audience's attention. Bring in some sample broadcasts and play them for the class. **Ask:** What makes the speakers' voices different from ordinary voices?

As a further exercise, bring in some examples of comedians imitating newscasters or deejays, pointing out the ways in which comedians exaggerate the distinctive characteristics of professional broadcasters. Be sure that the comedians' material is appropriate for students. **OL**

Speaking, Listening, and Viewing Workshop

Persuasive Presentation

Delivering a Persuasive Presentation as a Radio or Television Broadcast

Connecting to Literature Arthur C. Clarke wrote "The Sentinel" and later received an Oscar nomination for co-writing the screenplay for the movie *2001: A Space Odyssey*, based on his story. He has appeared on television shows and hosted a Japanese television series based on one of his books. Although he is much sought after for interviews, he rarely gives them. One of his most memorable quotes is about the challenge of exploring the unknown: "The only way of discovering the limits of the possible is to venture a little way past them into the impossible."

Assignment **Deliver a persuasive presentation on the issue you chose for your editorial.**

Planning Your Persuasive Presentation

In your editorial, you chose an issue of importance and presented your opinion on it. You stated your opinion, acknowledged the concerns of others on the issue, and supplied examples and facts to support your proposed solution. Look to your editorial for ideas as you plan your persuasive presentation. Remember that your purpose is to win support for your opinion. To do this, supply convincing arguments and evidence.

- Begin by knowing the issue well. Read articles and reports, and make sure you have solid reasons for your opinion.
- Know your audience. Will your presentation be for a radio or television broadcast? How will the medium affect your planning and delivery?
- Choose one or two significant points to give focus to your presentation. It is not necessary to cover every aspect of the issue.
- Propose a solution for the issue.

Ideas for visuals
—paper plate (recycling)
—photo of unusual rain forest animal (habitat loss)

Additional Support

Skills Practice

LISTENING AND VIEWING: Persuasive Appeals An effective persuasive presentation is anchored by a logical argument but also makes emotional appeals. Have students listen to or watch a sample editorial broadcast from radio or television. Suggest that students keep in mind the following questions as they listen or watch.

Write on the board:

- What logical arguments does the speaker present?
- How does the speaker appeal to the audience's emotions?

Then have small groups discuss their responses to the appeal. **OL**

Use a Cause-and-Effect Chart As you think about your solution for the issue, you could jot your ideas in a cause-and-effect chart to clarify the connection between the problem and the solution.

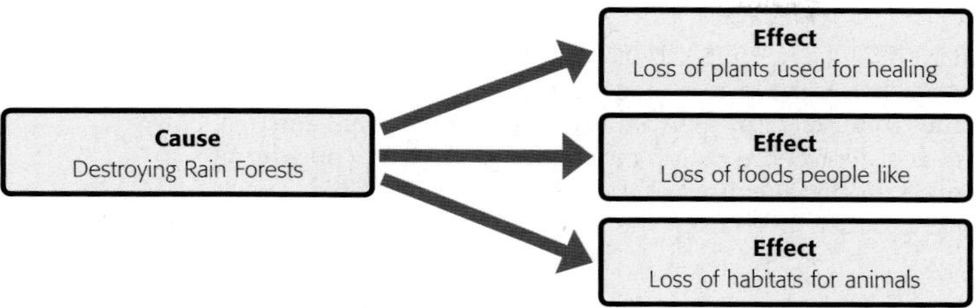

Developing Your Presentation

Adjust Your Format to the Medium If you are planning a television broadcast, consider using visuals. You could use props that are symbolic of your issue. You could also prepare a graph or chart to illustrate a statistic that supports your view. In contrast, a radio broadcast has no need for visuals. You will have to rely on effective word choice and tone of voice to communicate.

Develop Your Argument As in your editorial, include background information, a statement of your opinion, supporting evidence, audience concerns, and a proposed solution. End with your conclusion.

The "Hook" Ask yourself what will immediately interest your audience. Begin with a statement to grab their attention.

Delivering Your Presentation

Use the chart below to practice and deliver your persuasive presentation. Try not to rely on notes, especially for a television broadcast.

Goals	Strategies
☑ To speak convincingly	☑ Give facts and details. Acknowledge and challenge opposing views.
☑ To keep the attention of your audience	☑ Vary the pitch of your voice and the speed at which you speak.
☑ To match your presentation format to a radio or television broadcast	☑ Rely on your tone of voice for a radio broadcast. Look at the camera and use facial expressions and visuals for a television broadcast.
☑ To persuade your audience	☑ Use appeals to emotion, logic, or authority.

Variety Is the Key

Using your voice is important in delivering a presentation, especially during a radio broadcast. Vary the tone and pitch of your voice to keep your listeners interested. If you speak in a flat, monotonous voice, you will lose your audience quickly. Raise your voice to show enthusiasm and lower it to show a more objective view.

Persuasive Appeals

Appeal to the emotions of your audience to encourage responses to feelings and sentiments, such as joy, fear, horror, and love. Appeal to logic when you want your audience to consider serious matters. You can also appeal to authority by referring to an expert on the subject.

ACADEMIC STANDARDS (pages 1266–1267)

9.7.18 Deliver persuasive arguments...

9.7.3 Recognize and use elements of classical speech forms...in formulating rational arguments and applying the art of persuasion...

Teach

Speaking Skills

Persuading an Audience

The first step in persuading an audience is developing a powerful argument. Remind students to

- grab the audience's attention with a bold statement or surprising piece of information
- focus on their most important points
- propose a solution in clear, convincing language **OL**

Listening Skills

Active Listening Encourage students to listen to presentations with a critical and attentive ear. Have them take notes during the presentations of other students and write down objections, counterarguments, questions, or further thoughts they have on the issues presented. Allow time for a question-and-answer period after each presentation, in which students can further discuss and explore the important themes. **OL**

English Language Coach

Pronunciation English language learners may have difficulty pronouncing some of the words in their essays. Have them lightly circle difficult words and then work on the pronunciations with more proficient speakers before they give their presentations. **EL**

Differentiated Instruction

Speech Practice Provide extra time for less proficient readers and learning disabled students to practice their presentations. Have small groups listen to and critique the presentations. Some students may benefit from making and listening to recordings of themselves. **BL**

Academic Standards

Additional Support activities on pp. 1266 and 1267 cover the following standards:

Skills Practice: **9.7.12** Analyze the types of arguments used by the speaker...

English Language Coach: **9.7** [Develop] speaking skills...

Differentiated Instruction: **9.7.11** Evaluate the clarity, quality, effectiveness, and general coherence of a speaker's... delivery...

Focus

Summary

In this lesson, students will be introduced to a variety of genre fiction, including mysteries and science fiction. They will also be introduced to two novels relating to the Big Ideas of Our World and Beyond and Revealing the Concealed. Encourage students to read these works, which are related to themes they learned about in this unit.

Teach

★ Literary History

Du Maurier and Hitchcock Both born in London, England, Daphne du Maurier (1907–1989) and Alfred Hitchcock (1899–1980) became legends of the modern suspense story, she in literature, he in film. Hitchcock's first American film, *Rebecca* (1940), was based on du Maurier's 1938 novel. His masterpiece *The Birds* (1963) was based on a du Maurier short story. Her macabre, imaginative stories were the perfect prototypes for Hitchcock's films. **AS**

INDEPENDENT READING

Genre Fiction

THERE ARE MANY VARIETIES OF FICTION. ONE OF THEM IS SCIENCE FICTION, which presents imagined events related to science or technology. Mysteries, in which characters use clues to puzzle out the solution to a problem, make up another well-known fiction category. For genre fiction on a range of themes, consider the first three suggestions. For genre fiction that expresses the Big Ideas of *Our World and Beyond* and *Revealing the Concealed,* try the titles from the Glencoe Literature Library on the next page.

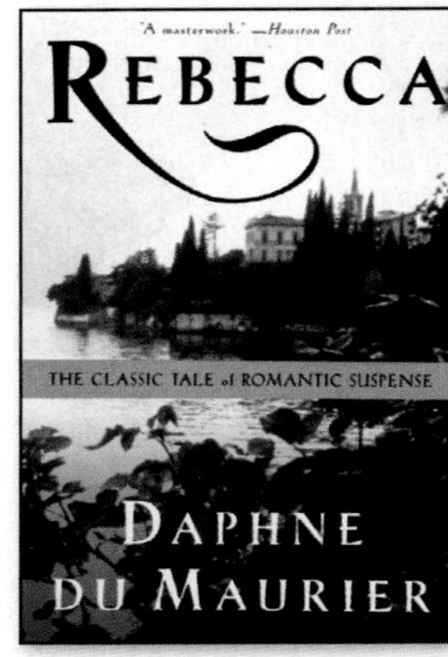

Rebecca

by Daphne du Maurier

This novel combines the haunting setting of a remote seacoast estate with romance, jealousy, suspense, and mystery. As the novel opens, a young wife finds herself overshadowed by a former wife's reputation for beauty and grace. Yet the new wife can learn nothing about the mysterious death of the first wife. A formal, dashing, and secretive husband and a forbidding housekeeper add layers of suspense and mystery. So full of psychological tension is this tale that Alfred Hitchcock turned it into a thriller movie. ★

The Beekeeper's Apprentice

by Laurie R. King

When Sir Arthur Conan Doyle retired Sherlock Holmes, he left him in Sussex raising bees. It is there that fifteen-year-old American Mary Russell finds him. In this feminist tale, the bright, clever, self-confident Mary represents a dramatic shift from Dr. Watson. As the story unfolds, she and Holmes match wits with great criminal minds. One of them turns out to be the evil daughter of Holmes's old archrival, Professor Moriarty. The book combines mystery, humor, and history for an exciting and original read.

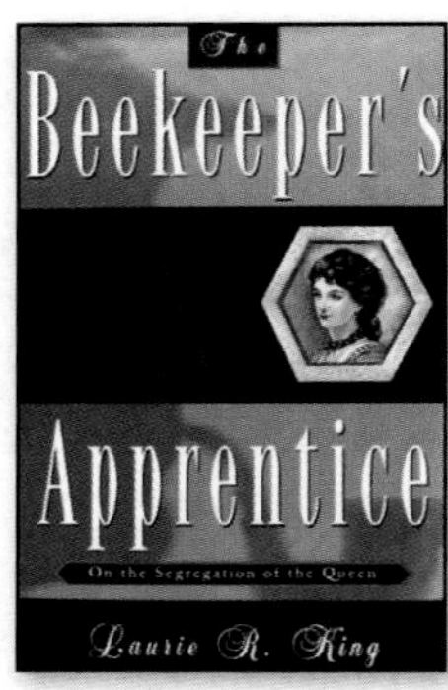

Additional Support

Skills Practice

SPEAKING, LISTENING, AND VIEWING: Watching an Adaptation Encourage students to read du Maurier's *Rebecca* and then watch Alfred Hitchcock's film adaptation of the novel. Ask them to consider the following questions:

- What might a director take into consideration when making a film adaptation of a short story or novel?
- What are some reasons for reading the novel instead of watching the film?

Have small groups discuss their views on these questions. Invite a volunteer from each group to present an oral statement to the class. **OL**

CRITICS' CORNER

"The end of Fahrenheit 451 *is essentially optimistic, despite the horrifying vision of an apocalyptic near-future presented earlier in the novel. Even though machines have produced the situation whereby books are banned and men and women are hunted for reading them, Bradbury is never simplistically antimachine and never illustrates a blind . . . prejudice when writing of the impediments of science or technology."*

—Willis E. McNelly, *Science Fiction Writers*

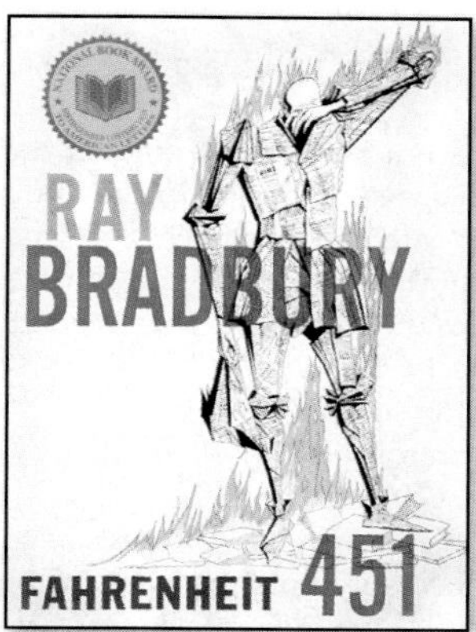

Fahrenheit 451

by Ray Bradbury ★

The first page of this novel begins with the sentence, "It was a pleasure to burn." This is what the main character, a fireman, is thinking as he routinely carries out his job of setting fire to the homes of people who illegally have books. Set in an unspecified time in the future, the novel has many themes. One of them is a celebration of books and readers. Another theme is the increasing isolation of humans in the modern world and their separation from nature. In addition, the novel depicts the menacing and controlling power of television.

From the Glencoe Literature Library

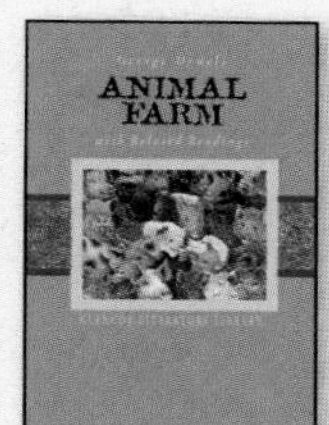

Animal Farm

by George Orwell

In this modern fable set in a world different from our own, animals who are a lot like humans revolt against the owner who mistreats them.

Frankenstein

by Mary Shelley

This early science fiction story explores the idea of creating life by scientific means and reveals something about what it means to be human.

Teach

★ Political History

Totalitarianism The word *totalitarianism* refers to a government so repressive that it has total control over all political and cultural opposition. The twentieth century saw the emergence of totalitarian or near-totalitarian states across Europe and Asia, notably Nazi Germany, Joseph Stalin's Soviet Union, and Mao Zedong's China. Both *Fahrenheit 451* and *Animal Farm* address the consequences of such government repression. **AS**

Glencoe Literature Library

Glencoe Literature Library offers an extensive collection of hardcover books that help you encourage your students to read independently. Choose among the more than 120 full-length literary works—novels, novellas, plays, and nonfiction. Each book includes related readings from a broad range of genres. Go to www.Glencoe.com for more information.

Reading in the Real World

Citizenship Many of the novels described in this lesson—*Fahrenheit 451, Animal Farm,* and *Frankenstein*—address serious philosophical and political questions. **Ask:** Do you think a story can change the way people think? Have you ever read a book that changed the way you thought about the world? Encourage students to read these novels and report back to the class on what they learned. Ask them to connect the books to the unit's Big Ideas of Our World and Beyond and Revealing the Concealed. **OL**

Academic Standards

Additional Support activities on pp. 1268 and 1269 cover the following standards:

Skills Practice: **9.3.2** Compare and contrast the presentation of a similar theme or topic across genres... **9.7.13** Identify the artistic effects of a media presentation...

Reading in the Real World: **9.3.5** Compare works that express a universal theme and provide evidence to support the views expressed in each work.

Focus

BELLRINGER

Ask: Do you experience anxiety before taking a test? Your feelings are normal and common to many. The best solution for test anxiety is preparation. Have students brainstorm lists of ways they can prepare for tests. Encourage them to list things such as getting a good night's sleep and specific study techniques.

Test Preparation and Practice

English Language Arts

ISTEP+ GQE/Core 40 Practice

READING: Vocabulary, Comprehension, and Analysis

Read the following passage. Then, on a separate sheet of paper, answer the questions on page 1272.

from "Wasps' Nest" by Agatha Christie

And at that moment the garden door opened and Claude Langton stepped quickly out into the road. He started when he saw Poirot.

"Oh—er—good evening."

"Good evening, Monsieur[1] Langton. You are early."

Langton stared at him. "I don't know what you mean."

"You have taken the wasps' nest?"

"As a matter of fact, I didn't."

"Oh!" said Poirot softly. "So you did not take the wasps' nest. What did you do then?"

"Oh, just sat and yarned[2] a bit with old Harrison. I really must hurry along now, Monsieur Poirot. I'd no idea you were remaining in this part of the world."

"I had business here, you see."

"Oh! Well, you'll find Harrison on the terrace. Sorry I can't stop."[3]

He hurried away. Poirot looked after him. A nervous young fellow, good looking with a weak mouth!

"So I shall find Harrison on the terrace," murmured Poirot. "I wonder." He went in through the garden door and up the path. Harrison was sitting in a chair by the table. He sat motionless and did not even turn his head as Poirot came up to him!

[1]**Monsieur:** French for "Mister"
[2]**yarned:** chatted
[3]**stop:** stay; remain

"Ah! *Mon ami,*"[4] said Poirot. "You are all right, eh?"

There was a long pause and then Harrison said in a queer, dazed voice, "What did you say?"

"I said—are you all right?"

"All right? Yes, I'm all right. Why not?"

"You feel no ill effects? That is good."

"Ill effects? From what?"

"Washing soda."[5]

Harrison roused himself suddenly. "Washing soda? What do you mean?"

Poirot made an apologetic gesture. "I infinitely regret the necessity, but I put some in your pocket."

"You put some in my pocket? What on earth for?"

Harrison stared at him. Poirot spoke quietly and impersonally like a lecturer coming down to the level of a small child.

"You see, one of the advantages, or disadvantages, of being a detective is that it brings you into contact with the criminal classes. And the criminal classes, they can teach you some very interesting and curious things. There was a pickpocket once—I interested myself in him because for once in a way he has not done what they say he has done—and so I get him off. And because he is grateful he pays me in the only way he can think of—which is to show me the tricks of his trade.

[4]***mon ami:*** French for "my friend"
[5]**washing soda:** sodium carbonate, a nonpoisonous substance once commonly used in making soaps

Writing

Punctuating Dialogue Point out to students that Christie has correctly punctuated the lines of dialogue in this excerpt from "Wasps' Nest." Quotation marks enclose the spoken words, and commas set off the speaker tags. Have students take a portion of this excerpt and copy the story exactly as it was published but without the punctuation. Then tell students to exchange papers and use proofreading marks to indicate where the quotation marks and other punctuation should be inserted without looking at the original. **OL**

"And it so happens that I can pick a man's pocket if I choose without his ever suspecting the fact. I lay one hand on his shoulder, I excite myself, and he feels nothing. But all the same I have managed to transfer what is in his pocket to my pocket and leave washing soda in its place.

"You see," continued Poirot dreamily, "if a man wants to get at some poison quickly to put in a glass, unobserved, he positively must keep it in his right-hand coat pocket; there is nowhere else. I knew it would be there."

He dropped his hand into his pocket and brought out a few white, lumpy crystals. "Exceedingly dangerous," he murmured, "to carry it like that—loose."

Calmly and without hurrying himself, he took from another pocket a wide-mouthed bottle. He slipped in the crystals, stepped to the table and filled up the bottle with plain water. Then carefully corking it, he shook it until all the crystals were dissolved. Harrison watched him as though fascinated.

Satisfied with his solution, Poirot stepped across to the nest. He uncorked the bottle, turned his head aside, and poured the solution into the wasps' nest, then stood back a pace or two watching.

Some wasps that were returning alighted, quivered a little and then lay still. Other wasps crawled out of the hole only to die. Poirot watched for a minute or two and then nodded his head and came back to the veranda.[6]

"A quick death," he said. "A very quick death."

Harrison found his voice. "How much do you know?"

Poirot looked straight ahead. "As I told you, I saw Claude Langton's name in the book.[7] What I did not tell you was that almost immediately afterwards, I happened to meet him. He told me he had been buying cyanide of potassium at your request—to take a wasps' nest. That struck me as a little odd, my friend, because I remember that at that dinner of which you spoke, you held forth[8] on the superior merits of petrol and denounced the buying of cyanide as dangerous and unnecessary."

"Go on."

"I knew something else. I had seen Claude Langton and Molly Deane together when they thought no one saw them. I do not know what lovers' quarrel it was that originally parted them and drove her into your arms, but I realized that misunderstandings were over and that Miss Deane was drifting back to her love."

"Go on."

"I knew something more, my friend. I was in Harley Street the other day, and I saw you come out of a certain doctor's house. I know that doctor and for what disease one consults him, and I read the expression on your face. I have seen it only once or twice in my lifetime, but it is not easily mistaken. It was the face of a man under sentence of death. I am right, am I not?"

"Quite right. He gave me two months."

"You did not see me, my friend, for you had other things to think about. I saw something else on your face—the thing that I told you this afternoon men try to conceal. I saw hate there, my friend. You did not trouble to conceal it, because you thought there were none to observe."

"Go on," said Harrison.

"There is not much more to say. I came down here, saw Langton's name by accident in the poison book as I tell you, met him, and came here to you. I laid traps for you. You denied having asked Langton to get cyanide, or rather you expressed surprise at his having done so. You were taken aback at first at my appearance, but presently, you saw how well it would fit in and you encouraged my suspicions. I knew from Langton himself that he was coming at half past eight. You told me nine o'clock, thinking I should come and find everything over. And so I knew everything."

"Why did you come?" cried Harrison. "If only you hadn't come!"

Poirot drew himself up. "I told you," he said, "murder is my business."

"Murder? Suicide, you mean."

"No." Poirot's voice rang out sharply and clearly. "I mean murder. Your death was to be quick and easy, but the death you planned for Langton was the worst death any man can die.

[6]**veranda:** porch
[7]**name in the book:** a records book at a pharmacy, which lists customers who bought poison
[8]**held forth:** spoke at length; lectured

Test Preparation and Practice

English Language Arts

Teach

Assessment Explain to students that this Test Preparation and Practice lesson is designed to develop test-taking strategies as well as to test their mastery of the skills covered in this unit. The lesson is modeled on tests they will be required to pass to be eligible to receive a high school diploma. Students will read one or two grade-level-appropriate selections and answer vocabulary, comprehension, and literary analysis questions, including multiple-choice, constructed-response, and extended-response items. In other sections, students' ability to use Standard English in their writing is assessed, and they are given an extended-writing prompt. **OL**

Assess

1. **D** is the correct answer.
2. **B** is the correct answer. Harrison denounced cyanide as dangerous at a dinner Poirot had attended before Harrison asked Langton to purchase some cyanide.
3. **C** is the correct answer. Poirot speaks "quietly and impersonally like a lecturer coming down to the level of a small child."
4. **D** is the correct answer. Harrison planned to make it appear that he had been poisoned by Langton, after which Langton would likely be hanged for the crime.
5. Rubric:

   2 points — versions of two exemplars

   1 point — version of one exemplar

   0 points — other

   Exemplars:
   - He sees Harrison leave a doctor's office with a grim expression on his face and concludes that Harrison is gravely ill.
   - He sees Claude Langton and Molly Deane together and concludes that they have resumed their relationship.
   - He sees hate on Harrison's face and concludes that Harrison is up to no good.
6. **B** is the correct answer. The crystals are cyanide of potassium.

He bought the poison; he comes to see you, and he is alone with you. You die suddenly, and the cyanide is found in your glass, and Claude Langton hangs. That was your plan."

Again Harrison moaned.

"Why did you come? Why did you come?"

"I have told you, but there is another reason. I liked you. Listen, *mon ami,* you are a dying man; you have lost the girl you loved, but there is one thing that you are not: you are not a murderer. Tell me now: are you glad or sorry that I came?"

There was a moment's pause and then Harrison drew himself up. There was a new dignity in his face—the look of a man who has conquered his own baser self.[9] He stretched out his hand across the table.

"Thank goodness you came," he cried. "Oh! Thank goodness you came."

[9] **baser self:** dishonorable part of his personality

1 Read this sentence from the story.

> **And the criminal classes, they can teach you some very interesting and curious things.**

Which of these definitions BEST fits *curious* as used in this sentence?

A eager to know or learn
B made carefully
C nosy
D unusual

2 Which of these events happened FIRST in the lives of the characters?

A Poirot replaced the cyanide with washing soda.
B Harrison denounced cyanide as dangerous.
C Poirot saw Langton's name in the poison book.
D Harrison asked Langton to buy the cyanide.

3 Early in the story, Poirot's manner of speaking to Harrison is compared to

A a detective grilling a criminal
B buzzing wasps in a nest
C a lecturer talking to a child
D cyanide crystals dissolving in water

4 How does the author reveal that Harrison intends to deceive Poirot even after Poirot uncovers Harrison's plan to poison himself?

A Harrison denies that he asked Langton to buy cyanide.
B Poirot sees Harrison leaving his doctor's office with an expression of hate on his face.
C Langton tells Poirot that he and Molly Deane have renewed their relationship.
D Harrison claims that he was planning a suicide, not a murder.

5 Give TWO specific details from the story that demonstrate Poirot's ability to draw conclusions from his observations.

6 How did Poirot prove that the white crystals were poisonous?

A He mixed them with wine.
B He poured them into a wasps' nest.
C He put them in Harrison's pocket.
D He gave them to a criminal.

7 Agatha Christie said, "Evil is not something superhuman; it's something less than human." Do you agree with this statement? **Write a reflective essay in which you discuss Christie's opinion and your ideas about evil. Include at least TWO details from the story to support your ideas.**

Use a separate sheet of paper to plan your writing.

Writing Checklist

The following checklist will help you write your essay. Be sure to

- ❑ brainstorm for ideas and develop a plan before you start writing
- ❑ organize your writing with an introduction, a body, and a conclusion
- ❑ pay attention to your word choice and voice
- ❑ edit for sentence fluency and conventions
- ❑ have a neat and organized presentation

7. Refer to the Reading Comprehension, Writing Applications, and Language Conventions rubrics provided by the State of Indiana Department of Education.

Student essays should include the following:
- a clearly stated and defended position supported by relevant evidence from the passage
- effective voice, word choice, and sentence variety
- effective presentation, with attention to grammar and spelling conventions

WRITING: Writing Process

The following passage is from the first draft of a student's essay. Read the passage and use it to answer numbers 8–11 on a separate sheet of paper.

> [1]I remember the first time I got to be a detective, when I was just nine years old. [2]A family living a few doors down had a daughter and she couldn't find her dog. [3]She had looked everywhere, and so had her parents. [4]Soon, the neighbors were helping too. [5]I felt sorry for the family. [6]So I really wanted to help. [7]My mother said that I was very good at finding things.

8 Choose the BEST way to revise Sentence 2.

- **A** A family living a few doors down whose daughter couldn't find her dog.
- **B** There was a family living a few doors down. The daughter of the family couldn't find her dog.
- **C** The daughter in a family living a few doors down couldn't find her dog.
- **D** The dog of a daughter in a family living a few doors down couldn't be found.

9 The Modern Library Association (MLA) recommends these guidelines for citing works used for reference.

1. List entries by author name. Write the author's last name first.
2. Underline the title of a book.
3. Place a colon after the place of publication, followed by the name of the publisher.
4. Include the year of publication last.

The student who wrote the paragraph above had been reading about detectives. According to the MLA recommendations above, which is the correct way for the student to cite this source?

- **A** The Great Detectives, Lindsay R. Dowd. London: Exeter Publishing, 2006.
- **B** Dowd, Lindsay R. The Great Detectives. Exeter Publishing: London, 2006.
- **C** Lindsay R. Dowd. The Great Detectives. Exeter Publishing, London: 2006.
- **D** Dowd, Lindsay R. The Great Detectives. London: Exeter Publishing, 2006.

10 Choose the BEST way to combine Sentences 5 and 6.

- **A** I felt sorry for the family, but I really wanted to help.
- **B** I felt sorry for the family, so I really wanted to help.
- **C** I felt sorry for the family because I really wanted to help.
- **D** I felt sorry for the family, then I really wanted to help.

11 The writer wants to replace the underlined phrase in Sentence 7 with a more formal expression. Which of these is the BEST replacement?

- **A** adept
- **B** dependable
- **C** virtuous
- **D** ethical

LiteratureOnline **Unit Assessment** To prepare for the Unit test, go to www.glencoe.com.

Test Preparation and Practice

English Language Arts

8. C is the correct answer. Option A is a fragment. The other options are wordy or awkward.

9. D is the correct answer. It is the only option that meets all four requirements.

10. B is the correct answer. The coordinating conjunction *so* means "with the result that."

11. A is the correct answer. *Adept* means "highly skilled" or "proficient."

Unit Assessment Have students access the Web site to prepare for the Unit Six test.

Test Preparation and Practice

English Language Arts

Assess

12. **C** is the correct answer. The nonessential clause should be set off with commas.
13. **C** is the correct answer. A colon is used to introduce a list of appositives.
14. **D** is the correct answer. There is no subject.
15. **B** is the correct answer. The future perfect tense expresses a future action (completion of the searches) that will begin and end before another future event (sunset) starts.
16. **D** is the correct answer.
17. **A** is the correct answer. An appositive should be set off with commas.
18. **C** is the correct answer. Capitalize verbs in book titles.

WRITING: English Language Conventions

Answer numbers 12–18 on a separate sheet of paper.

12 Choose the sentence that is punctuated correctly.

A Detectives, even fictional ones such as Hercule Poirot are always looking for clues.
B Detectives even fictional ones such as Hercule Poirot, are always looking for clues.
C Detectives, even fictional ones such as Hercule Poirot, are always looking for clues.
D Detectives, even fictional ones, such as Hercule Poirot are always looking for clues.

13 Decide which punctuation mark is needed in the sentence.

I looked for the dog in the following places under the porch, in the basement, behind the garage, and in the attic.

A .
B ,
C :
D ;

14 What type of an error has the writer of this sentence made?

Walked around the outside of the house thoughtfully, expecting to find more clues.

A spelling
B run-on sentence construction
C pronoun-antecedent agreement
D sentence fragment

15 Read this sentence.

By the time the sun goes down, the neighbors <u>had completed</u> their searches.

Choose the word or group of words that BEST replaces the underlined part of the sentence.

A will complete
B will have completed
C completed
D have completed

16 Choose the word that is spelled correctly.

Although the suspect's explanation was ______, it proved to be incorrect.

A plausable
B plossible
C plasible
D plausible

17 Read this sentence.

<u>Hercule Poirot the great Belgian detective</u> agreed to take the case, especially after he heard it involved a stolen necklace.

Choose the correct way to punctuate the underlined part of the sentence.

A Hercule Poirot, the great Belgian detective,
B Hercule Poirot–the great Belgian detective,
C Hercule Poirot: the great Belgian detective,
D Hercule Poirot the great Belgian detective,

18 What additional word in the sentence should be capitalized?

Agatha Christie is a well-known author of more than sixty mystery novels, including *And Then There were None* and *Murder on the Orient Express.*

A author
B mystery
C were
D the

1274 UNIT 6 GENRE FICTION

Writing

Outlining To help students organize their ideas for the essay assignment, have them follow the pattern of the sample outline below.

I. Introduction
  A. Get reader's attention
  B. Thesis statement
II. First supporting paragraph
  A. Evidence and support
  B. Evidence and support
III. Second supporting paragraph
  A. Evidence and support
  B. Evidence and support
IV. Second supporting paragraph
  A. Evidence and support
  B. Evidence and support
V. Memorable conclusion **OL**

WRITING: Writing Applications

Complete the writing activity below. Do your planning and writing on separate sheets of paper.

Character

> "Character cannot be developed in ease and quiet. Only through experience of trial and suffering can the soul be strengthened, ambition inspired, and success achieved."
>
> —Helen Keller (1880–1968)
> American author, activist, and lecturer

Do you agree or disagree with this quotation? Write an essay in which you explain to your teacher your beliefs about the quotation. Support your viewpoint with examples and reasons based on your own experiences, observations, and/or readings.

Be sure to include
- five paragraphs, including an introduction, a body, and a conclusion
- an interpretation that completes the assigned task
- examples and reasons that support your interpretation

Use a separate sheet of paper to plan your writing. As you write, keep in mind that your essay will be evaluated for **ideas and content, organization, style, voice,** and **language conventions.**

Writing Checklist

Before you begin writing, be sure to
- ❑ brainstorm for ideas
- ❑ organize your ideas into a logical pattern
- ❑ develop a plan for an introduction, a body, and a conclusion

As you write your essay, be sure to
- ❑ respond to the quotation and clearly state your interpretation
- ❑ provide reasons for your interpretation
- ❑ use language and vocabulary that will help convey a clear and interesting message
- ❑ maintain a tone that is appropriate for your intended audience
- ❑ use correct sentence structure, grammar, and punctuation

Test Preparation and Practice

English Language Arts

Assess

Assessment of writing prompts should focus on four elements:
- **Ideas and Content,** the message or theme and the details that develop it
- **Organization,** the arrangement of main ideas and supporting details
- **Style,** the word choices that a writer uses to convey meaning and the fluency, or rhythm and flow, of sentences
- **Voice,** the writer's unique way of using tone and style

Students' writing should also be assessed for correct **capitalization, punctuation, spelling, grammar and usage, paragraphing,** and **sentence structure.**

In addition, student essays should:
- fully complete the assigned task
- include complete, thorough, relevant, and logically organized ideas
- exhibit correct word usage
- demonstrate exceptional writing technique
- use language and tone appropriate for the task and audience

REFERENCE SECTION

LITERARY TERMS HANDBOOK

A

Abstract language Language that expresses an idea or intangible reality, as opposed to a specific object or occurrence or a concrete reality. Words such as *dog* and *sky* are concrete, whereas words such as *truth* and *evil* are abstract.

See also CONCRETE LANGUAGE.

Absurd, Theater of the *See THEATER OF THE ABSURD.*

Act A major unit of a drama, or play. Modern dramas generally have one, two, or three acts. Older dramas often have five acts. Although Shakespeare did not separate his plays into acts, each play was later divided into five acts. Acts may be divided into one or more scenes.

See page 821.

See also DRAMA, SCENE.

Allegory A literary work in which all or most of the characters, settings, and events stand for ideas, qualities, or figures beyond themselves. The overall purpose of an allegory is to teach a moral lesson.

See pages 1179 and 1184.

See also SYMBOL.

Alliteration The repetition of consonant sounds, generally at the beginnings of words. Alliteration can be used to emphasize words, reinforce meaning, or create a musical effect. Note the repeated *s* and *f* sounds in the following line from Mary Oliver's poem "The Black Snake":

> It is what sent the snake coiling and flowing
> forward . . .

See pages 621, 659, and 661.

See also SOUND DEVICES.

Allusion A reference to a well-known character, place, or situation from history, music, art, or another work of literature. Discovering the meaning of an allusion can often be essential to understanding a work. Edna St. Vincent Millay alludes to Penelope, Odysseus's wife in Homer's *Odyssey*, in her poem "An Ancient Gesture":

> I thought, as I wiped my eyes on the corner of
> my apron:
> Penelope did this too.

Ambiguity The state of having more than one meaning. The richness of literary language lies in its ability to evoke multiple layers of meaning.

See also CONNOTATION.

Analogy A comparison that shows similarities between two things that are otherwise dissimilar. A writer may use an analogy to explain something unfamiliar by comparing it to something familiar. Chitra Banerjee Divakaruni makes the following analogies in these lines from her poem "My Mother Combs My Hair":

> We hold the silence
> tight between us
> like a live wire,
> like a strip of gold
> torn from a wedding brocade.

See also METAPHOR, RHETORICAL DEVICES, SIMILE.

Anecdote A short written or oral account of an event from a person's life. Essayists often use anecdotes to support their opinions, clarify their ideas, grab the reader's attention, or entertain. In "Field Trip," Naomi Shihab Nye's story about her time at camp is an anecdote.

See pages 341, 348, and 398.

Antagonist A person or a force in society or nature that opposes the *protagonist*, or central character, in a story or drama. The reader is generally meant not to sympathize with the antagonist. Polyphemus, the Cyclops, is Odysseus's antagonist in one episode of Homer's *Odyssey*.

See pages 109 and 119.

See also CHARACTER, CONFLICT, PROTAGONIST.

Anthropomorphism The assignment of human characteristics to gods, animals, or inanimate objects. It is a key element in fables and folktales, in which the main characters are often animals. The animals in "Baker's Bluejay Yarn" have human characteristics.

See also FABLE.

Antithesis The technique of putting opposite ideas side by side in order to point out their differences or to draw attention to the superiority of one. Antithesis is often used in logical argument. Michel de Montaigne makes frequent use of antithesis in his essay "That One Man's Profit Is Another's Loss," as when he writes, "No profit can be made except at another's expense."

See pages 447–449.

See also ARGUMENT, PERSUASION.

Aphorism A short, pointed statement that expresses a wise or clever observation about human experience. Naomi Shihab Nye concludes her essay "Field Trip" with an aphorism:

> **The things we worry about are never the things that happen. And the things that happen are the things we never could have dreamed.**

See pages 394 and 398.

Apostrophe A literary device in which a speaker addresses an inanimate object, an idea, or an absent person. In Act 3, Scene 2, of *The Tragedy of Romeo and Juliet*, Juliet addresses the night:

> **Spread thy close curtain, love-performing night,**
> **That th' runaway's eyes may wink, and Romeo**
> **Leap to these arms untalk'd of and unseen!**

See also PERSONIFICATION.

Archetype An idea, a character, a story, or an image that is common to human experience across cultures and throughout the world. In their purest form, archetypes occur in oral tradition, but they also appear in written works of literature. They can be divided into the following categories:

Character archetype: Includes familiar individuals such as the wise leader, the rebel, the damsel in distress, and the traitor. Coyote, the trickster of Native American folklore, is a character archetype.

Image archetype: An object or a place that has a universal symbolism. For example, a rose symbolizes love.

Plot pattern archetype: A story that occurs in many cultures. Making the long journey home, completing the "impossible" task, and outwitting the formidable enemy are all archetypal plots.

Theme archetype: An idea that occurs wherever people tell stories. The ideas that good can overcome evil, that people can redeem themselves, and that an underworld exists are all archetypal themes.

See pages 947–952 and 1054–1055.

See also FOLKLORE, MYTH, ORAL TRADITION, STOCK CHARACTER, SYMBOL.

Argument A type of persuasive writing in which logic or reason is used to try to influence a reader's ideas or actions. Anna Quindlen presents an argument against being perfect in "Put Down the Backpack."

See pages 436–437, 447, 449, 451, 1138.

See also PERSUASION.

Aside In a play, a comment that a character makes to the audience, which other characters onstage do not hear. The speaker turns to one side—or "aside"—away from the action onstage. Asides, which are rare in modern drama, reveal what a character is thinking or feeling. For example, in Act 2, Scene 2, of Shakespeare's *Romeo and Juliet*, Romeo makes two asides to the audience as he decides whether to make his presence known to Juliet, who is standing on the balcony above him.

See pages 746 and 773.

See also SOLILOQUY.

Assonance The repetition of same or similar vowel sounds within nonrhyming words. In the following lines from Rita Dove's poem "Grape Sherbet," the long *i* sound is repeated in *I've* and *trying,* and the short *i* sound is repeated in *it* and *exist.*

> **I've been trying / to remember the taste, / but it doesn't exist.**

See pages 621, 623, and 625.

See also SOUND DEVICES.

Atmosphere The dominant emotional feeling of a literary work that contributes to the mood. Authors create atmosphere primarily through details of setting, such as time, place, and weather. In "The Cask of Amontillado,"

Edgar Allan Poe creates atmosphere by describing the eerie setting:

> **We had passed through walls of piled bones, with casks and puncheons intermingling, into the inmost recesses of the catacombs.**

See pages 2–8.

See also MOOD.

Author's purpose An author's intent in writing a literary work. For example, the author may want to persuade, inform, describe a process, entertain, or express an opinion. Anna Quindlen's purpose in "Put Down the Backpack" is to persuade and inspire.

See pages 300–306, 320, 362, and 479.

See also DICTION, STYLE, THEME.

Autobiography A person's account of his or her life. The author typically focuses on the most significant events in his or her life. Autobiographies can give insights into the author's view or himself or herself and of the society in which he or she lived. For example, in *The Story of My Life,* Helen Keller traces the importance of education in her life.

See pages 300–306 and 308–309.

See also BIOGRAPHY, MEMOIR, NONFICTION.

B

Ballad A musical narrative song or poem that in most cases recounts a single exciting or dramatic episode. Folk ballads were passed down by word of mouth for generations before being written down. Literary ballads are written in imitation of folk ballads and have a known author. Many ballads include elements of plot, such as exposition, conflict, climax, and resolution. "Sweet Betsy from Pike" is a folk ballad.

See pages 1088 and 1090.

See also FOLKLORE, NARRATIVE POETRY, ORAL TRADITION, PLOT.

Bias An inclination toward a certain opinion or position on a topic, possibly stemming from prejudice.

See pages 439, 444, and 1186.

See also NONFICTION.

Biography A nonfiction account of a person's life written by another person. Biographies can vary in length, from brief encyclopedia entries to works that span several volumes. James Cross Giblin's "A Brother's Crime" is an excerpt from a biography of John Wilkes Booth's brother Edwin.

See pages 317 and 335.

See also AUTOBIOGRAPHY, JOURNAL, MEMOIR.

Blank verse Unrhymed poetry or dramatic verse written in a meter known as *iambic pentameter.* Each line of iambic pentameter has five units, or feet; each foot is made up of an unstressed syllable followed by a stressed syllable. Much of Shakespeare's work is written in blank verse. The following line from *Romeo and Juliet*, spoken by Friar Lawrence, is an example of blank verse.

˘ ´ ˘ ´ ˘ ´ ˘ ´ ˘ ´

Be pa / tient, for / the world / is broad / and wide.

See page 690.

See also FOOT, IAMB, METER, RHYTHM.

C

Cadence The rhythmic rise and fall of language when it is spoken or read aloud.

See also FREE VERSE, METER.

Catalog The listing of images, details, people, or events in a literary work. In "The Drums of Washington," Arthur M. Schlesinger Jr. catalogs the responses of world leaders and artists on hearing that President Kennedy had been assassinated.

See page 242.

Character An individual in a literary work. *Main characters* are central to the story and are typically fully developed. *Minor characters* display few personality traits and are used to help develop the story. In James Hurst's "The Scarlet Ibis," Brother and Doodle are main characters, and Mama, Daddy, and Aunt Nicey are minor characters. A character who shows varied and sometimes contradictory traits, such as Walter Mitty in James Thurber's "The Secret Life of Walter Mitty," is a *round character*. A character who reveals only one personality trait, such as the vengeful murderer in Edgar Allan Poe's "The Cask of Amontillado," is a *flat character.* A *stock* *character* is a flat character of a familiar and often-repeated type, such as the hard-boiled detective. A *dynamic character* changes during the story. A *static character*—such as the king in Frank R. Stockton's "The Lady, or the Tiger?"—remains the same throughout the story.

See pages 2–8 and 106–107.

See also ANTAGONIST, CHARACTERIZATION, FOIL, PROTAGONIST, STEREOTYPE, STOCK CHARACTER.

Character archetype *See ARCHETYPE.*

Characterization The methods a writer uses to reveal the personality of a character. In *direct characterization,* the writer makes explicit statements about a character. In *indirect characterization,* the writer reveals a character through that individual's words, thoughts, and actions and through what other characters think and say about that character. In his play *The Bear,* Anton Chekhov uses indirect characterization to create Smírnoff, a bold, brazen egotist who becomes sentimental when he falls in love with Popóva.

See pages 161 and 189.

See also CHARACTER.

Climax The point of greatest emotional intensity, interest, or suspense in the plot of a literary work. Also called the *turning point,* the climax usually comes near the end of a story or drama. For example, in Amy Tan's "Rules of the Game," the climax occurs when Meimei and her mother exchange harsh words and Meimei runs away.

See pages 10–11 and 2008.

See also CONFLICT, PLOT.

Colloquialism Informal language used in everyday conversation but not in formal writing or speech. The narrator's speech in Mark Twain's short story "Baker's Bluejay Yarn" is peppered with colloquialisms, as when he says:

> **He glances up perfectly joyful, this time; winks his wings and his tail both, and says, 'Oh, no, this ain't no fat thing, I reckon! If I ain't in luck!—why it's a perfectly elegant hole!'**

See pages 248 and 255.

See also DIALECT.

Comedy A type of drama that is humorous and typically has a happy ending. Comedy can be divided into two categories: high and low. *High comedy* makes fun of human behavior in a witty, sophisticated manner. *Low comedy* involves physical humor and simple, often vulgar, wordplay. Eudora Welty's play *Bye-Bye Brevoort* is an example of high comedy.

See pages 683–688.

See also DRAMA, FARCE, HUMOR, PARODY, SATIRE.

Comic relief A humorous scene, event, or speech in an otherwise serious drama. It provides relief from emotional intensity while at the same time highlighting the seriousness of the story. In Paddy Chayefsky's *Marty,* there is a moment of comic relief when Marty's mother uses the slang word *tomatoes* to describe the young women who will be at the Waverly Ballroom.

> **MOTHER. I say, why don't you go to the Waverly Ballroom? It's loaded with tomatoes.**

Conceit An elaborate figure of speech that makes a comparison between two significantly different things. The conceit draws an analogy between some object from nature or everyday life and the subject or theme of a poem. Emily Dickinson's poem "'Hope' is the thing with feathers—" is a conceit.

See pages 590 and 593.

See also ANALOGY, EXTENDED METAPHOR.

Concrete language Specific language about actual things or occurrences. Words such as *dog* and *sky* are concrete, while words such as *truth* and *evil* are abstract.

See also ABSTRACT LANGUAGE.

Conflict The struggle between opposing forces in a story or drama. An *external conflict* exists when a character struggles against some outside force, such as another person, nature, society, or fate. In Homer's *Odyssey*, for example, Odysseus is involved in external conflicts with Polyphemus, Scylla and Charbydis, and the suitors. An *internal conflict* is a struggle that takes place within the mind of a character who is torn between opposing feelings or goals. In W. D. Wetherell's "The Bass, the River, and Sheila Mant," the narrator is torn between reeling in the fish (and losing the potential affections of Sheila) and letting it go (and losing the catch of a lifetime).

See pages 2–8, 42, 980.

See also ANTAGONIST, PLOT, PROTAGONIST.

Connotation The suggested or implied meanings associated with a word beyond its dictionary definition, or *denotation.* A word can have a positive or negative connotation, or no connotation.

See pages 475 and 1186.

See also AMBIGUITY, DENOTATION, FIGURATIVE LANGUAGE.

Consonance The repetition of consonant sounds, typically within or at the end of words that do not rhyme and preceded by different vowel sounds.

See pages 621 and 625.

See also SOUND DEVICES.

Couplet Two consecutive lines of rhymed verse that work together as a unit to make a point or to express an idea. Paul Laurence Dunbar's poem "Sympathy" contains many couplets, such as:

> And the faint perfume from its chalice steals–
> I know what the caged bird feels!

See also RHYME, SONNET, STANZA.

D

Denotation The literal, or dictionary, meaning of a word.

See page 1186.

See also CONNOTATION.

Denouement The resolution of a story. *Denouement* is a French word meaning "unknotting." The denouement comes after the climax of a story and often ties in with the falling action.

See pages 10–11 and 185.

See also FALLING ACTION, PLOT, RESOLUTION.

Description A detailed portrayal of a person, a place, an object, or an event. Good descriptive writing helps readers to see, hear, smell, taste, or feel the subject. The opening paragraph of James Hurst's "The Scarlet Ibis" contains this rich description:

> The last graveyard flowers were blooming, and their smell drifted across the cotton field and through every room of our house, speaking softly the names of our dead.

See pages 10–11, 94, and 1138.

See also FIGURATIVE LANGUAGE, IMAGERY.

Descriptive essay *See ESSAY.*

Dialect A variation of a language spoken by a group of people, often within a particular region. Dialects may differ from the standard form of a language in vocabulary, pronunciation, or grammatical form. For example, the following lines from Robert Burns's "A Red, Red Rose" make use of Scottish dialect:

> Till a' the seas gang dry, my dear,
>
> And the rocks melt wi' the sun!

See pages 68, 255, and 1163.

Dialogue Conversation between characters in a literary work. Dialogue brings characters to life by revealing their personalities and by showing what they are thinking and feeling as they react to other characters. Dialogue can also create mood, advance the plot, and develop theme. Plays are composed almost completely of dialogue. This dialogue takes place between Friar Lawrence and Romeo in Act 3, Scene 3 of *Romeo and Juliet*:

> FRIAR. O, then I see that madmen have no ears.
>
> ROMEO. How should they, when that wise men have no eyes?
>
> FRIAR. Let me dispute with thee of thy estate.

See pages 189, 427, and 682–688.

See also MONOLOGUE.

Diction A writer's choice of words; an important element in the writer's voice or style. Skilled writers choose their words carefully to convey a particular meaning or feeling.

See pages 209, 570, and 646.

See also AUTHOR'S PURPOSE, CONNOTATION, STYLE, TONE, VOICE.

Drama A story written to be performed by actors before an audience. The script of a dramatic work, or play, often includes the author's instructions to the actors and director, known as stage directions. A drama may be divided into acts, which may also be broken up into scenes, indicating changes in location or the passage of time.

See pages 680–939.

See also ACT, COMEDY, DIALOGUE, SCENE, STAGE DIRECTIONS, TRAGEDY.

Dramatic irony *See IRONY.*

Dynamic character *See CHARACTER.*

E

End rhyme The rhyming of words at the ends of lines as in William Wordsworth's "I Wandered Lonely as a Cloud."

See page 520.

End-stopped line A line of poetry that ends in a punctuation mark. An end-stopped line usually contains a complete thought or image. Emily Dickinson's "I'm Nobody! Who are you?" contains the following end-stopped lines:

> **I'm Nobody! Who are you?**
> **Are you—Nobody—Too?**

See page 592.

See also ENJAMBMENT.

Enjambment The continuation of a sentence or phrase from one line of a poem to the next, without a pause between the lines. The following lines from William Wordsworth's "I Wandered Lonely as a Cloud" are an example of enjambment:

> **The waves beside them danced; but they**
> **Outdid the sparkling waves in glee . . .**

See pages 557 and 559.

See also END-STOPPED LINE.

Epic A long narrative poem that recounts, in formal language, the exploits of a larger-than-life figure. This *epic hero* is usually a person of high social status who embodies the ideals of his or her people. He or she is often of historical or legendary importance. Epic plots typically involve supernatural events, long time periods, distant journeys, and life-and-death struggles between good and evil. Folk epics have no known author and usually arise through storytelling and collective experiences of people, while literary epics are written by known authors.

See pages 946–952, 959, and 979.

See also FOLKLORE, HERO, MYTH, NARRATIVE POETRY, ORAL TRADITION.

Epic hero *See EPIC, HERO.*

Epic simile A long, elaborate comparison that continues for several lines. It is a feature of epic poems but occurs in other poems as well. In the *Odyssey*, for example, Homer compares Scylla plucking her victims from Odysseus's ship to an angler catching fish.

See pages 960–1018.

See also EPIC, SIMILE.

Epiphany A sudden understanding of the meaning or essence of something. In William Wordsworth's "I Wandered Lonely as a Cloud," the speaker has an epiphany when he sees a field of wild daffodils and recognizes nature's power to bring joy.

See pages 520, 629, and 631.

Epithet A brief phrase used to characterize a person, place, or thing. A *Homeric epithet* is a formulaic or stock phrase specific to epic poetry. Homeric epithets fit the meter of the poem and appear throughout. Before poems were written, these epithets functioned as mnemonic devices, helping the poet remember the lines during his or her performance. For example, in the *Odyssey*, Homer repeatedly uses "bleating ewes" to describe the Cyclops's flock and "fingertips of rose" to describe the dawn.

See pages 960–1018.

Essay A short work of nonfiction on a single topic. *Descriptive essays* describe a person, place, or thing. *Narrative essays* relate true stories. *Persuasive essays* promote an opinion. *Reflective essays* reveal an author's observations on a subject. All of these types of essays fall into two general categories, according to their style. A *formal essay* is serious and impersonal, often with the purpose of instructing or persuading. Typically, the author strikes a serious tone and develops a main idea, or *thesis,* in a logical, highly organized way. An *informal* or *personal essay* entertains while it informs, usually in light, conversational style.

See pages 301–306 and 380–381.

See also NONFICTION.

Exaggeration *See HYPERBOLE.*

Exposition An author's introduction of the characters, setting, and situation at the beginning of a story, novel, or play.

See pages 10, 20, and 1204.

See also PLOT.

Extended metaphor A metaphor that compares two unlike things in various ways throughout a paragraph, a stanza, or an entire selection. Emily Dickinson uses an extended metaphor in "'Hope' is the thing with feathers–."

See pages 590 and 593.

See also CONCEIT, METAPHOR.

F

Fable A short, usually simple tale that teaches a moral and sometimes uses animal characters. Themes in fables are often directly stated. Pär Lagerkvist's "The Princess and All the Kingdom" is a modern fable.

See pages 1114–1120.

See also LEGEND, MORAL, PARABLE, THEME.

Falling action In a play or story, the action that follows the climax. The falling action may show the results of the climax. It may also include the *denouement,* a French word meaning "unknotting." The denouement, or *resolution,* explains the plot or unravels the mystery.

See pages 10 and 185.

See also CLIMAX, PLOT.

Fantasy A highly imaginative genre of fiction, usually set in an unfamiliar world or a distant, heroic past. Fantasy stories commonly take place in imaginary worlds and may include gnomes, elves, or other fantastical beings and forces. The use of some type of magic is common in fantasy stories.

See pages 1114–1120.

See also SCIENCE FICTION.

Farce A type of comedy with stereotyped characters in ridiculous situations. Anton Chekhov's play *The Bear* contains many farcical situations, such as when Smírnoff challenges Popóva to a duel.

See pages 823 and 884.

See also COMEDY, HUMOR, PARODY, SATIRE.

Fiction Literature in which situations and characters are invented by the writer. Fiction includes both short stories, such as James Thurber's "The Secret Life of Walter Mitty," and novels, such as Willa Cather's *My Ántonia*. Aspects of a fictional work may be based on fact or experience.

See also DRAMA, NONFICTION, NOVEL, SHORT STORY.

Figurative language Language that uses figures of speech, or expressions that are not literally true but express some truth beyond the literal level. Types of figurative language include hyperbole, metaphor, personification, simile, and understatement.

See pages 508–514, 722, and 806.

See also HYPERBOLE, IMAGERY, METAPHOR, OXYMORON, PERSONIFICATION, SIMILE, SYMBOL, UNDERSTATEMENT.

Figures of speech *See FIGURATIVE LANGUAGE.*

Flashback An interruption in the chronological order of a narrative to describe an event that happened earlier. A flashback gives readers information that may help explain the main events of the story. There are examples of flashback in Louise Erdrich's "The Leap," a story that is told from the point of view of a woman who is remembering various events in her life and her mother's life.

See pages 45 and 1204.

Flat character *See CHARACTER.*

Foil A character who provides a strong contrast to another character, usually a main character. By using a foil, a writer calls attention to the strengths or weaknesses of a character. In *Romeo and Juliet*, the fun-loving Mercutio is a foil to the love-struck Romeo.

See pages 695 and 721.

See also CHARACTER.

Folklore The traditional beliefs, customs, stories, songs, and dances of a culture. Folklore is based on the concerns of ordinary people and is passed down through oral tradition.

See pages 1090 and 1093.

See also BALLAD, EPIC, FOLKTALE, MYTH, ORAL TRADITION, TALL TALE.

Folktale An anonymous traditional story passed down orally long before being written down. Folktales include animal stories, trickster stories, fairy tales, myths, legends, and tall tales.

See also EPIC, FOLKLORE, LEGEND, MYTH, ORAL TRADITION, TALL TALE.

Foot The basic unit in the measurement of rhythm in poetry. A foot usually contains one stressed syllable (´) and one or more unstressed syllables (˘).

See also METER, RHYTHM, SCANSION.

Foreshadowing An author's use of clues to prepare readers for events that will happen later in a story. The pistol shots and jarring cries that Rainsford hears at the beginning of Richard Connell's short story "The Most Dangerous Game" foreshadow Rainsford's fate: he will be hunted on the island.

See pages 43 and 1228.

See also PLOT, RISING ACTION, SUSPENSE.

Form The structure of a poem. Many modern writers use loosely structured poetic forms instead of following traditional or formal patterns. These poets vary the lengths of lines and stanzas, relying on emphasis, rhythm, pattern, or the placement of words and phrases to convey meaning.

See pages 516 and 621.

See also RHYTHM, STANZA, STRUCTURE.

Formal essay *See ESSAY.*

Frame story A plot structure that includes the telling of a story within a story. The frame is the outer story, which usually precedes and follows the inner, more important story. Twain uses a frame in "Baker's Bluejay Yarn." Some literary works have frames that bind together many different stories.

Free verse Poetry that has no fixed pattern of meter, rhyme, line length, or stanza arrangement. Alma Luz Villanueva's poem "I Was a Skinny Tomboy Kid" is composed in free verse.

See pages 533, 581, 617 and 646.

See also POETRY, RHYTHM.

G

Genre A category or type of literature. Examples of genres are poetry, drama, fiction, nonfiction, essay, and epic. The term also refers to subcategories of literary work. For example, fantasy, magical realism, mystery, romance, and science fiction are genres of fiction. Ursula K. Le Guin's short story "The Rule of Names," for example, belongs to both the fiction and fantasy genres.

H

Haiku A traditional Japanese form of poetry that has three lines and seventeen syllables. The first and third lines have five syllables each; the second line has seven syllables. The purpose of traditional haiku is to capture a flash of insight that occurs during an observation of nature.

See pages 567 and 570.

Hero The main character in a literary work, typically a character whose admirable qualities or noble deeds arouse admiration. For example, Ivan is the hero in the Russian tale "Vasilisa of the Golden Braid and Ivan the Pea." In contemporary usage, the term can refer to either a female or male.

See pages 946–952.

See also EPIC, MYTH, PROTAGONIST, TRAGEDY.

High comedy *See COMEDY.*

Historical narrative A work of nonfiction that tells the story of important historical events or developments. James Cross Giblin's "A Brother's Crime" is an example of a historical narrative.

See pages 328 and 360.

Homeric epithet *See EPITHET.*

Humor The quality of a literary work that makes the characters and their situations seem funny, amusing, or ludicrous. Humor often points out human failings and the irony found in many situations. Humorous language includes sarcasm, exaggeration, and verbal irony. Humorous writing can be equally effective in fiction and nonfiction.

See also COMEDY, FARCE, PARODY, PUN, SATIRE.

Hyperbole A figure of speech that uses exaggeration to express strong emotion, make a point, or evoke humor. "You've asked me a million times" is an example of hyperbole.

See page 1186.

See also FIGURATIVE LANGUAGE, UNDERSTATEMENT.

I

Iamb A two-syllable metrical foot consisting of one unstressed syllable (˘) followed by one stressed syllable (ʹ), as in the word *divide.*

Iambic pentameter A specific poetic meter in which each line has five metric units, or feet, and each foot consists of an unstressed syllable (˘) followed by a stressed syllable (ʹ). The rhythm of a line of iambic pentameter would be indicated as shown in this example from Shakespeare's *Romeo and Juliet*:

> **Be pa / tient, for / the world / is broad / and wide.**

See page 690.

See also BLANK VERSE, METER, SCANSION.

Idiom An expression whose meaning is different from its literal meaning. Idioms are readily understood by native speakers but are often puzzling to nonnative speakers. Phrases such as "catch his eye," "turn the tables," "over the hill," and "keep tabs on" are idiomatic expressions in English. Idioms can add realism to dialogue in a story and contribute to characterization.

See page 1163.

See also COLLOQUIALISM, DIALECT.

Image archetype *See ARCHETYPE.*

Imagery Descriptive language that appeals to one or more of the five senses: sight, hearing, touch, taste, and smell. This use of sensory detail helps create an emotional response in the reader. For example, the following lines from Chitra Banerjee Divakaruni's "My Mother Combs My Hair" use imagery to make *silence* concrete:

> **We hold the silence**
> **tight between us**
> **like a live wire,**
> **like a strip of gold**
> **torn from a wedding brocade.**

See pages 6–7 and 508–514.

See also FIGURATIVE LANGUAGE.

Informal essay *See ESSAY.*

In medias res Latin phrase meaning "in the middle of things." A work of literature is said to start in medias res when the story begins in the middle of the action. A work of literature that starts in medias res skips the exposition and moves directly to the rising action.

Internal conflict *See CONFLICT.*

Inversion The reversal of the usual word order in a prose sentence or line of poetry. Writers use inversion to maintain rhyme scheme or meter, or to emphasize certain words or phrases. The following line from Shakespeare's *Romeo and Juliet* contains an example of inversion:

> **JULIET. So Romeo would, were he not <u>Romeo call'd</u>.**

See page 65.

See also STYLE.

Irony A contrast or discrepancy between appearance and reality, or between what is expected and what actually happens.

In *situational irony,* the actual outcome of a situation is the opposite of what is expected—as in the ending of O. Henry's "The Gift of the Magi."

In *verbal irony,* a person says one thing and means another. For example, in Poe's "The Cask of Amontillado," as Montresor leads Fortunato to his doom in the vaults, he says, "Come, we will go back ere it is too late. Your cough—," as if he were genuinely concerned about Fortunato.

In *dramatic irony,* the audience or reader knows information that characters do not. In Shakespeare's *Romeo and Juliet*, for example, the audience knows that Juliet is alive, while Romeo is convinced that she is dead.

See pages 78, 103, and 774.

See also PARADOX.

J

Journal A daily record of events kept by a participant in those events or a witness to them. A journal is usually less intimate than a diary and often emphasizes events rather than emotions. Patricia Hampl's "North Shore Mornings" is an example of a journal.

See pages 546–550.

See also NONFICTION.

Juxtaposition The placement of two or more distinct elements side by side in order to contrast or compare them. It is commonly used to evoke an emotional response in the reader. In her essay "Sayonara," Anne Morrow Lindbergh juxtaposes the way to say "good-bye" in several languages to prove that *Sayonara* is the most eloquent.

> **For *Sayonara,* literally translated, "Since it must be so," of all the good-byes I have heard is the most beautiful. Unlike the *Auf Wiedersehens* and *Au revoirs,* it does not try to cheat itself by any bravado "Till we meet again . . ."**

See page 487.

L

Language *See DICTION, FIGURATIVE LANGUAGE, IMAGERY, SENSORY DETAILS.*

Legend A traditional story handed down from past generations and believed to be based on real people and events. Legends usually celebrate the heroic qualities of a national or cultural leader. Because legends are the stories of the people, they are often expressions of the values or character of a nation.

See also EPIC, FABLE, FOLKLORE, HERO, MYTH, ORAL TRADITION.

Line The basic unit of poetry. A line consists of a word or a row of words. In metered poems, lines are measured by the number of feet they contain.

See pages 543 and 555.

See also FOOT, STANZA.

Literal language Language that is simple, straightforward, and free of embellishment. It is the opposite of figurative language, which conveys ideas indirectly.

See also DENOTATION.

Local color The use of specific details to re-create the language, customs, geography, and habits of a particular area. Isaac Bashevis Singer's short story "The Son from America" has many examples of local color.

> **The more prosperous villagers had kerosene lamps, but Berl and his wife did not believe in newfangled gadgets. What was wrong with a wick in a dish of oil? Only for the Sabbath would Berlcha buy three tallow candles at the store.**

See also DIALECT.

Low comedy *See COMEDY.*

Lyric poetry Poetry that expresses a speaker's personal thoughts and feelings. Lyric poems are usually short and musical. While the subject of a lyric poem might be an object, a person, or an event, the emphasis of the poem is on the experience of emotion. William Wordsworth's "I Wandered Lonely as a Cloud" is an example of a lyric poem.

See pages 610 and 612.

See also POETRY.

M

Magical realism Fiction that combines fantasy and realism. Magical realism inserts fantastic, sometimes humorous, events and details into a believable reality. Diana García's "The Flat of the Land" is an example of magical realism.

See page 268.

See also GENRE.

Memoir A type of narrative nonfiction that presents an author's personal experience of an event or a period in the writer's life. A memoir is usually written from the first-person point of view. It often emphasizes the person's thoughts and feelings, his or her relationships with other people, or the impact of significant historical events on his or her life. James Herriot's "A Case of Cruelty" is an example of a memoir.

See pages 364 and 374.

See also AUTOBIOGRAPHY.

Metaphor A figure of speech that makes a comparison between two seemingly unlike things. Unlike a *simile,* a metaphor implies an underlying similarity between the two and does not use the word *like* or *as.* In the following lines from Shakespeare's *Romeo and Juliet*, Romeo uses a metaphor to compare his lips to religious pilgrims:

> **My lips, two blushing pilgrims, ready stand**
> **To smooth that rough touch with a tender kiss.**

See pages 508–514, 575, 594, 625, and 1092.

See also ANALOGY, FIGURATIVE LANGUAGE, SIMILE.

Meter A regular pattern of stressed and unstressed syllables that gives a line of poetry a predictable rhythm. The unit of meter within a line is the *foot.* Each type of foot has a unique pattern of stressed (´) and unstressed (˘) syllables:

iamb (˘´) as in *complete*
trochee (/´) as in *trouble*
anapest (˘˘´) as *intervene*
dactyl (´˘˘) as in *majesty*
spondee (´´) as in *blue-green*

A particular meter is named for the type of foot and the number of feet per line. For example, *trimeter* has three feet per line, *tetrameter* has four feet, *pentameter* has five feet, and *hexameter* has six feet. William Wordsworth wrote "I Wandered Lonely as a Cloud" in iambic tetrameter:

> **I wan / dered lone / ly as / a cloud**
>
> **That floats / on high / o'er vales / and hills**

See pages 509–514, 529, and 1092.

See also FOOT, IAMBIC PENTAMETER, RHYTHM, SCANSION.

Monologue A long speech or written expression of thoughts by a character in a literary work. Friar Lawrence's summary of events in the final scene of Shakespeare's *Romeo and Juliet* is a monologue.

See pages 333, 746, and 773.

See also DIALOGUE, SOLILOQUY.

Mood The emotional quality of a literary work. A writer's choice of language, subject matter, setting, diction, and tone, as well as sound devices such as rhyme and rhythm, contributes to mood. Richard Connell sustains a tense, eerie mood throughout much of his short story "The Most Dangerous Game":

> **An apprehensive night crawled slowly by like a wounded snake, and sleep did not visit Rainsford, although the silence of a dead world was on the jungle.**

See pages 56, 64, and 86.

See also ATMOSPHERE, SETTING, TONE.

Moral A practical lesson about right and wrong conduct. In fables, the moral is stated directly; in other literary forms, it is often implied.

See also FABLE, PARABLE, THEME.

Motif A significant word, phrase, image, description, idea, or other element that is repeated throughout a literary work and is related to the theme. Fishing is a motif in W. D. Wetherell's "The Bass, the River, and Sheila Mant."

See pages 117 and 1036.

Motivation The stated or implied reason a character acts, thinks, or feels a certain way. Motivation may be an external circumstance or an internal moral or emotional impulse. In O. Henry's "The Gift of the Magi," Della is motivated to sell her hair by the desire to buy her husband a beautiful gift.

See pages 134, 721, and 1191.

Mystery A genre of fiction that follows a standard plot pattern—a crime is committed, and a detective searches for clues that will lead him or her to the criminal. Any story that relies on the unknown or the terrifying can be considered a mystery. "The Mystery of Hunter's Lodge" is an example of a mystery.

See pages 1112–1257.

See also FICTION, GENRE.

Myth A traditional story that deals with goddesses, gods, heroes, and supernatural forces. A myth may explain a belief, a custom, or a force of nature. Homer's *Odyssey* incorporates some of the most famous traditional myths of ancient Greece, such as the myth of the Sirens.

See pages 946–952, 1059, and 1067.

See also EPIC, FOLKLORE, LEGEND, ORAL TRADITION.

N

Narrative Writing or speech that tells a story. Driven by a *conflict,* or problem, a narrative unfolds event by event and leads to a *resolution.* The story is narrated, or told, by a *narrator* and can take the form of a novel, an essay, a poem, or a short story.

See also NARRATIVE POETRY, NARRATOR, PLOT.

Narrative essay *See ESSAY.*

Narrative poetry Verse that tells a story. Narrative poems are usually contrasted with *lyric poetry. Ballads, epics,* and *romances* are all types of narrative poetry. Robert Frost's "The Road Not Taken" is a narrative poem.

See also BALLAD, EPIC, LYRIC POETRY, NARRATIVE.

Narrator The person who tells a story. The narrator may be a character in the story, as in Truman Capote's "A Christmas Memory," or a character outside the story, as in Frank R. Stockton's "The Lady, or the Tiger?" Narrators are not always truthful. A narrator in a work of literature may be *reliable* or *unreliable.* Some unreliable narrators intentionally mislead readers. Others fail to understand the true meaning of the events they describe. Most stories with unreliable narrators are written in the first person.

See pages 3–8.

See also NARRATIVE, POINT OF VIEW, SPEAKER.

Nonfiction Literature about real people, places, and events. Among the categories of nonfiction are biographies, autobiographies, and essays. Maya Angelou's *All God's Children Need Traveling Shoes* is an example of nonfiction.

See also AUTOBIOGRAPHY, BIOGRAPHY, ESSAY, FICTION, MEMOIR.

Novel A book-length fictional prose narrative. Because of its length, a novel has greater potential to develop plot, character, setting, and theme than does a short story.

See also FICTION, PLOT, SHORT STORY.

O

Onomatopoeia The use of a word or phrase that imitates or suggests the sound of what it describes. Some examples are *mew, hiss, crack, swish, murmur,* and *buzz.*

See also SOUND DEVICES.

Oral tradition Literature that passes by word of mouth from one generation to the next. Oral literature was a way of recording the past, glorifying leaders, and teaching morals and traditions to young people. Epics such as Homer's *Odyssey* were originally passed on in this manner.

See also BALLAD, EPIC, FOLKLORE, LEGEND, MYTH.

Oxymoron A figure of speech in which opposite ideas are combined. For example, the following line from Act 1, Scene 1 of Shakespeare's *Romeo and Juliet* contains two oxymorons:

> **Why then, O brawling love, O loving hate . . .**

See also FIGURATIVE LANGUAGE, PARADOX.

P

Parable A simple story pointing to a moral or religious lesson. It differs from a fable in that the characters are usually people instead of animals. Shinichi Hoshi's "He–y, Come on Ou–t!" is a modern parable.

See also FABLE, MORAL.

Paradox A situation or statement that appears to be contradictory but is actually true, either in fact or in a figurative sense. These lines from Denise Levertov's "The Secret" contain a paradox:

> **I who don't know the**
> **secret wrote**
> **the line.**

See pages 318 and 615.

See also OXYMORON.

Parallelism The use of a series of words, phrases, or sentences that have similar grammatical form. Parallelism shows the relationship between ideas and helps emphasize thoughts. In his inaugural address, John F. Kennedy used many fine examples of parallelism, including the famous line:

And so, my fellow Americans, ask not what your country can do for you—ask what you can do for your country.

See pages 439, 445, and 553.

See also REPETITION.

Parody A humorous imitation of a literary work that aims to point out the work's shortcomings. A parody may imitate the plot, characters, or style of another work, usually through exaggeration. Bret Harte's "The Stolen Cigar Case" is a parody of Sherlock Holmes stories.

See pages 1249 and 1257.

See also COMEDY, FARCE, HUMOR, SATIRE.

Persona The person who is understood to be speaking or telling a story or another work. Whether the story is told by an omniscient narrator, as in Guy de Maupassant's "The Necklace," or by one of the characters, as in Amy Tan's "Rules of the Game," the narrator is not the author. The attitudes and beliefs of the persona may not be the same as those of the author.

See pages 248 and 255.

See also NARRATOR, POINT OF VIEW.

Personification A figure of speech in which an animal, an object, a force of nature, or an idea is given human characteristics. Juliet personifies night in this line from Act 3, Scene 2 of Shakespeare's *Romeo and Juliet*:

Come, gentle night; come, loving, black-brow'd night

See pages 578, 586, and 588.

See also APOSTROPHE, FIGURATIVE LANGUAGE.

Persuasion A type of writing, usually nonfiction, that attempts to convince readers to think or act in a particular way. Writers of persuasive works use appeals to logic, emotion, morality, and authority to sway their readers. John Dos Passos's "The American Cause" is an example of persuasive writing.

See pages 436–437.

See also ARGUMENT.

Persuasive essay *See ESSAY.*

Play A literary work of any length intended for performance onstage with actors assuming the roles of the characters and speaking the lines from a playwright's script.

See also DRAMA.

Plot The sequence of events in a narrative work. *Conflicts* are introduced in the *exposition,* the first stage of the plot. As the work progresses, *rising action* builds suspense and adds complications, which lead to the *climax,* or turning point. After the climax, which is the moment of highest emotional pitch or greatest suspense, come *the falling action* and *resolution,* sometimes called the *denouement,* which reveal the logical results of the climax.

See pages 2–8, 10–11, and 20.

See also CLIMAX, CONFLICT, DENOUEMENT, EXPOSITION, FALLING ACTION, FORESHADOWING, RESOLUTION, RISING ACTION.

Plot pattern archetype *See ARCHETYPE.*

Poetry A form of literary expression that differs from prose in emphasizing the line, rather than the sentence, as the unit of composition. Many other traditional characteristics of poetry apply to some poems but not to others. Some of these characteristics are emotional, imaginative language; use of figures of speech; division into stanzas; and the use of rhyme and regular meter.

See also FIGURATIVE LANGUAGE, METER, PROSE, RHYME, STANZA.

Point of view The perspective from which a story is told. In a story with *first-person* point of view, the narrator is a character in the story, referred to as "I." The reader sees everything through that character's eyes. Truman Capote's "A Christmas Memory" is told from the first-person point of view. In a story with *third-person limited* point of view, the narrator reveals the thoughts, feelings, and observations of only one character, referring to that character as "he" or "she," as in Diana García's "The Flat of the Land." In a story with *third-person omniscient,* or all-knowing, point of view, the narrator is not a character in the story but rather someone who stands outside the story and comments on the action. A third-person omniscient narrator knows everything about the characters and the events and may reveal details that the characters themselves could not reveal. Guy de Maupassant's "The Necklace" is told from the third-person omniscient point of view. Occasionally an author uses *second-person* point of view, addressing the reader or a character as "you."

See pages 3–8 and 206–207.

See also NARRATOR, SPEAKER.

Prologue An introductory section of a play, a speech, or another literary work. Shakespeare's *Romeo and Juliet* begins with a prologue.

Propaganda Written or spoken material designed to bring about a change or to damage a cause through use of emotionally charged words, name-calling, or other techniques.

Props A theater term (a shortened form of *properties*) for objects and elements of the scenery used in a stage play, movie, or television show.

See also STAGE DIRECTIONS.

Prose Literature that is written in sentence and paragraph form (as distinguished from poetry, which is arranged in lines and stanzas). Essays, short stories, novels, magazine articles, and most plays are examples of prose.

See also POETRY.

Protagonist The central character in a literary work, around whom the main conflict revolves. During the course of the literary work, the protagonist undergoes a conflict that is crucial to the plot. Generally, the reader or audience is meant to sympathize with the protagonist. Walter Mitty is the protagonist in James Thurber's story "The Secret Life of Walter Mitty."

See pages 106, 119, and 157.

See also ANTAGONIST, CHARACTER, CONFLICT, HERO.

Pun A humorous play on words. Puns usually involve words that are similar in sound (*merry* and *marry*) or a word that has several meanings. In Act 3, Scene 1 of Shakespeare's *Romeo and Juliet*, when Mercutio is fatally wounded, he says, "Ask for me tomorrow, and you shall find me a grave man," meaning both serious and dead.

See also HUMOR.

Q

Quatrain A four-line stanza. The quatrain is the most common stanza form in English poetry. It may be unrhymed or have a variety of rhyme schemes.

See also COUPLET, SONNET, STANZA.

R

Reflective essay *See ESSAY.*

Refrain A line or lines repeated at intervals in a poem or song, usually at the end of a stanza. In Paul Laurence Dunbar's "I Know Why the Caged Bird Sings," the line "I know why the caged bird sings" serves as a refrain.

See page 603.

See also REPETITION.

Reliable narrator *See NARRATOR.*

Repetition The recurrence of sounds, words, phrases, lines, or stanzas in a speech or literary work. Writers use repetition to emphasize an important point, to expand upon an idea, to help create rhythm, and to increase the feeling of unity in a work. In her poem "Remember," Joy Harjo uses repetition to emphasize the importance of remembering where one comes from.

See pages 439 and 606.

See also PARALLELISM, RHETORICAL DEVICES, RHYME.

Resolution Also called the *denouement,* a French word meaning "unknotting," the resolution is the part of a plot that concludes the falling action by revealing or suggesting the outcome of the conflict.

See also CONFLICT, FALLING ACTION, PLOT.

Rhetorical devices Persuasive techniques used by public speakers and writers of literary works, especially those written to persuade. Rhetorical devices include repetition, parallelism, analogy, logic, and the skillful use of connotation and anecdote. Effective rhetoric often appeals to logic, emotion, morality, or authority.

See pages 439, 444, and 456.

See also ANALOGY, ANECDOTE, ARGUMENT, CONNOTATION, PARALLELISM, PERSUASION, REPETITION.

Rhyme The repetition of the same stressed vowel sounds and any succeeding sounds in two or more words. *End rhyme* occurs at the ends of lines of poetry. *Internal rhyme* occurs within a single line. *Slant rhyme* occurs when words include sounds that are similar but not identical (*jackal* and *buckle*). Slant rhyme typically involves some variation of *consonance* (the repetition of similar consonant sounds) or *assonance* (the repetition of similar vowel sounds).

See pages 509–514 and 522.

See also ASSONANCE, CONSONANCE, RHYME SCHEME, SOUND DEVICES.

Rhyme scheme The pattern that end rhymes form in a stanza or poem. Rhyme scheme is designated by the assignment of a different letter of the alphabet to each new rhyme. William Wordsworth used the following rhyme scheme for his six-line stanzas in "I Wandered Lonely as a Cloud":

I wandered lonely as a cloud	a
That floats on high o'er vales and hills,	b
When all at once I saw a crowd,	a
A host, of golden daffodils;	b
Beside the lake, beneath the trees,	c
Fluttering and dancing in the breeze.	c

See page 517.

See also RHYME.

Rhythm The pattern of beats created by the arrangement of stressed and unstressed syllables, especially in poetry. Rhythm gives poetry a musical quality. It can also emphasize certain words or ideas to help convey meaning. Rhythm can be *regular,* with a predictable pattern or meter, or *irregular.*

See pages 509–514 and 1092.

See also BLANK VERSE, FOOT, IAMBIC PENTAMETER, METER, SCANSION.

Rising action The part of a plot where complications to the conflict develop and increase reader interest.

See also PLOT.

Round character *See CHARACTER.*

S

Satire Writing that uses humor or wit to ridicule the vices or follies of people or societies, often to bring about change or improvement. Satire uses devices such as *exaggeration, understatement,* and *irony.* Eugène Ionesco's play *The Leader* is a satire.

See also COMEDY, FARCE, HUMOR, PARODY, SARCASM, WIT.

Scansion The analysis of the meter of a line of verse. To scan a line of poetry means to note the stressed (´) and unstressed (˘) syllables and to divide the line into its feet, or rhythmic units. Note the scansion of these lines from William Wordsworth's "I Wandered Lonely as a Cloud":

I wan / dered lone / ly as / a cloud

That floats / on high / o'er vales / and hills

See page 517.

See also FOOT, METER, RHYTHM.

Scene A subdivision of an act in a play. Each scene usually takes place in a specific setting and time.

See page 821.

See also ACT, DRAMA.

Science fiction Fiction that deals with the impact of science and technology–real or imagined–on society and on individuals. Sometimes occurring in the future, science fiction commonly portrays space travel, exploration of other planets, and future societies. Arthur C. Clarke's short story "The Sentinel" is an example of science fiction.

See also FANTASY, GENRE.

Sensory details Evocative words or phrases that convey sensory experiences–seeing, hearing, tasting, touching, and smelling. Sensory details make writing come alive by helping readers experience what is being described.

See also IMAGERY.

Setting The time and place in which the events of a literary work occur. Setting includes not only the physical surroundings but also the ideas, customs, values, and beliefs of a particular time and place. Setting often helps create an atmosphere or a mood. Judith Ortiz Cofer's "American History" is set in Paterson, New Jersey, on November 22, 1963, the day John F. Kennedy was assassinated.

See pages 10, 75, 240, and 904.

See also ATMOSPHERE, MOOD.

Short story A brief fictional narrative in prose. A short story usually focuses on a single event and has only a few characters. Elements of the short story include *setting, characters, plot, point of view,* and *theme.*

See also FICTION, NOVEL, PLOT.

Simile A figure of speech that uses *like* or *as* to compare seemingly unlike things. For example, this simile appears in Truman Capote's "A Christmas Memory":

She is small and sprightly, like a bantam hen.

See pages 575, 597, 649, and 652.

See also ANALOGY, EPIC SIMILE, FIGURATIVE LANGUAGE, METAPHOR.

Situational irony *See IRONY.*

Slant rhyme *See RHYME.*

Soliloquy A dramatic device in which a character, alone onstage (or while under the impression of being alone), reveals his or her private thoughts and feelings as if thinking aloud. An example of a soliloquy may be found in Act 2, Scene 2 of Shakespeare's *Romeo and Juliet*, in the speech by Romeo that begins: "But soft! What light through yonder window breaks?"

See pages 746 and 773.

See also ASIDE, MONOLOGUE.

Sonnet A lyric poem of fourteen lines, typically written in iambic pentameter and usually following strict patterns of stanza division and rhyme.

The *Shakespearean sonnet,* also called the *English sonnet,* consists of three *quatrains,* or four-line stanzas, followed by a *couplet,* or pair of rhyming lines. The rhyme scheme is typically *abab cdcd efef gg.* The couplet often presents a conclusion to the issues or questions presented in the three quatrains.

In the *Petrarchan sonnet,* also called the *Italian sonnet,* fourteen lines are divided into two stanzas, the eight-line *octave* and the six-line *sestet.* The sestet usually responds to a question or situation posed by the octave. The rhyme scheme is typically *abbaabba cdcdcd* or *abbaabba cdecde.*

See also COUPLET, LYRIC POETRY, RHYME SCHEME, STANZA.

Sound devices Techniques used to emphasize particular sounds in writing. Writers use sound devices, such as *alliteration* or *rhyme,* to underscore the meaning of certain words, to enhance rhythm, and to add to the musical quality of the work.

See pages 509–514, 621, and 806.

See also ALLITERATION, ASSONANCE, CONSONANCE, ONOMATOPOEIA, RHYME, RHYTHM.

Speaker The voice that communicates with the reader of a poem, similar to the narrator in a work of prose. Sometimes the speaker's voice is that of the poet, sometimes that of a fictional person or even a thing. The speaker's words communicate a particular tone, or attitude, toward the subject of the poem. One should never assume that the speaker and the writer are the same. The speaker in Margaret Walker's poem "Lineage" is a granddaughter who is in awe of the strength of her grandmothers.

See pages 525, 527, and 594.

See also NARRATOR, TONE.

Stage directions Instructions written by a playwright that describe the appearance and actions of characters, as well as the sets, props, costumes, sound effects, and lighting for a play.

See pages 682–688.

See also DRAMA, PROPS.

Stanza A group of lines forming a unit in a poem or song. A stanza in a poem is similar to a paragraph in prose. Typically, stanzas in a poem are separated by a line of space.

See pages 508–514, 516, and 543.

See also COUPLET, QUATRAIN, SONNET.

Stereotype A generalization about a group of people that is made without regard for individual differences. In literature, this term is often used to describe a conventional or flat character who conforms to an expected, fixed pattern of behavior. The rebellious teenager is a stereotype.

See also CHARACTER.

Stock character A character who represents a type that is recognizable as belonging to a particular genre. For example, a cruel stepmother or charming prince is often found in fairy tales. Valiant knights and heroes are found in legends and myths. The hard-boiled detective is found in detective stories. Stock characters have conventional traits and mannerisms shared by all members of their type. Gandalf in J. R. R. Tolkien's *The Hobbit* is an example of a stock character: the wise wizard.

See pages 107, 837, and 1036.

See also ARCHETYPE, CHARACTER, STEREOTYPE.

Stream of consciousness The literary representation of an author's or a character's free-flowing thoughts, feelings, and memories. Stream-of-consciousness writing does not always employ conventional sentence structure or other rules of grammar and usage.

Structure The particular order or pattern a writer uses to present ideas. For example, narratives sometimes follow a chronological order. Listing detailed information, comparing and contrasting, analyzing cause-and-effect relationships, or describing a problem and then offering a solution are some other ways a writer can structure a text. Poetic structure—more commonly known as *form*—refers to the organization of words, lines, and images, as well as of ideas.

See pages 10–11, 416, and 516–517.

See also FORM.

Style The expressive qualities that distinguish an author's work, including word choice, sentence structure, and figures of speech.

See pages 43, 65, 349, 807, and 1221.

See also AUTHOR'S PURPOSE, DICTION, IMAGERY, TONE, VOICE.

Subject The topic of a literary work.

Surprise ending An unexpected plot twist at the end of a story. The ending might surprise readers because the author provided misleading clues or withheld important information. O. Henry's "The Gift of the Magi" and Richard Connell's "The Most Dangerous Game" both have surprise endings.

See pages 23–43 and 121–130.

Suspense A feeling of curiosity, uncertainty, or even dread about what is going to happen next in a story. To build suspense, an author may create a threat to the central character or use *foreshadowing*. Suspense is especially important in the plot of an adventure or a mystery story. Edgar Allan Poe's "The Cask of Amontillado" is an example of a suspenseful story. The reader, like Fortunato, is led through the catacombs and is kept "in the dark" until the very end about what sort of revenge the narrator will take.

See pages 2–8 and 23.

See also FORESHADOWING, MOOD.

Symbol Any person, animal, place, object, or event that exists on a literal level within a work but also represents something on a figurative level. In O. Henry's story "The Gift of the Magi," Della's hair is the symbol of her beauty.

See pages 122, 130, and 229.

See also ALLEGORY, FIGURATIVE LANGUAGE.

T

Tall tale A wildly imaginative story, usually passed down orally, about the fantastic adventures or amazing feats of folk heroes in realistic local settings. Mark Twain's "Baker's Bluejay Yarn" is an example of a tall tale.

See also FOLKLORE.

Teleplay The script of a drama written for television, which, in addition to dialogue and stage directions, usually contains detailed instructions about camera shots and angles. Paddy Chayefsky wrote *Marty* for television, so the script contains instructions about how the play should be filmed.

> ***Dissolve to: Live shot—a row of stags along a wall. Camera is looking lengthwise down the row.***

See also STAGE DIRECTIONS.

Theater of the absurd Drama, primarily of the 1950s and 1960s, that does not contain a plot but instead presents a series of scenes in which the characters speak in meaningless conversations or perform actions with little purpose. The central concern of this drama is to show that people are helpless or confused in an alienating world. French playwright Eugène Ionesco was a leading writer of this type of drama.

See pages 887 and 894.

See also DRAMA.

Theme The main idea or message of a story, poem, novel, or play often expressed as a general statement about life. Some works have a *stated theme,* which is expressed directly. More commonly, works have an *implied theme,* which is revealed gradually through other elements such as plot, character, setting, point of view, and symbol. A literary work may have more than one theme. Themes and subjects are different. The subject of a work might be love; the theme would be what the writer says about love—for example, love is cruel; love is wonderful; or love is fleeting.

See pages 2–8, 140, 270, and 278.

See also AUTHOR'S PURPOSE, FABLE, MORAL.

Theme archetype *See ARCHETYPE.*

Thesis The main idea of an essay or another work of nonfiction. The thesis may be implied but is commonly stated directly.

See pages 410 and 413.

See also ESSAY, NONFICTION.

Title The name given to a literary work. The title can help explain the setting, provide insight into the theme, or describe the action that will take place in the work.

See pages 311 and 317.

Tone An author's attitude toward his or her subject matter. Tone is conveyed through elements such as word choice, rhythm, sentence structure, and figures of speech. A writer's tone may convey a variety of attitudes, such as sympathy, objectivity, seriousness, irony, sadness, bitterness, or humor. James Thurber's amused, affectionate tone in "The Secret Life of Walter Mitty" contrasts with Margaret Atwood's ironic tone in "Waiting."

See pages 258, 352, 462, and 536.

See also ATMOSPHERE, AUTHOR'S PURPOSE, DICTION, MOOD, NARRATOR, SPEAKER, STYLE, VOICE.

Tragedy A play in which a main character suffers a downfall. That character, the *tragic hero*, is typically a person of dignified or heroic stature. The downfall may result from outside forces or from a weakness within the character, which is known as a *tragic flaw.* In Shakespeare's *Romeo and Juliet,* the two young lovers—joint heroes of the play—meet their fates in part because of their own uncontrolled passions.

See pages 690–691.

See also DRAMA, HERO.

Tragic Hero See TRAGEDY.

U

Understatement Language that makes something seem less important than it really is. Understatement may be used to add humor or to focus the reader's attention on something the author wants to emphasize. In "Field Trip," Naomi Shihab Nye uses understatement when she says that the woman who cut off her finger was "distracted."

See also HYPERBOLE.

Unreliable narrator *See NARRATOR.*

V

Verbal irony *See IRONY.*

Verse paragraph A group of lines in a poem that form a unit. Unlike a stanza, a verse paragraph does not have a fixed number of lines. While poems written before the twentieth century usually contain stanzas, many contemporary poems are made up of verse paragraphs. Verse paragraphs help to organize a poem into thoughts, as paragraphs help to organize prose.

See also FREE VERSE, STANZA.

Voice The distinctive use of language that conveys the author's or narrator's personality to the reader. Voice is determined by elements of style such as word choice and tone.

See page 278.

See also DICTION, NARRATOR, STYLE, TONE.

W

Word choice *See DICTION.*

The Reading Process

Being an active reader is a crucial part of being a lifelong learner. It is also an ongoing task. Good reading skills are recursive; that is, they build on each other, providing the tools you'll need to understand text, to connect selections to your own life, to interpret ideas and themes, and to read critically.

Vocabulary Development

To develop a rich vocabulary, consider these four important steps:

- **Read** a wide variety of texts.
- **Enjoy** and engage in wordplay and word investigation.
- **Listen** carefully to how others use words.
- **Participate** regularly in good classroom discussions.

Using context to discover meaning

When you look at the words and sentences surrounding a new word, you are using context. **Look** before, at, and after a new word or phrase. **Connect** what you know with what an author has written. Then **guess** at a possible meaning. **Try again** if your guess does not make sense. Consider these strategies for using context:

- Look for a synonym or an antonym nearby to provide a clue to the word's meaning.
- Notice if the text relates the word's meaning to another word.
- Check for a description of an action associated with the word.
- Try to find a general topic or idea related to the word.

Using word parts and word origins

Consider these basic elements when taking a word apart to determine meaning:

- **Base words** Locate the most basic part of a word to predict a core meaning.
- **Prefixes** Look at syllables attached before a base that add to or change a meaning.
- **Suffixes** Look at syllables added to the end of a base word that create new meanings.

Also consider **word origins**—Latin, Greek, and Anglo-Saxon roots—that are the basis for much of English vocabulary. Knowing these roots can help you determine derivations and spellings, as well as meanings in English.

Using reference materials

When using context and analyzing word parts do not help to unlock the meaning of a word, go to a reference source such as a dictionary, a glossary, a thesaurus, or even the Internet. Use these tips:

- **Locate** a word by using the guide words at the top of the pages.
- **Look** at the parts of the reference entry, such as part of speech, definition, or synonym.
- **Choose** between multiple meanings by thinking about what makes sense.
- **Apply** the meaning to what you're reading.

Distinguishing between meanings

Determining subtle differences between word meanings also aids comprehension. **Denotation** refers to the dictionary meaning or meanings of a word. **Connotation** refers to an emotion or underlying value that accompanies a word's dictionary meaning. The word *fragrance* has a different connotation from the word *odor,* even though the denotation of both words is "smell."

Comprehension Strategies

Because understanding is the most critical reading task, lifelong learners use a variety of reading strategies before, during, and after reading to ensure their comprehension.

Establishing and adjusting purposes for reading

To establish a purpose for reading, preview or **skim** a selection by glancing quickly over the entire piece, reading headings and subheadings, and noticing the organizational pattern of the text.

If you are reading to learn, solve a problem, or perform a task involving complex directions, consider these tips:

- Read slowly and carefully.
- Reread difficult passages.
- Take careful notes or construct a graphic.

Adjust your strategies as your purpose changes. To locate specific information in a longer selection, or to enjoy an entertaining plot, you might allow yourself a faster pace. Know when to speed up or slow down to maintain your understanding.

Drawing on personal background

When you recall information and personal experiences that are uniquely your own, you **draw on your personal background.** By thus **activating prior knowledge,** and combining it with the words on a page, you create meaning in a selection. To expand and extend your prior knowledge, share it interactively in classroom discussions.

Monitoring and modifying reading strategies

Check or **monitor your understanding** as you read, using the following strategies:

- Summarize
- Clarify
- Question
- Predict what will come next

You can use these four important steps once or twice in an easy, entertaining passage or after every paragraph in a conceptually dense nonfiction selection. As you read, think about asking interesting questions, rather than passively waiting to answer questions your teacher may ask later.

All readers find that understanding sometimes breaks down when material is difficult. Consider these steps to modify or change your reading strategies when you don't understand what you've read:

- Reread the passage.
- Consult other sources, including text resources, teachers, and other students.
- Write comments or questions on another piece of paper for later review or discussion.

Constructing graphic organizers

Graphic organizers, such as charts, maps, and diagrams, help you construct ideas in a visual way so you can remember them later. Look at the following model. Like a Venn diagram, which compares and contrasts two ideas or characters, a **semantic features analysis** focuses on the discriminating features of ideas or words. The items or ideas you want to compare are listed down the side, and the discriminating features are listed across the top. In each box, use a + if the feature or characteristic applies to the item or a – if the feature or characteristic does not apply.

People in Government	Elected	Appointed	Passes Laws	Vetoes Laws
President	+	–	–	+
State Governor	+	–	–	+
Supreme Court Justice	–	+	–	–
Secretary of Defense	–	+	–	–

A **flowchart** helps you keep track of the sequence of events. Arrange ideas or events in a logical, sequential order. Then draw arrows between your ideas to indicate how one idea or event flows into another. Look at the following flowchart to see how you might show the chronological sequence of a story. Use a flowchart to make a **change frame,** recording causes and effects in sequence to illustrate how something changed.

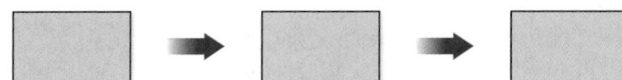

A **web** can be used for a variety of purposes as you read a selection.

- To **map out the main idea and details** of a selection, put the main idea in the middle circle and, as you read, add supporting details around the main thought.
- To **analyze a character in a story,** put the character's name in the middle and add that character's actions, thoughts, reputation, plot involvement, and personal development in the surrounding circles.
- To **define a concept,** put a word or an idea in the middle circle and then add a more general category, descriptions, examples, and non-examples in the surrounding circles.

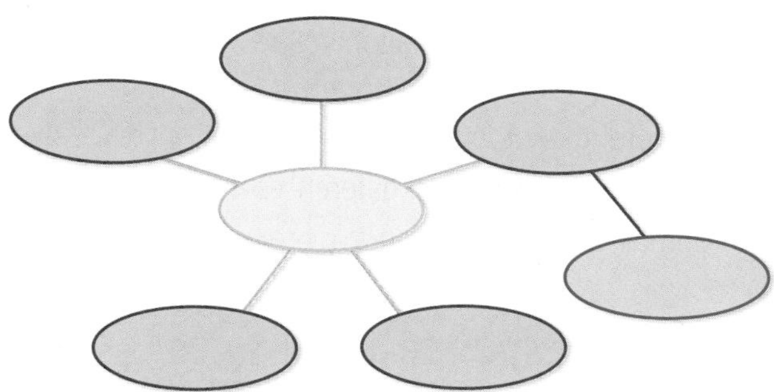

Analyzing text structures

To follow the logic and message of a selection and to remember it, analyze the **text structure,** or organization of ideas, within a writer's work. In narrative as well as in informational text, writers may embed one structure within another, but it is usually possible to identify one main pattern of organization. Recognizing the pattern of organization can help you discover the writer's purpose and will focus your attention on the important ideas in the selection. **Look for signal words** to point you to the structure.

- **Chronological order** often uses words such as *first, then, after, later*, and *finally*.
- **Cause-and-effect order** can include words or phrases such as *therefore, because, subsequently,* or *as a result of*.
- **Comparison-contrast order** may use words or phrases such as *similarly, in contrast, likewise,* or *on the other hand*.

Interpreting graphic aids

Graphic aids provide an opportunity to see and analyze information at a glance. Charts, tables, maps, and diagrams allow you to analyze and compare information. Maps include a compass rose, legend, and scale to help you interpret direction, symbols, and size. Charts and graphs compare information in categories running horizontally and vertically.

Tips for Reading Graphic Aids

- Examine the title, labels, and other explanatory features.
- Apply the labels to the graphic aid.
- Interpret the information.

Look carefully at the models below.

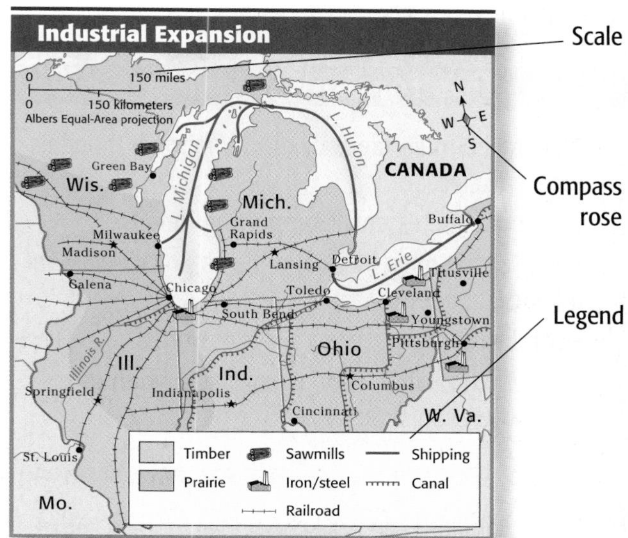

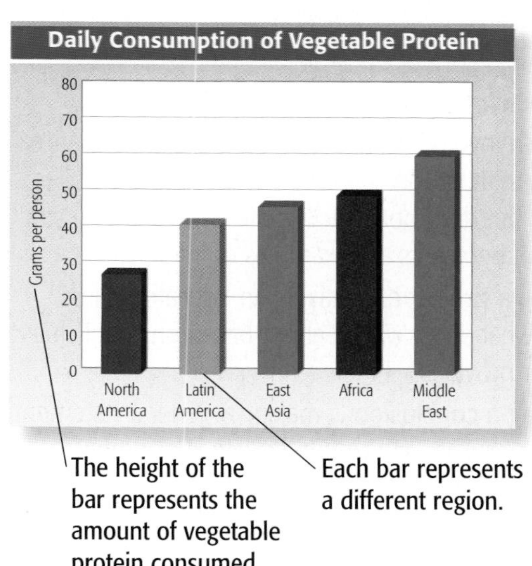

Sequencing

The order in which thoughts are arranged is called a **sequence**. A good sequence is one that is logical, given the ideas in a selection. **Chronological order, spatial order,** and **order of importance** are common forms of sequencing. Think about the order of a writer's thoughts as you read and pay particular attention to sequence when **following complex written directions**.

Summarizing

A summary is a short restatement of the main ideas and important details of a selection. Summarizing what you have read is an excellent tool for understanding and remembering a passage.

Tips for Summarizing

- Identify the **main ideas** or most important thoughts within a selection.
- Determine the essential **supporting details.**
- Relate all the main ideas and the essential details in a **logical sequence.**
- **Paraphrase**–that is, use your own words.
- Answer **who, what, why, where,** and **when** questions when you summarize.

The best summaries can easily be understood by someone who has not read the selection. If you're not sure whether an idea is a main idea or a detail, try taking it out of your summary. Does your summary still sound complete?

Drawing inferences and supporting them

An **inference** involves using your reason and experience to come up with an idea based on what a writer implies or suggests but does not directly state. The following strategic reading behaviors are examples of inference:

- **Making a prediction** is taking an educated guess about what a text will be about based on initial clues a writer provides.
- **Drawing a conclusion** is making a general statement you can explain with reason or with supporting details from a text.
- **Making a generalization** is generating a statement that can apply to more than one item or group.

What is most important when inferring is to be sure that you have accurately based your thoughts on supporting details from the text as well as on your own knowledge.

Reading silently for sustained periods

When you read for long periods of time, your task is to avoid distractions. Check your comprehension regularly by summarizing what you've read so far. Using study guides or graphic organizers can help get you through difficult passages. Take regular breaks when you need them and vary your reading rate with the demands of the task.

Synthesizing information

You will often need to read across texts; that is, in different sources, combining or **synthesizing** what you've learned from varied sources to suit your purposes. Follow these suggestions:

- Understand the information you've read in each source.
- Interpret the information.
- Identify similarities and differences in ideas or logic.
- Combine like thoughts in a logical sequence.

Literary Response

Whenever you share your thoughts and feelings about something you've read, you are responding to text. While the way you respond may vary with the type of text you read and with your individual learning style, as a strategic reader you will always need to adequately support your responses with proof from the text.

Responding to informational and aesthetic elements

When you respond both intellectually *and* emotionally, you connect yourself with a writer and with other people. To respond in an intellectual way, ask yourself if the ideas you have read are logical and well supported. To respond emotionally, ask yourself how you feel about those ideas and events. Choose a way to respond that fits your learning style. Class discussions, journal entries, oral interpretations, enactments, and graphic displays are some of the many ways to share your thoughts and emotions about a writer's work.

Comparing responses with authoritative views

Critics' reviews may encourage you to read a book, see a movie, or attend an event. They may also warn you that whatever is reviewed is not acceptable entertainment or is not valued by the reviewer. Deciding whether to value a review depends on the credibility of the reviewer and also on your own personal views and feelings. Ask yourself the following questions:

- What is the reviewer's background?
- What qualifies the reviewer to write this evaluation?
- Is the review balanced? Does it include both positive and negative responses?
- Are arguments presented logically?
- Are opinions supported with facts?
- What bias does this reviewer show?
- Do I agree? Why or why not?

Analysis and Evaluation

Good readers want to do more than recall information or interpret thoughts and ideas. When you read, read critically, forming opinions about characters and ideas, and making judgments using your own prior knowledge and information from the text.

Analyzing characteristics of texts

To be a critical reader and thinker, start by analyzing the characteristics of the text. Think about what specific characteristics make a particular selection clear, concise, and complete. Ask yourself these questions:

- What **pattern of organization** has this writer used to present his or her thoughts? Cause/effect? Comparison/contrast? Problem/solution? Does this organization make the main ideas clear or vague? Why?
- What word order, or **syntax,** gives force and emphasis to this writer's ideas? Does the grammatical order of the words make ideas sound complete, or is the sentence structure confusing?
- What **word choices** reveal this writer's tone, or attitude about the topic? Is the language precise or too general? Is it economical and yet descriptive?

Evaluating the credibility of sources

Evaluating the credibility of a source involves making a judgment about whether a writer is knowledgeable and truthful. Consider the following steps:

- **Decide on the writer's purpose or motive.** What will the writer gain if you accept his or her ideas or if you act on his or her suggestions?
- **Investigate the writer's background.** How has the writer become an authority in his or her field? Do others value what he or she says?
- **Evaluate the writer's statements.** Is the writer's information factual? Can it be proved? Are opinions clearly stated as such? Are they adequately supported with details so that they are valid? Are any statements nonfactual? Check to be sure.

Analyzing logical arguments and modes of reasoning

When you analyze works you've read, ask yourself whether the reasoning behind a writer's works is logical. Two kinds of logical reasoning are

Inductive Reasoning By observing a limited number of particular cases, a reader arrives at a general or universal statement. This logic moves from the specific to the general.

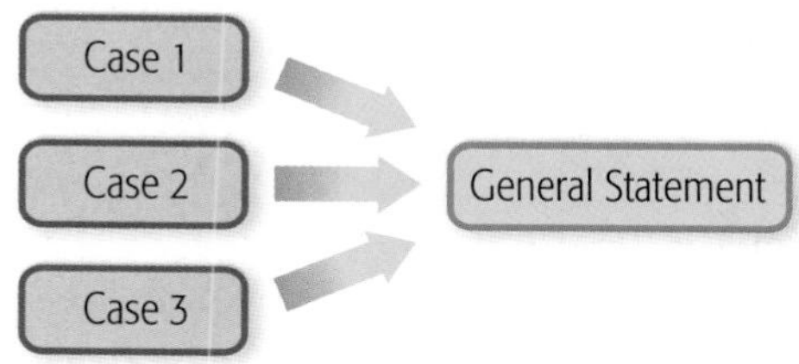

Deductive Reasoning This logic moves from the general to the specific. The reader takes a general statement and, through reasoning, applies it to specific situations.

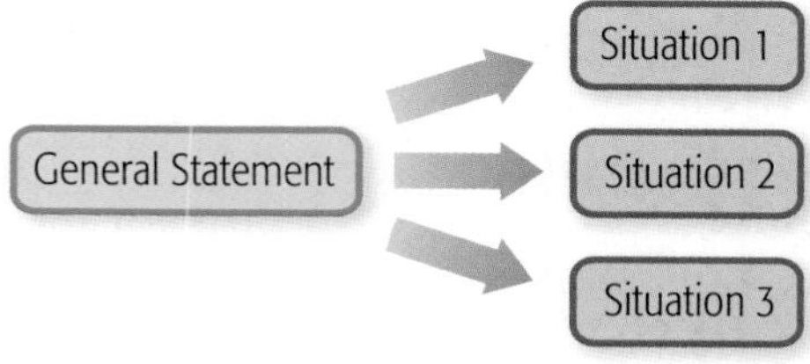

READING HANDBOOK

READING HANDBOOK

Faulty reasoning, on the other hand, is vague and illogical. Look for either/or reasoning or oversimplified statements when analyzing faulty reasoning. Failure to understand a writer's work may be the result of poorly presented, unsupported arguments, sequenced in a haphazard way.

A writer shows **bias** when he or she demonstrates a strong personal, and sometimes unreasonable, opinion. Look for bias when evaluating editorials, documentaries, and advertisements.

Writers use **persuasive techniques** when they try to get readers to believe a certain thing or act in a particular way. A writer may have a strong personal bias and still compose a persuasive essay that is logical and well supported. On the other hand, deceptive arguments can be less than accurate in order to be persuasive. Read carefully to judge whether a writer's bias influences his or her writing in negative or positive ways.

by Dinah Zike, M.Ed., Creator of Foldables™

Reading and Thinking with Foldables™

by Dinah Zike, M.Ed., Creator of Foldables™

Using Foldables™ Makes Learning Easy and Enjoyable

Anyone who has paper, scissors, and a stapler or some glue can use Foldables in the classroom. Just follow the illustrated step-by-step directions. Check out the following sample:

Reading Objective: to understand how one character's actions affect other characters in a short story

Use this Foldable to keep track of what the main character does and how his or her actions affect the other characters.

Practice reading and following step-by-step directions.

1. Place a sheet of paper in front of you so that the short side is at the top. Fold the paper in half from top to bottom.
2. Fold in half again, from side to side, to divide the paper into two columns. Unfold the paper so that the two columns show.
3. Draw a line along the column crease. Then, through the top layer of paper, cut along the line you drew, forming two tabs.
4. Label the tabs ***Main character's actions*** and ***Effects on others.***
5. As you read, record the main character's actions under the first tab. Record how each of those actions affects other characters under the second tab.

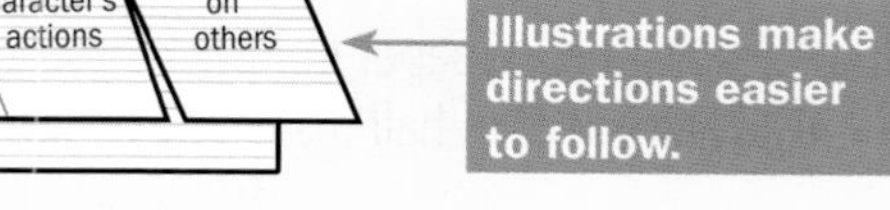

Illustrations make directions easier to follow.

Become an active reader, tracking and reorganizing information so that you can better comprehend the selection.

Short Story

Reading Objective: to analyze a short story on the basis of its literary elements

As you read, use the following Foldable to keep track of five literary elements in the short story.

1. Stack three sheets of paper with their top edges about a half-inch apart. Be sure to keep the side edges straight.
2. Fold up the bottom edges of the paper to form six tabs, five of which will be the same size.
3. Crease the paper to hold the tabs in place and staple the sheets together along the crease.
4. Turn the sheets so that the stapled side is at the top. Write the title of the story on the top tab. Label the five remaining tabs ***Setting, Characters, Plot, Point of View,*** and ***Theme.***
5. Use your Foldable as you read the short story. Under each labeled tab, jot down notes about the story in terms of that element.

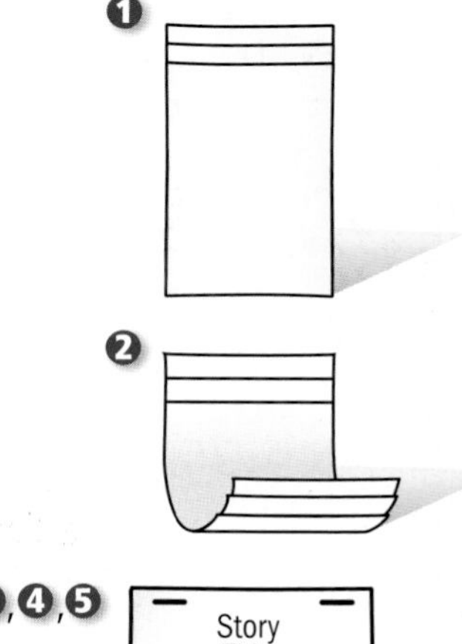

You may adapt this simple Foldable in several ways.

- Use it with dramas, longer works of fiction, and some narrative poems—wherever five literary elements are present in the story.
- Change the labels to focus on something different. For example, if a story or a play has several settings, characters, acts, or scenes, you could devote a tab to each one.

Drama

Reading Objective: to understand conflict and plot in a drama

As you read the drama, use the following Foldable to keep track of conflicts that arise and ways that those conflicts are resolved.

1. Place a sheet of paper in front of you so that the short side is at the top. Fold the paper in half from side to side.
2. Fold the paper again, one inch from the top as shown here.
3. Unfold the paper and draw lines along all of the folds. This will be your chart.
4. At the top, label the left column ***Conflicts*** and the right column ***Resolutions.***
5. As you read, record in the left column the various conflicts that arise in the drama. In the right column, explain how each conflict is resolved by the end of the drama.

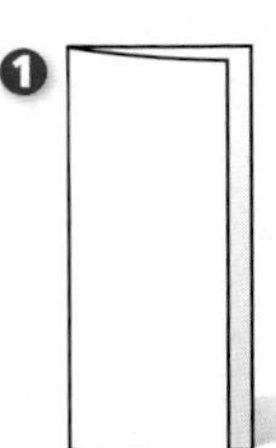

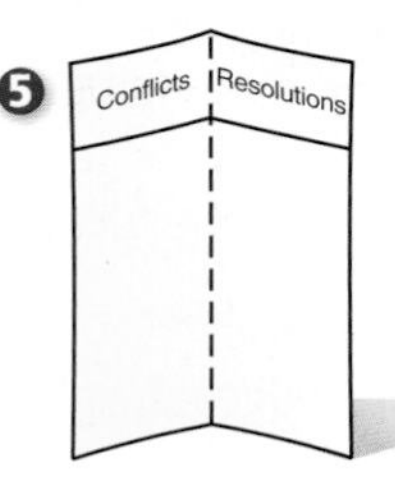

You may adapt this simple Foldable in several ways.

- Use it with short stories, longer works of fiction, and many poems—wherever conflicts and their resolutions are important.
- Change the labels to focus on something different. For example, you could record the actions of two characters, or you could record the thoughts and feelings of a character before and after the story's climax.

Lyric Poem

Reading Objective: to interpret the poet's message by understanding the speaker's thoughts and feelings

As you read the poem, use the following Foldable to help you distinguish between what the speaker *says* and what the poet *means*.

1. Place a sheet of paper in front of you so that the short side is at the top. Fold the paper in half from top to bottom.
2. Fold the paper in half again from left to right.
3. Unfold and cut through the top layer of paper along the fold line. This will make two tabs.
4. Label the left tab ***Speaker's Words.*** Label the right tab ***Poet's Meaning.***
5. Use your Foldable to jot down notes on as you read the poem. Under the left tab, write down key things the speaker says. Under the right tab, write down what you think the poet means by having the speaker say those things.

You may adapt this simple Foldable in several ways.

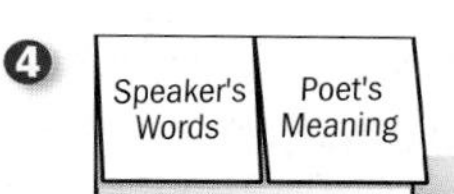

- Use it to help you visualize the images in a poem. Just replace ***Speaker's Words*** with ***Imagery*** and replace ***Poet's Meaning*** with ***What I See.***
- Replace the label ***Speaker's Words*** with ***Speaker's Tone*** and under that tab write adjectives that describe the tone of the speaker's words.
- If the poem you are reading has two stanzas, you might devote each tab to notes about one stanza.

Informational Text

Reading Objective: to understand and remember ideas in informational text

As you read a nonfiction selection, use this Foldable to help you identify what you already know about the topic, what you might want to know about it, and what you learn about it from the selection.

1. Hold a sheet of paper in front of you so that the short side is at the top. Fold the bottom of the paper up and the top down to divide the paper into thirds.
2. Unfold the paper and turn it so that the long side is at the top. Draw lines along the folds and label the three columns ***Know, Want to Know,*** and ***Learned.***
3. Before you read the selection, write what you already know about the topic under the left heading and what you want to know about it under the middle heading. As you read, jot down what you learn about the topic under the last heading.

❶

❷,❸

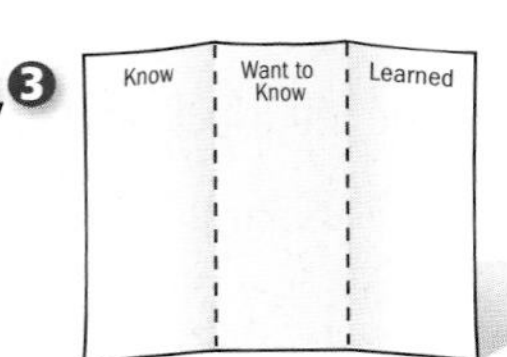

You may adapt this simple Foldable in several ways.

- Use it with magazine and newspaper articles, textbook chapters, reference articles, and informational Web sites–anything you might read to look for information.
- Use this three-part Foldable to record information from three sources. Label each column with the name of one source and write notes from that source under its heading.
- For a two-column Foldable, just fold the sheet of paper in half. For four columns, fold it in half and then in half again.

The Writing Process

Writing is a process with five stages: *prewriting, drafting, revising, editing/ proofreading,* and *publishing/presenting.* These stages often overlap, and their importance, weight, and even their order vary according to your needs and goals. Because writing is recursive, you almost always have to double back somewhere in this process, perhaps to gather more information or to reevaluate your ideas.

The Writing Process

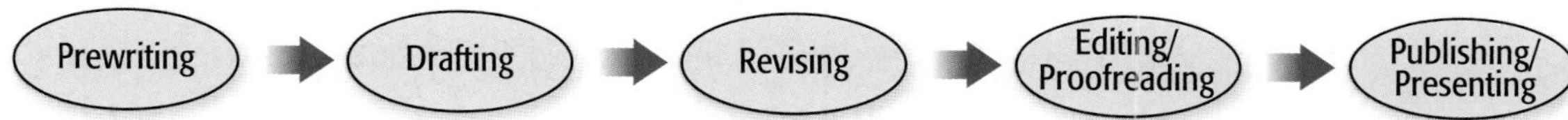

Prewriting

The prewriting stage includes coming up with ideas, making connections, gathering information, defining and refining the topic, and making a plan for a piece of writing.

Tips for prewriting

- Begin with an interesting idea (*what* you will write about).
- Decide the purpose of the writing (*why* you are writing).
- Identify the audience (for *whom* you are writing).
- Explore your idea through a technique such as freewriting, clustering, making diagrams, or brainstorming.

  Freewriting is writing nonstop for a set time, usually only five or ten minutes. The idea is to keep pace with your thoughts, getting them on paper before they vanish. Freewriting can start anywhere and go anywhere.

  Clustering begins with writing a word or phrase in the middle of a sheet of paper. Circle the word or phrase; then think of related words and ideas. Write them in bubbles connected to the central bubble. As you cluster, connect related ideas. The finished cluster will be a diagram of how your ideas can be organized.

  Brainstorming is creating a free flow of ideas with a group of people–it's like freewriting with others. Start with a topic or question; encourage everyone to join in freely. Accept all ideas without judgment and follow each idea as far as it goes. You can evaluate the ideas later.
- Search for information in print and nonprint sources.
- If you are writing a personal essay, all of the information may come from your own experiences and feelings. If you are writing a report or a persuasive essay, you will probably need to locate pertinent factual information and take notes on it. Besides library materials, such as books, magazines, and newspapers, you will want to use the Internet and other online resources. You may also want to interview people with experience or specialized knowledge related to your topic.
- As you gather ideas and information, jot them down on note cards to use as you draft.
- Evaluate all ideas and information to determine or fine-tune the topic.
- Organize information and ideas into a plan that serves as the basis for writing.
- Develop a rough outline reflecting the method of organization you have chosen. Include your main points and supporting details.
- Find and include missing information or ideas that might add interest or help accomplish the purpose of the writing.

Drafting

In this stage, you translate into writing the ideas and information you gathered during prewriting. Drafting is an opportunity to explore and develop your ideas.

Tips for drafting

- Follow the plan made during prewriting but be flexible. New and better ideas may come to you as you develop your ideas; be open to them.
- Transform notes and ideas into related sentences and paragraphs, but don't worry about grammar or mechanics. At this point, it is usually better to concentrate on getting your ideas on paper. You might want to circle or annotate ideas or sections that need more work.
- Determine the tone or attitude of the writing.
- Try to formulate an introduction that will catch the interest of your intended audience.

Revising

In this stage, review and evaluate your draft to make sure it accomplishes its purpose and speaks to its intended audience. When revising, interacting with a peer reviewer can be especially helpful.

Using peer review

Ask one or more of your classmates to read your draft. Here are some specific ways in which you can direct their responses:

- Have readers tell you in their own words what they have read. If you do not hear your ideas restated, you will want to revise for clarity.
- Ask readers to tell you what parts of your writing they liked best and why.
- Discuss the ideas in your writing with your readers. Add any new insights you gain to your revision.
- Ask readers for suggestions about things such as organization and word choice.

You may want to take notes on your readers' suggestions so you will have a handy reference as you revise.

Tips for the peer reviewer

When you are asked to act as a reviewer for a classmate's writing, the following tips will help you do the most effective job:

- Read the piece all the way through—without commenting—to judge its overall effect.
- Tell the writer how you responded to the piece. For example, did you find it informative? interesting? amusing?
- Ask the writer about parts you don't understand.
- Think of questions to ask that will help the writer improve the piece.
- Be sure that your suggestions are constructive.
- Help the writer make improvements.
- Answer the writer's questions honestly. Think about how you would like someone to respond to you.

Tips for revising

- Be sure you have said everything you wanted to say. If not, *add.*
- If you find a section that does not relate to your topic, *cut it.*
- If your ideas are not in a logical order, *rearrange* sentences and paragraphs.
- *Rewrite* any unclear sentences.
- Evaluate your introduction to be sure it creates interest, leads the reader smoothly into your topic, and states your main idea. Also evaluate your conclusion to be sure it either summarizes your writing or effectively brings it to an end.
- Evaluate your word choices. Choose vivid verbs and precise nouns. Use a thesaurus to help you.
- Consider the comments of your peer reviewer. Evaluate them carefully and apply those that will help you create a more effective piece of writing.

Editing/Proofreading

In the editing/proofreading stage, you polish your revised draft and proofread it for errors in grammar and spelling. Use this proofreading checklist to help you check for errors and use the proofreading symbols in the chart below to mark places that need corrections.

- ☑ Have I avoided run-on sentences and sentence fragments and punctuated sentences correctly?
- ☑ Have I used every word correctly, including plurals, possessives, and frequently confused words?
- ☑ Do verbs and subjects agree? Are verb tenses correct?
- ☑ Do pronouns refer clearly to their antecedents and agree with them in person, number, and gender?
- ☑ Have I used adverb and adjective forms and modifying phrases correctly?
- ☑ Have I spelled every word correctly and checked the unfamiliar ones in a dictionary?

Publishing/Presenting

There are a number of ways you can share your work. You could publish it in a magazine, a class anthology, or another publication, or read your writing aloud to a group. You could also join a writers' group and read one another's works.

Proofreading Symbols		
⊙	Lt Brown	Insert a period.
∧	No one came the party.	Insert a letter or a word.
≡	I enjoyed paris.	Capitalize a letter.
/	The Class ran a bake sale.	Make a capital letter lowercase.
⁀ ‿	The campers are home sick.	Close up a space.
(sp)	They visited N.Y.	Spell out.
∧ ;	Sue please come I need your help.	Insert a comma or a semicolon.
∩∪	He enjoyed feild day.	Transpose the position of letters or words.
#	alltogether	Insert a space.
℘	We went to to Boston.	Delete letters or words.
∨ ∨ ∨	She asked, Whos coming?	Insert quotation marks or an apostrophe.
/=/	mid January	Insert a hyphen.
¶	"Where?" asked Karl. "Over there," said Ray.	Begin a new paragraph.

WRITING HANDBOOK

Using the Traits of Strong Writing

What are some basic terms you can use to discuss your writing with your teacher or classmates? What should you focus on as you revise and edit your compositions? Check out the following seven terms, or traits, that describe the qualities of strong writing. Learn the meaning of each trait and find out how using the traits can improve your writing.

Ideas The message or the theme and the details that develop it

Writing is clear when readers can grasp the meaning of your ideas right away. Check to see whether you're getting your message across.

- ☑ Does the title suggest the theme of the composition?
- ☑ Does the composition focus on a single narrow topic?
- ☑ Is the thesis—the main point or central idea—clearly stated?
- ☑ Do well-chosen details elaborate your main point?

Organization The arrangement of main ideas and supporting details

An effective plan of organization points your readers in the right direction and guides them easily through your composition from start to finish. Find a structure, or order, that best suits your topic and writing purpose. Check to see whether you've ordered your key ideas and details in a way that keeps your readers on track.

- ☑ Are the beginning, middle, and end clearly linked?
- ☑ Is the internal order of ideas easy to follow?
- ☑ Does the introduction capture your readers' attention?
- ☑ Do sentences and paragraphs flow from one to the next in a way that makes sense?
- ☑ Does the conclusion wrap up the composition?

Voice A writer's unique way of using tone and style

Your writing voice comes through when your readers sense that a real person is communicating with them. Readers will respond to the **tone** (or attitude) that you express toward a topic and to the **style** (the way that you use language and shape your sentences). Read your work aloud to see whether your writing voice comes through.

- ☑ Does your writing sound interesting?
- ☑ Does your writing reveal your attitude toward your topic?
- ☑ Does your writing sound like you—or does it sound like you're imitating someone else?

Word Choice The vocabulary a writer uses to convey meaning

Words work hard. They carry the weight of your meaning, so make sure you choose them carefully. Check to see whether the words you choose are doing their jobs well.

- ☑ Do you use lively verbs to show action?
- ☑ Do you use vivid words to create word pictures in your readers' minds?
- ☑ Do you use precise words to explain your ideas simply and clearly?

Sentence Fluency The smooth rhythm and flow of sentences that vary in length and style

The best writing is made up of sentences that flow smoothly from one sentence to the next. Writing that is graceful also sounds musical–rhythmical rather than choppy. Check for sentence fluency by reading your writing aloud.

- ☑ Do your sentences vary in length and structure?
- ☑ Do transition words and phrases show connections between ideas and sentences?
- ☑ Does parallelism help balance and unify related ideas?

Conventions Correct spelling, grammar, usage, and mechanics

A composition free of errors makes a good impression on your readers. Mistakes can be distracting, and they can blur your message. Try working with a partner to spot errors and correct them. Use this checklist to help you.

- ☑ Are all words spelled correctly?
- ☑ Are all proper nouns—as well as the first word of every sentence—capitalized?
- ☑ Is your composition free of sentence fragments?
- ☑ Is your composition free of run-on sentences?
- ☑ Are punctuation marks—such as apostrophes, commas, and end marks—inserted in the right places?

Presentation The way words and design elements look on a page

Appearance matters, so make your compositions inviting to read. Handwritten papers should be neat and legible. If you're using a word processor, double-space the lines of text and choose a readable font. Other design elements–such as boldfaced headings, bulleted lists, pictures, and charts–can help you present information effectively as well as make your papers look good.

Preparing a manuscript

Follow the guidelines of the Modern Language Association when you prepare the final copy of your research paper.

- **Heading** On separate lines in the upper left-hand corner of the first page, include your name, your teacher's name, the course name, and the date.
- **Title** Center the title on the line below the heading.
- **Numbering** Number the pages one-half inch from the top of the page in the right-hand corner. Write your last name before each page number after the first page.
- **Spacing** Use double spacing throughout.
- **Margins** Leave one-inch margins on all sides of every page.

Writing Modes

Writing may be classified as expository, descriptive, narrative, or persuasive. Each of these classifications, or modes, has its own purpose.

Expository Writing

Expository writing gives instructions, defines or explains new terms or ideas, explains relationships, compares one thing or opinion with another, or explains how to do something. Expository essays usually include a thesis statement in the introduction.

- ☑ Does the opening contain attention-grabbing details or intriguing questions to hook the reader?
- ☑ Have I provided sufficient information to my audience in a clear and interesting way?
- ☑ Have I checked the accuracy of the information I have provided?
- ☑ Are my comparisons and contrasts clear and logical?

Descriptive Writing

Description re-creates an experience primarily through the use of sensory details. A writer should strive to create a single impression that all the details support. To do so requires careful planning as well as choices about order of information, topic sentences, and figurative language.

- ☑ Did I create interest in my introduction?
- ☑ Are my perspective and my subject clearly stated in my topic sentence?
- ☑ Did I organize details carefully and consistently?
- ☑ Did I order information effectively?
- ☑ Have I chosen precise, vivid words?
- ☑ Do transitions clearly and logically connect the ideas?
- ☑ Have I created a strong, unified impression?

Narrative Writing

Narrative writing, whether factual or fictional, tells a story and has these elements: characters, plot, point of view, theme, and setting. The plot usually involves a conflict between a character and an opposing character or force.

- ☑ Did I introduce characters and a setting?
- ☑ Did I develop a plot that begins with an interesting problem or conflict?
- ☑ Did I build suspense, lead the reader to a climax, and end with a resolution?
- ☑ Did I use dialogue to move the story along?

Persuasive Writing

Persuasive writing expresses a writer's opinion. The goal of persuasion is to make an audience change its opinion and, perhaps, take action. Effective persuasive writing uses strong, relative evidence to support its claims. This kind of writing often requires careful research, organization, and attention to language.

- ☑ Did I keep my audience's knowledge and attitudes in mind from start to finish?
- ☑ Did I state my position in a clear thesis statement?
- ☑ Have I included ample supporting evidence?
- ☑ Have I addressed opposing viewpoints?
- ☑ Have I avoided errors in logic?

Research Paper Writing

More than any other type of paper, research papers are the product of a search—a search for data, for facts, for informed opinions, for insights, and for new information.

Selecting a topic

- If a specific topic is not assigned, choose a topic. Begin with the assigned subject or a subject that interests you. Read general sources of information about that subject and narrow your focus to some aspect of it that interests you. Good places to start are encyclopedia articles and the tables of contents of books on the subject. A computerized library catalog will also display many subheads related to general topics. Find out if sufficient information about your topic is available.
- As you read about the topic, develop your paper's central idea, which is the purpose of your research. Even though this idea might change as you do more research, it can begin to guide your efforts. For example, if you were assigned the subject of the Civil War, you might find that you're interested in women's roles during that war. As you read, you might narrow your topic down to women who went to war, women who served as nurses for the Union, or women who took over farms and plantations in the South.

Conducting a broad search for information

- Generate a series of researchable questions about your chosen topic. Then research to find answers to your questions.
- Among the many sources you might use are the card catalog, the computer catalog, the *Reader's Guide to Periodical Literature* (or an electronic equivalent), newspaper indexes, and specialized references such as biographical encyclopedias.
- If possible, use primary sources as well as secondary sources. A **primary source** is a firsthand account of an event–for example, the diary of a woman who served in the army in the Civil War is a primary source. **Secondary sources** are sources written by people who did not experience or influence the event. Locate specific information efficiently by using the table of contents, indexes, chapter headings, and graphic aids.

Developing a working bibliography

If a work seems useful, write a **bibliography card** for it. On an index card, write down the author, title, city of publication, publisher, date of publication, and any other information you will need to identify the source. Number your cards in the upper right-hand corner so you can keep them in order.

Following are model bibliography, or source, cards.

Book

❶ **Settle, Mary Lee** ❷ 6
❸ **All the Brave Promises.**
❹ **Columbia: University of South Carolina Press, 1995.** ❺

❻ Evanston Public Library ❼ D810.W754

❶ Author
❷ Source number
❸ Title
❹ City of publication/Publisher
❺ Date of publication
❻ Location of source
❼ Library call number

Periodical

❶ Chelminski, R. ❷ 2
❸ "The Maginot Line"
❹ *Smithsonian*, June 1997: 90–99

❶ Author
❷ Source number
❸ Title
❹ Title of magazine/date/page number(s)

Online source

❶ "Job Hunting Resources"	❷ 6
❸ The Career Building Network	
❹ CareerBuilder	
❺ 14 Feb. 2002	
❻ **http://www.careerbuilder.com**	

❶ Title ❹ Sponsoring organization
❷ Source number ❺ Date of access
❸ Title of database ❻ URL

Evaluating your sources

Your sources should be **a**uthoritative, **r**eliable, **t**imely, and **s**uitable **(arts)**.

- The source should be **authoritative.** The author should be well-known in the field. An author who has written several books or articles about a subject or who is frequently quoted may be considered an authority. You might also consult *Book Review Index* and *Book Review Digest* to find out how other experts in the field have evaluated a book or an article.
- The source should be **reliable.** If possible, avoid material from popular magazines in favor of that from more scholarly journals. Be especially careful to evaluate material from online sources. For example, the Web site of a well-known university is more reliable than that of an individual. (You might also consult a librarian or your instructor for guidance in selecting reliable online sources.)
- The source should be **timely.** Use the most recent material available, particularly for subjects of current importance. Check the publication date of books as well as the month and year of periodicals.
- The source should be **suitable,** or **appropriate.** Consider only material that is relevant to the purpose of your paper. Do not waste time on books or articles that have little bearing on your topic. If you are writing on a controversial topic, you should include material that represents more than one point of view.

Compiling and organizing note cards

Careful notes will help you to organize the material for your paper.

- As you reread and study sources, write useful information on index cards. Be sure that each note card identifies the source (use the number of the bibliography card that corresponds to each source).
- In the lower right-hand corner of the card, write the page number on which you found the information. If one card contains several notes, write the page number in parentheses after the relevant material.
- Three helpful ways to take notes are paraphrasing, summarizing, and quoting directly.

  1. **Paraphrase** important details that you want to remember; that is, use your own words to restate specific information.
  2. **Summarize** main ideas that an author presents. When you summarize several pages, be sure to note the page on which the material begins and the page on which it ends–for example, 213–221.
  3. **Quote** the exact words of an author only when the actual wording is important. Be careful about placing the author's words in quotation marks.

- Identify the subject of each note card with a short phrase written in the upper left.

> Avoid **plagiarism**–presenting an author's words or ideas as if they were your own. Remember that you must credit the source not only for material directly quoted but also for any facts or ideas obtained from the source.

See the sample note card below, which includes information about careers and goals from three pages.

Careers and goals 12
Many people "crave work that will spark... excitement and energy."
(5) Sher recognizes that a career does not necessarily satisfy a person's aim in life. (24) She also offers advice on how to overcome obstacles that people experience in defining their goals. (101)

- Organize your note cards to develop a **working outline.** Begin by sorting them into piles of related cards. Try putting the piles together in different ways that suggest an organizational pattern. (If, at this point, you discover that you do not have enough information, go back and do further research.) Many methods of organization are possible. You might also combine methods of organization.

Developing a thesis statement

A thesis statement tells what your topic is and what you intend to say about it—for example, "World War II changed the lives of African Americans and contributed to the rise of the civil rights movement."

- Start by examining your central idea.
- Refine it to reflect the information that you gathered in your research.
- Next, consider your approach to the topic. What is the purpose of your research? Are you proving or disproving something? illustrating a cause-and-effect relationship? offering a solution to a problem? examining one aspect of the topic thoroughly? predicting an outcome?
- Revise your central idea to reflect your approach.
- Be prepared to revise your thesis statement if necessary.

Drafting your paper

Consult your working outline and your notes as you start to draft your paper.

- Concentrate on getting your ideas down in a complete and logical order.
- Write an introduction and a conclusion. An effective introduction creates interest, perhaps by beginning with a question or a controversial quotation; it should also contain your thesis statement. An effective conclusion will summarize main points, restate your thesis, explain how the research points to important new questions to explore, and bring closure to the paper.

Documenting sources

Since a research paper, by its nature, is built on the work of others, you must carefully document all the sources you have used.

- Name the sources of words, ideas, and facts that you borrow.
- In addition to citing books and periodicals from which you take information, cite song lyrics, letters, and excerpts from literature.
- Also credit original ideas that are expressed graphically in tables, charts, and diagrams, as well as the sources of any visual aids you may include, such as photographs.
- You need not cite the source of any information that is common knowledge, such as "John F. Kennedy was assassinated in 1963 in Dallas, Texas."

In-text citations The most common method of crediting sources is with parenthetical documentation within the text. Generally a reference to the source and page number is included in parentheses at the end of each quotation, paraphrase, or summary of information borrowed from a source. An in-text citation points readers to a corresponding entry in your **works-cited list**—a list of all your sources, complete with publication information, that will appear as the final page of your paper. The Modern Language Association (MLA) recommends the following guidelines for crediting sources in text. You may wish to refer to the *MLA Handbook for Writers of Research Papers* by Joseph Gibaldi for more information and examples.

- **Put in parentheses the author's last name and the page number where you found the information.**

  An art historian has noted, "In Wood's idyllic farmscapes, man lives in complete harmony with Nature; he is the earth's caretaker" (Corn 90).

- **If the author's name is mentioned in the sentence, put only the page number in parentheses.**

  Art historian Wanda Corn has noted, "In Wood's idyllic farmscapes, man lives in complete harmony with Nature; he is the earth's caretaker" (90).

- **If no author is listed, put the title or a shortened version of the title in parentheses. Include a page number if you have one.**

  Some critics believe that Grant Wood's famous painting *American Gothic* pokes fun at small-town life and traditional American values ("Gothic").

Compiling a list of works cited

At the end of your text, provide an alphabetized list of published works or other sources cited.

- Include complete publishing information for each source.
- For magazine and newspaper articles, include the page numbers. If an article is continued on a different page, use + after the first page number.
- For online sources, include the date accessed.
- Cite only those sources from which you actually use information.
- Arrange entries in alphabetical order according to the author's last name. Write the last name first. If no author is given, alphabetize by title.
- For long entries, indent five spaces every line after the first.

How to cite sources

On the next three pages, you'll find sample style sheets that can help you prepare your list of sources–the final page of the research paper. Use the one your teacher prefers.

MLA Style

MLA style is most often used in English and social studies classes. Center the title *Works Cited* at the top of your list.

Source	Style
Book with one author	Witham, Barry B. *The Federal Theatre Project: A Case Study.* New York: Cambridge UP, 2003. ["UP" is an abbreviation for "University Press."]
Book with two or three authors	Hoy, Pat C., II, Esther H. Schor, and Robert DiYanni. *Women's Voices: Visions and Perspectives.* New York: McGraw-Hill, 1990. [If a book has more than three authors, name only the first author and then write "et al." (Latin abbreviation for "and others").]
Book with editor(s)	Komunyakaa, Yusef, and David Lehman, eds. *The Best American Poetry 2003.* New York: Scribners, 2003.
Book with an organization or a group as author or editor	Smithsonian Institution. *Aircraft of the National Air and Space Museum.* Washington: Smithsonian Institution Press, 1998.
Work from an anthology	Cofer, Judith Ortiz. "Tales Told Under the Mango Tree." *Hispanic American Literature.* Ed. Nicolas Kanellos. New York: HarperCollins, 1995. 34–44.
Introduction in a published book	Weintraub, Stanley. Introduction. *Great Expectations.* By Charles Dickens. New York: Signet, 1998. v–xii.
Encyclopedia article	"Jazz." *Encyclopaedia Britannica.* 15th ed. 1998.
Weekly magazine article	Franzen, Jonathan. "The Listener." *New Yorker* 6 Oct. 2003: 85–99.
Monthly magazine article	Quammen, David. "Saving Africa's Eden." *National Geographic* Sept. 2003: 50–77.
Newspaper article	Dionne, E. J., Jr. "California's Great Debate." *Washington Post* 26 Sept. 2003: A27. [If no author is named, begin the entry with the title of the article.]
Internet	"Visit Your Parks." *National Park Service.* 1 Oct. 2003. National Park Service, U.S. Dept. of the Interior. 3 Nov. 2003 <http://www.nps.gov/parks.html>.
Online magazine article	Martin, Richard. "How Ravenous Soviet Viruses Will Save the World." *Wired Magazine* 11.10 (October 2003). 17 Oct. 2003 <http://www.wired.com/wired/archive/11.10/phages.html>.
Radio or TV program	"Orcas." *Champions of the Wild.* Animal Planet. Discovery Channel. 21 Oct. 2003.
Videotape or DVD	Hafner, Craig, dir. *The True Story of Seabiscuit.* DVD. A & E Home Video, 2003. [For a videotape (VHS) version, replace "DVD" with "Videocassette."]
Interview	Campeche, Tanya. E-mail interview. 25 Feb. 2004. [If an interview takes place in person, replace "E-mail" with "Personal"; if it takes place on the telephone, use "Telephone."]

CMS Style

CMS style was created by the University of Chicago Press to meet its publishing needs. This style, which is detailed in *The Chicago Manual of Style* (CMS), is used in a number of subject areas. Center the title *Bibliography* at the top of your list.

Source	Style
Book with one author	Witham, Barry B. *The Federal Theatre Project: A Case Study.* New York: Cambridge University Press, 2003.
Book with multiple authors	Hoy, Pat C., II, Esther H. Schor, and Robert DiYanni. *Women's Voices: Visions and Perspectives.* New York: McGraw-Hill, 1990. [If a book has more than ten authors, name only the first seven and then write "et al." (Latin abbreviation for "and others").]
Book with editor(s)	Komunyakaa, Yusef, and David Lehman, eds. *The Best American Poetry 2003.* New York: Scribners, 2003.
Book with an organization or a group as author or editor	Smithsonian Institution. *Aircraft of the National Air and Space Museum.* Washington, DC: Smithsonian Institution Press, 1998.
Work from an anthology	Cofer, Judith Ortiz. "Tales Told Under the Mango Tree." *Hispanic American Literature,* edited by Nicolas Kanellos, 34–44. New York: HarperCollins, 1995.
Introduction in a published book	Dickens, Charles. *Great Expectations.* New introduction by Stanley Weintraub. New York: Signet, 1998.
Encyclopedia article	[Credit for encyclopedia articles goes in your text, not in your bibliography.]
Weekly magazine article	Franzen, Jonathan. "The Listener." *New Yorker,* October 6, 2003, 85–99.
Monthly magazine article	Quammen, David. "Saving Africa's Eden." *National Geographic,* September 2003, 50–77.
Newspaper article	Dionne, E. J., Jr. "California's Great Debate." *Washington Post,* September 26, 2003, A27. [Credit for unsigned newspaper articles goes in your text, not in your bibliography.]
Internet	U.S. Dept. of the Interior. "Visit Your Parks." *National Park Service.* http://www.nps.gov/parks.html.
Online magazine article	Martin, Richard. "How Ravenous Soviet Viruses Will Save the World." *Wired Magazine* 11.10 (October 2003). http://www.wired.com/wired/archive/11.10/phages.html.
Radio or TV program	[Credit for radio and TV programs goes in your text, not in your bibliography.]
Videotape or DVD	Hafner, Craig, dir. *The True Story of Seabiscuit.* A & E Home Video, 2003. DVD. [For a videotape (VHS) version, replace "DVD" with "Videocassette."]
Interview	[Credit for interviews goes in your text, not in your bibliography.]

APA Style

The American Psychological Association (APA) style is commonly used in the sciences. Center the title *References* at the top of your list.

Source	Style
Book with one author	Witham, B. B. (2003). *The federal theatre project: A case study.* New York: Cambridge University Press.
Book with multiple authors	Hoy, P. C., II, Schor, E. H., & DiYanni, R. (1990). *Women's voices: Visions and perspectives.* New York: McGraw-Hill. [If a book has more than six authors, list the first six authors and then write "et al." (Latin abbreviation for "and others").]
Book with editor(s)	Komunyakaa, Y., & Lehman, D. (Eds.). (2003). *The best American poetry 2003.* New York: Scribners.
Book with an organization or a group as author or editor	Smithsonian Institution. (1998). *Aircraft of the National Air and Space Museum.* Washington, DC: Smithsonian Institution Press.
Work from an anthology	Cofer, J. O. (1995). Tales told under the mango tree. In N. Kanellos (Ed.), *Hispanic American Literature* (pp. 34–44). New York: HarperCollins.
Introduction in a published book	[Credit for introductions goes in your text, not in your references.]
Encyclopedia article	Jazz. (1998). In *Encyclopaedia Britannica.* (Vol. 6, pp. 519–520). Chicago: Encyclopaedia Britannica.
Weekly magazine article	Franzen, J. (2003, October 6). The listener. *The New Yorker,* 85–99.
Monthly magazine article	Quammen, D. (2003, September). Saving Africa's Eden. *National Geographic,* 204, 50–77.
Newspaper article	Dionne, E. J., Jr. (2003, September 26). California's great debate. *The Washington Post,* p. A27. [If no author is named, begin the entry with the title of the article.]
Internet	U.S. Dept. of Interior, National Park Service. (2003, October 1). *National Park Service.* Visit your parks. Retrieved October 17, 2003, from http://www.nps.gov/parks.html
Online magazine article	Martin, R. (2003, October). How ravenous Soviet viruses will save the world. *Wired Magazine,* 11.10. Retrieved October 17, 2003, from http://www.wired.com/wired/archive/11.10/phages.html
Radio or TV program	Orcas. (2003, October 21). *Champions of the wild* [Television series episode]. Animal Planet. Silver Spring, MD: Discovery Channel.
Videotape or DVD	Hafner, C. (Director). (2003). *The true story of Seabiscuit* [DVD]. A & E Home Video. [For a videotape (VHS) version, replace "DVD" with "Videocassette."]
Interview	[Credit for interviews goes in your text, not in your references.]

BUSINESS WRITING

Business writing is a specialized form of expository writing. Business writing might include documents such as letters, memorandums, reports, briefs, proposals, and articles for business publications. Business writing must be clear, concise, accurate, and correct in style and usage.

Letter of Application

One form of business writing that follows a conventional format is a letter of application. A letter of application can be used when applying for a job, an internship, or a scholarship. In most cases, the letter is intended to accompany a résumé or an application. Because detailed information is usually included in the accompanying form, a letter of application should provide a general overview of your qualifications and the reasons you are submitting an application. A letter of application should be concise. You should clearly state which position you are applying for and then explain why you are interested and what makes you qualified. The accompanying material should speak for itself.

32 South Street
Austin, Texas 78746
May 6, 20__

Melissa Reyes
City Life magazine
2301 Davis Avenue
Austin, Texas 78764

❶ Re: Internship

Dear Ms. Reyes:

I am a junior at City High School and editor of the City High Herald. I
❷ am writing to apply for your summer internship at City Life magazine. As
a journalism student and a longtime fan of your magazine, I feel that an
internship with your magazine would provide me with valuable experience
in the field of journalism. I believe that my role with the City High Herald
❸ has given me the skills necessary to be a useful contributor to your
magazine this summer. In addition, my enclosed application shows that I
❹ am also a diligent worker.

I thank you for considering my application for your summer internship, and I hope to be working with you in the coming months.

Sincerely,
Anne Moris
Anne Moris

❶ The optional subject line indicates the topic of the letter.

❷ The writer states her purpose directly and immediately.

❸ The writer comments briefly on her qualifications.

❹ The writer makes reference to the accompanying material.

Activity: Choose a local business where you might like to work. Write a letter of application for an internship at that business. Assume that you will be submitting this letter along with a résumé or an internship application that details your experience and qualifications.

Résumé

The purpose of a résumé is to provide the employer with a comprehensive record of your background information, related experience, and qualifications. Although a résumé is intended to provide a great deal of information, the format is designed to provide this information in the most efficient way possible.

All résumés should include the following information: a heading that provides your name and contact information; a job goal or a career objective; your education information; your work experience; other related experience; and relevant activities, associations, organizations, or projects that you have participated in. You may also want to include honors that you have received and list individuals whom the employer can contact for a reference. When listing work experience, be sure to give the name of the employer, your job title, and a few brief bulleted points describing your responsibilities.

❶ Jane Wiley
909 West Main Street, Apt. #1
Urbana, Illinois 61802
(217) 555-0489 • jane@internet.edu

Goal
Seeking position in television news production

❷ **Education**
Junior standing in the College of Communications at the University of Illinois, Urbana-Champaign
2000 Graduate of City High School

Honors
Member of National Honor Society

Activities
❸ Member, Asian American Association: 2001–Present
Environmental Committee Chairperson, Asian American Association: August 2002–May 2003

Work Experience
❹ Radio Reporter, WPGU, 107.1 FM, Champaign, Illinois: May 2002–Present
❺ • Rewrote and read stories for afternoon newscasts
• Served as field reporter for general assignments

Cashier, Del's Restaurant, Champaign, Illinois: May 2002–August 2002
• Responsible for taking phone orders
• Cashier for pickup orders

Assistant Secretary, Office of Dr. George Wright, Woodstock, Illinois: May 2001–August 2001
• Answered phones
• Made appointments

❶ Header includes all important contact information.

❷ All important education background is included.

❸ Related dates are included for all listed activities.

❹ Job title is included along with the place of employment.

❺ Job responsibilities are briefly listed.

Activity: Create an outline that lists the information that you would want to include in a résumé. Use a word processor if possible.

Job Application

When applying for a job, you usually need to fill out a job application. When you fill out the application, read the instructions carefully. Examine the entire form before beginning to fill it out. Write neatly and fill out the form completely, providing all information directly and honestly.

If a question does not apply to you, indicate that by writing *n/a,* short for "not applicable." Keep in mind that you will have the opportunity to provide additional information in your résumé, in your letter of application, or during the interview process.

❶ **Please type or print neatly in blue or black ink.**

❷ **Name:** ______________________ **Today's date:** __________

Address: ____

Phone #: ______ **Birth date:** ____ **Sex:** ___ **Soc. Sec. #:** ______

****

Job History (List each job held, starting with the most recent job.)

❸ 1. Employer: ______________________ Phone #: __________

Dates of employment: ______________________________

Position held: ___________________________________

Duties: ____

❹ 2. Employer: ______________________ Phone #: __________

Dates of employment: ______________________________

Position held: ___________________________________

Duties: ____

****

Education (List the most recent level of education completed.)

____

****

Personal References:

1. Name: ______________________ Phone #: __________

Relationship: ___________________________________

2. Name: ______________________ Phone #: __________

Relationship: ___________________________________

❶ The application provides specific instructions.

❷ All of the information requested should be provided in its entirety.

❸ The information should be provided neatly and succinctly.

❹ Experience should be stated accurately and without embellishment.

Activity: Pick up a job application from a local business or use the sample application above. Complete the application thoroughly. Fill out the application as if you were actually applying for the job. Be sure to pay close attention to the guidelines mentioned above.

Memos

A memorandum (memo) conveys precise information to another person or a group of people. A memo begins with a leading block. It is followed by the text of the message. A memo does not have a formal closing.

TO: All Employees
FROM: Jordan Tyne, Human Resources Manager
❶ SUBJECT: New Human Resources Assistant Director
DATE: November 3, 20__

❷ Please join me in congratulating Leslie Daly on her appointment as assistant director in the Human Resources Department. Leslie comes to our company with five years of experience in the field. Leslie begins work on Monday, ❸ November 10. All future general human resource inquiries should be directed to Leslie.

Please welcome Leslie when she arrives next week.

❶ The topic of the memo is stated clearly in the subject line.

❷ The announcement is made in the first sentence.

❸ All of the important information is included briefly in the memo.

Business E-mail

E-mail is quickly becoming the most common form of business communication. While e-mail may be the least formal and most conversational method of business writing, it shouldn't be written carelessly or too casually. The conventions of business writing–clarity, attention to your audience, proper grammar, and the inclusion of relevant information–apply to e-mail.

An accurate subject line should state your purpose briefly and directly. Use concise language and avoid rambling sentences.

To: LiamS@internet.com
From: LisaB@internet.com
CC: EricC@internet.com
Date: January 7, 8:13 A.M.
❶ Subject: New Product Conference Call

Liam,

❷ I just wanted to make sure that arrangements have been made for next week's conference call to discuss our new product. The East Coast sales team has already scheduled three sales meetings at the end of the month with potential buyers, so it's important that our sales team is prepared to talk about the ❸ product. Please schedule the call when the manufacturing director is available, since he will have important information for the sales team.

Lisa

❶ Subject line clearly states the topic.

❷ The purpose is stated immediately and in a conversational tone.

❸ Important details are included in a brief, direct fashion.

Activity: Write an e-mail to your co-workers. Inform them of a change in company procedure that will affect them. State the specific information that they need to know. Indicate to your co-workers whether action needs to be taken on their part.

Grammar Glossary

This glossary will help you quickly locate information on parts of speech and sentence structure.

A

Absolute phrase. *See* Phrase.

Abstract noun. *See* Noun chart.

Action verb. *See* Verb.

Active voice. *See* Voice.

Adjective A word that modifies a noun or pronoun by limiting its meaning. Adjectives appear in various positions in a sentence. (The *gray* cat purred. The cat is *gray*.)

Many adjectives have different forms to indicate **degree of comparison**. *(short, shorter, shortest)*

The **positive degree** is the simple form of the adjective. *(easy, interesting, good)*

The **comparative degree** compares two persons, places, things, or ideas. *(easier, more interesting, better)*

The **superlative degree** compares more than two persons, places, things, or ideas. *(easiest, most interesting, best)*

A **predicate adjective** follows a linking verb and further identifies or describes the subject. (The child is *happy*.)

A **proper adjective** is formed from a proper noun and begins with a capital letter. Many proper adjectives are created by adding these suffixes: *-an, -ian, -n, -ese,* and *-ish. (Chinese, African)*

Adjective clause. *See* Clause chart.

Adverb A word that modifies a verb, an adjective, or another adverb by making its meaning more specific. When modifying a verb, an adverb may appear in various positions in a sentence. (Cats *generally* eat less than dogs. *Generally,* cats eat less than dogs.) When modifying an adjective or another adverb, an adverb appears directly before the modified word. (I was *quite* pleased that they got along *so* well.) The word *not* and the contraction *-n't* are adverbs. (Mike *wasn't* ready for the test today.) Certain adverbs of time, place, and degree also have a negative meaning. (He's *never* ready.)

Some adverbs have different forms to indicate degree of comparison. *(soon, sooner, soonest)*

The **comparative** degree compares two actions. *(better, more quickly)*

The **superlative** degree compares three or more actions. *(fastest, most patiently, least rapidly)*

Adverb clause. *See* Clause chart.

Antecedent. *See* Pronoun.

Appositive A noun or a pronoun that further identifies another noun or pronoun. (My friend *Julie* lives next door.)

Appositive phrase. *See* Phrase.

Article The adjective *a, an,* or *the.*

Indefinite articles *(a* and *an)* refer to one of a general group of persons, places, or things. (I eat *an* apple *a* day.)

The **definite article** *(the)* indicates that the noun is a specific person, place, or thing. (*The* alarm woke me up.)

Auxiliary verb. *See* Verb.

B

Base form. *See* Verb tense.

C

Clause A group of words that has a subject and a predicate and that is used as part of a sentence. Clauses fall into two categories: *main clauses,* which are also called *independent clauses,* and *subordinate clauses,* which are also called *dependent clauses.*

A **main clause** can stand alone as a sentence. There must be at least one main clause in every sentence. *(The rooster crowed,* and *the dog barked.)*

A **subordinate clause** cannot stand alone as a sentence. A subordinate clause needs a main clause to complete its meaning. Many subordinate clauses begin with subordinating conjunctions or relative pronouns. (*When Geri sang her solo,* the audience became quiet.) The chart on the next page shows the main types of subordinate clauses.

TYPES OF SUBORDINATE CLAUSES			
Clause	**Function**	**Example**	**Begins with . . .**
Adjective clause	Modifies a noun or pronoun	Songs *that have a strong beat* make me want to dance.	A relative pronoun such as *which, who, whom, whose,* or *that*
Adverb clause	Modifies a verb, an adjective, or an adverb	*Whenever Al calls me,* he asks to borrow my bike.	A subordinating conjuction such as *after, although, because, if, since, when,* or *where*
Noun clause	Serves as a subject, an object, or a predicate nominative	*What Philip did* surprised us.	Words such as *how, that, what, whatever, when, where, which, who, whom, whoever, whose,* or *why*

Collective noun. *See* Noun chart.

Common noun. *See* Noun chart.

Comparative degree. *See* Adjective; Adverb.

Complement A word or phrase that completes the meaning of a verb. The four basic kinds of complements are *direct objects, indirect objects, object complements,* and *subject complements.*

A **direct object** answers the question *What?* or *Whom?* after an action verb. (Kari found a *dollar.* Larry saw *Denise.*)

An **indirect object** answers the question *To whom? For whom? To what?* or *For what?* after an action verb. (Do *me* a favor. She gave the *child* a toy.)

An **object complement** answers the question *What?* after a direct object. An object complement is a noun, a pronoun, or an adjective that completes the meaning of a direct object by identifying or describing it. (The director made me the *understudy* for the role. The little girl called the puppy *hers.*)

A **subject complement** follows a subject and a linking verb. It identifies or describes a subject. The two kinds of subject complements are *predicate nominatives* and *predicate adjectives.*

A **predicate nominative** is a noun or pronoun that follows a linking verb and tells more about the subject. (The author of "The Raven" is *Poe.*)

A **predicate adjective** is an adjective that follows a linking verb and gives more information about the subject. (Ian became *angry* at the bully.)

Complex sentence. *See* Sentence.

Compound preposition. *See* Preposition.

Compound sentence. *See* Sentence.

Compound-complex sentence. *See* Sentence.

Conjunction A word that joins single words or groups of words.

A **coordinating conjunction** *(and, but, or, nor, for, yet, so)* joins words or groups of words that are equal in grammatical importance. (David *and* Ruth are twins. I was bored, *so* I left.)

Correlative conjunctions *(both . . . and, just as . . . so, not only . . . but also, either . . . or, neither . . . nor, whether . . . or)* work in pairs to join words and groups of words of equal importance. (Choose *either* the muffin *or* the bagel.)

A **subordinating conjunction** *(after, although, as if, because, before, if, since, so that, than, though, until, when, while)* joins a dependent idea or clause to a main clause. (Beth acted *as if* she felt ill.)

Conjunctive adverb An adverb used to clarify the relationship between clauses of equal weight in a sentence. Conjunctive adverbs are used to replace *and (also, besides, furthermore, moreover)*; to replace *but (however, nevertheless, still)*; to state a result *(consequently, therefore, so, thus)*; or to state equality *(equally, likewise, similarly)*. (Ana was determined to get an A; *therefore*, she studied often.)

Coordinating conjunction. *See* Conjunction.

Correlative conjunction. *See* Conjunction.

D

Declarative sentence. *See* Sentence.

Definite article. *See* Article.

Demonstrative pronoun. *See* Pronoun.

Direct object. *See* Complement.

E

Emphatic form. *See* Verb tense.

F

Future tense. *See* Verb tense.

G

Gerund A verb form that ends in *-ing* and is used as a noun. A gerund may function as a subject, the object of a verb, or the object of a preposition. (*Smiling* uses fewer muscles than *frowning*. Marie enjoys *walking.*)

Gerund phrase. *See* Phrase.

I

Imperative mood. *See* Mood of verb.

Imperative sentence. *See* Sentence chart.

Indicative mood. *See* Mood of verb.

Indirect object. *See* Complement.

Infinitive A verb form that begins with the word *to* and functions as a noun, an adjective, or an adverb. (No one wanted *to answer.*) Note: When *to* precedes a verb, it is not a preposition but instead signals an infinitive.

Infinitive phrase. *See* Phrase.

Intensive pronoun. *See* Pronoun.

Interjection A word or phrase that expresses emotion or exclamation. An interjection has no grammatical connection to other words. Commas follow mild ones; exclamation points follow stronger ones. (*Well,* have a good day. *Wow!*)

Interrogative pronoun. *See* Pronoun.

Intransitive verb. *See* Verb.

Inverted order In a sentence written in *inverted order,* the predicate comes before the subject. Some sentences are written in inverted order for variety or special emphasis. (Up the beanstalk *scampered Jack.*) The subject also generally follows the predicate in a sentence that begins with *here* or *there.* (*Here was* the solution to his problem.) Questions, or interrogative sentences, are generally written in inverted order. In many questions, an auxiliary verb precedes the subject, and the main verb follows it. (*Has* anyone *seen* Susan?) Questions that begin with *who* or *what* follow normal word order.

Irregular verb. *See* Verb tense.

L

Linking verb. *See* Verb.

M

Main clause. *See* Clause.

Mood of verb A verb expresses one of three moods: indicative, imperative, or subjunctive.

The **indicative mood** is the most common. It makes a statement or asks a question. (We *are* out of bread. *Will* you *buy* it?)

The **imperative mood** expresses a command or makes a request. (*Stop* acting like a child! Please *return* my sweater.)

The **subjunctive mood** is used to express, indirectly, a demand, suggestion, or statement of necessity (I demand that he *stop* acting like a child. It's necessary that she *buy* more bread.) The subjunctive is also used to state a condition or wish that is contrary to fact. This use of the subjunctive requires the past tense. (If you *were* a nice person, you *would return* my sweater.)

N

Nominative pronoun. *See* Pronoun.

Noun A word that names a person, a place, a thing, or an idea. The chart on this page shows the main types of nouns.

TYPES OF NOUNS

Noun	Function	Examples
Abstract noun	Names an idea, a quality, or a characteristic	capitalism, terror
Collective noun	Names a group of things or persons	herd, troop
Common noun	Names a general type of person, place, thing, or idea	city, building
Compound noun	Is made up of two or more words	checkerboard, globe-trotter
Noun of direct address	Identifies the person or persons being spoken to	*Maria,* please stand.
Possessive noun	Shows possession, ownership, or the relationship between two nouns	my *sister's* room
Proper noun	Names a particular person, place, thing, or idea	Cleopatra, Italy, Christianity

Noun clause. *See* Clause chart.

Noun of direct address. *See* Noun chart.

Number A noun, pronoun, or verb is *singular* in number if it refers to one; *plural* if it refers to more than one.

O

Object. *See* Complement.

P

Participle A verb form that can function as an adjective. Present participles always end in *-ing.* (The woman comforted the *crying* child.) Many past participles end in *-ed.* (We bought the beautifully *painted* chair.) However, irregular verbs form their past participles in some other way. (Cato was Caesar's *sworn* enemy.)

Passive voice. *See* Voice.

Past tense. *See* Verb tense.

Perfect tense. *See* Verb tense.

Personal pronoun. *See* Pronoun, Pronoun chart.

Phrase A group of words that acts in a sentence as a single part of speech.

An **absolute phrase** consists of a noun or pronoun that is modified by a participle or participial phrase but has no grammatical relation to the complete subject or predicate. *(The vegetables being done,* we finally sat down to eat dinner.*)*

An **appositive phrase** is an appositive along with any modifiers. If not essential to the meaning of the sentence, an appositive phrase is set off by commas. (Jack plans to go to the jazz concert, *an important musical event.*)

A **gerund phrase** includes a gerund plus its complements and modifiers. *(Playing the flute* is her hobby.*)*

An **infinitive phrase** contains the infinitive plus its complements and modifiers. (It is time *to leave for school.*)

A **participial phrase** contains a participle and any modifiers necessary to complete its meaning. (The woman *sitting over there* is my grandmother.)

A **prepositional phrase** consists of a preposition, its object, and any modifiers of the object. A prepositional phrase can function as an adjective, modifying a noun or a pronoun. (The dog *in the yard* is very gentle.) A prepositional phrase may also function as an adverb when it modifies a verb, an adverb, or an adjective. (The baby slept *on my lap.*)

A **verb phrase** consists of one or more auxiliary verbs followed by a main verb. (The job *will have been completed* by noon tomorrow.)

Positive degree. *See* Adjective.

Possessive noun. *See* Noun chart.

Predicate The verb or verb phrase and any objects, complements, or modifiers that express the essential thought about the subject of a sentence.

A **simple predicate** is a verb or verb phrase that tells something about the subject. *(We ran.)*

A **complete predicate** includes the simple predicate and any words that modify or complete it. *(We solved the problem in a short time.)*

A **compound predicate** has two or more verbs or verb phrases that are joined by a conjunction and share the same subject. (We *ran to the park and began to play baseball.*)

Predicate adjective. *See* Adjective; Complement.

Predicate nominative. *See* Complement.

Preposition A word that shows the relationship of a noun or pronoun to some other word in the sentence. Prepositions include *about, above, across, among, as, behind, below, beyond, but, by, down, during, except, for, from, into, like, near, of, on, outside, over, since, through, to, under, until, with.* (I usually eat breakfast *before* school.)

A **compound preposition** is made up of more than one word. *(according to, ahead of, as to, because of, by means of, in addition to, in spite of, on account of)* (We played the game *in spite of* the snow.)

Prepositional phrase. *See* Phrase.

Present tense. *See* Verb tense.

Progressive form. *See* Verb tense.

Pronoun A word that takes the place of a noun, a group of words acting as a noun, or another pronoun. The word or group of words that a pronoun refers to is called its **antecedent**. (In the following sentence, *Mari* is the antecedent of *she*. *Mari likes Mexican food, but she doesn't like Italian food.*)

A **demonstrative pronoun** points out specific persons, places, things, or ideas. *(this, that, these, those)*

An **indefinite pronoun** refers to persons, places, or things in a more general way than a noun does. *(all, another, any, both, each, either, enough, everything, few, many, most, much, neither, nobody, none, one, other, others, plenty, several, some)*

An **intensive pronoun** adds emphasis to another noun or pronoun. If an intensive pronoun is omitted, the meaning of the sentence will be the same. (Rebecca *herself* decided to look for a part-time job.)

An **interrogative pronoun** is used to form questions. *(who? whom? whose? what? which?)*

A **personal pronoun** refers to a specific person or thing. Personal pronouns have three cases: nominative, possessive, and objective. The case depends upon the function of the pronoun in a sentence. The first chart on this page shows the case forms of personal pronouns.

A **reflexive pronoun** reflects back to a noun or pronoun used earlier in the sentence, indicating that the same person or thing is involved. (We told *ourselves* to be patient.)

A **relative pronoun** is used to begin a subordinate clause. *(who, whose, that, what, whom, whoever, whomever, whichever, whatever)*

Proper adjective. *See* Adjective.

Proper noun. *See* Noun chart.

R

Reflexive pronoun. *See* Pronoun.

Relative pronoun. *See* Pronoun.

S

Sentence A group of words expressing a complete thought. Every sentence has a subject and a predicate. Sentences can be classified by function or by structure. The second chart on this page shows the categories by function; the following subentries describe the categories by structure. *See also* Subject; Predicate; Clause.

A **simple sentence** has only one main clause and no subordinate clauses. *(Alan found an old violin.)* A simple sentence may contain a compound subject or a compound predicate or both. *(Alan and Teri found an old violin. Alan found an old violin and tried to play it. Alan and Teri found an old violin and tried to play it.)* The subject and the predicate can be expanded with adjectives, adverbs, prepositional phrases, appositives, and verbal phrases. As long as the sentence has only one main clause, however, it remains a simple sentence. *(Alan, rummaging in the attic, found an old violin.)*

A **compound sentence** has two or more main clauses. Each main clause has its own subject and predicate, and these main clauses are usually joined by a comma and a coordinating conjunction. *(Cats meow, and dogs bark, but ducks quack.)* Semicolons may also be used to join the main clauses in a compound sentence. *(The helicopter landed; the pilot had saved four passengers.)*

A **complex sentence** has one main clause and one or more

PERSONAL PRONOUNS

Case	Singular Pronouns	Plural Pronouns	Function in Sentence
Nominative	I, you, she, he, it	we, you, they	subject or predicate nominative
Objective	me, you, her, him, it	us, you, them	direct object, indirect object, or object of a preposition
Possessive	my, mine, your, yours, her, hers, his, its	our, ours, your, yours, their, theirs	replacement for the possessive form of a noun

TYPES OF SENTENCES

Sentence Type	Function	Ends with . . .	Examples
Declarative sentence	Makes a statement	A period	I did not enjoy the movie.
Exclamatory sentence	Expresses strong emotion	An exclamation point	What a good writer Consuela is!
Imperative sentence	Makes a request or gives a command	A period or an exclamation point	Please come to the party. Stop!
Interrogative sentence	Asks a question	A question mark	Is the composition due today?

subordinate clauses. *(Since the movie starts at eight, we should leave here by seven-thirty.)*

A **compound-complex sentence** has two or more main clauses and at least one subordinate clause. *(If we leave any later, we may miss the previews, and I want to see them.)*

Simple predicate. *See* Predicate.

Simple subject. *See* Subject.

Subject The part of a sentence that tells what the sentence is about.

A **simple subject** is the main noun or pronoun in the subject. *(Babies* crawl.*)*

A **complete subject** includes the simple subject and any words that modify it. *(The man from New Jersey* won the race.*)* In some sentences, the simple subject and the complete subject are the same. *(Birds* fly.*)*

A **compound subject** has two or more simple subjects joined by a conjunction. The subjects share the same verb. *(Firefighters* and *police officers* protect the community.*)*

Subjunctive mood. *See* Mood of verb.

Subordinate clause. *See* Clause.

Subordinating conjunction. *See* Conjunction.

Superlative degree. *See* Adjective; Adverb.

T

Tense. *See* Verb tense.

Transitive verb. *See* Verb.

V

Verb A word that expresses action or a state of being. *(cooks, seem, laughed)*

An **action verb** tells what someone or something does. Action verbs can express either physical or mental action. (Crystal *decided* to *change* the tire herself.)

A **transitive verb** is an action verb that is followed by a word or words that answer the question *What?* or *Whom?* (I *held* the baby.)

An **intransitive verb** is an action verb that is not followed by a word that answers the question *What?* or *Whom?* (The baby *laughed.*)

A **linking verb** expresses a state of being by linking the subject of a sentence with a word or an expression that identifies or describes the subject. (The lemonade *tastes* sweet. He *is* our new principal.) The most commonly used linking verb is *be* in all its forms *(am, is, are, was, were, will be, been, being)*. Other linking verbs include *appear, become, feel, grow, look, remain, seem, sound, smell, stay, taste.*

An **auxiliary verb**, or helping verb, is a verb that accompanies the main verb to form a verb phrase. (I *have been* swimming.) The forms of *be* and *have* are the most common auxiliary verbs: *(am, is, are, was, were, being, been; has, have, had, having).* Other auxiliaries include *can, could, do, does, did, may, might, must, shall, should, will, would.*

Verbal A verb form that functions in a sentence as a noun, an adjective, or an adverb. The three kinds of verbals are gerunds, infinitives, and participles. *See* Gerund; Infinitive; Participle.

Verb tense The tense of a verb indicates when the action or state of being occurs. All the verb tenses are formed from the four principal parts of a verb: a base form *(talk)*, a present participle *(talking)*, a simple past form *(talked)*, and a past participle *(talked)*. A **regular verb** forms its simple past and past participle by adding *-ed* to the base form. *(climb, climbed)* An **irregular verb** forms its past and past participle in some other way. *(get, got, gotten)*

In addition to present, past, and future tenses, there are three perfect tenses.

The **present perfect tense** expresses an action or a condition that occurred at some indefinite time in the past. This tense also shows an action or a condition that began in the past and continues into the present. (She *has played* the piano for four years.)

The **past perfect tense** indicates that one past action or condition began *and* ended before another past action started. (Andy *had finished* his homework before I even began mine.)

The **future perfect tense** indicates that one future action or condition will begin *and* end before another future event starts. Use *will have* or *shall have* with the past participle of a verb. (By tomorrow, I *will have finished* my homework, too.)

The **progressive form** of a verb expresses a continuing action with any of the six tenses. To make the progressive forms, use the appropriate tense of the verb *be* with the present participle of the main verb. (She *is swimming*. She *has been swimming.*)

The **emphatic form** adds special force, or emphasis, to the present and past tense of a verb. For the emphatic form, use *do, does,* or *did* with the base form. (Toshi *did want* that camera.)

Voice The **voice** of a verb shows whether the subject performs the action or receives the action of the verb.

A verb is in the **active voice** if the subject of the sentence performs the action. (The referee *blew* the whistle.)

A verb is in the **passive voice** if the subject of the sentence receives the action of the verb. (The whistle *was blown* by the referee.)

Mechanics

This section will help you use correct capitalization, punctuation, and abbreviations in your writing.

Capitalization

This section will help you recognize and use correct capitalization in sentences.

Rule: Capitalize the first word in any sentence, including direct quotations and sentences in parentheses unless they are included in another sentence.

Example: She said, "Come back soon."

Example: Emily Dickinson became famous only after her death. (She published only six poems during her lifetime.)

Rule: Always capitalize the pronoun *I* no matter where it appears in the sentence.

Example: Some of my relatives think that I should become a doctor.

Rule: Capitalize proper nouns, including

a. names of individuals and titles used in direct address preceding a name or describing a relationship.

Example: George Washington; Dr. Morgan; Aunt Margaret

b. names of ethnic groups, national groups, political parties and their members, and languages.

Example: Italian Americans; Aztec; the Republican Party; a Democrat; Spanish

c. names of organizations, institutions, firms, monuments, bridges, buildings, and other structures.

Example: Red Cross; Stanford University; General Electric; Lincoln Memorial; Tappan Zee Bridge; Chrysler Building; Museum of Natural History

d. trade names and names of documents, awards, and laws.

Example: Microsoft; Declaration of Independence; Pulitzer Prize; Sixteenth Amendment

e. geographical terms and regions or localities.

Example: Hudson River; Pennsylvania Avenue; Grand Canyon; Texas; the Midwest

f. names of planets and other heavenly bodies.

Example: Venus; Earth; the Milky Way

g. names of ships, planes, trains, and spacecraft.

Example: USS *Constitution; Spirit of St. Louis; Apollo 11*

h. names of most historical events, eras, calendar items, and religious names and items.

Example: World War II; Age of Enlightenment; June; Christianity; Buddhists; Bible; Easter; God

i. titles of literary works, works of art, and musical compositions.

Example: "Why I Live at the P.O."; *The Starry Night; Rhapsody in Blue*

j. names of specific school courses.

Example: Advanced Physics; American History

Rule: Capitalize proper adjectives (adjectives formed from proper nouns).

Example: Christmas tree; Hanukkah candles; Freudian psychology; American flag

Punctuation

This section will help you use these elements of punctuation correctly.

Rule: Use a **period** at the end of a declarative sentence or a polite command.

Example: I'm thirsty.

Example: Please bring me a glass of water.

Rule: Use an **exclamation point** to show strong feeling or after a forceful command.

Example: I can't believe my eyes!

Example: Watch your step!

Rule: Use a **question mark** to indicate a direct question.

Example: Who is in charge here?

Rule: Use a **colon**

a. to introduce a list (especially after words such as *these, the following,* or *as follows*) and to introduce material that explains, restates, or illustrates previous material.

Example: The following states voted for the amendment: Texas, California, Georgia, and Florida.

Example: The sunset was colorful: purple, orange, and red lit up the sky.

b. to introduce a long or formal quotation.

Example: It was Mark Twain who stated the following proverb: "Man is the only animal that blushes. Or needs to."

c. in precise time measurements, biblical chapter and verse references, and business letter salutations.

Example:

3:35 P.M.	7:50 A.M.
Gen. 1:10–11	Matt. 2:23
Dear Ms. Samuels:	Dear Sir:

Rule: Use a **semicolon**

a. to separate main clauses that are not joined by a coordinating conjunction.

Example: There were two speakers at Gettysburg that day; only Lincoln's speech is remembered.

b. to separate main clauses joined by a conjunctive adverb or by *for example* or *that is*.

Example: Because of the ice storm, most students could not get to school; consequently, the principal canceled all classes for the day.

c. to separate the items in a series when these items contain commas.

Example: The students at the rally came from Senn High School, in Chicago, Illinois; Niles Township High School, in Skokie, Illinois; and Evanston Township High School, in Evanston, Illinois.

d. to separate two main clauses joined by a coordinating conjunction when such clauses already contain several commas.

Example: The designer combined the blue silk, brown linen, and beige cotton into a suit; but she decided to use the yellow chiffon, yellow silk, and white lace for an evening gown.

Rule: Use a **comma**

a. between the main clauses of a compound sentence.

Example: Ryan was late getting to study hall, and his footsteps echoed in the empty corridor.

b. to separate three or more words, phrases, or clauses in a series.

Example: Mel bought carrots, beans, pears, and onions.

c. between coordinate modifiers.

Example: That is a lyrical, moving poem.

d. to set off parenthetical expressions, interjections, and conjunctive adverbs.

Example: Well, we missed the bus again.

Example: The weather is beautiful today; however, it is supposed to rain this weekend.

e. to set off nonessential words, clauses, and phrases, such as:
–adverbial clauses

Example: Since Ellen is so tall, the coach assumed she would be a good basketball player.

–adjective clauses

Example: Scott, who had been sleeping, finally woke up.

–participles and participial phrases

Example: Having found what he was looking for, he left.

–prepositional phrases

Example: On Saturdays during the fall, I rake leaves.

–infinitive phrases

Example: To be honest, I'd like to stay awhile longer.

–appositives and appositive phrases

Example: Ms. Kwan, a soft-spoken woman, ran into the street to hail a cab.

f. to set off direct quotations.

Example: "My concert," Molly replied, "is tonight."

g. to set off an antithetical phrase.

Example: Unlike Tom, Rob enjoys skiing.

h. to set off a title after a person's name.

Example: Margaret Thomas, Ph.D., was the guest speaker.

i. to separate the various parts of an address, a geographical term, or a date.

Example: My new address is 324 Indian School Road, Albuquerque, New Mexico 85350.

Example: I moved on March 13, 1998.

j. after the salutation of an informal letter and after the closing of all letters.

Example: Dear Helen, Sincerely,

k. to set off parts of a reference that direct the reader to the exact source.

Example: You can find the article in the *Washington Post*, April 4, 1997, pages 33–34.

l. to set off words or names used in direct address and in tag questions.

Example: Yuri, will you bring me my calculator?

Example: Lottie became a lawyer, didn't she?

Rule: Use a **dash** to signal a change in thought or to emphasize parenthetical material.

Example: During the play, Maureen—and she'd be the first to admit it—forgot her lines.

Example: There are only two juniors attending—Mike Ramos and Ron Kim.

Rule: Use **parentheses** to set off supplemental material. Punctuate within the parentheses only if the punctuation is part of the parenthetical expression.

Example: If you like jazz (and I assume you do), you will like this CD. (The soloist is Miles Davis.)

Example: The upper Midwest (which states does that include?) was hit by terrible floods last year.

Rule: Use **brackets** to enclose information that you insert into a quotation for clarity or to enclose a parenthetical phrase that already appears within parentheses.

Example: "He serves his [political] party best who serves the country best."
—*Rutherford B. Hayes*

Example: The staircase (which was designed by a famous architect [Frank Lloyd Wright]) was inlaid with ceramic tile.

Rule: Use **ellipsis points** to indicate the omission of material from a quotation.

Example: ". . . Neither an individual nor a nation can commit the least act of injustice against the obscurest individual. . . ."
—*Henry David Thoreau*

Rule: Use **quotation marks**

a. to enclose a direct quotation, as follows:

Example: "Hurry up!" shouted Lisa.

When a quotation is interrupted, use two sets of quotation marks.

Example: "A cynic," wrote Oscar Wilde, "is someone who knows the price of everything and the value of nothing."

Use single quotation marks for a quotation within a quotation.

Example: "Did you say 'turn left' or 'turn right'?" asked Leon.

In writing dialogue, begin a new paragraph and use a new set of quotation marks every time the speaker changes.

Example: "Do you really think the spaceship can take off?" asked the first officer.
"Our engineer assures me that we have enough power," the captain replied.

b. to enclose titles of short works, such as stories, poems, essays, articles, chapters, and songs.

Example: "The Lottery" [short story]
"Provide, Provide" [poem]
"Civil Disobedience" [essay]

c. to enclose unfamiliar slang terms and unusual expressions.

Example: The man called his grandson a "rapscallion."

d. to enclose a definition that is stated directly.

Example: *Gauche* is a French word meaning "left."

Rule: Use **italics**

a. for titles of books, lengthy poems, plays, films, television series, paintings and sculptures, long musical compositions, court cases, names of newspapers and magazines, ships, trains, airplanes, and spacecraft. Italicize and capitalize articles *(a, an, the)* at the beginning of a title only when they are part of the title.

Example: *E.T.* [film]; *The Piano Lesson* [play]
The Starry Night [painting]
the *New Yorker* [magazine]
Challenger [spacecraft]
The Great Gatsby [book]
the *Chicago Tribune* [newspaper]

b. for foreign words and expressions that are not used frequently in English.

Example: Luciano waved good-bye, saying, *"Arrivederci."*

c. for words, letters, and numerals used to represent themselves.

Example: There is no *Q* on the telephone keypad.

Example: Number your paper from *1* through *10*.

Rule: Use an **apostrophe**

a. for a possessive form, as follows:

Add an apostrophe and *-s* to all singular nouns, plural nouns not ending in *-s*, singular indefinite pronouns, and compound nouns. Add only an apostrophe to a plural noun that ends in *-s*.

Example: the tree's leaves
the man's belt
the bus's tires
the children's pets
everyone's favorite
my mother-in-law's job
the attorney general's decision
the baseball player's error
the cats' bowls

If two or more persons possess something jointly, use the possessive form for the last person named. If they possess it individually, use the possessive form for each one's name.

Example: Ted and Harriet's family
Ted's and Harriet's bosses
Lewis and Clark's expedition
Lewis's and Clark's clothes

b. to express amounts of money or time that modify a noun.

Example: two cents' worth

Example: three days' drive (You can use a hyphenated adjective instead: a three-day drive.)

c. in place of omitted letters or numerals.

Example: haven't [have not] the winter of '95

d. to form the plural of letters, numerals, symbols, and words used to represent themselves. Use an apostrophe and *-s*.

Example: You wrote two *5*'s instead of one.

Example: How many *s*'s are there in Mississippi?

Example: Why did he use three *!*'s at the end of the sentence?

Rule: Use a **hyphen**

a. after any prefix joined to a proper noun or proper adjective.

Example: all-American pre-Columbian

b. after the prefixes *all-, ex-,* and *self-* joined to any noun or adjective, after the prefix *anti-* when it joins a word beginning with *i,* after the prefix *vice-* (except in some instances such as *vice president*), and to avoid confusion between words that begin with *re-* and look like another word.

Example: ex-president
self-important
anti-inflammatory
vice-principal
re-creation of the event
recreation time
re-pair the socks
repair the computer

c. in a compound adjective that precedes a noun.

Example: a bitter-tasting liquid

d. in any spelled-out cardinal or ordinal numbers up to *ninety-nine* or *ninety-ninth,* and with a fraction used as an adjective.

Example: twenty-three eighty-fifth
one-half cup

e. to divide a word at the end of a line between syllables.

Example: air-port scis-sors
fill-ing fin-est

Abbreviations

Abbreviations are shortened forms of words.

Rule: Use only one period if an abbreviation occurs at the end of a sentence. If the sentence ends with a question mark or an exclamation point, use the period and the second mark of punctuation.

Example: We didn't get home until 3:30 A.M.

Example: Did you get home before 4:00 A.M.?

Example: I can't believe you didn't get home until 3:30 A.M.!

Rule: Capitalize abbreviations of proper nouns and abbreviations related to historical dates.

Example: John Kennedy Jr. P.O. Box 333
800 B.C. A.D. 456 1066 C.E.

Rule: Use all capital letters and no periods for most abbreviations of organizations and government agencies.

Example: CBS CIA IBM
NFL MADD GE
FBI

Spelling

The following basic rules, examples, and exceptions will help you master the spellings of many words.

Forming Plurals

English words form plurals in many ways. Most nouns simply add *-s*. The following chart shows other ways of forming plural nouns and some common exceptions to the pattern.

General Rules for Forming Plurals		
If the word ends in	**Rule**	**Examples**
ch, s, sh, x, z	add *-es*	glass, glasses
a consonant + *y*	change *y* to *i* and add *-es*	caddy, caddies
a vowel + *y* or *o*	add only *-s*	cameo, cameos monkey, monkeys
a consonant + *o* common exceptions	generally add *-es* but sometimes add only *-s*	potato, potatoes cello, cellos
f or *ff* common exceptions	add *-s* change *f* to *v* and add *-es*	cliff, cliffs hoof, hooves
lf	change *f* to *v* and add *-es*	half, halves

A few plurals are exceptions to the rules in the previous chart, but they are easy to remember. The following chart lists these plurals and some examples.

Special Rules for Forming Plurals	
Rule	**Examples**
To form the plural of most proper names and one-word compound nouns, follow the general rules for plurals.	Cruz, Cruzes Mancuso, Mancusos crossroad, crossroads
To form the plural of hyphenated compound nouns or compound nouns of more than one word, make the most important word plural.	mother-in-law, mothers-in-law attorney general, attorneys general
Some nouns have unusual plural forms.	goose, geese child, children
Some nouns have the same singular and plural forms.	moose scissors pants

Adding Prefixes

When adding a prefix to a word, keep the original spelling of the word. Use a hyphen only when the original word is capitalized or with the prefixes *all-*, *ex-*, and *self-* joined to a noun or an adjective.

co + operative = cooperative
inter + change = interchange
pro + African = pro-African
ex + partner = ex-partner

Suffixes and the Silent *e*

Many English words end in a silent letter *e*. Sometimes the *e* is dropped when a suffix is added. When adding a suffix that begins with a consonant to a word that ends in silent *e*, keep the *e*.

like + ness = likeness   sure + ly = surely
COMMON EXCEPTIONS awe + ful = awful;
judge + ment = judgment

When adding a suffix that begins with a vowel to a word that ends in silent *e*, usually drop the *e*.

believe + able = believable
expense + ive = expensive
COMMON EXCEPTION mile + age = mileage

When adding a suffix that begins with *a* or *o* to a word that ends in *ce* or *ge*, keep the *e* so the word will retain the soft *c* or *g* sound.

notice + able = noticeable
courage + ous = courageous

When adding a suffix that begins with a vowel to a word that ends in *ee* or *oe*, keep the final *e*.

see + ing = seeing   toe + ing = toeing

Drop the final silent *e* after the letters *u* or *w*.

argue + ment = argument
owe + ing = owing

Keep the final silent *e* before the suffix *-ing* when necessary to avoid ambiguity.

singe + ing = singeing

Suffixes and the Final *y*

When adding a suffix to a word that ends in a consonant + *y*, change the *y* to *i* unless the suffix begins with *i*. Keep the *y* in a word that ends in a vowel + *y*.

try + ed = tried   fry + ed = fried
stay + ing = staying   display + ed = displayed
copy + ing = copying   joy + ous = joyous

Adding *-ly* and *-ness*

When adding *-ly* to a word that ends in a single *l*, keep the *l*, but when the word ends in a double *l*, drop one *l*. When the word ends in a consonant + *le*, drop the *le*. When adding *-ness* to a word that ends in *n*, keep the *n*.

casual + ly = casually
practical + ly = practically
dull + ly = dully
probable + ly = probably
open + ness = openness
mean + ness = meanness

Doubling the Final Consonant

Double the final consonant in words that end in a consonant preceded by a single vowel if the word is one syllable, if it has an accent on the last syllable that remains there even after the suffix is added, or if it is a word made up of a prefix and a one-syllable word.

stop + ing = stopping
admit + ed = admitted
replan + ed = replanned

Do not double the final consonant if the accent is not on the last syllable or if the accent shifts when the suffix is added. Also do not double the final consonant if the final consonant is *x* or *w*. If the word ends in a consonant and the suffix begins with a consonant, do not double the final consonant.

benefit + ed = benefited
similar + ly = similarly
raw + er = rawer
box + like = boxlike
friend + less = friendless
rest + ful = restful

Forming Compound Words

When joining a word that ends in a consonant to a word that begins with a consonant, keep both consonants.

out + line = outline
after + noon = afternoon
post + card = postcard
pepper + mint = peppermint

ie and *ei*

Learning this rhyme can save you many misspellings: "Write *i* before *e* except after *c*, or when sounded like *a* as in *neighbor* and *weigh*." There are many exceptions to this rule, including *seize, seizure, leisure, weird, height, either, neither, forfeit.*

-cede, -ceed, and *-sede*

Because of the relatively few words with *sēd* sounds, these words are worth memorizing.

These words use *-cede:* **accede, precede, secede.**

One word uses *-sede:* **supersede.**

Three words use *-ceed:* **exceed, proceed, succeed.**

LANGUAGE HANDBOOK

Succeeding on Tests

This section is designed to help you prepare for both classroom and standardized tests. You will become familiar with the various formats of tests and the types of questions you will be required to answer.

Preparing for Classroom Tests

This section will help you learn how to prepare for classroom tests.

Thinking ahead

- Write down information about an upcoming test—when it will be given, what it will cover, and so on—so you can plan your study time effectively.
- Review your textbook, quizzes, homework assignments, class notes, and handouts. End-of-chapter review questions often highlight key points from your textbook.
- Develop your own questions about main ideas and important details, and practice answering them. Writing your own practice tests is an excellent way to get ready for a real test.
- Make studying into an active process. Rather than simply rereading your notes or a chapter in your textbook, try to create a summary of the material. This can be an outline, a list of characters, or a time line. Try to include details from both your lecture notes and your textbook reading so you will be able to see connections between the two.
- Form study groups. Explaining information to a peer is one of the best ways to learn the material.
- Sleep well the night before a test. Spreading your study time over several days should have given you enough confidence to go to bed at your regular time the night before a test.
- Remember that eating well helps you remain alert. Students who eat a regular meal on the morning of a test generally score higher than those who do not.

Taking objective tests

Many of the tests you take in your high school classes will be objective tests, meaning that they ask questions that have specific correct answers. Time is often limited for these tests, so be sure to use your time efficiently.

- First, read the directions carefully. If anything is unclear, ask questions.
- Try to respond to each item on the test, starting with the easier ones.
- Skip difficult questions rather than dwelling on them. You can always come back to them at the end of the test.
- Try to include some time to review your test before turning it in.

Below are tips for answering specific kinds of objective test items:

Kind of item	Tips
Multiple-choice	Read all the answer choices provided before choosing one; even if the first one seems nearly correct, a later choice may be a better answer. Be cautious when choosing responses that contain absolute words such as *always, never, all,* or *none*. Since most generalizations have exceptions, absolute statements are often incorrect.
True/False	If *any* part of the item is false, the correct answer must be "false."
Short-answer	Use complete sentences to help you write a clear response.
Fill-in	Restate fill-ins as regular questions if you are not sure what is being asked.
Matching	Note in the directions whether some responses can be used more than once or not used at all.

Taking subjective (essay) tests

You will also take subjective tests during high school. Typically, these tests ask questions that require you to write an essay. Your grade is based more on how well you are able to make your point than on whether you choose a correct answer.

- When you receive the test, first read it through. If there are several questions, determine how much time to spend on each question.
- Begin your answer by jotting down ideas on scratch paper for several minutes. Read the test question again to make sure you are answering it. Then create a rough outline from which you can create your essay.
- Start your essay with a thesis statement in the first paragraph and follow with paragraphs that provide supporting evidence. Give as much information as possible, including examples and illustrations where appropriate.
- Finish your essay with a conclusion, highlighting the evidence you have provided and restating your thesis.
- You will probably not have time to revise and recopy your essay. After you are finished writing, spend any remaining time proofreading your answer and neatly making any necessary corrections.

Preparing for Standardized Tests

Standardized tests are designed to be administered to very large groups of students, not just those in a particular class. Three of the most widely known standardized tests, all part of the college application process, are the ACT, the PSAT, and the SAT. The strategies in this handbook refer specifically to the PSAT and SAT tests, but they also can apply to preparing for the ACT and other standardized tests.

The PSAT is generally administered to students in the eleventh grade, though some schools offer it to students in the tenth grade as well. This test is designed to predict how well you will do on the SAT. For most students, the PSAT is simply a practice test. Those who perform exceptionally well on the eleventh grade PSAT, however, will qualify for National Merit Scholarship competition.

The SAT consists of the SAT-I: Reasoning Test and a variety of SAT-II: Subject Tests. The SAT-I is a three-hour test that evaluates your general verbal and mathematics skills. The SAT-II: Subject Tests are hour-long tests given in specific subjects and are designed to show specifically how much you have learned in a particular subject area.

Tips for taking standardized tests

Standardized tests are often administered outside of regular class time and require registration. Ask your teacher or guidance counselor how you can register early to ensure that you can take the test at a time and location most convenient for you. In addition, follow these tips:

- Skip difficult questions at first. Standardized tests are usually timed, so first answer items you know. You can return later to those you skipped.
- Mark only your answers on the answer sheet. Most standardized tests are scored by a computer, so stray marks can be read as incorrect answers.
- Frequently compare the question numbers on your test with those on your answer sheet to avoid putting answers in the wrong spaces.
- If time permits, check your answers. If you are not penalized for guessing, fill in answers for any items you might have skipped.

Preparing for the PSAT and the SAT-I

The verbal sections of the PSAT and SAT-I contain sentence completion items and reading comprehension questions.

Sentence completion

Sentence completion items provide a sentence with one or two blanks and ask you to select the word or pair of words that best fits in the blank(s). Here is some general information to help you with these questions on the PSAT and SAT-I.

- Start by reading the sentence and filling in your own word to replace the blank. Look for words that show how the word in the blank is related to the rest of the sentence–*and, but, since, therefore, although.*
- Do not read the sentence with the words from each answer choice inserted. This may leave you with several choices that "sound good."
- Once you have chosen your own word to fill in the blank, pick the word from the answer choices that is closest in meaning to your word.

- If you have trouble coming up with a specific word to fill in the blank, try to determine whether the word should be positive or negative. Even this bit of information can help you eliminate some answer choices. If you can eliminate even one answer choice, take a guess at the correct answer.

Reading comprehension

Reading comprehension questions on the PSAT and SAT-I measure your ability to understand and interpret what you read. Each reading passage is followed by a series of questions. Here are some points to keep in mind when working with these questions:

- You get points for answering questions correctly, not for reading passages thoroughly. Therefore, it is to your advantage to read the passages quickly and spend your time working on the questions.
- After quickly reading a passage, briefly summarize it. This will help you answer general questions, which are based on the passage as a whole.
- To answer specific questions based on details included in the passage, return to the passage to find the correct answers. Reading Comprehension is like an open-book test: you are expected to look at the passage while answering the questions.
- Reading Comprehension passages almost never include controversial opinions. Therefore, an answer choice like "advocated the overthrow of the government" is very likely to be incorrect.
- If you can eliminate even one answer choice, take a guess at the correct answer.

Taking Essay Tests

Writing prompts, or long essay questions, include key words that signal the strategy you will use to bring your ideas into sharp focus. Similarly, these key words also appear in constructed responses, or short essay questions.

Key Word	Strategy
Analyze	To **analyze** means to systematically and critically examine all parts of an issue or event.
Classify or categorize	To **classify** or **categorize** means to put people, things, or ideas into groups, based on a common set of characteristics.
Compare and contrast	To **compare** is to show how things are similar or alike. To **contrast** is to show how things are different.
Describe	To **describe** means to present a sketch or an impression. Rich detail, especially details that appeal to the senses, flesh out a description.
Discuss	To **discuss** means to systematically write about all sides of an issue or event.
Evaluate	To **evaluate** means to make a judgment and support it with evidence.
Explain	To **explain** means to clarify or make plain.
Illustrate	To **illustrate** means to provide examples or to show with a picture or other graphic.
Infer	To **infer** means to read between the lines or to use knowledge or experience to draw conclusions, make generalizations, or form a prediction.
Justify	To **justify** means to prove or to support a position with specific facts and reasons.
Predict	To **predict** means to tell what will happen in the future based on an understanding of prior events and behaviors.
State	To **state** means to briefly and concisely present information.
Summarize	To **summarize** means to give a brief overview of the main points of an event or issue.
Trace	To **trace** means to present the steps or stages in a process or an event in sequential or chronological order.

GLOSSARY/GLOSARIO

Pronunciation Key

This glossary lists the vocabulary words found in the selections in this book. The definition given is for the word as it is used in the selection; you may wish to consult a dictionary for other meanings of these words. The key below is a guide to the pronunciation symbols used in each entry.

a	at	**ō**	hope	**ng**	sing
ā	ape	**ô**	fork, all	**th**	thin
ä	father	**oo**	wood, put	**t͟h**	this
e	end	**o͞o**	fool	**zh**	treasure
ē	me	**oi**	oil	**ə**	ago, taken, pencil, lemon, circus
i	it	**ou**	out	**′**	indicates primary stress
ī	ice	**u**	up	**′**	indicates secondary stress
o	hot	**ū**	use		

ENGLISH

A

abash (ə bash′) *v.* to make ashamed or uneasy; to embarrass **p. 591**

absurdity (ab sur′də tē) *n.* something that is ridiculous; a piece of nonsense **p. 253**

accost (ə kôst′) *v.* to approach and speak to, especially in an aggressive manner **p. 58**

acquiesce (ak′ wē es′) *v.* to consent or agree to without protest **p. 79**

acquiescence (ak′ wē es′ əns) *n.* passive acceptance; compliance **p. 1168**

adamant (ad′ ə mənt) *adj.* rigidly determined **p. 366**

adjacent (ə jā′ sənt) *adj.* next to or close to; neighboring **p. 724**

admonition (ad′ mə nish′ ən) *n.* cautionary advice; warning **p. 137**

adversary (ad′ vər ser′ē) *n.* an opponent or enemy **p. 114**

ESPAÑOL

A

abash/avergonzar(se) *v.* producir vergüenza; abochornar; **p. 591**

absurdity/absurdo *s.* lo que no tiene sentido; que es irracional; **p. 253**

accost/abordar *v.* acercarse a alguien para hablar, especialmente en una manera agresiva **p. 58**

acquiesce/acceder *v.* mostrarse de acuerdo en lo que alguien solicita o quiere; **p. 79**

acquiescence/aquiescencia *s.* la acomodación a las opiniones o a los gustos ajenos; sumisión; **p. 1168**

adamant/inflexible *adj.* que no acepta cambios; **p. 366**

adjacent/adyacente *adj.* situado en las proximidades; contiguo; **p. 724**

admonition/advertencia *s.* llamarle a alguien la atención sobre algo; amonestación; **p. 137**

adversary/adversario(a) *s.* enemigo; persona o grupo que están en contra; **p. 114**

adversity (ad vur′ sə tē) *n.* hardship **p. 759**

affluence (af′ lo͞o əns) *n.* wealth; abundance of property **p. 403**

aghast (ə gast′) *adj.* filled with fear, horror, or amazement **p. 225**

aloof (ə lo͞of′) *adj.* emotionally distant; uninvolved; disinterested; standoffish **p. 1016**

amiability (ā′ mē ə bil′ə tē) *n.* the state of being friendly, sociable, and generally agreeable **p. 893**

anguish (ang′ gwish) *n.* extreme suffering; agony **p. 707**

anthology (an thol′ə jē) *n.* a collection of written works, such as poems, stories, or essays, in a single book or set **p. 321**

antiquity (an tik′ wə tē) *n.* an ancient time or times **p. 151**

apparition (ap′ ə rish′ ən) *n.* an unexpected or unusual sight **p. 883**

archetypal (är′ kə tī′ pəl) *adj.* serving as an ideal model or perfect example **p. 598**

ardor (är′ dər) *n.* passion; intensity of emotion; enthusiasm **p. 982**

augment (ôg ment′) *v.* to become greater; increase; grow **p. 346**

B

baleful (bāl′fəl) *adj.* threatening evil or intending harm **p. 894**

belittle (bi lit′ əl) *v.* to cause to seem less important; to scorn **p. 265**

belligerent (be lij′ ər ənt) *adj.* inclined or eager to fight **p. 578**

benediction (ben′ ə dik′ shən) *n.* short prayer used as a blessing **p. 274**

benevolently (bə nev′ ə lənt lē) *adv.* kindly **p. 115**

bestow (bi stō′) *v.* to give as a gift **p. 276**

bewildered (bi wil′ dərd) *adj.* perplexed or confused **p. 1172**

blatantly (blāt′ ənt lē) *adv.* obviously or conspicuously **p. 907**

blighted (blīt′ əd) *adj.* damaged or spoiled **p. 168**

adversity/adversidad *s.* infortunio; penalidad; **p. 759**

affluence/afluencia *s.* riqueza; abundancia de bienes; **p. 403**

aghast/espantado(a) *adj.* lleno de miedo, horror, o asombro **p. 225**

aloof/apartado(a) *adj.* distante emocionalmente; desinteresado; retraído **p. 1016**

amiability/amabilidad *s.* trato amable, agrado y afecto con los demás; **p. 893**

anguish/angustia *s.* sufrimiento extremo; agonía; **p. 707**

anthology/antología *s.* una colección de obras escritas, como poemas, historias, o ensayos, en un libro singular **p. 321**

antiquity/antigüedad *s.* un tiempo o unn época antigua **p. 151**

apparition/aparición *s.* manifestación de algo que antes no estaba o era desconocido; **p. 883**

archetypal/arquetípico(a) *adj.* que sirve como modelo o forma ideal; **p. 598**

ardor/ardor *s.* pasión; intensidad de emoción; entusiasmo **p. 982**

augment/aumentar *v.* hacer mayor en tamaño, en cantidad o intensidad; acrecentar; **p. 346**

B

baleful/funesto(a) *adj.* fiero, temible que causa espanto; **p. 894**

belittle/empequeñecer *v.* hacer que parecer menos importante; desdeñar **p. 265**

belligerent/belicoso(a) *adj.* que tiende a la violencia; que está impaciente luchar; **p. 578**

benediction/bendición *s.* petición de la protección divina; **p. 274**

benevolently/benévolamente *adv.* con cariño **p. 115**

bestow/conceder *v.* dar regalos; **p. 276**

bewildered/perplejo(a) *adj.* confundido, confuso; **p. 1172**

blatantly/obviamente *adv.* evidentemente o visiblemente **p. 907**

blighted/marchitado(a) *adj.* dañado o estropeado **p. 168**

bog (bog) *n.* a wetland ecosystem where shrubs and peat moss grow and various animals live **p. 592**

bravado (brə vä′ dō) *n.* pretended courage or confidence **p. 412**

brocade (brō kād′) *n.* a silk fabric with raised patterns embroidered on it **p. 651**

brood (bro͞od) *n.* the young of a family **p. 1069**

C

cadaverous (kə dav′ ər əs) *adj.* resembling a corpse in appearance; pale and thin **p. 1209**

calamity (kə lam′ ə tē) *n.* a disastrous event **p. 331**

calligraphy (kə lig′ re fē) *n.* artistic, decorative, or stylized writing or lettering **p. 568**

callousness (kal′ əs nes) *n.* state or attitude of feeling no emotion or sympathy **p. 365**

campaign (kam pān′) *n.* a series of related actions with the purpose of a specific goal, such as an election campaign **p. 70**

careen (kə ren′) *v.* to tilt or sway while moving, as if out of control **p. 164**

cataract (kat′ ə rakt′) *n.* a waterfall **p. 1159**

cathedral (ke thē′drəl) *n.* a large, important church; sometimes used to describe something of great importance **p. 467**

ceaselessly (sēs′ lis lē) *adv.* without stopping; continually **p. 534**

chalice (chal′ is) *n.* drinking cup; a cup-shaped interior of a flower **p. 602**

chamber (chām′ bər) *n.* a room, especially a bedroom **p. 1080**

chide (chīd) *v.* to express disapproval **p. 359**

cohort (kō′ hôrt) *n.* a companion, an associate, or a member of the same group **p. 1146**

collective (kə lek′ tiv) *adj.* having to do with a group of persons or things; common; shared **p. 150**

commemorate (kə mem′ ə rāt′) *v.* to preserve the memory of **p. 47**

bog/pantano *s.* ecosistema de tierra húmeda en que crece arbustos y musgo de pantano y donde animales varios viven; **p. 592**

bravado/bravuconada *s.* hecho con lo que parece valentía pero no lo es; **p. 412**

brocade/brocado *s.* tejido de seda con dibujos entretejidos; **p. 651**

brood/cría *s.* los jóvenes de una familia **p. 1069**

C

cadaverous/cadavérico(a) *adj.* pálido o flaco; con las características de un cadáver; **p. 1209**

calamity/calamidad *s.* situación desastrosa; **p. 331**

calligraphy/caligrafía *s.* técnica de escribir con letra bella según diferentes estilos; **p. 568**

callousness/callosidad *s.* insensibilidad; falta de compasión, humanidad y ternura; dureza de corazón; **p. 365**

campaign/campaña *s.* serie de actividades que se aplican para conseguir un fin, como una campaña electoral; **p. 70**

careen/carenar *v.* inclinar o oscilar cuando está moviendo, como si no tiene control **p. 164**

cataract/catarata *s.* cascada o salto de agua; **p. 1159**

cathedral/catedral *s.* iglesia principal de una zona que es sede de una diócesis; **p. 467**

ceaselessly/incesantemente *adv.* sin parar; continuamente; **p. 534**

chalice/cáliz *s.* copa o vaso; parte exterior de una flor formada por varias hojas, comúnmente verdes, que se unen al tallo (bot.); **p. 602**

chamber/cámara *s.* habitación, especialmente de uso privado y restringido; **p. 1080**

chide/regañar *v.* reprender o llamar la atención; comunicar desaprobación; **p. 359**

cohort/cohorte *s.* compañero o miembro del mismo grupo **p. 1146**

collective/colectivo(a) *adj.* de un grupo de personas o cosas; común; repartido **p. 150**

commemorate/conmemorar *v.* guardar la memoria de **p. 47**

commonplace (kom′ən plās′) *adj.* ordinary; not original or interesting **p. 251**

condemn (kən dem′) *v.* to declare to be wrong; to pronounce guilty **p. 448**

condone (ken doñ′) *v.* to excuse or overlook an offense, usually a serious one, without criticism **p. 31**

confidant (kon′ fə dant′) *n.* a person to whom secrets are entrusted **p. 313**

confiscate (kon′fis kāt′) *v.* to seize or take away **p. 101**

conglomerate (kən glom′ər it) *adj.* made up of separate parts collected together as one **p. 411**

console (kən sōl′) *v.* to comfort someone experiencing sorrow or disappointment **p. 397**

conspiracy (kən spir′ə sē) *n.* the act of secretly planning together **p. 193**

conspiratorial (kən spir′ə tôr′ ē əl) *adj.* suggesting a secret plot or plan **p. 917**

constricting (kən strikt′ ing) *adj.* restricting; limiting **p. 50**

contention (kən tən′shən) *n.* a point advanced in a debate or an argument **p. 448**

contour (kon′ toor) *n.* outline or general shape **p. 274**

contrive (kən trīv) *v.* to plan creatively; to bring about by scheming **p. 895**

cower (kou′ ər) *v.* to crouch or shrink back, as in fear or shame **p. 995**

craven (krā vən) *adj.* extremely cowardly **p. 212**

D

degenerate (di jen′ə rāt′) *v.* to decline or deteriorate **p. 101**

denigrate (den′ə grāt′) *v.* to criticize or belittle **p. 483**

depreciate (di prē′ shē āt′) *v.* to lessen the price or value of **p. 125**

detached (di tacht′) *adj.* separated; apart **p. 534**

detachment (di tach′mənt) *n.* indifference; a state of being apart from **p. 424**

diffidence (dif′ə dəns) *n.* shyness **p. 905**

commonplace/común *adj.* ordinario; vulgar o no selecto; **p. 251**

condemn/condenar *v.* desaprobar; decir que es malo; imponer un castigo; **p. 448**

condone/perdonar *v.* olvidar una ofensa, usualmente alguna seria, sin crítica **p. 31**

confidant/confidente *s.* una persona quien reciba secretos **p. 313**

confiscate/decomisar *v.* asir; incautar algo como pena; **p. 101**

conglomerate/conglomerado *s.* compuesto de partes distintos congregados junto como uno; **p. 411**

console/consolar *v.* confortar a alguien quiene tiene trizteza o frustración **p. 397**

conspiracy/conspiracíon *s.* el acto de planear juntos secretamente **p. 193**

conspiratorial/clandestino(a) *adj.* que sugiere una conspiración o un plan secreto; **p. 917**

constricting/constreñido(a) *adj.* restrictido; limitador **p. 50**

contention/argumento *s.* razonamiento que se usa para provar o demostrar algo; **p. 448**

contour/contorno *s.* líneas generales; perfil; **p. 274**

contrive/idear *v.* alcanzar lo que se intenta o desea; trazar; **p. 895**

cower/agacharse *v.* agazaparshe o retroceder, como si tiene miedo o vergüenza **p. 995**

craven/acobardado(n) *adj.* cobardísmo **p. 212**

D

degenerate/degenerar *v.* decaer o deteriorarse; **p. 101**

denigrate/denigrar *v.* ofender la reputación o la buena fama; menospreciar; **p. 483**

depreciate/depreciar *v.* aminorar el precio o el valor de algo **p. 125**

detached/separado(a) *adj.* aislado; suelto; **p. 534**

detachment/aislamiento *s.* separación de algo; indiferencia; **p. 424**

diffidence/timidez *s.* falta de seguridad o confianza en uno mismo; **p. 905**

diligent (dil′ ə jənt) *adj.* steady; responsible **p. 367**

dire (dīr) *adj.* dreadful; terrible **p. 15**

discern (di surn′) *v.* to detect or recognize; to make out **p. 27**

disconsolate (dis kon′ sə lit) *adj.* so unhappy that nothing can comfort; hopeless and depressed **p. 222**

discreet (dis krēt′) *adj.* showing good judgment; cautious **p. 235**

disdainful (dis dān′ fəl) *adj.* showing scorn for something or someone regarded as unworthy **p. 214**

dismantling (dis mant′ əl ing) *v.* taking apart; tearing down **p. 866**

disperse (dis purs′) *v.* to go off in different directions; to scatter **p. 1145**

distracted (dis trakt′ əd) *adj.* unable to pay attention; agitated **p. 136**

distraught (dis trôt′) *adj.* very upset; confused **p. 211**

diverge (di vurj′) *v.* to lead in different directions away from a common starting point **p. 610**

dollop (dol′ əp) *n.* a glob of a soft, mushy substance **p. 624**

dreary (drēr′ ē) *adj.* sad; depressing; dull; uninteresting **p. 592**

dubious (dōō′ bē əs) *adj.* skeptical; feeling doubt **p. 181**

E

ebb (eb) *v.* to become less or weaker; decline; fail **p. 1131**

ebulliently (i bul′ yent lē) *adv.* with overflowing enthusiasm **p. 918**

effusive (i fū′siv) *adj.* showing feeling freely **p. 897**

elation (i lā′ shən) *n.* a feeling of great joy; ecstasy **p. 238**

elixir (i lik′ sər) *n.* magical cure **p. 1152**

diligent/diligente *adj.* cuidadoso, exacto y activo; **p. 367**

dire/espantoso(a) *adj.* que causa terror, asombro, consternación; **p. 15**

discern/discernir *v.* detectar o reconocir, redactar **p. 27**

disconsolate/desconsolado(a) *adj.* tan infeliz que mada puede confortar; sin esperanza; deprimido **p. 222**

discreet/discreto(a) *adj.* juicioso; prudente; que muestra buen juicio **p. 235**

disdainful/desdeñoso(a) *adj.* que muestra desdén para algo o a alguien indignol o con una reputación sin valor **p. 214**

dismantling/desmantelando *v.* derribando o desmontando; **p. 866**

disperse/dispersar *v.* ir por direcciones diferentes; poner en fuga **p. 1145**

distracted/distraído(a) *adj.* que no presta atención a lo que sucede a su alrededor; **p. 136**

distraught/consternado(a) *adj.* conturbado y abatido; **p. 211**

diverge/divergir *v.* llevar en direcciones diferentes lejos de un punto de partida común; **p. 610**

dollop/porción (de masa) *s.* cantidad separada de otra mayor; **p. 624**

dreary/lóbrego(a) *adj.* triste; melancólico; sombrío; **p. 592**

dubious/dudoso(a) *adj.* escéptico; que siente incertidumbre **p. 181**

E

ebb/disminuir *v.* hacerse menos poderoso; decaer; faltar **p. 1131**

ebulliently/hirvientemente *adv.* con una superabundancia de entusiasmo **p. 918**

effusive/efusivo(a) *adj.* que manifiesta con intensidad los afectos o los sentimientos alegres; **p. 897**

elation/elación *s.* un sentimiento de alegría intensa; éxtasis **p. 238**

elixir/elixir *s.* medicamento o remedio maravilloso; **p. 1152**

eloquence (el′ə kwəns) *n.* the quality of persuasive, inspirational speech **p. 754**

emanate (em′ ə nāt′) *v.* to come forth **p. 15**

embroider (em broi′ dər) *v.* to make a story more interesting with imaginary details or exaggerations **p. 322**

endeavor (en dev′ ər) *n.* a serious or strenuous attempt to accomplish something **p. 83**

engrossed (in grōst′) *adj.* completely drawn in; absorbed **p. 1206**

enigma (i nig′ mə) *n.* a mystery; a baffling person or thing **p. 1128**

enthrall (en thrôl′) *v.* to hold spellbound; fascinate **p. 236**

eradicate (i rad′ ə kāt′) *v.* to get rid of completely **p. 442**

estuaries (es′choo͞ er′ ēz) *n.* places where rivers feed into the sea **p. 461**

exacerbate (ig zas′ər bāt′) *v.* to make worse, more violent, or more bitter **p. 421**

exalted (eg′ zôl təd) *adj.* noble; exaggerated **p. 880**

excruciating (iks kroo͞′ shē ā′ ting) *adj.* agonizing; intensely painful **p. 396**

exhilarated (ig zil′ ə rāt′ əd) *adj.* cheerful, lively, or excited **p. 315**

expedient (ik spē′ dē ənt) *adj.* fulfilling a specific need in a pressing situation; serving as a means to an end **p. 1207**

explicit (eks plis′ it) *adj.* definitely stated; clearly expressed **p. 59**

extricate (eks′ trə kāt′) *v.* to release from entanglement or difficulty; to set free **p. 48**

F

fervent (fur′ vənt) *adj.* having or showing great intensity of feeling; passionate **p. 16**

fetter (fet′ ər) *v.* to chain **p. 1070**

fickle (fik′ əl) *adj.* given to frequent changes of thought or mood; unreliable; inconstant **p. 767**

eloquence/elocuencia *s.* la facultad de persuadir, conmover o delitar con palabras habladas o escritas; **p. 754**

emanate/emanar *v.* desprenderse o salir de algo; **p. 15**

embroider/embellecer *v.* hacerun cuento más interesante con detalles imaginarios o exageraciones **p. 322**

endeavor/empeño *s.* esfuerzo en lo que se hace; **p. 83**

engrossed/absorbido(a) *adj.* muy atento o pendiente de una cosa; **p. 1206**

enigma/enigma *s.* un misterio; una persona o cosa desconcertante **p. 1128**

enthrall/esclavizar *v.* fascinar; tener encantado **p. 236**

eradicate/erradicar *v.* eliminar por completo; **p. 442**

estuaries/estuarios *s.* pl. desembocadura de un río en el mar; **p. 461**

exacerbate/exacerbar *v.* causar gran enfado o enojo, irritar; **p. 421**

exalted/exaltado(a) *adj.* noble; elevado; digno de admiración y respeto; **p. 880**

excruciating/angustioso(a) *adj.* doloroso intensamente; torturador **p. 396**

exhilarated/animado(a) *adj.* alegre, vivo, o excitado **p. 315**

expedient/conveniente *adj.* útil, adecuado u oportuno; **p. 1207**

explicit/explícito(a) *adj.* claro; expresado definitivamente **p. 59**

extricate/desembarazar *v.* liberar de enredo o dificultad; hacer libre **p. 48**

F

fervent/ardiente *adj.* que muestra una intensidad de sentimiento; apasionado **p. 16**

fetter/encadenar *v.* poner en cadenas **p. 1070**

fickle/caprichoso(a) *adj.* que obra arbitrariamente, según el humor o por antojo; inconstante; **p. 767**

fluidity (flo͞o i′ də tē) *n.* the ability, as of a liquid, to flow and change shape **p. 266**

forethought (for′ thôt′) *n.* thinking or planning beforehand **p. 558**

forge (fôrj) *v.* to form or make, especially by heating or hammering **p. 1070**

formidable (fôr′ mi də bəl) *adj.* impressive; awe-inspiring **p. 1240**

fugitive (fū′ jə tiv) *adj.* intending flight; running away or fleeing **p. 404**

fulfill (fo͞ol fil′) *v.* to measure up to, or satisfy; to bring to pass **p. 322**

furled (furld) *adj.* rolled up and secured **p. 867**

futilely (fū′ til ē) *adv.* uselessly; vainly; hopelessly **p. 152**

G

gale (gāl) *n.* a very strong wind **p. 591**

gamut (gam′ ət) *n.* the entire range or series of something **p. 226**

gelled (jeld) *adj.* in a semisolid state after having been liquid **p. 624**

glutton (glut′ ən) *n.* someone who eats greedily **p. 841**

gratification (grat′ ə fi kā′ shən) *n.* the condition of being pleased or satisfied **p. 252**

guile (gīl) *n.* slyness; craftiness; skillful deception **p. 965**

guise (gīz) *n.* outward appearance; false appearance **p. 1000**

H

haggard (hag′ ərd) *adj.* having a worn and tired look **p. 211**

haphazardly (hap′ haz′ ərd lē) *adv.* in a random or disorderly manner **p. 403**

haughty (hô′ tē) *adj.* very proud; scornful of others **p. 795**

horde (hôrd) *n.* crowd, throng, or swarm **p. 1044**

fluidity/fluidez *s.* la habilidad, como de un líquido, de fluir y cambiar forma **p. 266**

forethought/providencia *s.* cuidado que se pone al hacer algo para evitar problemas; precaución; **p. 558**

forge/forjar *v.* formar o hacer, especialmente por califacción o martilleo **p. 1070**

formidable/formidable *adj.* que infunde asombro y miedo; que causa respeto y tenor; **p. 1240**

fugitive/fugitivo(a) *adj.* que huye o se esconde; **p. 404**

fulfill/cumplir *v.* realizar; satisfacer **p. 322**

furled/aferrado(a) *adj.* plegar las velas y asegurarlas; **p. 867**

futilely/vanamente *adv.* desperadamente; inútilmente **p. 152**

G

gale/vendaval *s.* viento muy fuerte; **p. 591**

gamut/gama *s.* la escala entera o una serie de algo **p. 226**

gelled/en estado de gel frase *adj.* que la parte líquida está coagulada; **p. 624**

glutton/glotón(ona) *s.* que come mucho y con ansia; **p. 841**

gratification/satisfacción *s.* gusto o placer que se siente por algo **p. 252**

guile/astucia *s.* travesura; artería; engaño hábil **p. 965**

guise/guisa *s.* apariencia física; apariencia falsa **p. 1000**

H

haggard/macilento(a) *adj.* que tiene una apariencia cansada y usada **p. 211**

haphazard/casual *adj.* que sucede por casualidad; **p. 403**

haughty/orgulloso(a) *adj.* desdeñoso de los otros y con demasiado orgullo **p. 795**

horde/horda *n.* multitude, muchedumbre, o enjambre; **p. 1044**

host (hōst) *n.* a great number; a multitude **p. 520**

hyperactive (hī′ pər ak′ tiv) *adj.* overly energetic; very lively **p. 136**

I

impart (im pärt′) *v.* to make known; to tell **p. 110**

impartial (im pär′ shəl) *adj.* not favoring one side more than another; fair **p. 15**

impenetrable (im pen′ ə trə bəl) *adj.* inaccessible, or incapable of being **p. 260**

imperative (im per′ ə tiv) *adj.* absolutely necessary **p. 36**

imperious (im pēr′ ē əs) *adj.* commanding; dominant **p. 908**

impervious (im pur′ vē əs) *adj.* incapable of being passed through, affected, or disturbed **p. 386**

implacable (im plak′ ə bəl) *adj.* impossible to satisfy or soothe; unyielding **p. 1011**

implicitly (im plis′ it lē) *adv.* without question or reservation **p. 1193**

implore (im plôr′) *v.* to ask earnestly; to beg **p. 61**

imposing (im pō′ zing) *adj.* impressive in appearance or manner **p. 314**

impudence (im′ pyə dəns) *n.* speech or behavior that is aggressively forward or rude **p. 999**

impunity (im pū′ nə tē) *n.* freedom from punishment, harm, or bad consequences **p. 57**

imputation (im′ pyə tā′ shən) *n.* an accusation **p. 123**

inaugurate (in ô′ gyə rāt′) *v.* to make a formal beginning **p. 191**

incessantly (in ses′ ənt lē) *adv.* endlessly; constantly **p. 221**

inconsolable (in kən sō′ lə bəl) *adj.* heartbroken; impossible to comfort **p. 140**

incriminating (in krim′ ə nāt′ ing) *adj.* showing involvement in a crime **p. 332**

indiscernible (in′ di sur′ nə bəl) *adj.* difficult or impossible to see **p. 264**

infallibility (in fal′ ə bil′ ə tē) *n.* state of being incapable of error **p. 1256**

host/multitud *s.* gran cantidad de personas, animales o cosas; **p. 520**

hyperactive/hiperactivo(a) *adj.* que tiene exceso de actividad; **p. 136**

I

impart/impartir *v.* dar a conocer; decir **p. 110**

impartial/imparcial *adj.* que no favorece un lado más que el otro; justo **p. 15**

impenetrable/impenetrable *adj.* que no se puede penetrar o imposible de entender; **p. 260**

imperative/imperativo *adj.* absolutamente necesario **p. 36**

imperious/imperioso(a) *adj.* que manda o se comporta con claro autoritarismo; **p. 908**

impervious/ impenetrable *adj.* incapaz de ser permeado, afectado, o perturbado **p. 386**

implacable/implacable *adj.* imposible de satisfacer o aliviar; inflexible **p. 1011**

implicitly/implícitamente *adj.* de manera callada o silenciosa; **p. 1193**

implore/implorar *v.* preguntar seriamente; rogar **p. 61**

imposing/imponente *adj.* impresivo por la apararienca o la manera **p. 314**

impudence/aplomo *s.* dicho o comportamiento que es grosero o agresivamente delantero **p. 999**

impunity/impunidad *s.* libertad de castigo, daño, o consequencias malas **p. 57**

imputation/imputación *s.* una acusación **p. 123**

inaugurate/inaugurar *v.* hacer un comienzo formal **p. 191**

incessantly/incesantemente *adv.* que se repite con mucha frecuencia; **p. 221**

inconsolable/inconsolable *adj.* doloroso; imposible de consolar; **p. 140**

incriminating/inculpatorio(a) *adj.* que muestra que ha actuado en un delito; **p. 332**

indiscernible/imperceptible *adj.* que no se puede distinguir o identificar; **p. 264**

infallibility/infalibilidad *s.* estado de ser incapaz de hacer errores **p. 1256**

ingenious (in jēn′ yəs) *adj.* especially clever, inventive, or original **p. 1041**

inherent (in her′ ənt) *adj.* existing naturally in someone or something. **p. 461**

inhibition (in′ i bish′ ən) *n.* a restraint on one's natural impulses **p. 182**

inscrutable (in skrōō′ tə bəl) *adj.* not readily understood or interpreted **p. 1250**

intimation (in′ tə mā′ shən) *n.* a suggestion or hint **p. 330**

invincible (in vin′ sə bəl) *adj.* not able to be beaten or overcome **p. 421**

irreverent (i rev′ ər ənt) *adj.* showing a lack of proper respect **p. 316**

irrevocably (i rev′ ə kə blē) *adv.* in a way that cannot be revoked or undone **p. 1133**

isolated (ī′sə lāt′əd) *adj.* alone; cut off from others **p. 534**

itinerary (ī tin′ ər er′ ē) *n.* the planned route for a journey **p. 880**

J

jostle (jos′ əl) *v.* to bump, push, or shove roughly, as with elbows in a crowd **p. 1009**

K

keen (kēn) *adj.* sharp; intense **p. 602**

kindred (kin′drid) *n.* people who are related; family **p. 1058**

L

lament (lə ment′) *v.* to express deep sorrow **p. 787**

languid (lang′ gwid) *adj.* drooping; weak and listless **p. 1239**

languor (lang′ gər) *n.* weakness; fatigue **p. 82**

lavish (lav′ ish) *v.* to give generously; provide in abundance **p. 1016**

literate (lit′ ər it) *adj.* able to read and write **p. 1153**

ingenious/ingenioso(a) *adj.* especialmente listo, inventivo, u original; **p. 1041**

inherent/inherente *adj.* propio o característico de algo; algo que existo naturalmente en alguien o algo; **p. 461**

inhibition/prohibición *s.* una restricción sobre los impulsos naturales **p. 182**

inscrutable/inescrutable *adj.* que no se puede entender o interpretar fácilmente **p. 1250**

intimation/insinuación *s.* hecho que permite suponer algo; **p. 330**

invincible/invencible *adj.* que no puede ser vencido; **p. 421**

irreverent/irreverente *adj.* que muestra una falta de respeto **p. 316**

irrevocably/irrevocablemente *adv.* en una manera que no se puede revocar **p. 1133**

isolated/aislado(a) *adj.* solitario; separado de otros; **p. 534**

itinerary/itinerario *s.* la ruta planeada por un viaje **p. 880**

J

jostle/empujar *v.* empellar mientras se camina, como en una multitud **p. 1009**

K

keen/penetrante *adj.* agudo, intenso; **p. 602**

kindred/pariente *s.* de la familia ya sea por consanguinidad o afinidad; **p. 1058**

L

lament/lamentar *v.* expresar dolor profundo; **p. 787**

languid/lánguido(a) *adj.* débil o sin fuerzas; **p. 1239**

languor/languidez *s.* debilidad o falta de fuerza; falta de ánimo; **p. 82**

lavish/prodigar *v.* dar en gran cantidad o abundancia; **p. 1016**

literate/instruido(a) *adj.* que sabe leer y escribir; **p. 1153**

lithe (līth) *adj.* limber; bending easily **p. 183**

livelong (liv′ lông′) *adj.* complete; whole; used to emphasize the length of a period of time **p. 592**

logic (loj′ ik) *n.* a method of reasoning **p. 827**

lurk (lurk) *v.* to conceal oneself; to move about in a sneaky manner **p. 778**

M

magnitude (mag′ nə tōōd′) *n.* great size, volume, or extent; importance; significance **p. 475**

malodorous (mal ō′ dər əs) *adj.* bad-smelling; stinky **p. 117**

meticulous (mi tik′ yə ləs) *adj.* characterized by extreme or excessive care in the treatment of details **p. 1169**

misadventure (mis′ əd ven′ chər) *n.* a mishap; an unfortunate event **p. 791**

mock (mok) *v.* to make fun of or ridicule **p. 271**

molasses (mə las′ iz) *n.* a thick, dark brown syrup created by boiling down raw sugar **p. 74**

monogrammed (mon′ ə gramd) *adj.* decorated with a design of one or more letters, usually the initials of a name **p. 480**

monopoly (mə nop′ ə lē) *n.* exclusive possession or control **p. 829**

monotony (mə not′ ən ē) *n.* undesirable sameness **p. 1183**

mortal (môrt′ əl) *adj.* deadly **p. 71**

mourn (môrn) *v.* to feel or express grief or sorrow **p. 824**

muse (mūz) *v.* to think or reflect, especially in an idle, dreamy manner **p. 197**

N

negations (ni gā′ shənz) *n.* acts of denying; negative statements or denials **p. 460**

lithe/flexible *adj.* ágil; que dobla fácilmente **p. 183**

livelong/todo(a) *adj.* enteramente o completamente; usado para dar énfasis a la duración de un tiempo **p. 592**

logic/lógica *s.* razonamiento, método o sentido común; **p. 827**

lurk/acechar *v.* observar o esperar cautelosamente con algún propósito; merodear; **p. 778**

M

magnitude/magnitud *s.* tamaño o importancia; **p. 475**

malodorous/maloliente *adj.* férido; que ole malo **p. 117**

meticulous/meticuloso(a) *adj.* muy puntual, escrupuloso o concienzudo; **p. 1169**

misadventure/desgracia *s.* un contratiempo; un suceso infortunado **p. 791**

mock/burlar(se) *v.* reírse de algo o poner en ridículo; **p. 271**

molasses/melaza *s.* jarabe saturado obtenido entre dos cristalizaciones o cocciones sucesivas en la fabricación del azúcar; **p. 74**

monogrammed/con monograma *frase prep adj.* decorado con las letras de un nombre, generalmente las iniciales; **p. 480**

monopoly/monopolio *s.* ejercicio exclusivo de una actividad; **p. 829**

monotony/monotonía *s.* falta de variedad; **p. 1183**

mortal/mortal *adj.* que puede producir la muerte; que tiene que morir; muy fuerte o muy grande; **p. 71**

mourn/deplorar *v.* sentir o expresar pena o dolor **p. 824**

muse/ruminar *v.* discurrir fantásticamente y dar por cierto lo que no lo es; pensar; **p. 197**

N

negations/negaciones *s pl.* actos que niegan la veracidad de algo; **p. 460**

negligently (neg′ li jənt lē) *adv.* in a carelessly inattentive manner **p. 453**

negotiate (ni gō′ shē āt′) *v.* to discuss or compromise **p. 442**

nominal (nom′ ən əl) *adj.* insignificant **p. 1231**

nonchalant (non′ shə länt′) *adj.* having an air of easy unconcern or indifference **p. 905**

nostalgia (nos tal′ jə) *n.* a feeling of longing experienced when remembering the past; an overly sentimental feeling **p. 468**

novel (nov′ əl) *adj.* new and unusual **p. 16**

O

obstinately (ob′ stə nit lē) *adv.* stubbornly; in spite of reason or persuasion **p. 454**

ordain (ôr dān′) *v.* to appoint; to establish **p. 96**

P

pandemonium (pan′ də mō′ nē əm) *n.* wild uproar **p. 213**

pang (pang) *n.* a sudden sharp feeling of pain or distress **p. 385**

paperweight (pāp′ ər wāt′) *n.* a heavy, often decorative object traditionally used to hold down loose papers **p. 69**

paraphernalia (par′ ə fər nāl′ yə) *n.* personal items or equipment **p. 1040**

parasol (par′ ə sôl) *n.* small, decorative umbrella used for protection from the sun **p. 840**

parched (pärcht) *adj.* severely dry **p. 397**

parsimony (pär′sə mō′ nē) *n.* stinginess **p. 123**

pensive (pen′ siv) *adj.* thinking deeply, often sadly **p. 178**

perfidious (pər fi′ dē əs) *adj.* characterized by or related to betrayal; treacherous **p. 1214**

pernicious (pər nish′ əs) *adj.* destructive; deadly **p. 701**

perpetrator (pur′ pə trā′ tər) *n.* one who commits a crime or another similar act **p. 331**

negligently/negligentemente *adv.* en una manera sin atencíon o cuidado **p. 453**

negotiate/negociar *v.* referido a un asunto tratarlo o resolverlo; **p. 442**

nominal/nominal *adj.* pequeño y de poca importancia; insignificante; **p. 1231**

nonchalant/indiferente *adj.* que no importa que sea o se haga de una manera u otra; **p. 905**

nostalgia/nostalgia *s.* un sentimiento de añoranza cuando estaba recordando el pasado; un sentimiento demasiado sentimental **p. 468**

novel/nuevo(a) *adj.* raro o lo que no conocido antes **p. 16**

O

obstinately/obstinadamente *adv.* de forma perseverante o firme y decidida **p. 454**

ordain/decretar *v.* decidir o determinar por quien tiene autoridad; establecer; **p. 96**

P

pandemonium/pandemónium *s.* lugar en el que hay mucho ruido y confusión; **p. 213**

pang/punzada *s.* un sentimiento súbito y afilado, de daño o dolor **p. 385**

paperweight/pisapapeles *s.* objeto pesado que se coloca sobre los papeles para que no se muevan; **p. 69**

paraphernalia/bienes parafernales *s.* utensilios, herramientas o instrumentos de un oficio o arte; **p. 1040**

parasol/sombrilla *s.* tipo de paraguas que sirve para protegerse del sol; **p. 840**

parched/tostado(a) *adj.* severamente seco **p. 397**

parsimony/parsimonia *s.* tacañería; avaricia **p. 123**

pensive/pensativo(a) *adj.* que piensa profundamente, muchas veces con tristeza **p. 178**

perfidious/pérfido(a) *adj.* desleal, traidor, infiel; **p. 1214**

pernicious/pernicioso(a) *adj.* extremadamente malo o perjudicial; **p. 701**

perpetrator/perpetrador(a) *s.* que comete o consume un delito; **p. 331**

perpetually (pər pech′ o͞o əl ē) *adv.* constantly; unceasingly **p. 50**

perspicacity (pur′ spə kas′ ə tē) *n.* acute mental powers or perception **p. 1252**

pervade (pər vād′) *v.* to go through or fill every part of **p. 355**

perverse (pər vurs′) *adj.* deliberately unreasonable or wrong; stubborn **p. 728**

philosopher (fi los′ ə fər) *n.* thinker **p. 841**

pious (pī′ əs) *adj.* having either genuine or pretended religious devotion **p. 81**

placidly (plas′ id lē) *adv.* calmly; serenely **p. 373**

plait (plāt) *n.* a braid of material or hair **p. 651**

plausible (plô′ zə bəl) *adj.* apparently true or acceptable; likely **p. 1145**

plunder (plun′ dər) *v.* to take (property) by force, especially in warfare **p. 963**

ponderous (pon′ dər əs) *adj.* having great weight or bulk; heavy **p. 970**

portent (pôr′ tent) *n.* something that foreshadows a coming event **p. 1180**

posterity (pos ter′ ə tē) *n.* future generations **p. 705**

potent (pōt′ ənt) *adj.* having or exercising force, power, or authority; strong and powerful **p. 196**

precariously (pri kār′ ē əs lē) *adv.* dangerously; insecurely **p. 170**

preclude (pri klo͞od′) *v.* to prevent; to make impossible **p. 57**

predicament (pri dik′ ə mənt) *n.* a difficult or tricky situation **p. 760**

premonition (prē′ mə nish′ ən) *n.* anticipation of an event without outside warning or reason **p. 329**

pretentious (pri ten′ shəs) *adj.* expressing exaggerated importance or worth **p. 829**

pretext (prē′ tekst′) *n.* a claimed purpose, usually given to hide another purpose **p. 1200**

principle (prin′ sə pəl) *n.* a basic law, truth, or belief **p. 251**

perpetually/perpetuamente *adv.* constantamente; incesantemente **p. 50**

perspicacity/perspicacia *s.* agudeza mental, penetración o entendimiento; **p. 1252**

pervade/difundir(se) *v.* propagar, esparcir, extender; **p. 355**

perverse/obstinado(a) *adj.* perseverante y porfiado; **p. 728**

philosopher/filósofo *s.* persona que medita o reflexiona; **p. 841**

pious/piadoso(a) *adj.* religioso, devoto; **p. 81**

placidly/plácidamente *adv.* con quietud, sin perturbación; **p. 373**

plait/trenza *s.* conjunto de tres o más mechones que se cruzan entre sí alternativamente; de cabello u otra matera; **p. 651**

plausible/creíble *adj.* alparecer es verdad o aceptable; probable **p. 1145**

plunder/saquear *v.* apoderarse por la fuerza de lo que se encuentra en un lugar, especialmente en la guerra **p. 963**

ponderous/ponderoso(a) *adj.* que tiene peso grandre o bulto; pesado **p. 970**

portent/presagio *s.* adivinación o conocimiento de las cosas futuras; **p. 1180**

posterity/posteridad *s.* generaciones futuras; **p. 705**

potent/potente *adj.* que tiene capacidad para producir un efecto; grande o fuerte; **p. 196**

precariously/precariamente *adv.* peligrosamente; inseguramente **p. 170**

preclude/impedir *v.* prevenir; hacer imposible **p. 57**

predicament/apuro *s.* aprieto o situación difícil; **p. 760**

premonition/premonición *s.* presentimiento de que algo va a ocurrir; **p. 329**

pretentious/pretencioso(a) *adj.* que pretende ser más que lo que en realidad es; **p. 829**

pretext/pretexto *s.* motivo o causa simulada o aparente; **p. 1200**

principle/principio *s.* norma o idea fundamental que rige el pensamiento o la conducta; cada una de las ideas fundamentales en las que se basa un estudio; **p. 251**

privation (prī vā′ shən) *n.* the lack of the comforts or basic necessities of life **p. 226**

prodigal (prod′ i gəl) *adj.* dangerously extravagant; wasteful **p. 1193**

profane (prō fān′) *v.* to degrade or disrespect something holy or important **p. 719**

profound (prə found′) *adj.* significant; deep; intense **p. 233**

prowess (prau′ əs) *n.* incredible or superior talent or ability **p. 1215**

prudence (pro͞od′ əns) *n.* caution, good judgment **p. 126**

prudent (pro͞od′ ənt) *adj.* showing wisdom and good judgment **p. 455**

putrid (pū′ trid) *adj.* very nasty; disgusting **p. 137**

Q

quandary (kwon′ drē) *n.* state of indecision or doubt **p. 353**

R

rancor (rang′ kər) *n.* bitter resentment against someone; long-lasting spite **p. 734**

ravenous (rav′ ə nəs) *adj.* extremely hungry **p. 1181**

reconciliation (rek′ ən sil′ ē ā′ shən) *n.* a settlement of a controversy or disagreement **p. 84**

redundant (ri dun′ dənt) *adj.* unnecessarily repetitive; without a purpose **p. 482**

reiterate (rē it′ ə rāt′) *v.* to say again or do again; repeat **p. 170**

relent (ri lent′) *v.* to become less harsh or strict; to yield **p. 113**

renowned (ri nound′) *adj.* famous; widely known **p. 1002**

replenish (ri plen′ ish) *v.* to fill, supply, or build up again **p. 402**

repulsive (ri pul′ siv) *adj.* arousing aversion or disgust **p. 1170**

résumé (rez′oo mā′) *n.* a listing of one's accomplishments; a summary **p. 919**

privation/privación *s.* la falta de comodidades o necesidades basicas de vivir **p. 226**

prodigal/pródigo *adj.* que desperdicia en gastos inútiles; **p. 1193**

profane/profanar *v.* referido a algo sagrado o importante tratarlo sin respeto o deshonrarlo; **p. 719**

profound/profundo(a) *adj.* significante; hondo; intenso **p. 233**

prowess/destreza *s.* habilidad o arte para hacer algo bien hecho; **p. 1215**

prudence/prudencia *s.* aviso; buen juicio **p. 126**

prudent/prudente *adj.* que actúa con cautela y tiene sensatez y buen juicio; **p. 455**

putrid/pútrido(a) *adj.* podrido, dañado, echado a perder; **p. 137**

Q

quandary/incertidumbre *s.* estado de duda o con temor de errar; **p. 353**

R

rancor/rencor *s.* resentimiento arraigado y que resulta difícil de quitar; **p. 734**

ravenous/famélico(a) *adj.* hambriento; **p. 1181**

reconciliation/reconciliación *s.* restablecimiento de buenas relaciones; **p. 84**

redundant/redundante *adj.* que sobra; que se repite innecesariamente; **p. 482**

reiterate/reiterar *v.* decir otravez o hacer otra vez; repetir **p. 170**

relent/ceder *v.* hacerse menos áspero o estricto; rendir **p. 113**

renowned/renombrado(a) *adj.* famoso; conocido extensamente **p. 1002**

replenish/rellenar *v.* abastecer, poner de nuevo, reemplazar; **p. 402**

repulsive/repulsivo(a) *adj.* que produce asco o rechazo; **p. 1170**

résumé/resumen *n.* una lista o inscripción de sus logros o éxitos; un sumario; **p. 919**

retain (ri tān′) *v.* to keep possession of **p. 726**

retrospect (ret′ rə spekt′) *n.* the act of looking back or thinking about the past **p. 322**

reverberate (ri vur′ bə rāt′) *v.* to echo; resound **p. 389**

reverent (rev′ ər ənt) *adj.* feeling or expressing respect or courtesy **p. 598**

reverie (rev′ ər ē) *n.* fanciful thinking, especially of pleasant things; a daydream **p. 1147**

revive (ri vīv′) *v.* to bring back to life; to give new strength **p. 784**

riveted (riv′ it əd) *adj.* fixed or secured firmly **p. 878**

rosin (roz′ in) *n.* a resin made from the sap of various pine trees and used to increase sliding friction on the bows of certain stringed instruments **p. 578**

S

sanction (sangk′ shən) *v.* to give official approval or permission **p. 870**

scrutinize (skrōōt′ ən īz′) *v.* to scan, inspect, or examine **p. 97**

serene (sə ren′) *adj.* calm; peaceful; undisturbed **p. 167**

severance (sev′ ər əns) *n.* the act of cutting off or apart **p. 395**

shrill (shril) *adj.* loud; piercing **p. 1059**

shroud (shroud) *v.* to cover, as with a veil or burial cloth; conceal **p. 988**

shun (shun) *v.* to keep away from; avoid **p. 982**

signify (sig′ nə fī′) *v.* to represent or mean; to indicate **p. 252**

singular (sing′ gyə lər) *adj.* unusual or out of the ordinary; odd **p. 1230**

solicitude (sə lis′ ə tōōd′) *n.* care or concern **p. 908**

solitude (sol′ ə tōōd′) *n.* isolation; the state of being alone **p. 520**

sow (sō) *v.* to plant by scattering seeds **p. 660**

retain/retener *v.* conservar en la memoria; conservar; **p. 726**

retrospect/mirada retrospectiva *s.* el acto de reflexionar sobre el pasado **p. 322**

reverberate/reflejar *v.* hacer un eco; resonar **p. 389**

reverent/reverente *adj.* que muestra o expresa respeto; **p. 598**

reverie/ensueño *s.* pensamiento imaginativo, especialmente de cosas agradables; fantasía **p. 1147**

revive/revivir *v.* resucitar; recuperar la vitalidad; **p. 784**

riveted/remachado(a) *adj.* sujeto con remaches; **p. 878**

rosin/colofonia *s.* resina obtenida en la destilación de la trementina de pinos y otros árboles; **p. 578**

S

sanction/sancionar *v.* autorizar o aprobar un acto; **p. 870**

scrutinize/escrutar *v.* explorar, indagar o examinar atentamente; **p. 97**

serene/sereno(a) *adj.* tranquilo; pacífico; quieto **p. 167**

severance/separación *s.* el acto de cortar o separar algo **p. 395**

shrill/chillón(ona) *adj.* sonido con una frecuencia de vibración grande; **p. 1059**

shroud/amortajar *v.* cubrir, como con un velo o tela de entierro; ocultar **p. 988**

shun/eludir *v.* apartarse de; evitar **p. 982**

signify/significar *v.* expresar o querer decir; **p. 252**

singular/singular *adj.* raro, excelente o extraordinario; peculiar; **p. 1230**

solicitude/preocupación *s.* lo que despierta interés, cuidado o atención; **p. 908**

solitude/soledad *s.* falta de compañía, estar solo; **p. 520**

sow/sembrar *v.* arrojar, esparcir o colocar la semilla en la tierra para que crezca; **p. 660**

spew (spū) *v.* to emerge forcefully, in a stream **p. 1159**

spurn (spurn) *v.* to reject with disdain or contempt **p. 1181**

staff (staf) *n.* a long stick used for assistance with walking or as a weapon **p. 1081**

staggering (stag′ ər ing) *adj.* shocking; overwhelming **p. 470**

stead (sted) *n.* place **p. 1084**

stifle (stī′ fəl) *v.* to smother for lack of air; to prevent from developing properly **p. 782**

stoke (stōk) *v.* to stir up; to cause to increase **p. 356**

subsequent (sub′ sə kwənt) *adj.* following in time, order, or place **p. 453**

suffuse (sə fūz′) *v.* to spread through or over **p. 385**

suitor (so͞o′ tər) *n.* a man who courts a woman in hope of marrying her **p. 1080**

supplicant (sup′ lə kənt) *n.* one who asks humbly and earnestly **p. 598**

surge (surj) *v.* to move suddenly in a wave **p. 355**

surreptitiously (sur′ əp tish′ əs lē) *adv.* secretly or slyly **p. 182**

symmetrical (si met′ ri kəl) *adj.* exactly agreeing in size, form, and arrangement on both sides of something **p. 345**

T

tangible (tan′ jə bəl) *adj.* capable of being touched or felt **p. 25**

tantalize (tant′ əl īz′) *v.* to torment or tease by tempting with something and then withholding it **p. 1129**

tax (taks) *v.* to place a heavy burden on; to strain **p. 558**

tedious (tē′ dē əs) *adj.* tiresome; boring **p. 802**

template (tem′ plāt) *n.* a pattern that serves as a guide to making something accurately **p. 481**

tentative (ten′ tə tiv) *adj.* hesitant; uncertain **p. 52**

spewing/salir *v.* salir de forma acelerada, apresurada o atropellada; **p. 1159**

spurn/rechazar *v.* mostrar oposición o desprecio; **p. 1181**

staff/bastón *s.* vara que sirve para apoyarse al andar; **p. 1081**

staggering/asombroso(a) *adj.* que causa admiración, susto o espanto; **p. 470**

stead/lugar *s.* sitio; espacio ocupado o que puede ser ocupado; **p. 1084**

stifle/sofocar *v.* impedir la respiración; **p. 782**

stoke/avivar *v.* aumentar la fuerza de algo; animar, excitar; **p. 356**

subsequent/subsiguiente *adj.* que sigue inmediatamente; en tiempo, orden o lugar; **p. 453**

suffuse/esparcir *v.* extender o bañar; diseminar **p. 385**

suitor/pretendiente *s.* persona que aspira a casarse con otra; **p. 1080**

supplicant/suplicante *s.* persona que pide con humildad y sumisión; **p. 598**

surge/levantar(se) *v.* empezar a producirse como un oleaje; **p. 355**

surreptitiously/subrepticiamente *adv.* secretamente o furtivamente **p. 182**

symmetrical/simétrico(a) *adj.* exactamente lo mismo (en el tamaño, la forma, y el arreglo de algo) **p. 345**

T

tangible/tangible *adj.* capaz de ser tocado o sentido **p. 25**

tantalize/atormentar *v.* tortutar o fastidiar por temptar con algo (y entonces lo detener) **p. 1129**

tax/fatigar *v.* someter a un esfuerzo; **p. 558**

tedious/tedioso(a) *adj.* cansado; aburrido **p. 802**

template/plantilla *s.* pieza que se coloca sobre otra y que sirve como guía para cortar o dibujar; **p. 481**

tentative/tentativo(a) *adj.* vacilante; incierto **p. 52**

tenuously (ten′ ū əs lē) *adv.* uncertainly; shakily **p. 418**

terrain (tə rān′) *n.* the physical features of the land **p. 423**

testimony (tes′ tə mō′ nē) *n.* a solemn declaration **p. 442**

throng (thrông) *n.* a large number of people or things crowded together **p. 384**

tiered (tērd) *adj.* arranged in layers or levels **p. 868**

toil (toil) *v.* to work very hard or for long hours **p. 660**

transcend (tran send′) *v.* to go beyond **p. 366**

traverse (trav′ ərs) *v.* to pass across or through **p. 345**

treacherous (trech′ ər əs) *adj.* marked by betrayal of fidelity, confidence, or trust **p. 98**

tread (tred) *n.* step or footstep **p. 276**

trifle (trī′ fəl) *n.* something of little value or importance **p. 1251**

tumult (tōō′ məlt) *n.* commotion; uproar **p. 983**

twine (twīn) *v.* to coil around **p. 568**

U

ubiquitous (ū bik′ wə təs) *adj.* seeming to be everywhere at once **p. 151**

uncanny (un kan′ ē) *adj.* not normal or natural; seemingly supernatural in origin **p. 1037**

unintelligible (un′ in tel′ ə jə bəl) *adj.* not able to be understood **p. 412**

unsavory (un sā′ vər ē) *adj.* unpleasant in character; disagreeable to the taste **p. 798**

unstratified (un strat′ ə fīd) *adj.* not structured into different social classes **p. 461**

V

valor (val′ ər) *n.* great courage, especially in battle **p. 963**

vanquished (vang′ kwishd) *n.* people who have been defeated in battle **p. 881**

tenuously/débilmente *adv.* con poco vigor con poca fuerza; **p. 418**

terrain/terreno *s.* características físicas de la tierra ; **p. 423**

testimony/testimonio *s.* declaración o explicación de alguien que afirma o asegura algo; prueba de la verdad de algo; **p. 442**

throng/muchedumbre *s.* un gran número de gente o cosas; una peña **p. 384**

tiered/por niveles *frase prep.* adj. organizado en diferentes alturas; **p. 868**

toil/trabajar duro *frase verbal* trabajar con gran esfuerza; **p. 660**

transcend/exceder *v.* sobrepasar o superar; **p. 366**

traverse/atravesar *v.* cruzar o pasar por **p. 345**

treacherous/traicionero(a) *adj.* que denota traición o falsedad; **p. 98**

tread/pisada *s.* paso, golpe dado con el pie; **p. 276**

trifle/bagatela *s.* de poco valor o importancia; **p. 1251**

tumult/tumulto *s.* conmoción; alboroto **p. 983**

twine/enroscar *v.* colocar en forma de rosca; **p. 568**

U

ubiquitous/obicuo(a) *adj.* que parecer estar por todas partes ahora mismo **p. 151**

uncanny/extraño(a) *adj.* que es raro o distinto de lo normal; **p. 1037**

unintelligible/ininteligible *adj.* que no se puede entender; **p. 412**

unsavory/insípido(a) *adj.* desagradable en carácter; desagradable en sabor **p. 798**

unstratified/no por estratos frase *adj.* sin capas o niveles en la sociedad; **p. 461**

V

valor/valor *s.* valería, especialmente en batalla **p. 963**

vanquished/vencido(a) *adj.* pueblo o individuo que ha sido derrotado; **p. 881**

venture (ven′ chər) *n.* an undertaking involving chance, risk, or danger **p. 441**

verbatim (vər bā′ tim) *adv.* word for word; in exactly the same words **p. 346**

veritably (ver′ i tə blē) *adv.* truly **p. 1199**

vice (vīs) *n.* a moral fault or failing **p. 448**

vigilant (vij′ əl ənt) *adj.* alert and watchful for danger or trouble **p. 236**

W

want (wont) *v.* to fail to possess; to lack **p. 610**

withered (wi<u>th</u>′ ərd) *adj.* shriveled or dried up **p. 1061**

writhe (rīth) *v.* to twist in pain **p. 1071**

Z

zealous (zel′ əs) *adj.* very eager; enthusiastic **p. 37**

venture/empresa *s.* acción o tarea que conlleva dificultad o riesgo; **p. 441**

verbatim/literalmente *adv.* palabra por palabra; en las mismas palabras **p. 346**

veritably/verdaderamente *adv.* realmente; sinceramente **p. 1199**

vice/vicio *s.* mal hábito que se repite con frecuencia; costumbre gusto o necesidad censurable, especialmente en sentido moral; **p. 448**

viligant/vigilante *adj.* alerta y en vela por peligro o problemas **p. 236**

W

want/carecer de *v.* no tener algo; **p. 610**

withered/marchito(a) *adj.* falto de frescura, vigor o vitalidad; **p. 1061**

writhe/torcer *v.* retorcer a causa de dolor **p. 1071**

Z

zealous/fervoroso(a) *adj.* entusiasta; muy ávido **p. 37**

ACADEMIC WORD LIST

The list of words that appears on this page and the following pages represents a research-based collection of words that are commonly used in academic texts. The purpose of the list is to present students with the basics of a working academic vocabulary, one that will prove useful in reading, writing, and research in many areas of study. Many of these words also appear throughout the Glencoe Language Arts program.

Sublist One

analysis
approach
area
assessment
assume
authority
available
benefit
concept
consistent
constitutional
context
contract
create
data
definition
derived
distribution
economic
environment
established
estimate
evidence
export
factors
financial
formula
function
identified
income
indicate
individual
interpretation
involved
issues
labor
legal
legislation
major
method
occur
percent
period
policy
principle
procedure
process
required
research
response
role
section
sector
significant
similar
source
specific
structure
theory
variables

Sublist Two

achieve
acquisition
administration
affect
appropriate
aspects
assistance
categories
chapter
commission
community
complex
computer
conclusion
conduct
consequences
construction
consumer
credit
cultural
design
distinction
elements
equation
evaluation
features
final
focus
impact
injury
institute
investment
items
journal
maintenance
normal
obtained
participation
perceived
positive
potential
previous
primary
purchase
range
region
regulations
relevant
resident
resources
restricted
security
select
site
sought
strategies
survey
text
traditional
transfer

Sublist Three

alternative
circumstances
comments
compensation
components
consent
considerable
constant
constraints
contribution
convention
coordination
core
corporate
corresponding
criteria
deduction
demonstrate
document
dominant
emphasis
ensure
excluded
framework
funds
illustrated
immigration
implies
initial
instance
interaction
justification
layer
link
location
maximum
minorities
negative
outcomes
partnership

philosophy
physical
proportion
published
reaction
registered
reliance
removed
scheme
sequence
sex
shift
specified
sufficient
task
technical
techniques
technology
validity
volume

Sublist Four

access
adequate
annual
apparent
approximated
attitudes
attributed
civil
code
commitment
communication
concentration
conference
contrast
cycle
debate
despite
dimensions
domestic
emerged
error
ethnic
goals
granted
hence
hypothesis
implementation
implications
imposed
integration
internal
investigation
job
label
mechanism
obvious
occupational
option
output
overall
parallel
parameters
phase
predicted
principal
prior
professional
project
promote
regime
resolution
retained
series
statistics
status
stress
subsequent
sum
summary
undertaken

Sublist Five

academic
adjustment
alter
amendment
aware
capacity
challenge
clause
compounds
conflict
consultation
contact
decline
discretion
draft
enable
energy
enforcement
entities
equivalent
evolution
expansion
exposure
external
facilitate
fundamental
generated
generation
image
liberal
license
logic
marginal
medical
mental
modified
monitoring
network
notion
objective
orientation
perspective
precise
prime
psychology
pursue
ratio
rejected
revenue
stability
styles
substitution
sustainable
symbolic
target
transition
trend
version
welfare
whereas

Sublist Six

abstract
accurate
acknowledged
aggregate
allocation
assigned
attached
author
bond
brief
capable
cited
cooperative
discrimination
display
diversity
domain
edition
enhanced
estate
exceed
expert
explicit
federal
fees
flexibility
furthermore
gender
ignored
incentive
incidence
incorporated
index
inhibition
initiatives
input
instructions
intelligence
interval
lecture
migration
minimum
ministry
motivation
neutral
nevertheless
overseas
preceding
presumption
rational
recovery
revealed
scope
subsidiary
tapes
trace
transformation
transport
underlying
utility

Sublist Seven

adaptation
adults
advocate
aid
channel
chemical
classical

comprehensive
comprise
confirmed
contrary
converted
couple
decades
definite
deny
differentiation
disposal
dynamic
eliminate
empirical
equipment
extract
file
finite
foundation
global
grade
guarantee
hierarchical
identical
ideology
inferred
innovation
insert
intervention
isolated
media
mode
paradigm
phenomenon
priority
prohibited
publication
quotation
release
reverse
simulation
solely
somewhat
submitted
successive
survive
thesis
topic
transmission
ultimately
unique
visible
voluntary

Sublist Eight

abandon
accompanied
accumulation
ambiguous
appendix
appreciation
arbitrary
automatically
bias
chart
clarity
conformity
commodity
complement
contemporary
contradiction
crucial
currency
denote
detected
deviation
displacement
dramatic
eventually
exhibit
exploitation
fluctuations
guidelines
highlighted
implicit
induced
inevitably
infrastructure
inspection
intensity
manipulation
minimized
nuclear
offset
paragraph
plus
practitioners
predominantly
prospect
radical
random
reinforced
restore
revision
schedule
tension
termination
theme
thereby
uniform
vehicle
via
virtually
visual
widespread

Sublist Nine

accommodation
analogous
anticipated
assurance
attained
behalf
bulk
ceases
coherence
coincide
commenced
concurrent
confined
controversy
conversely
device
devoted
diminished
distorted
duration
erosion
ethical
format
founded
incompatible
inherent
insights
integral
intermediate
manual
mature
mediation
medium
military
minimal
mutual
norms
overlap
passive
portion
preliminary
protocol
qualitative
refine
relaxed
restraints
revolution
rigid
route
scenario
sphere
subordinate
supplementary
suspended
team
temporary
trigger
unified
violation
vision

Sublist Ten

adjacent
albeit
assembly
collapse
colleagues
compiled
conceived
convinced
depression
encountered
enormous
forthcoming
inclination
integrity
intrinsic
invoked
levy
likewise
nonetheless
notwithstanding
odd
ongoing
panel
persistent
posed
reluctant
so-called
straightforward
undergo
whereby

INDEX OF SKILLS

References beginning with R refer to handbook pages.

Literary Concepts

Reading and Critical Thinking

Vocabulary

Writing

Grammar

Speaking, Listening, and Viewing

Research, Test-Taking, and Study Skills

Interdisciplinary Activities

INDEX OF AUTHORS AND TITLES

INDEX OF ART AND ARTISTS

S

T

U

V

W

Y

Z

ACKNOWLEDGMENTS

Unit 1

"The Most Dangerous Game" by Richard Connell. Copyright © 1924 by Richard Connell. Copyright renewed © 1952 by Louise Fox Connell. Used by permission of Brandt & Hochman Literary Agents, Inc. Any electronic copying or distribution of this text is expressly forbidden.

"The Leap" by Louise Erdrich. First published in *Harper's* magazine, March 1990. Later adapted for inclusion in *Tales of Burning Love* (HarperCollins, 1996). Copyright © 1990 and 1996 by Louise Erdrich, reprinted by permission of The Wylie Agency.

"Blues Ain't No Mockin Bird", copyright © 1971 by Toni Cade Bambara, from *Gorilla, My Love* by Toni Cade Bambara. Used by permission of Random House, Inc.

"The Garden of Stubborn Cats" from *Marcovaldo or the Seasons in the City* by Italo Calvino, copyright © 1963 by Giulio Einaudi editore s.p.a., Torino, English translation by William Weaver, copyright © 1983 by Harcourt, Inc. and Martin Secker & Warburg, Ltd., reprinted by permission of Harcourt, Inc.

"Rules of the Game" from *The Joy Luck Club* by Amy Tan. Copyright © 1989 by Amy Tan. Used by permission of G. P. Putnam's Sons, a division of Penguin Group (USA) Inc.

"Liberty" by Julia Alvarez. Copyright © 1996 by Julia Alvarez. First published in *Writer's Harvest 2,* edited by Ethan Canin, published by Harcourt Brace and Company, 1996. Reprinted by permission of Susan Bergholz Literary Services, New York. All rights reserved.

"The Struggle to Be an All-American Girl" by Elizabeth Wong. Reprinted by permission of the author, www.elizabethwong.net.

"Grudnow" from *The Imperfect Paradise* by Linda Pastan. Copyright © 1988 by Linda Pastan. Used by permission of W. W. Norton & Company, Inc.

"Sweet Potato Pie" by Eugenia Collier. Reprinted by permission of the author.

"The Scarlet Ibis" by James Hurst. Reprinted by permission of the author.

"The Bass, the River, and Sheila Mant" is from *The Man Who Loved Levittown,* by W. D. Wetherell, © 1985. Used by permission of the University of Pittsburgh Press.

"A Christmas Memory" by Truman Capote, copyright © 1956 by Truman Capote. Used by permission of Random House, Inc.

"The Secret Life of Walter Mitty" from *My World–And Welcome to It* © 1942 by James Thurber. Copyright renewed 1971 by James Thurber. Reprinted by permission of Rosemary A. Thurber and The Barbara Hogenson Agency. All rights reserved.

Calvin and Hobbes, © 1995 Watterson. Dist. by Universal Press Syndicate. Reprinted with permission. All rights reserved.

"American History" from *The Latin Deli: Prose and Poetry* by Judith Ortiz Cofer. Copyright © 1993 by Judith Ortiz Cofer. Reprinted by permission of The University of Georgia Press.

"The Drums of Washington" from *A Thousand Days: John F. Kennedy in the White House* by Arthur M. Schlesinger, Jr. Copyright © 1965, and renewed 1993 by Arthur M. Schlesinger, Jr. Reprinted by permission of Houghton Mifflin Company. All rights reserved.

"The Flat of the Land" by Diana Garcia. Reprinted by permission of the author.

Unit 2

Copyright © 1995 by Julia Alvarez. From "On Finding a Latino Voice," first published in Washington Post Book World, May 14, 1995, and later published in *Something to Declare,* by Plume, an imprint of Penguin Group (USA), in 1999 and originally in hardcover by Algonquin Books of Chapel Hill. Reprinted by permission of Susan Bergholz Literary Services, New York. All rights reserved.

"Of Dry Goods and Black Bow Ties" by Yoshiko Uchida, courtesy of the Bancroft Library, University of California, Berkeley.

"Only Daughter" by Sandra Cisneros. Copyright © 1990 by Sandra Cisneros. First published in *Glamour,* November 1990. Reprinted by permission of Susan Bergholz Literary Services, New York. All rights reserved.

"A Brother's Crime" from *Good Brother, Bad Brother: The Story of Edwin Booth and John Wilkes Booth* by James Cross Giblin. Copyright © 2005 by James Cross Giblin. Reprinted by permission of Clarion Books, an imprint of Houghton Mifflin Company. All rights reserved.

Reprinted with the permission of Simon Spotlight Entertainment, an imprint of Simon & Schuster, from *The Story of My Life: An Afghan Girl on the Other Side of the Sky* by Farah Ahmedi with Tamim Ansary. Text copyright © 2005 Nestegg Productions LLC.

From *All Things Bright and Beautiful* by James Herriot, copyright © 1974 by the author and reprinted by permission of St. Martin's Press, LLC.

"Ali" by W. S. Merwin. Copyright © 2003 by W. S. Merwin. Used by permission of The Wylie Agency.

From *All God's Children Need Traveling Shoes* by Maya Angelou, copyright © 1986 by Maya Angelou. Used by permission of Random House, Inc.

"Field Trip" by Naomi Shihab Nye. Reprinted by permission of the author.

"The Solace of Open Spaces" from *The Solace of Open Spaces* by Gretel Ehrlich, copyright © 1985 by Gretel Ehrlich. Used by permission of Viking Penguin, a division of Penguin Group (USA) Inc.

"Sayonara" from *North to the Orient,* copyright 1935 and renewed 1963 by Anne Morrow Lindbergh, reprinted by permission of Harcourt, Inc.

From *Into Thin Air* by Jon Krakauer, copyright © 1997 by Jon Krakauer. Used by permission of Villard Books, a division of Random House, Inc.

"That One Man's Profit Is Another's Loss" from *Essays* by Michel de Montaigne, translated with an introduction by J. M. Cohen (Penguin Classics, 1958). Copyright © J. M. Cohen, 1958. Reprinted by permission of Penguin Group (UK).

"The American Cause" from *The Theme Is Freedom* by John Dos Passos. Reprinted by permission of Lucy Dos Passos Coggin, owner and assigned of copyright.

From "Thoughts on Fenway Park," by Jayson Stark. ESPN.com. Copyright © 2005 ESPN Internet Ventures. Reprinted by permission.

From "Being Perfect" by Anna Quindlen. Copyright © 1999 by Anna Quindlen. Reprinted by permission of International Creative Management, Inc.

Unit 3

"who are you,little i" copyright © 1963, 1991 by the Trustees for the E. E. Cummings Trust, from *Complete Poems: 1904–1962* by E. E. Cummings. Edited by George J. Firmage. Used by permission of Liveright Publishing Corporation.

"Earth Your Dancing Place" from *Nature: Poems Old and New* by May Swenson. Copyright © 1994 by the Literary Estate of May Swenson. Reprinted by permission of Houghton Mifflin Company. All rights reserved.

"The Black Snake" from *Twelve Moons* by Mary Oliver. Copyright © 1972, 1973, 1974, 1976, 1978, 1979 by Mary Oliver. By permission of Little, Brown and Co., Inc.

"The Peace of Wild Things" from *Openings,* copyright © 1968 and renewed 1996 by Wendell Berry, reprinted by permission of Harcourt Brace & Company.

From *The Devil in the White City* by Erik Larson, copyright © 2003 by Erik Larson. Used by permission of Crown Publishers, a division of Random House, Inc.

Haiku by Bashō and haiku by Chiyo, from *Zen Art for Meditation* by Stewart W. Holmes and Chimyo Horioko. Reprinted by permission of Charles E. Tuttle Co., Inc.

"Haiku" by Katy Peake, from *Shared Sightings,* copyright © 1995 by Sheila Golburgh Johnson. Reprinted by permission of Daniel & Daniel Publishers, Inc.

"Peace" by Paula Yup. Reprinted by permission of the author.

"How Things Work" from *A Fire In My Hands,* copyright © 2006, 1999 by Gary Soto, reprinted by permission of Harcourt, Inc.

"I Was a Skinny Tomboy Kid" by Alma Luz Villanueva. Reprinted by permission of the author.

"The World Is Not A Pleasant Place to Be" from *My House* by Nikki Giovanni. Copyright © 1972 by Nikki Giovanni. Reprinted by permission of HarperCollins Publishers.

"Hope is the thing with feathers" and "I'm Nobody! Who are you?" reprinted by permission of the publishers, and the Trustees of Amherst College from *The Poems of Emily Dickinson,* Thomas H. Johnson, ed., Cambridge, Mass: The Belknap Press of Harvard University Press, copyright © 1951, 1955, 1979, 1983 by the President and Fellows of Harvard College.

"Defining the Grateful Gesture" by Yvonne Sapia. Reprinted by permission of the author.

"Remember" by Joy Harjo, from the book *She Had Some Horses.* Copyright © 1983. Appears by permission of the publisher, Thunder's Mouth Press, A Division of Avalon Publishing Group, Inc.

"The Road Not Taken" from *The Poetry of Robert Frost,* edited by Edward Connery Latham. Copyright 1916, 1969 by Henry Holt and Company. Copyright 1944 by Robert Frost. Reprinted by permission of Henry Holt and Company, LLC.

"The Secret" by Denise Levertov, from *Poems 1960–1967,* copyright © 1964 by Denise Levertov. Reprinted by permission of New Directions Publishing Corp.

"Grape Sherbet" from *Museum,* Carnegie Mellon University Press, © 1983 by Rita Dove. Reprinted by permission of the author.

"Goodnight Willie Lee, I'll See You in the Morning," copyright © 1975 by Alice Walker, from *Goodnight Willie Lee, I'll See You in the Morning* by Alice Walker. Used by permission of Doubleday, a division of Random House, Inc.

"Elena" is reprinted with permission from the publisher of *Chants* by Pat Mora (Houston: Arte Publico Press, University of Houston, © 1984).

"My Mother Combs My Hair" by Chitra Banerjee Divakaruni, from *Black Candle,* copyright © 1991 by Chitra Banerjee Divakaruni. Reprinted by permission of CALYX Books.

"Lineage" from *This Is My Century: New and Collected Poems* by Margaret Walker Alexander. Copyright © 1989 by Margaret Walker Alexander. Reprinted by permission of The University of Georgia Press.

"Good Use for Bad Weather" from *Here at Eagle Pond* by Donald Hall. Copyright © 1990 by Donald Hall. Reprinted by permission of Houghton Mifflin Company. All rights reserved.

"Possum Crossing" from *Quilting the Black-Eyed Pea* by Nikki Giovanni. Copyright © 2002 by Nikki Giovanni. Reprinted by permission of HarperCollins Publishers.

Unit 4

"The Taxi" from *The Complete Poetical Works of Amy Lowell.* Copyright © 1955 by Houghton Mifflin Company. Copyright © renewed 1983 by Houghton Mifflin Company, Brinton P. Roberts, and G. D'Andelot Belin, Esquire. Reprinted by permission of Houghton Mifflin Company. All rights reserved.

"Counting the Beats" from *Complete Poems in One Volume* by Robert Graves. Reprinted by permission of Carcanet Press Ltd.

"The Bear" from *The Plays of Anton Chekhov* by Paul Schmidt. Copyright © 1997 by Paul Schmidt. Reprinted by permission of HarperCollins Publishers.

"About Two Nice People" copyright © 1951 by Shirley Jackson, from *Just an Ordinary Day: The Uncollected Stories* by Shirley Jackson. Used by permission of Bantam Books, a division of Random House, Inc. and The Linda Allen Agency.

"Simile" by N. Scott Momaday. Reprinted by permission of the author.

"Bye-Bye Brevoort" by Eudora Welty. Reprinted by the permission of Russell & Volkening as agents for the author. Copyright © 1980 by Eudora Welty.

"Marty" from *The Collected Works of Paddy Chayefsky The Television Plays* by Paddy Chayefsky. Copyright © 1954 by Paddy Chayefsky. Copyright renewed 1982 by Susan Chayefsky and Dan Chayefsky. International Copyright Secured. All rights reserved. Reprinted by permission of Applause Theatre & Cinema Books, LLC.

From *Introduction to Shakespeare* by Marchette Chute, copyright 1951, renewed © 1979 by Marchette Chute. Used by permission of Dutton, A Division of Penguin Young Readers Group, A Member of Penguin Group (USA) Inc., 345 Hudson Street, New York, NY 10014. All rights reserved.

"The Traveling Bear" from *The Complete Poetical Works of Amy Lowell.* Copyright © 1955 by Houghton Mifflin Company. Copyright © renewed 1983 by Houghton Mifflin Company, Brinton P. Roberts, and G. D'Andelot Belin, Esquire. Reprinted by permission of Houghton Mifflin Company. All rights reserved.

Unit 5

From *The Ramayana: A Shortened Modern Prose Version of the Indian Epic* by R. K. Narayan (First published by Viking Penguin Inc. 1972, Penguin Books 1977). Copyright © R. K. Narayan, 1972. Reprinted by permission of Penguin Group (UK) and Viking Penguin, a division of Penguin Group (USA) Inc.

"Ithaca" from *The Complete Poems of Cavafy,* copyright © 1961 and renewed 1989 by Rae Dalven, reprinted by permission of Harcourt, Inc.

"An Ancient Gesture" by Edna St. Vincent Millay. From *Collected Poems,* HarperCollins. Copyright © 1954, 1982 by Edna St. Vincent Millay and Norma Millay Ellis. All rights reserved. Used by permission of Elizabeth Barnett, literary executor.

"Waiting" from *The Penelopiad* by Margaret Atwood. Copyright © 2005 by O. W. Toad Ltd. Used by permission of Grove/Atlantic, Inc.

"Over Hill and Under Hill" from *The Hobbit* by J. R. R. Tolkien. Copyright © 1966 by J. R. R. Tolkien. Copyright © renewed 1994 by Christopher R. Tolkien, John F. R. Tolkien and Priscilla M. A. R. Tolkien. Reprinted by permission of Houghton Mifflin Company. All rights reserved.

"Perseus" from *Mythology* by Edith Hamilton. Copyright © 1942 by Edith Hamilton; copyright © renewed 1969 by Dorian Fielding Reid and Doris Fielding Reid. By permission of Little, Brown and Co., Inc.

"The Fenris Wolf" from *Legends of the North* by Olivia E. Coolidge. Copyright © 1951, renewed 1979 by Olivia E. Coolidge. Reprinted by permission of Houghton Mifflin Company. All rights reserved.

"Coyote and Crow" from *Indian Legends of the Pacific Northwest,* by Ella Clark. Copyright © 1953 The Regents of the University of California; © renewed 1981 by Ella E. Clark. Reprinted by permission of the University of California Press.

Unit 6

From "Buy Jupiter" by Isaac Asimov. Published by permission of The Estate of Isaac Asimov c/o Ralph M. Vicinanza Ltd.

"The Sentinel" by Arthur C. Clarke. Reprinted by permission of the author and the author's agents, Scovil Chichak Galen Literary Agency, Inc.

"2001: A Space Odyssey" by Roger Ebert. Copyright © The Ebert Co. Ltd. Reprinted by permission.

"He-y, Come on Ou-t!" by Sinichi Hoshi. Reprinted by permission of the translator, Stanleigh H. Jones.

"The Rule of Names" copyright © 1964, 1992 by Ursula K. Le Guin, first appeared in *Fantastic,* from *The Winds of Twelve Quarters,* reprinted by permission of the author and the author's agents; the Virginia Kidd Agency, Inc.

"In Memoriam" by Nancy Kress. Reprinted by permission of the author.

"Purchase" by Naomi Long Madgett, from *Remembrances of Spring: Collected Early Poems* (Michigan State University Press, 1993). Reprinted by permission of the author.

From *Einstein's Dreams* by Alan Lightman, copyright © 1993 by Alan Lightman. Illustrations copyright © 1993 by Chris Costello. Used by permission of Pantheon Books, a division of Random House, Inc.

"The Golden Kite, the Silver Wind" by Ray Bradbury. Copyright © 1953 by Epoch Associates, renewed 1981 by Ray Bradbury. Reprinted by permission of Don Congdon Associates, Inc.

"The President's Half Disme" by Ellery Queen. Copyright © 1947 by Ellery Queen. Copyright renewed by Ellery Queen. Reproduced here with the permission of the Frederic Dannay and Manfred B. Lee Literary Property Trusts and their agent, JackTime, 3 Erold Court, Allendale, NJ 07401, USA.

"The Mystery of Hunter's Lodge" from *Poirot Investigates* by Agatha Christie. Copyright © 1924 by Agatha Christie. Reprinted by permission of Harold Ober Associates Incorporated.

"Wasps' Nest" from *Double Sin and Other Stories* by Agatha Christie, copyright 1925, 1926, 1929, 1954 © 1957, 1958, 1960, 1961 by Agatha Christie Ltd., copyright renewed. Used by permission of G.P. Putnam's sons, a division of Penguin Group (USA) Inc.

Reference Section

Content from The Academic Word List, developed at the School of Linguistics and Applied Language Studies at Victoria University of Wellington, New Zealand, is reprinted by permission of Averil Coxhead.

http://language.massey.ac.nz/staff/awl/index.shtml.

Maps

Mapping Specialists Inc.

Photography

COVER (t)CORBIS; **COVER** (c)Getty Images; **COVER** (b)Peter Christopher/Masterfile; **IN24** Private Collection/Bridgeman Art Library; **IN25** Edward Hopper/Indianapolis Museum of Art/Bridgeman Art Library; **IN26** Seamas Culligan/ZUMA/CORBIS; **IN27** Bridgeman Art Library; **IN28** Bridgeman Art Library; **IN29** Mary Evans Picture Library/The Image Works; **IN30** Neal Beidleman/Woodfin Camp and Associates; **IN31** Images.com/CORBIS; **IN32** Leslie Hinrichs/SuperStock; **IN34** Diana Ong/SuperStock; **IN35** Private Collection/Bridgeman Art Library; **IN36** Private Collection, By courtesy of Julian Hartnoll/Bridgeman Art Library; **IN38** Springville Museum of Art, Utah/Bridgeman Art Library; **IN39** Scala/Art Resource, NY; **IN40** Royal Library, Copenhagen, Denmark/Bridgeman Art Library; **IN42** (t)Thomas Baines/Bridgeman Art Library/Getty Images; **IN42** (b)Stapleton Collection/CORBIS; **IN44** CNAC/MNAM/Dist. Réunion des Musées Nationaux/Art Resource, NY; **IN45** SuperStock, Inc./SuperStock; **IN46** CORBIS; **IN48** Scala/Art Resource, NY; **IN49** Underwood and Underwood/CORBIS; **IN50** Andrew Brookes/CORBIS; **IN50** Getty Images; **IN50** Stockbyte; **IN55** Peter Christopher/Masterfile; **IN55** Photodisc/Getty Images; **IN55** Steven Allen/Getty Images; **1** Private Collection/Bridgeman Art Library; **3** CORBIS; **5** HIP/Art Resource, NY; **6** Louis K. Meisel Gallery, Inc./CORBIS; **9** Private Collection/Bridgeman Art Library; **10** Southampton City Art Gallery, Hampshire, UK/Bridgeman Art Library; **12** (t)Bettmann/CORBIS; **12** (b)St. Nicholas Center, www.stnicholascenter.org.; **14** Vanni/Art Resource, NY; **17** Tate Gallery, London/Art Resource, NY; **18** Stalking Tiger, Rosa Bonheur. Private Collection. Gavin Graham Gallery, London, UK. Bridgeman Art Library; **22** New York Times Pictures; **24** Bridgeman Art Library; **25** Henri Cleenewerck/Private Collection/Bridgeman Art Library; **27** Paul Almasy/CORBIS; **28** The Museum of Modern Art/Licensed by SCALA/Art Resource, NY; **30** Bridgeman Art Library; **31** Henri Cleenewerck/Private Collection/Bridgeman Art Library; **32** Bettmann/CORBIS; **33** Bo Zaunders/CORBIS; **34** Aaron Haupt Photography; **36** Erich Lessing/Art Resource, NY; **38** Aaron Haupt Photography; **39** The Butler Institute of American Art; **40** Henri Cleenewerck/Private Collection/Bridgeman Art Library; **44** Nancy Crampton; **46** Christie's Images. ©1998 Artists Rights Society (ARS), New York/ADAGP, Paris; **49** Réunion des Musées Nationaux/Art Resource, NY; **50** George Hall/CORBIS; **51** Christie's Images/SuperStock. ©1998 Estate of Pablo Picasso/Artists Rights Society (ARS), New York; **55** Bettmann/CORBIS; **57** Erich Lessing/Art Resource, NY; **58** Bettmann/CORBIS; **60** Seamas Culligan/ZUMA/CORBIS; **62** North Wind Picture Archives; **63** Blue Lantern Studio/CORBIS; **67** 1998 Bill Gaskins; **69** Royalty-Free/CORBIS; **70** Hampton University Art Museum, Hampton, VA/Elizabeth Catlett/VAGA; **72** Private Collection/Jessie Coates/SuperStock; **73** Robert Franz/CORBIS; **74** Anthony Bannister/CORBIS; **77** Mansell/Time Inc.; **79** Nationalmuseum 1992/E. Cornelius ©Estate of Bruno Liljefors/Licensed by VAGA, New York, NY; **80** Bridgeman Art Library; **82** Christie's Images/SuperStock; **89** Rick Farrell/TIME; **90** Rick Farrell/TIME; **93** Sophie Bassouls/CORBIS SYGMA; **95** Bridgeman Art Library; **96** Mary Iverson/CORBIS; **99** SuperStock, Inc./SuperStock; **101** Bridgeman Art Library; **103** Ditz/Private Collection/Bridgeman Art Library; **105** Private Collection/Bridgeman Art Library; **106** Calvin and Hobbes © 1986 Watterson. Dist. By Universal Press Syndicate. Reprinted with permission. All rights reserved.; **108** James Wilson/Woodfin Camp & Associates;

110 Royalty-Free/CORBIS; **111** W.B. Finch/Stock Boston; **112** Bridgeman Art Library; **116** Charles Moore/Black Star; **117** CNAC/MNAM/Dist. Réunion des Musées Nationaux/Art Resource, NY; **121** Bettmann/CORBIS; **123** The Newark Museum Art Resource, NY; **124** Scala/The Hermitage, St. Petersburg, Russia/ Art Resource, NY; **125** Bettmann/CORBIS; **127** Everett Shinn, Cross Streets of New York, 1899; **128** Bettmann/CORBIS; **129** Bettmann/CORBIS; **129** The Art Archive/Victoria and Albert Museum London/Sally Chappell; **132** (t)T. F. Chen Cultural Center/SuperStock; **132** (b)Bridgeman Art Library; **133** Theo Westernberger/Gamma-Liaison Network; **135** T. F. Chen Cultural Center/ SuperStock; **139** Bridgeman Art Library; **142** (l)Art Explosion; **145** Bridgeman Art Library; **146** Fred Otnes/Images.com; **147** file photo; **149** Patti Mollica/ SuperStock; **150** National Museum of American Art, Washington, DC/Art Resource, NY; **151** N. Carter/North Wind Picture Archives; **155** Hirshhorn Museum and Sculpture Garden, Smithsonian Institution. Gift of Joseph W. Hirshhorn, 1966. Photographer; Ricardo Blanc.; **156** file photo; **160** MedioImages/Punchstock; **162** Burstein Collection/CORBIS; **163** Sylvia Martin/Photo Researchers; **165** Private Collection/Christie's Images; **167** Mark Steinmetz; **168** Private Collection/Christie's Images; **169** Robert Finken/Photo Researchers; **171** Christie's Images/SuperStock; **176** Celeste Wetherell and University of Pittsburgh Press; **180** Ed Labadie/Stock Illustration Source; **182** David David Gallery/SuperStock; **184** Winslow Homer/SuperStock; **188** Hulton-Deutsch Collection/CORBIS; **190** Bridgeman Art Library; **191** Ditz/Private Collection/Bridgeman Art Library; **194** (t)Fine Art Photographic Library/CORBIS; **194** (b)Bettmann/CORBIS; **195** Matt Meadows; **196** Matt Meadows; **197** Manfred Danegger/Photo Researchers; **198** The Metropolitan Museum of Art, gift of Dr. and Mrs. Robert E. Carroll, 1979; **199** Matt Meadows; **200** Munson-Williams-Proctor Institute Museum of Art, Utica, New York, Edward W. Root Bequest, 57.104; **203** Bridgeman Art Library; **205** The Museum of Modern Art/Licensed by SCALA/Art Resource, NY; **206** Jeanne White/Photo Researchers; **208** Martha Holmes/Getty Images; **210** The Art Archive/Imperial War Museum; **212** Hulton Archive/Getty Images; **213** Edward Hopper/Indianapolis Museum of Art/Bridgeman Art Library; **215** Calvin and Hobbes © 1995 Watterson. Dist. By Universal Press Syndicate. Reprinted with permission. All rights reserved.; **219** Hulton-Deutsch Collection/CORBIS; **221** Victoria & Albert Museum, London/Art Resource, NY; **222** Mark Steinmetz; **224** Julius L. Stewart/SuperStock; **226** Georges Stein/ Gavin Graham Gallery, London, UK/Bridgeman Art Library; **229** Royalty-Free/ Corbis; **231** Miriam Berkley; **233** The Newark Museum/Art Resource, NY; **235** Patti Mollica/CORBIS; **237** ©The Andy Warhol Foundation, Inc./Art Resource, NY; **242** AP Images; **242** Bettmann/CORBIS; **243** Carl Mydans/ Time Life Pictures/Getty Images; **244** CORBIS; **247** National Portrait Gallery, Smithsonian Institution/Art Resource; **249** Bridgeman Art Library; **250** Academy of Natural Sciences of Philadelphia/CORBIS; **257** Courtesy Diana Garcia; **259** Bridgeman Art Library; **261** © The Georgia O'Keefe Museum. Gift of The Burnett Foundation; **262** Raymond Gehman/CORBIS; **263** Amanda Merullo/Stock Boston; **264** Susanne Schuenke/SuperStock; **269** Nancy R. Schiff/Getty Images; **271** Bridgeman Art Library; **275** Erich Lessing/Art Resource, NY; **276** Erich Lessing/Art Resource, NY; **277** akg-images; **282** The Fleming-Wyfold Art Foundation/Bridgeman Art Library International; **285** Images.com/CORBIS; **288** Charles Gupton/CORBIS; **290** (l)file photo; **290** (r)file photo; **291** (l)file photo; **291** (t)1998 Bill Gaskins; **291** (1)file photo; **291** (2)file photo; **291** (3)file photo; **298–299** The Three Graces/Freeman/ Private Collection/David Findlay Jr Fine Art, NYC, USA/Bridgeman Art Library; **300** Canadian War Museum, Ottawa, Canada/Bridgeman Art Library; **301** Private Collection/Bridgeman Art Library; **302** Theo Westernberger/Gamma-Liaison Network; **304** Private Collection/Bridgeman Art Library; **305** Louis K. Meisel Gallery, Inc./CORBIS; **307** Private Collection/Bridgeman Art Library; **308** Foxtrot © 2006 Bill Amend. Reprinted with permission of Universal Press Syndicate. All rights reserved.; **309** Fine Art Photographic Library/CORBIS; **310** file photo; **312** Museum of History and Industry, Seattle, Washington; **314** California Historical Society; **316** E.O. Hoppe/CORBIS; **319** Dana Tynan, Stringer/AP Images; **321** Kactus Foto, Santiago, Chile/SuperStock; **324** Kim Karpeles/Alamy Images; **327** Alejandra Villa; **329** Mary Evans Picture Library/ The Image Works; **331** CORBIS; **335** Excerpt from The Murder of Abraham Lincoln, © 2005 Rick Geary, published by permission from NBM Publishing.; **336** Excerpt from The Murder of Abraham Lincoln, © 2005 Rick Geary, published by permission from NBM Publishing.; **337** Excerpt from The Murder of Abraham Lincoln, © 2005 Rick Geary, published by permission from NBM Publishing.; **338** Excerpt from The Murder of Abraham Lincoln, © 2005 Rick Geary, published by permission from NBM Publishing.; **339** Excerpt from The Murder of Abraham Lincoln, © 2005 Rick Geary, published by permission from NBM Publishing.; **340** Oscar White/CORBIS; **342** Topical Press Agency/Hulton Archive/Getty Images; **344** Library of Congress/CORBIS; **347** Bettmann/ CORBIS; **351** David Bartolomi Photography; **353** Shepard Sherbell/CORBIS; **354** Art Explosion; **355** Teru Kuwayama/CORBIS; **357** Michael S. Yamashita/ CORBIS; **358** AP Images; **362** (t)Louis K. Meisel Gallery, Inc./CORBIS; **362** (c)Darrell Lecorre/Masterfile; **362** (b)Fine Art Photographic Library, London/Art Resource, NY; **363** Alan Band/Getty Images; **365** Christie's Images/CORBIS; **367** Louis K. Meisel Gallery, Inc./CORBIS; **371** Holly Roberts/ Getty Images; **375** Darrell Lecorre/Masterfile; **377** Fine Art Photographic Library, London/Art Resource, NY; **379** Smithsonian American Art Museum, Washington, DC/Art Resource, NY; **380** Elizabeth Barakah Hodges/SuperStock; **381** Pam Ingalls/CORBIS; **382** AP Images; **385** John Shaw/Tom Stack & Associates; **386** Rosemary Woods/Getty Images; **388** Tilly Willis/Getty Images; **390** Dennis Stock/Magnum Photos; **393** Gerardo Somoza/CORBIS; **395** Franklin McMahon/CORBIS; **397** William Henry Huddle/Texas State Library and Archives Commission; **400** David McLain/Getty Images; **402** The Art Archive/Gift of Paul Krogman and Claude Rauch in Memory of Bill Cody; **404** Geoffrey Clements/CORBIS; **405** Americana Images/SuperStock; **409** Bettmann/CORBIS; **411** The Art Archive/Private Collection/Chris Deakes; **415** Time Life Pictures/Getty Images; **417** Neal Beidleman/Woodfin Camp and Associates; **419** Scott Fischer/Woodfin Camp and Associates; **420** Neal Beidleman/Woodfin Camp and Associates; **423** Scott Fischer/Woodfin Camp and Associates; **426** Time Life Pictures/Getty Images; **429** Onne Van Der Wal/ TIME; **430** Onne Van Der Wal/TIME; **431** Onne Van Der Wal/TIME; **432** Onne Van Der Wal/TIME; **433** (l)Onne Van Der Wal/TIME; **433** (r)Onne Van Der Wal/TIME; **434** Andrew Brookes/CORBIS; **435** Schalkwijk/Art Resource, NY; **436** National Portrait Gallery, Smithsonian Institution/Art Resource, NY; **438** Bettmann/CORBIS; **440** Bettmann/CORBIS; **443** Bettmann/CORBIS; **446** Bettmann/CORBIS; **448** akg-images; **450** The Corcoran Gallery of Art/CORBIS; **452** Pam Ingalls/CORBIS; **455** Erich Lessing/ Art Resource, NY; **456** Comstock Images/Alamy; **458** Bettmann/CORBIS; **460** T. F. Chen Cultural Center/SuperStock; **464** (t)CORBIS; **464** (c)Mike Segar/Reuters/CORBIS; **464** (b)Icon SMI/CORBIS; **467** CORBIS; **469** Ed Quinn/CORBIS; **470** Ezra Shaw/Getty Images; **471** Mike Segar/Reuters/ CORBIS; **473** Icon SMI/CORBIS; **477** Jed Jacobsohn/Getty Images; **478** AP Images; **483** Giraudon/Art Resource, NY; **484** Images.com/CORBIS; **490** © Christie's Images Ltd; **496** Charles Gupton/CORBIS; **498** (l)Aaron Haupt Photography; **498** (r)Aaron Haupt Photography; **499** (l)file photo; **499** (t)Underwood and Underwood/CORBIS; **499** (1)file photo; **499** (2)file photo; **499** (3)file photo; **506–507** Vincent van Gogh. Rijksmuseum Kroeller-Mueller, Otterio, The Netherlands/Art Resource, NY; **510** Mary Evans Picture Library; **511** The Art Archive/National Archives Washington DC; **513** Private Collection/Bridgeman Art Library; **515** Scala/Art Resource, Inc.; **516** Calvin and Hobbes © 1995 Watterson. Dist. By Universal Press Syndicate. Reprinted with permission. All rights reserved.; **518** Bettmann/ CORBIS; **520** John Newcomb/SuperStock; **521** Tom Stock/Stone/Getty Images; **523** Getty Images; **524** The Art Archive/Culver Pictures; **526** Leslie Hinrichs/SuperStock; **528** William Harry Warren Bicknell/Bettmann/CORBIS; **529** FOXTROT © Bill Amend. Reprinted with permission of UNIVERSAL PRESS SYNDICATE. All rights reserved.; **530** Bridgeman Art Library; **532** The National Portrait Gallery, Smithsonian Institution/Art Resource, NY; **534** Maison de Victor Hugo/Musée de la Ville de Paris/Giraudon/Art Resource, NY; **538** (l)Brian Doben/TIME; **538** (r)Brian Doben/TIME; **539** (l)Brian Doben/ TIME; **539** (r)Brian Doben/TIME; **541** (t)Getty Images; **541** (c)CORBIS; **541** (b)Fine Art Photographic Library, London/Art Resource, NY; **542** Library of Congress; **543** Getty Images; **544** Getty Images; **546** Conrad Zobel/CORBIS; **547** Bridgeman Art Library; **549** CORBIS; **551** Scala/Art Resource, NY; **552** Barbara Savage Cheresh; **553** Charles & Josette Lenars/CORBIS; **554** Courtesy Ismael Frigerio; **556** file photo; **558** Fine Art Photographic Library, London/Art Resource, NY; **560** (c)Mark Lennihan/AP Images; **560** Terra Foundation for American Art, Chicago/Art Resource, NY; **561** Roger Viollet Collection/Getty Images; **562** Bridgeman Art Library; **563** Stock Montage/Stock Montage/Getty Images; **566** Snark/Art Resource; **568** Asian Art & Archaeology, Inc./CORBIS; **569** Yoshitoshi/Asian Art & Archaeology, Inc./CORBIS; **572** Andrew Brookes/CORBIS; **573** Private Collection/Bridgeman Art Library; **574** Non Sequitur © Wiley Miller. Dist. By Universal Press Syndicate. Reprinted with permission. All rights reserved.; **576** Courtesy Carolyn Soto; **578** Erich Lessing/Art Resource, NY; **580** Courtesy Alma Luz Villanueva; **581** Brand X/SuperStock; **583** Bridgeman Art Library; **585** Judie Burstein/Globe Photos; **586** Jim Corwin/Stock Boston; **587** Elizabeth Catlett/Licensed by VAGA, New York, NY; **589** Hulton Archive/Getty Images; **591** Mimmo Jodice/CORBIS; **592** Diana Ong/SuperStock; **594** Max Pechstein/Art Resource, NY; **596** Joan Fetchen; **600** Hulton Archive/Getty Images; **602** Bridgeman Art Library; **604** Paul Abdoo/MPI/Getty; **605** Marilyn "Angel" Wynn/Native Stock; **606** Tim Nicola courtesy Artistic Gallery, Santa Fe. Photography by Jerry Jacka.; **608** Eric Schaal/Getty Images; **610** Sotheby's/akg-images; **611** GET FUZZY: © Darby Conley/Dist. by United Feature Syndicate, Inc.; **614** Christopher Felver/CORBIS; **615** David Lees/Hulton Archive/Getty Images; **616** Bildarchiv Preussischer Kulturbesitz/Art Resource, NY; **617** Erich Lessing/Art Resource, NY; **619** Michael Escoffery/Art Resource, NY; **620** Fine Art Photographic Library/CORBIS; **622** Ted Thai/Getty Images; **624** Anna Belle Lee Washington/SuperStock; **625** Anna Belle Lee Washington/SuperStock; **627** (t)Alphonse Osbert/Art Resource, NY; **627** (c)Grace Cossington Smith/Art Gallery of New South Wales, Sydney, Australia/Bridgeman Art Library; **627** (b)Darlene Hammond/Getty Images; **628** Adam Scull/Globe Photos; **629** Images.com/CORBIS; **630** Alphonse Osbert/Art Resource, NY; **632** Images.com/CORBIS; **634** Grace Cossington Smith/Art Gallery of New South Wales, Sydney, Australia/Bridgeman Art Library; **637** George Tooker/Delaware Art Museum, Wilmington/Bridgeman Art Library; **638** © Banco de Mexico Trust/Bridgeman-Giraudon/Art Resource, NY; **640** Private Collection/Bridgeman Art Library International; **642** The Barnes Foundation, Merion Station, Pennsylvania/CORBIS; **643** Cheron Bayna; **644** Dex Images/CORBIS; **645** Private Collection/Christie's Images; **647** Private Collection/Christie's Images; **648** CALYX Books; **650** Private Collection/Bridgeman Art Library; **652** AFP/Getty Images; **656** From BONE ®: OUT FROM BONEVILLE by Jeff Smith. Published by Graphix, an imprint of Scholastic Inc. Copyright © 2005, 1992, 1991; **657** From BONE ®: OUT FROM BONEVILLE by Jeff Smith. Published by Graphix, an imprint of Scholastic Inc. Copyright © 2005, 1992, 1991; **658** Nancy Crampton; **660** Smithsonian American Art Museum, Washington, DC/Art Resource, NY; **667** CORBIS; **670** Charles Gupton/CORBIS; **672** (l)Aaron Haupt Photography; **672** (r)Aaron Haupt Photography; **673** (t)Bettmann/CORBIS; **673** (cl)Aaron Haupt Photography; **673** (cr)file photo; **673** (bl)file photo; **673** (br)file photo; **675** Academy of Natural Sciences of Philadelphia/CORBIS; **680** Andre Rouillard/SuperStock; **684** The Art Archive; **685** Miramax/Dimension Films/The Kobal Collection/Paul Chedlow; **686** Mary Evans Picture Library; **687** Private Collection/Art Resource, NY; **689** Private Collection/Bridgeman Art Library; **690** Gustavo Tomsich/CORBIS; **692** Hulton Archive/Getty Images; **693** From Shakespeare and His Theatre by John Russell Brown. Illustrated by David Gentleman. Originally published by Penguin Books Ltd.; **694** Martin Droeshout/Art Resource, NY; **696** Private Collection/Christie's Images; **699** Palazzo Ducale, Mantua, Italy/SuperStock; **704** Geoffrey Clements/CORBIS; **713** Hermitage, St. Petersburg, Russia/Bridgeman Art Library; **718** Musee des Beaux-Arts, Nimes, France, Giraudon/Bridgeman Art Library; **718** Private Collection/Christie's Images; **726** akg-images; **732** Ashmolean Museum, Oxford; **737** Private Collection/Christie's Images; **741** Private Collection, By courtesy of Julian Hartnoll/Bridgeman Art Library; **744** ArenaPal /Topham/The Image Works; **750** Private Collection/Christie's Images; **754–755** Fine Art Photographic Library/CORBIS; **761** Birmingham Museums and Art Gallery/Bridgeman Art Library; **766** Bridgeman Art Library, London/SuperStock; **777** From the RSC Collection with the permission of the Governors of the Royal Shakespeare Theatre. Photo by Brian Glover.; **783** Master of the Jarves Cassonie/SuperStock; **786** Art Gallery of South Australia, Adelaide. Elder Bequest Fund 1899.; **796** Folger Shakespeare Library, Washington, DC/Art Resource, NY; **800** Derby Museum & Art Gallery, England/Bridgeman Art Library; **804** Frederick Leighton/From the collection of Agnes Scott College; **805** akg-images; **809** Ed Bradshaw/TIME; **810** KAVEH GOLESTAN/TIME; **811** THE GRANGER COLLECTION; **813** (1)Bridgeman Art Library, London/SuperStock; **813** (2)Max Furguson/Bridgeman Art Library/Getty Images; **813** (3)Joe Baker/Stock Illustration Source; **813** (4)Illustration Works; **814** Max Furguson/Bridgeman Art Library/Getty Images; **816** Illustration Works; **818** Joe Baker/Stock Illustration Source; **819** Louis K. Meisel Gallery, Inc./CORBIS; **820** Mark di Vincenzo/Stock Illustration Source; **822** Topham/The Image Works; **824** Christie's Images/CORBIS; **829** Christie's Images Ltd; **832** Christie's Images Ltd; **834** Elaina McBroom; **837** (t)Francis G. Mayer/CORBIS; **837** (c) Christie's Images Ltd; **837** (b)Bridgeman Art Library; **838** Peter Adams/zefa/CORBIS; **840** Erich Lessing/Art Resource, NY; **842** Christie's Images Ltd; **845** Francis G. Mayer/CORBIS; **846** Bridgeman Art Library/Getty Images; **848** Réunion de Musées Nationaux/Art Resource, NY; **852** Lina Chesak/Images.com; **852** Images.com/CORBIS; **854** Lina Chesak/Images.com; **855** Scala/Art Resource, NY; **857** The Grand Design/SuperStock; **858** (Detail-pull quote): Royal Academy of Arts, London, UK/Bridgeman Art Library; **859** Royal Academy of Arts, London, UK/Bridgeman Art Library; **860** The Grand Design/SuperStock; **861** Images.com/CORBIS; **862** Suzi Kennett/Private Collection/Bridgeman Art Library; **863** Images.com/CORBIS; **864** Hulton Archive/Getty Images; **866** Tate Gallery, London/Art Resource, NY; **870** SuperStock, Inc./SuperStock; **872** Galleria Narciso, Turin, Italy/Bridgeman Art Library; **875** Andrew Brookes/CORBIS; **876** Getty Images; **878** © Historical Picture Archive/CORBIS; **881** The Museum of Modern Art/Licensed by SCALA/Art Resource, NY; **882** SuperStock, Inc./SuperStock; **886** Bridgeman Art Library; **888** Sophie Bassouls/CORBIS SYGMA; **890** Bettmann/CORBIS; **892** Bridgeman Art Library; **896** Bridgeman Art Library; **899** Metropolitan Museum of Art, New York, USA/Bridgeman Art Library; **906** Bridgeman Art Library; **909** Sandra Speidel/Images.com; **912** Springville Museum of Art, Utah, USA/Bridgeman Art Library; **919** Bridgeman Art Library; **921** Chisholm Gallery/SuperStock; **925** UNITED ARTISTS/THE KOBAL COLLECTION; **928** Paramount Pictures/Hulton Archive/Getty Images; **934** Charles Gupton/CORBIS; **936** (l)Aaron Haupt Photography; **936** (r)Aaron Haupt Photography; **937** (l)Jonathan Magee/Trinity University; **937** (tr)Pirie MacDonald/CORBIS; **937** (cr)Aaron Haupt Photography; **937** (br)Aaron Haupt Photography; **944** Archivo Iconografico, S.A./CORBIS; **944** Archivo Iconografico, S.A./CORBIS; **946** CORBIS; **949** Art Resource, NY; **950** Scala/Art Resource, NY; **951** (t)The Philadelphia Museum of Art/Art Resource, NY; **951** (b)Réunion des Musées Nationaux/Art Resource, NY; **953** Erich Lessing/Art Resource, NY; **954** Private Collection/Bridgeman Art Library; **956** SuperStock; **957** Erich Lessing/Louvre, Paris, France/Art Resource, NY; **958** Bettmann/CORBIS; **960–961** Kevin Fleming; **964** The Art Archive/Dagli Orti; **966** Stapleton Collection/CORBIS; **973** Erich Lessing/Art Resource, NY; **974** Pushkin Museum, Moscow/Bridgeman Art Library; **976** akg-images; **983** © National Gallery of Victoria, Melbourne, Australia/Bridgeman Art Library; **985** akg-images/Peter Connolly; **987** Scala/Palazzo Poggi, Bologna, Italy/Art Resource, NY; **992** Erich Lessing/Art Resource, NY; **995** National Archaeological Museum, Athens/Bridgeman Art Library; **998** The Stapleton Collection/Bridgeman Art Library; **1001** Erich Lessing/Art Resource, NY; **1003** National Gallery Collection; By kind permission of the Trustees of the National Gallery, London/CORBIS; **1006** © Erich Lessing/Art Resource, NY; **1010** Ancient Art & Architecture Collection; **1013** Erich Lessing/Art Resource, NY; **1015** The Metropolitan Museum of Art, Fletcher Fund, 1956 (56.171.38). Photograph ©1989 The Metropolitan Museum of Art; **1018** Bettmann/CORBIS; **1019** David Lees/CORBIS; **1022** Andrew Brookes/CORBIS; **1023** (1)The Stapleton Collection/Bridgeman Art Library; **1023** (2)Scala/Art Resource, NY; **1023** (3)Tate Gallery, London/Art Resource, NY; **1023** (4)Penelope (w/c on paper), Dicksee, Sir Frank (1853–1928)/Private Collection, The Maas Gallery, London, UK/Bridgeman Art Library; **1024** Scala/Art Resource, NY; **1026** Tate Gallery, London/Art Resource, NY; **1027** Penelope (w/c on paper), Dicksee, Sir Frank (1853–1928)/Private

Collection, The Maas Gallery, London, UK/Bridgeman Art Library; **1029** The Art Archive/Private Collection London; **1031** (t)Mark Leong/TIME; **1031** (b)Mark Leong/TIME; **1032** Mark Leong/TIME; **1033** Mark Leong/TIME; **1034** Mark Leong/TIME; **1035** Haywood Magee/Getty Images; **1037** Private Collection/Bridgeman Art Library; **1039** akg-images; **1043** Musée Jeanne d'Aboville, La Fère, France, Lauros/Giraudon/Bridgeman Art Library; **1045** Mikhail Belomlinsky/Private Collection/Bridgeman Art Library; **1049** Reprinted by permission of HarperCollins Publishers Ltd. © 1937 JRR Tolkien; **1050** Reprinted by permission of HarperCollins Publishers Ltd. © 1937 JRR Tolkien; **1051** Reprinted by permission of HarperCollins Publishers Ltd. © 1937 JRR Tolkien; **1052** Reprinted by permission of HarperCollins Publishers Ltd. © 1937 JRR Tolkien; **1053** Private Collection/Bridgeman Art Library; **1054** Images.com/CORBIS; **1056** Gjon Mili/Getty Images; **1058** Bridgeman Art Library; **1063** Giraudon/Art Resource, NY; **1064** akg-images/Rabatti-Domingie; **1066** Araldo de Luca/CORBIS; **1067** National Museum of Iceland, Reykjavik, Iceland/Bridgeman Art Library; **1069** Werner Forman/Art Resource, NY; **1071** Royal Library, Copenhagen, Denmark/Bridgeman Art Library; **1073** Andrew Brookes/CORBIS; **1074** Connie Ricca/CORBIS; **1075** Jay Syverson/CORBIS; **1076** Academy of Natural Sciences of Philadelphia/CORBIS; **1078** Russian School/Bibliotheque des Arts Decoratifs, Paris, France, Archives Charmet/Bridgeman Art Library; **1080** Metropolitan Museum of Art, New York, USA/Bridgeman Art Library; **1082** Fitzwilliam Museum, University of Cambridge, UK/Bridgeman Art Library; **1084** Art Museum of Ryasan, Russia/Bridgeman Art Library; **1088** Butler Institute of American Art, Youngstown, OH, USA/Bridgeman Art Library; **1089** Newberry Library/SuperStock; **1091** Alexander Gardner/CORBIS; **1099** J. Howard Miller/CORBIS; **1102** Charles Gupton/CORBIS; **1104** (l)Aaron Haupt Photography; **1104** (r)file photo; **1105** (l)Robbie Jack/CORBIS; **1105** (tr)Barnabas Bosshart/CORBIS; **1105** (cr)file photo; **1105** (br)file photo; **1112** George Tooker/Metropolitan Museum of Art, New York/Bridgeman Art Library; **1116** Douglas Kirkland/CORBIS; **1117** Tim Bird/CORBIS; **1118** Private Collection/Bridgeman Art Library; **1119** Forrest J. Ackerman Collection/CORBIS; **1121** Private Collection/Bridgeman Art Library; **1122** Scala/Art Resource, NY; **1124** Dana Fineman/Sygma/CORBIS; **1127** Paul Anderson/Images.com/CORBIS; **1128** Paul Anderson/Images.com/CORBIS; **1129** Sean Sexton Collection/CORBIS; **1130** Paul Anderson/Images.com/CORBIS; **1131** Paul Anderson/Images.com/CORBIS; **1132** Georgia O'Keeffe Museum, Santa Fe/Art Resource, NY; **1134** Paul Anderson/Images.com/CORBIS; **1137** Paul Anderson/Images.com/CORBIS; **1138** AP Images; **1138** SUNSET BOULEVARD/CORBIS SYGMA; **1139** akg-images; **1140** akg-images; **1142** Japan Foreign-Rights Centre; **1144** Mary Evans Picture Library/The Image Works; **1145** Bob Daemmrich/Stock Boston; **1147** Christie's Images/Bridgeman Art Library. ©1998 Charly Herscovici, Brussels/Artists Rights Society(ARS), New York; **1150** Bettmann/CORBIS; **1152** Blue Lantern Studio/CORBIS; **1155** Thomas Baines/Bridgeman Art Library/Getty Images; **1156** Blue Lantern Studio/CORBIS; **1157** Blue Lantern Studio/CORBIS; **1158** Private Collection/Bridgeman Art Library; **1160** Bridgeman Library/Getty Images; **1161** (l)Mary Evans Picture Library; **1161** (r)Mary Evans Picture Library; **1164** (t)Bildarchiv Preussischer Kulturbesitz/Art Resource, NY; **1164** Caroline Burrows/Illustration Works/Getty Images; **1164** Geoffrey Clements/CORBIS; **1165** Henry Koningisor; **1167** A. Belov/CORBIS; **1168** A. Belov/CORBIS; **1169** A. Belov/CORBIS; **1171** Bildarchiv Preussischer Kulturbesitz/Art Resource, NY; **1174** Caroline Burrows/Illustration Works/Getty Images; **1175** Geoffrey Clements/CORBIS; **1177** Caroline Burrows/Illustration Works/Getty Images; **1178** Vince Bucci/Getty Images; **1180** Scala/Art Resource, NY; **1183** SEF/Art Resource, NY; **1186** Andrew Brookes/CORBIS; **1187** Getty Images; **1188** Private Collection/Bridgeman Art Library; **1190** Hulton Archive/Getty; **1192** Swim Ink 2, LLC/CORBIS; **1194** Bridgeman Art Library; **1197** Lake County Museum/CORBIS; **1203** Eric Schaal/Getty Images; **1205** Images courtesy of HeritageAuctions.com; **1208** Bridgeman Art Library; **1211** Stapleton Collection/CORBIS; **1217** Philadelphia Museum of Art/CORBIS; **1220** Christie's Images/CORBIS; **1221** Bettmann/CORBIS; **1224** Karl Ammann/TIME; **1225** Mark Leong/TIME; **1227** Keystone/Getty Images; **1229** Peter Ruck/BIPs/Getty Images; **1231** Time Life Pictures/Mansell/Time Life Pictures/Getty Images; **1235** Time Life Pictures/Mansell/Time Life Pictures/Getty Images; **1237** Time Life Pictures/Mansell/Time Life Pictures/Getty Images; **1238** Peter Ruck/BIPs/Getty Images; **1241** Peter Ruck/BIPs/Getty Images; **1243** Peter Ruck/BIPs/Getty Images; **1244** Peter Ruck/BIPs/Getty Images; **1245** H. Armstrong Roberts/CORBIS; **1248** W. and D. Downey/Getty Images; **1250** Images.com/CORBIS; **1253** Images.com/CORBIS; **1256** Images.com/CORBIS; **1260** (tl)Brand X Pictures/PunchStock; **1263** Keren Su/CORBIS; **1266** Charles Gupton/CORBIS; **1268** (l)file photo; **1268** (r)file photo; **1269** (t)Don Farall/Getty Images; **1269** (cl)file photo; **1269** (cr)Aaron Haupt Photography; **1269** (b)Aaron Haupt Photography.